CONTENTS

A, a The first letter of the English alphabet; the highest grade, meaning excellent or best.

AA *abbr.* Alcoholics Anonymous.

aard-vark *n.*

A burrowing African animal, which resembles the anteater and feeds on ants and termites.

aard-wolf *n.* A hyena-like mammal, feeding chiefly on carrion and insects.

AB *abbr.* One of the major blood types. One who possesses it may donate blood to type AB and receive blood from types A, B, AB, and O.

AB *abbr.* Bachelor of Arts; academic degree.

ab-a-ca *n.* A plant from the Philippines whose leafstalks are the source of Manila hemp.

a-back *adv.* Unexpectedly; by surprise; startled.

ab-a-cus *n.* A frame holding parallel rods with beads, used for manual computation, especially by the Chinese.

a-baft *adv.* On or toward the stern, aft, or hind part of a ship.

a-ban-don *v.* To yield utterly; to desert; to forsake; to withdraw protection, support, or help. abandoned *adj.*, abandonment *n.*, abandonedly *adv.*

a-base *v.* To lower in rank, prestige, position, or estimation; to cast down, to humble.

a-base-ment *n.* A state of depression, degradation, or humiliation.

a-bash *v.* To embarrass; to disconcert; to make ashamed or uneasy.

a-bate *v.* To deduct; to make less; to reduce in quantity, value, force, or intensity. -er *n.*, abatable, abated *adj.*

ab-be *n.* A French title given to a priest.

ab-bey *n.* An abbey church, a monastery, or convent.

ab-bre-vi-ate *v.* To make briefer; to abridge; to shorten; to reduce to a briefer form, as a word or phrase.

ab-bre-vi-a-tion *n.* A shortened form of a word or phrase, used to represent the full form. -or *n.*, -ory *adj.*

ab-di-cate *v.* To relinquish power or responsibility formally. abdication *v.*

ab-do-men *n.* That part of the human body that lies between the thorax and the pelvis. abdominal *adj.*, -ally *adv.*

ab-duct *v.* To carry away wrongfully, as by force or fraud; to kidnap; to draw aside or away. -or, abduction *n.*

a-beam *adv.* At right angles to the keel of a ship.

a-bed *adv.* In bed; on a bed; to bed.

ab-er-rant *adj.* Straying from the right way or usual course. aberrantly *adv.*

a-bet *v.* To incite, encourage, or assist. abetment *n.*

ab-hor *v.* To dislike intensely; to loathe. abhorrer, abhorrence *n.*

a-bide *v.* To tolerate; to bear; to remain; to last; to conform to; to comply with.

a-bil-i-ty *n.* State of being able; possession of qualities necessary; competence; skill.

ab-ject *adj.* Sunk to a low condition; groveling; mean; despicable. abjection, abjectness *n.*

ab-jure *v.* To renounce solemnly or on oath; to repudiate; to forswear. -er *n.*

a-blaze *adv.* On fire; brilliantly lighted up; very excited; angry.

a-ble *adj.* Having sufficient ability; capable or talented. -ness *n.*, -y *adv.*

a-ble--bodied *adj.* Having a sound, strong body; competent for physical service.

ab-lu-tion *n.* The act of washing, cleansing, or purification by a liquid, usually water; specifically, a washing of the body as a part of religious rites. ablutionary *adj.*

ab-ne-gate *v.* To deny; to refuse or renounce; to relinquish or surrender.

ab-nor-mal *adj.* Not normal; irregular; unnatural. -ity *n.*, abnormally *adv.*

a-board *adv.* On board a ship or other vehicle.

a-bode *n.* A dwelling place; home.

a-bol-ish *v.* To put an end to; to annul. abolisher, -ment *n.*, abolishable *adj.*

A--Bomb *n.* An atomic bomb; a very destructive bomb where energy is released in an explosion with enormous force and heat.

a-bom-i-na-ble *adj.* Detestable; loathsome. -bly *adv.*, abominableness *n.*

a-bort *v.* To terminate or cause to terminate an operation or procedure before completion.

a-bor-tion *n.* Induced termination of pregnancy before the fetus can survive; something malformed.

a-bound *v.* To have plenty; to exist in large numbers.

a-bout *adv.* Approximately; on every side, here and there.

a-bove *adv.* Higher or greater than; in or at a higher place.

ab-ra-ca-dab-ra *n.* A word believed by some to have magical powers, used in casting spells; nonsense, foolish talk.

a-brade *v.* To wear or rub off; to grate off; abrasive, scouring.

a-re-ac-tion *n.* To eliminate a bad experience by reliving it.

a-breast *adv.* or *adj.* Side by side.

a-bridge *v.* To make smaller, fewer, or shorter while maintaining essential contents. abridger *n.*, abridgable, abridgeable *adj.*

a-broad *adv.* Widely; in many places; outside one's country; at large.

ab-ro-gate *v.* To cancel; to put an end to; to repeal. abrogation *n.*, abrogable, abrogative *adj.*

ab-rupt *adj.* Happening or coming suddenly with no warning. abruptness *n.*, abruptly *adv.*

ab-scess *n.* An infected place in the body

which becomes sore and swollen and contains pus. **abscessed** *adj.*

ab-scind *v.* To cut off; to sever; to pare away; to separate.

ab-scond *v.* To remove oneself, as to flee from justice. **absconder** *n.*

ab-sence *n.* Being absent, not present; inattention.

ab-sent *adj.* Not present; away; lacking; nonexistent. **absently** *adv.*

ab-sent--mind-ed *adj.* Always forgetting things; dreaming or thinking of something else; not paying attention.

ab-so-lute *adj.* Unconditional; without restraint; perfect. **absoluteness** *n.*, **absolutely** *adv.*

ab-solve *v.* To set free or release from duties, guilt, or penalty. **absolver** *n.*, **absolvable** *adj.*

ab-sorb *v.* To take in; to take up the full attention; to engage one's whole attention. **absorbability** *n.*, **absorbable** *adj.*

ab-sorp-tion *n.* The act of giving full attention or having great interest.

ab-stain *v.* To refrain from doing something. **abstainer** *n.*

ab-ste-mi-ous *adj.* Showing moderation in the use of drink and food. **abstemiousness** *n.*, **abstemiously** *adv.*

ab-sten-tion *n.* The act of holding off from using or doing something.

ab-stract *v.* To remove from, reduce, or summarize. **abstractedness** *n.*

ab-struse *adj.* Hard or difficult to understand. **-ness** *n.*, **abstrusely** *adv.*

ab-surd *adj.* Contrary to reason; clearly untrue or unreasonable. **absurdity**, **absurdness** *n.*

a-bun-dance *n.* Ample supply; plenty; amount more than enough.

a-buse *v.* To use in an improper or wrong way. *n.* Improper treatment.

a-but *v.* To border; to touch at one end.

a-but-ment *n.* Support at the end of an arch or bridge.

a-bys-mal *adj.* Immeasurably deep or low.

a-byss *n.* A deep crack or gap in the earth. **abyssal** *adj.*

a-ca-cia *n.* Thorny tree or shrub of warm climates.

a-cad-e-my *n.* A private school for special training, as in music, art, or military.

a-can-thus *n.* A prickly plant, native to the Mediterranean region.

a-cap-pel-la *adj.* Singing without instrumental accompaniment.

a-cat-a-lec-tic *adj.* Not stopping short; having the complete number or syllables, in a line of verse.

ac-cede *v.* To consent; to agree; to arrive at a certain condition or state.

ac-cel-er--ate *v.* To make run or work faster; to increase the speed. **-tion** *n.*

ac-cent *n.* An effort to make one syllable more prominent than the others.

ac-cept *v.* To take what is given; to believe to be true; to agree. **accepter**, **acceptor** *n.*

ac-cept-able *adj.* Satisfactory; proper; good enough. **acceptableness**,

acceptability *n.*, acceptably *adv.*

ac-cep-tance *n.* Approval or belief; an accepting or being accepted.

ac-cess *n.* Admission, entrance; attack. **accessibility** *n.*, **accessible** *adj.*

ac-ces-sion *n.* In Computer Science, the act of obtaining data from storage.

ac-ces-si-ble *adj.* Easy access or approach.

ac-ces-sory *n.*, *pl.* **-ies** Aiding or contributing.

ac-ci-dent *n.* A happening that is not planned or expected. **accidental** *adj.*, **accidentally** *adv.*

ac-claim *v.* To greet with strong approval or loud applause; to hail or cheer.

ac-cli-mate *v.* To get used to a different climate or new surroundings.

ac-co-lade *n.* Award; praise; ceremony used in conferring knighthood.

ac-com-mo-date *v.* To give room or lodging; to make fit; to adjust.

ac-com-mo-dat-ing *adj.* Ready to help; willing to please; obliging.

ac-com-mo-da-tion *n.* Adjustment; change to fit new conditions; help or convenience.

ac-com-pa-ni-ment *n.* Something that goes well with another.

ac-com-pa-nist *n.* A person who plays a musical accompaniment.

ac-com-pa-ny *v.* To be together with; to go along with.

ac-com-plice *n.* Companion who helps another break the law.

ac-com-plish *v.* To perform; to carry out; to complete; to do. **accomplisher** *n.*, **accomplishable** *adj.*

ac-com-plish-ment *n.* Finish; completion.

ac-cord *n.* Harmony; agreement. *v.* To grant or award. **accordance** *n.*

ac-cord-ing-ly *adv.* In a way that is proper and fitting.

ac-cor-di-on *n.* A musical instrument fitted with bellows and button keyboard, played by pulling out and pressing together the bellows to force air through the reeds. **accordionist** *n.*

ac-cost *v.* To come close to and to speak first in an unfriendly manner.

ac-count *n.* A description; a statement of debts and credits in money transactions; a record; a report. **account** *v.*

ac-count-able *adj.* Liable to be held responsible; able to be explained. **accountableness** *n.*, **accountably** *adv.*

ac-coun-tan-cy *n.* The profession of an accountant.

ac-count-ing *n.* A report on how accounts have been balanced; the system of keeping business records or accounts.

ac-cred-it *v.* To authorize someone; to give official power. **accreditation** *n.*

ac-crete *v.* To grow together or join. **accretive** *adj.*

ac-crue *v.* To result naturally; to increase at certain times.

ac-cu-mu-late *v.* To collect or gather over a period of time; to pile up. **-or** *n.*

ac-cu-ra-cy *n.* **-cies** Exactness; precision; the fact of being accurate or without mistakes.

ac-cu-rate *adj.* Without mistakes or errors; careful and exact; correct. **accurately** *adv.*

ac-curs-ed *adj.* Sure to end badly; under a curse; unpleasant or annoying; very bad. **accursedness** *n.*, **accursedly** *adv.*

ac-cu-sa-tion *n.* A charge that a person is guilty of breaking the law.

ac-cu-sa-tive *adj.* Relating to the direct object of a preposition or of a verb.

ac-cuse *v.* To find fault with; to blame; to charge someone with doing wrong or breaking the law. **accuser** *n.*

ac-custom *v.* To familiarize by habit.

ac-custom-ed *adj.* Customary; usual.

ace *n.* The face of a die or a playing card marked with one spot; in tennis and some other sports, a score made by a serve that is not returned.

ac-e-tate *n.* Salt formed by union of acetic acid with a base, used in making rayon and plastics.

a-ce-tic acid *n.* The main ingredient of vinegar; a sour, colorless liquid that has a sharp smell.

a-cet-y-lene *n.* A highly inflammable, poisonous, colorless gas that burns brightly with a hot flame, used in blowtorches for cutting metal.

ache *v.* To give or have a dull, steady pain; to want very much; to long for.

ache *n.* A dull, continuous pain.

a-chieve *v.* To set or reach by trying hard; to do; to succeed in doing; to accomplish. **achiever** *n.*

a-chieve-ment *n.* Something achieved by work, courage, or skill.

A-chil-les ten-don *n*

The tendon that connects the heelbone and calf muscles.

achro-ma-tism *n.* A quality of giving of images practically free from extraneous colors.

ac-id *n.* A chemical compound containing hydrogen that forms a salt when combined with a base; dissolves in water, has a very sour taste, makes litmus paper turn red.

ac-id head *n.* A user of the drug LSD.

a-cid-i-ty *n.* Condition or quality of being acid.

acid rain *n.* Acid precipitation that falls as rain.

a-cid-u-late *v.* To become or make somewhat acid.

ack *abbr.* Acknowledge; acknowledgment.

ack-ack *n.* Antiaircraft fire.

ac-know-ledge *v.* To admit the truth, existence or reality. **-ment** *n.*, **-able** *adj.*

ac-me *n.* The highest point of attainment; peak.

ac-ne *n.* A common inflammatory disease of young people in which pimples continue to appear on the body.

ac-o-lyte *n.* An altar boy or someone who assists a priest at Mass.

ac-o-nite *n.* A poisonous plant with flowers resembling hoods.

a-corn *n.* A fern or moss-type plant that has no seed leaves.

a-corn squash *n.* An acorn-shaped squash with yellow flesh and a ridged rind.

a-cot-y-ledon *n.* A plant as a fern or moss, which does not have seed leaves.

a-cous-tic *adj.* Having to do with sound or the sense of hearing; the sense of sound; absorbing sound. **acoustical** *n.*, **acoustically** *adv.*

a-cous-tics *n.* The scientific study of sound; total effect of sound, especially in an enclosed space. **acoustician** *n.*

ac-quaint *v.* To make familiar; to let know, to make aware; to inform.

ac-quaint-ance *n.* A person whom one knows but not as a close friend. **acquaintanceship** *n.*

ac-qui-esce *v.* To agree without arguing; to comply without protest. **-ent** *adj.*

ac-quire *v.* To secure control or possession; to become the owner. **acquirer** *n.*

ac-quire-ment *n.* The act of acquiring something, as a skill gained by learning.

ac-quir-ed im-mun-ity *n.* Immunity against diseases that one develops during a lifetime.

ac-qui-si-tion *n.* Something that is acquired; the act of acquiring.

ac-quis-i-tive *adj.* Eager to gain and possess things; greedy.

ac-quit *v.* To rule that a person accused of something is not guilty; to conduct oneself; to behave. **acquittal** *n.*

a-cre *n.* A measurement of land that equals 43,560 square feet.

a-cre-age *n.* The total number of acres in a section of land.

ac-rid *adj.* Having a sharp, bitter, or irritating taste or smell. **acridity**, **acridness** *n.*, **acridly** *adv.*

ac-ri-mo-ni-ous *adj.* Sharp or bitter in speech or manner. **acrimoniousness** *n.*, **acrimoniously** *adv.*

ac-ro-bat *n.* One who is skilled in gymnastic feats. **acrobatic** *adj.*

ac-ro-pho-bi-a *n.* Unusual fear of heights.

a-cross *prep.* From side to side; to one side from the other.

across the board *adj.* Designates win, place, and show in one bet on the same contestant.

a-cros-tic *n.* A series of lines or a poem in which certain letters in each line form a name or motto. **-ally** *adv.*

a-cryl-ic *n.* Relating to or of acrylic acid or its derivatives.

acrylic fiber *n.* A fiber which is made of chemicals, used in making fabrics.

ac-ry-lo-ni-trile *n.* A liquid organic compound used to make acrylic fibers and rubber.

act *n.* Doing something; a thing done; deed; an action; a showing of emotion which is not real or true; a law; decree; one of the main parts of a play, opera, etc. -ability *n.*, -able *adj.*

act-ing *adj.* Temporarily performing the duties, services; or functions of another person.

ac-tin-o-gen *n.* An element which is radioactive.

ac-tion *n.* The process of doing or acting; an effect produced by something; a lawsuit.

ac-ti-vate *v.* To put into action. -tion *n.*

ac-tive *adj.* Working; full of action; busy; lively; quick. activeness *n.*, -ly *adv.*

ac-tiv-ism *n.* A practice based on direct action to affect changes in government and social conditions.

ac-tiv-ity *n.* Being active, in motion; normal power of body or mind.

act of God *n.* An enforceable, uncontrollable happening caused by nature.

ac-tor *n.* A person who acts in movies, plays, television shows, etc.

ac-tress *n.* A female actor.

ac-tu-al *adj.* Acting or existing in fact or reality; as it really is, true, real. actualness *n.*

ac-tu-ate *v.* To put into motion or action. actuation *n.*

ac-u-punc-ture *n.* A traditional Chinese means of treating some illnesses or of lessening pain by putting thin needles into certain parts of the body.

a-cute *adj.* Extremely sensitive; sharp and quick, as pain; shrewd. acuteness *n.*, acutely *adv.*

acute accent *n.* A mark to indicate heavy stress on a syllable.

ad *n.* An advertisement.

AD *abbr.* *Anno Domini*, Latin for "in the year of the Lord".

ad-age *n.* A proverb; a wise or true saying.

a-da-gi-o *adj.* Term used in music to tell how fast a piece should be played.

Ad-am *n.* The first man named in the Bible, the husband of Eve.

ad-a-mant *adj.* Standing firm; not giving in easily; unyielding. adamantly *adv.*

a-dapt *v.* To fit or suit; to change oneself as to adjust to new conditions. -ness *n.*

ad-ap-ta-tion *n.* An act of changing so as to fit or become suitable.

add *v.* To join or put something with another so that there will be more; to cause an increase. add up *v.* To make sense; to be reasonable. add up to *v.* To indicate; to mean. addable, addible *adj.*

ad-dax *n.* An African antelope with spiral twisted horns.

ad-der *n.*

A common poisonous snake found in America and Europe.

ad-dict *n.* A person with a habit so strong that he cannot easily give it up. addiction *n.*, addicted *v.*

ad-di-tion *n.* An adding of numbers to find their total; the act of joining one thing to another. additional *adj.*, additionally *adv.*

ad-di-tive *n.* A substance added to another in small amounts to alter it.

ad-dle *v.* To become or make confused; to spoil.

ad-dress *v.* To direct or aim; to speak to; to give attention to. *n.* The location to which mail or goods can be sent to a person.

ad-duce *v.* To offer as proof or give as a reason. adducer *n.*, adducible *adj.*

ad-e-noids *n.* Lymphoid tissue growths in the upper part of the throat behind the nose; may need to be removed surgically.

a-dept *adj.* Highly skilled; expert. adeptly *adv.*, adeptness *n.*

ad-e-qua-cy *n.* The state of being good enough to fill a requirement.

ad-e-quate *adj.* Sufficient; good enough for what is needed. adequateness *n.*, adequately *adv.*

ad-here *v.* To stay attached; to stick and not come loose; to stay firm in support.

ad-her-ent *n.* A person who follows a leader, party, or belief; a believer or supporter.

ad-he-sion *n.* The act or state of sticking to something or of being stuck together.

ad-he-sive *adj.* Tending to stick and not come loose; cling; having a sticky surface.

a-dieu *n.* A word for good-by.

a-di-os *interj.* Spanish for good-by.

ad-in-ter-im *adj.* In the meantime.

adj *abbr.* Adjective; adjacent; adjourned.

ad-ja-cent *adj.* Close to or nearby.

ad-ja-cent an-gles *n.* Two angles with a side in common, having the same vertex.

ad-jec-tive *n.* A word used to describe a noun or pronoun.

ad-join *v.* To be next to; to be in or nearly in contact with.

ad-journ *v.* To close a meeting or session for a time. adjournment *n.*

ad-judge *v.* To decide by judicial procedure.

ad-junct *n.* Something less important added to something with more importance. adjunctly *adv.*, adjunctive *adj.*

ad-jure *v.* To ask urgently; to command solemnly. adjuration *n.*

adjust *v.* To arrange or change; to make work correctly; to regulate. -ability *n.*

ad-just-a-ble *adj.* Anything that can be adjusted.

ad-just-ment *n.* The act or process of changing; a settlement of a suit or claim.

ad-ju-tant *n.* An administrative staff officer who serves as a secretary to the commanding officer.

ad-lib *v.* To improvise; to compose or make up spontaneously.

ad-man *n.* A person who works in the business of advertising.

ad-min-is-ter *v.* To direct or manage; to give or carry out instructions. **administrable** *adj.*

ad-min-is-tra-tion *n.* The people who manage a school, company, or organization.

ad-min-is-tra-tor *n.* A person who administers or directs, an executive; a manager.

ad-mi-ra-ble *adj.* Worthy of being admired or praised; excellent.

ad-mi-ral *n.* The highest rank for a naval officer; the commanding officer of a navy.

ad-mi-ral-ty *n.* The department of the British navy; the court and law dealing with ships and shipping.

ad-mire *v.* To hold a high opinion; to regard with wonder, delight, and pleased approval. **admiringly** *adv.*, **admirer** *n.*

ad-mis-si-ble *adj.* Capable of being admitted, accepted or allowed.

ad-mis-sion *n.* The right or act of being admitted; an admitting of the truth of something; a confession.

ad-mit *v.* To take or accept as being the truth; to permit or give the right to enter. **admittedly** *adv.*

ad-mit-tance *n.* Permission to enter.

ad-mit-ted-ly *adv.* One's own admission or confession.

ad-mix-ture *n.* Blend; mingling.

ad-mon-ish *v.* To warn a person to correct a fault; to criticize in a gentle way. **admonisher** *n.*

ad-mo-ni-tion *n.* A mild criticism or warning.

a-do-be *n.* A brick or building material made from clay and straw and then dried in the sun.

ad-o-les-cence *n.* The period of physical and psychological development between childhood and adulthood; also known as youth.

ad-o-les-cent *n.* A person in the transitional period between childhood and adulthood.

a-dopt *v.* To legally take into one's family and raise as their own. **-ion** *n.*

a-dor-a-ble *adj.* Very likable; charming. **adorably** *adv.*, **adorableness** *n.*

a-dore *v.* To love greatly; to worship or honor highly; to like very much.

a-dorn *v.* To add splendor or beauty.

a-dorn-ment *n.* Something that adorns; decoration; ornament; the act of adorning.

ad rem *adj.* Relevant to a point at issue.

a-dre-nal gland *n.* A small endocrine gland that consist of a medulla and cortex, located near the kidney.

a-drift *adv.* Drifting; floating freely without being steered; having no clear purpose or aim.

a-droit *adj.* Skillful and clever in difficult circumstances. **adroitly** *adv.*

ad-sorb *v.* To collect and hold as molecules of gases, liquids; to become adsorbed. **adsorbable** *adj.*

ad-ulate *v.* To give greater praise or flattery than is proper or deserved. **-ion** *n.*

a-dult *n.* A man or woman who is fully grown; a mature person. *adj.* Having reached full size and strength. **-hood** *n.*

a-dul-ter-ate *v.* To make impure or of less quality by adding improper ingredients.

a-dul-tery *n.* The act of sexual intercourse between a married person and someone other than the husband or wife.

adv *abbr.* Adverb; advertisement.

ad-vance *v.* To move ahead; to make or become higher; to increase in value or price.

ad-vanced *adj.* Ahead in time; beyond beginning status.

ad-vance-ment *n.* A promotion in position; progression; money ahead of time.

ad-van-tage *n.* A better chance or more forcible position; a condition, thing or event that can help or benefit; the first point, after deuce scored in the game of tennis.

ad-van-ta-geous *adj.* Giving advantage; favorable.

ad-vent *n.* A coming or arrival; the four Sundays before Christmas.

ad-ven-ture *n.* An exciting and dangerous experience that is remembered; an unusual experience. **adventure** *v.*

ad-ven-tur-er *n.* A person who looks for adventure; one who seeks wealth and social position. **adventurous** *adj.*

ad-verb *n.* A word used with a verb, adjective, or another adverb to tell when, where, how, what kind, or how much. **adverbial** *adj.*, **abverbially** *adv.*

ad-verse *adj.* Opposed; not helpful; against someone or something. **adverseness** *n.*, **adversely** *adv.*

ad-ver-si-ty *n.* Bad luck or misfortune.

ad-ver-tise *v.* To draw public attention to a product you wish to sell. **-er** *n.*

ad-ver-tise-ment *n.* A public notice designed to advertise something.

ad-ver-tis-ing *n.* The job of preparing advertisements for publication or broadcast.

ad-vice *n.* Suggestion or recommendation regarding a course of action or decision.

ad-vis-a-ble *adj.* Fit to be done or advised. **advisability**, **advisableness** *n.*

ad-vis-ed-ly *adv.* Deliberately; with consideration.

ad-vise-ment *n.* Careful thought and consideration.

ad-viser *n.* A person who gives an opinion or advises.

ad-vis-so-ry *adj.* Exercising or having the power to advise; giving or containing advice.

ad-vo-cate *v.* To write or speak in favor of or support. **advocate** *n.*

AEC *abbr.* Atomic Energy Commission.

a-e-des *n.* A mosquito that transmits yellow fever.

ae-gis *n.* Protection; support or sponsorship.

aer-ate *v.* To purify by exposing to the open air.

aer-i-al *adj.* Of or in the air; pertaining to aircraft. *n.* An antenna for television or radio. **aerially** *adv.*

aer-i-al-ist *n.* An acrobat who does stunts high above the ground on a wire or trapeze.

aer-ie *n.* The nest of a predatory bird, built on a cliff or other high places.

aer-o-bics *n.* Strenuous exercise that increases oxygen to the heart and lungs, therefore strengthening them.

aer-o-nau-tics *pl., n.* The science of designing and constructing aircraft. **aeronautic** *adj.*

aer-o-pause *n.* The region in the upper atmosphere where aircraft cannot fly.

aer-o-plane *n.* British word for airplane.

aer-o-sol *n.* A liquid substance under pressure within a metal container.

Ae-sop *n.* Greek writer of fables from the sixth century B.C.

aes-thet-ic *adj.* Having a love for beauty.

aes-thet-ics *n.* The study of the nature of beauty. **aesthetically** *adv.*

a-far *adv.* Far off; far away.

af-fa-ble *adj.* Good natured, easy to talk to; friendly. **affably** *adv.*

af-fair *n.* An event or happening; matters of business or public concern.

af-fect *v.* To move emotionally; to feel sympathetic or sad; to bring about a change in. **affecting, affected** *adj.*

af-fec-ta-tion *n.* Artificial behavior that is meant to impress others.

af-fec-tion *n.* A tender or fond feeling towards another.

af-fec-tion-ate *adj.* Loving and gentle. **affectionately** *adv.*

af-fi-da-vit *n.* A written statement by a person swearing that something is the truth.

af-fil-i-ate *v.* To join in, connect, or associate with. **affiliation** *n.*

af-fin-i-ty *n.* A special attraction with kinship; a natural attraction or liking.

af-firm *v.* To declare positively and be willing to stand by the truth. **affirmation** *n.*

af-firm-a-tive *adj.* Asserting the fact is true. **affirmative** *n.*

af-fix *n.* To attach; to fasten; to add at the end. *n.* A prefix or suffix added to a word.

af-flict *v.* To cause suffering or pain; to cause mental suffering. **affliction** *n.*

af-flu-ence *n.* Wealth; riches; abundance.

af-flu-ent *adj.* Prosperous; rich; having all the wealth or money needed.

af-ford *v.* To be able to provide; to have enough money to spare.

af-for-est *v.* To turn open land into forest. **afforestation** *n.*

af-fray *n.* Brawl or noisy fight.

af-front *v.* To insult one to his face; to confront.

af-ghan *n.* A crocheted or knitted cover in colorful designs.

a-field *adv.* Away from home or the usual path.

a-fire *adv.* Burning.

AFL-CIO *abbr.* American Federation of Labor and Congress of Industrial Organizations.

a-flame *adj.* Burning; in flames; glowing.

a-float *adv.* Floating on the surface of water; circulating.

a-flut-ter *adj.* Nervously excited.

a-foot *adj.* In the progress of happening; walking; on foot.

a-fore-men-tioned *adj.* Mentioned before.

a-fore-said *adj.* Having spoken of something before.

a-fore-thought *adj.* Premeditated; planned beforehand.

a-foul *adv.* Tangled; entangled in a collision.

a-fraid *adj.* Hesitant; filled with fear; reluctant.

a-fresh *adj.* Once more; again.

Af-ri-ca *n.* A continent located in the Eastern Hemisphere, south of Europe and between the Atlantic and Indian Oceans.

Af-ri-kaans *n.* The spoken language of the Republic of South Africa.

aft *adv.* At, close to, near, or toward the rear of an aircraft or stern of a ship.

af-ter *adv.* In the rear. *prep.* Following.

af-ter-birth *n.* The placenta and fetal matter released by the uterus after childbirth.

af-ter-ef-fect *n.* An effect coming after.

af-ter-math *n.* Consequence; result.

af-ter-thought *n.* An idea occurring later.

a-gain *adv.* Moreover; another time; once more.

a-gainst *prep.* In exchange for; in preparation for.

a-gape *adv.* With expectation; in wonder; open-mouthed.

ag-ate *n.* The type of quartz that has bands of colors.

a-ga-ve *n.* Fleshy-leaved tropical American plant.

age *n.* The length of time from beginning to a certain date; the time of life when a person has full legal rights; the age of 21. *v.* To grow or become old; to mature.

aged *adj.* Grown or become old. **agedness** *n.,* **agedly** *adv.*

age-ism *n.* Discrimination based on a person's age.

age-less *adj.* Existing forever; never seems to grow old.

a-gen-cy *n.* A business or service that acts for others; action; active influence; power.

a-gen-da *n.* Program or list of things to be done.

a-gent *n.* One who acts as the representative of another; one who acts or exerts power.

ag-gior-na-men-to *n.* Bringing up to date.

ag-glom-er-ate *v.* To collect; to form into a mass. **agglomerate** *n.*

ag-glu-ti-nate *v.* To join by adhesion; to cause red blood cells to clump together.

ag-glu-ti-nin *n.* A substance that causes agglutination; a group or mass formed by the union of separate elements.

ag-gran-dize *n.* To enlarge, to extend; to increase. **aggrandizement** *n.*

ag-gra-vate *v.* To annoy; to make worse.

ag-gre-gate *adj.* To gather together into a mass or whole. **aggregate** *adj.*

ag-gres-sion *n.* Hostile action or behavior; an unprovoked assault.

ag-gres-sive *adj.* Offensive; distressing; pushy; afflicting. **aggressiveness** *n.*

a-ghast *adj.* Appalled; struck with amazement.

ag-ile *adj.* Marked by the ability to move quickly and easily; nimble. **agility** *n.*

ag-itate *v.* To disturb; to upset; to stir or move with violence; to try to arouse the public interest. **-ion, -or** *n.*

a-gleam *adj.* Gleaming.

a-glim-mer *adv.* Glimmering.

a-glitter *adj.* Glittering.

a-glow *adj.* Glowing.

ag-nos-tic *n.* One who doubts that there is a God or life hereafter. **-ism** *n.*

a-go *adj. & adv.* In the past; gone by.

a-gog *adj.* Excited; eagerly expectant.

ag-o-nize *v.* To afflict with great anguish or to suffer. **agonized, agonizing** *adj.*

ag-o-ny *n., pl.* **-nies** Intense mental distress or physical pain; anguish.

ag-o-ra-pho-bi-a *n.* Fear of open spaces.

agr *or* **agric** *abbr.* Agricultural; agriculture.

a-grar-i-an *adj.* Pertaining to or of land and its ownership; pertaining to farming; agricultural.

a-gree *v.* To give assent; to consent; to share an understanding or opinion; to be beneficial or suitable; to correspond.

a-gree-a-ble *adj.* Pleasant; pleasing; willing; ready to consent. **agreeableness** *n.*, **agreeably** *adv.*

a-gree-ment *n.* Harmony; concord; state or act of agreeing.

ag-ri-busi-ness *n.* Big business farming, embracing the product, distribution, and processing of farm products and the manufacture of farm equipment.

ag-ri-cul-ture *n.* Raising of livestock; farming and cultivating the crops. **agriculturalist, agriculturist** *n.*

a-ground *adv. & adj.* Stranded; on the ground; to run ashore; beached.

a-gue *n.* Fever accompanied by chills or shivering and sweating. **aguish** *adj.*

a-head *adv.* Before; in advance; to or at the front of something.

a-hoy *interj.* A nautical call or greeting.

aid *v.* To give help or assistance. **-er** *n.*

AIDS *n.* Disease that destroys the body's immunological system; Acquired Immune Deficiency Syndrome.

ail *v.* To feel sick; to make ill or uneasy. **ailing** *adj.*

ai-lan-thus *n.* A tree with numerous pointed leaves.

ai-ler-on *v.* Movable control flap on the trailing edge of an airplane wing.

ail-ment *n.* A mild illness.

aim *v.* To direct a weapon; to direct purpose. *n.* Intention.

aim-less *adj.* Lacking of purpose.

ain't *contr.* Am not, are not, is not, has not, or have not.

ai-o-li *n.* Rich garlic flavored mayonnaise.

air *n.* An odorless, tasteless, colorless, gaseous mixture; primarily composed of nitrogen (78%) and oxygen (21%); the sky; a breeze. **on the air** Broadcast.

air-borne *adj.* Carried through or by the air.

air brake *n.* Brake operated by the power of compressed air.

air-brush *n.* Machine using compressed air to spray paint and other liquids on a surface.

air con-di-tion-er *n.* Equipment used to lower the temperature and humidity of an enclosure.

air-craft *n.* A machine that flies, such as a helicopter, airplane, or glider.

air-craft car-rier *n.* A large ship which carries airplanes on which they can be landed and launched.

air-crew *n.* A crew that mans an airplane.

air-drop *n.* Delivery of supplies made by parachute from an airplane while in flight.

air-dry *v.* To dry by exposing to the air.

air-field *n.* Paved runways at an airport; landing strip.

air-flow *n.*

The motion of air around a body as relative to the surface of a body immersed in it.

air-foil *n.* Part of an airplane which controls stability, lift, thrust, etc.

Air Force *n.* Aviation branch of armed forces.

air-frame *n.* The structure of a rocket or airplane without an engine.

air-freight *n.* Freight that is transported from one location to another by air.

air gun *n.* Gun which is operated by compressed air.

air-hole *n.* A hole that is used to discharge or admit air into an area.

air-ing *n.* Exposing something in the open air.

air lane *n.* The regular route of travel for airplanes.

air letter *n.* A letter that is transmitted by means of an aircraft.

air-lift *n.* System of transporting supplies or troops by air when ground routes are blocked.

air-line *n.* An air transportation company or system.

air-lin-er *n.* A large passenger airline.

air lock *n.* Airtight compartment between regions of unequal pressure.

air-mail & air mail *n.* Mail sent by means of air.

air-man *n.* A person enlisted in the air force.

air-man-ship *n.* The skill in navigating or piloting an airplane.

air-plane *n.* A vehicle capable of flight, heavier than air, and propelled by jet engines or propellers.

air pocket *n.* A condition in the atmosphere that can cause an airplane to loose altitude quickly.

air-port *n.* A terminal station for passengers where aircraft take off and land.

air raid *n.* Bombing attack by military aircraft.

air-ship *n.* Dirigible; a self-propelled lighter-than-air aircraft.

air-sick-ness *n.* Nausea resulting from flight in an aircraft. **airsick** *adj.*

air--speed *n.* Speed of an aircraft while airborne.

air-strip *n.* Concrete runway on an airfield; minimally equipped airfield.

air-tight *adj.* Impermeable by air or gas. **airtightness** *n.*

air-wave *n.* The medium of television and radio transmission and communication.

air-wor-thy *adj.* Fit to fly. **-iness** *n.*

air-y *adj.* Open to the air; breezy; light as air; graceful or delicate. **airiness** *n.*, **airily** *adv.*

aisle *n.* Passageway between rows of seats, as in a church, auditorium, or airplane. **aisled** *adj.*

a-jar *adv. & adj.* Partially opened.

a-kim-bo *adj. & adv.* Bent; with a crook.

a-kin *adj.* Related, as in family; similar in quality or character.

al-a-bas-ter *n.* A dense, translucent, tinted or white, fine-grained gypsum. **alabastrine** *adj.*

a la carte *n.* Separate price for each item on the menu.

a-lack *interj.* An exclamation expressive of sorrow.

a-lac-ri-ty *n.* Readiness; cheerfulness; eagerness; briskness.

a la mode *n.* Served with ice cream, as pie; fashionable.

a-larm *n.* A warning of danger; sudden feeling of fear; the bell or buzzer of a clock. *v.* To frighten or warn by an alarm. **alarming** *adv.*, **alarmingly** *adj.*

a-larm-ist *n.* Someone who needlessly alarms others. **alarmism** *n.*

a-las *interj.* Expressive of anxiety or regret.

a-late *or* **alated** *adj.* Winged; having wings. **alation** *n.*

alb *n.* White linen robe worn by clergy during Mass.

al-ba-core *n.* Large marine fish; major source of canned tuna.

al-ba-tross *n.* Large, web-footed, long-winged sea bird.

al-be-it *conj.* Although; even though.

al-bi-no *n.* An animal or person with an abnormal whiteness of the skin and hair and pink colored eyes.

al-bum *n.* A book for photographs, autographs, stamps; a book of collections.

al-bu-men *n.* White of an egg.

al-bu-min *n.* Several proteins found in the white of eggs, blood serum, milk, and plant and animal tissue.

al-bu-min-ous *adj.* Relating to, having the properties of or containing albumen.

al-caz-ar *n.* A Spanish fortress or palace.

al-che-my *n.* Traditional chemical philosophy concerned primarily with changing base metals into gold.

al-co-hol *n.* Intoxicating liquor containing alcohol; ethanol; a series of related organic compounds.

al-co-hol-ic *adj.* Resulting from alcohol; containing or preserved in alcohol; suffering from alcoholism. **alcoholic** *n.*

al-co-hol-ism *n.* Excessive alcohol consumption; a habit or addiction.

al-co-hol-ize *v.* Saturate or treat something with alcohol.

al-cove *n.* Recess or partly enclosed extension of a room.

al-de-hyde *n.* Any of a class of highly reactive compounds obtained by oxidation of alcohols.

al-der *n.* Tree of the birch family, grows in marshy soil.

al-der-man *n.* Member of a municipal legislative body.

ale *n.* Beverage similar to, but more bitter than beer, made from malt by fermentation.

a-lem-bic *n.* A glass or metal vessel formerly used in distillation.

a-lert *adj.* Vigilant; brisk; watchful; active. *n.* A signal by siren of air attack. **alertly** *adv.*, **alertness** *n.*

al-ex-an-drine *n.* Line of English verse in iambic hexameter; probably from poems dealing with Alexander the Great.

al-fal-fa *n.* Plant with purple flowers, widely resembling the clover widely grown for forage.

al-fres-co *adv. & adj.* In the fresh air; outside.

al-gae *pl., n.* Various primitive, chiefly aquatic, one-celled or multicellular plants, as the seaweed.

al-ge-bra *n.* Generalization of math in which symbols represent members of a specified set of numbers and are related by operations that hold for all numbers in the set. **algebraic**, **algebraically** *adv.*, **algebraist** *n.*

a-li-as *n., pl.* aliases Assumed name. *adv.* Otherwise known as.

al-i-bi *n.* A form of defense, an attempt by a defendant to prove he was elsewhere when a crime was committed; an excuse.

a-li-en *adj.* Owing allegiance to a government or country, not one's own; unfamiliar; repugnant; a member of another region, or country. *n.* A stranger; a foreigner.

al-ien-a-ble *adj.* Able to be transferred to the ownership of another. **-bility** *n.*

al-ien-ate v. To cause to become indifferent or unfriendly. **alienation** n.

al-ien-ist n. A psychiatrist accepted by a court as an expert on mental stability.

a-light v. To settle; to come down; to dismount. adj. or adv. Burning, lighted.

a-lign v. To arrange in a line; to take one side of an argument or cause. **aline** v.

a-lign-ment or **alinement** n. Arrange or position in a straight line.

a-like adj. Similar, having close resemblance. adv. In the same manner, way, or degree.

al-i-ment n. Nourishment; food. **alimentation** n., **alimental** adj.

al-i-men-ta-ry adj. Pertaining to nutrition or food.

al-i-men-ta-ry canal n. The tube of the digestive system from the mouth to the anus, including the pharynx, esophagus, stomach, and intestines.

al-i-men-ta-tion n. The process or act of affording nutriment. -tive adj.

al-i-mo-ny n., pl. -nies Court ordered allowance for support, usually given by a man to his former wife following a divorce or legal separation.

A-line adj. Having a close-fitting top and a flared bottom.

al-i-phat-ic adj. Having to do with organic chemical compounds where the carbon atoms are linked in open chains.

a-live adj. Living; having life; in existence or effect; full of life. -ness n.

a-li-yah n. Immigration of Jewish people to Israel.

a-liz-a-rin n. A red-orange compound used in dyes.

al-ka-li n., pl. -lies or -lis A hydroxide or carbonate of an alkali metal, whose aqueous solution is slippery, bitter, caustic, and basic in reactions.

al-ka-li metal n. Any of the mostly basic metals comprising lithium, sodium, potassium, francium, etc.

al-ka-line adj. Of, relating to, or containing an alkali. **alkalinity** n.

al-ka-lin-ize adj. To make alkaline.

al-ka-loid n. Any of various nitrogen containing organic bases obtained from plants. **alkaloidal** adj.

al-ka-lo-sis n. Unusually high alkali content in the blood and tissues.

all adj. Total extent or total entity; being a whole number, amount, or quantity; every.

Al-lah n. The Moslem supreme being.

all-a-round n. Variance of all-round.

al-lay v. To relieve; to lessen; to calm; to pacify. **allayer** n.

al-le-ga-tion n. The act or result of alleging.

al-lege v. To affirm; to assert to be true; to declare without proof.

Al-le-ghe-ny Mountains n. Section of the Appalachians extending from Pennsylvania to Virginia.

al-le-giance n. Loyalty to one's nation, cause, or sovereign; obligations of a vassal to an overlord. **allegiant** adj.

al-le-go-ry n., pl. -ries A dramatic, literary, or pictorial device in which each object, character, and event symbolically illustrates a moral or religious principle. **allegoric**, **allegorical** adj., -ally adv., -ist n.

al-le-gret-to adv., Mus. Slower than allegro but faster than andante. **allegretto** adj.

al-le-gro adv., Mus. Faster than allegretto but slower than presto. **allegro** adj. & n.

al-lele n. Any of a group of possible mutational forms of a gene. **allelic** adj., **allelism** n.

al-le-lu-ia interj. Expressing praise to God or of thanksgiving.

al-ler-gen n. Substance which causes an allergy. **allergenic** adj.

al-ler-gist n. A doctor specializing in allergies.

al-ler-gy n. -gies Pathological or abnormal reaction to environmental substances, as foods, dust, pollens, or microorganisms. **allergic** adj.

al-le-vi-ate v. To make more bearable. **alleviation**, **alleviator** n.

al-ley n., pl. -leys Narrow passageway between or behind buildings.

al-li-ance n. A union, relationship, or connection by kinship, marriage, or common interest; a confederation of nations by a formal treaty; an affinity.

al-li-ga-tor n. Large amphibious reptile with very sharp teeth, powerful jaws, and a shorter snout than the related crocodile.

al-li-ga-tor pear n. An avocado.

al-lit-er-ate v. To arrange or form words beginning with the same sound. -or n.

al-lit-er-a-tion n. Occurrence of two or more words having the same initial sound. **alliterative** adj.

al-lo-cate v. To assign; to allot. **allocation** n.

al-lot v. To distribute or set aside as a share of something. -ment, **allotter** n.

all out adv. With every possible effort or resource.

al-low v. To make a provision for, to permit; to permit to have; to admit; to concede allowable adj., **allowably** adv.

al-low-ance n. The act of allowing something, a regular amount of money, food, etc.; a price discount.

al-loy v. Something that has been added to; item reduced purity or value.

all right adj. Meets satisfaction, certainly. adv. Satisfactory; correct; unhurt. adj., Slang Good; of sound character; dependable.

all-round adj. Versatile, including all aspects.

all-spice n. Tropical American tree bearing aromatic berries, used as a spice.

all-star adj. Composed entirely of star performers.

all-time adj. Of all time.

all told adv. Everything taken into account.

al-lude n. To refer to something indirectly. **allusion** n., **allusive** adj., allusively *adv.*

al-lure *v.* To entice; to tempt. *n.* Attraction; charm; enticement; the prospect of attracting.

allurement, allurer *n.*, alluringly *adv.*

al-lu-sion *n.* The act of referring to something indirectly; an hint.

al-lu-vi-um *n.* Sediment deposited by flowing water as in a river bed.

alluvial *adj.*

al-ly *v.* To connect or unite in a formal or close relationship or bond. *n.* One united with another in a formal or personal relationship.

al-ma ma-ter *n.* College, school, or university one has attended; the anthem of that college, school, or university.

al-ma-nac *n.* Annual publication having calendars with weather forecasts, astronomical information, and other useful facts.

al-might-y *adj.* Having absolute power. Almighty *n.* The Almighty God.

al-mond *n.* An oval, edible nut with a soft, light-brown shell; tree bearing such nuts.

al-most *adv.* Not quite; slightly short of.

alms *pl., n.* Goods or money given to the poor in charity.

alms-house *n.* A poorhouse.

al-oe *n.* Any of various mostly African plants having fleshy, spiny-toothed leaves; a cathartic drug made from the juice of the leaves of this plant.

a-loft *adv.* Toward the upper rigging of a ship; in or into a high place; in the air.

a-lo-ha *interj.* Hawaiian expression of greeting or farewell.

a-lone *adj.* Away from other people; single; solitary; excluding anyone or anything else; with nothing further; sole; only. alone *adv.*

a-long *adv.* In a line with; following the length or path; in association; together; as a companion.

a-long-shore *adv.* Near, along, or by the shore, either on land or in the water.

a-long-side *adv.* Along, at, near, or to the side of; side by side with.

a-loof *adj.* Indifferent; distant.

aloofness *n.*, aloofly *adv.*

a-loud *adv.* Orally; audibly.

alp *n.* High mountain.

al-pac-a *n.* South American mammal related to the llama; the wool of the alpaca.

al-pen-horn *n.* Long curved horn used to call cows to pasture.

al-pen-stock *n.* Long staff with an iron point used by mountain climbers.

al-pha *n.* First letter of the Greek alphabet.

al-pha-bet *n.* The letters of a language, arranged in an order fixed by custom.

al-pha-bet-i-cal *adj.* Arranged in the traditional order of the letters of a language. alphabetically *adv.*

al-pha-bet-ize *v.* To arrange in alphabetical order.

al-pha de-cay *n.* Decay of an atomic

nucleus as it emits an alpha particle.

Al-pha ray *n.* A stream of alpha particles.

Alps *n.* The major mountain system of south-central Europe, forming an arc from Southern France to Albania.

al-read-y *adv.* By this or a specified time.

al-so *adv.* Likewise; besides; in addition.

al-so-ran *n.* One defeated in a competition.

alt *abbr.* Alteration; alternate; altitude.

Al-ta-ic *adj.* A language family of Europe and Asia. Altaian *n.*

al-tar *n.* An elevated structure before which religious ceremonies may be held or sacrifices offered.

al-tar-piece *n.* A carving or painting placed above and behind an altar.

al-ter *v.* To make change or become different; to modify; to castrate or spay, as an animal. -ability, alteration *n.*

al-ter-a-tive *adj.* Tending to alter or produce alterations.

al-ter-ca-tion *n.* Noisy and heated quarrel.

al-ter e-go *v.* An intimate friend; another aspect of oneself.

al-ter-nate *v.* To happen or follow in turn; to occur in successive turns. *n.* Substitute.

alternately *adv.*, alternation *n.*

al-ter-nat-ing cur-rent *n.* Electric current that reverses direction at regular intervals.

al-ter-na-tive *n.* A choice between two or more possibilities; one of the possibilities to be chosen. -ly *adv.*

al-ter-na-tive *adj.* Allowing a choice.

al-ter-na-tor *n.* Electric generator producing alternating current.

al-though *conj.* Even though.

al-tim-e-ter *n.* Instrument for measuring and indicating altitude.

al-ti-tude *n.* The height of a thing above a reference level; above the earth's surface; above sea level.

al-to *n.* Low female singing voice; the range between soprano and tenor.

al-to-geth-er *adv.* Entirely; with all included or counted.

al-tru-ism *n.* Selfless concern for the welfare of others. altruist *n.*,

altruistic *adj.*, altruistically *adv.*

al-um *n.* Any one of several similar double sulfates.

a-lu-mi-na *n.* Any of several forms of aluminum oxide.

a-lu-mi-num *n.* A silvery-white, ductile metallic element used to form many hard, light, corrosion resistant alloys.

a-lum-na *n., pl.* -nae Female graduate or former student of a school, college, or university.

a-lum-nus *n., pl.* -ni A male graduate or former student of a school, college, or university.

al-ways *adv.* Continuously; forever; on every occasion; at all times.

am *n.* First person, singular, present tense of be.

AM *abbr.* Ante meridian, Latin for "before noon".

AMA *abbr.* American Medical Association.

a-mal-gam *n.* An alloy of mercury with other metals, as with tin or silver; a blend of diverse elements. **amalgramable** *adj.*

a-mal-ga-mate *v.* To mix so as to make a unified whole; to blend. **amalgamation, amalgamator** *n.*

a-man-dine *adj.* Made or garnished with almonds.

am-a-ranth *n.* Various weedy plants with greenish or purplish flowers; an imaginary flower that never fades. **amaranthine** *adj.*

am-a-ryl-lis *n.* A bulbous plant with large, lily-like, reddish or white flowers.

am-a-teur *n.* One who engages in an activity as a pastime rather than as a profession; one who lacks expertise. **amateurish** *adj.,* **amateurism** *n.*

am-a-to-ry *adj.* Of or expressive of sexual love.

a-maze *v.* To astound; to affect with surprise or wonder. **amazingly** *adv.,* **amazedness, -ment** *n.,* **amazing** *adj.*

Am-a-zon *n.* Member of a nation of female warriors in a region near the Black Sea; a tall vigorous, aggressive woman.

Am-a-zon *n.* A river of South America, beginning in the Andes and flowing through North Brazil to the Atlantic.

amb *abbr.* Ambassador.

am-bass-a-dor *n.* Official representative of the highest rank, accredited by one government to another. **ambassadorial** *adj.,* **-ship.** *n.*

am-ber *n.* A hard, translucent, yellow, brownish-yellow, or orange fossil resin, used for jewelry and ornaments; medium to dark orange yellow.

am-ber-gris *n.* A waxy, grayish substance produced by sperm whales, and used in making perfumes.

am-bi-ance *n.* Environment; atmosphere.

am-bi-dex-trous *adj.* Able to use both hands with equal facility.

am-bi-ent *adj.* Surrounding.

am-big-u-ous *adj.* Doubtful; uncertain. **ambiguousness** *n.,* **ambiguously** *adv.*

am-bi-tion *n.* Strong desire to achieve; will to succeed; the goal or object desired.

am-bi-tious *adj.* Challenging. **ambitiousness** *n.,* **ambitiously** *adv.*

am-biv-a-lence *n.* Existence of mutually different feelings about a person or thing.

am-ble *v.* To move at a leisurely pace. **ambler** *n.*

am-bro-sia *n.* Food of the Greek Gods and immortals; food having exquisite flavor or fragrance. **ambrosial** *adj.*

am-bu-lance *n.* Vehicle equipped to transport the injured or sick.

am-bu-la-to-ry *adj.* Moving about; movable; or to do with walking.

am-bus-cade *n.* Ambush.

am-bush *n.* Surprise attack made from a hidden position. **ambush** *v.,*

ambusher, ambushment *n.*

A-me-ba also **Amoeba** *n.*

Single-celled semifluid living animal

a-me-lio-rate *v.* To become or make better. **ameliorator, amelioration** *n.,* **ameliorative** *adj.*

a-men *interj.* Used at the end of a prayer to express solemn approval.

a-me-na-ble *adj.* Responsive; tractable; accountable. **amenableness, amenability** *n.*

a-mend *v.* To correct; to improve; to rectify. **amendable** *adj.,* **amender** *n.*

a-mend-ment *n.* Correction, reformation or improvement; the parliamentary procedure where such alteration is made.

a-mends *pl., n.* Compensation for insult or injury.

a-men-i-ty *n., pl.* **-ties** Agreeableness; means of comfort or convenience.

Amer *abbr.* America; American.

a-merce *v.* To punish. **amercment** *n.*

America *n.* United States of America; North America; South America.

A-mer-ica-n *n.* A native of one of the Americas or a U.S. citizen.

American eagle *n.* The bald eagle.

A-mer-i-can-ism *n.* Language usage, trait, or tradition of the U.S.

American plan *n.* A hotel plan where a guest is charged a fixed daily rate for service, room, and meals.

Am-er-ind *n.* American Indian or an Eskimo.

am-e-thyst *n.* Violet or purple form of transparent corundum or quartz, used as a gemstone. **amethystine** *adj.*

a-mi-a-ble *adj.* Friendly and pleasant. **amiableness, amiability** *n.,* **-ly** *adv.*

am-i-ca-ble *adj.* Harmonious; friendly. **amicability, amicableness** *n.,* **-ly** *adv.*

a-mid *prep.* In the middle of; surrounded by.

a-mid-ships *adv.* Halfway between the bow and the stern.

a-midst *prep.* In the middle of; surrounded by; during.

a-mi-go *n.* A friend.

A-mish *pl., n.* Mennonites that settled mostly in southeastern Pennsylvania in the late 1600's. **Amish** *adj.*

a-miss *adj.* Out of order or place; in an improper or wrong way.

am-i-ty *n.* Relationships that are friendly, as between two states.

am-me-ter *n.* A tool measuring electric current.

am-mo *n.* Ammunition.

am-mo-nia *n.* Colorless, pungent gas.

am-mo-nium hy-drox-ide *n.* A colorless, basic aqueous solution of ammonia.

am-mu-ni-tion *n.* Projectiles that can be propelled or discharged from guns; any means of defense.

am-ne-sia *n.* The loss of memory. **-iac** *n.*

am-nes-ty *n., pl.* **-ties** Pardon for political offenders.

a-moe-ba *n., pl.* **-bas** *or* **-bae** Various

minute one-celled organisms having an indefinite, changeable form. **amoebic** *adj.*

a-mong *prep.* In or through the midst of; between one another.

a-mon-til-la-do *n., pl.* **-dos** A pale, dry sherry.

a-mor-al *adj.* Neither moral nor immoral. **amorality** *n.*, **amorally** *adv.*

am-o-rous *adj.* Inclined to or indicative of sexual love. **amorousness** *n.*

a-mor-phous *adj.* Lacking definite form; shapeless; general; vague.

am-or-tize *v.* To liquidate a loan by installment payments; a loan. **-tion** *n.*

a-mount *n.* Aggregate, sum or total quantity. *v.* To be equivalent.

a-mour *n.* A forbidden love affair.

a-mour--pro-pre *n.* Self-respect.

am-per-age *n.* Strength of an electric current, expressed in amperes.

am-pere *n.* Unit of electric current equal to a flow of one amp per second.

am-per-sand *n.* The character or sign that represents and (&).

am-phet-a-mine *n.* Colorless volatile liquid; a drug.

amphi *prefix.* Around, on both sides, all around on all sides.

am-phib-i-an *n.* An organism, as a frog or toad, developing from an aquatic state into an air-breathing state; aircraft that can take off and land on land or water; a vehicle that can take off or land on land or water.

am-phi-the-a-ter *n.* A round or oval building having tiers of seats rising around an arena.

am-pho-ra *n., pl.* **-rae** *or* **-ras** Ancient Greek jar with two handles and a narrow neck, used to carry oil or wine.

am-ple *adj.* Sufficient; abundant; large. **ampleness** *n.*, **amply** *adv.*

am-pli-tude *n.* Maximum value of a periodically varying quantity; greatness of size; fullness.

am-pli-tude mod-u-la-tion *n.* The encoding of a carrier wave by variation of its amplitude in accordance with a signal.

am-pul *or* **am-pule** *n.* A small, sealed vial containing a hypodermic injection solution.

am-pu-tate *v.* To cut off; to remove, as a limb from one's body. **amputation** *n.*

am-pu-tee *n.* A person who has had one or more limbs amputated.

amt *abbr.* Amount.

amu *n., Phys.* Atomic mass unit.

a-muck *adv.* In an uncontrolled manner; a murderous frenzy; out of control.

am-u-let *n.* A charm worn as protection against evil or injury.

A-mur *n.* A river of East Asia.

a-muse *v.* To entertain in an agreeable, pleasing way. **-ment** *n.*, **amusable** *adj.*

an *adj.* One; one sort of; each; form of "a" used before words beginning with a vowel or with an unpronounced "h" as an elephant or honor.

a-nach-ro-nism *n.* Connecting of a thing, of a person or happening with another that came alter in history; anything that seems to be out of place in history.

an-a-con-da *n.* A large tropical American snake which kills its prey by crushing it to death in its coils.

an-a-dem *n.* A wreath for the head.

an-ad-ro-mous *adj.* Migrating up river from the sea to breed in fresh water, as a salmon.

a-nae-mi-a *n.* Variant of anemia.

an-aes-the-sia *n.* Variant of anesthesia.

an-a-gram *n.* Word formed by transposing the letters of another word. **anagrammatical, anagrammatic** *adj.*

a-nal *adj.* Of or relating to the anus.

anal *abbr.* Analogous; analogy; analysis; analytic.

an-al-ge-sia *n.* Inability to feel pain while awake. **analgesic** *adj. & n.*

an-al-og com-puter *n.* A computer where numerical data are represented by measurable quantities as lengths, electrical signals, or voltage.

a-nal-o-gous *adj.* Similar; corresponding in certain ways. **analogously** *adv.*

an-a-logue *n.* Something that bears resemblance to something else.

a-nal-o-gy *n., pl.* **-gies** Connection between things that are otherwise dissimilar; a conclusion or opinion that if two things are alike in some respects they must be alike in others.

a-nal-y-sis *n.* Breaking up or separation of something into its parts so as to examine them and see how they fit together; result.

an-a-lyst *n.* A person who analyzes or who is skilled in analysis.

an-a-lyze *v.* To make an analysis of.

an-a-pest *n.* Metrical foot make up of two short syllables followed by one long one. **anapestic** *adj.*

an-ar-chic *adj.* Of, like, or promoting confusion or disorder.

an-ar-chism *n.* Belief that all forms of government act in an unfair way against the liberty of a person and should be done away with.

an-ar-chy *n.* Lack of political authority, disorder and confusion; the absence of any purpose or standard.

a-nas-to-mo-sis *n.* Connection or union of branches, as of rivers, leaf veins, or blood vessels. **anastomotic** *adj.*

a-nas-tro-phe *n.* Changing the normal syntactic order of words.

a-nath-e-ma *n.* Curse; ban; or excommunication. **anathematize** *v.*

a-nat-o-mize *v.* To examine in great detail; to analyze; in biology, to dissect. **anatomization** *n.*

a-nat-o-my *n., pl.* **-mies** Structure of an organ or organism; a detailed analysis. **anatomical, anatomic** *adj.*

an-ces-try *n., pl.* **-tries** Line of descent; lineage ancestors collectively.

an-ces-tor *n.* A person who comes before one in a family line; someone earlier than a grandparent; forefather. **ancestral** *adj.*

an-chor *n.*

Heavy metal device lowered into the water by a chain to keep a ship from drifting. *v.* To attach or fix firmly.

an-chor-age *n.* A place for anchoring a ship; a strong support that keeps something steady.

an-cho-rite *n.* A religious hermit.

anchor man *n.* The main member of a team of newscasters.

an-cho-vy *n.*

A very small fish of the herring family; usually salted, canned in oil, and used for making sauces and relishes.

an-cient *adj.* Anything belonging to the early history of people; very old. **ancientness** *n.*, **anciently** *adv.*

and *conj.* Together with; along with; as well as; added to; as a result; plus; also.

an-dan-te *adv.*, *Mus.* Rather slow in tempo. **andante** *adj.*

an-dan-ti-no *adj.*, *Mus.* Slightly faster in tempo than andante.

An-des *n.* A mountain system stretching the length of west South American, from Venezuela to Tierra del Fuego.

and-i-ron *n.* Heavy metal support for logs or wood in a fireplace.

andr *n.* The male sex; masculine.

an-dro-gen *n.* Hormone that develops and maintains masculine characteristics. **androgenic** *adj.*

an-drog-y-nous *adj.* Having the characteristics or nature of both male and female; having both staminate and pistillate flowers in the same cluster with the male flowers uppermost. **androgynal**, **androgyny** *n.*

an-droid *n.* In science fiction; a synthetic man made to look like a human being.

an-ec-dote *n.* Short account of a story of some happening or about some person. **anecdotal**, **-tic** *adj.*, **anecdotist** *n.*

an-echo-ic *adj.* Neither having or producing echoes.

a-ne-mi-a *n.* The condition in which a person's blood does not have enough red corpuscles or hemoglobin and, therefore, does not carry a normal amount of oxygen.

a-ne-mic *adj.* Of or having anemia.

an-e-mom-e-ter *n.* Instrument for measuring wind force and speed.

a-nem-o-ne *n.* A plant with purple, white, or red cup-shaped flowers.

a-nent *prep.* Regarding; concerning.

an-es-the-sia *n.* Condition in which one has no feeling of heat, touch, or pain in all or part of the body.

an-es-the-si-ol-o-gy *n.* The medical study and use of anesthetics. **-ist** *n.*

an-es-thet-ic *adj.* Taking away the feeling of pain. *n.* Drug, gas, etc. used to bring on anesthesia before surgery. **-ally** *adv.*

an-es-the-tize *v.* To bring on unconsciousness by giving anesthetics; to remove the capacity to feel pain in a localized area.

a-new *adv.* Again; once more; in a new way.

an-gel *n.* An immortal being attendant upon God; a very kind and lovable person; a helping or guiding spirit. **angelic** *adj.*

an-gel-fish *n.* Several tropical fishes with a flattened body.

an-gel-i-ca *n.* A plant with aromatic seed, used as flavoring.

an-ger *n.* Feeling of extreme hostility; rage; wanting to fight back.

an-gi-na *n.* A disease marked by painful choking spasms and attacks of suffocation pain. **anginous**, **anginose** *adj.*, **anginal** *adj.*

angina pec-to-ris *n.* Severe pain in the chest, associated with feelings of apprehension and suffocation.

an-gle *v.*

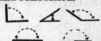

A shape made by two straight lines meeting in a point or two surfaces meeting along a line.

an-gle-worm *n.* Earthworm, used as fishing bait.

An-gli-can *n.* Member of the church of England or any of its related churches.

an-gli-cize *v.* To make English in form, idiom, or character. **anglicization** *n.*

an-gling *n.* The act of fishing with a hook and line.

An-glo *n.* A root word meaning "English".

An-glo--Sax-on *n.* A member of one of the Germanic peoples who settled in Britain in the 5th and 6th centuries A.D.

an-go-ra *n.* The long silky hair of the Angora rabbit or Angora goat; yarn or fabric made from the hair of an Angora goat or rabbit.

an-gry *adj.* Feeling or showing anger; having a menacing aspect; inflamed. **angrily** *adv.*

an-guish *n.* Great suffering, from worry, grief, or pain; agony.

an-gu-lar *adj.* Having angles or sharp corners; measured by an angle or degrees of an arc; gaunt, bony, lean. **angularity** *n.*, **angularly** *adv.*

an-hy-dride *n.* Chemical compound formed from another by removing the water.

an-hy-drous *adj.* Does not contain any water.

an-i-line *n.* Colorless, oily, poisonous liquid, used to make rubber, dyes, resins, pharmaceuticals, and varnishes.

an-i-mad-vert *v.* To comment with disapproval. **animadversion** *n.*

an-i-mal *n.* Any being other than a human being; any four-footed creature; beast. **animalize** *v.*

an-i-mal-cule *n.* Microscopic or minute

animal.

an-i-mate *v.* To give liveliness, life or spirit to; to cause to act; to inspire. animatedly *adv.*, animation *n.*

a-ni-ma-to *adv.*, *Mus.* In a lively or animated manner; used as a direction. animato *adj.*

an-i-ma-tor *n.* One who animates, such as an artist or technician who produces an animation, as a cartoon.

an-i-mism *n.* A belief in primitive tribes that natural objects and forces have souls. animist *n.*, animistic *adj.*

an-i-mos-i-ty *n.*, *pl.* -ties Hostility; bitterness; hatred.

an-i-mus *n.* Feeling of animosity.

an-i-on *n.* An ion with a negative charge that is attracted to an anode; electrolysis.

an-ise *n.* A plant with yellowish-white flower clusters and licorice-flavored seeds; aniseed.

an-i-seed *n.* Seed used for flavoring and in medicine.

an-i-sette *n.* Anise-flavored liqueur.

an-kle *n.* Joint that connects the foot with the leg; slender section of the leg immediately above this joint.

an-klet *n.* A short sock, an ornament worn around the ankle.

ann *abbr.* Annals; annual; annuity.

an-nals *pl.*, *n.* Descriptive record; history. annalist *n.*

an-neal *v.* To heat and then cool glass slowly to make it less brittle.

an-nex *v.* To add or join a smaller thing to a larger one. annexation *n.*

an-ni-hi-late *v.* To destroy completely; totally. annihilator, annihilation *n.*

an-ni-ver-sa-ry *n.*, *pl.* -ries The date on which something happened at an earlier time; this event celebrated on this date each year.

an-no-tate *v.* To use notes to give one's opinions. annotation, annotator *n.*, annotative *adj.*

an-nounce *v.* To proclaim; to give notice. announcement *n.*

an-nounc-er *n.* A performer on radio or television who provides program continuity and gives commercial and other points of interest.

an-noy *v.* To bother; to irritate; to make slightly angry. -ing *adj.*, -ingly *adv.*

an-noy-ance *n.* A nuisance; irritation; act of annoying.

an-nu-al *adj.* Recurring or done at the same time each year; a yearly publication, as a yearbook. annually *adv.*

an-nu-i-tant *n.* Person who receives an annuity.

an-nu-i-ty *n.*, *pl.* -ties Annual payment of an income or allowance.

an-nul *v.* To cancel a marriage or a law; to do away with; to put an end to. annullable *adj.*, annulment *n.*

an-nu-lar *adj.* Shaped like or forming a ring. annularity *n.*, annularly *adv.*

an-nun-ci-ate *v.* To proclaim; to announce.

an-nun-ci-a-tion *n.* An announcement; the act of announcing.

an-ode *n.* Positively charged electrode. anodic *adj.*, anodically *adv.*

an-o-dize *v.* To coat a metallic surface by electrolysis with a protective oxide.

a-noint *v.* To apply oil in a religious ceremony. anointer, anointment *n.*

a-nomaly *n.*, *pl.* -lies Anything irregular or abnormal. anomalistic, -lous *adj.*

a-non *adv.* Soon; in a short period of time.

a-non-y-mous *adj.* An unknown or withheld name, agency. anonymity, anonymousness *n.*, anonymously *adv.*

an-oth-er *adj.* Additional; one more different, but of the same character.

ans *abbr.* Answer.

an-swer *n.* A written or spoken reply, as to a question; a result or solution, as to a problem. *v.* To respond correctly; to be responsible for. answerable *adj.*

ant *n.*

A small insect, usually without wings; which lives in or on the ground, or in wood in large colonies.

ant *abbr.* Antenna; antonym.

ant-ac-id *n.* A substance which neutralizes or weakens acids.

an-tag-o-nism *n.* Hostility; condition of being against; the feeling of unfriendliness toward.

an-tag-o-nize *v.* To arouse hostility; to make an enemy of someone.

Ant-arc-tic *n.* Large area of land completely covered with ice; the South Pole.

ant-eat-er *n.* Animal with a long snout and a long, sticky tongue, feeding mainly on ants.

an-te-ce-dent *adj.* One event that precedes another; previous.

an-te-date *v.* To precede in time; to give an earlier date than the actual date.

an-te-lope *n.* A slender, long-horned, swift-running, hoofed mammal.

an-te me-rid-i-em *n.* Time before noon, abbreviated as "A.M.".

an-ten-na *n.*, *pl.* -nae Slender feelers on the head of an insect, lobster, crab, etc.; wire or set of wires used in radio and television to send and receive signals.

an-te-pe-nult *n.* The third syllable from the end of a word. -timate *adj.* & *n.*

an-te-ri-or *adj.* Toward or at the front; coming before; earlier.

an-te-room *n.* Waiting room; a room leading to a larger more, important room.

an-them *n.* Hymn of praise or loyalty; an official song of a country, school, etc.

an-ther *n.* The part of the flower where the pollen is located at the end of a stamen.

an-thol-o-gy *n.* A collection of stories, poems, or other writings.

an-thra-cite *n.* Coal with a high carbon content and low volatile matter; hard coal. **anthracitic** *adj.*

an-thrax *n.* The infectious, usually fatal disease found in animals such as cattle and sheep; disease that can be transmitted to man.

an-thro-po-cen-tric *adj.* To interpret reality in terms of human experience and values.

an-thro-poid *n.* Gorillas or chimpanzees resembling man.

an-thro-pol-o-gy *n.* The science that studies the origin, culture, and development of man. **anthropologic, anthropological** *adj.*, **-ally** *adv.*, **anthropologist** *n.*

an-thro-po-mor-phism *n.* The ascribing of human motivation and human characteristics to something that is not human. **anthropomorphic** *adj.*

an-ti *n.* One who opposes a group, policy, practice, or proposal.

an-ti-anx-i-ety *adj.* Preventing or relieving anxiety.

an-ti-bal-lis-tic missile *n.* A missile designed to destroy a ballistic missile.

an-ti-bi-ot-ic *n.* A substance, as streptomycin or penicillin, that is produced by organisms, as fungi and bacteria, effective in the destruction of microorganisms and used widely to prevent or treat diseases.

an-ti-bod-y *n.* Proteins generated in the blood that react to foreign proteins or carbohydrates of certain types, neutralizing them and producing immunity against certain microorganisms or their toxins.

an-tic *n.* Mischievous caper or act.

An-ti-christ *n.* A great enemy of Christ. **Antichristian** *adj.*

an-tic-i-pate *v.* To look forward; to act in advance of; to foresee. **anticipation, anticipator** *n.*, **anticipatory** *adj.*

an-ti-cli-max *n.* A letdown or decline; a commonplace conclusion; a series of significant events or happenings. **anticlimactic** *adj.*, **-cally** *adv.*

an-ti-dote *n.* A substance that counteracts an injury or poison. **-al** *adj.*

an-ti-freeze *n.* Substance, as ethylene glycol, that is mixed with water or liquid to lower the freezing point.

an-ti-gen *n.* Substance, when introduced into the body, stimulates the production of antibodies. **antigenic** *adj.*, **antigenically** *adv.*, **antigenicity** *n.*

an-ti-his-ta-mine *n.* A drug used to relieve the symptoms of allergies and colds by interfering with the production of histamines. **antihistaminic** *adj.*

an-ti-knock *n.* Substance added to gasoline to reduce engine knock, making the vehicle run smoother.

An-til-les *n.* The main group of islands in the West Indies, forming a chain that separates the Caribbean from the Atlantic.

an-ti-log-a-rithm *n.* The number corresponding to a given logarithm. **antilog** *abbr.* Antilogarithm.

an-ti-ma-cas-sar *n.* A protective covering for the backs and arms of chairs and sofas, used to prevent soiling.

an-ti-mat-ter *n.* A form of matter that is composed of antiparticles.

an-ti-mo-ni-al *adj.* Containing or of antimony.

an-ti-mo-ny *n.* Silver-white metallic element used in chemistry, medicine, and alloys, etc.

an-tin-o-my *n.* An opposition or contradiction.

an-ti-par-ti-cle *n.* Identically matched atomic particles, but with exactly opposite electrically charged magnetic properties and spin.

an-ti-pasto *n.* Appetizer including cheese, fish, vegetables, and smoked meat served with oil and vinegar.

an-tip-a-thy *n.*, *pl.* **-thies** Feeling of repugnance or opposition. **antipathetic, -al** *adj.*, **-ally** *adv.*

an-ti-per-spi-rant *n.* Substance applied to the underarm to reduce excessive perspiration.

an-tiph-o-ny *n.* One that echoes or answers another; responsive chanting or singing.

an-ti-pode *n.* A direct opposite. **antipodal** *adj.*

an-ti-pro-ton *n.* The antiparticle of a proton.

an-tique *adj.* Belonging to or of ancient times. *n.* An object that is over 100 years old. **antique** *v.*

an-tiquity *n.*, *pl.* **-ties** Quality of being ancient or old.

an-ti-Sem-ite *n.* A person hostile toward Jews. **anti-Semitic** *adj.*, **-Semitism** *n.*

an-ti-sep-sis *n.* Condition of being free from pathogenic bacteria and the method of obtaining this condition.

an-ti-sep-tic *adj.* Pertaining or capable of producing antisepsis; thoroughly clean. **antiseptically** *adv.*

an-ti-so-cial *adj.* Unsociable; opposed to society.

an-tith-e-sis *n.*, *pl.* **-e -ses** Direct opposition or contrast. **antithetical, antithetic** *adj.*

an-ti-trust *adj.* Having to do with the regulation of trusts, monopolies, and cartels.

ant-ler *n.*

One of a pair of bony growths on the head of a member of the deer family. **-ed** *adj.*

an-to-nym *n.* A word opposite in meaning to another word.

an-uria *n.* The inability to urinate.

a-nus *n.* The lower opening of the alimentary canal.

an-vil *n.* A heavy block of steel or iron on which metal is formed.

anx-i-e-ty *n.* A state of uncertainty; disturbance of the mind regarding uncertain events.

anx-ious *adj.* Troubled in mind or worried about some uncertain matter or event. **-ness** *n.*, **anxiously** *adv.*

any *adj.* One; no matter which; some; every; and quantity or part.

any-body *pron., pl.* -bodies Anyone; any person.

any-how *adv.* By any means; in any why; whatever.

any-more *adv.* At present and from now on.

any-one *pron.* Any person; anybody.

any-place *adv.* Anywhere.

any-thing *pron.* Any occurrence, object or matter.

any-time *adv.* At any time whatever.

any-way *adv.* Nevertheless; anyhow; in any manner; carelessly.

any-where *adv.* In, at, or to any place; to any degree or extent.

a-or-ta *n., pl.* -tas *or* -tae The main artery that carries blood away from the heart; distributes blood to all of the body except the lungs. aortal, -ic *adj.*

a-ou-dad *n.* Wild sheep of North Africa having long curved horns and a growth of hair on the neck and chest similar to a beard.

AP *abbr.* Associated Press.

APA *abbr.* American Psychiatric Association.

a-pace *adv.* Rapid in pace; quickly.

A-pache *n., pl.* -es A member of the Athapaskan-speaking tribe of Indians in North America, settled in the Southwest U.S. and North Mexico.

a-part *adv.* Separate or at a distance; in pieces; to pieces; to set aside. apartness *n.*

a-part-heid *n.* In the Republic of South Africa, an official policy of political, social, and economic discrimination and segregation against nonwhites.

a-part-ment *n.* A suite or room in a building equipped for individual living.

ap-a-thy *n.* The lack of emotions or feelings. apathetic *adj.*, apathetically *adv.*

ap-a-tite *n.* Mineral used as a source of phosphorus compounds.

ape *n.* A large mammal such as a gorilla, chimpanzee, or monkey; a very clumsy, coarse person. aped *v.*

Ap-en-nines *n.* A mountain range in Italy extending the length of the peninsula.

a-pe-ri-tif *n.* A drink of alcoholic liquor consumed before a meal.

ap-er-ture *n.* An opening.

a-pex *n., pl.* apexes *or* apices The highest point; tip; top.

a-pha-sia *n.* Any partial or total loss of the ability to express ideas, resulting from brain damage. aphasiac *n.*, aphasic *adj. & n.*

aphe-lion *n.* The point in an orbit farthest from the sun.

aphid *n.* Small insects that suck sap from plants.

aph-o-rism *n.* Brief statement of truth or principal. aphorist *n.*, aphoristically *adv.*, aphoristic *adj.*

apho-tic *adj.* Without light.

aph-ro-dis-i-ac *adj.* Increasing or arousing the sexual desire or potency.

Aph-ro-di-te *n.* Greek goddess of love and beauty.

a-pi-ary *n.* Place where bees are kept and raised for their honey.

a-piece *adv.* For or to each one.

a-plomb *n.* Assurance; poise; self-confidence.

apmt *abbr.* Appointment.

apo- *pref.* Lack of; separation of; being away from.

A-poc-a-lypse *n.* The last book of the New Testament; Revelation. apocalyptical, apocalyptic *adj.*

a-poc-ry-pha *n.* Fourteen books not included in the Old Testament by Protestants, considered uncanonical because they are not part of the Hebrew scriptures; eleven of the books are accepted in the Roman Catholic Church.

a-poc-ry-phal *adj.* False; of questionable authenticity. apocryphally *adv.*

ap-o-gee *n.* The point most distant from earth in the moon's orbit.

A-pol-lo *n.* Greek sun god; very handsome young man.

a-pol-o-get-ic *adj.* Making an expression of apology. apologetical, -ally *adv.*

a-pol-o-gize *v.* To make an apology.-er *n.*

a-pol-o-gy *n., pl.* -gies A statement expressing regret for an action or fault; a formal justification or defense.

ap-o-plex-y *n.* Sudden loss of muscular control, consciousness, and sensation resulting from a rupture or blockage of the blood vessel in the brain.

a-pos-ta-sy *n., pl.* -sies Desertion of one's political party, religious faith, or cause.

a-pos-tate *n.* One who forsakes his faith or principles.

apos-te-ri-o-ri *adj., L.* Inductive; reasoning from facts to principles or from effect to cause.

a-pos-tle *n.* A person sent on a mission; the first Christian missionary to go into a new area or group; the person who first initiates a moral reform or introduces an important system or belief; a member of a Mormon council of twelve men. apostleship *n.*

Apostles' Creed *n.* A Christian statement of belief in God, used in public worship.

a-pos-to-late *n.* A group of people dedicated to spreading a religion or a doctrine.

ap-os-tol-ic *adj.* Relating to an apostle; living by the teachings of the New Testament and the apostles. -ity *n.*

a-pos-tro-phe *n.* The mark (') used to indicate the removal of letters or figures, the plural of letters or figures, and the possessive case; the act of turning away; addressing the usually absent person or a usually personified thing rhetorically.

a-pos-tro-phize *v.* To make use of apostrophe.

a-poth-e-car-ies' mea-sure *pl., n.* A measurement used mainly by pharmacists; a measurement of capacity.

a-poth-e-car-y *n., pl.* -caries A person

who prepares drugs for medical uses.

apo-the-ci-um *n.* A single-celled structure in many lichens and fungi that consists of a cupped body bearing asci on the exposed flat or concave surface.

ap-o-thegm *n.* A short, essential, and instructive formulation or saying. **apothegmatical, apothegmatic** *adj.*

apo-the-o-sis *n.* The perfect way to explain or define something or someone.

ap-pall *v.* To overcome by shock or dismay; to weaken; to fail; to become pale.

ap-pall-ing *adj.* Dismay or disgust caused by an event or a circumstance.

ap-pa-nage *n.* A rightful adjunct; provision for a younger offspring or child; a section of property or privilege appropriated by or to a person as his share.

ap-pa-ra-tchik *n.* A member of the Communist party.

ap-pa-ra-tus *n.*, *pl.* -tuses Appliance or an instrument designed and used for a specific operation.

ap-par-el *v.* To dress or put on clothing; to adorn or embellish. *n.* Clothing. *Naut.* The sails and rigging of a ship.

ap-par-ent *adj.* Clear and opened to the eye and mind; open to view, visible. **apparently** *adv.*, **apparentness** *n.*

ap-par-ent time *n.* Time of day so indicated by a sundial or the sun.

ap-pa-ri-tion *n.* An unusual or unexpected appearance; the act of being visible; a ghostly figure. **-al** *adj.*

ap-par-i-tor *n.* An official person sent to carry out the order of a judge, court, or magistrate.

ap-peal *n.* Power to arouse a sympathetic response; an earnest plea; a legal preceding where a case is brought from a lower court to a higher court for a rehearing. *v.* To make a request; to ask another person for corroboration, vindication, or decision on a matter of importance. **-able** *adj*

ap-pear *v.* To come into existence; to come into public view; to come formally before an authorized person.

ap-pear-ance *n.* The action or process of appearing; an outward indication or showing.

ap-pease *v.* To give peace; to cause to stop or subside; to calm; to pacify. **appeasable** *adj.*, **appeasement** *n.*

ap-pel-late *adj.* Having the power to hear and review the decisions of the lower courts.

ap-pel-la-tion *n.* Identifying by a name or title.

ap-pel-la-tive *adj.* Having to do with the giving of names; relating to or of a common noun. **-tive** *n.*, **-ly** *adv.*

ap-pend *v.* To add an appendix or supplement, as to a book; to attach.

ap-pend-age *n.* Something added to something more important or larger; a subordinate or a dependent person.

ap-pen-dec-to-my *n.* The surgical removal of the appendix.

ap-pen-dix *n. Med.*

Ascending colon

Cecum

Appendix

medical term that refers to a small hollow blind process or the vermiform appendix.

ap-per-cep-tion *n.* The mental understanding of something perceived in terms of previous experience. **apperceptively** *adv.*, **apperceptive** *adj.*

ap-per-tain *v.* To belong to or connect with, as a rightful part.

ap-petite *n.* The craving or desire for food. **appetitive** *adj.*

ap-plaud *v.* To express or show approval by clapping the hands. **-able** *adj.*

ap-plause *n.* The expression of public approval. **applausive** *adj.*

ap-pli-ance *n.* A piece of equipment or device designed for a particular use.

ap-pli-ca-ble *adj.* Appropriate; suitable; capable of being applied. **-bility** *n.*

ap-pli-cant *n.* A person who applies for a job or position.

ap-pli-ca-tion *n.* The act of putting something to use; the act of superposing or administering; request or petition; a form used to make a request.

ap-pli-ca-tor *n.* A device used to apply a substance; one who applies.

ap-plies *adj.* Putting something to practical use to solve definite problems.

ap-ply *v.* To make a request in the form of a written application; to put into use for a practical purpose or reason; to put into operation or to bring into action; to employ with close attention.

ap-pog-gia-tu-ra *n.* A music note or tone that precedes an essential melodic note or tone and usually is written as a note of smaller size.

ap-point *v.* To arrange something; to fix or set officially. **-able** *adj.*, **-er** *n.*

ap-point-ment *n.* The act of appointing or designating; arrangement for a meeting; a nonelective position or office; engagement or meeting.

ap-por-tion *v.* To divide and share according to a plan. **apportionment** *n.*

ap-pose *v.* To apply one thing to another; to put before. **apposable** *adj.*

ap-po-site *adj.* Highly appropriate or pertinent. **-ness** *n.*, **appositely** *adv.*

ap-po-si-tion *n.* A grammatical construction where a noun or noun phrase is followed by another; the explanatory equivalent. **appositional** *adj.*

ap-prais-al *n.* The evaluation of property by an authorized person.

ap-praise *v.* To estimate the value, worth, or status of a particular item. **-ment**, **appraiser** *n.*, **appraising** *adj.*

ap-pre-cia-ble *adj.* Capable of being measured or perceived, noticed, or estimated. **appreciably** *adv.*

ap-pre-ci-ate *v.* To recognize the worth, quality, or significance; to value very highly; to be aware of; to realize; to increase in price or value. -tory *adj.*

ap-pre-ci-a-tion *n.* The expression of admiration, gratitude, or approval; increase in value. **ap-pre-cia-tive** *adj.*

ap-pre-hend *v.* To anticipate with anxiety, dread or fear; to recognize the meaning of; to grasp; to understand.

ap-pre-hen-si-ble *adj.* Capable of being apprehended.

ap-pre-hen-sion *n.* The act of or comprehending power to comprehend; suspicion or fear of future events.

ap-pre-hen-sive *adj.* Viewing the future with anxiety or fear. -ly *adv.*

ap-pren-tice *n.* A person who is learning a trade, art, or occupation under a skilled worker for a prescribed period of time. *v.* To work as an apprentice under the supervision of a skilled worker. **apprenticeship** *n.*

ap-pressed *adj.* Pressed close to or lying flat against.

ap-prise *v.* To inform; to give notice.

ap-proach *v.* To come near to or draw closer; to be close in appearance. *n.* Access to or reaching something.

ap-pro-ba-tion *n.* A formal approval.

ap-pro-pri-ate *v.* To take possession of; to take without permission. *adj.* Suitable for a use or occasion; fitting. **appropriately** *adv.*, -or, -ness *n.*

ap-pro-pri-a-tion *n.* Money set apart for a particular use; the act or instance of appropriating.

ap-prov-al *n.* The act of approving; subject to acceptance or refusal.

ap-prove *v.* To regard or express a favorable opinion; to give formal or official approval. **approvingly** *adv.*

ap-prox-i-mate *adj.* Located close together; almost accurate or exact. *v.* To bring close or near to; to approach; to estimate; to be near the same. **approximately** *adv.*

ap-pur-te-nance *n.* Something that belongs with another more important thing; an accessory that is passed along with.

ap-pur-te-nant *adj.* Constitutes a legal attachment.

aprax-ia *n.* Inability to execute complex coordinate movement. **apraxic** *adj.*

apri-o-ri *adj.* Based on theory rather than personal experience; deductive.

ap-ro-pos *adv.* At a good time; by the way.

apse *n.* A semicircular or polygonal projection of a building or church.

ap-si-dal *adj.* Relating to an apse.

apt *adj.* Unusually qualified or fitting; appropriate; having a tendency; suitable; quick to understand. **aptly** *adv.*, **aptness** *n.*

ap-ti-tude *n.* A natural talent or ability; quickness in learning

aqua *n.*, *pl.* **aquae**, **aquas** Water; aquamarine.

aqua-cade *n.* Water entertainment, con-

sisting of swimming and diving exhibitions, with musical accompaniment.

aqua-lunger *n.* A scuba diver.

aqua-marine *n.* A color of pale blue to light green; a mineral that is blue, blue-green, or green in color.

aqua-naut *n.* A scuba diver who lives inside and outside of an underwater shelter for an extended period of time.

aqua pura *n.* Very pure water.

aqua regia *n.* Mixture of hydrochloric and nitric acids that dissolves platinum or gold.

aqua-relle *n.* A transparent water-color drawing.

aquar-i-um *n.* An artificial pond where living plants and aquatic animals are maintained and exhibited.

Aquar-i-us *n.* The eleventh sign of the zodiac; a person born under this sign; (Jan. 20 - Feb. 18).

a-quat-ic *adj.* Anything occurring on or in the water.

aqua-vitae *n.* A very strong liquor; alcohol.

aq-ue-duct *n.* A conduit for carrying a large quantity of flowing water; a bridge-like structure supporting a canal over a river.

aq-ue-ous *adj.* Like or resembling water; dissolved in water; watery.

aqueous humor *n.* The clear fluid in the chamber of the eye between the cornea and lens.

aq-ui-cul-ture or **aqua-cul-ture** *n.* The culti-vation of produce in natural water; hydroponics. **aquicultural** *adj.*

aq-ui-fer *n.* The layer of underground gravel, sand, or rocks where water collects.

aq-ui-line *adj.* Resembling or related to an eagle; hooked or curved like the beak on an eagle.

a-quiv-er *adj.*, *Slang* Trembling or quivering.

ar-a-besque *n.* An intricate style or design of interwoven leaves, flowers, and geometric forms.

ar-a-ble *adj.* Land that is suitable for cultivation by plowing.

a-rach-nid *n.* Arthropods that are mostly air-breathing, having four pairs of legs but no antennae; an insect as a spider. **arachnidan** *n.*, **arachnid** *adj.*

Ar-a-ma-ic *n.* A Semitic language used in Southwestern Asia, known since the nineth century B.C. This commercial language was adopted by non-Aramaean people.

Aramaic alphabet *n.* The commercial alphabet for many countries of southwest Asia, dating from the ninth century B.C.

ara-ne-id *n.* A breed of spider.

ar-ba-lest *n.* Military weapon from medieval times with a steel bow, used to throw balls and stones **arbalester** *n.*

ar-bi-ter *n.* A person chosen to decide a dispute, having absolute power of determining and judging.

ar-bi-tra-ble *adj.* Subject to arbitration.

ar-bit-ra-ment *adj.* The settling of a dispute; the power or right of deciding.

ar-bi-trar-y *adj.* Something based on whim or impulse. **-ily** *adv.*, **-iness** *n.*

ar-bi-tra-tor *n.* A person chosen to settle a dispute or controversy between parties.

ar-bor *n.* A garden shelter that is shady and covered with or made of climbing plants. **arborous** *adj.*

ar-bo-re-al *adj.* Resembling or related to a tree; living in trees. **arboreally** *adv.*

ar-bo-re-tum *n.* A place for studying and exhibiting trees, shrubs, and plants cultivated for educational and for scientific purposes.

ar-bo-ri-cul-ture *n.* The ornamental cultivation of shrubs and trees. **arboriculturist** *n.*

ar-bor-ist *n.* A specialist in the maintenance and care of trees.

ar-bo-ri-za-tion *n.* The formation of an arrangement or figure of a bush or shrub.

ar-bo-rize *v.* To branch repeatedly and freely.

ar-bor-vi-tae *n.* An evergreen tree of the pine family that has closely overlapping or compressed scale leaves, often grown for hedges and for ornamental decorations.

ar-bo-vi-rus *n.* Various viruses transmitted by arthropods, including the causative agents for yellow fever and encephalitis.

ar-bu-tus *n.* A fragrant pinkish flower that blossoms early in the spring.

arc *n.* Something that is curved or arched; the luminous discharge of electric current across a gap of two electrodes.

ARC *abbr.* American Red Cross.

ar-cade *n.* An arched covered passageway supported by columns; a long arched gallery or building.

ar-cad-ed *adj.* Furnished with arcades or arches.

ar-ca-dia *n.* The ancient Greek area usually chosen as background for poetry; region of simple quiet and pleasure.

arch *n.*

A structure that spans over an open area and gives support. **archly** *adv.*, **archness** *n.*

ar-chae-ol-o-gy *n.* Scientific study of ancient times and ancient peoples. **archaeological** *adj.*, **archaeologist** *n.*

ar-cha-ic *adj.* Something that belongs to an earlier time; characteristic of an earlier language, now used only in special cases.

ar-cha-ism *n.* Something that is outdated or old fashioned, as an expression or word. **archaistic** *adj.*, **archaist** *n.*

arch-an-gel *n.* The highest in order of angels. **archangelic** *adj.*

arch-bishop *n.* A bishop of the highest rank.

arch-dea-con *n.* A clergyman who has the duty of assisting a bishop. **archdeaconate** *n.*

arch-di-o-cese *n.* The territory or district of an archbishop. **archdiocesan** *adj.*

arch-duch-ess *n.* A woman who has a rank and right equal to that of an archduke; the wife or widow of an archduke.

arch-duchy *n.* The territory of an archduchess or of an archduke.

arch-duke *n.* A royal prince of the imperial family of Austria. **-dom** *n.*

arch-en-e-my *n.* One who is a chief enemy.

ar-cher-y *n.* The practice or art of shooting with a bow and arrow. **archer** *n.*

ar-che-spore *n.* A single cell or group of cells from which a mother spore is formed.

ar-che-type *n.* An original from which other things are patterned.

arch-fiend *n.* A chief or principal friend; a person of great wickedness, especially Satan.

ar-chi-tect *n.* A person who may design and or supervise the construction of large structures.

ar-chi-tec-ton-ic *adj.* To resemble architecture in organization or structure. **architectonically** *adv.*

ar-chi-tec-ture *n.* The art or science of designing and building structures; a method or style of construction or building. **architectural** *adj.*

ar-chi-trave *n.* In classical architecture, a horizontal piece supported by the columns of a building.

ar-chives *pl., n.* Public documents or records; the place where archives are kept. **archival** *adj.*, **archivist** *n.*

arch-way *n.* A passage or way under an arch; an arch over a passage.

arc lamp *n.* Electric lamp which produces light as when a current passes between two incandescent electrodes.

arc-tic *adj.* Extremely cold or frigid; relating to the territory north of the Arctic Circle.

Arc-tic Cir-cle *n.* Parallel of the latitude that is approximately 66.5 degrees north of the equator.

-ard *or* **-art** *suff.* A person who is characterized by performing something excessively.

ar-dor *n.* Extreme warmth or passion; emotion; intense heat.

ar-du-ous *adj.* Taking much effort to bring forth; difficult. **arduously** *adv.*

are *v.* First, second, and third person plural and second person singular of the verb "to be".

ar-e-a *n.* A flat or level piece of ground. **areal** *adj.*

area code *n.* The three-digit number assigned to each telephone area in the United States, used to call another area in the U.S.

area-way *n.* A sunken area in a basement that offers access, light and air.

a-re-ca *n.* Tall palm of southeast Asia

that has white flowers and red or orange egg-shaped nuts.

a-re-na *n.* Enclosed area for public entertainment, such as football games, concerts, etc.

a-re-na the-ater *n.* A theater with the stage located in the center and the audience seated around the stage.

aren't *contr.* Are not.

Ar-gen-ti-na *n.* Country of southeastern South America. **Argentinean** *adj. & n.*

ar-gen-tite *n.* A lustrous ore.

ar-gil-la-ceous *adj.* Resembling or containing clay.

ar-go-sy *n., pl.* **-sies** A fleet of ships; a large merchant ship.

ar-got *n.* A secret, specialized vocabulary.

ar-gu-able *adj.* Open to argument.

ar-gue *v.* To debate, to offer reason for or against a subject; to dispute, argue, or quarrel; to persuade or influence. **argument, arguer** *n.*

ar-gu-men-ta-tion *n.* The process or art of arguing; debating.

ar-gu-men-ta-tive *adj.* Given to argument.

ar-gus pheasant *n.* A large South Asian bird with long tail feathers brilliantly colored with eye-like spots.

ar-gyle *or* **argyll** *n.* A pattern knitted with varicolored, diamond-shaped designs.

a-ri-a *n.* A vocal piece with accompaniment sung in solo; part of an opera.

ar-id *adj.* Insufficient rain; dry; lacking in interest or feeling; dull. **aridity** *n.*

Aries *n.* The first sign of the zodiac; a person born under this sign: (March 21 - April 19).

a-right *adv.* Correctly; rightly.

a-rise *v.* To come from a source; to come to attention.

aris-ta *n., pl.* **-tae** *or* **-tas** Bristle-like appendage or structure.

ar-is-toc-ra-cy *n.* A government by the best individuals or by a small privileged class; a class or group viewed as superior; the hereditary privileged ruling nobility or class. **aristocratic** *adj.*

a-rith-me-tic *adj.* Branch of math that deals with addition, subtraction, multiplication, division. **arithmetical** *adj.,* **arithmetically** *adv.*

a-rith-met-ic mean *n.* The number received by dividing the sum of a set of quantities by the number of quantities in the set.

a-rith-met-ic pro-gres-sion *n.* A progression in which the difference between any term and the one before or after is constant, as 2,4,6,8, etc.

-ar-i-um *suff.* The place or thing connected to or relating with.

ark *n.* The ship Noah built for survival during the Great Flood; the chest which contained the Ten Commandments on stone tables, carried by the Jews; something that gives protection.

arm *n.* The part between the shoulder and the wrist; upper limb of the human body. *v.* To furnish with protection against danger. **armer** *n.*

ar-ma-da *n.* A fleet of warships; a large force of moving things.

ar-ma-dil-lo *n.* A burrowing nocturnal animal with an armor-like covering of jointed, bony plates.

Ar-ma-ged-don *n.* A final battle between the forces of good and evil.

ar-ma-ment *n.* Military supplies and weapons; the process of preparing for battle.

ar-ma-ture *n.* The main moving part of an electric device or machine; a piece of soft iron that connects the poles of a magnet.

arm-chair *n.* A chair with armrests or supports. *adj.* Remote from the direct dealing with problems.

arm-ed for-ces *n.* The combined air, military, and naval forces of a nation.

arm-ful *n., pl.* **armfuls** *or* **armsful** As much as the arm can hold.

arm-hole *n.* The opening in a garment for the arm.

ar-mi-stice *n.* The temporary suspension of combat by mutual agreement; truce.

Armistice Day *n.* The armistice ending of World War I; title used before the official adoption of Veterans Day in 1954.

arm-let *n.* A band worn on the upper arm.

ar-moire *n.* A large wardrobe or cupboard.

ar-mor *n.* Covering used in combat to protect the body, made from a heavy metal. **armor** *v.,* **armored** *adj.*

ar-mor-er *n.* A person who makes armor; one who assembles, repairs, and tests firearms.

ar-mory *n., pl.* **-mories** The supply of arms for attack or defense; the place where military equipment is stored.

arm-pit *n.* The hollow area under the arm where it joins the shoulder.

arm-rest *n.* The support for the arm, as on a chair.

arm-twist-ing *n.* The use of direct personal pressure to achieve a desired effect.

arm wrestling *n.* A game in which two opponents sit face to face gripping right hands, with elbows securely on a table, making an attempt to bring the opponent's arm down flat onto the table.

ar-my *n., pl.* **-mies** A group of persons organized for a country's protection; the land forces of a country.

ar-my-worm *n.* Moth whose larvae travels in multitudes from one area to another destroying grain and grass.

ar-ni-ca *n.* Plant of the genus Arnica with yellow flowers from which a form of a tincture, as a liniment, is made.

a-ro-ma *n.* A distinctive fragrance or pleasant odor. **-tical, aromatic** *adj.*

a-round *adv.* To or on all sides; in succession or rotation; from one place to another; in a circle or circular movement.

around-the-clock *adj.* Lasting continuously for a period of 24 hours.

arouse *v.* To wake up from a sleep; to stir; to excite. **arousal** *n.*

ar-peg-gi-o *n.* Tones of a chord produced in succession and not simultaneously.

arr *abbr.* Arranged; arrival; arrive.

ar-rack *n.* An alcoholic beverage distilled from the juices of the coconut palm, from the Far or Near East.

ar-raign *v.* To called before a court to answer a charge or indictment; to accuse of imperfection, inadequacy, or of wrong doing. **arraignment** *n.*

ar-range *v.* To put in correct order or proper sequence; to prepare for something; to take steps to organize something; to bring about an understanding or an agreement; to prepare or change a musical composition for instruments or voices other than those that is was written for.

ar-range-ment *n.* The state or being arranged; something made by arranging things or parts together.

ar-rant *adj.* Extreme; being notoriously without moderation. **arrantly** *adv.*

ar-ras *n.* A screen or wall hanging of tapestry.

ar-ray *v.* To place or set in order; to draw up; to decorate or dress in an impressive attire. **arrayer** *n.*

ar-rears *n., pl.* The state of being behind something, as an obligation, payment, etc.; an unfinished duty.

ar-rear-age *n.* The condition of having something unpaid or overdue.

ar-rest *n.* To stop or to bring an end to; to capture; to seize; to hold in custody by the authority of law. **arrester, arrestor, arrestment** *n.*

arrest-ee *n.* A person under arrest.

ar-rest-ing *adj.* Very impressive or striking; catching the attention. **-ly** *adv.*

ar-rhyth-mia *n.* The alteration in rhythm of the heartbeat, either in force or time.

ar-rhyth-mic *adj.* Lacking regularity or rhythm.

ar-riv-al *n.* The act of arriving.

ar-rive *v.* To reach or get to a destination.

ar-ro-gance *n.* An overbearing manner, intolerable presumption; an insolent pride. **arrogant, arrogantly** *adv.*

ar-row *n.* A weapon shot from a bow; a sign or mark to show direction.

ar-row-head *n.* The striking end of an arrow, usually shaped like a wedge. **arrowheaded** *adj.*

ar-row-root *n.* A starch-yielding plant of tropical America.

ar-row-wood *n.* Shrubs with tough pliant shoots that were formerly used in making arrowheads.

ar-rowy *adj.* To move swiftly; something that resembles an arrow.

ARS *abbr.* Agricultural Research Service.

ar-se-nal *n.* A collection of weapons; a place where arms and military equipment are manufactured or stored.

ar-se-nic *n.* A solid, poisonous element, steel-gray in color, used to make insecticide or weed killer. **arsenic, arsenical** *adj.*

ar-son *n.* The fraudulent burning of property. **arsonist** *n.*, **arsonous** *adj.*

art *n.* A human skill of expression of other objects by painting, drawing, sculpture, etc.; a branch of learning.

ar-te-ri-ole *n.* One of the small terminal twigs of an artery that ends in capillaries.

ar-ter-y *n., pl.* **-teries** A blood vessel that carries blood from the heart to the other parts of the body; a major means for transportation. **arterial** *adj.*

ar-te-sian well *n.*

A well that produces water without a pump.

art form *n.* The recognized form of an artistic expression.

art-ful *adj.* Showing or performed with skill or art. **artfully** *adv.*, **artfulness** *n.*

art glass *n.* Glass designed for decorative purposes; novelty glassware.

ar-thral-gia *n.* Pain that occurs in one or more joints. **arthralgic** *adj.*

ar-thrit-ic *n.* A person who has arthritis. *adj.* Affected with arthritis; showing effects associated with aging.

ar-thri-tis *n.* Inflammation of joints due to infectious or metabolic causes.

ar-thro-pod *n.* An animal with jointed limbs and segmented body, as a spider. **arthropodal, arthropodan, arthropodous** *adj.*

ar-ti-choke *n.* A plant with a thistle-like head, which can be cooked and eaten as a vegetable.

ar-ti-cle *n.* A term or clause in a contract; a paragraph or section; a condition or rule; an object, item or commodity.

ar-tic-u-lar *adj.* Related to or of a joint.

ar-tic-u-late *adj.* Able to express oneself clearly, effectively, or readily; speaking in distinct words, or syllables. **-ness, articulator** *n.*, **articulately** *adv.*

ar-ti-fact *n.* Something made by man showing human modification or workmanship.

ar-ti-fice *n.* An artful or clever skill; ingenuity.

ar-ti-fi-cial *adj.* Not genuine; made by man; not found in nature. **artificially** *adv.*

ar-til-lery *n.* Weapons, especially cannons; troops that are trained in the use of guns and other means of defense.

ar-ti-san *n*. A mechanic or a craftsman.

art-ist *n*. A person who practices the fine arts of painting, sculpture, etc.

ar-tiste *n*. One who is an expert in the theatrical profession.

ar-tis-tic *adj*. Relating to the characteristic of an artist or art. artistically *adv*.

art-ist-ry *n*. The artistic ability, or quality of workmanship or effect.

art-less *adj*. Lacking knowledge, art, or skill; crude; natural; simple. artlessly *adv*., artlessness *n*.

art-mobile *n*. A trailer that carries an art collection for exhibition on road tours.

art-work *n*. The artistic work of an artist.

ARV *abbr*. American Revised Version.

Ar-y-an *adj*. Relating to or of the Indo-European family of languages.

as *adv*. In the manner like; of the same degree or amount; similar to.

AS *abbr*. After sight, airspeed, Anglo-Saxon.

ASA *abbr*. American Society of Appraisers; American Statistical Association.

asb *abbr*. Asbestos.

as-bes-tos *n*. A noncombustible, fibrous, mineral form of magnesium silicate that is used especially in fireproofing. asbestine *adj*.

ASCAP *abbr*. American Society of Composers, Authors, and Publishers.

ASCE *abbr*. American Society of Civil Engineers.

as-cend *v*. To rise up from a lower level; to climb; to mount; to walk up. ascendible, ascendable *adj*.

as-cen-dant *or* ascsendent *adj*. Rising; moving up.

as-cent *n*. A way up; a slope; the act of rising.

as-cer-tain *v*. To find out for certain; to make sure. -ment *n*., -able *adj*.

as-cet-icism *n*. The practice of strict self-denial through personal and spiritual discipline.

as-cot *n*. A scarf or broad tie that is placed under the chin.

as-cribe *v*. To assign or attribute to something. ascribable, ascription *v*.

ASCU *abbr*. Association of State Colleges and Universities.

ASE *abbr*. American Stock Exchange.

a-sex-u-al *adj*. Lacking sexual reproductive organs; without sex. asexuality *n*.

asg *abbr*. Assigned, assignment.

ash *n*. A type of tree with a hard, tough elastic wood; the grayish dust remaining after something has burned.

a-shamed *adj*. Feeling guilt, disgrace, or shame; feeling unworthy or inferior. ashamedly *adv*.

a-shore *adv*. On or to the shore.

ash-tray *n*. A container or receptacle for discarding tobacco ashes and cigarette and cigar butts.

Ash Wednesday *n*. The first day of Lent.

ASI *abbr*. Airspeed indicator.

aside *adv*. Out of the way; to a side; to one side; something that is said in an undertone and not meant to be heard by someone.

ask *v*. To request; to require or seek information. asker *n*.

askance *adv*. With a side glance; with suspicion or distrust.

askew *adv. or adj*. Out of line, not straight.

a-slant *adv*. In a slanting direction.

a-sleep *adv*. In a state of sleep; lacking sensation; numb; not alert.

a-slope *adv*. In a slanting or sloping position or direction.

ASME *abbr*. American Society of Mechanical Engineers.

a-so-cial *adj*. Selfish, not social.

as-par-a-gus *n*. A vegetable with tender shoots, very succulent when cooked.

as-pect *n*. The situation, position, view, or appearance of something.

as-pen *n*. A tree known as the trembling poplar, having leaves that flutter even in a very light breeze.

as-peri-ty *n., pl*. -ties Roughness in manner.

as-persion *v*. False charges or slander; defamation; maligning.

as-phalt *n*. A sticky, thick, blackish-brown mixture of petroleum tar used in paving roads and roofing buildings. asphaltic *adj*.

as-phyx-i-ate *v*. To suffocate, to prevent from breathing. asphyxiation *n*.

as-pic *n*. A savory jelly made from fish, meat, or vegetable juices.

as-pi-rate *v*. To give pronunciation with a full breathing sound; to draw out using suction. aspiration *n*.

as-pire *v*. To desire with ambition; to strive towards something that is higher. aspiringly *adv*., aspirer *n*.

as-pi-rin *n*. Medication used for the relief of pain and fever.

ASR *abbr*. Airport surveillance radar; air-sea rescue.

ass *n*. A hoofed animal; a donkey; a stupid or foolish person.

as-sail *v*. To attack violently with words or blows. assailant *n*.

as-sas-sin *n*. Murderer especially one that murders a politically important person either for fanatical motives or for hire.

as-sas-si-nate *v*. To murder a prominent person by secret or sudden attack. assassination, assassinator *n*.

as-sault *n*. A very violent physical or verbal attack on a person. assaulter *n*.

as-say *n*. To evaluate or to assess; to try; to attempt. assayer *n*.

as-sem-blage *n*. A collection of things or people; artistic composition made from junk, scraps; and miscellaneous materials.

as-sem-ble *v*. To put together the parts of something; to come together as a group. assembly *n*.

as-sem-bly line *n*. The arrangement of workers, machines, and equipment which allows work to pass from operation to operation in the correct order until the product is assembled.

as-sem-bly-man *n*. A member of an assembly line.

as-sent *v.* To agree on something. -er *n.*

as-sert *v.* To declare or state positively; to maintain; to defend. **asserter, assertor** *n.*

as-sess *v.* To fix or assign a value to something. **assessor** *n.*

as-sess-ment *n.* The official determination of value for tax purposes.

as-set *n.* A valuable quality or possession; all of the property of a business or a person that can be used to cover liabilities.

as-sev-er-ate *v.* To state positively, firmly, and seriously. **asseveration** *n.*

as-sign *v.* To designate as to duty; to give or allot; to attribute. **assignable** *adj.*

as-sign-ed risk *n.* A poor risk for insuring; one that insurance companies would normally refuse but are forced to insure by state law.

as-sign-ee *n.* The person appointed to act for another; the person to whom property or the right to something is legally transferred.

as-sign-ment *n.* A given amount of work or task to undertake; a post, position, or office to which one is assigned.

as-sim-i-late *v.* To take in, to understand; to make similar; to digest or to absorb into the system. **assimilator, assimilation** *n.*

as-sist *v.* To give support, to aid, to give help. **assistance, assistant** *n.*

as-size *n.* A fixed or customary standard.

assoc *abbr.* Associate.

assn *abbr.* Association.

as-so-ci-ate *v.* To connect or join together. *n.* A partner, colleague, or companion.

as-so-ci-a-tion *n.* An organized body of people having a common interest; a society. **associational** *adj.*

as-so-nance *n.* The repetition of sound in words or syllables.

as-sort *v.* To distribute into groups of a classification or kind. **assorter** *n.*, **assortative** *adj.*

as-sort-ed *adj.* Made up of different or various kinds.

as-sort-ment *n.* The act or state of being assorted; a collection of different things.

ASSR *abbr.* Autonomous Soviet Socialist Republic.

asst *abbr.* Assistant.

as-suage *v.* To quiet, pacify; to put an end to by satisfying. **assuagement** *n.*

as-sua-sive *adj.* Having a smooth, pleasant effect or quality.

as-sume *v.* To take upon oneself to complete a job or duty; to take responsibility for; to take for granted. **assumable** *adj.*, **assumably** *adv.*

as-sump-tion *n.* An idea or statement believed to be true without proof.

as-sur-ance *n.* A statement made to inspire confidence of mind or manner; freedom from uncertainty or self-doubt.

as-sure *v.* To give the feeling of confidence; to make sure or certain.

as-sured *adj.* Satisfied as to the truth or certainty. **assuredly** *adv.*

as-sur-er *n.* A person who gives assurance.

assy *abbr.* Assembly.

as-ter *n.*

A plant having white, bluish, purple, or pink daisy-like flowers.

as-ter-isk *n.* The character (*) used to indicate letters omitted or as a reference to a footnote.

a-stern *adv. & adj.* Toward the rear or back of an aircraft or ship.

as-ter-oid *n.* One of thousands of small planets between Jupiter and Mars.

asth-ma *n.* A respiratory disease marked by labored breathing, accompanied by wheezing, and often coughing and gasping. **asthmatic** *adj.*, **-ally** *adv.*

as though *conj.* As if.

astig-ma-tism *n.* A defect of the lens of an eye resulting in blurred or imperfect images.

a-stir *adj.* To be out of bed, awake; in motion.

ASTM *abbr.* American Society for Testing and Materials.

as to *prep.* With reference to or regard to; concerning; according to.

as-ton-ish *v.* To strike with sudden fear, wonder, or surprise.

as-ton-ish-ing *adj.* Causing surprise or astonishment. **astonishingly** *adv.*

as-ton-ish-ment *n.* The state of being amazed or astonished.

as-tound *v.* To fill with wonder and bewilderment. **-ing** *adj.* **-ingly** *adv.*

ASTP *abbr.* Army Specialized Training Program.

as-tra-khan *n.* The curly fur from a young lamb of the southeast U.S.S.R.

as-tral *adj.* Resembling, or related to the stars.

a-stray *adv.* Away from a desirable or proper path or development.

a-stride *prep.* One leg on either side of something; placed or lying on both sides of; extending across or over.

as-trin-gent *adj.* Able to draw together or to constricting tissue. **astringency** *n.*

as-tro-dome *n.* A large stadium covered by a dome.

as-tro-labe *n.* Instrument formerly used to determine the altitude of a celestial body.

as-trol-o-gy *n.* The study of the supposed influences of the planets and stars and their movements and positions on human affairs. **-ical** *adj.*, **-er** *n.*

astron *abbr.* Astronomer; Astronomy.

as-tro-naut *n.* A person who travels in a spacecraft beyond the earth's atmosphere.

as-tro-nau-tics *n.* The technology and science of the construction and operation of a spacecraft. **astronautical** *adj.* **astronautically** *adv.*

as-tro-nom-i-cal *adj.* Relating to astronomy; something inconceivable or enormously large. **-ally** *adv.*

as-tron-o-my *n.* The science of the celestial bodies and their motion, magnitudes, and constitution **-er** *n.*

as-tro-phys-ics *n.* Branch of astronomy dealing with the chemical and physical constitution of the celestial bodies. **astrophysical** *adj.*, **astrophysicist** *n.*

as-tute *adj.* Sharp in discernment; very shrewd. **astutely** *adv.*, **astuteness** *n.*

a-sun-der *adv.* Separate into parts or positions apart from each other.

ASV *abbr.* American Standard Version.

asy-lum *n.* A refuge or institution for the care of the needy or sick; a place of security and retreat; an institution providing help and care for the destitute or insane.

a-sym-metric *adj.* Something that is not symmetrical. **asymmetry** *n.*

at *prep.* To indicate presence, occurrence, or condition; used as a function word to indicate a certain time.

at-a-vism *n.* The reappearance a hereditary characteristic that skipped several generations. **atavistic** *adj.*

atax-ia *n.* Any nervous disorder with an inability to coordinate voluntary muscular movements. **ataxic** *adj.*

at-el-ier *n.* An artist's workshop.

a-the-ism *n.* The disbelief that God exists.

athe-ist *n.* A person who does not believe in God. **-ic, atheistical** *adj.*

Ath-ens *n.* The capital city of Greece.

a-thirst *adj.* Having a strong, eager desire for something.

ath-lete *n.* A person who participates in sports, as football, basketball, soccer, etc.

ath-lete's foot *n.* A contagious skin infection of the feet.

ath-let-ic *adj.* Relating to athletes; physically strong and active.

a-thwart *adv.* Opposition to the expected or right; from one side to another.

a-tilt *adj. & adv.* Inclined upward or tilted in some way.

At-lan-tic Ocean *n.* The second largest ocean.

at-las *n.* A collection or book of maps.

at-mos-phere *n.* A gaseous mass that surrounds a celestial body, as the earth; a predominant mood or feeling.

at-oll *n.* An island of coral that encircles a lagoon either partially or completely.

at-om *n.*

A tiny particle, the smallest unit of an element.

atom bomb *or* **atomic bomb** *n.* A bomb that explodes violently due to the sudden release of atomic energy, occurring from the splitting of nuclei of a heavy chemical element.

at-om-ic en-er-gy *n.* Energy that is released by changes in the nucleus of an atom.

a-ton-al *adj.* Marked by the deliberate avoidance of a traditional key or tonal center. **atonality** *n.*, **atonally** *adv.*

a-tone *v.* To give satisfaction; to make amends.

a-tone-ment *n.* Amends for an injury or a wrongdoing; the reconciliation between God and man.

atop *adj.* On the top of something.

atri-um *n.* One of the heart chambers; the main hall of a Roman house. **atrial** *adj.*

a-tro-cious *adj.* Exceedingly cruel or evil.

a-troc-i-ty *n.*, *pl.* **-ties** The condition of being atrocious; an atrocious act.

a-tro-phy *v.* To decrease in size or a wasting away.

att *abbr.* Attached; attention; attorney.

at-tach *v.* To bring together; to fasten or become fastened; to bind by personal attachments. **attachable** *adj.*

at-ta-che *n.* An expert on the diplomatic staff of an embassy.

attache case *n.* A briefcase or a small suitcase.

at-tach-ment *n.* The state of being attached; a tie of affection or loyalty; the supplementary part of something.

at-tack *v.* To threaten with force, to assault; to start to work on with vigor.

at-tain *v.* To arrive at or reach a goal. **attainability** *n.*, **-able** *adj.* **-ness** *n.*

at-tain-der *n.* The loss of civil rights that occurs following a criminal conviction.

at-tain-ment *n.* Accomplishment; an achievement.

at-taint *v.* To disgrace or stain; to achieve or obtain by effort.

at-tar *n.* The fragrant oil from flowers.

at-tempt *v.* To make an effort to do something. **attempt** *n.*

at-tend *v.* To be present; to take charge of or to look after.

at-ten-dance *n.* The fact or act of attending; the number of times a person attends.

at-ten-dant *n.* One who provides a service for another.

at-ten-tion *n.* Observation, notice, or mental concentration. **attentive** *adj.*, **attentively** *adv.*, **attentiveness** *n.*

at-ten-u-ate *v.* To lessen the force, amount or value; to become thin; to weaken. **attenuation** *n.*

at-test *v.* To give testimony or to sign one's name as a witness. **attestation** *n.*

at-tic *n.* The space directly below the roof of a building.

at-tire *n.* A person's dress or clothing. *v.* To clothe; to dress.

at-ti-tude *n.* A mental position; the feeling one has for oneself.

attn *abbr.* Attention.

at-tor-ney *n.*, *pl.* **-neys** A person with legal training who is appointed by another to transact business for him. **attorneyship** *n.*

at-torn-ey gen-er-al *n.* The chief law officer of a state or nation.

at-tract *v.* To draw by appeal; to cause to draw near by appealing qualities.

at-trac-tion *n.* The capability of attracting; something that attracts or is meant to attract.

at-trac-tive *adj.* Having the power of charming, or quality of attracting. **attractively** *adv.*, **attractiveness** *n.*

at-trib-ute *v.* To explain by showing a cause. *n.* A characteristic of a thing or person. **attributable** *adj.*

at-tune *v.* To bring something into harmony; to put in tune; to adjust.

a-typ-i-cal *adj.* Not confirming to the typical type. **atypically** *adv.*

atty *abbr.* Attorney.

atty gen *abbr.* Attorney general.

atwit-ter *adj.* Very excited; or nervously concerned about something.

at wt *abbr.* Atomic Weight.

au-bade *n.* A poem or song for lovers who part at dawn; a love song in the morning.

au-burn *adj.* A reddish brown color; moderately brown; used in describing the color of a person's hair.

au cou-rant *adj.* Fully familiar or informed.

auc-tion *n.* A public sale of merchandise to the highest bidder. **auctioneer** *n.*

auction bridge *n.* A variation in the game of bridge in which tricks made in excess of the contract are scored toward game.

auc-to-ri-al *adj.* Having to do with an author.

au-da-cious *adj.* Bold, daring, or fearless; insolent. **-ly** *adv.*, **-ity** *n.*

au-di-ble *adj.* Capable of being heard.

au-di-ence *n.* A group of spectators or listeners; the opportunity to express views; a formal hearing or conference.

au-di-o *adj.* Of or relating to sound or its high-fidelity reproduction.

au-dit *n.* Verification or examination of financial accounts or records.

au-di-tion *n.* A trial performance given by an entertainer as to demonstrate ability.

au-di-tor *n.* A person who listens or hears; one who audits accounts.

au-di-to-ri-um *n.* A large room in a public building or a school that holds many people.

au-di-to-ry *adj.* Related to the organs or sense of hearing.

au-ger *n.* The tool which is used for the purpose of putting holes in the ground or wood.

aught *n.* Zero (0).

aug-ment *v.* To add to or increase; to enlarge. **augmentation, augmenter** *n.*, **augmentative, augmentable** *adj.*

au jus *adj.* Served in the juices obtained from roasting.

auk *n.* Sea bird with a stocky body and short wings, living in the arctic regions.

au na-tu-rel *adj.* Of a natural state.

aunt *n.* A sister of a person's father or mother; the wife of one's uncle.

au-ra *n.*, *pl.* **-ras, -rae** An emanation said to come from a person's or an animal's body.

au-ral *adj.* Relating to the ear or the sense of hearing. **aurally** *adv.*

au-re-ate *adj.* Of a brilliant golden color.

au-re-ole *n.* A halo.

au re-voir *interj.* Used in expressing farewell to someone.

au-ri-cle *n.* The two upper chambers of the heart.

au-ric-u-lar *adj.* Dealing with the sense of hearing or of being in the shape of the ear.

au-ro-ra *n.* The brilliant display of moving and flashing lights in the night sky, believed to be caused by electrically charged particles. **auroral** *adj.*

aus-tere *adj.* Stern in manner and appearance. **austerity** *n.*

aus-tral *adj.* Southern.

Aus-tri-a *n.* Country of central Europe.

au-then-tic *adj.* Real; genuine; worthy of acceptance.

au-then-ti-cate *v.* To prove something is true or genuine. **authentication, authenticity, authenticator** *n.*

author *n.* A person who writes an original literary work. **author** *v.*

au-thor-i-tar-i-an *adj.* Blind submission and absolute, unquestioned obedience to authority. **authoritarianism, authoritorian** *n.* **authoritative** *adj.*

au-thor-i-ty *n.*, *pl.* **-ties** A group or person with power; a government; an expert.

au-thor-i-za-tion *n.* The act of authorizing something.

au-thor-ize *v.* To give authority, to approve, to justify.

au-tism *n.* Absorption in a self-centered mental state, such as fantasies, daydreams or hallucinations in order to escape from reality. **autistic** *adj.*

auto *abbr.* Automatic; automobile.

au-to-bahn *n.* Highway in Germany.

au-to-bi-og-ra-phy *n.*, *pl.* **-phies** The life story of a person, written by that person. **autobiographer** *n.*

au-toch-tho-nous *adj.* Native to an area.

au-toc-ra-cy *n.* Government by one person who has unlimited power. **autocrat** *n.*, **autocratic** *adj.*

au-to-di-dact *n.* A person who has taught himself. **autodidactic** *adj.*

au-to-graph *n.* A handwritten signature.

au-to-in-tox-i-ca-tion *n.* Self-poisoning caused by metabolic wastes of other toxins in the body.

au-to-mate *v.* To operate by automation; To convert something to automation.

au-to-mat-ic *adj.* Operating with very little control; self-regulating.

au-ton-o-my *n.* Independence; self-government.

au-to-pilot *n.* The device for automatically steering aircraft and ships.

au-to-ma-tion *n.* The equipment and techniques used to acquire automation.

au-to-mo-bile *n.* A four-wheeled passenger vehicle commonly propelled by an internal-combustion engine.

au-to-mo-tive *adj.* Relating to self-propelled vehicles.

au-to-nom-ic *adj.* Pertaining to the autonomic system of the nervous system.

au-to-nom-ic ner-vous sys-tem *n.* The part of the body's nervous system which is regulated involuntarily.

au-top-sy *n., pl.* -sies Postmortem examination; the examination of a body after death to find the cause of death. autopsic, autopsical *adj.*

au-to-stra-da *n.* An expressway in Italy.

au-tumn *n.* The season between summer and winter. autumnal *adj.*

aux-il-ia-ry *adj.* Providing help or assistance to someone; giving support.

aux-il-ia-ry verb *n.* Verbs that accompany a main verb and express the mood, voice, or tense.

auxin *n.* The hormone in a plant that stimulates growth.

av *or* **ave** *abbr.* Avenue.

a-vail *v.* To be of advantage or use; to use. *n.* The advantage toward attaining a purpose or goal.

a-vail-abil-i-ty *n.* The state of being available.

a-vail-able *adj.* Ready or present for immediate use. -ness *adj.*, -ly *adv.*

av-a-lanche *n.* A large amount of rock or snow that slides down a mountainside.

a-vant--garde *n.* The people who apply and invent new ideas and styles in a certain field.

av-a-rice *n.* One's desire to have wealth and riches.

a-vast *interj., Naut.* A command to stop or cease.

a-venge *v.* To take revenge for something. avenger *n.*

av-e-nue *n.* A street lined with trees; a way of achieving something; sometimes called an "avenue of attack".

a-ver *v.* To be firm and to state positively. averment *n.*

av-er-age *n.* Something that is typical or usual, not being exceptional; common.

a-verse *adj.* Having a feeling of distaste or repugnance. -ness *n.*, aversely *adv.*

a-ver-sion *n.* A feeling of strong dislike, or distaste for something.

a-vert *v.* To prevent or keep from happening; to turn aside or away from.

av *abbr.* Average.

a-vi-ary *n.* A place where birds are kept. aviarist *n.*

a-vi-a-tion *n.* The operation of planes and other aircraft.

a-vi-a-tor *n.* Pilot of an aircraft.

av-id *adj.* Greedy; eager; enthusiastic.

av-o-ca-do *n.*

The pear-shaped edible fruit from the avocado tree, having a large seed and yellowish-green pulp.

av-o-ca-tion *n.* A pleasurable activity that is in addition to the regular work a

person must do; a hobby.

a-void *v.* To stay away from; to shun; to prevent or keep from happening. avoidable *adj.*, avoidably *adv.*

a-void-ance *n.* The act of making something void

a-vouch *v.* To assert; to guarantee.

a-vow *v.* To state openly on a subject. avower, avowal *n.*, avowedly *adv.*

a-wait *v.* To wait for something.

a-wake *v.* To wake up; to be alert or watchful.

a-ward *v.* To give or confer as being deserved needed, or merited. *n.* A judgment or decision; a prize. awardable *adj.*, awarder *n.*

a-ware *adj.* Being conscious or mindful of something. awareness *n.*

a-wash *adj.* Flooded; afloat; to be washed by water.

a-way *adv.* At a distance; apart from.

awe *n.* A feeling of wonder mixed with reverence. awe *v.*

a-wea-ry *adj.* Tired.

a-weigh *adj.* To hang just clear of a ship's anchor.

awe-some *adj.* Expressive of awe. awesomely *adv.*, awsomeness *n.*

aw-ful *adj.* Very unpleasant or dreadful.

a-while *adv.* For a short time.

a-whirl *adj.* To spin around.

awk-ward *adj.* Not graceful; clumsy. awkwardly *adv.*, awkwardness *n.*

awl *n.* Tool used to make holes in leather.

awn *n.* The part of a piece a grass which resembles a bristle. -ed, awnless *adj.*

awn-ing *n.* Structure that serves as a shelter over a window; roof-like.

AWOL *abbr.* Absent without leave.

a-wry *adv.* In a twisted or turned position.

ax *or* **axe** *n.* Tool used to split wood.

ax-i-om *n.* Statement recognized as being true; something assumed to be true without proof. -atic *adj.*, -cally *adv.*

ax-is *n., pl.* **axes**

The line around an object or body that rotates or may be thought to rotate.

ax-le *n.* A spindle or shaft around which a wheel or pair of wheels revolve.

a-yah *n.* A native nursemaid or maid in India.

a-zal-ea *n.* A shrub of the genus Rhododendron group grown for their many colored flowers.

a-zo-ic *adj.* Time period which occured before life first appeared on the earth.

AZT *abbr.* Azidothymidine; a drug that improves the symptoms of AIDS;, (Acquired Immune Deficiency Syndrome), allowing a longer and better life. Approved early 1987 by the Federal Government for prescription use.

Az-tec *n.* The Indian people of Mexico.

az-ure *n.* The blue color of the sky.

B, b The second letter of the English alphabet; a student's grade rating of good, but not excellent.

BA *abbr.* Bachelor of Arts.

babble *v.* To reveal secrets; to chatter senselessly; to talk foolishly.

babe *n.* A very young child or infant.

ba-bel *n.* Babbling noise of many people talking at the same time.

ba-boon *n.* A species of the monkey family with a large body and big canine teeth.

ba-by *n., pl.* **babies** A young child; infant. **babyish** *adj.*

bac-ca-lau-re-ate *n.* A degree given by universities and colleges.

Bac-chus *n.* The Greek god of wine.

bach-e-lor *n.* An unmarried male; the first degree one can receive from a four year university.

ba-cil-lus *n., pl.* **bacilli** A rod-like microscopic organism which can cause certain diseases.

back *n.* The rear part of the human body from the neck to the end of the spine; also the rear part of an animal.

back-ache *n.* A pain in the back.

back-bite *v.* To gossip or speak in a nasty way about a person who is not present.

back-board *n.* A board that gives support when placed under or behind something.

back-bone *n.* The spinal column or spine of the vertebrates; the strongest support, or strength.

back-drop *n.* A curtain or scene behind the back of a stage set.

back-er *n.* One who gives support to a cause.

back-field *n.* Football players who are positioned behind the line of scrimmage.

back-fire *n.* Premature explosion of unburned exhaust gases or ignited fuel of an internal-combustion engine.

back-gam-mon *n.* A game played by two people wherein each player tries to move his counters on the board, at the same time trying to block his opponent.

back-ground *n.* The area or surface behind which objects are represented; conditions leading up to a happening; the collection of a person's complete experience.

back-hand *n.* A stroke in the game of tennis, made with the back of the hand facing outward. **backhand** *v.,* **backhanded** *adj.*

back-ing *n.* Support or aid; a supply in reserve.

back-lash *n.* A violent backward movement or reaction.

back-log *n.* An accumulation of unfinished work; a reserve supply.

back-pack *n.* A piece of equipment used to carry items on the back, mounted on a lightweight frame, and constructed of nylon or canvas.

back-pedal *v.* To move backward or retreat.

back-rest *n.* A support given to the back.

back room *n.* A room in the rear of a building for inconspicuous group meetings.

back-saw *n.* Saw with metal ribs on its back side.

back-seat *n.* The seat in the back of an auto-mobile, etc.; an inferior position.

back-side *n.* The buttocks.

back-slide *v.* To lapse back into a less desirable condition, as in a religious practice. **backsliding** *v.,* **backslider** *n.*

back-spin *n.* A spin which rotates in the reverse direction.

back-stage *n.* The area behind the performing area in a theatre.

back-stop *n.* Something that prevents a ball from being hit out of play.

back-stretch *n.* The opposite of the homestretch on a racecourse.

back-stroke *n.* A swimming stroke performed while on the back.

back-swept *adj.* Slanting or swept backward.

back-talk *n.* A smart or insolent reply.

back-track *v.* To reverse a policy; to retrace previous steps. **backtracking** *v.*

back-up *n.* One that serves as an alternative or substitute.

back-ward *adv.* Toward the back; to or at the back. **backwardness** *n.,* **backwards** *adv.*

back-wash *n.* A backward flow of water.

back-wa-ter *n.* A body of water turned back by an obstruction.

back-woods *n., pl.* A sparsely populated, heavily wooded area. **backwoodsman** *n.*

ba-con *n.* Side and back of a pig, salted and smoked.

bac-ter-ia *pl., n.* The plural of bacterium.

bac-te-ri-cide *n.* A substance that kills bacteria.

bac-te-ri-ol-o-gy *n.* Scientific study of bacteria.

bac-te-ri-um *n., pl.* **-ria** Any of various forms of numerous unicellular micro organisms that cause disease. **bacterial** *adj.*

bad *adj.* Naughty or disobedient; unfavorable; inferior; poor; spoiled; invalid. **badly** *adv.*

badger *n.*

A sturdy burrowing mammal. *v.* To harass or trouble persistently.

bad-lands *pl., n.* Area with sparse life, peaks, and eroded ridges.

bad-min-ton *n.* A court game played with long-handled rackets and a shuttlecock.

baf-fle *v.* To puzzle; to perplex. *n.* A device that checks or regulates the flow of gas, sound, or liquids etc. **baffled, baffling** *v.*

bag *n.* A flexible container used for

holding, storing, or carrying something. **bag** v. **bagful** n., **baggy** adj.

ba-gasse n. Plant residue.

ba-gel n. A hard, glazed, round roll with a chewy texture and a hole in the middle.

bag-gage n. The personal belongings of a traveler.

bag-gy adj. Loose. **baggily** adv.

Bagh-dad n. The capital of Iraq.

bag-man n. A person who collects illicit payments for another.

bag-pipe n. A wind instrument with a leather bag and melody pipes. **bagpiper** n.

ba-guette n. A gem in the shape of a long, narrow rectangle.

bag-wig n. An 18th century wig with the hair in the back contained in a small silk bag.

bag-worm n. A type of moth larva that lives in a silk case covered with plant debris, very destructive to evergreens.

Ba-ha-ma Islands n. Islands in the Atlantic Ocean, southeast of Florida.

bail n. The security or money given to guarantee the appearance of a person for trial. v. To remove water from a boat by dipping and emptying the water overboard. **bailor, bailer** n.

bail-iff n. The officer who guards prisoners and keeps order in a courtroom.

bail-i-wick n. The office or district of a bailiff.

bails-man n. The person who puts up the bail for another.

bait v. To lure; to entice. n. Food that is used to catch or trap an animal.

baize n. A coarse woolen or cotton cloth.

bake v. To cook in an oven; to harden or dry. **baking, baked** v., **baker** n.

baker's dozen n. Thirteen.

bak-ing pow-der n. A leavening agent used in baking consisting of carbonate, an acid substance, and flour or starch.

bak-ing soda n. Sodium bicarbonate.

bak-sheesh n. A tip or gratuity.

bal-a-lai-ka n. A three-stringed musical instrument.

bal-ance n. Device for determining the weight of something; the agreement of totals in the debit and credit of an account.

bal-co-ny n., pl. -nies Gallery or platform projecting from the wall of a building.

bald adj. Lacking hair on the head.

bal-der-dash n. Nonsense.

bale n. A large, bound package or bundle.

ba-leen n. A whalebone.

balk v. To refuse to go on; to stop short of something. n. A rafter or crossbeam extending from wall to wall. **balking** v., **balky** adj.

ball n. A round body or mass; a pitched baseball that is delivered outside of the strike zone.

bal-lad n. A narrative story or poem of folk origin; a romantic song.

bal-last n. Heavy material placed in a vehicle to give stability and weight.

ball bear-ing n A bearing that reduces friction by separating the stationary parts from the moving ones.

bal-le-ri-na n. A female ballet dancer in a company.

bal-let n. An artistic expression of dance by choreographic design.

bal-lis-tic missile n. A projectile that is self-powered, is guided during ascent, and has a free fall trajectory at descent.

bal-loon n. A bag inflated with gas lighter than air which allows it to float in the atmosphere, used as a child's toy.

bal-lot n. A slip of paper used in secret voting. v. To vote by ballot.

ball-park n. A stadium where ball games are played.

ball-point n. A pen that has a small self-inking writing point.

bal-ly-hoo n. Exaggerated advertising.

balm n. A fragrant ointment that soothes, comforts, and heals.

ba-lo-ney n., Slang Nonsense.

bal-sa n. American tree that is very light in weight.

bal-sam n. A fragrant ointment from different trees; a plant cultivated for its colorful flowers.

bal-us-ter n. The upright post that supports a handrail.

bam-boo n. Tropical, tall grass with hollow, pointed stems.

bam-boo-zle v. To trick or deceive. **bamboozled, bamboozling** v.

ban v. To prohibit; to forbid. **banning, banned** v.

ba-nal adj. Trite; lacking freshness.

ba-nan-a n. The crescent-shaped usually yellow, edible fruit of a tropical plant.

band n. A strip used to trim, finish, encircle, or bind; the range of a radio wave length; a group of musicians who join together to play their instruments.

band-age n. A strip of cloth used to protect an injury. **bandage** v.

ban-dan-na n. A brightly colored cotton or silk handkerchief.

ban-deau n. A narrow band worn in the hair; a narrow brassiere.

ban-dit n., pl. bandits, banditti A gangster or robber. **banditry** n.

ban-do-leer n. A belt worn over the shoulder with pockets for cartridges.

ban-dy adv. Bent; crooked; curved outward.

bane n. A cause of destruction. -ful adj.

bang n. A sudden loud noise; short hair cut across the forehead. v. To move or hit with a loud noise.

Bang-kok n. The capital of Thailand.

ban-gle n. A bracelet worn around the wrist or ankle.

ban-ish v. To leave; to drive away.

banished, banishing v., -er, -ment n.

ban-jo n. A stringed instrument similar to a guitar. banjoist n.

bank n. A slope of land adjoining water; an establishment that performs financial transactions. bankable adj.

bank-rupt n., pl. -cies One who is legally insolvent and whose remaining property is divided among creditors. bankrupt v., bankruptcy n.

ban-ner n. A piece of cloth, such as a flag, that is used as a standard by a commander or monarch.

ban-nock n. Unleavened or flat cake made from barley or oatmeal.

banns pl., n. The announcement of a forthcoming marriage.

ban-quet n. An elaborate dinner or feast.

ban-yan n. A tree from the tropics whose aerial roots grow downward to form additional roots.

bap-tism n. A Christian sacrament of spiritual rebirth through the application of water. baptismal adj.

bap-tize v. To immerse in water during baptism. baptized, -ing v., baptizer n.

bar n. A rigid piece of material used as a support; a counter where a person can receive drinks. v. To prohibit or exclude.

barb n. A sharp projection that extends backward making it difficult to remove. barbed adj.

bar-bar-i-an n. A person or culture thought to be primitive and therefore inferior. barbarous, barbaric adj.

bar-be-cue n. An outdoor fireplace or pit for roasting meat. barbecue v.

bar-bell n. A bar with weights at both ends, used for exercise.

bar-ber n. A person whose business is cutting and dressing hair and shaving and trimming beards.

bar-ber-shop n. The place of business where hair is cut.

bard n. A poet. bardic adj.

bare adj. Exposed to view; without coloring. bare v., bareness n.

bare-back adv. & adj. Riding a horse without a saddle.

bare-ly adv. Sparsely; by a very little amount.

barf v. Slang To vomit.

bar-gain n. A contract or agreement on the purchase or sale of an item; a purchase made at a favorable or good price. bargainer n.

barge n. A flat-bottomed boat. v. To intrude abruptly.

bar-i-tone n. A male voice in the range between tenor and bass.

bark n. The outer covering of a tree; the abrupt, harsh sound made by a dog. barker n.

bar-ley n. A type of grain used for food and for making whiskey and beer.

bar mitz-vah n. A Jewish boy who, having reached the age of 13, assumes the moral and religious duties of an adult.

barn n. A farm building used to shelter animals and to store farm equipment and products.

bar-na-cle n. A fish with a hard shell that remains attached to an underwater surface.

ba-rom-et-er n. An instrument that records the weight and pressure of the atmosphere.

bar-on n. The lowest rank of nobility in Great Britain. -ness n., baronial adj.

ba-roque adj. An artistic style characterized by elaborate and ornate forms.

bar-rack n. A building for housing soldiers.

bar-ra-cu-da n., pl. -da, -das A fish with a large, narrow body, found in the Atlantic Ocean.

bar-rage n. A concentrated outpouring or discharge of missiles from small arms.

bar-ra-try n. The unlawful breach of duty by a ship's crew that results in injury to the ship's owner.

bar-rel n. Wooden container with round, flat ends of equal size and sides that bulge.

bar-ren adj. Lacking vegetation; sterile.

bar-rette n. A clasp or small bar used to hold hair in place.

bar-ri-cade n. Barrier.

bar-ri-er n. A structure that restricts or bars entrance.

bar-room n. A building or room where a person can purchase alcoholic beverages sold at a counter.

bar-row n. A rectangular, flat frame with handles; a wheelbarrow.

bar-tend-er n. A person who serves alcoholic drinks and other refreshments at a bar.

bar-ter v. To trade something for something else without the exchange of money. -ing, bartered v., barterer n.

Barton, Clara n. The founder of the American Red Cross.

ba-salt n. A greenish-black volcanic rock.

base n. The fundamental part; the lowest part; the bottom. base v.

base-ball n. A game played with a ball and bat; the ball used in a baseball game.

base-board n. A molding that covers the area where the wall meets the floor.

base-ment n. The foundation of a building or home.

bash v. To smash with a heavy blow; Slang A party. bashed, bashing v.

bash-ful adj. Socially shy. bashfully adv.

ba-sic adj. Forming the basis; fundamental. basically adv.

BASIC n. A common computer programming language.

bas-il n. An herb used as seasoning in cooking.

bas-o-lisk n. A tropical American lizard.

ba-sin n. A sink; a washbowl; a round open container used for washing; an area that has been drained by a river system.

ba-sis n., pl. bases The main part; foundation.

bask v. To relax in the warmth of the

sun. **basking, basked** v.

bas-ket n. An object made of woven material, as straw, cane, or other flexible items. **basketry** n.

bas-ket-ball n. A game played on a court with two teams; each team trying to throw the ball through the basketball hoop at the opponents' end of the court.

bas mitz-vah n. A Jewish girl who having reached the age of thirteen, assumes the moral and religious duties of an adult.

bass n., pl. **basses**

A fresh water fish, one of the perch family.

bas-si-net n. A basket on legs used as an infant's crib.

bas-soon n. A woodwind instrument with a low-pitched sound.

bas-tard n. An illegitimate child. *Slang* A disagreeable, nasty, or mean person. **bastardize** v.

baste v. To run a loose stitch to hold a piece of material in place for a short time. **-ed, -ing** v.

bat n. A wooden stick made from strong wood; a nocturnal flying mammal. **bat** v., **batter** n.

bath n., pl. **-baths** The act of washing the body.

bathe v. To take a bath. **bathing** v.

bat-tal-ion n. A military unit consisting of a headquarters and three or more companies.

bat-ten v. To secure; to fasten together.

bat-ter v. To beat or strike continuously; to assault. n. A cricket or baseball player at bat. **battering, battered** v.

bat-tery n. A group of heavy guns.

bat-tle n. A struggle; combat between opposing forces. v. To engage in a war or battle. **battled, battling** v.

bawd n. A prostitute. **bawdy** adj.

bawl v. To cry out loudly.

bay n. The inlet of a body of water; a main division or compartment.

bay-berry n. Evergreen shrub used for decorations and making candles.

bay-o-net n. A spear-like weapon.

ba-zaar n. A fair where a variety of items are sold as a money-making project for charity, clubs, churches, or other such organizations.

ba-zooka n. Weapon for firing rockets.

BBA abbr. Bachelor of Business Administration.

BC abbr. Before Christ.

BD abbr. Bank draft.

be v. To occupy a position; to exist; used with the present participle of a verb to show action; used as a prefix to construct compound words, as behind, before, because, etc.

beach n. Pebbly or sandy shore of a lake, ocean, sea, or river.

bea-con n. A coastal guiding or signaling device.

bead n. A small round piece of material with a hole for threading. **beading** n.

beak n. The bill of a bird. **beaked** adj.

beak-er n. Large, widemouthed cup for drinking; a cylindrical, glass laboratory vessel with a lip for pouring.

beam n. Large, oblong piece of wood or metal used in construction. v. To shine.

bean n. An edible seed or seed pod.

bear n., pl. **bears**

A carnivorous mammal. v. To endure; to carry; to support. **bearable**, adj.

beard n. Hair growing on the chin and cheeks. **bearded, beardless** adj.

beast n. A four-legged animal. **-ly** adj.

beat v. To strike repeatedly; to defeat. adj. Exhausted, very tired. **beaten** adj., **beat, beater** n.

be-a-tif-ic adj. Giving or showing extreme bliss or joy.

be-at-i-tude n. The highest form of happiness; heavenly bliss.

beau n. Sweetheart; dandy.

beau-ty n. Quality that is pleasing to the eye. **beautiful** adj., **beautifully**, adv.

be-bop n. *Slang* Jazz music.

be-calm v. To make quiet. **becalming** v.

be-cause conj. For a reason; since.

beck n. A summons; a call.

be-come v. To come, to be, or to grow. **becoming** adj.

bed n. Furniture for sleeping; a piece of planted or cultivated ground. **-ding** n.

be-dazzle v. To confuse with bright lights. **bedazzling, bedazzled** v.

bed-bug n. A wingless insect that sucks blood and infests human homes, especially beds.

bed-fast adj. Confined to a bed; bedridden.

bed-lam n. A state or situation of confusion.

be-drag-gled adj. Limp and wet; soiled as though pulled through mud.

bee n. A hairy-bodied insect characterized by structures for gathering pollen and nectar from flowers.

beech n. A tree of light-colored bark, with edible nuts.

beef n., pl. **beefs, beeves** A cow, steer, or bull that has been fattened for consumption. **beefy** adj.

beer n. An alcoholic beverage.

bees-wax n. The wax from bees that is used for their honeycombs.

beet n. The root from a cultivated plant that can be used as a vegetable or a source of sugar.

bee-tle n. An insect with modified, horny front wings, which cover the membranous back wings when it is not in flight.

be-fit *v.* To be suitable. **befitting** *adj.*

be-fore *adv.* Earlier; previously. *prep.* In front of.

be-friend *v.* To be a friend to someone.

beg *v.* To make a living by asking for charity. **beggar** *n.*, **beggarly** *adj.*

be-gan *v.* The past tense of begin.

be-get *v.* To cause or produce.

be-gin *v.* To start; to come into being; to commence. **beginner, beginning** *n.*

be-gone *v.*, *interj.* Go away; depart.

be-go-nia *n.* A tropical plant with waxy flowers and showy leaves.

be-grime *v.* To soiled with grime.

be-grudge *v.* To envy someone's possessions or enjoyment.

be-guile *v.* To deceive; to delight; to charm. **beguiled** *v.*

be-gun *v.* The past participle of begin.

be-half *n.* The support or interest of another person.

be-have *v.* To function in a certain manner; to conduct oneself in a proper manner. **behaving** *v.*, **behavior,** *n.*

be-head *v.* To remove the head from the body; to decapitate.

be-held *v.* Past participle of behold.

be-hind *adv.* To or at the back; late or slow in arriving.

be-hold *v.* To look at; to see.

be-hoove *v.* To benefit or give advantage.

beige *n.* or *adj.* A light brownish, grey color.

being *n.* One's existence.

be-la-bor *v.* To work on or to discuss beyond the point where it is necessary; to carry to absurd lengths.

be-lat-ed *adj.* Tardy; late. **belatedly** *adv.*

bel can-to *n.* Operatic singing with rich lyricism and brilliant vocal means.

belch *v.* To expel stomach gas through the mouth.

bel-fry *n.*, *pl.* **belfries** The tower that contains the bell of a church.

Bel-grade *n.* Capital of Yugoslavia.

be-lief *n.* Something that is trusted or believed.

be-lieve *v.* To accept as true or real; to hold onto religious beliefs. **believable** *adj.*, **believer** *n.*

be-lit-tle *v.* To think or speak in a slighting manner of someone or something. **belittled, belittling** *v.*

bell *n.* A metal instrument that gives a metallic sound when struck.

Bell, Alexander Graham *n.* Inventor of the telephone.

bel-la-don-na *n.* A poisonous plant with black berries; a medicine extracted from the belladonna plant.

bell--bot-toms *pl.*, *n.* Pants with legs that flare at the bottom.

belles--let-tres *pl.*, *n.* Literature that is regarded not for its value, but for its artistic quality.

bel-lig-er-ent *adj.* Hostile and inclined to be aggressive. **belligerence** *n.*, **belligerent** *n.*

bel-low *v.* To make a deep, powerful roar like a bull. **bellowed, bellowing** *v.*

bel-lows *n.* An instrument that produces air in a chamber and expels it through a short tube.

bel-ly *n.*, *pl.* **bellies** The abdomen or the stomach.

be-long *v.*, *pl.* **belongings** *n.* To be a part of. **belonging** *n.*

be-loved *adj.* To be dearly loved.

be-low *adv.* At a lower level or place. *prep.* To be inferior to.

belt *n.* A band worn around the waist; a zone or region that is distinctive in a special way.

belt-way *n.* A highway that encircles an urban area.

be-muse *v.* To bewilder or confuse; to be lost in thought. **bemusing** *v.*, **bemused** *adj.*

bench *n.* A long seat for more than two people; the seat of the judge in a court of law.

bend *v.* To arch; to change the direct course; to deflect. **-ing** *v.*, **bender** *n.*

beneath *adv.* To or in a lower position; below; underneath.

ben-e-dict *n.* A previously confirmed bachelor who was recently married.

ben-e-dic-tion *n.* A blessing given at the end of a religious service.

ben-e-fac-tion *n.* A charitable donation; a gift. **benefactor** *n.*

ben-e-fice *n.* Fixed capital assets of a church that provide a living.

be-nef-i-cence *n.* The quality of being kind or charitable.

ben-e-fi-cial *adj.* Advantageous; helpful. **beneficially** *adv.*

ben-e-fit *n.* Aid; help; an act of kindness; a social event or entertainment to raise money for a person or cause.

be-nev-o-lence *n.* The inclination to be charitable. **benevolent** *adj.*

be-night-ed *adj.* Overtaken by night.

be-nign *adj.*, *pl.* **-ities.** Having a gentle and kind disposition; gracious; not malignant. **benignly** *adv.*

ben-i-son *n.* A blessing; benediction

bent *adj.* Curved, not straight. *n.* A fixed determination; purpose.

be-numb *v.* To dull; to make numb.

be-queath *v.* To give or leave to someone by will; to hand down. **-al** *n.*

be-quest *n.* Something that is bequeathed.

be-rate *v.* To scold severely.

be-reave *v.* To deprive; to suffer the loss of a loved one. **bereft** *adj.*, **bereavement** *n.*

be-ret *n.* A round, woolen cap that has no brim.

berg *n.* A large mass of ice; iceberg.

ber-i-ber-i *n.* Nervous disorder from the deficiency of vitamin B producing partial paralysis of the extremities.

berry *n.*, *pl.* **berries** An edible fruit, such as a strawberry or blackberry.

ber-serk *adj.* Destructively violent.

berth *n.* Space at a wharf for a ship or boat to dock; a built-in bunk or bed on a train or ship.

ber-yl *n.* A mineral composed of silicon, oxygen, and beryllium that is the major source of beryllium.

be-ryl-li-um *n.* A corrosion-resistant, rigid, light-weight metallic element.

be-seech *v.* To ask or request earnestly.

be-side *prep.* At the side of; next to.

be-siege *v.* To surround with troops; to harass with requests.

be-sit *v.* To surround on all sides.

be-smear *v.* To soil; to smear.

be-som *n.* A broom made of twigs that are attached to a handle, used to sweep floors.

be-spat-ter *v.* To splash; to soil.

be-speak *v.* To indicate; to speak.

best *adj.* Exceeding all others in quality or excellence; most suitable, desirable, or useful.

bes-tial *adj.*, *pl.* -ities Of or relating to an animal; brutish. -ly *adv.*, bestiality *n.*

bes-ti-ar-y *n.* A medieval collection of fables about imaginary and real animals, each with a moral.

be-stir *v.* To rouse into action.

best man *n.* The attendant of a bridegroom at a wedding.

be-stow *v.* To present or to give honor.

be-stride *v.* To step over or to straddle.

bet *n.* An amount risked on a stake or wager.

be-take *v.* To cause oneself to make one's way; move or to go.

beta particle *n.* High-speed positron or electron coming from an atomic nucleus that is undergoing radioactive decay.

be-ta-tron *n.* Accelerator in which electrons are propelled by the inductive action of a rapidly varying magnetic field.

be-think *v.* To remember or to remind oneself.

Beth-le-hem *n.* The birthplace of Jesus.

be-tide *v.* To happen to; to take place.

be-to-ken *v.* To show by a visible sign.

be-tray *v.* To be disloyal or unfaithful; to indicate; to deceive. betrayal *n.*

be-troth *v.* To promise to take or give in marriage. betrothal *n.*

be-trothed *n.* A person to whom one is engaged to marry.

bet-ter *adj.* More suitable, useful, desirable, or higher in quality. *v.* To improve oneself. betterment *n.*

be-tween *prep.* The position or time that separates; in the middle or shared by two.

be-twixt *prep.* Not knowing which way one should go; between.

bev-el *n.* The angle at which one surface meets another when they are not at right angles.

bev-er-age *n.* A refreshing liquid for drinking other than water.

bev-y *n.*, *pl.* -bevies A collection or group; a flock of birds.

be-wail *v.* To express regret or sorrow.

be-ware *v.* To be cautious; to be on guard.

be-wilder *v.* To confuse; to perplex or puzzle. bewilderment *n.*

be-witch *v.* To fascinate or captivate completely. -ery *n.*, bewitchment *v.*

bey *n.* The Turkish title of respect and honor.

be-yond *prep.* Outside the reach or scope of; something past or to the far side.

bez-el *n.* A flange or groove that holds the beveled edge of an object such as a gem in a ring mounting.

be-zique *n.* A card game that uses a deck of 64 cards, similar to pinochle.

bi *pref.* Two; occurring two times; used when constructing nouns.

bi-a-ly *n.* A baked roll with onions on the top.

bi-an-nu-al *adj.* Taking place twice a year; semiannual. biannually *adv.*

bi-as *n.* A line cut diagonally across the grain of fabric; prejudice. *v.* To be or to show prejudice.

bib *n.* A cloth that is tied under the chin of small children to protect their clothing.

Bi-ble *n.* The holy book of Christianity, containing the Old and New Testaments. Biblical *adj.*, Biblically *adv.*

bib-li-og-ra-phy *n.*, *pl.* -phies A list of work by a publisher or writer; a list of sources of information. -her *n.*

bib-u-lous *adj.* Inclined to drink, of or related to drinking.

bi-cen-ten-ni-al *adj.* Happening once every 200 years. *n.* Anniversary or celebration of 200 years.

bi-ceps *n.*

Large muscle in the front of the upper arm and at the back of the thigh. bicipital *adj.*

bick-er *v.* To quarrel or argue. bicker *n.*

bi-con-cave *adj.* Bowing in on two sides.

bi-cul-tur-al *adj.* Having or containing two distinct cultures.

bi-cus-pid *n.* A tooth with two roots.

bi-cy-cle *n.* A two-wheeled vehicle propelled by pedals. bicyclist *n.*

bid *v.* To request something; to offer to pay a certain price. *n.* One's intention in a card game. bidder *n.*

bid-dy *n.* A young chicken; hen. *Slang* A fussy woman.

bide *v.* To remain; to wait.

bi-det *n.* A basin for bathing the genital and anal areas.

bi-en-ni-al *adj.* Occurring every two years; lasting for only two years. biennially *adv.*

bier *n.* A stand on which a coffin is placed before burial.

bi-fo-cal *adj.* Having two different focal lengths.

bifocals *pl.*, *n.* Lenses used to correct both close and distant vision.

bi-fur-cate *v.* To divide into two parts.

big *adj.* Very large in dimensions, intensity, and extent; grown-up; bountiful. bigness *n.*

big-a-my *n.*, *pl.* bigamies The act of marrying one person while still married to another. bigamist *n.*

Big Dipper *n.* Cluster of seven stars that

form a bowl and handle.

big head *adj.* A conceited person. **bigheadedness** *n.*

big--hearted *adj.* Being generous and kind.

bighorn *n.* A sheep from the mountainous western part of North America.

bight *n.* The slack in a rope; a bend in the shoreline.

big-ot *n., pl.* **-ries** A person who is fanatically devoted to one group, religion, politics, or race. **bigoted** *adj.*, **bigotry** *n.*

big-wig *n.* A person of authority.

bike *n.* A bicycle. **bike** *v.*, **biker** *n.*

bi-ki-ni *n.* A scanty, two-piece bathing suit.

bi-lat-er-al *adj.* Having or relating to two sides.

bile *n.* A brownish-yellow alkaline liquid that is secreted by the liver. **biliary** *adj.*

bilge *n.* Lowest inside part of the hull of a ship.

bi-lin-gual *adj.* Able to speak two languages with equal ability.

bil-ious *adj.* Undergoing gastric distress from a sluggish gallbladder or liver.

bilk *v.* To cheat or swindle.

bill *n.* Itemized list of fees for services rendered; a document presented containing a formal statement of a case complaint or petition; the beak of a bird. **bill** *v.*, **biller** *n.*

bill-board *n.* A place for displaying advertise-ments.

bill-fold *n.* Pocket-sized wallet for holding money and personal information.

bil-liards *n.* Game played on a table with cushioned edges.

bil-lion *n.* A thousand million.

bil-lion-aire *n.* A person whose wealth equals at least one billion dollars.

bill of lading *n.* A form issued by the carrier for promise of delivery of merchandise listed.

Bill of Rights *n.* The first ten amendments to the United States Constitution.

bil-low *n.* Large swell of water or smoke; wave. **billowy** *adj.*

bil-ly club *n.* A short wooden club used for protection or defense.

billy goat *n.* A male goat.

bi-met-al-lism *n.* The use of two metals, gold and silver, as legal tenders.

bi-month-ly *adj., pl.* **-lies** Occurring every two months.

bin *n.* An enclosed place for storage.

bi-na-ry *adj.* Made of two different components or parts.

bind *v.* To hold with a belt or rope; to bandage; to fasten and enclose pages of a book between covers. **binding** *n.*

bind-er *n.* A notebook for holding paper; payment or written statement legally binding an agreement.

bind-er-y *n., pl.* **-eries** The place where books are taken to be bound.

binge *n.* Uncontrollable selfindulgence; a spree.

bin-go *n.* A game of chance in which a person places markers on numbered cards in accordance with numbers drawn by a caller.

bin-na-cle *n.* A place where a ship's compass is contained.

bin-oc-u-lar *n.* A device designed for both eyes to bring objects far away into focus.

bi-o-chem-is-try *n.* Chemistry of substances and biological processes.

bi-o-de-grad-a-ble *adj.* Decomposable by natural processes.

bi-o-feed-back *n.* The technique of controlling involuntary bodily functions.

bi-o-haz-ard *n.* Biological material that threatens humans and or their environment if infective.

biological warfare *n.* Warfare that uses organic biocides or diseaseproducing microorganisms to destroy crops, livestock, or human life.

bi-ol-o-gy *n.* Science of living organisms and the study of their structure, reproduction, and growth. **biological** *adj.*, **biologist** *n.*

bi-o-med-i-cine *n.* Medicine that has to do with human response to environmental stress.

bi-on-ics *n.* Application of biological principles to the study and design of engineering systems, as electronic systems.

bi-o-phys-ics *n.* The physics of living organisms.

bi-op-sy *n., pl.* **biopsies** The examination for the detection of a disease in tissues removed from a living organism.

bi-ot-ic *adj.* Related to specific life conditions or to life itself.

bi-o-tin *n.* Part of the vitamin B complex found in liver, milk, yeast, and egg yolk.

bi-par-ti-san *adj.* Support by two political parties. **bipartisanship** *n.*

bi-plane *n.* A glider or airplane with wings on two levels.

bi-polar *adj.* Having or related to two poles; concerning the earth's North and South Poles.

bi-racial *adj.* Composed of or for members of two races.

birch *n.* A tree providing hard, close-grained wood.

bird *n.* A warm-blooded, egg-laying animal whose body is covered by feathers.

bird-brain *n., Slang* A person who acts in a silly fashion.

bird-ie *n.* A stroke under par in the game of golf; a shuttlecock.

bi-ret-ta *n.* Cap worn by Roman Catholic clergy, square in shape.

birl-ing *n.* A game of skill in which two lumberjacks try to balance on a floating log while spinning the log with their feet.

birth *n.* The beginning of existence. *v.* To bring forth a baby from the womb.

birth con-trol *n.* A technique used to control or prevent the number of children born by lessening the chances of conception.

birth-day *n.* The day a person is born and the anniversary of that day.

birth-mark *n.* A blemish or mark on the skin present at birth.

birth-place *n.* The place of birth.

birth-rate *n.* The ratio of the number of births to a given population over a specified period of time.

birth-right *n.* Privilege granted by virtue of birth especially to the first-born.

birth-stone *n.* A gemstone that represents the month a person was born in.

bis *adv.* Again; encore.

bis-cuit *n.* Small piece of bread made with baking soda or baking powder; a cookie.

bi-sect *v.* To divide or cut into two equal parts. **bisection** *n.*

bi-sex-u-al *adj.* Sexually relating to both sexes.

bish-op *n.* A Christian clergyman with high rank. **bishopric** *n.*

bis-muth *n.* A white, crystalline metallic element.

bi-son *n.*

A large buffalo of northwestern America, with a dark-brown coat and short, curved horns.

bisque *n.* A creamy soup made from fish or vegetables; unglazed clay.

bis-sex-tile *adj.* Related to the extra day occurring in a leap year.

bis-tro *n., pl.* **bistros** A bar or small nightclub.

bit *n.* A tiny piece or amount of something; a tool designed for boring or drilling especially, drilling for oil; in computer science, either of two characters, as the binary digits zero and one, of a language that has only two characters; a unit of information; storage capacity, as of a computer memory.

bitch *n.* A female dog; a spiteful woman. *v.* To complain.

bite *v.* To cut, tear, or crush with the teeth. **bite** *n.*, **bitingly** *adv.*

bit-stock *n.* A brace that secures a drilling bit.

bit-ter *adj.* Having a sharp, unpleasant taste. **bitterly** *adv.*, **bitterness** *n.*

bit-ter-sweet *n.* A woody vine whose root, when chewed, has first a bitter, then a sweet taste.

bi-tu-mi-nous coal *n.* Coal that contains a high ratio of bituminous material and burns with a smoky flame.

bi-valve *n.* A mollusk that has a hinged two-part shell, a clam or oyster.

biv-ou-ac *n.* A temporary military camp in the open air.

bi-week-ly *n.* Occurring every two weeks.

bi-year-ly *n.* Occurring every two years.

bi-zarre *adj.* Extremely strange or odd.

bkpg *abbr.* Bookkeeping.

bkpt *abbr.* Bankrupt.

blab *v.* To reveal a secret by indiscreetly talking; to gossip.

blab-ber *v.* To chatter; to blab. **blabber** *n.*

blab-ber-mouth *n., Slang* A person who gossips.

black *adj.* Very dark in color; depressing; cheerless; darkness, the absence of light. **blackness** *n.*, **blackly** *adv.*

black--and--blue *adj.* Discolored skin caused by bruising.

black-ball *n.* A vote that prevents a person's admission to an organization or club.

black belt *n.* The rank of expert in karate.

black-berry *n., pl.* **berries** A thorny plant with black edible berries that have small seeds.

black-bird *n.* A small bird, the males of the species having mostly all black feathers.

black-board *n.* Hard, slate-like board written on with chalk.

black box *n.* The container that protects the tape recordings of airline pilots from water and fire, normally recoverable in the event of an accident.

black eye *n.* A bruise or discoloration around the eye.

black--eyed Susan *n.* North American plant with orange-yellow petals and dark brown centers; state flower of Maryland.

black-head *n.* A small mass of dirt that clogs the pore of the skin.

black-jack *n.* A card game in which each player tries to accumulate cards with points higher than that of the dealer, but not more than 21 points.

black-light *n.* Ultraviolet or invisible infrared light.

black magic *n.* Witchcraft.

black-mail *n.* The threat of exposing a past discreditable act or crime; money paid to avoid exposure. **blackmailer** *n.*

black market *n.* The illegal buying or selling of merchandise or items.

Black Muslim *n.* A member of a Black religious organization that supports the establishment of a Black nation.

black-out *n.* The temporary loss of electrical power. *v.* To conceal lights that might be seen by enemy aircraft.

Black Power *n.* The movement by Black Americans to emphasize their social, economic, and political powers.

Black Sea *n.* The inland sea between Asia Minor and Europe.

black sheep *n.* A person who is considered a loser by a respectable family.

black-smith *n.* A person who shapes iron with heat and a hammer.

black-top *n.* Asphalt, used to pave or surface roads.

black widow *n.* A spider that is extremely poisonous.

blad-der *n.* The expandable sac in the pelvis that holds urine.

blade *n.* The cutting part of a knife; the

leaf of a plant or a piece of grass.

blame v. To hold someone guilty for something; to find fault. **blameless** n.

blanch v. To remove the color from something, as to bleach; to pour scalding hot water over fresh vegetables.

bland adj. Lacking taste or style. **blandly** adv., **blandness** n.

blan-dish v. To coax by flattery.

blank adj. Having no markings or writing; empty; confused. **blankly** adv., **blankness** n.

blank check n. Carte blanche; freedom of action.

blan-ket n. A woven covering used on a bed.

blank verse n. A poem of lines that have rhythm but do not rhyme.

blare v. To make or cause a loud sound.

blar-ney n. Talk that is deceptive or nonsense.

blast n. A strong gust of air; the sound produced when a horn is blown. **blasted** adj.

blast-off n. The launching of a space ship.

bla-tant adj. Unpleasant; offensively loud; shameless. **blatancy** n.

blath-er v. To talk, but not making sense.

blaze n. A bright burst of fire; a sudden outburst of anger; a trail marker; a white mark on an animal's face.

bla-zon v. To make known. **blazoner** n.

bldg abbr. Building.

bleach v. To remove the color from a fabric; to become white.

bleach-ers pl., n. Seating for spectators in a stadium.

bleak adj. Discouraging and depressing; barren; cold; harsh. **bleakness** n., **bleakly** adv.

bleat n. The cry of a sheep or goat.

bleed v. To lose blood, as from an injury; to extort money; to mix or allow dyes to run together.

bleed-ing heart n. A plant with pink flowers; a person who feels very sympathetic toward the underprivileged.

bleep n. A signal with a quick, loud sound.

blem-ish n. A flaw or defect.

blend v. To mix together smoothly, to obtain a new substance. **blender** n.

bless v. To honor or praise; to confer prosperity or well-being.

bless-ed adj. Holy; enjoying happiness.

bless-ing n. A short prayer before a meal.

blight n. A disease of plants that can cause complete destruction.

blimp n. A large aircraft with a nonrigid gas-filled hull.

blind adj. Not having eyesight; something that is not based on facts. n. A shelter that conceals hunters.

blind date n. A date between two strangers that has been arranged by a third party.

blind-ers pl., n. Flaps that are attached to the bridle of a horse, restricting side vision.

blind-fold v. To cover the eyes with a cloth; to block the vision. **blindfolded** adj.

blink v. To squint; to open and close the eyes quickly; to take a quick glance.

blink-er n. A signaling light that displays a message; a light on a car used to indicate turns.

blintz n. A very thin pancake rolled and stuffed with cottage cheese or other fillings.

blip v. To remove; erase sounds from a recording. n. The brief interruption as the result of blipping.

bliss n. To have great happiness or joy. **blissful** adj., **blissfully** adv.

blis-ter n. The swelling of a thin layer of skin that contains a watery liquid.

blithe adj. Carefree or casual. **blithery** adv., **blitheness** n.

blitz n. A sudden attack; an intensive and forceful campaign.

bliz-zard n. A severe winter storm characterized by wind and snow.

blk abbr. Black, block.

bloat v. To swell or puff out.

blob n. A small shapeless mass.

bloc n. A united group formed for a common action or purpose.

block n. A solid piece of matter; the act of obstructing or hindering something. **blockage** n., **blocker** n.

block-ade n. The closure of an area. **blockader** n., **blockade** v.

blond adj. A golden or flaxen color. **blondish** adj.

blonde adj. A woman or girl with blond hair.

blood n. The red fluid circulated by the heart throughout the body that carries oxygen and nutrients to all parts of the body.

blood bank n. A place where blood is processed, typed, and stored for future needs.

blood count n. The determination of the number of white and red corpuscles in a specific amount of blood.

blood-cur-dling adj. Terrifying; horrifying.

blood-hound n. A breed of dogs with a very keen sense of smell.

blood-let-ting n. The act of bleeding a vein as part of medical therapy.

blood-mobile n. A portable blood bank that visits different locations, drawing and collecting blood from donors.

blood poisoning n. The invasion of the blood by toxin produced by bacteria; septicemia.

blood-shot adj. Redness; irritation especially of the eyes.

blood-stream n. The circulation of blood in the vascular system.

blood-sucker n. An animal that sucks blood.

blood vessel n. Any canal in which blood circulates, such as a vein, artery, or capillary.

blood-y adj. Stained with blood; having the characteristics of containing blood. **bloodiness** n., **bloodied** adj.

bloom v. To bear flowers; to flourish; to have a healthy look. **blooming** adj.

bloom-ers n., pl. Loose trousers that are gathered at the knee or just below.

bloop-er n. An embarrassing blunder made in public.

blos-som n. A flower or a group of flowers of a plant that bears fruit. v. To flourish; to grow.

blot n. A spot or stain. v. To dry with an absorbent material.

blotch n. An area of a person's skin that is discolored. **blotch** v., **blotchily** adj.

blouse n. A loosely fitting shirt or top.

blow v. To move or be in motion because of a current of air. n. A sudden hit with a hand or fist. **blower** n.

blow—by—blow adj. Minutely detailed in description.

blow dry v. To dry one's hair with a hand-held hair dryer.

blow-hole n. A hole in the ice that enables aquatic mammals to come up and breathe; the nostril of a whale and other cetaceans.

blow-out n. The sudden deflation of a tire that occurs while driving.

blow-torch n. A hand-held tool that generates a flame hot enough to melt soft metals.

blow-up n. An enlargement; a photograph; an explosion of a violent temper.

BLT abbr. Bacon, lettuce, and tomato sandwich.

blubber n. The fat removed from whales and other marine mammals. **blubbery** adj.

blue n. A color the same as the color of a clear sky; the hue that is between violet and green; the color worn by the Union Army during the Civil War.

blue baby n. An infant with a bluish colored skin, caused by inadequate oxygen in the blood.

blue-fish n. A game fish of the tropical waters of the Atlantic and Indian Oceans.

blue-grass n. Folk music of the southern United States, played on guitars and banjos.

blue jay n. A bird having mostly blue colored feathers.

blue-nose n. A person who advocates a rigorous moral code.

blue-print n. A reproduction of technical drawings or plans, using white lines on a blue background.

blue ribbon n. The award given for placing first in a contest.

blues pl., n. A style of jazz from American Negro songs; a state of depression.

blue spruce n. An evergreen tree from the Rocky Mountains.

bluff v. To deceive or mislead; to intimidate by showing more confidence than the facts can support. n. A steep and ridged cliff.

blun-der n. An error or mistake caused by ignorance. v. To move clumsily. **blunderer** n.

blun-der-buss n. A short gun with a flared muzzle.

blunt adj. Frank and abrupt; a dull end or edge. **bluntly** adv.

blur v. To smudge or smear; to become hazy.

blurt v. To speak impulsively.

blush v. To be embarrassed from modesty or humiliation and to turn red in the face; to feel ashamed. n. Make-up used to give color to the cheekbones. **-ful** adj., **blushingly** adv.

blus-ter n. A violent and noisy wind in a storm. **bluster** v., **blusterer** n.

blvd abbr. Boulevard

bo-a n.

A large nonvenomous snake of the Boidea family which coils around prey and crushes it.

boar n.

A male pig; wild pig.

board n. A flat piece of sawed lumber; a flat area on which games are played. v. To receive lodging, meals or both, usually for pay; to enter a ship, train, or plane. **boarder** n.

board-walk n. A wooden walkway along a beach.

boast v. To brag about one's own accomplishments. **-er** n., **boastful** adj.

boat n. A small open craft or ship.

boat-swain n. Warrant or petty officer in charge of the rigging, anchors, and crew of a ship.

bob v. To cause to move up and down in a quick, jerky movement.

bob-bin n. A spool that holds thread in a sewing machine.

bob-by n. An English police officer.

bob-by socks pl., n. An ankle sock, usually worn by teenaged girls.

bob-cat n. A wildcat of North America, with reddish-brown fur, small ears, and a short tail.

bob-o-link n. An American song bird, the male has black, yellowish and white feathers.

bob-sled n. Racing sled which has steering controls on the front runners.

bode v. To foretell by omen or sign.

bod-ice n. The piece of a dress that extends from the shoulder to the waist.

bod-kin n. A small instrument with a sharp point for making holes in fabric.

bod-y n. The main part of something; the physical part of a person. **bodily** adv.

bod-y build-ing n. The development and toning of the body through diet and exercise.

body-guard n. A person hired to protect another person.

body-surf v. To ride on a wave without a

surfboard. **bodysurfer** *n.*

bo-gey *n.* In golf, one stroke over par for a hole.

bog-gle *v.* To pull away from with astonishment.

Bo-go-ta *n.* The capital of Colombia.

bo-gus *adj.* Something that is counterfeit; worthless in value.

Bo-he-mi-an *n.* An inhabitant or native of Bohemia.

bo-he-mi-an *n.* A person whose life-style is unconventional.

boil *v.* To raise the temperature of water or other liquid until it bubbles; to evaporate; reduce in size by boiling. *n.* A very painful, pus-filled swollen area of the skin caused by bacteria in the skin.

boil-er *n.* A vessel that contains water and is heated for power.

bois-ter-ous *adj.* Violent, rough and stormy; undisciplined. **boisterously** *adv.*

bold *adj.* Courageous; showing courage; distinct and clear. **boldly** *adv.*, **boldness** *n.*

bold-face *n.* A style of printing type with heavy thick lines.

bole *n.* A tree trunk.

bo-le-ro *n.* A short jacket without sleeves, worn open in the front.

boll *n.* A rounded capsule that contains seeds, as from the cotton plant.

boll wee-vil *n.* A small beetle whose larvae damage cotton bolls.

bo-lo-gna *n.* A seasoned, smoked sausage.

bol-ster *n.* A long, round pillow.

bolt *n.* A threaded metal pin designed with a head at one end and a removable nut at the other; a thunderbolt; a large roll of material. *v.* To run or move suddenly.

bomb *n.* A weapon that is detonated upon impact releasing destructive material as gas or smoke. *Slang* A complete and total failure.

bom-bard *v.* To attack repeatedly with missiles or bombs. **bombarder** *n.*, **bombardment** *n.*

bom-bast *n.* Very ornate speech. **bombastic** *adj.*

bom-ba-zine *n.* Silk or cotton fabric woven with diagonal ribbing.

bombed *adj.*, *Slang* Drunk.

bomber *n.* A military aircraft that carries and drops bombs.

bo-na fide *adj.* Performed in good faith; genuine; authentic.

bo-nan-za *n.* A profitable pocket or vein of ore; great prosperity.

bon-bon *n.* Chocolate or fondant candy with a creamy, fruity, or nutty center.

bond *n.* Something that fastens or binds together; a duty or binding agreement; an insurance agreement in which the agency guarantees to pay the employer in the event an employee is accused of causing financial loss. **bonded** *adj.*

bond-age *n.* Slavery; servitude.

bond ser-vant *n.* One who agrees to work without pay.

bonds-man *n.* One who agrees to provide bond for someone else.

bone *n.*

The calcified connecting tissue of the skeleton. **bone** *v.*

bone—dry *adj.* Completely without water.

bone-head *n.*, *Slang* A stupid person. **boneheaded** *adj.*

bon-er *n.*, *Slang* A mistake or blunder.

bon-fire *n.* An open outdoor fire.

bo-ni-to *n.* A game fish related to the tuna.

bon-kers *adj.*, *Slang* Acting in a crazy fashion.

Bonn *n.* Capital of West Germany.

bon-net *n.* A woman's hat that ties under the chin.

bon-ny *adj.* Attractive or pleasing; pretty.

bon-sai *n.* A small ornamental shrub grown in a shallow pot.

bo-nus *n.*, *pl.* **-nuses** Something that is given over and above what is expected.

bon voyage *n.* A farewell wish for a traveler to have a pleasant and safe journey.

boo *n.* Verbal expression showing disapproval or contempt.

boo—boo *n.*, *Slang* A mistake, blunder, or minor injury.

boog-ie *v.*, *Slang* To dance especially to rock and roll music.

book *n.* A group of pages fastened along the left side and bound between a protective cover; literary work that is written or printed.

book-ie *n.*, *Slang* A bookmaker.

book-ing *n.* A scheduled engagement.

book-keep-ing *n.* The business of recording the accounts and transactions of a business. **bookkeeper** *n.*

boom *n.* A deep, resonant sound; a long pole extending to the top of a derrick giving support to guide lifted objects. *v.* To cause to flourish or grow swiftly.

boo-mer-ang *n.* A curved, flat missile that can be thrown so that it returns to the thrower.

boon *n.* Something that is pleasant or beneficial; a blessing; favor.

boon-docks *pl.*, *n.* *Slang* Back country.

boon-dog-gle *n.* A useless activity; a waste of time.

Boone, Daniel *n.* The American pioneer who explored and settled in Kentucky.

boor *n.* A person with clumsy manners and little refinement; rude person.

boost *v.* To increase; to raise or lift by pushing up from below. *n.* An increase in something.

boost-er *n.* A promoter; a supplementary or additional dose of vaccine.

boot *n.* A protective covering for the foot; any protective sheath or covering. In computer science, to load a computer with an operating system or other software.

boo-tee *n.* A soft, knitted sock for a baby.

booth *n.* A small enclosed compartment or area; display area at trade shows for displaying merchandise for sale; an area in a restaurant with a table and benches.

boot-leg v., *Slang.* To sell, make, or transport liquor illegally.

booze n., *Slang.* An alcoholic drink.

bo-rax n. A crystalline compound used in manufacturing detergents and phar-maceuticals.

bor-der n. A surrounding margin or edge; a political or geographic boundary.

bor-der-land n. Land near or on a border; an indeterminate situation.

bor-derline n. A line or mark indicating a border.

bore v. To make a hole through or in something using a drill; to become tired, repetitious, or dull. **boredom** n.

bo-re-al adj. Located in or of the north.

bo-ric acid n. A colorless or white mixture that is used as a preservative and as a weak antiseptic.

born adj. Brought into life or being; having an innate talent.

born-again adj. Having accepted Jesus Christ as a person's personal savior.

Bor-ne-o n. An island in the western Pacific Ocean divided by Indonesia, Brunei, and Malaysia.

bo-ron n. A soft, brown nonmetallic element used in nuclear reactor control elements, abrasives, and flares.

bor-ough n. A self-governing incorporated town, found in some United States cities; an incorporated British town that sends one or more representatives to Parliament.

bor-row v. To receive money with the intentions of returning it; to use another idea as one's own.

borscht n. Hot or cold beet soup.

BOS abbr. Basic Operating System; the program that handles the routine functions of computer operations, such as accessing the disk drive, displaying information on the screen, handling input and output, etc.

bos-ky adj. Thickly covered with trees or shrubs; related to a wooded area.

bos-om n. The female's breasts; the human chest; the heart or center of something.

Bos-po-rus n. The strait which link the Marmara and Black Seas.

boss n. An employer or supervisor for whom one works. v. To command; to supervise. **bossiness** n., **bossy** adj.

Bos-ton n. Capital of Massachusetts.

bot abbr. Botany; botanical; botanist.

bot-a-ny n. The science of plants. **botanical** adj., **botanist** n.

botch v. To ruin something by clumsiness; to repair clumsily. **botcher** n.

both adj. Two in conjunction with one another.

both-er v. To pester, harass, or irritate; to be concerned about something. **bothersome** adj.

bot-tle n. A receptacle, usually made of glass, with a narrow neck and a top that can be capped or corked; formula

or milk that is fed to a baby.

bot-tle-neck n. A narrow, obstructed passage, highway, road, etc.; a hindrance to progress or production.

bot-tom n. The lowest or deepest part of anything; the base; underside; the last; the land below a body of water. *Informal* The buttocks. **bottomless** adj.

bottom line n. The end result; lowest line of a financial statement, showing net loss or gain.

bot-u-lism n. Food poisoning, often fatal, caused by bacteria that grows in improperly prepared food.

bouf-fant adj. Full; puffed out.

bough n. The large branch of a tree.

bouil-lon n. A clear broth made from meat.

boul-der n. A large round rock.

boul-e-vard n. A broad city street lined with trees.

bounce v. To rebound or cause to rebound; to leap or spring suddenly; to be returned by a bank as being worthless or having no value.

bounc-er n. A person who removes disorderly people from a public place.

bounc-ing adj. Healthy; vigorous; robust; lively and spirited.

bound n. A leap or bounce. v. To limit; to be tied.

bound-a-ry n., pl. -ries A limit or border.

bound-en adj. Under an obligation or agreement.

bound-er n. A vulgar person.

bound-less adj. Without limits. **boundlessly** adv.

boun-te-ous adj. Plentiful or generous; giving freely. **bounteously** adv., **bounteousness** n.

boun-ti-ful adj. Abundant; plentiful. **bountifully** adv.

bounty n. Generosity; an inducement or reward given for the return of something; a good harvest.

bou-quet n. A group of cut flowers; the aroma of wine.

bour-bon n. Whiskey distilled from fermented corn mash.

bour-geois pl., n. A member of the middle class. **bourgeois** adj.

bout n. A contest or match; the length of time spent in a certain way.

bou-tique n. A small retail shop that sells specialized gifts, accessories, and fashionable clothes.

bou-ton-niere n. A flower worn in the buttonhole of a man's jacket.

bo-vine adj. Of or relating to an ox or cow.

bow n. The front section of a boat or ship; bending of the head or waist to express a greeting or courtesy; a weapon made from a curved stave and strung taut to launch arrows; a rod strung with horsehair, used for playing stringed instruments.

bowd-ler-ize v. To expurgate. **bowdlerization** n.

bow-el n. The digestive tract located below the stomach; the intestines.

bow-ie knife *n.* A single-edged thick-bladed hunting knife.

bowl *n.* A hemispherical container for food or liquids; a bowl-shaped part, as of a spoon or ladle; a bowl-shaped stadium. *v.* To participate in the game of bowling.

bow-leg *n.* An outward curvature of the leg at the knee.

bowl-er *n.* A person that bowls.

bowl-ing *n.* A game in which a person rolls a ball down a wooden alley in order to knock down a triangular group of ten wooden bowling pins.

bowling alley *n.* A building containing alleys for the game of bowling.

bowl over *v.* To astound; to be astounded.

bow-sprit *n.* A spar that projects forward from the stem of a ship.

box *n.* A small container or chest, usually with a lid; a special area in a theater that holds a small group of people; a shrub or evergreen with leaves and hard wood that is yellow in color. *v.* to fight with the fists.

box-car *n.* An enclosed railway car used for the transportation of freight.

box-er *n.* A person who boxes professionally; a German breed of dog with short hair, brownish coat, and a square nose or muzzle.

box-ing *n.* A sport in which two opponents hit each other using padded gloves on their hands, forming fists.

box office *n.* An office where theatre tickets are purchased.

boy *n.* A male youth or child. **boyhood** *n.*

boy-cott *v.* To abstain from dealing with, buying, or using as a means of protest.

Boy Scout *n.* A boy who belongs to a worldwide organization that emphasizes citizenship training and character development.

B P *abbr.* Bills payable.

B P O E *abbr.* Benevolent and Protective Order of Elks.

Br *abbr.* Britain.

B R *abbr.* Bills receivable.

bra *n.* Brassiere.

brace *n.* A device that supports or steadies something. **brace** *v.*

brace-let *n.* An ornamental band for the wrist.

brack-en *n.* A large species of fern with tough stems and finely divided fronds.

brack-et *n.* A support attached to a vertical surface that projects in order to hold a shelf or other weight. *v.* To enclose a word in brackets ( ).

brack-ish *adj.* Containing salt; distasteful.

bract *n.* A leaf-like plant below a flower cluster or flower.

brad *n.* A nail that tapers to a small head.

brag *v.* To assert or talk boastfully.

brag-ga-do-ci-o *n., pl.* A cockiness or arrogant manner; empty bragging.

brag-gart *n.* A person who brags.

Brah-ma *n.* A member of the Hindu group that created the universe.

Brah-man-ism *n.* The religious beliefs and practices of ancient India; strict Hinduism.

braid *v.* To interweave three or more strands of something; to plait.

braille *n.* A system of printing for the blind, consisting of six dots, two across and four directly under the first two. Numbers and letters are represented by raising certain dots in each group of six.

brain *n.* The large mass of nerve tissue enclosed in the cranium, responsible for the interpretation of sensory impulses, control of the body, and coordination; the center of thought and emotion in the body. **braininess** *n.*, **brainless** *adj.*, **brainlessness** *n.*

brain-storm *n.* A sudden idea or inspiration.

brain-wash-ing *n.* Intensive indoctrination to radically change a person's convictions.

brain wave *n.* The rhythmic fluctuation of voltage between parts of the brain.

braise *v.* To cook by first browning in a small amount of fat, adding a liquid such as water, and then simmering in a covered container.

brake *n.* A device designed to stop or slow the motion of a vehicle or machine. **brake** *v.*

brake fluid *n.* The liquid contained in hydraulic brake cylinders.

bram-ble *n.* A prickly shrub or plant such as the raspberry or blackberry bush.

bran *n.* The husk of cereal grains that is separated from the flour.

branch *n.* An extension from the main trunk of a tree. *v.* To divide into different subdivisions.

brand *n.* A trademark or label that names a product; a mark of disgrace or shame; a piece of charred or burning wood; a mark made by a hot iron to show ownership. **brand** *v.*

bran-dish *v.* To wave or flourish a weapon.

brand name *n.* A company's trademark.

brand-new *adj.* Unused and new.

bran-dy *n., pl.* **-dies** An alcoholic liquor distilled from fermented fruit juices or wine. **brandied** *adj.*, **brandy** *v.*

brash *adj.* Hasty, rash, and unthinking; insolent; impudent.

brass *n.* An alloy of zinc, copper and other metals in lesser amounts. *Slang.* A high-ranking officer in the military.

bras-siere *n.* A woman's undergarment with cups to support the breasts.

brass tacks *pl., n.* The details of immediate, practical importance.

brat *n.* An ill-mannered child.

brat-wurst *n.* A fresh pork sausage.

braun-schweig-er *n.* Smoked liverwurst.

bra-va-do *n.* A false showing of bravery.

brave *adj.* Having or displaying courage. *n.* An American Indian warrior.

brav-er-y *n.* The quality of or state of being brave.

bra-vo *Interj.* Expressing approval.

brawl *n.* A noisy argument or fight.

brawn *n.* Well-developed and solid muscles. **brawniness** *n.*, **brawny** *adj.*

bray *v.* To make a loud cry like a donkey.

braze *v.* To solder using a nonferrous alloy that melts at a lower temperature than that of the metals being joined together.

bra-zen *adj.* Made of brass; shameless or impudent.

bra-zier *n.* A person who works with brass; a metal pan that holds burning charcoal or coals.

Bra-zil *n.* A large South American country.

breach *n.* Ruptured, broken, or torn condition or area; a break in friendly relations. *v.* To break the law or obligation.

breach of promise *n.* The violation of a promise.

bread *n.* A leavened food made from a flour or meal mixture and baked. *Slang* Money. *v.* To cover with bread crumbs before cooking.

bread--and--butter *adj.* Being the basis of one's livelihood.

bread-basket *adj.* A major grain producing region of the United States. *Slang* The stomach.

bread-board *n.* A board used for cutting bread; a board on which electric or electronic circuit diagrams may be laid out.

bread-fruit *n.* A tropical tree with lobed leaves and edible fruit.

bread-stuff *n.* Bread; a cereal product; meal, grain, or flour.

breadth *n.* The distance or measurement from side to side; width.

bread-win-ner *n.* The one whose pay supports a household.

break *v.* To separate into parts with violence or suddenness; to collapse or give way; to change suddenly. *Informal* A stroke of good luck.

break-age *n.* Things that are broken.

break-down *n.* Failure to function.

break-er *n.* A wave that breaks into foam.

break-fast *n.* The first meal of the day.

break-through *n.* A sudden advance in know-ledge or technique; a thrust that goes farther than anticipated or expected.

break-water *n.* A barrier that protects a beach from the full force of waves.

breast *n.* The milk-producing glandular organs on a woman's chest; the area of the body from the neck to the abdomen.

breast-bone *n.* The sternum.

breast-plate *n.* A metal plate worn on the chest for protection.

breast-stroke *n.* A stroke in swimming for which a person lies face down and extends the arms in front of the head, drawing the knees forward and outward and then sweeping the arms back while kicking outward and backward. **breaststroker** *n.*

breath *n.* The air inhaled and exhaled in breathing; a very slight whisper, fragrance, or breeze.

breathe *v.* To draw air into and expel from the lungs; to take a short rest.

breather *n.* A small opening in an otherwise air-tight enclosure; one that breathes.

breath-tak-ing *adj.* Astonishing; awesome. **breathtakingly** *adv.*

breech *n.*, *pl.* **-es** The buttocks; the hind end of the body; the part of a gun or firearm located at the rear of the bore. *plural* Trousers that fit tightly around the knees.

breed *v.* The genetic strain of domestic animals, developed and maintained by mankind. **breeding** *n.*

breeze *n.* A slight gentle wind; something that is accomplished with very little effort. **breezy** *adj.*

breeze-way *n.* A roofed connection between two buildings or walls.

Bre-men *n.* A city in West Germany.

breve *n.* The curved mark over a vowel to indicate a short or unstressed syllable.

bre-vi-ar-y *n.* A book that contains prayers and psalms for the canonical hours.

brev-i-ty *n.*, *pl.* **-ties** A brief duration; conciseness.

brew *v.* To make beer from malt and hops by boiling, infusion, and germentation. **brewer** *n.*

brew-er-y *n.* A building or plant where beer or ale is brewed.

bribe *v.* To influence or induce by giving a token or anything of value for a service. **bribe** *n.*

brib-ery *n.* The practice of giving or receiving a bribe.

bric--a--brac *n.* A collection of small objects.

brick *n.* A molded block of baked clay, usually rectangular in shape.

brick-bat *n.* A piece of a brick used as a weapon when thrown as a missile.

brick-lay-er *n.* A person who lays bricks as a profession.

bri-dal *adj.* Relating to a bride or a nuptial ceremony.

bride *n.* A women just married or about to be married.

bride-groom *n.* A man just married or about to be married.

brides-maid *n.* A woman who attends a bride at her wedding.

bridge *n.* A structure that provides passage over a depression or obstacle; a card game for four players.

bridge-head *n.* A military position secured by advance troops in enemy territory, giving protection for the main attack force.

bridge-work *n.* The construction of dental work.

bri-dle *n.* A harness used to restrain or guide a horse **bridler** *n.*

brief *n.* A concise, formal statement of a client's case. *adj.* Short in duration. *v.* To summarize or inform in a short statement. -ly *adv.*, briefness *n.*

brief-case *n.* A small, flat, flexible case for holding and carrying papers or books.

bri-er *n.* A woody, thorny, or prickly plant.

brig *n.* A prison on a ship; a twin-masted, square-rigged sailing ship.

bri-gade *n.* A military unit organized for a specific purpose.

brig-and *n.* A person who lives as a robber; bandit.

bright *adj.* Brilliant in color; vivid; shining and emitting or reflecting light; happy; cheerful; lovely. brightness *n.*

bril-liant *adj.* Very bright and shiny; sparkling; radiant; extraordinarily intelligent.

brim *n.* The edge or rim of a cup.

brim-ful *adj.* Completely full.

brim-stone *n.* Sulfur.

brin-dle *adj.* Having dark streaks or flecks on a gray or tawny background.

brine *n.* Water saturated with salt; the water contained in the oceans and seas.

bring *v.* To carry with oneself to a certain place; to cause, act, or move in a special direction.

brink *n.* The upper edge or margin of a very steep slope.

bri-oche *n.* A roll made from flour, eggs, butter, and yeast.

bri-quette *n.* A small brick-shaped piece of charcoal.

brisk *adj.* Moving or acting quickly; being sharp in tone or manner; energetic, invigorating or fresh. briskly *adv.*, briskness *n.*

bris-ket *n.* The meat from the lower chest or breast of an animal.

bris-ling *n.* A small fish that is processed like a sardine.

bris-tle *n.* Short, stiff, coarse hair. *v.* To react in angry defiance. bristly *adj.*

britch-es *pl.*, *n.* Trousers; breeches.

Brit-ish *n.* The people and the language spoken in Great Britain.

brit-tle *adj.* Very easy to break; fragile. brittleness *n.*

bro *abbr.* Brother.

broach *n.* A tapered and serrated tool used for enlarging and shaping a hole.

broad *adj.* Covering a wide area; from side to side; clear; bright. broadly *adv.*

broad-cast *v.* To transmit a program by television; to make widely known. broadcaster *n.*

broad-cloth *n.* A textured woolen cloth with a lustrous finish.

broad-en *v.* To become or make broad or broader.

broad-loom *adj.* Woven on a wide loom. *n.* Carpet woven in this manner.

broad-mind-ed *adj.* Tolerant of varied views; liberal. broadmindedness *n.*

broad-side *n.* The side of a ship that is above the water line; a sheet of paper printed on both sides and then folded.

bro-cade *n.* A silk fabric with raised patterns in silver and gold.

broc-co-li *n.* A green vegetable from the cauliflower family, eaten before the small buds open.

bro-chure *n.* A booklet or pamphlet.

bro-gan *n.* A sturdy oxford shoe.

brogue *n.* A strong regional accent.

broil *v.* To cook by exposure to direct radiant heat.

broil-er *n.* A device, usually a part of a stove, that is used for broiling meat; a young chicken.

broke *adj.* Penniless; completely without money.

bro-ken *adj.* Separated violently into parts.

bro-ken-hearted *adj.* Overcome by despair or grief.

bro-ken home *n.* A family situation in which the parents are not living together.

bro-ker *n.* A person who acts as a negotiating agent for contracts, sales, or purchases in return for payment.

bro-ker-age *n.* The establishment of a broker.

bro-mide *n.* A compound of bromine with other elements; a sedative; a commonplace idea or notion. bromidic *adj.*

bro-mine *n.* A nonmetallic element of a deep red, toxic liquid that gives off a disagreeable odor.

bron-chi-al *adj.* Pertaining to the bronchi or their extensions. bronchially *adv.*

bron-chus *n.* Either of two main branches of the trachea that lead directly to the lungs.

bron-co *n.* A wild horse of western North America.

bron-to-saur *n.* A very large dinosaur.

bronze *n.* An alloy of tin, copper, and zinc; moderate olive brown to yellow in color. bronze *v.*, bronze *adj.*

Bronze Age *n.* Human culture between the Iron Age and the Stone Age.

brooch *n.* A large decorative pin.

brood *n.* The young of an animal ; a family of young. *v.* To produce by incubation; to hatch; to think about at length.

brood-er *n.* An enclosed heated area for raising young chickens.

brook *n.* A small fresh-water stream that contains many rocks.

broom *n.* A long-handled implement used for sweeping; a shrub with small leaves and yellow flowers.

bros *abbr.* Brothers.

broth *n.* The liquid in which fish, meat, or vegetables have been cooked; also called stock.

broth-el *n.* A house of prostitution; a whorehouse.

broth-er *n.* A male who shares the same parents as another person. brotherly *adj.*, brotherliness *n.*

brother-hood *n.* The state of being brothers; one that is related to another for a particular purpose.

brother--in--law *n.* The brother of one's spouse; the husband of one's sister; the husband of one's spouse's sister.

broug-ham *n.* A vehicle without a cover over the driver's seat.

brought *v.* The past tense of bring.

brow *n.* The ridge above the eye where the eyebrow grows.

brow-beat *v.* To bully; dominate; intimidate.

brown *n.* A color between yellow and red; a dark or tanned complexion.

brown bag-ging *n.* The practice of bringing one's lunch to work.

Brown Betty *n.* A pudding baked with apples, spices, and bread crumbs.

brown bread *n.* Bread made from whole wheat flour.

brown-ie *n.* A good-natured elf believed to perform helpful services; a square, chewy piece of chocolate cake.

Brownie A member of the Girl Scouts from 7 to 9 years of age.

brown-out *n.* An interruption of electrical power.

brown-stone *n.* A reddish-brown sandstone used for construction; a building faced with brownstone.

brown study *n.* A state of being total absorbed.

brown sugar *n.* Sugar with crystals covered by a film or refined dark syrup.

browse *v.* To look over something in a leisurely and casual way.

bruise *n.* An injury that ruptures small blood vessels and discolors the skin without breaking it.

brunch *n.* A combination of a late breakfast and an early lunch.

bru-net *or* **bru-nette** A person with dark brown hair.

brunt *n.* The principal shock, or force.

brush *n.* A device consisting of bristles used for applying paint, scrubbing or grooming the hair; a very dense growth of bushes. *v.* To touch lightly in passing.

brush-off *Slang* To dismiss abruptly.

brussels sprout *n.* The small head of a green vegetable, resembling the cabbage.

bru-tal *adj.* Very harsh or cruel treatment. **brutality** *n.*, **brutally** *adv.*, **brutalize** *v.*

brute *n.* A person characterized by physical power rather than intelligence; a person who behaves like an animal. **brutish** *adj.*

BS *abbr.* Bachelor of Science

BSA *abbr.* Boy Scouts of America.

bsh *abbr.* bushel.

bsk *abbr.* basket.

bu *abbr.* bureau.

bub-ble *n.* A small round object, usually hollow; a small body of gas contained in a liquid. *v.* To produce bubbles.

bubble gum *n.* A chewing gum that can be blown into bubbles.

bub-bly *adj.* Something full of bubbles. *Slang* Champagne.

bu-bo *n.* Inflammatory swelling of the lymphatic glands, especially in the area of the groin or armpits.

bu-bon-ic plague *n.* The contagious and normally fatal disease that is transmitted by fleas from infected rats, characterized by fever, diarrhea, chills, and vomiting.

buck *n.* The adult male deer; the lowest grade in the military category. *v.* To throw a rider; to oppose the system. *Slang* A dollar.

buck-board *n.* An open carriage with four wheels and a seat attached to a flexible board.

buck-et *n.* A vessel used to carry liquids or solids; a pail.

buck-et seat *n.* A separate seat with a rounded or molded back.

buck-eye *n.* A tree with flower clusters and glossy brown nuts.

buck-le *v.* To warp, crumple, or bend under pressure. *n.* Metal clasp for fastening one end to another.

buck-ram *n.* A coarse, stiff fabric that is sized with glue and used for interlinings in garments and in bookbindings.

buck-shot *n.* A coarse lead shot for shotgun shells.

buck-tooth *n.* A large, prominently projecting front tooth. **-ed** *adj.*

buck-wheat *n.* A plant with small edible seeds that are often ground into flour and used as a cereal grain.

bud *n.* Something that has not developed completely; a small structure that contains flowers or leaves that have not developed.

Bu-da-pest *n.* Capital of Hungary.

Bud-dhism *n.* A religion that teaches that suffering is inherited and that one can be released from it by moral and mental self-purification. **Buddhist** *n.*

bud-dy *n.* A good companion, partner, or friend.

budge *v.* To give way to; to cause to move slightly.

bud-get *n.* The total amount of money allocated for a certain purpose.

buff *n.* A leather made mostly from skins of buffalo, elk, or oxen, having the color of light to moderate yellow.

buf-fa-lo *n.* A wild ox with heavy forequarters, short horns, and a large muscular hump. *v.* To bewilder, to intimidate.

buff-er *n.* A tool used to polish or shine; in computer science, a part of the memory used to hold information temporarily while data transfers from one place to another. *v.* To lessen, absorb, or protect against the shock of an impact.

buf-fet *n.* A meal placed on a side table so that people may serve themselves; a side table for serving food. *v.* To strike sharply with the hand.

buf-foon *n.* A clown; a stupid person; an uneducated person.

bug *n.* Any small insect; a concealed listening device. *v.* To bother or annoy.

bug-gy *n.* A small carriage pulled behind a horse.

bu-gle *n.* A brass instrument without keys or valves. **bugle** *v.*, **bugler** *n.*

build *v.* To erect by uniting materials

into a composite whole; to fashion or create; to develop or add to. *n.* The form or structure of a person.

build-ing *n.* A roofed and walled structure for permanent use.

built--in *adj.* Containing something within a structure.

bulb *n.* A rounded underground plant such as a tulip that lies dormant in the winter and blooms in the spring; an incandescent light for electric lamps. **bulbous** *adj* Resembling a bulb in shape.

Bulg *abbr.* Bulgaria

bulge *n.* A swelling of the surface caused by pressure from within. **bulgy** *adj.*

bulk *n.* A large mass; anything that has great size, volume, or units. **bulky** *adj.*

bulk-age *n.* A substance that increases the bulk of material in the intestine, therefore stimulating peristalsis.

bulk-head *n.* The partition that divides a ship into compartments; a retaining wall along a waterfront.

bull *n.* The adult male in cattle and other large mammals. *Slang* Nonsense talk.

bull *abbr.* Bulletin.

bull-dog *n.* A short-haired dog with a stocky build and an undershot lower jaw.

bull-doze *v.* To move or dig up with a bulldozer. *Slang* To bully.

bull-dozer *n.* A tractor-like machine with a large metal blade in front for moving earth and rocks.

bul-let *n.* A cylindrical projectile that is fired from a gun.

bul-le-tin *n.* A broadcasted statement of public interest; a public notice.

bull-fight *n.* A Spanish or Mexican spectacle in which men known as matadors engage in fighting bulls.

bull-head-ed *adj.* Headstrong and stubborn.

bul-lion *n.* Refined gold or silver in the uncoined state.

bull-ish *adj.* Tending to cause or hopeful of rising prices, as in the stock market.

bull-pen *n.* The area where pitchers warm up during a baseball game.

bull's eye *n.* The center of a target.

bul-ly *n., pl.* -ies A person who is mean or cruel to weaker people.

bul-rush *n.* Tall grass as found in a marsh.

bul-wark *n.* A strong protection or support.

bum *n.* One who begs from others; one who spends time unemployed. *v.* To loaf.

bum-mer *Slang* Depressing.

bum-ble-bee *n.*

A large hairy bee.

bump *v.* To collide with, knock, or strike something. *n.* A swelling or lump on a person's body.

bump-er *n.* A device on the front of vehicles that absorbs shock and prevents damage.

bumper--to--bumper *adj.* A long line of cars or other vehicles moving very slowly.

bump-kin *n.* An awkward, stupid, or unsophisticated country person.

bump-tious *adj.* Crudely self-assertive and forward; pushy.

bun *n.* Any of a variety of plain or sweet small breads; tightly rolled hair that resembles a bun.

bunch *n.* A cluster or group of items that are the same.

bun-co *n.* A game of confidence; a swindling scheme.

bun-dle *n.* Anything wrapped or held together. *Slang* A large amount of money. **bundler** *n.*

bundle up. *v.* To dress warmly, usually using many layers of clothing.

bun-ga-low *n.* A small one-story cottage.

bun-gle *v.* To work or act awkwardly or clumsily. **bungler** *n.*

bun-ion *n.* An inflamed, painful swelling of the first joint of the big toe.

bunk *n.* A narrow bed that is built in; one of a tier of berths on a ship.

bun-ker *n.* A tank for storing fuel on a ship; an embankment or a sand trap creating a hazard on a golf course.

bun-kum *n.* Meaningless talk.

bun-ny *n., pl.* -nies A small rabbit.

Bun-sen burner *n.* An adjustable gas-burning laboratory burner.

bunt *v.* To tap a pitched ball with a half swing. *n.* The center of a square sail.

bunt-ing *n.* A hooded blanket for a baby.

buoy *n.* A floating object to mark a channel or danger. *v.* To stay afloat.

buoy-an-cy *n.* The tendency of an object or body to remain afloat in liquid or to rise in gas or air.

bur. *abbr.* Bureau

bur-den *n.* Something that is hard to bear; a duty or responsibility; a ship's capacity for carrying cargo.

bur-dock *n.* A coarse plant with purplish flowers.

bu-reau *n., pl.* **bureaus, bureaux.** A low chest for storing clothes; a branch of the government or a subdivision of a department.

bu-reauc-ra-cy *n., pl.* -cies. A body of nonelected officials in a government; the administration of a government through bureaus.

burg *n.* A town or city.

bur-geon *v.* To put forth new life as in leaves, buds, etc.

burg-er *n., Slang* A hamburger.

bur-glar *n.* A person who steals personal items from another person's home.

bur-glar-ize *v.* To commit burglary.

bur-glar-proof *adj.* Protected and secure against burglary.

bur-gla-ry *n.* The breaking into and entering of a private home with the intent to steal.

Bur-gun-dy *n.* A white or red wine produced in Burgundy, an area in southeast France.

bur-i-al *n.* The process or act of burying.

burl *n.* A woody, often flat and hard, hemispherical growth on a tree.

bur-lap *n.* A coarse cloth woven from hemp or jute.

bur-lesque *n.* Theatrical entertainment with comedy and mocking imitations.

bur-ly *adj.* Very heavy and strong.

burn *v.* To be destroyed by fire; to consume fuel and give off heat. *n.* An injury produced by fire, heat, or steam; the firing of a rocket engine in space.

burn-er *n.* The part of a fuel-burning device where the fire is contained.

bur-nish *v.* To make shiny by rubbing; to polish.

burnt *adj.* Affected by burning.

burp *n.* A belch.

bur-ro *n.* A small donkey.

bur-row *n.* A tunnel dug in the ground by an animal.

bur-sar *n.* The person or official in charge of monies at a college.

bur-si-tis *n.* An inflammation of the small sac between a tendon of the knee, elbow, or shoulder joints.

burst *adj.* To explode or experience a sudden outbreak; to very suddenly become visible or audible. *n.* A sudden explosion or outburst.

bus *n., pl.* **busses** A large passenger vehicle. **bus** *v.*

bus *abbr.* Business.

bus boy *n.* A waiter's assistant; one who removes dirty dishes from a table and the resets it.

bus-by *n.* A fur hat that is worn in certain regiments of the British Army.

bush *n.* A low plant with branches near the ground; a dense tuft or growth; land that is covered intensely with undergrowth.

bushed *adj., Slang* Extremely exhausted; tired.

bush-el *n.* A unit of dry measurement which equals four pecks or 2,150.42 cubic inches; a container that holds a bushel.

bush-mas-ter *n.* The largest New World venomous snake.

bush-whack *v.* To travel through thick woods by cutting bushes and small trees; to ambush. **bushwacker** *n.*

busi-ness *n.* A person's professional dealings or occupation; an industrial or commercial establishment.

bus-kin *n.* A boot that reaches halfway to the knee; tragedy as that of an ancient Greek drama.

bus-man's holiday *n.* Vacation or holiday where a person follows the same practice of his usual occupation.

bust *n.* A sculpture that resembles the upper part of a human body; the breasts of a women. *v.* To break or burst; to become short of money.

bus-tle *n.* A padding that gives extra bulk to the back of a woman's skirt.

bus-y *adj.* Full of activity; engaged in work. **busily** *adv.*, **-ness** *n.*

busy-body *n.* An inquisitive person who interferes with someone else's business.

but *conj.* On the contrary to; other than; if not; except for the fact.

bu-tane *n.* A gas produced from petroleum, used as a fuel refrigerant and aerosol propellant.

butch-er *n.* One who slaughters animals and dresses them for food.

but-ler *n.* A male servant of a household.

butt *n.* The object of ridicule; the thick large or blunt end of something. *v.* To hit with horns or the head; to be joined at the end.

but-ter *n.* A yellow substance churned from milk.

but-ter-fat *n.* The natural fat from milk that floats to the top of unpasteurized milk.

but-ter-fin-gers *n.* An awkward, clumsy person.

but-ter-fly *n., pl.* **-flies**

A narrow-bodied insect with four broad, colorful wings.

but-ter-milk *n.* The liquid that remains after butter has been churned from milk.

but-ter-scotch *n.* A candy made from brown sugar and melted butter.

but-tocks *pl., n.* The two round fleshy parts of the rump.

but-ton *n.* A small disk that interlocks with a buttonhole to close a piece of garment.

but-ton-hole *n.* The slit through which a button is inserted to close a piece of garment.

but-tress *n.* A support made of brick or stone.

bux-om *adj.* Lively; happy. **buxomness** *n.*

buy *v.* To purchase in exchange for money. *n.* Anything that is bought.

buy-er *v.* A person who buys from a store or an individual.

buzz *v.* To make a low vibrating sound, as a bee.

buz-zard *n.* A broad-winged vulture from the same family as the hawk.

buzz-er *n.* An electrical signaling device that makes a buzzing sound.

bx *abbr.* Box.

by *prep.* Up to and beyond; to go past; not later than; next to; according to.

bye *n.* A position in which a contestant has no opponent after pairs are drawn for a tournament, and, therefore, advances to the next round.

bye-bye *Slang* Farewell.

by-gone *adj.* Gone by; past.

by-law *n.* A rule or law governing internal affairs of a group or organization.

by--product *n.* Material that is left over when something is manufactured but also has a market value of its own.

byte *n.* In computer science, a sequence of adjacent binary digits operated on as a unit.

by-word *n.* A well-known proverb.

By-zan-ti-um *n.* An ancient Greek city on the site of Constantinople.

C, c The third letter of the English alphabet; the Roman numeral for 100.

cab *n.* A taxicab; the compartment where a person sits to drive a large truck or machinery.

ca-bal *n.* A group that conspires against a government or other public institution.

ca-ban-a *n.* A small building or shelter on the beach or at the side of a pool.

cab-a-ret *n.* A restaurant that provides dancing and live entertainment.

cab-bage *n.*

A plant with large, edible green leaves, eaten as a vegetable.

cab-in *n.* A small, roughly-built house, especially one made from logs; the living quarters on a ship; the area of an airplane for the passengers and crew members.

cab-i-net *n.* A unit for displaying and storing dishes and other objects; a selected group of people appointed by the head of state to officially advise and to take charge of the different government departments.

ca-ble *n.* A heavy rope made from fiber or steel; a bound group of insulated conductors.

ca-boo-dle *n., Slang* The entire unit, amount, or collection.

ca-boose *n.* The last car of a train, that contains the eating and sleeping quarters for the crew.

ca-ca-o *n.* Any tree of the chocolate family; the dried seed of the cacao tree from which chocolate and cocoa are made.

cach-a-lot *n.* A sperm whale.

cache *n.* A safe place to hide and conceal goods.

ca-chet *n.* A mark of distinction or authenticity.

cack-le *v.* To laugh with the characteristic shrill noise a hen makes after laying an egg; to talk or laugh with a similar sound. cackler *n.*

ca-coph-o-ny *n.* A harsh and disagreeable sound. cacophonous *adj.*

cac-tus *n., pl.* -es, -ti A leafless plant with a thick, prickly surface, which grows primarily in hot and dry regions.

ca-dav-er *n.* The body of a person who has died; pale and gaunt.

cad-die *n., pl.* caddies A person employed by a golfer to assist him by carrying his clubs during the game of golf.

ca-dence *n.* A rhythmic movement or flow.

ca-den-za *n.* An elaborate ornamental section for a soloist near the end of a concerto.

ca-det *n.* A student in training at a naval or military academy. cadetship *n.*

cadge *v.* To beg or to receive by begging; to mooch. cadger *n.*

ca-dre *n.* The group of trained personnel that forms the heart of an organization.

ca-du-ce-us *n.* The symbol of the medical profession, a winged staff entwined with two serpents entwined around it.

cae-su-ra *n.* A pause or break in a line of verse or poetry.

caf-e-te-ri-a *n.* A restaurant where a person chooses his own food and then carries it on a tray to his table.

caf-feine *n.* A stimulant found in coffee, tea, and dark colas.

caf-tan *n.* A loose-fitting, full-length garment worn in the Near East.

cage *n.* A box-like structure enclosed with bars or grating for the confinement of animals.

ca-gey *adj.* Shrewd, wary, or cautious.

ca-hoot *n.* A questionable relationship with an associate.

cais-son *n.* A waterproof structure that is used for construction work underwater.

ca-jole *v.* To wheedle or coax someone into doing something.

Ca-jun *n.* A native of Louisiana descended from French-speaking immigrants.

cake *n.* A sweet food made from flour, eggs, and shortening. cake *v.*

cal-a-bash *n.* A large hard-shelled gourd that can be used as a utensil.

cal-a-boose *n., Slang* A jail.

cal-a-mine *n.* A pink powder of zinc oxide and ferric oxide mixed with mineral oils to form a lotion for skin irritations such as poison ivy.

ca-lam-i-ty *n., pl.* -ies Misfortune or great distress. -tous *adj.*, -ly *adv.*

cal-ci-fy *v.* To become or make chalky or stony. calcification *n.*

cal-cine *v.* To heat to a high temperature without melting, but causing loss of moisture and reduction. calcination *n.*

cal-ci-um *n.* The alkaline element that is found in teeth and bones; the element symbolized by Ca.

cal-cu-late *v.* To figure by a mathematical process, to evaluate; to estimate. calculable *adj.*, calculably *adv.*

cal-cu-lat-ed *adj.* Worked out beforehand with careful estimation. calculatedly *adv.*

cal-cu-lat-ing *adj.* Shrewd consideration of self-interest.

cal-cu-la-tor *n.* A machine with a keyboard for automatic mathematical operation.

cal-cu-lus *n., pl.* -es A stone in the gallbladder or kidneys; the mathematics of integral and differential calculus.

cal-dron *n.* A large boiler or kettle.

cal-en-dar *n.* A system for showing time divisions by years, months, weeks, and days; the twelve months in a year.

cal-en-der *n.* A machine that makes paper and cloth smooth and glossy.

cal-ends *n.* The first day of the new moon.

calf *n., pl.* calves The young offspring of the domestic cow; the young of large animals as the whale and elephant.

cal-i-ber *n.* The inner diameter of a tube or gun; the quality or worth of something.

cal-i-co *n.* Cotton fabric with figured patterns.

Cal-i-for-nia *n.* A state located on the western coast of the United States.

cal-i-per *n.* An instrument with two curved, hinged legs, used to measure inner and outer dimensions.

ca-liph *n.* A religious and secular head in Islam. **caliphate** *n.*

cal-is-then-ics *n.* Exercises that develop muscular tone and promote good physical condition.

call *v.* To call out to someone; to name or designate; to telephone; to pay a short visit; to demand payment; in card games, to demand the opponent show his cards.

cal-la *or* **cal-la lilly** *n.* A family of white and yellow flowers enclosing a club-like flower stalk.

cal-lig-ra-phy *n.* The art of writing with a pen using different slants and positions.

call-ing *n.* The occupation or profession of a person.

cal-liope *n.* A keyboard musical instrument that is fitted with steam whistles.

Cal-lis-to *n.* The largest of Jupiter's moons.

cal-lous *adj.* Having calluses; to be without emotional feelings. **callously** *adv.*, **callousness** *n.*

cal-lus *n., pl.* **-luses** A thickening of the horny layer of the skin.

calm *adj.* Absence of motion; having little or no wind, storms, or rough water.

cal-o-mel *n.* A white, tasteless compound used as a purgative.

cal-o-rie *n., pl.* **-ries** A measurement of the amount of heat or energy produced by food. **caloric** *adj.*

cal-u-met *n.* A pipe used by the North American Indians during ceremonies; also known as a peace pipe.

ca-lum-ni-ate *v., pl.* **-nies** To slander; to malign.

cal-um-ny *n., pl.* **-ies** A statement that is malicious, false, and damaging to someone's reputation.

Cal-va-ry *n.* The location where Jesus Christ was crucified.

Cal-vin-ism *n.* The doctrine of John Calvin, marked by a strong emphasis on the sovereignty of God.

ca-lyp-so *n., pl.* **calypsos** Improvised ballad of the West Indies with lyrics on topical or humorous subjects.

ca-lyx *n., pl.* **calyxes, calyces** The outer cover of a flower.

cam *n.* A curved wheel used to produce a reciprocating motion.

ca-ma-ra-de-rie *n* Good will among friends.

cam-ber *n.* A slight curve upward in the middle.

cam-bric *n.* A cotton fabric or white linen.

came *n.* A grooved lead bar that is used to hold together the panes of glass in latticework or stained-glass windows. *v.* Past tense of to come.

cam-el *n.*

An animal used in desert regions, having either one or two humps on its back.

ca-mel-lia *n.* A shrub with shiny green leaves and various colored flowers.

ca-mel-o-pard *n.* A giraffe.

cam-e-o *n.* A gem usually cut with one layer contrasting another, serving as a background; a brief appearance by a famous performer in a single scene on a television show or in a movie.

cam-er-a *n.* An apparatus for taking photographs in a lightproof enclosure with an aperture and shuttered lens through which the image is focused and recorded on photosensitive film.

cam-i-sole *n.* A woman's short, sleeveless undergarment.

cam-ou-flage *v.* To disguise by creating the effect of being part of the natural surroundings.

camp *n.* A temporary lodging or makeshift shelter.

cam-paign *n.* An organized operation designed to bring about a particular political, commercial, or social goal. **campaigner** *n.*

cam-pa-ni-le *n., pl.* **-iles** A free-standing bell tower that is associated with a church.

camp-er *n.* A person who camps in makeshift shelters for recreation; a vehicle specially equipped for casual travel and camping.

camp-fire *n.* An outdoor fire used for cooking and for heat while camping.

camp-ground *n.* A specially prepared area for camping.

cam-phor *n.* A crystalline compound used as an insect repellent. **camphoric** *adj.*

camp-site *n.* The area used for camping.

cam-pus *n.* The buildings and grounds of a college, school, or university.

cam-shaft *n.* The shaft of an engine that is fitted with cams.

can *v.* To know how to do something; to be physically or mentally able; to have the ability to do something; to preserve fruit or vegetables by sealing in an airtight container. *n.* An airtight container.

Ca-naan *n.* In biblical times, known as the Promised Land. **Canaanite** *n.*

Can-a-da *n.* The Commonwealth nation located in the northern half of North America. **Canadian** *adj. & n.*

ca-nal *n.* A man-made water channel for irrigating land.

ca-nal-ize *v.* To convert into canals; to make new canals.

ca-nar-y *n., pl.* **-ies** A green or yellow

songbird which is popular as a caged bird.

ca-nas-ta *n.* A card game using two decks of cards which each player or partnership tries to meld in groups of three or more cards of the same rank; a meld of seven cards that are of the same rank in canasta.

can-can *n.* A dance performed by women, characterized by high kicking while holding up the front of a full skirt.

can-cel *v.* To invalidate or annul; to cross out; to neutralize; in mathematics, to remove a common factor from the numerator and the denominator of a fraction; in computer science, to abort or stop a procedure or program. **cancellation** *n.*

can-cer *n.* A malignant tumor that invades healthy tissue and spreads to other areas; the disease marked by such tumors. **cancerous** *adj.*

Cancer *n.* The fourth sign of the zodiac; a person born between June 21 - July 22.

can-de-la-bra *n., pl.* **candelabrum** A decorative candlestick with several branching arms for candles.

can-did *adj.* Free from bias, malice, or prejudice; honest and sincere.

can-di-date *n., pl.* A person who is aspires to or is nominated or qualified for a membership, award, or office. **candidacy, candidature** *n.*

can-dle *n.* A slender, cylindrical mass of wax or tallow containing a linen or cotton wick which is burned to produce light. *v.* To hold something between the eye and a light, as to test eggs for blood clots, growths, or fertility. **candler** *n.*

can-dle-light *n.* The light emitted from a candle.

can-dor *n.* Straightforwardness; frankness of expression.

can-dy *n., pl.* **-ies** A confection made from sugar and flavored in a variety of ways. *v.* To preserve, cook, coat, or saturate with syrup or sugar.

can-dy-tuft *n.* A variety of plants with white, purple, or reddish flower clusters.

cane *n.* A pithy or hollow, flexible, jointed stem of bamboo or rattan that is split for basketry or wickerwork; a walking stick.

ca-nine *adj.* Relating to or resembling a dog; of the dog family.

Ca-nis Ma-jor *n.* A constellation in the Southern Hemisphere that contains the Dog Star.

can-is-ter *n.* A container made of thin metal, used to store dry foods, such as flour, sugar, coffee, and tea; the cylinder that explodes and scatters shot when fired from a gun.

can-ker *n.* An ulcerated sore in the mouth.

canned *adj.* Preserved and sealed under pressure.

can-ner-y *n., pl.* **-ies** A company that processes canned meat, vegetables, and other foods.

can-ni-bal *n.* Any animal who survives by eating one of its own kind; a person who survives by eating the flesh of human beings. **cannibalism** *n.*, **cannibalization** *n.*, **cannibalistic** *adj.*

can-ni-bal-ize *v.* To remove parts from a plane for use as replacements in another plane.

can-non *n., pl.* **cannons** A heavy war weapon made of metal and mounted on wheels or a base for discharging projectiles.

can-non-ball *n.* An iron projectile fired from a cannon.

can-ny *adj.* Thrifty; careful; cautious; shrewd.

ca-noe *n.*

A lightweight, slender boat with pointed ends which moves by paddling. **canoe** *v.*, **canoeist** *n.*

can-on *n.* The laws established by a church council; a priest serving in a collegiate church or cathedral. **canonical** *adj.*

can-on-ize *v.* To officially declare a deceased person a saint. **canonization** *n.*

can-o-py *n., pl.* **-ies** A cloth covering used as an ornamental structure over a bed; the supporting surface of a parachute; the transparent cover over the cockpit of an airplane.

cant *n.* The external angle of a building. *v.* To throw off by tilting.

can-ta-bi-le *n.* A lyrical, flowing style of music.

can-ta-loupe *n.* A sweet-tasting, orange-colored muskmelon.

can-tan-ker-ous *adj.* Bad-tempered and argumentative. **cantakerously** *adv.*

can-ta-ta *n.* A drama that is sung but not acted.

can-ter *n.* An easy lope just a little slower than a gallop, but faster than a trot.

can-ti-cle *n.* A hymn or chant sung in church.

can-ti-lev-er *n.* A long structure, such as a beam, supported only at one end.

can-ton *n.* A small area of a country divided into parts. **cantonal** *adj.*

can-ton-ment *n.* One or more temporary billets for troops.

can-tor *n.* The chief singer in a synagogue.

can-vas *n.* A heavy fabric used in making tents and sails for boats; a piece of canvas that is used for oil paintings.

can-vass *v.* To travel through a region to solicit opinions or votes; to take a poll or survey. **canvasser** *n.*

can-yon *n.* A deep and narrow gorge with steep sides.

cap *n.* A covering for the head, usually brimless and made of a soft material; the final or finishing touch to something; a small explosive charge that is used in cap guns. **cap** *v.*

ca-pa-ble *adj.* Having the ability to perform in an efficient way; qualified. **capability,** *n.,* **capably** *adv.*

ca-pa-cious *adj.* Having a lot of room or space.

ca-pac-i-tance *n.* The property of a body or circuit which allows it to store an electrical charge. **capacitive** *adj.*

ca-pac-i-tor *n.* The circuit element composed of metallic plates that are separated by a dielectric and are used to store a charge temporarily.

ca-pac-i-ty *n., pl.* **-ies** The ability to contain, receive, or absorb; having the aptitude or ability to do something; the maximum production or output; in computer science, the total amount of data or information that can be processed, stored, or generated.

ca-par-i-son *n.* An ornamental covering for a horse, saddle, or harness.

cape *n.* A sleeveless covering for the shoulders that fastens at the neck; a point of land that extends into a lake or sea.

cap-il-lary *n., pl.* **-ies** Any of the small vessels that connect the veins and arteries. *adj.* Having a hair-like bore; very fine or small in size.

cap-i-tal *n.* The town or city that is designated as the seat of government for a nation or state; material wealth in the form of money or property that is used to produce more wealth; funds that are contributed to a business by the stockholders or owners; net worth of a company or business.

cap-i-tal-ism *n.* The economic system in which the means of distribution and production are privately owned and operated for private profit.

capitalist *n.* A person who invests in a business. **capitalistic** *adj.*

cap-i-ta-tion *n.* A census or tax of equal amount for each person.

ca-pit-u-late *v.* To surrender under terms of an agreement. **-tor** *n.,* **-tory** *adj.*

ca-pon *n.* A young rooster that has been castrated to improve the meat for eating.

ca-price *n.* A sudden change of action or mind without adequate reason; a whim. **capricious** *adj.,* **-ness** *n.*

Capricorn *n.* The tenth sign of the zodiac; a person born between (December 22 - January 19.)

cap-size *v.* To overturn in a boat.

cap-stan *n., Naut.* A drum-like apparatus rotated to hoist weights by winding in a cable on a ship or boat.

cap-su-lated *adj.* Formed or in a capsule-like state. **capsulation** *n.*

cap-sule *n.* A small gelatinous case for a dose of oral medicine; a fatty sac that surrounds an organ of the body, as the kidney, and protects it; a summary in a brief form. **capsular** *adj.*

cap-tain *n.* The chief leader of a group; the commander or master of a ship. *Naval* The commissioned naval officer who ranks below a commodore or rear admiral; the designated spokesperson of a team.

cap-tion *n.* A subtitle; a description of an illustration or picture.

cap-tious *adj.* Deceptive; critical.

cap-ti-vate *v.* To hold the attention, fascinate, or charm a person or group of people. **captivation** *n.,* **captivator** *n.*

cap-tive *n.* A person being held as a prisoner.

cap-ture *v.* To take something or someone by force. **capturer** *n.*

car *n.* An automobile; an enclosed vehicle, as a railroad car.

ca-rafe *n.* A glass bottle for serving wine or water.

car-a-mel *n.* A chewy substance primarily composed of sugar, butter, and milk.

car-a-mel-ize *v.* To make into caramel.

car-at *n.* The unit of weight for gems that equals 200 milligrams.

car-a-way *n.* An aromatic seed used in cooking.

car-bide *n.* A carbon compound with a more electropositive element.

car-bine *n.* A short-barreled rifle, light in weight.

car-bo-hy-drate *n.* A group of compounds, including starches, celluloses, and sugars that contain carbon, hydrogen, and oxygen.

car-bon *n.* A nonmetallic element that occurs as a powdery noncrystalline solid; the element symbolized by C. **carbonization** *n.,* **carbonize** *v.*

car-bon-ate *v.* To add or charge with carbon dioxide gas, as in a beverage. **carbonation** *n.*

car-bon copy *n.* The copy of an original made with carbon paper. *Slang* An exact copy.

car-bon di-ox-ide *n.* An odorless, colorless, nonflammable gas, removed from the atmosphere by the photosynthesis of plants and returned by the respiration of animals.

car-bon mon-ox-ide *n.* An odorless, colorless gas that is formed by the incomplete oxidation of carbon, burns with a blue flame, an is highly poisonous when inhaled.

car-bon tet-ra-chlo-ride *n.* A nonflammable, colorless, poisonous liquid used as a cleaning fluid and in fire extinguishers.

car-bun-cle *n.* An infection of the skin and deeper tissue which is red, inflamed, full of pus, and painful.

car-bu-re-tor *n.* The device in gasoline engines that mixes vapor, fuel, and air for efficient combustion.

car-cass *n.* The dead body of an animal; something that no longer has life.

car-ci-no-ma *n.* A malignant tumor; cancer. **carcinomatous** *adj.*

card *n.* A small piece of pasteboard or very stiff paper, used in a wide variety of ways, as a greeting card, a business card, a postcard, etc.

car-di-ac *adj.* Relating to the heart.

car-di-ac mas-sage *n.* A procedure performed by a physician to restore proper circulation and respiration for someone in distress.

car-di-gan *n.* A sweater with an opening down the front.

car-di-nal *adj.* Of prime importance; principal. *n.* An official of the Catholic Church who ranks just below the Pope and who is appointed by him.

car-di-o-gram *n.* The curve recorded by a cardiograph and is used in the diagnosis of heart defects.

car-di-ol-o-gy *n.* The study of the heart, its diseases, and treatments. -ist *n.*

car-di-o-pul-mo-nary *adj.* Relating to the heart and lungs.

car-di-o-pul-mo-nary re-sus-ci-ta-tion *n.* A procedure used to restore breathing after cardiac arrest by using mouth-to-mouth resuscitation.

car-di-o-vas-cu-lar *adj.* Involving and relating to the heart and the blood vessels.

care *n.* A feeling of concern, anxiety, or worry; guardianship or custody. *v.* To show interest or regard.

ca-reen *v.* To lurch or twist from one side to another while moving rapidly.

ca-reer *n.* The profession or occupation a person takes in life. career *n.*

care-free *adj.* Free from all cares, worries, and concerns.

care-ful *adj.* Exercising care; cautious; watchful.

ca-ress *v.* To gently show affection by touching or stroking. caress *n.*

car-go *n.* Freight; the goods and merchandise carried on a ship, plane, or other vehicle.

car-hop *n.* A person who waits on customers at a drive-in restaurant.

Carib-bean Sea *n.* An arm of the Atlantic Ocean bounded by the coasts of South and Central America and the West Indies.

car-i-bou *n.*

A large antlered deer of northern North America.

car-il-lon *n.* A set of tuned bells in a tower, that are usually played by a keyboard.

car-mine *n.* A vivid red color; crimson; deep purplish red.

car-nage *n.* A bloody slaughter; war; massacre.

car-nal *adj.* Relating to sensual desires. carnality *n.*, carnally *adv.*

car-na-tion *n.* A fragrant perennial flower in a variety of colors.

car-nel-ian *n.* A clear red chalcedony that is used as a gem.

car-ni-val *n.* A traveling amusement show with side shows, a Ferris wheel, and merry-go-rounds; any kind of a happy celebration.

car-ni-vore *n.* A flesh-eating animal.

carnivorous *adj.*, carnivorously *adv.*

car-ol *n* A song to celebrate joy or praise. caroler *n.*, carol *v.*

ca-rouse *v.* To be rowdy and to be in a drunken state. carouser *n.*

car-pal *adj.* Pertaining to the wrist and the bones in the wrist.

car-pel *n.*, *Bot.* A seed vessel or pistil.

car-pen-ter *n.* A person who builds and repairs wooden structures. -ry *n.*

car-pet *n.* A thick, woven or felt floor covering that helps to insulate the floors. carpeting *n.*

car-pet bag *n.* An old-fashioned traveling bag made from carpet.

car-rot *n.* An orange vegetable that is a root.

car-rou-sel *n.* A merry-go-round.

car-ry *v.* To transport from one place to another; to bear the burden, weight, or responsibility of; to keep or have available for sale; to maintain on business books for future settlement.

cart *n.* A two-wheeled vehicle for moving heavy goods; a small lightweight vehicle that can be moved around by hand.

car-tel *n.* A group of independent companies that have organized to control prices, production, etc.

Carter, James Earl Jr. (Jimmy) *n.* The 39th president of the United States 1977-1981.

car-ti-lage *n.* A tough, elastic substance of connective tissue attached to the surface of bones near the joints. cartilaginous *adj.*

car-tog-ra-phy *n.* The art of developing charts and maps. cartographer *n.*, cartographic *adj.*

carton *n.* A container made from cardboard.

car-toon *n.* A caricature depicting a humorous situation; animated cartoons produced by photographing a series of action drawings. cartoonist *n.*

car-tridge *n.* A case made of metal, pasteboard, etc., that contains a charge of powder; the primer and shot or projectile for a firearm.

carve *v.* To slice meat or poultry; to cut into something; to create, as sculpture.

cary-at-id *n.* A supporting column sculptured in the form of a female figure.

cas-cade *n.* A waterfall that flows over steep rocks.

case *n.* A particular occurrence or instance; an injury or disease; an argument, supporting facts, or reasons that justify a situation; a box or housing to carry things in, as a briefcase; in the law, a suit of action brought against a person.

cas-ing *n.* A protective covering or container; the framework of a window or door.

ca-sein *n.* A dairy protein that is used in foods and in manufacturing adhesives and plastics.

cash-ew *n.* A tropical American tree that produces an edible nut that can be eaten raw or roasted.

cash-ier *n.* An employee who handles cash as part of his job description; an officer in a bank in charge of receiving or distributing money.

cash-mere *n.* The wool from the Kashmir goat; the yarn made from this wool.

ca-si-no *n.*, *pl.* **-nos** A public establishment open especially for gambling.

cask *n.* A large wooden vessel or barrel; the quantity that a cask will hold.

cas-ket *n.* A coffin; a small chest or box.

cas-que *n.* A helmet. **casqued** *adj.*

cas-se-role *n.* A dish in which the food is baked and also served; food cooked and served in this manner.

cas-sette *n.* A cartridge of magnetic tape used in tape recorders to play and record.

cas-sock *n.* A close-fitting garment worn by members of the clergy.

cast *v.* To hurl or throw with force; to direct or turn; to shed; to give a certain part or role; to deposit or give a vote on something; to make or throw, as with a fishing line. *Naut.* To fall off, to veer; to be shipwrecked or marooned at sea. *n.* A dressing made from plaster of paris used on a broken bone.

cas-ta-net *n.*, *pl.* **-nets** An instrument made from a pair of ivory or hardwood shells, held in the palm of the hand and clapped together with the fingers.

cast-a-way *adj.* Throw away. *n.* One who is shipwrecked or discarded.

caste *n.* A social separation based on a profession, hereditary, or financial hierarchy.

cas-tel-lat-ed *adj.* Adorned by battlements and turrets.

cast-er *n.* A small set of swiveling rollers that are fastened under pieces of furniture and the like.

cas-ti-gate *v.* To punish or criticize severely. **castigation, castigator** *n.*

cast-ing *n.* The act of one that casts.

cas-tle *n.* A fort or fortified dwelling for nobility; any large house or place of refuge; a stronghold.

cast-off *adj.* Discarded; thrown away.

castor oil *n.* An oil from the seeds of a tropical plant used as a cathartic and lubricant.

cas-trate *v.* To remove the testicles; to remove the ovaries; to spay. **-tion** *n.*

ca-su-al *adj.* Informal; occurring by chance. **casually** *adv.*, **casualness** *n.*

ca-su-al-ty *n.*, *pl.* **-ies** One who is injured or killed in an accident. *Milit.* A soldier who is killed, wounded, taken prisoner by the enemy, or missing in action.

cat *n.* A small domesticated animal, a pet; any of the animals in the cat family, such as the lion, lynx, tiger, etc.

cat-a-clysm *n.* A sudden and violent disaster. **cataclysmic, cataclysmal** *adj.*

cat-a-combs *n.* An underground passage with small rooms for coffins.

cat-a-falque *n.* The structure that supports a coffin during a state funeral.

cat-a-lep-sy *n.* A condition in which there is a rigidity of the muscles, causing the patient to remain in a fixed position or posture.

cat-a-log *or* **cat-a-logue** *n.* A publication containing a list of names, objects, etc.

cat-a-lyst *n.*, *Chem.* Any substance that alters and decreases the time it takes a chemical reaction to occur.

cat-a-ma-ran *n.* A boat with twin hulls.

cat-a-pult *n.* An ancient military device for throwing arrows or stones; a device for launching aircraft from the deck of a ship.

cat-a-ract *n.* A large waterfall or downpour. *Pathol.* A disease of the lens of the eye, causing total or partial blindness.

ca-tarrh *n.*, *Pathol.* Inflammation of the nose and throat. **catarrhal** *adj.*

ca-tas-tro-phe *n.* A terrible and sudden disaster. **catastophic** *adj.*

catch *v.* To take; to seize or capture; to reach in time; to intercept; to become entangled or fastened. **catch** *n.*

catch-all *n.* A container or bag for odds and ends.

catch-er *n.* A person who catches a ball.

cat-e-gor-i-cal *adj.* Absolute; certain; related to or included in a category without qualification. **-ly** *adv.*

cat-e-go-rize *v.* To place in categories.

cat-e-go-ry *n.*, *pl.* **-ries** A general group to which something belongs.

ca-ter *v.* To provide a food service; to bring directly to a location. **caterer** *n.*

cat-er-pil-lar *n.* The very fuzzy, wormlike, brightly-colored spiny larva of a moth or butterfly.

cat-er-waul *n.* The harsh cry made by cats at mating time. **caterwaul** *v.*

ca-the-dral *n.* A large and important church, containing the seat of a bishop.

cath-e-ter *n.*, *Med.* A thin, flexible tube that is inserted into body cavities for drainage and to draw urine from the bladder. **catheterize** *v.*

cath-ode *n.* The negatively charged electrode which receives positively charged ions during electrolysis.

cath-ode ray tube *n.* The vacuum tube on which images are found, used in a computer screen.

Catholic *n.* A member of the Roman Catholic Church.

cat-i-on *n.* A positively charged ion that is attracted in electrolytes to a negative electrode. **cationic** *adj.*

cat-nap *n.* A short nap. **catnap** *v.*

CAT scan *n.* A cross-sectional picture produced by a scanner, used to x-ray the body by using computerized axial tomography.

cat-tail *n.* A long marsh plant that has minute brown flowers and long leaves, used in making chair seats and in dried flower arrangements.

cat-tle *n.*, *pl.* Farm animals raised for meat and dairy products.

cat-ty-cor-nered *adj.* Not straight; sitting at an angle.

Cau-ca-sian *n.* An inhabitant of Caucasus. *adj.* Relating to a major ethnic division of the human race; of or relating to the white race.

cau-cus *n.* A meeting of a political party to make policy decisions and to select candidates.

cau-li-flow-er *n.* A vegetable related to broccoli and cabbage.

caulk *v.* To seal seams and edges against leakage of water and air. **caulker** *n.*

cause *v.* To produce a result, consequence, or effect. *n.* A goal, principle; a reason; motive. **causer** *n.*

cau-se-rie *n.* A short informal conversation or chat.

cause-way *n.* A paved highway through a marsh tract; raised road over water.

cau-ter-ize *v.* To sear or burn with a hot instrument. **cauterization** *n.*

cau-ter-y *n.* A very hot instrument used to destroy tissue that does not seem normal.

cau-tion *n.* A warning careful planning.

cau-tious *adj.* Very careful.

cav-al-cade *n.* A group of horse-drawn carriages or riders, forming a procession.

cav-a-lier *n.* A very gallant gentleman; a knight.

cav-al-ry *n.*, *pl.* -ies Army troops trained to fight on horseback or in armored vehicles. **cavalryman** *n.*

cave *n.* An underground tomb or chamber with an opening at the ground surface.

ca-ve-at *n.* A formal legal notice to stop the proceedings until both sides have a hearing; a warning or caution.

ca-vern *n.* A very large underground cave. **cavernous** *adj.*

cav-i-ar *or* **cav-i-are** *n.* The eggs of large fish, eaten as an appetizer.

cav-i-ty *n.*, *pl* -ies A decayed place in a tooth; a hollow or hole.

CD *abbr.* Compact disk; civil defense; certificate of deposit.

cease *v.* To come to an end or put an end to; to stop.

cease-fire *v.* To stop fighting, usually as a result of a truce.

cease-less *adj.* Endless. **ceaselessly** *adv.*

ce-cum *or* **cae-cum** *n.*, *Anat.* The pouch where the large intestine begins.

ce-dar *n.* An evergreen tree with fragrant, reddish wood.

ce-dil-la *n.* A diacritical mark placed under the letter c in the French vocabulary to indicate a modification or alteration of the usual phonetic sound.

ceil-ing *n.* The overhead covering of a room; the maximum limit to something; the maximum height for visibility under specified conditions for aircraft.

cel-e-brate *v.* To observe with ceremonies, rejoicing, or festivity. **celebration** *n.*

cel-leb-ri-ty *n.*, *pl.* -ies A famous person.

cel-er-y *n.* A green vegetable with an edible stalk.

ce-les-ta *n.* A musical instrument which produces bell-like tones when the keyboard and metal plates are struck by hammers.

ce-les-tial *adj.* Heavenly; spiritual.

cel-i-bate *n.* A person who remains unmarried because of religious vows; one who is sexually abstinent. **celibacy** *n.*, **celibate** *adj.*

cell *n.*

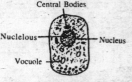

Central Bodies

Nuclelous — Nucleus

Vocuole

A typical cell

The smallest unit of any organism that is capable of independent function, is composed of a small mass of cytoplasm, usually encloses a central nucleus, and is surrounded by a membrane or a rigid cell wall; a cavity of an ovary or pericarp that is seed-bearing. *Electr.* The part of a battery that generates the electricity; in computer science, the location in memory that holds a single unit of information; a byte. A prison; a small room.

cel-lar *n.* An underground area, beneath a building, used for storage.

cel-lo *n.* A base instrument of the violin family. **cellist** *n.*

cel-lo-phane *n.* A transparent paper-like material made from treated cellulose that has been processed in thin, clear strips.

cel-lu-lar *adj.* Consisting of cells.

cel-lu-lite *n.* A fatty deposit or area under the skin.

cel-lu-lose *n.* A carbohydrate that is insoluble in ordinary solvents and forms the fundamental material for the structure of plants.

ce-ment *n.* A construction material made up of powdered, calcined rock and clay materials which when added with water, set up as a hard, solid mass.

cem-e-ter-y *n.*, *pl.* -ies The place for burying the dead.

cen-ser *n.* A vessel or container for burning incense.

cen-sor *n.* A person who examines films and printed materials to determine what might be objectionable. **-ship** *n.*

cen-sure *n.* An expression of criticism and/or disapproval.

cen-sus *n.* An official count of the population.

cent *n.* One; one hundredth of a dollar.

cen-te-nar-i-an *n.* A person who has reached the age of 100 or more.

cen-ter *n.* The place of equal distance from all sides; the heart; in sports, a person who holds the middle position, as in the forward line.

cen-ti-pede *n.* A flat arthropod with numerous body segments and legs.

cen-tral *adj.* In, near, or at the center; of

primary importance. -ly *adv.*, -ize *v.*

cen-tral ner-vous sys-tem *n.* The nervous system that consists of the spinal cord and the brain.

cen-trif-u-gal *adj.* Moving or directing away from a center location.

cen-tu-ry *n.*, *pl.* -ies A period consisting of 100 years.

ce-ram-ic *adj.* Of or relating to a brittle material made by firing a nonmetallic mineral, such as clay. **ceramics** *n.*

ce-re-al *n.* An edible grain eaten as a breakfast food.

cer-e-bel-lum *n.*, *pl.* -bellums The part of the brain responsible for the coordination of voluntary muscular movements.

cer-e-bral hem-or-rhage *n.* The rupture of an artery in the brain, which allows blood to escape.

cer-e-bral pal-sy *n.* A variety of chronic conditions in which brain damage, usually occurring at birth, impairs motor function and control.

cer-e-brum *n.*, *pl.* -brums *or* -bra The brain structure that is divided into two cerebral hemisphere's and occupies most of the cranial cavity.

cer-e-mo-ni-al *adj.* Mark by or relating to a ceremony. **ceremonially** *adv.*

cer-e-mo-ny *n.*, *pl.* -ies A ritual or formal act performed in a certain manner.

ce-rise *n.* The color of deep purplish red.

cer-tain *adj.*, *pl.* -ties Being very sure of something; without any doubt; inevitable; not mentioned but assumed. **certainly** *adv.*

cer-tif-i-cate *n.* A document stating the truth or accuracy of something; a document that certifies fulfillment of duties or requirements, as of a course of study.

cer-tif-i-ca-tion *n.* A certified statement.

cer-ti-fy *v.* To testify in writing that something is true or a fact.

cer-vi-cal *adj.* Relating to the neck of the cervix.

ce-si-um *n.* An electrometal, white in color, from the alkali group, used in photoelectric cells.

ces-sa-tion *n.* The act of stopping or ceasing.

ces-sion *n.* The act of giving up territory or rights to another.

chafe *v.* To become sore by rubbing; to irritate.

cha-grin *n.* A feeling of distress caused by disappointment, failure, or humiliation.

chain *n.* A connection of several links; anything that confines or restrains. **chain gang** Prisoners that are chained together. **chain reaction** Series of events that directly affect one another.

chair *n.* A seat with four legs and a back, intended for one person; a seat of office; the chairman. *Slang* Electric chair. **chair lift** A chair suspended from cables that is used to carry people and snow equipment up or down the ski slopes.

chair-man *n.*, *pl.* -men The person presiding over a committee, board, or other meeting.

chaise *n.* A one-horse vehicle for two people.

cha-let *n.* A cottage that has a gently sloping and overhanging roof.

chal-ice *n.* A drinking goblet or cup.

chalk *n.* A soft mineral made from fossil seashells, used for marking on a surface, such as a slate board. **chalky** *adj.*

chalk-board *n.* A blackboard made from slate.

chal-lah *or* **cha-lah** A loaf of braided bread made with extra eggs, traditionally eaten by Jews on holidays and the Sabbath.

chal-lenge *n.* A demand for a contest; a protest. *v.* To call into question.

chal-lis *n.* A lightweight printed cloth in rayon, cotton, or wool.

cham-ber *n.* A bedroom in a large home; a judge's office; a meeting place or hall for a legislative body; the compartment of a gun that holds the charge.

cham-ber-lain *n.* The high-ranking person or official of a royal court.

cham-ber-maid *n.* A maid who takes care of bedrooms at a hotel.

cham-pagne *n.* A white sparkling wine.

cham-pi-on *n.* The holder of first place in a contest; one who defends another person.

cham-pi-on-ship *n.* The competition that determines a winner.

chance *n.* The random existence of something happening; a gamble or a risk.

chan-cel *n.* The area of a church that contains the altar and choir.

chan-cel-lor *n.* The chief director or minister of state in certain countries in Europe. **chancellorship** *n.*

chan-cer-y *n.* The office for the safekeeping of official records.

chan-cre *n.* A lesion that is the first indication of syphilis.

chan-croid *n.* A sore or lesion in the genital area that is similar to a chancre, but does not involve syphilis.

chanc-y *adj.* Risky; dangerous.

chan-de-lier *n.* A light fixture with many branches for lights that is suspended from the ceiling.

chan-dler *n.* A person who makes and sells candles. **chandlery** *n.*

change *v.* To become or make different; to alter; to put with another; to use to take the place of another; to freshen a bed by putting clean coverings on. *n.* Coins; money given back when the payment exceeds the bill. **changeable** *adj.*, **changeably** *adv.*

chan-nel *n.* The deepest part of a stream, river, or harbor; the course that anything moves through or past; a groove.

chant *n.* A melody in which all words are sung on the same note. *v.* To celebrate with a song. **chanter** *n.*

Cha-nu-kah *n.* *Variation of* Hanukkah

cha-os *n.* Total disorder. **chaotic** *adj.*, **chaotically** *adv.*

chap n., Slang A fellow; a man. v. To dry and split open from the cold and wind.

chap-el n. A place to worship, usually contained in a church.

chap-er-on or chap-er-one n. An older woman who supervises younger people. chaperone v.

chap-lain n. A clergyman who conducts religious services for a group.

chap-let n. A garland for the head; a string of beads.

chap-ter n. One division of a book; a branch of a fraternity, religious order, or society.

char-ac-ter n. A quality or trait that distinguishes an individual or group; a person that is portrayed in a play; a distinctive quality or trait. adj. Distinctive; peculiar.

cha-rades pl., n. A game in which the syllables of words are acted out by each player.

chard n. On edible white beet with large, succulent leaves.

charge v. To give responsibility; to ask a price; to accuse; to impute something to; to command; to record a debt owed. n. Management; custody; supervision; an expense or price. Slang A thrill. chargeable adj.

charg-er n. An apparatus for recharging a battery.

char-i-ot n. An ancient horse-drawn vehicle used to fight battles. -eer n.

char-i-ty n. Money or help given to aid the needy; an organization, fund, or institution whose purpose is to aid those in need.

cha-ri-va-ri n. A mock serenade to newlyweds, performed with horns, tin pans, etc.

char-la-tan n. One who falsely claims to possess knowledge or a skill he does not have. charlatanism n.

charm n. The ability to delight or please; a small ornament that has a special meaning, usually worn on a bracelet.

char-nel n. A special room or building that contains the bones or bodies of the dead.

chart n. A map, graph, or table that gives information in a form that is easy to read.

char-ter n. An official document that grants certain privileges and rights. v. To lease or hire a vehicle or aircraft.

char-treuse n. A light yellowish green.

char-y adj. Wary; cautious; not wasting time, resources, or money. charily adv., chariness n.

chase v. To follow quickly; to pursue; to run after. chase, chaser n.

chasm n. A very deep crack in the earth's surface.

chas-sis n. The rectangular framework that supports the body and engine of a motor vehicle.

chaste adj. Morally pure; modest; not guilty of participating in sexual intercourse.

chas-tise v. To severely reprimand; to punish by beating. chastisement n.

chas-u-ble n. The vestment without sleeves worn over the alb by a priest when celebrating Mass.

chat v. To converse in a friendly manner.

chat-tel n. An item of movable personal property.

chauf-feur n. A person who is hired to drive an automobile for another person.

chau-vin-ism n. The unreasonable belief in the superiority of one's own group. chauvinist n., chauvinistic adj.

cheap adj. Inexpensive; low in cost; of poor quality. cheaply adv., -ness n.

cheap-en v. To lessen the value; to make cheap.

cheat v. To deprive of by deceit; to break the rules. cheater n.

check v. To control or restrain; to examine for correctness or condition. n. The act of verifying, comparing, or testing; a bill one receives at a restaurant; a written order on one's bank to pay money from funds on deposit; the act of comparing item to item; a move in chess which threatens a king and which forces the opponent to move the king to safety.

check-up n. A complete physical examination.

ched-dar n. A firm, smooth cheese which ranges in flavor from mild to sharp.

cheek n. The fleshy part of the face just below the eye and above and to the side of the mouth.

cheek-bone n. The facial bone below the eyes

cheep n. To utter high-pitched sounds.

cheer v. To give courage to; to instill with courage or hope; to make glad or happy; to shout with encouragement or applause. n. Good spirits; happiness.

cheer-ful adj. Having good spirits.

cheer-leader n. Someone who leads cheers at a sporting event.

cheese n. A food made from the curd of milk that is seasoned and aged.

cheese-cloth n. A loosely-woven cotton gauze.

chee-tah n. A swift-running, long-legged African wildcat.

chef n. A male cook who manages a kitchen; the head cook.

che-la n. The pincer-like claw of an arachnid.

chem-i-cal adj. Of or related to chemistry. chemically adv.

che-mise n. A woman's loose undergarment which resembles a slip; a loose-fitting dress that hangs straight down from the shoulders.

chem-ist n. A person who is versed in chemistry.

chem-is-try n. The scientific study of the composition, structure, and properties of substances and their reactions.

che-mo-ther-a-py n. The treatment of a disease, such as cancer, with chemicals. chemotherapeutic adj.

che-nille n. A fuzzy, soft cord used to

make rugs, bedspreads, and other fabrics.

cher-ish v. To treat with love; to hold dear.

Cher-o-kee n. A tribe of Iroquoian Indians who formerly lived in northern Georgia and North Carolina, now living in the state of Oklahoma.

che-root n. A cigar that is cut off square at both ends.

cher-ry n., pl. -ies A fruit tree bearing a small, round, deep, or purplish red fruit with a small, hard stone.

cher-ub n., pl. -cherubs A beautiful young child; a representation of an angel resembling a child with a rosy face and wings.

chess n. A game played on a chessboard by two people, each of whom has sixteen pieces and tries to checkmate his opponent's king in order to win the game.

chess-board n. A board with sixty-four squares, which can be used to play chess or checkers.

chess-man n., pl. chessmen Any of the pieces necessary to play chess.

chest n. The part of the upper body that is enclosed by the thorax; the ribs; a box usually having a hinged lid, used for storage.

ches-ter-field n. An overcoat with concealed buttons and a velvet collar.

chest-nut n. A tree bearing edible reddish-brown nuts; a nut from a chestnut tree.

chew v. To crush or grind with the teeth; to masticate. n. The act of chewing. chewer n., chewy adj.

chi-a-ro-scu-ro n. The distribution of shade and light in a picture.

Chi-ca-na n. An American woman with Mexican ancestry.

chick n.

A young chicken or bird. Slang A young woman.

chick-en n. A domestic fowl; the edible meat of a chicken. Slang Cowardly; afraid; losing one's nerve.

chick-en feed n. Food for chickens. Slang Very little money.

chick-en--heart-ed adj. Timid or cowardly.

chic-le n. The milky juice of a tropical tree; the principal ingredient of chewing gum.

chic-o-ry n., pl. -ies An herb with blue flowers used in salads, the dried, roasted roots of which are used as a coffee substitute.

chide v. To scold or find fault. chider n.

chief n. The person of highest rank. chiefly adv., -or adj.

chief-tain n. The head of a group, clan, or tribe.

chif-fon n. A sheer fabric made from rayon or silk. adj. In cooking, having a fluffy texture.

chif-fo-nier n. A tall chest of drawers

with a mirror at the top.

chig-ger n. A mite that attaches itself to the skin and causes intense itching.

chi-gnon n. A roll of hair worn at the back of the neck.

chil-blain n. An inflammation of the hands and feet caused by exposure to cold.

child n., pl. children A young person of either sex; adolescent; a person between infancy and youth. childish adj.

child abuse n. Sexual or physical maltreatment of a child by a guardian, parent, or other adult.

child-birth n. The act of giving birth.

child-hood n. The time or period of being a child.

child-like adj. Characteristic of a child.

chil-i or chile or chil-li n. A hot pepper; a sauce made of meet and chili or chili powder.

chill v. To be cold, often with shivering; to reduce to a lower temperature. n. A feeling of cold.

chill-y adj. Very cold; without warmth of temperature or feeling.

chime n. A group or set of bells tuned to a scale. v. To announce on the hour, by sounding a chime.

chi-me-ra n. An absurd fantasy; an imaginary monster with a goat's body, a lion's head, and a serpent's tail.

chim-ney n. A flue for smoke to escape, as from a fireplace.

chim-pan-zee n. An anthropoid ape with large ears and dark brown hair, smaller and more intelligent than the gorilla.

chin n. The lower part of the face. v. To lift oneself up while grasping an overhead bar until the chin is level with the bar.

chin-chil-la n. A rodent from South America raised for its soft fur.

chine n. The spine or backbone of animals.

chink n. A narrow crack.

chintz n. A printed cotton fabric which is glazed.

chintz-y adj. Cheap.

chip n. A small piece that has been broken or cut from another source; a disk used in the game of poker; in Computer Science, an integrated circuit engraved on a silicone substrate.

chip-munk n.

A striped rodent of the squirrel family.

chi-ro-prac-tic n. A method of therapy in which the body is manipulated to adjust the spine. chiropractor n.

chirp n. The high-pitched sound made by a cricket or a small bird. chirp v.

chis-el n. A tool with a sharp edge which is used to shape and cut metal, wood, or stone.

chit n. A voucher indicating the amount

owed for food or drink; a lively girl.

chit-chat *n.* Casual conversation or small talk.

chi-tin *n.* The substance that forms the hard outer cover of insects.

chit-ter-lings *pl., n.* The small intestines of a pig, used as food.

chiv-al-ry *n., pl.* **-ies** The brave and courteous qualities of an ideal knight.

chive *n.* An herb used as flavoring in cooking.

chlo-ride *n.* A compound of chlorine with a double positive element.

chlo-rine *n.* A greenish-yellow compound used to purify water, bleach, and disinfectant.

chlo-ro-phyll *n.* The green pigment that is found in photosynthetic organisms.

chock *n.* A wedge or block placed under a wheel to prevent motion. **chock** *v.*

choc-o-late *n.* A preparation of ground and roasted cacao nuts that is usually sweetened; a candy or beverage made from chocolate. **chocolaty** *adj.*

Choc-taw *n.* A member of the tribe of North American Indians from the Muskhogean group, now residing in Oklahoma.

choice *n.* To select or choose; the opportunity, right, or power to choose.

choir *n.* An organized group of singers that usually perform in a church.

chok-er *n.* A necklace that fits tightly around the neck.

cho-les-ter-ol *n.* A fatty crystalline substance that is derived from bile and is present in most gallstones, the brain, and blood cells.

choose *v.* To select or pick out; to prefer; to make a choice. **chosen** *adj.*, **choosy** *or* **choosey** *adj.*

chop *v.* To cut by making a sharp downward stroke; to cut into bits or small pieces.

chop-per *n., Slang* A helicopter.

chop-pers *pl., n., Slang* False teeth.

chop-py *adj.* Rough; irregular; jerky.

chop-sticks *pl., n.* Slender sticks of ivory or wood, Chinese in origin, used in pairs of two as eating utensils.

cho-ral *adj.* Pertaining to, written for, or sung by a choir or chorus. **chorally** *adv.*

cho-rale *n.* A Protestant hymn with a simple melody, sung in unison.

chore *n.* A daily task; a task that becomes unpleasant or burdensome.

cho-re-a *n.* An acute nervous disease especially of children, marked by irregular and uncontrollable movement of muscles.

cho-re-og-ra-phy *n.* The creation of a dance routine. **choreograph** *v.*, **choreographer** *n.*, **choreographic** *adj.*

chor-is-ter *n.* A choirboy or a member of a choir.

chor-tle *v.* To chuckle with glee, especially in triumph or joy. **chortle**, **chortler** *n.*

cho-rus *n., pl.* **-ses** A group of people who sing together; repeated verses of a song.

cho-sen *adj.* Selected or preferred above all.

chow-der *n.* A soup dish made with fish or clams, often having a milk base.

Christ *n.* Jesus; The Messiah; God's son who died to save Christians from sin.

chris-ten *v.* To baptize; to give a Christian name at baptism; to use for the first time. **christening** *n.*

Chris-tian *n.* A believer and follower of the teachings of Jesus. **Christianly** *adv.*, **Christianity** *n.*

Christ-mas *n.* December 25th, the anniversary of the birth of Jesus Christ, observed as a holiday or holy day.

chro-mat-ic *adj.* Relating to color.

chro-mo-some *n.* One of several small bodies in the nucleus of a cell, containing genes responsible for the determination and transmission of hereditary characteristics.

chron-ic *adj.* Frequently recurring; continuing for long periods of time; affected by a disease for a long time. **chronically** *adv.*

chron-i-cle *n.* A record of events written in the order in which they occurred. **chronicle** *v.*, **chronicler** *n.*

chrys-a-lis *n., pl.* **-ses** The enclosed pupa from which a moth or butterfly develops.

chry-san-the-mum *n.* A cultivated plant having large, showy flowers.

chub *n.* A freshwater fish related to the carp.

chub-by *adj.* Plumb; rounded.

chuck *v.* To tap or pat affectionately under the chin. *Slang* To throw out or to throw away; to quit; to give up. *n.* A cut of beef extending from the neck to the ribs.

chuck-hole *n.* A hole in the street or the pavement.

chuck-le *v.* To laugh quietly with satisfaction. **chuckler** *n.*

chum *n.* A close friend or pal.

chunk *n.* A thick piece of anything; a large quantity of something; a lump.

church *n.* A building for Christian worship; a congregation of public Christian worship.

churl *n.* A rude or rustic person. **churlish** *adj.*, **churlishness** *n.*

churn *n.* The container in which cream or milk is beaten vigorously to make butter. *v.* To agitate in a churn in order to make butter; to agitate violently.

chute *n.* An incline passage through which water, coal, etc., may travel to a destination. *Slang* A parachute.

chut-ney *n.* An agreeable condiment of fruit, spices, and herbs.

ci-der *n.* The juice from apples.

ci-gar *n.* Rolled tobacco leaves used for smoking.

cig-a-rette *n. or* **cig-a-ret** A small amount of tobacco rolled in thin paper for smoking.

cinch *n.* The strap for holding a saddle. *v.* To assure. *Slang* Something easy to do.

cin-cho-na *n.* A tree in South America whose bark yields quinine.

cinc-ture *n.* A belt or cord to put around the waist. *v.* To encircle or surround with a cincture.

cin-der *n.* A piece of something that is partially burned. **cindery** *adj.*

cin-e-ma *n., pl.* **-mas** A motion picture; a motion picture theatre; the business of making a motion picture.

cin-e-mat-o-graph *n.* A movie projector or camera.

cin-e-ma-tog-ra-phy *n.* The art of photographing a motion picture. **cinematographer** *n.*

cin-na-bar *n.* A mineral which is the principal source of mercury.

cin-na-mon *n.* The aromatic inner bark of a tropical Asian tree, used as a spice, reddish brown in color.

ci-pher *n.* The symbol for the absence of quantity; O; secret writing that has a prearranged key or scheme.

cir-cle *n.* A process that ends at its starting point; a group of people having a common interest or activity.

cir-cuit *n.* The closed path through which an electric current flows.

cir-cuit break-er *n.* A relay switch that automatically stops the flow of an electric current in an overloaded circuit.

cir-cuit court *n.* The lowest court of record, located in various counties or districts over which its jurisdiction extends.

cir-cu-lar *adj.* Moving in a circle or round-like fashion; relating to something in a circle; having free motion, as the air.

cir-cu-late *v.* To pass from place to place or person to person; to distribute in a wide area. **circulation, circulator** *n.,* **circulatory** *adj.*

cir-cum-cise *v.* To remove the foreskin on the male penis. **circumcision** *n.*

cir-cum-fer-ence *n.* The perimeter or boundary of a circle. **circumferential** *adj.*

cir-cum-flex *n.* A mark indicating the quality or sound of vowels as they appear in words.

cir-cum-scribe *v.* To confine something within drawn boundaries; to surround.

cir-cum-stance *n.* A fact or condition that must be considered when making a decision.

cir-cum-stan-tial *adj.* Incidental; not essential; dependent on circumstances.

cir-cum-stan-ti-ate *adj.* Providing support or circumstantial evidence.

cir-cum-vent *v.* To outwit or gain advantage; to avoid or go around. **circumvention** *n.,* **circumventive** *adj.*

cir-cus *n., pl.* **-cuses** Entertainment featuring clowns, acrobats, and trained animals.

cir-rho-sis *n.* A liver disease that is ultimately fatal. **cirrhotic** *adj.*

cir-rus *n., pl.* **-cirri** A high altitude, white, wispy cloud.

cis-tern *n.* A man-made tank or artificial reservoir for holding rain water.

cit-a-del *n.* A fortress commanding a city; a stronghold.

cit-ta-tion *n.* An official summons from a court; a quotation used in literary or legal material; an honor.

cite *v.* To bring forward as proof; to summon to action; to rouse; to summon to appear in court. **citeable** *adj., n.*

cit-i-zen *n.* A resident of a town or city; a native or naturalized person entitled to protection from a government. **citizenship** *n.*

citizen's band *n.* A two-way radio frequency band for private use.

citric acid *n.* A colorless acid found in lime, lemon, and other juices.

cit-ron *n.* A fruit resembling a lemon, but less acidic and larger in size.

cit-rus *n., pl.* **citrus, citruses** Any of a variety of trees bearing fruit with thick skins, as limes, oranges, lemons, and grapefruits.

cit-y *n.* A place larger than a town.

civ-et *n.* A cat-like mammal that secretes a musky fluid from the genital glands, which is used in perfumery.

civ-ic *adj.* Relating to or of a citizen, city, or citizenship.

civ-il *adj.* Relating to citizens; relating to the legal proceedings concerned with the rights of private individuals.

civ-il de-fense *n.* A civilian program of volunteers ready to take action in case of a natural disaster, invasion, or enemy attack.

ci-vil-ian *n.* A person not serving in the military, as a firefighter, or as a policeman.

civ-i-li-za-tion *n.* A high level of social, cultural, and political development.

civ-i-lize *v.* To bring out of a state of savagery into one of education and refinement.

civ-il rights *pl., n.* Rights guaranteed to citizens; the rights provided by the 13th and 14th amendments of the United States Constitution.

civ-il ser-vice *n.* The administrative or executive service of a government.

civ-il war *n.* A war between two regions of the same country; English Civil War (1642-1646); United States Civil War (1861-1865); Spanish Civil War (1936-1939).

claim *v.* To ask for one's due; to hold something to be true; to make a statement that something is true. **claim, claimant** *n.*

clair-voy-ance *n.* The ability to visualize in the mind distant objects or objects hidden from the senses. **clairvoyant** *n.*

clam *n.* Any of various marine and freshwater bivalve mollusks. *Slang* To become silent; to clam up.

clam-bake *n.* An outside gathering in which clams are cooked over hot coals.

clam-ber *v.* To climb by using both the hands and feet. **clamberer** *n.*

clam-my *adj.* Damp, cold, and sticky.

clam-or *n.* A loud noise or outcry; a vehement protest or demand. **clamourous** *adj.*, **clamorously** *adv.*

clamp *n.* A device for holding or fastening things together.

clan *n.* A large group of people who are related to one another by a common ancestor. **-nish** *adj.*, **clannishly** *adv.*, **clansman** *n.*

clan-des-tine *adj.* Kept or done in secrecy for a purpose.

clang *v.* To cause or make a loud, ringing, metallic sound.

clan-gor *n.* A loud series of clangs.

clap *v.* To applaud; to strike the hands together with an explosive sound.

clap-board *n.* A narrow board with one end thicker than the other, used to cover the outside of buildings so as to weatherproof the inside.

clap-per *n.* The part of a bell that hits against the side.

clar-i-fy *v.* To become or make clearer. **clarification** *n.*

clar-i-net *n.* A woodwind instrument with a single reed. **clarinetist** *n.*

clar-i-ty *n.* The state or quality of being clear.

clash *v.* To bring or strike together; to collide; to conflict.

clasp *n.* A hook to hold parts of objects together; a grasp or grip of the hands. **clasp** *v.*

class *n.* A group or set that has certain social or other interests in common; a group of students who graduate at the same time.

clas-sic *adj.* Belonging in a certain category of excellence; having a lasting artistic worth.

clas-si-cal *adj.* Relating to the style of the ancient Roman or Greek classics; standard and authoritative, not experimental or new.

clas-si-cism *n.* A belief in the esthetic principles of ancient Rome and Greece. **classicist** *n.*

clas-si-fy *v.* To arrange or assign items, people, etc., into the same class or category. **classification** *n.*

clat-ter *v.* To make or to cause a rattling sound. **clatter** *n.*

clause *n.* A group of words which are part of a simple compound, or complex sentence, containing a subject and predicate.

claus-tro-pho-bia *n.* A fear of small or enclosed places.

clav-i-chord *n.* A keyboard instrument which is one step down from the piano.

clav-i-cle *n.* The bone that connects the breastbone and the shoulder blade.

cla-vier *n.* An instrument with a keyboard, such as the harpsichord.

claw *n.* A sharp, curved nail on the foot of an animal; the pincer of certain crustaceans, such as the crab, lobster, etc.

clay *n.* A fine-grained, pliable earth that hardens when fired, used to make pottery, bricks, and tiles.

clay pig-eon *n.* A clay disk that is hurled into the air as a target for trapshooting and skeet.

clean *adj.* Free from impurities, dirt, or contamination; neat in habits.

cleanse *v.* To make pure or clean. **cleanser** *n.*

clear *adj.* Free from precipitation and clouds; able to hear, see, or think easily; free from doubt or confusion; free from a burden, obligation, or guilt. **clearly** *adv.*, **clearness** *n.*

clearance *n.* The distance that one object clears another by; a permission to proceed.

cleat *n.* A metal projection that provides support, grips, or prevents slipping.

cleav-age *n.* The process, act, or result of splitting; the cleft a woman displays in low-cut clothes.

cleav-er *n.* A knife used by butchers.

clef *n.* A symbol indicating which pitch each line and space represents on a musical staff.

clem-ent *adj.* Merciful; mild.

cler-gy *n.* The group of men and women who are ordained as religious leaders and servants of God.

cler-gy-man *n.* A member of the clergy.

cler-i-cal *adj.* Trained to handle office duties.

clerk *n.* A worker in an office who keeps accounts, records, and correspondence up to date; a person who works in the sales department of a store.

Cleveland, Stephen Grover *n.* The 22nd and 24th president of the United States from 1885-1889 and 1893-1897.

clev-er *adj.* Mentally quick; showing dexterity and skill. **cleverly** *adv.*, **cleverness** *n.*

cli-ent *n.* A person who secures the professional services of another.

cli-en-tele *n.* A collection of patients, customers, or clients.

cliff *n.* A high, steep edge or face of a rock.

cliff-hanger *n.* Anything which causes suspense and anticipation until the final outcome is known.

cli-mac-ter-ic *n.* A time in life when physiological changes.

cli-mate *n.* The weather conditions of a certain region generalized or averaged over a period of years; the prevailing atmosphere. **climatic** *adj.*

cli-max *n.* The point of greatest intensity and fullest suspense; the culmination.

climb *v.* To move to a higher or lower location; to advance in rank or status. **climbable** *adj.*, **climber** *n.*

clinch *v.* To secure; to fasten; to settle definitively. **clinch** *n.*

cling *v.* To hold fast to; to grasp or stick; to hold on and resist emotional separation. **clinger** *n.*

clin-ic *n.* A medical establishment connected with a hospital; a center that offers instruction or counseling.

clink *v.* To cause a light ringing sound.

clip *v.* To cut off; to curtail; to cut short. *n.* Something that grips, holds, or clasps articles together.

clip-per *n.* A sailing vessel that travels at a high rate of speed.

clique *n.* A small and exclusive group of people.

cloak *n.* A loose outer garment that conceals or covers.

clob-ber *v., Slang* To hit repeatedly and violently.

cloche *n.* A bell-shaped, close-fitting hat.

clock *n.* An instrument that measures time. *v.* To time with a clock, stopwatch, etc.

clod *n.* A large piece or lump of earth; a stupid, ignorant person.

clog *v.* To choke up. *n.* A shoe with a wooden sole.

clone *n.* An identical reproduction grown from a single cell of the original. **clone** *v.*

close *adj.* Near, as in time, space, or relationship; nearly even, as in competition; fitting tightly. *v.* To shut. **closeness** *n.*

clos-et *n.* A small cabinet, compartment, or room for storage. **closet** *v.*

close-up *n.* A picture that is taken at close range; a close view or examination of something.

clot *n.* A thick or solid mass, as of blood.

cloth *n., pl.* **cloths** A knitted, woven, or matted piece of fabric, used to cover a table; the professional clothing of the clergy.

clothe *v.* To provide clothes; to cover with clothes; to wrap.

clo-ture *n.* A parliamentary action that calls for an immediate vote.

cloud *n.* A visible body of water or ice particles floating in the atmosphere; something that obscures. **cloudy** *adj.*, **cloudiness** *n.*

clout *n.* A heavy blow with the hand. *Slang* The amount of influence or pull a person may have. **clout** *v.*

clove *n.* A spice from an evergreen tree; a small bud that is part of a larger group, as a clove of garlic.

clo-ver *n.* A plant that has a dense flower and trifoliolate leaves.

clover-leaf *n.* A junction of highways that cross each other at different levels and are connected by curving ramps.

clown *n.* A professional comedian who entertains by jokes, tricks, and funny jest; a circus comedian who dresses in outlandish costumes and wears heavy makeup on his face. **clownish** *adj.*

cloy *v.* To make one sick or disgusted with too much sweetness. **cloyingly** *adv.*

club *n.* A heavy wooden stick, used as a weapon; a group of people who have organized themselves with or for a common purpose.

clump *n.* A very thick cluster or group; a dull, heavy sound. *v.* To plant or place in a clump.

clum-sy *adj.* Lacking coordination, grace, or dexterity; not tactful or skillful. **clumsily** *adv.*, **clumsiness** *n.*

clus-ter *n.* A bunch; a group.

clutch *v.* To seize or attempt to seize and hold tightly. *n.* A tight grasp; a device for connecting and disconnecting the engine and the drive shaft in an automobile or other mechanism.

clut-ter *n.* A confused mass of disorder.

coach *n.* An automobile that is closed and usually has four doors and four wheels; a trainer and/or director of athletics, drama, etc.

co-ad-ju-tor *n.* An assistant.

co-ag-u-lant *n.* A substance that causes coagulation.

co-ag-u-late *v.* To clot. **coagulation** *n.*

coal *n.* A mineral widely used as a natural fuel; an ember.

co-a-lesce *v.* To come together or to grow as one.

co-ali-tion *n.* A temporary alliance.

coarse *adj.* Lacks refinement; of inferior or low quality; having large particles; harsh. **coarseness** *v.*

coast *v.* To move without propelling oneself; to use the force of gravity alone; to slide or glide along. *n.* The land bordering the sea.

coat *n.* An outer garment with sleeves, worn over other clothing; a layer that covers a surface. **coat** *v.*, **coating** *n.*

coax *v.* To persuade by tact, gentleness, or flattery. **coaxingly** *adv.*

co-ax-i-al *adj.* Having common coincident axes.

co-ax-i-al cable *n.* A cable that has two or more insulated conductors that are capable of transmitting television or radio signals or multiple telephone or telegraph messages.

cob *n.* A male swan; a corncob; a thickset horse that has short legs.

co-balt *n.* A hard, lustrous metallic element that resembles iron and nickel.

cob-ble *v.* To make or repair shoes; to make or put together roughly. **cobble** *n.*

CO-BOL *n.* In Computer Science, computer programming that is simple and based on English.

co-bra *n.* A venomous snake from Asia or Africa. When excited, the neck dilates into a broad hood.

cob-web *n.* The fine thread from a spider which is spun into a web and used to catch prey.

co-caine *n.* An alkaloid used as an anesthetic and narcotic.

coc-cyx *n.* The small bone at the bottom of the spinal column.

coch-i-neal *n.* A brilliant scarlet dye prepared from the dried, pulverized bodies of certain female insects of tropical America.

coch-le-a *n.* The spiral tube of the inner ear, forming an essential part for hearing.

cock *n.* The adult male in the domestic fowl family; the rooster; the hammer of a firearm and the readiness for firing. *v.* To raise in preparation for hitting; to ready a firearm for firing.

cock-ade *n.* A knot of ribbon or something similar worn on a hat as a badge.

cock-a-too *n.* A crested parrot of the East Indies.

cock-a-trice *n.* A mythical serpent said to be hatched from a cock's egg, deadly to those who meet its glance or feel its breath.

cock-le *n.* European bivalve mollusk of the edible species, having ridged, somewhat heart-shaped shells.

cock-pit *n.* The compartment of an airplane where the pilot and the crew sit.

cock-roach *n.* A flat-bodied, fast running, chiefly nocturnal insect, many of which are household pests.

co-co *n.* The fruit obtained from the coconut palm.

co-coa *n.* The powder from the roasted husked seed kernels of the cacao.

co-coon *n.* The protective fiber or silk pupal case that is spun by insect larvae.

cod *n.* A large fish of the North Atlantic that is important as food.

cod-dle *v.* To cook just below the boiling point; to simmer.

code *n.* A system of set rules; a set of secret words, numbers, or letters used as a means of communication; in Computer Science, the method of representing information or data by using a set sequence of characters, symbols, or words. **code** *v.*

co-dex *n.* An ancient manuscript of the classics or Scriptures.

co-ed-u-ca-tion *n.* An educational system for both men and women at the same institution. **coeducational** *adj.*

co-erce *v.* To restrain or dominate with force; to compel by law, authority, fear, or force.

co-e-val *adj.* Of the same time period.

co-ex-ist *v.* To exist at the same time or together; the ability to live peaceably with others in spite of differences. **coexistence** *n.*

cof-fee *n.* A beverage prepared from ground beans of the coffee tree.

cof-fee cake *n.* A sweet dough containing raisins or nuts and shaped into a ring or braid.

cof-fer *n.* A strongbox or chest made for valuables.

cof-fin *n.* A box in which a corpse is buried.

cog *n.* A tooth or one of series of a teeth on the rim of wheel in a machine or a mechanical device.

co-gent *adj.* Compelling; forceful; convincing.

cog-i-tate *v.* To think carefully about or to ponder. **cogitation** *n.*

co-gnac *n.* A fine brandy made in France.

cog-nate *adj.* From a common ancestor; identical or similar in nature; related.

cog-ni-zance *n.* Perception of fact; awareness; recognition; observation.

cog-no-men *n., pl.* **cognomens** A person's surname; nickname.

co-hab-it *v.* To live together as husband and wife.

co-here *v.* To stick or hold together.

co-hort *n.* A group of people who are united in one effort; an accomplice.

coif *n.* A close-fitting hat that is worn under a nun's veil.

coil *n.* A series of connecting rings. *v.* To wind in spirals.

coin *n.* A flat, rounded piece of metal used as money. *v.* To invent or make a new phrase or word.

co-in-cide *v.* To happen at the same time; to agree exactly.

co-in-ci-dence *n.* Two events happening at the same time by accident but appearing to have some connection.

co-i-tus *n.* Physical union of male and female sexual organs; sexual intercourse.

coke *n.* A solid, carbonaceous fuel made by heating soft coal until some of its gases have been removed. *Slang* Cocaine.

cold *adj.* Having a low temperature; feeling uncomfortable; without sufficient warmth; lacking in affection or sexual desire; frigid. *n.* An infection of the upper respiratory tract resulting in coughing, sneezing, etc. **coldness** *n.*

cold--blooded *adj.* Done without feeling; having a body temperature that varies according to the temperature of the surroundings. **cold-bloodedly** *adv.*

cold boot *n.* In Computer Science, the boot performed when power is turned on for the first time each day.

cold cuts *pl., n.* A selection of freshly sliced cold meats.

cole *n.* A plant such as the cabbage or a vegetable of the same family.

col-ic *n.* A sharp pain in the abdomen caused by muscular cramps or spasms, occurring most often in very young babies.

col-i-se-um *n.* A large amphitheater used for sporting games.

col-lab-o-rate *v.* To cooperate or work with another person. **collaboration,** **collaborator** *n.*

col-lapse *v.* To fall; to give way; to fold and assume a smaller size; to lose all or part of the air in a lung.

col-lar *n.* The upper part of a garment that encircles the neck and is often folded over.

col-lar-bone *n., Anat.* The clavicle, located near the neck.

col-late *v.* To compare in a critical fashion; to assemble in correct sequence or order.

col-lat-er-al *adj.* Serving to support; guaranteed by stocks, property, bonds, etc.

col-league *n.* Someone who works in the same profession or official body.

col-lect *v.* To gather or assemble; to gather donations or payments. **collectible, collection** *n.*

col-lege *n.* An institution of higher education which grants a bachelor's degree; a school of special instruction or special fields.

col-lide *v.* To come together with a

direct impact; to clash; to come into conflict.

col-lo-cate *v.* To compare facts and arrange in correct order.

col-lo-di-on *n.* A highly flammable spray solution used to protect wounds and used for photographic plates.

col-loid *n.* A glue-like substance, such as gelatin, that cannot pass through animal membranes.

col-lo-quy *n., pl.* **-quies** A formal conversation or conference.

col-lu-sion *n.* A secret agreement between two or more people for an illegal purpose.

co-lon *n.* A punctuation mark (:) used to introduce an example or series; the section of the large intestine that extends from the cecum to the rectum. **colonic** *adj.*

colo-nel *n.* An officer in the armed forces that ranks above a lieutenant colonel and below a brigadier general. **colonelcy** *n.*

col-o-ny *n., pl* **-ies** A group of emigrants living in a new land away from, but under the control of, the parent country; a group of insects, as ants.

col-o-phon *n.* The inscription at the end of a book that gives the publication facts.

col-or *n.* The aspect of things apart from the shape, size, and solidity; a hue or tint that is caused by the different degrees of light that are reflected or emitted by them. **colored**, **colorful** *adj.*, **coloring** *n.*, **color** *v.*

col-or-a-tion *n.* The arrangement of different colors or shades.

col-or-blind *adj.* Unable to distinguish colors, either totally or partially.

col-or-fast *adj.* Color that will not run or fade with washing or wearing. **colorfastness** *n.*

co-los-sal *adj.* Very large or gigantic in degree or size.

co-los-sus *n.* Something that is very large, as a huge state, thing, or person.

colt *n.* A very young male horse. **coltish** *adj.*

Columbus, Christopher *n.* The person credited with finding the New World.

col-umn *n.* A decorative and/or supporting pillar used in construction; a vertical division of typed or printed lines on paper. **columnar** *adj.*

col-um-nist *n.* A person who writes a newspaper or magazine column.

co-ma *n.* A deep sleep or unconsciousness caused by an illness or injury.

co-ma-tose *adj.* Unconscious.

comb *n.* A toothed instrument made from a material such as plastic used for smoothing and arranging the hair; the fleshy crest on the head of a fowl.

com-bat *v.* To fight against; to oppose; to contend. *n.* A struggle; a fight or contest especially with armed conflict, as a battle.

com-bi-na-tion *n.* The process of combining or the state of being combined; a series of numbers or letters needed

to open certain locks.

com-bine *v.* To unite; to merge. *n.* A farm machine that harvest by cutting, threshing, and cleaning the grain.

com-bus-ti-ble *adj.* Having the capability of burning. *n.* A combustible material as paper or wood.

com-bus-tion *n.* The chemical change that occurs rapidly and produces heat and light; a burning. **combustive** *adj.*

come *v.* To arrive; to approach; to reach a certain position, state, or result; to appear; to come into view.

com-e-dy *n., pl.* **-ies** A humorous, entertaining performance with a happy ending; a real-life comical situation. **comedic** *adj.*

co-mes-ti-ble *n.* Something that is fit to eat. *adj.* Fit to eat.

com-et *n.* A celestial body that moves in an orbit around the sun, consisting of a solid head that is surrounded by a bright cloud with a long vaporous tail.

com-fort *v.* To console in time of grief or fear; to make someone feel better; to help; to assist. **comfort** *n.*, **comfortingly** *adv.*

com-fort-a-ble *adj.* In a state of comfort; financially secure. **comfortably** *adv.*

com-fort-er *n.* A heavy blanket or quilt; someone who comforts.

com-ic *adj.* Characteristic of comedy. *n.* A comedian. **Comics** Comic strips.

com-i-cal *adj.* Amusing; humorous.

com-ma *n.* The punctuation mark (,) used to indicate separation of ideas or a series in a sentence.

com-mand *v.* To rule; to give orders; to dominate. *n.* In computer science, the instruction given that specifies an operation to be performed.

com-mand-ing *adj.* Dominating by size or position.

com-mem-o-rate *v.* To honor the memory of; to create a memorial to. **commemoration, commemorator** *n.*

com-mence *v.* To begin; to start.

com-mence-ment *n.* A graduation ceremony.

com-mend *v.* To give praise; to applaud. **commendable** *adj.*, **commendation** *n.*

com-men-su-rate *adj.* Equal in duration, extent, or size. **commensuration** *n.*

com-ment *n.* A statement of criticism, analysis, or observation.

com-merce *n.* The exchanging of products or materials; buying and selling.

com-mer-cial *adj.* Of or relating to a product; supported by advertising. *n.* An advertisement on radio or television.

com-mis-er-ate *v.* To display or feel sympathy for someone.

com-mis-sar *n.* An official of the Communist Party whose duties include enforcement of party loyalty and political indoctrination.

com-mis-sar-y *n., pl.* **-ies** A store that sells food and supplies on a military base.

com-mis-sion *n.* The moneys paid to a

person for his service in the area of sales; the act of entrusting to another; the command or authorization to act as specified.

com-mit-tee *n.* A group of persons appointed or elected to perform a particular task or function.
committeeman, committeewoman *n.*

com-mode *n.* A movable washstand with storage underneath; a toilet; a low chest of drawers or bureau.

com-mo-di-ous *adj.* Roomy; spacious. commodiously *adv.*

com-mo-dore *n.* A naval officer ranking above a captain and below a rear admiral; the senior captain of a naval squadron or of a merchant fleet.

com-mon *adj.* Having to do with, belonging to, or used by an entire community or public; vulgar; unrefined.

com-mon de-nom-i-na-tor *n.* A number that can be evenly divided by all the denominators of a set of fractions.

com-mon frac-tion *n.* A fraction with both the denominator and numerator being whole numbers.

com-mon law *n.* The unwritten system of law that is based on judicial decisions, customs, and usages.

com-mon-weal-th *n.* The common good of the whole group of people.

com-mu-ni-ca-ble *adj.* Capable of being transmitted, as with a disease. communicability *n.*

com-mu-ni-cate *v.* To make known; to cause others to partake or share something.

com-mu-ni-ca-tion *n.* The act of transmitting ideas through writing or speech; the means to transmit messages between person or places.

com-mun-ion *n.* The mutual sharing of feelings and thoughts; a religious fellowship between members of a church.

com-mun-ion *n.* A sacrament in which bread and wine are consumed to commemorate the death of Christ.

com-mu-nism *n.* A system of government in which goods and production are commonly owned; the theory of social change and struggle toward communism through revolution.

com-mu-ni-ty *n., pl.* -ies A group of people living in the same area and under the same government; a class or group having common interests and likes.

com-mu-ni-ty pro-per-ty *n.* Property not belonging to only a husband or wife but owned jointly.

com-mute *v.* To travel a long distance to one's job each day; to exchange or to substitute.

com-muter *n.* One who travels a long distance on a regular basis.

com-pact *adj.* Packed together or solidly united; firmly and closely united.

com-pac-tor *n.* A device for compressing trash into a small mass for disposal.

com-pan-ion *n.* An associate; a person employed to accompany or assist

another; one hired to travel or live with another. companionship *n.*

com-pan-ion-a-ble *adj.* Friendly; sociable. companionably *adv.*

com-pan-ion-way *n., Naut.* A stairway leading from a ship's deck to the cabin below.

com-pa-ny *n., pl.* -ies The gathering of persons for a social purpose; a number of persons who are associated for a common purpose, as in business; a business.

com-pa-ra-ble *adj.* Capable of comparison; worthy of comparison; similar. comparability *n.*, comparably *adv.*, comparative *adj.*

com-pare *v.* To speak of or represent as similar or equal to; to note the similarities or likenesses of.

com-par-i-son *n.* Likeness; similarity. *Gram.* Modification of an verb or adjective that indicates the positive, comparative, or superlative degree.

comparison--shop *v.* To shop and look for bargains by comparing the prices of different brands found available in different stores.

com-part-ment *n.* One of the sections into which an enclosed area is divided.

com-pass *n.* An instrument used to determine geographic direction; an enclosed area or space; the extent of reach of something; range or area; scope. a pair of compasses A device shaped like a V that is used for drawing circles.

com-pas-sion *n.* Sympathy for someone who is suffering or distressed in some way. compassionate *adj.*

com-pat-i-ble *adj.* Able to function, exist, or live together harmoniously. compatibility *n.*, compatibly *adv.*

com-pa-tri-ot *n.* A person of the same country.

com-peer *n.* A person that is a peer or equal.

com-pel *v.* To urge or force action.

com-pen-di-um *n., pl.* -diums A short summary.

com-pen-sate *v.* To make up for; to make amends; to pay; to neutralize or counterbalance. compensation *n.*, compensatory *adj.*

com-pete *v.* To contend with others; to engage in a contest or competition.

com-pe-tent *adj.* Having sufficient ability; being capable. competence, competency *n.*

com-pe-ti-tion *n.* The act of rivalry or competing; a trial of skill or ability; a contest between teams or individuals. competitive *adj.*

com-pet-i-tor *n.* One who competes against another.

com-pile *v.* To put together material gathered from a number of sources; in Computer Science, to convert our language into machine language. compilation *n.*, compiler *n.*

com-plain-ant *n.* A person filing a formal charge.

com-plaint *n.* An expression of pain,

dissatisfaction, or resentment; a cause or reason for complaining; a grievances.

com-plai-sance *n.* The willingness to please, to oblige. **complaisant** *adj.*

com-ple-ment *n.* Something that perfects, completes, or adds to. **-ary** *adj.*

com-plete *adj.* Having all the necessary parts; whole; concluded. **completion** *n.*

com-plex *adj.* Consisting of various intricate parts. **complexity** *n.*, **complexly** *adv.*

com-plex-ion *n.* The natural color and texture of the skin. **complexioned** *adj.*

com-pli-ance *n.* The act of agreeing passively to a request, rule, or demand; the tendency to yield to others. **compliant** *adj.*, **compliancy** *n.*

com-pli-cate *v.* To make or become involved or complex.

com-plic-i-ty *n.* An involvement or association with a crime.

com-pli-ment *n.* An expression of praise or admiration.

com-pli-men-ta-ry *adj.* Conveying a compliment.

com-ply *v.* To agree, to consent to, or obey a command or wish. **complier** *n.*

com-po-nent *n.* A constituent part.

com-port *v.* To behave or conduct oneself in a certain way.

com-pose *v.* To make up from elements or parts; to produce or create a song; to arrange, as to typeset. **composer** *n.*

com-posed *adj.* Calm.

com-pos-ite *adj.* Made up from separate elements or parts; combined or compounded. *Bot.* Characteristic of a plant with densely clustered flowers.

com-po-si-tion *n.* The act of putting together artistic or literary work; a short essay written for an assignment in school. **compositional** *adj.*

com-post *n.* A fertilizing mixture that consists of decomposed vegetable matter.

com-po-sure *n.* Tranquillity; calm self-possession.

com-pote *n.* Fruit that is preserved or stewed in syrup; a dish used for holding fruit, candy, etc.

com-pound *n.* The combination of two or more parts, elements, or ingredients; in grammar, a new word that is composed of two or more words joined with a hyphen or written as a solid word. *Chem.* A definite substance that results form combining specific radicals or elements in certain or fixed proportions. *v.* To combine; to increase. **compoundable** *adj.*

com-pound frac-ture *n.* A fracture (broken bone) that breaks and protrudes through the skin.

com-pre-hend *v.* To perceive, to grasp mentally, or to understand fully; to comprise; to include. **comprehension** *n.*

com-pre-hen-si-ble *adj.* Capable of being understood. **comprehensibility** *n.*, **comprehensibly** *adv.*

com-pre-hen-sive *adj.* Large in content

or scope.

com-press *v.* To press together into a smaller space; to condense. *n.* A soft pad sometimes medicated, for applying cold, heat, moisture, or pressure to a part of the body. **compressibility**, **compression** *n.*, **compressible** *adj.*

com-pres-sed air *n.* Air that is under greater pressure than the atmosphere.

com-pres-sor *n.* Something that compresses; a machine that is used for compressing air to utilize its expansion.

com-prise *v.* To consist of; to be made up of. **comprisable** *adj.*

com-pro-mise *n.* The process of settling or the settlement of differences between opposing sides, with each side making concessions. **compromiser** *n.*, **compromise** *v.*

comp-trol-ler *n.* A person appointed to examine and verify accounts.

com-pul-sion *n.* The act or state of being compelled; an irresistible urge or impulse to act irrationally. **compulsive** *adj.*

com-pute *v.* To ascertain or determine by the use of mathematics; to determine something by the use of a computer. **computability**, **comutation** *n.*, **computable** *adj.*

com-puter *n.* A person who computes; a high speed, electronic machine which performs logical calculations, processes, stores, and retrieves programmed information.

com-puter-ize *v.* To process or store information on a computer; to switch from manual operations to computers.

com-puter lan-guage *n.* The various codes and information that are used to give data and instructions to computers.

com-rade *n.* An associate, friend, or companion who shares one's interest or occupation. **comradeship** *n.*

con *v.* To study carefully. *Slang* To swindle or trick.

con-cat-e-nate *v.* To join, connect, or link together. **concatenate** *adj.*, **concatenation** *n.*

con-cave *adj.* Hollowed and curved inward. **concavely** *adv.*, **concave** *n.*

con-ceal *v.* To keep from disclosure, sight, or knowledge; to hide. **concealable** *adj.*, **concealment** *n.*

con-cede *v.* To grant or yield to a right or privilege; to acknowledge as true. **conceder** *n.*, **conceded** *adj.*

con-ceive *v.* To become pregnant; to create a mental image. **conceivability** *n.*, **conceivable** *adj.*, **conceivably** *adv.*

con-cen-trate *v.* To give intense thought to; to draw to a common point; to intensify by removing certain elements; to become compact. **concentrative** *adj.*, **concentrator** *n.*

con-cen-tra-tion *n.* The state of being concentrated or the act of concentrating; the process or act of giving complete attention to a certain problem or task.

con-cen-tra-tion camp *n.* An enclosed camp for the confinement of political dissidents, aliens, or prisoners of war.

con-cept *n.* A generalized idea formed from particular occurrences or instances; an opinion. **conceptual** *adj.*

con-cep-tion *n.* The union of sperm and egg; a mental thought or plan.

con-cern *n.* Something to consider; sincere interest; something that affects one's business or affairs. *v.* To be interested in; to be involved with. **concerned** *adj.*

con-cert *n.* A musical performance for a group of people; agreement in purpose, action, or feeling. *v.* To act or plan together. **concerted** *adj.*

con-cer-to *n., pl.* -tos, -ti A composition that features one or more solo instruments.

con-ces-sion *n.* The act of conceding; something that has been conceded; a tract of land that is granted by a government for a particular use.

con-ces-sion-aire *n.* The operator or holder of a concession.

conch *n.* A tropical marine mollusk having a large spiral shell and flesh that is edible.

con-chol-o-gy *n.* The study of mollusks and shells. **conchological** *adj.*, **conchologist** *n.*

con-cil-i-ate *v.* To win over or to gain a friendship. **conciliation, conciliator** *n.*, **conciliatory** *adj.*

con-cise *adj.* Short and to the point.

con-clave *n.* A private or secret meeting; the private meeting of the Roman Catholic cardinals to elect a new pope.

con-clude *v.* To close or bring to an end; to bring about an agreement; to arrive at a decision; to resolve. **conclusion** *n.*

con-clu-sive *adj.* Putting an end to any questions or doubt.

con-coct *v.* To make by combining ingredients; to devise or to plan. **concoction** *n.*

con-com-i-tant *adj.* Accompanying. **concomitance** *n.*, **concomitantly** *adv.*

con-cord *n.* Accord; harmony; friendly and peaceful relationships.

con-cor-dance *n.* A condition of concord or agreement; the alphabetical index of major words used by an author, listed in the order of use in a book.

con-cor-dant *adj.* Exist in agreement; harmonious. **concordantly** *adv.*

con-course *n.* A large, open space for the assembling or passage of crowds.

con-cres-cence *n.* Increase by the addition of particles; growing together.

con-crete *adj.* Pertaining to a specific instance or thing; naming a specific class of things. *n.* A construction material made from sand, gravel, and cement. *v.* To bring together in one body or mass. **concretely** *adv.*, **concreteness** *n.*

con-cu-bine *n.* A woman living with a man and not being legally married to him. **concubinage** *n.*

con-cu-pis-cence *n.* A strong sexual desire; lust. **concupiscent** *adj.*

con-cur *v.* To agree or express approval; to cooperate; to happen at the same time; to coincide. **concurrence** *n.*

con-cur-rent *adj.* Referring to an event that happens at the same time as another; acting together.

con-cus-sion *n.* A sudden and violent jolt; a violent injury to an organ, especially the brain. **concussive** *adj.*

con-demn *v.* To find to be wrong; to show the guilt; to announce judgment upon; to officially declare unfit for use. **condemnable, condemnatory** *adj.*, **condemnation, condemner** *n.*

con-dense *v.* To make more concentrated or compact; to change something from a liquid state to a solid state or from a gaseous to a liquid state. **condensation, condenser** *n.*, **condensible** *adj.*

con-di-ment *n.* A relish, spice, or sauce used to season food.

con-di-tion *n.* The mode or state of existence of a thing or person; a circumstance that is found to be necessary to the occurrence of another; a provision in a contract or will that leaves room for modification or changes at a future date. *Slang* A sickness or ailment. **condition** *v.*

con-di-tion-al *adj.* Tentative; depending on a condition; implying or expressing a condition. *Gram.* A mood, clause, tense, or condition. **conditionality** *n.*, **conditionally** *adv.*

con-di-tioned *adj.* Prepared for a certain process or action by past experience.

con-di-tion-er *n.* An application that improves the usability of a substance.

con-do *n., Slang* Condominium.

con-dom *n.* A thin rubber sheath used to cover the penis, serving as an antivenereal or contraceptive purpose during sexual intercourse.

con-do-min-i-um *n.* A joint ownership; an apartment in which all units are owned separately; a building in which the units are owned by each tenant.

con-done *n.* To overlook; to forgive; to disregard. **condoner** *n.*

con-dor *v.* One of the largest flying birds, with a bare head and a white downy neck.

con-du-cive *adj.* Contributing towards or promotion; helpful. **conduce** *v.*

con-duct *v.* To lead and direct a performance of a band or orchestra; to guide or show the way; to lead; to direct or control the course of; to transmit heat, electricity, or sound. *n.* Behavior. **conductibility, conduction** *n.*, **conductible** *adj.*

con-duc-tor *n.* A person who conducts a musical ensemble; one who is in charge of a railroad or streetcar. *Phys.* Any substance that conducts light, electricity, heat, or sound.

con-duit *n.* A pipe used to pass electric wires or cable through; a channel or pipe that water passes through.

cone *n.* A solid body that is tapered

evenly to a point from a base that is circular; a wafer that is cone-shaped and used for holding ice cream.

con-fab-u-late *v.* To chat or speak informally. **confabulation, confabulator** *n.,* **confabulatory** *adj.*

con-fec-tion-er-y *n.* Candy and sweets as a whole; a store that sells candy and sweets. **confection** *n.*

con-fed-er-a-cy *n., pl.* **-ies** The union of eleven southern states that seceded from the United States during the Civil War of 1861-1865 and established the Confederate Sate of America.

con-fed-er-ate *n.* An ally or friend; a person who supports the Confederacy. **confederate** *v.*

con-fer *v.* To consult with another; to hold a conference; to give or grant. **conferment, conferral, conferrer** *n.,* **conferrable** *adj.*

con-fer-ence *n.* A formal meeting for discussion; a league of churches, schools, or athletic teams.

con-fess *v.* To disclose or admit to a crime, fault, sin, or guilt; to tell a priest or God of one's sins. **confessedly** *adv.*

con-fes-sion *n.* The act of confessing.

con-fes-sion-al *n.* The small enclosure where a priest hears confessions.

con-fet-ti *pl., n.* Small pieces of paper thrown during a happy occasion.

con-fide *v.* To entrust a secret to another. **confider** *n.,* **confiding** *adj.,* **confidingly** *adv.*

con-fi-dence *n.* A feeling of selfassurance; a feeling of trust in a person; reliance; good faith. **confident** *adj.*

con-fi-den-tial *adj.* Hold as a secret; having another's entrusted confidence. **confidentiality** *n.,* **confidentially** *adv.*

con-fig-u-ra-tion *n.* An arrangement of pats or things; the arrangement of elements. **configurationally** *adv.*

con-fine *v.* To keep within a certain boundary or limit. **confines, confinement, confiner** *n.*

con-firm *v.* To establish or support the truth of something; to make stronger; to ratify and bind by a formal approval. **confirmable, confirmatory** *adj.*

con-fir-ma-tion *n.* The act of confirming to show proof; a religious rite that admits a person to full membership in a church.

con-fis-cate *v.* To seize for public use; to officially seize. **confiscation, confiscator** *n.*

con-flate *v.* To combine two different ideas into a whole. **conflation** *n.*

con-flict *n.* A battle; clash; a disagreement of ideas, or interests. **conflict** *v.,* **conflictive** *adj.*

con-flu-ence *n.* The flowing together of two streams or rivers; the point where the two join. **confluent** *adj. & n.,* **confluently** *adv.*

con-form *v.* To be similar in form or character; to adhere to prevailing customs or modes. **conformable** *adj.,*

conformably *adv.*

con-for-ma-tion *n.* The manner in which something is shaped, structured, or arranged.

con-found *v.* To amaze, confuse, or perplex; to confuse one thing for another.

con-front *v.* To put or stand face to face with defiance. **confrontation** *n.,* **confrontational** *adj.*

con-fuse *v.* To mislead or bewilder; to jumble or mix up. **confusedness** *n.,* **confusingly** *adv.*

con-fu-sion *n.* The state of being confused.

con-fute *v.* To prove to be invalid or false. **confutable** *adj.,* **confutation** *n.*

con-geal *v.* To jell; to solidify; to change from a liquid to a solid form.

con-gen-ial *adj.* Having similar character habits, or tastes; sociable; friendly. **congeniality** *n.,* **congenially** *adv.*

con-gen-i-tal *adj.* Existing from the time of birth, but not from heredity.

con-gest *v.* To enlarge with an excessive accumulation of blood; to clog. **congestion** *n.,* **congestive** *adj.*

con-glom-er-ate *n.* A business consisting of many different companies; gravel that is embedded in cement material.

con-grat-u-late *v.* To acknowledge an achievement with praise. **congratulation, congratulatory** *adj.*

con-grat-u-la-tions *pl., n.* The expression of or the act of congratulating.

con-gre-gate *v.* To assemble together in a crowd. **congregator** *n.*

con-gre-ga-tion *n.* A group of people meeting together for worship.

Con-gress *n.* The United States legislative body, consisting of the Senate and the House of Representatives. **Congressional** *adj.*

con-gress-man *n.* An elected member of the United States House of Representatives.

con-gress-wom-an *n.* A woman elected as a member of the United States House of Representatives.

con-gru-ent *adj.* Agreeing to conform; in mathematics, having exactly the same size and shape.

con-ic *or* **con-i-cal** *adj.* Related to and shaped like a cone.

conj *abbr.* Conjunction.

con-jec-ture *n.* A guess or conclusion based on incomplete evidence. **conjecturable, conjectural** *adj.,* **conjecture** *v.*

con-join *v.* To unite; join to together. **conjoint** *adj.*

con-ju-gal *adj.* Pertaining to the relationship or marriage of husband and wife. **conjugally** *adv.*

con-ju-gate *adj.* To change the form of a verb; to join in pairs. **conjugately** *adv.,* **conjugative** *adj.,* **conjugator** *n.*

con-junct *adj.* Combined; joined together.

con-junc-tion *n.* The act of joining; the state of being joined. *Gram.* A word used to join or connect other words, phrases, sentences, or clauses.

con-junc-ti-va *n., pl.* -vas, -vae The membrane lining of the eyelids. **conjunctival** *adj.*

con-junc-tive *adj.* Connective; joining. *Gram.* Serving as a conjunction.

con-junc-ti-vi-tis *n., Pathol.* Inflammation of the membrane that lines the eyelids.

con-jure *v.* To bring into the mind; to appeal or call on solemnly; to practice magic.

con-nect *v.* To join; to unite; to associate, as to relate. **connectedly** *adv.*, **connector, connecter** *n.*

Con-nect-i-cut *n.* A state located in the northeastern part of the United States.

con-nec-tion *n.* An association of one person or thing to another; a union, link, or bond; an influential group of friends or associates.

con-nec-tive *adj.* Capable of connecting; tending to connect. *n.* Something that connects as a word. **connectivity** *n.*

con-nive *v.* To ignore a known wrong, therefore implying sanction; to conspire; to cooperate in secret. **connivance** *n.*

con-nois-seur *n.* A person whose expertise in an area of art or taste allows him to be a judge; an expert. **connoisseurship** *n.*

con-no-ta-tion *n.* The associative meaning of a word in addition to the literal meaning. **connotative** *adj.*

con-note *v.* To imply along with the literal meaning.

con-nu-bi-al *adj.* Having to do with marriage or the state of marriage. **connubiality** *n.*, **connubially** *adv.*

con-quer *v.* To subdue; to win; to overcome by physical force.

con-quis-ta-dor *n., pl.* -dors A Spanish conquer+or of the sixteenth century.

con-san-guin-e-ous *adj.* Having the same blood; descended from the same ancestor. **consanguineously** *adv.*

con-science *n.* The ability to recognize right and wrong regarding one's own behavior.

con-sci-en-tious *adj.* Honest; scrupulous; careful.

con-scious *adj.* Aware on one's own existence and environment; aware of facts or objects.

con-script *n.* One who is drafted or forced to enroll for a service or a job.

con-se-crate *v.* To declare something to be holy; to dedicate to sacred uses. **consecration, consecrator** *n.*

con-sec-u-tive *adj.* Following in uninterrupted succession. **consecutively** *adv.*, **consecutiveness** *n.*

con-sen-sus *n.* A general agreement; a collective opinion.

con-sent *v.* To agree; an acceptance. **consenter** *n.*

con-se-quence *n.* The natural result from a preceding condition or action; the effect.

con-se-quent *adj.* Following as a natural result or effect. **consequently** *adv.*

con-se-quen-tial *adj.* Having or showing self-importance. **consequentially** *adv.*

con-serv-a-tive *adj.* Opposed to change; desiring the preservation of the existing order of things; moderate; cautious; wanting to conserve. **conservatively** *adv.*, **conservativeness** *n.*

con-ser-va-to-ry *n., pl.* -ries A school of dramatic art or music; a greenhouse.

con-serve *v.* To save something from decay, loss, or depletion; to maintain; to preserve fruits with sugar. *n.* A mixture of several fruits cooked together with sugar and sometimes raisins or nuts. **conservable** *adj.*, **conserver** *n.*

con-sid-er *v.* To seriously think about; to examine mentally; to believe or hold as an opinion; to deliberate.

con-sid-er-a-ble *adj.* Large in amount or extent; important; worthy of consideration. **considerably** *adv.*

con-sid-er-a-tion *n.* The taking into account of circumstance before forming an opinion; care and thought; a kind or thoughtful treatment or feeling. **considering** *prep.*

con-sign *v.* To commit to the care of another; to deliver or forward, as merchandise; to put aside, as for specific use. **consignee** *n.*, **consignable** *adj.*, **consignor, consignment** *n.*

con-sist *v.* To be made up of.

con-sis-ten-cy *n., pl.* -cies Agreement or compatibility among ideas, events, or successive acts; the degree of texture, viscosity, or density. **consistent** *adj.*

con-sis-to-ry *n., pl.* -ries In the Roman Catholic Church, the assembly of all cardinals with the pope presiding over them.

con-sole *v.* To give comfort to someone. **consolable** *adj.*, **consolation** *n.*, **consolingly** *adv.*

con-sol-i-date *v.* To combine in one or to form a union of; to form a compact mass. **consolidation, consolidator** *n.*

con-so-nant *n.* A sound produced by complete or partial blockage of the air from the mouth, as the sound of b, f, k, s, t; the letter of the alphabet that represents such a sound. *adj.* In agreement. **consonantal** *adj.*, **consonantly** *adv.*

con-sort *n.* A spouse; companion or partner. *v.* To unite or keep in company.

con-sor-ti-um *n., pl.* -tia *n.* An association with banks or corporations that require vast resources.

con-spic-u-ous *adj.* Noticeable. **conspicuously** *adv.*, **conspicuousness** *n.*

con-spir-a-cy *n., pl.* -ies A plan or act of two or more persons to do an evil act.

con-spire *v.* To plan a wrongful act in secret; to work or act together. **conspirator** *n.*

con-sta-ble *n.* A peace officer.

con-stant *adj.* Faithful; unchanging; steady in action, purpose, and affection. *Math.* A quantity that remains the same throughout a given problem. **constancy** *n.*, **constantly** *adv.*

con-ster-na-tion *n.* Sudden confusion or amazement.

con-sti-pa-tion *n.* A condition of the bowels characterized by difficult or infrequent evacuation. **constipate** *v.*

con-stit-u-en-cy *n., pl.* **-cies** A group of voters that is represented by an elected legislator.

con-stit-u-ent *adj.* Having the power to elect a representative. *n.* A necessary element or part.

con-sti-tu-tion *n.* The fundamental laws that govern a nation; structure or composition. **constitutional** *adj.*, **constitutionality** *n.*

con-strain *v.* To restrain by physical or moral means. **constrained** *adj.*

con-straint *n.* The threat or use of force; confinement; restriction.

con-strict *v.* To squeeze, compress, or contract. **constriction** *n.*, **constrictive** *adj.*, **constrictively** *adv.*

con-struct *v.* To create, make, or build. **constructor, constructer** *n.*

con-struc-tion *n.* The act of constructing or building something. *Gram.* The arrangement of words in a meaningful clause or sentence. **constructional** *adj.*

con-struc-tive *adj.* Useful; helpful; building, advancing, or improving; resulting in a positive conclusion. **constructively** *adv.*, **constructiveness** *n.*

con-strue *v.* To interpret; to translate; to analyze grammatical structure.

con-sul *n.* An official that resides in a foreign country and represents his or her government's commercial interests and citizens. **consular** *adj.*, **consulship** *n.*

con-sul-ate *n.* The official premises occupied by a consul.

con-sult *v.* To seek advice or information from; to compare views. **consultant, consultation** *n.*

con-sume *v.* To ingest; to eat or drink; to destroy completely; to absorb; to engross. **consumable** *adj.* & *n.*

con-sum-er *n.* A person who buys services or goods.

con-sum-mate *v.* To conclude; to make a marriage complete by the initial act of sexual intercourse.

con-sump-tion *n.* Fulfillment; the act of consuming; the quantity consumed; tuberculosis.

con-sump-tive *adj.* Tending to destroy or waste away; affected with or pertaining to pulmonary tuberculosis. **consumptively** *adv.*, **consumptiveness** *n.*

con-tact *n.* The place, spot, or junction where two or more surfaces or objects touch; the connection between two electric conductors. **contacts** *Slang* Contact lens; thin lens of plastic or glass with an optical prescription, worn directly on the cornea of the eye.

con-ta-gion *n.* The transmitting of a disease by contact. **contagious** *adj.*, **contagiously** *adv.*, **contagiousness** *n.*

con-tain *v.* To include or enclose; to restrain or hold back. **containable** *adj.*, **containment** *n.*

con-tain-er *v.* Something that holds or carries, as a box or can.

con-tain-er ship *n.* A ship that is designed to carry containerized cargo.

con-tam-i-nate *v.* To pollute or make inferior by adding undesireable elements; to taint; to infect; to make dirty or to soil. **contamination** *n.*

con-temn *v.* To scorn or despise.

con-tem-plate *v.* To look over; to ponder; to consider thoughtfully. **contemplation** *n.*, **contemplative** *adj.*

con-tem-po-ra-ne-ous *adj.* Occurring or living at the same time; contemporary. **contemporaneously** *adv.*

con-tempt *n.* The act of viewing something as mean, vile, or worthless scorn; legally, the willful disrespect or disregard of authority. **contemptible** *adj.*, **contemptibleness** *n.*, **contemptibly** *adv.*

con-temp-tu-ous *adj.* Feeling or showing contempt. **contemptuously** *adv.*

con-tend *v.* To dispute; to fight; to debate; to argue. **contender** *n.*

con-tent *n.* Something contained within; the subject matter of a book or document; the proportion of a specified part. *adj.* Satisfied. **contentment** *n.*, **contentedly** *adv.*, **contented** *adj.*

con-ten-tion *n.* Competition; rivalry; controversy; argument. **contentious** *adj.*, **contentiously** *adv.*

con-test *n.* A competition; strife; conflict. *v.* To challenge. **contestable** *adj.*, **contestant, contester** *n.*

con-text *n.* A sentence, phrase, or passage so closely connected to a word or words that it affects their meaning; the environment in which an event occurs.

con-ti-nent *n.* One of the seven large masses of the earth: Asia, Africa, Australia, Europe, North America, South America and Antarctica.

con-ti-nen-tal *adj.* Of or characteristic of a continent.

con-ti-nen-tal di-vide *n.* A divide separating rivers or streams that flow to opposite sides of a continent.

con-tin-ue *v.* To maintain without interruption a course or condition; to resume; to postpone or adjourn a judicial proceeding. **continuance, continuer** *n.*

con-ti-nu-i-ty *n., pl.* **-ties** The quality of being continuous.

con-tin-u-ous *adj.* Uninterrupted. **continuously** *adv.*, **continuousness** *n.*

con-tort *v.* To severely twist out of shape.

con-tor-tion-ist *n.* An acrobat who exhibits unnatural body positions.

con-tour *n.* The outline of a body, figure, or mass.

con-tra-band *n.* Illegal or prohibited traffic; smuggled goods.

con-tra-bass *n.* A double bass, also called a contrabassoon.

con-tra-cep-tion *n.* The voluntary prevention of impregation. **contraceptive** *adj.*

con-tract *n.* A formal agreement between two or more parties to perform the duties as stated.

con-trac-tion *n.* The act of contracting; a shortening of a word by omitting a letter or letters and replacing them with an apostrophe (').

con-trac-tile *adj.* Having the power to contract.

con-tra-dict *v.* To express the opposite side or idea; to be inconsistent. **contradictable, contradictory** *adj.*, **contradicter, contradictor** *n.*

con-tral-to *n., pl.* **-tos** The lowest female singing voice.

con-trap-tion *n.* A gadget.

con-tra-puntal *adj.* Relating to counterpoint. **contrapuntally** *adv.*

con-trar-y *adj.* Unfavorable; incompatible with another. **contrarily** *adv.*, **contrariness** *n.*

con-trast *v.* To note the differences between two or more people, things, etc. **contrastable** *adj.*

con-tra-vene *v.* To be contrary; to violate; to oppose; to go against.

con-trib-ute *v.* To give something to someone; to submit for publication. **contribution** *n.*, **contributive, contributory** *adj.*, **contributively** *adv.*

con-trite *adj.* Grieving for sin or shortcoming. **contritely** *adv.*, **contrition** *n.*

con-trol *v.* To have the authority or ability to regulate, direct, or dominate a situation. **controllable** *adj.*

con-trol-ler *n.* The chief accounting officer of a business, also called the comptroller.

con-tro-ver-sy *n.* A dispute; a debate; a quarrel. **controversial** *adj.*

con-tro-vert *v.* To contradict; to deny.

con-tu-me-ly *n., pl* **-lies** Rude treatment. **contumelious** *adj.*

co-nun-drum *n.* A riddle with an answer that involves a pun; a question or problem with only a surmise for an answer.

con-va-lesce *v.* To grow strong after a long illness. **convalescence** *n.*, **convalescent** *adj.*

con-vec-tion *n.* The transfer of heat by the movement of air, gas, or heated liquid between areas of unequal density. **convectional** *adj.*

con-vene *v.* To meet or assemble formally. **convenable** *adj.*, **convener** *n.*

con-ven-ience *n.* The quality of being convenient or suitable.

con-vent *n.* A local house or community of a religious order, especially for nuns.

con-ven-ti-cle *n.* A secret meeting for religious study or worship.

con-ven-tion *n.* A formal meeting; a regulatory meeting between people, states, or nations on matters that affect all of them.

con-ven-tion-al *adj.* Commonplace, ordinary.

con-verge *v.* To come to a common point. **convergence** *n.*, **covergent** *adj.*

con-ver-sa-tion *n.* An informal talk. **conversational** *adj.*

converse *v.* To involve oneself in conversation with another.

con-ver-sion *n.* The act or state of changing to adopt new opinions or beliefs; a formal acceptance of a different religion. **conversional** *adj.*

con-vert-i-ble *adj.* A car with a top that folds back or can be removed completely.

con-vex *adj.* Curved outward like the outer surface of a ball. **convexity** *n.*

con-vey *v.* To transport; to pass information on to someone else; to conduct. **conveyable** *adj.*

con-vey-ance *n.* The action of conveying; the legal transfer of property or the document effecting it.

con-vict *v.* To prove someone guilty. *n.* A prisoner.

con-vic-tion *n.* The act of being convicted.

con-vince *v.* To cause to believe without doubt. **convincingly** *adv.*

con-vo-ca-tion *n.* A formal or ceremonial assembly or meeting.

con-voke *v.* To call together for a formal meeting.

con-voy *n.* A group of cars, trucks, etc., traveling together. *v.* To escort or guide.

con-vulse *v.* To move or shake violently. **convulsive** *adj.*, **convulsively** *adv.*

con-vul-sion *n.* A violent involuntary muscular contraction.

cook *v.* To apply heat to food before eating; to prepare food for a meal. *n.* A person who prepares food.

cook-book *n.* A book containing directions for preparing and cooking food.

cook-ie *n., pl.* **-ies** A sweet, flat cake.

cool *adj.* Without warmth; indifferent or unenthusiastic. *Slang* First-rate; composure.

cool-ant *n.* The cooling agent that circulates through a machine.

Coolidge, John Calvin *n.* The 30th president of the United States, from 1923-1929.

coon *n., Informal* A raccoon.

coop *n.* A cage or enclosed area to contain animals, as chickens.

co--op *n.* A cooperative.

co-op-er-ate *v.* To work together toward a common cause. **cooperation, cooperator** *n.*

co-op-er-a-tive *adj.* Willing to cooperate with others. **cooperatively** *adv.*, **cooperativeness** *n.*

co--opt *v.* To elect or choose as a new member.

co-or-di-nate *v.* To be equal in rank, importance, or degree; to plan a wardrobe or outfit so that it goes well together. *n.* Any of a set of numbers which establishes position on a graph, map, etc. **coordinately** *adv.*, **coordinator** *n.*

co-or-di-na-tion *n.* The state of being coordinated.

coot *n.* A short-winged bird. *Slang* A silly old man.

coot-ie *n., Slang* A body louse.

cop *n., Informal* A police officer.

cope *v.* To strive; to struggle or contend with something. *n.* The long cape worn by a priest on special ceremonial occasions.

cop-ier *n.* A machine that makes copies of original material.

co-pi-lot *n.* The assistant pilot on an aircraft.

co-pi-ous *n.* Large in quantity; abundant. **copiously** *adv.*

cop—out *n.*, *Slang* A way to avoid responsibility.

cop-per *n.* A metallic element that is a good conductor of electricity and heat, reddish-brown in color.

cop-per-head *n.* A venomous snake found in the eastern United States, having brownish-red markings.

cop-ra *n.* Dried coconut meat that yields coconut oil.

copse *n.* A thicket made up of trees or small bushes.

cop-ter *n.*, *Slang* A helicopter.

cop-u-la *n.*, *Gram.* A word or words which connect a subject and predicate.

cop-u-late *v.* To have sexual intercourse. **copulation** *n.*

copy *v.*, *pl.* **-ies** To reproduce an original. *n.* A single printed text. **copyist** *n.*

copy edit *v.* To edit and correct a written copy for publication. **copy editor** *n.*

copy-right *n.* The statutory right to sell, publish, or distribute a literary or artistic work.

copy writer *n.* A person who writes copy for advertisements.

coq au vin *n.* Chicken cooked in wine.

co-quette *n.* A woman who flirts. **coquettish** *adj.*

cor-al *n.* The stony skeleton of a small sea creature, often used for jewelry.

Cor-al Sea *n.* An arm of the southwest Pacific, located southeast of New Guinea and northeast of Australia.

cor-al reef *n.* A marine mound formed chiefly of broken pieces and grains of coral that have become a hard mass.

cor-al snake *n.* A venomous snake of tropical America and the southern United States, brightly colored with red, black, and yellow rings.

cord *n.* A string or twine; an insulated wire used to supply electricity to another source; a measurement for firewood that equals 128 cubic feet; a raised rib of fabric, as corduroy. **cord** *v.*, **corder** *n.*

cor-dial *adj.* Warm-hearted and sincere. *n.* A liqueur. **cordiality** *n.*, **cordially** *adv.*

cord-ite *n.* A smokeless gunpowder.

cor-don *n.* A circle of men or ships positioned to guard or enclose an area; an ornamental ribbon or braid worn as an insignia of honor.

cor-du-roy *n.* A durable cotton fabric which has a ribbed pile.

core *n.* The innermost or central part of something; the inedible center of a fruit that contains the seeds. *v.* To remove the core from a piece of fruit.

co-re-spon-dent *n.* A person charged with having committed adultery with the defendant in a divorce case.

cork *n.* The elastic bark of the oak tree used for bottle stoppers and craft projects.

cork-age *n.* The fee that must be paid when one consumes a bottle of liquor not purchased on the premises.

cork-screw *n.* A pointed metal spiral attached to a handle used for removing corks from bottles.

corn *n.* An American-cultivated cereal plant bearing seeds on a large ear or cob; the seed of this plant; a horny thickening of the skin, usually on the toe.

Corn Belt *n.* The major corn growing states of the United States; Illinois, Indiana, Iowa, Kansas, Missouri, Nebraska, and Ohio.

corn bread *n.* A bread made from crushed cornmeal, eggs, flour, and milk.

corn cob *n.* The woody core around which the corn kernels grow.

corn-crib *n.* The building used for storing and drying corn.

cor-ne-a *n.* The transparent membrane of the eyeball. **corneal** *adj.*

cor-ner *n.* The point formed when two surfaces or lines meet and form an angle; the location where two streets meet.

corner-back *or* **corner back** *n.* In football, the defensive halfback who defends the flank and covers the pass receiver.

corner-stone *n.* A stone that forms part of the corner of a building, usually laid in place with a special ceremony.

cor-net *n.* A three valved, brass musical instrument. **cornetist** *n.*

corn-meal *n.* Meal made from corn.

corn-row *v.* To braid the hair in rows very close to the head.

corn-stalk *n.* A stalk of corn.

corn-starch *n.* A starch made from corn and used to thicken food while cooking.

corn syrup *n.* A sweet syrup made from cornstarch, containing maltose, dextrins, and dextrose.

cor-nu-co-pi-a *n.* A curved goat's horn overflowing with flowers, fruit, and corn to signify prosperity.

corn-y *adj.*, *Slang* Trite or mawkishly old-fashioned.

co-rol-la *n.* The petals of a flower.

cor-ol-lary *n.*, *pl.* **-ies** Something that naturally or incidentally follows or accompanies.

cor-o-nar-y *adj.* Of or relating to the two arteries that supply blood to the heart muscles. **coronary** *n.*

cor-o-nary throm-bo-sis *n.* A blockage of the coronary artery of the heart.

cor-po-ral *n.* A noncommissioned officer who ranks above a private first class but below a sergeant. *adj.* Relating to the body.

cor-po-rate *adj.* Combined into one joint body; relating to a corporation.

cor-po-ra-tion *n.* A group of merchants united in a trade guild; any group or persons that act as one.

cor-po-re-al *adj.* Of a physical nature.

corps *n., pl.* **corps** A branch of the armed forces; the body of persons under common direction.

corpse *n.* A dead body.

cor-pu-lence *n.* The excessive accumulation of body fat; obesity. **corpulent** *adj.*

cor-pus-cle *n.* A minute particle or living cell, especially as one in the blood. **corpuscular** *adj.*

cor-pus de-lic-ti *n.* The essential evidence pertaining to a crime.

cor-ral *n.* An enclosure for containing animals. *v., Slang* To take possession of.

cor-rect *v.* To make free from fault or mistakes. **correctable, correctible** *adj.*, **correctional, correction, correctness** *n.*, **corrective** *adj. & n.*, **correctly** *adv.*

cor-rel-a-tive *adj.* Having a mutual relation.

cor-re-spond *v.* To communicate by letter or written words; to be harmonious, equal or similar. **correspondingly** *adv.*

cor-ri-dor *n.* A long hall with rooms on either side; a piece of land that forms a passage through a foreign land.

cor-ri-gen-dum *n., pl.* **-da** An error in print that is accompanied by its correction.

cor-ri-gi-ble *adj.* Able to correct; capable of being corrected.

cor-rob-o-rate *v.* To support a position or statement with evidence. **corroboration** *n.*, **corroborative** *adj.*

cor-rode *v.* To eat away through chemical action. **corrodible** *adj.*, **corrosion** *n.*, **corrosive** *adj. & n.*

cor-rupt *adj.* Dishonest; evil. *v.* To become or make corrupt. **corrupter** *n.*

cor-sage *n.* A small bouquet of flowers worn on a woman's shoulder or wrist.

cor-sair *n.* A pirate; a fast moving vessel.

cor-set *n.* An undergarment that is tightened with laces and reinforced with stays, worn to give shape and support to a woman's body. **corsetiere** *n.*

cor-tege *n.* A ceremonial procession; a funeral procession.

cor-tex *n., pl.* **-tices** The external layer of an organ, especially the gray matter that covers the brain; the bark of trees and the rinds of fruits.

cor-ti-sone *n.* A hormone produced by the adrenal cortex, used in the treatment of rheumatoid arthritis.

co-run-dum *n.* An aluminum oxide used as an abrasive.

cor-us-cate *v.* To sparkle. **coruscation** *n.*

cor-vette *n.* An armed warship smaller than a destroyer, used as an escort vessel.

co-ry-za *n.* An acute inflammation of the upper respiratory system.

co-sign *v.* To sign a document jointly.

co-sig-na-to-ry *n., pl.* **-ies** One who jointly cosigns a document.

cos-met-ic *n.* A preparation designed to beautify the face. **cosmetically** *adv.*

cos-me-tol-o-gy *n.* The study of cosmetics and their use. **cosmetologist** *n.*

cos-mog-o-ny *n.* The creation of the universe.

cos-mo-naut *n.* A Soviet astronaut.

cos-mo-pol-i-tan *adj.* Being at home anywhere in the world.

cos-mop-o-lite *n.* A cosmopolitan person.

cos-mos *n.* An orderly and harmoniously systematic universe.

Cos-sack *n.* A member of a group of people of southern Russia, famous as horsemen.

cos-set *v.* To pamper; pet.

cost *n.* The amount paid or charged for a purchase. **cost** *v.*, **costly** *adj.*

cos-tive *adj.* Affected with or causing constipation.

cos-tume *n.* A suit, dress, or set of clothes characteristic of a particular season or occasion; clothes worn by a person playing a part or dressing up in a disguise.

cot *n.* A small, often collapsible bed.

cot-tage *n.* A small house, usually for vacation use.

cot-ter pin *n.* A metal pin whose ends can be flared after being inserted through a slot or hole.

cot-ton *n.* A plant or shrub cultivated the fiber surrounding its seeds; a fabric created by the weaving of cotton fibers; yarn spun from cotton fibers.

cot-ton can-dy *n.* Spun sugar.

cot-ton-mouth *n.* The water moccasin. *Slang* Having a dry mouth.

couch *n.* A piece of furniture, such as a sofa or bed on which one may sit or recline for rest or sleep. *v.* To phrase in a certain manner; to lie in ambush.

cou-gar *n.* A large brown cat, also called a mountain lion, panther, and puma.

cough *v.* To suddenly expel air from the lungs with an explosive noise.

could *v.* Past tense of can.

could-n't *contr.* Could not.

cou-lomb *n.* The unit of quantity used to measure electricity; the amount conveyed by one amphere in one second.

coun-cil *n.* A group of people assembled for consultation or discussion; an official legislative or advisory body. **councilman, councilor** *n.*

coun-sel *n.* Advice given through consultation; a lawyer engaged in the management or trial of a court case.

coun-sel-or *n.* One who gives advice; a lawyer.

count *v.* To name or number so as to find the total number of units involved; to name numbers in order; to take account of in a tally or reckoning; to rely or depend on something or someone; to have significance. *n.* A nobleman found in various countries throughout Europe, having rank corresponding to that of a British earl; a tally.

count-down *n.* An audible counting in descending order to mark the time remaining before an event.

coun-te-nance *n.* The face as an indication of mood or character; bearing or expression that would suggest approval or sanction.

coun-ter *n.* A level surface over which transactions are conducted, on which food is served, or on which articles are displayed; a person or device that counts to determine a number or amount. *v.* To move or act in a contrary, or opposing direction or wrong way

coun-ter-act *v.* To oppose and, by contrary action, make ineffective.

coun-ter-attack *n.* An attack made in response to an enemy attack. **counterattack** *v.*

coun-ter-bal-ance *n.* A force or influence that balances another; a weight that balances another. **counterbalance** *v.*

coun-ter-claim *n.* A contrary claim made to offset another.

coun-ter-clock-wise *adj. & adv.* In a direction contrary to that in which the hands of a clock move.

coun-ter-cul-ture *n.* A culture with values opposite those of traditional society.

coun-ter-es-pi-o-nage *n.* Espionage aimed at discovering and thwarting enemy espionage.

coun-ter-feit *v.* To closely imitate or copy with the intent to deceive; to forge. *adj.* Marked by false pretense. *n.* Something counterfeit.

coun-ter-foil *n.* A stub, as on a check or ticket, usually serving as a record of the transaction.

coun-ter-in-tel-li-gence *n.* An intelligence agency function designed to block information, deceive the enemy, prevent sabotage, and gather military and political material and information.

coun-ter-ir-ri-tant *n.* An irritation that diverts attention from another. **counterirritant** *adj.*

coun-ter-man *n.* One who works at a counter.

coun-ter-mand *v.* To reverse or revoke a command by issuing a contrary order. *n.* An order which reverses or contradicts a previous order.

coun-ter-of-fen-sive *n.* A military offensive designed to thwart an enemy attack.

coun-terpane *n.* A covering.

coun-terpart *n.* One that matches or complements another.

coun-ter-plea *n.* A plea made in answer to a previous plea.

coun-ter-point *n., Mus.* The combining of melodies into a harmonic relationship while retaining the linear character.

coun-ter-pro-duc-tive *adj.* Tending to hinder rather than aid in the attainment of a goal.

coun-ter-re-vo-lu-tion *n.* A revolution designed to overthrow a government previously seated by a revolution.

coun-ter-sign *n.* A signature confirming the authenticity of a document already signed by another; a sign or signal given in response to another. **countersign** *v.*

coun-ter-sink *n.* A funnel-shaped enlargement on the outer end of a drilled hole designed to allow the head of a nail or screw to lie flush with or below the surface; a tool for making a countersink. *v.* To set the head, as of a nail or screw at or below the surface.

coun-ter-ten-or *n.* An adult tenor with a very high range, higher than that of the average tenor.

coun-ter-vail *v.* To counteract.

coun-ter-weight *n.* An equivalent weight, used as a counterbalance. **counterweight** *v.*

count-ess *n.* The wife or widow of an earl or count; a woman who, in her own right, holds the rank of earl or count.

count-ing house *n.* A building or room used for keeping books and doing business.

count-less *adj.* Too many or too numerous to be counted.

coun-tri-fied *adj.* Of or relating to country life; rural; unsophisticated.

coun-try *n., pl.* **-ies** A given area or region; the land of one's birth, residence, or citizenship; a state, nation, or its territory.

coun-try club *n.* A suburban club for social and recreational activities.

coun-try-man *n.* A compatriot; one living in the country or having country ways.

coun-try music *n.* Music derived from the folk style of the southern United States and from the cowboy.

coun-try-side *n.* A rural area or its inhabitants.

coun-ty *n., pl.* **-ies** A territorial division for local government within a state.

coup *n.* A brilliant, sudden move that is usually highly successful.

cou-ple *n.* A pair; something that joins two things together; a few. *v.* To join in marriage or sexual union.

cou-plet *n.* Two rhyming lines of poetry in succession.

cou-pon *n.* A statement of interest due, to be removed from a bearer bond and presented for payment when it is payable; a form surrendered to obtain a product, service, or discount on same; a form to be clipped from a magazine or paper and mailed for discounts or gifts.

cour-age *n.* Mental or moral strength to face danger without fear. **courageous** *adj.,* **courageously** *adv.*

cou-ri-er *n.* A messenger; a person who carries contraband for another.

course *n.* The act of moving in a path from one point to another; the path over which something moves; a period of time; a series or sequence; a series of studies.

court *n.* The residence of a sovereign or similar dignitary; a sovereign's family and advisors; an assembly for the transaction of judicial business; a place where trials are conducted; an area marked off for game playing. *v.* To try to win favor or dispel hostility.

cour-te-ous *adj.* Marked by respect for and consideration of others.

cour-te-san *n.* A prostitute one who associates with or caters to high-ranking or wealthy men.

cour-te-sy *n., pl.* -ies Courteous behavior; general allowance despite facts.

court-house *n.* A building for holding courts of law.

court-i-er *n.* One in attendance at a royal court.

court-yard *n.* An open space enclosed by walls.

cous-in *n.* A child of one's uncle or aunt; a member of a culturally similar race or nationality.

cove *n.* A small inlet or bay, generally sheltered; a deep recess or small valley in the side of a mountain.

cov-e-nant *n.* A formal, binding agreement; a promise or pledge.

cov-er *v.* To place something on or over; to lie over; to spread over; to guard from attack; to hide or conceal. *Slang* To be all-encompassing; to act as a stand-in during another's absence; to have within one's gun sights. **cover** *n.*

cov-et *v.* To wish for enviously; to crave possession of that which belongs to someone else.

cov-ey *n.* A small group of birds, especially quail or partridges.

cow *n., pl.* cows The mature female of cattle or of any species when the adult male is referred to as a bull.

cow-ard *n.* One who shows great fear or timidity. **cowardice** *n.*

cowl *n.* A hood or long hooded cloak such as that of a monk; a covering for a chimney that is designed to improve the air draft; the top portion at the front of an automobile where the windshield and dashboard are attached.

cow-slip *n.* A common British primrose with yellow or purple flowers.

cox-comb *n.* A conceited foolish person.

cox-swain *n.* One who steers a boat or racing shell.

coy *adj.* Quieting or shy, or to pretending to be so. **coyness** *n.*

coy-o-te *n.* A small wolf-life animal that is native to North America.

coz-en *v.* To swindle, cheat, deceive, win over, or induce to do something by coaxing or trickery. **cozener** *n.*

co-zy *adj.* Comfortable and warm; snug. *n.* A cover placed over a teapot to retain the warmth. **cozily** *adv.*, **coziness** *n.*

crab *n., pl.* crabs Any one of numerous chiefly marine crustaceans with a short, broad shell, four pairs of legs, and one pair of pincers; sideways motion of an airplane headed into a crosswind. **crabs** Infestation with crab lice. **crabber** *n.*

crab-bed *adj.* Morose or peevish; difficult to read or understand. **crabbedly** *adv.*, **crabbedness** *n.*

crab-by *adj.* Being ill-tempered and cross.

crack *v.* To make a loud explosive sound; to break, snap, or split apart; to break without completely separating; to lose control under pressure (often used with up); to go at a good speed; to break with a sudden, sharp sound; to solve; to reduce petroleum compounds to simpler forms by heating. *n.* A sharp, witty remark; a weakness caused by decay or age; an attempt or try. *Slang* A highly dangerous and addictive form of cocaine.

crack-le *v.* To make sharp, sudden, repeated noises; to develop a network of fine cracks.

cra-dle *n.* A small bed for infants, usually on rockers or rollers; a framework of support, such as that for a telephone receiver; a small platform on casters used by mechanics when working under a vehicle; a device used for rocking in panning for gold.

craft *n.* A special skill or ability; a trade that requires dexterity or artistic skill; the ability to use cunning and skill in deceiving; an aircraft, boat, or ship.

crag *n.* A steep, jagged rock or cliff. **cragged, craggy** *adj.*

cram *v.* To pack tightly or stuff; to thrust in a forceful manner; to eat in a greedy fashion; to prepare hastily for an exam.

cramp *n.* A painful involuntary contraction of a muscle; sharp abdominal pain.

cran-ber-ry *n., pl.* -berries A North American shrub which grows in damp soil and bears edible, tart red berries.

crane *n.* A large bird with long legs and a long neck; a machine used for lifting or moving heavy objects. *v.* To strain or stretch the neck.

cra-ni-um *n., pl.* crania The skull, especially the part in which the brain is enclosed. **cranial** *adj.*

crank *n.* An arm bent at right angles to a shaft and turned to transmit motion; an eccentric person; a bad-tempered person; a grouch. *v.* To operate or start by crank.

crank-case *n.* The housing of a crankshaft.

crank-shaft *n.* A shaft propelled by a crank.

crank-y *adj.* Grouchy, irritable. **crankiness** *n.*

cran-ny *n., pl.* -ies A small break or crevice; an obscure nook or corner.

craps *v.* A gambling game played with two dice.

crap-shoot-er *n.* A person who plays craps.

crash *v.* To break violently or noisily; to damage in landing, usually an airplane; to collapse suddenly, usually a business; to cause to make a loud noise; to enter into without an invitation. *Slang* To spend the night in a particular place; to return to normalcy from a drug-induced state. *n.* In computer science, the unplanned termination of a computer operation or program.

crass *adj.* Insensitive and unrefined.

crate *n.* A container, usually made of wooden slats, for protection during shipping or storage. **crate** *v.*

cra-ter *n.* A bowl-shaped depression at the mouth of a volcano; a depression formed by a meteorite; a hole made by an explosion. **cratered** *adj.*

cra-vat *n.* A necktie.

crave *v.* To desire intensely.

cra-ven *adj.* Completely lacking courage.

crav-ing *n.* An intense longing or desire.

craw *n.* The crop of a bird; the stomach of a lower animal.

craw-fish *n.* A crayfish.

crawl *v.* To move slowly by dragging the body along the ground in a prone position; to move on hands and knees; to progress slowly.

cray-on *n.* A stick of white or colored chalk or wax used for writing or drawing.

craze *v.* To make insane or as if insane; to become insane; to develop a fine mesh of narrow cracks. *n.* Something that lasts for a short period of time; a fad.

cra-zy *adj.* Insane; impractical; unusually fond. **crazily** *adv.,* **craziness** *n.*

creak *v.* A squeaking or grating noise. **creaky** *adj.,* **creakily** *adv.*

cream *n.* The yellowish, fatty part of milk, containing a great amount of butterfat; something having the consistency of cream; the best part; a pale yellow-white color. **creaminess** *n.,* **creamy** *adj.*

crease *n.* A line or mark made by folding and pressing a pliable substance. **crease** *v.*

cre-ate *v.* To bring something into existence; to give rise to.

cre-a-tion *n.* The act of creating; something that is created; the universe.

cre-a-tive *adj.* Marked by the ability to create; inventive; imaginative. **creatively** *adv.,* **creativeness** *n.*

crea-tor *n.* One that creates. **The Creator.** God.

crea-ture *n.* Something created; a living being.

cre-dence *n.* Belief.

cre-den-za *n.* A buffet or sideboard, usually without legs.

cred-i-ble *adj.* Offering reasonable grounds for belief. **credibility** *n.,* **credibly** *adv.*

cred-it *n.* An amount at a person's disposal in a bank; recognition by name for a contribution; acknowledgment; recognition by a learning institution that a student has completed a requirement leading to a degree.

cred-u-lous *adj.* Gullible; ready to believe on slight or uncertain evidence. **credulously** *adv.*

creed *n.* A brief authoritative statement of religious belief.

creek *n.* A narrow stream. **up the creek** In a difficult or perplexing situation.

creel *n.* A wicker basket for holding fish.

creep *v.* To advance at a slow pace; to go timidly or cautiously; to grow along a surface, clinging by means of tendrils or aerial roots.

cre-mate *v.* To reduce to ashes by burning.

cre-o-sote *n.* An oily liquid mixture obtained by distilling coal tar, used especially as a wood preservative.

crept *v.* The past tense of creep.

cre-pus-cu-lar *adj.* Of, resembling, or relating to twilight.

cre-scen-do *adv.* In music, gradually increasing in loudness.

cres-cent *n.* The shape of the moon in its first and fourth quarters, defined with a convex and a concave edge.

cress *n.* Any of numerous plants with sharp-tasting edible leaves.

crest *n.* A tuft or comb on the head of a bird or animal; the top line of a mountain or hill.

cre-tin *n.* One afflicted with cretinism; a person with marked mental deficiency.

cre-tin-ism *n.* A condition marked by physical stunting and mental deficiency.

cre-tonne *n.* A strong cotton or linen cloth, used especially for curtains and upholstery.

cre-vasse *n.* A deep crack or crevice.

crev-ice *n.* A narrow crack.

crew *n.* A group of people that work together; the whole company belonging to an aircraft or ship.

crew-el *n.* Slackly twisted worsted yarn, used in embroidery.

crib *n.* A small bed with high sides for an infant; a feeding bin for animals.

cri-er *n.* One who calls out public notices.

crime *n.* An act or the commission of an act that is forbidden by law.

crimp *v.* To cause to become bent or crinkled; to pinch in or together.

crim-son *n.* A deep purplish color. *v.* To make or become crimson.

cringe *v.* To shrink or recoil in fear.

crin-kle *v.* To wrinkle. **crinkly** *adj.*

crin-o-line *n.* An open-weave fabric used for lining and stiffening garments.

crip-ple *n.* One who is lame or partially disabled; something flawed or imperfect. *adj.* Being a cripple. *v.* To deprive one of the use of a limb or limbs.

cri-sis *n., pl.* **crises** An unstable or uncertain time or state of affairs, the outcome of which will have a major impact; the turning point for better or worse in a disease or fever.

crisp *adj.* Easily broken; brittle; brisk or cold; sharp; clear. *v.* To make or become crisp. **crisply** *adv.,* **crispness** *n.*

crisp-er *n.* A compartment within a

refrigerator used to keep fruits and vegetables fresh.

cri-te-ri-on *n.*, *pl.* **criteria** A standard by which something can be judged.

crit-ic *n.* A person who is critical; a person who examines a subject and expresses an opinion as to its value; a person who judges or evaluates art or artistic creations, as a theatre critic.

crit-i-cal *adj.* Very important, as a critical decision; tending to criticize harshly. **critically** *adv.*

crit-i-cism *n.* The act of criticizing, usually in a severe or negative fashion.

crit-i-cize *v.* To be a critic; to find fault with; to judge critically; to blame.

croak *n.* A hoarse, raspy cry such as that made by a frog. *v.* To utter a croak. *Slang* To die.

cro-chet *n.* The needlework achieved by looping thread with a hooked needle. **crochet** *v.*

crock *n.* An earthenware pot or jar most often used for cooking or storing food.

croc-o-dile *n.*

Any of various large, thick-skinned, long-bodied reptiles of tropical and subtropical regions.

croc-o-dile tears *n.*, *pl.* Insincere grief.

cro-cus *n.*, *pl.* **crocuses** A plant having solitary, long-tubed flowers and slender, linear leaves.

crone *n.* A witch-like, withered old woman.

cro-ny *n.*, *pl.* **-ies** A close friend.

crook *n.* A bent or hooked implement; a bend or curve; a person given to dishonest acts. *v.* To bend or curve.

croon *v.* To sing in a gentle, low voice; to make a continued moaning sound. **croon** *n.*

crop *n.* A plant which is grown and then harvested for use or for sale; a riding whip. *v.* To cut off short; to appear unexpectedly.

cro-quet *n.* An outdoor game played by driving wooden balls through hoops with long-handled mallets.

cro-quette *n.* A small patty or roll of minced food that is breaded and deep fried.

cross *n.*

A structure consisting of an upright post and a crossbar, used especially by the Romans for execution, such as the cross on which Jesus was crucified; something that tries one's virtue or patience; a medal with the shape of the cross, such as the one used as a Christian emblem; a mark formed by the intersection of two lines. *v.* In biology, to interbreed a plant or an animal

with one of a different kind; to go over; to intersect; to turn against; to go against. *adj.* Ill-tempered.

cross-bar *n.* A horizontal bar or line.

crotch *n.* The angle formed by the junction of two parts, such as legs or branches. **crotched** *adj.*

crotch-et *n.* A peculiar opinion or preference.

crouch *v.* To bend at the knees and lower the body close to the ground.

croup *n.* A spasmodic laryngitis, especially of children, marked by a loud, harsh cough and difficulty in breathing. **croupy** *adj.*

crou-pi-er *n.* One who collects and pays bets at a gambling table.

crou-ton *n.* A small piece of toasted or fried bread.

crow *n.* A large, black bird.

crowd *n.* A large group of people gathered together. *v.* To assemble in large numbers; to press close.

crown *n.* A circular ornament or head covering made of precious metal and jewels, worn as the headdress of a sovereign; the highest point; the topmost part of the skull; the title representing the championship of a sport; a reward or honor for achievement; the part of a tooth that rises above the gum line. *v.* To place a checker on another checker to make a king; to adorn something with a crown; to hit on the head.

CRT *abbr.* Cathode Ray Tube.

cru-cial *adj.* Extremely important; critical.

cru-ci-ble *n.* A vessel used for melting and calcining materials at high temperatures; a hard test of someone.

cru-ci-fy *v.* To put to death by nailing to a cross; to treat cruelly; to torment.

crude *adj.* Unrefined; lacking refinement or tact; haphazardly made. *n.* Unrefined petroleum. **-ly** *adv.*, **-ness** *n.*

cruel *adj.* Inflicting suffering; causing pain. **cruelly** *adv.*, **cruelty** *n.*

cru-et *n.* A small glass bottle normally used as a container for oil or vinegar.

cruise *v.* To drive or sail about for pleasure; to move about the streets at leisure; to travel at a speed that provides maximum efficiency.

crumb *n.* A small fragment of material, particularly bread.

crum-ble *v.* To break into small pieces. **crumbly** *adj.*

crum-ple *v.* To bend or crush out of shape; to cause to collapse; to be crumpled.

crunch *v.* To chew with a crackling noise; to run, walk, etc., with a crushing noise. **crunch** *n.*

cru-sade *n.* Any of the military expeditions undertaken by Christian leaders during the 11th, 12th, and 13th centuries to recover the Holy Land from the Moslems. **crusade** *v.*

crush *v.* To squeeze or force by pressure so as to damage or injure; to reduce to particles by pounding or grinding; to put down or suppress. -able *adj.*, -er *n.*

crust *n.* The hardened exterior or surface of bread; a hard or brittle surface layer; the outer layer of the earth; the shell of a pie, normally made of pastry. *v.* To cover or become covered with crust.

crus-ta-cean *n.* Any one of a large class of aquatic arthropods, including lobsters and crabs, with a segmented body and paired, jointed limbs.

crutch *n.* A support usually designed to fit in the armpit and to be used as an aid in walking; any support or prop.

crux *n.* An essential or vital moment; a main or central feature.

cry *v.* To shed tears; to call out loudly; to utter a characteristic call or sound; to proclaim publicly. **cry** *n.*

crypt *n.* An underground chamber or vault primarily used to bury the dead.

cryp-tic *adj.* Intended to be obscure; serving to conceal.

cryp-tog-ra-phy *n.* The writing and deciphering of messages in secret code. **cryptographer** *n.*

crys-tal *n.* Quartz that is transparent or nearly transparent; a body that is formed by the solidification of a chemical element; a clear, high-quality glass. **crystalline** *adj.*

crys-tal ball *n.* A glass globe for fore-telling the future.

crys-tal-lize *v.* To cause to form crystals or assume crystalline form; to cause to take a definite form; to coat with crystals, especially sugar crystals.

cub *n.* The young of the lion, wolf, or bear; an awkward child or youth.

cub-by-hole *n.* A small enclosed area.

cube *n.* A regular solid with six equal squares, having all its angles right angles. **cube** *v.*

cube root *n.* A number whose cube is a given number.

cubic *adj.* Having the shape of a cube; having three dimensions; having the volume of a cube with the edges of a specified unit.

cu-bi-cle *n.* A small partitioned area.

cub-ism *n.* An art style that portrays the subject matter with geometric forms. **cubist** *n.*

cu-bit *n.* An ancient unit of measurement that equals approximately eighteen to twenty inches.

Cub Scout *n.* A member of the Boy Scout organization from the ages of eight to ten.

cuck-oo *n., pl.* **cuckoos** A European bird, gray in color, which lays its eggs in the nests of other birds. *Slang* Silly.

cu-cum-ber *n.* A fruit with a green rind and white, seedy flesh.

cud *n.* Food forced up into the mouth of a ruminating animal from the first stomach and chewed again.

cud-dle *v.* To caress fondly and hold close; to snuggle. **cuddle** *n.*, -y *adj.*

cue *n.* A signal given to an actor or someone making a speech, letting him know it is his turn; a long rod for play-ing pool and billiards.

cue ball *n.* The white ball that is struck with the cue in billiards and pool.

cuff *n.* The lower part of a sleeve; the part of the pant legs which is turned up. *v.* To strike someone.

cuffs *n.* Handcuffs.

cui-rass *n.* A piece of armor for the breast and back, used for protection.

cui-sine *n.* A style of cooking and preparing food; the food prepared.

cu-li-nar-y *adj.* Relating to cooking.

cull *v.* To select the best from a group. **culler** *n.*

cul-mi-nate *v.* To reach or rise to the highest point. **culmination** *n.*

cu-lotte *n.* A woman's full pants made to look like a skirt.

cul-pa-ble *adj.* Meriting blame. **culpability** *n.*

cul-prit *n.* A person guilty of a crime.

cult *n.* A group or system of religious worship. **cultic** *adj.*, **cultist** *n.*

cul-ti-vate *v.* To improve land for planting by fertilizing and plowing; to improve by study; to encourage. **cultivatable** *adj.*, **cultivator** *n.*

cul-ture *n.* The act of developing intellectual ability with education; a form of civilization, particularly the beliefs, arts, and customs. *Biol.* The growth of living material in a prepared nutrient media. **culture** *v.*

cul-vert *n.* A drain that runs under a road or railroad.

cum-ber-some *adj.* Clumsy; unwieldy.

cum-mer-bund *n.* A wide sash worn by men in formal attire.

cu-mu-lus *n., pl.* **cumuli** A white, fluffy cloud with a rounded top and a flat base.

cu-ne-i-form *n.* Wedge-shaped characters used in ancient Babylonian, Assyrian, and Sumerian writing.

cun-ning *adj.* Crafty; sly. **cunningly** *adv.*

cup *n.* A small, open container with a handle, used for drinking; a measure of capacity that equals 1/2 pint, 8 ounces, or 16 tablespoons.

Cu-pid *n.* The god of love in Roman mythology.

cu-pid-i-ty *n.* An excessive desire for material gain.

cu-po-la *n.* A rounded roof; a small vaulted structure that usually rises above a roof.

cur *n.* A mongrel; a dog of mixed breeds.

cu-rate *n.* A member of the clergy that assists the priest.

cu-ra-tor *n.* A person in charge of a museum.

curb *n.* Something that restrains or controls; the raised border along the edge of a street. **curb** *v.*

curd *n.* The coagulated portion of milk used for making cheese.

cure *n.* Recovery from a sickness; a medical treatment; the process of preserving food with the use of salt, smoke, or aging.

cu-ret-tage *n.* Surgical cleaning and scraping.

cur-few *n.* An order for people to clear the streets at a certain hour; the hour at which an adolescent has been told to be home by his or her parents.

cu-ri-o *n.* An unusual or rare object.

cu-ri-ous *adj.* Questioning; inquisitive; eager for information. curiousity *n.,* curiously *adv.*

curl *v.* To twist into curves; shape like a coil. *n.* A ringlet of hair. curler, curliness *n.,* curly *adj.*

cur-mudg-eon *n.* An ill-tempered person.

cur-rant *n.* A small seedless raisin.

cur-ren-cy *n., pl.* -cies Money in circulation.

cur-rent *adj.* Belonging or occurring in the present time. *n.* Water or air that has a steady flow in a definite direction. currently *adv.*

cur-ric-u-lum *n., pl.* -la, -lums The courses offered in a school.

cur-ry *v.* To groom a horse with a brush. *n.* A pungent spice used in cooking.

cur-ry-comb *n.* A special comb used to curry a horse.

curse *n.* A prayer or wish for harm to come to someone or something.

cursor *n.* In computer science, the flashing square, underline, or other indicator on the CRT screen of a computer that shows where the next character will be deleted or inserted.

cur-sive *n.* A flowing writing in which the letters are joined together. -ly *adv.*

curt *adj.* Abrupt; rude. curtly *adv.,* curtness *n.*

cur-tail *v.* To shorten. curtailment *n.*

cur-tain *n.* A piece of material that covers a window and can be either drawn to the sides or raised.

curt-sy *n., pl.* -sies A respectful gesture made by bending the knees and lowering the body.

cush-ion *n.* A pillow with a soft filling. *v.* To absorb the shock or effect.

cus-pid *n.* A pointed canine tooth.

cus-pi-dor *n.* A spittoon.

cuss *v.* To use profanity.

cus-tard *n.* A mixture of milk, eggs, sugar, and flavoring that is baked.

cus-to-di-an *n.* One who has the custody or care of something or someone.

cus-to-dy *n., pl.* -dies The act of guarding; the care and protection of a minor.

cus-tom *n.* An accepted practice of a community or people; the usual manner of doing something. customs The tax one must pay on imported goods. customary *adj.*

custom--built *adj.* Built to one's special order.

cus-tomer *n.* A person with whom a merchant or business person must deal, usually on a regular basis.

cus-tom house *n.* An office of business where customs are paid and ships are cleared for entering or leaving a country.

cut *v.* To penetrate with a sharp edge, as with a knife; to omit or leave something out; to reap or harvest crops in the fields. *Slang* To cut class; to share in the profits. cut *n.*

cut back *v.* To reduce; to prune.

cute *adj.* Attractive in a delightful way.

cut glass *n.* Glass shaped and decorated by using a cutting instrument.

cut-lass *or* cut-las *n.* A thick, short, curved sword.

cut-lery *n.* Cutting instruments used at the dinner table and used to prepare food for cooking.

cut-let *n.* A thin piece of meat for broiling or frying, usually lamb or veal.

cut-off *n.* A short cut; the act of cutting something off.

cut-out *n.* Something intended to be cut or already cut out. *v.* To shape by cutting; to eliminate. *Slang* cut it out Stop it.

cut-rate *adj.* Offering merchandise at a lower than normal price.

cut-ter *n., Naut.* A fast-sailing vessel with a single mast.

cut-throat *n.* A murderer; a thug.

cut up *v.* To act foolishly; to behave like a clown; to cut into pieces.

cy-a-nide *n., Chem.* A compound of cyanogen with a metallic element; a poison.

cyc-la-men *n.* A plant with red, white, or pink flowers.

cy-cle *n.* A recurring time in which an event occurs repeatedly; a bicycle or motorcycle. cyclical *adj.,* cyclically *adv.*

cy-clist *n.* A person who rides a cycle.

cy-clone *n.* A storm with wind rotating about a low pressure center, accompanied by destructive weather. cyclonic *adj.*

cy-clo-tron *n.* Machine that obtains high-energy electrified particles by whirling at a high speed in a strong magnetic field.

cyl-in-der *n.*

A long, round body that is either hollow or solid. cylindrical *adj.*

cyn-ic *n.* One who believes that all people have selfish motives. cynical *adj.,* cynicism *n.*

cy-no-sure *n.* A person or object that attracts admiration and interest.

cy-press *n.* An evergreen tree that grows in a warm climate and bears small, scale-like needles.

cyst *n.* An abnormal sac or vesicle which may collect and retain fluid. cystic *adj.*

cyst-ic fi-bro-sis *n.* A congenital disease, usually developing in childhood and resulting in disorders of the lungs and pancreas.

cys-ti-tis *n.* An inflammation of the bladder.

cy-tol-o-gy *n.* The scientific study of cell formation, function, and structure. cytological, cytologic *adj.,* cytologist *n.*

czar *n.* An emperor or king or one of the former emperors or kings of Russia. *Slang* One who has authority.

D, d The fourth letter of the English alphabet; the Roman numeral for 500.

DA *abbr.* District Attorney.

dab *v.* To touch quickly with light, short strokes.

dab-ble *v.* To play in a liquid, as water, with the hands; to work in or play with in a minor way. **dabbler** *n.*

dachs-hund *n.* A small dog with very short legs, drooping ears, and a long body.

dad *n., Informal* Father.

dad-dy *n., pl.* **-dies** *Informal* Father.

dad-dy-long-legs *n.* An insect with very long legs and a rounded body that resembles a spider.

daf-fo-dil *n.* A bulbous plant with solitary yellow flowers.

daft *adj.* Insane; crazy; foolish. **daftly** *adv.*, **daftness** *n.*

dag-ger *n.* A pointed, short-edged weapon which is used for stabbing.

da-querre-o-type *n.* A very early photographic process which used silver-coated metallic plates that were sensitive to light.

dahl-ia *n.* A perennial plant having tuberous roots and showy purple, red, yellow, or white flowers.

dai-ly *adj., pl.* **-lies** To occur, appear, or happen every day of the week. *n.* A newspaper which is published daily.

dai-ly dou-ble *n.* A bet that is won by picking the winners of two specified races occurring on the same day.

dain-ty *adj., pl.* **-ties** Having or showing refined taste; delicately beautiful. **daintily** *adv.*, **daintiness** *n.*

dai-qui-ri *n.* A cocktail made with rum and lime juice.

dair-y *n., pl.* **-ies** A commercial establishment which processes milk for resale. **dairymaid**, **dairyman** *n.*

dai-sy *n., pl.* **-ies** A plant having flowers with yellow disks and white rays.

dale *n.* A small valley.

dal-ly *v.* To waste time; to dawdle; to flirt. **dallier**, **dalliance** *n.*

Dal-ma-tian *n.* A breed of dog with short, smooth white hair with black spots. *adj.* Pertaining to Dalmatia or its people.

dam *n.* A barrier constructed for controlling or raising the level of water; female animal who has had offspring.

dam-age *n.* An injury to person or property; in law, the compensation given for loss or injury. **damageable** *adj.*, **damagingly** *adv.*

dam-ask *n.* An elaborately patterned, reversible fabric, originally made of silk.

dame *n.* A mature woman or matron. *Slang* A woman. **Dame** *Brit.* A title given to a woman, the female equivalent of a British Lord.

damn *v.* To swear or curse at; to pronounce as bad, worthless, or a failure. **damnation**, **damnableness** *n.*

damp *adj.* Between dry and wet; of or relating to poisonous gas or foul air found in a mine. **dampish** *adj.*, **damply** *adv.*

dam-sel *n.* A maiden; a young unmarried woman.

dam-son *n.* The tree that produces an oval purple plum of the same name.

dance *v.* To move rhythmically to music using improvised or planned steps and gestures. **dance**, **dancer** *n.*

dan-de-lion *n.* A plant considered a weed in North America, having yellow flowers and green notched leaves, sometimes used in salads and in making wines.

dan-dle *v.* To move a child or infant up and down on the knees or in the arms with a gentle movement. **dandler** *n.*

dan-druff *n.* A scaly material which forms on the scalp and is shed from time to time.

dan-dy *n., pl.* **-dies** A man who is very interested in an elegant appearance and fine clothes. *Informal adj.* Excellent, very fine. **dandify** *v.*, **dandy**, **dandyish** *adj.*, **dandyism** *n.*

dan-ger *n.* An exposure to injury, evil, or loss.

dan-ger-ous *adj.* Unsafe. **dangerously** *adv.*, **dangerousness** *n.*

dan-gle *v.* To hang loosely and swing to and fro; to have an unclear grammatical relation in a sentence.

dank *adj.* Uncomfortably damp; wet and cold. **dankly** *adv.*, **dankness** *n.*

dan-seuse *n., pl.* **-seuses** A female ballet dancer.

dap-per *adj.* Stylishly dressed.

dap-ple *v.* To make variegated or spotted in color.

dare *v.* To have the boldness or courage to undertake an adventure; to challenge a person as to show proof of courage. **dare** *n.*, **daring** *adj.*, **daringly** *adv.*

dare-devil *n.* A person who is bold or reckless. **daredevilry**, **daredeviltry** *n.*

dark *adj.* Dim; to have little or no light; to be difficult to comprehend; of a deep shade of color, as black or almost black. **in the dark** To do in secret; to be in a state of ignorance.

Dark Ages *n.* The early part of the Middle Ages.

dark-en *v.* To become or make dark or darker. **darkish** *adj.*, **darkly** *adv.*

dar-ling *n.* A favorite person; someone who is very dear; a person tenderly loved. **darlingly** *adv.*, **darlingness** *n.*

darn *v.* To mend a hole by filling the gap with interlacing stitches. **darner** *n.*

dart *n.* A pointed missile either shot or thrown. **darts** *pl.* The game of throwing darts at a usually round target.

dash *v.* To break or shatter with a striking violent blow; to move quickly; to rush; to finish or perform a duty in haste. **dash**, **dasher** *n.*

das-tard *n.* A coward; a sneak. **dastardliness** *n.*, **dastardly** *adj.*

da-ta *pl., n.* The figures or facts from which conclusions may be drawn.

da-ta bank *n.* In computer science, the location in a computer where information is stored.

da-ta

da-ta pro-cess-ing *n.* In computer science, the business of handling and storing information using computers and other available machines.

date *n.* A particular point in time; a day, month, or year; the exact time at which something happens; a social engagement; a person's partner on such an occasion. **date** *v.*

date-line *n.* The line or phrase at the beginning of a periodical giving the date and place of publication; the 180th meridian on a map or globe which is where a day begins.

da-tum *n., pl.* -ta A single piece of information.

daub *v.* To coat or smear with grease, plaster, or an adhesive substance. **dauber** *n.*

daugh-ter *n.* The female offspring of a man or woman; a female descendant. **daughterly** *adj.*

daughter—in—law *n.* One's son's wife.

daunt *v.* To intimidate or discourage.

Davis, Jefferson *n.* President of the Confederate States of America, from 1861-1865.

dav-it *n.* A small crane on the side of a ship, for lifting its boats.

daw-dle *v.* To waste; to take more time than is needed. **dawdler** *n.*

dawn *n.* The beginning of a new day; to begin to understand, expand, or develop. **dawning** *n.*

day *n.* The period of time that falls between dawn and nightfall; the time that is represented by one rotation of the earth upon its axis, twenty-four hours; the large portion of a day spent in a particular way.

day-care *n.* A service provided for working mothers and fathers, offering daytime supervision, training, and safe keeping for their children while they work.

day-light sav-ings time *n.* The period of the year, beginning in the spring, when clocks are moved ahead by one hour.

Day of A-tone-ment *n.* Yom Kippur.

daze *v.* To bewilder or stun with a heavy blow or shock. **dazedly** *adv.*

DBA *abbr.* Doing business as.

DC *abbr.* District of Columbia.

D—Day *n., Milit.* June 6, 1944, the day on which the Allies invaded France in World War II.

dea-con *n.* The clergyman who ranks immediately below a priest. **deaconess, deaconry, deaconship** *n.*

dead *adj.* Without life; no longer in existence or use; dormant; quiet; in law, no longer in force.

dead-beat *n., Slang* A person who avoids paying his debts.

dead-end *n.* A point from which one cannot progress; a street having no outlet.

dead-eye *n.* A sharpshooter.

dead heat *n.* A contest where two or more entrants finish at the same time.

dead-line *n.* A time limit when something must be finished.

dead-ly *adj.* Very dangerous; likely to cause death.

dead pan *adj., Slang* Having no expression on one's face.

dead reck-on-ing *n., Naut.* A method of computing a vessel's position by compass and log without the use of astronomical observation.

Dead Sea *n.* The salt lake between Jordan and Israel.

deaf *adj.* Totally or partially unable to hear; refusing or unwilling to listen.

deal *v.* To distribute or pass out playing cards; to be occupied or concerned with a certain matter; to discuss, consider, or take affirmative action. *n.* An indefinite amount; a business transaction. **dealer** *n.*

deal-er-ship *n.* A franchise to sell a certain item in a specified area, as a car dealer.

deal-ing *n., Slang* Involved in the buying and selling of illegal drugs.

dean *n.* The head administrator of a college, high school, or university. **deanship** *n.*

dear *adj.* Greatly cherished; loved. **dearly** *adv.*, **dearness** *n.*

death *n.* Termination; the permanent cessation of all vital functions.

death-bed *n.* The bed on which a person dies; the last hours.

death-blow *n.* An event or blow that is fatal.

death-cup *n.* A poisonous mushroom.

death-less *adj.* Immortal; not subject to death.

death-ly *adj.* Fatal; causing death.

death rate *n.* Ratio of deaths to the population of a certain area.

death-trap *n.* An unsafe structure.

death-watch *n.* A vigil kept on a person who is dying.

de-ba-cle *n.* A sudden downfall, failure, or collapse.

de-bark *v.* To disembark.

de-base *v.* To lower in character or value; demean. **debasement** *n.*

de-bate *v.* To discuss or argue opposing points; to consider; to deliberate. **debatable** *adj.*, **debatably** *adv.*

de-bauch *v.* To lead away from morals; to corrupt. **debauchery, -ment** *n.*

de-ben-ture *n.* A voucher given as an acknowledgment of debt.

de-bil-i-tate *v.* To make feeble or weak. **debilitation** *n.*, **debilitative** *adj.*

deb-it *n.* A debt or item recorded in an account. *v.* To enter a debt in a ledger.

de-brief *v.* To interrogate or question in order to obtain information.

de-bris *n.* Scattered or discarded remains or waste.

debt *n.* That which someone owes, as money, services, or goods; an obligation to pay or render something to another.

debt-or *n.* A person owing a debt to another.

de-bug *v.* To find and remove a concealed electronic listening device; in computer science, to remove errors in a computer program.

de-bunk *v.*, *Informal* To expose false pretensions.

de-but *n.* A first public appearance; the formal introduction to society; the beginning of a new career. debut *v.*

deb-u-tante *n.* A young woman making her debut in society.

dec-ade *n.* A period of ten years; a set or group of ten.

de-ca-dence *n.* A process of decay or deterioration; a period or condition of decline, as in morals. decadent *adj.*, decadently *adv.*

de-caf-fein-at-ed *adj.* Having the caffeine removed.

dec-a-gon *n.*, *Geom.* A polygon with ten sides and ten angles. decagonal *adj.*, decagonally *adv.*

dec-a-gram *or* **del-a-gram** *n.* In the metric system, a measure of weight equal to 10 grams.

de-cal *n.* A design or picture transferred by decalcomania.

de-cal-co-ma-ni-a *n.* The process of transferring pictures or designs printed on special paper to glass, wood, and other materials.

dec-a-li-ter *or* **dek-a-li-ter** *n.* In the metric system, a measure of capacity equal to 10 liters.

dec-a-logue *or* **dec-a-log** *n.* The Ten Commandments.

dec-a-me-ter *or* **dek-a-me-ter** *n.* In the metric system, a measure of length equal to 10 meters.

de-camp *v.* To break camp; to leave or depart suddenly.

de-cant *v.* To pour off liquid without disturbing the sediments; to pour from one container to another. decantation *n.*

de-cant-er *n.* A decorative stoppered bottle for serving wine or other liquids.

de-cap-i-tate *v.* To cut off the head; to behead. decapitation, decapitator *n.*

de-cath-lon *n.* An athletic event with ten different track and field events in all of which each contestant participates.

de-cay *v.* To decline in quantity or quality; to rot. *Phys.* To diminish or disintegrate by radioactive decomposition.

de-cease *v.* To die. decedent *n.*, deceased *adj.*

de-ceit *n.* Deception; the quality of being deceptive; falseness. deceitful *adj.*, deceitfully *adv.*

de-ceive *v.* To mislead by falsehood; to lead into error; to delude. deceivable *adj.*, deceiver *n.*

de-cel-er-ate *v.* To decrease in velocity. deceleration, decelerator *n.*

De-cem-ber *n.* The 12th month of the year, having 31 days.

de-cen-ni-al *adj.* Happening once every 10 years; continuing for ten years. decennially *adv.*

de-cent *adj.* Adequate; satisfactory; kind; generous; characterized by propriety of conduct, speech, or dress; respectable. *Informal* Properly or adequately clothed. decently *adv.*, decentness *n.*

de-cen-tral-ize *v.* To divide the administrative functions of a central authority among several local authorities; to reorganize into smaller and more dispersed parts. decentralization *n.*

de-cep-tion *n.* The act of deceiving; the fact or state of being deceived; anything which deceives or deludes.

de-cep-tive *adj.* Having the tendency or power to deceive. deceptively *adv.*, deceptiveness *n.*

dec-i-are *n.* In the metric system, one tenth of an are.

de-ci-bel *n.* A measurement of sound; one tenth of a bel.

de-cide *v.* To settle; to determine, as a controversy or contest; to determine the conclusion or issue of; to make up one's mind. decider *n.*

de-cid-ed *adj.* Definite or unquestionable; exhibiting determination. decidedly *adv.*, decidedness *n.*

de-cid-u-ous *adj.*, *Biol.* Shedding or falling off at maturity or at a certain season, such as fruit, leaves, petals, antlers, or snake skins.

dec-i-gram *n.* In the metric system, the tenth part of a gram.

dec-i-li-ter *n.* In the metric system, the tenth part of a liter.

de-cil-lion *n.* The cardinal number written as one followed by thirty-three zeros; a thousand nonillions. decillionth *adj. & n.*

dec-i-mal *n.* A proper fraction based on the number 10 and indicated by the use of a decimal point; every decimal place indicating a multiple of a power of 10; a number with a decimal point; a decimal fraction or one of its digits. decimally *adv.*

de-c-i-mal point *n.* A period placed to the left of a decimal fraction.

dec-i-mate *v.* To destroy or kill a large proportion of something; to select by lot and kill one out of every ten. decimation *n.*

dec-i-meter *n.* In the metric system, the tenth part of a meter.

de-ci-pher *v.* To determine the meaning of something obscure, as a poor handwriting; to translate from code or cipher into plain text; to decode. decipherable *adj.*

de-ci-sion *n.* The act of deciding; a judgment or conclusion reached by deciding; in boxing, a victory decided when there has not been a knockout.

de-ci-sive *adj.* Ending uncertainty or dispute; conclusive; characterized by firmness; unquestionable; unmistakable. decisively *adv.*

dec-i-stere *n.* In the metric system, a cubic decimeter, or the tenth part of a stere.

deck *n.* A set of playing cards. *Naut.* A

horizontal platform that covers or extends across a vessel, and serves as both a floor and a roof. **hit the deck** To rise from bed; to get up early; to be ready for action. **on deck** Present and ready for action. **all decked out** To decorate or dress elegantly. v. To knock someone or something down with a punch.

deck hand or **deck-hand** n. A member of a ship's crew assigned to work on deck.

de-claim v. To speak or deliver loudly and rhetorically; to give a formal speech; to attack verbally. **declamation** n., **declamatory** adj.

de-clare v. To make known or clear; to state formally or officially; to say emphatically; to avow; to assert; to make full claim to, as goods liable to duty; to proclaim an opinion or choice for or against something. **declarer**, **declaration** n., **declarative** adj.

de-clas-si-fy v. To remove the security classification of a document. **declassification** n.

de-clen-sion n. A descent; a sloping downward; a decline; a deviation, as from a belief. *Gram.* The inflection of nouns, pronouns, and adjectives according to case, number, and gender. **declensional** adj.

dec-li-na-tion n. The act of bending downward or inclining; deviation, as in conduct or direction; the angle formed between the direction of a compass needle and the true north; a polite refusal.

de-cline v. To reject or refuse something; to grow frail gradually, as in health; to bend or incline to the side or downward; to refuse politely. *Gram.* To give the inflected form of a noun, pronoun, or adjective. n. The act or result of deterioration. **declinable**, **declinational** adj., **declination**, **decliner**, **decline** n.

de-cliv-i-ty n., pl. -ties A steep downward slope or surface. **declivitous**, **declivous** adj.

de-coct v. To extract by boiling; to condense. **decoction** n.

de-code v. To convert from a coded message into plain language. **decoder** n.

de-com-pose v. To decay; to separate into constituent parts. -able adj., **decomposer**, **decomposition** n.

de-com-press v. To relieve of pressure; to bring a person back to normal air pressure, as divers or caisson workers. **decompression** n.

de-con-ges-tant n. An agent that relieves congestion.

de-con-tam-i-nate v. To make free of contamination by destroying or neutralizing poisonous chemicals, radioactivity, or other harmful elements. -tion, **decontaminator** n.

de-con-trol v. To free from the control of, especially from governmental control.

de-cor n. The style of decorating a room, office, or home.

dec-o-rate v. To adorn or furnish with fashionable or beautiful things; to confer a decoration or medal upon. **decorator** n.

dec-o-ra-tion n. The process, art, or act of decorating; a thing or group of things which decorate; an emblem, badge, medal, or award.

Dec-o-ra-tion Day n. Memorial Day, the day set aside to honor all fallen soldiers with special services and flowers placed on their graves.

dec-o-ra-tive adj. Suitable for decoration; ornamental. **decoratively** adv., **decorativeness** n.

dec-o-rous adj. Marked by decorum; seemly; proper. **decorously** adv., **decorousness** n.

de-co-rum n. Proper behavior; good or fitting conduct.

de-coy n. An artificial animal used to lure game, especially ducks; a means to mislead, trap, or lure into danger.

de-crease v. To grow or cause to grow gradually less or smaller; to diminish. n. The process or act of decreasing or the resulting state; a decline.

de-cree n. An authoritative and formal order or decision; a judicial judgment.

dec-re-ment n. The process or act of decreasing; the amount lost by gradual waste or diminution. **decremental** adj.

de-crep-it adj. Broken down or worn out by old age or excessive use. **decrepitly** adv., **decrepitude** n.

de-cre-scen-do n., pl. -dos *Mus.* A gradual decrease in force or loudness. **decrescendo** adj. & adv.

de-crim-i-nal-ize v. To remove the criminal classification of; to no longer prohibit.

de-cry v. To disparage or condemn openly; to denounce. **decrier** n.

ded-i-cate v. To set apart, as for sacred uses; to set apart for special use, duty, or purpose; to address or inscribe a work of literature, art or music to someone; to commit oneself to a certain cause, course of action, or thought; to unveil or open to the public. **dedication** n., **dedicatory** adj.

de-duce v. To derive a conclusion by reasoning. **deducible** adj.

de-duct v. To subtract or take away from. **deductible** adj.

de-duc-tion n. The act of deducing or subtracting; an amount that is or may be deducted; the process or act of deducting. -tive adj., **deductively** adv.

deed n. Anything performed or done; a notable achievement or feat; in law, a legal document, especially one relating to the transference of property. **deedless** adj.

deem v. To judge or consider.

deep adj. Extending far below a surface; extending far backward from front to rear or far inward from an outer surface; penetrating to or coming from a depth; hard to understand; extreme; intense; vivid and rich in shade; low in

pitch; resonant. *n., Naut.* The interval between two fathoms marked in succession. **to go off the deep end** To become excited or hysterical. **the deep** *Poet.* The ocean or sea.
deep-ly *adv.,* **deepness** *n.*

deep-en *v.* To become or make deep or deeper.

deep-freeze *v.* To quick-freeze. *Slang* An appliance for storing frozen foods.

deep-root-ed *adj.* Firmly implanted, said of beliefs; of or relating to a plant with very long roots.

deep-six *v., Slang* To throw overboard; to get rid of; to toss out.

deer *n., pl.* **deer**

A hoofed ruminant mammal having deciduous antlers, usually in the male only, as the elk, moose, and reindeer.

deer fly *n.* Any of the various bloodsucking flies.

deer-skin *n.* A deer's hide or the leather made from it.

de-es-ca-late *v.* To decrease or be decreased gradually, as in intensity, scope, or effect.

de-face *v.* To spoil or mar the appearance or surface of something.

de fac-to *adj.* Really or actually exercising authority.

de-fal-cate *v.* To embezzle; to misuse funds. **defalcation** *n.*

de-fame *v.* To slander or libel.
defamation, defamatory *adj.,* **-er** *n.*

de-fault *v.* To neglect to fulfill an obligation or requirement, as to pay money due or to appear in court; to forfeit by default. *n.* The failure to participate or compete in a competition. **defaulter** *n.*

de-feat *v.* To win a victory; to beat; to prevent the successful outcome of; to frustrate; to baffle; in law, to make void; to annul.

de-feat-ism *n.* The practice of those accepting defeat as inevitable.
defeatist *n. & adj.*

def-e-cate *v.* To discharge feces from the bowels. **defecation, defecator** *n.*

de-fect *n.* The lack of something desirable or necessary for completeness or perfection; a fault or imperfection. **defection, defector** *n.*

de-fec-tive *adj.* Having a defect; imperfect. *Gram.* Lacking one or more of the infected forms normal for its class. *Psychol.* Having less than normal intelligence. **-ly** *adv.,* **defectiveness** *n.*

de-fend *v.* Protect.

de-fend-ant *n.* The person charged in a criminal or civil lawsuit.

de-fense *n.* The action of defending.

de-fer *v.* To delay or postpone.
deferment *n.*

de-fi-ance *n.* The instance or act of defy-

ing; a challenge. **defiant** *adj.,* **-ly** *adv.*

de-fi-cient *adj.* Lacking in a necessary element.

def-i-cit *n.* Deficiency in amount.

de-flate *v.* To cause to collapse by removing gas or air; to remove self-esteem or conceit. *Econ.* To reduce or restrict money or spending so that prices decline.
deflation *n.,* **deflationary** *adj.*

de-flect *v.* To turn aside; to swerve from a course. **deflectable,**
deflective *adj.,* **deflection, deflector** *n.*

de-flower *v.* To rob one's virginity; to violate; to rob of charm or beauty.

de-fog *v.* To remove fog from, as from the inside of an automobile.
defogger *n.*

de-fo-li-ant *n.* A chemical sprayed or dusted on plants or trees to cause the leaves to drop off. **defoliate** *v.*

de-for-est *v.* To clear of forests or trees.
deforestation *n.*

de-form *v.* To distort the form of; to be distorted; to mar the beauty or excellence of; to spoil the natural form of.
deformable *adj.,* **deformation** *n.*

de-fraud *v.* To cheat; to swindle. **-er** *n.*

de-fray *v.* To provide for or to make payment on something.
defrayable *adj.,* **defrayal** *n.*

de-frost *v.* To cause to thaw out; to remove the ice or frost from. **-er** *n.*

deft *adj.* Skillful and neat in one's actions. **deftly** *adv.,* **deftness** *n.*

de-funct *adj.* Dead; deceased.
defunctive *adj.,* **defunctness** *n.*

de-fuse *v.* To remove the detonator or fuse from; to remove or make less dangerous, tense, or hostile.

de-fy *v., pl.* **-fies** To confront or resist boldly and openly; to challenge someone to do something or not do something; to dare. **defier** *n.*

deg *abbr.* Degree.

de-gauss *v.* To neutralize the magnetic field of something.

de-gen-er-ate *v.* To decline in quality, value, or desirability; to deteriorate; to become worse. *adj.* Morally depraved or sexually deviant. **degenerate,**
degeneracy *n.,* **-ly** *adv.,* **-ive** *adj.*

de-grade *v.* To reduce in rank, status, or grade; to demote; to reduce in quality or intensity. **degraded** *adj.,*
degradedly *adv.,* **degradedness** *n.*

de-gree *n.* One of a succession of stages and/or steps; relative manner, condition or respect; the academic title given by an institution of learning upon completion of a course of study or as an honorary distinction; a unit on a temperature or thermometer scale; in law, a measure of severity, as murder in the first degree. *Gram.* A form used in the comparison of adjectives and adverbs. **by degrees** Little by little. **to a degree** Somewhat.

de-horn *v.* To remove the horns from an animal.

de-hu-man-ize *v.* To deprive of human qualities, especially to make mechanical and routine.

de-hu-mid-i-fy *v.* To remove the moisture from. **dehumidifier** *n.*

de-hy-drate *v.* To cause to lose moisture or water. **dehydration** *n.*

de-ice *v.* To rid of or keep free of ice. **deicer** *n.*

de-i-fy *v.* To glorify or idealize; to raise in high regard; to worship as a god. **deification** *n.*

deign *v.* To think it barely worthy of one's dignity; to condescend.

De-i gra-ti-a *adv., L.* By the grace of God.

de-ism *n.* A belief in the existence of God but a denial of the validity of revelation. **deist** *n.*

de-ject *v.* To lower the spirits; to dishearten. **-ion, -edness** *n.,* **dejectedly** *adv.*

de-jec-tion *n.* The state or condition of being dejected; depression; melancholy.

de ju-re *adv., L.* By right; legally or rightfully.

deka- *or* **deca-** *combining form* In the metric system, ten times a specified unit.

dek-a-gram *n.* See decagram.

dek-a-liter *n.* See decaliter.

dek-a-meter *n.* See decameter.

dek-are *or* **dec-are** *n.* In the metric system, a thousand square meters or 10 ares.

dek-a-stere *or* **dec-a-stere** *n.* In the metric system, a measure of volume equal to 10 steres.

deke *v., Slang* In hockey, to outmaneuver an opponent by faking a shot or movement.

del *abbr.* Delete.

de-lay *v.* To put off until a later time; to defer; to cause to be late or detained; to linger; to waste time; to procrastinate. *n.* The time period that someone is delayed. **delayer** *n.*

de-le *n., Print.* A mark in typesetting which indicates something is to be deleted or taken out of the manuscript.

de-lec-ta-ble *adj.* Giving great pleasure; delightful; savory: delicious. **delectability** *n.*

de-lec-ta-tion *n.* Enjoyment or pleasure.

del-e-ga-tion *n.* The act of delegating or the state of being delegated; a person or group of people appointed to represent others.

de-lete *v.* To cancel; to take out. **-ion** *n.*

del-e-te-ri-ous *adj.* Causing moral or physical injury; harmful. **deleteriously** *adv.,* **deleteriousness** *n.*

delft *n.* A glazed earthenware, usually blue and white in color, originating in Delft, Holland, in 1310.

Del-hi *n.* A city in north central India.

del-i *n., Slang* A delicatessen.

de-lib-er-ate *v.* To say or do something intentionally; to plan in advance. *adj.* Premeditated; to be leisurely or slow in manner or motion. **deliberateness, deliberation** *n.,* **deliberately** *adv.,* **deliberative** *adj.*

del-i-ca-cy *n., pl.* **-cies** A select or choice food; the quality or state of being delicate.

del-i-cate *adj.* Pleasing to the senses; exquisite and fine in workmanship, texture, or construction; pleasing, as in color, taste, or aroma; sensitive and subtle in perception, feeling, or expression; frail in constitution; easily broken or damaged; considerate of the feelings of others. **delicately** *adv.,* **delicateness** *n.*

del-i-ca-tes-sen *n.* A store which sells cooked meats, preserved cheeses, pickles, and other delicacies.

de-li-cious *adj.* Extremely enjoyable and pleasant to the taste. **deliciously** *adv.,* **deliciousness** *n.*

de-li-cious *n.* A variety of red, sweet apples.

de-light *n.* A great joy or pleasure. *v.* To give or take great pleasure; to rejoice; to gratify or please highly. **delighted** *adj.,* **delightedly** *adv.*

de-light-ful *adj.* Extremely pleasing. **delightfully** *adv.,* **delightfulness** *n.*

de-lim-it *v.* To give or prescribe the limits of.

de-lin-e-ate *v.* To represent by a drawing; to draw or trace the outline of something; to sketch; to represent in gestures or words. **delineation** *n.*

de-lin-quent *adj.* Neglecting to do what is required by obligation or law; falling behind in a payment. *n.* A juvenile who is out of control, as violating the law. **delinquency, delinquent** *n.,* **delinquently** *adv.*

del-i-quesce *v., Chem.* To become liquid by absorbing atmospheric moisture; to melt. **deliquescent** *adj.*

de-lir-i-um *n.* A temporary or sporadic mental disturbance associated with fever, shock, or intoxication and marked by excitement, incoherence, and hallucination; uncontrolled excitement and emotion. **delirious** *adj.,* **deliriously** *adv.,* **deliriousness** *n.*

de-lir-i-um tre-mens *n.* Acute delirium resulting from chronic and excessive use of alcohol.

de-liv-er *v.* To surrender; to hand over; to set free; to liberate; to give or send forth; to assist in the birth of an offspring; to do what is expected or desired; to take to the intended recipient. to be delivered of To give birth. **deliverable** *adj.,* **deliverance, deliverer** *n.*

de-liv-er-y *n., pl.* **-ies** The act of conveying or delivering; a transferring or handing over; the process or act of giving birth, as parturition; the act or manner of throwing.

dell *n.* A small, secluded, usually wooded valley.

del-phin-ium *n.* Any of a genus of perennial plants of the crowfoot with spurred flowers which are usually blue.

del-ta *n.* The fourth letter in the Greek alphabet; a typically triangular-shaped silt deposit at or in the mouth of a river; anything triangular in shape.

del-ta ray *n.* An electron ejected from matter ionizing radiation.

del-ta wing *n.* An aircraft with wings that sweep back.

de-lude *v.* To mislead the mind or judgment; to deceive; to cause to be deceived.

del-uge *v.* To flood with water; to overwhelm; to destroy. *n.* A great flood.

de-lu-sion *n.* A false, fixed belief held in spite of contrary evidence. **delusional, delusive** *adj.*

de luxe *or* **de-luxe** *adj.* High elegance or luxury.

delve *v.* To search for information with careful investigation.

Dem *abbr.* Democratic; Democrat.

de-mag-net-ize *v.* To remove the magnetic properties of. **-ation** *n.*

dem-a-gogue *n.* A person who leads the populace by appealing to emotions and prejudices. **demagoguery, demagogy** *n.*

de-mand *v.* To ask for in a firm tone; to claim as due; to have the need or requirement for; in law, to summon to court; to make a formal claim to property. *Econ.* The ability and desire to purchase something; the quantity of merchandise wanted at a certain price. **in demand** Sought after; desired. **on demand** On request or presentation; a note payable whenever the lender demands it. **-able** *adj.*, **demander** *n.*

de-mar-cate *v.* To set boundaries or limits; to separate or limit. **-tion** *n.*

de-mean *v.* To behave or conduct oneself in a particular manner; to degrade; to humble oneself or another.

de-mean-or *n.* A person's conduct toward others; a person's general behavior.

de-ment-ed *adj.* Insane.

de-men-tia *n.* An irreversible deterioration of intellectual faculties.

de-mer-it *n.* A fault; a defect; a mark against one's record, especially for bad conduct in school.

de-mesne *n.* A manor house with the adjoining lands; a domain; a region; in law, lands held in one's own power.

dem-i-god *n.* A mythological, semidivine being, especially the offspring of a mortal and a god.

dem-i-john *n.* A large, narrow-necked bottle usually enclosed in wicker.

de-mil-i-ta-rize *v.* To remove the military characteristics from. **-ation** *n.*

dem-i-mon-daine *n.* A woman who belongs to the demimonde.

dem-i-monde *n.* A class of women who are supported by wealthy protectors or lovers.

de-mise *n.* Death; in law, a transfer of an estate by lease or will.

dem-i-tasse *n.* A small cup of very strong coffee; the name of the cup used to hold this beverage.

dem-o *n., pl.* **-os** *Slang* A demonstration to show product use and purpose.

de-mo-bi-lize *v.* To disband; to release from the military service.

de-moc-ra-cy *n., pl.* **-cies** A form of government exercised either directly by the people or through their elected representatives; rule by the majority; the practice of legal, political, or social equality.

dem-o-crat *n.* One who prefers a democracy; one who believes in social and political equality. *adj.* Marked by or advocating democracy. **democratically** *adv.*, **democratize** *v.*

de-mog-ra-phy *n.* Study of the characteristics of human population, such as growth, size, and vital statistics. **-ic** *adj.*, **demographically** *adv.*

de-mol-ish *v.* To tear down; to raze; to completely do away with; to end. **demolisher, demolishment** *n.*

dem-o-li-tion *n.* The process of demolishing, especially destruction with explosives.

de-mon *n.* An evil spirit; a devil. *Informal* A person of great skill or zeal. **demonic** *adj.*

de-mon-e-tize *v.* To deprive the currency of its standard value; to withdraw currency from use. **demonetization** *n.*

de-mo-ni-ac *adj.* Like or befitting a demon; to be influenced or possessed by or as by demons; of, resembling, or suggestive of a demon.

de-mon-ol-o-gy *n.* The belief or study in demons.

de-mon-stra-ble *adj.* Obvious or apparent. **demonstrability** *n.*, **-ably** *adv.*

dem-on-strate *v.* To show or prove by reasoning or evidence; to make a public protest. **-tion, demonstrator** *n.*

de-mon-stra-tive *adj.* Serving to point out or demonstrate; able to prove beyond any doubt; conclusive and convincing. *Gram.* Indicating the object or person referred to; a demonstrative pronoun. **-ly** *adv.*, **demonstrativeness** *n.*

de-mor-al-ize *v.* To undermine the morale or confidence of someone; to degrade; to corrupt. **-ation, -er** *n.*

de-mote *v.* To reduce in rank, grade, or position. **demotion** *n.*

de-mul-cent *n.* A soothing substance. **demulcent** *adj.*

de-mur *v.* To take issue; to object. **-ral** *n.*

de-mure *adj.* Reserved and modest; coy. **demurely** *adv.*

de-murrer *n.* In law, a plea to dismiss a lawsuit on the grounds that the plaintiff's statements are insufficient to prove claim.

den *n.* The shelter for a wild animal; a small room in a home used for private study or relaxation.

de-na-ture *v.* To change the nature or natural qualities of, especially to make unfit for consumption. **denaturant, denaturation** *n.*

den-drite *n., Physiol.* The branching process of a nerve cell which conducts impulses toward the cell body. **dendritic** *adj.*, **dendritically** *adv.*

den-drol-ogy *n.* The botanical study of trees.

den-gue *n., Pathol.* An infectious tropical disease transmitted by mosquitoes, characterized by severe joint pains and fever.

de-ni-al *n.* A refusal to comply with a request; refusal to acknowledge the truth of a statement; abstinence; self-denial.

den-i-grate *v.* To slander; to defame.

den-im *n.* A strong, twilled cotton used for jeans, overalls, and work clothes.

Den-mark *n.* A country of northern Europe consisting of an archipelago and a peninsula between the Baltic and North seas.

de-nom-i-nate *v.* To give a name to; to designate.

de-nom-i-na-tion *n.* The name of a group or classificatio

denomination the act of calling by name or naming; an organization of similar religious congregations. -al *adj.*

de-nom-i-na-tor *n.* In mathematics, the term for the bottom half of a fraction, which indicates the number of equal parts into which the unit is divided; a common characteristic or trait.

de-no-ta-tion *n.* The meaning of, or the object or objects designated by a word; an indication, as a sign.

de-note *v.* To make known; to point out; to indicate; to signify; to designate; to mean, said of symbols or words. denotable, denotative *adj.*

de-noue-ment *n.* The final solution of a novel, play, or plot.

de-nounce *v.* To attack or condemn openly and vehemently; to accuse formally; to announce the ending of something in a formal way. -er *n.*

dense *adj.* Compact; thick; close; slow to understand; stupid. -ly *adv.*, -ness *n.*

den-si-ty *n., pl.* -ties The state or quality of being dense or close in parts; the quantity or amount of something per unit measure, area, volume, or length.

dent *n.* A small surface depression made by striking or pressing. *v.* To put adent in something; to make meaningful progress or headway.

den-tal *adj.* Pertaining to the teeth; of or pertaining to dentistry.

den-tal floss *n.* A strong thread, either waxed or unwaxed, used to clean between the teeth.

den-tal hy-gien-ist *n.* A licensed dental professional who provides preventive dental care, as cleaning and instruction on how to care for teeth at home.

den-ti-frice *n.* A preparation in powder or paste form for cleaning the teeth.

den-tine *or* **den-tin** *n.* The hard, calcified part of the tooth beneath the enamel, containing the pulp chamber and root canals.

den-tist *n.* A licensed person whose profession is the diagnosis, treatment, and prevention of diseases of the gums and teeth. dentistry *n.*

den-ti-tion *n.* The kind, number, and arrangement of teeth, as in humans and other animals; the process of cutting teeth.

den-ture *n.* A set of artificial teeth either partial or full; also called a dental plate.

de-nude *v.* To remove all covering; to be or cause to be naked. *Geol.* To come into view by erosion. denudation *n.*

de-nun-ci-a-tion *n.* Open disapproval of a person or action; an accusation; warning or threat.

Den-ver *n.* The capital of the state of Colorado.

de-ny *v.* To declare untrue; to refuse to acknowledge or recognize; to withhold; to refuse to grant. **to deny oneself** To refuse oneself something desired; self-denial.

de-o-dor-ant *n.* A product designed to prevent, mask, or destroy unpleasant odors.

de-o-dor-ize *v.* To destroy, modify, or disguise the odor of. deodorization, deodorizer *n.*

de-ox-i-dize *v.* To remove the oxygen from; to reduce from the state of an oxide. deoxidization, deoxidizer *n.*

de-ox-y-ri-bo-nu-cle-ic acid *n.* A nucleic acid which forms a principal constituent of the genes and is known to play a role of importance in the genetic action of the chromosomes, also known as DNA.

de-part *v.* To leave; to go away; to deviate.

de-part-ment *n.* The distinct division or part of something, as in a business, college, or store. *Informal* An area of special activity or knowledge. -al *adj.*

de-part-men-tal-ize *v.* To divide into organized departments. -ation *n.*

de-part-ment store *n.* A large retail store selling various types of merchandise and services.

de-par-ture *n.* The act of taking leave or going away; a divergence; a deviation; the act of starting out on a new course of action or going on a trip.

de-pend *v.* To rely on; to trust with responsibilities; to be determined or conditioned.

de-pend-a-ble *adj.* Capable of being depended upon; trustworthy. dependability, -ness *n.*, -y *adv.*

de-pend-ence *or* **de-pend-ance** *n.* The quality or state of being dependent; trust or reliance; the state of being contingent on or determined by something else.

de-pend-en-cy *or* **de-pend-an-cy** *n., pl.* -cies The state of being dependent; a territory separate from but still subject to another state, territory, or country.

de-pend-ent *adj.* Depending or needing the help of another for support; determined by or contingent on something or someone else. *n., also* **de-pend-ant** A person who depends on another person for financial support. -ly *adv.*

de-pict *v.* To represent in a sculpture or a picture; to describe or represent in words. **depiction** n.

dep-i-late v. To remove the hair from. **depilation, depilator** n.

de-pil-a-to-ry n., pl. -ries A chemical which removes hair, usually in cream or liquid form.

de-plete v. To exhaust, empty, or use up a supply of something. **depletion** n.

de-plor-a-ble adj. Grievous; lamentable; very bad; wretched. **deplorably** adv.

de-plore v. To have, show, or feel great disapproval of something.

de-ploy v. To spread out; to place or position according to plans. -ment n.

de-po-lit-i-cize v. To remove the political status or aspect from.

de-po-nent n. A person who testifies under oath giving sworn testimony, especially in writing.

de-pop-u-late v. To quickly remove or lower the population greatly, as by massacre or disease. **depopulation** n.

de-port v. To banish or expel someone from a country; to behave in a specified manner. -ation, **deportee** n.

de-port-ment n. One's conduct; behavior.

de-pose v. To remove from a powerful position or office; in law, to declare or give testimony under oath. **deposable** adj., **deposal** n.

de-pos-it v. To put, place, or set something down; to entrust money to a bank; to put down in the form of a layer, as silt; to give as security or partial payment. **deposit, depositor** n.

dep-o-si-tion n. The act of deposing, as from an office; that which is deposited; in law, written testimony given under oath.

de-pos-i-to-ry n., pl. -ries A place where anything is deposited for safekeeping.

de-pot n. A railroad station. *Milit.* The place where military materials are manufactured, stored, and repaired; an installation for processing personnel; a warehouse or storehouse.

de-prave v. To render bad or worse; in morals, to corrupt or pervert. **depraved** adj., **depravity** n.

dep-re-cate v. To express regret for or disapproval of; to belittle. **deprecatingly** adv., -ion, **deprecator** n.

de-pre-ci-ate v. To lessen in value or price. **depreciator** n., **depreciative, depreciatory** adj.

de-pre-ci-a-tion n. A loss in efficiency or value resulting from age or usage; the decline in the purchasing value of money.

de-press v. To make gloomy; to lower the spirits of; to lessen in energy or vigor; to press down; to lower; to diminish in value or price. -or n.

de-pres-sant adj. Acting to lower the nervous or functional activities. n. A sedative; a depressant agent.

de-pres-sed adj. Dejected; sad; low in spirits; lower than, even with, or below the surface; reduced in amount, value, or power.

de-pres-sion n. The state of being or the act of depressing; a severe decline in business, accompanied by increasing unemployment and falling prices. *Psych.* A condition of deep dejection characterized by lack of response to stimulation and withdrawal.

de-pres-sive adj. Tending to depress; related to psychological depression. **depressively** adv.

de-prive v. To take something away from; to keep from using, acquiring, or enjoying. **deprivable** adj.

depth n. The degree or state of being deep; the distance or extent backward, downward, or inward; the most intense part of something; intensity or richness of sound or color; the range of one's comprehension. **depths** pl. A deep part or place; an intense state of feeling or being.

dep-u-ta-tion n. A person or persons who are acting for another or others; the act of deputing or the state of being deputed.

de-pute v. To appoint as a deputy, an agent, or other figure of authority; to delegate; to transfer.

dep-u-tize v. To act as a deputy; to appoint as a deputy.

dep-u-ty n., pl. -ties The person designated or authorized to act for in the absence of, or to assist another, generally a sheriff; a member of a legislative body in certain countries.

de-rail v. To run off the rails; to cause a train to run off the rails. **derailment** n.

de-range v. To disturb the arrangement or normal order of; to unbalance the reason; to make insane. -ment n.

der-by n., pl. -bies An annual horse race especially for 3-year-olds; a race open to all contestants; a stiff hat made from felt with a round crown and a narrow, curved brim.

de-reg-u-late v. To decontrol or remove from regulation or control. -ion n.

der-e-lict adj. Neglectful of obligations; remiss. n. Abandoned or deserted, as a ship at sea; a vagrant; a social outcast.

der-e-lic-tion n. Voluntary neglect, as of responsibility; the fact or state of being abandoned.

de-ride v. To ridicule; to treat with scornful mirth. **derider, derision** n., **deridingly** adv., **derisive** adj.

de ri-gueur adj. Prescribed or required by manners, custom, or fashion.

der-i-va-tion n. The act of or process of deriving; the process used to form new words by the addition of affixes to roots, stems, or words.

de-riv-a-tive adj. Of or relating to something derived.

de-rive v. To receive or obtain from a source. *Chem.* To produce a compound from other substances by chemical reaction.

der-mal or **der-mic** adj. Relating to or of the skin.

der-ma-ti-tis n., *Pathol.* An inflammation of the skin.

der-ma-tol-o-gy n. The medical study of the skin and the diseases related it.

dermatologist *n.*

der-o-gate *v.* To take or cause to take away from; to distract; to cause to become inferior. derogation *n.*

de-rog-a-tory *adj.* Having the effect of belittling; lessening. derogatorily *adv.*

der-ri-ere *n.* The buttocks.

der-ring--do *n.* A courageous or daring action or spirit.

der-rin-ger *n.* A short-barreled, large-bored, pocket-sized pistol.

des-cant *v.* To play or sing a varied melody.

de-scend *v.* To move from a higher to a lower level; to pass through inheritance; to come from a particular family. *Astron.* Moving toward the horizon.

de-scen-dent *n.* One who descends from another individual; an offspring.

de-scen-dant *or* de-scen-dent *adj.* Proceeding downward; descending from an ancestor.

de-scent *n.* A slope; lowering or decline, as in level or status.

de-scribe *v.* To explain in written or spoken words; to draw or trace the figure of. describable *adj.*, describer *n.*

de-scrip-tion *n.* The technique or act of describing; an account or statement that describes. descriptive *adj.*

de-scry *v.* To catch sight of; to discover by observation. descrier *n.*

des-e-crate *v.* To violate something sacred, turning it into something common or profane. desecration *n.*

de-seg-re-gate *v.* To remove or eliminate racial segregation in. desegregation *n.*

de-sen-si-tize *v.* To make less sensitive; to eliminate the sensitivity of an individual, tissue, or organ, as to an allergen. desensitizer, desensitization *n.*

des-ert *v.* To abandon or forsake. *Milit.* To be absent without leave with the plan of not returning, AWOL. *n.* A dry, barren region incapable of supporting any considerable population or vegetation without an artificial water supply.

de-ser-tion *n.* The act of deserting or leaving; in law, the willful abandonment of one's spouse, children, or both.

de-serve *v.* To be worthy of or entitled to.

de-served *adj.* Merited; earned. deserving *adj.*, deservingly *adv.*

des-ic-cant *n.* A silica gel used to absorb moisture; any material used to absorb moisture.

des-ic-cate *v.* To preserve by drying, such as food; dehydrate. desiccation *n.*, desiccative *adj.*

de-sid-er-a-tum *n., pl.* -ta A desired and necessary thing.

de-sign *v.* To draw and sketch preliminary outlines; to invent or create in the mind; to have as an intention or goal. *n.* An artistic or decorative piece of work; a project; a plan; a well thoughtout intention. designedly *adv.*, designer *n.*

des-ig-nate *v.* To assign a name or title to; to point out; to specify; to appoint or select, as to an office. designate *adj.*, designation *n.*

de-sign-ing *adj.* Of or relating to the art or act of making designs; scheming or plotting; crafty. designingly *adv.*

de-sir-a-ble *adj.* Pleasing, attractive, or valuable; worthy of desire. desirability, desirableness *n.*

de-sire *v.* To long for; to wish; to crave; to request or ask for; to have sexual appetite.

de-sir-ous *adj.* Having a craving or strong desire.

de-sist *v.* To stop doing something; to cease from an action.

desk *n.*

A table or piece of furniture usually with drawers or compartments and a top for writing; a stand or table to hold reading materials; a department in a newspaper office, as the copy desk.

Des Moines *n.* The capital of the state of Iowa.

des-o-late *adj.* Made unfit for habitation; useless; forlorn; forsaken. desolately *adv.*

des-o-la-tion *n.* A wasteland; the condition of being ruined or deserted; loneliness.

de-spair *v.* To lose or give up hope; to abandon all purpose. despair *n.*, despairing *adj.*, despairingly *adv.*

des-per-a-do *n., pl.* -does *or* -dos A dangerous, desperate, or violent criminal.

des-per-ate *adj.* Rash, violent, reckless, and without care, as from despair; intense; overpowering.

des-per-a-tion *n.* The state of being desperate.

des-pi-ca-ble *adj.* Deserving scorn or contempt. despicably *adv.*

de-spise *v.* To regard with contempt; to regard as worthless. despiser *n.*

de-spite *prep.* Notwithstanding; in spite of.

de-spoil *v.* To rob; to strip of property or possessions by force. despoiler, despoilment, despoliation *n.*

de-spond *v.* To lose hope, courage, or spirit. despondently *adv.*

de-spon-den-cy *n.* A dejection of spirits from loss of courage or hope. despondent *adj.*

des-pot *n.* An absolute ruler; a tyrant. despotic *adj.*, despotically *adv.*, despotism *n.*

des-sert *n.* A serving of sweet food, as pastry, ice cream, or fruit, as the last course of a meal.

des-ti-na-tion *n.* The point or place to which something or someone is directed; the purpose or end for which something is created or intended.

des-tine *v.* To be determined in advance;

to design or appoint a distinct purpose. **destined** *adj.*

des-ti-ny *n., pl.* **-nies** The inevitable loss or fate to which a person or thing is destined; fate; a predetermined course of events.

des-ti-tute *adj.* Utterly impoverished; not having; extremely poor. **destitution** *n.*

de-stroy *v.* To ruin; to tear down; to demolish; to kill; to make useless or ineffective.

de-stroy-er *n.* One that destroys. *Milit.* A small maneuverable warship.

de-struct *n., Aeros.* The deliberate destruction of a defective or dangerous missile or rocket after launch.

de-struc-ti-ble *adj.* Capable of being destroyed. **destructibility** *n.*

de-struc-tion *n.* The state of or the act of being destroyed. **destructive** *adj.*, **destructively** *adv.*, **destructiveness** *n.*

des-ue-tude *n.* A condition or state of disuse.

de-sul-fur-ize *v.* To remove sulfur from. **desulfurizer, desulfurizationer** *n.*

des-ul-to-ry *adj.* Something that occurs by chance; lacking continuity; aimless.

de-tach *v.* To unfasten, disconnect, or separate; to extricate oneself; to withdraw.

de-tached *adj.* Separate; apart.

de-tach-ment *n.* The process of separating. *Milit.* A shipment of military equipment or personnel from a larger unit for special duty.

de-tail *n.* A part or item considered separately. *Milit.* Military personnel selected for a particular duty.

de-tain *v.* To stop; to keep from proceeding; to delay.

de-tect *v.* To find out or perceive; to expose or uncover, as a crime. **detectable, detectible** *adj.*, **detection, detector** *n.*

de-tec-tive *n.* A person whose work is to investigate crimes, discover evidence, and capture criminals.

de-tent *n.* A pawl.

de-ten-tion *n.* The act of or state of being detained; in law, a time or period of temporary custody which precedes disposition by a court.

de-ter *v.* To prevent or discourage someone from acting by arousing fear, uncertainty, intimidation, or other strong emotion. **determent** *n.*

de-ter-gent *n.* A cleansing agent which is chemically different from soap. **detergency, detergence** *n.*

de-te-ri-o-rate *v.* To worsen; to depreciate. **deterioration** *n.*, **deteriorative** *adj.*

de-ter-mi-nate *adj.* Definitely fixed or limited; conclusive. *Bot.* The terminating in a bud or flower, as each axis of an inflorescence. **determinately** *adv.*, **determinateness** *n.*

de-ter-mine *v.* To settle or decide conclusively or authoritatively; to limit to extent or scope; to fix or ascertain; to give direction or purpose to; in law, to come to an end.

determinable *adj.*, **determinably** *adv.*, **determination** *n.*

de-ter-mined *adj.* Showing or having a fixed purpose; resolute; firm. **determinedly** *adv.*

de-ter-rent *n.* Something which deters. *adj.* Serving to deter. **deterrently** *adv.*

de-test *v.* To dislike strongly. **detestable** *adj.*, **detestably** *adv.*, **detestation** *n.*

de-throne *v.* To remove from the throne, to depose, as a king.

det-o-nate *v.* To explode suddenly and violently. **detonation** *n.*

det-o-na-tor *n.* The device, such as a fuse or percussion cap, used to detonate an explosive.

de-tour *n.* A road used temporarily instead of a main road; a deviation from a direct route or course of action.

de-tox-i-fy *v.* To free oneself from dependence on drugs or alcohol. **detoxification** *n.*

de-tract *v.* To take away from; to diminish; to divert. **detraction, detractor** *n.*, **detractive** *adj.*

de-train *v.* To leave or cause to leave a railroad train. **detrainment** *n.*

det-ri-ment *n.* Damage; injury; loss; something which causes damage, injury, or loss. **detrimental** *adj.*, **detrimentally** *adv.*

de-tri-tus *n.* Loose fragments or particles formed by erosion, glacial action, and other forces; debris.

deuce *n.* Two; a playing card or the side of a die with two spots or figures; in tennis, a tie in which each side has 40 points. *Informal* The devil, bad luck, or a mild oath.

De-us *n., L.* God.

deu-te-ri-um *n.* The isotope of hydrogen which contains one more neutron in its nucleus than hydrogen does.

Deu-ter-on-o-my *n.* The fifth book of the Old Testament.

deut-sche mark *n.* The standard monetary unit of East and West Germany, equivalent to 100 pfennigs.

de-val-u-ate *v.* To reduce or lessen the value of. **devaluation** *n.*

dev-as-tate *v.* To destroy; to ruin; to overwhelm; to overpower. **devastation** *n.*

de-vel-op *v.* To bring out or expand the potentialities; to make more elaborate; to enlarge; to advance from a lower to a higher stage or from an earlier to a later stage of maturation. *Photog.* To process an image upon a sensitized plate that has been exposed to the action of light. **developer, development** *n.*, **developmental** *adj.*

de-vi-ant *adj.* Anything which deviates from a norm, especially from an accepted standard. **deviance, deviant** *n.*

de-vi-ate *v.* To turn away from a specified prescribed behavior or course. **deviation** *n.*

de-vice *n.* Something constructed and used for a specific purpose, as a machine; a crafty or evil scheme or plan; an ornamental design; a motto or an emblem.

dev-il *or* **Devil** *n.* The spirit of evil, the ruler of Hell; Satan; a wicked or malevolent person; a daring, clever, and energetic person; a printer's apprentice, also called a printer's devil. the devil to pay Trouble to be expected as a consequence of something.

dev-il-fish *n., pl.* **-fishes** Any of the large cephalopods, as the octopus.

dev-il-ish *adj.* To resemble or have the characteristics of a devil. *Informal* Extreme.

dev-il-may-care *adj.* Reckless; careless.

dev-il-ment *n.* Mischief.

dev-il's ad-vo-cate *n.* One who argues about something with which he or she may not disagree, as for the sake of argument.

devil's food cake *n.* A chocolate cake made from dark chocolate, flour, and eggs.

dev-il-try *n., pl.* **-tries** Malicious mischief; cruelty or wickedness.

de-vi-ous *adj.* Leading away from the straight, regular, or direct course; rambling; straying from the proper way. *Slang* Underhanded. **deviously** *adv.*, **deviousness** *n.*

de-vise *v.* To form in the mind; to contrive; to plan; to invent; in law, to transmit or give by will. *n.* The act of bequeathing lands; a clause in a will conveying real estate.

de-vi-see *n.* In law, the person to whom a devise is made.

de-vi-sor *n.* In law, the person who devises property.

de-vi-tal-ize *v.* To make weak; to destroy the vitality. **devitalization** *n.*

de-void *adj.* Empty; utterly lacking; without.

de-voir *n.* The act or expression of courtesy or respect; duty or responsibility.

de-volve *v.* To pass duty or authority on to a successor.

de-vote *v.* To apply time or oneself completely to some activity, purpose, or cause. **devotement** *n.*

de-vot-ed *adj.* Feeling or showing devotion; set apart, as by a vow; consecrated. **devotedly** *adv.*, **devotedness** *n.*

dev-o-tee *n.* An enthusiastic supporter; one who is deeply devoted to anything; one marked by religious ardor.

de-vo-tion *n.* A strong attachment or affection, as to a person or cause; zeal or ardor in the performance of religious duties or acts; the state or act of being devoted. **devotional** *adj.*, **devotionally** *adv.*

de-vour *v.* To destroy or waste; to eat up greedily; to engulf. **devourer** *n.*

de-vout *adj.* Extremely and earnestly religious; showing sincerity; displaying piety or reverence. **devoutly** *adv.*, **devoutness** *n.*

dew *n.* Moisture condensed from the atmosphere in minute drops onto cool surfaces; something which is refreshing or pure.

dew-ber-ry *n.* The fruit of many species of trailing blackberries; the plant which bears such fruit.

dew-claw *n.* A rudimentary toe in some dogs and other mammals.

dew-lap *n.* The loose skin under the throat and neck of cattle and certain dogs.

dew point *n.* The temperature at which condensation of vapor occurs.

dex-ter-i-ty *n.* Proficiency or skill in using the hands or body; cleverness.

dex-ter-ous *or* **dex-trous** *adj.* Skillful or adroit in the use of the hands, body, or mind. **dexterously** *adv.*, **dexterousness** *n.*

dex-trose *n.* Sugar found in animal and plant tissue and derived synthetically from starches.

dia *abbr.* Diameter.

di-a-be-tes *n., Pathol.* A metabolic disorder characterized by deficient insulin secretion, leading to excess sugar in the urine and blood, extreme hunger, and thirst.

di-a-bet-ic *adj., Med.* Pertaining to, or affected with diabetes. **diabetic** *n.*

di-a-bol-ic *or* **di-a-bol-i-cal** *adj.* Wicked; proceeding from the devil; satanic or infernal. **diabolically** *adv.*, **-ness** *n.*

di-a-crit-ic *n.* A mark near or through a phonetic character or combination of characters, to indicate a special phonetic value or to distinguish words otherwise graphically identical. **diacritical, diacritic** *adj.*

di-a-dem *n.* A crown or headband worn to symbolize or indicate royalty or honor.

di-aer-e-sis *n.* Variation of dieresis.

di-ag-no-sis *n., pl.* **-ses** An analysis and examination to identify a disease; the result of diagnosis. **diagnose** *v.*, **diagnostic** *adj.*, **diagnostician** *n.*

di-ag-o-nal *adj.* In mathematics, joining two opposite corners of a polygon which are not adjacent. *n.* A diagonal or slanting plane or line. **diagonally** *adv.*

di-a-gram *n.* A sketch, plan, drawing, or outline designed to demonstrate or clarify the similarity among parts of a whole or to illustrate how something works. **diagram** *v.*, **diagrammatic, diagrammatical** *adj.*, **-ly** *adv.*

di-al *n.* Any graduated circular plate or face upon which a measurement, as pressure or temperature, is indicated by means of a needle or pointer; the face of a clock, watch, or sundial; a control for selecting a radio or television station. *v.* To make a call by means of a dial telephone.

di-a-lec-tic *n.* The act or practice of argument or exposition in which the conflict between contradictory facts or ideas is resolved. **dialectical, dialectic** *adj.*

di-a-logue *or* **dialog** *n.* A conversation involving two or more persons; a conversational passage in a literary work.

di-al-y-sis *n., pl.* **-ses** The separation of substances in solution, which is accomplished by passing them through membranes or filters. **kidney dialysis** A form of *dialysis* used to cleanse the blood of impurities and wastes when the kidneys are unable to perform this function.

di-am-e-ter *n.* In mathematics, a straight line which passes through the center of a circle or sphere and stops at the circumference or surface; a measurement of that distance.

di-a-met-ri-cal *or* **diametric** *adj.* Along or relating to a diameter; exactly opposite; contrary. **diametrically** *adv.*

dia-mond *n., pl.* **-s** A very hard, highly refractive, colorless, or white crystalline of carbon used as a gem; a playing card with a red, lozenge-shaped figure; a precious gem; in baseball, the shape of a baseball field.

dia-mond an-ni-ver-sa-ry *n.* The 60th or 75th anniversary.

dia-mond-back *n.* A large, venomous rattlesnake of the south and western United States and Mexico; an edible turtle of the southern United States.

Dia-mond State *n.* The nickname of the state of Delaware.

di-a-pa-son *n.* The full range of a voice or an instrument; in a pipe organ, either of two principal stops which form the tonal basis for the entire scale.

di-a-per *n.* A folded piece of soft, absorbent material placed between a baby's legs and fastened at the waist. *v.* To put a diaper on.

di-aph-a-nous *adj.* Of such fine texture as to be transparent or translucent; delicate. **diaphanously** *adv.*

di-a-phragm *n., Anat.* The muscular wall which separates the abdominal and thoracic cavities. *Photog.* The disk with an adjustable aperture that can control the amount of light which passes through the lens of a telescope, camera, etc.; a contraceptive device usually made of a rubber or rubberlike material and shaped like a cap to cover the uterine cervix.

di-ar-rhe-a *or* **di-ar-rhoe-a** *n., Pathol.* A disorder of the intestines causing excessively frequent, loose bowel movements.

di-a-ry *n., pl.* **-ries** A daily record, especially a personal record of one's activities, experiences, or observations; a journal; a book for keeping such records. **diarist** *n.*

di-as-to-le *n., Physiol.* The normal rhythmic dilatation and relaxation of the heart cavities during which they fill with blood. **diastolic** *adj.*

di-as-tro-phism *n., Geol.* Any of the processes through which the earth's crust, as mountains and continents, are formed.

di-a-ther-my *n., pl.* **-mies** *Med.* The generation of heat in the body tissues by high-frequency electromagnetic waves. **diathermic** *adj.*

di-a-tom *n.* Any of various tiny planktonic algae whose walls contain silica.

di-a-tom-ic *adj.* Having two atoms in a molecule.

di-a-ton-ic *adj., Mus.* Relating to a standard major or minor scale of eight tones without the chromatic intervals.

di-a-tribe *n.* A bitter, often malicious criticism or denunciation.

dib-ble *n.* A gardener's pointed tool used to make holes in soil, especially for planting bulbs or seedlings. **dibble** *v.*

dice *pl., n.*

Two or more small cubes of wood, bone, or ivory having the sides marked with dots from one to six; a game of chance. *v.* To gamble with dice; to cut food into small cubes.

di-chot-o-my *n., pl.* **-mies** A division into two mutually exclusive subclasses. *Bot.* The branching of something in which each successive axis forks into two equally developed branches. **dichotomous** *adj.*

di-chro-mate *n., Chem.* A chemical compound with two chromium atoms per anion.

di-chro-mat-ic *adj., Zool.* Having two color phases within the species apart from the changes due to age or sex. *Pathol.* Having the ability to see only two of the three primary colors.

Dickens, Charles John Huffam *n.* (1812-1870). English novelist.

dick-er *v.* To haggle or work towards a deal or bargain.

dick-ey *or* **dick-ie** *or* **dick-y** *n., pl.* **-eys** *or* **-ies** A woman's blouse front worn under a jacket or low-necked dress; the detachable shirtfront for a man; a small bird.

di-cot-y-le-don *n.* A plant which has two seed leaves. **dicotyledonous** *adj.*

dic-tate *v.* To read or speak aloud for another to record or transcribe; to give commands, terms, rules, or other orders with authority. *n.* A directive or guiding principle. **dictation** *n.*

dic-ta-ting ma-chine *n.* A phonographic machine which records and reproduces speech, as for dictation.

dic-ta-tor *n.* A person having absolute authority and supreme governmental powers; one who dictates. **dictatorship** *n.*

dic-ta-to-ri-al *adj.* Tending to dictate; relating to or characteristic of a dictator. **dictatorially** *adv.*

dic-tion *n.* The selection and arrangement of words in speaking and writing; the manner of uttering speech sounds.

dic-tion-ar-y *n., pl.* **-ies** A reference book containing alphabetically arranged words together with their definitions and usages.

dic-tum *n., pl.* **-ta** *or* **-tums** An authoritative or positive utterance; a pronouncement; a saying that is popular.

did *v.* Past tense of do.

di-dac-tic *or* **didactical** *adj.* Being inclined to teach or moralize excessively. **didactically** *adv.*, **didacticism** *n.*

did-dle *v.* To cheat; to swindle; to waste valuable time.

did-n't *contr.* Did not.

di-do *n., pl.* **-dos** *or* **-does** *Informal* A mischievous caper; an antic.

die *v.* To expire; to stop living; to cease to exist; to fade away; to cease operation or functioning, as an engine. **to die hard** To resist defeat or death to the end. **to die off** To be removed one after another by death.

die cast-ing *n.* The process of giving an alloy or metal a desired shape; the act of cutting, stamping, or shaping with or as with a die.

diel-drin *n.* A highly toxic and persistent chemical which is used as an insecticide.

di-e-lec-tric *n., Elect.* A nonconductor of electricity.

di-er-e-sis *n., pl.* **-ses** The mark over a vowel indicating that it is to be pronounced in a separate syllable.

die-sel *n.* A diesel engine or a vehicle driven by a diesel engine.

die-sel en-gine *n.* An internal-combustion engine in which an air-fuel mixture is ignited by the heat generated from the high compression in the cylinder.

die-sink-er *n.* A person who engraves metal dies.

di-et *n.* A regulated selection of food and drink, especially one followed for medical or hygienic reasons; something that is taken or provided regularly; an assembly or legislature.

di-e-tet-ics *pl., n.* The study of diet and or the regulations of a diet. **dietetical, dietetic** *adj.* **dietetically** *adv.*, **dietitian, -ian** *n.*

di-eth-yl-stil-bes-trol *n.* A synthetic estrogen used especially to treat menstrual disorders.

dif-fer *v.* To have different opinions; to disagree.

dif-fer-ence *n.* The quality, state, or degree of being different or unlike; a controversy or cause for a disagreement; in mathematics, the amount by which a number or quantity is less or greater than another.

dif-fer-ent *adj.* Not the same; separate; other; marked by a difference; unlike; differing from the ordinary. **differently** *adv.*, **differentness** *n.*

dif-fer-en-tia *n., pl.* **-tiae** A specific difference; something that distinguishes a species from others of the same genus.

dif-fer-en-tial *adj.* Relating to or showing a difference or differences. *n.* The amount or degree to which similar things differ.

dif-fer-en-tial cal-cu-lus *n.* In mathematics, the difference or variation of a function with respect to changes in independent variables.

dif-fer-en-tial gear *n., Mech.* A coupling consisting of a train of gears used to connect two or more shafts to allow different rates of wheel rotation, as on curves.

dif-fer-en-ti-ate *v.* To show, state, or distinguish the difference; to become or make different. **differentiation** *n.*

dif-fi-cult *adj.* Hard to do, deal with, or accomplish; hard to please.

dif-fi-cul-ty *n., pl.* **-ties** The quality or state of being difficult; something that requires great effort; conflicts or problems.

dif-fi-dent *adj.* Lacking confidence in oneself; timid. **diffidence** *n.*, **diffidently** *adv.*

dif-frac-tion *n., Phys.* A modification of light rays, especially a beam of light as it passes an aperture or obstacle.

dif-fuse *v.* To pour out and spread freely in all directions; to scatter. **diffusion** *n.*

dig *v.* To turn up, break up, or remove the earth with a shovel; to discover or learn by investigation or research. *Slang* To understand, like, appreciate or enjoy. *Informal* To work intensively.

di-gest *v.* To change ingested food into usable form; to mentally assimilate; to endure; to tolerate patiently; to decompose or soften with moisture or heat. **digestibility** *n.*, **digestible, digestive** *adj.*

di-gest-ion *n.* The chemical and muscular action of transforming food into an assimilable state.

dig-it *n.* A toe or finger; the Arabic numerals 0 through 9.

dig-i-tal *adj.* Pertaining to or like the fingers or digits; expressed in digits, especially for computer use; reading in digits, as a clock.

dig-i-tal com-put-er *n.* In computer science, a computer using data that is represented as digits to perform operations.

dig-i-tal-is *n.* The foxglove plant; a drug prepared from dried leaves of foxglove, used as a heart stimulant.

dig-ni-fied *adj.* Showing or possessing dignity; poised.

dig-ni-fy *v.* To give dignity or distinction to something.

dig-ni-tary *n., pl.* **-ies** A person of high rank, notability, and influence.

dig-ni-ty *n., pl.* **-ties** The quality or state of being excellent; the quality of being poised or formally reserved in appearance and demeanor; a high rank, office, or title.

di-graph *n.* A pair of letters, as the ea in seat or oa in boat, that represents a single sound. **digraphic** *adj.*

di-gress *v.* To turn away or aside from the main subject in a discourse; to wander. **digression** *n.*, **digressive** *adj.*, **digressively** *adv.*

dik-dik *n.* A very small African antelope.

dike *n.* An embankment made of earth, built to hold and control flood waters, also known as a levee.

di-lap-i-dat-ed *adj.* Being in a state of decay or disrepair. **dilapidation** *n.*

di-late *v.* To become or make enlarged; to expand. **dilatable** *adj.*, **dilation**, **dilator** *n.*

dil-a-to-ry *adj.* Tending to cause decay; characterized by delay; slow; tardy. **dilatorily** *adv.*

di-lem-ma *n.* A predicament requiring a choice between equally undesirable alternatives.

dil-et-tante *n.*, *pl.* -tantes *or* -tanti One who has an amateurish and superficial interest in something.

dil-i-gent *adj.* Showing painstaking effort and application in whatever is undertaken; industrious. **diligence** *n.*, **diligently** *adv.*

dill *n.* An aromatic herb with aromatic leaves and seeds used as seasoning.

dil-ly *n.*, *pl.* -lies *Slang* Someone or something that is extraordinary.

dil-ly--dal-ly *v.* To waste time with indecision or hesitation.

di-lute *v.* To weaken, thin, or reduce the concentration of by adding a liquid. **dilution** *n.*

dim *adj.* Dull; lacking sharp perception or clarity of understanding; obscured or darkened from faintness of light; pessimistic or negative. **dim** *v.*, **dimly** *adv.*, **dimness** *n.*

dim *abbr.* Dimension.

dime *n.* A United States coin worth ten cents or one tenth of a dollar.

di-men-sion *n.* A measurable extent, as length, thickness, or breadth. **dimensions** *pl.* The magnitude or scope of something. **dimensional** *adj.*, **dimensionality** *n.*

di-min-ish *v.* To become or make smaller or less; to reduce in power, rank, or authority; to decrease; to taper. **diminishable** *adj.*, **diminishment**, **diminution** *n.*

dim-in-ished *adj.* Reduced; lessened.

di-min-u-en-do *adv.* Gradually lessening in volume. **diminuendo** *adj. & n.*

di-min-u-tive *adj.* Very small; tiny.

dim-i-ty *n.*, *pl.* -ties A sheer cotton fabric woven with cords, stripes, or checks.

dim-mer *n.* A rheostat used to reduce the intensity of an electric light.

dim-ple *n.* A slight depression in the surface of the skin, especially one made visible in the cheek by smiling; a slight surface depression. **dimple** *v.*

dim-wit *n.*, *Slang* A simpleminded or stupid person. **dimwitted** *adj.*, **dimwittedly** *adv.*, **dimwittedness** *n.*

din *n.* A loud, confused, harsh noise.

dine *v.* To eat dinner.

din-er *n.* A dining car on a train; a restaurant usually shaped like a railroad car.

di-nette *n.* A small room or alcove which is used as a dining room.

ding-a-ling *n.*, *Slang* A silly person.

din-ghy *n.*, *pl.* -ghies A small rowboat; an inflatable rubber raft.

din-ky *adj.*, *Informal* Insignificant or small.

din-ner *n.* The last meal of the day, taken usually between the hours of 5:00 and 7:00 P.M.; a banquet or formal meal.

din-ner-ware *n.* The tableware used in serving a meal.

di-no-saur *n.*, *Paleon.*

A group of extinct reptiles from the Mesozoic period, some of which were the largest land animals known to exist.

Coelosaurus

dint *n.* Means; force; effort. *v.* To drive with force.

di-oc-ese *n.* The territory under the jurisdiction of a bishop. **diocesan** *adj. & n.*

di-ode *n.* An electron tube which permits electrons to pass in only one direction, used as a rectifier.

di-o-ra-ma *n.* A miniature scene in three dimensions.

dip *v.* To let or put down into a liquid momentarily; to lift up and out by scooping or bailing; to be baptized by immersion; to make candles by repeatedly immersing wicks in wax or tallow; to sink or go down suddenly. *n.* A sauce made of liquid, into which something is to be dipped; a depression or hollow. *Slang* A silly person.

diph-the-ri-a *n.*, *Pathol.* An acute contagious disease caused by bacillus and characterized by formation of a false membrane in the throat and other air passages by weakness and fever.

diph-thong *n.*, *Phon.* A blend of a single speech sound which begins with one vowel sound and moves to another in the same syllable, as oi in oil, oi in coil or oy in toy.

di-plo-ma *n.* A document issued by a college, school, or university testifying that a student has earned a degree or completed a course of study.

di-plo-ma-cy *n.*, *pl.* -cies The art or practice of conducting international negotiations; skill and tact in dealing with people.

dip-lo-mat *n.* A person employed in diplomacy. **diplomatic** *adj.*

dip-per *n.* One that dips; a container for dipping; a long-handled cup for dipping water. *Astron.* The Big Dipper and the Little Dipper, two northern constellations.

dip-so-ma-ni-a *n.* An insatiable craving for alcohol. **dipsomaniac** *n. & adj.*

dip-ter-ous *adj.* Pertaining to or of animals having a single pair of wings such as the fly, gnat, and mosquito.

dip-tych *n.* A pair of painted or carved panels which are hinged together.

dir *abbr.* Director.

dire *adj.* Dreadful or terrible in consequence. **direly, direfully** *adv.*, **direness** *n.*

di-rect *v.* To control or regulate the affairs of; to command or order; to direct or tell someone the way; to cause something to move in a given or direct course; to indicate the destination of a letter; to supervise or instruct the performance of a job; to move or lie in a straight line; to do something immediate. *adj.* Without compromise; absolute; in the exact words of a person, as a direct quote.

di-rect cur-rent *n.* An electrical current which flows in only one direction.

di-rec-tion *n.* The act of directing; an order or command; the path or line along which something points, travels, or lies. **directional** *adj.*

di-rec-tive *n.* A regulation or order from someone with authority.

di-rect-ly *adv.* Immediately; at once; in a direct manner or line; doing without an agent, medium, or go-between.

di-rec-tor *n.* A person who manages or directs; one of a group of persons who supervises the affairs of an institute, corporation or business. **directorship** *n.*

di-rec-to-ry *n.*, *pl.* **-ries** A book listing data, alphabetically or classified, containing the names and addresses of a specific group, persons, organizations, inhabitants, or businesses.

di-rect tax *n.* A tax which is charged directly to the taxpayer.

dirge *n.* A slow mournful song; a funeral hymn.

dir-i-gi-ble *n.* A lighter-than-air plane which may be steered by means of its own motive power.

dirk *n.* A dagger.

dirn-dl *n.* A lady's full-skirted dress with a gathered waistband.

dirt *n.* Soil or earth; obscene or profane language; scandalous or hateful gossip. *Min.* Broken ore or rock; washed-down earth, containing precious metal. **dirt-bike** A lightweight motorbike used on rough roads, surfaces, or trails. **dirt-cheap** Extremely cheap.

dirty *adj.* Not clean; grimy; indecent; obscene; mean; despicable; lacking in brightness or clarity; relating to excessive radioactive fallout. *v.* To become or make soiled. **dirtiness** *n.*

dirty tricks *pl.*, *n.*, *Informal* Unethical behavior, especially in politics.

dis-a-ble *v.* To make powerless or to incapacitate; to disqualify legally. **disability** *n.*

dis-a-buse *v.* To free from delusion, misunderstanding, or misconception.

dis-ad-van-tage *n.* A circumstance that is unfavorable; loss or damage; detriment. **disadvantage** *v.*

dis-af-fect *v.* To weaken or destroy the affection or loyalty of. **disaffection** *n.*, **disaffectedly** *adv.*, **disaffected** *adj.*

dis-a-gree *v.* To vary in opinion; to differ; to argue; to quarrel; to be unfavorable or unacceptable.

dis-a-gree-able *adj.* Offensive or unpleasant. **disagreeably** *adv.*

dis-al-low *v.* To refuse to allow; to reject as invalid or untrue. **disallowance** *n.*

dis-ap-pear *v.* To vanish; to drop from sight. **disappearance** *n.*

dis-ap-point *v.* To fail to satisfy the desires, hopes, or expectations of. **disappointment** *n.*

dis-ap-pro-ba-tion *n.* Disapproval; condemnation.

dis-ap-prove *v.* To refuse to approve; to reject; to condemn. **disapproval** *n.*

dis-arm *v.* To make harmless; to deprive or take away the weapons or any means of attack or defense. **disarmament** *n.*

dis-ar-range *v.* To disturb the order of something. **disarrangement** *n.*

dis-ar-ray *n.* A state of confusion or disorder; an upset or turmoil.

dis-as-sem-ble *v.* To take apart.

dis-as-so-ci-ate *v.* To break away from or to detach oneself from an association. **disassociation** *n.*

dis-as-ter *n.* An event that causes great ruin or distress; a sudden and crushing misfortune. **disastrous** *adj.*, **disastrously** *adv.*

dis-a-vow *v.* To disclaim or deny any responsibility for or knowledge of. **disavowal** *n.*

dis-band *v.* To disperse; to break up. **disbandment** *n.*

dis-bar *v.* In law, to be expelled officially from the legal profession. **disbarment** *n.*

dis-be-lieve *v.* To refuse to believe in something. **disbelief, disbeliever** *n.*

dis-burse *v.* To pay out. **disbursement, disbursal, disburser** *n.*

disc *or* **disk** *n.*, *Informal* A phonograph record.

disc *abbr.* Discount.

dis-card *v.* To remove a playing card from one's hand; to throw out. *n.* The act of discarding; something which is cast aside or rejected. **discarder** *n.*

dis-cern *v.* To detect visually; to detect with senses other than that of vision; to comprehend mentally; to perceive as separate and distinct. **discerner, discernment** *n.*, **discernible** *adj.*

dis-charge *v.* To relieve of a charge, duty, load, or burden; to release as from confinement, custody, care, or duty; to dismiss from employment; to send forth; to shoot or fire a weapon; to get rid of; to release from service or duty; to fulfill an obligation, duty, or debt. *n.* The act of discharging or the condition of being discharged.

dis-ci-ple *n.* One who accepts and assists in spreading the doctrines of another. **Disciple** One of Christ's followers.

dis-ci-pline *n.* Training which corrects, molds, or perfects the mental faculties or moral character; behavior which results from such training; obedience to authority or rules; punishment meant to correct poor behavior. *v.* To train or develop by teaching and by control; to bring order to; to penalize.

dis-ci-pli-nary *adj.*

dis-claim *v.* To disavow any claim to or association with. **disclaimer** *n.*

dis-close *v.* To make known; to bring into view.

disclosure *n.*

dis-co *n., pl.* **-cos** A discotheque.

dis-color *v.* To alter or change the color of.

discoloration *n.*

dis-com-fit *v.* To defeat in battle; to make upset or uneasy. **discomfiture** *n.*

dis-com-fort *n.* Physical or mental uneasiness; pain; an inconvenience. *v.* To make uncomfortable.

dis-com-mode *v.* To inconvenience.

dis-com-pose *v.* To disrupt the composure or serenity of; to unsettle; to destroy the order of. **discomposure** *n.*

dis-con-cert *v.* To upset; to discompose; to perturb. **disconcertingly** *adv.*

dis-con-nect *v.* To sever or break the connection of or between.

disconnection *n.*

dis-con-nect-ed *adj.* Not connected.

dis-con-so-late *adj.* Without consolation; dejected; cheerless; sorrowful. **disconsolately** *adv.*

dis-con-tent *n.* Lack of contentment; dissatisfaction. *v.* To make unhappy. **discontent** *v.,* **discontentedly** *adv.,* **discontented** *adj.*

dis-con-tin-ue *v.* To come or bring to an end; to break the continuity of; to interrupt; to stop trying, taking, or using. **discontinuance, discontinuation** *n.*

dis-cord *n.* Lacking accord or harmony; a harsh combination of musical sounds. **discordant** *adj.*

dis-co-theque *n.* A nightclub where music is provided for dancing.

dis-count *v.* To sell or offer for sale at a price lower than usual; to leave out of account; to disregard; to give discounts; to underestimate the importance of something. *n.* A reduction from the full amount of a debt or from the standard price; the act or practice of discounting; a deduction taken or an allowance made. **discountable** *adj.*

dis-coun-te-nance *v.* To look upon with disfavor; to make uneasy.

dis-cour-age *v.* To deprive or be deprived of enthusiasm or courage; to hinder by disfavoring. **discouragement** *n.,* **discouragingly** *adv.*

dis-course *n.* A conversation; a formal and lengthy discussion of a subject. *v.* To write or converse extensively.

discourser *n.*

dis-cour-te-ous *adj.* Lacking consideration or courteous manners. **discourteously** *adv.,* **discourtesy** *n.*

dis-cov-er *v.* To make known or visible; to observe or learn of for the first time. **discoverable** *adj.,* **discoverer, discovery** *n.*

dis-cred-it *v.* To mar the reputation of or disgrace someone or something; to injure the reputation of. *n.* Loss of credit or reputation; doubt; disbelief. **discreditable** *adj.,* **discreditably** *adv.*

dis-creet *adj.* Tactful; careful of appearances; modest. **discreetly** *adv.,* **discreetness** *n.*

dis-crep-an-cy *n., pl.* **-cies** A difference in facts; an instance of being discrepant. **discrepant** *adj.*

dis-crete *adj.* Separate; made up of distinct parts.

dis-cre-tion *n.* The quality or act of being discreet; the ability to make responsible choices; power to decide; the result of separating or distinguishing. **discretionary** *adj.*

dis-crim-i-nate *v.* To distinguish or differentiate between someone or something on the basis of race, sex, class, or religion; to act prejudicially. **discriminatingly** *adv.,* **discrimination** *n.,* **discriminative** *adj.*

dis-cur-sive *adj.* Covering a wide field of subjects in a quick manner; rambling from subject to subject. **discursively** *adv.,* **discursiveness** *n.*

dis-cus *n.* A heavy disk made of wood, rubber, or metal, which is hurled for distance in athletic competitions; a brightly-colored, disk-shaped fresh water fish of South America.

dis-cuss *v.* To investigate by argument or debate; to consider or examine something through discourse. **discussible** *adj.,* **discussion** *n.*

dis-cus-sant *n.* A participant in a discussion.

dis-dain *v.* To treat contemptuously; to look on with scorn. **disdainfully** *adv.*

dis-ease *n.* A condition of the living animal, plant body, or one of its parts which impairs normal functioning; a condition of ill health. **diseased** *adj.*

dis-em-bark *v.* To go or put ashore from a ship; unload.

dis-em-body *v.* To release or free the soul or physical existence.

dis-em-bow-el *v.* To remove the bowels or entrails; to eviscerate. **disembowelment** *n.*

dis-en-chant *v.* To free from false beliefs or enchantment. **disenchantingly** *adv.,* **disenchanting** *adj.*

dis-en-cum-ber *v.* To relieve of hardships; to free from encumbrance; unburden.

dis-en-fran-chise *v.* To disfranchise. **disenfranchisement** *n.*

dis-en-gage *v.* To free from something that holds or otherwise engages; to set free. **disengagement** *n.*

dis-en-tan-gle *v.* To relieve of entanglement, confusion, etc. **disentanglement** *n.*

dis-es-teem *v.* To regard with little esteem. *n.* Lack of esteem.

dis-fa-vor *n.* Disapproval; the state of being disliked. **disfavor** *v.*

dis-fig-ure *v.* To mar, deface, or deform the appearance of something or someone. **disfigurement** *n.*

dis-fran-chise *v.* To deprive of a legal right or privilege, especially the right to vote. **disfranchisement** n.

dis-gorge v. To discharge by the throat or mouth; to regurgitate; to give up on request or under pressure; to discharge violently or as a result of force; to discharge the contents of; to spew forth violently.

dis-grace n. The state of having lost grace, favor, respect, or honor; something that disgraces. v. To bring reproach or shame to; to humiliate by a superior showing; to cause to lose favor or standing.
disgracer, disgracefulness n.,
disgraceful adj., **disgracefully** adv.

dis-grun-tle v. To make dissatisfied or discontented.

dis-guise v. To alter the customary appearance or character of in order to prevent recognition; to conceal the actual existence or character of. n. Clothes and or make-up assumed to disguise one's identity or to copy that of another; an artificial manner; the act of disguising. **disguisedly** adv., **disguiser** n., **disguisable** adj.

dis-gust v. To affect with nausea, repugnance, or aversion; to cause one to become impatient or lose attention. n. A marked aversion to something distasteful; repugnance. **disgustedly, disgustfully, disgustingly** adv., **disgusted, disgusting, disgustful** adj.

dish n. A concave vessel on which food is served; the amount a dish holds; the food served in a dish; a particularly prepared food; fashion; a directional microwave antenna having a concave reflector. _Slang_ Something that is favored; an attractive woman. v. To make sarcastic, cutting remarks; to put food into a dish.

dis-ha-bille n. The state of being carelessly dressed; undress.

dis-har-mo-ny n. Lack of harmony or agreement; discord.

dish-cloth n. A cloth used for washing dishes; also called a dishrag.

dis-heart-en v. To cause to lose spirit or courage; to discourage, demoralize, or dispirit.

di-shev-el v. To mess up or disarrange; to throw into disorder or disarray.

dis-hon-est adj. Lack of honesty; arising from or showing fraud or falseness.
dishonesty n., **dishonestly** adv.

dis-hon-or n. The deprivation of honor; disgrace; the state of one who has lost honor; a cause of disgrace; failure to pay a financial obligation. v. To bring disgrace on something or someone; to fail to pay.

dish-rag n. A dishcloth.

dish-washer n. A person or a machine which washes dishes.

dis-il-lu-sion v. To deprive of illusion; to disenchant.

dis-in-cline v. To make or to be unwilling; to be or cause to be not interested.

dis-in-fect v. To cleanse and make free from infection, especially by destroying harmful microorganisms; to sterilize. **disinfection** n.

dis-in-gen-u-ous adj. Lacking frankness, sincerity, or simplicity; crafty; not straightforward.

dis-in-her-it v. To deliberately deprive of inheritance; to depose of previously held privileges.

dis-in-te-grate v. To break or reduce into separate elements, parts, or small particles; to destroy the unity or integrity of; to explode; to undergo a change in structure, as an atomic nucleus.
disintegration, disintegrator n.

dis-inter v. To exhume or dig up something buried; to bring to light, disclose, uncover, or expose.

dis-in-ter-est-ed adj. The state of being unbiased, impartial, unselfish, or not interested; free from selfish motive or interest. **disinterest** n., **disinterestedly** adv.

dis-join v. To end the joining of; to become detached; to disconnect.

disk or **disc** n. A thin, flat, circular object; in computer science, a round, flat plate coated with a magnetic substance on which data for a computer is stored; a fairly flat, circular, metal object used to break up soil; the implement employing such tools.

disk op-er-at-ing sys-tem n. In computer science, the software which controls the disk drives and disk accessing; abbreviated as DOS.

disk pack n. In computer science, a computer storage device which has several magnetic disks to use and store as a unit.

dis-like v. To regard with aversion or disapproval. n. Distaste.

dis-lo-cate v. To put out of place or proper position. _Med._ To displace a bone from a socket or joint.

dis-lodge v. To remove or drive out from a dwelling or position; to force out of a settled position.

dis-loy-al adj. Not loyal; untrue to personal obligations or duty.
disloyally adv., **disloyalty** n.

dis-mal adj. Causing gloom or depression; depressing; lacking in interest or merit. **dismally** adv., **dismalness** n.

dis-man-tle v. To strip of dress or covering or to strip of furniture and equipment; to take apart. **dismantlement** n.

dis-may v. To deprive or be deprived of courage or resolution through the pressure of sudden fear or anxiety.
dismay n., **dismayingly** adv.

dis-mem-ber v. To cut, pull off or disjoin the limbs, members, or parts of.
dismemberment n.

dis-miss v. To discharge or allow to leave; to remove from position or service; to bar from attention or serious consideration; in law, to disallow or reject any further judicial consideration on a claim or action.
dismissal n., **dismissible** adj.

dis-mount v. To get down from; to remove from a seat, setting, or support; to take apart; to disassemble. **dismount** *n.*

dis-o-bey *v.* To refuse or fail to obey; to be disobedient. **disobedient** *adj.*, **disobediently** *adv.*

dis-o-blige *v.* To act contrary to the wishes of; to neglect or refuse to act in accordance with the wishes of; to offend; to inconvenience. **disobligingly** *adv.*

dis-or-der *n.* Breach of peace or public order; lack of good order; an abnormal physical or mental condition; an ailment. *v.* To disturb the order of; to disturb the normal or regular functions of. **disorderly** *adj.*, **disorderliness** *n.*

dis-or-gan-ize *v.* To destroy or break up the organization, unity, or structure of. **disorganization** *n.*

dis-own *v.* To refuse to acknowledge or claim as one's own.

dis-pa-rate *adj.* Altogether dissimilar; unequal. **disparately** *adv.*, **disparateness** *n.*

dis-pas-sion-ate *adj.* Free from bias or passion. **dispassionately** *adv.*

dis-patch *or* **des-patch** *v.* To send off to a particular destination or on specific business; to dispose of quickly; to kill summarily. *n.* The act of dispatching; a message sent with speed; a message; a news story sent to a newspaper. **dispatcher** *n.*

dis-pel *v.* To drive off or away.

dis-pense *v.* To give out; to distribute; to administer; to let go or exempt. **dispense with** To get rid of; to forgo. **dispenser** *n.*

dis-perse *v.* To break up or scatter in various directions; to spread or distribute from a common source; to distribute. **dispersible** *adj.*, **dispersion**, **dispersal** *n.*

di-spir-it *v.* To deprive of or be deprived of spirit; to discourage or be discouraged. **dispiritedly** *adv.*

dis-place *v.* To change the position of; to take the place of; to discharge from an office; to cause a physical displacement of. **displacement** *n.*

dis-play *v.* To put forth or spread; to put in view; to show off. *n.* The act of displaying; in computer science, a device which gives information in a visual form such as on a cathode-ray tube (computer screen or CRT).

dis-please *v.* To cause the disapproval or annoyance of; to cause displeasure. **displeasingly** *adv.*, **displeasure** *n.*

dis-pose *v.* To put in place; to finally settle or come to terms. **dispose of** To get rid of; to attend to or settle; to transfer or part with, as by selling. **disposable** *adj.*

dis-pos-sess *v.* To deprive of possession or ownership of land, possessions, or property. **dispossession** *n.*

dis-pro-por-tion *n.* Lack of proportion, symmetry or proper relation. **disproportion** *v.*, **disproportional**, **disproportionate** *adj.*,

disproportionately *adv.*

dis-prove *v.* Prove to be false or erroneous. **disproof** *n.*, **disprovable** *adj.*

dis-pu-ta-tion *n.* The act of disputing; a debate.

dis-pute *v.* To debate or argue; to question the validity of; to strive against or to resist. *n.* A verbal controversy; a quarrel. **disputable** *adj.*, **disputably** *adv.*, **disputant**, **disputer** *n.*

dis-qual-i-fy *v.* To deprive of the required properties or conditions; to deprive of a power or privilege; to make ineligible for a prize or further competition. **disqualification** *n.*

dis-quiet *v.* To take away the tranquillity of; to trouble. **disquieting** *adj.*, **disquietingly** *adv.*

dis-qui-si-tion *n.* A formal inquiry into or discussion of a subject.

dis-re-gard *v.* To ignore; to neglect; to pay no attention to; to treat without proper attention. **disregard** *n.*, **disregardful** *adj.*

dis-re-pair *n.* The state of being in need of repair, usually due to neglect.

dis-re-pute *n.* A state of being held in low esteem; loss of a good reputation; disgrace. **disreputable** *adj.*

dis-re-spect *n.* Lack of respect or reverence. **disrespect** *v.*, **disrespectful** *adj.*, **disrespectfully** *adv.*

dis-robe *v.* To undress.

dis-rupt *v.* To throw into disorder or confusion; upset; to cause to break down. **disruption** *n.*, **disruptive** *adj.*

dis-sat-is-fy *v.* To fail to satisfy; to disappoint. **dissatisfaction** *n.*, **dissatisfied** *adj.*

dis-sect *v.* To cut into pieces; to expose the parts of something, such as an animal, for examination; to analyze in detail. **dissector** *n.*

dis-sem-ble *v.* To conceal or hide the actual nature of; to put on a false appearance; to conceal facts. **dissembler** *n.*

dis-sem-i-nate *v.* To scatter or spread, as if by sowing, over a wide area. **dissemination**, **disseminator** *n.*

dis-sen-sion *n.* Difference of opinion; discord; strife.

dis-sent *v.* To differ in opinion or thought. *n.* Difference of opinion; refusal to go along with an established church.

dis-ser-ta-tion *n.* A formal written discourse or treaties, especially one submitted for a doctorate.

dis-serv-ice *n.* An ill turn; an ill service, injury, or harm.

dis-sev-er *v.* To sever; to divide; to separate disseverance, disseverment *n.*

dis-si-dent *adj.* Strong and open difference with an opinion or group. **dissident**, **dissidence** *n.*

dis-sim-i-lar *adj.* Different; not the same; unlike. **dissimilarity** *n.*

dis-si-mil-i-tude *n.* Lack of resemblance; unlikeness.

dis-sim-u-late *v.* To conceal under a

false appearance; to dissemble.

dis-si-pate *v.* To disperse or drive away; to squander or waste; to separate into parts and scatter or vanish; to become dispersed; to lose irreversibly. **dissipation** *n.*

dis-so-ci-ate *v.* To break from the association with another. **dissociation** *n.*

dis-so-lute *adj.* Loose in morals; lacking moral restraint. **dissolutely** *adv.*, **dissoluteness** *n.*

dis-so-lu-tion *n.* The act or process of changing from a solid to a fluid form; the separation of body and soul; death.

dis-solve *v.* To pass into solution, such as dissolving sugar in water; to overcome, as by emotion; to fade away; to become decomposed; to terminate. **dissolvable** *adj.*

dis-so-nance *n., Mus.* Lack of agreement; a conflict. *Mus.* A harsh or disagreeable combination of sounds; discord. **dissonant** *adj.*, **dissonantly** *adv.*

dis-suade *v.* To alter the course of action; to turn from something by persuasion or advice. **dissuader**, **dissuasion** *n.*, **dissuasive** *adj.*

dis-taff *n.* A staff rotation for holding the flax, tow, or wool in spinning; the female side of a family; women in general.

dis-tal *n.* Relatively remote from the point of attachment or origin. **distally** *adv.*

dis-tance *n.* Separation in time or space; the degree of separation between two points; the space that separates any two specified points in time; the quality or state of being distant; aloofness. *v.* To put space between; to keep at a distance.

dis-tant *adj.* Apart or separate by a specified amount of time or space; situated at a great distance; coming from, going to, or located at a distance; remotely related. **distantly** *adv.*, **distantness** *n.*

dis-taste *v.* To feel aversion to; to have an offensive taste; dislike. **distastefully** *adv.*, **distastefulness** *n.*

dis-tem-per *n.* Bad humor or temper; a highly contagious viral disease of dogs, marked by fever and by respiratory and sometimes nervous symptoms. *v.* To throw out of order.

dis-tend *v.* To expand from internal pressure. **distensible** *adj.*, **distention**, **distension** *n.*

dis-till *v.* To extract by distillation; to give off in drops. **distiller**, **distillery** *n.*

dis-til-late *n.* The condensed substance separated by distillation.

dis-til-la-tion *n.* The act or process of heating a liquid or other substance until it sends off a gas or vapor and then cooling the gas or vapor until it returns to a liquid or solid form, thus separating impurities.

dis-tinct *adj.* Distinguished from all others; clearly seen; unquestionable. **distinctly** *adv.*, **distinctness** *n.*

dis-tinc-tion *n.* The act of distinguishing; a difference; a special honor or recognition.

dis-tinc-tive *adj.* Serving to give style or distinction to. **distinctiveness** *n.*

dis-tin-guish *v.* To recognize as being different; to discriminate; to make something different or noticeable. **distinguishable**, **distinguished** *adj.*, **distinguishably** *adv.*

dis-tort *v.* To twist or bend out of shape; to twist the true meaning of; to give a misleading account of. **distortion** *n.*

dis-tract *v.* To draw or divert one's attention away from something; to cause one to feel conflicting emotions. **distraction** *n.*

dis-trait *adj.* Absent-minded.

dis-traught *adj.* Deeply agitated with doubt or anxiety; crazed.

dis-tress *v.* To cause suffering of mind or body. *n.* Pain or suffering; severe physical or mental strain; a very painful situation; a state of danger or desperate need. **distressingly** *adv.*

dis-trib-ute *v.* To divide among many; to deliver or give out; to classify. **distribution** *n.*, **distributive** *adj.*

dis-trib-u-tor *n.* A person that distributes, such as a wholesaler; a device which directs electrical current to the spark plugs of a gasoline engine.

dis-trict *n.* An administrative or political section of a territory; a distinctive area. **district** *v.*

dis-trict at-tor-ney *n.* The public prosecuting officer of a judicial district.

Dis-trict of Co-lum-bi-a *n.* The capital of the United States of America; the only part of the continental United States which is not a state.

dis-trust *n.* Suspicion; doubt. *v.* To doubt; to suspect. **distrustful** *adj.*, **distrustfully** *adv.*

dis-turb *v.* To destroy the tranquillity or composure of; to unsettle mentally or emotionally; to interrupt or interfere with; to bother. **disturbance**, **disturber** *n.*

dis-u-nite *v.* To divide or separate.

dis-u-ni-ty *n.* Discord; unrest.

dis-use *n.* The state of not using; out of use.

ditch *n.* A trench in the earth. *v.* To dig a ditch in; to surround with a ditch. *Slang* To discard; to get rid of something; to land a disabled aircraft on water.

ditch dig-ger *n.* One that digs ditches.

dith-er *n.* A state of nervousness or indecision; commotion.

dit-to *n., pl.* -tos An exact copy; the same as stated before. **ditto mark** The pair of marks (" ") used to substitute the word *ditto.* *adv.* As before.

dit-ty *n., pl.* -ties A short, simple song.

dit-ty bag *n.* A small bag used by sailors to hold small articles, such as thread, buttons, and other small personal effects.

di-u-ret-ic *adj.* Tending to cause an increase in the flow of urine. *n.* A drug given to increase the amount of urine produced.

di-ur-nal *adj.* Having a daily cycle or recurring every day; of, relating to, or occurring in the daytime; opening in the daytime and closing at night. **diurnally** *adv.*

di-va *n., pl.* **-vas** or **-ve** A prima donna; a female opera star.

di-van *n.* A long, backless and armless sofa or couch.

dive *v.* To plunge into water headfirst; to plunge downward at a sharp angle; to submerge; to rush headlong. *n.* The act or an instance of diving; a submerging of a submarine; a sharp decline. *Slang* A disreputable bar; in boxing, a faked knockout; in football, an offensive play in which the ball carrier plunges into the line for short yardage. **diver** *n.*

dive--bomb *v.* To bomb something from an airplane by making a steep dive toward the target and releasing the bomb. **dive-bomber** *n.*

div-er *n.* A person who dives; a person who stays underwater for prolonged periods by having air supplied either from the surface or from compressed air tanks.

di-verge *v.*

Light rays

Lens

To move or extend in different directions from a common point; (diverging rays of light); to differ in opinion or manner. **divergent** *adj.*

di-vers *adj.* Various; several.

di-verse *adj.* Unlike in characteristics; having various forms or qualities. **diversely** *adv.*, **diverseness** *n.*

di-ver-si-fy *v.* To give variety to something; to engage in varied operations; to distribute over a wide range of types or classes. **diversification** *n.*

di-ver-sion *n.* The act of diverting from a course, activity or use; something that diverts or amuses. **diversionary** *adj.*

di-ver-si-ty *n., pl.* **-ties** A difference; variety; unlikeness.

di-vert *v.* To turn from a set course; to give pleasure by distracting the attention from something that is burdensome or oppressive. **diversionary** *adj.*, **diversion, diversity** *n.*

di-vest *v.* To undress or strip, especially of clothing or equipment; to deprive or dispossess of property, authority, or title; to take away from a person. **divestment** *n.*

di-ves-ti-ture *n.* The act of divesting; the compulsory transfer of title or disposal of interests upon government order.

di-vide *v.* To separate into parts, areas, or groups; to separate into pieces or portions and give out in shares; to cause to be apart; in mathematics, to

perform mathematical division on a number. *n.* An act of dividing; a dividing ridge between drainage areas. **dividable** *adj.*

div-i-dend *n.* An individual share of something distributed; a bonus; a number to be divided; a sum or fund to be divided and distributed.

di-vine *adj.* Of, relating to, preceding from, or pertaining to God. *Informal* Extremely pleasing. *n.* A clergyman or theologian. *v.* To foretell. **divineness** *n.*, **divinely** *adv.*

di-vin-ing rod *n.* A forked branch or stick that supposedly indicates the location of underground water or minerals by bending downward when held over a source.

di-vi-sion *n.* Separation; something which divides, separates, or marks off; the act, process, or instance of separating or keeping apart; the condition or an instance of being divided in opinion; in mathematics, the process of discovering how many times one quantity is contained in another. *Milit.* A self-sufficient tactical unit capable of independent action. **divisional** *adj.*

di-vi-sive *adj.* Tending to create dissension or disunity. **divisiveness** *n.*

di-vi-sor *n.* In mathematics, the number by which a dividend is to be divided.

di-vorce *n.* The legal dissolution of a marriage; the complete separation of things. **divorce** *v.*, **divorcee** *n.*

div-ot *n.* A square of turf or sod; a piece of turf torn up by a golf club while making a shot.

di-vulge *v.* To reveal or make known; to disclose; to reveal a secret.

Dix-ie *n.* The southern states of the continental U.S.

dix-ie-land *n.* Distinctly American jazz music, usually played by a small band and characterized by ensemble and solo improvisation.

diz-zy *adj.* Having a whirling sensation in the head with loss of proper balance; mentally confused; caused by or marked by giddiness; extremely rapid. **dizzily** *adv.*, **dizzy** *v.*

DMZ *abbr.* Demilitarized zone.

do *v.* To bring to pass; to bring about; to perform or execute; to put forth; to exert; to bring to an end. *n.* A festive get-together; a command to do something. *Mus.* The first tone of a scale. **do away with** To destroy; to kill. **do in** To tire completely; to kill. **do up** To adorn or dress lavishly; to wrap and tie.

Do-ber-man pin-scher *n.* A medium-sized, slender, smooth-coated dog.

do-cent *n.* A teacher at a college or university; a guide or lecturer in a museum.

doc-ile *adj.* Easily led, taught, or managed. **docilily** *n.*

dock *n.* A landing slip or pier for ships or boats; a loading area for trucks or trains; an enclosure where the defendant sits or stands in a criminal trail. *Bot.* A weedy plant with small flower clusters. *v.* To haul or guide into a dock; to become docked. *Aeros.* To connect, as in two or more spacecrafts.

dock-age *n.* A charge for the use of a dock; docking facilities.

dock-et *n.* A brief written summary of a document; an agenda; an identifying statement about a document placed on its cover.

dock-yard *n.* A shipyard; a place where ships are repaired or built.

doc-tor *n.* A person trained and licensed to practice medicine, such as a physician, surgeon, dentist, or veterinarian; a person holding the highest degree offered by a university. *v.* To restore to good condition; to practice medicine; to administer medical treatment; to tamper with; to alter for a desired end. **doctoral** *adj.*

doc-tor-ate *n.* The degree, status, or title of a doctor.

doc-trine *n.* Something taught as a body of principles; a statement of fundamental government policy especially in international relations. **doctrinal** *adj.*

doc-u-ment *n.* An official paper utilized as the basis, proof, or support of something. *v.* To furnish documentary evidence of; to prove with, support by, or provide by documents. **documentation** *n.*

doc-u-men-ta-ry *adj.* Relating to or based on documents; an artistic way of presenting facts. **documentary** *n.*

dod-der *v.* To tremble, shake, or totter from weakness or age. *n., Bot.* A parasitic, twining vine.

dodge *v.* To avoid by moving suddenly; to evade a responsibility by trickery or deceit; to shift suddenly. **dodge** *n.*

do-do *n., pl.* **-does** *or* **-dos** An extinct flightless bird, formerly present on the island of Mauritius. *Informal* One hopelessly behind the times. *Slang* A stupid person; an unimaginative person.

doe *n., pl.* **does** *or* **doe** A mature female deer; any of various mammals, as the hare or kangaroo.

does-n't *contr.* Does not.

dog *n.* A usually domesticated carnivorous mammal, raised in a variety of breeds, probably descended from the common wolf; any of various animals, such as the dingo. *Informal* A mean, worthless person; a fellow; an undesirable piece of merchandise. *Slang* An unattractive woman or girl; a theatrical flop.

dog days *pl., n.* The hot, sultry part of summer between mid-July and September.

dog-fight *n.* An aerial combat between planes.

dog-ged *adj.* Stubbornly determined; obstinate **doggedly** *adv.*, **doggedness** *n.*

dog-gie bag *n.* A container used to carry home leftover food from a meal eaten at a restaurant.

dog-ma *n.* A rigidly held doctrine proclaimed to be true by a religious group; a principle or idea considered to be the absolute truth.

dog-mat-ic *adj.* Marked by an authoritative assertion of unproved or unprovable principles. **dogmatically** *adv.*

do--good-er *n., Informal* An earnest but usually impractical and often naive and ineffectual humanitarian or reformer.

dog paddle *n.* A beginner's swimming stroke in which the arms and legs move up and down. **dog-paddle** *v.*

do-jo *n.* A school of instruction in the Japanese martial arts.

dol-drums *pl., n.* A period of listlessness or despondency. *Naut.* The ocean region near the equator where there is very little wind.

dole *n.* The distribution of food, money, or clothing to the needy; a grant of government funds to the unemployed; something portioned out and distributed bit by bit. **dole** *adj.*

dole-ful *adj.* Filled with grief or sadness. **dolefully** *adv.*, **dolefulness** *n.*

doll *n.* A child's toy having a human form. *Slang* A woman; an attractive person. **dolled up** To dress up elegantly, as for a special occasion.

dol-lar *n.* A coin, note, or token representing one dollar; the standard monetary unit of the U.S.

dol-lop *n.* A lump or blob of a semiliquid substance; an indefinite amount or form.

dol-ly *n., pl.* **-lies** A doll; a low, flat frame on wheels or rollers used to move heavy loads; a wheeled apparatus for moving a motion picture or television camera toward or away from the action.

dol-men *n.* A prehistoric monument made up of a huge stone set on upright stone.

do-lor-ous *adj.* Marked by grief or pain; sad; mournful. **dolorously** *adv.*, **dolorousness** *n.*

dol-phin *n.*

Any of various small cetaceans with the snout in the shape of a beak and the neck vertebrae partially fused.

dolt *n.* A stupid person.

do-main *n.* A territory under one government; a field of activity or interest.

dome *n.* A roof resembling a hemisphere; something suggesting a dome.

do-mes-tic *adj.* Of or relating to the home, household or family life; interested in household affairs and home life; tame or domesticated; of or relating to policies of one's country; originated in a particular country. *n.* A

household servant.
domestically *adv.*, **domesticity** *n*.
dom-i-cile *n*. A dwelling place, house, or home. **domicile** *v*., **domiciliary** *adj*.
dom-i-nant *adj*. Having the most control or influence; most overwhelming; in genetics, producing a typical effect even when paired with an unlike gene for the same characteristic.
dominance *n*., **dominantly** *adv*.
dom-i-nate *v*. To rule or control; to exert the supreme determining or guiding influence on; to occupy the most prominent position in or over.
domination, dominator *n*.
dom-i-no *n.*, *pl.* **-noes** *or* **-nos** A long, loose, hooded cloak usually worn with a half mask as a masquerade costume; a person wearing a domino; the mask itself; a small rectangular block of wood or plastic with the face marked with dots. *pl.* A game containing 28 of such pieces.
dom-i-no the-o-ry *n*. The theory that if a certain event occurs, a series of similar events will follow.
Don *n*. Sir; used as a courtesy title with a man's name in Spanish-speaking countries; a Spanish gentleman; a head, fellow, or tutor at an English university; a Mafia leader.
don *v*. To put something on; to dress.
done *adj*. Completely finished or through; doomed to failure, defeat, or death; cooked adequately.
do-nee *n*. A recipient of a gift.
done for *adj*. Mortally stricken; doomed; left with no opportunity for recovery; ruined.
don-key *n.*, *pl.* **-keys** The domesticated ass. *Informal* A stubborn person.
do-nor *n*. One who gives, donates, or contributes.
don't *contr*. Do not.
doo-dle *v*. To scribble, design, or sketch aimlessly, especially when preoccupied. **doodle** *n*.
doom *n*. To pronounce judgment, particularly an official condemnation to a severe penalty or death; an unhappy destiny. *v*. To condemn; to make certain the destruction of.
dooms-day *n*. Judgment day; a dreaded day of judgment or reckoning; the end of the world.
door *n*. A barrier, normally swinging or sliding, by which an entry is closed and opened; a means of entrance or exit.
dope *n*. A preparation for giving a desired quality to a substance or surface, such as an antiknock added to gasoline. *Slang* A narcotic, especially one that is addictive; a stupid person; facts and details; all the details.
dor-mant *adj*. Asleep; a state of inactivity or rest. **dormancy** *n*.
dor-sal *adj.*, *Anat*. Of, relating to, or situated on or near the back.
do-ry *n.*, *pl.* **-ries** A small flat-bottomed boat with high, flaring sides and a sharp bow.

DOS *abbr*. Disk operating system.
dose *n*. The measured quantity of a therapeutic agent to be taken at one time or at stated intervals. *Med*. The prescribed amount of radiation to which a certain part of the body is exposed. **dosage** *n.*, **dose** *v*.
dos-si-er *n*. A complete file of documents or papers giving detailed information about a person or affair.
dot *n*. A small round spot; a mark made by or as if by a writing implement; a small round mark used in punctuation; a precise moment in time; a short click or buzz forming a letter or part of a letter in the Morse code. **dot** *v*.
dote *v*. To show excessive affection or fondness; to exhibit mental decline, especially as a result of senility. **doter** *n*.
dou-ble *adj*. Twice as much; composed of two like parts; designed for two. *Bot*. Having more than the usual number of petals. *n*. An actor who takes the place of another for scenes calling for special skill; in baseball, a two-base hit. *v*. In baseball, to make a double; to make or become twice as great; to fold in two; to turn and go back; to serve an additional purpose. **doubly** *adv*.
dou-ble--breast-ed *adj*. Having two rows of buttons and one row of buttonholes and fastening so as to give a double thickness of cloth across one's chest.
dou-ble--cross *v.*, *Slang* To betray.
dou-ble--deck-er *n*. A vehicle, as a ship or other means of transportation, with two decks for passengers; a sandwich with three slices of bread and two layers of filling.
dou-ble dip *n*. A person holding a salaried position while receiving a pension from a previous job.
dou-ble-head-er *n*. Two games played consecutively on the same day or night.
dou-ble joint-ed *adj*. Having unusually flexible joints which allow connected parts to bend at abnormal angles.
dou-ble play *n*. In baseball, a play in which two runners are put out during one continuous play of the ball.
dou-ble take *n*. A delayed reaction to something unusual.
dou-ble talk *n*. Speech which is meaningless despite the use of intelligible words; evasive or ambiguous language.
doubt *v*. To be uncertain or mistrustful about something; to distrust. **doubt, doubter** *n*.
dough *n*. A soft mixture of flour, liquids, and other ingredients which is baked to make bread, pastry, and other foods. *Slang* Money. **doughy** *adj*.
dough-nut *or* **donut** *n*. A small cake made of rich, light dough which is deep fried.
dough-ty *adj*. Marked by valor; brave.
dour *adj*. Stern and forbidding; morose and ill-tempered.

douse v. To plunge into liquid; to throw water on; to drench; to extinguish. **douser** n.

dove n. Any of numerous pigeons; a gentle, innocent person. **dovish** adj.

dow-a-ger n. A widow holding a title or property from her dead husband; a dignified, elderly woman.

dow-dy adj. Not neat or tidy; old-fashioned. **dowdier, dowdiest** adj.

dow-el n. A round wooden pin which fits tightly into an adjacent hole to fasten together the two pieces.

dow-er n. The part of a deceased man's estate that is given to his widow by law. v. To provide with a dower.

down adv. Toward or in a lower physical condition; from a higher to a lower position; the direction that is opposite of up; a lower or worse condition or status; from a past time or past generations of people; partial payment at the time of purchase. v. To put something in writing; to bring, strike, put, or throw down; in football, any of a series of plays during which a team must advance at least ten yards in order to retain possession of the ball. n. A grassy highland used for grazing; soft, fluffy feathers of a young bird; a soft hairy growth, such as that on a peach.

down-er n., Slang A depressant or seda-tive drug; a barbiturate; something that is depressing.

down--home adj. Of, or typically pertaining to, the southern United States.

Down's syn-drome n. Extreme mental deficiency; a condition in which a child is born with a broad, short skull, slanting eyes, and broad hands with short fingers; Mongolism.

down-ward or **down-wards** adv. From a higher to a lower place. **downward** adj.

down-wind adv. & adj. In the direction toward which the wind blows.

dowse v. To search for with a divining rod to find underground water or minerals. **dowser** n.

dox-ol-o-gy n., pl. -gies A hymn or verse in praise of God.

doz-en n. Twelve of a kind; a set of twelve things. **dozen, dozenth** adj.

Dr abbr. Doctor; drive.

drab adj. Of a light, dull brown or olive brown color; commonplace or dull. **drabness** n.

drach-ma n., pl. -mas or -mae A silver coin of ancient Greece.

draft n. A current of air; a sketch or plan of something to be made; a note for the transfer of money; the depth of water a ship draws with a certain load. Milit. A mandatory selection of men for service. v. To draw a tentative plan or sketch. adj. The drawing of a liquid from a keg or tap. **draftee** n.

drag v. To pull along or haul by force; to move with painful or undue slowness; to bring by force; to proceed slowly; to lag behind. Slang To puff on a pipe,

cigarette, or cigar. n. Something which retards motion or action; a tool used under water to detect or collect objects; something which is boring or dull. Slang Someone or something that is bothersome; a street; a race. **dragger** n.

drag-on n.

An mythical, giant, serpent-like, winged, fire-breathing monster.

drag-on-fly n.

A large insect which holds it's wings in a horizontal position and during it's naiad stage has rectal gills.

drain v. To draw off liquid gradually; to use up; to exhaust physically or emo-tionally; to flow off gradually. n. A means, such as a trench or channel, by which liquid matter is drained; some-thing which causes depletion. **drainer** n.

drake n. A male duck.

dram n. A small drink; a small portion; a measurement equaling approximately .06 ounces.

dra-ma n. A composition in prose or verse, especially one recounting a serious story; dramatic art of a par-ticular period.

drank v. Past tense of drink.

drape v. To cover or adorn with some-thing; to arrange or hang in loose folds. n. The manner in which cloth hangs or falls.

dras-tic adj. Acting extremely harsh or severe. **drastically** adv.

draught n. & v. A variation of draft.

draughts pl., n. The game of checkers, as referred to by the British.

draw v. To move or cause to move toward a direction or to a position as if by leading; to take out for use; to withdraw funds; to take in air; to sketch; to elicit a response; to attract; to formulate from evidence at hand; to displace water in floating; to provoke; to end something undecided or tied; to write in a set form.

draw-back n. An undesirable feature.

draw-bridge n. A bridge that can be raised or lowered to allow ships and boats to pass.

drawer n. One that draws pictures; a sliding box or receptacle in furniture. **drawers** pl. An article of clothing for the lower body.

draw-ing n. An act of drawing; the process of deciding something by choosing lots; the art of representing something or someone by means of lines; the amount drawn from an ac-count.

drawl *v.* To speak slowly with prolonged vowels.

dray *n.* A low, heavy cart without sides, used for hauling.

dread *v.* To fear greatly; to anticipate with alarm, anxiety, or reluctance. *n.* A great fear.

dread-ful *adj.* Inspiring dread; very distasteful or shocking; awful. **dreadfully** *adv.*, **dreadfulness** *n.*

dream *n.* A series of thoughts, images, or emotions which occur during the rapid eye movement or REM state of sleep; an experience in waking life that has the characteristics of a dream; a daydream; something notable for its beauty or enjoyable quality; something that is strongly desired; something that fully satisfies a desire. **dream** *v.*, **dreamful, dreamlike** *adj.*, **dreamfully** *adv.*, **dreamfulness** *n.*

drea-ry *adj.* Bleak and gloomy; dull. **drearily** *adv.*, **dreariness** *n.*

dredge *n.* An apparatus used to remove sand or mud from the bottom of a body of water; a boat or barge equipped with a dredge. *v.* To dig, gather, or deepen with a dredging machine; to use a dredge. **dredger** *n.*

dregs *pl., n.* The sediment of a liquid; the least desirable part.

drench *v.* To wet thoroughly; to throw water on. **drencher** *n.*

dress *n.* An outer garment for women and girls; covering or appearance appropriate to a particular time. *v.* To set straight; to put clothes on; to arrange in a straight line at proper intervals; to provide with clothing; to kill and prepare for market; to put on or wear formal or fancy clothes.

drew *v.* Past tense of draw.

drib-ble *v.* To drip; to slobber or drool; to bounce a ball repeatedly; to move in short bounces. **dribbler** *n.*

drift *v.* To be driven or carried along by or as if by currents of air or water; to move along the line of least resistance; to move about aimlessly; to be carried along with no guidance or control; to accumulate in piles, as sand; to deviate from a set course; in the western U.S., to drive livestock slowly to allow grazing.

drill *n.* A tool used in boring holes; the act of training soldiers in marching and the manual of arms; a physical or mental exercise to perfect a skill by regular practice; a marine snail which is destructive to oysters by boring through their shells and feeding on them. *v.* To make a hole with a drill; to train by repeated exercise.

drill-mas-ter *n.* *Milit.* A non-commissioned officer who instructs in military drill.

drink *v.* To take liquid into the mouth and swallow; to take in or suck up; to receive into one's consciousness; to partake of alcoholic beverages. *n.* A liquid suitable for swallowing; al-

coholic beverages; a sizable body of water. **drinkable** *adj.*, **drinker** *n.*

drip *v.* To fall in drops. *n.* Liquid or moisture which falls in drops; the sound made by falling drops. *Slang* A dull or unattractive person.

drip coffee *n.* Coffee made by allowing boiling water to drip slowly through ground coffee.

drip-dry *adj.* Made of a washable fabric which dries without wrinkling and needs no ironing. **drip-dry** *v.*

drive *v.* To propel, push, or press onward; to repulse by authority; to force into a particular act or state; to operate or be conveyed in a vehicle; to supply a moving force; to impress convincingly with force; in sports, to hit a ball hard in a game; to rush or advance violently. *n.* The act of driving; a trip taken in a vehicle; the means or apparatus by which motion is transmitted to a machine; an organized movement or campaign to accomplish something; initiative; the act of urging together animals. *Milit.* A full-scale military offensive.

drive-in *n.* A place of business which allows consumers to be accommodated while remaining in their vehicles.

driv-el *v.* To slobber; to talk nonsensically. **drivel** *n.*

driz-zle *n.* A fine, quiet, gentle rain. **drizzle** *v.*

droll *adj.* Whimsically comical. **drollery** *n.*

drom-e-dar-y *n., pl.* -ies A one-humped camel, widely used in northern Africa and western Asia as a beast of burden.

drone *n.* A male bee, especially a honey bee, which has no sting, performs no work, and produces no honey; a person who depends on others for his survival; an unmanned boat or aircraft controlled by a remote control device. *v.* To make a low, continuous humming sound; to speak monotonously. **droner** *n.*

drool *v.* To let saliva dribble from the mouth. *Informal* To make an exaggerated expression of desire. **drool** *n.*

droop *v.* To hang or bend downward; to become depressed. **droop, droopiness** *n.*, **droopy** *adj.*

drop *n.* A tiny, pear-shaped or rounded mass of liquid; a small quantity of a substance; the smallest unit of liquid measure; the act of falling; a swift decline; the vertical distance from a higher to a lower level; a delivery of something by parachute. *v.* To fall in drops; to descend from one area or level to another; to fall into a state of collapse or death; to pass into a given state or condition; to end or terminate an association or relationship with; to deposit at a specified place. **drop behind** To fall behind. **drop by** To pay a brief visit. **drop out** To quit school without graduating; to withdraw from society.

drop-sy *n., Med.* A diseased condition in

which large amounts of fluid collect in the body tissues and cavities.

dross *n.* An impurity which forms on the surface of molten metal; inferior, trivial, or worthless matter.

drought *or* **drouth** *n.* A prolonged period of dryness; a chronic shortage of something.

drove *n.* A herd being driven in a body; a crowd. *v.* Past tense of drive.

drown *v.* To kill or die by suffocating in a liquid; to cause not to be heard by making a loud noise; to drive out.

drowse *v.* To doze. **drowse** *n.*

drows-y *adj.* Sleepy; tending to induce sleep. **drowsiness** *n.*

drub *v.* To hit with a stick; to abuse with words; to defeat decisively.

drudge *n.* A person who does tiresome or menial tasks. **drudge** *v.*, **drudgery** *n.*

drug *n.* A substance used in the treatment of disease or illness; a narcotic. *v.* To take drugs for narcotic effect; to mix or dose with drugs.

drum *n.*

A musical percussion instrument consisting of a hollow frame with a cover stretched across one or both ends, played by beating with sticks or the hands; something with the shape of a drum; a cylindrical container; a metal container holding a capacity between 12 and 110 gallons; any of various percoid fishes that make a drumming noise. *v.* To beat a drum; to tap rhythmically or incessantly; to instill by repetition; to dismiss in disgrace. **drum up** To invent or devise; to go out and actively pursue new accounts or business.

drunk *adj.* Intoxicated with alcohol which impairs the physical and mental faculties of a person; overwhelmed by strong feeling or emotion. *n.* A drunkard.

drunk-ard *adj.* A person who is intoxicated by liquor.

drupe *n.* A fruit, as the peach, usually having one large pit or seed.

dry *adj.* Free from moisture or liquid; having little or no rain; devoid of running water; not liquid; thirsty; eaten without a garnish, such as jelly; humorous in a shrewd, impersonal way; not sweet, as in dry wines. *Informal* Opposed to the sale or consumption of alcoholic beverages. *v.* To remove the water from. **dryly** *adv.*, **dryness** *n.*

dry-ad *n.* A wood nymph.

dry--clean *v.* To clean cloth or fabrics with chemical solvents, as benzenes, rather than water.

dry goods *pl.*, *n.* Textile fabrics as distinguished from foodstuffs and hardware.

du-al *adj.* Made up or composed of two parts; having a double purpose.

dub *v.* To confer knighthood upon; to nickname; to give a new sound track to; to add to a film, radio, or television production; to transpose a sound already recorded. **dub, dubber** *n.*

du-bi-ous *adj.* Causing doubt; unsettled in judgment; reluctant to agree; question as to quality or validity; verging on impropriety. **dubiously** *adv.*

du-cal *adj.* Pertaining to a duke or dukedom.

duch-ess *n.* The wife or widow of a duke; a female holding a ducal title in her own right.

duck *n.*

Any of various swimming birds with short necks and legs; the flesh of any of these birds used as food. *Slang* A person. *v.* To lower the head and body quickly; to evade; to plunge quickly under water.

duct *n.* A bodily tube or canal, especially one carrying a secretion; a tubular passage through which something flows.

duc-tile *adj.* Capable of being drawn into a fine strand or wire; easily influenced or persuaded.

dud *n.*, *Informal* A bomb, shell, or explosive round which fails to detonate; something which turns out to be a failure. **duds** *pl.* Clothing; personal belongings.

dude *n.*, *Informal* A city person vacationing on a ranch; a man who is a fancy dresser. *Slang* A fellow.

dudg-eon *n.* A sullen, displeased, or indignant mood.

due *adj.* Owed; payable; owed or owing as a natural or moral right; scheduled or expected to occur. *n.* Something that is deserved or owed. **dues** *pl.* A fee or charge for membership.

du-el *n.* A premeditated combat between two people, usually fought to resolve a point of honor; a struggle which resembles a duel. **duel** *v.*, **duelist** *n.*

du-et *n.* A musical composition for two performers or musical instruments.

duf-fel bag *n.* A large cloth bag for carrying personal belongings.

duke *n.* A noble ranking below a prince and above a marquis. **dukes** *pl.*, *Slang* The fists. **dukedom** *n.*

dul-cet *adj.* Melodious; pleasing to the ear; having an agreeable, soothing quality.

dul-ci-mer *n.* A musical stringed instrument played with two small picks or by plucking.

dull *adj.* Stupid; lacking in intelligence or understanding; insensitive; having a blunt edge or point; not intensely felt; arousing no interest or curiosity; not bright; overcast or gloomy; unclear. *v.* To make or become dull; to blunt or to make blunt. **dullness** *n.*, **dully** *adv.*

du-ly *adv.* In a proper or due manner.

dumb *adj.* Unable to speak; temporarily speechless. *Informal* Stupid.

dumbly adv., **dumbness** n.

dumb-bell n. A short bar with two adjustable weighted disks attached to each end, used in pairs for calisthenic exercise.

dumb-waiter n. A small elevator, usually found in the kitchen of a home, which is used to convey goods, as food or dishes, from one floor to another.

dum-dum bullet n. A soft-nosed, small-arms bullet designed to expand on contact.

dum-found or **dumb-found** v. To confound with amazement.

dum-my n., pl. **-mies** One who is habitually silent; one who is stupid; the exposed hand in bridge; a bridge player whose hand is a dummy; an imitation or copy of something, used as a substitute; a person or agency secretly in the service of another.

dump v. To throw down or discard in a mass; to empty material out of a container or vehicle; in computer science, to reproduce data stored in the working memory onto an external storage medium. n. A place where garbage or trash is dumped. Milit. A military storage facility. Slang A disreputable or messy place.

dump-ling n. A small mass of dough cooked in soup or stew; sweetened dough wrapped around fruit, baked, and served as desert.

dun v. To press a debtor for payment. n. A brownish gray to dull grayish brown color. **dun** adj.

dunce n. A slow-witted person.

dune n. A ridge or hill of sand blown or drifted by the wind.

dung n. The excrement of animals; manure.

dun-ga-ree n. A sturdy, coarse, cotton fabric, especially blue denim; pants or overalls made from this material.

dun-geon n. A dark, confining, underground prison chamber.

dunk v. To dip a piece of food into liquid before eating; to submerge someone in a playful fashion.

du-o n., pl. **-os** An instrument duet; two people in close association.

du-o-de-num n., pl. **-dena** or **-denums** The first portion of the small intestine, extending from the lower end of the stomach to the jejunum. duodenal adj.

dupe n. A person who is easily manipulated or deceived. v. To deceive or trick.

du-plex adj. Double. n. An apartment with rooms on two adjoining floors; having two parts.

du-pli-cate adj. Identical with another; existing in or consisting of two corresponding parts. n. Either of two things which are identical; an exact copy of an original. v. To make an exact copy of. duplication n.

du-ra-ble adj. Able to continue for a prolonged period of time without deterioration. durability n.

du-ra-tion n. The period of time during which something exists or lasts.

du-ress n. Constraint by fear or force; in law, coercion illegally applied; forced restraint.

dur-ing prep. Throughout the time of; within the time of.

dusk n. The earliest part of the evening, just before darkness.

dust n. Fine, dry particles of matter; the earth, as a place of burial; the surface of the ground; a scorned condition. v. To remove the dust from; to sprinkle or cover with a powdery material. **dusty** adj.

Dutch n. The people of the Netherlands; the language of the Netherlands. **Dutch** adj., **Dutchman** n.

Dutch elm disease n. A fungus which affects elm trees, eventually killing them.

Dutch treat n. A date during which each person pays his own way.

duty n., pl. **-ties** Something which a person must or ought to do; a moral obligation; a service, action, or task assigned to one, especially in the military; a government tax on imports.

dwarf n., pl. **-rfs** or **-rves** A human being, plant, or animal of a much smaller than normal size. v. To stunt the natural growth of; to cause to seem small by comparison. **dwarfish** adj.

dwell v. To live, as an inhabitant; to continue in a given place or condition; to focus one's attention. **dweller** n.

dwell-ing n. A house or building in which one lives.

DWI abbr. Driving while intoxicated.

dwin-dle v. To waste away; to become steadily less.

dye v. To fix a color in or stain materials; to color with or become colored by a dye. n. A color imparted by a dye.

dying adj. Coming to the end of life.

dy-nam-ic adj. Marked by energy and productive activity or change; of or relating to energy, motion, or force. **dynamically** adv.

dy-nam-ics n., Phys. The part of physics which deals with force, energy, and motion and the relationship between them.

dy-na-mite n. An explosive composed of nitroglycerin or ammonium nitrate and an absorbent material, usually packaged in stick form. v. To blow up with or as if with dynamite.

dy-nas-ty n., pl. **-ties** A succession of rulers from the same family; a family or group which maintains great power, wealth, or position for many years. **dynastic** adj.

dys-en-ter-y n. An infection of the lower intestinal tract which produces pain, fever, and severe diarrhea.

dys-lex-i-a n. An impairment in one's ability to read. **dyslexic** adj.

dys-pep-sia n. Indigestion. **dyspeptic** adj.

dys-pro-si-um n. A metallic element used in nuclear research, symbolized by Dy.

dys-tro-phy n. Atrophy of muscle tissue; any of various neuromuscular disorders, especially muscular dystrophy.

E, e The fifth letter of the English alphabet. *Mus.* The third tone in the natural scale of C.

ea *abbr.* Each.

each *adj.* Everyone of two or more considered separately. *adv.* To or for each; apiece.

each other *pron.* Each in reciprocal action or relation; one another.

ea-ger *adj.* Marked by enthusiastic interest or desire; having a great desire or wanting something. -ly *adv.*, -ness *n.*

ea-gle *n.* A large, powerful bird of prey having a powerful bill, broad strong wings, and soaring flight; a U.S. gold coin worth ten dollars; a score of two under par on a hole in golf.

eagle--eyed *adj.* Having exceptional vision.

ear *n., Anat.*

The hearing organ in vertebrates, located on either side of the head; any of various organs capable of detecting vibratory motion; the ability to hear keenly; attention or heed; something that resembles the external ear. **all ears** Listen closely. **by ear** Without reference to written music.

earl *n.* A British title for a nobleman ranking above a viscount and below a marquis. **earldom** *n.*

ear-ly *adj.* Occurring near the beginning of a period of time; a development or a series; distant in past time; before the usual or expected time; occurring in the near future. *adv.* Near the beginning of time; far back in time. **earlier, earliest** *adj.*

early bird *n.* An early riser; a person who arrives early.

earn *v.* To receive payment in return for work done or services rendered; to gain as a result of one's efforts.

ear-nest *n.* A serious mental state; payment in advance to bind an agreement; a pledge. *adj.* Characterized by an intense and serious state of mind; having serious intent. **earnestly** *adv.*, **earnestness** *n.*

earn-ings *pl., n.* Something earned, such as a salary.

earth *n.* The third planet from the sun and the planet on which there is life; the outer layer of the world; ground; soil; dirt.

ease *n.* A state of being comfortable; freedom from pain, discomfort, or care; freedom from labor or difficulty; an act of easing or a state of being eased. *v.* To free from pain or discomfort; to lessen the pressure or tension; to make less difficult; to move or pass with freedom. **at ease** Free from discomfort. *Milit.* Standing silently with the feet apart, as in a military formation. **easeful** *adj.*, **easefully** *adv.*

ea-sel *n.* A frame used by artists to support a canvas or picture.

east *n.* The direction opposite of west; the direction in which the sun rises. **-erly** *adj. & adv.*, **-ward** *adj.*, **-ds** *adv.*

East Berlin *n.* The capital of East Germany.

Easter *n.* A Christian festival which celebrates the resurrection of Christ.

easy *adj.* Capable of being accomplished with little difficulty; free from worry or pain; not hurried or strenuous; something readily obtainable. **easily** *adv.*, **easiness** *n.*

easy going *adj.* Taking life easy; without worry, concern, or haste.

eat *v.* To chew and swallow food; to erode; to consume with distress or agitation; to take a meal. **eat crow** To accept what one has been fighting against. **eat one's heart out** To grieve bitterly. **eat one's words** To retract what has been said. **eat out of one's hand** To accept the domination of another. **eater** *n.*

eaves *pl., n.* The overhanging edge of a roof.

ebb *n.* The return of the tide towards the sea; a time of decline. *v.* To recede, as the tide does; to fall or flow back; to weaken.

ebb tide *n.* The tide while at ebb; a period of decline.

eb-o-ny *n., pl.* **-nies** The dark, hard, colored wood from the center of the ebony tree of Asia and Africa. *adj.* Resembling ebony; black.

e-bul-lient *adj.* Filled with enthusiasm. **ebullience** *n.*, **ebulliently** *adv.*

eb-ul-li-tion *n.* The process of boiling or bubbling; a sudden release of emotion.

ec-cen-tric *adj.* Differing from an established pattern or accepted norm; deviating from a perfect circle; not located at the geometrical center. *n.* An odd or erratic person; a disk or wheel with its axis not situated in the center. **eccentrically** *adv.*, **eccentricity** *n.*

ec-cle-si-as-ti-cal *n.* A clergyman; a person officially serving a church. *adj.* Of or relating to a church.

ech-e-lon *n.* A formation, as of military aircraft or naval vessels, resembling a series of steps where each rank is positioned slightly to the right or left of the preceding one; a level of command or authority; a hierarchy.

ech-o *n., pl.* **-oes** Repetition of a sound by reflecting sound waves from a surface; the sound produced by such a reflection; a repetition; the reflection of transmitted radar signals by an object. *v.* To repeat or be repeated by; to imitate.

ec-lec-tic *adj.* Having components from diverse sources or styles. **eclectic** *n.*

e-clipse *n.* A total or partial blocking of one celestial body by another. *v.* To fall into obscurity or decline; to cause an eclipse of.

e-clip-tic *n., Astron.* The circle formed by the intersection of the plane of the earth's orbit and the celestial sphere.

ec-logue *n.* A short pastoral poem in the

form of a dialogue.

ec-o-cide *n.* The deliberate destruction of the natural environment, caused by pollutants.

e-col-o-gy *n.* The branch of science concerned with the interrelationship of organisms and their environments; the relationship between living organisms and their environments. **ecologic** *adj.*, **ecologically** *adv.*, **ecologist** *n.*

ec-o-nom-ic *adj.* The science relating to the development, production, and manage-ment of material wealth; relating to the necessities of life.

ec-o-nom-i-cal *adj.* Not wasteful; frugal; operating with little waste. **-ly** *adv.*

ec-o-nom-ics *pl., n.* The science which treats production, distribution, and consumption of commodities. **-ist** *n.*

e-con-o-mize *v.* To manage thriftily; to use sparingly. **economizer** *n.*

e-con-o-my *n., pl.* **-mies** Careful management of money, materials, and resources; a reduction in expenses; a system or structure for the management of resources and production of goods and services.

ec-ru *n.* A light yellowish brown, as the color of unbleached linen.

ec-sta-sy *n., pl.* **-sies** The state of intense joy or delight. **ecstatic** *adj.*, **ecstatically** *adv.*

Ec-ua-dor *n.* A country located in northwestern South America. **Ecuadorian** *adj. & n.*

ec-u-men-i-cal *adj.* Worldwide or general in extent, application, or influence; promoting unity among Christian churches or religions. **ecumenically** *adv.*, **ecumenism** *n.*

ec-ze-ma *n.* A noncontagious inflammatory skin condition, marked by itching and scaly patches. **eczematous** *adj.*

ed-dy *n., pl.* **-dies** A current, as of water, running against the direction of the main current, especially in a circular motion. **eddy** *v.*

e-del-weiss *n.* An Alpine plant having woolly leaves and small flowers.

E-den *n.* The garden which was the first home of Adam and Eve; a delightful area; a paradise.

edge *n.* The thin, sharp, cutting side of a blade; keenness; sharpness; the border where an object or area begins or ends; an advantage. *v.* To furnish with an edge or border; to sharpen; to move gradually. **on edge** Tense.

ed-i-ble *adj.* Safe or fit for consumption. **edibility**, **edible** *n.*

e-dict *n.* A public decree; an order or command officially proclaimed.

ed-i-fy *v.* To benefit and enlighten, morally or spiritually. **edification**, **edifier** *n.*

Edison, Thomas Alva *n.* (1847-1931). An American inventor.

ed-it *v.* To prepare and correct for publication; to compile for an edition; to delete or change. **editor** *n.*

e-di-tion *n.* The form in which a book is published; the total number of copies printed at one time; one similar to an original version.

ed-i-to-ri-al *n.* An article in a newspaper or magazine which expresses the opinion of a publisher or editor. *adj.* Of or relating to an editor or an editor's work; being or resembling an editorial. **editorially** *adv.*

ed-u-cate *v.* To supply with training or schooling; to supervise the mental or moral growth of. **educator** *n.*

e-duce *v.* To call forth or bring out; to develop from given facts.

eel *n., pl.* **eel** *or* **eels** A snake-like marine or freshwater fish without scales or pelvic fins.

ee-rie *or* **ee-ry** *adj.* Suggesting or inspiring the supernatural or strange; spooky. **eerily** *adv.*, **eeriness** *n.*

ef-face *v.* To remove or rub out. **effacer**, **effacement** *n.*

ef-fect *n.* Something produced by a cause; the power to produce a desired result; the reaction something has on an object; a technique which produces an intended impression. **take effect** To become operative. **effecter** *n.*

ef-fec-tive *adj.* Producing an expected effect or proper result. **effectiveness** *n.*

ef-fem-i-nate *adj.* Having a more woman-like quality or trait than a man. **effeminacy** *n.*, **effeminately** *adv.*

ef-fer-ent *adj., Physiol.* Carrying away or outward from a central organ or part. **efferent** *n.*, **efferently** *adv.*

ef-fete *adj.* Exhausted of effectiveness or force; worn-out; decadent.

ef-fi-ca-cious *adj.* Producing an intended effect. **efficaciously** *adv.*

ef-fi-cient *adj.* Adequate in performance with a minimum of waste or effort; giving a high ratio of output.

ef-fi-gy *n., pl.* **-gies** A life-size sculpture or painting representing a crude image or dummy of a hated person.

ef-flo-res-cence *n.* A time of flowering; a slow process of development; the highest point. **efflorescent** *adj.*

ef-flu-ence *n.* An act of flowing out; something that flows out or forth. **effluent** *adj. & n.*

ef-flu-vi-um *n., pl.* **-via** *or* **-viums** An unpleasant vapor from something. **effluvial** *adj.*

ef-fort *n.* Voluntary exertion of physical or mental energy; a difficult exertion; a normally earnest attempt or achievement; something done through exertion. *Phys.* A force applied against inertia. **effortless** *adj.*

ef-fron-ter-y *n., pl.* **-ies** Shameless boldness; impudence.

ef-ful-gent *adj.* Shining brilliantly; radiant. **effulgence** *n.*

ef-fu-sion *n.* An instance of pouring forth; an unrestrained outpouring of feeling. **effuse** *v.*, **effusive** *adj.*, **effusively** *adv.*

egg *n.* The hard-shelled reproductive cell of female animals, especially one produced by a chicken, used as food.

v. To incite to action.

egg-beat-er *n.* A kitchen tool with rotating blades used to mix, blend, or beat food.

egg-head *n.*, *Informal* An intellectual; highbrow.

egg-nog *n.* A drink of beaten eggs, sugar, and milk or cream, often mixed with alcohol.

egg-plant *n.* A widely cultivated perennial plant which yields an egg-shaped edible fruit.

egg-roll *n.* A thin egg-dough casing filled with minced vegetables and sometimes meat or seafood which is fried.

eg-lan-tine *n.* The sweetbrier, a type of rose.

e-go *n.* The self thinking, feeling, and acting distinct from the external world. *Physiol.* The conscious aspect that most directly controls behavior and is most in touch with reality.

e-go-cen-tric *adj.* Thinking, observing, and regarding oneself as the object of all experiences. egocentric, egocentricity *n.*

e-go-ma-ni-a *n.* Self obsession. egomaniac *n.*, egomaniacal *adj.*

ego trip *n.* *Slang* Something which satisfies the ego.

e-gre-gious *adj.* Outstandingly or remarkably bad; flagrant. -ly *adv.*

e-gress *n.* The act of coming out; emergence; a means of departing; exit.

e-gret *n.*

Any of several species of white wading birds having long, drooping plumes.

E-gypt *n.* A country located in northeast Africa and southwest Asia.
Egyptian *adj. & n.*

ei-der *n.* A large sea duck found in northern regions, having soft down which is used for comforters, pillows, etc.

eight *n.* The cardinal number which follows seven. eighth *n.*, *adj. & adv.*

eight ball *n.* The black ball with the number eight in the game of pool. behind the eight ball *Slang* In a bad spot.

Einstein, Albert *n.* (1879-1955). A German born American physicist.

Eisenhower, Dwight David *n.* (1890-1969). The 34th president of the United States, from 1953-1961.

ei-ther *pron.* One or the other. *conj.* Used before the first of two or more alternatives linked by or. *adj.* One or the other of two. *adv.* Likewise; also.

e-jac-u-late *v.* To eject abruptly, as in semen; to utter suddenly and briefly; to exclaim.
ejaculation *n.*, ejaculatory *adj.*

e-ject *v.* To throw out; to expel.
ejection, ejector *n.*

eke out *v.* To obtain with great effort.

e-lab-o-rate *adj.* Planned or carried out with great detail; very complex; intricate. *v.* To work out or complete with great detail; to give more detail.
elaborateness, -tion *n.*, -ly *adv.*

e-land *n.* A large African antelope with a tan coat and large spiral horns.

e-lapse *v.* To slip or glide away.

e-las-tic *adj.* Complying with changing circumstances; capable of easy adjustment. elastically *adv.*, elasticity *n.*

e-late *v.* To make proud of. elation *n.*

el-bow *n.* A sharp turn, as in a river or road, which resembles an elbow. *Anat.* The outer joint of the arm between the upper arm and forearm.

elbow-room *n.* Ample room to move about; enough space for comfort.

eld-er *adj.* Older. *n.* One who is older than others; a person of great influence; an official of the church. *Bot.* A shrub bearing reddish fruit.

e-lect *v.* To choose or select by vote, as for an office; to make a choice. *adj.* Singled out on purpose; elected but not yet inaugurated. *n.* One chosen or set apart, especially for spiritual salvation.

e-lec-tric *or* **e-lec-tri-cal** *adj.* Relating to electricity. electrically *adv.*

e-lec-tri-cian *n.* A person whose job it is to install or maintain electric equipment.

e-lec-tric-i-ty *n.*, *Phys.*, *Chem.* A force that causes bodies to attract or repel each other, responsible for a natural phenomena as lightning; electric current as a power source; emotional excitement.

e-lec-tro-car-di-o-gram *n.* The record produced by an electrocardiograph machine.

e-lec-tro-car-di-o-graph *n.* An electric instrument which detects and records the heartbeat.

e-lec-tro-cute *v.* To kill or execute by the use of electric current. electrocution *n.*

e-lec-trode *n.* A conductor by which an electric current enters or leaves.

e-lec-tro-dy-nam-ics *n.*, *Phys.* The study of the interactions of moving electric charges. electrodynamic *adj.*

e-lec-trol-y-sis *n.*, *Chem.*, *Phys.* A chemical decomposition by an electric current; destruction of tumors or hair roots by an electric current.

e-lec-tro-mag-net *n.* A magnet consisting of a soft iron core magnetized by an electric current passing through a wire which is coiled around the core.

e-lec-trom-e-ter *n.* An instrument for detecting or measuring electric potential or differences between two conductors.

e-lec-tro-mo-tive *adj.* Of, pertaining to, or tending to produce electric current.

e-lec-tron *n.*, *Elect.* A subatomic particle with a negative electric charge found outside of an atoms nucleus.

e-lec-tro-stat-ic *adj.* Pertaining to static electric charges.

e-lec-tro-stat-ics *pl.*, *n.*, *Phys.* The physics

of static electric charges.

e-lec-tro-type *n.* A duplicate metal plate made by electroplating a mold of the original plate which is used in printing. **electrotype** *v.*

el-ee-mos-y-nar-y *adj.* Of, pertaining to, or contributed as charity.

el-e-gance *n.* Refinement in appearance, movement, or manners. **elegant** *adj.*

el-e-gy *n., pl.* **-gies** A poem expressing sorrow and lamentation for one who is dead.

el-e-ment *n.* A constituent part. *Chem. & Phys.* A substance not separable into less complex substances by chemical means. **elements** *pl.* The conditions of the weather.

el-e-men-ta-ry *adj.* Fundamental, essential; referring to elementary school; introducing fundamental principles.

el-e-phant *n.*

A large mammal having a long, flexible trunk and curved tusks.

el-e-phan-ti-a-sis *n., Pathol.* The enormous enlargement of affected parts along with hardening, caused by obstruction of lymphatics from parasitic worms.

el-e-vate *v.* To lift up or raise; to promote to a higher rank.

e-lev-en *n.* A cardinal number with a sum equal to ten plus one. **eleventh** *n.*

elf *n., pl.* **elves** An imaginary being with magical powers, often mischievous; a small, mischievous child. **elfish** *adj.*

e-lic-it *v.* To bring or draw out; to evoke.

e-lide *v.* To omit, especially to slur over in pronunciation, as a vowel, consonant, or syllable. **elision** *n.*

e-lim-i-nate *v.* To get rid of, remove; to leave out, to omit; to excrete, as waste. **elimination, -tor** *n.,* **-ive, -ory** *adj.*

e-lite *n.* The most skilled members of a group; a small, powerful group; a type size yielding twelve characters to the inch. **elite** *adj.*

e-lix-ir *n., Phar.* A sweetened aromatic liquid of alcohol and water, used as a vehicle for medicine; a medicine regarded as a cure-all.

elk *n., pl.* **elks** *or* **elk** The largest deer of Europe and Asia.

ell *n.* An extension of a building at right angles to the main structure.

el-lipse *n., Geom.* A closed curve, somewhat oval in shape.

el-lip-tic *or* **el-lip-ti-cal** *adj.* Of, pertaining to, or shaped like an ellipse.

elm *n.* Any of various valuable timber and shade trees with arching branches.

el-o-cu-tion *n.* The art of effective public speaking. **-ary** *adj.,* **elocutionist** *n.*

e-lope *v.* To run away, especially in order to get married, usually without parental permission. **elopement, eloper** *n.*

el-o-quent *adj.* Having the power to speak fluently and persuasively; vividly expressive. **eloquence** *n.,* **-ly** *adv.*

else *adj.* Different; other; more; additional. *adv.* In addition; besides.

else-where *adv.* To or in another place.

e-lu-ci-date *v.* To make clear, clarify; to explain. **elucidator, elucidation** *n.*

e-lude *v.* To evade or avoid; to escape understanding.

e-ma-ci-ate *v.* To become or cause to become extremely thin from the loss of appetite. **emaciation** *n.*

em-a-nate *v.* To come or give forth, as from a source. **emanation** *n.*

e-man-ci-pate *v.* To liberate; to set free from bondage. **emancipation, emancipator** *n.*

e-mas-cu-late *v.* To castrate; to deprive of masculine vigor. **emasculation, emasculator** *n.*

em-balm *v.* To treat a corpse with preservatives in order to protect from decay. **embalmer** *n.*

em-bank *v.* To support, protect, or defend with a bank of earth or stone. **embankment** *n.*

em-bar-go *n., pl.* **-goes** A prohibition or restraint on trade, as a government order forbidding the entry or departure of merchant vessels, for example the oil embargo of 1973. **embargo** *v.*

em-bark *v.* To board a ship; to set out on a venture. **embarkation** *n.*

em-bar-rass *v.* To cause to feel self-conscious; to confuse; to burden with financial difficulties **embarrassment** *n.*

em-bas-sy *n., pl.* **-sies** The head-quarters of an ambassador.

em-bat-tle *v.* To prepare or arrange for battle.

em-bed *v.* To fix or enclose tightly in a surrounding mass.

em-bel-lish *v.* To adorn or make beautiful with ornamentation; to decorate; to heighten the attractiveness by adding ornamental details. **-ment** *n.*

em-ber *n.* A small piece of glowing coal or wood, as in a dying fire. **embers** *pl.* The smoldering ashes or remains of a fire.

em-bez-zle *v.* To take money or other items fraudulently. **embezzlement** *n.*

em-bit-ter *v.* To make bitter; to create feelings of hostility. **embitterment** *n.*

em-bla-zon *v.* To decorate in bright colors.

em-blem *n.* A symbol of something; a distinctive design. **emblematic, emblematical** *adj.*

em-bod-y *v.* To give a bodily form to; to personify. **embodiment** *n.*

em-bold-en *v.* To encourage; to make bold.

em-bo-lism *n., Med.* The blockage of a blood vessel, as by an air bubble or a detached clot.

em-bon-point *n.* Plumpness; stoutness.

em-boss *v.* To shape or decorate in relief; to represent in relief.

em-bou-chure *n., Mus.* The part of a wind instrument which is applied to the lips to produce a musical tone.

em-bow-er v. To enclose, cover, or shelter.

em-brace v. To clasp or hold in the arms; to hug; to surround; to take in mentally or visually. n. The act of embracing; a hug.

em-bra-sure n., Arch. A flared opening in a wall, as for a door or window.

em-bro-cate v. To moisten and rub an injured part of the body with a liquid medicine. embrocation n.

em-broi-der v. To decorate with ornamental needlework; to add fictitious details. embroidery n.

em-broil v. To involve in contention or violent actions; to throw into confusion. embroilment n.

em-bry-o n., pl. -os An organism in its early developmental stage, before it has a distinctive form; in the human species, the first eight weeks of development, especially before birth or germination; a rudimentary stage. embryonic adj.

em-bry-ol-o-gy n. The science concerned with the origin, structure, and growth of embryos. embryological adj., embryologist n.

em-cee n., Informal A master of ceremonies.

e-mend v. To correct or remove faults. emendation, emender n.

em-er-ald n. A bright-green, transparent variety of beryl, used as a gemstone.

e-merge v. To rise into view; to come into existence. emergence n., -ent adj.

e-mer-gen-cy n., pl. -cies A sudden and unexpected situation requiring prompt action.

e-mer-i-tus adj. Retired from active duty but retaining the honorary title held immediately before retirement. emeritus n.

em-er-y n. A grainy, mineral substance having impure corundum, used for polishing and grinding.

e-met-ic adj. A medicine used to induce vomiting. emetic n.

em-i-grate v. To move from one country or region to settle elsewhere. emigrant, n.

e-mi-gre n. A refugee.

em-i-nent adj. High in esteem, rank, or office; conspicuous; outstanding. eminently adv.

eminent domain n. The right of a government to take or control property for public use.

e-mir n. A Moslem prince.

em-is-sar-y n., pl. -ies A person sent out on a mission.

e-mit v. To send forth; to throw or give out.

e-mol-lient n. A substance for the soothing and softening of the skin. emollient adj.

e-mol-u-ment n. Profit; compensation, as a salary or perquisite.

e-mote v. To show emotion, as in acting.

e-mo-tion n. A strong surge of feeling; any of the feelings of fear, sorrow, joy,

hate, or love; a particular feeling, as love or hate.

em-pa-thy n., Physiol. Identification with and understanding the feelings of another person. empathetic, empathic adj.

em-pen-nage n. The rear section or tail of an aircraft.

em-per-or n. The ruler of an empire.

em-pha-sis n., pl. -ses Significance or importance attached to anything.

em-phat-ic adj. Expressed or spoken with emphasis. emphatically adv.

em-pire n. The territories or nations governed by a single supreme authority.

em-pir-i-cal or **em-pir-ic** adj. Depending on or gained from observation or experiment rather than from theory and science. empirically adv.

em-place-ment n. A platform for guns or military equipment.

em-ploy v. To engage the service or use of; to devote time to an activity. employable adj., employer, -ment n.

em-ploy-ee or **em-ploy-e** n. A person who works for another in return for salary or wages.

em-po-ri-um n., pl. -riums or -ria A large store which carries general merchandise.

em-pow-er v. To authorize; to delegate; to license.

em-press n. A woman who rules an empire; an emperor's wife or widow.

emp-ty adj. Containing nothing; vacant; lacking substance. emptily adv., emptiness n.

em-py-re-an n. Pertaining to the highest part of heaven; the sky.

e-mu n. A swift-running Australian bird which is related to the ostrich.

em-u-late v. To strive to equal, especially by imitating. emulation n., emulous adj.

e-mul-sion n., Chem. A suspended mixture of small droplets, one within the other. Photog. A light-sensitive coating on photographic paper, film, or plates. emulsive adj.

en-a-ble v. To supply with adequate power, knowledge, or opportunity; to give legal power to another.

en-act v. To make into law. enactment n.

en-nam-el n. A decorative or protective coating fused on a surface, as of pottery; a paint that dries to a hard, glossy surface; the hard outermost covering of a tooth. v. To apply, inlay, or decorate with enamel.

en-am-or v. To inflame with love; to charm.

en-camp v. To form or stay in a camp. encampment n.

en-cap-su-late v. To enclose or encase in a capsule. encapsulation n.

en-ceph-a-li-tis n., Pathol. Inflammation of the brain.

en-chain v. To put in chains.

en-chant v. To put under a spell; to bewitch; to charm; to delight greatly. enchantment n.

en-cir-cle v. To form a circle around; to move around. encirclement n.

en-clave n. A country surrounded by a foreign country; a cultural group living within a larger group.

en-close v. To surround on all sides; to put in the same envelope or package with something else. enclosure n.

en-co-mi-um n., pl. -miums or -mia High praise.

en-com-pass v. To surround; to form a circle; to enclose.

en-core n. An audience's demand for a repeat performance; a performance in response to an encore. v. To call for an encore.

en-coun-ter n. An unplanned or unexpected meeting or conflict. v. To come upon unexpectedly; to confront in a hostile situation.

encounter group n. A therapy group formed to increase people's sensitivity and to reveal their feelings so that they openly relate to others.

en-cour-age v. To inspire with courage or hope. -ment n., encouragingly adv.

en-croach v. To intrude upon the rights or possessions of another. encroacher, encroachment n.

en-crust v. To cover with a crust; to crust. encrustation n.

en-cum-ber v. To hinder or burden with difficulties or obligations. encumbrance n.

en-cy-cli-cal n., Rom. Cath. Ch. A papal letter to the bishops of the world.

en-cy-clo-pe-di-a n. A comprehensive work with articles covering a broad range of subjects. encyclopedic adj.

en-cyst v. To become enclosed in a sac. encystment n.

end n. A part lying at a boundary; the terminal point at which something concludes; the point in time at which something ceases; a goal; a fragment; a remainder; in football, either of the players in the outermost position on the line of scrimmage. v. To come or bring to a termination; to ruin or destroy; to die.

en-dan-ger v. To expose or put into danger or imperil. endangerment n.

en-dan-gered adj. Threatened with extinction.

en-dear v. To make beloved or dear. endearingly adv.

en-dear-ment n. The state of being endeared.

en-deav-or n. An attempt to attain or do something. endeavor v.

en-dem-ic adj. Peculiar to a particular area or people.

en-dive n. A herb with crisp succulent leaves, used in salads; a plant related to the endive.

en-do-cri-nol-o-gy n. The area of science or study of the endocrine glands and various secretions. endocrinologist n.

en-dog-e-nous adj., Biol. Originating or growing from within.

en-dor-phin n. Hormones with tranquilizing and pain-killing capabilities, secreted by the brain.

en-dorse v. To write one's signature on the back of a check, so as to obtain the cash indicated on the front, or on the back of a car title, so as to show transfer of ownership. endorsee, endorsement n.

en-do-scope n., Med. An instrument used to examine a bodily canal or hollow organ. endoscopic adj., endoscopy n.

en-dow v. To supply with a permanent income or income-producing property; to bestow upon. endowment n.

en-dure v. To undergo; to sustain; to put up with; to tolerate; to bear. endurable adj.

end-wise or end-ways adv. On end; lengthwise.

en-e-ma n. The injection of a liquid into the rectum for cleansing; the liquid injected.

en-e-my n., pl. -mies One who seeks to inflict injury on another; a foe; a hostile force or power.

en-er-gy n., pl. -gies Capacity or tendency for working or acting; vigor; strength; vitality of expression. Phys. The capacity for doing work; usable heat or electric power.

en-er-vate v. To deprive of vitality or strength; to weaken. enervation n.

en-fee-ble v. To weaken; to make feeble. enfeeblement n.

en-fold v. To enclose; to wrap in layers; to embrace.

en-force v. To compel obedience; to impose by force or firmness. enforcer n. enforceable adj., enforcement,

en-fran-chise v. To grant with civil rights, as the right to vote; to give a franchise to. enfranchisement n.

en-gage v. To employ or hire; to secure or bind, as by a contract; to pledge oneself, especially to marry; to undertake conflict; to participate. Mech. To interlock.

en-gen-der v. To give rise to; to exist; to cause.

en-gine n. A machine which converts energy into mechanical motion; a mechanical instrument; a locomotive.

Eng-land n. Great Britian, also a part of the United Kingdom.

Eng-lish adj. Of, relating to, or characteristic of England, its people, language, and customs. n. The English language; the language of the United States and other countries that are or were formerly under English control. Englishman, Englishwoman n.

Eng-lish Chan-nel n. A section of the Atlantic Ocean which separates England from France.

en-gorge v. To swallow greedily. Pathol. To fill an artery with blood. engorgement n.

en-graft v., Bot. To join or fasten, as if by grafting.

en-grave v. To carve or etch into a surface; to carve, cut, or etch into a stone, metal, or wood for printing; to print from plates made by such a process.

engraver *n.*

en-grav-ing *n.* The act or technique of one that engraves; the impression printed from an engraved plate.

en-gross *v.* To occupy the complete attention of; to copy or write in a large, clear hand. **engrossingly** *adv.*

en-gulf *v.* To enclose completely; to submerge; to swallow.

en-hance *v.* To make greater; to raise to a higher degree. **enhancement** *n.*

e-nig-ma *n.* One that baffles; anything puzzling; a riddle.

en-jamb-ment *or* **en-jambe-ment** *n.* Con-struction of a sentence from one line of a poem to the next, allowing related words to fall on different lines.

en-join *v.* To command to do something; to prohibit, especially by legal action. **enjoiner** *n.*

en-joy *v.* To feel joy or find pleasure in; to have the use or possession of. **enjoyable** *adj.,* **enjoyably** *adv.*

en-large *v.* To make larger; to speak or write in greater detail. **enlargement,** **enlarger** *n.*

en-light-en *v.* To give a broadening or revealing knowledge; to give spiritual guidance or light to. **enlightenment** *n.*

en-list *v.* To secure the help or active aid of. *Milit.* To sign-up for service with the armed forces. **enlistment** *n.*

en-liv-en *v.* To make livelier, cheerful or vigorous. **enlivener** *n.*

en masse *adv., Fr.* All together; grouped.

en-mesh *v.* To catch in a net; to entangle.

en-mi-ty *n., pl.* **-ties** Deep hatred; hostility.

en-no-ble *v.* To make noble or honorable in quality or nature; to confer the rank of nobility. **ennoblement** *n.*

en-nui *n.* Boredom; weariness.

e-nor-mity *n., pl.* **-ties** Excessive wickedness; an outrageous offense or crime.

e-nor-mous *adj.* Very great in size or degree. **enormously** *adv.,* **-ness** *n.*

e-nough *adj.* Adequate to satisfy demands or needs. *adv.* To a satisfactory degree.

en-quire *v.* Variation of inquire.

en-rage *v.* To put or throw into a rage.

en-rap-ture *v.* To enter into a state of rapture; to delight.

en-rich *v.* To make rich or richer; to make more productive.

en-roll *or* **en-rol** *v.* To enter, place, or write one's name on a roll, register, or record. **enrollment, enrollment** *n.*

en-sconce *v.* To settle securely; to shelter.

en-sem-ble *n.* A group of complementary parts that are in harmony; a coordinated outfit of clothing; a group of people performing together; music for two or more performers.

en-shrine *v.* To place in a shrine; to hold sacred. **enshrinement** *n.*

en-shroud *v.* To cover with a shroud.

en-sign *n.* An identifying flag or banner, as one displayed on a ship or aircraft. *Milit.* A commissioned officer of the lowest rank in the U.S. Navy or Coast Guard.

en-si-lage *n.* The process of storing and preserving green fodder in a silo; fodder that has been stored. **ensile** *v.*

en-slave *v.* To make a slave of; to put in bondage. **enslavement** *n.*

en-snare *v.* To catch; to trap.

en-sue *v.* To follow as a consequence.

en-sure *v.* To make certain of.

en-tail *v.* To have as a necessary accompaniment or result; to restrict the inheritance of property to a certain line of heirs. **entailment** *n.*

en-tan-gle *v.* To tangle; to complicate; to confuse. **entanglement** *n.*

en-tente *n., Fr.* A mutual agreement between governments for cooperative action; the parties to an entente.

en-ter *v.* To go or come into; to penetrate; to begin; to become a member of or participant in; in law, to make a record of.

en-ter-prise *n.* A large or risky undertaking; a business organization; boldness and energy in practical affairs.

en-ter-tain *v.* To harbor or give heed to; to accommodate; receive as a guest; to amuse. **entertainer, entertainment** *n.*

en-thrall *v.* To fascinate; to captivate. **enthrallment** *n.*

en-throne *v.* To place on a throne. **enthronement** *n.*

en-thu-si-asm *n.* Intense feeling for a cause; eagerness. **enthusiast** *n.,* **enthusiastic** *adj.*

en-tice *v.* To attract by arousing desire. **enticer, enticement** *n.*

en-tire *adj.* Having no part left out; whole; complete. **entirely** *adv.*

en-ti-tle *v.* To give a name to; to furnish with a right. **entitlement** *n.*

en-ti-ty *n., pl.* **-ties** The fact of real existence; something that exists alone.

en-tomb *v.* To place in a tomb. **-ment** *n.*

en-to-mol-o-gy *n.* The study of insects. **entomologist** *n.,* **entomologic** *adj.*

en-trails *pl., n.* Internal organs of man or animals.

en-trance *n.* The act of entering; the means or place of entry; the first appearance of an actor in a play.

en-trance *v.* To fascinate; enchant. **entrancement** *n.,* **entrancingly** *adv.*

en-trap *v.* To catch in a trap. **-ment** *n.*

en-treat *v.* To make an earnest request of or for.

en-trench *v.* To dig a trench, as for defense; to fix or sit firmly. **-ment** *n.*

en-tre-pre-neur *n., Fr.* A person who launches or manages a business venture. **entrepreneurial** *adj.*

en-trust *v.* To transfer to another for care or performance; to give as a trust or responsibility.

en-try *n., pl.* **-tries** An opening or place for entering; an item entered in a book, list, or register.

en-twine *v.* To twine about or together.

e-nu-mer-ate *v.* To count off one by one. **enumeration, enumerator** *n.*

e-nun-ci-ate *v.* To pronounce with clarity; to announce; proclaim.

enunciation n.

en-ve-lope n. Something that covers or encloses; a paper case, especially for a letter, having a flap for sealing. v. To completely enclose.

en-ven-om v. To make poisonous; to embitter.

en-vi-a-ble adj. Highly desirable. -ly adv.

en-vi-ron-ment n. Surroundings; the combination of external conditions which affect the development and existence of an individual, group, or organism. -al adj., -ly adv.

en-vi-ron-men-tal-ist n. A person who seeks to preserve the natural environment.

en-vi-rons pl., n. A surrounding region; a place; outskirts, especially of a city.

en-vis-age v. To have or form a mental image of.

en-voy n. A messenger or agent; a diplomatic representative who is dispatched on a special mission.

en-vy n., pl. -vies A feeling of discontent or resentment for someone else's possessions or advantages; any object of envy. v. To feel envy because of or toward. envious adj.

en-zyme n., Biochem. Proteins produced by living organisms that function as biochemical catalysts in animals and plants. enzymatic adj.

e-o-li-an adj., Geol. Caused by or transmitted by the wind.

e-on n. An indefinite period of time.

ep-au-let or ep-au-lette n. A shoulder ornament, as on a military uniform.

e-pergne n. An ornamental centerpiece for holding flowers or fruit, used on a dinner table.

e-phed-rine n., Chem. A white, odorless alkaloid used to relieve nasal congestion.

e-phem-er-al adj. Lasting a very short time. ephemerally adv.

ep-ic n. A long narrative poem celebrating the adventures and achievements of a hero. epic adj.

ep-i-cen-ter n. The part of the earth's surface directly above the focus of an earthquake.

ep-i-cure n. One having refined tastes, especially in food and wine.

ep-i-dem-ic adj. Breaking out suddenly and affecting many individuals at the same time in a particular area, especially true of a contagious disease; anything that is temporarily widespread, as a fad. epidemic n.

ep-i-der-mis n., Anat.

Epidermis

Dermis

The outer, nonvascular layer of the skin. epidermal adj.

ep-i-glot-tis n., Anat. The leaf-shaped, elastic cartilage at the base of the tongue that covers the windpipe during the act of swallowing. epiglottal adj.

ep-i-gram n. A clever, brief, pointed remark or observation; a terse, witty poem or saying. epigrammatic adj.

ep-i-graph n. An inscription on a tomb, monument, etc.; a motto or quotation placed at the beginning of a literary work.

e-pig-ra-phy n. The study and interpretation of inscriptions. epigrapher n.

ep-i-lep-sy n., Pathol. A nervous disorder marked by attacks of unconsciousness with or without convulsions. epileptic n. & adj.

ep-i-logue or ep-i-log n. A short speech given by an actor to the audience at the end of a play; an appended chapter placed at the end of a novel or book, etc.

ep-i-neph-rine or ep-i-neph-rin n., Biochem. A hormone secreted by the adrenal medulla of the adrenal glands that raises the blood pressure and quickens the pulse, used in synthesized form as a cardiovascular stimulant.

e-piph-a-ny n. The Christian festival held on January 6th, celebrating the manifestation of Christ to the Gentiles as represented by the Magi; also known as the Twelfth Day.

ep-i-phyte n., Bot. A plant that receives its nourishment from the air and rain while growing on another plant, as an orchid, moss, or lichen. epiphytic adj.

e-pis-co-pa-cy n., pl. -cies The government of a church by bishops; an episcopate.

e-pis-co-pal adj. Pertaining to or governed by bishops.

E-pis-co-pa-lian n. A member of the Protestant Episcopal Church.

e-pis-co-pate n. The term, rank, or position of a bishop; bishops as a group.

ep-i-sode n. A section of a poem, novel, etc., that is complete in itself; an occurrence; an incident. episodic adj.

e-pis-tle n. A formal letter. Epistle One of the letters in the New Testament. epistolary adj.

ep-i-taph n. An inscription, as on a tomb or gravestone, in memory of a deceased person.

ep-i-the-li-um n., pl. -liums or -lia Biol. The thin, membranous tissue consisting of one or more layers of cells, forming the covering of the outer bodily surface and most of the internal surfaces and organs. epithelial, epithelioid adj.

ep-i-thet n. A term, word, or phrase used to characterize a person or thing; an abusive phrase or word.

e-pit-o-me n. A concise summary, as of a book; an extreme or typical example.

e-pit-o-mize v. To be a perfect example.

ep-och n. A point in time marking the beginning of a new era. epochal adj.

ep-ox-y n., pl. -ies Chem. A durable, corrosion-resistant resin used especially in surface glues and coatings.

Ep-som salts *pl., n.* A hydrated magnesium sulfate, used as a purge or to reduce inflammation.

eq-ua-ble *adj.* Not changing or varying; free from extremes; evenly proportioned; uniform; not easily upset. **equability** *n.*

e-qual *adj.* Of the same measurement, quantity, or value as another; having the same privileges or rights.

e-qual-ize *v.* To become or make equal or uniform equalization, equalizer *n.*

e-qual op-por-tu-ni-ty em-ploy-er *n.* An employer who does not discriminate on the basis of age, race, sex, religion, etc.

e-qua-nim-i-ty *n.* Composure.

e-quate *v.* To consider or make equal.

e-qua-tion *n.* The act or process of being equal; a mathematical statement expressing the equality of two quantities, usually shown as (=).

e-qua-tor *n.* The great imaginary circle around the earth; a line lying in a plane perpendicular to the earth's polar axis. **equatorial** *adj.*

eq-uer-ry *n., pl.* **-ries** The officer in charge of the horses of royalty; the personal attendant to a member of the British royal family.

e-ques-tri-an *adj.* Pertaining or relating to horsemanship. *n.* The person who rides or performs on a horse. **equestrienne** *n.*

e-qui-an-gu-lar *adj., Geom.* Having all angles equal.

e-qui-dis-tant *adj.* Having equal distances.

e-qui-lat-er-al *adj.* Having all sides equal. **equilateral** *n.*

e-qui-lib-ri-um *n., pl.* **-ums** *Phys.* The state of balance between two opposing forces or influences; any state of compromise, adjustment, or balance.

e-quine *adj.* Pertaining to or like a horse.

e-qui-nox *n.* Either of the two times a year when the sun crosses the celestial equator and the days and nights are equal in time. **equinoctial** *adj.*

e-quip *v.* To furnish or fit with whatever is needed for any undertaking or purpose; to dress for a certain purpose or reason.

eq-ui-page *n.* A carriage that is equipped with horses and attendants.

e-quip-ment *n.* The state or act of being equipped; the material one is provided with for a special purpose.

eq-ui-ta-ble *adj., pl.* **-ties** Being impartial in treatment or judgment. **equitableness** *n.,* **equitably** *adv.*

eq-ui-ta-tion *n.* The art or act of horse riding.

eq-ui-ty *n., pl.* **-ties** Fairness or impartiality; the value of property beyond a mortgage or liability; in law, justice based on the concepts of fairness and ethics.

e-quiv-a-lent *adj.* Being equal or virtually equal, as in effect or meaning. **equivalence, equivalency,**

equivalent *n.,* **equivalently** *adv.*

e-quiv-o-cal *adj.* Ambiguous; questionable. **equivocally** *adv.*

e-quiv-o-cate *v.* To use intentionally evasive or vague language. **equivocation, equivocator** *n.*

-er *n., suff.* A thing or person that performs the action of the root verb; a person concerned with a trade or profession, as a banker, teacher, etc.; one who lives in or comes from a certain area, as a northerner, midwesterner, etc.; used to form the comparative usage degree of adverbs and adjectives.

e-ra *n.* An extended period of time that is reckoned from a specific date or point in the past and used as the basis of a chronology.

e-rad-i-cate *v.* To destroy utterly; to remove by the roots. **eradicator, eradication** *n.,* **eradicable** *adj.*

e-rase *v.* To remove something written. *Slang* To kill. **erasable** *adj.,* **eraser, erasure** *n.*

er-bi-um *n., Chem.* A soft, metallic, silvery, rare-earth element, symbolized by Er.

ere *prep., Poet.* Prior to; before.

e-rect *adj.* In a vertical position; standing up straight. *v.* To construct; build. *Physiol.* The state of erectile tissue, as through an influx of blood. **erectly** *adv.,* **erectness, erector, erection** *n.*

ere-long *adv., Archaic* Before long.

er-e-mite *n.* A hermit.

erg *n., Phys.* A unit of work or energy.

er-go *conj. & adv.* Consequently; therefore.

er-gos-ter-ol *n., Biochem.* A steroid alcohol synthesized by yeast from sugars, converted under ultraviolet radiation to vitamin D.

er-got *n.* The disease of rye and other cereal plants; a drug used to contract involuntary muscles and to control hemorrhage.

E-rie *n.* One of America's five Great Lakes.

er-mine *n.*

A weasel whose fur changes from brown to white depending on the season.

e-rode *v.* To wear away gradually by constant friction; to corrode; to eat away.

e-rog-e-nous *adj.* Responsive to sexual stimulation.

e-ro-sion *n.* The state or process of being eroded. **erosional** *adj.*

e-ro-sive *adj.* Eroding or tending to erode. **erosiveness** *n.*

e-rot-ic *adj.* Pertaining to or promoting sexual desire. **erotically** *adv.,* **eroticism** *n.*

e-rot-ica *pl., n.* Art or literature with an erotic quality.

err *v.* To make a mistake; to sin.

er-rand *n.* A short trip to carry a message or to perform a specified task, usually for someone else.

er-rant *adj.* Wandering or traveling about in search of adventure; straying from what is proper or customary. **errantry** *n.*

er-rat-ic *adj.* Lacking a fixed course. *Med.* Irregular; inconsistent. **erratically** *adv.*

er-ra-tum *n., pl.* **-ta** An error in writing or printing.

er-ro-ne-ous *adj.* To have or contain an error. **-ly** *adv.*, **erroneousness** *n.*

er-ror *n.* Something said, believed, or done incorrectly; a mistake; the state of being wrong or mistaken; in baseball, a misplay by a team member who is not batting.

er-satz *adj.* A substitute that is usually inferior; artificial.

erst-while *adj., Archaic* Former.

er-u-dite *adj.* Scholarly.

er-u-di-tion *n.* Great learning.

e-rupt *v.* To burst forth violently and suddenly; to explode with steam, lava, etc., as a volcano or geyser; to break out in a skin rash or pimples.

-ery *n., suff.* A place of business; a business, or a place where something is performed or done: bakery; the collection of things; practice or act of something; the qualities or characteristics of something; slavery.

er-y-sip-e-las *n.* An acute, inflammatory, and very uncomfortable skin disease resulting from streptococcus.

e-ryth-ro-cyte *n.* A disk-shaped blood cell that contains hemoglobin and is responsible for the red color of blood.

es-ca-late *v.* To intensify, increase, or enlarge. **escalation** *n.*

es-ca-la-tor *n.* A moving stairway with steps attached to an endless belt.

es-cal-lop *n. & v.* Variation of scallop.

es-ca-pade *n.* Reckless or playful behavior; a prankish trick.

es-cape *v.* To break free from capture, confinement, restraint, etc; to fade from the memory; to enjoy temporary freedom from unpleasant realities. **escape, escapee, escaper** *n.*

es-cape-ment *n., Mech.* A device used in timepieces to control the movement of the wheel and supply energy impulses to a pendulum or balance; a typewriter mechanism that controls the horizontal movement of the carriage.

escape velocity *n., Phys.* The minimum velocity that a rocket or anybody must attain to escape or overcome the gravitational field.

escape wheel *n., Mech.* The rotating notched wheel in an escapement.

es-cap-ism *n.* An escape from unpleasant realities through daydreams or other mental diversions. **escapist** *n. & adj.*

es-ca-role *n.* Endive leaves used for salads.

es-carp-ment *n.* A steep slope or drop; a long cliff formed by erosion.

-escense *n., suff.* To give off light in a cer-

tain way, as florescence.

-escent *adj., suff.* To give off light in a special way, as phosphorescent; beginning to be.

es-chew *v.* To shun or avoid. **eschewal** *n.*

es-cort *n.* A group or individual person accompanying another so as to give protection or guidance; a male who accompanies a female in public.

es-cri-toire *n.* A writing desk.

es-crow *n.* In law, a written deed, contract, or money placed in the custody of a third party until specified conditions are met.

es-cu-do *n., pl.* **-dos** The monetary unit of Portugal.

es-cutch-eon *n.* A shield-shaped surface with an emblem bearing a coat of arms; a protective plate, as for a keyhole.

-ese *n. & adj., suff.* An inhabitant or native of; in the language or style of.

Es-ki-mo *n., pl.* **-mo** *or* **-mos** One of a Mongoloid people living in the Arctic.

Eskimo dog *n.* A large dog of a sturdy, broad-chested breed used to draw sleds.

e-soph-a-gus *n., pl.* **-gi** *Anat.* The muscular, membranous tube through which food passes on the way from the mouth to the stomach. **esophageal** *adj.*

es-o-ter-ic *adj.* Confidential; kept secret; understood or meant for only a particular and often very small group.

es-pa-drille *n.* A shoe with a canvas upper and a flexible sole.

es-pal-ier *n.* A flat framework used to train shrubs to grow a particular way. **espalier** *v.*

es-pe-cial *adj.* Having a very special place; apart or above others; exceptional. **especially** *adv.*

Es-pe-ran-to *n.* An artificial language with a vocabulary based on words in many European languages.

es-pi-o-nage *n.* The act or practice of spying to obtain secret intelligence.

es-pla-nade *n.* A flat, open stretch of land along a shoreline.

es-pou-sal *n.* Support or adoption, as of a cause; a wedding.

es-pouse *v.* To make something one's own; to take as a spouse; to marry; to give in marriage.

es-pres-so *n., pl.* **-sos** A strong coffee brewed by steam pressure from darkly-roasted beans.

es-prit *n.* Spirit; wit; mental liveliness.

es-prit de corps *n., Fr.* A group's spirit of enthusiasm and devotion to the common goals of the group.

es-py *v.* To catch a quick view or sight of.

Esq *abbr.* Esquire.

-esque *adj., suff.* Resembling.

es-quire *n.* The title of courtesy or respect; sometimes written as Esq. behind a man's last name.

-ess *n., suff.* Female.

es-say *n.* A short composition that deals with a single topic and expresses the author's viewpoint on a subject; an effort or attempt.

essayer, essayist n., **essay** v.

es-sene n. The real nature in which something consists; the most important element; an immaterial spirit; being.

Es-sene n. A member of an ascetic Jewish sect of ancient Palestine.

es-sen-tial adj. Necessary; indispensable; containing, of, or being an essence. **essential, essentially** adv. **essentiality, essentialness** n.

EST abbr. Eastern Standard Time.

-est adj. & adv., suff. Used to form the superlative degree of adverbs and adjectives.

es-tab-lish v. To make permanent, stable, or secure; to install; to create or find; to cause to be accepted or recognized; to prove.

es-tab-lish-ment n. The state of being established; a place of business or residence; those collectively who occupy positions of influence and status in a society.

es-tate n. A usually large or extensive piece of land containing a large house; in law, the nature, degree, and extent of ownership or use of property.

es-teem v. To regard with respect.

es-ter n., Chem. Any of a class of organic compounds formed by the reaction of an acid with an alcohol.

Esther n. In the Old Testament, the Jewish queen and wife of King Ahasuerus of Persia, who saved her people from massacre.

es-thet-ic adj. Variation of aesthetic.

es-ti-ma-ble adj. Worthy of respect or admiration. **-ness** n., **estimably** adv.

es-ti-mate v. To form or give an approximate opinion or calculation. n. A preliminary opinion or statement of the approximate cost for certain work. **estimation** n.

es-ti-val adj. Pertaining to or of summer.

es-ti-vate v. To pass the summer in a state of dormancy.

Es-to-ni-a n. A former country located in western Europe, now a part of the U.S.S.R.

Es-to-ni-an adj. Of or pertaining to Estonia. **Estonian** n.

es-trange v. To arouse hated or indifference where there had been love and caring; to disassociate or remove oneself. **estrangement** n.

es-tro-gen n., Biochem. Any of various steroid hormones that regulate female reproductive functions and secondary sex characteristics. **estrogenic** adj.

es-tu-ar-y n., pl. **-ies** The wide mouth of a river where the current meets the sea and is influenced by tides.

ET abbr. Eastern Time; extra terrestrial.

etc abbr. And so forth.

etch v. To engrave or cut into the surface by the action of acid; to sketch or outline by scratching lines with a pointed instrument. **etcher** n.

etch-ing n. The process of engraving in which lines are scratched with a sharp

instrument on a plate covered with wax or other coating after which the exposed parts are subjected to the corrosive action of an acid; a picture or impression made from an etched plate.

e-ter-nal adj. Existing without beginning or end; unending; meant to last indefinitely. **eternal, eternality, eternalness** n., **eternally** adv.

e-ter-ni-ty n., pl. **-ties** Existence without beginning or end; forever; the immeasurable extent of time; the endless time after a person dies.

eth-ane n., Chem. An odorless, colorless, gaseous hydrocarbon from the methane series that is contained in crude petroleum and in illuminating gas.

eth-a-nol n., Chem. The alcohol obtained after the distillation of certain fermented sugars or starches; the intoxicant in liquors, wines, and beers; alcohol.

e-ther n., Chem. A highly flammable liquid compound with a characteristic odor, used as a solvent and an anesthetic; the clear upper regions of space.

e-the-re-al adj. Very airy and light; highly refined; delicate; heavenly. **ethereally** adv., **ethereally** adv.

eth-ic n., pl. **-ics** The system of moral values; the principle of right or good conduct.

eth-i-cal adj. Relating to or of ethics; conforming to right principles of conduct as accepted by a specific profession, as medicine. **ethically** adv.

E-thi-o-pi-a n. A country located in Eastern Africa.

eth-nic adj. Relating to or of a national, cultural, or racial group. **ethnicity** n.

eth-nog-ra-phy n., pl. **-phies** The branch of anthropology dealing with the classification and description of primitive human cultures.

eth-nol-o-gy n., pl. **-gies** The branch of anthropology that is concerned with the study of ethnic and racial groups, their cultures, origins, and distribution.

eth-yl n., Chem. An organic radical occurring in ether and alcohol; a univalent hydrocarbon radical; any gasoline that is treated with tetraethyl lead to reduce engine knock. **-ic** adj.

eth-yl-ene n., Chem. A colorless, flammable gas refined from natural gas and petroleum and used as a fuel.

ethylene glycol n., Chem. A colorless, syrupy alcohol used as an antifreeze, solvent, and lubricant.

ethyl ether n., Chem. Ether.

e-ti-ol-o-gy n. The science and study of causes or origins. Med. The theory of the cause of a particular disease. **etiologic, etiological** adj., **etiologically** adv., **etiologist** n.

et-i-quette n. The prescribed rules, forms and practices, established for behavior in polite society or in official or professional life.

E-trus-can *adj.* Relating to or of Etruria, its language, or people.

Et-na, Mount *n.* An active volcano located in eastern Sicily.

-ette *n., suff.* Small; female.

et-y-mol-o-gy *n., pl.* **-gies** The history of a word as shown by breaking it down into basic parts, tracing it back to the earliest known form, and indicating its changes in form and meaning; the branch of linguistics that deals with etymologies. **etymological**, **etymologic** *adj.*, **etymologist** *n.*

et-y-mon *n., pl.* **-mons** *or* **-ma** The earlier form of a word in the same language or in the ancestral language.

eu-ca-lyp-tus *n., pl.* **-tuses** *or* **-ti** A large, native Australian tree with very aromatic leaves that yield an oil used medicinally.

Eu-cha-rist *n.* The Christian sacrament of Communion in which bread and wine are consecrated and received in the remembrance of the passion and death of Christ. **Eucharistic** *adj.*

eu-chre *n.* A card game for two to four players played with 32 cards in which the winning side must take three of five tricks. *Informal* To trick or cheat.

eu-gen-ics *n.* The science of improving the physical and mental qualities of human beings through genetics. **eugenic** *adj.*, **eugenicist** *n.*

eu-lo-gize *v.* To write or deliver a eulogy for. **eulogist, eulogizer** *n.*

eu-lo-gy *n., pl.* **-gies** A speech that honors a person or thing, usually delivered at a funeral; high praise. **eulogistic** *adj.*, **eulogistically** *adv.*

eu-nuch *n.* A castrated man.

eu-phe-mism *n.* A substitution for a word or expression that is thought to be too strong, blunt, or painful for another person. **euphemistic** *adj.*, **euphemistically** *adv.*

eu-pho-ny *n., pl.* **-nies** The agreeable sound of spoken words. **euphonious** *adj.*, **euphoniously** *adv.*

eu-pho-ri-a *n.* A very strong feeling of elation or well-being. **euphoric** *adj.*

Eur *abbr.* Europe, European.

Eur-a-sian *adj.* Pertaining to the land mass comprising the continents of Asia and Europe; relating to people who are a mixture of European and Asian heritage.

eu-re-ka *interj.* An expression of triumph or achievement.

Eu-ro-dol-lar *n.* A United States dollar deposited in a foreign bank, especially a bank in Europe.

Eu-ro-pe-an *adj.* Derived from or related to Europe or its inhabitants; relating to a person of European descent.

European plan *n.* A rate for a hotel that covers only the cost of the room.

eu-ro-pi-um *n., Chem.* A soft, silvery-white, rare-earth element used in nuclear research, symbolized by Eu.

eu-sta-chian tube *n., Anat.* The passage between the middle ear and the

pharynx that equalizes the air pressure between the tympanic cavity and the atmosphere.

eu-tha-na-sia *n.* The act or practice of putting to death painlessly a person suffering from an incurable disease; also called mercy killing.

eu-then-ics *n.* The study of improving the physical and mental qualities of human beings by controlling the environmental factors. **euthenist** *n.*

e-vac-u-ate *v.* To leave a threatened area, town, building, etc.; to empty; to remove the contents. *Physiol.* To discharge or eject, as from the bowels. **evacuation, evacuator** *n.*

e-vac-u-ee *n.* A person who is evacuated from a hazardous place.

e-vade *v.* To baffle; to elude; to get away from by using cleverness or tricks.

e-val-u-ate *v.* To examine carefully; to determine the value of; to appraise. **evaluation, evaluator** *n.*

ev-a-nesce *v.* To disappear; to fade away.

ev-a-nes-cent *adj.* Vanishing or passing quickly; fleeting. **evanescence** *n.*, **evanescently** *adv.*

e-van-gel-i-cal *or* **e-van-gel-ic** *adj.* Relating to the Christian gospel, especially the four Gospels of the New Testament; maintaining the doctrine that the Bible is the only rule of faith. **evangelicalism** *n.*, **evangelically** *adv.*

e-van-gel-ism *n.* The zealous preaching and spreading of the gospel.

e-van-gel-ist *or* **Evangelist** *n.* One of the four writers of the New Testament Gospels: Matthew, Mark, Luke, or John; a zealous Protestant preacher or missionary. **-ic** *adj.*, **-ally** *adv.*

e-van-gel-ize *v.* To preach the gospel; to convert to Christianity. **-ation** *n.*

e-vap-o-rate *v.* To convert into vapor; to remove the liquid or moisture from fruit, milk, etc., so as to concentrate or dry it. **evaporative** *adj.*, **evaporator** *n.*

e-va-sion *n.* The act or means of evading.

e-va-sive *adj.* Being intentionally vague; equivocal. **-ly** *adv.*, **evasiveness** *n.*

eve *n.* The evening before a special day or holiday; the period immediately preceding some event; evening.

Eve *n.* The first woman created by God; the wife of Adam.

e-ven *adj.* Having a flat, smooth, and level surface; having no irregularities; smooth; on the same line or plane; equally matched; not owing or having anything owed to one; exactly divisible by 2; opposed to odd. to break even *Informal* To end with neither profit or loss, as in business. to get even One's full measure of revenge. **evenly** *adv.*, **evenness** *n.*

e-ven-hand-ed *adj.* Fair; impartial. **evenhandedly** *adv.*, **evenhandedness** *n.*

eve-ning *n.* The time between sunset and bedtime.

eve-ning dress *n.* Formal attire for evening.

eve-ning prim-rose *n.* A biennial herb with conspicuous yellow flowers that open in the evening.

evening star *n.* The brightest planet visible in the west just after sunset, especially Venus.

e-ven-song *n.* An evening prayer.

e-vent *n.* A significant occurrence; something that takes place; the actual or possible set of circumstances; a real or contingent situation; the final outcome; one of the parts of a sports program. **eventful** *adj.* **eventfully** *adv.,* **eventfulness** *n.*

e-ven-tide *n.* Evening.

e-ven-tu-al *adj.* Happening or expected to happen in due course of time. **eventually** *adv.*

e-ven-tu-al-i-ty *n., pl.* **-ties** A likely or possible occurrence; the conceivable outcome.

e-ven-tu-ate *v.* To result ultimately; to come out eventually.

ev-er *adv.* At any time; on any occasion; by any possible chance or conceivable way; at all times; throughout the entire course of time.

Ev-er-est Mount *n.* A mountain in the Himalayas, measuring 29,028 feet high.

ev-er-glade *n.* A tract of low, swampy land.

ev-er-green *adj.* A tree that has green foliage throughout the year.

ev-er-last-ing *adj.* Lasting or existing forever; eternal. *n.* One of several plants, chiefly of the aster family, whose flowers keep their form and color when dried. **everlastingly** *adv.*

ev-er-more *adv.,* *Poet.* For and at all time to come; always.

e-vert *v.* To turn inside out or outward.

eve-ry *adj.* Without exceptions; the utmost; all possible. **every now and then** From time to time; occasionally. **every other** Each alternate. **every which way** *Informal* In every way or direction and with very little order.

eve-ry-body *pron.* Every person.

eve-ry-day *adj.* Happening every day; daily; suitable for ordinary days.

eve-ry-one *pron.* Everybody; every person.

eve-ry-place *adv.* Everywhere.

eve-ry-thing *pron.* All things; whatever exists; whatever is needed, relevant, or important; the essential thing; the only thing that really matters.

eve-ry-where *adv.* In, at, or to everyplace.

e-vict *v.* To put out or expel a tenant by legal process. **evictor, eviction** *n.*

ev-i-dence *n.* Signs or facts on which a conclusion can be based. *v.* To indicate clearly. **in evidence** Clearly present; evident.

ev-i-dent *adj.* Easily understood or seen; obvious. **evidently** *adv.*

e-vil *adj.* Morally bad or wrong; causing injury or any other undesirable result; marked by misfortune or distress; low in public esteem. **The Evil One** Satan.

e-vil-do-er *n.* A person who does evil to another. **evildoing** *n.*

e-vil–mind-ed *adj.* Obsessed with vicious

or evil thoughts or intentions. **evil-mindedly** *adv.,* **evil-mindedness** *n.*

e-vince *v.* To demonstrate or indicate clearly; to give an outward sign of having a quality or feeling.

e-vis-cer-ate *v.* To remove the vital part of something; to remove the entrails. **evisceration** *n.*

e-voke *v.* To call or summon forth; to draw forth or produce a reaction; to summon up the spirits by or as by incantations. **evocation** *n.,* **evocative** *adj.,* **evocatively** *adv.*

ev-o-lu-tion *n.* The gradual process of development or change. *Biol.* The theory that all forms of life originated by descent from earlier forms. **-ary** *adj.,* **evolutionism, evolutionist** *n.*

e-volve *v.* To develop or change gradually. *Biol.* To be developed by evolutionary processes; to develop or work out. **evolvement** *n.*

ewe *n.* A female sheep.

ew-er *n.*
A large, wide-mouthed pitcher or jug.

ex *n.* The letter x. *Slang* A former spouse.

ex- *pref.* Out of; former.

ex *abbr.* Example; exchange.

ex-ac-er-bate *v.* To make more severe or worse; to aggravate. **exacerbation** *n.*

ex-act *adj.* Perfectly complete and clear in every detail; accurate in every detail with something taken as a model; similar. *v.* To be extremely careful about accuracy and detail; to force unjustly for the payment of something; to insist upon as a strict right or obligation; to call for or require. **exaction, exactness** *n.,* **exactly** *adv.*

ex-act-ing *adj.* Making severe demands; rigorous; involving constant attention, hard work, etc. **exactingly** *adv.,* **exactingness** *n.*

ex-act-i-tude *n.* The quality of being exact.

ex-ag-ger-ate *v.* To look upon or to represent something as being greater than it really is; to make greater in intensity or size than would be normal or expected. **exaggerated, -tive** *adj.,* **exaggeration, exaggerator** *n.*

ex-alt *v.* To raise in character, honor, rank, etc.; to praise or glorify; to increase the intensity of. **exalted** *adj.,* **exaltedly** *adv.,* **exalter, exaltation** *n.*

ex-am *n., Slang* An examination.

ex-am-i-na-tion *n.* A test of skill or knowledge; the act of examining or the state of being examined; medical testing and scrutiny. **-al** *adj.*

ex-am-ine *v.* To observe or inspect; to test by questions or exercises, as to fitness or qualification. **examinee, examiner** *n.*

ex-ample *n.* One that is representative as a sample; one worthy of imitation; an object or instance of punishment, reprimand, etc.; a previous instance or case that is identical with or similar to something that is under consideration; a problem or exercise in algebra, arithmetic, etc. to set an example To act in such a way as to arouse others to imitation.

ex-as-per-ate *v.* To make frustrated or angry; to irritate. **exasperatingly** *adv.*, **exasperation** *n.*

ex-ca-vate *v.* To dig a hole or cavity; to form or make a tunnel, hole, etc., by digging, scooping, or hollowing out; to remove or uncover by digging; to unearth. **excavation, excavator** *n.*

ex-ceed *v.* To surpass in quality or quantity; to go beyond the limit. **exceeding** *adj.*

ex-ceed-ing-ly *adv.* Greater than; to an extraordinary degree or extreme.

ex-cel *v.* To surpass or to do better than others.

ex-cel-lence *n.* The state or quality of being superior or excellent; a superior trait or quality.

Ex-cel-len-cy *n., pl.* -cies An honorary title or form of address for high officials, as bishops or ambassadors.

ex-cel-lent *adj.* The best quality; exceptionally good. **excellently** *adv.*

ex-cel-si-or *n.* Long, firm wood shavings used in packing to protect delicate materials. *adj.* Upward; higher.

ex-cept *prep.* With the omission or exclusion of; aside from; not including; leaving out.

ex-cept-ing *prep.* With the exception that.

ex-cep-tion *n.* The act of or state of being excepted; something that is excluded from or does not conform to a general class, rule, or principle; criticism or objection.

ex-cep-tion-a-ble *adj.* Open to objection or exception. **exceptionability** *n.*, **exceptionably** *adv.*

ex-cep-tion-al *adj.* Being an exception to the rule; well above average. **exceptionally** *adv.*

ex-cerpt *n.* A passage from a book, speech, etc. *v.* To select and cite.

ex-cess *n.* The amount or condition of going beyond what is necessary, usual, or proper; overindulgence, as in drink or food.

ex-ces-sive *adj.* Exceeding what is usual, necessary, or proper; extreme. **excessively** *adv.*, **excessiveness** *n.*

ex-change *v.* To give in return for something else; to trade; to return as unsatisfactory and get a replacement. *n.* The substitution of one thing for another; a place where brokers meet to buy, sell, or trade; the mutual receiving and giving of equal sums or money. **exchangeable** *adj.*

ex-cheq-uer *n.* The treasury of a nation or organization; financial resources; funds. *Slang* One's total financial resources.

ex-cise *n.* The indirect or internal tax on the production, consumption, or sale of a commodity, such as liquor or tobacco, that is produced, sold, and used or transported within a country.

ex-cise *v.* To remove surgically. **excision** *n.*

ex-cit-a-ble *adj.* To be easily excited. **-ly** *adv.*, **excitability, excitableness** *n.*

ex-cite *v.* To stir up strong feeling, action, or emotion; to stimulate the emotions of; to bring about; to induce. **-ation, -ment** *n.*, **-edly, excitingly** *adv.*

ex-claim *v.* To cry out abruptly; to utter suddenly, as from emotion.

ex-cla-ma-tion *n.* An abrupt or sudden forceful utterance. **exclamatory** *adj.*

exclamation point *n.* A punctuation mark (!) used after an interjection or exclamation.

ex-clude *v.* To keep out; to omit from consideration; to put out. **exclusion** *n.*

ex-clu-sive *adj.* Intended for the sole use and purpose of a single individual or group; intended for or possessed by a single source; having no duplicate; the only one; complete. **exclusively** *adv.*, **exclusiveness, exclusivity** *n.*

ex-com-mu-ni-cate *v.* To deprive the right of church membership. **excommunication** *n.*

ex-co-ri-ate *v.* To tear the skin or wear off; to censure harshly. **excoriation** *n.*

ex-cre-ment *n.* Bodily waste, especially feces. **excremental** *adj.*

ex-cre-ta *pl., n.* Excretions from the body such as sweat, urine, etc.

ex-crete *v.* To throw off or eliminate waste matter by normal discharge from the body. **excretion** *n.*, **excretory** *adj.*

ex-cru-ci-at-ing *adj.* Intensely painful; agonizing. **excruciatingly** *adv.*

ex-cul-pate *v.* To free from wrong doing; to prove innocent of guilt. **exculpation** *n.*, **exculpatory** *adj.*

ex-cur-sion *n.* A short trip, usually made for pleasure; a trip available at a special reduced fare. *Phys.* The oscillating movement between two points; also, half of this total distance. **excursionist** *n.*

ex-cur-sive *adj.* To go in one direction and then another; rambling; digressive.

ex-cuse *v.* To ask forgiveness or pardon for oneself; to grant pardon or forgiveness; to overlook or accept; to apologize for; to justify; to allow one to leave; to release. *n.* A reason, justification, or explanation. **poor excuse** *Informal* An inferior example for something. **-able** *adj.*, **excusably** *adv.*

exec *abbr.* Executive; executor.

ex-e-cra-ble *adj.* Extremely bad; detestable; revolting. **execrableness** *n.*, **execrably** *adv.*

ex-e-crate *v.* To detest; to feel or express detestation for; to abhor. **execration, execrator** *n.*

ex-e-cute *v.* To carry out; to put into effect; to validate, as by signing; to carry out what has been called for in a will; to put to death by the legal authority.

ex-e-cu-tion *n.* The act of executing a job or task; a putting to death as a result of a legal decision, as the death penalty.

ex-e-cu-tion-er *n.* A person who puts others to death; a person who carries out a legal execution.

ex-ec-u-tive *n.* A manager or administrator in an organization; the branch of the government responsible for activating or putting the laws of a country into effect and for carrying out plans or policies. **executively** *adv.*

executive Council *n.* The cabinet of a provincial government in Canada.

ex-ec-u-tor *n.* The person appointed to carry out the reading and execution of a will. **executorial** *adj.*

ex-e-ge-sis *n., pl.* **-ses** An interpretation or explanation of a text. **exegetic** *adj.*, **exegetically** *adv.*

ex-em-plar *n.* Something that serves as a worthy model or imitation; a typical example.

ex-em-pla-ry *adj.* Serving as a model; worthy of imitation; commendable.

ex-em-pli-fy *v.* To show by giving examples; to be an example of. **exemplification** *n.*

ex-empt *v.* To free or excuse from an obligation or duty to which others are subject. **exempt** *adj.*, **exemption** *n.*

ex-er-cise *n.* The act of performing drills; the act of training or developing oneself; something that is done to maintain or increase a skill, such as practice on the piano. **exercises** *pl.* A ceremony, etc., such as a graduation. **exercise** *v.*, **exerciser** *n.*

ex-ert *v.* To put into action, as influence or force; to put oneself through a strenuous effort. **exertion** *n.*

ex-hale *v.* To breathe out; the opposite of inhale; to breathe forth or give off, as air, vapor, or aroma.

ex-haust *v.* To make extremely tired; to drain oneself of resources, strength, etc. *n.* The escape or discharge of waste gases, working fluid, etc.; the waste gases, etc. that escape; the device through which waste gases are released or expelled. **exhaustible** *adj.*, **exhaustion** *n.*

ex-haus-tive *adj.* Tending to exhaust or that which exhausts. **exhaustively** *adv.*

ex-hib-it *v.* To display, as to put up for public view; to bring documents or evidence into a court of law. **exhibition, exhibitor** *n.*

ex-hi-bi-tion-ism *n.* The practice of deliberately drawing undue attention to oneself. **-ist** *n.*, **exhibitionistic** *adj.*

ex-hil-a-rate *v.* To elate, make cheerful, or refresh. **-tion** *n.*, **-tive** *adj.*

ex-hort *v.* To urge by earnest appeal or argument; to advise or recommend strongly. **exhortation** *n.*

ex-hume *v.* To dig up and remove from a grave; to disinter. **exhumation** *n.*

ex-i-gen-cy *n., pl.* **-cies** The quality or state of being exigent. *usually pl.* A pressing need or necessity.

exigence *n.*, **exigent** *adj.*

ex-ig-u-ous *adj.* Extremely small. **-ity** *n.*

ex-ile *n.* The separation by necessity or choice from one's native country or home; banishment; one who has left or been driven from his or her country. *v.* To banish or expel from one's native country or home.

ex-ist *v.* To have actual being or reality; to live.

ex-is-tence *n.* The fact or state of existing, living, or occurring; the manner of existing. **existent** *adj.*

ex-is-ten-tial *adj.* Based on experience; of or relating to existentialism. **existentially** *adv.*

ex-is-ten-tial-ism *n.* A philosophy that stresses the active role of the will rather than of reason in facing problems posed by a hostile universe. **existentialist** *n.*

ex-it *n.* A way or passage out; the act of going away or out; the departure from a stage, as in a play. **exit** *v.*

ex-o-bi-ol-o-gy *n.* The search for and study of extraterrestrial life. **exobiologist** *n.*

ex-o-dus *n.* A going forth; a departure of large numbers of people, as that of Moses and the Israelites as described in Exodus, the second book of the Old Testament.

ex officio *adj. & adv., L.* By virtue of or because of office or position.

ex-og-e-nous *n., Biol.* That which is derived from external causes.

ex-on-er-ate *v.* To free or clear one from accusation or blame; to relieve or free from responsibility. **exoneration** *n.*

ex-or-bi-tant *adj.* Beyond usual and proper limits, as in price or demand. **exorbitance** *n.*, **exorbitantly** *adv.*

ex-or-cise *v.* To cast out or expel an evil spirit by prayers or incantations; to free from an evil spirit. **exorciser, exorcism, exorcist** *n.*

ex-o-sphere *n., Meteor.* The region of the earth's atmosphere starting about 400 miles up.

ex-o-ther-mic *or* **ex-o-ther-mal** *adj.* Releasing rather than absorbing heat.

ex-ot-ic *adj.* Belonging by nature or origin to another part of the world; foreign; strangely different and fascinating. **exotically** *adv.*

ex-pand *v.* To increase the scope, range, volume, or size; to open up or spread out; to develop more fully in form or details. **expandable** *adj.*, **expander** *n.*

ex-panse *n.* A wide, open stretch.

ex-pan-sion *n.* The act of or state of being expanded; the amount of increase in range, size, or volume.

ex-pan-sive *adj.* Capable of expanding or inclined to expand; characterized by expansion; broad and extensive; open and generous; outgoing. **expansively** *adv.*, **expansiveness** *n.*

ex par-te *adj. & adv.* In law, giving only one side or point of view.

ex-pa-ti-ate *v.* To elaborate; to talk or write at length. **expatiation** *n.*

ex-pa-tri-ate v. To leave one's country and reside in another; to send into exile; to banish. expatriate, expatriation n.

ex-pect v. To look forward to something as probable or certain; to look for as proper, right, or necessary. Slang To presume or suppose.

ex-pec-tan-cy n., pl. -cies The action or state of expecting; expectation; an object or amount of expectation.

ex-pec-tant adj. Expecting; pregnant. expectantly adv.

ex-pec-ta-tion n. The state or act of expecting; something that is expected and looked forward to. expectations pl. Something expected in the future.

ex-pec-to-rant adj. Promoting the discharge by spitting of the mucus from the respiratory tract. n. Any medicine that is used to promote expectoration.

ex-pec-to-rate v. To spit. expectoration n.

ex-pe-di-en-cy n., pl. -cies The state or quality of being expedient.

ex-pe-di-ent adj. Promoting narrow or selfish interests; pertaining to or prompted by interest rather than by what is right. expediently adv.

ex-pe-dite v. To speed up the progress or process of something; to do with quick efficiency. expediter, expeditor n.

ex-pe-di-tion n. A journey of some length for a definite purpose; the person or group and equipment that engage in such a journey; promptness.

ex-pe-di-tion-ar-y adj. Relating to or being an expedition; sent on military service abroad.

ex-pe-di-tious adj. Quick; speedy. expeditiously adv., expeditiousness n.

ex-pel v. To drive or force out, as to dismiss from a school. expellable adj., expeller, expulsion n.

ex-pend v. To consume; to pay out or use up.

ex-pend-a-ble adj. Available for spending. Milit. Equipment or supplies that can be sacrificed. expendability n.

ex-pen-di-ture n. An amount spent; the act or process of expending.

ex-pense n. The outlay or consumption of money; the amount of money required to buy or do something. expenses pl. The funds that have been allotted or spent to cover incidental costs; the charges incurred by an employee while at or pertaining to work. Informal The reimbursement for such charges incurred.

ex-pen-sive adj. Costing a lot of money; high-priced. -ly adv., -ness n.

ex-pe-ri-ence n. The actual participation in something or the direct contact with; the knowledge or skill acquired from actual participation or training in an activity or event; one's total judgments or reactions based on one's past. experience v.

ex-pe-ri-enced adj. To be knowledgeable through actual practices, etc.

ex-per-i-ment n. The act or test performed to demonstrate or illustrate a truth; the conducting of such operations. -al adj., experimentally adv., experimentation, experimenter n.

ex-pert n. A person having great knowledge, experience, or skill in a certain field. adj. Skilled as the result of training or experience. expertly adv., expertness n.

ex-per-tise n. A specialized knowledge, ability, or skill in a particular area.

ex-pi-ate v. To atone for; to make amends for. expiation, expiator n., expiatory adj.

ex-pi-ra-tion n. The emission of breath; the act of breathing out.

ex-pire v. To come to an end; to breathe out, as from the mouth; to exhale. expiration n.

ex-plain v. To make understandable; to clarify; to give reasons for; to account for; to give an explanation for. explainable, explanatory adj., explainer, explanation n.

ex-ple-tive n. An exclamation, often profane. adj. A word added merely to fill out a sentence.

ex-pli-ca-ble adj. Capable of explanation.

ex-pli-cate v. To clear up the meaning of. -tion, explicator n., explicative adj.

ex-plic-it adj. Plainly expressed; specific; unreserved in expression; straightforward. explicitly adv., explicitness n.

ex-plode v. To cause to burst or blow up violently with a loud noise; to increase rapidly without control; to show to be false.

ex-ploit n. A deed or act that is notable. v. To use to the best advantage of; to make use of in a selfish or unethical way. exploitable, exploitative adj., exploitation, exploiter n.

ex-plore v. To examine and investigate in a systematic way; to travel through unfamiliar territory. exploration, explorer n., exploratory adj.

ex-plo-sion n. A sudden, violent release of energy; the sudden, violent outbreak of personal feelings.

ex-plo-sive adj. Marked by or pertaining to an explosion. n. A chemical preparation that explodes. explosively adv., explosiveness n.

ex-po-nent n. A person who represents or speaks for a cause or group; in mathematics, a number or symbol that indicates the number of times an expression is used as a factor. exponential adj., exponentially adv.

ex-port v. To carry or send merchandise or raw materials to other countries for resale or trade. n. A commodity exported. exportable adj., exportation, exporter n.

ex-pose v. To lay open, as to criticism or ridicule; to lay bare and uncovered; to reveal the identity of someone; to deprive of the necessities of heat, shelter, and protection. Photog. To admit light to a sensitized film or plate. exposer n.

ex-po-si-tion n. A statement of intent or

meaning; a detailed presentation of subject matter; a commentary or interpretation; a large public exhibition. **expositor** *n.*, **expository** *adj.*

ex post facto *adj., L.* After the fact and retroactive.

ex-pos-tu-late *v.* To reason earnstly with someone about the inadvisability of his or her actions in an effort to correct or dissuade that person. **-tion, -or** *n.*, **expostulatory** *adj.*

ex-po-sure *n.* The act or state of being exposed; an indication of which way something faces. *Photog.* The act of exposing a sensitive plate or film; the time required for the film or plate to be exposed.

ex-pound *v.* To give a detailed statement of something; to explain the meaning at length. **expounder** *n.*

ex-press *v.* To formulate in words; to verbalize; to state; to comunicate through some medium other than words or signs; to squeeze or press out, as juice from fruit; to send goods, etc., by a fast or rapid means of delivery. *adj.* Explicit; precise. **expressly** *adv.*

ex-pres-sion *n.* Communication of opinion, thought, or feeling; the outward indication or manifestation of a condition, feeling, or quality; a particular phrase or word from a certain region of the country; a facial aspect or look that conveys a feeling; in mathematics, a symbol, sign, or set of that indicates something.

ex-pres-sion-ism *n.* An early 20th Century movement in the fine arts that emphasizes subjective expression of the artist's inner experiences rather than realistic representation. **expressionistic** *adj.*, **expressionist** *n.*

ex-pres-sive *adj.* Of or characterized by expression; serving to indicate or express; full of expression. **expressively** *adv.*, **expressiveness** *n.*

ex-press-ly *adv.* Plainly; in direct terms.

ex-press-way *n.* A multilane highway designed for rapid travel.

ex-pro-pri-ate *v.* To transfer or take property from the owner for public use; to deprive a person of property or ownership. **expropriation, -or** *n.*

ex-pul-sion *n.* The act of expelling or the state of being expelled.

ex-punge *v.* To delete or remove; to erase. **expunger** *n.*

ex-pur-gate *v.* To remove obscene or objectionable material from a play, book, etc., before it is available to the public. **expurgation, expurgator** *n.*

ex-qui-site *adj.* Delicately or intricately beautiful in design or craftsmanship; highly sensitive; keen or acute, as in pain or pleasure. **exquisitely** *adv.*, **exquisiteness** *n.*

ex-tant *adj.* Still in existence; not lost or destroyed; surviving.

ex-tem-po-ra-ne-ous *adj.* Acting or performing with little or no advance preparation; spoken with regard to content, but not memorized or read word for word. **extemporaneously** *adv.*

ex-tem-po-re *adj.* Extemporaneously.

ex-tem-po-rize *v.* To make, do, or perform with little or no advance preparation; to improvise to meet circumstances. **-ation, extemporizer** *n.*

ex-tend *v.* To stretch or open to full length; to make longer, broader, or wider; to continue; to prolong; to put forth or hold out, as the hand; to exert to full capacity; to offer something. **extendible** *adj.*

ex-tend-ed *adj.* Pulled or extended out; stretched out.

ex-tend-er *n.* A substance added to another to dilute, modify, or adulterate.

ex-ten-sion *n.* The act or state of being extended; an agreement with a creditor that allows a debtor further time to pay a debt. *Phys.* The property of matter by virtue of which it occupies space. **extensional** *adj.*

ex-ten-sive *adj.* Widespread; far-reaching; having a wide range; broad in scope. **-ly** *adv.*, **extensiveness** *n.*

ex-tent *n.* The degree, dimension, or limit to which anything is extended; the area over which something extends; the size.

ex-ten-u-ate *v.* To minimize the seriousness of something as a crime or fault. **extenuation** *n.*, **extenuating** *adj.*

ex-te-ri-or *adj.* Pertaining to or of the outside; the external layer.

ex-ter-mi-nate *v.* To annihilate; to destroy completely. **extermination, exterminator** *n.*

ex-tern *or* **externe** *n.* A person that is associated with but not officially residing in a hospital or an institution.

ex-ter-nal *adj.* For, of, or on the outside; acting from the outside; pertaining to foreign countries; outside; exterior. **externals** *pl.* Outward or superficial circumstances. **externally** *adv.*

ex-tinct *adj.* Inactive; no longer existing; extinguished. **extinction** *n.*

ex-tin-guish *v.* To put an end to; to put out; to make extinct. **extinguishable** *adj.*, **extinguisher** *n.*

ex-tir-pate *v.* To pull up by the roots; to destroy wholly, completely. **-tion, extirpator** *n.*, **extirpative** *adj.*

ex-tol *also* **ex-toll** *v.* To praise highly. **extoller, extolment** *n.*

ex-tort *v.* To obtain money from a person by threat, oppression, or abuse of authority. **extortion, extortionist** *n.*, **extortionate** *adj.*

ex-tra *adj.* Over and above what is normal, required, or expected. *n.* An extra edition of a newspaper that covers news of special importance; a performer hired for a small part in a movie.

ex-tract *v.* To pull or draw out by force; to obtain in spite of resistance; to obtain from a substance as by pressure or distillation; in mathematics, to determine the root of a number.

-able, **extractible** *adj.*, **extractor** *n.*

ex-trac-tion *n.* The process or act of extracting;
person's origin or ancestry.

ex-tra-cur-ric-u-lar *adj.* Pertaining to or of activities not directly a part of the curriculum of a school or college.

ex-tra-dite *v.* To obtain or surrender by extradition. **extraditable** *adj.*

ex-tra-di-tion *n.* The legal surrender of an alleged criminal to the jurisdiction of another country, government, or state for trial.

ex-tra-dos *n., pl.* -dos *or* -doses The exterior or upper curve of an arch.

ex-tra-ga-lac-tic *adj.* Coming from beyond the galaxy; situated beyond the galaxy.

ex-tra-mar-i-tal *adj.* Adulterous.

ex-tra-mu-ral *adj.* Taking place outside of an educational building or institution; involving teams from different schools.

ex-tra-ne-ous *adj.* Coming from without; foreign; not vital or essential.
extraneously *adv.*

ex-tra-or-di-nar-y *adj.* Beyond what is usual or common; remarkable.
extraordinarily *adv.*

ex-trap-o-late *v.* To infer the possibility beyond the strict evidence of a series of events, facts, or observations; in mathematics, to infer the unknown information by projecting or extending known information. **extrapolation**,
extrapolator *n.*, **extrapolative** *adj.*

ex-tra-sen-so-ry *adj.* Beyond the range of normal sensory perception.

ex-tra-ter-res-tri-al *adj.* Occurring or originating outside the earth or its atmosphere. **extraterrestrial** *n.*

ex-tra-ter-ri-to-ri-al *adj.* Pertaining to or of extraterritoriality; situated outside of the territorial limits.

ex-tra-ter-ri-to-ri-al-i-ty *n.* An exemption from local legal jurisdiction, as that extended to foreign diplomats.

ex-trav-a-gant *adj.* Overly lavish in expenditure; wasteful; exceeding reasonable limits; immoderate; unrestrained. **extravagance** *n.*, -ly *adv.*

ex-trav-a-gan-za *n.* A lavish, spectacular, showy entertainment.

ex-tra-ve-hic-u-lar *adj.* Occurring or done outside a vehicle, especially a spacecraft in flight.

ex-treme *adj.* Greatly exceeding; going far beyond the bounds of moderation; exceeding what is considered moderate, usual, or reasonable; final; last; of the highest or utmost degree; one of the two ends of farthest limits of anything; in mathematics, the first or last term of a proportion or series; a drastic measure. -ly *adv.*, **extremeness** *n.*

ex-trem-ist *n.* A person who advocates or resorts to extreme measures or holds extreme views. **extremism** *n.*

ex-trem-i-ty *n., pl.* -ties The utmost or farthest point; the greatest degree of distress or peril; an extreme measure; an appendage or limb of the body; a

hand or foot.

ex-tri-cate *v.* To free from hindrance, entanglement, or difficulties; to disengage. **extrication** *n.*

ex-trin-sic *adj.* Not inherent; outside the nature of something; from the outside; external. **extrinsically** *adv.*

ex-tro-vert *or* extravert *n.*, *Psychol.* A person who is more interested in people and things outside himself than in his own private feelings and thoughts. **extroversion** *n.*

ex-trude *v.* To push or thrust out; to shape by forcing through dies under pressure; to project or protrude.
extrusion *n.*, **extrusive** *adj.*

ex-u-ber-ant *adj.* Full of high spirits, vitality, vigor, and joy; plentiful; abundant. **exuberance** *n.*, **exuberantly** *adv.*

ex-ude *v.* To give off; to ooze or trickle forth, as sweat. **exudation**, **exudate** *n.*

ex-ult *v.* To be jubilant; to rejoice greatly. **exultant** *adj.*, **exultation** *n.*, **exultantly**, **exultingly** *adv.*

ex-ur-bi-a *n.* The often well-to-do residential area outside the suburbs of a large city. **exurbanite** *n.*

eye *n.* An organ of sight consisting of the cornea, iris, pupil, retina, and lens; a look; gaze; the ability to judge, perceive, or discriminate. **eye of the storm** *Meteor.* The central area of a hurricane or cyclone. **eye of the wind** *Naut.* The direction from which the wind blows. **to catch one's eye** To get someone's attention. **see eye to eye** To be in complete agreement.

eye-ball *n.* The ball of the eye, enclosed by the socket and eyelids and connected at the rear to the optic nerve.

eye-brow *n.* The short hairs covering the bony ridge over the eye.

eye-ful *n., pl.* -fuls A satisfying or complete view.

eye-glass *n.* A corrective lens used to assist vision. **eyeglasses** *pl.* A pair of corrective lenses set in a frame.

eye-lash *n.* The stiff, curved hairs growing from the edge of the eyelids.

eye-let *n.* A small perforation or hole for a hook or cord to fit through in closing a fastening; the metal ring reinforcing an eyelet.

eye-lid *n.* Either of two folds of skin and muscle that open and close over an eye.

eye-sight *n.* The faculty or power of sight; the range of vision.

eye-strain *n.* Fatigue or discomfort of the eyes, caused by excessive or improper use and marked by symptoms such as pain and headache.

eye-tooth *n., pl.* **teeth**

One of the canine teeth of the upper jaw.

Ezekiel *n.* A Hebrew prophet; a book in the Old Testament written by him.

Ezra *n.* Hebrew high priest; a book in the Old Testament written in part by him.

F, f The sixth letter of the English alphabet; in music, the fourth tone in the scale of C major; a failing grade.

fa-ble n. A brief, fictitious story embodying a moral and using persons, animals, or inanimate objects as characters; a falsehood; a lie. fabulist, fabler n., fabled adj.

fab-ric n. A cloth produced by knitting, weaving, or spinning fibers; a structure or framework, as the social fabric.

fab-ri-cate v. To make or manufacture; to build; to construct by combining or assembling parts; to make up in order to deceive; to invent, as a lie or story. fabricated v., fabrication, fabricator n.

fab-u-lous adj. Past the limits of belief; incredible. fabulously adv.

fa-cade n., Arch. The face or front of a building; an artificial or false appearance.

face n. The front surface of the head from ear to ear and from forehead to chin; external appearance, look, or aspect; the value written on the printed surface of a note or bond; the principal, front, finished, or working surface of anything; the most prominent or significant surface of an object. v. To confront with awareness. **face up to** To recognize the existence of something and confront it bravely. faced, facing v.

fac-et n. One of the flat, polished surfaces cut upon a gemstone; the small, smooth surface on a bone or tooth; a phase, aspect, or side of a person or subject. faceted or facetted adj.

fa-ce-ti-ae n. Humorous or witty writings or remarks.

fa-ce-tious adj. Given to or marked by playful jocularity; humorous. facetiously adv., facetiousness n.

face value n. The apparent value of something; the value printed on the face of a bill or bond.

fa-cial adj. Near, of, or for the face; a massage or other cosmetic treatment for the face. facially adv.

fac-ile adj. Requiring little effort; easily achieved or performed; arrived at without due care, effort, or examination; superficial. -ly adv., facileness n.

fa-cil-i-tate v. To make easier or less difficult. facilitating, facilitated v., facilitation, facilitator n.

fa-cil-i-ty n., pl. -ies Ease in performance, moving, or doing something; something that makes an operation or action easier.

fac-ing n. The lining or covering sewn to a garment; any outer protective or decorative layer applied to a surface.

fac-sim-i-le n. An exact copy, as of a document; the method of transmitting drawings, messages, or such by an electronic method.

fact n. Something that actually occurred or exists; something that has real and demonstrable existence; actuality.

fac-tion n. A group or party within a government that is often self-seeking and usually in opposition to a larger group; discord. -al adv., -alism n.

fac-tious adj. Given to dissension; creating friction; divisive. factiously adv.

fac-ti-tious adj. Produced artificially; lacking authenticity or genuineness. factitiously adv., factitiousness n.

fac-tor n. One who transacts business for another person on a commission basis; one of the elements or causes that contribute to produce the result; in mathematics, one of two or more quantities that when multiplied together give or yield a given product; in biology, a gene. factorship n., factorable adj., factorage n.

fac-to-ry n., pl. -ies An establishment where goods are manufactured; a plant.

fac-to-tum n. An employee who performs all types of work.

fac-tu-al adj. Containing or consisting of facts, literal and exact. factually adv.,

fac-ture n. The process, manner or act of construction; making.

fac-ul-ty n., pl. -ies A natural ability or power; the inherent powers or capabilities of the body or mind; the complete teaching staff of a school or any other educational institution.

fad n. A temporary fashion adopted with wide enthusiasm. faddish adj.,

fade v. To lose brightness, brilliance, or loudness gradually; to vanish slowly; to lose freshness, vigor, or youth; to disappear gradually. faded, fading v.

Fahr-en-heit adj. Of or relating to the temperature scale in which the freezing point of water is 32 degrees and the boiling point of water is 212 degrees under normal atmospheric pressure.

fa-ience n. Earthenware that is decorated with a colorful opaque glaze.

fail v. To be totally ineffective, unsuccessful; to go bankrupt; to receive an academic grade below the acceptable standards; to issue such a grade; to omit or neglect. failing, failed v.

fail-ing n. A minor fault; a defect.

faille n. A ribbed material of cotton, silk, or rayon.

fail-ure n. The fact or state of failing; a breaking down in health, action, strength, or efficiency; a situation in which a business becomes insolvent or bankrupt; in school, a failing grade.

faint adj. Having little strength or vigor; feeble; lacking brightness or clarity; dim. n. A sudden, temporary loss of consciousness; a swoon. faintly adv., faintness n.

fair adj. Visually light in coloring; pleasing to the eye; beautiful; impartial; free from blemish or imperfection; moderately large or good; not stormy; without precipitation.

fair-y n., pl. -ies A tiny imaginary being, capable of working good or ill. Slang A male homosexual.

fair-y-land n. Any delightful, enchanting place; the land of the fairies.

fair-y tale *n.* An incredible or fictitious tale of fanciful creatures; a tale about fairies.

faith *n.* A belief in the value, truth, or trustworthiness of someone or something; belief and trust in God, the Scriptures, or other religious writings; a system of religious beliefs.

faith-ful *adj.* True and trustworthy in the performance of duty, the fulfillment of promises or obligations, etc. **faithfully** *adv.,* **faithfulness** *n.*

faith-less *adj.* Not being true to one's obligations or duties; lacking a religious faith; unworthy of belief or trust. **faithlessly** *adv.,* **faithlessness** *n.*

fake *adj.* Having a false or misleading appearance; not genuine. *v.* To make a brief, deceptive movement in order to mislead one's opponent in certain sports. **fake, faker, fakery** *n.*

fall *v.* To drop down from a higher place or position due to the removal of support or loss of hold or attachment; to collapse; to become less in rank or importance; to drop when wounded or slain; to be overthrown by another government; to come as though descending, as night falls; to pass into a specified condition, as to fall asleep; to cut down or fell, as a tree; to surrender, as a city or fort. **to fall back on** To recede; to retreat. **to fall down on** To fail in. **to fall for** *Slang* To be deceived by. **to fall in** In the military, to meet and go along with. **to fall out** In the military, to leave ranks. **to fall short of** To fail to meet a standard or to reach a particular place. **to fall under** To be classified, as to be included. **the fall of man** The disobedience of Adam and Eve that began or resulted in original sin. *n.* A moral lapse or loss of innocence; autumn. **falling** *v.*

fal-la-cious *adj.* Containing or based on fundamental errors in reasoning; deceptive. **-ness** *n.,* **-ly** *adv.*

fal-la-cy *n., pl.* **-ies** A deception; an error.

fall-back *n.* A place or position to which one can retreat.

fall guy *n., Slang* A person left to receive the blame or penalties; scapegoat.

fal-li-ble *adj.* Capable of making an error; liable to be deceived or misled; apt to be erroneous. **fallibility** *n.,* **fallibly** *adv.*

fall-ing-out *n.* A fight, disagreement, or quarrel.

fall-off *n.* A decrease in something.

fal-lo-pi-an tube *n.* One of a pair of long, slender ducts serving as a passage for the ovum from the ovary to the uterus.

fal-low *n.* Ground that has been plowed but left unseeded during the growing season. **fallowness** *n.*

fal-low *adj.* Light yellowish-brown in color.

false *adj.* Contrary to truth or fact; incorrect; deliberately untrue or deceptive; treacherous; unfaithful; not natural or real; artificial; in music, an

incorrect pitch.

falsely *adv.,* **falseness, falsity** *n.*

false face *n.* A mask used for a disguise at Halloween.

false-hood *n.* The act of lying; an intentional untruth.

false ribs *pl., n.* Ribs that are not united directly with the sternum. In man there are five on each side.

fal-set-to *n.* A high singing voice, usually male, that is artificially high. **falsetto** *adv.*

fal-si-fy *v.* To give an untruthful account of; to misrepresent; to alter or tamper with in order to deceive; to forge. **falsified** *v.,* **falsification, falsifier** *n.*

fal-ter *v.* To be uncertain or hesitant in action or voice; to waver; to move with unsteadiness. **-ing** *adj.*

fame *n.* Public esteem; a good reputation. **famed** *adj.*

fa-mil-iar *adj.* Being well-acquainted with; common; having good and complete knowledge of something; unconstrained or informal. **-ly** *adv.*

fa-mil-i-ar-i-ty *n., pl.* **-ties** An acquaintance with or the knowledge of something; an established friendship; an undue liberty or informality.

fa-mil-iar-ize *v.* To make oneself or someone familiar with something. **-ing, familiarized** *v.,* **familiarization** *n.*

fam-i-ly *n., pl.* **-ies** Parents and their children; a group of people connected by blood or marriage and sharing common ancestry; the members of a household; a group or class of like things; in science, a taxonomic category higher than a genus and below an order. **family** *adj.*

family name *n.* A surname or last name.

family tree *n.* A genealogical diagram showing family descent; the ancestors and descendants of a family.

fam-ine *n.* A widespread scarcity of food; a drastic shortage of or scarcity of anything; severe hunger; starvation.

fam-ish *v.* To starve or cause to starve. **famished** *adj.*

fa-mous *adj.* Well-known; renowned. *Slang* admirable. **-ly** *adv.,* **-ness** *n.*

fan *n.* A device for putting air into motion, especially a flat, lightweight, collapsible, wedge-like shape; a machine that rotates thin, rigid vanes. *Slang* an enthusiastic devotee or admirer of a sport, celebrity, diversion, etc. *v.* To move or stir up air with a fan; to direct air upon; to cool or refresh with or as with a fan; to spread like a fan; in baseball, to strike out. **-ned, fanning** *v.*

fa-nat-ic *n.* One who is moved by a frenzy of enthusiasm or zeal. **-al, fanatically** *adv.,* **fanaticism** *n.*

fan-ci-er *n.* A person having a special enthusiasm for or interest in something.

fan-ci-ful *adj.* Existing or produced only in the fancy; indulging in fancies; exhibiting invention or whimsy in design. **fancifully** *adv.,* **fancifulness** *n.*

fan-cy *n., pl.* **-cies** Imagination of a fantastic or whimsical nature; a notion or idea not based on evidence or fact; a whim or caprice; judgment or taste in art, style, etc. *adj.* Adapted to please the fancy; highly decorated. *v.* To imagine; to visualize; to believe without proof or conviction; to suppose; to breed, as animals, for conventional points of beauty. **fanciness** *n.*

fan-dan-go *n.* A Spanish or Spanish-American dance in triple time; the music for this dance.

fan-fare *n.* A short, loud trumpet flourish; a spectacular public display.

fang *n.*

A long, pointed tooth or tusk an animal uses to seize or tear at its prey; one of the hollow, grooved teeth with which a poisonous snake injects its venom. **fanged** *adj.*

fan-jet *n.* An aircraft with turbojet engines.

fan-ny *n., pl.* -ies *Slang* The buttocks.

fan mail *n.* Mail received by a public figure from admirers.

fan-tail *n.* Any fanshaped tail or end; a variety of domestic pigeons having fan-like tail feathers. **fantailed** *adj.*

fan-ta-sia *n.* A composition structured according to the composer's fancy and not observing any strict musical form.

fan-ta-size *v.* To create mental fantasies; to imagine or indulge in fantasies. **fantasizing, fantasized** *v.*

fan-tas-tic *adj.* Existing only in the fancy; unreal; wildly fanciful or exaggerated; impulsive or capricious; coming from the imagination or fancy. *Slang* Superb. **fantastically** *adv.*

fan-ta-sy *n., pl.* -ies A creative imagination; a creation of the fancy; an unreal or odd mental image; a whimsical or odd notion; a highly or ingeniously imaginative creation; in psychology, the sequence of pleasant mental images fulfilling a wish.

far *adv.* From, to, or at a considerable distance; to or at a certain distance, degree, or point; very remote in time, quality, or degree. *adj. & adv.* Remote in space or time; extending widely or at great lengths; extensive or lengthy. **far and away** Decidedly. **far and wide** Everywhere.

far-away *adj.* Very distant; remote; absent-minded; dreamy.

fare *v.* To be in a specific state; to turn out. *n.* A fee paid for hired transportation; food or a variety of foods.

fare--thee--well *n.* The most extreme degree; perfection.

fare-well *n.* Good-by; a departure. *adj.* Closing; parting.

far--fetched *adj.* Neither natural nor obvious; highly improbable.

far--flung *adj.* Widely distributed over a great distance.

fa-ri-na *n.* A fine meal obtained chiefly from nuts, cereals, potatoes, or Indian corn, used as a breakfast food or in puddings.

far-i-na-ceous *adj.* Made from, rich in, or composed of starch; mealy.

farm *n.* Land that is cultivated for agricultural production; land used to breed and raise domestic animals; the area of water used for the breeding and raising of a particular type of aquatic animal, such as fish; the raising of livestock or crops as a business; in baseball, a minor league club used by a major league club for training its recruits. **farm out** To send work out to be done. **farmer** *n.*

farm-house *n.* The homestead on a farm.

farm-land *n.* Land that is suitable for agricultural production.

farm-stead *n.* A farm, including its land and all of the buildings.

farm team *n.* A minor league baseball team.

farm-yard *n.* The area surrounded by farm buildings and enclosed for confining stock.

far--off *adj.* Distant; remote.

far--out *adj., Slang* Very unconventional.

far-ra-go *n., pl.* goes A confused mixture.

far--reach-ing *adj.* Having a wide range, effect, or influence.

far-row *n.* A litter of pigs.

far--see-ing *adj.* Having foresight; prudent; wise; having the ability to see distant objects clearly.

far--sight-ed *adj.* Able to see things at a distance more clearly than things nearby; wise. **-ly** *adv.,* **-ness** *n.*

far-ther *adv.* To or at a more distant point. *adj.* More remote or distant.

far-ther-most *adj.* Most distant; farthest.

far-thest *adj.* To or at the greatest distance.

far-thing *n.* Something of little worth; a former British coin worth 1/4 of a penny.

fas-ci-nate *v.* To attract irresistibly, as by beauty or other qualities; to captivate; to hold motionless; to spellbind. **fascinating** *adj.,* **fascinatingly** *adv.,* **fascination, fascinator** *n.*

fas-cism *n.* A one-party system of government marked by a centralized dictatorship, stringent socioeconomic controls, and often belligerent nationalism. **fascist** *n.,* **fascistic** *adj.*

fashion *n.* The mode or manner of dress, living, and style that prevails in society, especially in high society; good form or style; current style or custom; a piece of clothing made up in the current style. **fashionable, fashionableness** *adj.,* **fashionably** *adv.*

fast *adj.* Swift; rapid; performed quickly; constant; steadfast; firmly secured; sound or deep, as sleep; permitting or suitable for quick movement; requiring rapidity of motion or action; acting or moving quickly. *v.* To give up food, especially for a religious reason. **fast-back** *n.* A car with a downward slope from the roof to the rear.

fast-en v. To join something else; to connect; to securely fix something; to shut or close; to focus steadily. fastener n.

fas-tid-i-ous adj. Exceedingly delicate or refined; hard to please in matters of taste. fastidiously adv., -ness n.

fast--track adj. High-powered and aggressive.

fat adj. Having superfluous flesh or fat; obese; plump; containing much fat or oil; rich or fertile, as land; abundant; plentiful; profitable; thick; broad. a fat chance Slang. Very little or no chance at all. n. Any of a large class of yellowish to white, greasy liquid or solid substances that are widely distributed in animal and plant tissues; consisting of various fatty acids and glycerol generally odorless, tasteless, and color-less; the richest or most desirable part. fatness, fattiness n., fatty adj.

fat-al adj. Causing death; deadly; bringing ruin or disaster; destructive; decisively important; fateful; brought about by fate; destined; inevitable. fatally adv.

fa-tal-ism n. The belief that events or things are predetermined by fate and cannot be altered. fatalist n., fatalistic adj., fatalistically adv.

fa-tal-i-ty n., pl. -ies A death caused by a disaster or accident; the capability of causing death or disaster; the quality or state of being subject to or determined by fate.

fat-back n. The strip of unsmoked salt pork taken from the upper part of a pork side.

fate n. The force or power held to predetermine events; fortune; inevitability; the final result or outcome; unfortunate destiny; fated adj.

fate-ful adj. Determining destiny; governed by fate; bringing death or disaster. fatefully adv., fatefulness n.

fa-ther n. The male parent; any male forefather; ancestor; a male who establishes or founds something. Father A priest; one of the early Christian writers who formulated doctrines and codified observances. fatherhood, fatherliness n., fatherly adj.

fa-ther--in--law n. The father of one's spouse.

fa-ther-land n. The land where one was born; the native country of one's ancestors.

Father's Day n. A day set aside to honor all fathers, occurring on the third Sunday in June.

fath-om-less adj. Too deep to measure; too difficult to understand.

fa-tigue n. The state or condition of extreme tiredness or weariness from prolonged physical or mental exertion. fatigues Military clothes for heavy work and field duty. v. To become or make tired. fatiguing, fatigued v.

fat-ten v. To make or become fat; to increase the amount of something. fattening, fattened v.

fat-ty adj. Greasy; oily; having an excess of fat.

fa-tu-i-ty n. Stupidity; foolishness.

fat-u-ous adj. Silly and foolish in a self-satisfied way. -ly adv., fatuousness n.

fau-cet n. A fixture with an adjustable valve used to draw liquids from a pipe or cask.

fault n. An impairment or defect; a weakness; a minor offense or mistake; a break in the earth's crust allowing adjoining surfaces to shift in a direction parallel to the crack; a bad serve, as in tennis. v. To criticize. at fault Open to blame; in the wrong. faultily, faultlessly adv., faultless, faulty adj.

fault-find-er n. One who finds fault; a petty critic. faultfinding n. & adj.

faun n. A woodland deity represented in Roman mythology as part goat and part man.

fau-na n., pl. faunas or faunae Animals living within a given area or environment. faunal adj.

fau-vism n. An art movement noted for the use of very flamboyant colors and bold, often distorted forms.

faux pas n. A false step; a social blunder.

fa-vor n. A helpful or considerate act; the attitude of friendliness or approbation; the condition of being held in the regard; approval or support. favors Consent to sexual intimacy, especially as granted by a woman; a token of love or remembrance; a small gift given to each guest at a party. v. To benefit; to give advantage; to prefer or like one more than another; to support or approve; to look like or resemble; to treat with special care. favorer n., favoringly adv.

fa-vor-a-ble adj. Beneficial; antageous; building up hope or confidence; approving; promising. -ness n., -ly adv.

fa-vor-ite n. Anything regarded with special favor or preferred above all others; in sports, the contestant considered to be the most likely winner.

fa-vor-it-ism n. Preferential treatment; a display of often unjust partiality.

fa-vour n. & y. British variety of favor.

fawn n. A young deer less than a year old; a light yellowish-brown color. fawningly adv.

fay n. A fairy or elf.

faze v. To worry; to disconcert. fazed, fazing v.

FBI abbr. Federal Bureau of Investigation.

fe-al-ty n., pl. -ies The obligation of allegiance owed to a feudal lord by his vassal or tenant; faithfulness; loyalty.

fear n. The agitated feeling caused by the anticipation or the realization of danger; an uneasy feeling that something may happen contrary to one's hopes; a feeling of deep, reverential awe and dread. v. To be apprehensive; to suspect. fearfulness n., fearful adj., fearfully adv.

fear-less adj. Without fear; brave; courageous. -ness n., -ly adv.

fear-some *adj.* Causing fear; timid. **fearsomely** *adv.*, **fearsomeness** *n.*

fea-si-ble *adj.* Capable of being put into effect or accomplished; practical. **feasibility** *n.*, **feasibly** *adv.*

feast *n.* A delicious meal; a banquet; a day or days of celebration set aside for a religious purpose or in honor of some person, event, or thing. *v.* To provide with pleasure. **-ing** *v.*, **-er** *n.*

feat *n.* A notable act or achievement.

feath-er *n.* One of the light, hollow-shafted structures that form the covering of birds. **a feather in one's cap** An achievement one should be proud of; in rowing, to turn the oar blade following each stroke so that the blade is more or less horizontal as it is carried back to the position for reentering the water. **feathery** *adj.*

feather bed *n.* A mattress stuffed with feathers; a bed with a feather mattress.

feather-edge *n.* A very thin, fragile edge.

feather-stitch *n.* An embroidery stitch that resembles a feather, accomplished by taking one or more short stitches alternately on either side of a straight line.

feather-weight *n.* A boxer weighting between 118 and 127 pounds; any person or thing that is light in weight.

fea-ture *n.* The appearance or shape of the face; the main presentation at a movie theater; a special article in a magazine or newspaper that is given special prominence. **feature** *v.*

feb-ri-fuge *n.* A medicine used to reduce fever.

feb-rile *adj.* Feverish.

Feb-ru-ar-y *n.* The second month of the year, having 28 days or, in a leap year, 29 days.

fe-ces *pl. n.* Waste that is excreted from the bowels; excrement. **fecal** *adj.*

feck-less *adj.* Ineffective; weak; careless and irresponsible. **fecklessly** *adv.*

fe-cund *adj.* Fruitful; productive. **-ity** *n.*

fe-cun-date *v.* To make fertile. **fecundating**, **-ed** *v.*, **fecundation** *n.*

fed *v.* Past tense of feed.

fed *abbr.* Federal, federated.

fed-er-al *adj.* Of, relating to, or formed by an agreement between two or more states or groups in which each retains certain controlling powers while being united under a central authority; of or pertaining to the United States central government. Federal Pertaining to or of the central government of Canada; of or supporting the Union in the American Civil War. **federally** *adv.*

fed-er-al-ism *n.* The organization or system of a federal government; the advocacy or support of this system. **federalist** *n.*

Federalist Party *n.* The political party of 1787-1830 which advocated the adoption of the U.S. Constitution and the formation of a strong national government.

fed-er-a-l-ize *v.* To join or unite in a federal union; to bring under the control of the federal government. **-ing**, **federalized** *v.*, **federalization** *n.*

fed-er-ate *v.* To unite in a federal union or alliance. **federating**, **federated** *v.*

fe-do-ra *n.* A soft hat with a low crown creased lengthwise and a brim that can be turned up or down.

fed up *adj.* Extremely annoyed or disgusted.

fee *n.* A fixed charge, compensation, or payment for something; a charge for professional services; an inherited estate in land.

fee-ble *adj.* Very weak; lacking in strength; ineffective. **-ness** *n.*, **-ly** *adv.*

feeble minded *adj.* Mentally deficient; intellectually subnormal. **-ness** *n.*

feed *v.* To supply with food; to provide as food; to consume food; to keep supplied, as with fuel for a fire; to enter data into a computing machine; to draw support or encouragement. *n.* The mechanical part, as of a sewing machine, that keeps supplying material to be worked on. *Slang* A meal.

feed-back *n.* The return to the input of a portion of the output of a machine; the return of data for corrections or control.

feed-stock *n.* Raw materials required for an industrial process.

feel *v.* To examine, explore, or perceive through the sense of touch; to perceive as a physical sensation; to believe; to consider; to be aware of; to be emotionally affected by; to think; to suppose; to judge; to experience the full force or impact of; to produce a sensory impression of being soft, hard, hot or cold; to produce an indicated overall condition, impression, or reaction. **feeling** *v.*

feet *n.* The plural of foot.

feign *v.* To make a false show of; to dream up a false story and tell it as the truth; to fabricate; to imitate so as to deceive. **feigned** *adj.*

feint *n.* A deceptive or misleading movement intended to draw defensive action away from the real target.

fe-lic-i-tate *v.* To congratulate. **felicitating**, **felicitating** *v.*, **felicitation** *n.*

fe-lic-i-tous *adj.* Most appropriate; well chosen; pertinent or effective in manner or style. **felicitously** *adv.*

fe-lic-i-ty *n.*, *pl.* **-ies** Happiness; bliss; an instance or source of happiness; an agreeably pertinent or effective style.

fe-line *adj.* Of or relating to cats, including wild and domestic cats; resembling a cat, as in stealth or agility. **felinity**, **feline** *n.*, **felinely** *adv.*

fell *v.* Past tense of fall; to strike or cause to fall down; to finish a seam with a flat, smooth strip made by joining edges, then folding under and stitching flat. *n.* Timber cut down during one season; an animal's hide; pelt. *adj.* Cruel and fierce; lethal.

fel-lah *n.*, *pl.* **fellahin** *or* **fellaheen** An Arab peasant or laborer.

fel-low *n.* A boy or man; an associate, comrade; the counterpart; one of a pair. *Informal* A boyfriend.

fel-low-ship *n.* A friendly relationship; the condition or fact of having common interests, ideals, or experiences; the status of being a fellow at a college or university, also the financial grant made to a fellow.

fel-ly *n.*, *pl.* -ies

The rim of a wooden wheel, into which spokes are inserted.

fel-on *n.* A person who has committed a felony; an inflammation in the terminal joint or at the cuticle of a finger or toe.

fel-o-ny *n.*, *pl.* -ies A serious crime, such as rape, murder, or burglary, punishable by a severe sentence. **felonious** *adj.*, **-ly** *adv.*, **feloniousness** *n.*

felt *v.* Past tense of feel. *n.* An unwoven fabric made from pressed animal fibers, as wool or fur; a piece of fabric or material made of felt.

fe-male *n.* The sex that produces ova or bears young; a plant with a pistil but no stamen, which is capable of being fertilized and producing fruit. *adj.* Of or relating to the sex that produces ova or bears young; suitable to this sex having a bore, slot, or hollow part designed to receive a projecting part, as a plug or prong.

fem-i-nine *adj.* Pertaining to or of the female sex; female; characterized by qualities generally attributed to women; lacking in manly qualities. *Gram.* Applicable to females only or to persons or things classified as female. **femininely** *adv.*, **feminineness, femininity** *n.*

fem-i-nism *n.* The movement advocating the granting of the same social, political, and economic rights to women as the ones granted to men. **feminist** *n.*, **feministic** *adj.*

femme fa-tale *n.*, *pl.* **femmes fatales** A seductive or charming woman.

fe-mur *n.*, *pl.* **femurs** *or* **femora** The bone extending from the pelvis to the knee. **femoral** *adj.*

fen *n.* A low, marshy land; a bog.

fence *n.* A structure made from rails, stakes, or strung wire that functions as a boundary or barrier. *Slang* A seller and recipient of stolen goods; the location where such goods are sold. *v.* To close in, surround, or separate as if by a fence. **on the fence** Neutral or undecided. **fencer** *n.*

fenc-ing *n.* The sport of using a foil or saber; the practice of making quick, effective remarks or retorts, as in a debate; the material used to make fences; fences collectively.

fend *v.* To ward off or to keep off; to offer resistance. **fending, fended** *v.*

fend-er *n.* The protective device over the wheel of a car or other vehicle; a

metal guard set in front of an open fireplace; the projection on the front of a locomotive or streetcar, designed to push obstructions from the tracks, also known as cow-catcher.

fen-es-tra-tion *n.* The design and position of doors and windows in a building.

fen-nel *n.* A tall herb from the parsley family which produces an edible stalk and aromatic seeds used as a flavoring.

fe-ral *adj.* Not tame nor domesticated; returned to a wild state; existing in a untamed state.

fer--de--lance *n.* A large, venomous snake of tropical America, with gray and brown markings.

fer-ment *n.* Any substance or agent producing fermentation, as yeast, mold, or enzyme; excitement; unrest; agitation. **fermentability, fermenter** *n.*, **fermentable** *adj.*

fer-men-ta-tion *n.* The decomposition of complex organic compounds into simpler substances; the conversion of glucose into ethyl alcohol through the action of zymase; great agitation; commotion.

fer-mi-um *n.* A metallic radioactive element, symbolized by Fm.

fern *n.* Any of a number of flowerless, seedless plants, having fronds with divided leaflets and reproducing by spores. **ferny** *adj.*

fe-ro-cious *adj.* Extremely savage, fierce, cruel, or bloodthirsty. *Slang* Very intense. **ferociously** *adv.*, **ferociousness, ferocity** *n.*

fer-ret *n.* A small, red-eyed polecat of Europe, often domesticated and trained to hunt rodents or rabbits. *v.* To search out by careful investigation; to drive out of hiding. **ferreter** *n.*, **ferrety** *adj.*

fer-ric *adj.* Pertaining to or containing iron.

fer-ric ox-ide *n.* A dark compound that occurs as hematite ore and rust.

Fer-ris wheel *n.* A large, power-driven wheel with suspended compartments in which passengers ride for amusement.

fer-ro-mag-net-ic *adj.* Relating to or being typical of substances, as iron and nickel, that are readily magnetized. **ferromagnetism** *n.*

fer-rous *adj.* Pertaining to or containing iron.

fer-rule *n.* A cap or ring used near or at the end of a stick, as a walking cane, to reinforce it or prevent splitting.

fer-ry *n.*, *pl.* -ies A boat or other craft used to transport people, vehicles, and other things across a body of water.

fer-ry-boat *n.* A boat used to transport passengers or goods.

fer-tile *adj.*, *Biol.* Having the ability to reproduce; rich in material required to maintain plant growth. **fertility, fertileness** *n.*

fer-til-ize *v.* To make fertile; to cause to

be productive or fruitful; to begin the biological reproduction by supplying with sperm or pollen; to make fertile by spreading or adding fertilizer.

fertilized, fertilizing *v.*,
fertilizable *adj.*, **fertilization** *n.*

fer-til-iz-er *n.* A material that fertilizes, such as nitrates or manure which enriches soil.

fer-ule *n.* A flat stick sometimes used to punish children. **ferule** *v.*

fer-vent *adj.* Passionate; ardent; very hot. **fervency, ferventness** *n.*, **fervently** *adv.*

fer-vid *adj.* Fervent to an extreme degree; impassioned; very hot; burning. **fervidly** *adv.*, **fervidness** *n.*

fer-vor *n.* Great emotional warmth or intensity.

fes-cue *n.* A type of tough grass, often used as pasturage.

fes-tal *adj.* Pertaining to or typical of a festival, holiday, or feast.

fes-ter *v.* To develop or generate pus; to be a constant source of irritation or resentment.

fes-ti-val *n.* A particular holiday or celebration; a regularly occurring occasion.

fes-tive *adj.* Relating to or suitable for a feast or other celebration. **festively** *adv.*, **festiveness** *n.*

fes-tiv-i-ty *n.*, *pl.* -ies A festival; gladness and rejoicing.

fet-a *n.* A white Greek cheese made of goat's or ewe's milk and preserved in brine.

fe-tal *adj.* Relating to or like a fetus.

fe-tal po-si-tion *n.* The bodily position of a fetus with the spine curved, the head bowed forward, and the arms and legs drawn in toward the chest.

fetch *v.* To go after and return with; to draw forth; to elicit; to bring as a price; to sell for.

fetching, fetched *v.*, **fetcher** *n.*

fete *n.* A festival or feast; a very elaborate outdoor celebration. **fete** *v.*

fet-id *adj.* Having a foul odor; stinking.
fetidly *adv.*, **fetidness** *n.*

fet-ish *n.* An object that is regarded as having magical powers; something that one is devoted to excessively or irrationally. *Psychiatry* A nonsexual object that arouses or gratifies sexual desires. **fetishistic** *adj.*, **fetishist** *n.*

fet-lock *n.* A tuft of hair that grows just above the hoof at the back of the leg of a horse.

fe-tol-o-gy *n.* The medical study of a fetus. **fetologist** *n.*

fet-tuc-ci-ne *n.* Narrow strips of pasta.

fe-tus *n.* The individual unborn organism carried within the womb from the time major features appear; especially in humans, the unborn young after the eighth week of development.

feud *n.* A bitter quarrel between two families, usually lasting over a long period of time.

feu-dal *adj.* Relating to or characteristic of feudalism. **-ize** *v.*, **feudally** *adv.*

feu-dal-ism *n.* The political, social, and economic organization produced by the feudal system.
feudalist *n.*, **feudalistic** *adj.*

feu-da-to-ry *n.*, *pl.* -ies One holding a feudal fee. *adj.* Owing feudal homage or allegiance.

fe-ver *n.* Abnormally high body temperature and rapid pulse; a craze; a heightened emotion or activity.
-ish *adj.*, **feverishly** *adv.*, **feverishness** *n.*

fever blister *n.* A cold sore.

few *adj.* Small in number; not many. *n.* A select or limited group.

fey *adj.* Seemingly spellbound; having clairvoyance; acting as if under a spell.

fez *n.* A red felt, black-tasseled hat worn by Egyptian men.

fi-an-ce *n.* A man to whom a woman is engaged to be married.

fi-an-cee *n.* A woman to whom a man is engaged to be married.

fi-as-co *n.*, *pl.* fiascoes A complete or total failure.

fi-at *n.* A positive and authoritative order or decree.

fib *n.* A trivial lie. **fib** *v.*, **fibber** *n.*

fi-ber *n.* A fine, long, continuous piece of natural or synthetic material made from a filament of asbestos, spun glass, textile, or fabric; internal strength; character. **fibrous** *adj.*

fi-ber-glass *n.* A flexible, nonflammable material of spun glass used for textiles, insulation, and other purposes.

fi-ber op-tics *pl.*, *n.* Light optics transmitted through very fine, flexible glass rods by internal reflection.
fiber optic *adj.*

fi-ber-scope *n.* The flexible fiber optic instrument used to view otherwise inaccessible objects.

fib-ril-la-tion *n.*, *Pathol.* The rapid and uncoordinated contraction of the muscle fibers of the heart.

fi-brin *n.*, *Biochem.* An insoluble protein that promotes the clotting of blood.
fibrinous *adj.*

fi-brin-o-gen *n.*, *Biochem.* A complex blood plasma protein that is converted to fibrin during the process of blood clotting.

fi-broid *adj.* Made up or resembling fibrous tissue.

fib-u-la *n. Anat.*

The outer and smaller bone of the lower limb or hind leg in humans located between the knee and ankle.

Fibula

-fic *adj.*, *suffix* Making; causing; rendering.

-fication *n.*, *suffix* Making; production.

fi-chu *n.* A lightweight triangular scarf, worn about the neck and fastened loosely in front.

fick-le *adj.* Inconstant in purpose or feeling; changeable. **fickleness** *n.*

fic-tion *n.* Something that is created or imaginary; a literary work that is produced by the imagination and not based on fact. **fictional** *adj.*

fic-ti-tious *adj.* Nonexistent; imaginary; not genuine; false; not real. **fictitiously** *adv.*, **fictitiousness** *n.*

fid-dle *n.* A violin. *v.* To play the violin; to fidget or make nervous or restless movements; to spend time in a careless way. *Naut.* A rack used at the table to prevent things from sliding off. **fit as a fiddle** To enjoy good or perfect health. **to play second fiddle** To be put into a position subordinate to that of another. **fiddling, fiddled** *v.*, **fiddler** *n.*

fiddler catfish *n.* A freshwater, scaleless fish with long whisker-like feelers used for navigation; ranging in size from 8 to 14 inches in length and having a light taste and tender texture.

fiddler crab *n.* A small burrowing crab found mostly off the Atlantic coast of the United States, the male being much larger than the female.

fi-del-i-ty *n.*, *pl.* **-ies** Faithfulness or loyalty to obligations, vows, or duties. *Elect.* The degree to which a phonograph, tape recorder, or other electronic equipment receives and transmits input signals without distortion.

fidg-et *v.* To move nervously or restlessly. **fidgets** *pl.*, *n.* The condition of being nervous or restless. **fidgeter, fidgetiness** *n.*, **fidgety** *adj.*

fie *interj.* An expression of disgust or impatience in response to an unpleasant surprise.

fief *n.* A feudal estate in land.

field *n.* A piece of land with few or no trees; a cultivated piece of land devoted to the growing of crops; an area in which a natural resource such as oil is found; an airport; the complete extent of knowledge, research, or study in a given area; in sports, the bounded area in which an event is played; the members of a team actually engaged in active play; in business, the area away from the home office. *Milit.* A region of active operations or maneuvers. *Physics* A region of space that is marked by a physical property, as electromagnetic force, with a determinable value at each point in the region. **fielder** *n.*

field ar-til-lery *n.* Artillery that has been mounted for use in the fields.

field e-vent *n.* An event at an athletic meet other than races, such as jumping and throwing.

field glass *n.*, *often* **field glasses** A compact, portable binocular instrument for viewing distant objects.

field mag-net *n.* A magnet providing the magnetic field in a generator or electric motor.

field of force *n.* A region where the force of a single agent, as an electric current, is operative.

fierce *adj.* Savage and violent in nature. *Slang* Very difficult or disagreeable.

fiercely *adv.*, **fierceness** *n.*

fier-y *adj.* Containing or composed of fire; brightly glowing; blazing; hot and inflamed; full of spirit or intense with emotion. **fieriness** *n.*

fi-es-ta *n.* A religious holiday or festival.

fife *n.* A small, shrill-toned instrument similar to a flute.

fif-teen *n.* The cardinal number equal to 14 + 1. **fifteen** *adj.*, **-th** *n.*, *adj.* & *adv.*

fifth *n.* The ordinal of five; one of five equal parts. *Mus.* The space between a tone and another tone five steps from it. **fifth** *adj.* & *adv.*

Fifth Amendment *n.* An amendment to the United States Constitution, ratified in 1791, guaranteeing due process of law and that no person shall be forced to testify against himself".

fifth wheel *n.* A superfluous thing or person.

fif-ty *n.* The cardinal number equal to 5 X 10. **fiftieth** *n.*, *adj.* & *adv.*, **fifty** *adj.*

fifty-fifty *adj.*, *Slang* Divided into two equal portions or parts.

fig *n.* A tree or shrub bearing a sweet, pear-shaped, edible fruit; the fruit of the fig tree.

fight *v.* To struggle against; to quarrel; to argue; to make one's way by struggling; to participate in wrestling or boxing until a final decision is reached. *n.* A physical battle; struggle; strife; conflict; combat. **fighting** *v.*

fight-er *n.* A person who fights. *Milit.* A fast, highly maneuverable airplane used in combat.

fig-ment *n.* An invention or fabrication.

fig-ure *n.* A symbol or character that represents a number; anything other than a letter; the visible form, silhouette, shape, or line of something; the human form or body; an individual, especially a prominent one; the impression or appearance that a person makes; a design or pattern, as in a fabric; a figure of speech; a series of movements, as in a dance. **fig-ures** *pl.* In mathematics, calculations; an amount shown in numbers. *v.* To represent; to depict; to compute. **figured, figuring** *v.*

fig-ure eight *n.* A skating maneuver shaped like an 8; anything shaped like the number 8.

fig-ure-head *n.* A person with nominal leadership but no real power; a carved figure on a ship's prow.

fig-ure of speech *n.* An expression, as a metaphor or hyperbole, where words are used in a more forceful, dramatic, or illuminating way.

fig-u-rine *n.* A small sculptured or molded figure; a statuette.

Fi-ji *n.* A native of the Fiji Islands.

fil-a-ment *n.* A very thing, finely spun fiber, wire, or thread; the fine wire enclosed in an electric lamp bulb which is heated electrically to incandescence. **-ary, filamentous** *adj.*

fil-bert *n.* The edible nut of the hazel

tree or the tree it grows on.

filch v. To steal. **filcher** n.

file n. A device for storing papers in proper order; a collection of papers so arranged; a line of persons, animals, or things placed one behind another; a hard, steel instrument with ridged cutting surfaces, used to smooth or polish. v. To march as soldiers; to make an application, as for a job. **filing, filed** v.

fi-let n. A filet of meat or fish; lace or net with a pattern of squares.

fi-let mi-gnon n. A small, tender cut of beef from the inside of the loin.

fil-i-al adj. Of or relating to a son or daughter; pertaining to the generation following the parents. **filially** adv.

fil-i-buster n. An attempt to prolong, prevent, or hinder legislative action by using delaying tactics such as long speeches. **filibuster** v., **filibusterer** n.

fil-i-gree n. Delicate, lace-like ornamental work made of silver or gold intertwisted wire. **filigree** v. & adj.

fil-ing n., often **fil-ings** Particles removed by a file.

Fil-i-pi-no n. A native or inhabitant of the Philippines. **Filipino** adj.

fill v. To put into or hold as much of something as can be contained; to supply fully, as with food; to put together or make up what is indicated in an order or prescription; to meet or satisfy a requirement or need; to occupy an office or position; to insert something, as to fill in a name or address. *Naut.* To trim the yards so the sails will catch the wind. n. A built-up piece of land or the material, as earth or gravel, used for it. **to fill in on** To give someone additional information of facts about something. **to fill out** To become or make fuller or more rounded. **filling** v.

fill-er n. Something that is added to increase weight or bulk or to take up space; a material used to fill cracks, pores, or holes in a surface before it is completed.

fil-let *or* **fi-let** n. A narrow ribbon or band for holding the hair; a strip of boneless fish or meat. v. To slice, bone, or make into fillets.

fill-ing n. That which is used to fill something, especially the substance put into a prepared cavity in a tooth; the horizontal threads crossing the warp in weaving.

fill-ing sta-tion n. A retail business where vehicles are serviced with gasoline, oil, water, and air for tires.

fil-lip n. A snap of the finger that has been pressed down by the thumb and then suddenly released; something that arouses or excites. **fillip** v.

Fill-more, Mil-lard n. The 13th president of the United States, from 1850-1853.

fil-ly n. A young female horse.

film n. A thin covering, layer, or membrane. *Photog.* A photosensitive strip or sheet of flexible cellulose material that is used to make photographic negatives or transparencies; the film containing the pictures projected on a large screen; the motion picture itself. v. To cover with or as if with a film; to make a movie. **filmy** adj.

film-dom n. The movie industry or business.

film-strip n. A strip of film containing graphic matter for still projection on a screen.

fil-ter n. A device, as cloth, paper, charcoal, or any other porous substance, through which a liquid or gas can be passed to separate outsuspended matter. *Photog.* A colored screen that controls the kind and intensity of light waves in an exposure. v. To pass liquids through a filter; to strain. **filterability** n., **filterable, filtrable** adj.

filth n. Anything that is dirty or foul; something that is considered offensive.

filth-y adj. Highly unpleasant; morally foul; obscene. **filthily** adv., **filthiness** n.

fil-trate v. To pass or cause to pass through something. n. Anything which has passed through the filter. **filtrating, filtrated** v., **filtration** n.

fin n.

A thin membranous extension of the body of a fish or other aquatic animal, used for swimming and balancing. *Slang* A five dollar bill.

fi-na-gle v., *Slang* To get something by trickery or deceit. **finagled** v., **finagling** adj., **finagler** n.

fi-nal adj. Pertaining to or coming to the end; last or terminal. **finality** n., **finally** adv.

finals pl., n. Something decisively final, as the last of a series of athletic contests; the final academic examination.

fi-na-le n. The last part, as the final scene in a play or the last part of a musical composition.

fi-nal-ist n. A contestant taking part in the final round of a contest.

fi-nal-ize v. To put into final and complete form. **finalized, finalizing** v., **finalization, finalizer** n.

fi-nance n. The science of monetary affairs. **finances** Monetary resources; funds. v. To supply the capital or funds for something; to sell or provide on a credit basis. **financial** adj., **financially** adv.

fin-an-cier n. An expert who deals with large-scale financial affairs.

finch n. A small bird, as a grosbeak, canary, or goldfinch, having a short stout bill.

find v. To come upon unexpectedly; to achieve; to attain; to ascertain; to determine; to consider; to regard; to recover or regain something; to detect the true identity or nature of something or someone. finding v.

find-er n. A person who finds; the device on a camera that indicates what will be in the picture.

find-ing n. Something that is found or discovered. findings pl., n. Conclusions or statistics that are the result of a study, examination, or investigation.

fine adj. Superior in skill or quality; very enjoyable and pleasant; light and delicate in workmanship, texture, or structure; made up or composed of very small parts. Slang To be in good health; very well. n. The sum of money required as the penalty for an offense. fineness n. fine v. finely adv.

fi-ne n., Mus. The end.

fine arts pl., n. The arts of drawing, painting, sculpture, architecture, literature, music, and drama.

fin-er-y n., pl. -ies Elaborate jewels and clothes.

fi-nesse n. A highly refined skill; the skillful handling of a situation.

fin-ger n. One of the digits of the hand, usually excluding the thumb; that part of a glove made to fit the finger; anything resembling the finger. Mus. The use of the fingers in playing an instrument.

fin-ger-board n. The strip of wood on the neck of a stringed instrument against which the strings are pressed by the fingers in order to play.

fin-ger bowl n. A small bowl which contains water for cleansing the fingers at the table after eating.

fin-ger-ing n., Mus. The technique of using the fingers in order to play a musical instrument; the marking that indicates which fingers are to be used.

fin-ger-nail n. The transparent covering on the dorsal surface of the tip of each finger.

fin-ger-print n. An inked impression of the pattern formed by the ridges of the skin on the tips of each finger and thumb. fingerprint v.

fin-ger-tip n. The extreme end of a finger.

fin-i-al n. The ornamental projection or terminating part, as on a lamp shade.

fin-ick-y adj. Hard to please; choosy. finickiness n.

fi-nis n. The end.

fin-ish v. To bring to an end; to conclude; to reach the end; to consume all. Slang To kill, defeat, or destroy. n. The last stage or conclusion of anything; the perfection or polish in manners, speech, or education; the surface quality or appearance of paint, textiles, or other materials. adj. Having a glossy polish. finishing v., finisher n., finished adj.

fi-nite adj. Having bounds or limits; of or relating to a number which can be determined, counted, or measured. finitely adv., finiteness n.

fink n., Slang A person that breaks a strike; an unsavory person.

fin-nan had-die n. Smoked haddock.

fin-ny adj. Having or suggesting fins or fin-like extensions.

fir n. An evergreen tree with flat needles and erect cones.

fire n. The chemical reaction of burning, which releases heat and light. v. To have great enthusiasm; to ignite or cause to become ignited; to bake in a kiln; to discharge a firearm or explosive; to let a person go from a job; to dismiss. fired, firing v.

fire a-larm n. A safety device to signal the outbreak of a fire.

fire-arm n. A small weapon used for firing a missile; a pistol or rifle using an explosive charge.

fire-ball n. A very bright meteor; a hot, incandescent sphere of air and vaporized debris. Slang A remarkably energetic person or thing.

fire-box n. A box that contains a fire alarm; the compartment in which the fuel of a locomotive or furnace is burned.

fire-brand n. A piece of glowing or burning wood; one who stirs up or agitates conflict or trouble.

fire-break n. A strip of land that is cleared to prevent a fire from spreading.

fire-brick n. A highly heat-resistant brick, used to line furnaces and fireplaces.

fire-bug n. One who enjoys setting fire to buildings or homes; a pyromaniac.

fire-crack-er n. A small paper cylinder charged with an explosive that is set off to make noise.

fire-damp n. Gas, mainly methane, occurring naturally in coal mines and forming explosive mixtures with air.

fire en-gine n. A large motor vehicle equipped to carry firefighters and their equipment to a fire.

fire es-cape n. A structure, often metal, used as an emergency exit from a building.

fire ex-tin-guish-er n. A portable apparatus that contains fire extinguishing chemicals, which are ejected through a short nozzle and hose.

fire fight-er n. A person who fights fires as an occupation.

fire-fly n. A beetle that flies at night, having an abdominal organ that gives off a flashing light.

fire-house n. The building used to house fire fighting equipment and personnel.

fire irons pl. n. Equipment that includes tongs, shovel, and a poker used to tend a fire, usually in a fireplace.

fire-man n., pl. -men A person employed to prevent or extinguish fires; one who tends fires.

fire-place n. An open recess in which a fire is built, especially the base of a chimney that opens into a room.

fire-plug n. A hydrant for supplying water in the event of a fire.

fire-pow-er n., Milit. The capacity to deliver fire or missiles, as from a weapon, military unit, or ship.

fire-proof *adj.* Resistant to fires.

fire tow-er *n.* A forest fire lookout station.

fire-trap *n.* A building made from such construction or built in such a way that it would be hard to escape from if there were a fire.

fire wall *n.* A fireproof wall in a building used as a barrier to forestall or prevent a fire from spreading.

fire-works *pl. n.* Explosives used to generate colored lights, smoke, and noise for entertainment or celebrations.

fir-ing line *n.* In combat, the front line from which gunfire is delivered; the vulnerable front position of a pursuit or activity.

firm *adj.* Relatively solid, compact, or unyielding to pressure or touch; steadfast and constant; strong and sure. *n.* A partnership of two or more persons for conducting a business. *v.* To become or make firm or firmer.

firm-ly *adv.* Unwaveringly; resolutely. **firmness** *n.*

fir-ma-ment *n.* The expanse of the heavens; the sky.

firn *n.* Snow that is partially consolidated by thawing and freezing but has not converted to glacial ice.

first *adj.* Preceding all others in the order of numbering; taking place or acting prior to all others; earliest; ranking above all in importance or quality; foremost. *adv.* Above or before all others in time, order, rank, or importance; for the very first time. *n.* The ordinal number that matches the number 1 in a series, 1st; the transmission gear producing the lowest driving speed in an automotive vehicle. **firstly** *adv.*

first aid *n.* The emergency care given to a person before full treatment and medical care can be obtained.

First Amend-ment *n.* The amendment to the Constitution of the United States which forbids Congress to interfere with religion, free speech, free press, the right to assemble peaceably, or the right to petition the government, ratified in 1791.

first-born *adj.* First in order. *n.* The child who is born first.

first class *n.* The best quality or highest rank; a class of sealed mail that consists partly or wholly of written matter; the best or most luxurious accommodations on a plane, ship, etc.

first-de-gree burn *n.* A mild burn characterized by heat, pain, and redness of the skin surface but not exhibiting blistering or charring of tissues.

first-hand *adj.* Coming directly from the original source. **firsthand** *adv.*

first la-dy *or* **First La-dy** *n.* The wife of the President of the United States or the wife or hostess of the chief executive of a state, city, or other country.

first lieu-ten-ant *n., Milit.* A commis-

sioned officer ranking above a 2nd lieutenant and below a captain.

first per-son *n.* A category for verbs or pronouns indicating the speaker or writer of a sentence in which they are used.

first-rate *adj.* Of the finest rank, quality, or importance. **first-rate** *adv.*

firth *n.* A narrow inlet or arm of the sea.

fis-cal *adj.* Relating to or of the finances or treasury of a nation or a branch of government; financial. **fiscally** *adv.*

fish *n., pl.* **fish** *or* **fishes**

A cold-blooded, vertebrated aquatic animal having fins, gills for breathing, and usually scales; the flesh of fish used as food. **like a fish out of water** Not at ease or comfortable. *v.* To try to catch fish; to seek or find one's way; to grope; to try and obtain something in an artful or indirect way. **fishing** *n.*

fish bowl *n.* A bowl usually made of glass, serving as a small aquarium for fish; a lack of privacy.

fish-er-man *n., pl.* **-men** A person who fishes commercially or for sport and relaxation; a commercial fishing boat.

fish-er-y *n., pl.* **-ies** The business of catching, processing, or selling fish; a fish nursery or hatchery.

fish sto-ry *n.* An extravagant, boastful story that is probably not true.

fish-tail *v.* To swing from side to side while moving forward, as the motion of the rear end of a vehicle.

fish-wife *n., pl.* **-wives** A very coarse, abusive woman.

fish-y *adj.* Resembling fish, as in taste or odor; improbable; highly suspicious. **fishily** *adv.*, **fishiness** *n.*

fis-sile *adj.* Capable of being separated or split. *Physics* Fissionable. **fissility** *n.*

fis-sion *n.* The process or act of splitting into parts. *Physics* The exploding of the nucleus of an atom that leads to the formation of more stable atoms and the release of large quantities of energy. **fissionable** *adj.*

fis-sure *n.* A narrow opening, crack, or cleft in a rock. **fissure** *v.*

fist *n.* The hand closed tightly with the fingers bent into the palm. *Slang* The hand.

fist-fight *n.* A fight between two or more people without protection for the hands.

fist-ful *n., pl.* **-fuls** A hand full.

fis-tu-la *n., pl.* **-las** *or* **-lae** *Pathol.* A duct or other passage formed by the imperfect closing of a wound or abscess and leading either to the body surface or to another hollow organ. **-ous** *adj.*

fit *v.* To be the proper size and shape; to be in good physical condition; to possess the proper qualifications; to be competent; to provide a time or place for something; to belong. *adj.*

Adapted or adequate for a particular circumstance or purpose. *Med.* A convulsion; an impulsive and irregular exertion or action. **fitter, fitness** *n.*

fitch *n.* The polecat of the Old World or its fur.

fit-ful *adj.* Characterized by irregular actions; capricious; restless. **fitfully** *adv.,* **fitfulness** *n.*

fit-ing *adj.* Suitable or proper. *n.* The act of trying on clothes for alteration; a piece of equipment or an appliance used in an adjustment. **fittingly** *adv.,* **fittingness** *n.*

five *n.* The cardinal number equal to 4 + 1; any symbol of this number, as 5; anything with five units, parts, or members. **five** *adj. & pron.*

fix *v.* To make stationary, firm, or stable; to direct or hold steadily; to place or set definitely; to make rigid; to arrange or adjust; to prepare, as a meal. *n.* A position of embarrassment or difficulty. *Naut.* The position of a ship determined by observations, radio, or bearings. *Slang* The injection of a narcotic, such as heroin. **fixing, fixed** *v.*

fix-a-tion *n.* The act or state of being fixed; a strong, often unhealthy preoccupation. **fixate** *v.*

fix-ture *n.* Anything that is fixed or installed, as a part or appendage of a house; any article of personal property affixed to reality to become a part of and governed by the law of real property.

fizz *n.* A hissing or bubbling sound; effervescence; tiny gas bubbles. **fizz** *v.*

flab *n.* Excessive, loose, and flaccid body tissue. **flabby** *adj.,* **flabbiness** *n.*

flab-ber-gast *v.* To astound; to amaze. **flabbergasting, flabbergasted** *v.*

flac-cid *adj.* Lacking resilience or firmness. **flaccidity** *n.,* **flaccidly** *adv.*

flac-on *n.* A small, stoppered decorative bottle.

flag *n.* A piece of cloth, usually oblong, bearing distinctive colors and designs to designate a nation, state, city, or organization. *Bot.* Any of various iris or cattail plants with long blade-shaped leaves. *v.* To mark with or adorn with flags for identification or orna-mentation; to grow weak or tired.

Flag Day *n.* June 14, 1777, the day on which Congress proclaimed the Stars and Stripes the national standard of the United States.

flag-el-lant *n.* One who whips himself or has himself whipped by another for religious motives or for sexual excitement. **flagellation** *n.*

flag-on *n.* A vessel or container with a handle, spout, and hinged lid, used for holding wines or liquors.

fla-grant *adj.* Obvious; glaring; disgraceful; notorious; outrageous. **flagrance, flagrancy** *n.,* **flagrantly** *adv.*

flair *n.* An aptitude or talent for something; a dashing style.

flak *n.* Antiaircraft fire; abusive or excessive criticism.

flake *n.* A small, flat, thin piece which has split or peeled off from a surface. *Slang* Oddball; eccentric. **flake** *v.,* **flakily** *adv.,* **flakiness** *n.,* **flaky** *adj.*

flam-boy-ant *adj.* Extravagantly ornate; showy; florid; brilliant and rich in color. **flamboyance, flamboyancy** *n.,* **flamboyantly** *adv.*

flame *n.* A mass of burning vapor or gas rising from a fire, often having a bright color and forming a tongue-shaped area of light; something that resembles a flame in motion, intensity, or appearance; a bright, red-yellow color; violent and intense emotion or passion. *Slang* A sweetheart. **flaming, flamed, flame** *v.*

fla-men-co *n.* A fiery percussive dance of the Andalusian gypsies with strong and often improvised rhythms.

flame-out *n.* The combustion failure of a jet aircraft engine while in flight.

fla-min-go *n.* A large, long-necked, tropical wading bird, having very long legs, and pink or red plumage.

flam-ma-ble *adj.* Capable of catching fire and burning rapidly. **flammability, flammable** *n.*

flange *n.* A projecting rim or collar used to strengthen or guide a wheel or other object, keeping it on a fixed track. **flange** *v.*

flank *n.* The fleshy part between the ribs and the hip on either side of the body of an animal or human being; the lateral part of something. *Milit.* The right or left side of a military bastion or formation. *v.* To be stationed at the side of something. **flanker** *n.*

flan-nel *n.* A woven fabric made of wool or a wool, cotton, or synthetic blend. **flannels** *pl., n.* Trousers made of flannel. **flannelly** *adj.*

flan-nel-ette *n.* Cotton flannel.

flap-per *n.* A young woman of the 1920's whose dress and behavior were considered unconventional; a young bird unable to fly.

flare *v.* To blaze up or burn with a bright light; to break out suddenly or violently, as with emotion or action; to open or spread outward. **flaring, flared** *v.,* **flare** *n.*

flash *v.* To burst forth repeatedly or suddenly into a brilliant fire or light; to occur or appear briefly or suddenly. *n.* A short and important news break or transmission. **flashed, flashing** *v.*

flash-back *n.* The interruption in the continuity of a story, motion picture, drama, or novel to give a scene that happened earlier.

flash card *n.* A card printed with numbers or words and displayed briefly as a learning drill.

flash flood *n.* A violent and sudden flood occurring after a heavy rain.

flash point *n.* The lowest temperature at which the vapor of a combustible liquid will ignite or burn.

flash-y *adj.* Showing brilliance for a

moment; tastelessly showy; gaudy. **flashily** *adv.*, **flashiness** *n.*

flask *n.* A small container made of glass and used in laboratories.

flat *adj.* Extending horizontally with no curvature or tilt; stretched out level, prostrate or prone; lacking flavor or zest; deflated. *Mus.* Below the correct pitch. *n.* An apartment that is entirely on one floor of a building. **flat broke** Having little or no money. **to fall flat** Failing to achieve. **flatly** *adv.*, **-ness** *n.*

flat-bed *n.* A truck that has a shallow rear platform without sides.

flat-car *n.* A railroad car having no roof or sides.

flat-foot *n.*, *pl.* **-feet** A condition in which the arch of the foot is flat. *Slang* A police officer. **flat-footed** *adj.*

flat--out *adv.* In a direct way; at top speed. *adj.* Out-and-out.

flat-ten *v.* To make flat; to knock down. **flattener** *n.*

flat-ter *v.* To praise extravagantly, especially without sincerity; to gratify the vanity of; to portray favorably; to show as more attractive. **flatterer** *n.*, **flattering** *adj.*, **flatteringly** *adv.*

flat-ter-y *n.* Excessive, often insincere compliments.

flat-top *n.* A United States aircraft carrier; a short haircut having a flat crown.

flat-u-lent *adj.* Marked by or affected with gases generated in the intestine or stomach; pretentious without real worth or substance. **flatulence** *n.*, **flatulently** *adv.*

flat-ware *n.* Tableware that is fairly flat and designed usually of a single piece, as plates; table utensils, as knives, forks, and spoons.

flaunt *v.* To display showily. **flaunting** *v.*, **flaunter** *n.*, **flauntingly** *adv.*

flau-tist *n.* A flutist.

fla-vor *n.* A distinctive element in the taste of something; a distinctive, characteristic quality; a flavoring. *v.* To impart flavor to. **flavorful**, **flavorsome** *adj.*

fla-vor-ing *n.* A substance, as an extract or something else that is used to increase the flavor.

flaw *n.* A defect or blemish that is often hidden and that may cause failure under stress; a weakness in character; a fault in a legal paper that may nullify it. **flaw** *v.*

flaw-less *adj.* Without flaws or defects; perfect. **flawlessly** *adv.*, **flawlessness** *n.*

flax *n.* A plant with blue flowers, seeds that yield linseed oil, and slender stems from which a fine textile fiber is derived.

flax-en *adj.* Made of or pertaining to flax; pale yellow or golden as flax fiber.

flay *v.* To remove the skin of; to scold harshly.

flea *n.* A small, wingless, bloodsucking, parasitic jumping insect; a parasite of warm-blooded animals.

flea--bit-ten *adj.* Bitten or covered by fleas. *Slang* Shabby.

flea mar-ket *n.* A place where antiques and used items goods are sold.

fleck *n.* A tiny spot or streak; a small flake or bit. *v.* To mark with flecks.

fledg-ling *or* **fledge-ling** *n.* A young bird with newly acquired feathers; a person who is inexperienced; a beginner.

flee *v.* To run away; to move swiftly away. **fleeing** *v.*, **fleer** *n.*

fleece *n.* A coat of wool covering a sheep; the soft wool covering a sheep. *v.* To shear the fleece from; to swindle; to cover with fleece. **-er**, **fleeciness** *n.*, **fleecily** *adv.*, **fleecy** *adj.*

fleet *n.* A number of warships operating together under the same command; a number of vehicles, as taxicabs or fishing boats, operated under one command. *adj.* Moving rapidly or nimbly. **fleetly** *adv.*, **fleetness** *n.*

flesh *n.* Soft tissue of the body of a human or animal, especially skeletal muscle; the meat of animals as distinguished from fish or fowl; the pulpy substance of a fruit or vegetable; the body as opposed to the mind or soul; mankind in general; one's family. *v.* To arouse the hunting instinct of dogs by feeding fresh meat.

flesh and blood *n.* Human nature together with its weaknesses; one biologically connected to another.

flesh-ly *adj.* Of or pertaining to the body; sensual; worldly. **fleshliness** *n.*

flesh-pot *n.* A place were physical gratification is received.

flesh-y *adj.* Of, resembling, or suggestive of flesh; firm and pulpy; juicy as fruit. **fleshiness** *n.*

fleur-de-lis *n.*, *pl.* **fleurs-de-lis**

A heraldic emblem consisting of a three-petaled iris, at one time used as the armorial emblem of French sovereigns; the emblem of Quebec Province.

flew *v.* Past tense of fly.

flex *v.* To bend the arm repeatedly; to contract a muscle. **flexing**, **flexed** *v.*

flex-i-ble *adj.* Capable of being bent or flexed; pliable; responsive to change; easily yielding. **flexibility** *n.*, **flexibly** *adv.*

flex time *n.* A system which allows employees to set their own work schedules within a wide range of hours.

flick *n.* A light, quick snapping movement or the sound accompanying it. *v.* To strike or hit with a quick, light stroke; to cause to move with a quick movement. *Slang* A movie.

flick-er *v.* To burn or shine unsteadily, as a candle. *n.* A wavering or unsteady light; a North American woodpecker having a brownish back and a spotted breast. **flickering** *v.*

fli-er *or* **fly-er** *n.* One who or that which flies, especially an aviator; a daring or risky venture; a printed advertisement or handbill for mass distribution.

flight *n.* The act or manner of flying; a scheduled airline trip; a group that flies together; a swift or rapid passage or movement, as of time; a group of stairs leading from one floor to another; an instance of fleeing.

flight at-ten-dant *n.* A person employed to assist passengers on an aircraft.

flight bag *n.* A lightweight piece of luggage having flexible sides and outside pockets.

flight-y *adj.* Inclined to act in a fickle fashion; marked by irresponsible behavior, impulse, or whim; easily excited, skittish. **flightiness** *n.*

flim-flam *n. Slang* A swindle; trick; hoax.

flim-sy *adj.* Lacking in physical strength or substance; unconvincing. **flimsiness** *n.*, **flimsily** *adv.*

flinch *v.* To wince or pull back, as from pain; to draw away. **flincher** *n.*

fling *v.* To throw or toss violently; to throw oneself completely into an activity. *n.* An act of casting away; a casual attempt; a period devoted to self-indulgence; unrestraint.

flint *n.* A hard quartz that produces a spark when struck by steel; an implement used by primitive man; an alloy which used in lighters to ignite the fuel. **flinty** *adj.*

flip *v.* To turn or throw suddenly with a jerk; to strike or snap quickly and lightly. *Slang* To go crazy; to become upset or angry; to react enthusiastically. **flip** *n.*, **flipper** *adj.*

flip--flop *n.* The sound or motion of something flapping loosely; a backward somersault; a sudden reversal of direction or point of view; an electronic device or a circuit capable of assuming either of two stable states.

flip-pant *adj.* Marked by or showing disrespect, impudence, or the lack of seriousness. **flippancy** *n.*, **-ly** *adv.*

flip-per *n.* A broad flat limb, as of a seal, adapted for swimming; a paddle-like rubber shoe used by skin divers and other swimmers.

flip side *n.* The reverse or opposite side.

flirt *v.* To make teasing romantic or sexual overtures; to act so as to attract attention; to move abruptly; to dart. *n.* A person who flirts; a snappy, quick, jerky movement. **flirtation**, **flirtatiousness** *n.*, **flirtatious** *adj.*

flit *v.* To move rapidly or abruptly.

flit-ter *v.* To flutter. **flitter** *n.*

float *n.* An act or instance of floating; something that floats on the surface of or in a liquid; a device used to buoy the baited end of a fishing line; a floating platform anchored near a shoreline, which is used by swimmers or boats; a vehicle with a platform used to carry an exhibit in a parade; a drink consisting of ice cream floating in a beverage. *v.* To be or cause to be suspended within or on the surface of a liquid; to be or cause to be suspended in or move through the air as if supported by water; to drift randomly from place to place; to move lightly and easily; to place a security on the market; to obtain money for the establishment or development of an enterprise by issuing and selling securities. **floating** *v.*, **floatable** *adj.*, **floater** *n.*

float-ing rib *n.* One of the four lower ribs in the human being that are not attached to the other ribs.

flock *n.* A group of animals of all the same kind, especially birds, sheep, geese, etc., living, feeding or kept together; a group under the direction of a single person, especially the members of a church; a large number. *v.* To travel as if in a flock.

floe *n.* A large, flat mass of floating ice or a detached part of such a mass.

flog *v.* To beat hard with a whip or stick. **flogger** *n.*

flood *n.* The great deluge depicted in the Old Testament; an overflow of water onto land that is normally dry; an overwhelming quantity. *v.* To overwhelm with or as if with a flood; to fill abundantly or overwhelm; to supply the carburetor of an engine with an excessive amount of fuel; in football, to send more than one pass receiver into the same defensive area.

flood-gate *n.* A valve for controlling the flow or depth of a large body of water.

flood-light *n.* An electric lamp that gives off a broad and intensely bright beam of light. **floodlight** *v.*

floor *n.* The level base of a room; the lower inside surface of a structure; a ground surface; the right, as granted under parliamentary rules, to speak to a meeting or assembly; an area dividing a building into stories. *v.* To cover or furnish with a floor; to knock down; to overwhelm; to puzzle; to press the accelerator of a vehicle to the floorboard.

floor ex-er-cise *n.* A competitive gymnastics event with tumbling maneuvers performed on a mat.

floor show *n.* Entertainment consisting of singing, dancing; nightclub acts.

floor-walk-er *n.* A department store employee who supervises the sales force and gives assistance to customers.

floo-zy *n., pl.* **-ies** *Slang* A sleazy, loose woman; a prostitute.

flop *v.* To fall down clumsily; to move about in a clumsy way. *Slang* To completely fail; to go to bed. **flop** *n.*

flop house *n.* A cheap, rundown hotel.

flop-py *adj.* Flexible and loose. **floppily** *adv.*, **floppiness** *n.*

flop-py disk *n.* In computer science, a flexible plastic disk which is coated with magnetic material, used to record and store computer data.

flo-ra *n., pl.* **-ras** *or* **-rae** Plants growing

in a specific region or season.

flo-ral *adj.* Of or pertaining to flowers.

flo-res-cence *n.* A state or process of blossoming. **florescent** *adj.*

flor-id *adj.* Flushed with a rosy color or redness; ornate. **-ness** *n.*, **floridly** *adv.*

flo-rist *n.* One who grows or sells flowers and also artificial ones which are made of silk or silk-like fibers.

floss *n.* A loosely-twisted embroidery thread; a soft, silky fiber, such as the tassel on corn; dental floss. *v.* To clean between the teeth with dental floss. **flossed, flossing** *v.*

flo-ta-tion *n.* The act or state of floating.

flo-til-la *n.* A fleet of small vessels; a group resembling a small fleet.

flot-sam *n.* Any goods remaining afloat after a ship has sunk.

flounce *n.* A gathered piece of material attached to the upper edge of another surface, as on a curtain. *v.* To move with exaggerated tosses of the body. **flouncy** *adj.*

floun-der *v.* To struggle clumsily, as to gain footing; to act or speak in a confused way. *n.* Any of various edible marine flatfish. **-ed, floundering** *v.*

flour *n.* A soft, fine, powder-like substance obtained by grinding the meal of grain, especially wheat. *v.* To coat or sprinkle with flour. **flourly** *adj.*

flour-ish *v.* To thrive; to fare well; to prosper and succeed. *n.* A decorative touch or stroke, especially in handwriting; a dramatic act or gesture; a musical fanfare, as of trumpets. **flourished, flourishing** *v.*

flout *v.* To have or show open contempt for. **floutingly** *adv.*

flow *v.* To move freely, as a fluid; to circulate, as blood; to proceed or move steadily and easily; to rise; to derive; to be abundant in something; to hang in a loose, free way. **flow** *n.*

flow chart *n.* A chart or diagram showing the sequence and progress of a series of operations on a specific project.

flow-er *n.* A cluster of petals, bright in color, near or at the tip of a seed-bearing plant; blossoms; the condition of highest development; the peak; the best example or representative of something. *v.* To produce flowers; to bloom; to develop fully.

fl oz *abbr.* Fluid ounce.

flu *n.*, *Informal* Influenza.

flub *v.* To bungle or botch; to make a mess of. **flub** *n.*

fluc-tu-ate *v.* To shift irregularly; to change; to undulate. **fluctuation** *n.*

flue *n.* A conduit or passage through which air, gas, steam, or smoke can pass.

flu-ent *adj.* Having an understanding of a language use; flowing smoothly and naturally; flowing or capable of flowing. **fluency** *n.*, **fluently** *adv.*

fluff *n.* A ball, tuft, or light cluster of loosely gathered fibers of cotton or wool. *Slang* A mistake made by an actor or announcer in reading or an-

nouncing something. *v.* To make or become fluffy by patting with the hands. *Informal* To make an error in speaking or reading.

flu-id *n.* A substance, as water or gas, capable of flowing. *adj.* Changing readily, as a liquid. **fluidity, fluidness** *n.*, **fluidly** *adv.*

fluke *n.* A flatfish, especially a flounder; a flattened, parasitic trematode worm; the triangular head of an anchor at the end of either of its arms; a barb or point on an arrow; an unexpected piece of good luck. **fluky** *adj.*

flung *v.* Past tense of fling.

flunk *v.*, *Slang* To fail in, as an examination or course; to give a failing grade to. **flunking, flunked** *v.*

flun-ky *or* **flun-key** *n.* A liveried servant; a person who does menial work.

flu-o-res-cence *n.*, *Chem.*, *Phys.* Emission of electromagnetic radiation, especially of visible light, resulting from and occurring during the absorption of radiation from another source; the radiation emitted. **fluorescence** *v.*, **fluorescent** *adj.*

fluorescent lamp *n.* A tubular electric lamp in which ultraviolet light is reradiated as visible light.

fluor-i-date *v.* To add a sodium compound to water in order to prevent tooth decay. **flouridating, flouridated** *v.*, **fluoridation** *n.*

flu-o-ride *n.* A compound of fluorine with another element or a radical.

flu-o-rine *n.* A pale yellow, corrosive, and extremely reactive gaseous element, symbolized by F.

fluor-o-scope *n.* A device for observing shadows projected upon a flourescent screen of an optically opaque object, as the human body, which may be viewed by transmission of x-rays through the object. **fluoroscope** *v.*, **fluoroscopic** *adj.*, **fluoroscopy** *n.*

flur-ry *n.*, *pl.* **-ies** A sudden gust of wind; a brief, light fall of snow or rain, accompanied by small gusts; a sudden burst of activity or commotion.

flush *v.* To flow or rush out suddenly and abundantly; to become red in the face; to blush; to glow with a reddish color; to purify or wash out with a brief, rapid gush of water; to cause to flee from cover, as a game animal or bird. *n.* Glowing freshness or vigor; a hand in certain card games, as poker, in which all the cards are the same suit. *adj.* Having a heightened reddish color; abundant; affluent, prosperous; having surfaces that are even; arranged with adjacent sides close together; having margins aligned with no indentations; direct as a blow. *adv.* In an even position with another surface. **flushed, flushing** *v.*

flus-ter *v.* To make or become nervous or confused.

flute *n.* A high-pitched, tubular woodwind instrument equipped with finger holes and keys; a decorative groove in the shaft of a column; a small grooved pleat, as in cloth. **fluting** *n.*, **-ed** *adj.*

flut-ist *n.* A flute player.

flut-ter *v.* To flap or wave rapidly and irregularly; to fly as with a light, rapid beating of the wings; to beat erratically, as one's heart; to move about in a restless way. **flutter** *n.*, **fluttery** *adj.*

flux *n.* A flowing or discharge; a constant flow or movement; a state of constant fluctuation or change; a substance that promotes the fusing of metals and prevents oxide formation. *v.* To make fluid; to melt; to apply a flux to.

fly *v.*

To move through the air on wings or wing-like parts; to travel by air; to float or cause to float in the air; to escape; to flee; to pass by swiftly or quickly; to hit a fly ball. *n.* A folded piece of cloth that covers the fastening of a garment, especially trousers; a fly ball one has batted over the field; any of numerous winged insects, including the housefly and the tsetse; a fishing lure that resembles an insect. **fly off the handle** To react explosively.

flyable *adj.*

fly--by--night *adj.* Unstable or temporary; financially unsound.

fly-weight *n.* A boxer who belongs to the lightest weight class, weighing 112 pounds or less.

fly-wheel *n.* A rotating wheel heavy enough to regulate the speed of a machine shaft.

FM *abbr.* Field manual; frequency modulation.

foal *n.* The young animal, as a horse, especially one under a year old. *v.* To give birth to a foal.

foam *n.* A mass of bubbles produced on the surface of a liquid by agitation; froth; a firm, spongy material used especially for insulation and upholstery. *v.* To cause to form foam. **foam at the mouth** To be very angry.

foaminess *n.*, **foamy** *adj.*

fob *n.* A chain or ribbon attached to a pocket watch and worn dangling from a pocket; an ornament or seal worn on a fob. *v.* To dispose of by fraud, deceit, or trickery; to put off by excuse.

focal length *n.* The distance to the focus from a lens surface or concave mirror.

fo-cus *n.*, *pl.* **cuses** *or* **ci** A point in an optical system at which rays converge or from which they appear to diverge; the clarity with which an optical system delivers an image; adjustment for clarity; a center of activity or interest *v.* To produce a sharp, clear image of; to adjust a lens in order to produce a clean image; to direct; to come together at a point of focus.

focal *adj.*, **focally** *adv.*

fod-der *n.* A coarse feed for livestock, made from chopped stalks of corn and hay.

foe *n.* An enemy in war; an opponent or adversary.

foe-tal *adj.* Variation of fetal.

foe-tus *n.* Variation of fetus.

fog *n.* A vapor mass of condensed water which lies close to the ground; a state of mental confusion or bewilderment. *v.* To obscure or cover with, as if with fog. **foggily** *adv.*, **-iness** *n.*, **foggy** *adj.*

fog-horn *n.* A horn sounded in fog to give warning.

fo-gy *or* **fo-gey** *n.* A person with old-fashioned attitudes and ideas. **-ish** *adj.*

foi-ble *n.* A minor flaw, weakness, or failing.

foil *v.* To prevent from being successful; to thwart. *n.* A very thin, flexible sheet of metal; one that serves as a contrast; a fencing sword having a light, thin, flexible blade and a blunt point.

foiled, foiling *v.*

foist *v.* To pass off something as valuable or genuine.

fold *v.* To double or lay one part over another; to bring from an opened to a closed position; to put together and intertwine; to envelop or wrap; to blend in by gently turning one part over another. *Slang* To give in; to stop production; to fail in business. *n.* A line, layer, pleat or crease formed by folding; a folded edge; an enclosed area for domestic animals; a flock of sheep; a people united by common aims and beliefs; a church and its members. **folding, folded** *v.*

fol-de-rol *n.* Nonsense; a pretty but useless ornament.

fo-li-age *n.* The leaves of growing plants and trees; a cluster of flowers and branches.

fo-li-o *n.* A large sheet of paper folded once in the middle; a folder for loose papers; a book that consists of folios; a page number.

folk *n.*, *pl.* **folk** *or* **folks** An ethnic group of people forming a nation or tribe; people of a specified group. *Slang* A person's parents, family, or relatives.

fol-li-cle *n.* A small anatomical cavity or sac.

fol-low *v.* To proceed or come after; to pursue; to follow the course of; to obey; to come after in time or position; to ensue; to result; to attend to closely; to understand the meaning of. **following, followed** *v.*

fol-ly *n.*, *pl.* **-ies** Lack of good judgment; an instance of foolishness; an excessively costly and often unprofitable undertaking.

fo-ment *v.* To rouse; to incite; to treat therapeutically with moist heat.

foment, fomentation *n.*

fond *adj.* Affectionate liking; cherished with great affection; deeply felt.

fondly *adv.*, **fondness** *n.*

fon-dant *n.* A sweet, soft preparation of sugar used in candies and icings; a candy made chiefly of fondant.

fon-dle *v.* To stroke, handle, or caress affectionately and tenderly. -ed, -ling *v.*

font *n.* A receptacle in a church that holds baptismal or holy water; an assortment of printing type of the same size and face.

food *n.* A substance consisting essentially of carbohydrates and protein used to sustain life and growth in the body of an organism; nourishment, as in solid form; something that sustains or nourishes. food for thought Something to think about, something to ponder.

food-stuff *n.* A substance having food value.

fool *n.* One lacking good sense or judgment; one who can easily be tricked or made to look foolish. *v.* To dupe; to act in jest; to joke. *Slang* To amuse oneself. fooling *v.*

foot *n.*, *pl.* **feet**

The lower extremity of the vertebrate leg upon which one stands; a unit of measurement equal to 12 inches; a basic unit of verse meter that consists of a group of syllables; the end lower or opposite the head; the lowest part. *v.* To go on foot; to walk or run. *Slang* To pay the bill. on foot Walking rather than riding.

foot-ball *n.* A game played by two teams on a long rectangular field having goals at either end whose object is to get the ball over a goal line or between goalposts by running, passing or kicking; the oval ball used in the game of football.

foot-bridge *n.* A bridge for pedestrians.

foot-fall *n.* A footstep; the sound of a footstep.

foot-hill *n.* A low hill at or near the foot of a mountain or a higher hill.

foot-hold *n.* A place providing support for the foot, as in climbing; a position usable as a base for advancement.

foot-ing *n.* Secure and stable position for placement of the feet; a foundation.

foot-less *adj.* Without feet.

foot-locker *n.* A small trunk for personal belongings, designed to be placed at the foot of a bed.

foot-loose *adj.* Free to move as one pleases; having no ties.

foot-note *n.* A note of reference, explanation, or comment usually below the text on a printed page; a commentary. footnote *v.*

foot-path *n.* A narrow path for people on foot.

foot-print *n.* The outline or impression of the foot on a surface.

foot-stool *n.* A low stool for resting the feet.

foot-wear *n.* Articles, as shoes or boots, worn on the feet.

foot-work *n.* The use of the feet, as in boxing.

fop *n.* A man unduly concerned with his clothes or appearance; a dandy.

foppery, **foppishness** *n.*, **foppish** *adj.*

for *prep.* Used to indicate the extent of something; used to indicate the number or amount of; considering the usual characteristics of; on behalf of someone; to be in favor of. *conj.* Because; in as much as; with the purpose of.

for-age *n.* Food for cattle or other domestic animals; a search for supplies or food. *v.* To make a raid so as to find supplies; to plunder or rummage through, especially in search of provisions. forager *n.*

for-ay *n.* A raid to plunder. foray *v.*

for-bade *or* **for-bad** *v.* Past tense of forbid.

for-bear *v.* To refrain from; to cease from. forbearance *n.*

for-bid *v.* To command someone not to do something; to prohibit by law; to prevent.

forbidding *adj.* Very difficult; disagreeable.

force *n.* Energy or power; strength; the use of such power; intellectual influence; a group organized for a certain purpose. *Physics* Something that changes the state of rest or the body motion or influence. *v.* To compel to do something or to act; to obtain by coercion; to bring forth, as with effort; to move or drive against resistance; to break down by force; to press or impose, as one's will. in force In large numbers; in effect. forceable, forceful *adj.*, forcer *n.*, forcefully *adv.*

force-meat *n.* Finely ground meat, fish, or poultry, used in stuffing or served separately.

for-ceps *n.* forceps *pl.* An instrument resembling a pair of tongs used for manipulating, grasping or extracting, especially in surgery.

forc-i-ble *adj.* Accomplished or achieved by force; marked by force. -ly *adv.*

ford *n.* A shallow place in a body of water that can be crossed without a boat. *v.* To wade across a body of water.

Ford, Gerald Rudolph *n.* The 38th president of the United States from, 1974-1977.

Ford, Henry *n.* (1863-1947). American automobile maker.

fore *adj.* & *adv.* Situated in, at, or toward the front; forward. *n.* The front of something. *interj.* A cry used by a golfer to warn others that a ball is about to land in their direction.

fore--and--aft *adj.* Lying or going lengthwise on a ship; from stem to stern.

fore-arm *v.* To prepare in advance, as for a battle. *n.* The part of the arm between the elbow and the wrist.

fore-bear *or* **for-bear** *n.* An ancestor.

fore-bode *v.* To give an indication or warning in advance; to have a premonition of something evil. foreboding *n.*, forbodingly *adv.*

fore-cast *v.* To estimate or calculate in advance, especially to predict the weather. **forecast, forecaster** *n.*

fore-cas-tle *n.* The part of a ship's upper deck located forward of the foremast; living quarters for the crew at the bow of a merchant ship.

fore-close *v.* To recall a mortgage in default and take legal possession of the mortgaged property; to exclude; to shut out. **foreclosure** *n.*

fore-fa-ther *n.* An ancestor.

fore-fin-ger *n.* The finger next to the thumb.

fore-foot *n.* A front foot of an animal, insect, etc.

fore-front *n.* The foremost or very front of something; the vanguard.

fore-go *v.* To go before; to precede in time, place, etc. **foregoing** *v.*

fore-go-ing *adj.* Before; previous.

fore-gone *adj.* Already finished or gone.

fore-ground *n.* The part of a picture or landscape represented as nearest to the viewer.

fore-hand *n.* A stroke in tennis in which the palm of the hand holding the racket faces toward the direction of the stroke. **forehand** *adj. & adv.*

fore-head *n.* The part of the face that is above the eyebrows and extends to the hair.

for-eign *adj.* Situated outside one's native country; belonging to; located in or concerned with a country or region other than one's own; involved with other nations; occurring in a place or body in which it is not normally located.

for-eign-er *n.* A person from a different place or country; an alien.

fore-knowl-edge *n.* Prior knowledge of something; knowledge beforehand.

fore-lock *n.* A lock of hair growing from the front of the scalp and hanging over the forehead.

fore-man *n.* The person who oversees a group of people; the spokesperson for a jury. **forewoman** *n.*

fore-mast *n., Naut.* The forward mast of a sailing vessel; the mast nearest the bow of a ship.

fore-most *adj. & adv.* First in rank, position, time, or order.

fore-noon *n.* The period between sunrise and noon.

fo-ren-sic *adj.* Of, relating to, or used in courts of justice or formal debate. **forensically** *adv.*

fo-ren-sic med-i-cine *n.* A science dealing with the application of medicine in legal problems.

fore-or-dain *v.* Appoint or dispose of in advance; predestine.

fore-part *n.* The first or earliest part of a period of time.

fore-run-ner *n.* One sent or going before to give notice of the approach of others; a harbinger.

fore-sail *n., Naut.* The sail carried on the foremast of a square-rigged vessel.

fore-see *v.* To know or see beforehand.

foreseeable *adj.,* **foreseer** *n.*

fore-shad-ow *v.* To represent or warn of beforehand.

fore-shore *n.* The part of a shore uncovered at low tide.

fore-short-en *v.* To shorten parts of an object in order to give the illusion of depth.

fore-sight *n.* The act or capacity of foreseeing; the act of looking forward; concern for the future; prudence. **foresighted** *adj.,* **foresightedness** *n.*

fore-skin *n.* A fold of skin that covers the glans of the penis.

for-est *n.* A large tract of land covered with trees; something resembling a forest, as in quantity or density. *v.* To cover with trees. **-ed** *adj.,* **-land** *n.*

fore-stall *v.* To exclude, hinder, or prevent by prior measures.

for-est ran-ger *n.* An officer in charge of patrolling or protecting a public forest.

fore-taste *v.* To sample or indicate beforehand. **foretasting, foretasted** *v.,* **foretaste** *n.*

fore-tell *v.* To tell about in advance; to predict. **foretelling** *v.,* **foreteller** *n.*

fore-thought *n.* Prior thought or planning; a plan for the future.

fore-to-ken *v.* To warn beforehand.

for-ev-er *adv.* For eternity; without end.

fore-warn *v.* To warn in advance. **-ed** *v.*

fore-word *n.* An introductory statement preceding the text of a book.

for-feit *n.* Something taken away as punishment; a penalty; something that is placed in escrow and redeemed on payment of a fine; a forfeiture. *v.* To lose or give up the right to by some offense or error. **-er** *n.,* **-able** *adj.*

for-fei-ture *n.* The act of forfeiting; something forfeited; a penalty.

for-gath-er *v.* To come together; to convene; to assemble. **-ing, -ed** *v.*

forge *n.* A furnace where metals are heated and wrought; a smithy; a workshop that produces wrought iron. *v.* To form by heating and hammering; to give shape to; to imitate falsely; to advance slowly but steadily; to defraud; to counterfeit. **forging, forged** *v.,* **forger, forgery** *n.*

for-get *v.* To lose the memory of; to fail to become mindful or aware of at the right time. **forgetful, forgetable** *adj.,* **forgetfully** *adv.,* **forgetfulness** *n.*

for-give *v.* To pardon; to give up resentment of; to cease to feel resentment against. **-ness** *n.,* **-able** *adj.*

for-go *or* **fore-go** *v.* To give up or refrain from. **forgoer** *n.*

fork *n.* A tool consisting of a handle at one end of which are two or more prongs; the division of something into two or more parts that continue, as in a river or road.

forked *adj.* Shaped like or having a fork.

fork lift *n.* A self-propelled industrial vehicle with a pronged platform for hoisting and transporting heavy objects.

for-lorn *adj.* Abandoned or left in distress; hopeless; being in a poor condition. **forlornly** *adv.*, **forlornness** *n.*

form *n.* The shape or contour of something; a body of a living being; the basic nature or particular state of something; the way in which something exists; variety; manner, as established by custom or regulation; the style or manner determined by etiquette or custom; performance according to established criteria; fitness with regard to training or health; procedure of words, as in a ceremony; a document having blanks for insertion of information; style in musical or literary composition; the design or style of a work of art. *v.* To construct or conceive in the mind. *suffix* Having the form or shape of; cuneiform.

for-mal *adj.* Of or pertaining to the outward aspect of something; relating or concerned with the outward form of something; adhering to convention, rule, or etiquette; based on accepted conventions. **formally** *adv.*

for-mal-de-hyde *n.* A colorless, gaseous chemical used chiefly as a preservative and disinfectant in synthesizing other compounds.

for-mat *n.* A general style of a publication; the general form or layout of a publication. *v.* In computer science, to produce data in a specified form.

for-ma-tion *n.* The act or process of forming or the state of being formed; the manner in which something is formed; a given arrangement, as of troops, as a square or in a column.

for-ma-tive *adj.* Forming or having the power to form; of or pertaining to formation, growth, or development.

for-mer *adj.* Previous; preceding in place; being the first of two persons or things mentioned or referred to.

for-mer-ly *adv.* Previously.

form--fit-ting *adj.* Following closely to the contours of the body.

for-mi-da-ble *adj.* Extremely difficult; exciting fear by reason of size or strength. **formidably** *adv.*

form letter *n.* A standarized format of an impersonal letter sent to different people or to a large number of people.

for-mu-la *n.*, *pl.* -las *or* -lae A prescribed method of words or rules for use in a certain ceremony or procedure; a nutritious food for an infant in liquid form. *Math.* A combination or rule used to express an algebraic or symbolic form. *Chem.* A symbolic representation of the composition of a chemical compound. **formulaic** *adj.*

for-mu-late *v.* To state or express as a formula. **formulation, formulator** *n.* **formulating, formulated** *v.*

for-ni-ca-tion *n.* Voluntary sexual intercourse between two unmarried people. **fornicate** *v.*, **fornicator** *n.*

for-sake *v.* To abandon or renounce; to give up. **forsaking** *v.*

for-sooth *adv.* In truth; certainly.

for-swear *v.* To renounce emphatically or upon oath; to forsake; to swear falsely; to perjure oneself. -ing *v.*

for-syth-i-a *n.* An Asian shrub cultivated for its early-blooming, bright, yellow flowers.

fort *n.* A fortified structure or enclosure capable of defense against an enemy; a permanent army post.

forte *n.* An activity one does with excellence; a person's strong point; the part of a sword blade between the middle and the hilt.

forth *adv.* Out into plain sight, as from seclusion; forward in order, place, or time.

forth-com-ing *adj.* Ready or about to appear or occur; readily available.

forth-right *adj.* Straightforward; direct; frank. -ly *adv.*, **forthrightness** *n.*

forth-with *adv.* At once; promptly; immediately.

for-ti-fy *v.* To strengthen and secure with military fortifications; to provide physical strength or courage to; to strengthen; to enrich food, as by adding vitamins, minerals, etc. **fortification, fortifier** *n.*, **fortifying, fortified** *v.*

for-tis-si-mo *adv.*, *Music.* Very loudly (used as a direction). **fortissimo** *adj.*

for-ti-tude *n.* Strength of mind in adversity, pain, or peril, allowing a person to withstand pain.

fort-night *n.* A period of two weeks. **fortnightly** *adj. & adv.*

FOR-TRAN *n.* In computer science, a programming language for problems that are expressed in algebraic terms.

for-tress *n.* A fort.

for-tu-i-tous *adj.* Occurring by chance; lucky; fortunate. **fortuitously** *adv.*

for-tu-nate *adj.* Brought about by good fortune; having good fortune.

for-tune *n.* A hypothetical force that unpredictably determines events and issues favorably and unfavorably; success that results from luck; possession of material goods; a very large amount of money.

for-tune hunt-er *n.* A person who seeks wealth through marriage.

for-tune--tell-er *n.* A person who claims to predict the future. **fortune-telling** *n. & adj.*

for-ty *n.*, *pl.* -ies The cardinal number equal to four times ten. **fortieth** *n.*, *adj. & adv.*, **forty** *adj. & pron.*

for-ty--nin-er *n.* A United States pioneer in the 1849 California gold rush.

forty winks *n.*, *Slang* A short nap.

fo-rum *n.*, *pl.* -rums *or* -ra A public marketplace in an ancient Rome city, where most legal and political business was transacted; a judicial assembly.

for-ward *adj.* At, near, or toward a place or time in advance; oversteping the usual bounds in an insolent or presumptuous way; extremely unconventional, as in political opinions; so-

cially advanced. *n.* A player in football at the front line of offense or defense. *v.* To send forward or ahead; to help advance onward.
forwardly *adv.*, forwardness *n.*

fos-sil *n.* The remains of an animal or plant of a past geologic age preserved in the rocks of the earth's surface; one that is outdated.
fossilization *n.*, fossilize *v.*

fos-ter *v.* To give parental care to; to nurture; to encourage. *adj.* Giving or receiving parental care.

foul *adj.* Revolting to the senses; spoiled or rotten; covered with offensive matter; morally offensive; vulgar or obscene; unfavorable; dishonorable; indicating the limiting lines of a playing area. *adj.* In a foul way. *v.* To physically contact or entangle; to become foul or dirty; to dishonor; to obstruct; to entangle; to make or hit a foul. foul up *Slang* To make a mistake.
foully *adv.*, foulness *n.*

found *v.* To establish; to set up, often with funds to permit continuation and maintenance; to establish the basis or lay the foundation of; to melt metal and pour into a mold; to make by casting molten metal. founder *n.*

foun-da-tion *n.* The act of founding or establishing; the basis on which anything is founded; an institution supported by an endowment; a cosmetic base for make up.

foun-dry *n.*, *pl.* ries An establishment where metal is cast.

fount *n.* A fountain; an abundant source.

foun-tain *n.* A natural spring or jet of water coming from the earth; an artificially created spray of water; a basin-like structure from which such a stream comes; a point of origin or source.

foun-tain pen *n.* A pen having a reservoir of ink that automatically feeds the writing point.

four *n.* The cardinal number that equals 3 + 1; anything consisting of four units. four *adj. & pron.*

four-score *adj.* Being four times twenty; eighty.

four-teen *n.* The cardinal number that equals 13 + 1; anything consisting of fourteen units.
fourteen *adj. & pron.*,
fourteenth *n.*, *adj. & adv.*

fourth *n.* The ordinal number matching the number four in a series; the fourth forward gear of a transmission in a motor vehicle. fourth *adj. & adv.*

Fourth of July *n.* American Independence Day celebrated as a national holiday.

four-wheel *adj.* An automotive transmission in which all four wheels are linked to the source of driving power.

fowl *n.*, *pl.* fowl *or* fowls A bird used as food or hunted as game, as the duck, goose, etc.; the edible flesh of a fowl. *v.* To hunt or catch wild fowl. fowler *n.*

fox *n.*

A wild mammal having a pointed snout, upright ears, and a long bushy tail; the fur of a fox; a sly or crafty person. *v.* To outwit; to trick.

fox-hole *n.* A shallow pit dug by a soldier as cover against enemy fire.

fox-hound *n.* A large dog breed developed for fox hunting.

fox terrier *n.* A small dog having a wiry or smooth white coat with dark markings.

fox-trot *n.* A ballroom dance in 4/4 or 2/4 time consisting of a variety of rhythmic steps.

fox-y *adj.* Like a fox; sly or crafty; sharp *Slang* Very pretty. foxily *adv.*

foy-er *n.* The public lobby of a hotel, theater, etc.; an entrance hall.

fpm *abbr.* Feet per minute.

fps *abbr.* Feet per second.

Fr *abbr.* Father (clergyman).

fra-cas *n.* A noisy quarrel or disturbance; fight or dispute.

frac-tion *n.* A small part; a disconnected part or fragment of anything; in mathematics, an indicated quantity less than a whole number that is expressed as a decimal. *Chem.* A component of a compound separated from a substance by distilling. fractional *adj.*

frac-ture *n.* The act of breaking; the state of being broken. *Med.* The breaking or cracking, as in a bone.

frag-ile *adj.* Easily damaged or broken; frail; tenuous; flimsy.
fragilely *adv.*, fragility *n.*

frag-ment *n.* A part detached or broken; part unfinished or incomplete. *v.* To break into fragments. fragmentation *n.*

fra-grant *adj.* Having an agreeable, especially sweet odor. fragrance *n.*, fragrantly *adv.*

frail *adj.* Delicate; weak; easily damaged. frailly *adv.*, frailness *n.*

frame *v.* To put into a frame, as a picture; to build; to design; to adjust or adapt for a given purpose; to provide with a frame. *Slang* To incriminate so as to make a person appear guilty. *n.* Something made up of parts and joined together, such as a skeletal structure of a body; the pieces of wood or metal which surround a picture, photograph, or work of art; general structure; one exposure on a roll of film. frame-up *Slang* An act or actions which serve to frame someone or to make someone appear guilty when he is not. -er *n.*, -ing, framed *v.*

France *n.* A country located in western Europe.

fran-chise *n.* A privilege or right granted to a person or group by a government; the constitutional right to vote; authorization to sell a manufacturer's products; the territory within which a privilege or immunity is authorized.

franchise v., **franchisee, franchiser** n.

Franco, Francisco n. (1892-1975). Spanish dictator.

fran-gi-ble adj. Breakable. **frangibility** n.

frank adj. Sincere and straightforward. v. To mark mail officially so that no charge is made for delivery. n. The right to send mail without charge; a signature or mark on mail indicating that mail can be sent without charge; mail sent without charge; to mail free. **frankly** adv., **frankness** n.

frank-furt-er n. A smoked sausage made of beef or beef and pork.

frank-in-cense n. An aromatic gum resin obtained from African and Asian trees used as incense and in medicine.

Frank-lin, Benjamin n. (1706-1790). American statesman, scientist and inventor.

fran-tic adj. Emotionally out of control with worry or fear. **frantically, franticly** adv.

fra-ter-nal adj. Pertaining to or relating to brothers; of, pertaining to, or befitting a fraternity. Biol. Of or relating to a twin or twins that developed from separately fertilized ova. **fraternalism** n., **fraternally** adv.

frat-er-nize v. To associate with others in a friendly way; to mingle intimately with the enemy, often in violation of military law. -**ing**, **fraternized** v.

frat-ri-cide n. The killing of one's brother or sister; one who has killed his brother or sister. **fratricidal** adj.

fraud n. A deliberate and willful deception perpetrated for unlawful gain; a trick or swindle; an impostor; a cheat.

fraud-u-lent adj. Marked by or practicing fraud. -**ence** n., **fraudulently** adv.

fraught adj. Full of or accompanied by something specified.

fray n. A brawl, or fight; a heated argument or dispute. v. To wear out by rubbing; to irritate one's nerves.

fraz-zle v., Slang To wear out; to completely fatigue. **frazzle** n., **frazzling, frazzled** v.

freak n. A seemingly capricious event; a whimsical quality or disposition. Slang A drug addict; a highly individualistic rebel; a person with an extreme physical abnormality; a fan or enthusiast. **freak out** To experience hallucinations or paranoia induced by a drug; to make or become highly excited. **freakish, freaky** adj., **freakily** adv., **freakishness** n.

freck-le n. One of the small, brownish, often sun induced spots on the skin usually due to precipitation of pigment increasing in number and intensity on exposure to the sun.

free adj. Not imprisoned; not under obligation; politically independent; possessing political liberties; not affected by a specified circumstance or condition; exempt; costing nothing; not being occupied or used; too familiar; forward; liberal, as with money. adv. In a free way; without charge. v. To set at liberty; to release or rid; to untangle. -**ly** adv., -**ness** n.

free-dom n. The condition or state of being free; political independence; possession of political rights; boldness of expression; liberty; unrestricted access or use.

free lance n. One whose services are without long-term commitments to any one employer.

free--standing adj. Standing alone without any support.

free trade n. International exchange between nations or states which is unrestricted.

free-way n. A highway with more than two lanes.

free will n. The ability to choose freely; the belief that a human being's choices can be made freely, without external constraint. adj. Done willingly.

freeze v. To become ice or a similar solid through loss of heat; to preserve by cooling at an extremely low temperature; to become nonfunctional through the formation of ice or frost; to feel uncomfortably cold; to make or become rigid; to become suddenly motionless, rigid or inactive, as though through fear; to set prices at a certain level; to forbid further use of. n. An act of freezing or the state of being frozen; a cold snap. **freezing** v.

freeze--dry v. To preserve by drying in a frozen state under a high vacuum. **freeze-dried** adj.

freez-er n. One that freezes or keeps cold; an insulated cabinet for freezing and storing perishable foods.

freight n. A service of transporting commodities by air, land or water; the price paid such transportation; a train that transports goods only. v. To carry as cargo.

freight-er n. A ship used for transporting cargo.

French n. The language of France; of or pertaining to the people of France. **French** adj., -**man**, -**woman** n.

fren-zy n., pl. -**ies** A state of extreme excitement or violent agitation; temporary insanity or delirium. -**ied** adj.

fre-quent adj. Happening or appearing often or time after time. v. To go to a place repeatedly. **frequenter, frequentness** n., **frequently** adv.

fres-co n., pl. -**coes** or -**cos** The art of painting on moist plaster with water-based paint; a picture so painted.

fresh adj. Newly-made, gathered, or obtained; not spoiled, musty, or stale; new; different; not soiled; pure and clean; having just arrived; refreshed; revived. Slang Impudent; disrespectful. **freshly** adv., **freshness** n.

fresh-man n. A student in the first year of studies in a high school, university, or college; a beginner.

fret v. To be anxious or irritated; to wear away; to make by erosion; to ripple water. *n.* An ornamental design, composed of repeated symmetric figures; a ridge of metal fixed across the fingerboard of a stringed instrument, as a guitar.

Freud, Sigmund *n.* (1856-1939). Austrian psychoanalyst. **Freudian** *adj. & n.*

fri-a-ble *adj.* Easily crumbled or pulverized brittle. **friability, friableness** *n.*

fri-ar *n.* A member of a mendicant Roman Catholic order.

fric-as-see *n.* A dish of meat or poultry stewed in gravy. **fricassee** *v.*

fric-tion *n.* The rubbing of one surface or object against another; a conflict or clash. *Phys.* A force that retards the relative motion of two touching objects. **frictional** *adj.*

friend *n.* Someone who is personally well known by oneself and for whom one holds warm regards; a supporter of a cause or group. **Friend** A member of the Society of Friends; a Quaker. **friendless** *adj.*, **friendship** *n.*

frieze *n.* A decorative horizontal band along the upper part of a wall in a room.

frig-ate *n.* A square-rigged warship of the 17th to mid 19th centuries; U.S. warship smaller than a cruiser but larger than a destroyer.

fright *n.* Sudden violent alarm or fear; a feeling of alarm. *Slang* Something very unsightly or ugly.

fright-en *v.* To fill with fear; to force by arousing fear. **-ing** *adj.*, **-ingly** *adv.*

frig-id *adj.* Very cold; lacking warmth of feeling or emotional warmth; sexually unresponsive. **-ity, -ness** *n.*, **-ly** *adv.*

frill *n.* A decorative ruffled or gathered border. *Slang* A superfluous item. **frilly** *adj.*

fringe *n.* An edging that consists of hanging threads, cords, or loops. **fringe** *v.*

frip-per-y *n.*, *pl.* **-ies** Showy and often cheap ornamentation; a pretentious display.

frisk *v.* To skip or leap about playfully; to search someone for a concealed weapon by running the hands over the clothing quickly.

frit-ter *v.* To squander or waste little by little. *n.* A small fried cake made of plain batter, often containing fruits vegetables, or fish. **-ed, -ing** *v.*

friv-o-lous *adj.* Trivial; insignificant; lacking importance; not serious; silly. **frivolousness** *n.*, **frivolously** *adv.*

frizz *v.* To form into small, tight curls. **frizziness** *n.*, **frizzily** *adv.*, **frizzy** *adj.*

fro *adv.* Away from; back, as running to and fro.

frock *n.* A smock or loose-fitting robe; a robe worn by monks.

frog *n.*

Any of various small, smooth-skinned, web-footed, largely aquatic, tailless, leaping amphibians; an ornamental braid or cord; an arrange-

ment of intersecting railroad tracks designed to permit wheels to pass over the intersection without difficulty; a perforated holder for flower stems. *Slang* Hoarseness in the throat.

frol-ic *n.* Merriness; a playful, carefree occasion. *v.* To romp about playfully; to have fun. **-ker** *n.*, **frolicsome** *adj.*

from *prep.* Starting at a particular time or place; used to indicate a specific point; used to indicate a source; used to indicate separation or removal; used to indicate differentiation, as knowing right from left.

frond *n.* A large leaf, as of a tropical fern, usually divided into smaller leaflets.

front *n.* The forward surface of an object or body; the area or position located before or ahead; a position of leadership; a field of activity for disguising objectionable or illegal activities; an apparently respectable person, group, or business used as a cover for illegal or secret activities. *Meteor.* The line of separation between air masses of different temperatures. **frontal** *adj.*, **frontally** *adv.*

front money *n.* Money paid in advance for a service or product that has been promised.

fron-tier *n.* A part of an international border or the area adjacent to it; an unexplored area of knowledge or thought. **frontiersman** *n.*

fron-tis-piece *n.* An illustration that usually precedes the title page of a book or periodical.

frost *n.* A feathery covering of minute ice crystals on a cold surface; the act or process of freezing. *v.* To cover with frost; to apply frosting to a cake. **frostily** *adv.*, **frostiness** *n.*, **frosty** *adj.*

Frost, Robert Lee *n.* (1874-1963). American poet.

frost-bite *n.* The local destruction of bodily tissue due to exposure to freezing temperatures, often resulting in gangrene. **frostbite** *v.*

frost-ing *n.* Icing; a mixture of egg whites, sugar, butter, etc.; a lusterless or frosted surface on glass or metal.

froth *n.* A mass of bubbles on or in a liquid, resulting from agitation or fermentation; a salivary foam, as of an animal, resulting from disease or exhaustion; anything unsubstantial or trivial. *v.* To expel froth. **frothily** *adv.*, **frothiness** *n.*, **frothy** *adj.*

frou-frou *n.* A rustling sound, as of silk; a frilly dress or decoration.

for-ward *adj.* Obstinate. **forwardness** *n.*

frown *v.* To contract the brow as in displeasure or concentration; to look on with distaste or disapproval. **frown** *n.*, **frowningly** *adv.*, **frowned, frowning** *v.*

frow-zy *or* **frow-sy** *adj.* Appearing unkempt.

fro-zen *adj.* Covered with, changed into, surrounded by, or made into ice; extremely cold, as a climate; immobilized or made rigid, as by fear; coldly reserved; unfriendly; kept at a fixed level, as wages; not readily available for withdrawal, sale, or liquidation, as from a bank.

fru-gal *adj.* Economical; thrifty. frugality, frugalness *n.*, frugally *adv.*

fruit *n.*, *pl.* fruit *or* fruits The ripened, mature, seed-bearing part of a flowering plant, as a pod or berry; the edible, fleshy plant part of this kind, as an apple or plum; the fertile structure of a plant that does not bear seeds; the outcome or result. *v.* To produce or cause to produce fruit. fruitage *n.*, fruitful, fruitless *adj.*

fru-i-tion *n.* Achievement or accomplishment of something worked for or desired; the state of bearing fruit.

frump-y *adj.* Unfashionable; dowdy. frump, frumpiness *n.*

frus-trate *v.* To keep from attaining a goal or fulfilling a desire; to thwart; to prevent the fruition of; to nullify. frustration *n.*, frustratingly *adv.*, frustrating, frustrated *v.*

fuch-sia *n.* A chiefly tropical plant widely grown for its drooping, four-petaled flowers of purple, red, or white.

fuel *n.* A combustible matter consumed to generate energy, especially a material such as wood, coal, or oil burned to generate heat. *v.* To take in or supply with fuel; to stimulate, as an argument. fueler *n.*

fu-gi-tive *adj.* Fleeing or having fled, as from arrest, pursuit, etc. *n.* One who flees or tries to escape.

fugue *n.*, *Mus.* A musical composition in which the theme is elaborately repeated by different voices or instruments; a psychological disturbance in which actions are not remembered after returning to a normal state.

ful-crum *n.*, *pl.* -crums *or* -cra The point on which a lever turns.

ful-fill *or* **ful-fil** *v.* To convert into actuality; to effect; to carry out; to satisfy. fulfillment, fulfilment *n.*

ful-minate *v.* To condemn severely; to explode. fulmination, fulminator *n.*, fulminated, fulminating *v.*

ful-some *adj.* Offensively insincere. fulsomely *adv.*, fulsomeness *n.*

fum-ble *v.* To handle idly; to blunder; to mishandle a baseball or football. *n.* The act of fumbling; a fumbled ball. fumbler *n.*, fumbling, fumbled *v.*

fume *n.*, *often* fumes An irritating smoke, gas, or vapor. *v.* To treat with or subject to fumes; to show or feel anger or distress.

fu-mi-gate *v.* To subject to fumes in order to exterminate vermin or insects. -ation, -tor *n.*, -ed, -ing *v.*

func-tion *n.* The characteristics or proper activity of a person or thing; specific occupation, duty, or role; an official ceremony; something depending upon or varying with another; in math, a quantity whose value is dependent on the value of another. *v.* To serve or

perform a function as required or expected.

fun-da-men-tal *adj.* Basic or essential; of major significance; anything serving as the primary origin; most important. fundamental *n.*, fundamentally *adv.*

fu-ner-al *n.* The service performed in conjunction with the burial or cremation of a dead person.

fun-gus *n.*, *pl.* -gi *or* -guses 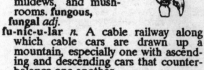 Any of numerous spore-bearing plants which have no chlorophyll that include yeasts, molds, mildews, and mushrooms. fungous, fungal *adj.*

fu-nic-u-lar *n.* A cable railway along which cable cars are drawn up a mountain, especially one with ascending and descending cars that counterbalance one another.

fun-nel *n.* A cone-shaped utensil having a tube for channeling a substance into a container. *v.* To pass or cause to pass through a funnel.

fur-be-low *n.* A ruffle or frill on clothing; a piece of showy decoration or ornamentation.

fur-bish *v.* To make bright, as by rubbing; to polish; to renovate. furbishing, furbished *v.*

fu-ri-ous *adj.* Extremely angry; marked by rage or activity. furiously *adv.*

furl *v.* To roll up and secure to something, as a pole or mast; to curl or fold. furl *n.*

fur-nace *n.* A large enclosure designed to produce intense heat.

fur-nish *v.* To outfit or equip, as with fittings or furniture. -er *n.*, furnishing *v.*

fu-ror *n.* Violent anger; rage; great excitement; commotion; an uproar.

fur-row *n.* A long, narrow trench in the ground, made by a plow or other tool; a deep wrinkle in the skin, especially of the forehead. furrow *v.*

fur-tive *adj.* Done in secret; surreptitious; obtained underhandedly; stolen.

fu-ry *n.*, *pl.* -ies Uncontrolled anger; turbulence; an angry or spiteful woman.

fu-sil-lage *n.* The central section of an airplane, containing the wings and tail assembly.

fu-sion *n.* The act or procedure of melting together by heat; a blend produced by fusion; a nuclear reaction in which nuclei of a light element combine to form more massive nuclei, with the release of huge amounts of energy.

fus-tian *n.* A sturdy, stout cotton cloth. *adj.* Pompous, pretentious language; bombastic.

fu-tile *adj.* Ineffectual; being of no avail; without useful result; serving no useful purpose.

fuzz *n.* A mass of fine, loose particles, fibers, or hairs.

G, g The seventh letter of the English alphabet. *Mus.* The fifth tone in the scale of C major. *Slang* One thousand dollars; a grand. *Physiol* A unit of force equal to that due to the earth's gravity.

gab-ar-dine *n.* A firm cotton, wool, or rayon material, having a diagonal raised weave, used for suits and coats.

gab-ble *v.* To speak rapidly or incoherently. **gabble** *n.*

gab-bro *n.* a granular igneous rock. **gabbroci, gabbroitic** *adj.*

Gabriel *n.* A special messenger of God mentioned in the Bible.

ga-boon *n.* An African tree with reddish-brown whood and is used mainly in furniture.

gad *v.* To wander about restlessly with little or no purpose. **gadder** *n.*

gad-a-bout *n., Slang* A person seeking fun.

gad-fly *n.* A fly that bites or annoys cattle and horses; an irritating, critical, but often constructively provocative person.

gadg-et *n., Slang* A small device or tool used in performing miscellaneous jobs, especially in the kitchen.

gad-o-lin-i-um *n.* A metallic element, silvery-white in color, of the lanthanide series, symbolized by Gd.

Gae-a *n.* In Greek mythology, the mother and wife of Uranus, the goddess of earth.

gaff *n.* A sharp iron hook used for landing fish. *Naut.* A spar on the top edge of a fore-and-aft sail. *Slang* Abuse or harsh treatment.

gag *n.* Something, as a wadded cloth, forced into or over the mouth to prevent someone from speaking or crying out; an obstacle to or any restraint of free speech, such as by censorship. *Slang* A practical joke or hoax. **to pull a gag** To perform a practical joke or trick on someone. *v.* To keep a person from speaking out by means of a gag; to choke on something. **gagger** *n.*

gage *n.* Something that is given as security for an action to be performed; a pledge; anything, as a glove, thrown down as a challenge to fight.

gag-gle *n.* A flock of geese; a group; a cluster.

gai-e-ty *n., pl.* **-ies** The state of being happy; cheerfulness; fun.

gai-ly *adv.* A gay or cheerful manner; showily or brightly.

gain *v.* To earn or acquire possession of something; to succeed in winning a victory; to develop an increase of; to put on weight; to secure as a profit; to improve progress; to draw nearer to.

gain-ful *adj.* Producing profits; lucrative. **gainfully** *adv.*, **gainfulness** *n.*

gain-say *v.* To deny; to contradict; dispute. **gainsayer** *n.*

gait *n.* A way or manner of moving on foot; one of the foot movements in which a horse steps or runs.

ga-la *n.* A festive celebration. **gala** *adj.*

ga-lac-tose *n.* The sugar typically occurring in lactose.

gal-ax-y *n., pl.* **-ies** *Astron.* Any of the very large systems of stars, nebulae, or other celestial bodies that constitute the universe; a brilliant, distinguished group or assembly. **Galaxy** The Milky Way. **galactic** *adj.*

gale *n., Meteor.* A very powerful wind stronger than a stiff breeze; an outburst, as of hilarity.

ga-le-na *n.* A metallic, dull gray mineral that is the principal ore of lead.

Gal-i-lee, Sea of *n.* The freshwater lake that is bordered by Syria, Israel, and Jordan.

gall *n., Physiol.* The bitter fluid secreted by the liver; bile; bitterness of feeling; animosity; impudence; something that irritates. *v.* To injure the skin by friction; to chafe. **-ing** *adj.*, **-ingly** *adv.*

gal-lant *adj.* Dashing in appearance or dress; majestic; stately; chivalrously attentive to women; courteous. **-ly** *adv.*

gal-lant-ry *n., pl.* **-ries** Nobility and bravery; a gallant act.

gall-blad-der *or* **gall bladder** *n.*

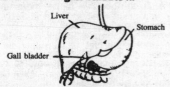

The small sac under the right lobe of the liver that stores bile.

gal-le-on *n.* A large three-masted sailing ship.

gal-ler-y *n., pl.* **-ries** A long, narrow passageway, as a corridor, with a roofed promenade, especially an open-sided one extending along an inner or outer wall of a building; a group of spectators, as at a golf tournament; a building where statues, paintings, and other works of art are displayed; a room or building where articles are sold to the highest bidder; an underground passage in a mine. **galleried** *adj.*, **gallery** *v.*

gal-ley *n., pl.* **-leys** A long medieval ship that was propelled by sails and oars; the long tray used by printers to hold set type; a printer's proof made from composed type, used to detect and correct errors.

gal-li-nule *n.* A wading bird with dark iridescent plumage.

gal-li-um *n.* A silvery metallic element used in semiconductor technology and as a component of various low-melting alloys, symbolized by Ga.

gal-li-vant *v.* To roam about in search of amusement or pleasure.

gal-lon *n.* A liquid measurement used in the U.S., equal to 4 quarts; in Great Britain, a liquid measurement which equals 4 imperial quarts; a dry measurement that equals 1/8 bushel.

gal-lop *n.* A horse's gait that is faster than a canter and characterized by regular leaps during which all four feet are off the ground at once.

gal-lows *n.* A framework of two or more upright beams and a crossbeam, used for execution by hanging.

gall-stone *n., Pathol.* A small, hard concretion of cholesterol crystals that sometimes form in the gall bladder or bile passages.

ga-lore *adj.* In great numbers; abundant; plentiful.

ga-losh *pl., n.* galoshes Waterproof overshoes which are worn in bad weather.

gal-va-nism *n.* Electricity that is produced by chemical action. *Med.* A therapeutic application of continuous electric current from voltaic cells.

gal-va-nize *v.* To stimulate or shock muscular action by an electric current; to protect iron or steel with rust resistant zinc. *Slang* To infuse with energy. **galvanization, galvanizer**.

gal-va-nom-e-ter *n., Electr.* An apparatus for detecting the presence of an electric current and for determining its strength and direction. **-metric** *adj.*

gam-bit *n.* In chess, an opening in which a piece is sacrificed for a favorable position; a maneuver that is carefully planned.

gam-ble *v.* To take a chance on an uncertain outcome as a contest or a weekly lottery number. *n.* Any risky venture. **gambler** *n.*

gam-bol *v.* To frolic, skip, or leap about in play.

gam-brel roof *Archit.* A ridged roof with the slope broken on each side, the lower slope steeper than the upper.

game *n.* A contest governed by specific rules; a way of entertaining oneself; amusement; a calculated way to do something; animals, fish, or birds that are hunted for sport or food.
-er, -est *adj.,* **-ly** *adv.,* **-ness** *n.*

game-cock *n.* A rooster bred and trained for cockfighting.

game-keep-er *n.* A person in charge of protecting and maintaining wildlife on a private preserve.

gam-ete *n., Biol.* Either of two mature reproductive cells, an ovum or sperm, which produce a zygote when united.

gam-in *n.* A homeless child who wanders about the streets of a town or city.

gam-ma globulin *n., Biochem.* A globulin that is present in blood plasma and contains antibodies effective against certain infectious diseases.

gamma ray *n., Phys.* Electromagnetic radiation that has energy greater than several hundred thousand electron volts.

gam-mon *n.* A cured ham; in the game of backgammon, a double victory in which a player removes all his pieces before the other player removes any.

gam-ut *n.* The whole range or extent of anything.

gam-y *adj.* Having the strong flavor of game, especially when slightly tainted; scandalous.

gan-der *n.* A male goose. *Slang* A quick glance; a look or peek.

Gandhi, Mohandas Karamchand "Mahatma" *n.* Hindu leader of India, who was assassinated in 1948.

gang *n.* A group of persons who are organized and work together or socialize regularly; a group of adolescent hoodlums or criminals. **gang up on** To attack as a group.

gan-gling *adj.* Tall and thin; lanky.

gan-gli-on *n., pl.* **-glia** *or* **-ons** *Physiol.* A collection of nerve cells located outside the spinal cord or brain. **ganglionic** *adj.*

gang-plank *n.* A temporary board or ramp used to board or leave a ship.

gan-grene *n., Pathol.* The death and decay of tissue in the body caused by a failure in the circulation of the blood supply. **gangrene** *v.,* **gangrenous** *adj.*

gang-ster *n.* A member of a criminal gang.

gang-way *n.* A passageway through, into, or out of an obstructed area. *Naut.* A passage on a ship's deck offering entrance to passengers or freight; gangplank.

gan-net *n.* A large sea bird with white plumage and black wing tips, related to the pelican and heron.

gan-try *n., pl.* **-ies** *Aeros.* A bridge-like framework support, especially a movable vertical structure with platforms, that is used in assembling or servicing rockets before they are launched.

gap *n.* An opening or wide crack, as in a wall; a cleft; a deep notch or ravine in a mountain ridge, offering passage.

gape *v.* To open the mouth wide, as in yawning; to stare in amazement with the mouth wide open; to become widely separated or open. **gaper** *n.*

gar *n.* A fish having a spearlike snout and elongated body covered with bony plates; a garfish.

ga-rage *n.* A building or structure in which motor vehicles are stored, repaired, or serviced.

gar-bage *n.* Food wastes, consisting of unwanted or unusable pieces of meat, vegetables, and other food products; any unwanted or worthless material; trash.

gar-ble *v.* To mix up or confuse; to change or distort the meaning of with the intent to mislead or misrepresent. **garble, garbler** *n.*

gar-den *n.* A place for growing flowers, vegetables, or fruit; a piece of ground commonly used as a public resort. *v.* To work in or make into a garden. **gardener, gardening** *n.*

gar-de-nia *n.* A tropical shrub with glossy evergreen leaves and fragrant white flowers.

Garfield, James Abram n. (1831-1881). The 20th president of the United States, assassinated in 1881, after serving from March through September of 1881.

gar-gan-tu-an adj. Of enormous size; immense.

gar-gle v. To force air from the lungs through a liquid held in the back of the mouth and throat. gargle n.

gar-goyle n. A waterspout made or carved to represent a grotesque animal or human figure, projecting from a gutter to throw rain away from the side of a building.

gar-ish adj. Too showy and bright; gaudy. garishly adv., garishness n.

gar-land n. A wreath, chain, or rope of flowers or leaves. v. To decorate with or form into a garland. Naut. A ring of rope attached to a spar to aid in hoisting or to prevent chafing.

gar-lic n. A plant related to the onion with a compound bulb which contains a strong odor and flavor, used as a seasoning.

gar-ment n. An article of clothing.

gar-ner v. To gather and store; to accumulate.

gar-net n. A dark-red silicate mineral used as a gemstone and as an abrasive.

gar-nish v. To add something to, as to decorate or embellish; to add decorative or flavorful touches to food or drink. garnish n.

gar-nish-ee v., Law To attach a debt or property with notice that no return or disposal is to be made until a court judgment is issued; to take a debtor's wages by legal authority.

gar-nish-ment n. The act of garnishing; the legal proceeding that turns property belonging to a debtor over to his creditor.

gar-ni-ture n. Anything that is used to garnish.

gar-ret n. A room in an attic.

gar-ri-son n. The military force that is permanently placed in a fort or town; a military post.

gar-rote or **gar-rotte** n. The former Spanish method of execution by strangulation with an iron collar tightened by a screw-like device. garrote v.

gar-ru-lous adj. Given to continual talkativeness; chatty. garrulity, garrulousness n.

gar-ter n. A band or strap that is worn to hold a stocking in place.

garter snake n. A nonvenomous North American snake which is small, harmless and has brightly colored stripes.

gas n., pl. **gases** A form of matter capable of expanding to fill a container and taking on the shape of the container; a combustible mixture used as fuel; gasoline; a gas used to produce an irritating, poisonous, or asphyxiating atmosphere. gas v.

gash n. A long, deep cut. gash v.

gas-ket n., Mech. A rubber seal, disk, or ring used between matched machine parts or around pipe joints to prevent the escape of fluid or gas.

gas-light n. A light produced by burning illuminating gas.

gas mask n. A protective respirator which covers the face and contains a chemical air filter to protect against poisonous gases.

gas-o-hol n. A fuel blended from unleaded gasoline and ethanol.

gas-o-line or **gas-o-lene** n. A colorless, highly flammable mixture of liquid hydrocarbons made from crude petroleum and used as a fuel and a solvent.

gasp v. To inhale suddenly and sharply, as from fear or surprise; to make labored or violent attempts to breathe.

gas-tric adj. Of or pertaining to the stomach.

gas-tric juice n., Biochem. The digestive fluid secreted by the stomach glands, containing several enzymes.

gas-tric ul-cer n., Pathol. An ulcer formed on the stomach lining, often caused by excessive secretion of gastric juices.

gas-tri-tis n., Pathol. Inflammation of the stomach lining. gastritic adj.

gas-tro-en-ter-ol-o-gy n. The medical study of the stomach and intestines. gastroenterologist n.

gas-tron-o-my n. The art of good eating. gastronome n., gastronomical adj.

gas-tro-pod n. One of the large class of aquatic and terrestrial mollusks, including snails, slugs, limpets, having a single shell and a broad, muscular organ of locomotion. -ous adj.

gas-works n., pl. -works An establishment where gas is manufactured.

gat n., Slang A pistol; short for Gatling gun.

gate n. A movable opening in a wall or fence, commonly swinging on hinges, that closes or opens; a valve-like device for controlling the passage of gas or water through a conduit or dam; the total paid admission receipts or number in attendance at a public performance.

gate--crash-er n. One who gains admittance without an invitation or without paying.

gate-leg ta-ble n. A table with legs that swing out to support drop leaves, the legs folding against the frame when the leaves are let down.

gath-er v. To bring or come together into one place or group; to harvest or pick; to increase or gain; to accumulate slowly; to fold or pleat a cloth by pulling it along a thread. gather, gathering n.

Gat-ling gun n. An early machine gun.

gauche adj. Socially awkward; clumsy; boorish. gauchely adv., gaucheness n.

gaud-y adj. Too highly decorated to be in good taste. gaudiness n.

gauge *or* **gage** *n.* A standard measurement, dimension, or capacity; an instrument used for measuring, testing, or registering; the distance between rails of a railroad; the diameter of the bore of a shotgun barrel. *v.* To determine the capacity, contents or volume of; to estimate; to evaluate. **gauger** *n.*

gaunt *adj.* Thin and bony; haggard; gloomy or desolate in appearance.

gaunt-let *or* **gant-let** *n.*

A challenge to fight; a glove to protect the hand; a former military punishment which forced an offender to run between two lines of men armed with clubs with which to strike him; criticism from all sides.

gauze *n.* A loosely-woven, transarent material used for surgical bandages; any thin, open-mesh material; a mist. **gauzy** *adj.*, **gauziness** *n.*

gav-el *n.* A mallet used by a presiding officer or by a person in charge to call for order or attention. **gavel** *v.*

ga-vi-al *n.* A large crocodile found in India, with long, slender jaws.

ga-votte *n.* A French dance resembling a quick-moving minuet.

gawk *v.* To gape; to stare stupidly.

gay *adj.* Merry; happy and carefree; brightly ornamental or colorful; *n.* A homosexual. **gayness** *n.*

gaze *v.* To look steadily or intently at something in admiration or wonder; to stare.

ga-zelle *n.* A small, gracefully formed antelope of northern Arabia and Africa, having curved horns and large eyes.

ga-zette *n.* A newspaper; an official publication. *v.* To publish or announce in a gazette.

gaz-et-teer *n.* A dictionary consisting of geographical facts.

gear *n.*, *Mech.* A toothed wheel which interacts with another toothed part to transmit motion; an assembly of parts that work together for a special purpose; equipment. *v.* To regulate, match, or suit something. **gearing** *n.*

gear-shift *n.*, *Mech.* A mechanism used for engaging or disengaging the gears in a power transmission system.

gear-wheel *or* **gear wheel** *n.*, *Mech.* A cogwheel.

geck-o *n.*, *pl.* **-os** *or* **-oes** Any of various small lizards of warm regions having toes with adhesive pads enabling them to climb up or down vertical surfaces.

Ge-hen-na *n.* In the New Testament, hell; a place of torment.

ge-fil-te fish *n.* Chopped fish mixed with crumbs, seasoning, and eggs, then cooked in a broth and served chilled in oval-shaped cakes or balls.

Gei-ger coun-ter *n.*, *Phys.* An instrument used to measure, detect, and record cosmic rays and nuclear radiation.

gei-sha *n.*, *pl.* **-sha** *or* **-shas** A Japanese girl who furnishes entertainment and companionship for men.

gel *n.*, *Chem.* A colloid that is in a more solid than liquid form. *v.* To change into or take on the form of a gel.

gel-a-tin *or* **gel-a-tine** *n.* An almost tasteless, odorless, dried protein, soluble in water and derived from boiled animal tissues, used in making foods, drugs, and photographic film; a jelly made from gelatin. **-ous** *adj.*

geld *v.* To castrate or spay, especially a horse.

geld-ing *n.* A gelded animal.

gel-id *adj.* Very cold; frigid. **gelidity** *n.*

gem *n.* A cut and polished precious or semiprecious stone; one that is highly treasured. *v.* To set or decorate with or as with gems.

Gem-i-ni *n.* The third sign of the zodiac; a person born between May 21 and June 20.

gem-ol-o-gy *or* **gem-mol-o-gy** *n.* The study of gems. **-ical** *adj.*, **-ist** *n.*

gen-darme *n.*, *pl.* **gendarmes** An armed policeman in France.

gen-der *n.*, *Gram.* Any of two or more categories, as feminine, masculine, and neuter, into which words are divided and which determine agreement with or selection of modifiers or grammatical forms; the quality of being of the male or female sex.

gene *n.*, *Biol.* A functional hereditary unit which occupies a fixed location on a chromosome and controls or acts in the transmission of hereditary characteristics.

ge-ne-al-o-gy *n.*, *pl.* **-ies** A record, table, or account showing the descent of a family, group, or person from an ancestor; the study of ancestry. **genealogical** *adj.*, **-ically** *adv.*, **-ist** *n.*

gen-er-al *adj.* Pertaining to, including, or affecting the whole or every member of a group or class; common to or typical of most; not being limited to a special class; miscellaneous; not detailed or precise. *n.*, *Milit.* An officer in the United States Army, Air Force, or Marine Corps ranking above a colonel. **generally** *adv.*

gen-er-al as-sem-bly *n.* A legislative body. General Assembly The supreme deliberative body of the United Nations.

gen-er-al-i-ty *n.*, *pl.* **-ies** The state or quality of being general; an inadequate, inexact or vague statement or idea.

gen-er-al-ize *v.* To draw a general conclusion from particular facts, experiences, or observations.

gen-er-al-i-za-tion *n.* Something arrived at by generalizing such as a broad, overall statement or conclusion.

gen-er-al prac-ti-tion-er *n.* A doctor who treats a variety of medical problems rather than specializing in one.

gen-er-al-ship *n.* The office or rank of a general; leadership or management of any type.

gen-er-al staff *n., Milit.* A group of officers who assist the commander in planning and supervising military operations.

gen-er-al store *n.* A retail store selling a large variety of merchandise but not subdivided into departments.

gen-er-ate *v.* To cause to be; to produce; to bring into existence, especially by a chemical or physical process. **generative** *adj.*

gen-er-a-tion *n.* A group of individuals born at about the same time; the average time interval between the birth of parents and that of their offspring. **generational** *adj.*

gen-er-a-tor *n., Mech.* A machine that changes mechanical energy into electrical energy.

ge-ner-ic *adj.* Relating to or indicating an entire class or group; general; pertaining to a genus or class of related things; of or relating to a class of product, or merchandise that does not bear a trademark or trade name. **generically** *adv.*

gen-er-ous *adj.* Sharing freely; abundant; overflowing. -ity *n.*, generously *adv.*

gen-e-sis *n., pl.* -ses The act or state of originating. Genesis The first book of the Old Testament.

ge-net-ic *adj.* Of or pertaining to the origin or development of something; of or relating to genetics. **genetically** *adv.*

ge-net-ic code *n., Biochem.* The biochemical basis of heredity that specifies the amino acid sequence in the synthesis of proteins and on which heredity is based.

Ge-ne-va Con-ven-tion *n.* The international agreement signed at Geneva in 1864 which governs the wartime treatment of prisoners of war and of the wounded, sick, and the dead.

gen-ial *adj.* Cheerful, kind, pleasant and good-humored in disposition or manner. **geniality** *n.*, genially *adv.*

ge-nie *n.* A supernatural creature, capable of taking on human form, who does one's bidding.

ge-nii *n.* In ancient mythology, a guardian spirit appointed to guide a person through life.

gen-i-tal *adj.* Of or pertaining to the reproductive organs or the process of reproduction.

gen-i-tals *pl.,n.* The external sexual organs. **genitalia** *n.*

gen-i-tive *adj., Gram.* Indicating origin, source, or possession. *n.* The genitive case. **genitival** *adj.*

gen-i-to-u-ri-nar-y *adj., Anat.* Of or pertaining to the genital and urinary organs or their functions.

gen-ius *n., pl.* -ses Exceptional intellectual ability or creative power; a strong, natural talent.

gen-o-cide *n.* The systematic extermination or destruction of a political, racial, or cultural group. **genocidal** *adj.*

gens *n., pl.* gentes In ancient Rome, a clan that included families of the same name that have descended through the male line.

gen-teel *adj.* Refined or well-bred; elegant; polite; stylish or fashionable. **genteelly** *adv.*, **genteelness** *n.*

gen-tian *n.* An annual or perennial plant with showy blue, red, yellow, or white flowers.

Gen-tile *n.* A person, especially a Christian, who is not a Jew; of or relating to nonMormons.

gen-til-i-ty *n.* The quality of being genteel; the members of the upper class; wellborn or well-bred persons collectively.

gen-tle *adj.* Not harsh, severe, rough, or loud; easily handled or managed; docile; not sudden or steep; from a good family of high social standing. *Meteor.* A soft, moderate breeze. *v.* To tame. **gently** *adv.*, **gentleness** *n.*

gen-tle-folk *or* **gen-tle-folks** *pl., n.* Persons from good family backgrounds.

gen-tle-man *n.* A man of noble birth and social position; a courteous or polite man; used as a form of address.

gen-tle-wom-an *n.* A woman of noble birth and social position; a woman attendant upon a lady of rank; a well-bred or polite woman.

gen-try *n.* People of good family or high social standing; the aristocracy; in England, the social class that is considered the upper ranks of the middle class.

gen-u-flect *v.* To bend down on one knee, as in worship. **genuflection** *n.*

gen-u-ine *adj.* Real; authentic; not counterfeit or spurious; not hypocritical; sincere. **genuinely** *adv.*, **genuineness** *n.*

ge-nus *n., pl.* nera *Biol.* A group or category of plants and animals usually including several species.

ge-o-cen-tric *adj.* Of or relating to the earth's center; formulated on the assumption that the earth is the center of the universe. -ally *adv.*, -al *adj.*

ge-o-chem-is-try *n.* A branch of chemistry that deals with the chemical composition of the earth's crust. **geochemical** *adj.*, **geochemist** *n.*

ge-o-des-ic dome *n.* A vaulted or domed structure of lightweight straight elements that form interlocking polygons.

ge-o-des-ic line *n.* In mathematics, the shortest line that connects two points on a given surface.

ge-od-e-sy *n.* The geologic science dealing with the determination of the shape, area, and curvature of the earth. **geodesist** *n.*, **geodetic** *adj.*

ge-og-ra-phy *n., pl.* -hies The science that deals with the earth's natural climate, resources, and population.

geographer n., **geographic,**
geographical adj., **geographically** adv.

ge-ol-o-gy n., pl. -ies The science that deals with the history, origin, and structure of the earth. **geologic, geological** adj., **geologically** adv., **geologist** n.

ge-o-met-ric adj. According to or pertaining to the rules and principles of geometry; increasing in a geometric progression.

ge-o-met-ric pro-gres-sion n. A sequence of numbers, as 4, 8, 16, 32 where each term is the product of a constant factor and the term that precedes it.

ge-om-e-try n., pl. ies The branch of mathematics that deals with the measurement, properties, and relationships of lines, angles, points, surfaces and solids.

ge-o-phys-ics pl., n. The study of the earth as the product of complex forces that act upon it internally from outer space, with reference to exploration of the less accessible regions.

ge-o-pol-i-tics pl., n. The study of the influence of economic and geographical factors on the politics and policies of a nation or region. **geopolitical** adj.

ge-o-ther-mal or **ge-o-ther-mic** adj. Relating to the internal heat of the earth.

ge-ra-ni-um n. A plant having rounded leaves and clusters of pink, red, or white flowers; a plant of the genus Pelargonium, with divided leaves and purplish or pink flowers.

ger-bil n. An animal of the rodent family found in the desert regions of Africa and Asia Minor, having long hind legs and a long tail; a popular pet.

ger-i-at-rics pl., n. The medical study that deals with the structural changes, diseases, physiology, and hygiene of old age. -ic adj., **geriatrician** n.

germ n. A small cell or organic structure from which a new organism may develop; a microorganism which causes disease. Biol. A reproductive cell.

Ger-man n. The language of Germany; an inhabitant or native of Germany. **German** adj.

ger-mane adj. Relevant to what is being considered or discussed.

Ger-man-ic n. Relating to the language or customs of the Dutch, German, English, Afrikaans, Flemish or Scandinavians. **Germanic** adj.

ger-ma-ni-um n. A grayish-white element widely used in electronics and optics, symbolized by Ge.

Ger-man meas-les n., Pathol. A contagious viral disease accompanied by sore throat, fever and a skin rash; a disease capable of causing defects in infants born to mothers infected during the first stages of pregnancy.

Ger-man shep-herd n. A large breed of dog, which is often trained to help the police and the blind.

germ cell n. An egg or sperm cell.

ger-mi-cide n. An agent used to destroy microorganisms or disease germs. **germicidal** adj.

ger-mi-nal adj. Of or relating to a germ or germ cell; of or in the earliest stage of development.

ger-mi-nate v. To begin to grow, develop, or sprout. **germination** n.

germ plasm n., Biol. The part of the protoplasm of a germ cell containing the chromosomes and genes.

ger-on-tol-gy n. The study of the processes and phenomena of aging. **gerontological, -ic** adj., **gerontologist** n.

ger-ry-man-der v. To divide a voting area so as to advance unfairly the interests of a political party; to adjust or adapt to one's advantage.

ger-und n., Gram. A verb form that is used as a noun.

gest n. A notable deed or feat.

ge-sta-po n. The secret police in Germany under the Nazi regime, known for its brutality.

ges-ta-tion n. The carrying of a developing offspring in the uterus; pregnancy. **gestate** v., **gestational** adj.

ges-tic-u-late v. To make expressive or emphatic gestures, as in speaking.

ges-ture n. A bodily motion, especially with the hands in speaking, to emphasize some idea or emotion. v. To make gestures. **gesturer** n.

ge-sund-heit interj. German A phrase used to wish good health to a person who has just sneezed.

get v. To come into possession of, as by receiving, winning, earning or, buying. to get ahead To attain success. to get back at To revenge oneself on. to get by To manage; to survive.

get-a-way n. The act of or instance of escaping by a criminal; a start, as of a race.

gew-gaw n. A little ornamental article of small value.

gey-ser n. A natural hot spring that intermittently ejects hot water and steam.

ghast-ly adj. Horrible; terrifying; very unpleasant or bad; ghost-like in appearance; deathly pale.

ghat n. A broad flight of steps that leads down to the edge of a river; a mountain pass, range, or chain.

gher-kin n. A very small, prickly cucumber pickled as a relish.

ghet-to n. A run-down section of a city in which a minority group lives because of poverty or social pressure.

ghost n. The spirit of a dead person which is believed to appear to or haunt living persons; a spirit; a ghostwriter; a false, faint secondary television image. **ghostly** adj.

ghost-writer n. A person hired to write for another person and to give credit for the writing to that other person.

ghoul n. A person who robs graves; in Moslem legend, an evil spirit which plunders graves and feeds on corpses. -ish adj., -ishly adv., **ghoulishness** n.

GI n., pl. GIs or GI's An enlisted person

in the United States armed forces. *adj.* In conformity with military regulations or customs. *v.* To clean or scrub in preparation for or as if for a military inspection.

gi-ant *n.* A legendary man-like being of supernatural size and strength; one of great power, importance, or size. **giantess** *n.*

gib-ber *v.* To talk or chatter incoherently or unintelligibly.

gib-ber-ish *n.* Meaningless speech.

gib-bet *n.* A gallows. *v.* To execute by hanging on a gibbet.

gib-bon *n.* A slender, long-armed Asian ape.

gib-bous *adj.* The moon or a planet which is seen with more than half but not all of the apparent disk illuminated. **gibbously** *adv.*, **-ness** *n.*

gibe *v.* To ridicule or make taunting remarks. **gibe, giber** *n.*

gib-let *n.*, *or* **giblets** The heart, liver, and gizzard of a fowl.

gid-dy *adj.* Affected by a reeling or whirling sensation; dizzy; frivolous and silly; flighty. **-ily** *adv.*, **-iness** *n.*

gift *n.* Something that is given from one person to another; a natural aptitude; a talent.

gifted *adj.* The state of having a special talent or ability.

gig *n.* A light, two-wheeled carriage drawn by one horse. *Naut.* A speedy, light rowboat; a spear with forks or prongs used for fishing. *Slang* A job, especially an engagement to play music. *Milit., Slang* A demerit; a punishment to military personnel.

gi-gan-tic *adj.* Of tremendous or extraordinary size; huge. **gigantically** *adv.*

gig-gle *v.* To laugh in high-pitched, repeated, short sounds. **giggle, giggler** *n.*, **giggly** *adj.*

gig-o-lo *n.* A man who is supported by a woman not his wife; a man who is paid to be an escort or dancing partner.

Gi-la mon-ster *n.* A large, venomous lizard of the southwestern United States desert, having an orange and black body.

gild *v.* To coat with a thin layer of gold; to brighten or adorn. **gilded** *adj.*, **gilding, gilder** *n.*

gill *n.*, *Zool.* The organ, as of fishes and various other aquatic invertebrates, used for taking oxygen from water. *n.* A liquid measure that equals 1/4 pint.

gilt *adj.* Covered with or of the color of gold. *n.* A thin layer of gold or a gold-colored substance which is applied to a surface.

gilt-edge *or* **gilt-edged** *adj.* Of the highest value or the best quality.

gim-bal *n.* A three ringed device that keeps an object supported on it level, as the compass of a ship.

gim-crack *n.* A cheap and useless object of little or no value.

gim-let *n.* A small, sharp tool with a bar handle and a pointed, spiral tip which is used for boring holes.

gim-mick *n.* A tricky feature that is obscured or misrepresented; a tricky device, especially when used dishonestly or secretly; a gadget. **gimmickry** *n.*, **gimmicky** *adj.*

gin *n.* An aromatic, clear, alcoholic liquor distilled from grain and flavored with juniper berries; a machine used to separate seeds from cotton fibers. *v.* To remove the seeds from cotton with a gin.

gin-ger *n.* A tropical Asian plant that has a pungent aromatic root, used in medicine and cooking.

gin-ger-bread *n.* A dark, ginger and molasses flavored cake or cookie.

gin-ger-ly *adv.* Doing something very cautiously. **-iness** *n.*, **gingerly** *adj.*

ging-ham *n.* A cotton fabric woven in solid colors and checks.

gin-gi-vi-tis *n.*, *Pathol.* Inflammation of the gums.

gink-go *n.*, *pl.* **-goes** *or* **-koes** A large Chinese shade tree cultivated in the United States, with edible fruits and nuts.

gin rum-my *n.* A variety of the card game rummy.

gin-seng *n.* A herb native to China and North America with an aromatic root believed to have medicinal properties.

gi-raffe *n.*, *pl.* **-fes** *or* **-fe**

The tallest of all mammals, having an extremely long neck and very long legs, found in Africa.

gird *v.* To surround, encircle, or attach with or as if with a belt.

gird-er *n.* A strong, horizontal beam, as of steel or wood, which is the main support in a building.

gir-dle *n.* A cord or belt worn around the waist; a supporting undergarment worn by women to give support and to shape. **girdle** *v.*

girl *n.* A female child or infant; a young, unmarried woman; any woman of any age; one's sweetheart. **girlish** *adj.*, **girlishly** *adv.*, **girlishness** *n.*

girl Fri-day *n.* A woman employee responsible for a variety of tasks.

girl friend *n.* A female friend; a regular or frequent female companion of a boy or man.

Girl Scout *n.* A member of the Girl Scouts of the United States, an organization for girls between 7 and 17 years of age.

girth *n.* The circumference or distance around something; a strap that encircles an animal's body to secure something on its back, as a saddle.

gis-mo *n.*, *Slang* A part or device whose name is unknown or forgotten; a gadget.

gist *n.* The central or main substance, as

of an argument or question.

give *v.* To make a present of; to bestow; to accord or yield to another; to put into the possession of another; to convey to another; to donate or contribute; to apply; to devote; to yield as to pressure; to collapse; to furnish or provide; to deliver in exchange; to pay. **give away** To hand over the bride to the bridegroom at a wedding ceremony. **give out** To collapse; to be exhausted. **give up** To surrender; to submit oneself. **giver** *n.*

giv-en *adj.* Bestowed; presented; specified or assumed.

giv-en name *n.* The name bestowed or given at birth or baptism.

giz-zard *n.* The second stomach in birds, where partly digested food is finely ground.

gla-brous *adj.*, *Biol.* Having no hair or down; having a smooth surface. **glabrousness** *n.*

gla-cial *adj.* Of or pertaining to, caused by, or marked by glaciers; extremely cold. **glacially** *adv.*

gla-cial e-poch *Geol.* A portion of geological time when ice sheets covered much of the earth's surface.

gla-cier *n.* A large mass of compacted snow that moves slowly until it either breaks off to form icebergs or melts when it reaches warmer climates.

glad *adj.* Displaying, experiencing, or affording joy and pleasure; a state of being happy; being willing to help; grateful. *n.* Short for gladiolus.

glad-den *v.* To make glad.

glade *n.* A clearing in a forest or woods.

glad-i-a-tor *n.* An ancient Roman slave, captive, or paid freeman who entertained the public by fighting to the death; one who engages in an intense struggle or controversy. **gladiatorial** *adj.*

glad-i-o-lus *.*, *pl.* -li *or* -luses A plant with fleshy bulbs, sword-shaped leaves, and spikes of colorful flowers.

glad-some *adj.* Giving cheer; showing joy. **gladsomely** *adv.*, **gladsomeness** *n.*

glam-or-ize *or* **glam-our-ize** *v.* To make glamorous; to portray or treat in a romantic way.

glam-our *or* **glam-or** *n.* Alluring fascination or charm. **glamourous** *adj.*

glance *v.* To take a brief or quick look at something; to obliquely strike a surface at an angle and be deflected; to give a light, brief touch; to brush against.

gland *n.*, *Anat.* Any of various body organs which excrete or secrete substances. **glandular** *adj.*

glare *v.* To stare fiercely or angrily; to shine intensely; to dazzle. *n.* An uncomfortably harsh or bright light.

glass *n.* A hard, amorphous, brittle, usually transparent material which hardens from the molten state, preceded by rapid cooling to prevent crystallization; any substance made of or resembling glass; a mirror, tumbler,

windowpane, lens, or other material made of glass. **glasses** A pair of eyeglasses used as an aid to vision; glassware. **glass, glassy** *adj.*

glass blowing *n.* The art or process of shaping objects from molten glass by gently blowing air into them through a glass tube.

glau-co-ma *n.*, *Pathol.* A disease of the eye characterized by abnormally high pressure within the eyeball and partial or complete loss of vision.

glaze *n.* A thin, smooth coating as on ceramics. *v.* To become covered with a thin glassy coating of ice; to coat or cover with a glaze; to fit with glass, as to glaze a window. **glazer** *n.*, **glazing, glazed** *v.*

gleam *n.* A momentary ray or beam of light. *v.* To shine or emit light softly; to appear briefly. **gleamy** *adj.*

glean *v.* To collect or gather facts by patient effort; to collect part by part; to pick bits of a crop left by a reaper. **gleaner** *n.*, **gleanings** *pl.*, *n.*

glee *n.* Joy; merriment; an unaccompanied song for male voices. **gleeful** *adj.*, **gleefully** *adv.*

glee club *n.* A singing group that is organized to sing short pieces of choral music.

glen *n.* A small, secluded valley.

glib *adj.* Spoken easily and fluently; superficial. **glibly** *adv.*, **glibness** *n.*

glide *v.* To pass or move smoothly with little or no effort; to fly without motor power. **glidingly** *adv.*, **gliding** *v.*

glid-er *n.* One that glides; a swing gliding in a metal frame. *Aeron.* An aircraft without an engine, constructed to soar on air currents.

glim-mer *n.* A faint suggestion; an indication; a dim unsteady light. **glimmering** *v.*

glimpse *n.* A momentary look.

glis-sade *n.* A gliding ballet step; a controlled slide in either a sitting or standing position, used to descend a steep, snowy, or icy incline. **glissade** *v.*, **glissader** *n.*

glis-san-do *n.*, *pl.* -di A rapid passing from one tone to another by a continuous change of pitch.

glis-ten *v.* To shine softly as reflected by light. **glisten** *n.*, -**ing**, **glistened** *v.*

glitch *n.* A minor mishap or malfunction. *Elect.* A false signal caused by an unwanted surge of power.

glit-ter *n.* A brilliant sparkle; small bits of light-reflecting material used for decoration. *v.* To sparkle with brilliance. **glittery** *adj.*, **glittering, glittered** *v.*

gloat *v.* To express, feel, or observe with great malicious pleasure or self-satisfaction. **gloater** *n.*, **gloating** *v.*

glob-al *adj.* Spherical; involving the whole world. **globalize** *v.*, **globally** *adv.*

globe *n.* A spherical object; anything that is perfectly rounded; the earth; anything like a sphere, such as a fishbowl;

a spherical representation of the earth, usually including geographical and political boundaries.

globe--trot-ter *n.* One who travels all over the world.

glob-u-lin *n., Biochem.* Any of a class of simple proteins found widely in blood, milk, tissue, muscle and plant seeds.

gloom *n.* Partial or total darkness; depression of the mind or spirits. **gloomily** *adv.*, **-iness** *n.*, **gloomy** *adj.*

glo-ri-fy *v.* To worship and give glory to; to give high praise. **glorification** *n.*

glo-ri-ous *adj.* Magnificent; resplendent; delightful; illustrious; full of glory. **gloriously** *adv.*

glory *n., pl.* **-ies** Distinguished praise or honor; exalted reputation; adoration and praise offered in worship; a wonderful asset; the height of one's triumph, achievement, or prosperity. *v.* To rejoice with jubilation.

gloss *n.* The sheen or luster of a polished surface; a deceptively or superficially attractive appearance; a note that explains or translates a difficult or hard to understand expression. *v.* To cover over by falsehood in an attempt to excuse or ignore.

glos-sa-ry *n., pl.* **-ries** A list of words and their meanings.

gloss-y *adj.* Having a bright sheen; lustrous; superficially attractive. *n.* A photo print on smooth, shiny paper. **glossily** *adv.*, **glossiness** *n.*

glot-tis *n., pl.* **-ises** or **-ides** *Anat.* The opening or cleft between the vocal cords at the upper part of the larynx. **glottal** *adj.*

glove *n.* A covering for the hand with a separate section for each finger; an oversized protective covering for the hand, as that used in baseball, boxing, or hockey. **gloved** *adj.*

glow *v.* To give off heat and light, especially without a flame; to have a bright, warm, ruddy color. *n.* A warm feeling of emotion. **glowing** *adj.*, **glowingly** *adv.*

glow-er *v.* To look sullenly or angrily at; to glare. **glower** *n.*, **gloweringly** *adv.*

glow-worm *n.* A European beetle; the luminous larva or grub-like female of an insect which displays phosphorescent light; the firefly.

glox-in-i-a *n.* A tropical South American plant with large, bell-shaped flowers.

glu-cose *n., Chem.* A substance less sweet than cane sugar, found as dextrose in plants and animals and obtained by hydrolysis; a yellowish to colorless syrupy mixture of dextrose, maltose, and dextrins with a small amount of water, used especially in confectionery and baking.

glue *n.* Any of various adhesives in the form of a gelatin, made from animal substances, as bones or skins, and used to stick and hold items together. **glue** *v.*, **gluey** *adj.*

glum *adj.* Moody and silent.

glut *v.* To feed or supply beyond capacity; to provide with a supply that exceeds demand.

glu-ten *n.* A mixture of plant proteins that is used as an adhesive and as a substitute for flour. **glutenous** *adj.*

glut-ton *n.* Someone who eats immoderately; one who has a large capacity for work or punishment. **-ous** *adj.*, **gluttonously** *adv.*, **gluttony** *n.*

glyc-er-ol *n., Chem.* A sweet, oily, syrupy liquid derived from fats and oils and used as a solvent, sweetener, antifreeze, and lubricant.

gly-co-side *n., Chem.* Any of a group of carbohydrates which, when decomposed, produce glucose or other sugar.

G--man *n., pl.* **-men.** An agent of the Federal Bureau of Investigation.

gnarl *n.* A hard, protruding knot on a tree. **gnarled** *adj.*

gnash *v.* To grind or strike the teeth together, as in a rage or pain.

gnat *n.* A small, winged insect, specially one that bites or stings.

gnaw *v.* To bite or eat away with persistence; to consume or wear away.

gneiss *n.* A banded, coarse-grained rock with minerals arranged in layers.

gnome *n.* In folklore, a dwarf-like creature who lives underground and guards precious metals and treasures.

gnu *n., pl.* **gnus** or **gnu** South African antelope with an ox-like head, curved horns, a long tail, and a mane.

go *v.* To proceed or pass along; to leave; to move away from; to follow a certain course of action; to function; to function correctly; to be in operation; to be awarded or given; to have recourse; to resort to; to pass, as of time; to be abolished or given up; to pass to someone, as by a will. *n.* An attempt; a try. **go back** on To abandon. **go** for To try; to try to obtain. **go places** To be on the road to success. **go under** To suffer destruction or defeat. **going** *v.*

go--a-head *n.* Permission; a signal to move ahead or proceed.

goal *n.* A purpose; the terminal point of a race or journey; in some games, the area, space, or object into which participants must direct play in order to score.

goal-ie *n.* A goalkeeper.

goal-keep-er *n.* The player responsible for defending the goal in hockey, soccer, and other games, preventing the ball or puck from passing over the goal for a score; a goal tender.

goat *n.* A horned, cud-chewing mammal related to the sheep; a lecherous man. *Slang* One who is a scapegoat. **goatish** *adj.*, **goatishly** *adv.*, **-ness** *n.*

goat-ee *n.* A short, pointed beard on a man's chin.

goat-skin *n.* The skin of a goat, often used for leather.

gob-ble *v.* To eat and swallow food greedily; to take greedily; to grab.

gob-ble-dy-gook *n., Informal* Wordy and often unintelligible language.

gob-bler *n.* A male turkey.

go--be-tween *n.* A person who acts as an agent between two parties.

gob-let *n.* A drinking glass, typically with a base and stem.

gob-lin *n.* In folklore, an ugly, grotesque creature said to be mischievous and evil.

god *n.* Someone considered to be extremely important or valuable; an image, symbol, or statue of such a being.

God *n.* The Supreme Being; the ruler of life and the universe.

god-child *n.* A child for whom an adult serves as sponsor at baptism, circumcision, and other rites.

god-dess *n.* A female of exceptional charm, beauty, or grace.

god-father *n.* A man who sponsors a child at his or her baptism or other such ceremony.

god-head *n.* Godhood; divinity. **Godhead** The essential and divine nature of God.

god-hood *n.* The state or quality of being a god; divinity.

god-less *adj.* Not recognizing a god. **godlessness** *n.*

god-ly *adj.* Filled with love for God.

god-mother *n.* A woman who sponsors a child at his or her baptism or other such ceremony.

god-par-ent *n.* A godfather or godmother.

god-send *n.* Something received unexpectedly that is needed or wanted.

god-son *n.* A male godchild.

God-speed *n.* Best wishes for someone's venture or journey.

go--get-ter *n.* An enterprising, aggressive person.

gog-gle *n., pl.* **-gles**

Spectacles or eyeglasses to protect the eyes against dust, wind, sparks, and other debris. *v.* To gaze or stare with bulging eyes.

go-ing *n.* The act of moving, leaving, or departing; the condition of roads or ground that affects walking, riding, and other movement; a condition influencing activity or progress. **goings on** Actions or behavior, used to express disapproval.

goi-ter *n., Pathol.* Any abnormal enlargement of the thyroid gland, visible as a swelling in the front of the neck. **goitrous** *adj.*

gold *n.* A soft, yellow, metallic element that is highly ductile and resistant to oxidation; used especially in coins and jewelry; a precious metal; a bright, vivid yellow; money; the element symbolized by Au.

gold-en an-ni-ver-sa-ry *n.* The 50th anniversary.

gold-en-rod *n.* A North American plant with small yellow flowers; the state flower of Alabama, Kentucky, and Nebraska.

gold--fill-ed *adj.* Made of a hard base metal over which a thick covering of gold is laid.

gold-finch *n.* A small bird, the male of which has yellow plumage with black forehead, tail, and wings.

gold-fish *n.* A reddish or brass-colored freshwater fish, cultivated as an aquarium fish.

gold mine *n.* A mine which produces gold ore; any source of great riches or profit.

gold stand-ard *n.* The monetary system based on gold of a specified weight and fineness as the unit of value and exchange.

golf *n.* A game played outdoors with a hard ball and various clubs, on a grassy course with 9 or 18 holes. **golf** *v.,* **golfer** *n.*

Gol-go-tha *n.* The place near Jerusalem where Jesus was crucified; also known as Calvary.

Go-li-ath *n.* In the Bible, a giant Philistine killed by David with a stone from a sling shot.

gon-ad *n., Anat.* The male or female sex gland where the reproductive cells develop; an ovary or testis. **gonadal, gonadial, gonadic** *adj.*

gon-do-la *n.* A long, narrow, flat-bottomed boat propelled by a single oar and used on the canals of Venice.

gone *adj.* Past; bygone; dead; beyond hope; marked by faintness or weakness. **far gone** Exhausted; wearied; almost dead.

gon-er *n., Slang* One that is ruined, close to death, or beyond all hope of saving.

gon-fa-lon *n.* A banner hung from a crosspiece and cut so as to end in streamers.

gong *n.* A heavy metal disk which produces a deep resonant tone when struck.

gon-o-coc-cus *n., pl.* **-cocci** The bacterium which causes gonorrhea. **gonococcal, gonococcic** *adj.*

gon-or-rhe-a *n., Pathol.* A contagious venereal infection transmitted chiefly by sexual intercourse. **gonorrheal** *adj.*

goo-ber *n., Regional* A peanut.

good *adj.* Having desirable or favorable qualities or characteristics; morally excellent; virtuous; well-behaved; tractable; proper; excellent in degree or quality; unspoiled; fresh; healthy; striking or attractive. **goods** Merchandise or wares; personal belongings; cloth; fabric. **for good** Forever; permanently. **better, best** *adj.*

Good Book *n.* The Bible.

good--by *or* **good--bye** *interj.* Used to express farewell. *n.* A farewell; a parting word; an expression of farewell. *adj.* Final.

good--for--noth-ing *n.* A person of little worth or usefulness.

Good Fri-day *n.* The Friday before Easter, a day observed by Christians as a commemoration of the crucifixion of Jesus.

good--heart-ed *adj.* Having a kind and generous disposition. -ness *n.*

good--hu-mored *adj.* Having a cheerful temper or mood; amiable.

good-humoredly *adv.,* -humoredness *n.*

good--na-tured *adj.* Having an easygoing and pleasant disposition.

good-naturedly *adv.,* -naturedness *n.*

good-will *n.* A desire for the well-being of others; the pleasant feeling or relationship between a business and its customers.

good-y *n., pl.* -ies Something that is good to eat; a prissy person.

goof *n., Slang* A stupid or dull-witted person; a mistake. *v.* To blunder; to make a mistake.

gook *n., Slang* A slimy, sludgy, or dirty substance.

goon *n., Slang* A thug or hoodlum hired to intimidate or injure someone; a person hired to break strikes; a stupid person.

goose *n., pl.* **geese**

A large water bird related to swans and ducks; a female goose. *Informal* A silly person.

goose-ber-ry *n., pl.* -ies The edible greenish berry of a spiny shrub used for pies, jams, and other foods.

goose bumps *pl., n.* A prickling sensation of the skin caused by fear or cold, also known as goose pimples and goose skin.

goose-neck *n.* Any various devices curved like a goose's neck.

go-pher *n.* A burrowing North American rodent with large cheek pouches.

gore *v.* To stab or pierce. *n.* Blood that has been shed; a triangular or tapering piece of cloth as in a sail or skirt.

gorge *n.* A deep, narrow ravine; deep or violent disgust. *v.* To eat or devour something greedily. **gorger** *n.*

gor-geous *adj.* Beautiful; dazzling; extremely beautiful; magnificent.

gorgeously *adv.,* **gorgeousness** *n.*

Gor-gon-zo-la *n.* A pungent, strongly flavored Italian cheese.

go-ril-la *n.*

A large African jungle ape, having a massive, stocky body, long arms, and tusklike canine teeth.

gorse *n.* A spiny plant bearing fragrant yellow flowers.

go-ry *adj.* Covered or stained with blood; marked by much bloodshed or violence.

gos-hawk *n.* A large, shortwinged hawk formerly used in falconry.

gos-ling *n.* A young goose.

gos-pel *or* **Gos-pel** *n.* The teachings of Christ and the apostles; any information which is accepted as unquestionably true; any of the first four books of the New Testament.

gos-pel mus-ic *n.* American religious music based on simple folk melodies blended with rhythmic and melodic elements of spirituals and jazz.

gos-sa-mer *n.* The fine film or strands of a spider's web floating in the air; anything sheer, delicate, light, or flimsy. **gossamer** *adj.*

gos-sip *n.* Idle, often malicious talk; a person who spreads sensational or intimate facts. *v.* To spread or engage in gossip. **gossiper** *n.,* **gossipy** *adj.*

Goth *n.* A member of a Germanic people that invaded the Roman Empire early in the Christian era; a barbarian.

Goth-am *n.* A nickname for New York City.

Goth-ic *adj.* Of or pertaining to the Goths or to their language; of or relating to an architectural style popular from about 1200 to 1500, which was characterized by pointed arches and ribbed vaulting.

Gou-da cheese *n.* A mild, yellow Dutch cheese made from milk.

gouge *n.* A chisel with a scoop-shaped blade used for woodcarving; a groove or hole made with or as if with a gouge *v.* To make a hole or groove with a gouge; to cheat, as to charge exorbitant prices. **gouger** *n.*

gou-lash *n.* A stew made from beef or veal and vegetables seasoned chiefly with paprika.

gourd *n.* A vine fruit related to the pumpkin, squash, and cucumber and bearing inedible fruit with a hard rind; the dried, hollowed-out shell can be used as a drinking utensil.

gour-mand *n.* A person who takes excessive pleasure in eating.

gour-met *n.* Someone who appreciates and understands fine food and drink.

gout *n., Pathol.* A disease caused by a defect in metabolism and characterized by painful inflammation of the joints. **gouty** *adj.*

gov-ern *v.* To guide, rule, or control by right or authority; to control or guide the action of something; to restrain.

governable *adj.,* **governance** *n.*

gov-ern-ess *n.* A woman employed in a private household to train and instruct children.

gov-ern-ment *n.* The authoritative admin-istration of public policy and affairs of a nation, state or city; the system or policy by which a political unit is governed; any governed territory, district, or area.

governmental *adj.,* **governmentally** *adv.*

gov-er-nor *n.* Someone who governs, as the elected chief executive of any state in the United States; an official appointed to exercise political authority over a territory. *Mech.* A device which will automatically controls the speed of a machine. **governorship** *n.*

govt *abbr.* Government.

gown *n.* A woman's dress, especially for a formal affair; any long, loose-fitting garment; a robe worn by certain officials, scholars, and clergymen.

GP *abbr.* General practitioner.

GPO *abbr.* General Post Office.

gr *abbr.* Grade; gross; grain.

grab *v.* To snatch or take suddenly; to take possession of by force or by dishonest means. *Slang* To capture the attention of someone or something. **grab, grabber** *n.*, **grabby** *adj.*

grab bag *n.* A bag or container full of miscellaneous unidentified articles from which one may draw an object at random.

gra-ben *n.*, *Geol.* An elongated depression in the earth, caused by the downward faulting of a portion of the earth's crust.

grace *n.* Seemingly effortless beauty, ease, and charm of movement, proportion, or form; a charming quality or characteristic; an extension of time that is granted after a set date, as for paying a debt. **graceful, graceless** *adj.*, **gracefully** *adv.*, **gracefulness** *n.*

gra-cious *adj.* Marked by having or showing kindness and courtesy; full of compassion; merciful. **graciously** *adv.*, **graciousness** *n.*

grack-le *n.* Any of various New World blackbirds having long tails and iridescent blackish plumage.

grad *n.*, *Slang* A graduate.

gra-da-tion *n.* A gradual and orderly arrangement or progression according to quality, size, rank, or other value; the act of grading. **gradational** *adj.*

grade *n.* A step or degree in a process or series; a group or category; a level of progress in school, usually constituting a year's work; a letter or number indicating a level of achievement in school work; the degree to which something slopes, as a road, track, or other surface. *Milit.* Rank or rating. **grade** *v.*

grade school *n.* Elementary school, which will usually teach from kindergarten to grade 6 or grade 8.

gra-di-ent *n.* A slope or degree of inclination. *Phys.* A rate of change in variable factors, as temperature or pressure.

grad-u-al *adj.* Moving or changing slowly by degrees; not steep or abrupt. **gradually** *adv.*, **gradualness** *n.*

grad-u-ate *v.* To receive or be granted an academic diploma or degree upon completion of a course of study; to divide into categories, grades or steps. *n.* A person who holds an academic degree; a type container or beaker marked in units or degrees, used for measuring liquids.

grad-u-ate stu-dent A student who has received a college degree and is working toward an advanced or higher degree.

grad-u-a-tion *n.* The state of graduating;

a commencement ceremony; issuing of diplomas or degrees.

graf-fi-to *n.*, *pl.* **graf-fi-ti** An inscription or drawing made on a public wall, subway train, rock, or any other surface.

graft *v.* To insert a shoot from a plant into another living plant so that the two will grow together as a single plant. *Surg.* To transplant a piece of tissue or an organ. *n.* Living tissue or skin used to replace damaged or destroyed tissue or skin; the act of acquiring or getting personal profit or advantage by dishonest or unfair means through one's public position.

gra-ham *n.* Whole wheat flour.

grail *n.* The legendary cup used by Christ at the Last Supper; also called the Holy Grail.

grain *n.* A small, hard seed or kernel of cereal, wheat, or oats; the seeds or fruits of such plants as a group; a very small amount; a small, hard particle, as a grain of sand; the side of a piece of leather from which the hair has been removed; the characteristic markings or pattern of this side; texture; basic nature. **against the grain** Contrary to one's inclinations or temperament. **grainer** *n.*, **grainless** *adj.*

grain al-co-hol *n.* Ethanol.

grain el-e-va-tor *n.* A building used to store grain.

grain-y *adj.* Having a granular texture; resembling the grain of wood. **graininess** *n.*

gram *n.* A metric unit of mass and weight equal to 1/1000 kilogram and nearly equal to one cubic centimeter of water at its maximum density.

gram-mar *n.* The study and description of the classes of words, their relations to each other, and their arrangement into sentences; the inflectional and syntactic rules of a language. **-ian** *n.*, **grammatical** *adj.*, **grammatically** *adv.*

gram-mar school *n.* An elementary school. *Brit.* A secondary or preparatory school.

gram mol-e-cule *n.*, *Chem.* The quantity of a compound, expressed in grams, that is equal to the molecular weight of that compound.

gran-a-ry *n.*, *pl.* **ries** A building for storing threshed grain; an area or region where grain grows in abundance.

grand *adj.* To be large in size, extent, or scope; magnificent; of high rank or great importance; lofty; admirable; main or principal; highly satisfactory; excellent. *Slang* A thousand dollars. **grandly** *adv.*, **grandness** *n.*

grand-child *n.* The child of one's son or daughter.

grand-dad *n.* The father of one's mother or father.

grand-daugh-ter *n.* The daughter of one's son or daughter.

gran-deur *n.* The quality or condition of being grand; splendor; magnificence.

grand-fa-ther *n.* The father of one's

father or mother; an ancestor.

grandfatherly *adv.*

grand-fa-ther clock *n.* A pendulum clock enclosed in a tall narrow cabinet.

gran-dil-o-quent *adj.* Speaking in or characterized by a pompous or bombastic style. **grandiloquence** *n.*

gran-di-ose *adj.* Impressive and grand; pretentiously pompous; bombastic. **grandiosely** *adv.*, **grandiosity** *n.*

grand mal *n.*, *Pathol.* A form of epilepsy characterized by severe convulsions and loss of consciousness.

grand-moth-er *n.* The mother of one's father or mother; a female ancestor.

grand op-era *n.* A form of opera having a serious and complex plot with the complete text set to music.

grand-par-ent *n.* A parent of one's mother or father.

grand pi-ano *n.* A piano with the strings which are arranged horizontally in a curved, wooden case.

grand slam *n.* In bridge, the taking of all the tricks; in baseball, a home run hit with runners on first, second, and third bases.

grand-son *n.* A son of one's son or daughter.

grand-stand *n.* A raised stand of seats, usually roofed, for spectators at a racetrack or sports event.

gran-ite *n.* A hard, coarse-grained igneous rock composed chiefly of quartz, mica, and orthoclase, which is used for building material and in sculpture. **granitic** *adj.*

gran-ite-ware *n.* Ironware utensils coated with hard enamel.

gran-ny *or* **gran-nie** *n.* A grandmother; an old woman; a fussy person.

gra-no-la *n.* Rolled oats mixed with dried fruit and seeds and eaten as a snack.

grant *v.* To allow; to consent to; to admit something as being the truth; in law, to transfer property by a deed. *n.* That which is granted. **grantee**, **granter**, **grantor** *n.*

Grant, Ulysses S. *n.* The 18th president of the United States, from 1869-1877.

gran-u-lar *adj.* The state of being composed or seeming to be composed or containing grains or granules. **granularity** *n.*

gran-u-late *v.* To make or form into granules or crystals; to become or cause to become rough and grainy. **granulation** *n.*

gran-ule *n.* A very small grain or particle.

grape *n.* Any of numerous woody vines bearing clusters of smooth-skinned, juicy, edible berries, having a dark purplish blue, red, or green color, eaten raw or dried and used in making wine.

grape-fruit *n.* A tropical, large, round citrus fruit with a pale yellow rind and tart, juicy pulp; the tree bearing this fruit.

grape-shot *n.* A shot consisting of a cluster of small iron balls, formerly used to charge a cannon.

grape sug-ar *n.* Dextrose.

grape-vine *n.* A climbing vine that produces grapes; a secret or informal means of transmitting information or rumor from person to person.

graph *n.* A diagram representing the relationship between sets of things.

graph-ic *or* **graph-i-cal** *adj.* Describing in full detail; of or pertaining to drawings or blueprints, as in architecture.

graph-ite *n.* A soft black form of carbon having a metallic luster and slippery texture, used in lead pencils, lubricants, paints, and coatings. **graphitic** *adj.*

graph-ol-o-gy *n.* The study of handwriting for the purpose of analyzing a person's character or personality. **graphologist** *n.*

grap-nel *n.* A small anchor with several flukes at the end.

grap-ple *n.* An instrument with iron claws used to fasten an enemy ship alongside for boarding. *v.* To struggle or contend with; to fasten, seize or drag as with a grapple. **grappler** *n.*

grasp *v.* To seize and grip firmly; to comprehend; to understand. *n.* The power to seize and hold. **graspable** *adj.*, **grasper** *n.*

grasp-ing *adj.* Urgently desiring material possessions; greedy. **graspingly** *adv.*, **graspingness** *n.*

grass *n.* Any of numerous plants having narrow leaves and jointed stems; the ground on which grass is growing. *Slang* Marijuana. **-iness** *n.*, **grassy** *adj.*

grass-hop-per *n.*

Any of several jumping insects that has long powerful hind legs. *Slang* Any type of small, lightweight airplane which can be used for dusting crops and military observation.

grass-land *n.* Land in which grasses are the main vegetation, as a prairie.

grass-roots *pl.*, *n.* A society of common people, thought of as having practical and highly independent views or interests. **grassroots** *adj.*

grass wi-dow *n.* A woman who is separated or divorced from her husband.

grate *v.* To reduce, shred or pulverize by rubbing against a rough or sharp surface; to make or cause to make a harsh sound. *n.* A rasping noise. **grater** *n.*, **grating** *adj.*, **gratingly** *adv.*

grate *n.* A framework or bars placed over a window or other opening; an iron frame to hold burning fuel in a fireplace or furnace.

grate-ful *adj.* The state of being thankful or appreciative for benefits or kindnesses; expressing gratitude. **gratefully** *adv.*, **gratefulness** *n.*

grat-i-fy *v.* To give pleasure or satisfaction to; to fulfill the desires of; to indulge. **gratification** *n.*

grat-ing *n.* A grate.

grat-is *adv. & adj.* Without requiring payment; free.

grat-i-tude *n.* The state of appreciation and gratefulness; thankfulness.

gra-tu-i-tous *adj.* Given or obtained without payment; unjustified; unwarranted. **-ly** *adv.*, **gratuitousness** *n.*

gra-tu-i-ty *n., pl.* **-ies** A gift, as money, given in return for a service rendered; a tip.

gra-va-men *n., pl.* **-mens** *or* **-mina** In law, the part of an accusation or charge weighing most heavily against the accused.

grave *n.* A burial place for a dead body, usually an excavation in the earth. *adj.* Very serious or important in nature; filled with danger; critical. *v.* To sculpt or carve; to engrave. *Mus.* Solemn and slow. **gravely** *adv.*, **-ness, -er** *n.*

grav-el *n.* Loose rock fragments often with sand. *Pathol.* The deposit of sand-like crystals that form in the kidneys; also known as kidney stones.

grave-stone *n.* A stone that marks a grave; a tombstone.

grave-yard *n.* An area set aside as a burial place; a cemetery.

grave-yard shift *n. Slang* A work shift that usually begins at midnight.

gra-vim-e-ter *n.* An implement for determining specific gravity. **gravimetry** *n.*

grav-i-tate *v.* To be drawn as if by an irresistible force; to sink or settle to a lower level.

grav-i-ta-tion *n., Physics* The force or attraction any two bodies exert towards each other. **gravitational, gravitative** *adj.*, **gravitationally** *adv.*

grav-i-ty *n., pl.* **-ies** The gravitational force manifested by the tendency of material bodies to fall toward the center of the earth; gravitation in general; weight; importance; seriousness.

gra-vy *n., pl.* **-ies** The juices exuded by cooking meat; a sauce made by seasoning and thickening these juices. *Slang* Money or profit which is easily acquired.

gray *or* **grey** *adj.* A neutral color between black and white; gloomy; dismal; having gray hair; characteristic of old age. **grayish** *adj.*, **grayness** *n.*

gray-beard *n., Slang* An old man.

gray-ling *n., pl.* **-ling** *or* **-lings** Any of several freshwater food and game fish with a small mouth and a large dorsal fin.

gray mat-ter *n.* The grayish-brown nerve tissue of the spinal cord and brain, consisting mainly of nerve cells and fibers; brains.

graze *v.* To feed upon growing grasses or herbage; to put livestock to feed on grass or pasturage; to brush against lightly in passing; to abrade or scrape slightly.

gra-zier *n.* One who grazes cattle.

grease *n.* Melted or soft animal fat; any thick fatty or oily substance, as a lubricant. *v.* To lubricate or coat with grease. **greasiness** *n.*, **greasy** *adj.*

grease paint *n.* Makeup used for theatre performances.

great *adj.* Very large in size or volume; prolonged in duration or extent; more than ordinary; considerable; remarkable; impressive; eminent; renowned; very good or first-rate; a generation removed from a relative. **greatly** *adv.*, **greatness** *n.*

great--aunt *n.* An aunt of either of one's parents.

Great Bear *n.* The constellation Ursa Major.

Great Brit-ain *n.* The island which is located off the west coast of Europe, made up of England, Scotland and Wales; the United Kingdom.

great--grand-child *n.* A child of a grandchild.

great--grand-daugh-ter *n.* A daughter of a grandchild.

great--grand-fa-ther *n.* The father of a grandparent.

great--grand-mo-ther *n.* The mother of a grandparent.

great--grand-par-ent *n.* The father or mother of a grandparent.

great--grand-son *n.* The son of a grandchild.

great-heart-ed *adj.* Noble or generous in spirit; magnanimous. **-ly** *adv.*, **-ness** *n.*

Great Lakes *n.* The group of five freshwater lakes of central North America located on either side of the boundary between the United States and Canada and including Lake Superior, Lake Michigan, Lake Huron, Lake Erie, and Lake Ontario.

great--neph-ew *n.* A grandnephew.

great--niece *n.* A grandniece.

Great Salt Lake *n.* A lake composed of salt water located in the state of Utah.

great seal *n.* The chief seal of a government.

great--un-cle *n.* An uncle of either of one's parents; granduncle.

grebe *n.* Any of various swimming and diving birds having partially webbed feet, very short tails, and a pointed bill.

Greece *n.* A country of southeast Europe. **Grecian** *adj. & n.*

greed *n.* Selfish desire to acquire more than one needs or deserves.

greed-y *adj.* Excessively eager to acquire or gain something; having an excessive appetite for drink and food; gluttonous. **greedily** *adv.*, **greediness** *n.*

Greek *n.* An inhabitant or native of Greece; the modern or ancient language of Greece. *adj.* Pertaining to or of the Greek Church; of or pertaining to the culture of Greece.

green *adj.* Of the color between yellow and blue in the spectrum; not fully matured or developed; lacking in skill or experience. *n.* A grassy plot or lawn, especially an area of closely mowed grass at the end of a golf fairway. **greenish** *adj.*, **greenness** *n.*

green-back *n.* A U.S. legaltender currency note.

green bean *n.* A string bean; a vegetable commonly grown in private gardens.

green-er-y *n., pl.* **-ies** Green foliage or plants.

green--eyed *adj.* Jealous.

green-horn *n.* An inexperienced person; a beginner; a person who is easily fooled.

green-house *n.* An enclosed structure equipped with heat and moisture designed for the cultivation of plants.

green pep-per *n.* The unripened fruit of various pepper plants.

green-room *n.* The room or lounge in a theatre used by performers when they are offstage.

green thumb *n.* A special skill for making plants thrive.

greet *v.* To address someone in a friendly way; to welcome; to meet or receive in a specified manner. **greeter** *n.*

greet-ing *n.* A word of salutation on meeting.

gre-gar-i-ous *adj.* Habitually associating with others as in groups, flocks, or herds; enjoying the company of others; sociable. **-ly** *adv.,* **-ness** *n.*

grem-lin *n.* A mischievous elf said to cause mechanical trouble in airplanes.

Gre-na-da *n.* An island in the West Indies.

gre-nade *n.* A small explosive device detonated by a fuse and thrown by hand or projected from a rifle.

gren-a-dier *n.* A member of a special European corps which was formerly armed with grenades.

gren-a-dine *n.* A syrup made from pomegranates or red currants and used as a flavoring in mixed drinks.

grew *v.* Past tense of grow.

grey *n., & adj.* Variation of gray.

grey-hound *n.* One of a breed of slender, swift-running dogs with long legs.

grid *n.* An arrangement of regularly spaced bars; the system of intersecting parallel lines that divide maps, charts, and aerial photographs, used as a reference for locating points.

grid-dle *n.* A flat pan used for cooking.

grid-i-ron *n.* A metal framework used for broiling meat, fish, and other foods; a football field.

grief *n.* Deep sadness or mental distress caused by a loss, remorse, or bereavement.

griev-ance *n.* A real or imagined wrong which is regarded as cause for complaint or resentment; a complaint of unfair treatment.

grieve *v.* To cause or feel grief or sorrow.

griev-ous *adj.* Causing grief, sorrow, anguish, or pain; causing physical suffering. **grievously** *adv.*

grif-fin *or* **grif-fon** *n.* In Greek mythology, a fabulous beast with a lion's body, an eagle's head, and wings.

grill *n.* A cooking utensil made from parallel metal bars; a gridiron; food cooked on a grill; a restaurant where grilled foods are a specialty. *v.* To broil on a grill.

grille *or* **grill** *n.* A grating with open metalwork used as a decorative screen or room divider.

grim *adj.* Stern or forbidding in appearance or character; unyielding; relentless; grisly; gloomy; dismal. **grimly** *adv.,* **grimness** *n.*

grim-ace *n.* A facial expression of pain, disgust, or disapproval. **grimace** *v.*

grime *n.* Dirt, especially soot clinging to or coating a surface. **griminess** *n.,* **grimy** *adj.*

grin *v.* To smile broadly. **grin** *n.*

grind *v.* To reduce to fine particles; to sharpen, polish, or shape by friction; to press or rub together; to work or study hard. *n.* A person who works hard or who studies very hard.

grind-er *n.* One that grinds.

grind-ers *pl.,n. Slang* The teeth.

grind-stone *n.* A flat, circular stone which revolves on an axle and is used for polishing, sharpening, or grinding.

grip *n.* A firm hold; a grasp; the ability to seize or maintain a hold; the mental or intellectual grasp; a suitcase. *v.* To grasp and keep a firm hold on; to capture the imagination or attention. **gripper** *n.,* **grippingly** *adv.*

gripe *v.* To cause sharp pain or cramps in the bowels; to anger; to annoy; to complain.

grippe *n.* Influenza. **grippy** *adj.*

gris-ly *adj.* Ghastly; gruesome.

grist *n.* Grain that is to be ground; a batch of such grain.

gris-tle *n.* Cartilage of meat. **gristly** *adj.*

grist-mill *n.* A mill for grinding grain.

grit *n.* Small, rough granules, as of sand or stone; having great courage and fortitude. *v.* To clamp the teeth together. **gritty** *adj.*

grits *pl., n.* Coarsely ground hominy; coarse meal; eaten primarily in the southern states of the U.S.

griz-zle *v.* To become or cause to become gray.

grizzly bear *n.*

A large, grayish bear of western North America. **grizzlies** *pl.,n., Slang* Grizzly bears.

groan *v.* To utter a deep, prolonged sound of or as of disapproval or pain. **groan** *n.,* **groaningly** *adv.*

groat *n.* A former British coin worth four-pence; any grain without its hull; a tiny sum.

gro-cer *n.* A storekeeper who deals in foodstuffs and various household supplies.

gro-cer-y *n., pl.* **-ies** A store in which foodstuffs and household staples are sold.

groceries *pl., n.* The merchandise sold in a grocery.

grog *n.* Any alcoholic liquor, especially rum, mixed with water.

grog-gy *adj.* To be dazed, weak, or not fully conscious, such as from a blow or exhaustion; drunk. **groggily** *adv.*, **grogginess** *n.*

groin *n., Anat.* The crease or fold where the thigh meets the abdomen. *Archit.* The curved edge of a building formed by two intersecting vaults.

grom-met *n.* A reinforcing eyelet through which a rope, cord, or fastening may be passed. *Naut.* A ring of rope or metal used to secure the edge of a sail.

groom *n.* A male person hired to tend horses; a stableman; a bridegroom. *v.* To make neat in appearance; to prepare for a particular position, as for a political office.

grooms-man *n., pl.* **-men** The best man at a wedding; any one of a bridegroom's attendants.

groove *n.* A long, narrow channel or indentation; a fixed, settled habit or routine; a rut. **groove** *v.*

groovy *adj., Slang* A state or condition of being wonderful; delightful.

grope *v.* The act of feeling about with or as with the hands, as in the dark; to look for uncertainly or blindly. **grope** *n.*, **gropingly** *adv.*

gros-beck *n.* Any of several colorful birds which are related to the finch, having a stout, short beak.

gros-grain *n.* A heavy, horizontally corded silk or rayon fabric, woven as a ribbon.

gross *adj.* Exclusive of deductions; of or relating to the total amount received; excessively large or fat; lacking refinement or delicacy; coarse; vulgar. *n.* The entire amount without deduction; an amount that equals 12 dozen or 144 items. **grossly** *adv.*, **grossness** *n.*

gross na-tion-al pro-duct *n.* The total market value of all goods and services produced by a nation in a year.

gro-tesque *adj.* Distorted, incongruous or ludicrous in appearance or style; bizarre; outlandish. **grotesque**, **grotesqueness** *n.*, **grotesquely** *adv.*

grot-to *n., pl.* **-toes** *or* **-tos** A cave or cave-like structure.

grouch *n.* An habitually irritable or complaining person. **grouch** *v.*, **-ily** *adv.*, **grouchiness** *n.*, **grouchy** *adj.*

ground *n.* The surface of the earth; soil, sand, and other natural material at or near the earth's surface; the connecting of an electric current to the earth through a conductor.

grounds *n.* The land that surrounds a building; the basis for an argument, action or belief; the sediment at the bottom of a liquid, such as coffee or tea. *v.* To prevent an aircraft or pilot from flying. *Naut.* To run a boat aground.

ground *v.* Past tense of grind.

ground cov-er *n.* A low-growing plant which forms a dense, extensive growth and tends to prevent soil erosion.

ground glass *n.* Glass that has been treated so that it is not fully transparent.

ground hog *n.* A woodchuck.

Ground-hog Day *n.* February 2nd, on which, if the ground hog sees his shadow, he goes underground again because there will be six more weeks of winter.

ground-less *adj.* Without foundation or basis.

ground rule *n.* A basic rule; the rule in sports that modifies play on a particular field, course, or court.

ground sheet *n.* A waterproof cover to protect an area of ground, such as a baseball or football field.

ground ze-ro *n.* The point on the ground vertically beneath or above the point of detonation of an atomic bomb.

group *n.* A collection or assemblage of people, objects, or things having something in common.

grou-per *n.* A large fish related to the sea bass.

group-ie *n., Slang* A female follower of a rock group, especially when it is on tour.

group ther-a-py *n.* Psychotherapy which in-volves sessions guided by a therapist and attended by several patients who discuss their problems.

grouse *n., pl.* **grouse** Any of a family of game birds characterized by mottled, brownish plumage and rounded bodies. *v.* To complain; to grumble.

grout *n.* A material used to fill cracks in masonry or spaces between tiles. **grout** *v.*, **grouter** *n.*

grove *n.* A small group of trees, lacking undergrowth.

grov-el *v.* To lie or crawl face downward, as in fear; to act with abject humility. **groveler** *n.*, **grovelingly** *adv.*

grow *v.* To increase in size, develop, and reach maturity; to expand; to increase; to come into existence. **to grow on** To become increasingly acceptable, necessary, or pleasing to. **grower** *n.*, **growing** *v.*

growl *v.* To utter a deep, guttural, threatening sound, as that made by a hostile or agitated animal. **growling** *v.*

grown-up *n.* A mature adult.

growth *n.* The act or process of growing; a gradual increase in size or amount. *Pathol.* An abnormal formation of bodily tissue, as a tumor.

grub *v.* To dig up by the roots; to lead a dreary existence; to drudge. *n.* The thick, worm-like larva of certain insects, as of the June beetle. *Slang* Food; to scrounge. **grubbing** *v.*

grub-by *adj.* Sloppy, unkempt. **grubbily** *adv.*, **grubbiness** *n.*

grudge *n.* A feeling of ill will, rancor, or deep resentment. *v.* To be displeased, resentful, or envious of the possessions or good fortune of another person. **grudger** *n.*, **grudgingly** *adv.*

gru-el *n.* A thin liquid made by boiling

meal in water or milk.

gru-el-ing or **gru-el-ling** *adj.* Extremely tiring; exhausting. **gruelingly** *adv.*

grue-some *adj.* The state of causing horror or fright. **gruesomely** *adv.*, **gruesomeness** *n.*

gruff *adj.* Brusque and rough in manner; harsh in sound; hoarse. **gruffly** *adv.*, **gruffness** *n.*

grum-ble *v.* To complain in low, throaty sounds; to growl. **grumble**, **grumbler** *n.*, **grumbly** *adj.*

grump-y *adj.* Irritable and moody; ill tempered. **grumpily** *adv.*, **-iness** *n.*

grun-gy *adj.*, *Slang* Dirty, run-down, or inferior in condition or appearance.

grunt *n.* The deep, guttural sound of a hog. **grunt** *v.*

G-string *n.* A very narrow loincloth with a waistband, worn by strip-teasers.

G-suit *n.* A flight garment designed to counteract the effects of high acceleration on a person by exerting pressure on the body parts.

GU *abbr.* Guam.

gua-no *n.* The excrement of sea birds, used as a fertilizer.

guar *abbr.* Guaranteed.

guar-an-tee *n.* The promise or assurance of the durability or quality of a product; something held or given as a pledge or security. *v.* To assume responsibility for the default or debt of; to certify; to vouch for.

guar-an-tor *n.* One who gives a guarantee or guaranty.

guar-an-ty *n.*, *pl.* **-ies** A pledge or promise to be responsible for the debt, duty, or contract of another person in case of default; something that guarantees.

guard *v.* To watch over or shield from danger or harm; to keep watch as to prevent escape, violence, or indiscretion. *n.* A defensive position, as in boxing or fencing; in football, one of two linemen on either side of the center; in basketball, one of the two players stationed near the middle of the court; a device or piece of equipment that protects against damage, loss, or harm. **guarding, guarded** *v.*

guard-i-an *n.* One who is legally assigned responsibility for the care of the person and property of an infant, minor or person unable to be do for himself because of physical or mental disability. **guardianship** *n.*

guard-rail *n.* The protective rail, as on a highway or any area that proposes a threat or danger.

guards-man *n.* A member of the U.S. National Guard.

gua-va *n.* A tree or shrub of the myrtle family bearing small, pear-shaped, edible, yellow-skinned fruit.

gub-ba *v.*, *Slang* To tickle the neck area, especially of children and babies.

gu-ber-na-to-ri-al *adj.* Of or pertaining to a governor.

guern-sey *n.*, *pl.* **-seys** A breed of brown and white dairy cattle.

guer-ril-la *n.* A member of an irregular military force that is capable of great speed and mobility, often operating behind enemy lines.

guess *v.* To make a judgment or form an opinion on uncertain or incomplete knowledge; to suppose; to believe.

guest *n.* A person who is the recipient of hospitality from another; a customer who pays for lodging.

guff *n.*, *Slang* Nonsense or empty talk.

guf-faw *n.* A loud burst of laughter.

guid-ance *n.* The act, process, or result of guiding.

guide *n.* One who leads or directs another, as in a course of action; a person employed to conduct others on trips through museums and sightseeing tours. **-able** *adj.*, **guider** *n.*

guide-book *n.* A handbook containing directions and other information for tourists and visitors.

guid-ed mis-sile *n.*, *Mil.* An unmanned missile that can be controlled by radio signals while in flight.

guide-line *n.* Any suggestion, statement, or outline of policy or procedure.

guild *n.* An association of persons of the same trade or occupation.

guil-lo-tine *n.* An instrument of capital punishment in France, used for beheading condemned prisoners.

guilt *n.* The condition or fact of having committed a crime or wrongdoing; the feeling of responsibility for having done something wrong.

guilt-y *adj.* Deserving of blame for an offense that has been committed; convicted of some offense; pertaining to, involving or showing guilt. **guiltily** *adv.*, **guiltiness** *n.*

guin-ea *n.* Formerly, a British gold coin worth one pound and five pence.

guin-ea fowl *n.* A widely domesticated bird of African origin with dark gray plumage speckled with white.

guin-ea hen *n.* The female guinea fowl.

guin-ea pig *n.* A small, domesticated rodent usually with a short white tail, widely used for biological experimentation.

gui-tar *n.* A musical instrument with six strings, played by plucking or strumming.

gulf *n.* A large area of ocean or sea partially enclosed by land; a wide, impassable separation, as in social position or education.

gull *n.* A long-winged, web-footed sea bird, usually white and gray with a hooked upper mandible.

gull *n.* A gullible person; one who is easily tricked.

gul-let *n.*, *Pathol.* The passage from the mouth to the stomach; esophagus; the throat; the pharynx.

gul-li-ble *adj.* Easily cheated or fooled. **gullibility** *n.*, **gullibly** *adv.*

gul-ly *n.*, *pl.* **-ies** A ditch or channel cut in the earth by running water.

gulp *v.* To swallow rapidly or in large amounts; to gasp or choke, as in nervousness; in computer science, small group of bytes that may be either data or instructions. **gulping, gluped** v.

gum n. A sticky, viscous substance exuded from various trees and plants, soluble in water and hardening on exposure to air; chewing gum; the firm connective fleshly tissue that surrounds the base of the teeth. v., Slang To bungle. **gummy** adj.

gum-bo n. A thick soup or stew containing okra.

gum-boil n. A type of small boil or abscess on the gum.

gump-tion n., Slang Boldness; initiative; enterprise.

gum-shoe n., Slang A detective.

gun n. A weapon made of metal from which a projectile is thrown by the force of an explosion; a portable firearm. v. To shoot; to open up the throttle of an engine in order to accelerate. **gun for** To try to ruin, catch, or acquire.

gung ho adj., Slang Extremely enthusiastic.

gun-man n., pl. -men One who is armed with a gun, especially an armed criminal.

gun-ner-y n. The science and art of constructing and operating guns; the use of guns in general.

gun-ny n., pl. -ies A type of coarse, heavy fabric made of jute or hemp and used for making sacks.

gun-pow-der n. An explosive powder used in blasting, fireworks, and guns.

gun-shot n. A shot fired from a gun.

gun--shy adj. Afraid of loud noises, as gunfire; wary.

gun-smith n. A person who makes or repairs guns.

gun-wale or **gun-nel** n. The upper edge of a ship's side.

gup-py n., pl. -ies

A small, tropical freshwater fish, popular in home aquariums.

gur-gle v. To flow in a broken, uneven current, making low, bubbling sounds. **gurgle** n., **gurglingly** adv.

gu-ru n. A spiritual teacher of Hinduism.

gush v. To flow forth in volume and with sudden force; to be overly sentimental or enthusiastic. **gush** n., **gushy** adj.

gush-er n. An oil well with a plentiful natural flow of oil; a person who gushes.

gust n. A sudden, violent rush of wind or air; a sudden outburst, as of emotion. v. To blow in gusts. **gustily** adv., **gustiness** n., **gusty** adj.

gus-ta-to-ry adj. Of or pertaining to the sense of taste or the act of tasting.

gus-to n. Hearty enjoyment or enthusiasm.

gut n. The alimentary canal or part of it. v. To disembowel. **guts** Bowels; entrails; the prepared intestines of cer-

tain animals, used as strings for musical instruments and surgical sutures; fortitude; courage.

gut-less adj., Slang Lacking courage.

guts-y n., Slang Courageous.

gut-ter n. A channel or ditch at the side of a street for carrying off surface water; a trough attached below or along the eaves of a house for carrying off rain water from the roof.

gut-ter-snipe n. A person of the lowest class; a street urchin.

gut-tur-al adj. Pertaining to the throat; having a harsh, muffled, or grating quality. **guttural** n., **gutturally** adv.

guy n., Slang A man; a fellow.

guz-zle v. To drink greedily or to excess.

guzzler n., **guzzling, guzzled** v.

gym n., Informal A gymnasium.

gym-na-si-um n., pl. -ums or -sia A room or building equipped for indoor sports.

gym-nas-tics pl., n. A sport or physical exercises, especially those performed with special apparatus in a gym. **gymnast** n., **gymnastic** adj.

gym-no-sperm n. One of a class of plants whose seeds are not enclosed within an ovary.

gy-ne-col-o-gy n. The branch of medicine dealing with the female reproductive organs, female diseases, and female organs. **gynecological** adj.

gyp v., Informal To swindle, cheat, or defraud. n. A fraud. **gypper** n.

gyp-sum n. A mineral, hydrous calcium sulfate, used to make plaster of Paris, gypsum plaster, and plasterboard.

Gyp-sy n., pl. -ies A person who looks like or leads the life of a Gypsy. v. To wander or live like a Gypsy or the Gypsies.

Gyp-sy n., pl. -ies A member of a wandering, dark-haired, dark-skinned, Caucasian people originally from India and now living mainly in Europe and the U.S.

gyp-sy moth n. A moth whose larvae are destructive to foliage.

gy-rate v. To rotate or revolve around a fixed point or axis; to move or turn in a spiral motion. adj. Coiled or winding about. **gyrator** n., **gyratory** adj.

gyr-fal-con n. A falcon with color phases ranging from black to white.

gy-ro n. A gyroscope or gyrocompass.

gy-ro-com-pass n. A type of compass which has a motor-driven gyroscope so mounted that its axis of rotation maintains a constant position with reference to the true or the geographic north.

gy-ro pi-lot n., Aeron. An automatic pilot.

gy-ro-scope n. A spinning wheel or disk whose spin axis maintains its angular orientation when not subjected to external torques. **gyroscopic** adj.

gy-ro-sta-bi-liz-er n. A gyroscopic instrument designed to reduce the rolling motion of ships.

H, h The eighth letter of the English alphabet.

ha-be-as cor-pus *n.* In law, a writ commanding a person to appear before a judge or court for the purpose of releasing that person from unlawful detention or restraint.

hab-er-dash-er *n.* A person who deals in men's clothing and men's furnishings.

hab-er-dash-er-y *n., pl.* **-ies** The goods sold by a haberdasher.

ha-bil-i-ment *n., pl.* **-ments** Clothing characteristic of an office, rank, or occasion.

hab-it *n.* Involuntary pattern of behavior acquired by frequent repetition; manner of conducting oneself; an addiction.

hab-it-a-ble *adj.* Suitable for habitation. **habitability,** **-ness** *n.,* **habitably** *adv.*

hab-i-tat *n.* The region in which an animal or plant lives or grows; the place of residence of a person or group.

hab-i-ta-tion *n.* A place of residence.

hab-it--form-ing *adj.* Producing physiological addiction.

ha-bit-u-al *adj.* Practicing by or acting according to habit; resorted to on a regular basis; regular. **habitually** *adv.,* **habitualness** *n.*

ha-ci-en-da *n.* A large estate or ranch in Spanish-speaking countries; the main building of a hacienda.

hack *v.* To cut with repeated irregular blows; to manage successfully. *n.* A tool used for hacking; a rough, dry cough; a taxi driver.

hack-le *n.* One of the long, slender, often narrow glossy feathers on the neck of a rooster; the hair on the back of the neck, especially of a dog, that rise in anger or fear.

hack-ney *n.* A horse of medium size for ordinary driving or riding; a carriage or coach available for hire. *v.* To make common or frequent use of.

hack-neyed *adj.* Trite; commonplace.

hack-saw *n.* A saw in a narrow frame for cutting metal.

had-dock *n.* A food fish that is usually smaller than the related cod and is found on both sides of the Atlantic.

Ha-des *n.* The underground abode of the dead in Greek mythology; hell.

had-n't *contraction* Had not.

haft *n.* A handle of a weapon or tool.

hag *n.* A malicious, ugly old woman; a witch. **haggish** *adj.*

Hag-ga-dah *n.* Ancient Jewish lore forming especially the nonlegal part of the Talmud; the Jewish ritual for the Seder.

hag-gard A worn-out, exhausted, and gaunt look, as from hunger or fatigue. **haggardly** *adv.,* **haggardness** *n.*

hag-gle *v.* To argue or bargain on price or terms. **-er** *n.,* **haggling, haggled** *v.*

hag-i-og-ra-phy *n., pl.* **-phies** Biography of the lives of saints or revered persons. **hagiographer** *n.,* **hagiographic, hagiographical** *adj.*

hai-ku *n.* An unrhymed Japanese verse form with three short lines.

hail *n.* Precipitation of small, hard lumps of ice and snow; a hailstone; an exclamation, greeting, acclamation; *v.* To pour down as hail; to call loudly in greeting or welcome; to shout with enthusiasm; to signal in order to draw the attention of.

hail-stone *n.* A type of hard pellet made of frozen snow & ice.

hair *n.* One of the pigmented filaments that grow from the skin of most mammals; a covering of such structures, as on the human head and on the skin; a slender margin. **hairy** *adj.*

hair-breadth *adj.* Extremely close or narrow. *n.* An extremely small space or margin.

hair-brush *n.* A instrument used for grooming the hair.

hair-cloth *n.* A wiry, stiff fabric of horsehair.

hair--raising *adj.* Causing fear or horror. **hairraiser** *n.*

bair-split-ing *n.* The process of making petty distinctions. **hairsplitter** *n.*

hair-spring *n.* A fine, coiled spring that regulates and controls the movement of the balance wheel in a clock or watch.

hair trig-ger *n.* A gun trigger set to react to the slightest pressure. **hair trigger** *adj.* Reacting immediately to the slightest provocation.

hake *n.* A marine food fish related to the cod.

hal-berd *n.* A medieval weapon used in the 15th and 16th centuries, having both an ax-like blade and a steel spike on the end of a long pole.

hal-cy-on *adj.* Calm and tranquil; peaceful;

hale *adj.* Healthy and robust; free from defect. *v.* To compel to go. **haleness** *n.*

half *n., pl.* **halves** One of two equal parts into which a thing is divisible; art of a thing approximately equal to the remainder; one of a pair. *adj.* Being one of two equal parts; being partial or incomplete. **half** *adv.*

half-back *n.* In football, either of two players who, along with the fullback and quarterback, make up the backfield; a player positioned behind the front line in any of various sports.

half--caste *n.* A person having one European and one Asian parent. **half--caste** *adj.*

half step *n., Mus.* A semitone.

half--track *n.* A vehicle propelled by continuous rear treads and front wheels.

half--wit *n.* A mentally disturbed person; a feeble-minded person. **--witted** *adj.*

hal-i-but *n.* Any of the edible flat fishes of the North Atlantic or Pacific waters.

hal-ite *n.* Large crystal or masses of salt.

hal-i-to-sis *n.* A condition or state of having bad breath.

hal-le-lu-jah *interj.* Used to express joy,

praise, or jubilation. **hallelujah** *n.*

hall-mark *n.* An official mark placed on gold and silver products to attest to their purity; an indication of quality or superiority; a distinctive characteristic.

hal-low *v.* To sanctify; to make holy; to honor.

Hal-low-een *n.* October 31, the eve of All Saints' Day, celebrated particularly by children.

hal-lu-ci-na-tion *n.* An illusion of seeing something that is nonexistent; something one thinks is seen during a hallucination; a delusion. **hallucinate** *v.*, **hallcuinational, hallucinative,** *adj.* **hallucinatory** *adj.*

hal-lu-ci-no-gen *n.* A drug or other agent which causes hallucination. **hallucinogenic** *adj.*

ha-lo *n.* A ring of colored light surrounding the head; an aura of glory. **halo** *v.*

hal-o-gen *n.* Any of the group of nonmentallic elements including flourine, chlorine, bromine, iodine, and astatine. **halogenous** *adj.*

hal-ter *n.* A rope or strap for leading or tying an animal; a noose for hanging a person; a woman's upper garment tied behind the neck and across the back.

halve *v.* To divide into two equal parts; to lessen by half. *Informal* Share equally.

hal-yard *n.* A rope for hoisting or lowering a sail, flag, or yard.

ham *n.* The meat of a hog's thigh; the back of the knee or thigh. **ham** *v.*

Ham-il-ton, Alexander *n.* (1755-1804) American Revolutionary statesman.

ham-let *n.* A small rural village or town.

ham-mer *n.*

A hand tool with a heavy head used to drive or strike forcefully, especially nails; the part of a gun which strikes the primer or firing pin; any of the padded wooden levers which strike the strings of a piano. *v.* To strike or pound forcibly and repeatedly. **hammerer** *n.*

ham-mer-head *n.* A large, predatory shark of warm seas, whose eyes are set in long, fleshy projections at the sides of the head.

ham-mer-lock *n.* A hold in wrestling in which the opponent's arm is twisted upward behind his back.

ham-mer-toe *n.* A toe that is bent downward and malformed.

ham-mock *n.* A hanging bed or couch of fabric or heavy netting, suspended from supports at each end.

ham-per *v.* To interfere with movement or progress of. *n.* A large, usually covered, receptacle used to store dirty laundry.

ham-ster *n.* Any of various rodents with large cheek pouches and a short tail.

ham-string *n.* Either of two tendons located at the back of the human knee; the large tendon at the back of the hock of four-footed animals. *v.* To cripple by cutting the hamstring; to frustrate.

hand *n.* The part of the arm below the wrist, consisting of the palm, four fingers and a thumb; a unit of measure, four inches, used especially to state the height of a horse; a pointer on a dial, as of a clock, meter, or gauge; the cards dealt to or held by a player in one round of a game; a manual laborer, worker, or employee. *v.* To give, offer, or transmit with the hand; direct with the hands.

hand-ball *n.* A court game in which the players bat a small rubber ball against the wall with their hands.

hand-bar-row *n.* A flat rectangular frame with handles at both ends for carrying loads.

hand-bill *n.* A hand-distributed ad-vertisement.

hand-book *n.* A small guide or reference book giving information or instructions.

hand-car *n.* A small open four-wheeled railroad car propelled by a small motor or by hand.

hand-cuff *v.* To put handcuffs on; to make ineffective. **handcuffs** *pl., n.* A pair of circular metal shackles chained together that can be fastened around the wrists.

hand-gun *n.* A gun that can be held and fired with one hand.

hand-i-cap *n.* A race or contest in which advantages or penalties are given to individual contestants to equalize the odds; any disadvantage that makes achievement unusually difficult; physical disability; an obstacle. *v.* To give a handicap to.

hand-i-craft *or* **hand-craft** *n.* Skill and expertise in working with the hands; an occupation requiring manual dexterity; skilled work produced by the hands.

hand-ker-chief *n.* A type of small piece of cloth used for wiping the face or nose; a kerchief or scarf.

han-dle *v.* To touch, pick up, or hold with the hands; to represent; to trade or deal in. **handler** *n.*

hand-made *adj.* Made by hand or by a hand process.

hand-maid *or* **hand-maid-en** *n.* A female maid or personal servant.

hand--me--down *n.* Something, such as an article of clothing, used by a person after being outgrown or is carded by another. **hand-me-down** *adj.*

hand-out *n.* Free food, clothing, or cash given to the needy; a folder distributed free of charge; a flyer; a press release for publicity.

hand-pick *v.* To select with care.

hand-set *n.* A telephone receiver and transmitter combined in a single unit.

hand-shake *n.* The act of clasping hands by two people, as in greeting, agreement, or parting.

hand-some *adj.* Very good-looking or attractive; very generous, as with money. -ly *adv.*, **handsomeness** *n.*

hand-spring *n.* An acrobatic feat in which the body flips entirely backward or forward, while the feet pass quickly in an arc over the head.

hand-stand *n.* The feat of supporting the body on the hands with the feet balanced in the air.

hand--to--mouth *adj.* Providing or having barely enough to exist.

hand-work *n.* Work which is done by hand.

hand-writ-ing *n.* Writing performed with the hand, especially cursive; the type of writing of a person. **handwriting on the wall.** An omen of one's unpleasant fate.

hand-y *adj.* Easy to use or reach; helpful or useful. **handily** *adv.*, **handiness** *n.*

handy-man *n.* A person who does odd jobs.

hang *v.* To be attached to from above and unsupported from below; to fasten or be suspended so as to swing freely; to be put to death by hanging by the neck; to fasten or attach something as a picture to a wall. **hangout** *Slang* To spend one's time in a particular place.

han-gar *n.* A building for housing aircraft.

han-ger *n.* A device from which something may be hung or on which something hangs.

hang gli-der *n.* A device shaped like a kite from which a person hangs suspended in a harness while gliding through the air.

hang gliding *n.*, **hang glide** *v.*

hang-man *n., pl.* -men One hired to execute people by hanging.

hang-nail *n.* The small piece of skin that hangs loose from the side or root of a fingernail.

hang-over *n.* Something remaining from what has passed; the effects of excessive alcohol intake.

hang--up *n., Slang* A psychological or emotional problem; an obstacle.

hank *n.* A loop, coil, or piece of hair, thread, or yarn.

han-ker *v.* To have a yearning or craving for something. **hankerer, hankering** *n.*

Ha-nuk-kah *or* **Ha-nu-kah** *n.* An eight-day Jewish holiday remembering the re-dedication of the Temple in Jerusalem.

hao-le *n.* A person who is not of the Hawaiian race, especially a Caucasian.

hap-haz-ard *adj.* Occurring by accident; happening by chance or at random; hit-or-miss. -ly *adv.*, **haphazardness** *n.*

hap-less *adj.* Unfortunate; unlucky. **haplessly** *adv.*, **haplessness** *n.*

hap-pen *v.* To occur or come to pass; to take place; to discover by chance; to turn up or appear by chance.

hap-pen-ing *n.* A spontaneous event or performance; an important event.

happen-stance *n.* An event occurring by chance.

hap-py *adj.* Enjoying contentment and well-being; glad, joyous, satisfied or pleased. **happily** *adv.*, **happiness** *n.*

hap-py--go--luck-y *adj.* Carefree and unconcerned.

ha-ra--ki-ri *n.* A Japanese suicide ritual committed by ripping open the abdomen with a knife.

ha-rangue *n.* A long, extravagant speech; a lecture. -er *n.*

ha-rass *v.* To disturb or annoy constantly; to torment persistently. **harassment, harasser** *n.*

har-bin-ger *n.* A person that initiates or pioneers a major change; something that foreshadows what is to come.

har-bor *n.* A place of refuge or shelter; a bay or cove; an anchorage for ships. *v.* To provide shelter; to entertain, as a feeling or thought. -age, -er *n.*

hard *adj.* Difficult to perform, endure, or comprehend; solid in texture or substance; resistant to cutting or penetration; containing salts which make lathering with soap difficult; high in alcoholic content. **hardness** *n.*

hard-back *adj.* Text bound between hard covers as opposed to paper ones.

hard--bit-ten *adj.* Tough or seasoned by hard experiences.

hard--boiled *adj.* Boiled or cooked in the shell to a hard or solid state.

hard co-py *n.* In computer science, the printed information or data from a computer.

hard--core *or* **hard-core** *adj.* Extremely graphic in presentation; obstinately resistant to change.

hard disk *n.* In computer science, magnetic storage consisting of a rigid disk of aluminum coated with a magnetic recording substance; contained within a removable cartridge or mounted in the hard disk of a microcomputer.

hard-en *v.* To make or become hard or harder; to make or become physically or mentally tough; to make or become callous or unsympathetic.

hard hat *n.* A protective head covering made of rigid material, worn by construction workers.

hard-head-ed *adj.* Having a stubborn character; obstinate. **hardheadedly** *adv.*, **hardheadedness** *n.*

hard-heart-ed *adj.* Heartless; unfeeling. **hardheartedly** *adv.*, **hardheartedness** *n.*

har-di-hood *n.* Resolute courage; audacious boldness; vitality; vigor.

Hard-ing, Warren Gamaliel *n.* (1865-1923) The 29th President of the United States, from 1921-1923, died in office.

hard-ly *adj., Slang* Very little; almost certainly not. *adv.* Forcefully; painfully; barely.

hard--nosed *adj.* Stubborn; hard-headed; unyielding.

hard pal-ate *n.* The bony forward part of the palate that forms the roof of the mouth.

hard-pan *n.* A layer of very hard clay-like matter or subsoil which roots cannot penetrate.

hard rock *n.* Rock music featuring amplified sound and modulations, and feedback.

hard-ship *n.* A painful, difficult condition.

hard-tack *n.* A hard, cracker-like biscuit made with flour and water.

hard-wood *n.* The wood of an angiosermous tree as opposed to that of a coniferous tree; a tree that yields hardwood.

har-dy *adj.* Bold and robust; able to survive very unfavorable conditions, as extreme cold; daring -iness *n.*, -ily *adv.*

hare *n.*

Various mammals related to the rabbits but having longer ears and legs.

hare-brained *adj.* Foolish or silly.

hare-lip *n.* A congenital deformity in which the upper lip is split. -ed *adj.*

har-em *n.* The women living in a Muslim residence; the living quarters of a harem.

hark *v.* To listen closely. **hark back** To retrace one's steps; to go back to earlier times.

har-le-quin *n.* A jester; a clown. *adj.* Patterned with vividly colored diamond shapes.

har-lot *n.* A prostitute.

harm *n.* Emotional or physical damage or injury. *v.* To cause harm to. **harmful** *adj.*, -ly *adv.*, **harmfulness** *n.*

harm-less *adj.* Without harm; not harmful.

har-mon-ic *adj.* Relating to musical harmony; in harmony; concordant. **harmonically** *adv.*

har-mon-i-ca *n.* A small, rectangular musical instrument having a series of tuned metal reeds that vibrate with the player's breath.

har-mo-ni-ous *adj.* Pleasing to the ear; characterized by agreement and accord; having components agreeably combined. -ly *adv.*, **harmonious** *n.*

har-mo-ny *n.*, *pl.* -ies Complete agreement, as of feeling or opinion; an agreeable combination of component parts; pleasing sounds; a combination of musical tones into chords. **harmonize** *v.*, **harmonizer** *n.*

har-ness *n.* The working gear, other than a yoke, of a horse or other draft animal. **harnesser** *n.*

harp *n.* A musical instrument having a triangular upright frame with strings plucked with the fingers. *v.* To play a harp. **harp on** To write or talk about excessively. **harpist** *n.*

har-poon *n.* A barbed spear used in hunting whales and large fish.

harp-si-chord *n.* A piano-like instrument whose strings are plucked by using quills or leather points. -ist *n.*

har-py *n.*, *pl.* -pies A vicious woman; a predatory person.

har-ri-dan *n.* A mean, hateful old woman.

har-ri-er *n.* A slender, narrow-winged hawk that preys on small animals; a hunting dog; a cross-country runner.

Har-ri-son, Benjamin *n.* (1833-1901). The 23rd president of the United States from 1889-1893.

Har-ri-son, William Henry *n.* (1773-1841) The 9th president of the United States, from March 4th - April 4th 1841; died in office.

har-row *n.* A tool with sharp teeth for breaking up and smoothing soil.

har-ry *v.* To harass.

harsh *adj.* Disagreeable; extremely severe. **harshly** *adv.*, **harshness** *n.*

hart *n.* A fully grown male deer after it has passed its fifth year.

har-um--scar-um *adj.* Reckless; irresponsible.

har-vest *n.* The process or act of gathering a crop; the season or time for gathering crops. *v.* To reap; to obtain as if by gathering. **harvester** *n.*

hash *n.* A fried or baked mixture of chopped meat and potatoes. *v.* To chop up into small pieces. *Slang* To make a mess of; to discuss at great length.

hash-ish *n.* The leaves and flowering tops of the hemp plant, which are chewed, drunk, or smoked for their intoxicating and narcotic effect.

hasp *n.* A clasp or hinged fastener that passes over a staple and is secured by a pin, bolt, or padlock.

has-sle *n.*, *Slang* A type of quarrel or argument. **hassle** *v.*

has-sock *n.* A firm upholstered cushion used as a footstool.

haste *n.* Speed; swiftness of motion or action; excessive eagerness to act. **make haste** To hurry.

has-ten *v.* To act or move with haste or speed.

hast-y *adj.* Rapid; swift; made or done with excessive speed. -iness *n.*

hat *n.* A covering for the head with a crown and brim.

hat-box *n.* A container or box used for storing or carrying hats.

hatch *n.* A small opening or door, as in a ship's deck. *v.* To bring forth, as young from an egg; to devise; to contrive secretly. **hatchery** *n.*

hatch-et *n.* A small ax with a short handle.

hatch-way *n.* An opening covered by a hatch in a ship's deck.

hate *v.* To feel hostility or animosity

toward; to dislike intensely.

hatefully *adv.*, **hatefulness, hater** *n.*

hat-ter *n.* A person who makes, sells, or repairs hats.

haugh-ty *adj.* Arrogantly proud; disdainful. **-ily** *adv.*, **haughtiness** *n.*

haul *v.* To pull or draw with force; to move or transport, as in a truck or cart. *n.* The distance over which someone travels or something is transported; an amount collected at one time.

haul-age *n.* The process or act of hauling; a charge for hauling.

haunch *n.* The hip; the buttock and upper thigh of a human or animal; the loin and leg of a four-footed animal.

haunt *v.* To appear to or visit as a ghost or spirit; to visit frequently; to linger in the mind. **haunting** *adj.*

haut-bois *or* **haut-boy** *n.* An oboe.

hau-teur *n.* A disdainful arrogance.

have *v.* To hold or own, as a possession or as property. **have to** Need to; must. **have had it** Suffered or endured all that one can tolerate.

hav-er-sack *n.* A bag for carrying supplies on a hike or march.

hav-oc *n.* Mass confusion; widespread destruction; devastation.

haw *n.* A hesitating sound made by a speaker who is groping for words. *v.* To hesitate in speaking; to falter in speaking.

hawk *n.*

Any of several predatory birds, with a short, hooked bill and strong claws for seizing small prey; one who advocates a war-like foreign policy; one having an aggressive attitude.

hawkish *adj.*, **-ly** *adv.*, **hawkishness** *n.*

haw-ser *n.* A heavy cable or rope for towing or securing a ship.

haw-thorn *n.* A thorny shrub or tree bearing white or pink flowers and red fruit.

hay *n.* Alfalfa or grass that has been cut and dried for animal food.

Hayes, Rutherford Birchard *n.* (1822-1893) The 19th president of the United States from 1877-1881.

hay fe-ver *n.* An acute allergy to certain airborne pollens, marked by severe irritation of the upper respiratory tract and the eyes.

hay-fork *n.* A hand tool used to move hay.

hay-loft *n.* A upper loft in a barn or stable used to store hay.

hay-mow *n.* A large mound of hay stored in a loft.

hay-stack *n.* A pile of hay stored outdoors.

hay-wire *adj.*, *Slang* Broken; emotionally out of control; crazy.

haz-ard *n.* A risk; chance; an accident; a anger or source of danger. *v.* To take a chance on; to venture. **hazardous** *adj.*

haze *n.* A fog-like suspension of dust, smoke, and vapor in the air; a confused or vague state of mind. *v.* To harass with disagreeable tasks.

ha-zel *n.* A small tree or shrub bearing edible brown nuts with smooth shells; a light brown or yellowish brown.

ha-zel-nut *n.* The edible nut of the hazel.

haz-y *adj.* Lacking clarity; vague. **hazily** *adv.*, **haziness** *n.*

hdqrs. *abbr.* Headquarters.

H--Bomb *n.* Hydrogen bomb.

head *n.* The upper part of a human or animal body, containing the brain, the principal nerve centers, the eyes, ears, nose and mouth. **headed** *adj.*

head-ache *n.* A pain or ache in the head. *Slang* A bothersome problem. **-y** *adj.*

head-band *n.* A band of cloth worn around the head.

head-first *adv.* With the head in a forward position; headlong.

head-hunt-ing *n.* A tribal custom of decapitating slain enemies and preserving the heads as trophies. **headhunter** *n.*

head-ing *n.* A title or caption that acts as a front, beginning, or upper part of anything; the direction or course of a ship or aircraft.

head-land *n.* A high ridge or cliff projecting into the water.

head-line *n.* A title, caption, or summarizing words of a newspaper story or article printed in large type. *v.* To provide with a headline; to serve as the star performer. **headliner** *n.*

head-lock *n.* A wrestling hold in which the head of a wrestler is locked under the arm of his opponent.

head-long *adv.* Headfirst; not having deliberation. **headlong** *adj.*

head-mas-ter *n.* A school principal of a private school.

head-mis-tress *n.* A female school principal of a private school.

head-piece *n.* A helmet, cap or other covering for the head; a headset.

head-quar-ters *pl.*, *n.* The official location from which a leader directs a military unit.

head-set *n.* A pair of headphones.

head-stall *n.* The part of a bridle that goes over a horse's head.

head-stand *n.* The act of balancing the body's weight on the top of the head, with the aid of the arms.

head start *n.* An early or advance start; an advantage.

head-stone *n.* A memorial stone marker at the head of a grave, indicating a name, date of birth and date of death.

head-wat-er *n.* The source of a river or stream.

head-way *n.* Motion in a forward direction; progress toward a goal; clearance beneath an arch or ceiling.

head wind *n.* A wind blowing in the direction opposite the course of a ship or aircraft.

head-y *adj.* Tending to intoxicate;

affecting the senses; headstrong.
head-i-ly *adv.*, **head-i-ness** *n.*

heal *v.* To restore to good health; to mend. **healable** *adj.*, **healer** *n.*

health *n.* The overall sound condition or function of a living organism at a particular time; freedom from disease or defect. **healthful** *adj.*, **healthfully** *adv.*, **healthfulness** *n.*

health-y *adj.* In a state of or having good health; characteristic of a sound condition. **-ily** *adv.*, **healthiness** *n.*

heap *n.* A haphazard assortment of things; a large number or quantity. *v.* To throw or pile into a heap.

hear *v.* To perceive by the ear; to listen with careful attention; to be informed of; to listen to officially or formally, as in a court of law. **hearer** *n.*

hear-ing *n.* One of the five senses; the range by which sound can be heard; an opportunity to be heard; in law, a preliminary examination of an accused person.

hear-ing aid *n.* An electronic device used to amplify the hearing of partially deaf persons.

heark-en *v.* To listen carefully.

hear-say *n.* Information heard from another; common talk; rumor.

hearse *n.* A vehicle for conveying a dead body to the place of burial.

heart *n.*

The hollow, primary muscular organ of vertebrates which circulates blood throughout the body; the emotional center, such as in love, hate, consideration, or compassion; the most essential part of something;

heart-ache *n.* Emotional grief; sorrow;

heart at-tack *n.* An acute malfunction or interrupted heart function.

heart-beat *n.* A pulsation of the heart, consisting of one contraction and one relaxation.

heart-break *n.* Great sorrow; deep grief. **heartbreaking** *adj.*, **-breakingly** *adv.*

heart-burn *n.* A sensation of burning in the stomach and esophagus, usually caused by excess acid in the stomach.

heart-en *v.* To give courage to.

heart-felt *adj.* Deeply felt; sincere.

hearth *n.* The floor of a fireplace, furnace; the stone that forms the front of a fireplace.

heart-land *n.* A strategically important central region, one regarded as vital to a nation's economy or defense.

heart-less *adj.* Having no sympathy; lacking compassion. **heartlessness** *n.*, **heartlessly** *adv.*

heart-rend-ing *adj.* Causing great distress, suffering emotional anguish.

heart-sick *adj.* Profoundly dejected. **heartsickness** *n.*

heart-throb *n.* One pulsation of the heart; tender emotion; a loved one.

heart--to--heart *adj.* Sincere; frank.

heart--warm-ing *adj.* A feeling of warm sympathy.

heart-wood *n.* The older, no longer active central wood of a tree.

heart-y *adj.* Marked by exuberant warmth; full of vigor; nourishing; substantial. **-ily** *adv.*, **heartiness** *n.*

heat *n.* A quality of being hot or warm; a degree of warmth; depth of feeling; a period of sexual ardor in female animals. *Slang* Pressure or stress. **heater** *n.*

heat ex-haus-tion *n.* A reaction to intense heat, a mild form of heat stroke.

heath *n.* An open tract of uncultivated wasteland covered with low-growing shrubs and plants.

hea-then *n.* A person or nation that does not recognize the God of Christianity, Judaism, or Islam; in the Old Testament, a Gentile; non-Jew. **heathenish** *adj.*, **-dom**, **heathenism** *n.*

heath-er *n.* A shrub that grows in dense masses and has small evergreen leaves and small pinkish flowers. **heather**, **heathery** *adj.*

heat stroke *n.* A state of collapse or exhaustion, accompanied by fever and marked by clammy skin, caused by excessive heat.

heave *v.* To raise or lift, especially forcibly; to hurl or throw. *Naut.* To push, pull, or haul, as by a rope. *Slang* To vomit. *n.* The act of throwing.

heaves *n.* A disease of horses affecting the lungs and marked by coughing and difficult breathing.

heav-en *n.* The sky; the region above and around the earth; the abode of God, the angels, and the blessed souls of the dead; a state or place of blissful happiness. **heavenliness** *n.*, **heavenly** *adj.*, **heavenward** *adv.* & *adj.*

heav-y *adj.* Of great weight; very thick or dense; forceful; powerful; rough and violent, as stormy weather; of great significance; grave; painful, as bad news; oppressive. **heavily** *adv.*, **heaviness** *n.*

heavy--du-ty *adj.* Designed for hard use.

heavy--hand-ed *adj.* Clumsy; not tactful; oppressive. **heavy-handedly** *adv.*, **heavy-handedness** *n.*

heavy--heart-ed *adj.* Melancholy; depressed; sad. **heavyheartedly** *adv.*, **heavyheartedness** *n.*

heavy--set *adj.* Having a stocky build.

heavy--weight *n.* A person of above average weight; a competitor in the heaviest class; a boxer weighing more that 175 pounds.

He-bra-ic *or* **He-bra-i-cal** *adj.* Of or relating to the Hebrews or their language or culture. **Hebraist** *n.*

He-brew *n.* A member of a Semitic people claiming descent from Abraham, Isaac, and Jacob; the modern form of the language of the Hebrews. **Hebrew** *adj.*

heck-le *v.* To badger or annoy, as with

questions, comments, or gibes. -er *n.*

hec-tic *adj.* Intensely active, rushed, or excited; marked by a persistent and fluctuating fever caused by a disease, such as tuberculosis; feverish; flushed.

he'd *conj.* He had; he would.

hedge *n.* A boundary or fence formed of shrubs or low-growing trees; a means to guard against financial loss; a deliberately ambiguous statement.

hedge *v.,* **hedger** *n.*

hedge-hog *n.* A small nocturnal mammal with dense, erectile spines on the back, which are presented when the animal rolls itself into a ball in self-defense; a porcupine.

hedge-hop *v.* To fly an aircraft close to the ground, as in spraying crops. **hedgehopper** *n.*

hedge-row *n.* A dense row of bushes, shrubs, or trees forming a hedge.

he-don-ism *n.* The doctrine devoted to the pursuit of pleasure; the philosophy that pleasure is the principal good in life. **hedonist** *n.,* **hedonistic** *adj.*

heed *v.* To pay attention; to take notice of something. *n.* Attention. -ful *adj.,* **heedfully** *adv.,* **heedfulness** *n.*

heel *n.* The rounded back part of the human foot under and behind the ankle; the part of a shoe supporting or covering the heel; a lower or bottom part; the crusty ends of a loaf of bread.

heft *n., Slang* Weight; bulk. *v.* To gauge or estimate the weight of by lifting; to lift up.

heft-y *adj.* Bulky; heavy; sizable.

he-gem-o-ny *n.* Dominance or leadership, as of one country over another.

he-gi-ra *n.* A journey or departure to flee an undesirable situation.

heif-er *n.* A young cow, particularly one that has not produced a calf.

height *n.* The quality of being high; the highest or most advanced point; the distance from the base of something; the apex; the distance above a specified level; altitude; the distance from head to foot.

height-en *v.* To increase or become high in quantity or degree; to raise or lift.

Heim-lich ma-neu-ver *n.* An emergency maneuver used to dislodge food from a choking person's throat; the closed fist is placed below the rib cage and pressed inward to force air from the lungs upward.

hei-nous *adj.* Extremely wicked; hateful or shockingly wicked. **heinously** *adv.,* **heinousness** *n.*

heir *n.* A person who inherits another's property or title.

heir-ess *n.* A female heir, especially to a large fortune.

heir-loom *n.* A family possession handed down from generation to generation; an article of personal property acquired by legal inheritance.

heist *v., Slang* To take from; to steal. *n.* A robbery.

hel-i-cal *adj.* Of or pertaining to the shape of a helix. **helically** *adv.*

hel-i-con *n.* A large, circular tuba that encircles the player's shoulder.

hel-i-cop-ter *n.*

An aircraft propelled by rotors which can take off vertically rather than needing an approach or a rolling start.

hel-i-port *n.* A designated area where helicopters land and take off.

he-li-um *n.* An extremely light, nonflammable, odorless, gaseous element, symbolized by He.

hell *or* **Hell** *n.* The abode of the dead souls condemned to eternal punishment; a place of evil, torment, or destruction; great distress; anguish; a cause of trouble or misery.

hellish *adj.,* **hellishly** *adv.*

he'll *contr.* He will.

hel-le-bore *n.* A North American plant bearing white or greenish flowers and yielding a toxic alkaloid used in medicine.

Hel-le-nism *n.* Ancient Greek civilization, character or culture; adoption of Greek thought, style, or cultural customs. **Hellenist** *n.,* **Hellenistic** *adj.*

hell hole *n.* A place of extreme wretchedness or horror.

helm *n.* A wheel or steering apparatus for a ship; a position or any place of control or command.

hel-met *n.* A protective covering for the head made of metal, leather, or plastic.

helms-man *n.* One who guides a ship.

hel-ot *n.* A serf; a slave. **helotry** *n.*

help *v.* To assist or aid. *n.* Assistance; relief; one that assists; one hired to help. **helper** *n.,* -ful *adj.,* -fully *adv.*

help-ing *n.* A single serving of food.

help-less *adj.* Without help; powerless; lacking strength.

Hel-sin-ki *n.* The capital of Finland.

hel-ter--skel-ter *adv.* In a confused or hurried manner; in an aimless way. *adj.* Rushed and confused. *n.* Great confusion; a tumult.

helve *n.* A handle on a tool such as an axe or hatchet.

hem *n.* A finished edge of fabric folded under and stitched. *interj.* A sound made as in clearing the throat, used especially to attract attention or to fill a pause in speech. *v.* To fold under and stitch down the edge of; to confine and surround.

he--man *n. Slang* A man marked by strength; a muscular man.

he-ma-tol-o-gy *n.* The branch of biological science that deals with blood and blood-generating organs. -ist *n.*

hem-i-sphere *n.* A half sphere that is divided by a plane passing through its center; either symmetrical half of an approximately spherical shape; the northern or southern half of the earth divided by the equator or the eastern or western half divided by a meridian. **hemispherical** *adj.*

hem-lock *n.* An evergreen tree of North America and eastern Asia, having flat needles and small cones; the wood of a hemlock; any of several poisonous herbaceous plants, having compound leaves and small whitish flowers; a poison obtained from the hemlock plant.

he-mo-glo-bin *n.* The respiratory pigment in the red blood cells of vertebrates containing iron and carrying oxygen to body tissues.

he-mo-phil-i-a *n., Pathol.* An inherited blood disease characterized by severe, protracted, sometimes spontaneous bleeding. **hemophiliac** *n.*

hem-or-rhage *n.* Bleeding, especially excessive bleeding. **hemorrhage** *v.*

hem-or-rhoid *n., Pathol.* A painful mass of dilated veins in swollen anal tissue.

hem-or-rhoids *pl., n.* A condition in which hemorrhoids occur.

he-mo-stat *n.* An agent that stops bleeding; a clamp-like instrument for preventing or reducing bleeding.

hemp *n.* An Asian herb; the female plant from which hashish and marijuana are produced; the tough fiber of the male plant from which coarse fabrics and rope are made. **hempen** *adj.*

hem-stitch *n.* An ornamental stitch, made by pulling out several threads and tying the remaining threads together in groups. **hemstitch** *v.*

hen *n.* A mature female bird, especially an adult female domestic fowl.

hence-forth / hence-for-ward *adv.* From this time on.

hench-man *n.* A loyal and faithful follower; one who supports a political figure chiefly for personal gain.

hen-na *n.* An Asian and North African ornamental tree bearing fragrant white or reddish flowers; a brownish-red dye derived from henna leaves and used as a cosmetic dye; a strong reddish brown.

hen-peck *v.* To domineer over one's husband by persistent nagging.

Hen-ry, Patrick *n.* (1736-1799). An American Revolutionary leader.

hep-a-rin *n., Biochem* A substance found especially in liver tissue having the power to slow or prevent blood clotting.

he-pat-ic *adj.* Of or like the liver.

he-pat-i-ca *n.* A small perennial herb having three-lobed leaves and white or lavender flowers.

hep-a-ti-tis *n., Pathol.* Inflammation of the liver causing jaundice.

her-ald *n.* A person who announces important news; one that comes before as a sign of what is to follow.

he-ral-dic *adj.* An official whose duty is to grant royal proclamations. *v.* To announce.

her-ald-ry *n., pl.* -ries The art or science of tracing genealogies and devising

and granting coats of arms.

herb *n.* A soft-stemmed plant without woody tissue that usually withers and dies each year; an often pleasant-smelling plant. **herbal** *adj. & n.*

her-ba-ceous *adj.* Like, or consisting of herbs; green and leaf-like.

herb-age *n.* Grass or vegetation used especially for grazing; the succulent edible parts of plants.

herb-al-ist *n.* One who gathers, grows, and deals in herbs.

her-bar-i-um *n., pl.* -iums *or* -ia A collection of dried plant specimens that are scientifically arranged for study; a place housing a herbarium.

her-bi-cide *n.* A chemical agent used to kill weeds. **herbicidal** *adj.*

her-bi-vore *n.* A type of herbivorous animal.

her-biv-o-rous *adj.* Feeding chiefly on plant life or vegetables. **-ly** *adv.*

her-cu-le-an *adj.* Of unusual size, force, or difficulty; having great strength.

herd *n.* A number of cattle or other animals of the same kind, kept or staying together as a group; a large crowd of people. *v.* To bring together in a herd. **herder, herdsman** *n.*

here-af-ter *adv.* From now on; at some future time. *n.* Existence after death.

here-by *adv.* By means or by virtue of this.

he-red-i-tar-y *adj.* Passing or transmitted from an ancestor to a legal heir; having an inherited title or possession; transmitted or transmissible by genetic inheritance. **hereditarily** *adv.*

he-red-i-ty *n.* The genetic transmission of physical traits from parents to offspring.

here-in *adv.* In or into this place.

here-of *adv.* Relating to or in regard to this.

her-e-sy *n., pl.* -sies A belief in conflict with orthodox religious beliefs; any belief contrary to set doctrine.

her-e-tic *n.* A person holding opinions different from orthodox beliefs, especially religious beliefs. **heretical** *adj.*

here-to *adv.* To this matter, proposition, or thing.

here-to-fore *adv.* Up to the present time; previously.

here-un-to *adv.* Hereto; to this.

here-up-on *adv.* Immediately following or resulting from this.

here-with *adv.* Together or along with this; hereby.

her-i-ta-ble *adj.* Something capable of being inherited.

her-i-tage *n.* Property that is inherited; something handed down from past generations; a legacy.

her-maph-ro-dite *n.* A person having both male and female reproductive organs. **hermaphroditic** *adj.*

her-met-ic *or* **her-met-i-cal** *adj.* Tightly sealed against air and liquids; made impervious to outside influences. **hermetically** *adv.*

her-mit *n.* A person who lives in seclusion, often for religious reasons.

her-mit-age *n.* The dwelling place or retreat of a hermit; a secluded hideaway.

her-ni-a *n.* The protrusion of a bodily organ, as the intestine, through an abnormally weakened wall that usually surrounds it; a rupture. **hernial** *adj.*

he-ro *n., pl.* **-roes** A figure in mythology and legend renowned for exceptional courage and fortitude. **heroic** *adj.,* **heroically** *adv.*

he-ro-ic coup-let *n.* A verse consisting of two rhyming lines of iambic pentameter.

her-o-in *n.* A highly addictive narcotic derivative of morphine.

her-o-ine *n.* A woman of heroic character; the principal female character in a story or play.

her-o-ism *n.* Heroic behavior.

her-on *n.* A bird having a long slender bill, long legs, and a long neck.

her-pes *n., Pathol.* A viral infection, characterized by small blisters on the skin or mucous membranes. **-etic** *adj.*

her-pe-tol-o-gy *n.* The scientific study and treatment of reptiles and amphibians. **-ic, herpetological** *adj.,* **herpetologically** *adv.,* **herpetologist** *n.*

her-ring *n.* A valuable food fish of the North Atlantic, the young of which are prepared as sardines, the adults are pickled, salted, or smoked.

hertz *n.* A unit of frequency equaling one cycle per second.

he's *contr.* He has; he is.

hes-i-tant *adj.* Given to hesitating; lacking decisiveness. **hesitancy** *n.*

hes-i-tate *v.* To pause or to be slow before acting, speaking, or deciding; to be uncertain. **hesitatingly** *adv.,* **hesitation** *n.,* **hesitating** *v.*

het-er-o-dox *adj.* Not in accord with established beliefs or religious doctrine; holding unorthodox opinions or beliefs. **heterodoxy** *n.*

het-er-o-sex-u-al *adj.* Of or having sexual desire to the opposite sex; involving different sexes. **-ity** *n.*

hew *v.* To make or shape with or as if with an axe; to adhere strictly; to conform.

hex *n.* One held to bring bad luck; a jinx. *v.* To put under an evil spell; to bewitch.

hex-a-gon *n.*

A polygon having six sides and six angles. **-al** *adj.,* **-ally** *adv.*

hex-am-e-ter *n.* A line of verse containing six metrical feet.

hey-day *n.* A time of great power, prosperity or popularity; a peak.

hi-a-tus *n.* A slight gap, break, or lapse in time from which something is missing; a break.

hi-ba-chi *n., pl.* **-chis** A deep, portable charcoal grill used for cooking food.

hi-ber-nate *v.* To pass the winter in an

inactive, dormant, sleep-like state. **hibernation, hibernator** *n.*

hi-bis-cus *n.* A chiefly tropical shrub or tree, bearing large colorful flowers.

hic-cup *or* **hic-cough** *n.* An involuntary contraction of the diaphragm that occurs on inhalation and spasmodically closes the glottis, producing a short, sharp sound. **hiccup** *v.*

hick *n., Slang* A clumsy, unsophisticated country person. *adj.* Typical of hicks.

hick-o-ry *n., pl.* **-ries** A North American tree with a smooth or shaggy bark, hard edible nuts, and heavy, tough wood.

hi-dal-go *n., pl.* **-goes** A Spanish nobleman of lesser nobility.

hide *v.* To put, or keep out of sight; to keep secret; to obscure from sight; to seek shelter. *n.* The skin of an animal.

hide-bound *adj.* Obstinately narrowminded or inflexible.

hid-e-ous *adj.* Physically repulsive; extremely ugly. **-ly** *adv.,* **-ness** *n.*

hi-er-ar-chy *n., pl.* **-chies** An authoritative body or group of things or persons arranged in successive order; a ranked series of persons or things. **-ical, -ic** *adj.,* **hierarchically** *adv.*

hi-er-o-glyph-ic *n.* A pictorial symbol representing an idea, object, or sound. **hieroglyphically** *adv.*

hi--fi *n.* High fidelity; electronic equipment, such as a phonograph, radio, or recording equipment capable of reproducing high-fidelity sound.

high *adj.* Extending upward; located at a distance above the ground; more than normal in degree or amount.

high-ball *n.* A mixed drink often served in a tall glass.

high-born *adj.* Of noble birth or ancestry.

high-boy *n.* A tall chest of drawers often in two sections with the lower one mounted on four legs.

high-bred *adj.* Highborn; descending from superior breeding stock.

high-brow *n., Slang* One who claims to have superior knowledge or culture. **highbrow, highbrowed** *adj.*

high-er--up *n., Slang* A person having superior rank or status.

high-fa-lu-tin *adj.* Pretentious or extravagant in manner or speech.

high fash-ion *n.* The newest in fashion, style, or design.

high fi-del-ity *n., Elect.* The reproduction of sound with minimal distortion, as on records or tapes.

high--flown *adj.* Pretentious in language or style.

high fre-quen-cy *n.* A radio frequency in the band from three to thirty megacycles.

high--hand-ed *adj.* Overbearing and arbitrary. **-ly** *adv.,* **highhandedness** *n.*

high--hat *adj., Slang* Supercilious; patronizing; snobbish; fashionable.

high jump *n.* A jump for height in athletics.

high-land *n.* Land elevated as a plateau.

highlands *pl.* A hilly or mountainous region.

high-light *n.* A significant event or detail of special importance *v.* To give emphasis to; to provide with highlights.

high--mind-ed *adj.* Possessing noble principles or behavior. -mindedness *n.*

high-ness *n.* The state of being high. Highness A title used for royalty.

high--pres-sure *adj., Informal* Using insistent persuasive methods or tactics. *v.* To try to persuade by using high-pressure techniques.

high--rise *n.* An extremely tall building.

high-road *n.* A main road; a direct or guaranteed method or course.

high school *n.* A secondary school of grades nine through twelve or grades ten through twelve. high schooler *n.*

high seas *pl., n.* The open waters of an ocean or sea that are beyond the territorial jurisdiction of any one nation.

high--sound-ing *adj.* Pretentious or imposing in implication or sound.

high--spirited *adj.* Unbroken in spirit; proud.

high--stick-ing *n.* In hockey, an offense in which a player holds the stick above the shoulders of other players or himself.

high--strung *adj.* A state of being very nervous and excitable.

high tech *n.* An interior design that incorporates industrial materials or motifs; high technology.

high tech-nol-o-gy *n.* The technology that involves highly advanced or specialized systems or devices.

high--test *adj.* Relating to gasoline with a high octane number.

high tide *n.* The highest level reached by the incoming tide each day.

high-way *n.* A main or principal road or thoroughfare of some length which connects towns and cities and is open to the public.

high-way-man *n.* Formerly, a robber who waylaid travelers on highways.

hi-jack *v., Slang* To seize illegally or steal while in transit; to coerce or compel someone; to commandeer a vehicle, especially an airplane in flight. hijacker *n.*

hike *v.* To walk for a lengthy amount of time usually through rugged terrain or woods; to pull up clothing with a sudden motion. hike, hiker *n.*

hi-lar-i-ous *adj.* Boisterously happy or cheerful. hilariously *adv.,* hilarity *n.*

hill *n.* A rounded, elevation of the earth's surface, smaller than a mountain; a pile or heap; a small pile or mound, as of soil. *v.* To surround or cover with hills, as potatoes. hilliness *n.,* hilly *adj.*

hill-bil-ly *n., pl.* -lies *Slang* A person living or coming from an isolated rural region, as from the mountains or a backwoods area, especially of the southern U.S.

hill-ock *n.* A small or low hill or mound. hillocky *adj.*

hill-side *n.* The side or slope of a hill.

hill-top *n.* The summit or top of a hill.

hilt *n.* The handle of a dagger or sword. to the hilt Fully; completely; thoroughly.

him *pron.* The objective case of the pronoun he.

Hi-ma-la-yas *n.* A mountain range in Asia.

him-self *pron.* That identical male one; a form of the third person, singular masculine pronoun.

hind *adj.* Located at or toward the rear part; posterior.

hin-der *v.* To interfere with the progress or action of. hinderer *n.*

hind-most *adj.* Farthest to the rear or back.

hin-drance *n.* The act of hindering or state of being hindered.

hind-sight *n.* Comprehension or understanding of an event after it has happened.

Hin-du *n.* A native of India; a person whose religion is Hinduism.

hinge *n.* A jointed device which allows a part, as a door or gate, to swing or turn on another frame. *v.* To attach by or to equip with a hinge or hinges.

hint *n.* An indirect indication or suggestion. *v.* To make something known by a hint.

hin-ter-land *n.* A region remote from cities; an inland area immediately adjacent to a coastal area.

hip *n.* The part of the human body that projects outward below the waist and thigh; the hip joint.

hip *n.* The bright, red seed case of a rose.

hip *adj., Slang* Said to be aware of or informed about current goings on.

hip-bone *n.* The large, flat bone which forms a lateral half of the pelvis.

hip joint *n.* The joint between the hipbone and the thighbone.

hip-pie *or* **hip-py** *n., pl.* -ies A young person who adopts unconventional dress and behavior along with the use of drugs to express withdrawal from middle class life and indifference to its values.

hip-po-pot-a-mus *n.*

A large, aquatic mammal, native to Africa, having short legs, a massive, thick-skinned hairless body, and a broad wide-mouthed muzzle.

hire *v.* To obtain the service of another for pay. hirer *n.*

his *adj.* The possessive case of the pronoun he.

hir-sute *adj.* Covered with hair.

His-pan-ic *adj.* Of or relating to the language, people, or culture of Spain or Latin America.

hiss *n.* A sound resembling a prolonged, sibilant sound, as that of *sss* *v.* To emit such a sound as an expression of disapproval. **hisser** n.

his-ta-mine n., Biochem. A white, crystalline substance that occurs in plant and animal tissue, found to reduce blood pressure and to have a contracting action on the uterus and believed to cause allergic reactions. -ic adj.

his-tol-o-gy n., pl. -ies The study of the minute structures of animal and plant tissues as seen through a microscope. **histological** adj., **histologist** n.

his-to-ri-an n. A person who specializes in the writing or study of history.

his-tor-ic adj. Significant or famous in history; historical.

his-tor-i-cal adj. Relating to or taking place in history; serving as a source of knowledge of the past; historic. **historically** adv., **historicalness** adj.

his-to-ry n., pl. -ries Past events, especially those involving human affairs; an account or record of past events that is written in chronological order, especially those concerning a particular nation, people, activity, or knowledge; the study of the past and its significance.

his-tri-on-ics pl., n. Theatrical arts; feigned emotional display.

hit v. To give a blow to; to strike with force; to come forcibly in contact with; to collide with; to inflict a blow on; to move or set in motion by striking; in baseball, to make a successful hit while at bat. **hitter** n.

hitch v. To fasten or tie temporarily, with a hook or knot. Slang To unite in marriage; to obtain a ride by hitchhiking. n. A delay or difficulty. Milit. A period of time in the armed forces.

hitch-hike v. To travel by signaling and obtaining rides from a passing driver. **hitchhiker** n.

hith-er adv. To this place. adj. Situated toward this side.

hith-er-to adv. Up to now.

hive n. A natural or man-made structure serving as a habitation for honeybees; a beehive.

hives pl., n. Any of various allergic conditions marked by itching welts.

hoar adj. Having white or gray hair; grayish or white, as with frost. **hoariness** n.

hoard n. The accumulation of something stored away for safekeeping or future use. v. To amass and hide or store valuables, money. **hoarder** n.

hoard-frost n. The deposit of ice crystals that form on a cold surface exposed to moist air.

hoarse adj. Having a husky, gruff, or croaking voice. -ly adv., **hoarseness** n.

hoars-en v. To become or make hoarse.

hoar-y adj. Ancient; aged; gray or white with age.

hoax n. A trick or deception. v. To deceive by a hoax. **hoaxer** n.

hob n. The projection at the side or interior of a fireplace used to keep things warm; an elf or hobgoblin.

hob-ble v. To limp or walk with a limp; to progress irregularly or clumsily; to fetter a horse or other animal. n. A hobbling gait or walk.

hob-by n., pl. -bies An activity or interest undertaken for pleasure during one's leisure time.

hob-by-horse n. A child's rocking horse; a long stick surmounted by a horse's head.

hob-gob-lin n. An imaginary cause of terror or dread.

hob-nail n. A short, broad-headed nail used to stud the soles of heavy shoes against wear or slipping.

hob-nob n. To associate in a friendly manner; to be on familiar terms.

ho-bo n., pl. **ho-boes** or **ho-bos** A vagrant who travels aimlessly about; a tramp.

hock n. The joint of the hind leg of a horse, ox, or other animal which corresponds to the ankle in man.

hock-ey n. A game played on ice between two teams of skaters whose object is to drive a puck into the opponent's goal using curved wooden sticks; a similar kind of hockey played on a field with a small ball instead of a puck.

ho-cus--po-cus n. Any deception or trickery, as misleading gestures; nonsense words or phrases used in conjuring or sleight of hand.

hod n. A V-shaped trough held over the shoulder to carry loads, as bricks or mortar.

hodge-podge n. A jumbled mixture or collection.

Hodg-kin's dis-ease n., Pathol. A disease characterized by progressive enlargement of the lymph nodes, lymphoid tissue, and spleen, generally fatal.

hoe n. A tool with a long handle and flat blade used for weeding, cultivating, and loosening the soil. **hoe** v., **hoer** n.

hoe-cake n. A thin, flat cake made of cornmeal.

hoe-down n., Slang A lively country square dance; party.

hog n. A pig, especially one weighing more than 120 pounds and raised for the market; a greedy, selfish, or dirty person. v. To take something selfishly; to take more than one's share. **hoggish** adj., **hoggishly** adv., -ness n.

hog-nose snake n. Any of several nonvenomous American snakes with flat heads and prominent snouts.

hogs-head n. A large barrel or cask that holds from 63 to 140 gallons.

hog--tie v. To tie together the four feet of an animal or the hands and feet of a person.

hog-wash n. Kitchen scraps fed to hogs; any nonsense; false or ridiculous talk or writing.

hoi pol-loi n. The common people; the masses.

hoist v. To haul or raise up. n. A machine used for raising large objects. **hoister** n.

hold v. To take and keep as in one's

hand; to grasp; to possess; to put or keep in a particular place, position, or relationship; to suppress; to keep under control. *n.* A cargo storage area inside a ship or aircraft.

hold-ing *n.* Property, as land, money, or stocks.

hold-ing pat-tern *n.* A usually circular course that is flown by an aircraft awaiting clearance to land at an airport.

hold-o-ver *n.* Something that remains from an earlier time.

hold-up *n.* A robbery at gun point; a delay.

hole *n.* A cavity or opening in a solid mass or body. **hole** *v.*

hol-i-day *n.* A day set aside by law to commemorate a special person or event; a day set aside for religious observance; a day free from work; any day of rest.

ho-li-ness *n.* The state of being holy.

hol-lan-daise sauce *n.* A creamy sauce made from butter, egg yolks, and lemon juice or vinegar.

hol-ler *v.* To shout loudly; to yell.

hol-low *adj.* Having a cavity or space within; concaved or sunken; lacking significance or substance; not genuine; empty; meaningless. **-ly** *adv.*, **-ness** *n.*

hol-ly *n.*, *pl.* **-ies** A tree or shrub that bears glossy spiny leaves and bright-red berries.

hol-ly-hock *n.* A tall, cultivated plant of the mallow family, widely cultivated for its tall spikes of large, variously colored flowers.

hol-mi-um *n.* A metallic element of the rare-earth group, symbolized by Ho.

hol-o-caust *n.* A widespread or total destruction, especially by fire.

hol-o-grah *n.* A handwritten document, as a letter or will, signed by the person who wrote it. **holographical** *adj.*

Hol-stein *n.* One of a breed of black-and-white dairy cattle.

hol-ster *n.* A leather case designed to hold a pistol or gun. **holstered** *adj.*

ho-ly *adj.* Regarded with or characterized by divine power; sacred.

Ho-ly Com-mu-nion *n.* The Eucharist.

Ho-ly Ghost *n.* The third person of the Trinity.

Ho-ly Land *n.* Palestine.

Ho-ly Spir-it *n.* The Holy Ghost.

hom-age *n.* Great respect or honor, especially when expressed publicly.

home *n.* The place where one resides; a place of origin; one's birthplace or residence during the formative years; a place one holds dear because of personal feelings or relationships; a place of security and comfort.

home-bod-y *n.*, *pl.* **-ies** One who prefers to stay at home or whose main interest centers around the home.

home-com-ing *n.* A return to one's home; a yearly celebration during which alumni return to visit their old schools.

home eco-nom-ics *n.* The principles of home management.

home-ly *adj.* Having a simple, familiar, everyday character; having plain or ugly features; unattractive. **-lness** *n.*

ho-me-op-a-thy *n.* A system of treating a disease with minute doses of medicines that produce the symptoms of the disease being treated. **homeopath** *n.*, **homeopathic** *adj.*

ho-me-o-sta-sis *n., Biol.* A state of equilibrium that occurs between different but related functions or elements. **homeostatic** *adj.*

home plate *n.* In baseball, the rubber slab or plate at which a batter stands.

home run *n.* In baseball, a hit that allows the batter to circle all the bases and to score.

home-sick *adj.* Longing or yearning for home and family. **homesickness** *n.*

home-spun *adj.* Something made, woven, or spun at home; anything that is simple and plain.

home-stead *n.* A house and its land. *v.* To occupy land granted under the Homestead Act. **homesteader** *n.*

home-stretch *n.* The straight portion of a racecourse between the last turn and the finish line; the last or final stage of anything.

home-work *n.* Work done at home, especially school assignments.

home-y *or* **hom-y** *adj.* Suggesting the coziness, intimacy, and comforts of home. **homeyness** *or* **hominess** *n.*

hom-i-cide *n.* The killing of one person by another; a person killed by another.

hom-i-let-ic *n.* Pertaining to the nature of a sermon.

hom-i-ly *n.*, *pl.* **-ies** A sermon, particularly one based on a Biblical text.

hom-i-ny *n.* Kernels of hulled and dried corn, often ground into a coarse white meal and boiled.

ho-mo-ge-ne-ous *adj.* Of the same or similar nature or kind. **homogeneity, homogeneousness** *n.*, **-ly** *adv.*

ho-mog-e-nize *v.* To process milk by breaking up fat globules and dispersing them uniformly. **-ation, -er** *n.*

hom-o-graph *n.* A word that is identical to another in spelling, but different from it in origin and meaning.

hom-o-nym *n.* A word that has the same sound and often the same spelling as another but a different meaning and origin.

hom-o-phone *n.* One of two or more words that have the same sound but different spelling, origin, and meaning.

Ho-mo sa-pi-ens *n.* The scientific name for the human race.

ho-mo-sex-u-al *adj.* Having sexual attraction or desire for persons of the same sex. **homosexual, homosexuality** *n.*

bon-cho *n.*, *pl.* **-chos** The main person in charge; the boss; the manager.

hone *n.* A fine-grained stone used to sharpen cutting tools, such as knives or razors. *v.* To perfect something; to sharpen.

hon-est *adj.* Not lying, cheating, or stealing; having or giving full worth or value. **honestly** *adv.*, **honesty** *n.*

hon-ey *n., pl.* **hon-eys** A sweet, sticky substance made by bees from the nectar gathered from flowers; sweetness. *Slang* Dear; darling. **-ed** *or* **-ied** *adj.*

hon-ey-bee *n.* Any of various bees living in colonies and producing honey.

hon-ey-comb *n.* A structure consisting of a series of hexagonal cells made by bees for the storage of honey, pollen, or their eggs.

hon-ey-moon *n.* A trip taken by a newly-married couple. **honeymooner** *n.*

hon-ey-suck-le *n.* A shrub or vine bearing a tubular, highly fragrant flower.

honk *n.* The harsh, loud sound made by a goose; the sound made by an automobile horn. **honk** *v.*, **honker** *n.*

hon-ky--tonk *n., Slang* A cheap bar or nightclub.

hon-or *n.* High regard or respect; personal integrity; reputation; privilege; used as a title for mayors and judges. *v.* To accept something as valid. **honorer** *n.*

hon-or-a-ble *adj.* Worthy of honor.

hon-or-ar-y *adj.* Relating to an office or title bestowed as an honor, without the customary powers, duties, or salaries.

hon-or-if-ic *adj.* Giving or conveying respect or honor.

hood *n.* A covering for the head and neck, often attached to a garment; the movable metal hinged cover of an automobile engine. **hooded** *adj.*

-hood *suff.* The quality or state of; sharing a given quality or state.

hood-lum *n.* A young, tough, wild, or destructive fellow.

hoo-doo *n.* Voodoo. *Slang* One who is thought to bring bad luck.

hood-wink *v.* To deceive; to blindfold.

hoo-ey *n., & interj., Slang* Nonsense.

hoof *n., pl.* **hooves** The horny covering of the foot in various mammals, as horses, cattle, and oxen. *Slang* To dance; to walk. **on the hoof** Alive; not butchered. **hoofed** *adj.*

hook *n.* A curved or bent piece of metal used to catch, drag, suspend, or fasten something; in golf, a stroke that sends the ball curving to the left; in boxing, to strike with a short, swinging blow; in hockey, to check illegally with the hockey stick. *Slang v.* To cause to become dependent or addicted. *Naut., Slang* An anchor. **by hook or by crook** In one way or another. **hook, line, and sinker** Unreservedly; entirely. **to hookup with** To marry; to form an association.

hoo-kah *n.* A smoking pipe having a long, flexible tube that passes through a vessel of water which cools the smoke as it is drawn through.

hook-er *n., Slang* A prostitute.

hook-worm *n.* A parasitic intestinal worm with hooked mouth parts.

hook-y *n., Slang* Truant. **to play hooky** To be out of school without permis-

sion.

hoop *n.* A circular band of metal or wood used to hold staves of a cask or barrel together; in basketball, the basket.

hoop-la *n., Slang* Noise and excitement.

hoose-gow *n., Slang* A jail.

hoot *n.* The loud sound or cry of an owl. **hooter** *n.*, **hoot** *v.*

hoot *n., Slang* A very insignificant amount. **not give a hoot** Not caring.

hoot-en-an-ny *n., pl.* **-ies** An informal gathering of folk singers for a public performance.

hop *n.* A perennial herb with lobed leaves and green flowers that resemble pine cones; the dried flowers of the plant, yielding an oil used in brewing beer. *Slang* A dance; a quick trip on a plane. *v.* To move by making short leaps on one foot; to move with light springing motions.

hope *v.* To want or wish for something with a feeling of confident expectation. **to hope against hope** To continue hoping for something even when it may be in vain. **-fully** *adv.*

hope-ful *adj.* Manifesting or full of hope. *n.* A young person who shows signs of succeeding. **hope-less** *adj.*

hop-ped--up *adj., Slang* Stimulated by narcotics; drugged.

horde *adj.* A large crowd.

hore-hound *n.* A whitish, bitter, aromatic plant, whose leaves yield a bitter extract used as a flavoring in candy.

ho-ri-zon *n.* The line along which the earth and sky seem to meet; the bounds or limit of one's knowledge, experience or interest.

hor-i-zon-tal *adj.* Parallel to the horizon. **horizontal** *n.*, **horizontally** *adv.*

hor-mone *n., Physiol.* An internal secretion carried by the bloodstream to other parts of the body where it has a specific effect.

horn *n.*

A hard, bone-like, permanent projection on the heads of certain hoofed animals, as cattle, sheep, or deer; the two antlers of a deer which are shed annually. *Mus.* Any of the various brass instruments, formerly made from animal horns. **horn in** To join in a conversation or other activities without being invited. **-y** *adj.*

horn-ed toad *n.* A lizard with a flat body, a short tail, and horn-like projections on the head.

hor-net *n.* Any of various wasps which are capable inflicting a severe sting.

horn-pout *n.* A freshwater catfish with a large head and barbels for navigation.

horn-swog-gle *v.* To deceive.

hor-o-scope *n.* A chart or diagram of the relative positions of the planets and signs of the zodiac at a certain time, as that of a person's birth; used to predict the future.

hor-ri-ble *adj.* Shocking; inducing or producing horror. *Informal* Excessive; inordinate. **horribly** *adv.*

hor-rid *adj.* Horrible. **horridly** *adv.*

hor-ri-fy *v.* To cause a feeling of horror; to dismay or shock.

hor-ror *n.* The painful, strong emotion caused by extreme dread, fear, or repugnance. *Informal* Something that is disagreeable or ugly.

hors d'oeuvre *n.* An appetizer served with cocktails before dinner.

horse *n.*

A large, strong, hoofed quadruped mammal with a long mane and tail, used for riding and for pulling heavy objects; a device that generally has four legs, used for holding or supporting something; in gymnastics, a wooden, leather-covered block of wood on four legs, used for vaulting and other exercises.

horse chest-nut *n.* Any of several Eurasian trees with digitate leaves, clusters of flowers, and chestnut-like fruit.

horse-fly *n.* A large fly, the female of which sucks the blood of various mammals, such as horses and cattle.

horse-hair *n.* The hair from a horse's tail or mane; a fabric made from such hair; haircloth.

horse-hide *n.* The hide of a horse; leather made from a horse's hide. *Informal* A baseball.

horse-laugh *n.* A loud, scornful laugh.

horse-man *n.* A person who rides horseback; one who breeds or raises horses. **horsemanship** *n.*

horse-play *n.* Rough, boisterous fun or play.

horse-pow-er *n., Mech.* A unit of power that is equal to 746 watts and nearly equivalent to the gravitational unit that equals 550 foot-pounds per second.

horse-rad-ish *n.* A tall, coarse, white-flowered herb from the mustard family; the pungent root of this plant is used as a condiment.

horse sense *n., Slang* Common sense.

horse-shoe *n.* A protective U-shaped shoe for a horse, consisting of a narrow plate of iron shaped to fit the rim of a horse's hoof. **horseshoes** A game in which the object is to encircle a stake with tossed horseshoes.

horse-shoe crab *n.* Any closely related marine arthropod with a rounded body and a stiff pointed tail.

horse-whip *n.* A whip used to control horses. *v.* To whip or flog.

hort *abbr.* Horticultural; horticulture.

hor-ti-cul-ture *n.* The art or science of raising and tending fruits, vegetables, flowers, or ornamental plants.

horticultural *adj.*, **horticulturist** *n.*

ho-san-na *interj.* Used to praise or glorify God.

hose *n.* A sock; a stocking; a flexible tube for carrying fluids or gases under pressure. *v.* To wash; to water; to squirt with a hose.

ho-sier-y *n.* Stockings and socks.

hosp *abbr.* Hospital.

hos-pice *n.* A lodging for travelers or the needy.

hos-pi-ta-ble *adj.* Treating guests with warmth and generosity; receptive. **hospitably** *adv.*

hos-pi-tal *n.* An institution where the injured or sick receive medical, surgical, and emergency care.

hos-pi-tal-i-ty *n.* Hospitable treatment, disposition, or reception.

hos-pi-tal-ize *v.* To place or admit in a hospital as a patient for care or treatment. **hospitalization** *n.*

host *n.* One who receives or entertains guests; one who provides a room or building for an event or function. *Biol.* A living organism, as a plant or an animal, on or in which a parasite lives.

hos-tage *n.* A person held as security that promises will be kept or terms met by a third party.

host-ess *n.* A woman who entertains socially; a woman who greets patrons at a restaurant and escorts them to their tables.

hos-tile *adj.* Of or relating to an enemy; antagonistic. **hostilely** *adv.*

hos-til-i-ty *n., pl.* -**ies** A very deep-seated opposition or hatred; war.

hot *adj.* Having heat that exceeds normal body temperature; sexually excited or receptive; electrically charged, as a hot wire. *Slang* Recently and or illegally obtained.

hot air *n., Slang* Idle talk.

hot cake *n.* A pancake.

hot dog *n.* A cooked frankfurter, served in a long roll. *Slang* A person who enjoys showing off.

hot-el *n.* A business that provides lodging, meals, entertainment, and other services for the public.

hot-foot *v.* To hasten.

hot-head-ed *adj.* To have a fiery temper. **hotheadedly** *adv.*, **hotheadedness** *n.*

hot-house *n.* A heated greenhouse used to raise plants.

hot line *n.* A direct telephone line that is in constant operation and ready to facilitate immediate communication.

hot plate *n.* A portable electric appliance for heating or cooking food.

hot po-ta-to *n.* An issue or problem that involves unpleasant or dangerous consequences for anyone dealing with it.

hot rod *n.* An automobile modified or rebuilt for greater power and speed. **hot rodder** *n.*

hot seat *n., Slang* An electric chair; a position of embarrassment, anxiety, or uneasiness.

hot spring *n.* A natural spring with water

temperature above 98 degrees.

hound *n.* Any of several kinds of long-eared dogs with deep voices which follow their prey by scent; a person unusually devoted to something; a fan. *v.* To pursue or drive without letting up; to nag continuously.

hour *n.* A measure of time equal to 60 minutes; one 24th of a day; the time of day or night. **hours** *pl.* A specific or certain period of time.

hour-glass *n.*

A glass instrument having two compartments from which sand, mercury, or water flows from the top compartment to the bottom.

hour-ly *adj.* Something that happens or is done every hour. **hourly** *adv.*

house *n.* A building that serves as living quarters for one or more families; home; the shelter or refuge.

how *adv.* In what manner or way; to what effect; in what condition or state; for what reason; with what meaning.

how-dy *interj.* A word used to express a greeting.

how-ev-er *adj.* In whatever way. *conj.* Nevertheless.

how-it-zer *n.* A short cannon that fires projectiles at a high trajectory.

howl *v.* To utter a loud, sustained, plaintive sound, as the wolf.

howl-er *n.* One that howls; a ridiculous or stupid blunder.

how-so-ev-er *adv.* To whatever degree or extent.

hua-ra-che *n.* A sandal with a low heel and an upper made of interwoven leather thongs.

hub *n.* The center of a wheel; the center of activity.

hub-cap *n.* The removable metal cap that covers the end of an axle, such as one used on the wheel of a motor vehicle.

huck-le-ber-ry *n.* A type of bush, related to the blueberry and bearing glossy, blackish, usually acidic berries.

HUD *abbr.* Department of Housing and Urban Development.

hud-dle *n.* A crowd together; in football, a brief meeting of teammates to prepare for the next play. *v.* To nestle or crowd together; to confer.

hue *n.* A gradation of color running from red through yellow, green, and blue to violet; a particular color; a shade. **hued** *adj.*

huff *n.* A fit of resentment or of ill temper. *v.* To exhale or breathe heavily, as from extreme exertion. **huffily** *adv.*, **huffiness** *n.*, **huffy** *adj.*

hug *v.* To embrace; to hold fast; to keep, cling, or stay close to. **-er** *n.*

huge *adj.* Of great quantity, size, or extent. **hugely** *adv.*, **hugeness** *n.*

hu-la *n.* A Hawaiian dance characterized by beautiful rhythmic movement of the hips and gestures with the hands.

hulk *n.* A heavy, bulky ship; the body of an old ship no longer fit for service.

hulk-ing *adj.* Unwieldy or awkward.

hull *n.* The outer cover of a fruit or seed; the framework of a boat; the external covering of a rocket, spaceship, or guided missile.

hul-la-ba-loo *n.* A confused noise; a great uproar.

hum *v.* To make a continuous low-pitched sound; to be busily active; to sing with the lips closed. **hummer** *n.*

hu-man *adj.* Of, relating to, or typical of man; having or manifesting human form or attributes. **-ly** *adv.*, **-ness** *n.*

hu-mane *adj.* To be marked by compassion, sympathy, or consideration for other people or animals. **humanely** *adv.*, **humaneness** *n.*

hu-man-i-tar-i-an *n.* A person who is concerned for human welfare, especially through philanthropy. **humanitarian** *adj.*, **humanitarianism** *n.*

hu-man-i-ty *n.*, *pl.* **-ies** The quality or state of being human; humankind.

hum-ble *adj.* Marked by meekness or modesty; unpretentious; lowly. *v.* To make humble. **-ness**, **-er** *n.*, **-ly** *adv.*

hum-bug *n.* A person who passes himself off as something he is not; a fraud; a hoax.

hum-din-ger *n.*, *Slang* Someone or something that is marked as superior.

hum-drum *n.*, *Slang* Boring; dull.

hu-mer-us *n.*, *pl.* **meri** The long bone of the upper arm or forelimb extending from the shoulder to the elbow. **humeral** *adj.*

hu-mid *adj.* Containing or characterized by a large amount of moisture; damp.

hu-mid-i-fy *v.* To make humid or more moist. **humidifier** *n.*

hu-mid-i-ty *n.* A moderate amount of wetness in the air; dampness.

hu-mi-dor *n.* A container used to keep cigars in which the air is kept properly humidified by a special device.

hu-mil-i-ate *v.* To reduce one's dignity or pride to a lower position. **-ation** *n.*

hum-ming-bird *n.* A very small bird with narrow wings, long primaries, a slender bill, and a very extensile tongue.

hum-mock *n.* A rounded knoll or hill of snow or dirt. **hummocky** *adj.*

hu-mor *n.* Something that is or has the ability to be comical or amusing. *Physiol.* Fluid contained in the body such as blood or lymph. **humorous** *adj.*, **humorously** *adv.*

hump *n.* The rounded lump or protuberance, as on the back of a camel. **over the hump** To be past the difficult or most critical state.

hunch *n.* A strong, intuitive feeling about a future event or result. *v.* To bend into a crooked position or posture.

hun-dred *n.*, *pl.* **-dreds** *or* **-dred** The cardinal number equal to 10 X 10. **hundred** *adj.* & *pron.*, **hundredth** *n.*, *adj.* & *adv.*

hun-ger *n.* A strong need or desire for food. **hungrily** *adv.*, **hungry** *adj.*

hunt v. To search or look for food; to pursue with the intent of capture; to look in an attempt to find.
hunter, huntress n.
hur-dle n. A portable barrier used to jump over in a race; an obstacle one must overcome. v. To leap over.
hurdler n.
hurl v. To throw something with great force; in baseball, to pitch.
hurl, hurler n.
hur-rah interj. Used to express approval, pleasure, or exultation. **hurrah** n. & v.
hur-ri-cane n. A tropical cyclone with winds exceeding 74 miles per hour, usually accompanied by rain, thunder, and lightning.
hur-ry v. To move or cause to move with haste. **hurriedly** adv., **hurriedness** n.
hurt v. To experience or inflict with physical pain; to cause physical or emotional harm to; to damage.
hurtful adj.
hus-band n. A man who is married.
hush v. To make or become quiet; to calm; to keep secret; to suppress. n. A silence.
hush--pup-py n., pl -ies A mixture of cornmeal that is shaped into small balls and deep fried.
husk n. The dry or membranous outer cover of certain vegetables, fruits, and seeds, often considered worthless.
husker n.
husk-y adj. Having a dry cough or grating sound; burly or robust.
huskily adv., **huskiness** n.
husk-y n., pl. -ies A heavy-coated working dog of the arctic region.
hus-sy n., pl -ies A saucy or mischievous girl; a woman with doubtful morals.
hus-tle v. To urge or move hurriedly along; to work busily and quickly. Slang To make energetic efforts to solicit business or make money.
hustle, hustler n.
hut n. An often small and temporary dwelling made of simple construction; a shack.
hutch n. A compartment or chest for storage.
hy-a-cinth n. A bulbous plant that has a cluster of variously colored, highly fragrant, bell-shaped flowers.
hy-brid n. An offspring of two dissimilar plants or of two animals of different races, breeds, varieties, or species; something made up of mixed origin or makeup. **hybrid** adj.
hy-drant n. A pipe with a valve and spout which supplies water from a main source.
hy-drate n. A chemical compound formed by the union of water with another substance in definite proportions. **hydrate** v., **hydration** n.
hy-drau-lic adj. Operated, moved, or effected by the means of water; hardening or setting under water.
hy-drau-lics pl., n. The scientific study that deals with practical applications of liquids in motion.

hy-dro-gen n. A colorless, normally odorless, highly flammable gas that is the simplest and lightest of the elements, symbolized by H. -nous adj.
hy-dro-gen per-ox-ide n. A colorless, unstable, liquid compound that is used as an antiseptic solution and as a bleach.
hy-dro-pho-bi-a n. A fear of water; rabies. **hydrophobic** adj.
hy-dro-plane v. To skim over water with only the hull more or less touching the surface.

hy-e-na n.

Any of several strong carnivorous mammals of Africa and Asia, with coarse hair and very powerful jaws.
hy-giene n. The science of the establishment and maintenance of good health and the prevention of disease.
hygienic adj., -ically adv., -ist n.
hy-men n. The thin membrane that partly closes the external vaginal orifice.
hymn n. A song of praise giving thanks to God; a song of joy. **hymn** v.
hype v., Slang To put on; to stimulate; to promote or publicize extravagantly.
hy-per pref. Excessive in anything that is performed or done physically.
hy-per-ac-tive adj. Abnormally active.
hy-per-ten-sion n. The condition of abnormally high blood pressure.
hypertensive adj. & n.
hy-phen n. A punctuation mark (-) used to show connection between two or more words. **hyphen** v.
hy-phen-ate v. To separate or join with a hyphen. **hyphenation** n.
hyp-no-sis n., pl. **hypnoses** A state that resembles sleep but is brought on or induced by another person whose suggestions are accepted by the subject.
hyp-not-ic adj. Inducing sleep. n. An agent, such as a drug, which induces sleep. **hypnotically** adv.
hyp-no-tism n. The study or act of inducing hypnosis. **hypnotist** n.
hyp-no-tize v. To induce hypnosis; to be dazzled by; to be overcome by suggestion.
hy-po n., pl. **hypos** Slang A hypodermic needle or syringe.
hy-po-chon-dri-a n. A mental depression accompanied by imaginary physical ailments. **hypochondriac** n.
hy-po-der-mic sy-ringe n. A syringe and hypodermic needle used for injecting a substance into one's body.
hys-ter-ec-to-my n., pl. -ies Surgery on a female which partially or completely removes the uterus.
hys-ter-ia n. A psychological condition characterized by emotional excess and or unreasonable fear.
hys-ter-ic n. A person suffering from hysteria. pl., n. A fit of uncontrollable laughter or crying; hysteria.

I, i The ninth letter of the English alphabet; the Roman numeral for one.

I *pron.* The person speaking or writing. *n.* The self; the ego.

I or **i** *abbr.* Island; isle.

i-amb or **i-am-bus** *n.* A metrical foot consisting of a short or unstressed syllable followed by an accented syllable. **iambic** *adj. & n.*

i-at-ric *adj.* Pertaining to medicine or a physician.

i-at-ro-gen-ic *adj.* Induced inadvertently by a physician or his treatment. **iatrogenically** *adv.*

ib or **ibid** *abbr., L.* Ibidem, in the same place.

i-bex *n.*

An Old World mountain goat with long curved horns.

i-bi-dem *adv.* Used in footnotes to indicate a part of literary work that was just mentioned.

i-bis *n.* A long-billed wading bird related to the heron and stork.

ice *n.* Solidly frozen water; a dessert of crushed ice which is flavored and sweetened. *Informal* Extreme coldness of manner. *v.* To change into ice; to cool or chill; to cover with icing. **icily** *adv.,* **iciness** *n.,* **icy** *adj.*

ice age *n., Geol.* A time of widespread glaciation.

ice-boat *n.* A vehicle with runners and usually a sail, used for sailing over ice; an icebreaker.

ice-box *n.* A structure designed for holding ice in which food and other perishables are stored.

ice-break-er *n.* A sturdy vessel for breaking a path through icebound waters; a pier or dock apron for deflecting floating ice from the base of a pier or bridge.

ice cap *n.* An extensive perennial covering of ice and snow that covers a large area of land.

ice hock-ey *n.* A version of hockey played on ice.

ice-house *n.* A building where ice is stored.

Ice-land *n.* An island country in the North Atlantic near the Arctic Circle. **Icelander** *n.,* **Icelandic** *adj.*

ice pack *n.* A large mass of floating, compacted ice; a folded bag filled with ice and applied to sore parts of the body.

ice water *n.* Water cooled by ice.

ich-thy-ol-o-gy *n.* The zoological study of fishes. **ichthyologic, ichthyological** *adj.,* **ichthyologist** *n.*

i-ci-cle *n.* A hanging spike of ice formed by dripping water that freezes.

ic-ing *n.* A sweet preparation for coating cakes and cookies.

i-con or **i-kon** *n.* A sacred Christian pictorial representation of Jesus Christ, the Virgin Mary, or other sacred figures.

i-con-o-clast *n.* One who opposes the use of sacred images; one who attacks traditional or cherished beliefs. **iconoclasm** *n.,* **iconoclastic** *adj.*

id *n., Psychol..* The unconscious part of the psyche associated with instinctual needs and drives.

I'd *contr.* I had; I should; I would.

ID *abbr.* Identification.

i-de-a *n.* Something existing in the mind; conception or thought; an opinion; a plan of action.

i-de-al *n.* A concept or imagined state of perfection; highly desirable; perfect; an ultimate objective; an honorable principle or motive. *adj.* Conforming to absolute excellence. **ideally** *adv.*

i-de-al-ism *n.* The practice or tendency of seeing things in ideal form; pursuit of an ideal; a philosophical system believing that reality consists of ideas or perceptions. **-ist** *n.,* **idealistic** *adj.*

i-de-al-ize *v.* To regard or represent as ideal. **idealization** *n.*

i-dem *pron. & adj., L.* The same; used to indicate a previously mentioned reference.

i-den-ti-cal *adj.* Being the same; exactly equal or much alike; designating a twin or twins developed from the same ovum. **identically** *adv.*

i-den-ti-fy *v.* To recognize the identity of; to establish as the same or similar; to equate; to associate oneself closely with an individual or group. **-iable** *adj.*

i-den-ti-ty *n., pl.* **-ties** The condition or state of being a specific person or thing and recognizable as such; the condition or fact of being the same as something else.

id-e-o-gram or **id-e-o-graph** *n.* A pictorial symbol used in a writing system to represent an idea or thing, as Chinese characters; a graphic symbol, as $.

i-de-ol-o-gy *n., pl.* **-gies** A body of ideas that influence a person, group, culture, or political party. **-ical** *adj.*

ides *pl., n.* In the ancient Roman calendar, the fifteenth day of March, May, July, and October or the thirteenth day of the other months.

id-i-o-cy *n., pl.* **-cies** A condition of an idiot.

id-i-om *n.* A form of expression having a meaning that is not readily understood from the meaning of its component words; the dialect of people or a region; a kind of language or vocabulary. **-atic** *adj.,* **-atically** *adv.*

id-i-o-syn-cra-sy *n., pl.* **-sies** A peculiarity, as of behavior. **idiosyncratic** *adj.,* **-ally** *adv.*

id-i-ot *n.* A mentally deficient person; an extremely foolish or stupid person. **idiotic** *adj.,* **idiotically** *adv.*

i-dle *adj.* Doing nothing; inactive; moving lazily; slowly; running at a slow speed or out of gear; unemployed or inactive.

idleness, **idler** *n.*, **idly** *adv.*

i-dol *n.* A symbol or representation of a god or deity that is worshiped; a person or thing adored.

i-dol-a-tr *n.* The worship of idols; blind adoration; devotion. **-ter** *n.*, **-ous** *adj.*

i-dol-ize *v.* To admire with excessive admiration or devotion; to worship as an idol. **idolization, idolizer** *n.*

i-dyll *or* **i-dyl** *n.* A poem or prose piece about country life; a scene, event, or condition of rural simplicity; a romantic interlude.

idyllic *adj.*, **idyllically** *adv.*

if-fy *adj.*, *Slang* Marked by unknown qualities or conditions.

ig-loo *n.* A dome-shaped Eskimo dwelling often made of blocks of snow.

ig-ne-ous *adj.*, *Geol.* Relating to fire; formed by solidification from a molten magma.

ig-nite *v.* To start or set a fire; to render luminous by heat.

ig-ni-tion *n.* An act or action of igniting; a process or means for igniting the fuel mixture in an engine.

ig-no-ble *adj.* Dishonorable in character or purpose; not of noble rank. **-ly** *adv.*

ig-no-min-i-ous *adj.* Marked by or characterized by shame or disgrace; dishonorable. **ignominy** *n.*

ig-no-ra-mus *n.* A totally ignorant person.

ig-no-rant *adj.* Lacking education or knowledge; not aware; lacking comprehension. **ignorance** *n.*

ig-nore *v.* To pay no attention to; to reject. **ignorable** *adj.*

i-gua-na *n.*

A large, dark-colored tropical American lizard.

il-e-i-tis *n.* Inflammation of the ileum.

il-e-um *n., pl.* **ilea** The lower part of the small intestine between the jejunum and the large intestine.*

ill *adj.* Not healthy; sick; destructive in effect; harmful; hostile; unfriendly; not favorable; not up to standards. *adv.* In an ill manner; with difficulty; scarcely. *n.* Evil; injury or harm; something causing suffering.

I'll *contr.* I will; I shall.

Ill *abbr.* Illinois.

ill-ad-vised *adj.* Done without careful thought or sufficient advice.

ill-bred *adj.* Ill-mannered; impolite; rude.

il-le-gal *adj.* Contrary to law or official rules. **illegality** *n.*, **illegally** *adv.*

il-leg-i-ble *adj.* Not readable; not legible. **illegibly** *adv.*, **illegibility** *n.*

il-le-git-i-mate *adj.* Against the law; unlawful; born out of wedlock. **illegitimacy** *n.*, **illegitimately** *adv.*

ill-fat-ed *adj.* Destined for misfortune; doomed; unlucky.

ill-fa-vored *adj.* Unattractive; objectionable; offensive; unpleasant.

ill-got-ten *adj.* Obtained in an illegal or dishonest way.

ill-hu-mored *adj.* Irritable; cross. **ill-humoredly** *adv.*

il-lic-it *adj.* Not permitted by custom or law; unlawful. **illicitly** *adv.*

il-lit-er-ate *adj.* Unable to read and write; uneducated. **illiteracy, -ate** *n.*

ill-man-nered *adj.* Lacking or showing a lack of good manners; rude.

ill-na-tured *adj.* Disagreeable or unpleasant disposition.

ill-ness *n.* Sickness; a state of being in poor health.

il-log-i-cal *adj.* Contrary to the principles of logic; not logical. **illogicality** *n.*, **illogically** *adv.*

ill-tem-pered *adj.* Having or showing a cross temper or disposition.

il-lu-mi-nate *v.* To give light; to make clear; to provide with understanding; to decorate with pictures or designs. **illumination, illuminator** *n.*

ill-use *v.* To treat cruelly or unjustly. *n.* Unjust treatment.

il-lu-sion *n.* A misleading perception of reality; an overly optimistic idea or belief; misconception. **-ive, -ory** *adj.*

il-lus-trate *v.* To explain or clarify, especially by the use of examples; to clarify by serving as an example; to provide a publication with explanatory features. **illustrator** *n.*

il-lus-tra-tion *n.* The act of illustrating; an example or comparison used to illustrate.

il-lus-tra-tive *adj.* Serving to illustrate.

il-lus-tri-ous *adj.* Greatly celebrated; renowned. **illustriousness** *n.*

ill will *n.* Unfriendly or hostile feelings; malice.

I'm *contr.* I am.

im-age *n.* A representation of the form and features of someone or something; an optically formed representation of an object made by a mirror or lens; a mental picture of something imaginary. *v.* To make a likeness of; to reflect; to depict vividly.

im-age-ry *n., pl.* **-ies** Mental pictures; existing only in the imagination.

im-ag-in-a-ble *adj.* Capable of being imagined. **imaginably** *adv.*

im-ag-i-nar-y *adj.* Existing only in the imagination.

im-ag-i-na-tion *n.* The power of forming mental images of unreal or absent objects; such power used creatively; resourcefulness.

imaginative *adj.*, **imaginatively** *adv.*

im-ag-ine *v.* To form a mental picture or idea of; to suppose; to guess.

i-ma-go *n., pl.* **-goes** *or* **-gines** An insect in its sexually mature adult stage.

i-mam *n.* A prayer leader of Islam; rulers that claim descent from Muhammad.

im-bal-ance *n.* A lack of functional balance; defective coordination.

im-be-cile *n.* A mentally deficient person. **imbecilic** *adj.*, **imbecility** *n.*

im-bibe *v.* To drink; to take in. **-er** *n.*

im-bri-cate *adj.* With edges over-lapping in a regular arrangement, as roof tiles or fish scales.

im-bro-glio *n., pl.* -glios A complicated situation or disagreement; a confused heap; a tangle.

im-bue *v.* To saturate, as with a stain or dye.

im-i-ta-ble *adj.* Capable or worthy of imitation.

im-i-tate *v.* To copy the actions or appearance of another; to adopt the style of; to duplicate; to appear like. **imitator** *n.*

im-i-ta-tion *n.* An act of imitating; something copied from an original.

im-mac-u-late *adj.* Free from sin, stain, or fault; impeccably clean. **immaculately** *adv.*

im-ma-nent *adj.* Existing within; restricted to the mind; subjective. **immanence, immanency** *n.,* -ly *adv.*

im-ma-te-ri-al *adj.* Lacking material body or form; of no importance or relevance. -ly *adv.,* **immaterialness** *n.*

im-ma-ture *adj.* Not fully grown; undeveloped; suggesting a lack of maturity. -ly *adv.,* **immaturity** *n.*

im-meas-ur-a-ble *adj.* Not capable of being measured. **immeasurably** *adv.*

im-me-di-a-cy *n., pl.* -ies The quality of being immediate; directness; something of urgent importance.

im-me-di-ate *adj.* Acting or happening without an intervening object, agent, or cause; directly perceived; occurring at once; close in time, location, or relation. **immediately** *adv.*

im-me-mo-ri-al *adj.* Beyond the limits of memory, tradition, or records.

im-mense *adj.* Exceptionally large. **immensely** *adv.,* **immensity** *n.*

im-merse *v.* To put into a liquid; to baptize by submerging in water; to engross; to absorb. -ible *adj.,* -ion *n.*

im-mi-grant *n.* One who leaves his country to settle in another.

im-mi-grate *v.* To leave one country and settle in another. **immigration** *n.*

im-mi-nent *adj.* About to happen. **imminence** *n.*

im-mo-bile *adj.* Not moving or incapable of motion **immobility** *n.*

im-mo-bi-lize *v.* To render motionless. **immobilization** *n.*

im-mod-er-ate *adj.* Exceeding normal bounds. **immoderately** *adv.*

im-mod-est *adj.* Lacking modesty; indecent; boastful. -ly *adv.,* - y *n.*

im-mo-late *v.* To kill, as a sacrifice; to destroy completely. **immolator** *n.*

im-mor-al *adj.* Not moral. -ly *adv.*

im-mo-ral-i-ty *n., pl.* -ies Lack of morality; an immoral act or practice.

im-mor-tal *adj.* Exempt from death; lasting forever, as in fame. *n.* A person of lasting fame. **immortality** *n.,* **immortally** *adv.*

im-mov-a-ble *adj.* Not capable of moving or being moved. -ly *adv.*

im-mune *adj.* Not affected or responsive; resistant, as to a disease. **immunity** *n.*

im-mu-nize *v.* To make immune. **immunization** *n.*

im-mu-nol-o-gy *n.* The study of immunity to diseases. -ic, -ical *adj.,* -ly *adv.*

im-mu-no-sup-pres-sive *adj.* Acting to suppress a natural immune response to an antigen.

im-mure *v.* To confine by or as if by walls; to build into a wall.

im-mu-ta-ble *adj.* Unchanging or unchangeable. **immutability** *n.,* -y *adv.*

imp *n.* A mischievous child.

im-pact *n.* A collision; the impetus or force produced by a collision; an initial, usually strong effect. *v.* To pack firmly together; to strike or affect forcefully.

im-pac-ted *adj.* Wedged together at the broken ends, as an impacted bone; wedged inside the gum in such a way that normal eruption is prevented, as an impacted tooth.

im-pac-tion *n.* Something wedged in a part of the body.

im-pair *v.* To diminish in strength, value, quantity, or quality. **impairment** *n.*

im-pa-la *n.* A large African antelope, the male of which has slender curved horns.

im-pale *v.* To pierce with a sharp stake or point; to kill by piercing in this fashion. **impalement** *n.*

im-pal-pa-ble *adj.* Not perceptible to touch; not easily distinguished. **impalpability** *n.,* **impalpably** *adv.*

im-part *v.* To grant; to bestow; to make known; to communicate.

im-par-tial *adj.* Not partial; unbiased. **impartiality** *n.,* **impartially** *adv.*

im-pass-a-ble *adj.* Impossible to travel over or across.

im-passe *n.* A road or passage having no exit; a difficult situation with no apparent way out; a deadlock.

im-pas-sioned *adj.* Filled with passion.

im-pas-sive *adj.* Unemotional; showing no emotion; expressionless. **impassively** *adv.*

im-pa-tient *adj.* Unwilling to wait or tolerate delay; expressing or caused by irritation at having to wait; restlessly eager; intolerant. **impatiently** *adv.*

im-peach *v.* To charge with misconduct in public office before a proper court of justice; to make an accusation against. -able *adj.,* **impeachment** *n.*

im-pec-ca-ble *adj.* Having no flaws; perfect; not capable of sin. -ly *adv.*

im-pe-cu-ni-ous *adj.* Having no money. **impecuniousness** *n.*

im-ped-ance *n.* A measure of the total opposition to the flow of an electric current, especially in an alternating current circuit.

im-pede *v.* To obstruct or slow down the progress of.

im-ped-i-ment *n.* One that stands in the way; something that impedes, especially an organic speech defect.

im-ped-i-men-ta *pl., n.* Things that impede or encumber, such as baggage.

im-pel *v.* To spur to action; to provoke;

to drive forward; to propel. **impeller** n.

im-pend v. To hover threateningly; to be about to happen.

im-pen-e-tra-ble adj. Not capable of being penetrated; not capable of being seen through or understood; unfathomable. **-ility** n., **-ly** adv.

im-pen-i-tent adj. Not sorry; unrepentant. **impenitence** n.

im-per-a-tive adj. Expressing a command or request; empowered to command or control; compulsory. **imperative** n., **imperatively** adv.

im-per-cep-ti-ble adj. Not perceptible by the mind or senses; extremely small or slight. **imperceptibly** adv.

im-per-fect adj. Not perfect; of or being a verb tense which shows an uncompleted or continuous action or condition. n. The imperfect tense. **imperfectly** adv.

im-per-fec-tion n. The quality or condition of being imperfect; a defect.

im-pe-ri-al adj. Of or relating to an empire or emperor; designating a nation or government having dependent colonies; majestic; regal. n. A pointed beard on the lower lip or chin. **imperially** adv.

im-pe-ri-al-ism n. The national policy or practice of acquiring foreign territories or establishing dominance over other nations. **imperialist** n., **imperialistic** adj.

imperial moth n. A large New World moth with yellow wings and brownish or purplish markings.

im-per-il v. To put in peril; endanger.

im-pe-ri-ous adj. Commanding; domineering; urgent. **imperiousness** n., **imperiously** adv.

im-per-ish-a-ble adj. Not perishable. **imperishably** adv.

im-per-ma-nent adj. Not permanent; temporary. **impermanence** n., **impermanently** adv.

im-per-me-a-ble adj. Not permeable. **impermeability** n., **impermeably** adv.

im-per-mis-si-ble adj. Not permissible; not allowed.

im-per-son-al adj. Having no personal reference or connection; showing no emotion or personality. **-ly** adv.

im-per-son-ate v. To assume the character or manner of. **-ation**, **-tor** n.

im-per-ti-nent adj. Overly bold or disrespectful; not pertinent; irrelevant. **impertinence** n., **impertinently** adv.

im-per-turb-a-ble adj. Unshakably calm. **imperturbability** n., **imperturbably** adv.

im-per-vi-ous adj. Incapable of being penetrated or affected. **imperviously** adv., **imperviousness** n.

im-pe-ti-go n. A contagious skin disease marked by pustules.

im-pet-u-ous adj. Marked by sudden action or emotion; impulsive. **impetuosity** n., **impetuously** adv.

im-pe-tus n. A driving force; an incitement; a stimulus; momentum.

im-pi-e-ty n., pl. **-ies** The quality of being impious; irreverence.

im-pinge v. To strike or collide; to impact; to encroach. **impingement** n.

im-pi-ous adj. Not pious; irreverent; disrespectful. **impiously** adv.

imp-ish adj. Mischievous. **impishly** adv., **impishness** n.

im-pla-ca-ble adj. Not capable of being placated or appeased. **implacability** n., **implacably** adv.

im-plant v. To set in firmly; to fix in the mind; to insert surgically. **-ation** n.

im-plau-si-ble adj. Difficult to believe; unlikely. **implausibility** n., **-ly** adv.

im-ple-ment n. A utensil or tool. v. To put into effect; to carry out; to furnish with implements. **implementation** n.

im-pli-cate v. To involve, especially in illegal activity; to imply.

im-pli-ca-tion n. The act of implicating or state of being implicated; the act of implying; an indirect expression; something implied.

im-plic-it adj. Contained in the nature of someone or something but not readily apparent; understood but not directly expressed; complete; absolute.

im-plode v. To collapse or burst violently inward. **implosion** n.

im-plore v. To appeal urgently to. **implorer** n., **imploringly** adv.

im-ply v. To involve by logical necessity; to express indirectly; to suggest.

im-po-lite adj. Rude.

im-pon-der-a-ble adj. Incapable of being weighed or evaluated precisely. **imponderable** n.

im-port v. To bring in goods from a foreign country for trade or sale; to mean; to signify; to be significant. n. Something imported; meaning; significance; importance. **importer** n.

im-por-tance n. The quality of being important; significance.

im-por-tant adj. Likely to determine or influence events; significant; having fame or authority. **importantly** adv.

im-por-ta-tion n. The act or business of importing goods; something imported.

im-por-tu-nate adj. Persistent in pressing demands or requests. **-ly** adv.

im-por-tune v. To press with repeated requests. **importunity**, **importuner** n.

im-pose v. To enact or apply as compulsory; to obtrude or force oneself or a burden on another; to take unfair advantage; to palm off. **imposition** n.

im-pos-ing adj. Awesome; impressive. **imposingly** adv.

im-pos-si-ble adj. Not capable of existing or happening; unlikely to take place or be done; unacceptable; difficult to tolerate or deal with. **impossibility** n., **impossibly** adv.

im-post n. A tax or duty.

im-pos-tor or **im-pos-ter** n. One who assumes a false identity or title for the purpose of deception.

im-pos-ture n. Deception by the assumption of a false identity.

im-po-tent adj. Without strength or vigor; having no power; ineffectual; incapable of sexual intercourse.

impotence, impotency *n.*, **-ly** *adv.*

im-pound *v.* To confine in or as if in a pound; to seize and keep in legal custody; to hold water, as in a reservoir. **impoundment** *n.*

im-pov-er-ish *v.* To make poor; to deprive or be deprived of natural richness or fertility. **impoverishment** *n.*

im-prac-ti-ca-ble *adj.* Incapable of being done or put into practice. **-ness, impracticability** *n.*, **impracticably** *adv.*

im-prac-ti-cal *adj.* Unwise to put into effect; unable to deal with practical or financial matters efficiently. **impracticality** *n.*

im-pre-cise *adj.* Not precise.

im-preg-nate *v.* To make pregnant; to fertilize, as an ovum; to fill throughout; to saturate. **-ion, -or** *n.*

im-pre-sa-ri-o *n.*, *pl.* **-os** A theatrical manager or producer, especially the director of an opera company.

im-press *v.* To apply or produce with pressure; to stamp or mark with or as if with pressure; to fix firmly in the mind; to affect strongly and usually favorably. *n.* The act of impressing; a mark made by impressing; a stamp or seal for impressing. **impressible** *adj.*, **impresser** *n.*

im-pres-sion *n.* A mark or design made on a surface by pressure; an effect or feeling retained in the mind as a result of experience; an indistinct notion or recollection; a satiric or humorous imitation; the copies of a publication printed at one time.

im-pres-sion-a-ble *adj.* Easily influenced.

im-pres-sion-ism *n.* A style of late nineteenth century painting in which the immediate appearance of scenes is depicted with unmixed primary colors applied in small strokes to simulate reflected light. **impressionist** *n.*, **impressionistic** *adj.*

im-pres-sive *adj.* Making a strong impression; striking. **impressively** *adv.*, **impressiveness** *n.*

im-pri-ma-tur *n.* Official permission to print or publish; authorization.

im-print *v.* To make or impress a mark or design on a surface; to make or stamp a mark on; to fix firmly in the mind. *n.* A mark or design made by imprinting; a lasting influence or effect; a publisher's name, often with the date and place of publication, printed at the bottom of a title page.

im-pris-on *v.* To put in prison. **imprisonment** *n.*

im-prob-a-ble *adj.* Not likely to occur or be true. **improbability** *n.*, **improbably** *adv.*

im-promp-tu *adj.* Devised or performed without prior planning or preparation. **impromptu** *adv.*

im-prop-er *adj.* Unsuitable; indecorous; incorrect. **improperly** *adv.*

improper fraction *n.* A fraction having a numerator larger than or the same as the denominator.

im-pro-pri-e-ty *n.*, *pl.* **-ies** The quality or state of being improper; an improper act or remark.

im-prove *v.* To make or become better; to increase something's productivity or value. **improvable** *adj.*

im-prove-ment *n.* The act or process of improving or the condition of being improved; a change that improves.

im-prov-i-dent *adj.* Not providing for the future. **-ence** *n.*, **improvidently** *adv.*

im-pro-vise *v.* To make up, compose, or perform without preparation; to make from available materials. **-ation, -er, -or** *n.*, **-ory, -orial** *adj.*, **-ally** *adv.*

im-pru-dent *adj.* Not prudent; unwise. **imprudence** *n.*, **imprudently** *adv.*

im-pu-dent *adj.* Marked by rude boldness or disrespect. **-ence** *n.*, **-ly** *adv.*

im-pugn *v.* To attack as false; to cast doubt on.

im-pulse *n.* A driving force or the motion produced by it; a sudden spontaneous urge; a motivating force; a general tendency. *Physiol.* A transfer of energy from one neuron to another.

im-pul-sive *adj.* Acting on impulse rather than thought; resulting from impulse; uncalculated. **impulsively** *adv.*, **impulsiveness** *n.*

im-pu-ni-ty *n.* Exemption from punishment.

im-pure *adj.* Not pure; unclean; unchaste or obscene; mixed with another substance; adulterated; deriving from more than one source or style. **impurely** *adv.*, **impurity** *n.*

im-pute *v.* To attribute something as a mistake, to another; to charge. **imputation** *n.*

in ab-sen-tia *adv.* In the absence of.

in-ac-ces-si-ble *adj.* Not accessible. **inaccessibility** *n.*, **inaccessibly** *adv.*

in-ac-tive *adj.* Not active or inclined to be active; out of current use or service. **inactively** *adv.*, **inactivity, -ness** *n.*

in-ad-e-quate *adj.* Not adequate. **inadequacy** *n.*, **inadequately** *adv.*

in-ad-ver-tent *adj.* Unintentional; accidental; inattentive. **-ly** *adv.*

in-al-ien-a-ble *adj.* Not capable of being given up or transferred. **inalienably** *adv.*, **inalienability** *n.*

in-ane *adj.* Without sense or substance. **inanely** *adv.*, **inanity** *n.*

in-an-i-mate *adj.* Not having the qualities of life; not animated. **inanimately** *adv.*, **inanimateness** *n.*

in-a-ni-tion *n.* Exhaustion, especially from malnourishment.

in-ap-pre-cia-ble *adj.* Too slight to be significant. **inappreciably** *adv.*

in-ar-tic-u-late *adj.* Not uttering or forming intelligible words or syllables; unable to speak; speechless; unable to speak clearly or effectively; unexpressed. **-ly** *adv.*, **inarticulateness** *n.*

in-as-much as *conj.* Because of the fact that; since.

in-au-gu-rate *v.* To put into office with a formal ceremony; to begin officially. **inauguration, inaugurator** *n.*

in--be-tween *adj.* Intermediate. *n.* An intermediate or intermediary.

in between *adv. & prep.* Between.

in-bound *adj.* Incoming.

in-cal-cu-la-ble *adj.* Not calculable; indeterminate; unpredictable; very large. **incalculably** *adv.*

in-can-des-cent *adj.* Giving off visible light when heated; shining brightly; ardently emotional or intense. **incandescence** *n.*

incandescent lamp *n.*

A lamp in which a filament is heated to incandescence by an electric current.

in-can-ta-tion *n.* A recitation of magic charms or spells; a magic formula for chanting or reciting.

in-ca-pac-i-tate *v.* To render incapable; to disable; in law, to disqualify. **incapacitation** *n.*

in-ca-pac-i-ty *n., pl.* -ies Inadequate ability or strength; a defect; in law, a disqualification.

in-car-cer-ate *v.* To place in jail. **incarceration** *n.*

in-car-na-tion *n.* The act of incarnating or state of being incarnated; the embodiment of God in the human form of Jesus; one regarded as personifying a given abstract quality or idea.

in-cen-di-ary *adj.* Causing or capable of causing fires; of or relating to arson; tending to inflame; inflammatory. **incendiary** *n.*

in-cense *v.* To make angry. *n.* A substance, as a gum or wood, burned to produce a pleasant smell; the smoke or odor produced.

in-cen-tive *n.* Something inciting one to action or effort; a stimulus.

in-cep-tion *n.* A beginning; an origin. **inceptive** *adj.*

in-cer-ti-tude *n.* Uncertainty; lack of confidence; instability.

in-ces-sant *adj.* Occurring without interruption; continuous. **incessantly** *adv.*

in-cest *n.* Sexual intercourse between persons so closely related that they are forbidden by law to marry. **incestuous** *adj.*, **incestuously** *adv.*

inch *n.* A unit of measurement equal to 1/12th of a foot. *v.* To move slowly.

in-cho-ate *adj.* In an early stage; incipient. -ly *adv.*, **inchoateness** *n.*

in-ci-dence *n.* The extent or rate of occurrence.

in-ci-dent *n.* An event; an event that disrupts normal procedure or causes a crisis.

in-ci-den-tal *adj.* Occurring or likely to occur at the same time or as a result; minor; subordinate. *n.* A minor attendant occurrence or condition. **incidentally** *adv.*

in-cin-er-ate *v.* To burn up. -ation *n.*

in-cin-er-a-tor *n.* One that incinerates; a furnace for burning waste.

in-cip-i-ent *adj.* Just beginning to appear or occur. **incipience** *n.*, -ly *adv.*

in-cise *v.* To make or cut into with a sharp tool; to carve into a surface; to engrave.

in-ci-sion *n.* The act of incising; a cut or notch, especially a surgical cut.

in-ci-sive *adj.* Having or suggesting sharp intellect; penetrating; cogent and effective; telling. -ly *adv.*, -ness *n.*

in-ci-sor *n.*

A cutting tooth at the front of the mouth.

in-cite *v.* To provoke to action. **incitement**, **inciter** *n.*

in-clem-ent *adj.* Stormy or rainy; unmerciful. **inclemency** *n.*

in-cli-na-tion *n.* An attitude; a disposition; a tendency to act or think in a certain way; a preference; a bow or tilt; a slope.

in-cline *v.* To deviate or cause to deviate from the horizontal or vertical; to slant; to dispose or be disposed; to bow or nod. *n.* An inclined surface.

in-clude *v.* To have as a part or member; to contain; to put into a group or total. **inclusion** *n.*, **inclusive** *adj.*, -ly *adv.*

in-cog-ni-to *adv. & adj.* With one's identity hidden.

in-co-her-ent *adj.* Lacking order, connection, or harmony; unable to think or speak clearly or consecutively. **incoherence** *n.*, **incoherently** *adv.*

in-com-bus-ti-ble *adj.* Incapable of burning. **incombustible** *n.*

in-come *n.* Money or its equivalent received in return for work or as profit from investments.

income tax *n.* A tax on income earned by an individual or business.

in-com-ing *adj.* Coming in or soon to come in.

in-com-men-su-rate *adj.* Not commensurate; disproportionate. -ly *adv.*

in-com-mode *v.* To inconvenience; to disturb.

in-com-mu-ni-ca-do *adv. & adj.* Without being able to communicate with others.

in-com-pa-ra-ble *adj.* Incapable of being compared; without rival. **incomparably** *adv.*

in-com-pat-i-ble *adj.* Not suited for combination or association; inconsistent. **incompatibility** *n.*, **incompatibly** *adv.*

in-com-pe-tent *adj.* Not competent. **incompetence**, **incompetency**,

in-com-plete *adj.* Not complete. **incompletely** *adv.*, **incompleteness** *n.*

in-con-gru-ous *adj.* Not corresponding; disagreeing; made up of diverse or discordant elements; unsuited to the surrounding or setting. -ity *n.*, -ly *adv.*

in-con-se-quen-tial *adj.* Without importance; petty. **inconsequentially** *adv.*

in-con-sid-er-a-ble *adj.* Unimportant; trivial. **inconsiderably** *adv.*

in-con-sid-er-ate *adj.* Not considerate;

thoughtless. -ly *adv.*, -ness *n.*

in-con-sol-a-ble *adj.* Not capable of being consoled. inconsolably *adv.*

in-con-spic-u-ous *adj.* Not readily seen or noticed. -ly *adv.*, -ness *n.*

in-con-stant *adj.* Likely to change; unpredictable; faithless; fickle. inconstancy *n.*, inconstantly *adv.*

in-con-ti-nent *adj.* Not restrained; uncontrolled; unable to contain or restrain something specified; incapable of controlling the excretory functions. -ence *n.*, incontinently *adv.*

in-con-tro-vert-i-ble *adj.* Unquestionable; indisputable. -ly *adv.*

in-con-ven-ience *n.* The quality or state of being inconvenient; something inconvenient. *v.* To cause inconvenience to; to bother.

in-con-ven-ient *adj.* Not convenient. inconveniently *adv.*

in-cor-po-rate *v.* To combine into a unified whole; to unite; to form or cause to form a legal corporation; to give a physical form to; to embody. incorporation, incorporator *n.*

in-cor-po-re-al *adj.* Without material form or substance. incorporeally *adv.*

in-cor-ri-gi-ble *adj.* Incapable of being reformed or corrected. incorrigibility, incorrigible *n.*, incorrigibly *adv.*

in-cor-rupt-i-ble *adj.* Not capable of being corrupted morally; not subject to decay. -ility *n.*, incorruptibly *adv.*

in-crease *v.* To make or become greater or larger; to have offspring; to reproduce. *n.* The act of increasing; the amount or rate of increasing. increasingly *adv.*

in-cred-i-ble *adj.* Too unlikely to be believed; unbelievable; extraordinary; astonishing. -ility *n.*, incredibly *adv.*

in-cred-u-lous *adj.* Skeptical; disbelieving; expressive of disbelief. incredulity *n.*, incredulously *adv.*

in-cre-ment *n.* An increase; something gained or added, especially one of a series of regular additions. -al *adj.*

in-crim-i-nate *v.* To involve in or charge with a wrongful act, as a crime. incrimination *n.*, incriminatory *adj.*

in-cu-bus *n., pl.* -buses *or* -bi An evil spirit believed to seize or harm sleeping persons; a nightmare; a nightmarish burden.

in-cul-cate *v.* To impress on the mind by frequent repetition or instruction. inculcation, inculcator *n.*

in-cul-pate *v.* To incriminate.

in-cum-bent *adj.* Lying or resting on something else; imposed as an obligation; obligatory; currently in office. *n.* A person who is currently in office. incumbency *n.*, incumbently *adv.*

in-cu-nab-u-lum *n., pl.* -la A book printed before 1501.

in-cur *v.* To become liable or subject to, especially because of one's own actions. incurrence *n.*

in-cu-ri-ous *adj.* Lacking interest; detached.

in-cur-sion *n.* A sudden hostile intrusion into another's territory.

in-cus *n., pl.* incudes An anvil-shaped bone in the middle ear of mammals.

in-debt-ed *adj.* Obligated to another, as for money or a favor; beholden. indebtedness *n.*

in-de-cent *adj.* Morally offensive or contrary to good taste. -cy *n.*, -ly *adv.*

in-de-ci-pher-a-ble *adj.* Not capable of being deciphered or interpreted.

in-de-ci-sion *n.* Inability to make up one's mind; irresolution.

in-de-ci-sive *adj.* Without a clear-cut result; marked by indecision. indecisively *adv.*, indecisiveness *n.*

in-dec-o-rous *adj.* Lacking good taste or propriety. -ly *adv.*, indecorousness *n.*

in-deed *adv.* Most certainly; without doubt; in reality; in fact. *interj.* Used to express surprise, irony, or disbelief.

in-de-fat-i-ga-ble *adj.* Tireless. indefatigably *adv.*

in-de-fin-a-ble *adj.* Not capable of being defined. -ness *n.*, indefinably *adv.*

in-def-i-nite *adj.* Not decided or specified; vague; unclear; lacking fixed limits. -ly *adv.*, indefiniteness *n.*

in-del-i-ble *adj.* Not able to be erased or washed away; permanent. -ly *adv.*

in-del-i-cate *adj.* Lacking sensitivity; tactless. indelicacy *n.*, indelicately *adv.*

in-dem-ni-fy *v.* To secure against hurt, loss, or damage; to make compensation for hurt, loss, or damage. indemnification, indemnifier *n.*

in-dem-ni-ty *n., pl.* -ties Security against hurt, loss, or damage; a legal exemption from liability for damages; compensation for hurt, loss, or damage.

in-dent *v.* To set in from the margin, as the first line of a paragraph; to notch the edge of; to serrate; to make a dent or depression in; to impress; to stamp. *n.* An indentation.

in-den-ta-tion *n.* The act of indenting or the state of being indented; an angular cut in an edge; a recess in a surface.

in-den-ture *n.* A legal deed or contract; a contract obligating one party to work for another for a specified period of time. *v.* To bind into the service of another.

in-de-pend-ence *n.* The quality or state of being independent.

in-de-pend-ent *adj.* Politically self-governing; free from the control of others; not committed to a political party or faction; not relying on others, especially for financial support; providing or having enough income to enable one to live without working. *n.* One who is independent, especially a candidate or voter not committed to a political party. independently *adv.*

in-depth *adj.* Thorough; detailed.

in-de-scrib-a-ble *adj.* Surpassing description; incapable of being described. indescribably *adv.*

in-de-ter-mi-nate *adj.* Not determined; not able to be determined; unclear or vague. indeterminacy *n.*, indeterminately *adv.*

in-dex *n.*, *pl.* **-dexes** *or* **-dices** A list for aiding reference, especially an alphabetized listing in a printed work which gives the pages on which various names, places, and subjects are mentioned; something serving to guide or point out, especially a printed character calling attention to a paragraph or section; something that measures or indicates; a pointer, as in an instrument; in mathematics, a small number just above and to the left of a radical sign indicating what root is to be extracted; any number or symbol indicating an operation to be performed on a expression; a number or scale indicating change in magnitude, as of prices, relative to the magnitude at some specified point usually taken as one hundred (100). *v.* To provide with or enter in an index; to indicate; to adjust through.

in-dex-a-tion *n.* The linkage of economic factors, as wages or prices, to a cost-of-living index so they rise and fall within the rate of inflation.

in-dex fin-ger *n.*

The finger next to the thumb.

in-dex of re-frac-tion *n.* The quotient of the speed of light in a vacuum divided by the speed of light in a medium under consideration.

In-di-a *n.* A country in southern Asia.

In-di-an *n.* A native or inhabitant of India; a member of any of various aboriginal peoples of the Americas. **Indian** *adj.*

Indian Ocean *n.* An ocean that extends from southern Asia to Antarctica and from eastern Africa to southeastern Australia.

in-di-cate *v.* To point out; to show; to serve as a sign or symptom; to signify; to suggest the advisability of; to call for. **indication, indicator** *n.*

in-dic-a-tive *adj.* Serving to indicate; of or being a verb mood used to express actions and conditions that are objective facts. *n.* The indicative mood; a verb in the indicative mood.

in-dict *v.* To accuse of an offense; to charge; to make a formal accusation against by the findings of a grand jury. **indictable** *adj.*, **indicter, indictor, indictment** *n.*

in-dif-fer-ent *adj.* Having no marked feeling or preference; impartial; neither good nor bad. **indifference** *n.*, **indifferently** *adv.*

in-dig-e-nous *adj.* Living or occurring naturally in an area; native.

in-di-gent *adj.* Impoverished; needy. **indigence** *n.*

in-di-ges-tion *n.* Difficulty or discomfort in digesting food.

in-dig-nant *adj.* Marked by or filled with indignation. **indignantly** *adv.*

in-dig-na-tion *n.* Anger aroused by injustice, unworthiness, or unfairness.

in-dig-ni-ty *n.*, *pl.* **-ies** Humiliating treatment; something that offends one's pride.

in-di-go *n.*, *pl.* **-gos** *or* **-goes** A blue dye obtained from a plant or produced synthetically; a dark blue.

in-di-go bunt-ing *n.* A small North American bird, the male of which has deep-blue plumage.

in-di-go snake *n.* A non-venomous bluish-black snake found in the southern United States and northern Mexico.

in-di-rect *adj.* Not taking a direct course; not straight to the point. **indirection** *n.*, **indirectly** *adv.*

in-dis-creet *adj.* Lacking discretion. **indiscreetly** *adv.*, **indiscretion** *n.*

in-dis-pen-sa-ble *adj* Necessary; essential. **indispensability, indispensable** *n.*

in-dis-posed *adj.* Mildly ill. **indisposition** *n.*

in-dite *v.* To write; to compose; to put down in writing. **inditer** *n.*

in-di-um *n.* A soft, silver-white, metallic element used for mirrors and transistor compounds, symbolized by In.

in-di-vid-u-al *adj.* Of, for, or relating to a single human being. **individually** *adv.*

in-di-vis-i-ble *adj.* Not able to be divided.

In-do-chi-na *n.* The southeastern peninsula of Asia.

in-doc-tri-nate *v.* To instruct in a doctrine or belief; to train to accept a system of thought uncritically. **indoctrination** *n.*

In-do--Eu-ro-pe-an *n.* A family of languages comprising most of the languages of Europe and parts of southern Asia. **Indo-European** *adj.*

in-do-lent *adj.* Disinclined to exert oneself; lazy. **indolence** *n.*

in-dom-i-ta-ble *adj.* Incapable of being subdued or defeated. **indomitably** *adv.*

In-do-ne-sia *n.* A country of southeastern Asia. **Indonesian** *adj. & n.*

in-du-bi-ta-ble *adj.* Too evident to be doubted. **indubitably** *adv.*

in-duce *v.* To move by persuasion or influence; to cause to occur; to infer by inductive reasoning. **inducer** *n.*

in-duce-ment *n.* The act of inducing; something that induces.

in-duct *v.* To place formally in office; to admit as a new member; to summon into military service. **inductee** *n.*

in-duc-tance *n.* A circuit element, usually a conducting coil, in which electromagnetic induction generates electromotive force.

in-duc-tion *n.* The act of inducting or of being inducted; reasoning in which conclusions are drawn from particular instances or facts; the generation of electromotive force in a closed circuit by a magnetic field that changes with time; the production of an electric charge in an uncharged body by bringing a charged body close to it.

in-dulge v. To give in to the desires of, especially to excess; to yield to; to allow oneself a special pleasure. **indulger** n.

in-dus-tri-al adj. Of, relating to, or used in industry. **industrially** adv.

in-dus-tri-ous adj. Working steadily and hard; diligent. -ly adv., -ness n.

in-dus-try n., pl. -tries The commercial production and sale of goods and services; a branch of manufacture and trade; industrial management as distinguished from labor; diligence.

in-e-bri-ate v. To make drunk; to intoxicate. -ed, -iant adj., inebriation n.

in-ef-fa-ble adj. Beyond expression; indescribable. **ineffably** adv.

in-ef-fi-cient adj. Wasteful of time, energy, or materials. **inefficiency** n., **inefficiently** adv.

in-e-luc-ta-ble adj. Not capable of being avoided or overcome. **ineluctably** adv.

in-ept adj. Awkward or incompetent; not suitable. **ineptitude**, **ineptness** n., **ineptly** adv.

in-e-qual-i-ty n., pl. -ies The condition or an instance of being unequal; social or economic disparity; lack of regularity; in mathematics, an algebraic statement that a quantity is greater than or less than another quantity.

in-eq-ui-ty n., pl. -ies Injustice; unfairness.

in-ert adj. Not able to move or act; slow to move or act; sluggish; displaying no chemical activity. -ly adv., -ness n.

in-er-tia n. The tendency of a body to remain at rest or to stay in motion unless acted upon by an external force; resistance to motion or change. **inertial** adj., **inertially** adv.

in-ev-i-ta-ble adj. Not able to be avoided or prevented. **inevitably** adv.

in-ex-o-ra-ble adj. Not capable of being moved by entreaty; unyielding. **inexorably** adv.

in-ex-pe-ri-ence n. Lack of experience.

in-ex-pli-ca-ble adj. Not capable of being explained. **inexplicably** adv.

in ex-tre-mis adv. At the point of death.

in-ex-tri-ca-ble adj. Not capable of being untied or untangled; too complex to resolve. **inextricably** adv.

in-fal-li-ble adj. Not capable of making mistakes; not capable of failing; never wrong. **infallibility** n., **infallibly** adv.

in-fa-mous adj. Having a very bad reputation; shocking or disgraceful. **infamously** adv.

in-fa-my n., pl. -ies Evil notoriety or reputation; the state of being infamous; a disgraceful, publicly known act.

in-fan-cy n., pl. -ies The condition or time of being an infant; an early stage of existence; in law, minority.

in-fant n. A child in the first period of life; a very young child; in law, a minor.

in-fan-ti-cide n. The killing of an infant.

in-fan-tile adj. Of or relating to infants or infancy; immature; childish.

in-fan-tile pa-ra-ly-sis n. Poliomyelitis.

in-fan-try n., pl. -ries The branch of an army made up of soldiers who are trained to fight on foot. **infantryman** n.

in-farct n. An area of dead tissue caused by an insufficient supply of blood. **infarcted** adj., **infarction** n.

in-fat-u-ate v. To arouse an extravagant or foolish love in. **infatuated** adj., **infatuation** n.

in-fect v. To contaminate with disease-causing microorganisms; to transmit a disease to; to affect as if by contagion. **infective** adj.

in-fec-tion n. Invasion of a bodily part by disease-causing microorganisms; the condition resulting from such an invasion; an infectious disease.

in-fe-lic-i-tous adj. Not happy; unfortunate; not apt, as in expression. **infelicity** n., **infelicitously** adv.

in-fer v. To conclude by reasoning; to deduce; to have as a logical consequence; to lead to as a result or conclusion. **inferable** adj.

in-fer-ence n. A conclusion based on facts and premises.

in-fe-ri-or adj. Located under or below; low or lower in order, rank, or quality. **inferior, inferiority** n.

in-fer-nal adj. Of, like, or relating to hell; damnable; abominable. **infernally** adv.

in-fer-no n. A place or condition suggestive of hell.

in-fest v. To spread in or over so as to be harmful or offensive. **infestation** n.

in-fi-del n. One who has no religion; an unbeliever in a religion, especially Christianity.

in-field n. In baseball, the part of a playing field within the base lines. **infielder** n.

in-fil-trate v. To pass or cause to pass into something through pores or small openings; to pass through or enter gradually or stealthily. **infiltration** n.

in-fi-nite adj. Without boundaries; limitless; immeasurably great or large; in mathematics, greater in value than any specified number, however large; having measure that is infinite. **infinite** n., **infinitely** adv.

in-fin-i-tes-i-mal adj. Immeasurably small. **infinitesimally** adv.

in-fin-i-ty n., pl. -ies The quality or state of being infinite; unbounded space, time, or amount; an indefinitely large number.

in-firm adj. Physically weak, especially from age; feeble; not sound or valid.

in-fir-ma-ry n., pl. -ries An institution for the care of the sick or disabled.

in-flame v. To set on fire; to arouse to strong or excessive feeling; to intensify; to produce, affect or be affected by inflammation.

in-flam-ma-ble adj. Tending to catch fire easily; easily excited.

in-flam-ma-tion n. Localized redness,

swelling, heat, and pain in response to an injury or infection.

in-flate *v.* To fill and expand with a gas; to increase unsoundly; to puff up; to raise prices abnormally. **inflatable** *adj.*

in-fla-tion *n.* The act or process of inflating; a period during which there is an increase in the monetary supply, causing a continuous rise in the price of goods.

in-flect *v.* To turn; to veer; to vary the tone or pitch of the voice, especially in speaking; to change the form of a word to indicate number, tense, or person. **inflective** *adj.*, **inflection** *n.*

in-flex-i-ble *adj.* Not flexible; rigid; not subject to change; unalterable. **inflexibility** *n.*, **inflexibly** *adv.*

in-flict *v.* To cause to be suffered; to impose. **inflicter, inflictor, infliction** *n.*

in-flo-res-cence *n.*

A characteristic arrangement of flowers on a stalk. **inflorescent** *adj.*

in-flu-ence *n.* The power to produce effects, especially indirectly or through an intermediary; the condition of being affected; one exercising indirect power to sway or affect. *v.* To exert influence over; to modify. **influential** *adj.*

in-flu-en-za *n.* An acute, infectious viral disease marked by respiratory inflammation, fever, muscular pain, and often intestinal discomfort; the flu.

in-flux *n.* A stream of people or things coming in.

in-form-ant *n.* One who discloses or furnishes information which should remain secret.

in-for-ma-tive *adj.* Providing information; instructive.

in-frac-tion *n.* A violation of a rule.

in-fra-red *adj.* Of, being, or using electromagnetic radiation with wave lengths longer than those of visible light and shorter than those of microwaves.

in-fra-son-ic *adj.* Producing or using waves or vibrations with frequencies below that of audible sound.

in-fra-struc-ture *n.* An underlying base or foundation; the basic facilities needed for the functioning of a system.

in-fringe *v.* To break a law; to violate; to encroach; to trespass. **infringement** *n.*

in-fu-ri-ate *v.* To make very angry or furious; to enrage. **-ly** *adv.*, **-ation** *n.*

in-fuse *v.* To introduce, instill or inculcate, as principles; to obtain a liquid extract by soaking a substance in water. **infusion** *n.*

-ing *suff* Used in forming the present participle of verbs and adjectives resembling participles; activity or action; the result or a product of an action.

in-gen-ious *adj.* Showing great ingenuity; to have inventive ability; clever. **ingeniously** *adv.*, **ingeniousness** *n.*

in-ge-nu-i-ty *n., pl.* **-ies** Cleverness; inventive skill.

in-gen-u-ous *adj.* Frank and straightforward; lacking sophistication.

in-gest *v.* To take or put food into the body by swallowing. **-ion** *n.*, **-ive** *adj.*

in-gle-nook *n.* A recessed area or corner near or beside a fireplace.

in-glo-ri-ous *adj.* Not showing courage or honor; dishonorable. **-ly** *adv.*

in-got *n.* A mass of cast metal shaped in a bar or block.

in-grain *v.* To impress firmly on the mind or nature. *n.* Fiber or yarn that is dyed before being spun or woven.

in-grained *adj.* To be worked into the inmost texture; deep-seated.

in-grate *n.* A person who is ungrateful.

in-gra-ti-ate *v.* To gain favor or confidence of others by deliberate effort or manipulation. **ingratiatingly** *adv.*, **ingratiation** *n.*, **ingratiatory** *adj.*

in-grat-i-tude *n.* Lack of gratitude.

in-gre-di-ent *n.* An element that enters into the composition of a mixture; a part of anything.

in-gress *n.* A going in or entering of a building. **ingression** *n.*, **ingressive** *adj.*

in-grown *adj.* Growing into the flesh; growing abnormally within or into. **ingrowing** *adj.*

in-gui-nal *adj., Anat.* Of, pertaining to, or located in the groin.

in-hab-it *v.* To reside in; to occupy as a home. **inhabitability, inhabiter, inhabitation** *n.*, **inhabitable** *adj.*

in-hab-i-tant *n.* A person who resides permanently, as distinguished from a visitor.

in-ha-la-tion *n.* The act of inhaling.

in-ha-la-tor *n.* A device that enables a person to inhale air, anesthetics, medicated vapors, or other matter.

in-hale *v.* To breathe or draw into the lungs, as air or tobacco smoke; the opposite of exhale. **inhalation** *n.*

in-hal-er *n.* One that inhales; a respirator.

in-here *v.* To be an essential or permanent feature; to belong.

in-her-ent *adj.* Forming an essential element or quality of something. **inherently** *adv.*

in-her-it *v.* To receive something, as property, money, or other valuables, by legal succession or will. *Biol.* To receive traits or qualities from one's ancestors or parents. **inheritable** *adj.*, **inheritor** *n.*

in-her-i-tance *n.* The act of inheriting; that which is inherited or to be inherited by legal transmission to a heir.

in-her-i-tance tax *n.* A tax imposed on an inherited estate.

in-hib-it *v.* To restrain or hold back; to prevent full expression. **inhibitable** *adj.*, **inhibitor,**

inhibiter *n.*, inhibitive, inhibitory *adj.*

in-hi-bi-tion *n.* The act of restraining, especially a self-imposed restriction on one's behavior; a mental or psychological restraint.

in--house *adj.* Of, relating to, or carried on within an organization.

in-hu-man *adj.* Lacking pity, emotional warmth, or kindness; monstrous; not being of the ordinary human type. inhumanly *adv.*

in-hu-mane *adj.* Lacking compassion or pity; cruel. inhumanely *adv.*

in-hu-man-i-ty *n.*, *pl.* -ties The lack of compassion or pity; an inhumane or cruel act.

in-im-i-cal *adj.* Harmful opposition; hostile; malign. inimically *adv.*

in-im-i-ta-ble *adj.* Incapable of being matched; unique. inimitably *adv.*

in-iq-ui-ty *n.*, *pl.* -ies The grievous violation of justice; wickedness; sinfulness. iniquitous *adj.*

in-i-tial *adj.* Of or pertaining to the beginning. *n.* The first letter of a name or word. *v.* To mark or sign with initials. initially *adv.*

in-i-ti-ate *v.* To begin or start; to admit someone to membership in an organization, fraternity, or group; to instruct in fundamentals. *adj.* Initiated. initiator *n.*, initiatory *adj.*

in-i-ti-a-tive *n.* The ability to originate or follow through with a plan of action; the action of taking the first or leading step. *Govt.* The power or right to propose legislative measures.

in-ject *v.* To force a drug or fluid into the body through a blood vessel or the skin with a hypodermic syringe; to throw in or introduce a comment abruptly. injection *n.*

in-junc-tion *n.* An authoritative command or order; in law, a court order requiring the party to do or to refrain from some specified action. injunctive *adj.*

in-jure *v.* To cause physical harm, damage, or pain.

in-ju-ri-ous *adj.* Causing injury, damage or hurt; slanderous; abusive. injuriously *adv.*, injuriousness *n.*

in-ju-ry *n.*, *pl.* -ies Damage or harm inflicted or suffered.

in-jus-tice *n.* The violation of another person's rights; an unjust act; a wrong.

ink *n.* Any of variously colored liquids or paste, used for writing, drawing, and printing. inker *n.*

ink-ling *n.* A slight suggestion or hint; a vague idea or notion.

ink-stand *n.* A stand or device for holding writing tools and ink.

ink-well *n.* A small container or reservoir for holding ink.

ink-y *adj.* Resembling ink in color; dark; black; containing or pertaining to ink.

in-laid *adj.* Ornamented with wood, ivory, or other materials embedded flush with the surface.

in-land *adj.* Pertaining to or located in the interior of a country. inlander *n.*

in--law *n.* A relative by marriage.

in-lay *v.* To set or embed something, as gold or ivory, into the surface of a decorative design.

in-let *n.* A bay or stream that leads into land; a passage between nearby islands.

in-mate *n.* A person who dwells in a building with another; one confined in a prison, asylum, or hospital.

inn *n.* A place of lodging where a traveler may obtain meals and/or lodging.

in-nards *pl. n.*, *Slang* The internal organs or parts of the body; the inner parts of a machine.

in-nate *adj.* Inborn and not acquired; having as an essential part; inherent. innately *adv.*

in-ner *adj.* Situated or occurring farther inside; relating to or of the mind or spirit.

in-ner ear *n.* The part of the ear which includes the semicircular canals, vestibule, and cochlea.

in-ner-most *adj.* Most intimate; farthest within.

in-ner tube *n.* A flexible, inflatable rubber tube placed inside a tire.

in-ning *n.* In baseball, one of nine divisions of a regulation baseball game, in which each team has a turn at bat. innings *pl.* In the game of cricket, the time or period during which one side bats.

inn-keep-er *n.* The proprietor or manager of an inn.

in-no-cent *adj.* Free from sin, evil, or moral wrong; pure; legally free from blame or guilt; not maliciously intended; lacking in experience or knowledge; naive. innocence, innocent *n.*, innocently *adv.*

in-noc-u-ous *adj.* Having no harmful qualities or ill effect; harmless.

in-nom-i-nate bone *n.*, *Anat.* One of the two large, irregular bones which form the sides of the pelvis.

in-no-vate *v.* To introduce or begin something new. innovative *adj.*, innovator *n.*

in-nu-en-do *n.*, *pl.* -dos or -does An indirect or oblique comment, suggestion or hint.

in-nu-mer-a-ble *adj.* Too numerous or too much to be counted; countless.

in-oc-u-late *v.* To introduce a mild form of a disease or virus to a person or animal in order to produce immunity. inoculation *n.*

in-op-er-a-ble *adj.* Unworkable; incapable of being treated or improved by surgery.

in-op-er-a-tive *adj.* Not working; not functioning.

in-op-por-tune *adj.* Inappropriate; untimely; unsuitable. -ly *adv.*, inopportuneness *n.*

in-or-di-nate *adj.* Exceeding proper or normal limits; not regulated; unrestrained. inordinately *adv.*

in-or-gan-ic *adj.* Not having or involving

living organisms, their remains, or products.

in-pa-tient *n.* A patient admitted to a hospital for medical treatment.

in-put *n.* The amount of energy delivered to a machine; in computer science, information that is put into a data processing system. *Elect.* The voltage, current, or power that is delivered to a circuit.

in-quest *n.* A legal investigation into the cause of death.

in-quire *v.* To ask a question; to make an investigation. **inquirer** *n.*, **inquiringly** *adv.*

in-quir-y *n., pl.* **-ies** The act of seeking or inquiring; a request or question for information; a very close examination; an investigation or examination of facts or evidence.

in-qui-si-tion *n.* A former Roman Catholic tribunal established to seek out and punish heretics; an interrogation that violates individual rights; an investigation. **inquisitor** *n.*, **inquisitorial** *adj.*

in-quis-i-tive *adj.* Curious; probing; questioning. **inquisitively** *adv.*, **inquisitiveness** *n.*

in-sane *adj.* Afflicted with a serious mental disorder impairing a person's ability to function; the characteristic of a person who is not sane. **insanely** *adv.*, **insanity** *n.*

in-san-i-tar-y *adj.* Not sanitary; not hygienic and dangerous to one's health.

in-scribe *v.* To write, mark, or engrave on a surface; to enter a name in a register or on a formal list; to write a short note on a card. *Geom.* To enclose one figure in another so that the latter encloses the former. **inscriber** *n.*

in-scru-ta-ble *adj.* Difficult to interpret or understand; incomprehensible. **inscrutability,** **-ness** *n.*, **-ly** *adv.*

in-sect *n., Zool.* Any of a numerous cosmopolitan class of small to minute winged invertebrate animals with 3 pairs of legs, a segmented body, and usually 2 pairs of wings.

in-sec-ti-cide *n.* A substance for killing insects.

in-sec-tiv-o-rous *adj.* Feeding on insects.

in-se-cure *adj.* Troubled by anxiety and apprehension; threatened; not securely guarded; unsafe; liable to break, fail, or collapse. **insecurely** *adv.*, **insecurity** *n.*

in-sem-i-nate *v.* To introduce semen into the uterus of; to make pregnant; to sow seed. **-ion, inseminator** *n.*

in-sen-sate *adj.* Showing a lack of humane feeling; unconscious.

in-sen-si-ble *adj.* Deprived of consciousness; unconscious; incapable of perceiving or feeling; unmindful; unaware. **insensibility** *n.*, **insensibly** *adv.*

in-sen-ti-ent *adj.* Without sensation or consciousness. **insentience** *n.*

in-sep-a-ra-ble *adj.* Incapable of being separated or parted. **inseparability** *n.*, **inseparably** *adv.*

in-sert *v.* To put in place; to set. *n.* In printing, something inserted or to be inserted. **insertion** *n.*

in-set *v.* To set in; to implant; to insert.

in-shore *adj.* Near or moving toward the shore. **inshore** *adv.*

in-side *n.* The part, surface, or space that lies within. **insides** *n.* The internal parts or organs. **inside** *adj.*

in-sid-er *n.* One having special knowledge or access to confidential information.

in-sid-i-ous *adj.* Cunning or deceitful; treacherous; seductive; attractive but harmful. **-ly** *adv.*, **insidiousness** *n.*

in-sight *n.* Perception into the true or hidden nature of things. **insightful** *adj.*, **insightfully** *adv.*

in-sig-ni-a *n., pl.* **-nia** *or* **-nias** A badge or emblem used to mark membership, honor, or office.

in-sin-cere *adj.* Not sincere; hypocritical. **insincerely** *adv.*, **insincerity** *n.*

in-sin-u-ate *v.* To suggest something by giving a hint; to introduce by using ingenious and sly means. **insinuating** *adv.*, **insinuation** *n.*

in-sip-id *adj.* Lacking of flavor; tasteless; flat; dull; lacking interest. **insipidly** *adv.*, **insipidness** *n.*

in-sist *v.* To demand or assert in a firm way; to dwell on something repeatedly, as to emphasize. **insistence** *n.*, **insistent** *adj.*, **-ly** *adv.*

in-so-far *adv.* To such an extent.

in-sole *n.* The fixed inside sole of a shoe or boot; a removable strip of material put inside a shoe for protection or comfort.

in-sol-u-ble *adj.* Incapable of being dissolved; not soluble; not capable of being solved. **insolubility,** **insolubleness** *n.*, **insolubly** *adv.*

in-sol-vent *adj.* In law, unable to meet debts; bankrupt.

in-som-ni-a *n.* The chronic inability to sleep. **insomniac** *n.*

in-sou-ci-ant *adj.* Lighthearted and cheerful; unconcerned; not bothered. **insouciance** *n.*

in-spect *v.* To examine or look at very carefully for flaws; to examine or review officially. **inspection, inspector** *n.*

in-spi-ra-tion *n.* The stimulation within the mind of some idea, feeling, or impulse which leads to creative action; a divine or holy presence which inspires; the act of inhaling air. **inspirational** *adj.*, **inspirationally** *adv.*

in-spire *v.* To exert or guide by a divine influence; to arouse and create high emotion; to exalt; to inhale; breathe in. **inspirer** *n.*, **inspiringly** *adv.*

in-sta-bil-i-ty *n., pl.* **-ties** Lacking stability.

in-stall *or* **in-stal** *v.* To put in position for service; to place into an office or position; to settle. **installation,**

installer n.

in-stall-ment or in-stal-ment n. One of several payments due in specified amounts at specified intervals.

in-stance n. An illustrative case or example; a step in proceedings. v. To illustrate.

in-stant n. A very short time; a moment; a certain or specific point in time. adj. Instantaneously; immediate; urgent.

in-stan-ta-ne-ous adj. Happening with no delay; instantly; completed in a moment. instantaneously adv.

in-stant-ly adv. Immediately; at once.

in-stead adv. In lieu of that just mentioned.

in-step n., Anat.

The arched upper part of the human foot.

in-sti-gate v. To urge forward; to stir up; to foment; to provoke. instigation, instigator n.

in-still or in-stil v. To introduce by gradual instruction or effort; to pour in slowly by drops. instillation, instiller n.

in-stinct n. The complex and normal tendency or response of a given species to act in ways essential to its existence, development, and survival. instinctive, instinctual adj., -ly adv.

in-sti-tute v. To establish or set up; to find; to initiate; to set in operation; to start. n. An organization set up to promote or further a cause; an institution for educating.

in-sti-tu-tion n. The principle custom that forms part of a society or civilization; an organization which performs a particular job or function, such as research, charity, or education; a place of confinement such as a prison or mental hospital. -ize v., institutional adj., institutionally adv.

in-struct v. To impart skill or knowledge; to teach; to give orders or direction. instructive adj.

in-struc-tion n. The act of teaching or instructing; important knowledge; a lesson; an order or direction.

in-struc-tor n. One who instructs; a teacher; a low-rank college teacher, not having tenure. instructorship, instructress n.

in-stru-ment n. A mechanical tool or implement; a device used to produce music; a person who is controlled by another; a dupe; in law, a formal legal document, deed, or contract.

in-stru-men-tal adj. Acting or serving as a means; pertaining to, composed for, or performed on a musical instrument. instrumentally adv.

in-stru-men-tal-ist n. A person who plays or performs with a musical instrument.

in-stru-men-tal-i-ty n., pl. -ies Anything that serves to accomplish a purpose; means or agency.

in-stru-men-ta-tion n. The use of instruments or work performed with instruments. Mus. The arrangement of music for instruments.

in-sub-or-di-nate adj. Not obedient; not obeying orders. insubordinately adv., insubordination n.

in-sub-stan-tial adj. Unreal; imaginary; not solid or firm; flimsy. insubstantiality n.

in-suf-fi-cient adj. Inadequate; not enough. -ly adv., insufficiency n.

in-su-lar adj. Of or related to an island; typical or suggestive of life on an island; narrow-minded; limited in customs, opinions, and ideas. insularity n.

in-su-late v. To isolate; to wrap or surround with nonconducting material in order to prevent the passage of heat, electricity, or sound into or out of; to protect with wrapping or insulation. insulation, insulator n.

in-su-lin n., Biochem. The hormone released by the pancreas, essential in regulating the metabolism of sugar; a preparation of this hormone removed from the pancreas of a pig or an ox, used in the treatment of diabetes.

in-sult v. To speak or to treat with insolence or contempt; to abuse verbally. n. An act or remark that offends someone. insulter n., insulting adj., insultingly adv.

in-su-per-a-ble adj. Insurmountable; not able to be overcome. insuperability n., insuperably adv.

in-sur-ance n. Protection against risk, loss, or ruin; the coverage an insurer guarantees to pay in the event of death, loss, or medical bills; a contract guaranteeing such protection on future specified losses in return for annual payments; any safeguard against risk or harm. insurability n., insurable adj.

in-sure v. To guarantee against loss of life, property, or other types of losses; to make certain; to ensure; to buy or issue insurance. insurability n., insurable adj.

in-sured n. A person protected by an insurance policy.

in-sur-er n. The person or company which insures someone against loss or damage.

in-sur-mount-a-ble adj. Incapable of being overcome. insurmountably adv.

in-sur-rec-tion n. An open revolt against an established government. -al adj., insurrectionary adj., insurrectionist n.

in-sus-cep-ti-ble adj. Immune; incapable of being infected. insusceptibility n.

in-tact adj. Remaining whole and not damaged in any way. intactness n.

in-take n. The act of taking in or absorbing; the amount or quantity taken in or absorbed.

in-tan-gi-ble adj. Incapable of being touched; vague or indefinite to the mind. -ility, -ness n., intangibly adv.

in-te-ger n. Any of the numbers 1, 2, 3, etc., including all the positive whole numbers and all the negative numbers and zero; a whole entity.

in-te-gral *adj.* Being an essential and indispensable part of a whole; made up, from, or formed of parts that constitute a unity.

in-te-grate *v.* To make into a whole by joining parts together; to unify; to be open to people of all races or ethnic groups. -ion *n.*, integrative *adj.*

in-teg-ri-ty *n.* Uprightness of character; honesty; the condition, quality, or state of being complete or undivided.

in-tel-lect *n.* The power of the mind to understand and to accept knowledge; the state of having a strong or brilliant mind; a person of notable intellect.

in-tel-lec-tu-al *adj.* Pertaining to, possessing, or showing intellect; inclined to rational or creative thought. *n.* A person who pursues and enjoys matters of the intellect and of refined taste. -ity *n.*, intellectually *adv.*

in-tel-lec-tu-al-ize *v.* To examine objectively so as not to become emotionally involved. -ation, intellectualizer *n.*

in-tel-li-gence *n.* The capacity to perceive and comprehend meaning; information; news; the gathering of secret information, as by military or police authorities; information so collected.

in-tel-li-gent *adj.* Having or showing intelligence. intelligently *adv.*

in-tel-li-gi-ble *adj.* Having the capabilities of being understood; understanding.

in-tend *v.* To have a plan or purpose in mind; to design for a particular use. intended *adj.*

in-tense *adj.* Extreme in strength, effect, or degree; expressing strong emotion, concentration, or strain; profound. intensely *adv.*, intenseness *n.*

in-ten-si-fy *v.* To become or make more intense or acute. intensification *n.*

in-ten-si-ty *n.*, *pl.* -ies The quality of being intense or acute; a great effect, concentration, or force.

in-ten-sive *adj.* Forceful and concentrated; marked by a full and complete application of all resources. intensively *adv.*

intensive care *n.* The hospital care provided for a gravely ill patient in specially designed rooms with monitoring devices and life-support systems.

in-tent *n.* A purpose, goal, aim, or design. intently *adv.*, intentness *n.*

in-ten-tion *n.* A plan of action; purpose, either immediate or ultimate.

in-ten-tion-al *adj.* Deliberately intended or done. -ity *n.*, intentionally *adv.*

in-ter *v.* To place in a grave; bury. interment *n.*

inter- *pref.* Mutually; with each other; together; among or between.

in-ter-act *v.* To act on each other or with each other. -ion *n.*, interactive *adj.*

in-ter-breed *v.* To crossbreed; to breed together two different species.

in-ter-cede *v.* To argue or plead on another's behalf. interceder *n.*

in-ter-cept *v.* To interrupt the path or course of; to seize or stop. intercept, interception *n.*

in-ter-cep-tor *or* **in-ter-cept-er** *n.* One who or that which intercepts; a fighter plane designed for the pursuit and interception of enemy aircraft.

in-ter-ces-sion *n.* An entreaty or prayer on behalf of others. intercessor *n.*, intercessional, intercessory *adj.*

in-ter-change *v.* To put each in the place of another; to give and receive in return. *n.* The intersection of a highway which allows traffic to enter or turn off without obstructing other traffic. -able *adj.*, -ably *adv.*, -er *n.*

in-ter-col-le-gi-ate *adj.* Involving or pertaining to two or more colleges.

in-ter-com *n.*, *Informal* A two-way communication system, as used in different areas of a home or business.

in-ter-com-mu-ni-cate *v.* To communicate with each other. -tion *n.*, intercommunicative *adj.*

in-ter-con-ti-nen-tal *adj.* Pertaining to or involving two or more continents.

in-ter-course *n.* Mutual exchange between persons or groups; communication; sexual intercourse.

in-ter-dict *v.* To forbid or prohibit by official decree. -tion, -or *n.*, -ory *adj.*

in-ter-est *n.* Curiosity or concern about something; that which is to one's benefit; legal or financial right, claim, or share, as in a business; a charge for a loan of money, usually a percent of the amount borrowed.

in-ter-est-ed *adj.* Having or displaying curiosity; having a right to share in something. interestedly *adv.*

in-ter-est-ing *adj.* Stimulating interest, attention, or curiosity. interesting *adv.*, interestingness *n.*

in-ter-face *n.* A surface forming a common boundary between adjacent areas; in computer science, the software or hardware connecting one device or system to another. interface *v.*, interfacial *adj.*

in-ter-fere *v.* To come between; to get in the way; to be an obstacle or obstruction. interference *n.*

in-ter-ga-lac-tic *adj.* Between galaxies.

in-ter-im *n.* A time between events or periods. *adj.* Temporary.

in-te-ri-or *adj.* Of, or contained in the inside; inner; away from the coast or border; inland; private; not exposed to view.

in-ter-ject *v.* To go between other parts or elements; to add something between other things. interjector *n.*, interjectory *adj.*

in-ter-jec-tion *n.* A word used as an exclamation to express emotion, as *Oh! Heavens! Super!* interjectional *adj.*

in-ter-lace *v.* To join by weaving together; to intertwine; to blend.

in-ter-lin-e-ar *adj.* Situated or inserted between lines of a text.

in-ter-lock *v.* To join closely.

in-ter-loc-u-tor *n.* One who takes part in a conversation.

in-ter-loc-u-to-ry *adj.* Having the nature of a dialogue; in law, pronounced while a suit is pending and temporarily in effect.

in-ter-lope *v.* To intrude or interfere in the rights of others.

in-ter-lude *n.* A period of time that occurs in and divides some longer process; light entertainment between the acts of a show, play, or other more serious entertainment.

in-ter-mar-ry *v.* To marry someone who is not a member of one's own religion, class, race, or ethnic group. **intermarriage** *n.*

in-ter-me-di-ar-y *n., pl.* **-ies** A mediator. *adj.* Coming between; intermediate.

in-ter-me-di-ate *adj.* Situated or occurring in the middle or between. **intermediately** *adv.* **intermediateness** *n.*

in-ter-min-gle *v.* To blend or become mixed together.

in-ter-mis-sion *n.* A temporary interval of time between events or activities; the pause in the middle of a performance.

in-ter-mit-tent *adj.* Ceasing from time to time; coming at intervals.

in-tern *or* **in-terne** *n.* A medical school graduate undergoing supervised practical training in a hospital. *v.* To confine, as in wartime. **internship** *n.*

in-ter-nal *adj.* Of or pertaining to the inside; pertaining to the domestic affairs of a country; intended to be consumed by the body from the inside.

in-ter-nal--com-bus-tion en-gine *n.* An engine in which fuel is burned inside the engine.

in-ter-nal med-i-cine *n.* The branch of medicine that studies and treats the nonsurgical diseases.

in-ter-na-tion-al *adj.* Pertaining to or involving two or more nations. **-ly** *adv.*

in-ter-na-tion-al-ism *n.* The policy of cooperation among nations where politics and economics are concerned. **internationalist** *n.*

in-ter-nec-ine *adj.* Mutually destructive to both sides; involving struggle within a group.

in-tern-ee *n.* A person who is confined or interned.

in-ter-nist *n.* A physician who is a specialist in internal medicine.

in-ter-play *n.* Action, movement, or influence between or among people.

in-ter-po-late *v.* To insert between other things or elements; to change something by introducing additions or insertions. **interpolation, interpolator** *n.*

in-ter-pose *v.* To put between parts; to put in or inject a comment into a conversation or speech; to intervene. **interposer, interposition** *n.*

in-ter-pret *v.* To convey the meaning of something by explaining or restating; to present the meaning of something, as in a picture; to take words spoken or written in one language and put them into another language. **-able** *adj.,* **interpretation, interpreter** *n.*

in-ter-pre-ta-tive *or* **in-ter-pre-tive** *adj.* Of or based on interpreting; to provide an interpretation. **-ly** *adv.*

in-ter-ra-cial *adj.* Between, among, or affecting different races.

in-ter-reg-num *n., pl.* **-nums** *or* **-na** An interval between two successive reigns; a break in continuity.

in-ter-re-late *v.* To have or to put into a mutual reltionship. **-ationship** *n.*

in-ter-ro-gate *v.* To question formally. **interrogation, interrogator** *n.*

in-ter-rog-a-tive *adj.* Asking or having the nature of a question. *n.* A word used to ask a question. **-ly** *adv.*

in-ter-rupt *v.* To break the continuity of something; to intervene abruptly while someone else is speaking or performing. **-er, -ion** *n.,* **interruptive** *adj.*

in-ter-scho-las-tic *adj.* Conducted between or among schools.

in-ter-sect *v.* To divide by cutting through or across; to form an intersection; to cross.

in-ter-sperse *v.* To scatter among other things. **interspersion** *n.*

in-ter-state *adj.* Between, involving, or among two or more states.

in-ter-stel-lar *adj.* Among or between the stars.

in-ter-stice *n.* The small space between things. **interstitial** *adj.*

in-ter-twine *v.* To unite by twisting together. **intertwinement** *n.*

in-ter-ur-ban *adj.* Between or among connecting urban areas.

in-ter-val *n.* The time coming between two points or objects; a period of time between events or moments. *Mus.* The difference in pitch between two tones.

in-ter-vene *v.* To interfere or take a decisive role so as to modify or settle something; to interfere with force in a conflict. **intervention** *n.*

in-ter-view *n.* A conversation conducted by a reporter to elicit information from someone; a conversation led by an employer who is trying to decide whether to hire someone. **interview** *v.,* **interviewer** *n.*

in-ter-weave *v.* To weave together; to intertwine.

in-tes-tate *adj.* Having made no valid will; not disposed of by a will. **intestacy** *n.*

in-tes-tine *or* **in-tes-tines** *n. Anat.*

The section of the alimentary canal from the stomach to the anus. **intestinal** *adj.,* **intestinally** *adv.*

in-ti-mate *adj.* Characterized by close friendship or association. **-ly** *adv.,* **intimacy, intimateness** *n.*

in-tim-i-date *v.* To make timid or fearful; to frighten; to discourage or suppress by threats or by violence.

intimidation, intimidator *n.*

in-to *prep.* To the inside of; to a form or condition of; to a time in the midst of.

in-tol-er-a-ble *adj.* Not tolerable; unbearable. **-ility, -ness** *n.,* **-ly** *adv.*

in-tol-er-ant *adj.* Not able to endure; not tolerant of the rights or beliefs of others. **intolerance** *n.,* **-ly** *adv.*

in-to-na-tion *n.* The manner of speaking, especially the meaning and melody given to speech by changing levels of pitch.

in-tone *v.* To utter or recite in a monotone; to chant. **intoner** *n.*

in-tox-i-cate *v.* To make drunk; to elate or excite. **intoxicant, intoxication** *n.*

intra- *prefix* Within.

in-tra-cel-lu-lar *adj.* Within a cell or cells.

in-tra-cra-ni-al *adj.* Within the skull.

in-trac-ta-ble *adj.* Hard to manage; difficult to cure or treat.

in-tra-dos *n., pl.* **-dos** *or* **-doses** The interior curve of an arch or vault.

in-tra-mu-ral *adj.* Taking place within a school, college, or institution; competition limited to a school community.

in-tra-mus-cu-lar *adj.* Within a muscle.

in-tran-si-gent *adj.* Refusing to moderate a position; uncompromising. **intransigence, intransigency,** *n.*

in-tra-oc-u-lar *adj.* Within the eyeball.

in-tra-state *adj.* Within a state.

in-tra-u-ter-ine *adj.* Within the uterus.

in-tra-u-ter-ine de-vice *n.* A metal or plastic loop, ring, or spiral inserted into the uterus as a means of contraception.

in-tra-ve-nous *adj.* Within a vein. **intravenously** *adv.*

in-trep-id *adj.* Courageous; unshaken by fear; bold. **-y** *adv.,* **intrepidness** *n.*

in-tri-cate *adj.* Having many perplexingly entangled parts or elements; complex; difficult to solve or understand. **intricacy** *n.,* **intricately** *adv.*

in-trigue *v.* To arouse the curiosity or interest; to fascinate; to plot; to conspire; to engage in intrigues. *n.* A secret or illicit love affair; a secret plot or plan. **intriguer** *n.*

in-trin-sic *adj.* Belonging to the true or fundamental nature of a thing; inherent. **intrinsically** *adv.*

in-tro-duce *v.* To present a person face to face to another; to make acquainted; to bring into use or practice for the first time; to bring to the attention of. **-er, -tion** *n.,* **-tory** *adj.*

in-tro-it *or* **In-tro-it** *n.* A hymn or psalm sung at the beginning of a Roman Catholic Mass.

in-tro-vert *n., Psychol.* A person who directs his interest to himself and not to friends or social activities. **introversion** *n.,* **introversive, -ed** *adj.*

in-trude *v.* To thrust or push oneself in; to come in without being asked or wanted.

in-tu-it *v.* To understand through intui-

tion.

in-tu-i-tion *n.* The direct knowledge or awareness of something without conscious attention or reasoning; knowledge that is acquired in this way. **intuitive** *adj.,* **intuitively** *adv.*

in-un-date *v.* To overwhelm with abundance or excess, as with work. **inundation** *n.*

in-ure *v.* To become used to accepting something which is undesirable. **inurement** *n.*

in-vade *v.* To enter by force with the intent to conquer or pillage; to penetrate and overrun harmfully; to violate; to encroach upon. **invader** *n.*

in-va-lid *n.* A chronically sick, bedridden, or disabled person. **invalid** *adj. & v.*

in-val-id *adj.* Disabled by injury or disease; not valid; unsound. **invalidity** *n.,* **invalidly** *adv.*

in-val-i-date *v.* To nullify; to make invalid. **invalidation, invalidator** *n.*

in-val-u-able *adj.* Priceless; of great value; to be of great help or use. **invaluably** *adv.,* **invaluableness** *n.*

in-var-i-a-ble *adj.* Constant and not changing. **invariably** *adv.*

in-va-sion *n.* The act of invading; an entrance made with the intent of overrunning or occupying. **invasive** *adj.*

in-veigh *v.* To angrily protest. **inveigher** *n.*

in-vei-gle *v.* To win over by flattery. **inveiglement, inveigler** *n.*

in-vent *v.* To devise or create by original effort or design. **inventor** *n.*

in-ven-tion *n.* The act or process of inventing; a new process, method, or device conceived from study and testing.

in-ven-tive *adj.* Skillful at invention or contrivance; ingenious.

in-ven-to-ry *n., pl.* **-ies** A list of items with descriptions and quantities of each; the process of making such a list. **inventory** *v.*

in-verse *adj.* Reversed in order or sequence; inverted. *n.* Something opposite. **inversely** *adv.*

in-ver-sion *n.* The act of inverting or the state of being inverted; that which is inverted.

in-vert *v.* To turn upside down; to reverse the position, condition, or order of something. **-er** *n.,* **-ible** *adj.*

in-ver-te-brate *adj.* Lacking a backbone or spinal column. **invertebrate** *n.*

in-vest *v.* To use money for the purchase of stocks or property in order to obtain profit or interest; to place in office formally; to install; to make an investment. **investor** *n.*

in-ves-ti-gate *v.* To search or inquire into; to examine carefully. **investigative** *adj.,* **-tion, investigator** *n.*

in-ves-ti-ture *n.* The ceremony or act of investing or installing someone in a high office.

in-vest-ment *n.* The act of investing money or capital to gain interest or income; property acquired and kept for future benefit.

in-vig-o-rate *v.* To give strength or vitality to. -ingly *adv.*, invigoration *n.*

in-vin-ci-ble *adj.* Incapable of being defeated. -ility *n.*, invincibly *adv.*

in-vi-o-la-ble *adj.* Secure from profanation; safe from assault. inviolability *n.*

in-vi-o-late *adj.* Not violated. inviolately *adv.*, inviolateness *n.*

in-vis-i-ble *adj.* Not capable of being seen; not visible; not open to view; hidden. invisibility *n.*, invisibly *adv.*

in-vi-ta-tion *n.* The act of inviting; the means or words that request someone's presence or participation.

in-vite *v.* To request the presence or participation of; to make a formal or polite request for; to provoke; to entice; to issue an invitation.

in-vit-ing *adj.* Tempting; attractive. invitingly *adv.*

in-vo-ca-tion *n.* An appeal to a deity or other agent for inspiration, witness, or help; a prayer used at the opening of a ceremony or service.

in-voice *n.* An itemized list of merchandise shipped or services rendered, including prices, shipping instructions, and other costs; a bill. invoice *v.*

in-voke *v.* To call upon for aid, support, or inspiration; to conjure. invoker *n.*

in-vol-un-tar-y *adj.* Not done by choice or willingly. *n. Physiol.* Muscles which function without an individual's control. involuntariness *n.*

in-volve *v.* To include as a part; to make

in-vul-ner-a-ble *adj.* To be immune to attack; impregnable; not able to be physically injured or wounded. invulnerability *n.*, invulnerably *adv.*

in-ward *adj.* Situated toward the inside, center, or interior; of or existing in the mind or thoughts. -ness *n.*, -ly *adv.*

i-o-dine *n.* A grayish-black, corrosive, poisonous element, symbolized by I; a solution made up of iodine, alcohol, and sodium iodide or potassium iodide which is used as an antiseptic.

i-on *n., Physics.* An atom or group of atoms which carries a positive or negative electric charge as a result of having lost or gained one or more electrons.

i-on-ize *v.* To convert completely or partially into ions. ionization *n.*

IOU *abbr.* I owe you.

ip-so fac-to *adv., L.* By that very fact or act.

i-ras-ci-ble *adj.* Easily provoked to anger; quick-tempered. irascibly *adv.*

i-rate *adj.* Raging; angry. irately *adv.*

ir-i-des-cent *adj.* Displaying the colors of the rainbow in shifting hues and patterns. iridescence *n.*

i-ris *n., pl.* irises *or* irides

The pigmented part of the eye which regulates the size of the pupil by contracting and expanding around it. *Bot.* A plant with narrow sword-shaped leaves and large, handsome flowers, as the gladiolus and crocus.

I-rish *adj.* Pertaining to Ireland and its people or their language.

irk *v.* To annoy or to weary.

Iron Age *n.* The most recent of three early stages of human progress, following the Stone Age and the Bronze Age.

i-ron-bound *adj.* Bound with iron; unyielding.

i-ron-clad *adj.* Covered with protective iron plates; strict; unbreakable.

iron curtain *n.* An impenetrable political and ideological barrier between the Soviet bloc and the rest of the world.

i-ron-ic *adj.* Marked by or characterized by irony. ironical *adj.*, ironically *adv.*

iron lung *n.* A tank which encloses the entire body with the exception of the head and regulates the respiration of a patient by alternately increasing and decreasing air pressure.

i-ron-stone *n.* A heavy, white, glazed pottery.

i-ro-ny *n., pl.* -ies A literary device for conveying meaning by saying the direct opposite of what is really meant.

ir-ra-di-ate *v.* To subject to ultraviolet light, radiation, or similar rays.

ir-ra-tion-al *adj.* Unable to reason; contrary to reason; absurd; in mathematics, a number which is not expressible as an integer or a quotient of integers. -ity *n.*, irrationally *adv.*

ir-rec-on-cil-a-ble *adj.* Not able or willing to be reconciled.

ir-re-deem-a-ble *adj.* Not capable of being recovered, bought back, or paid off; not convertible into coin.

ir-re-duc-i-ble *adj.* Not having the capabilities of reduction, as to a smaller amount. -ility *n.*, -ly *adv.*

ir-ref-ra-ga-ble *adj.* Cannot be refuted or disproved. irrefragably *adv.*

ir-re-fut-able *adj.* Cannot be disproved

ir-reg-u-lar *adj.* Not according to the general rule or practice; not straight, uniform, or orderly; uneven. *n.* One who is irregular. -ity *n.*, -ly *adv.*

ir-rel-e-vant *adj.* Not pertinent or related to the subject matter. -ly *adv.*, irrelevance, irrelevancy *n.*

ir-re-lig-ious *adj.* Lacking in religion; opposed to religion. irreligiously *adv.*

ir-re-mis-si-ble *adj.* Unpardonable, as for sin. irremissibility *n.*

ir-re-mov-a-ble *adj.* Not removable.

ir-rep-a-ra-ble *adj.* Unable to be set right or repaired. -ility *n.*, -ly *adv.*

ir-re-place-a-ble *adj.* Unable to be replaced.

ir-re-press-i-ble *adj.* Impossible to hold back or restrain. -ility *n.*, -ly *adv.*

ir-re-proach-a-ble *adj.* Blameless; not meriting reproach. -ness *n.*, -ly *adv.*

ir-re-sist-i-ble *adj.* Completely fascinating; impossible to resist. -bility *n.*

ir-res-o-lute *adj*. Lacking resolution; indecisive; lacking firmness of purpose.

ir-re-spec-tive *adj*. Regardless of.

ir-re-spon-si-ble *adj*. Lacking in responsibility; not accountable.

ir-re-triev-a-ble *adj*. Unable to be retrieved or recovered.

ir-rev-er-ence *n*. A lack of reverence; a disrespectful action. irreverent *adj*.

ir-re-vers-i-ble *adj*. Impossible to reverse. -ility *n*., irreversibly *adv*.

ir-rev-o-ca-ble *adj*. Unable or incapable of being turned in the other direction; incapable of being repealed, annulled or undone. -ility *n*., irrevocably *adv*.

ir-ri-gate *v*. To water the land or crops artificially, as by means of ditches or sprinklers; to refresh with water. *Med*. To wash out with a medicated fluid or water. -ation, -or *n*., irrigational *adj*.

ir-ri-ta-ble *adj*. Easily annoyed; ill-tempered. *Pathol*. To respond abnormally to stimuli.

ir-ri-tate *v*. To annoy or bother; to provoke; to be sore, chafed, or inflamed. -ation *n*., -ant *adj*., -ingly *adv*.

ir-rupt *v*. To burst or rush in; to invade. -ion *n*., irruptive *adj*., irruptively *adv*.

IRS *abbr*. Internal Revenue Service.

is *v*. Third person, singular, present tense of the verb to be.

-ish *suffix* Of or belonging to a nationality or ethnic group; characteristic of; the approximate age of; the approximate time of; somewhat.

is-land *n*. A piece of land smaller than a continent, completely surrounded by water. islander *n*.

isle *n*. A small island.

-ism *suffix* Practice; process; a manner of behavior characteristic of person or thing; a system of principles.

is-n't *contr*. Is not.

i-so-late *v*. To set apart from the others; to put by itself; to place or be placed in quarantine. isolation, isolator *n*.

i-so-la-tion-ism *n*. A national policy of avoiding political or economic alliances or relations with other countries. isolationist *n*.

i-so-mer *n*. A compound having the same kinds and numbers of atoms as another compound but differing in chemical or physical properties due to the linkage or arrangement of the atoms. isomeric *adj*.

i-sos-ce-les tri-an-gle *n*.

A triangle which has two equal sides.

i-so-therm *n*. A line on a map linking points that have the same t e m p e r a t u r e. isothermal *adj*.

i-so-tope *n*. Any of two or more species of atoms of a chemical element which contain in their nuclei the same number of protons but different numbers of neutrons. -ic *adj*., -ically *adv*.

i-so-trop-ic *adj*. Having the same value in all directions. isotropy *n*.

Is-rae-li *adj*. Of or pertaining to the country of Israel or its inhabitants.

Is-ra-el-ite *n*. A Hebrew. Israelite *adj*.

is-sue *n*. The act of giving out; something that is given out or published; a matter of importance to solve. *Med*. A discharge as of pus or blood. *v*. To come forth; to flow out; to emerge; to distribute or give out, as supplies.

isth-mus *n*. A narrow strip of land which connects two larger pieces of land.

it *pron*. Used as a substitute for a specific noun or name when referring to places, things, or animals of unspecified sex; used to refer to the general state of something.

I-tal-ian *adj*. Italian in character. *n*. A person living in Italy.

i-tal-ic *adj*. A style of printing type in which the letters slant to the right. Italics *pl*. Italic typeface.

i-tal-i-cize *v*. To print in italics.

It-a-ly *n*. A country in southern Europe, bordered by the Mediterranean Ocean. Italian *adj*. & *n*.

itch *n*. A skin irritation which causes a desire to scratch; a contagious skin disease accompanied by a desire to scratch; a restless desire or craving.

-ite *suffix* A native or inhabitant of; an adherent of; a sympathizer or follower; a descendant of; a rock or mineral.

i-tem *n*. A separately-noted unit or article included in a category or series; a short article, as in a magazine or newspaper.

i-tem-ize *v*. To specify by item; to list. itemizer, itemization *n*.

it-er-ate *v*. To state or do again; to repeat. iteration *n*.

i-tin-er-ant *adj*. Traveling from place to place; wandering. itinerant *n*.

i-tin-er-ar-y *n*., *pl*. -ies A scheduled route of a trip.

it'll *contr*. It will; it shall.

its *adj*. The possessive case of the pronoun it.

IUD *abbr*. Interuterine device.

I've *contr*. I have.

i-vo-ry *n*., *pl*. -ies A hard, smooth, yellowish-white material which forms the tusks of elephants, walruses, and other animals; any substance similar to ivory. ivories The teeth; the keys on a piano. ivory *adj*.

i-vo-ry-billed wood-peck-er *n*. A type of large and almost extinct woodpecker living in the southeastern U.S.

i-vo-ry black *n*. A type of black pigment which can be made by calcining ivory.

i-vo-ry tow-er *n*. A condition or attitude of withdrawal from the world and reality.

i-vo-ry tow-ered *adj*. To be divorced from practical matters.

i-vy *n*., *pl*. -ies A climbing plant having glossy evergreen leaves.

iz-zard *n*. The letter Z.

J, j *n.* The tenth letter of the English alphabet.

JA *abbr.* Joint account; judge advocate.

jab *v.* To poke or thrust sharply with short blows; a rapid punch.

jab-ber *v.* To speak quickly or without making sense.

Jab-ber-wock-y *n.* A poem characterized by meaningless speech and nonsense syllables; an imitation of this in speech or in writing; gibberish.

jab-ot *n.* A ruffle or decoration on the front of a blouse, dress, or shirt.

ja-cal *n.* A small hut found in the southwestern United States and Mexico, with wall made of rows and rows of thin vertical poles filled in with mud.

jac-a-mar *n.* A tropical, brilliantly colored, insectivorous bird.

jack *n.* The playing card that ranks just below a queen and bears a representation of a knave; any of various tools or devices used for raising heavy objects; the male of certain animals; a man or boy; fellow; a small flag on a ship that indicates nationality. *Electr* A socket into which a plug is inserted to make an electric circuit.

jacks *n.* A game played with a set of six-pronged metal pieces and a small ball.

jack-al *n.* An African or Asian dog-like, carnivorous mammal.

jack-ass *n.*

A male donkey or ass; a stupid person or one who acts in a stupid fashion.

jack-et *n.* A short coat worn by men and women; an outer protective cover for a book; the skin of a cooked potato.

Jack Frost *n.* A name given to frost or winter weather.

jack-hammer *n.* A tool operated by air pressure, used to break pavement and to drill rock.

jack--in--the--box *n.* A toy consisting of a small box from which a puppet springs up when the lid is unfastened.

jack--in--the--pul-pit *n.* A common herb which grows from a turnip-shaped bulb.

Jack Ketch *n.* An executioner.

jack-knife *n.* A large pocketknife; a dive executed by doubling the body forward with the knees unbent and the hands touching the ankles and then straightening before entering the water. *v.* To bend in the manner of a jackknife.

jack-leg *adj.* Deficient in skill or training; having questionable practices; below professional quality or standards.

jack-light *n.* A light used for hunting or fishing at night. *v.* To fish or hunt with a light. **jacklighter** *n.*

jack--of--all--trades *n.* A person who is able to do many types of work.

jack--o--lan-tern *n.* A lantern made from a hollowed out pumpkin which has been carved to resemble a face.

jack-pot *n.* Any post, prize, or pool in which the amount won is cumulative.

jack rabbit *n.*

A large American hare with long back legs and long ears.

Jackson, Andrew *n.* (1767-1845) The seventh president of the United States from 1829-1837.

Ja-cob *n.* A Hebrew patriarch.

Ja-cob's ladder *n.* The ladder Jacob saw in his dreams, which extended from earth to heaven. *Naut.* A ladder with wooden or metal rungs and nonrigid sides. *Bot.* A plant with blue flowers and ladder-like leaflets.

jade *n.* A hard, translucent, green gemstone; an old, worn-out unmanageable horse; a mean old woman; hussy. *adj.* Worn-out; exhausted. **jade** *v.*

jag *n.* A very sharp projection or point. *Slang* A binge or spree.

jag-ged *adj.* Having jags or sharp notches; serrated. **jaggedness** *n.*

jag-uar *n.* A large, spotted, feline mammal of tropical America with a tawny coat and black spots.

jai alai *n.* A game similar to handball in which players catch and throw a ball with long, curved, wicker baskets strapped to their arms.

jail *n.* A place of confinement for incarceration

jail-bird *n.*, *Slang* A prisoner or ex-prisoner.

jail-er *n.* The officer in charge of a jail and its prisoners.

ja-lop-y *n.*, *pl.* **-ies** *Slang* An old, run-down automobile.

ja-lou-sie *n.* A window, blind, or door having adjustable horizontal slats.

jam *v.* To force or wedge into a tight position; to apply the brakes of a car suddenly; to be locked in a position; to block; to crush. *Mus.* To be a participant in a jazz session. *Slang* To be in a difficult situation or to be crowded together, as of people, cars; a difficult situation. **jam** *v.*

jam *n.* A preserve of whole fruit boiled with sugar.

jamb *n.* The vertical sidepiece of a door.

jam-bo-ree *n.* A large, festive gathering.

jam session *n.* An informal gathering of a group of jazz musicians.

jan-gle *v.* To make a harsh unmusical sound. *n.* A discordant sound. **-er** *n.*

jan-i-tor *n.* A person who cleans and cares for a building. **janitorial** *adj.*

Jan-u-ar-y *n.* The first month of the year, having thirty-one days.

ja-pan *n.* A black varnish used for coating objects.

Jap-a-nese *adj.* Pertaining to Japan, its people, or their language.

Jap-a-nese bee-tle *n.* A green and brown beetle which is very damaging to plants.

jape *v.* To joke; to make fun of or mock by words or actions. **jape, -er, -ery** *n.*

jar *n.* A deep, cylindrical vessel with a wide mouth; a harsh sound. *v.* To strike against or bump into; to affect one's feelings unpleasantly.

jar-di-niere *n.* A decorative pot or stand for flowers or plants.

jar-gon *n.* The technical or specialized vocabulary used among members of a particular profession. **jargonistic** *adj.*

jas-mine *or* **jes-sa-mine** *n.* A shrub with fragrant yellow or white flowers.

jas-per *n.* An opaque red, brown, or yellow variety of quartz, having a high polish.

ja-to *n.* A takeoff of an airplane which is assisted by an auxiliary rocket engine.

jaun-dice *n., Pathol.* A diseased condition of the liver due to the presence of bile pigments in the blood and characterized by yellowish staining of the eyes, skin, and body fluids. **jaun-diced** *adj.* To be affected with jaundice.

jaunt *n.* A short journey for pleasure.

jaun-ty *adj.* Having a buoyantly carefree and self-confident air or matter about oneself. **jauntily** *adv.,* **jauntiness** *n.*

Ja-va *n., Slang* Coffee.

jave-lin *n.* A light spear thrown as a weapon; a long spear with a wooden shaft, used in competitions of distance throwing.

jaw *n., Anat.* Either of the two bony structures forming the framework of the mouth and holding the teeth.

jaw-bone *n.* One of the bones of the jaw, especially the lower jaw.

jaw-break-er *n.* A very hard piece of candy. *Slang* A word which is hard to pronounce.

Jaws of Life *n.* A trademark for a metal device having pincer-like arms used to provide access to persons trapped inside a crushed vehicle.

jay *n.* Any of various corvine birds of brilliant coloring, as the blue jay.

Jay-cee *n.* A young man belonging to an organization connected with a city's chamber of commerce.

jay-walk *v., Slang* To cross a street carelessly, violating traffic regulations and or signals. **jaywalker** *n.*

jazz *n.* A kind of music which has a strong rhythmic structure with frequent syncopation and often involving ensemble and solo improvisation. *Slang* Lying and exaggerated talk; idle and foolish talk; liveliness. *Jazz up* To make more interesting; to enliven.

jct *abbr.* Junction.

jeal-ous *adj.* Suspicious or fearful of being replaced by a rival; resentful or bitter in rivalry; demanding exclusive love. **-ly** *adv.,* **jealousness, jealousy** *n.*

jean *n.* A strong, twilled cotton cloth. **jeans** Pants made of denim.

jeep *n.* A trademark for a small, military, and civilian vehicle with four-wheel drive.

jeer *v.* To speak or shout derisively.

Je-ho-vah *n.* God, in the Christian translations of the Old Testament.

je-june *adj.* Lacking in substance or nourishment; immature.

je-ju-num *n., pl.* **-na** *Anat.* The part of the small intestine which extends from the duodenum to the ileum.

jel-ly *n. pl.* **-ies** Any food preparation made with pectin or gelatin and having a somewhat elastic consistency; a food made of boiled and sweetened fruit juice and used as a filler or spread. *v.* To make into jelly; to become or take the form of jelly; to become gelatinous; to assume or cause to assume definite form.

jel-lybean *n.* A small candy having a hard, colored coating over a gelatinous center.

jel-ly-fish *n., pl.* **fishes** Any of a number of freeswimming marine animals of jellylike substance, often having bell or umbrella-shaped bodies with trailing tentacles. *Slang* A person lacking determination; a spineless weakling.

jeop-ard-ize *v.* To put in jeopardy; to expose to loss or danger.

jeop-ard-y *n.* Exposure to loss or danger.

jer-bo-a *n.*

Any of a type of small, nocturnal rodent of Asia and Africa with long hind legs.

jer-e-mi-ad *n.* A lament or prolonged complaint.

Jer-emi-ah *n.* A Hebrew prophet of the seventh century B.C.

jerk *v.* To give a sharp twist or pull to. *n.* A sudden movement, as a tug or twist. *Physiol.* An involuntary contraction of a muscle resulting from a reflex action. *Slang* An annoying or foolish person. **jerky, -ily** *adv.,* **jerkiness** *n.*

jer-kin *n.* A close-fitting jacket, usually sleeveless.

jerk-wa-ter *adj.* Of little importance.

jer-ry--build *v.* To build flimsily and cheaply. **jerry--builder** *n.*

jer-sey *n., pl.* **-seys** A soft ribbed fabric of wool, cotton, or other material; a knitted sweater, jacket, or shirt; fawn-colored, small dairy cattle which yield milk rich in butter fat.

Je-ru-sa-lem *n.* Capital of Israel.

jest *n.* An action or remark intended to provoke laughter; a joke; a playful mood. **jester** *n.*

Jes-u-it *n.* A member of the Society of Jesus, a religious order founded in 1534.

Je-sus *n.* The founder of Christianity, son of Mary and regarded in the Christian faith as Christ the son of God, the Messiah; also referred to as Jesus Christ or Jesus of Nazareth.

jet *n.*

A sudden spurt or gush of liquid or gas emitted through a narrow opening; a jet airplane; a hard, black mineral which takes a high polish and is used in jewelry; a deep glossy black.

jet lag *n.* Mental and physical fatigue resulting from rapid travel through several time zones.

jet set *n.* An international social group of wealthy individuals who travel from one fashionable place to another for pleasure. **jet setter** *n.*

jet stream *n.* A high-velocity wind near the troposphere, generally moving from west to east often at speeds exceeding 250 mph.; a high-speed stream of gas or other fluid expelled from a jet engine or rocket.

jet-ti-son *v.* To throw cargo overboard; to discard a useless or hampering item.

jet-ty *n., pl.* **-ies** A wall made of piling rocks, or other material which extends into a body of water to protect a harbor or influence the current; a pier.

Jew *n.* A descendant of the ancient Hebrew people; a person believing in Judaism. **Jewess** *n.*

jew-el *n.* A precious stone used for personal adornment; a person or thing of very rare excellence or value. *v.* To furnish with jewels. **jewelry** *n.*

jew-eler *or* **jew-el-ler** *n.* A person who makes or deals in jewelry.

Jew-ish *adj.* Of, relating to, or resembling the Jews, their customs, or their religion. **Jewishness** *n.*

Jew's harp *n.* A small musical instrument held between the teeth when played, consisting of a U-shaped frame with a flexible metal piece attached which is plucked with the finger to produce twanging sounds.

Jez-e-bel *n.* The wife of Ahab, queen of Israel in the 9th century B.C., notorious for her evil actions.

jib *n., Naut.* A triangular sail set on a stay extending from the head of the foremast to the bowsprit. *v.* To swing or shift from one side of a vessel to the other.

jif-fy *or* **jiff** *n., pl.* **-ies, jiffs** A very short time.

jig *n.* Any of a variety of fast, lively dances; the music for such a dance. *Mech.* A device used to hold and guide a tool. **jig** *v.*

jig-ger *n.* A small measure holding 1 1/2 oz. used for measuring liquor. *Naut.* A small sail in the stern of a sailing craft. *Slang* Any small item which does not have a particular name.

jig-gle *v.* To move or jerk lightly up and down. *n.* A jerky, unsteady movement.

jig-saw *n.* A saw having a slim blade set vertically, used for cutting curved or irregular lines.

jig-saw puz-zle *n.* A puzzle consisting of many irregularly shaped pieces which fit together and form a picture.

jilt *v.* To discard a lover. *n.* A woman or girl who discards a lover.

jim-my *n., pl.* **-ies** A short crowbar, often used by a burglar. *v.* To force open or break into with a jimmy.

jim-son-weed *n.* A tall, coarse, foul-smelling, poisonous annual weed with large, trumpet-shaped purplish or white flowers.

jin-gle *v.* To make a light clinking or ringing sound. *n.* A short, catchy song or poem, as one used for advertising.

jin-go-ism *n.* Extreme nationalism which is marked by a belligerent foreign policy. **jingoist** *n.,* **jingoistic** *adj.*

jinn *n., pl.* **jin-ni** In the Moslem legend, a spirit with supernatural powers.

jinx *n., Slang* A person or thing thought to bring bad luck; a period of bad luck.

jit-ney *n.* A vehicle carrying passengers for a small fee.

jit-ter *v., Slang* To be intensely nervous.

jit-ter-bug *n., Slang* A lively dance or one who performs this dance.

jit-ters *n.* Nervousness.

jive *n., Slang* Jazz or swing music and musicians.

job *n.* Anything that is done; work that is done for a set fee; the project worked on; a position of employment.

job-ber *n.* One who buys goods in bulk from the manufacturer and sells them to retailers; a person who works by the job; a pieceworker.

job-name *n.* Computer Science. A code that is assigned to a specific job instruction in a computer program, for the operator's use.

jock *n., Slang* A male athlete in college; a person who participates in athletics.

jock-ey *n.* A person who rides a horse as a professional in a race; one who works with a specific object or device.

joc-u-lar *adj.* Marked by joking; playful.

joc-und *adj.* Cheerful; merry; suggestive of high spirits and lively mirthfulness.

jog *n.* A slight movement or a slight shake; the slow steady trot of a horse, especially when exercising or participating in a sport; a projecting or retreating part in a surface or line. *v.* To shift direction abruptly; to exercise by running at a slow but steady pace.

jog-gle *v.* To move or shake slightly.

john *n., Slang* Toilet; a prostitute's client.

John *n.* One of the twelve Apostles.

John Doe *n., Law* A person in a legal proceeding whose true name is unknown.

John Hancock *n.* One of the signer's of the Declaration of Independence.

Slang A signature.

john-ny-cake *n.* A thin bread made with cornmeal.

john-ny--come--late-ly *n.,* *pl.* -ies Slang A late or recent arrival.

Johnson, Lyndon Baines (1908-1973) The 36th president of the United States from 1963-1969.

John the Bap-tist *n.* The baptizer of Jesus Christ.

join *v.* To bring or put together so as to form a unit; to become a member of an organization; to participate.

join-er *n.* A person whose occupation is to build articles by joining pieces of wood; a cabinetmaker; a carpenter.

joint *n.*

The place where two or more things or parts are joined; a point where bones are connected. *Slang* A disreputable or shabby place of entertainment.   **adj.** Marked by cooperation, as a joint effort.

join-ture *n.,* *Law* A settlement of property arranged by a husband which is to be used for the support of his wife after his death.

joist *n.* Any of a number of small parallel beams set from wall to wall to support a floor.

joke *n.* Something said or done to cause laughter, such as a brief story with a punch line; something not taken seriously. *v.* To tell or play jokes.

jok-er *n.* A person who jokes; a playing card, used in certain card games as a wild card; an unsuspected or unapparent fact which nullifies a seeming advantage.

jol-li-fi-ca-tion *n.* Merrymaking; festivity.

jol-ly *adj.* Full of good humor; merry.

jolt *v.* To knock or shake about. *n.* A sudden bump or jar, as from a blow.

Jon-ah *n.* An 8th or 9th century B.C. Hebrew prophet who was swallowed by a whale and then cast on the shore alive three days later; a person who brings bad luck.

jon-quil *n.* A widely grown species of narcissus related to the daffodil, having fragrant white or yellow flowers and long narrow leaves.

Joseph *n.* The husband of Mary, the mother of Jesus.

Joseph of Arimathea *n.* A very wealthy disciple of Christ who provided the tomb for his burial.

josh *v., Slang* To make good-humored fun of someone; to tease; to joke.

Jos-hu-a *n.* The successor to Moses.

joss *n.* A Chinese idol or image.

joss stick *n.* A stick of incense burnt by the Chinese.

jos-tle *v.* To make one's way through a crowd by pushing, elbowing, or shoving. **jostler** *n.*

jot *v.* To make a brief note of some-

thing. *n.* A tiny bit.

jounce *v.* To bounce; to bump; to shake. **jounce** *n.,* **jouncy** *adj.*

jour *abbr.* Journal; journalist.

jour-nal *n.* A diary or personal daily record of observations and experiences; in bookkeeping, a book in which daily financial transactions are recorded. *Mech.* The part of an axle which rotates in or against a bearing.

jour-nal-ese *n.* The vocabulary and style of writing supposedly characteristic of most newspapers.

jour-nal-ism *n.* The occupation, collection, writing, editing, and publishing of newspapers and other periodicals. **journalist** *n.,* **journalistic** *adj.,* **journalistically** *adv.*

jour-ney *n.* A trip from one place to another over a long distance; the distance that is traveled. *v.* to make a trip; to travel a long distance.

jour-ney-man *n., pl.* -men A worker who has served an apprenticeship in a skilled trade.

joust *n.* A formal combat between two knights on horseback as a part of a medieval tournament.

Jove *Interj.* A mild expression of surprise or emphasis.

jo-vi-al *adj.* Good-natured; good-humored; jolly. **joviality** *n.*

jowl *n.* The fleshy part of the lower jaw; the cheek. **jowly** *adj.*

joy *n.* A strong feeling of great happiness; delight; a state or source of contentment or satisfaction; anything which makes one delighted or happy. **joyfully** *adv.,* **joyfulness** *n.,* **joyless** *adj.,* **joylessly** *adv.,* **joylessness** *n.*

joy-ous *adj.* Joyful; causing or feeling joy. **joyously** *adv.,* **joyousness** *n.*

joy ride *Slang* A ride taken for pleasure only.

joy stick *Slang* The control stick of an airplane or video game.

ju-bi-lant *adj.* Exultantly joyful or triumphant; expressing joy. **jubilance** *n.,* **jubilantly** *adv.*

ju-bi-la-tion *n.* Rejoicing; exultation.

ju-bi-lee *n.* A special anniversary of an event; any time of rejoicing.

Ju-dah *n.* In the Old Testament, a son of Jacob and Leah; the ancient kingdom in southern Palestine.

Ju-da-ic *or* **Judaical** *adj.* Of or pertaining to Jews. **Judaically** *adv.*

Ju-da-ism *n.* The religious practices or beliefs of the Jews; a religion based on the belief in one God.

Ju-das *n.* One of the twelve Apostles; the betrayer of Jesus; one who betrays another under the guise of friendship.

Ju-de-a *or* **Ju-dea-a** *n.* The southern part of ancient Palestine. **Judea, Judecan** *adj. & n.*

judge *v., Law* A public officer who passes judgment in a court. *v.* To decide authoritatively after deliberation.

judg-ment *or* **judge-ment** *n.* The ability to make a wise decision or to form an opinion; the act of judging. *Law* The sentence or determination of a court. **judgmental** *adj.*

ju-di-ca-ture *n.* The function or action of administration of justice; law, courts, or judges as a whole.

ju-di-cial *adj.* Pertaining to the administering of justice, to courts of law, or to judges; enforced or decreed by a court of law. **judicially** *adv.*

ju-di-ci-ar-y *adj.* Of or pertaining to judges, courts, or judgments. *n.* The department of the government which administers the law; a system of courts of law.

ju-di-cious *adj.* Having, showing, or exercising good sound judgment. **judiciously** *adv.*, **judiciousness** *n.*

Judith *n.* A Jewish heroine who rescued her countrymen by slaying the Assyrian general, Holofernes.

ju-do *n.* A system or form of self-defense, developed from jujitsu in Japan in 1882, which emphasizes principles of balance and leverage.

jug *n.* A small pitcher or similar vessel for holding liquids. *Slang* A jail.

jug-gle *v.* To keep several objects continuously moving from the hand into the air; to practice fraud or deception. **juggler** *n.*

jug-u-lar *adj.*, *Anat.* Of or pertaining to the region of the throat or the jugular vein.

jug-u-lar vein *n.*, *Anat.* One of the large veins on either side of the neck.

juice *n.* The liquid part of a vegetable, fruit, or animal. *Slang* Electric current.

juic-er *n.* A device for extracting juice from fruit.

juic-y *adj.* Full of; abounding with juice; full of interest; richly rewarding, especially financially. **juiciness** *n.*

juke box *n.* A large, automatic, coin-operated record player equipped with push buttons for the selection of records.

ju-lep *n.* A mint julep.

July *n.* The seventh month of the year, having 31 days.

jum-ble *v.* To mix in a confused mass; to throw together without order; to confuse or mix something up in the mind.

jump *v.* To spring from the ground, floor, or other surface into the air by using a muscular effort of the legs and feet; to move in astonishment; to leap over; to increase greatly, as prices. *Informal* To attack by surprise. *Computer Science* To move from one set of instructions in a program to another set further behind or ahead.

jump-er *n.* One who or that which jumps; a sleeveless dress, usually worn over a blouse. *Electr.* A short wire used to bypass or join parts of a circuit.

jump shot *n.*, *Basketball* A shot made at the highest point of a jump.

jump-y *adj.* Nervous; jittery. **-iness** *n.*

junc-tion *n.* The place where lines or routes meet, as roads or railways; the

process of joining or the act of joining.

June *n.* The sixth month of the year, having 30 days.

June beetle *or* **June bug** *n.* A large, brightly colored beetle which flies in June and has larvae that live in the soil and often destroy crops.

jun-gle *n.* A densely covered land with tropical vegetation, usually inhabited by wild animals. **jungle** *adj.*

jun-ior *adj.* Younger in years or rank, used to distinguish the son from the father of the same first name; the younger of two. *n.* The third year of high school or college.

ju-ni-per *n.* An evergreen shrub or tree of Europe and America with dark blue berries, prickly foliage, and fragrant wood.

junk *n.* Discarded material, as glass, scrap iron, paper, or rags; a flat-bottomed Chinese ship with battened sails; rubbish; worthless matter. *Slang* Heroin, narcotics or dope.

jun-ket *n.* A party, banquet, or trip; a trip taken by a public official with all expenses paid for by public funds; a custard-like dessert of flavored milk set with rennet. **junket** *v.*, **junketeer** *n.*

junk-ie *or* **junk-y** *n.* Slang A drug addict that uses heroin.

Juno *n.* In Roman mythology, the queen of heaven.

jun-ta *n.* A body of men or persons, as military officers, in power following a coup d'etat.

Ju-pi-ter *n.*, *Astron.* The fifth planet from the sun; the largest planet in the solar system.

ju-rid-i-cal *or* **ju-rid-ic** *adj.* Of or pertaining to the law and to the administration of justice.

ju-ris-dic-tion *n.* The lawful right or power to interpret and apply the law; the territory within which power is exercised. **jurisdictional** *adj.*

ju-ror *n.* A person who serves on a jury.

ju-ry *n.*, *pl.* **-ies** A group of legally qualified persons summoned to serve on a judicial tribunal to give a verdict according to evidence presented.

just *adj.* Fair and impartial in acting or judging; morally right; merited; deserved; based on sound reason. *adv.* To the exact point; precisely; exactly right. **justly** *adv.*, **justness** *n.*

jus-tice *n.* The principle of moral or ideal rightness; conformity to the law; the abstract principle by which right and wrong are defined; a judge.

justified margin *n.* A typing or typesetting margin with all the characters at the ends of the lines vertically aligned.

jus-ti-fy *v.* To be just, right, or valid; to declare guiltless; to adjust or space lines to the proper length. **-iable** *adj.*,

jut *v.* To extend beyond the main portion; to project.

ju-ve-nile *adj.* Young; youthful; not yet an adult. *n.* A young person; an actor who plays youthful roles; a child's book.

K, k The eleventh letter of the English alphabet. In Computer science, a unit of storage capacity equal to 1024 bytes.

Kaa-ba *n.* Building in the Great Mosque at Mecca.

ka-bob *n.* Cubed meat and vegetables placed on a skewer.

ka-bu-ki *n.* A traditional Japanese drama in which dances and songs are performed in a stylized fashion.

kaf-fee klatsch *n.* An informal get-together to drink coffee and talk.

kai-nite *n.* A mineral that is used as a fertilizer and a source of magnesium and potassium.

kai-ser *n.* An Austrian ruler from 1804-1918; an emperor.

ka-ka-po *n.* A large parrot.

ka-lie-do-scope *n.* A tubular instrument rotated to make successive symmetrical designs by using mirrors reflecting the changing patterns made by pieces of loose colored glass at the end of a tube. -ic, -ical *adj.*, -ally *adv.*

kame *n.* A short ridge of gravel and sand that remains after glacial ice melts.

kam-ik *n.* Boot made of sealskin, knee-high in length.

ka-mi-ka-ze *n.* A Japanese pilot in World War II trained to make a suicidal crash; an aircraft loaded with explosives used in a suicide attack.

kan-ga-roo *n.*, *pl.* -roo, roos

Any of various herbivorous marsupials, of Australia, with short forelegs, large hind limbs, capable of jumping, and a large tail.

ka-o-lin *or* **ka-o-line** *n.* A fine clay used in ceramics.

ka-pok *n.* A silky fiber manufactured from the fruit of the silk-cotton tree and used for stuffing cushions and life preservers.

ka-put *adj.*, *Slang* Destroyed or out of order.

kar-a-kul *n.* Any of a breed of fat-tailed sheep of central Asia having a narrow body and coarse wiry, brown fur.

kar-at *n.* A unit of measure for the fineness of gold; a measure of weight for precious gems.

ka-ra-te *n.* A Japanese art of self-defense.

kar-ma *n.* The over-all effect of one's behavior, held in Hinduism and Buddhism to determine one's destiny in a future existence. **karmic** *adj.*

ka-ross *n.* Animal skins sewn together worn by natives.

ka-ty-did *n.* Any of various green insects related to grasshoppers and crickets, having specialized organs on the wings of the male that make a shrill sound when rubbed together.

katz-en-jam-mer *n.* A feeling of uneasiness, worry, or nervousness.

kay-ak *n.* A watertight Eskimo boat with a light frame and covered with sealskin.

kay-o *n.* To knock our an opponent, in boxing.

ka-zoo *n.* A toy musical instrument with a paper membrane which vibrates when a player hums into the tube.

ke-a *n.* A New Zealand parrot.

kedge *n.* A small anchor. *v.* Pull a ship by the rope of an anchor.

keel *n.* The central main stem on a ship or aircraft which runs lengthwise along the center line from bow to stern, to which a frame is built upwards. *v.* To capsize. *keel over.* To fall over suddenly; turn upside down.

keen *adj.* Having a sharp edge or point; acutely painful or harsh; intellectually acute; strong; intense. *Slang* Great. -ly *adv.*, **keenness** *n.*, **keener** *n.*

keep *v.* To have and hold; to not let go; to maintain, as business records; to know a secret and not divulge it; to protect and defend. -er *n.*, -ing *n.*

keep back *v.* To withhold things; to prevent one from coming forward.

keep-er *n.* One who keeps, guards, or maintains something; a person who respects or observes a requirement; a device for holding something in place, as a latch, or clasp.

keep-ing *n.* Charge or possession; conformity or harmony; maintenance or support; be consistent with.

keep off *v.* To fend or avert off. *v.* To stay back or remain at a distance.

keep-sake *n.* A memento or souvenir; a token or remembrance of friendship.

kef *n.* A tranquil and dreamy state; a narcotic.

keg *n.* A small barrel usually having the capacity of five to ten gallons; the unit of measure for nails which equals 100 pounds.

Keller, Helen *n.* 1880-1968 American author and lecturer who was deaf, mute, and blind.

kelp *n.* Any of a large brown seaweeds.

kel-pie *n.* A sheep dog originally bred in Australia.

Kel-vin *adj.* Designating or relating to the temperature scale having a zero point of approximately -273. 15 degree C.

kemp *n.* A course hairlike fiber used in the making of carpet.

ken-nel *n.* A shelter for or a place where dogs or cats are bred, boarded, or trained. **kenneled, kenneling.** *v.*

Ken-ny meth-od *n.*, *Med.* A treatment for poliomyelitis that involves both exercise and hot applications.

ke-no *n.* A game of chance resembling bingo; a lottery game.

kep-i *n.* a French military cap having a flat, round top and a visor.

ker-a-tin *n.* A fibrous protein which forms the basic substance of nails, hair, horns, and hoofs. **keratinous** *adj.*

ker-chief *n.* A piece of cloth usually

worn around the neck or on the head; scarf. **kerchiefed, kerchieft** *adj.*

ker-mis *n.* An annual fair of the Netherlands.

ker-nel *n.* A grain or seed, as of corn, enclosed in a hard husk; the inner substance of a nut; the central, most important part. **kernelly** *adj.*

ker-o-sene *or* **ker-o-sine** *n.* An oil distilled from petroleum or coal and used for illumination.

kes-trel *n.* A small falcon, with gray and brown plumage.

ketch *n.* A small sailing vessel with two masts.

ketch-up *n.* A thick, smooth sauce made form tomatoes.

ke-tene *n.* A gas which is colorless and poisonous.

ke-to *adj.* Having a ketone.

ke-tol *n.* Organic compound having a ketone and alcohol group.

ke-tone *n.* An organic compound; used as a solvent; acetone. **-ic** *adj.*, **-sis** *n.*

ket-tle *n.* A pot, usually made of metal, used for stewing or boiling.

ket-tle-drum *n.* A musical instrument with a parchment head which can be tuned by adjusting the tension.

ket-tle of fisk *n.* A mess; an awkward situation; matter of consideration.

key *n.* An object used to open a lock; button or level pushed on a keyboard of a typewriter, piano, etc.; the crucial or main element. **keyed** *adj.*

Key, Francis Scott *n.* 1779-1843. American poet and lawyer.

key-board *n.* A bank of keys, as on a piano, typewriter, or computer terminal. *v.* To set by means of a keyed typesetting machine; to generate letters by means of a word processor.

key club *n.* A private club that offers entertainment and serves liquor.

key-hole *n.* Lock; area that a key is inserted into.

key-note *n.*, *Mus.* The first and harmonically fundamental tone of a scale; main principle or theme.

key-note ad-dress *n.* An opening speech that outlines issues for discussion.

key-punch *n.* A machine operated from a keyboard that uses punched holes in tapes or cards for data processing systems. **keypunch** *n.*, **keypuncher** *v.*

key-stone *n.* The wedge-shaped stone at the center of an arch that locks its parts together; an essential part.

key-stroke *n.* A stroke of a key, as of a typewriter.

kg *abbr.* Kilogram.

khad-dar *n.* Cloth made from cotton.

khak-i *n.* A yellowish brown or olive-drab color; a sturdy cloth being khaki in color. **khakis** A uniform of khaki cloth. **khaki** *adj.*

khan *n.* An Asiatic title of respect; a medieval Turkish, Mongolian or Tartar ruler. **khanate** *n.*

khe-dive *n.* A ruler of Egypt from 1867 to 1914 governing as a viceroy of the sultan of Turkey.

kib-itz *v.* Slang To look on and offer meddlesome advice to others. **kibitzer** *n.*

kick *v.* To strike something with a force by the foot. **kick in** To put in money. **kick out** To expel with force. **kicker** *n.*

kick-back *n.* A secret payment to a person who can influence a source of income; repercussion; a strong reaction.

kick-off *n.* The play that begins a game of soccer or football.

kick-stand *n.* The swiveling bar for holding a two-wheeled vehicle upright.

kid *n.* A young goat; leather made from the skin of a young goat. *Slang* A child; youngster *v.* To mock or tease playfully to deceive for fun; to fool. **kiddish** *adj.*, **kiddishness, kidder** *n.*

kid-nap *v.* To seize and hold a person; unlawfully, often for ransom. **kidnapper** *n.*, **kidnaping, kidnapping** *v.*

kid-ney *n.*, *pl.* **-neys**

Either of two organs situated in the abdominal cavity of vertebrates whose function is to keep proper water balance in the body and to excrete wastes in the form of urine.

kidney bean *n.* A bean grown for its edible seeds.

kidvid *n.*, *Slang* Television programming for kids.

kiel-ba-sa *n.* A smoked Polish sausage.

kill *n.* To put to death; nullify; cancel; to slaughter for food; to deprive of life; to neutralize or destroy the active qualities. **killer** *n.*

kill-deer *n.*, *pl.* **-deer, -deers** A bird characterized by a plaintive, penetrating cry.

kill-er whale *n.* A black and white carnivorous whale, found in the colder waters of the seas.

kil-lick *n.* An anchor for a boat sometimes consisting of a stone secured by wood.

kil-li-fish *n.* A fish found in North America belonging to the family Cyprinodontidea.

kill-ing *n.* The act of a person who kills; a slaying. **killingly** *adv.*

kill-joy *n.* One who spoils the enjoyment of others.

kiln *n.* An oven or furnace for hardening or drying a substance, especially one for firing ceramics, pottery, etc.

ki-lo *n.* A kilogram.

kil-o-bit *n.* In computer science, one thousand binary digits.

kil-o-cal-o-rie *n.* One thousand gram calories.

ki-lo-cy-cle *n.* A unit equal to one thousand cycles, one thousand cycles per second.

kil-o-gram *n.* A measurement of weight in the meteoric system equal to slightly more than one third of a pound.

kil-o-li-ter *n.* Metric measurement equal

to one thousand liters.

kil-o-me-ter *n.* Metric measurement equal to one thousand meters.

kil-o-ton *n.* One thousand tons; an explosive power equal to that of one thousand tons of TNT.

kil-o-volt *n.* One thousand volts.

kil-o-watt *n.* A unit of power equal to one thousand watts.

kil-o-watt-hour *n.* A unit of electric power consumption of one thousand watts throughout one hour.

kilt *n.* A knee-length wool skirt with deep pleats, usually of tartan, worn especially by men in the Scottish Highlands.

kil-ter *n.* Good condition; proper or working order.

ki-mo-no *n.* A loose, Japanese robe with a wide sash; a loose robe worn chiefly by women.

kin *n.* One's relatives by blood; relatives collectively.

kind *n.* A characteristic; a variety.

kind *adj.* Of a friendly, or good-natured disposition; coming from a good-natured readiness to please others. **kindness** *n.*

kin-der-gar-ten *n.* A school or class for young children from the ages of four to six to further their social, mental and physical development.

kin-der-gart-ner *n.* A child who attends kindergarten.

kind-heart-ed *adj.* Having much generosity and kindness.

kin-dle *v.* To ignite; to catch fire; to stir up; to arouse; to excite, as the feelings.

kind-less *adj.* Mean, cruel, unkind, unfriendly. **kindlessly** *adv.*

kin-dling *n.* Easily ignited material such as, sticks, wood chips, etc. used to start a fire.

kind-ly *adv.* A kind nature, disposition, or character; benevolent. **kindliness** *n.*

kind-ness *n.* An act of good will; state or quality of being kind.

kin-dred *n.* A person's relatives by blood. *adj.* Having a like nature; similar. **kindredness** *n.*

kin-e-mat-ics *n.* The branch of dynamics that deals with motion considered apart from force and mass. **kinematic, kinematical** *adj.*, **kinematically** *adv.*

kin-e-scope *n.* A cathode-ray tube in a television set which translates received electrical into a visible picture on a screen; a film of a television on broadcast.

ki-ne-sics *n.* To study the relationship between communication and body language. **kinesic** *adj.*, **-ally** *adv.*

ki-ne-si-ol-o-gy *n.* Science that investigates organic and anatomy process in reference to human motion.

kin-es-the-sia *n.* The sense of muscular movement or effort. **-is, -tic** *adj.*

ki-net-ic *adj.* Of, or pertaining to, or produced by motion.

ki-net-ic art *n.* The type of modern abstract art that attempts to present or indicate a sense of motion.

ki-ne-to-scope *n.* The early form of the motion picture, where a series of pictures pass beneath a small opening for viewing, at a high rate of speed.

king *n.* One who rules over a country; a male ruler; a playing card with a picture of a king; the main piece in the game of chess; a crowned checker in the game of checkers. **kingship** *n.*

king-bird *n.* A North American bird belonging to the genus Tyrannus.

king-bolt *n.* A vertical central vehicle to the front axle.

king crab *n.* A large crab-like crustacean common in the coastal waters of Japan, Alaska, and Siberia.

king-craft *n.* The art of ruling as a king; the profession and techniques used by a king.

king-dom *n.* The area or the country which is ruled by a king or queen. **kingdomless** *adj.*

king-fish *n.* A large fish used for food.

king-fish-er *n.* A bright colored bird having a long stout bill and short tails and feeds on fish and insects.

King James Bible *n.* An English translation of the Bible from Hebrew and Greek published in 1611 authorized by King James I of England.

king-let *n.* A very small bird; a king of little importance.

king-ly *adj.* Pertaining to or belonging to a king or kings; monarchical; splendid; befitting a king.

king-pin *n.* The foremost pin of a set arranged in order for playing bowling or tenpins; the most important or essential person.

king post *n.* A post located between the tie beam and the apex of a roof truss.

king-ship *n.* A monarchy; the state, or dignity of a king.

king--size *adj.* Very large; larger than the standard size.

king snake *n.* Large snake found in the southern United States which is non-poisonous.

king-wood *n.* Wood of Brazil with violet-colored stripes.

kink *n.* A tight twist or knot-like curl; a sharp painful muscle cramp; a mental quirk. *v.* To form or cause to form a kink.

kink-y *adj.* Tightly curled; sexually uninhibited. **kinkily** *adv.*, **kinkiness** *n.*

kin-ka-jou *n.* A tropical American mammal having large eyes, brown fur and a long prehensile tail.

ki-osk *n.* A small building used as a refreshment booth or newsstand.

kip *n.* The untanned skin of a calf, a lamb and or an adult of any small breed; a bundle of such hides.

kip-per *n.* A salted and smoked herring or salmon. *v.* To cure by salting, smoking, or drying.

kirk *n.* The Presbyterian Church of Scotland as opposed to the Episcopal Church of Scotland.

Kir-man *n.* An elaborate Persian rug having elaborate floral designs and soft colors.

kir-tle *n.* A woman's long skirt or petticoat; a man's tunic or coat.

kis-met *n.* Fate; appointed lot.

kiss *v.* To touch two lips together in greeting, between two people.
kissable *adj.*

kit *n.* A collection of tools, supplies, or items for a special purpose.

kitch-en *n.* A room in a house or building used to prepare and cook food.

kitch-en-ette *n.* A small area that functions ar a kitchen.

kitch-en-ware *n.* Dishes, pots, pans, and other utensils that are used in a kitchen.

kite *n.* A light-weight framework of wood and paper designed to fly in a steady breeze at the end of a string; any of various predatory birds of the hawk family having a long, usually forked tail.

kith *or* **kin** *n.* Acquaintances or family.

kitsch *n.* Anything that is pretentious and in poor taste.

kit-ten *n.*

A young cat. -ish *adj.*

kit-ty *n.* A small collection or accumulation of objects or money; a young cat or kitten.

kit-ty-cor-nered *adj.* Diagonally; catty-cornered.

ki-va *n.* A Pueblo Indian chamber, used in ceremonies, often underground.

Ki-wa-ni-an *n.* A member of a major national and international service club organized to promote higher business standards and provides service to the community.

ki-wi *n.* A flightless bird, of New Zealand having vestigial wings and a long, slender bill; a vine, native to Asia, which yields a fuzzy-skinned, edible fruit; the fruit of this vine; a student who has not piloted a plane solo.

ki *abbr.* Kiloliter.

klatch, klatsch *n.* A social gathering devoted primarily to small talk and gossip.

klep-to-ma-ni-a *n.* Obsessive desire to steal or impulse to steal, especially without economic motive. -iac *n.*

kloof *n.* A ravine; gorge; deep mountain cleft.

klutz *n., Slang* A stupid or clumsy person. **klutziness** *n.*, **klutzy** *adj.*

km *abbr.* Kilometer.

knack *n.* A natural talent; aptitude.

knack-wurst *or* **knock-wurst** *n.* A thick or short, heavily seasoned sausage.

knap-sack *n.* A supply or equipment bag, as of canvas or nylon, worn strapped across the shoulders.

knave *n.* Tricky; or dishonest person; a rascal. -ish *adj.*, -ly *adv.*, -ry *n.*

knead *v.* To work dough into a uniform mass; to shape by or as if by kneading.

knee *n.* The joint in the human body which connects the calf with the thigh.

knee-cap *n.* Patella; bone covering the joint of the knee.

knee-deep *adj.* So deep that it reaches ones knees.

kneel *v.* To go down upon one's knees. **kneeler** *n.*

knell *v.* To sound a bell, especially when rung for a funeral; to tolr. *n.* An act or instance of knelling; a signal of disaster.

knick-ers *pl. n.* Short loose-fitting pants gathered at the knee.

knick-knack *n.* A trinket; trifling article.

knife *n.* An instrument used to cut an item. knifed, knifing *v.*

knife edge *n.* A very sharp edge; the edge of a knife.

knife switch *n.* A switch used to close a circuit.

knight *n.* A medieval soldier serving a monarch; a chess piece bearing the shape of a horse's head.

knight-hood *n.* The character of a knight.

knight-ly *adj.* Dealing with a knight.

knish *n.* Baked or fried dough stuffed with meat, cheese, or potatoes.

knit *v.*

To form by intertwining thread or yarn, by interlocking loops of a single yarn by means of needles; to fasten securely; to draw together.

knitting needle *n.* A long, slender, pointed rod for knitting.

knob *n.* A rounded protuberance; a lump; a rounded mountain; a rounded handle. knobbed *adj.*, knobby *adj.*

knock *v.* To hit or strike with a hard blow; to criticize; to collide; to make a noise, as that of a defective engine.

knock-down *adj.* Designed to be easily assembled for storage or shipment. knockdown *n.*

knock down *v.* To strike to the ground with or as with a sharp blow.

knock down drag out *adj.* Extremely violent or bitter.

knock-er *n.* One who or that which knocks; as a metal ring for knocking on a door.

knock-knee *n.* A condition in which one or both knees turn inward and knock or rub together while walking.

knoll *n.* A small round hill; a mound.

knot *n.* A interwinding as of string or rope; a fastening made by tying together lengths of material, as string; a unifying bond, especially of marriage; a hard node on a tree from which a branch grows. *Naut.* A unit of speed, also called a nautical mile which equals approximately 1.15 statute miles per hour. -ted, -ting *v.*

knot-hole *n.* A hole in lumber left by the falling out of a knot.

knout *n.* A whip or scourge for flogging criminals. **knout** *v.*

know *v.* To perceive directly as fact or truth; to believe to be true; to be certain of; to be familiar with or have experience of. **-able** *adj.*, **-ledge, -er** *n.*

know-how *n.* Knowing how to do something.

know-ing *adj.* To be astute; to know secret knowledge. **knowingly** *adv.*

knowl-edge *n.* Having ability to know facts, information.

knowl-edge-a-ble *adj.* The state of being intelligent.

know--noth-ing *n.* An extremely stupid person.

knuck-le *n.* On the finger; the joint of the finger. **knuckly** *adj.*

knuck-le ball *n.* A pitch used in baseball that is a slow pitch.

knuck-le-bone *n.* The bone of the finger which forms the knuckle.

knuck-le-head *n.* A person who is not very smart; dumb.

knur *n.* A lump or knot of a tree.

knurl *n.* A ridge. **knurled, knurly** *adj.*

ko-a-la *n.*

An Australian marsupial which has large hairy ears, gray fur, and feeds on eucalyptus leaves.

Ko-di-ak- bear *n.* A type of large bear that is found in Alaska.

kohl *n.* Dark powder used as cosmetics to darken under the eyes.

kohl-ra-bi *n., pl.* **-ies** A variety of cabbage having a thick stem and eaten as a vegetable.

ko-la *n.* The tree which produce: the kola nut.

ko-la nut *n.* The brownish nut used as a tonic and stimulant.

ko-lin-sky *n.* A mink found in Asia.

kook *n., Slang* A crazy or eccentric person. **kookiness** *n.*, **kooky** *adj.*

Ko-ran *n.* The sacred book of Islam, accepted as containing the revelations made to Mohammed by Allah through the angel Gabriel.

ko-sher *adj.* Conformant to eat according to Jewish dietary laws. *Slang* Appropriate; proper.

kow-tow *v.* To show servile deference.

kph *abbr.* Kilometers per hour.

kraal *n.* A village of southern African natives; and enclosure for animals in southern Africa.

kryp-ton *n.* A white, inert gaseous chemical used mainly in fluorescent lamps; symbolized by Kr.

kum-quat *n.* A small, round orange fruit having a sour pulp and edible rind.

kung fu *n.* A Japanese art of self-defense similar to karate.

ku-miss *n.* The fermented camel's milk drank by Asiatic nomads.

ky-pho-sis *n.* Abnormal curving of the spine.

L, l *n.* The twelfth letter of the English alphabet; the Roman numeral for fifty.

la-bel *n.* Something that identifies or describes. **label** *v.* To attach a label to.

la-bi-al *adj.* Pertaining to or of the labia or lips.

la-bi-um *n., pl.* **labia** Any of the four folds of the vulva.

la-bor *n.* Physical or manual work done for hire. *Med.* The physical pain and efforts involved in childbirth. *v.* To work; to progress with great effort.

lab-o-ra-to-ry *n., pl.* **-ies** A place equipped for conducting scientific experiments, research, or testing; a place where drugs and chemicals are produced.

lab-y-rinth *n.*

A system of winding, intricate passages; a maze. **-ine** *adj.*

lac *n.* The resinous secretion left on certain trees by the lac insect and used in making paints and varnishes.

lace *n.* A delicate open-work fabric of silk, cotton, or linen made by hand or on a machine; a cord or string used to fasten two edges together. *v.* To fasten or tie together; to interlace or intertwine. **lacy** *adj.*

lac-er-ate *v.* To open with a jagged tear; to wound the flesh by tearing. **-tion** *n.*

lach-ry-mal or **lac-ri-mal** *adj.* Relating to or producing tears; relating to the glands that produce tears.

lack *n.* The deficiency or complete absence of something. *v.* To have little of something or to be completely without.

lack-ey *n.* A male servant of very low status.

lack-lus-ter *adj.* Lacking sheen; dull.

lac-quer *n.* A transparent varnish which is dis-solved in a volatile solution and dries to give surfaces a glossy finish.

lac-tate *v.* To secrete or to milk. **-tion** *n.*

lac-te-al *adj.* Of, resembling, or like milk. *n., Anat.* Any of the lymphatic vessels carrying chyle from the small intestine to the blood.

lac-tic acid *n.* A limpid, syrupy acid that is present in sour milk, molasses, some fruits, and wines.

lac-tose *n., Biochem.* A white, odorless crystal-line sugar that is found in milk.

la-cu-na *n., pl.* **-nas, -nae** A space from which something is missing; a gap.

lad *n.* A boy or young man.

lad-der *n.* An implement used for climbing up or down in order to reach another place or area.

lad-en *adj.* Heavily burdened; oppressed; weighed down; loaded. **laden** *v.*

lad-ing *n.* Cargo; freight.

la-dle *n.*

A cup-shaped vessel with a deep bowl and a long handle, used for dipping or conveying liquids. **ladle** v.

la-dy n., pl. **ladies** A woman showing refinement, cultivation, and often high social position; the woman at the head of a household; an address or term of reference for any woman.

lag v. To stray or fall behind; to move slowly; to weaken gradually. n. The process or act of retardation or falling behind; the amount or period of lagging.

la-gniappe n. A small gift which is given to a purchaser by a storekeeper. *Informal* Anything given as an extra bonus.

la-goon n. A body of shallow water separated from the ocean by a coral reef or sandbars. **lagoonal** adj.

laid Past tense of lay.

lain v. Past tense of lie.

lais-sez-faire n. A policy stating that a government should exercise very little control in trade and industrial affairs; noninterference.

la-i-ty n. Laymen, as distinguished from clergy.

lake n. A large inland body of either salt or fresh water.

La-maze meth-od n. A method of childbirth in which the mother is prepared psychologically and physically to give birth without the use of drugs.

lamb n. A young sheep; the meat of a lamb used as food; a gentle person.

lam-baste or lambast v., *Slang* To thrash or beat.

lam-bent adj. Lightly and playfully brilliant; flickering gently; softly radiant. **lambency** n., **lambently** adv.

lame adj. Disabled or crippled, especially in the legs or feet so as to impair free movement; weak; ineffective; unsatisfactory. -ly adv., **lameness** n.

la-me n. A brocaded fabric woven with gold or silver thread, sometimes mixed with other fiber.

la-ment v. To express sorrow; to mourn. n. An expression of regret or sorrow. **lamentable** adj., -ably adv., -ation n.

lam-i-na n., pl. -nae, -nas A thin scale or layer. *Bot.* The blade or flat part of a leaf.

lam-i-nate v. To form or press into thin sheets; to form layers by the action of pressure and heat. **lamination** n., **laminated** adj., **laminator** n.

lamp n. A device for generating heat or light.

lam-poon n. A satirical, but often humorous, attack in verse or prose, especially one that ridicules a group, person, or institution. **lampoonery** n.

lam-prey n., pl. preys An eel-like fish having a circular, suctorial mouth with rasping teeth and no jaw.

lance n. A spear-like implement used as a weapon by mounted knights or soldiers. *lance* v.

land n. The solid, exposed surface of the earth as distinguished from the waters. v. To arrive at a destination; to catch a fish; to receive a new job. **landless** adj.

lan-dau n. A four-wheeled vehicle with a closed carriage and a back seat with a collapsible top.

land-er n. A space vehicle for landing on a celestial body.

land-ing n. The act of coming, going, or placing ashore from any kind of vessel or craft; the act of descending and settling on the ground in an airplane.

land-locked adj. Almost or completely surrounded by land.

land-mark n. A fixed object that serves as a boundary marker.

land-scape n. A view or vista of natural scenery as seen from a single point. v. To change or improve the features of a section of ground by contouring the land and planting shrubs, trees, or flowers.

lane n. A small or narrow path between walls, fences, or hedges.

lan-guage n. The words, sounds, pronunciation and method of combining words used and understood by people.

lan-guid adj. Lacking in energy; drooping; weak. -ly adv., **languidness** n.

lan-guish v. To become weak; to be or live in a state of depression. **languisher** n., **languishment** n.

lank adj. Slender; lean. -y adv., -ness n.

lan-o-lin n. Wool grease obtained from sheep's wool and refined for use in ointments and cosmetics.

lan-tern n. A portable light having transparent or translucent sides.

lan-yard n. A piece of rope or line used to secure objects on ships.

la-pel n.

The front part of a garment, especially that of a coat, that is turned back, usually a continuation of the collar.

lap-in n. Rabbit fur that is sheared and dyed.

lap-is laz-u-li n. A semi-precious stone that is azure blue in color.

lap-pet n. A flap or fold on a headdress or on a garment.

lapse n. A temporary deviation or fall to a less desirable state. lapse v.

lar-ce-ny n., pl. -ies The unlawful taking of another person's property. -ous adj.

lard n. The soft, white, solid or semi-solid fat obtained after rendering the fatty tissue of the hog.

lar-der n. A place, such as a pantry or room, where food is stored.

large adj. Greater than usual or average in amount or size. at large To be free and not confined.

large in-tes-tine n. The portion of the intestine that extends from the end of the small intestine to the anus.

large-scale adj. Larger than others of the same kind; extensive; of or relating to a scale drawing to show detail.

lar-gess or lar-gesse n. Liberal or excessive giving to an inferior; generosity.

lar-go *adv., Mus.* In a very slow, broad, and solemn manner. **largo** *adj. & n.*

lar-i-at *n.* A long, light rope with a running noose at one end to catch livestock.

lark *n.* A bird having a melodious ability to sing; a merry or carefree adventure.

lar-va *n., pl.* **larvae** The immature, wingless, often worm-like form of a newly hatched insect; the early form of an animal that differs greatly from the adult, such as the tadpole. **larval** *adj.*

lar-yn-gi-tis *n.* Inflammation of the larynx.

lar-ynx *n., pl.* **larynges** *or* **larynxes** The upper portion of the trachea which contains the vocal cords. **-al** *adj.*

la-sa-gna *or* **la-sa-gne** *n.* Traditional Italian dish of wide flat noodles baked with a sauce of tomatoes, meat, and cheese.

la-ser *n.* A device which utilizes the natural oscillations of molecules or atoms between energy levels for generating coherent electromagnetic radiation in the visible, ultraviolet, or infrared parts of the spectrum.

lash *v.* To strike or move violently or suddenly; to attack verbally; to whip. *n.* Eyelash. **lasher** *n.*

lass *n.* A young girl or woman.

las-si-tude *n.* A condition of weariness; fatigue.

las-so *n., pl.* **-sos, -soes** A long rope or long leather thong with a running noose used to catch horses and cattle. **lasso** *v.*

last *adj.* Following all the rest; of or relating to the final stages, as of life; worst; lowest in rank. *adv.* After all others in sequence or chronology. *v.* To continue. *n.* A form in the shape of a foot used to hold a shoe while it is repaired or to shape a shoe as it is being made.

Last Rites *n., Eccl.* Sacraments of the Roman Catholic Church given to a person near death.

Last Sup-per *n.* The last meal eaten by Jesus Christ and his disciples, before his crucifixion.

latch *n.* A device used to secure a gate or door, consisting of a bar that usually fits into a notch. **latch onto** To grab onto.

latch-et *n.* A narrow leather strap or thong used to fasten a shoe or sandal.

latch-key *n.* A key for opening an outside door.

latch-key child *n* A child whose parent or parents work during the day and who carries a key to the front door because he or she returns home from school to an empty house.

late *adj.* Coming, staying, happening after the proper or usual time; having recently died. **lateness** *n.*, **lately** *adv.*

lat-er-al *adj.* Relating to or of the side. *n.* In football, an underhand pass thrown sideways or away from the line of scrimmage. **laterally** *adv.*

la-tex *n.* The milky, white fluid that is produced by certain plants, such as the rubber tree; a water emulsion of synthetic rubber or plastic globules used in paints and adhesives.

lath *n.* A thin, narrow strip of wood nailed to joists, rafters, or studding and used as a supporting structure for plaster.

lathe *n.* A machine for holding material while it is spun and shaped by a tool.

lath-er *n.* A foam formed by detergent or soap and water. **-er** *n.*, **lathery** *adj.*

lat-i-tude *n.* The angular distance of the earth's surface north or south of the equator, measured in degrees along a meridian; freedom to act and to choose.

la-trine *n.* A public toilet, as in a camp or in a barracks.

lat-ter *adj.* Being the second of two persons or two things.

lat-tice *n.* A structure made of strips of wood, metal, or other materials, interlaced or crossed, framing regularly spaced openings. **lattice** *v.*

laud *v.* To praise; to extol. **laudable** *adj.*

laugh *v.* To express amusement, satisfaction, or pleasure with a smile and inarticulate sounds. **laughable** *adj.*

laugh-ter *n.* The expression, sound, or act produced by laughing.

launch *v.* To push or move a vessel into the water for the first time; to set a rocket or missile into flight. **-er** *n.*

launch *n.* A large boat carried by a ship.

laun-der *v.* To wash clothes or other materials in soap and water. **laundrer, laundress** *n.*

laun-dro-mat *n.* A place to wash and dry clothes in coin operated automatic machines.

laun-dry *n., pl.* **-ies** An establishment where laundering is done professionally; clothes or other articles to be or that have been laundered.

lau-re-ate A person honored for his accomplishment. **laureate** *v.*

la-va *n.* Molten rock which erupts or flows from an active volcano; the rock formed after lava has cooled and hardened.

lav-a-to-ry *n., pl.* **-ies** A room with permanently installed washing and toilet facilities.

lav-en-der *n.* An aromatic plant having spikes of pale violet flowers; light purple in color. **lavender** *adj.*

lav-ish *adj.* Generous and extravagant in giving or spending. **lavisher** *n.*, **lavishly** *adv.*, **lavishness** *n.*

law *n.* A rule of conduct or action, recognized by custom or decreed by formal enactment, considered binding on the members of a nation, community, or group; a system or body of such rules.

law-a-bid-ing *adj.* Abiding by the laws.

lawn *n.* A stretch of ground covered with grass that is mowed regularly near a house, park, or building.

law-ren-ci-um *n.* A short-lived radioactive element, symbolized by LR.

law-suit *n.* A case or proceeding brought before a court of law for settlement.

law-yer *n.* A person trained in the legal profession who acts for and advises clients or pleads in court.

lax *adj.* Lacking disciplinary control; lacking rigidity or firmness. laxity, laxness *n.*, laxly *adv.*

lax-a-tive *n.* A medicine taken to stimulate evacuation of the bowels. laxative *adj.*

lay *v.* To cause to lie; to place on a surface; past tense of lie.

lay-er *n.* A single thickness, coating, or covering that lies over or under another. layered *adj.*, layer *v.*

lay-ette *n.* The clothing, bedding, and equipment for a newborn child.

lay-man *n.* A person not belonging to a particular profession or specialty; one who is not a member of the clergy.

lay-off *n.* A temporary dismissal of employees.

lay-out *n.* A planned arrangement of something, such as a street, room, park, or building.

la-zy *adj.* Unwilling to work; moving slowly; sluggish. lazily *adv.*, laziness *n.*

la-zy-bones *n. Slang* A lazy person.

lb *abbr.* Pound

L--do-pa *n.* A drug used in treating Parkinson's disease.

lea *n., Poetic.* A grassy field or meadow.

leach *v.* To cause a liquid to pass through a filter; to remove or wash out by filtering. leachable *adj.*

lead *v.* To go ahead so as to show the way; to control the affairs or action of. *n.* A soft, malleable, heavy, dull gray metallic element symbolized by Pb, used in solder, paints, and bullets; a graphite stick used as the writing material in pencils; in printing, the thin strip of type metal used to provide space between printed lines. leadenness *n.*, leading, leaden *adj.*

lead poisoning *n.* Poisoning of a person's system by the absorption of lead or any of its salts.

leaf *n., pl.* **leaves**

A flat outgrowth from a plant structure or tree, usually green in color and functioning as the principal area of photosynthesis; a single page in a book. *v.* To turn the pages of a book. leafless, leafy *adj.*

leaf-let *n.* A part or a segment of a compound leaf; a small printed handbill or circular, often folded.

league *n.* An association of persons, organizations, or states for common action or interest; an association of athletic competition; an underwater measurement of distance that equals 3 miles or approximately 4.8 km.

leak *n.* An opening, as a flaw or small crack, permitting an escape or entrance of light or fluid. leakage *n.*,

leakiness *n.*, leaky *adj.*

lean *v.* To rest or incline the weight of the body for support; to rest or incline anything against a large object or wall; to rely or depend on; to have a tendency or preference for; to tend towards a suggestion or action. *adj.* having little or no fat; thin. leanly *adv.*, leanness *n.*

lean-ing *n.* An inclination; a predispositon.

lean--to *n.* A structure of branches, sloping to the ground from a raised support, usually an outside wall.

leap *v.* To rise or project oneself by a sudden thrust from the ground with a spring of the legs; to spring, to jump. leap, leaper *n.*

leap-frog *n.* A game in which two players leap over each other by placing one's hands on the back of another who is bending over and leaping over him in a straddling position.

leap year *n.* A year containing 366 days, occurring every 4th year, with the extra day added to make 29 days in February.

learn *n.* The process of acquiring knowledge, understanding, or mastery of a study or experience. learner *n.*, learnable *adj.*, learn *v.*

lease *n.* A contract for the temporary use or occupation of property or premises in exchange for payment of rent.

leash *n.* A strong cord or rope for restraining a dog or other animal.

least-wise *adv., Slang* At least; at any rate.

leath-er *n.* An animal skin or hide with the hair removed, prepared for use by tanning.

leath-er-neck *n., Slang* A United States Marine.

leave *v.* To go or depart from; to permit to remain behind or in a specified place or condition; to forsake; to abandon; to bequeath, as in a will. *n.* Official permission for absence from duty.

leav-en *n.* An agent of fermentation, as yeast, used to cause batters and doughs to rise; any pervasive influence that produces a significant change.

lech-er-y *n.* Unrestrained indulgence in sexual activity. lecher *n.*, lecherous *adj.*, lecherously *adv.*

lec-i-thin *n.* Any of a group of phosphorus containing compounds found in plant and animal tissues, commercially derived from egg yolks, corn, and soybeans, and used in the production of foods, cosmetics, pharmaceuticals, and plastics.

lec-tern *n.* A stand or tall desk, usually with a slanted top, on which a speaker or instructor may place books or papers.

lec-ture *n.* A speech on a specific subject, delivered to an audience for information or instruction. *v.* To give a speech or lecture; to criticize or reprimand.

led *v., p.t. & p.p.* Past tense of lead.

ledge *n.* A narrow, shelf-like projection forming a shelf, as on a wall or the side of a rocky formation.

ledg-er *n.* A book in which sums of money received and paid out are recorded.

lee *n.* The side of a ship sheltered from the wind.

Lee, Robert E. (Edward) *n.* (1807-1870) A commander and general of the American Confederacy during the American Civil War.

leech *n.* Any of various carnivorous or bloodsucking worms; a person who clings or preys on others.

leek *n.* A culinary herb of the lily family, related to the onion, with a slender, edible bulb.

leer *n.* A sly look or sideways glance expressing desire or malicious intent.

lee-way *n., Naut.* The lateral drift of a plane or ship away from the correct course.

left *adj.* Pertaining to or being on the side of the body that faces north when the subject is facing east.

leg *n.* A limb or appendage serving as a means of support and movement in animals and man; a part or division of a journey or trip. leg *v.*

leg-a-cy *n., pl.* -ies Personal property, money, and other valuables that are bequeathed by will; anything that is handed down from an ancestor, predecessor, or earlier era.

le-gal *adj.* Of, pertaining to, or concerned with the law or lawyers; something based on or authorized by law. -ity, -ization *n.*, -ize *v.*, -ly *adv.*

le-gal-ism *n.* A strict conformity to the law, especially when stressing the letter and forms of the law rather than the spirit of justice. -ist *n.*, -istic *adj.*

le-ga-tion *n.* The official diplomatic mission in a foreign country, headed by a minister; the official residence or business premises of a diplomatic minister of lower rank than an ambassador.

le-ga-to *adv., Music* Smooth and flowing with successive notes connected. legato *adj. & n.*

leg-end *n.* An unverifiable story handed down from the past; a body of such stories, as those connected with a culture or people.

leg-en-dar-y *adj.* Presented as, based on, or of the nature of a legend. legendary *adv.*

leg-horn *n.* A hat made from finely plaited wheat straw.

leg-i-ble *adj.* Capable of being read or deciphered. legibility *n.*, legibly *adv.*

le-gion *n.* In ancient Rome, an army unit that comprised between 4,200 and 6,000 men; any of various honorary or military organizations, usually national in character.

leg-is-late *v.* To pass or make laws.

leg-is-la-tion *n.* The act or procedures of passing laws; lawmaking; an officially enacted law.

leg-is-la-tive *adj.* Of or pertaining to legislation or a legislature; having the power to legislate.

leg-is-la-ture *n.* A body of persons officially constituted and empowered to make and change laws.

leg-ume *n.* A plant of the pea or bean family, that bears pods which split when mature; the seeds or pod of a legume used as food. leguminous *adj.*

leg-work *n., Slang* A chore, task, or gathering of information accomplished by going about on foot.

lei *n., pl.* leis

A wreath of flowers worn around the neck; the customary greeting of welcome in the state of Hawaii.

lei-sure *n.* The time of freedom from work or duty. leisured *adj.*

LEM *abbr.* Lunar excursion module.

lem-on *n.* An oval citrus fruit grown on a tree, having juicy, acid pulp and a yellow rind that yields an essential oil used as a flavoring and as a perfuming agent. *Slang* Something, as an automobile, that proves to be defective or unsatisfactory.

lem-on-ade *n.* A drink made from water, lemon juice, and sugar.

lend *v.* To allow the temporary use or possession of something with the understanding that it is to be returned; to offer oneself as to a specific purpose. lender *n.*

length *n.* The linear extent of something from end to end, usually the longest dimension of a thing as distinguished from its thickness and width; the measurement of something to estimate distance. lengthy *adj.*

length-en *v.* To make or become longer.

length-wise *adv. & adj.* Of or in the direction or dimension of length; longitudinally.

le-ni-ent *adj.* Gentle, forgiving, and mild; merciful; undemanding; tolerant. leniency, lenience *n.*

len-i-tive *adj.* Having the ability to ease pain or discomfort. lenitive *n.*

lens *n.*

In optics, the curved piece of glass or other transparent substance that is used to refract light rays so that they converge or diverge to form an image; the transparent structure in the eye, situated behind the iris, which serves to focus an image on the retina.

lent *v.* Past tense of lend.

Lent *n., Eccl.* The period of forty days, excluding Sundays, of fasting and penitence observed by many Christians from Ash Wednesday until Easter. Lenten *adj.*

len-til *n.* A leguminous plant, having

broad pods and containing edible seeds.

Leo *n.* The fifth sign of the zodiac; a person born between (July 23 - August 22.)

leop-ard *n.*

A large member of the cat family of Africa and Asia, having a tawny coat with dark brown or black spots grouped in rounded clusters, also called a panther. **leopardess** *n.*

le-o-tard *n.* A close-fitting garment worn by dancers and acrobats.

lep-er *n.* One who suffers from leprosy.

lep-re-chaun *n.* A mischief-making elf of Irish folklore, supposed to own hidden treasure.

lep-ro-sy *n., Pathol.* A chronic communicable disease characterized by nodular skin lesions and the progressive destruction of tissue. -otic *adj.*

les-bi-an *n.* A homosexual woman. **lesbian** *adj.*

lese maj-es-ty *or n.* An offense against a ruler or supreme power of state.

le-sion *n., Pathol.* An injury; a wound; any well-defined bodily area where the tissue has changed in a way that is characteristic of a disease.

less *adj.* Smaller; of smaller or lower importance or degree. *prep.* With the subtraction of; minus.

-less *suffix.* Without; lacking.

les-see *n.* One who leases a property.

les-son *n.* An instance from which something is to be or has been learned; an assignment to be learned or studied as by a student.

les-sor *n.* One who grants a lease to another.

let *v.* To give permission; to allow. *n.* An invalid stroke in a game such as tennis, that must be repeated because of some interruption or hindrance of playing conditions.

let-down *n.* A decrease or slackening, as in energy or effort. *Slang* A disappointment.

le-thal *adj.* Pertaining to or being able to cause death. **lethally** *adv.*

leth-ar-gy *n., Pathol.* A state of excessive drowsiness or abnormally deep sleep; laziness. -ic *adj.*, -ically *adv.*

let's *contr.* Let us.

let-ter *n.* A standard character or sign used in writing or printing to represent an alphabetical unit or speech sound; a written or printed means of communication sent to another person.

let-ter-head *n.* Stationery printed with a name and address, usually of a company or business establishment.

let-ter--perfect *adj.* Absolutely correct; perfect.

let-tuce *n.* A plant having crisp, edible leaves that are used especially in salads.

leu-ke-mi-a *n., Pathol.* A generally fatal disease of the blood in which white blood cells multiply in uncontrolled numbers. **leukemic** *adj.*

le-vee *n.* An embankment along the shore of a body of water, especially a river, built to prevent over-flowing.

lev-el *n.* A relative position, rank, or height on a scale; a standard position from which other heights and depths are measured. *adj.* Balanced in height; even. *v.* To make or become flat or level. -er, levelness *n.*, levelly *adv.*

lev-el--head-ed *adj.* Showing good judgment and common sense. -ness *n.*

lever *n.* A handle that projects and is used to operate or adjust a mechanism.

lever-age *n.* The use of a lever; the mechanical advantage gained by using a lever; power to act effectively.

lev-i-tate *v.* To rise and float in the air in apparent defiance of gravity. -ion *n.*

Le-vit-i-cus *n.* The third book of the Old Testament.

lev-i-ty *n., pl.* -ies Lack of seriousness; frivolity; lightness.

lev-y *v.* To impose and collect by authority or force, as a fine or tax; to draft for military service; to prepare for, begin, or wage war. **levy** *n.*

lewd *adj.* Preoccupied with sex; lustful. **lewdly** *adv.*, **lewdness** *n.*

lex-i-cog-ra-phy *n.* The practice or profession of compiling dictionaries. **lexicographer** *n.*, **lexicographical** *adj.*

lex-i-con *n.* A dictionary; a vocabulary or list of words that relate to a certain subject, occupation, or activity. **lexical** *adj.*

li-a-bil-i-ty *n., pl.* -ies The condition or state of being liable; that which is owed to another.

li-a-ble *adj.* Legally or rightly responsible.

li-ai-son *n.* A communication, as between different parts of an armed force or departments of a government; a close connection or relationship; an illicit love affair.

li-ar *n.* A person who tells falsehoods.

lib *n. Slang* Liberation.

li-bel *n., Law* A written statement in published form that damages a person's character or reputation. **libel** *v.*, **libelous** *adj.*

lib-er-al *adj.* Characterized by generosity or lavishness in giving; abundant; ample; inclining toward opinions or policies that favor progress or reform, such as religion or politics. **liberalism, liberality** *n.*, **-ize** *v.*, **liberally** *adv.*

liberal arts *pl. n.* Academic courses that include literature, philosophy, history, languages, etc., which provide general cultural information.

lib-er-ate *v.* To set free, as from bondage, oppression, or foreign control. **liberation** *n.*

lib-er-ty *n., pl.* -ies The state of being free from oppression, tyranny, confinement, or slavery; freedom; in Navy terms, the permission to be absent from one's ship or duty for less that 48 hours.

Lib-er-ty Bell *n.* The bell rung July 4, 1776, to celebrate the adoption of the Declaration of Independence and cracked in 1835; located in Philadelphia, Pennsylvania.

li-bi-do *n.* One's sexual desire or impulse; the psychic energy drive that is behind all human activities. -inous *adj.*

Libra *n.* The seventh sign of the Zodiac; a person born between (September 23 - October 22.)

li-brar-i-an *n.* A person in charge of a library; one who specializes in library work.

li-brar-y *n., pl.* -ies A collection of books, pamphlets, magazines, and reference books kept for reading reference, or borrowing; a commercial establishment, usually in connection with a city or school, which rents books.

lice *n.* Plural of louse.

li-cense *n.* An official document that gives permission to engage in a specified activity or to perform a specified act. license *v.*, licenser *n.*

li-cen-ti-ate *n.* A person licensed to practice a specified profession.

li-cen-tious *adj.* Lacking in moral restraint; immoral. licentiously *adv.*, licentiousness *n.*

li-chen *n.* Any of various flowerless plants consisting of fungi, commonly growing in flat patches on trees and rocks. lichened, lichenous *adj.*

lic-it *adj.* Lawful. -ly *adv.*, licitness *n.*

lick *v.* To pass the tongue over or along the surface of. *Slang* To beat; to thrash.

lick-e-ty-split *adv.* Full speed; rapidly.

lic-o-rice *n.* A perennial herb of Europe, the dried root of which is used to flavor medicines and candy.

lid *n.* A hinged or removable cover for a container; an eyelid. lidded, lidless *adj.*

lie *v.* To be in or take a horizontal recumbent position; to recline. *n.* A false or untrue statement.

liege *n.* A feudal lord or sovereign. *adj.* Loyal; faithful.

lien *n.* The legal right to claim, hold, or sell the property of another to satisfy a debt or obligation.

lieu *n.* Place; stead. in lieu of In place of.

lieu-ten-ant *n.* A commissioned officer in the U.S. Army, Air Force, or Marine Corps who ranks below a captain.

life *n., pl.* lives The form of existence that distinguishes living organisms from dead organisms or inanimate matter in the ability to carry on metabolism, respond to stimuli, reproduce, and grow.

life-guard *n.* An expert swimmer employed to protect people in and around water.

lifer *n.* Slang A person sentenced to life in prison.

life--sup-port sy-stem *n.* A system giving a person all or some of the items, such as oxygen, water, food, and control of temperature, necessary for a person's life and health while in a spacecraft or while exploring the surface of the moon; a system used to sustain life in a critical health situation.

life-time *n.* The period between one's birth and death.

life-work *n.* The main work of a person's lifetime.

life zone *n.* A biogeographic zone.

lift *v.* To raise from a lower to a higher position; to elevate; to take from; to steal. *n.* The act or process of lifting; force or power available for lifting; an elevation of spirits; a device or machine designed to pick up, raise, or carry something; an elevator. lifter *n.*

lift-off *n.* The vertical takeoff or the instant of takeoff of an aircraft or spacecraft.

lig-a-ment *n.* A tough band of tissue joining bones or holding a body organ in place. ligamentous *adj.*

li-gate *v.* To tie with a ligature.

lig-a-ture *n.*

Something, as a cord, that is used to bind; a thread used in surgery; something that unites or connects; a printing character that combines two or more letters.

light *n.* Electromagnetic radiation that can be seen by the naked eye; brightness; a source of light; spiritual illumination; enlightenment; a source of fire, such as a match. *adj.* Having light; bright; of less force, quantity, intensity, weight, than normal; having less calories or alcoholic content; dizzy; giddy. light *v.*, lightness *n.*

light-er *n.* A device used to light a pipe, cigar or cigarette; a barge used to load and unload a cargo ship.

light-ning *n.* The flash of light produced by a high-tension natural electric discharge into the atmosphere. *adj.* Moving with or as if with the suddenness of lightning.

light-ning bug *n.* A firefly.

light-ning rod *n.* A grounded metal rod positioned high on a building to protect it from lightning.

light op-er-a *n.* An operetta.

lights *pl.* *n.* The lungs, especially of a slaughtered animal.

light-ship *n.* A ship, having a powerful light or horn, that is anchored in dangerous waters to warn other vessels.

light show *n.* A display of colored lights in kaleidoscopic patterns, often accompanied by film, slides, or music.

light-weight *n.* A person who weighs very little; a boxer or wrestler weighting between 127 and 135 pounds.

light--year *or* **light year** *n.* A measure equal to the distance light travels in one year, approximately 5.878 trillion miles.

lig-ne-ous *adj*. Of or resembling wood; woody.

lig-ni-fy *v*. To make or become woody or wood-like.

lig-nite *n*. A brownish-black soft coal, especially one in which the texture of the original wood is distinct.

lig-ro-in *n*. A volatile, flammable fraction of petroleum used as a solvent.

lik-en *v*. To describe as being like; to compare.

like-ness *n*. Resemblance; a copy.

like-wise *adv*. In a similar way.

li-lac *n*. A shrub widely grown for its large, fragrant purplish or white flower cluster; a pale purple. lilac *adj*.

Lil-li-pu-tian *n*. A very small person. *adj*. Tiny.

lilt *n*. A light song; a rhythmical way of speaking.

lil-y *n*., *pl*. -ies

Any of various plants bearing trumpet-shaped flowers; a plant similar or related to the lily, as the water lily.

lil-y--liv-ered *adj*. Timid; cowardly.

lily of the valley *n*., *pl*. lilies A widely cultivated plant which bears fragrant, bell-shaped white flowers on a short stem.

Li-ma *n*. The capital of Peru.

li-ma bean *n*. Any of several varieties of tropical American plants having flat pods with light green edible seeds.

limb *n*. A large bough of a tree; an animal's appendage used for movement or grasping; an arm or leg.

lim-ber *adj*. Bending easily; pliable; moving easily; agile. *v*. To make or become limber. -ly *adv*., limberness *n*.

lim-bo or **Lim-bo** *n*. The abode of souls kept from entering Heaven; a place or condition of oblivion or neglect.

Lim-burg-er *n*. A soft white cheese having a strong odor and flavor.

lime *n*. A tropical citrus tree with evergreen leaves, fragrant white flowers, and edible green fruit; calcium oxide. limy *adj*.

lime-light *n*. A focus of public attention; the center of attention.

lim-er-ick *n*. A humorous verse of five lines.

lime-stone *n*. A form of sedimentary rock composed mainly of calcium carbonate which is used in building and in making lime and cement.

lim-it *n*. A boundary; a maximum or a minimum number or amount; a restriction on frequency or amount. *v*. To restrict; to establish bounds or boundaries. limitation *n*.

li-mo-nite *n*. A natural iron oxide used as an ore of iron.

lim-ou-sine *n*. A luxurious large vehicle; a small bus used to carry passengers to airports and hotels.

limp *v*. To walk lamely. *adj*. Lacking or having lost rigidity; not firm or strong.

limply *adv*., **limpness** *n*.

lim-pet *n*. Any of numerous marine gastropod mollusks having a conical shell and adhering to tidal rocks.

lim-pid *adj*. Transparently clear. limpidity *n*., limpidly *adv*.

linch-pin *n*. A locking pin inserted through a shaft to keep a wheel from slipping off.

Lincoln, Abraham *n*. The 16th president of the United States from 1861-1865, who was assassinated.

Lind-berg, Charles A. *n*. (1902-1974) American aviator; the first man to make a nonstop flight across the Atlantic Ocean, linking the United States and France.

lin-den *n*. Any of various shade trees having heart-shaped leaves.

lin-e-age *n*. A direct line of descent from an ancestor.

lin-e-a-ment *n*. A contour, shape, or feature of the body and especially of the the face.

lin-e-ar *adj*. Of, pertaining to, or resembling a line; long and narrow.

lin-e-ar per-spec-tive *n*. A technique in painting and drawing in which parallel lines converge to give the illusion of distance and depth.

line-back-er *n*. In football, one of the defensive players positioned directly behind the line of scrimmage.

line drive *n*. In baseball, a ball hit with force whose path approximates a straight line parallel or nearly parallel to the ground.

line-man *n*. A person who works on telephone or electric power lines; a player on the forward line of a team, especially football.

lin-en *n*. Thread, yarn, or fabric made of flax; household articles, such as sheets and pillow cases, made of linen or a similar fabric. linen *adj*.

line of scrim-mage *n*. In football, an imaginary line that extends across the field from the position of the football on any given play.

lin-er *n*. A ship belonging to a ship line or an aircraft belonging to an airline; one that lines or serves as a lining.

line score *n*. In baseball, a statistical record of each inning of a game.

lines-man *n*. An official in a court game, as tennis or volleyball, who calls shots which fall out-of-bounds; an official in football who marks the downs.

line--up *n*. A line of persons formed for the purpose of inspection or identification; the members of a team who take part in a game; a group of television programs that are aired sequentially.

ling *n*. Any of various marine food fishes related to the cod.

lin-ger *v*. To be slow in parting or reluctant to leave; to be slow in acting; to procrastinate. -er *n*., lingeringly *adv*.

lin-ge-rie *n*. Women's undergarments.

lingo *n*., *pl*. goes Language that is unfamiliar; a specialized vocabulary.

lin-guist *n.* One who is fluent in more than one language; A person specializing in linguistics.

lin-i-ment *n.* A liquid or semi-liquid medicine applied to the skin.

lin-ing *n.* A material which is used to cover an inside surface.

link *n.* One of the rings forming a chain; something in the form of a link; a tie or bond; a cuff link. *v.* To connect by or as if by a link or links.

link-age *n.* The act or process of linking; a system of connecting structures.

links *pl., n.* A golf course.

li-no-le-um *n.* A floor covering consisting of a surface of hardened linseed oil and a filler, as wood or powdered cork, on a canvas or burlap backing.

lin-seed *n.* The seed of flax, used in paints and varnishes.

lin-sey--wool-sey *n.* A coarse, sturdy fabric of wool and linen or cotton.

lin-tel *n.* A horizontal beam across the top of a door which supports the weight of the structure above it.

li-on *n.*

A large carnivorous mammal of the cat family, found in Africa and India, having a short, tawny coat and a long, heavy mane in the male; a person of great importance or prestige. **lioness** *n.*

li-on--heart-ed *adj.* Very courageous.

li-on-ize *v.* To treat someone as a celebrity.

lip service *n.* An expression of acquiescence that is not acted upon.

liq-ue-fy *or* **liq-ui-fy** *v.* To make liquid. **liquefaction, liquefier** *n.*

li-queur *n.* A sweet alcoholic beverage; a cordial.

liq-ui-date *v.* To settle a debt by payment or other settlement; to close a business by settling accounts and dividing up assets; to get rid of, especially to kill. -ion, liquidator *n.*

liq-uor *n.* A distilled alcoholic beverage; a liquid substance, as a watery solution of a drug.

Lis-bon *n.* The capital of Portugal.

lisle *n.* A fine, tightly twisted cotton thread.

lisp *n.* A speech defect or mannerism marked by lisping. *v.* To mispronounce the s and z sounds, usually as th. **lisper** *n.*

lis-some *adj.* Nimble. **lissomely** *adv.*, **lissomeness** *n.*

list *n.* A series of numbers or words; a tilt to one side. **list** *v.*

list-less *adj.* Lacking energy or enthusiasm. -ly *adv.*, **listlessness** *n.*

lit *abbr.* Literary; literature.

lit-a-ny *n., pl.* -ies A prayer in which phrases recited by a leader are alternated with answers from a congregation.

li-tchi *or* **li-chee** *n.* A Chinese tree, bearing edible fruit; the fruit of the tree.

lit-er-al *adj.* Conforming to the exact meaning of a word; concerned primarily with facts; without embellishment or exaggeration.

literally *adv.*, **literalistic** *adj.*

lit-er-al-ism *n.* Adherence to the explicit sense of a given test; literal portrayal; realism. -ist *n.*, **literalistic** *adj.*

lit-er-ar-y *adj.* Pertaining to literature; appropriate to or used in literature; of or relating to the knowledge of literature. **literarily** *adv.*

lit-er-ate *adj.* Having the ability to read and write; showing skill in using words. **literacy, literate** *n.*

lit-er-a-ti *pl., n.* The educated class.

lit-er-a-ture *n.* Printed material, as leaflets for a political campaign; written words of lasting excellence.

lithe *adj.* Bending easily; supple.

lithely *adv.*, **litheness** *n.*

lith-i-um *n.* A silver-white, soft metallic element symbolized by Li.

li-thog-ra-phy *n.* A printing process in which a flat surface is treated so that the ink adheres only to the portions that are to be printed.

lithograph *n. & v.*, **lithographer** *n.*, **lithographic, lithographical** *adj.*

li-thol-o-gy *n.* The microscopic study and classification of rocks. **lithologist** *n.*

lit-i-gate *v.* To conduct a legal contest by judicial process. -ant, -ion, -or *n.*

lit-mus *n.* A blue powder obtained from lichens which turns red in acid solutions and blue in alkaline solutions, used as an acid-base indicator.

lit-mus pa-per *n.* Unsized paper that is treated with litmus and used as an indicator.

lit-ter *n.* A covered and curtained couch, mounted on shafts and used to carry a single passenger; a stretcher used to carry a sick or injured person; material used as bedding for animals; the offspring at one birth of a multiparous animal; an accumulation of waste material. **litter** *v.*, **litterer** *n.*

lit-ter-bug *n.* One who litters a public area.

Little Dipper *n.* Ursa Minor.

lit-to-ral *adj.* Relating to or existing on a shore. *n.* A shore.

lit-ur-gy *n., pl.* -ies A prescribed rite or body of rites for public worship.

liturgical *adj.*, **liturgically** *adv.*

live-li-hood *n.* A means of support or subsistence.

live-ly *adj.* Vigorous. **liveliness** *n.*

liv-er *n.* The large, very vascular, glandular organ of vertebrates which secretes bile.

liv-er-wurst *n.* A kind of sausage made primarily of liver.

liv-er-y *n., pl.* -ies A uniform worn by servants; the care and boarding of horses for pay; a concern offering horses and vehicles for rent. -ied *adj.*

liv-er-y-man *n.* A keeper or employee of a livery stable.

live-stock *n.* Farm animals raised for human use.

live wire *n., Slang* An energetic person.

liv-id *adj.* Discolored from a bruise; very angry.

liz-ard *n.*

One of various reptiles, usually with an elongated scaly body, four legs, and a tapering tail.

liz-ard fish *n.* A bottom-dwelling fish, having a lizard-like head and dwelling in warm waters of the seas.

lla-ma *n.* A South American ruminant, related to the camel family and raised for its soft wool.

load *n.* A mass or weight that is lifted or supported; anything, as cargo, put in a ship, aircraft, or vehicle for conveyance; something that is a heavy responsibility; a burden. **loader, loading** *n.* **load** *v.*

load-ed *adj.* Intended to trick or trap. *Slang* Drunk; rich.

loaf *n., pl.* **loaves** A food, especially bread, that is shaped into a mass. *v.* To spend time in idleness. **loafer** *n.*

loam *n.* Soil that consists chiefly of sand, clay, and decayed plant matter. **-y** *adj.*

loan *n.* Money lent with interest to be repaid; something borrowed for temporary use. *v.* To lend.

loath *adj.* Averse.

loathe *v.* To dislike intensely.

loath-ing *n.* Intense dislike; abhorrence.

loath-some *adj.* Arousing disgust. **loathsomely** *adv.*, **loathsomeness** *n.*

lob *v.* To hit or throw in a high arc.

lob-by *n., pl.* **-ies** A foyer, as in a hotel or theatre; a group of private persons trying to influence legislators. **lobbyist** *n.* **lobby** *v.*

lobe *n.* A curved or rounded projection or division, as the fleshy lower part of the ear. **lobar, lobed** *adj.*

lob-lol-ly *n., pl.* **-ies** A mudhole; mire.

lo-bo *n.* The gray wolf, as referred to by those who reside in the western United States.

lo-bot-o-my *n., pl.* **-mies** Surgical severance of nerve fibers by incision into the brain.

lob-ster *n.*

Any of several large, edible marine crustaceans with five pairs of legs, the first pair being large and claw-like.

lob-ule *n.* A small lobe; a subdivision of a lobe. **lobular** *adj.*

lo-cal *adj.* Pertaining to, being in, or serving a particular area or place. **locally** *adv.*

lo-cale *n.* A locality where a particular event takes place; the setting or scene, as of a novel.

lo-cal-i-ty *n., pl.* **-ties** A specific neighborhood, place, or district.

lo-cate *v.* To determine the place, position, or boundaries of; to look for and find; to establish or become established; to settle. **locator** *n.*

lo-ca-tion *n.* The act or process of locating; a place where something is or can be located; a site outside a motion picture or television studio where a movie is shot.

loch *n., Scot.* A lake.

lock *n.* A device used, as on a door, to secure or fasten; a part of a waterway closed off with gates to allow the raising or lowering of boats by changing the level of the water; a strand or curl of hair. **lock** *v.*

lock-et *n.* A small, ornamental case for a keepsake, often a picture, worn as a pendant on a necklace.

lock-jaw *n.* Tetanus; a form of tetanus in which a spasm of the jaw muscles locks the jaws closed.

lock-smith *n.* A person who makes or repairs locks.

lo-co *adj., Slang* Insane.

lo-co-mo-tion *n.* The act of moving; the power to move from place to place.

lo-co-mo-tive *n.* A self-propelled vehicle that is generally electric or diesel-powered and is used for moving railroad cars.

lo-co-weed *n.* Any of several plants found throughout the western and central United States which are poisonous to livestock.

lo-cust *n.* Any of numerous grasshoppers which often travel in swarms and damage vegetation; any of various hardwooded leguminous trees, such as carob, black locust, or honey locust.

lode-star *n.* A star; the North Star, used as a reference point.

lodge *n.* A house, such as a cabin, used as a temporary or seasonal dwelling or shelter; an inn; the den of an animal, such as a beaver; a local chapter of a fraternal organization; the meeting hall of such a chapter. **lodge** *v.*

lodg-er *n.* One who rents a room in another's house.

lodg-ment *or* **lodge-ment** *n.* An act of lodging; a place for lodging; an accumulation or deposit.

loft *n.* One of the upper, generally unpartitioned floors of an industrial or commercial building, such as a warehouse; an attic; a gallery in a church or hall.

lo-gan-ber-ry *n.* A prickly plant cultivated for its edible, acidic, red fruit.

loge *n.* A small compartment, especially a box in a theatre; a small partitioned area, as a separate forward section of a theatre mezzanine or balcony.

log-ger-head *n.* Any of various large marine turtles, especially the carnivorous turtle found in the warm waters of the western Atlantic. **at loggerheads** In a state of contention; at odds.

log-gi-a *n.* A roofed but open arcade along the front of a building; an open balcony in a theatre.

log-ic *n.* The science dealing with the principles of reasoning, especially of the method and validity of deductive reasoning; something that forces a decision apart from or in opposition to reason. **logician** *n.*

log-i-cal *adj.* Relating to; or in accordance with logic; something marked by consistency of reasoning. **logically** *adv.*

lo-gis-tics *pl., n.* The methods of procuring, maintaining, and replacing material and personnel, as in a military operation. **logistic** *adj.*

lo-go-type *n.* Identifying symbol for a company or publication.

lo-gy *adj.* Something marked by sluggishness. **loginess** *n.*

loin *n.* The area of the body located between the ribs and pelvis; a cut of meat from an animal.

loin-cloth *n.* A cloth worn about the loins.

loins The thighs and groin; the reproductive organs.

loi-ter *v.* To stay for no apparent reason; to dawdle or delay. **loiterer** *n.*

loll *v.* To move or act in a lax, lazy or indolent manner; to hang loosely or laxly. **loller** *n.*

lol-li-pop *or* **lol-ly-pop** *n.* A piece of flavored hard candy on a stick.

lol-ly-gag *v., Slang* To fool around.

Lon-don *n.* The capital of England.

lone *adj.* Single; isolated; sole; unfrequented.

lone-ly *adj.* Being without companions; dejected from being alone. **-iness** *n.*

lon-er *n.* A person who avoids the company of others.

lone-some *adj.* Dejected because of the lack of companionship. **-ness** *n.*

long-bow *n.* A wooden bow that is approximately five to six feet in length.

lon-gev-i-ty *n.* Long life; long duration; seniority.

Longfellow, Henry Wadsworth *n.* (1807-1882) American poet.

long-hair *n.* A lover of the arts, especially classical music; a person with long hair.

long-hand *n.* Cursive handwriting.

long-horn *n.* One of the long-horned cattle of Spanish derivation, formerly common in the southwestern United States; a firm-textured cheddar cheese ranging from white to orange in color and from mild to sharp in flavor.

lon-gi-tude *n.* The angular distance that is east and west of the prime meridian at Greenwich, England.

lon-gi-tu-di-nal *adj.* Of or relating to the length; relating to longitude. **-ly** *adv.*

long-shore-man *n.* A dock hand who loads and unloads cargo.

look *v.* To examine with the eyes; to see; to glance, gaze, or stare at. *n.* The act of looking; the physical appearance of something or someone.

loom *v.* To come into view as an image; to seem to be threatening. *n.* A machine used for interweaving thread or yarn to produce cloth.

loop *n.* A circular length of line folded over and joined at the ends; a loop-shaped pattern, figure, or path. *v.* To form into a loop; to join, fasten, or encircle with a loop.

loop-hole *n.* A means of escape; a legal way to circumvent the intent of a law.

loose *adj.* Not tightly fastened; not confined or fitting; free.

loot *n.* Goods, usually of significant value, taken in time of war; goods that have been stolen. *v.* To plunder; to steal. **looter** *n.*

lop *v.* To remove branches from; to trim.

lope *v.* To run with a steady gait. **lope, lopper** *n.*

lop-sid-ed *adj.* Larger or heavier on one side than on the other; tilting to one side. **lopsidedly** *adv.*, **lopsidedness** *n.*

lo-qua-cious *adj.* Overly talkative. **loquaciously** *adv.*, **loquacity** *n.*

Lord *n.* God. A man having dominion and power over other people; the owner of a feudal estate.

Lord's Sup-per *n.* Communion.

lore *n.* Traditional fact; knowledge that has been gained through education or experience.

lor-gnette *n.* A pair of opera glasses with a handle.

lose *v.* To mislay; to fail to keep. **loser** *n.*

loss *n.* The suffering or damage used by losing; someone or something that is lost. **losses** *pl. n.* Killed, wounded, or captured soldiers; casualties.

lost *adj.* Unable to find one's way.

lot *n.* Fate; fortune; a parcel of land having boundaries; a plot.

lo-tion *n.* A liquid medicine for external use on the hands and body.

lot-ter-y *n., pl.* **-ies** A contest in which winners are selected by a random drawing.

lo-tus *n.* An aquatic plant having fragrant pinkish flowers and large leaves; any of several plants similar or related to the lotus.

lo-tus-eater *n.* One of a people represented in the Odyssey of Homer as eating the lotus fruit and living in the dreamy indolence it produced.

loud *adj.* Marked by intense sound and high volume. **loudly** *adv.*, **loudness** *n.*

Louis XIV *n.* (1638-1715) King of France from 1643 to 1715.

lounge *v.* To move or act in a lazy, relaxed manner. *n.* A room, as in a hotel or theatre, where people may wait; a couch. **lounger** *n.*

louse *n., pl.* **lice**

A small, wingless biting or sucking insect which lives as a parasites on various animals and also on human beings. *Slang* A mean, contemptible person.

lous-y *adj.* Lice-infested. *Slang* Mean; poor; inferior; abundantly supplied. **lousily** *adv.*

lout *n.* An awkward, stupid person. **loutish** *adj.*

lou-ver *or* **lou-vre** *n.* An opening in a wall fitted with movable, slanted slats which let air in, but keep precipitation out; one of the slats used in a louver. **louvered** *adj.*

love *n.* Intense affection for another arising out of kinship or personal ties; a strong feeling of attraction resulting from sexual desire; enthusiasm or fondness; a score of zero in tennis. **love** *v.*, **lovable**, **loving** *adj.*

love-bird *n.* Any of various Old World parrots which show great affection for their mates.

love-ly *adj.* Beautiful. **loveliness**, **lovely** *n.*

lov-er *n.* A person who loves another; a sexual partner.

love seat *n.* A small couch which seats two.

love-sick *adj.* Languishing with love; expressing a lover's yearning. **-ness** *n.*

loving cup *n.* A large, ornamental cup with two or more handles, often given as an award or trophy.

low *adj.* Not high; being below or under normal height, rank, or level; depressed. *v.* To moo, as a cow.

low-brow *n.* An uncultured person.

low-down *n.* The whole truth; all the facts *adj.* Despicable; mean; depressed.

low-er--case *adj.* Having as its typical form a, b, c, or u, v, w rather than A, B, C, or U, V, W.

low-er class *n.* The group in society that ranks below the middle class in social and economic status.

low-est com-mon de-nom-i-na-tor *n.* The least common multiple of the denominators of a set of fractions.

low-est com-mon mul-ti-ple *n.* Least common multiple.

low fre-quen-cy *n.* A radio-wave frequency between 30 and 300 kilohertz.

low-land *n.* Land that is low and level in relation to the surrounding countryside.

low-ly *adj.* Low in position or rank.

low--rise *adj.* Having one or two stories and no elevator.

low--ten-sion *adj.* Having a low voltage; built to be used at low voltage.

lox *n.* Smoked salmon; liquid oxygen.

loy-al *adj.* Faithful in allegiance to one's country and government; faithful to a person, cause, ideal, or custom.

loy-al-ist *n.* One who is or remains loyal to political cause, party, government, or sovereign.

loz-enge *n.* Small medicated candy, normally having the shape of a lozenge.

lu-au *n.* A traditional Hawaiian feast.

lub-ber *n.* An awkward, clumsy or stupid person; an inexperienced sailor.

lu-bri-cant *n.* A material, as grease or oil, applied to moving parts to reduce friction.

lu-bri-cious *or* **lu-bri-cous** *adj.* Smooth, unstable; shifty. **lubricity** *n.*

lu-cid *adj.* Easily understood; mentally clear; rational; shining. **lucidity**, **lucidness** *n.*, **lucidly** *adv.*

luck *n.* Good fortune; the force or power which controls odds and which brings good fortune or bad fortune. **lucky** *adj.*, **luckily** *adv.*, **luckiness** *n.*

lu-cra-tive *adj.* Producing profits or great wealth. **lucratively** *adv.*

lu-cre *n.* Money; profit.

lu-cu-brate *v.* To study or work laboriously.

lu-di-crous *adj.* Amusing or laughable through obvious absurdity; ridiculous. **ludicrously** *adv.*, **ludicrousness** *n.*

luff *v.* To turn a sailing vessel toward the wind.

lug *n.* An ear-like handle or projection used as a hold; a tab. *v.* To carry with difficulty.

luge *n.* A small sled similar to a toboggan which is ridden in a supine position and used especially in competition.

lu-gu-bri-ous *adj.* Mournful; dejected; especially exaggeratedly or affectedly so. **-ly** *adv.*, **lugubriousness** *n.*

luke-warm *adj.* Mildly warm; tepid; unenthusiastic; soothing. **-ly** *adv.*

lull *v.* To cause to rest or sleep; to cause to have a false sense of security. *n.* A temporary period of quiet or rest.

lul-la-by *n., pl.* **-bies** A song to lull a child to sleep.

lum-ba-go *n.* Painful rheumatic pain of the muscles and tendons of the lumbar region.

lum-bar *adj.* Part of the back and sides between the lowest ribs and the pelvis.

lu-mi-nar-y *n., pl.* **-ies** A celestial body, as the sun; a notable person.

lu-mi-nes-cence *n.* An emission of light without heat, as in fluorescence.

lu-mi-nous *adj.* Emitting or reflecting light; bathed in steady light; illuminated; easily understood; clear.

lum-mox *n.* A clumsy oaf.

lump *n.* A projection; a protuberance; a swelling, as from a bruise or infection. *v.* To group things together. **-y** *adj.*

lu-na-cy *n., pl.* **-ies** Insanity.

lu-nar *adj.* Of, relating to, caused by the moon.

lu-nar e-clipse *n.* An eclipse where the moon passes partially or wholly through the umbra of the earth's shadow.

lu-na-tic *n.* A crazy person.

lunch-eon *n.* A lunch.

lunch-eon-ette *n.* A modest restaurant at which light meals are served.

lung *n.*

One of the two spongy organs that

constitute the basic respiratory organ of air-breathing vertebrates.

lunge *n.* A sudden forward movement.

lu-pus *n.* A bacterial disease of the skin.

lure *n.* A decoy; something appealing; an artificial bait to catch fish. *v.* To attract or entice with the prospect of reward or pleasure.

lurk *v.* To lie in concealment, as in an ambush.

lus-cious *adj.* Very pleasant to smell or taste; appealing to the senses. **lusciously** *adv.*, **lusciousness** *n.*

lush *adj.* Producing luxuriant growth or vegetation. *Slang* An alcoholic. **lushly** *adv.*, **lushness** *n.*

lust *n.* Intense sexual desire; an intense longing; a craving. **-ful** *adj.*

lus-ter *or* **lus-tre** *n.* A glow of reflected light; sheen; brilliance or radiance; brightness. **lustrous, lusterless** *adj.*

lust-y *adj.* Vigorous; healthy; robust; lively. **lustily** *adv.*, **lustiness** *n.*

lute *n.* A medieval musical stringed instrument with a fretted finger board, a pear-shaped body, and usually a bent neck.

lu-te-ti-um *or* **lu-te-ci-um** *n.* A silvery rare-earth metallic element symbolized by Lu.

Luther, Martin (1483-1546) German religious leader.

Lu-ther-an *n.* A member of a Protestant church that was founded by and adheres to the teachings of Martin Luther. **Lutheran** *adj.*, **Lutheranism** *n.*

lux-u-ri-ant *adj.* Growing or producing abundantly; lush; plentiful.

lux-u-ri-ate *v.* To enjoy luxury or abundance; to grow abundantly.

ly-ce-um *n.* A hall where public programs are presented; an organization which sponsors such programs as lectures and concerts.

lye *n.* A powerful caustic solution yielded by leaching wood ashes; potassium hydroxide; sodium hydroxide.

ly-ing-in *n.* Confinement in childbirth.

lymph node *n.* A roundish body of lymphoid tissue; lymph gland.

lynch *v.* To execute without authority or the due process of law.

lynx *n.*

A wildcat. *adj.* Having acute eyesight.

lyre *n.* An ancient Greek stringed instrument related to the harp.

lyr-ic *adj.* Concerned with thoughts and feelings; romantic; appropriate for singing. *n.* A lyric poem. **lyrics** The words of a song. **-al** *adj.*, **-ally** *adv.*

ly-ser-gic acid di-eth-yl-am-ide *n.* An organic compound which induces psychotic symptoms similar to those of schizophernia; LSD.

M, m The thirteenth letter of the English alphabet; the Roman numeral for 1,000.

MA *abbr.* Master of Arts.

ma'am *n.* Madam.

mac *n.* An address for a man whose name is unknown.

ma-ca-bre *adj.* Suggesting death and decay.

mac-ad-am *n.* Pavement for roads consisting of layers of compacted, broken stone, usually cemented with asphalt and tar. **macadamize** *v.*

mac-a-ro-ni *n.* Dried pasta made into short tubes and prepared as food.

mac-a-roon *n.* A small cookie made of sugar, egg whites, coconut, and ground almonds.

ma-caw *n.* Any of various tropical American parrots with long tails, brilliant plumage, and harsh voices.

mace *n.* An aromatic spice made by grinding the cover of the nutmeg.

mac-er-ate *v.* To make a solid substance soft by soaking in liquid; to cause to grow thin. **maceration** *n.*

ma-chet-e *n.* A large, heavy knife with a broad blade, used as a weapon.

mach-i-nate *v.* To plot. **machination, machinator** *n.*

ma-chine *n.* A device or system built to use energy to do work; a political organization. *v.* To produce precision tools.

ma-chine lan-guage *n.*, In Computer Science, the system of numbers or instructions for coding input data.

ma-chin-er-y *n.*, *pl.* **-ies** A collection of machines as a whole; the mechanism or operating parts of a machine.

ma-chin-ist *n.* One skilled in the operation or repair of machines.

ma-chis-mo *n.* An exaggerated sense of masculinity.

ma-cho *adj.*, *Slang* Exhibiting machismo.

mack-er-el *n.* A fish with dark, wavy bars on the back and a silvery belly, found in the Atlantic Ocean.

mac-ra-me *n.* The craft or hobby of tying knots into a pattern.

mac-ro-bi-ot-ic *adj.* Relating to or being an extremely restricted diet to promote longevity, consisting mainly of whole grain, vegetables and fish.

ma-cron *n.* A mark (-) placed over a vowel to indicate a long sound.

mac-ro-scop-ic *or* **mac-ro-scop-ic-al** *adj.* Large enough to be seen by the naked eye.

mad *adj.* Angry; afflicted with a mental disorder; insane.

mad-am *n.*, *pl.* **mes-dames** A title used to address a married woman; used without a name as a courtesy title when addressing a woman.

mad-cap *adj.* Impulsive, rash or reckless.

mad-den *v.* To craze; to enrage; to make mad. *v.* To become mad.

mad-ding *adj.* Behaving senselessly; acting mad.

made *v.* Past tense of make.

mad-e-moi-selle *n.*, *pl.* **mademoiselles** *or*

mesdemoiselles An unmarried French girl or woman.

made--up adj. Fabricated; invented; having only makeup on.

mad-house n., Slang A place of confusion and disorder.

Mad-i-son, James n. (1751-1836). The 4th U.S. president of the United States from (1809-1817).

mad-ri-gal n., Music An unaccompanied song, usually for four to six voices, developed during the early Renaissance.

mael-strom n. Any irresistible or dangerous force.

maes-tro n., pl. -tros or -tri A person mastering any art, but especially a famous conductor of music.

Ma-fi-a n. A secret criminal organization in Sicily; an international criminal organization believed to exist in many countries, including the U.S.

mag-a-zine n. A publication with a paper cover containing articles, stories, illustrations and advertising; the part of a gun which holds ammunition ready for feeding into the chamber.

ma-gen-ta n. A purplish red color.

mag-got n. The legless larva of any of various insects, as the housefly, often found in decaying matter.

Ma-gi pl., n. Magus The three wise men of the East who traveled to Bethlehem to pay homage to the baby Jesus.

mag-ic n. The art which seemingly controls foresight of natural events and forces by means of supernatural agencies. -al adj., -ly adv., -ian n.

mag-is-trate n. A civil officer with the power to enforce the law.

Mag-na Car-ta n. The Great Charter of English liberties which the barons forced King John to sign on June 19, 1215; any document constituting a guarantee of rights and privileges.

mag-nan-i-mous adj. Generous in forgiving insults or injuries. magnanimity, magnanimousness n., -ly adv.

mag-nate n. A person notable or powerful, especially in business.

mag-ne-sia n., Chem. A light, white powder used in medicine as an antacid and laxative.

mag-ne-si-um n. A light, silvery metallic element which burns with a very hot, bright flame and is used in lightweight alloys, symbolized by Mg.

mag-net n.

A body having the property of attracting iron and other magnetic material. magnetism n.

mag-net-ic adj. Pertaining to magnetism or a magnet; capable of being attracted by a magnet; having the power or ability to attract. magnetically adv.

magnetic field n. The area in the neighborhood of a magnet or of an electric current, marked by the existence of a detectable magnetic force in every part of the region.

mag-net-ite n. A black iron oxide in mineral form, which is an important iron ore.

mag-net-ize v. To have magnetic properties; to attract by personal charm or influence. magnetizable adj., magnetization, magnetizer n.

mag-ne-to n. A small alternator which works by means of magnets that are permanently attached, inducing an electric current for the spark in some engines.

mag-ne-tom-e-ter n. An instrument used for measuring the direction and intensity of magnetic forces.

mag-ne-to-sphere n., Physics A region of the upper atmosphere extending from about 500 to several thousand km above the surface, forming a band of ionized particles trapped by the earth's magnetic field.

mag-nif-i-cent adj. Having an extraordinarily imposing appearance; beautiful; outstanding; exceptionally pleasing.

mag-ni-fy v. To increase in size; to cause to seem more important or greater; to glorify or praise someone or something. magnification, magnifier n.

mag-nil-o-quent adj. Speaking or spoken in a lofty and extravagant manner. magniloquence n., magniloquently adv.

mag-ni-tude n. Greatness or importance in size or extent. Astron. The relative brightness of a star expressed on a numerical scale, ranging from one for the brightest to six for those just visible.

mag-no-lia n. An ornamental flowering tree or shrub with large, fragrant flowers of white, pink, purple, or yellow.

mag-num n. A wine bottle holding about two quarts or approximately 2/5 gallon.

mag-num o-pus n. A great work of art; literary or artistic masterpiece; the greatest single work of an artist, writer, or other creative person.

mag-pie n. Any of a variety of large, noisy bird found the world over having long tapering tails and black and white plumage.

ma-ha-ra-ja or ma-ha-ra-jah n. A king or prince who rules an Indian state.

ma-ha-ra-ni or ma-ha-ra-nee n. The wife of a maharajah.

ma-hat-ma n. In some Asian religions, a person venerated for great knowledge; a title of respect.

ma-hog-a-ny n., pl. -ies Any of various tropical trees having hard, reddish-brown wood, much used for cabinet work and furniture.

maid n. A young unmarried woman or girl; a female servant. maiden n.

maid-en-hair n. A delicate fern with dark stems and light-green, feathery fronds.

maid-en name n. A woman's family name before marriage.

maid of hon-or *n.* An unmarried woman who is the main attendant of a bride at a wedding.

mail *n.* Letter, printed matter, or parcel handled by the postal system. -er *n.*

mail or-der *n.* Goods which are ordered and sent by mail.

maim *v.* To disable or to deprive of the use of a bodily part; to impair.

main *adj.* Being the most important part of something. *n.* A large pipe used to carry water, oil, or gas. **mainly** *adv.*

Maine *n.* A state located in the northeastern corner of the United States.

main-land *n.* The land part of a country as distinguished from an island.

main-line *v., Slang* To inject a drug directly into a vein.

main-stream *n.* A main direction or line of thought. **mainstream** *adj. & v.*

main-tain *v.* To carry on or to keep in existence; to preserve in a desirable condition. -able *adj.*, **maintenance** *n.*

maize *n.* Corn.

maj-es-ty *n., pl.* -ies Stateliness; exalted dignity. **majestic** *adj.*, -ically *adv.*

ma-jor *adj.* Greater in importance, quantity, number, or rank; serious. *n.* An officer in the U.S. Army, Air Force or Marines who ranks above a captain and below a lieutenant colonel; a subject or field of academic study. *Music* A major musical scale, interval, key, or mode.

ma-jor-ette *n.* A young woman or girl who marches and twirls a baton with a band.

ma-jor-i-ty *n., pl.* -ies The greater number of something; more than half; the age at which a person is considered to be an adult, usually 21 years old.

make *v.* To cause something to happen; to create; to provide, as time; to manufacture a line of goods. *n.* A brand name, as a make of a car. **make a-way with** To carry off. **make hay** To take advantage of a given opportunity in the early stages. **make no bones** To perform unhesitating.

make--be-lieve *n.* A pretending to believe. *v.* To pretend.

make up *n.* The manner in which something is formed together or assembled; con-structions; the qualities of physical or mental constitution; cosmetics. *v.* To invent a story.

mal-a-chite *n.* A green basic copper carbonate, used as a common ore of copper and for decorating stoneware.

mal-a-droit *adj.* Lacking skill; awkward; clumsy. -ly *adv.*, **maladroitness** *n.*

mal-a-dy *n., pl.* -ies A chronic disease or sickness.

mal-aise *n.* The vague discomfort sometimes indicating the beginning of an illness.

mal-a-prop-ism *n.* A foolish misuse of a word.

mal-ap-ro-pos *adj.* Not appropriate.

ma-lar-i-a *n., Pathol.* The infectious disease introduced into the blood by the bite of the infected female anopheles mosquito and characterized by cycles of fever, chills, and profuse sweating. **malarial** *adj.*

ma-lar-key *n., Slang* Foolish or insincere talk; nonsense.

mal-con-tent *adj.* Unhappy with existing conditions or affairs. **malcontent** *n.*

mal de mer *n.* Seasickness.

male *adj.* Of or belonging to the sex that has organs to produce spermatozoa. *Bot.* A plant with stamens but no pistil. *n.* A male person or animal.

mal-e-dic-tion *n.* A curse; execration. **maledictory** *adj.*

mal-e-fac-tor *n.* A person who commits a crime or an unlawful act; a criminal. **malefaction** *n.*

ma-lev-o-lent *adj.* Full of spite or ill will for another; malicious. **malevolently** *adv.*, **malevolence** *n.*

mal-func-tion *n.* Failure to function correctly. **malfunction** *v.*

mal-ice *n.* The direct intention or desire to harm others. *Law* The willfully formed design to injure another without just reason or cause.

ma-lign *v.* To speak slander or evil of. **maligner** *n.*

ma-lig-nant *adj., Pathol.* Of or relating to tumors and abnormal or rapid growth, and tending to metastasize; opposed to benign; causing death or great harm. **malignancy**, **malignity** *n.*, **malignantly** *adv.*

mall *n.* A walk or other shaded public promenade; a street with shops, restaurants, and businesses which is closed to vehicles.

mal-lard *n., pl.* **mallard** *or* -ards. A wild duck having brownish plumage, the male of which has a green head and neck.

mal-le-a-ble *adj.* Able to be bent, shaped, or hammered without breaking; capable of being molded, altered, or influenced. **malleability**, **malleableness** *n.*, **malleably** *adv.*

mal-let *n.* A hammer with a head made of wood or rubber and a short handle; a tool for striking an object without marring it.

mal-le-us *n., pl.* -lei *Anat.* The club-shaped bone of the middle ear or the largest of three small bones; also called the hammer.

mal-nour-ished *adj.* Undernourished.

mal-nu-tri-tion *n.* Insufficient nutrition.

mal-oc-clu-sion *n.* Improper alignment of the teeth.

mal-o-dor-ous *adj.* Having a disagreeable or foul odor. -ly *adv.*, -ness *n.*

mal-prac-tice *n.* Improper treatment of a patient by his doctor during surgery or treatment which results in damage or injury; failure to perform a professional duty in a proper, careful, or correct fashion, resulting in injury, loss, or other problems.

malt *n.* Grain, usually barley, used chiefly in brewing and distilling; an alcoholic beverage.

mal-tose *n.* A white, crystalline sugar

found in malt.

mal-treat v. To treat badly, unkindly, or roughly. **maltreatment** n.

ma-ma n. Mother.

mam-ba n. A venomous snake found in the tropics and in southern Africa.

mam-bo n. A dance resembling the rumba of Latin America.

mam-mal n. Any member of a class whose females secrete milk for nourishing their young, including man. **mammalian** adj. & n.

mam-ma-ry gland n. The milk-producing organ of the female mammal, consisting of small cavity clusters with ducts ending in a nipple.

mam-mog-ra-phy n. An x-ray examination of the breast for early detection of cancer.

mam-moth n. An extinct, early form of elephant whose tusks curved upwards and whose body was covered with long hair; anything of great or huge size.

man n., pl. **men** An adult or fully-grown male; the human race; any human being, regardless of sex. Slang Husband; an expression of pleasure or surprise.

man-a-cle n. A device for restraining the hands; handcuffs. **manacle** v.

man-age v. To direct or control the affairs or use of; to organize. **manageability** n., **-able** adj., **-ably** adv.

man-ag-er n. One in charge of managing an enterprise or business. **managerial** adj., **managership** n.

man-a-tee n. An aquatic mammal of the coastal waters of Florida, West Indies, and the Gulf of Mexico.

man-date n. An authoritative order or command. Law A judicial order issued by a higher court to a lower one. **mandate** v.

man-da-to-ry adj. Required by, having the nature of, or relating to a mandate; obligatory.

man-di-ble n. The lower jaw bone. Biol. Either part of the beak of a bird. **mandibular** adj.

man-do-lin n. A musical instrument having a pear-shaped body and a fretted neck.

man-drake n. A plant having purplish flowers and a branched root sometimes resembling the human form.

man-drel or **man-dril** n. A spindle or shaft on which material is held for working on a lathe.

man-drill n. A large, fierce West African baboon.

mane n.

The long hair growing on the neck of some animals, as the lion, and horse.

man--eat-er n. An animal which feeds on human flesh, such as a shark or a tiger.

ma-nege n. The art of training and riding horses; the performance of a horse so trained.

ma-neu-ver n., Milit. A planned strategic movement or shift, as of warships, or troops; any planned, skillful, or calculated move. **maneuver** v., **maneuverability** n., **maneuverable** adj.

man Fri-day n. A person devoted to another as a servant, aide, or employee.

man-ful adj. Having a manly spirit. **manfully** adv., **manfulness** n.

man-ga-nese n. A hard, brittle, gray-white metallic element which forms an important component of steel alloys, symbolized by Mn.

mange n. A contagious skin disease of dogs and other domestic animals caused by parasitic mites and marked by itching and hair loss. **mangy** adj.

man-ger n. A trough or box which holds livestock feed.

man-gle v. To disfigure or mutilate by bruising, battering, or crushing; to spoil. **mangler** n.

man-go n., pl. **-goes** or **-gos** A tropical evergreen tree that produces a fruit having a slightly acid taste.

man-grove n. A tropical evergreen tree or shrub having aerial roots which form dense thickets along tidal shores.

man-han-dle v. To handle very roughly.

man-hole n. A circular covered, opening usually in a street, through which one may enter a sewer, drain, or conduit.

man-hood n. The state of being an adult male.

man--hour n. The amount of work that one person can complete in one hour.

ma-ni-a n. An extraordinary enthusiasm or craving for something; intense excitement and physical overactivity, often a symptom of manic-depressive psychosis.

-mania suffix. Unreasonable or intense desire or infatuation with.

ma-ni-ac n. A violently insane person. **maniac, maniacal** adj.

man-ic--de-pres-sive adj. Of a mental disorder characterized by alternating periods of manic excitation and depression. **manic-depressive** n.

man-i-cot-ti n. Pasta shaped like a tube, filled with meat or ricotta cheese and served with hot tomato sauce.

man-i-cure n. The cosmetic care of the hands and fingernails. **manicurist** n.

man-i-fest adj. Clearly apparent; obvious. v. To display, reveal or show. n. A list of cargo or passengers. **manifestly** adv.

man-i-fes-ta-tion n. The act or state of being manifest.

man-i-fes-to n., pl. **-toes** or **-tos** A public or formal explanation of principles or intentions, usually of a political nature.

man-i-fold adj. Having many and varied parts, forms, or types; having an assortment of features. Mech. A pipe with several or many openings, as for the escaping of exhaust gas.

manifoldly *adv.*, **manifoldness** *n.*

man-i-kin *or* **man-ni-kin** *n.* A little man; a dwarf; a mannequin.

Ma-nil-a *n.* The capital of the Philippines.

Manila hemp *n.* The fiber of the banana plant, used for making paper, rope, and cord.

Manila paper *n.* Strong, light brown paper, originally made from Manila hemp but now made of various fibers.

ma-nip-u-late *v.* To handle or manage shrewdly and deviously for one's own profit. **manipulation, manipulator** *n.*, **manipulative** *adj.*

man-kind *n.* The human race; men collectively, as opposed to women.

man-ly *adj.* Pertaining to or having qualities which are traditionally attributed to a man. **manliness** *n.*

man--made *adj.* Made by human beings and not developed by nature.

man-na *n.* The food which was miraculously given to the Israelites in the wilderness on their flight from Egypt; anything of value that one receives unexpectedly.

manned *adj.* Operated by a human being.

man-ne-quin *n.* A life-sized model of a human figure, used to fit or display clothes; a woman who models clothes.

man-ner *n.* The way in which something happens or is done; an action or style of speech; one's social conduct and etiquette. **mannered** *adj.*

man-ner-ism *n.* A person's distinctive behavioral trait or traits. **mannerist** *n.* **manneristic, manneristical** *adj.*

man-ner-ly *adj.* Well-behaved; polite. **mannerliness** *n.*

man-nish *adj.* Resembling a man; masculine. **-ly** *adv.*, **mannishness** *n.*

man--of--war *n.*, *pl.* **men--of--war** A warship.

ma-nom-e-ter *n.* An instrument used to measure pressure, as of gases or liquids. **manometric** *adj.*

man-or *n.* A landed estate; the house or hall of an estate. **manorial** *adj.*

man pow-er *n.* The force of human physical power; the number of men whose strength and skill are readily available to a nation, army, project, or other venture.

man-que *adj.* Lacking fulfillment; frustrated.

man-sard *n.*, *Archit.* A curved roof with the lower slope almost vertical and the upper almost horizontal.

manse *n.* The house of a clergyman.

man-sion *n.* A very large, impressive house.

man--size *or* **man--sized** *adj.*, *Slang* Quite large.

man-slaugh-ter *n.*, *Law* The unlawful killing without malice of a person by another.

man-ta *n.* A rough-textured cotton fabric; any of several very large fishes having large, very flat bodies with winglike fins.

man-teau *n.*, *pl.* **-teaus** *or* **-teaux** A robe or cloak.

man-tel *also* **man-tle** *n.* A shelf over a fireplace; the ornamental brick or stone around a fireplace.

man-til-la *n.* A light scarf worn over the head and shoulders by women in Latin America and Spain.

man-tis *n.*, *pl.* **mantises** *or* **mantes** A tropical insect with a long body, large eyes, and swiveling head, which stands with its forelegs folded as if in prayer.

man-tle *n.* A loose-fitting coat which is usually sleeveless; something that covers or conceals; a device consisting of a sheath of threads, used in gas lamps to give off brilliant illumination when heated by a flame. **mantle** *v.*

man-u-al *adj.* Used or operated by the hands. *n.* A small reference book which gives instructions on how to operate or work something. **-ly** *adv.*

man-u-fac-ture *v.* To make a product; to invent or produce something. **-er** *n.*

ma-nure *n.* The fertilizer used to fertilize land, obtained from animal dung.

man-u-script *n.* A typed or written material copy of an article, book, or document, which is being prepared for publication.

man-y *adj.* Amounting to a large or indefinite number or amount.

map *n.* A plane surface representation of a region. *v.* To plan anything in detail. **mapmaker, mapper** *n.*

ma-ple *n.* A tall tree having lobed leaves and a fruit of two joined samaras; the wood of this tree, amber-yellow in color when finished and used for furniture and flooring.

ma-ple su-gar *n.* Sugar made from the sap of the maple tree.

ma-ple sy-rup *n.* The refined sap of the sugar maple.

mar *v.* To scratch or deface; to blemish; to ruin; to spoil.

mar-a-bou *n.* A stork of Africa, whose soft down is used for trimming women's garments.

ma-ra-ca *n.*

A percussion instrument made from gourds containing dried beans or pebbles.

mar-a-schi-no *n.* A cherry preserved in a cordial distilled from the fermented juice of the small wild cherry and flavored with cracked cherry pits.

mar-a-thon *n.* A foot race of 26 miles, usually run on the streets of a city; any contest of endurance.

mar-ble *n.* A limestone which is partly crystallized and irregular in color. *v.* To contain sections of fat, as in meat. **marbles** A game played with balls of glass. *Slang* A person's common sense or sanity **marble** *v.*, **marbly** *adj.*

march *v.* To walk with measured, regular steps in a solemn or dignified manner.

Mus. A musical composition.

March *n.* The third month of the year, containing 31 days.

Mar-di Gras *n.* The Tuesday before Ash Wednesday, often celebrated with parades and costumed merrymaking.

mare *n.* The female of the horse and other equine animals.

ma-re *n., pl. Astron.* Any of the dark areas on the surface of the moon.

mar-ga-rine *n.* A butter substitute made from vegetable oils and milk.

mar-gin *n.* The edge or border around the body of written or printed text; the difference between the selling price and cost of an item.

mar-gi-na-li-a *pl., n.* The notes in the margin of a book.

ma-ri-a-chi *n.* A Mexican band; the music performed by a musician playing in a mariachi.

Marie Antoinette *n.* (1755-1793). The queen of Louis XVI of France from 1774-1793.

mar-i-gold *n.* Any of a variety of plants having golden-yellow flowers.

mar-i-jua-na *or* **marihuana** *n.* Hemp; the dried flower tops and leaves of this plant, capable of producing disorienting or hallucinogenic effects when smoked in cigarettes or ingested.

ma-ri-na *n.* A docking area for boats, furnishing moorings and supplies for small boats.

mar-i-nade *n.* A brine made from vinegar or wine and oil with various herbs and spices for soaking meat, fowl, or fish before cooking.

mar-i-nate *v.* To soak meat in a marinade.

ma-rine *adj.* Of, pertaining to, existing in, or formed by the sea. *n.* A soldier trained for service on land and at sea. **Marine** *n.* A member of the Marine Corps.

mar-i-tal *adj.* Pertaining to marriage. **maritally** *adv.*

mar-i-time *adj.* Located or situated on or near the sea; pertaining to the sea and its navigation and commerce.

mark *n.* A visible impression, trace, dent, or stain; an identifying seal, inscription, or label.

Mark *n.* The evangelist who wrote the second Gospel narratives in the New Testament; the second Gospel of the New Testament; Saint Mark.

mar-ket *n.* The trade and commerce in a certain service or commodity; a public place for purchasing and selling merchandise; the possible consumers of a particular product. *v.* To sell. **marketability** *n.,* **marketable** *adj.*

mar-ket-place *n.* A place, such as a public square, where ideas, opinions, and works are traded and tested.

marks-man *n.* A person skilled in firing a gun and hitting the mark. **-woman** *n.*

mark-up *n.* The amount of increase in price from the cost to the selling price. *v.* To raise the price.

mar-lin *n.* A large marine game fish of the Atlantic; the striped marlin found in the Pacific.

mar-line-spike *n., Naut.* A pointed tool used in splicing ropes.

mar-ma-lade *n.* A preserve made from the pulp and rind of fruits.

ma-roon *v.* To put ashore and abandon on a desolate shore. *n.* A dull purplish red.

mar-que-try *n.* Inlaid work of wood or ivory used for decorating furniture.

mar-quis *n.* The title of a nobleman ranking below a duke.

mar-qui-sette *n.* A fabric of cotton, silk, nylon, or a combination of these, used in curtains, clothing, and mosquito nets.

mar-riage *n.* The state of being married; wedlock; the act of marrying or the ceremony entered into by a man and woman so as to live together as husband and wife. **-ability** *n.,* **-able** *adj.*

mar-row *n.* The soft, vascular tissue which fills bone cavities; the main part or essence of anything.

mar-ry *v.* To take or join as husband or wife; to unite closely.

Mars *n.* The 4th planet from the sun.

marsh *n.* An area of low, wet land; a swamp. **marshy** *adj.*

mar-shal *n.* A military officer of high rank in foreign countries; the person in the U.S. in charge of a police or fire department. *v.* To bring troops together to prepare for a battle.

marsh-mal-low *n.* A soft, white confection made of sugar, corn syrup, starch, and gelatin and coated with powdered sugar.

mar-su-pi-al *n.* An animal, such as a kangaroo, koala, or opossum, which has no placenta, but which in the female has an abdominal pouch with teats to feed and carry the offspring.

mart *n.* A trading market; a center.

mar-ten *n.*

A weasel-like mammal of eastern North America with arboreal habits; the valuable brown fur of the marten.

mar-tial *adj.* Of, pertaining to, or concerned with war or the military life.

mar-tial arts *pl., n.* Oriental arts of self-defense, such as karate or judo, which are practiced as sports.

mar-tial law *n.* Temporary rule by military forces over the citizens in an area where civil law and order no longer exist.

mar-tin *n.* A bird of the swallow family with a tail that is less forked than that of the common swallow.

mar-ti-ni *n., pl.* **-nis** A cocktail of gin and dry vermouth, served with an olive or lemon peel.

mar-tyr *n.* A person who would rather

die than renounce his religious principles; one making great sacrifices to advance a cause, belief, or principle. **martyr** v., **martyrdom** n.

mar-vel n. Anything causing surprise, wonder, or astonishment. **marvel** v.

mar-vel-ous or **marvellous** adj. Causing astonishment and wonder; wondrous. Informal Excellent; very good, admirable. -ly adv., **marvelousness** n.

Marx-ism n. The body of socialist doctrines developed by Karl Marx. **Marxist** n.

Mary n. The mother of Jesus.

mar-zi-pan n. A confection of grated almonds, sugar, and egg whites.

masc abbr. Masculine.

mas-car-a n. A cosmetic preparation used for coloring or darkening the eyelashes.

mas-cot n. A person, animal, or object thought to bring good luck.

mas-cu-line adj. Of or pertaining to the male sex; male; the masculine gender. **masculinity** n.

ma-ser n., Physics One of several devices which are similar to the laser but which operate with microwaves rather than light.

mash n. A soft, pulpy mass or mixture used to distill alcohol or spirits. v. To crush into a soft, pulpy mass. -er n.

mask n. A covering used to conceal the face in order to disguise or protect. v. To hide or conceal.

mas-o-chism n. A condition in which sexual gratification is marked by pleasure in being subjected to physical pain or abuse. -ist n., -istic adj.

ma-son n. A person working with brick or stone.

ma-son-ic adj. Pertaining to or like freemasonry or Freemasons.

masque n. An elaborately staged dramatic performance, popular during the 16th and 17th centuries in England; a masquerade.

mas-quer-ade n. A costume party in which the guests are masked and dressed in fancy costumes. v. To disguise oneself. **masquerader** n.

mass n. A body of matter that does not have definite shape but is relatively large in size; physical volume; the measure of a body's resistance to acceleration.

Mass or **mass** n. A celebration in the Roman Catholic and some Protestant churches; the service including this celebration.

mas-sa-cre n. The indiscriminate and savage killing of human beings in large numbers. **massacre** v.

mas-sage n. The manual or mechanical manipulation of the skin to improve circulation and to relax muscles.

mas-seur n. A man who gives massages.

mas-seuse n. A woman who gives massages.

mas-sive adj. Of great intensity, degree, and size. -ly adv., **massiveness** n.

mast n. The upright pole or spar which supports the sails and running rigging of a sail boat.

mas-tec-to-my n., pl. -ies The surgical removal of breast.

mas-ter n. A person with control or authority over others; one who is exceptionally gifted or skilled in an art, science, or craft; the title given for respect or in address. v. To learn a skill, craft, or job; to overcome defeat. **mastership** n.

mas-ter key n. A key which will open many different locks whose keys are not the same.

mas-ter-ly adj. Characteristic of a master. **masterliness** n.

mas-ter-mind n. A person who plans and directs at the highest levels of policy and strategy. v. To plan or direct an undertaking.

mas-ter of cer-e-mo-nies n. A person who hosts a formal event or program.

mas-ter-piece n. Something having notable excellence; an unusually brilliant achievement which is considered the greatest achievement of its creator.

mas-ter plan n. A plan providing complete instructions.

mast-head n. The top of a mast; the listing in a periodical giving the names of the editors, staff, and owners.

mas-ti-cate v. To chew. **mastication** n.

mas-to-don n. A large, extinct mammal which resembles an elephant.

mas-toid n., Anat. The nipple shaped portion at the rear of the temporal bone behind the ear.

mas-tur-ba-tion n. The act of stimulating the sexual organs by hand or other means without sexual intercourse. **masturbate** v., **masturbator** n.

mat n. A flat piece of material made of fiber, rubber, rushes, or other material and used to cover floors; the border around a picture, which serves as a contrast between the picture and the frame.

mat-a-dor n. A bullfighter who kills the bull after completing various maneuvers with a cape.

match n. Anything that is similar or identical to another; a short, thin piece of wood or cardboard with a specially treated tip which ignites as a result of friction. v. To equal; to oppose successfully. -able adj., -er n.

match-maker n. A person who arranges a marriage.

mate n. A spouse; something matched, joined, or paired with another; in chess, a move which puts the opponent's king in jeopardy. Naval A petty officer. **mate** v.

ma-te-ri-al n. The substance from which anything is or may be composed or constructed of; anything that is used in creating, working up, or developing something.

ma-te-ri-al-ism n. The doctrine that physical matter is the only reality and that everything, including thought, feeling, will, and mind, is explainable in terms of matter; a preference for material objects as opposed to spiritual or intellectual pursuits. **materialist** *n.*, **materialistic** *adj.*, **materialistically** *adv.*

ma-te-ri-al-ize *v.* To give material or actual form to something; to assume material or visible appearance; to take form or shape. **-ation, materializer** *n.*

ma-te-ri-el *n.* The equipment and supplies of a military force, including guns and ammunition.

ma-ter-nal *adj.* Relating to a mother or motherhood; inherited from one's mother.

ma-ter-ni-ty *n.* The state of being a mother; the qualities of a mother; the department in a hospital for the prenatal and postnatal care of babies and their mothers.

math *n.* Mathematics.

math-e-mat-ics *n.* The study of form, arrangement, quantity, and magnitude of numbers and operational symbols. **-al** *adj.*, **-ally** *adv.*, **mathematician** *n.*

mat-i-nee *n.* An afternoon performance of a play, concert, movie, etc.

ma-tri-arch *n.* A woman ruler of a family, tribe, or clan. **-al** *adj.*, **-y** *n.*

mat-ri-cide *n.* The killing of one's own mother; one who kills his mother. **matricidal** *adj.*

ma-tric-u-late *v.* To enroll, or to be admitted into a college or university. **matriculation** *n.*

mat-ri-mo-ny *n.* The condition of being married; the act, sacrament, or ceremony of marriage. **matrimonial** *adj.*, **matrimonially** *adv.*

ma-trix *n.*, *pl.* **-rixes** *or* **-rices.** Something within which something else develops, originates, or takes shape; a mold or die.

ma-tron *n.* A married woman or widow of dignity and social position; the woman supervisor in a prison. **matronliness** *n.*, **matronly** *adj. & adv.*

mat-ter *n.* Something that makes up the substance of anything; that which is material and physical, occupies space, and is perceived by the senses; something that is sent by mail; something that is written or printed.

mat-tock *n.* A tool having a blade on one side and a pick on the other or one with a blade on each side.

mat-tress *n.* A large cloth case filled with soft material and used on or as a bed.

mat-u-rate *v.* To ripen or mature.

ma-ture *adj.* Completely developed; at full growth; something, as a bond at a bank, that is due and payable. **mature** *v.*, **maturely** *adv.*, **maturity** *n.*

mat-zo *n.*, *pl.* **-zos** *or* **-zot** A large, flat piece of unleavened bread eaten during Passover.

maud-lin *adj.* Overly sentimental; tearfully and overwhelmingly emotional.

maul *n.* A heavy hammer or mallet used to drive wedges, piles, and other materials. *v.* To handle roughly; to abuse.

maun-der *v.* To wander or talk in an incoherent manner.

mau-so-le-um *n.*, *pl.* **-leums** *or* **-lea** A large and stately tomb.

mauve *n.* A purplish rose shade; a moderately reddish to gray purple.

mav-er-ick *n.* An unbranded or orphaned calf or colt. *Slang* A person who is unorthodox in his ideas or attitudes.

maw *n.* The jaws, mouth, or gullet of a hungry or ferocious animal; the stomach.

mawk-ish *adj.* Disgustingly sentimental; sickening or insipid. **mawkishly** *adv.* **mawkishness** *n.*

max *abbr.* Maximum.

max-i *n.* A floor-length garment, such as a skirt or coat.

max-il-la *n.*, *pl.* **-lae** *or* **-las** The upper jaw or jawbone. **maxillary** *adj.*

max-im *n.* A brief statement of truth, general principle, or rule of conduct.

max-i-mize *v.* To increase as greatly as possible; to intensify to the maximum.

max-i-mum *n.*, *pl.* **-mums** *or* **-ma** The greatest possible number, measure, degree, or quantity. **maximum** *adj.*

may *v.* To be permitted or allowed; used to express a wish, purpose, desire, contingency, or result.

May *n.* The fifth month of the year, having 31 days.

may-be *adv.* Perhaps; possibly.

May Day *n.* The first day of May, traditionally celebrated as a spring festival and in some countries as a holiday honoring the labor force.

may-flow-er *n.* A wide variety of plants which blossom in May.

Mayflower *n.* The ship on which the Pilgrims came to America in 1620.

may-hem *n.*, *Law* The offense of injuring a person's body; any situation brought on by violence, confusion, noise, or disorder.

may-o *n.*, *Slang* Mayonnaise.

may-on-naise *n.* A dressing for salads, made by beating raw egg yolk, oil, lemon juice, or vinegar and seasonings.

may-or *n.* The chief magistrate of a town borough, municipality, or city. **mayoral** *adj.*, **mayoralty, mayorship** *n.*

may-pole *n.* A decorated pole hung with streamers around which May Day dancing takes place.

maze *n.* A complicated, intricate network of passages or pathways; a labyrinth; a state of uncertainty, bewilderment, or perplexity. **maze** *v.*

MBA *abbr.* Master of Business Administration.

MC *abbr.* Master of ceremonies.

McKinley, William *N.* (1843-1901). The 25th president of the United States from 1897-1901, assassinated while in office.

MD *abbr.* Doctor of Medicine.

mdse *abbr.* Merchandise.

me *pron.* The objective case of the pronoun I.

mead *n.* An alcoholic beverage made from fermented honey and water with yeast and spices added.

mead-ow *n.* A tract of grassland used for grazing or growing hay.

mead-ow-lark *n.* A songbird of North America.

mea-ger *or* **mea-gre** *adj.* Thin; lean; deficient in quantity, richness, vigor, or fertility. **-ly** *adv.*, **meagerness** *n.*

meal *n.* The edible seeds of coarsely ground grain; any powdery material; the food served or eaten at one sitting at certain times during the day; the time or occasion of taking such food.

meal-tick-et *n.*, *Slang* One who is a source of financial support for another; a ticket or card bought for a specified price and redeemable at a restaurant for food.

meal-y--mouthed *adj.* Unable to speak plainly and frankly; evasive.

mean *v.* To have in mind as a purpose or intent; to be of a specified importance or significance. *adj.* Poor or inferior in appearance or quality. *n.* The medium point. **means** The method or instrument by which some end is or may be accomplished; the available resources.

me-an-der *v.* To wander about without a certain course or a fixed direction.

mean-ing *n.* That which is meant or intended; the aim, end, or purpose; the significance; an interpretation. **meaningful, meaningfulness** *adj.*

mean-time *n.* The time or period between or during the intervening time.

mean-while *adv.* At the same time.

mea-sles *n.* A contagious viral disease usually occurring in children, characterized by the eruption of red spots.

mea-sly *adj.*, *Slang* Very small; meager.

meas-ure *n.* The range, dimension, extent, or capacity of anything. *Mus.* The group of beats marked off by regularly recurring primary accents; the notes and rests between two successive bars on a musical staff. *v.* To determine the range, dimension, extent, volume, or capacity of anything. **measurable** *adj.*, **measurably** *adv.*, **measurer** *n.*

meas-ure-ment *n.* The process or act of measuring.

neat *n.* The flesh of an animal which is used as food; the core or essential part of something. **-iness** *n.*, **meaty** *adj.*

nech *abbr.* Mechanical; mechanics.

ne-chan-ic *n.* A person skilled in the making, operation, or repair of machines or tools.

ne-chan-i-cal *adj.* Involving or having to do with the construction, operation, or design of tools or machines; produced or operated by a machine. **-ly** *adv.*

ne-chan-i-cal draw-ing *n.* A drawing done with the aid of squares, compasses, or other instruments.

ne-chan-ics *pl.*, *n.* The scientific study and analysis of the action of forces and motion on material bodies.

nech-a-nism *n.* The arrangement or parts of a machine; the technique or process by which something works.

mech-a-nize *v.* To make mechanical; to equip with tanks, trucks, mechanical and other equipment, as in the military. **mechanization** *n.*

med *abbr.* Medical.

med-al *n.*

A small piece of metal with a commemorative image or inscription which is presented as an award.

med-al-ist *n.* A person who designs, collects, or makes medals; one who has been awarded or received a medal.

me-dal-lion *n.* A large circular or oval medal which is used as a decorative element.

med-dle *v.* To interfere or participate in another person's business or affairs. **meddler** *n.*, **meddlesome** *adj.*

med-i-a *pl.*, *n.* The instruments of news communication, as radio, television, and newspapers.

me-di-al *adj.* Pertaining to or situated in the middle; ordinary.

me-di-an *n.* Something that is halfway between two different parts. *adj.* Relating to or constituting the median of a set of numbers.

me-di-an strip *n.* The strip which divides highway traffic lanes which are going in opposite directions.

me-di-ate *v.* To help settle or reconcile opposing sides in a dispute. **mediation, mediator** *n.*

med-ic *n.*, *Slang* A physician or intern; a medical student; in the armed forces, a corpsman or enlisted person trained to give first aid.

Med-i-caid *or* **medicaid** *n.* A governmental medical care or health insurance program providing medical aid for people who are unable to pay their own medical expenses.

med-i-cal *adj.* Relating to the study or practice of medicine. **medically** *adv.*

medical examiner *n.* A physician who is authorized by a governmental body to ascertain causes of death.

Med-i-care *or* **medicare** *n.* The program under the Social Security Administration which provides medical care for elderly people.

med-i-cate *v.* To treat an injury or illness with medicine. **medication** *n.*

med-i-cine *n.* Any agent or substance used in the treatment of disease or in the relief of pain; the science of diagnosing and treating disease; the profession of medicine.

med-i-cine ball *n.* A large, heavy ball used for physical exercise.

med-i-cine man *n.* In primitive cultures, a person believed to have supernatural powers for healing.

me-di-e-val *or* **mediaeval** *adj.* Like or characteristic of the Middle Ages. **-ism, medievalist** *n.*, **medievally** *adv.*

me-di-o-cre *adj.* Common; fair; undistinguished.

med-i-tate *v.* To be in continuous, contemplative thought; to think about doing something. **-tive** *adj.,* **-tion** *n.*

Med-i-ter-ra-ne-an *n.* A sea bounded by Africa, Asia, and Europe, which connects with the Atlantic Ocean through the Straits of Gibraltar. *adj.* Of or relating to the people or countries bounded by the Mediterranean.

me-di-um *n., pl.* **-dia** *or* **-ums** Something which occupies a middle position between two extremes; the means of communicating information or ideas through publishing, radio, or television.

med-ley *n.* A mixture or confused mass of elements; a jumble. *Music* A musical composition made up of parts of different songs.

me-dul-la *n., pl.* **-las** *or* **-lae** *Anat.* The center of certain vertebrate structures, such as bone marrow.

me-dul-la ob-lon-ga-ta The mass of nerve tissue found at the base of the brain, controlling bodily functions such as breathing and circulation.

meek *adj.* Showing patience and a gentle disposition; lacking spirit or backbone; submissive. **-ly** *adv.,* **-ness** *n.*

meet *v.* To come upon; to encounter; to come into conjunction or contact with someone or something; to cope or deal with; to handle; to fulfill an obligation or need.

meet-ing *n.* An assembly or gathering of persons; a coming together.

meg-a-bucks *n., Slang* One million dollars; a lot of money.

meg-a-hertz *n., pl.* **-hertz** *Physics.* One million cycles per second, used as a radio-frequency unit.

meg-a-lo-ma-ni-a *n., Psychiatry* A mental disorder marked by fantasies of power, wealth, or omnipotence. **megalomaniac** *n.,* **megalomaniacal** *adj.*

meg-a-lop-o-lis *n.* A very large urban complex.

meg-a-phone *n.* A funnel-shaped device which is used to amplify or direct the voice.

meg-a-ton *n.* One million tons; the unit equal to the explosive power of one million tons of TNT.

meg-a-watt *n.* A unit of electrical power equal to one million watts.

mei-o-sis *n., pl.* **-ses** *Biol.* The process by which undeveloped sex cells, sperm and ovum, mature by reduction division so that they contain only half of the full number of chromosomes. **meiotic** *adj.*

mel-an-cho-li-a *n., Psychiatry* A mental disorder of great depression of spirits and excessive brooding without apparent cause. **melancholiac** *adj. & n.*

mel-an-chol-ic *adj.* Depressed; sad.

mel-an-chol-y *adj.* Excessively gloomy or sad.

me-lange *n., French* A medley or mixture.

mel-a-nin *n., Biochem.* The brownish-black pigment which is contained in animal tissues, as the hair and skin.

mel-a-nism *n.* An abnormally dark pigmentation of the skin.

mel-a-no-ma *n., pl.* **-mas** *or* **-mata** A dark-colored tumor or malignant mole.

meld *v.* In pinochle and other card games, to declare or announce a combination of cards for inclusion in one's total score. *n.* The card or combination of cards declared for a score.

me-lee *n.* The confused and tumultuous mingling of a crowd.

mel-io-rate *v.* To cause to improve or to improve. **melioration** *n.,* **-ive** *adj.*

mel-lif-er-ous *adj.* Producing or bearing honey.

mel-lo *adj.* Sweet and soft; rich and full-flavored; rich and soft in quality, as in sounds or colors.

me-lo-di-ous *adj.* Characterized by a melody; tuneful; pleasant to hear. **melodiously** *adv.*

mel-o-dra-ma *n.* A very dramatic presentation which is marked by suspense and romantic sentiment; sensational and highly emotional language or behavior. **-tic** *adj.,* **-tically** *adv.*

mel-o-dy *n., pl.* **-ies** An agreeable succession of pleasing sounds. **melodic** *adj.,* **melodically** *adv.*

mel-on *n.* The large fruit of any of various plants of the gourd family, as the watermelon.

melt *v.* To change from a solid to a liquid as a result of pressure or heat.

melt-down *n.* The melting of a nuclear-reactor core.

melt-ing pot *n.* A place where immigrants of different cultures or races are assimilated.

mem-ber *n.* A person who belongs to a society, party, club, or other organization. *Biol.* An organ or part of an animal or person's body, especially a limb.

mem-ber-ship *n.* The state or fact of being a member.

mem-brane *n.* A thin, pliable, sheet-like layer of tissue which covers body surfaces and separates or connects body parts. **membranous** *adj.*

me-men-to *n., pl.* **-tos** *or* **-toes** A keepsake.

mem-o *n.* A memorandum.

mem-oir *n.* Personal records or reminiscences; an autobiography.

mem-o-ra-ble *adj.* Worth remembering or noting. **memorably** *adv.*

mem-o-ran-dum *n., pl.* **-dums** *or* **-da** A brief, informal note written as a reminder.

me-mo-ri-al *n.* Something that serves to keep in remembrance, as a person or event. *adj.* Perpetuating remembrance. **memorialize** *v.*

Memorial Day *n.* The holiday that recognizes members of the armed forces killed in wars, celebrated on the last Monday in May.

mem-o-rize v. To commit something to memory. **memorization, memorizer** n.

mem-ory n., pl. **-ries** The mental function or capacity of recalling or recognizing something that has been previously learned or experienced.

men pl. n. The plural of man.

men-ace n. Something or someone who threatens; an annoying person. **menace** v., **menacingly** adv.

me-nar-che n. The beginning or the first occurrence of menstruation.

mend v. To fix; to repair; to correct.

men-da-cious adj. Prone to lying; deceitful; untrue; false. **-ly** adv., **-ity** n.

men-de-le-vi-um n. A short-lived radioactive element of the actinide series, symbolized by Md.

me-ni-al adj. Relating to a household servant or household chores requiring little responsibility or skill. **menially** adv.

men-in-gi-tis n., Pathol. An inflammation of the membranes which enclose the brain and spinal cord.

me-ninx n., pl. **meninges** The membrane which encloses the spinal cord and brain. **meningeal** adj.

men-o-pause n., Physiol. The time of final menstruation, occurring normally between the ages of 45 and 50 **menopausal** adj.

men-ses pl., n. The blood and dead cell debris which are discharged from the uterus through the vagina by women who are not pregnant; menstruation, occurring at monthly intervals between puberty and menopause.

men-stru-ate v. To discharge the menses, approximately every 28 days. **menstrual** adj.

men-stru-a-tion n., Physiol. The process, act, or periodical flow of bloody fluid from the uterus, also called period.

-ment suffix The result or product of achievement; action; process.

men-tal adj. Relating to or of the mind. **mentally** adv.

men-tal de-fi-cien-cy n. Subnormal intellectual development, marked by deficiencies ranging from impaired learning ability to social incompetence.

men-tal-i-ty n., pl. **-ies** Mental faculties or powers; mental activity; habit of mind.

men-tal re-tar-da-tion n. A mental deficiency.

men-thol n., Chem. The white, waxy crystalline alcohol which is obtained from and has the odor of peppermint oil. **mentholated** adj.

men-tion v. To refer to incidentally, in passing, or briefly. **-able** adj., **-er** n.

men-tor n. A wise and trusted person.

men-u n. A list of food or dishes available at a restaurant; in Computer Science, a list of options displayed on the screen from which the operator may choose.

me-ow n. The cry of a cat. **meow** v.

me-phi-tis n. A sickening or foul smell; a stench emitted from the earth.

mer-can-tile adj. Of or relating to merchants, trading, or commerce.

mer-ce-nar-y n. A person who is concerned only with making money and obtaining material gain; a person paid to serve as a soldier in a foreign country. **mercenary** adj.

mer-cer-ize v. To treat cotton yarn or thread with sodium hydroxide so as to give strength and receptiveness to dyes.

mer-chan-dise n. Commodities or goods that are bought and sold. v. To buy and sell.

mer-chant n. A person who operates a retail business for profit.

mer-chant-man n. A ship used for commercial shipments.

mer-cu-ry n. A silvery, metallic, liquid element used in thermometers and barometers, symbolized by Hg.

mer-cy n., pl. **-ies** Compassionate and kind treatment. **merciful, merciless** adj., **-ifully, mercilessly** adv.

mere adj. Absolute; no more than what is stated. **merest** adj., **merely** adv.

merge v. To unite or bring together as one; in Computer Science, to combine two or more files into one, retaining the internal order of both.

mer-ger n. The act of combining two or more corporations into one.

me-ringue n. A mixture of stiffly beaten egg whites and sugar, used as a topping for cakes and pies or baked into crisp shells.

me-ri-no n., pl. **-nos** A Spanish breed of hardy, white, fine-wooled sheep; a soft, lightweight fabric originally made of merino wool. **merino** adj.

mer-it n. A characteristic act or trait which is worthy of praise. v. To earn; to be worthy of.

mer-i-toc-ra-cy n., pl. **-ies** A system which bases advancement on ability or achievement.

mer-i-to-ri-ous adj. Deserving honor, praise or reward. **meritoriously** adv.

mer-maid n. An imaginary sea creature having the upper body of a woman and the tail of a fish. **merman** n.

mer-ry adj. Delightful; gay; entertaining; festive; happy; joyous. **merrily** adv., **merriness** n.

mer-ry--go--round n. A circular, revolving platform often with benches and animal figures, usually found in circuses and amusement parks.

me-sa n. A flat-topped hill or small plateau with steep sides.

mesh n. Open spaces in a thread, wire or cord net; something that entraps or snares; the fitting or coming together of gear teeth for transmitting power. **mesh** v.

mes-mer-ize v. To hypnotize or put into a trance.

Mes-o-po-ta-mi-a n. The area between the Euphrates and Tigris rivers.

mes-quite n. A thorny, deep-rooted shrub or small tree which grows in the southwestern United States and in Mexico.

mess *n., pl.* **messes** A disorderly or confused heap; a jumble; a dish or portion of soft or liquid food; a meal eaten by a group of persons, usually in the military.

mes-sage *n.* Any information, command, or news transmitted from one person to another.

mes-sen-ger *n.* A person who carries a message or does an errand for another person or company.

Mes-si-ah *n.* The anticipated or expected king of the Jews; Jesus Christ.

mess-y *adj.* Untidy; upset; dirty; lacking neatness. **messily** *adv.,* **messiness** *n.*

met *v., p.t. & p.p.* Past tense of meet.

me-tab-o-lism *n.* The chemical and physical changes in living cells which involve the maintenance of life. **metabolic** *adj.,* **metabolize** *v.*

meta-car-pus *n.* The part of the forefoot or hand which connects the bones of the toes or fingers to the ankle or wrist.

met-a-gal-ax-y *n.* The universe; the entire system of galaxies.

metal *n.* One of a category of opaque, fusible, ductile, and typically lustrous elements. **-lic** *adj.,* **metallically** *adv.*

met-al-lur-gy *n.* The technology and science which studies methods of extracting metals from their ores and of preparing them for use. **metallurgical** *adj.,* **metallurgist** *n.*

met-a-mor-pho-sis *n.* The transformation and change in the structure and habits of an animal during normal growth, as the metamorphosis of a tadpole into a frog. **-ism** *n.,* **metamorphose** *v.*

met-a-phor *n.* A figure of speech in which the context demands that a word or phrase not be taken literally, as the sun is smiling; a comparison which doesn't use like or as.

me-tas-ta-sis *n.* A spread of cancer cells from the original tumor to one or more additional sites within the body. **metastasize** *v.,* **metastatic** *adj.*

met-a-tar-sus *n., pl.* **-si** The part of the human foot which forms the instep and contains five bones between the ankle and the toes; the hind foot of four-legged animals. **metatarsal** *adj.*

me-te-or *n.* A moving particle in the solar system which appears as a trail or streak in the sky as it comes into contact with the atmosphere of the earth.

me-te-or-ic *adj.* Of or relating to a meteor or meteors; resembling a meteor in speed, brilliance, or brevity.

me-te-or-ite *n.* A stony or metallic mass of a meteor which reaches the earth after partially burning in the atmosphere.

me-te-or-ol-o-gy *n.* The science concerned with the study of weather, weather conditions and weather forecasting. **-ical, meteorologic** *adj.,* **meteorologically** *adv.,* **meteorologist** *n.*

me-ter *n.* The arrangement of words, syllables, or stanzas in verse or poetry; a measure equaling 39.37 inches.

meth-a-done *n.* A man-made narcotic used in the treatment of heroin addiction.

meth-ane *n.* A colorless, odorless flammable gas used as a fuel; a product of the decomposition of organic matter.

meth-a-nol *n.* A colorless, odorless flammable alcohol that is used as an antifreeze, as a fuel, and as a raw material in chemical synthesis.

me-thinks *v.* It seems to me.

meth-od *n.* A manner, a process, or the regular way of doing something; the orderly arrangement, development, or classification.

Methuselah *n.* A Biblical ancestor of Noah who is said to have lived to the age of 969.

meth-yl *n.* An alkyl radical derived from methane which occurs in several organic compounds.

me-tic-u-lous *adj.* Very precise; careful; concerned with small details. **meticulously** *adv.,* **meticulousness** *n.*

me-tis *n.* A person of mixed blood, usually of French and Indian ancestry.

met-ric *adj.* Of or relating to the metric system. **metrical** *adj.,* **metrication** *n.*

met-ric sys-tem *n.* A decimal system of weights and measures based on the meter as a unit of length and the kilogram as a unit of mass, originated in France around 1790.

met-ri-fy *v.* To adopt or convert to the metric system. **metrification** *n.*

met-ro *n.* A subway system for transportation.

met-ro-nome *n.* An instrument designed to mark time by means of a series of clicks at exact intervals. **-ic** *adj.*

me-trop-o-lis *n.* A large or capital city of a state, region, or country. **metropolitan** *adj.*

mew *n.* A hideaway; a secret place.

Mexico *n.* A large country located in southwestern North America.

mez-za-nine *n.* A low story between two main stories of a building; the lowest balcony in a theatre.

MIA *abbr.* Missing in action.

mice *pl. n.* The plural of mouse.

Michelangelo *n.* Italian Renaissance painter and sculptor.

mi-crobe *n.* A germ, plant, or animal so small that is can be seen only with the aid of a microscope.

mi-cro-bi-ol-o-gy *n.* The scientific study of microorganisms. **microbiological** *adj.,* **microbiologist** *n.*

mi-cro-ceph-a-ly *n.* A condition of abnormal smallness of the head, usually associated with mental defects.

mi-cro-cir-cuit *n.* An electronic circuit composed of very small components.

mi-cro-com-put-er *n.* A computer which uses a microprocessor.

mi-cro-film *n.* A film used to photograph printed matter at a greatly reduced size.

mi-cro-or-gan-ism *n.* An organism too small to see without the aid of a microscope.

mi-cro-phone *n.*

An instrument which converts acoustical waves into electrical signals and feeds them into a recorder, amplifier or broadcasting transmitter. -ic *adj.*

mi-cro-proc-es-sor *n.* In Computer Science, a semiconductor processing unit which is contained on an integrated circuit chip.

mi-cro-scope *n.*

An optical instrument consisting of a lens or combination of lenses, used to produce magnified images of very small objects.

mi-cro-scop-ic *adj.* Too small to be seen by the eye alone. microscopical *adv.*

mi-cro-sur-ger-y *n.* Surgery performed by means of a microscope and laser beam. microsurgical *adj.*

mi-cro-wave *n.* A very short electromagnetic wave.

mid *adj.* In the middle or center; central.

mid-air *n.* A point in the air just above the ground surface.

mid-day *n.* Noon; the middle of the day.

mid-den *n.* A refuse heap or dunghill.

mid-dle *adj.* Being equally distant from extremes or limits; the central. *n.* Anything which occupies a middle position; the waist.

mid-dle age *n.* A period of life from about 40 to 60 years.

Middle Ages *pl. n.* The period of European history from about 500 to 1500.

mid-dle class *n.* The social class of people between a high income and low income status.

mid-dle ear *n.* A small membrane-lined cavity between the tympanic membrane and the inner ear through which sound waves are carried.

mid-dle-man *n.* A person who serves as an agent between the producer of a product and the consumer.

midg-et *n.* A very small person.

mid-i *n.* *Slang* A dress, skirt, or coat which extends to the calf.

mid-night *n.* 12 o'clock p.m.; the middle of the night.

mid-point *n.* A point at or near the middle.

mid-riff *n.* The midsection of the human torso; the diaphragm.

midst *n.* The central or middle part or position; a person positioned among others in a group.

mid-sum-mer *n.* The middle of summer.

mid-term *n.* The middle of an academic term.

mid-way *n.* The section of a carnival or fair where shows and rides are located.

mid-wife *n.* A woman who gives assistance in the birth of a baby.

mid-year *n.* The middle of a calendar year; academic examinations which are given in the middle of the academic year.

miff *n.* Ill humor; displeasure. miff *v.*

might *n.* Force, power, or physical strength. *v.* To indicate a present condition contrary to fact; to ask permission politely.

might-y *adj.* Showing or having great power.

mi-graine *n.* A condition of severe, recurring headaches often accompanied by nausea.

mi-grant *n.* A person who moves from one place to another to find work in the fields.

mi-grate *v.* To move from one place to another or from one climate to another. -ion *n.*, -ional, -ory *adj.*

mike *n.*, *Slang* Microphone.

mil *n.* A unit of measure equal to 1/1000 of an inch, used in measuring wire.

milch *adj.* Giving milk.

mild *adj.* Gentle in manner, behavior, or disposition; not severe or extreme. mildly *adv.*, mildness *n.*

mil-dew *n.* A fungal growth which is usually white in color. mildew *v.*, mildewy *adj.*

mile *n.* A unit of measurement equaling 5,280 feet.

mile-age *n.* The distance traveled or measured in miles; an allowance given for traveling expenses at a set rate per mile; the average distance of miles a vehicle will travel on a gallon of gas.

mil-i-tant *adj.* Engaged in warfare or combat; aggressive. militancy,

mil-i-ta-rize *v.* To train or equip for war.

mil-i-tar-y *adj.* Of or related to arms, war, or soldiers. *n.* A nation's armed forces. militarily *adv.*

mi-li-tia *n.* A military service or armed forces called upon in case of an emergency.

milk *n.* A whitish fluid produced by the mammary glands of all mature female mammals as a source of food for their young. *v.* To draw milk from the breast or udder. *Slang* To take advantage of every possibility in a given situation. milkiness *n.*, milky *adj.*

milk-sop *n.* A man who lacks manly qualities.

milk-weed *n.* Any of various plants which secrete latex and have pointed pods that open to release seeds and downy flowers.

Milk-y Way *n.* The broad, luminous galaxy in which the solar system is located.

mill *n.* A building housing machinery for grinding grain into meal or flour; any of various machines which grind, crush, or press; a unit of money which equals 1/1000 of a U.S. dollar. *v.* To grind.

mill-er *n.* A person who operates, works, or owns a grain mill; a moth whose wings are covered with a powdery substance.

mil-li-ner *n.* Someone who designs, sells, or makes women's hats.

mil-lion *n.* A very large number equal to 1,000 x 1,000. **million** *adj.*, **millionth** *n., adj.*

mime *v.* To act a part or performance without using words. *n.* An actor who portrays a part, emotion, or situation using only gestures and body language. **mimer** *n.*

mim-e-o-graph *n.* A duplicating machine that makes duplicates of typed or drawn information from a stencil through which ink is pressed.

mim-ic *v.* To imitate another person's behavior or speech.

mince *v.* To cut or chop something into small pieces.

mind *n.* The element of a human being which controls perception, thought, feeling, memory, and imagination. *v.* To obey; to take care of; to bring; to remember; to object to.

mine *n.* A pit or underground excavation from which metals or coal can be uncovered and removed. **miner** *n.*

mine *pron.* The one that belongs to me.

min-er-al *n.* A solid inorganic substance, such as silver, diamond, or quartz, which is taken from the earth. **mineral** *adj.*, **mineralize** *v.*

min-e-stro-ne *n.* A very thick vegetable soup that may contain pasta and beans.

min-gle *v.* To mix or come together. **-er** *n.*

min-i-a-ture *n.* A copy or model of something that has been greatly reduced in size.

min-i-com-put-er *n.* In Computer Science, a computer designed on a very small scale.

mini-disk *n. Computer Science* The 5 1/4 inch floppy disk which is used for storing information.

min-i-mum *n., pl.* **-ums** *or* **-uma** The least, smallest, or lowest amount, degree, number, or position.

min-is-ter *n.* The pastor of a Protestant church; a high officer of state who is in charge of a governmental division.

mink *n., pl.* **mink** *or* **minks**

A semiaquatic animal of the weasel family whose thick, lustrous fur is used for making fur coats.

min-now *n.* A small, fresh-water fish used as bait.

mi-nor *adj.* Not of legal age; lesser in degree, size or importance.

mi-nor-i-ty *n., pl.* **-ies** The smaller in number of two groups constituting a whole; a part of the population that differs, as in race, sex, or religion.

min-ster *n.* A large cathedral or church.

min-strel *n.* A medieval traveling musician or poet.

mint *n.* A place where coins are made by a government; any of a variety of aromatic plants used for flavoring; candy flavored by such a plant. **-y** *adj.*

min-u-end *n.* A number of quantity from which another is to be subtracted.

min-u-et *n.* A slow, stately dance.

mi-nus *prep., Math.* Reduced by subtraction. *n.* The minus sign (-); a negative number.

min-ute *n.* The unit of time which equals 60 seconds.

mi-nute *adj.* Extremely small in size.

mir-a-cle *n.* A supernatural event or happening regarded as an act of God.

mi-rage *n.* An optical illusion in which nonexistent bodies of water with reflections of objects are seen.

mire *n.* Soil or heavy mud.

mir-ror *n.* A surface of glass which reflects light, forming the image of an object.

mirth *n.* Merriment or joyousness expressed by laughter.

mis- *prefix* Wrong, bad, or ill.

mis-ad-ven-ture *n.* An unlucky mishap; a misfortune.

mis-an-thrope *n.* Someone who hates mankind.

mis-ap-pre-hend *v.* To understand something incorrectly; to misunderstand. **misapprehension** *n.*

mis-ap-pro-pri-ate *v.* To embezzle money; to use wrongly for one's own benefit. **misappropriation** *n.*

misc *abbr.* Miscellaneous.

mis-car-riage *n.* The premature birth of a fetus from the uterus.

mis-ce-ge-na-tion *n.* The marriage between two people of different races.

mis-cel-la-ne-ous *adj.* Consisting of a mixed variety of parts, elements, or characteristics.

mis-chance *n.* Bad luck or mishap.

mis-chief *n.* Behavior which causes harm, damage, or annoyance.

mis-chie-vous *adj.* Tending to behave in a playfully annoying way. **-ly** *adv.*

mis-ci-ble *adj. Chem.* Capable of being mixed. **miscibility** *n.*

mis-con-ceive *v.* To misunderstand the meaning. **misconceiver, -eption** *n.*

mis-con-duct *n.* Improper conduct or behavior; bad management.

mis-count *v.* To count incorrectly; to miscalculate.

mis-cre-ant *n.* A person who is involved in criminal or evil acts; a heretic. **miscreant** *adj.*

mis-cue *n.* An error; a mistake.

mis-deed *n.* A wrong or improper act; an evil deed.

mis-de-mean-or *n., Law* A crime less serious than a felony.

mis-er *n.* A person who hoards money; a person who lives a meager life in order to hoard his money.

mis-er-a-ble *adj.* Very uncomfortable or unhappy; causing misery. **miserableness** *n.*, **miserably** *adv.*

mis-er-y *n.* A state of great unhappiness, distress, or pain.

mis-feed *n.* In computer science, the failure of paper or other media to pass through a printer or other device properly.

mis-fire *v.* To fail to explode, ignite, or fire. **misfire** *n.*

mis-fit *n.* A person who is not adjusted to his environment; anything which does not fit correctly.

mis-for-tune *n.* Bad luck or fortune.

mis-giv-ing *n.* A feeling of doubt.

mis-guide *v.* To guide incorrectly; to misdirect. **-ance** *n.*, **misguidedly** *adv.*

mis-han-dle *v.* To handle clumsily; to manage inefficiently.

mis-hap *n.* An unfortunate accident; bad luck.

mish-mash *n.* A jumble or hodgepodge.

mis-in-ter-pret *v.* To understand or explain incorrectly. **misinterpretation** *n.*

mis-judge *v.* To make a mistake in judgment. **misjudgment** *n.*

mis-lay *v.* To lose; to put something in a place and not remember where.

mis-lead *v.* To lead in a wrong direction; to deliberately deceive. **misleader** *n.*, **misleading** *adj.*

mis-no-mer *n.* A wrong or inappropriate name.

mis-pro-nounce *v.* To pronounce a word incorrectly.

mi-sog-a-my *n.* Hatred of marriage.

mi-sog-y-ny *n.* Hatred of women.

mis-place *v.* To mislay; to put in a wrong place.

mis-read *v.* To read or interpret incorrectly.

mis-rep-re-sent *v.* To represent wrongly, misleadingly, or falsely. **-ation** *n.*

mis-rule *n.* Misruling; the condition of being misruled; disorder.

Miss *n.* The proper title for an unmarried woman or girl. *v.* To fail to hit, reach, or make contact with something; to omit; to feel the absence or loss of.

mis-sal *n.* A book containing prayers and services, used in the Roman Catholic Church throughout the year.

mis-shape *v.* To deform; to shape badly; to distort. **misshapen** *adj.*

mis-sile *n.* An object that is thrown or shot at a target. **missilery** *n.*

mis-sion *n.* An instance or the act of sending; an assignment or task to be carried out.

mis-sion-ar-y *n., pl.* **-ies** A person sent to do religious or charitable work, usually in a foreign country.

mis-spell *v.* To spell a word incorrectly. **misspelling** *n.*

mis-take *n.* A wrong statement, action, or decision. **mistaken**, **mistakable** *adj.*, **-ably** *adv.*, **mistake** *v.*

Mis-ter *n.* A courtesy title used before a man's name, abbreviated as Mr.

mis-tle-toe *n.* A parasitic plant with thick leaves, small yellowish flowers and white berries.

mis-treat *v.* To treat badly or wrongly. **mistreatment** *n.*

mis-tress *n.* A woman having authority, ownership, or a position of control; a woman having a sexual relationship with a man who is not her husband.

mis-tri-al *n.* A trial that is invalid because of an error during the procedure.

mis-trust *v.* To have doubt; to lack trust in something or someone. **mistrust** *n.* **mistrustful** *adj.*, **mistrustfully** *adv.*

mis-un-der-stand *v.* To interpret incorrectly; to fail to understand.

mite *n.* A very small insect; a small amount of money.

mi-ter *n.*

A joint made by cutting two pieces at an angle and then fitting them together.

mit-i-gate *v.* To make or become less severe or painful.

mi-to-sis *n., pl.* **mitoses** A process of cell division in which chromatin divides into chromo-somes.

mitt *n.* A women's glove that covers only the wrist and hand, leaving the fingers exposed; in baseball, a glove for a catcher or first baseman made in the style of a mitten.

mix *v.* To blend or combine into one; to come or bring together. **mixable** *adj.*

mixed num-ber *n.* A number representing the sum of an integer and a fraction, such as 5 1/2.

mix-ture *n.* The state of being mixed; the process or act of mixing; a combination of two or two substances.

mix-up *n.* An instance or state of confusion.

mo *abbr.* Money order; mail order.

moan *n.* A very low, dull sound indicative of pain or grief.

moat *n.* A deep and wide trench surrounding a castle, usually filled with water.

mob *n.* A large, unruly crowd. *v.* To overcrowd.

mo-bi-lize *v.* To put into motion; to make ready. **mobilization** *n.*

moc-ca-sin *n.* A shoe or slipper made of a soft leather.

mo-cha *n.* An Arabian coffee of superior quality; a flavoring with coffee, often used with chocolate.

mock *v.* To treat with contempt or scorn; to imitate a mannerism or sound closely; to mimic. *adv.* In an insincere manner. *n.* An imitation; a copy. **mockingly** *adv.*

mock-er-y *n., pl.* **-ies** Insulting or contemptuous action or speech; a subject of laughter or sport; a false appearance.

mock--he-ro-ic *n.* A satirical imitation of the heroic manner or style.

mock-ing-bird *n.* A common bird that is remarkable for its exact imitations of the notes of other birds.

mock orange *n.* Any of several deciduous shrubs.

mock-up *or* **mock--up** *n.* A model of a structure used for study, testing, or demonstration.

mod *n.* A modern and unusual style of dress. *adj.* Modern.

mode *n.* A way or method of doing something; a particular manner or form; the value or score that occurs most frequently in a set of data; the current fashion or style, as in dress.

mod-el *n.* A small representation of an object; a pattern that something will be based on; a design or type; one serving as an example; one who poses for an artist or photographer. model *v.*, modeler *n.*

mod-er-ate *adj.* Not excessive; tending toward the mean or average extent or quality; opposed to extreme political views. moderate *v.*, moderation *n.*

mod-er-a-tor *n.* A person who moderates; a person who presides over a discussion or meeting but takes no sides.

mod-ern *adj.* Typical of the recent past or the present; advanced or up-to-date. modernity *n.*, modernly *adv.*

mod-ern-ism *n.* A thought, action, or belief characteristic of modern times. modernistic *adj.*

mod-ern-ize *v.* To make or become modern. modernization *n.*

mod-est *adj.* Placing a moderate estimate on one's abilities or worth; retiring or reserved; limited in size or amount. modesty *n.*

mod-i-cum *n.* A small amount.

mod-i-fy *v.* To alter; to make different in character or form; to change to less extreme; to moderate. modified, modifiable *adj.*, -ication, modifier *n.*

mod-ish *adj.* Fashionable. modishly *adv.*, modishness *n.*

mo-diste *n.* A person dealing in fashionable clothing for women.

mod-u-late *v.* To soften; to temper; to vary the intensity of. *Music* To change from one key to another; to vary the tone or intensity of. -ation, -or *n.*, modulative, modulatory *adj.*

mod-ule *n.* One of a series of standardized components which work together in a system. *Electr.* A self-contained subassembly of electronic components, as a computer stage; the self-contained area of a spacecraft for performing a particular task. -ar *adj.*

mod-us op-er-an-di *n.* A method of operating or proceeding.

mod-us vi-ven-di *n.* A compromise which avoids difficulties.

mo-gul *n.* A very great or important person; a small hill or bump of ice and snow on a ski slope.

mo-hair *n.* The fabric or yarn made from the silky hair of the Angora goat.

Mo-ham-med *n.* The Arab founder of Islam.

Mohs scale *n.* A scale that classifies the hardness of minerals ranging from one for the softest, which is talc, to fifteen for the hardest, which is diamond.

moi-e-ty *n., pl.* **-ies** A half; any portion; part or share.

moil *v.* To work hard; to drudge. moil *n.*

moi-re *n.* Fabric, especially silk or rayon having a wavy pattern.

moist *adj.* Slightly wet; damp; saturated with moisture or liquid. moistly *adv.*, moistness *n.*

mois-ten *v.* To make or become moist or slightly wet. moistener *n.*

mois-ture *n.* Liquid diffused or condensed in a relatively small quantity; dampness. -ize *v.*, moisturizer *n.*

Mo-ja-ve *or* **Mo-ha-ve** *n.* A desert region located in southern California.

mol *abbr.* Molecular; molecule.

mo-lar *n.* A grinding tooth which has a broad surface for grinding food, located in the back of the mouth.

mo-las-ses *n.* A thick, dark syrup produced when sugar is refined.

mold *n.* A superficial, often woolly growth produced on damp or decaying organic matter or on living organisms; a fungus that produces such a growth; crumbling, soft, friable earth suited to plant growth; distinctive nature or character; the frame on or around which an object is constructed; a cavity in which an object is shaped; general shape; form. moldable *adj.*

mold-board *n.* The curved blade of a plow.

mold-er *v.* To crumble or decay gradually and turn to dust.

mole *n.* A pigmented spot or mark on the human skin; a small, insectivorous mammal that lives mostly underground and has a narrow snout, small eyes, and silky fur; a large wall of stone or masonry used as a breakwater or pier.

mo-lec-u-lar *adj.* Of, relating to, or caused by molecules.

mo-lec-u-lar bi-ol-o-gy *n.* The branch of biology dealing with the structure and development of biological systems which are studied in terms of their molecular constituents.

mol-e-cule *n.* The simplest structural unit into which a substance can be divided and still retain its identity.

mo-lest *v.* To bother, annoy, or persecute; to accost sexually. molestation, molester *n.*

mol-li-fy *v.* To make less angry; to soften; to make less intense or severe. mollification *n.*

mol-lusk *or* **mol-lusc** *n.* Any of various largely marine invertebrates, including the edible shellfish.

mol-ly-cod-dle *v.* To spoil by pampering; to coddle.

molt *v.* To cast off or shed an external covering, as horns, feathers, or skin, which is periodically replaced by new growth. molt *n.*

mol-ten *adj.* Transformed to liquid form by heat.

mo-lyb-de-num *n.* A hard, gray metallic element used to harden steel alloys, symbolized by Mo.

mo-men-tar-i-ly *adv.* For just a moment; soon; from moment to moment.

mo-men-tar-y *adj.* Lasting just a moment; occurring presently or at every moment.

mo-men-tous *adj.* Of great importance or consequence; significant. momentously *adv.*, momentousness *n.*

mo-men-tum *n., pl.* -ta *or* -tums A property of a moving body which determines the length of time required to bring it to rest when under the action of a constant force.

mon-arch *n.* A person who reigns over a kingdom or empire; a large orange and black butterfly. monarchic, monarchical *adj.*

mon-ar-chism *n.* The principles or system of a monarchic government. monarchist *n.*, monarchistic *adj.*

mon-ar-chy *n., pl.* -chies Government by a monarch; sovereign control; a government or nation ruled by a monarch.

mon-as-ter-y *n., pl.* -ies A house for persons under religious vows. -ial *adj.*

mo-nas-tic *adj.* Of, relating to, or typical of monasteries, monks, or life in monasteries.

mo-nas-ti-cism *n.* The monastic lifestyle or system.

mon-au-ral *adj.* Of or relating to a system of transmitting or recording sound by techniques in which one or more sources are channeled into one carrier.

Mon-day *n.* The second day of the week.

Monet, Claude *n.* (1840-1926). French Impressionist painter.

mon-e-tar-y *adj.* Of or relating to money or how it is circulated. -ily *adv.*

mon-ey *n.* Anything which has or is assigned value and is used as a medium of exchange.

mon-ey-lend-er *n.* Someone whose business is lending money to others with interest.

mon-ger *n.* One who attempts to stir up or spread something that is undesirable; one who deals.

Mon-go-li-a *n.* A region of Asia that extends from Siberia to northern China; a country in Asia.

Mon-go-li-an *n.* A native or inhabitant of Mongolia; a member of the Mongoloid ethnic division. Mongolian *adj.*

Mon-gol-ism *n.* Down's syndrome.

Mon-gol-oid *adj.* Of, constituting, or characteristic of a people native to Asia, including peoples of northern and eastern Asia, Malaysians, Eskimos, and American Indians. Mongoloid Of, affected with, or pertaining to Down's syndrome. Mongoloid *n.*

mon-goose *n., pl.* -ses A chiefly African or Asian mammal which has the ability to kill venomous snakes.

mon-grel *n.* An animal or plant, especially a dog, produced by interbreeding.

mo-ni-tion *n.* A caution or warning, as for an impending danger.

mon-i-tor *n.* A student assigned to assist a teacher; a receiver used to view the picture being picked up by a television camera; the image being generated by a computer. monitorial *adj.*

mon-i-to-ry *adj.* Giving a caution or conveying a warning.

monk *n.* A man who is a member of a religious order and lives in a monastery. monkish *adj.*, monkishly *adv.*, monkishness *n.*

mon-key *n., pl.* -keys

A member of the older primates, excluding man, having a long-tail; a smaller species as distin guished from the larger apes. *v.* To play or fool around; to tamper with.

monk's cloth *n.* A sturdy cotton cloth having a coarse basket weave.

monks-hood *n.* A normally poisonous plant of the genus Aconitum, having variously colored hooded flowers.

mon-o *n.* Mononucleosis.

mon-o-chro-mat-ic *adj.* Of, consisting of, or having one color. -ally *adv.*

mon-o-cle *n.* An eyeglass for one eye.

mon-o-cot-y-le-don *n.* Any of various plants having a single embryonic seed leaf appearing at germination. monocotyledonous *adj.*

mo-noc-u-lar *adj.* Of, relating to, or having one eye.

mo-nog-a-my *n.* Marriage or sexual relationship with only one person at a time. monogamist *n.*, -ous *adj.*

mon-o-gram *n.* A design consisting of one or more initials. monogram *v.*

mon-o-graph *n.* A scholarly pamphlet or book on a particular and usually limited subject. monographic *adj.*

mon-o-lin-gual *adj.* Knowing only one language.

mon-o-lith *n.* A single block of stone, as one used in architecture or sculpture. monolithic *adj.*

mon-o-logue *or* **mon-o-log** *n.* A speech by one person which precludes conversation; a series of jokes and stories delivered by a comedian. -ist *n.*

mon-o-ma-ni-a *n.* A pathological obsession or mental disorder in which a person is totally obsessed with a single idea. -c *n.*, monomaniacal *adj.*

mo-no-mi-al *n.* An algebraic expression consisting of only one term.

mon-o-nu-cle-ar *adj.* Having only one nucleus.

mon-o-nu-cle-o-sis *n.* An infectious disease marked by an abnormal increase of too many cells having one nucleus.

mon-o-nu-cle-o-tide *n.* A nucleotide containing one molecule each of a phosphoric acid, a pentose, and either a purine or pyrimidine base.

mon·o·phon·ic *adj.* Having only one part; a solo voice with accompaniment, as a piano.

mon·o·plane *n.* An aircraft with one wing or one set of wings.

mo·nop·o·ly *n., pl.* **-ies** Exclusive ownership or control, as of a service or commodity, by a single group, person, or company; a group, person, or company having a monopoly; exclusive possession; a service or commodity controlled by a single group. **-ist, -ization** *n.,* **-istic** *adj.,* monopolize *v.*

mon·o·rail *n.* A single rail serving as a track on which a wheeled vehicle can travel; a vehicle that travels on such a rail.

mon·o·so·di·um glu·ta·mate *n.* Sodium glutamate used as a seasoning, abbreviated as MSG.

mon·o·syl·la·ble *n.* A word of one syllable. **-ic** *adj.,* monosyllabically *adv.*

mon·o·the·ism *n.* The belief that there is just one God. monotheist *n.,* monotheistic *adj.*

mon·o·tone *n.* The utterance of sounds, syllables, or words in a single unvarying tone.

mo·not·o·nous *adj.* Spoken in a monotone; lacking in variety. monotonously *adv.,* monotony *n.*

mon·ox·ide *n.* An oxide that contains one oxygen atom per molecule.

Monroe, James *N.* (1758-1831). The 5th President of the United States.

Mon·si·gnor *n., pl.* **-ors** *or* **-ori** A title given to Roman Catholic priests who have received papal honors.

mon·soon *n.* A periodic wind, especially in the Indian Ocean and southern Asia; the season of the monsoon in India and parts of Asia.

mon·ster *n.* An animal or plant having an abnormal form or structure; an animal, plant, or object having a frightening or deformed shape; one unusually large for its kind. **-ity, -ousness** *n.,* **-ous** *adj.,* **-ously** *adv.*

mon·tage *n.* A composite picture made by combining several separate pictures or parts of several pictures; a rapid succession of images in a motion picture, designed to illustrate an association of ideas.

month *n.* One of the twelve divisions of a calendar year.

month·ly *adj.* Occurring, done, or payable each month. *n.* A publication issued once a month. monthly *adv.*

mon·u·ment *n.* An object, such as a statue, built as a memorial to a person or an event; a burial vault; an area set aside for public use by a government because of its aesthetic, historical, or ecological significance.

mon·u·men·tal *adj.* Serving as or similar to a monument; massive; extremely important. monumentally *adv.*

mooch *v. Slang* To acquire by begging; to steal. moocher *n.*

mood *n.* A conscious yet temporary state of mind or emotion; the prevailing spirit; a verb form or set of verb forms inflected to show the understanding of the person speaking regarding the condition expressed.

mood·y *adj.* Subject to moods, especially depression; gloomy. -ily *adv.,* -iness *n.*

moon *n.* The earth's only natural satellite; a natural satellite which revolves around a planet. *v.* To dream.

moon·beam *n.* A ray of moonlight.

moon·light *n.* The light of the moon. *v.* To hold a second job in addition to a regular one. moonlighter *n.*

moon·lit *adj.* Lit by the moon.

moon·rise *n.* The rising of the moon above the horizon; the time of the moon's rising.

moon·scape *n.* The surface of the moon as seen or as depicted.

moon·set *n.* The descent of the moon below the horizon; the time of the moon's setting.

moon·shine *n.* Moonlight; empty talk; nonsense; intoxicating liquor, especially illegally distilled corn whiskey.

moor *v.* To make fast with cables, lines, or anchors. *n.* An expanse of open, rolling, infertile land. moorage *n.*

moor·ing *n.* A place where a ship or aircraft can be secured; a stabilizing device.

moose *n., pl.* **moose**

A very large North American deer having a large broad muzzle.

moot *v.* To bring up as for debate or discussion; to argue. *adj.* Open to debate; having no legal significance.

mope *v.* To be uncaring or dejected; to move in a leisurely manner. moper *n.*

mop·pet *n.* A child; a darling baby.

mop--up *n.* The process of completing a task.

mo·raine *n.* An accumulation of earth and stones carried and finally deposited by a glacier.

mor·al *adj.* Of or pertaining to conduct or character from the point of right and wrong; teaching a conception of right behavior. *n.* The lesson to be learned from a story, event, or teaching. morals Standards of right and wrong. morally *adv.*

mo·rale *n.* An individual's state of mind with respect to the tasks he or she is expected to perform; esprit de corps.

mor·al·ist *n.* Someone concerned with moral principles and questions; someone who practices morality. moralism *n.,* -ic *adj.,* -ally *adv.*

mo·ral·i·ty *n., pl.* **-ies** The quality of being morally right; moral behavior.

mor·al·ize *v.* To think, discuss, or judge in a moral sense. moralization, moralizer *n.*

mo·rass *n.* A marsh or bog; low-lying wet, soft ground; something which hinders or overwhelms.

mor-a-to-ri-um n., pl. -iums or -ia A temporary pause in activity; an authorization given legally to a debtor to suspend payments for a period of time.

mo-ray n. Any of various marine eels found usually in tropical waters.

mor-bid adj. Of, pertaining to, or affected by disease; suggesting an unhealthy mental state of being; gruesome. -ity, -ness n., -ly adv.

mor-da-cious adj. Violent in action; prone to biting. mordacity n.

mor-dant adj. Biting and caustic in thought, manner, or style. mordancy n., mordantly adv.

more adj. Greater number, size, or degree; additional. n. An additional or greater number, degree, or amount. adv. To a greater extent or degree; in addition. pron. Additional things or persons.

mo-rel n. An edible mushroom having a sponge-like cap or hood.

more-o-ver adv. Furthermore; besides.

mo-res n., pl. The moral customs and traditional customs of a social group.

morgue n. A place in which dead bodies are kept until claimed or identified; the reference file at a newspaper or magazine office.

mor-i-bund adj. Approaching extinction; at the point of death. moribundity n.

morn n. Morning.

morn-ing n. The early part of the day; the time from midnight to noon.

morn-ing--glo-ry n. A usually twining, climbing plant with funnel-shaped flowers which are open in the morning, but closed later in the day.

morn-ing star n. A planet seen in the eastern part of the sky just before or at sunrise.

Mo-roc-co n. A country located in northwestern Africa.

mo-roc-co n. A soft, textured leather made of goatskin.

mo-ron n. An adult exhibiting an intelligence equal to that of a seven to twelve year old child; a very stupid person. -ic adj., moronically adv.

mo-rose adj. Having a sullen disposition; marked by gloom. morosely adv., moroseness n.

mor-pheme n. A meaningful unit which cannot be divided into smaller meaningful parts. morphemic adj., morphemically adv.

mor-phi-a n. Morphine.

mor-phine n. A highly addictive narcotic derived from opium which can be used as either a sedative or to dull pain.

mor-phol-o-gy n. The study of the form and structure of living organisms, considered separate from function; the study and description of word formation in a language. morphological adj., morphologically adv., morphologist n.

mor-ris n. An old English folk dance.

mor-row n. The next day.

Morse code n. Either of two codes, developed by S. F. B. Morse, consisting of dots and dashes, long and short sounds, or long and short flashes of light.

mor-sel n. A small piece or quantity of food; a tasty dish.

mor-tal adj. Having caused or about to cause death; fatal; subject to death; very tedious or prolonged; unrelentingly hostile; of, relating to, or connected with death. n. A human being. mortally adv.

mor-tal-i-ty n., pl. -ies The state or condition of being mortal; the death rate; deaths.

mor-tar n. A strong vessel in which materials can be crushed or ground with a pestle; a muzzle-loading cannon for firing shells at short ranges and at high angles; a mixed building material, as cement with sand and water, which hardens and is used with masonry or plaster.

mor-tar-board n.

A square board with a handle, for holding mortar; an academic cap topped by a stiff, flat square.

mort-gage n. A temporary conveyance of property to a creditor as security for the repayment of a debt; a contract or deed defining the terms of a mortgage. v. To pledge or transfer by means of a mortgage. mortgagee, mortgagor n.

mor-ti-cian n. An undertaker.

mor-ti-fy v. To destroy the strength or functioning of; to subdue or deaden through pain or self-denial; to subject to severe humiliation; to become gangrenous. -ication n., -ingly adv.

mor-tise n. A usually hollowed out rectangular hole in a piece of wood which receives a tenon of another piece to form a joint.

mor-tu-ar-y n., pl. -ies A place in which dead bodies are temporarily held until burial or cremation.

mo-sa-ic n. A decorative inlaid design of small pieces, as of colored glass or tile, in cement. mosaic adj.

Mos-es n. Hebrew prophet and lawgiver; in the Old Testament, the person who lead the Israelites out of Egypt to the Promised Land; the person whom God presented the Ten Commandments to.

mo-sey v. Slang To move slowly; to shuffle along.

Mos-lem n. A believer of Islam. Moslem adj.

mosque n. A Moslem house of worship.

mos-qui-to n., pl. -toes or -tos Any of various winged insects of which the females suck the blood of animals or humans.

mos-qui-to net n. A fine net or screen to keep out mosquitoes.

moss n. Delicate, small green plants which often form a dense, mat-like growth. mossiness n., mossy adj.

moss-back *n.* An old-fashioned person.

moss rose *n.* An old-fashioned garden rose which has a glandular, mossy calyx and flower stalk.

most *adj.* The majority of. *n.* The greatest amount. *pron.* The largest part or number. *adv.* In or to the highest degree.

most-ly *adv.* For the most part; principally.

mot *n.* A short, witty saying.

mote *n.* A particle, as of dust; a speck of dust.

mo-tel *n.* A temporary, roadside dwelling for motorists with rooms opening directly onto a parking area.

mo-tet *n.* A polyphonic vocal composition, based on a religious text and usually sung without accompaniment.

moth *n.* A usually nocturnal insect of the order Lepidoptera, having antennae that are often feathered, duller in color and with wings smaller than the butterflies.

moth-ball *n.* A ball, usually of camphor, used to repel moths from clothing during storage.

moth--eat-en *adj.* Partially eaten by moths; in a state of disrepair.

moth-er *n.* A female parent; one who holds a maternal relationship toward another; an old or elderly woman; a woman in a position of authority. *adj.* Of, relating to, or being a mother. *v.* To give birth to; to care for or protect like a mother. motherhood.

motherliness *n.*, mothery *adj.*

moth-er--in--law *n.* The mother of one's spouse.

moth-er-land *n.* The country or land of one's birth.

moth-er--of--pearl *n.* The pearly iridescent internal layer of a mollusk shell.

mo-tif *n.* An underlying main element or theme that recurs in a musical, artistic, or literary work.

mo-tile *adj.* Exhibiting or capable of movement.

mo-tion *n.* The act or process of changing position; a purposeful movement of the body or a bodily part; a formal proposal or suggestion that action be taken. motion *v.*, motionless *adj.*

mo-tion pic-ture *n.* A sequence of filmed pictures that gives the illusion of continuous movement, when projected on a screen.

mo-tion sick-ness *n.* Dizziness; nausea brought on by motion as traveling by land or water.

mo-ti-vate *v.* Causing to act.

mo-tive *n.* Something, as a need or desire, which causes a person to act; a musical motif. *adj.* Causing or having the power to cause motion.

mot-ley *adj.* Composed of a variety of components.

mo-tor *n.* Any of various devices which develop energy or impart motion. *adj.* Imparting or producing motion; driven by or equipped with a motor; of, relating to or designed for motor vehicles; of, relating to, or involving muscular movement. *v.* To travel or transport by motor vehicle. motorist *n.*

mo-tor-bike *n.* A small motorcycle.

mo-tor-boat *n.* A boat propelled by an internal-combustion engine or an electric motor.

mo-tor-cade *n.* A procession of motor vehicles.

mo-tor-car *n.* An automobile.

mo-tor-cy-cle *n.* A two-wheeled automotive vehicle. motorcycle *v.*, motorcyclist *n.*

mo-tor home *n.* A motor vehicle built on a truck frame and equipped to provide a self-contained home during travel.

mo-tor-ize *v.* To equip with a motor; to supply with motor-propelled vehicles. motorization *n.*

mo-tor-man *n.* An operator of a locomotive engine, streetcar, or subway train.

mo-tor scoo-ter *n.* A small two-wheeled vehicle similar to a scooter but having a low-powered gasoline engine.

mo-tor ve-hi-cle *n.* A motor-powered vehicle which travels freely without the need for rails.

mot-tle *v.* To mark or be marked with spots or streaks of different colors or shades; to blotch. *n.* A blotch.

mot-to *n., pl.* -toes *or* -tos A sentence, phrase, or word expressing purpose, character, or conduct; an appropriate phrase inscribed on something.

moue *n.* A grimace, as of disapproval or disdain.

mound *n.* A small hill of earth, sand, gravel or debris; the slightly elevated ground in the middle of a baseball diamond on which the pitcher stands.

mount *v.* To rise or ascend; to get up on; climb upon; to increase in amount or extent; to organize and equip; to launch and carry out. *n.* A horse or other animal used for riding; a support to which something is fixed.

moun-tain *n.* A land mass that rises above its surroundings and is higher than a hill.

moun-tain ash *n.* Any of various deciduous trees bearing clusters of small white flowers and orange-red berries.

moun-tain-eer *n.* An inhabitant of a mountainous region; one who climbs mountains for sport. mountaineer *v.*

moun-tain goat *n.* A long-haired Rocky Mountain goat.

moun-tain laurel *n.* A low-growing evergreen shrub with poisonous leaves and clusters of pink or white flowers.

moun-tain lion *n.* A large wildcat; puma.

moun-tain-ous *adj.* Of or relating to a region with many mountains.

moun-tain-side *n.* The side of a mountain.

moun-tain-top *n.* The top of a mountain.

moun-te-bank *n.* A quack doctor; a false and boastful pretender; a charlatan.

Mount-ie *n.* or **Mounty** A member of the Canadian Mounted Police.

mount-ing *n.* A supporting frame or

structure of an article.

mourn v. To express grief; to feel grief or sorrow; to follow the religious customs and rituals surrounding the death of a loved one.

mouse n., pl. **mice**

A small rodent that frequents human habitations; a timid person.

mousse n. A light frozen dessert.

mouth n., pl. **mouths** The bodily opening through which food is taken in.

mouth-off v. To speak disrespectfully.

mouth--to--mouth adj. Pertaining to a method of artificial resuscitation.

move v. To set in motion; to change one's place or location; to make a recommendation in a formal manner. **movable**, **moveable** adj., **moveably** adv.

move-ment n. The act of moving; a part of a musical composition; an excretion of the bowels.

mov-er n. One that moves; a person employed to help in moving the contents of a home or business.

mov-ie n. A motion picture; motion picture industry.

mow v. To cut down, as with a machine. n. The part of the barn where hay or grain is stored. **mower** n.

Mozart, Wolfgang Amadeus N. (1756-1791). Austrian composer.

moz-za-rel-la n. A soft white cheese with a mild flavor.

MP abbr. Military Police.

npg abbr. Miles per gallon.

mph abbr. Miles per hour.

Mr abbr. Mister.

Mrs abbr. Mistress.

Ms abbr. A form of address used for a woman when her marital status is irrelevant or unknown.

MST abbr. Mountain Standard Time.

much adj. In great amount, quantity, degree, or extent. adv. To a great extent. n. Something impressive.

mu-ci-lage n. A sticky substance that is similar to plant gums.

muck n. Moist farmyard manure; moist, sticky soil or filth. v. To dirty with or as with muck. **mucky** adj.

muck-rake v. To search out and publicly expose real or apparent misconduct on the part of well-known persons. **muckraker** n.

mu-co-sa n. A mucous membrane.

mu-cous adj. Of, pertaining to, or secreting mucus.

mu-cous mem-brane n. A membrane secreting mucus which lines bodily channels that come into contact with air.

mu-cus n. The viscous liquid secreted by glands by the mucous membrane.

mud n. A mixture of water and earth. Slang A slanderous remark. **muddily** adv., **muddiness** n., **muddy** adj. & v.

mud-dle v. To make muddy; to mix up or confuse; to make a mess of; to think or act in a confused way. -er n.

muff n. A warm, tubular covering for the hands; a bungling performance. v. To handle awkwardly; to act or do something stupidly or clumsily.

muf-fle v. To wrap up so as to conceal or protect; to deaden the sound of; to suppress.

muf-fler n. A scarf worn around the neck; a device which deadens noise, especially one forming part of the exhaust system of an automotive vehicle.

mug n. A large drinking cup; a person's face; a photograph of someone's face. v. To make funny faces; to assault viciously, usually with the intent to rob.

mug-gy adj. Warm, humid and sultry. **muggily** adv., **mugginess** n.

mug-wump n. A defector from the Republican Party in 1884; anyone who acts independently, especially in politics.

muk-luk n. A boot made from the skin of seals or reindeer, worn by Eskimos; a slipper that resembles a mukluk.

mu-lat-to n., pl. -tos or -toes A person with one white parent and one black parent; a person of mixed black and white ancestry.

mul-ber-ry n. Any of several trees having an edible, berry-like fruit.

mulch n. A loose protective covering, as of sawdust or compost, or wood chips spread on the ground to prevent moisture evaporation, to protect roots from freezing, and to retard the growth of weeds. **mulch** v.

mulct n. A financial penalty or fine. v. To punish by fining; to obtain by fraud or theft.

mule n. A hybrid animal that is the offspring of a female horse and a male ass. Slang A stubborn person. **mulish** adj., -ly adv., **mulishness** n.

mule deer n. A long-eared deer of western North America, heavier built and larger than the white-tail deer.

mule--foot adj. Having a solid foot; not cleft.

mule-skin-ner n. A muleteer.

mu-le-teer n. A person who drives mules.

mu-ley adj. Naturally without horns.

mull v. To mix or grind thoroughly; to ponder; to think about.

mul-lah n. A Muslim leader and clergyman.

mul-lein n. A plant having yellow flowers and downy leaves.

mul-let n. An edible marine and freshwater fish.

mul-li-gan stew n. A stew made of various vegetables and meats.

multi- prefix Much, many, multiple; more than two.

mul-ti-dis-ci-plin-ary adj. Using or related to a combination of several disciplines for a common cause.

mul-ti-far-i-ous adj. Having much diversity. **multifariously** adv.

mul-ti-form adj. Having many appearances or forms. **multiformity** *n.*

mul-ti-lane *adj.* Having several lanes.

mul-ti-lat-er-al *adj.* Having many sides; involving or participated in by more than two parties or nations. **-ly** *adv.*

mul-ti-lin-gual *adj.* Expressed in several languages. **multilingualism** *n.*

mul-ti-mil-lion-aire *n.* A person whose fortune is worth many millions of dollars.

mul-ti-na-tion-al *adj.* Involving or relating to several countries.

mul-tip-a-rous *adj.* Producing more than one at a birth.

mul-ti-ple *adj.* Relating to or consisting of more than one individual, part, or element. *Math.* A number into which another number can be divided with no remainders.

mul-ti-ple scle-ro-sis *n.* A degenerative condition marked by patches of hardened tissue in the spinal cord or the brain.

mul-ti-plex *n.* A communications system in which two or more messages can be transmitted simultaneously on the same circuit. **multiplex** *v.*

mul-ti-pli-ca-tion *n.* The mathematical operation by which a number indicates how many times another number is to be added to itself.

mul-ti-plic-i-ty *n., pl.* **-ies** A large number or variety.

mul-ti-pli-er *n.* A number that is or is to be multiplied by another number.

mul-ti-ply *v.* To increase in amount or number; to combine by multiplication.

mul-ti-sense *adj.* Having several meanings.

mul-ti-stage *adj.* Consisting of propulsion units which operate in turn.

mul-ti-tude *n.* A very large amount or number. **multitudinous** *adj.*

mul-ti-vi-ta-min *n.* A pill containing several vitamins that are essential to health.

mum *adj.* Silent, not speaking.

mum-ble *v.* To speak or utter in a low, confused manner. **mumbler** *n.*

mum-ble-ty--peg or **mum-ble--the--peg** *n.* A game in which players try to throw a knife from various positions so that the blade will stick into the ground.

mum-bo jum-bo *n.* A complicated or obscure ritual; a confusing and complicated language or activity.

mum-mer *n.* A performer who acts in a pantomime.

mum-mery *n., pl.* **-ies** A hypocritical or ridiculous ceremony.

mum-mi-fy *v.* To dry and embalm as a mummy; to cause to shrivel and dry up. **mummification** *n.*

mum-my *n., pl.* **-ies** A body embalmed or treated for burial in the manner of the ancient Egyptians.

mumps *pl. n.* An acute, contagious viral disease marked by fever and swelling of the salivary glands.

munch *v.* To chew noisily. **muncher** *v.*

mun-dane *adj.* Pertaining to or relating to the world; characterized by the ordinary and practical. **mundanely** *adv.*

Mu-nich *n.* A city located in southwest Germany.

mu-nic-i-pal *adj.* Relating to or typical of a municipality; having self-government in local affairs. **municipally** *adv.*, **municipality** *n.*

mu-nif-i-cent *adj.* Very liberal in giving; lavish. **-ence** *n.*, **munificently** *adv.*

mu-ni-tions *pl. n.* Guns and ammunition.

mu-ral *n.* A painting created on a wall.

mur-der *n.* The crime of unlawfully killing a person. *Slang* Something very dangerous, difficult, or uncomfortable. *v.* To kill a person unlawfully and with premeditated malice. **murderer** *n.*

mur-der-ous *adj.* Intending or having the purpose or capability of murder. **murderously** *adv.*

murk *n.* Darkness; gloom. **murkily** *adv.*, **murkiness** *n.*, **murky** *adj.*

mur-mur *n.* A low, indistinct, and often continuous sound; a gentle or soft utterance. **murmur** *v.*

mur-mur-ous *adj.* Characterized by murmurs. **murmurously** *adv.*

mur-rain *n.* A plague affecting plants or domestic animals.

mur-rey *n.* Mulberry colored; purplish-black.

mus *abbr.* Museum; musical; musician.

mus-cae vo-li-tan-tes *n.* A condition of spots before the eyes due to cells and cell fragments in the vitreous humor and lens.

mus-cle *n.* Bodily tissue which consists of long cells that contract when stimulated. **muscle** *v.*

mus-cle--bound *adj.* Having muscles which are overdeveloped and lack the capacity to flex fully, usually caused by too much exercise.

mus-cu-lar *adj.* Relating to or consisting of muscle; brawny; having well-developed muscles. **muscularity** *n.*

mus-cu-lar dys-tro-phy *n.* A noncontagious hereditary disease characterized by gradual but irreversible muscular deterioration.

mus-cu-la-ture *n.* The muscles of an animal's body.

muse *n.* A state of deep thought.

Muse *n.* One of the nine Greek goddesses in mythology, who are the inspiration for creativity, as music and art.

mu-sette *n.* A small bagpipe having a soft, sweet tone or sound; a small bag with a shoulder strap.

mush *n.* A thick porridge of cornmeal boiled in water or milk; soft matter. **mushiness** *n.*, **mushy** *adj.*

mush-room *n.*

A fungus having an umbrella-shaped cap on a stalk. *v.* To grow or multiply quickly.

mu-sic *n.* Organized tones in sequences and combinations which make up a continuous composition. **musical** *adj.*

mu-si-cian *n.* A composer or performer of music. **-ly** *adj.*, **musicianship** *n.*

mu-si-col-o-gy *n.* The scientific and historical study of music. **musicological** *adj.*, **musicologist** *n.*

musk *n.* A substance with a strong, powerful odor which is secreted by the male musk deer. **muskiness** *n.*, **-y** *adj.*

mus-keg *n.* A bog formed by moss, leaves, and decayed matter resembling peat.

mus-ket *n.* A heavy, large-caliber shoulder gun with a long barrel. **musketeer** *n.*

musk-mel-on *n.* A sweet melon having a rough rind and juicy, edible flesh.

musk-rat *n.*

A rodent of North America with brown fur.

mus-lin *n.* A plain-woven, sheer, or coarse fabric.

muss *v.* To make messy or untidy. *Slang* A confused conflict. **mussily** *adv.*, **mussiness** *n.*, **mussy** *adj.*

mus-sel *n.* A freshwater bivalve mollusk.

must *v.* To be forced to; to have to; to be obligated to do something; to be necessary to do something. *n.* A requirement; absolute; something indispensable.

mus-tache *also* **mous-tache** *n.* The hair growing on the human upper lip, especially on the male upper lip.

mus-tang *n.* A wild horse of the western plains.

mus-ter *v.* To come or bring together; to convene; to bring or call forth.

mustn't *contr.* Must not.

mus-ty *adj.* Moldy or stale in odor or taste. **mustily** *adv.*, **mustiness** *n.*

mu-ta-ble *adj.* Prone to or capable of change. **mutability, mutableness** *n.*

mu-tant *n.* An individual or organism which differs from the parental strain as a result of mutation. **mutant** *adj.*

mu-tate *v.* To undergo or cause to undergo mutation. **mutative** *adj.*

mu-ta-tion *n.* A change in form. *Biol.* A sudden change in the hereditary makeup of an organism in which there is a physical or chemical change in the genes.

mute *adj.* Unable to speak. *n.* A person who cannot speak. **-ly** *adv.*, **-ness** *n.*

mu-ti-late *v.* To deprive of an essential part, as a limb of the body; to maim or cripple; to make imperfect. **mutilation, mutilator** *n.*

mu-ti-ny *n.*, *pl.* **-ies** Open revolt against lawful authority. **mutineer** *n.*, **mutinous** *adj.*, **mutiny** *v.*

mutt *n.*, *Slang* A mongrel; a dog of mixed breed.

mut-ter *v.* To speak or utter in a low voice; to grumble; to complain.

mut-ton *n.* The flesh of a fully grown sheep, used for food. **muttony** *adj.*

mu-tu-al *adj.* Having the same relationship; received and directed in equal amounts. **mutuality** *n.*

my *adj.* Relating to or of myself or one. *interj.* Used to express surprise, dismay, or pleasure.

my-ce-li-um *n.*, *pl.* **-lia** A mass of interwoven filaments which form the main growing structure of a fungus. **-ial** *adj.*

my-col-o-gy *n.* A branch of botany; the scientific study of fungi. **mycological** *adj.*, **mycologist** *n.*

my-e-li-tis *n.* An inflammation of the spinal cord or bone marrow.

my-elo-ma *n.* A tumor of the bone marrow.

my-na *or* **my-nah** *n.* A dark brown, slightly crested bird of south-eastern Asia.

myo-car-dio-graph *n.* A recording tool which traces the action of the heart muscles.

myo-car-di-um *n.* The muscular layer of the heart, located in the middle of the heart wall.

my-o-pia *n.* A visual defect in which visual images come to a focus in front of the retina of the eye rather than on the retina, causing fuzzy images. **myopic** *adj.*, **myopically** *adv.*

myr-i-ad *adj.* Having extremely large, indefinite aspects or elements.

myr-i-a-pod *n.* An arthropod, having a segmented body and many legs.

myr-mi-don *n.* A loyal follower.

myrrh *n.* An aromatic gum resin yielded from shrubs and trees, used in incense and perfumes.

myr-tle *n.* An evergreen shrub.

my-self *pron.* The one identical with me; used reflexively; my normal, healthy state or condition.

mys-te-ri-ous *adj.* Relating to or being a mystery; impossible or difficult to comprehend. **-ly** *adv.*, **-ness** *n.*

mys-ter-y *n.*, *pl.* **-ies** Something not understood; a problem or puzzle; an enigma; a Christian sacrament.

mys-tic *adj.* Relating to mystics, mysticism, or mysteries. *n.* A person practicing or believing in mysticism. **mystical** *adj.*, **mystically** *adv.*

mys-ti-cism *n.* The spiritual discipline of communion with God.

mys-ti-fy *v.* To perplex, to bewilder. **mystification** *n.*, **mystifyingly** *adv.*

mys-tique *n.* A body of beliefs connected with a group, person, idea, or thing.

myth *n.* A traditional story dealing with supernatural ancestors; a person or thing having only an unverifiable or imaginary existence. **mythical, mythic** *adj.*, **mythically** *adv.*

my-thol-o-gy *n.*, *pl.* **-ies** A body of myths dealing with gods and heroes. **mythological** *adj.*, **mythologist** *n.*

myx-e-de-ma *n.* A disease caused by decreased activity of the thyroid gland and marked by loss of mental and physical vigor.

N, n The fourteenth letter of the English alphabet.

nab v., *Slang* To seize; to arrest.

na-cho n. A tortilla, often small and triangular in shape, topped with cheese or chili sauce and baked.

nag v. To bother by scolding or constant complaining. n. A worthless horse. **nagger** n., **nagging** adj., **naggingly** adv.

nai-ad n., Gr. Mythol. A nymph presiding over and living in springs, brooks, and fountains.

nail n. A thin pointed piece of metal for hammering into wood and other materials to hold pieces together.

nail-brush n. A small brush with frim bristles used to clean the hands and nails.

nail file n. A small instrument with a rough surface, used to shape the fingernails.

na-ive adj. Simple and trusting; not sophisticated. **-ly** adv., **naiveness** n.

na-ked adj. Without clothes on the body; nude. **nakedly** adv., **nakedness** n.

nam-by--pam-by adj. Weak; indecisive.

name n. A title or word by which something or someone is known. v. To give a name. **namable, namable** adj.

name--call-ing n. The use of offending names to induce condemnation or rejection.

name-less adj. Having no name; anonymous. **namelessly** adv., **-ness** n.

nan-ny n. A child's nurse; one who cares for small children.

nan-ny goat n. A female domestic goat.

nap n. A short rest or sleep, often during the day. v. The surface of a piece of leather or fabric. **napless, napped** adj.

na-palm n. A mixture of aluminum soaps used in jelling gasoline for use in bombs or by flame throwers.

nape n. The back of the neck.

nar-cis-sus n. A widely grown type of bulbous plant which includes the jonquil, narcissus, and daffodil.

nar-co-sis n. A deep drug induced state of stupor or unconsciousness.

nar-cot-ic n. A drug which dulls the senses, relieves pain, and induces a deep sleep; if abused, it can become habit-forming and cause convulsions or comas. **narcotically** adv.

nar-rate v. To tell a story or give a description in detail. **narration** n., **narrator** v.

nar-row adj. Slender or small in width; of less than standard width. **narrowly** adj., **narrowness** n.

nar-whal n.

An aquatic mammal of the Arctic regions, closely related to the white whale, having a long, twisted, protruding tusk in the male.

na-sal adj. Of or pertaining to the nose.

na-stur-tium n. A five-petaled garden plant usually having red, yellow, or orange flowers.

nas-ty adj. Dirty, filthy, or indecent; unpleasant. **nastily** adv., **nastiness** n.

na-tal adj. Pertaining to or associated with birth.

na-tion n. A group of people made up of one or more nationalities under one government. **-al** adj., **-ally** adv.

na-tion-al-ism n. Devotion to or concern for one's nation.

na-tion-al-i-ty n. The fact or condition of belonging to a nation.

na-tion-al-ize v. To place a nation's resources and industries under the control of the state.

na-tive n. A person born in a country or place.

na-tiv-i-ty n. Birth, circumstances, or conditions.

nat-ty adj. Tidy and trimly neat. **nattily** adv., **nattiness** n.

nat-u-ral adj. Produced or existing by nature. *Mus.* A note that is not sharp or flat. **naturalness** n., **naturally** adv.

nat-u-ral child-birth n. Childbirth with little stress or pain, requiring training for the mother and father and medical supervision, but without the use of drugs, anesthesia, or surgery.

nat-u-ral-ize v. To confer the privileges and rights of full citizenship. **naturalization** n.

na-ture n. The universe and its phenomena; one's own character or temperament. **natured** adj.

naught n. Nothing; the number 0; zero.

naugh-ty adj. Unruly; not proper; ill-behaved. **naughtily** adv., **-iness** n.

nau-se-a n. An upset stomach with a feeling that one needs to vomit. **-ous** adj., **nauseate** v., **-tingly** adv.

nau-ti-cal adj. Pertaining to ships or seamanship. **nautically** adv.

na-val adj. Of or relating to ships; maritime.

na-vel n. A small mark or scar on the abdomen where the umbilical cord was attached.

nav-i-ga-ble adj. Sufficiently deep and wide enough to allow ships to pass. **navigableness** n., **navigably** adv.

nav-i-gate v. To plan the course of a ship or aircraft; to steer a course. **-tion, navigator** n., **navigational** adj.

na-vy n. One of a nation's organizations for defense; a nation's fleet of ships; a very dark blue.

Na-zi n., pl. nazis A member of the German fascist party which controlled Germany from 1933-1945 under Adolf Hitler. **Nazi** adj., **nazification** n.

NBA abbr. National Basketball Association; National Boxing Association.

Ne-an-der-thal adj. Suggesting a caveman in behavior or appearance; primitive or crude. **Neanderthal** n.

neap tide n. A tide in the minimum range which occurs during the first and third quarter of the moon.

near adv. At, to, or within a short time or distance. **nearness** n.

near-by *adj. & adv.* Close by; near at hand; adjacent.

near-sight-ed *adj.* Able to see clearly at short distances only. **-ly** *adv.,* **nearsightedness** *n.*

neat *adj.* Tidy and clean; free from disorder and dirt. **neatly** *adv.,* **neatness** *n.*

neat-en *v.* To make neat; to set in order.

neb-u-lous *adj.* Confused or vague; hazy. **-ly** *adv.,* **nebulousness** *n.*

nec-es-sar-y *adj.* Unavoidable; required; essential; needed. **necessarily** *adv.*

ne-ces-si-tate *v.* To make necessary; to oblige.

ne-ces-si-ty *n., pl.* **-ies** The condition of being necessary; the condition making a particular course of action necessary.

neck *n.* The part of the body which connects the head and trunk; a narrow part or projection, as of land, a stringed instrument, or bottle. *v.* To caress and kiss.

neck-tie *n.* A narrow strip of material worn around the neck and tied.

nec-tar *n.* A sweet fluid in various flowers, gathered by bees to help make honey. **nectarous** *adj.*

nee *n.* The surname a woman was born with.

need *n.* The lack of something desirable, useful, or necessary.

need-ful *adj.* Necessary. *n.* Something needed. **needfully** *adv.,* **needfulness** *n.*

nee-dle *n.* A slender, pointed steel implement which contains an eye through which thread is passed. *v.* To tease. **needlelike** *adj.*

needle-point *n.* Decorative stitching done on canvas in even stitches across counted threads. **needlepoint** *adj.*

need-less *adj.* Unnecessary; not needed. **needlessly** *adv.,* **needlessness** *n.*

need-n't *contr.* Need not.

ne-far-i-ous *adj.* Extremely wicked; despicable. **-le** *adv.,* **-ness** *n.*

neg *abbr.* Negative.

ne-gate *v.* To nullify; to deny. **-tor** *n.*

ne-ga-tion *n.* A judgement; a negative statement, or doctrine.

neg-a-tive *adj.* Expressing denial or disapproval; not positive. *n.* In photography, a negative photo. **negatively** *adj.,* **negativeness** *n.*

neglect *v.* To ignore; to pay no attention to; to fail to perform. **neglectful** *adj.*

neg-li-gee *n.* A woman's loose-fitting dressing gown.

neg-li-gent *adj.* To neglect what needs to be done.

ne-go-ti-ate *v.* To confer with another person to reach an agreement. **negotiation, negotiator** *n.*

ne-groid *adj.* Of or relating to the Black race.

neigh-bor *n.* One who lives near another. **neighboring** *adj.* **neighbor** *v.*

neigh-bor-hood *n.* A section or small region that possesses a specific quality.

neigh-bor-ly *adj.* Characteristic of congenial neighbors; friendly. **neighborliness** *n.*

nei-ther *adj.* Not one or the other. *pron.* Not the one or the other.

nel-son *n.* A wrestling hold using the application of leverage against an opponent's arm, head, and neck.

neo *prefix* Recent; new.

neo-dym-i-um *n.* A metallic element of the rare-earth group, symbolized by Nd.

ne-on *n.* An inert gaseous element used in lighting fixtures, symbolized by Ne. **neon, neoned** *adj.*

ne-o-nate *n.* A newborn child less than a month old.

ne-o-na-tol-o-gy *n.* The medical study of the first 60 days of a baby's life.

neo-phyte *n.* A novice; a beginner.

ne-o-plasm *n.* A tumor tissue serving no physiologic function. **neoplastic** *adj.*

neph-ew *n.* The son of one's sister, brother, sister-in-law, or brother-in-law.

ne-phrit-ic *adj.* Relating to the kidneys; afflicted with an inflammation of the kidneys.

nep-o-tism *n.* The act of showing favoritism to relatives or friends in the work force. **nepotist** *n.*

Nep-tune *n.* The planet 8th in order from the sun.

nep-tu-ni-um *n.* A radioactive metallic element.

nerve *n.* The bundles of fibers which convey sensation and originate motion through the body. *Slang* Impudent.

nerve-less *adj.* Lacking courage or strength. **-ly** *adv.,* **nervelessness** *n.*

nerv-ous *adj.* Affecting the nerves or the nervous system; agitated; worried. **nervously** *adv.,* **nervousness** *n.*

nervous system *n., Physiol.* The body system that coordinates, regulates, and controls the various internal functions and responses to stimuli.

nest *n.* A place, shelter, or home built by a bird to hold its eggs and young.

nest egg *n.* A supply of money accumulated or saved for future use.

nes-tle *v.* To lie close to. **nestler** *n.*

net *n.* A meshed fabric made of cords, ropes, threads, or other material knotted or woven together; the profit, weight, or price which remains after all additions, subtractions, or adjustments have been made. **net** *v.*

neth-er *adj.* Situated below or beneath.

neth-er-most *adj.* Lowest; farthest down.

net-tle *n.* A plant having toothed leaves covered with stinging hairs.

net-work *n.* A system of interlacing tracks, channels, or lines; an interconnected system.

neu-ral *adj.* Relating to a nerve or the nervous system. **neurally** *adv.*

neu-ral-gia *n.* Pain that occurs along the course of a nerve.

neu-ri-tis *n.* An inflammation of a nerve which causes pain, the loss of reflexes, and muscular decline. **neurotic** *adj.*

neu-rol-o-gy *n.* The medical and scientific study of the nervous system and disorders. **neurological** *adj.,* **neurologist** *n.*

neu-ron *or* **neu-rone** *n., Anat.*
A granular cell nerve which is the main functional unit of the nervous system.

neu-ro-sis *n.* Any one of various functional disorders of the mind or emotions having no physical cause. **neurotic** *adj. n.*, **neurotically** *adv.*

neu-ro-sur-geon *n.* A surgeon that specializes in neurosurgery.

neu-ro-surgery *n.* Surgery of the brain.

neu-ter *adj.* Neither feminine nor masculine. *n.* A castrated animal. **neuter** *v.*

neu-tral *adj.* Not supporting either side of a debate, quarrel, or party; a color which does not contain a decided hue. *Chem.* Neither alkaline nor acid. **neutrality** *n.*, **neutrally** *adv.*

neu-tral-ize *v.* To make or declare neutral.

neu-tron *n.* An uncharged particle in the nucleus of an atom present in all atomic nuclei except the hydrogen nucleus.

nev-er *adv.* Not ever; absolutely not.

nev-er-the-less *adv.* Nonetheless; however.

new *adj.* Not used before; unaccustomed; unfamiliar. **newness** *n.*

New Deal *n.* The legislative and social programs of President F.D. Roosevelt designed for relief, economic recovery, and social security during the 1930's.

news *n., pl.* Current information and happenings.

news-cast *n.* A television or radio news broad-cast.

news-pa-per *n.* A weekly or daily publication which contains recent news and information.

news-print *n.* An inexpensive machine-finished paper made from wood pulp and used chiefly for newspapers and some paperback books.

New Test-a-ment *n.* The second part of the Christian Bible containing the Gospels, Acts, Epistles, and the Book of Revelation.

New World *n.* North and South America.

next *adj.* Immediately following or proceeding; nearest in space or position.

nib-ble *v.* To bite a little at a time; to take small bites. **nibble, nibbler** *n.*

nice *adj.* Pleasing; enjoyable; polite and courteous; refined. **-ly** *adv.*,

niche *n.* A recess or alcove in a wall.

nick *n.* A small chip or cut on a surface; the final critical moment.

nick-el *n.* A hard, silver, metallic element used in alloys and symbolized by Ni; a United States coin worth five cents.

nick-el-o-de-on *n.* A movie theatre which charged five cents for admission; a coin-operated juke box.

nick-name *n.* The familiar form of a proper name, expressed in a shortened form. **nickname** *v.*

nic-o-tine *or* **nicotin** *n.* A poisonous alkaloid found in tobacco and used in insecticides and medicine.

niece *n.* A daughter of one's sister or brother or one's sister-in-law or brother-in-law.

nigh *adv.* Near in relationship, time, or space.

night *n.* The time between dusk and dawn or the hours of darkness.

night-cap *n.* An alcoholic drink usually taken before retiring for the night.

night-in-gale *n.*
A songbird with brownish plumage, noted for the sweet, nocturnal song of the male.

night-mare *n.* A frightening and horrible dream.

nim-ble *adj.* Marked by a quick, light movement; quick-witted. **nimbleness** *n.*, **nimbly** *adv.*

nin-com-poop *n.* A silly or stupid person.

nine *n.* The cardinal number that is equal to 8 + 1. **nine** *adj., pron.*

ni-o-bi-um *n.* A gray, metallic element used in alloys, symbolized by Nb.

nip *v.* To pinch, bite, or grab something. *n.* A pinch, bite, or grab; a sharp, stinging feeling caused by cold temperatures. **nipper** *n.*

nip-ple *n.* The small projection of a mammary gland through which milk passes; an artificial teat usually made from a type of rubber which a bottle-fed baby nurses.

ni-tro-gen *n.* A nonmetallic gaseous element which is essential to life.

ni-tro-glyc-er-in *n.* A highly flammable, explosive liquid, used to make dynamite and, in medicine, to dilate blood vessels.

Nixon Richard M. *n.* Born in 1913, the 37th president of the United States from 1969-1974 resigned August 9, 1974 due to Watergate scandal.

no *adv.* Used to express rejection, disagreement, or denial; not so; not at all.

no-bel-i-um *n.* A radioactive element.

Nobel prize *n.* An award given to people with achievements in literature, economics, medicine, and other fields, established by the last will and testament of Alfred Nobel.

no-bil-i-ty *n., pl.* **ies** The state or quality of being noble.

no-ble *adj.* Morally good; superior in character or nature. *n.* A person of rank or noble birth. **noblemen, nobleness** *n.*, **nobly** *adv.*

no-bod-y *pron.* Not anybody; no person.

noc-tur-nal *adj.* Pertaining to or occurring during the night. **nocturnally** *adv.*

nod *n.* A quick downward motion of the head as one falls off to sleep; a downward motion of the head indicating acceptance or approval.

node *n.* A swollen or thickened enlargement.

no-el *n.* A Christmas carol.

noise *n.* A sound which is disagreeable or loud; in computer science, unwanted data in an electronic signal. **noisy** *adj.*, **noisily** *adv.*

no-mad *n.* A member of a group of people who wander from place to place. **nomadic** *adj.*, **nomadism** *n.*

no-men-cla-ture *n.* The set of names used to describe the elements of art, science, and other fields.

nom-i-nal *adj.* Of or relating to something that is in name or form only. **nominally** *adv.*

nom-i-nate *v.* To select a candidate for an elective office. **-tion, -tor** *n.*

nom-i-nee *n.* A person nominated for a position or office.

non- *prefix* Not.

non-a-ge-nar-i-an *adj.* A person between the ages of 90 and 100 years.

non-cha-lant *adj.* Giving an effect of casual unconcern. **nonchalance** *n.*, **nonchalantly** *adv.*

non com-pos men-tis *adj.* Mentally unbalanced.

non-con-form-ist *n.* A person who does not feel compelled to follow or accept his community's traditions. **-ity** *n.*

none *pron.* Not any; not one.

non-sec-tar-i-an *adj.* Not associated with or restricted to one religion, faction, or sect.

non-sense *n.* Something that seems senseless or foolish. **nonsensical** *adj.*

non seq-ui-tur *n.* An inference that does not follow as the logical result of what has preceded it.

non-sex-ist *adj.* Not discriminating on the basis of gender.

noo-dle *n.* A flat strip of dried dough made with eggs and flour.

nook *n.* A corner, recess, or secluded place.

noon *n.* The middle of the day; 12:00 o'clock.

noose *n.* A loop of rope secured by a slipknot, allowing it to decrease in size as the rope is pulled.

nor *conj.* Not either; or not.

norm *n.* A rule, model, or pattern typical for a particular group.

nor-mal *adj.* Ordinary, average, usual; having average intelligence. **normalcy**, **normality** *n.*, **normally** *adv.*

north *n.* The direction to a person's left while facing east.

nose *n.* The facial feature containing the nostrils; the sense of smell.

nose-dive *n.* A sudden plunge as made by an aircraft.

nos-tal-gia *n.* A yearning to return to the past. **nostalgic** *adj.*

nos-tril *n.* The external openings of the nose.

nos-y *or* **nos-ey** *adj.* Snoopy; inquisitive; prying.

not *adv.* In no manner; used to express refusal or denial.

no-ta-ble *adj.* Remarkable, distin-guished. **notably** *adv.*

no-ta-rize *v.* To acknowledge and certify as a notary public.

notary public *n.* A person who is legally authorized as a public officer to witness and certify documents.

no-ta-tion *n.* A process or system of figures or symbols used in specialized fields to represent quantities, numbers, or values. **notational** *adj.*

notch *n.* A v-shaped indentation or cut.

note *n.*

A record or message in short form. *Mus.* A tone or written character. **note** *v.*

not-ed *adj.* Famous; well-known.

noth-ing *n.* Not any thing; no part or portion.

no-tice *n.* An announcement; a notification. **noticeable** *adj.*, **noticeably** *adv.*

no-ti-fy *v.* To give notice of; to announce. **notifier**, **notification** *n.*

no-tion *n.* An opinion; a general concept; an idea.

notions *pl.*, *n.* Small useful articles, as thread or buttons.

no-to-ri-ous *adj.* Having a widely known and usually bad reputation.

not-with-stand-ing *prep.* In spite of. *adv.* Nevertheless; anyway. *conj.* Although.

noun *n.* A word which names a person, place, or thing.

nour-ish *v.* To furnish with the nutriment and other substances needed for growth and life; to support. **nourishing** *adj.*, **nourishment** *n.*

nou-veau riche *n.* A person who has recently become rich.

no-va *n.*, *pl.* **-vae** *or* **-vas** A star which flares up and fades away after a few years or months.

nov-el *n.* An inventive narrative dealing with human experiences; a book. **-ist** *n.*

nov-el-ty *n.*, *pl.* **-ies** Something unusual or new.

No-vem-ber *n.* The 11th month of the calendar year, having 30 days.

nov-ice *n.* A person who is new and unfamiliar with an activity or business.

now *adv.* At the present time; immediately.

no-where *adv.* Not in or at any place.

nox-ious *adj.* Harmful; obnoxious; corrupt.

nu-ance *n.* A slight variation.

nub *n.* A knob; a small piece or lump.

nu-bile *adj.* Suitable or ready for marriage.

nu-cle-ar *adj.* Pertaining to and resembling a nucleus; relating to atomic energy.

nu-cle-us *n.*, *pl.* **-clei** *or* **-cleuses** A central element around which other elements are grouped.

nude *adj.* Unclothed; naked. **-ity**, **-ist** *n.*

nudge *v.* To poke or push gently.

nug-get *n.* A lump, as of precious metal.

nui-sance *n.* A source of annoyance.

null *adj.* Invalid; having no value or

consequence. **nullification** *n.*

nul-li-fy *v.* To counteract.

numb *adj.* Lacking physical sensation. **numb** *v.*, **numbness** *n.*

num-ber *n.* A word or symbol which is used in counting or which indicates how many or which one is in a series.

number-less *adj.* Too many to be counted.

nu-meral *n.* A symbol, figure, letter, word, or a group of these which represents a number.

nu-mer-a-tor *n.* The term in mathematics indicating how many parts are to be taken; the number in a fraction which appears above the line.

nu-mer-ous *adj.* Consisting or made up of many units.

nun *n.* A woman who has joined a religious group and has taken vows to give up worldly goods and never to marry.

nup-tial *adj.* Of or pertaining to a wedding.

nuptials *pl.*, *n.* A wedding.

nurse *n.* A person who is specially trained to care for disabled or sick persons. *v.* To feed a baby from a mother's breast.

nurs-er-y *n.*, *pl.* **-ies** A room reserved for the special use of infants or small children; a business or place where trees, shrubs, and flowers are raised.

nur-ture *n.* The upbringing, care, or training of a child. **nurture** *v.*, **nurturer** *n.*

nut *n.* A hard-shelled fruit or seed which contains an inner, often edible kernal.

nut-crack-er *n.* A hinged tool for cracking nuts.

nut-gall *n.* A type of gall that looks like a nut.

nut grass *n.* A type of perennial sedge that has a rootstock which is slender and will bear small tubers which are edible.

nut-hatch *n.* A type of small tree climbing bird that has a small and compact body.

nut-let *n.* A type of small fruit that is similar to a nut.

nut-meg *n.* The hard seed of a tropical ever-green tree, which is grated and used as a spice.

nu-tri-ent *n.* A substance which nourishes. **nutrient** *adj.*

nu-tri-tion *n.* The process by which a living being takes in food and uses it to live and grow. **-tive**, **-tional** *adj.*, **nutritionally** *adv.*, **nutritionist** *n.*

nuts *adj.*, *Slang* Foolish, crazy.

nuz-zle *v.* To gently rub against something with the nose; to cuddle.

ny-lon *n.* A strong, elastic material; yarn or fabric made from nylon. **nylons** Stockings made of nylon.

nymph *n.*, *Gr. & Rom. Mythol.* Nature goddesses who lived in woods, rivers, and trees; various immature insects, especially the larva which undergoes incomplete metamorphosis. **-al** *adj.*

O, o The 15th letter of the English alphabet.

O *n* A word used before a name when talking to that person; an interjection.

O' *abbr.* o'clock.

oaf *n.* A stupid or clumsy person. **oafish** *adj.*, **oafishly** *adv.*

oak *n.* A large tree of durable wood bearing acorns. **oaken** *adj.*

oak apple *n.* The round gall which is made on oak leaves by the gall wasp.

oak-moss *n.* A type of lichens that will grow on oak trees.

oak wilt *n.* A type of disease of the oak tree that will cause wilting and defoliation and is caused by a fungus.

oar *n.* A long pole, flat at one end, used in rowing a boat.

oars-man *n.* A person who rows in a racing crew. **oarsmanship** *n.*

oa-sis *n.*, *pl.* **oases** A fertile section in the desert which contains water.

oat *n.* A cultivated cereal grass whose grain or seed is used as food.

oat-en *adj.* To be pertaining to oats.

oath *n.* A solemn promise in the name of God or on a Bible that a person will speak only the truth.

oat-meal *n.* A cooked cereal food made from rolled oats.

ob-du-rate *adj.* Stubborn; hard-hearted; not giving in. **obduracy** *n.*

o-be-di-ent *adj.* Obeying or willing to do what one is told. **obedience** *n.*

ob-e-lisk *n.* A tall, four-sided stone pillar which slopes from a pointed top.

o-bese *adj.* Very fat. **obesity** *n.*

o-bey *v.* To carry out instructions; to be guided or controlled; to follow directions. **obeyer** *n.*

o-bit *n.* *Slang* An obituary.

o-bit-u-ar-y *n.*, *pl.* **-ies** A published announcement that a person has died, often containing a short biography of the person's life. **obituary** *adj.*

ob-ject *v.* To voice disapproval; to protest. *n.* Something that is visible or can be touched. *Grammar* A word in a sentence which explains who or what is acted upon. **objectless** *adj.*

ob-jec-tion *n.* A feeling of opposition or disagreement, etc.; the reason for a disagreement. **objective** *adj.*

ob-la-tion *n.* A religious offering or the act of sacrifice; that which is offered.

ob-li-ga-tion *n.* A promise or feeling of duty; something one must do because one's conscience or the law demands it; a debt which must be repaid.

o-blige *v.* To constrain; to put in one's debt by a service or favor; to do a favor. **obliger** *n.*, **obligingly** *adv.*

ob-li-gee *n.* The person to whom another is obligated.

o-blique *adj.*

Inclined; not level or straight up and down; slanting; indirect. **-ness**, **obliquity** *n.*

o-blit-er-ate *v.* To blot out or eliminate completely; to wipe out. **obliteration**,

obliterator *n.*, **obliterative** *adj.*

o-bliv-i-on *n.* The condition of being utterly forgotten; the act of forgetting.

ob-liv-i-ous *adj.* Not aware or conscious of what is happening; unmindful. **obliviously** *adv.*, **obliviousness** *n.*

ob-long *adj.* Rectangular; longer in one direction than the other; normally, the horizontal dimension; the greater in length. **oblong** *n.*

ob-lo-quy *n.* Abusinve language; a stonly condemnatory utterance.

ob-nox-ious *adj.* Very unpleasant; repugnant. **obnoxiousness** *n.*

o-boe *n.* A double-reed, tube-shaped woodwind instrument. **oboist** *n.*

ob-scene *adj.* Indecent; disgusting. **obscenity** *n.*

ob-scure *adj.* Remote; not clear; faint. *v.* To make dim; to conceal by covering. **-ly** *adv.*, **obscurity, obscureness** *n.*

ob-serve *v.* To pay attention; to watch. **observable, observant** *adj.*, **observably** *adv.*, **observer** *n.*

ob-ser-vant *adj.* Paying strict attention to someting. **observantly** *adv.*

ob-ser-va-tion *n.* The act of observing some-thing; that which is observed; a judgment or opinion. **observational** *adj.*, **-ly** *adv.*

ob-ser-va-to-ry *n.*, *pl.* **-ies** A building or station furnished with instruments for studying the natural phenomenon; a high tower affording a panoramic view.

ob-sess *v.* To preoccupy the mind with an idea or emotion; to be abnormally preoccupied. **obsession** *n.*

ob-so-lete *adj.* No longer in use; out-of-date. **obsolescence** *n.*, **obsolescent** *adj.*

ob-sta-cle *n.* An obstruction; anything which opposes or stands in the way of.

ob-ste-tri-cian *n.* A physician who specializes in the care of a woman during pregnancy and childbirth.

ob-stet-rics *pl.*, *n.* The branch of medicine which deals with pregnancy and childbirth.

ob-sti-nate *adj.* Stubbornly set to an opinion or course of action; difficult to control or manage; hardheaded. **obstinacy** *n.*, **obstinately** *adv.*

ob-strep-er-ous *adj.* Noisy, unruly, or boisterous in resistance to advice or control. **obstreperousness** *n.*

ob-struct *v.* To block, hinder or impede. **obstructor, obstruction** *n.*, **-ive** *adj.*

ob-struc-tion-ism *n.* The deliberate interference the progress or business. **obstructionist** *n.*, **obstructionistic** *adj.*

ob-tain *v.* To acquire or gain possession of. **obtainable** *adj.*, **obtainer** *n.*

ob-trude *v.* To thrust forward without request or warrant; to call attention to oneself. **obtruder, obtrusion** *n.*

ob-tuse *adj.* Lacking acuteness of feeling; insensitive; not distinct or clear to the senses, as pain or sound. *Bot.* Rounded or blunt at the end, as a petal or leaf. **-ly** *adv.*, **obtuseness** *n.*

ob-vert *v.* To turn in order to present a different view or surface.

ob-vi-ate *v.* To counter or prevent by effectiye measures; to provide for.

ob-vi-ous *adj.* Easily seen, discovered, or understood. **obviously** *adv.*, **-ness** *n.*

oc-ca-sion *n.* The time an event occurs; the event itself; a celebration. *v.* To bring about; to cause.

oc-ca-sion-al *adj.* Appearing or occurring irregularly or now and then; intended, made, or suitable for a certain occasion; incidental

oc-ci-den-tal *adj.* Western. **-ly** *adv.*

oc-cip-i-tal bone *n. Anat.* The bone which forms the back of the skull.

oc-cult *adj.* Concealed. *n.* The action or influence of supernatural agencies or secret knowledge of them. **occultist** *n.*

oc-cult-ism *n.* Study or belief in the influence or action of supernatural powers.

oc-cu-pan-cy *n.* The state or act of being occupied; the act of holding in possession; the time or term during which something is occupied.

oc-cu-pant *n.* A person who acquires title by occupancy

oc-cu-pa-tion *n.* A job, profession, or vocation; a foreign military force which controls an area.

oc-cu-pa-tion-al ther-a-py *n. Med.* The treatment of mental, nervous, or physical disabilities by means of work designed to promote recovery or re-adjustment. **occupational therapist** *n.*

oc-cu-py *v.* To take and retain possession of; to live in. **occupier** *n.*

oc-cur *v.* To suggest; to have something come to mind; to happen. **occurrence** *n.*, **occurrent** *adj.*

o-cean *n.* An immense body of salt water which covers 3/4 of the earth's sur-face; one of the oceans. **oceanic** *adj.*

ocean-ar-i-um *n.* A large contained marine aquarium.

o-ce-an-og-ra-phy *n.* The science of oceanic phenomena dealing with un-derwater research. **oceanographer** *n.*, **oceanographic** *adj.*

o'clock *adv.* Of, or according to the clock.

oc-ta-gon *n.* A polygon with eight angles and eight sides. **octagonal** *adj.*, **octagonally** *adv.*

oc-tane *n.* Any of several hydrocarbon compounds which occur in petroleum.

oc-tave *n., Music* A tone on the eighth degree above or below another tone.

Oc-to-ber *n.* The 10th month of the calendar year, having 31 days.

oc-to-ge-nar-i-an *n.* A person between the ages of 80 and 90.

oc-to-pus *n., pl.* **-es** *or* **-pi**

A cephalopod with a sac-like body and eight tentacles con-taining double rows of suckers.

oc-u-lar *adj.* Of or relating to the eye; perceived or done by the eye.

OD *n. Slang* An overdose of a drug; one who has taken an overdose. *v.* To overdose; to die from an overdose.

odd *adj.* Unusual; strange; singular; left over; not even. **oddly** *adv.*, **oddness** *n.*

odd-ball *n.* One who displays an eccentric behavior.

odds *pl.* *n.* An equalizing advantage given to a weaker opponent; a ratio between the probability against and the probability for something happening or being true.

odds and ends *n.* Miscellaneous things; remnants; scraps.

ode *n.* A lyric poem usually honoring a person or event.

o-dom-e-ter *n.* A device in a vehicle used to measure distance traveled. **odometry** *n.*

o-dor *n.* A smell; a sensation which occurs when the sense of smell is stimulated.

od-ys-sey *n.* A long voyage marked by many changes of fortune; a spiritual quest.

Oedipus complex *n.* An unconscious sexual feeling a child develops towards the parent of the opposite sex.

of *prep.* Proceeding; composed of; relating to.

off *adv.* From a position or place; no longer connected or on. *adj.* Canceled. *prep.* Away from. *interj.* Go away.

of-fend *v.* To make angry; to arouse resentment; to break a law. **offender** *n.*

of-fense *n.* A violation of a duty, rule, or a propriety; the act of causing displeasure; the act of assaulting or attacking; in football and other sports, the team having possession of the ball.

of-fen-sive *adj.* Disagreeable or unpleasant; causing resentment; insulting.

of-fer *v.* To present for acceptance or rejection; to present as an act of worship; to make available; to present in order to satisfy a requirement.

of-fer-ing *n.* The act of one who offers; a contribution, as money, given to the support of a church.

off-hand *adv. or adj.* Without preparation or premeditation.

of-fice *n.* A place where business or professional duties are conducted; an important job, duty, or position.

of-fi-cer *n.* A person who holds a title, position of authority, or office; a policeman.

of-fi-cial *adj.* Something derived from proper authority. *n.* One who holds a position or office; a person who referees a game such as football, basketball, or soccer. **officialism** *n.*, **officially** *adv.*

of-fi-ci-ate *v.* To carry out the duties and functions of a position or office.

of-fi-cious *adj.* Offering one's services or advice in an unduly forward manner. **officiously** *adv.*, **officiousness** *n.*

off-spring *n., pl.* **-springs** The descen-

dants of a person, plant, or animal.

of-ten *adv.* Frequently; many times.

oh *interj.* Used to express surprise, fear, or pain.

ohm *n.* A unit of electrical resistance equal to the resistance of a conductor in which one volt produces a current of one ampere.

oil *n.* Any of various substances, usually thick, which can be burned or easily melted; a lubricant. *v.* To lubricate.

oil-cloth *n.* A cloth treated with oil which therefore becomes waterproof.

oil field *n.* An area rich in petroleum; an area which has been made ready for oil production.

oil slick *n.* A layer of oil floating on water.

oint-ment *n.* An oily substance used on the skin as an aid to healing or to soften the skin.

o-kra *n.* A tall tropical and semitropical plant with green pods that can be either fried or cooked in soups.

old *adj.* Having lived or existed for a long time; of a certain age. *n.* Former times.

old-en *adj.* Of or relating to times long past; ancient.

old--fash-ioned *adj.* Pertaining to or characteristic of former times or old customs; not modern or up-to-date.

Old Glo-ry *n.* The flag of the United States of America.

Old Tes-ta-ment *n.* The first of two parts of the Christian Bible, containing the history of the Hebrews, the laws of Moses, the writings of the prophets, the Holy Scriptures of Judaism, and other material.

Old World *n.* The eastern hemisphere, including Asia, Europe, and Africa.

ol-fac-tory *adj.* Pertaining to the sense of smell.

oli-gar-chy *pl., n.* **-ies** A government controlled by a small group for corrupt and selfish purposes; the group exercising such control.

ol-ive *n.*

A small oval fruit from an evergreen tree with leathery leaves and yellow flowers, valuable as a source of oil.

O-lym-pic Games *pl., n.* International athletic competition held every four years, based on an ancient Greek festival.

om-buds-man *pl. n.* **-men** A government official appointed to report and receive grievances against the government.

om-e-let *or* **om-e-lette** *n.* A dish made from eggs and other items, such as bacon, cheese, and ham, and cooked until set.

o-men *n.* A phenomenon which is thought of as a sign of something to come, whether good or bad.

om-i-nous *adj.* Foreshadowed by an

omen or by a presentiment of evil; threatening.

o-mis-sion *n.* The state or act of being omitted; anything neglected or left out.

o-mit *v.* To neglect; to leave out; to overlook.

om-ni-bus *n.* A public vehicle designed to carry a large number of people; a bus. *adj.* Covering a complete collection of objects or cases.

om-nip-o-tent *adj.* Having unlimited or infinite power or authority.

om-nis-cient *adj.* Knowing all things; having universal or complete knowledge.

om-niv-or-ous *adj.* Feeding on both vegetable and animal substances; absorbing everything. **omnivorously** *adv.*

on *prep.* Positioned upon; indicating proximity; indicating direction toward; with respect to. *adv.* In a position of covering; forward.

once *adv.* A single time; at any one time. *conj.* As soon as.

once-over *n., Slang* A swift but comprehensive glance.

on-col-o-gy *n.* The study of tumors. **oncological, oncologic** *adj.*, **-ist** *n.*

one *adj.* Single; undivided. *n.* A single person; a unit; the first cardinal number (1).

one-self *pron.* One's own self.

one--sid-ed *adj.* Partial to one side; unjust. **one-sidedness** *n.*

on-ion *n.* An edible bulb plant having a pungent taste and odor.

on--line *adj. Computer Science* Controlled directly by a computer.

on-ly *adj.* Sole; for one purpose alone. *adv.* Without anyone or anything else. *conj.* Except; but.

on-o-mat-o-poe-ia *n.* The use of a word, as buzz or hiss, which vocally imitates the sound it denotes. **onomatopoeic, onomatopoetic** *adj.*

on-shore *adj.* Moving or coming near or onto the shore. **onshore** *adv.*

on-slaught *n.* A fierce attack.

on-to *prep.* To a position or place; aware of.

o-nus *n.* A burden; a responsibility or duty which is difficult or unpleasant; the blame.

on-ward *adv.* Moving forward in time or space. **onwards** *adj.*

on-yx *n.* A gemstone; a chalcedony in layers of different colors.

oo-dles *pl., n., Slang* A great or large quantity.

ooze *n.* A soft deposit of slimy mud on the bottom of a body of water; muddy or marshy ground; a bog. *v.* To flow or leak slowly; to disappear little by little.

o-pal *n.* A translucent mineral composed of silicon, often marked with an iridescent play of colors. **opaline** *adj.*

o-paque *adj.* Not transparent; dull; obscure. **opacity, opaqueness** *n.*

OPEC *abbr.* Organization of Petroleum Exporting Countries.

o-pen *adj.* Having no barrier; not covered, sealed, locked, or fastened. *n.* A contest for both amateurs and professionals. *v.* To begin or start. **openness** *n.*, **openly** *adv.*

open--and--shut *adj.* Easily settled; simple to decide.

op-era *n.* A drama having music as a dominant factor, an orchestral accompaniment, acting, and scenery.

op-er-ate *v.* To function, act, or work effectively; to perform an operation, as surgery. **operative** *adj.*

op-er-a-tion *n.* The process of operating; the system or method of operating; a series of acts to effect a certain purpose; a process; a procedure performed on the human body with surgical instruments to restore health; various mathematical or logical processes.

op-er-a-tor *n.* A person who operates a machine; the owner or person in charge of a business. *Slang* A shrewd person.

oph-thal-mol-o-gy *n.* A branch of medical science dealing with diseases of the eye, its structure, and functions.

o-pin-ion *n.* A judgment held with confidence; a conclusion held without positive knowledge.

o-pi-um *n.* A bitter, highly addictive drug; a narcotic.

o-pos-sum *n., pl.* **-sum** *or* **-sums**

A nocturnal animal which hangs by its tail and carries its young in a pouch.

op-po-nent *n.* An adversary; one who opposes another.

op-por-tune *adj.* Occurring at the right or appropriate time. **opportunist** *n.*, **opportunely** *adv.*

op-por-tu-ni-ty *n., pl.* **-ies** A favorable position; a chance for advancement.

op-pose *v.* To be in direct contention with; to resist; to be against. **opposable** *adj.*, **opposition** *n.*

op-po-site *adj.* Situated or placed on opposing sides. **oppositeness** *n.*

op-press *v.* To worry or trouble the mind; to weigh down; to burden as if to enslave. **oppression, oppressor** *n.*

op-pres-sive *adj.* Unreasonably severe or burdensome.

op-tic *adj.* Pertaining or referring to sight or the eye.

op-ti-cal *adj.* Pertaining to sight; constructed or designed to assist vision. **optically** *adv.*

op-ti-cian *n.* A person who makes eyeglasses and other optical articles.

op-ti-mism *n.* A doctrine which emphasizes that everything is for the best.

op-ti-mum *n., pl.* **-ma** The degree or condition producing the most favorable result. *adj.* Conducive to the best result.

op-tion n. The act of choosing or the power of choice; a choice. **optionally** adv.

op-tion-al adj. Left to one's decision; elective; not required.

op-tom-e-try n. The occupation or profession of examining the eyes and prescribing corrective lenses.

op-u-lence n. Wealth in abundance; affluence.

or conj. A word used to connect the second of two choices or possibilities, indicating uncertainty. suffix Indicating a person or thing which does something.

or-a-cle n. A seat of worship where ancient Romans and Greeks consulted the gods for answers; a person of unquestioned wisdom. **oracular** adj.

o-ral adj. Spoken or uttered through the mouth; taken or administered through the mouth. **orally** adv.

o-ral con-tra-cep-tive n. A pill containing hormones, taken monthly to prevent pregnancy.

or-ange n. A citrus fruit which is round and orange in color. adj. Yellowish red.

o-rang-u-tan n., pl. -tans A large, anthropoid ape, having brownish-red hair and very long arms.

o-rate v. To speak in an elevated manner.

orb n. A globe or sphere.

or-bit n. The path of a celestial body or a manmade object. v. To revolve or move in an orbit; to circle. **orbital** adj.

or-chard n. Land that is devoted to the growing of fruit trees.

or-ches-tra n. A group of musicians performing together on various instruments. **orchestral** adj.

or-ches-tra pit n. In theatres, the space reserved for musicians.

or-chid n. A plant found the world over having three petals in various colors.

or-dain v. To appoint as a minister, priest, or rabbi by a special ceremony; to decree.

or-deal n. A painful or severe test of character or endurance.

or-der n. A condition where there is a logical arrangement or disposition of things; sequence or succession; method; an instruction for a person to follow; a request for certain objects. v. To command; to demand.

or-der-ly adj. Neat, tidy.

or-di-nance n. A command, rule, or order; a law issued by a municipal body.

or-di-nar-y adj. Normal; having no exceptional quality; common; average; plain.

ore n. A natural underground substance, as a mineral or rock, from which valuable matter is extracted.

o-reg-a-no n. A bushy perennial herb of the mint family, used as a seasoning for food.

or-gan n. A musical instrument of pipes, reeds, and keyboards which produces sound by means of compressed air; a part of an animal, human, or plant that performs a definite function, as the heart, a kidney, or a stamen.

or-gan-dy or **or-gan-die** n., pl. -ies A translucent, stiff fabric of cotton or silk.

or-gan-ic adj. Effecting or pertaining to the organs of an animal or plant; of or relating to the process of growing plants with natural fertilizers with no chemical additives. **organically** adv.

or-gan-i-za-tion n. The state of being organized or the act of organizing; a group of people united for a particular purpose. **organizational** adj.

or-gan-ize v. To assemble or arrange with an orderly manner; to arrange by planning. **organization** n.

or-gasm n. Physiol. Intensive emotional excitement; the culmination of a sexual act.

o-ri-ent v. To determine the bearings or right direction with respect to another source.

O-ri-ent n. The countries located east of Europe. **Oriental** adj.

or-i-fice n. An opening through which something may pass; a mouth.

or-i-gin n. The cause or beginning of something; the source; a beginning place.

o-rig-i-nal adj. Belonging to the first or beginning. n. A new idea produced by one's own imagination; the first of a kind. **originality** n., **originally** adv.

or-i-ole n. A songbird having brightly colored yellow and black plumage in the males.

or-na-ment n. A decoration. v. To adorn or beautify. **ornamental** adj., **ornamentally** adv., **ornamentation** n.

or-nate adj. Excessively ornamental; elaborate; showy, as a style of writing.

or-phan n. A child whose parents are deceased. **orphan** v., **orphanage** n.

or-ris n. Any of several species having a fragrant root and used in medicine, perfumes, and cosmetics.

or-tho-don-tics n. The branch of dentistry dealing with the correction and prevention of irregularities of the teeth.

or-tho-dox adj. Following established traditions and beliefs, especially in religion.

Or-tho-dox Ju-da-ism n. The branch of Jewish faith which accepts the Mosaic Laws as interpreted in the Talmud.

or-tho-pe-dics or **or-tho-pae-dics** n. The branch of surgery or manipulative treatment concerned with the disorders of the bones, joints, and muscles. **orthopedist** n.

os-cil-late v. To swing back and forth with regular motion, as a pendulum. **oscillation, -tor** n., **oscillatory** adj.

os-mi-um n. A hard, but brittle metallic element symbolized as OS.

os-mo-sis n. The tendency of fluids separated by a semipermeable membrane to pass through it and become mixed and equal in strength.

osmotic *adj.*

os-ten-ta-tion *n.* The act of displaying pretentiously in order to excite.

os-teo *n. comb. form* Bone; pertaining to the bones.

os-te-op-a-thy *n.* A medical practice based on the theory that diseases are due chiefly to abnormalities of the body, which can be restored by manipulation of the parts by therapeutic measures.

os-teo-po-ro-sis *n.* A disorder causing gradual deterioration of bone tissue, usually occurring in older women.

os-tra-cize *v.* To exile or exclude from a group; to shut out.

oth-er *adj.* Additional; alternate; different from what is implied or specified. *pron.* A different person or thing.

oth-er-wise *adv.* Under different conditions of circumstances.

ot-ter *n., pl.* **-ter** *or* **-ters** web-footed aquatic mammals, related to the weasel.

ouch *n. interj.* An exclamation to express sudden pain.

ought *v.* Used to show or express a moral duty or obligation; to be advisable or correct.

ounce *n.* A unit of weight which equals 1/16 of a pound.

our *adj.* Of or relating to us ourselves. *pron.* The possessive case of the pronoun we. **ourselves** Our own selves.

oust *v.* To eject; to remove with force.

out *adv.* Away from the center or inside. *adj.* Away. *n.* A means of escape. *prep.* Through; forward from.

out-age *n.* A loss of electricity.

out-break *n.* A sudden outburst; an occurrence.

out-cast *n.* A person who is excluded; a homeless person.

out-come *n.* A consequence or result.

out-dated *adj.* Old-fashioned and obsolete.

out-do *v.* To excel in achievement.

out-fit *n.* The equipment or tools required for a specialized purpose; the clothes a person is dressed in. *v.* To supply.

out-land-ish *adj.* Extremely ridiculous, unusual, or strange.

out-law *n.* A person who habitually defies or breaks the law; a criminal. *v.* To ban; prohibit; to deprive of legal protection.

out-let *n.* An exit.

out-line *n.* A rough draft showing the main features of something. **outline** *v.*

out-look *n.* A person's point of view; an area offering a view of something.

out-num-ber *v.* To go over or exceed in number.

out-pa-tient *n.* A patient who visits a clinic or hospital for treatment but does not spend the night.

out-post *n.* Troops stationed at a distance away from the main group as a guard against attack; a frontier or outlying settlement.

out-put *n.* Production or yield during a given time.

out-rage *n.* An extremely violent act of violence or cruelty; the violent emotion such an act engenders. **outrageous** *adj.*, **outrage** *v.*

out-right *adj.* Free from reservations or complications; complete; entire.

out-side *n.* The area beyond the boundary lines or surface; extreme. *adv.* Outdoors.

out-spo-ken *adj.* Spoken without reserve; candid. **outspokenly** *adv.*

out-stand-ing *adj.* Excellent; prominent; unsettled, as a bill owed; projecting.

out-ward *adj.* Pertaining to the outside or exterior; superficial. **outwards** *adv.*

out-wit *v.* To trick, baffle, or outsmart with ingenuity.

o-val *adj.* Having the shape of an egg; an ellipse.

o-va-ry *n., pl.* **-ies** One of the pair of female reproductive glands. **ovarian** *adj.*

o-va-tion *n.* An enthusiastic display of approval for a person or a performance; applause.

ov-en *n.* An enclosed chamber used for baking, drying, or heating.

o-ver *prep.* Above; across; upon. *adv.* Covering completely; thoroughly; again; repetition. *adj.* Higher; upper. *prefix* Excessive, as overstuffed or overcrowded.

o-ver-act *v.* To act in an exaggerated way.

o-ver-all *adj.* Including or covering everything; from one side or end to another; generally. *n.* Pants with a bib and shoulder straps.

o-ver-arm *adj.* Thrown or executed with the arms raised above the shoulders.

o-ver-bear *v.* To crush or bear down by superior force or weight. **overbearing** *adj.*

o-ver-board *adv.* Over the side of a boat or ship into the water.

o-ver-cast *adj.* Gloomy; obscured. *Meteor.* Clouds covering more than 9/10 of the sky.

o-ver-coat *n.* A coat worn over a suit for extra warmth.

o-ver-come *v.* To prevail; to conquer or defeat. **overcomer** *n.*

o-ver-con-fi-dence *n.* Extreme or excessive confidence.

o-ver-do *v.* To do anything excessively; to overcook.

o-ver-dose *n.* To take an excessive dose of medication, especially narcotics.

o-ver-draw *v.* To withdraw money over the limits of one's credit.

o-ver-drive *n.* A gearing device in a vehicle that turns a drive shaft at a greater speed than that of the engine, therefore decreasing power output.

o-ver-due *adj.* Past the time of return or payment.

o-ver-flow *v.* To flow beyond the limits of capacity; to overfill.

o-ver-hand v. To execute something with the hand above the level of the elbow or shoulder. over-handed adv.

o-ver-haul v. To make all needed repairs.

o-ver-head n. The operating expenses of a company, including utilities, rent, and up-keep. adj. Situated above the level of one's head.

o-ver-look v. To disregard or fail to notice something purposely; to ignore.

o-ver-night adj. Lasting the whole night; from dusk to dawn. overnight adv.

o-ver-pass n. A raised section of highway which crosses other lines of traffic. v. To cross, pass over, or go through something; to overlook.

o-ver-ride v. To disregard; to take precedence over; to declare null and void.

o-ver-rule v. To put aside by virtue of higher authority.

o-ver-run v. To spread out; to extend or run beyond.

o-ver-see v. To supervise workers; to direct. overseer n.

o-ver-shoe n. A cover worn over a shoe for protection from snow or water.

o-ver-sight n. A mistake made inadvertently.

o-ver-size or o-ver-sized adj. Larger than the average size of something.

o-ver-step v. To go beyond a limit or restriction.

o-vert adj. Open to view.

o-ver-whelm v. To overcome completely; to make helpless.

o-void adj. Having the shape of an egg.

ovu-late n. To discharge or produce eggs from an ovary.

o-vum n., pl. ova The female reproductive cell.

owe v. To be in debt for a certain amount; to have a moral obligation.

owl n.

A predatory nocturnal bird, having large eyes, a short hooked bill, and long powerful claws. owlish adj.

own adj. Belonging to oneself. v. To possess; to confess; to admit. owner n.

ox n., pl. oxen A bovine animal used domestically in much the same way as a horse; an adult castrated bull.

ox-ford n. A shoe which is laced and tied over the instep.

ox-ide n. A compound of oxygen and another element.

ox-y-gen n. A colorless, odorless, tasteless gaseous element essential to life, symbolized by O.

ox-y-gen mask n. A device worn over the mouth and nose through which a person can receive oxygen as an aid to breathing.

oys-ter n. An edible marine mollusk.

o-zone n. A pale-blue gas formed of oxygen with an odor like chlorine, formed by an electrical discharge in the air. Slang Fresh air.

P, p The 16th letter of the English alphabet.

pace n. A person's step in walking or the length of a person's step; stride; the gait of a horse in which the legs on the same side are moved at the same time. pace v., pacer n.

pace-mak-er n. The person who sets the pace for another in a race; a surgically implanted electronic instrument used to stabilize or stimulate the heartbeat.

pac-er n. One that sets a particular speed or pace.

Pa-cif-ic n. The largest ocean on the earth, extending from North & South America westward to Asia and Australia.

pac-i-fy v. To quiet or soothe anger or distress; to calm. pacification n.

pack n. A bundle; a group or number of things tied or wrapped up; a full set of associated or like things, such as a pack of cards; a group of wolves or wild dogs that hunt together. v. To put things together in a trunk, box, or suitcase; to put away for storage. to send packing To force to leave with haste and without ceremony. packability n., packable adj.

pack-age n. Something tied up, wrapped or bound together.

pack-age store n. A retail establishment that sells alcoholic beverages only in sealed containers.

pack animal n. An animal used to carry heavy packs.

pack-board n. A metal frame that is usually covered with canvas, used to carry goods and equipment over ones shoulder.

pact n. An agreement between nations, groups, or people.

pad n. Anything stuffed with soft material and used to protect against blows; a cushion; a drawing or writing tablet of paper gummed together at one edge; the cushion-like part of the foot on some animals, as the dog. Slang A person's home. v. To stuff, line, or protect with soft material; to extend or lengthen something by inserting unnecessary matter; to travel by foot in a soft and nearly inaudible way.

pad-dle n. A broad-bladed implement usually made from wood, used to steer and propel a small boat; a tool used for mixing, turning, or stirring; a small wooden, rounded racket used in table tennis. paddle v., paddler n.

paddle-wheel n. A wheel with boards for propelling vessels.

pad-dy wag-on n., Slang A police vehicle for transporting suspects.

pad-lock n. A detachable lock, having a pivoted u-shaped hasp which can be inserted through a ring and then locked. padlock v.

pa-dre n. A title used in Spain and Italy for a priest.

pa-gan n. A person who does not acknowledge God in any religion; a heathen. **pagan** *adj.*, **paganism** *n.*

page *n.* A person hired to deliver messages or run errands; one side of the leaf of a book or letter. *v.* To call or summon a person.

pag-eant *n.* An elaborate exhibition or spectacular parade for public celebration. **pageantry** *n.*

pa-go-da *n.* A sacred Buddhist tower built as a memorial or shrine.

paid *v.* Past tense of pay.

pail *n.* A cylindrical container usually having a handle; a bucket.

pain *n.* The unpleasant feeling resulting from injury or disease; any distress or suffering of the mind; sorrow. *v.* To cause or experience pain.

painful, painless *adj.*

pain-kell-er *n.* Medication that relieves pain. **painkilling** *adj.*

paint *n.* A mixture of colors or pigments which are spread on a surface as protection or as a decorative coating; makeup for the face, as rouge. *v.* To apply paint to a surface; the practice of using paint to express oneself on canvas. **painter, painting** *n.*

pair *n., pl.* **pairs** *or* **pair** Two things which are similar and used together; something made of two parts which are used together; two persons or animals which live or work together.

pa-ja-mas *pl. n.* A loose fitting garment for sleeping, consisting of a jacket and pants.

pal-ace *n.* The royal residence of a sovereign, as of a king; a mansion. **palatial** *adj.*

pal-at-a-ble *adj.* Pleasant to the taste; agreeable to one's feelings or mind.

pale *n.* The pointed stake of a fence; a picket; an area that is enclosed within bounds. *adj.* Having a whitish or lighter than normal complexion; pallid; weak. **palely,** *adv.*

pal-ette *n.* A thin oval board with a hole for the thumb, on which an artist lays and mixes colors.

pal-in-drome *n.* A word, number, or sentence which reads the same backward or forward, such as toot or 1991.

pal-i-sade *n.* A fence made of stakes for protection. **palisade** *v.*

pall *n.* A heavy cloth used to cover a bier or coffin; a very gloomy atmosphere.

pal-la-di-um *n.* A silvery-white metallic element symbolized by Pd.

pall-bear-er *n.* A person who assists in carrying a coffin at a funeral.

pal-let *n.* A wooden platform on which material for freight shipments can be moved or stored.

pal-lid *adj.* Deficient in color; lacking sparkle. **pallidly** *adv.*, **pallidness** *n.*

pal-lor *n.* Lacking color; paleness.

palm *n.* The inner area of the hand between the fingers and the wrist; any of a large group of tropical evergreen trees, having an unbranched trunk with a top or crown of fan-like leaves. *v.* To hide something small in or about the hand.

Palm Sunday *n.* The Sunday before Easter; celebrated as Christ's triumphal entry into Jerusalem.

pal-sy *n., pl.* **-ies** Paralysis; the loss of ability to control one's movements.

pam-per *v.* To treat with extreme care.

pam-phlet *n.* A brief publication which is not permanently bound.

pan-a-ce-a *n.* A remedy for all diseases, difficulties, or ills; a cure-all.

pan-cake *n.* A thin, flat cake made from batter and fried on a griddle, served with butter, powdered sugar, syrup, and other toppings.

pan-cre-as *n., Anat.* A large, irregularly shaped gland situated behind the stomach which releases digestive enzymes and produces insulin.**-tic** *adj.*

pan-cre-atec-to-my *n.* The surgical removal of any part or all of the pancreas.

pan-da *n.*

A large bear-like animal of China and Tibet with black and white fur and rings around the eyes; a racoon-like animal of the south-eastern Himalayas with a ringed tail and reddish fur.

pan-de-mo-ni-um *n.* A place marked with disorder and wild confusion; disorder; confusion.

pan-der *or* **panderer** *n.* A go-between in sexual affairs; a pimp; one who profits from the base desires or passions of others. *v.* To act as a panderer for someone.

pan-el *n.* A flat, rectangular piece of material, often wood, which forms a part of a surface; a group of people selected to participate in a discussion group or to serve on a jury.

panelist *n.*, **panel** *v.*

pan-ic *n.* A sudden unreasonable fear which overpowers. *v.* To cause or to experience panic. **panicky** *adj.*

pan-nier *n.* One of a pair of large baskets which are carried on either side of an animal or over a person's back.

pan-ni-kin *n.* A small cup or pan.

pan-o-ply *n., pl.* **-lies** The complete equipment of a warrior, including his armor and weapons.

pan-o-ram-a *n.* An unlimited or complete view in all directions of what is visible.

pan-sy *n., pl.* **-ies** A garden plant with flowers bearing blossoms in a variety of colors.

pant *v.* To breathe in rapid or short gasps; to yearn. *n.* A short breath.

pan-the-ism *n.* The belief that the laws and forces of nature are all manifestations of God.

pantheist *n.*, **pantheistic** *adj.*

pan-ther *n.* A black leopard in its unspotted form. **pantheress** *n.*

pan-to-mime *n.* Communication done solely by means of facial and body gestures. *v.* To express or act in pantomime.

pan-try *n., pl.* **-ies** A closet or room for the storage of food, dishes, and other kitchen items.

pants *pl, n.* Trousers; underpants.

pap *n.* A soft food for invalids or babies.

pa-pa-cy *n., pl.* **-ies** The dignity or jurisdiction of a pope; a pope's term in office.

pa-per *n.* A substance made of pulp from wood and rags, formed into sheets for printing, wrapping and writing.

pa-pier--ma-che *n.* A material consisting of wastepaper mixed with glue or paste which can be molded when wet and becomes hard when dry.

pa-poose *n.* A North American Indian child or baby.

pa-pri-ka *n.* A dark red seasoning powder made by grinding red peppers.

Pap test *n.* A test in which a smear of bodily secretion from the uterus is examined for the early detection of cancer.

par-a-ble *n.* A short, fictitious story which illustrates a moral lesson.

par-a-chute *n.*

A folding umbrella shaped apparatus of light fabric used to make a safe landing after a free fall from an airplane. **parachute** *v.*, **parachutist** *n.*

pa-rade *n.* An organized public procession; a march. **parader** *n.*

par-a-dise *n.* A state or place of beauty, bliss or delight; heaven. **paradisiac, paradisiacal** *adj.*

par-a-dox *n.* A statement which seems opposed to common sense or contradicts itself, but is perhaps true. **paradoxical** *adj.*, **paradoxically** *adv.*

par-af-fin *n.* A white, waxy substance derived from petroleum and used to make lubricants, candles, and sealing materials. **paraffin** *v.*

par-a-gon *n.* A pattern or model of excellence or perfection.

par-a-graph *n.* A section of a composition dealing with a single idea, containing one or more sentences with the first line usually indented.

par-a-keet *n.*

A small parrot with a long, wedge-shaped tail.

par-al-lel *adj.* Moving in the same direction but separated by a distance, as railroad tracks. *n.* A parallel curve, line, or surface; a comparison; one of the imaginary lines which circle the earth paralleling the equator and mark the latitude. **parallel** *v.*, **parallelism** *n.*

par-al-lel-o-gram *n.* A four-sided figure having parallel opposite sides which are equal.

pa-ral-y-sis *n., pl.* **-ses** Complete or partial loss of the ability to feel any sensation or to move.

paralytic *adj. & n.*

par-a-lyze *v.* To cause to be inoperative or powerless.

par-a-med-ic *n.* A person trained to give emergency medical treatment until a doctor is available.

par-a-mount *adj.* Superior to all others in rank, importance, and power.

par-a-noi-a *n.* Mental insanity marked by systematic delusions of persecution or grandeur.

par-a-pher-na-lia *n.* Personal effects or belongings; the apparatus or articles used in some activities; equipment.

par-a-phrase *v.* To put something written or spoken into different words while retaining the same meaning.

par-a-site *n., Biol.* An organism which lives, grows, feeds, and takes shelter in or on another organism; a person depending entirely on another without providing something in return.

par-a-sol *n.* A small umbrella used as protection from the sun.

par-a-troops *pl., n.* Troops which are equipped and trained to parachute behind enemy lines.

par-boil *v.* To precook something in boiling water.

par-cel *n.* A wrapped package; a bundle; a portion or plat of land. **parcel** *v.*

parch *v.* To become very dry from intense heat; to become dry from thirst or the lack of water.

parch-ment *n.* Goatskin or sheepskin prepared with a pumice stone and used as a material for writing or drawing.

par-don *v.* To forgive someone for an offense. In law, to allow a convicted person freedom from the penalties of an office or crime. **pardonable** *adj.*, **pardonably** *adv.*, **pardon** *n.*

pare *v.* To cut away or remove the outer surface gradually. **parer** *n.*

par-e-go-ric *n.* A medication used to relieve stomach pains.

par-ent *n.* A mother or father; a forefather; an ancestor; a source; a cause. **parentage, parenthood** *n.*, **parental** *adj.*

pa-ren-the-sis *n., pl.* **-ses** One of a pair of curved lines () used to enclose a qualifying or explanatory remark.

par-ish *n.* In association with the Roman Catholic Church, the district under the charge of a priest; the members of a parish.

park *n.* A tract of land used for recreation. *v.* To leave something temporarily in a parking garage or lot, as a car. **parker** *n.*

par-ka *n.* A cloth jacket with an attached hood.

Par-kin-son's disease *n., Pathol.* A progressive disease marked by partial facial paralysis, muscular tremor, weakness, and impaired muscular control.

par-lia-ment *n.* The assembly which

constitutes the lawmaking body of various countries, as the United Kingdom.

par-lor *n.* A room for entertaining visitors or guests; a business offering a personal service, as beauty parlor, ice cream parlor, or funeral parlor.

pa-ro-chi-al *adj.* Belonging to a local parish; having to do with a parish.

par-o-dy *n., pl.* -ies A composition, song, or poem which mimics another in a ridiculous way.

pa-role *n.* The conditional release of a prisoner before his sentence expires. parole *v. & adj.*

par-ox-ysm *n.* A violent attack or outburst; a spasm.

par-ri-cide *n.* A person who murders his mother or father; the crime of murdering one's parents. -al *adj.*

par-rot *n.*

A brightly colored, semitropical bird with a strong, hooked bill. *v.* To imitate or repeat.

par-ry *v.* To avoid something; to turnaside. parry *n.*

parse *v.* To identify the parts of speech in a sentence and to indicate their relationship to each other.

par-si-mo-ny *n.* Extreme reluctance to use one's resources or to spend money. parsimonious *adj.*, -ly *adv.*

pars-ley *n.* An herb with curly leaves which is used for seasoning and garnishing.

pars-nip *n.* A plant from the carrot family cultivated for its long, edible root.

par-son *n.* A pastor or clergyman.

par-son-age *n.* The home provided by a church for its parson.

part *n.* A segment, portion, or division of a whole; a component for a machine; the role of a character, as in a play; the line which forms where the hair is parted by combing or brushing. *v.* To leave or go away from; to be separated into pieces; to give up control or possession.

par-take *v.* To have a share or part; to take; to take a part in something.

par-tial *adj.* Incomplete; inclined to favor one side more than the other. partiality *n.*, partially *adv.*

par-tic-i-pate *v.* To join in or share; to take part. participant, participation, participator *n.*, participatory *adj.*

par-ti-cle *n.* A very small piece of solid matter. *Gram.* A group of words, such as articles, prepositions, and conjunctions which convey very little meaning but help to connect, specify, or limit the meanings of other words.

par-tic-u-lar *adj.* Having to do with a specific person, group, thing, or category; noteworthy; precise. particularly *adv.*

part-ing *n.* A division; a separation; the place where a division or separation occurs. *adj.* Done, given, or said on departing.

par-ti-tion *n.* A separation or division. *v.* To divide.

part-ner *n.* One who shares something with another.

part-ner-ship *n.* Two or more persons who run a business together and share in the profits and losses.

par-tridge *n., pl.* partridges A plump or stout-bodied game bird.

par-ty *n., pl.* -ies A group of persons who gather for pleasure or entertainment; a group of persons associated together for a common purpose; a group which unites to promote or maintain a policy, a cause, or other purposes, as a political group. In law, a person or group of people involved in a legal proceeding.

pass *v.* To proceed; to move; to transfer; to go away or come to an end; to get through a course, trial or test; to approve; to vote for; to give as an opinion or judgment; to hit or throw a ball to another player. *n.* A ticket or note that allows a person to come and go freely. come to pass To happen. pass away To die or cease to live. pass over To leave out, to ignore.

pas-sage *n.* The act of going, proceeding, or passing; the enactment by a legislature of a bill into law; a small portion or part of a whole book or speech; something, as a path or channel, through, over or along which something else may pass.

pas-sen-ger *n.* One who travels in a vehicle, car, plane, boat, or other conveyance.

pas-sion *n.* A powerful feeling; lust; sexual desire; an outburst of strong feeling; violence or anger. Passion The suffering of Christ which followed the Last Supper to the time of his death. passionless, passionate *adj.*

pas-sive *adj.* Not working, acting, or operating; inactive; acted upon, influenced; or affected by something external. *Gram.* Designating the form of a verb which indicates the subject is receiving the action. passively *adv.*, passivity, passiveness *n.*

Pass-o-ver *n.* The Jewish holiday which commemorates the Exodus from Egypt.

pass-port *n.* An official permission issued to a person allowing him to travel out of this country and to return; a document of identification.

past *adj.* Having to do with or existing at a former time. *n.* Before the present time; a person's history or background. *adv.* To go by. *prep.* After; beyond in time; beyond the power, reach, or influence.

paste *n.* A mixture usually made from water and flour, used to stick things together; dough used in making pastry; a brilliant glass used in imitating precious stones. paste *v.*

pas-tel *n.* A crayon made of ground pigments; a drawing made with crayons of this kind. *adj.* Pale and light in color or shade.

Pasteur, Louis *n.* (1822-1895.) A French scientist who discovered a treatment for rabies and for killing bacteria in milk.

pas-teur-i-za-tion *n.* The process of killing disease-producing microorganisms by heating the liquid to a high temperature for a period of time.

pas-time *n.* Spending spare time in a pleasant way; a diversion.

pas-tor *n.* A Christian clergyman in charge of a church or congregation.

pas-tor-al *adj.* Referring to the duties of a pastor; pertaining to life in the country; rural or rustic. *n.* A poem dealing with country life.

past par-ti-ci-ple *n.* A participle used with reference to actions and conditions in the past.

pas-try *n.* Food made with dough or having a crust made of dough, as pies, tarts, or other desserts.

pas-ture *n.* An area for grazing of domestic animals. pastured, pasturing *v.*, pasturage, pasturer *n.*

pat *v.* To tap lightly with something flat. *n.* A soft, caressing stroke.

patch *n.* A piece of fabric used to repair a weakened or torn area in a garment; a piece of cloth with an insignia which represents an accomplishment. *v.* to repair or put together hastily. patchy, patchable *adj.*, patcher *n.*

pat-ent *n.* A governmental protection assuring an inventor the exclusive right of manufacturing, using, exploiting, and selling an invention. *adj.* Evident; obvious. patentee, patency *n.* patently *adv.*

pa-ter-nal *adj.* Relating to or characteristic of a father; inherited from a father. -ly *adv.*, -ism *n.*

pa-thet-ic *adj.* Arousing pity, tenderness, or sympathy. pathetically *adv.*

pa-thol-o-gy *n.* The science that deals with facts about diseases, their nature and causes. pathologic, pathological *adj.*, pathologist *n.*

pa-thos *n.* A quality in a person that evokes sadness or pity.

pa-tience *n.* The quality, state, or fact of being patient; the ability to be patient.

pa-tient *adj.* Demonstrating uncomplaining endurance under distress. *n.* A person under medical care. -ly *adv.*

pa-tri-arch *n.* The leader of a tribe or family who rules by paternal right; a very old and revered man. patriarchal *adj.*, patriarchy *n.*

pa-tri-ot *n.* A person who loves and defends his country. patriotic *adj.*, patriotically *adv.*, patriotism *n.*

pa-trol *n.* Walking around an area for the purpose of maintaining or observing security; a person or group carrying out this action. patrol *v.*

pa-tron *n.* A person who fosters, protects, or supports some person, enterprise, or thing; a regular customer.

pat-sy *n., pl.* -ies *Slang* A person who is taken advantage of.

pat-tern *n.* Anything designed or shaped to serve as a guide in making something else; a sample. *v.* To make according to a pattern.

pat-ty *n., pl.* -ies A small, flat piece of chopped meat.

pau-per *n.* A very poor person who depends on charity. pauperism *n.*, pauperize *v.*

pause *v.* To linger, hesitate, or stop for a time. pause *n.*

pave *v.* To surface with gravel, concrete, asphalt, or other material.

pave-ment *n.* A surface that has been paved.

pa-vil-ion *n.* A large, roofed structure used for shelter.

paw *n.* The foot of an animal. *v.* To handle clumsily or rudely.

pawn *n.* Something given as security for a loan; a hostage; a chessman of little value. pawn *v.*

pay *v.* To give a person what is due for a debt, purchase, or work completed; to compensate; to suffer the consequences.

pay-ment *n.* The act of paying.

pea *n.* A round edible seed contained in a pod and grown on a vine.

peace *n.* A state of physical or mental tranquillity; calm; serenity; the absence of war; the state of harmony between people. peaceable, -ful *adj.*, peaceably, peacefully *adv.*

peach *n.* A round, sweet, juicy fruit having a thin, downy skin, a pulpy yellow flesh, and a hard, rough single seed.

pea-cock *n.*

A male bird with brilliant blue or green plumage and a long iridescent tail that fans out to approximately six feet.

peak *n.* A projecting edge or point; the summit of a mountain; the top. *v.* To bring to the maximum.

peal *n.* The ring of bells; the long, loud sound of thunder or laughter. *v.* To ring.

pea-nut *n.* A nut-like seed which ripens underground; the plant bearing this nut.

pear *n.* A juicy, edible fruit which grows on a tree.

pearl *n.* A smooth, rounded deposit formed around a grain of sand in the shell of various mollusks, especially the oyster; anything which is precious, rare, or fine. pearly *adj.*

peas-ant *n.* A farmhand or rustic workman; an uneducated person of the lowest class. *Slang* Uneducated or uncouth.

peat *n.* The black substance formed when plants begin to decay in wet ground, as bogs. **peaty** *adj.*

peat moss *n.* A moss which grows in very wet areas, used as plant food and mulch.

peb-ble *n.* A small, smooth stone. *v.* To treat, as to give a rough texture.

pe-can *n.* A large tree of the central and southern United States with an edible oval, thin-shelled nut.

peck *v.* To strike with the beak; to eat without any appetite, taking only small bites. *n.* A measure which equals 1/4 of a bushel.

pec-tin *n.* A complex carbohydrate found in ripe fruits and used in making jelly. **pectic** *adj.*

pe-cu-liar *adj.* Odd; strange. **peculiarity** *n.,* **peculiarly** *adv.*

ped-al *n.* A lever usually operated by the foot. **pedal** *v.*

ped-dle *v.* To travel around in an attempt to sell merchandise.

ped-es-tal *n.* A support or base for a statue. **to put on a pedestal** To hold something in high respect.

pe-des-tri-an *n.* A person traveling by foot.

pe-di-at-rics *n.* The branch of medicine dealing with the care of children and infants. **pediatric** *adj.,* **pediatrician** *n.*

ped-i-cure *n.* The cosmetic care of the toenails and feet. **pedicurist** *n.*

ped-i-gree *n.* A line of ancestors, especially of an animal of pure breed.

ped-i-ment *n.* A broad, triangular architectural or decorative part above a door.

pe-dom-e-ter *n.* An instrument which indicates the number of miles one has walked.

pe-dun-cle *n., Biol.* A stalk-like support in some plants and animals.

peek *v.* To look shyly or quickly from a place of hiding; to glance. **peek** *n.*

peel *n.* The natural rind or skin of a fruit. *v.* To pull or strip the skin or bark off; to remove in thin layers. *Slang* To undress. **peeler** *n.*

peen *n.* The ball-shaped end of a hammer opposite the flat, striking surface.

peep *v.* To utter a very small and weak sound, as of a young bird.

peer *v.* To look searchingly; to come partially into one's view. *n.* An equal; a member of the British nobility, as a duke or earl.

pee-vish *adj.* Irritable in mood; cross. **peevishly** *adv.,* **peevishness** *n.*

peg *n.* A small pin, usually of wood or metal; a projecting pin on which something may be hung. *Slang* An artificial leg, often made of wood. **peg** *v.*

pei-gnoir *n.* A woman's loose fitting dressing gown.

pe-koe *n.* A superior black tea made from young or small leaves.

pel-i-can *n.* A large, web-footed bird with a large pouch under the lower bill for the temporary storage of fish.

pel-let *n.* A small round ball made from paper or wax; a small bullet or shot.

pelt *n.* The skin of an animal with the fur.

pel-vis *n., pl.* **-vises** *or* **-ves** The structure of the vertebrate skeleton which rests on the lower limbs, supporting the spinal column.

pen *n.* An instrument used for writing.

pe-nal *adj.* Of or pertaining to punishment or penalties.

pen-al-ty *n., pl.* **-ties.** The legal punishment for an offense or crime; something which is forfeited when a person fails to meet a commitment; in sports, a punishment or handicap imposed for breaking a rule.

pen-ance *n.* A voluntary act to show sorrow or repentance for sin.

pen-dant *or* **pen-dent** *n.* An ornament which hangs from a necklace.

pend-ing *adj.* Not yet decided; imminent. *prep.* During; until.

pen-du-lous *adj.* Hanging downward so as to swing; wavering.

pen-du-lum *n.* A suspended object free to swing back and forth.

pen-e-trate *v.* To force a way through or into; to pierce; to enter; to pass through something. **penetrable, penetrating** *adj.,* **penetration** *n.*

pen-guin *n.* A web-footed, flightless, marine bird of the southern hemisphere.

pen-i-cil-lin *n.* A powerful antibiotic derived from mold and used to treat certain types of bacterial infections.

pen-in-su-la *n.* A piece of land projecting into water from a larger land mass. **peninsular** *adj.*

pe-nis *n., pl.* **-nises** *or* **-nes** The male sex organ; the male organ through which urine leaves the body.

pen-i-tent *adj.* Having a feeling of guilt or remorse for one's sins or misdeeds; sorry. **penitence** *n.,* **penitential** *adj.*

pen-ny *n., pl.* **-ies** A United States coin worth one cent ($.01).

pen-sion *n.* The amount of money a person receives regularly after retirement. **pensioner** *n.*

pen-sive *adj.* Involved in serious, quiet reflection; causing melancholy thought. **pensively** *adv.,* **pensiveness** *n.*

pen-ta-gon *n.* Any object or building having five sides and five interior angles. **Pentagon** The five-sided office building in Arlington, Va. which houses the Defense Department.

pent-house *n.* An apartment built on the roof of a building.

pe-o-ny *n., pl.* **-nies** A plant with a large, fragrant red, white, or pink flower.

peo-ple *n., pl.* **people** Human beings; a body of persons living in the same country, under the same government, and speaking the same language; one's relatives or family. **people** *v.*

pep-per *n.* A strong, aromatic condiment. *v.* To pelt or sprinkle.

pep-tic *adj.* Pertaining to or aiding digestion.

per an-num *adv.* For, by, or in each year; annually.

per-cale *n.* A closely woven cotton fabric.

per--cap-i-ta *adj. & adv., Latin* Of each individual.

per-ceive *v.* To become aware of by the senses; to understand; to feel or observe. -able *adj.*, perceivably *adv.*

per-cent-age *n.* The rate per hundred; a part or proportion in relation to a whole. *Slang* Profit; advantage.

per-cept *n.* A mental impression of something perceived; the immediate knowledge obtained from perceiving.

perch *n.* A place on which birds rest or alight; any place for standing or sitting; a small, edible freshwater fish having tender white meat.

per-cip-i-ent *adj.* Having the power of perception. percipience, percipiency *n.*

per-co-late *v.* To pass or cause to pass through a porous substance; to filter. percolation, percolator *n.*

per-cus-sion *n.* The sharp striking together of one body against another; the striking of a cap in a firearm. *Music.* An instrument which makes music when it is struck, as a drum or cymbal.

per-en-ni-al *adj.* Lasting from year to year; perpetual. *n.* A plant which lives through the winter and blooms again in the spring. perennially *adv.*

per-fect *adj.* Having no defect or fault; flawless; accurate; absolute. *v.* To make perfect. -ly *adv.*, perfectness *n.*

per-form *v.* To execute or carry out an action; to act or function in a certain way; to act; to give a performance or exhibition. performable *adj.*, performer, performance *n.*

per-fume *n.* A fragrant substance which emits a pleasant scent; one distilled from flowers. perfume *v.*

per-haps *adv.* Possibly; maybe; not sure.

per-i-gee *n.* The point of an orbit when a satellite of the earth is closest to the earth; the lowest part of an orbit.

per-il *n.* A source of danger; exposure to the chance of injury; danger. perilous *adj.*, perilously *adv.*

pe-ri-od *n.* An interval of time marked by certain conditions; an interval of time that is regarded as a phase in development; menstruation; the punctuation mark (.) which indicates the end of a sentence or an abbreviation.

pe-riph-er-y *n., pl.* -ies The outer part, boundary, or surface. peripheral *adj.*

per-ish *v.* To ruin or spoil; to suffer an untimely or violent death.

per-i-win-kle *n.* Any of several edible marine snails; a trailing evergreen plant with blue and sometimes white flowers.

per-jure *v.* To give false testimony while under oath. perjury *n.*

per-ma-nent *adj.* Continuing in the same state; lasting indefinitely; enduring. *n.*

A hair wave which gives long lasting curls or body to the hair. permanence, permanency *n.*, permanently *adv.*

per-me-ate *v.* To spread through; to pervade; to pass through the pores. permeation *n.* permeable *adj.*

per-mis-sion *n.* The act of permitting something; consent.

per-mit *v.* To consent to; to allow. *n.* An official document giving permission for a specific activity.

per-ni-cious *adj.* Very harmful; malicious. -ly *adv.*, perniciousness *n.*

per-ox-ide *n., Chem.* Oxide containing the highest proportion of oxygen for a given series; a chemical used with other ingredients to bleach the hair.

per-pen-dic-u-lar *adj.* Being at right angles to the plane of the horizon. *Math.* Meeting a plane or given line at right angles. perpendicular, perpendicularity *n.*, -ly *adv.*

per-pe-trate *v.* To perform; to commit; to be guilty. petration, perpetrator *n.*

per-pet-u-al *adj.* Lasting or continuing forever or an unlimited time. perpetually *adv.*

per-plex *v.* To confuse or be confused; to make complicated. perplexing *adj.*, -ly, perplexedly *adv.*, perplexity *n.*

per-se-cute *v.* To harass or annoy persistently; to oppress because of one's religion, beliefs, or race. persecution, persecutor *n.*, persecutive *adj.*

per-se-vere *v.* To persist in any purpose or idea; to strive in spite of difficulties or obstacles. perseverance *n.*, perseveringly *adv.*

per-sim-mon *n.* A tree having reddish orange, edible fruit.

per-sist *v.* To continue firmly despite obstacles; to endure. persistence, persistency *n.*, persistent *adj.*, persistently *adv.*

per-son *n.* A human being; an individual; the personality of a human being. *Law* Any human being, corporation, or other entity having legal rights and duties.

per-son-al *adj.* Belonging to a person or persons; of the body or person; relating to oneself; done by oneself.

per-son-i-fy *v.* To think of or represent as having human qualities or life; to be a symbol of. personifier, -fication *n.*

per-son-nel *n.* The body of people working for a business or service.

per-spec-tive *n.*

A painting or drawing technique in which objects seem to have depth and distance.

per-spi-ra-tion *n.* The salty fluid excreted from the body by the sweat glands.

per-spire *v.* To give off perspiration.

per-suade *v.* To cause to convince or believe by means of reasoning or argument. persuader, persuasiveness *n.*, persuasive *adj.*

per-tain *v.* To relate to; to refer to; to

belong as a function, adjunct or quality; to be appropriate or fitting.

per-ti-na-cious *adj.* Adhering firmly to an opinion, belief, or purpose; stubbornly persistent. **pertinaciously** *adv.*, **pertinacity** *n.*

per-ti-nent *adj.* Relating to the matter being discussed.

per-turb *v.* To disturb, make anxious, or make uneasy; to cause confusion. **perturbation** *n.*

per-vade *v.* To spread through every part of something; to permeate. **pervasive** *adj.*

per-ver-sion *n.* The act of being led away from the accepted course; a deviant form of sexual behavior.

per-vert *v.* To lead away from the proper cause; to use in an improper way. *n.* A person practicing or characterized by sexual perversion. **perverted**, **pervertible** *adj.*

pes-si-mism *n.* The tendency to take a gloomy view of affairs or situations and to anticipate the worst. **-ist** *n.*, **pessimistic** *adj.*, **pessimistically** *adv.*

pest *n.* A person or thing which is a nuisance; an annoying person or thing; a destructive insect, plant, or animal.

pes-ter *v.* To harass with persistent annoyance; to bother.

pes-ti-cide *n.* A chemical substance used to destroy rodents, insects, and pests. **pesticidal** *adj.*

pes-ti-lence *n.* A widespread and often fatal infectious disease, as bubonic plague or cholera.

pet *n.* An animal, bird, or fish one keeps for companionship; any favorite or treasured thing. *adj.* Treated or tamed as a pet. *v.* To stroke or caress gently. *Slang* To make love by fondling and caressing.

pet-al *n.*, *Bot.* One of the leaf-like parts of a flower.

pe-tite *adj.* Small in size; little. **petiteness** *n.*

pet-it four *n.*, *pl.* **petits fours** *or* **petit fours** A small decorated cake.

pe-ti-tion *n.* A solemn request or prayer; a formal written request addressed to a group or person in authority. **petitioner** *n.*

pet-ri-fy *v.* To convert into a stony mass; to make fixed or immobilize, as in the face of danger or surprise. **petrification** *n.* **petrifactive** *adj.*

pe-tro-le-um *n.* An oily, thick liquid which develops naturally below the ground surface, used in products such as gasoline, fuel oil, and kerosene.

pet-ti-coat *n.* A woman's skirt-like garment worn as an underskirt.

pet-ty *adj.* To have little importance or value; insignificant; trivial; having a low position or rank; minor; small-minded. **pettiness** *n.*

pet-ty cash *n.* Cash held on hand for minor bills or expenditures.

pe-tu-nia *n.* A widely grown tropical plant having a funnel-shaped flower in various colors.

pew *n.* A row of bench-like seats for seating people in church.

pew-ter *n.* An alloy of tin with copper, silver-gray in color and used for tableware and kitchen utensils.

pfen-nig *n.*, *pl.* **-nigs** *or* **-nige** A small coin of Germany, equal to one hundredth of a Deutschemark.

phal-lus *n.*, *pl.* **-li** *or* **-luses** A representation of the penis, often as a symbol of generative power. **phallic** *adj.*

phan-tasm *n.* The creation of an imaginary image; a fantasy; a phantom. **phantasmal**, **phantasmic** *adj.*

phan-tom *n.* Something which exists but has no physical reality; a ghost. **phantom** *adj.*

phar-ma-ceu-ti-cal *adj.* Pertaining or relating to a pharmacy or pharmacists.

phar-ma-cy *n.*, *pl.* **-cies.** A place of business which specializes in preparing, identifying, and disbursing drugs; a drugstore.

phar-ynx *n.*, *pl.* **-ynges** *or* **-ynxes.** The part of the throat located between the palate and the esophagus, serving as a passage for air and food. **pharyngeal** *adj.*

phase *n.* Any decisive stage in development or growth. *Astron.* One of the forms or appearances of a planet.

pheas-ant *n.* A long-tailed game bird noted for the beautiful plumage of the male.

phe-nom-e-non *n.*, *pl.* **-na** *or* **-nons.** Something that can be observed or perceived; a rare occurrence. *Slang* An outstanding person with remarkable power, ability, or talent.

phi-lan-der *v.* To make love without feeling or serious intentions. **-er** *n.*

phi-lat-e-ly *n.* The collection and study of postage stamps and postmarked material. **philatelic** *adj.*, **philatelist** *n.*

phil-har-mon-ic *adj.* Pertaining to a symphony orchestra. **philharmonic** *n.*

phi-los-o-phy *n.*, *pl.* **-ies** The logical study of the nature and source of human knowledge or human values; the set of values, opinions, and ideas of a group or individual.

pho-bi-a *n.* A compulsive fear of a specified situation or object.

phone *n.*, *Slang* A telephone. *v.* To call or communicate by telephone.

phon-ic *adj.* Pertaining to sounds in speech; using the same symbol for each sound. **-ally** *adv.*, **phonetics** *n.*

pho-no-graph *n.* A machine which uses a needle to reproduce sound from a grooved disc or record.

pho-ny *adj.* *Informal* Counterfeit; fraudulent; not real or genuine.

phos-phate *n.*, *Chem.* A salt or phosphoric acid which contains mostly phosphorus and oxygen.

phos-pho-rus *n.* A highly flammable, poisonous, nonmetallic element used in safety matches, symbolized by P.

pho-to *n.* *Slang* A photograph.

pho-to-cop-y *v.* To reproduce printed material using a photographic process. **photocopier, photocopy** *n.*

pho-to-graph *n.* A picture or image recorded by a camera and then reproduced on a photosensitive surface. **photography** *n.*

pho-to-stat *n.* A trademark for a camera designed to reproduce documents and graphic material.

pho-to-syn-the-sis *n., Biochem.* The chemical process by which plants use light to change carbon dioxide and water into carbohydrates, releasing oxygen as a by-product. **photosynthesize** *v.,* **photosynthetic** *adj.*

phrase *n., Gram.* A brief or concise expression which does not contain a predicate.

phre-nol-o-gy *n.* The study of or the theory that the conformation of the human skull indicates the degree of intelligence and character.

phys-i-cal *adj.* Relating to the human body apart from the mind or emotions; pertaining to material rather than imaginary subjects. *n.* A medical exam to determine a person's physical condition. **physically** *adv.*

phy-si-cian *n.* A person licensed to practice medicine.

phys-ics *n.* The scientific study which deals with energy, matter, motion, and related areas of science.

phys-i-ol-o-gy *n., pl.* **-ies** The scientific study of living animals, plants, and their activities and functions; the vital functions and processes of an organism. **physiological, physiologic** *adj.,* **physiologist** *n.*

phys-i-o-ther-a-py *n.* The treatment of disease or physical defects by the use of heat and massage.

pi-an-o *n.* A musical instrument with a manual keyboard and felt-covered hammers which produce musical tones when struck upon steel wires.

pi-az-za *n.* A public square or an open area in an Italian town or city.

pi-ca *n.* A printer's type size of 12 points, equal to about 1/6 inch; a typewriter type size with 10 characters to an inch.

pic-co-lo *n.* A small flute with a brilliant sound pitched an octave above the flute.

pick *v.* To select or choose from a number or group; to remove the outer area of something with the fingers or a pointed instrument; to remove by tearing away little by little; to open a lock without using a key; to harass or tease someone or something; to pluck a musical instrument. *n.* A pointed metal tool sharpened at both ends, used to break up hard surfaces. *Music* A small flat piece of plastic or of bone, used to pluck or strum the strings of an instrument, as a guitar or banjo.

pick-et *n.* A pointed stake driven into the ground as support for a fence; a person positioned outside of a place of employment during a strike. *Mil.* A soldier posted to guard a camp.

pick-le *n.* A cucumber preserved in a solution of brine or vinegar. *Slang* A troublesome situation.

pick-pock-et *n.* A person who steals from another's purse or pocket.

pic-nic *n.* An outdoor social gathering where food is provided usually by the people attending. **picnicker** *n.*

pic-ture *n.* A visual representation on a surface, which is printed, drawn or photographed; the mental image or impression of an event or situation.

piece *n.* An element, unit, or part of a whole; a musical or literary work. *Slang* A firearm.

piecemeal *adv.* Gradually, bit by bit.

pier *n.* A structure extending into the water, used to secure, protect, and provide access to vessels.

pierce *v.* To penetrate or make a hole in something; to force into or through. **piercing** *adj.*

Pierce, Franklin *n.* The 14th president of the United States, from 1853-1857.

pi-e-ty *n., pl.* **-ties.** Devoutness toward God.

pig *n.*

A cloven-hoofed mammal with short legs, bristly hair, and a snout for rooting; the edible meat of a pig; pork. *Slang* A greedy or gross person.

pi-geon *n.* A bird with short legs, a sturdy body, and a small head.

pig-gy-back *adv.* Carried on the back and shoulders. **piggyback** *adj.*

pig-head-ed *adj.* Stubborn. **-ly** *adv.*

pig-ment *n.* A material used as coloring matter, suitable for making paint. *Biol.* Any substance such as melanin and chlorophyll which imparts color to vegetable tissue or animals.

pig-skin *n.* Something made from the skin of a pig. *Slang* A football.

pike *n.* A long pole with a sharp, pointed steel head; a large edible fresh-water fish with a long snout and a slender body. *Slang* A turnpike or a major highway.

pile *n.* A quantity of anything thrown in a heap; a massive or very large building or a group of buildings.

pil-fer *v.* To steal in little quantities; to steal items of little value. **pilferage** *n.*

pil-grim *n.* A person who travels to a sacred place; a wanderer. **Pilgrims** The English Puritans who founded the Plymouth colony in New England in the year 1620.

pill *n.* A small tablet containing medicine which is taken by mouth; someone or something which is disagreeable but must be dealt with. **the pill** *Slang* An oral contraceptive drug taken by women.

pil-lar *n.* A freestanding column which serves as a support.

pil-low *n.* A cloth case filled with feathers or other soft material, used to cushion the head during sleep.

pi-lot *n.* A person who is licensed to operate an aircraft; someone who is trained and licensed to guide ships in and out of port. *v.* To act or serve as a pilot.

pi-men-to *n.* A sweet pepper used as a stuffing for olives or as a relish.

pimp *n.* A person who arranges customers for prostitutes in exchange for a share of their money.

pim-ple *n.* A small eruption of the skin, having an inflamed base. **pimpled, pimply** *adj.*

pin *n.* A small, stiff piece of wire with a blunt head and a sharp point, used to fasten something, usually temporarily; one of the rounded wooden clubs serving as the target in bowling.

pin-a-fore *n.* A sleeveless apron-like garment.

pin-cer *n.* An implement having two handles and a pair of jaws working on a pivot, used to hold objects.

pinch *v.* To squeeze between a finger and thumb causing pain or discomfort; to be miserly. *n.* The small amount that can be held between the thumb and forefinger.

pine *n., Bot.* Any of various cone-bearing evergreen trees; the wood of such a tree.

pine-ap-ple *n.* A tropical American plant with spiny, curved leaves bearing a large edible fruit. *Slang* A hand grenade.

pink *n.* Any of various plants related to the carnation, having fragrant flowers; a light or pale hue of crimson; the highest or best possible degree.

pink-eye *n., Pathol.* An acute, contagious conjunctivitis of the eye.

pin-na-cle *n.* The highest peak; a sharp point; a pointed summit.

pi-noch-le *or* **pi-noc-le** *n.* A card game for two, three, or four people, played with a double deck of 48 cards.

pint *n.* A liquid or dry measurement equal to half of a quart or two cups.

pin-to *n., pl.* -tos *or* -toes A horse with spots; a spotted bean of the southwestern United States.

pin-wheel *n.* A toy with revolving paper or plastic fastened to a stick; a fireworks display featuring a revolving wheel of colored flames.

pin-worm *n.* A nematode parasite which infests the human intestines and rectum.

pi-o-neer *n.* One of the first settlers of a new region or country; the first developer or investigator in a new field of enterprise, research, or other endeavor.

pi-ous *adj.* Reverently religious; devout. **piously** *adv.*, **piousness** *n.*

pipe *n.* A hollow cylinder for conveying fluids; a small bowl with a hollow stem for smoking tobacco. *Music* A tubular flute.

pipe-line *n.* A pipe used to transfer gas or oil over long distances; a means for conveying information.

pique *n.* A feeling of resentment or irritation.

pi-rate *n.* A robber of the high seas. *Slang* Someone who uses or reproduces someone else's work without authorization. **piracy** *n.*, **pirate** *v.*, **piratical** *adj.*

Pis-ces *n.* The 12th sign of the zodiac; one born between February 19-March 20.

pis-ta-chi-o *n.* A small tree of western Asia; the edible fruit from this tree.

pis-til *n.* The seed-producing female reproductive organ of a flower.

pis-tol *n.* A small hand-held firearm.

pis-ton *n., Mech.* A solid cylinder fitted into a larger cylinder, moving back and forth under liquid pressure.

pit *n.* An artificial or manmade hole in the ground; a slight indentation in the skin, as a scar from the chicken pox; an area for refueling or repair at a car race; the stone in the middle of some fruit, as peaches. *the pits* Anything at its worst.

pitch *n.* A thick, sticky, dark substance which is the residue of the distillation of petroleum or coal tar; the degree of slope of an incline; the property of a musical tone which makes it high or low. *v.* To cover with pitch; to throw; to throw out; to slope.

pitch-black *adj.* Extremely dark.

pitch-er *n.* The person who throws the ball to the batter; a container for holding and pouring liquids.

pitch-fork *n.* A large fork with a wide prong span, used as a garden or farm tool.

pith *n., Bot.* The sponge-like soft tissue at the center of the branch or stem of many plants.

pit-i-ful *adj.* Evoking or meriting pity. **pitifully** *adv.*

pit-y *n., pl.* -ies. A feeling of compassion or sorrow for another's misfortune.

piv-ot *n.* A thing or person upon which development, direction, or effect depends. *v.* To turn.

piz-za *n.* An Italian food consisting of a doughy crust covered with tomato sauce, cheese, and other toppings and then baked.

place *n.* A region; an area; a building or location used for a special purpose; the position of something in a series or sequence. *v.* To put in a particular order or place.

place-ment *n.* The act of being placed; a business or service which finds positions of employment for applicants.

pla-cen-ta *n., pl.* -tas *or* -tae *Anat.* The vascular, membranous structure which supplies a fetus with nourishment before its birth.

plague *n.* Anything that is troublesome. *Pathol.* A highly contagious and often fatal epidemic disease, as the bubonic plague.

plaid n. A rectangular wool cloth or garment, usually worn by men and women, having a crisscross or checkered design.

plain adj. Level; flat; clear; open, as in view; not rich or luxurious; not highly gifted or cultivated.

plainly adv., **plainness** n.

plain-tiff n. A person who brings suit.

plan n. A scheme or method for achieving something; a drawing to show proportion and relationship to parts. v. To have in mind as an intention or purpose.

plane n. A tool for smoothing or leveling a wood surface. *Geom.* A surface as a straight line that joins any two points on it. *Slang* Airplane. **plane** v.

plan-et n., *Astron.* A celestial body which is illuminated by light from the star around which it revolves. **-tary** adj.

plan-e-tar-i-um n., pl. **-iums** or **-ia** A device for exhibiting celestial bodies as they exist at any time and for any place on earth.

plank n. A broad piece of wood; one of the issues or principles of a political platform.

plant n. A living organism belonging to the vegetable kingdom, having cellulose cell walls. v. To place a living organism in the ground for growing; to place so as to deceive or to spy.

plaque n. A flat piece, made from metal, porcelain, ivory, or other materials, engraved for mounting; the bacteria deposit which builds up on the teeth.

plas-ma n. The clear fluid part of blood, used for transfusions.

plas-ter-board n. A building material of layered gypsum bonded to outer layers of paper.

plas-tic adj. Pliable; capable of being molded. n. A synthetically made material which is molded and then hardened into objects.

plasticity n. **plasticize** v.

plastic surgery n. Surgery dealing with the restoration or repair of deformed or destroyed parts of the body or skin.

plate n. A flat flexible, thin piece of material, as metal; a shallow, flat vessel made from glass, crockery, plastic, or other material from which food is served or eaten; a piece of plastic, metal, or vulcanite fitted to the mouth to hold one or more artificial teeth. *Baseball* The place or object marking home base. v. To cover something, as jewelry, with a thin layer of gold, silver, or other metal.

pla-teau n. An extensive level expanse of elevated land; a period or stage of stability.

plat-form n. Any elevated or raised surface used by speakers, or by other performers or for display purposes; a formal declaration of principles or policy of a political party.

plat-i-num n. A silver-white, metallic element which is corrosive-resistant, used in jewelry; symbolized by Pt.

Pla-to n. Greek philosopher.

pla-toon n. A military unit subdivision commanded by a lieutenant.

plat-ter n. A large, oblong, shallow dish for serving food.

plau-si-ble adj. Seeming to be probable; appearing to be trustworthy or believable.

play v. To amuse or entertain oneself, as in recreation; to take part in a game; to perform in a dramatic role; to perform with a musical instrument; in fishing, to allow a hooked fish to tire itself out; to pretend to do something. n. A dramatic presentaton.

play-ful adj. Lightly humorous; full of high spirits.

play-ground n. The area set aside for children's recreation.

play--off n. A sports contest to break a tie; a series of games to decide the winner or championship.

pla-za n. An open-air marketplace or square; a shopping mall.

plea n. An urgent request. In law, an allegation made by either party in a law suit.

plead v. To argue for or against something in court; to ask earnestly.

pleas-ant adj. Giving or promoting the feeling of pleasure; very agreeable.

pleasantly adv. **pleasantness** n.

please v. To make happy; to give pleasure; to be the will or wish of; to prefer.

pleas-ur-a-ble adj. Pleasant; gratifying.

pleas-ure n. A feeling of satisfaction or enjoyment; one's preference or wish.

pleat n. A fold in a cloth made by doubling the cloth back and fastening it down.

plebe n. A freshman or first year student at the United States Naval Academy.

pledge n. A solemn promise; a deposit of something as security for a loan; a promise to join a fraternity; a person who is pledged to join a fraternity. v. To promise or vow.

plen-ti-ful adj. Having great abundance.

plentifully adv. **plentifulness** n.

plen-ty n. An ample amount; prosperity or abundance.

pleu-ra n., pl. **pleurae** *Anat.* The membranous sac which envelops the lungs and provides a lining for the thoracic cavity.

pli-a-ble adj. Flexible; easily controlled or persuaded. **pliability,**

pliableness n. **pliably** adv.

pli-ers pl. n. A pincers-like implement used for holding, bending, or cutting.

plight n. A distressing circumstance, situation, or condition.

plod n. To walk in a heavy, slow way.

plot n. A small piece of ground usually used for a special purpose; the main story line in a piece of fiction; a plan; an intrigue; a conspiracy. v. To represent something by using a map or chart; to scheme secretly. **plotter** n.

plow n. An implement for breaking up or turning over the soil. v. To dig out.

Slang To hit with force.

pluck *v.* To remove by pulling out or off; to pull and release the strings on a musical instrument. *Slang* To swindle.

plug *n.* Anything used to stop or close a hole or drain. *Electr.* A two-pronged device attached to a cord and used in a jack or socket to make an electrical connection. *Slang* To advertise favorably; to give a recommendation or a piece of publicity for someone.

plum *n.* A small tree bearing an edible fruit with a smooth skin and a single hard seed; the fruit from such a tree.

plum-age *n.* The feathers of a bird.

plumb *n.* A lead weight tied to the end of a string, used to test the exact perpendicular line of something.

plumb-er *n.* A person who repairs or installs plumbing in a home or business.

plume *n.* A feather used as an ornament.

plun-der *v.* To deprive of goods or property in a violent way. plunderer *n.*

plunge *v.* To thrust or cast something, as into water; to submerge; to descend sharply or steeply.

plunk *v.* To put down or place suddenly; to pluck or strum a banjo.

plunk, plunker *n.*

plu-ral *adj.* Consisting of or containing more than one. plural *n.*

plus *prep.* Add the symbol (+) which indicates addition; increase; extra quantity.

Plu-to *n.* The planet which is ninth in order from the sun.

plu-to-ni-um *n.* A radioactive metallic element symbolized by Pu.

ply *v.* To mold, bend, or shape. *n.* A layer of thickness; the twisted strands of thread, yarn,, or rope.

ply-wood *n.* A structural material consisting of thin layers of wood which have been glued and pressed together.

PM *abbr.* Prime Minster; Post meridiem.

pneu-mo-nia- *n.* An inflammation caused by bacteria, virus of the lungs, or irritation.

poach *v.* To cook in a liquid just at the boiling point; to trespass on another's property with the intent of taking fish or wild game. poacher *n.*

pock-et *n.* A small pouch within a garment, having an open top and used for carrying items. *v.* To put in or deposit in a pocket.

pod *n.*, *Bot.*

A seed vessel, as of a bean or pea. *Aeron* A separate and detachable compartment in a spacecraft.

po-di-a-try *n.* Professional care and treatment of the feet.

po-di-um *n.,pl.* -ia *or* -iums A small raised platform for an orchestra conductor or a speaker.

po-em *n.* A composition in verse with language selected for its beauty and sound.

po-et *n.* A person who writes poetry.

po-et-ry *n.* The art of writing stories, poems, and thoughts into verse.

point *n.* The sharp or tapered end of something; a mark of punctuation, as a period (.); a geometric object which does not have property or dimensions other than locaton; a degree, condition, or stage; a particular or definite spot in time. *v.* To aim; to indicate direction by using the finger.

poin-set-ti-a *n.* A tropical plant having large scarlet leaves, used in Christmas decorations.

poise *v.* To bring into or hold one's balance. *n.* Equilibrium; self-confidence; the ability to stay calm in all social situations.

poi-son *n.* A substance which kills, injures, or destroys.
poisoner *n.*, poisonous *adj.*

poke *v.* To push or prod at something with a finger or other implement.

po-lar *adj.* Having to do with the poles of a magnet or sphere; relating to the geographical poles of the earth.

po-lar-ize *v.* To cause something to vibrate in an exact pattern; to break up into opposite groups. -ation *n.*

pole *n.* Either of the two ends of the axis of a sphere, as the earth; the two points called the North and South Poles, where the axis of the earth's rotation meets the surface; a long, slender rod.

pol-i-o-my-e-li-tis *n.* Inflammation of the spinal cord causing paralysis; also *polio.*

po-lice *n.* A division or department organized to maintain order; the members of such a department. *v.* To patrol; to enforce the law and maintain order.

po-liceman *n.* A member of the police force. policewoman *n.*

pol-i-cy *n.*, *pl.* -ies Any plan or principle which guides decision making.

pol-ish *v.*

To make lustrous and smooth by rubbing; to become refined or elegant.

po-lite *adj.* Refined, mannerly, and courteous.

po-lit-i-cal *adj.* Concerned with or pertaining to government; involved in politics.

pol-i-ti-cian *n.* A person active in governmental affairs or politics.

pol-i-tics *n.* The activities and methods of a political party.

Polk, James K. *n.* The 11th president of the United States from 1845-1849.

poll *n.* The recording of votes in an election; a public survey taken on a given topic. poll *v.*

pol-len *n.* The yellow dust-like powder which contains the male reproductive cells of a flowering plant.

pol-lute *v.* To contaminate; to make unclear or impure; to dirty. pollution *n.*

po-lo-ni-um *n.* A radioactive metallic element symbolized by PO.

pol-ter-geist *n.* A mischievous ghost or spirit which makes much noise.

pol-y-es-ter *n.* A strong lightweight synthetic resin used in fibers.

pol-y-graph *n.* A machine designed to record different signals given off by the body, as respiration, blood pressure, or heartbeats; may be used to detect a person who may be lying.

pol-y-he-dron *n.*, *pl.* -dra *or* -drons *Geom.* A solid bounded by polygons.

pom-pa-dour *n.* A hairstyle which is puffed over the forehead.

pomp-ous *adj.* A showing or appearance of dignity or importance.

pond *n.* A body of still water, smaller in size than a lake.

pon-der *v.* To weigh or think about very carefully; to meditate.

pon-der-ous *adj.* Massive; having great weight.

pon-tiff *n.* A pope.

po-ny *n.*, *pl.* -ies A small horse.

poor *adj.* Lacking possessions and money; not satisfactory; broke; needy; destitute.

pop *v.* To cause something to burst; to make a sharp, explosive sound. *Slang* Soda. popper *n.*

pope *n.* The head of the Roman Catholic Church.

pop-lar *n.* A rapid growing tree having a light, soft wood.

pop-u-lar *adj.* Approved of; widely liked; suited to the means of the people.

pop-u-la-tion *n.* The total number of people in a given area, country, or city.

por-ce-lain *n.* A hard, translucent ceramic which has been fired and glazed.

porch *n.* A covered structure forming the entrance to a house.

por-cu-pine *n.*

A clumsy rodent covered with long sharp quills.

pore *v.* To ponder or meditate on something. *n.* A minute opening, as in the skin.

pork *n.* The edible flesh of swine. *Informal* Favors given by a government for political reasons and not public necessity.

por-nog-ra-phy *n.* Pictures, films, or writing which deliberately arouse sexual excitement.

por-poise *n.*

An aquatic mammal with a blunt, rounded snout.

port *n.* A city or town with a harbor for loading and unloading cargo from ships; the left side of a ship; a dark-red, sweet, fortified wine.

port-a-ble *adj.* Capable of being moved easily.

por-ter *n.* A person hired to carry baggage.

port-fo-li-o *n.* A carrying case for holding papers, drawings, and other flat items.

port-hole *n.* A small opening in the side of a ship providing light and ventilation.

por-tion *n.* A section or part of a whole; a share. *v.* To allot; to assign.

por-tray *v.* To represent by drawing, writing, or acting.

pose *v.* To place or assume a position, as for a picture.

po-si-tion *n.* The manner in which something is placed; an attitude; a viewpoint; a job; employment. *v.* To place in proper order.

pos-i-tive *adj.* Containing, expressing, or characterized by affirmation; very confident; absolutely certain; not negative. positively *adv.*, positiveness *n.*

pos-se *n.* A deputized group or squad.

pos-ses-sion *n.* The fact or act of possessing property; the state of being possessed, as by an evil spirit.

pos-ses-sive *adj.* Having a strong desire to possess; not wanting to share. *n.* The noun or pronoun case which indicates ownership.

pos-si-ble *adj.* Capable of being true, happening, or being accomplished. possibility *n.*, possibly *adv.*

post *n.* An upright piece of wood or metal support; a position or employment. *v.* To put up information in a public place. *prefix.* After; in order; or time; behind.

post-age *n.* The charge or fee for mailing something.

pos-te-ri-or *adj.* Located in the back. *n.* The buttocks.

post-mor-tem *adj.* The examination of a body after death; an autopsy.

post-op-er-a-tive *adj.* Following surgery.

post-pone *v.* To put off; to defer to a later time. postponable *adj.*, postponement, postponer *n.*

post-script *n.* A short message added at the end of a letter.

pos-ture *n.* The carriage or position of the body.

pot *n.* A rounded, deep container used for cooking and other domestic purposes. *Slang* A large sum of money which is shared by all members of a group; marijuana. pot *v.*, potful *n.*

po-tas-si-um *n.* A silvery-white, highly reactive metallic element symbolized by K.

po-ta-to *n.*, *pl.* -toes A thick, edible, underground tuber plant native to America.

po-tent *adj.* Having great strength or physical powers; having a great influence on the mind or morals; sexually competent.

po-ten-tial *adj.* Possible, but not yet actual; having the capacity to be developed. *Electr.* The potential energy of an electric charge that depends on its position in an electric field. **potentiality** n., **potentially** adv.

pot-pour-ri n. A mixture of sweet-smelling dried flower petals and spices, kept in an airtight jar.

pot-ter-y n., pl. -ies Objects molded from clay and fired by intense heat.

pouch n. A small bag or other container for holding or carrying money, tobacco, and other small articles. Zool. The sac-like structure in which some animals carry their young.

poul-try n. Domestic fowl as ducks and hens, which are raised for eggs or meat.

pound n., pl. pounds or pound A measure of weight equal to sixteen ounces; a public enclosure where stray animals are fed and housed. v. To strike repeatedly or with force; to throb or beat violently or rapidly.

pov-er-ty n. The condition or state of being poor and needing money.

POW abbr. Prisoner of war.

pow-der n. A dry substance which has been finely ground or pulverized; dust; an explosive, such as gunpowder. v. To dust or cover.

pow-er-ful adj. Possessing energy or great force; having authority.

power of attorney n. A legal document in which one person gives another the authority to act for him.

prac-ti-cal adj. Serving an actual use or purpose; inclined to act instead of thinking or talking about something; useful.

pract-ice n. A custom or habit of doing something. v. To work at a profession; to apply; to put into effect; to exercise or rehearse.

prai-rie n. A wide area of level or rolling land with grass and weeds but no trees.

praise v. To express approval; to glorify.

prank n. A mischievous, playful action or trick. **prankster** n.

pra-seo-dym-i-um n. A metallic element of the rare-earth group, symbolized by Pr.

prawn n. An edible shrimp-like crustacean found in both salt and fresh water.

pray v. To address prayers to God; to ask or request.

prayer n. A devout request; the act of praying; a formal or set group of words used in praying.

praying mantis n. An insect which holds its front legs folded as, in prayer.

pre- pref Earlier or prior to something; in front.

preach v. To advocate; to proclaim; to deliver a sermon. **preacher**, **preachment** n., **preachy** adj.

pre-am-ble n. An introduction to something, as a law, which states the purpose and reasons for the matter which follows.

pre-cau-tion n. A measure of caution or care taken in advance to guard against harm.

pre-cede v. To be or go before in time, position, or rank. **precedence** n.

prec-e-dent n. An instance which may serve as a rule or example in the future.

pre-cept n. A rule, order, or commandment meant to guide one's conduct.

pre-cinct n. An electoral district of a county, township, city, or town; an enclosure with definite boundaries.

pre-cious adj. Having great worth or value; beloved; cherished.

pre-cip-i-ta-tion n. Condensed water vapor which falls as snow, rain, sleet or hail. Chem. The act of causing crystals to separate and fall to the bottom of a liquid.

pre-cip-i-tous adj. Very steep; marked with very steep cliffs.

pre-cise adj. Exact; definite; strictly following rules; very strict.

pre-ci-sion n. Exactness; the quality of being precise; accuracy.

pre-clude v. To shut out; to make impossible; to prevent.

pre-co-cious adj. Showing and developing skills and abilities very early in life.

pre-con-ceive v. To form a notion or conception before knowing all the facts. **preconception** n.

pre-da-cious adj. Living by preying on other animals.

pred-a-tor n. A person who lives or gains by stealing from another person; an animal that survives by killing and eating other animals.

pre-des-ti-na-tion n. Destiny; fate; the act by which God has predestined all events.

pred-i-ca-ble adj. Capable of being predicated: to foretell.

pred-i-cate n. Gram. The word or words which say something about the subject of a clause or sentence; the part of a sentence which contains the verb. v. To establish.

pre-dict v. To tell beforehand; to foretell; to forcast. **predictability** n., **-able** adj., **-ably** adv., **prediction** n.

pre-dom-i-nant adj. Superior in strength, authority, number, or other qualities.

pree-mie n. Slang A baby born before the expected due date.

pre-empt v. To take or get hold of before someone else; to take the place of; to do something before someone else has a chance to do it. **-ion** n., **-ive** adj.

pre-fab-ri-cate v. To construct in sections beforehand. **prefabrication** n.

pref-ace n. The introduction at the beginning of a book or speech.

pre-fect n. A high administrative official. **prefecture** n.

pre-fer v. To select as being the favorite; to promote; to present.

pref-er-ence n. A choice; a special liking for anything over another. **preferential** adj.

pre-fix v. To put at the beginning; to put before.

preg-nant adj. Carrying an unborn fetus; significant. **pregnancy** n.

pre-his-tor-i-cal *adj.* Of or related to the period before recorded history.

pre-judge *v.* To judge before one knows all the facts. **prejudgment** *n.*

prej-u-dice *n.* A biased opinion based on emotion rather than reason; bias against a group, race, or creed.

pre-lim-i-nar-y *adj.* Leading up to the main action. **preliminaries** *n.*

prel-ude *n.* An introductory action. *Music* The movement at the beginning of a piece of music.

pre-ma-ture *adj.* Occurring or born before the natural or proper time. **prematurely** *adv.*

pre-med-i-tate *v.* To plan in advance or beforehand.

pre-mi-er *adj.* First in rank or importance. *n.* The chief executive of a government. **premiership** *n.*

pre-mi-um *n.* An object offered free as an inducement to buy; the fee or amount payable for insurance; an additional amount of money charged above the nominal value.

pre-na-tal *adj.* Existing prior to birth.

pre-oc-cu-py *v.* To engage the mind or attention completely.

prep *Slang* Preparatory school; preparation.

prep-a-ra-tion *n.* The process of preparing for something.

pre-par-a-to-ry *adj.* Serving as preparation.

pre-pare *v* To make ready or qualified; to equip. **preparedly** *adv.*

pre-pay *v.* To pay for in advance.

pre-pon-der-ate *v.* To have superior importance, weight, force, influence, or other qualities. **preponderance**, **preponderancy** *n.*, **preponderantly** *adv.*

prep-o-si-tion *n.*, *Gram.* A word placed in front of a noun or pronoun to show a connection with or to something or someone.

pre-pos-ter-ous *adj.* Absurd; ridiculous; beyond all reason.

prep-pie *n.* *Slang* A student attending a prep school; a young adult who behaves and dresses very traditionally.

pre-rog-a-tive *n.* The unquestionable right belonging to a person.

pres-age *n.* An omen or indication of something to come; a premonition. **presage** *v.*

pre-school *adj.* Of or for children usually between the ages of two and five. **preschooler** *n.*

pre-scribe *v.* To impose as a guide; to recommend.

pre-scrip-tion *n.*, *Med.* A physician's written order for medicine.

pres-ence *n.* The state of being present; the immediate area surrounding a person or thing; poise.

pres-ent *adj.* Now going on; not past or future. *Gram.* Denoting a tense or verb form which expresses a current state or action. *v.* To bring into the acquaintance of another; to introduce; to make a gift of. *n.* A gift. *adv.* Currently.

pres-en-ta-tion *n.* A formal introduction of one person to another; to present something as an exhibition, show, or product.

pre-serv-a-tive *adj.* Keeping something from decay or injury. **preservation** *n.*, **preservable** *adj.*

pre-serve *v.* To keep or save from destruction or injury; to prepare fruits or vegetables to prevent spoilage or decay. **preserves** Fruit which has been preserved with sugar.

pre-shrunk *adj.* Material which has been washed during the manufacturing process to minimize shrinkage later.

pre-side *v.* To have a position of authority or control; to run or control a meeting.

pres-i-dent *n.* The chief executive officer of a government, corporation, or association. **presidency** *n.*, **-ial** *adj.*

press *v.* To act upon or exert steady pressure or force; to squeeze out or extract by pressure; to smooth by heat and pressure; to iron clothes. *n.* A machine used to produce printed material. **presser** *n.*

pres-sure *n.* The act of or the state of being pressed; a constraining moral force; any burden, force, painful feeling, or influence; the depressing effect of something hard to bear.

pres-tige *n.* Importance based on past reputation and achievements.

pres-to *adv.*, *Music* Very fast and quick; at once.

pre-sume *v.* To take for granted; to take upon oneself without permission; to proceed overconfidently. **-able** *adj.*, **presumably** *adv.*, **presumer** *n.*

pre-sump-tion *n.* Arrogant conductor speech; something that can be logically assumed true until disproved.

pre-tend *v.* To make believe; to act in a false way. **pretender** *n.*

pre-tense *n.* A deceptive and false action or appearance; a false purpose.

pre-ten-tions *n.* Having or making claims to worth, excellence, etc.; showy.

pre-text *n.* A motive assumed in order to conceal the true purpose.

pret-ty *adj.* Pleasant; attractive; characterized by gracefulness; pleasing to look at. **sitting pretty** In a favorable position; good circumstances. **prettier**, **prettiest** *adj.*

pre-vail *v.* To succeed; to win control over something; to predominate. **prevailer** *n.*, **prevailingly** *adv.*

pre-vent *v.* To keep something from happening; to keep from doing something.

pre-ven-tive *or* **preventative** *adj.* Protecting or serving to ward off harm, disease, or other problems. **preventive** *n.*

pre-view *or* **prevue** *n.* An advance showing or viewing to invited guests.

pre-vi-ous *adj.* Existing or occurring earlier. **previously** *adv.*

price *n.* The set amount of money expected or given for the sale of something.

prick *n.* A small hole made by a sharp point. *v.* To pierce something lightly.

pride *n.* A sense of personal dignity; a feeling of pleasure because of something achieved, done, or owned.

priest *n.* A clergyman in the Catholic church who serves as mediator between God and His worshipers.

pri-ma-ry *adj.* First in origin, time, series, or sequence; basic; fundamental.

prime *adj.* First in importance, time, or rank. *n.* A period of full vigor, success, or beauty. *v.* To make ready by putting something on before the final coat, as to prime wood before painting.

prim-i-tive *adj.* Of or pertaining to the beginning or earliest time; resembling the style or manners of an earlier time.

primp *v.* To dress or arrange with superfluous attention to detail.

prince *n.* The son of a king; a king.

prin-cess *n.* The daughter of a king.

prin-ci-pal *adj.* Chief; most important. *n.* The head-master or chief official of a school; a sum of money invested or owed which is separate from the interest.

prin-ci-ple *n.* The fundamental law or truth upon which others are based; a moral standard.

print *n.* An impression or mark made with ink; the design or picture which is transferred from an engraved plate or other impression. *v.* To stamp designs; to publish something in print, as a book or magazine.

print-er *n.* A person whose occupation is printing.

print-out *n.* *Computer Science* The output of a computer, printed on paper.

pri-or *adj.* Previous in order or time.

pri-or-i-ty *n.* Something which takes precedence; something which must be done or taken care of first.

prism *n.*

A solid figure with triangular ends and rectangular sides, used to disperse light into a spectrum.

pris-on *n.* A place of confinement where people are kept while waiting for a trial or while serving time for breaking the law; jail. **prisoner** *n.*

pri-vate *adj.* Secluded or removed from the public view; secret; intimate; owned or controlled by a group or person rather than by the public or government. *n.* An enlisted person holding the lowest rank in military service.

priv-i-lege *n.* A special right or benefit granted to a person. **privileged** *adj.*

prize *n.* An award or something given to the winner of a contest; something exceptional or outstanding.

pro *n.* An argument in favor of or supporting something. *Slang* A professional or an expert in a given field.

prob-a-bil-i-ty *n., pl.* -ies The state or quality of being probable; a mathe-matical statement or prediction of the odds of something happening or not happening.

prob-a-ble *adj.* Likely to become a reality, but not certain or proved.

pro-bate *n.* The act of legally proving that a will is genuine.

pro-ba-tion *n.* A period used to test the qualifications and character of a new employee; the early release of lawbreakers who must be under supervision and must report as requested to a probation officer.

probe *n.* An instrument used for investigating an unknown environment; a careful investigation or examination.

prob-lem *n.* A perplexing situation or question; a question presented for consideration, solution, or discussion. **problem, problematic** *adj.*

pro-ce-dure *n.* A certain pattern or way of doing something; the normal methods or forms to be followed.

pro-ceed *v.* To carry on or continue an action or process. *Law* To begin or institute legal action.

pro-ceeds *pl., n.* The profits received from a fund-raising venture.

proc-ess *n.* The course, steps, or methods toward a desired result. *Law* Any judicial request or order. *Computer Science* The sequence of operations which gives a desired result. *v.* To compile, compute, or assemble; data.

pro-ces-sion *n.* A group which moves along in a formal manner; a parade.

pro-ces-sion-al *n.* A hymn sung during a procession; *adj.* the opening of a church service; of or relating to a procession.

pro-ces-sor *n.* *Computer Science* The central unit of a computer which processes data.

pro-claim *v.* To announce publicly.

proc-la-ma-tion *n.* An official public declaration or announcement.

pro-cras-ti-nate *v.* To put off, defer, or postpone to a later time. **procrastination, procrastinator** *n.*

proc-tor *n.* A person in a university or college whose job it is to see that order is maintained during exams. **proctorial** *adj.*

pro-cure *v.* To acquire; to accomplish.

prod *v.* To arouse mentally; to poke with a pointed instrument. *n.* A pointed implement used to prod or poke.

prod-i-gal *adj.* Wasteful expenditure of money, strength, or time; extravagance. *n.* One who is a spendthrift or is wasteful.

pro-duce *v.* To bear or bring forth by a natural process; to manufacture; to make; to present or bring into view.

prod-uct *n.* Something produced, manufactured, or obtained. *Math.* The answer obtained by multiplying.

pro-duc-tion *n.* The process or act of producing; something produced, as a play.

pro-fane *adj.* Manifesting disrespect toward sacred things; vulgar.

pro-fess *v.* To admit or declare openly; to make an open vow.

pro-fes-sor *n.* A faculty member of the highest rank in a college or university; a highly skilled teacher.

pro-fi-cient *adj.* Highly skilled in a field of knowledge. **proficiency** *n.*, **proficiently** *adv.*

pro-file *n.* The outline of a person's face or figure as seen from the side; a short biographical sketch indicating the most striking characteristics.

prof-it *n.* The financial return after all expenses have been accounted for. *v.* To gain an advantage or a financial reward. **profitable** *adj.*

pro-found *adj.* Deeply held or felt; intellectually penetrating.

pro-fuse *adj.* Extravagant; giving forth lavishly; overflowing. **profusely** *adv.*, **profuseness** *n.*

prog-e-ny *n.*, *pl.* **-ies** One's offspring, children, or descendants.

prog-no-sis *n.*, *pl.* **-noses** A prediction of the outcome and course a disease may take.

pro-gram *n.* Any prearranged plan or course; a show or performance, as one given at a scheduled time. *Computer Science* A sequence of commands which tell a computer how to perform a task or sequence of tasks. **program** *v.*

prog-ress *n.* Forward motion or advancement to a higher goal; an advance; steady improvement.

pro-hib-it *v.* To forbid legally; to prevent.

pro-ject *n.* A plan or course of action; a proposal; a large job. *v.* To give an estimation on something.

pro-jec-tile *n.* Anything hurled forward through the air.

pro-jec-tion *n.* The act or state of being projected; the state or part that sticks out.

pro-lif-er-ate *v.* To grow or produce with great speed, as cells in tissue formation.

pro-logue *n.* An introductory statement at the beginning of a poem, song, or play.

pro-long *v.* To extend or lengthen in time.

prom-e-nade *n.* An unhurried walk for exercise or amusement; a public place for such a walk, as the deck of a ship.

prom-i-nent *adj.* Jutting out; widely known; held in high esteem.

pro-mis-cu-ous *adj.* Lacking selectivity or discrimination, especially in sexual relationships.

prom-ise *n.* An assurance given that one will or will not do something; a pledge. **promise** *v.*

prompt *adj.* Arriving on time; punctual; immediate. *v.* To suggest or inspire.

prone *adj.* Lying flat; face down. **pronely** *adv.*, **proneness** *n.*

pro-noun *n.*, *Gram.* A word which can be used in the place of a noun or noun phrase.

pro-nounce *v.* To deliver officially; to ar-

ticulate the sounds.

proof *n.* The establishment of a fact by evidence; the act of showing that something is true; a trial impression from the negative of a photograph. *v.* To proofread; to mark and make corrections.

proof-read *v.* To read in order to detect and mark errors in a printer's proof.

prop *n.* A support to keep something upright. *v.* To sustain.

prop-a-gate *v.* To reproduce or multiply by natural causes; to pass on qualities or traits. **propagation** *n.*

prop-er *adj.* Appropriate; especially adapted or suited; conforming to social convention; correct.

prop-er-ty *n.*, *pl.* **-ies** Any object of value owned or lawfully acquired, as real estate; a piece of land.

proph-e-cy *n.*, *pl.* **-ies** A prediction made under divine influence.

proph-et *n.* One who delivers divine messages; one who foretells the future. **prophetess** *n.*

pro-pi-ti-ate *v.* To win the goodwill of; to stop from being angry. **propitiation** *n.*

pro-po-nent *n.* One who supports or advocates a cause.

pro-por-tion *n.* The relation of one thing to another in size, degree, or amount. *v.* To adjust or arrange with balance and harmony. **proportional,** **-ate** *adj.*, **proportionally** *adv.*

pro-pose *v.* To present or put forward for consideration or action; to suggest someone for an office or position; to make an offer; to offer marriage. **proposal** *n.*

prop-o-si-tion *n.* A scheme or plan offered for consideration; a subject or idea to be proved or discussed. *v.* To make a sexual suggestion.

pro-pri-e-ty *n.*, *pl.* **-ies** The quality or state of being proper in accordance with recognized principles or usage.

pro-pul-sion *n.* The act or process of propelling. **propulsive** *adj.*

pro-rate *v.* To distribute or divide proportionately. **proration** *n.*

pro-scribe *v.* To banish; to outlaw; to prohibit.

prose *n.* Ordinary language, speech, or writing which is not poetry.

pros-e-cute *v.* To carry on. *Law* To bring suit against a person; to seek enforcement for legal process. **prosecution** *n.*

pros-pect *n.* Something that has the possibility of future success; a possible customer. *v.* To explore. **prospective** *adj.*, **prospectively** *adv.*

pros-per *v.* To be successful; to achieve success. **prosperous** *adj.*

pros-tate *n.* A small gland at the base of the male bladder.

pros-ti-tute *n.* One who sells the body for the purpose of sexual intercourse.

pros-trate *adj.* Lying with the face down to the ground. *v.* To overcome; to adopt a submissive posture. **prostrative** *adj.*, **prostrator** *n.*

pro-tect *v.* To guard or shield from attack or injury; to shield.

protective *adj.*, **protectively** *adv.*

pro-tein *n., Biochem.* Any of a very large group of highly complex nitrogenous compounds occurring in living matter and composed of amino acids which are essential for tissue repair and growth.

pro-test *v.* To make a strong formal objection; to object to. *n.* The act of protesting. **protester** *n.*

Prot-es-tant *n.* A member of any of the Christian churches who believes Jesus is the son of God and died for man's sins.

pro-to-col *n.* The code and rules of diplomatic and state etiquette.

pro-ton *n., Physics* A unit of positive charge equal in magnitude to an electron.

pro-tract *v.* To extend in space; to protrude.

pro-trude *v.* To project; to thrust outward. **protrusion** *n.*

proud *adj.* Showing or having a feeling that one is better than the others; having a feeling of satisfaction; having proper self-respect or proper self-esteem.

prove *v.* To show with valid evidence that something is true.

provable *adj.*, **provably** *adv.*

prov-erb *n.* An old saying which illustrates a truth. **Proverbs** *n.* The book contained in the Bible which has many sayings supposed to have come from Solomon and others.

pro-vide *v.* To supply or furnish with what is needed.

pro-vi-sion *n.* A supply of food or needed equipment.

pro-voke *v.* To cause to be angry; to annoy. **provocation** *n.*

prox-i-mate *adj.* Immediate; direct; close.

prox-y *n., pl.* **-ies** The authority, usually written, to act for another.

prude *n.* A person who is very modest, especially in matters related to sex. **prudery, prudishness** *n.*, **prudish** *adj.*

pru-dent *adj.* Cautious; discreet; managing very carefully.

salm *n.* A sacred hymn, taken from the Book of Psalms in the Old Testament.

so-ri-a-sis *n., Pathol.* A non-contagious, chronic, inflammatory skin disease characterized by reddish patches and white scales.

ST *abbr.* Pacific Standard Time.

sych *v., Slang* To prepare oneself emotionally or mentally; to outwit or out-guess.

sy-chi-a-try *n.* The branch of medicine which deals with the diagnosis and treatment of mental disorders.

sy-chic *adj.* Cannot be explained by natural or physical laws. *n.* A person who communicates with the spirit world.

sy-chol-o-gy *n., pl.* **-ies** The science of emotions, behavior, and the mind.

psychological *adj.*, **psychologist** *n.*

psy-cho-path *n.* A person suffering from a mental disorder characterized by aggressive antisocial behavior. **-ic** *adj.*

pu-ber-ty *n.* The stage of development in which sexual reproduction can first occur; the process of the body which culminates in sexual maturity. **pubertal, puberal** *adj.*

pub-lic *adj.* Pertaining to or affecting the people or community; for everyone's use; widely or well known.

pub-lic do-main *n.* Public property; a published work whose copyrights have expired.

pub-li-ca-tion *n.* The business of publishing; any pamphlet, book, or magazine.

pub-lic-i-ty *n.* The state of being known to the public; common knowledge.

pub-lish *v.* To print and distribute a book, magazine, or any printed matter to the public. **-able** *adj.*, **-er** *n.*

puck *n.* A hard rubber disk used in playing ice hockey.

pud-dle *n.* A small pool of water.

puff *n.* A brief discharge of air or smoke. *v.* To breathe in short heavy breaths.

pull *v.* To apply force; to cause motion toward or in the same direction of; to remove from a fixed place; to stretch.

pulp *n.* The soft juicy part of a fruit; a soft moist mass; inexpensive paper.

pul-pit *n.* The elevated platform lectern used in a church from which a service is conducted.

pul-sate *v.* To beat rhythmically. **pulsation, pulsator** *n.*

pulse *n., Physiol.* The rhythmical beating of the arteries caused by the action of the heart. **pulse** *v.*

pul-ver-ize *v.* To be reduced to dust or powder by crushing.

punch *n.* A tool used for perforating or piercing; a blow with the fist; a drink made of an alcoholic beverage and a fruit juice or other non-alcoholic beverage. *v.* To use a punch on something; to hit sharply with the hand or fist.

punc-tu-al *adj.* Prompt; arriving on time.

pun-ish *v.* To subject a person to confinement or impose a penalty for a crime.

punishment *n.* A penalty which is imposed for breaking the law or a rule.

punk *n., Slang* A young, inexperienced boy. *adj.* Of or relating to a bizarre style of clothing; relating to punk rock bands.

punt *n.* A narrow, long, flat-bottomed boat; in football, a kick of a football dropped from the hands. *v.* To kick a football.

pup *n.*

A puppy, young dog, or the young of other animals.

pupil *n.* A person who attends school and receives instruction by a teacher.

pup-pet *n.* A small figure of an animal or person which is manipulated by hand or by strings. **puppeteer, puppetry** *n.*

pur-chase *v.* To receive by paying money as an exchange. **purchaser** *n.*

pure *adj.* Free from anything that damages, weakens, or contaminates; innocent; clean.

purge *v.* To make clean; to free from guilt or sin; to rid of anything undesirable, as unwanted persons. *Med.* To cause or induce emptying of the bowels. **purge** *n.*

pu-ri-fy *v.* To make clean or pure. **purification, purifier** *n.*

pu-ri-ty *n.* The quality of being pure; freedom from guilt or sin.

pur-ple *n.* A color between red and violet. **purplish** *adj.*

pur-port *v.* To give the appearance of intending; to imply, usually with the intent to deceive.

pur-pose *n.* A desired goal; an intention. **-ful, purposeless** *adj.,* **purposely** *adv.*

purr *n.* The low, murmuring sound characteristic of a cat. **purr** *v.*

pur-sue *v.* To seek to achieve; to follow in an attempt to capture. **pursuer** *n.*

pur-suit *n.* The act of pursuing an occupation.

pur-vey *v.* To supply provisions as a service. **purveyance, purveyor** *n.*

pus *n.* A yellowish secretion formed in infected tissue which contains bacteria.

put *v.* To cause to be in a location; to bring into a specific relation or state; to bring forward for debate or consideration, as to put up for. **put down** To humiliate.

pu-ta-tive *adj.* Commonly supposed.

pu-tre-fy *v.* To cause to decay; to decay. **putrefaction** *n.,* **putrefactive** *adj.*

putt *n.* In golf, a light stroke made on a putting green to get the ball into the hole.

pyg-my *n., pl.* **-ies** A very small person or animal; a dwarf.

py-lon *n.* A tower serving as a support for electrical power lines.

py-or-rhe-a *n., Pathol.* Inflammation of the gums and sockets of the teeth.

pyr-a-mid *n.*

A solid structure with a square base and triangular sides which meet at a point.

pyre *n.* A pile of combustible material for burning a dead body.

py-ro-ma-ni-a *n.* A compulsion to set fires.

Pyr-rhic vic-to-ry *n.* A victory acquired at too great of a cost.

py-thon *n.* A large nonvenomous snake which crushes its prey.

py-u-ri-a *n. Pathol.* The condition where there is pus in the urine.

pyx-ie *n.* A type of evergreen plant that is located in the eastern U.S.

Q, q The seventeenth letter of the English alphabet.

qua *adv.* The character or capacity of.

quack *n.* To make crying sounds as of a duck; someone who pretends of makes believe he knows how to perform something.

qat *n.* A small plant found in Africa, the fresh leaf is chewed for a stimulating effect.

qi-vi-ut *n.* Yarn spun from the fine, soft hair of the musk ox.

quack *n.* The harsh, croaking cry of a duck; someone who pretends to be a doctor. **quack** *v.,* **quackery** *n.*

quack grass *n.* A quickly growing weed.

quack-sal-ver *n.* A doctor who is quacked.

quad-ran-gle *n., Math* A plane figure with four sides and four angles.

quad-rant *n.*

A quarter section of a circle, subtending or enclosing a central angle of 90 degrees.

quad-rate *adj.* Being square.

quad-ri-ceps *n.* The great muscle of the front of the thigh.

quad-rille *n.* A square dance consisting of four couples.

quad-ril-lion *n.* A thousand trillions; one followed by fifteen zeros.

quad-ru-ple *adj.* Consisting of four parts; multiplied by four.

quaff *v.* To drink with abundance.

quag-mire *n.* An area of soft muddy land that gives away underfoot; a marsh.

quail *n., pl.* A small game bird.

quaint *adj.* Pleasing in an old-fashioned, unusual way.

quake *v.* To shake or tremble violently.

quak-er *n.* The religious sect called the Society of Friends.

qual-i-fi-ca-tion *n.* An act of qualifying; the ability, skill, or quality which makes something suitable for a given position.

qual-i-fy *v.* To prove something able.

qual-i-ty *n., pl.,* **ties** A distinguishing character which makes something such as it is; a high degree of excellence.

qualm *n.* A sudden feeling of sickness; sensation of uneasiness or doubt.

quan-da-ry *n.* A state of perplexity.

quan-ti-ty *n.* Number; amount; bulk; weight; a portion; as a large amount.

quar-an-tine *n.* A period of enforced isolation for a specified period of time used to prevent the spread of a contagious disease. **quarantine** *v.*

quar-rel *n.* An unfriendly, angry dis agreement.

quar-ry *n., pl.* **quar-ries** An anima hunted for food; an open pit or ex cavation from which limestone o other material is being extracted.

quart *n.* A unit of measurement equal ing four cups.

quar-ter *n.* One of four equal parts int

which anything may be divided; a place of lodging, as a barracks; a U.S. coin equal to 1/4 of a dollar.

quar-ter-back n., *Football* The offensive player who directs the plays for his team.

quar-ter-mas-ter n. The officer in charge of supplies for army troops; a navy Od officer who steers a ship and handles signaling equipment.

quar-tet n. A musical composition for four voices or instruments; any group or set of four.

quartz n. A hard, transparent crystallized mineral.

qua-sar n. One of the most distant and brightest bodies in the universe; a quasar producing intense visible radiation but not emitting radio signals.

quea-sy adj. Nauseated; sick. -iness n.

queen n. The wife of a king; a woman sovereign or monarch; in chess, the most powerful piece on the board, which can move any number of squares in any direction; the fertile female in a colony of social insects.

queer adj. Strange; unusual; different from the normal. *Slang* Homosexual.

quell v. To put down with force; to quiet; to pacify.

quench v. To extinguish or put out; to cool metal by thrusting into water; to drink to satisfy a thirst.

quer-u-lous adj. Complaining or fretting; expressing complaints.

que-ry n. An injury; a question. v. To question.

quest n. A search; pursuit; an expedition to find something.

ques-tion n. An expression of inquiry which requires an answer; a problem; an unresolved matter; the act of inquiring or asking.

ques-tion mark n. A mark of punctuation, (?), used in writing to indicate a question.

ques-tion-naire n. A written series of questions to gather statistical information often used for a survey.

queue n., *Computer Science* A sequence of stored programs or data on hold for processing.

quib-ble v. To raise trivial objection. **quibble, quibbler** n.

quiche n. Unsweetened custard baked in a pastry shell, usually with vegetables or seafood.

quick adj. Moving swiftly; occurring in a short time; responding, thinking, or understanding something rapidly and easily. **quickly** adv., **quickness** n.

quick-sand n. A bog of very fine, wet sand of considerable depth, that engulfs and sucks down objects, people, or animals.

quid n. A small portion of tobacco; a cow's cud.

qui-es-cent adj. Being in a state of quiet repose.

qui-et adj. Silent; making very little sound; still; tranquil; calm. v. To become or make quiet. n. The state of being quiet.

quill n.

A strong bird feather; a spine from a porcupine; a writing instrument made from a long stiff feather.

quilt n. A bed coverlet made of two layers of cloth with a soft substance between and held in place by lines of stitching.

qui-nine n., *Chem.* A very bitter, colorless, crystalline powder used in the treatment of malaria.

quin-sy n., *Pathol.* A severe inflammation of the tonsils, which is accompanied by fever.

quin-tes-sence n. The most essential and purest form of anything.

quin-tet n. A musical composition written for five people; any group of five.

quin-til-lion n. A thousand quadrillions, one followed by eighteen zeros.

quin-tu-ple adj. Increased five times; multiplied by five; consisting of five parts.

quip n. A sarcastic remark. **quipster** n.

quirk n. A sudden, sharp bend or twist; a personal mannerism.

quis-ling n. A person who is a traitor, working against his own country from within.

quit v. To cease; to give up; to depart; to abandon; to resign or leave a job or position.

quite adv. To the fullest degree; really; actually; to a great extent.

quiv-er v. To shake with a trembling motion. n. The arrows used in archery; the case in which arrows are kept.

quix-ot-ic adj. Extravagantly romantic; impractical.

quiz v. To question, as with an informal oral or written examination. **quiz, quizzer** n.

quiz-zi-cal adj. Being odd; teasing; questioning.

quod n. *Slang* For a jail.

quoit n. A game in which a metal ring connected to a rope is thrown in an attempt to encircle a stake.

quon-dam adj. Former.

quo-rum n. The number of members needed in order to validate a meeting.

quot-a-ble adj. To be suitable for being quoted.

quo-ta-tion n. The exact quoting of words as a passage; the stated current price.

quo-ta-tion mark n. The marks of punctuation (" ") showing a direct quote.

quote v. To repeat exactly what someone else has previously stated.

quo-tid-i-an adj. Occurring or recurring daily.

quo-tient n., *Math* The amount or number which results when one number is divided by another.

R, r The eighteenth letter of the English alphabet.

rab-bet n. A recess or groove along the edge of a piece of wood cut to fit another piece to form a joint. -ed v.

rab-bi n. An ordained leader of Jews; the leader and teacher of a Jewish congregation. **rabbinic** adj.

rab-bin-i-cal adj. To be referring or pertaining to the rabbis. **rabbinically** adv.

rab-bit n.

A burrowing mammal related to but smaller than the hare.

rab-ble n. A disorderly crowd. -ing, -ed v.

rab-id adj. Affected with rabies; mad; furious. **rabidly** adv. **rabidness** n.

ra-bies n. An acute, infectious viral disease of the central nervous system, often fatal, which is transmitted by the bite of an infected animal.

rac-coon n., pl. **-coons, -coon**

A nocturnal mammal with a black, masklike face and a black-and-white ringed, bushy tail.

race n. The zoological division of the human population having common origin and other physical traits, such as hair form and pigmentation; a group of people having such common characteristics or appearances; people united by a common nationality.

race n. A contest which is judged by speed; any contest, such as a race for an elective office. **raced, racer** n.

ra-ceme n. A type of plant bearing flowers along its stalk.

ra-chis n. A type of axial structure.

ra-cial adj. A characteristic of a race of people.

rac-ism n. A thought or belief that one race is better than another race. -ist n.

rack n. An open framework or stand for displaying or holding something; an instrument of torture used to stretch the body; a triangular frame used to arrange the balls on a pool table. Mech. A metal bar with teeth designed to move a cogged bar and produce a rotary or linear motion. v. to strain, as with great effort in thinking.

rack-et or **racquet** n. A light-weight batlike object with netting stretched over an oval frame, used in striking a tennis ball or a shuttlecock.

rack-et-eer n. A person who engages in acts which are illegal.

rac-on-teur n. One who is skilled in the act of telling stories.

rac-y adj. Having a spirited or strongly marked quality; slightly improper or immodest. **racily** adv., **raciness** n.

ra-dar n. A system which uses radio signals to detect the presence of an object or the speed the object is traveling.

ra-dar as-tron-o-my n. Astronomy that deals with investigations of the celestial bodies of the solar system by comparing characteristics of reflected radar wave with characteristics of ones transmitted from earth.

ra-dar-scope n. A screen or oscilloscope that serves as a visual indicator in a radar receiver.

rad-dled adj. To be in a state of confusion; broken down; worn; lacking composure.

ra-di-al adj. Pertaining to or resembling a ray or radius; developing from a center axis.

ra-di-ance n. The quality of being shiny; the state of being radiant; relating or emitting to radiant heat.

ra-di-ant adj. Emitting rays of heat or light; beaming with kindness or love; projecting a strong quality. -ly adv.

ra-di-ant heat n. Heat that is transmitted by radiation.

ra-di-ate v. To move out in rays, such as heat moving through the air. -ly adv.

ra-di-a-tion n. An act of radiating; the process or action of radiating; the process of emitting radiant energy in the form of particles or waves. **radiationless** adj., **radiative** adj.

ra-di-a-tor n. Something which radiates.

rad-i-cal adj. Proceeding from a foundation or root; drastic; making extreme changes in views, conditions, or habits; carrying convictions or theories to their fullest application. **radically** adv., **radicalness** n.

ra-di-o n. The technique of communicating by radio waves; the business of broadcasting programmed material to the public via radio waves. **radioing, radioed** v.

ra-di-o-ac-tive adj. Exhibiting radioactivity. **radioactively** adv.

ra-di-o-ac-tiv-i-ty n., Physics A spontaneous emission of electromagnetic radiation, as from a nuclear reaction.

ra-di-o-fre-quen-cy n. A frequency which is above 15,000 cycles per second that is used in radio transmission.

ra-di-o-gram n. A type of radiograph.

ra-di-ol-o-gy n. A science which deals with rays for a radioactive substance and use for medical diagnosis. -ist n.

ra-di-um n A radioactive metallic element symbolized by Ra.

ra-di-us n., pl. **-dii** or **-uses**

A line from the center of a circle to its sur face or circumference.

ra-don n. A heavy, colorless, radioactive gaseous element symbolized by Rn.

raf-fi-a n. A fiber from an African palm tree used for making baskets, hats, and other woven articles.

raff-ish adj. Something that is marked by crudeness or flashy vulgarity. **raffishly** adv., **raffishness** n.

raf-fle n. A game of chance; a lottery in

which one buys chances to win something.

raft *n.* A floating structure made from logs or planks and used for water transportation.

raft-er *n.* A timber of a roof which slopes.

rag *n.* A cloth which is useless and sometimes used for cleaning purposes.

rag-a-muf-fin *n.* A child who is unkempt.

rag-bag *n.* A miscellaneous grouping or collection; a bag for holding scrap pieces of material.

rag doll *n.* A child's doll that is usually made from scrap material and has a hand painted face.

rage *n.* Violent anger. **-ing** *adj.,* **-ly** *adv.*

rag-ged *adj.* To be torn or ripped. **raggedness** *n.,* **raggedly** *adv.*

rag-weed *n.* A type of plant whose pollen can cause hay fever.

raid *n.* A sudden invasion or seizure.

rail *n.* A horizontal bar of metal, wood, or other strong material supported at both ends or at intervals; the steel bars used to support a track on a railroad.

rail-ing *n.* A barrier of wood.

rain *n.* The condensed water from atmospheric vapor, which falls to earth in the form of drops.

rain-bow *n.* An arc that contains bands of colors of the spectrum and is formed opposite the sun and reflects the sun's rays, usually visible after a light rain shower.

rain check *n.* A coupon or stub for merchandise which is out of stock; the assurance of entrance or availability at a later date.

rain-coat *n.* A water-resistant or waterproof coat.

rain-fall *n.* The amount of measurable precipitation.

rain gauge *n.* An instrument used to measure rain fall.

rain-making *n.* The act or process of producing or attempting to produce rain by the use of artificial means.

raise *v.* To cause to move upward; to build; to make greater in size, price, or amount; to increase the status; to grow; as plants; to rear as children; to stir ones emotions; to obtain or collect as funds or money.

rai-sin *n.* A grape dried for eating.

rake *n.* A tool with a long handle at the end and a set of teeth at the other end used to gather leaves and other matter; a slope or incline, as the rake of an auditorium. **rake** *v.*

ral-ly *v.* To call together for a purpose. *n.* A rapid recovery, as from depression, exhaustion, or any setback; in a meeting whose purpose is to rouse or create support.

ram *n.* A male sheep; an implement used to drive or crush by impact; to cram or force into place.

RAM *abbr.* Random access memory.

ram-ble *v.* To stroll or walk without a special destination in mind; to talk without sequence of ideas. **ramble** *n.,* **ramblingly** *adv.*

ram-bunc-tious *adj.* Rough or boisterous. **rambunctiousness** *n.*

ramp *n.* An incline which connects two different levels; movable staircase allows passengers to enter or leave an aircraft.

ram-page *n.* A course of destruction or violent behavior. *v.* To storm about in a rampage. **rampageous** *adj.,* **rampageously** *adv.,* **rampageousness** *n.*

ram-pan-cy *n.* The state or quality of being rampant.

ram-pant *adj.* Exceeding or growing without control; wild in actions; standing on the hind legs and elevating both forelegs. **rampantly** *adv.*

ram-rod *n.* A metal rod used to drive or plunge the charge into a muzzle-loading gun or pistol; the rod used for cleaning the barrels of a rifle or other firearm.

ram-shack-le *adj.* Likely to fall apart from poor construction or maintenance.

ranch *n.* A large establishment for raising cattle, sheep, or other livestock; a large farm that specializes in a certain crop or animals. **rancher** *n.*

ran-cid *adj.* Having a rank taste or smell. **rancidness** *n.*

ran-dom *adj.* Done or made in a way that has no specific pattern or purpose; to select from a group whose members all had an even chance of being chosen.

rang *v.* Past tense of ring.

range *n.* An area over which anything moves; an area of activity; a tract of land over which animals such as cattle and horses graze; an extended line or row especially of mountains; an open area for shooting at a target; large cooking stove with burners and oven. *v.* to arrange in a certain order; to extend or proceed in a particular direction.

range finder *n.* Instrument that is used in gunnery to determine the distance of a target.

rank *n.* A degree of official position or status. *v.* To place in order, class, or rank. *adj.* A strong and disagreeable odor, smell, or taste.

ran-sack *v.* To search or plunder through every part of something.

ran-som *n.* The price demanded or paid for the release of a kidnaped person; the payment for the release of a person or property detained. **ransom** *v.*

rant *v.* To talk in a wild, loud way.

ra-pa-cious *adj.* Living on prey seized alive; taking by force; plundering. **rapaciously** *adv.,* **-ness, rapacity** *n.*

rape *n.* The crime of forcible sexual intercourse; abusive treatment.

rap-id *adj.* Having great speed; completed quickly or in a short time. **rapidity, rapidness** *n.*

ra-pi-er *n.* A long, slender, straight sword with two edges.

rap-ine *n.* The forcible taking of another's property.

rap-port *n.* A harmonious relationship.

rapt *adj.* Deeply absorbed or carried away with something and not to noticing anything else; engrossed.
raptness *n.*, raptly *adv.*

rare *adj.* Scarce; infrequent; often held in high esteem or admiration because of infrequency. rareness *n.*

ras-cal *n.* A person full of mischief; a person who is not honest. rascally *adj.*

rash *adj.* Acting without consideration or caution. *n.* A skin irritation or eruption caused by an allergic reaction.

rasp *n.*

A file with course raised and pointed projections. *v.* To scrape or rub with a course file; to utter something in a rough, grating voice.
rasper *n.*, raspy *adj.*

rasp-berry *n.* A small edible fruit, red or black in color and having many small seeds. *Slang* Contemptuous sound made by expelling air with the tongue between the lips in order to make a vibration.

raspy *adj.* Grating; irritable.

rat *n.*

A rodent similar to the mouse, but having a longer tail.
Slang A despicable person who betrays his friends or associates.

rat-a-tat *n.* A sharp tapping, or repeated knocking.

ratch-et *n.* A mechanism consisting of a pawl that allows a wheel or bar to move in one direction only.

ratch-et wheel *n.* A wheel with teeth that is held place with a engaging handle.

rate *n.* The measure of something to a fixed unit; the degree of price or value; a fixed ratio or amount. *v.* To appraise.

rath-er *adv.* Preferably; with more reason or justice; more accurate or precise.

rat-i-fy *v.* To approve something in an official way. ratification *n.*

rat-ing *n.* A relative evaluation or estimate of something.

ra-tio *n.*, *pl.* -tios The relationship between two things in amount, size, degree, expressed as a proportion.

ra-tion *n.* A fixed portion or share. *v.* To provide or allot in rations. rationing *n.*

ra-tio-nal *adj.* Having the faculty of reasoning; being of sound mind.
-ity *n.*, rationally *adv.*, rationalness *n.*

rat-tan *n.* An Asian palm whose strong stems are used to make wickerworks.

rat-tle *v.* To make a series of rapid, sharp noises in quick succession; to talk rapidly; chatter. *n.* A baby's toy made to rattle when shaken.

rat-tler *n.*, *Slang* A venomous snake which has a series of horny, modified joints which make a rattling sound when moved; a rattlesnake; one that rattle.

rat-tle-trap *n.* Something that is rickety or rattly.

rau-cous *adj.* Loud and rowdy; having a rough hoarse sound; disorderly.
raucously *adv.*, raucousness *n.*

rav-age *v.* To bring on heavy destruction; devastate.

rave *v.* To speak incoherently; to speak with enthusiasm. *n.* The act of raving.

rav-el *v.* To separate fibers or threads; to unravel. ravelment *n.*

ra-ven *n.* A large bird, with shiny black feathers. *adj.* Of or relating to the glossy sheen or color of the raven.

ra-vine *n.* A deep gorge with steep sides in the earth's surface, usually created by flowing water.

rav-ish *v.* To seize and carry off; to rape. ravishment *n.*, ravisher *n.*

raw *adj.* Uncooked; in natural condition; not processed. inexperienced; damp, sharp, or chilly. rawly *adv.*, rawness *n.*

ray *n.* A thin line of radiation or light; a small trace or amount; one of several lines coming from a point.

ray-on *n.* A synthetic cellulose yarn; any fabric made from such yarn.

ra-zor *n.* A sharp cutting instrument used especially for shaving.

ra-zor-back *n.* A wild hog of the southeastern United States; the mascot of the University of Arkansas.

razz *v.*, *Slang* To heckle; to tease.

raz-zle--daz-zel *n.* A state of complete confusion.

re- *prefix* Again, anew or reverse action.

reach *v.* To stretch out; to be able to grasp. *n.* The act of stretching out.

re-act *v.* To act in response to. *Chem* To undergo a chemical change; to experience a chemical reaction.

re-ac-tor *n.* A person, object, device, or substance which reacts to something.

read *v.* To visually go over something, a book, and to understand its meaning; to learn or be informed; to perceive something in a meaning which may or may not actually be there.

read-y *adj.* Prepared for use or action; quick or prompt; willing.

Rea-gan, Ronald Wilson *n.* The 40th president of the United States in augurated in 1981.

re-a-gent *n* Any substance which cause a chemical reaction.

re-al *adj.* Something which is existing, genuine, true, or authentic. *La* Property which is regarded as permanent or immovable.

reel-to-reel *adj.* Pertaining to magnetic tape which is threaded to a take-up reel, which moves from one reel to another.

real estate *n.* Land and whatever is attached such as natural resources or buildings.

re-al-ism *n.* Concern or interest with actual facts and things as they really are realist *n.*, -tic *adj.*, realistically *adv.*

re-al-i-ty *n.*, *pl.* The fact or state of being real or genuine; an actual situation or event.

re-al-ize *v.* To understand correctly; to make real. realizable *adj.*, realization *n.*, realizer *n.*

re-al-ly *adv.* Actually; truly; indeed.

realm *n.* A scope or field of any power or influence.

ream *n.* A quantity of paper containing 500 sheets.

reap *v.* To harvest a crop with a sickle or other implement.

rear *n.* The back. *adj.* Of or at the rear. *v.* To raise up on the hind legs; to raise as an animal or child.

rea-son *n.* A statement given to confirm or justify a belief, promise, or excuse; the ability to decide things, to obtain ideas, to think clearly, and to make logical and rational choices and decisions. *v.* To discuss something logically. reasoning *n.*

rea-son-a-ble *adj.* Moderate; rational. reasonableness *n.*, reasonably *adv.*

re-a-sur-ance *n.* The act of reassuring; reinsurance.

re-bate *n.* A deduction allowed on items sold; a discount; money which is returned to the purchaser from the original payment. *v.* To return part of the payment. rebater *n.*

re-bel *v.* To refuse allegiance; to resist any authority; to react with violence.

re-bel-lion *n.* An organized uprising to change or overthrow an existing authority.

re-bel-lious *adj.* Engaged in rebellion; relating to a rebel or rebellion. rebelliously *adv.*, rebelliousness *n.*

re-birth *n.* A revival or renaissance; reincarnation.

re-bound *v.* To spring back; to recover from a setback or frustration. *n.* Recoil.

re-broad-cast *v.* To repeat or broadcast again. rebroadcast *n.*

re-buff *v.* To refuse abruptly; to snub.

re-build *v.* To make extensive repairs to something; to reconstruct; remodel.

re-buke *v.* To criticize something sharply; to turn back. rebuker *n.*

re-but *v.* To try and prove someone wrong by argument or evidence. rebuttal *n.*, rebutable *adj.*

re-call *v.* To order or summon to return to ask for something to be returned; so that defects can be fixed or repaired; to remember; to recollect.

re-cant *v.* To formally admit that a previously held belief was wrong by making public confession.

re-cap *v.* To restore an old tire; to review or summarize something.

re-cede *v.* To move back; as floodwater; to withdraw from an agreement.

re-ceipt *n.* The written acknowledgment of something received. *pl.*, receipts The amount of money received.

re-ceive *v.* To take or get something; to greet customers or guests; to accept as true or correct. receiver *n.*

re-cent *adj.* Happening at a time just before the present. recently *adv.*

re-cep-ta-cle *n.* Anything which holds something; an electrical outlet designed to receive a plug.

re-cep-tion *n.* The act or manner of receiving something; a formal entertainment of guests, as a wedding reception.

re-cep-tion-ist *n.* An employee who greets callers and answers the telephone for a business.

re-cep-tive *adj.* Able to receive. -ly *adv.*, receptiveness, receptivity *n.*

re-cess *n.* A break in the normal routine of something; a depression or niche in a smooth surface.

re-ces-sion *n.* The act of receding; withdrawal; a period or time of reduced economic activity. -ary *adj.*

rec-i-pe *n.* The directions and a list of ingredients for preparing food.

re-cip-ro-cate *v.* To give and return mutually, one gift or favor for another.

re-cite *v.* To repeat something from memory; give an account of something in detail.

reck-less *adj.* State of being careless and rash when doing something. -ness *n.*

reck-on *v.* To calculate; to compute; to estimate; to consider; to assume.

reck-on-ing *n.* The act of calculation or counting.

re-claim *v.* To redeem; to reform; to recall; to change to a more desirable condition or state.

rec-la-ma-tion *n.* The state of being reclaimed.

re-cline *v.* To assume a prone position. recliner *n.*

rec-luse *n.* A person who chooses to live in seclusion.

rec-og-ni-tion *n.* An acknowledgment which is formal.

re-cog-ni-zance *n.* An amount of money which will be forfeited for a nonperformance of an obligation.

rec-og-nize *v.* To experience or identify something or someone as having been known previously; to appreciative. recognizable *adj.*, recognizably *adv.*

re-coil *v.* To fall back or to rebound. recoilless *adj.*

rec-ol-lect *v.* To remember or recall to the mind. recollection *n.*

rec-om-mend *v.* To suggest to another as desirable; advise. recommendation *n.*, recommedable *adj.*

rec-om-pense *v.* To reward with something for a service.

rec-on-cile *v.* To restore a friendship after an estrangement. -ably *adv.*

rec-on-dite *adj.* Being obscure.

re-con-di-tion *v.* To return to a good condition.

re-con-firm *v.* Confirm something again.

re-con-nais-sance *n.* An observation of territory such as that of the enemy.

re-con-noi-ter *v.* To survey a region.

re-con-sid-er *v.* To think about again with a view to changing a previous action or decision. **reconsideration** *n.*

re-con-struct *v.* To build something again.

re-con-struc-tion *n.* Something which has been reconstructed or rebuilt.

re-cord *v.* To write down for future use or permanent reference; to preserve sound on a tape or disk for replay; a phonograph record. *n.* Information which is recorded and kept permanently.

re-cord-er *n.* A person who records things such as official transactions.

re-cord-ing *n.* The act of making a transcription of sounds.

rec-ord play-er *n.* The machine which is used to play recordings.

re-count *v.* To tell the facts; narrate or describe in detail; to count again. *n.* A second count to check the results of the first count.

re-coup *v.* To be reimbursed; to recover.

re-course *n.* A turning to or an appeal for help.

re-cov-er *v.* To regain something which was lost; to be restored to good health. *Law* To obtain a judgment for damages.

re-cov-er-y *n.* The power to regain something.

rec-re-ant *adj.* Cowardly; unfaithful. **recreant** *n.*

re-cre-ate *v.* To create again.

rec-re-a-tion *n.* Refreshment of body and mind; a pleasurable occupation or exercise. **recreational** *adj.*

re-crim-i-nate *v.* The charging of another of the same account. **-tory,** **recriminative** *adj.,* **recrimination** *n.*

re-cruit *v.* To enlist someone for military or naval purposes; to look for someone as for a service or employment. *n.* A newly enlisted person.

rec-tal *adj.* Referring to the rectum of the body.

rec-tan-gle *n.*

A parallelogram with all right angles. **rectangular** *adj.,* **rectangularity** *n.*

rec-ti-fi-er *n.* That which rectifies something.

rec-ti-fy *v.* To make correct. *Chem.* To purify by repeated distillations. *Electr.* To make an alternating current a direct current.

rec-ti-lin-e-ar *adj.* Made up of or indicated by straight lines; bounded by straight lines.

rec-ti-tude *n.* Rightness in principles and conduct; correctness.

rec-to *n.* The right-hand page of a book.

rec-tor *n.* A member of the clergy in charge of a parish; a priest in charge of a congregation, church, or parish; the principal or head of a school or of a college.

rec-tum *n., pl.* **-tums, -ta** *Anat.* The lower terminal portion of the large intestine connecting the colon and anus.

re-cum-bent *adj.* Lying down or reclin-

ing.

re-cu-per-ate *v.* To regain strength or to regain one's health; to recover from a financial loss.

recuperation *n.,* **recuperative** *adj.*

re-cur *v.* To happen, to return, or to appear again. **recurrence, recurrent** *adj.*

red *n.* Having the color which resembles blood, as pigment or dye which colors red. *Slang* A communist; one who is in favor of the overthrow of an existing political of social order; a condition indicating a loss, as in the red.

Red Cross *n.* An organization which helps people in need, collects and preserves human blood for use in emergencies, and responds with help in time of disaster.

re-deem *v.* To buy back; to pay off; to turn something in, as coupons or rain checks and receive something in exchange.

re-demp-tion *n.* The act of redeeming; rescue; ransom; that which redeems; salvation.

re-doubt *n.* A small enclosed fortification.

re-doubt-a-ble *adj.* To be dreaded. **redoubtably** *adv.*

re-dound *v.* To have an effect on something.

re-dress *v.* To put something right.

red snap-per *n.* A saltwater fish which is red in color and can be found in the Gulf of Mexico and near Florida.

red-start *n.* An American warbler which is brightly colored.

red tape *n.* Routines which are rigid and may cause a delay in a process.

re-duce *v.* To decrease; lessen in number, degree, or amount; to put into order; to lower in rank; to lose weight by dieting.

re-duc-tion *n.* The state of being reduced.

re-dun-dant *adj.* Exceeding what is necessary; repetitive.

re-du-pli-cate *v.* To repeat something. **reduplication** *n.*

red-wood *n.* A tree found in California which is very tall and wide.

re-ech-o *v.* To reverberate again.

reed *n.* Tall grass with a slender stem, which grows in wet areas; a thin tongue of wood, metal, cane, or plastic; placed in the mouthpiece of an instrument to produce sounds by vibrating. **reediness** *n.,* **reedy** *adj.*

reef *n.* A chain of rocks, coral, or sand at or near the surface of the water.

reef-er *n.* A jacket which is close-fitting.

reek *v.* To emit vapor or smoke; to give off a strong offensive odor.

reel *n.* A device which revolves on an axis and is used for winding up or letting out fishing line, rope, or other string-like material; a lively and fast dance.

re-e-lect *v.* The act of electing someone again for an office.

re-em-pha-size *v.* To stress something or an idea again.

re-en-list v. To enlist or join a group or an armed force again. **reenlistment** n.

re-enter v. To enter a room or area again.

re-ex-am-ine v. Examine something or someone another time or again. **reexamination** n.

re-fec-to-ry n. The place in colleges where the students dine.

re-fer v. To direct for treatment, information, or help.

ref-er-ee n. A person who supervises a game, making sure all the rules are followed.

ref-er-ence n. The act of referring someone to someplace or to something.

ref-er-en-dum n. A public vote on an item for final approval or for rejection.

ref-er-ent n. What is referred to such as a person.

re-fill v. To fill something with an item again.

re-fine v. To purify by removing unwanted substances or material; to improve. **refined** adj., **refinement** n.

re-fin-er-y n. A place or location which is used for the purpose of refining, such as sugar.

re-fin-ish v. The act of putting a new surface onto something, such as wood.

re-fit v. To repair something.

re-flect v. To throw back rays of light from a surface; to give an image, as from a mirror; to ponder or think carefully about something. **reflection** n. **reflective** adj.

re-flec-tor n. Something which is able to reflect things, such as light.

re-flex adj. Turning, casting, or bending backward. n. An involuntary reaction of the nervous system to a stimulus.

re-for-est v. The act of replanting a forest or wooded area with trees. **reforestation** n.

re-form v. To reconstruct, make over, or change something for the better; improve; to abandon or give up evil ways. **reformer** n., **reformed** adj.

re-for-ma-to-ry n. A jail-like institution for young criminals.

re-fract v. The deflecting something, such as a ray of light. **refractive** adj.

re-frac-tion n. The state of being refracted or deflected.

re-frac-to-ry adj. Unmanageable; obstinate; difficult to melt; resistant to heat. n. Something which does not change significantly when exposed to high temperatures.

re-frain v. To hold back.

re-fresh v. To freshen something again. **refreshing** adj.

re-fresh-ment n. Something which will refresh someone, such as a cold drink or snack.

re-frig-er-ant n. An agent which cools something.

re-frig-er-ate v. To chill or cool; to preserve food by chilling; to place in a refrigerator.

re-frig-er-a-tor n. A box-like piece of equipment which chills food and other matter.

re-fu-el v. To put fuel into something again.

ref-uge n. Shelter or protection from harm; any place one may turn for relief or help.

ref-u-gee n. A person who flees to find safety.

re-ful-gent adj. State of being radiant or putting off a bright light.

re-fund v. To return or pay back; to reimburse. **refundable** adj. **refund** n.

re-fur-bish v. To make clean; to renovate.

re-fus-al n. The denial of something which is demanded.

re-fuse v. To decline; to reject; to deny.

ref-use n. Rubbish; trash.

re-fute v. To overthrow or to disprove with the use of evidence.

re-gain v. To recover; to reach again.

re-gal adj. Of or appropriate for royalty. **regally** adv.

re-gale v. To entertain or delight; to give pleasure.

re-ga-li-a n. Something which represents royalty such as a septer.

re-gard v. To look upon closely; to consider; to have great affection for. n. Careful attention or thought; esteem or affection. **regards** Greetings of good wishes.

re-gard-ful adj. State of being mindful.

re-gard-less adj. State of being careless or showing no regard towards something or someone.

re-gat-ta n. A boat race.

re-gen-cy n., pl. **-ies** The jurisdiction or office of a regent.

re-gen-er-ate v. To reform spiritually or morally; to make or create anew; to refresh or restore.

re-gent n. One who rules and acts as a ruler during the absence of a sovereign, or when the ruler is underage.

re-gime n. An administration.

reg-i-men n. Government control; therapy.

reg-i-ment n. A military unit of ground troops which is composed of several battalions. **-al** adj., **regimentation** n.

re-gion n. An administrative, political, social, or geographical area.

re-gion-al adj. Typical or pertaining to a geographic region; limited to a particular region.

reg-is-ter n. Something which contains names or occurrences.

reg-is-trar n. The person who keeps a register.

reg-is-tra-tion n. An act of recording things or names.

re-gress v. To return to a previous state or condition. **regress, regression** n.

re-gret v. To feel disappointed or distressed about. n. A sense of loss or expression of grief; a feeling of sorrow. **regretfully, regretably** adv., **regretful, regretable** adj.

reg-u-lar *adj.* Usual; normal; customary; conforming to set principles, procedures, or discipline; well-ordered; not varying. **regularity** *n.*, **regularly** *adv.*

reg-u-late *v.* To adjust to a specification or requirement. **regulative, regulatory** *adj.*, **regulator** *n.*

reg-u-la-tion *n.* A rule that is set down in order to govern an area or people.

re-gur-gi-tate *v.* To pour something forth.

re-ha-bil-i-tate *v.* To restore; to a former state, by education and therapy. **rehabilitation** *n.*, **rehabilitative** *adj.*

re-hash *v.* To rework or go over old material.

re-hears-al *n.* The act of practicing for a performance. **rehearse** *v.*

reign *n.* The period in time when the monarch rules over an area.

re-im-burse *v.* To repay. **-ment** *n.*

rein *n.* One of a pair of narrow, leather straps attached to the bit of a bridle and used to control a horse.

rein-deer *n.* A large deer found in northern regions, both sexes having antlers.

re-in-force *v.* To support; to strengthen with additional people or equipment. **reinforcement** *n.*

re-in-state *v.* To restore something to its former position or condition. **-ment** *n.*

re-it-er-ate *v.* To say or do something over and over again.

re-ject *v.* To refuse; to discard as useless. **reject, rejection** *n.*

re-joice *v.* To fill with joy; to be filled with joy.

re-join *v.* To respond or to answer someone.

re-join-der *n.* The answer to a reply made by someone to another.

re-ju-ve-nate *v.* To restore to youthful appearance or vigor. **rejuvenation** *n.*

re-kin-dle *v.* To inflame something again.

re-lapse *v.* To fall back or revert to an earlier condition. **relapse** *n.*

re-late *v.* To tell the events of; to narrate; to bring into natural association.

re-lat-ed *adj.* To be in the same family; connected to each other by blood or by marriage.

re-la-tion *n.* The relationship between people by marriage or blood lines. **relational** *adj.*

re-la-tion-ship *n.* A connection by blood or family; kinship; friendship; a natural association.

rel-a-tive *adj.* Relevant; connected; considered in comparison or relationship to other. *n.* A member of one's family.

rel-a-tiv-i-ty *n.* A condition or state of being relative.

re-lax *v.* To make loose or lax; to relieve something from effort or strain; to become less formal or less reserved. **relaxation** *n.*, **relaxedly** *adv.*

re-lay *n.* A race in which a fresh team replaces another. *v.* To pass from one group to another.

re-lease *v.* To set free from confinement; to unfasten; to free; to relinquish a claim on something. **releaser** *n.*

rel-e-gate *v.* To banish someone or something.

re-lent *v.* To soften in temper, attitude, or determination; to slacken. **relentless** *adj.*

rel-e-vant *adj.* Related to matters at hand.

re-li-a-ble *adj.* Dependable; capable of being relied upon.

re-li-ance *n.* Confidence and trust; something which is relied upon.

re-li-ant *adj.* State of being confident or having reliance.

re-lic *n.* Something which is very old; a keepsake; an object whose cultural environment has disappeared.

re-lief *n.* Anything which decreases or lessens anxiety, pain, discomfort, or other unpleasant conditions or feelings.

re-lief map *n.* A map which outlines the contours of the land.

re-lieve *v.* To lessen or ease pain, anxiety, embarrassment, or other problems; to release or free from a duty by providing a replacement. **reliever** *n.*, **relievable** *adj.*

re-lig-ion *n.* An organized system of beliefs, rites, and celebrations centered on a supernatural being power; belief pursued with devotion **-ious** *adj.*

re-lin-quish *v.* To release something or someone.

re-lish *n.* Pleasure; a spicy condiment taken with food to lend it flavor.

re-live *v.* To experience something again.

re-lo-cate *v.* To move to another area. **relocation** *n.*

re-luc-tance *n.* An unwillingness.

re-luc-tant *adj.* Unwilling; not yielding.

re-ly *v.* To trust or depend.

re-main *v.* To continue without change; to stay after the departure of others.

remainder *n.* Something left over. *Math* The difference which remains after division or subtraction.

re-mains *pl.*, *n.* What is left after all other parts have been taken away; corpse.

re-mand *n.* State of being remanded.

re-mark *n.* A brief expression or comment; to take notice; to observe; to comment.

re-mark-a-ble *adj.* Extraordinary. **remarkably** *adv.*

re-me-di-a-ble *adj.* Being able to be remedied.

rem-e-dy *n.*, *pl.* **-ies** A therapy or medicine which relieves pain; something which corrects an error or fault. *v.* To cure or relieve. To rectify.

re-mem-ber *v.* To bring back or recall to the mind; to retain in the mind carefully; to keep a person in one's thought; to recall a person to another as a means of greetings.

re-mem-brance *n.* Something which is remembered by someone.

re-mind *v.* To cause or help to remember.

rem-i-nisce *v.* To recall the past things which have happened.

rem-i-nis-cence *n.* The practice or process of recalling the past. **reminiscent** *adj.*

re-miss *adj.* Lax in performing one's duties; negligent. **remissness** *n.*

re-mis-sion *n.* A forgiveness; act of remitting.

re-mit *v.* To send money as payment for goods; to forgive, as a crime or sin; to slacken, make less violent, or less intense. **remittance** *n.*

rem-nant *n.* A small piece or a scrap or something.

re-mod-el *v.* To reconstruct something making it like new.

re-mon-strance *n.* Statement of reasons against an idea or something.

re-mon-strate *v.* Giving strong reasons against an act or an idea.

re-morse *n.* Deep moral regret for past misdeeds. **remorseful** *adj.*

re-mote *adj.* Distant in time; space or relation. **remotely** *adv.,* **remoteness** *n.*

re-mount *v.* To mount something again.

re-mov-a-ble *adj.* Being able to be removed.

re-mov-al *n.* The change of a site or place.

re-move *v.* To get rid of; to extract; to dismiss from office; to change one's business or residence. An act of moving. **removable** *adj.,* **removal** *n.*

re-moved *adj.* State of being separate from others.

re-mu-ner-ate *v.* Pay an equivalent for a service.

ren-ais-sance *n.* A revival or rebirth; the humanistic revival of classical art, literature, and learning in Europe which occurred during the 14th through the 16th centuries.

re-nal *adj.* Of or relating to the kidneys.

re-nas-cence *n.* A revival or a rebirth.

rend *v.* To remove from with violence; to split.

ren-der *v.* To give or make something available; to submit or give; to represent artistically; to liquefy or melt fat by means of heat. **rendering** *n.*

ren-dez-vous *n.* A meeting place that has been prearranged. *v.* To meet at a particular time and place.

ren-di-tion *n.* An interpretation or a translation.

ren-e-gade *n.* A person who rejects one allegiance for another; an outlaw; a traitor. **renegade** *adj.*

re-nege *v.* To fail to keep one's word.

re-new *v.* To make new or nearly new by restoring; to resume. **renewable** *adj.,* **renewal** *n.*

ren-net *n.* An extract taken from a calf's stomach and used to curdle milk for making cheese.

re-nounce *v.* To reject something or someone.

ren-o-vate *v.* To return or to restore to a good condition.

re-nown *n.* The quality of being widely honored. **renowned** *adj.*

rent *n.* The payment made for the use of another's property. *v.* To obtain occupancy in exchange for payment. **rental** *n.*

re-nun-ci-a-tion *n.* Renouncing.

re-or-gan-i-za-tion *n.* The process of reorganizing something.

rep. *n., Slang* Representative. *v.* Represent.

re-pair *v.* To restore to good or usable condition; to renew; refresh. **repairable** *adj.*

re-pair-man *n.* The person who makes repairs of things that are broken.

rep-a-ra-ble *adj.* Being able to be corrected.

rep-a-ra-tion *n.* The act of repairing something.

rep-ar-tee *n.* A quick, witty response or reply.

re-pa-tri-ate *v.* To go back to one's own country.

re-pay *v.* To pay back money; to do something in return.

re-peal *v.* To withdraw officially. **repeal** *n.,* **repealer** *n.*

re-peat *v.* To utter something again; to do an action again.

re-pel *v.* To discourage; to force away; to create aversion.

re-pel-lent *adj.* Able to repel.

re-pent *v.* To feel regret for something which has occurred; to change one's sinful way. **-ance** *n.,* **repentant** *adj.*

re-per-cus-sion *n.* An unforeseen effect produced by an action. **-ive** *adj.*

rep-er-toire *n.* The accomplishments or skills of a person.

rep-er-to-ry *n.* A collection of things.

rep-e-ti-tion *n.* The act of doing something over and over again; the act of repeating.

re-place *v.* To return something to its previous place. **replaceable** *adj.,* **replacement** *n.,* **replacer** *n.*

re-plen-ish *v.* To add to something to replace what has gone or been used.

re-plete *adj.* Having plenty; abounding; full.

rep-li-ca *n.* A reproduction or copy of something. **replicate** *v.*

re-ply *v.* To give an answer to either verbally or in writing. **reply** *n.*

re-port *n.* A detailed account; usually in a formal way. *v.* To tell about; to make oneself available; to give details of. **reportable** *adj.,* **reporter** *n.*

re-port-ed-ly *adv.* To be according to a report.

re-pose *n.* The act of being at rest. *v.* To lie at rest. **reposeful** *adj.*

re-pos-i-tor-y *n.* The location where things may be placed for preservation.

re-pos-sess *v.* To restore ownership of something.

rep-re-hend *v.* To show or express disapproval of. **reprehension** *n.,* **-sible** *adj.*

rep-re-sent *v.* To stand for something; to serve as the official representative for.

rep-re-sen-ta-tion *n.* The act of representing.

rep-re-sent-a-tive *n.* A person or thing

serving as an example or type. *adj.* Of or relating to government by representation; typical.

re-press *v.* To restrain; hold back; to remove from the conscious mind. repression *n.*, repressive *adj.*

re-prieve *v.* To postpone punishment; to provide temporary relief. -able *adj.*, reprieve *n.*, reprieve, reprieving *v.*

rep-ri-mand *v.* To censure severely; rebuke. reprimand *n.*

re-print *n.* An additional printing of a book exactly as the previous one. reprint *v.*, reprinter *n.*

re-pri-sal *n.* Retaliation with intent to inflect injury in return for injury received.

re-proach *v.* To blame; to rebuke. reproachful *adj.*

rep-ro-bate *adj.* The state of being morally depraved.

re-pro-duce *v.* To produce an image or copy. *Biol.* To produce an offspring; to recreate or produce again. -er *n.*, reproducible *adj.*, reproduction *n.*

re-proof *n.* A censure.

re-prove *v.* To tell or express a disapproval of something.

rep-tile *n.*

A cold-blooded, egg-laying vertebrate, as a snake, lizard, or turtle. reptilian *n.*, *adj.*

re-pub-lic *n.* A political unit or state where representatives are elected to exercise the power.

re-pub-li-can *adj.* Having the character of a republic.

re-pub-li-can-ism *n.* The Republican principles.

Republican Party *n.* One of the two political parties in the United States.

re-pu-di-ate *v.* To cast away; to refuse to pay something.

re-pug-nance *n.* The state or condition of being opposed.

re-pug-nant *adj.* Distasteful; repulsive; offensive.

re-pulse *v.* To repel or drive back; to repel or reject rudely; to disgust or be disgusted. repulsion *n.*

re-pul-sive *adj.* State of causing aversion.

rep-u-ta-ble *adj.* To be honorable. reputability *n.*

re-put-a-tion *n.* The commonly held evaluation of a person's character.

re-pute *v.* To account or to consider something.

re-quest *v.* To ask for something.

re-qui-em *n.* The Roman Catholic mass for a deceased person.

re-quire *v.* To demand or insist upon. requirement *n.*

req-ui-site *adj.* Absolutely needed; necessary.

req-ui-si-tion *n.* A demand or a request.

re-quit-al *n.* The act of requiting something.

re-quite *v.* To reward; to repay someone.

re-run *n.* A television show which is shown again.

re-sale *n.* The act of selling something again.

re-scind *v.* To repeal; to void. rescindable *adj.*, rescission *n.*

res-cue *v.* To free from danger. *n.* An act of deliverance. rescuer *n.*

re-search *n.* A scientific or scholarly investigation; to carefully seek out. researcher *n.*

re-sem-ble *v.* To have similarity to something. resemblance *n.*

re-sent *v.* To feel angry about. -ful *adj.*, resentfully *adv.*, resentment *n.*

res-er-va-tion *n.* The act of keeping something back.

re-serve *v.* To save for a special reason; to set apart; to retain; to put off. *n.* Something that is saved for a future point in time; the portion of a country's fighting force kept inactive until called upon.

res-er-voir *n.* A body of water stored for the future; large reserve; a supply.

re-side *v.* To dwell permanently; to exist as a quality or attribute. residence *n.*

res-i-due *n.* Matter remaining after treatment or removal of a part; something which remains.

re-sign *v.* To give up; to submit to something as being unavoidable; to quit. resignation *n.*

res-in *n.* A plant substance from certain plants and trees used in varnishes and lacquers. resinous *adj.*

re-sist *v.* To work against or actively oppose; to withstand. resistible *adj.*

res-o-lute *adj.* Coming from or characterized by determination. resolutely *adv.*, resolution *n.*

re-solve *v.* To make a firm decision on something; to find a solution. resolvable *adj.*, resolver *n.*, -tion *n.*

re-sort *v.* To go frequently or customarily. *n.* A place, or recreation, for rest, and for a vacation.

re-sound *v.* To be filled with echoing sounds; to reverberate; to ring or sound loudly. resounding *adj.*, resoundingly *adv.*

re-source *n.* A source of aid or support which can be drawn upon if needed. resources One's available capital or assets. resourceful *adj.*

re-spect *v.* To show consideration or esteem for; to relate to. *n.* Courtesy or considerate treatment. respectfully *adv.* respectful *adj.*

res-pi-ra-tion *n.* The process or act of inhaling and exhaling; the act of breathing; the process in which an animal or person takes in oxygen from the air and releases carbon dioxide. respirator *n.*

res-pite *n.* A temporary postponement.

re-spond *v.* To answer or reply; to act when promted by something or someone.

re-sponse *n.* A reply; the act of replying. responsive *adj.*

re-spon-si-ble *adj.* Trustworthy; in

charge; having authority; being answerable for one's actions or the actions of others. **responsibility** *n.*

rest *n.* A cessation of all work, activity, or motion. *Mus.* An interval of silence equal in time to a note of same value. *v.* To stop work; to place or lay. **restful** *adj.*, **restfully** *adv.*

res-tau-rant *n.* A place which serves meals to the public.

res-ti-tu-tion *n.* The act of restoring something to its rightful owner; compensation for injury, loss, or damage.

res-tive *adj.* Nervous or impatient because of a delay. **restively** *adv.*, **restiveness** *n.*

re-store *v.* To bring back to a former condition; to make restitution of. **restoration** *n.*

re-strain *v.* To hold back or be held back; to control, limit, or restrict. **restraint** *n.*

re-strict *v.* To confine within limits. **restriction** *n.*, **restrictive** *adj.*, **restrictively** *adv.*

re-sult *v.* To happen or exist in a particular way. *n.* The consequence of an action, course, or operation.

re-sume *v.* To start again after an interruption. **resumption** *n.*

res-u-me *n.* A summary of one's personal history, background, work, and education.

re-sus-ci-ate *v.* To return to life; to revive. **resuscitation** *n.*, **resuscitator** *n.*

re-tail *v.* The sale of goods or commodities to the public. To sell to the consumer. **retail** *adj.*, **retailer** *n.*

re-tain *v.* To hold in one's possession; to remember; to employ someone, as for his services.

re-tain-er *n.* A person or thing that retains; a fee paid for one's services.

re-tard *v.* To delay or slow the progress of. **retardant** *n. & adj.*

re-tar-da-tion *n.* A condition in which mental development is slow or delayed; a condition of mental slowness.

re-ten-tion *n.* The act or condition of being retained.

ret-i-na *n., pl.* **-nas,- nae** The light sensitive membrane lining the inner eyeball connected by the optic nerve to the brain. **retinal** *adj.*

re-tire *v.* To depart for rest; to remove oneself from the daily routine of working. *Baseball* To put a batter out. **retirement** *n.*, **retired** *adj.*, **retiree** *n.*

re-trace *v.* To go back over.

re-tract *v.* To draw back or to take back something that has been said. **retractable** *adj.*, **retraction** *n.*

re-tread *v.* To replace the tread of a worn tire. **retread** *n.*

re-treat *n.* The act of withdrawing from danger; a time of study; prayer; and meditation in a quiet; isolated location.

re-trieve *v.* To regain; to find something and carry it back. **retrievable** *adj.*, **retrieval** *n.*

ret-ro-ac-tive *adj.* Taking effect on a date prior to enactment.

ret-ro-spect *n.* A review of things in the past. **-ively** *adv.*, **retrospective** *adj.*

re-turn *v.* To come back to an earlier condition; to reciprocate. *n.* The act of sending, bringing, or coming back. **returns** *n.* A yield or profit from investments; a report on the results of an election. **returnable** *adj.*, **returnee** *n.*, **returner** *n.*

re-un-ion *n.* A reuniting; the coming together of a group which has been separated for a period of time.

re-veal *v.* To disclose or make known; to expose or bring into view.

rev-eil-le *n.* The sounding of a bugle used to awaken soldiers in the morning.

rev-el *v.* To take great delight in. **-er** *n.*

rev-e-la-tion *n.* An act of or something revealed; a manifestation of divine truth. **Revelation** The last book in the New Testament.

re-venge *v.* To impose injury in return for injury received. **revengeful** *adj.*, **revenger** *n.*

re-verse *adj.* Turned backward in position. *n.* The opposite of something; a change in fortune usually from better to worse; change or turn to the opposite direction; to transpose or exchange the positions of. *Law* To revoke a decision. **reverser** *n.*

re-vert *v.* To return to a former practice or belief. **reversion** *n.*

re-view *v.* To study or look over something again; to give a report on. *n.* A reexamination; a study which gives a critical estimate of something. **reviewer** *n.*

re-vise *v.* To look over something again with the intention of improving or correcting it. **reviser** *n.*, **revision** *n.*

re-viv-al *n.* The act or condition or reviving; the return of a film or play which was formerly presented; a meeting whose purpose is religious reawakening.

re-vive *v.* To restore, refresh, or recall; to return to consciousness or life.

re-voke *v.* To nullify or make void by recalling. **revocation** *n.*

re-volt *n.* To try to overthrow authority; to fill with disgust.

rev-o-lu-tion *n.* The act or state of orbital motion around a point; the abrupt overthrow of a government; a sudden change in a system.

re-volve *v.* To move around a central point; to spin; to rotate. **-able** *adj.*

re-vue *n.* A musical show consisting of songs, dances, skits, and other similar entertainment.

re-ward *n.* Something given for a special service. *v.* To give a reward.

R.F.D. *abbr.* Rural free delivery.

rhap-so-dy *n., pl.* **-ies** An excessive display of enthusiasm.

rhe-ni-um *n.* A metallic element symbolized by Re.

rhet-o-ric *n.* Effective expression in writing or speech; language which is not sincere.

Rh fac-tor *n.* A substance found in the red blood cells of 85% of all humans; the presence of this factor is referred to as PH positive; the absence as PH negative.

rhi-noc-er-os *n.*

A very large mammal with one or two upright horns on the snout.

Rhode Is-land *n.* A state located in the northeastern part of the United States.

rho-di-um *n.* A metallic element symbolized by Rh.

rhu-barb *n.* A garden plant with large leaves and edible stalks used for pies.

rhyme *or* **rime** *n.* A word or verse whose terminal sound corresponds with another. rhyme *v.*, rhymer *n.*

rhy-thm *n.* Music, speech, or movements which are characterized by equal or regularly alternating beats. rhythmical, rhythmic *adj.* -ly *adv.*

rib *n.* One of a series of curved bones enclosed in the chest of man and animals. *Slang* To tease.

rib-bon *n.* A narrow band or strip of fabric, such as satin, used for trimming.

rice *n.* A cereal grass grown extensively in warm climates.

rich *adj.* Having great wealth; of great value; satisfying and pleasing in voice, color, tone, or other qualities; extremely productive; as soil or land.

rick-ets *n.*, *Pathol.* A disease occurring in early childhood resulting from a lack of vitamin D and insufficient sunlight, characterized by defective bone growth and deformity.

rid *v.* To make free from anything objectionable.

rid-dle *v.* To perforate with numerous holes. *n.* A puzzling problem or question which requires a clever solution.

ride *v.* To travel in a vehicle or on an animal; to sit on and drive, as a motorcycle.

rid-er *n.* One who rides as a passenger; a clause, usually having little relevance, which is added to a document.

ridge *n.* A long, narrow crest; a horizontal line formed where two sloping surfaces meet. ridge *v.*

rid-i-cule *n.* Actions or words intended to make a person or thing the object of mockery.

ri-dic-u-lous *adj.* To be causing derision or ridicule.

rife *adj.* State of being abundant or abounding.

rif-fle *n.* Ripply water which is caused by a ridge.

riff-raff *n.* The rabble; low persons in society.

ri-fle *n.* A firearm having a grooved bore designed to be fired from the shoulder.

ri-fling *n.* The act of putting or cutting spiral grooves in the barrel of a gun.

rift *n.* A fault; disagreement; a lack of harmony.

rig *v.* To outfit with necessary equipment. *n.* The arrangement of sails, masts, and other equipment on a ship; the apparatus used for drilling water or oil wells.

right *adj.* In accordance with or conformable to law, justice, or morality; proper and fitting; properly adjusted, disposed, or placed; orderly; sound in body or mind. *n.* The right side, hand, or direction; the direction opposite left. *adv.* Immediately; completely; according to justice, morality, or law. rightness *n.*

right an-gle *n.*, *Geom.*

An angle of 90 degrees; an angle with two sides perpendicular to each other.

rig-id *adj.* Not bending; inflexible; severe; stern. rigidity, rigidness *n.*

rig-or *n.* The condition of being rigid or stiff; stiffness of temper; harshness. rigorous *adj.*, rigorously *adv.*

rind *n.* A tough outer layer which may be taken off or pealed off.

ring *n.* A circular mark, line, or object; a small circular band worn on a finger; a group of persons acting together; especially in an illegal way. *v.* To make a clear resonant sound, as a bell when struck. *n.* The sound made by a bell.

ring-worm *n.*, *Pathol.* A contagious skin disease caused by fungi and marked by discolored, ring-shaped, scaly patches on the skin.

ri-ot *n.* A wild and turbulent public disturbance. *Slang* An irresistibly amusing person. riotous *adj.*

rip *v.* To tear apart violently; to move violently or quickly. *n.* A torn place.

rip-off *Slang* To steal.

rip-cord *n.* A cord which, when pulled, releases a parachute from its pack.

ripe *adj.* Fully developed or aged; mature. ripeness *n.*

rip-ple *v.* To cause to form small waves on the surface of water; to waver gently.

ris-i-ble *adj.* Being inclined to or causing laughter.

risk *n.* A chance of suffering or encountering harm or loss; danger. risky *adj.*

rite *n.* A formal religious ceremony; any formal custom or practice.

rit-u-al *n.* A prescribed method for performing a religious ceremony. *adj.* Pertaining to or practiced as a rite. ritual *adj.*, ritualism *n.*

ri-val *n.* One who strives to compete with another; one who equals or almost equals another.

riv-er *n.* A relatively large natural stream of water, usually fed by another body of water.

ri-vet *n.* A metal bolt used to secure two or more objects.

RN *abbr.* Registered Nurse.

roach *n.* A European freshwater fish; cockroach. *Slang* The butt of a marijuana cigarette.

roam *v.* To travel aimlessly or without a purpose. **roamer** *n.*

roar *v.* To utter a deep prolonged sound of excitement; to laugh loudly. **roar, roarer** *n.*

roast *v.* To cook meat by using dry heat in an oven. *n.* A cut of meat.

rob *v.* To take property unlawfully from another person. **robber** *n.*, **robbery** *n.*

robe *n.* A long loose garment usually worn over night clothes; a long flowing garment worn on ceremonial occasions.

rob-in *n.* A large North American bird with a black head and reddish breast.

ro-bot *n.* A machine capable of performing human duties.

ro-bust *adj.* Full of strength and health; rich; vigorous. **robustly** *adv.*, **-ness** *n.*

rock *n.* A hard naturally formed material. *Slang* One who is dependable.

rock-et *n.*

A device propelled with the thrust from a gaseous combustion. *v.* To move rapidly.

rode *v.* Past tense of ride.

ro-dent *n.* A mammal, such as a rat, mouse, or beaver having large incisors used for gnawing.

ro-de-o *n.* A public show, contest, or demonstration of ranching skills, as riding and roping.

roe *n.* The eggs of a female fish.

rogue *n.* A scoundrel or dishonest person; an innocently or playful person.

roll *v.* To move in any direction by turning over and over; to sway or rock from side to side, as a ship; to make a deep prolonged sound as thunder. *n.* A list of names. *Slang* A large amount of money.

roll-er *n.* A cylinder for crushing, smoothing or rolling something; any of a number of various cylindrical devices.

Roman Catholic Church *n.* The Christian church having priests and bishops and recognizing the Pope as its supreme head.

ro-mance *n.* A love affair, usually of the young, characterized by ideals of devotion and purity; a fictitious story filled with extravagant adventures. **romance** *v.*, **romancer** *n.*

Ro-man nu-mer-al *n.* The letter or letters of the Roman system of numbering still used in formal contexts, as: V = 5, X = 10, L = 50, C = 100, D = 500, M = 1000.

romp *v.* To run, play, or frolic in a carefree way.

rood *n.* A measurement of land which equals 1/4 acre.

rook-ie *n.* An untrained person; a novice or inexperienced person.

room *n.* A section or area of a building set off by partitions or walls. *v.* To occupy or live in a room.

roast *n.* A place or perch on which birds sleep or rest; a piece of meat which has been or is to be roasted.

root *n.*

The part of a plant which grows in the ground. *Math* A number which, when multiplied by itself, will produce a given quantity. *v.* To search or rummage for something; to turn up the earth with the snout, as a hog. **rootless** *adj.*, **rootless** *adj.*

rope *n.* A heavy cord of twisted fiber. **know the ropes.** To be familiar with all of the conditions at hand.

ro-sa-ry *n., pl.* **-ies** A string of beads for counting prayers; a series of prayers.

rose *n.* A shrub or climbing vine having sharp prickly stems and variously colored fragrant flowers.

ro-sette *n.* An ornament gathered to resemble a rose and made of silk or ribbon.

Rosh Ha-sha-nah *n.* The Jewish New Year.

ros-ter *n.* A list of names.

ro-ta-ry *adj.* Turning or designed to turn; of or relating to axial rotation.

ro-tate *v.* To turn on an axis; to alternate something in sequence. **rotatable** *adj.*, **rotation, rotator** *n.*, **rotatory** *adj.*

ro-tis-ser-ie *n.* A rotation device with spits for roasting food.

ro-tor *n.* A rotating part of a mechanical device.

rot-ten *adj.* Decomposed; morally corrupt; very bad.

ro-tund *adj.* Plump; rounded.

rouge *n.* A cosmetic coloring for the cheeks.

rough *adj.* Having an uneven surface; violent or harsh. *n.* The part of a golf course with tall grass. *v.* To treat roughly. *adv.* In a very rude manner. **roughly** *adv.*, **roughness** *n.*

round *adj.* Curved; circular; spherical. *v.* To become round; to surround. *adv.* Throughout; prescribed duties, places, or actions. **roundness** *n.*

rouse *v.* To awaken or stir up.

route *n.* A course of travel. *v.* To send in a certain direction.

rou-tine *n.* Activities done regularly. *adj.* Ordinary.

rove *v.* To wander over a wide area. **rover** *n.*, **roving** *adj.*

row *n.* A number of things positioned next to each other; a continuous line. *v.* To propel a boat with oars.

roy-al *adj.* Relating to a king or queen.

roy-al-ty *n., pl.* **-ies** Monarchs and or their families; a payment to someone for the use of his invention, copyright, or services.

R.S.V.P. *abbr.* Respondez s'il vous plait; please reply.

rub *v.* To move over a surface with friction and pressure; to cause to become worn or frayed.

rub-ber *n.* A resinous elastic material obtained from the coagulated and processed sap of tropical plants or produced synthetically. **rubbery** *adj.*

rub-ber ce-ment *n.* A type of adhesive that is liquid and made of rubber.

rub-ber-ize *v.* Coat or cover something with rubber.

rub-ber plant *n.* Type of plant that is found in East India and yields rubber.

rub-bish *n.* Worthless trash; nonsense. **rubbishy** *adj.*

rub-ble *n.* The pieces of broken material or stones.

ru-bel-la *n.* The German measles.

ru-bi-cund *adj.* State of being of a red color or hue.

ru-bid-i-um *n., Symbol* A silvery, highly reactive element symbolized by Rb.

ru-bric *n.* A heading, title, or initial letter of a manuscript which appears in red.

ru-by *n., pl.* **-ies** A deep-red precious stone.

ruck-us *n., Slang* A noisy uproar, or commotion.

rud-der *n., Naut.* A broad, flat, hinged device attached to the stern of a boat used for steering.

rud-dy *adj.* Being red in color or hue. **ruddiness** *n.*

rude *adj.* Discourteous; offensively blunt. **rudeness** *n.*

ru-di-ment *n.* A first step, element, skill, or principle. *Biol.* An undeveloped organ.

rue *v.* To repent.

rue-ful *adj.* To be causing sorrow or remorse.

ruff *n.* A stiff collar which has pleats in it.

ruf-fi-an *n.* A lawless, rowdy person.

ruf-fle *n.* A pleated strip or frill; a decorative band. *v.* To disturb or destroy the smoothness.

rug *n.* A heavy textile fabric used to cover a floor.

rug-ged *adj.* Strong; rough; having an uneven or rough surface. **ruggedness** *n.*, **ruggedly** *adv.*

ru-in *n.* Total destruction. *v.* To destroy. **ruination** *n.*, **ruinous** *adj.*

rule *n.* Controlling power; an authoritative direction or statement which regulates the method of doing something; a standard procedure. *v.* To have control over; to make a straight line using a ruler; to be in command.

rum *n.* A type of liquor made from molasses and is distilled.

rum-ba *n.* A type of dance which has a complex rhythm.

rum-ble *v.* To make a heavy, continuous sound. *n.* A long deep rolling sound.

ru-mi-nant *n.* A cud-chewing animal; as a cow, deer, sheep, or giraffe; an animal which chews something which was swallowed.

ru-mi-nate *v.* To chew a cud; to ponder at length. **rumination** *n.*, **ruminative** *adj.*, **ruminator** *n.*

rum-mage *v.* To look or search thoroughly by digging or turning things over; to ransack.

rum-mage sale *n.* A sale of second-hand objects, conducted to make money.

ru-mor *n.* An uncertain truth which is circulated from one person to another; gossip. *v.* To speed by rumor.

ru-mor-mon-ger *n.* One who aids in the spreading of rumors.

rump *n.* The fleshy hind quarter of an animal; the human buttocks.

rum-ple *v.* To form into creases or folds; to wrinkle.

rum-pus room *n.* A type of room which is used for parties.

run *v.* To hurry busily from place to place; to move quickly in such a way that both feet leave the ground for a portion of each step; to make a rapid journey; to be a candidate seeking an office; to drain or discharge. *Law* To be effective, concurrent with. *n.* A speed faster than a walk; a streak, as of luck; the continuous extent or length of something; an outdoor area used to exercise animals. In baseball, the method of scoring a point by running the bases and returning to home plate.

rund-let *n.* A type of barrel which is small in size.

rung *n.* A bar or board which forms a step of a ladder.

run of the mill *adj.* Ordinary; average.

runt *n.* The smallest animal in a litter.

run-through *n.* The rehearsal of a play.

rup-ture *n.* A state of being broken; the act of bursting.

ru-ral *adj.* Pertaining to the country or country life.

ruse *n.* A type of trick.

rush *v.* To move quickly; to hurry; to be in a hurry.

rus-set *n.* A reddish or yellowish brown color. **rust** *n.* Ferric oxide which forms a coating on iron material exposed to moisture and oxygen; deterioration through neglect. *v.* To form rust.

rus-tic *adj.* Characteristic of country life. *n.* A simple person. **rustically** *adv.*

rus-ti-cate *v.* Living and staying in the country or rural area. **rusticator**, **rusticity** *n.*

rus-tle *v.* To move making soft sounds, such as those made by leaves of a tree.

rus-tler *n.* A person who steals cattle.

rust-proof *adj.* Being unable to rust.

rust-y *adj.* To be covered by rust. **rustiness** *n.*, **rustily** *adv.*

rut *n.* An indented track made by the wheels of vehicles.

ru-the-ni-um *n.* A metallic element symbolized by Ru.

ruth-less *adj.* Merciless. **ruthlessly** *adv.*

rye *n.* A cultivated cereal grass whose seeds are used to make flour and whiskey.

S, s The nineteenth letter of the English alphabet.

Sab-bath *n.* The seventh day of the week; sundown on Friday to sundown on Saturday; a day set apart as the day of worship for Jews and some Christians; Sunday, the first day of the week, a day set apart as the day of worship by most Christians.

sa-ber *n.* A lightweight sword.

sa-ber rat-tling *n.* An aggressive show of military force or power.

sa-ber--toothed ti-ger *n.* A cat like animal with excessively long upper canine teeth, having a saverlike look or appearance.

sa-ble *n.* A carnivorous mammal having soft, black or dark fur.

sab-o-tage *n.* An act of malicious destruction, intended to obstruct production of war material by the opposing side.

sab-o-teur *n.* A person who practices or commits sabotage.

sac *n., Biol.* A membranous pouch in an animal or plant, containing a liquid.

sac-cha-rin *n.* A white, crystalline powder used as a noncaloric sugar substitute.

sa-chet *n.* A small bag of a sweet-smelling powder used to scent clothes.

sack *n.* A strong bag for holding articles. *Slang* Dismissal from a position or job; sleeping bag or bed.

sac-ra-ment *n., Eccl.* A formal Christian rite performed in a church, as a baptism. **Sacrament** The consecrated bread and wine of the Eucharist; the Lord's Supper.

sa-cred *adj.* Dedicated to worship; holy. **sacredly** *adv.*, **sacredness** *n.*

sac-ri-fice *n.* The practice of offering something, as an animal's life, to a deity. *v.* To give up something of value for something else. **sacrificial** *adj.*

sad *adj.* Marked by sorrow; unhappy; causing sorrow; deplorable. **sadly** *adv.*, **sadness** *n.*

sad-dle *n.*

A seat for a rider, as on the back of a horse or bicycle; a cut of meat which includes the backbone. *v.* To put a saddle on; to load down; to burden.

sa-dism *n., Psychol.* A condition in which sexual gratification comes from inflicting pain on others; cruelty. **sadist** *n.*, **sadistic** *adj.*, **-ly** *adv.*

sa-fa-ri *n., pl.* **-ris.** A trip or journey; a hunting expedition in Africa.

safe *adj.* Secure from danger, harm, or evil. *n.* A strong metal container used to protect and store important documents or money. **safely** *adv.*, **safeness** *n.*

sag *v.* To droop; to sink from pressure or weight; to lose strength. **sag** *n.*

sa-ga *n.* A long heroic story.

sage *n.* A person recognized for judgment and wisdom. **sage** *adj.*

Sag-it-ta-ri-us *n.* The ninth sign of the zodiac; a person born between (November 22 - December 21.)

said *v.* Past tense of say.

sail *n.* A strong fabric used to catch the wind and cause a ship to move; a trip on a sailing vessel or boat. *v.* To travel on a sailing vessel.

saint *n.* A person of great purity who has been officially recognized as such by the Roman Catholic Church; a person who has died and is in heaven. **sainted** *adj.* **sainthood** *n.*

sake *n.* Motive or reason for doing something.

sal-ad *n.* A dish usually made of green vegetables, fruit, or meat tossed with dressing.

sal-a-man-der *n.* A lizard-like amphibian with porous, scaleless skin.

sa-la-mi *n.* A spiced sausage made of beef and pork.

sa-la-ry *n., pl.* **-ies** A set compensation paid on a regular basis for services rendered. **salaried** *adj.*

sale *n.* An exchange of goods for a price; disposal of items at reduced prices. **salable** *adj.*

sa-li-ent *adj.* Projecting beyond a line; conspicuous.

sa-li-va *n.* Tasteless fluid secreted in the mouth which aids in digestion.

Salk vac-cine *n.* A vaccine used to immunize against polio.

salm-on *n., pl.* **-on** *or* **-ons** A large game fish with pinkish flesh.

sa-lon *n.* A large drawing room; a business establishment pertaining to fashion.

sa-loon *n.* A place where alcoholic drinks are sold; a barroom.

salt *n.* A white crystalline solid, mainly sodium chloride, found in the earth and sea water, used as a preservative and a seasoning. *adj.* Containing salt. **salty** *adj.*

salt-pe-ter *n.* Potassium nitrate.

sal-u-tar-y *adj.* Wholesome; healthful.

sal-u-ta-tion *n.* An expression; a greeting of good will, as used to open a letter.

sa-lute *v.* To show honor to a superior officer by raising the right hand to the forehead. *n.* An act of respect or greeting by saluting.

sal-vage *v.* The act of rescuing a ship, its cargo, or its crew; property which has been saved. *v.* To save from destruction; to rescue.

salve *n.* A medicated ointment used to soothe the pain of a burn or wound.

sal-vo *n., pl.* **-vos** *or* **-voes** The discharge of a number of guns at the same time.

same *adj.* Identical; exactly alike; similar; not changing. *pron.* The very same one or thing. **sameness** *n.*

sam-ple *n.* A portion which represents the whole. *v.* To try a little.

san-a-to-ri-um *n., pl.* **-ums** *or* **-ria** An institution for treating chronic diseases.

sanc-ti-fy v. To make holy. -fication n.

sanc-tion n. Permission from a person of authority; a penalty to ensure compliance. v. To officially approve an action.

sanc-tu-ar-y n., pl. -ies. A sacred, holy place, as the part of a church, where services are held; a safe place; a refuge.

sand n. Fine grains of disintegrated rock found in deserts and on beaches. v. To smooth or polish with sandpaper. **sandy** adj.

san-dal n.

A shoe which is fastened to the foot by straps attached to the sole; a low shoe or slipper with an ankle strap.

san-dal-wood n. A fragrant Asian tree used in wood carving and cabinet making.

sand-bag n. A sand-filled bag, used to hold back water.

sand-wich n. Two or more slices of bread between which a filling, such as cheese or meat, is placed.

sane adj. Having a healthy, sound mind; showing good judgment. **sanely** adv., **sanity** n.

san-i-tar-y adj. Free from bacteria or filth which endanger health.

san-i-tize v. To make sanitary; to make clean or free of germs.

sap n. The liquid which flows or circulates through plants and trees. v. To weaken or wear away gradually. Slang A gullible person; fool.

sa-pi-ent adj. Wise.

sap-phire n. A clear, deep-blue gem, used in jewelry.

sar-casm n. An insulting or mocking statement or remark. **sarcastic**, **sarcastically** adj.

sar-dine n. A small edible fish of the herring family, often canned in oil.

sar-don-ic adj. Scornful; mockingly cynical.

sa-ri n. A garment consisting of a long piece of lightweight material wrapped around the body and over the shoulder of Hindu women.

sar-sa-pa-ril-la n. The dried root of a tropical American plant, which is used as flavoring.

sash n. A band worn over the shoulder or around the waist.

sass n., Slang Rudeness; a disrespectful manner of speech. v. To talk with disrespect.

sas-sa-fras n. The dried root of a North American tree, used as flavoring.

Sa-tan n. The devil.

sat-el-lite n. A natural or man-made object which orbits a celestial body.

sat-in n. A smooth, shiny fabric made of silk, nylon, or rayon, having a glossy face and dull back.

sat-ire n. The use of mockery, sarcasm, or humor in a literary work to ridicule or attack human vice.

sat-is-fac-tion n. Anything which brings about a happy feeling; the fulfillment of a need, appetite, or desire; a source of gratification.

sat-is-fy v. To fulfill; to give assurance to.

sat-u-rate v. To make completely wet; to soak or load to capacity. **saturable** adj., **saturation** n.

Sat-urn n. The sixth planet from the sun.

sat-yr n., Gr. Myth. A Greek woodland god having a human body and the legs, horns, and ears of a goat.

sauce n. A liquid or dressing served as an accompaniment to food. **saucing** v.

sau-cer n. A small shallow dish for holding a cup.

sau-er-kraut n. Shredded and salted cabbage cooked in its own juices until tender and sour.

sau-na n. A steam bath in which one is subjected to heat produced by water poured over heated rocks.

sau-sage n. Chopped meat, usually pork, which is highly seasoned, stuffed into a casing and cooked.

sav-age adj. Wild; not domesticated; uncivilized; brutal. **savagely** adv., **savagery** n.

save v. To rescue from danger, loss, or harm; to prevent loss or waste; to keep for another time in the future; to be delivered from sin. **saver** n.

sav-ior n. One who saves. Christ Savior.

sa-voir-faire n. Social skill; the ability to say and do the right thing.

sa-vor n. The taste or smell of something. v. To have a particular smell; to truly enjoy. **savory** adj.

saw n. A tool with a sharp metal blade edged with teeth-like points for cutting. v. Past tense of see; to cut with a saw.

sax-o-phone n. A brass wind instrument having finger keys and a reed mouthpiece. **saxophonist** n.

say v. To speak aloud; to express oneself in words; to indicate; to show. n. The chance to speak; the right to make a decision.

scab n. The stiff, crusty covering which forms over a healing wound. Slang A person who continues to work while others are on strike.

sca-bies n. A contagious skin disease characterized by severe itching, caused by a mite under the skin.

scaf-fold n. A temporary support of metal or wood erected for workers who are building or working on a large structure.

scal-a-wag n., Slang A rascal.

scald v. To burn with steam or a hot liquid; to heat a liquid to a temperature just under boiling.

scale n. A flat plate which covers certain animals, especially fish and reptiles; a device for weighing; a series of marks indicating the relationship between a map or model and the actual dimensions. Music A sequence of eight musical notes in accordance with a specified scheme of intervals. -ly *adj.*

scal-lop *n.* A marine shellfish with a fan-shaped, fluted bivalve shell; the fleshy edible muscle of the scallop.

scalp *n.* The skin which covers the top of the human head where hair normally grows. *v.* To tear or remove the scalp from. *Slang* To buy or sell something at a greatly inflated price. **scalper** *n.*

scal-pel *n.* A small, straight knife with a narrow, pointed blade, used in surgery.

scamp *n.* A scheming or tricky person.

scan *v.* To examine all parts closely; to look at quickly; to analyze the rhythm of a poem. *Electron.* To move a beam of radar in search of a target. **scan, scanner** *n.*

scan-dal *n.* Something which brings disgrace when exposed to the public; gossip.

scan-di-um *n.* A metallic element symbolized by Sc.

scant *adj.* Not plentiful or abundant; inadequate. **scantly** *adv.,* **scantness** *n.*

scant-ling *n.* The dimensions of material used in building, as wood and brick.

scap-u-la *n., pl.* **-lae** One pair of large, flat, triangular bones which form the back of the shoulder. **scapular** *adj.*

scar *n.* A permanent mark which remains on the skin after a sore or injury has healed. **scar** *v.*

scarce *adj.* Not common or plentiful; rare. **scarceness** *n.*

scarf *n.* A wide piece of cloth worn around the head, neck, and shoulders for warmth.

scar-la-ti-na *n.* A mild form of scarlet fever.

scar-let *n.* A bright or vivid red.

scarlet fever *n.* A communicable disease caused by streptococcus and characterized by a sore throat, vomiting, high fever, and a rash.

scat-ter *v.* To spread around; to distribute in different directions.

scav-en-ger *n.* An animal, as a vulture, which feeds on decaying or dead animals or plant matter.

sce-nar-i-o *n.* A synopsis of a dramatic plot.

scene *n.* A view; the time and place where an event occurs; a public display of temper; a part of a play.

scent *n.* A smell; an odor. *v.* To smell; to give something a scent.

scep-ter *n.* A rod or staff carried by a king as a sign of authority.

sched-ule *n.* A list or written chart which shows the times at which events will happen, including a plan given for work and specified deadlines.

scheme *n.* A plan of action; an orderly combination of related parts; a secret plot.

schol-ar *n.* A student with a strong interest in learning. **scholarly** *adj.*

school *n.* A place for teaching and learning; a group of persons devoted to similar principles.

schoon-er *n.* A sailing vessel with two or more masts.

sci-ence *n.* The study and theoretical explanation of natural phenomena in an orderly way; knowledge acquired through experience. **scientific** *adj.,* **scientifically** *adv.,* **scientist** *n.*

scis-sors *pl., n.* A cutting tool consisting of two blades joined and pivoted so that the edges are close to each other.

scle-ro-sis *n., pl.* **-ses** A hardening of a part of the body, as an artery.

scold *v.* To accuse or reprimand harshly.

sconce *n.* A wall bracket for holding candles.

scoop *n.* A small, shovel-like tool. *v.* To lift up or out. *Slang* An exclusive news report.

scoot *v.* To go suddenly and quickly.

scope *n.* The range or extent of one's actions; the space to function or operate in.

-scope *suff.* A device for seeing or discovering.

scorch *v.* To burn slightly, changing the color and taste of something; to parch with heat.

scorcher *n., Slang* A very hot day.

score *n.* A numerical record of total points won in a game or other contest; the result of an examination; a grouping of twenty items; a written musical composition which indicates the part to be performed by each person; a groove made with a pointed tool. *v.* To achieve or win; to arrange a musical score for.

scorn *n.* Contempt; disdain. *v.* To treat with scorn. **scornful** *adj.*

Scor-pi-o *n.* The eighth sign of the zodiac; a person born between (October 23 - November 21.)

scor-pi-on *n.*

An arachnid having an upright tail tipped with a poisonous sting.

scour *v.* To clean by rubbing with an abrasive agent; to clean thoroughly.

scout *v.* To observe activities in order to obtain information. *n.* A person whose job is to obtain information; a member of the Boy Scouts or Girl Scouts.

scow *n.* A large barge with a flat bottom and square ends, used to transport freight, gravel, or other cargo.

scowl *v.* To make an angry look; to frown. **scowl** *n.*

scrab-ble *v.* To scratch about frantically, as if searching for something. **scrabble, scrabbler** *n.*

scrag-gly *adj.* Messy; irregular.

scrap *n.* A small section or piece. *v.* To throw away waste.

scrape *v.* To rub a surface with a sharp object in order to clean. *Slang* An embarrassing situation.

scratch *v.* To mark or make a slight cut on; to mark with the fingernails. *n.* The mark made by scratching; a harsh, unpleasant sound.

scrawl v. To write or draw quickly and often illegibly. **scrawl** n.

scraw-ny adj. Very thin; skinny.

scream v. To utter a long, sharp cry, as of fear or pain. n. A long piercing cry. Slang A very funny person.

screech v. To make a shrill, harsh noise. **screech** n.

screen n. A movable object used to keep something from view, to divide, or to decorate; a flat reflecting surface on which a picture is projected. v. To keep from view.

screw n.

A metal piece that resembles a nail, having a spiral thread which is used for fastening things together; a propeller on a ship. v. To join by twisting. **screw up** To make a mess of.

scribe n. A person whose profession is to copy documents and manuscripts.

scrim-mage n. In football, a practice game. **scrimmage** v.

scrim-shaw n. The art of carving designs on whale ivory or whalebone.

scrip-ture n. A sacred writing. Scriptures The Bible.

scroll n. A roll of parchment or similar material used in place of paper.

scro-tum n., pl. -ta The external sac of skin which encloses the testes. -al adj.

scrub v. To clean something by rubbing. Slang To cancel.

scrump-tious adj., Slang Delightful.

scru-ple n. A principle which governs one's actions. **scrupulous** adj.

scu-ba n. An apparatus used by divers for underwater breathing; from the initials for self-contained underwater breathing apparatus.

scuff v. To drag or scrape the feet while walking. n. A rough spot.

scuf-fle v. To struggle in a confused manner. **scuffle** n.

scull n. An oar mounted at the stern of a boat, which is moved back and forth to produce forward motion.

sculp-tor n. A person who creates statues from clay, marble, or other material.

scum n. A thin layer of waste matter floating on top of a liquid.

scurf n. Flaky dry skin; dandruff.

scur-ry v. To move quickly; to scamper.

scythe n. A tool with a long handle and curved, single-edged blade, used for cutting hay, grain and grass.

seal n.

A device having a raised emblem, displaying word or symbol, used to certify a signature or the authenticity of a document; a tight closure which secures; a large aquatic mammal with a sleek body and large flippers; the fur or pelt of a seal. v. To hunt seals.

sealer, sealant n.

sea level n. The level of the sea's surface, used as a standard reference point in measuring the height of land or the depth of the sea.

seam n. The line formed at the joint of two pieces of material.

sear v. To wither or dry up; to shrivel; to burn or scorch.

search v. To look over carefully; to find something; to probe. **searcher** n.

sea-son n. One of the four parts of the year; spring, summer, fall or autumn and winter; a time marked by particular activities or cele-brations. v. To add flavorings or spices; to add interest or enjoyment. **seasonal** adj., **seasonally** adj.

seat n. A place or spot, as a chair, stool, or bench, on which to sit; the part of the body used for sitting; the buttocks.

se-cede v. To withdraw from an organization or group. **secession**, **secessionist** n.

se-clude v. To isolate; to keep apart.

sec-ond n. A unit of time equal to 1/60 of a minute; a very short period of time; an object which does not meet first class standards. Math A unit of measure equal to 1/60 of a minute of angular measurement.

sec-on-dar-y adj. Not being first in importance; inferior; pertaining to a secondary school; high school.

se-cret n. Knowledge kept from others; a mystery. **secretly** adv. **secret**, **secrecy** n.

sec-re-tary n., pl. -ies A person hired to write and keep records for an executive or an organization; the head of a government department. **secretarial** adj.

se-crete v. To produce and give off; to release or discharge.

sec-tion n. A part or division of something; a separate part. v. To divide or separate into sections.

sec-tor n. An area or zone in which a military unit operates; the part of a circle bounded by two radii and the arc they cut. Math v. To divide.

sec-u-lar adj. Relating to something worldly; not sacred or religious.

se-cure adj. Safe and free from doubt or fear; sturdy or strong; not likely to fail. v. To tie down, fasten, lock, or otherwise protect from risk or harm; to ensure. **securely** adv.

se-cu-ri-ty n., pl. -ies The state of being safe and free from danger or risk; protection; an object given to assure the fulfillment of an obligation; in computer science, the prevention of unauthorized use of a device or program.

se-dan n. A closed, hardtop automobile with a front and back seat.

se-date adj. Serene and composed. v. To keep or be kept calm through the use of drugs. **sedative** n.

sed-i-ment n. Material which floats in or settles to the bottom of a liquid. **sedimentary** adj., **sedimentation** n.

se-duce *v.* To tempt and draw away from proper conduct; to entice someone to have sexual intercourse. **seducer, seduction** *n.*, **seductive** *adj.*

see *v.* To have the power of sight; to understand; to experience; to imagine; to predict. **see red** To be extremely angry.

seed *n.* A fertilized plant ovule with an embryo, capable of producing an offspring. *v.* To plant seeds; to remove the seeds from.

seek *v.* To search for; to try to reach; to attempt. **seeker** *n.*

seem *v.* To appear to be; to have the look of. **seeming** *adj.*, **seemingly** *adv.*

seep *v.* To leak or pass through slowly. **seepage** *n.*

seer *n.* A person who predicts the future.

see-saw *n.* A board supported in the center which allows children to alternate being up and down.

seg-ment *n.* Any of the parts into which a thing is divided. *v.* To divide. **segmental** *adj.*, **segmentation** *n.*

seg-re-gate *v.* To separate or isolate from others.

seg-re-ga-tion *n.* The act of separating people based on the color of their skin.

seine *n.* A fishing net with weights on one edge and floats on the other.

seize *v.* To grasp or take possession forcibly.

sel-dom *adv.* Not often.

se-lect *v.* To choose from a large group; to make a choice. **select, selection** *adj.*, **selector, selectness** *n.*

se-le-ni-um *n.* An element symbolized by Se.

self *n.*, *pl.* **-selves.** The complete and essential being of a person; personal interest, advantage or welfare.

self--de-fense *n.* To act of defending oneself or one's belongings.

sell *v.* To exchange a product or service for money; to offer for sale. **seller** *n.*

se-man-tics *n.* The study of word meanings and the relationships between symbols and signs.

sem-a-phore *n.* A system for signaling by using flags, lights or arms in various positions. **semaphore** *v.*

se-men *n.* The secretion of the male reproductive system, thick and whitish in color and containing sperm.

se-mes-ter *n.* One of two periods of time in which a school year is divided.

sem-i-an-nu-al *adj.* Occurring twice a year.

sem-i-co-lon *n.* A punctuation mark (;) having a degree of separation stronger than a comma but less than a period.

sem-i-nar *n.* A course of study for students engaged in advanced study of a particular subject.

sem-i-nar-y *n.*, *pl.* **-ies** A school that prepares ministers, rabbis, or priests for their religious careers. **seminarian** *n.*

sen-ate *n.* The upper house of a legislature, as the United States Senate.

send *v.* To cause something to be conveyed from one place to another; to dispatch.

se-nile *adj.* Having a mental deterioration often associated with old age. **senility** *n.*

sen-ior *adj.* Being the older of two; of higher office or rank; referring to the last year of high school or college. *n.* One who is older or of higher rank.

sen-ior-i-ty *n.* Priority over others based on the length of time of service.

sen-sa-tion *n.* An awareness associated with a mental or bodily feeling; something that causes a condition of strong interest.

sense *n.* Sensation; feeling; the physical ability which allows a person to be aware of things around him; the five senses: taste, smell, touch, sight, and hearing; an ethical or moral attitude; the meaning of a word; *v.* To feel through the senses; to have a feeling about.

sen-si-bil-i-ty *n.*, *pl.* **-ies** The ability to receive sensations.

sen-si-ble *adj.* Capable of being perceived through the senses; sensitive; having good judgment. **sensibly** *adv.*

sen-si-tive *adj.* Capable of intense feelings; affected by the emotions or circumstances of others; tender-hearted; of or relating to secret affairs of state. **sensitively** *adv.*, **sensitivity, sensitiveness** *n.*

sen-sor *n.* A device which responds to a signal.

sen-su-al *adj.* Preoccupied with the gratification of the senses. **sensualist, sensuality** *n.*, **sensuous** *adj.*

sent *v.* Past tense of send.

sen-tence *n.* A series of words arranged to express a single complete thought; a prison term for a convicted person, determined by a judge or jury. *v.* To impose or set the terms of punishment.

sen-ti-ment *n.* Feelings of affection; an idea, opinion, thought, or attitude based on emotion rather than reason.

sen-ti-men-tal *adj.* Emotional; affected by sentiment.

sen-ti-nel *n.* One who guards.

se-pal *n.* One of the leaves which forms a calyx in a flower.

sep-a-rate *v.* To divide or keep apart by placing a barrier between; to go in different directions; to set apart from others. *adj.* Single; individual.

sep-a-ra-tion *n.* The process of separating or being separated; an interval which separates.

Sept *abbr.* September.

Sep-tem-ber *n.* The ninth month of the calendar year, having 30 days.

se-quel *n.* A new story which follows or comes after an earlier one and which uses the same characters.

se-quence *n.* A set arrangement; a number of connected events; the regular order; the order in which something is done. **sequential** *adj.*, **sequentially** *adv.*

ser-e-nade *n.* Music performed as a romantic expression of love.

se-rene *adj.* Calm; peaceful. **serenity** *n.*

serf *n.* A slave owned by a lord during the Middle Ages.

serge *n.* A twilled, durable woolen cloth.

ser-geant *n.* A noncommissioned officer who ranks above a corporal but below a lieutenant.

se-ri-al *adj.* Arranged in a series with one part presented at a time.

se-ries *pl. n.* A number of related items which follow one another.

se-ri-ous *adj.* Sober; grave; not trivial; important. **seriously** *adv.*, **-ness** *n.*

ser-mon *n.* A message or speech delivered by a clergyman during a religious service.

ser-pent *n.* A snake.

ser-rate *adj.* Having sharp teeth; having a notched edge. **serrate** *v.*, **serration** *n.*

se-rum *n.*, *pl.* **-rums** *or* **-ra** The yellowish fluid part of the blood which remains after clotting; the fluid extracted from immunized animals and used for the prevention of disease.

ser-vant *n.* One employed to care for someone or his property.

serve *v.* To take care of; to wait on; to prepare and supply; to complete a term of duty; to act in a certain capacity; to start the play in some sports. *n.* The manner of serving or delivering a ball.

serv-ice *n.* Help given to others; a religious gathering; the military; a set of dishes or utensils. *v.* To repair; to furnish a service to something or someone.

ses-a-me *n.* A tropical plant and its edible seeds.

ses-sion *n.* A meeting or series of meetings; a meeting set for a specific purpose; the period during the day or year during which a meeting takes place.

set *v.* To put or place; to cause to do; to regulate; to adjust; to arrange; to place in a frame or mounting; to go below the horizon; to establish or fix. *n.* A group of things which belong together; a piece of equipment made up of many pieces; a young plant. *adj.* Established; ready.

set-tee *n.* A small couch or bench with arms and a back.

set-ting *n.* The act of placing or putting something somewhere; the scenery for a show or other production; the place where a novel, play, or other fictional work takes place; a jewelry mounting.

set-tle *v.* To arrange or put in order; to restore calm or tranquillity to; to come to an agreement on something; to resolve a problem or argument; to establish in a new home or business.

sev-en *n.* The cardinal number 7, after 6 and before 8. **seven** *adj. & pron.*, **seventh** *adj.*, *adv. & n.*

sev-en-teen *n.* The cardinal number 17, after 16 and before 18. **seventeen** *adj.*, **seventeenth** *adj.*, *adv. & n.*

sev-en-ty *n.*, *pl.* **-ies** The cardinal number 70, after 69 and before 71. **seventy** *adj.* **seventieth** *adj.*, *adv. & n.*

sev-er *v.* To cut off or separate. **severance** *n.*

sev-er-al *adj.* Being more than one or two, but not many; separate. **-ly** *adv.*

se-vere *adj.* Strict; stern; hard; not fancy; extremely painful; intense. **severely** *adv.*, **severity** *n.*

sew *v.* To fasten or fix; to make stitches with thread and needle.

sew-age *n.* The solid waste material carried away by a sewer.

sew-er *n.* A conduit or drain pipe used to carry away waste.

sex *n.* One of two divisions, male and female, into which most living things are grouped; sexual intercourse.

sex-tet *n.* A group of six people or things; music written for six performers.

sgt *abbr.* Sergeant.

shab-by *adj.* Worn-out; ragged. **shabbily** *adv.*, **shabbiness** *n.*

shack *n.* A small, poorly built building.

shack-le *n.* A metal band locked around the ankle or wrist of a prisoner; anything that restrains or holds. *v.* To restrain with shackles.

shad *n.*, *pl.* **shad** *or* **shads** An edible fish which swims upstream to spawn.

shad-ow *n.* An area from which light is blocked; a shaded area. *v.* To cast or throw a shadow on. **shadowy** *adj.*

shaft *n.* A long, narrow part of something; a beam or ray of light; a long, narrow underground passage; a tunnel; a narrow, vertical opening in a building for an elevator.

shake *v.* To move or to cause a back-and-forth or up and down motion; to tremble; to clasp hands with another, as to welcome or say farewell; to upset or disturb. **shake** *n.*, **shaky** *adj.*

shall *v.*, *p.t.* Past tense of should; used with the pronouns I or we to express future tense; with other nouns or pronouns to indicate promise, determination or a command.

shal-low *adj.* Not deep; lacking intellectual depth.

sham *n.* A person who is not genuine but pretends to be; a cover for pillows. *v.* To pretend to have or feel something.

sham-ble *v.* To walk while dragging one's feet.

shambles A scene or state of complete destruction.

shame *n.* A painful feeling of embarrassment or disgrace brought on by doing something wrong; dishonor; disgrace; a disappointment.

sham-poo *n.* A soap used to cleanse the hair and scalp; a liquid preparation used to clean upholstery and rugs.

sham-rock *n.* A form of clover with three leaflets on a single stem; regarded as the national flower and emblem of Ireland.

shank *n.* The portion of the leg between the ankle and the knee; a cut of meat from the leg of an animal, such as a lamb.

shape *n.* The outline or configuration of something; the form of a human body; the condition of something; the finished form in which something may appear. *v.* To cause to take a particular form.

share *n.* A part or portion given to or by one person; one of equal parts, as the capital stock in a corporation **sharer** *n.*

shark *n.*

A large marine fish which eats other fish and is dangerous to man; a greedy, crafty person.

sharp *adj.* Having a thin edge or a fine point; capable of piercing or cutting; clever; quick-witted; intense; painful. *Slang* Nice looking. *n. Music* A note raised half a tone above a given tone. **sharpness** *n.*, **sharply** *adv.*

shat-ter *v.* To burst suddenly into pieces.

shave *v.* To remove a thin layer; to cut body hair, as the beard, by using a razor; to come close to.

shawl *n.* An oblong or square piece of fabric worn over the head or shoulders.

she *pron.* A female previously indicated by name.

shear *v.* To trim, cut, or remove the fleece or hair with a sharp instrument; to clip. **shearer** *n.*

sheath *n.* A cover or case for a blade, as a sword.

shed *v.* To pour out or cause to pour; to throw off without penetrating; to cast off or leave behind, especially by a natural process. *n.* A small building for shelter or storage.

sheen *n.* Luster.

sheep *n.*, *pl.* **sheep**

A cud-chewing thick-fleeced mammal, widely domesticated for meat and wool; a meek or timid person.

sheer *adj.* Very thin; almost transparent; complete; absolute; very steep, almost perpendicular.

sheet *n.* A large piece of cloth for covering a bed; a single piece of paper; a continuous, thin piece of anything.

shelf *n.*, *pl.* **shelves** A flat piece of wood, metal, plastic, or other rigid material attached to a wall or within another structure, used to hold or store things; something which resembles a shelf, as a ledge of rocks.

shell *n.* The hard outer covering of certain organisms; something light and hollow which resembles a shell; the framework of a building under construction; a case containing explosives which are fired from a gun. **sheller** *n.*

shel-lac *n.* A clear varnish used to give a smooth, shiny finish to furniture and floors. *Slang* To defeat. **shellac** *v.*

shel-ter *n.* Something which gives protection or cover. *v.* To give protection.

shelve *v.* To put aside; to place on a shelf.

shep-herd *n.* A person who takes care of a flock of sheep; a person who takes care of others.

sher-bet *n.* A sweet frozen dessert made with fruit juices, milk or water, egg white, and gelatin.

sher-iff *n.* A high ranking law-enforcement officer.

shield *n.* A piece of protective metal or wood held in front of the body; anything which serves to conceal or protect; a badge or emblem. **shield** *v.*, **shielder** *n.*

shift *n.* A group of people who work together; a woman's loose-fitting dress. *v.* To change direction or place; to change or move the gears in an automobile.

shim-mer *v.* To shine with a faint sparkle. **shimmer** *n.*, **shimmery** *adj.*

shin *n.* The front part of the leg from the knee to the ankle. *v.* To climb a rope or pole by gripping and pulling with the hands and legs.

shine *v.* To give off light; to direct light; to make bright or glossy; to polish shoes. *n.* Brightness.

shiner *n.* A black eye.

shin-gle *n.* A thin piece of material, as asbestos, used to cover a roof or side of a house. *v.* To apply shingles to. **shingler** *n.*

shin-gles *pl.*, *n., Pathol.* An acute, inflammatory viral infection, characterized by skin eruptions along a nerve path.

ship *n.* A large vessel for deep-water travel or transport. *v.* To send or transport.

ship-wreck *n.* The loss of a ship; destruction; ruin. *v.* To wreck.

ship-yard *n.* A place where ships are built or repaired.

shirt *n.* A garment worn on the upper part of the body.

shiv-er *v.* To tremble or shake with excitement or chill **shiver** *n.*, **-ery** *adj.*

shock *n.* A sudden blow or violent impact; an unexpected, sudden upset of mental or emotional balance; a serious weakening of the body caused by the loss of blood pressure or sudden injury. *v.* To strike with great surprise, disgust, or outrage; to give an electric shock.

shoe *n.* An outer cover for a foot; the part of a brake which presses against the drum or wheel to slow or stop the motion. *v.* To put on shoes.

shone *v.* Past tense of shine.

shoot *v.* To kill or wound with a missile, as a bullet, fired from a weapon; to discharge or throw rapidly; to push forward or begin to grow by germinating. *Slang* To inject drugs directly into the veins. **shooter** *n.*

shop *n.* A small business or small retail store; a place where certain goods are produced. *v.* To visit a store in order to examine or buy things. **shopper** *n.*

shore *n.* The land bordering a body of water.

short *adj.* Having little height or length; less than normal in distance, time, or other qualities; less than the needed amount. **shorts** Underpants or outerpants which end at the knee or above. **shortage** A lack in the amount needed. **short-change** To give less than the correct amount, as change for money. **short circuit** An electrical malfunction.

short-en-ing *n* A fat, such as butter, used to make pastry rich and light.

short order *n.* An order, usually for food, which can be quickly prepared and served.

shot *n.* The discharging of a gun, rocket, or other device; an attempt; a try; an injection; a photogragh. *Slang* Useless; ruined.

should *v.* Past tense of shall, used to express obligation, duty, or expectation.

shoul-der *n.* The part of the body located between the neck and upper arm; the side of the road. *v.* To use the shoulder to push or carry something; to take upon oneself.

should-n't *contr.* Should not.

shout *v.* To yell. *n.* A loud cry.

shov-el *n.* A tool with a long handle and a scoop, used for picking up material or for digging. *v.* To move, dig, or scoop up with a shovel; to push or move large amounts rapidly.

show *v.* To put within sight; to point out; to explain; to put on display. *n.* A display; a movie, play or similar entertainment.

show-er *n.* A short period of rain; a party with gifts given in honor of someone; a bath with water spraying down on the bather. *v.* To take a shower; to be extremely generous. **showery** *adj.*

shrank *v.* Past tense of shrink.

shrap-nel *n.*, *pl.* **shrapnel** A large shell containing metal fragments; fragments of metal that are exploded with great force.

shed *n.* A narrow strip or torn fragment; a small amount. *v.* To rip, tear, or cut into shreds.

shrew *n.* A small mouse-like mammal, having a narrow, pointed snout.

shriek *n.* A loud, sharp scream or noise.

shrill *adj.* A high-pitched, sharp sound.

shrimp *n.*, *pl.* **shrimp** *or* **shrimps** A small, edible shellfish. *Slang* A small person.

shrine *n.* A place for sacred relics; a place considered sacred because of an event or person associated with it.

shrink *v.* To make or become less or smaller; to pull back from; to flinch. *Slang* A psychiatrist.

shroud *n.* A cloth in which a body is wrapped for burial. *v.* To cover.

shrub *n.* A woody plant which grows close to the ground and has several stems beginning at its base.

shrug *v.* To raise the shoulders briefly to indicate doubt or indifference **shrug** *n.*

shrunk *v.* Past tense of shrink.

shuck *n.* The outer husk that covers an ear of corn. **shuck** *v.*

shud-der *v.* To tremble uncontrollably, as from fear. **shudder** *n.*

shuf-fle *v.* To drag or slide the feet; to mix together in a haphazard fashion; to rearrange or change the order of cards. **shuffle** *n.*

shun *v.* To avoid deliberately.

shut *v.* To move a door, drawer, or other object to close an opening; to block an entrance; to lock up; to cease or halt operations.

shut-tle *n.* A device used to move thread in weaving; a vehicle, as a train or plane, which travels back and forth from one location to another.

shy *adj.* Bashful; timid; easily frightened. *v.* To move suddenly from fear. **shyly** *adv.*, **shyness** *n.*

sib-ling *n.* One of two or more children from the same parents.

sick *adj.* In poor health; ill; nauseated; morbid. **sickness** *n.*

sick-le *n.*

A tool with a curved blade attached to a handle, used for cutting grass or grain.

side *n.* A surface between the front and back or top and bottom of an object; either surface of a flat object; the part to the left or right of a vertical axis; the right or left portion of the human body; the space beside someone or something; an opinion or point of view which is the opposite of another. *v.* To take a stand and support the opinion of a particular side. *adj.* Supplementary; peripheral.

SIDS *abbr.*, *n.* Sudden infant death syndrome; an unexpected death of a seemingly healthy baby, occurring during sleep sometime in the first four months of life.

siege *n.* The action of surrounding a town or port in order to capture it; a prolonged sickness.

si-er-ra *n.* A rugged chain of mountains or hills.

si-es-ta *n.* A rest or short nap.

sieve *n.* A meshed or perforated device which allows small particles to pass through but which holds back larger particles; a device for separating liquids from solids. **sieve** *v.*

sift *v.* To separate coarse particles from small or fine ones by passing through a sieve. **sift through** To carefully examine. **sifter** n.

sigh v. To exhale a long, deep breath, usually when tired, sad, or relieved.

sight n. The ability to see with the eyes; the range or distance one can see; a view; a device mounted on a firearm used to guide the eye or aim.

sign n. A piece of paper, wood, metal, etc., with information written on it; a gesture that tells or means something. v. To write one's name on.

sig-nal n. A sign which gives a warning; the image or sound sent by television or radio.

sig-na-ture n. The name of a person, written by that person; a distinctive mark which indicates identity. *Music* A symbol indicating the time and key.

sig-nif-i-cance n. The quality of being important; the meaning of something which is considered important.

sig-ni-fy v. To express or make known by a sign; to indicate. **signification** n., **significant** adj.

sign language n. A means of communicating by using hand gestures; the language of deaf people.

si-lence n. The state or quality of being silent; quiet. v. To make quiet. **silencer** n.

silent adj. Making no sound; not speaking; mute; unable to speak; an unpronounced letter, as the "g" in gnat. **silently** adv.

sil-hou-ette n.

The outline of something, as a human profile, filled in with a solid color, as black; the outline of an object.

sil-i-con n. The second most common chemical element, found only in combination with another substance, symbolized as Si.

silk n. A soft, thread-like fiber spun by silkworms; thread or fabric made from silk. **silken**, **silky** adj.

sill n. The horizontal support that forms the bottom part of the frame of a window or door.

sil-ly adj. Foolish; lacking good sense, seriousness, or substance. **silliness** n.

si-lo n. A tall, cylindrical structure for storing food for farm animals; an underground shelter or storage for guided missiles.

sil-ver n. A soft, white metallic element used in tableware, jewelry, and coins, symbolized by Ag. v. To coat with silver. adj. Of the color silver.

sim-i-lar adj. Almost the same, but not identical.

sim-mer v. To cook just below boiling; to be near the point of breaking, as with emotion.

sim-ple adj. Easy to do or understand; not complicated; ordinary; not showy; lacking intelligence or education.

simpleness n., **simply** adv.

sim-plic-i-ty n. The state of being easy to understand; naturalness; sincerity.

sim-pli-fy v. To make easy or simple. **simplification** n.

sim-u-late v. To have the appearance, effect, or form of. **-tion**, **simulator** n.

si-mul-ta-ne-ous adj. Occurring at exactly the same time. **-ly** adj.

sin n. The breaking of a religious law or a law of God. v. To do something which is morally wrong. **sinless** adj., **sinner** n.

since adv. At a time before the present. prep. During the time later than; continuously from the time when something occurs.

sin-cere adj. Honest; not deceitful; genuine; true. **sincerely** adv., **sincerity** n.

sing v. To use the voice to make musical tones; to make a humming or whistling sound. **singer** n.

singe v. To slightly burn the surface of something; to remove feathers.

sin-gle adj. Of or referring to only one, separate; individual; unmarried. n. A separate, individual person or item; a dollar bill; in baseball, a hit that allows the batter to progress to first base. **singly** adv.

sin-gu-lar adj. Separate; one; extraordinary; denoting a single unit, thing or person.

sink v. To submerge beneath a surface; to go down slowly; to become less forceful or weaker. n. A basin for holding water, attached to a wall and connected to a drain. **sinkable** adj.

si-nus n., pl. sinuses Anat. A body cavity; one of eight air spaces in the bones of the face which drain into the nasal cavity.

sip v. To drink in small amounts. **sip** n.

si-phon also syphon n. A tube through which liquid from one container can be drawn into another by forced air pressure. **siphon** v.

sir n. A respectful term used when addressing a man.

si-ren n. A whistle which makes a loud wailing noise, as a warning or signal; a seductive woman.

sis-ter n. A female having the same parents as another; a woman in membership with others, as in a church group or sorority. **sisterly** adj., **sisterhood** n.

sit v. To rest the body with the weight on the buttocks; to cover eggs for hatching; to pose for a portrait.

six n. The cardinal number 6, after five and before seven.

six-teen n. The cardinal number 16, after fifteen and before seventeen.

six-ty n. The cardinal number 60, after fifty nine and before sixty one.

siz-a-ble adj. Large in size or dimensions.

size n. The measurement or dimensions of something; a sticky substance used to glaze walls, before applying wall paper.

siz·zle v. To make a hissing sound, as of fat frying. **sizzle** n.

skate n. A device with rollers which attaches to the shoe and allows one to glide over ice or roll over a wooden or cement surface; a shoe fitted with rollers. **ice skate, roller skate** v.

skate-board n. A narrow piece of wood with wheels attached.

skel·e·ton n. The framework of bones that protects and supports the soft tissues and organs.

skep·tic n. A person who doubts or questions. **skepticism** n., **skeptical** adj., **skeptically** adv.

sketch n. A rough drawing or outline; a brief literary composition. **sketchy** adj.

skew v. To turn or slant. n. A slant.

ski n., pl. **skis** One of a pair of long, narrow pieces of wood worn on the feet for gliding over snow or water. v. To travel on skis. **skier** n.

skid v. To slide to the side of the road; to slide along without rotating. **skid** n.

skill n. Ability gained through practice; expertise. **skilled** adj.

skim v. To remove the top layer; to remove floating matter; to read over material quickly; to travel over lightly and quickly. **skimmer** n.

skimp v. To economize; to hold back. **skimpy** adj.

skin n. The tough, outside covering of man and some animals; the outside layer of a vegetable or fruit; the fur or pelt of an animal. **skin** v., **skinless** adj.

skip v. To move in light jumps or leaps; to go from one place to another, missing what is between. **skip** n.

skirt n. A piece of clothing that extends down from the waist. v. To extend along the boundary; to avoid the issue.

skull n. The bony part of the skeleton which protects the brain.

skunk n.

A black mammal with white streaks down its back, which sprays an unpleasant smelling liquid when annoyed or frightened.

sky n., pl. **skies** The upper atmosphere above the earth; the celestial regions.

slab n. A thick piece or slice.

slack adj. Not taut or tense; sluggish; lacking in strength. v. To make slack. n. A part of something which hangs loose. **slacks** Long pants or trousers.

slain v. Past tense of slay.

slam v. To shut with force; to strike with a loud impact. n. A loud noise produced by an impact.

slam-mer n., Slang Jail or prison.

slan-der n. A false statement that deliberately does harm to another's reputation. **slanderous** adj.

slang n. Informal language that contains made-up words or common words used in a different or uncommon way.

slant v. To lie in an oblique position; to slope; to report on something giving only one side or viewpoint. n. An incline or slope.

slap n. A sharp blow with an open hand.

slash v. To cut with a fast sweeping stroke; to reduce or limit greatly. n. A long cut.

slate n. A fine grained rock that splits into thin layers, often used as a writing surface or roofing material. **slate** v.

slaugh-ter v. To kill livestock for food; to kill in great numbers. Slang To soundly defeat. **slaughterer** n.

slave n. A person held against his will and made to work for another.

sled n. A vehicle with runners, used to travel on snow or ice.

sleek adj. Smooth and shiny; neat and trim. **sleekly** adv., **sleekness** n.

sleep n. A natural state of rest for the mind and body. v. To rest in sleep.

sleet n. Rain that is partially frozen; a combination of snow and rain. **sleet** v., **sleety** adj.

sleeve n. The part of a garment which covers the arm; a case for something.

sleigh n. A vehicle mounted on runners, usually pulled over ice and snow by horses.

slen-der adj. Slim; inadequate in amount. **slenderly** adv., **slenderness** n.

slept v. Past tense of sleep.

slice n. A thin cut; a portion or share; in sports, a ball in flight that curves off to the right of its target. v. To cut into slices. **slicer** n.

slick adj. Smooth and slippery; quick; smart; clever; attractive for the present time but without quality or depth. n. Water with a thin layer of oil floating on top.

slick-er n. A raincoat made of yellow oilcloth.

slide v. To move smoothly across a surface without losing contact. n. The act of sliding; a slanted smooth surface usually found on playgrounds; a transparent picture which can be projected on a screen; a small glass plate for examining specimens under a microscope.

slight adj. Minor in degree; unimportant. v. To ignore. **-ly** adv.

slim adj. Slender; meager; not much. **slimness** n.

slime n. A wet, slippery substance. **slimy** adj.

sling n. A piece of material, as leather, or a strap which secures something; a piece of fabric worn around the neck used to support an injured hand or arm; a weapon made of a strap, used to throw a stone.

slip v. To move in a smooth, quiet way; to fall or lose one's balance. Slang To become less active, alert, or strong. n. The action of slipping; the place between two piers used for docking a boat; a woman's undergarment; a small piece of paper; a portion of a plant used for grafting.

slith-er v. To slide or slip in an indirect manner; to move like a snake. **slithery** adj.

sliv-er n. A thin, narrow piece of something that has been broken off.

slob-ber v. To dribble from the mouth. **slobber** n.

slo-gan n. A phrase used to express the aims of a cause.

slope v. To slant upward or downward. n. An upward or downward incline, as a ski slope.

slosh v. To splash in a liquid, as water. **sloshy** adj.

slot n. A narrow, thin groove or opening. *Slang* A place or scheduled time for an event.

sloth n. Laziness; a slow mammal found in South America.

slouch n. A drooping or sagging posture; a lazy person. v. To sit or walk with poor posture.

slow adj. Moving at a low rate of speed; requiring more time than usual; not lively; sluggish; not interesting. adv. At less speed; in a slow manner. **slowly** adv., **slowness** n.

slug n. A slow animal related to the snail; a bullet or a lump of metal. v. To strike forcefully with the fist or a heavy object.

sluice n. A man-made ditch used to move water; a sloping trough used for floating logs. v. To wash with flowing water.

slum n. A crowded urban neighborhood marked by poverty. **slum** v.

slum-ber v. To sleep; to doze. **-er** n.

slump v. To fall or sink suddenly.

slung v. Past tense of sling.

slur v. To slide over without careful consideration; to pronounce unclearly. n. An insult. *Music* Two or more notes connected with a curved line to indicate they are to be slurred.

slush n. Melting snow; snow which is partially melted. **slushy** adj.

slut n. A woman of bad character; a prostitute. **sluttish** adj.

sly adj. Cunning; clever; sneaky; underhanded. **slyly** adv., **slyness** n.

smack v. To slap; to press and open the lips with a sharp noise. n. The act or noise of slapping something. adv. Directly.

small adj. Little in size, quantity, or extent; unimportant. n. The part that is less than the other. **smallness** n.

small-pox n. An acute, contagious disease marked by high fever and sores on the skin.

smart adj. Intelligent; clever.

smash v. To break into small pieces; to move forward violently, as to shatter; to ruin. n. The act or sound of crashing. adj. Outstanding. **smasher** n.

smear v. To spread or cover with a sticky, oily, or moist substance. *Slang* To discredit one's reputation. **smear** n.

smell v. To notice an odor by means of the olfactory sense organs. n. An odor; the ability to perceive an odor; the scent of something.

smelt v. To heat metals or their ores to a high temperature in order to obtain pure metallic constituents.

smile n. A grin; a facial expression in which the corners of the mouth turn upward, indicating pleasure. **smile** v.

smirk v. To smile in a conceited way. **smirk, smirker** n.

smite v. To hit with great force using the hand.

smith n. One who repairs or shapes metal.

smock n. A loose-fitting garment worn as a protection for one's clothes while working. v. To gather fabric into very small pleats or gathers.

smog n. A mixture of smoke and fog. **smoggy** adj.

smoke n. A cloud of vapor released into the air when something is burning. v. To preserve or flavor meat by exposing it to smoke. **smokeless, smoky** adj., **smoker** n.

smolder v. To burn slowly without a flame and with little smoke.

smooth adj. Not irregular; flat; without lumps, as in gravy; without obstructions or impediments. adv. Evenly. v. To make less difficult; to remove obstructions.

smor-gas-bord n. A buffet meal with a variety of foods to choose from.

smother n. Failure to receive enough oxygen to survive. v. To conceal; to be overly protective. **smothery** adj.

smudge v. To soil by smearing with dirt. n. A dirty mark or smear.

smug adj. Complacent with oneself; self-satisfied. **smugly** adv., **smugness** n.

smug-gle v. To import or export goods illegally without paying duty fees. **smuggler** n.

snack n. A small amount of food taken between meals. **snack** v.

snag n. A stump or part of a tree that is partly hidden under the surface of water; a pull in a piece of fabric. v. To tear on a rough place. *Slang* To catch unexpectedly; to snatch.

snake n. Any of a large variety of scaly reptiles, having a long tapering body. *Slang* An untrustworthy person.

snap v. To break suddenly with a sharp, quick sound; to fly off under tension; to snatch something suddenly.

snare n. Anything that entangles or entraps; a trap with a noose, used to catch small animals.

snarl v. To speak in an angry way; to cause confusion; to tangle or be tangled. n. A growl.

snatch v. To seize or grasp something suddenly. n. The act of taking something; a brief or small part.

sneak v. To act or move in a quiet, sly way. n. A person who acts in a secret, underhanded way.

sneer v. To express scorn by the look on one's face.

sneeze v. To expel air from the nose suddenly and without control.

sniff *v.* To inhale through the nose in short breaths with a noise; to show scorn. **sniff** *n.*

snip *v.* To cut off in small pieces and with quick strokes. *n.* A small piece.

snipe *n.*, *pl.* snipe *or* snipes A bird with a long bill which lives in marshy places. *v.* To shoot at people from a hidden position. **sniper** *n.*

snob *n.* A person who considers himself better than anyone else and who looks down on those he considers to be his inferiors.

snoop *v.*, *Slang* To prowl or spy. *n.* One who snoops.

snore *v.* To breath with a harsh noise while sleeping. **snore, snorer** *n.*

snor-kel *n.* A tube that extends above the water, used for breathing while swimming face down.

snort *n.* To force air through the nostrils with a loud, harsh noise. *Slang* To inhale a narcotic through the nose.

snow *n.* Vapor that forms crystals in cold air and falls to the ground in white flakes. *Slang* To charm or overwhelm.

snub *v.* To treat with contempt or in an unfriendly way. **snub** *n.*

snuff *v.* To draw air in through the nostrils. **snuff** *n.*

snug *adj.* Warm, pleasant, comfortable and safe.

so *adv.* To a degree or extent as a result; likewise; also; indeed. *conj.* In order that; therefore.

soap *n.* A cleansing agent made of an alkali and a fat, and used for washing. *v.* To rub with soap.

soar *v.* To glide or fly high without any noticeable movement; to rise higher than usual.

sob *v.* To weep with short, quick gasps.

so-ber *adj.* Not drunk or intoxicated; serious; solemn; quiet. **soberly** *adv.*, **soberness** *n.*

soc-cer *n.* A game in which two teams of eleven men each try to kick a ball into the opposing team's goal.

so-cia-ble *adj.* Capable of friendly social relations; enjoying the company of others. **sociableness** *n.*, **sociably** *adv.*

so-cial *adj.* Having to do with people living in groups; enjoying friendly companionship with others. *n.* An informal party or gathering.

so-cial-ism *n.* A system in which people as a whole, and not individuals, control and own all property.

so-ci-e-ty *n.*, *pl.* -ies People working together for a common purpose; companionship.

so-ci-ol-o-gy *n.* The study of society and the development of human society. **sociologic, sociological** *adj.*

sock *n.* A short covering for the foot, ankle, and lower part of the leg; a hard blow. *Slang* To hit with force.

sock-et *n.* A hollow opening into which something is fitted.

Soc-ra-tes *n.* Greek philosopher.

so-da *n.* Sodium carbonate; a flavored, carbonated drink.

sod-den *adj.* Completely saturated; very wet; lacking in expression.

so-di-um *n.* A metallic element symbolized by Na.

sod-om-y *n.* Anal sexual intercourse.

so-fa *n.* An upholstered couch with arms and a back.

soft *adj.* Not stiff or hard; not glaring or harsh; mild or pleasant; gentle in sound.

soft-ball *n.* A game played on a smaller diamond than baseball, with a larger, softer ball.

soft-ware *n.* In computer science, data, as routines, programs and languages, which is essential to the operation of computers.

sog-gy *adj.* Saturated with a liquid or moisture.

sol-ace *n.* Comfort in a time of trouble, grief, or misfortune. **solacer** *n.*

so-lar *adj.* Relating to or connected with the sun; utilizing the sun for power or light; measured by the earth's movement around the sun.

so-lar-i-um *n.*, *pl.* -ia *or* -ums A glassed-in room exposed to the sun's rays.

solar system *n.* The sun and the planets, asteroids, and comets that orbit it.

sol-der *n.* Any alloy, as lead or tin, which is melted and used to mend or join other pieces of metal. **soldered** *adj.*

soldier *n.* An enlisted person who serves in the military.

sole *n.* The bottom of a foot or shoe; single, the only one; a flat fish very popular as seafood.

sol-emn *adj.* Very serious; characterized by dignity; sacred. **solemnity, solemnness** *n.*

so-lic-it *v.* To try to obtain; to ask earnestly; to beg or entice a person persistently. **solicitation** *n.*

sol-id *adj.* Having a definite firm shape and volume; having no crevices; not hollow; having height, weight and length; without interruption; reliable, sound and upstanding. *n.* A solid substance. **solidification, solidness** *n.*, **solidify** *v.*

sol-i-taire *n.* A single gemstone set by itself; a card game played by one person.

sol-i-tude *n.* The act of being alone or secluded; isolation.

so-lo *n.* A musical composition written for and performed by one single person or played by one instrument.

sol-stice *n.* Either of the two times in a twelve month period at which the sun reaches an extreme north or south position.

sol-u-ble *adj.* Capable of being dissolved; able to be solved or explained. **solubility** *n.*, **solubly** *adv.*

solve *v.* To find the answer to. **solvable** *adj.*

som-ber *adj.* Dark; gloomy; melancholy.

some *adj.* Being an indefinite number or quantity; unspecified. *pron.* An undetermined or indefinite quantity. *adv.* An approximate degree. **some-**

body *n.* A person unknown. someday *adv.* At an unspecified future time. somehow *adv.* In a way.

som-er-sault *n.* The act or acrobatic stunt in which one rolls the body in a complete circle, with heels over head.

som-nam-bu-lism *n.* The act of walking during sleep. somnambulant *adj.*

son *n.* A male offspring.

so-na-ta *n.* An instrumental composition with movements contrasting in tempo and mood but related in key.

song *n.* A piece of poetry put to music; the act or sound of singing.

son-ic *adj.* Pertaining to sound or the speed of sound.

son-net *n.* A poem made up of fourteen lines.

soon *adv.* In a short time; in the near future; quickly.

soot *n.* The black powder generated by incomplete combustion of a fuel, such as coal or wood.

soothe *v.* To make comfortable; to calm.

sop *v.* To soak up a liquid; to absorb. *n.* Anything softened by a liquid; something given as a conciliatory offering.

soph-o-more *n.* A second year college or high school student.

so-pran-o *n., pl.* -nos *or* -ni The highest female singing voice.

sor-cery *n.* The use of supernatural powers.

sor-did *adj.* Filthy, very dirty; morally corrupt.

sore *adj.* Tender or painful to the touch, as an injured part of the body; severe or extreme. *n.* A place on the body which has been bruised, inflamed, or injured in some way. sorely *adv.*

sor-ghum *n.* A cane-like grass grown for its sweet juices and used as fodder for animals; the syrup prepared from the sweet juices.

so-ror-i-ty *n., pl.* -ies A social organization for women.

sor-rel *n.* Any of several herbs with sour-tasting leaves, used in salads.

sor-row *n.* Anguish; mental suffering; an expression of grief. sorrowful *adj.*, sorrowfully *adv.*

sor-ry *adj.* Feeling or showing sympathy or regret; worthless.

sort *n.* A collection of things having common attributes or similar qualities. *v.* to arrange according to class, kind, or size.

sor-tie *n., Mil.* An attack on enemy forces; a combat mission flown by an aircraft.

souf-fle *n.* A fluffy dish made of egg yolks, whipped egg whites, and other ingredients, served as a main dish or sweetened as a dessert.

sought *v.* Past tense of seek.

soul *n.* The spirit in man that is believed to be separate from the body and is the source of a person's emotional, spiritual, and moral nature. *Slang* A spirit or attitude derived from Blacks and their culture.

sound *n.* A sensation received by the ears from air, water, noise, and other sources. *v.* To make a sound; to make noise. *adj.* Free from flaw, injury, disease, or damage. -less *adj.*, -ly *adv.*

soup *n.* A liquid food made by boiling meat and/or vegetables, in water.

sour *adj.* Sharp to the taste; acid; unpleasant; disagreeable. *v.* To become sour or spoiled. sourly *adv.*

source *n.* Any point of origin or beginning; the beginning or place of origin of a stream or river.

south *n.* The direction opposite of north. *adv.* To or towards the south. *adj.* From the south southerly *adj. & adv.*, southern, southward *adj.*, -er *n.*

South Car-o-li-na *n.* A state located in the southeastern part of the United States.

South Da-ko-ta *n.* A state located in the central northwestern part of the United States.

south-paw *n.* A left-handed person.

South Pole *n.* The southernmost part of the earth.

south-west *n.* The direction between south and west. southwestern *adj.*

sou-ve-nir *n.* An item kept as a remembrance of something or someplace.

sov-er-eign *n.* A ruler with supreme power; a monarch. *adj.* Possessing supreme jurisdiction or authority.

sow *v.* To scatter or throw seeds on the ground for growth. *n.* A female pig.

space *n.* The unlimited area in all directions in which events occur and have relative direction; an interval of time; the area beyond the earth's atmosphere. space *v.*

spade *n.* A tool with a flat blade used for digging, heavier than a shovel spade *v.*

spa-ghet-ti *n.* Pasta made in long, thin pieces.

span *n.* The extent of space from the end of the thumb to the end of the little finger of a spread hand; the section between two limits or supports. *v.* To extend across.

span-iel *n.* A dog with large drooping ears and short legs.

spank *v.* To strike or slap the buttocks with an open hand as a means of punishment.

spare *v.* To refrain from injuring, harming or destroying; to refrain from using; to do without. *n.* An extra, as a spare tire.

spar-kle *v.* To emit or reflect light.

spar-row *n.* A small bird with grayish or brown plumage.

sparse *adj.* Scant; thinly distributed. sparsely *adv.*, sparsify *n.*

spasm *n.* An involuntary muscle contraction.

spat-ter *v.* To scatter or splash a liquid.

spat-u-la *n.* A kitchen utensil with a flexible blade for mixing soft substances.

spawn *n.* The eggs of fish or other water animals, as oysters or frogs. *v.* To lay eggs.

speak *v.* To utter words; to express a thought in words. **speaker** *n.*

spear *n.* A weapon with a long shaft and a sharply pointed head. *v.* To strike, pierce, or stab with a spear.

spear-mint *n.* A mint plant yielding an aromatic oil used as a flavoring.

spe-cial-ist *n.* A person, such as a doctor, who devotes his practice to one particular field. **spe-cial-ize** *v.*

spec-i-men *n.* A sample; a representative of a particular thing.

speck *n.* A small particle, mark, or spot. *v.* To cover or dot with specks.

spec-ta-cle *n.* A public display of something unusual. *pl.* Eyeglasses. **spectacled** *adj.*

spec-trum *n.*, *Physics* The band of colors produced when light is passed through a prism or other means, separating the light into different wave lengths.

spec-u-late *v.* To reflect and think deeply; to take a chance on a business venture in hopes of making a large profit. **speculation** *n.*

speech *n.* The ability, manner, or act of speaking; a talk before the public. **speechless** *adj.*

speed *n.* Rate of action or movement; quickness; rapid motion. *Slang* A drug used strictly as a stimulant.

spell *v.* To say out loud or write in proper order the letters which make up a word; to relieve. *n.* The state of being controlled by magic; a short period of time; a time or period of illness; an attack.

spend *v.* To give out; to use up; to pay; to exhaust.

sperm *n.* The male cell of reproduction; semen. **spermatic** *adj.*

sphere *n.*, *Math* A round object with all points the same distance from a given point; globe, ball, or other rounded object. **spherical** *adj.*, **spherically** *adv.*

sphinx *n.*, *pl.* **sphinxes** *or* **sphinges** An ancient Egyptian figure having the head of a man, male sheep, or hawk and the body of a lion; a very mysterious person.

spice *n.* A pungently aromatic plant used as flavoring in food, as nutmeg, cinnamon, pepper, or curry. **spicy** *adj.*

spi-der *n.*

An eight-legged insect with a body divided into two parts spinning webs as a means of capturing and holding its prey.

spike *n.* A large, thick nail; a pointed metal piece on the sole of a shoe to prevent slipping, as on a sports shoe.

spill *v.* To allow or cause something to flow or run out of something. *Slang n.* A fall from a horse; to make known.

spin *v.* To draw out fibers and twist into thread; to run something around and around; to resolve. *Slang* A short drive or ride in an auto. **spinner** *n.*

spin-ach *n.* A widely cultivated plant

with dark green leaves which are used in salads.

spin-dle *n.* A rod with a slit in the top and a piece of wood at the other end, used to hold yarn or thread; a needle-like rod mounted on a base, used to hold papers.

spine *n.* The spinal column; the backbone; the back of a bound book, inscribed with the title.

spin-ster *n.* An unmarried woman; an old maid.

spir-it *n.* The vital essence of man, considered divine in origin; the part of a human being characterized by personality and self-consciousness; the mind; the Holy Ghost; the creative power of God; a supernatural being, as a ghost or angel.

spir-i-tual *adj.* Of, like, or pertaining to the nature of spirit; relating to religion; sacred. *n.* A religious song originating among the Negroes of the southern United States. **spirituality** *n.*, **spiritualize** *v.*

spite *n.* Hatred or malicious bitterness; a grudge. **spite** *v.*, **spiteful** *adj.*, **spitefully** *adv.*

spit-toon *n.* A cuspidor or receptacle for spit.

spitz *n.* A small dog with a tail which curls over its back.

splash *v.* To spatter a liquid; to wet or soil with liquid; to make a splash. **splash** *n.*, **splashy** *adj.*

splash-down *n.* The landing of a missile or spacecraft in the ocean.

spleen *n.*, *Anat.* A highly vascular, flattened organ which filters and stores blood, located below the diaphragm.

splen-did *adj.* Illustrious; magnificent.

splice *v.* To join together by wearing, overlapping, and binding the ends. **splice** *n.*

splint *n.* A device used to hold a fractured or injured limb in the proper position for healing. **splint** *v.*

splutter *v.* To make a slight, short spitting sound. **splutter** *n.*

spoil *v.* To destroy the value, quality, or usefulness; to overindulge as to harm the character. **spoils, spoilage, -er** *n.*

spoke *n.* One of the rods that serve to connect and support the rim of a wheel.

spokes-man *n.* One who speaks on behalf of another.

sponge *n.* Any of a number of marine creatures with a soft, porous skeleton which soaks up liquid. *v.* To clean with a sponge. **sponger** *n.*, **spongy** *adj.*

spon-sor *n.* A person who is responsible for a debt or duty of another; a business that finances a television or radio program that in turn advertises its product. **sponsor** *v.*, **sponsorship** *n.*

spon-ta-ne-ous *adj.* Done from one's own impulse without apparent external cause. **spontaneity** *n.*, **spontaneously** *adv.*

spook *n.*, *Slang* A ghost. *v.* To scare or frighten. **spooky** *adj.*

spool *n.* A small cylinder for holding thread, tape or wire.

spoon *n.* An eating or cooking utensil; a shiny metallic fishing lure. *Slang* To make love, as by kissing or caressing. **spoonful** *n.*

spo-rad-ic *adj.* Occurring occasionally or at irregular intervals. **sporadically** *adv.*

spore *n.*, *Bot.* The reproductive singlecelled structure produced by nonflowering plants; any cell capable of developing into a new organism, seed, or germ.

sport *n.* An interesting diversion; a particular game or physical activity with set rules; a person who leads a fast life. *Slang* To amuse and have a good time. **sporting** *adj.*

sport-ing *adj.* Of or relating to risk taking or gambling; displaying sportsmanship.

sports-man-ship *n.* Fair play; the ability to win or lose graciously.

spot *n.* A small area that differs in size, portion, or color. *adj.* Delivered or made immediately. *Slang* A dangerous or difficult situation. **spot** *v.*, **spotless** *adj.*, **spotlessly** *adv.*

spot-light *n.* A powerful light thrown directly at one area.

spouse *n.* One's husband or wife; a marriage partner.

spout *v.* To pour out forcibly, as under pressure; to cause to shoot forth. *Slang* To orate pompously; to declaim. **spouter** *n.*

sprain *n.* A wrenching or twisting of a muscle or joint.

sprawl *v.* To sit or lie in an ungraceful manner; to develop haphazardly. **sprawl, sprawler** *n.*

spray *n.* A liquid dispersed in a fine mist or droplets. **sprayer** *n.*

spread *v.* To unfold or open fully; to apply or distribute over an area; to force apart; to extend or expand.

spree *n.* An excessive indulgence in an activity; a binge.

sprin-kle *v.* To scatter in small particles or drops; to rain in small drops.

sprint *n.* A short, fast race. **sprinter** *n.*

sprock-et *n.*, *Mech.* A tooth-like projection from the rim of a wheel.

spruce *n.* An evergreen tree with needle-like foliage, cones, and soft wood.

spry *adj.* Quick; brisk; energetic.

spud *n.*, *Slang* A potato.

spur *n.* A sharp, projecting device worn on a rider's boot, used to nudge a horse.

sput-nik *n.* An unmanned Soviet earth satellite.

sput-ter *v.* To throw off small particles in short bursts; to speak in a confused or agitated manner.

spy *n.*, *pl.* **spies** A secret agent who obtains information; one who watches other people secretly.

squab-ble *v.* To engage in a petty argument. **squabble** *n.*

squad *n.* A small group organized to perform a specific job.

squan-der *v.* To spend extravagantly or wastefully.

square *n.* A parallelogram with four equal sides; an implement having a T or L shape used to measure right angles. *Math.* To multiply a number by itself. *Slang* An unsophisticated person; a person who is not aware of the latest fads or trends.

square root *n.* A number which when multiplied by itself gives the given number.

squash *n.*

An edible fruit of the gourd family; a sport played in a walled court with a hard rubber ball and racket. *v.* To press or squeeze into a soft pulp.

squat *v.* To sit on the heels; to crouch; to settle on a piece of land in order to obtain legal title **squatter, squatness** *n.*

squaw *n.* An American Indian woman.

squeak *v.* To utter a sharp, penetrating sound. **squeak** *n.*, **squeaky** *adj.*

squea-mish *adj.* Easily shocked or nauseated. **-ly** *adv.*, **squeamishness** *n.*

squee-gee *n.* A tool having a stout rubber blade across a wooden handle, used to wash windows. **squeegee** *v.*

squeeze *v.* To press together; to extract by using pressure. *n.* An instance of squeezing for pleasure; a hug.

squib *n.* A firecracker that does not explode.

squint *v.* To view through partly closed eyes; to close the eyes in this manner.

squire *n.* An old-fashioned title for a rural justice of the peace, lawyer, or judge; a man who escorts a woman; a young man who ranks just below a knight. **squire** *v.*

squirm *n.* To twist the body in a wiggling motion. **squirm** *v.*

squir-rel *n.*

A rodent with gray or brown fur, having a long bushy tail and dark eyes. **squirrel** *v.*

squirt *v.* To eject in a thin stream or jet; to wet with a squirt. *n.* The act of squirting.

sta-bi-lize *v.* To make firm; to keep from changing. **stabilization, stabilizer** *n.*

sta-ble *n.* A building for lodging and feeding horses or other farm animals. *adj.* Standing firm and resisting change. **stable** *v.*

stac-ca-to *adj.*, *Music* Marked by sharp emphasis. **staccato** *n. & adv.*

stack *n.* A large pile of straw or hay; any systematic heap or pile; a chimney. *v.* To fix cards so as to cheat.

sta-di-um *n.*, *pl.* **-dia** A large structure for holding athletic events or other large gatherings.

staff *n.*, *pl.* **staffs** *or* **staves** A pole or rod used for a specific purpose; the people employed to assist in the day-to-day affairs of running a business, organization, or government. *Mil.* A group of people on an executive or advisory board. *Music* The horizontal lines on which notes are written.

stag *n.* The adult male of various animals; a man who attends a social gathering without a woman companion; a social event for men only. *adj.* For men only.

stag-ger *v.* To walk unsteadily; to totter. *adj.* Strongly affected by defeat, misfortune, or loss of strength.

stag-nant *adj.* Not flowing; standing still; foul from not moving; inactive. **stagnate** *v.*

stair *n.* A step or a series of steps.

stair-case *n.* A series or a flight of steps that connect one level to another.

stake *n.* A bet placed on a game of chance; a sharpened piece of wood for driving into the ground. **stake** *v.*

stale *adj.* Having lost freshness; deteriorated; lacking in interest; dull; inactive.

stale-mate *n.* A position in chess when a player cannot move without placing his king in check.

stalk *n.* The main axis of a plant. *v.* To approach in a stealthy manner.

stall *n.* An enclosure in a barn, used as a place to feed and confine animals; a sudden loss of power in an engine; a booth used to display and sell. *v.* To try to put off doing something; to delay.

stal-lion *n.* An uncastrated, fully grown male horse.

sta-men *n.*, *pl.* stamens *Bot.* The pollen-producing organs of a flower.

stam-i-na *n.* Physical or moral endurance.

stam-mer *v.* To make involuntary halts or repetitions of a sound or syllable while speaking **stammerer** *n.*

stamp *v.* To put the foot down with force; to imprint or impress with a die, mark, or design. *n.* The act of stamping; the impression or pattern made by a stamp; a postage stamp.

stam-pede *n.* A sudden rush of panic, as of a herd of horses or cattle. *v.* To cause a stampede.

stance *n.* The posture or position of a standing person or animal.

stand *v.* To be placed in or maintain an erect or upright position; to take an upright position; to remain unchanged; to maintain a conviction; to resist. *n.* The act of standing; a device on which something rests; a small booth for selling or displaying items.

stand-ard *n.* A model which stands for or is accepted as a basis for comparison. **standard** *adj.*

stand-ing *n.* A status, reputation, or achievement; a measure of esteem. *adj.* Unchanging; stationary; not moving.

sta-ple *n.* A principle commodity grown in an area; a major element; a metal fastener designed to hold materials such as cloth or paper. **staple** *v.*, **stapler** *n.*

star *n.*, *Astron.* A self-luminous body that is a source of light; any of the celestial bodies that can be seen in the night sky; a symbol having five or six points and resembling a star.

star-board *n.* The right side of a ship or boat. **starboard** *adj.* & *adv.*

starch *n.* Nutrient carbohydrates that are found in foods such as rice and potatoes. *v.* To stiffen clothing by using starch. **-iness** *n.*, **starchy** *adj.*

stare *v.* To look with an intent, direct gaze. **stare**, **starer** *n.*

stark *adj.* Bare; total; complete; forbidding in appearance. **starkness** *n.*, **starkly** *adv.*

star-ling *n.* A common black or brown bird.

star-tle *v.* To cause a sudden surprise; to shock. **startle** *n.*

starve *v.* To suffer or die from not having food or love. **starvation** *n.*

state *n.* A situation, mode, or condition of something; a nation; the governing power or authority of; one of the subdivisions or areas of a federal government, as the United States. *v.* To make known verbally.

stat-ic *adj.* Not moving. *n.* A random noise heard on a radio. **statically** *adv.*

sta-tion-ar-y *adj.* Not movable; unchanging.

sta-tion-er-y *n.* Writing paper and envelopes.

sta-tis-tic *n.* An estimate using an average or mean on the basis of a sample taken; numerical data.

stat-ue *n.* A form sculpted from wood, clay, metal, or stone.

stave *n.* A narrow piece of wood used in forming part of a container, as a barrel. **stave** *v.*

stay *v.* To remain; to pause; to maintain a position; to halt or stop; to postpone or delay an execution. *n.* A short visit.

stead-fast *adj.* Not changing or moving; firm in purpose; true. **steadfastly** *adv.*, **steadfastness** *n.*

stead-y *adj.* Firmly placed, fixed or set; not changing; constant; uninterrupted.

steal *v.* To take another person's property; to move in a sly way; to move secretly. *Baseball* To take a base without the ball being hit. *Slang* A real bargain.

steam *n.* Water in the form of vapor; the visible mist into which vapor is condensed by cooling. **steamy** *adj.*

steel *n.* A various mixture of iron, carbon, and other elements; a strong material that can be shaped when heated. **steely** *adj.*

stem *n.* The main stalk of a plant; the main part of a word to which prefixes and suffixes may be added. *v.* To stop or retard the progress or flow of something.

sten-cil *n.* A form cut into a sheet of

material, as cardboard or plastic, so that when ink or paint is applied, the pattern will reproduce on paper or another material.

ste-nog-ra-phy *n.* The skill of writing in shorthand. **stenographer** *n.*

ste-re-o *n.* A record player with stereophonic sound. **stereo** *adj.*

ste-reo-phon-ic *adj.* Relating to or giving a three-dimensional effect of auditory perspective.

ster-e-o-type *n.* A conventional opinion or belief; a metal printing plate.

ster-ile *adj.* Free from microorganisms; sanitary; unable to reproduce.

ster-ling *n.* An alloy of 92.5% silver and another metal, as copper.

stern *adj.* Inflexible; harsh. *n.* The rear of a boat or ship. **sternly** *adv.*, **sternness** *n.*

ster-num *n., pl.* -nums *or* -na A long, flat bone located in the chest wall, connecting the collarbones and the cartilage of the first seven pairs of ribs. **sternal** *adj.*

steth-o-scope *n.*

An instrument used to listen to the internal sounds of the body.

stew *v.* To cook slowly; to simmer; to boil. *n.* A dish of stewed meat and potatoes. *Slang* To worry.

stew-ard *n.* A manager of another's financial affairs; a person responsible for maintaining household affairs; a male attendant on an airplane or ship. **stewardess, stewardship** *n.*

stick *n.* A slender piece of wood; a club, rod, or walking stick. *v.* To put a hole in something; to pierce; to cling; to become jammed.

stiff *adj.* Not flexible; not easily bent; awkward. *n., Slang* A dead body. **stiffness** *n.*

sti-fle *v.* To suffocate; to cut off; to suppress; to keep back.

stig-ma *n., pl.* -mata *or* -mas A mark of disgrace. **stigmata** The part of a flower where pollen is deposited at pollination; wounds resembling the crucifixion scars of Jesus Christ. **stigmatic** *adj.*

still *adj.* Silent; calm; peaceful; until now or another time. **still** *v.*, **stillness** *n.*

still-birth *n.* The birth of a dead fetus.

stilt *n.* One of a pair of long poles with foot supports, used for walking.

stim-u-lant *n.* An agent which arouses or accelerates physiological activity.

stim-u-late *v.* To excite to a heightened activity; to quicken. **stimulation** *n.*

stim-u-lus *n., pl.* -li Something that excites to action.

sting *v.* To prick with something sharp; to feel or cause to feel a smarting pain; to cause or feel sharp pain, either physical or mental. *n.* The act of stinging; the injury or pain caused by the stinger of a bee or wasp. **stinger** *n.*

stin-gy *adj.* Not giving freely; cheap.

stink *v.* To give off a foul odor that is highly offensive.

stip-u-late *v.* To settle something by agreement; to establish conditions of agreement. **stipulation** *n.*

stir *v.* To mix a substance by moving round and round; to agitate or provoke. **stirrer** *n.*

stir-rup *n.* A loop extending from a horse's saddle, used to support the rider's foot.

stitch *n.* In sewing, a single loop formed by a needle and thread; the section of loop of thread, as in sewing. *v.* To join with a stitch.

stock *n.* A supply of goods kept on hand; animals living on a farm; a share in ownership, as in a company or corporation; the raw material or the base used to make something. *v.* To provide with stock. *adj.* Regular, common, or typical.

stock-ade *n.* A barrier placed around a fort for protection.

stock-ing *n.* A knitted covering for the foot.

stock-y *adj.* Short and plump; built sturdily.

stole *n.* A long, narrow scarf that is usually worn around a woman's shoulders, as a mink stole. *v.* Past tense of steal.

stom-ach *n., Anat.* The organ into which food passes from the esophagus; one of the primary organs of digestion. *v.* To tolerate or stand; to put up with.

stone *n.* Rock; compacted earth or mineral matter; a gem or jewel; the seed or pit of certain fruits. *Med.* A hard rock that forms inside a body organ, as the kidney. **stoned** To be overcome by an excessive amount of alcohol or drugs.

stool *n.* A seat without a backrest and arms; a small version of this on which to rest the feet; a bowel movement.

stoop *v.* To bend the body forward and downward from the waist. *n.* A porch attached to a house.

stop *v.* To cease; to halt; to refrain from moving, operating, or acting; to block or obstruct; to visit for a short time. *v.* A location where a bus, train, or other means of mass transportation may pick up or drop off passengers. **stoppage** *n.*

stor-age *n.* The act of storing or keeping; in Computer Science, the part of a computer in which all information is held; the memory.

store *n.* A business offering merchandise for sale; a supply to be used in the future. *v.* To supply; to accumulate.

stork *n.* A large, wading bird.

storm *n.* An atmospheric condition marked by strong winds with rain, sleet, hail, or snow. *v.* To attack with a powerful force. **stormy** *adj.*

sto-ry *n., pl.* -ies. A narration of a fictional tale or account; a lie; a level in a building.

stout *adj.* Strong; sturdy; substantial; courageous. **stoutly** *adv.*

stove *n.* An apparatus in which oil, electricity, gas, or other fuels are consumed to provide the heat for cooking.

stow *v.* To pack or put away.

strad-dle *v.* To sit or stand with the legs on either side of something; to favor both sides of an issue. **straddler** *n.*

straight *adj.* Being without bends, angles, or curves; upright; erect; honest; undiluted; unmodified; heterosexual. *n.* In poker, a numerical sequence of five cards not of the same suit. **straightly** *adv.*, **straightness** *n.*

strain *v.* To stretch beyond a proper limit; to injure by putting forth too much effort; to pass through a sieve to separate small particles from larger ones.

strait *n.* A narrow passageway which connects two bodies of water.

strand *n.* Land that borders a body of water; one of the threads that are twisted together to form a rope. *v.* To leave in a difficult situation.

strange *adj.* Not previously known or experienced; odd; peculiar; inexperienced; alien. **strangely** *adv.*, **strangeness** *n.*

stran-ger *n.* A person unknown; a newcomer.

stran-gle *v.* To kill by choking. **-er** *n.*

strap *n.* A long, narrow strip of leather or other material used to secure objects. **strap** *v.*

strat-e-gy *n.*, *pl.* **-ies** The skillful planning and managing of an activity. **strategic** *adj.*, **strategist** *n.*

stra-tum *n.*, *pl.* **-ta** *or* **-tums** A horizontal layer, as of the earth's crust.

straw *n.* A stalk of dried, threshed grain; a slender, plastic or paper straw used to suck up a liquid. *adj.* Yellowish brown.

straw-ber-ry *n.*

A low plant with white flowers and red fruit; the fruit of this plant.

stray *v.* To roam or wander. *n.* A lost or wandering animal or person. **strayer** *n.*

streak *n.* A narrow line or stripe that is different from the surrounding area; a run of good or bad luck. *v.* To rush or move rapidly; to make a streak. **streaky** *adj.*

stream *n.* A small body of flowing water; a steady or continuous succession or procession. *v.* To flow in or like a stream.

street *n.* A public thoroughfare in a town or city with buildings on either or both sides.

strength *n.* The quality of being strong; power in general; degree of concentration or potency.

stren-u-ous *adj.* Necessitating or characterized by vigorous effort or exertion. strenuously *adv.*

stress *n.* Special significance; an emphasis given to a specific syllable, word, action, or plan; strain or pressure. **stressful** *adj.*

stretch *v.* To extend fully; to extend forcibly beyond proper limits; to prolong. *n.* The state or act of stretching. **stretchable**, **stretchy** *adj.*

strick-en *adj.* Suffering, as from an emotion, illness, or trouble.

strict *adj.* Holding to or observing rules exactly; imposing absolute standards. **strictly** *adv.* **strictness** *n.*

stride *v.* To walk with a long, sweeping step.

strike *v.* To hit with the hand; to ignite, as with a match; to afflict suddenly with a disease; to discover; to conclude or make; to stop working as a protest against something or in favor of rules or demands presented to an employer. **strike** *n.*

string *n.* A strip of thin twine, wire, or catgut used on stringed musical instruments; a series of related acts, items, or events; in Computer Science, data arranged in an ascending or descending sequence according to a command within the data.

strin-gent *adj.* Of or relating to strict requirements; marked by obstructions or scarcity. **stringency** *n.*, **-ly** *adv.*

strip *v.* To take off the outer covering; to divest or pull rank; to remove one's clothes; to rob. **strip**, **stripper** *n.*

stripe *n.* A streak, band, or strip of a different color or texture; a piece of material or cloth worn on the sleeve of a uniform to indicate rank, award, or service.

stroke *n.* The movement of striking; a sudden action with a powerful effect; a single movement made by the hand or as if by a brush or pen. *Path.* A sudden interruption of the blood supply to the brain. *v.* To pass the hand over gently.

stroll *v.* To walk in a slow, leisurely way.

strong *adj.* Exerting or possessing physical power; durable; difficult to break. **strongly** *adv.*

stron-ti-um *n.* A metallic element symbolized by Sr.

struc-ture *n.* A construction made up of a combination of related parts. **structure** *v.*, **structural** *adj.*

strug-gle *v.* To put forth effort against opposition. **struggle**, **struggler** *n.*, **strugglingly** *adv.*

stub *n.* A short, projecting part; the short end of something after the main part has been removed or used. **stub** *v.*

stub-born *adj.* Inflexible; difficult to control, handle, or manage.

stuc-co *n.*, *pl.* **-coes** *or* **-cos** Fine plaster used to coat exterior walls and to decorate interior walls.

stud *n.* An upright post, as in a building frame, to which sheets of wallboard or paneling are fastened; a male horse used for breeding. **stud** *v.*

stu-dent *n.* A person who studies at a school or college.

stu-di-o *n.* The place of work for an artist, photographer, or other creative person; a place for filming movies.

stud-y *n., pl.* **-ies** The process of applying the mind to acquire knowledge.

stum-ble *v.* To trip and nearly fall over something; to come upon unexpectedly. **stumble** *n.*

stump *n.* The part of a tree which remains after the top is cut down. *v.* To puzzle or be puzzled; to walk heavily; to campaign.

stun *v.* To render senseless by or as if by a blow.

stu-pen-dous *adj.* Astonishing or impressive. **-ness** *n.*, **-ly** *adv.*

stu-pid *adj.* Slow in apprehension or understanding. **stupidity** *n.*

stur-dy *adj.* Possessing robust strength and health. **sturdily** *adv.*, **sturdiness** *n.*

stur-geon *n.* A large freshwater fish highly valued as a source of caviar.

stut-ter *v.* To speak with involuntary repetitions of sound. **stutter** *n.*

sty *n., pl.* **sties** An inflammation of the edge of an eyelid.

style *n.* A method, manner, or way of performing, speaking, or clothing; elegance, grace, or excellence in performance or appearance. **style** *v.* **stylish** *adj.*

suave *adj.* Ingratiating; smoothly pleasant in manner.

sub-con-scious *adj.* Below the level of consciousness. **subconscious** *n.*

sub-due *v.* To bring under control by influence, training, persuasion or force.

sub-ject *n.* The word in a sentence that defines a person or thing; a person who is under the control of another's governing power. *v.* To subdue or gain control over. **subjection** *n.*

sub-jec-tive *adj.* Taking place within, relating to or preceding from an individual's emotions or mind. **subjectively** *adv.*, **subjectivity** *n.*

sub-ma-rine *adj.* Operating or existing beneath the surface of the sea. *n.* A ship that travels underwater. **-er** *n.*

sub-merge *v.* To plunge under the surface of the water. **submergible** *adj.*, **submergence** *n.*

sub-mit *v.* To give into or surrender to another's authority. **submission, submittal** *n.*

sub-or-di-nate *adj.* Being of lower class or rank; minor; inferior. **subordination** *n.*, **subordinative** *adj.*

sub-poe-na *n.* A legal document requiring a person to appear in court for testimony.

sub-se-quent *adj.* Following in time, place, or order. **subsequently** *adv.*, **subsequentness** *n.*

sub-side *v.* To move to a lower level or sink; to become less intense.

sub-sid-i-ar-y *adj., pl., n.* **-ies.** Providing assistance in a lesser capacity. **subsidiaries** *pl., n.*

sub-si-dy *n., pl.* **-dies.** Financial aid granted directly to a private commercial enterprise from the government.

sub-sist *v.* To have continued existence.

sub-soil *n.* The layer of earth that comes after the surface soil. **subsoiler** *n.*

sub-stance *n.* Matter or material of which anything consists.

sub-sti-tute *n.* Something or someone that takes the place of another.

sub-ten-ant *n.* A person who rents property from a tenant.

sub-ter-ra-ne-an *adj.* Located, situated, or operating underground.

sub-ti-tle *n.* An explanatory title, as in a document, book, etc.; a written translation that appears at the bottom of a foreign motion picture screen.

sub-tract *v.* To deduct or take away from.

sub-trop-i-cal *adj.* Pertaining to regions adjacent to the tropics.

sub-urb *n.* A residential community near a large city. **suburban** *adj.*

sub-way *n.* An underground electrically-powered train, usually used as a means of transportation.

suc-ceed *v.* To accomplish what is attempted; to come next or to follow.

suc-cess *n.* Achievement of something intended or desired; attaining wealth, or fame.

suc-ces-sion *n.* The act or process of following in order; sequence; series; the order, sequence or act by which something changes hands.

suc-ces-sive *adj.* Following in order or sequence. **-ly** *adv.*, **successiveness** *n.*

suc-cu-lent *adj.* Juicy; full of juice or sap. **succulence** *n.*, **succulently** *adv.*

such *adj.* Of this or that kind or thing; a great degree or extent in quality. *pron.* Of a particular degree or kind; a person or thing of such.

suck *v.* To pull liquid in the mouth by means of a vacuum created by the lips and tongue. *n.* The action of sucking.

su-crose *n.* Sugar obtained from the sugar beet or sugar cane.

suc-tion *n.* The process or act of sucking.

sud-den *adj.* Happening very quickly without warning or notice; sharp; abrupt; marked by haste. **suddenly** *adv.*, **suddenness** *n.*

suede *n.* Leather with a soft, napped finish.

su-et *n.* The hard fat around the kidney and loins of sheep.

suf-fer *v.* To feel pain or distress; to sustain injury, loss, or damage. **sufferer** *n.*

suf-fi-cient *adj.* As much that is needed or desired. **sufficiency** *n.*, **-ly** *adv.*

suf-fix *n.* A form affixed to the end of a word.

suf-fo-cate *v.* To kill by depriving something or someone of oxygen. **-tion** *n.*

sugar *n.* A sweet, watersoluble, crystalline carbohydrate. *Slang* A nickname for someone.

sug-gest *v.* To give an idea for action or consideration; to imply; hint or intimate.

sug-ges-tion *n.* The act of suggesting; a

slight insinuation; hint.

su-i-cide *n.* The act of taking one's own life. **suicidal** *adj.*

suit *n.* A set of articles, as clothing, to be used or worn together; in cards, one of the four sets: spades, hearts, clubs, and diamonds that make up a deck. *v.* To meet the requirements of; to satisfy.

sul-fur *also* **sulphur** *n.* A light, yellow, nonmetallic element occurring naturally in both combined and free form, used in making matches, gunpowder and medicines.

sulk *v.* To be sullenly silent.

sul-len *adj.* Ill-humored, melancholy; gloomy; depressing.

sul-try *adj.* Hot and humid; muggy.

sum *n.* The result obtained by adding; the whole amount, quantity, or number; summary.

sum-ma-ry *n., pl.* **-ries.** Giving the sum or substance. *adj.* A statement covering the main points. **summarily** *adv.*

sum-mer *n.* The warmest of the four seasons, following spring and coming before autumn. **summery** *adj.*

sum-mit *n.* The top and highest point, or degree.

sum-mons *n., pl.* **-monses.** An order or command to perform a duty; a notice to appear at a certain place.

sun *n.* The star around which other planets of the solar system orbit; the energy, visible light, and heat, that is emitted by the sun; sunshine.

Sun-day *n.* The Christian holy day; the first day of the week.

sun-down *n.* The time of day the sun sets.

sunk-en *adj.* Submerged or deeply depressed in.

su-per *adj.* Exceeding a norm; in excessive intensity or degree; surpassing most others; superior in rank, status or position; excellent. *n. Slang* Superintendent of a building.

su-perb *adj.* Of first-rate quality. **superbly** *adv.*

su-per-fi-cial *adj.* Pertaining to a surface; concerned only with what is not necessarily real.

su-pe-ri-or *adj.* Of higher rank, grade, or dignity. *n.* A person who surpasses another in rank or excellence. **superiority** *n.,* **superiorly** *adv.*

su-per-la-tive *adj.* Of the highest degree of excellence; pertaining to the degree of comparison of an adverb or adjective that shows extreme extent or level. **superlatively** *adv.*

su-per-nat-u-ral *adj.* An order of existence beyond the natural world; pertaining to a divine power. **-ly** *adv.*

su-per-sede *v.* To take the place of; to set aside.

su-per-son-ic *adj., Aero.* Characterized by a speed greater than that of sound.

su-per-sti-tion *n.* A belief founded, despite evidence that it is irrational; a belief, resulting from faith in magic or chance. **-tious** *adj.,* **-ly** *adv.*

su-per-vise *v.* To have charge in directing the work of other people. **supervision, supervisor** *n.,* **supervisory** *adj.*

sup-per *n.* The last or evening meal of the day.

sup-ple-ment *n.* A part that compensates for what is lacking. **supplementary, supplemental** *adj.*

sup-ply *v., pl., n.* **-plies.** To provide with what is needed; to make available. **supplier** *n.*

sup-port *v.* To bear or hold the weight of; to tolerate; to give assistance or approval. **supportable, supportive** *adj.,* **supporter** *n.*

sup-pose *v.* To think or assume as true; to consider probable. **supposed** *adj.,* **supposedly** *adv.*

sup-pos-i-to-ry *n., pl.* **-ries.** A medication, in solid form, that melts when inserted into the body cavity, as the rectum.

sup-press *v.* To put an end to something by force.

su-preme *adj.* Of the highest authority, rank, or power.

sur-charge *n.* An extra fee added to the cost of something; to overcharge.

sure *adj.* Firm and sturdy; being impossible to doubt; inevitable; not liable to fail. **surer, surest** *adj.,* **surely** *adv.*

sur-face *n.* The exterior or outside boundary of something; outward appearance. **surface** *v.*

surge *v.* To increase suddenly. *n.* A large swell of water.

sur-geon *n.* A physician who practices surgery.

sur-ger-y *n., pl.* **-ies.** The branch of medicine in which physical deformity or disease is treated by an operative procedure.

sur-mise *v.* To guess; to conjecture.

sur-mount *v.* To overcome; to be at the top.

sur-name *n.* A person's family's last name.

sur-pass *v.* To go beyond the limits of; to be greater than. **surpassingly** *adv.*

sur-plus *n.* An amount beyond what is needed.

sur-prise *v.* To come upon unexpectedly or suddenly. **-er** *n.,* **surprisingly** *adv.*

sur-ren-der *v.* To give up or yield possession or power. *n.* The act of surrendering.

sur-rey *n., pl.* **-reys.** A four-wheeled, horse-driven carriage.

sur-ro-gate *n.* A person who puts himself in the place of another. **surrogate** *v.*

sur-round *v.* To extend around all edges of something; to enclose or shut in.

sur-veil-lance *n.* Close observation kept over one, especially as a suspect.

sur-vey *v., pl., n.* **-veys.** To examine in detail; to determine area, boundaries, or position and elevation of a section of the earth's surface. **surveyor** *n.*

sur-vive *v.* To continue to exist; to outlast; to outlive. **surviving** *adj.,* **survival, survivor** *n.*

su-shi *n.* A Japanese dish of thin slices of fresh, raw fish.

sus-pect v. To have doubt or distrust.

sus-pend v. To bar from a privilege for a certain time, as a means of punishment; to hang so as to allow free movement.

sus-pense n. The feeling of being insecure or undecided, resulting from uncertainty.

sus-pi-cion n. The instance of suspecting something wrong without proof. **suspicious** adj., **suspiciously** adv.

sus-tain v. To hold up and keep from falling; to suffer or undergo an injury.

su-ture n. The stitching together or joining the edges of an incision or cut.

swab n. A small stick with a wad of cotton on both ends, used to apply medication. *Slang* A sailor. **swab** v.

swad-dle v. To wrap closely, using a long strip of flannel or linen.

swag-ger v. To walk with a proud or conceited air.

swal-low v. To cause food to pass from the mouth to the stomach; to retract or take back, as words spoken. n. The act of swallowing.

swan n.

A mostly pure white bird having a long neck and heavy body, related to geese.

swap v. To trade something for something in return. **swap** n.

swarm n. A large number of insects, as bees; a large group of persons or things. **swarm** v., **swarmer** n.

swat v. To hit something with a sharp blow.

swath n. The area or width of grass cut by a machine. **swathe** v.

sway v. To move or swing from right to left or side by side; to exert influence or control.

swear v. To make an affirmation under oath. **swearer** n.

sweat v. To excrete a salty moisture from the pores of the skin. *Informal* To work hard; to cause to sweat. *Slang* Being impatient; having anxiety.

sweat gland n., *Anat.* One of the tubular glands that secrete sweat externally through pores.

swift adj. Moving with great speed; accomplished or occurring quickly. **swiftly** adv., **swiftness** n.

swin-dle v. To cheat out of property or money; to practice fraud. **swindle**, **swindler** n.

swine n., pl. **swine** A hoofed mammal with a snout, related to pigs and hogs; a low, despicable person. **swinish** adj.

swing v. To move freely back and forth; to hang or to be suspended. n. The act of a swing; a seat that hangs from chains or ropes. *Music* Jazz played by a larger band and developed by using simple harmonic patterns.

swirl v. To move with a whirling, rotating motion. **swirl** n., **swirly** adj.

switch n. A small, thin, flexible stick, twig or rod. *Electr.* A device for opening or closing an electric circuit; to shift to another train track by using a switch; to exchange.

swiv-el n. A coupling device, ring, or pivot that allows attached parts to rotate or move freely. **swivel** v.

sword n. A weapon with a long, pointed cutting blade.

syc-a-more n. A North American tree that is used widely for shade.

syl-la-ble n., *Phonet.* A word or part of one that consists of a single vocal impulse, usually consisting of one or more vowels or consonants.

syl-lo-gism n. An argument with a major premise, a minor premise and a conclusion that is logically drawn from the premises.

sym-bol n. Something that stands for or represents something else. **symbolic**, **symbolical** adj., **symbolically** adv.

sym-me-try n., pl. **-tries**. Balance in form, size, and position of parts that are on two sides of an axis.

sym-pa-thet-ic adj. Having or showing kindness or sympathy for others. **sympathetically** adv., **sympathize** v.

sym-pa-thy n., pl. **-thies**. Mutual understanding or affection during a time of sadness or loss.

sym-pho-ny n., pl. **-nies**. A large orchestra with wind, percussion and string sections. **symphonic** adj.

symp-tom n. A sign of change in a body's functions or appearance. **-tic** adj.

syn-a-gogue n. A place for Jewish worship and prayer.

syn-chro-nize v. To operate or take place at the same time.

syn-di-cate n. An organization set up to carry out business transactions; a company that sells materials for simultaneous publication at a number of different locations.

syn-drome n. A set of concurrent symptoms that indicate or characterize a disorder or disease.

syn-o-nym n. A word that means the same or nearly the same as another. **synonymous** adj., **synonymy** n.

syn-op-sis n., pl. **-ses**. A shortened statement or narrative.

syn-tax n. The way in which words are put together or arranged to form sentences and phrases. **syntactic**, **syntactical** adj.

syph-i-lis n. An infectious venereal disease transmissible by direct contact and usually progressing in severity.

sy-ringe n. A medical instrument used to inject or draw fluids from the body.

syr-up n. A sticky, thick, sweet liquid, used as a topping for food.

sys-tem n. A method or way of doing something; the human body or related parts of the body that perform vital functions; an orderly arrangement. **systematic** adj., **systematically** adv.

sys-to-le n., *Physiol.* The regular rhythmic contraction of the heart that pumps blood through the aorta and pulmonary artery. **systolic** adj.

T, t The twentieth letter of the English alphabet.

tab *n.* A strip, flap, or small loop that projects from something. *Slang* A bill or total.

tab-er-na-cle *n.* A portable shelter or structure used by the Jews during their journey out of Egypt; a place of worship.

ta-ble *n.* An article of furniture having a flat top, supported by legs; a collection of related signs, values, or items. *v.* To put off or postpone.

ta-ble-spoon *n.* A unit of measure; a large spoon for serving food. **tablespoonful** *n., pl.,* **tablespoonsful**

tab-leau *n., pl.* **-leaux** *or* **-leaus** A vivid representation; a stage scene represented by motionless and silent people who stand in an appropriate arrangement.

tab-let *n.* A pad used for writing; a thin, flat piece of stone or wood which is fit for or has an inscription.

tab-loid *n.* A small newspaper.

ta-boo *n.* A custom or rule against doing, using, or mentioning something. *adj.* Forbidden by social authority, convention, or custom.

tab-u-lar *adj.* Pertaining to or arranged in a table or list. **tabularly** *adv.*

ta-chom-e-ter *n.* An instrument for measuring velocity and speed.

tac-it *adj.* Understood; expressed or implied nonverbally; implicit. **tacitly** *adv.,* **tacitness** *n.*

tack *n.* A small, short nail with a flat head; a sewing stitch used to hold something temporarily; the changing of a sailboat from one direction to another. *v.* to change the direction in which a sailboat is going. **tacker** *n.*

tack claw *n.* A small tool used to remove tacks.

tacki-ness *n.* The state of being tacky.

tack-le *n.* Equipment used for fishing or other sports or occupations; an apparatus of ropes and pulley blocks for pulling and hoisting heavy loads. In football, a position on a football team; the lineman between the guard and end. **tackled** *v.,* **tackler** *n.*

tack-y *adj.* Slightly sticky; shabby; lacking style or good taste; flashy.

tact *n.* Having the ability to avoid what would disturb someone. **tactful, tactless** *adj.,* **tactfully, tactlessly** *adv.,* **tactfulness, -nessness** *n.*

tac-tic *n.* A way or method of working toward a goal; the art of using strategy to gain military objectives or other goals. **tactical** *adj.,* **tactician** *n.*

tad *n.* A small boy; an insignificant degree or amount.

tad-pole *n.*

The early stage in the growth of a frog or toad during which it breathes by external gills, has a long tail, and lives in the water; a polliwog.

taf-fe-ta *n.* A stiff, smooth fabric of rayon, nylon, or silk. **taffetized** *adj.*

taff-rail *n.* The rail around the stern of a boat or ship.

Taft, William H. *n.* The 27th president of the United States from 1909-1913.

tag *n.* A piece of plastic, metal, paper, or other material that is attached to something in order to identify it; a children's game in which one child is "it" and tries to catch another child, who then becomes "it." **tag** *v.,* **-ger** *n.*

tail *n.* The posterior extremity, extending from the end or back of an animal. **Tails** The opposite side of a coin from heads; formal evening dress for men. *v.* To follow or keep close watch on someone.

tail-gate *n.* The hinged gate at the back of a truck or automobile for loading and unloading. *v.* To follow very closely in a car.

tai-lor *n.* One whose profession is making, mending, and altering clothing. *v.* To adapt for a specific purpose.

taint *v.* To spoil, contaminate, or pollute. *n.* A blemish or stain.

take *v.* To seize or capture; to get possession of; to receive, swallow, absorb, or accept willingly; to attack and surmount; to move, convey, or conduct to a different place; to require; to choose or pick. *n.* The process of acquiring; the total receipts for admission at an event. *Slang* To cheat; to subtract.

talc *n.* A soft, fine-grained, smooth mineral used in making talcum powder.

tal-ent *n.* The aptitude, disposition, or characteristic ability of a person. **talented, talentless** *adj.*

tal-ent scout *n.* A person who discovers and recruits people with talent for a specialized activity or field.

talk *v.* To communicate by words or speech; to engage in chatter or gossip. *n.* A speech or lecture, usually given to a group of people. *Slang* To boast; to brag. **talker, talkativeness** *n.,* **talkative** *adj.,* **talkatively** *adv.*

tall *adj.* Of greater than average height; of a designated or specified height; imaginary, as a tall tale. **tallness** *n.,* **tallish** *adj.*

tal-low *n.* Hard fat rendered from sheep or cattle, used to make candles, lubricants, and soap. **tallow** *adj.*

tal-ly *n., pl.* **-ies** A record or counting of money, amounts, or scores. *v.* To agree with; to reckon or figure a score; to count.

tal-on *n.* A long, curved claw found on birds or animals. **taloned** *adj.*

tam-bou-rine *n.*

A percussion instrument made of a small drum with jingling metal disks around the rim.

tame *adj.* Not wild or ferocious; domesticated or manageable. *v.* To make

docile or calm. **tamely** *adv.*,
tamer, tameness *n.*

tam-per *v.* To change, meddle, or alter something; to use corrupt measures to scheme. **tamperproof** *adj.*, **tamperer** *n.*

tan *v.* To cure a hide into leather by using chemicals. *n.* A brownish skin tone caused by exposure to the sun.

tan-dem *n.* Any arrangement that involves two or more things, animals or persons arranged one behind the other.

tang *n.* A sharp, distinct taste, smell, or quality; a slender shank that projects from a tool and connects to a handle. **tangy** *adv.*

tan-gent *n.* A line that touches a curved line but does not intersect or cross it; a sudden change from one course to another. **tangency** *n.*, **tangential** *adj.*

tan-ger-ine *n.* A small citrus fruit with an easily peeled orange skin, resembling an orange.

tan-gi-ble *adj.* Capable of being appreciated or felt by the sense of touch; capable of being realized. **tangibility, tangibleness** *n.*, **tangibly** *adv.*

tan-gle *v.* To mix, twist, or unite in a confused manner making separation difficult. **tangle, tanglement** *n.*

tan-go *n.* A ballroom dance with long, gliding steps. **tango** *v.*

tank *n.* A large container for holding or storing a gas or liquid. **tankful** *n.*

tank-ard *n.* A large drinking mug, usually with a hinged top.

tan-ta-lize *v.* To tease or tempt by holding or keeping something just out of one's reach. **tantalizer** *n.*, **-ingly** *adv.*

tan-ta-lum *n.* A metallic element symbolized by Ta.

tan-trum *n.* A fit; an outburst or a rage of bad temper.

tap *v.* To strike repeatedly, usually while making a small noise; to strike or touch gently; to make secret contact with something. In medicine, to remove fluids from the body. **tapper** *n.*

tape *n.* A narrow strip of woven fabric; a string or ribbon stretched across the finish line of a race. **tape** *v.*

ta-per *n.*

A very slender candle. *v.* To become gradually smaller or thinner at one end.

tap-es-try *n.*, *pl.* **-ies** A thick fabric woven with designs and figures.

tap-i-o-ca *n.* A bead-like substance used for thickening and for puddings.

taps *n.* *pl.* *Mil.* A bugle call that signals lights out, also sounded at memorial and funeral services.

tar-dy *adj.* Late; not on time. **tardily** *adv.*, **tardiness** *n.*

tar-get *n.* An object marked to shoot at; an aim or goal.

tar-iff *n.* Duty or tax on merchandise coming into or going out of a country.

tar-nish *v.* To become discolored or dull; to lose luster; to spoil. **tarnish** *n.*, **tarnishable** *adj.*

tar-ot *n.* A set of 22 cards used for fortune-telling, each card showing a virtue, an elemental force, or a vice.

tar-pau-lin *n.* A sheet of waterproof canvas used as a protective covering.

tar-ry *v.* To linger, delay, or hesitate.

tart *adj.* Sharp; sour; cutting, biting in tone or meaning. **tartly** *adv.*, **-ness** *n.*

tar-tan *n.* A plaid fabric pattern of Scottish origin. **tartan** *adj.*

tar-tar *n.* The reddish, acidic, crust-like deposit which forms as grape juice turns to wine; a hard deposit which forms on the teeth, composed of secretions, food, and calcium salts. **tartaric** *adj.*

task *n.* A bit of work, usually assigned by another; a job.

tas-sel *n.*

An ornamental decoration made from a bunch of string or thread.

taste *n.* The ability to sense or determine flavor in the mouth; a personal liking or disliking. *v.* To test or sense flavors in the mouth. **tasteful, tasteless** *adj.*, **taster** *n.*

tat-ter *n.* A torn scrap of cloth. *v.* To become or make ragged.

tat-tle *v.* To reveal the secrets of another by gossiping. **tattler** *n.*

tat-tle-tale *n.* One who betrays secrets concerning others; a person, usually a child, who informs on others.

tat-too *n.* A permanent design or mark made on the skin by pricking and inserting an indelible dye. **tattoo** *v.*, **tattooer** *n.*

taught *v.* Past tense of teach.

Tau-rus *n.* The second sign of the zodiac; a person born between April 20 - May 20.

taut *adj.* Tight; emotionally strained. **tautly** *adv.*, **tautness** *n.*

tau-tol-o-gy *n.*, *pl.* **-ies** Redundancy; a statement which is an unnecessary repetition of the same idea.

tav-ern *n.* An inn; an establishment or business licensed to sell alcoholic drinks. **taverner** *n.*

tax *n.* A payment imposed and collected from individuals or businesses by the government. *v.* To strain. **taxable** *adj.*, **taxation, taxer, taxpayer** *n.*

tax--ex-empt *adj.* Exempted from tax; bearing tax-free interest on federal or state income.

tax shel-ter *n.* A credit or allowance that reduces taxes on current earnings for an individual investor or corporation.

tax-i *v.* To move along the ground or water surface on its own power before taking off.

taxi-cab *n.* A vehicle for carrying passengers for money.

tax-i-der-my *n.* The art or profession of preparing, stuffing, and mounting animal skins. **taxidermist** *n.*

Taylor, Zachary *n.* The 12th president of the United States from 1849-1850, died in office.

tea *n.* A small tree or bush which grows where the climate is very hot and damp; a drink made by steeping the dried leaves of this shrub in boiling water.

teach *v.* To communicate skill or knowledge; to give instruction or insight. **teachability, teachableness, teaching** *n.,* **teachable** *adj.*

teach-er *n.* A person who teaches; one who instructs.

team *n.* Two or more players on one side in a game; a group of people trained or organized to work together; two or more animals harnessed to the same implement. *v.* To join or work together.

team-ster *n.* A person who drives a team of animals or a vehicle as an occupation.

tear *v.* To become divided into pieces; to separate; to rip into parts or pieces; to move fast; to rush. *n.* A rip or torn place.

tear *n.* A fluid secreted by the eye to moisten and cleanse. *v.* To cry. **teary** *adj.*

tease *v.* To make fun of; to bother; to annoy; to tantalize. *n.* A person who teases. **teaser** *n.,* **teasingly** *adv.*

tech *abbr.* Technical; technician.

tech-ne-tium *n.* A metallic element symbolized by Tc.

tech-ni-cal *adj.* Expert; derived or relating to technique; relating to industry or mechanics. **technically** *adv.*

tech-nique *n.* A technical procedure or method of doing something.

tech-nol-o-gy *n., pl.* **-ies** The application of scientific knowledge to serve man in industry, commerce, medicine and other fields.

te-di-ous *adj.* Boring; taking a long time. **tediously** *adv.*

tee *n.*

A peg used to hold a golf ball on the first stroke toward a hole or goal post; a peg used to support a football during a field goal attempt. **tee** *v.*

teem *v.* To abound; to be full of; to swarm or crowd.

teens *pl., n.* The ages between 13 and 19; the years of one's life between 13 and 19.

teeth *pl., n.* The plural of tooth.

tel-e-cast *n.* A television broadcast.

tel-e-gram *n.* A message sent or received by telegraph. **telegram** *v.*

tel-e-graph *n.* A system for communicating; a transmission sent by wire or radio. *v.* To send messages by electricity over wire. **telegrapher, telegraphist** *n.,* **telegraphic** *adj.*

te-lep-a-thy *n.* Communication by means of mental processes rather than ordinary means. **telepathic** *adj.,* **-ist** *n.*

tel-e-phone *n.* A system or device for transmitting conversations by wire. **telephone** *v.,* **telephoner** *n.*

tel-e-pho-to *adj.* Relating to a camera lens which produces a large image of a distant object. **telephotograph** *n.*

tel-e-scope *n.* An instrument which contains a lens system which makes distant objects appear larger and nearer. **telescopic** *adj.*

tel-e-thon *n.* A long telecast used to raise money for a worthy cause.

tel-e-vi-sion *n.* Reception and transmission of images on a screen with sound; the device that reproduces television sounds and images.

tel-ex *n.* Teletype communications by means of automatic exchanges.

tell *v.* To relate or describe; to command or order. **tellable, telling** *adj.,* **teller** *n.*

tel-lu-ri-um *n.* An element symbolized by Te.

temp *abbr.* Temperature.

tem-per *n.* The state of one's feelings. *v.* To modify something, making it flexible or hard. **temperable** *adj.*

tem-per-a-ment *n.* Personality; a characteristic way of thinking, reacting, or behaving. **temperamental** *adj.*

tem-per-ance *n.* Moderation; restraint; moderation or abstinence from drinking alcoholic beverages.

tem-per-ate *adj.* Avoiding extremes; moderate. **-ly** *adv.,* **temperateness** *n.*

tem-per-a-ture *n.* A measure of heat or cold in relation to the body or environment; an elevation in body temperature above the normal 98.6 degrees Fahrenheit.

tem-pest *n.* A severe storm, usually with snow, hail, rain, or sleet.

tem-ple *n.* A place of worship; the flat area on either side of the forehead.

tem-po *n., pl.* **-pos** *or* **-pi** *Mus.* The rate of speed at which a musical composition is to be played.

tem-po-rar-y *adj.* Lasting for a limited amount of time; not permanent.

tempt *n.* To encourage or draw into a foolish or wrong course of action; to lure. **temptation, tempter** *n.*

ten *n.* The cardinal number equal to 9 + 1; the number before eleven.

te-na-cious *adj.* Persistent; stubborn. **tenaciously** *adv.,* **tenaciousness** *n.*

ten-ant *n.* A person who pays rent to occupy another's property. **tenantless, tenantable** *adj.*

Ten Commandments *n.* The ten rules of moral behavior which were given to Moses by God.

tend *v.* To be inclined or disposed; to be directed; to look after.

ten-den-cy *n., pl.* **-ies** A disposition to act or behave in a particular way; a particular dir-ection, mode, outcome, or direction.

ten-der *adj.* Fragile; soft; not hard or tough; painful or sore when touched. *n.* Something offered as a formal bid or offer; compassionate; a supply ship.

v. To make an offer to buy or purchase; to present, as a resignation. -hearted, tenderly *adv.*, tenderness *n.*

ten-der-loin *n.* A cut of tender pork or beef.

ten-don *n.* A band of tough, fibrous tissues that connect, a muscle and bone.

ten-dril *n.*

A thread-like part of a climbing plant which attaches itself to a support. -led *or* tendrilled *adj.*

ten-nis *n.* A sport played with a ball and racket by 2 or 4 people on a rectangular court.

ten-or *n.* An adult male singing voice, above a baritone.

tense *adj.* Taut or stretched tightly; nervous; under strain. tense *v.*

ten-sion *n.* The condition of stretching or the state of being stretched. tensional, tensionless *adj.*

tent *n.* A portable shelter made by stretching material over a supporting framework.

ten-ta-cle *n.* A long, unjointed, flexible body part that projects from certain invertebrates, as the octopus. tentacular, tentacled *adj.*

ten-ta-tive *adj.* Experimental; subject to change; not definite. tentatively *adv.*

ten-ure *n.* The right, state, or period of holding something, as an office or property. -ed, -ial *adj.*, tenurially *adv.*

te-pee *n.* A tent made of hides or bark used by the Indians of North America.

tep-id *adj.* Lukewarm. -ly *adv.*, -ness *n.*

ter-bi-um *n.* A metallic element of the rare-earth group symbolized by Tb.

ter-cen-ten-a-ry *n., pl.* -ries. The time span of 300 years; a 300th anniversary. tercentenary *adj.*

term *n.* A phrase or word; a limited time or duration; a phrase having a precise meaning. *Math* The quantity of two numbers either added together or subtracted.

ter-mi-nal *adj.* Of, forming, or located at the end; final. *n.* A station at the end of a bus line, railway, or airline; In Computer Science, the instrument through which data enters or leaves a computer.

ter-mi-nate *v.* To bring to a conclusion or end; to finish. termination *n.*

ter-mite *n.* The winged or wingless insect which lives in large colonies feeding on wood.

ter-race *n.* An open balcony or porch; a level piece of land that is higher than the surrounding area; a row of houses built on a sloping or raised site.

ter-ra cot-ta *n.* A hard, baked clay used in ceramic pottery.

ter-rain *n.* The surface of an area, as land.

ter-ra-pin *n.* An edible turtle of North America, living in both fresh and salt water.

ter-res-tri-al *adj.* Something earthly; not heavenly; growing or living on land.

ter-ri-ble *adj.* Causing fear or terror; intense; extreme; horrid; difficult. terribly *adv.*, terribleness *n.*

ter-ri-er *n.* A very active small dog, originally bred by hunters to dig for burrowing game, now kept as a family pet.

ter-rif-ic *adj.* Terrifying. *Informal* Excellent; causing amazement. -ally *adv.*

ter-ri-fy *v.* To fill with fear or terror; to frighten; to menace. terrified, terrifying *adj.*

ter-ri-to-ry *n., pl.* -ies An area, usually of great size, which is controlled by a particular government; a district or area assigned to one person or group. territorial *adj.*, territorially *adv.*

ter-ror *n.* Extreme fear; one who causes terror.

ter-ror-ism *n.* The state of being terrorized or the act of terrorizing; the use of intimidation to attain one's goals or to advance one's cause.

terse *adj.* Brief; using as few words as possible without loss of force or clearness. tersely *adj.*, terseness *n.*

test *n.* An examination or evaluation of something or someone; an examination to determine one's knowledge, skill, intelligence or other qualities. test *v.*, tester *n.*

tes-ta-ment *n.* A legal document which states how one's personal property is to be distributed upon his death.

Testament *n.* One of the two sections of the Bible: the Old Testament and the New Testament.

tes-tate *adj.* Having left a valid will.

tes-ti-fy *v.* To give evidence while under oath; to serve as proof. testifier *n.*

tes-ti-mo-ni-al *n.* A formal statement; a gift, dinner, reception, or other sign of appreciation given to a person as a token of esteem. testimonial *adj.*

tes-ti-mo-ny *n., pl.* -ies A solemn affirmation made under oath; an outward expression of a religious experience.

tes-tis *n., pl.* testes The sperm producing gland of the male.

test tube *n.*

A thin glass tube closed at one end, used in biology and chemistry.

test--tube ba-by *n.* A baby conceived outside of a mother's womb by fertilizing an egg removed from the mother and then returning the fertilized egg to the mother's womb.

tet-a-nus *n., Pathol* An often fatal disease marked by muscular spasms, commonly known as lockjaw.

teth-er *n.* A rope or chain which fastens an animal to something but allows limited freedom to wander within its range.

text *n.* The actual wording of an author's work distinguished his from notes; the main part or body of a book.

textual *adj.*, **textually** *adv.*

text-book *n.* A book used by students to prepare their lessons.

tex-tile *n.* A cloth made by weaving; yarn or fiber for making cloth. **textile** *adj.*

tex-ture *n.* The look, surface, or feel of something; the basic makeup.

textural *adj.*, **texturally** *adv.*

thal-li-um *n.* A metallic element resembling lead, symbolized by Tl.

than *conj.* In comparison with or to something.

thank *v.* To express one's gratitude; to credit.

thank-ful *adj.* Feeling or showing gratitude; grateful. **thankfully** *adv.*, **thankfulness** *n.*, **thankless** *adj.*

thanks *pl.*, *n.* An expression of one's gratitude.

Thanks-giv-ing Day *n.* A United States holiday, set apart as a legal holiday for public thanksgiving, celebrated on the fourth Thursday of November.

that *adj.*, *pl.* **those** The person or thing present or being mentioned. *conj.* Used to introduce a clause stating what is said.

thatch *n.* Grass, straw, or similar material used to make a roof. *v.* To overlay or cover with or as if with thatch.

thaw *v.* To change from a frozen state to a liquid or soft state; to grow warmer; to melt. **thaw** *n.*

the *definite adj. or article* Used before nouns and noun phrases as a determiner, designating particular persons or things. *adv.* Used to modify words in the comparative degree; by so much; by that much.

the-a-tre *n.* A building adapted to present dramas, motion pictures, plays, or other performances; a performance.

the-at-ri-cal *adj.* Extravagant; designed for show, display, or effect.

theft *n.* The act or crime of stealing; larceny.

their *adj. & pron.* The possessive case of they; belonging to two or more things or beings previously named.

the-ism *n.* The belief in the existence of God. **theist** *n.*, **theistic** *adj.*

them *pron.* The objective case of they.

theme *n.* The topic or subject of something. *Mus.* A short melody of a musical composition. **thematic** *adj.*

them-selves *pron.* Them or they; a form of the third person plural pronoun.

then *adv.* At that time; soon or immediately. *adj.* Being or acting in or belonging to or at that time.

thence *adv.* From that place, event, fact, or origin.

thenceforth, thence-for-ward *adv.* From that time on.

the-oc-ra-cy *n.*, *pl.* **-ies** Government by God or by clergymen who think of themselves as representatives of God. **theocrat** *n.*, **theocratic** *adj.*, **-ically** *adv.*

the-ol-o-gy *n.*, *pl.* **-ies** The religious study

of the nature of God, beliefs, practices, and ideas. **theologian** *n.*

the-o-rize *v.* To analyze theories. **theoretician, -ation, -er, theorist** *n.*

the-o-ry *n.*, *pl.* **-ies** A general principle or explanation which covers the known facts; an offered opinion which may possibly, but not positively, be true.

ther-a-peu-tics *n.* The medical treatment of disease. **therapeutist** *n.*

ther-a-py *n.*, *pl.* **-ies** The treatment of certain diseases; treatment intended to remedy an undesirable condition. **therapist** *n.*

there *adv.* In, at, or about that place; toward, into, or to.

thereabouts, thereafter, thereby, therefore, therefrom, therein *adv.*

ther-mal *adj.* Having to do with or producing heat.

ther-mom-e-ter *n.* A glass tube containing mercury which rises and falls with temperature changes. **-metric** *adj.*

ther-mo-plas-tic *adj.* Pliable and soft when heated or warm but hard when cooled. **thermoplastic** *n.*

ther-mo-stat *n.*

A device that automatically responds to temperature changes and activates equipment such as air conditioners and furnaces to adjust the temperature to correspond with the setting on the device.

the-sau-rus *n.*, *pl.* **-ruses** *or* **-ri** A book which contains synonyms.

these *pron.* The plural of this.

the-sis *n.*, *pl.* **-ses** A formal argument or idea; a paper written by a student that develops an idea or point of view.

they *pron.* The two or more beings just mentioned.

they'd *contr.* They had.

they'll *contr.* They will.

they're *contr.* They are.

they've *contr.* They have.

thick *adj.* Having a heavy or dense consistency; having a considerable extent or depth from one surface to its opposite. *Slang* Excessive.

thickly *adv.*, **thickness, thicken** *n.*

thief *n.*, *pl.* **thieves** A person who steals.

thieve *v.* To take by theft. **thievery** *n.*

thigh *n.* The part of the leg between the hip and the knee of man.

thim-ble *n.*

A small cap-like protection for the finger, worn while sewing.

thimbleful *n.*

thin *adj.* Having very little depth or extent from one side or surface to the other; not fat; slender.

thinly *adv.*, **thinness** *n.*

thing *n.* Something not recognized or named; an idea, conception, or utterance; a material or real object.

things One's belongings.

think v. To exercise thought; to use the mind; to reason and work out in the mind; to visualize. **thinkable** adj., **thinker** n.

third n. Next to the second in time or place; the last in a series of three.

Third World n. The underdeveloped or nonaligned nations of the world, especially in Asia and Africa.

thirst n. An uncomfortably dry feeling in the throat and mouth accompanied by an urgent desire for liquids. -y adj.

thir-teen n. The cardinal number equal to 12 + 1.

this pron., pl. **these** The person or thing that is near, present, or just mentioned; the one under discussion.

this-tle n. A prickly plant usually producing a purplish or yellowish flower.

thith-er adv. To that place; there; on the farthest side.

thong n. A narrow strip of leather used for binding.

tho-rax n., pl. **-raxes** or **-races** The section or part of the human body between the neck and abdomen, supported by the ribs and breastbone. **thoracic** adj.

tho-ri-um n. A radioactive metallic element symbolized by Th.

thorn n. A sharp, pointed, woody projection on a plant stem. **thorniness** n., **thorny** adj.

thor-ough adj. Complete; intensive; accurate; very careful; absolute. **thoroughness** n., **thoroughly** adv.

thor-ough-bred adj. Being of a pure breed of stock.

thor-ough-fare n. A public highway, road or street.

those adj. & pron. The plural of that.

though adv. Nevertheless; in spite of.

thought n. The process, act, or power of thinking; a possibility; an idea. **thoughtful, thoughtless** adj.

thou-sand n. The cardinal number equal to 10 X 100. **thousand** adj. & pron.

thrash v. To beat or strike with a whip; to move violently about; to defeat.

thread n. A thin cord of cotton or other fiber; the ridge going around a bolt, nut or screw. v. To pass a thread through, as to thread a needle.

thread-bare adj. Shabby.

threads pl., n. Slang Clothes.

threat n. An expression or warning of intent to do harm; anything holding a possible source of danger. **threaten** v., **threatener** n., **threateningly** adv.

three n. The cardinal number equal to 2 + 1.

three-D or **3-D** n. A three-dimensional form.

thresh v. To separate seed from a harvested plant mechanically; to strike severely.

thresh-old n. A horizontal piece of wood or other material which forms a doorsill; a beginning point.

threw v. Past tense of throw.

thrice adv. Three times.

thrift n. The careful use of money and other resources. **thriftily** adv., **thriftiness** n., **thrifty** adj.

thrill n. A feeling of sudden intense excitement, fear, or joy. **thrilling** adj., **thrillingly** adv.

thrive v. To prosper; to be healthy; to do well in a position.

throat n. The front section or part of the neck containing passages for food and air.

throb v. To beat, move, or vibrate in a pulsating way; to pulsate. **throb** n.

throm-bo-sis n., pl. **-ses** The development of a blood clot in a blood vessel or in the heart cavity.

throng n. A large group or crowd. v. To crowd around or into.

throt-tle n. The valve which controls the flow of fuel to an engine. v. To control the speed or fuel with a throttle.

through prep. From the beginning to the end; in one side and out the opposite side. Slang Completed; finished.

through-out prep., adv. In every place; everywhere; at all times.

throw v. To toss or fling through the air with a motion of the arm; to hurl with force. Slang To entertain, as to throw a party. **throw up** To vomit. **throw out** To discard something.

thru prep., adv., & adj. Through.

thrush n. A small songbird having a brownish upper body and spotted breast.

thrust v. To push; to shove with sudden or vigorous force. n. A sudden stab or push.

thru-way or **through-way** n. A major highway; an expressway.

thud n. A heavy, dull thumping sound.

thug n. A tough or violent gangster. **thuggish** adj.

thumb n. The short first digit of the hand; the part of the glove that fits over the thumb. v. To browse through something quickly.

thump n. A blow with something blunt or heavy. **thump** v.

thun-der n. The loud explosive sound made as air is suddenly expanded by heat and then quickly contracted again.

thun-der-bolt n. A flash of lightning immediately followed by thunder.

thun-der-cloud n. A dark cloud carrying an electric charge and producing lightning and thunder.

thun-der-show-er n. A brief rainstorm with thunder and lightning.

Thurs-day n. The fifth day of the week.

thus adv. In this or that way; therefore.

thwack v. To strike hard, using something flat.

thwart v. To prevent from happening; to prevent from doing something. n. A seat positioned crosswise in a boat.

thy adj. Pertaining to oneself; your.

thyme n. An aromatic mint herb whose leaves are used in cooking.

thy-roid adj. Anat. Pertaining to the thyroid gland. n. The gland in the neck of man that produces hormones which regulate food use and body growth.

thy-rox-ine *n.* A hormone secreted by the thyroid gland.

ti-ar-a *n.* A bejeweled crown in the form of a half circle and worn by women at formal occasions.

tick *n.* One of a series of rhythmical tapping sounds made by a clock; a small bloodsucking parasite, many of which are carriers of disease.

tick-et *n.* A printed slip of paper or cardboard allowing its holder to enter a specified event or to enjoy a privilege; a list of candidates who represent a political party.

tick-le *v.* To stroke lightly so as to cause laughter; to amuse or delight.
tickle, tickler *n.*

tidal wave *n.* An enormous rise of destructive ocean water caused by a storm or earthquake.

tid-bit *n.* A choice bit of food, news, or gossip.

tide *n.* The rise and fall of the surface level of the ocean which occurs twice a day due to the gravitational pull of the sun and moon on the earth.

tid-ings *pl., n.* News; information about events.

ti-dy *adj.* Well arranged; neat; orderly. *v.* To make orderly and neat.
tidily *adv.*, **tidiness** *n.*

tie *v.* To secure or bind with a rope, line, cord or other similar material; to make secure or fasten with a rope; to make a bow or knot in; to match an opponent's score. *n.* A string, rope, cord or other material used to join parts or hold something in place. A necktie; a beam that gives structural support. **railroad tie** A device, as timber, laid crosswise to support train tracks.

tier *n.* A layer or row placed one above the other. **tiered** *adj.*

ti-ger *n.*

A large carnivorous cat having tawny fur with black stripes.

tiger-eye *n.* A yellow-brown gemstone.

tight *adj.* Set closely together; bound or securely firm; not loose; taut; difficult. *adv.* Firmly. *Slang* Intoxicated.

tight-en *v.* To become or make tighter. **tightener** *n.*

tight-rope *n.* A tightly stretched horizontal rope high above the ground for the use of acrobats.

tights *pl., n.* A skintight stretchable garment, covering the lower half of the body.

tile *n.* A thin, hard, flat piece of plastic, asphalt, baked clay, or stone used to cover walls, floors, and roofs. *v.* To cover with tile.

till *prep. & conj.* Until; unless or before. *v.* To cultivate; to plow. *n.* A small cash register or drawer for holding money.

till-er *n.* A machine or person that tills land.

tilt *v.* To tip, as by raising one end. *n.* The state of tilting or being tilted.

tim-ber *n.* Wood prepared for building; a finished piece of wood or plank.

tim-ber line *n.* The height on a mountain beyond which trees cannot grow.

time *n.* A continuous period measured by clocks, watches, and calendars; the period or moment in which something happens or takes place. *adj.* Of or pertaining to time; pertaining to paying in installments. *Slang* A period of imprisonment.

time--shar-ing *n.* The joint ownership of property with each individual sharing the use of the property.

time tri-al *n.* A race or competition where each participant is timed individually over a set distance.

tim-id *adj.* Lacking self-confidence; shy.

tin *n.* A white, soft, malleable metallic element, symbolized by Sn; a container made of tin. *adj.* Made of tin.

tinc-ture *n.* A tinge of color; an alcohol solution of some medicinal substance. *v.* To tint.

tin-der *n.* A readily combustible substance or material used for kindling.

tin-der-box *n.* A portable metal box for holding tinder; a building which is a fire hazard; a situation which is about to explode with violence.

tine *n.* A narrow pointed spike or prong, as of a fork or antler.

tinge *v.* To impart a faint trace of color; to tint. *n.* A slight trace of added color.

tin-gle *v.* To feel a stinging or prickling sensation. **tingle** *n.*, **tingly** *adj.*

tink-er *n.* A person who mends domestic household utensils; one who does repair work of any kind. *v.* To work as a tinker; to attempt to fix, mend, or repair something in a bumbling, unprofessional manner.

tin-kle *v.* To produce a slight, sharp series of metallic ringing sounds.

tin-ny *adj.* Pertaining to or composed of tin.

tin-sel *n.* Thin strips of glittering material used for decorations.

tint *n.* A slight amount or trace of color. *v.* To color.

ti-ny *adj.* Minute; very small.

tip *v.* To slant from the horizontal or vertical. *n.* Extra money given as an acknowledgment of a service; a gratuity; a helpful hint.

tip-ple *v.* To drink an alcoholic beverage to excess.

tip-sy *adj.* Partially intoxicated **-iness** *n.*

ti-rade *n.* A long, violent speech or outpouring, as of censure.

tire *v.* To become or make weary; to be fatigued; to become bored. *n.* The outer covering for a wheel, usually made of rubber, serving to absorb shock and to provide traction.

tire-less *adj.* Untiring. **tirelessly** *adv.*

tis-sue *n.*, *Biol.* Similar cells and their products developed by plants and animals; a soft, absorbent piece of paper, consisting of two layers.

tis-sue pa-per *n.* Thin, almost transparent paper used for wrapping or protecting delicate articles.

ti-ta-ni-um *n.* A metallic element symbolized by Ti.

tithe *n.* A tenth of one's income given voluntarily for the support of a church. **tithe** *v.*, **tither** *n.*

tit-il-late *v.* To excite or stimulate in a pleasurable way. **titilating, titillative** *adj.*, **titillatingly** *adv.*, **titillation** *n.*

ti-tle *n.* An identifying name of a book, poem, play, or other creative work; a name or mark of distinction indicating a rank or an office. In law, the evidence giving legal right of possession or control of something. In sports, a championship. *v.* To give a title or name to.

to *prep.* Toward, opposite or near; in contact with; as far as; used as a function word indicating an action, movement, or condition suggestive of movement; indicating correspondence, dissimilarity, similarity, or proportion; indicating the one for which something is done or exists. *adv.* In the state, direction, or condition.

toad *n.* A tailless amphibian, resembling the frog but without teeth in the upper jaw and having a rougher, drier skin.

toad-stool *n.* A poisonous mushroom or inedible fungus, shaped like an umbrella.

toast *v.* To heat and brown over a fire or in a toaster. *n.* Sliced bread browned in a toaster. **toasty** *adj.*

toaster *n.* A device for toasting bread.

to-bac-co *n.* A tropical American plant widely cultivated for its leaves, which are prepared in various ways, as for chewing or smoking.

to-bog-gan *n.* A long sled-like vehicle without runners, having long thin boards curved upwards at the forward end. **tobogganist** *n.*, **toboggan** *v.*

to-day *adv.* On or during the present day. *n.* The present time, period, or day.

tod-dle *v.* To walk unsteadily with short steps.

tod-dler *n.* A small child learning to walk.

tod-dy *n.*, *pl.* **-ies** A drink made with hot water, sugar, spices, and liquor.

toe *n.* One of the extensions from the front part of a foot; the part of a stocking, boot or shoe that covers the toes.

tof-fee *n.* A chewy candy made of butter and brown sugar.

to-geth-er *adv.* In or into one group, mass, or body; regarded jointly; in time with what is happening or going on. **togetherness** *n.*

toil *v.* To labor very hard and continuously. *n.* A difficult task -some *adj.*

toi-let *n.* A porcelain apparatus with a flushing device, used as a means of disposing body wastes.

toi-lette *n.* The act of washing, dressing, or grooming oneself.

toi-let wa-ter *n.* A liquid with a scent stronger than cologne and weaker than perfume.

to-ken *n.* A keepsake; a symbol of authority or identity; a piece of imprinted metal used in place of money. *adj.* Done as a pledge or indication.

tol-er-ate *v.* To put up with; to recognize and respect the opinions and rights of others; to endure; to suffer. **toleration** *n.*, **tolerance, tolerant** *adj.*

toll *n.* A fixed charge for travel across a bridge or along a road. *v.* To sound a bell in repeated single, slow tones.

tom *n.* A male turkey or cat.

tom-a-hawk *n.* An ax used as a weapon or tool by North American Indians.

to-ma-to *n.*, *pl.* **-toes** A garden plant cultivated for its edible fruit; the fruit of such a plant.

tomb *n.* A vault for burying the dead; a grave.

tom-boy *n.* A girl whose behavior is characteristic of a boy. **tomboyish** *adj.*

tomb-stone *n.* A stone used to mark a grave.

tom-cat *n.* A male cat.

to-mor-row *n.* The day after the present day. *adv.* On the day following today.

ton *n.* A measurement of weight equal to 2,000 pounds. *Slang* A large amount.

tone *n.* A vocal or musical sound that has a distinct pitch, loudness, quality, and duration; the condition of the body and muscles when at rest.

tongs *pl.*, *n.* An implement with two long arms joined at one end, used for picking up or lifting.

tongue *n.* The muscular organ attached to the floor of the mouth, used in tasting, chewing, and speaking; anything shaped like a tongue, as the material under the laces or buckles of a shoe.

ton-ic *n.* A medicine or other agent used to restore health. In music, the first note of a scale. *Slang* Flavored carbonated soda.

to-night *n.* This night; the night of this day; the night that is coming. *adv.* On or during the present or coming night.

ton-sil *n.* One of a pair of tissue similar to lymph nodes, found on either side of the throat.

ton-sil-lec-to-my *n.* The surgical removal of tonsils.

too *adv.* Also; as well; more than is needed.

tool *n.* An implement used to perform a task; anything needed to do one's work. *v.* To make or shape with a tool. **tooling** *n.*

tooth *n.*, *pl.* **teeth** One of the hard, white structures rooted in the jaw and used for chewing and biting; the small, notched, projecting part of any object, such as a gear, comb or saw.

toothed, toothless *adj.*

top *n.* The highest part or surface of anything; a covering or lid; the aboveground part of a rooted plant; the highest degree; a toy having a symmetric body with a tapered end upon which it spins. **top** *v.*

to-paz *n.* A gemstone, usually yellow in color.

top-coat *n.* An outer coat.

top-ic *n.* The subject discussed in an essay, thesis, speech or other discourse; the theme.

top-most *adj.* Uppermost.

to-pog-ra-phy *n., pl.* **-ies** A detailed description of a region or place; a physical outline showing the features of a region or place.

top-ple *v.* To fall; to overturn.

top-sy--tur-vy *adv.* With the top side down; upside down. *adj.* In a confused state. *n.* Confusion.

To-rah *n.* The body of law and wisdom contained in Jewish Scripture and oral tradition; a parchment scroll that contains the first five books of the Old Testament.

torch *n.* A stick of resinous wood which is burned to give light; any portable device which produces hot flame. *Slang* To set fire to.

tor-ment *n.* Extreme mental anguish or physical pain; a source of trouble or pain. *v.* To cause terrible pain; to pester, harass, or annoy. **tormentingly** *adv.*, **tormentor** *n.*

tor-na-do *n., pl.* **-does** *or* **-dos** A whirling, violent windstorm accompanied by a funnel-shaped cloud that travels a narrow path over land; a whirlwind.

tor-pe-do *n., pl.* **-oes** A large, self-propelled, underwater missile launched from a ship, containing an explosive charge.

tor-pid *adj.* Having lost the power of motion or feeling; dormant. **torpidity** *n.*, **torpidly** *adv.*

tor-rent *n.* A swift, violent stream; a raging flood. **torrential** *adj.*

tor-rid *adj.* Parched and dried by the heat. **torridly** *adv.*

tor-sion *n.* The act or result of twisting; the stress produced when one end is held fast and the other turned. **torsional** *adj.*

tor-so *n., pl.* **-sos** *or* **-si** The trunk of the human body.

tort *n., Law* A wrongful act requiring compensation for damages.

tor-toise *n.* A turtle that lives on the land; a person or thing regarded as slow.

tor-tu-ous *adj.* Marked by repeated bends, turns, or twists; devious. **tortuousness** *n.*

tor-ture *n.* The infliction of intense pain as punishment; something causing anguish or pain. *v.* To subject or cause intense suffering; to wrench or twist out of shape. **-er** *n.*, **torturously** *adv.*

toss *v.* To fling or throw about con-

tinuously; to throw up in the air. *n.* A throw.

tot *n.* A young child; a toddler.

to-tal *n.* The whole amount or sum; the entire quantity. *adj.* Absolute; complete. **total** *v.*, **totally** *adv.*

to-tal-i-tar-i-an *adj.* Characteristic of a government controlled completely by one party; exercising complete political control. **totalitarian** *n.*

tote *v.* To carry something on one's arm or back.

to-tem *n.* An animal or plant regarded as having a close relationship to some family clan or group; a representation or symbol.

tot-ter *v.* To walk unsteadily; to shake or sway as if about to fall.

tou-can *n.*

A brightly colored tropical bird having a very large thin bill.

touch *v.* To allow a part of the body, as the hands, to feel or come into contact with; to hit or tap lightly; to eat or drink; to join; to come next to; to have an effect on; to move emotionally. *n.* An instance or act of touching; the feeling, fact, or act of touching or being touched; a trace; a tiny amount; a method, manner, or style of striking the keys of an instrument with a keyboard. **touchable** *adj.*

tough *adj.* Resilient and strong enough to withstand great strain without breaking or tearing; strong; hardy; very difficult; difficult to cut or chew. *n.* An unruly person; a thug. **toughly** *adv.*, **toughness** *n.*

tou-pee *n.* A wig worn to cover a bald spot on one's head.

tour *n.* A trip with visits to points of interest; a journey; a period or length of service at a single place or job. **tourism, tourist** *n.*

tour-na-ment *n.* A contest involving a number of competitors for a title or championship.

tour-ni-quet *n.* A device used to temporarily stop the flow of blood through an artery.

tou-sle *v.* To mess up; to disarrange.

tout *v.* To solicit customers. *Slang* In horse racing, a person who obtains information on racehorses and sells it to bettors. **touter** *n.*

tow *v.* To drag or pull, as by a chain or rope. *n.* An act of being pulled; a rope or line for pulling or dragging; coarse broken flax, hemp, or jute fiber prepared for spinning.

to-ward *or* **to-wards** *prep.* In the direction of; just before; somewhat before; regarding; with respect to.

tow-el *n.* An absorbent piece of cloth used for drying or wiping. **towel** *v.*

tow-er *n.* A very tall building or structure; a skyscraper; a place of security or defense. **towering** adj.

town n. A collection of houses and other buildings larger than a village and smaller than a city.

town-ship n. A subdivision of a county having corporate powers of municipal government.

tox-e-mi-a n., Pathol. Blood poisoning; a condition in which the blood contains toxins.

tox-ic adj. Relating to a toxin; destructive, deadly, or harmful.

tox-in n. A poisonous substance produced by chemical changes in plant and animal tissue.

toy n. An object designed for the enjoyment of children; any object having little value or importance; a small trinket; a bauble; a dog of a very small breed. v. To amuse or entertain oneself.

trace n. A visible mark or sign of a thing, person, or event; something left by some past agent or event. v. To follow the course or track of; to copy by drawing over the lines visible through a sheet of transparent paper. **traceable** adj., **traceably** adv., **tracer** n.

track n. A mark, as a footprint, left by the passage of anything; a regular course; a set of rails on which a train runs; a circular or oval course for racing. v. To follow the trail of footprints of. **trackable** adj., **tracker** n.

tract n. An extended area, as a stretch of land. Anat. An extensive region of the body, one comprising body organs and tissues that together perform a specialized function.

trac-tion n. The act of drawing, as a load over a surface; the state of being drawn or pulled; rolling friction that prevents a wheel from skidding over the surface on which it runs.

trac-tor n. A diesel or gasoline-powered vehicle used in farming to pull another piece of machinery.

trac-tor trail-er n. A large truck having a cab and no body, used to pull large trailers.

trade n. A business or occupation; skilled labor; a craft; an instance of selling or buying; a swap. **trade** v., **tradeable** adj., **trader** n.

trade-mark n. A brand name which is legally the possession of one company and cannot be used by another.

trade-off n. A compromise of possibilities when all cannot be attained at the same time; a surrender of one consideration in order to obtain another.

tra-di-tion n. The doctrines, knowledge, practices, and customs passed down from one generation to another. **traditional** adj., **traditionally** adv.

tra-duce v. To betray. **traducement**, **traducer** n.

traf-fic n. The passage or movement of vehicles; trade, buying and selling; the signals handled by a communications system. **trafficker** n.

trag-e-dy n., pl. -ies An extremely sad or fatal event or course of events; a story, play, or other literary work which arouses terror or pity by a series of misfortunes or sad events.

trail v. To draw, drag, or stream along behind; to follow in the tracks of; to follow slowly behind or in the rear; to let hang so as to touch the ground. n. Something that hangs or follows along behind; a rough path through a wooded area.

trail-er n. One who trails; a large vehicle that transports objects and is pulled by another vehicle.

train n. The part of a long gown that trails behind the wearer; a long moving line of vehicles or persons; a group of railroad cars. v. To instruct so as to make skillful or capable of doing something; to aim; to direct. **trainable** adj., -er, **training**, **trainee** n.

trait n. A quality or distinguishing feature, such as one's character.

trai-tor n. A person who betrays his country, a cause, or another's confidence.

tra-jec-to-ry n., pl. -ies The curved line or path of a moving object.

tram-mel n. A long, large net used to catch birds or fish; something that impedes movement. **trammeler** n.

tramp v. To plod or walk with a heavy step. n. A homeless person or vagrant who travels about aimlessly.

tram-ple v. To tread heavily; to stomp; to inflict injury, pain, or loss by heartless or brutal treatment. **trample**, **trampler** n.

tram-po-line n. A canvas device on which an athlete or acrobat may perform. **trampolinist** n.

trance n. A stupor, daze, mental state, or condition, such as produced by drugs or hypnosis.

tran-quil adj. Very calm, quiet, and free from disturbance. **tranquillity** n., **tranquilly** adv., **tranquilize** v.

trans-act v. To perform, carry out, conduct, or manage business in some way. **transaction**, **transactor** n.

tran-scend v. To pass beyond; to exceed; to surpass. **transcendent** adj., **transcendence** n.

tran-scribe v. To make copies of something; to adopt or arrange.

tran-script n. A written copy.

trans-crip-tion n. The process or act of transcribing.

trans-fer v. To remove, shift, or carry from one position to another. **transferable** adj., -ence, **transferer** n.

trans-fig-ure v. To change the outward appearance or form; to exalt; to glorify. **transfiguration** n.

trans-fix v. To pierce; to hold motionless, as with terror, awe or amazement. **transfixion** n.

trans-form v. To change or alter completely in nature, form or function. **-able** adj., **-ation**, **transformer** n.

trans-fuse v. To transfer liquid by pouring from one place to another. *Med.* To pass blood from the blood vessels of one person into the vessels of another. **transfusion, transfuser** *n.*

trans-gress *v.* To go beyond the limit or boundaries; to sin against or violate. **transgression, -or** *n.,* **transgressive** *adj.*

tran-sient *adj.* Not staying or lasting very long; moving from one location to another. **transient** *n.,* **transiently** *adv.*

tran-sit *n.* Passage or travel from one point to another; an instrument for surveying that measures horizontal and vertical angles.

trans-late *v.* To change from one language to another while retaining the original meaning; to explain. **translation, translator** *n.*

trans-lu-cent *adj.* Diffusing and admitting light but not allowing a clear view of the object.

trans-mis-sion *n.* The act or state of transmitting. *Mech.* The gears and associated parts of an engine which transmit power to the driving wheels of an automobile or other vehicle.

trans-mit *v.* To dispatch or convey from one thing, person, or place to another. **transmissible, -table** *adj.,* **-ter** *n.*

trans-mute *v.* To change in nature, kind, or substance. **transmutation** *n.*

tran-som *n.* A small, hinged window over a doorway; the horizontal crossbar in a window.

trans-par-ent *adj.* Admitting light so that images and objects can be clearly viewed; easy to understand; obvious. **transparency** *n.,* **transparently** *adv.*

tran-spire *v.* To give off waste products through plant or animal pores in the form of vapor; to happen; to take place. **transpiration** *n.*

trans-plant *v.* To remove a living plant from where it is growing and plant it in another place; to remove a body organ from one person and implant it in the body of another, as a kidney transplant; to remove skin from one area of the body and move it to another area of the body, as a skin graft. **transplantable** *adj.*

trans-port *v.* To carry or move from one place to another. *n.* A vessel or ship used to carry military supplies and troops; the process or act of transporting. **transportable** *adj.,* **transportation, transporter** *n.*

trans-pose *v.* To reverse the place or order of. *Mus.* To perform or write music in a key different from the one it was originally written in.

trans-sex-u-al *n.* A person whose sex has been changed surgically.

trap *n.* A device for holding or catching animals; a device which hurls clay pigeons, disks, or balls into the air to be fired upon by sportsmen; anything which deliberately catches or stops people or things. *v.* To catch in a trap; to place in an embarrassing position. *Slang* The mouth.

tra-peze *n.* A short horizontal bar suspended by two ropes, used for acrobatic exercise or stunts.

trap-shoot-ing *n.* The hobby or sport of shooting at clay pigeons, disks, and other objects hurled into the air.

trau-ma *n., pl.* **-mas** *or* **-mata** A severe wound caused by a sudden physical injury; an emotional shock causing lasting and substantial damage to a person's psychological development.

tra-vail *n.* Strenuous mental or physical exertion; labor in childbirth. *v.* To undergo the sudden sharp pain of childbirth.

trav-el *v.* To journey or move from one place to another. *n.* The process or act of traveling. **traveler** *n.*

tra-verse *v.* To pass over, across, or through. *n.* A path or route across; something that lies across something else. **traversable** *adj.,* **traversal, traverser** *n.*

trawl *n.* A strong fishing net which is dragged through water.

tray *n.* A flat container having a low rim, used for carrying, holding, or displaying something.

treach-er-ous *adj.* Disloyal; deceptive; unreliable. **-ly** *adv.,* **treachery** *n.*

tread *v.* To walk along, on, or over; to trample. *n.* The act or manner of treading; the part of a wheel which comes into contact with the ground.

trea-son *n.* Violation of one's allegiance to a sovereign or country, as giving or selling state secrets to another country or attempting to overthrow the government. **-able, treasonous** *adj.*

treas-ure *n.* Hidden riches; something regarded as valuable. *v.* To save and accumulate for future use; to value.

treasurer *n.* A person having charge and responsibilities for funds.

treas-ur-y *n., pl.* **-ies** A place where public or private funds are kept. **Treasury** The executive department of the United States Government in charge of collection, management, and expenditure of public revenue.

treat *v.* To behave or act toward; to regard in a given manner; to provide entertainment or food for another at one's own expense or cost. *n.* A pleasant surprise; something enjoyable which was unexpected. **treatable** *adj.,* **treater** *n.*

treat-ment *n.* The manner or act of treating; medical care.

treb-le *adj.* Multiplied by three; having three. *Mus.* Performing or having the highest range, part, or voice. *n.* A high-pitched sound or voice. **treble** *v.*

tree *n.* A tall woody plant, usually having a single trunk of considerable height; a diagram resembling a tree, as one used to show family descent. *Slang* To get the advantage of something. **tree** *v.,* **treeless** *adj.*

tre-foil *n.* Any of various plants having three leaflets with red, purple, yellow, or pink flowers.

trek *v.* To make a slow and arduous journey. **trek, trekker** *n.*

trel-lis *n.* A latticework frame used for supporting vines and other climbing plants.

trem-ble *v.* To shake involuntarily, as with fear or from cold; to express or feel anxiety. **tremble, trembler** *n.*, **trembly** *adj.*

tre-men-dous *adj.* Extremely huge, large, or vast. *Slang* Wonderful.

trem-or *n.* A quick, shaking movement; any continued and involuntary trembling or quavering of the body.

trench *n.* A ditch; a long, narrow excavation in the ground. *v.* To cut deep furrows for protection. **trencher** *n.*

trend *n.* A general inclination, direction, or course; a fad. *v.* To have or take a specified direction. **trendsetter** *n.*

tres-pass *v.* To infringe upon another's property. In law, to invade the rights, property, or privacy of another without consent or knowledge.

tres-tle *n.* A bar or beam supported by four legs, used as a support, as for a table.

tri-al *n.* In law, the examination and hearing of a case before a court of law in order to determine the case; an attempt or effort; an experimental treatment or action to determine a result. *adj.* Pertaining to or of a trial; performed or used during an experiment or test.

tri-an-gle *n.*, *Geom.*

A plane figure bounded by three sides and having three angles. **triangular** *adj.*, **triangularity** *n.*

tribe *n.* A group of people composed of several villages, districts, or other groups which share a common language, culture, and name.

trib-u-la-tion *n.* Great distress or suffering caused by oppression.

trib-un-al *n.* A decision-making body.

trib-ute *n.* An action of respect or gratitude to someone; money or other goods given by one country to another showing obedience and insuring against invasion.

tri-ceps *n.*, *Anat.* The large muscle at the back of the upper arm.

trick *n.* An action meant to fool, as a scheme; a prank; a feat of magic. *v.* To deceive or cheat. **tricky** *adj.*

trick-er-y *n.* Deception.

trick-le *v.* To flow in droplets or a small stream. **trickle** *n.*

tri-col-or *n.* The French color in the flag. **tricolored** *adj.*

tri-cy-cle *n.* A small vehicle having three wheels, propelled by pedals.

tri-dent *n.* A long spear with three prongs, used as a weapon.

tried *adj.* Tested and proven reliable or useful.

tri-en-ni-al *adj.* Happening every third year; lasting for a time period of three years. **triennial** *n.*, **triennially** *adv.*

tri-fle *n.* Something of little value or importance; a dessert made with cake, jelly, wine, and custard. *v.* To use or treat without proper concern.

trig-ger *n.* A lever pulled to fire a gun; a device used to release or start an action. *v.* To start.

trill *n.* A tremulous utterance of successive tones. *v.* To utter with a fluttering sound.

tril-lion *n.* The cardinal number equal to one thousand billion.

trim *v.* To clip or cut off small amounts in order to make neater; to decorate. *adj.* Neat. **trim** *n.*

tri-ni-tro-tol-u-ene *n.* A very powerful explosive, abbreviated as TNT.

trin-ket *n.* A small piece of jewelry.

tri-o *n.* A set or group of three.

trip *n.* Travel from one place to another; a journey; a loss of balance. *v.* To stumble. *Slang* A hallucinatory effect induced by drugs.

tripe *n.* The stomach lining of oxen or similar animals, used as food. *Slang* Nonsense.

trip-le *adj.* Having three parts. *v.* To multiply by three; in baseball, a three-base hit.

trip-let *n.* One of three born at the same time.

trip-li-cate *n.* A group of three identical things. **triplicate** *v.*

tri-pod *n.* A three-legged stand or frame.

trite *adj.* Used too often; common.

tri-umph *v.* To be victorious. *n.* A victory. **triumphant** *adj.*, **-ly** *adv.*

triv-i-al *adj.* Insignificant; of little value or importance; ordinary.

Tro-jan *n.* A determined, courageous person.

troll *v.* To fish by pulling a baited line slowly behind a boat; to sing with a loud, full voice. *n.* The act of trolling for fish; dwarf or elf.

trol-ley *n.* A streetcar powered by electricity from overhead lines; a small container or basket used to convey material, as in an underground tunnel or mine.

trom-bone *n.* A brass musical instrument, larger and lower in pitch than a trumpet.

troop *n.* A group or assembly of people or animals; a group of Boy Scouts or Girl Scouts having an adult leader; a military unit. **trooper** *n.*

tro-phy *n.*, *pl.* **-ies** A prize or object, such as a plaque, awarded to someone for his success, victory, or achievement.

trop-ic *n.* Either of two imaginary parallel lines which constitute the Torrid Zone. **Tropics** The very warm region of the earth's surface between the Tropic of Cancer and the Tropic of Capricorn. **tropical** *adj.*

tro-po-sphere *n.* The lowest atmosphere between the earth's surface and the stratosphere.

trot *n.* The gait of a horse or other four-footed animal, between a walk and a run, in which the hind leg and opposite front leg move at about the same time. trot *v.*

trou-ble *n.* Danger; affliction; need; distress; an effort; physical pain, disease or malfunction. *v.* To bother; to worry; to be bothered; to be worried.
troubler *n.*, troublingly *adv.*

trough *n.* A long, narrow, shallow container, especially one that holds food or water for animals.

trounce *v.* To whip or beat; to defeat decisively.

troupe *n.* A group, especially of the performing arts. troupe *v.*

trou-sers *pl., n.* An outer garment that covers the body from the waist down.

trous-seau *n., pl.* -seaux *or* -seaus The wardrobe, linens, and other similar articles of a bride.

trout *n.* A freshwater game or food fish.

trowel *n.* A flat-bladed garden tool with a pointed blade, used for digging.
trowel *v.*, troweler *n.*

tru-ant *n.* A person who is absent from school without permission.
truancy *n.*, truant *adj.*

truce *n.* An agreement to stop fighting; a cease fire.

truck *n.* An automotive vehicle used to carry heavy loads; any of various devices with wheels designed to move heavy loads; garden vegetables for sale. trucker *n.*

trudge *v.* To walk heavily; to plod.

true *adj.* In accordance with reality or fact; not false; real; loyal; faithful. *adv.* Truthfully. truly *adv.*

Truman, Harry S *n.* The 33rd president of the United States from 1945-1953.

trump *n.* In cards, a suit of any cards which outrank all other cards for a selected period of time.

trum-pet *n., Mus.* A brass instrument having a flared bell, valves, and a mouthpiece. *v.* To proclaim something loudly.

trunk *n.*

The main part of a tree; the human body, excluding the head, arms and legs; a sturdy box for packing clothing, as for travel or storage; the long snout of an elephant. trunks Men's clothing worn for swimming or athletics.

truss *v.* To fasten or tie securely. *Med.* A support or device worn to keep a hernia in place.

trust *n.* Confidence or faith in a person or thing; care or charge. *Law* The confidence or arrangement by which property is managed and held for the good or benefit of another person. *v.* To have confidence or faith in; to believe; to expect; to entrust; to depend on.

truth *n., pl.* truths The facts correspond-

ing with actual events or happenings; sincerity or honesty. truthful *adj.*, truthfully *adv.*, truthfulness *n.*

try *v.* To make an attempt; to make an effort; to strain; to hear or conduct a trial; to place on trial.
trying *adj.*, tryout *n.*

tsu-na-mi *n.* An extensive and destructive ocean wave caused by an underwater earthquake.

tub *n.* A round, low, flat-bottomed, vessel with handles on the side, as one used for washing.

tu-ba *n.* A large, brass wind instrument having a low range.

tube *n.* A hollow cylinder, made of metal, rubber, glass or other material, used to pass or convey something through. tube, tubal *adj.*

tu-ber *n.*

The underground stem of certain plants, as the potato, with buds from which new plants arise.

tu-ber-cu-lo-sis *n.* A contagious lung disease of humans and animals caused by microorganisms; abbreviated as TB.

tuck *n.* A flattened fold of material, usually stitched in place. *v.* To sew or make a tuck in material; to put in a safe place; to make secure.

Tues-day *n.* The third day of the week.

tuft *n.* A small cluster of feathers, threads, hair, or other material fastened or growing closely together.

tug *v.* To strain and pull vigorously. *n.* A hard pull; a strong force.

tu-i-tion *n.* Payment for instruction, as at a private school or college.

tu-lip *n.* A bulb-bearing plant, having upright cup-like blossoms.

tum-ble *v.* To fall or cause to fall; to perform acrobatic rolls, somersaults, and similar maneuvers; to mix up; to turn over and over. tumbler, tumble *n.*

tum-ble-down *adj.* Ramshackle; in need of repair.

tum-brel *n.* A cart which can discharge its load by tilting.

tu-mor *n., Pathol.* A swelling on or in any part of the body; an abnormal growth which may be malignant or benign.

tu-mult *n.* The confusion and noise of a crowd; a riot; any violent commotion.
tumultuous *adj.*

tu-na *n., pl.* -na *or* -nas Any of several large marine food fish.

tun-dra *n.* A treeless area in the arctic regions having a subsoil which is permanently frozen.

tune *n.* A melody which is simple and easy to remember; agreement; harmony. *v.* To adjust. tunable *adj.*, tunably *adv.*, tuner *n.*

tu-nic *n.* A loose garment extending to the knees, worn by ancient Romans and Greeks.

tun-nel *n.* An underground or underwater passageway. **tunnel** *v.*

tur-ban *n.* A Moslem headdress that consists of a long scarf wound around the head.

tur-bu-lent *adj.* Marked by a violent disturbance.

turf *n.* A layer of earth with its dense growth of grass and matted roots. *Slang* Home territory or ground.

tur-key *n.* A large game bird of North America, having a bare head and extensible tail; the meat of this bird. *Slang* A failure.

tur-moil *n.* A state of confusion or commotion.

turn *v.* To move or cause to move around a center point; to revolve or rotate; to transform or change; to move so that the bottom side of something becomes the top and the top becomes the bottom; to strain or sprain; to translate; to go beyond or to pass; to become 40; to make sour; to spoil, as food; to change or reverse the position or direction of; to become or cause to become hostile. **turn to** To seek comfort or advice from; to open a book to a certain page. **turn down** To refuse or deny. **turn in** To go to bed. **turn off** To be or cause to be disgusted with something. **in turn** One after another. **turn over** To ponder; to think about; to give up or transfer to another. **turn up** To arrive; to appear; to find. **turner** *n.*

tur-nip *n.* An edible root from the mustard family of plants.

tur-pen-tine *n.* The thick sap of certain pine trees; a clear liquid manufactured from this sap, used to thin paint.

tur-quoise *n.* A blue-green gemstone; a light bluish-green color. **turquoise** *adj.*

tur-tle *n.*

A scaly-skinned animal having a soft body covered with a hard shell into which the head, legs, and tail can be retracted.

tur-tle-neck *n.* A high collar that fits closely around the neck.

tusk *n.* A long, curved tooth, as of an elephant or walrus.

tus-sle *n.* A hard fight or struggle with a problem or person. **tussle** *v.*

tu-tor *n.* A person who teaches another person privately. *v.* To teach, coach, or instruct privately.

tu-tu *n.* A very short ballet skirt.

tux-e-do *n.* A semiformal dress suit worn by men.

twain *n.* Two.

twang *n.* A sharp, ringing sound like that of a violin or other stringed instrument. *v.* To cause or make a twang.

tweak *v.* To pinch and twist sharply.

tweez-ers *pl., n.* A small, pincer-like implement used to grasp or pluck small objects.

twelve *n.* The cardinal number equal to 11 + 1. **twelve** *adj. & pron.*

twen-ty *n.* The cardinal number equal to 19 + 1 or 2 X 10. **twenty** *adj. & pron.*

twice *adv.* Double; two times.

twid-dle *v.* To turn or twirl in an aimless way.

twig *n.* A small branch which grows from a larger branch on a tree.

twi-light *n.* The soft light of the sky between sunset and complete darkness.

twill *n.* A weave that produces the parallel rib on the surface of a fabric.

twine *v.* To weave or twist together. *n.* A strong cord or thread made by twisting many threads together.

twinge *n.* A sudden, sharp pain; a brief emotional or mental pang. **twinged** *v.*

twin-kle *v.* To gleam or shine with quick flashes; to sparkle. **twinkle** *n.*

twirl *v.* To rotate or cause to turn around and around. **twirl** *n.*

twist *v.* To wind two or more pieces of thread, twine, or other materials together to make a single strand; to curve; to bend; to distort or change the meaning of; to injure and wrench.

twit *v.* To tease about a mistake. *n.* A taunting reproach.

twitch *v.* To move or cause to move with a jerky movement. *n.* A sudden tug.

twit-ter *v.* To utter a series of chirping sounds; to chatter nervously.

two *n.* The cardinal number of 1 + 1; the second in a sequence.

ty-coon *n., Slang* A business person of wealth and power.

tyke *n.* A small child.

Tyler, John *n.* The 10th president of the United States from 1841-1845.

ty-phoid *n., Path.* An acute, infectious disease caused by germs in drink or food, resulting in high fever and intestinal hemorrhaging. **typhoid** *adj.*

typ-i-cal *adj.* Exhibiting the characteristics of a certain class or group. **typically** *adv.*

typ-i-fy *v.* To be characteristic or typical of; to show all the traits or qualities of. **typified, typifying** *adj.*

typ-ist *n.* The operator of a typewriter.

ty-po *n., Slang* An error in typewriting or in setting type; any printed error which was not the fault of the author.

ty-ran-no-sau-rus *n.*

A large, flesh-eating dinosaur which walked on its hind legs.

tyr-an-ny *n.* Harsh, absolute, and unfair rule by a king or other ruler; complete control.

tyr-an-nize *v.* To rule or control completely.

ty-rant *n.* An absolute, unjust, or cruel ruler; one who exercises power, authority, or control unfairly.

ty-ro *also* **ti-ro** *n.* A novice or a beginner.

U, u The twenty-first letter of the English alphabet.

ud-der *n.* The milk-producing organ pouch of some female animals, having two or more teats.

ugh *interj.* Used to express disgust or horror.

ug-ly *adj.* Offensive; unpleasant to look at -lily *adv.* -liest, -lier *adj.*, -liness *n.*

uh *interj.* To express hesitation.

u-ku-le-le *n.* A small, four-stringed musical instrument, orginally from Hawaii.

ul-cer *n.* A festering, inflamed sore on a mucous membrane or on the skin that results in the destruction of the tissue. ulcerous *adj.* ulceration *n.*, ulcerate *v.*

ul-na *n.*, *Anat.* One of the two bones of the forearm.

ul-ti-mate *adj.* Final; ending; most extreme. ultimately *adv.*, ultimateness *n.*, ultimacy *n.*

ul-ti-ma-tum *n.*, *pl* -tums, -ta A final demand, proposal, or choice, as in-egotiating.

ultra- *prefix.* Beyond the scope, range, or limit of something.

ul-tra-mod-ern *adj.* Extremely advanced or modern in style or ideas.

ul-tra-son-ic *adj.* Relating to sound frequencies inaudible to humans.

ul-tra-vi-o-let *adj.* Producing radiation having wave-lengths just shorter than those of visible light and longer than those of X rays. ultraviolet *n.*

um-bil-i-cal cord *n.*

The structure by which a fetus is attached to its mother, serving to supply food and dispose of waste.

um-brel-la *n.* A collapsible frame covered with plastic or cloth, held above the head as protection from sun or rain.

um-pire *n.* In sports, the person who rules on plays in a game. *v.* To act as an umpire.

ump-teen *adj.*, *Slang* An indefinitely large number. umpteenth *adj.*

un-prefix The reverse or opposite of an act; removal or release from.

un-able *adj.* Not having the mental capabilities.

un-ac-com-pa-nied *adj.* Alone; without a companion. *Mus.* Solo.

un-ac-count-a-ble *adj.* Without an explanation; mysterious; not responsible. unaccountably *adv.*, -bility *n.*

un-ac-cus-tomed *adj.* Not used to or in the habit of; not ordinary.

u-nan-i-mous *adj.* Agreed to completely; based on the agreement of all. unanimously *adv.*

un-armed *adj.* Lacking means for protection.

un-as-sum-ing *adj.* Modest and not showy. unassumingness *n.*

un-at-tach-ed *adj.* Not engaged, going steady, or married.

un-a-void-a-ble *adj.* Inevitable; unstoppable. unavoidably *adv.*

un-a-ware *adj.* Not realizing. -ness *n.*

un-bear-a-ble *adj.* Not possible to endure; intolerable. unbearably *adv.*

un-be-com-ing *adj.* Unattractive; not pleasing; notproper. -ness *n.*,

un-be-known *or* unbeknownst *adj.* Not known; without one's knowledge.

un-be-liev-a-ble *adj.* Incredible; hard to accept; not to be believed. -ly *adv.*

un-called for *adj.* Not necessary or needed; not requested.

un-can-ny *adj.* Strange, odd, or mysterious; exceptional. uncannily *adv.*, uncanniness *n.*

un-cer-tain *adj.* Doubtful; not sure; not known; hard to predict. uncertainly *adv.*, uncertainness *n.*

un-changed *adj.* Having nothing new or different.

un-civ-i-lized *adj.* Without culture or refinement; without an established cultural and social way of living.

un-cle *n.* The brother of one's mother or father; the husband of an aunt.

un-clean *adj.* Immoral; dirty; not decent. uncleanness *n.*, uncleanly *adv.*

un-clothe *v.* To uncover or undress. unclothed *adj.*

un-com-fort-a-ble *adj.* Disturbed; not at ease physically or mentally; causing discomfort. uncomfortably *adv.*

un-com-mon *adj.* Rare; odd; unusual. uncommonly *adv.*, uncommonness *n.*

un-com-pro-mis-ing *adj.* Firm; unwilling to give in or to compromise. uncompromisingly *adv.*

un-con-cern *n.* Lack of interest; disinterest; indifference.

un-con-cerned *adj.* the state of not having any interest in something or someone. -ness *n.*, -ly *adv.*

un-con-di-tion-al *adj.* Without conditions or limits. unconditionally *adv.*

un-con-scious *adj.* Not mentally aware; done without thought; not on purpose. unconsciously *adv.* unconsciousness *n.*

un-con-sti-tu-tion-al *adj.* Contrary to the constitution or the basic laws of a state or country.

un-couth *adj.* Acting or speaking crudely, unrefined; clumsy or awkward. uncouthness *n.*, -ly *adv.*

un-cov-er *v.* To remove the cover from something; to disclose. uncovered *adj.*

un-de-cid-ed *adj.* Unsettled; having made no firm decision; open to change. undecidedly *adv.*

un-de-ni-able *adj.* Not open to doubt or denial; not possible to contradict. undeniably *adv.*

un-der *prep.* Below, in place or position; in a place lower than another; less in degree, number, or other quality; inferior in rank, quality, or character; during the reign or period; in accordance with. less than the required amount; insufficient.

un-der *prefix.* Location beneath or below; lower in importance or rank, degree or amount.

un-der-brush *n.* Small bushes, vines, and plants that grow under tall trees.

un-der-clothes *pl., n.* Clothes worn next to the skin; underwear.

un-der-de-vel-oped *adj.* Not fully mature or grown; lacking modern communications and industry.

un-der-foot *adj.* Underneath or below the feet; being so close to one's feet as to be in the way.

un-der-go *v.* To have the experience of; to be subjected to.

un-der-grad-u-ate *n.* A college or university student studying for a bachelor's degree.

un-der-hand *adj.* Done deceitfully and secretly; sneaky. -ed *adj.* -edly *adv.*

un-der-line *v.* To draw a line directly under something. underline *n.*

un-der-mine *v.* To weaken; to make less strong.

un-der-neath *adv.* Beneath or below; on the under side; lower. *prep.* Under; below.

un-der-priv-i-leged *adj.* Deprived of economic and social advantages.

un-der-rate *v.* To rate or value below the true worth.

un-der-score *v.* To emphasize.

un-der-sell *v.* To sell for less than a competitor.

un-der-side *n.* The side or part on the bottom.

un-der-stand *v.* To comprehend; to realize; to know the feelings and thoughts of. understanding *v.*

un-der-stand-a-ble *adj.* Able to sympathize or comprehend. -ably *adv.*

un-der-state *v.* To make too little of the actual situation. understatement *n.*

un-der-stood *adj.* Agreed upon by all.

un-der-stud-y *v.* To learn another person's part or role in order to be able to replace him if necessary.

un-der-take *v.* To set about to do a task; to pledge oneself to a certain job; to attempt. undertaking *n.*

un-der-tak-er *n.* A person who prepares the dead for burial.

un-der-tone *n.* A low, quiet voice; a pale or subdued color visible through other colors.

un-der-tow *n.* The underwater current which runs in the opposite direction of the surface current.

un-der-wa-ter *adj.* Occurring, happening or used beneath the surface of the water. underwater *adv.*

un-de-sir-a-ble *adj.* Offensive; not wanted. undesirably *adv.*

un-do *v.* To cancel; to reverse; to loosen or unfasten; to open a package.

un-done *adj.* Not finished; unfastened; ruined.

un-du-late *v.* To move from side to side with a flowing motion; to have a wavy shape. undulation *n.*

un-dy-ing *adj.* Without end.

un-earth *v.* To dig up from the earth; to find or discover.

un-earth-ly *adj.* Strange; not from this world.

un-eas-y *adj.* Feeling or causing distress or discomfort; embarrassed; awkward; uncertain. uneasily *adv.*, uneasiness *n.*

un-em-ployed *adj.* Without a job; without work. unemployment *n.* .

un-e-qual *adj.* Not even; not fair; not of the same size or time; lacking sufficient ability. unequaled *adj.*

un-e-ven *adj.* Not equal; varying in consistency or form; not balanced. -ly *adv.*

un-e-vent-ful *adj.* Lacking in significance; calm. uneventfully *adv.*

un-expect-ed *adj.* Surprising; happening without warning. unexpectedly *adv.*

un-fail-ing *adj.* Constant, unchanging.

un-fair *adj.* Not honest; marked by a lack of justice. -ly *adv.*, unfairness *n.*

un-faith-ful *adj.* Breaking a promise or agreement; without loyalty; guilty of adultery. -ness *n.*, unfaithfully *adv.*

un-fa-mil-iar *adj.* Not knowing; strange; foreign. unfamiliarity *n.*

un-fa-vor-able *adj.*, Not desired; harmful; unpleasant.

un-feel-ing *adj.* Without sympathy; hardhearted; without sensation. unfeelingly *adv.*

un-fit *adj.* Not suitable; not qualified; in poor body or mental health. unfitly *adv.*, unfitness *n.*

un-fold *v.* To open up the folds of and lay flat; to reveal gradually. -ment *n.*

un-fore-seen *adj.* Not anticipated or expected.

un-for-get-ta-ble *adj.* Impossible or hard to forget; memorable. -ably *adv.*

un-for-tu-nate *adj.* Causing or having bad luck, damage, or harm. *n.* A person who has no luck. -ly *adv.*

un-found-ed *adj.* Not founded or based on fact; groundless; lacking a factual basis.

un-friend-ly *adj.* Showing a lack of kindness; not friendly; not favorable. unfriendliness *n.*

un-furl *v.* To unroll or unfold; to open up or out.

un-fur-nished *adj.* Without furniture.

un-god-ly *adj.* Wicked; evil; lacking reverence for God. ungodliness *n.*

un-grate-ful *adj.* Not thankful; showing no appreciation. ungratefully *adv.*

un-guent *n.* A healing or soothing salve; ointment.

un-heard *adj.* Not heard; not listened to.

un-heard--of *adj.* Not known or done before; without precedent.

un-hook *v.* To release or undo from a hook.

u-ni-corn *n.*

A mythical animal resembling a horse, with a horn in the center of its forehead.

u-ni-cy-cle *n.* A one wheeled vehicle with pedals.

un-i-den-ti-fied fly-ing ob-ject *n.* A flying object that cannot be explained or identified, abbreviated as UFO.

u-ni-form *n.* Identical clothing worn by the members of a group to distinguish them from the general population. **uniformly** *adv.*

u-ni-fy *v.* To come together as one; to unite. **unifier** *n.*

un-in-hab-it-ed *adj.* Not lived in; empty.

un-in-ter-est-ed *adj.* Having no interest or concern in; not interested.

un-ion *n.* The act of joining together of two or more groups or things; a group of countries or states joined under one government; a marriage; an organized body of employees who work together to upgrade their working conditions and wages. **Union** The United States, especially the federal government during the Civil War.

u-nique *adj.* Unlike any other; sole. **uniqueness** *n.*, **uniquely** *adv.*

u-ni-sex *adj.* Adaptable and appropriate for both sexes.

u-ni-son *n.* In music, the exact sameness of pitch, as of a tone; harmonious agreement.

u-nit *n.* Any one of several parts regarded as a whole; an exact quantity that is used as a standard of measurement; a special section or part of a machine.

u-nite *v.* To join or come together for a common purpose.

United Nations *n.* An international organization formed in 1945.

United States of America *n.* A country bordering the Atlantic and Pacific Oceans, Mexico, and Canada.

u-ni-ty *n.*, *pl.* **-ies** The fact or state of being one; accord; agreement; harmony.

u-ni-valve *n.* A mollusk having a one-piece shell, such as a snail.

u-ni-ver-sal *adj.* Having to do with the world or the universe in its entirety. **universally** *adv.*, **universalness** *n.*

u-ni-verse *n.* The world, stars, planets, space, and all that is contained.

u-ni-ver-si-ty *n.*, *pl.* **-ies** An educational institution offering undergraduate and graduate degrees in a variety of academic areas.

un-just *adj.* Not fair; lacking justice or fairness. **unjustly** *adv.*

un-kempt *adj.* Poorly groomed; messy; untidy.

un-kind *adj.* Harsh; lacking in sympathy, concern, or understanding. **unkindly** *adj.* **unkindness** *n.*

un-known *adj.* Strange; unidentified; not known; not familiar or famous.

un-lead-ed *adj.* Containing no lead.

un-like *prep.* Dissimilar; not alike; not equal in strength or quantity; not usual for.

un-lim-it-ed *adj.* Having no boundaries or limitations.

un-load *v.* To take or remove the load; to unburden; to dispose or get rid of by selling in volume.

un-lock *v.* To open, release, or unfasten a lock; open with a key.

un-loose *v.* To loosen or undo; to release.

un-luck-y *adj.* Unfortunate; having bad luck; disappointing or unsuitable.

un-manned *adj.* Designed to operate or be operated without a crew of people.

un-men-tion-a-ble *adj.* Improper or unsuitable.

un-mis-tak-a-ble *adj.* Very clear and evident; understood; obvious.

un-mor-al *adj.* Having no moral knowledge.

un-nat-u-ral *adj.* Abnormal or unusual; strange; artificial. **unnaturally** *adv.*

un-nec-es-sar-y *adj.* Not needed; not appropriate. **unnecessarily** *adv.*

un-nerve *v.* To frighten; to upset. **unnervingly** *adv.*

un-num-bered *adj.* Countless; not identified by number.

un-oc-cu-pied *adj.* Empty; not occupied.

un-pack *v.* To remove articles out of trunks, suitcases, boxes, or other storage places.

un-pleas-ant *adj.* Not agreeable; not pleasant. **-tly** *adv.*, **unpleasantness** *n.*

un-pop-u-lar *adj.* Not approved or liked. **unpopularity** *n.*

un-pre-dict-a-ble *adj.* Not capable or being foretold; not reliable. **unpredictably** *adj.*

un-pre-pared *adj.* Not equipped or ready.

un-pro-fes-sion-al *adj.* Contrary to the standards of a profession; having no professional status.

un-prof-it-a-ble *adj.* Showing or giving no profit; serving no purpose.

un-qual-i-fied *adj.* Lacking the proper qualifications; unreserved.

un-rav-el *v.* To separate threads; to solve; to clarify; to come apart.

un-re-al *adj.* Having no substance or reality.

un-rea-son-a-ble *adj.* Not according to reason; exceeding all reasonable limits.

un-re-li-a-ble *adj.* Unable to be trusted; not dependable.

un-re-served *adj.* Done or given without reserve; unlimited.

un-re-strained *adj.* Not held back, forced, or affected.

un-ru-ly *adj.* Disorderly; difficult to subdue or control.

un-sat-is-fac-to-ry *adj.* Unacceptable; not pleasing.

un-screw *v.* To loosen or unfasten by removing screws from.

un-scru-pu-lous *adj.* Without morals, guiding principles, or rules. **unscrupulously** *adv.*, **-ness** *n.*

un-seat *v.* To cause to lose one's seat; to force out of office.

un-sel-fish *adj.* Willing to share; thinking of another's well-being before one's own. **unselfishly** *adv.*, **unselfishness** *n.*

un-set-tle *v.* To cause to be upset or excited; to disturb. **unsettled** *adj.*

un-sheathe *v.* To draw a sword from a

sheath or other case.

un-sight-ly *adj.* Not pleasant to look at; ugly.

un-skilled *adj.* Having no skills or training in a given kind of work.

un-skill-ful *adj.* Lacking in proficiency. unskillfully *adv.*, unskillfulness *n.*

un-sound *adj.* Having defects; not solidly made; unhealthy in body or mind. unsoundly *adv.*, unsoundness *n.*

un-speak-a-ble *adj.* Of or relating to something which cannot be expressed or described. unspeakably *adv.*

un-sta-ble *adj.* Not steady or firmly fixed; having the tendency to fluctuate or change.

un-stead-y *adj.* Not secure; unstable; variable. unsteadily *adv.*, -diness *n.*

un-sub-stan-tial *adj.* Lacking strength, weight, or solidity; unreal.

un-suit-a-ble *adj.* Unfitting; not suitable; not appropriate for a specific circumstance. -bly *adv.*, -ness *n.*

un-tan-gle *v.* To free from snarls or entanglements.

un-thank-ful *adj.* Ungrateful.

un-think-a-ble *adj.* Unimaginable.

un-ti-dy *adj.* Messy; showing a lack of tidiness. untidily *adv.*, untidiness *n.*

un-tie *v.* To unfasten or loosen; to free from a restraint or bond.

un-til *prep.* Up to the time of. *conj.* To the time when; to the degree or place.

un-time-ly *adj.* Premature; before the expected time.

un-told *adj.* Not revealed; not told; inexpressible; cannot be described or revealed.

un-touch-a-ble *adj.* Cannot be touched; incapable of being obtained or reached.

un-true *adj.* Not true; contrary to the truth; not faithful; disloyal.

un-truth *n.* Something which is not true; the state of being false. untruthful *adj.*, -fully *adv.*, -ness *n.*

un-used *adj.* Not put to use; never having been used.

un-u-su-al *adj.* Not usual; uncommon. unusually *adv.*, unusualness *n.*

un-ut-ter-a-ble *adj.* Incapable of being described or expressed; unpronounceable. unutterably *adv.*

un-veil *v.* To remove a veil from; to uncover; to reveal.

un-war-y *adj.* Not cautious or careful; careless.

un-whole-some *adj.* Unhealthy; morally corrupt or harmful.

un-will-ing *adj.* Reluctant; not willing. unwillingly *adv.*, unwillingness *n.*

un-wind *v.* To undo or reverse the winding of; to untangle.

un-wise *adj.* Lacking good judgment or common sense. unwisely *adv.*

un-wor-thy *adj.* Not deserving; not becoming or befitting; lacking merit or worth; shameful. unworthiness *n.*

up *adv.* From a lower position to a higher one; on, in, or to a higher level, position, or place; to a greater degree or amount; in or into a specific action

or an excited state, as they stirred up trouble; to be even with in time, degree, or space, as up to date; under consideration, as up for discussion; in a safe, protected place, as vegetable are put up in jars; totally, completely, as the building was burned up; in baseball, at bat or, as up to bat. up front To be honest.

up-beat *n.*, *Mus.* The relatively unaccented beat preceding the down beat. *adj.* Optimistic; happy.

up-bring-ing *n.* The process of teaching and rearing a child.

up-com-ing *adj.* About to take place or appear.

up-date *v.* To revise or bring up-to-date; to modernize. update *n.*

up-draft *n.* An upward current of air.

up-grade *v.* To increase the grade, rank, or standard of. *n.* An upward slope.

up-hill *adv.* Up an incline. *adj.* Hard to accomplish; going up a hill or incline.

up-hol-ster *v.* To cover furniture with fabric covering, cushions, and padding. upholsterer, upholstery *n.*

up-keep *n.* The cost and work needed to keep something in good condition.

up-land *n.* A piece of land which is elevated or higher than the land around it.

up-lift *v.* To raise or lift up; to improve the social, economic, and moral level of a group or of a society.

up-on *prep.* On.

up-per *adj.* Higher in status, position or location. *n.* The part of a shoe to which the sole is attached. *Slang* A drug used as a stimulant. upper case *n.* The large or capital case of letters.

up-per--class *adj.* Economically or socially superior.

up-per-class-man *n.* A junior or senior at a high school or college.

up-right *adj.* Having a vertical direction or position; honest. *n.* Something standing vertically, such as a beam in a building.

up-ris-ing *n.* A revolt; a rebellion; an insurrection.

up-roar *n.* A confused, loud noise; a commotion.

up-root *v.* To detach completely by pulling up the roots. uprooter *n.*

up-set *v.* To capsize; to turn over; to throw into confusion or disorder; to overcome; to beat unexpectedly. *adj.* Capsized; overturned; distressed; troubled. upsetter *n.*

up-stage *adj. & adv.* Toward or at the back part of a stage. *Slang* To steal the show or scene from.

up-stairs *adv.* Up one or more flights of stairs. *adj.* Situated on the upper floor.

up-stand-ing *adj.* Straightforward; honest; upright.

up-tight *adv.* Nervous, tense, or anxious.

up--to--date *adj.* Most current or recent; appropriate to the present time.

up-town *adv.* Toward or in the upper part of town. uptown *adv.*

up-ward *or* **up-wards** *adv.* From a lower

position to or toward a higher one. *adj.* Directed toward a higher positon. **upwardly** *adv.*

u-ra-ni-um *n.* A hard, heavy, shiny metallic element that is radioactive, used especially in research and in nuclear weapons and fuels, symbolized by U.

U-ra-nus *n.* The seventh planet of the solar system in distance from the sun.

ur-ban *adj.* Pertaining to a city or having characteristics of a city; living or being in a city. **urbanite** *n.*, **urbanize** *v.*

urge *v.* To encourage, push, or drive; to recommend persistently and strongly. *n.* An influence, impulse, or force.

ur-gent *adj.* Requiring immediate attention. **urgency** *n.*, **urgently** *adv.*

urine *n.* In man and other mammals, the yellowish fluid waste produced by the kidneys.

Ur-sa Ma-jor *n.* The constellation of seven stars forming the Big Dipper.

Ur-sa Mi-nor *n.* The constellation of seven stars forming the Little Dipper.

Us *pl.*, *pron.* The objective case of we; used as an indirect object, direct object, or object of a preposition.

US *abbr.* United States.

USA *abbr.* United States of America.

us-a-ble *or* **use-a-ble** *adj.* Fit or capable of being used. **usability** *n.*, **usably** *adv.*

us-age *n.* The way or act of using something; the way words are used.

use *v.* To put into action; to emply for a special purpose; to employ on a regular basis; to exploit for one's own advantage. *n.* The state or fact of being used; the act or way of using something; the reason or purpose for which something is used; the function of something; the occupation or utilization of property. **used** *adj.*, **useful** *adj.*, **useless** *adj.*

ush-er *n.* A person who directs people to the correct seats in a theatre. *v.* To show or escort someone to a place; to go before as a representative or sign of something that comes later.

u-su-al *adj.* Ordinary or common; regular; customary. **usually** *adv.*, **usualness** *n.*

u-surp *v.* To take over by force without authority. **usurpation**, **usurper** *n.*

u-ten-sil *n.* A tool, implement, or container, especially one for the kitchen.

u-ter-us *n.* An organ of female mammals within which young develop and grow before birth. **uterine** *adj.*

u-til-i-ty *n.*, *pl.* **-ies** The state or quality of being useful; a company which offers a public service, as water, heat, or electricity.

u-til-ize *v.* To make or put to use.

ut-most *adj.* Of the greatest amount or degree; most distant. **utmost** *n.*

ut-ter *v.* To say or express verbally; to speak. *adv.* Absolute; complete. **utterly** *adv.*, **utterance** *n.*

u-vu-la *n.* The fleshy projection which hangs above the back of the tongue. **uvular** *adj.*

V, v The twenty-second letter of the English alphabet; the Roman numeral for 5.

va-cant *adj.* Empty; not occupied; without expression or thought.

va-cate *v.* To leave; to cease to occupy.

va-ca-tion *n.* A period of time away from work for pleasure, relaxation, or rest.

vac-ci-nate *v.* To inject with a vaccine so as to produce immunity to an infectious disease, as measles or smallpox.

vac-ci-na-tion *n.* The inoculation with a vaccine.

vac-cine *n.* A solution of weakened or killed microorganisms, as bacteria or viruses, injected into the body to produce immunity to a disease.

vac-u-um *n.*, *pl.* **-ums**, **-ua** A space which is absolutely empty; a void; a vacuum cleaner.

vag-a-bond *n.* A homeless person who wanders from place to place; a tramp.

va-gar-y *n.*, *pl.* **-ies** An eccentric or capricious action or idea. **vagarious** *adj.*

va-gi-na *n.*, *pl.* **-nas**, **-nae** *Anat.* The canal or passage extending from the uterus to the external opening of the female reproductive system.

vag-i-ni-tis *n.* An inflammation of the vagina.

va-grant *n.* A person who wanders from place to place. *adj.* Roaming from one area to another without a job. **vagrancy** *n.*

vague *adj.* Not clearly expressed; not sharp or definite. **vaguely** *adv.*

vain *adj.* Conceited; lacking worth or substance; having too much pride in oneself. **in vain** Irreverently. **-ly** *adv.*

val-ance *n.* A decorative drapery across the top of a window.

vale *n.* A valley.

val-e-dic-to-ri-an *n.* The student ranking highest in a graduating class, who delivers a speech at the commencement.

val-en-tine *n.* A card or gift sent to one's sweetheart on Valentine's Day, February 14th.

val-et *n.* A man who takes care of another man's clothes and other personal needs; a hotel employee who attends to personal services for guests.

val-iant *adj.* Brave; exhibiting valor. **valiance**, **valor** *n.*

val-id *adj.* Founded on facts or truth. *Law* Binding; having legal force. **validity**, **validate** *n.*

val-ley *n.*, *pl.* **-leys** Low land between ranges of hills or mountains.

val-or *n.* Bravery. **-ous** *adj.*, **-ously** *adv.*

val-u-a-ble *adj.* Of great value or importance; having a high monetary value.

val-ue *n.* The quality or worth of something that makes it valuable; material worth; a principle regarded as worthwhile or desirable. *Math* A calculated numerical quantity. *v.* To estimate the value or worth of; to regard very highly; to rate according to importance, worth, or usefulness. **valueless** *adj.*

valve *n.* The movable mechanism which opens and closes to control the flow of a substance through a pipe or other passageway. *Anat.* A membranous structure in a vein or artery that prevents or slows the backward movement of fluid.

va-moose *v.* *Slang* To leave in a hurry.

vam-pire *n.* In folklore, a dead person believed to rise from the grave at night to suck the blood of sleeping persons; a person who preys on others.

vam-pire bat *n.*

A tropical bat that feeds on the blood of living mammals.

van *n.* A large closed wagon or truck.

va-na-di-um *n.* A metallic element symbolized by V.

Van Buren, Martin *n.* 1782-1862 The 8th president of the United States from 1837-1841.

van-dal-ism *n.* The malicious defacement or destruction of private or public property.

vane *n.* A metal device that turns in the direction the wind is blowing; a thin rigid blade of an electric fan, propeller, or windmill.

va-nil-la *n.* A flavoring extract used in cooking and baking; prepared from the vanilla bean.

van-ish *v.* To disappear suddenly; to drop out of sight; to go out of existence.

van-i-ty *n., pl.,* -ies Conceit; extreme pride in one's ability, possessions, or appearance.

van-tage *n.* A superior position; an advantage.

va-por *n.* Moisture or smoke suspended in air, as mist or fog. **vaporish, vaporous** *adj.,* **vaporize** *v.*

var-i-able *adj.* Changeable; tending to vary; inconstant. *n.* A quantity or thing which can vary. **-ness** *n.,* **-ly** *adv.*

var-i-ance *n.* The state or act of varying; difference; conflict.

var-i-a-tion *n.* The result or process of varying; the degree or extent of varying. *Mus.* A different form or version of a given theme, with modifications in rhythm, key, or melody.

var-i-e-gat-ed *adj.* Having marks of different colors. **variegate** *v.*

va-ri-e-ty *n., pl.,* -ies The state or character of being varied or various; a number of different kinds; an assortment.

var-i-ous *adj.* Of different kinds. **variousness** *n.*

var-mint *n., Slang* A troublesome animal; an obnoxious person.

var-nish *n.* A solution paint used to coat or cover a surface with a hard, transparent, shiny film. *v.* To put varnish on.

var-si-ty *n., pl.,* -ies The best team representing a college, university, or school.

var-y *v.* To change; to make or become

different; to be different; to make of different kinds.

vas-cu-lar *adj., Biol.* Having to do with vessels circulating fluids, as blood.

va-sec-to-my *n., pl.* -ies Method of male sterilization involving the surgical excision of a part of the tube which conveys semen.

vast *adj.* Very large or great in size. **vastly** *adv.,* **vastness** *n.*

vault *n.* An arched structure that forms a ceiling or roof; a room for storage and safekeeping, as in a bank, usually made of steel; a burial chamber. *v.* To supply or construct with a vault; to jump or leap with the aid of a pole.

veg-e-ta-ble *n.* A plant, as the tomato, green beans, lettuce, raised for the edible part. *adj.* Resembling a vegetable in activity; passive; dull.

veg-e-tar-i-an *n.* A person whose diet is limited to vegetables. *adj.* Consuming only plant products. **vegetarianism** *n.*

veg-e-ta-tion *n.* Plants or plant life which grow from the soil.

ve-hi-cle *n.* A motorized device for transporting goods, equipment, or passengers; any means by which something is transferred, expressed, or applied.

veil *n.* A piece of transparent cloth worn on the head or face for concealment or protection; anything that conceals from view. *v.* To cover or conceal, as with a veil.

vein *n., Anat.*

A vessel which transports blood back to the heart after passing through the body; one of the branching support tubes of an insect's wing; a long wavy, ir regularly colored streak, as in marble, or wood. **vein** *v.*

ve-lour *n.* A soft velvet-like woven cloth having a short, thick nap.

vel-vet *n.* A fabric made of rayon, cotton, or silk, having a smooth, dense pile. **velvety** *adj.*

vend-er *or* **vend-or** *n.* A person who sells, as a peddler.

ven-det-ta *n.* A fight or feud between blood-related persons, involving revenge killings.

ven-er-a-ble *adj.* Meriting or worthy of respect by reason of dignity, position, or age.

ve-ne-re-al dis-ease *n.* A contagious disease, as syphilis, or gonorrhea, which is typically acquired through sexual intercourse.

ve-ne-tian blind *n.* A window blind having thin, horizontal slats which can be adjusted to desired angles so as to vary the amount of light admitted.

ven-i-son *n.* The edible flesh of a deer.

ven-om *n.* A poisonous substance secreted by some animals, as scorpions or snakes, usually transmitted to their prey or an enemy through a bite or sting. **venomous** *adj.*

ve-nous *adj.* Of or relating to veins. *Physiol.* Returning blood to the heart after passing through the capillaries, supplying oxygen for the tissues, and becoming charged with carbon dioxide. **venously** *adv.*

vent *n.* A means of escape or passage from a restricted area; an opening which allows the escape of vapor, heat, gas, or liquid.

ven-ti-late *v.* To expose to a flow of fresh air for refreshing, curing, or purifying purposes; to cause fresh air to circulate through an area; to expose to public discussion or examination. **ventilation, ventilator** *n.*

ven-ture *n.* A course of action involving risk, chance, or danger, especially a business investment. *v.* To take a risk.

ven-ue *n.* The place where a crime or other cause of legal action occurs; the locale of a gathering or public event.

Ve-nus *n.* The planet second in order from the sun.

verb *n.* The part of speech which expresses action, existence, or occurrence.

ver-bal *adj.* Expressed in speech; expressed orally; not written; relating to or derived from a verb. *n.* An adjective, noun, or other word which is based on a verb and retains some characteristics of a verb. **verbally** *adv.*, **verbalize** *v.*

ver-ba-tim *adv.* Word for word.

ver-be-na *n.* An American garden plant having variously colored flower clusters.

verge *n.* The extreme edge or rim; margin; the point beyond which something begins. *v.* To border on.

ver-min *n.*, *pl.* **vermins** A destructive, annoying animal which is harmful to one's health.

ver-sa-tile *adj.* Having the capabilities of doing many different things; having many functions or uses. **versatility** *n.*

verse *n.* Writing that has a rhyme; poetry; a subdivision of a chapter of the Bible. *v.* To make verse; to tell or celebrate in verse; to familiarize by close association or study.

ver-sion *n.* An account or description told from a particular point of view; a translation from another language, especially a translation of the Bible; a form or particular point of view; a condition in which an organ, such as the uterus, is turned; manual turning of a fetus in the uterus to aid delivery. **versional** *adj.*

ver-so *n.*, *pl.* -**sos** The left-hand page.

ver-sus *prep.* Against; in contrast to; as an alternative of.

ver-te-bra *n.*, *pl.* -**brae**, -**bras** One of the bony or cartilaginous segments making up the spinal column. -**al** *adj.*

ver-tex *n.*, *pl.* -**es**, -**tices** The highest or topmost point; the pointed top of a triangle, opposite the base; the point at which two lines meet to form an angle.

ver-ti-cal *adj.* In a straight up-and-down direction; being perpendicular to the plane of the horizon or to a primary axis; upright. **vertically** *adv.*

ver-y *adv.* To a high or great degree; truly; absolutely; exactly; actually; in actual fact.

ves-per *n.* An evening prayer service; a bell to call people to such a service.

ves-sel *n.* A hollow or concave utensil, as a bottle, kettle, container, or jar; a hollow craft designed for navigation on water, one larger than a rowboat. *Anat.* A tube or duct for circulating a bodily fluid.

vest *n.* A sleeveless garment open or fastening in front, worn over a shirt.

ves-tige *n.* A trace or visible sign of something that no longer exists. **vestigial** *adj.*, **vestigially** *adv.*

ves-try *n.*, *pl.* **vestries** A room in a church used for meetings and classes.

vet *n.*, *Slang* A veterinarian; a veteran.

vet-er-an *n.* A person with a long record or experience in a certain field; one who has served in the military.

Veterans Day *n.* A day set aside to commemorate the end of World War I in 1918, celebrated on November 11th of each year.

vet-er-i-nar-i-an *n.* One who is trained and authorized to give medical treatment to animals.

vet-er-i-nar-y *adj.* Pertaining to or being the science and art of prevention and treatment of animals.

ve-to- *n.*, *pl.* **vetoes** The power of a government executive, as the President or a governor, to reject a bill passed by the legislature. *v.* To reject a bill passed by the legislature.

vex *v.* To bother; or annoy. **vexation** *n.*

vi-a *prep.* By way of; by means of.

vi-a-duct *n.* A bridge, resting on a series of arches, carrying a road or railroad.

vi-al *n.* A small, closed container used especially for liquids.

vi-brate *v.* To move or make move back and forth or up and down. **vibration** *n.*

vi-car-i-ous *adj.* Undergoing or serving in the place of someone or something else; experienced through sympathetic or imaginative participation in the experience of another.

vice *n.* An immoral habit or practice; evil conduct. *prefix* One who takes the place of another.

vi-ce ver-sa *adv.* With the order or meaning of something reversed.

vi-chy-ssoise *n.* A soup made from potatoes, chicken stock, and cream, flavored with leeks or onions and usually served cold.

vi-cin-i-ty *n.*, *pl.* -**ies** The surrounding area or district; the state of being near in relationship or space.

vi-cious *adj.* Dangerously aggressive; having the quality of immorality. **viciously** *adv.*, **viciousness** *n.*

vic-tim *n.* A person who is harmed or killed by another; a living creature which is slain and offered as sacrifice; one harmed by circumstance or condition. **victimize** *v.*

vic-tor *n.* A person who conquers; the winner.

vic-to-ri-ous *adj.* Being the winner in a contest. **victoriously** *adv.*

vic-to-ry *n.*, *pl.* **-ies** A defeat of those on the opposite side.

vid-e-o *adj.* Being, related to, or used in the reception or transmission of television.

vid-e-o disc *n.* A disc containing recorded images and sounds which may be played on a television set.

vid-e-o game *n.* A computerized game displaying on a display screen, controlled by a player or players.

vid-e-o ter-mi-nal *n.* *Computer Science* A computer device having a cathoderay tube for displaying data on a screen.

vie *v.* To strive for superiority.

Vi-et-nam *n.* A country located in southeastern Asia.

view *n.* The act of examining or seeing; a judgment or opinion; the range or extent of one's sight; something that is kept in sight. *v.* To watch or look at attentively; to consider.

vig-il *n.* A watch with prayers kept on the night before a religious feast; a period of surveillance.

vig-or *n.* Energy or physical strength; intensity of effect or action. **-ous** *adj.*

Vi-king *n.* One of the pirate Scandinavian people who plundered the coasts of Europe from the eighth to the tenth century.

vile *adj.* Morally disgusting, miserable, and unpleasant. **vilely** *adv.*, **vileness** *n.*

vil-la *n.* A luxurious home in the country; a country estate.

vil-lage *n.* An incorporated settlement, usually smaller than a town. **villager** *n.*

vil-lain *n.* An evil or wicked person; a criminal; an uncouth person. **villainous** *adj.*, **villainy** *n.*

vin-ai-grette *n.* A small ornamental bottle with a perforated top, used for holding an aromatic preparation such as smelling salts.

vin-di-cate *v.* To clear of suspicion; to set free; to provide a defense or justification for. **vindication** *n.*

vin-dic-tive *adj.* Showing or possessing a desire for revenge; spiteful.

vine *n.* A plant whose stem needs support as it climbs or clings to a surface.

vin-e-gar *n.* A tart, sour liquid derived from cider or wine and used in flavoring and preserving food. **-y** *adj.*

vin-tage *n.* The grapes or wine produced from a particular district in one season.

vi-nyl *n.* A variety of shiny plastics, similar to leather, often used for clothing and for covering furniture.

vi-o-la *n.* A stringed instrument, slightly larger and deeper in tone than a violin.

vi-o-late *v.* To break the law or a rule; to disrupt or disturb a person's privacy. **violation** *n.*

vi-o-lence *n.* Physical force or activity used to cause harm, damage, or abuse.

vi-o-let *n.* A small, low-growing plant with blue, purple, or white flowers; a purplish-blue color.

vi-o-lin *n.* A small stringed instrument, played with a bow.

vi-per *n.* A poisonous snake; an evil or treacherous person.

vir-gin *n.* A person who has never had sexual intercourse. *adj.* In an unchanged or natural state.

Virgo *n.* The sixth sign of the zodiac; a person born between August 23rd and September 22nd.

vir-ile *adj.* Having the qualities and nature of a man; capable of sexual performance in the male. **virility** *n.*

vir-tu *n.* The love or knowledge of fine objects of art.

vir-tue *n.* Morality, goodness or uprightness; a special type of goodness. **virtuous** *adj.*, **virtuously** *adv.*

vi-rus *n.* Any of a variety of microscopic organisms which cause diseases.

vi-sa *n.* An official authorization giving permission on a passport to enter a specific country.

vis-cid *adj.* Sticky; having an adhesive quality.

vise *or* **vice** *n.* A tool in carpentry and metalwork having two jaws to hold things in position.

vis-i-bil-i-ty *n.*, *pl.* **-ies** The degree or state of being visible; the distance that one is able to see clearly.

vis-i-ble *adj.* Apparent; exposed to view.

vi-sion *n.* The power of sight; the ability to see; an image created in the imagination; a supernatural appearance.

vis-it *v.* To journey to or come to see a person or place. *n.* A professional or social call. *Slang* To chat. **visitor**, **visitation** *n.*

vi-sor *n.* A brim on the front of a hat which protects the eyes from glare, the sun, wind, and rain.

vi-su-al *adj.* Visible; relating to seeing or sight.

vi-tal *adj.* Essential to life; very important. **vitally** *adv.*

vi-tal signs *pl.*, *n.*, *Med.* The pulse rate, body temperature, blood pressure, and respiratory rate of a person.

vi-ta-min *n.* Any of various substances which are found in foods and are essential to good health.

vit-re-ous *adj.* Related to or similar to glass.

vit-ri-fy *v.* To convert into glass or a substance similar to glass, by heat and fusion.

vi-va-cious *adj.* Filled with vitality or animation; lively. **vivaciously** *adv.*

viv-id *adj.* Bright; brilliant; intense; having clear, lively, bright colors. **vividly** *adv.*

viv-i-fy v. To give life to. **vivifiction** n.

vo-cab-u-lar-y n., pl. **-ies** A list or group of words and phrases, usually in alphabetical order; all the words that a person uses or understands.

vo-cal adj. Of or related to the voice; uttered by the voice; to speak freely and loudly. n. A vocal sound. **-ly** adv.

vo-ca-tion n. A career, occupation, or profession.

vo-cif-er-ate v. To utter or cry out loudly; to shout. **vociferation** n., **vociferous** adj., **vociferously** adv.

vogue n. The leading style or fashion; popularity. **vogue** adj.

voice n. The sounds produced by speaking; the ability or power to produce musical tones. v. To express; to utter; to give voice.

void adj. Containing nothing; empty; not inhabited; useless; vain; without legal force or effect; null. n. Empty space; the quality or state of being lonely. v. To make void; to discharge; to emit.

voile n. A fine, soft, sheer fabric used for making light clothing and curtains.

volt-age n. The amount of electrical power, given in terms of the number of volts.

vol-ume n. The capacity or amount of space or room; a book; a quantity; the loudness of a sound.

vol-un-tar-y adj. Done cooperatively or willingly; from one's own choice.

vol-un-teer n. One who offers himself for a service of his own free will. adj. Consisting of volunteers. v. To offer voluntarily.

vo-lup-tuous adj. Full of pleasure; delighting the senses; sensuous; luxury. **voluptuousness** n.

vom-it v. To eject contents of the stomach through the mouth. n. The food or matter ejected from the stomach by vomiting.

vo-ra-cious adj. Having a large appetite; insatiable. **voraciously** adv.

vote n. The expression of one's choice by voice, by raising one's hand, or by secret ballot. v. To express one's views. **voteless** adj., **voter** n.

vo-tive adj. Performed in fulfillment of a vow or in devotion.

vouch v. To verify or support as true; to guarantee. **voucher** n.

vow n. A solemn pledge or promise, especially one made to God; a marriage vow.

vow-el n. A sound of speech made by voicing the flow of breath within the mouth; a letter representing a vowel, as a, e, i, o, u, and sometimes y.

voy-age n. A long trip or journey.

vul-gar adj. Showing poor manners; crude; improper; immoral or indecent. **vulgarity** n.

vul-ner-a-ble adj. Open to physical injury or attack. **vulnerability** n., **-ably** adv.

vul-ture n. A large bird of the hawk family, living on dead animals; a greedy person; one who feeds on the mistakes or bad luck of others.

W, w The twenty-third letter of the English alphabet.

wacky adj. Amusingly or absurdly irrational. **wackily** adj., **wackiness** n.

wad n. A small crumpled mass or bundle; a soft plug used to hold shot or gunpowder charge in place. Slang A large roll of money. **wad** v.

wad-dle v. To walk with short steps and swing from side to side. **waddle, waddler** n.

wade v. To walk through a substance as mud or water which hampers one's steps.

wa-fer n. A small, thin, crisp cracker, cookie, or candy.

waf-fle n. Pancake batter cooked in a waffle iron.

waft-age n. The state or act of being wafted.

wag v. To move quickly from side to side or up and down. n. A playful, witty person. **waggish** adj., **wagger** n.

wage n. A payment of money for labor or services. v. To conduct. **-less** adj.

wa-ger v. To make a bet. **wager** n.

wag-on n. A four-wheeled vehicle used to transport goods; a station wagon; a child's four-wheeled cart with a long handle.

wail n. A loud, mournful cry or weep. n. To make such a sound.

waist n. The narrow part of the body between the thorax and hips; the middle part or section of something which is narrower than the rest. **waisted** adj.

wait-er n. A man who serves food at a restaurant.

wait-ress n. A woman who serves food at a restaurant.

wake v. To come to consciousness, as from sleep. n. A vigil for a dead body; the surface turbulence caused by a vessel moving through water.

walk v. To move on foot over a surface; to pass over, go on, or go through by walking; in baseball, to advance to first base after four balls have been pitched. **walker** n.

walk-out n. A labor strike against a company.

wall n. A vertical structure to separate or enclose an area. v. To provide or close up, as with a wall.

wal-la-by n. A small or medium-sized kangaroo.

wal-let n. A flat folding case for carrying paper money.

wal-lop n. A powerful blow; an impact. v. To move with disorganized haste. **walloper** n.

wal-nut n. An edible nut with a hard, light-brown shell; the tree on which this nut grows.

wal-rus n.

A large marine mammal of the seal family, having flippers, tusks, and a tough hide.

waltz n. A ballroom dance in 3/4 time;

music for a waltz. *v.* To dance a waltz; to advance successfully and easily.

wam-pum *n.* Polished shells, once used as currency by North American Indians. *Slang* Money.

wand *n.* A slender rod used by a magician.

wan-der *v.* To travel about aimlessly; to roam; to stray. **wanderer** *n.*

wane *v.* To decrease in size or extent; to decrease gradually. *n.* A gradual deterioration.

wan-gle *v.* To resort to devious methods in order to obtain something wanted. **wangler** *n.*

want *v.* To wish for or desire; to need; to lack; to fail to possess a required amount; to hunt in order to apprehend. *n.* The state of lacking a required or usual amount. **wanting** *adj.*

war *n.* An armed conflict among states or nations; a state of discord; the science of military techniques or procedures.

ward *n.* A section in a hospital for certain patients requiring similar treatment; a person under protection or surveillance. *v.* To keep watch over someone or something.

ware *n.* Manufactured items of the same general kind; items or goods for sale.

ware-house *n.* A large building used to store merchandise. **warehouse** *v.*

warm *adj.* Moderate heat; neither hot or cold; comfortably established; marked by a strong feeling; having pleasant feelings.

warn *v.* To give notice or inform beforehand; to call to one's attention; to alert.

warp *v.* To become bent out of shape; to deviate from a proper course. *n.* The condition of being twisted or bent; threads running down the length of a fabric.

war-rant *n.* A written authorization giving the holder legal power to search, seize, or arrest. *v.* To provide a reason; to give proof. **warrantable** *adj.*, **warrantor** *n.*

war-ri-or *n.* One who fights in a war or battle.

war-y *adj.* Marked by caution.

wash *v.* To cleanse by the use of water; to remove dirt; to move or deposit as if by the force of water. *n.* A process or instance of washing; a group of soiled clothes or linens.

wash--and--wear *adj.* Requiring little or no ironing after washing.

wash-board *n.* A corrugated board on which clothes are rubbed in the process of washing; an uneven surface as a washboard.

washed--out *adj.*, *Slang* Tired.

wash-er *n.* A small disk usually made of rubber or metal having a hole in the center, used with nuts and bolts; a washing machine.

wash-ing *n.* Clothes and other articles that are washed or to be washed; cleaning.

Washington, George *n.* (1732-1799) The first president of the United States from 1789-1797.

was-n't *contr.* Was not.

wasp *n.* Any of various insects, having a slim body with a constricted abdomen, the female capable of inflicting a painful sting.

waste *v.* To be thrown away; to be available but not used completely. *n.* A barren region; the instance of wasting; useless material produced as a byproduct. *Slang* To destroy or murder. **wasteful** *adj.*, **waster** *n.*

watch *v.* To view carefully; to guard; to keep informed. *n.* The act of staying awake to guard or protect; a small timepiece worn on the wrist, designed to keep the correct time of day.

watch-dog *n.* A dog trained to guard someone or his property.

watch-ful *adj.* Carefully observant or attentive. **watchfully** *adv.*

watch-man *n.* A person hired to keep watch; a guard.

wa-ter *n.* The clear liquid making up oceans, lakes, and streams; the body fluids as tears or urine. *v.* To pour or spray on water on something or someone; to give water to drink; to weaken or dilute with water.

wa-ter moc-ca-sin *n.* A venomous snake from the lowlands and swampy areas of the southern United States.

wa-ter po-lo *n.* A water game between two teams, the object of which is to get a ball into the opponent's goal.

wa-ter pow-er *n.* The power or energy produced by swift-moving water.

wa-ter-proof *adj.* Capable of preventing water from penetrating. *v.* To make or treat in order to make waterproof. *n.* A material or fabric which is waterproof.

wa-ter--re-pel-lant *adj.* A material or product treated to resist water, but not completely waterproof.

wa-ter-shed *n.* The raised area between two regions that divides two sections drained by different river sources.

wa-ter--ski *v.* To travel over water on a pair of short, broad skis while being pulled by a motorboat.

wa-ter-spout *n.* A tube or pipe through which water is discharged; a funnel-shaped column of spray and mist whirling over an ocean or lake.

wa-ter ta-ble *n.* The upper limit of the portion of the ground completely saturated with water.

wa-ter-tight *adj.* Closed or sealed so tightly that no water can enter, leaving no chance for evasion.

wa-ter-way *n.* A navigable body of water; a channel for water.

wa-ter-y *adj.* Containing water; diluted; lacking effectiveness. **wateriness** *n.*

watt *n.* A unit of electrical power represented by current of one ampere, produced by the electromotive force of one volt.

wave *v.* To move back and forth or up

and down; to motion with the hand. *n.*
A swell or moving ridge of water; a
curve or curl, as in the hair.

wa-ver *v.* To sway unsteadily; to move
back and forth; to weaken in force.
waver *n.*, **waveringly** *adv.*

wax *n.* A natural yellowish substance
made by bees, solid when cold and
easily melted or softened when
heated. **waxy** *adj.*

way *n.* A manner of doing something; a
tendency or characteristic; a habit or
customary manner of acting or living;
a direction; freedom to do as one
chooses.

way-lay *v.* To attack by ambush.

way-ward *adj.* Unruly; unpredictable.

we *pl.*, *pron.* Used to refer to the person
speaking and one or more other
people.

weak *adj.* Having little energy or
strength; easily broken; having
inadequate skills; not reasonable or
convincing. **weakness** *n.*, **weakly** *adv.*

wealth *n.* An abundance of valuable
possessions or property; all goods and
resources having monetary value.

wealth-y *adj.* Having much wealth or
money; abundant; rich.

wean *v.* To accustom an infant or small
child to food other than a mother's
milk or bottle.

weap-on *n.* A device used in fighting a
war; a device which can be used to
harm another person.

wear *v.* To have on or put something on
the body; to display. *n.* The act of
wearing out or using up; the act of
wearing, as clothing. **wearable** *adj.*

wea-ri-some *adj.* Tedious, boring or
tiresome.

wea-ry *adj.* Exhausted; tired; feeling
fatigued. *v.* To make or become tired;
to become fatigued. **-ily** *adv.*, **-iness** *n.*

wea-sel *n.* A mammal with a long tail
and short legs; a sly, sneaky person.

weath-er *n.* The condition of the air or
atmosphere in terms of humidity,
temperature, and similar features. *v.*
To become worn by the actions of
weather; to survive.

weather vane *n.*

A device that turns,
indicating the
direction of the wind.

weave *v.* To make a
basket, cloth, or
other item by interlacing threads or
other strands of material. **weaver** *n.*

web *n.*

A cobweb; a piece of
interlacing material
which forms a woven
structure; something
constructed as an
entanglement; a thin
membrane that joins the toes of
certain water birds.

wed *v.* To take as a spouse; to marry.

we'd *contr.* We had; we should.

wed-ding *n.* A marriage ceremony; an act
of joining together in close
association.

wedge *n.* A tapered, triangular piece of
wood or metal used to split logs, to
add leverage, and to hold something
open or ajar. *v.* To force or make
something fit tightly.

wed-lock *n.* Marriage; the state of being
married.

weed *n.* An unwanted plant which
interferes with the growth of grass,
vegetables, or flowers.

week *n.* A period of seven days,
beginning with Sunday and ending
with Saturday; the time or days
normally spent at school or work.

week-day *n.* Any day of the week except
Saturday or Sunday.

week-end *n.* The end of the week from
the period of Friday evening through
Sunday evening.

week-ly *adv.* Every week; once a week.
adj. Taking place or done every week
of or relating to a week.

weep *v.* To shed tears; to express sorrow,
joy, or emotion; by shedding tears; to
cry. **weeper** *n.*

wee-vil *n.* A small beetle having a
downwardcurving snout, which damages plants.

weigh *v.* To determine the heaviness of
an object by using a scale; to consider
carefully in one's mind; to be of a particular weight; to oppress or burden.

weight *n.* The amount that something
weighs; heaviness; a heavy object used
to hold or pull something down; an
overpowering force; the quality of a
garment for a particular season. *v.* To
make heavy.

weight-less *adj.* Lacking the pull of
gravity; having little weight.

weight-y *adj.* Burdensome; important.

weird *adj.* Having an extraordinary or
strange character. **weirdly** *adv.*

weird-o *n.*, *Slang* A person who is very
strange.

wel-come *v.* To extend warm hospitality;
to accept gladly. *adj.* Received
warmly. *n.* A greeting upon one's arrival.

weld *v.* To unite metallic parts by applying heat and sometimes pressure, allowing the metals to bond together. *n.*
A joint formed by welding.

wel-fare *n.* The state of doing well;
governmental aid to help the disabled
or disadvantaged.

well *n.* A hole in the ground which contains a supply of water; a shaft in the
ground through which gas and oil are
obtained. *adj.* Being in good health; in
an agreeable state.

we'll *contr.* We will; we shall.

well--be-ing *n.* The state of being healthy, happy, or prosperous.

well--done *adj.* Completely cooked; done
properly.

well--groomed *adj.* Clean, neat, and

properly cared for.

well--known *adj.* Widely known.

well--man-nered *adj.* Polite; having good manners.

well--mean-ing *adj.* Having good intentions.

well--to--do *adj.* Having more than enough wealth.

welsh *v.*, *Slang* To cheat by avoiding a payment to someone; to neglect an obligation. **welsher** *n.*

welt *n.* A strip between the sole and upper part of a shoe; a slight swelling on the body, usually caused by a blow to the area. *v.* To hit severly.

wel-ter-weight *n.* A boxer weighing between 136 and 147 pounds.

went *v.* Past tense of go.

wept *v.* Past tense of weep.

were *v.* Second person singular past plural of be.

we're *contr.* We are.

were-n't *contr.* Were not.

west *n.* The direction of the setting sun; the direction to the left of a person standing north. *adj.* At, of, or from the west. *adv.* To or toward the west.

western *adj.*

whack *v.* To strike with a hard blow, to slap. *n.* An attempt.

whale *n.*

A very large mammal resembling a fish which lives in salt water. *Slang* An outstanding or impressive example.

wharf *n.* A pier or platform built at the edge of water so that ships can load and unload.

what *pron.* Which one; which things; which type or kind. *adv.* In which way. *adj.* Which particular one.

what-ev-er *pron.* Everything or anything. *adj.* No matter what. *Slang* Which thing or things.

what's *contr.* What is.

wheat *n.* A grain ground into flour, used to make breads and similar foods.

wheel *n.* A circular disk which turns on an axle; an apparatus having the same principles of a wheel; something which resembles the motion or shape of a wheel. *v.* To move on or as if by wheels; to turn around a central axis; to rotate, pivot, or turn around.

wheel-bar-row *n.* A vehicle having one wheel, used to transport small loads.

wheel-chair *n.* A mobile chair for disabled persons.

wheel-er *n.* Anything that has wheels.

wheeze *v.* To breathe with a hoarse whistling sound. *n.* A high whistling sound.

whelk *v.* Any of various large water snails, sometimes edible.

when *adv.* At what time; at which time. *pron.* What or which time. *conj.* While; at the time that; although.

whence *adv.* From what source or place; from which.

when-ev-er *adv.* At any time; when. *conj.* At whatever time.

where *adv.* At or in what direction or place; in what direction or place.

where-a-bouts *adv.* Near, at, or in a particular location. *n.* The approximate location.

where-as *conj.* It being true or the fact; on the contrary.

where-by *conj.* Through or by which.

wher-ev-er *adv.* In any situation or place.

whet *v.* To make sharp; to stimulate.

wheth-er *conj.* Indicating a choice; alternative possibilities; either.

whet-stone *n.* A stone used to sharpen scissors, knives, and other implements.

whew *n.*, *interj.* Used to express relief; or tiredness.

whey *n.* The clear, water-like part of milk that separates from the curd.

which *pron.* What one or ones; the one previously; whatever one or ones; whichever. *adj.* What one; any one of.

which-ev-er *pron.* Any; no matter which or what.

whiff *n.* A slight puff; a light current of air; a slight breath or odor.

while *n.* A length or period of time. *conj.* During the time that; even though; at the same time; although.

whim *n.* A sudden desire or impulse.

whim-per *v.* To make a weak, soft crying sound. **whimper** *n.*

whim-si-cal *adj.* Impulsive; erratic; light and spontaneous. **whimsically** *adv.*

whine *v.* To make a squealing, plaintive sound; to complain in an irritating, childish fashion.

whin-ny *v.* To neigh in a soft gentle way.

whip *v.* To spank repeatedly with a rod or stick; to punish by whipping; to move in a motion similar to whipping or beating. *n.* A flexible stick or rod used to herd or beat animals; a dessert made by whipping ingredients; the utensil used to do so. *Slang* To overcome. **whipper** *n.*

whip-lash *n.* An injury to the spine or neck caused by a sudden jerking motion of the head.

whip-poor-will *n.* A brownish nocturnal bird of North America.

whir *v.* To move with a low purring sound.

whirl *v.* To rotate or move in circles; to twirl; to move, drive, or go very fast. *n.* A rapid whirling motion. **whirler** *n.*

whirl-pool *n.* A circular current of water.

whirl-wind *n.* A violently whirling mass of air; a tornado.

whirl-y-bird *n.*, *Slang* A helicopter.

whisk *v.* To move with a sweeping motion; to move quickly or lightly. *n.* A sweeping movement; a utensil used in cooking; to stir.

whisk-er *n.*

The hair that grows on a man's face; the long hair near the mouth of dogs, cats, and other animals. **whiskers** A man's beard.

whis-key *n.* An alcoholic beverage distilled from rye, barley, or corn.

whis-per *v.* To speak in a very low tone; to tell in secret. *n.* A low rustling sound; the act of whispering.

whis-tle *v.* To make a clear shrill sound by blowing air through the teeth, through puckered lips, or through a special instrument. *n.* A device used to make a whistling sound. **whistler** *n.*

white *n.* The color opposite of black; the part of something that is white or light in color, as an egg or the eyeball; a member of the Caucasian group of people. *adj.* Having a light color; pale; pure; blameless, without sin.

white-cap *n.* A wave having a top of white foam.

white--col-lar *adj.* Relating to an employee whose job does not require manual labor.

White House *n.* The official residence of the President of the United States, located in Washington, D.C.

white-wash *n.* A mixture made of lime and other ingredients and used for whitening fences and exterior walls. *v.* To cover up a problem; to pronounce someone as being innocent without really investigating.

whith-er *adv.* To what state, place, or circumstance; wherever.

whit-tle *v.* To cut or carve off small shavings from wood with a knife; to remove or reduce gradually. **-ler** *n.*

whiz *v.* To make a whirring or buzzing sound, a projectile passing at a high rate of speed through the air. *Slang* A person having notable expertise, as with a computer.

who *pron.* Which or what certain individual, person, or group; referring to a person previously mentioned.

who'd *contr.* Who would; who had.

who-ev-er *pron.* Whatever person; all or any persons.

whole *adj.* Complete; having nothing missing; not divided or in pieces; a complete system or unity; everything considered. *Math* Not a fraction. **wholeness** *n.*

whole-heart-ed *adj.* Sincere; totally committed; holding nothing back.

whole-sale *n.* The sale of goods in large amounts to a retailer. *adj.* Relating to or having to do with such a sale. *v.* To sell wholesale. **wholesaler** *n.*

whole-some *adj.* Contributing to good mental or physical health. **wholesomely** *adv.*, **wholesomeness** *n.*

whole wheat *adj.* Made from the wheat kernel with nothing removed.

who'll *contr.* Who shall; who will.

whol-ly *adv.* Totally; exclusively.

whom *pron.* The form of who used as the direct object of a verb or the object of the preposition.

whom-ev-er *pron.* The form of whoever used as the object of a preposition or the direct object of a verb.

whoop-ing cough *n.* An infectious disease of the throat and breathing passages in which the patient has spasms of coughing often followed by gasps for breath.

whoop-ing crane *n.* A large bird of North America, nearly extinct, having long legs and a high, shrill cry.

whoosh *v.* To make a rushing or gushing sound, as a rush of air.

whop-per *n.* Something of extraordinary size. *Slang* A lie.

whore *n.* A prostitute.

who's *contr.* Who is; who has.

whose *pron.* Belonging to or having to do with one's belongings. *adj.* Relating to which or whom.

why *adv.* For what reason or purpose. *conj.* The cause, purpose, or reason for which. *interj.* Expressing surprise or disagreement.

wick *n.* The soft strand of fibers which extends from a candle or lamp and draws up the fuel for burning.

wick-er *n.* A thin, pliable twig used to make furniture and baskets.

wick-et *n.* A wire hoop in the game of croquet; a small door, window, or opening used as a box office.

wide *adj.* Broad; covering a large area; completely extended or open. *adv.* Over a large area; full extent.

wide-spread *adj.* Fully spread out; over a broad area.

wid-ow *n.* A woman whose husband is no longer living.

wid-ow-er *n.* A man whose wife is no longer living.

width *n.* The distance or extent of something from side to side.

wield *v.* To use or handle something skillfully; to employ power effectively.

wie-ner *n.* A frankfurter; a hot dog.

wife *n.* A married female.

wig *n.* Artificial or human hair woven together to cover baldness or a bald spot on the head.

wig-gle *v.* To squirm; to move with rapid side-to-side motions. **wiggler** *n.*

wig-wam *n.* An Indian dwelling place.

wild *adj.* Living in a natural, untamed state; not occupied by man; not civilized; strange and unusual. *adv.* Out of control. *n.* A wilderness region not cultivated or settled by man.

wild-cat *n.* A medium-sized wild, feline animal; one with a quick temper. *v.* To drill for oil or gas in an area where such products are not usually found. *adj.* Not approved or legal.

wil-der-ness *n.* An unsettled area; a region left in its uncultivated or natural state.

wild-life *n.* Animals and plants living in their natural environments.

will *n.* The mental ability to decide or choose for oneself; strong desire or determination; a legal document stating how one's property is to be distributed after death. *v.* To bring about by an act of a will; to decide as by decree; to give or bequeath something in a will.

wil-low *n.* A large tree, usually having

narrow leaves and slender flexible twigs.

Wilson, Woodrow *n.* (1856-1924) The 28th president of the United States from 1913-1921.

wilt *v.* To cause or to become limp; to lose force; to deprive of courage or energy.

win *v.* To defeat others; to gain victory in a contest; to receive. *n.* Victory; the act of winning. **winner** *n.*

winch *n.* An apparatus with one or more drums on which a cable or rope is wound, used to lift heavy loads.

wind *n.* A natural movement of air. *v.* To become short of breath. **windy** *adj.*

wind *v.* To wrap around and around something; to turn, to crank. *n.* A turning or twisting.

wind-fall *n.* A sudden or unexpected stroke of good luck.

wind in-stru-ment *n.* A musical instrument which produces sound when a person forces his breath into it.

wind-mill *n.* A machine operated or powered by the wind.

win-dow *n.* An opening built into a wall for light and air; a pane of glass.

win-dow--shop *v.* To look at merchandise in store windows without going inside to buy. **window-shopper** *n.*

wind-pipe *n.* The passage in the neck used for breathing; the trachea.

wine *n.* A drink containing 10-15% alcohol by volume, made by fermenting grapes.

wing *n.* One of the movable appendages that allow a bird or insect to fly; one of the airfoils on either side of an aircraft, allowing it to glide or travel through the air. *v.* To move as if on wings; to fly.

wing-spread *n.* The extreme measurement from the tips or outer edges of the wings of an aircraft, bird, or other insect.

wink *v.* To shut one eye as a signal or message; to blink rapidly. *n.* The act of winking; a short period of rest; a nap.

win-ning *adj.* Defeating others; captivating. *n.* Victory.

win-some *adj.* Very pleasant; charming.

win-ter *n.* The coldest season, coming between autumn and spring. *adj.* Relating to or typically of winter.

win-ter-green *n.* A small plant having aromatic evergreen leaves which yield an oil, used as flavoring or medicine.

wipe *v.* To clean by rubbing; to take off by rubbing. *n.* The act or instance of wiping.

wire *n.* A small metal rod used to conduct electricity; thin strands of metal twisted together to form a cable; the telephone or telegraph system; the finish line of a race. *v.* To equip with wiring. *Slang* To convey a message by telegram or telegraph; something completed at the last possible time.

wis-dom *n.* The ability to understand what is right, true, or enduring; good judgment; knowledge.

wise *adj.* Having superior intelligence; having great learning; having a capacity for sound judgment marked by deep understanding. **wisely** *adv.*

wise-crack *n.*, *Slang* A witty remark or joke usually showing a lack of respect.

wish *v.* To desire or long for something; to command or request. *n.* A longing or desire.

wish-bone *n.* The bone of a bird, which, according to the superstition, when broken brings good luck to the person who has the longer end.

wish-ful *adj.* Having or expressing a wish; hopeful. **wishfully** *adv.*

wisp *n.* A tuft or small bundle of hay, straw, or hair; a thin piece. **wispy** *adj.*

wit *n.* The ability to use words in a clever way; a sense of humor.

witch *n.* A person believed to have magical powers; a mean, ugly, old woman.

with *prep.* In the company of; near or alongside; having, wearing or bearing; in the judgment or opinion of; containing; in the possession or care of; supporting; among; occurring at the same time. *v.* To take away or back; to retreat.

with-draw *v.* To take away; to take back; to remove; to retreat.

whither *v.* To dry up or wilt from a lack of moisture; to lose freshness or vigor.

with-hold *n.* To hold back or keep.

withholding tax *n.* The tax on income held back by an employer in payment of one's income tax.

with-in *adv.* Inside the inner part; inside the limits; inside the limits of time, distance, or degree. *n.* An inside area.

with-out *adv.* On the outside; not in possession of. *prep.* Something or someone lacking.

with-stand *v.* To endure.

wit-ness *n.* A person who has seen, experienced, or heard something; something serving as proof or evidence. *v.* To see or hear something; to give proof or evidence of; to give testimony.

wit-ty *adj.* Amusing or cleverly humorous.

wiz-ard *n.* A very clever person; a person thought to have magical powers. *Slang* One with amazing skill.

wob-ble *v.* To move unsteadily from side to side, as a rocking motion.

woe *n.* Great sorrow or grief; misfortune.

wok *n.* A convex metal cooker for stir-frying food.

woke *v.* Past tense of wake.

wolf *n.* A carnivorous animal found in northern areas; a fierce person. *v.* To eat quickly and with greed. **wolfish** *adj.*, **wolfishly** *adv.*

woman *n.* The mature adult human female; a person who has feminine qualities.

womanhood *n.* The state of being a woman.

womb *n.* The uterus; the place where development occurs.

won *v.* Past tense of win.

won-der *n.* A feeling of amazement or admiration. *v.* To feel admiration; to feel uncertainty. **wonderful** *adj.*

won-der-ment *n.* A feeling or state of amazement.

won-drous *adj.* Wonderful; marvelous.

won't *contr.* Will not.

won-ton *n.* A noodle dumpling filled with minced pork and served in soup.

wood *n.* The hard substance which makes up the main part of trees. *adj.* Made of wood. **woods** *n.* A growth of trees smaller than a forest.

wood-chuck *n.*

A rodent having short legs and a heavyset body, which lives in a burrow.

wood-en *adj.* Made of wood; resembling wood; stiff; lifeless; lacking flexibility.

wood-peck-er *n.* A bird which uses its bill for drilling holes in trees looking for insects to eat.

wood-wind *n.* A group of musical instruments which produce sounds when air is blown through the mouthpiece, as the clarinet, flute, and oboe.

wool *n.* The soft, thick hair of sheep and other such mammals; a fabric made from such hair.

word *n.* A meaningful sound which stands for an idea; a comment; a brief talk; an order or command. *v.* To express orally. **wording** *n.*

word proc-ess-ing *n.* A system which produces typewritten documents with automated type and editing equipment.

work *n.* The action or labor required to accomplish something; employment; a job; a project or assignment; something requiring physical or mental effort. *v.* To engage in mental or physical exertion; to labor to have a job; to arrange. **worker** *n.*

work-out *n.* A period of strenuous exercise.

world *n.* The planet Earth; the universe; the human race; a field of human interest or effort.

worldly *adj.* Interested in pleasure rather than religious or spiritual matters.

worm *n.*

A small, thin animal having a long, flexible, rounded or flattened body. *Slang* A crude person.

worn *adj.* Made weak or thin from use; exhausted.

wor-ry *v.* To be concerned or troubled; to tug at repeatedly; to annoy; to irritate. *n.* Distress or mental anxiety.

wor-ship *n.* Reverence for a sacred object; high esteem or devotion for a person. *v.* To revere; attend a religious service. **worshiper** *n.*

worst *adj.* Bad; most inferior; most disagreeable *adv.* In the worst degree.

worth *n.* The quality or value of something; personal merit; the quantity that can be purchased for a certain amount of money.

wor-thy *adj.* Valuable or useful; deserving admiration or honor.

would-n't *contr.* Would not.

wound *n.* A laceration of the skin. *v.* To injure by tearing, cutting, or piercing the skin.

wow *interj.* An expression of amazement, surprise, or excitement.

wran-gle *v.* To quarrel noisily. **-ler** *n.*

wrath *n.* Violent anger or fury.

wreak *v.* To inflict punishment upon another person.

wreath *n.* A decorative ring-like form of intertwined flowers, bows, and other articles.

wreck *v.* To ruin or damage by accident or deliberately; to spoil. *n.* Destruction; the remains of something wrecked or ruined; someone in poor condition.

wren *n.* A small brown songbird having a slender beak, short tail, and rounded wings.

wrench *n.*

A tool used to grip, turn, or twist an object as a bolt or nut. *v.* To turn or twist violently; to give emotional pain.

wrest *v.* To twist or pull away in a violent way. *n.* A forcible twist.

wres-tle *v.* To struggle with an opponent in order to pin him down. *n.* The instance of wrestling. **wrestler** *n.*

wretch *n.* An extremely unhappy person; a miserable person. **wretched** *adj.*

wrig-gle *v.* To squirm; to move by turning and twisting.

wring *v.* To squeeze and twist by hand or machine; to press together.

wrin-kle *n.* A small crease on the skin or on fabric. *v.* To have or make wrinkles.

wrist *n.*, *Anat.* The joint of the body between the hand and forearm; the part of a sleeve which encircles the wrist.

writ *n.*, *Law* A written court document directed to a public official or individual ordering a specific action.

write *v.* To form symbols or letters; to form words on a surface.

writhe *v.* To twist, as in pain; to suffer greatly with pain.

writ-ing *n.* A book or other written work; handwriting; the process of forming letters into words; the occupation of a writer.

wrong *adj.* Incorrect; against moral standards; not suitable; immoral; unsuitable; inappropriate. *n.* An act which is wicked or immoral. *v.* To do wrong; to injure or hurt. **wrongly** *adv.*

wrote *v.* Past tense of write.

wrought *adj.* Fashioned; formed; beaten or hammered into shape.

wrung *v.* Past tense of *wring*.

X, x The twenty-fourth letter of the English alphabet.

Xan-a-du *n.* A place having idyllic beauty.

xan-thate *n.* Ester or slat of a xanthic acid.

xan-thic *adj.* The color yellow or all colors that tend toward the color yellow when relating to flowers.

xan-thin *n.* A carotenoid pigment that is soluble in alcohol.

xan-thine *n.* A crystalline nitrogen compound, closely related to uric acid, found in blood, urine and certain plant and animal tissues.

xan-tho-chroid *adj.* Pertaining to the light-complexioned caucasoid race.

xan-tho-ma *n.* A skin condition of the eyelids marked by small, yellow, raised nodules or plates.

X chro-mo-some *n.* The sex female chromosome, associated with female characteristics; occurs paired in the female and single in the male chromosome pair.

xe-bec *n.* A small vessel with three-masts having both leteen and square sails.

xe-nic *adj.* Relating to, or employing a culture medium that contains one or more unidentified organisms.

xe-non *n.* The colorless, odorless gaseous element found in small quantities in the air, symbolized by Xe.

xe-no-phile *n.* One attracted to foreign people, styles, manners, etc.

xen-o-phobe *n.* A person who dislikes, fears, and mistrusts foreigners or anything strange. **xenophobia** *n.*

xe-rarch *adj.* Originating or developing in a dry place.

xe-ric *adj.* Relating to or requiring only a small amount of moisture. **-ally** *adv.*

xe-roph-i-lous *adj.* Tolerant or characteristic of xeric environments.

xerophily *n.*

xe-roph-thal-mi-a *n.* A itching soreness of the eyes that is caused by an insufficient amount of vitamin A. **-ic** *adj.*

xe-ro-phyte *n.* A plant that can live in a surrounding of extreme heat and drought. **xerophytic** *adj.*,

xerophytically *adv.*, **xerophytism** *n.*

X--ra-di-a-tion *n.* Treatment with X-rays.

X ray *n.* Energy that is radiated with a short wavelength and high penetrating power; a black and white negative image or picture of the interior of the body.

x--sec-tion *n.* Cross section of something. **x-sectional** *adj.*

y-lo-phone *n.*

A musical instrument consisting of mounted wooden bars which produce a ringing musical sound when struck with two small wooden hammers.

y-lose *n.* A crystalline aldose sugar.

y-lot-o-mous *adj.* Capable of cutting or boring wood. **xylotomic** *adj.*

Y, y The twenty-fifth letter of the English alphabet.

yacht *n.* A small sailing vessel powdered by wind or motor, used for pleasure cruises. **yacht** *v.*

yacht-ing *n.* The sport of sailing in a yacht.

yachts-man *n.* A person who sails a yacht. **yachtmanship** *n.*

yak *n.* A longhaired ox of Tibet and the mountains of central Asia.

yam *n.*

An edible root; a variety of the sweet potato.

Yan-kee *n.* A native of the northern United States. **Yankee** *adj.*

yap *v.* To bark in a high pitched, sharp way. *Slang* To talk in a relentess, loud, or stupid manner.

yard *n.* A unit of measure that equals 36 inches or 3 feet; the ground around or near a house or building.

yard goods *n.* Fabric that is sold by the yard.

yard-man *n.* A person employed as a worker in a railroad yard.

yard-mas-ter *n.* A person in charge of a railroad yard.

yard-stick *n.* A graduated measuring stick that equals 1 yard or 36 inches; standard of measurement.

yarn *n.* Twisted fibers, as of wool, used in knitting or weaving. *Slang* An involved tale or story.

yawn *v.* To inhale a deep breath with the mouth open wide. **yawn, yawner** *n.*

yawn-ing *adj.* Expressing tiredness by a yawn.

Y-Chro-mo-some *n.* The sex chromosome associated with male characteristics.

ye *pron.* You, used especially in religious contexts, as hymns.

yea *adv.* Yes; indeed; truly.

yeah *adv.*, *Slang* Yes.

year *n.* A period of time starting on January 1st and continuing through December 31st, consisting of 365 days or 366 days in a leap year.

year-book *n.* A book printed each year giving facts about the year; a book printed each year for a high school, college, etc.

year-ling *n.* An animal that is one year old.

year-ly *adj.* Pertaining to something that happens, appears, or comes once a year, every year.

yearn *v.* To feel a strong craving; deep desire; a wistful feeling.

yearner, yearning *n.*

year--round *adj.* Lasting or continuing for an entire year.

yeast *n.* Fungi or plant cells used to make baked goods rise or fruit juices ferment.

yell *v.* To cry out loudly. *n.* A loud cry; a cheer to show support for an athletic team.

yel-low n. The bright color of a lemon; the yolk of an egg. v. To make or become yellow. adj. Of the color yellow. Slang Cowardly.

yel-low fev-er n. An acute infectious disease of the tropics, spread by the bite of a mosquito.

yel-low-jack-et n. A small wasp, having bright yellow markings, and usually makes its nest below ground level.

yelp n. A quick, sharp, shrill cry, as from pain.

yen n. An intense craving or longing.

yeo-man n. The owner of a small farm; a petty officer who acts as a clerk.

yes adv. To express agreement.

yes-ter-day n. The day before today; a former or recent time. adv. On the day before the present day.

yet adv. Up to now; at this time; even now; more so. conj. Nevertheless; but.

yew n. An evergreen tree having poisonous flat, dark-green needles and poisonous red berries.

Yid-dish n. A language spoken by Jews combining German and Hebrew; spoken by Jews. **Yiddish** adj.

yield v. To bear or bring forward; to give up the possession of something; to give way to. n. An amount that is produced.

yield-ing adj. Ready to yield, comply, or submit; unresisting. **yieldingly** adv.

YMCA abbr., n. Young Men's Christian Association.

yo-del v. To sing in a way so that the voice changes from normal to a high shrill sound and then back again. **yodeler** n.

yo-ga n. A system of exercises which helps the mind and the body in order to achieve tranquillity and spiritual insight.

yo-gurt n. A thick custard-like food made from curdled milk and often mixed with fruit.

yoke n. A wooden bar used to join together two oxen or other animals working together; the section of a garment fitting closely around the shoulders. v. To join with a yoke.

yo-del n. A very unsophisticated country person; a bumpkin.

yolk n. The yellow nutritive part of an egg.

Yom Kip-pur n. The Jewish holiday observed with fasting and prayer for the forgiveness of sins.

you pron. The person or persons addressed.

you all pron., Slang y'all A southern variation used for two or more people in direct address.

you'd contr. You had; you would.

you'll contr. You will; you shall.

young adj. Of or relating to the early stage of life; not old. n. The offspring of an animal. **youngster** n.

your adj. Belonging to you or yourself or the person spoken to.

you're contr. You are.

your-self pron. A form of you for emphasis when the object of a verb and the subject is the same.

youth n. The appearance or state of being young; the time of life when one is not considered an adult; a young person.

youth-ful adj. Being of a young age or early stage in life. **youthfully** adv., **youthfulness** n.

you've contr. You have.

yowl v. To make a loud, long cry or howl. **yowl** n.

yo--yo n. A grooved spool toy with a string wrapped around the spool so it can be spun or moved up and down.

yt-ter-bi-um n. A metallic element of the rare-earth group symbolized by Yb.

yt-tri-um n. A metallic element symbolized by Y.

yuc-ca n. A tropical plant having large, white flowers and long, pointed leaves.

yule n. Christmas.

yule-tide n. The Christmas season.

YWCA abbr. Young Women's Christian Association.

Z, z The twenty-sixth letter of the English alphabet.

za-ny n., pl -nies A clown; a person who acts silly or foolish. adj. Typical of being clownish. **zaniness** n., **zannily** adv.

zap v., Slang To destroy; to do away with.

zeal n. Great interest or eagerness.

zeal-ot n. A fanatical person; a fanatic.

zeal-ous adj. Full of interest; eager; passionate. **-ly** adv., **zealousness** n.

ze-bra n.

An African mammal of the horse family having black or brown stripes on a white body.

zeph-yr n. A gentle breeze.

ze-ro n., pl. -ros, -roes The number or symbol "0"; nothing; the point from which degrees or measurements on a scale begin; the lowest point. v. To aim, point at, or close in on. adj. Pertaining to zero; nonexisting.

zest n. Enthusiasm; a keen quality. **zestful** adj., **zestfully** adv., **zesty** adj.

zig-zag n. A pattern with sharp turns in alternating directions. adv. To move in a zigzag course or path. **zigzag** v.

zilch n., Slang Nothing; zero.

zil-lion n., Slang An extremely large number.

zinc n. A bluish-white crystalline metallic element, used as a protective coating for steel and iron, symbolized by Zn.

Zi-on n. The Jewish homeland, symbolic of Judaism; the Jewish people.

zip n. To act or move with vigor or speed. v. To move with energy, speed or facility; to open or close with a zipper. Slang Energy; zero; nothing.

WEBSTER'S THESAURUS

DICTIONARY FORMAT

OF

SYNONYMS AND ANTONYNMS

DEFINITION OF THESAURUS

SYNONYMS:
Words having the same meaning.

Example:
Give *(syn.)* offer, present, supply

ANTONYMS:
Words having the opposite meaning

Example:
Cold *(ant.)* hot, warm, heated

a (*SYN.*) any, one.

abandon (*SYN.*) relinquish, resign, surrender, leave, give up, cease, forsake.
(*ANT.*) *support, keep, fulfill, uphold, depend, stay, maintain, embrace.*

abandoned (*SYN.*) depraved, wicked, deserted, desolate, forsaken, rejected.
(*ANT.*) *befriended, cherished, chaste, moral, respectable, virtuous, righteous.*

abate (*SYN.*) lessen, curtail, reduce, decrease, restrain, decline, stop.
(*ANT.*) *grow, prolong, increase, extend.*

abbey (*SYN.*) nunnery, convent, cloisters, monastery.

abbot (*SYN.*) friar, monk.

abbreviate (*SYN.*) shorten, lessen, abridge, condense, curtail, reduce, cut.
(*ANT.*) *lengthen, increase, expand.*

abbreviation (*SYN.*) abridgment, reduction, shortening, condensation.
(*ANT.*) *expansion, extension, amplification, lengthening, dilation.*

abdicate (*SYN.*) relinquish, renounce, vacate, waive, desert, forsake, abolish.
(*ANT.*) *maintain, defend, retain, uphold.*

abdomen (*SYN.*) paunch, belly, stomach.

abduct (*SYN.*) carry off, take, kidnap.

abettor *SYN.*) accomplice, ally, confederate, associate, accessory.
(*ANT.*) *opponent, rival, enemy.*

abhor (*SYN.*) dislike, hate, loathe, execrate, avoid, scorn, detest, despise.

abhorrent (*SYN.*) loathsome, horrible, detestable, nauseating, hateful.

abide (*SYN.*) obey, accept, tolerate, endure, dwell, stay, reside.

ability (*SYN.*) aptness, capability, skill, dexterity, faculty, power, talent.
(*ANT.*) *incapacity, weakness, inability.*

abject (*SYN.*) sordid, infamous, miserable, wretched, mean, contempt.

able (*SYN.*) qualified, competent, fit, capable, skilled, having power.
(*ANT.*) *inadequate, trained, efficient, incapable, weak, incompetent, unable.*

abnormal (*SYN.*) uncommon, unnatural, odd, irregular, monstrous, eccentric, unusual, weird, strange.
(*ANT.*) *standard, natural, usual, normal, average.*

aboard (*SYN.*) on board.

abolish (*SYN.*) end, eradicate, annul, cancel, revoke, destroy, invalidate.
(*ANT.*) *promote, restore, continue, establish, sustain.*

abominable (*SYN.*) foul, dreadful, hateful, revolting, vile, odious, loathsome.
(*ANT.*) *delightful, pleasant, agreeable.*

abominate (*SYN.*) despise, detest, hate, dislike, abhor, loathe.
(*ANT.*) *love, cherish, approve, admire.*

abomination (*SYN.*) detestation, hatred, disgust, revulsion, antipathy, horror.

abort (*SYN.*) flop, fizzle, miscarry, abandon, cancel.

abortion (*SYN.*) disaster, failure, defeat.

abound (*SYN.*) swarm, plentiful, filled.
(*ANT.*) *scarce, lack.*

about (*SYN.*) relating to, involving, concerning, near, around, upon, almost.

above (*SYN.*) higher than, overhead, on, upon, over, superior to.

(*ANT.*) *under, beneath, below.*

abrasion (*SYN.*) rubbing, roughness, scratching, scraping, friction, chap.

abrasive (*SYN.*) hurtful, sharp, galling, annoying, grating, irritating, caustic.
(*ANT.*) *pleasant, soothing, comforting.*

abreast (*SYN.*) side by side, alongside.

abridge (*SYN.*) condense, cut, abbreviate, make shorter, contract.
(*ANT.*) *increase, lengthen, extend.*

abroad (*SYN.*) away, overseas, widely.
(*ANT.*) *at home, privately, secretly.*

abrogate (*SYN.*) rescind, withdraw, revoke, annul, cancel, abolish, repeal.

abrupt (*SYN.*) sudden, unexpected, blunt, curt, craggy, precipitous, sharp.
(*ANT.*) *foreseen, smooth, warm, courteous, gradual, smooth, expected.*

abscess (*SYN.*) pustule, sore, wound, inflammation.

absence (*SYN.*) nonexistence, deficiency, lack, need, shortcoming.
(*ANT.*) *attendance, completeness, existence, presence.*

absent (*SYN.*) away, truant, abroad, departed, inattentive, lacking out, off.
(*ANT.*) *attending, watchful, present.*

absolute (*SYN.*) unconditional, entire, actual, complete, thorough, total.
(*ANT.*) *partial, conditional, dependent accountable, restricted, qualified.*

absolutely (*SYN.*) positively, really, doubtlessly.
(*ANT.*) *doubtfully, uncertainly.*

absolution (*SYN.*) pardon, forgiveness, acquittal, mercy, dispensation.

absolve (*SYN.*) exonerate, discharge, acquit, pardon, forgive, clear, excuse.
(*ANT.*) *blame, convict, charge, accuse.*

absorb (*SYN.*) consume, swallow up, engulf, assimilate, imbibe, engage.
(*ANT.*) *discharge, dispense, emit, exude, leak, eliminate, bore, tire, weary, drain.*

absorbent (*SYN.*) permeable, spongy, pervious, porous.
(*ANT.*) *moisture-proof, impervious.*

abstemious (*SYN.*) abstinent, sparing, cautious, temperate, ascetic.
(*ANT.*) *uncontrolled, indulgent.*

abstinence (*SYN.*) fasting, self-denial, continence, do without, sobriety.
(*ANT.*) *greed, excess, self-indulgence.*

abstract (*SYN.*) part, appropriate, steal, remove, draw from, separate, abridge.
(*ANT.*) *return, unite, add, replace.*

abstracted (*SYN.*) parted, removed, stolen, abridged, taken away.
(*ANT.*) *replaced, returned, added.*

abstraction (*SYN.*) idea, image, generalization, thought, opinion.
(*ANT.*) *matter, object, thing, substance.*

absurd (*SYN.*) ridiculous, silly, foolish, irrational, nonsensical, impossible.
(*ANT.*) *rational, sensible, sound, meaningful, consistent, reasonable.*

abundance (*SYN.*) ampleness, profusion, copiousness, plenty.
(*ANT.*) *insufficiency, want, absence, dearth, scarcity.*

abundant (*SYN.*) ample, overflowing, plentiful, rich, teeming, large amount, profuse, abounding.
(*ANT.*) *insufficient, scant, not enough,*

scarce, deficient, uncommon, absent.

abuse *(SYN.)* maltreatment, misuse, reproach, defamation, dishonor, mistreat, damage, ill-use, reviling, aspersion, desecration, invective, insult, outrage, profanation, perversion, upbraiding, disparagement, misemploy, misapply, hurt, harm, injure, berate.
(ANT.) plaudit, respect, appreciate, commendation. protect, praise, cherish.

abusive *(SYN.)* harmful, insulting, libelous, hurtful, slanderous, nasty, defamatory, injurious, scathing, derogatory.
(ANT.) supportive, helpful, laudatory, complimentary.

abut *(SYN.)* touch, border, meet, join, verge on, connect with.

abutment *(SYN.)* pier, buttress, bulwark, brace, support.

abysmal *(SYN.)* immeasurable, boundless, endless, stupendous, profound, unbelievable, infinite, overwhelming, consummate.

abyss *(SYN.)* depth, chasm, void, infinitude, limbo, unknowable.

academic *(SYN.)* learned, scholarly, theoretical, erudite, bookish, formal, pedantic.
(ANT.) ignorant, practical, simple, uneducated.

academy *(SYN.)* college, school.

accede *(SYN.)* grant, agree, comply, consent, yield, endorse, accept, admit.
(ANT.) dissent, disagree, differ, oppose.

accelerate *(SYN.)* quicken, dispatch, facilitate, hurry, rush, speed up, forward, hasten, push, expedite.
(ANT.) hinder, retard, slow, delay, quicken.

accent *(SYN.)* tone, emphasis, inflection, stress, consent.

accept *(SYN.)* take, approve, receive, allow, consent to, believe, adopt, admit.
(ANT.) ignore, reject, refuse.

acceptable *(SYN.)* passable, satisfactory, fair, adequate, standard, par, tolerable, unobjectionable.
(ANT.) poor, substandard, inadmissible.

access *(SYN.)* entrance, approach, course, gateway, door, avenue.

accessible *(SYN.)* nearby, attainable, achievable, affable, democratic, accommodating.
(ANT.) remote, unobtainable, unachievable, standoffish, forbidding, unfriendly.

accessory *(SYN.)* extra, addition, assistant, supplement, contributory, accomplice.

accident *(SYN.)* casualty, disaster, misfortune, mishap, chance, calamity, contingency, fortuity, misadventure, mischance, injury, event, catastrophe.
(ANT.) purpose, intention, calculation.

accidental *(SYN.)* unintended, chance, casual, fortuitous, contingent, unplanned, unexpected, unforeseen.
(ANT.) calculated, planned, willed, intended, intentional, on purpose, deliberate.

acclaim *(SYN.)* eminence, fame, glory, honor, reputation, credit, applaud, distinction, approve, notoriety.
(ANT.) infamy, obscurity, disapprove, reject, disrepute.

acclimated *(SYN.)* adapted, habituated, acclimatized, accommodated, seasoned, inured, used to, weathered, reconciled.

accolade *(SYN.)* praise, honor, acclaim, recognition, applause, kudos, bouquet, crown, testimonial, acclamation, salute.

accommodate *(SYN.)* help, assist, aid, provide for, serve, oblige, hold, house.
(ANT.) inconvenience.

accommodating *(SYN.)* obliging, helpful, willing, kind, cooperative, gracious, cordial, sympathetic, unselfish.
(ANT.) unfriendly, selfish, hostile, uncooperative.

accommodation *(SYN.)* change, alteration, adaptation, convenience, adjustment, acclimatization, aid, help, boon, kindness, service, courtesy.
(ANT.) inflexibility, rigidity, disservice, stubbornness, disadvantage.

accommodations *(SYN.)* housing, lodgings, room, place, quarters, board.

accompany *(SYN.)* chaperon, consort with, escort, go with, associate with, attend, join.
(ANT.) abandon, quit, leave, desert, avoid, forsake.

accomplice *(SYN.* accessory, ally, associate, partner in crime, assistant, sidekick, confederate.
(ANT.) opponent, rival, enemy, adversary.

accomplish *(SYN.)* attain, consummate, achieve, do, execute, carry out, fulfill, complete, effect, perform, finish.
(ANT.) fail, frustrate, spoil, neglect, defeat.

accomplished *(SYN.)* proficient, skilled, finished, well-trained, gifted, masterly, polished, able.
(ANT.) unskilled, amateurish, crude.

accomplishment *(SYN.)* deed, feat, statute, operation, performance, action, achievement, transaction.
(ANT.) cessation, inhibition, intention, deliberation.

accord *(SYN.)* concur, agree, award, harmony, conformity, agreement, give, tale, sum, statement, record, grant.
(ANT.) difference, quarrel, disagreement.

accordingly *(SYN.)* consequently, therefore, whereupon, hence, so, thus.

accost *(SYN.)* approach, greet, speak to, address.
(ANT.) avoid, shun.

account *(SYN.)* description, chronicle, history, narration, reckoning, rate, computation, detail, narrative, relation, recital, consider, believe, deem, record, explanation, report, tale, story, anecdote, reason, statement, tale, ledger.
(ANT.) confusion, misrepresentation, distortion.

accountable *(SYN.)* chargeable, answerable, beholden, responsible, obliged, liable.

account for (SYN.) justify, explain, substantiate, illuminate, clarify, elucidate.

accredited (SYN.) qualified, licensed, deputized, certified, commissioned, vouched for, empowered.
(ANT.) illicit, unofficial, unauthorized.

accrue (SYN.) amass, collect, heap, increase, accumulate, gather, hoard.
(ANT.) disperse, dissipate, waste, diminish.

accrued (SYN.) accumulated, totaled, increased, added, enlarged, amassed, expanded.

accumulate (SYN.) gather, collect, heap, increase, accrue, assemble, compile, hoard, amass.
(ANT.) spend, give away, diminish, dissipate.

accumulation (SYN.) heap, collection, pile, store, hoard, stack, aggregation.

accurate (SYN.) perfect, just, truthful, unerring, meticulous, correct, all right.
(ANT.) incorrect, mistaken, false, wrong.

accursed (SYN.) ill-fated, cursed, condemned, doomed, bedeviled, ruined.
(ANT.) fortunate, hopeful.

accusation (SYN.) charge, incrimination, indictment, arraignment.
(ANT.) pardon, exoneration, absolve.

accuse (SYN.) incriminate, indict, censure, tattle, denounce, charge, arraign, impeach, blame.
(ANT.) release, vindicate, exonerate, acquit, absolve, clear.

accustom (SYN.) addict, familiarize, condition.

accustomed (SYN.) familiar with, used to, comfortable with.
(ANT.) strange, unusual, rare, unfamiliar.

ace (SYN.) champion, star, king, queen, winner, head.

acerbity (SYN.) bitterness, harshness, unkindness, sourness, acidity, unfriendliness, acrimony, coldness, sharpness.
(ANT.) sweetness, gentleness, kindness, tenderness.

ache (SYN.) hurt, pain, throb.

achieve (SYN.) do, execute, gain, obtain, acquire, accomplish, realize, perform, complete, accomplish, finish, fulfill, reach, attain, secure, procure.
(ANT.) fail, lose, fall short.

achievement (SYN.) feat, accomplishment, attainment, exploit, realization, performance, completion, deed.
(ANT.) botch, dud, mess, omission, defeat, failure.

acid (SYN.) tart, sour, bitter, mordant, biting, biting.
(ANT.) pleasant, friendly, bland, mild, sweet.

acknowledge (SYN.) allow, admit, agree to, concede, recognize, answer, grant, accept, receive.
(ANT.) reject, refuse, disavow, refute, deny.

acme (SYN.) summit, top, zenith, peak, crown.
(ANT.) bottom.

acquaint (SYN.) inform, teach, enlighten, notify, tell.

acquaintance (SYN.) fellowship, friendship, cognizance, knowledge, intimacy, familiarity, companionship, associate, colleague, companion.
(ANT.) inexperience, unfamiliarity, ignorance.

acquiesce (SYN.) submit, agree, concur, assent, comply, consent, succumb.
(ANT.) refuse, disagree, rebel, argue.

acquire (SYN.) attain, earn, get, procure, assimilate, obtain, secure, gain, appropriate.
(ANT.) miss, surrender, lose, forego, forfeit.

acquirement (SYN.) training, skill, learning, achievement, attainment, education, information.

acquisition (SYN.) procurement, gain, gift, purchase, proceeds, possession, grant.

acquisitive (SYN.) greedy, avid, hoarding, covetous.

acquit (SYN.) forgive, exonerate, absolve, cleanse, pardon, excuse, excuse, discharge, found not guilty.
(ANT.) doom, saddle, sentence, condemn.

acrid (SYN.) bitter, sharp, nasty, stinging, harsh.
(ANT.) pleasant, sweet.

acrimonious (SYN.) sharp, sarcastic, acerb, waspish, cutting, stinging, testy.
(ANT.) soft, kind, sweet, pleasant, soothing.

acrobat (SYN.) athlete, gymnast.

act (SYN.) deed, doing, feat, execution, accomplishment, performance, action, operation, transaction, law, decree, statute, edict, achievement, exploit, statute, judgment, routine, pretense.
(ANT.) inactivity, deliberation, intention, cessation.

acting (SYN.) officiating, substituting, surrogate, temporary, delegated.

action (SYN.) deed, achievement, feat, activity, exploit, movement, motion, play, behavior, battle, performance, exercise.
(ANT.) idleness, inertia, repose, inactivity, rest.

activate (SYN.) mobilize, energize, start, propel, nudge, push.
(ANT.) paralyze, immobilize, stop, deaden.

active (SYN.) working, operative, alert, agile, nimble, supple, sprightly, busy, brisk, lively, quick, industrious, energetic, vigorous, industrious, occupied, vivacious, dynamic, engaged.
(ANT.) passive, inactive, idle, dormant, lazy, lethargic.

activism (SYN.) engagement, confrontation, agitation, commitment, aggression, fervor, zeal.
(ANT.) detachment, lethargy, disengagement.

activist (SYN.) militant, doer, enthusiast.

activity (SYN.) action, liveliness, motion, vigor, agility, exercise, energy, quickness, enterprise, movement, briskness.
(ANT.) idleness, inactivity, dullness,

sloth.

actor *(SYN.)* performer, trouper, entertainer.

actual *(SYN.)* true, genuine, certain, factual, authentic, concrete, real.
(ANT.) unreal, fake, bogus, nonexistent, false.

actuality *(SYN.)* reality, truth, deed, occurrence, fact, certainty.
(ANT.) theory, fiction, falsehood, supposition.

acute *(SYN.)* piercing, severe, sudden, keen, sharp, perceptive, discerning, shrewd, astute, smart, intelligent.
(ANT.) bland, mild, dull, obtuse, insensitive.

adamant *(SYN.)* unyielding, firm, obstinate.
(ANT.) yielding.

adapt *(SYN.)* adjust, conform, accommodate, change, fit, alter, vary, modify.
(ANT.) misapply, disturb.

add *(SYN.)* attach, increase, total, append, sum, affix, augment, adjoin, put together, unite, supplement.
(ANT.) remove, reduce, deduct, subtract, detach, withdraw.

address *(SYN.)* greet, hail, accost, speak to, location, residence, home, abode, dwelling, speech, lecture, greeting, oration, presentation.
(ANT.) avoid, pass by.

adept *(SYN.)* expert, skillful, proficient.
(ANT.) unskillful.

adequate *(SYN.)* capable, commensurate, fitting, satisfactory, sufficient, enough, ample, suitable, plenty, fit.
(ANT.) lacking, scant, insufficient, inadequate.

adhere *(SYN.)* stick fast, grasp, hold, keep, retain, cling, stick to, keep, cleave.
(ANT.) surrender, abandon, release, separate, loosen.

adherent *(SYN.)* follower, supporter.
(ANT.) renegade, dropout, defector.

adjacent *(SYN.)* next to, near, bordering, adjoining, touching, neighboring.
(ANT.) separate, distant, apart.

adjoin *(SYN.)* connect, be close to, affix, attach.
(ANT.) detach, remove.

adjoining *(SYN.)* near to, next, next to, close to, touching, bordering.
(ANT.) distant, remote, separate.

adjourn *(SYN.)* postpone, defer, delay, suspend, discontinue, put off.
(ANT.) begin, convene, assemble.

adjust *(SYN.)* repair, fix, change, set, regulate, settle, arrange, adapt, suit, accommodate, modify, very, alter, fit.

administer *(SYN.)* supervise, oversee, direct, manage, rule, govern, control, conduct, provide, give, execute, preside, apply, contribute, help.

administration *(SYN.)* conduct, direction, management, supervision.

admirable *(SYN.)* worthy, fine, praise-deserving, commendable, excellent.

admiration *(SYN.)* pleasure, wonder, esteem, approval.
(ANT.) disdain, disrespect, contempt.

admire *(SYN.)* approve, venerate, appreciate, respect, revere. esteem, like.
(ANT.) abhor, dislike, despise, loathe, detest, hate.

admissible *(SYN.)* fair, justifiable, tolerable, allowable, permissible.
(ANT.) unsuitable, unfair, inadmissible.

admission *(SYN.)* access, admittance, entrance, pass, ticket.

admit *(SYN.)* allow, assent, permit, acknowledge, welcome, concede, agree, confess, accept, grant, own up to.
(ANT.) deny, reject, dismiss, shun, obstruct.

admittance *(SYN.)* access, entry, entrance.

admonish *(SYN.)* caution, advise against, warn, rebuke, reprove, censure.
(ANT.) glorify, praise.

admonition *(SYN.)* advice, warning, caution, reminder, tip.

ado *(SYN.)* trouble, other, fuss, bustle, activity, excitement, commotion, action, hubbub, upset, confusion, turmoil.
(ANT.) tranquillity, quietude.

adolescent *(SYN.)* young, youthful, immature, teenage.
(ANT.) grown, mature, adult.

adoration *(SYN.)* veneration, reverence, glorification, worship homage.

adore *(SYN.)* revere, venerate, idolize, respect, love, cherish, esteem, honor.
(ANT.) loathe, hate, despise.

adorn *(SYN.)* trim, bedeck, decorate, ornament, beautify, embellish, glamorize, enhance, garnish, embellish.
(ANT.) mar, spoil, deform, deface, strip, bare.

adrift *(SYN.)* floating, afloat, drifting, aimless, purposeless, unsettled.
(ANT.) purposeful, stable, secure, well-organized.

adroit *(SYN.)* adept, apt, dexterous, skillful, clever, ingenious, expert.
(ANT.) awkward, clumsy, graceless, unskillful, oafish.

adult *(SYN.)* full-grown, mature.
(ANT.) infantile, immature.

advance *(SYN.)* further, promote, bring forward, propound, proceed, aggrandize, elevate, improve, adduce, allege, propose, progress, move, advancement, improvement, promotion, upgrade.
(ANT.) retard, retreat, oppose, hinder, revert, withdraw, flee, retardation.

advantage *(SYN.)* edge, profit, superiority, benefit, mastery, leverage, favor, vantage, gain.
(ANT.) handicap, impediment, obstruction, disadvantage, detriment, hindrance, loss.

adventure *(SYN.)* undertaking, occurrence, enterprise, happening, event, project, occurrence, incident, exploit.

adventurous *(SYN.)* daring, enterprising, rash, bold, chivalrous.
(ANT.) cautious, timid, hesitating.

adversary *(SYN.)* foe, enemy, contestant, opponent, antagonist.

(ANT.) *ally, friend.*

adverse *(SYN.)* hostile, counteractive, unfavorable, opposed, disastrous, contrary, antagonistic, opposite, unlucky, unfriendly, unfortunate.
(ANT.) *favorable, propitious, fortunate, friendly, beneficial.*

adversity *(SYN.)* misfortune, trouble, calamity, distress, hardship, disaster.
(ANT.) *benefit, happiness.*

advertise *(SYN.)* promote, publicize, make known, announce, promulgate.

advertisement *(SYN.)* commercial, billboard, want ad, handbill, flyer, poster, brochure, blurb.

advice *(SYN.)* counsel, instruction, suggestion, warning, information, caution, exhortation, admonition, recommendation, plan, tip, guidance, opinion.

advisable *(SYN.)* wise, sensible, prudent, suitable, fit, proper, fitting.
(ANT.) *ill-considered, imprudent, inadvisable.*

advise *(SYN.)* recommend, suggest, counsel, caution, warn, admonish.

adviser *(SYN.)* coach, guide, mentor, counselor.

advocate *(SYN.)* defend, recommend, support.
(ANT.) *opponent, adversary, oppose, opponent.*

aesthetic *(SYN.)* literary, artistic, sensitive, tasteful, well-composed.
(ANT.) *tasteless.*

affable *(SYN.)* pleasant, courteous, sociable, friendly, amiable, gracious, approachable, communicative.
(ANT.) *unfriendly, unsociable.*

affair *(SYN.)* event, occasion, happening, party, occurrence, matter, festivity, business, concern.

affect *(SYN.)* alter, modify, concern, regard, move, touch, feign, pretend, influence, sway, transform, change, impress.

affected *(SYN.)* pretended, fake, sham, false.

affection *(SYN.)* fondness, kindness, emotion, love, feeling, tenderness, attachment, disposition, endearment, liking, friendliness, warmth.
(ANT.) *aversion, indifference, repulsion, hatred, repugnance, dislike, antipathy.*

affectionate *(SYN.)* warm, loving, tender, fond, attached.
(ANT.) *distant, unfeeling, cold.*

affirm *(SYN.)* aver, declare, swear, maintain, endorse, certify, state, assert, ratify, pronounce, say, confirm, establish.
(ANT.) *deny, dispute, oppose, contradict, demur, disclaim.*

afflict *(SYN.)* trouble, disturb, bother, agitate, perturb.
(ANT.) *soothe.*

affliction *(SYN.)* distress, grief, misfortune, trouble.
(ANT.) *relief, benefit, easement.*

affluent *(SYN.)* wealthy, prosperous, rich, abundant, ample, plentiful, well-off, bountiful, well-to-do.
(ANT.) *poor.*

afford *(SYN.)* supply, yield, furnish.

affront *(SYN.)* offense, slur, slight, provocation, insult.

afraid *(SYN.)* faint-hearted, frightened, scared, timid, fearful, apprehensive, cowardly, terrified.
(ANT.) *assured, composed, courageous, bold, confident.*

after *(SYN.)* following, subsequently, behind, despite, next.
(ANT.) *before.*

again *(SYN.)* anew, repeatedly, afresh.

against *(SYN.)* versus, hostile to, opposed to, in disagreement.
(ANT.) *pro, with, for, in favor of.*

age *(SYN.)* antiquity, date, period, generation, time, senility, grow old, senescence, mature, dotage, ripen, mature, era, epoch.
(ANT.) *youth, childhood.*

aged *(SYN.)* ancient, elderly, old.
(ANT.) *youthful, young.*

agency *(SYN.)* office, operation.

agent *(SYN.)* performer, doer, worker, actor, operator.

aggravate *(SYN.)* intensify, magnify, annoy, irritate, increase, heighten, nettle, make worse, irk, vex, provoke, embitter, worsen.
(ANT.) *soften, soothe, appease, pacify, mitigate, ease, relieve.*

aggregate *(SYN.)* collection, entirety, sum, accumulate, total, amount to, compile, conglomeration.
(ANT.) *part, unit, ingredient, element.*

aggression *(SYN.)* assault, attack, invasion, offense.
(ANT.) *defense.*

aggressive *(SYN.)* offensive, belligerent, hostile, attacking, militant, pugnacious.
(ANT.) *timid, withdrawn, passive, peaceful, shy.*

aghast *(SYN.)* surprised, astonished, astounded, awed, thunderstruck, flabbergasted, bewildered.

agile *(SYN.)* nimble, graceful, lively, active, alert, fast, quick, athletic, spry.
(ANT.) *inept, awkward, clumsy.*

agility *(ANT.)* quickness, vigor, liveliness, energy, activity, motion.
(ANT.) *dullness, inertia, idleness, inactivity.*

agitate *(SYN.)* disturb, excite, perturb, rouse, shake, arouse, disconcert, instigate, inflame, provoke, jar, incite, stir up, toss.
(ANT.) *calm, placate, quiet, ease, soothe.*

agitated *(SYN.)* jumpy, jittery, nervous, restless, restive, upset, disturbed, ruffled.

agony *(SYN.)* anguish, misery, pain, suffering, torture, ache, distress, throe, woe, torment, grief.
(ANT.) *relief, ease, comfort.*

agree *(SYN.)* comply, coincide, conform, assent, accede, tally, settle, harmonize, unite, yield, consent.
(ANT.) *differ, disagree, protest, contradict, argue, refuse.*

agreeable *(SYN.)* amiable, charming, gratifying, pleasant, suitable, pleasur-

able, welcome, pleasing, acceptable, friendly, cooperative.
(ANT.) obnoxious, offensive, unpleasant, disagreeable, quarrelsome, contentious, touchy.
agreement (SYN.) harmony, understanding, unison, contract, pact, stipulation, alliance, deal, bargain, treaty, contract, arrangement, settlement, accord, concord.
(ANT.) variance, dissension, discord, disagreement, difference, misunderstanding.
agriculture (SYN.) farming, gardening, tillage, husbandry, cultivation, agronomy.
ahead (SYN.) before, leading, forward, winning, inadvance.
(ANT.) behind.
aid (SYN.) remedy, assist, helper, service, support, assistant, relief, help.
(ANT.) obstruct, hinder, obstacle, impede, hindrance.
ail (SYN.) bother, trouble, perturb, disturb, suffer, feel sick.
ailing (SYN.) sick, ill.
(ANT.) hearty, hale, well.
ailment (SYN.) illness, disease, affliction, sickness.
aim (SYN.) direction, point, goal, object, target, direct, try, intend, intention, end, objective.
aimless (SYN.) directionless, adrift, purposeless.
air (SYN.) atmosphere, display, reveal, expose, publicize.
(ANT.) conceal, hide.
airy (SYN.) breezy, light, gay, lighthearted, graceful, fanciful.
aisle (SYN.) corridor, passageway, lane, alley, opening, artery.
ajar (SYN.) gaping, open.
akin (SYN.) alike, related, connected, similar, affiliated, allied.
alarm (SYN.) dismay, fright, signal, warning, terror, apprehension, affright, consternation, fear, siren, arouse, startle, bell.
(ANT.) tranquillity, composure, security, quiet, calm, soothe, comfort.
alarming (SYN.) appalling, daunting, shocking.
(ANT.) comforting, calming, soothing.
alcoholic (SYN.) sot, drunkard, tippler, inebriate.
alert (SYN.) attentive, keen, clearwitted, ready, nimble, vigilant, watchful, observant.
(ANT.) logy, sluggish, dulled, listless.
alias (SYN.) anonym, assumed name.
alibi (SYN.) story, excuse.
alien (SYN.) adverse, foreigner, strange, remote, stranger, different, extraneous.
(ANT.) germane, kindred, relevant, akin, familiar, accustomed.
alight (SYN.) debark, deplane, detrain, disembark.
(ANT.) embark, board.
alive (SYN.) existing, breathing, living, live, lively, vivacious, animated.
(ANT.) inactive, dead, moribund.
allay (SYN.) soothe, check, lessen, calm, lighten, relieve, soften, moderate,

quite.
(ANT.) excite, intensify, worsen, arouse.
allege (SYN.) affirm, cite, claim, declare, maintain, state, assert.
(ANT.) deny, disprove, refute, contradict, gainsay.
allegiance (SYN.) faithfulness, duty, devotion, loyalty, fidelity, obligation.
(ANT.) treachery, disloyalty.
allegory (SYN.) fable, fiction, myth, saga, parable, legend.
(ANT.) history, fact.
alleviate (SYN.) diminish, soothe, solace, abate, assuage, allay, soften, mitigate, extenuate, relieve, let up, ease, slacken, relax, weaken.
(ANT.) increase, aggravate, augment, irritate.
alley (SYN.) footway, byway, path, passageway, aisle, corridor, opening, lane.
alliance (SYN.) combination, partnership, union, treaty, coalition, association, confederacy, marriage, pact, agreement, relation, interrelation, understanding, relationship.
(ANT.) separation, divorce, schism.
allot (SYN.) divide, mete, assign, give, measure, distribute, allocate, share, grant, dispense, deal, apportion.
(ANT.) withhold, retain, keep, confiscate, refuse.
allow (SYN.) authorize, grant, acknowledge, admit, let, permit, sanction, consent, concede, mete, allocate.
(ANT.) protest, resist, refuse, forbid, object, prohibit.
allowance (SYN.) grant, fee, portion, ration, allotment.
allude (SYN.) intimate, refer, insinuate, hint, advert, suggest, imply, mention.
(ANT.) demonstrate, specify, state, declare.
allure (SYN.) attract, fascinate, tempt, charm, infatuate, captivate.
ally (SYN.) accomplice, associate, confederate, abettor, assistant, friend, partner.
(ANT.) rival, enemy, opponent, foe, adversary.
almighty (SYN.) omnipotent, powerful.
almost (SYN.) somewhat, nearly.
(ANT.) completely, absolutely.
alms (SYN.) dole, charity, donation, contribution.
aloft (SYN.) overhead.
alone (SYN.) desolate, unaided, only, isolated, unaided, lone, secluded, lonely, deserted, solitary, single, apart, solo, separate.
(ANT.) surrounded, attended, accompanied, together.
aloof (SYN.) uninterested, uninvolved, apart, away, remote, unsociable, standoffish, separate, disdainful, distant.
(ANT.) warm, outgoing, friendly, cordial.
also (SYN.) in addition, likewise, too, besides, furthermore, moreover, further.
alter (SYN.) adjust, vary, deviate, modify, reserved, change.
(ANT.) maintain, preserve, keep.
alteration (SYN.) difference, adjust-

ment, change, modification.
(ANT.) maintenance, preservation.
altercation *(SYN.)* controversy, dispute, argument, quarrel.
alternate *(SYN.)* rotate, switch, spell, interchange.
(ANT.) fix.
alternative *(SYN.)* substitute, selection, option, choice, replacement, possibility.
although *(SYN.)* though, even if, even though, despite, notwithstanding.
altitude *(SYN.)* elevation, height.
(ANT.) depth.
altogether *(SYN.)* totally, wholly, quite, entirely, thoroughly, completely.
(ANT.) partly.
altruism *(SYN.)* kindness, tenderness, generosity, charity, benevolence, liberality.
(ANT.) selfishness, unkindness, cruelty, inhumanity.
always *(SYN.)* evermore, forever, perpetually, ever, unceasingly, continually, constantly, eternally, everlastingly.
(ANT.) never, rarely, sometimes, occasionally.
amalgamate *(SYN.)* fuse, unify, unite, commingle, merge, blend, combine, consolidate.
(ANT.) decompose, disintegrate, separate.
amass *(SYN.)* collect, accumulate, heap up, gather, increase, compile, assemble, store up.
(ANT.) disperse, dissipate, spend.
amateur *(SYN.)* beginner, dilettante, learner, dabbler, neophyte, apprentice, novice, nonprofessional, tyro.
(ANT.) expert, master, adept, professional, authority.
amaze *(SYN.)* surprise, flabbergast, stun, dumbfound, astound, bewilder, aghast, thunderstruck, astonish.
(ANT.) bore, disinterest, tire.
ambiguous *(SYN.)* uncertain, vague, obscure, dubious, equivocal, unclear, deceptive.
(ANT.) plain, clear, explicit, obvious, unequivocal, unmistakable, certain.
ambition *(SYN.)* eagerness, goal, incentive, aspiration, yearning, longing, desire.
(ANT.) indifference, satisfaction, indolence, resignation.
ambitious *(SYN.)* aspiring, intent upon.
(ANT.) indifferent.
amble *(SYN.)* saunter, stroll.
ambush *(SYN.)* trap, hiding place.
amend *(SYN.)* change, mend, better, correct, improve.
(ANT.) worsen.
amends *(SYN.)* compensation, restitution, payment, reparation, remedy, redress.
amiable *(SYN.)* friendly, good-natured, gracious, pleasing, agreeable, outgoing, kindhearted, kind, pleasant.
(ANT.) surly, hateful, churlish, disagreeable, ill-natured, ill-tempered, cross, captious, touchy.
amid *(SYN.)* among, amidst, sur-

rounded by.
amiss *(SYN.)* wrongly, improperly, astray, awry.
(ANT.) properly, rightly, right, correctly, correct.
ammunition *(SYN.)* shot, powder, shells, bullets.
among *(SYN.)* between, mingled, mixed amidst, amid, betwixt, surrounded by.
(ANT.) separate, apart.
amorous *(SYN.)* amatory, affectionate, loving.
amount *(SYN.)* sum, total, quantity, number, price, value, measure.
ample *(SYN.)* broad, large, profuse, spacious, copious, liberal, plentiful, full, bountiful, abundant, great, extensive, generous, wide, enough, sufficient, roomy.
(ANT.) limited, insufficient, meager, small, lacking, cramped, confined, inadequate.
amplification *(SYN.)* magnification, growth, waxing, accrual, enhancement, enlargement, heightening, increase.
(ANT.) decrease, diminishing, reduction, contraction.
amplify *(SYN.)* broaden, develop, expand, enlarge, extend.
(ANT.) confine, restrict, abridge, narrow.
amuse *(SYN.)* divert, please, delight, entertain, charm.
(ANT.) tire, bore.
amusement *(SYN.)* diversion, pastime, entertainment, pleasure, enjoyment, recreation.
(ANT.) tedium, boredom.
amusing *(SYN.)* pleasant, funny, pleasing, entertaining, comical.
(ANT.) tiring, tedious, boring.
analogous *(SYN.)* comparable, corresponding, like, similar, correspondent, alike, correlative, parallel, allied, akin.
(ANT.) different, opposed, incongruous, divergent.
analysis *(SYN.)* separation, investigation, examination.
analyze *(SYN.)* explain, investigate, examine, separate.
ancestral *(SYN.)* hereditary, inherited.
ancestry *(SYN.)* family, line, descent, lineage.
(ANT.) posterity.
anchor *(SYN.)* fix, attach, secure, fasten.
(ANT.) detach, free, loosen.
ancient *(SYN.)* aged, old-fashioned, archaic, elderly, antique, old, primitive.
(ANT.) new, recent, current, fresh.
anecdote *(SYN.)* account, narrative, story, tale.
anesthetic *(SYN.)* opiate, narcotic, sedative, painkiller, analgesic.
angel *(SYN.)* cherub, archangel, seraph.
(ANT.) demon, devil.
angelic *(SYN.)* pure, lovely, heavenly, good, virtuous, innocent, godly, saintly.
(ANT.) devilish.
anger *(SYN.)* exasperation, fury, ire, passion, rage, resentment, temper, indignation, animosity, irritation, wrath,

displeasure, infuriate, arouse, nettle, annoyance, exasperate.
(ANT.) forbearance, patience, peace, self-control.

angry *(SYN.)* provoked, wrathful, furious, enraged, incensed, exasperated, maddened, indignant, irate, mad, inflamed.
(ANT.) happy, pleased, calm, satisfied, content, tranquil.

anguish *(SYN.)* suffering, torment, torture, distress, pain, heartache, grief, agony, misery.
(ANT.) solace, relief, joy, comfort, peace, ecstasy, pleasure.

animal *(SYN.)* beast, creature.

animate *(SYN.)* vitalize, invigorate, stimulate, enliven, alive, vital, vigorous.
(ANT.) dead, inanimate.

animated *(SYN.)* gay, lively, spry, vivacious, active, vigorous, chipper, snappy.
(ANT.) inactive.

animosity *(SYN.)* grudge, hatred, rancor, spite, bitterness, enmity, opposition, dislike, hostility, antipathy.
(ANT.) good will, love, friendliness, kindliness.

annex *(SYN.)* join, attach, add, addition, wing, append.

annihilate *(SYN.)* destroy, demolish, end, wreck, abolish.

announce *(SYN.)* proclaim, give out, make known, notify, publish, report, herald, promulgate, advertise, broadcast, state, tell, declare, publicize.
(ANT.) conceal, withhold, suppress, bury, stifle.

announcement *(SYN.)* notification, report, declaration, bulletin, advertisement, broadcast, promulgation, notice, message.
(ANT.) silence, hush, muteness, speechlessness.

annoy *(SYN.)* bother, irk, pester, tease, trouble, vex, disturb, inconvenience, molest, irritate, harry, harass.
(ANT.) console, gratify, soothe, accommodate, please, calm, comfort.

annually *(SYN.)* once a year.

anoint *(SYN.)* grease, oil.

answer *(SYN.)* reply, rejoinder, response, retort, rebuttal, respond.
(ANT.) summoning, argument, questioning, inquiry, query, ask, inquire.

antagonism *(SYN.)* opposition, conflict, enmity, hostility, animosity.
(ANT.) geniality, cordiality, friendliness.

antagonist *(SYN.)* adversary, rival, enemy, foe, opponent.
(ANT.) ally, friend.

antagonize *(SYN.)* against, provoke, counter, oppose, embitter.
(ANT.) soothe.

anthology *(SYN.)* garland, treasury, collection.

anticipate *(SYN.)* await, foresee, forecast, hope for, expect.

anticipated *(SYN.)* expected, foresight, hoped, preconceived.
(ANT.) dreaded, reared, worried, doubted.

antics *(SYN.)* horseplay, fun, merrymaking, pranks, capers, tricks, clowning.

antipathy *(SYN.)* hatred.

antiquated *(SYN.)* old, out-of-date, outdated, old-fashion.

antique *(SYN.)* rarity, curio, old, ancient, old-fashioned, archaic, out-of-date.
(ANT.) new, recent, fresh.

anxiety *(SYN.)* care, disquiet, fear, concern, solicitude, trouble, worry, apprehension, uneasiness, distress, foreboding.
(ANT.) nonchalance, assurance, confidence, contentment, peacefulness, placidity, tranquillity.

anxious *(SYN.)* troubled, uneasy, perturbed, apprehensive, worried, concerned, desirous, bothered, agitated, eager, fearful.
(ANT.) tranquil, calm, peaceful.

anyway *(SYN.)* nevertheless, anyhow.

apartment *(SYN.)* suite, flat, dormitory.

apathy *(SYN.)* unconcern, indifference, lethargy.
(ANT.) interest, feeling.

aperture *(SYN.)* gap, pore, opening, cavity, chasm, abyss, hole, void.
(ANT.) connection, bridge, link.

apex *(SYN.)* acme, tip, summit, crown, top.

apologize *(SYN.)* ask forgiveness.

apology *(SYN.)* defense, excuse, confession, justification, alibi, explanation, plea.
(ANT.) denial, complaint, dissimulation, accusation.

apostate *(SYN.)* nonconformist, unbeliever, dissenter, heretic, schismatic.
(ANT.) saint, conformist, believer.

appall *(SYN.)* shock, stun, dismay, frighten, terrify, horrify.
(ANT.) edify, please.

appalling *(SYN.)* fearful, frightful, ghastly, horrid, repulsive, terrible, dire, awful.
(ANT.) fascinating, beautiful, enchanting, enjoyable.

apparatus *(SYN.)* rig, equipment, furnishings, gear, tackle.

apparel *(SYN.)* clothes, attire, garb, clothing, garments, dress, robes.

apparent *(SYN.)* obvious, plain, self-evident, clear, manifest, transparent, unmistakable, palpable, unambiguous, ostensible, illusory, visible, seeming, evident, understandable.
(ANT.) uncertain, indistinct, dubious, hidden, mysterious.

apparition *(SYN.)* illusion, ghost, phantom, vision, fantasy, dream.

appeal *(SYN.)* plea, petition, request, entreaty, request, plead, petition, beseech, beg, entreat, attract.
(ANT.) repulse, repel.

appear *(SYN.)* look, arrive, emanate, emerge, arise, seem, turn up.
(ANT.) vanish, withdraw, exist, disappear, evaporate.

appearance *(SYN.)* advent, arrival, aspect, demeanor, fashion, guise, apparition, manner, mien, look, presence.

(ANT.) disappearance, reality, departure, vanishing.

appease *(SYN.)* calm, compose, lull, quiet, relieve, assuage, pacify, satisfy, restraint, lesson, soothe, check, ease, alleviate, still, allay, tranquilize.

(ANT.) excite, arouse, incense, irritate, inflame.

append *(SYN.)* supplement, attach, add.

appendage *(SYN.)* addition, tail, supplement.

appetite *(SYN.)* zest, craving, desire, liking, longing, stomach, inclination, hunger, thirst, relish, passion.

(ANT.) satiety, disgust, distaste, repugnance.

appetizer *(SYN.)* hors d'oeuvre.

applaud *(SYN.)* cheer, clap, hail, approve, praise, acclaim.

(ANT.) disapprove, denounce, reject, criticize, condemn.

appliance *(SYN.)* machine, tool, instrument, device, utensil, implement.

applicable *(SYN.)* fitting, suitable, proper, fit, usable, appropriate, suited.

(ANT.) inappropriate, inapplicable.

apply *(SYN.)* affix, allot, appropriate, use, employ, petition, request, devote, avail, pertain, attach, ask, administer, petition, assign, relate, utilize.

(ANT.) give away, demand, detach, neglect, ignore.

appoint *(SYN.)* name, choose, nominate, designate, elect, establish, assign, place.

(ANT.) discharge, fire, dismiss.

appointment *(SYN.)* rendezvous, meeting, designation, position, engagement, assignment.

(ANT.) discharge, dismissal.

appraise *(SYN.)* value, evaluate, place a value on.

appreciate *(SYN.)* enjoy, regard, value, prize, cherish, admire, go up, improve, rise, respect, think highly of, esteem, appraise.

(ANT.) belittle, misunderstand, apprehend, degrade, scorn, depreciate, undervalue.

apprehend *(SYN.)* seize, capture, arrest, understand, dread, fear, grasp, perceive.

(ANT.) release, lose.

apprehension *(SYN.)* fear, misgiving, dread, uneasiness, worry, fearfulness, anticipation, capture, seizure.

(ANT.) confidence, composure, self-assuredness.

apprehensive *(SYN.)* worried, afraid, uneasy, bothered, anxious, concerned, perturbed, troubled, fearful.

(ANT.) relaxed.

apprentice *(SYN.)* amateur, recruit, novice, learner, beginner.

(ANT.) experienced, professional, master.

approach *(SYN.)* greet, inlet, come near, advance, access, passageway.

(ANT.) avoid, pass by, retreat.

appropriate *(SYN.)* apt, particular, proper, fitting, suitable, applicable, loot, pillage, purloin, rob, steal, embezzle, assign, becoming, apportion, authorize.

(ANT.) improper, contrary, inappropriate, buy, repay, restore, return, unfit, inapt.

approval *(SYN.)* commendation, consent, praise, approbation, sanction, assent, endorsement, support.

(ANT.) reproach, censure, reprimand, disapprove.

approve *(SYN.)* like, praise, authorize, confirm, endorse, appreciate, think well of, ratify, commend, sanction.

(ANT.) criticize, nullify, disparage, frown on, disapprove, deny.

approximate *(SYN.)* near, approach, roughly, close.

(ANT.) correct.

apt *(SYN.)* suitable, proper, appropriate, fit, suited, disposed, liable, inclined, prone, clever, bright, alert, intelligent, receptive.

(ANT.) ill-becoming, unsuitable, unlikely, slow, retarded, dense.

aptness *(SYN.)* capability, dexterity, power, qualification, skill, ability, aptitude.

(ANT.) incompetency, unreadiness, incapacity.

aptitude *(SYN.)* knack, talent, gift, ability.

aqueduct *(SYN.)* gully, pipe, canal, waterway, channel.

arbitrary *(SYN.)* unrestricted, absolute, despotic, willful, unreasonable, unconditional, authoritative.

(ANT.) contingent, qualified, fair, reasonable, dependent, accountable.

arbitrate *(SYN.)* referee, settle, mediate, umpire, negotiate.

architecture *(SYN.)* structure, building, construction.

ardent *(SYN.)* fervent, fiery, glowing, intense, keen, impassioned, fervid, hot, passionate, earnest, eager, zealous, enthusiastic.

(ANT.) cool, indifferent, nonchalant, apathetic.

ardor *(SYN.)* enthusiasm, rapture, spirit, zeal, fervent, eager, glowing, eagerness.

(ANT.) unconcern, apathy, disinterest, indifference.

arduous *(SYN.)* laborious, hard, difficult, burdensome, strenuous, strained.

(ANT.) easy.

area *(SYN.)* space, extent, region, zone, section, expanse, district, neighborhood, size.

argue *(SYN.)* plead, reason, wrangle, indicate, prove, show, dispute, denote.

(ANT.) reject, spurn, ignore, overlook.

argument *(SYN.)* debate, dispute, discussion, controversy.

(ANT.) harmony, accord, agreement.

arid *(SYN.)* waterless, dry, flat, dull, unimaginative, stuffy.

(ANT.) fertile, wet, colorful.

arise *(SYN.)* enter, institute, originate, start, open, commence, emerge.

(ANT.) terminate, end, finish, complete, close.

aristocrat *(SYN.)* noble, gentleman, peer, lord, nobleman.
(ANT.) peasant, commoner.

arm *(SYN.)* weapon, defend, equip, empower, fortify.

armistice *(SYN.)* truce, pact, deal, understanding, peace, treaty, contract.

army *(SYN.)* troops, legion, military, forces, militia.

aroma *(SYN.)* smell, odor, fragrance, perfume, scent.

arouse *(SYN.)* stir, animate, move, pique, provoke, kindle, disturb, excite.
(ANT.) settle, soothe, calm.

arraign *(SYN.)* charge, censure, incriminate, indict, accuse.
(ANT.) acquit, release, vindicate, exonerate, absolve.

arraignment *(SYN.)* imputation, charge, accusation, incrimination.
(ANT.) pardon, exoneration, exculpation.

arrange *(SYN.)* classify, assort, organize, place, plan, prepare, devise, adjust, dispose, regulate, group, prepare.
(ANT.) jumble, scatter, disorder, confuse, disturb, disarrange.

arrangement *(SYN.)* display, grouping, order, array.

array *(SYN.)* dress, adorn, attire, clothe, arrange, order, distribute, exhibit.
(ANT.) disorder, disorganization, disarray.

arrest *(SYN.)* detain, hinder, restrain, seize, withhold, stop, check, obstruct, apprehend, interrupt, catch, capture.
(ANT.) free, release, discharge, liberate.

arrival *(SYN.)* advent, coming.
(ANT.) leaving, departure.

arrive *(SYN.)* come, emerge, reach, visit, land, appear.
(ANT.) exit, leave, depart, go.

arrogance *(SYN.)* pride, insolence.
(ANT.) humbleness, modesty, humility.

arrogant *(SYN.)* insolent, prideful, scornful, haughty, cavalier, proud.
(ANT.) modest, humble.

art *(SYN.)* cunning, tact, artifice, skill, aptitude, adroitness, painting, drawing.
(ANT.) clumsiness, innocence, unskillfulness, honesty.

artful *(SYN.)* clever, sly, skillful, knowing, deceitful, tricky, crafty, cunning.
(ANT.) artless.

article *(SYN.)* story, composition, treatise, essay, thing, report, object.

artificial *(SYN.)* bogus, fake, affected, feigned, phony, sham, unreal.
(ANT.) genuine, true, real, authentic.

artist *(SYN.)* actor, actress, painter, sculptor, singer, designer.

artless *(SYN.)* innocent, open, frank, simple, honest, candid, natural, unskilled, ignorant, truthful, sincere.
(ANT.) artful.

ascend *(SYN.)* rise, scale, tower, mount, go up, climb.
(ANT.) fall, sink, descend, go down.

ascertain *(SYN.)* solve, learn, clear up, answer.

ascribe *(SYN.)* attribute, assign.

ashamed *(SYN.)* shamefaced, humiliated, abashed, mortified, embarrassed.
(ANT.) proud.

ask *(SYN.)* invite, request, inquire, query, question, beg, solicit, demand.
(ANT.) order, reply, insist, answer.

askance *(SYN.)* sideways.

askew *(SYN.)* disorderly, crooked, awry, twisted.
(ANT.) straight.

asleep *(SYN.)* inactive, sleeping.
(ANT.) alert, awake.

aspect *(SYN.)* appearance, look, view, outlook, attitude, viewpoint, phase, part, feature, side.

asphyxiate *(SYN.)* suffocate, stifle, smother, choke, strangle, throttle.

aspiration *(SYN.)* craving, desire, hope, longing, objective, passion, ambition.

aspire *(SYN.)* seek, aim, wish for, strive, desire, yearn for.

ass *(SYN.)* mule, donkey, burro, silly, dunce, stubborn, stupid, fool.

assail *(SYN.)* assault, attack.

assassinate *(SYN.)* purge, kill, murder.

assault *(SYN.)* invade, strike, attack, assail, charge, bombard, onslaught.
(ANT.) protect, defend.

assemble *(SYN.)* collect, gather, meet, congregate, connect, manufacture.
(ANT.) disperse, disassemble, scatter.

assembly *(SYN.)* legislature, congress, council, parliament.

assent *(SYN.)* consent to, concede, agree, approval, accept, comply.
(ANT.) deny, dissent, refusal, denial, refuse.

assert *(SYN.)* declare, maintain, state, claim, express, defend, press, support.
(ANT.) deny, refute, contradict, decline.

assess *(SYN.)* calculate, compute, estimate, levy, reckon, tax, appraise.

asset *(SYN.)* property, wealth, capitol, resources, goods.

assign *(SYN.)* apportion, ascribe, attribute, cast, allot, choose, appropriate, name, elect, appoint, distribute.
(ANT.) release, relieve, unburden, discharge.

assignment *(SYN.)* task, job, responsibility, duty.

assist *(SYN.)* help, promote, serve, support, sustain, abet, aid, back.
(ANT.) prevent, impede, hinder, hamper.

assistance *(SYN.)* backing, help, patronage, relief, succor, support.
(ANT.) hostility, resistance, antagonism, counteraction.

assistant *(SYN.)* accomplice, ally, associate, confederate, abettor.
(ANT.) rival, enemy, adversary.

associate *(SYN.)* affiliate, ally, join, connect, unite, combine, link, mingle, partner, mix.
(ANT.) separate, disconnect, divide, disrupt, estrange.

association *(SYN.)* organization, club, union, society, fraternity, sorority, companionship, fellowship.

assorted *(SYN.)* varied, miscellaneous, classified, different, several, grouped.
(ANT.) alike, same.

assortment *(SYN.)* collection, variety, mixture, conglomeration.

assume (SYN.) arrogate, affect, suspect, believe, appropriate, take, pretend.
(ANT.) doff, demonstrate, prove, grant, concede.

assumption (SYN.) presumption, guess, theory, supposition, conjecture.

assurance (SYN.) confidence, conviction, self-reliance, surety, firmness, courage, promise, pledge, certainty, assertion.
(ANT.) humility, shyness, suspicion, modesty.

assure (SYN.) promise, convince, warrant, guarantee, pledge.
(ANT.) equivocate, deny.

astonish (SYN.) astound, amaze, surprise, shock.
(ANT.) tire, bore.

astound (SYN.) shock, amaze, astonish, stun, surprise, floor.

asylum (SYN.) shelter, refuge, home, madhouse, institution.

athletic (SYN.) strong, active, able-bodied, gymnastic, muscular.

atone (SYN.) repay, make up.

attach (SYN.) connect, adjoin, annex, join, append, stick, unite, adjoin, affix.
(ANT.) unfasten, untie, detach, separate, disengage.

attachment (SYN.) friendship, liking, regard, adherence, affection, devotion.
(ANT.) estrangement, opposition, alienation, aversion.

attack (SYN.) raid, assault, besiege, abuse, censure, offense, seige, invade.
(ANT.) surrender, defense, opposition, aid, defend, protect, repel.

attain (SYN.) achieve, acquire, accomplish, gain, get, reach, win.
(ANT.) relinquish, discard, abandon, desert.

attempt (SYN.) essay, experiment, trial, try, undertaking, endeavor, effort.
(ANT.) laziness, neglect, inaction.

attend (SYN.) accompany, escort, watch, be serve, care for, follow, lackey.
(ANT.) desert, abandon, avoid.

attendant (SYN.) waiter, servant, valet.

attention (SYN.) consideration, heed, circumspection, notice, watchfulness.
(ANT.) negligence, omission, oversight.

attentive (SYN.) careful, awake, alive, considerate, heedful, mindful, wary.
(ANT.) indifferent, unaware, oblivious.

attest (SYN.) testify, swear, certify.

attire (SYN.) apparel, dress, clothe.

attitude (SYN.) standpoint, viewpoint, stand, pose, aspect, position, posture.

attorney (SYN.) lawyer.

attract (SYN.) enchant, interest, pull, fascinate, draw, tempt, infatuate.
(ANT.) deter, repel, repulse, alienate.

attractive (SYN.) enchanting, winning, engaging, pleasant, pleasing, seductive.
(ANT.) unattractive, obnoxious, repellent, repulsive, forbidding.

attribute (SYN.) give, apply, place, trait, characteristic, feature, nature, credit.

audible (SYN.) distinct, bearable, plain, clear.
(ANT.) inaudible.

augment (SYN.) enlarge, increase, raise, expand, broaden, extend.

auspicious (SYN.) lucky, timely, favorable, promising, fortunate.
(ANT.) untimely, unfortunate.

authentic (SYN.) real, true, genuine, pure, accurate, reliable, legitimate.
(ANT.) false, spurious, artificial.

authenticate (SYN.) validate, warrant, guarantee, verify, certify.

author (SYN.) father, inventor, maker, originator, writer, composer.

authority (SYN.) dominion, justification, power, permission, authorization.
(ANT.) incapacity, denial, prohibition.

authorize (SYN.) permit, sanction, legalize, assign, enable, approve, empower.
(ANT.) forbid, prohibit.

autocrat (SYN.) monarch, ruler, tyrant.

autograph (SYN.) endorse, sign, approve.

automatic (SYN.) self-acting, mechanical, involuntary, self-working.
(ANT.) hand-operated, intentional, deliberate, manual.

automobile (SYN.) auto, car.

auxiliary (SYN.) assisting, helping, aiding.

avail (SYN.) help, profit, use, value, benefit, serve, advantage.

available (SYN.) obtainable, convenient, ready, handy, accessible, prepared.
(ANT.) unavailable, out of reach, inaccessible, unobtainable.

average (SYN. moderate, ordinary, usual, passable, fair, intermediate.
(ANT.) outstanding, exceptional, extraordinary, unusual.

averse (SYN.) unwilling, opposed, forced, against, involuntary.
(ANT.) willing.

aversion (SYN.) disgust, dislike, distaste, loathing, abhorrence, antipathy.
(ANT.) devotion, enthusiasm, affection, love.

avert (SYN.) avoid, prevent, prohibit.
(ANT.) invite.

avid (SYN.) greedy, eager.

avocation (SYN.) sideline, hobby, minor occupation.

avoid (SYN.) elude, forestall, evade, escape, avert, eschew, free, shun.
(ANT.) oppose, meet, confront, encounter, seek.

award (SYN.) reward, prize, medal, gift.

aware (SYN.) mindful, perceptive, informed, apprised, realizing.
(ANT.) unaware, insensible, ignorant.

away (SYN.) absent, departed, distracted, gone, not at home.
(ANT.) present, attentive, attending.

awe (SYN.) surprise, respect, dread, astonishment, alarm, fear and wonder.

awful (SYN.) frightful, horrible, awe-inspiring, dire, terrible, unpleasant, imposing, solemn, appalling, cruel.
(ANT.) humble, lowly, pleasant, nice, commonplace.

awkward (SYN.) unpolished, clumsy, ungraceful, ungainly, cumbersome.
(ANT.) adroit, graceful, skillful.

awry (SYN.) askew, wrong, twisted, crooked, disorderly.
(ANT.) straight, right.

axiom (SYN.) fundamental, maxim, principle, theorem, adage, apothegm.

babble *(SYN.)* twaddle, nonsense, gibberish, prattle, balderdash, rubbish, chatter, baby talk, poppycock, jabber, maunder, piffle.

baby *(SYN.)* newborn, infant, neonate, babe, teeny, small, wee, little, undersized, midget, papoose, protect, cosset, pamper.

babyish *(SYN.)* infantile, childish, baby, whiny, unreasonable, immature, puerile, foolish, dependent.
(ANT.) mature, adult, sensible, reasonable, grownup.

back *(SYN.)* help, assist, endorse, support, second, ratify, approve, stand by, approve, posterior, rear.
(ANT.) anterior, front, face, undercut, veto, undermine, progress, flow, leading, close, accessible, near.

backbiting *(SYN.)* gossip, slander, abuse, malice, cattiness, aspersion, derogation, belittling, badmouthing.
(ANT.) compliments, praise, loyalty, friendliness, approval.

backbone *(SYN.)* vertebrae, spine, pillar, support, staff, mainstay, basis, courage, determination, toughness, character.
(ANT.) timidity, weakness, cowardice, spinelessness.

backbreaking *(SYN.)* exhausting, fatiguing, tough, tiring, demanding, wearying, wearing, difficult.
(ANT.) light, relaxing, undemanding, slight.

back down *(SYN.)* accede, concede, acquiesce, yield, withdraw, renege.
(ANT.) persevere, insist.

backer *(SYN.)* underwriter, benefactor, investor, patron, sponsor, supporter.

backfire *(SYN.)* flop, boomerang, fail, founder, disappoint.
(ANT.) succeed.

background *(SYN.)* training, training, practice, knowledge, experience.

backing *(SYN.)* help, support, funds, money, assistance, grant, advocacy, subsidy, sympathy, endorsement.
(ANT.) criticism, detraction, faultfinding.

backlog *(SYN.)* inventory, reserve, hoard, amassment, accumulation.

backslide *(SYN.)* relapse, revert, return, weaken, regress, renege.

backward *(SYN.)* dull, sluggish, stupid, loath, regressive, rearward, underdeveloped, slow, retarded.
(ANT.) progressive, precocious, civilized, advanced, forward.

bad *(SYN.)* unfavorable, wrong, evil, immoral, sinful, faulty, improper, unwholesome, wicked, corrupt, tainted, harmful, injurious, defective, poor, imperfect, inferior, substandard, contaminated, inappropriate, unsuited, rotten, unsuitable, sorry, upset, sick, suffering, unpleasant, disagreeable.
(ANT.) good, honorable, reputable, moral, excellent.

badger *(SYN.)* tease, question, annoy, pester, bother, taunt, bait, provoke, torment, harass, hector.

baffle *(SYN.)* confound bewilder, perplex, puzzle, mystify, confuse, frustrate, bewilder.
(ANT.) inform, enlighten.

bag *(SYN.)* catch, snare, poke, sack.

bait *(SYN.)* enticement, captivate, ensnare, tease, torment, pester, worry, entrap, question, entice, lure, trap, harass, tempt, badger.

balance *(SYN.)* poise, stability, composure, remains, residue, equilibrium, compare, weigh, equalize.
(ANT.) unsteadiness, instability.

bald *(SYN.)* bare, hairless, nude, open, uncovered, simple.
(ANT.) covered, hairy.

baleful *(SYN.)* evil immoral sinful, destructive, detrimental, noxious, wicked, bad, villainous, injurious.
(ANT.) good, moral, reputable, excellent, harmless.

balk *(SYN.)* unwilling, obstinate, stubborn, hesitate, check, stop.
(ANT.) willing.

ball *(SYN.)* cotillion, dance, globe, sphere, spheroid.

ballad *(SYN.)* poem, song, ditty.

balloon *(SYN.)* puff up, enlarge, swell.
(ANT.) shrivel, shrink.

ballot *(SYN.)* choice, vote, poll.

balmy *(SYN.)* soft, gentle, soothing, fragrant, mild.
(ANT.) tempestuous, stormy.

ban *(SYN.)* prohibit, outlaw, disallow, block, bar, exclude, obstruct, prohibition, taboo, forbid.
(ANT.) allow, permit.

banal *(SYN.)* hackneyed, corny, vapid, trite, overused, humdrum.
(ANT.) striking, original, fresh, stimulating, novel.

band *(SYN.)* company, association, crew, group, society, belt, strip, unite, gang.

bandit *(SYN.)* thief, robber, highwayman, outlaw, marauder.

bang *(SYN.)* hit, strike, slam.

banish *(SYN.)* drive away, eject, exile, oust, deport, dismiss, expel.
(ANT.) receive, accept, shelter, admit, harbor, embrace, welcome.

bank *(SYN.)* barrier, slope, storage, treasury, row, series, string, shore.

banner *(SYN.)* colors, standard, pennant, flag.

banquet *(SYN.)* feast, celebration, festival, dinner, affair.

banter *(SYN.)* joke, tease, jest.

bar *(SYN.)* counter, impediment, saloon, exclude, obstacle, barricade, obstruct, shut out, hindrance, forbid, block, barrier, obstruction.
(ANT.) allow, permit, aid, encouragement.

barbarian *(SYN.)* brute, savage, boor, ruffian, rude, uncivilized, primitive, uncultured, coarse, cruel, barbaric, crude.
(ANT.) permit, allow, encouragement.

barbarous *(SYN.)* savage, remorseless, cruel, uncivilized, rude, unrelenting, merciless, crude, ruthless, inhuman.
(ANT.) kind, civilized, polite, humane, refined, tasteful, cultivated.

barber *(SYN.)* coiffeur, hairdresser.
bare *(SYN.)* naked, nude, uncovered, undressed, unclothed, unfurnished, plain, barren, empty, disclose, reveal, publicize, bald, expose, scarce, mere.
(ANT.) dressed, garbed, conceal, covered, hide, disguise, clothed.
barefaced *(SYN.)* impudent, bold, insolent, brazen, shameless, audacious, impertinent, rude.
barely *(SYN.)* hardly, scarcely, just.
bargain *(SYN.)* agreement, arrangement, deal, contract, arrange, sale.
baroque *(SYN.)* ornamented, elaborate, embellished, ornate.
barren *(SYN.)* unproductive, bare, unfruitful, infertile, sterile, childless.
(ANT.) productive, fruitful, fertile.
barricade *(SYN.)* fence, obstruction, shut in, fortification, barrier.
(ANT.) free, open, release.
barrier *(SYN.)* fence, wall, bar, railing, obstacle, hindrance, fortification, restraint, impediment, limit, barricade.
(ANT.) assistance, aid, encouragement.
barter *(SYN.)* exchange, deal, trade.
base *(SYN.)* bottom, rest, foundation, establish, found, immoral, evil, bad, wicked, depraved, selfish, worthless, cheap, debased, poor, support, stand, low, abject, menial.
(ANT.) exalted, righteous, lofty, esteemed, noble, honored, refined, valuable.
bashful *(SYN.)* timorous, abashed, shy, coy, timid, diffident, modest, sheepish, embarrassed, humble, recoiling, uneasy, awkward, ashamed.
(ANT.) fearless, outgoing, adventurous, gregarious, aggressive, daring.
basic *(SYN.)* underlying, chief, essential, main, fundamental.
(ANT.) subsidiary, subordinate.
basis *(SYN.)* presumption, support, base, principle, groundwork, presupposition, foundation, postulate, ground, assumption, premise, essential.
(ANT.) implication, trimming, derivative, superstructure.
basket *(SYN.)* hamper, creel, dossier, bassinet.
bastion *(SYN.)* mainstay, support, staff, tower, stronghold.
bat *(SYN.)* strike, hit, clout, stick, club, knock, crack.
batch *(SYN.)* group, set, collection, lot, cluster, bunch, mass, combination.
bath *(SYN.)* washing, shower, tub, wash, dip, soaping.
bathe *(SYN.)* launder, drench, swim, cover, medicate, immerse, wet, dip, soak, suffuse, rinse, saturate.
bathing suit *(SYN.)* maillot, swimsuit, trunks.
bathos *(SYN.)* mawkishness, soppiness, slush, sentimentality.
bathroom *(SYN.)* powder room, toilet, bath, lavatory.
baton *(SYN.)* mace, rod, staff, billy, crook, stick, fasces.
battalion *(SYN.)* mass, army, swarm, mob, drove, horde, gang, legion, regiment.

batten *(SYN.)* thrive, flourish, fatten, wax, expand, bloom, boom, grow.
(ANT.) decrease, weaken, fail.
batter *(SYN.)* pound, beat, hit, pommel, wallop, bash, smash, mixture, strike.
battery *(SYN.)* series, troop, force, rally, muster, set.
battle *(SYN.)* strife, fray, combat, struggle, contest, skirmish, conflict, fight, war, flight, warfare, action, campaign, strive against.
(ANT.) truce, concord, agreement, settlement, harmony, accept, concur, peace.
battlement *(SYN.)* parapet, rampart, fort, bastion, stronghold, escarpment.
bauble *(SYN.)* plaything, toy, trinket.
bawd *(SYN.)* procuress, prostitute.
bawdy *(SYN.)* vulgar, smutty, filthy, dirty, obscene, pornographic.
bawl *(SYN.)* sob, shout, wail, cry loudly, bellow, weep, cry.
bawl out *(SYN.)* scold, upbraid, censure, berate, reprove, reprimand.
bay *(SYN.)* inlet, bayou, harbor, lagoon, cove, sound, gulf.
bazaar *(SYN.)* fair, market, marketplace.
beach *(SYN.)* sands, seashore, waterfront, seaside, strand, coast, shore.
beacon *(SYN.)* light, signal, watchtower, guide, flare, warning, alarm.
bead *(SYN.)* globule, drop, pill, blob.
beak *(SYN.)* nose, bill, proboscis.
beam *(SYN.)* gleam, ray, girder, crossmember, pencil, shine, glisten, smile, glitter, gleam.
beaming *(SYN.)* joyful, bright, happy, radiant, grinning.
(ANT.) sullen, gloomy, threatening, scowling.
bear *(SYN.)* carry, support, take, uphold, suffer, convey, allow, stand, yield, endure, tolerate, produce, sustain, brook, transport, undergo, permit, suffer, abide, tolerate.
(ANT.) evade, shun, avoid, refuse, dodge.
bearable *(SYN.)* sufferable, supportable, manageable, tolerable.
(ANT.) terrible, painful, unbearable, awful, intolerable.
bearing *(SYN.)* course, direction, position, posture, behavior, manner, carriage, relation, reference, connection, application, deportment, air, way, conduct.
bearings *(SYN.)* orientation, whereabouts, location, direction, position, reading, course.
bear on *(SYN.)* affect, relate to.
bear out *(SYN.)* confirm, substantiate, justify, verify, prove.
bear up *(SYN.)* carry on, endure.
bear with *(SYN.)* tolerate, forbear.
beast *(SYN.)* monster, savage, brute, creature, animal.
beastly *(SYN.)* detestable, mean, low, hateful, loathsome, nasty, unpleasant, despicable, obnoxious, brutal, brutish, offensive.

(ANT.) *considerate, sympathetic, refined, humane, fine, pleasant.*

beat *(SYN.)* pulse, buffet, pound, defeat, palpitate, hit, thump, belabor, knock, overthrow, thrash, pummel, rout, smite, throb, punch, subdue, pulsate, dash, strike, overpower, vanquish, conquer, batter, conquer, overcome, blow.

(ANT.) *stroke, fail, defend, surrender, shield.*

beaten *(SYN.)* disheartened, dejected, licked, discouraged, hopeless, downcast, down, depressed.

(ANT.) eager, hopeful, cheerful.

beatific *(SYN.)* uplifted, blissful, elated, happy, wonderful, joyful, divine.

(ANT.) *awful, hellish, ill-fated, accursed.*

beating *(SYN.)* whipping, drubbing, flogging, lashing, scourging, walloping.

beau *(SYN.)* lover, suitor, swain, admirer.

beautiful *(SYN.)* pretty, fair, lovely, charming, comely, handsome, elegant, attractive.

(ANT.) *repulsive, hideous, unsightly, foul, homely, plainness, unattractive, ugly, ugliness.*

beauty *(SYN.)* handsomeness, fairness, charm, pulchritude, attractiveness, loveliness, comeliness, grace, allegiance.

(ANT.) ugliness, disfigurement, homeliness, plainness, deformity, eyesore.

becalm *(SYN.)* calm, quiet, smooth, still, hush, repose, settle.

because *(SYN.)* inasmuch as, as, since, for.

because of *(SYN.)* as a result of, as a consequence of.

beckon *(SYN.)* call, signal, summon, motion, gesture, wave.

becloud *(SYN.)* obfuscate, confuse, befog, confound, obscure, muddle.

(ANT.) illuminate, clarify, solve.

become *(SYN.)* change, grow, suit, be appropriate, befit.

becoming *(SYN.)* suitable, meet, befitting, appropriate, fitting, seemly, enhancing, attractive, pleasing, flattering, tasteful, smart, adorning, ornamental.

(ANT.) unsuitable, inappropriate, incongruent, ugly, unattractive, improper.

bed *(SYN.)* layer, cot, vein, berth, stratum, couch, accumulation, bunk, deposit, cradle.

bedazzle *(SYN.)* glare, blind, dumbfound, flabbergast, bewilder, furbish, festoon.

bedeck *(SYN.)* deck, adorn, beautify, smarten, festoon, garnish.

bedevil *(SYN.)* worry, fret, irk, torment, harass, pester, nettle, tease, vex, plague.

(ANT.) soothe, calm, delight, please.

bedlam *(SYN.)* tumult, uproar, madhouse, commotion, confusion, racket, rumpus, pandemonium.

(ANT.) calm, peace.

bedraggled *(SYN.)* shabby, muddy, sodden, messy, sloppy.

(ANT.) dry, neat, clean, well-groomed.

bedrock *(SYN.)* basis, foundation, roots, basics, essentials, fundamentals, bottom, bed, substratum, core.

(ANT.) top, dome, apex, nonessentials.

bedroom *(SYN.)* chamber, bedchamber.

beef *(SYN.)* brawn, strength, heft, gripe, sinew, fitness, huskiness, might.

beef up *(SYN.)* reinforce, vitalize, nerve, buttress, strengthen.

(ANT.) sap, weaken, enervate, drain.

beefy *(SYN.)* solid, strong, muscular, heavy, stocky.

befall *(SYN.)* occur, come about, happen.

before *(SYN.)* prior, earlier, in advance, formerly.

(ANT.) *behind, following, afterward, latterly, after.*

befriend *(SYN.)* welcome, encourage, aid, stand by.

(ANT.) dislike, shun, desert, avoid.

befuddle *(SYN.)* stupefy, addle, confuse, rattle, disorient.

beg *(SYN.)* solicit, ask, implore, supplicate, entreat, adjure, petition, beseech, request, importune, entreat, implore.

(ANT.) grant, cede, give, bestow, favor.

beget *(SYN.)* sire, engender, produce, create, propagate, originate, breed, generate, procreate, father.

(ANT.) *murder, destroy, kill, abort, prevent, extinguish.*

beggar *(SYN.)* scrub, tatterdemalion, pauper, wretch, ragamuffin, vagabond, starveling.

begin *(SYN.)* open, enter, arise, initiate, commence, start, inaugurate, originate, institute, create.

(ANT.) *terminate, complete, finish, close, end, stop.*

beginner *(SYN.)* nonprofessional, amateur, apprentice.

(ANT.) veteran, professional.

beginning *(SYN.)* outset, inception, origin, source, commencement, start, opening, initiation, inauguration.

(ANT.) *termination, completion, end, close, consummation, closing, ending, finish.*

begrime *(SYN.)* soil, dirty, smear, muddy, splotch, tarnish.

(ANT.) wash, clean, freshen, launder.

begrudge *(SYN.)* resent, envy, stint, withhold, grudge.

begrudging *(SYN.)* hesitant, reluctant, resentful, unwilling, forced.

(ANT.) *willing, eager, quick, spontaneous.*

beguiling *(SYN.)* enchanting, interesting, delightful, intriguing, engaging, bewitching, attractive, enthralling, captivating.

(ANT.) *boring, dull, unattractive, tedious.*

behalf *(SYN.)* benefit, welfare, support, aid, part, interest.

behave *(SYN.)* deport, comport, manage, act, demean, bear, interact, carry, operate, conduct.

(ANT.) rebel, misbehave.

behavior *(SYN.)* manners, carriage, disposition, action, deed, bearing,

deportment, conduct, demeanor.
(ANT.) rebelliousness, misbehavior.
behead *(SYN.)* decapitate, guillotine, decollate.
behest *(SYN.)* order, command, decree, mandate, bidding.
behind *(SYN.)* after, backward, at the back, in back of.
(ANT.) frontward, ahead, before.
behold *(SYN.)* look, see, view, notice, observe, perceive, sight.
(ANT.) overlook, ignore.
being *(SYN.)* life, existing, existence, living, actuality, organism, individual.
(ANT.) death, nonexistence, expiration.
belabor *(SYN.)* repeat, reiterate, pound, explain, expatiate, din.
belated *(SYN.)* late, delayed, overdue, tardy.
(ANT.) well-timed, early.
belch *(SYN.)* emit, erupt, gush, disgorge, bubble, eructation, burp.
beleaguered *(SYN.)* bothered, beset, annoyed, beset, harassed, badgered, vexed, plagued, victimized.
belie *(SYN.)* distort, misrepresent, twist, disappoint.
belief *(SYN.)* trust, feeling, certitude, opinion, conviction, persuasion, credence, confidence, reliance, faith, view, creed, assurance.
(ANT.) heresy, denial, incredulity, distrust, skepticism, doubt.
believe *(SYN.)* hold, apprehend, fancy, support, accept, conceive, suppose, imagine, trust, credit.
(ANT.) doubt, reject, distrust, disbelieve, question.
believer *(SYN.)* adherent, follower, devotee, convert, zealot.
(ANT.) doubter, critic, scoffer, skeptic.
belittle *(SYN.)* underrate, depreciate, minimize, decry, disparage, diminish, demean, slight, discredit, militant, depreciate, humiliate.
(ANT.) esteem, admire, flatter, overrate, commend.
bell *(SYN.)* pealing, ringing, signal, tolling, buzzer, chime.
belligerent *(SYN.)* aggressive, warlike, hostile, offensive, combative, militant.
(ANT.) easygoing, compromising, peaceful.
bellow *(SYN.)* thunder, roar, scream, shout, yell, howl.
bellwether *(SYN.)* leader, pilot, guide, ringleader, boss, shepherd.
belly *(SYN.)* stomach, abdomen, paunch.
belonging *(SYN.)* loyalty, relationship, kinship, acceptance, rapport.
belongings *(SYN.)* property, effects, possessions.
beloved *(SYN.)* adored, sweet, loved, cherished, prized, esteemed, valued, darling.
below *(SYN.)* under, less, beneath, underneath, lower.
(ANT.) aloft, overhead, above, over.
belt *(SYN.)* girdle, sash, strap, cummerbund, band, waistband, whack, hit, wallop, punch.
bemoan *(SYN.)* mourn, lament, grieve,

sorrow, regret, deplore.
bend *(SYN.)* turn, curve, incline, submit, bow, lean, crook, twist, yield, stoop, crouch, agree, suppress, oppress, mold, kneel, deflect, subdue, influence.
(ANT.) resist, straighten, break, stiffen.
beneath *(SYN.)* under, below.
(ANT.) above, over.
benediction *(SYN.)* thanks, blessing, prayer.
beneficial *(SYN.)* salutary, good, wholesome, advantageous, useful, helpful, serviceable, profitable.
(ANT.) harmful, destructive, injurious, disadvantageous, unwholesome, deleterious, detrimental.
benefit *(SYN.)* support, help, gain, avail, profit, account, favor, aid, good, advantage, serve, interest, behalf, service.
(ANT.) handicap, calamity, trouble, disadvantage, distress.
benevolence *(SYN.)* magnanimity, charity, tenderness, altruism, humanity, philanthropy, generosity, liberality, beneficence, good will.
(ANT.) malevolence, unkindness, cruelty, selfishness, inhumanity.
benevolent *(SYN.)* kindhearted, tender, merciful, generous, altruistic, obliging, kind, good, well-wishing, philanthropy, liberal, unselfish, kindly, disposed, openhearted, humane, benign, friendly.
(ANT.) malevolent, greedy, wicked, harsh.
bent *(SYN.)* curved, crooked, resolved, determined, set, inclined, firm, decided.
(ANT.) straight.
berate *(SYN.)* scold.
beseech *(SYN.)* appeal, entreat, plead, ask, beg, implore.
beset *(SYN.)* surround, attack.
besides *(SYN.)* moreover, further, except for, also, as well, furthermore.
besiege *(SYN.)* assault, attack, siege, bombard, raid, charge.
bespeak *(SYN.)* engage, reserve, indicate, show, signify, express.
best *(SYN.)* choice, prime, select.
(ANT.) worst.
bestial *(SYN.)* brutal, beastly, savage, cruel.
bestow *(SYN.)* confer, place, put, award, give, present.
(ANT.) withdraw, withhold.
bet *(SYN.)* gamble, give, stake, wager, pledge, ante.
betray *(SYN.)* reveal, deliver, expose, mislead, trick, deceive, exhibit, show.
(ANT.) shelter, protect, safeguard.
betrothal *(SYN.)* marriage, engagement, contract.
better *(SYN.)* superior, preferable, improve.
(ANT.) worsen.
between *(SYN.)* among, betwixt.
beware *(SYN.)* take care, watch out, look sharp, be careful.
bewilder *(SYN.)* perplex, confuse, mystify, baffle, puzzle, overwhelm.
(ANT.) clarify, enlighten.

bewitch *(SYN.)* captivate, charm, delight, enchant.

beyond *(SYN.)* past, farther, exceeding.

bias *(SYN.)* slant, inclination, proneness, turn, bent, penchant, tendency, disposition, propensity, partiality, predisposition, leaning, proclivity, prejudice, influence, warp, slanting, predilection.
(ANT.) fairness, justice, evenhandedness, equity, detachment, impartiality.

bible *(SYN.)* guide, handbook, gospel, manual, sourcebook, guidebook.

bibulous *(SYN.)* guzzling, intemperate, sottish, alcoholic.
(ANT.) sober, moderate.

bicker *(SYN.)* dispute, argue, wrangle, quarrel.
(ANT.) go along with, agree.

bid *(SYN.)* order, command, direct, wish, greet, say, offer, instruct, invite, purpose, tender, proposal.

bidding *(SYN.)* behest, request, decree, call, charge, beck, summons, solicitation, invitation, instruction, mandate.

bide *(SYN.)* stay, tarry, delay, wait, remain.

big *(SYN.)* large, huge, bulky, immense, colossal, majestic, august, monstrous, hulking, gigantic, massive, great, enormous, tremendous, outgoing, important, kind, bighearted, considerable, generous, grand.
(ANT.) small, little, tiny, immature, petite.

big-hearted *(SYN.)* good-natured, liberal, generous, unselfish, openhanded, unstinting, charitable, magnanimous.
(ANT.) cold, selfish, mean, uncharitable.

bigoted *(SYN.)* intolerant, partial, prejudiced, biased, unfair, chauvinist.

bigotry *(SYN.)* bias, blindness, intolerance, unfairness, prejudice, ignorance, passion, sectarianism.
(ANT.) acceptance, open-mindedness.

big-shot *(SYN.)* somebody, brass hat, big gun.
(ANT.) underling, nobody, nebbish, cipher.

bijou *(SYN.)* gem, bauble, jewel, ornament.

bile *(SYN.)* spleen, rancor, anger, bitterness, peevishness, ill-humor, nastiness, resentment, discontent, irascibility.
(ANT.) cheerfulness, affability, pleasantness.

bilge *(SYN.)* hogwash, drivel, gibberish, rubbish, bosh, foolishness, twaddle.

bilious *(SYN.)* petulant, crabby, ill-natured, cross, peevish, crotchety, cranky.
(ANT.) happy, agreeable, pleasant, good-natured.

bilk *(SYN.)* defraud, trick, cheat, hoodwink, deceive, fleece, rook, bamboozle.

bill *(SYN.)* charge, invoice, account, statement.

billet *(SYN.)* housing, quarters, berth, shelter, barrack, installation.

billingsgate *(SYN.)* swearing, scurrility, cursing, abuse, vulgarity, gutter, profanity.

billow *(SYN.)* surge, swell, rise, rush, peaking, magnification, amplification, augmentation, increase, intensification.
(ANT.) lowering, decrease.

bin *(SYN.)* cubbyhole, box, container, chest, cubicle, crib, receptacle, can.

bind *(SYN.)* connect, restrain, band, fasten, oblige, obligate, engage, wrap, connect, weld, attach, tie, require, restrict.
(ANT.) unlace, loose, unfasten, untie, free.

binding *(SYN.)* compulsory, obligatory, mandatory, compelling, unalterable, imperative, indissoluble, unconditional, unchangeable.
(ANT.) adjustable, flexible, elastic, changeable.

binge *(SYN.)* fling, spree, carousal, toot.

birth *(SYN.)* origin, beginning, infancy, inception.
(ANT.) finish, decline, death, disappearance, end.

biscuit *(SYN.)* bun, roll, cake, muffin, bread, rusk.

bit *(SYN.)* fraction, portion, scrap, fragment, particle, drop, speck, harness, small amount, restraint, morsel, sum.

bite *(SYN.)* gnaw, chew, nip, sting, pierce, mouthful, snack, morsel.

biting *(SYN.)* cutting, sharp, acid, sneering, sarcastic.
(ANT.) soothing, kind, gentle, agreeable.

bitter *(SYN.)* distasteful, sour, acrid, pungent, piercing, vicious, severe, biting, distressful, stinging, distressing, ruthless, hated, hostile, grievous, harsh, painful, tart.
(ANT.) sweet, mellow, pleasant, delicious.

bizarre *(SYN.)* peculiar, strange, odd, uncommon, queer, unusual.
(ANT.) usual, everyday, ordinary, inconspicuous.

black *(SYN.)* sooty, dark, ebony, inky, swarthy, soiled, filthy, dirty, stained, somber, depressing, sad, dismal, gloomy.
(ANT.) white, clean, pristine, glowing, pure, cheerful, sunny, bright.

blackball *(SYN.)* turn down, ban, blacklist, exclude, snub, reject, debar.
(ANT.) accept, include, invite, ask, bid.

blacken *(SYN.)* tar, ink, black, darken, besoot, smudge, begrime, discredit, defile, dull, dim, tarnish, ebonize, denounce, sully, libel, blemish, defame.
(ANT.) exalt, honor, whiten, brighten, shine, bleach.

blackmail *(SYN.)* bribe, payment, bribery, extortion, shakedown, coercion.

blackout *(SYN.)* faint, coma, unconsciousness, oblivion, amnesia, stupor, swoon.

bladder *(SYN.)* saccule, sac, vesicle, pouch, pod, cell, blister, container, cyst.

blade *(SYN.)* cutter, lancet, knife, sword.

blah *(SYN.)* lifeless, flat, jejune, lukewarm, stale, insipid, tasteless, pedestrian, tedious, dreary, uninteresting.
(ANT.) spirited, fascinating, vibrant, vigorous.

blame *(SYN.)* upbraid, criticize, fault, guilt, accuse, rebuke, charge, implicate, impeach, tattle, condemn, indict, responsibility, censure, denounce, reproach.
(ANT.) exonerate, credit, honor, absolve.

blameless *(SYN.)* moral, innocent, worthy, faultless.
(ANT.) blameworthy, culpable, guilty.

blanch *(SYN.)* whiten, bleach, decolorize, peroxide, fade, wash out, dim, dull.

bland *(SYN.)* soft, smooth, gentle, agreeable, vapid, insipid, mild, polite.
(ANT.) harsh, outspoken, disagreeable.

blandish *(SYN.)* praise, compliment, overpraise, cajole, puff, adulate, salve, fawn, court, toady, butter up, please, jolly.
(ANT.) insult, deride, criticize, belittle.

blandisher *(SYN.)* adulator, booster, sycophant, eulogist, apple polisher, flunkey.
(ANT.) knocker, faultfinder, belittler.

blandishment *(SYN.)* applause, cajolery, honey, adulation, plaudits, acclaim, fawning, compliments.
(ANT.) carping, belittling, criticism, deprecation.

blank *(SYN.)* unmarked, expressionless, uninterested, form, area, void, vacant, empty.
(ANT.) marked, filled, alert, animated.

blanket *(SYN.)* quilt, coverlet, cover, comforter, robe, padding, carpet, wrapper, mantle, envelope, housing, coat, comprehensive, universal, across-the-board, panoramic, omnibus.
(ANT.) limited, detailed, restricted, precise.

blare *(SYN.)* roar, blast, resound, jar, scream, swell, clang, peal, trumpet, toot, hoot.

blasphemous *(SYN.)* profane, irreverent, impious, godless, ungodly, sacrilegious, irreligious.
(ANT.) reverent, reverential, religious, pious.

blasphemy *(SYN.)* profanation, impiousness, cursing, irreverence, sacrilege, abuse, ecration, swearing, contempt.
(ANT.) respect, piety, reverence, devotion.

blast *(SYN.)* burst, explosion, discharge, blowout.

blasted *(SYN.)* blighted, withered, ravaged, decomposed, spoiled, destroyed.

blastoff *(SYN.)* launching, expulsion, launch, shot, projection.

blatant *(SYN.)* shameless, notorious, brazen, flagrant, glaring, bold, obvious.
(ANT.) deft, subtle, insidious, devious.

blaze *(SYN.)* inferno, shine, flare, marking, fire, outburst, holocaust, notch, flame.
(ANT.) die, dwindle.

bleach *(SYN.)* pale, whiten, blanch, whitener.
(ANT.) darken, blacken.

bleak *(SYN.)* dreary, barren, cheerless, depressing, gloomy, windswept, bare, cold, dismal, desolate, raw, chilly.
(ANT.) lush, hopeful, promising, cheerful.

bleary *(SYN.)* hazy, groggy, blurry, fuzzy, misty, clouded, overcast, dim, blear.
(ANT.) clear, vivid, precise, clear-cut.

bleed *(syn.)* pity, lose blood, grieve, sorrow.

blemish *(SYN.)* injury, speck, flaw, scar, disgrace, imperfection, stain, fault, blot.
(ANT.) purity, embellishment, adornment, perfection.

blend *(SYN.)* beat, intermingle, combine, fuse, unify, consolidate, unite, amalgamate, conjoin, mix, coalesce, intermix, join, merge, compound, combination, stir, mixture, commingle, mingle.
(ANT.) separate, decompose, analyze, disintegrate.

bless *(SYN.)* thank, celebrate, extol, glorify, adore, delight, praise, gladden, exalt.
(ANT.) denounce, blaspheme, slander, curse.

blessed *(SYN.)* sacred, holy, consecrated, dedicated, hallowed, sacrosanct, beatified, joyful, delighted, joyous, sainted, canonized, blissful.
(ANT.) miserable, sad, dispirited, cheerless.

blessing *(SYN.)* benison, sanction, favor, grace, benediction, invocation, approbation, approval, compliment, bounty, windfall, gift, benefit, advantage, kindness, felicitation, invocation.
(ANT.) disapproval, execration, curse, denunciation, malediction, rebuke, displeasure, condemnation, adversity, misfortune, mishap, calamity.

blight *(SYN.)* decay, disease, spoil, sickness, wither, ruin, damage, harm, decaying, epidemic, affliction, destroy.

blind *(SYN.)* sightless, unmindful, rash, visionless, ignorant, unsighted, unconscious, discerning, heedless, oblivious, purblind, unknowing, screen, unaware, thoughtless, shade, unthinking, cover, curtain, without thought, headlong.
(ANT.) discerning, sensible, calculated, perceiving, perceptive, aware.

blink *(SYN.)* bat, glance, flicker, wink, twinkle.

bliss *(SYN.)* ecstasy, rapture, glee, elation, joy, blessedness, gladness, happiness, delight, felicity, blissfulness.
(ANT.) woe, sadness, sorrow, grief,

unhappiness, torment, wretchedness, misery.

blissful *(SYN.)* happy, elated, rapturous, esctatic, paradisiacal, joyous, enraptured.

blister *(SYN.)* bleb, swelling, welt, sore, blob, bubble, inflammation, boil, canker.

blithe *(SYN.)* breezy, merry, airy, lighthearted, light, gay, fanciful, graceful.
(ANT.) morose, grouchy, low-spirited, gloomy.

blitz *(SYN.)* strike, onslaught, thrust, raid, lunge, drive, incursion, assault, sally.

blizzard *(SYN.)* storm, snowstorm, snowfall, gale, tempest, blast, blow, swirl.

bloat *(SYN.)* distend, puff up, inflate, swell.
(ANT.) deflate.

blob *(SYN.)* bubble, blister, pellet, globule.

block *(SYN.)* clog, hinder, bar, impede, close, obstruct, barricade, blockade, obstruction, hindrance, obstacle, impediment, retard, check, stop.
(ANT.) forward, promote, aid, clear, advance, advantage, assist, further, open.

blockade *(SYN.)* barrier, fortification, obstruction, barricade.

blockhead *(SYN.)* dunce, dolt, fool, sap, idiot, simpleton, chump, booby, bonehead, woodenhead.

blood *(SYN.)* murder, gore, slaughter, bloodshed, ancestry, lineage, heritage.

bloodcurdling *(SYN.)* hair-raising, terrifying, alarming, chilling, stunning, scary.

bloodless *(SYN.)* dead, torpid, dull, drab, cold, colorless, passionless, lackluster.
(ANT.) passionate, vital, ebullient, animated, vivacious.

bloodshed *(SYN.)* murder, killing, slaying, blood bath, massacre, carnage.

bloodthirsty *(SYN.)* murderous, cruel.

bloody *(SYN.)* cruel, pitiless, bloodthirsty, inhuman, ruthless, ferocious, murderous.
(ANT.) kind, gentle.

bloom *(SYN.)* thrive, glow, flourish, blossom, flower.
(ANT.) wane, decay, dwindle, shrivel, wither.

blooming *(SYN.)* flush, green, vigorous, thriving, vital, abloom, healthy, fresh, booming.
(ANT.) flagging, declining, whithering.

blooper *(SYN.)* muff, fluff, error, bungle, botch, blunder, fumble, howler, indiscretion.

blossom *(SYN.)* bloom, flower, flourish.
(ANT.) shrink, wither, dwindle, fade.

blot *(SYN.)* stain, inkblot, spot, inkstain, blemish, dishonor, disgrace, spatter, obliterate, soil, dry.

blot out *(SYN.)* wipe out, destroy, obliterate, abolish, annihilate, cancel, expunge, strike out, shade, darken,

shadow, overshadow, obfuscate, cloud, eclipse.

blow *(SYN.)* hit, thump, slap, cuff, box, shock, move, drive, spread, breeze, puff, whistle, inflate, enlarge.

blowout *(SYN.)* blast, explosion, burst.

blue *(SYN.)* sapphire, azure, gloomy, sad, unhappy, depressed, dejected, melancholy.
(ANT.) cheerful, optimistic, happy.

blueprint *(SYN.)* design, plan, scheme, chart, draft, prospectus, outline, proposal, conception, project, layout.

blues *(SYN.)* dumps, melancholy, depression, doldrums, moodiness, dejection, despondency, gloominess, moroseness.

bluff *(SYN.)* steep, perpendicular, vertical, abrupt, precipitous, rough, open, frank, hearty, blunt, fool, mislead, pretend, deceive, fraud, lie, fake, deceit.

blunder *(SYN.)* error, flounder, mistake, stumble.

blunt *(SYN.)* solid, abrupt, rough, dull, pointless, plain, bluff, edgeless, unceremonious, obtuse, rude, outspoken, unsharpened, rounded, worn, crude, direct, impolite, short, curt, gruff.
(ANT.) tactful, polite, subtle, polished, suave, sharp, keen, pointed, diplomatic.

blur *(SYN.)* sully, dim, obscure, stain, dull, confuse, cloud, smear, stain, smudge.
(ANT.) clear, clarify.

blush *(SYN.)* redden.

board *(SYN.)* embark, committee, wood, mount, cabinet, food, get on, lumber.

boast *(SYN.)* vaunt, flaunt, brag, glory, crow, exaggerate, bragging.
(ANT.) humble, apologize, minimize, deprecate.

body *(SYN.)* remains, bulk, mass, carcass, form, company, corpus, society, firmness, group, torso, substance, collection, cadaver, trunk, group, throng, company, crowd, band.
(ANT.) spirit, intellect, soul.

bogus *(SYN.)* counterfeit, false, pretend, fake, phony.
(ANT.) genuine.

boil *(SYN.)* seethe, bubble, pimple, fume, pimple, cook, swelling, rage, foam, simmer, stew.

boisterous *(SYN.)* rough, violent, rowdy, noisy, tumultuous.
(ANT.) serene.

bold *(SYN.)* daring, forward, pushy, striking, brave, dauntless, rude, prominent, adventurous, fearless, insolent, conspicuous, defiant, arrogant, cavalier, brazen, unafraid, intrepid, courageous, valiant, heroic, gallant, disrespectful, impudent, shameless.
(ANT.) modest, bashful, cowardly, timid, retiring, flinching, fearful, timorous, polite, courteous, deferential.

bolt *(SYN.)* break away, fastener, flee, take flight, lock.

bombard *(SYN.)* shell, open fire, bomb, rake, assail, attack.

bond *(SYN.)* fastener, rope, tie, cord, connection, attachment, link, tie, promise.
(ANT.) sever, separate, untie, disconnect.

bondage *(SYN.)* slavery, thralldom, captivity, imprisonment, servitude, confinement, vassalage, enslavement.
(ANT.) liberation, emancipation, free, independence, freedom.

bonds *(SYN.)* chains, cuffs, fetters, shackles, irons, bracelets.

bone up *(SYN.)* learn, master, study, relearn.

bonus *(SYN.)* more, extra, premium, gift, reward, bounty.

bony *(SYN.)* lean, lank, thin, lanky, rawboned, fleshless, skinny, gangling, weight.
(ANT.) plump, fleshy, stout.

book *(SYN.)* manual, textbook, work, booklet, monograph, brochure, tract, volume, pamphlet, treatise, publication, hardcover, paperback, novel, workbook, text.

bookish *(SYN.)* formal, scholarly, theoretical, academic, learned, scholastic, erudite.
(ANT.) simple, ignorant.

boom *(SYN.)* advance, grow, flourish, progress, gain, increase, roar, beam, rumble, reverberate, thunder, prosper, swell, thrive, pole, rush.
(ANT.) decline, fail, recession.

booming *(SYN.)* flourishing, blooming, thriving, vigorous, prospering, exuberant.
(ANT.) waning, dying, failing, declining.

boon *(SYN.)* gift, jolly, blessing, pleasant, godsend, windfall.

boondocks *(SYN.)* sticks, backwoods.

boor *(SYN.)* lout, clown, oaf, yokel, rustic, vulgarian, ruffian.

boorish *(SYN.)* coarse, churlish, uncivil, ill-mannered, ill-bred, uncivilized, crude, uncouth.
(ANT.) polite, cultivated, cultivated, well-mannered.

boost *(SYN.)* push, lift, help, hoist, shove.
(ANT.) depress, lower, belittle, submerge, disparage, decrease, decline, reduction, downturn.

booster *(SYN.)* supporter, fan, rooter, plugger, follower.

boot *(SYN.)* shoe, kick.

booth *(SYN.)* enclosure, cubicle, stand, compartment, box.

bootless *(SYN.)* purposeless, ineffective, profitless, useless.
(ANT.) favorable, successful, useful.

bootlicker *(SYN.)* flunky, fawner, toady, sycophant.

booty *(SYN.)* prize, plunder, loot.

booze *(SYN.)* spirits, drink, liquor, alcohol.

border *(SYN.)* fringe, rim, verge, boundary, edge, termination, brink, limit, brim, outskirts, frontier, margin.
(ANT.) interior, center, mainland, core, middle.

borderline *(SYN.)* indeterminate, halfway, obscure, inexact, indefinite,
unclear.
(ANT.) precise, absolute, definite.

border on *(SYN.)* approximate, approach, resemble, echo, parallel, connect.

bore *(SYN.)* tire, weary, hole, perforate, pierce, drill.
(ANT.) arouse, captivate, excite, interest.

boredom *(SYN.)* ennui, doldrums, weariness, dullness, tedium.
(ANT.) stimulation, motive, activity, stimulus, excitement.

boring *(SYN.)* monotonous, dull, dead, flat, tedious, wearisome, trite, prosaic, humdrum, long-winded.

born *(SYN.)* hatched, produced.

borrow *(SYN.)* copy, adopt, simulate, mirror, assume, usurp, plagiarize, take.
(ANT.) allow, advance, invent, originate, credit, lend.

bosom *(SYN.)* chest, breast, feelings, thoughts, mind, interior, marrow, heart.

boss *(SYN.)* director, employer, oversee, direct, foreman, supervisor, manager.
(ANT.) worker, employee, underling.

bossy *(SYN.)* overbearing, arrogant, domineering, lordly, tyrannical, highhanded, arbitrary, oppress.
(ANT.) flexible, easygoing, cooperative.

botch *(SYN.)* blunder, bungle, fumble, goof, muff, mishandle, mismanage.
(ANT.) perform, realize.

bother *(SYN.)* haunt, molest, trouble, annoy, upset, fleeting, transient, harass, inconvenience, momentary, disturb, passing, pester, tease, irritate, worry, vex.
(ANT.) prolonged, extended, long, protracted, lengthy, comfort, solace.

bothersome *(SYN.)* irritating, vexatious, worrisome, annoying, distressing, troublesome, disturbing.

bottle *(SYN.)* container, flask, vessel, decanter, vial, ewer, jar.

bottleneck *(SYN.)* obstacle, obstruction, barrier, block, blockage, detour.

bottom *(SYN.)* basis, fundament, base, groundwork, foot, depths, lowest part, underside, foundation, seat, buttocks, rear, behind.
(ANT.) top, peak, apex, summit, topside.

bough *(SYN.)* branch, arm, limb.

bounce *(SYN.)* recoil, ricochet, rebound.

bound *(SYN.)* spring, vault, hop, leap, start, surrounded, jump, limit, jerk, boundary, bounce, skip, tied, shackled, trussed, fettered, certain, sure, destined, compelled, required.
(ANT.) unfettered, free.

boundary *(SYN.)* bound, limit, border, margin, outline, circumference, perimeter, division, frontier, edge.

boundless *(SYN.)* limitless, endless, inexhaustible, unlimited, eternal, infinite.
(ANT.) restricted, narrow, limited.

bounteous *(SYN.)* plentiful, generous, liberal, abundant.
(ANT.) scarce.

bountiful *(SYN.)* bounteous, fertile,

plentiful, generous, abundant.
(*ANT.*) *sparing, infertile, scarce.*
bounty *(SYN.)* generosity, gift, award, bonus, reward, prize, premium.
bourgeois *(SYN.)* common, ordinary, commonplace, middle-class, conventional.
(*ANT.*) *upper-class, unconventional, loose, aristocratic.*
bout *(SYN.)* round, contest, conflict, test, struggle, match, spell, fight.
bow *(SYN.)* bend, yield, kneel, submit, stoop.
bowels *(SYN.)* entrails, intestines, innards, guts, stomach.
bowl *(SYN.)* container, dish, pot, pottery, crock, jug, vase.
bowl over *(SYN.)* fell, floor, overturn, astound, nonplus, stagger, jar.
bow out *(SYN.)* give up, withdraw, retire, resign, abandon.
box *(SYN.)* hit, fight, crate, case, container.
boxer *(SYN.)* prizefighter, fighter.
boy *(SYN.)* male, youngster, lad, kid, fellow, buddy, youth.
(*ANT.*) *girl, man.*
boycott *(SYN.)* picket, strike, ban, revolt, blackball.
boy friend *(SYN.)* date, young man, sweetheart, courtier, beau.
brace *(SYN.)* strengthen, tie, prop, support, tighten, stay, strut, bind, truss, crutch.
bracelet *(SYN.)* armband, bangle, circlet.
bracing *(SYN.)* stimulating, refreshing, restorative, fortifying, invigorating.
bracket *(SYN.)* join, couple, enclose, relate, brace, support.
brag *(SYN.)* boast, flaunt, vaunt, bluster, swagger.
(*ANT.*) *demean, debase, denigrate, degrade, depreciate, deprecate.*
braid *(SYN.)* weave, twine, wreath, plait.
brain *(SYN.)* sense, intelligence, intellect, common sense, understanding, reason.
(*ANT.*) *stupid, stupidity.*
brake *(SYN.)* decelerate, stop, curb.
(*ANT.*) *accelerate.*
branch *(SYN.)* shoot, limb, bough, tributary, offshoot, part, division, expand, department, divide, spread, subdivision.
brand *(SYN.)* make, trademark, label, kind, burn, trade name, mark, stamp, blaze.
brave *(SYN.)* bold, daring, gallant, valorous, adventurous, heroic, magnanimous, chivalrous, audacious, valiant, courageous, fearless, intrepid, unafraid.
(*ANT.*) *weak, cringing, timid, cowardly, fearful, craven.*
brawl *(SYN.)* racket, quarrel, fracas, riot, fight, melee, fray, disturbance, dispute, disagreement.
brawn *(SYN.)* strength, muscle.
(*ANT.*) *weakness.*
brazen *(SYN.)* immodest, forward, shameless, bold, brassy, impudent, insolent, rude.

(*ANT.*) *retiring, self-effacing, modest, shy.*
breach *(SYN.)* rupture, fracture, rift, break, crack, gap, opening, breaking, quarrel, violation.
(*ANT.*) *observation.*
break *(SYN.)* demolish, pound, rack, smash, burst, rupture, disobey, violate, crack, infringe, crush, squeeze, transgress, fracture, shatter, wreck, crash, atomize, disintegrate, collapse, splinter, crack, gap, breach, opening, rupture.
(*ANT.*) *restore, heal, join, renovate, mend, repair.*
breed *(SYN.)* engender, bear, propagate, father, beget, rear, conceive, train, generate, raise, procreate, nurture, create, mother, produce, originate, generate, raise, train, nurture.
(*ANT.*) *murder, abort, kill.*
breeze *(SYN.)* air, wind, zephyr, breath.
(*ANT.*) *calm.*
breezy *(SYN.)* jolly, spry, active, brisk, energetic, lively, carefree, spirited.
brevity *(SYN.)* briefness, conciseness.
(*ANT.*) *length.*
brew *(SYN.)* plot, plan, cook, ferment, prepare, scheme.
bribe *(SYN.)* buy off.
bridle *(SYN.)* control, hold, restrain, check, harness, curb, restraint, halter.
(*ANT.*) *release, free, loose.*
brief *(SYN.)* curt, short, fleeting, passing, compendious, terse, laconic, succinct, momentary, transient, temporary, concise, compact, condensed.
(*ANT.*) *long, extended, prolonged, lengthy, protracted, comprehensive, extensive, exhaustive.*
brigand *(SYN.)* bandit, robber, thief.
bright *(SYN.)* luminous, gleaming, clever, witty, brilliant, lucid, vivid, clear, smart, intelligent, lustrous, clever, shining, shiny, sparkling, shimmering, radiant, cheerful, lively, gay, happy, lighthearted, keen, promising, favorable, encouraging.
(*ANT.*) *sullen, dull, murky, dark, gloomy, dim, lusterless, boring, colorless, stupid, backward, slow.*
brilliant *(SYN.)* bright, clear, smart, intelligent, sparkling, shining, alert, vivid, splendid, radiant, glittering, talented, ingenious, gifted.
(*ANT.*) *mediocre, dull, lusterless, second-rate.*
brim *(SYN.)* border, margin, lip, rim, edge.
(*ANT.*) *middle, center.*
bring *(SYN.)* fetch, take, carry, raise, introduce, propose.
(*ANT.*) *remove, withdraw.*
brink *(SYN.)* limit, verge, rim, margin, edge.
brisk *(SYN.)* fresh, breezy, cool, lively, spry, refreshing, spirited, jolly, energetic, quick, active, animated, nimble, spry, agile, sharp, keen, stimulating, invigorating.
(*ANT.*) *musty, faded, stagnant, decayed, hackneyed, slow, lethargic, sluggish, still, dull, oppressive.*

briskness *(SYN.)* energy, exercise, motion, rapidity, agility, action, quickness, activity, vigor, liveliness, movement.

(ANT.) inertia, idleness, sloth, dullness, inactivity.

bristle *(SYN.)* flare up, anger, rage, seethe, get mad.

brittle *(SYN.)* crumbling, frail, breakable, delicate, splintery, crisp, fragile, weak.

(ANT.) tough, enduring, unbreakable, thick, strong, sturdy, flexible, elastic, supple.

broach *(SYN.)* set afoot, introduce, inaugurate, start, mention, launch, advance.

broad *(SYN.)* large, wide, tolerant, expanded, vast, liberal, sweeping, roomy, expansive, extended, general, extensive, full.

(ANT.) restricted, confined, narrow, constricted, slim, tight, limited, negligible.

broadcast *(SYN.)* distribute, announce, publish, scatter, circulate, spread, send, transmit, relay.

broaden *(SYN.)* spread, widen, amplify, enlarge, extend, increase, add to, expand, stretch, deepen, magnify.

(ANT.) tighted, narrow, constrict, straiten.

broad-minded *(SYN.)* unprejudiced, tolerant, liberal, unbigoted.

(ANT.) prejudiced, petty, narrowminded.

brochure *(SYN.)* booklet, pamphlet, leaflet, mailing, circular, tract, flier.

broil *(SYN.)* cook, burn, heat, roast, bake, scorch, fire, grill, singe, sear, toast.

broken *(SYN.)* flattened, rent, shattered, wrecked, destroyed, reduced, smashed, crushed, fractured, ruptured, interrupted, burst, separated.

(ANT.) whole, integral, united, repaired.

brokenhearted *(SYN.)* disconsolate, forlorn, heartbroken, sad, grieving.

bromide *(SYN.)* banality, platitude, stereotype, commonplace, slogan, proverb.

brooch *(SYN.)* clasp, pin, breastpin, broach.

brood *(SYN.)* study, consider, ponder, reflect, contemplate, meditate, young, litter, offspring, think, muse, deliberate.

brook *(SYN.)* rivulet, run, branch, stream, creek.

brother *(SYN.)* comrade, man, kinsman, sibling.

(ANT.) sister.

brotherhood *(SYN.)* kinship, kindness, fraternity, fellowship, clan, society, brotherliness, bond, association, relationship, solidarity.

(ANT.) strife, discord, acrimony, opposition.

brotherly *(SYN.)* affectionate, fraternal, cordial, sympathetic, benevolent, philanthropic, humane, kindred, communal, altruistic.

brow *(SYN.)* forehead, eyebrow.

browbeat *(SYN.)* bully, domineer, bulldoze, intimidate, henpeck, oppress, grind.

brown study *(SYN.)* contemplation, reflection, reverie, musing, thoughtfulness, deliberation, rumination, selfcommunion.

browse *(SYN.)* scan, graze, read, feed.

bruise *(SYN.)* hurt, injure, wound, damage, abrasion, injury, contusion, mark, damage, harm, wound.

brunt *(SYN.)* force, impact, shock, strain, oppression, severity.

brush *(SYN.)* rub, wipe, clean, bushes, remove, shrubs, broom, whisk, paintbrush, hairbrush, underbrush, thicket.

brush-off *(SYN.)* dismissal, snub, slight, rebuff, turndown.

brusque *(SYN.)* sudden, curt, hasty, blunt, rough, steep, precipitate, rugged, craggy, gruff, surly, abrupt, short, bluff.

(ANT.) smooth, anticipated, courteous, expected, gradual, personable.

brutal *(SYN.)* brute, cruel, inhuman, rude, barbarous, gross, sensual, ferocious, brutish, coarse, bestial, carnal, remorseless, ruthless, savage, mean, savage, pitiless, barbaric.

(ANT.) kind, courteous, humane, civilized, gentle, kindhearted, mild.

brute *(SYN.)* monster, barbarian, beast, animal, wild, savage.

bubble *(SYN.)* boil, foam, seethe, froth.

buccaneer *(SYN.)* sea robber, privateer, pirate.

buck *(SYN.)* spring, jump, vault, leap.

bucket *(SYN.)* pot, pail, canister, can.

buckle *(SYN.)* hook, fastening, fastener, bend, wrinkle, clip, clasp, distort, catch, strap, fasten, collapse, yield, warp.

bud *(SYN.)* develop, sprout.

buddy *(SYN.)* companion, friend, partner, pal.

budge *(SYN.)* stir, move.

budget *(SYN.)* schedule, ration.

buff *(SYN.)* shine, polish, burnish, rub.

buffet *(SYN.)* bat, strike, clout, blow, knock, beat, crack, hit, slap, cabinet, counter, server.

buffoon *(SYN.)* jester, fool, clown, jokester, zany, comedian, chump, boor, dolt.

bug *(SYN.)* fault, hitch, defect, catch, snag, failing, rub, flaw, snarl, weakness, annoy, pester, hector, vex, nag.

bugbear *(SYN.)* bogy, specter, demon, devil, fiend.

build *(SYN.)* found, rear, establish, constructed, raise, set up, erect, assemble.

(ANT.) raze, destroy, overthrow, demolish, undermine.

building *(SYN.)* residence, structure, house, edifice.

build-up *(SYN.)* gain, enlargement, increase, praise, commendation, promotion, jump, expansion, uptrend, testimonial, plug, puff, blurb, endorsement, compliment.

(ANT.) reduction, decrease, decline.

bulge *(SYN.)* lump, protuberance, bump, swelling, extend, protrude.

(ANT.) hollow, shrink, contract.

bulk *(SYN.)* lump, magnitude, volume, size, mass, most, majority.

bulky *(SYN.)* great, big, huge, large, enormous, massive, immense, monstrous, clumsy, cumbersome.

(ANT.) tiny, little, small, petite, handy.

bull *(SYN.)* push, force, press, drive, thrust, bump.

bulldoze *(SYN.)* cow, bully, coerce, thrust, push.

bulletin *(SYN.)* news, flash, message, statement, newsletter, circular.

bullheaded *(SYN.)* dogged, stiff-necked, stubborn, mulish, rigid, pigheaded, willful, tenacious, unyielding.

(ANT.) flexible, submissive, compliant.

bully *(SYN.)* pester, tease, intimidate, harass, domineer.

bulwark *(SYN.)* wall, bastion, abutment, bank, dam, rampart, shoulder, parapet, backing, maintainer, embankment, safeguard, reinforcement.

bum *(SYN.)* idler, loafer, drifter, hobo, wretch, dwadler, beggar, vagrant.

bumbling *(SYN.)* bungling, inept, blundering, clumsy, incompetent, awkward, maladroit, lumbering, ungainly.

(ANT.) facile, handy, dexterous.

bump *(SYN.)* shake, push, hit, shove, prod, collide, knock, bang, strike.

bumpkin *(SYN.)* hick, yokel, rustic.

bumptious *(SYN.)* arrogant, self-assertive, conceited, forward, over-bearing, pushy, boastful, obtrusive.

(ANT.) sheepish, self-effacing, retiring, shrinking, unobtrusive, diffident.

bumpy *(SYN.)* uneven, jolting, rough, jarring, rocky, coarse, craggy, irregular.

(ANT.) flat, smooth, flush, polished.

bunch *(SYN.)* batch, bundle, cluster, company, collection, flock, group.

bundle *(SYN.)* package, mass, collection, batch, parcel, packet, box, carton.

bungalow *(SYN.)* ranch house, cabana, cabin, cottage, lodge, summer house.

bungle *(SYN.)* tumble, botch, foul up, boggle, mess up, louse up, blunder.

bunk *(SYN.)* berth, rubbish, nonsense, couch, bed, cot.

buoyant *(SYN.)* light, jolly, spirited, effervescent, blithe, sprightly, lively, resilient, vivacious, afloat, floating, cheery, cheerful.

(ANT.) hopeless, dejected, sullen, depressed, heavy, despondent, sinking, low, pessimistic, downcast, glum.

burden *(SYN.)* oppress, afflict, trouble, encumber, tax, weight, load, worry, contents, trial, lade, overload.

(ANT.) lighten, alleviate, ease, mitigate, console, disburden.

burdensome *(SYN.)* arduous, cumbersome, bothersome, oppressive, irksome, trying, hard, difficult.

bureau *(SYN.)* office, division, department, unit, commission, board, chest.

bureaucrat *(SYN.)* clerk, official, functionary, servant, politician.

burglar *(SYN.)* thief, robber.

burial *(SYN.)* interment, funeral.

burly *(SYN.)* husky, beefy, heavyset,

brawny, strapping.

(ANT.) skinny, scrawny.

burn *(SYN.)* scorch, blaze, scald, sear, char, incinerate, fire, flare, combust, flame, consume.

(ANT.) quench, extinguish.

burnish *(SYN.)* polish, shine, buff, wax.

burrow *(SYN.)* tunnel, search, seek, dig, excavate, hunt, den, hole.

burst *(SYN.)* exploded, broken, erupt.

bury *(SYN.)* hide, inhume, conceal, immure, cover, inter, entomb, secrete.

(ANT.) reveal, display, open, raise.

business *(SYN.)* employment, profession, trade, work, art, engagement, vocation, occupation, company, concern, firm, partnership, corporation.

(ANT.) hobby, avocation, pastime.

bustle *(SYN.)* noise, flurry, action, trouble, fuss, ado, stir, excitement, commotion.

(ANT.) calmness, composure, serenity, peacefulness.

bustling *(SYN.)* humming, busy, stirring, vibrant, bubbling, alive, active, moving, jumping, astir, zealous.

busy *(SYN.)* careful, industrious, active, patient, assiduous, diligent, perseverant, hardworking, employed.

(ANT.) unconcerned, indifferent, apathetic, lethargic, careless, inactive, unemployed, lazy, indolent.

busybody *(SYN.)* gossip, tattletale, pry, meddler, snoop.

but *(SYN.)* nevertheless, yet, however, though, although, still.

butcher *(SYN.)* kill, murder, slaughter, assassinate, slay, massacre.

(ANT.) save, protect, vivify, animate, resuscitate.

butt *(SYN.)* bump, ram, bunt, shove, jam, drive, punch, blow, push, thrust, propulsion.

buttocks *(SYN.)* hind end, rump, posterior, backside, behind, bottom, rear.

button *(SYN.)* clasp, close, fasten, hook.

buttress *(SYN.)* support, brace, stay, frame, prop, reinforcement, bulwark, backing, encourage, sustain, reassure, boost, bolster, steel.

buxom *(SYN.)* well-developed, chesty, ample, fleshy, full figured, zaftig.

buy *(SYN.)* procure, get, purchase, acquire, obtain.

(ANT.) vend, sell.

buzz *(SYN.)* whir, hum, thrum, drone.

by *(SYN.)* near, through, beside, with, from, at, close to.

bygone *(SYN.)* bypast, former, earlier, past, older, onetime, forgotten.

(ANT.) immediate, present, current, modern.

bypass *(SYN.)* deviate from, go around, detour around.

by-product *(SYN.)* offshoot, spin-off, effect, extra, outgrowth, bonus, appendage, side effect, supplement, extension, side issue, rider.

bystander *(SYN.)* onlooker, watcher, viewer, observer, witness, kibitzer.

byway *(SYN.)* passage, detour, path.

byword *(SYN.)* adage, proverb, axiom, shibboleth, apothegm, motto, slogan.

cab *(SYN.)* coach, taxi, car, hack, taxicab, carriage.

cabin *(SYN.)* cottage, shack, shanty, hut.

cabinet *(SYN.)* ministry, council, committee, case, cupboard.

cable *(SYN.)* wire, cord, rope, telegraph.

cafeteria *(SYN.)* cafe, diner, restaurant.

calculate *(SYN.)* count, compute, figure, estimate, consider, tally, determine.
(ANT.) guess, miscalculate, assume.

calculating *(SYN.)* crafty, shrewd, scheming, cunning.
(ANT.) simple, guileless, direct, ingenuous.

calculation *(SYN.)* figuring, reckoning, computation, estimation.

calendar *(SYN.)* timetable, schedule, diary.

call *(SYN.)* designate, name, yell, cry, ask, shout, speak, cry out, exclaim.

calling *(SYN.)* occupation, profession, trade.

callous *(SYN.)* insensitive, impenitent, obdurate, unfeeling, hard, heartless.
(ANT.) soft, compassionate, tender.

calm *(SYN.)* appease, lull, quiet, soothe, composed, tranquilize, tranquil.
(ANT.) disturbed, emotional, turmoil.

campaign *(SYN.)* cause, crusade, movement.

canal *(SYN.)* gully, tube, waterway.

cancel *(SYN.)* eliminate, erase, delete, repeal, revoke, void.
(ANT.) perpetuate, confirm, ratify.

candid *(SYN.)* free, blunt, frank, plain, open, sincere, honest, straightforward.
(ANT.) sly, contrived, wily, scheming.

candidate *(SYN.)* applicant, aspirant, nominee.

canine *(SYN.)* pooch, dog, puppy.

canny *(SYN.)* artful, skillful, shrewd, cautious, careful, cunning.

canopy *(SYN.)* awning, screen, shelter.

canyon *(SYN.)* gully, arroyo, ravine.

cap *(SYN.)* top, cover, crown, lid.

capability *(SYN.)* ability, capacity, dexterity, qualification.
(ANT.) incapacity, disability.

capable *(SYN.)* clever, qualified, able.
(ANT.) unfitted, incapable, inept.

capacity *(SYN.)* capability, power, ability, talent, content, skill, volume.
(ANT.) inability, stupidity, incapacity.

capital *(SYN.)* important, property, wealth, money, city, cash, assets.
(ANT.) unimportant, trivial, secondary.

captain *(SYN.)* commander, authority, supervisor, leader, commander.

captivate *(SYN.)* fascinate, charm, delight.

captivity *(SYN.)* detention, imprisonment, custody, confinement, bondage.
(ANT.) liberty, freedom.

capture *(SYN.)* catch, grip, apprehend, clutch, arrest, snare, seize, nab.
(ANT.) set free, lose, liberate, throw.

cardinal *(SYN.)* chief, primary, important, prime, leading, major, essential.
(ANT.) secondary, auxiliary.

care *(SYN.)* concern, anxiety, worry, caution, solicitude, attention, regard, charge, ward, attention, regard.
(ANT.) neglect, disregard, indifference.

career *(SYN.)* occupation, profession, job, calling, vocation, trade.

carefree *(SYN.)* lighthearted, happy, unconcerned, breezy, jolly, lively.

careful *(SYN.)* prudent, thoughtful, attentive, cautious, painstaking, scrupulous, discreet, watchful.
(ANT.) nice, careful, heedless, messy.

careless *(SYN.)* imprudent, heedless, unconcerned, inattentive, lax.
(ANT.) careful, cautious, painstaking.

cargo *(SYN.)* freight, load, freightload, shipment.

carriage *(SYN.)* bearing, conduct, action, deed, behavior, demeanor, disposition, deportment.

carry *(SYN.)* convey, transport, support, bring, sustain, bear, hold, move, transfer, take.
(ANT.) drop, abandon.

carve *(SYN.)* hew, shape, cut, whittle, chisel, sculpt.

case *(SYN.)* state, covering, receptacle, condition, instance, example, occurrence, illustration, sample.

cast *(SYN.)* fling, toss, throw, pitch, form, company, shape, mold, hurl.

castle *(SYN.)* mansion, palace, chateau.

casual *(SYN.)* chance, unexpected, informal, accidental, incidental, offhand, unplanned, spontaneous.
(ANT.) planned, expected, calculated, formal, deliberate, dressy.

casualty *(SYN.)* calamity, fortuity, mishap, loss, injured, dead, wounded, accident, misfortune.
(ANT.) purpose, intention, calculation.

catalog *(SYN.)* classify, roll, group, list, inventory, directory, index, record.

catastrophe *(SYN.)* mishap, calamity, disaster, adversity, accident, ruin.
(ANT.) fortune, boon, triumph, blessing, advantage, welfare.

catch *(SYN.)* hook, snare, entrap, ensnare, capture, grip, apprehend.
(ANT.) lose, free, liberate, throw, release.

category *(SYN.)* class, caste, kind, order, genre, rank, classification.

cause *(SYN.)* effect, incite, create, induce, inducement, occasion, incentive, prompt, reason, motive.

caution *(SYN.)* heed, vigilance, care, prudence, counsel, warning, wariness.
(ANT.) carelessness, abandon, recklessness.

cautious *(SYN.)* heedful, scrupulous, attentive, prudent, thoughtful, discreet.
(ANT.) improvident, headstrong, heedless, foolish, forgetful, indifferent.

cave *(SYN.)* grotto, hole, shelter, lair, den, cavern.

cave in *(SYN.)* fall in, collapse.

cavity *(SYN.)* pit, hole, crater.

cavort *(SYN.)* caper, leap, frolic, hop, prance.

cease *(SYN.)* desist, stop, abandon, discontinue, relinquish, end, terminate, leave, surrender, resign.
(ANT.) occupy, continue, persist, begin, endure, stay.

cede *(SYN.)* surrender, relinquish, yield.

celebrate *(SYN.)* honor, glorify, com-

memorate, keep, solemnize, extol, observe, commend, praise.
(ANT.) *decry, overlook, profane, disregard, disgrace.*
celebrated *(SYN.)* eminent, glorious, distinguished, noted, illustrious, famed, well-known, popular, renowned, famous.
(ANT.) *obscure, hidden, anonymous, infamous, unknown.*
celebrity *(SYN.)* somebody, personage, heroine, hero, dignitary, notable.
celestial *(SYN.)* godlike, holy, supernatural, divine, paradisiacal, utopian, transcendent, superhuman.
(ANT.) *diabolical, profane, mundane, wicked.*
cement *(SYN.)* solidify, weld, fasten, secure.
cemetery *(SYN.)* graveyard.
censure *(SYN.)* denounce, reproach, upbraid, blame, disapproval, reprehend, condemn, criticism, disapprove, criticize, reprove.
(ANT.) *commend, approval, forgive, approve, praise, applaud, condone.*
center *(SYN.)* heart, core, midpoint, middle, nucleus, inside, hub, focus.
(ANT.) *rim, boundary, edge, border, periphery, outskirts.*
central *(SYN.)* chief, necessary, main, halfway, dominant, mid, middle, inner, focal, leading, fundamental, principal.
(ANT.) *side, secondary, incidental, auxiliary.*
ceremonious *(SYN.)* correct, exact, precise, stiff, outward, external, solemn, formal.
(ANT.) *material, unconventional, easy, heartfelt.*
ceremony *(SYN.)* observance, rite, parade, formality, pomp, ritual, protocol, solemnity.
(ANT.) *informality, casualness.*
certain *(SYN.)* definite, assured, fixed, inevitable, sure, undeniable, positive, confident, particular, special, indubitable, secure, unquestionable.
(ANT.) *probable, uncertain, doubtful, questionable.*
certainly *(SYN.)* absolutely, surely, definitely.
(ANT.) *dubiously, doubtfully, questionably.*
certainty *(SYN.)* confidence, courage, security, assuredness, firmness, assertion, statement.
(ANT.) *humility, bashfulness, modest, shyness.*
certificate *(SYN.)* affidavit, document.
certify *(SYN.)* validate, affirm, verify, confirm, authenticate, substantiate.
certitude *(SYN.)* confidence, belief, conviction, feeling, faith, persuasion, trust.
(ANT.) *doubt, incredulity, denial, heresy.*
cessation *(SYN.)* ending, finish, stoppage, termination, conclusion, end.
chafe *(SYN.)* heat, rub, warm, annoy, disturb.
chagrin *(SYN.)* irritation, mortification, embarrassment, annoyance, vexation, worry, bother, shame, annoy, irk,

humiliation, irritate, vex, frustrate, humiliate, embarrass, mortify, exasperate, disappoint, disappointment.
chain *(SYN.)* fasten, bind, shackle, restrain.
chairman *(SYN.)* speaker.
challenge *(SYN.)* question, dare, call, summon, threat, invite, threaten, demand.
chamber *(SYN.)* cell, salon, room.
champion *(SYN.)* victor, winner, choice, best, conqueror, hero, support, select.
chance *(SYN.)* befall, accident, betide, disaster, opportunity, calamity, occur, possibility, prospect, happen, luck, fate, take place.
(ANT.) *design, purpose, inevitability, calculation, certainty, intention.*
change *(SYN.)* modification, alternation, alteration, mutation, variety, exchange, shift, alter, transfigure, veer, vary, variation, substitution, substitute, vicissitude.
(ANT.) *uniformity, monotony, settle, remain, endure, retain, preserve, steadfastness, endurance, immutability, stability.*
changeable *(SYN.)* fitful, fickle, inconstant, unstable, shifting, wavering.
(ANT.) *stable, uniform, constant, unchanging.*
channel *(SYN.)* strait, corridor, waterway, artery, duct, canal, way, trough, groove, passageway.
chant *(SYN.)* singing, incantation, hymn, intone, sing, carol, psalm, song, ballad.
chaos *(SYN.)* confusion, jumble, turmoil, anarchy, disorder, muddle.
(ANT.) *organization, order, tranquillity, tidiness, system.*
chaotic *(SYN.)* confused, disorganized, disordered, messy.
(ANT.) *neat, ordered, systematic, organized.*
chap *(SYN.)* break, fellow, person, crack, split, man, rough, individual, boy.
chaperon *(SYN.)* associate with, escort, convoy, accompany, consort with.
(ANT.) *avoid, desert, leave, abandon, quit.*
chapter *(SYN.)* part, section, division.
char *(SYN.)* scorch, singe, burn, sear.
character *(SYN.)* description, class, kind, repute, mark, individuality, disposition, traits, personality, reputation, symbol, features, qualify, eccentric, nature.
characteristic *(SYN.)* exclusive, distinctive, special, mark, feature, property, typical, unique, attribute, distinguishing, trait, quality.
charge *(SYN.)* arraignment, indictment, accusation, sell for, attack, assail, assault, indict, blame, allegation, care, custody, imputation.
(ANT.) *pardon, flee, exculpation, excuse, absolve, retreat, exoneration.*
charitable *(SYN.)* benevolent, generous, liberal, altruistic, kind, obliging, considerate, unselfish.
(ANT.) *petty, mean, harsh, wicked,*

greedy, narrow-minded, stingy, malevolent.

charity *(SYN.)* benevolence, kindness, magnanimity, altruism, generosity.

(ANT.) malevolence, cruelty, selfishness.

charm *(SYN.)* allure, spell, enchantment, attractiveness, magic, witchery, amulet, talisman, lure, enchant, bewitch, fascinate, captivate.

charmer *(SYN.)* siren, temptress, enchantress, vamp, seductress, seducer, enchanter.

charming *(SYN.)* attractive, enchanting, fascinating, alluring, appealing, winsome, agreeable, bewitching, winning.

(ANT.) revolting, repugnant, repulsive.

chart *(SYN.)* design, plan, cabal, plot, sketch, stratagem, map, diagram, conspiracy, graph, intrigue.

charter *(SYN.)* lease, hire, rent, alliance.

chase *(SYN.)* hunt, run after, pursue, trail, follow, persist, scheme.

(ANT.) escape, flee, abandon, elude, evade.

chasm *(SYN.)* ravine, abyss, canyon, gorge.

chaste *(SYN.)* clear, immaculate, innocent, sincere, bare, clean, modest, pure, decent, virtuous, virginal, sheer, absolute, spotless.

(ANT.) polluted, tainted, foul, impure, sinful, worldly, sullied, defiled.

chasten *(SYN.)* chastise, restrain, punish, discipline.

chastise *(SYN.)* punish, castigate, correct.

(ANT.) release, acquit, free, exonerate.

chat *(SYN.)* argue, jabber, blab, plead, consult, converse, lecture, discuss, talk, conversation, tattle.

chatter *(SYN.)* dialogue, lecture, speech, conference, talk, discourse.

(ANT.) silence, correspondence, writing.

cheap *(SYN.)* poor, common, inexpensive, shabby, low-priced, beggary, low-cost, shoddy, mean, inferior.

(ANT.) honorable, dear, noble, expensive, costly, well-made, elegant, dignified.

cheat *(SYN.)* deceive, fool, bilk, outwit, victimize, dupe, gull, hoodwink, circumvent, swindler, cheater, trickster, phony, fraud, defraud, charlatan, crook, chiseler, con artist, hoax, swindle.

check *(SYN.)* dissect, interrogate, analyze, contemplate, inquire, question, scrutinize, arrest, stop, halt, block, curb, control, investigate, review, examine, test, counterfoil, stub, barrier, watch.

(ANT.) overlook, disregard, advance, foster, continue, promote, omit, neglect.

checkup *(SYN.)* medical examination, physical.

cheek *(SYN.)* nerve, effrontery, impudence, gall, impertinence.

cheer *(SYN.)* console, gladden, comfort, encourage, applause, encouragement, joy, glee, gaiety, mirth, soothe, sympathize, approval, solace.

(ANT.) depress, sadden, discourage, derision, dishearten, discouragement,

antagonize.

cheerful *(SYN.)* glad, jolly, joyful, gay, happy, cherry, merry, joyous, lighthearted.

(ANT.) mournful, sad, glum, depressed, gloomy, sullen.

cherish *(SYN.)* prize, treasure, appreciate, nurse, value, comfort, hold dear, foster, nurture, sustain.

(ANT.) disregard, neglect, deprecate, scorn, reject, undervalue, abandon.

chest *(SYN.)* bosom, breast, coffer, box, case, trunk, casket, dresser, commode, cabinet, chifforobe.

chew *(SYN.)* gnaw, munch, bite, nibble.

chic *(SYN.)* fashionable, modish, smart, stylish, trendy.

chide *(SYN.)* admonish, rebuke, scold, reprimand, criticize, reprove.

(ANT.) extol, praise, commend.

chief *(SYN.)* chieftain, head, commander, captain, leader, principal, master, boss, leading, ruler.

(ANT.) servant, subordinate, secondary, follower, incidental, accidental, auxiliary, attendant.

chiefly *(SYN.)* mainly, especially, mostly.

childish *(SYN.)* immature, childlike, infantile, babyish.

(ANT.) mature, adult, seasoned, grownup.

chill *(SYN.)* coolness, cold, cool, coldness, brisk, frosty.

(ANT.) hot, warm, heat, heated, warmth.

chilly *(SYN.)* cold, frigid, freezing, arctic, cool, icy, passionless, wintry, unfeeling.

(ANT.) fiery, heated, passionate, ardent.

chirp *(SYN.)* peep, cheep, twitter, tweet, chirrup.

chivalrous *(SYN.)* noble, brave, polite, valorous, gallant, gentlemanly, courteous.

(ANT.) crude, rude, impolite, uncivil.

chivalry *(SYN.)* courtesy, nobility, gallantry, knighthood.

choice *(SYN.)* delicate, elegant, fine, dainty, exquisite, pure, refined, subtle, splendid, handsome, option, selection, beautiful, minute, pretty, pick, select, uncommon, rare, precious, valuable, thin, small.

(ANT.) coarse, rough, thick, blunt, large.

choke *(SYN.)* throttle, gag, strange.

choose *(SYN.)* elect, decide between, pick, select, cull, opt.

(ANT.) reject, refuse.

chop *(SYN.)* hew, cut, fell, mince.

chore *(SYN.)* routine, task, job, duty, work.

chronic *(SYN.)* persistent, constant, lingering, continuing, perennial, unending, sustained, permanent.

(ANT.) fleeting, acute, temporary.

chronicle *(SYN.)* detail, history, narrative, account, description, narration, recital.

(ANT.) misrepresentation, confusion, distortion.

chuckle *(SYN.)* titter, laugh, giggle.

chum *(SYN.)* friend, pal, buddy, companion.

cinema *(SYN.)* effigy, film, etching, appearance, drawing, engraving, illustration, likeness, image, panorama, painting, picture, photograph.

circle *(SYN.)* disk, ring, set, group. class, club, surround, encircle, enclose, round.

circuit *(SYN.)* circle, course, journey, orbit, revolution, tour.

circuitous *(SYN.)* distorted, devious, indirect, roundabout swerving, crooked, tortuous.
(ANT.) straightforward, straight, direct, honest.

circular *(SYN.)* chubby, complete, curved, bulbous, cylindrical, round, ringlike, globular, entire, rotund.
(ANT.) straight.

circumference *(SYN.)* border, perimeter, periphery, edge.

circumspection *(SYN.)* care, worry, solicitude, anxiety, concern, caution, attention, vigilance.
(ANT.) neglect, negligence, indifference.

circumstance *(SYN.)* fact, event, incident, condition, happening, position, occurrence, situation.

circumstances *(SYN.)* facts, conditions, factors, situation, background, grounds, means, capital, assets, rank, class.

cite *(SYN.)* affirm, assign, allege, advance, quote, mention, declare, claim, maintain.
(ANT.) refute, gainsay, deny, contradict.

citizen *(SYN.)* native, inhabitant, national, denizen, subject, dweller, resident.

city *(SYN.)* metropolis, municipality, town.

civil *(SYN.)* courteous, cultivated, accomplished, public, municipal, respectful, genteel, polite, considerate, gracious, urban.
(ANT.) uncouth, uncivil, impertinent, impolite, boorish.

civilization *(SYN.)* cultivation, culture, education, breeding, enlightenment, society, refinement.
(ANT.) ignorance, vulgarity.

civilize *(SYN.)* refine, tame, polish, cultivate, instruct, teach.

claim *(SYN.)* aver, declare, allege, assert, affirm, express, state, demand, maintain, defend, uphold.
(ANT.) refute, deny, contradict.

clamor *(SYN.)* cry, din, babel, noise, racket, outcry, row, sound tumult, shouting, shout, uproar.
(ANT.) hush, serenity, silence, tranquility, stillness, quiet.

clan *(SYN.)* fellowship, kindness, solidarity, family, brotherliness, association, fraternity.
(ANT.) discord, strife, opposition, acrimony.

clandestine *(SYN.)* covert, hidden, latent, private, concealed, secret, unknown.
(ANT.) exposed, known, conspicuous, obvious.

clarify *(SYN.)* educate, explain, expound, decipher, illustrate, clear, resolve, define, interpret, unfold.
(ANT.) darken, obscure, baffle, confuse.

clash *(SYN.)* clank, crash, clang, conflict, disagreement, opposition, collision, struggle, mismatch, contrast, disagree, collide, interfere.
(ANT.) accord, agreement, harmony, blend, harmonize, match, agree.

clasp *(SYN.)* grip, hold, grasp, adhere, clutch, keep, have, maintain, possess, occupy, retain, support, confine, embrace, fastening, check, detain, curb, receive.
(ANT.) relinquish, vacate, surrender, abandon.

class *(SYN.)* category, denomination, caste, kind, genre, grade, rank, order, elegance, classification, division, sort, family, species, set, excellence.

classic *(SYN.)* masterpiece.

classification *(SYN.)* order, category, class, arrangement, ordering, grouping, organization.

classify *(SYN.)* arrange, class, order, sort, grade, group, index.

clause *(SYN.)* condition, paragraph, limitation, article.

claw *(SYN.)* hook, talon, nail, scratch.

clean *(SYN.)* mop, tidy, neat, dustless, clear, unsoiled, immaculate, unstained, untainted, pure, dust, vacuum, scour, decontaminate, wipe, sterilize, cleanse, scrub, purify, wash, sweep.
(ANT.) stain, soil, pollute, soiled, impure, dirty, stain.

cleanse *(SYN.)* mop, purify, wash, sweep.
(ANT.) stain, soil, dirty, pollute.

clear *(SYN.)* fair, sunny, cloudless, transparent, apparent, limpid, distinct, intelligible, evident, unmistakable, understandable, unclouded, uncloudy, light, bright, certain, manifest, lucid, plain, obvious, unobstructed.
(ANT.) obscure, unclear, muddled, confused, dark, cloudy, blocked, obstructed, questionable, dubious, blockaded, foul, overcast.

clearly *(SYN.)* plainly, obviously, evidently, definitely, surely, certainly.
(ANT.) questionably, dubiously.

clemency *(SYN.)* forgiveness, charity, compassion, grace, mercy, leniency, pity, mildness.
(ANT.) punishment, vengeance, retribution.

clerical *(SYN.)* ministerial, pastoral, priestly, celestial, holy, sacred, secretarial.

clerk *(SYN.)* typist, office worker, office girl, saleslady, salesperson, salesclerk.

clever *(SYN.)* apt, dexterous, quick, adroit, quick-witted, talented, bright, skillful, witty, ingenious, smart, intelligent, shrewd, gifted, expert, sharp.
(ANT.) unskilled, slow, stupid, backward, maladroit, bungling, dull, clumsy.

cleverness *(SYN.)* intellect, intelligence, comprehension, mind, perspicacity, sagacity, fun.
(ANT.) sobriety, stupidity, solemnity,

commonplace, platitude.

client *(SYN.)* patron, customer.

cliff *(SYN.)* scar, bluff, crag, precipice, escarpment.

climate *(SYN.)* aura, atmosphere, air, ambience.

climax *(SYN.)* apex, culmination, peak, summit, consummation, height, acme, zenith.
(ANT.) depth, base, anticlimax, floor.

climb *(SYN.)* mount, scale, ascend.
(ANT.) descend.

clip *(SYN.)* snip, crop, cut, mow, clasp.

cloak *(SYN.)* conceal, cover, disguise, clothe, cape, guard, envelop, hide, mask, protect, shield.
(ANT.) divulge, expose, reveal, bare, unveil.

clod *(SYN.)* wad, hunk, gobbet, lump, chunk, clot, gob, dunce, dolt, oaf, fool.

clog *(SYN.)* crowd, congest, cram, over-fill, stuff.

cloister *(SYN.)* monastery, priory, hermitage, abbey, convent.

close *(SYN.)* adjacent, adjoining, immediate, unventilated, stuffy, abutting, neighboring, dear, oppressive, mean, impending, nearby, near, devoted.
(ANT.) afar, faraway, removed, distant.

close *(SYN.)* seal, shut, clog, stop, obstruct, cease, conclude, complete, end, terminate, occlude, finish.
(ANT.) unlock, begin, open, unbar, inaugurate, commence, start.

closet *(SYN.)* cabinet, locker, wardrobe, cupboard.

cloth *(SYN.)* fabric, goods, material, textile.

clothe *(SYN.)* garb, dress, apparel.
(ANT.) strip, undress.

clothes *(SYN.)* array, attire, apparel, clothing, dress, garb, dress, garments, raiment, drapery, vestments.
(ANT.) nudity, nakedness.

clothing *(SYN.)* attire, clothes, apparel, array, dress, drapery, garments, garb, vestments.
(ANT.) nudity, nakedness.

cloud *(SYN.)* fog, mist, haze, mass, collection, obscure, dim, shadow.

cloudy *(SYN.)* dim, dark, indistinct, murky, mysterious, indefinite, vague, sunless, clouded, obscure, overcast, shadowy.
(ANT.) sunny, clear, distinct, limpid, lucid, clarified, cloudless, clearheaded, brilliant, bright.

club *(SYN.)* society, association, set, circle, organization, bat, cudgel, stick, blackjack.

clue *(SYN.)* sign, trace, hint, suggestion.

clumsy *(SYN.)* bungling, inept, rough, unpolished, bumbling, awkward, ungraceful, gauche, ungainly, unskillful, untoward.
(ANT.) polished, skillful, neat, graceful, dexterous, adroit.

cluster *(SYN.)* batch, clutch, group, bunch, gather, pack, assemble, crowd.

clutch *(SYN.)* grip, grab, seize, hold.

coalition *(SYN.)* combination, association, alliance, confederacy, entente, league, treaty.

(ANT.) schism, separation, divorce.

coarse *(SYN.)* unpolished, vulgar, refined, rough, smooth, impure, rude, crude, gruff, gross, cultivated, delicate, cultured.
(ANT.) delicate, smooth, refined, polished, genteel, cultivated, suave, fine, cultured.

coast *(SYN.)* seaboard, seashore, beach, shore, drift, glide, ride.

coax *(SYN.)* urge, persuade, wheedle, cajole.
(ANT.) force, bully, coerce.

coddle *(SYN.)* pamper, baby, spoil, indulge.

code *(SYN.)* crypt, cryptogram, cipher.

coerce *(SYN.)* constrain, compel, enforce, force, drive, oblige, impel.
(ANT.) prevent, persuade, convince, induce.

coercion *(SYN.)* emphasis, intensity, energy, dint, might, potency, power, vigor, strength, compulsion, force, constraint, violence.
(ANT.) impotence, frailty, feebleness, weakness, persuasion.

cognizance *(SYN.)* apprehension, erudition, acquaintance, information, learning, knowledge, lore, science, scholarship, understanding.
(ANT.) illiteracy, misunderstanding, ignorance.

cognizant *(SYN.)* conscious, aware, apprised informed, mindful, observant, perceptive.
(ANT.) unaware, ignorant, oblivious, insensible.

coherent *(SYN.)* logical, intelligible, sensible, rational, commonsensical, reasonable.

coiffeur *(SYN.)* hairdresser.

coiffure *(SYN.)* haircut, hairdo.

coincide *(SYN.)* acquiesce, agree, accede, assent, consent, comply, correspond, concur, match, tally, harmonize, conform.
(ANT.) differ, disagree, protest, contradict.

coincidence *(SYN.)* accident, chance.
(ANT.) plot, plan, prearrangement, scheme.

coincident *(SYN.)* identical, equal, equivalent, distinguishable, same, like.
(ANT.) distinct, contrary, disparate, opposed.

coincidental *(SYN.)* unpredicted, unexpected, chance, unforeseen, accidental, fortuitous.

cold *(SYN.)* cool, freezing, chilly, frigid, icy, frozen, wintry, arctic, unfriendly, indifferent, phlegmatic, stoical, passionless, chill, unemotional, heartless, unfeeling.
(ANT.) hot, torrid, fiery, burning, ardent, friendly, temperate, warm, passionate.

collapse *(SYN.)* descend, decrease, diminish, fail, downfall, failure, decline, fall, drop, sink, subside, topple.
(ANT.) soar, steady, limb, mount, arise.

colleague *(SYN.)* companion, attendant, comrade, associate, crony, coworker,

mate, friend, partner.
(ANT.) *enemy, stranger, adversary.*
collect (SYN.) assemble, amass, concentrate, pile, accumulate, congregate, obtain, heap, gather, solicit, secure, procure, raise, get, mass, hoard, consolidate.
(ANT.) *divide, dole, assort, dispel, distribute, disperse.*
collected (SYN.) cool, calm, composed, peaceful, imperturbable, placid, sedate, quiet.
(ANT.) *excited, violent, aroused, agitated.*
collection (SYN.) amount, conglomeration, sum, entirety, aggregation, hoard, accumulation, pile, store, aggregate, total, whole.
(ANT.) *part, unit, particular, element, ingredient.*
collide (SYN.) hit, smash, crash, strike.
collision (SYN.) conflict, combat, duel, battle, encounter, crash, smash, fight, contention, struggle, discord.
(ANT.) *concord, amity, harmony, consonance.*
collusion (SYN.) combination, cabal, intrigue, conspiracy, plot, treason, treachery.
color (SYN.) hue, paint, pigment, complexion, dye, shade, tone, tincture, stain, tint, tinge.
(ANT.) *paleness, transparency, achromatism.*
colorful (SYN.) impressive, vivid, striking, full-color, multicolored, offbeat, weird, unusual.
(ANT.) *flat, dull, uninteresting.*
colossal (SYN.) enormous, elephantine, gargantuan, huge, immense, gigantic, prodigious.
(ANT.) *little, minute, small, miniature, diminutive, microscopic, tiny.*
combat (SYN.) conflict, duel, battle, collision, encounter, fight, contest, oppose, war, contention, struggle, discord.
(ANT.) *consonance, harmony, concord, yield, surrender, succumb, amity.*
combination (SYN.) association, confederacy, alliance, entente, league, compounding, mixture, blend, composite, federation, mixing, compound, blending, union.
(ANT.) *separation, division, schism, divorce.*
combine (SYN.) adjoin, associate, accompany, conjoin, connect, link, mix, blend, couple, unite, join.
(ANT.) *detach, disjoin, divide, separate, disconnect.*
come (SYN.) near, approach, reach, arrive, advance.
(ANT.) *depart, leave, go.*
comedian (SYN.) comic, wit, humorist, gagman, wag.
comely (SYN.) charming, elegant, beauteous, beautiful, fine, lovely, pretty, handsome lovely.
(ANT.) *hideous, repulsive, foul, unsightly.*
come-on (SYN.) lure, inducement, enticement, temptation, premium.

comfort (SYN.) contentment, ease, enjoyment, relieve, consolation, relief, cheer, console, calm, satisfaction, soothe, encourage, succor, luxury, solace.
(ANT.) *depress, torture, discomfort, upset, misery, disturb, agitate, affliction, discompose, uncertainty, suffering.*
comfortable (SYN.) pleasing, agreeable, convenient, cozy, welcome, acceptable, relaxed, restful, cozy, gratifying, easy, contented, rested, satisfying, pleasurable.
(ANT.) *miserable, distressing, tense, strained, troubling, edgy, uncomfortable.*
comical (SYN.) droll, funny, humorous, amusing, ludicrous, witty, ridiculous, odd, queer.
(ANT.) *sober, solemn, sad, serious, melancholy.*
command (SYN.) class, method, plan regularity, rank, arrangement, series, sequence, point, aim, conduct, manage, guide, bid, system, succession, bidding, direct, order, demand, direction, rule, dictate, decree.
(ANT.) *consent, obey, misdirect, distract, deceive, misguide, license, confusion.*
commandeer (SYN.) take, possession, seize, confiscate, appropriate.
commanding (SYN.) imposing, masterful, assertive, authoritative, positive.
commence (SYN.) open, start.
(ANT.) *stop, end, terminate, finish.*
commend (SYN.) laud, praise, applaud, recommend.
(ANT.) *censure, blame, criticize.*
commendable (SYN.) deserving, praiseworthy.
(ANT.) *bad, deplorable, lamentable.*
commendation (SYN.) approval, applause, praise, recommendation, honor, medal.
(ANT.) *criticism, condemnation, censure.*
commensurate (SYN.) keep, celebrate, observe, honor, commend, extol, glorify, laud, praise, honor.
(ANT.) *decry, disgrace, disregard, overlook, profane, dishonor.*
comment (SYN.) assertion, declaration, annotation, explanation, review, commentary, report, remark, observation, utterance, criticism, statement.
commerce (SYN.) business, engagement, employment, art, trade, marketing, enterprise, occupation.
(ANT.) *hobby, pastime, avocation.*
commission (SYN.) board, committee, command, permit, order, permission, delegate, authorize, deputize, entrust.
commit (SYN.) perpetrate, perform, obligate, do, commend, consign, relegate, bind, delegate, empower, pledge, entrust, authorize, trust.
(ANT.) *neglect, mistrust, release, free, miscarry, fail, loose.*
commitment (SYN.) duty, promise, responsibility, pledge.
committee (SYN.) commission, bureau, board, delegate, council.

commodious *(SYN.)* appropriate, accessible, adapted, favorable, handy, fitting, timely.
(ANT.) inconvenient, troublesome, awkward.

commodity *(SYN.)* article, merchandise, wares, goods.

common *(SYN.)* ordinary, popular, familiar, mean, low, general, vulgar, communal, mutual, shared, natural, frequent, prevalent, joint, conventional, plain, usual, universal.
(ANT.) odd, exceptional, scarce, noble, extraordinary, different, separate, outstanding, rare, unusual, distinctive, refined.

commonplace *(SYN.)* common, usual, frequent, ordinary, everyday.
(ANT.) distinctive, unusual, original.

commonsense *(SYN.)* perceptible, alive, apprehensible, aware, awake, cognizant, conscious, comprehending, perceptible.
(ANT.) unaware, impalpable, imperceptible.

commotion *(SYN.)* confusion, chaos, disarray, ferment, disorder, stir, tumult, agitation.
(ANT.) tranquillity, peace, certainty, order.

communicable *(SYN.)* infectious, virulent, catching, transferable, contagious.
(ANT.) hygienic, noncommunicable, healthful.

communicate *(SYN.)* convey, impart, inform, confer, disclose, reveal, relate, tell, advertise, publish, transmit, publicize, divulge.
(ANT.) withhold, hide, conceal.

communication *(SYN.)* disclosure, transmission, declaration, announcement, notification, publication, message, report, news, information.

communicative *(SYN.)* unreserved, open, frank, free, straightforward, unrestrained.
(ANT.) close-mouthed, secretive.

communion *(SYN.)* intercourse, fellowship, participation, association, sacrament, union.
(ANT.) nonparticipation, alienation.

community *(SYN.)* public, society, city, town, village, township.

compact *(SYN.)* contracted, firm, narrow, snug, close, constricted, packed, vanity, treaty, agreement, tense, taught, tight, niggardly, close-fisted, parsimonious, compressed, stingy.
(ANT.) slack, open, loose, relaxed, unconfined, unfretted, sprawling, lax.

companion *(SYN.)* attendant, comrade, consort, friend, colleague, partner, crony, mate, associate.
(ANT.) stranger, enemy, adversary.

companionship *(SYN.)* familiarity, cognizance, acquaintance, fellowship, knowledge, intimacy.
(ANT.) unfamiliarity, inexperience, ignorance.

company *(SYN.)* crew, group, band, party, throng, house, assemblage, troop, fellowship, association, business, concern, partnership, corporation, companionship, firm.
(ANT.) seclusion, individual, solitude, dispersion.

comparable *(SYN.)* allied, analogous, alike, akin, like, correspondent, correlative, parallel.
(ANT.) opposed, incongruous, dissimilar, unlike, different, divergent.

compare *(SYN.)* discriminate, match, differentiate, contrast, oppose.

comparison *(SYN.)* likening, contrasting, judgment.

compartment *(SYN.)* division, section.

compassion *(SYN.)* mercy, sympathy, pity, commiseration, condolence.
(ANT.) ruthlessness, hardness, brutality, inhumanity, cruelty.

compassionate *(SYN.)* sympathizing, benign, forbearing, good, tender, affable, humane, indulgent, kind, sympathetic, kindly.
(ANT.) inhuman, merciless, unkind, cold-hearted, unsympathetic, cruel.

compatible *(SYN.)* consistent, agreeing, conforming, accordant, congruous, harmonious, cooperative, agreeable, constant, consonant, correspondent.
(ANT.) discrepant, paradoxical, disagreeable, contradictory.

compel *(SYN.)* drive, enforce, coerce, constrain, force, oblige, impel.
(ANT.) induce, coax, prevent, wheedle, persuade, cajole, convince.

compensate *(SYN.)* remunerate, repay, reimburse, recompense, balance.

compensation *(SYN.)* fee, earnings, pay, payment, recompense, allowance, remuneration, remittance, settlement, stipend, repayment, salary, wages.
(ANT.) present, gratuity, gift.

compete *(SYN.)* rival, contest, oppose, vie.
(ANT.) reconcile, accord.

competence *(SYN.)* skill, ability, capability.

competent *(SYN.)* efficient, clever, capable, able, apt, proficient, skillful, fitted, qualified.
(ANT.) inept, incapable, unfitted, awkward, incompetent, inadequate.

competition *(SYN.)* contest, match, rivalry, tournament.

competitor *(SYN.)* rival, contestant, opponent.
(ANT.) ally, friend, colleague.

complain *(SYN.)* lament, murmur, protest, grouch, grumble, regret, moan, remonstrate, whine, repine.
(ANT.) rejoice, praise, applaud, approve.

complaint *(SYN.)* protest, objection, grievance.

complement *(SYN.)* supplement, complete.
(ANT.) clash, conflict.

complete *(SYN.)* consummate, entire, ended, full, thorough, finished, full, whole, concluded, over, done, terminate, unbroken, total, undivided.
(ANT.) unfinished, imperfect, incomplete, start, partial, begin, commence, lacking.

completion *(SYN.)* achievement, attainment, end, conclusion, close, finish, wind-up, accomplishment, realization.
(ANT.) omission, neglect, failure, defeat.

complex *(SYN.)* sophisticated, compound, intricate, involved, perplexing, elaborate, complicated.
(ANT.) basic, simple, rudimentary, uncompounded, uncomplicated, plain.

complexion *(SYN.)* paint, pigment hue, color, dye, stain, tincture, tinge, tint, shade.
(ANT.) paleness, transparency, achromatism.

compliant *(SYN.)* meek, modest, lowly, plain, submissive, simple, unostentatious, unassuming, unpretentious.
(ANT.) proud, vain, arrogant, haughty, boastful.

complicated *(SYN.)* intricate, involved, complex, compound, perplexing.
(ANT.) simple, plain, uncompounded.

compliment *(SYN.)* eulogy, flattery, praise, admiration, honor, adulation, flatter, commendation, tribute.
(ANT.) taunt, affront, aspersion, insult, disparage, criticism.

complimentary *(SYN.)* gratis, free.

comply *(SYN.)* assent, consent, accede, acquiesce, coincide, conform, concur, tally.
(ANT.) differ, dissent, protest, disagree.

component *(SYN.)* division, fragment, allotment, moiety, apportionment, scrap, portion, section, share, segment, ingredient, organ.
(ANT.) whole, entirety.

comport *(SYN.)* carry, conduct, behave, act, deport, interact, operate, manage.

compose *(SYN.)* forge, fashion, mold, make, construct, create, produce, shape, form, constitute, arrange, organize, make up, write, invent, devise, frame.
(ANT.) misshape, dismantle, disfigure, destroy.

composed *(SYN.)* calm, cool, imperturbable, placid, quiet, unmoved, sedate, peaceful, collected, tranquil.
(ANT.) aroused, violent, nervous, agitated, perturbed, excited.

composer *(SYN.)* author, inventor, creator, maker, originator.

composition *(SYN.)* paper, theme, work, essay, compound, mixture, mix.

composure *(SYN.)* calmness, poise, control, self-control, self-possession.
(ANT.) anger, rage, turbulence, agitation.

compound *(SYN.)* blend, confound, jumble, consort, aggregate, complicated, combination, combined, mixture, complex, join.
(ANT.) segregate, separate, divide, simple, sort.

comprehend *(SYN.)* apprehend, discern, learn, perceive, see, grasp, understand.
(ANT.) mistake, misunderstand, ignore.

comprehension *(SYN.)* insight, perception, understanding, awareness, discernment.
(ANT.) misconception, insensibility.

comprehensive *(SYN.)* wide, inclusive, complete, broad, full.
(ANT.) fragmentary, partial, limited, incomplete.

compress *(SYN.)* press, compact, squeeze, pack, crowd.
(ANT.) spread, stretch, expand.

comprise *(SYN.)* contain, hold, embrace.
(ANT.) emit, encourage, yield, discharge.

compulsion *(SYN.)* might, energy, potency, strength, vigor.
(ANT.) persuasion, impotence, frailty.

compulsory *(SYN.)* required, obligatory, necessary, unavoidable.
(ANT.) elective, optional, free, unrestricted.

computation *(SYN.)* reckoning, record.
(ANT.) misrepresentation.

compute *(SYN.)* count, calculate, determine, figure, reckon.
(ANT.) conjecture, guess, miscalculate.

comrade *(SYN.)* attendant, companion, colleague, associate, friend.
(ANT.) stranger, enemy, adversary.

con *(SYN.)* cheat, bamboozle, trick, swindle.

conceal *(SYN.)* disguise, cover, hide, mask, screen, secrete, veil, withhold.
(ANT.) reveal, show, disclose, expose.

concede *(SYN.)* permit, suffer, tolerate, grant, give, admit, acknowledge, allow, yield.
(ANT.) forbid, contradict, protest, refuse, deny, negate, resist.

conceit *(SYN.)* pride, vanity, complacency, conception, idea, egotism, self-esteem, caprice, fancy, whim.
(ANT.) humility, meekness, humbleness, modesty.

conceited *(SYN.)* proud, arrogant, vain, smug, egotistical.
(ANT.) humble, modest, self-effacing.

conceive *(SYN.)* design, create, imagine, understand, devise, concoct, perceive, frame, grasp, invent.
(ANT.) imitate, reproduce, copy.

concentrate *(SYN.)* localize, focus, condense, ponder, meditate, center, scrutinize.
(ANT.) scatter, diffuse, dissipate, disperse.

concentrated *(SYN.)* compressed, thick, dense.
(ANT.) sparse, quick, dispersed.

concept *(SYN.)* fancy, conception, image, notion, idea, sentiment, thought.
(ANT.) thing, matter, substance, entity.

conception *(SYN.)* consideration, deliberation, fancy, idea, notion, regard, thought, view.

concern *(SYN.)* matter, anxiety, affair, disturb, care, business, solicitude, interest, affect, involve, touch, trouble, interest, worry.
(ANT.) unconcern, negligence, disinterest, tire, bore, calm, soothe, indifference.

concerning *(SYN.)* regarding, about, respecting.

concerted *(SYN.)* united, joint, com

bined.
(ANT.) *individual, unorganized, separate.*
concession *(SYN.)* admission, yielding, granting.
(ANT.) *insistence, demand.*
concise *(SYN.)* pity, neat, brief, compact, succinct, terse.
(ANT.) *wordy, lengthy, verbose, prolix.*
conclude *(SYN.)* decide, achieve, close, complete, end, finish, terminate, arrange, determine, settle, perfect, perform.
(ANT.) *start, begin, commence.*
concluding *(SYN.)* extreme, final, last, terminal, utmost.
(ANT.) *first, foremost, opening, initial.*
conclusion *(SYN.)* end, finale, termination, deduction, close, settlement, decision, finish, resolution, determination, completion, issue, judgment.
(ANT.) *commencement, inception, opening, start, beginning.*
conclusive *(SYN.)* decisive, eventual, final, terminal, ultimate.
(ANT.) *original, first, inaugural.*
concord *(SYN.)* agreement, unison, understanding, accordance, stipulation.
(ANT.) *disagreement, discord, dissension.*
concrete *(SYN.)* solid, firm, precise, definite, specific.
(ANT.) *undetermined, vague, general.*
concur *(SYN.)* agree, assent, consent, accede.
(ANT.) *dissent, protest, differ.*
condemn *(SYN.)* denounce, reproach, blame, upbraid, convict, rebuke, doom, judge, censure, reprehend, punish, reprobate, sentence.
(ANT.) *condone, forgive, absolve, praise, applaud, extol, approve, pardon, laud, excuse, commend.*
condense *(SYN.)* shorten, reduce, abridge, abbreviate, concentrate, digest, compress, diminish.
(ANT.) *enlarge, increase, swell, expand.*
condition *(SYN.)* circumstance, state, situation, case, plight, requirement, position, necessity, stipulation, predicament, provision, term.
conditional *(SYN.)* dependent, relying.
(ANT.) *casual, original, absolute.*
condolence *(SYN.)* commiseration, concord, harmony, pity, sympathy, warmth.
(ANT.) *harshness, indifference, unconcern.*
conduct *(SYN.)* control, deportment, supervise, manage, behavior, deed, actions, act, behave, manners, deportment.
confederate *(SYN.)* ally, abettor, assistant.
(ANT.) *enemy, rival, opponent, adversary.*
confederation *(SYN.)* combination, league, union, marriage, treaty.
(ANT.) *separation, divorce.*
confer *(SYN.)* gossip, grant, speak, tattle, blab, chat, deliberate, consult, award, give, bestow, talk, mutter.
(ANT.) *retrieve, withdraw.*

confess *(SYN.)* avow, acknowledge, admit, concede, grant, divulge, reveal.
(ANT.) *disown, renounce, deny, conceal.*
confession *(SYN.)* defense, justification, excuse, apology.
(ANT.) *dissimulation, denial, complaint.*
confidence *(SYN.)* firmness, self-reliance, assurance, faith, trust, pledge, declaration, self-confidence, reliance, self-assurance, courage, statement.
(ANT.) *distrust, shyness, mistrust, bashfulness, diffidence, doubt, modesty, suspicion.*
confident *(SYN.)* certain, sure, dauntless, self-assured.
(ANT.) *uncertain, timid, shy.*
confine *(SYN.)* enclose, restrict, hinder, fence, limit, bound.
(ANT.) *release, expose, free, expand, open.*
confirm acknowledge, establish, settle, substantiate, approve, fix, verify, assure, validate, ratify, corroborate, strengthen.
(ANT.) *disclaim, deny, disavow.*
confirmation *(SYN.)* demonstration, experiment, test, trail, verification.
(ANT.) *fallacy, invalidity.*
confirmed *(SYN.)* regular, established, habitual, chronic.
(ANT.) *occasional, infrequent.*
conflict *(SYN.)* duel, combat, fight, collision, discord, encounter, interference, inconsistency, contention, struggle, opposition, clash, oppose, battle, controversy, contend, engagement, contest, variance.
(ANT.) *consonance, harmony, amity.*
confiscate *(SYN.)* capture, catch, gain, purloin, steal, take, clutch, grip, seize, get, obtain, bear.
conflagration *(SYN.)* flame, glow, heat, warmth, fervor, passion, vigor.
(ANT.) *apathy, cold, quiescence.*
conform *(SYN.)* adapt, comply, yield, submit, obey, adjust, agree, fit, suit.
(ANT.) *misapply, misfit, rebel, vary, disagree, disturb.*
conformity *(SYN.)* congruence, accord, agreement, correspondence.
confound *(SYN.)* confuse, baffle, perplex, puzzle, bewilder.
confront *(SYN.)* confront, defy, hinder, resist, thwart, withstand, bar.
(ANT.) *submit, agree, support, succumb.*
confuse *(SYN.)* confound, perplex, mystify, dumbfound, baffle, puzzle, jumble, mislead, mix up, mistake, bewilder.
(ANT.) *explain, instruct, edify, illumine, enlighten, illuminate, solve.*
confused *(SYN.)* deranged, indistinct, disordered, muddled, bewildered, disconcerted, disorganized, perplexed.
(ANT.) *organized, plain, clear, obvious.*
confusion *(SYN.)* commotion, disarray, agitation, disorder, chaos, ferment, stir, perplexity, tumult, bewilderment, disarrangement, uncertainty, muss, mess, turmoil.

(ANT.) order, tranquillity, enlightenment, comprehension, understanding, tidiness, organization, peace.

congregate *(SYN.)* gather, forgather, meet, convene.
(ANT.) scatter, dispel, disperse, dissipate.

congress *(SYN.)* parliament, legislature, assembly.

congruous *(SYN.)* agreeing, conforming, constant, correspondent.
(ANT.) incongruous, inconsistent, discrepant.

conjecture *(SYN.)* law, supposition, theory.
(ANT.) proof, fact, certainty.

conjunction *(SYN.)* combination, junction, connection, link.
(ANT.) separation, disconnection, separation, diversion.

connect *(SYN.)* adjoin, link, combine, relate, join, attach, unite, associate, attribute, affix.
(ANT.) detach, separate, disjoin, untie, dissociation, disconnect, disassociation, unfasten.

connection *(SYN.)* conjunction, alliance, link, affinity, bond, tie, association, relationship, union.
(ANT.) isolation, dissociation, separation, disassociation, disunion.

conquer *(SYN.)* master, beat, humble, defeat, overcome, rout, win, succeed, achieve, gain, overpower, quell, subdue, crush, vanquish.
(ANT.) cede, yield, retreat, surrender.

conquest *(SYN.)* triumph, victory, achievement.
(ANT.) surrender, failure, defeat.

conscientious *(SYN.)* upright, straight, honest, incorruptible, scrupulous.
(ANT.) careless, irresponsible, slovenly.

conscious *(SYN.)* cognizant, informed, perceptive, aware, intentional, sensible, awake, purposeful, deliberate, sensible.
(ANT.) unaware, insensible, asleep, comatose, ignorant.

consecrate *(SYN.)* exalt, extol, hallow, honor.
(ANT.) mock, degrade, debase, abuse.

consecrated *(SYN.)* holy, divine, devout, spiritual.
(ANT.) evil, worldly, secular.

consent *(SYN.)* permission, leave, agree, let, assent, agreement, license, permit.
(ANT.) refusal, opposition, denial, dissent, prohibition.

consequence *(SYN.)* outcome, issue, result, effect, significance, importance.
(ANT.) impetus, cause.

consequential *(SYN.)* significant, important, weighty.
(ANT.) trivial, unimportant, minor, insignificant.

consequently *(SYN.)* hence, thence, therefore.

conservative *(SYN.)* conventional, reactionary, cautious, moderate, careful.
(ANT.) radical, liberal, rash, foolhardy, reckless.

conserve *(SYN.)* save, retain, reserve, guard, keep, support, sustain.

(ANT.) dismiss, neglect, waste, reject, discard.

consider *(SYN.)* heed, ponder, contemplate, examine, study, weigh, reflect, think about, regard, deliberate, respect.
(ANT.) ignore, overlook, disdain, disregard, neglect.

considerable *(SYN.)* much, noteworthy, worthwhile, significant, important.

considerate *(SYN.)* careful, considerate, heedful, prudent, kind, thoughtful, polite, introspective, reflective.
(ANT.) thoughtless, heedless, inconsiderate, selfish, rash.

consideration *(SYN.)* kindness, care, heed, politeness, empathy, notice, watchfulness, kindliness, thoughtfulness, courtesy, concern, sympathy, thought, attention, reflection, fee, pay, study.
(ANT.) omission, oversight, negligence.

consistent *(SYN.)* conforming, accordant, compatible, agreeing, faithful, constant, harmonious, expected, regular, congruous, correspondent.
(ANT.) paradoxical, discrepant, contrary, antagonistic, opposed, eccentric, inconsistent, incongruous.

consolation *(SYN.)* enjoyment, sympathy, relief, ease, contentment, comfort, solace.
(ANT.) discomfort, suffering, discouragement, torture, burden, misery.

console *(SYN.)* solace, comfort, sympathize with, assuage, soothe.
(ANT.) worry, annoy, upset, disturb, distress.

consolidate *(SYN.)* blend, combine, conjoin, fuse, mix, merge, unite.
(ANT.) decompose, separate, analyze, disintegrate.

consort *(SYN.)* companion, comrade, friend.
(ANT.) stranger, enemy, adversary.

conspicuous *(SYN.)* distinguished, clear, manifest, salient, noticeable, striking, obvious, prominent, visible.
(ANT.) hidden, obscure, neutral, common, inconspicuous.

conspiracy *(SYN.)* machination, combination, treason, intrigue, cabal, treachery, plot, collusion.

conspire *(SYN.)* plan, intrigue, plot, scheme.

constancy *(SYN.)* devotion, faithfulness, accuracy, precision, exactness.
(ANT.) faithlessness, treachery, perfidy.

constant *(SYN.)* continual, invariable, abiding, permanent, faithful, invariant, true, ceaseless, enduring, unchanging, steadfast, unchangeable, loyal, stable, immutable, staunch, steady, fixed.
(ANT.) fickle, irregular, wavering, off-and-on, infrequent, occasional, mutable.

constantly *(SYN.)* eternally, ever, evermore, forever, unceasingly.
(ANT.) rarely, sometimes, never, occasionally.

consternation *(SYN.)* apprehension, dismay, alarm, fear, fright, dread, horror, terror.

(ANT.) *bravery, courage, boldness, assurance.*

constitute (SYN.) compose, found, form, establish, organize, create, appoint, delegate, authorize, commission.

constitution (SYN.) law, code, physique, health, vitality.

constrain (SYN.) necessity, indigence, need, want, poverty.
(ANT.) *luxury, freedom, uncertainty.*

construct (SYN.) build, form, erect, make, fabricate, raise, frame.
(ANT.) *raze, demolish, destroy.*

construction (SYN.) raising, building, fabricating.

constructive (SYN.) useful, helpful, valuable.
(ANT.) *ruinous, destructive.*

construe (SYN.) explain, interpret, solve, render, translate.
(ANT.) *distort, confuse, misconstrue.*

consult (SYN.) discuss, chatter, discourse, gossip, confer, report, rumor, deliberate, speech, talk.
(ANT.) *writing, correspondence, silence.*

consume (SYN.) engulf, absorb, use up, use, expend, exhaust, devour, devastate, destroy, engross.
(ANT.) *emit, expel, exude, discharge.*

consumer (SYN.) user, buyer, purchaser.

consummate (SYN.) close, conclude, do finish, perfect, terminate.

consummation (SYN.) climax, apex, culmination, peak.
(ANT.) *depth, base, floor.*

contact (SYN.) meeting, touching.

contagious (SYN.) infectious, virulent, communicable, catching.
(ANT.) *noncommunicable, healthful, hygienic.*

contain (SYN.) embody, hold, embrace, include, accommodate, repress, restrain.
(ANT.) *emit, encourage, yield, discharge.*

contaminate (SYN.) corrupt, sully, taint, defile, soil, pollute, dirty, infect, poison.
(ANT.) *purify.*

contemplate (SYN.) imagine, recollect, consider, study, reflect upon, observe, deliberate, muse, ponder, plan, intend, view, regard, think about, reflect, think, mean.
(ANT.) *forget, guess, conjecture.*

contemplative (SYN.) simultaneous, meditative, thoughtful, contemporaneous, pensive, studious.
(ANT.) *inattentive, indifferent, thoughtless.*

contemporary (SYN.) modern, present, simultaneous, fashionable, coexisting, contemporaneous, up-to-date.
(ANT.) *old, antecedent, past, ancient, succeeding, bygone.*

contempt (SYN.) detestation, malice, contumely, disdain, derision, scorn.
(ANT.) *respect, reverence, admiration, esteem, awe.*

contemptible (SYN.) base, mean, vile, vulgar, nasty, low, detestable, selfish,
miserable, offensive.
(ANT.) *generous, honorable, noble, exalted, admirable.*

contemptuous (SYN.) disdainful, sneering, scornful, insolent.
(ANT.) *modest, humble.*

contend (SYN.) dispute, combat, contest, assert, claim, argue, maintain.

content (SYN.) pleased, happy, contented, satisfied.
(ANT.) *restless, dissatisfied, discontented.*

contented (SYN.) delighted, fortunate, gay, happy, joyous, lucky, merry.
(ANT.) *gloomy, blue, depressed.*

contention (SYN.) combat, duel, struggle, discord, battle, variance.
(ANT.) *concord, harmony, amity, consonance.*

contentment (SYN.) delight, happiness, gladness, pleasure, satisfaction.
(ANT.) *misery, sorrow, grief, sadness, despair.*

contest (SYN.) dispute, debate, competition, tournament, oppose, discuss, quarrel, squabble.
(ANT.) *allow, concede, agree, assent.*

continence (SYN.) forbearance, temperance.
(ANT.) *self-indulgence, excess, intoxication.*

contingency (SYN.) likelihood, possibility, occasion, circumstance.

contingent (SYN.) depending, subject.
(ANT.) *independent, original, casual.*

continual (SYN.) constant, unceasing, everlasting, unremitting, endless, continuous, uninterrupted, regular, connected, consecutive, ceaseless.
(ANT.) *periodic, rare, irregular, occasional, interrupted.*

continue (SYN.) proceed, extend, endure, persist, resume, renew, recommence, last, remain, last, prolong, pursue.
(ANT.) *check, cease, discontinue, stop, suspend.*

continuous (SYN.) continuing, uninterrupted, ceaseless, unceasing, incessant, constant.
(ANT.) *intermittent, irregular, sporadic.*

contract (SYN.) condense, diminish, reduce, bargain, restrict, agreement, compact, pact, shrink, get, treaty, shorten.
(ANT.) *lengthen, extend, swell, expand, elongate.*

contraction (SYN.) reduction, shortening.
(ANT.) *enlargement, expansion, extension.*

contradict (SYN.) gainsay, counter, oppose, confute, dispute.
(ANT.) *verify, confirm, agree, support.*

contradictory (SYN.) inconsistent, conflicting, incompatible, paradoxical, unsteady.
(ANT.) *congruous, consistent, correspondent.*

contrary (SYN.) disagreeable, perverse, hostile, stubborn, opposite, opposing, opposed, disagreeing, disastrous, conflicting, headstrong, unlucky.

contrast *(SYN.)* differentiate, compare, distinction, disagreement, distinguish, differ, discriminate, difference, oppose.
(ANT.) agreement, similarity, likeness.

contribute *(SYN.)* grant, give, donate, bestow, provide, offer.
(ANT.) deny, withhold.

contribution *(SYN.)* grant, gift, offering, donation.

contrition *(SYN.)* grief, regret, self-reproach.
(ANT.) self-satisfaction, complacency.

contrive *(SYN.)* devise, intend, plan, make, invent, plot, hatch, form, project, arrange, manage, maneuver, scheme, sketch.

control *(SYN.)* govern, regulate, rule, command, dominate, direct, manage, check, repress, curb, management, mastery, direction, restraint, superintend, restrain.
(ANT.) ignore, forsake, follow, submit, abandon.

controversy *(SYN.)* disagreement, dispute, debate.
(ANT.) agreement, harmony, accord, concord, decision.

convenience *(SYN.)* accessibility, aid, benefit, help, service, availability.
(ANT.) inconvenience.

convenient *(SYN.)* adapted, appropriate, fitting, favorable, handy, suitable, accessible, nearby, ready, available, advantageous, timely.
(ANT.) inconvenient, troublesome, awkward.

convention *(SYN.)* meeting, conference, assembly, practice, custom, rule.

conventional *(SYN.)* common, regular, usual, everyday, habitual, routine, accustomed.
(ANT.) exotic, unusual, bizarre, extraordinary.

conversant *(SYN.)* aware, intimate, familiar, versed, close, friendly, sociable.
(ANT.) affected, distant, cold, reserved.

conversation *(SYN.)* colloquy, dialogue, chat, parley, discussion, talk.

converse *(SYN.)* jabber, talk, argue, comment, harangue, plead, rant, spout, discuss, chat, talk, speak, reason.

conversion *(SYN.)* alteration, change, mutation, modification, metamorphosis.

convert *(SYN.)* change, alter, alter, turn, transform, shift, modify, exchange, win over, vary, veer.
(ANT.) establish, stabilize, settle, retain.

convey *(SYN.)* carry, bear, communicate, transport, transmit, support, sustain.
(ANT.) drop, abandon.

conveyance *(SYN.)* van, car, train, truck, plane.

convict *(SYN.)* felon, offender, criminal.

conviction *(SYN.)* opinion, position, view, faith, belief, confidence,

feeling, reliance, trust.
(ANT.) doubt, heresy, incredulity, denial.

convince *(SYN.)* persuade, assure, exhort, induce, influence.
(ANT.) deter, compel, restrain, dissuade.

convivial *(SYN.)* jolly, social, jovial, gregarious.
(ANT.) solemn, stern, unsociable.

convoy *(SYN.)* with, attend, chaperon.
(ANT.) avoid, desert, quit, leave.

cool *(SYN.)* frosty, chilly, icy, cold, wintry, quiet, composed, collected, distant, unfriendly, quiet, moderate.
(ANT.) hot, warm, heated, overwrought, excited, hysterical, friendly, outgoing.

cooperate *(SYN.)* unite, combine, help, contribute, support.

coordinate *(SYN.)* attune, harmonize, adapt, match, balance.

copious *(SYN.)* ample, abundant, bountiful, overflowing, plentiful, profuse, rich.
(ANT.) scant, scarce, insufficient, meager, deficient.

copy *(SYN.)* facsimile, exemplar, imitation, duplicate, reproduction, likeness, print, carbon, transcript.
(ANT.) prototype, original.

cordial *(SYN.)* polite, friendly, affable, genial, earnest, gracious, warm, ardent, warmhearted, hearty, sincere.
(ANT.) unfriendly, cool, aloof, hostile, ill-tempered, reserved.

core *(SYN.)* midpoint, heart, kernel, center, middle.
(ANT.) outskirts, border, surface, outside, boundary, rim.

corporation *(SYN.)* business, organization, crew, group, troop, society, company, conglomerate, firm.
(ANT.) individual, dispersion, seclusion.

corpse *(SYN.)* cadaver, carcass, remains, body, form.
(ANT.) spirit, soul, mind, intellect.

corpulent *(SYN.)* obese, portly, chubby, stout.
(ANT.) slim, thin, slender, lean, gaunt.

correct *(SYN.)* true, set right, faultless, impeccable, proper, accurate, precise, mend, right, rebuke, punish, amend, rectify, better, emend, caution, discipline, exact, strict.
(ANT.) condone, aggravate, false, inaccurate, wrong, untrue, faulty.

correction *(SYN.)* order, improvement, regulation, instruction, amendment, emendation, remedy, rectification, repair, training, punishment.
(ANT.) confusion, turbulence, chaos.

correlative *(SYN.)* allied, correspondent, like, similar, parallel.
(ANT.) different, opposed, divergent.

correspond *(SYN.)* compare, coincide, match, agree, suit, fit, write.
(ANT.) differ, diverge, vary.

correspondent *(SYN.)* allied, alike, comparable, like, parallel, similar.
(ANT.) different, opposed, divergent, dissimilar.

corridor *(SYN.)* hallway, hall, foyer,

passage, lobby, passageway.
corrode *(SYN.)* erode.
corrupt *(SYN.)* crooked, untrustworthy, treacherous, debased, unscrupulous, wicked, evil, low, contaminated, perverted, bribe, depraved, corrupted, demoralize, degrade, venal, putrid, tainted, dishonest, impure.
(ANT.) upright, honest, pure, sanctify, edify, purify, sanctified, scrupulous.
corrupted *(SYN.)* crooked, dishonest, impure, spoiled, unsound.
cost *(SYN.)* price, value, damage, charge, loss, sacrifice, penalty, worth.
costly *(SYN.)* dear, expensive.
(ANT.) cheap, inexpensive.
costume *(SYN.)* dress, clothes, apparel, clothing, garb.
couch *(SYN.)* davenport, sofa, loveseat.
council *(SYN.)* caution, instruction, committee, cabinet, board, suggestion.
counsel *(SYN.)* guidance, attorney, lawyer, counselor, hint, imply, opinion, advice, offer, advise.
(ANT.) declare, dictate, insist.
count *(SYN.)* consider, number, enumerate, total, figure, compute, tally, estimate.
(ANT.) conjecture, guess, miscalculate.
countenance *(SYN.)* visage, face, aspect, support, appearance, approval, encouragement, favor.
(ANT.) forbid, prohibit.
counteract *(SYN.)* thwart, neutralize, offset, counterbalance, defeat.
counterfeit *(SYN.)* false, fraudulent, pretended, pretend, sham, imitate, forgery, artificial, bogus, fake, spurious, imitation, unreal.
(ANT.) authentic, natural, real, genuine, true.
country *(SYN.)* state, nation, forest, farmland.
(ANT.) city.
couple *(SYN.)* team, pair, accompany, associate, attach, combine, connect, brace, join, link, unite.
(ANT.) detach, separate, disjoin, disconnect.
courage *(SYN.)* fearlessness, boldness, chivalry, fortitude, mettle, spirit, daring, bravery, prowess, intrepidity, valor, resolution.
(ANT.) fear, timidity, cowardice.
courageous *(SYN.)* bold, dauntless, brave, daring, intrepid, valorous, plucky, fearless, heroic, valiant.
(ANT.) fearful, weak, timid, cowardly.
course *(SYN.)* passage, advance, path, road, progress, way, direction, bearing, route, street, track, trail, way.
courteous *(SYN.)* civil, respectful, polite, genteel, well-mannered, gracious, refined.
(ANT.) discourteous, rude, uncivil, impolite, boorish.
courtesy *(SYN.)* graciousness, politeness, respect.
(ANT.) discourtesy, rudeness.
covenant *(SYN.)* agreement, concord, harmony, unison, compact, stipulation.

(ANT.) variance, discord, dissension, difference.
cover *(SYN.)* clothe, conceal, disguise, curtain, guard, envelop, mask, cloak, shield, hide, screen, protect, embrace, top, lid, covering, stopper, protection, refuge, spread, overlay, include, veil.
(ANT.) bare, expose, reveal.
covert *(SYN.)* potential, undeveloped, concealed, dormant.
(ANT.) explicit, visible, manifest.
covetous *(SYN.)* grasping, greedy, acquisitive, avaricious.
(ANT.) generous.
coward *(SYN.)* milquetoast, cad.
(ANT.) hero.
cowardice *(SYN.)* dread, dismay, fright, dismay, panic, terror, timidity.
(ANT.) fearlessness, courage, bravery.
cowardly *(SYN.)* fearful, timorous, afraid, faint-hearted, yellow, pusillanimous, spineless.
cower *(SYN.)* wince, flinch, cringe, quail, tremble.
coy *(SYN.)* embarrassed, sheepish, shy, timid.
(ANT.) fearless, outgoing, bold, adventurous, daring.
crack *(SYN.)* snap, break, split.
cracker *(SYN.)* wafer, biscuit, saltine.
craft *(SYN.)* talent, skill, expertness, ability, cunning, guile, deceit, trade, profession, occupation.
crafty *(SYN.)* covert, clever, cunning, skillful, foxy, tricky, sly, underhand, shrewd.
(ANT.) frank, sincere, gullible, open, guileless, ingenuous.
craggy *(SYN.)* rough, rugged, irregular, uneven.
(ANT.) level, sleek, smooth, fine, polished.
crank *(SYN.)* cross, irritable, bad-tempered, testy.
(ANT.) cheerful, happy.
crash *(SYN.)* smash, shatter, dash.
crave *(SYN.)* want, desire, hunger for.
(ANT.) relinquish, renounce.
craving *(SYN.)* relish appetite, desire, liking, longing, passion.
(ANT.) renunciation, distaste, disgust.
crazy *(SYN.)* delirious, deranged, idiotic, mad, insane, demented, foolish, maniacal.
(ANT.) sane, sensible, sound, rational, reasonable.
creak *(SYN.)* squeak.
create *(SYN.)* fashion, form, generate, engender, formulate, make, originate, produce, cause, ordain, invent, beget, design, construct, constitute.
(ANT.) disband, abolish, terminate, destroy, demolish.
creative *(SYN.)* imaginative, ingenious, original, resourceful, clever, inventive, innovative, mystical.
(ANT.) unromantic, dull, literal.
credence *(SYN.)* confidence, faith, feeling, opinion, trust.
(ANT.) doubt, incredulity, denial.
credible *(SYN.)* conceivable, believable.
(ANT.) inconceivable, unbelievable.
credit *(SYN.)* believe, accept, belief,

trust, faith, merit, honor, apprehend, fancy, hold, support.
(ANT.) doubt, reject, question, distrust.
creditable (SYN.) worthy, praiseworthy.
(ANT.) dishonorable, discreditable, shameful.
credulous (SYN.) trusting, naive, believing, gullible, unsuspicious.
(ANT.) suspicious.
creed (SYN.) belief, precept, credo, faith, teaching.
(ANT.) practice, deed, conduct, performance.
creek (SYN.) brook, spring, stream, rivulet.
crime (SYN.) offense, insult, aggression, wrongdoing, wrong, misdeed.
(ANT.) right, gentleness, innocence, morality.
criminal (SYN.) unlawful, crook, gangster, outlaw, illegal, convict, delinquent, offender, malefactor, culprit, felonious, felon, transgressor.
cripple (SYN.) hurt, maim, damage, injure.
crippled (SYN.) deformed, disabled, maimed, hobbling, limping, unconvincing, unsatisfactory.
(ANT.) robust, sound, vigorous, athletic.
crisis (SYN.) conjuncture, emergency, pass, pinch, acme, climax, contingency, juncture, exigency, strait.
(ANT.) calm, normality, stability, equilibrium.
crisp (SYN.) crumbling, delicate, frail, brittle.
(ANT.) calm, normality, stability.
criterion (SYN.) measure, law, rule, principle, gauge, proof.
(ANT.) fancy guess, chance, supposition.
critic (SYN.) reviewer, judge, commentator, censor, defamer, slanderer, faultfinder.
critical (SYN.) exact, fastidious, caviling, faultfinding, accurate, risky.
(ANT.) shallow, uncritical, approving, insignificant, trivial, unimportant.
criticize (SYN.) examine, analyze, inspect, blame, censure, appraise.
(ANT.) neglect, overlook, approve.
crooked (SYN.) twisted, corrupt, hooked, curved, criminal, dishonest.
(ANT.) improved, raised, straight.
crop (SYN.) fruit, produce, harvest, cut, mow, reaping, result, yield.
cross (SYN.) mix, mingle, traverse, interbreed, annoyed, irritable, cranky.
(ANT.) cheerful.
crouch (SYN.) duck, stoop.
crow (SYN.) boast, brag.
crowd (SYN.) masses, flock, host, squeeze, mob, multitude, press.
crown (SYN.) coronet, apex, crest, circlet, pinnacle, tiara, skull, head.
(ANT.) base, bottom, foundation, foot.
crude (SYN.) rude, graceless, unpolished, green, harsh, rough, coarse.
(ANT.) finished, refined, polished.
cruel (SYN.) ferocious, mean, heartless, unmerciful, malignant, savage, brutal.
(ANT.) humane, forbearing, kind, compassionate, merciful, benevolent.

cruelty (SYN.) harshness, meanness, savagery, brutality.
(ANT.) compassion, kindness.
crumb (SYN.) jot, grain, mite, particle, shred.
(ANT.) mass, bulk, quantity.
crunch (SYN.) champ, gnaw, nibble.
crush (SYN.) smash, break, crash.
cry (SYN.) yowl, yell, roar, shout, bellow, scream, wail, weep, bawl, sob.
culprit (SYN.) delinquent, felon, offender.
cultivate (SYN.) plant, seed, farm, till, refine, educate, teach.
cultivation (SYN.) farming, horticulture, tillage, agriculture.
cultural (SYN.) civilizing, educational, elevating, instructive.
culture (SYN.) humanism, upbringing, cultivation, breeding, education.
(ANT.) illiteracy, vulgarity, ignorance.
cultured (SYN.) sophisticated, worldly.
(ANT.) crude, simple, uncouth.
cumbersome (SYN.) clumsy, awkward.
(ANT.) handy.
cunning (SYN.) clever, wily, crafty, foxy, skillful, tricky, ingenious, foxiness, ability, skill, wiliness, devious, shrewdness, slyness, cleverness, crooked.
(ANT.) gullible, honest, naive, openness, straightforward, simple, direct.
curb (SYN.) check, restraint, hinder.
(ANT.) aid, loosen, incite, encourage.
cure (SYN.) help, treatment, heal.
curiosity (SYN.) wonder, marvel, rarity.
(ANT.) apathy, indifference.
curious (SYN.) interrogative, interested.
(ANT.) unconcerned, incurious.
current (SYN.) up-to-date, modern.
(ANT.) antiquated, old, ancient, past.
curse (SYN.) ban, oath, denounce.
(ANT.) boon, blessing, advantage.
cursory (SYN.) frivolous, shallow, slight.
(ANT.) complete, deep, profound.
curt (SYN.) hasty, short, abrupt, blunt, rude, harsh.
(ANT.) friendly, smooth, gradual, polite.
curtail (SYN.) condense, reduce, limit, abbreviate.
(ANT.) lengthen, extend.
curtain (SYN.) blind, drapery, drape.
curve (SYN.) crook, deflect, bend, twist.
(ANT.) resist, stiffen, straighten.
cushion (SYN.) pillow, pad, check.
custodian (SYN.) guard, keeper, guardian, watchman.
custody (SYN.) guardianship, care.
(ANT.) neglect, disregard, indifference.
custom (SYN.) fashion, rule, routine, practice, usage.
customary (SYN.) common, usual.
(ANT.) exceptional, irregular, rare.
customer (SYN.) patron, client, buyer.
cut (SYN.) slash, gash, prick, slit, sever.
cut back (SYN.) decrease, reduce.
cut in (SYN.) butt in, interfere.
cut off (SYN.) cease, end, stop, terminate.
cut short (SYN.) stop, finish, end, quit.
cutting (SYN.) bitter, stern, caustic, scathing, harsh, acerbic.
cylindrical (SYN.) circular, curved, plump, rotund, spherical, round.

dab *(SYN.)* coat, pat, smear.

dabble *(SYN.)* splatter, toy, splash, fiddle, putter.

daft *(SYN.)* crazy, foolish, insane.

dagger *(SYN.)* knife, dirk, blade.

daily *(SYN.)* every day, diurnal, regularly.

dainty *(SYN.)* slender, pleasing, delicate, frail, pleasant, pretty, petite.
(ANT.) uncouth, vulgar, coarse, tough.

dam *(SYN.)* dike, levee, barrier, slow, stop, check, obstruct, block.
(ANT.) free, release, loose, unleash.

damage *(SYN.)* spoil, deface, impair, mar, hurt, injury, impairment, destruction, harm, injure.
(ANT.) repair, benefit, mend, rebuild, improve, ameliorate.

dame *(SYN.)* woman, lady.

damp *(SYN.)* humid, dank, moisture, wetness, dampness, humidity.
(ANT.) arid, dry.

dampen *(SYN.)* wet, depressed, moisten, dull, suppress, sprinkle, discouraged, retard, slow, muffle, inhibit.
(ANT.) dehumidify, increase, encourage.

dance *(SYN.)* bounce, flit, skip, sway, prance, bob, glide, caper, cavort, frisk.

dandle *(SYN.)* jounce, joggle, bounce, jiggle, nestle, cuddle, caress.

danger *(SYN.)* jeopardy, risk, threat, hazard, uncertainty, peril.
(ANT.) safety, immunity, security.

dangerous *(SYN.)* risky, insecure, threatening, critical, perilous, unsafe.
(ANT.) trustworthy, protected, safe.

dangle *(SYN.)* droop, swing, flap, hang.

dare *(SYN.)* brave, call, question, defy, risk, challenge, summon.

daring *(SYN.)* foolhardy, chivalrous, rash, fearless, courageous, intrepid.
(ANT.) timid, cowardice, timidity.

dark *(SYN.)* somber, obscure, gloomy, black, dim, evil, hidden, secret.
(ANT.) lucid, light, happy, cheerful.

darling *(SYN.)* dear, adored, sweetheart, favorite, cherished.
(ANT.) unlovable, rejected, forlorn.

darn *(SYN.)* repair, mend.

dart *(SYN.)* scurry, arrow, barb, hurry, dash, throw, missile, run, hasten.

dash *(SYN.)* pound, thump, beat, smite, buffet, thrash, smash, break, scurry.
(ANT.) stroke, encourage, defend.

data *(SYN.)* information, statistics.

date *(SYN.)* interview, appointment.

dated *(SYN.)* out-of-date, old-fashioned.
(ANT.) latest, current, fashionable, hot.

dawn *(SYN.)* sunrise, start, outset.
(ANT.) dusk, sunset, nightfall, end.

daze *(SYN.)* perplex, stun, puzzle, bewilder, upset, confuse, confusion.

dazzle *(SYN.)* surprise, stun, astonish, impress, bewilder, stupefy.

dead *(SYN.)* lifeless, deceased, dull.
(ANT.) animate, functioning, active.

deadly *(SYN.)* lethal, mortal, fatal.

deaf *(SYN.)* unhearing, unaware.
(ANT.) aware, conscious.

deal *(SYN.)* act, treat, attend, cope, barter, trade, bargain, apportion, give.

dear *(SYN.)* valued, esteemed, expensive, beloved, costly, darling.

(ANT.) hateful, reasonable, unwanted.

death *(SYN.)* decease, extinction, demise, passing.
(ANT.) life.

debase *(SYN.)* lower, degrade, alloy, adulterate, defile, humiliate, depress.
(ANT.) restore, improve, vitalize.

debris *(SYN.)* rubbish, litter, junk.

debt *(SYN.)* amount due, liability, obligation.

decay *(SYN.)* spoil, waste, disintegrate, perish, rot, collapse, decompose.
(ANT.) progress, increase, grow, flourish.

deceased *(SYN.)* lifeless, departed, dead.
(ANT.) living, alive.

deceit *(SYN.)* duplicity, cheat, fraud, chicanery, trick, cunning, deception.
(ANT.) truthfulness, openness.

deceitful *(SYN.)* false, fraudulent, insincere, dishonest, deceptive.
(ANT.) sincere, honest.

deceive *(SYN.)* cheat, defraud, hoodwink, mislead, swindle.

decency *(SYN.)* decorum, dignity, propriety, respectability.

decent *(SYN.)* befitting, fit, suitable, becoming, respectable, adequate, seemly.
(ANT.) vulgar, gross, improper, unsuitable, indecorous, indecent, coarse.

deception *(SYN.)* trick, cheat, sham, deceit, trickery, craftiness, treachery.
(ANT.) openness, frankness, candor, probity, truthfulness, honesty.

deceptive *(SYN.)* specious, fallacious, deceitful, false, delusive, unreliable.
(ANT.) honest, real, genuine, true, truthful, authentic.

decide *(SYN.)* resolve, determine, terminate, conclude, close, settle.
(ANT.) waver, hesitate, vacillate, doubt, suspend.

decipher *(SYN.)* render, unravel, construe, solve, decode, translate.
(ANT.) misconstrue, distort, misinterpret, confuse.

decision *(SYN.)* resolution, determination, settlement.

decisive *(SYN.)* determined, firm, decided, unhesitating, resolute.

declaration *(SYN.)* pronouncement, notice, affirmation, statement.

declare *(SYN.)* assert, promulate, affirm, tell, broadcast, express, proclaim,
(ANT.) deny, withhold, conceal.

decline *(SYN.)* descend, decay, dwindle, refuse, incline, wane, sink, depreciate.
(ANT.) accept, ascend, ameliorate, increase.

decompose *(SYN.)* rot, disintegrate, molder, decay, crumble.

decorate *(SYN.)* trim, paint, deck, enrich, color, beautify, enhance, furbish.
(ANT.) uncover, mar, deface, defame.

decoration *(SYN.)* ornamentation, embellishment, adornment, furnishing.

decoy *(SYN.)* lure, bait.

decrease *(SYN.)* lessen, wane, deduct, diminish, curtail, deduct, remove.
(ANT.) expansion, increase, enlarge, expand, grow.

decree *(SYN.)* order, edict, statute, declaration, announce, act.

decrepit *(SYN.)* feeble, weakened, rick-

ety, weak, run-down, tumble-down.
(ANT.) strong, forceful, vigorous, energetic, lusty.

decry (SYN.) lower, belittle, derogate, minimize, undervalue.
(ANT.) praise, commend, magnify.

dedicate (SYN.) sanctify, consecrate, hallow, devote, assign.

dedicated (SYN.) disposed, true, affectionate, fond, wedded.
(ANT.) indisposed, detached, untrammeled, disinclined.

deduct (SYN.) lessen, shorten, abate, remove, eliminate, curtail, subtract.
(ANT.) grow, enlarge, add, increase, amplify, expand.

deed (SYN.) feat, action, performance, act, operation, achievement, document, certificate, title.
(ANT.) intention, cessation, inactivity, deliberation.

deem (SYN.) hold, determine, believe, regard, reckon, judge, consider.

deep (SYN.) bottomless, low, unplumbed, acute, obscure, involved.
(ANT.) shallow.

deface (SYN.) spoil, impair, damage, mar, hurt, scratch, mutilate, disfigure.
(ANT.) mend, benefit, repair, enhance.

defamation (SYN.) invective, reproach, upbraiding, abuse, insult, outrage.
(ANT.) respect, approval, laudation, commendation.

default (SYN.) loss, omission, lack, failure, want, dereliction.
(ANT.) victory, achievement, sufficiency, success.

defeat (SYN.) quell, vanquish, beat, overcome, overthrow, subdue.
(ANT.) submit, retreat, cede, yield, surrender, capitulate, lose.

defect (SYN.) shortcoming, fault, omission, blemish, imperfection, forsake.
(ANT.) perfection, flawlessness, support, join, completeness.

defective (SYN.) faulty, imperfect, inoperative, flawed, inoperable.
(ANT.) flawless, perfect, faultless.

defend (SYN.) screen, espouse, justify, protect, vindicate, fortify, assert.
(ANT.) oppose, assault, submit, attack, deny.

defense (SYN.) resistance, protection, bulwark, fort, barricade, trench.

defer (SYN.) postpone, delay.
(ANT.) speed, hurry, expedite.

deference (SYN.) fame, worship, adoration, reverence, admiration, respect.
(ANT.) dishonor, derision, reproach, contempt.

defiant (SYN.) rebellious, antagonistic, obstinate.
(ANT.) yielding, submissive.

deficient (SYN.) lacking, short, incomplete, defective, scanty, insufficient.
(ANT.) enough, ample, sufficient, adequate.

defile (SYN.) pollute, march, corrupt, dirty, file, debase, contaminate.
(ANT.) purify.

define (SYN.) describe, fix, establish, label, designate, set, name, explain.

definite (SYN.) fixed, prescribed, certain, specific, exact, determined.
(ANT.) indefinite, confused, undetermined, equivocal.

definitely (SYN.) certainly, assuredly, absolutely, positively, surely.

definition (SYN.) sense, interpretation, meaning, explanation.

deft (SYN.) handy, adroit, clever, adept, dexterous, skillful, skilled.
(ANT.) inept, clumsy, maladroit, awkward.

defunct (SYN.) lifeless, dead, departed, expired, extinct, spiritless, inanimate.
(ANT.) living, alive, stirring.

defy (SYN.) hinder, oppose, withstand, attack, resist, confront, challenge.
(ANT.) yield, allow, relent, surrender, submit, accede.

degenerate (SYN.) dwindle, decline, weaken, deteriorate, decrease.
(ANT.) ascend, ameliorate, increase, appreciate.

degrade (SYN.) crush, reduce, subdue, abash, humble, lower, shame, demote.
(ANT.) praise, elevate, honor.

degree (SYN.) grade, amount, step, measure, rank, honor, extent.

deign (SYN.) condescend, stoop.

dejected (SYN.) depressed, downcast, sad, disheartened, blue, discouraged.
(ANT.) cheerful, happy, optimistic.

delectable (SYN.) tasty, delicious, savory, delightful, sweet, luscious.
(ANT.) unsavory, distasteful, unpalatable, acrid.

delegate (SYN.) emissary, envoy, ambassador, representative, commission.

delete (SYN.) erase, cancel, remove.
(ANT.) add.

deliberate (SYN.) studied, willful, intended, contemplated, premeditated.
(ANT.) fortuitous, hasty, accidental.

delicate (SYN.) frail, critical, slender, dainty, pleasing, fastidious, exquisite.
(ANT.) tough, strong, coarse, clumsy, hearty, hale, vulgar, rude.

delicious (SYN.) tasty, luscious, delectable, sweet, savory.
(ANT.) unsavory, distasteful, unpalatable, unpleasant, acrid.

delight (SYN.) joy, bliss, gladness, pleasure, ecstasy, happiness, rapture.
(ANT.) revolt, sorrow, annoyance, displeasure, disgust, displease, revulsion.

delightful (SYN.) pleasing, pleasant, charming, refreshing, pleasurable.
(ANT.) nasty, disagreeable, unpleasant.

delirious (SYN.) raving, mad, giddy, frantic, hysterical, violent.

deliver (SYN.) impart, publish, rescue, commit, communicate, free, address.
(ANT.) restrict, confine, capture, enslave, withhold, imprison.

deluge (SYN.) overflow, flood.

delusion (SYN.) mirage, fantasy, phantasm, vision, dream, illusion, phantom.
(ANT.) substance, actuality.

delve (SYN.) dig, look, search, scoop, explore, hunt.

demand (SYN.) claim, inquire, ask, need, require, obligation, requirement.
(ANT.) tender, give, present, waive, relinquish, offer.

demean *(SYN.)* comport, bear, operate, carry, act, manage, deport.

demeanor *(SYN.)* manner, way, conduct, actions, behavior.

demented *(SYN.)* insane, crazy, mad, mental, psychotic, lunatic.

demolish *(SYN.)* ruin, devastate, ravage, annihilate, wreck, destroy, raze.
(ANT.) erect, make, save, construct, preserve, build, establish.

demolition *(SYN.)* wrecking, destruction.
(ANT.) erection, construction.

demon *(SYN.)* fiend, monster, devil, ogre, spirit.

demonstrate *(SYN.)* evince, show, prove, display, illustrate, describe.
(ANT.) hide, conceal.

demonstration *(SYN.)* exhibit, show, presentation, exhibition, display, rally.

demur *(SYN.)* waver, falter, delay, stutter, doubt, vacillate, hesitate, scruple.
(ANT.) proceed, decide, resolve.

demure *(SYN.)* meek, shy, modest, diffident, retiring, bashful, coy.

den *(SYN.)* cave, lair, cavern.

denial *(SYN.)* disallowance, proscription, refusal, prohibition.

denounce *(SYN.)* condemn, blame, reprove, reprehend, censure, reproach.
(ANT.) condone, approve, forgive, commend, praise.

dense *(SYN.)* crowded, slow, close, obtuse, compact, dull, stupid.
(ANT.) sparse, quick, dispersed, clever, dissipated, empty, smart, bright.

dent *(SYN.)* notch, impress, pit, nick.

deny *(SYN.)* refuse, withhold, dispute, disavow, forbid, refute, contradict.
(ANT.) confirm, affirm, admit, confess, permit, allow, concede, assert.

depart *(SYN.)* quit, forsake, withdraw, renounce, desert, relinquish, die, perish, decease.
(ANT.) tarry, remain, come, abide, stay, arrive.

departure *(SYN.)* valediction, farewell.

depend *(SYN.)* trust, rely, confide.

dependable *(SYN.)* secure, trustworthy, certain, safe, trusty, reliable, tried.
(ANT.) unreliable, fallible, dubious, uncertain.

dependent *(SYN.)* relying, contingent, subordinate, conditional.
(ANT.) original, casual, absolute, independent.

depict *(SYN.)* explain, recount, describe, portray, characterize, relate, narrate.

deplore *(SYN.)* repine, lament, bemoan, wail, bewail, weep, grieve, regret.

deport *(SYN.)* exile, eject, oust, banish, expel, dismiss, ostracize, dispel, exclude.
(ANT.) receive, admit, shelter, accept, harbor.

deportment *(SYN.)* deed, behavior, manner, action, carriage, disposition, bearing, demeanor.

deposit *(SYN.)* place, put, bank, save, store, sediment, dregs, addition, entry.
(ANT.) withdraw, withdrawal.

depreciate *(SYN.)* dwindle, decrease, decay, belittle, disparage, weaken,

minimize, descend, deteriorate.
(ANT.) ascend, ameliorate, praise, increase, applaud, appreciate.

depress *(SYN.)* deject, dishearten, sadden, dampen, devaluate, devalue, lessen, lower, cheapen, reduce, dispirit, discourage, sink.
(ANT.) exalt, cheer, exhilarate.

depression *(SYN.)* hopelessness, despondency, pessimism, dip, cavity, pothole, hole, despair, gloom, melancholy, sadness, sorrow, recession, decline, desperation, discouragement.
(ANT.) eminence, elation, optimism, happiness, confidence, elevation, hope.

deprive *(SYN.)* bereave, deny, strip.
(ANT.) provision, supply, provide.

derelict *(SYN.)* decrepit, shabby, dilapidated, neglected, forsaken, deserted, remiss, abandoned, lax.

dereliction *(SYN.)* want, lack, failure, miscarriage, loss, default, deficiency, omission, fiasco.
(ANT.) sufficiency, success, achievement, victory.

derision *(SYN.)* irony, satire, banter, raillery, sneering, gibe, ridicule.

derivation *(SYN.)* source, birth, inception, start, beginning, spring, commencement, foundation, origin.
(ANT.) issue, end, outcome, harvest, product.

derive *(SYN.)* obtain, acquire, get, receive.

descend *(SYN.)* wane, lower, move, slope, incline, decline, slant, sink.
(ANT.) increase, appreciate, ameliorate, ascend.

descendant *(SYN.)* child, issue, progeny, offspring.

describe *(SYN.)* portray, picture, recount, depict, relate, characterize, represent, narrate.

description *(SYN.)* history, record, recital, account, computation, chronicle, reckoning, narration, detail, narrative.
(ANT.) misrepresentation, confusion, caricature.

desecration *(SYN.)* profanation, insult, defamation, reviling, abuse, maltreatment, aspersion, perversion, dishonor.
(ANT.) respect, commendation, approval, laudation.

desert *(SYN.)* forsake, wilderness, resign, abjure, abandon, wasteland, waste, leave, surrender, abdicate, quit, barren, uninhabited.
(ANT.) uphold, defend, stay, maintain, accompany, join, support.

deserter *(SYN.)* runaway, renegade, fugitive, defector.

deserts *(SYN.)* right, compensation, due, reward, requital, condign.

deserve *(SYN.)* earn, warrant, merit.

design *(SYN.)* drawing, purpose, outline, devise, intend, draw, contrive, draft, cunning, plan, artfulness, delineation, scheming, sketch, intent, invent, objective, mean, contrivance, plotting, intention, create.
(ANT.) candor, accident, result, chance.

designate *(SYN.)* manifest, indicate,

show, specify, denote, reveal, name, appoint, select, assign, disclose, signify, imply, nominate, intimate.
(ANT.) divert, mislead, conceal, falsify, distract.

desirable (SYN.) coveted, wanted.

desire (SYN.) longing, craving, yearning, appetite, lust, long for, crave, covet, want, request, ask, need, wish, aspiration, urge.
(ANT.) hate, aversion, loathing, abomination, detest, loathe, abhor, distaste.

desist (SYN.) cork, stop, cease, hinder, terminate, abstain, halt, interrupt, seal, arrest, plug, bar.
(ANT.) promote, begin, speed, proceed, start.

desolate (SYN.) forlorn, waste, bare, lonely, abandoned, wild, deserted, uninhabited, empty, sad, miserable, wretched, unhappy, bleak, forsaken.
(ANT.) crowded, teeming, populous, happy, cheerful, fertile, attended.

despair (SYN.) discouragement, pessimism, depression, hopelessness, despondency, gloom, desperation.
(ANT.) elation, optimism, hope, joy, confidence.

desperado (SYN.) criminal, crook, thug, gangster, hoodlum.

desperate (SYN.) reckless, determined, despairing, wild, daring, hopeless, despondent, audacious.
(ANT.) optimistic, composed, hopeful, collected, calm, assured.

despicable (SYN.) vulgar, offensive, base, vile, contemptible, selfish, low, mean, worthless, nasty.
(ANT.) noble, exalted, admirable, generous, worthy, dignified.

despise (SYN.) hate, scorn, detest, loathe, disdain, abhor, condemn, dislike, abominate.
(ANT.) honor, love, approve, like, admire.

despite (SYN.) notwithstanding.

despoil (SYN.) plunder, rob, loot.

despondent (SYN.) sad, dismal, depressed, somber, ejected, melancholy, doleful, sorrowful.
(ANT.) joyous, cheerful, merry, happy.

despot (SYN.) tyrant, ruler, oppressor, dictator.

despotic (SYN.) authoritative, unconditional, absolute, tyrannous, entire, unrestricted.
(ANT.) dependent, conditional, qualified, accountable.

destiny (SYN.) fate, portion, outcome, consequence, result, fortune, doom, lot.

destitute (SYN.) poor, penurious, needy, impecunious, poverty-stricken, impoverished, indigent.
(ANT.) opulent, wealthy, affluent, rich.

destroy (SYN.) raze, devastate, ruin, end, demolish, wreck, extinguish, annihilate, exterminate, obliterate, waste, slay, kill, eradicate.
(ANT.) make, construct, start, create, save, establish.

destroyed (SYN.) rent, smashed, interrupted, flattened, wrecked, broken, ruptured, crushed.
(ANT.) whole, repaired, integral, united.

destruction (SYN.) ruin, devastation, extinction, demolition.
(ANT.) beginning, creation.

destructive (SYN.) deadly, baneful, noxious, deleterious, injurious, pernicious, fatal, detrimental.
(ANT.) salutary, beneficial, creative.

detach (SYN.) deduct, remove, subtract, curtail, divide, shorten, decrease, disengage, reduce, separate, diminish.
(ANT.) hitch, grow, enlarge, increase, connect, amplify, attack, expand.

detail (SYN.) elaborate, commission, part, itemize, portion, division, fragment, assign, circumstance, segment.

detain (SYN.) impede, delay, hold back, retard, arrest, restrain, stay.
(ANT.) quicken, hasten, expedite, forward, precipitate.

detect (SYN.) discover, reveal, find, ascertain, determine, learn, originate, devise.
(ANT.) hide, screen, lose, cover, mask.

determinant (SYN.) reason, incentive, source, agent, principle, inducement.
(ANT.) result, effect, consequence, end.

determine (SYN.) decide, settle, end, conclude, ascertain, induce, fix, verify, resolve, establish, necessitate.

detest (SYN.) loathe, hate, despise.
(ANT.) savor, appreciate, like, love.

detriment (SYN.) injury, harm, disadvantage, damage.
(ANT.) benefit.

detrimental (SYN.) hurtful, mischievous, damaging, harmful.
(ANT.) salutary, advantageous, profitable, beneficial.

develop (SYN.) evolve, unfold, enlarge, amplify, expand, create, grow, advance, reveal, unfold, mature, elaborate.
(ANT.) wither, contract, degenerate, stunt, deteriorate, compress.

development (SYN.) growth, expansion, progress, unraveling, elaboration, evolution, maturing, unfolding.
(ANT.) compression, abbreviation, curtailment.

deviate (SYN.) deflect, stray, divert, diverge, wander, sidetrack, digress.
(ANT.) preserve, follow, remain, continue, persist.

device (SYN.) tool, utensil, means, channel, machine, agent, vehicle, gadget, apparatus, tools, instrument, contrivance.
(ANT.) preventive, impediment, hindrance, obstruction.

devilish (SYN.) diabolical, fiendish, diabolic, satanic, demonic.

devious (SYN.) tortuous, winding, distorted, circuitous, tricky, crooked, roundabout, cunning, erratic, indirect.
(ANT.) straight, direct, straightforward, honest.

devise (SYN.) create, concoct, invent, originate.

devote (SYN.) assign, dedicate, give, apply.

(ANT.) *withhold, relinquish, ignore, withdraw.*

devoted *(SYN.)* attached, dedicated, prone, wedded, addicted, ardent, earnest, loyal, disposed, inclined, fond, affectionate, faithful.
(ANT.) *untrammeled, disinclined, detached, indisposed.*

devotion *(SYN.)* piety, zeal, ardor, loyalty, dedication, religiousness, consecration, affection, love, devoutness, fidelity, attachment.
(ANT.) *unfaithfulness, aversion, alienation, indifference.*

devour *(SYN.)* consume, gulp, gorge, waste, eat, ruin, swallow, destroy.

devout *(SYN.)* sacred, religious, spiritual, holy, theological, pietistic, pious, sanctimonious, reverent.
(ANT.) *profane, skeptical, atheistic, secular, impious.*

dexterity *(SYN.)* talent, capability, qualification, aptness, skill, ability.
(ANT.) *unreadiness, incapacity, disability, incompetency.*

dexterous *(SYN.)* clever, adroit, handy, deft, facile, skillful, skilled, proficient.
(ANT.) *awkward, clumsy.*

dialect *(SYN.)* slang, jargon, cant, speech, idiom, tongue, diction, vernacular.
(ANT.) *nonsense, drivel, babble, gibberish.*

dialogue *(SYN.)* interview, chat, discussion, conference, exchange, talk, conversation.

diary *(SYN.)* memo, account, journal, words.

dicker *(SYN.)* haggle, bargain, negotiate.

dictate *(SYN.)* deliver, speak, record, command, order, direct.

dictator *(SYN.)* oppressor, tyrant, despot, persecutor, overlord, autocrat.

die *(SYN.)* fade, wane, cease, depart, wither, decay, decline, sink, expire, perish, decease, go, diminish, fail, languish, decrease.
(ANT.) *live, begin, grow, survive, flourish.*

difference *(SYN.)* inequality, variety, disparity, discord, distinction, dissension, dissimilarity, disagreement, contrast, separation.
(ANT.) *harmony, similarity, identity, agreement, likeness, compatibility, kinship, resemblance.*

different *(SYN.)* unlike, various, distinct, miscellaneous, divergent, sundry, contrary, differing, diverse, variant, incongruous, divers, unlike, changed, dissimilar, opposite.
(ANT.) *similar, congruous, same, alike, identical.*

differentiate *(SYN.)* separate, discriminate, distinguish, perceive, detect, recognize, discern.
(ANT.) *confuse, omit, mingle, confound, overlook.*

difficult *(SYN.)* involved, demanding, arduous, trying, complicated, hard, laborious, perplexing, hard, intricate.
(ANT.) *simple, easy, facile, effortless.*

difficulty *(SYN.)* trouble, hardship, fix, predicament, trouble.
(ANT.) *ease.*

diffuse *(SYN.)* spread, sparse, scattered, scanty, dispersed, thin, rare.
(ANT.) *concentrated.*

dig *(SYN.)* burrow, excavate, appreciate, understand.

digest *(SYN.)* consume, eat, reflect on, study, shorten, consider, summarize, abridge, abstract, abridgment, synopsis.

dignified *(SYN.)* serious, solemn, noble, stately, elegant.

dignify *(SYN.)* honor, elevate.
(ANT.) *shame, degrade, humiliate.*

dignity *(SYN.)* stateliness, distinction, bearing.

digress *(SYN.)* divert, wander, bend, stray, deflect, sidetrack, crook.
(ANT.) *preserve, continue, remain, follow, persist.*

dilate *(SYN.)* increase, widen, amplify, enlarge, augment, expand.
(ANT.) *shrink, contract, restrict, abridge.*

dilemma *(SYN.)* fix, strait, condition, scrape, difficulty, plight.
(ANT.) *ease, calmness, satisfaction, comfort.*

diligent *(SYN.)* patient, busy, hardworking, active, perseverant, assiduous, industrious, careful.
(ANT.) *unconcerned, indifferent, apathetic, lethargic, careless.*

dim *(SYN.)* pale, shadowy, faint, faded, unclear, vague, darken, dull, indistinct.
(ANT.) *brighten, brilliant, bright, illuminate, glaring.*

dimension *(SYN.)* size, importance, measure, extent.

diminish *(SYN.)* suppress, lower, decrease, shrink, wane, abate, reduce, lessen, assuage.
(ANT.) *enlarge, revive, amplify, increase.*

diminutive *(SYN.)* small, wee, tiny, little, minute.
(ANT.) *large, big, great, gigantic, huge.*

din *(SYN.)* tumult, clamor, sound, babble, outcry, row, noise, racket.
(ANT.) *quiet, stillness, hush.*

dine *(SYN.)* lunch, eat, sup, feed.

dingy *(SYN.)* dull, dark, dismal, dirty, drab, murky, gray.
(ANT.) *cheerful, bright.*

dip *(SYN.)* immerse, plunge, submerge, wet, swim.

diplomacy *(SYN.)* knack, dexterity, skill, address, poise, tact, finesse.
(ANT.) *vulgarity, blunder, awkwardness, incompetence.*

diplomatic *(SYN.)* politic, adroit, tactful, discreet, judicious, gracious, polite, discriminating.
(ANT.) *rude, churlish, gruff, boorish, impolite, coarse.*

dire *(SYN.)* horrible, terrible, appalling, fearful, harrowing, grievous, ghastly, awful, horrid, terrifying, dreadful, frightful, horrifying, monstrous, horrendous, repulsive.
(ANT.) *lovely, enchanting, fascinating,*

beautiful, enjoyable.

direct *(SYN.)* rule, manage, bid, order, level, command, conduct, regulate, point, indicate, show, aim, control, sight, guide, instruct, train, govern.
(ANT.) swerving, untruthful, misguide, distract, indirect, crooked, deceive.

direction *(SYN.)* way, order, course, instruction, tendency, management, route, trend, guidance, administration, supervision, inclination.

directly *(SYN.)* immediately, straight.

dirt *(SYN.)* pollution, soil, filthiness, filth.
(ANT.) cleanliness, cleanness.

dirty *(SYN.)* muddy, base, pitiful, filthy, shabby, foul, soiled, nasty, mean, grimy, low, obscene, untidy, indecent, unclean, messy, squalid, contemptible, sloppy.
(ANT.) pure, neat, wholesome, clean, presentable.

disability *(SYN.)* inability, weakness, handicap, incapacity, injury, unfitness, incompetence, impotence.
(ANT.) power, ability, strength, capability.

disable *(SYN.)* weaken, incapacitate, cripple.
(ANT.) strengthen.

disabled *(SYN.)* deformed, limping, weak, crippled, maimed, defective, unsatisfactory, halt, unconvincing, feeble.
(ANT.) vigorous, athletic, sound, agile, robust.

disadvantage *(SYN.)* drawback, hindrance, handicap, inconvenience, obstacle.
(ANT.) advantage, benefit, convenience.

disagree *(SYN.)* quarrel, dispute, differ, conflict.
(ANT.) agree.

disagreement *(SYN.)* nonconformity, variance, difference, objection, challenge, remonstrance, dissent.
(ANT.) assent, acceptance, compliance, agreement.

disappear *(SYN.)* end, fade out, vanish.
(ANT.) emerge, appear.

disappoint *(SYN.)* fail, displease, mislead, dissatisfy.
(ANT.) please, satisfy, gratify.

disappointment *(SYN.)* dissatisfaction, defeat, discouragement, failure.
(ANT.) pleasure, satisfaction, gratification.

disapprove *(SYN.)* object to, disfavor, oppose.
(ANT.) approve.

disarm *(SYN.)* paralyze, demilitarize.

disaster *(SYN.)* casualty, mishap, misfortune, catastrophe, accident, adversity, ruin, calamity.
(ANT.) fortune, advantage, welfare.

disavow *(SYN.)* reject, revoke, disclaim, retract, disown.
(ANT.) recognize, acknowledge.

disband *(SYN.)* scatter, split, dismiss, separate.

disbelief *(SYN.)* doubt, incredulity, skepticism.
(ANT.) certainty, credulity.

discard *(SYN.)* scrap, reject.

discern *(SYN.)* distinguish, see, descry, separate, differentiate, perceive, discriminate, detect, observe, recognize.
(ANT.) omit, confuse, overlook, mingle, confound.

discernment *(SYN.)* perception, sharpness, intelligence, perspicacity, acuity, keenness.
(ANT.) dullness, stupidity.

discharge *(SYN.)* remove, relieve, dismiss, banish, unburden, shoot, fire, explosion, eject, detonation, liberation, release, unload, discard, send.
(ANT.) retain, employ, enlist, hire, accept, recall, detain.

disciple *(SYN.)* learner, follower, student, adherent, supporter, scholar, pupil, votary, devotee.
(ANT.) guide, leader.

discipline *(SYN.)* training, order, instruction, drill, restraint, regulation, practice, correction, control, self-control, train, teach, exercise.
(ANT.) carelessness, sloppiness, confusion, negligence, messiness, chaos, turbulence.

disclaim *(SYN.)* retract, reject, deny, renounce, disavow, revoke.
(ANT.) recognize, acknowledge.

disclose *(SYN.)* show, divulge, betray, uncover, discover, reveal, expose.
(ANT.) hide, cloak, mask, cover, obscure, conceal.

discomfit *(SYN.)* malaise, concern, confuse, baffle, perplex, disconcert.

discomfort *(SYN.)* malaise, concern, anxiety, uneasiness.

disconcerted *(SYN.)* disturbed, agitated, upset.

disconnect *(SYN.)* divide, separate, unhook, disengage, detach.
(ANT.) connect, bind, attach, unify, engage.

disconsolate *(SYN.)* depressed, downcast, sorrowful, dejected, dismal, sad, unhappy, wretched, somber, cheerless, morose, lugubrious, miserable, mournful.
(ANT.) delightful, merry, glad, cheerful, happy.

discontent *(SYN.)* displeased, disgruntled, unhappy, dissatisfied, vexed.

discontinue *(SYN.)* postpone, delay, adjourn, stay, stop, defer, suspend, end, cease, interrupt.
(ANT.) prolong, persist, continue, start, begin, proceed, maintain.

discord *(SYN.)* disagreement, conflict.
(ANT.) concord, accord, agreement.

discourage *(SYN.)* hamper, obstruct, restrain, block, dishearten, retard, check, dispirit, thwart, depress, hinder, stop.
(ANT.) expedite, inspire, encourage, promote, inspirit, assist, further.

discourteous *(SYN.)* gruff, rude, vulgar, blunt, impolite, saucy, uncivil, boorish, rough.
(ANT.) stately, courtly, civil, dignified, genteel.

discover *(SYN.)* find out, invent, expose, ascertain, devise, reveal, learn, determine, detect.

(ANT.) *hide, screen, cover, conceal, lose.*

discredit *(SYN.)* disbelieve, dishonor, doubt, disgrace, shame.

discreet *(SYN.)* politic, discriminating, judicious, adroit, prudent, cautious, wise, tactful, careful, diplomatic.
(ANT.) *incautious, rude, coarse, boorish, tactless, imprudent, indiscreet, careless, gruff.*

discrepant *(SYN.)* incompatible, wavering, contrary, irreconcilable, unsteady, illogical, contradictory.
(ANT.) *correspondent, compatible, consistent.*

discriminating *(SYN.)* exact, particular, critical, accurate, discerning.
(ANT.) *unimportant, shallow, insignificant, superficial.*

discrimination *(SYN.)* perspicacity, discernment, racism, wisdom, bias, sagacity, intolerance, prejudice, intelligence, understanding.
(ANT.) *thoughtlessness, senselessness, arbitrariness.*

discuss *(SYN.)* gossip, plead, discourse, blab, lecture, talk, chat, spout, mutter, deliberate, consider, reason, comment.

discussion *(SYN.)* speech, chatter, lecture, conference, talk, dialogue, conversation, rumor.
(ANT.) *silence, correspondence, writing.*

disdain *(SYN.)* derision, hatred, contempt, scorn, contumely, reject, haughtiness, detestation.
(ANT.) *respect, esteem, reverence, admire, prize, honor, admiration, awe, regard.*

disdainful *(SYN.)* haughty, scornful, arrogant, contemptuous.
(ANT.) *awed, admiring, regardful.*

disease *(SYN.)* malady, disorder, ailment, illness, affliction, infirmity, complaint, sickness.
(ANT.) *soundness, health, vigor.*

disentangle *(SYN.)* unwind, untie, clear, unravel, unknot, unsnarl, untangle.

disfigured *(SYN.)* deformed, marred, defaced, scarred.

disgrace *(SYN.)* odium, chagrin, shame, mortification, embarrassment, humiliate, scandal, dishonor, mortification.
(ANT.) *renown, glory, respect, praise, dignity, honor.*

disgraceful *(SYN.)* ignominious, shameful, discreditable, disreputable, scandalous, dishonorable.
(ANT.) *renowned, esteemed, respectable, honorable.*

disguise *(SYN.)* excuse, simulation, pretension, hide, camouflage, makeup, cover-up, mask, conceal, screen, affectation, pretext.
(ANT.) *show, reality, actuality, display, reveal, sincerity, fact.*

disgust *(SYN.)* offend, repulse, nauseate, revolt, sicken.
(ANT.) *admiration, liking.*

disgusting *(SYN.)* repulsive, nauseating, revolting, nauseous, repugnant

dish *(SYN.)* serve, container, give, receptacle.

dishearten *(SYN.)* depress, sadden, dis-

courage.

disheveled *(SYN.)* mussed, sloppy, rumpled, untidy.

dishonest *(SYN.)* crooked, impure, unsound, false, contaminated, venal, corrupt, putrid, thievish, vitiated, tainted.
(ANT.) *upright, honest, straightforward.*

dishonor *(SYN.)* disrepute, scandal, indignity, chagrin, mortification, shame, obloquy, defamation, humiliation, disgrace, scandal.
(ANT.) *renown, glory, praise, honor, dignity.*

disinclined *(SYN.)* unwilling, reluctant, loath.

disingenuous *(SYN.)* tricky, deceitful, scheming, dishonest, underhanded, cunning, artful, crafty, insidious.

disintegrate *(SYN.)* decompose, dwindle, spoil, decay, wane, ebb, decline, rot.
(ANT.) *increase, flourish, rise, grow.*

disinterested *(SYN.)* unbiased, openminded, neutral, impartial, unprejudiced.

dislike *(SYN.)* aversion, dread, reluctance, abhorrence, disinclination, hatred, repugnance.
(ANT.) *devotion, affection, enthusiasm, attachment.*

disloyal *(SYN.)* false, treasonable, apostate, unfaithful, recreant, treacherous, untrue, perfidious, traitorous, faithless.
(ANT.) *true, devoted, constant, loyal.*

dismal *(SYN.)* dark, lonesome, somber, bleak, dull, sad, doleful, sorrowful, cheerless, depressing, dreary, funeral, gloomy, melancholy.
(ANT.) *lively, gay, happy, lighthearted, charming, cheerful.*

dismantle *(SYN.)* take apart, wreck, disassemble.

dismay *(SYN.)* disturb, bother, dishearten, horror, alarm, bewilder, frighten, scare, discourage, confuse.
(ANT.) *encourage, hearten.*

dismiss *(SYN.)* remove, discharge, discard, release, liberate, exile, banish, eject, oust.
(ANT.) *retain, detain, engage, hire, accept, recall.*

disobedient *(SYN.)* refractory, forward, unruly, insubordinate, defiant, rebellious, undutiful.
(ANT.) *submissive, compliant, obedient.*

disobey *(SYN.)* invade, break, violate, infringe, defile.

disorder *(SYN.)* tumult, chaos, jumble, confusion, muddle, turmoil, anarchy.
(ANT.) *organization, neatness, system, order.*

disorganization *(SYN.)* jumble, confusion, muddle, anarchy.
(ANT.) *system, order.*

disorganized *(SYN.)* muddled, confused, indistinct, bewildered, mixed.
(ANT.) *organized, lucid, clear, plain.*

disown *(SYN.)* deny, renounce, reject, repudiate, forsake, disinherit.

disparaging *(SYN.)* belittling, deprecatory, discrediting, deprecating.

disparage *(SYN.)* undervalue, depreciate, lower, belittle, derogate,

minimize, decry, discredit.
(ANT.) *exalting, praise, aggrandize, magnify, commend.*
disparagement (SYN.) lowering, decrying, undervaluing, belittling, minimizing.
(ANT.) *praise, exalting, aggrandizement, magnification.*
dispassionate (SYN.) calm, cool, composed, controlled, unemotional, imperturbable.
dispatch (SYN.) throw, impel, transmit, emit, cast, finish, report, message, send, speed, achieve, conclude, communication, promptness, discharge.
(ANT.) *reluctance, get, retain, bring, slowness, hold.*
dispel (SYN.) disseminate, scatter, disperse, separate, diffuse.
(ANT.) *collect, accumulate, gather.*
dispense (SYN.) deal, give, allot, assign, apportion, mete, distribute, grant, allocate, measure.
(ANT.) *refuse, withhold, confiscate, retain, keep.*
disperse (SYN.) dissipate, scatter, disseminate, diffuse, separate, dispel.
(ANT.) *collect, amass, gather, assemble, accumulate.*
dispirited (SYN.) downhearted, unhappy, dejected, disheartened, sad, depressed, melancholy.
(ANT.) *cheerful, happy, optimistic.*
displace (SYN.) remove, transport, lodge, shift, move.
(ANT.) *retain, leave, stay, remain.*
display (SYN.) parade, exhibit, show, expose, reveal, demonstrate, showing, uncover, flaunt.
(ANT.) *hide, cover, conceal.*
displeasure (SYN.) dislike, disapproval, dissatisfaction, distaste, discontentment.
disposal (SYN.) elimination, adjustment, removal, release, arrangement, administration, settlement.
dispose (SYN.) settle, adjust, arrange.
disposition (SYN.) behavior, character, deed, deportment, action, manner, bearing, temperament, nature, demeanor, personality, carriage.
dispossess (SYN.) eject, expel, evict, oust, dislodge.
disprove (SYN.) refute, deny, invalidate, controvert.
dispute (SYN.) squabble, debate, argument, controversy, contention, disagreement, bicker, contest, argue, contend, quarrel, contradict, discuss, deny, oppose, altercate.
(ANT.) *harmony, concord, agreement, allow, concur, agree, concede, decision.*
disregard (SYN.) slight, omit, ignore, inattention, oversight, skip, neglect, overlook.
(ANT.) *regard, include.*
disrepair (SYN.) ruin, decay, dilapidation, destruction.
disreputable (SYN.) dishonored, notorious, dishonorable, disgraced.
disrespectful (SYN.) fresh, impertinent, rude, impolite, impudent.
(ANT.) *polite, respectful, courteous.*

dissect (SYN.) examine, cut, analyze.
disseminate (SYN.) publish, circulate, spread, publish, broadcast.
dissent (SYN.) objection, challenge, disagreement, protest, remonstrance, difference, nonconformity, variance, noncompliance.
(ANT.) *assent, acceptance, compliance, agreement.*
dissertation (SYN.) thesis, treatise, disquisition.
dissimilar (SYN.) diverse, unlike, various, distinct, contrary, sundry, different, miscellaneous.
(ANT.) *same, alike, similar, congruous.*
dissimulation (SYN.) pretense, deceit, sanctimony, hypocrisy, cant.
(ANT.) *honesty, candor, openness, frankness, truth.*
dissipate (SYN.) misuse, squander, dwindle, consume, waste, lavish, diminish.
(ANT.) *save, conserve, preserve, accumulate, economize.*
dissolve (SYN.) liquefy, end, cease, melt, fade, disappear.
distant (SYN.) stiff, cold, removed, far, afar, unfriendly, remote, faraway, separated, aloof, reserved.
(ANT.) *nigh, friendly, close, cordial, near.*
distasteful (SYN.) disagreeable, unpleasant, objectionable.
distend (SYN.) swell, widen, magnify, expand, enlarge.
distinct (SYN.) plain, evident, lucid, visible, apparent, different, separate, individual, obvious, manifest, clear.
(ANT.) *vague, indistinct, uncertain, obscure, ambiguous.*
distinction (SYN.) importance, peculiarity, trait, honor, fame, characteristic, repute, quality, renown, prominence, attribute, property.
(ANT.) *nature, substance, essence, being.*
distinctive (SYN.) odd, exceptional, rare, individual, eccentric, special, strange.
(ANT.) *ordinary, general, common, normal.*
distinguish (SYN.) recognize, differentiate, divide, classify, descry, discern, separate, perceive, detect.
(ANT.) *mingle, conjoin, blend, found, omit, confuse, overlook.*
distinguished (SYN.) eminent, illustrious, renowned, celebrated, elevated, noted, important, famous, prominent.
(ANT.) *ordinary, common, unknown, undistinguished, obscure, unimportant.*
distort (SYN.) contort, falsify, twist, misrepresent.
distract (SYN.) occupy, bewilder, disturb, divert, confuse.
(ANT.) *focus, concentrate.*
distracted (SYN.) abstracted, preoccupied, absent.
(ANT.) *attentive, attending, watchful, present.*
distraction (SYN.) entertainment, confusion, amusement, diversion.

entreat *(SYN.)* implore, beg, plead.

entreaty *(SYN.)* plea, appeal.

entrust *(SYN.)* commit, charge, assign, delegate, consign, commission.

enumerate *(SYN.)* count, tally, list, number.

enunciate *(SYN.)* announce, express, speak, state.

envelop *(SYN.)* embrace, cover, conceal, surround, wrap.

environment *(SYN.)* neighborhood, habitat, surroundings, setting.

envision *(SYN.)* picture, imagine, visualize.

envoy *(SYN.)* delegate, emissary, representative, agent, messenger.

envy *(SYN.)* covetousness, jealousy, spitefulness, covet.
(ANT.) indifference, generosity.

epicure *(SYN.)* gourmand, gourmet, connoisseur, gastronome, epicurean, aesthete.

epidemic *(SYN.)* prevalent, scourge, plague, catching, widespread, pestilence, infectious.

episode *(SYN.)* happening, affair, occurrence, event, experience.

epoch *(SYN.)* age.

equal *(SYN.)* even, uniform, like, alike, equitable, same, identical, commensurate, equivalent, regular, parallel.
(ANT.) different, unequal, irregular, uneven.

equilibrium *(SYN.)* stability, steadiness, balance, firmness.

equip *(SYN.)* fit, rig, provide, outfit, prepare, furnish.

equipment *(SYN.)* utensils, material, apparatus.

equitable *(SYN.)* square, rightful, fair, due, just, fit.
(ANT.) partial, biased, unjust, uneven.

equity *(SYN.)* impartiality, fairness, justness, justice, fair-mindedness, evenhandedness.

equivalent *(SYN.)* match, rival, equal, like, replacement.

equivocal *(SYN.)* oblique, ambiguous, vague, indeterminate, uncertain, obscure.
(ANT.) clear, precise, explicit, certain, clear-cut, definite.

equivocate *(SYN.)* temporize, evade, hedge, quibble, fudge, waffle, straddle.

era *(SYN.)* epoch, cycle, age, time, period.

eradicate *(SYN.)* remove, demolish, eliminate.

erase *(SYN.)* obliterate, remove, cancel.
(ANT.) add, include.

erect *(SYN.)* upright, build, straight, raise, construct, vertical.
(ANT.) flat, horizontal, raze, flatten, demolish.

erection *(SYN.)* building, construction, raising, fabrication.

erode *(SYN.)* rust, consume, disintegrate.

erotic *(SYN.)* carnal, fleshy, amatory, prurient, lewd, wanton, passionate, lecherous.

err *(SYN.)* slip, misjudge.

errand *(SYN.)* chore, duty, task, exercise.

errant *(SYN.)* roving, rambling, wandering, vagrant.

erratic *(SYN.)* irregular, abnormal, uneven, occasional, sporadic, changeable, unsteady, odd, eccentric, strange, extraordinary, unconventional, bizarre, peculiar, uncertain, unusual, unstable.
(ANT.) regular, steady, normal, ordinary.

erroneous *(SYN.)* wrong, mistaken, incorrect, inaccurate, false, untrue.
(ANT.) true, right, correct, accurate.

error *(SYN.)* inaccuracy, fault, slip, oversight, fallacy, mistake, blunder.

erudite *(SYN.)* sage, wise, learned, deep, profound.

erupt *(SYN.)* vomit.

escapade *(SYN.)* caper, antic, stunt, trick, prank.

escape *(SYN.)* shun, avoid, flee, decamp, elude, flight, avert, departure, abscond, fly, evade.
(ANT.) meet, confront, invite, catch.

escort *(SYN.)* conduct, lead, attend, accompany, protection, guard, guide, convoy, usher, squire.

especially *(SYN.)* unusually, principally, mainly, particularly, primarily.

essay *(SYN.)* test, thesis, undertake, paper, try.

essence *(SYN.)* substance, character, nature, principle, odor, meaning, basis, smell, perfume.

essential *(SYN.)* vital, intrinsic, basic, requisite, fundamental, indispensable, critical, requirement, necessity, necessary, important.
(ANT.) dispensable, unimportant, inessential.

establish *(SYN.)* prove, fix, found, settle, institute, raise, verify, conform, form, sanction, ordain, begin, organize.
(ANT.) upset, discontinue, scatter, disperse, refute, abolish, unsettle.

esteem *(SYN.)* revere, deem, appreciate, honor, value, think, admire, respect, hold, prize, reverence, regard.
(ANT.) scorn, disdain, depreciate, disregard, contempt, abhor.

estimate *(SYN.)* calculate, gauge, judge, rate, evaluate, compute, value, figure.

estimation *(SYN.)* judgment, viewpoint, opinion.

etch *(SYN.)* stamp, engrave, impress.

eternal *(SYN.)* undying, immortal, ceaseless, infinite, everlasting, deathless, perpetual, endless, timeless.
(ANT.) mortal, transient, finite, brief, temporary, passing.

etiquette *(SYN.)* decorum, formality.

evacuate *(SYN.)* withdraw, depart, leave, vacate.

evade *(SYN.)* miss, avoid, bypass.
(ANT.) confront, meet, face.

evaluate *(SYN.)* value, appraise, assay.

evaporate *(SYN.)* disappear, vanish.
(ANT.) condense, appear.

even *(SYN.)* smooth, level, still, square, same, flat, balanced, equal, parallel, identical.

(ANT.) *irregular, bumpy, unbalanced, unequal, divergent.*

evening *(SYN.)* twilight, dusk, sunset.
(ANT.) *sunrise, dawn.*

event *(SYN.)* issue, end, result, circumstance, occurrence, incident, consequence, happening, episode, outcome.

even-tempered *(SYN.)* composed, calm, cool.
(ANT.) *hotheaded.*

eventual *(SYN.)* consequent, ultimate.
(ANT.) *present, current.*

eventually *(SYN.)* ultimately.

ever *(SYN.)* continuously, always, constantly.
(ANT.) *never.*

everlasting *(SYN.)* permanent, ceaseless, endless, continual.

evermore *(SYN.)* always.

everyday *(SYN.)* commonplace, common, usual, ordinary, customary.
(ANT.) *rare.*

evict *(SYN.)* oust, put out, expel.

evidence *(SYN.)* grounds, clue, facts, testimony, data, sign, proof.

evident *(SYN.)* apparent, clear, obvious, indubitable, plain, conspicuous, patent, manifest, open, unmistakable.
(ANT.) *hidden, unclear, uncertain, obscure, concealed.*

evil *(SYN.)* immoral, harmful, badness, sinful, injurious, woe, bad, wicked.
(ANT.) *goodness, moral, useful, upright, virtuous, beneficial, virtue, advantageous.*

evoke *(SYN.)* summon, prompt.

evolve *(SYN.)* grow, advance, develop, result, emerge, unfold.

exact *(SYN.)* correct, faultless, errorless, detailed, accurate.
(ANT.) *inaccurate, inexact, faulty.*

exaggerate *(SYN.)* stretch, expand, amplify, embroider, heighten, overstate, caricature, magnify, enlarge.
(ANT.) *understate, minimize, diminish, depreciate.*

exalt *(SYN.)* erect, consecrate, raise, elevate, extol, dignify.
(ANT.) *humble, degrade, humiliate.*

examination *(SYN.)* investigation, inspection, test, scrutiny.

examine *(SYN.)* assess, contemplate, question, review, audit, notice, inquire, analyze, check, investigate, dissect, inspect, survey.
(ANT.) *omit, disregard, overlook.*

example *(SYN.)* pattern, archetype, specimen, illustration, model, instance, prototype, sample.
(ANT.) *rule, concept, principle.*

exasperate *(SYN.)* aggravate, anger, madden, irritate.

excavate *(SYN.)* unearth, dig, burrow.

exceed *(SYN.)* excel, beat, surpass, top.

exceedingly *(SYN.)* extremely, very, especially, unusually, surprisingly.

excel *(SYN.)* better, beat, surpass.

excellence *(SYN.)* distinction, superiority.
(ANT.) *poorness, inferiority, badness.*

excellent *(SYN.)* wonderful, fine, marvelous, superior.

(ANT.) *poor, terrible, bad, inferior.*

except *(SYN.)* omitting, barring, but, reject, excluding, save, exclude.

exception *(SYN.)* affront, offense, exclusion, deviation, omission, anomaly.

exceptional *(SYN.)* different, irregular, strange, unusual, abnormal.

excerpt *(SYN.)* abstract, extract.

excess *(SYN.)* surplus, intemperance, extravagance, immoderation, profusion, abundant, profuse, superfluity.
(ANT.) *want, sparse, lack, dearth.*

exchange *(SYN.)* barter, interchange, substitute, trade, change, swap.

excite *(SYN.)* arouse, incite, agitate, stimulate, awaken, disquiet.
(ANT.) *lull, quiet, bore, pacify.*

exclaim *(SYN.)* vociferate, cry, call out, cry out, ejaculate, shout.

exclamation *(SYN.)* shout, outcry, clamor.

exclude *(SYN.)* omit, restrain, hinder, bar, except, prevent.
(ANT.) *welcome, involve, embrace, admit, accept, include.*

exclusion *(SYN.)* exception, bar, rejection.
(ANT.) *inclusion.*

exclusive *(SYN.)* restricted, limited, restrictive, choice, selective, fashionable.
(ANT.) *common, general, ordinary, unrestricted, unfashionable.*

excursion *(SYN.)* voyage, tour, trip.

excuse *(SYN.)* exculpate, forgive, remit, acquit, free, pardon, condone, explanation, overlook, exempt, reason, justify, absolve.
(ANT.) *revenge, punish, convict.*

execute *(SYN.)* complete, accomplish, do, achieve, kill, perform.

exemplify *(SYN.)* show, illustrate.

exempt *(SYN.)* excuse, free, except, release.

exercise *(SYN.)* drill, task, use, activity, lesson, training, exertion, application, gymnastics, operation, practice.
(ANT.) *rest, indolence, repose.*

exertion *(SYN.)* attempt, effort, strain, endeavor.

exhale *(SYN.)* blow, breathe out.

exhaust *(SYN.)* drain, tire, empty, wear out, use, finish, fatigue.
(ANT.) *renew, refresh, replace.*

exhaustive *(SYN.)* comprehensive, thorough, extensive, complete.
(ANT.) *incomplete.*

exhibit *(SYN.)* demonstrate, display, reveal, betray, present, show, flaunt.
(ANT.) *hide conceal, disguise.*

exhilarate *(SYN.)* gladden, refresh, cheer, excite, stimulate.

exhort *(SYN.)* advise, urge, prompt.

exile *(SYN.)* expulsion, proscription, deportation, ostracism, expatriation, deport, extradition, expel, banishment.
(ANT.) *retrieval, welcome, recall, admittance, reinstatement.*

exist *(SYN.)* stand, live, occur, be.

exit *(SYN.)* leave, depart.

exodus *(SYN.)* leaving, exit, departure.

exonerate *(SYN.)* acquit, clear.

exorbitant *(SYN.)* unreasonable, outrageous, overpriced, preposterous, ex-

cessive.
(ANT.) normal, reasonable.
exotic (SYN.) strange, vivid, foreign.
(ANT.) dull, native.
expand (SYN.) unfold, enlarge, broaden, spread, inflate, swell, grow.
(ANT.) contract, shrivel, shrink.
expect (SYN.) await, think, hope.
expedient (SYN.) helpful, desirable, rush, hasten, useful, fitting, sensible.
(ANT.) delay.
expedition (SYN.) trek, speed, trip, haste, voyage, journey, hurry.
expel (SYN.) exile, dislodge, discharge, excommunicate, oust, eject, dismiss, banish, disown.
(ANT.) favor, recall, invite, admit.
expend (SYN.) consume, waste, spend.
(ANT.) ration, reserve, conserve.
expense (SYN.) charge, payment, price.
expensive (SYN.) costly, dear.
(ANT.) modest, inexpensive, cheap.
experience (SYN.) occurrence, episode, sensation, happening, existence, background, feeling, living, knowledge.
experienced (SYN.) expert, qualified, accomplished, skilled, practiced.
(ANT.) untutored, inexperienced, naive.
experiment (SYN.) trial, test, prove, research, examine, try, verify.
expert (SYN.) adept, handy, skillful, clever, specialist, authority, skilled, knowledgeable, ingenious.
(ANT.) unskilled, inexperienced.
expire (SYN.) terminate, die, cease, perish, pass, end, disappear.
(ANT.) commence, continue.
explain (SYN.) illustrate, decipher, expound, clarify, resolve, define, unravel, elucidate, unfold, justify, interpret.
(ANT.) darken, baffle, obscure.
explanation (SYN.) definition, description, interpretation, account, reason, justification, excuse.
explicit (SYN.) lucid, definitive, specific, express, clear, manifest.
(ANT.) vague, implicit, ambiguous.
exploit (SYN.) feat, deed, accomplishment, adventure.
explore (SYN.) research, hunt, probe, search, investigate, look, examine.
explosion (SYN.) bang, boom, blowup, flare-up, blast, detonation, outbreak, convulsion, furor, tantrum, paroxysm.
explosive (SYN.) fiery, rabid, eruptive, volcanic, fulminatory, inflammatory.
(ANT.) stable, inert, peaceful, calm.
exponent (SYN.) explicator, spokesman, supporter, expounder, interpreter.
expose (SYN.) uncover, display, bare, open, unmask, reveal.
(ANT.) hide, conceal, mask, covered.
exposition (SYN.) fair, bazaar, show, expo, exhibition.
expound (SYN.) clarify, present, explain, lecture, demonstrate.
express (SYN.) voice, tell, send, say, ship, declare, precise, specific, swift.
expression (SYN.) declaration, statement, look.
expressive (SYN.) suggestive, meaningful, telling, significant, thoughtful.
(ANT.) meaningless, nondescript.

expressly (SYN.) precisely, exactly, definitely, clearly.
(ANT.) tentatively, ambiguously.
expulsion (SYN.) ejection, discharge, removal, elimination.
expunge (SYN.) blot out, erase, cancel, obliterate, delete, efface, remove.
expurgate (SYN.) cleanse, purge, censor, edit, emasculate, abridge, blip.
exquisite (SYN.) delicate, delightful, attractive, dainty, beautiful, elegant, fine, superb, lovely, excellent, perfect.
(ANT.) vulgar, dull, ugly, unattractive.
extant (SYN.) subsisting, remaining, surviving, present, existing.
(ANT.) lost, defunct, extinct, vanished.
extemporaneous (SYN.) casual, impromptu, offhand.
extemporize (SYN.) improvise, devise.
extend (SYN.) lengthen, stretch, increase, offer, give, grant, expand.
(ANT.) abbreviate, shorten, curtail.
extension (SYN.) expansion, increase, stretching, enlargement.
extensive (SYN.) vast, wide, spacious, broad.
(ANT.) narrow, cramped, confined, restricted.
extent (SYN.) length, degree, range, amount, measure, size, compass, reach, magnitude, expanse, area.
extenuating (SYN.) exculpating, excusable, qualifying, justifying.
exterior (SYN.) surface, face, outside, covering, outer, external.
(ANT.) inside, lining, interior, inner.
exterminate (SYN.) slay, kill, destroy.
external (SYN.) outer, exterior, outside.
(ANT.) inner, internal, inside, interior.
externals (SYN.) images, effects, look, appearance, veneer, aspect.
extinct (SYN.) lost, dead, gone, vanished.
(ANT.) present, flourishing, alive, extant.
extinction (SYN.) eclipse, annihilation, obliteration, death, extirpation.
extinguish (SYN.) suppress, smother, quench.
extol (SYN.) laud, exalt, praise.
(ANT.) denounce, discredit, disparage.
extra (SYN.) surplus, spare, additional.
extract (SYN.) remove, essence.
(ANT.) penetrate, introduce.
extraordinary (SYN.) unusual, wonderful, marvelous, peculiar, noteworthy, remarkable, uncommon, exceptional.
(ANT.) commonplace, ordinary, usual.
extravagant (SYN.) excessive, exaggerated, lavish, wasteful, extreme.
(ANT.) prudent, frugal, thrifty, economical, provident.
extreme (SYN.) excessive, overdone, outermost, limit, greatest, utmost, furthest, extravagant.
(ANT.) reasonable, modest, moderate.
extricate (SYN.) rescue, free, clear, release, liberate.
exuberant (SYN.) ebullient, vivacious.
(ANT.) sad, depressed.
exult (SYN.) rejoice, delight.
eye (SYN.) watch, view, stare, look, inspect, glance.

fable *(SYN.)* legend, parable, myth, fib, falsehood, fiction, tale, story.

fabled *(SYN.)* legendary, famous, famed, historic.

fabric *(SYN.)* goods, textile, material, cloth, yard goods.

fabricate *(SYN.)* assemble, make, construct, create, manufacture, form.
(ANT.) raze, destroy, demolish.

fabrication *(SYN.)* deceit, lie, falsehood, untruth, forgery, deception.
(ANT.) reality, actuality, truth, fact.

fabulous *(SYN.)* amazing, marvelous, unbelievable, fantastic, astounding.
(ANT.) ordinary, commonplace, credible, proven, factual.

facade *(SYN.)* deception, mask, front, show, pose, veneer, guise, affectation.

face *(SYN.)* cover, mug, front, assurance, countenance, audacity, visage, expression, look, features, facade, encounter, meet, surface.
(ANT.) rear, shun, avoid, evade, back.

facet *(SYN.)* perspective, view, side.

facetious *(SYN.)* jocular, pungent, humorous, funny, clever, droll, witty, playful, jesting.
(ANT.) sober, serious, grave, weighty.

face to face *(SYN.)* opposing, confronting.

facile *(SYN.)* simple, easy, quick, uncomplicated, clever, fluent, skillful.
(ANT.) complex, difficult, complicated, laborious, hard, ponderous, painstaking, arduous.

facilitate *(SYN.)* help, speed, ease, promote, accelerate, expedite.

facilities *(SYN.)* aid, means, resources, conveniences.

facility *(SYN.)* ability, skill, ease, skillfulness, material.
(ANT.) effort, difficulty, labor.

facsimile *(SYN.)* reproduction, replica.

fact *(SYN.)* reality, deed, certainty, act, incident, circumstance, occurrence, event, truth, actuality.
(ANT.) falsehood, fiction, delusion.

faction *(SYN.)* clique, party, sect.

factitious *(SYN.)* false, sham, artificial, spurious, unnatural, affected.
(ANT.) natural, real, genuine, artless.

factor *(SYN.)* part, certain, element, basis, cause.

factory *(SYN.)* installation, plant, works.

factual *(SYN.)* true, correct, accurate, sure, genuine, authentic.
(ANT.) incorrect, erroneous, invented.

faculty *(SYN.)* power, capacity, talent, staff, gift, ability, qualification, ability, skill.

fad *(SYN.)* fashion, vogue, mania, rage.

faddish *(SYN.)* ephemeral, modish, temporary, passing, fleeting.
(ANT.) lasting, permanent, enduring.

fade *(SYN.)* pale, bleach, weaken, dim, decline, sink, discolor, fail, diminish.

fagged *(SYN.)* exhausted, tired, weary, jaded, pooped, worn.

fail *(SYN.)* neglect, weaken, flunk, miss, decline, disappoint, fade.
(ANT.) succeed, achieve, accomplish.

failing *(SYN.)* fault, foible, imperfection, frailty, defect, shortcoming.

(ANT.) steadiness, strength, integrity.

failure *(SYN.)* miscarriage, omission, decline, deficiency, fiasco, lack, dereliction, failing, unsuccessfulness, loss, default, want, insufficiency.
(ANT.) conquest, accomplishment, success, triumph, victory, hit, luck.

faint *(SYN.)* timid, faded, languid, halfhearted, dim, pale, wearied, feeble, indistinct, weak.
(ANT.) strong, sharp, forceful, glaring, clear, distinct, conspicuous, brave.

faint-hearted *(SYN.)* shy, cowardly, timid, bashful.
(ANT.) fearless, brave, stouthearted, courageous.

fair *(SYN.)* pale, average, light, sunny, mediocre, bright, just, clear, lovely, market, blond, honest, equitable, impartial, reasonable, comely.
(ANT.) ugly, fraudulent, foul, outstanding, dishonorable, unfair.

fairly *(SYN.)* equally, evenly, rather, impartially, passably, justly, somewhat.

fair-minded *(SYN.)* reasonable, fair, just, open-minded, honest, unprejudiced, impartial, evenhanded.
(ANT.) bigoted, narrow-minded, unjust, close-minded, partisan.

fairness *(SYN.)* equity, justice, evenhandedness, honesty.
(ANT.) favoritism, partiality, bias, onesidedness.

fairy *(SYN.)* gnome, elf, pixie, sprite.

faith *(SYN.)* dependence, trust, reliance, creed, loyalty, doctrine, confidence, dogma, tenet, persuasion, constancy, credence, fidelity, religion, belief.
(ANT.) disbelief, doubt, infidelity.

faithful *(SYN.)* staunch, true, devoted, trusty, loyal, constant, credible, steadfast, strict, trust-worthy, accurate.
(ANT.) untrustworthy, faithless, inaccurate, wrong, false, disloyal, erroneous.

faithless *(SYN.)* treacherous, unfaithful, disloyal, perfidious, untrue.
(ANT.) loyal, true, unwavering, constant, faithful.

fake *(SYN.)* falsify, distort, pretend, feign, fraud, counterfeit, cheat, false, artificial, phony, imitation, forgery.
(ANT.) honest, pure, real, genuine, authentic.

falderal *(SYN.)* foolery, jargon, nonsense, gibberish, blather, balderdash.

fall *(SYN.)* drop, decline, diminish, droop, topple, decrease, sink, hang, descend, subside, plunge, collapse.
(ANT.) soar, climb, steady, rise, ascend.

fallacious *(SYN.)* untrue, false, wrong, erroneous, deceptive, illusory.
(ANT.) accurate, true, exact, real.

fallacy *(SYN.)* mistake, error, illusion, sophism, misconception, deception.

fall back *(SYN.)* retreat, recede, retire, withdraw, concede.
(ANT.) progress, advance, gain, prosper, proceed.

fallow *(SYN.)* idle, unprepared, unproductive, inactive.
(ANT.) prepared, productive, cultivated.

false *(SYN.)* incorrect, wrong, deceitful, fake, imitation, counterfeit.

(ANT.) genuine, loyal, true, honest.

falsehood *(SYN.)* untruth, lie, fib, story.
(ANT.) truth.

falsify *(SYN.)* misquote, distort, misstate, mislead, adulterate.

falter *(SYN.)* stumble, tremble, waver, hesitate, flounder.

fame *(SYN.)* distinction, glory, mane, eminence, credit, reputation, renown, acclaim, notoriety.
(ANT.) infamy, obscurity, anonymity, disrepute.

famed *(SYN.)* known, renowned, famous.
(ANT.) obscure, unknown, anonymous.

familiar *(SYN.)* informal, intimate, close, acquainted, amicable, knowing, cognizant, well-acquainted, versed, unreserved, friendly, sociable, affable, aware, known, courteous, intimate.
(ANT.) unfamiliar, distant, affected, reserved.

familiarity *(SYN.)* sociability, acquaintance, awareness, frankness, intimacy, understanding, knowledge, fellowship.
(ANT.) distance, ignorance, reserve, presumption, constraint, haughtiness.

family *(SYN.)* kin, tribe, folks, group, relatives.

famine *(SYN.)* want, deficiency, starvation, need.
(ANT.) excess, plenty.

famous *(SYN.)* distinguished, noted, glorious, illustrious, famed, celebrated, well-known, eminent, renowned, prominent, esteemed.
(ANT.) obscure, hidden, unknown.

fan *(SYN.)* arouse, spread, admirer, enthusiast, devotee, stir, aficionado, whip, follower.

fanatic *(SYN.)* bigot, enthusiast, zealot.

fancy *(SYN.)* love, dream, ornate, imagine, suppose, imagination, taste, fantasy, ornamented, elaborate, think.
(ANT.) plain, undecorated, simple, unadorned.

fantastic *(SYN.)* strange, unusual, odd, wild, unimaginable, incredible, unbelievable, unreal, bizarre, capricious.
(ANT.) mundane, ordinary, staid, humdrum.

fantasy *(SYN.)* illusion, dream, whim, hallucination, delusion, caprice, mirage, daydream, fancy.
(ANT.) bore.

far *(SYN.)* removed, much, distant, remote, estranged, alienated.
(ANT.) close, near.

fare *(SYN.)* prosper, eat, passenger, thrive, toll, progress, succeed.

farewell *(SYN.)* good-by, valediction, departure, leaving.
(ANT.) welcome, greeting.

farm *(SYN.)* grow, harvest, cultivate, ranch, hire, charter, plantation.

fascinate *(SYN.)* charm, enchant, bewitch, attract, enthrall.

fashion *(SYN.)* create, shape, style, mode, make, custom, form, manner, method, way, vogue.

fashionable *(SYN.)* chic, smart, stylish, modish, elegant, voguish.
(ANT.) dowdy, unfashionable.

fast *(SYN.)* fleet, firm, quick, swift, inflexible, stable, secure, expeditious, rapid, steady, solid, constant, speedy.
(ANT.) insecure, sluggish, unstable, loose, slow, unsteady.

fasten *(SYN.)* secure, bind, tie, join, fix, connect, attach, unite.
(ANT.) open, loose, free, loosen, release, separate.

fastidious *(SYN.)* choosy, selective, discriminating, picky, meticulous.

fat *(SYN.)* stout, plump, chubby, pudgy, obese, oily, fleshy, greasy, fatty, portly, corpulent, paunchy, wide, thick, rotund.
(ANT.) slim, gaunt, emaciated, thin, slender.

fatal *(SYN.)* killing, lethal, doomed, disastrous, deadly, fateful, mortal.
(ANT.) nonfatal.

fate *(SYN.)* end, fortune, doom, issue, destiny, necessity, portion, result, lot, chance, luck, outcome, consequence, kismet.

father *(SYN.)* cause, sire, breed, originate, founder, inventor.

fatherly *(SYN.)* protective, paternal, kind, paternalistic.

fathom *(SYN.)* penetrate, understand, interpret, comprehend.

fatigue *(SYN.)* weariness, lassitude, exhaustion, enervation, languor, tiredness.
(ANT.) vivacity, rejuvenation, energy, vigor.

fault *(SYN.)* defect, flaw, mistake, imperfection, shortcoming, error, weakness, responsibility, omission, blemish, blame, failure.
(ANT.) perfection, completeness.

faultfinding *(SYN.)* carping, censorious, critical, caviling, nit-picking.

faulty *(SYN.)* imperfect, broken, defective, damaged, impaired.
(ANT.) flawless, perfect, whole.

favor *(SYN.)* rather, resemble, liking, service, prefer, approval, like, support, patronize, benefit.
(ANT.) deplore, disapprove.

favorite *(SYN.)* prized, pet, choice, darling, treasured, preferred.

favoritism *(SYN.)* prejudice, bias, partiality.
(ANT.) fairness, impartiality.

fear *(SYN.)* horror, terror, fright, trepidation, alarm, consternation, dismay, cowardice, panic, anxiety, dread, scare, apprehension.
(ANT.) fearlessness, boldness, courage, assurance.

fearless *(SYN.)* bold, brave, courageous, gallant, dauntless, confident.
(ANT.) timid, fearful, cowardly.

feast *(SYN.)* dinner, banquet, barbecue.

feat *(SYN.)* performance, act, operation, accomplishment, achievement, doing, transaction, deed.
(ANT.) intention, deliberation, cessation.

feature *(SYN.)* trait, quality, characteristic, highlight, attribute.

fee *(SYN.)* payment, pay, remuneration, charge, recompense.

feeble *(SYN.)* faint, puny, exhausted, impair, delicate, weak, enervated, frail, powerless, forceless, sickly, decrepit, ailing.
(ANT.) strong, forceful, powerful, vigorous, stout.

feed *(SYN.)* satisfy, nourish, food, fodder, forage.

feel *(SYN.)* sense, experience, perceive.

feeling *(SYN.)* opinion, sensibility, tenderness, affection, impression, belief, sensation, sympathy, thought, passion, sentiment, attitude, emotion.
(ANT.) fact, imperturbability, anesthesia, insensibility.

fellowship *(SYN.)* clan, society, brotherhood, fraternity, camaraderie, companionship, comradeship, association.
(ANT.) dislike, discord, distrust, enmity, strife, acrimony.

felonious *(SYN.)* murderous, criminal, larcenous.

feminine *(SYN.)* womanly, girlish, ladylike, female, maidenly, womanish.
(ANT.) masculine, male, virile.

ferocious *(SYN.)* savage, fierce, wild, blood-thirsty, brutal.
(ANT.) playful, gentle, harmless, calm.

fertile *(SYN.)* rich, fruitful, teeming, plenteous, bountiful, prolific, luxuriant, productive, fecund.
(ANT.) unproductive, barren, sterile.

festival *(SYN.)* feast, banquet, regalement, celebration.

festive *(SYN.)* joyful, gay, joyous, merry, gala, jovial, jubilant.
(ANT.) sad, gloomy, mournful, morose.

fetching *(SYN.)* charming, attractive, pleasing, captivating, winsome.

feud *(SYN.)* dispute, quarrel, strife, argument, conflict, controversy.
(ANT.) amity, understanding, harmony, peace.

fiber *(SYN.)* line, strand, thread, string.

fickle *(SYN.)* unstable, capricious, restless, changeable, inconstant, variable.
(ANT.) stable, constant, trustworthy, steady, reliable, dependable.

fiction *(SYN.)* fabrication, romance, falsehood, tale, allegory, narrative, fable, novel, story, invention.
(ANT.) verity, reality, fact, truth.

fictitious *(SYN.)* invented, make-believe, imaginary, fabricated, unreal, counterfeit, feigned.
(ANT.) real, true, genuine, actual, proven.

fidelity *(SYN.)* fealty, devotion, precision, allegiance, exactness, constancy, accuracy, faithfulness, loyalty.
(ANT.) treachery, disloyalty.

fidget *(SYN.)* squirm, twitch, wriggle.

fiendish *(SYN.)* devilish, demonic, diabolical, savage, satanic.

fierce *(SYN.)* furious, wild, savage, violent, ferocious, vehement.
(ANT.) calm, meek, mild, gentle, placid.

fight *(SYN.)* contend, scuffle, struggle, battle, wrangle, combat, brawl, quarrel, dispute, war, skirmish, conflict.

figure *(SYN.)* design, pattern, mold, shape, form, frame, reckon, calculate, compute, determine.

fill *(SYN.)* glut, furnish, store, stuff, occupy, gorge, pervade, content, stock, fill up, supply, sate, replenish, satisfy.
(ANT.) void, drain, exhaust, deplete, empty.

filter *(SYN.)* screen, strainer, sieve.

filth *(SYN.)* pollution, dirt, sewage, foulness.
(ANT.) cleanliness, innocence, purity.

filthy *(SYN.)* foul, polluted, dirty, stained, unwashed, squalid.
(ANT.) pure, clean, unspoiled.

final *(SYN.)* ultimate, decisive, concluding, ending, terminal, last, conclusive, eventual, latest.
(ANT.) inaugural, rudimentary, beginning, initial, incipient, first, original.

finally *(SYN.)* at last, eventually, ultimately.

find *(SYN.)* observe, detect, discover, locate.

fine *(SYN.)* thin, pure, choice, small, elegant, dainty, splendid, handsome, delicate, nice, powdered, beautiful, minute, exquisite, subtle, pretty, refined.
(ANT.) thick, coarse, rough, blunt, large.

finicky *(SYN.)* fussy, meticulous, finical, fastidious, prim.

finish *(SYN.)* consummate, close, get done, terminate, accomplish, conclude, execute, perform, complete, end, achieve, fulfill, do, perfect.
(ANT.) open, begin, start, beginning.

fire *(SYN.)* vigor, glow, combustion, passion, burning, conflagration, ardor, flame, blaze, intensity, fervor.
(ANT.) apathy, cold.

firm *(SYN.)* solid, rigid, inflexible, stiff, unchanging, steadfast, dense, hard, unshakable, compact, business, company, corporation, partnership.
(ANT.) weak, limp, soft, drooping.

first *(SYN.)* chief, primary, initial, pristine, beginning, foremost, primeval, earliest, prime, primitive, original.
(ANT.) subordinate, last, least, hindmost, latest.

fishy *(SYN.)* suspicious, questionable, doubtful.
(ANT.) believable, credible.

fit *(SYN.)* adjust, suit, suitable, accommodate, conform, robust, harmonize, belong, seizure, spasm, attack, suited, appropriate, healthy, agree, adapt.
(ANT.) misfit, disturb, improper.

fitful *(SYN.)* variable, restless, fickle, capricious, unstable, changeable.
(ANT.) trustworthy, stable, constant, steady.

fitting *(SYN.)* apt, due, suitable, proper.
(ANT.) improper, unsuitable, inappropriate.

fix *(SYN.)* mend, regulate, affix, set, tie, repair, attach, settle, link, bind, determine, establish, define, place, rectify, stick, limit, adjust, fasten.
(ANT.) damage, change, mistreat, displace, alter, disturb, mutilate.

fixation *(SYN.)* fetish, obsession, infatuation, compulsion.

flair *(SYN.)* style, dash, flamboyance, drama, gift, knack, aptitude.

flamboyant *(SYN.)* showy, flashy, ostentatious, gaudy, ostentatious.

flame *(SYN.)* blaze, fire.

flash *(SYN.)* flare, flame, wink, twinkling, instant, gleam.

flashy *(SYN.)* tawdry, tasteless, pretentious, garish, flamboyant.

flat *(SYN.)* vapid, stale, even, smooth, tasteless, horizontal, dull, level, insipid, uninteresting, lifeless, boring.
(ANT.) tasty, racy, hilly, savory, stimulating, interesting, broken, sloping.

flattery *(SYN.)* compliment, praise, applause, blarney, acclaim.

flaunt *(SYN.)* exhibit, show off, display, parade.
(ANT.) conceal, hide, disguise.

flavor *(SYN.)* tang, taste, savor, essence, quality, character, season, spice.

flaw *(SYN.)* spot, imperfection, blemish, fault, deformity, blotch.

flee *(SYN.)* fly, abscond, hasten, escape, run away, decamp, evade.
(ANT.) remain, appear, stay, arrive.

fleece *(SYN.)* filch, rob, purloin, swindle, defraud, pilfer, cheat.

fleet *(SYN.)* rapid, swift, quick, fast.
(ANT.) unhurried, sluggish, slow.

fleeting *(SYN.)* brief, swift, passing, temporary.
(ANT.) stable, fixed, lasting, permanent.

fleshy *(SYN.)* overweight, chubby, stocky, plump, obese, stout.
(ANT.) spare, underweight, skinny.

flexible *(SYN.)* lithe, resilient, pliable, tractable, complaint, elastic, yielding, adaptable, agreeable, supple, pliant, easy, ductile.
(ANT.) hard, unbending, firm, brittle, inflexible, rigid, fixed.

flighty *(SYN.)* giddy, light-headed, frivolous, irresponsible.
(ANT.) solid, responsible, steady.

flimsy *(SYN.)* wobbly, weak, frail, fragile, unsteady, delicate, thin.
(ANT.) durable, stable, firm, strong.

fling *(SYN.)* pitch, throw, toss, fun, celebration, party.

flippant *(SYN.)* disrespectful, sassy, insolent, brazen, rude, impertinent.
(ANT.) courteous, polite, mannerly.

flit *(SYN.)* flutter, scurry, hasten, dart, skim.

flock *(SYN.)* gathering, group, flight, swarm, herd, school.

flog *(SYN.)* thrash, lash, switch, strike, paddle.

flood *(SYN.)* overflow, deluge, inundate, cascade.

florid *(SYN.)* gaudy, fancy, ornate, embellished.
(ANT.) spare, simple, plain, unadorned.

flourish *(SYN.)* succeed, grow, prosper, wave, thrive, bloom.
(ANT.) wither, wane, die, decline.

flout *(SYN.)* disdain, scorn, spurn, ignore, taunt, ridicule, mock.

flow *(SYN.)* proceed, abound, spout, come, stream, run, originate, emanate, result, pour, squirt, issue, gush, spurt.

fluctuate *(SYN.)* vary, oscillate, change,

waver, hesitate, vacillate.
(ANT.) persist, stick, adhere, resolve.

fluent *(SYN.)* graceful, glib, flowing.

fluid *(SYN.)* liquid, running, liquefied.

flush *(SYN.)* abundant, flat, even, level.

fluster *(SYN.)* rattle, flurry, agitate, upset, perturb, quiver, vibrate.

fly *(SYN.)* flee, mount, shoot, decamp, hover, soar, flit, flutter, sail, escape, rush, spring, glide, abscond, dart, float.
(ANT.) sink, descend, plummet.

foam *(SYN.)* suds, froth, lather.

foe *(SYN.)* opponent, enemy, antagonist, adversary.
(ANT.) associate, ally, friend, comrade.

fog *(SYN.)* haze, mist, cloud, daze, confusion, stupor, vapor, smog.

foible *(SYN.)* frailty, weakness, failing, shortcoming, kink.

foist *(SYN.)* misrepresent, insinuate, falsify.

fold *(SYN.)* lap, double, overlap, clasp, pleat, tuck.

follow *(SYN.)* trail, observe, succeed, ensue, obey, chase, comply, accompany, copy, result, imitate, heed, adopt.
(ANT.) elude, cause, precede, avoid, flee.

follower *(SYN.)* supporter, devotee, henchman, adherent, partisan, votary, attendant, disciple, successor.
(ANT.) master, head, chief, dissenter.

following *(SYN.)* public, disciples, supporters, clientele, customers.

folly *(SYN.)* imprudence, silliness, foolishness, indiscretion, absurdity, imprudence, imbecility, stupidity, extravagance.
(ANT.) reasonableness, judgment, sense, prudence, wisdom.

fond *(SYN.)* affectionate, loving, attached, tender, devoted.
(ANT.) hostile, cool, distant, unfriendly.

fondness *(SYN.)* partiality, liking, affection.
(ANT.) hostility, unfriendliness.

food *(SYN.)* viands, edibles, feed, repast, nutriment, sustenance, diet, bread, provisions, meal, rations, victuals, fare.
(ANT.) want, hunger, drink, starvation.

fool *(SYN.)* oak, dunce, jester, idiot, simpleton, buffoon, harlequin, dolt, blockhead, numskull, clown, dope, trick, deceive, nincompoop.
(ANT.) scholar, genius, sage.

foolish *(SYN.)* senseless, irrational, crazy, silly, brainless, idiotic, simple, nonsensical, stupid, preposterous, asinine.
(ANT.) sane, sound, sensible, rational, judicious, wise, reasonable, prudent.

footing *(SYN.)* base, basis, foundation.

footloose *(SYN.)* uncommitted, free, detached, independent.
(ANT.) engaged, rooted, involved.

forbearance *(SYN.)* moderation, abstinence, abstention, continence.
(ANT.) greed, excess, intoxication.

forbid *(SYN.)* disallow, prevent, ban, prohibit, taboo, outlaw.
(ANT.) approve, let, allow, permit.

forbidding *(SYN.)* evil, hostile, un-

friendly, sinister, scary, repulsive.
(ANT.) pleasant, beneficent, friendly.
force *(SYN.)* energy, might, violence, vigor, intensity, dint, power, constraint, coercion, vigor, compel, compulsion, oblige, make, coerce, strength.
(ANT.) weakness, frailty, persuasion, feebleness, impotence, ineffectiveness.
forceful *(SYN.)* dynamic, vigorous, energetic, potent, drastic, intense.
(ANT.) lackadaisical, insipid, weak.
foreboding *(SYN.)* misgiving, suspicion, apprehension, presage, intuition.
forecast *(SYN.)* prophesy, predict, predetermine.
foregoing *(SYN.)* above, former, preceding, previous, prior.
(ANT.) later, coming, below, follow.
foreign *(SYN.)* alien, strange, exotic, different, unfamiliar.
(ANT.) commonplace, ordinary, familiar.
foreigner *(SYN.)* outsider, alien, newcomer, stranger.
(ANT.) native.
foreman *(SYN.)* super, boss, overseer, supervisor.
forerunner *(SYN.)* harbinger, proclaimer, informant.
foresee *(SYN.)* forecast, expect, anticipate, surmise, envisage.
forest *(SYN.)* grove, woodland, wood, copse, woods.
forestall *(SYN.)* hinder, thwart, prevent, obstruct, repel.
foretell *(SYN.)* soothsay, divine, predict.
forever *(SYN.)* evermore, always, everlasting, hereafter, endlessly.
(ANT.) fleeting, temporarily.
forfeit *(SYN.)* yield, resign, lose, sacrifice.
forgive *(SYN.)* exonerate, clear, excuse, pardon.
(ANT.) impeach, accuse, blame, censure.
forgo *(SYN.)* relinquish, release, surrender, waive, abandon.
(ANT.) keep, retain, safeguard.
forlorn *(SYN.)* pitiable, desolate, dejected, woeful, wretched.
(ANT.) optimistic, cherished, cheerful.
form *(SYN.)* frame, compose, fashion, arrange, construct, make up, devise, create, invent, mold, shape, forge, organize, produce, constitute, make.
(ANT.) wreck, dismantle, destroy, misshape.
formal *(SYN.)* exact, stiff, correct, outward, conformist, conventional, affected, regular, proper, ceremonious, decorous, methodical, precise, solemn, external, perfunctory.
(ANT.) heartfelt, unconstrained, easy, unconventional.
former *(SYN.)* earlier, one-time, previous, erstwhile, prior.
formidable *(SYN.)* alarming, frightful, imposing, terrible, terrifying, dire, fearful, forbidding.
(ANT.) weak, unimpressive, ordinary.
forsake *(SYN.)* abandon, desert, forgo, quit, discard, neglect.

forte *(SYN.)* gift, capability, talent, specialty, aptitude, bulwark.
forth *(SYN.)* out, onward, forward.
forthright *(SYN.)* honest, direct, candid, outspoken, blunt, sincere, plain, explicit.
forthwith *(SYN.)* instantly, promptly, immediately.
(ANT.) afterward, later, ultimately, slowly.
fortify *(SYN.)* bolster, strengthen, buttress, barricade, defend.
fortuitous *(SYN.)* successful, benign, lucky, advantageous, propitious, happy, favored, chance.
(ANT.) unlucky, condemned, persecuted.
fortunate *(SYN.)* happy, auspicious, fortuitous, successful, favored, advantageous, benign, charmed, lucky, felicitous, blessed, propitious, blissful.
(ANT.) ill-fated, cheerless, unlucky, unfortunate, cursed, condemned.
fortune *(SYN.)* chance, fate, lot, luck, riches, wealth, kismet, destiny.
fortuneteller *(SYN.)* soothsayer, clairvoyant, forecaster, oracle, medium.
forward *(SYN.)* leading, front, promote, elevate, advance, first, ahead, onward, further, foremost, aggrandize.
(ANT.) withhold, retard, hinder, retreat, oppose.
foul *(SYN.)* base, soiled, dirty, mean, unclean, polluted, impure, vile, evil, muddy, wicked, rainy, stormy, despicable, filthy.
(ANT.) pure, neat, wholesome, clean.
found *(SYN.)* organize, establish.
foundation *(SYN.)* support, root, base, underpinning, groundwork, bottom, establishment, substructure, basis.
(ANT.) top, cover, building.
foxy *(SYN.)* cunning, sly, artful, crafty, wily, sharp, shrewd, slick.
fraction *(SYN.)* fragment, part, section, morsel, share, piece.
fracture *(SYN.)* crack, break, rupture.
fragile *(SYN.)* delicate, frail, weak, breakable, infirm, brittle, feeble.
(ANT.) tough, hardy, sturdy, strong, stout, durable.
fragment *(SYN.)* scrap, piece, bit, remnant, part, splinter, segment.
fragrance *(SYN.)* odor, smell, scent, perfume, aroma.
fragrant *(SYN.)* aromatic, scented, perfumed.
frail *(SYN.)* feeble, weak, delicate, breakable, fragile.
(ANT.) sturdy, strong, powerful.
frame *(SYN.)* support, framework, skeleton, molding, border, mount.
frank *(SYN.)* honest, candid, open, unreserved, direct, sincere, straightforward.
(ANT.) tricky, dishonest.
frantic *(SYN.)* frenzied, crazed, raving, panicky.
(ANT.) composed, stoic.
fraud *(SYN.)* deception, guile, swindle, deceit, artifice, imposture, trick, cheat, imposition, duplicity, chicanery.
(ANT.) sincerity, fairness, integrity.

fraudulent *(SYN.)* tricky, fake, dishonest, deceitful.

fray *(SYN.)* strife, fight, battle, struggle, tussle, combat, brawl, melee, skirmish.
(ANT.) truce, agreement, peace, concord.

freak *(SYN.)* curiosity, abnormality, monster, oddity.

free *(SYN.)* munificent, clear, autonomous, immune, open, freed, bountiful, liberated, unfastened, immune, emancipated, unconfined, unobstructed, easy, artless, loose, familiar, bounteous, unrestricted, liberal, independent, careless, frank, exempt.
(ANT.) stingy, clogged, illiberal, confined, parsimonious.

freedom *(SYN.)* independence, privilege, familiarity, unrestraint, liberty, exemption, liberation, immunity, license.
(ANT.) servitude, constraint, bondage, slavery, necessity.

freely *(SYN.)* liberally, generously, unstintingly.

freight *(SYN.)* chipping, cargo, load, shipment.

frenzy *(SYN.)* craze, agitation, excitement.

frequent *(SYN.)* usual, habitual, common, often, customary, general.
(ANT.) unique, rare, solitary, uncommon, exceptional, infrequent, scanty.

fresh *(SYN.)* recent, new, additional, further, refreshing, natural, brisk, novel, inexperienced, late, current, sweet, pure, cool.
(ANT.) stagnant, decayed, musty, faded.

fret *(SYN.)* torment, worry, grieve, anguish.

fretful *(SYN.)* testy, irritable, touchy, peevish, short-tempered.
(ANT.) calm.

friend *(SYN.)* crony, supporter, ally, companion, intimate, associate, advocate, comrade, mate, patron, acquaintance, chum, defender.
(ANT.) stranger, adversary.

friendly *(SYN.)* sociable, kindly, affable, genial, companionable, social, neighborly, amicable.
(ANT.) hostile, antagonistic, reserved.

friendship *(SYN.)* knowledge, familiarity, fraternity, acquaintance, intimacy, fellowship, comradeship, cognizance.
(ANT.) unfamiliarity, ignorance.

fright *(SYN.)* alarm, fear, panic, terror.

frighten *(SYN.)* scare, horrify, daunt, affright, appall, terrify, alarm, terrorize, astound, dismay, startle, panic.
(ANT.) soothe, embolden, compose, reassure.

frigid *(SYN.)* cold, wintry, icy, glacial, arctic, freezing.

fringe *(SYN.)* hem, edge, border, trimming, edging.

frisky *(SYN.)* animated, lively, peppy, vivacious.

frolic *(SYN.)* play, cavort, romp, frisk.

front *(SYN.)* facade, face, start, beginning, border, head.

(ANT.) rear, back.

frontier *(SYN.)* border, boundary.

frugal *(SYN.)* parsimonious, saving, stingy, provident, temperate, economical, sparing.
(ANT.) extravagant, wasteful, self-indulgent, intemperate.

fruitful *(SYN.)* fertile, rich, bountiful, teeming, fecund, productive, luxuriant.
(ANT.) lean, unproductive, barren, sterile.

fruitless *(SYN.)* barren, futile, vain, sterile, unproductive.
(ANT.) fertile, productive.

frustrate *(SYN.)* hinder, defeat, thwart, circumvent, outwit, foil, baffle, disappoint, balk, discourage, prevent.
(ANT.) promote, fulfill, accomplish.

fugitive *(SYN.)* deserter, runaway.

fulfill *(SYN.)* do, effect, complete, accomplish, realize.

full *(SYN.)* baggy, crammed, entire, satiated, flowing, perfect, gorged, soaked, complete, filled, packed, extensive, plentiful, replete, voluminous.
(ANT.) lacking, devoid, partial, empty.

full-grown *(SYN.)* ripe, adult, mature, developed, grown-up, complete.
(ANT.) green, young, unripe, adolescent.

fullness *(SYN.)* glut, repletion, enough, satiety, satiation, sufficiency, all, totality, satisfaction, overload, wholeness, aggregate, everything, sum.
(ANT.) need, want, hunger, lack, insufficiency, privation, emptiness, incompleteness.

full-scale *(SYN.)* major, all-out, lavish, comprehensive, unlimited, maximum.
(ANT.) indifferent, partial, minor.

fun *(SYN.)* merriment, pleasure, enjoyment, gaiety, sport, amusement.

function *(SYN.)* operation, activity, affair, ceremony, gathering, party.

fundamental *(SYN.)* basic, essential, primary, elementary.

funny *(SYN.)* odd, droll, ridiculous, queer, farcical, laughable, comic, curious, amusing, humorous, witty.
(ANT.) solemn, sad, sober, melancholy.

furious *(SYN.)* angry, enraged.
(ANT.) serene, calm.

furnish *(SYN.)* yield, give, endow, fit, produce, equip, afford, decorate, supply, appoint.
(ANT.) divest, denude, strip.

furthermore *(SYN.)* moreover, also.

furtive *(SYN.)* surreptitious, secret, hidden, clandestine.
(ANT.) honest, open.

fury *(SYN.)* wrath, anger, frenzy, rage, violence, fierceness.
(ANT.) calmness, serenity.

fuss *(SYN.)* commotion, bother, pester, annoy, irritate.

futile *(SYN.)* pointless, idle, vain, useless, worthless, minor.
(ANT.) weighty, important, worthwhile, serious, valuable.

future *(SYN.)* approaching, imminent, coming, impending.
(ANT.) former, past.

fuzzy *(SYN.)* indistinct, blurred.
(ANT.) lucid, clear.

gab *(SYN.)* jabber, babble, chatter, prattle, gossip.

gabble *(SYN.)* chatter, babble, jabber, blab, prate, gaggle, prattle, blather, gibberish.

gabby *(SYN.)* chatty, talkative, wordy, verbose.

gad *(SYN.)* wander, roam, rove, ramble, meander, cruise.

gadabout *(SYN.)* gypsy, wanderer, rambler.

gadget *(SYN.)* contrivance, device, doodad, jigger, thing, contraption.

gaffe *(SYN.)* blunder, boner, mistake, gaucherie, error, howler.

gag *(SYN.)* witticism, crack jest, joke.

gaiety *(SYN.)* joyousness, cheerfulness, high-spiritedness, joyfulness, light-heartedness.

(ANT.) melancholy, sadness, depression.

gain *(SYN.)* acquire, avail, account, good, interest, attain, favor, achieve, get, secure, advantage, earn, profit, procure, service, obtain, improvement, increase, behalf, net, reach, win, benefit.

(ANT.) trouble, lose, calamity, forfeit, handicap, lose, distress.

gainful *(SYN.)* lucrative, rewarding, profitable, beneficial, payable, productive.

(ANT.) unproductive, unprofitable, unrewarding.

gainsay *(SYN.)* refute, contradict, controvert, deny, refuse, inpugn, contravene, disavow, differ.

(ANT.) maintain, aver, affirm, asseverate.

gait *(SYN.)* stride, walk, tread, step.

gala *(SYN.)* ball, party, carnival, fete, festival.

gale *(SYN.)* burst, surge, outburst.

gall *(SYN.)* nerve, audacity, impudence, annoy, vex, anger, provoke, irritate.

gallant *(SYN.)* bold, brave, courageous, valorous, valiant, noble, polite, fearless, heroic, chivalrous.

gallantry *(SYN.)* valor, daring, courage, prowess, heroism, manliness, dauntlessness, graciousness, attentiveness, coquetry, gentleness, fearlessness, chivalrousness.

(ANT.) poltroonery, timidity, cowardice, cravenness, cloddishness.

gallery *(SYN.)* passageway, hall, aisle, hallway, passage, corridor.

galling *(SYN.)* vexing, irritating, annoying, distressful, irksome.

galore *(SYN.)* abounding, plentiful, profuse, rich, overflowing.

gamble *(SYN.)* game, wager, bet, hazard, risk, venture, chance.

gambol *(SYN.)* romp, dance, cavort, frolic.

game *(SYN.)* fun, contest, merriment, pastime, match, play, amusement, recreation, diversion, entertainment, competition, sport.

(ANT.) labor, hardship, work, business.

gamut *(SYN.)* extent, scope, sweep, horizon, range.

gang *(SYN.)* group, troop, band, company, horde, crew.

gangling *(SYN.)* rangy, lean, skinny, tall, lanky.

gangster *(SYN.)* crook, hoodlum, gunman, criminal.

gap *(SYN.)* cavity, chasm, pore, gulf, aperture, abyss, interval, space, hole, void, pore, break, opening.

gape *(SYN.)* ogle, stare, gawk.

garb *(SYN.)* clothing, dress, vesture, array, attire, clothes, drapery, apparel, garments, costume, raiment.

(ANT.) nudity, nakedness.

garbage *(SYN.)* refuse, waste, trash, rubbish.

garbled *(SYN.)* twisted, confused, distorted.

gargantuan *(SYN.)* colossal, monumental, giant, huge, large, enormous.

garments *(SYN.)* drapery, dress, garb, apparel, array, attire, clothes, vesture, raiment, clothing.

(ANT.) nakedness, nudity.

garnish *(SYN.)* decorate, embellish, trim, adorn, enrich, beautify, deck, ornament.

(ANT.) expose, strip, debase, uncover, defame.

garrulous *(SYN.)* chatty, glib, verbose, talkative, communicative, voluble.

(ANT.) silent, uncommunicative, laconic, reticent, taciturn.

gash *(SYN.)* lacerate, slash, pierce, cut, hew, slice.

gasp *(SYN.)* pant, puff, wheeze.

gather *(ANT.)* assemble, collect, garner, harvest, reap, deduce, judge, amass, congregate, muster, cull, glean, accumulate, convene.

(ANT.) scatter, disperse, distribute, disband, separate.

gathering *(SYN.)* meeting, crowd, throng, company, assembly.

gaudy *(SYN.)* showy, flashy, loud, bold, ostentatious.

gaunt *(ANT.)* lank, diaphanous, flimsy, gauzy, narrow, rare, scanty, meager, gossamer, emaciated, scrawny, tenuous, thin, fine, lean, skinny, spare, slim, slight, slender, diluted.

(ANT.) wide, fat, thick, broad, bulky.

gay *(SYN.)* merry, lighthearted, joyful, cheerful, sprightly, jolly, happy, joyous, gleeful, jovial, colorful, bright, glad.

(ANT.) glum, mournful, sad, depressed, sorrowful, somber, sullen.

gaze *(SYN.)* look, stare, view, watch, examine, observe, glance, behold, discern, seem, see, survey, witness, inspect, goggle, appear.

(ANT.) hide, overlook, avert, miss.

geld *(SYN.)* neuter, alter, spay, castrate.

gem *(SYN.)* jewel, semiprecious stone.

general *(SYN.)* ordinary, universal, usual, common, customary, regular, vague, miscellaneous, indefinite, inexact.

(ANT.) definite, particular, exceptional, singular, rare, particular, precise, exact, specific.

generally *(SYN.)* ordinarily, usually, customarily, normally, mainly.

(ANT.) seldom, infrequently, rare.

generate *(SYN.)* produce, bestow, impart, concede, permit, acquiesce, cede, relent, succumb, surrender, pay, supply, grant, relent, bear, afford, submit, waive, allow, breed, accord, accede, abdicate, resign, relinquish, surrender, quit.
(ANT.) assert, refuse, struggle, resist, dissent, oppose, deny, strive.

generation *(SYN.)* age, date, era, period, seniority, senescence, senility, time, epoch, dotage.
(ANT.) infancy, youth, childhood.

generosity *(SYN.)* magnanimity, benevolence, humanity, kindness, philanthropy, tenderness, altruism, liberality, charity, beneficence.
(ANT.) selfishness, malevolence, cruelty, inhumanity, unkindness.

generous *(SYN.)* giving, liberal, unselfish, magnanimous, bountiful, munificent, charitable, big, noble, beneficent.
(ANT.) greedy, stingy, selfish, covetous, mean, miserly.

genesis *(SYN.)* birth, root, creation, source, origin, beginning.

genius *(SYN.)* intellect, adept, intellectual, sagacity, proficient, creativity, ability, inspiration, faculty, originality, aptitude, brain, gift, prodigy, talent.
(ANT.) dullard, stupidity, dolt, shallowness, moron, ineptitude, obtuseness.

genre *(SYN.)* chaste, order, set, elegance, class, excellence, kind, caste, denomination, grade.

genteel *(SYN.)* cultured, polished, polite, refined, elegant.
(ANT.) discourteous, churlish, common.

gentle *(SYN.)* peaceful, placid, tame, serene, relaxed, docile, benign, soothing, calm, soft, mild, amiable, friendly, kindly, cultivated.
(ANT.) nasty, harsh, rough, fierce, mean, violent, savage.

genuine *(SYN.)* real, true, unaffected, authentic, sincere, bona fide, unadulterated, legitimate, actual, veritable, definite, proven.
(ANT.) false, sham, artificial, fake, counterfeit, bogus, pretended, insincere, sham.

genus *(SYN.)* kind, race, species, type, variety, character, family, breed, sort.

germ *(SYN.)* pest, virus, contamination, disease, pollution, taint, infection, contagion, poison, ailment.

germinate *(SYN.)* vegetate, pullulate, sprout, develop, grow.

gesture *(SYN.)* omen, signal, symbol, emblem, indication, note, token, symptom, movement, sign, motion, indication.

get *(SYN.)* obtain, receive, attain, gain, achieve, acquire, procure, earn, fetch, carry, remove, prepare, take, ready, urge, induce, secure.
(ANT.) lose, surrender, forfeit, leave, renounce.

ghastly *(SYN.)* frightful, horrible, horrifying, frightening, grisly, hideous, dreadful.

ghost *(SYN.)* phantom, spook, appari-

tion, specter, trace, hint, vestige, spirit.

ghoulish *(SYN.)* weird, eerie, horrifying, gruesome, sinister, scary.

giant *(SYN.)* monster, colossus, mammoth, superman, gigantic.
(ANT.) small, tiny, dwarf, runt, midget, infinitesimal.

gibe *(SYN.)* sneer, jeer, mock, scoff, boo, hoot, hiss.
(ANT.) approve.

giddy *(SYN.)* reeling, dizzy, flighty, silly, scatterbrained.
(ANT.) serious.

gift *(SYN.)* endowment, favor, gratuity, bequest, talent, charity, present, largess, donation, grant, aptitude, boon, offering, faculty, genius, benefaction.
(ANT.) purchase, loss, ineptitude, deprivation, earnings, incapacity.

gigantic *(SYN.)* huge, colossal, immense, large, vast, elephantine, gargantuan, prodigious, mammoth, monumental, enormous.
(ANT.) small, tiny, minute, diminutive, little.

giggle *(SYN.)* chuckle, jeer, laugh, roar, snicker, titter, cackle, guffaw, mock.

gild *(SYN.)* cover, coat, paint, embellish, sweeten, retouch, camouflage.

gingerly *(SYN.)* gentle, cautiously, carefully, gently.
(ANT.) roughly.

gird *(SYN.)* wrap, tie, bind, belt, encircle, surround, get set, prepare.
(ANT.) untie.

girl *(SYN.)* female, lass, miss, maiden, damsel.

girth *(SYN.)* measure, size, width, dimensions, expanse, proportions.

gist *(SYN.)* connotation, explanation, purpose, significance, acceptation, implication, interpretation, meaning.
(ANT.) redundancy.

give *(SYN.)* bestow, contribute, grant, impart, provide, donate, confer, deliver, present, furnish, yield, develop, offer, produce, hand over, award, allot, deal out, mete out, bend, sacrifice, supply.
(ANT.) withdraw, take, retain, keep, seize.

given *(SYN.)* handed over, presented, supposed, stated, disposed, assumed, inclined, bent.

glacier *(SYN.)* frigid, icy, iceberg.

glad *(SYN.)* happy, cheerful, gratified, delighted, joyous, merry, pleased, exulting, charmed, thrilled, satisfied, tickled, gay, bright.
(ANT.) sad, depressed, dejected, melancholy, unhappy, morose, somber, despondent.

gladness *(SYN.)* bliss, contentment, happiness, pleasure, well-being, beatitude, delight, satisfaction, blessedness.
(ANT.) sadness, sorrow, despair, misery, grief.

glade *(SYN.)* clearing.

gladiator *(SYN.)* battler, fighter, competitor, combatant, contender, contestant.

glamorous *(SYN.)* spellbinding, fascinating, alluring, charming, bewitching, entrancing, captivating, enchanting, attractive, appealing, enticing, enthralling.

glamour (SYN.) charm, allure, attraction, magnetism, fascination.

glance (SYN.) eye, gaze, survey, view, examine, inspect, discern, look, see, witness, peek, regard, skim, reflect, glimpse, behold, observe.
(ANT.) hide, miss, avert, overlook.

glare (SYN.) flash, dazzle, stare, glower, glow, shine, glaze, burn, brilliance, flare, blind, scowl.

glaring (SYN.) flagrant, obvious, blatant, prominent, dazzling.

glass (SYN.) cup, tumbler, goblet, pane, crystal.

glassy (SYN.) blank, empty, emotionless, vacant, fixed, expressionless.

glaze (SYN.) buff, luster, cover, wax, gloss, coat, polish, shellac.

gleam (SYN.) flash, glimmer, glisten, shimmer, sparkle, twinkle, glare, beam, glow, radiate, glimmering, shine, burn, reflection, blaze.

glean (SYN.) reap, gather, select, harvest, pick, separate, cull.

glee (SYN.) mirth, joy, gladness, enchantment, delight, cheer, bliss, elation, merriment.
(ANT.) depression, misery, dejection.

glen (SYN.) ravine, valley.

glib (SYN.) smooth, suave, flat, plain, polished, sleek, urbane.
(ANT.) rough, rugged, blunt, harsh, bluff.

glide (SYN.) sweep, sail, fly, flow, slip, coast, cruise, move easily, skim, slide.

glimmer (SYN.) blink, shimmer, flicker, indication, hint, clue, suggestion.

glimpse (SYN.) notice, glance, peek, see, impression, look, flash.

glint (SYN.) flash, gleam, peek, glance, glimpse, sparkle, glitter.

glisten (SYN.) shimmer, shine, glimmer, twinkle, glitter, glister, sparkle.

glitch (SYN.) mishap, snag, hitch, malfunction.

glitter (SYN.) glisten, glimmer, sparkle, shine, twinkle.

gloat (SYN.) triumph, exult, glory, rejoice, revel.

global (SYN.) universal, international, worldwise.

globe (SYN.) orb, ball, world, earth, map, universe, sphere.

gloom (SYN.) bleakness, despondency, misery, sadness, woe, darkness, dejection, obscurity, blackness, shadow, shade, dimness, shadows, melancholy.
(ANT.) joy, mirth, exultation, cheerfulness, light, happiness, brightness, frivolity.

gloomy (SYN.) despondent, dismal, glum, somber, sorrowful, sad, dejected, disconsolate, dim, dark, morose, dispirited, moody, grave, pensive.
(ANT.) happy, merry, cheerful, highspirited, bright, sunny, joyous.

glorify (SYN.) enthrone, exalt, honor, revere, adore, dignify, enshrine, consecrate, praise, worship, laud, venerate.

(ANT.) mock, dishonor, debase, abuse, degrade.

glorious (SYN.) exalted, high, noble, splendid, supreme, elevated, lofty, raised, majestic, famous, noted, stately, distinguished, celebrated, renowned, famed, magnificent, grand, proud, impressive, elegant, sublime.
(ANT.) ridiculous, low, base, ignoble, terrible, ordinary.

glory (SYN.) esteem, praise, respect, reverence, admiration, honor, dignity, worship, eminence, homage, deference.
(ANT.) dishonor, disgrace, contempt, reproach, derision.

gloss (SYN.) luster, shine, glow, sheen.

glossary (SYN.) dictionary, thesaurus, wordbook, lexicon.

glossy (SYN.) smooth, glistening, shiny, sleek, polished.
(ANT.) matte, dull.

glow (SYN.) beam, glisten, radiate, shimmer, sparkle, glare, blaze, scintillate, shine, light, gleam, burn, flare, flame, radiate, dazzle, blush, redden, heat, warmth, flicker.

glower (SYN.) scowl, stare, frown, glare.
(ANT.) beam, grin, smile.

glowing (SYN.) fiery, intense, passionate, zealous, enthusiastic, ardent, eager, fervent, favorable, impassioned, keen, complimentary, vehement.
(ANT.) cool, indifferent, apathetic, nonchalant.

glue (SYN.) bind, fasten, cement, paste.

glum (SYN.) morose, sulky, fretful, crabbed, sullen, dismal, dour, moody.
(ANT.) joyous, merry, amiable, gay, pleasant.

glut (SYN.) gorge, sate, content, furnish, fill, pervade, satiate, stuff, replenish, fill up, satisfy, stock.
(ANT.) empty, exhaust, deplete, void, drain.

glutton (SYN.) pig, hog, greedy eater.

gluttony (SYN.) ravenousness, piggishness, devouring, insatiability.
(ANT.) satisfaction, fullness.

gnarled (SYN.) twisted, knotted, rugged, knobby, nodular.

gnash (SYN.) gnaw, crunch, grind.

gnaw (SYN.) chew, eat, gnash, grind, erode.

go (SYN.) proceed, depart, flee, move, vanish, exit, walk, quit, fade, progress, travel, become, fit, agree, leave, suit, harmonize, pass, travel, function, operate, withdraw.
(ANT.) stay, arrive, enter, stand, come.

goad (SYN.) incite, prod, drive, urge, push, shove, jab, provoke, stimulate.

goal (SYN.) craving, destination, desire, longing, objective, finish, end, passion, aim, object, aspiration.

gobble (SYN.) devour, eat fast, gorge, gulp, stuff.

goblet (SYN.) cup, glass.

goblin (SYN.) troll, elf, dwarf, spirit.

godlike (SYN.) holy, supernatural, heavenly, celestial, divine, transcendent.
(ANT.) profane, wicked, blasphemous,

diabolical, mundane.

godly *(SYN.)* pious, religious, holy, pure, divine, spiritual, righteous, saintly.

golden *(SYN.)* shining, metallic, bright, fine, superior, nice, excellent, valuable. *(ANT.) dull, inferior.*

gong *(SYN.)* chimes, bells.

good *(SYN.)* honest, sound, valid, cheerful, honorable, worthy, conscientious, moral, genuine, humane, kind, fair, useful, skillful, adequate, friendly. *(ANT.) bad, imperfect, vicious, undesirable, unfriendly, unkind, evil.*

good-by *(SYN.)* so long, farewell.

good-bye *(SYN.)* farewell.

good-hearted *(SYN.)* good, kind, thoughtful, kindhearted, considerate. *(ANT.) evil-hearted.*

good-humored *(SYN.)* pleasant, good-natured, cheerful, sunny, amiable. *(ANT.) petulant, cranky.*

goodness *(SYN.)* good, honesty, integrity, virtue, righteousness. *(ANT.) sin, evil, dishonesty, corruption.*

goods *(SYN.)* property, belongings, holdings, possessions, merchandise.

good will *(SYN.)* agreeability, harmony, willingness, readiness.

gore *(SYN.)* impale, penetrate, puncture, gouge.

gorge *(SYN.)* ravine, devour, stuff, gobble, valley, defile, pass, cram, fill.

gorgeous *(SYN.)* grand, ravishing, glorious, stunning, brilliant, divine. *(ANT.) homely, ugly, squalid.*

gory *(SYN.)* bloody.

gossamer *(SYN.)* dainty, fine, filmy, delicate, sheer, transparent.

gossip *(SYN.)* prate, rumor, prattle, hearsay, meddler, tattler, chatter.

gouge *(SYN.)* scoop, dig, carve, burrow, excavate, chisel, notch.

gourmet *(SYN.)* gourmand, gastronome, connoisseur.

govern *(SYN.)* manage, oversee, reign, preside over, supervise, direct, command, sway, administer, control. *(ANT.) assent, submit, acquiesce.*

government *(SYN.)* control, direction, rule, command, authority.

governor *(SYN.)* controller, administrator, director, leader, manager.

gown *(SYN.)* garment, robe, frock, dress, costume, attire.

grab *(SYN.)* snatch, grip, clutch, seize, grasp, capture, pluck.

grace *(SYN.)* charm, beauty, handsomeness, loveliness, dignify, fairness, honor, distinguish, sympathy. *(ANT.) eyesore, homeliness, deformity, ugliness, disfigurement.*

graceful *(SYN.)* elegant, fluid, natural, supple, beautiful, comely, flowing. *(ANT.) clumsy, awkward, gawky, ungainly, deformed.*

gracious *(SYN.)* warm-hearted, pleasing, friendly, engaging, agreeable, kind, amiable, kindly, nice, good, courteous, polite, generous. *(ANT.) surly, hateful, churlish, rude, disagreeable, impolite, thoughtless, discourteous, ill-natured.*

grade *(SYN.)* kind, rank, elegance, denomination, sort, arrange, category, classify, rate, group, place, mark.

gradual *(SYN.)* deliberate, sluggish, dawdling, laggard, slow, leisurely, moderate, easy, delaying. *(ANT.) quick, swift, fast, speedy, rapid.*

graduate *(SYN.)* pass, finish, advance.

graft *(SYN.)* fraud, theft, cheating, bribery, dishonesty, transplant.

grain *(SYN.)* speck, particle, plant, bit, seed, temper, fiber, character, texture, markings, nature, tendency.

grand *(SYN.)* great, elaborate, splendid, royal, stately, noble, considerable. *(ANT.) unassuming, modest, insignificant, unimportant, humble.*

grandeur *(SYN.)* resplendence, majesty, distinction, glory.

grandiose *(SYN.)* grand, lofty, magnificent, stately, noble, pompous, dignified, imposing, sublime, majestic. *(ANT.) lowly, ordinary, common.*

grandstand *(SYN.)* bleachers, gallery.

granite *(SYN.)* stone, rock.

grant *(SYN.)* confer, allocate, deal, divide, mete, appropriation, assign, benefaction, distribute, allowance, donate, award, mete out, deal out. *(ANT.) refuse, withhold, confiscate, keep, retain.*

granular *(SYN.)* grainy, sandy, crumbly, rough, gritty.

graph *(SYN.)* design, plan, stratagem, draw up, chart, sketch, cabal, machination, outline, plot.

graphic *(SYN.)* vivid, lifelike, significant, meaningful, pictorial, descriptive.

grapple *(SYN.)* grip, seize, clutch, clasp, grasp, fight, struggle.

grasp *(SYN.)* clutch, grip, seize, apprehend, capture, snare, hold, clasp. *(ANT.) release, lose, throw, liberate.*

grasping *(SYN.)* possessive, greedy, selfish, acquisitive, mercenary. *(ANT.) liberal, unselfish, generous.*

grate *(SYN.)* file, pulverize, grind, scrape, scratch, scrape, annoy, irritate.

grateful *(SYN.)* beholden, obliged, appreciative, thankful, indebted. *(ANT.) ungrateful, unappreciative, grudging, thankless.*

gratify *(SYN.)* charm, please, satisfy. *(ANT.) frustrate.*

gratifying *(SYN.)* contentment, solace, relief, comfort, ease, succor, consolation, enjoyment. *(ANT.) suffering, torment, affliction, discomfort, torture, misery.*

grating *(SYN.)* harsh, rugged, severe, stringent, coarse, gruff, jarring, rigorous, strict. *(ANT.) smooth, melodious, gentle, soft.*

gratis *(SYN.)* complimentary, free.

gratitude *(SYN.)* gratefulness, thankfulness, appreciation. *(ANT.) ungratefulness.*

gratuity *(SYN.)* tip, bonus, gift.

grave *(SYN.)* sober, grim, earnest, serious, important, momentous, sedate, solemn, somber, imposing, vital, essential, staid, consequential, thoughtful.

(ANT.) light, flighty, trivial, insignificant, unimportant, trifling, merry, gay, cheery, frivolous.
gravel *(SYN.)* stones, pebbles, grain.
gravitate *(SYN.)* incline, tend, lean, approach, toward.
gravity *(SYN.)* concern, importance, seriousness, pull, movement.
(ANT.) triviality.
graze *(SYN.)* scrape, feed, rub, brush, contact, skim.
grease *(SYN.)* fat, oil, lubrication.
greasy *(SYN.)* messy, buttery.
great *(SYN.)* large, numerous, eminent, illustrious, big, gigantic enormous, immense, vast, weighty, fine.
(ANT.) minute, common, menial, ordinary, paltry, unknown.
greed *(SYN.)* piggishness, lust, desire, greediness, avarice, covetousness.
(ANT.) selflessness, generosity.
greedy *(SYN.)* selfish, devouring, ravenous, avaricious, covetous, rapacious, gluttonous, insatiable, voracious.
(ANT.) full, generous, munificent, giving, satisfied.
green *(SYN.)* inexperienced, modern, novel, recent, further, naive, fresh, natural, raw, unsophisticated, undeveloped, immature, unripe, additional, brisk, artless.
(ANT.) hackneyed, musty, decayed, faded, stagnant.
greenhorn *(SYN.)* tenderfoot, beginner, apprentice, amateur, novice.
greenhouse *(SYN.)* hothouse.
greet *(SYN.)* hail, accost, meet, address, talk to, speak to, welcome, approach.
(ANT.) pass by, avoid.
gregarious *(SYN.)* outgoing, civil, affable, hospitable, sociable.
(ANT.) inhospitable, antisocial, disagreeable, hermitic.
grief *(SYN.)* misery, sadness, tribulation, affliction, heartache, woe, trial, anguish, mourning, distress, lamentation.
(ANT.) happiness, solace, consolation, comfort, joy.
grief-stricken *(SYN.)* heartsick, ravaged, devastated, wretched, forlorn, desolate, wretched.
(ANT.) joyous, blissful, content.
grievance *(SYN.)* injury, wrong, injustice, detriment, complaint, damage, prejudice, evil, objection, protest, accusation, harm.
(ANT.) improvement, benefit, repair.
grieve *(SYN.)* lament, brood over, mourn, weep, wail, sorrow, distress, bemoan, hurt, deplore.
(ANT.) revel, carouse, celebrate, rejoice, gladden, soothe.
grieved *(SYN.)* contrite, remorseful, beggarly, mean, pitiful, shabby, vile, sorrowful, pained, hurt, sorry, contemptible, worthless.
(ANT.) splendid, delighted, cheerful, impenitent, unrepentant.
grievous *(SYN.)* gross, awful, outrageous, shameful, lamentable, regrettable.
(ANT.) agreeable, comforting, pleasur-

able.
grill *(SYN.)* cook, broil, question, interrogate, barbecue, grating, gridiron, cross-examine.
grim *(SYN.)* severe, harsh, strict, merciless, fierce, horrible, inflexible, adamant, ghastly, frightful, unyielding, rigid, stern.
(ANT.) pleasant, lenient, relaxed, amiable, congenial, smiling.
grimace *(SYN.)* expression, mope.
grimy *(SYN.)* unclean, grubby, soiled.
grin *(SYN.)* beam, smile, smirk.
grind *(SYN.)* mill, mash, powder, crush, crumble, pulverize, smooth, grate, sharpen, even.
grip *(SYN.)* catch, clutch, apprehend, trap, arrest, grasp, hold, bag, suitcase, lay hold of, clench, command, control, possession, domination, comprehension, understanding, seize.
(ANT.) release, liberate, lose, throw.
gripe *(SYN.)* protest, grumbling.
grit *(SYN.)* rub, grind, grate, sand, gravel, pluck, courage, stamina.
groan *(SYN.)* sob, wail, howl, moan, whimper, wail, complain.
groggy *(SYN.)* dazed, dopy, stupefied, stunned, drugged, unsteady.
(ANT.) alert.
groom *(SYN.)* tend, tidy, preen, curry, spouse, consort.
groove *(SYN.)* furrow, channel, track, routine, slot, scratch.
groovy *(SYN.)* marvelous, delightful, wonderful.
grope *(SYN.)* fumble, feel around.
gross *(SYN.)* glaring, coarse, indelicate, obscene, bulky, great, total, whole, brutal, grievous, aggregate, earthy, rude, vulgar, entire, enormous, plain, crass, rough, large.
(ANT.) appealing, delicate, refined, proper, polite, cultivated, slight, comely, trivial, decent.
grotesque *(SYN.)* strange, weird, odd, incredible, fantastic, monstrous, absurd, freakish, bizarre, peculiar, deformed, disfigured, queer.
grotto *(SYN.)* tunnel, cave, hole, cavern.
grouch *(SYN.)* protest, remonstrate, whine, complain, grumble, murmur, mope, mutter, repine.
(ANT.) praise, applaud, rejoice.
grouchy *(SYN.)* cantankerous, grumpy, surly.
(ANT.) cheerful, contented, pleasant.
ground *(SYN.)* foundation, presumption, surface, principle, underpinning, premise, base, bottom, fix, basis, soil, land, earth, set, root, support, establish, dirt, presupposition.
(ANT.) implication, superstructure, trimming, derivative.
groundless *(SYN.)* baseless, unfounded, unwarranted, needless.
grounds *(SYN.)* garden, lawns, dregs, foundation, leftovers, reason, sediment, cause, basis, premise, motive.
groundwork *(SYN.)* support, bottom, base, underpinning, premise, presupposition, principle, basis.
(ANT.) trimming, implication, deriva-

tive, superstructure.

group *(SYN.)* crowd, clock, party, troupe, swarm, bunch, brook, assembly, herd, band, mob, brood, class, throng, cluster, flock, lot, collection, pack, horde, gathering, aggregation.
(ANT.) disassemble.

grouse *(SYN.)* mutter, grumble, gripe, scold, growl, complain.

grovel *(SYN.)* creep, crawl, cower, cringe, slouch, stoop, scramble.

groveling *(SYN.)* dishonorable, lowly, sordid, vile, mean, abject, despicable, ignoble, menial, servile, vulgar, ignominious.
(ANT.) lofty, noble, esteemed, exalted, righteous.

grow *(SYN.)* extend, swell, advance, develop, enlarge, enlarge, germinate, mature, expand, flower, raise, become, cultivate, increase, distend.
(ANT.) wane, shrink, atrophy, decay, diminish, contract.

growl *(SYN.)* complain, snarl, grumble, gnarl, roar, clamor, bellow.

grown-up *(SYN.)* full-grown, adult, of age, mature, big, senior.
(ANT.) little, childish, junior, juvenile.

growth *(SYN.)* expansion, development, unfolding, maturing, progress, elaboration, evolution.
(ANT.) degeneration, deterioration, curtailment, abbreviation, compression.

grub *(SYN.)* gouge, dig, scoop out, burrow, tunnel, excavate, plod, toil, drudge.

grubby *(SYN.)* unkempt, grimy, slovenly, dirty.
(ANT.) tidy, spruce, neat, clean, well-groomed.

grudge *(SYN.)* malevolence, malice, resentment, bitterness, spite, animosity, enmity, rancor, ill will.
(ANT.) kindness, love, benevolence, affection, good will, friendliness.

grudgingly *(SYN.)* reluctantly, unwillingly, under protest, involuntarily.

grueling *(SYN.)* taxing, exhausting, excruciating, trying, arduous, grinding, crushing.
(ANT.) effortless, easy, light, simple.

gruesome *(SYN.)* hideous, frightful, horrible, loathsome, ghastly, grisly.
(ANT.) agreeable, soothing, delightful, charming.

gruff *(SYN.)* scratchy, crude, incomplete, unpolished, stormy, brusque, rude, rough, uncivil, churlish, violent, harsh, imperfect, craggy, irregular, deep, husky, approximate, tempestuous, blunt.
(ANT.) civil, courteous, polished, calm, even, sleek, smooth, finished, gentle, placid, pleasant, tranquil.

grumble *(SYN.)* protest, complain.

grumpy *(SYN.)* ill-tempered, cranky, grouchy, surly, cross-grained, crabbed, fractious, pettish, disgruntled, moody.
(ANT.) winsome, amiable, pleasant, cheery.

guarantee *(SYN.)* bond, pledge, token, warrant, earnest, surety, bail, commit-

ment, promise, secure, swear, assure, sponsor, certify, warranty, insure, endorse, security.

guarantor *(SYN.)* voucher, sponsor, warrantor, signatory, surety.

guaranty *(SYN.)* warranty, token, deposit, earnest, pledge, stake.

guard *(SYN.)* protect, shield, veil, cloak, conceal, disguise, envelop, preserve, hide, defend, cover, sentry, protector, shroud, curtain.
(ANT.) unveil, expose, ignore, neglect, bare, reveal, disregard, divulge.

guarded *(SYN.)* discreet, cautious.
(ANT.) audacious, reckless, careless.

guardian *(SYN.)* curator, keeper, protector, custodian, patron, watchdog, champion.

guess *(SYN.)* estimate, suppose, think, assume, reason, believe, reckon, speculate, notion, surmise, hypothesis, imagine, consider, opinion.
(ANT.) know.

guest *(SYN.)* caller, client, customer, patient, visitor, company.
(ANT.) host.

guide *(SYN.)* manage, supervise, conduct, direct, lead, steer, escort, pilot, show, squire, usher, control, affect, influence, regulate.
(ANT.) follower, follow.

guild *(SYN.)* association, union, society.

guile *(SYN.)* deceitfulness, fraud, wiliness, trick, deceit, chicanery, cunning, deception, craftiness, sneakiness.
(ANT.) sincerity, openness, honesty, truthfulness, candor, frankness.

guileless *(SYN.)* open, innocent, naive, sincere, simple, candid.
(ANT.) treacherous, plotting.

guilt *(SYN.)* sin, blame, fault, offense.

guilty *(SYN.)* culpable, to blame, responsible, criminal, blameworthy.
(ANT.) blameless, innocent, guiltless.

guise *(SYN.)* aspect, pretense, mien, look, air, advent, apparition, appearance, dress, garb, coat, cover, clothes, show, manner, form, demeanor, arrival.

gulch *(SYN.)* gorge, ravine, canyon.

gulf *(SYN.)* ravine, cut, break, crack, chasm, canyon, abyss, cleft, separation, bay, sound, inlet.

gullible *(SYN.)* trustful, naive, innocent, unsuspecting, deceivable, believing.
(ANT.) skeptical, sophisticated.

gully *(SYN.)* ditch, gorge, ravine, valley, gulch, gulf.

gulp *(SYN.)* devour, swallow, gasp.

gun *(SYN.)* fire, shoot, weapon, discharge, pistol, firearm, revolver.

gush *(SYN.)* pour, spurt, stream, rush out, spout, flood, flush, chatter.

gust *(SYN.)* blast, wind, outbreak.

gutter *(SYN.)* ditch, groove, drain, channel, trench, sewer, trough.

gymnasium *(SYN.)* playground, arena, court, athletic field.

gymnastics *(SYN.)* drill, exercise, acrobatics, calisthenics.

gyp *(SYN.)* swindle, cheat, defraud.

gypsy *(SYN.)* nomad.

habit *(SYN.)* usage, routine, compulsion, use, wont, custom, disposition, practice, addiction, fashion.

habitation *(SYN.)* abode, domicile, lodgings, dwelling, home.

habitual *(SYN.)* general, usual, common, frequent, persistent, customary, routine, regular, often.
(ANT.) solitary, unique, exceptional, occasional, unusual, scanty, rare.

habituated *(SYN.)* used, accustomed, adapted, acclimated, comfortable, familiarized, addicted, settled.

hack *(SYN.)* cleave, chop, slash, hew, slice, pick, sever, mangle.

hackneyed *(SYN.)* stale, stereotyped, trite, commonplace, ordinary, banal, common, unique.
(ANT.) novel, stimulating, modern, fresh, creative, momentous.

hag *(SYN.)* beldam, crone, vixen, granny, ogress, harridan, virage.

haggard *(SYN.)* drawn, careworn, debilitated, spent, gaunt, worn.
(ANT.) bright, fresh, clear-eyed, animated.

haggle *(SYN.)* dicker, bargain.

hail *(SYN.)* welcome, approach, accost, speak to, address, greet.
(ANT.) pass by, avoid.

hairdo *(SYN.)* hairstyle, coiffure, haircut.

hairdresser *(SYN.)* beautician, barber.

hairless *(SYN.)* shorn, bald, baldpated, depilitated.
(ANT.) hirsute, hairy, unshaven.

hair-raising *(SYN.)* horrifying, exciting, alarming, thrilling, startling, frightful, scary, breathtaking.

hairy *(SYN.)* bearded, shaggy, hirsute, bewhiskered.

hale *(SYN.)* robust, well, wholesome, hearty, healthy, sound, strong, vigorous, salubrious.
(ANT.) noxious, frail, diseased, delicate, infirm, injurious.

half-baked *(SYN.)* crude, premature, makeshift, illogical, shallow.

half-hearted *(SYN.)* uncaring, indifferent, unenthusiastic, cool.
(ANT.) eager, enthusiastic, earnest.

half-wit *(SYN.)* dope, simpleton, nitwit, dunce, idiot, fool.

hall *(SYN.)* corridor, lobby, passage, hallway, vestibule, foyer.

hallow *(SYN.)* glorify, exalt, dignify, aggrandize, consecrate, elevate, ennoble, raise, erect.
(ANT.) dishonor, humiliate, debase, degrade.

hallowed *(SYN.)* holy, sacred, beatified, sacrosanct, blessed, divine.

hallucination *(SYN.)* fantasy, mirage, dream, vision, phantasm, appearance, aberration, illusion.

halt *(SYN.)* impede, obstruct, terminate, stop, hinder, desist, check, arrest, abstain, discontinue, hold, end, cork, interrupt, bar, cease.
(ANT.) start, begin, proceed, speed, beginning, promote.

halting *(SYN.)* imperfect, awkward, stuttering, faltering, hobbling, doubtful, limping, wavering.
(ANT.) decisive, confident, smooth, graceful, facile.

hammer *(SYN.)* beat, bang, whack, pound, batter, drive, tap, cudgel.

hamper *(SYN.)* prevent, impede, thwart, restrain, hinder, obstruct.
(ANT.) help, assist, expedite, encourage, facilitate.

hamstrung *(SYN.)* disabled, helpless, paralyzed.

hand *(SYN.)* assistant, helper, support, aid, farmhand, laborer.

handicap *(SYN.)* retribution, penalty, disadvantage, forfeiture, hindrance, chastisement.
(ANT.) reward, pardon, compensation, remuneration.

handily *(SYN.)* readily, skillfully, easily, dexterously, smoothly, adroitly, deftly.

handkerchief *(SYN.)* bandanna, kerchief, scarf.

handle *(SYN.)* hold, touch, finger, clutch, grip, manipulate, feel, grasp, control, oversee, direct, treat, steer, supervise, run, regulate.

hand out *(SYN.)* disburse, distribute, deal, mete, circulate.

hand over *(SYN.)* release, surrender, deliver, yield, present, fork over.

handsome *(SYN.)* lovely, pretty, fair, comely, beautiful, charming, elegant, good-looking, large, generous, liberal, beauteous, fine.
(ANT.) repulsive, ugly, unattractive, stingy, small, mean, petty, unsightly, meager, homely, foul, hideous.

handy *(SYN.)* suitable, adapted, appropriate, favorable, fitting, near, ready, close, nearby, clever, helpful, useful, timely, accessible.
(ANT.) inopportune, troublesome, awkward, inconvenient.

hang *(SYN.)* drape, hover, dangle, suspend, kill, sag, execute, lynch.

hang in *(SYN.)* continue, endure, remain, perservere, resist, persist.

hang-up *(SYN.)* inhibition, difficulty, snag, hindrance, block.

hanker *(SYN.)* wish, yearn, long, desire, pine, thirst, covet.

haphazard *(SYN.)* aimless, random, purposeless, casual, indiscriminate, accidental.
(ANT.) determined, planned, designed, deliberate.

hapless *(SYN.)* ill-fated, unfortunate, jinxed, luckless, wretched.

happen *(SYN.)* occur, take place, bechance, betide, transpire, come to pass, chance, befall.

happening *(SYN.)* episode, event, scene, incident, affair, experience, phenomenon, transaction.

happiness *(SYN.)* pleasure, gladness, delight, beatitude, bliss, contentment, satisfaction, joy, joyousness, blessedness, joyfulness, felicity, elation, well-being.
(ANT.) sadness, sorrow, despair, misery, grief.

happy *(SYN.)* gay, joyous, cheerful, fortunate, glad, merry, contented,

satisfied, lucky, blessed, pleased, opportune, delighted.
(ANT.) *gloomy, morose, sad, sorrowful, miserable, inconvenient, unlucky, depressed, blue.*
happy-go-lucky (SYN.) easygoing, carefree, unconcerned.
(ANT.) *prudent, responsible, concerned.*
harangue (SYN.) oration, diatribe, lecture, tirade, exhortation.
harass (SYN.) badger, irritate, molest, pester, taunt, torment, provoke, tantalize, worry, aggravate, annoy, nag, plague, vex.
(ANT.) *please, soothe, comfort, delight, gratify.*
harbinger (SYN.) sign, messenger, proclaim, forerunner, herald.
harbor (SYN.) haven, port, anchorage, cherish, entertain, protect, shelter.
hard (SYN.) difficult, burdensome, arduous, rigid, puzzling, cruel, strict, unfeeling, severe, stern, impenetrable, compact, tough, solid, onerous, rigorous, firm, intricate, harsh, perplexing.
(ANT.) *fluid, brittle, effortless, gentle, tender, easy, simple, plastic, soft, lenient, flabby, elastic.*
hard-boiled (SYN.) unsympathetic, tough, harsh, unsentimental.
harden (SYN.) petrify, solidify.
(ANT.) *loose, soften.*
hardheaded (SYN.) stubborn, obstinate, unyielding, headstrong.
hardhearted (SYN.) merciless, hard, unmerciful, callous, pitiless, ruthless.
hardly (SYN.) barely, scarcely.
hard-nosed (SYN.) shrewd, tough, practical.
hardship (SYN.) ordeal, test, effort, affliction, misfortune, trouble, experiment, proof, essay, misery, examination, difficulty, tribulation.
(ANT.) *consolation, alleviation.*
hardy (SYN.) sturdy, strong, tough, vigorous.
(ANT.) *frail, decrepit, feeble, weak, fragile.*
harm (SYN.) hurt, mischief, misfortune, mishap, damage, wickedness, cripple, injury, evil, detriment, ill, infliction, wrong.
(ANT.) *favor, kindness, benefit, boon.*
harmful (SYN.) damaging, injurious, mischievous, detrimental, hurtful, deleterious.
(ANT.) *helpful, salutary, profitable,, advantageous, beneficial.*
harmless (SYN.) protected, secure, snag, dependable, certain, painless, innocent, trustworthy.
(ANT.) *perilous, hazardous, insecure, dangerous, unsafe.*
harmonious (SYN.) tuneful, melodious, congenial, amicable.
(ANT.) *dissonant, discordant, disagreeable.*
harmony (SYN.) unison, bargain, contract, stipulation, pact, agreement, accordance, concord, accord, understanding, unity, coincidence.
(ANT.) *discord, dissension, difference,*

variance, disagreement.
harness (SYN.) control, yoke.
harry (SYN.) vex, pester, harass, bother, plague.
harsh (SYN.) jarring, gruff, rugged, severe, stringent, blunt, grating, unpleasant, tough, stern, strict, unkind, rigorous, cruel, coarse.
(ANT.) *smooth, soft, gentle, melodious, soothing, easy, mild.*
harvest (SYN.) reap, gather, produce, yield, crop, gain, acquire, fruit, result, reaping, product, proceeds, glean, garner.
(ANT.) *plant, squander, lose, sow.*
haste (SYN.) speed, hurry, rush, rapidity, flurry, scramble.
(ANT.) *sloth, sluggishness.*
hasten (SYN.) hurry, sprint, quicken, rush, precipitate, accelerate, scurry, run, scamper, dispatch, press, urge, dash, expedite, speed.
(ANT.) *retard, tarry, detain, linger, dawdle, delay, hinder.*
hasty (SYN.) quick, swift, irascible, lively, nimble, brisk, active, speedy, impatient, testy, sharp, fast, rapid.
(ANT.) *slow, dull, sluggish.*
hat (SYN.) helmet, bonnet.
hatch (SYN.) breed, incubate, brood.
hate (SYN.) loathe, detest, despise, disfavor, hatred, abhorrence, abominate, abhor, dislike.
(ANT.) *love, cherish, approve, admire, like.*
hateful (SYN.) loathsome, detestable, offensive.
(ANT.) *likable, loving, admirable.*
hatred (SYN.) detestation, dislike, malevolence, enmity, rancor, ill will, loathing, hate, hostility, abhorrence, aversion, animosity.
(ANT.) *friendship, love, affection, attraction.*
haughty (SYN.) proud, stately, vainglorious, arrogant, disdainful, overbearing, supercilious, vain.
(ANT.) *meek, ashamed, lowly, humble.*
haul (SYN.) draw, pull, drag, tow.
have (SYN.) own, possess, seize, hold, control, occupy, acquire, undergo, maintain, experience, receive, gain, affect, include, contain, get, take, obtain.
(ANT.) *surrender, abandon, renounce, lose.*
havoc (SYN.) devastation, ruin, destruction.
hazard (SYN.) peril, chance, dare, risk, offer, conjecture, jeopardy, danger.
(ANT.) *safety, defense, protection, immunity.*
hazardous (SYN.) perilous, precarious, threatening, unsafe, dangerous, critical, menacing, risky.
(ANT.) *protected, secure, safe.*
hazy (SYN.) uncertain, unclear, ambiguous, dim, obscure, undetermined, vague, unsettled, indefinite.
(ANT.) *specific, clear, lucid, precise, explicit.*
head (SYN.) leader, summit, top, culmination, director, chief, master, commander, supervisor, start, source,

crest, beginning, crisis.
(ANT.) foot, base, bottom, follower, subordinate, underling.
headstrong *(SYN.)* obstinate, stubborn, willful.
(ANT.) easygoing, amenable.
headway *(SYN.)* movement, progress.
heady *(SYN.)* thrilling, intoxicating, exciting, electrifying.
heal *(SYN.)* restore, cure.
healthy *(SYN.)* wholesome, hale, robust, sound, well, vigorous, strong, hearty, healthful, hygienic, salubrious, salutary.
(ANT.) noxious, diseased, unhealthy, delicate, frail, infirm, injurious.
heap *(SYN.)* collection, mound, increase, store, stack, pile, gather, accumulate, amass, accrue, accumulation, collect.
(ANT.) dissipate, scatter, waste, diminish, disperse.
hear *(SYN.)* heed, listen, detect, harken, perceive, regard.
heart *(SYN.)* middle, center, sympathy, nucleus, midpoint, sentiment, core, feeling, midst.
(ANT.) outskirts, periphery, border, rim, boundary.
heartache *(SYN.)* anguish, mourning, sadness, sorrow, affliction, distress, grief, lamentation, tribulation.
(ANT.) happiness, joy, solace, comfort, consolation.
heartbroken *(SYN.)* distressed, forlorn, mean, paltry, worthless, contemptible, wretched, crestfallen, disconsolate, downhearted, comfortless, brokenhearted, low.
(ANT.) noble, fortunate, contented, significant.
hearten *(SYN.)* encourage, favor, impel, urge, promote, sanction, animate, cheer, exhilarate, cheer.
(ANT.) deter, dissuade, deject, discourage, dispirit.
heartless *(SYN.)* mean, cruel, ruthless, hardhearted, pitiless.
(ANT.) sympathetic, kind.
heart-rending *(SYN.)* heartbreaking, depressing, agonizing.
hearty *(SYN.)* warm, earnest, ardent, cordial, sincere, gracious, sociable.
(ANT.) taciturn, aloof, cool, reserved.
heat *(SYN.)* hotness, warmth, temperature, passion, ardor, zeal, inflame, cook, excitement, warm.
(ANT.) cool, chill, coolness, freeze, coldness, chilliness, iciness, cold.
heated *(SYN.)* vehement, fiery, intense, passionate.
heave *(SYN.)* boost, hoist, raise.
heaven *(SYN.)* empyrean, paradise.
heavenly *(SYN.)* superhuman, godlike, blissful, saintly, holy, divine, celestial, angelic, blessed.
(ANT.) wicked, mundane, profane, blasphemous, diabolical.
heavy *(SYN.)* weighty, massive, gloomy, serious, ponderous, cumbersome, trying, burdensome, harsh, grave, intense, dull, grievous, concentrated, severe, oppressive, sluggish.

(ANT.) brisk, light, animated.
heckle *(SYN.)* torment, harass, tease, hector, harry.
heed *(SYN.)* care, alertness, circumspection, mindfulness, consider, watchfulness, reflection, study, attention, notice, regard, obey, ponder, respect, meditate, mind, observe, deliberate, examine, contemplate, weigh, esteem, application.
(ANT.) negligence, oversight, over look, neglect, ignore, disregard, indifference, omission.
heedless *(SYN.)* sightless, headlong, rash, unmindful, deaf, unseeing, oblivious, ignorant, inattentive, disregardful, blind.
(ANT.) perceiving, sensible, aware, calculated, discerning.
height *(SYN.)* zenith, peak, summit, tallness, mountain, acme, apex, elevation, altitude, prominence, maximum, pinnacle, culmination.
(ANT.) base, depth, anticlimax.
heighten *(SYN.)* increase, magnify, annoy, chafe, intensify, amplify, aggravate, provoke, irritate, concentrate, nettle.
(ANT.) soothe, mitigate, palliate, soften, appease.
heinous *(SYN.)* abominable, grievous, atrocious.
hello *(SYN.)* greeting, good evening, good afternoon, good morning.
(ANT.) farewell, good-bye, so long.
help *(SYN.)* assist, support, promote, relieve, abet, succor, back, uphold, further, remedy, encourage, aid, facilitate, mitigate.
(ANT.) afflict, thwart, resist, hinder, impede.
helper *(SYN.)* aide, assistant, supporter.
helpful *(SYN.)* beneficial, serviceable, wholesome, useful, profitable, advantageous, good, salutary.
(ANT.) harmful, injurious, useless, worthless, destructive, deleterious, detrimental.
helpfulness *(SYN.)* assistance, cooperation, usefulness, serviceability, kindness, neighborliness, willingness, collaboration, supportiveness, readiness.
(ANT.) antagonism, hostility, opposition.
helpless *(SYN.)* weak, feeble, dependent, disabled, inept, unresourceful, incapable, incompetent.
(ANT.) resourceful, competent, enterprising.
helplessness *(SYN.)* impotence, feebleness, weakness, incapacity, ineptitude, invalidism, shiftless, awkwardness.
(ANT.) power, strength, might, potency.
helter-skelter *(SYN.)* haphazardly, chaotically, irregularly.
hem *(SYN.)* bottom, border, edge, rim, margin, pale, verge, flounce, boundary, fringe, brim, fence, hedge, frame.
hem in *(SYN.)* enclose, shut in, confine, restrict, limit.
hence *(SYN.)* consequently, thence, therefore, so, accordingly.
herald *(SYN.)* harbinger, crier, envoy,

forerunner, precursor, augury, forecast.

herculean *(SYN.)* demanding, heroic, titanic, mighty, prodigious, laborious, arduous, overwhelming, backbreaking.

herd *(SYN.)* group, pack, drove, crowd, flock, gather.

heretic *(SYN.)* nonconformist, sectarian, unbeliever, sectary, schismatic, apostate, dissenter.

heritage *(SYN.)* birthright, legacy, patrimony, inheritance.

hermit *(SYN.)* recluse, anchorite, eremite.

hero *(SYN.)* paladin, champion, idol.

heroic *(SYN.)* bold, courageous, fearless, gallant, valiant, valorous, brave, chivalrous, adventurous, dauntless, intrepid, magnanimous.
(ANT.) fearful, weak, cringing, timid, cowardly.

heroism *(SYN.)* valor, bravery, gallant, dauntless, bold, courageous, fearless.

hesitant *(SYN.)* reluctant, unwilling, disinclined, loath, slow, averse.
(ANT.) willing, inclined, eager, ready, disposed.

hesitate *(SYN.)* falter, waver, pause, doubt, demur, delay, vacillate, wait, stammer, stutter, scruple.
(ANT.) proceed, resolve, continue, decide, persevere.

hesitation *(SYN.)* distrust, scruple, suspense, uncertainty, unbelief, ambiguity, doubt, incredulity, skepticism.
(ANT.) determination, belief, certainty, faith, conviction.

hidden *(SYN.)* undeveloped, unseen, dormant, concealed, quiescent, latent, potential, inactive.
(ANT.) visible, explicit, conspicuous, evident.

hide *(SYN.)* disguise, mask, suppress, withhold, veil, cloak, conceal, screen, camouflage, shroud, pelt, skin, leather, cover.
(ANT.) reveal, show, expose, disclose, uncover, divulge.

hideous *(SYN.)* frightful, ugly, shocking, frightening, horrible, terrible, horrifying, terrifying, grisly, gross.
(ANT.) lovely, beautiful, beauteous.

high *(SYN.)* tall, eminent, exalted, elevated, high-pitched, sharp, lofty, proud, shrill, raised, strident, prominent, important, powerful, expensive, dear, high-priced, costly, grave, serious, extreme, towering.
(ANT.) low, mean, tiny, stunted, short, base, lowly, deep, insignificant, unimportant, inexpensive, reasonable, trivial, petty, small.

highly *(SYN.)* extremely, very, extraordinarily, exceedingly.

high-minded *(SYN.)* lofty, noble, honorable.
(ANT.) dishonorable, base.

high-priced *(SYN.)* dear, expensive, costly.
(ANT.) economical, cheap.

high-strung *(SYN.)* nervous, tense, wrought-up, intense.
(ANT.) calm.

highway *(SYN.)* parkway, speedway, turnpike, superhighway, freeway.

hilarious *(SYN.)* funny, side-splitting, hysterical.
(ANT.) depressing, sad.

hinder *(SYN.)* hamper, impede, block, retard, stop, resist, thwart, obstruct, check, prevent, interrupt, delay, slow, restrain.
(ANT.) promote, further, assist, expedite, advance, facilitate.

hindrance *(SYN.)* interruption, delay, interference, obstruction, obstacle, barrier.

hinge *(SYN.)* rely, depend, pivot.

hint *(SYN.)* reminder, allusion, suggestion, clue, tip, taste, whisper, implication, intimate, suspicion, mention, insinuation.
(ANT.) declaration, affirmation, statement.

hire *(SYN.)* employ, occupy, devote, apply, enlist, lease, rent, charter, rental, busy, engage, utilize, retain, let, avail.
(ANT.) reject, banish, discard, fire, dismiss, discharge.

history *(SYN.)* narration, relation, computation, record, account, chronicle, detail, description, narrative, tale, recital.
(ANT.) confusion, misrepresentation, distortion, caricature.

hit *(SYN.)* knock, pound, strike, hurt, pummel, beat, come upon, find, discover, blow, smite.

hitch *(SYN.)* tether, fasten, harness, interruption, hindrance, interference.

hoard *(SYN.)* amass, increase, accumulate, gather, save, secret, store, cache, store, accrue, heap.
(ANT.) dissipate, scatter, waste, diminish, squander, spend, disperse.

hoarse *(SYN.)* deep, rough, husky, raucous, grating, harsh.
(ANT.) clear.

hoax *(SYN.)* ploy, ruse, wile, device, cheat, deception, antic, imposture, stratagem, stunt, guile, fraud.
(ANT.) openness, sincerity, candor, exposure, honesty.

hobbling *(SYN.)* deformed, crippled, halt, lame, unconvincing, unsatisfactory, defective, feeble, disabled, maimed, weak.
(ANT.) robust, vigorous, agile, sound, athletic.

hobby *(SYN.)* diversion, pastime, avocation.
(ANT.) vocation, profession.

hobo *(SYN.)* derelict, vagrant, vagabond, tramp.

hoist *(SYN.)* heave, lift, elevate, raise, crane, elevator, derrick.

hold *(SYN.)* grasp, occupy, possess, curb, contain, stow, carry, adhere, have, clutch, keep, maintain, clasp, grip, retain, detain, accommodate, restrain, observe, conduct, check, support.
(ANT.) vacate, relinquish, surrender, abandon.

holdup *(SYN.)* heist, robbery, stickup,

delay, interruption, slowdown.

hole *(SYN.)* cavity, void, pore, opening, abyss, chasm, gulf, aperture, tear, pit, burrow, lair, den, gap.

hollow *(SYN.)* unfilled, vacant, vain, meaningless, flimsy, false, hole, cavity, depression, hypocritical, depressed, empty, pit, insincere.
(ANT.) sound, solid, genuine, sincere, full.

holocaust *(SYN.)* fire, burning, extermination, butchery, disaster, massacre.

holy *(SYN.)* devout, divine, blessed, consecrated, sacred, spiritual, pious, sainted, religious, saintly, hallowed.
(ANT.) worldly, sacrilegious, unconsecrated, evil, profane, secular.

homage *(SYN.)* reverence, honor, respect.

home *(SYN.)* dwelling, abode, residence, seat, quarters, hearth, domicile, family, house, habitat.

homely *(SYN.)* uncommonly, disagreeable, ill-natured, ugly, vicious, plain, hideous, unattractive, deformed, surly, repellent, spiteful.
(ANT.) fair, handsome, pretty, attractive, comely, beautiful.

homesick *(SYN.)* lonely, nostalgic.

honest *(SYN.)* sincere, trustworthy, truthful, fair, ingenuous, candid, conscientious, moral, upright, open, frank, forthright, honorable, just.
(ANT.) fraudulent, tricky, deceitful, dishonest, lying.

honesty *(SYN.)* frankness, openness, fairness, sincerity, trustworthiness, justice, candor, honor, integrity, responsibility, uprightness.
(ANT.) deceit, dishonesty, trickery, fraud, cheating.

honor *(SYN.)* esteem, praise, worship, admiration, homage, glory, respect, admire, heed, dignity, revere, value, deference, venerate, reverence, consider, distinction, character, principle, uprightness, honesty, adoration.
(ANT.) scorn, dishonor, despise, neglect, abuse, shame, reproach, disdain, contempt, derision, disgrace.

honorable *(SYN.)* fair, noble, creditable, proper, reputable, honest, admirable, true, trusty, eminent, respectable, esteemed, just, famed, illustrious, noble, virtuous, upright.
(ANT.) infamous, disgraceful, shameful, dishonorable, ignominious.

honorary *(SYN.)* gratuitous, complimentary.

hoodlum *(SYN.)* crook, gangster, criminal, hooligan, mobster.

hop *(SYN.)* jump, leap.

hope *(SYN.)* expectation, faith, optimism, anticipation, expectancy, confidence, desire, trust.
(ANT.) pessimism, despair, despondency.

hopeful *(SYN.)* optimistic, confident.
(ANT.) despairing, hopeless.

hopeless *(SYN.)* desperate, despairing, forlorn, fatal, incurable, disastrous.
(ANT.) promising, hopeful.

hopelessness *(SYN.)* gloom, discourage-

ment, depression, pessimism, despondency.
(ANT.) hope, optimism, confidence, elation.

horde *(SYN.)* host, masses, press, rabble, swarm, throng, bevy, crush, mob, multitude, crowd, populace.

horizontal *(SYN.)* even, level, plane, flat, straight, sideways.
(ANT.) upright, vertical.

horrendous *(SYN.)* awful, horrifying, terrible, dreadful, horrid, ghastly.
(ANT.) splendid, wonderful.

horrible *(SYN.)* awful, dire, ghastly, horrid, terrible, repulsive, frightful, appalling, horrifying, dreadful, ghastly, fearful.
(ANT.) enjoyable, enchanting, beautiful, lovely, fascinating.

horrid *(SYN.)* repulsive, terrible, appalling, dire, awful, frightful, fearful, shocking, horrible, horrifying, horrid, ghastly, dreadful, revolting, hideous.
(ANT.) fascinating, enchanting, enjoyable, lovely, beautiful.

horror *(SYN.)* dread, awe, hatred, loathing, foreboding, alarm, apprehension, aversion, terror.
(ANT.) courage, boldness, assurance, confidence.

horseplay *(SYN.)* tomfoolery, clowning, shenanigans.

hospital *(SYN.)* infirmary, clinic, sanatorium, rest home, sanitarium.

hospitality *(SYN.)* warmth, liberality, generosity, graciousness, welcome.

hostile *(SYN.)* unfriendly, opposed, antagonistic, inimical, adverse, warlike.
(ANT.) friendly, favorable, amicable, cordial.

hostility *(SYN.)* grudge, hatred, rancor, spite, bitterness, enmity, malevolence.
(ANT.) love, friendliness, good will.

hot *(SYN.)* scorching, fervent, hot-blooded, passionate, peppery, ardent, burning, fiery, impetuous, scalding, heated, sizzling, blazing, frying, roasting, warm, intense, torrid, pungent.
(ANT.) indifferent, apathetic, impassive, passionless, bland, frigid, cold, freezing, cool, phlegmatic.

hot air *(SYN.)* bombast, blather, jabber, gabble.

hotbed *(SYN.)* sink, nest, well, den, nursery, cradle, source, incubator, seedbed.

hot-blooded *(SYN.)* passionate, ardent, excitable, wild, fervent, fiery, impetuous, rash, brash, intense, impulsive.
(ANT.) stolid, impassive, cold, staid.

hotel *(SYN.)* hostel, motel, inn, hostelry.

hotheaded *(SYN.)* rash, touchy, short-tempered, reckless, unruly.
(ANT.) levelheaded, cool-headed, calm.

hound *(SYN.)* harry, pursue, pester, harass.

hourly *(SYN.)* frequently, steadily, constantly, unfailingly, periodically, perpetually, ceaselessly, continually, incessantly.
(ANT.) occasionally, seldom.

house *(SYN.)* building, residence,

abode, dwelling.

housebreaker *(SYN.)* robber, thief, prowler, cracksman, burglar.

household *(SYN.)* manage, family, home.

householder *(SYN.)* homeowner, occupant.

housing *(SYN.)* lodgings, shelter, dwelling, lodgment, case, casing, quarters, domicile, enclosure, console, bracket.

hovel *(SYN.)* cabin, hut, sty, shack, hole, shed.

hover *(SYN.)* hang, drift, poise, stand by, linger, impend, waver, hand around.

however *(SYN.)* notwithstanding, still, nevertheless, but, yet.

howl *(SYN.)* bellow, yowl, wail, yell, cry.

hub *(SYN.)* pivot, center, core, heart, axis, basis, focus, nucleus.

hubbub *(SYN.)* uproar, tumult, commotion, clamor, bustle, turmoil, racket, confusion.
(ANT.) peacefulness, stillness, silence, quiet, quiescence.

huckster *(SYN.)* peddler, adman, hawker, salesman, pitchman.

huddle *(SYN.)* mass, herd, bunch, crowd, cram, gather, shove, pack, flock, ball, conglomeration, knot, clump, medley, scrum.

hue *(SYN.)* pigment, tint, shade, dye, complexion, paint, stain, color, tone, tincture.
(ANT.) transparency, achromatism, paleness.

huffy *(SYN.)* sensitive, vulnerable, testy, offended, thin-skinned, touchy, irascible, cross, offended.
(ANT.) tough, placid, stolid, impassive.

hug *(SYN.)* embrace, coddle, caress, kiss, pet, press, clasp, fondle, cuddle.
(ANT.) tease, vex, spurn, buffet, annoy.

huge *(SYN.)* great, immense, vast, ample, big, capacious, extensive, gigantic, enormous, vast, tremendous, large, wide, colossal.
(ANT.) short, small, mean, little, tiny.

hulking *(SYN.)* massive, awkward, bulky, ponderous, unwieldy, overgrown, lumpish, oafish.

hullabaloo *(SYN.)* clamor, uproar, din, racket, tumult, hubbub, commotion, noise, blare.
(ANT.) calm, peace, silence.

hum *(SYN.)* whir, buzz, whiz, purr, croon, murmur, intone, vibrate.

human *(SYN.)* hominid, mortal, fleshly, individual, person.

humane *(SYN.)* lenient, tender, tolerant, compassionate, clement, forgiving, kind, forbearing, thoughtful, kindhearted, kindly, gentle, merciful.
(ANT.) remorseless, cruel, heartless, pitiless, unfeeling, brutal.

humanist *(SYN.)* scholar, sage, classicist, savant.

humanitarian *(SYN.)* benefactor, philanthropist.

humanitarianism *(SYN.)* good will, beneficence, philanthropy, welfarism, humanism.

humanity *(SYN.)* generosity, magnanimity, tenderness, altruism, beneficence, kindness, charity, philanthropy.
(ANT.) selfishness, unkindness, cruelty, inhumanity.

humble *(SYN.)* modest, crush, mortify, simple, shame, subdue, meek, abase, break, plain, submissive, compliant, unpretentious, unassuming, abash, unostentatious, lowly, polite, courteous, unpretending, degrade.
(ANT.) praise, arrogant, exalt, illustrious, boastful, honor, elevate.

humbly *(SYN.)* deferentially, meekly, respectfully, unassumingly, diffidently, modestly, subserviently, submissively.
(ANT.) insolently, proudly, grandly, arrogantly.

humbug *(SYN.)* drivel, gammon, bosh, nonsense, rubbish, inanity.

humdrum *(SYN.)* commonplace, prosy, mundane, insipid, tedious, routine, dull, boring.
(ANT.) interesting, stimulating, arresting, striking, exciting.

humid *(SYN.)* moist, damp, misty, muggy, wet, watery, vaporous.
(ANT.) parched, dry, desiccated.

humiliate *(SYN.)* corrupt, defile, depress, pervert, abase, degrade, disgrace, adulterate, humble, shame, lower, impair, deprave, depress.
(ANT.) restore, raise, enhance, improve, vitalize.

humiliation *(SYN.)* chagrin, dishonor, ignominy, scandal, abasement, mortification, disrepute, odium, disgrace, shame.
(ANT.) honor, praise, glory, dignity, renown.

humor *(SYN.)* jocularity, wit, temperament, sarcasm, irony, joking, amusement, joke, disposition, waggery, fun, clowning, satire, mood.
(ANT.) sorrow, gravity, seriousness.

humorous *(SYN.)* funny, ludicrous, witty, curious, queer, amusing, comical, farcical, laughable, droll.
(ANT.) sober, unfunny, melancholy, serious, sad, solemn.

hunger *(SYN.)* desire, longing, inclination, relish, stomach, zest, craving, liking, passion.
(ANT.) satiety, repugnance, disgust, distaste, renunciation.

hungry *(SYN.)* famished, thirsting, craving, avid, longing, starved, ravenous.
(ANT.) gorged, satisfied, full, sated.

hunt *(SYN.)* pursuit, investigation, examination, inquiry, pursue, track, chase, search, quest, seek, probe, scour, exploration.
(ANT.) cession, resignation, abandonment.

hurl *(SYN.)* throw, cast, propel, fling, toss, pitch, thrust.
(ANT.) retain, pull, draw, haul, hold.

hurried *(SYN.)* rushed, hasty, swift, headlong, slipshod, careless, impulsive, superficial.
(ANT.) deliberate, slow, dilatory, thorough, prolonged.

hurry *(SYN.)* quicken, speed, ado, rush,

accelerate, run, hasten, race, urge, bustle, expedite, precipitate.
(ANT.) *retard, tarry, hinder, linger, dawdle, delay, hinder.*

hurt (SYN.) damage, harm, grievance, detriment, pain, injustice, injure, abuse, distress, disfigured, mar, afflict, spoil, affront, insult, wound, dishonor, wrong, mischief.
(ANT.) *improvement, repair, compliment, help, praise, benefit.*

hurtful (SYN.) harmful, damaging, maleficent, injurious, baleful, noxious.
(ANT.) *remedial, beneficial, good, salutary.*

hurtle (SYN.) charge, collide, rush, crash, lunge, bump, fling.

husband (SYN.) spouse, mate.

hush (SYN.) quiet, silence, still.

husk (SYN.) shell, hull, pod, skin, covering, crust, bark.

husky (SYN.) strong, brawny, strapping, muscular.
(ANT.) *feeble, weak.*

hustle (SYN.) hasten, run, race, hurry, speed.

hut (SYN.) cottage, shanty, cabin, shed.

hutch (SYN.) box, chest, locker, trunk, coffer, bin.

hybrid (SYN.) mule, mixture, crossbreed, cross, mongrel, mutt, composite.

hygiene (SYN.) cleanliness, sanitation, health, hygienics, prophylaxis.

hygienic (SYN.) robust, strong, well, wholesome, hale, healthy, sound, salubrious.
(ANT.) *frail, noxious, infirm, delicate, diseased, injurious.*

hyperbole (SYN.) puffery, exaggeration, embellishment, overstatement, ballyhoo, amplification, magnification.

hypercritical (SYN.) faultfinding, captious, censorious, finicky, exacting, carping, querulous, nagging, finical, hairsplitting.
(ANT.) *lax, easygoing, indulgent, lenient, tolerant.*

hypnotic (SYN.) soothing, opiate, sedative, soporific, entrancing, spellbinding, arresting, charming, engaging, gripping.

hypnotize (SYN.) entrance, dazzle, mesmerize, fascinate, spellbind.

hypocrisy (SYN.) pretense, deceit, dissembling, fakery, feigning, pharisaism, sanctimony, cant, dissimulation.
(ANT.) *openness, candor, truth, directness, forthrightness, honesty, frankness.*

hypocrite (SYN.) cheat, deceiver, pretender, dissembler, fake, fraud, charlatan.

hypocritical (SYN.) dissembling, two-faced, insincere, dishonest, duplicitous, deceitful, phony.
(ANT.) *heartfelt, true, genuine, honest.*

hypothesis (SYN.) law, theory, supposition, conjecture.
(ANT.) *proof, fact, certainty.*

hypothetical (SYN.) conjectural, speculative, theoretical.

idea (SYN.) conception, image, opinion, sentiment, concept, fancy, notion, thought, impression.
(ANT.) *thing, matter, entity, object, substance.*

ideal (SYN.) imaginary, supreme, unreal, visionary, perfect, faultless, fancied, exemplary, utopian.
(ANT.) *imperfect, actual, material, real, faulty.*

idealistic (SYN.) extravagant, dreamy, fantastic, fanciful, ideal, maudlin, imaginative, mawkish, sentimental, poetic, picturesque.
(ANT.) *practical, literal, factual, prosaic.*

identify (ANT.) recollect, apprehend, perceive, remember, confess, acknowledge, name, describe, classify.
(ANT.) *ignore, forget, overlook, renounce, disown, repudiate.*

identity (SYN.) uniqueness, personality, character, individuality.

ideology (SYN.) credo, principles, belief.

idiom (SYN.) language, speech, vernacular, lingo, dialect, jargon, slang, tongue.
(ANT.) *babble, gibberish, drivel, nonsense.*

idiot (SYN.) buffoon, harlequin, dolt, jester, dunce, blockhead, imbecile, numb-skull, simpleton, oaf, nincompoop, fool, moron.
(ANT.) *philosopher, genius, scholar, sage.*

idiotic (SYN.) asinine, absurd, brainless, irrational, crazy, nonsensical, senseless, preposterous, silly, ridiculous, simple, stupid, foolish, inane, moronic, half-witted, simpleminded, dimwitted.
(ANT.) *prudent, wise, sagacious, judicious, sane, intelligent, bright, brilliant, smart.*

idle (SYN.) unemployed, dormant, lazy, inactive, unoccupied, indolent, slothful, inert, unused.
(ANT.) *occupied, working, employed, active, industrious, busy, engaged.*

idol (SYN.) unoccupied, unused, inactive, unemployed.

idolize (SYN.) revere, worship, adore.
(ANT.) *despise.*

ignoble (SYN.) dishonorable, ignominious, lowly, menial vile, sordid, vulgar, abject, base, despicable, groveling, mean, vile.
(ANT.) *righteous, lofty, honored, esteemed, noble, exalted.*

ignominious (SYN.) contemptible, abject, despicable, groveling, dishonorable, ignoble, lowly, low, menial, mean, sordid, servile, vulgar, vile.
(ANT.) *lofty, noble, esteemed, righteous, exalted.*

ignorant (SYN.) uneducated, untaught, uncultured, illiterate, uninformed, unlearned, unlettered, untrained, unaware, unmindful.
(ANT.) *cultured, literate, educated, erudite, informed, cultivated, schooled, learned, lettered.*

ignore (SYN.) omit, slight, disregard,

overlook, neglect, skip.
(ANT.) notice, regard, include.
ill *(SYN.)* diseased, ailing, indisposed, morbid, infirm, unwell, unhealthy, sick, unhealthy.
(ANT.) robust, strong, healthy, well, sound, fit.
ill-use *(SYN.)* defame, revile, vilify, misemploy, disparage, abuse, traduce, asperse, misapply, misuse.
(ANT.) protect, cherish, respect, honor, praise.
ill-advised *(SYN.)* injudicious, ill-considered, imprudent.
ill-at-ease *(SYN.)* nervous, uncomfortable, uneasy.
(ANT.) comfortable.
illegal *(SYN.)* prohibited, unlawful, criminal, illicit, outlawed, illegitimate.
(ANT.) permitted, lawful, honest, legal, legitimate.
illiberal *(SYN.)* fanatical, bigoted, intolerant, narrow-minded, dogmatic, prejudiced.
(ANT.) progressive, liberal radical.
illicit *(SYN.)* illegitimate, criminal, outlawed, unlawful, prohibited, illegal, unauthorized.
(ANT.) legal, honest, permitted, lawful, licit.
ill-natured *(SYN.)* crabby, cranky, grouchy, cross, irascible.
illness *(SYN.)* complaint, infirmity, ailment, disorder, malady, sickness.
(ANT.) healthiness, health, soundness, vigor.
illogical *(SYN.)* absurd, irrational, preposterous.
ill-tempered *(SYN.)* crabby, cranky, cross, grouchy.
ill-treated *(SYN.)* harmed, mistreated, abused, maltreated.
illuminate *(SYN.)* enlighten, clarify, irradiate, illustrate, light, lighten, explain, interpret, clarify, elucidate, brighten, illumine.
(ANT.) obscure, confuse, darken, obfuscate, shadow, complicate.
illusion *(SYN.)* hallucination, vision, phantom, delusion, fantasy, dream, mirage.
(ANT.) substance, actuality, reality.
illusive *(SYN.)* fallacious, delusive, false, specious, misleading, deceptive, deceitful, delusory.
(ANT.) real, truthful, authentic, genuine, honest.
illustrate *(SYN.)* decorate, illuminate, adorn, show, picture, embellish, demonstrate.
illustration *(SYN.)* likeness, painting, picture, print, scene, sketch, view, engraving, drawing, panorama, photograph, cinema, etching, effigy, film, appearance, portrayal, resemblance, image, portrait.
illustrator *(SYN.)* painter, artist.
illustrious *(SYN.)* prominent, eminent, renowned, famed, great, vital, elevated, majestic, noble, excellent, dignified, big, gigantic, enormous, immense, huge, vast, large, countless, numerous, celebrated, critical,

momentous, august, weighty, grand, fine, magnificent, serious, important.
(ANT.) menial, common, minute, diminutive, small, obscure, ordinary, little.
image *(SYN.)* reflection, likeness, idea, representation, notion, picture, conception.
imaginary *(SYN.)* fanciful, fantastic, unreal, whimsical.
(ANT.) actual, real.
imagination *(SYN.)* creation, invention, fancy, notion, conception, fantasy, idea.
imaginative *(SYN.)* inventive, poetical, fanciful, clever, creative, mystical, visionary.
(ANT.) prosaic, dull, unromantic, literal.
imagine *(SYN.)* assume, surmise, suppose, conceive, dream, pretend, conjecture, fancy, opine, envisage, think, envision, guess, picture.
imbecile *(SYN.)* idiot, numbskull, simpleton, blockhead, dolt, dunce, jester, buffoon, harlequin, nincompoop, clown, fool, oaf.
(ANT.) scholar, genius, philosopher, sage.
imbibe *(SYN.)* absorb, consume, assimilate, engulf, engage, occupy, engross.
(ANT.) dispense, exude, discharge, emit.
imitate *(SYN.)* duplicate, mimic, follow, reproduce, mock, ape, counterfeit, copy, simulate, impersonate.
(ANT.) invent, distort, alter, diverge.
imitation *(SYN.)* replica, reproduction, copy, duplicate, facsimile, transcript, exemplar.
(ANT.) prototype, original.
immaculate *(SYN.)* clean, spotless, unblemished.
(ANT.) dirty.
immature *(SYN.)* young, boyish, childish, youthful, childlike, puerile, girlish, juvenile, callow.
(ANT.) old, senile, aged, elderly, mature.
immeasurable *(SYN.)* unlimited, endless, eternal, immense, interminable, unbounded, immeasurable, boundless, illimitable, infinite.
(ANT.) limited, confined, bounded, finite, circumscribed.
immediate *(SYN.)* present, instant, instantaneous, near, close, next, prompt, direct.
(ANT.) distant, future.
immediately *(SYN.)* now, presently, instantly, promptly, straightway, directly, instantaneously, forthwith.
(ANT.) sometime, hereafter, later, shortly, distantly.
immense *(SYN.)* enormous, large, gigantic, huge, colossal, elephantine, great, gargantuan, vast.
(ANT.) small, diminutive, little, minuscule, minute, petit, tiny.
immensity *(SYN.)* hugeness, enormousness, vastness.
immerse *(SYN.)* plunge, dip, dunk, sink, submerge, engage, absorb, engross, douse.

(ANT.) uplift, elevate, recover.

immigration *(SYN.)* settlement, colonization.
(ANT.) exodus, emigration.

imminent *(SYN.)* nigh, impending, overhanging, approaching, menacing, threatening.
(ANT.) retreating, afar, distant, improbable, remote.

immoderation *(SYN.)* profusion, surplus, extravagance, excess, intemperance, superabundance.
(ANT.) lack, want, deficiency, dearth, paucity.

immoral *(SYN.)* sinful, wicked, corrupt, bad, indecent, profligate, unprincipled, antisocial, dissolute.
(ANT.) pure, high-minded, chaste, virtuous, noble.

immortal *(SYN.)* infinite, eternal, timeless, undying, perpetual, ceaseless, endless, deathless, everlasting.
(ANT.) mortal, transient, finite, ephemeral, temporal.

immune *(SYN.)* easy, open, autonomous, unobstructed, free, emancipated, clear, independent, unrestricted, exempt, liberated, familiar, loose, unconfined, frank, unfastened, careless, freed.
(ANT.) confined, impeded, restricted, subject.

immutable *(SYN.)* constant, faithful, invariant, persistent, unchanging, unalterable, continual, ceaseless, enduring, fixed, permanent, abiding, perpetual, unwavering.
(ANT.) mutable, vacillating, wavering, fickle.

impact *(SYN.)* striking, contact, collision.

impair *(SYN.)* harm, injure, spoil, deface, destroy, hurt, damage, mar.
(ANT.) repair, mend, ameliorate, enhance, benefit.

impart *(SYN.)* convey, disclose, inform, tell, reveal, transmit, notify, confer, divulge, communicate, relate.
(ANT.) hide, withhold, conceal.

impartial *(SYN.)* unbiased, just, honest, fair, reasonable, equitable.
(ANT.) fraudulent, dishonorable, partial.

impartiality *(SYN.)* indifference, unconcern, impartiality, neutrality, disinterestedness, apathy, insensibility.
(ANT.) passion, ardor, fervor, affection.

impasse *(SYN.)* standstill, deadlock, stalemate.

impede *(SYN.)* hamper, hinder, retard, thwart, check, encumber, interrupt, bar, clog, delay, obstruct, block, frustrate, restrain, stop.
(ANT.) assist, promote, help, advance, further.

impediment *(SYN.)* barrier, bar, block, difficulty, check, hindrance, snag, obstruction.
(ANT.) assistance, help, aid, encouragement.

impel *(SYN.)* oblige, enforce, drive, coerce, force, constrain.
(ANT.) induce, prevent, convince, persuade.

impending *(SYN.)* imminent, nigh, threatening, overhanging, approaching, menacing.
(ANT.) remote, improbable, afar, distant, retreating.

impenetrable *(SYN.)* rigid, tough, harsh, strict, unfeeling, rigorous, intricate, arduous, penetrable, cruel, difficult, severe, stern, firm, hard, compact.
(ANT.) soft, simple, gentle, tender, brittle, fluid, flabby, elastic, lenient, easy, effortless.

imperative *(SYN.)* critical, instant, important, necessary, serious, urgent, cogent, compelling, crucial, pressing, impelling, importunate, exigent, insistent.
(ANT.) trivial, insignificant, unimportant, petty.

imperceptible *(SYN.)* invisible, indiscernible, unseen, indistinguishable.
(ANT.) seen, evident, visible, perceptible.

imperfection *(SYN.)* flaw, shortcoming, vice, defect, blemish, failure, mistake, omission, fault, error.
(ANT.) correctness, perfection, completeness.

imperil *(SYN.)* jeopardize, risk, endanger, hazard, risk.
(ANT.) guard, insure.

impersonal *(SYN.)* objective, detached, disinterested.
(ANT.) personal.

impersonate *(SYN.)* mock, simulate, imitate, ape, counterfeit, mimic, copy, duplicate.
(ANT.) alter, invent, diverge, distort.

impertinence *(SYN)* impudence, presumption, sauciness, effrontery, audacity, rudeness, assurance, boldness, insolence.
(ANT.) truckling, politeness, diffidence, subserviency.

impertinent *(SYN.)* rude, offensive, insolent, disrespectful, arrogant, brazen, impudent, insulting, contemptuous, abusive.
(ANT.) polite, respectful, considerate, courteous.

impetuous *(SYN.)* rash, heedless, quick, hasty, careless, passionate, impulsive.
(ANT.) cautious, reasoning, careful, prudent, thoughtful, calculating.

implicate *(SYN.)* reproach, accuse, blame, involve, upbraid, condemn, incriminate, rebuke, censure.
(ANT.) exonerate, absolve, acquit.

implore *(SYN.)* beg, pray, request, solicit, crave, entreat, beseech, ask, importune, supplicate, adjure, appeal, petition.
(ANT.) give, cede, bestow, favor, grant.

imply *(SYN.)* mean, involve, suggest, connote, hint, mention, indicate, insinuate, signify.
(ANT.) state, assert, declare, express.

impolite *(SYN.)* rude, unpolished, impudent, boorish, blunt, discourteous, rough, saucy, surly, savage, insolent, gruff, uncivil, coarse, ignorant, crude, illiterate, raw, primitive, vulgar, un-

taught.
(ANT.) genteel, courteous, courtly, dignified, polite, stately, noble, civil.
import (SYN.) influence, significance, stress, emphasis, importance, value, weight.
(ANT.) triviality, insignificance.
important (SYN.) critical, grave, influential, momentous, well-known, pressing, relevant, prominent, primary, essential, weighty, material, considerable, famous, principle, famed, sequential, notable, significant, illustrious, decisive.
(ANT.) unimportant, trifling, petty, trivial, insignificant, secondary, anonymous, irrelevant.
impose (SYN.) levy, require, demand.
imposing (SYN.) lofty, noble, majestic, magnificent, august, dignified, grandiose, high, grand, impressive, pompous, stately.
(ANT.) ordinary, undignified, humble, common, lowly.
imposition (SYN.) load, onus, burden.
impossible (SYN.) preposterous.
impregnable (SYN.) safe, invulnerable, secure, unassailable.
(ANT.) vulnerable.
impress (SYN.) awe, emboss, affect, mark, imprint, indent, influence.
impression (SYN.) influence, indentation, feeling, opinion, mark, effect, depression, guess, thought, belief, dent, sensibility.
(ANT.) fact, insensibility.
impressive (SYN.) arresting, moving, remarkable, splendid, thrilling, striking, majestic, grandiose, imposing, commanding, affecting, exciting, touching, stirring.
(ANT.) regular, unimpressive, commonplace.
impromptu (SYN.) casual, unprepared, offhand, extemporaneous.
improper (SYN.) unfit, unsuitable, inappropriate, naughty, indecent, unbecoming.
(ANT.) fitting, proper, appropriate.
improve (SYN.) better, reform, refine, ameliorate, amend, help, upgrade, rectify.
(ANT.) debase, vitiate, impair, corrupt, damage.
improvement (SYN) growth, advance, progress, betterment, development, advancement, progression.
(ANT.) relapse, regression, decline, retrogression, delay.
imprudent (SYN.) indiscreet, thoughtless, desultory, lax, neglectful, remiss, careless, inattentive, heedless, inconsiderate, reckless, ill-advised, irresponsible, unconcerned.
(ANT.) careful, meticulous, accurate.
impudence (SYN.) boldness, insolence, rudeness, sauciness, assurance, effrontery, impertinence, presumption, audacity.
(ANT.) politeness, truckling, subserviency, diffidence.
impudent (SYN.) forward, rude, abrupt, prominent, striking, bold, fresh, impertinent, insolent, pushy, insulting, brazen.
(ANT.) bashful, flinching, polite, courteous, cowardly, retiring, timid.
impulse (SYN.) hunch, whim, fancy, urge, caprice, surge, pulse.
impulsive (SYN.) passionate, rash, spontaneous, heedless, careless, hasty, quick, impetuous.
(ANT.) reasoning, calculating, careful, prudent, cautious.
impure (SYN.) dishonest, spoiled, tainted, contaminated, debased, corrupt, profligate, unsound, putrid, corrupted, crooked, depraved, vitiated, venal.
imputation (SYN.) diary, incrimination, arraignment, indictment.
(ANT.) exoneration, pardon, exculpation.
inability (SYN.) incompetence, incapacity, handicap, disability, impotence, weakness.
(ANT.) power, strength, ability, capability.
inaccurate (SYN.) false, incorrect, mistaken, untrue, askew, wrong, awry, erroneous, fallacious, imprecise, faulty, amiss.
(ANT.) right, accurate, true, correct.
inactive (SYN.) lazy, unemployed, indolent, motionless, still, inert, dormant, idle, unoccupied.
(ANT.) employed, working, active, industrious, occupied.
inadequate (SYN.) insufficient, lacking, short, incomplete, defective, scanty.
(ANT.) satisfactory, enough, adequate, ample, sufficient.
inadvertent (SYN.) careless, negligent, unthinking, thoughtless.
inane (SYN.) trite, insipid, banal, absurd, silly, commonplace, vapid, foolish, stupid, hackneyed.
(ANT.) stimulating, novel, fresh, original, striking.
inanimate (SYN.) deceased, spiritless, lifeless, gone, dull, mineral, departed, dead, insensible, vegetable, unconscious.
(ANT.) living, stirring, alive, animate.
inattentive (SYN.) absent-minded, distracted, abstracted, preoccupied.
(ANT.) watchful, attending, attentive.
inaugurate (SYN.) commence, begin, open, originate, start, arise, launch, enter, initiate.
(ANT.) end, terminate, close, complete, finish.
incense (SYN.) anger, enrage, infuriate.
incentive (SYN.) impulse, stimulus, inducement, encouragement.
(ANT.) discouragement.
inception (SYN.) origin, start, source, opening, beginning, outset, commencement.
(ANT.) end, termination, close, completion, consummation.
incessant (SYN.) perennial, uninterrupted, continual, ceaseless, continuous, unremitting, eternal, constant, unceasing, unending, perpetual, everlasting.

(ANT.) *rare, occasional, periodic, interrupted.*

incident (SYN.) happening, situation, occurrence, circumstance, condition, event, fact.

incidental (SYN.) casual, contingent, trivial, undersigned, chance, fortuitous, accidental, secondary, unimportant, unintended.
(ANT.) *intended, fundamental, planned, calculated, willed, decreed.*

incidentally (SYN.) by the way.

incinerate (SYN.) sear, char, blaze, scald, singe, consume, scorch, burn.
(ANT.) *quench, put out, extinguish.*

incisive (SYN.) neat, succinct, terse, brief, compact, condensed, neat, summary, concise.
(ANT.) *wordy, prolix, verbose, lengthy.*

incite (SYN.) goad, provoke, urge, arouse, encourage, cause, stimulate, induce, instigate, foment.
(ANT.) *quiet, bore, pacify, soothe.*

inclination (SYN.) bent, preference, desire, slope, affection, bent, bias, disposition, bending, penchant, incline, attachment, predisposition, predication, tendency, prejudice, slant, lean, leaning.
(ANT.) *nonchalance, apathy, distaste, aversion, reluctance, disinclination, uprightness, repugnance.*

incline (SYN.) slope, nod, lean.
(ANT.) *straighten.*

include (SYN.) contain, hold, accommodate, embody, encompass, involve, comprise, embrace.
(ANT.) *omit, exclude, discharge.*

income (SYN.) earnings, salary, wages, revenue, pay, return, receipts.

incomparable (SYN.) peerless, matchless, unequaled.

incompetency (SYN.) inability, weakness, handicap, impotence, disability, incapacity.
(ANT.) *strength, ability, power, capability.*

incomprehensible (SYN.) unintelligible, indecipherable.

inconceivable (SYN.) unbelievable, unimaginable, impossible.
(ANT.) *possible, believable.*

incongruous (SYN.) inconsistent, contrary, incompatible, irreconcilable, contradictory, unsteady, incongruous, wavering, paradoxical, vacillating, discrepant, illogical.
(ANT.) *consistent, compatible, correspondent.*

inconsiderate (SYN.) unthinking, careless, unthoughtful, unmindful.
(ANT.) *logical, consistent.*

inconsistency (SYN) discord, variance, contention, conflict, controversy, interference.
(ANT.) *harmony, concord, amity, consonance.*

inconsistent (SYN.) fickle, wavering, variable, changeable, contrary, unstable, illogical, contradictory, irreconcilable, discrepant, paradoxical, incompatible, self-contradictory, incongruous, unsteady, fitful, shifting.

(ANT.) *unchanging, steady, logical, stable, uniform, constant.*

inconspicuous (SYN.) retiring, unnoticed, unostentatious.
(ANT.) *obvious, conspicuous.*

inconstant (SYN.) fickle, shifting, changeable, fitful, vacillating, unstable, wavering.
(ANT.) *stable, constant, steady, uniform, unchanging.*

inconvenient (SYN.) awkward, inappropriate, untimely, troublesome.
(ANT.) *handy, convenient.*

incorrect (SYN.) mistaken, wrong, erroneous, inaccurate.
(ANT.) *proper, accurate, suitable.*

increase (SYN.) amplify, enlarge, grow, magnify, multiply, augment, enhance, expand, intensify, swell, raise, greater, prolong, broaden, lengthen, expansion, accrue, extend, heighten.
(ANT.) *diminish, reduce, atrophy, shrink, shrinkage, decrease, lessening, lessen, contract.*

incredible (SYN.) improbable, unbelievable.
(ANT.) *plausible, credible, believable.*

incriminate (SYN.) charge, accuse, indict, arraign, censure.
(ANT.) *release, exonerate, acquit, absolve, vindicate.*

incrimination (SYN.) imputation, indictment, accusation, charge, arraignment.
(ANT.) *exoneration, pardon, exculpation.*

indebted (SYN.) obliged, grateful, beholden, thankful, appreciative.
(ANT.) *unappreciative, thankless.*

indecent (SYN.) impure, obscene, pornographic, coarse, dirty, filthy, smutty, gross, disgusting.
(ANT.) *modest, refined, decent, pure.*

indeed (SYN.) truthfully, really, honestly, surely.

indefinite (SYN.) unsure, uncertain, vague, confused, unsettled, confusing.
(ANT.) *decided, definite, equivocal.*

independence (SYN.) liberation, privilege, freedom, immunity, familiarity, liberty, exemption, license.
(ANT.) *necessity, constraint, compulsion, reliance, dependence, bondage, servitude.*

independent (SYN.) free, unrestrained, voluntary, autonomous, self-reliant, uncontrolled, unrestricted.
(ANT.) *enslaved, contingent, dependent, restricted.*

indestructible (SYN.) enduring, lasting, permanent, unchangeable, abiding, constant, fixed, stable, changeless.
(ANT.) *unstable, temporary, transitory, ephemeral.*

indicate (SYN.) imply, denote, signify, specify, intimate, designate, symbolize, show, manifest, disclose, mean, reveal.
(ANT.) *mislead, falsify, distract, conceal, falsify.*

indication (SYN.) proof, emblem, omen, sign, symbol, token, mark, portent, gesture, signal.

indict (SYN.) charge, accuse, in-

criminate, censure, arraign.
(ANT.) acquit, vindicate, absolve, exonerate.
indictment (SYN.) incrimination, arraignment, imputation, charge.
(ANT.) pardon, exoneration, exculpation.
indifference (SYN.) unconcern, apathy, impartiality, disinterestedness, insensibility, neutrality.
(ANT.) ardor, passion, affection, fervor.
indifferent (SYN.) uncaring, insensitive, cool, unconcerned.
(ANT.) caring, concerned, earnest.
indigence (SYN.) necessity, destitution, poverty, want, need, privation, penury.
(ANT.) wealth, abundance, plenty, riches, affluence.
indigenous (SYN.) inborn, native, inherent, domestic, aboriginal, plenty, endemic, innate, natural.
indigent (SYN.) wishing, covetous, demanding, lacking, requiring, wanting, claiming, craving.
indignant (SYN.) irritated, irate, angry, aroused, exasperated.
(ANT.) calm, serene, content.
indignation (SYN.) ire, petulance, passion, choler, anger, wrath, temper, irritation, exasperation, animosity, resentment, rage.
(ANT.) self-control, peace, forbearance, patience.
indignity (SYN.) insolence, insult, abuse, affront, offense.
(ANT.) homage, apology, salutation.
indirect (SYN.) winding, crooked, devious, roundabout, cunning, tricky, tortuous, circuitous, distorted, erratic, swerving.
(ANT.) straightforward, direct, straight, honest.
indiscretion (SYN.) imprudence, folly, absurdity, extravagance.
(ANT.) prudence, sense, wisdom, reasonableness, judgment.
indispensable (SYN.) necessary, fundamental, basic, essential, important, intrinsic, vital.
(ANT.) optional, expendable, peripheral, extrinsic.
indistinct (SYN.) cloudy, dark, mysterious, vague, blurry, ambiguous, cryptic, dim, obscure, enigmatic, abstruse, hazy, blurred, unintelligible.
(ANT.) clear, lucid, bright, distinct.
indistinguishable (SYN.) identical, like, coincident, equal, same, equivalent.
(ANT.) dissimilar, opposed, contrary, disparate, distinct.
individual (SYN.) singular, specific, unique, distinctive, single, particular, undivided, human, apart, marked, person, different, special, separate.
(ANT.) universal, common, general, ordinary.
individuality (SYN.) symbol, description, mark, kind, character, repute, class, standing, sort, nature, disposition, reputation, sign.
indolent (SYN.) slothful, lazy, idle, inactive, slow, sluggish, torpid, supine, inert.

(ANT.) diligent, active, assiduous, vigorous, zestful, alert.
indomitable (SYN.) insurmountable, unconquerable, invulnerable, impregnable, unassailable.
(ANT.) weak, puny, powerless, vulnerable.
induce (SYN.) evoke, cause, influence, persuade, effect, make, originate, prompt, incite, create.
inducement (SYN.) incentive, motive, purpose, stimulus, reason, impulse, cause, principle, spur, incitement.
(ANT.) result, attempt, action, effort, deed.
induct (SYN.) instate, establish, install.
(ANT.) eject, oust.
indulge (SYN.) humor, satisfy, gratify.
indulgent (SYN.) obliging, pampering, tolerant, easy.
indurate (SYN.) impenitent, hard, insensible, tough, obdurate, callous, unfeeling.
(ANT.) soft, compassionate, tender, sensitive.
industrious (SYN.) hard-working, perseverant, busy, active, diligent, assiduous, careful, patient.
(ANT.) unconcerned, indifferent, lethargic, careless, apathetic, lazy, indolent, shiftless.
inebriated (SYN.) drunk, tight, drunken, intoxicated, tipsy.
(ANT.) sober, clearheaded, temperate.
ineffective (SYN.) pliant, tender, vague, wavering, defenseless, weak, inadequate, poor, irresolute, frail, decrepit, delicate, vacillating, assailable, exposed, vulnerable.
(ANT.) sturdy, robust, strong, potent, powerful.
inept (SYN.) clumsy, awkward, improper, inappropriate.
(ANT.) adroit, dexterous, adept, appropriate, proper, apt, fitting.
inequity (SYN.) wrong, injustice, unfairness, grievance, injury.
(ANT.) righteousness, lawfulness, equity, justice.
inert (SYN.) lazy, dormant, slothful, inactive, idle, indolent, motionless, unmoving, fixed, static.
(ANT.) working, active, industrious, occupied.
inertia (SYN.) indolence, torpidity, idleness, slothfulness, indolence, sluggishness, supineness.
(ANT.) assiduousness, activity, alertness, diligence.
inevitable (SYN.) definite, fixed, positive, sure, undeniable, indubitable, certain, assured, unquestionable, secure.
(ANT.) uncertain, probable, doubtful, questionable.
inexpensive (SYN.) low-priced, cheap, inferior, mean, beggarly, common, poor, shabby, modest, economical.
(ANT.) expensive, costly, dear.
inexperienced (SYN.) naive, untrained, uninformed, green.
(ANT.) experienced, skilled, sophisticated, trained, seasoned.

inexplicable *(SYN.)* hidden, mysterious, obscure, secret, dark, cryptic, enigmatical, incomprehensible, occult, recondite, inscrutable, dim.
(ANT.) plain, simple, clear, obvious, explained.

infamous *(SYN.)* shocking, shameful, scandalous.

infantile *(SYN.)* babyish, naive, immature, childish.
(ANT.) mature, grownup, adult.

infect *(SYN.)* pollute, poison, contaminate, defile, sully, taint.
(ANT.) purify, disinfect.

infection *(SYN.)* virus, poison, ailment, disease, pollution, pest, germ, taint, contamination, contagion.

infectious *(SYN.)* contagious, virulent, catching, communicable, pestilential, transferable.
(ANT.) noncommunicable, hygienic, healthful.

infer *(SYN.)* understand, deduce, extract.

inference *(SYN.)* consequence, result, conclusion, corollary, judgment, deduction.
(ANT.) preconception, foreknowledge, assumption, presupposition.

inferior *(SYN.)* secondary, lower, poorer, minor, subordinate, mediocre.
(ANT.) greater, superior, better, higher.

infinite *(SYN.)* immeasurable, interminable, unlimited, unbounded, eternal, boundless, illimitable, immense, endless, vast, innumerable, numberless, limitless.
(ANT.) confined, limited, bounded, circumscribed, finite.

infinitesimal *(SYN.)* minute, microscopic, tiny, submicroscopic.
(ANT.) gigantic, huge, enormous.

infirm *(SYN.)* feeble, impaired, decrepit, forceless, languid, puny, powerless, enervated, weak, exhausted.
(ANT.) stout, vigorous, forceful, lusty, strong.

infirmity *(SYN.)* disease, illness, malady, ailment, sickness, disorder, complaint.
(ANT.) soundness, health, vigor, healthiness.

inflame *(SYN.)* fire, incite, excite, arouse.
(ANT.) soothe, calm.

inflammation *(SYN.)* infection, soreness, irritation.

inflammatory *(SYN.)* instigating, inciting, provocative.

inflate *(SYN.)* expand, swell, distend.
(ANT.) collapse, deflate.

inflexible *(SYN.)* firm, stubborn, headstrong, immovable, unyielding, uncompromising, dogged, contumacious, determined, obstinate, rigid, unbending, unyielding, steadfast.
(ANT.) submissive, compliant, docile, amenable, yielding, flexible, giving, elastic.

inflict *(SYN.)* deliver, deal, give, impose, apply.

influence *(SYN.)* weight, control, effect, sway.

influenced *(SYN.)* sway, affect, bias, control, actuate, impel, stir, incite.

influential *(SYN.)* important, weighty, prominent, significant, critical, decisive, momentous, relevant, material, pressing, consequential, grave.
(ANT.) petty, irrelevant, mean, trivial, insignificant.

inform *(SYN.)* apprise, instruct, tell, notify, advise, acquaint, enlighten, impart, warn, teach, advise, relate.
(ANT.) delude, mislead, distract, conceal.

informal *(SYN.)* simple, easy, natural, unofficial, familiar.
(ANT.) formal, distant, reserved, proper.

informality *(SYN.)* friendship, frankness, liberty, acquaintance, sociability, intimacy, unreserved.
(ANT.) presumption, constraint, reserve, distance, haughtiness.

information *(SYN.)* knowledge, data, intelligence, facts.

informative *(SYN.)* educational, enlightening, instructive.

informer *(SYN.)* tattler, traitor, betrayer.

infrequent *(SYN.)* unusual, rare, occasional, strange.
(ANT.) commonplace, abundant, usual, ordinary, customary, frequent, numerous.

ingenious *(SYN.)* clever, skillful, talented, adroit, dexterous, quick-witted, bright, smart, witty, sharp, apt, resourceful, imaginative, inventive, creative.
(ANT.) dull, slow, awkward, bungling, unskilled, stupid.

ingenuity *(SYN.)* cunning, inventiveness, resourcefulness, aptitude, faculty, cleverness, ingenuousness.
(ANT.) ineptitude, clumsiness, dullness, stupidity.

ingenuous *(SYN.)* open, sincere, honest, candid, straightforward, plain, frank, truthful, free, naive, simple, innocent, unsophisticated.
(ANT.) scheming, sly, contrived, wily.

ingredient *(SYN.)* component, element, constituent.

inhabit *(SYN.)* fill, possess, absorb, dwell, occupy, live.
(ANT.) relinquish, abandon, release.

inherent *(SYN.)* innate, native, congenital, inherent, intrinsic, inborn, inbred, natural, real.
(ANT.) extraneous, acquired, external, extrinsic.

inhibit *(SYN.)* curb, constrain, hold back, restrain, bridle, hinder, repress, suppress, stop, limit.
(ANT.) loosen, aid, incite, encourage.

inhuman *(SYN.)* merciless, cruel, brutal, ferocious, savage, ruthless, malignant, barbarous, barbaric, bestial.
(ANT.) kind, benevolent, forbearing, gentle, compassionate, merciful, humane, humane.

inimical *(SYN.)* hostile, warlike, adverse, antagonistic, opposed, unfriendly.
(ANT.) favorable, amicable, cordial.

iniquitous *(SYN.)* baleful, immoral, per-

nicious, sinful, wicked, base, bad, evil, noxious, unsound, villainous, unwholesome.
(ANT.) moral, good, excellent, honorable, reputable.
iniquity *(SYN.)* injustice, wrong, grievance, unfairness, injury.
(ANT.) lawful, equity, righteousness, justice.
initial *(SYN.)* original, first, prime, beginning, earliest, pristine, chief, primeval, primary, foremost, basic, elementary.
(ANT.) latest, subordinate, last, least, hindmost, final, terminal.
initiate *(SYN.)* institute, enter, arise, inaugurate, commence, originate, start, open, begin.
(ANT.) terminate, complete, end, finish, close, stop.
initiative *(SYN.)* enthusiasm, energy, vigor, enterprise.
injure *(SYN.)* harm, wound, abuse, dishonor, damage, hurt, impair, spoil, disfigure, affront, insult, mar.
(ANT.) praise, ameliorate, help, preserve, compliment, benefit.
injurious *(SYN.)* detrimental, harmful, mischievous, damaging, hurtful, deleterious, harmful, destructive.
(ANT.) profitable, helpful, advantageous, salutary, beneficial, useful.
injury *(SYN.)* harm, detriment, damage, injustice, wrong, prejudice, grievance, mischief.
(ANT.) repair, benefit, improvement.
injustice *(SYN.)* unfairness, grievance, iniquity, wrong, injury.
(ANT.) righteousness, justice, equity, lawfulness.
inmate *(SYN.)* patient, prisoner.
inn *(SYN.)* motel, lodge, hotel.
innate *(SYN.)* native, inherent, congenital, innate, real, inborn, natural, intrinsic, inbred.
(ANT.) extraneous, acquired, external, extrinsic.
innocent *(SYN.)* pure, sinless, blameless, innocuous, lawful, naive, faultless, virtuous, not guilty.
(ANT.) guilty, corrupt, sinful, culpable, sophisticated, wise, worldly.
innocuous *(SYN.)* naive, pure, innocent, blameless, virtuous, lawful, faultless, innocuous, sinless.
(ANT.) sinful, corrupt, unrighteous, culpable, guilty.
inquire *(SYN.)* ask, solicit, invite, demand, claim, entreat, interrogate, query, beg, request, question, investigate, examine.
(ANT.) dictate, insist, reply, command, order.
inquiring *(SYN.)* prying, searching, curious, inquisitive, peering, snoopy, peeping, meddling, interrogative.
(ANT.) unconcerned, indifferent, uninterested, incurious.
inquiry *(SYN.)* investigation, quest, research, examination, interrogation, exploration, query, question, scrutiny, study.
(ANT.) inattention, inactivity, disregard,

negligence.
inquisitive *(SYN.)* meddling, peeping, nosy, interrogative, peering, searching, prying, snoopy, inquiring, curious.
(ANT.) unconcerned, indifferent, incurious, uninterested.
insane *(SYN.)* deranged, mad, foolish, idiotic, demented, crazy, delirious, maniacal, lunatic.
(ANT.) sane, rational, reasonable, sound, sensible, coherent.
insanity *(SYN.)* delirium, aberration, dementia, psychosis, lunacy, madness, frenzy, mania, craziness, derangement.
(ANT.) stability, rationality, sanity.
insecure *(SYN.)* uneasy, nervous, uncertain, shaky.
(ANT.) secure.
insensitive *(SYN.)* unfeeling, impenitent, callous, hard, indurate, obdurate, tough.
(ANT.) soft, compassionate, tender, sensitive.
insight *(SYN.)* intuition, acumen, penetration, discernment, perspicuity.
(ANT.) obtuseness.
insignificant *(SYN.)* trivial, paltry, petty, small, frivolous, unimportant, insignificant, trifling.
(ANT.) momentous, serious, important, weighty.
insincere *(SYN.)* false, dishonest, deceitful.
(ANT.) honest, sincere.
insinuate *(SYN.)* imply, mean, suggest, connote, signify, involve.
(ANT.) express, state, assert.
insipid *(SYN.)* tasteless, dull, stale, flat, vapid.
(ANT.) racy, tasty, savory, exciting.
insist *(SYN.)* command, demand, require.
insolence *(SYN.)* boldness, presumption, sauciness, effrontery, audacity, assurance, impertinence, rudeness.
(ANT.) politeness, truckling, diffidence, subserviency.
insolent *(SYN.)* arrogant, impertinent, insulting, rude, brazen, contemptuous, abusive, offensive, disrespectful.
(ANT.) respectful, courteous, polite, considerate.
inspect *(SYN.)* observe, discern, eye, behold, glance, scan, stare, survey, view, regard, see, watch, witness, examine, investigate.
(ANT.) overlook, miss, avert, hide.
inspection *(SYN.)* examination, retrospect, survey, revision, reconsideration, critique, criticism, review.
inspiration *(SYN.)* creativity, aptitude, genius, originality, ability, faculty, sagacity, talent, proficient, master, gift, adept, intellectual, thought, impulse, idea, notion, hunch.
(ANT.) dullard, moron, shallowness, ineptitude, stupidity, obtuseness, dolt.
install *(SYN.)* establish.
instance *(SYN.)* occasion, illustration, occurrence, example, case.
instant *(SYN.)* flash, moment.
instantaneous *(SYN.)* hasty, sudden unexpected, rapid, abrupt, immediate.

(ANT.) slowly, anticipated, gradual.

instantly *(SYN.)* now, presently, directly, forthwith, immediately, rapidly straight-away, at once, instantaneously.

(ANT.) sometime, distantly, hereafter, later, shortly.

instinct *(SYN.)* intuition, feeling.

instinctive *(SYN.)* offhand, voluntary, willing, spontaneous, automatic, impulsive, extemporaneous.

(ANT.) rehearsed, planned, compulsory, prepared, forced.

institute *(SYN.)* ordain, establish, raise, form, organize, sanction, fix, found, launch, begin, initiate.

(ANT.) overthrow, upset, demolish, abolish, unsettle.

instruct *(SYN.)* teach, tutor, educate, inform, school, instill, train, inculcate, drill.

(ANT.) misinform, misguide.

instruction *(SYN.)* advise, warning, information, exhortation, notification, admonition, caution, recommendation, counsel, suggestion, teaching, training, education, command, order.

instrument *(SYN.)* channel, device, utensil, tool, agent, apparatus, means, vehicle, medium, agent, implement.

(ANT.) obstruction, hindrance, preventive, impediment.

insubordinate *(SYN.)* rebellious, unruly, defiant, disorderly, disobedient, undutiful, refractory, intractable, mutinous.

(ANT.) obedient, compliant, submissive, dutiful.

insufficient *(SYN.)* limited, lacking, deficient, short, inadequate.

(ANT.) ample, protracted, abundant, big, extended.

insulation *(SYN.)* quarantine, segregation, seclusion, withdrawal, isolation, loneliness, alienation, solitude.

(ANT.) union, communion, association, fellowship, connection.

insult *(SYN.)* insolence, offense, abuse, dishonor, affront, insult, indignity, offend, humiliate, outrage.

(ANT.) compliment, homage, apology, salutation, flatter, praise.

integrated *(SYN.)* mingled, mixed, combined, interspersed, desegregated, nonsectarian, interracial.

(ANT.) separated, divided, segregated.

integrity *(SYN.)* honesty, openness, trustworthiness, fairness, candor, justice, rectitude, sincerity, uprightness, soundness, wholeness, honor, principle, virtue.

(ANT.) fraud, deceit, cheating, trickery, dishonesty.

intellect *(SYN.)* understanding, judgment.

intellectual *(SYN.)* intelligent.

intelligence *(SYN.)* reason, sense, intellect, understanding, mind, ability, skill, aptitude.

(ANT.) feeling, passion, emotion.

intelligent *(SYN.)* clever, smart, knowledgeable, well-informed, alert, discerning, astute, quick, enlightened,

smart, bright, wise.

(ANT.) insipid, obtuse, dull, stupid, slow, foolish, unintelligent, dumb.

intend *(SYN.)* plan, prepare, scheme, contrive, outline, design, sketch, plot, project, delineate.

intense *(SYN.)* brilliant, animated, graphic, lucid, bright, expressive, vivid, deep, profound, concentrated, serious, earnest.

(ANT.) dull, vague, dusky, dim, dreary.

intensify *(SYN.)* accrue, augment, amplify, enlarge, enhance, extend, expand, heighten, grow, magnify, raise, multiply.

(ANT.) reduce, decrease, contract, diminish.

intent *(SYN.)* purpose, design, objective, intention, aim.

(ANT.) accidental, result, chance.

intensity *(SYN.)* force, potency, power, toughness, activity, durability, fortitude, vigor, stamina.

(ANT.) weakness, feebleness, infirmity, frailty.

intention *(SYN.)* intent, purpose, objective, plan, expectation, aim, object.

(ANT.) chance, accident.

intentional *(SYN.)* deliberate, intended, studied, willful, contemplated, premeditated, designed, voluntary, purposeful, planned.

(ANT.) fortuitous, accidental, chance.

intentionally *(SYN.)* purposefully, deliberately, maliciously.

(ANT.) accidentally.

interest *(SYN.)* attention, concern, care, advantage, benefit, profit, ownership, credit, attract, engage, amuse, entertain.

(ANT.) apathy, weary, disinterest.

interested *(SYN.)* affected, concerned.

(ANT.) unconcerned, indifferent, uninterested.

interesting *(SYN.)* engaging, inviting, fascinating, attractive.

(ANT.) boring, tedious, uninteresting, wearisome.

interfere *(SYN.)* meddle, monkey, interpose, interrupt, tamper, butt in, intervene.

interference *(SYN.)* prying, intrusion, meddling, obstacle, obstruction.

interior *(SYN.)* internal, inmost, inner, inward, inside, center.

(ANT.) outer, adjacent, exterior, external, outside.

interject *(SYN.)* intrude, introduce, insert, inject, interpose.

(ANT.) overlook, avoid, disregard.

interminable *(SYN)* immense, endless, immeasurable, unlimited, vast, unbounded, boundless, eternal, infinite.

(ANT.) limited, bounded, circumscribed, confined.

internal *(SYN.)* inner, interior, inside, intimate, private.

(ANT.) outer, external, surface.

interpose *(SYN.)* arbitrate, inject, intervene, meddle, insert, interject, introduce, intercede, intrude, interfere.

(ANT.) overlook, avoid, disregard.

interpret *(SYN.)* explain, solve, trans-

late, construe, elucidate, decode, explicate, render, unravel, define, understand.
(ANT.) misinterpret, falsify, confuse, distort, misconstrue.
interrogate *(SYN.)* quiz, analyze, inquire, audit, question, contemplate, assess, dissect, notice, scan, review, view, check, survey, scrutinize, examine.
(ANT.) overlook, omit, neglect, disregard.
interrupt *(SYN.)* suspend, delay, postpone, defer, adjourn, stay, discontinue, intrude, interfere.
(ANT.) prolong, persist, continue, maintain, proceed.
interval *(SYN.)* pause, gap.
intervene *(SYN.)* insert, intercede, meddle, inject, introduce, interpose, mediate, interfere, interrupt, intrude.
(ANT.) overlook, avoid, disregard.
intimacy *(SYN.)* fellowship, friendship, acquaintance, frankness, familiarity, unreserved, liberty.
(ANT.) presumption, distance, haughtiness, constraint, reserve.
intimate *(SYN.)* chummy, confidential, friendly, loving, affectionate, close, familiar, near, personal, private, secret.
(ANT.) conventional, formal, ceremonious, distant.
intimation *(SYN.)* reminder, implication, allusion, hint, insinuation.
(ANT.) declaration, statement, affirmation.
intolerant *(SYN.)* fanatical, narrow-minded, prejudiced, bigoted, illiberal, dogmatic, biased.
(ANT.) tolerant, radical, liberal, progressive, broad-minded, fair.
intoxicated *(SYN.)* inebriated, tipsy, drunk, tight, drunken, high.
(ANT.) sober, temperate, clearheaded.
intrepid *(SYN.)* brave, fearless, insolent, abrupt, rude, pushy, adventurous, daring, courageous, prominent, striking, forward, imprudent.
(ANT.) timid, bashful, flinching, cowardly, retiring.
intricate *(SYN.)* compound, perplexing, complex, involved, complicated.
(ANT.) simple, plain, uncompounded.
intrigue *(SYN.)* design, plot, cabal, machination, stratagem, scheme, attract, charm, interest, captivate.
intrinsic *(SYN.)* natural, inherent, inbred, congenital, inborn, native.
(ANT.) extraneous, acquired, external, extrinsic.
introduce *(SYN.)* acquaint, present, submit, present, offer, propose.
introduction *(SYN.)* preamble, prelude, beginning, prologue, start, preface.
(ANT.) finale, conclusion, end, epilogue, completion.
intrude *(SYN.)* invade, attack, encroach, trespass, penetrate, infringe, interrupt.
(ANT.) vacate, evacuate, abandon, relinquish.
intruder *(SYN.)* trespasser, thief, prowler, robber.

intuition *(SYN.)* insight, acumen, perspicuity, penetration, discernment, instinct, clairvoyance.
invade *(SYN.)* intrude, violate, infringe, attack, penetrate, encroach, trespass.
(ANT.) vacate, abandon, evacuate, relinquish.
invalidate *(SYN.)* annul, cancel, abolish, revoke, abrogate.
(ANT.) promote, restore, sustain, establish, continue.
invaluable *(SYN.)* priceless, precious, valuable.
(ANT.) worthless.
invasion *(SYN.)* assault, onslaught, aggression, attack, intrusion.
(ANT.) surrender, opposition, resistance, defense.
invective *(SYN.)* insult, abuse, disparagement, upbraiding, reproach, defamation, aspersion.
(ANT.) laudation, plaudit, commendation.
invent *(SYN.)* devise, fabricate, design, concoct, frame, conceive, contrive, create, originate, devise.
(SYN.) reproduce, copy, imitate.
inventive *(SYN.)* fanciful, imaginative, visionary, poetical, clever, creative.
(ANT.) unromantic, literal, dull, prosaic.
inventiveness *(SYN)* cunning, cleverness, ingeniousness, aptitude.
(ANT.) ineptitude, clumsiness, dullness, stupidity.
invert *(SYN.)* upset, turn about, transpose, countermand, revoke, reverse, overturn, repeal.
(ANT.) maintain, stabilize, endorse.
investigate *(SYN.)* look, probe, ransack, scrutinize, ferret, examine, seek, explore, search, scour, inspect, study.
investigation *(SYN.)* exploration, interrogation, quest, question, scrutiny, inquiry, query, examination, study, research.
(ANT.) inattention, disregard, inactivity, negligence.
invigorating *(SYN.)* bracing, fortifying, vitalizing, stimulating.
invincible *(SYN.)* insurmountable, unconquerable, impregnable, indomitable, invulnerable, unassailable.
(ANT.) powerless, weak, vulnerable.
invisible *(SYN.)* indistinguishable, unseen, imperceptible, indiscernible.
(ANT.) evident, visible, seen, perceptible.
invite *(SYN.)* bid, ask, encourage, request, urge.
inviting *(SYN.)* appealing, attractive, tempting, luring, alluring.
(ANT.) unattractive, uninviting.
involuntary *(SYN.)* reflex, uncontrolled, automatic, unintentional.
(SYN.) voluntary, willful.
involve *(SYN.)* include, embrace, entangle, envelop, incriminate, embroil, implicate, contain, complicate, confuse.
(ANT.) separate, disconnect, extricate, disengage.
involved *(SYN.)* compound, intricate,

complicated, complex, perplexing.
(ANT.) *plain, uncompounded, simple.*
invulnerable *(SYN.)* indomitable, unassailable, invincible, unconquerable, insurmountable, impregnable.
(ANT.) *weak, puny, powerless, vulnerable.*
irate *(SYN.)* incensed, enraged, angry.
ire *(SYN.)* indignation, irritation, wrath, anger, animosity, fury, passion, temper, exasperation, petulance, rage.
(ANT.) *peace, patience, conciliation, self-control, forbearance.*
irk *(SYN.)* irritate, bother, disturb, pester, trouble, vex, tease, chafe, annoy, inconvenience, provoke.
(ANT.) *console, soothe, accommodate, gratify.*
irrational *(SYN.)* inconsistent, preposterous, self-contradictory, unreasonable, absurd, foolish, nonsensical, ridiculous.
(ANT.) *sensible, sound, rational consistent, reasonable.*
irregular *(SYN.)* eccentric, unusual, aberrant, devious, abnormal, unnatural, capricious, variable, unequal, disorderly, unsettled, random, disorganized.
(ANT.) *regular, methodical, fixed, usual, ordinary, even.*
irrelevant *(SYN.)* foreign, unconnected, remote, alien, strange.
(ANT.) *germane, relevant, akin, kindred.*
irresolute *(SYN.)* frail, pliant, vacillating, ineffective, wavering, weak, yielding, fragile, pliable.
(ANT.) *robust, potent, sturdy, strong, powerful.*
irresponsible *(SYN.)* unreliable.
irritable *(SYN.)* hasty, hot, peevish, testy, irascible, fiery, snappish, petulant, choleric, excitable, touchy.
(ANT.) *composed, agreeable, tranquil, calm.*
irritate *(SYN.)* irk, molest, bother, annoy, tease, disturb, inconvenience, vex, trouble, pester, inflame, chafe.
(ANT.) *console, gratify, accommodate, soothe, pacify, calm.*
irritable *(SYN.)* peevish, testy, sensitive, touchy.
(ANT.) *happy, cheerful.*
irritation *(SYN.)* chagrin, mortification, vexation, annoyance, exasperation.
(ANT.) *pleasure, comfort, gratification, appeasement.*
isolate *(SYN.)* detach, segregate, separate, disconnect.
(ANT.) *happy, cheerful.*
isolated *(SYN.)* lone, single, alone, desolate, secluded, solitary, deserted.
(ANT.) *surrounded, accompanied.*
isolation *(SYN.)* quarantine, seclusion, separation, solitude, alienation, retirement, loneliness, withdrawal, segregation, detachment.
(ANT.) *fellowship, union, association, communion, connection.*
issue *(SYN.)* flow, proceed, result, come, emanate, originate, abound.
itemize *(SYN.)* register, detail, record.

jab *(SYN.)* thrust, poke, nudge, prod, shove, jolt, boost, tap, slap, rap.
jack *(SYN.)* fellow, guy, boy, toiler, guy, man, worker.
jacket *(SYN.)* wrapper, envelope, coat, sheath, cover, folder, enclosure, skin.
jade *(SYN.)* hussy, wanton, trollop.
jag *(SYN.)* notch, snag, protuberance, barb, dent, cut, nick, indentation.
jagged *(SYN.)* crooked, bent, ragged, pointy, notched, aquiline, furcated.
(ANT.) *smooth.*
jail *(SYN.)* stockade, prison, reformatory, penitentiary, keep, dungeon, brig, confine, lock up, detain.
jam *(SYN.)* force, pack, ram, crowd, push, wedge, squeeze, stuff, load.
jamboree *(SYN.)* celebration, fete, spree, festival, festivity, carousal.
janitor *(SYN.)* custodian, doorkeeper, caretaker, superintendent, gatekeeper.
jar *(SYN.)* rattle, shake, bounce, jolt.
jargon *(SYN.)* speech, idiom, dialect, vernacular, diction, argot.
(ANT.) *gibberish, babble, nonsense.*
jaunt *(SYN.)* journey, trip, tour, excursion, outing, voyage, expedition.
jazzy *(SYN.)* garish, vivacious, loud, splashy, exaggerated, flashy.
jealous *(SYN.)* covetous, envious.
jealousy *(SYN.)* suspicion, envy, resentfulness, greed, covetousness.
(ANT.) *tolerance, liberality.*
jeer *(SYN.)* taunt, mock, scoff, deride, make fun of, gibe, sneer.
(ANT.) *flatter, praise, compliment, laud.*
jeering *(SYN.)* mockery, sneering, derision, sarcasm, irony, ridicule.
jell *(SYN.)* finalize, congeal, set, solidify, shape up, take form.
jeopardize *(SYN.)* risk, dare, expose, imperil, chance, venture, hazard.
(ANT.) *know, guard, determine.*
jerk *(SYN.)* quiver, twitch, shake, spasm, jolt, yank, fool.
jet *(SYN.)* squirt, spurt, gush, inky, nozzle.
jetty *(SYN.)* pier, breakwater, buttress.
jewel *(SYN.)* ornament, gemstone, gem, bauble, stone.
jig *(SYN.)* caper, prance, jiggle, leap.
jiggle *(SYN.)* shimmy, agitate, jerk, twitch, wiggle.
jilt *(SYN.)* abandon, get rid of, reject, desert, forsake, leave.
jingle *(SYN.)* chime, ring, tinkle.
jinx *(SYN.)* hex, whammy, curse.
jittery *(SYN.)* jumpy, nervous, quivering, shaky, skittery.
job *(SYN.)* toil, business, occupation, post, chore, stint, career, duty.
jobless *(SYN.)* idle, unoccupied, inactive, unemployed.
jocularity *(SYN.)* humor, wit, joke, facetiousness, waggery.
(ANT.) *sorrow, gravity.*
jog *(SYN.)* gait, trot, sprint, run, lope.
join *(SYN.)* conjoin, unite, attach, ac company, associate, assemble, fit.
(ANT.) *separate, disconnect, split sunder, part, divide, detach.*
joint *(SYN.)* link, union, connection junction, coupling, common.

(ANT.) divided, separate.

joke (SYN.) game, jest, caper, prank, anecdote, quip, tease, banter, laugh.

joker (SYN.) wisecracker, humorist, comedian, trickster, comic, jester, wit.

jolly (SYN.) merry, joyful, gay, happy, sprightly, pleasant, jovial, gleeful. (ANT.) mournful, depressed, glum.

jolt (SYN.) sway, waver, startle, rock, jar, jerk, bounce, quake, bump, shake.

jot (SYN.) note, write, record.

jounce (SYN.) bounce, jolt, bump, jostle, jar, shake.

journal (SYN.) account, diary, log, chronicle, magazine, newspaper.

journey (SYN.) tour, passage, cruise, voyage, pilgrimage, jaunt, trip, outing.

joy (SYN.) pleasure, glee, bliss, elation, mirth, felicity, rapture, delight. (ANT.) grief, depression, unhappiness, sorrow, misery, gloom, affliction.

joyful (SYN.) gay, lucky, opportune, cheerful, happy, blissful, jovial, merry. (ANT.) gloomy, sad, blue, solemn, serious, grim, morose, glum, depressed.

joyous (SYN.) jolly, gay, blithe, merry, gleeful, cheerful, jovial. (ANT.) sad, gloomy, sorrowful.

jubilant (SYN.) exulting, rejoicing, overjoyed, triumphant, elated, delighted. (ANT.) dejected.

jubilee (SYN.) gala, holiday, celebration.

judge (SYN.) umpire, think, estimate, decide, arbitrator, condemn, decree.

judgment (SYN.) wisdom, perspicacity, discernment, decision, common sense. (ANT.) thoughtlessness, senselessness.

judicious (SYN.) sensible, wise, well-advised, thoughtful. (ANT.) ignorant.

jug (SYN.) bottle, jar, flask, flagon.

jumble (SYN.) disarrangement, tumult, agitation, ferment, turmoil. (ANT.) peace, arrange, compose.

jump (SYN.) leap, caper, skip, bound, jerk, vault, hop, spring.

junction (SYN.) coupling, joining, union, crossroads, intersection, weld. (ANT.) separation.

jungle (SYN.) woods, thicket, undergrowth, forest, bush.

junior (SYN.) secondary, inferior, minor, lower, younger.

junk (SYN.) rubbish, scraps, trash, waste, dump, discard, castoffs, debris.

junky (SYN.) tawdry, ramshackle, tattered, tacky, shoddy.

jurisdiction (SYN.) power, commission, warrant, authority, authorization.

just (SYN.) fair, trustworthy, precise, exact, candid, upright, honest. (ANT.) tricky, dishonest, unjust, corrupt.

justice (SYN.) justness, rectitude, equity, law, fairness, impartiality, right. (ANT.) unfairness, inequity, wrong.

justify (SYN.) uphold, excuse, defend, acquit, exonerate, absolve, clear, vindicate. (ANT.) convict.

jut (SYN.) project, protrude, stick out. (ANT.) indent, recess.

juvenile (SYN.) youthful, childish. (ANT.) old, aged, adult, mature.

kaiser (SYN.) czar, caesar, caliph, mogul, tycoon, khan, cazique.

kavass (SYN.) badel, macebearer, constable.

keck (SYN.) vomit, belch, retch.

keen (SYN.) clever, cunning, acute, penetrating, exact, severe, shrewd, wily, astute, sharp, bright, intelligent. (ANT.) stupid, shallow, dull, blunted, slow, bland, gentle, obtuse, blunt.

keep (SYN.) maintain, retain, observe, protect, confine, sustain, continue, preserve, save, guard, restrain, reserve. (ANT.) abandon, disobey, dismiss, discard, ignore, neglect, lose, reject, relinquish.

keeper (SYN.) warden, jailer, ranger, gaoler, guard, turnkey, watchman, escort, custodian.

keeping (SYN.) congeniality, uniformity.

keepsake (SYN.) reminder, memorial, relic, souvenir, memento, hint.

keg (SYN.) container, drum, tub, barrel, receptacle, reservatory, capsule, cask.

kelpie (SYN.) sprite, naiad, pixy.

kelson (SYN.) bottom, sole, toe, foot, root, keel.

kempt (SYN.) neat, trim, tidy, spruce.

ken (SYN.) field, view, vision, range, scope.

kennel (SYN.) swarm, flock, covy, drove, herd, pound, doghouse.

kerchief (SYN.) neckcloth, hankerchief, scarf, headpiece, babushka.

kern (SYN.) peasant, carle, serf, tike, tyke, countryman.

kernel (SYN.) marrow, pith, backbone, soul, heart, core, nucleus.

ketch (SYN.) lugger, cutter, clipper, ship, barge, sloop.

kettle (SYN.) pan, caldron, vat, pot, teapot, vessel, receptacle, receiver.

key (SYN.) opener, explanation, tone, lead, cause, source, note, pitch.

keynote (SYN.) core, model, theme, pattern, standard, gist.

keystone (SYN.) backbone, support.

khan (SYN.) master, czar, kaiser, padishah, caesar.

kick (SYN.) punt, remonstrate, boot.

kickback (SYN.) repercussion, backfire, rebound.

kickoff (SYN.) beginning, opening, commencement, outset, start.

kid (SYN.) joke, tease, fool, jest, tot, child.

kidnap (SYN.) abduct, snatch, shanghai.

kill (SYN.) execute, put to death, slay, butcher, assassinate, murder, cancel, destroy, slaughter, finish, end. (ANT.) save, protect, animate, resuscitate, vivify.

killing (SYN.) massacre, genocide, slaughter, carnage, butchery, bloodshed.

killjoy (SYN.) wet blanket, sourpuss, party-pooper.

kin (SYN.) relatives, family, folks, relations.

kind (SYN.) humane, affable, compassionate, benevolent, merciful, tender, sympathetic, breed, indulgent. (ANT.) unkind, cruel, merciless, severe, *mean, inhuman.*

kindle *(SYN.)* fire, ignite, light, arouse, excite, set afire, stir up, trigger, move, provoke, inflame.
(ANT.) pacify, extinguish, calm.

kindly *(SYN.)* warm, kindhearted, kind, warmhearted.
(ANT.) mean, cruel.

kindred *(SYN.)* family, relations, relatives, consanguinity, kinsfolk, affinity.
(ANT.) strangers, disconnection.

kinetic *(SYN.)* vigorous, active, dynamic, energetic, mobile, forceful.

king *(SYN.)* sovereign, ruler, chief, monarch, potentate.

kingdom *(SYN.)* realm, empire, monarchy, domain.

kingly *(SYN.)* kinglike, imperial, regal, royal, majestic.

kink *(SYN.)* twist, curl, quirk.

kinship *(SYN.)* lineage, blood, family, stock, relationship.

kismet *(SYN.)* fate, end, fortune.

kiss *(SYN.)* pet, caress, fondle, cuddle, osculate, embrace.
(ANT.) vex, spurn, annoy, tease, buffet.

kit *(SYN.)* outfit, collection, furnishings, equipment, rig, gear, set.

knack *(SYN.)* cleverness, readiness, deftness, ability, ingenuity, skill, talent, aptitude, talent, know-how, art, adroitness, skillfulness.
(ANT.) inability, clumsiness, awkwardness, ineptitude.

knave *(SYN.)* rogue, rascal, villain, scoundrel.

knead *(SYN.)* combine, massage, blend.

knickknack *(SYN.)* trinket, bric-a-brac, trifle.

knife *(SYN.)* sword, blade.

knightly *(SYN.)* valiant, courageous, gallant, chivalrous, noble.

knit *(SYN.)* unite, join, mend, fasten, connect, combine, heal.

knob *(SYN.)* doorknob, handle, protuberance, bump.

knock *(SYN.)* thump, tap, rap, strike, hit, jab, punch, beat, pound, bang, hammer, thwack.

knockout *(SYN.)* stunning, overpowering, stupefying, overwhelming.

knoll *(SYN.)* hill, elevation, hump, mound, butte.

knot *(SYN.)* cluster, gathering, collection, group, crowd, twist, snarl, tangle.

know *(SYN.)* perceive, comprehend, apprehend, recognize, understand, discern, discriminate, ascertain, identify.
(ANT.) doubt, suspect, dispute, ignore.

knowing *(SYN.)* sage, smart, wise, clever, sagacious, shrewd.

knowledge *(SYN.)* information, wisdom, erudition, learning, apprehension.
(ANT.) misunderstanding, ignorance, stupidity, illiteracy.

knurl *(SYN.)* gnarl, knot, projection, burl, node, lump.

kosher *(SYN.)* permitted, okay, fit, proper, acceptable.

kowtow *(SYN.)* stoop, bend, kneel, genuflect, bow.

kudos *(SYN.)* acclaim, praise, approbation, approval.

label *(SYN.)* mark, tag, title, name, marker, stamp, sticker, ticket, docket, identity.

labor *(SYN.)* toil, travail, effort, task, childbirth, work, parturition, striving, workers, effort, industry, workingmen.
(ANT.) recreation, indolence, idleness, leisure.

laboratory *(SYN.)* lab, workroom, workshop.

laborer *(SYN.)* wage earner, helper, worker, toiler, blue-collar worker.

laborious *(SYN.)* tiring, difficult, hard, burdensome, industrious, painstaking.
(ANT.) simple, easy, relaxing, restful.

labyrinth *(SYN.)* complex, maze, tangle.

lace *(SYN.)* openwork, fancywork, embroidery, edging.

lacerate *(SYN.)* mangle, tear roughly.

laceration *(SYN.)* cut, wound, puncture, gash, lesion, injury.

lack *(SYN.)* want, need, shortage, dearth, scarcity, require.
(ANT.) profusion, quantity.

lackey *(SYN.)* stooge, flatterer, flunky.

lacking *(SYN.)* insufficient, short, deficient, incomplete, defective, scanty.
(ANT.) satisfactory, enough, ample, sufficient, adequate.

lackluster *(SYN.)* dull, pallid, flat, lifeless, drab, dim.

laconic *(SYN.)* short, terse, compact, brief, curt, succinct, concise.

lacquer *(SYN.)* polish, varnish, gild.

lad *(SYN.)* youth, boy, fellow, stripling.

laden *(SYN.)* burdened, weighted.

ladle *(SYN.)* scoop, dipper.

lady *(SYN.)* matron, woman, dame, gentlewoman.

ladylike *(SYN.)* feminine, womanly, maidenly, womanish, female.
(ANT.) masculine, male, virile, mannish, manly.

lag *(SYN.)* dawdle, loiter, linger, poke, dilly-dally, delay, tarry, slowdown.

laggard *(SYN.)* dallier, idler, lingerer, slowpoke, dawdler.

lair *(SYN.)* retreat, burrow, den, nest, mew, hole.

lambaste *(SYN.)* berate, scold, censure.

lame *(SYN.)* feeble, maimed, disabled, crippled, deformed, hobbling, unconvincing, weak, poor, inadequate, halt.
(ANT.) vigorous, convincing, plausible, athletic, robust, agile, sound.

lament *(SYN.)* deplore, wail, bemoan, bewail, regret, grieve, mourning, lamentation, moaning, wailing, mourn.
(ANT.) celebrate, rejoice.

lamentable *(SYN.)* unfortunate.

lamp *(SYN.)* light, beam, illumination, shine, insight, knowledge, radiance.
(ANT.) shadow, darkness, obscurity, gloom.

lampoon *(SYN.)* skit, tirade, burlesque, parody, satire.

lance *(SYN.)* cut, pierce, perforate, stab, puncture, impale, knife.

land *(SYN.)* earth, continent, ground, soil, domain, estate, field, realm, plain, surface, arrive, descend, country, island, region, alight, shore, sod, tract.

landlord *(SYN.)* owner, landholde

landowner, proprietor.

landmark *(SYN.)* keystone, monument, milestone, point, cornerstone.

landscape *(SYN.)* panorama, environs, countryside, scenery, scene.

landslide *(SYN.)* rockfall, avalanche.

lane *(SYN.)* alley, way, road, path, aisle, pass, channel, avenue, artery, passage.

language *(SYN.)* dialect, tongue, speech, lingo, jargon, cant, diction, idiom, patter, phraseology, vernacular, words. *(ANT.)* gibberish, nonsense, babble, drivel.

languid *(SYN.)* feeble, drooping, irresolute, dull, lethargic, weak, faint. *(ANT.)* forceful, strong, vigorous.

languish *(SYN.)* decline, sink, droop, wither, waste, fail, wilt, weaken. *(ANT.)* revive, rejuvenate, refresh.

languor *(SYN.)* weariness, depression, torpor, inertia, apathy.

lanky *(SYN.)* skinny, gaunt, lean, scrawny, slender, thin. *(ANT.)* chunky, stocky, obese, fat.

lantern *(SYN.)* torch, light, lamp.

lap *(SYN.)* drink, lick, fold over.

lapse *(SYN.)* decline, sink, slump.

larceny *(SYN.)* pillage, robbery, stealing, theft, burglary, plunder.

lard *(SYN.)* grease, fat.

large *(SYN.)* great, vast, colossal, ample, extensive, capacious, sizable, broad, massive, grand, immense, big, enormous, huge, giant, mammoth, wide. *(ANT.)* tiny, little, short, small.

largely *(SYN.)* chiefly, mainly, principally, mostly.

lariat *(SYN.)* lasso, rope.

lark *(SYN.)* fling, frolic, play, fun, spree, joke, revel, celebration.

lascivious *(SYN.)* lecherous, raunchy, lustful, wanton, lewd.

lash *(SYN.)* thong, whip, rod, cane, blow, strike, hit, beat, knout.

lass *(SYN.)* maiden, girl, damsel. *(ANT.)* woman,

lasso *(SYN.)* lariat, rope, noose, snare.

last *(SYN.)* terminal, final, ultimate, remain, endure, concluding, latest, utmost, end, conclusive, hindmost, continue, extreme. *(ANT.)* first, initial, beginning, opening, starting, foremost.

latch *(SYN.)* clasp, hook, fastener, lock, closing, seal, catch.

late *(SYN.)* overdue, tardy, behind, advanced, delayed, new, slow, recent. *(ANT.)* timely, early.

lately *(SYN.)* recently, yesterday.

latent *(SYN.)* potential, undeveloped, unseen, dormant, secret, concealed, inactive, hidden, obscured, covered, quiescent. *(ANT.)* visible, evident, conspicuous, explicit, manifest.

lather *(SYN.)* suds, foam, froth.

lateral *(SYN.)* sideways, glancing, tangential, marginal, skirting, side.

latitude *(SYN.)* range, scope, freedom, extent.

latter *(SYN.)* more recent, later. *(ANT.)* former.

lattice *(SYN.)* grating, screen, frame, trellis, openwork, framework, grid.

laud *(SYN.)* commend, praise, extol, glorify, compliment. *(ANT.)* criticize, belittle.

laudable *(SYN.)* creditable, praiseworthy, commendable, admirable.

laudation *(SYN.)* applause, compliment, flattery, praise, commendation, acclaim, extolling, glorification. *(ANT.)* criticizing, condemnation, reproach, disparagement, censure.

laugh *(SYN.)* chuckle, giggle, snicker, cackle, titter, grin, smile, roar, guffaw, jeer, mock.

laughable *(SYN.)* funny, amusing, comical, humorous, ridiculous.

launch *(SYN.)* drive, fire, propel, start, begin, originate, set afloat, initiate. *(ANT.)* finish, stop, terminate.

launder *(SYN.)* bathe, wash, scrub, scour.

laurels *(SYN.)* glory, distinction, recognition, award, commendation, reward, honor.

lavatory *(SYN.)* toilet, washroom, bathroom, latrine.

lavish *(SYN.)* squander, waste, dissipate, scatter, abundant, free, plentiful, liberal, extravagant, ample, wear out, prodigal, generous, spend. *(ANT.)* economize, save, conserve, accumulate, sparing, stingy, preserve.

law *(SYN.)* decree, formula, statute, act, rule, ruling, standard, principle, ordinance, proclamation, regulation, order, edict.

lawful *(SYN.)* legal, permissible, allowable, legitimate, authorized, constitutional, rightful. *(ANT.)* prohibited, criminal, illicit, illegal, illegitimate.

lawless *(SYN.)* uncivilized, uncontrolled, wild, savage, untamed, violent. *(ANT.)* obedient, law-abiding, tame.

lawlessness *(SYN.)* chaos, anarchy.

lawn *(SYN.)* grass, meadow, turf.

lawyer *(SYN.)* counsel, attorney, counselor.

lax *(SYN.)* slack, loose, careless, vague, lenient, lazy. *(ANT.)* firm, rigid.

lay *(SYN.)* mundane, worldly, temporal, place, dispose, bet, wager, hazard, risk, stake, site, earthly, profane, laic, arrange, location, put, set, ballad, deposit, position, song, secular. *(ANT.)* spiritual, unworldly, remove, misplace, disturb, mislay, disarrange, ecclesiastical, religious.

lay off *(SYN.)* discharge, bounce, fire, dismiss.

layout *(SYN.)* plan, arrangement, design.

lazy *(SYN.)* slothful, supine, idle, inactive, sluggish, inert, indolent, torpid. *(ANT.)* alert, ambitious, forceful, diligent, active, assiduous.

lea *(SYN.)* pasture, meadow.

leach *(SYN.)* remove, extract, seep, dilute, wash out.

lead *(SYN.)* regulate, conduct, guide, escort, direct, supervise, command, come first, steer, control.

(ANT.) follow.

leader *(SYN.)* master, ruler, captain, chief, commander, principal, director, head, chieftain.

(ANT.) follower, servant, disciple, subordinate, attendant.

leading *(SYN.)* dominant, foremost, principal, first, main, primary.

league *(SYN.)* entente, partnership, association, confederacy, coalition, society, alliance, federation, union.

(ANT.) separation, schism.

leak *(SYN.)* dribble, flow, drip, opening, perforation.

lean *(SYN.)* rely, tilt, slim, slender, slope, incline, tend, trust, bend, tendency, slant, depend, spare, scant, lanky, thin, meager, inclination, narrow, sag.

(ANT.) rise, heavy, fat, erect, straighten, portly, raise.

leaning *(SYN.)* trend, proclivity, bias, tendency, bent, predisposition, proneness.

(ANT.) disinclination, aversion.

leap *(SYN.)* vault, skip, caper, dive, hurdle, jump, bound, start, hop, plunge, spring.

learn *(SYN.)* gain, find out, memorize, acquire, determine.

learned *(SYN.)* erudite, knowing, enlightened, deep, wise, discerning, scholarly, intelligent, educated, sagacious.

(ANT.) simple, uneducated, ignorant, illiterate, unlettered, foolish.

learning *(SYN.)* science, education, lore, apprehension, wisdom, knowledge, scholarship, erudition.

(ANT.) misunderstanding, ignorance, stupidity.

lease *(SYN.)* charter, let, rent, engage.

leash *(SYN.)* chain, strap, shackle, collar.

least *(SYN.)* minutest, smallest, tiniest, trivial, minimum, fewest, slightest.

(ANT.) most.

leave *(SYN.)* give up, retire, desert, abandon, withdraw, relinquish, will, depart, quit, liberty, renounce, go, bequeath, consent, allowance, permission, freedom, forsake.

(ANT.) come, stay, arrive, tarry, remain, abide.

lecherous *(SYN.)* lustful, sensual, carnal, lascivious.

lecture *(SYN.)* talk, discussion, lesson, instruct, speech, conference, sermon, report, recitation, address, oration, discourse.

(ANT.) writing, meditation, correspondence.

ledge *(SYN.)* eaves, ridge, shelf, rim, edge.

lee *(SYN.)* shelter, asylum, sanctuary, haven.

leech *(SYN.)* barnacle, bloodsucker, parasite.

leer *(SYN.)* eye, grimace, ogle, wink, squint.

leeway *(SYN.)* reserve, allowance, elbowroom, slack, clearance.

leftovers *(SYN.)* scraps, remains,

residue, remainder.

legacy *(SYN.)* bequest, inheritance, heirloom.

legal *(SYN.)* legitimate, rightful, honest, allowable, allowed, permissible, lawful, permitted, authorized.

(ANT.) illicit, illegal, prohibited, illegitimate.

legalize *(SYN.)* authorize, ordain, approve, sanction.

legate *(SYN.)* envoy, agent, representative, emissary.

legend *(SYN.)* saga, fable, allegory, myth, parable, tale, story, folklore, fiction, chronicle.

(ANT.) history, facts.

legendary *(SYN.)* fictitious, traditional, mythical, imaginary, fanciful.

legible *(SYN.)* plain, readable, clear, distinct.

(ANT.) illegible.

legion *(SYN.)* outfit, unit, troop, regiment, company, battalion, force, army, team, division.

legislation *(SYN.)* resolution, ruling, lawmaking, regulation, enactment, statute, decree.

legislator *(SYN.)* statesman, congressman, senator, politician, lawmaker.

legitimate *(SYN.)* true, real, bona fide, lawful, proper, right, valid, correct, unadulterated, authentic, rightful, legal, sincere.

(ANT.) sham, counterfeit, artificial, false.

leisure *(SYN.)* respite, intermission, ease, relaxation, rest, calm, tranquillity, recreation, peace, pause.

(ANT.) motion, commotion, tumult, agitation, disturbance.

leisurely *(SYN.)* sluggish, laggard, unhurried, relaxed, casual, dawdling, slow, deliberate.

(ANT.) hurried, swift, pressed, rushed, forced, fast, speedy, quick.

lend *(SYN.)* entrust, advance, confer.

length *(SYN.)* reach, measure, extent, distance, span, longness, stretch.

lengthen *(SYN.)* stretch, prolong, draw, reach, increase, grow, protract, extend.

(ANT.) shrink, contract, shorten.

leniency *(SYN.)* grace, pity, compassion, mildness, charity, mercy, clemency.

(ANT.) vengeance, punishment, cruelty.

lenient *(SYN.)* tender, humane, clement, tolerant, compassionate, merciful, relaxed, forgiving, gentle, mild, lax, kind.

(ANT.) unfeeling, pitiless, brutal, remorseless.

leprechaun *(SYN.)* gnome, imp, goblin, fairy, elf, sprite, banshee.

lesion *(SYN.)* wound, blemish, sore, trauma, injury.

less *(SYN.)* fewer, smaller, reduced, negative, stinted.

(ANT.) more.

lessen *(SYN.)* shorten, reduce, deduct, subtract, curtail, diminish, shrink, dwindle, decline, instruction, teaching, remove, decrease.

(ANT.) swell, grow, enlarge, increase.

expand, multiply, amplify.
lesson *(SYN.)* exercise, session, class, assignment, section, recitation.
let *(SYN.)* admit, hire out, contract, allow, permit, consent, leave, grant, rent. *(ANT.)* deny.
letdown *(SYN.)* disillusionment, disappointment.
lethal *(SYN.)* mortal, dangerous, deadly, fatal, devastating.
lethargic *(SYN.)* sluggish, logy, slow, listless, phlegmatic, lazy. *(ANT.) vivacious, energetic.*
lethargy *(SYN.)* numbness, stupor, daze, insensibility, torpor. *(ANT.) wakefulness, liveliness, activity, readiness.*
letter *(SYN.)* note, letter, mark, message, character, symbol, sign, memorandum.
letup *(SYN.)* slowdown, slackening, lessening, abatement, reduction.
levee *(SYN.)* dike, breakwater, dam, embankment.
level *(SYN.)* smooth, even, plane, equivalent, uniform, horizontal, equal, flatten, equalize, raze, demolish, flat. *(ANT.) uneven, sloping, hilly, broken.*
level-headed *(SYN.)* reasonable, sensible, calm, collected, cool.
leverage *(SYN.)* clout, power, influence, weight, rank.
levity *(SYN.)* humor, triviality, giddiness, hilarity, fun, frivolity.
levy *(SYN.)* tax, duty, tribute, rate, assessment, exaction, charge, custom. *(ANT.) wages, remuneration, gift.*
lewd *(SYN.)* indecent, smutty, course, gross, disgusting, impure. *(ANT.) pure, decent, refined.*
liability *(SYN.)* indebtedness, answerability, obligation, vulnerability.
liable *(SYN.)* answerable, responsible, likely, exposed to, subject, amenable, probable, accountable. *(ANT.) immune, exempt, independent.*
liaison *(SYN.)* union, coupling, link, connection, alliance.
liar *(SYN.)* fibber, falsifier, storyteller, fabricator, prevaricator.
libel *(SYN.)* slander, calumny, vilification, aspersion, defamation. *(ANT.) defense, praise, applause, flattery.*
liberal *(SYN.)* large, generous, unselfish, openhanded, broad, tolerant, kind, unprejudiced, open-minded, lavish, plentiful, ample, abundant, extravagant, extensive. *(ANT.) restricted, conservative, stingy, confined.*
liberality *(SYN.)* kindness, philanthropy, beneficence, humanity, altruism, benevolence, generosity, charity. *(ANT.) selfishness, cruelty, malevolence.*
liberate *(SYN.)* emancipate, loose, release, let go, deliver, free, discharge. *(ANT.) subjugate, oppress, jail, confine, restrict, imprison.*
liberated *(SYN.)* loose, frank, emancipated, careless, liberal, freed, autonomous, exempt, familiar.

(ANT.) subject, clogged, restricted, impeded.
liberty *(SYN.)* permission, independence, autonomy, license, privilege, emancipation, freedom. *(ANT.) constraint, imprisonment, bondage, captivity.*
license *(SYN.)* liberty, freedom, liberation, permission, exemption, authorization, warrant, allow, consent, permit, sanction, approval, unrestraint. *(ANT.) servitude, constraint, bondage, necessity.*
lick *(SYN.)* taste, lap, lave.
lid *(SYN.)* top, cover, cap, plug, cork, stopper.
lie *(SYN.)* untruth, fib, illusion, delusion, falsehood, fiction, equivocation, prevarication, repose, location, perjury, misinform, site, recline, similitude. *(ANT.) variance, truth, difference.*
life *(SYN.)* sparkle, being, spirit, vivacity, animation, buoyancy, vitality, existence, biography, energy, liveliness, vigor. *(ANT.) demise, lethargy, death, languor.*
lift *(SYN.)* hoist, pick up, elevate, raise, heft.
light *(SYN.)* brightness, illumination, beam, gleam, lamp, knowledge, brilliance, fixture, bulb, candle, fire, ignite, burn, dawn, incandescence, flame, airy, unsubstantial, dainty, luminosity, shine, radiance, giddy, enlightenment, weightless, understanding. *(ANT.) darken, gloom, shadow, extinguish, darkness.*
lighten *(SYN.)* diminish, unburden, reduce, brighten.
light-headed *(SYN.)* giddy, silly, dizzy, frivolous. *(ANT.) sober, clear-headed, rational.*
lighthearted *(SYN.)* carefree, merry, gay, cheerful, happy, glad. *(ANT.) somber, sad, serious, melancholy.*
like *(SYN.)* fancy, esteem, adore, love, admire, care for, prefer, cherish. *(ANT.) disapprove, loathe, hate, dislike.*
likely *(SYN.)* liable, reasonable, probable, possible.
likeness *(SYN.)* similarity, resemblance, representation, image, portrait. *(ANT.) difference.*
likewise *(SYN.)* besides, as well, also, too, similarly.
liking *(SYN.)* fondness, affection, partiality. *(ANT.) antipathy, dislike.*
limb *(SYN.)* arm, leg, member, appendage, part, bough.
limber *(SYN.)* bending, flexible, elastic, pliable. *(ANT.) inflexible, stiff.*
limbo *(SYN.)* exile, banishment, purgatory.
limelight *(SYN.)* spotlight, notice, notoriety, fame, prominence.
limerick *(SYN.)* jingle, rhyme.
limit *(SYN.)* terminus, bound, extent, confine, border, restriction, boundary,

restraint, edge, frontier, check, end, limitation.
(ANT.) *endlessness, vastness, boundlessness.*
limn (SYN.) depict, portray, sketch, paint, illustrate.
limp (SYN.) soft, flabby, drooping, walk, limber, supple, flexible, hobble, stagger.
(ANT.) *stiff.*
limpid (SYN.) clear, open, transparent, unobstructed.
(ANT.) *cloudy.*
line (SYN.) row, file, series, array, sequence, wire, seam, wrinkle, crease, boundary, arrangement, kind, type, division.
lineage (SYN.) race, family, tribe, nation, strain, folk, people, ancestry, clan.
linger (SYN.) wait, rest, bide, delay, dwadle, stay, loiter, remain, dilly-dally, tarry.
(ANT.) *leave, expedite.*
lingo (SYN.) vernacular, dialect, language, jargon, speech.
link (SYN.) unite, connector, loop, couple, attach, connective, connection, coupling, juncture, bond.
(ANT.) *separate, disconnect, split.*
lip (SYN.) edge, brim, rim.
liquid (SYN.) watery, fluent, fluid, flowing.
(ANT.) *solid, congealed.*
liquidate (SYN.) pay off, settle, defray.
liquor (SYN.) spirits, alcohol, drink, booze.
lissome (SYN.) nimble, quick, lively, flexible, agile.
list (SYN.) roll, register, slate, enumeration, series.
listen (SYN.) overhear, attend to, heed, hear, list, hearken.
(ANT.) *ignore, scorn, disregard, reject.*
listless (SYN.) uninterested, tired, lethargic, unconcerned, apathetic.
(ANT.) *active.*
literal (SYN.) exact, verbatim, precise, strict, faithful.
literally (SYN.) actually, exactly, really.
literate (SYN.) informed, educated, learned, intelligent, versed, knowledgeable.
(ANT.) *unread, illiterate, ignorant, unlettered.*
literature (SYN.) books, writings, publications.
lithe (SYN.) supple, flexible, bending, limber, pliable.
(ANT.) *stiff.*
litigious (SYN.) quarrelsome, disputatious, argumentative.
litter (SYN.) rubbish, trash, scatter, clutter, strew, debris, rubble, disorder.
little (SYN.) tiny, petty, miniature, diminutive, puny, wee, significant, small, short, brief, bit, trivial.
(ANT.) *huge, large, big, long, immense.*
liturgy (SYN.) ritual, sacrament, worship, service.
live (SYN.) dwell, reside, abide, survive, exist, alive, occupy, stay, active.
(ANT.) *die.*

livelihood (SYN.) keep, sustenance, support, subsistence, job, trade, profession, vocation.
lively (SYN.) blithe, vivaciousness, clear, vivid, active, frolicsome, brisk, fresh, animated, energetic, live, spry, vigorous, quick, nimble, bright, exciting, supple.
(ANT.) *stale, dull, listless, slow, vapid.*
livestock (SYN.) animals, cattle.
livid (SYN.) grayish, furious, pale, enraged.
living (SYN.) support, livelihood, existent, alive.
load (SYN.) oppress, trouble, burden, weight, freight, afflict, encumber, pack, shipment, cargo, lade, tax.
(ANT.) *lighten, console, unload, mitigate, empty, ease.*
loafer (SYN.) loiterer, bum, idler, sponger, deadbeat.
loan (SYN.) credit, advance, lend.
loath (SYN.) reluctant, unwilling, opposed.
loathe (SYN.) dislike, despise, hate, abhor, detest, abominate.
(ANT.) *love, approve, like, admire.*
loathsome (SYN.) foul, vile, detestable, revolting, abominable, atrocious, offensive, odious.
(ANT.) *pleasant, commendable, alluring, agreeable, delightful.*
lob (SYN.) toss, hurl, pitch, throw, heave.
lobby (SYN.) foyer, entry, entrance, vestibule, passageway, entryway.
local (SYN.) limited, regional, restricted, particular.
locality (SYN.) nearness, neighborhood, district, vicinity.
(ANT.) *remoteness.*
locate (SYN.) discover, find, unearth, site, situate, place.
located (SYN.) found, residing, positioned, situated, placed.
location (SYN.) spot, locale, station, locality, situation, place, area, site, vicinity, position, zone, region.
lock (SYN.) curl, hook, bolt, braid, ringlet, plait, close, latch, tuft, fastening, bar, hasp, fasten, tress.
(ANT.) *open.*
locker (SYN.) wardrobe, closet, cabinet, chest.
locket (SYN.) case, lavaliere, pendant.
locomotion (SYN.) movement, travel, transit, motion.
locution (SYN.) discourse, cadence, manner, accent.
lodge (SYN.) cabin, cottage, hut, club, chalet, society, room, reside, dwell, live, occupy, inhabit, abide, board, fix, settle.
lodger (SYN.) guest, tenant, boarder, occupant.
lofty (SYN.) high, stately, grandiose, towering, elevated, exalted, sublime, majestic, scornful, proud, grand, tall, pompous.
(ANT.) *undignified, lowly, common, ordinary.*
log (SYN.) lumber, wood, board register, record, album, account.

logical *(SYN.)* strong, effective, telling, convincing, reasonable, sensible, rational, sane, sound, cogent.
(ANT.) crazy, illogical, irrational, unreasonable, weak.

logy *(SYN.)* tired, inactive, lethargic, sleepy, weary.

loiter *(SYN.)* idle, linger, wait, stay, tarry, dilly-dally, dawdle.

loll *(SYN.)* hang, droop, recline, relax.

lone *(SYN.)* lonely, sole, unaided, single, deserted, isolated, secluded, apart, alone, solitary.
(ANT.) surrounded, accompanied.

loner *(SYN.)* recluse, maverick, outsider, hermit.

loneliness *(SYN.)* solitude, isolation, seclusion, alienation.

lonely *(SYN.)* unaided, isolated, single, solitary, lonesome, unaccompanied, deserted, alone, desolate.
(ANT.) surrounded, attended.

lonesome *(SYN.)* secluded, remote, unpopulated, barren, empty, desolate.

long *(SYN.)* lengthy, prolonged, wordy, elongated, extended, lingering, drawn out, lasting, protracted, extensive, length, prolix, far-reaching, extended.
(ANT.) terse, concise, abridged, short.

long-standing *(SYN.)* established.

long-winded *(SYN.)* boring, dull, wordy.
(ANT.) curt, terse.

look *(SYN.)* gaze, witness, seem, eye, behold, see, watch, scan, view, appear, stare, discern, glance, examine, examination, peep, expression, appearance, regard, study, survey.
(ANT.) overlook, hide, avert, miss.

loom *(SYN.)* emerge, appear, show up.

loop *(SYN.)* ringlet, noose, spiral, fastener.

loose *(SYN.)* untied, unbound, lax, vague, unrestrained, dissolute, limp, undone, baggy, disengaged, indefinite, slack, careless, heedless, unfastened, free, wanton.
(ANT.) restrained, steady, fastened, secure, tied, firm, fast, definite, inhibited.

loosen *(SYN.)* untie, undo, loose, unchain.
(ANT.) tie, tighten, secure.

loot *(SYN.)* booty, plunder, take, steal, rob, sack, rifle, pillage, ravage, devastate.

lope *(SYN.)* run, race, bound, gallop.

lopsided *(SYN.)* unequal, twisted, uneven, askew, distorted.

loquacious *(SYN.)* garrulous, wordy, profuse, chatty, verbose.

lord *(SYN.)* peer, ruler, proprietor, nobleman, master, owner, governor.

lore *(SYN.)* learning, knowledge, wisdom, stories, legends beliefs, teachings.

lose *(SYN.)* misplace, flop, fail, sacrifice, forfeit, mislay, vanish, surrender.
(ANT.) succeed, locate, place, win, discover, find.

loss *(SYN.)* injury, damage, want, hurt, need, bereavement, trouble, death, failure, deficiency.

lost *(SYN.)* dazed, wasted, astray, for-feited, preoccupied, used, adrift, bewildered, missing, distracted, consumed, misspent, absorbed, confused, mislaid, gone, destroyed.
(ANT.) found, anchored.

lot *(SYN.)* result, destiny, bunch, many, amount, fate, cluster, group, sum, portion, outcome, number, doom, issue.

lotion *(SYN.)* cosmetic, balm, cream.

lottery *(SYN.)* wager, chance, drawing, raffle.

loud *(SYN.)* vociferous, noisy, resounding, stentorian, clamorous, sonorous, thunderous, shrill, blaring, roaring, deafening.
(ANT.) soft, inaudible, murmuring, subdued, quiet, dulcet.

lounge *(SYN.)* idle, loaf, laze, sofa, couch, davenport, relax, rest, lobby, salon, divan.

louse *(SYN.)* scoundrel, knave, cad, rat.

lousy *(SYN.)* revolting, grimy, rotten, dirty, disgusting.

lovable *(SYN.)* charming, attractive, delightful, amiable, sweet, cuddly.

love *(SYN.)* attachment, endearment, affection, adoration, liking, devotion, warmth, tenderness, friendliness, adore, worship, like, cherish, fondness.
(ANT.) loathing, detest, indifference, dislike, hate, hatred.

loveliness *(SYN.)* grace, pulchritude, charm, attractiveness, comeliness, fairness, beauty.
(ANT.) ugliness, eyesore, disfigurement.

lovely *(SYN.)* handsome, fair, charming, pretty, attractive, delightful, beautiful, beauteous, exquisite, comely.
(ANT.) ugly, unsightly, homely, foul, hideous, repulsive.

lover *(SYN.)* fiance, suitor, courter, sweetheart, beau.

loving *(SYN.)* close, intimate, confidential, affectionate, friendly.
(ANT.) formal, conventional, ceremonious, distant.

low *(SYN.)* mean, vile, despicable, vulgar, abject, groveling, contemptible, lesser, menial.
(ANT.) righteous, lofty, esteemed, noble.

lower *(SYN.)* subordinate, minor, secondary, quiet, soften, disgrace, degrade, decrease, reduce, diminish, lessen, inferior.
(ANT.) greater, superior, increase.

low-key *(SYN.)* subdued, muted, calm, controlled, restrained, understated.

lowly *(SYN.)* lowborn, humble, base, low, mean, common, average, simple.
(ANT.) royal, noble.

loyal *(SYN.)* earnest, ardent, addicted, inclined, faithful, devoted, affectionate, prone, fond, patriotic, dependable, true.
(ANT.) indisposed, detached, disloyal, traitorous, untrammeled.

loyalty *(SYN.)* devotion, steadfastness, constancy, faithfulness, fidelity, patriotism, allegiance.
(ANT.) treachery, falseness, disloyalty.

lubricate *(SYN.)* oil, grease, anoint.

lucent *(SYN.)* radiant, beaming, vivid, illuminated, lustrous.

lucid *(SYN.)* plain, visible, clear, intelligible, unmistakable, transparent, limpid, translucent, open, shining, light, explicit, understandable, clear-cut, distinct.
(ANT.) unclear, vague, obscure.

luck *(SYN.)* chance, fortunate, fortune, lot, fate, fluke, destiny, karma.
(ANT.) misfortune.

lucky *(SYN.)* favored, favorable, auspicious, fortunate, successful, felicitous.
(ANT.) unlucky, condemned, unfortunate, persecuted.

lucrative *(SYN.)* well-paying, profitable, high-paying, productive, beneficial.

ludicrous *(SYN.)* absurd, ridiculous.

lug *(SYN.)* pull, haul, drag, tug.

luggage *(SYN.)* bags, valises, baggage, suitcases, trunks.

lugubrious *(SYN.)* mournful, sad, gloomy, somber, melancholy.

lukewarm *(SYN.)* unenthusiastic, tepid, spiritless, detached, apathetic, mild.

lull *(SYN.)* quiet, calm, soothe, rest, hush, stillness, pause, break, intermission, recess, respite, silence.

lumber *(SYN.)* logs, timber, wood.

luminous *(SYN.)* beaming, lustrous, shining, glowing, gleaming, bright, light, alight, clear, radiant.
(ANT.) murky, dull, dark.

lummox *(SYN.)* yokel, oaf, bumpkin, clown, klutz.

lump *(SYN.)* swelling, protuberance, mass, chunk, hunk, bump.

lunacy *(SYN.)* derangement, madness, aberration, psychosis, craziness.
(ANT.) stability, rationality.

lunge *(SYN.)* charge, stab, attack, push.

lurch *(SYN.)* topple, sway, toss, roll, rock, tip, pitch.

lure *(SYN.)* draw, tug, drag, entice, attraction, haul, attract, temptation, persuade, pull, draw on, allure.
(ANT.) drive, alienate, propel.

lurid *(SYN.)* sensational, terrible, melodramatic, startling.

lurk *(SYN.)* sneak, hide, prowl, creep.

luscious *(SYN.)* savory, delightful, juicy, sweet, pleasing, delicious, tasty.
(ANT.) unsavory, nauseous, acrid.

lush *(SYN.)* tender, succulent, ripe.

lust *(SYN.)* longing, desire, passion, appetite, craving, aspiration, urge.
(ANT.) hate, aversion, loathing.

luster *(SYN.)* radiance, brightness, glister, honor, fame, effulgence, gloss.
(ANT.) dullness, obscurity, darkness.

lustful *(SYN.)* amorous, sexy, desirous, passionate, wanton.

lusty *(SYN.)* healthy, strong, mighty, powerful, sturdy, strapping, hale.
(ANT.) weak.

luxuriant *(SYN.)* abundant, flourishing, dense, lush, rich.

luxurious *(SYN.)* rich, lavish, deluxe.
(ANT.) simple, crude, sparse.

luxury *(SYN.)* frills, comfort, extravagance, elegance, splendor, prosperity, swankiness, well-being.
(ANT.) poverty.

lyric *(SYN.)* musical, text, words.

lyrical *(SYN.)* poetic, musical.

macabre *(SYN.)* ghastly, grim, horrible, gruesome.

machine *(SYN.)* motor, mechanism, device, contrivance.

machinist *(SYN.)* engineer.

mad *(SYN.)* incensed, crazy, insane, angry, furious, delirious, provoked.
(ANT.) sane, calm, healthy, rational, lucid, cheerful, happy.

madam *(SYN.)* dame, woman, lady, matron, mistress.

madder *(SYN.)* ruddle.

madness *(SYN.)* derangement, delirium, aberration, mania, insanity, craziness.
(ANT.) stability, rationality.

magazine *(SYN.)* journal, periodical, arsenal, armory.

magic *(SYN.)* sorcery, wizardry, charm, legerdemain, enchantment, black art.

magical *(SYN.)* mystical, marvelous, magic, miraculous, bewitching.

magician *(SYN.)* conjuror, sorcerer, wizard, witch, artist, trickster.

magistrate *(SYN.)* judge, adjudicator.

magnet *(SYN.)* lure, temptation.

magnetic *(SYN.)* pulling, attractive, alluring, drawing, enthralling, seductive.

magnetism *(SYN.)* allure, irresistibility, attraction, appeal.

magnificence *(SYN.)* luxury, grandeur, splendor, majesty, dynamic.

magnificent *(SYN.)* rich, luxurious, splendid, wonderful, impressive.
(ANT.) simple, plain.

magnify *(SYN.)* heighten, exaggerate, amplify, expand, stretch, caricature.
(ANT.) compress understate, depreciate, belittle.

magnitude *(SYN.)* mass, bigness, size, area, volume, dimensions, greatness.

maid *(SYN.)* chambermaid, servant.

maiden *(SYN.)* original, foremost, first, damsel, lass, miss.
(ANT.) accessory, secondary.

mail *(SYN.)* dispatch, send, letters, post, correspondence.

main *(SYN.)* essential, chief, highest, principal, first, leading, cardinal.
(ANT.) supplemental, subordinate, auxiliary.

mainstay *(SYN.)* buttress, pillar, refuge, reinforcement, support, backbone.

maintain *(SYN.)* claim, support, uphold, defend, vindicate, sustain, continue.
(ANT.) neglect, oppose, discontinue.

maintenance *(SYN.)* subsistence, livelihood, living, support, preservation.

majestic *(SYN.)* magnificent, stately, noble, august, grand, imposing, sublime, lofty, high, grandiose, dignified.
(ANT.) humble, lowly, undignified.

majesty *(SYN.)* grandeur, dignity, nobility, splendor, distinction.

major *(SYN.)* important, superior, larger, chief, greater, uppermost.
(ANT.) inconsequential, minor.

make *(SYN.)* execute, cause, produce, establish, assemble, create, shape.
(ANT.) unmake, break, undo, demolish.

make-believe *(SYN.)* pretend, imagined, simulated, false, fake, unreal.

maker *(SYN.)* inventor, creator, producer, builder, manufacturer.

makeshift *(SYN.)* proxy, deputy, understudy, expedient, agent, alternate.
(ANT.) sovereign, head, principal.

make-up *(SYN.)* composition, formation, structure, cosmetics.

male *(SYN.)* masculine, virile.
(ANT.) female, womanly, feminine.

malfunction *(SYN.)* flaw, breakdown, snag, glitch, failure.

malice *(SYN.)* spite, grudge, enmity, ill will, malignity, animosity, rancor.
(ANT.) love, affection, toleration.

malicious *(SYN.)* hostile, malignant, virulent, bitter, rancorous, evil-minded, malevolent, spiteful, wicked.
(ANT.) kind, benevolent, affectionate.

malign *(SYN.)* misuse, defame, revile, abuse, traduce, asperse, misapply.
(ANT.) praise, cherish, protect, honor.

malignant *(SYN.)* harmful, deadly, killing, lethal, mortal, destructive, hurtful.
(ANT.) benign, harmless.

malodorous *(SYN.)* reeking, fetid, smelly, noxious, vile, rancid, offensive.

malpractice *(SYN.)* wrongdoing, misdeed, abuse, malfeasance, error, mismanagement, dereliction, fault, sin.

maltreat *(SYN.)* mistreat, ill-treatment, abuse.

maltreatment *(SYN.)* disparagement, perversion, aspersion, invective, defamation, profanation.
(ANT.) respect, approval, laudation, commendation.

mammoth *(SYN.)* enormous, immense, huge, colossal, gigantic, gargantuan.
(ANT.) minuscule, tiny, small.

man *(SYN.)* person, human being, society, folk, soul, individual, mortal.
(ANT.) woman.

manage *(SYN.)* curb, govern, direct, bridle, command, regulate, repress, check, restrain, dominate, guide.
(ANT.) forsake, submit, abandon, mismanage, bungle.

manageable *(SYN.)* willing, obedient, docile, controllable, tractable, submissive, governable, wieldy.
(ANT.) recalcitrant, unmanageable, wild.

management *(SYN.)* regulation, administration, supervision, direction.

manager *(SYN.)* overseer, superintendent, supervisor, director, boss, executive.

mandate *(SYN.)* order, injunction, command, referendum, dictate, writ.

mandatory *(SYN.)* compulsory, required, obligatory, imperative, necessary.
(ANT.) optional.

maneuver *(SYN.)* execution, effort, proceeding, enterprise, working, action, operation, agency, instrumentality.
(ANT.) rest, inaction, cessation.

mangle *(SYN.)* tear apart, cut, maim, wound, mutilate, injure, break. '

manhandle *(SYN.)* maltreat, maul, abuse, ill-treat.

manhood *(SYN.)* maturity, manliness.
(ANT.) youth.

manic *(SYN.)* excited, hyped up, agitated.

manifest *(SYN.)* open, evident, lucid, clear, distinct, unobstructed, cloudless, apparent, intelligible, apparent.
(ANT.) vague, overcast, unclear, cloudy, hidden, concealed.

manifesto *(SYN.)* pronouncement, edict, proclamation, statement, declaration.

manifold *(SYN.)* various, many, multiple, numerous, abundant, copious, profuse.
(ANT.) few.

manipulate *(SYN.)* manage, feel, work, operate, handle, touch, maneuver.

manly *(SYN.)* strong, brave, masculine, manful, courageous, stalwart.

man-made *(SYN.)* artificial.
(ANT.) natural.

manner *(SYN.)* air, demeanor, custom, style, method, deportment, mode, habit, practice, way, behavior, fashion.

mannerism *(SYN.)* eccentricity, quirk, habit, peculiarity, idiosyncrasy, trait.

mannerly *(SYN.)* well-bred, gentlemanly, courteous, suave, polite, genteel.

manor *(SYN.)* land, mansion, estate, domain, villa, castle, property, palace.

manslaughter *(SYN.)* murder, killing, assassination, homicide, elimination.

mantle *(SYN.)* serape, garment, overgarment, cover, cloak, wrap.

manual *(SYN.)* directory, guidebook, handbook, physical, laborious, menial.

manufacture *(SYN.)* construct, make, assemble, fabricate, produce, fashion, build.

manure *(SYN.)* fertilizer, droppings, waste, compost.

manuscript *(SYN.)* copy, writing, work, paper, composition, document.

many *(SYN.)* numerous, various, divers, multitudinous, sundry, multifarious, several, manifold, abundant, plentiful.
(ANT.) infrequent, meager, few, scanty.

map *(SYN.)* sketch, plan, chart, graph, itinerary.

mar *(SYN.)* spoil, hurt, damage, impair, harm, deface, injure.
(ANT.) repair, benefit, mend.

marathon *(SYN.)* relay, race, contest.

march *(SYN.)* promenade, parade, pace, hike, walk, tramp.

margin *(SYN.)* boundary, border, rim, edge.

marine *(SYN.)* naval, oceanic, nautical, ocean, maritime.

mariner *(SYN.)* seafarer, gob, seaman, sailor.

marionette *(SYN.)* doll, puppet.

maritime *(SYN.)* shore, coastal, nautical.

mark *(SYN.)* stain, badge, stigma, vestige, sign, feature, label, characteristic, trace, brand, trait, scar, indication.

marked *(SYN.)* plain, apparent, noticeable, evident, decided, noted, special, noteworthy.

market *(SYN.)* supermarket, store, bazaar, mart, stall, marketplace, plaza, emporium.

maroon *(SYN.)* desert, leave behind, forsake, abandon, jettison.

marriage *(SYN.)* wedding, matrimony, nuptials, espousal, union, alliance, association.
(ANT.) divorce, celibacy, separation.

marrow *(SYN.)* center, core, gist, essential, soul.

marry *(SYN.)* wed, espouse, betroth.

marsh *(SYN.)* bog, swamp, mire, everglade, estuary.

marshal *(SYN.)* adjutant, officer, order, arrange, rank.

mart *(SYN.)* shop, market, store.

martial *(SYN.)* warlike, combative, militant, belligerent.
(ANT.) peaceful.

martyr *(SYN.)* victim, sufferer, tortured, torment, plague, harass, persecute.

marvel *(SYN.)* phenomenon, wonder, miracle, astonishment, sensation.

marvelous *(SYN.)* rare, wonderful, extraordinary, unusual, exceptional, miraculous, wondrous, amazing.
(ANT.) usual, common, ordinary.

mascot *(SYN.)* pet, amulet, charm.

masculine *(SYN.)* robust, manly, virile, strong, bold, male, lusty, vigorous, hardy, mannish.
(ANT.) weak, emasculated, feminine, effeminate, womanish, female.

mash *(SYN.)* mix, pulverize, crush, grind, crumble, granulate.

mask *(SYN.)* veil, disguise, cloak, secrete, withhold, hide, cover.
(ANT.) uncover, reveal, disclose.

masquerade *(SYN.)* pretend, disguise, pose, impersonate, costume party.

mass *(SYN.)* society, torso, body, remains, association, carcass, bulk.
(ANT.) spirit, mind, intellect.

massacre *(SYN.)* butcher, murder, carnage, slaughter, execute, slay, genocide, killing, butchery, extermination.
(ANT.) save, protect, vivify, animate.

massage *(SYN.)* knead, rub, stroke.

massive *(SYN.)* grave, cumbersome, heavy, sluggish, ponderous, serious.
(ANT.) light, animated, small, tiny.

mast *(SYN.)* pole, post.

master *(SYN.)* owner, employer, leader, ruler, chief, head, lord, teacher.
(ANT.) slave, servant.

masterful *(SYN.)* commanding, bossy, domineering, dictatorial, cunning.

masterly *(SYN.)* adroit, superb, skillful, expert.
(ANT.) awkward, clumsy.

mastermind *(SYN.)* prodigy, sage, guru, mentor.

masterpiece *(SYN.)* prizewinner, classic, perfection, model.

mastery *(SYN.)* sway, sovereignty, domination, transcendence, ascendancy, influence, jurisdiction, prestige.

mat *(SYN.)* cover, rug, pallet, bedding, pad.

match *(SYN.)* equivalent, equal, contest, balance, resemble, peer, mate.

matchless *(SYN.)* peerless, incomparable, unequaled, unrivaled, excellent.
(ANT.) ordinary, unimpressive.

mate *(SYN.)* friend, colleague, associate, partner, companion, comrade.
(ANT.) stranger, adversary.

material *(SYN.)* sensible, momentous, germane, bodily, palpable, important, physical, essential, corporeal, tangible, substance, matter, fabric.
(ANT.) metaphysical, spiritual, insignificant, mental, immaterial, irrelevant, intangible.

materialize *(SYN.)* take shape, finalize, embody, incarnate, emerge, appear.

maternal *(SYN.)* motherly.
(ANT.) fatherly.

mathematics *(SYN.)* measurements, computations, numbers, calculation, figures.

matrimony *(SYN.)* marriage, wedding, espousal, union.
(ANT.) virginity, divorce.

matrix *(SYN.)* template, stamp, negative, stencil, mold, form, die, cutout.

matron *(SYN.)* lady.

matted *(SYN.)* tangled, clustered, rumpled, shaggy, knotted, gnarled, tousled.

matter *(SYN.)* cause, thing, substance, occasion, material, moment, topic, stuff, concern, theme, subject, consequence, affair, business, interest.
(ANT.) spirit, immateriality.

mature *(SYN.)* ready, matured, complete, ripe, consummate, mellow, aged, seasoned, full-grown.
(ANT.) raw, crude, undeveloped, young, immature, innocent.

maudlin *(SYN.)* emotional, mushy, sentimental, mawkish.

maul *(SYN.)* pummel, mistreat, manhandle, beat, batter, bruise, abuse.

mausoleum *(SYN.)* shrine, tomb, vault.

maverick *(SYN.)* nonconformist, oddball, outsider, dissenter, loner.

mawkish *(SYN.)* sentimental, emotional, nostalgic.

maxim *(SYN.)* rule, code, law, proverb, principle, saying, adage, motto.

maximum *(SYN.)* highest, largest, head, greatest, supremacy, climax.
(ANT.) minimum.

may *(SYN.)* can, be able.

maybe *(SYN.)* feasibly, perchance, perhaps, possibly.
(ANT.) definitely.

mayhem *(SYN.)* brutality, viciousness, ruthlessness.

maze *(SYN.)* complex, labyrinth, network, muddle, confusion, snarl, tangle.

meadow *(SYN.)* field, pasture, lea, range, grassland.

meager *(SYN.)* sparse, scanty, mean, frugal, deficient, slight, paltry, inadequate.
(ANT.) ample, plentiful, abundant, bountiful.

meal *(SYN.)* refreshment, dinner, lunch, repast, breakfast.

mean *(SYN.)* sordid, base, intend, plan, propose, expect, indicate, denote, say, signify, suggest, express, average, nasty, middle, contemptible, offensive, vulgar, unkind, cruel, despicable, vile, low, medium.
(ANT.) dignified, noble, exalted

thoughtful, gentle, openhanded, kind, generous, admirable.

meander *(SYN.)* wind, stray, wander, twist

meaning *(SYN.)* gist, connotation, intent, purport, drift, acceptation, implication, sense, import, interpretation, denotation, signification, explanation, purpose, significance.

meaningful *(SYN.)* profound, deep, expressive, important, crucial.

meaningless *(SYN.)* nonsensical, senseless, unreasonable, preposterous.

means *(SYN.)* utensil, channel, agent, money, riches, vehicle, apparatus, device, wealth, support, medium, instrument.
(ANT.) preventive, impediment, hindrance.

measly *(SYN.)* scanty, puny, skimpy, meager, petty.

measure *(SYN.)* law, bulk, rule, criterion, size, volume, weight, standard, dimension, breadth, depth, test, touchstone, trial, length, extent, gauge.
(ANT.) guess, chance, supposition.

measureless *(SYN.)* immeasurable, immense, boundless, limitless, infinite, vast.
(ANT.) figurable, ascertainable, measurable.

meat *(SYN.)* lean, flesh, food.

mecca *(SYN.)* target, shrine, goal, sanctuary, destination.

mechanic *(SYN.)* repairman, machinist.

mechanism *(SYN.)* device, contrivance, tool, machine, machinery.

medal *(SYN.)* decoration, award, badge, medallion, reward, ribbon, prize, honor.

meddle *(SYN.)* tamper, interpose, pry, snoop, intrude, interrupt, interfere, monkey.

meddlesome *(SYN.)* forward, bothersome, intrusive, obtrusive.

media *(SYN.)* tools, instruments, implements.

mediate *(SYN.)* settle, intercede, umpire, intervene, negotiate, arbitrate, referee.

medicinal *(SYN.)* helping, healing, remedial, therapeutic, corrective.

medicine *(SYN.)* drug, medication, remedy, cure, prescription, potion.

mediocre *(SYN.)* medium, mean, average, moderate, fair, ordinary.
(ANT.) outstanding, exceptional.

meditate *(SYN.)* remember, muse, think, judge, mean, conceive, contemplate, deem, suppose, purpose, consider, picture, reflect, believe, plan, reckon.

medium *(SYN.)* modicum, average, middling, median.
(ANT.) extreme.

medley *(SYN.)* hodgepodge, mixture, assortment, conglomeration, mishmash, miscellany.

meek *(SYN.)* subdued, dull, tedious, flat, docile, domesticated, tame, insipid, domestic.
(ANT.) spirited, exciting, savage, wild.

meet *(SYN.)* fulfill, suffer, find, collide,

gratify, engage, connect, converge, encounter, unite, join, satisfy, settle, greet, answer, undergo, answer, meeting, contest, match, assemble, discharge, gather, convene, congregate, confront, intersect.
(ANT.) scatter, disperse, separate, cleave.

melancholy *(SYN.)* disconsolate, dejected, despondent, glum, somber, pensive, moody, dispirited, depressed, gloomy, dismal, doleful, depression, downcast, gloom, sadness, sad, grave, downhearted, sorrowful.
(ANT.) happy, cheerful, merry.

meld *(SYN.)* unite, mix, combine, fuse, merge, blend, commingle, amalgamate.

melee *(SYN.)* battle royal, fight, brawl, free-for-all, fracas.

mellow *(SYN.)* mature, ripe, aged, cured, full-flavored, sweet, smooth, melodious, develop, soften.
(ANT.) unripened, immature.

melodious *(SYN.)* lilting, musical, lyric, dulcet, mellifluous, tuneful, melodic.

melodramatic *(SYN.)* dramatic, ceremonious, affected, stagy, histrionic, overwrought, sensational, stagy.
(ANT.) unemotional, subdued, modest.

melody *(SYN.)* strain, concord, music, air, song, tune, harmony.

melt *(SYN.)* dissolve, liquefy, blend, fade out, vanish, dwindle, disappear, thaw.
(ANT.) freeze, harden, solidify.

member *(SYN.)* share, part, allotment, moiety, element, concern, interest, lines, faction, role, apportionment.
(ANT.) whole.

membrane *(SYN.)* layer, sheath, tissue, covering.

memento *(SYN.)* keepsake, token, reminder, trophy, sign, souvenir, remembrance.

memoirs *(SYN.)* diary, reflections, experiences, autobiography, journal, confessions.

memorable *(SYN.)* important, historic, significant, unforgettable, noteworthy, momentous, crucial, impressive.
(ANT.) passing, forgettable, transitory, commonplace.

memorandum *(SYN.)* letter, mark, token, note, indication, remark, message.

memorial *(SYN.)* monument, souvenir, memento, remembrance, commemoration, reminiscent, ritual, testimonial.

memorize *(SYN.)* study, remember.

memory *(SYN.)* renown, remembrance, reminiscence, fame, retrospection, recollection, reputation.
(ANT.) oblivion.

menace *(SYN.)* warning, threat, intimidation, warn, threaten, imperil, forebode.

menagerie *(SYN.)* collection, zoo, kennel.

mend *(SYN.)* restore, better, refit, sew, remedy, patch, correct, repair, rectify, ameliorate, improve, reform, recover, fix.

(ANT.) hurt, deface, rend, destroy.

mendacious (SYN.) dishonest, false, lying, deceitful, deceptive, tricky.

(ANT.) honest, truthful, sincere, creditable.

mendicant (SYN.) ragamuffin, vagabond, beggar.

menial (SYN.) unskilled, lowly, degrading, tedious, humble, routine.

mental (SYN.) reasoning, intellectual, rational, thinking, conscious, reflective, thoughtful.

(ANT.) physical.

mentality (SYN.) intellect, reason, understanding, liking, disposition, judgment, brain, inclination, faculties, outlook.

(ANT.) materiality, corporeality.

mention (SYN.) introduce, refer to, reference, allude, enumerate, speak of.

mentor (SYN.) advisor, tutor, sponsor, guru, teacher, counselor, master, coach.

mercenary (SYN.) sordid, corrupt, venal, covetous, grasping, avaricious, greedy.

(ANT.) liberal, generous.

merchandise (SYN.) stock, wares, goods, sell, commodities, promote, staples, products.

merchant (SYN.) retailer, dealer, trader, storekeeper, salesman, businessman.

merciful (SYN.) humane, kindhearted, tender, clement, sympathetic, forgiving, tolerant, forbearing, lenient, compassionate, tenderhearted, kind.

(ANT.) remorseless, cruel, unjust, mean, harsh, unforgiving, vengeful, brutal, unfeeling, pitiless.

merciless (SYN.) carnal, ferocious, brute, barbarous, gross, ruthless, cruel, remorseless, bestial, savage, rough, pitiless, inhuman.

(ANT.) humane, courteous, merciful, openhearted, kind, civilized.

mercurial (SYN.) fickle, unstable, volatile, changeable, inconstant, capricious, flighty.

mercy (SYN.) grace, consideration, kindness, clemency, mildness, forgiveness, pity, charity, sympathy, leniency, compassion.

(ANT.) punishment, retribution, ruthlessness, cruelty, vengeance.

mere (SYN.) only, simple, scant, bare.

(ANT.) substantial, considerable.

merely (SYN.) only, barely, simply, hardly.

meretricious (SYN.) gaudy, sham, bogus, tawdry, flashy, garish.

merge (SYN.) unify, fuse, combine, amalgamate, unite, blend, commingle.

(ANT.) separate, decompose, analyze.

merger (SYN.) cartel, union, conglomerate, trust, incorporation, combine, pool.

meridian (SYN.) climax, summit, pinnacle, zenith, peak, acme, apex, culmination.

merit (SYN.) worthiness, earn, goodness, effectiveness, power, value, virtue, goodness, quality, deserve, excellence, worth.

(ANT.) sin, fault, lose, consume.

merited (SYN.) proper, deserved, suitable, adequate, earned.

(ANT.) unmerited, improper.

meritorious (SYN.) laudable, excellent, commendable, good, praise-worthy, deserving.

merry (SYN.) hilarious, lively, festive, joyous, sprightly, mirthful, blithe, gay, cheery, joyful, jolly, happy, gleeful, jovial, cheerful.

(ANT.) sorrowful, doleful, morose, gloomy, sad, melancholy.

mesh (SYN.) grid, screen, net, complex.

mesmerize (SYN.) enthrall, transfix, spellbind, bewitch, charm, fascinate, hypnotize.

mess (SYN.) dirtiness, untidiness, disorder, confusion, muddle, trouble, jumble, difficulty, predicament, confuse, dirty.

message (SYN.) letter, annotation, memo, symbol, indication, sign, note, communication, memorandum, observation, token.

messenger (SYN.) bearer, agent, runner, courier, liaison, delegate, page.

messy (SYN.) disorderly, dirty, confusing, confused, disordered, sloppy, untidy, slovenly.

(ANT.) orderly, neat, tidy.

metallic (SYN.) grating, harsh, clanging, brassy, brazen.

metamorphosis (SYN.) transfiguration, change, alteration, rebirth, mutation.

mete (SYN.) deal, assign, apportion, divide, give, allocate, allot, measure.

(ANT.) withhold, keep, retain.

meteoric (SYN.) flashing, blazing, swift, brilliant, spectacular, remarkable.

meter (SYN.) record, measure, gauge.

method (SYN.) order, manner, plan, way, mode, technique, fashion, approach, design, procedure.

(ANT.) disorder.

methodical (SYN.) exact, definite, ceremonious, stiff, accurate, distinct, unequivocal.

(ANT.) easy, loose, informal, rough.

meticulous (SYN.) precise, careful, exacting, fastidious, fussy, perfectionist.

metropolitan (SYN.) civic, city, municipal.

mettle (SYN.) intrepidity, resolution, boldness, prowess, bravery, fearlessness.

(ANT.) fear, timidity, cowardice.

microscopic (SYN.) tiny, precise, fine, detailed, minute, infinitesimal, minimal.

(ANT.) general, huge, enormous.

middle (SYN.) midpoint, nucleus, center, midst, median, central, intermediate, core.

(ANT.) end, rim, outskirts, beginning, border, periphery.

middleman (SYN.) dealer, agent, distributor, broker, representative, intermediary.

midget (SYN.) gnome, shrimp, pygmy, runt, dwarf.

(ANT.) giant.

midst *(SYN.)* center, heart, middle, thick.

midway *(SYN.)* halfway, midmost, inside, central, middle.

mien *(SYN.)* way, semblance, manner, behavior, demeanor, expression, deportment.

miff *(SYN.)* provoke, rile, chagrin, irk, irritate, affront, offend, annoy, exasperate.

might *(SYN.)* force, power, vigor, potency, ability, strength.
(ANT.) frailty, vulnerability, weakness.

mighty *(SYN.)* firm, fortified, powerful, athletic, potent, muscular, robust, strong, cogent.
(ANT.) feeble, weak, brittle, insipid, frail, delicate.

migrant *(SYN.)* traveling, roaming, straying, roving, rambling, transient, meandering.
(ANT.) stationary.

migrate *(SYN.)* resettle, move, emigrate, immigrate, relocate, journey.
(ANT.) stay, remain, settle.

migratory *(SYN.)* itinerant, roving, mobile, vagabond, unsettled, nomadic, wandering.

mild *(SYN.)* soothing, moderate, gentle, tender, bland, pleasant, kind, meek, calm, amiable, compassionate, temperate, peaceful, soft.
(ANT.) severe, turbulent, stormy, excitable, violent, harsh, bitter.

milieu *(SYN.)* environment, background, locale, setting, scene, circumstances.

militant *(SYN.)* warlike, belligerent, hostile, fighting, pugnacious, aggressive, combative.
(ANT.) peaceful.

military *(SYN.)* troops, army, service, soldiers.

milksop *(SYN.)* namby-pamby, weakling, sissy, coward.

mill *(SYN.)* foundry, shop, plant, factory, manufactory.

millstone *(SYN.)* load, impediment, burden, encumbrance, hindrance.

mimic *(SYN.)* simulate, duplicate, copy, imitate, mock, counterfeit, simulate.
(ANT.) invent, distort, alter.

mince *(SYN.)* shatter, fragment, chop, smash.

mind *(SYN.)* intelligence, psyche, disposition, intention, understanding, intellect, spirit, brain, inclination, mentality, soul, wit, liking, brain, sense, watch, faculties, judgment, reason.
(ANT.) matter, corporeality.

mindful *(SYN.)* alert, aware, watchful, cognizant, watchful, sensible, heedful.

mine *(SYN.)* shaft, lode, pit, excavation, drill, dig, quarry, source.

mingle *(SYN.)* unite, coalesce, fuse, merge, combine, amalgamate, unify, conjoin, mix, blend, commingle.
(ANT.) separate, analyze, sort, disintegrate.

miniature *(SYN.)* small, little, tiny, midget, minute, minuscule, wee, petite, diminutive.
(ANT.) outsize.

minimize *(SYN.)* shorten, deduct, belittle, decrease, reduce, curtail, lessen, diminish, subtract.
(ANT.) enlarge, increase, amplify.

minimum *(SYN.)* lowest, least, smallest, slightest.
(ANT.) maximum.

minister *(SYN.)* pastor, clergyman, vicar, parson, curate, preacher, prelate, chaplain, cleric, deacon, reverend.

minor *(SYN.)* poorer, lesser, petty, youth, inferior, secondary, smaller, unimportant, lower.
(ANT.) higher, superior, major, greater.

minority *(SYN.)* youth, childhood, immaturity.

minstrel *(SYN.)* bard, musician.

mint *(SYN.)* stamp, coin, strike, punch.

minus *(SYN.)* lacking, missing, less, absent, without.

minute *(SYN.)* tiny, particular, fine, precise, jiffy, instant, moment, wee, exact, detailed, microscopic.
(ANT.) large, general, huge, enormous.

miraculous *(SYN.)* spiritual, supernatural, wonderful, marvelous, incredible, preternatural.
(ANT.) commonplace, natural, common, plain, everyday, human.

mirage *(SYN.)* vision, illusion, fantasy, dream, phantom.
(ANT.) reality, actuality.

mire *(SYN.)* marsh, slush, slime, mud.

mirror *(SYN.)* glass, reflector, reflect.

mirth *(SYN.)* joy, glee, jollity, joyousness, gaiety, joyfulness, laughter, merriment.
(ANT.) sadness, gloom, seriousness.

misadventure *(SYN.)* accident, adversity, reverse, calamity, catastrophe, hardship, mischance, setback.

misappropriate *(SYN.)* embezzle, steal, purloin, plunder, cheat, filch, defraud.

misbehave *(SYN.)* trespass, act badly.
(ANT.) behave.

miscalculate *(SYN.)* miscount, blunder, confuse, err, mistake, misconstrue.

miscarriage *(SYN.)* omission, want, decay, fiasco, default, deficiency, loss, abortion, prematurity.
(ANT.) success, sufficiency, achievement.

miscarry *(SYN.)* flounder, fall short, falter, go wrong, fail.
(ANT.) succeed.

miscellaneous *(SYN.)* diverse, motley, indiscriminate, assorted, sundry, heterogeneous, mixed, varied.
(ANT.) classified, selected, homogeneous, alike, ordered.

miscellany *(SYN.)* medley, gallimaufry, jumble, potpourri, mixture, collection.

mischief *(SYN.)* injury, harm, damage, evil, ill, prankishness, rascality, roguishness, playfulness, wrong, detriment, hurt.
(ANT.) kindness, boon, benefit.

mischievous *(SYN.)* roguish, prankish, naughty, playful.
(ANT.) well-behaved, good.

misconduct *(SYN.)* transgression, delinquency, wrongdoing, negligence.

miscreant *(SYN.)* rascal, wretch, rogue, sinner, criminal, villain, scoundrel.

miscue *(SYN.)* blunder, fluff, mistake, error, lapse.

misdemeanor *(SYN.)* infringement, transgression, violation, offense, wrong.

miser *(SYN.)* cheapskate, tightwad.
(ANT.) philanthropist.

miserable *(SYN.)* abject, forlorn, comfortless, low, worthless, pitiable, distressed, heartbroken, disconsolate, despicable, wretched, uncomfortable, unhappy, poor, unlucky, paltry, contemptible, mean.
(ANT.) fortunate, happy, contented, joyful, content, wealthy, honorable, lucky, noble, significant.

miserly *(SYN.)* stingy, greedy, acquisitive, tight, tightfisted, cheap, mean, parsimonious, avaricious.
(ANT.) bountiful, generous, spendthrift, munificent, extravagant, openhanded, altruistic.

misery *(SYN.)* suffering, woe, evil, agony, torment, trouble, distress, anguish, grief, unhappiness, anguish, tribulation, calamity, sorrow.
(ANT.) fun, pleasure, delight, joy.

misfit *(SYN.)* crank, loner, deviate, fifth wheel, individualist.

misfortune *(SYN.)* adversity, distress, mishap, calamity, accident, catastrophe, hardship, ruin, disaster, affliction.
(ANT.) success, blessing, prosperity.

misgiving *(SYN.)* suspicion, doubt, mistrust, hesitation, uncertainty.

misguided *(SYN.)* misdirected, misled, misinformed, wrong, unwise, foolish, erroneous, unwarranted, ill-advised.

mishap *(SYN.)* misfortune, casualty, accident, disaster, adversity, reverse.
(ANT.) intention, calculation, purpose.

mishmash *(SYN.)* medley, muddle, gallimaufry, hodge-podge, hash.

misjudge *(SYN.)* err, mistake, miscalculate.

mislay *(SYN.)* misplace, lose.
(ANT.) discover, find.

mislead *(SYN.)* misdirect, deceive, misinform, deceive, delude.

misleading *(SYN.)* fallacious, delusive, deceitful, false, deceptive, illusive.
(ANT.) real, genuine, truthful, honest.

mismatched *(SYN.)* unfit, unsuitable, incompatible, unsuited.

misplace *(SYN.)* lose, mislay, miss.
(ANT.) find.

misrepresent *(SYN.)* misstate, distort, falsify, twist, belie, garble, disguise.

miss *(SYN.)* lose, want, crave, yearn for, fumble, drop, error, slip, default, omit, lack, need, desire, fail.
(ANT.) suffice, have, achieve, succeed.

misshapen *(SYN.)* disfigured, deformed, grotesque, malformed, ungainly, gnarled, contorted.

missile *(SYN.)* grenade, shot, projectile.

missing *(SYN.)* wanting, lacking, absent, lost, gone, vanished.

mission *(SYN.)* business, task, job, stint, work, errand, assignment, delegation.

missionary *(SYN.)* publicist, evangelist, propagandist.

mist *(SYN.)* cloud, fog, haze, steam, haze.

mistake *(SYN.)* slip, misjudge, fault, blunder, misunderstand, confuse, inaccuracy, misinterpret, error.
(ANT.) truth, accuracy.

mistaken *(SYN.)* false, amiss, incorrect, awry, wrong, misinformed, confused, inaccurate, askew.
(ANT.) true, correct, suitable, right.

mister *(SYN.)* young man, gentleman, esquire, fellow, buddy.

mistreat *(SYN.)* wrong, pervert, oppress, harm, maltreat, abuse.

mistrust *(SYN.)* suspect, doubt, distrust, dispute, question, skepticism, apprehension.
(ANT.) trust.

misunderstand *(SYN.)* misjudge, misinterpret, jumble, confuse, mistake.
(ANT.) perceive, comprehend.

misunderstanding *(SYN)* clash, disagreement, dispute, conflict, misinterpretation.

misuse *(SYN.)* defame, malign, abuse, misapply, traduce, asperse, revile, vilify.
(ANT.) protect, honor, respect, cherish.

mite *(SYN.)* particle, mote, smidgen, trifle, iota, corpuscle.

mitigate *(SYN.)* soften, soothe, abate, assuage, relieve, allay, diminish.
(ANT.) irritate, agitate, increase.

mix *(SYN.)* mingle, blend, consort, fuse, alloy, combine, jumble, fraternize, associate, concoct, commingle, amalgamate, confound, compound, join.
(ANT.) divide, sort, segregate, dissociate, separate.

mixture *(SYN.)* diversity, variety, strain, sort, change, kind, confusion, heterogeneity, jumble, mess, assortment, breed, mix, hodge-podge, subspecies.
(ANT.) likeness, sameness, homogeneity, monotony.

moan *(SYN.)* wail, groan, cry, lament.

moat *(SYN.)* fortification, ditch, trench, entrenchment.

mob *(SYN.)* crowd, host, populace, swarm, riot, bevy, horde, rabble, throng, multitude.

mobile *(SYN.)* free, movable, portable.
(ANT.) stationary, immobile, fixed.

mock *(SYN.)* taunt, jeer, deride, scoff, scorn, fleer, ridicule, tease, fake, imitation, sham, gibe, sneer, fraudulent, flout.
(ANT.) praise, applaud, real, genuine, honor, authentic, compliment.

mockery *(SYN.)* gibe, ridicule, satire, derision, sham, banter, irony, sneering, scorn, travesty, jeering.
(ANT.) admiration, praise.

mode *(SYN.)* method, fashion, procedure, design, manner, technique, way, style, practice, plan.
(ANT.) disorder, confusion.

model *(SYN.)* copy, prototype, type, example, ideal, imitation, version, facsimile, design, style, archetype, pattern, standard, mold.

(ANT.) *reproduction, imitation.*

moderate (SYN.) lower, decrease, average, fair, reasonable, abate, medium, conservative, referee, umpire, suppress, judge, lessen, assuage.
(ANT.) *intensify, enlarge, amplify.*

moderation (SYN.) sobriety, forbearance, self-control, restraint, continence, temperance.
(ANT.) *greed, excess, intoxication.*

moderator (SYN.) referee, leader, arbitrator, chairman, chairperson, master of cermonies, emcee.

modern (SYN.) modish, current, recent, novel, fresh, contemporary, new.
(ANT.) *old, antiquated, past, bygone, ancient.*

modernize (SYN.) refurnish, refurbish, improve, rebuild, renew, renovate.

modest (SYN.) unassuming, virtuous, bashful, meek, shy, humble, decent, demure, unpretentious, prudish, moderate, reserved.
(ANT.) *forward, bold, ostentatious, conceited, immodest, arrogant.*

modesty (SYN.) decency, humility, propriety, simplicity, shyness.
(ANT.) *conceit, vanity, pride.*

modicum (SYN.) particle, fragment, grain, trifle, smidgen, bit.

modification (SYN.) alternation, substitution, variety, change, alteration.
(ANT.) *uniformity, monotony.*

modify (SYN.) shift, vary, alter, change, convert, adjust, temper, moderate, curb, exchange, transform, veer.
(ANT.) *settle, establish, retain, stabilize.*

modish (SYN.) current, fashionable, chick, stylish, voguish.

modulate (SYN.) temper, align, balance, correct, regulate, adjust, modify.

module (SYN.) unit, measure, norm, dimension, component, gauge.

modus operandi (SYN.) method, technique, system, means, process, workings, procedure.

mogul (SYN.) bigwig, personage, figure, tycoon, magnate, potentate.

moiety (SYN.) part, scrap, share, allotment, piece, division, portion.

moist (SYN.) damp, humid, dank, muggy, clammy.

moisten (SYN.) wet, dampen, sponge.
(ANT.) *dry.*

moisture (SYN.) wetness, mist, dampness, condensation, evaporation, vapor, humidity.
(ANT.) *aridity, dryness.*

mold (SYN.) make, fashion, organize, produce, forge, constitute, create, combine, construct, form, pattern, format.
(ANT.) *wreck, dismantle, destroy, misshape.*

moldy (SYN.) dusty, crumbling, dank, old, deteriorating.

molest (SYN.) irk, disturb, trouble, annoy, pester, bother, vex, inconvenience.
(ANT.) *console, accommodate.*

mollify (SYN.) soothe, compose, quiet,

humor, appease, tranquilize, pacify.

molt (SYN.) slough off, shed, cast off.

molten (SYN.) fusible, melted, smelted, redhot.

moment (SYN.) flash, jiffy, instant, twinkling, gravity, importance, consequence, seriousness.

momentary (SYN.) concise, pithy, brief, curt, terse, laconic, compendious.
(ANT.) *long, extended, prolonged.*

momentous (SYN.) critical, serious, essential, grave, material, weighty, consequential, decisive, important.
(ANT.) *unimportant, trifling, mean, trivial, tribial, insignificant.*

momentum (SYN.) impetus, push, thrust, force, impulse, drive, vigor, propulsion, energy.

monarch (SYN.) ruler, king, queen, empress, emperor, sovereign.

monastic (SYN.) withdrawn, dedicated, austere, unworldly, celibate, abstinent, ascetic.

monastery (SYN.) convent, priory, abbey, hermitage, cloister.

money (SYN.) cash, bills, coin, notes, currency, funds, specie, capital.

monger (SYN.) seller, hawker, huckster, trader, merchant, shopkeeper, retailer, vendor.

mongrel (SYN.) mixed-breed, hybrid, mutt.

monitor (SYN.) director, supervisor, advisor, observe, watch, control.

monkey (SYN.) tamper, interfere, interrupt, interpose.

monogram (SYN.) mark, stamp, signature

monograph (SYN.) publication, report, thesis, biography, treatise, paper, dissertation.

monologue (SYN.) discourse, lecture, sermon, talk, speech, address, soliloquy, oration.

monomania (SYN.) obsessiveness, passion, single-mindedness, extremism.

monopoly (SYN.) corner, control, possession.

monotonous (SYN.) dull, slow, tiresome, boring, humdrum, dilatory, tiring, irksome, tedious, burdensome, wearisome.
(ANT.) *interesting, riveting, quick, fascinating, exciting, amusing.*

monsoon (SYN.) storm, rains.

monster (SYN.) brute, beast, villain, demon, fiend, wretch.

monstrous (SYN.) tremendous, huge, gigantic, immense, enormous, revolting, repulsive, shocking, horrible, hideous, terrible.
(ANT.) *diminutive, tiny, miniature, small.*

monument (SYN.) remembrance, memento, commemoration, souvenir, statue, shrine.

monumental (SYN.) enormous, huge, colossal, immense, gigantic, important, significant.
(ANT.) *trivial, insignificant, tiny, miniature.*

mood (SYN.) joke, irony, waggery, temper, disposition, temperament, sar-

casm.
(ANT.) sorrow, gravity.
moody *(SYN.)* morose, fretful, crabbed, changeable, sulky, dour, short-tempered, testy, temperamental, irritable, peevish, glum.
(ANT.) good-natured, even-tempered, merry, gay, pleasant, joyous.
moor *(SYN.)* tether, fasten, tie, dock, anchor, bind.
moorings *(SYN.)* marina, slip, harbor, basin, landing, dock, wharf, pier, anchorage.
moot *(SYN.)* unsettled, questionable, problematical, controversial, contestable.
mop *(SYN.)* wash, wipe, swab, scrub.
mope *(SYN.)* gloom, pout, whine, grumble, grieve, sulk, fret.
(ANT.) rejoice.
moral *(SYN.)* just, right, chaste, good, virtuous, pure, decent, honest, upright, ethical, righteous, honorable, scrupulous.
(ANT.) libertine, immoral, unethical, licentious, amoral, sinful.
morale *(SYN.)* confidence, spirit, assurance.
morality *(SYN.)* virtue, strength, worth, chastity, probity, force, merit.
(ANT.) fault, sin, corruption, vice.
morals *(SYN.)* conduct, scruples, guidelines, behavior, life style, standards.
morass *(SYN.)* fen, march, swamp, mire.
morbid *(SYN.)* sickly, unwholesome, unhealthy, ghastly, awful, horrible, shocking.
(ANT.) pleasant, healthy.
more *(SYN.)* further, greater, farther, extra, another.
(ANT.) less.
moreover *(SYN.)* further, in addition, also, furthermore, besides.
mores *(SYN.)* standards, rituals, rules, customs, conventions, traditions.
moron *(SYN.)* subnormal, dunce, blockhead, imbecile, retardate, simpleton.
morose *(SYN.)* gloomy, moody, fretful, crabbed, sulky, glum, dour, surly, downcast, sad, unhappy.
(ANT.) merry, gay, amiable, joyous, pleasant.
morsel *(SYN.)* portion, fragment, bite, bit, scrap, amount, piece, taste, tidbit.
(ANT.) whole, all, sum.
mortal *(SYN.)* fatal, destructive, human, perishable, deadly, temporary, momentary, final.
(ANT.) superficial, divine, immortal.
mortgage *(SYN.)* stake, post, promise, pledge.
mortician *(SYN.)* funeral director, embalmer.
mortified *(SYN.)* embarrassed, humiliated, abashed, ashamed.
mortify *(SYN.)* humiliate, crush, subdue, abase, degrade, shame.
(ANT.) praise, exalt, elevate.
mortuary *(SYN.)* morgue, crematory, funeral parlor.
most *(SYN.)* extreme, highest, supreme, greatest, majority.

(ANT.) least.
mostly *(SYN.)* chiefly, generally, largely, mainly, principally, especially.
mother *(SYN.)* bring about, produce, breed, mom, mama, watch, foster, mind, nurse, originate, nurture.
(ANT.) father.
motion *(SYN.)* change, activity, movement, proposition, action, signal, gesture, move, proposal.
(ANT.) stability, immobility, stillness.
motionless *(SYN.)* still, undisturbed, rigid, fixed, stationary, unresponsive.
motivate *(SYN.)* move, prompt, stimulate, induce, activate, propel, arouse.
motive *(SYN.)* inducement, purpose, cause, incentive, reason, incitement.
(ANT.) deed, result, attempt, effort.
motor *(SYN.)* engine, generator, machine.
motto *(SYN.)* proverb, saying, adage, byword, saw, slogan, catchword, aphorism.
mound *(SYN.)* hillock, hill, heap, pile, stack, knoll, accumulation, dune.
mount *(SYN.)* scale, climb, increase, rise, prepare, ready, steed, horse, tower.
(ANT.) sink, descend.
mountain *(SYN.)* alp, mount, pike, peak, ridge, height, range.
mounting *(SYN.)* backing, pedestal, easel, support, framework.
mourn *(SYN.)* suffer, grieve, bemoan, sorrow, lament, weep, bewail.
(ANT.) revel, celebrate, carouse.
mournful *(SYN.)* sorrowful, sad, melancholy, gloomy, woeful, rueful, disconsolate.
(ANT.) joyful, cheerful, happy.
mourning *(SYN.)* misery, trial, distress, affliction, tribulation, sorrow, woe.
(ANT.) happiness, solace, comfort, joy.
move *(SYN.)* impel, agitate, persuade, induce, push, instigate, advance, stir.
(ANT.) halt, stop, deter, rest.
movement *(SYN.)* activity, effort, gesture, move, proposition, crusade.
(ANT.) stillness, immobility.
moving *(SYN.)* poignant, stirring, touching.
mow *(SYN.)* prune, cut, shave, crop, clip.
much *(SYN.)* abundance, quantity, mass, ample, plenty, sufficient, substantial.
muck *(SYN.)* filth, mire, dirt, rot, sludge, sewage.
muddle *(SYN.)* disorder, chaos, mess.
muddled *(SYN.)* disconcerted, confused, mixed, bewildered, perplexed.
(ANT.) plain, lucid, organized.
muff *(SYN.)* blunder, bungle, spoil, mess, fumble.
muffle *(SYN.)* soften, deaden, mute, quiet, drape, shroud, veil, cover.
(ANT.) louden, amplify.
multiply *(SYN.)* double, treble, increase, triple, propagate, spread, expand.
(ANT.) lessen, decrease.
multitude *(SYN.)* crowd, throng, mass, swarm, host, mob, army, legion.
(ANT.) scarcity, handful.

mum *(SYN.)* mute, silent, quiet, still, close-mouthed, secretive.

mumble *(SYN.)* stammer, whisper, hesitate, mutter.
(ANT.) shout, yell.

municipal *(SYN.)* urban, metropolitan.

munificent *(SYN.)* bountiful, full, generous, forthcoming, satisfied.
(ANT.) voracious, insatiable, grasping, ravenous, devouring.

murder *(SYN.)* homicide, kill, slay, slaughter, butcher, killing, massacre, assassinate, execute.
(ANT.) save, protect, vivify, animate.

murderer *(SYN.)* slayer, killer, assassin.

murky *(SYN.)* gloomy, dark, obscure, unclear, impenetrable.
(ANT.) cheerful, light.

murmur *(SYN.)* mumble, whine, grumble, whimper, lament, mutter, complaint, remonstrate, complain, repine.
(ANT.) praise, applaud, rejoice.

muscle *(SYN.)* brawn, strength, power, fitness, vigor, vim, stamina, robustness.

museum *(SYN.)* exhibit hall, treasure house, gallery, repository.

mushroom *(SYN.)* multiply, proliferate, flourish, spread, grow, pullulate.

music *(SYN.)* symphony, harmony, consonance.

musical *(SYN.)* tuneful, melodious, dulcet, lyrical, harmonious.

must *(SYN.)* ought to, should, duty, obligation, ultimatum.

musty *(SYN.)* mildewed, rancid, airless, dank, stale, decayed, rotten, funky.

mute *(SYN.)* quiet, noiseless, dumb, taciturn, hushed, peaceful, speechless, uncommunicative, silent.
(ANT.) raucous, clamorous, noisy.

mutilate *(SYN.)* tear, cut, clip, amputate, lacerate, dismember, deform, castrate.

mutinous *(SYN.)* revolutionary, rebellious, unruly, insurgent, turbulent, riotous.
(ANT.) dutiful, obedient, complaint.

mutiny *(SYN.)* revolt, overthrow, rebellion, rebel, coup, uprising.

mutter *(SYN.)* complain, mumble, whisper, grumble, murmur.

mutual *(SYN.)* correlative, interchangeable, shared, alternate, joint, common.
(ANT.) unshared, unrequited, separate.

muzzle *(SYN.)* restrain, silence, bridle, bind, curb, suppress, gag, stifle.

myriad *(SYN.)* considerable, many.

mysterious *(SYN.)* hidden, mystical, secret, cryptic, incomprehensible.
(ANT.) simple, obvious, clear, plain.

mystery *(SYN.)* riddle, difficulty, enigma, puzzle, strangeness, conundrum.
(ANT.) solution, key, answer, resolution.

mystical *(SYN.)* secret, cryptic, hidden, dim, obscure, dark, cabalistic.
(ANT.) simple, explained, plain, clear.

mystify *(SYN.)* puzzle, confound, bewilder, stick, get, floor, bamboozle.

myth *(SYN.)* fable, parable, allegory, fiction, tradition, lie, saga, legend.
(ANT.) history.

nag *(SYN.)* badger, harry, provoke, tease, bother, annoy, molest, taunt, vex, torment, worry, annoy, pester, irritate, pick on, horse, torment.
(ANT.) please, comfort, soothe.

nail *(SYN.)* hold, fasten, secure, fix, seize, catch, snare, hook, capture.
(ANT.) release.

naive *(SYN.)* frank, unsophisticated, natural, artless, ingenuous, simple, candid, open, innocent.
(ANT.) worldly, cunning, crafty.

naked *(SYN.)* uncovered, unfurnished, nude, bare, open, unclad, stripped, exposed, plain, mere, simple, barren, unprotected, bald, defenseless, unclothed, undressed.
(ANT.) covered, protected, dressed, clothed, concealed, suppressed.

name *(SYN.)* title, reputation, appellation, style, fame, repute, renown, denomination, appoint, character, designation, surname, distinction, christen, denominate, mention, specify, epithet, entitle, call, label.
(ANT.) anonymity, misnomer, hint, misname.

nap *(SYN.)* nod, doze, sleep, snooze, catnap, siesta, slumber, drowse, forty winks.

narcissistic *(SYN.)* egotistical, egocentric, self-centered, egotistic.

narcotics *(SYN.)* opiates, drugs, sedatives, tranquilizers, barbiturates.

narrate *(SYN.)* recite, relate, declaim, detail, rehearse, deliver, review, tell, describe, recount.

narrative *(SYN.)* history, relation, account, record, chronicle, detail, recital, description, story, tale.
(ANT.) distortion, caricature, misrepresentation.

narrow *(SYN.)* narrow-minded, illiberal, bigoted, fanatical, prejudiced, close, restricted, slender, cramped, confined, meager, thin, tapering, tight.
(ANT.) progressive, liberal, wide.

narrow-minded *(SYN.)* close-minded, intolerant, partisan, arbitrary, bigoted.
(ANT.) tolerant, liberal, broad-minded.

nascent *(SYN.)* prime, introductory, emerging, elementary.

nasty *(SYN.)* offensive, malicious, selfish, mean, disagreeable, unpleasant, foul, dirty, filthy, loathsome, disgusting, polluted, obscene, indecent, sickening, nauseating, obnoxious, revolting, odious.
(ANT.) generous, dignified, noble, admirable, pleasant.

nation *(SYN.)* state, community, realm, nationality, commonwealth, kingdom, country, republic, land, society, tribe.

native *(SYN.)* domestic, inborn, inherent, natural, aboriginal, endemic, innate, inbred, indigenous, hereditary, original, local.
(ANT.) alien, stranger, foreigner, outsider, foreign.

natty *(SYN.)* chic, well-dressed, sharp, dapper.

natural *(SYN.)* innate, genuine, real,

unaffected, characteristic, native, normal, regular, inherent, original, simple, inbred, inborn, hereditary, typical, authentic, honest, legitimate, pure, customary.
(ANT.) irregular, false, unnatural, formal, abnormal.

naturally *(SYN.)* typically, ordinarily, usually, indeed, normally, plainly, of course, surely, certainly.
(ANT.) artificially.

nature *(SYN.)* kind, disposition, reputation, character, repute, world, quality, universe, essence, variety, features, traits.

naught *(SYN.)* nought, zero, nothing.

naughty *(SYN.)* unmanageable, insubordinate, disobedient, mischievous, unruly, bad, misbehaving, disorderly, wrong, evil, rude, improper, indecent.
(ANT.) obedient, good, well-behaved.

nausea *(SYN.)* sickness, vomiting, upset, queasiness, seasickness.

nauseated *(SYN.)* unwell, sick, queasy, squeamish.

nautical *(SYN.)* naval, oceanic, marine, ocean.

naval *(SYN.)* oceanic, marine, nautical, maritime.

navigate *(SYN.)* sail, cruise, pilot, guide, steer.

near *(SYN.)* close, nigh, dear, adjacent, familiar, at hand, neighboring, approaching, impending, proximate, imminent, bordering.
(ANT.) removed, distant, far, remote.

nearly *(SYN.)* practically, close to, approximately, almost.

neat *(SYN.)* trim, orderly, precise, clear, spruce, nice, tidy, clean, well-kept, clever, skillful, adept, apt, tidy, dapper, smart, proficient, expert, handy, well-done, shipshape, elegant, well-organized.
(ANT.) unkempt, sloppy, dirty, slovenly, messy, sloppy, disorganized.

nebulous *(SYN.)* fuzzy, indistinct, indefinite, clouded, hazy.
(ANT.) definite, distinct, clear.

necessary *(SYN.)* needed, expedient, unavoidable, required, essential, indispensable, urgent, imperative, inevitable, compelling, compulsory, obligatory, needed, exigent.
(ANT.) optional, nonessential, contingent, casual, accidental, unnecessary, dispensable, unneeded.

necessity *(SYN.)* requirement, fate, destiny, constraint, requisite, poverty, exigency, compulsion, want, essential, prerequisite.
(ANT.) option, luxury, freedom, choice, uncertainty.

necromancy *(SYN.)* witchcraft, charm, sorcery, conjuring, wizardry.

need *(SYN.)* crave, want, demand, claim, desire, covet, wish, lack, necessity, requirement, poverty, require, pennilessness.

needed *(SYN.)* necessary, indispensable, essential, requisite.
(ANT.) optional, contingent.

needle *(SYN.)* goad, badger, tease, nag, prod, provoke.

needless *(SYN.)* nonessential, unnecessary, superfluous, useless, purposeless.

needy *(SYN.)* poor, indigent, impoverished penniless, destitute.
(ANT.) affluent, well-off, wealthy, well-to-do.

nefarious *(SYN.)* detestable, vicious, wicked, atrocious, horrible, vile.

negate *(SYN.)* revoke, void, cancel, nullify.

neglect *(SYN.)* omission, default, heedlessness, carelessness, thoughtlessness, disregard, negligence, oversight, omission, ignore, slight, failure, overlook, omit, skip, pass over, be inattentive, miss.
(ANT.) diligence, do, protect, watchfulness, care, attention, careful, attend, regard, concern.

negligent *(SYN.)* imprudent, thoughtless, lax, careless, inattentive, indifferent, remiss, neglectful.
(ANT.) careful, nice, accurate, meticulous.

negligible *(SYN.)* trifling, insignificant, trivial, inconsiderable.
(ANT.) major, vital, important.

negotiate *(SYN.)* intervene, talk over, mediate, transact, umpire, referee, arbitrate, arrange, settle, bargain.

neighborhood *(SYN.)* environs, nearness, locality, district, vicinity, area, section, locality.
(ANT.) remoteness.

neighboring *(SYN.)* bordering, near, adjacent, next to, surrounding, adjoining.

neighborly *(SYN.)* friendly, sociable, amiable, affable, companionable, congenial, kind, cordial, amicable.
(ANT.) distant, reserved, cool, unfriendly, hostile.

neophyte *(SYN.)* greenhorn, rookie, amateur, beginner, apprentice, tyro, student.

nepotism *(SYN.)* bias, prejudice, patronage, favoritism.

nerve *(SYN.)* bravery, spirit, courage, boldness, rudeness, strength, stamina, bravado, daring, impudence, mettle, impertinence.
(ANT.) frailty, cowardice, weakness.

nervous *(SYN.)* agitated, restless, excited, shy, timid, upset, disturbed, shaken, rattle, high-strung, flustered, tense, jittery, strained, edgy, perturbed, fearful.
(ANT.) placid, courageous, confident, calm, tranquil, composed, bold.

nest *(SYN.)* den, refuge, hideaway.

nestle *(SYN.)* cuddle, snuggle.

net *(SYN.)* snare, trap, mesh, earn, gain, web, get, acquire, secure, obtain.

nettle *(SYN.)* irritate, vex, provoke, annoy, disturb, irk, needle, pester.

neurotic *(SYN.)* disturbed, psychoneurotic.

neutral *(SYN.)* nonpartisan, uninvolved, detached, impartial, cool, unprejudiced, indifferent, inactive.
(ANT.) involved, biased, partisan.

neutralize *(SYN.)* offset, counteract, nullify, negate.

nevertheless *(SYN.)* notwithstanding, however, although, anyway, but, regardless.

new *(SYN.)* modern, original, newfangled, late, recent, novel, young, firsthand, fresh, unique, unusual.
(ANT.) antiquated, old, ancient, obsolete, outmoded.

newborn *(SYN.)* baby, infant, cub, suckling.

news *(SYN.)* report, intelligence, information, copy, message, advice, tidings, knowledge, word, story, data.

next *(SYN.)* nearest, following, closest, successive, succeeding, subsequent.

nibble *(SYN.)* munch, chew, bit.

nice *(SYN.)* pleasing, pleasant, agreeable, thoughtful, satisfactory, friendly, enjoyable, gratifying, desirable, fine, good, cordial.
(ANT.) nasty, unpleasant, disagreeable, unkind, inexact, careless, thoughtless.

niche *(SYN.)* corner, nook, alcove, cranny, recess.

nick *(SYN.)* cut, notch, indentation, dash, score, mark.

nickname *(SYN.)* byname, sobriquet.

nigh *(SYN.)* close, imminent, near, adjacent, approaching, bordering, neighboring, impending.
(ANT.) removed, distant.

nightmare *(SYN.)* calamity, horror, torment, bad dream.

nil *(SYN.)* zero, none, nought, nothing.

nimble *(SYN.)* brisk, quick, active, supple, alert, lively, spry, light, fast, speedy, swift, agile.
(ANT.) slow, heavy, sluggish, clumsy.

nincompoop *(SYN.)* nitwit, idiot, fool, moron, blockhead, ninny, idiot, simpleton.

nip *(SYN.)* bite, pinch, chill, cold, squeeze, crispness, sip, small.

nippy *(SYN.)* chilly, sharp, bitter, cold, penetrating.

nit-picker *(SYN.)* fussbudget, precise, purist, perfectionist.

nitty-gritty *(SYN.)* essentials, substance, essence.

noble *(SYN.)* illustrious, exalted, dignified, stately, eminent, lofty, grand, elevated, honorable, honest, virtuous, great, distinguished, majestic, important, prominent, magnificent, grandiose, aristocratic, upright, well-born.
(ANT.) vile, low, base, mean, dishonest, common, ignoble.

nocturnal *(SYN.)* nightly.

nod *(SYN.)* bob, bow, bend, tip, signal.

node *(SYN.)* protuberance, growth, nodule, cyst, lump, wen.

noise *(SYN.)* cry, sound, din, babel, racket, uproar, clamor, outcry, tumult, outcry, sounds, hubbub, bedlam, commotion, rumpus, clatter.
(ANT.) quiet, stillness, hush, silence, peace.

noisome *(SYN.)* repulsive, disgusting, revolting, obnoxious, malodorous, rotten, rancid.

noisy *(SYN.)* resounding, loud, clamorous; vociferous, stentorian, tumul-

tuous.
(ANT.) soft, dulcet, subdued, quiet, silent, peaceful.

nomad *(SYN.)* gypsy, rover, traveler, roamer, migrant, vagrant, wanderer.

nominate *(SYN.)* propose, choose, select.

nomination *(SYN.)* appointment, naming, choice, selection, designation.

nominee *(SYN.)* aspirant, contestant, candidate, competitor.

nonbeliever *(SYN.)* skeptic, infidel, atheist, heathen.

nonchalant *(SYN.)* unconcerned, indifferent, cool, casual, easygoing.

noncommittal *(SYN.)* neutral, tepid, undecided, cautious, guarded, uncommunicative.

nonconformist *(SYN.)* protester, rebel, radical, dissenter, renegade, dissident, eccentric.

nondescript *(SYN.)* unclassifiable, indescribable, indefinite.

nonentity *(SYN.)* nothing, menial, nullity.

nonessential *(SYN.)* needless, unnecessary.

nonpareil *(SYN.)* unsurpassed, exceptional, paramount, unrivaled.

nonplus *(SYN.)* confuse, perplex, dumfound, mystify, confound, puzzle, baffle, bewilder.
(ANT.) illumine, clarify, solve, explain.

nonsense *(SYN.)* balderdash, rubbish, foolishness, folly, ridiculousness, stupidity, absurdity, poppycock, trash.

nonsensical *(SYN.)* silly, preposterous, absurd, unreasonable, foolish, irrational, ridiculous, stupid, senseless.
(ANT.) sound, consistent, reasonable.

nonstop *(SYN.)* constant, continuous, unceasing, endless.

nook *(SYN.)* niche, corner, recess, cranny, alcove.

noose *(SYN.)* snare, rope, lasso, loop.

normal *(SYN.)* ordinary, uniform, natural, unvaried, customary, regular, healthy, sound, whole, usual, typical, characteristic, routine, standard.
(ANT.) rare, erratic, unusual, abnormal.

normally *(SYN.)* regularly, frequently, usually, customarily.

nosy *(SYN.)* inquisitive, meddling, peering, searching, prying, snooping.
(ANT.) unconcerned, incurious, uninterested.

notable *(SYN.)* noted, unusual, uncommon, noteworthy, remarkable, conspicuous, distinguished, distinctive, celebrity, starts, important, striking, special, memorable, extraordinary, rare, exceptional, personality.
(ANT.) commonplace, ordinary, usual.

notch *(SYN.)* cut, nick, indentation, gash.

note *(SYN.)* sign, annotation, letter, indication, observation, mark, symbol, comment, remark, token, message, memorandum, record, memo, write, list, inscribe, notice.

noted *(SYN.)* renowned, glorious, celebrated, famous, illustrious, wellknown, distinguished, famed, notable.

(ANT.) unknown, hidden, infamous, ignominious.

noteworthy *(SYN.)* consequential, celebrated, exceptional, prominent.

notice *(SYN.)* heed, perceive, hold, mark, behold, descry, recognize, observe, attend to, remark, note, regard. *(ANT.)* overlook, disregard, skip.

notify *(SYN.)* apprise, acquaint, instruct, tell, advise, warn, teach, inform. *(ANT.)* mislead, delude, conceal.

notion *(SYN.)* image, conception, sentiment, abstraction, thought, idea. *(ANT.)* thing, matter, substance, entity.

notorious *(SYN.)* celebrated, renowned, famous, well-known, popular.

nourish *(SYN.)* strengthen, nurse, feed, supply, nurture, sustain, support.

nourishment *(SYN.)* nutriment, food, sustenance, support. *(ANT.)* starvation, deprivation.

novel *(SYN.)* fiction, narrative, allegory, tale, fable, story, romance, invention, different, unusual, strange, original, new, unique, fresh, firsthand, odd. *(ANT.)* verity, history, truth, fact.

novice *(SYN.)* beginner, amateur, newcomer, greenhorn, learner, apprentice. *(ANT.)* expert, professional, adept.

now *(SYN.)* today, at once, right away, immediately, at this time, present. *(ANT.)* later.

noxious *(SYN.)* poisonous, harmful, damaging, toxic, detrimental. *(ANT.)* harmless.

nucleus *(SYN.)* core, middle, heart, focus, hub, kernel.

nude *(SYN.)* naked, unclad, plain, open, defenseless, mere, bare, exposed. *(ANT.)* dressed, concealed, protected, clothed, covered.

nudge *(SYN.)* prod, push, jab, shove, poke, prompt.

nugget *(SYN.)* clump, mass, lump, wad, chunk, hunk.

nuisance *(SYN.)* annoyance, bother, irritation, pest.

nullify *(SYN.)* abolish, cross out, delete, invalidate, obliterate, cancel, expunge. *(ANT.)* perpetuate, confirm, enforce.

numb *(SYN.)* unfeeling, dull, insensitive, deadened, anesthetized, stupefied.

number *(SYN.)* quantity, sum, amount, volume, aggregate, total, collection. *(ANT.)* zero, nothing, nothingness.

numeral *(SYN.)* figure, symbol, digit.

numerous *(SYN.)* many, several, manifold, various, multitudinous, diverse. *(ANT.)* scanty, meager, few, scarce.

nuptials *(SYN.)* marriage, wedding, espousal, wedlock, matrimony. *(ANT.)* virginity, divorce, celibacy.

nurse *(SYN.)* tend, care for, nourish, nurture, feed, foster, train, mind, attend.

nurture *(SYN.)* hold dear, foster, sustain, appreciate, prize, bring up, rear. *(ANT.)* dislike, disregard, abandon.

nutriment *(SYN.)* food, diet, sustenance, repast, meal, fare, edibles. *(ANT.)* hunger, want, starvation.

nutrition *(SYN.)* nourishment, sustenance, food, nutriment.

oaf *(SYN.)* boor, clod, clown, lummox, fool, lout, dunce, bogtrotter.

oasis *(SYN.)* shelter, haven, retreat, refuge.

oath *(SYN.)* promise, pledge, vow, profanity, curse, agreement, commitment.

obdurate *(SYN.)* insensible, callous, hard, tough, unfeeling, insensitive. *(ANT.)* soft, compassionate, tender.

obedience *(SYN.)* docility, submission, subservience, compliance. *(ANT.)* rebelliousness, disobedience.

obedient *(SYN.)* dutiful, yielding, tractable, compliant, submissive. *(ANT.)* rebellious, intractable, insubordinate, obstinate.

obese *(SYN.)* portly, fat, pudgy, chubby, plump, rotund, stout, thickset. *(ANT.)* slim, gaunt, lean, thin, slender.

obey *(SYN.)* submit, yield, mind, comply, listen to, serve, conform. *(ANT.)* resist, disobey.

object *(SYN.)* thing, aim, intention, design, end, objective, particular, mark. *(ANT.)* assent, agree, concur, approve.

objection *(SYN.)* disagreement, protest, rejection, dissent, challenge. *(ANT.)* acceptance, compliance.

objectionable *(SYN.)* improper, offensive, unbecoming, deplorable.

objective *(SYN.)* aspiration, goal, passion, desire, aim, hope, purpose, drift. *(ANT.)* biased, subjective.

objectivity *(SYN.)* disinterest, neutrality, impartiality.

obligate *(SYN.)* oblige, require, pledge, bind, force, compel.

obligation *(SYN.)* duty, bond, engagement, compulsion, account, contract. *(ANT.)* freedom, choice, exemption.

oblige *(SYN.)* constrain, force, impel, enforce, coerce, drive, gratify. *(ANT.)* persuade, convince, allure, free, induce, disoblige, prevent.

obliging *(SYN.)* considerate, helpful, thoughtful, well-meaning, accommodating. *(ANT.)* discourteous.

obliterate *(SYN.)* terminate, destroy, eradicate, raze, extinguish. *(ANT.)* make, save, construct, establish.

oblivious *(SYN.)* sightless, unmindful, headlong, rash, blind, senseless. *(ANT.)* sensible, aware, calculated.

oblong *SYN.)* rectangular, elliptical, elongated.

obnoxious *(SYN.)* hateful, offensive, nasty, disagreeable, repulsive.

obscene *(SYN.)* indecent, filthy, impure, dirty, gross, lewd, pornographic, coarse, disgusting, bawdy, offensive, smutty. *(ANT.)* modest, pure, decent, refined.

obscure *(SYN.)* cloudy, enigmatic, mysterious, abstruse, cryptic, dim, indistinct, dusky, ambiguous, dark, indistinct, unintelligible, unclear, shadowy, fuzzy, blurred, vague. *(ANT.)* clear, famous, distinguished, noted, illumined, lucid, bright, distinct.

obsequious *(SYN.)* fawning, flattering, ingratiating.

observance *(SYN.)* protocol, ritual,

ceremony, rite, parade, pomp, solemnity, formality.
(ANT.) omission.
observant *(SYN.)* aware, alert, careful, mindful, watchful, heedful, considerate, attentive, anxious, circumspect, cautious, wary.
(ANT.) unaware, indifferent, oblivious.
observation *(SYN.)* attention, watching, comment, opinion, remark, notice, examination.
observe *(SYN.)* note, behold, discover, notice, perceive, eye, detect, inspect, keep, commemorate, mention, utter, watch, examine, mark, view, express, see, celebrate.
(ANT.) neglect, overlook, disregard, ignore.
observer *(SYN.)* examiner, overseer, lookout, spectator, bystander, witness, watcher.
obsession *(SYN.)* preoccupation, mania, compulsion, passion, fetish, infatuation.
obsolete *(SYN.)* old, out-of-date, ancient, archaic, extinct, old-fashioned, discontinued, obsolescent, venerable, dated, antiquated.
(ANT.) modern, stylish, current, recent, fashionable, extant.
obstacle *(SYN.)* block, hindrance, barrier, impediment, snag, check, deterrent, stoppage, hitch, bar, difficulty, obstruction.
(ANT.) help, aid, assistance, encouragement.
obstinate *(SYN.)* firm, headstrong, immovable, stubborn, determined, dogged, intractable, uncompromising, inflexible, willful, bullheaded, contumacious, obdurate, unbending, unyielding, pertinacious.
(ANT.) yielding, docile, amenable, submissive, pliable, flexible, compliant.
obstruct *(SYN.)* clog, barricade, impede, block, delay, hinder, stop, close, bar.
(ANT.) promote, clear, aid, help, open, further.
obstruction *(SYN.)* block, obstacle, barrier, blockage, interference.
obtain *(SYN.)* get, acquire, secure, win, procure, attain, earn, gain, receive, assimilate.
(ANT.) surrender, forfeit, lose, forego, miss.
obtrusive *(SYN.)* blatant, garish, conspicuous.
obtuse *(SYN.)* blunt, dull, slow-witted, unsharpened, stupid, dense, slow.
(ANT.) clear, interesting, lively, bright, animated, sharp.
obviate *(SYN.)* prevent, obstruct, forestall, preclude, intercept, avert, evade.
obvious *(SYN.)* plain, clear, evident, palpable, patent, self-evident, apparent, distinct, understandable, manifest, unmistakable.
(ANT.) concealed, hidden, abstruse, obscure.
obviously *(SYN.)* plainly, clearly, surely, evidently, certainly.
occasion *(SYN.)* occurrence, time, happening, excuse, opportunity, chance.

occasional *(SYN.)* random, irregular, sporadic, infrequent, periodically, spasmodic.
(ANT.) chronic, regular, constant.
occasionally *(SYN.)* seldom, now and then, infrequently, sometimes, irregularly.
(ANT.) regularly, often.
occlude *(SYN.)* clog, obstruct, choke, throttle.
occupant *(SYN.)* tenant, lodger, boarder, dweller, resident, inhabitant.
occupation *(SYN.)* employment, business, enterprise, job, trade, vocation, work, profession, matter, interest, concern, affair, activity, commerce, trading, engagement.
(ANT.) hobby, pastime, avocation.
occupy *(SYN.)* dwell, have, inhabit, absorb, hold, possess, fill, busy, keep.
(ANT.) relinquish, abandon, release.
occur *(SYN.)* take place, bechance, come about, befall, chance, transpire, betide, happen.
occurrence *(SYN.)* episode, event, issue, end, result, consequence, happening, circumstance, outcome.
ocean *(SYN.)* deep, sea, main, briny.
odd *(SYN.)* strange, bizarre, eccentric, unusual, single, uneven, unique, queer, quaint, peculiar, curious, unmatched, remaining, singular.
(ANT.) matched, common, typical, normal, familiar, even, usual, regular.
odious *(SYN.)* obscene, depraved, vulgar, despicable, mean, wicked, sordid, foul, base, loathsome, depraved, vicious, displeasing, hateful, revolting, offensive, repulsive, horrible, obnoxious, vile.
(ANT.) decent, upright, laudable, attractive, honorable.
odor *(SYN.)* fume, aroma, fragrance, redolence, smell, stink, scent, essence, stench.
odorous *(SYN.)* scented, aromatic, fragrant.
odyssey *(SYN.)* crusade, quest, journey, voyage.
offbeat *(SYN.)* uncommon, eccentric, strange, unconventional, peculiar.
off-color *(SYN.)* rude, improper, earthy, suggestive, salty.
offend *(SYN.)* annoy, anger, vex, irritate, displease, provoke, hurt, grieve, pain, disgust, wound, horrify, stricken, insult, outrage.
(ANT.) flatter, please, delight.
offender *(SYN.)* criminal, culprit, lawbreaker, miscreant.
offense *(SYN.)* indignity, injustice, transgression, affront, outrage, misdeed, sin, insult, atrocity, aggression, crime.
(ANT.) morality, gentleness, innocence, right.
offensive *(SYN.)* attacking, aggressive, unpleasant, revolting, disagreeable, nauseous, disgusting.
(ANT.) pleasing, defending, defensive, pleasant, attractive, agreeable.
offer *(SYN.)* suggestion, overture, proposal, present, suggest, propose, try, submit, attempt, tender.

(ANT.) withdrawal, denial, rejection.
offhand *(SYN.)* informal, unprepared, casual, impromptu, spontaneous.
(ANT.) considered, planned, calculated.
office *(SYN.)* position, job, situation, studio, berth, incumbency, capacity, headquarters, duty, task, function, work, post.
officiate *(SYN.)* regulate, administer, superintend, oversee, emcee.
offset *(SYN.)* compensate, counterbalance, cushion, counteract, neutralize, soften, balance.
offshoot *(SYN.)* outgrowth, addition, by-product, supplement, appendage, accessory, branch.
offspring *(SYN.)* issue, children, progeny, descendants.
often *(SYN.)* frequently, repeatedly, commonly, generally, many times, recurrently.
(ANT.) seldom, infrequently, rarely, occasionally, sporadically.
ogle *(SYN.)* gaze, stare, eye, leer.
ogre *(SYN.)* fiend, monster, devil, demon.
ointment *(SYN.)* lotion, pomade, balm, emollient.
old *(SYN.)* antique, senile, ancient, archaic, old-fashioned, superannuated, obsolete, venerable, antiquated, elderly, discontinued, abandoned, aged.
(ANT.) new, youthful, recent, modern, young.
old-fashioned *(SYN.)* outmoded, old, dated, ancient.
(ANT.) modern, fashionable, current, new.
olio *(SYN.)* potpourri, variety, mixture, jumble.
omen *(SYN.)* sign, gesture, indication, proof, portent, symbol, token, emblem, signal.
ominous *(SYN.)* unfavorable, threatening, sinister, menacing.
omission *(SYN.)* failure, neglect, oversight, default.
(ANT.) inclusion, notice, attention, insertion.
omit *(SYN.)* exclude, delete, cancel, eliminate, ignore, neglect, skip, leave out, drop, miss, bar, overlook, disregard.
(ANT.) insert, notice, enter, include, introduce.
omnipotent *(SYN.)* all-powerful, almighty, divine.
oncoming *(SYN.)* imminent, approaching, arriving, nearing.
onerous *(SYN.)* intricate, arduous, hard, perplexing, difficult, burdensome, puzzling.
(ANT.) simple, easy, facile, effortless.
one-sided *(SYN.)* unfair, partial, biased, prejudiced.
(ANT.) impartial, neutral.
ongoing *(SYN.)* advancing, developing, continuing, progressive.
onlooker *(SYN.)* witness, spectator, observer, bystander.
only *(SYN.)* lone, sole, solitary, single, merely, but, just.
onset *(SYN.)* commencement, begin-

ning, opening, start, assault, attack, charge, offense, onslaught.
(ANT.) end.
onslaught *(SYN.)* invasion, aggression, attack, assault, offense, drive, criticism, onset, charge, denunciation.
(ANT.) vindication, defense, surrender, opposition, resistance.
onus *(SYN.)* load, weight, burden, duty.
onward *(SYN.)* ahead, forward, frontward.
(ANT.) backward.
ooze *(SYN.)* seep, leak, drip, flow, filter.
opacity *(SYN.)* obscurity, thickness, imperviousness.
opaque *(SYN.)* murky, dull, cloudy, filmy, unilluminated, dim, obtuse, indistinct, shadowy, dark, obscure.
(ANT.) light, clear, bright.
open *(SYN.)* uncovered, overt, agape, unlocked, passable, accessible, unrestricted, candid, plain, clear, exposed, unclosed, unobstructed, free, disengaged, frank, unoccupied, public, honest, ajar, available.
open *(SYN.)* unbar, unfold, exhibit, spread, unseal, expand, unfasten.
(ANT.) close, shut, conceal, hide.
open-handed *(SYN.)* kind, generous, charitable, lavish, extravagant, bountiful.
(ANT.) mean, stingy.
openhearted *(SYN.)* frank, honest, candid, sincere, ingenuous, straightforward.
(ANT.) insincere, devious.
opening *(SYN.)* cavity, hole, void, abyss, aperture, chasm, pore, gap, loophole.
openly *(SYN.)* sincerely, frankly, freely.
(ANT.) secretly.
open-minded *(SYN.)* tolerant, fair, just, liberal, impartial, reasonable, unprejudiced.
(ANT.) prejudiced, bigoted.
operate *(SYN.)* comport, avail, behave, interact, apply, manage, utilize, demean, run, manipulate, employ, act, exploit, exert, exercise, practice, conduct.
(ANT.) neglect, waste.
operation *(SYN.)* effort, enterprise, mentality, maneuver, action, instrumentality, performance, working, proceeding, agency.
(ANT.) inaction, cessation, rest, inactivity.
operative *(SYN.)* busy, active, industrious, working, effective, functional.
(ANT.) inactive, dormant.
opiate *(SYN.)* hypnotic, tranquilizer, narcotic.
opinion *(SYN.)* decision, feeling, notion, view, idea, conviction, belief, judgment, sentiment, persuasion, impression.
(ANT.) knowledge, fact, misgiving, skepticism.
opinionated *(SYN.)* domineering, overbearing, arrogant, dogmatic, positive, magisterial, obstinate, pertinacious.
(ANT.) questioning, fluctuating, indecisive, skeptical, open-minded, indecisive.

opponent *(SYN.)* competitor, foe, adversary, contestant, enemy, rival, contender, combatant, antagonist.
(ANT.) comrade, team, ally, confederate.
opportune *(SYN.)* fitting, suitable, appropriate, proper, favorable, felicitous.
opportunity *(SYN.)* possibility, chance, occasion, time, contingency, opening.
(ANT.) obstacle, disadvantage, hindrance.
oppose *(SYN.)* defy, resist, withstand, combat, bar, counteract, confront, thwart, struggle, fight, contradict, hinder, obstruct.
(ANT.) submit, support, agree, cooperate, succumb.
opposed *(SYN.)* opposite, contrary, hostile, adverse, counteractive, unlucky, antagonistic, unfavorable, disastrous.
(ANT.) lucky, benign, propitious, fortunate, favorable.
opposite *(SYN.)* reverse, contrary, different, unlike, opposed.
(ANT.) like, same, similar.
opposition *(SYN.)* combat, struggle, discord, collision, conflict, battle, fight, encounter, discord, controversy, inconsistency, variance.
(ANT.) harmony, amity, concord, consonance.
oppress *(SYN.)* harass, torment, vex, afflict, annoy, harry, pester, hound, worry, persecute.
(ANT.) encourage, support, comfort, assist, aid.
oppression *(SYN.)* cruelty, tyranny, persecution, injustice, despotism, brutality, abuse.
(ANT.) liberty, freedom.
oppressive *(SYN.)* difficult, stifling, burdensome, severe, domineering, harsh, unjust, overbearing, overwhelming.
oppressor *(SYN.)* bully, scourge, slave-driver.
opprobrium *(SYN.)* disgrace, contempt, reproach, shame, discredit.
opt *(SYN.)* choose, prefer, pick, select.
optical *(SYN.)* seeing, visual.
optimism *(SYN.)* faith, expectation, optimism, anticipation, trust, expectancy, confidence, hope.
(ANT.) despair, pessimism, despondency.
optimistic *(SYN.)* happy, cheerful, bright, glad, pleasant, radiant, lighthearted.
(ANT.) pessimistic.
option *(SYN.)* preference, choice, selection, alternative, election, self-determination.
optional *(SYN.)* selective, elective, voluntary.
(ANT.) required.
opulence *(SYN.)* luxury, abundance, fortune, riches, wealth, plenty, affluence.
(ANT.) need, indigence, want, poverty.
opulent *(SYN.)* wealthy, rich, prosperous, well-off, affluent, well-heeled.
oracle *(SYN.)* authority, forecaster, wizard, seer, mastermind, clairvoyant.
oral *(SYN.)* voiced, sounded, vocalized,

said, uttered, verbal, vocal, spoken.
(ANT.) recorded, written, documentary.
orate *(SYN.)* preach, lecture, sermonize.
oration *(SYN.)* address, lecture, speech, sermon, discourse, recital, declamation.
orb *(SYN.)* globe, sphere, ball, moon.
orbit *(SYN.)* path, lap, course, circuit, revolution, revolve, circle.
orchestra *(SYN.)* ensemble, band.
orchestrate *(SYN.)* coordinate, direct, synchronize, organize.
ordain *(SYN.)* constitute, create, order, decree, decide, dictate, command, rule, bid, sanction, appoint.
(ANT.) terminate, disband.
ordeal *(SYN.)* hardship, suffering, test, affliction, trouble, fortune, proof, examination, trial, experiment, tribulation, misery.
(ANT.) consolation, alleviation.
order *(SYN.)* plan, series, decree, instruction, command, system, method, aim, arrangement, class, injuction, mandate, instruct, requirement, dictate, bidding.
(ANT.) consent, license, confusion, disarray, irregularity, permission.
order *(SYN.)* guide, command, rule, direct, govern, manage, regulate, bid, conduct.
(ANT.) misguide, deceive, misdirect, distract.
orderly *(SYN.)* regulated, neat, well-organized, disciplined, methodical, shipshape.
(ANT.) sloppy, messy, haphazard, disorganized.
ordinarily *(SYN.)* commonly, usually, generally, mostly, customarily, normally.
ordinary *(SYN.)* common, habitual, normal, typical, usual, conventional, familiar, accustomed, customary, average, standard, everyday, inferior, mediocre, regular, vulgar, plain.
(ANT.) uncommon, marvelous, extraordinary, remarkable, strange.
ordance *(SYN.)* munitions, artillery.
organ *(SYN.)* instrument, journal, voice.
organic *(SYN.)* living, biological, animate.
organism *(SYN.)* creature, plant, micro-organism.
organization *(SYN.)* order, rule, system, arrangement, method, plan, regularity, scheme, mode, process.
(ANT.) irregularity, chaos, disarrangement, chance, disorder, confusion.
organize *(SYN.)* assort, arrange, plan, regulate, systematize, devise, categorize, classify, prepare.
(ANT.) jumble, disorder, disturb, confuse, scatter.
organized *(SYN.)* planned, neat, orderly, arranged.
orient *(SYN.)* align, fit, accustom, adjust.
orifice *(SYN.)* vent, slot, opening, hole.
origin *(SYN.)* birth, foundation, source, start, commencement, inception, beginning, derivation, infancy, parentage, spring, cradle.

(ANT.) product, issue, outcome, end.

original *(SYN.)* primary, fresh, new, initial, pristine, creative, first, primordial, inventive, primeval, novel, introductory.
(ANT.) banal, trite, subsequent, derivative, later, modern, terminal.

originality *(SYN.)* unconventionality, genius, novelty, creativity, imagination.

originate *(SYN.)* fashion, invent, cause, create, make, initiate, inaugurate, organize, institute, produce, engender, commence, found, establish, form, begin, arise, generate, formulate.
(ANT.) demolish, terminate, annihilate, disband, destroy.

originator *(SYN.)* creator, inventor, discoverer.
(ANT.) follower, imitator.

ornament *(SYN.)* decoration, ornamentation, adornment, embellishment, trimming, garnish.

ornamental *(SYN.)* ornate, decorative.

ornate *SYN.)* florid, overdone, elaborate, showy, flowery, pretentious.

ornery *(SYN.)* disobedient, firm, unruly, stiff, rebellious, stubborn, headstrong, willful, contrary, rigid, mean, difficult, malicious, cross, disagreeable.
(ANT.) pleasant.

orthodox *(SYN.)* customary, usual, conventional, correct, proper, accepted.
(ANT.) different, unorthodox.

oscillate *(SYN.)* vary, change, hesitate, waver, undulate, fluctuate, vacillate.
(ANT.) persist, resolve, adhere, stick, decide.

ostentation *(SYN.)* parade, show, boasting, pageantry, vaunting, pomp, display, flourish.
(ANT.) reserve, humility, unobtrusiveness, modesty.

ostentatious *(SYN.)* flashy, showy, overdone, fancy, pretentious, garish.

ostracize *(SYN.)* hinder, omit, bar, exclude, blackball, expel, prohibit.

other *(SYN.)* distinct, different, extra, further, new, additional, supplementary.

ought *(SYN.)* must, should, be obliged.

oust *(SYN.)* eject, banish, exclude, expatriate, ostracize, dismiss, exile, expel.
(ANT.) shelter, accept, receive, admit, harbor.

outbreak *(SYN.)* riot, revolt, uprising, disturbance, torrent, eruption, outburst.

outburst *(SYN.)* outbreak, eruption, torrent, ejection, discharge.

outcast *(SYN.)* friendless, homeless, deserted, abandoned, forsaken, disowned, derelict, forlorn, rejected.

outcome *(SYN.)* fate, destiny, necessity, doom, portion, consequence, result, end, fortune, effect, issue, aftermath.

outcry *(SYN.)* scream, protest, clamor, noise, uproar.

outdated *(SYN.)* old-fashioned, unfashionable, old, outmoded.
(ANT.) stylish.

outdo *(SYN.)* outshine, defeat, excel, beat, surpass.

outer *(SYN.)* remote, exterior, external.

outfit *(SYN.)* garb, kit, gear, furnish, equip, rig, clothing, provisions.

outgoing *(SYN.)* leaving, departing, friendly, congenial, amicable.
(ANT.) unfriendly, incoming.

outing *(SYN.)* journey, trip, excursion, jaunt, expedition, junket.

outlandish *(SYN.)* peculiar, odd, weird, curious, strange, queer, exotic, bazaar.
(ANT.) ordinary, common.

outlast *(SYN.)* survive, endure, outlive.

outlaw *(SYN.)* exile, bandit, outcast, badman, convict, criminal, fugitive, desperado.

outlay *(SYN.)* expense, costs, spending, disbursement, expenditure, charge.

outlet *(SYN.)* spout, opening, passage.

outline *(SYN.)* form, sketch, brief, draft, figure, profile, contour, chart.

outlook *(SYN.)* viewpoint, view, prospect, opportunity, position, attitude, future.

outlying *(SYN.)* external, remote, outer, out-of-the-way, surburban, rural.

outnumber *(SYN.)* exceed.

output *(SYN.)* yield, crop, harvest, proceeds, productivity, production.

outrage *(SYN.)* aggression, transgression, vice, affront, offense, insult.
(ANT.) morality, right, gentleness.

outrageous *(SYN.)* shameful, shocking, disgraceful, insulting, nonsensical.
(ANT.) prudent, reasonable, sensible.

outright *(SYN.)* entirely, altogether, completely, quite, fully, thoroughly.

outside *(SYN.)* covering, exterior, surface, facade, externals, appearance.
(ANT.) intimate, insider.

outsider *(SYN.)* immigrant, stranger, foreigner, alien, newcomer, bystander.
(ANT.) countryman, friend, acquaintance, neighbor, associate.

outspoken *(SYN.)* rude, impolite, unceremonious, brusque, unrestrained, vocal, open, straight-forward, blunt.
(ANT.) suave, tactful, shy, polished, polite, subtle.

outstanding *(SYN.)* well-known, important, prominent, leading, eminent.
(ANT.) insignificant, unimportant.

outward *(SYN.)* apparent, outside, exterior, visible.

outweigh *(SYN.)* predominate, supersede, counteract, dwarf.

outwit *(SYN.)* baffle, trick, outsmart, bewilder, outdo, outmaneuver, confuse.

oval *(SYN.)* egg-shaped, elliptical, ovular.

ovation *(SYN.)* fanfare, homage, applause, tribute, cheers, acclamation.

overall *(SYN.)* comprehensive, complete, general, extensive, wide-spread, entire.

overbearing *(SYN.)* domineering, masterful, autocratic, dictatorial.
(ANT.) humble.

overcast *(SYN.)* dim, shadowy, cloudy, murky, dark, mysterious, gloomy, somber, dismal, hazy, indistinct.
(ANT.) sunny, bright, distinct, limpid, clear.

overcome *(SYN.)* quell, beat, crush, surmount, humble, conquer, defeat.
(ANT.) retreat, surrender, capitulate, cede, lose.

overdue *(SYN.)* tardy, advanced, slow, delayed, new.
(ANT.) timely, early, beforehand.

overflow *(SYN.)* run over, flood, spill, cascade, inundate.

overflowing *(SYN.)* ample, plentiful, teeming, abundant, copious, profuse.
(ANT.) insufficient, scant, deficient, scarce.

overhang *(SYN.)* protrude, extend, projection.

overhaul *(SYN.)* recondition, rebuild, service, repair, condition, revamp.

overhead *(SYN.)* high, above, aloft, expenses, costs.

overlap *(SYN.)* overhang, extend, superimpose.

overload *(SYN.)* burden, weight, oppress, afflict, weigh, trouble, encumber, tax.
(ANT.) ease, lighten, console, alleviate, mitigate.

overlook *(SYN.)* miss, disregard, exclude, cancel, omit, skip, ignore.
(ANT.) notice, enter, include, introduce.

overpass *(SYN.)* span, bridge, viaduct.

overpower *(SYN.)* overcome, conquer, defeat, surmount, overwhelm.
(ANT.) surrender.

overrated *(SYN.)* exaggerated, misrepresented.

overrule *(SYN.)* disallow, nullify, cancel, override, repeal, revoke.

overrun *(SYN.)* spread, exceed, beset, infest, flood, abound.

oversee *(SYN.)* direct, run, operate, administer, superintend, boss, manage, supervise.

overshadow *(SYN.)* dominate, control, outclass, surpass, domineer.

oversight *(SYN.)* omission, charge, superintendence, surveillance, inattention, error, inadvertence, neglect.
(ANT.) scrutiny, care, attention.

overstep *(SYN.)* surpass, exceed, trespass, transcend, impinge, violate.

overt *(SYN.)* honest, candid, frank, plain, open, apparent, straightforward.

overtake *(SYN.)* outdistance, reach, catch, pass.

overthrow *(SYN.)* defeat, demolish, overcome, destroy, ruin, rout.
(ANT.) revive, restore, construct.

overture *(SYN.)* offer, bid, proposal, prelude, introduction, presentation.
(ANT.) finale.

overturn *(SYN.)* demolish, overcome, vanquish, upset, supplant, destroy.
(ANT.) uphold, construct, build, preserve, conserve.

overweight *(SYN.)* pudgy, stout, heavy, obese, fat.

overwhelm *(SYN.)* crush, surmount, vanquish, conquer, astonish, surprise.

owe *(SYN.)* be liable, be indebted.

own *(SYN.)* monopolize, hold, possess, maintain, have.

owner *(SYN.)* landholder, partner, proprietor, possessor.

pace *(SYN.)* rate, gait, step.

pacific *(SYN.)* peaceful, calm, serene, undisturbed, composed.
(ANT.) turbulent, wild, excited, frantic.

pacify *(SYN.)* appease, lull, relieve, quell, soothe, allay, assuage, calm, satisfy, compose, placate, alleviate.
(ANT.) incense, inflame, arouse, excite.

pack *(SYN.)* prepare, stow, crowd, stuff, bundle, parcel, load, crowd, gang, mob.

package *(SYN.)* parcel, packet, load, bundle, box, bottle, crate.

packed *(SYN.)* filled, complete, plentiful, crammed, fall, replete, gorged, satiated, copious, entire, extensive.
(ANT.) lacking, depleted, devoid, vacant, insufficient, partial, empty.

pageant *(SYN.)* show, display, spectacle.

pain *(SYN.)* twinge, ache, pang, agony, distress, grief, anguish, throe, paroxysm, suffering, misery.
(ANT.) happiness, pleasure, comfort, relief, solace, ease, delight, joy.

painful *(SYN.)* hurting, galling, poignant, bitter, grievous, agonizing, aching.
(ANT.) sweet, pleasant, soothing.

painting *(SYN.)* image, picture, portrayal, scene, view, sketch, illustration, panorama, likeness, representation.

pair *(SYN.)* team, couple, mate, match.

pale *(SYN.)* colorless, white, pallid, dim, faint, whiten, blanch.
(ANT.) flushed, ruddy, bright, dark.

pamphlet *(SYN.)* leaflet, brochure.

pang *(SYN.)* throb, pain, hurt.

panic *(SYN.)* fear, terror, fright, alarm, apprehension, trembling, horror, dread.
(ANT.) tranquillity, composure, calmness, serenity, calm, soothe.

pant *(SYN.)* wheeze, puff, gasp.

pantry *(SYN.)* cupboard, storeroom.

paper *(SYN.)* journal, newspaper, document, article, essay.

parable *(SYN.)* fable, saga, legend, myth, allegory, chronicle, fiction.
(ANT.) history, fact.

parade *(SYN.)* procession, cavalcade, succession, train, file, cortege, retinue, sequence, march, review, pageant, strut.

paradise *(SYN.)* utopia, heaven.

parallel *(SYN.)* allied, analogous, comparable, corresponding, akin, similar.
(ANT.) opposed, different, incongruous.

paralyze *(SYN.)* numb, deaden.

parcel *(SYN.)* packet, package, bundle.

parched *(SYN.)* dry, arid, thirsty, drained, dehydrated, desiccated.
(ANT.) moist, damp.

pardon *(SYN.)* condone, overlook, remit, absolve, acquit, forgive, excuse.
(ANT.) punish, accuse, condemn.

parley *(SYN.)* interview, talk, conference, chat, dialogue, colloquy.

part *(SYN.)* piece, section, allotment, portion, segment, element, member.
(ANT.) whole, entirety.

partake *(SYN.)* dispense, parcel, allot, assign, distribute, partition, ap-

propriate, divide, portion, share.
(ANT.) *condense, aggregate, combine.*
partial *(SYN.)* unfinished, undone, incomplete, prejudiced, unfair.
(SYN.) comprehensive, complete.
participate *(SYN.)* join, share, partake.
participation *(SYN.)* communion, sacrament, union, intercourse, association, fellowship.
(ANT.) *nonparticipation, alienation.*
particle *(SYN.)* mite, crumb, scrap, atom, corpuscle, grain, iota, shred, smidgen, grain, speck, bit, spot.
(ANT.) *quantity, bulk, mass.*
particular *(SYN.)* peculiar, unusual, detailed, specific, fastidious.
(ANT.) *general, rough, universal, comprehensive, undiscriminating.*
partition *(SYN.)* distribution, division, separation, screen, barrier, separator, divider, wall.
(ANT.) *unification, joining.*
partner *(SYN.)* colleague, comrade, friend, crony, consort, associate, companion, mate, participant.
(ANT.) *stranger, enemy, adversary.*
pass *(SYN.)* proceed, continue, move, go, disregard, ignore, exceed, gap.
(ANT.) *note, consider, notice.*
passage *(SYN.)* section, passageway, corridor, section, voyage, tour.
passenger *(SYN.)* traveler, tourist, rider, voyager, commuter.
passion *(SYN.)* feeling, affection, turmoil, sentiment, perturbation.
(ANT.) *tranquillity, indifference, calm, restraint, dispassion, apathy, coolness.*
passionate *(SYN.)* fiery, ardent, burning, glowing, irascible, fervid.
(ANT.) *quiet, calm, cool, apathetic.*
passive *(SYN.)* relaxed, idle, stoical, enduring, inert, inactive, patient.
(ANT.) *dynamic, active, aggressive.*
past *(SYN.)* done, finished, gone, over, former.
(ANT.) *future, present, ahead.*
patch *(SYN.)* restore, fix, repair, ameliorate, correct, remedy, sew.
(ANT.) *rend, destroy, hurt, injure.*
path *(SYN.)* avenue, street, trail, walk, course, road, route, thoroughfare.
pathetic *(SYN.)* piteous, sad, affecting, moving, poignant, pitiable, touching.
(ANT.) *funny, comical, ludicrous.*
patience *(SYN.)* perseverance, composure, endurance, fortitude, longsuffering, forbearance, calmness, passiveness, serenity, courage, persistence.
(ANT.) *restlessness, nervousness, impatience, unquite, impetuosity.*
patient *(SYN.)* indulgent, forbearing, composed, passive, quiet, unexcited.
(ANT.) *high-strung, hysterical.*
patrol *(SYN.)* inspect, watch, guard.
patron *(SYN.)* purchaser, buyer, client, customer.
patronize *(SYN.)* support.
pattern *(SYN.)* guide, example, original, model, design, figure, decoration.
pause *(SYN.)* falter, hesitate, waver, demur, doubt, scruple, delay, rest.
(ANT.) *proceed, continue, decide,*

resolve, persevere, continuity.
pawn *(SYN.)* tool, puppet, stooge.
pay *(SYN.)* earnings, salary, allowance, stipend, wages, payment, compensation, recompense.
(ANT.) *gratuity, present, gift.*
payable *(SYN.)* unpaid, due, owed, owing.
peace *(SYN.)* hush, repose, serenity, tranquillity, silence, stillness, calmness.
(ANT.) *noise, tumult, disturbance.*
peaceable *(SYN.)* mild, calm, friendly, peaceful, amiable, gentle, pacific.
(ANT.) *aggressive, hostile, warlike.*
peaceful *(SYN.)* pacific, calm, undisturbed, quiet, serene, mild, placid.
(ANT.) *noisy, violent, agitated.*
peak *(SYN.)* climax, culmination, summit, zenith, height, acme, consummation, apex, top, point, crest.
(ANT.) *depth, floor, base, anticlimax, base, bottom.*
peculiar *(SYN.)* odd, eccentric, extraordinary, unusual, individual, particular.
(ANT.) *ordinary, common, normal.*
peculiarity *(SYN.)* characteristic, feature, mark, trait, quality, attribute, property, distinctiveness.
pedantic *(SYN.)* formal, scholastic, erudite, academic, learned, bookish, theoretical, scholarly.
(ANT.) *simple, common-sense, ignorant, practical, unlearned.*
peddle *(SYN.)* sell, vend, hawk.
pedestrian *(SYN.)* stroller, walker.
pedigree *(SYN.)* descent, line, parentage, lineage, ancestry, family.
peek *(SYN.)* glimpse, look, peer, peep.
peel *(SYN.)* rind, skin, peeling.
peep *(SYN.)* squeak, cheep, chirp.
peer *(SYN.)* match, rival, equal, parallel, peep, glimpse, examine, peek, scrutinize.
peeve *(SYN.)* nettle, irk, irritate, annoy, vex.
peevish *(SYN.)* ill-natured, irritable, waspish, touchy, petulant, snappish, fractious, ill-tempered, fretful.
(ANT.) *pleasant, affable, goodtempered, , genial, good-natured.*
pen *(SYN.)* coop, enclosure, cage.
penalize *(SYN.)* dock, punish.
penalty *(SYN.)* fine, retribution, handicap, punishment, chastisement, disadvantage, forfeiture, forfeit.
(ANT.) *remuneration, compensation, reward, pardon.*
penchant *(SYN.)* disposition, propensity, tendency, partiality, inclination, bent, tendency, slant, bias.
(ANT.) *justice, fairness, equity, impartiality.*
penetrate *(SYN.)* bore, hole, pierce, enter.
penetrating *(SYN.)* profound, recondite, abstruse, deep, solemn, piercing, puncturing, boring, sharp, acute.
(ANT.) *superficial, trivial, shallow, slight.*
peninsula *(SYN.)* spit, headland, neck, point.
penitent *(SYN.)* remorseful, sorrowful, regretful, contrite, sorry, repentant.

(ANT.) remorseless, objurgate.
penniless *(SYN.)* poor, destitute, impecunious, needy, poverty-stricken, needy.
(ANT.) rich, wealthy, affluent, opulent, prosperous, well-off.
pensive *(SYN.)* dreamy, meditative, thoughtful, introspective, reflective, contemplative.
(ANT.) thoughtless, heedless, inconsiderate, precipitous, rash.
penurious *(SYN.)* avaricious, greedy, parsimonious, miserly, stingy, acquisitive, tight.
(ANT.) munificent, extravagant, bountiful, generous, altruistic.
penury *(SYN.)* poverty, want, destitution, necessity, indigence, need, privation.
(ANT.) riches, affluence, abundance, plenty, wealth.
people *(SYN.)* humans, person.
perceive *(SYN.)* note, conceive, see, comprehend, understand, discern, recognize, apprehend, notice, observe, distinguish, understand, grasp.
(ANT.) overlook, ignore, miss.
perceptible *(SYN.)* sensible, appreciable, apprehensible.
(ANT.) imperceptible, absurd, impalpable.
perception *(SYN.)* understanding, apprehension, conception, insight, comprehension, discernment.
(ANT.) misconception, ignorance, misapprehension, insensibility.
perceptive *(SYN.)* informed, observant, apprised, cognizant, aware, conscious, sensible, mindful, discerning, sharp, acute, observant.
(ANT.) unaware, ignorant, oblivious, insensible.
perfect *(SYN.)* ideal, whole, faultless, immaculate, complete, superlative, absolute, unqualified, utter, sinless, holy, finished, blameless, entire, excellent, pure, flawless, ideal.
(ANT.) incomplete, defective, imperfect, deficient, blemished, lacking, faulty, flawed.
perfectionist *(SYN.)* purist, pedant.
perform *(SYN.)* impersonate, pretend, act, play, do, accomplish, achieve, complete.
performance *(SYN.)* parade, entertainment, demonstration, movie, show, production, ostentation, spectacle, presentation, offering.
performer *(SYN.)* entertainer, actress, actor.
perfume *(SYN.)* cologne, scent, essence.
perfunctory *(SYN.)* decorous, exact, formal, external, correct, affected, methodical, precise, stiff, outward, proper, solemn.
(ANT.) unconventional, easy, unconstrained, natural, heartfelt.
perhaps *(SYN.)* conceivable, possible, maybe.
(ANT.) absolutely, definitely.
peril *(SYN.)* jeopardy, risk, danger, hazard.
(ANT.) safety, immunity, protection,

defense, security.
perilous *(SYN.)* menacing, risky, hazardous, critical, dangerous, precarious, unsafe, insecure, threatening.
(ANT.) safe, firm, protected, secure.
period *(SYN.)* era, age, interval, span, tempo, time, epoch, duration, spell, date.
periodical *(SYN.)* uniform, customary, orderly, systematic, regular, steady.
(ANT.) exceptional, unusual, abnormal, rare, erratic.
perish *(SYN.)* die, sink cease, decline, decay, depart, wane, wither, languish, expire, cease, pass away.
(ANT.) grow, survive, flourish, begin, live.
perishable *(SYN.)* decomposable, decayable.
permanent *(SYN.)* constant, durable, enduring, abiding, fixed, changeless, unchangeable, lasting, indestructible, stable, continuing, long-lived, persistent, persisting, everlasting, unchanging, unaltered.
(ANT.) unstable, transient, ephemeral, temporary, transitory, passing, inconstant, fluctuating.
permeate *(SYN.)* penetrate, pervade, run through, diffuse, fill, saturate, infiltrate.
permissible *(SYN.)* allowable, fair, tolerable, admissible, justifiable, probable, warranted.
(ANT.) unsuitable, inadmissible, irrelevant.
permission *(SYN.)* authorization, liberty, permit, authority, consent, leave, license, freedom.
(ANT.) refusal, prohibition, denial, opposition.
permissive *(SYN.)* easy, tolerant, open-minded, unrestrictive.
(ANT.) restrictive.
permit *(SYN.)* let, tolerate, authorize, sanction, allow, grant, give.
(ANT.) refuse, resist, forbid, protest, object, prohibit, disallow.
perpendicular *(SYN.)* standing, upright, vertical.
(ANT.) horizontal.
perpetrate *(SYN.)* commit, perform, do.
(ANT.) neglect, fail, miscarry.
perpetual *(SYN.)* everlasting, immortal, ceaseless, endless, timeless, undying, infinite, eternal, unceasing, continuing, continual, continuous, permanent, constant, eternal.
(ANT.) transient, mortal, finite, temporal ephemeral, inconstant, intermittent, fluctuating.
perpetually *(SYN.)* continually, ever, incessantly, eternally, forever, always, constantly.
(ANT.) rarely, sometimes, never, occasionally, fitfully.
perplex *(SYN.)* confuse, dumbfound, mystify, puzzle, bewilder, confound, nonplus.
(ANT.) solve, explain, illumine, instruct, clarify.
perplexed *(SYN.)* confused, disorganized, mixed, bewildered, deranged,

disordered, muddled, disconcerted.
(ANT.) plain, obvious, clear, lucid, organized.
perplexing *(SYN.)* intricate, complex, involved, compound, complicated.
(ANT.) uncompounded, plain, simple.
persecute *(SYN.)* harass, hound, torment, worry, vex, torture, harry, afflict, annoy, oppress, pester, ill-treat, victimize, maltreat.
(ANT.) support, comfort, assist, encourage, aid.
persevere *(SYN.)* remain, abide, endure, last, persist, continue.
(ANT.) vacillate, desist, discontinue, cease, waver, lapse.
perseverance *(SYN.)* persistency, constancy, pertinacity, steadfastness, tenacity, industry.
(ANT.) sloth, cessation, laziness, idleness, rest.
persist *(SYN.)* endure, remain, abide, persevere, continue, last.
(ANT.) vacillate, waver, desist, cease, discontinue, stop.
persistence *(SYN.)* persistency, constancy, perseverance, steadfastness, tenacity.
(ANT.) cessation, rest, sloth, idleness.
persistent *(SYN.)* lasting, steady, obstinate, stubborn, fixed, enduring, immovable, constant, indefatigable, dogged.
(ANT.) wavering, unsure, hesitant, vacillating.
person *(SYN.)* human, individual, somebody, someone.
personal *(SYN.)* secret, private.
(ANT.) general, public.
personality *(SYN.)* make-up, nature, disposition, character.
perspicacity *(SYN.)* intelligence, understanding, discernment, judgment, wisdom, sagacity.
(ANT.) thoughtlessness, stupidity, arbitrariness, senselessness.
persuade *(SYN.)* entice, coax, exhort, prevail upon, urge, allure, induce, influence, win over, convince.
(ANT.) restrain, deter, compel, dissuade, coerce, discourage.
persuasion *(SYN.)* decision, feeling, notion, view, sentiment, conviction, belief, opinion.
(ANT.) knowledge, skepticism, fact, misgiving.
persuasive *(SYN.)* winning, alluring, compelling, convincing, stimulating, influential.
(ANT.) dubious, unconvincing.
pertain *(SYN.)* refer, relate, apply.
pertinacious *(SYN.)* firm, obstinate, contumacious, head-strong, dogged, inflexible, obdurate, uncompromising, determined, immovable, unyielding.
(ANT.) yielding, docile, amenable, submissive, compliant.
pertinent *(SYN.)* apt, material, relevant, relating, applicable, to the point, germane, apropos, apposite, appropriate.
(ANT.) unrelated, foreign, alien, extraneous.
perturbed *(SYN.)* agitated, disturbed,

upset, flustered.
pervade *(SYN.)* penetrate, saturate, fill, diffuse, infiltrate, run through, permeate.
perverse *(SYN.)* obstinate, ungovernable, sinful, contrary, fractious, peevish, forward, disobedient, wicked, intractable, petulant.
(ANT.) docile, agreeable, tractable, obliging.
perversion *(SYN.)* maltreatment, outrage, desecration, abuse, profanation, misuse, reviling.
(ANT.) respect.
pervert *(SYN.)* deprave, humiliate, impair, debase, corrupt, degrade, abase, defile.
(ANT.) improve, raise, enhance.
perverted *(SYN.)* wicked, perverse, sinful.
pest *(SYN.)* annoyance, bother, nuisance, bother, irritant, irritation.
pester *(SYN.)* disturb, annoy, irritate, tease, bother, chafe, inconvenience, molest, trouble, vex, harass, torment, worry.
(ANT.) console, soothe, accommodate, gratify.
pet *(SYN.)* darling, favorite, caress.
petition *(SYN.)* invocation, prayer, request, appeal, entreaty, supplication, suit, plea, application, solicitation, entreaty.
petty *(SYN.)* paltry, trivial, frivolous, small, unimportant, trifling, insignificant.
(ANT.) important, serious, weighty, momentous, grand, vital, significant, generous.
petulant *(SYN.)* irritable, ill-natured, fretful, snappish, peevish, ill-tempered, waspish, touchy.
(ANT.) pleasant, affable, good-tempered, genial, good-natured.
phantom *(SYN.)* apparition, ghost, specter.
phase *(SYN.)* period, stage, view, condition.
phenomenon *(SYN.)* occurrence, fact, happening, incident.
philanthropy *(SYN.)* kindness, benevolence, charity, generosity, tenderness, liberality, humanity, magnanimity, altruism.
(ANT.) unkindness, inhumanity, cruelty, malevolence, selfishness.
phlegmatic *(SYN.)* unfeeling, passionless, listless, cold, lethargic, sluggish, slow, lazy.
(ANT.) passionate, ardent, energetic.
phony *(SYN.)* counterfeit, artificial, ersatz, fake, synthetic, unreal, spurious, feigned, assumed, bogus, sham, false, forged.
(ANT.) real, genuine, natural, true.
phrase *(SYN.)* expression, term, word, name.
physical *(SYN.)* material, bodily, carnal, corporeal, natural, somatic, corporal.
(ANT.) spiritual, mental.
pick *(SYN.)* cull, opt, select, elect, choose.

(ANT.) reject, refuse.

picture *(SYN.)* etching, image, painting, portrait, print, representation, sketch, appearance, cinema, effigy, engraving, scene, view, illustration, panorama, resemblance, likeness, drawing, photo-graph.

piece *(SYN.)* portion, bit, fraction, morsel, scrap, fragment, amount, part, quantity, unit, section, portion.
(ANT.) sum, whole, entirety, all, total.

piecemeal *(SYN.)* gradually, partially.
(ANT.) whole, complete, entire.

pierce *(SYN.)* puncture, perforate.

pigheaded *(SYN.)* inflexible, stubborn, obstinate.

pigment *(SYN.)* shade, tint, color, dye, hue, complexion, tincture, stain, tinge.
(ANT.) transparency, paleness.

pile *(SYN.)* accumulation, heap, collection, amass.

pilgrim *(SYN.)* wanderer, traveler.

pilgrimage *(SYN.)* trip, journey, tour, expedition.

pillar *(SYN.)* support, prop, column, shaft.

pillow *(SYN.)* bolster, cushion, pad.

pilot *(SYN.)* helmsman, aviator, steersman.

pin *(SYN.)* clip, fastening, peg, fastener.

pinch *(SYN.)* squeeze, nip.

pinnacle *(SYN.)* crown, zenith, head, summit, chief, apex, crest, top.
(ANT.) bottom, foundation, base, foot.

pioneer *(SYN.)* guide, pilgrim, pathfinder, explorer.

pious *(SYN.)* devout, religious, spiritual, consecrated, divine, hallowed, holy, saintly, sacred, reverent.
(ANT.) worldly, sacrilegious, evil, secular, profane, irreligious, impious.

pirate *(SYN.)* plunderer, buccaneer, privateer.

pistol *(SYN.)* gun, revolver, weapon, handgun.

pit *(SYN.)* well, cavity, hole, excavation.

pitch *(SYN.)* throw, cast, toss, propel, hurl, fling, thrust, establish.
(ANT.) retain, draw, hold, pull, haul.

pitcher *(SYN.)* jug.

piteous *(SYN.)* poignant, touching, affecting, moving, pitiable, sad, pathetic.
(ANT.) funny, ludicrous, comical.

pitfall *(SYN.)* lure, snare, wile, ambush, bait, intrigue, trick, trap, artifice, net, snare.

pitiable *(SYN.)* poignant, touching, moving, affecting, sad.
(ANT.) ludicrous, funny, comical.

pitiful *(SYN.)* distressing, pathetic, pitiable.

pitiless *(SYN.)* unmerciful, mean, unpitying, merciless, cruel.
(ANT.) gentle, kind.

pity *(SYN.)* sympathy, commiseration, condolence, mercy, compassion, charity, mercy.
(ANT.) ruthlessness, hardness, cruelty, inhumanity, brutality, vindictiveness.

pivotal *(SYN.)* crucial, critical, essential, central.
(ANT.) peripheral, unimportant.

place *(SYN.)* lay, arrange, dispose, put, deposit, space, region, location, plot, area, spot.
(ANT.) mislay, remove, disarrange, disturb, misplace.

placid *(SYN.)* pacific, serene, tranquil, calm, imperturbable, composed, peaceful, quiet, still, undisturbed, unruffled.
(ANT.) wild, frantic, turbulent, stormy, excited.

plagiarize *(SYN.)* recite, adduce, cite, quote, paraphrase, repeat, extract.
(ANT.) retort, contradict, misquote, refute.

plague *(SYN.)* hound, pester, worry, harass, annoy, persecute, torment, vex, afflict, badger, torture, epidemic, trouble.
(ANT.) encourage, aid, comfort, assist, support.

plain *(SYN.)* candid, simple, flat, smooth, clear, evident, sincere, unpretentious, level, distinct, absolute, visible, open, frank, palpable, undecorated, ordinary, unembellished, unadorned.
(ANT.) embellished, abstruse, abrupt, rough, broken, insincere, adorned, fancy, elaborate, beautiful, ornamented.

plan *(SYN.)* design, purpose, sketch, devise, invent, contrive, intend, draw, create, scheme, plot, method, procedure.

plane *(SYN.)* level, airplane.

plastic *(SYN.)* pliable, moldable, supple, flexible, synthetic.

platform *(SYN.)* stage, pulpit.

plausible *(SYN.)* likely, practical, credible, feasible, possible, probable.
(ANT.) impracticable, impossible, visionary.

play *(SYN.)* entertainment, amusement, pastime, sport, game, fun, diversion, recreation, show, performance, drama, theatrical.
(ANT.) work, labor, boredom, toil.

playful *(SYN.)* sportive, frolicsome, frisky.

plaything *(SYN.)* game, trinket, toy, gadget.

playwright *(SYN.)* scriptwriter, dramatist.

plea *(SYN.)* invocation, request, appeal, entreaty, supplication, petition, suit.

plead *(SYN.)* beseech, defend, rejoin, supplicate, discuss, beg, appeal, ask, implore, argue, entreat.
(ANT.) deprecate, deny, refuse.

pleasant *(SYN.)* agreeable, welcome, suitable, charming, pleasing, amiable, gratifying, acceptable, pleasurable, enjoyable, nice, satisfying, satisfactory, acceptable, affable, mild, friendly.
(ANT.) offensive, disagreeable, obnoxious, unpleasant, horrid, sour, difficult, nasty.

please *(SYN.)* satisfy, suffice, fulfill, content, appease, gratify, satiate, compensate, remunerate.
(ANT.) dissatisfy, annoy, tantalize, frustrate, displease, vex.

pleasing *(SYN.)* luscious, melodious, sugary, delightful, agreeable, honeyed,

mellifluous, engaging, pleasant, charming, engaging.
(ANT.) repulsive, sour, acrid, bitter, offensive, irritating, annoying.
pleasure *(SYN.)* felicity, delight, amusement, enjoyment gratification, happiness, joy, satisfaction, gladness, well-being.
(ANT.) suffering, pain, vexation, trouble, affliction, discomfort, torment.
pledge *(SYN.)* promise, statement, assertion, declaration, assurance, agreement, oath, commitment, agree, vow, swear.
pledge *(SYN.)* bind, obligate, commit.
(ANT.) renounce, release, neglect, mistrust.
plentiful *(SYN.)* ample, profuse, replete, bountiful, abundant, plenteous, luxurious, fullness, fruitful, copious.
(ANT.) rare, scanty, deficient, scarce, insufficient.
plenty *(SYN.)* fruitfulness, bounty, fullness, abundance.
(ANT.) want, scarcity, need.
pliable *(SYN.)* elastic, supple, flexible, compliant, pliant, resilient, ductile.
(ANT.) rigid, unbending, hard, brittle, stiff.
plight *(SYN.)* dilemma, situation, difficulty, condition, predicament, fix, scrape, state.
(ANT.) satisfaction, ease, comfort, calmness.
plot *(SYN.)* design, plan, scheme, cabal, conspiracy, diagram, sketch, graph, chart, machination, intrigue.
plotting *(SYN.)* cunning, scheming, objective, artfulness, contrivance, purpose, intent, design.
(ANT.) accident, chance, result, candor, sincerity.
ploy *(SYN.)* ruse, guile, antic, deception, hoax, subterfuge, wile, cheat, artifice, fraud, trick.
(ANT.) honesty, sincerity, openness, exposure, candor.
pluck *(SYN.)* yank, snatch, jerk, pull.
plug *(SYN.)* cork, stopper.
plump *(SYN.)* obese, portly, stout, thickset, rotund, chubby, fat, paunchy, stocky, corpulent, pudgy, stout, fleshy.
(ANT.) slim, thin, gaunt, lean, slender, skinny.
plunder *(SYN.)* ravage, strip, sack, rob, pillage, raid, loot.
plunge *(SYN.)* immerse, dip, submerge.
pocketbook *(SYN.)* purse, handbag.
poem *(SYN.)* lyric, verse, poetry.
poetry *(SYN.)* rhyme, verse.
pogrom *(SYN.)* massacre, carnage, slaughter, butchery.
poignant *(SYN.)* pitiable, touching, affecting, impressive, sad, tender, moving, heart-rending.
point *(SYN.)* direct, level, train, aim, locality, position, spot, location.
(ANT.) distract, misguide, deceive, misdirect.
pointed *(SYN.)* keen, sharp, penetrating, shrewd, witty, quick, acute, penetrating, cutting, piercing, astute, severe.
(ANT.) shallow, stupid, bland, blunt,

gentle.
pointless *(SYN.)* vain, purposeless.
poise *(SYN.)* composure, self-possession, equanimity, equilibrium, carriage, calmness, balance, self-control, assurance, control, dignity.
(ANT.) rage, turbulence, agitation, anger, excitement.
poison *(SYN.)* corrupt, sully, taint, infect, befoul, defile, contaminate, venom, toxin, virus.
(ANT.) purify, disinfect.
poke *(SYN.)* punch, stab, thrust, jab.
policy *(SYN.)* procedure, system, rule, approach, tactic.
polish *(SYN.)* brighten, shine, finish, brightness, gloss.
(ANT.) tarnish, dull.
polished *(SYN.)* glib, diplomatic, urbane, refined, sleek, suave, slick.
(ANT.) rough, blunt, bluff, harsh, rugged.
polite *(SYN.)* civil, refined, well-mannered, accomplished, courteous, genteel, urbane, well-bred, cultivated, considerate, thoughtful, mannerly, respectful.
(ANT.) uncouth, impertinent, rude, boorish, uncivil, discourteous.
pollute *(SYN.)* contaminate, poison, taint, sully, infect, befoul, defile, dirty.
(ANT.) purify, disinfect, clean, clarify.
pomp *(SYN.)* flourish, pageantry, vaunting, show, boasting, ostentation, parade, display.
(ANT.) reserve, humility, modesty.
pompous *(SYN.)* high, magnificent, stately, august, dignified, grandiose, noble, majestic, lofty, imposing, arrogant, vain, pretentious.
(ANT.) lowly, undignified, humble, common, ordinary.
ponder *(SYN.)* examined, study, contemplate, investigate, meditate, muse, scrutinize, cogitate, reflect, weigh, deliberate, consider.
ponderous *(SYN.)* burdensome, trying, gloomy, serious, sluggish, massive, heavy, cumbersome, grievous, grave, dull, weighty.
(ANT.) light, animated, brisk.
poor *(SYN.)* penniless, bad, deficient, destitute, inferior, shabby, wrong, scanty, pecunious, indigent, needy, poverty-stricken, unfavorable, impoverished, penniless.
(ANT.) wealthy, prosperous, rich, fortunate, good, excellent.
poppycock *(SYN.)* rubbish, babble, twaddle, nonsense.
popular *(SYN.)* favorite, general, common, familiar, prevalent, liked, prevailing, well-liked, approved, accepted, celebrated, admired, ordinary.
(ANT.) unpopular, esoteric, restricted, exclusive.
populous *(SYN.)* dense, thronged, crowded.
porch *(SYN.)* patio, veranda.
pornographic *(SYN.)* impure, indecent, obscene, coarse, dirty, filthy, lewd, smutty, offensive, disgusting.
(ANT.) refined, modest, pure, decent.

port *(SYN.)* harbor, refuge, anchorage.

portable *(SYN.)* transportable, movable.

portal *(SYN.)* entry, doorway, opening, inlet, entrance.
(ANT.) exit, departure.

portend *(SYN.)* foreshadow, presage, foretoken.

portentous *(SYN.)* significant, critical, momentous.
(ANT.) trivial.

portion *(SYN.)* share, bit, parcel, part, piece, section, fragment, division, quota, segment, allotment.
(ANT.) whole, bulk.

portly *(SYN.)* majestic, grand, impressive, dignified, stout, fat, heavy, obese.
(ANT.) slender, thin, slim.

portrait *(SYN.)* painting, representation, picture, likeness.

portray *(SYN.)* depict, picture, represent, sketch, describe, delineate, paint.
(ANT.) misrepresent, caricature, suggest.

pose *(SYN.)* model.

position *(SYN.)* caste, site, locality, situation, condition, standing, incumbency, office, bearing, posture, berth, place, job, pose, rank, attitude, location, place, spot, station, job, situation, occupation.

positive *(SYN.)* sure, definite, fixed, inevitable, undeniable, indubitable, assured, certain, unquestionable, unmistakable.
(ANT.) uncertain, doubtful, questionable, probably, unsure, dubious, confused, negative, adverse.

positively *(SYN.)* unquestionably, surely, certainly, absolutely.

possess *(SYN.)* own, obtain, control, have, seize, hold, occupy, affect, hold, control.
(ANT.) surrender, abandon, lose, renounce.

possessed *(SYN.)* entranced, obsessed, consumer, haunted, enchanted.

possession *(SYN.)* custody, ownership, occupancy.

possessions *(SYN.)* commodities, effects, goods, property, merchandise, wares, wealth, belongings, stock.

possible *(SYN.)* likely, practical, probable, feasible, plausible, credible, practicable.
(ANT.) visionary, impossible, improbable.

possibility *(SYN.)* opportunity, chance, contingency, occasion.
(ANT.) obstacle, disadvantage, hindrance.

possible *(SYN.)* feasible, practical, practicable, doable.

possibly *(SYN.)* perchance, perhaps, maybe.

post *(SYN.)* position, job, berth, incumbency, situation, shaft, pole, fort, base, station.

postpone *(SYN.)* delay, stay, suspend, discontinue, defer, adjourn, interrupt, put off.
(ANT.) persist, prolong, maintain, continue, proceed.

postulate *(SYN.)* principle, adage, saying, proverb, truism, byword, aphorism, axiom, fundamental, maxim.

potency *(SYN.)* effectiveness, capability, skillfulness, efficiency, competency, ability.
(ANT.) wastefulness, inability, ineptitude.

potent *(SYN.)* mighty, influential, convincing, effective.
(ANT.) feeble, weak, powerless, impotent.

potential *(SYN.)* likely, possible, dormant, hidden, latent.

pouch *(SYN.)* container, bag, sack.

pound *(SYN.)* buffet, beat, punch, strike, thrash, defeat, subdue, pulse, smite, belabor, knock, thump, overpower, palpitate, rout, vanquish.
(ANT.) fail, surrender, stroke, defend, shield.

pour *(SYN.)* flow.

pout *(SYN.)* brood, sulk, mope.

poverty *(SYN.)* necessity, need, want, destitution, privation, indigence, distress.
(ANT.) plenty, abundance, wealth, riches, affluence, richness, comfort.

power *(SYN.)* potency, might, authority, control, predominance, capability, faculty, validity, force, vigor, command, influence, talent, ability, dominion, competency.
(ANT.) incapacity, fatigue, weakness, disablement, impotence, ineptitude.

powerful *(SYN.)* firm, strong, concentrated, enduring, forcible, robust, sturdy, tough, athletic, forceful, hale, impregnable, hardy, mighty, potent.
(ANT.) feeble, insipid, brittle, delicate, fragile, weak, ineffectual, powerless.

practical *(SYN.)* sensible, wise, prudent, reasonable, sagacious, sober, sound, workable, attainable.
(ANT.) stupid, unaware, impalpable, imperceptible, absurd, impractical.

practically *(SYN.)* almost, nearly.

practice *(SYN.)* exercise, habit, custom, manner, wont, usage, drill, tradition, performance, action, repetition.
(ANT.) inexperience, theory, disuse, idleness, speculation.

practiced *(SYN.)* able, expert, skilled, adept.
(ANT.) inept.

prairie *(SYN.)* plain, grassland.

praise *(SYN.)* applaud, compliment, extol, laud, glorify, commend, acclaim, eulogize, flatter, admire, celebrate, commendation, approval.
(ANT.) criticize, censure, reprove, condemn, disparage, disapprove, criticism, negation.

pray *(SYN.)* supplicate, importune, beseech, beg.

prayer *(SYN.)* plea, suit, appeal, invocation, supplication, petition, entreaty, request.

preach *(SYN.)* teach, urge, moralize, lecture.

preamble *(SYN.)* overture, prologue, beginning, introduction, prelude, start, foreword, preface.

(ANT.) *end, finale, completion, conclusion, epilogue.*

precarious (SYN.) dangerous, perilous, threatening, menacing, critical, risky, unsafe, hazardous.

(ANT.) *secure, firm, protected, safe.*

precaution (SYN.) foresight, forethought, care.

precedence (SYN.) preference, priority.

precedent (SYN.) model, example.

precept (SYN.) doctrine, tenet, belief, creed, teaching, dogma.

(ANT.) *practice, conduct, performance, deed.*

precious (SYN.) dear, useful, valuable, costly, esteemed, profitable, expensive, priceless, dear.

(ANT.) *poor, worthless, cheap, mean, trashy.*

precipice (SYN.) bluff, cliff.

precipitate (SYN.) speedy, swift, hasty, sudden.

precipitous (SYN.) unannounced, sudden, harsh, rough, unexpected, sharp, abrupt, hasty, craggy, steep, precipitate.

(ANT.) *expected, smooth, anticipated, gradual.*

precise (SYN.) strict, exact, formal, rigid, definite, unequivocal, prim, ceremonious, distinct, accurate, correct.

ANT.) *loose, easy, vague, informal, careless, erroneous.*

precisely (SYN.) specifically, exactly.

precision (SYN.) correction, accuracy, exactness.

preclude (SYN.) hinder, prevent, obstruct, forestall, obviate, thwart, impede.

(ANT.) *permit, aid, expedite, encourage, promote.*

preclusion (SYN.) omission, exception, exclusion.

(ANT.) *standard, rule, inclusion.*

predicament (SYN.) dilemma, plight, situation, condition, fix, difficulty, strait, scrape.

(ANT.) *satisfaction, comfort, east, calmness.*

predict (SYN.) forecast, foretell.

prediction (SYN.) forecast, prophecy.

predilection (SYN.) attachment, inclination, affection, bent, desire, penchant, disposition, preference.

ANT.) *repugnance, aversion, apathy, distaste, nonchalance.*

predominant (SYN.) highest, paramount, cardinal, foremost, main, first, leading, supreme, principal, essential, prevalent, dominant, prevailing.

(ANT.) *subsidiary, auxiliary, supplemental, minor, subordinate.*

predominate (SYN.) prevail, outweigh, rule.

preface (SYN.) foreword, introduction, preliminary, prelude, prologue, preamble.

prefer (SYN.) select, favor, elect, fancy.

preference (SYN.) election, choice, selection, alternative, option.

prejudice (SYN.) bias, favoritism, un-

fairness, partiality.

prejudiced (SYN.) fanatical, narrow-minded, dogmatic, bigoted, illiberal, intolerant.

(ANT.) *radical, liberal, tolerant, progressive.*

preliminary (SYN.) introductory, preparatory, prelude, preface.

premature (SYN.) early, untimely, unexpected.

(ANT.) *timely.*

premeditated (SYN.) intended, voluntary, contemplated, designed, intentional, willful, deliberate, studied.

(ANT.) *fortuitous, accidental.*

premeditation (SYN.) intention, deliberation, forethought, forecast.

(ANT.) *hazard, accident, impromptu, extemporization.*

premise (SYN.) basis, presupposition, assumption, postulate, principle, presumption.

(ANT.) *superstructure, derivative, trimming, implication.*

preoccupied (SYN.) abstracted, distracted, absorbed, meditative, inattentive, absent, absent-minded.

(ANT.) *attentive, alert, conscious, present, attending, watchful.*

prepare (SYN.) contrive, furnish, ready, predispose, condition, fit, arrange, plan, qualify, make ready, get ready.

preposterous (SYN.) foolish, nonsensical, silly, contradictory, unreasonable, absurd, inconsistent, irrational, self-contradictory.

(ANT.) *sensible, rational, consistent, sound, reasonable.*

prerequisite (SYN.) essential, requirement, necessity, condition, demand.

prerogative (SYN.) grant, right, license, authority, privilege.

(ANT.) *violation, encroachment, wrong, injustice.*

prescribe (SYN.) order, direct, designate.

presence (SYN.) nearness, attendance, closeness, vicinity, appearance, bearing, personality.

present (SYN.) donation, gift, today, now, existing, current, largess, donate, acquaint, introduce, being, give, gratuity, boon, grant.

(ANT.) *reject, spurn, accept, retain, receive.*

presentable (SYN.) polite, well-bred, respectable, well-mannered.

presently (SYN.) shortly, soon, directly, immediately.

preserve (SYN.) protect, save, conserve, maintain, secure, rescue, uphold, spare, keep, can, safeguard, defend, rescue.

(ANT.) *impair, abolish, destroy, abandon, squander, injure.*

preside (SYN.) officiate, direct, administrate.

press SYN.) impel, shove, urge, hasten, push, compress, squeeze, hug, crowd, propel, force, drive, embrace, smooth, iron, insist on, pressure, promote, urgency, jostle.

(ANT.) oppose, pull, falter, drag, retreat, ignore.

pressing *(SYN.)* impelling, insistent, necessary, urgent, compelling imperative, instant, serious, important, cogent, exigent, importunate.

(ANT.) unimportant, trifling, insignificant, petty, trivial.

pressure *(SYN.)* force, influence, stress, press, compulsion, urgency, constraint, compression.

(ANT.) relaxation, leniency, ease, recreation.

prestige *(SYN.)* importance, reputation, weight, influence, renown, fame, distinction.

presume *(SYN.)* guess, speculate, surmise, imagine, conjecture, apprehend, believe, think, assume, suppose, deduce.

(ANT.) prove, ascertain, demonstrate, know, conclude.

presumption *(SYN.)* boldness, impertinence, insolence, rudeness, assurance, effrontery, impudence, assumption, audacity, supposition, sauciness.

(ANT.) politeness, truckling, diffidence.

presumptuous *(SYN.)* bold, impertinent, fresh, imprudent, rude, forward, arrogant.

pretend *(SYN.)* feign, stimulate, act, profess, make believe, imagine, fake, sham, affect.

(ANT.) expose, reveal, display, exhibit.

pretense *(SYN.)* mask, pretext, show, affection, disguise, garb, semblance, simulation, fabrication, lie, excuse, falsification, deceit, subterfuge.

(ANT.) sincerity, actuality, truth, fact, reality.

pretentious *(SYN.)* gaudy, ostentatious.

(ANT.) simple, humble.

pretty *(SYN.)* charming, handsome, lovely, beauteous, fair, comely, attractive, beautiful, elegant.

(ANT.) repulsive, foul, unsightly, homely, plain, hideous.

prevail *(SYN.)* win, succeed, predominate, triumph.

(ANT.) yield, lose.

prevailing *(SYN.)* common, current, general, habitual, steady, regular, universal.

prevalent *(SYN.)* ordinary, usual, common, general, familiar, popular, prevailing, widespread, universal, frequent.

(ANT.) odd, scarce, exceptional, extraordinary.

prevent *(SYN.)* impede, preclude, forestall, stop, block, check, halt, interrupt, deter, slow, obviate, hinder, obstruct, thwart.

(ANT.) expedite, help, allow, abet, aid, permit, encourage, promote.

previous *(SYN.)* former, anterior, preceding, prior, antecedent, earlier, aforesaid, foregoing.

(ANT.) subsequent, following, consequent, succeeding, later.

prey *(SYN.)* raid, seize, victimize.

price *(SYN.)* worth, cost, expense, charge, value.

pride *(SYN.)* self-respect, vanity, glory, superciliousness, haughtiness, conceit, arrogance, self-importance, pretension, egotism, satisfaction, fulfillment, enjoyment, self-esteem.

(ANT.) modesty, shame, humbleness, lowliness, meekness, humility.

prim *(SYN.)* formal, puritanical, priggish, prudish.

primarily *(SYN.)* mainly, chiefly, firstly, essentially, originally.

(ANT.) secondarily.

primary *(SYN.)* first, principal, primeval, pristine, beginning, original, initial, fundamental, elementary, chief, foremost, earliest, main, prime.

(ANT.) subordinate, last, secondary, least, hindmost, latest.

prime *(SYN.)* first, primary, chief, excellent, best, superior, ready.

primeval *(SYN.)* fresh, primary, novel, inventive, creative, primordial, original, first, new, initial.

(ANT.) trite, modern, subsequent, banal, later, terminal, derivative.

primitive *(SYN.)* antiquated, early, primeval, prehistoric, uncivilized, uncultured, simple, pristine, old, aboriginal, unsophisticated, rude, rough, primary.

(ANT.) sophisticated, modish, civilized, cultured, cultivated, late.

principal *(SYN.)* first, leading, main, supreme, predominant, chief, foremost, highest, prime, primary, leader, headmaster, paramount, essential, cardinal.

(ANT.) supplemental, secondary, auxiliary, subsidiary, accessory, minor, subordinate.

principle *(SYN.)* law, method, axiom, rule, propriety, regulation, maxim, formula, order, statute.

(ANT.) exception, hazard, chance, deviation.

print *(SYN.)* issue, reprint, publish, letter, sign, fingerprint, mark, picture, lithograph, engraving, etching.

prior *(SYN.)* previous, aforesaid, antecedent, sooner, earlier, preceding, former, foregoing.

(ANT.) succeeding, following, later, consequent, subsequent.

prison *(SYN.)* brig, jail, stockade, penitentiary.

pristine *(SYN.)* primordial, creative, first, original, fresh, inventive, novel, primary, initial.

(ANT.) trite, terminal, derivative, modern, banal, subsequent, plagiarized, later.

private *(SYN.)* concealed, hidden, secret, clandestine, unknown, personal, surreptitious, covert, individual, particular, special, latent.

(ANT.) exposed, known, closed, general, public, conspicuous, disclosed, obvious.

privilege *(SYN.)* liberty, right, advantage, immunity, freedom, license, favor, sanction.

(ANT.) restriction, inhibition, prohibition, disallowance.

prize *(SYN.)* compensation, bonus, award, premium, remuneration, reward, bounty, esteem, value, rate, recompense, requital.
(ANT.) charge, punishment, wages, earnings, assessment.

probable *(SYN.)* presumable, likely.

probe *(SYN.)* stretch, reach, investigate, examine, examination, scrutiny, scrutinize, inquire, explore, inquiry, investigation, extend.
(ANT.) miss, short.

problem *(SYN.)* dilemma, question, predicament, riddle, difficulty, puzzle.

procedure *(SYN.)* process, way, fashion, form, mode, conduct, practice, manner, habit, system, operation, management, plan.

proceed *(SYN.)* progress, continue, issue, result, spring, thrive, improve, advance, emanate, rise.
(ANT.) retard, withhold, withdraw, hinder, retreat, oppose.

proceeding *(SYN.)* occurrence, business, affair, deal, negotiation, transaction, deed.

proceedings *(SYN.)* account, record, document.

proceeds *(SYN.)* result, produce, income, reward, intake, fruit, profit, store, yield, product, return, harvest, crop.

process *(SYN.)* method, course, system, procedure, operation, prepare, treat.

procession *(SYN.)* cortege, parade, sequence, train, cavalcade, file, retinue, succession.

proclaim *(SYN.)* declare, assert, make known, promulgate, state, assert, broadcast, express, announce, aver, advertise, tell, publish, profess.

proclamation *(SYN.)* declaration, announcement, promulgation.

procrastinate *(SYN.)* waver, vacillate, defer, hesitate, delay, postpone.

procreate *(SYN.)* generate, produce, beget, engender, originate, propagate, sire, create, father.
(ANT.) murder, destroy, abort, kill, extinguish.

procure *(SYN.)* secure, gain, win, attain, obtain, get, acquire, earn.
(ANT.) lose.

prod *(SYN.)* goad, nudge, jab, push.

produce *(SYN.)* harvest, reaping, bear, result, originate, bring about, store, supply, make, create, crop, proceeds.
(ANT.) conceal, reduce, destroy, consume, waste, hide.

product *(SYN.)* outcome, result, output, produce, goods, commodity, stock, merchandise.

productive *(SYN.)* fertile, luxuriant, rich, bountiful, fruitful, creative, fecund, teeming, plenteous, prolific.
(ANT.) wasteful, unproductive, barren, impotent, useless, sterile.

profanation *(SYN.)* dishonor, insult, outrage, defamation, abuse.
(ANT.) plaudit, commendation, laudation, respect, approval.

profane *(SYN.)* deflower, violate, desecrate, pollute, dishonor, ravish, debauch.

profess *(SYN.)* declare, assert, make known, state, protest, announce, aver, express, broadcast, avow, tell.
(ANT.) suppress, conceal, repress, withhold.

profession *(SYN.)* calling, occupation, vocation, employment.
(ANT.) hobby, avocation, pastime.

proffer *(SYN.)* extend, tender, volunteer, propose, advance.
(ANT.) reject, spurn, accept, receive, retain.

proficient *(SYN.)* competent, adept, clever, able, cunning, practiced, skilled, versed, ingenious, accomplished, skillful, expert.
(ANT.) untrained, inexpert, bungling, awkward, clumsy.

profit *(SYN.)* gain, service, advantage, return, earnings, emolument, improvement, benefit, better, improve, use, avail.
(ANT.) waste, loss, detriment, debit, lose, damage, ruin.

profitable *(SYN.)* beneficial, advantageous, helpful, wholesome, useful, gainful, favorable, beneficial, serviceable, salutary, productive, good.
(ANT.) harmful, destructive, injurious, deleterious, detrimental.

profound *(SYN.)* deep, serious, knowing, wise, intelligent, knowledgeable, recondite, solemn, abstruse, penetrating.
(ANT.) trivial, slight, shallow, superficial.

profuse *(SYN.)* lavish, excessive, extravagant, improvident, luxuriant, prodigal, wasteful, exuberant, immoderate, plentiful.
(ANT.) meager, poor, economical, sparse, skimpy.

profusion *(SYN.)* immoderation, superabundance, surplus, extravagance, intemperance, superfluity.
(ANT.) lack, paucity, death, want, deficiency.

program *(SYN.)* record, schedule, plan, agenda, calendar.

progress *(SYN.)* advancement, improvement, development, betterment, advance, movement, improve, progression.
(ANT.) delay, regression, relapse, retrogression, decline.

progression *(SYN.)* gradation, string, train, chain, arrangement, following, arrangement, order.

prohibit *(SYN.)* hinder, forbid, disallow, obstruct, prevent, stop, ban, interdict, debar.
(ANT.) help, tolerate, allow, sanction, encourage, permit.

prohibition *(SYN.)* prevention, ban, embargo, restriction.
(ANT.) allowance, permission.

prohibitive *(SYN.)* forbidding, restrictive.

project *(SYN.)* design, proposal, scheme, contrivance, outline, homework, activity, purpose, bulge, protrude, throw, cast, device, plan.

(ANT.) production, accomplishment, performance.
prolific *(SYN.)* fertile, rich, fruitful, teeming, fecund, bountiful, luxuriant, productive, plenteous.
(ANT.) unproductive, barren, sterile, impotent.
prolong *(SYN.)* extend, increase, protract, draw, stretch, lengthen.
(ANT.) shorten.
prominent *(SYN.)* distinguished, illustrious, outstanding, renowned, influential, famous, well-known, noted, notable, important, conspicuous, eminent, leading, celebrated.
(ANT.) low, vulgar, ordinary, common.
promise *(SYN.)* assurance, guarantee, pledge, undertaking, agreement, bestowal, word, contract, oath, vow.
promote *(SYN.)* advance, foster, encourage, assist, support, further, aid, help, elevate, raise, facilitate, forward.
(ANT.) obstruct, demote, hinder.
prompt *(SYN.)* punctual, timely, exact, arouse, evoke, occasion, induce, urge, ineffect, cite, suggest, hint, cause, mention, propose, make, precise, originate. *(ANT.) laggardly, slow, tardy, dilatory.*
promptly *(SYN.)* immediately, instantly, straightway, forthwith, directly, instantaneously, presently.
(ANT.) later, sometime, hereafter, distantly, shortly.
prone *(SYN.)* apt, inclined, disposed, likely, predisposed.
pronounce *(SYN.)* proclaim, utter, announce, articulate, enunciate.
pronounced *(SYN.)* clear, definite.
(ANT.) minor, unnoticeable.
proof *(SYN.)* evidence, verification, confirmation, experiment, demonstration, testimony, trial, protected, impenetrable, corroboration, test.
(ANT.) fallacy, invalidity, failure.
propel *(SYN.)* drive, push, transfer, actuate, induce, shift, persuade, move.
(ANT.) stay, deter, halt, rest, stop.
proper *(SYN.)* correct, suitable, decent, peculiar, legitimate, right, conventional, decent, just, well-mannered, seemly, fit, appropriate, fitting, respectable, special.
property *(SYN.)* real estate, effects, possessions, quality, characteristic.
(ANT.) poverty, destitution, want, deprivation.
prophecy *(SYN.)* augury, prediction.
prophet *(SYN.)* fortuneteller, oracle, seer, soothsayer, clairvoyant.
proportion *(SYN.)* steadiness, poise, composure, relation, balance, equilibrium, comparison, section, part, arrange, adjust, symmetry.
(ANT.) unsteadiness, imbalance, fall.
proposal *(SYN.)* plan, proposition, tender, scheme, program, offer, suggestion, overture.
(ANT.) rejection, acceptance, denial.
propose *(SYN.)* offer, proffer, recommend, plan, mean, expect, move, design, propound, present, tender.
(ANT.) fulfill, perform, effect.

proposition *(SYN.)* proposal, motion.
propound *(SYN.)* bring forward, offer, advance, allege, propose, assign.
(ANT.) retreat, hinder, withhold, retard.
proprietor *(SYN.)* master, owner.
(ANT.) slave, servant.
(ANT.) exciting, different, extraordinary.
proscribe *(SYN.)* forbid, ban, prohibit.
(ANT.) permit, allow.
prospect *(SYN.)* anticipation, expectation, candidate, buyer, explore, search.
prospective *(SYN.)* planned, proposed.
prosper *(SYN.)* succeed, win, achieve, gain, rise, prevail, flourish, thrive.
(ANT.) miscarry, wane, miss, fail.
prosperous *(SYN.)* rich, wealthy, affluent, well-to-do, sumptuous, well-off, flourishing, thriving, opulent.
(ANT.) impoverished, indigent, beggarly, needy, destitute, poor.
prostrate *(SYN.)* prone, supine, overcome, recumbent, crushed.
protect *(SYN.)* defend, preserve, save, keep, conserve, safeguard, maintain, guard, shield, secure.
(ANT.) impair, abandon, destroy, abolish, injure.
protection *(SYN.)* safeguard, shelter, security, bulwark, fence, guard, safety, assurance, defense, refuge, shield.
protest *(SYN.)* dissent, noncompliance, disagree, objection, disagreement.
(ANT.) acquiesce, assent, compliance, concur, comply, acceptance, approval.
prototype *(SYN.)* model, archetype, specimen, instance, illustration, example, pattern, sample.
(ANT.) rule, concept, precept, principle.
protract *(SYN.)* extend, strain, distend, expand, spread, stretch, elongate.
(ANT.) tighten, contract, loosen, shrink.
protuberance *(SYN.)* prominence, projection, bulge, protrusion, swelling.
proud *(SYN.)* overbearing, vain, arrogant, haughty, stately, vain, glorious.
(ANT.) humble, meek, ashamed, lowly.
prove *(SYN.)* manifest, verify, confirm, demonstrate, establish, show, affirm, examine, corroborate, try, test.
(ANT.) contradict, refute, disprove.
proverb *(SYN.)* maxim, byword, saying, adage, byword, saw, motto, apothegm.
provide *(SYN.)* supply, endow, afford, produce, yield, give, fit, equip, furnish, bestow, fit out.
(ANT.) strip, denude, divest, despoil.
provident *(SYN.)* saving, thrifty, economical, frugal, sparing.
(ANT.) wasteful, lavish, extravagant.
provision *(SYN.)* supply, fund, condition, arrangement, accumulation, reserve, store, hoard.
provisions *(SYN.)* stock, supplies, store.
provoke *(SYN.)* excite, stimulate, agitate, arouse, incite, stir up, vex, bother, disquiet, excite, irritate, annoy.
(ANT.) quell, allay, pacify, calm, quiet.
prowl *(SYN.)* sneak, slink, lurk.
proximate *(SYN.)* nigh, imminent, adjacent, neighboring, bordering, close, impending, approaching.
(ANT.) removed, distant, far.
proxy *(SYN.)* representative, equivalent,

makeshift, alternate, deputy, substitute, expedient, lieutenant.
(ANT.) sovereign, head, principal.
prudence *(SYN.)* watchfulness, care, heed, vigilance, wariness, carefulness, tact, judgment, wisdom, common, foresight, caution.
(ANT.) rashness, recklessness, abandon, foolishness, carelessness.
prudent *(SYN.)* reasonable, sensible, sound, discreet, practical, judicious, sagacious, sensible, provident, sage, intelligent, sober, careful, wise.
(ANT.) stupid, unaware, absurd.
pry *(SYN.)* peer, peep, meddle, peek.
prying *(SYN.)* inquisitive, meddling, curious, inquiring, nosy, peering, searching, interrogative, snoopy.
(ANT.) unconcerned, incurious, indifferent, uninterested.
psyche *(SYN.)* judgment, reason, understanding, brain, intellect, mentality, soul, mind, faculties, spirit.
(ANT.) materiality, body, matter.
public *(SYN.)* common, civil, governmental, federal, unrestricted, people, society, open.
publish *(SYN.)* distribute, issue, declare, announce, reveal, proclaim, publicize.
pull *(SYN.)* attract, induce, prolong, draw, tow, drag, remove, take out, persuade, allure, entice, extract.
(ANT.) shorten, alienate, drive, propel.
pulsate *(SYN.)* beat, throb, palpitate.
pump *(SYN.)* interrogate, question, ask, inquire, quiz, examine, query.
(ANT.) state, answer, respond, reply.
punish *(SYN.)* correct, pummel, chasten, reprove, strike, castigate, chastise.
(ANT.) release, exonerate, reward, pardon, acquit, free.
punishment *(SYN.)* correction, discipline.
(ANT.) turbulence, chaos, confusion.
pupil *(SYN.)* student, undergraduate.
purchase *(SYN.)* get, procure, buy, shopping, acquire, obtain.
(ANT.) sell, dispose of, vend.
pure *(SYN.)* chaste, absolute, clean, immaculate, untainted, spotless.
(ANT.) corrupt, mixed, defiled, foul, tainted, adulterated, polluted.
purify *(SYN.)* cleanse, wash, clean, mop.
(ANT.) soil, dirty, sully, stain, pollute.
purpose *(SYN.)* intention, end, goal, aim, objective, application, use, drift.
(ANT.) hazard, accident, fate.
pursue *(SYN.)* persist, track follow, hunt, hound, chase, trail.
(ANT.) evade, abandon, flee, elude.
pursuit *(SYN.)* hunt, chase.
push *(SYN.)* jostle, shove, urge, press, thrust, force, drive, crowd, hasten.
(ANT.) ignore, falter, halt, drag, oppose.
pushy *(SYN.)* impudent, abrupt, prominent, insolent, forward, brazen.
(ANT.) retiring, timid, cowardly.
put *(SYN.)* set, place, state, express, say, assign, attach, establish.
puzzle *(SYN.)* mystery, mystify, confound, perplex, riddle, conundrum.
(ANT.) key, solution, solve, explain, answer, resolution, illumine, clue.

quack *(SYN.)* faker, fake, fraud, gaggle, clack, gabble, bluffer, cackle, dissembler, charlatan, impostor.
quackery *(SYN.)* charlatanism, deceit, make-believe, fakery, duplicity, dissimulation, pretense, fraudulence, sham, counterfeiting, show.
(ANT.) integrity, probity, veracity, sincerity, honesty.
quaff *(SYN.)* swig, swill, swallow, lap up, sip, drink, ingurgitate, guzzle, imbibe.
quagmire *(SYN.)* swamp, bog, fen, ooze, morass, slough, marsh, plight, predicament, dilemma, impasse, fix, entanglement, quicksand, hole, quandary.
quail *(SYN.)* recoil, cower, flinch, blench, wince, falter, shrink, shake, hesitate, faint, droop.
(ANT.) brave, resist, defy, withstand.
quaint *(SYN.)* odd, uncommon, old-fashioned, antique, antiquated, queer, unusual, curious, eccentric, peculiar, picturesque, singular, whimsical, droll, charming, fanciful, droll, strange.
(ANT.) usual, normal, common, novel, ordinary, modern, current, commonplace, familiar.
quake *(SYN.)* shake, tremble, shudder, quiver, pulsate, stagger, shiver, temblor, vibrate, quaver, throb, earthquake.
qualification *(SYN.)* efficiency, adaptation, restriction, aptness, skill, ability, faculty, talent, power, aptitude, competence, suitability, capability, fitness, condition, dexterity.
(ANT.) unreadiness, incapacity, disability.
qualified *(SYN.)* clever, skillful, efficient, suitable, able, capable, fit, fitted, suited, bounded, limited, contingent, eligible, delimited, adept, circumscribed, equipped, modified, competent.
(ANT.) deficient, inept, impotent, categorical, unlimited, unfitted, unfit, incapable, unsuitable, inadequate.
qualify *(SYN.)* fit, suit, befit, ready, prepare, empower, lessen, moderate, soften, capacitate, condition, adapt, label, designate, name, call, equip, train, restrict, restrict, limit, change.
(ANT.) unfit, incapacitate, disable, disqualify, enlarge, reinforce, aggravate.
quality *(SYN.)* trait, feature, attribute, value, peculiarity, grade, caliber, character, distinction, rank, condition, status, characteristic, kind, nature, constitution, mark, type, property.
(ANT.) nature, inferiority, mediocrity, triviality, indifference, inferior, shoddy, second-rate, being, substance, essence.
qualm *(SYN.)* doubt, uneasiness, anxiety, suspicion, skepticism, question, pang, compunction, twinge, regret, uncertainty, demur, fear, remorse, misgiving.
(ANT.) security, comfort, confidence, easiness, invulnerability, firmness.
quandary *(SYN.)* predicament, perplexity, confusion, uncertainty, puzzle, plight, bewilderment, fix, difficulty, entanglement, impasse, doubt, dilemma.

(ANT.) *ease, relief, certainty, assurance.*

quantity (SYN.) sum, measure, volume, content, aggregate, bulk, mass, portion, amount, number, multitude, extent.
(ANT.) *zero, nothing.*

quarantine (SYN.) segregate, separate, confine, isolate, seclude.

quarrel (SYN.) contention, argument, affray, dispute, altercation, squabble, feud, difference, disagree, bicker, differ, spar, fight, bickering, tiff, argue, disagreement, spat.
(ANT.) *peace, friendliness, reconciliation, amity, agreement, sympathy, accord, concur, support, agree, unity, harmony.*

quarrelsome (SYN.) testy, contentious, edgy, peevish, irritable, snappish, argumentative, disputatious, cranky, belligerent, combative, disagreeable.
(ANT.) *genial, friendly, peaceful, easygoing, peaceable, tempered.*

quarry (SYN.) prey, quest, game, victim, goal, aim, prize, objective.

quarter (SYN.) place, source, fount, well, origin, mainspring, ruth, mercy, pity, compassion, clemency, spring, benevolence, forbearance.
(ANT.) *ruthlessness, brutality, cruelty, barbarity, harshness, ferocity.*

quarters (SYN.) residence, rooms, lodgings, dwelling, flat, billets, chambers, accommodations.

quash (SYN.) void, annul, overthrow, nullify, suppress, cancel, quench, quell, repress, invalidate.
(ANT.) *reinforce, sustain, authorize, sanction, validate, incite.*

quasi (SYN.) would-be, partial, synthetic, nominal, imitation, bogus, sham, counterfeit, mock.
(ANT.) *certified, real, legitimate.*

quaver (SYN.) tremble, shake, hesitate, trill, oscillate, waver, vibrate, shiver, quiver, falter, quake.

quay (SYN.) dock, wharf, pier, jetty, bank.

queasy (SYN.) sick, squeamish, nauseated, uneasy, queer, restless, nauseous, uncomfortable.
(ANT.) *untroubled, comfortable, easy, relaxed.*

queen (SYN.) empress, diva, doyenne, goddess, star.

queer (SYN.) odd, quaint, curious, unusual, droll, strange, peculiar, extraordinary, singular, uncommon, eccentric, weird, funny, nutty, screwy, wacky, deviant, whimsical.
(ANT.) *familiar, usual, normal, common, commonplace, plain, patent, conventional, ordinary.*

queerness (SYN.) oddity, oddness, freakishness, strangeness, singularity, outlandishness, anomaly, weirdness.
(ANT.) *normality, familiarity, commonness, standardization.*

quell (SYN.) subdue, calm, pacify, quiet, cool, hush, appease, lull, mollify, reduce, crush, smother, suppress, stifle, extinguish.
(ANT.) *encourage, foment, arouse,* foster, incite.

quench (SYN.) extinguish, stop, suppress, sate, allay, abate, stifle, slacken, put out, slake, satisfy.
(ANT.) *set, light, begin, start, kindle.*

querulous (SYN.) faultfinding, fretful, carping, critical, complaining, censorious, captious, petulant.
(ANT.) *pleased, easygoing, contented, carefree.*

query (SYN.) inquire, interrogate, demand, investigate, probe, examine, question, inquiry, ask.
(ANT.) *answer.*

quest (SYN.) investigation, interrogation, research, examination, search, question, exploration, seek, pursue, journey, hunt, pursuit, explore, query.
(ANT.) *negligence, inactivity, disregard.*

question (SYN.) interrogate, quiz, doubt, ask, pump, challenge, inquiry, uncertainty, interview, suspect, inquire, dispute, demand, examine, query.
(ANT.) *accept, solution, reply, assurance, rejoinder, state, answer, result, response, attest, avow, confidence, respond.*

questionable (SYN.) uncertain, doubtful, dubious, implausible, debatable, hypothetical, unlikely.
(ANT.) *obvious, assured, indubitable, proper, unimpeachable, seemly, conventional, sure, certain.*

queue (SYN.) file, row, line, series, chain, tier, sequence, string.

quibble (SYN.) cavil, shift, evasion, equivocation, dodge, sophism, prevaricate, quiddity, palter.

quick (SYN.) rapid, touchy, shrewd, active, hasty, testy, nimble, irascible, discerning, fast, swift, precipitate, excitable, speedy, sharp, impatient, acute, abrupt, curt, brisk, clever, keen, sensitive, lively.
(ANT.) *inattentive, dull, gradual, patient, slow, unaware, unhurried, backward, deliberate, sluggish.*

quicken (SYN.) expedite, forward, rush, hurry, accelerate, push, hasten, dispatch, facilitate, speed.
(ANT.) *slow, impede, hinder, hamper, delay, kill, deaden, retard, block.*

quickly (SYN.) soon, rapidly, fast, at once, promptly, presently, swiftly, hastily, fleety, headlong.
(ANT.) *deliberately, slowly, later, gradually.*

quickness (SYN.) energy, vigor, intensity, action, movement, briskness, exercise, motion, rapidity, agility, enterprise.
(ANT.) *sloth, idleness, inertia, dullness.*

quick-witted (SYN.) astute, shrewd, alert, keen, penetrating, quick, knowing, intelligent, clever.
(ANT.) *slow, dull, unintelligent, plodding.*

quiescent (SYN.) latent, resting, silent, tranquil, undeveloped, still, quiet, dormant, secret, unseen, inactive.
(ANT.) *visible, aroused, evident, active, patent, astir, manifest.*

quiet *(SYN.)* meek, passive, hushed, peaceful, calm, patient, quiescent, motionless, tranquil, gentle, undisturbed, mild, peace, silent, quiescence, hush, modest, quietude, rest, tranquillity, calmness, repose, silence, placid, serenity, soundless, immobile, still.
(ANT.) disturbed, agitation, excitement, loud, disturbance, restless, noisy, boisterous, anxious, perturbed, noise, agitated.

quietness *(SYN.)* tranquillity, repose, calm, silence, quietude, calmness, stillness, quietism, muteness, noiselessness, placidity, seclusion, soundlessness.
(ANT.) flurry, disturbance, fuss, turbulence, agitation, uproar, tumult.

quintessence *(SYN.)* heart, soul, extract, essence, distillation, core.
(ANT.) contingency, adjunct, excrescence, nonessential.

quip *(SYN.)* jest, sally, wisecrack, witticism, joke, jibe, pleasantry.

quirk *(SYN.)* mannerism, idiosyncrasy, foible, peculiarity, oddity, quiddity, vagary, habit, trait, eccentricity.

quirky *(SYN.)* odd, weird, whimsical, pe-culiar, pixilated, erratic, kinky.
(ANT.) normal, conventional, steady.

quisling *(SYN.)* collaborationist, traitor, subversive, betrayer.
(ANT.) partisan, loyalist.

quit *(SYN.)* leave, stop, desist, depart, abandon, resign, withdraw, refrain, retreat, cease, vacate, end, relinquish, discontinue, halt, lay off, surrender.
(ANT.) perservere, remain, stay, endure, persist, abide, continue.

quite *(SYN.)* somewhat, rather, completely, truly, absolutely, really, entirely.
(ANT.) hardly, merely, barely, somewhat.

quitter *(SYN.)* shirker, dropout, defeatist, piker, loser, malingerer.

quiver *(SYN.)* quake, shake, shudder, tremble, vibrate, shiver.

quixotic *(SYN.)* unrealistic, romantic, visionary, impractical, idealistic, chimerical, lofty, fantastic, fey.
(ANT.) pragmatic, realistic, prosaic, practical.

quiz *(SYN.)* challenge, interrogate, inquire, pump, doubt, question, ask, dispute, test, query, examine.
(ANT.) reply, say, inform, respond, accept, answer, state.

quizzical *(SYN.)* teasing, coy, mocking, derisive, insolent, arch, bantering, puzzled, questioning, baffled.
(ANT.) respectful, obsequious, uninterested, normal, everyday, usual, serious, attentive.

quota *(SYN.)* share, portion, apportionment, ratio, proportion, allotment.

quotation *(SYN.)* quote, selection, excerpt, repetition, cutting, reference.

quote *(SYN.)* refer to, recite, paraphrase, adduce, repeat, illustrate, cite, echo, plagiarize.
(ANT.) retort, contradict, refute.

rabble *(SYN.)* throng, mob, horde, crowd.

rabid *(SYN.)* frantic, frenzied, violent, raging, raving, zealous, fanatical.
(ANT.) normal, sound, sober, moderate.

race *(SYN.)* meet, run, clan, stock, lineage, strain, match, course, stream, hasten, compete, folk, competition, dash, contest, contend, hurry, speed, tribe.
(ANT.) linger, dawdle, dwell.

rack *(SYN.)* frame, framework, bracket, scaffold, skeleton.

racket *(SYN.)* sound, cry, babel, noise, uproar, hubbub, clamor, fuss, disturbance, din, tumult, fracas, clatter.
(ANT.) stillness, hush, silence, quiet, tranquillity, peace.

racy *(SYN.)* interesting, vigorous, lively, spirited, animated, entertaining.

radiance *(SYN.)* luster, brilliancy, brightness, splendor, effulgence, glowing.
(ANT.) gloom, darkness, obscurity.

radiant *(SYN.)* showy, superb, brilliant, illustrious, dazzling, grand, shining, bright, effulgent, beaming, sumptuous.
(ANT.) dark, unimpressive, dull, dim, lusterless, ordinary.

radiate *(SYN.)* spread, emit, diffuse, shed, irradiate, shine, gleam, illuminate.

radical *(SYN.)* ultra, innate, essential, organic, complete, revolutionary, insurgent, natural, total, fundamental, extreme, basic, original, thorough.
(ANT.) extraneous, moderate, conservative, superficial, shallow, established.

radius *(SYN.)* orbit, reach, extent, scope, sphere, range, sweep.

raft *(SYN.)* pontoon, platform, float.

rag *(SYN.)* dishcloth, dishrag, cloth.

ragamuffin *(SYN.)* tatterdemalion, wretch, beggar, vagabond, mendicant.

rage *(SYN.)* passion, ire, exasperation, fashion, fad, vogue, craze, anger, temper, fury, irritation, mania, rave, rant, storm, fume, overflow, wrath.
(ANT.) peace, forbearance, conciliation, patience.

raging *(SYN.)* raving, severe, passionate, boisterous, violent, fierce, wild, passionate, acute, intense, powerful.
(ANT.) feeble, soft, calm, quiet.

ragged *(SYN.)* tattered, torn, worn, shredded, seedy, threadbare, shabby.

raid *(SYN.)* assault, attack, invasion, arrest, invade, seizure, maraud, foray.

rail *(SYN.)* railing, fence, bar.

railing *(SYN.)* balustrade, banister, barrier, fence.

rain *(SYN.)* shower, drizzle, rainstorm, sprinkle, deluge, down-pour.

raise *(SYN.)* grow, muster, elevate, heave, cultivate, awake, rouse, excite, enlarge, increase, rise, breed, hoist, bring up, rear, gather, exalt, lift.
(ANT.) destroy, decrease, lessen, cut, depreciate, lower, abase, debase, drop, demolish, level.

rakish *(SYN.)* dapper, dashing, smart, debonair, natty, swanky, showy.

rally *(SYN.)* muster, convoke, summon,

convene, convention, assemblage.

ramble *(SYN.)* err, amble, saunter, wander, roam, saunter, walk, deviate, stroll, digress, stray.
(ANT.) stop, linger, stay, halt, settle.

rambling *(SYN.)* incoherent, erratic.
(ANT.) straightfoward, coherent.

rambunctious *(SYN.)* stubborn, defiant, unruly, aggressive, contrary.

ramification *(SYN.)* aftermath, extension, branch, offshoot, result, consequence.

rampage *(SYN.)* tumult, outbreak, uproar, rage, frenzy, ebullition, storm.

rampant *(SYN.)* excessive, flagrant, boisterous, menacing.
(ANT.) bland, calm, mild.

ramshackle *(SYN.)* rickety, decrepit, flimsy, dilapidated, shaky.

rancid *(SYN.)* spoiled, rank, tainted, sour, musty, putrid, rotten, purtrescent.
(ANT.) pure, fresh, wholesome, fragrant.

rancor *(SYN.)* spite, grudge, malice, animosity, malevolence, hostility.
(ANT.) kindness, toleration, affection.

random *(SYN.)* haphazard, chance, unscheduled, unplanned, casual.
(ANT.) intentional, specific, particular.

range *(SYN.)* expanse, extent, limit, area, grassland, pasture, plain, change, wander, roam, travel, rove.

rank *(SYN.)* estate, blood, range, grade, standing, hue, eminence, level, class, order, classify, dense, wild, rotten, degree, standing, arrange, sort, row.
(ANT.) shame, disrepute, stigma, humiliation.

ransack *(SYN.)* pillage, loot, rummage, plunder, despoil, ravish, search.

ransom *(SYN.)* release, deliverance, compensation, redeem.

rant *(SYN.)* declaim, rave, harangue.

rap *(SYN.)* thump, knock, blow, whack.

rapacious *(SYN.)* greedy, wolfish, avaricious, ravenous, grasping, predatory.

rapid *(SYN.)* speedy, quick, swift, fast.
(ANT.) deliberate, halting, sluggish, slow.

rapidity *(SYN.)* motion, enterprise, action, vigor, liveliness, activity, quickness, exercise, energy.
(ANT.) sloth, dullness, inertia, idleness.

rapine *(SYN.)* destruction, pillage, robbery, marauding, spoiling.

rapport *(SYN.)* harmony, fellowship, agreement, mutuality, accord, empathy.

rapture *(SYN.)* joy, gladness, ecstasy, bliss, transport, exultation, delight, happiness, enchantment, ravishment.
(ANT.) woe, misery, wretch, depression.

rare *(SYN.)* unique, strange, precious, uncommon, infrequent, choice, singular, occasional, unusual, fine, matchless, undone, incomparable, scarce.
(ANT.) worthless, common, commonplace, usual, everyday, customary.

rarely *(SYN.)* scarcely, hardly infrequently, occasionally, sparingly, barely.
(ANT.) usually, continually, often.

rascal *(SYN.)* scoundrel, villain, trickster, rogue, scamp, swindler, imp, prankster.

rash *(SYN.)* quick, careless, passionate, thoughtless, hotheaded, reckless, foolhardy, eruption, dermatitis, heedless.
(ANT.) thoughtful, considered, prudent, reasoning, calculating, careful.

raspy *(SYN.)* gruff, harsh, dissonant, grinding, hoarse, grating, strident.

rate *(SYN.)* try, adjudicate, consider, decide, condemn, decree, estimate, speed, pace, measure, judge, arbitrate, velocity, ratio, evaluate, evaluate.

ratify *(SYN.)* validate, certify, confirm, establish, support, endorse, uphold.

rating *(SYN.)* assessment, position, assignment, status, classification.

ration *(SYN.)* portion, allowance, distribute, measure, allotment, share, percentage.

rational *(SYN.)* sound, wise, sane, intelligent, sober, sensible, judicious, sober.
(ANT.) irrational, absurd, insane.

rationality *(SYN.)* cause, aim, intelligence, reason, basis, understanding, ground, argument, mind, sense.

raucous *(SYN.)* raspy, harsh, grating, hoarse, discordant, rowdy.
(ANT.) dulcet, pleasant, sweet.

ravage *(SYN.)* ruin, despoil, strip, waste, destroy, pillage, plunder, sack, havoc.
(ANT.) conserve, save, accumulate.

rave *(SYN.)* rage, storm, laud, praise.

ravenous *(SYN.)* hungry, voracious, craving, starved, gluttonous, famished.
(ANT.) replete, gorged, satiated, full.

ravine *(SYN.)* chasm, gorge, crevasse, canyon, abyss.

ravish *(SYN.)* violate, debauch.

ravishing *(SYN.)* enchanting, captivating, bewitching, fascinating, alluring.
(ANT.) loathsome, disgusting, repulsive.

raw *(SYN.)* harsh, rough, coarse, unrefined, undone, uncooked, unprocessed, crude, unpolished, natural.
(ANT.) finished, refined, processed.

ray *(SYN.)* beam.

raze *(SYN.)* ravage, wreck, destroy, flatten, annihilate, obliterate, demolish.
(ANT.) make, erect, construct, preserve, establish, save.

reach *(SYN.)* overtake, arrive at, extent, distance, scope, range, extend, attain, stretch.
(ANT.) fail, miss.

react *(SYN.)* result, reply, respond.
(ANT.) overlook, disregard.

reaction *(SYN.)* result, response, reception, repercussion.

readable *(SYN.)* understandable, distinct, legible, plain, clear, comprehensible.
(ANT.) obliterated, illegible, defaced.

readily *(SYN.)* quickly, promptly, easily.

ready *(SYN.)* mature, ripe, complete, seasonable, done, arrange, prompt, prepared, completed, quick, mellow.
(ANT.) undeveloped, immature, green.

real *(SYN.)* true, actual, positive, authentic, genuine, veritable.

(ANT.) counterfeit, unreal, fictitious, false, sham, supposed.

realization *(SYN.)* completion, achievement, performance, accomplishment, comprehension, insight.
(ANT.) failure.

realize *(SYN.)* discern, learn, comprehend, appreciate, perfect, actualize, understand, apprehend, know, see.
(ANT.) misunderstand, misapprehend.

really *(SYN.)* truly, actually, honestly, undoubtedly, positively, genuinely.
ANT.) questionably, possibly, doubtfully.

realm *(SYN.)* land, domain, farm, kingdom, sphere, department, estate, world.

reap *(SYN.)* gather, harvest, gain, glean, produce, cut, pick, acquire, garner.
(ANT.) plant, seed, sow, lose, squander.

reaping *(SYN.)* proceeds, result, crop, yield, fruit, produce.

rear *(SYN.)* posterior, raise, lift, train, nurture, rump, back, elevate, construct, build, foster.

reason *(SYN.)* intelligence, objective, understanding, mind, aim, argument, cause, aim, judgment, common sense, sanity, gather, assume, sake, motive.

reasonable *(SYN.)* prudent, rational, logical, sage, sound, moderate, intelligent, sensible, discreet.
(ANT.) unaware, imperceptible, insane, absurd, stupid, illogical, irrational.

rebel *(SYN.)* revolutionary, traitor, mutineer, mutiny, revolt, disobey.

rebellion *(SYN.)* revolt, uprising, coup, overthrow, insurrection, revolution.
(ANT.) submission, obedience, repression, peace.

rebellious *(SYN.)* unruly, forward, defiant, undutiful, disobedient.
(ANT.) obedient, compliant, submissive.

rebirth *(SYN.)* renascence, renaissance, revival.

rebuff *(SYN.)* snub, oppose, resist, reject, refuse, slight, opposition.
(ANT.) welcome, encourage, support.

rebuild *(SYN.)* restore, renew, refresh, reconstruct, renovate.

rebuke *(SYN.)* chide, scold, reproach, censure, upbraid, scolding, condemn.
(ANT.) praise, exonerate, absolve.

rebuttal *(SYN.)* contradiction, defense, answer.
(ANT.) argument, validation, corroboration.

recall *(SYN.)* recollect, remembrance, withdraw, retract, remember, recollection, reminisce, mind, memory, remind.
(ANT.) forget, overlook, ignore.

recede *(SYN.)* withdraw, ebb, retire, retreat.

receive *(SYN.)* entertain, acquire, admit, accept, shelter, greet, obtain, welcome.
(ANT.) reject, offer, give, bestow, discharge, impart.

recent *(SYN.)* novel, original, late, new, newfangled, fresh, modern, current.
(ANT.) old, antiquated, ancient.

reception *(SYN.)* gathering, party.

recess *(SYN.)* hollow, opening, nook, cranny, dent, respite, rest, break, pause.
(ANT.) gather, convene.

recession *(SYN.)* slump, depression.

recipe *(SYN.)* instructions, formula, prescriptions, procedure, method.

recital *(SYN.)* history, account, relation, chronicle, narrative, detail, narration.
(ANT.) distortion, confusion, misrepresentation.

recite *(SYN.)* describe, narrate, declaim, rehearse, tell, mention, repeat, detail, recapitulate, report, list, relate, deliver.

reckless *(SYN.)* thoughtless, inconsiderate, careless, imprudent, rash, indiscreet, unconcerned.
(ANT.) careful, nice, accurate.

reclaim *(SYN.)* reform, rescue, reinstate, regenerate, recycle.

recline *(SYN.)* stretch, sprawl, repose, rest, lounge, loll, incline.

recluse *(SYN.)* hermit, eremite, loner, anchorite.

recognize *(SYN.)* remember, avow, own, know, admit, apprehend, recollect, recall, concede, acknowledge, confess.
(ANT.) disown, ignore, renounce.

recollect *(SYN.)* recall, remember, memory, reflect, call to mind, reminisce.
(ANT.) forget.

recollection *(SYN.)* remembrance, retrospection, impression, recall.
(ANT.) forgetfulness, oblivion.

recommend *(SYN.)* hind, refer, advise, commend, suggest, counsel, allude, praise, approve, intimate, advocate.
(ANT.) disapprove, declare, insist.

recommendation *(SYN.)* instruction, justice, trustworthiness, counsel, admonition, caution, integrity, uprightness.
(ANT.) fraud, deceit, trickery, cheating.

reconcile *(SYN.)* meditate, unite, adapt, adjust, settle, reunite, appease.

recondition *(SYN.)* rebuild, overhaul, restore, service.

reconsider *(SYN.)* ponder, reevaluate, mull over, reflect, reassess.

record *(SYN.)* enter, write, register, chronicle, history, account, document.

recount *(SYN.)* report, convey, narrate, tell, detail, recite, describe, repeat.

recoup *(SYN.)* regain, recover, repay, retrieve.

recover *(SYN.)* regain, redeem, recapture, retrieve, salvage, better, improve, mend, heal.
(ANT.) debilitate, succumb, worsen.

recreation *(SYN.)* entertainment, amusement, enjoyment, diversion, fun.

recrimination *(SYN.)* vindication, reproach, dissension, accusation, countercharge.

recruit *(SYN.)* trainee, beginner, volunteer, draftee, select, enlist, novice.

recuperate *(SYN.)* regain, retrieve, cure, recapture, redeem, rally, convalesce, revive, recover, repossess, restore.
(ANT.) sicken, weaken, lose, regress, forfeit.

redeem *(SYN.)* claim, recover, repossess, regain, reclaim, cash in, retrieve.

reduce *(SYN.)* lessen, decrease, lower, downgrade, degrade, suppress, lower, abate, diminish.
(ANT.) enlarge, swell, raise, elevate, revive, increase, amplify.

reduction *(SYN.)* shortening, abridgment, abbreviation.
(ANT.) amplification, extension, enlargement.

reek *(SYN.)* odor, stench, stink, smell.

refer *(SYN.)* recommend, direct, commend, regard, concern, relate, suggest, mention.

referee *(SYN.)* judge, arbitrator, umpire, arbiter, moderator, mediator, intermediary.

reference *(SYN.)* allusion, direction, mention, concern, respect, referral.

refine *(SYN.)* purify, clarify, improve, clean.
(ANT.) pollute, debase, muddy, downgrade.

refined *(SYN.)* purified, cultured, cultivated, courteous, courtly.
(ANT.) rude, coarse, crude, vulgar.

refinement *(SYN.)* culture, enlightenment, education, civilization.
(ANT.) vulgarity, ignorance, boorishness.

reflect *(SYN.)* muse, mirror, deliberate, cogitate, think, reproduce, ponder, consider, reason, meditate, contemplate.

reflection *(SYN.)* warning, conception, intelligence, appearance, likeness, image, cogitation, notification.

reform *(SYN.)* right, improve, correction, change, amend, improvement, better, betterment, correct, rectify.
(ANT.) spoil, damage, aggravate, vitiate.

refresh *(SYN.)* exhilarate, renew, invigorate.
(ANT.) exhaust, tire.

refreshing *(SYN.)* bracing, cool, brisk, fresh.

refreshment *(SYN.)* food, snack, drink, nourishment, exhilaraton, stimulation.

refuge *(SYN.)* safety, retreat, shelter, asylum, sanctuary, harbor.
(ANT.) peril, exposure, jeopardy, danger.

refuse *(SYN.)* spurn, rebuff, decline, reject, trash, rubbish, withhold, disallow, waste, garbage, deny, demur.
(ANT.) allow, accept, welcome, grant.

refute *(SYN.)* rebut, disprove, confute, falsify, controvert, contradict.
(ANT.) prove, confirm, accept, establish.

regain *(SYN.)* redeem, retrieve, recover, repossess, recapture.
(ANT.) lose.

egalement *(SYN.)* feast, dinner, celebration, entertainment.

egard *(SYN.)* estimate, value, honor, affection, notice, care, consideration, consider, relation, respect, attend, thought, reference, care, attention, esteem, concern, liking.
(ANT.) neglect, disgust, antipathy.

egards *(SYN.)* salutations, greetings, good wishes, respects, remembrances.

regenerate *(SYN.)* improve, reconstruct, remedy, reestablish, rebuild.

regime *(SYN.)* direction, government, administration, management, dynasty, command, leadership.

regimented *(SYN.)* ordered, directed controlled, orderly, rigid, disciplined.
(ANT.) loose, free, unstructured.

region *(SYN.)* belt, place, spot, territory, climate, area, zone, locality, station, locale.

register *(SYN.)* catalog, record, book, list, roll, enter, roster, chronicle.

regressive *(SYN.)* revisionary, retrograde.
(ANT.) progressive, civilized, advanced.

regret *(SYN.)* sorrow, qualm, lament, grief, compunction, bemoan, concern, scruple, misgiving, remorse, contrition.
(ANT.) obduracy, complacency.

regular *(SYN.)* steady, orderly, natural, normal, customary, usual, habitual, even, uniform, systematic, unvaried, methodical, symmetrical.
(ANT.) odd, exceptional, unusual, irregular, abnormal, rare.

regulate *(SYN.)* control, manage, govern, direct, legislate, set, adjust, systematize.

regulation *(SYN.)* method, rule, axiom, guide, control, standard, canon, precept, restraint, requirement.
(ANT.) chaos, deviation, hazard, turbulence, confusion.

rehabilitate *(SYN.)* renew, restore, rebuild, reestablish, repair, reconstruct.

rehearse *(SYN.)* repeat, practice, train, learn, coach, prepare, perfect, direct.

reign *(SYN.)* dominion, power, rule, sovereignty, govern, domination.

reimburse *(SYN.)* recompense, remunerate, compensate, remit.

rein *(SYN.)* restriction, bridle, check, deterrent, curb, restraint, barrier, control.

reinforce *(SYN.)* brace, strengthen, fortify, intensify, support.

reiterate *(SYN.)* reproduce, recapitulate, duplicate, repeat, rephrase.

reject *(SYN.)* spurn, rebuff, decline, renounce, expel, discard, withhold, deny, refuse.
(ANT.) endorse, grant, welcome, accept.

rejection *(SYN.)* dissent, nonconformity, variance, challenge, remonstrance, difference, noncompliance.
(ANT.) assent, acceptance, compliance.

rejoice *(SYN.)* celebrate, delight, enjoy, revel, exhilarate, elate.

rejuvenate *(SYN.)* refresh, rekindle, overhaul, revitalize, animate, invigorate.
(ANT.) deplete, weaken, exhaust, eneverate.

relapse *(SYN.)* worsen, deteriorate, regress, weaken, fade, worsen, sink fail.
(ANT.) strengthen, progress, advance, get well, rehabilitate.

relate *(SYN.)* refer, beat, report, describe, tell, correlate, narrate, recount, compare, connect.

relation *(SYN.)* entente, compact, coalition, alliance, connection, relationship, association, partnership, similarity, kinsman, treaty, marriage.

(ANT.) separation, divorce.

relationship *(SYN.)* link, tie, alliance, connection, union, bond, affinity, conjunction.

(ANT.) separation, disunion.

relative *(SYN.)* dependent, proportional, about, pertinent, regarding.

relax *(SYN.)* slacken, loosen, repose, rest, recline, unwind.

(ANT.) increase, tighten, intensify.

relaxation *(SYN.)* comfort, ease, rest, enjoyment, lull, recess, breather, loafing.

relaxed *(SYN.)* welcome, pleasing, casual, acceptable, informal, restful, agreeable.

(ANT.) formal, planned, wretched, distressing, troubling.

release *(SYN.)* liberate, emancipate, relinquish, proclaim, publish, liberation, announce, deliver, free, discharge.

(ANT.) restrict, imprison, subjugate.

relegate *(SYN.)* entrust, authorize, remand, refer, assign.

relent *(SYN.)* cede, yield, surrender, give, relax, abdicate, relinquish, waive.

(ANT.) strive, assert, struggle.

relentless *(SYN.)* eternal, stubborn, tenacious, dogged, ceaseless, incessant, ceaseless, persistent, determined.

relevant *(SYN.)* related, material, apt, applicable, fit, relating, germane.

(ANT.) foreign, alien, unrelated.

reliable *(SYN.)* trusty, tried, certain, secure, trustworthy, dependable.

(ANT.) unreliable, eccentric, questionable, erratic, dubious.

reliance *(SYN.)* faith, confidence, trust.

(ANT.) mistrust, doubt, skepticism.

relic *(SYN.)* remains, fossil, throwback, heirloom, souvenir, keepsake, heirloom.

relief *(SYN.)* help, aid, comfort, ease, backing, patronage, alms, support.

(ANT.) hostility, defiance, antagonism, resistance.

relieve *(SYN.)* diminish, soothe, calm, abate, pacify, ease, lessen, replace, spell, lighten, comfort, alleviate.

(ANT.) disturb, irritate, agitate, trouble, aggravate, worry.

religion *(SYN.)* tenet, belief, dogma, faith, creed, persuasion.

religious *(SYN.)* godly, reverent, faithful, devout, zeal, pious, divine, holy, devoted, sacred, theological.

(ANT.) profane, irreligious, skeptical, impious, lax, atheistic.

religiousness *(SYN.)* love, zeal, affection, devoutness, fidelity, ardor.

(ANT.) indifference, apathy, unfaithfulness.

relinquish *(SYN.)* capitulate, submit, yield, abandon, cede, sacrifice, disclaim.

(ANT.) overcome, conquer, rout, resist.

relish *(SYN.)* enjoyment, satisfaction,

delight, gusto, appreciation, condiment, like, enjoy, enthusiasm.

(ANT.) distaste, antipathy, disfavor, dislike.

reluctance *(SYN.)* disgust, hatred, repulsion, abhorrence, distaste, repugnance, aversion.

(ANT.) enthusiasm, affection, devotion.

reluctant *(SYN.)* slow, averse, hesitant, unwilling, loath, disinclined, balky.

(ANT.) ready, eager, willing, disposed.

rely *(SYN.)* confide, trust, lean, depend.

(ANT.) mistrust, disbelieve, question, distrust.

remain *(SYN.)* survive, rest, stay, abide, halt, endure, dwell, tarry, continue, linger.

(ANT.) finish, leave, terminate, dissipate.

remainder *(SYN.)* leftover, residue, rest, surplus, balance, excess.

remains *(SYN.)* residue, balance, rest, remnants, relics, discards, waste, junk.

remark *(SYN.)* comment, state, utterance, mention, note, observe, observation, annotation, declaration, statement.

remarkable *(SYN.)* exciting, impressive, overpowering, unusual, affecting, thrilling, splendid, special, noteworthy, extraordinary, touching, august.

(ANT.) ordinary, unimpressive, commonplace, average, regular.

remedy *(SYN.)* redress, help, cure, relief, medicine, restorative, rectify, alleviate, medication, correct, reparation.

remember *(SYN.)* recollect, reminisce, recall, memorize, mind, retain, remind.

(ANT.) forget, overlook, disregard.

remembrance *(SYN.)* monument, memory, recollection, memento, recall, keepsake, souvenir, retrospection.

remiss *(SYN.)* delinquent, lax, careless, negligent, oblivious, forgetful, absentminded, sloppy, irresponsible.

remit *(SYN.)* send, pay, forward, forgive, pardon, overlook, excuse, reimburse.

remittance *(SYN.)* payment.

remnant *(SYN.)* remains, remainder, rest, residue, trace, relic.

remodel *(SYN.)* remake, reshape, rebuild, redecorate, renovate, modify, change, alter, convert, refurbish, update.

remonstrate *(SYN.)* grouch, protest, complain, grumble, murmur, repine, dispute.

(ANT.) rejoice, applaud, praise.

remorse *(SYN.)* sorrow, qualm, contrition, regret, compunction, repentance.

(ANT.) obduracy, complacency.

remorseless *(SYN.)* savage, unrelenting, crude, barbaric, merciless, cruel, fiendish, brutal, callous.

(ANT.) kind, refined, polite, civilized.

remote *(SYN.)* inconsiderable, removed, slight, far, unlikely, distant, inaccessible, unreachable, isolated, sequestered.

(ANT.) visible, nearby, current, near, close.

remove (SYN.) transport, eject, move, vacate, withdraw, dislodge, transfer, doff, displace, eliminate, murder, kill, oust, extract.
(ANT.) insert, retain, leave, stay, keep.

removed (SYN.) aloof, distant, cool, remote.

remuneration (SYN.) wages, payment, pay, salary, compensation, reimbursement, reward.

render (SYN.) become, make, perform, do, offer, present, give, submit.

rendition (SYN.) interpretation, version, depiction, expression, characterization.

renegade (SYN.) defector, insurgent, dissenter, rebel, maverick, mutineer, betrayer.

renege (SYN.) let down, doublecross, deceive.

renew (SYN.) restore, renovate, overhaul, revise, modernize, reshape, redo.

renounce (SYN.) resign, disown, revoke, abandon, quit, retract, forgo, leave, forsake, abdicate, reject, relinquish, deny.
(ANT.) assert, uphold, recognize, maintain.

renovate (SYN.) restore, rehabilitate, rebuild, refresh, renew, overhaul, redesign.

renown (SYN.) honor, reputation, eminence, acclaim, glory, repute, luster, fame, notability.
(ANT.) obscurity, anonymity, disgrace.

renowned (SYN.) noted, famous, distinguished, well-known, glorious, celebrated.
(ANT.) unknown, infamous, hidden, obscure.

rent (SYN.) payment, rental, let, lease, hire.

repair (SYN.) rebuilding, mend, renew, tinker, correct, patch, restore, adjust, reconstruction, remedy, amend, rehabilitation, retrieve.
(ANT.) harm, break.

repartee (SYN.) badinage, banter.

repast (SYN.) feast, banquet, meal, refreshment, snack.

repeal (SYN.) end, cancel, nullify, annul, quash, abolish, cancellation, rescind, abolition, abrogate.

repeat (SYN.) reiterate, restate, redo, rehearse, quote, remake, relate, iterate, reproduce.

repeated (SYN.) continuous, frequent, recurrent, continual.

repel (SYN.) check, repulse, rebuff, reject, decline, discourage.
(ANT.) lure, attract.

repellent (SYN.) sickening, offensive, disgusting, nauseating, repugnant, obnoxious.

repent (SYN.) deplore, regret, rue, lament.

repentance (SYN.) penitence, remorse, sorrow, compunction, qualm, grief.
(ANT.) obduracy, complacency.

repentant (SYN.) regretful, sorrowful, contrite, sorry, penitent.

(ANT.) remorseless, obdurate.

repetitious (SYN.) repeated, monotonous, boring, tiresome, humdrum.

repine (SYN.) protest, lament, complain, whine, regret, grouch, murmur, grumble.
(ANT.) rejoice, applaud, praise.

replace (SYN.) alternate, return, reinstate.

replacement (SYN.) understudy, proxy, second, alternate, substitute, replica, surrogate.

replenish (SYN.) store, pervade, fill, stock, occupy, supply.
(ANT.) empty, void, deplete, exhaust, drain.

replica (SYN.) reproduction, copy, exemplar, imitation, duplicate, facsimile.
(ANT.) prototype.

reply (SYN.) retort, rejoinder, answer, retaliate, respond, confirmation.
(ANT.) summoning, inquiry.

report (SYN.) declare, herald, publish, announce, summary, publish, advertise.
(ANT.) suppress, conceal, withhold, bury.

reporter (SYN.) journalist.

repose (SYN.) hush, quiet, tranquillity, rest, peace, slumber, calm, stillness, sleep, calmness, dormancy.
(ANT.) tumult, excitement, agitation.

reprehensible (SYN.) criminal, immoral, damnable, culpable, wrong, wicked.

represent (SYN.) picture, draw, delineate, portray, depict, denote, symbolize.
(ANT.) misrepresent, caricature.

representation (SYN.) effigy, film, likeness, portrait, print, scene, appearance, drawing, scene, view, cinema.

representative (SYN.) delegate, agent, substitute, surrogate.

repress (SYN.) limit, stop, check, bridle, curb, restrain, constrain, suppress.
(ANT.) loosen, aid, incite, liberate, encourage.

reprimand (SYN.) rate, scold, vituperate, berate, lecture, blame, admonish, upbraid.
(ANT.) praise, approve.

reproach (SYN.) defamation, dishonor, insult, profanation, abuse, disparagement, misuse, reviling.
(ANT.) respect, laudation, approval, plaudit.

reproduction (SYN.) replica, copy, exemplar, transcript, duplicate, photocopy.

reproof (SYN.) rebuke, punishment, blame, censure, disapproval, scorn, disdain, admonition.

repugnance (SYN.) disgust, hatred, reluctance, abhorrence, aversion, loathing, antipathy, distaste, repulsion.
(ANT.) devotion, affection, enthusiasm, attachment.

repulsive (SYN.) repellent, ugly, homely, deformed, horrid, offensive, plain, uncomely.
(ANT.) fair, pretty, attractive, hand-

some.

reputable *(SYN.)* honest, upstanding, trustworthy, straightforward, upright, reliable.
(ANT.) notorious, corrupt, disreputable.

reputation *(SYN.)* class, nature, standing, name, fame, kind, renown, prominence, character, distinction, disposition, repute.

repute *(SYN.)* class, nature, standing, kind, character, reputation, disposition, sort.

request *(SYN.)* sue, implore, petition, desire, appeal, question, entreaty, beseech, ask, pray, supplicate.
(ANT.) require.

require *(SYN.)* exact, need, order, command, order, lack, claim, demand, want.

requirement *(SYN.)* demand, need, necessity, condition, provision, prerequisite.

requisite *(SYN.)* vital, necessary, basic, fundamental, indispensable, essential, needed.
(ANT.) casual, nonessential, peripheral, accidental.

rescind *(SYN.)* annul, quash, revoke, abolish, invalidate, abrogate, withdraw.

rescue *(SYN.)* liberate, ransom, release, deliver, deliverance, liberation.

research *(SYN.)* exploration, quest, scrutiny, exploration, interrogation, query, examination, study, investigation.
(ANT.) inattention, disregard, negligence.

resemblance *(SYN.)* parity, similitude, analogy, likeness, correspondence.
(ANT.) distinction, difference.

resemble *(SYN.)* duplicate, mirror, look like.

resentfulness *(SYN.)* envy, jealousy, covetousness, suspicion.
(ANT.) liberality, geniality, tolerance, difference.

resentment *(SYN.)* displeasure, bitterness, indignation, rancor, outrage, hostility.
(ANT.) complacency, understanding, good will.

reservation *(SYN.)* skepticism, restriction, objection, limitation, doubt.

reserve *(SYN.)* fund, hold, keep, store, accumulation, save, stock, maintain, supply.
(ANT.) waste, squander.

reserved *(SYN.)* cautious, fearful, timorous, wary, aloof, chary, sheepish, restrained, proper, unfriendly, bashful, diffident.
(ANT.) forward, bold, wild, immodest, brazen, abandoned, friendly.

reside *(SYN.)* inhabit, dwell, abide, live, lie.

residence *(SYN.)* home, dwelling, stay, seat, abode, quarters, domicile, living quarters.

residue *(SYN.)* balance, remainder, rest, ashes, remnants, dregs, leftovers, ends.

resign *(SYN.)* vacate, withdraw, leave, surrender, quit.

resignation *(SYN.)* perseverance, endurance, fortitude, composure, forbearance.
(ANT.) unquiet, nervousness, impatience.

resigned *(SYN.)* forbearing, stoical, assiduous, passive, accepting, composed, uncomplaining.
(ANT.) turbulent, chafing.

resilience *(SYN.)* rubbery, springy, buoyant, elasticity.
(ANT.) unresponsive, fixed, rigid, stolid.

resist *(SYN.)* defy, attack, withstand, hinder, confront, oppose.
(ANT.) relent, allow, yield, accede.

resolute *(SYN.)* firm, resolved, set, determined, decided.
(ANT.) irresolute, wavering, vacillating.

resolution *(SYN.)* resolve, courage, determination, persistence, statement, verdict, recommendation, decision, steadfastness, dedication, perseverance.
(ANT.) indecision, inconstancy.

resolve *(SYN.)* determination, resolution, courage, settle, decide, persistence, determine, confirm, decision, steadfastness.
(ANT.) integrate, indecision, inconstancy.

resort *(SYN.)* motel, lodge, hotel, solve.

resound *(SYN.)* echoe, ring, reverberate.

resource *(SYN.)* store, source, supply, reserve.

resourceful *(SYN.)* inventive, ingenious, creative, clever, imaginative, skillful.

respect *(SYN.)* honor, approval, revere, heed, value, admire, esteem, point, detail, admiration, reverence, regard, feature, particular, venerate, consider.
(ANT.) disrespect, neglect, abuse, scorn, disregard, despise.

respectable *(SYN.)* becoming, respected, proper, seemly, tolerable, decent, acceptable, fair, adequate, passable, suitable, honorable, valuable.
(ANT.) unsavory, vulgar, gross, disreputable, reprehensible.

respectful *(SYN.)* courteous, polite, well-behaved, well-bred, compliant, submssive.
(ANT.) disobedient, impertinent, rude, flippant.

respite *(SYN.)* deferment, adjournment, suspension.

respond *(SYN.)* rejoin, answer, reply, acknowledge, retort.
(ANT.) overlook, disregard.

response *(SYN.)* reply, acknowledgment, answer, retort, rejoinder.
(ANT.) summoning, inquiry.

responsibility *(SYN.)* duty, obligation, accountability, trust-worthiness, trust, liability, commitment.

responsible *(SYN.)* answerable, chargeable, trustworthy, liable, accountable, able, capable, upstanding, reliable, solid, indebted, creditable.
(ANT.) careless, free, negligent.

rest *(SYN.)* ease, intermission, calm, quiet, balance, surplus, repose, lounge, inactivity, motionlessness, immobility

standstill, relax, remainder, excess, surplus, relaxation, slumber, peace, tranquillity, leisure.
(ANT.) tumult, commotion, motion, agitation.

restful (SYN.) peaceful, quiet, tranquil, calm.
(ANT.) tumultuous, upsetting, agitated, disturbed.

restitution (SYN.) recompense, satisfaction, refund, amends, retrieval.

restive (SYN.) balky, disobedient, fractious, impatient, unruly, fidgety, uneasy.

restless (SYN.) sleepless, unquiet, transient, active, agitated, disturbed, jumpy, nervous, uneasy, disquieted, irresolute.
(ANT.) quiet, tranquil, calm, peaceable.

restore (SYN.) repair, recover, rebuild, reestablish, renovate, return, renew, mend, reinstall, revive, rehabilitate, replace.

restrain (SYN.) limit, curb, constraint, stop, bridle, control, reserve, constrain, repress, check, suppress, hinder.
(ANT.) incite, aid, loosen.

restraint (SYN.) order, self-control, reserve, control, regulation, limitation, confinement.
(ANT.) freedom, liberty, confusion.

restrict (SYN.) fetter, restrain, confine, limit, engage, attach, connect, link, tie, bind.
(ANT.) broaden, enlarge, untie, loose, free.

restriction (SYN.) curb, handicap, check, boundary, ban, limitation, control, deterrent.

result (SYN.) effect, issue, outcome, resolve, end, consequence, happen, determination, conclusion, reward, aftermath.
(ANT.) cause, beginning, origin.

resume (SYN.) restart, continue, recommence, reassume.

resurgence (SYN.) rebirth, comeback, recovery, revival, resuscitation, rejuvenation, renewal.

resuscitate (SYN.) restore, revive, resurrect.

retain (SYN.) keep, hold, recall, remember, employ, hire, engage.

retainer (SYN.) aide, assistant, lackey, attendant, servant.

retaliate (SYN.) repay, revenge, return, avenge.
(ANT.) condone, forgive, overlook, excuse, forget.

retard (SYN.) detain, slacken, defer, impede, hold back, delay, postpone.
(ANT.) accelerate, speed, hasten, rush.

retention (SYN.) reservation, acquisition, holding, tenacity, possession.

reticent (SYN.) reserved, subdued, quiet, shy, withdrawn, restrained, bashful, silent.
(ANT.) outspoken, forward, opinionated.

retire (SYN.) resign, quit, abdicate, depart, vacate.

retiring (SYN.) timid, bashful, withdrawn, modest, reticent, quiet, reserved.
(ANT.) gregarious, assertive, bold.

retort (SYN.) reply, answer, response, respond, rejoin, rejoinder, retaliate.
(ANT.) summoning, inquiry.

retreat (SYN.) leave, depart, retire, withdraw, retirement, withdrawal, departure, shelter, refuge.
(ANT.) advanced.

retrench (SYN.) reduce, scrape, curtail.

retribution (SYN.) justice, vengeance, reprisal, punishment, comeuppance, vindictiveness, revenge, retaliation.

retrieve (SYN.) regain, recover, recapture, repossess, reclaim, salvage, recoup.

retrograde (SYN.) regressive, backward, declining, deteriorating, worsening.
(ANT.) onward, progression, advanced.

return (SYN.) restoration, replace, revert, recur, restore, retreat.
(ANT.) keep, take, retain.

reveal (SYN.) discover, publish, communicate, impart, uncover, tell, betray, divulge, disclose.
(ANT.) conceal, cover, obscure, cloak, hide.

revel (SYN.) rejoice, wallow, bask, enjoy, delight, savor, gloat, luxuriate, relish.

revenge (SYN.) vindictiveness, reprisal, requital, vengeance, repayment, repay, retribution, reparation.
(ANT.) reconcile, forgive, pity.

revenue (SYN.) take, proceeds, income, profit, return.

revere (SYN.) admire, honor, worship, respect, venerate, adore.
(ANT.) ignore, despise.

reverence (SYN.) glory, worship, homage, admiration, dignity, renown, respect, esteem, veneration, adoration.
(ANT.) dishonor, derision, reproach.

reverse (SYN.) overthrow, unmake rescind, opposite, invert, contrary, rear, back, misfortune, defeat, catastrophe, upset, countermand, revoke.
(ANT.) vouch, stabilize, endorse, affirm.

revert (SYN.) revive, relapse, backslide, rebound, retreat, recur, go back.
(ANT.) keep, take, appropriate.

review (SYN.) reconsideration, examination, commentary, retrospection.

revile (SYN.) defame, malign, vilify, abuse, traduce, asperse, scandalize.
(ANT.) honor, respect, cherish, protect.

revise (SYN.) change, alter, improve, correct, amend, update, rewrite, polish.

revision (SYN.) inspection, survey, retrospection, commentary, critique.

revival (SYN.) renaissance, exhumation, resurgence, renewal, revitalization.

revive (SYN.) refresh, lessen, decrease, renew, reduce, lower, abate, reanimate, diminish, reawaken, rejuvenate, suppress.
(ANT.) increase, amplify, intensify.

revoke (SYN.) nullify, cancel, abolish, quash, rescind, abrogate.

revolt (SYN.) mutiny, rebel, disgust, revolution, uprising, rebellion, upheaval, takeover, insurgence, abolish.

revolting *(SYN.)* hateful, odious, abominable, foul, vile, detestable.
(ANT.) delightful, agreeable, pleasant.

revolution *(SYN.)* rebellion, mutiny, turn, coup, revolt, overthrow, cycle.

revolutionary *(SYN.)* insurgent, extremist, radical, subversive, mutinous.

revolve *(SYN.)* spin, wheel, rotate, circle, circle, turn, whirl, gyrate.
(ANT.) travel, proceed, wander.

revolver *(SYN.)* gun, pistol.

revulsion *(SYN.)* reversal, rebound, backlash, withdrawal, recoil.

reward *(SYN.)* bounty, premium, meed, award, compensation, prize, recompense, bonus, remuneration, accolade, wages.
(ANT.) charge, wages, punishment.

rewarding *(SYN.)* pleasing, productive, fruitful, profitable, favorable, satisfying, gratifying, fulfilling.

rhetoric *(SYN.)* style, verbosity, expressiveness, eloquence, fluency, flamboyance.

rhyme *(SYN.)* poem, verse, poetry, ballad, ditty, rhapsody, sonnet.

ribald *(SYN.)* suggestive, off-color, indecent, spicy, rude, vulgar.

rich *(SYN.)* ample, costly, wealthy, fruitful, prolific, abundant, well-off, affluent, plentiful, fertile, bountiful, luxuriant.
(ANT.) poor, unfruitful, beggarly, barren, impoverished, scarce, scanty, unproductive, destitute.

rickety *(SYN.)* unsound, unsteady, flimsy, unstable, shaky, decrepit, wobbly.
(ANT.) steady, solid, sturdy.

ricochet *(SYN.)* recoil, backfire, rebound, bounce, deviate, boomerang.

rid *(SYN.)* free, clear, shed, delivered, eliminate, disperse, unload, purge.

riddle *(SYN.)* puzzle, mystery, conundrum, problem, question, enigma.
(ANT.) key, solution, answer, resolution.

ride *(SYN.)* tour, journey, motor, manage, drive, control, guide.

ridge *(SYN.)* hillock, backbone, spine, crest, mound, hump.

ridicule *(SYN.)* gibe, banter, mock, jeering, deride, tease, taunt, satire, mockery, derision.
(ANT.) praise, respect.

ridiculous *(SYN.)* silly, nonsensical, absurd, accurate, inconsistent, farcical, proper, laughable, apt, preposterous, foolish.
(ANT.) sound, reasonable, consistent.

rife *(SYN.)* widespread, abundant, innumerable, rampant, teeming.

rifle *(SYN.)* plunder, pillage, rummage, ransack, rob, steal.

rift *(SYN.)* crevice, fault, opening, crack, flaw, fissure, split, breach, opening.

right *(SYN.)* correct, appropriate, suitable, ethical, fit, real, legitimate, justice, factual, just, directly, virtue, true, definite, straight, honorably, seemly.
(ANT.) immoral, unfair, wrong, bad,

improper.

righteous *(SYN.)* ethical, chaste, honorable, good, virtuous, good, noble.
(ANT.) sinful, libertine, amoral, licentious.

rigid *(SYN.)* strict, unyielding, stiff, stern, austere, rigorous, inflexible, stringent, unbendable, severe, harsh, unbending.
(ANT.) supple, flexible, mild, compassionate, pliable, limp, relaxed.

rigorous *(SYN.)* unfeeling, rough, strict, blunt, cruel, hard, severe, grating, coarse, jarring, stern, stringent.
(ANT.) soft, mild, tender, gentle, smooth.

rile *(SYN.)* irritate, nettle, hector, exasperate, provoke, gripe.

rim *(SYN.)* verge, frontier, border, outskirts, edge, brink, lip, limit, termination, boundary, fringe, brim, margin.
(ANT.) core, mainland, center.

rind *(SYN.)* layer, cover, skin, hide, peel, crust, bark.

ring *(SYN.)* fillet, band, loop, circlet, circle, surround, encircle, peal, sound, resound, jingle, tinkle.

ringleader *(SYN.)* provoker, troublemaker, leader, instigator, chief, inciter, agitator.

rinse *(SYN.)* launder, cleanse, wash, soak, immerse, laundering, rinsing, immerse, bathe, clean.

riot *(SYN.)* disturbance, disorder, outburst, commotion, insurgence, uproar, panic, boisterousness, lark, hoot, wow, sensation, caper, roister, frolic, eruption, confusion, tumult, revolt.

riotous *(SYN.)* boisterous, wild, rambunctious, roisterous, tumultuous, turbulent, noisy, loud, rowdy, rollicking.

rip *(SYN.)* tear, rend, wound, rive, cleave, cut, slit, slash, lacerate, shred, scramble, dart, dash, split, disunite.
(ANT.) unite, join, repair.

ripe *(SYN.)* ready, finished, mature, complete, full-grown, develop, mellow, seasonable, full-fledged, primed, disposed, keen, avid, consummate.
(ANT.) raw, crude, undeveloped, premature, unprepared, unripe, immature.

ripen *(SYN.)* grow, season, age, mature, mellow, develop, progress, maturate.

rip into *(SYN.)* assail, lash out at, attack, charge.

rip-off *(SYN.)* fraud, dishonesty, gyp, racket, swindle, exploitation, heist, theft, extortion, thievery, larceny, shakedown.

riposte *(SYN.)* rejoinder, comeback, quip, retort, response, reply, wisecrack.

ripple *(SYN.)* wave, ruffle, wavelet, gurgle, undulate, gurgle, corrugation, rumple, crumple, spurtle, dribble, bubble.

rise *(SYN.)* thrive, awaken, ascend, climb, mount, tower, arise, wake, scale, flourish, prosper, advance, proceed, soar.
(ANT.) fall, drop, plunge, fade, slump,

decline, sinking, depression, waning, comedown, setback, retrogression, descend.

risk *(SYN.)* hazard, peril, danger, endanger, chance, jeopardy, threat, vulnerability, contingency, precariousness, shakiness.
(ANT.) protection, safety, immunity, defense.

risky *(SYN.)* menacing, chancy, threatening, critical, perilous, insecure, unsafe, dicey, unsound, dangerous.
(ANT.) guarded, safe, certain, firm, secure.

rite *(SYN.)* pomp, solemnity, ceremony, observance, ceremonial, formality.

ritual *(SYN.)* pomp, solemnity, ceremony, parade, rite, ritualism, prescription, routine, custom, tradition.

rival *(SYN.)* enemy, opponent, contestant, compete, foe, adversary, oppose.
(ANT.) colleague, confederate, allay.

rivalry *(SYN.)* contest, struggle, duel, race, vying, opposition, contention, competition.
(ANT.) alliance, collaboration, partnership, cooperation, teamwork, coalition.

river *(SYN.)* brook, stream, headstream, watercourse, tributary, creek.

rivet *(SYN.)* weld, bolt, fasten, attach, secure, bind, join, staple, nail, couple.

road *(SYN.)* street, way, highway, pike, drive, highway, expressway, boulevard.

roam *(SYN.)* err, saunter, deviate, rove, range, wander, digress, ramble, stroll.
(ANT.) stop, linger, stay, halt, settle.

roar *(SYN.)* cry, bellow, yell, shout, yowl, howl, bawl, hoot, bang, boom, blast, blare, scream, whoop, holler, yelp.

roast *(SYN.)* deride, ridicule, kid, ride, mock, tease, twit, parody, burlesque.

rob *(SYN.)* fleece, steal, despoil, pilfer, pillage, sack, loot, plunder, burglarize, ransack, hold up, rip off, thieve.

robbery *(SYN.)* larceny, plundering, thievery, stealing, theft, pillage, swiping, caper, snatching, burglary, plunder.

robe *(SYN.)* housecoat, bathrobe, dressing gown, caftan, muumuu, smock, cape.

robot *(SYN.)* computer, android, automaton, pawn, workhorse, drudge, laborer.

robust *(SYN.)* well, hearty, hale, sound, healthy, strong, able-bodied, stalwart.
(ANT.) fragile, feeble, debilitated, reserved, refined, puny, frail, delicate, infirm.

rock *(SYN.)* pebble, boulder, stone, gravel, granite, roll, sway, swagger, limestone.

rocky *(SYN.)* unstable, faint, rocklike, stony, pebbly, gravelly, trembly, rough.
(ANT.) effortless, easy, slight, simple, sound, rugged, stout, hardy, strong.

rod *(SYN.)* bar, pole, wand, stick, pike, staff, billy, baton.

rogue *(SYN.)* criminal, rascal, outlaw, scoundrel, scamp, good-for-nothing, villain.

roil *(SYN.)* churn, muddy, rile, mire,

disturb.

roister *(SYN.)* bluster, swagger, swashbuckle, vaunt, bluff, flourish, rollick.

role *(SYN.)* task, part, function, characterization, portrayal, face, character.

roll *(SYN.)* revolve, rotate, whirl, swing, rock, waver, reel, lumber, swagger, stagger, progress, proceed, turn, spin.

roll up *(SYN.)* amass, collect, accumulate, gather.

romance *(SYN.)* affair, enchantment, novel, tale, adventure, enterprise, daring, story.

romantic *(SYN.)* poetic, mental, dreamy, fanciful, imaginative.
(ANT.) homely, faint-hearted, familiar, unromantic, pessimistic, unemotional.

romp *(SYN.)* caper, gambol, frolic, play, conquer, triumph, horseplay, frisk.
(ANT.) defeat, rout.

room *(SYN.)* enclosure, cell, chamber, space, stay, lodge, cubicle, reside.

roomy *(SYN.)* broad, large, wide, sizable, generous, capacious, ample, spacious, extensive, commodious, vast.
(ANT.) tight, limited, crowded, confined, narrow.

roost *(SYN.)* coop, henhouse, perch, hutch, residence, abode, hearth, lodgings.

root *(SYN.)* reason, bottom, groundwork, cause, support, base, underpinning, beginning, mainspring, source, basis.
(ANT.) cover, top, building.

rooted *(SYN.)* fixed, fast, firm, steadfast, immovable, stationary.

root out *(SYN.)* dispose of, uproot, cut out, pluck out.

rope *(SYN.)* string, wire, cord, cable, line, strand, rigging, ropework, cordage.

roster *(SYN.)* list, census, muster, enrollment, listing, register.

rosy *(SYN.)* reddish, pink, healthy, fresh, cheerful, bright, happy, glowing, flushed, promising, favorable.
(ANT.) pale, pallid, gray, wan, disheartening, ashen, unfavorable, gloomy.

rot *(SYN.)* putrefy, waste, decay, mold, decompose, dwindle, spoil, decline, decomposition, wane, rotting, ebb.
(ANT.) increase, rise, grow, luxuriate.

rotary *(SYN.)* axial, rotating, turning, gyral, revolving, rolling, whirling, rotational.

rotate *(SYN.)* spin, twirl, wheel, circle, twist, orbit, invert, swivel, gyrate, wind, alternate, recur, intermit, pivot.
(ANT.) stop, arrest, stand.

rotation *(SYN.)* turning, rolling, succession, gyration, revolution, return, rhythm, swirling, spinning, whirling.

rotten *(SYN.)* decayed, decomposed, spoiled, putrid, contaminated, tainted.
(ANT.) unspoiled, pure, sweet, fresh.

rough *(SYN.)* jagged, scratchy, crude, incomplete, severe, craggy, stormy.
(ANT.) calm, polished, civil, mild.

roughly *(SYN.)* nearly, about, approximately.

round *(SYN.)* rotund, chubby, curved, bulbous, entire, complete, spherical, circular, bowed.

(ANT.) *slender, trim, slim, thin, lean.*

rouse (SYN.) waken, awaken, stimulate, excite, summon, arise, stir.

(ANT.) *rest, calm, sleep, restrain, sedate.*

rousing (SYN.) exciting, galvanic, stimulating, electric, moving, exhilarating, stirring, breathtaking, inciting.

(ANT.) *flat, uninteresting, drab, monotonous, boring, tiresome, slow.*

route (SYN.) street, course, trail, way, avenue, passage, thoroughfare, track, road, path.

routine (SYN.) way, habit, use, custom, practice, fashion, method, system, channel, circuit.

(ANT.) *unusual, rate, uncommon.*

rover (SYN.) traveler, adventurer, wanderer, voyager.

row (SYN.) file, order, series, rank, progression, sequence, arrangement.

rowdy (SYN.) disorderly, unruly, brawling, roughneck, scrapper.

royal (SYN.) lordly, regal, noble, courtly, ruling, stately, dignified.

(ANT.) *servile, common, low, humble.*

rub (SYN.) shine, polish, scour, scrape.

rubbish (SYN.) debris, garbage, trash, waste, junk, clutter.

rude (SYN.) gruff, impudent, blunt, impolite, boorish, insolent, saucy, rough.

(ANT.) *courtly, civil, stately, genteel, calm, dignified, polished, courteous.*

rudimentary (SYN. essential, primary, fundamental, original, imperfect.

ruffle (SYN.) rumple, disarrange, disorder, disturb, trimming, frill.

rug (SYN.) floor-covering, carpet.

rugged (SYN.) jagged, craggy, scratchy, irregular, uneven, harsh, severe, tough.

(ANT.) *smooth, level, even.*

ruin (SYN.) wreck, exterminate, devastate, annihilate, raze, demolish, spoil.

(ANT.) *save, establish, preserve.*

ruination (SYN.) obliteration, annihilation, havoc, catastrophe.

rule (SYN.) law, guide, order, regulation, dominion, sovereignty, control.

ruler (SYN.) commander, chief, leader, governor, yardstick.

ruling (SYN.) judgment, decision, decree.

rummage (SYN.) root, scour, ransack.

rumor (SYN.) innuendo, hearsay, gossip.

rumple (SYN.) tousle, furrow, crease, wrinkle, dishevel.

run (SYN.) race, hurry, speed, hasten, sprint, dart, scamper, dash.

runaway (SYN.) refugee, deserter, fugitive.

run-down (SYN.) ramshackle, dilapidated, tumble-down, weakened, unhealthy, summary, outline, draft.

rupture (SYN.) fracture, fissure, cleft, severance.

rural (SYN.) country, farm, rustic, backwoods.

(ANT.) *citified, urban.*

rush (SYN.) dash, speed, hurry, run.

(ANT.) *tarry, linger.*

sabotage (SYN.) subversion, treason, treachery, damage, disable, subvert.

sack (SYN.) pouch, bag.

sacrament (SYN.) communion, fellowship, association, intercourse.

(ANT.) *nonparticipation, alienation.*

sacred (SYN.) consecrated, blessed, devout, divine, holy, religious.

(ANT.) *profane, evil, sacrilegious, worldly, secular, blasphemous.*

sad (SYN.) dejected, cheerless, despondent, depressed, disconsolate, doleful.

(ANT.) *happy, cheerful, glad, merry.*

safe (SYN.) dependable, certain, harmless, secure, snug, trustworthy.

(ANT.) *hazardous, dangerous, unsafe, insecure, perilous.*

safeguard (SYN.) fence, bulwark, protection, shelter, refuge, shield, guard, defense, security.

sag (SYN.) incline, bend, lean, slant, tend, depend, rely, trust, fail.

(ANT.) *rise, raise, erect, straighten.*

saintly (SYN.) virtuous, moral, holy, devout, righteous, good.

sake (SYN.) motive, reason, purpose, benefit, advantage, welfare.

salary (SYN.) compensation, allowance, earnings, pay, fee, payment.

(ANT.) *gratuity, present, gift.*

saloon (SYN.) pub, bar.

salute (SYN.) receive, greet.

salvage (SYN.) retrieve, rescue, recover.

salvation (SYN.) release, rescue, deliverance.

same (SYN.) equal, coincident, equivalent, like, indistinguishable.

(ANT.) *disparate, contrary, dissimilar, opposed, distinct.*

sample (SYN.) example, case, illustration, model, instance, pattern.

sanction (SYN.) approval, approbation, authorization, authority, let, permit.

(ANT.) *reproach, reprimand, stricture, censure, object, forbid, refuse, resist.*

sanctuary (SYN.) harbor, haven, asylum, refuge, retreat, shelter.

(ANT.) *danger, hazard, exposure, jeopardy, peril.*

sane (SYN.) balanced, rational, normal, sound, reasonable.

(ANT.) *crazy, insane, irrational.*

sanitary (SYN.) purified, clean, hygienic, disinfected.

(ANT.) *soiled, fouled, unclean, dirty.*

sap (SYN.) undermine, exhausted, drain, weaken.

sarcastic (SYN.) biting, acrimonious, cutting, caustic, derisive, sardonic.

(ANT.) *agreeable, affable, pleasant.*

satire (SYN.) cleverness, fun, banter, humor, irony, raillery, pleasantry.

(ANT.) *platitude, sobriety, commonplace, solemnity, stupidity.*

satisfaction (SYN.) beatitude, bliss, delight, contentment, pleasure.

(ANT.) *grief, misery, sadness, despair.*

satisfactory (SYN.) ample, capable, adequate, commensurate, enough.

(ANT.) *scant, lacking, deficient, unsatisfactory, poor.*

satisfy (SYN.) compensate, appease, content, gratify, fulfill, suitable.

(ANT.) displease, dissatisfy, annoy, frustrate, tantalize.

saturate *(SYN.)* fill, diffuse, infiltrate, penetrate, permeate, run through.

saucy *(SYN.)* insolent, bold, impudent, impertinent.
(ANT.) shy, demure.

savage *(SYN.)* brutal, cruel, barbarous, ferocious, inhuman, merciless.
(ANT.) compassionate, forbearing, benevolent, gentle, humane, kind.

save *(SYN.)* defend, conserve, keep, maintain, guard, preserve, protect.
(ANT.) abolish, destroy, abandon, impair, injure.

savory *(SYN.)* delectable, delightful, delicious, palatable, luscious, tasty.
(ANT.) distasteful, nauseous, acrid, unpalatable, unsavory.

say *(SYN.)* converse, articulate, declare, express, discourse, harangue, talk.
(ANT.) hush, refrain, be silent.

saying *(SYN.)* aphorism, adage, byword, maxim, proverb, motto.

scalding *(SYN.)* hot, scorching, burning, torrid, warm, fervent, ardent.
(ANT.) cool, cold, freezing, passionless, frigid, bland.

scale *(SYN.)* balance, proportion, ration, range, climb, mount.

scamp *(SYN.)* troublemaker, rascal.

scan *(SYN.)* examine, study.

scandal *(SYN.)* chagrin, humiliation, abashment, mortification, dishonor.
(ANT.) glory, honor, dignity, praise.

scandalize *(SYN.)* asperse, defame, abuse, disparage, revile, vilify, traduce.
(ANT.) honor, respect, cherish.

scant *(SYN.)* succinct, summary, concise, terse, inadequate, deficient, insufficient, limited, lacking.
(ANT.) ample, big, extended, abundant, protracted.

scarce *(SYN.)* occasional, choice, infrequent, exceptional, rare, uncommon.
(ANT.) frequent, ordinary, usual, customary, abundant, numerous, worthless.

scare *(SYN.)* alarm, papal, affright, astound, dismay, daunt, frighten.
(ANT.) compose, reassure, soothe.

scared *(SYN.)* apprehensive, afraid, faint-hearted, frightened, fearful.
(ANT.) bold, assured, courageous, composed, sanguine.

scarf *(SYN.)* kerchief.

scatter *(SYN.)* dispel, disperse, diffuse, disseminate, separate, dissipate, spread.
(ANT.) assemble, accumulate, amass, gather, collect.

scene *(SYN.)* exhibition, view, display.

scent *(SYN.)* fragrance, fume, aroma, incense, perfume, odor, redolence.

schedule *(SYN.)* program, timetable.

scheme *(SYN.)* conspiracy, cabal, design, machination, intrigue, plot, plan, chart, stratage, diagram, graph.

scheming *(SYN.)* create, design, intend, mean, draw, sketch, purpose.

scholar *(SYN.)* intellectual, pupil, learner, disciple, sage, student, savant.
(ANT.) dunce, idiot, fool, ignoramus.

scholarly *(SYN.)* bookish, erudite, for-

mal, academic, learned, pedantic, theoretical, scholastic.
(ANT.) practical, simple, ignorant.

scholarship *(SYN.)* cognizance, erudition, apprehension, information, learning, knowledge, science, wisdom.
(ANT.) illiteracy, stupidity, ignorance.

science *(SYN.)* enlightenment, discipline, knowledge, scholarship.
(ANT.) superstition, ignorance.

scoff *(SYN.)* ridicule, belittle, mock.

scold *(SYN.)* berate, blame, lecture, rate, rebuke, censure, admonish, reprehend, upbraid, reprimand, criticize.
(ANT.) commend, praise, approve.

scorch *(SYN.)* burn, char, consume, blaze, incinerate, sear, singe, scald.
(ANT.) put out, quench, extinguish.

score *(SYN.)* reckoning, tally, record, mark, rating.

scorn *(SYN.)* contumely, derision, contempt, detestation, hatred, disdain.
(ANT.) esteem, respect, awe.

scoundrel *(SYN.)* rogue, villain, cad.

scour *(SYN.)* wash, clean, scrub.

scowl *(SYN.)* glower, frown, glare.

scrap *(SYN.)* fragment, rag, apportionment, part, portion, piece, section, share, segment, crumb, junk.
(ANT.) whole, entirety.

scrape *(SYN.)* difficulty, dilemma, condition, fix, predicament, plight, situation, strait, scour, rub, scratch.
(ANT.) comfort, ease, calmness.

scratch *(SYN.)* scrape, scar.

scrawny *(SYN.)* gaunt, skinny, spindly.
(ANT.) husky, burly.

scream *(SYN.)* screech, shriek, yell.

screech *(SYN.)* yell, cry, scream, shriek.

screen *(SYN.)* partition, cover, separation, protection.

script *(SYN.)* penmanship, hand, handwriting, text, lines.

scrub *(SYN.)* cleanse, mop, purify, clean, sweep, wash, scour.
(ANT.) pollute, dirty, stain, sully.

scrupulous *(SYN.)* conscientious, candid, honest, honorable, fair.
(ANT.) dishonest, fraudulent, lying deceitful, tricky, careless.

seal *(SYN.)* emblem, stamp, symbol, crest, signet.

search *(SYN.)* exploration, examination, investigation, inquiry, pursuit, hunt.
(ANT.) resignation, abandonment.

searching *(SYN.)* inquiring, inquisitive, interrogative, nosy, curious, peeping, peering, snoopy, prying.
(ANT.) indifferent, unconcerned, incurious, uninterested.

season *(SYN.)* mature, perfect, ripen, develop, age.

seasoned *(SYN.)* veteran, skilled.

secluded *(SYN.)* deserted, desolate, isolated, alone, lonely, lone, unaided.
(ANT.) attended, surrounded.

seclusion *(SYN.)* insulation, isolation, loneliness, alienation, quarantine, segregation, separation, retirement.
(ANT.) fellowship, union, connection, association, communion.

secondary *(SYN.)* minor, poorer, inferior, lower, subordinate.

(ANT.) greater, higher, superior.

secret *(SYN.)* concealed, hidden, latent, covert, private, surreptitious, unknown.
(ANT.) disclosed, exposed, known, obvious, conspicuous, open, public.

secrete *(SYN.)* clothe, conceal, cover, cloak, curtain, envelop, disguise, hide.
(ANT.) divulge, reveal, expose, unveil.

section *(SYN.)* district, country, domain, dominion, division, land, place.

secular *(SYN.)* lay earthly, laic, mundane, temporal, profane, worldly.
(ANT.) religious, spiritual, unworldly.

security *(SYN.)* bond, earnest, pawn, bail, guaranty, pledge, token, surety.

sedate *(SYN.)* controlled, serene, calm, composed, unruffled.

sediment *(SYN.)* residue, grounds.

see *(SYN.)* contemplate, descry, behold, discern, espy, distinguish, glimpse.

seek *(SYN.)* explore, hunt, examine, look, investigate, probe, ransack.

seem *(SYN.)* look, appeal.
(ANT.) exist, be, disappear, withdraw, vanish.

segment *(SYN.)* apportionment, division, fragment, moiety, allotment.
(ANT.) whole, entirety.

segregate *(SYN.)* exclude, separate.
(ANT.) include, combine.

seize *(SYN.)* check, detain, hinder, apprehend, arrest, obstruct, stop.
(ANT.) free, liberate, release, activate, discharge, loosen.

seldom *(SYN.)* infrequently, scarcely.

select *(SYN.)* cull, opt, pick, choose, elect, prefer.
(ANT.) reject, refuse.

selection *(SYN.)* election, choice, alternative, option, preference.

self-denial *(SYN.)* abstinence, continence, abstention, forbearance.
(ANT.) gluttony, excess, greed, intoxication, self-indulgence.

self-important *(SYN.)* egotistical, proud, conceited, egocentric.

self-indulgence *(SYN.)* egotism, narrowness, self-centeredness, self-seeking, stinginess, ungenerousness.
(ANT.) charity, magnanimity, altruism, liberality.

selfish *(SYN.)* illiberal, narrow, self-centered, self-seeking, mercenary, stingy, ungenerous, greedy, mean, miserly.
(ANT.) charitable.

self-satisfied *(SYN.)* smug, complacent.

sell *(SYN.)* market, retail, merchandise, vend, trade, barter.

send *(SYN.)* discharge, emit, dispatch, cast, propel, impel, throw, transmit, forward, ship, convey, mail.
(ANT.) get, hold, retain, receive, bring.

senile *(SYN.)* antiquated, antique, aged, ancient, archaic, obsolete, old, elderly, old-fashioned, venerable.
(ANT.) new, youthful, young, modern.

senior *(SYN.)* superior, older, elder.
(ANT.) minor, junior.

sensation *(SYN.)* feeling, image, impression, apprehension, sense, sensibility, perception, sensitiveness.

(ANT.) insensibility, torpor, stupor, apathy.

sensational *(SYN.)* exciting, marvelous, superb, thrilling, startling, spectacular.

sense *(SYN.)* perception, sensation, feeling, awareness, insight, consciousness, appreciate, discern, perceive.

senseless *(SYN.)* dense, dull, crass, brainless, dumb, foolish, stupid.
(ANT.) discerning, intelligent, alert, clever, bright.

sensibility *(SYN.)* sensation, emotion, feeling, passion, tenderness, sentiment.
(ANT.) imperturbability, anesthesia, insensibility, fact.

sensible *(SYN.)* apprehensible, perceptible, appreciable, alive, aware, awake, cognizant, comprehending, perceiving, conscious, sentient, intelligent, discreet, practical, judicious, prudent, sagacious, reasonable, sage, sober, wise, sound.
(ANT.) impalpable, imperceptible, absurd, stupid, unaware, foolish.

sensitive *(SYN.)* perceptive, prone, impressionable, responsive, tender, sore.
(ANT.) dull, hard, callous, insensitive.

sentence *(SYN.)* convict, condemn.
(ANT.) acquit, pardon, absolve acquit.

sentiment *(SYN.)* affection, emotion, sensation, feeling, sensibility, passion.
(ANT.) coldness, imperturbability, anesthesia, insensibility, fact.

sentimental *(SYN.)* extravagant, fanciful, fantastic, dreamy, fictitious, idealistic, ideal, maudlin, imaginative, mawkish, poetic, romantic, picturesque.
(ANT.) literal, practical, prosaic.

separate *(SYN.)* part sever, sunder, divide, allot, dispense, share.
(ANT.) convene, join, gather, combine.

separation *(SYN.)* insulation, isolation, loneliness, alienation, quarantine.
(ANT.) communion, fellowship, union, association, connection.

sequence *(SYN.)* chain, graduation, order, progression, arrangement, following, series, succession, train, string.

serene *(SYN.)* composed, imperturbable, calm, dispassionate, pacific, placid, peaceful, quiet, tranquil, still, undisturbed, unruffled.
(ANT.) frantic, turbulent, wild, excited, stormy, agitated, turbulent.

serenity *(SYN.)* calmness, hush, calm, quiet, peace, quiescence, rest, silence.
(ANT.) tumult, excitement, noise, agitation, disturbance.

series *(ANT.)* following, chain, arrangement, graduation, progression, order, sequence, train, string.

serious *(SYN.)* important, momentous, great, earnest, grave, sedate, sober.
(ANT.) trivial, informal, relaxed, small.

servant *(SYN.)* attendant, butler, domestic, valet, manservant, maid.

serve *(SYN.)* assist, attend, help, succor, advance, benefit, forward, answer.
(ANT.) command, direct, dictate, rule.

service *(SYN.)* advantage, account, avail, benefit, behalf, favor, good, gain.
(ANT.) distress, calamity, trouble.

set *(SYN.)* deposit, dispose, lay, arrange, place, put, position, pose, station, appoint, fix, assign, settle, establish.
(ANT.) mislay, misplace, disturb, remove, disarrange.

settle *(SYN.)* close, conclude, adjudicate, decide, end, resolve, agree upon, establish, satisfy, pay, lodge, locate, reside, determine, abide, terminate.
(ANT.) suspend, hesitate, doubt, vacillate, waver.

settlement *(SYN.)* completion, close, end, finale, issue, conclusion, termination, deduction, decision, inference.
(ANT.) commencement, prelude, start, inception, beginning.

sever *(SYN.)* part, divide, sunder, split, cut, separate.
(ANT.) convene, connect, gather, join, unite, combine.

several *(SYN.)* some, few, a handful.

severe *(SYN.)* arduous, distressing, acute, exacting, hard, harsh, intense.
(ANT.) genial, indulgent, lenient, yielding, merciful, considerate.

sew *(SYN.)* mend, patch, fix, stitch, refit, restore, repair.
(ANT.) destroy, hurt, deface, injure.

shabby *(SYN.)* indigent, impecunious, needy, penniless, worn, ragged, destitute, poor, threadbare, deficient, inferior, scanty.
(ANT.) rich, wealthy, ample, affluent, opulent, right, sufficient, good.

shack *(SYN.)* hovel, hut, shanty, shed.

shackle *(SYN.)* chain, fetter, handcuff.

shade *(SYN.)* complexion, dye, hue, paint, color, stain, pigment, darkness, shadow, tincture, dusk, gloom, blacken, darken, conceal, screen, tint, tinge.
(ANT.) transparency, paleness.

shady *(SYN.)* shifty, shaded, questionable, doubtful, devious.

shaggy *(SYN.)* hairy, unkempt, uncombed, woolly.

shake *(SYN.)* flutter, jar, jolt, quake, agitate, quiver, shiver, shudder, rock, totter, sway, tremble, vibrate, waver.

shaky *(SYN.)* questionable, uncertain, iffy, faltering, unsteady.
(ANT.) sure, definite, positive, certain.

shallow *(SYN.)* exterior, cursory, flimsy, frivolous, slight, imperfect, superficial.
(ANT.) complete, deep, abstruse, profound, thorough.

sham *(SYN.)* affect, act, feign, assume, pretend, simulate, profess.
(ANT.) exhibit, display, reveal, expose.

shame *(SYN.)* chagrin, humiliation, abashment, disgrace, mortification.
(ANT.) pride, glory, praise, honor.

shameful *(SYN.)* disgraceful, dishonorable, disreputable.
(ANT.) honorable, renowned, respectable, esteemed.

shameless *(SYN.)* unembarrassed, unashamed, brazen, bold, impudent.
(ANT.) demure, modest.

shape *(SYN.)* create, construct, forge, fashion, form, make, mold, figure.
(ANT.) disfigure, misshape, dismantle.

shapeless *(SYN.)* rough, amorphous, vague.

shapely *(SYN.)* attractive, well-formed, curvy, alluring.
(ANT.) shapeless.

share *(SYN.)* parcel, bit, part, division, portion, ration, piece, fragment, allotment, partake, apportion, participate, divide, section.
(ANT.) whole.

shared *(SYN.)* joint, common, reciprocal, correlative, mutual.
(ANT.) unrequited, dissociated.

sharp *(SYN.)* biting, pointed, cunning, acute, keen, rough, fine, cutting, shrill.
(ANT.) gentle, bland, shallow, smooth, blunt.

sharpen *(SYN.)* whet, hone, strop.

shatter *(SYN.)* crack, rend, break, pound, smash, burst, demolish, shiver, infringe.
(ANT.) renovate, join, repair, mend.

shattered *(SYN.)* fractured, destroyed, reduced, separated, broken, smashed, flattened, rent, wrecked.
(ANT.) united, integral, whole.

shawl *(SYN.)* stole, scarf.

sheepish *(SYN.)* coy, embarrassed, shy, humble, abashed, diffident, timid.
(ANT.) daring, outgoing, adventurous.

sheer *(SYN.)* thin, transparent, clear, simple, utter, absolute, abrupt, steep, see through.

sheet *(SYN.)* leaf, layer, coating, film.

shelter *(SYN.)* retreat, safety, cover, asylum, protection, sanctuary, harbor, guard, haven, security.
(ANT.) unveil, expose, bare, reveal.

shield *(SYN.)* envelop, cover, clothe, curtain, protest, protection, cloak, guard, conceal, defense, shelter, hide, screen, veil, shroud.
(ANT.) unveil, divulge, reveal, bare.

shift *(SYN.)* move, modify, transfer, substitute, vary, change, alter, spell, turn, transfigure.
(ANT.) settle, establish, stabilize.

shifting *(SYN.)* wavering, inconstant, changeable, fitful, variable, fickle.
(ANT.) uniform, stable, unchanging.

shiftless *(SYN.)* idle, lazy, slothful.
(ANT.) energetic.

shifty *(SYN.)* shrewd, crafty, tricky.

shimmer *(SYN.)* glimmer, shine, gleam.
(ANT.) dull.

shine *(SYN.)* flicker, glisten, glow, blaze, glare, flash, beam, shimmer, glimmer, radiate, brush, polish, twinkle, buff, luster, gloss, scintillate, radiance, gleam.

shining *(SYN.)* dazzling, illustrious, showy, superb, brilliant, effulgent, magnificent, splendid, bright.
(ANT.) ordinary, dull, unimpressive.

shiny *(SYN.)* bright, glossy, polished, glistening.
(ANT.) lusterless, dull.

shipshape *(SYN.)* clean, neat.
(ANT.) sloppy, messy.

shiver *(SYN.)* quiver, quake, quaver, tremble, shudder, shake, break, shatter.

shock *(SYN.)* disconcert, astonish, surprise, astound, amaze, clash, distur-

bance, bewilder, outrage, horrify, revolt, agitation, stagger, blow, impact, collision, surprise, startle, upset, stun.
(ANT.) prepare, caution, admonish.
shocking (SYN.) hideous, frightful, severe, appalling, horrible, awful.
(ANT.) safe, happy, secure, joyous.
shore (SYN.) seaside, beach, coast.
(ANT.) inland.
short (SYN.) abrupt, squat, concise, brief, low, curtailed, dumpy, small.
(ANT.) extended, ample, protracted.
shortage (SYN.) deficiency, deficit, shortfall.
(ANT.) surplus, enough.
shorten (SYN.) curtail, limit, cut, abbreviate, reduce, abridge, lessen, restrict.
(ANT.) lengthen, elongate.
shortening (SYN.) reduction, abridgment, abbreviation.
(ANT.) enlargement, amplification.
short-handed (SYN.) understaffed.
shortly (SYN.) soon, directly, presently.
shortsighted (SYN.) myopic, nearsighted, unimaginative, unthinking, thoughtless.
shout (SYN.) ejaculate, cry, yell, roar, vociferate, bellow, exclaim.
(ANT.) whisper, intimate.
shove (SYN.) propel, drive, urge, crowd, jostle, force, push, promote.
(ANT.) retreat, falter, oppose, drag, halt.
shovel (SYN.) spade.
show (SYN.) flourish, parade, point, reveal, explain, array, movie, production, display, exhibit, note, spectacle, demonstrate, entertainment, tell, usher, guide, prove, indicate, present, lead, demonstration.
showy (SYN.) ceremonious, stagy, affected, theatrical, artificial.
(ANT.) unaffected, modest, unemotional, subdued.
shred (SYN.) particle, speck, iota, mite, bit, smidgen, tear, slit, cleave, rip, disunite, wound, rend, mince, tatter, lacerate.
(ANT.) bulk, unite, quantity, mend, aggregate, repair.
shrewd (SYN.) cunning, covert, artful, stealthy, foxy, astute, ingenious, guileful, crafty, sly, surreptitious, wily, tricky, clever, intelligent, clandestine.
(ANT.) frank, sincere, candid, open.
shriek (SYN.) screech, scream, howl, yell.
shrill (SYN.) keen, penetrating, sharp, acute, piercing, severe.
(ANT.) gentle, bland, shallow.
shrink (SYN.) diminish, shrivel, dwindle.
shrivel (SYN.) wizen, waste, droop, decline, sink, dry, languish, wither.
(ANT.) renew, refresh, revive, rejuvenate.
shun (SYN.) escape, avert, forestall, avoid, forbear, evade, ward, elude, dodge, free.
(ANT.) encounter, confront, meet.
shut (SYN.) seal, finish, stop, close, terminate, conclude, clog, end, obstruct.

(ANT.) begin, open, start, unbar, inaugurate, unlock, commence.
shy (SYN.) reserved, fearful, bashful, retiring, cautious, demure, timid, shrinking, wary, chary.
(ANT.) brazen, bold, immodest, self-confident, audacious.
sick (SYN.) ill, morbid, ailing, unhealthy, diseased, unwell, infirm.
(ANT.) sound, well, robust, strong.
sickness (SYN.) illness, ailment, disease, complaint, disorder.
(ANT.) soundness, healthiness, vigor.
side (SYN.) surface, face, foe, opponent, rival, indirect, secondary, unimportant.
siege (SYN.) blockade.
sieve (SYN.) screen, strainer, riddle, colander.
sight (SYN.) eyesight, vision, scene, view, display, spectacle, eyesore.
sightless (SYN.) unmindful, oblivious, blind, unseeing, heedless, ignorant.
(ANT.) sensible, discerning, aware, perceiving.
sign (SYN.) omen, mark, emblem, token, suggestion, indication, clue, hint, approve, authorize, signal, gesture, symbol, portent.
signal (SYN.) beacon, sign, alarm.
significance (SYN.) connotation, drift, acceptation, explanation, implication, gist, importance, interpretation, intent, weight, meaning, purpose, purport, sense, signification.
significant (SYN.) grave, important, critical, material, indicative, meaningful, crucial, momentous, telling, vital, weighty.
(ANT.) irrelevant, insignificant, meaningless, unimportant, negligible.
signify (SYN.) designate, imply, denote, intimate, reveal, indicate, manifest, mean, communicate, show, specify.
(ANT.) distract, divert, mislead, conceal, conceal.
silence (SYN.) motionless, peaceful, placid, hushed, stillness, quiescent, still, soundlessness, quiet, tranquil, noiselessness, hush, muteness, undisturbed.
(ANT.) strident, loud, racket, disturbed, clamor, agitated, perturbed.
silent (SYN.) dumb, hushed, mute, calm, noiseless, quiet, peaceful, still, soundless, speechless, tranquil, uncommunicative, taciturn.
(ANT.) communicative, loud, noisy, raucous, talkative, clamorous.
silhouette (SYN.) contour, delineation, brief, draft, form, figure, outline, profile, plan, sketch.
silly (SYN.) asinine, brainless, crazy, absurd, foolish, irrational, witless, nonsensical, simple, ridiculous, stupid.
(ANT.) sane, wise, judicious, prudent.
similar (SYN.) alike, akin, allied, comparable, analogous, correlative, corresponding, correspondent, parallel, resembling, like.
(ANT.) dissimilar, divergent, opposed, different, incongruous.
similarity (SYN.) likeness, parity, analogy, correspondence, resemblance,

similitude.

(ANT.) *distinction, variance, difference.*

simple (SYN.) effortless, elementary, pure, easy, facile, mere, single, uncompounded, homely, humble, unmixed, plain, artless, naïve, frank, natural, unsophisticated, open, asinine, foolish, credulous, silly.

(ANT.) *artful, complex, intricate, adorned, wise.*

simpleton (SYN.) idiot, fool, ignoramus.

simulate (SYN.) copy, counterfeit, duplicate, ape, imitate, impersonate, mock, mimic.

(ANT.) *distort, diverge, alter, invent.*

sin (SYN.) evil, crime, iniquity, transgress, guilt, offense, ungodliness, trespass, vice, transgression, wickedness, wrong.

(ANT.) *purity, goodness, purity, virtue, righteousness.*

sincere (SYN.) earnest, frank, heartfelt, genuine, candid, honest, open, true, straightforward, faithful, truthful, upright, trustworthy, unfeigned.

(ANT.) *hypocritical, insincere, affected, dishonest, untruthful.*

sincerity (SYN.) fairness, frankness, honesty, justice, candor, integrity, openness, responsibility, rectitude, uprightness.

(ANT.) *deceit, dishonesty, cheating.*

sinful (SYN.) bad, corrupt, dissolute, antisocial, immoral, licentious, profligate, evil, indecent, unprincipled, vicious.

(ANT.) *pure, noble, virtuous.*

sing (SYN.) chant, croon, hum, carol, intone, lilt, warble.

singe (SYN.) burn, char, consume, blaze, incinerate, scorch, sear, scald.

(ANT.) *put out, quench, extinguish.*

single (SYN.) individual, marked, particular, distinctive, separate, special, specific, lone, one, solitary, sole, unwed, unmarried, singular, unique.

(ANT.) *ordinary, universal, general.*

singular (SYN.) exceptional, eccentric, odd, peculiar, rate, extraordinary, strange, unusual, striking, characteristic, remarkable, rare, individual, distinctive, uncommon, special.

(ANT.) *general, normal, ordinary.*

sink (SYN.) diminish, droop, subside, hang, decline, fall, extend, downward, drop, descend.

(ANT.) *mount, climb, soar, steady, arise.*

sinless (SYN.) faultless, holy, immaculate, perfect, blameless, holy, consummate, ideal, excellent, superlative, supreme.

(ANT.) *defective, faulty, blemished, imperfect.*

sip (SYN.) drink, taste, swallow.

sire (SYN.) breed, create, father, engender, beget, generate, procreate, originate, produce, propagate.

(ANT.) *destroy, ill, extinguish, murder, abort.*

site (SYN.) place, position, location, situation, station, locality.

situation (SYN.) circumstance, plight,

state, site, location, placement, locale, predicament, position, state, condition.

size (SYN.) bigness, bulk, dimensions, expanse, amplitude, measurement, area, extent, largeness, magnitude, mass, greatness, volume.

skeptic (SYN.) doubter, infidel, agnostic, deist, questioner, unbeliever.

(ANT.) *believer, worshiper, adorer.*

skepticism (SYN.) hesitation, questioning, wavering, doubting, distrust, mistrust, suspicion.

(ANT.) *confidence, reliance, trust.*

sketch (SYN.) draft, figure, form, outline, contour, delineation, drawing, picture, represent, silhouette, draw, profile.

sketchy (SYN.) indefinite, vague, incomplete, indistinct.

(ANT.) *definite, detailed, complete.*

skill (SYN.) cunning, deftness, dexterity, ability, adroitness, cleverness, talent, readiness, skillfulness.

(ANT.) *ineptitude, inability.*

skillful (SYN.) adept, clever, able, accomplished, competent, expert, ingenious, cunning, proficient, practiced, versed, skilled.

(ANT.) *untrained, inept, clumsy, inexpert, bungling, awkward.*

skimpy (SYN.) cheap, scanty, meager.

(ANT.) *abundant, generous.*

skin (SYN.) outside, covering, peel, rind, shell, pare.

skinny (SYN.) gaunt, thin, raw-boned.

(ANT.) *fat, hefty, heavy.*

skip (SYN.) drop, eliminate, ignore, exclude, cancel, delete, disregard, omit, overlook neglect, miss.

(ANT.) *notice, introduce, include, insert.*

skirmish (SYN.) brawl, battle, conflict, combat, dispute, encounter, contend, quarrel, squabble, scuffle, wrangle, struggle.

slack (SYN.) lax, limp, indefinite, free, disengaged, unbound, untied, unfastened, vague, dissolute, heedless, careless, unrestrained, limp, lazy, loose, inactive, sluggish, wanton.

(ANT.) *restrained, tied, right, stiff, taunt, rigid, fast, inhibited.*

slander (SYN.) libel, calumny, backbiting, aspersion, scandal, vilification.

(ANT.) *praise, flattery, commendation, defense.*

slang (SYN.) jargon, dialect.

slant (SYN.) disposition, inclination, bias, bent, partiality, slope, tilt, pitch, penchant, prejudice, proneness, proclivity, turn, incline, lean, tendency.

(ANT.) *justice, fairness, impartiality, equity.*

slash (SYN.) gash, cut, slit, lower, reduce.

slaughter (SYN.) butcher, kill, massacre, slay, butchering, killing.

slave (SYN.) bondservant, serf.

slavery (SYN.) captivity, imprisonment, serfdom, confinement, bondage, thralldom, servitude, enslavement.

(ANT.) *freedom, liberation.*

slay *(SYN.)* assassinate, kill, murder.

sleek *(SYN.)* smooth, polished, slick.
(ANT.) blunt, harsh, rough, rugged.

sleep *(SYN.)* drowse, nap, nod, catnap, repose, doze, rest, slumber, snooze.

sleepy *(SYN.)* tired, drowsy, nodding.

slender *(SYN.)* lank, lean, meager, emaciated, gaunt, scanty, rare, skinny, scrawny, slight, spare, trim, slim, tenuous, thin.
(ANT.) fat, broad, overweight, thick, wide, bulky.

slide *(SYN.)* glide, slip, skim, skid.

slight *(SYN.)* lank, lean, meager, emaciated, gaunt, fine, narrow, scanty, scrawny, skinny, sparse, small, rare, slender, spare, insignificant, tenuous, unimportant, slim, thin.
(ANT.) regard, notice, enormous, large, major, huge, include.

slim *(SYN.)* thin, slender, lank, slight, weak, insignificant, unimportant.

slip *(SYN.)* error, fault, inaccuracy, shift, err, slide, mistake, glide, blunder.
(ANT.) precision, truth, accuracy.

slipshod *(SYN.)* sloppy, careless.
(ANT.) careful.

slit *(SYN.)* slash, cut, tear, slot.

slogan *(SYN.)* catchword, motto.

slope *(SYN.)* incline, leaning, inclination, bending, slant.

sloth *(SYN.)* indolence, idleness, inactivity, inertia, supineness, sluggishness, torpidity.
(ANT.) alertness, assiduousness, diligence, activity.

slothful *(SYN.)* indolent, idle, inactive, lazy, inert, supine, sluggish, torpid.
(ANT.) alert, diligent, active, assiduous.

slovenly *(SYN.)* sloppy, bedraggled, unkempt, messy.
(ANT.) meticulous, neat.

slow *(SYN.)* deliberate, dull, delaying, dawdling, gradual, leisurely, tired, sluggish, unhurried, late, behindhand, delayed.
(ANT.) rapid, quick, swift, speedy, fast.

sluggish *(SYN.)* dull, deliberate, dawdling, delaying, laggard, gradual, leisurely, tired, slow, lethargic.
(ANT.) quick, rapid, fast, speedy, swift, energetic, vivacious.

slumber *(SYN.)* drowse, catnap, nod, doze, repose, sleep, rest, snooze.

slump *(SYN.)* drop, decline, descent.

sly *(SYN.)* covert, artful, astute, crafty, clandestine, foxy, furtive, cunning, insidious, guileful, stealthy, subtle, shrewd, tricky, surreptitious, underhand, wily, secretive.
(ANT.) sincere, ingenuous, open, candid.

small *(SYN.)* little, minute, petty, diminutive, puny, wee, tiny, trivial, slight, miniature.
(ANT.) immense, enormous, large, huge.

smart *(SYN.)* dexterous, quick, skillful, adroit, apt, clever, bright, witty, ingenious, sharp, intelligent.
(ANT.) foolish, stupid, unskilled, awkward, clumsy, bungling, slow, dumb.

smash *(SYN.)* burst, crush, demolish, destroy, break, crack, fracture, pound, fringe, rack, rupture, shatter, rend.
(ANT.) mend, renovate, restore, repair.

smear *(SYN.)* wipe, rub, spread.

smell *(SYN.)* fragrance, fume, odor, perfume, incense, aroma, fetidness, stench, stink, scent, sniff, detect, bouquet.

smidgen *(SYN.)* crumb, mite, small, bit, particle, shred, speck, scrap.
(ANT.) bulk, mass, quantity, aggregate.

smile grin.
(ANT.) frown.

smite *(SYN.)* knock, hit, dash, beat, belabor, buffet, pound, punch, pummel, thrash, thump, defeat, overthrow, overpower, subdue, vanquish, rout.
(ANT.) surrender, fail, defend, shield, stroke.

smooth *(SYN.)* polished, sleek, slick, glib, diplomatic, flat, level, plain, suave, urbane, even, unwrinkled.
(ANT.) rugged, harsh, rough, blunt, bluff, uneven.

smother *(SYN.)* suffocate, asphyxiate, stifle.

smutty *(SYN.)* disgusting, filthy, impure, coarse, dirty, lewd, offensive, obscene, pornographic.
(ANT.) modest, refined, decent, pure.

snag *(SYN.)* difficulty, bar, barrier, check, hindrance, obstruction.
(ANT.) assistance, help, encouragement.

snappish *(SYN.)* ill-natured, ill-tempered, fractious, irritable, fretful, peevish, testy, touchy, petulant.
(ANT.) good-tempered, pleasant, good-natured, affable, genial.

snappy *(SYN.)* quick, stylish, chic.

snare *(SYN.)* capture, catch, arrest, clutch, grasp, grip, lay, apprehend, seize, trap, net.
(ANT.) throw, release, lose, liberate.

snarl *(SYN.)* growl.

snatch *(SYN.)* grasp, seize, grab.

sneak *(SYN.)* steal, skulk, slink.

sneer *(SYN.)* fleer, flout, jeer, mock, gibe, deride, taunt, scoff, scorn.
(ANT.) laud, flatter, praise, compliment.

sneering *(SYN.)* derision, gibe, banter, jeering, mockery, raillery, sarcasm, ridicule, satire.

sniveling *(SYN.)* whimpering, sniffling, weepy, whining, blubbering.

snobbish *(SYN.)* uppity, conceited, snooty, snobby, snotty.

snoopy *(SYN.)* inquisitive, interrogative, curious, inquiring, meddling, peeping, prying, peering.
(ANT.) uninterested, incurious, unconcerned, indifferent.

snub *(SYN.)* rebuke, insult, slight.

snug *(SYN.)* constricted, close, contracted, compact, firm, narrow, taut, tense, stretched, tight, cozy, comfortable, sheltered.
(ANT.) loose, lax, slack, relaxed, open.

soak *(SYN.)* saturate, drench, steep, wet.

soar *(SYN.)* flutter, fly, flit, float, glide, sail, hover, mount.
(ANT.) plummet, sink, fall, descend.

sob *(SYN.)* weep, cry, lament.

sober *(SYN.)* sedate, serious, staid, earnest, grave, solemn, moderate.
(ANT.) ordinary, joyful, informal, boisterous, drunk, fuddled, inebriated.

sobriety *(SYN.)* forbearance, abstinence, abstention, self-denial, moderation, temperance.
(ANT.) self-indulgence, excess, intoxication.

social *(SYN.)* friendly, civil, gregarious, affable, communicative, hospitable, sociable, group, common, genial, polite.
(ANT.) inhospitable, hermitic, antisocial, disagreeable.

society *(SYN.)* nation, community, civilization, organization, club, association, fraternity, circle, association, company, companionship.

soft *(SYN.)* gentle, lenient, flexible, compassionate, malleable, meek, mellow, subdued, mild, tender, supple, yielding, pliable, elastic, pliant.
(ANT.) unyielding, rough, hard, tough, rigid.

soften *(SYN.)* assuage, diminish, abate, allay, alleviate, mitigate, relieve, soothe, solace.
(ANT.) irritate, increase, aggravate, agitate.

soil *(SYN.)* defile, discolor, spot, befoul, blemish, blight, stain, sully, earth, dirt, loam, dirty.
(ANT.) purify, honor, cleanse, bleach, decorate.

solace *(SYN.)* contentment, ease, enjoyment, comfort, consolation, relief, succor.
(ANT.) torture, torment, misery, affliction, discomfort.

sole *(SYN.)* isolated, desolate, deserted, secluded, unaided, lone, alone, only, single, solitary.
(ANT.) surrounded, accompanied, attended.

solemn *(SYN.)* ceremonious, imposing, formal, impressive, reverential, ritualistic, grave, sedate, earnest, sober, staid, serious, dignified.
(ANT.) ordinary, joyful, informal, boisterous, cheerful, gay, happy.

solicit *(SYN.)* beg, beseech, request, seek, pray.

solicitous *(SYN.)* anxious, concerned.

solicitude *(SYN.)* concern, worry, anxiety, care, attention, regard, vigilance, caution, wariness.
(ANT.) indifference, disregard, neglect, negligence.

solid *(SYN.)* hard, dense, compact, firm.
(ANT.) loose.

solitary *(SYN.)* isolated, alone, lonely, deserted, unaided, secluded, only, single, lone, sole.
(ANT.) surrounded, attended, accompanied.

solitude *(SYN.)* loneliness, privacy, refuge, retirement, seclusion, retreat, alienation, asylum, concealment.
(ANT.) publicity, exposure, notoriety.

solution *(SYN.)* explanation, answer.

solve *(SYN.)* explain, answer, unravel.

somatic *(SYN.)* corporeal, corporal, natural, material, bodily, physical.
(ANT.) spiritual, mental.

somber *(SYN.)* dismal, dark, bleak, doleful, cheerless, natural, physical, serious, sober, gloomy, grave.
(ANT.) lively, joyous, cheerful, happy.

sometimes *(SYN.)* occasionally.
(ANT.) invariably, always.

soon *(SYN.)* shortly, early, betimes, beforehand.
(ANT.) tardy, late, overdue, belated.

soothe *(SYN.)* encourage, console, solace, comfort, cheer, gladden, sympathize, calm, pacify.
(ANT.) dishearten, depress, antagonize, aggravate, disquiet, upset, unnerve.

soothing *(SYN.)* gentle, benign, docile, calm, mild, placid, peaceful, serene, soft, relaxed, tractable, tame.
(ANT.) violent, savage, fierce, harsh.

sophisticated *(SYN.)* cultured, worldly, blase, cultivated, urbane, cosmopolitan, suave, intricate, complex, advanced.
(ANT.) uncouth, ingenuous, simple, naive, crude.

sorcery *(SYN.)* enchantment, conjuring, art, charm, black, magic, voodoo, witchcraft, wizardry.

sordid *(SYN.)* vicious, odious, revolting, obscene, foul, loathsome, base, depraved, debased, vile, vulgar, abject, wicked, ignoble, despicable, mean, low, worthless, wretched, dirty, unclean.
(ANT.) upright, decent, honorable.

sore *(SYN.)* tender, sensitive, aching, hurting, painful.

sorrow *(SYN.)* grief, distress, heartache, anguish, misery, sadness, mourning, trial, tribulation, gloom, depression.
(ANT.) consolation, solace, joy, happiness, comfort.

sorrowful *(SYN.)* dismal, doleful, dejected, despondent, depressed, disconsolate, gloomy, melancholy, glum, moody, somber, sad, grave, aggrieved.
(ANT.) merry, happy, cheerful, joyous.

sorry *(SYN.)* hurt, pained, sorrowful, afflicted, grieved, contrite, repentant, paltry, poor, wretched, remorseful, mean, shabby, contemptible, worthless, vile, regretful, apologetic.
(ANT.) delighted, impenitent, cheerful, unrepentant, splendid.

sort *(SYN.)* class, stamp, category, description, nature, character, kind, type, variety.
(ANT.) peculiarity, deviation.

sound *(SYN.)* effective, logical, telling, binding, powerful, weighty, legal, strong, conclusive, valid.
(ANT.) weak, null, counterfeit.

sour *(SYN.)* glum, sullen, bitter, peevish, acid, rancid, tart, acrimonious, sharp, bad-tempered, unpleasant, cranky.
(ANT.) wholesome, kindly, genial, benevolent, sweet.

source *(SYN.)* birth, foundation, agent, determinant, reason, origin, cause, start, incentive, motive, spring, induce-

ment, principle, beginning.
(ANT.) *product, harvest, outcome, issue, consequence, end.*
souvenir (SYN.) memento, monument, commemoration, remembrance.
sovereign (SYN.) monarch, king, emperor, queen, empress.
sovereignty (SYN.) command, influence, authority, predominance, control, sway.
(ANT.) *debility, incapacity, disablement, ineptitude, impotence.*
space (SYN.) room, area, location.
spacious (SYN.) capacious, large, vast, ample, extensive, wide, roomy, large.
(ANT.) *limited, confined, narrow, small, cramped.*
span (SYN.) spread, extent.
spare (SYN.) preserve, safeguard, uphold, conserve, protect, defend, rescue, reserve, additional, unoccupied.
(ANT.) *impair, abolish, injure, abandon.*
sparing (SYN.) economical, thrifty, frugal.
(ANT.) *lavish.*
sparkle (SYN.) gleam, glitter, twinkle, beam, glisten, radiate, shine, blaze.
spat (SYN.) quarrel, dispute, affray, wrangle, altercation.
(ANT.) *peace, friendliness, agreement, reconciliation.*
spawn (SYN.) yield, bear.
speak (SYN.) declare, express, say, articulate, harangue, converse, talk, utter.
(ANT.) *refrain, hush, quiet.*
special (SYN.) individual, uncommon, distinctive, peculiar, exceptional, unusual, extraordinary, different, particular.
(ANT.) *general, widespread, broad, prevailing, average, ordinary.*
specialist (SYN.) authority, expert.
species (SYN.) variety, type, kind, class, sort.
specific (SYN.) limited, characteristic, definite, peculiar, explicit, categorical, particular, distinct, precise.
(ANT.) *generic, general, nonspecific.*
specify (SYN.) name, call, mention, appoint, denominate, designate, define.
(ANT.) *miscall, hint.*
specimen (SYN.) prototype, example, sample, model, pattern, type.
speck (SYN.) scrap, jot, bit, mite, smidgen, crumb, iota, particle, spot.
(ANT.) *quantity, bulk, aggregate.*
spectacle (SYN.) demonstration, ostentation, movie, array, exhibition, show, display, performance, parade, splurge.
spectator (SYN.) viewer, observer.
speculate (SYN.) assume, deduce, surmise, apprehend, imagine, consider, view, think, guess, suppose, conjecture.
(ANT.) *prove, demonstrate, conclude.*
speech (SYN.) gossip, discourse, talk, chatter, lecture, conference, discussion, address, dialogue, articulation, accent.
(ANT.) *silence, correspondence, writing,*

meditation.
speed (SYN.) forward, push, accelerate, hasten, rapidity, dispatch, swiftness.
(ANT.) *impede, slow, block, retard.*
spellbound (SYN.) fascinated, entranced, hypnotized, mesmerized, rapt.
spend (SYN.) pay, disburse, consume.
(ANT.) *hoard, save.*
spendthrift (SYN.) squanderer, profligate.
sphere (SYN.) globe, orb, ball, environment, area, domain.
spherical (SYN.) round, curved, globular.
spicy (SYN.) indecent, off-color, suggestive, indelicate.
spin (SYN.) revolve, turn, rotate, whirl, twirl, tell, narrate, relate.
spine (SYN.) vertebrae, backbone.
spineless (SYN.) weak, limp, cowardly.
(ANT.) *brave, strong, courageous.*
spirit (SYN.) courage, phantom, verve, fortitude, apparition, mood, soul, ghost.
(ANT.) *listlessness, substance, languor.*
spirited (SYN.) excited, animated, lively, active, vigorous, energetic.
(ANT.) *indolent, lazy, sleepy.*
spiritless (SYN.) gone, lifeless, departed, dead, insensible, deceased, unconscious.
(ANT.) *stirring, alive, living.*
spiritual (SYN.) sacred, unearthly, holy, divine, immaterial, supernatural.
(ANT.) *material, physical, corporeal.*
spite (SYN.) grudge, rancor, malice, animosity, malevolence, malignity.
(ANT.) *kindness, toleration, affection.*
spiteful (SYN.) vicious, disagreeable, surly, ill-natured.
(ANT.) *pretty, beautiful, attractive, fair.*
splendid (SYN.) glorious, illustrious, radiant, brilliant, showy, superb, bright.
(ANT.) *ordinary, mediocre, dull.*
splendor (SYN.) effulgence, radiance, brightness, luster, magnificence, display.
(ANT.) *darkness, obscurity, dullness.*
splinter (SYN.) fragment, piece, sliver, chip, shiver.
split (SYN.) rend, shred, cleave, disunite, sever, break, divide, opening, lacerate.
(ANT.) *repair, unite, join, sew.*
spoil (SYN.) rot, disintegrate, waste, decay, ruin, damage, mold, destroy.
(ANT.) *luxuriate, grow, flourish.*
spoken (SYN.) verbal, pronounced, articulated, vocal, uttered, oral.
(ANT.) *written, documentary.*
spokesman (SYN.) agent, representative.
spontaneous (SYN.) impulsive, voluntary, automatic, instinctive, willing, extemporaneous, natural, unconscious.
(ANT.) *planned, rehearsed, forced, studied, prepared.*
sport (SYN.) match, play, amusement, fun, pastime, entertainment, athletics.
sporting (SYN.) considerate, fair, sportsmanlike.
spot (SYN.) blemish, mark, stain, flaw,

blot, location, place, site, splatter.

spotty *(SYN.)* erratic, uneven, irregular, inconsistent.

(ANT.) regular, even.

spout *(SYN.)* spurt, squirt, tube, nozzle.

spray *(SYN.)* splash, spatter, sprinkle.

spread *(SYN.)* unfold, distribute, open, disperse, unroll, unfurl, scatter, jelly.

(ANT.) shut, close, hide, conceal.

sprightly *(SYN.)* blithe, hopeful, vivacious, buoyant, lively, light, nimble.

(ANT.) hopeless, depressed, sullen, dejected, despondent.

spring *(SYN.)* commencement, foundation, start, beginning, inception, jump, cradle, begin, birth, bound, originate.

(ANT.) issue, product, end.

sprinkle *(SYN.)* strew, spread, scatter, rain.

spruce *(SYN.)* orderly, neat, trim, clear, nice.

(ANT.) unkempt, sloppy, dirty.

spry *(SYN.)* brisk, quick, agile, nimble, energetic, supple, alert, active, lively.

(ANT.) heavy, sluggish, inert, clumsy.

spur *(SYN.)* inducement, purpose, cause, motive, impulse, reason, incitement.

(ANT.) effort, action, result, attempt.

squabble *(SYN.)* bicker, debate, altercate, contend, discuss, argue, quarrel.

(ANT.) concede, agree, assent.

squalid *(SYN.)* base, indecent, grimy, dirty, pitiful, filthy, muddy, nasty.

(ANT.) wholesome, clean, pure.

squander *(SYN.)* scatter, lavish, consume, dissipate, misuse.

(ANT.) preserve, conserve, save, accumulate.

squeamish *(SYN.)* particular, careful.

stab *(SYN.)* stick, gore, pierce, knife, spear, bayonet.

stability *(SYN.)* steadiness, balance, proportion, composure, symmetry.

(ANT.) imbalance, fall, unsteadiness.

stable *(SYN.)* firm, enduring, constant, fixed, unwavering, steadfast, steady.

(ANT.) irresolute, variable, changeable.

stack *(SYN.)* mass, pile, mound, heap, accumulate.

staff *(SYN.)* pole, stick, club, personnel, crew, employees.

stage *(SYN.)* frame, platform, boards, theater, scaffold, period, phase, step, direct, produce, present.

stagger *(SYN.)* totter, sway, reel, vary, falter, alternate.

staid *(SYN.)* solemn, sedate, earnest, sober, grave.

(ANT.) joyful, informal, ordinary.

stain *(SYN.)* blight, dye, tint, befoul, spot, defile, mark, dishonor, disgrace, smirch, blot, tint, blemish, discolor, color, tinge.

(ANT.) honor, bleach, decorate, purify.

stair *(SYN.)* staircase, stairway, steps.

stake *(SYN.)* rod, pole, picket, post, pale, bet, wager, concern, interest.

stale *(SYN.)* tasteless, spoiled, old, inedible, dry, uninteresting, trite, flat, dull, vapid, insipid.

(ANT.) new, fresh, tasty.

stalk *(SYN.)* dog, follow, track, shadow, hunt.

stall *(SYN.)* hesitate, stop, delay, postpone.

stammer *(SYN.)* falter, stutter.

stamp *(SYN.)* crush, trample, imprint, mark, brand, block, seal, die.

stand *(SYN.)* tolerate, suffer, stay, stand up, endure, bear, abide, halt, arise, rise, remain, sustain, rest.

(ANT.) run, yield, advance.

standard *(SYN.)* law, proof, pennant, emblem, touchstone, measure, example, gauge, model, banner, symbol, test.

(ANT.) guess, chance, irregular, unusual, supposition.

standing *(SYN.)* rank, position, station, status.

standpoint *(SYN.)* position, viewpoint, attitude.

staple *(SYN.)* main, principal, chief, essential, necessary.

stare *(SYN.)* gaze.

stark *(SYN.)* utter, absolute, sheer, complete, rough, severe, harsh, grim.

start *(SYN.)* opening, source, commence, onset, surprise, shock, beginning, origin, begin, initiate, jerk, jump, advantage, lead, commencement, outset.

(ANT.) end, completion, termination, close.

startle *(SYN.)* astonish, disconcert, aback, alarm, shock, agitate, surprise, astound, amaze, stun.

(ANT.) caution, prepare, admonish, forewarn.

starved *(SYN.)* longing, voracious, hungry, craving, avid, famished.

(ANT.) satisfied, sated, gorged, full.

state *(SYN.)* circumstance, predicament, case, situation, condition, affirm, declare, express, nation, country, status, assert, recite, tell, recount.

(ANT.) imply, conceal, retract.

stately *(SYN.)* lordly, elegant, regal, sovereign, impressive, magnificent, courtly, grand, imposing, majestic, noble, supreme, dignified.

(ANT.) low, common, mean, servile, humble, vulgar.

statement *(SYN.)* announcement, mention, allegation, declaration, thesis, assertion, report.

station *(SYN.)* post, depot, terminal, position, place.

status *(SYN.)* place, caste, standing, condition, state, rank, position.

statute *(SYN.)* law, ruling, decree, rule.

(ANT.) intention, deliberation.

stay *(SYN.)* delay, continue, hinder, check, hold, hindrance, support, brace, line, rope, linger, sojourn, abide, halt, stand, rest, remain, tarry, arrest, wait.

(ANT.) hasten, progress, go, depart, advance, leave.

stead *(SYN.)* place.

steadfast *(SYN.)* solid, inflexible, constant, stable, unyielding, secure.

(ANT.) unstable, insecure, unsteady.

steadfastness *(SYN.)* persistence, industry, tenacity, constancy, persistency.

(ANT.) laziness, sloth, cessation.

steady (SYN.) regular, even, unremitting, stable, steadfast, firm, reliable, solid.

steal (SYN.) loot, rob, swipe, burglarize, pilfer, shoplift, embezzle, snitch.

(ANT.) restore, buy, return, refund.

stealthy (SYN.) sly, secret, furtive.

(ANT.) direct, open, obvious.

steep (SYN.) sharp, hilly, sheer, abrupt, perpendicular, precipitous.

(ANT.) gradual, level, flat.

steer (SYN.) manage, guide, conduct, lead, supervise, escort, navigate, drive, control, direct.

stem (SYN.) stalk, trunk, arise, check, stop, originate, hinder.

stench (SYN.) odor, fetor, fetidness, stink, aroma, smell, fume, scent.

step (SYN.) stride, pace, stage, move, action, measure, come, go, walk.

stern (SYN.) harsh, rigid, exacting, rigorous, sharp, severe, strict, hard, unyielding, unmitigated, stringent.

(ANT.) indulgent, forgiving, yielding, lenient, considerate.

stew (SYN.) ragout, goulash, boil, simmer.

stick (SYN.) stalk, twig, rod, staff, pole, pierce, spear, stab, puncture, gore, cling, adhere, hold, catch, abide, remain, persist.

stickler (SYN.) nitpicker, perfectionist, disciplinarian.

sticky (SYN.) tricky, delicate, awkward.

stiff (SYN.) severe, unbendable, unyielding, harsh, inflexible, unbending, rigid, firm, hard, solid, rigorous.

(ANT.) supple, yielding, compassionate, mild, lenient, resilient.

stifle (SYN.) choke, strangle, suffocate.

stigma (SYN.) trace, scar, blot, stain, mark, vestige.

still (SYN.) peaceful, undisturbed, but, mild, hushed, calm, patient, modest, nevertheless, motionless, meek, quiescent, stationary, besides, however, quiet, hush, tranquil, serene, placid.

(ANT.) agitated, perturbed, loud.

stimulate (SYN.) irritate, excite, arouse, disquiet, rouse, activate, urge, invigorate, animate, provoke.

(ANT.) quell, calm, quiet, allay.

stimulus (SYN.) motive, goad, arousal, provocation, encouragement.

(ANT.) discouragement, depressant.

stingy (SYN.) greedy, penurious, avaricious, mean, penny-pinching, cheap, selfish, miserly, tight, tightfisted.

(ANT.) munificent, generous, giving, extravagant, openhanded, bountiful.

stipulate (SYN.) require, demand.

stir (SYN.) instigate, impel, push, agitate, induce, mix, rouse, move, propel.

(ANT.) halt, stop, deter.

stock (SYN.) hoard, store, strain, accumulation, supply, carry, keep, provision, fund, breed, sort.

(ANT.) sameness, likeness, homogeneity, uniformity.

stolid (SYN.) obtuse, unsharpened, dull,

blunt, edgeless.

(ANT.) suave, tactful, polished, subtle.

stone (SYN.) pebble, gravel, rock.

stony (SYN.) insensitive, unsentimental, cold.

stoop (SYN.) bow, bend, lean, crouch.

stop (SYN.) terminate, check, abstain, hinder, arrest, close, bar, cork, halt, end, conclude, obstruct, finish, quit, pause, discontinue, stay, impede, cease.

(ANT.) start, proceed, speed, begin.

store (SYN.) amass, hoard, collect, market, shop, reserve, supply, deposit, bank, save, accrue, increase, stock.

(ANT.) dissipate, waste, disperse.

storm (SYN.) gale, tempest, tornado, thunderstorm, hurricane, rage, rant, assault, besiege.

stormy (SYN.) rough, inclement, windy, blustery, roaring, tempestuous.

(ANT.) quiet, calm, tranquil, peaceful.

story (SYN.) yarn, novel, history, tale, falsehood, account, fable, anecdote, narrative, fabrication, lie, level, floor, fiction, report.

stout (SYN.) plump, obese, chubby, fat, paunchy, overweight, portly, heavy, sturdy, strong, pudgy, thickset.

(ANT.) thin, slender, flimsy, gaunt, slim.

straight (SYN.) erect, honorable, square, just, direct, undeviating, unbent, right, upright, honest, uncurving, directly, moral, correct, orderly, vertical.

(ANT.) dishonest, bent, circuitous, twisted, crooked.

straightforward (SYN.) forthright, direct, open, candid, aboveboard.

(ANT.) devious.

strain (SYN.) stock, kind, variety, stretch, breed, tighten, harm, injure, screen, filter, sprain, sort.

strainer (SYN.) colander, sieve, filter.

strait (SYN.) fix, situation, passage, condition, dilemma, channel, trouble, predicament, difficulty, distress, crisis.

(ANT.) ease, calmness, satisfaction, comfort.

strange (SYN.) bizarre, peculiar, odd, abnormal, irregular, unusual, curious, uncommon, singular, extraordinary, foreign, eccentric, unfamiliar, queer.

(ANT.) regular, common, familiar, conventional.

stranger (SYN.) foreigner, outsider, newcomer, alien, outlander, immigrant.

(ANT.) friend, associate, acquaintance.

strap (SYN.) strip, belt, thong, band.

strategy (SYN.) technique, management, tactics, approach.

stray (SYN.) ramble, rove, deviate, lost, strayed, wander, digress, roam, stroll.

(ANT.) linger, stop, halt, settle.

stream (SYN.) issue, proceed, flow, come, abound, spout, run, brook.

street (SYN.) way, road, boulevard, avenue.

strength (SYN.) power, might, toughness, durability, lustiness, soundness, vigor, potency.

(ANT.) weakness, frailty, feebleness.
strengthen *(SYN.)* verify, assure, confirm, fix, sanction, ratify, substantiate.
strenuous *(SYN.)* forceful, energetic, active, vigorous, determined.
stress *(SYN.)* urgency, press, emphasize, accentuate, accent, weight, strain, importance, compulsion, pressure.
(ANT.) relaxation, lenience, ease.
stretch *(SYN.)* strain, expand, elongate, extend, lengthen, spread, distend, protract, distort.
(ANT.) tighten, loosen, slacken, contract.
strict *(SYN.)* rough, stiff, stringent, harsh, unbending, severe, rigorous.
(ANT.) easygoing, lenient, mild.
strife *(SYN.)* disagreement, conflict, discord, quarrel, difference, unrest.
(ANT.) tranquillity, peace, concord.
strike *(SYN.)* pound, hit, smite, beat, assault, attack, affect, impress, overwhelm, sitdown, walkout, slowdown.
striking *(SYN.)* arresting, imposing, splendid, august, impressive, thrilling, stirring, awesome, aweinspiring.
(ANT.) ordinary, unimpressive, commonplace, regular.
strip *(SYN.)* disrobe, undress, remove, uncover, peel, ribbon, band, piece.
stripped *(SYN.)* open, simple, bare, nude, uncovered, exposed, bald, plain, naked, barren, defenseless.
(ANT.) protected, dressed, concealed.
strive *(SYN.)* aim, struggle, attempt, undertake, design, endeavor, try.
(ANT.) omit, abandon, neglect, decline.
stroke *(SYN.)* rap, blow, tap, knock, feat, achievement, accomplishment, caress.
troll *(SYN.)* amble, walk, ramble.
strong *(SYN.)* potent, hale, athletic, mighty, sturdy, impregnable, resistant.
(ANT.) feeble, insipid, brittle, weak, bland, fragile.
structure *(SYN.)* construction, framework, arrangement.
struggle *(SYN.)* fray, strive, fight, contest, battle, skirmish, oppose, clash.
(ANT.) peace, agreement, truce.
stubborn *(SYN.)* obstinate, firm, determined, inflexible, obdurate.
(ANT.) docile, yielding, amenable.
student *(SYN.)* pupil, observer, disciple, scholar, learner.
studio *(SYN.)* workroom, workshop.
study *(SYN.)* weigh, muse, master, contemplate, reflect, examination, examine.
stuff *(SYN.)* thing, subject, material, theme, matter, substance, fill, ram, cram, pack, textile, cloth, topic.
(ANT.) spirit, immateriality.
stumble *(SYN.)* sink, collapse, tumble, drop, topple, lurch, trip, fall.
(ANT.) steady, climb, soar, arise.
stun *(SYN.)* shock, knock out, dumbfound, take, amaze, alarm.
(ANT.) forewarn, caution, prepare.
stunning *(SYN.)* brilliant, dazzling, exquisite, ravishing.
(ANT.) drab, ugly.
stunt *(SYN.)* check, restrict, hinder.

stupid *(SYN.)* dull, obtuse, half-witted, brainless, foolish, dumb, witless, idiotic.
(ANT.) smart, intelligent, clever, quick, bright, alert, discerning.
stupor *(SYN.)* lethargy, torpor, daze, languor, drowsiness, numbness.
(ANT.) wakefulness, liveliness, activity.
sturdy *(SYN.)* hale, strong, rugged, stout, mighty, enduring, hardy, well-built.
(ANT.) fragile, brittle, insipid, delicate.
style *(SYN.)* sort, type, kind, chic, smartness, elegance.
subdue *(SYN.)* crush, overcome, rout, beat, reduce, lower, defeat, vanquish.
(ANT.) retreat, cede, surrender.
subject *(SYN.)* subordinate, theme, case, topic, dependent, citizen, matter.
sublime *(SYN.)* lofty, raised, elevated, supreme, exalted, splendid, grand.
(ANT.) ordinary, vase, low, ridiculous.
submerge *(SYN.)* submerse, dunk, sink, dip, immerse, engage, douse, engross.
(ANT.) surface, rise, uplift, elevate.
submissive *(SYN.)* deferential, yielding, dutiful, compliant.
(ANT.) rebellious, intractable, insubordinate.
submit *(SYN.)* quit, resign, waive, yield, tender, offer, abdicate, cede, surrender.
(ANT.) fight, oppose, resist, struggle, deny, refuse.
subordinate *(SYN.)* demean, reduce, inferior, assistant, citizen, liegeman.
(ANT.) superior.
subsequent *(SYN.)* later, following.
(ANT.) preceding, previous.
subside *(SYN.)* decrease, lower, sink, droop, hang, collapse, downward.
(ANT.) mount, steady, arise, climb.
subsidy *(SYN.)* support, aid, grant.
substance *(SYN.)* stuff, essence, importance, material, moment, matter.
(ANT.) spirit, immaterial.
substantial *(SYN.)* large, considerable, sizable, actual, real, tangible, influential.
(ANT.) unimportant, trivial.
substitute *(SYN.)* proxy, expedient, deputy, makeshift, replacement, alternate, lieutenant, representative, surrogate, displace, exchange, equivalent.
(ANT.) sovereign, master, head.
substitution *(SYN.)* change, mutation, vicissitude, alteration, modification.
(ANT.) uniformity, monotony.
subterfuge *(SYN.)* pretext, excuse, cloak, simulation, disguise, garb, pretension.
(ANT.) reality, truth, actuality, sincerity.
subtle *(SYN.)* suggestive, indirect.
(ANT.) overt, obvious.
subtract *(SYN.)* decrease, reduce, curtail, deduct, diminish, remove, lessen.
(ANT.) expand, increase, add, enlarge, grow.
succeed *(SYN.)* thrive, follow, replace, achieve, win, flourish, prevail, inherit.
(ANT.) flop, miscarry, anticipate, fail.
success *(SYN.)* prosperity, luck.
(ANT.) failure.
successful *(SYN.)* fortunate, favorable,

lucky, triumphant.

succession *(SYN.)* chain, course, series, order, string, arrangement, progression, train, following.

successive *(SYN.)* serial, sequential.

succinct *(SYN.)* pithy, curt, brief, short, compendious, terse.
(ANT.) prolonged, extended, long, protracted.

sudden *(SYN.)* rapid, swift, immediate, abrupt, unexpected, unforeseen, hasty.
(ANT.) slowly, anticipated.

suffer *(SYN.)* stand, experience, endure, bear, feel, allow, let, permit, sustain.
(ANT.) exclude, banish, overcome.

suffering *(SYN.)* distress, ache, anguish, pain, woe, misery, torment.
(ANT.) ease, relief, comfort.

sufficient *(SYN.)* fitting, enough, adequate, commensurate, satisfactory.
(ANT.) scant, deficient.

suffix *(SYN.)* ending.
(ANT.) prefix.

suggest *(SYN.)* propose, offer, refer, advise, hint, insinuate, recommend.
(ANT.) dictate, declare, insist.

suggestion *(SYN.)* exhortation, recommendation, intelligence, caution, admonition, warning, advice.

suit *(SYN.)* conform, accommodate, fit.
(ANT.) misapply, disturb.

suitable *(SYN.)* welcome, agreeable, acceptable, gratifying.
(ANT.) offensive, disagreeable.

sullen *(SYN.)* moody, fretful, surly, crabbed, morose, dour.
(ANT.) merry, gay, pleasant, amiable.

sullen *(SYN.)* fretful, morose, crabbed, dismal, silent, sulky, bitter, sad, somber, glum, gloomy, dour, moody.
(ANT.) pleasant, joyous, merry.

sultry *(SYN.)* close, hot, stifling.

sum *(SYN.)* amount, total, aggregate, whole, increase, append, add.
(ANT.) sample, fraction, reduce.

summarize *(SYN.)* abstract, abridge.
(ANT.) restore, add, unite, return.

summary *(SYN.)* digest, outline, abstract, synopsis, concise, brief, short.

summit *(SYN.)* peak, top, head, crest, zenith, apex, crown, pinnacle.
(ANT.) bottom, foundation, base, foot.

summon *(SYN.)* invoke, call, invite.
(ANT.) dismiss.

sundry *(SYN.)* miscellaneous, several, different, various, divers.
(ANT.) similar, identical, alike, same.

sunny *(SYN.)* cheery, cheerful, fair, joyful, happy, cloudless.
(ANT.) overcast, cloudy.

superb *(SYN.)* splendid, wonderful, extraordinary, marvelous.

superficial *(SYN.)* flimsy, shallow, cursory, slight, exterior.
(ANT.) thorough, deep, abstruse.

superintendent *(SYN.)* manager, supervisor, overseer, director, administrator.

superior *(SYN.)* greater, finer, better, employer, boss.
(ANT.) inferior.

superiority *(SYN.)* profit, mastery, advantage, good, service, edge, utility.
(ANT.) obstruction, harm, impediment.

supervise *(SYN.)* rule, oversee, govern, command, direct, superintend.
(ANT.) submit, forsake, abandon.

supervision *(SYN.)* oversight, inspection, surveillance, management.

supervisor *(SYN.)* manager, boss, foreman, director.

supplant *(SYN.)* overturn, overcome.
(ANT.) uphold, conserve.

supple *(SYN.)* lithe, pliant, flexible, limber, elastic, pliable.
(ANT.) stiff, brittle, rigid, unbending.

supplement *(SYN.)* extension, complement, addition, extend, add.

supplicate *(SYN.)* beg, petition, solicit, adjure, beseech, entreat, ask, pray.
(ANT.) cede, give, bestow, grant.

supplication *(SYN.)* invocation, plea, appeal, request, entreaty.

supply *(SYN.)* provide, inventory, hoard, reserve, store, accumulation.

support *(SYN.)* groundwork, aid, favor, base, prop, assistance, comfort, basis.
(ANT.) discourage, abandon, oppose.

supporter *(SYN.)* follower, devotee, adherent, henchman, attendant, disciple, votary.
(ANT.) master, head, chief.

suppose *(SYN.)* believe, presume, deduce, apprehend, think, assume, imagine, speculate, guess, conjecture.
(ANT.) prove, demonstrate, ascertain.

supposition *(SYN.)* theory, conjecture.
(ANT.) proof, fact.

suppress *(SYN.)* diminish, reduce, overpower, abate, lessen, decrease, subdue, lower.
(ANT.) revive, amplify, intensify.

supreme *(SYN.)* greatest, best, highest, main, principal, cardinal, first, chief, foremost, paramount.
(ANT.) supplemental, minor, subsidiary.

sure *(SYN.)* confident, fixed, inevitable, certain, positive, trustworthy.
(ANT.) probable, uncertain, doubtful.

surface *(SYN.)* outside, exterior, cover.

surge *(SYN.)* heave, swell, grow.
(ANT.) wane, ebb, diminish.

surname *(SYN.)* denomination, epithet, title, name, appellation, designation.

surpass *(SYN.)* pass, exceed, excel, outstrip, outdo.

surplus *(SYN.)* extravagance, intemperance, superabundance, excess, immoderation, remainder, extra, profusion, superfluity.
(ANT.) want, lack, dearth, paucity.

surprise *(SYN.)* miracle, prodigy, wonder, awe, phenomenon, marvel, bewilderment, wonderment, rarity.
(ANT.) expectation, triviality, indifference, familiarity.

surrender *(SYN.)* relinquish, resign, yield, abandon, sacrifice, submit, cede.
(ANT.) overcome, rout, conquer.

surround *(SYN.)* confine, encompass, circle, encircle, girdle, fence, circumscribe, limit, envelop.
(ANT.) open, distend, expose, enlarge.

surveillance *(SYN.)* inspection, oversight, supervision, management.

survey *(SYN.)* scan, inspect, view, examine, inspection, examination.

survive *(SYN.)* live, remain, continue.
(ANT.) die, fail, succumb.

suspect *(SYN.)* waver, disbelieve, presume, suppose, mistrust, distrust, question, suspected, assume, defendant, questionable, suspicious, doubt.
(ANT.) decide, believe, trust.

suspend *(SYN.)* delay, hang, withhold, interrupt, postpone, dangle, adjourn, poise, defer, swing.
(ANT.) persist, proceed, maintain.

suspicious *(SYN.)* suspecting, distrustful, doubtful, doubting, questioning, suspect, skeptical, unusual.

suspicion *(SYN.)* unbelief, distrust, suspense, uncertainty, doubt.
(ANT.) determination, conviction.

sustain *(SYN.)* bear, carry, undergo, foster, keep, prop, help, advocate, back, encourage, maintain, assist, suffer, approve, uphold, support.
(ANT.) betray, oppose, destroy.

swallow *(SYN.)* gorge, gulp, eat.

swamp *(SYN.)* fen, bog, marsh, quagmire, morass, flood, overcome, deluge.

swarm *(SYN.)* throng, horde, crowd.

sway *(SYN.)* control, affect, stir, actuate, impel, impress, bend, wave, swing, persuade, influence.

swear *(SYN.)* declare, state, affirm, vouchsafe, curse, maintain.
(ANT.) demur, oppose, deny.

sweat *(SYN.)* perspiration, perspire.

sweeping *(SYN.)* extensive, wide, general, broad, tolerant, comprehensive, vast.
(ANT.) restricted, confined.

sweet *(SYN.)* engaging, luscious, pure, clean, fresh, melodious, winning.
(ANT.) bitter, harsh, nasty, irascible.

swell *(SYN.)* increase, grow, expand.
(ANT.) diminish, shrink.

swift *(SYN.)* quick, fast, fleet, speedy, rapid, expeditious.

swindle *(SYN.)* bilk, defraud, con, deceive, cheat, guile, imposture, deception, artifice, deceit, trick.
(ANT.) sincerity, honesty, fairness.

swing *(SYN.)* rock, sway, wave.

switch *(SYN.)* shift, change, turn.

swoon *(SYN.)* faint.

symbol *(SYN.)* sign, character.

sympathetic *(SYN.)* considerate, compassionate, gentle, benevolent, good.
(ANT.) unkind, merciless, unsympathetic, indifferent, intolerant, cruel.

sympathize *(SYN.)* gladden, sheer, solace, comfort, encourage, soothe.
(ANT.) depress, antagonize.

sympathy *(SYN.)* compassion, agreement, tenderness, commiseration, pity.
(ANT.) indifference, unconcern, antipathy, malevolence.

symptom *(SYN.)* indication, sign.

synopsis *(SYN.)* outline, digest.

synthetic *(SYN.)* counterfeit, artificial, phony, unreal, bogus, sham.
(ANT.) natural, true, genuine.

system *(SYN.)* organization, procedure, regularity, arrangement, mode, order.
(ANT.) confusion, chance, disorder.

systematic *(SYN.)* orderly, organized.
(ANT.) irregular, random.

table *(SYN.)* catalog, list, schedule, postpone, chart, index, delay, put off.

tablet *(SYN.)* pad, notebook, capsule, sketchpad, pill, lozenge.

taboo *(SYN.)* banned, prohibited, forbidden, restriction.
(ANT.) accepted, allowed, sanctioned.

tack *(SYN.)* add, join, attach, clasp.

tackle *(SYN.)* rigging, gear, apparatus, equipment, grab, seize, catch, down.

tacky *(SYN.)* gummy, sticky, gooey.

tact *(SYN.)* dexterity, poise, diplomacy, judgment, savoir faire, skill, finesse.
(ANT.) incompetence, vulgarity, blunder, rudeness, awkwardness.

tactful *(SYN.)* discreet, considerate, judicious, adroit, sensitive, diplomatic.
(ANT.) coarse, gruff, tactless, boorish, unfeeling, churlish, rude.

tag *(SYN.)* sticker, label, mark, identification, marker, name.

tail *(SYN.)* rear, back, follow, end, shadow, pursue, trail, heel.

tailor *(SYN.)* modiste, couturier, modify, redo, shape, fashion.

taint *(SYN.)* spot, stain, tarnish, soil, mark, discolor.
(ANT.) cleanse, disinfect, clean.

tainted *(SYN.)* crooked, impure, vitiated, profligate, debased, spoiled.

take *(SYN.)* accept, grasp, catch, confiscate, clutch, adopt, assume.

taking *(SYN.)* charming, captivating, winning, attractive.

takeover *(SYN.)* revolution, merger, usurpation, confiscation.

tale *(SYN.)* falsehood, history, yarn, chronicle, account, fable, fiction.

talent *(SYN.)* capability, knack, skill, endowment, gift, cleverness, aptitude.
(ANT.) ineptitude, incompetence.

talented *(SYN.)* skillful, smart, adroit, dexterous, clever, apt, quick-witted.
(ANT.) dull, clumsy, awkward, unskilled.

talk *(SYN.)* conversation, gossip, report, speech, communicate, discuss, confer.
(ANT.) silence, correspondence, meditation, writing.

tall *(SYN.)* elevated, high, towering, big, lofty, imposing, gigantic.
(ANT.) tiny, low, short, small, stunted.

tally *(SYN.)* score, count, compute, reckon, calculate, estimate, list, figure.

tamper *(SYN.)* mix in, interrupt, interfere, meddle, interpose.

tang *(SYN.)* zest, sharpness, tartness.

tangible *(SYN.)* material, sensible, palpable, corporeal, bodily.
(ANT.) metaphysical, mental, spiritual.

tangle *(SYN.)* confuse, knot, snarl, twist, ensnare, embroil, implicate.

tangy *(SYN.)* pungent, seasoned, sharp.

tantalize *(SYN.)* tease, tempt, entice, titillate, stimulate, frustrate.

tantrum *(SYN.)* outburst, fit, fury, conniption, rampage.

tap *(SYN.)* pat, rap, hit, strike, blow, faucet, spout, spigot, bunghole.

tape *(SYN.)* ribbon, strip, fasten, bandage, bind, record, tie.

taper *(SYN.)* narrow, candle, decrease, lessen.

tardy *(SYN.)* slow, delayed, overdue,

late, belated.
(ANT.) prompt, timely, punctual, early.
target *(SYN.)* aim, goal, object, objective.
tariff *(SYN.)* duty, tax, levy, rate.
tarnish *(SYN.)* discolor, blight, defile, sully, spot, befoul, disgrace, stain.
(ANT.) honor, purify, cleanse, bleach.
tarry *(SYN.)* dawdle, loiter, linger, dally, remain, delay, procrastinate.
tart *(SYN.)* sour, acrid, pungent, acid, sharp, distasteful, bitter.
(ANT.) sweet, delicious, pleasant.
task *(SYN.)* work, job, undertaking, labor, chore, duty, stint.
taste *(SYN.)* tang, inclination, liking, sensibility, flavor, savor, try, sip.
(ANT.) indelicacy, disinclination, antipathy, insipidity.
tasteful *(SYN.)* elegant, choice, refined, suitable, artistic.
(ANT.) offensive, unbecoming.
tasteless *(SYN.)* flavorless, insipid, unpalatable, rude, unrefined.
tasty *(SYN.)* delectable, delicious, luscious, palatable, tempting.
tattered *(SYN.)* ragged, torn, shoddy, shabby, frazzled, frayed, tacky, seedy.
taunt *(SYN.)* tease, deride, flout, scoff, sneer, annoy, bother, ridicule, jeer.
(ANT.) praise, compliment, laud, flatter.
taunting *(SYN.)* ironic, caustic, cutting, sardonic, derisive, biting, acrimonious.
(ANT.) pleasant, agreeable, affable.
taut *(SYN.)* tight, constricted, firm, stretched, snug, tense, extended.
(ANT.) slack, loose, relaxed, open, lax.
tavern *(SYN.)* pub, bar, cocktail lounge.
tax *(SYN.)* duty, assessment, excise, levy, toll, burden, strain, tribute, tariff.
(ANT.) reward, gift, remuneration
taxi *(SYN.)* cab, taxicab.
teach *(SYN.)* inform, school, educate, train, inculcate, instruct, instill, tutor.
(ANT.) misinform, misguide.
teacher *(SYN.)* tutor, instructor.
team *(SYN.)* company, band, party, crew, gang, group.
tear *(SYN.)* rend, shred, sunder, cleave, rip, lacerate, teardrop, disunite, rend, divide, drop, wound, split, slit, sever.
(ANT.) mend, repair, join, unite, sew.
tease *(SYN.)* badger, harry, bother, irritate, nag, pester, taunt, vex, annoy.
(ANT.) please, delight, soothe, comfort.
technical *(SYN.)* industrial, technological, specialized, mechanical.
technique *(SYN.)* system, method, routine, approach, procedure.
teem *(SYN.)* abound, swarm.
teeter *(SYN.)* sway, hesitate, hem and haw, waver.
telecast *(SYN.)* broadcast.
televise *(SYN.)* telecast.
tell *(SYN.)* report, mention, state, betray, announce, recount, relate, narrate, rehearse, mention, utter, confess.
telling *(SYN.)* persuasive, convincing, forceful, effective.
temper *(SYN.)* fury, choler, exasperation, anger, passion, petulance, disposition, nature, rage, soothe, soften, wrath, indignation, irritation, pacify,

animosity, mood, resentment.
(ANT.) peace, self-control, forbearance, conciliation.
temperament *(SYN.)* humor, mood, temper, nature, disposition.
temperamental *(SYN.)* testy, moody, touchy, sensitive, irritable.
(ANT.) calm, unruffled, serene.
temperance *(SYN.)* abstinence, sobriety, self-denial, forbearance, abstention.
(ANT.) intoxication, excess, self-indulgence, gluttony, wantonness.
temperate *(SYN.)* controlled, moderate, cool, calm, restrained.
(ANT.) excessive, extreme, prodigal.
tempest *(SYN.)* draft, squall, wind, blast, gust, storm, hurricane, commotion, tumult, zephyr.
(ANT.) calm, tranquillity, peace.
tempo *(SYN.)* measure, beat, cadence, rhythm.
temporal *(SYN.)* mundane, earthly, lay, profane, worldly, terrestrial, laic.
(ANT.) spiritual, ecclesiastical, unworldly, religious, heavenly.
temporary *(SYN.)* brief, momentary, shortlived, fleeting, ephemeral, passing, short, transient.
(ANT.) lasting, permanent, immortal, everlasting, timeless, abiding.
tempt *(SYN.)* entice, allure, lure, attract, seduce, invite, magnetize.
tenacious *(SYN.)* persistent, determined, unchanging, unyielding.
tenable *(SYN.)* correct, practical, rational, reasonable, sensible, defensible.
tenacity *(SYN.)* perseverance, steadfastness, industry, constancy, persistence, pertinacity.
(ANT.) laziness, rest, cessation, idleness, sloth.
tenant *(SYN.)* renter, lessee, lodger, leaseholder, dweller, resident.
tend *(SYN.)* escort, follow, care for, lackey, watch, protect, take care of, attend, guard, serve.
tendency *(SYN.)* drift, inclination, proneness, leaning, bias, aim, leaning, disposition, predisposition, propensity, trend, impulse.
(ANT.) disinclination, aversion, deviation.
tender *(SYN.)* sympathetic, sore, sensitive, painful, gentle, meek, delicate, fragile, proffer, bland, mild, loving, offer, affectionate, soothing, propose, moderate, soft.
(ANT.) rough, severe, fierce, chewy, tough, cruel, unfeeling, harsh.
tenderfoot *(SYN.)* novice, apprentice, beginner, amateur.
tenderhearted *(SYN.)* kind, sympathetic, merciful, softhearted, understanding, sentimental, affectionate, gentle, sensitive.
tenderness *(SYN.)* attachment, kindness, love, affection, endearment.
(ANT.) repugnance, indifference, aversion, hatred, repulsive.
tenet *(SYN.)* dogma, belief, precept, doctrine, creed, opinion.
(ANT.) deed, conduct, practice, perfor-

mance.

tense _(SYN.)_ strained, stretched, excited, tight, nervous.
(ANT.) _loose, placid, lax, relaxed._
tension _(SYN.)_ stress, strain, pressure, anxiety, apprehension, distress.
tentative _(SYN.)_ hypothetical, indefinite, probationary, conditional.
tenure _(SYN.)_ administration, time, regime, term.
tepid _(SYN.)_ temperate, mild, lukewarm.
(ANT.) _boiling, scalding, passionate, hot._
term _(SYN.)_ period, limit, time, boundary, duration, name, phrase, interval, session, semester, expression, word.
terminal _(SYN.)_ eventual, final, concluding, decisive, ending, fatal, latest, last, ultimate, conclusive.
(ANT.) _original, first, rudimentary, incipient, inaugural._
terminate _(SYN.)_ close, end, finish, abolish, complete, cease, stop, conclude, expire, culminate.
(ANT.) _establish, begin, initiate, start, commence._
terminology _(SYN.)_ vocabulary, nomenclature, terms, phraseology.
terms _(SYN.)_ stipulations, agreement, conditions, provisions.
terrible _(SYN.)_ frightful, dire, awful, gruesome, horrible shocking, horrifying, terrifying, horrid, hideous, appalling, shocking.
(ANT.) _secure, happy, joyous, pleasing, safe._
terrific _(SYN.)_ superb, wonderful, glorious, great, magnificent, divine, colossal, sensational, marvelous.
terrify _(SYN.)_ dismay, intimidate, startle, terrorize, appall, frighten, petrify, astound, alarm, affright, horrify, scare.
(ANT.) _soothe, allay, reassure, compose, embolden._
territory _(SYN.)_ dominion, province, quarter, section, country, division, region, domain, area, place, district.
error _(SYN.)_ fear, alarm, dismay, horror, dread, consternation, fright, panic.
(ANT.) _calm, security, assurance, peace._
erse _(SYN.)_ concise, incisive, succinct, summary, condensed, compact, neat, pithy, summary.
(ANT.) _verbose, wordy, lengthy, prolix._
est _(SYN.)_ exam, examination, trial, quiz, analyze, verify, validate.
estify _(SYN.)_ depose, warrant, witness, state, attest, swear.
estimony _(SYN.)_ evidence, attestation, declaration, proof, witness, confirmation.
(ANT.) _refutation, argument, disproof, contradiction._
sty _(SYN.)_ ill-natured, irritable, snappish, waspish, fractious, fretful, touchy, ill-tempered, peevish, petulant.
(ANT.) _pleasant, affable, good-tempered, genial, good-natured._
ther _(SYN.)_ tie, hamper, restraint, bridle.
xt _(SYN.)_ textbook, book, manual.

textile _(SYN.)_ material, cloth, goods, fabric.
texture _(SYN.)_ construction, structure, makeup, composition, grain, finish.
thankful _(SYN.)_ obliged, grateful, appreciative.
(ANT.) _thankless, ungrateful, resenting._
thaw _(SYN.)_ liquefy, melt, dissolve.
(ANT.) _solidify, freeze._
theater _(SYN.)_ arena, playhouse, battlefield, stadium, hall.
theatrical _(SYN.)_ ceremonious, melodramatic, stagy, artificial, affected, dramatic, showy, dramatic, compelling.
(ANT.) _unemotional, subdued, modest, unaffected._
theft _(SYN.)_ larceny, robbery, stealing, plunder, burglary, pillage, thievery, depredation.
theme _(SYN.)_ motive, topic, argument, subject, thesis, text, point, paper, essay, composition.
theoretical _(SYN.)_ bookish, learned, scholarly, pedantic, academic, formal, erudite, scholastic.
(ANT.) _practical, ignorant, commonsense, simple._
theory _(SYN.)_ doctrine, guess, presupposition, postulate, assumption, hypothesis, speculation.
(ANT.) _practice, verity, fact, proof._
therefore _(SYN.)_ consequently, thence so, accordingly, hence, then.
thick _(SYN.)_ compressed, heavy, compact, viscous, close, concentrated, crowded, syrupy, dense.
(ANT.) _watery, slim, thin, sparse, dispersed, dissipated._
thief _(SYN.)_ burglar, robber, criminal.
thin _(SYN.)_ diluted, flimsy, lean, narrow, slender, spare, emaciated, diaphanous, gauzy, meager, slender, tenuous, slim, rare, sparse, scanty, lank, gossamer, scanty, slight.
(ANT.) _fat, wide, broad, thick, bulky._
think _(SYN.)_ picture, contemplate, ponder, esteem, intend, mean, imagine, deliberate, contemplate, recall, speculate, recollect, deem, apprehend, consider, devise, plan, judge, purpose, reflect, suppose, assume, meditate, muse.
(ANT.) _forget, conjecture, guess._
thirst _(SYN.)_ appetite, desire, craving, longing.
thirsty _(SYN.)_ arid, dry, dehydrated, parched, craving, desirous.
(ANT.) _satisfied._
thorn _(SYN.)_ spine, barb, prickle, nettle, bramble.
thorough _(SYN.)_ entire, complete, perfect, total, finished, unbroken, perfect, careful, thoroughgoing, consummate, undivided.
(ANT.) _unfinished, careless, slapdash, imperfect, haphazard, lacking._
thoroughfare _(SYN.)_ avenue, street, parkway, highway, boulevard.
(ANT.) _byway._
though _(SYN.)_ in any case, notwithstanding, however, nevertheless.
thought _(SYN.)_ consideration, pensive,

attentive, heedful, prudent, dreamy, reflective, introspective, meditation, notion, view, deliberation, sentiment, fancy, idea, impression, reasoning, contemplation, judgment, regard.
(ANT.) *thoughtlessness.*

thoughtful (SYN.) considerate, attentive, dreamy, pensive, provident, introspective, meditative, cautious, heedful, kind, courteous, friendly, pensive.
(ANT.) *thoughtless, heedless, inconsiderate, rash, precipitous, selfish.*

thoughtless (SYN.) inattentive, unconcerned, negligent, lax, desultory, inconsiderate, careless, imprudent, inaccurate, neglectful, indiscreet, remiss.
(ANT.) *meticulous, accurate, nice, careful.*

thrash (SYN.) whip, beat, defeat, flog, punish, flog, strap, thresh.

thread (SYN.) yarn, strand, filament, fiber, string, cord.

threadbare (SYN.) shabby, tacky, worn, ragged, frayed.

threat (SYN.) menace, warning, danger, hazard, jeopardy, omen.

threaten (SYN.) caution, warning, forewarn, menace, intimidate, loom.

threatening (SYN.) imminent, nigh, approaching, impending, overhanging, sinister, foreboding.
(ANT.) *improbable, retreating, afar, distant, remote.*

threshold (SYN.) edge, verge, start, beginning, doorsill, commencement.

thrift (SYN.) prudence, conservation, saving, economy.

thrifty (SYN.) saving, economical, sparing, frugal, provident, stingy, saving, parsimonious.
(ANT.) *wasteful, spendthrift, intemperate, self-indulgent, extravagant.*

thrill (SYN.) arouse, rouse, excite, stimulation, excitement, tingle.
(ANT.) *bore.*

thrive (SYN.) succeed, flourish, grow, prosper.
(ANT.) *expire, fade, shrivel, die, fail, languish.*

throb (SYN.) pound, pulsate, palpitate, beat, pulse.

throe (SYN.) pang, twinge, distress, suffering, pain, ache, grief, agony.
(ANT.) *pleasure, relief, ease, solace, comfort.*

throng (SYN.) masses, press, crowd, bevy, populace, swarm, rabble, horde, host, mass, teem, mob, multitude.

throttle (SYN.) smother, choke, strangle.

through (SYN.) completed, done, finished, over.

throughout (SYN.) all over, everywhere, during.

throw (SYN.) propel, cast, pitch, toss, hurl, send, thrust, fling.
(ANT.) *retain, pull, draw, haul, hold*

thrust (SYN.) jostle, push, promote, crowd, force, drive, hasten, push, press, shove, urge.
(ANT.) *ignore, falter, retreat, drag, oppose, halt.*

thug (SYN.) mobster, hoodlum, mugger,

gangster, assassin, gunman.

thump (SYN.) blow, strike, knock, jab, poke, pound, beat, clout, bat, rap, bang.

thunderstruck (SYN.) amazed, astounded, astonished, awed, flabbergasted, surprised, dumbfounded, bewildered, spellbound.

thus (SYN.) hence, therefore, accordingly, so, consequently.

thwart (SYN.) defeat, frustrate, prevent, foil, stop, baffle, circumvent hinder, obstruct, disappoint, balk, outwit.
(ANT.) *promote, accomplish, fulfill, help, further.*

ticket (SYN.) stamp, label, tag, seal, token, pass, summons, certificate, ballot, sticker, slate, citation.

tickle (SYN.) delight, entertain, thrill, amuse, titillate, excite.

ticklish (SYN.) fragile, delicate, tough, difficult.

tidings (SYN.) message, report, information, word, intelligence, news.

tidy (SYN.) trim, clear, neat, precise, spruce, orderly, shipshape.
(ANT.) *disheveled, unkempt, sloppy, dirty, slovenly.*

tie (SYN.) bond, join, relationship, bind, restrict, fetter, connect, conjunction, association, alliance, union, fasten, engage, attach, restrain, oblige, link, affinity.
(ANT.) *separation, disunion, unfasten, open, loose, untie, free, isolation.*

tier (SYN.) line, row, level, deck, layer.

tiff (SYN.) bicker, squabble, argue, row, clash, dispute, altercation.

tight (SYN.) firm, taut, penny-pinching, constricted, snug, taut, parsimonious, secure, fast, strong, sealed, fastened, watertight, locked, close, compact, stingy.
(ANT.) *slack, lax, open, relaxed, loose.*

till (SYN.) plow, work, moneybox, depository, cultivate, vault.

tilt (SYN.) slant, slope, incline, tip, lean.

timber (SYN.) lumber, wood, logs.

time (SYN.) epoch, span, term, age, duration, interim, period, tempo, interval, space, spell, season.

timeless (SYN.) unending, lasting, perpetual, endless, immemorial.
(ANT.) *temporary, mortal, temporal.*

timely (SYN.) prompt, exact, punctual, ready, precise.
(ANT.) *slow, dilatory, tardy, late.*

timepiece (SYN.) clock, watch.

timetable (SYN.) list, schedule.

timid (SYN.) coy, humble, sheepish, abashed, embarrassed, modest, bashful, diffident, shamefaced, retiring, fearful, faint-hearted, shy, timorous.
(ANT.) *gregarious, bold, daring, adventurous, fearless, outgoing.*

tinge (SYN.) color, tint, dye, stain, flavor, imbue, season, impregnate.

tingle (SYN.) shiver, chime, prickle.

tinker (SYN.) potter, putter, fiddle with, dawdle, dally, dabble.

tinkle (SYN.) sound, peal, ring, jingle, chime, toll.

tint (SYN.) color, tinge, dye, stain, hue

tone, shade.

tiny *(SYN.)* minute, little, petty, wee, slight, diminutive, miniature, small, insignificant, trivial, puny.
(ANT.) huge, large, immense, big, enormous.

tip *(SYN.)* point, end, top, peak, upset, tilt, reward, gift, gratuity, clue, hint, suggestion, inkling.

tirade *(SYN.)* outburst, harangue, scolding.

tire *(SYN.)* jade, tucker, bore, weary, exhaust, weaken, wear out, fatigue.
(ANT.) restore, revive, exhilarate, amuse, invigorate, refresh.

tired *(SYN.)* weary, exhausted, fatigued, run-down, sleepy, faint, spent, wearied, worn, jaded.
(ANT.) rested, fresh, hearty, invigorated, energetic, tireless, eager.

tireless *(SYN.)* active, enthusiastic, energetic, strenuous.
(ANT.) exhausted, wearied, fatigued.

tiresome *(SYN.)* dull, boring, monotonous, tedious.
(ANT.) interesting.

titan *SYN.)* colossus, powerhouse, mammoth.

title *(SYN.)* epithet, privilege, name, appellation, claim, denomination, due, heading, ownership, right, deed, designation.

toast *(SYN.)* salutation, pledge, celebration.

toddle *(SYN.)* stumble, wobble, shuffle.

toil *(SYN.)* labor, drudgery, work, travail, performance, business, achievement, employment, occupation, slave, sweat, effort.
(ANT.) recreation, ease, vacation, relax, loll, play, leisure, repose.

token *(SYN.)* mark, sign, sample, indication, evidence, symbol.

tolerant *(SYN.)* extensive, vast, considerate, broad, patient, large, sweeping, liberal, wide.
(ANT.) intolerant, bigoted, biased, restricted, narrow, confined.

tolerate *(SYN.)* endure, allow, bear, authorize, permit, brook, stand, abide.
(ANT.) forbid, protest, prohibit, discriminating, unreasonable.

toll *(SYN.)* impost, burden, rate, assessment, duty, custom, excise, tribute, levy, burden, strain.
(ANT.) reward, wages, gift, remuneration.

tomb *(SYN.)* vault, monument, catacomb, grave, mausoleum.

tone *(SYN.)* noise, sound, mood, manner, expression, cadence.

tongs *(SYN.)* tweezers, hook, grapnel, forceps.

tongue *(SYN.)* diction, lingo, cant, jargon, vernacular, dialect, idiom, speech, phraseology.
(ANT.) nonsense, drivel, babble, gibberish.

too *(SYN.)* furthermore, moreover, similarly, also, in addition, besides, likewise.

tool *(SYN.)* devise, medium, apparatus, agent, implement, utensil, agent,

vehicle, instrument.
(ANT.) preventive, hindrance, impediment, obstruction.

top *(SYN.)* crown, pinnacle, peak, tip, cover, cap, zenith, apex, crest, chief, head, summit.
(ANT.) bottom, foundation, base, foot.

topic *(SYN.)* subject, thesis, issue, argument, matter, theme, point.

topple *(SYN.)* collapse, sink, fall, tumble.

torment *(SYN.)* pain, woe, pester, ache, distress, misery, harass, throe, annoy, vex, torture, anguish, suffering, misery.
(ANT.) relief, comfort, ease, gratify, delight.

torpid *(SYN.)* sluggish, idle, lazy, inert, inactive, supine, slothful, indolent, motionless, lethargic.
(ANT.) alert, assiduous, diligent, active.

torpor *(SYN.)* lethargy, daze, numbness, stupor, drowsiness, insensibility, languor.
(ANT.) wakefulness, liveliness, activity, alertness, readiness.

torrent *(SYN.)* flood, downpour, deluge.

torrid *(SYN.)* scorching, ardent, impetuous, passionate, scalding, warm, fiery, sultry, tropical, intense, sweltering, burning, hot.
(ANT.) passionless, impassive, cold, frigid, apathetic, freezing, phlegmatic, indifferent, temperate.

torso *(SYN.)* form, frame, body.
(ANT.) soul, mind, spirit, intellect.

torture *(SYN.)* anguish, badger, plague, distress, ache, torment, pester, pain, hound, agony, woe, worry, vex, persecute, suffering, throe, afflict, misery.
(ANT.) aid, relief, comfort, ease, support, encourage, mitigation.

toss *(SYN.)* throw, cast, hurl, pitch, tumble, thrust, pitch, fling, propel.
(ANT.) retain, pull, draw, haul, hold.

total *(SYN.)* entire, complete, concluded, finished, thorough, whole, entirely, collection, aggregate, conglomeration, unbroken, perfect, undivided, consummate, full.
(ANT.) part, element, imperfect, unfinished, ingredient, particular, lacking.

tote *(SYN.)* move, transfer, convey, drag, carry.

totter *(SYN.)* falter, stagger, reel, sway, waver, stumble, wobble.

touch *(SYN.)* finger, feel, handle, move, affect, concern, mention, hint, trace, suggestion, knack, skill, ability, talent.

touch-and-go *(SYN.)* dangerous, risky, perilous, hazardous.

touching *(SYN.)* pitiable, affecting, moving, sad, adjunct, bordering, tangent, poignant, tender, effective, impressive, adjacent.
(ANT.) removed, enlivening, animated, exhilarating.

touchy *(SYN.)* snappish, irritable, fiery, choleric, testy, hot, irascible, nervous, excitable, petulant, sensitive, short-tempered, jumpy, peevish.
(ANT.) composed, agreeable, tranquil, calm, serene, stolid, cool.

tough *(SYN.)* sturdy, difficult, trying, vi-

cious, incorrigible, troublesome, hard, stout, leathery, strong, laborious, inedible, sinewy, cohesive, firm, callous, obdurate, vicious.
(ANT.) *vulnerable, submissive, easy, brittle, facile, weak, fragile, compliant, tender, frail.*

toughness *(SYN.)* stamina, sturdiness, fortitude, durability, intensity, force, might, stoutness, power, sturdiness, vigor.
(ANT.) *weakness, feebleness, infirmity, frailty.*

tour *(SYN.)* rove, travel, go, visit, excursion, ramble, journey, roam.
(ANT.) *stop, stay.*

tourist *(SYN.)* traveler, sightseer, vagabond, voyager.

tournament *(SYN.)* tourney, match, contest, competition.

tout *(SYN.)* vend, importune, peddle, solicit, sell, hawk.

tow *(SYN.)* tug, take out, unsheathe, haul, draw, remove, extract, pull, drag.
(ANT.) *propel, drive.*

towering *(SYN.)* elevated, exalted, high, lofty, tall, proud, eminent.
(ANT.) *base, mean, stunted, small, tiny, low.*

town *(SYN.)* hamlet, village, community, municipality.

toxic *(SYN.)* deadly, poisonous, fatal, lethal, harmful.
(ANT.) *beneficial.*

toy *(SYN.)* play, romp, frolic, gamble, stake, caper, plaything, wager, revel.

trace *(SYN.)* stigma, feature, indication, trait, mark, stain, scar, sign, trial, trace, suggestion, characteristic, vestige, symptoms.

track *(SYN.)* persist, pursue, follow, sign, mark, spoor, trace, path, route, road, carry, hunt, chase.
(ANT.) *escape, evade, abandon, flee, elude.*

tract *(SYN.)* area, region, territory, district, expanse, domain.

tractable *(SYN.)* yielding, deferential, submissive, dutiful, compliant, obedient.
(ANT.) *rebellious, intractable, insubordinate, obstinate.*

trade *(SYN.)* business, traffic, commerce, dealing, craft, occupation, profession, livelihood, swap, barter, exchange.

trademark *(SYN.)* logo, brand name, identification, emblem, insignia, monogram.

tradition *(SYN.)* custom, legend, folklore, belief, rite, practice.

traduce *(SYN.)* defame, malign, vilify, revile, abuse, asperse, scandalize, disparage.
(ANT.) *protect, honor, cherish, praise, respect, support, extol.*

tragedy *(SYN.)* unhappiness, misfortune, misery, adversity, catastrophe.

tragic *(SYN.)* miserable, unfortunate, depressing, melancholy, mournful.
(ANT.) *happy, cheerful, comic.*

trail *(SYN.)* persist, pursue, chase, follow, drag, draw, hunt, track.

(ANT.) *evade, flee, abandon, elude, escape.*

train *(SYN.)* direct, prepare, aim, point, level, teach, drill, tutor, bid, instruct, order, command.
(ANT.) *distract, deceive, misguide, misdirect.*

traipse *(SYN.)* roam, wander, saunter, meander.

trait *(SYN.)* characteristic, feature, attribute, peculiarity, mark, quality, property.

traitor *(SYN.)* turncoat, betrayer, spy, double-dealer, conspirator.

traitorous *(SYN.)* disloyal, faithless, apostate, false, recreant, perfidious, treasonable, treacherous.
(ANT.) *devoted, true, loyal, constant.*

tramp *(SYN.)* bum, beggar, rover, hobo, march, stamp, stomp, vagabond, wanderer, vagrant.
(ANT.) *laborer, worker, gentleman.*

trample *(SYN.)* crush, stomp, squash.

tranquil *(SYN.)* composed, calm, dispassionate, imperturbable, peaceful, pacific, placid, quiet, still, serene, undisturbed, unruffled.
(ANT.) *frantic, stormy, excited, disturbed, upset, turbulent, wild.*

tranquillity *(SYN.)* calmness, calm, hush, peace, quiet, quiescence, quietude, repose, serenity, rest, stillness, silence, placid.
(ANT.) *disturbance, agitation, excitement, tumult, noise.*

transact *(SYN.)* conduct, manage, execute, treat, perform.

transaction *(SYN.)* business, deal, affair, deed, settlement, occurrence, negotiation, proceeding.

transcend *(SYN.)* overstep, overshadow, exceed.

transcribe *(SYN.)* write, copy, rewrite, record.

transfer *(SYN.)* dispatch, send, transmit, remove, transport, transplant, consign, move, shift, reassign, assign, relegate.

transform *(SYN.)* change, convert, alter, modify, transfigure, shift, vary, veer.
(ANT.) *establish, continue, settle, preserve, stabilize.*

transgression *(SYN.)* atrocity, indignity, offense, insult, outrage, aggression, injustice, crime, misdeed, trespass, sin, wrong, vice.
(ANT.) *innocence, morality, gentleness, right.*

transient *(SYN.)* ephemeral, evanescent, brief, fleeting, momentary, temporary, short-lived.
(ANT.) *immortal, abiding, permanent, lasting, timeless, established.*

transition *(SYN.)* change, variation, modification.

translate *(SYN.)* decipher, construe, decode, elucidate, explicate, explain, interpret, solve, render, unravel.
(ANT.) *distort, falsify, misinterpret, confuse, misconstrue.*

transmit *(SYN.)* confer, convey, communicate, divulge, disclose, impart, send, inform, relate, notify, reveal, dispatch, tell.

(ANT.) withhold, hide, conceal.
transparent *(SYN.)* crystalline, clear, limpid, lucid, translucent, thin, evident, manifest, plain, evident, explicit, obvious, open.
(ANT.) opaque, muddy, turbid, thick, questionable, ambiguous.
transpire *(SYN.)* befall, bechance, betide, happen, chance, occur.
transport *(SYN.)* carry, bear, convey, remove, move, shift, enrapture, transfer, lift, entrance, ravish, stimulate.
transpose *(SYN.)* change, switch, reverse.
trap *(SYN.)* artifice, bait, ambush, intrigue, net, lure, pitfall, ensnare, deadfall, snare, ruse, entrap, bag, trick, stratagem, wile.
trash *(SYN.)* refuse, garbage, rubbish, waste.
trashy *(SYN.)* insignificant, worthless, slight.
trauma *(SYN.)* ordeal, upheaval, jolt, shock, disturbance.
travail *(SYN.)* suffering, torment, anxiety, distress, anguish, misery, ordeal.
travel *(SYN.)* journey, go, touring, ramble, rove, voyage, cruise, tour, roam.
(ANT.) stop, stay, remain, hibernate.
travesty *(SYN.)* farce, joke, misrepresentation, counterfeit, mimicry.
treachery *(SYN.)* collusion, cabal, combination, intrigue, conspiracy, machination, disloyalty, betrayal, treason, plot.
(ANT.) allegiance, steadfastness, loyalty.
treason *(SYN.)* cabal, combination, betrayal, sedition, collusion, intrigue, conspiracy, machination, disloyalty, treachery, plot.
treasure *(SYN.)* cherish, hold dear, abundance, guard, prize, appreciate, value, riches, wealth, foster, sustain, nurture.
(ANT.) disregard, neglect, dislike, abandon, reject.
treat *(SYN.)* employ, avail, manipulate, exploit, operate, utilize, exert, act, exercise, practice, handle, manage, deal, entertain, indulge, host, negotiate, tend, attend, heal, use.
(ANT.) neglect, overlook, ignore, waste.
treaty *(SYN.)* compact, agreement, pact, bargain, covenant, alliance, marriage.
(ANT.) schism, separation, divorce.
trek *(SYN.)* tramp, hike, plod, trudge.
tremble *(SYN.)* flutter, jolt, jar, agitate, quake, quiver, quaver, rock, shake, shudder, shiver, totter, sway, vibrate, waver.
trembling *(SYN.)* apprehension, alarm, dread, fright, fear, horror, terror, panic.
(ANT.) composure, calmness, tranquility, serenity.
tremendous *(SYN.)* enormous, huge, colossal, gigantic, great, large.
tremor *(SYN.)* flutter, vibration, palpitation.
trench *(SYN.)* gully, gorge, ditch, gulch,

moat, dugout, trough.
trenchant *(SYN.)* clear, emphatic, forceful, impressive, meaningful.
trend *(SYN.)* inclination, tendency, drift, course, tendency, direction.
trendy *(SYN.)* modish, faddish, stylish, voguish, popular, current.
trepidation *(SYN.)* apprehension, alarm, dread, fright, fear, horror, panic, terror.
(ANT.) boldness, bravery, fearlessness, courage, assurance.
trespass *(SYN.)* atrocity, indignity, affront, insult, outrage, offense, aggression, crime, misdeed, injustice, vice, wrong, sin.
(ANT.) evacuate, vacate, relinquish, abandon.
trespasser *(SYN.)* invader, intruder, encroacher.
trial *(SYN.)* experiment, ordeal, proof, test, examination, attempt, effort, endeavor, essay, affliction, misery, hardship, suffering, difficulty, misfortune, tribulation, trouble.
(ANT.) consolation, alleviation.
tribe *(SYN.)* group, race, clan, bunch.
tribulation *(SYN.)* anguish, distress, agony, grief, misery, sorrow, torment, suffering, woe, disaster, calamity, evil, trouble, misfortune.
(ANT.) elation, delight, joy, fun, pleasure.
tribunal *(SYN.)* arbitrators, judges, decision-makers, judiciary.
trick *(SYN.)* artifice, antic, deception, device, cheat, fraud, hoax, guile, imposture, ruse, ploy, stratagem, trickery, deceit, jest, joke, prank, defraud, subterfuge, wile, stunt.
(ANT.) exposure, candor, openness, honesty, sincerity.
trickle *(SYN.)* drip, drop, dribble, leak, seep.
tricky *(SYN.)* artifice, antic, covert, cunning, foxy, crafty, furtive, guileful, insidious, sly, shrews, stealthy, surreptitious, subtle, underhand, wily.
(ANT.) frank, candid, ingenuous, sincere, open.
trifling *(SYN.)* insignificant, frivolous, paltry, petty, trivial, small, unimportant.
(ANT.) momentous, serious, important, weighty.
trigger *(SYN.)* generate, provoke, prompt, motivate, activate.
trim *(SYN.)* nice, clear, orderly, precise, tidy, spruce, adorn, bedeck, clip, shave, prune, cut, shear, compact, neat, decorate, embellish, garnish.
(ANT.) deface, deform, spoil, mar, important, serious, momentous, weighty.
trimmings *(SYN.)* accessories, adornments, decorations, garnish, ornaments.
trinket *(SYN.)* bead, token, memento, bauble, charm, knickknack.
trio *(SYN.)* threesome, triad, triple.
trip *(SYN.)* expedition, cruise, stumble, err, journey, jaunt, passage, blunder, bungle, slip, excursion, tour, pilgrimage, voyage, travel.

trite (SYN.) common, banal, hackneyed, ordinary, stereotyped, stale.
(ANT.) modern, fresh, momentous, stimulating, novel, new.

triumph (SYN.) conquest, achievement, success, prevail, win, jubilation, victory, ovation.
(ANT.) succumb, failure, defeat.

triumphant (SYN.) celebrating, exultant, joyful, exhilarated, smug.

trivial (SYN.) insignificant, frivolous, paltry, petty, trifling, small, unimportant.
(ANT.) momentous, important weighty, serious.

troops (SYN.) militia, troopers, recruits, soldiers, enlisted men.

trophy (SYN.) award, memento, honor, testimonial, prize.

tropical (SYN.) sultry, sweltering, humid, torrid.

trouble (SYN.) anxiety, affliction, calamity, distress, hardship, grief, pain, misery, sorrow, woe, annoyance.
(ANT.) console, accommodate, gratify, soothe, joy, peace.

troublemaker (SYN.) rebel, scamp, agitator, demon, devil, ruffian.

troublesome (SYN.) bothersome, annoying, distressing, irksome, disturbing, trying, arduous, vexatious, arduous.
(ANT.) amusing, accommodating, gratifying, easy, pleasant.

truant (SYN.) delinquent, absentee, vagrant, malingerer.

truce (SYN.) armistice, cease-fire, interval, break, intermission, respite.

true (SYN.) actual, authentic, accurate, correct, exact, genuine, real, veracious, veritable, constant, honest, faithful.
(ANT.) erroneous, counterfeit, false, spurious, fictitious, faithless, inconstant.

truly (SYN.) indeed, actually, precisely, literally, really, factually.

truncate (SYN.) prune, clip, pare.

truss (SYN.) girder, brace, framework, shoring.

trust (SYN.) credence, confidence, dependence, reliance, faith.
(ANT.) incredulity, doubt, skepticism, mistrust.

trusted (SYN.) trustworthy, reliable, true, loyal, staunch, devoted.

trustworthy (SYN.) dependable, certain, reliable, secure, safe, sure, tried.
(ANT.) fallible, dubious, questionable, unreliable, uncertain.

truth (SYN.) actuality, authenticity, accuracy, correctness, exactness.
(ANT.) falsity, falsehood, fiction, lie, untruth.

truthful (SYN.) frank, candid, honest, sincere, open, veracious, accurate, correct, exact, reliable.
(ANT.) misleading, sly, deceitful.

try (SYN.) endeavor, attempt, strive, struggle, undertake, afflict, test, prove, torment, trouble, essay, examine.
(ANT.) decline, ignore, abandon, omit, neglect, comfort, console.

trying (SYN.) bothersome, annoying, distressing, irksome, disturbing.
(ANT.) amusing, easy, accommodating,

pleasant, gratifying.

tryout (SYN.) audition, trial, chance, test.

tryst (SYN.) rendezvous, meeting, appointment.

tub (SYN.) basin, vessel, sink, bowl.

tube (SYN.) hose, pipe, reed.

tubular (SYN.) hollow, cylindrical.

tuck (SYN.) crease, fold, gather, bend.

tuft (SYN.) bunch, group, cluster.

tug (SYN.) pull, wrench, tow, haul, draw, yank, jerk.

tuition (SYN.) instruction, schooling, teaching, education.

tumble (SYN.) toss, trip, fall, sprawl, wallow, lurch, flounder, plunge.

tumble-down (SYN.) ramshackle, decrepit, broken-down, dilapidated.

tumult (SYN.) chaos, agitation, commotion, confusion, disarrangement.
(ANT.) peacefulness, order, peace, certainty, tranquillity.

tune (SYN.) song, concord, harmony, air, melody, strain.
(ANT.) aversion, discord, antipathy.

tunnel (SYN.) passage, grotto, cave.

turbulent (SYN.) gusty, blustery, inclement, rough, roaring, stormy.
(ANT.) clear, calm, quiet, peaceful.

turf (SYN.) lawn, grassland, sod, grass.

turmoil (SYN.) chaos, agitation, commotion, confusion, disarray.
(ANT.) order, peace, certainty, quiet, tranquillity.

turn (SYN.) circulate, circle, invert, rotate, revolve, spin, twist, twirl, whirl.
(ANT.) fix, stand, arrest, stop, continue, endure, proceed, perpetuate.

turret (SYN.) watchtower, belfry, steeple, tower, cupola, lookout.

tussle (SYN.) wrestle, struggle, contend, battle, fight, scuffle.

tutor (SYN.) instruct, prime, school, teach, train, prepare, drill.

twig (SYN.) sprig, branch, shoot, stem.

twilight (SYN.) sunset, sundown, nightfall, eventide, dusk.

twin (SYN.) lookalike, imitation, copy, double, replica.

twine (SYN.) string, cordage, rope, cord.

twinge (SYN.) smart, pang, pain.

twinkle (SYN.) shine, gleam, glisten, sparkle, glitter, shimmer, scintillate.

twirl (SYN.) rotate, spin, wind, turn, pivot, wheel, swivel, whirl.

twist (SYN.) bow, bend, crook, intertwine, curve, incline, deflect, braid.
(ANT.) resist, break, straighten, stiffen.

twitch (SYN.) fidget, shudder, jerk.

tycoon (SYN.) millionaire, industrialist, businessman.

tyke (SYN.) rascal, urchin, brat, ragamuffin, imp.

type (SYN.) mark, emblem, sign, category, symbol, kind, class.
(ANT.) deviation, monstrosity, eccentricity, peculiarity.

typhoon (SYN.) hurricane, cyclone, storm, tornado, whirlwind, twister.

typical (SYN.) common, accustomed, conventional, familiar, customary.
(ANT.) marvelous, extraordinary.

tyrant (SYN.) dictator, autocrat, despot.

ugly *(SYN.)* hideous, homely, plain, deformed, repellent, uncomely, repulsive, unsightly, nasty, unpleasant.
(ANT.) beautiful, fair, pretty, attractive, handsome, comely, good.

ultimate *(SYN.)* extreme, latest, final, concluding, decisive, hindmost, last.
(ANT.) foremost, opening, first, beginning, initial.

umbrage *(SYN.)* anger, displeasure.

umpire *(SYN.)* judge, referee, arbitrator.

unadulterated *(SYN.)* genuine, clear, clean, immaculate, spotless, pure.
(ANT.) foul, sullied, corrupt, tainted, polluted, tarnished, defiled.

unalterable *(SYN.)* fixed, unchangeable, steadfast, inflexible.

unanimity *(SYN.)* accord, agreement.

unannounced *(SYN.)* hasty, precipitate, abrupt, unexpected.
(ANT.) courteous, expected, anticipated.

unassuming *(SYN.)* humble, lowly, compliant, modest, plain, meek, simple, unostentatious, retiring, submissive.
(ANT.) haughty, showy, pompous, proud, vain, arrogant, boastful.

unattached *(SYN.)* apart, separate, unmarried, single, free, independent.
(ANT.) committed, involved, entangled.

unavoidable *(SYN.)* inescapable, certain, inevitable, unpreventable.

unawares *(SYN.)* abruptly, suddenly, unexpectedly, off guard.

unbalanced *(SYN.)* crazy, mad, insane.

unbearable *(SYN.)* insufferable, intolerable.
(ANT.) tolerable, acceptable.

unbeliever *(SYN.)* dissenter, apostate, heretic, schismatic, nonconformist.

unbending *(SYN.)* firm, inflexible, decided, determined, obstinate.
(ANT.) flexible.

unbiased *(SYN.)* honest, equitable, fair, impartial, reasonable, unprejudiced.
(ANT.) partial, fraudulent, dishonorable.

unbroken *(SYN.)* complete, uninterrupted, continuous, whole.

unburden *(SYN.)* clear, disentangle, divest, free.

uncanny *(SYN.)* amazing, remarkable, extraordinary, strange.

uncertain *(SYN.)* dim, hazy, indefinite, obscure, indistinct, unclear, undetermined, unsettled, ambiguous, unsure, doubtful, questionable, dubious.
(ANT.) explicit, lucid, specific, certain, unmistakable, precise, clear.

uncertainty *(SYN.)* distrust, doubt, hesitation, incredulity, scruple, ambiguity, skepticism, uncertainty, suspense, suspicion, unbelief.
(ANT.) faith, belief, certainty, conviction, determination.

uncivil *(SYN.)* impolite, rude, discourteous.
(ANT.) polite.

uncivilized *(SYN.)* barbaric, barbarous, barbarian, brutal, crude, inhuman, cruel, merciless, rude, remorseless, uncultured, savage, unrelenting.
(ANT.) humane, kind, polite, refined.

unclad *(SYN.)* exposed, nude, naked, bare, stripped, defenseless, uncovered.

(ANT.) concealed, protected, clothed, covered, dressed.

uncommon *(SYN.)* unusual, rare, odd, scarce, strange, peculiar, queer, exceptional, remarkable.
(ANT.) ordinary, usual.

uncompromising *(SYN.)* determined, dogged, firm, immovable, contumacious, headstrong, inflexible, obdurate, intractable, obstinate, pertinacious.
(ANT.) docile, compliant, amenable, yielding, submissive, pliable.

unconcern *(SYN.)* disinterestedness, impartiality, indifference, apathy, insensibility, neutrality.
(ANT.) affection, fervor, passion, ardor.

unconditional *(SYN.)* unqualified, unrestricted, arbitrary, absolute, pure, complete, actual, authoritative, perfect, entire, ultimate, tyrannous.
(ANT.) conditional, contingent, accountable, dependent, qualified.

unconscious *(SYN.)* lethargic, numb, comatose.

uncouth *(SYN.)* green, harsh, crude, coarse, ill-prepared, rough, raw, unfinished, unrefined, vulgar, rude, impolite, discourteous, unpolished, ill-mannered, crass.
(ANT.) well-prepared, cultivated, refined, civilized, finished.

uncover *(SYN.)* disclose, discover, betray, divulge, expose, reveal, impart, show.
(ANT.) conceal, hide, cover, obscure, cloak.

undependable *(SYN.)* changeable, unstable, uncertain, shifty, irresponsible.
(ANT.) stable, dependable, trustworthy.

under *(SYN.)* beneath, underneath, following, below, lower, downward.
(ANT.) over, above, up, higher.

undercover *(SYN.)* hidden, secret.

undergo *(SYN.)* endure, feel, stand, bear, indulge, suffer, sustain, experience, let, allow, permit, feel, tolerate.
(ANT.) overcome, discard, exclude, banish.

underhand *(SYN.)* sly, secret, sneaky, secretive, stealthy, crafty.
(ANT.) honest, open, direct, frank.

undermine *(SYN.)* demoralize, thwart, erode, weaken, subvert, sabotage.

underscore *(SYN.)* emphasize, stress.

understand *(SYN.)* apprehend, comprehend, appreciate, conceive, discern, know, grasp, hear, learn, realize, see, perceive.
(ANT.) misunderstand, mistake, misapprehend, ignore.

understanding *(SYN.)* agreement, coincidence, concord, accordance, concurrence, harmony, unison, compact, contract, arrangement, bargain, covenant, stipulation.
(ANT.) variance, difference, discord, dissension, disagreement.

understudy *(SYN.)* deputy, agent, proxy, representative, agent, alternate, lieutenant, substitute.
(ANT.) head, principal, sovereign, master.

undertake *(SYN.)* venture, attempt.

undertaking *(SYN.)* effort, endeavor, attempt, experiment, trial, essay.
(ANT.) laziness, neglect, inaction.

undersigned *(SYN.)* casual, chance, contingent, accidental, fortuitous, incidental, unintended.
(ANT.) decreed, planned, willed, calculated.

undesirable *(SYN.)* obnoxious, distasteful, objectionable, repugnant.
(ANT.) appealing, inviting, attractive.

undivided *(SYN.)* complete, intact, entire, integral, total, perfect, unimpaired, whole.
(ANT.) partial, incomplete.

undoing *(SYN.)* ruin, downfall, destruction, failure, disgrace.

undying *(SYN.)* endless, deathless, eternal, everlasting, ceaseless, immortal, infinite, perpetual, timeless.
(ANT.) transient, mortal, temporal, ephemeral, finite, impermanent.

unearthly *(SYN.)* metaphysical, ghostly, miraculous, marvelous, preternatural, superhuman, spiritual, foreign, strange, weird, supernatural.
(ANT.) physical, plain, human, natural, common, mundane.

uneducated *(SYN.)* uncultured, ignorant, illiterate, uninformed, unlearned, untaught, unlettered.
(ANT.) erudite, cultured, educated, literate, formed.

unemployed *(SYN.)* inert, inactive, idle, jobless, unoccupied.
(ANT.) working, occupied, active, industrious, employed.

uneven *(SYN.)* remaining, single, odd, unmatched, rugged, gnarled, irregular.
(ANT.) matched, even, flat, smooth.

unexceptional *(SYN.)* commonplace, trivial, customary.

unexpected *(SYN.)* immediate, hasty, surprising, instantaneous, unforeseen, abrupt, rapid, startling, sudden.
(ANT.) slowly, expected, gradual, predicted, anticipated, planned.

unfaithful *(SYN.)* treacherous, disloyal, deceitful, capricious.
(ANT.) true, loyal, steadfast, faithful.

unfasten *(SYN.)* open, expand, spread, exhibit, unbar, unlock, unfold, unseal.
(ANT.) shut, hide, conceal, close.

unfavorable *(SYN.)* antagonistic, contrary, adverse, opposed, opposite, disastrous, counteractive, unlucky.
(ANT.) benign, fortunate, lucky, propitious.

unfeeling *(SYN.)* hard, rigorous, cruel, stern, callous, numb, hard, strict, unsympathetic, severe.
(ANT.) tender, gentle, lenient. humane.

unfold *(SYN.)* develop, create, elaborate, amplify, evolve, mature, expand.
(ANT.) wither, restrict, contract, stunt, compress.

unfurnished *(SYN.)* naked, mere, bare, exposed, stripped, plain, open, simple.
(ANT.) concealed, protected, covered.

ungainly *(SYN.)* clumsy, awkward, bungling, clownish, gawky.

(ANT.) dexterous, graceful, elegant.

unhappy *(SYN.)* sad, miserable, wretched, melancholy, distressed, depressed, wretched.
(ANT.) joyful, happy, joyous, cheerful.

unhealthy *(SYN.)* infirm, sick, diseased, sickly.
(ANT.) vigorous, well, healthy, hale.

uniform *(SYN.)* methodical, natural, customary, orderly, normal, consistent, ordinary, regular, unvarying, unchanging, systematic, steady, unvaried.
(ANT.) rare, unusual, erratic, abnormal, exceptional, changeable.

unimportant *(SYN.)* petty, trivial, paltry, trifling, insignificant, indifferent, minor, petty.

uninformed *(SYN.)* illiterate, uncultured, uneducated, ignorant, unlearned, untaught, unlettered.
(ANT.) informed, literate, erudite, cultured, educated.

uninhibited *(SYN.)* loose, open, liberated, free.
(ANT.) constrained, tense, suppressed.

unintelligible *(SYN.)* ambiguous, cryptic, dark, cloudy, abstruse, dusky, mysterious, indistinct, obscure, vague.
(ANT.) lucid, distinct, bright, clear.

uninteresting *(SYN.)* burdensome, dilatory, dreary, dull, boring, slow humdrum, monotonous, sluggish, tedious, tardy, wearisome, tiresome.
(ANT.) entertaining, exciting, quick, amusing.

union *(SYN.)* fusion, incorporation, combination, joining, concurrence, solidarity, agreement, unification, concord, harmony, alliance, unanimity, coalition, confederacy, amalgamation, league, concert, marriage.
(ANT.) schism, disagreement, separation, discord.

unique *(SYN.)* exceptional, matchless, distinctive, choice, peculiar, singular, rare, sole, single, incomparable, uncommon, solitary, unequaled.
(ANT.) typical, ordinary, commonplace, frequent, common.

unison *(SYN.)* harmony, concurrence, understanding, accordance, concord, agreeable, coincidence.
(ANT.) disagreement, difference, discord, variance.

unite *(SYN.)* attach, blend, amalgamate, combine, conjoin, associate, connect, embody, consolidate, join, link, fuse, unify, merge.
(ANT.) sever, divide, separate, sever, disrupt, disconnect.

universal *(SYN.)* frequent, general, popular, common, familiar, prevailing, prevalent, usual.
(ANT.) scarce, odd, regional, local, extraordinary, exceptional.

unkempt *(SYN.)* sloppy, rumpled, untidy, messy, bedraggled.
(ANT.) presentable, well-groomed, tidy, neat.

unkind *(SYN.)* unfeeling, unsympathetic, unpleasant, cruel, harsh.
(ANT.) considerate, sympathetic, amiable, kind.

unlawful *(SYN.)* illegitimate, illicit, illegal, outlawed, criminal, prohibited.
(ANT.) permitted, law, honest, legal, legitimate, authorized.

unlike *(SYN.)* dissimilar, different, distinct, contrary, diverse, divergent, opposite, incongruous, variant, miscellaneous, divers.
(ANT.) conditional, accountable, contingent, qualified, dependent.

unlucky *(SYN.)* cursed, inauspicious, unfortunate.
(ANT.) prosperous, fortunate, blessed.

unmerciful *(SYN.)* cruel, merciless, heartless, brutal.

unmistakable *(SYN.)* clear, patent, plain, visible, obvious.

unnecessary *(SYN.)* pointless, needless, superfluous, purposeless.

unoccupied *(SYN.)* empty, vacant, uninhabited.

unparalleled *(SYN.)* peerless, unequaled, rare, unique, unmatched.

unpleasant *(SYN.)* offensive, disagreeable, repulsive, obnoxious, unpleasing.

unqualified *(SYN.)* inept, unfit, incapable, incompetent, unquestioned, absolute, utter.

unreasonable *(SYN.)* foolish, absurd, irrational, inconsistent, nonsensical, ridiculous, silly.
(ANT.) reasonable, sensible, sound, consistent, rational.

unruffled *(SYN.)* calm, smooth, serene, unperturbed.

unruly *(SYN.)* unmanageable, disorganized, disorderly, disobedient.
(ANT.) orderly.

unsafe *(SYN.)* hazardous, insecure, critical, dangerous, perilous, menacing, risky, precarious, threatening.
(ANT.) protected, secure, firm, safe.

unselfish *(SYN.)* bountiful, generous, liberal, giving, beneficent, magnanimous, openhanded, munificent.
(ANT.) miserly, stingy, greedy, selfish, covetous.

unsightly *(SYN.)* ugly, unattractive, hideous.

unsophisticated *(SYN.)* frank, candid, artless, ingenuous, naive, open, simple.
(ANT.) sophisticated, cunning, crafty.

unsound *(SYN.)* feeble, flimsy, weak, fragile, sick, unhealthy, diseased, invalid, faulty, false.

unstable *(SYN.)* fickle, fitful, inconstant, capricious, changeable, restless.
(ANT.) steady, stable, constant.

unswerving *(SYN.)* fast, firm, inflexible, constant, secure, stable, solid, steady.
(ANT.) sluggish, insecure, unsteady, unstable, loose, slow.

untainted *(SYN.)* genuine, pure, spotless, clean, clear, unadulterated.
(ANT.) polluted, tainted, sullied, tarnished, defiled, corrupt, foul.

untamed *(SYN.)* fierce, savage, uncivilized, barbarous, outlandish, rude, undomesticated, desert, wild, frenzied.
(ANT.) quiet, calm, civilized, placid.

untidy *(SYN.)* messy, sloppy, disorderly.

unusual *(SYN.)* capricious, abnormal, devious, eccentric, aberrant, irregular.

(ANT.) methodical, regular, usual, fixed, ordinary.

unyielding *(SYN.)* fast, firm, inflexible, constant, solid, secure, stable, steadfast, unswerving, steady.
(ANT.) sluggish, slow, insecure, loose, unsteady, unstable.

upbraid *(SYN.)* blame, censure, berate, admonish, rate, lecture, rebuke.
(ANT.) praise, commend, approve.

uphold *(SYN.)* justify, espouse, assert, defend, maintain, vindicate.
(ANT.) oppose, submit, deny, attack.

upright *(SYN.)* undeviating, right, unswerving, direct, erect, unbent.
(ANT.) bent, dishonest, crooked, circuitous, winding.

uprising *(SYN.)* revolution, mutiny, revolt, rebellion.

uproar *(SYN.)* noise, disorder, commotion, tumult, disturbance.

upset *(SYN.)* disturb, harass, bother, annoy, haunt, molest, inconvenience, perplex, pester, tease, plague, trouble.
(ANT.) soothe, relieve, please, gratify.

upshot *(SYN.)* conclusion, result.

urbane *(SYN.)* civil, considerate, cultivated, courteous, genteel, polite, accomplished, refined, well-mannered.
(ANT.) rude, uncouth, boorish, uncivil.

urge *(SYN.)* craving, desire, longing, lust, appetite, aspiration, yearning.
(ANT.) loathing, hate, distaste, aversion, compel, dissuade, discourage.

urgency *(SYN.)* emergency, exigency, pass, pinch, strait, crisis.

urgent *(SYN.)* critical, crucial, exigent, imperative, impelling, insistent.
(ANT.) trivial, petty, insignificant.

usage *(SYN.)* use, treatment, custom, practice, tradition.

use *(SYN.)* custom, practice, habit, training, usage, manner, apply, avail, employ, operate, utilize, exert, exhaust, handle, manage, accustom.
(ANT.) disuse, neglect, waste, ignore, overlook, idleness.

useful *(SYN.)* beneficial, helpful, good, serviceable, wholesome, advantageous.
(ANT.) harmful, injurious, deleterious, destructive, detrimental.

useless *(SYN.)* bootless, empty, idle, pointless, vain, valueless, worthless.
(ANT.) profitable, potent, effective.

usher *(SYN.)* guide, lead.

usual *(SYN.)* customary, common, familiar, general, normal, habitual, accustomed, everyday, ordinary, regular.
(ANT.) irregular, exceptional, rare, extraordinary, abnormal.

utensil *(SYN.)* instrument, tool, vehicle, apparatus, device, implement.
(ANT.) hindrance, obstruction.

utilize *(SYN.)* use, apply, devote, busy, employ, occupy, avail.
(ANT.) reject, banish, discard.

utopian *(SYN.)* perfect, ideal, faultless, exemplary, supreme, visionary, unreal.
(ANT.) real, imperfect, actual, faulty.

utter *(SYN.)* full, perfect, whole, finished, entire, speak, say, complete.
(ANT.) imperfect, deficient, lacking, faulty, incomplete.

vacancy *(SYN.)* void, emptiness, vacuum, hollowness, blankness, vacuity, depletion, nothingness.
(ANT.) plenitude, fullness, profusion, completeness.

vacant *(SYN.)* barren, empty, blank, bare, unoccupied, void, vacuous.
(ANT.) filled, packed, employed, full, replete, busy, engaged.

vacate *(SYN.)* abjure, relinquish, abdicate, renounce, abandon, resign, surrender, desert, waive, quit, leave.
(ANT.) stay, support, uphold, maintain.

vacation rest, holiday, recess, break.
(ANT.) labor, work, routine.

vacillate *(SYN.)* hesitate, oscillate, undulate, change, fluctuate, vary, waver.
(ANT.) adhere, persist, stick, decide.

vacillating *(SYN.)* contrary, illogical, contradictory, contrary, inconsistent, incongruous, incompatible, paradoxical, irreconcilable, unsteady, wavering.
(ANT.) correspondent, congruous, consistent, compatible.

vacuity *(SYN.)* space, emptiness, vacuum, void, blank, nothingness, ignorance, unawareness, senselessness, mindlessness, chatter, nonsense, froth, absurdity.
(ANT.) matter, fullness, content, substance, knowledge, intelligence.

vacuous *(SYN.)* dull, blank, uncomprehending, imbecillic, foolish, thoughtless, distracted, absent-minded.
(ANT.) responsive, alert, attentive, bright, intelligent, aware.

vacuum *(SYN.)* void, gap, emptiness, hole, chasm, nothingness, abyss.

vagabond *(SYN.)* pauper, ragamuffin, scrub, beggar, mendicant, starveling, wretch, tatterdemalion, hobo, tramp.
(ANT.) responsible, established, rooted, installed, reliable.

vagary *(SYN.)* notion, whim, fantasy, fancy, daydream, caprice, conceit, quirk, whimsy, impulse.

vagrant *(SYN.)* hobo, rover, tramp, beggar, bum, wanderer, vagabond.
(ANT.) settled, worker, laborer, rooted, ambitious, gentleman.

vague *(SYN.)* indefinite, hazy, dim, indistinct, ambiguous, obscure, undetermined, unclear, unsure, unsettled.
(ANT.) certain, spelled out, specific, lucid, clear, definite, distinct, explicit, precise, unequivocal.

vain *(SYN.)* fruitless, empty, bootless, futile, idle, abortive, ineffectual, unavailing, vapid, pointless, valueless, useless, trivial, unfruitful, worthless, unsuccessful, proud, conceited.
(ANT.) meek, modest, potent, rewarding, self-effacing, diffident, profitable, effective, humble.

vainglory *(SYN.)* conceit, pride, self-esteem, arrogance, self-respect, superciliousness, haughtiness, vanity.
(ANT.) shame, modesty, meekness, humility, lowliness.

valet *(SYN.)* groom, dresser, attendant, manservant.

valiant *(SYN.)* bold, brave, courageous, adventurous, audacious, chivalrous, daring, fearless, dauntless, heroic, brave, gallant, magnanimous, intrepid, unafraid, valorous, dauntless.
(ANT.) weak, fearful, cowardly, timid.

valid *(SYN.)* cogent, conclusive, effective, convincing, binding, efficacious, logical, powerful, legal, sound, weighty, well-founded, real, genuine, actual, true, trustworthy, authentic, strong, telling, logical, authentic.
(ANT.) weak, unconvincing, void, unproved, null, spurious, counterfeit.

validate *(SYN.)* corroborate, substantiate, support, confirm, prove, uphold, sustain, authenticate.
(ANT.) disprove, contradict, cancel.

valise *(SYN.)* satchel, bag, baggage.

valley *(SYN.)* dale, dell, lowland, basin, gully, vale, ravine.
(ANT.) highland, hill, upland, headland.

valor *(SYN.)* courage, heroism, bravery, boldness, intrepidity, fearlessness.

valuable *(SYN.)* profitable, useful, costly, precious, dear, expensive, worthy, important, high-priced, esteemed.
(ANT.) trashy, poor, cheap, worthless.

value *(SYN.)* price, merit, usefulness, value, virtue, utility, appreciate, prize, hold dear, treasure, excellence, benefit, cost, rate, evaluate, appraise, esteem, importance, worth, worthiness.
(ANT.) valuelessness, uselessness, cheapness.

vanish *(SYN.)* evaporate, disappear.
(ANT.) appear.

vanity *(SYN.)* complacency, egotism, pride, self-esteem, conceit, caprice, fancy, idea, conception, notion, haughtiness, self-respect, whim, smugness, vainglory, arrogance, imagination.
(ANT.) meekness, humility, diffidence.

vanquish *(SYN.)* defeat, crush, humble, surmount, master, beat, conquer, overcome, rout, quell, subjugate, subdue.
(ANT.) surrender, cede, lose, retreat, capitulate.

vapid *(SYN.)* hackneyed, inane, insipid, trite, banal, commonplace.
(ANT.) striking, novel, fresh, original, stimulating.

vapor *(SYN.)* steam, fog, mist, smog, haze, steam.

variable *(SYN.)* fickle, fitful, inconstant, unstable, shifting, changeable, unsteady, wavering, vacillating.
(ANT.) unchanging, uniform, stable, un-wavering, steady, constant.

variant *(SYN.)* dissimilar, different, distinct, contrary, diverse, divergent, opposite, unlike, incongruous, divers, sundry, various, miscellaneous.
(ANT.) similar, same, congruous, identical, alike.

variation *(SYN.)* change, alternation, alteration, substitution, variety, substitute, mutation, exchange, vicissitude.

(ANT.) uniformity, stability, monotony.

variety *(SYN.)* dissimilarity, diversity, heterogeneity, assortment, change, difference, medley, mixture, miscellany, variousness, form, type, class, breed, sort, kind, strain, stock.
(ANT.) likeness, monotony, uniformity, sameness, homogeneity.

various *(SYN.)* miscellaneous, sundry, divers, several, contrary, distinct, dissimilar, divergent, unlike, incongruous, opposite, different.
(ANT.) identical, similar, same, alike, congruous.

vary *(SYN.)* exchange, substitute, alter, change, modify, shift, convert, transform, transfigure, diversify, veer.
(ANT.) settle, stabilize, continue, establish, preserve.

vassalage *(SYN.)* confinement, captivity, imprisonment, slavery, thralldom.
(ANT.) liberation, freedom.

vast *(SYN.)* big, capacious, extensive, huge, great, ample, immense, wide, unlimited, enormous, measureless, large.
(ANT.) tiny, small, short, little.

vault *(SYN.)* caper, jerk, jump, leap, bound, crypt, sepulcher, hop, spring, safe, start, tomb, grave, catacomb, skip.

vaunt *(SYN.)* crow, flaunt, glory, boast.
(ANT.) minimize, humble, deprecate, apologize.

vaunting *(SYN.)* flourish, display, ostentation, parade, show, pomp.
(ANT.) modesty, reserve, humility.

vehement *(SYN.)* excitable, fervent, ardent, burning, fiery, glowing, impetuous, hot, irascible, passionate.
(ANT.) calm, quiet, cool, apathetic, deliberate.

veil *(SYN.)* clothe, conceal, cover, cloak, web, hide, curtain, disguise, gauze, film, envelop, screen, mask, shield, film.
(ANT.) reveal, unveil, bare, divulge.

velocity *(SYN.)* quickness, rapidity, speed, swiftness.

venal *(SYN.)* greedy, mercenary, sordid, corrupt.
(ANT.) liberal, honorable, generous.

venerable *(SYN.)* antiquated, aged, antique, ancient, elderly, old, superannuated, old-fashion.
(ANT.) young, new, youthful, modern.

venerate *(SYN.)* approve, esteem, admire, appreciate, wonder, respect.
(ANT.) dislike, despise.

vengeance *(SYN.)* requital, reprisal, reparation, retribution, revenge.
(ANT.) forgiveness, remission, pardon, mercy.

venom *(SYN.)* toxin, poison, bitterness, spite, hate.

vent *(SYN.)* eject, emit, expel, shoot, spurt, emanate, hurl, shed, belch, discharge, breathe.

venture *(ANT.)* speculate, attempt, test, dare, hazard, gamble, chance, risk.
(ANT.) insure, secure, protect.

verbal *(SYN.)* oral, spoken, literal, unwritten, vocal.

(ANT.) printed, written, recorded.

verbose *(SYN.)* communicative, glib, chattering, chatty, garrulous, loquacious, talkative.
(ANT.) uncommunicative, silent.

verbosity *(SYN.)* long-windedness, verboseness, redundancy, wordiness.
(ANT.) terseness, laconic, conciseness.

verdict *(SYN.)* judgment, finding, opinion, decision.

verge *(SYN.)* lip, rim, edge, margin, brink, brim.

verification *(SYN.)* confirmation, demonstration, evidence, proof, test, experiment, testimony, trial.
(ANT.) terseness, laconic, conciseness.

verify *(SYN.)* confirm, substantiate, acknowledge, determine, assure, establish, approve, fix, settle, ratify, strengthen, corroborate, affirm, sanction.

veritable *(SYN.)* authentic, correct, genuine, real, true, accurate, actual.
(ANT.) false, fictitious, spurious, erroneous, counterfeit.

versed *(SYN.)* conversant, familiar, intimate, knowing, acquainted, aware.
(ANT.) inclined, level, prone, oblique.

version *(SYN.)* interpretation, rendition.

vertical *(SYN.)* erect, perpendicular, upright.
(ANT.) horizontal.

very *(SYN.)* exceedingly, extremely, greatly, considerably.

vessel *(SYN.)* craft, boat, ship.

vestige *(SYN.)* stain, scar, mark, brand, stigma, characteristic, trace, feature, trait, symptoms, hint, token, suggestion, indication.

veto *(SYN.)* refusal, denial, refuse, deny, negate, forbid, prohibit.
(ANT.) approve, approval.

vex *(SYN.)* embitter, exasperate, aggravate, annoy, chafe, bother, provoke, pester, plague, anger, nettle, anger.
(ANT.) soften soothe, palliate, mitigate.

vexation *(SYN.)* chagrin, irritation, annoyance, mortification, irritation, pique.
(ANT.) comfort, pleasure, appeasement, gratification.

vibrate *(SYN.)* flutter, jar, quake, jolt, quaver, agitate, transgression, wickedness, ungodliness, tremble, wrong.

vice *(SYN.)* iniquity, crime, offense, evil, guilt, sin, ungodliness, wickedness, depravity, corruption, wrong.
(ANT.) righteousness, virtue, goodness, innocence, purity.

vicinity *(SYN.)* district, area, locality, neighborhood, environs, proximity, nearness, adjacency.
(ANT.) remoteness, distance.

vicious *(SYN.)* bad, evil, wicked, sinful, corrupt, cruel, savage, dangerous.

victimize *(SYN.)* cheat, dupe, swindle, deceive, take advantage of.

victor *(SYN.)* champion, winner.
(ANT.) loser.

victory *(SYN.)* conquest, jubilation, triumph, success, achievement, ovation.
(ANT.) defeat, failure.

view *(SYN.)* discern, gaze, glance, be-

hold, eye, discern, stare, watch, examine, witness, prospect, vision, vista, sight, look, panorama, opinion, judgment, belief, impression, perspective, range, regard, thought, observation, survey, scene, conception, outlook, inspect, observe.
(ANT.) miss, overlook, avert, hide.

viewpoint *(SYN.)* attitude, standpoint, aspect, pose, disposition, position, stand, posture.

vigilant *(SYN.)* anxious, attentive, careful, alert, circumspect, cautious, observant, wary, watchful, wakeful.
(ANT.) inattentive, neglectful, careless.

vigor *(SYN.)* spirit, verve, energy, zeal, fortitude, vitality, strength, liveliness.
(ANT.) listlessness.

vigorous *(SYN.)* brisk, energetic, active, blithe, animated, frolicsome, strong, spirited, lively, forceful, sprightly, vivacious, powerful, supple.
(ANT.) vapid, dull, listless, insipid.

vile *(SYN.)* foul, loathsome, base, depraved, debased, sordid, vulgar, wicked, abject, ignoble, mean, worthless, sinful, bad, low, wretched, evil, offensive, objectionable, disgusting.
(ANT.) honorable, upright, decent, laudable, attractive.

vilify *(SYN.)* asperse, defame, disparage, abuse, malign, revile, scandalize.
(ANT.) protect, honor, praise, cherish.

village *(SYN.)* hamlet, town.
(ANT.) metropolis, city.

villain *(SYN.)* rascal, rogue, cad, brute, scoundrel, devil, scamp.

villainous *(SYN.)* deleterious, evil, bad, base, iniquitous, unsound, sinful, unwholesome, wicked.
(ANT.) honorable, reputable, moral, good, excellent.

violate *(SYN.)* infringe, break.

violent *(SYN.)* strong, forcible, forceful.
(ANT.) gentle.

vindicate clear, assert, defend, absolve, excuse, acquit, uphold, support.
(ANT.) accuse, convict, abandon.

violate *(SYN.)* disobey, invade, defile, break, desecrate, pollute, dishonor, debauch, profane, deflower, ravish.

violence *(SYN.)* constraint, force, compulsion, coercion.
(ANT.) weakness, persuasion, feebleness, impotence, frailty.

violent *(SYN.)* strong, forceful, powerful, forcible, angry, fierce, savage, passionate, furious.
(ANT.) gentle.

virgin *(SYN.)* immaculate, genuine, spotless, clean, chaste, untainted, innocent, guiltless, pure, untouched, modest, unused, undefiled, pure.
(ANT.) foul, tainted, defiled, sullied, polluted, corrupt.

virtue *(SYN.)* integrity, probity, purity, chastity, goodness, rectitude, effectiveness, force, honor, power, efficacy, quality, strength, merit, righteousness, advantage, excellence, advantage.
(ANT.) fault, vice, lewdness, corruption.

virulent *(SYN.)* hostile, malevolent, malignant, bitter, spiteful, wicked.

(ANT.) kind, affectionate, benevolent.

vision *(SYN.)* dream, hallucination, mirage, eyesight, sight, fantasy, illusion, specter, revelation, phantom, spook, ghost, imagination, farsightedness, keenness, foresight, apparition.
(ANT.) verity, reality.

visit *(SYN.)* attend, see, call on, appointment.

visitor *(SYN.)* caller, guest.

vista *(SYN.)* view, scene, aspect.

vital *(SYN.)* cardinal, living, paramount, alive, essential, critical, basic, indispensable, urgent, life-and-death.
(ANT.) lifeless, unimportant, inanimate, nonessential.

vitality *(SYN.)* buoyancy, being, life, liveliness, existence, spirit, vigor.
(ANT.) death, lethargy, dullness, demise.

vivacious *(SYN.)* lively, spirited.

vivid *(SYN.)* brilliant, striking, clear, bright, intense, lively, strong, graphic.
(ANT.) dim, dusky, vague, dull, dreary.

vocal *(SYN.)* said, uttered, oral, spoken, definite, outspoken, specific.

vocation *(SYN.)* commerce, employment, business, art, job, profession, trade, occupation, career, calling, work, trading.
(ANT.) pastime, hobby, avocation.

void *(SYN.)* barren, emptiness, space, annul, cancel, empty, bare, unoccupied, meaningless, invalid, useless.
(ANT.) employed, full, replete, engaged.

volatile *(SYN.)* effervescent, resilient, buoyant, animated, cheerful, hopeful.
(ANT.) depressed, sullen, hopeless, dejected, despondent.

volition *(SYN.)* desire, intention, pleasure, preference, choice, decision, resolution, testament, wish, will.
(ANT.) disinterest, compulsion, indifference.

voluble *(SYN.)* glib, communicative, verbose, loquacious, chatty, chattering.
(ANT.) uncommunicative, laconic, taciturn, silent.

volume *(SYN.)* capacity, skill, power, talent, faculty, magnitude, mass, book.
(ANT.) stupidity, inability, impotence, incapacity.

voluntary *(SYN.)* extemporaneous, free, automatic, spontaneous, offhand.
(ANT.) forced, planned, required, rehearsed, compulsory, prepared.

volunteer *(SYN.)* extend, offer, present, advance, propose, tender, sacrifice.
(ANT.) receive, spurn, reject, accept, retain.

voodoo *(SYN.)* art, conjuring, legerdemain, magic, witchcraft, wizardry.

voracious *(SYN.)* insatiable, ravenous.

vow *(SYN.)* oath, pledge, swear, promise.

voyage *(SYN.)* tour, journey, excursion.

vulgar *(SYN.)* ordinary, popular, common, general, crude, coarse, low.
(ANT.) polite, refined, select, aristocratic.

vulnerable *(SYN.)* unguarded, defenseless, unprotected.

wacky *(SYN.)* strange, crazy, peculiar.

wad *(SYN.)* hunk, clump, chunk.

wafer *(SYN.)* cracker, lozenge.

waft *(SYN.)* convey, glide, sail, float.

wage *(SYN.)* conduct, pursue, make.

wager *(SYN.)* stake, bet, play, gamble, speculate, risk, chance.

wages *(SYN.)* payment, compensation, fee, allowance, pay, salary, earnings.

wagon *(SYN.)* carriage, buggy, cart, surrey, stagecoach.

waif *(SYN.)* guttersnipe, ragamuffin, tramp, vagrant, urchin.

wail *(SYN.)* mourn, moan, cry, bewail, lament, bemoan, sorrow.

wait *(SYN.)* linger, tarry, attend, bide, watch, delay, await, abide, stay, serve, pause, remain, rest, minister, expect.
(ANT.) hasten, act leave, expedite.

waive *(SYN.)* renounce, abandon, surrender, relinquish, forgo.
(ANT.) uphold, maintain.

wake *(SYN.)* awaken, rouse, waken, arouse, stimulate, activate.
(ANT.) doze, sleep.

waken *(SYN.)* wake, arouse, rouse, awaken, stimulate, activate.
(ANT.) doze, sleep.

walk *(SYN.)* step, stroll, march, amble, saunter, hike, lane, path, passage.

wall *(SYN.)* barricade, divider, partition, panel, stockade.

wallow *(SYN.)* plunge, roll, flounder.

wan *(SYN.)* colorless, haggard, gaunt, pale, pallid, pasty, pale.

wander *(SYN.)* rove, stroll, deviate, ramble, digress, roam, range, err.
(ANT.) linger, stop, settle.

wane *(SYN.)* abate, weaken, fade, ebb, decrease, wither, subside.

want *(SYN.)* penury, destitution, crave, desire, requirement, poverty, wish, require, need, privation.
(ANT.) wealth, plenty, abundance.

wanton *(SYN.)* lecherous, immoral, loose, lewd, salacious, lustful.

war *(SYN.)* battle, hostilities, combat, fight, strife, contention.

warble *(SYN.)* sing, trill, chirp.

ward *(SYN.)* annex, wing, section.

warden *(SYN.)* custodian, guard, guardian, keeper, turnkey, jailer, curator.

ward off *(SYN.)* repel, thwart, deflect, foil, deter, forestall, repulse.

wardrobe *(SYN.)* chiffonier, bureau, closet, armoire.

warehouse *(SYN.)* arsenal, store-house, depository.

wares *(SYN.)* merchandise, staples, inventory, commodities, goods.

wariness *(SYN.)* heed, care, watchfulness, caution, vigilance.
(ANT.) carelessness, abandon.

warlike *(SYN.)* hostile, unfriendly, combative, belligerent, antagonistic, pugnacious, opposed, aggressive.
(ANT.) cordial, peaceful, amicable.

warm *(SYN.)* sincere, cordial, hearty, earnest, sympathetic, ardent, heated, gracious, temperate, enthusiastic.
(ANT.) cool, aloof, brisk, indifferent.

warmhearted *(SYN.)* loving, kind, kindhearted, friendly, generous.

warmth *(SYN.)* friendliness, cordiality, geniality, understanding, compassion.

warn *(SYN.)* apprise, notify, admonish, caution, advise, inform.

warning *(SYN.)* advice, information, caution, portent, admonition, indication, notice, sign.

warp *(SYN.)* turn, bend, twist, distort.

warrant *(SYN.)* pledge, assurance, warranty, guarantee, authorize, approve, mandate, sanction.

warrior *(SYN.)* combatant, fighter, soldier, mercenary, guerrilla.

wary *(SYN.)* careful, awake, watchful, heedful, attentive, alive, mindful.
(ANT.) unaware, indifferent, apathetic.

wash *(SYN.)* launder, cleanse, rub, touch, reach, border, wet, clean, scrub.
(ANT.) soil, dirty, stain.

waspish *(SYN.)* irritable, petulant, fractious, testy, snappish, touchy.
(ANT.) pleasant, genial.

waste *(SYN.)* forlorn, bleak, wild, solitary, dissipate, abandoned, spend, deserted, bare, consume, dwindle, decay, misspend, decrease, wither.
(ANT.) cultivated, attended.

wasteful *(SYN.)* wanton, costly, lavish, extravagant.

watch *(SYN.)* inspect, descry, behold, distinguish, guard, attend, observe, contemplate, espy, perceive, look at, protect, chronometer, timepiece.

watchful *(SYN.)* alert, careful, attentive, vigilant, wary, cautious.

waterfall *(SYN.)* cascade, cataract.

wave *(SYN.)* ripple, whitecap, undulation, breaker, surf, swell, sea, surge.

waver *(SYN.)* question, suspect, flicker, deliberate, doubt, distrust, hesitate.
(ANT.) confide, trust, believe, decide.

wavering *(SYN.)* fickle, shifting, variable, changeable, vacillating, fitful.
(ANT.) unchanging, constant, uniform.

wavy *(SYN.)* rippling, serpentine, curly.

wax *(SYN.)* raise, heighten, expand, accrue, enhance, extend, multiply, enlarge, augment, amplify.
(ANT.) contract, reduce, atrophy, diminish.

way *(SYN.)* habit, road, course, avenue, route, mode, system, channel, track, fashion, method, walk, approach.

waylay *(SYN.)* surprise, accost, ambush, attack, pounce, intercept.

wayward *(SYN.)* stubborn, headstrong, contrary, obstinate, naughty, disobedient, rebellious, refractory.

weak *(SYN.)* frail, debilitated, delicate, poor, wavering, infirm, bending, lame, defenseless, vulnerable, fragile, pliant.
(ANT.) strong, potent, sturdy, powerful.

weaken *(SYN.)* exhaust, sap, disable, devitalize.

weakness *(SYN.)* incompetence, inability, impotence, handicap, fondness, liking, affection, disability, incapacity.
(ANT.) strength, ability, dislike, power.

wealth *(SYN.)* fortune, money, riches, possessions, abundance, opulence, affluence, property, quantity, luxury.
(ANT.) want, need.

wealthy *(SYN.)* rich, exorbitant,

prosperous, affluent, successful.
(ANT.) poverty-stricken, poor, indigent, impoverished, beggarly, destitute, needy.
wear (SYN.) erode, fray, grind, apparel, clothes, garb, attire.
wearied (SYN.) weak, languid, faint, irresolute, feeble, timid.
(ANT.) brave, vigorous.
weary (SYN.) faint, spent, worn, tired, fatigued, exhausted, tiresome, bored.
(ANT.) rested, hearty, fresh.
weasel (SYN.) cheat, traitor, be-trayer.
weave (SYN.) lace, interlace, plait, intertwine, braid, knit.
web (SYN.) netting, network, net, cobweb, trap, entanglement.
wed (SYN.) espouse, marry.
wedlock (SYN.) marriage, union, espousal, wedding, matrimony.
wedge (SYN.) chock, jam, lodge.
wee (SYN.) small, tiny, miniature, petite, microscopic, minute.
weep (SYN.) mourn, sob, bemoan, cry, lament, whimper, wail.
weigh (SYN.) heed, deliberate, consider, study, ponder, contemplate.
(ANT.) neglect, ignore.
weight (SYN.) importance, emphasis, load, burden, import, stress, influence, heaviness, pressure, value.
(ANT.) triviality, levity, insignificance, lightness, buoyancy.
weird (SYN.) odd, eerie, strange, unnatural, peculiar, spooky.
welcome (SYN.) take, entertain, greet, accept, receive, reception, gain, greeting, shelter.
(ANT.) reject, impart, discharge.
weld (SYN.) solder, connect, fuse, bond.
welfare (SYN.) good, prosperity.
well (SYN.) hearty, happy, sound, hale, beneficial, good, convenient, expedient, healthy, favorably, fully, thoroughly, surely, adequately, satisfactorily, competently, certainly.
(ANT.) infirm, depressed, weak.
well-being (SYN.) delight, happiness, satisfaction, contentment, gladness.
(ANT.) sorrow, grief, sadness, despair.
well-bred (SYN.) cultured, polite, genteel, courtly, refined, cultivated.
(ANT.) crude, vulgar, boorish, rude.
well-known (SYN.) famous, illustrious, celebrated, noted, eminent, renowned.
(ANT.) unknown, ignominious, obscure, hidden.
wet (SYN.) moist, dank, soaked, damp, drenched, dampen, moisten.
(ANT.) arid, dry, parched.
wharf (SYN.) pier, dock.
wheedle (SYN.) coax, cajole, persuade.
whim (SYN.) fancy, notion, humor, quirk, caprice, whimsy, inclination.
whimsical (SYN.) quaint, strange, curious, odd, unusual, droll, eccentric.
(ANT.) normal, usual, familiar.
whine (SYN.) whimper, moan, complain.
whip (SYN.) scourge, thrash, beat, lash.
whirl (SYN.) rotate, twirl, spin, revolve, reel.
whole (SYN.) total, sound, all, intact, complete, well, hale, integral, unimpaired, healed, entire, uncut, un-

divided, unbroken, undamaged, intact.
(ANT.) partial, defective, imperfect, deficient.
wholesome (SYN.) robust, well, hale, healthy, sound, salubrious, good, hygienic, salutary, nourishing, healthful, strong, nutritious, hearty.
(ANT.) frail, noxious, infirm, delicate, injurious, diseased.
wicked (SYN.) deleterious, iniquitous, immoral, bad, evil, base, ungodly, unsound, sinful, bitter, blasphemous, malicious, evil-minded, profane.
(ANT.) moral, good, reputable, honorable.
wide (SYN.) large, broad, sweeping, extensive, vast, expanded.
(ANT.) restricted, narrow.
width (SYN.) wideness, extensiveness, breadth.
wield (SYN.) handle, brandish.
wild (SYN.) outlandish, uncivilized, untamed, irregular, wanton, foolish, mad, barbarous, rough, waste, desert, uncultivated, boisterous, unruly, savage, primitive, giddy, unrestrained, silly, wayward, uncontrolled, impetuous, crazy, ferocious, undomesticated, desolate.
(ANT.) quiet, gentle, placid, tame, restrained, civilized.
willful (SYN.) intentional, designed, contemplated, studied, premedi-tated.
(ANT.) fortuitous.
will (SYN.) intention, desire, volition, decision, resolution, wish, resoluteness, choice, determination, pleasure.
(ANT.) disinterest, coercion, indifference.
willing (SYN.) agreeing, energetic, enthusiastic, consenting, agreeable, eager.
wilt (SYN.) sag, droop, weaken.
wily (SYN.) cunning, foxy, sly, crafty.
win (SYN.) gain, succeed, prevail, achieve, thrive, obtain, get, acquire, earn, flourish.
(ANT.) lose, miss, forfeit, fail.
wind (SYN.) gale, breeze, storm, gust, blast, air, breath, flurry, puff, blow, hurricane, typhoon, cyclone, tornado, suggestion, hint, clue, zephyr, squall, coil, crank, screw, meander, wander, twist, weave, draft.
winsome (SYN.) winning, charming, agreeable.
wisdom (SYN.) insight, judgment, learning, sense, discretion, reason, prudence, erudition, foresight, intelligence, sageness, knowledge, information, sagacity.
(ANT.) nonsense, foolishness, stupidity, ignorance.
wise (SYN.) informed, sagacious, learned, penetrating, enlightened, advisable, prudent, profound, deep, erudite, scholarly, knowing, sound, intelligent, expedient, discerning.
(ANT.) simple, shallow, foolish.
wish (SYN.) crave, hanker, long, hunger, yearning, lust, craving, yearn, want, appetite, covet, longing, desire, urge.
(ANT.) hate, aversion, loathing, dis-

taste.

wit *(SYN.)* sense, humor, pleasantry, satire, intelligence, comprehension, understanding, banter, mind, wisdom, intellect, wittiness, fun, drollery, humorist, wag, comedian, raillery, irony, witticism.
(ANT.) solemnity, commonplace, sobriety.

witch *(SYN.)* magician, sorcerer, enchanter, sorceress, enchantress, warlock.

witchcraft *(SYN.)* enchantment, magic, wizardry, conjuring, voodoo.

withdraw *(SYN.)* renounce, leave, abandon, recall, retreat, go, secede, desert, quit, retire, depart, retract, remove, forsake.
(ANT.) enter, tarry, abide, place, stay.

wither *(SYN.)* wilt, languish, dry, shrivel, decline, fade, decay, sear, waste, wizen, weaken, droop, sink, fail, shrink.
(ANT.) renew, refresh, revive.

withhold *(SYN.)* forbear, abstain, repress, check, refrain.
(ANT.) persist, continue.

withstand *(SYN.)* defy, contradict, bar, thwart, oppose, hinder, combat, resist, counteract.
(ANT.) succumb, cooperate, support.

witness *(SYN.)* perceive, proof, spectator, confirmation, see, attestation, watch, observe, eyewitness, declaration, notice, testimony.
(ANT.) refutation, contradiction, argument.

witty *(SYN.)* funny, talented, apt, bright, adroit, sharp, clever.
(ANT.) foolish, slow, dull, clumsy, awkward.

wizard *(SYN.)* magician, conjuror, sorcerer.

wizardry *(SYN.)* voodoo, legerdemain, conjuring, witchcraft, charm.

woe *(SYN.)* sorrow, disaster, trouble, evil, agony, suffering, anguish, sadness, grief, distress, misery, torment, misfortune.
(ANT.) pleasure, delight, fun.

womanly *(SYN.)* girlish, womanish, female, ladylike.
(ANT.) mannish, virile, male, masculine.

wonder *(SYN.)* awe, curiosity, miracle, admiration, surprise, wonderment, marvel, conjecture, amazement, question, astonishment.
(ANT.) expectation, familiarity, indifference, apathy, triviality.

wonderful *(SYN.)* extraordinary, marvelous, astonishing, amazing, remarkable, astounding.

wont *(SYN.)* practice, use, custom, training, habit, usage, manner.
(ANT.) inexperience, disuse.

word *(SYN.)* phrase, term, utterance, expression, articulate.

wordy *(SYN.)* talkative, verbose, garrulous.

work *(SYN.)* opus, employment, achievement, performance, toil, business, exertion, occupation, labor, job,

product, accomplishment, travail, effort.
(ANT.) recreation, leisure, vacation, ease.

working *(SYN.)* busy, active, industrious.
(ANT.) lazy, dormant, passive, inactive.

world *(SYN.)* globe, earth, universe.

worldly *(SYN.)* bodily, fleshy, animal, carnal, corporeal, gross, voluptuous, base.
(ANT.) refined, temperate, exalted, spiritual.

worn *(SYN.)* tired, jaded, exhausted, wearied, faint, weary.
(ANT.) invigorated, fresh, rested.

worry *(SYN.)* concern, trouble, disquiet, anxiety, fear, pain, harry, gall, grieve, persecute, annoy, disturb, fidget, chafe, agonize, bother, haze, pester, uneasiness, fret.
(ANT.) console, comfort, contentment, satisfaction, peace.

worship *(SYN.)* honor, revere, adore, idolize, reverence, glorify, respect, deify, venerate.
(ANT.) curse, scorn, blaspheme, despise.

worth *(SYN.)* value, price, deserving, excellence, utility, worthiness, merit.
(ANT.) uselessness, cheapness.

worthless *(SYN.)* empty, idle, abortive, ineffectual, bootless, vain, unavailing.
(ANT.) meek, effective, modest, potent.

wound *(SYN.)* mar, harm, damage, hurt, dishonor, injure, injury, spoil, wrong.
(ANT.) compliment, benefit, help.

wrangle *(SYN.)* spat, bickering, affray, argument, dispute, quarrel, altercation, contention, squabble.
(ANT.) peace, friendliness, reconciliation, harmony.

wrap *(SYN.)* cover, protect, shield, cloak, mask, clothe, curtain, guard.
(ANT.) reveal, bare, unveil, expose.

wrath *(SYN.)* fury, anger, irritation, rage, animosity, passion, temper, petulance, choler, resentment.
(ANT.) patience, conciliation, peace.

wreck *(SYN.)* ravage, devastation, extinguish, destroy, annihilate, damage, raze, demolish, destruction, ruin.
(ANT.) construct, preserve, establish.

wrench *(SYN.)* tug, jerk, twist.

wrestle *(SYN.)* fight, tussle, grapple.

wretch *(SYN.)* cad, knave, scoundrel.

wretched *(SYN.)* forlorn, miserable, comfortless, despicable, paltry, low, worthless, disconsolate, sorry, mean.
(ANT.) noble, contented, happy, significant.

wring *(SYN.)* twist, extract.

writer *(SYN.)* creator, maker, author, father, composer.

writhe *(SYN.)* twist, squirm.

wrong *(SYN.)* awry, incorrect, improper, amiss, naughty, inappropriate, criminal, faulty, erroneous, bad, evil, imprecise, inaccurate, askew, sin, incorrectness, false, unsuitable, impropriety, wickedness, immoral.
(ANT.) proper, true, correct, suitable.

wry *(SYN.)* amusing, witty, dry, droll.

yacht *(SYN.)* sailboat, boat, cruiser.

yak *(SYN.)* chatter, babble, jabber, talk.

yank *(SYN.)* pull, wrest, draw, haul, tug, jerk, wrench, heave, extract, grab, wrest, snatch, nab, twitch, wring, extract.

yap *(SYN.)* howl, bark.

yard *(SYN.)* pen, confine, court, enclosure, compound, garden, courtyard.

yardstick *(SYN.)* measure, criterion, gauge.

yarn *(SYN.)* wool, tale, narrative, thread, story, fiber, anecdote, spiel.

yaw *(SYN.)* tack, change course, pitch, toss, roll.

yawn *(SYN.)* open, gape.

yearly *(SYN.)* annually.

yearn *(SYN.)* pine, long for, want, desire, crave, wish for, hope for.

yearning *(SYN.)* hungering, craving, desire, longing, appetite, lust, urge, aspiration, wish.

(ANT.) distaste, loathing, abomination, hate.

yell *(SYN.)* call, scream, shout, whoop, howl, roar, holler, wail, bawl.

yellow *(SYN.)* fearful, cowardly, chicken.

(ANT.) bold, brave.

yelp *(SYN.)* screech, squeal, howl, bark, yap.

yen *(SYN.)* longing, craving, fancy, appetite, desire, lust, hunger.

yet *(SYN.)* moreover, also, additionally, besides.

yield *(SYN.)* produce, afford, breed, grant, accord, cede, relent, succumb, bestow, allow, permit, give way, submit, bear, surrender, supply, fruits, give up, abdicate, return, impart, harvest, permit, accede, acquiesce, crop, capitulate, pay, concede, generate, relinquish.

(ANT.) assert, deny, refuse, resist, struggle, oppose, strive.

yielding *(SYN.)* dutiful, submissive, compliant, obedient, tractable.

(ANT.) rebellious, intractable, insubordinate.

yoke *(SYN.)* tether, leash, bridle, harness.

yokel *(SYN.)* hick, peasant, hayseed, innocent.

young *(SYN.)* immature, undeveloped, youthful, underdeveloped, juvenile, junior, underage.

(ANT.) old, mature, elderly.

youngster *(SYN.)* kid, lad, stripling, minor, youth, child, fledgling.

(ANT.) adult, elder.

youthful *(SYN.)* childish, immature, young, boyish, childlike, callow, girlish, puerile, juvenile, adolescent, growing, robust, active, peppy.

(ANT.) old, elderly, senile, aged, mature.

yowl *(SYN.)* yell, shriek, cry, wail, whoop, howl, scream.

zany *(SYN.)* clownish, comical, foolish, silly, scatterbrained.

zap *(SYN.)* drive, vim, pep, determination.

zeal *(SYN.)* fervor, eagerness, passion, feverency, vehemence, devotion, intensity, excitement, earnestness, inspiration, warmth, ardor, fanaticism, enthusiasm.

(ANT.) unconcern, ennui, apathy, indifference.

zealot *(SYN.)* champion, crank, fanatic, bigot.

zealous *(SYN.)* enthusiastic, fiery, keen, eager, fervid, ardent, intense, vehement, fervent, glowing, hot, impassioned, passionate.

(ANT.) cool, nonchalant, apathetic.

zenith *(SYN.)* culmination, apex, height, acme, consummation, top, summit, pinnacle, climax, peak.

(ANT.) floor, nadir, depth, base, anticlimax.

zero *(SYN.)* nonexistent, nil, nothing, none.

zest *(SYN.)* enjoyment, savor, eagerness, relish, satisfaction, gusto, spice, tang, pleasure, exhilaration.

zestful *(SYN.)* delightful, thrilling, exciting, stimulating, enjoyable.

zip *(SYN.)* vigor, vim, energy, vitality, spirited, animation, provocative.

zone *(SYN.)* region, climate, tract, belt, sector, section, district, locality, precinct, territory.

zoo *(SYN.)* menagerie.

zoom *(SYN.)* zip, fly, speed, whiz, roar, race.

BUSINESS DICTIONARY

abandonment *Law* The deliberate surrender of property or rights without conveying ownership to another as in abandonment of a rental property before the lease is up.

abatement *Accounting* Cancellation, all or in part, of a levy, such as for taxes, or a special assessment. *Law* Termination of a **cause of action.**

abend, abnormal ending *Computers* The termination of computer processing caused by a program or system fault.

ability to pay *Labor Relations* Descriptive of a company's pay capacity to absorb the cost of wage or fringe benefit increases demanded by a union; a company rejecting demands during contract negotiations on the basis that they cannot afford the cost may be forced to open its books to the union.

abort *Computers* To terminate the processing of data before completion.

above the line *Accounting, Finance* Any item on a financial report that affects *the line,* or **bottom line** of the report which is income before taxes, such as income subject to tax and expenses that are deductible.

absorbed *Accounting* Descriptive of fixed expenses such as for rent and administration, so described because they are *absorbed* into manufacturing costs according to a formula based on budgeted units. The condition of a fixed expense that has been completely charged off to manufacturing cost for the accounting period. See also **absorption costing.**

absorption costing *Accounting* A method of calculating the cost of manufactured units by assigning all costs to those units: variable costs are applied directly; fixed costs are assigned based on the absorption rate.

absorption rate *Accounting* The standard by which fixed costs are allocated to variable costs, as by number of units, hours of operation, etc.

accelerated depreciation *Accounting* Any of a number of systems for calculating the reduction in the **book value** of an asset based on a larger reduction in the early years.

access *Computers* To load a program or call up data for processing.

access code *Computers* A user's name or series of characters that are required to log onto a computer, program or certain files; a security code.

access time *Computers* The time required for a computer to retrieve information from storage or to return it to storage.

account, accounts *Accounting* The records of a company's financial transactions, grouped by type, as *Assets, Expenses, Liabilities, Sales,* etc. *Commerce* A company's contracts with customers and vendors, often allowing payment at a later date; the record of that contract.

accountability In general, the chain of command through which may be determined the person held accountable for an action, a project or some other phase of company activity; responsibility for some facet of the company operation.

account aging *Accounting* The classification of open accounts, receivable or payable, by the lapsed time since the transaction was recorded, usually in thirty day increments.

accountant One trained in the management of financial records and reporting of the financial aspects of an organization.

account executive *Marketing* Generally, a company executive, the primary link with a company's clients, who is often the mediator between the interests of the company and the needs of the client.

accounting The science of providing meaningful information about a company's finances as a tool for management.

accounting check *Accounting, Computers* A routine, such as totaling columns across a spreadsheet, to assure that data has been entered accurately.

accounting cycle Any set of procedures with a specific beginning and ending, such as for an accounts payable that begins with a journal entry and ends when a check is written.

accounting method The system used by a business for maintaining financial records as **cash basis** or **accrual basis.**

accounting principles Generally accepted procedures for recording and reporting financial transactions, often influenced or governed by tax law.

accounting procedure The step by step process used to record and report the financial transactions of an organization.

accounting system The means by which the financial transactions of an organization are recorded, including personnel, equipment and programs.

account number *Accounting* A numeric or alphanumeric number assigned to an **account** for easy reference; usually, a particular series represents a type of account, such as 1000 for *Expense,* 2000 for *Income,* etc. and numbers within the series represent subsets, as 1100 for *Supplies,* 1200 for *Utilities,* etc. *Commerce* The number that identifies the company's accounts with outside vendors or services, as a *bank account.*

accounts payable *Accounting* The record of amounts owed to suppliers of goods or services.

accounts receivable *Accounting* The record of amounts owed to the company for goods or services rendered.

accrual *Accounting* The accumulation of charges against accounts, whether or not anything of value is exchanged.

accrual accounts *Accounting* The records, on a company's books, of charges that are due or anticipated, as accrued liability for rent or taxes.

accrual basis An **accounting method** wherein payables and receivables are recorded as they are incurred, with an adjusting entry made to the ledger when they are actually paid or received. See also **cash basis.**

accumulated depreciation *Accounting* A compilation of the amount that has been charged off to depreciation that, when deducted from the original cost of the item being depreciated, shows the **adjusted basis** or **book value** of the item.

acknowledgment *Commerce, Law* Affirmation by signature of agreement to the terms and conditions of a contract or other document

acoustic coupler *Computers* A device that connects a telephone handset to a computer modem.

acquisition That obtained by a company, usually to improve or expand operations, as a piece of property, another company or new equipment.

across the board Affecting everything in a group the same way, as an across-the-board price increase.

active file *Computers* A computer file visible to the user and ready for processing.

active window *Computers* The screen area where the active file is viewed.

act of God *Law* A phrase used in contracts to describe an event caused by forces of nature for which the parties to the contract cannot be held responsible.

actual cost *Accounting* The amount paid, as for equipment, as distinguished from **residual value, market value** or **resale value.**

actual damages *Law* Losses directly relating to the matter at hand and that can be corroborated, as distinguished from indirect losses, as from pain and suffering.

adapter *Computers* A device, program, or routine for making disparate hardware or software elements compatible.

adaptive system *Computers* A computer program that learns by keeping a record of corrections to its activity, such as for correcting errors in optical character recognition.

ADC, analog to digital converter *Computers* A device that converts analog signals to digital data.

add-on *Computers* A peripheral device or program to enhance performance of an existing device or program

ADP, automatic data processing *Computers* The manipulation of data with the use of a computer.

addendum something added, as a commentary to a report or additional terms to a contract.

adjudicate *Law* To hear both sides of a dispute and render a judgment.

adjusted basis *Accounting* The cost of an asset, reduced by accumulated depreciation.

adjuster *Insurance* Employee of an insurance company responsible for evaluating and settling claims.

adjusting entry *Accounting* An account entry that corrects an earlier, incorrect entry.

administer To provide the guidance and control required for a group or organization to achieve a stated objective.

administrative expense *Accounting* Costs associated with the guidance and control of the operations of a company, such as management, accounting and general office personnel and supplies, that are not directly associated with manufacturing cost.

ad valorem *Latin* According to value; an assessment, such as taxes or insurance based on the value of the commodity involved.

advance A prepayment in anticipation of an obligation as against expenses, commissions or work to be performed.

advertising Any means by which an organization seeks to influence the thoughts or actions of an individual, usually used to sell a product or to promote good will.

affiliate An organization that is in some way connected to another, as through ownership, working agreement, etc.

affirmative action Action taken to correct past discrimination by seeking to hire minorities, trade with minority vendors, etc.

after market *Commerce* The sale of replacement parts or add-ons after the original product is sold; the trade in used or recovered material or equipment. *Marketing* A target audience or audiences that may be sought for a product in addition to the primary market.

after tax *Finance* Descriptive of a value adjusted for real or anticipated tax liability, as profits after tax from company operations or an investment.

age discrimination *Law* Unfair denial of employment or employment benefits based on age.

aged accounts *Accounting* A listing of accounts, receivable or payable, in categories by date due or past due, often designated as current, *30 days, 60 days, 90 days* and *over 90 days.*

agent One who acts as the representative of another, such as a company sales representative or an insurance adjuster.

aggregate A universe of information or things, considered as a whole, such as *aggregate sales* that represents all sales from all divisions of a company for the defined period.

agreement *Law* An understanding between two or more parties that is a basic requirement for a contract. *Labor Relations* The contract between employees in a **bargaining unit** and their **employer.**

agribusiness Agriculture, or farming, as a big business, often involving company divisions or affiliates that process the farm products

air bill Documentation for an air shipment.

air freight Commodities moved by air when speed is the overriding consideration.

algorithm A set of very precise instructions for completing a specific task. *Computers* A finite set of instructions with a distinct stopping place.

alias *Computers* A name assigned to a file, a location, a block of data, etc., used to address it for processing.

allocate, allocation *Accounting* The assignment, by formula, of fixed costs to the cost of manufactured product; the allowance for the purchase of various assets, goods and services. *Computers* The assignment of computer resources for a specific purpose, such as setting aside an area of memory for the operation of a TSR. *Manufacturing* The allotment of resources, materials and equipment time, to the fabrication of various products. *Marketing* The quota set for different products or prospects.

allowance *Accounting* Amount set aside for contingencies, as an allowance for bad debt. *Manufacturing* Time included in production standards for delays, as down time or operator fatigue. *Marketing* A rebate offered by a manufacturer to a distributor or retailer, as for advertising or promotion.

alphameric *Computers* See **alphanumeric**.

alphanumeric *Computers* Characters that are alphabetic or numerical, excluding symbols; short for alphabetic/numeric.

ALT, alternate key *Computers* a shift key that is used in conjunction with another key or keys to execute a command.

ALU, arithmetic and logic unit *Computers* The part of the CPU, or central processing unit, that performs arithmetic and logic functions.

AMA, American Management Association A professional organization that publishes information and sponsors seminars for managers.

American Marketing Association A professional organization that promotes sound and ethical practices in the areas of sales, advertising and marketing.

ambiguous *Computers* Imprecise; descriptive of a program command or formula that is stated in such a way that it may yield an undesirable result.

amend To revise by correcting or modifying, as a statute or a contract.

amendment A revision or addition that serves to correct or improve.

amenity That which gives added comfort or pleasure, as a privilege or facility available to employees of a company or to those of a certain rank.

amortization, amortization schedule *Accounting* The division of debt into periodic payments that include interest and other charges associated with the debt.

analog *Computers* Descriptive of data represented as a continuous variable, such as sound.

analog to digital converter *Computer* A device that converts analog data to digital data.

analyst One who specializes in the study of various aspects of business, reports on deficiencies and makes recommendations for their improvement.

AND operator *Computers* A Boolean operator used to return a value of true if the statements it joins are both true, as in a spreadsheet formula.

annotation *Computers* An explanatory note in a program or document; a feature in some word processing programs that allows commentary within a document without changing the original document.

annualize To extrapolate data from a limited period to fit an annual model, with consideration given to highs and lows that occur throughout the year.

annual meeting Meeting shortly after the end of the fiscal year at which time the company managers report to the stockholders and members of the board of directors stand for election.

annual report *Finance* The statement of a company's finances and, often, prospects for the future.

annuity *Insurance* A type of life insurance contract that guarantees periodic payments to the insured at some future time, usually retirement.

ANSI, American National Standards Institute An organization that establishes standards affecting most industries.

antitrust *Law* Descriptive of a set of laws that regulate business to prevent monopolies, price fixing, price discrimination, etc.

anti-virus *Computers* A program or routine designed to detect unauthorized alteration of a computer program or files.

application *Computers* A computer program designed for a particular use, such as a word processor or spreadsheet; a particular use to which a program is applied, as for compiling financial transactions or inventory records.

application generator *Computers* A program or utility that assists the user in creating custom designed applications.

applied cost *Accounting* The amount of overhead expense that is charged to a department, manufacturing operation or job.

appreciate *Finance* To increase in value.

appropriation *Accounting, Manufacturing* Money or materials set aside for a specific purpose. See also **allocate, allocation**.

arbitration *Labor Relations* A means of settling disputes in which the parties to the dispute agree to present their arguments to a mutually agreeable impartial third party called an *arbitrator*. See also, binding arbitration.

architecture *Computers* The design of a computer that defines such things as type of processor, speed, bus size, etc.

archives Generally, storage for inactive records. *Computers* Database records saved as inactive files after deletion from the active database.

arithmetic expression *Computers* A formula that uses a mathematical operator and returns a numeric value.

arithmetic relation *Computers* an expression that uses a mathematical operator to show the relationship between two values, such as = (equal to), ≠ (not equal to), > (greater than), etc.

arm's length transaction *Law* A business deal between unrelated persons or organizations in which there is no conflict of interest for either party; a measure of the legitimacy of a contract or other business arrangement.

array *Computers* An arrangement of data in named rows, columns and layers—a financial spreadsheet, for example may be a two dimensional array in which the rows represent items of expense for a company and the columns, different calendar periods; a three dimensional array might consist of layers containing similar data for various divisions or departments in the company.

arrears *Accounting* A payment that is past due.

articles of incorporation *Law* The document filed with a state that sets forth the objectives of the corporation and other information as required by law.

artificial intelligence *Computers* Descriptive of the ability of a computer to simulate human intelligence, as by recording corrections to its output and adjusting for future transactions.

artificial language *Computers* A programming language with a distinct set of rules and vocabulary.

ASCII, American Standard Code for Information Interchange *Computers* A basic system for representing printable and control characters for the microcomputer as binary digits.

as is *Commerce* An offer to sell goods in their present condition, without changes or repairs.

assembler *Computers* A program that translates a programming language into instructions that are understood directly by the computer.

assembly line *Manufacturing* A manufacturing technique that involves moving a product through a series of contiguous stations where partial assembly of a product, or a part for a product, is performed.

assembly plant *Manufacturing* Descriptive of a manufacturing operation where few, if any, of the parts used are formed internally, that is, all or most of the parts are bought from another plant or from outside suppliers, either standard or custom made. See also **fabricator**.

assessment A determination of the estimated value of property; insight into the status of a situation. *Accounting* A special charge or portion of a common expense that is charged to a company entity, as a department or division.

asset Any item of value, often descriptive of the strong points of a person or company. *Accounting* The balance sheet entries that express the worth of a company, as cash, accounts receivable, equipment, good will, etc. *Law* The property of a person or business available for discharge of debt.

assign To designate for a specific purpose, as to assign materials to a job; to delegate, as an individual to perform a task. *Law* To transfer ownership.

assignment That is assigned, as materials, resources, etc. *Law* To transfer rights, as for security for a debt; an instrument of transfer, such as a deed.

attest To affirm as true by sworn statement or signature.

attractive nuisance *Law* That which serves to draw attention and may be dangerous, especially to children, such as a pond or a vacant house.

attrition Uncontrolled loss of personnel, as by illness or retirement, or of equipment, as by wear and tear.

audience *Marketing* Descriptive of those who are considered potential buyers for a product or service; those who might be reached by a particular type of advertising; see also **target market**.

audio system *Computer* Any of the programs or devices that allow the use of a computer for the reproduction of sound or make it capable of responding to voice commands.

audit Any thorough analysis, as of a procedure or problem. *Accounting* A periodic review of a company's financial records and accounting procedures.

auditor *Accounting* One who is responsible for the review of a company's financial records.

audit trail *Accounting* The orderly recording of financial transactions so that any record in the system can be tracked back to its source.

automatic backup *Computers* A program that creates a backup copy of files as they are saved; a program that makes a copy of data in the computer at a predetermined time.

automatic link *Computers* A connection between embedded objects in documents or files that provides for the update of all instances of the object when a change is made in one.

automatic load *Computers* A program in computer memory that is brought on line by a predetermined signal, as of a timer, often used to create backup files during the night.

average cost *Accounting* The total cost to manufacture a given lot of goods divided by the number of units manufactured; the total value of a group of items in inventory, bought at different prices, divided by the number of items.

average balance *Finance* A system for calculating finance charges that calls for applying the interest rate to the total of the daily balances of the account for a set period by the number of days in the period.

axis A straight reference line on a graph, horizontal, vertical, or on a plane that is perpendicular to both the horizontal and vertical lines.

B

background check The process of verifying a prospective employee's references and job history.

background noise *Computers* Extraneous matter in a scanned image or in electronic transmission.

background processing *Computers* The performance of tasks by a computer without interaction with the user, such as printing a document or sorting a database, often while other work is being done in the foreground.

back haul *Commerce* The return trip of a commercial vehicle after making a delivery, often empty; see also **deadhead**.

backlog *Marketing* Orders received by a company that have not been filled. Backlog is often used to measure the relative strength of a company or a market by comparing the value or volume of backlog for different periods or different companies.

back pay Wages or salary owed from a prior period. *Labor Relations* Payment to employees who continue to work without a contract while negotiating; the back pay covers any increases in the new agreement, retroactive to the date of the termination of the old contract.

back up *Computers* The process of making a copy of data for safe keeping; the copy so made.

backup copy *Computers* A copy of data files and programs held as protection against corruption of the originals.

backup system *Computers* Computer hardware designed to take over processing in the event of a failure in the primary system; the procedure for recording and manipulating data in the event of a primary system failure. A device that provides power to the computer in the event of an outage. A system of hardware and software for making a copy of the data in a computer; see **automatic backup**.

backward compatibility *Computers* An upgraded program's ability to use files created by an earlier version.

bad debt *Accounting* An account that is written off because it is considered not collectible; see also, **reserve for bad debts**.

bait and switch *Marketing* The practice of advertising a product at a very attractive price, then attempting to convince the buyer to purchase another product at a higher price.

balance sheet *Accounting* A report that shows the financial condition of a company at a specific point in time. The report lists the *assets* of a company, such as cash, accounts receivable, inventory and equipment, and *liabilities*, such as accounts payable, loans, and mortgages. The difference between the *assets* and *liabilities* is *owner* or *stockholder's equity*.

balloon payment *Finance* A final payment on an installment loan that is significantly larger than the periodic installments that include only interest and little or none of the principle. Such an arrangement is acceptable to the lender when the loan is secured by an asset of greater value than the outstanding debt and is often desirable to suit the needs of a new business that has little cash, but anticipates having it by the time the final payment is due.

bankrupt, bankruptcy *Finance* The state of being judged unable to pay ones debts. A business may be forced into a Chapter 7 or involuntary bankruptcy when creditors petition the court to appoint a trustee to manage the company finances and liquidate the company, if necessary, to protect their interests. A Chapter 11 bankruptcy is the result of a petition by the business for protection from creditors while it reorganizes under court supervision.

bar chart A diagram that shows quantities as columns of varying length according to their relative magnitude.

bar code *Computers* A pattern of vertical stripes of varying widths representing codes that can be read by a scanner and recorded by a computer. Commonly used to identify consumer products at the point of sale, bar codes are also applied to mailing pieces for automated sorting and in manufacturing operations to identify raw materials, operation codes, employee time cards, etc. See also, **shop floor collection** and **Universal Product Code**.

bargaining agent *Labor Relations* An organization or individual authorized to negotiate pay scales, fringe benefits, working conditions, etc. with an employer as the sole representative of a group of workers comprising a bargaining unit.

bargaining unit *Labor Relations* A group of employees who have elected to bargain with management as a single entity through a duly elected representative and, by a majority vote, to accept or reject any offer made to them through their representative. See also, **collective bargaining.**

base pay The regular hourly wage of an employee, exclusive of **overtime pay, shift differential** or **fringe benefits.**

BASIC, Beginner's All-purpose Symbolic Instruction Code *Computers* A programming language.

basis *Accounting, Finance* The cost at which an asset is carried on the company books, and that is the number used to calculate depreciation for tax purposes. Such basis includes the cost of the asset itself, and in the case of equipment, may also include the cost of delivery and installation.

batch *Computers* A set of files or commands that are processed as a unit.

batch command *Computers* A single command that causes the execution of a number of commands contained in a **batch file.**

batch file *Computers* A program file containing a series of commands that are processed in order.

batch processing *Accounting* A cost accounting technique in which an item is manufactured in *batches*, expressed in pounds, gallons, units, etc. and costs are compared based on final output. See also **job processing.** *Computers* Processing of data that, once started, takes place without further input from the operator, as contrasted to **interactive processing.**

baud *Computers* A measure of transmission speed over telephone lines.

BBS, Bulletin Board Service *Computers* A message center that may be accessed by computer users via telephone lines.

before tax *Finance* Descriptive of a value that has not been adjusted for tax liability, as *before tax profits* from company operations or an investment.

benchmark A clearly defined standard for comparison, as for a value or performance; *benchmark testing* involves comparing results, such as the timed operation of a computer, with known results of a specific unit's performance when processing identical material to that used in the test.

benefit Anything that improves conditions; see **fringe benefits.** A company sponsored event to raise money or goods for a worthy cause.

biannual Descriptive of an event that takes place twice a year; semiannual; see **biennial.**

bid bond *Commerce* A guarantee in the form of a **certified check, surety bond,** or similar instrument by a person or company bidding, as a contractor for construction or manufacturing work, or for the purchase of goods. The bid bond is required to offer some assurance that the bidder is financially sound, or as protection to the party seeking bids for costs incurred by default of the bidder.

bi-directional printer *Computers* A computer printer head that prints while traveling in either direction across the paper, thus improving output speed.

biennial Descriptive of an event that takes place once every two years; see **biannual.**

billing cycle *Accounting* The precise procedure of reporting and recording transactions from the original sale to the rendering of an invoice or statement to the client. The time between periodic billing for the sale of goods or services.

bill of lading *Commerce* The record of goods transferred to a common carrier for delivery to a third party, expressing the contract between shipper and carrier.

bimonthly Once every two months; of that which occurs six times a year.

binary code *Computers* The representation of characters by the use of the **binary system.**

binary digit *Computers* The digits in a binary system, 0 or 1.

binary logic *Computers* A type of reasoning in computer formulae that returns one of two possible variables, as true or false, yes or no.

binary system *Computers* A number system in base 2.

binder *Law* A temporary agreement or contract, usually for some consideration, pending execution of a formal contract, such as a binder on an insurance policy or real estate that protects the buyer until a contract can be drawn.

binding arbitration A means of settling disputes in which the parties to the dispute agree to present their arguments to a mutually agreeable impartial third party called an *arbitrator* and agree to be bound by his or her decision.

BIOS, Basic Input/Output System *Computers* That part of the operating system that controls communication between the various elements of the computer and peripherals.

bit *Computers* Short for binary digit, the basic unit in the binary system.

bit mapping *Computers* The creation of a graphic image composed of tiny dots, or pixels, each of which is assigned a series of bits to record its precise location.

B/L or **b/l** See **bill of lading.**

blacklist A list of individuals or organizations considered undesirable for employment, transacting business, etc.

bleed *Colloq., Commerce* To charge at an excessive rate. *Finance* To take money, often illegally, from the working capital of an organization.

blister pack A firm, clear, bubble of plastic, often shaped to conform somewhat to that of the product it contains, affixed to a rigid backing, usually used for small items sold from hanging racks. See also, **shrink pack.**

block *Computers* A section of data, files, etc. that are manipulated as a unit.

block command *Computers* An instruction that acts on all elements in a particular section of text or files.

blue collar *Manufacturing* Descriptive of industrial workers, without regard to skills.

blue laws Any local ordinance that prohibits the conduct of business on a Sunday.

blue pencil To revise or edit, as a report.

blueprint An architect or engineers drawing; a type of printer's proof. Any detailed plan of action.

board of directors A group of individuals, elected by the stockholders of a corporation, responsible for appointing the chief executive officers and monitoring their performance.

boilerplate *Law* A preprinted contract form, as for a lease or a sales contract. Standardized language in a contract listing terms, rights and obligation of each party, etc. A standard contract used by a company for its sales or lease agreements.

bomb *Computers* A situation wherein the computer locks up and must be restarted.

bond *Commerce* A contract wherein a bonding agency guarantees payment for specific goods damaged in storage or in shipment, or for the dishonest or careless act of an employee. *Finance* An interest bearing document used as a means for the government or business to raise money. *Law* A written obligation to guarantee performance.

book *Accounting* To confirm a transaction by recording it.

bookkeeper *Accounting* One who records accounting transactions for a business.

bookmark *Computers* A user-inserted reference marker in a data file that allows instant return from another location.

books *Accounting* Collectively, the accounting records of an organization, as journals and ledgers.

book value *Accounting* The cost of an asset, reduced by accumulated depreciation.

Boolean algebra *Computers* a system of calculation used in computer programming based on **Boolean logic**.

Boolean logic *Computers* A logic system used in computer programming based on a return of one of two variables, as true or false, yes or no.

boot *Computers* To start up a computer by loading the operating system, called a *cold boot*. Restarting once the operating system has been loaded is called a *warm boot*.

bootleg software *Computers* A program obtained outside of normal channels, such as proprietary software transferred illegally to a second user.

bootstrap *Computers* A disc or device that loads the operating system onto a computer, enabling it to function.

bottom line A brief summary of a situation or report. *Accounting* Net profit or loss.

boycott To refuse to traffic with a particular organization or product and to encourage others to follow suit; often an organized effort to punish, or bring pressure to bear for the correction of perceived wrongs.

brainstorming A meeting open to the expression of all ideas, however bizarre, for the solution to a specific problem, without evaluating their merit. Later, the suggestions are evaluated and a plan of action is established. Often used to describe any discussion of a problem solving nature.

branch *Computers* A command to jump to another section of a program; an *unconditional branch* directs a move to a specific location; a *conditional branch* first calls for a test, then directs a move when certain conditions are met.

branch, branch office Any facility at a distance from the main plant or home office of a company.

brand *Marketing* A distinctive mark used by a company to identify its products.

brand loyalty *Marketing* A measure of the extent to which a consumer will seek out and repeatedly purchase a particular brand of a product.

brand manager *Marketing* An executive responsible for the advertising and marketing of one of a company's brands.

brand name The unique name of a particular product. Usually used to infer a well-known product.

BRC, business reply card A response card, usually with postage paid, designed for convenience so as to elicit maximum response from the consumer.

breach A break, as of a violation of the law or of a contract.

breach of contract *Law* The wrongful violation, or breaking, of a contract, as by not fulfilling a promise contained in the contract, by disclaiming the duty to perform, by illegally assigning any part of the contract, etc.

breach of promise The breaking of a promise, usually undocumented.

breach of trust *Law* A violation of duty by a trustee, as through fraud or carelessness.

break even analysis *Finance* A technique for establishing the point at which income equals expense. Calculations may involve an estimate of overhead and operating expense for a given period to determine how much income must be generated over that same period in order to break even. Based on units of production, the cost of materials, manufacturing and overhead is weighed against the number of units to determine selling price per unit; when the market determines selling price, fixed costs, such as overhead and set up are the deciding factors, defining how many units must be manufactured and sold to cover costs.

break-even point *Finance* The production or sales level at which all costs are recovered. Once **fixed cost** is recovered, only **variable cost** is incurred for additional units, so that additional sales at the same price will produce a **profit**. See also, **marginal cost**.

BRE, business reply envelope A response vehicle, self-addressed, often postage paid, furnished to a client or prospect in hope of a timely reply.

budget Generally, a detailed plan for a measured period, setting goals and outlining resources needed to meet those goals. *Accounting* A projection of anticipated sales and expense for an organization; a projection of costs associated with an acquisition; a projection of cash flow. *Manufacturing* A projection of manpower or material needs for a given level of production; *Marketing* A sales projection; an estimate of cost for the advertising and promotion of a product.

buffer *Computers* An area of memory reserved for holding signals received or to be transmitted in order to compensate for variance in transmission speed and operation of different devices. See also, **print buffer**.

bug *Computers* A malfunction in computer processing, caused by a program error, a read/write error or a fault in the CPU, a connector or a peripheral device.

building code The regulations established in local ordinance that govern structural requirements, as for building materials, plumbing, electricity, etc.

building permit A license granted by a local government to erect or modify a particular structure.

bundled *Computers* Descriptive of computer hardware and software sold together as a package.

burden of proof *Law* The responsibility of a party to a law suit to substantiate the items of contention that are the basis for the suit.

bus *Computers* The collection of lines along which data travels.

business An enterprise established to provide a product or service in the hope of earning a profit. Such an enterprise may be a **sole proprietorship, a partnership** or a **corporation**.

business cycle Generally, the regular alternation of periods of prosperity and periods of recession in industry. *Accounting* The period, often one month, for which reports that measure the performance of a business are tendered and compared with other like periods. The period, usually one year, during which a business normally passes through a complete cycle of busy and slow periods.

business ethics Descriptive of a standard of ideals in the conduct of business: that of dealing in an honest manner with suppliers and customers.

business etiquette The manner in which one person deals with another in a business setting, not so different from a private setting, such as the exercise of courtesy and punctuality.

business interruption insurance Security against possible loss by the temporary closing of a business, as by fire, usually covering continuing overhead expense as well as lost profits.

buyback An agreement to accept the return of goods held on consignment. *Finance* Corporate purchase of its own stock in order to reduce the outstanding shares on the market.

buyer's market Generally, a condition that exists when supply exceeds demand so that quantities are plentiful and prices are low. In business, often descriptive of a situation in which a particular seller must attract a buyer in order to dispose of overstock, fill in production down time, generate cash flow, etc.

buy in Financial backing in return for at least partial control of the operation of a business. *Colloq.* Acceptance of an offer to take part in a joint venture.

buyout Purchase of a business or of a controlling interest in a corporation's stock.

buy-sell agreement An agreement between individuals that a business, partnership interest, etc. will be traded contingent on something, as the death of one of the parties to the agreement. Such an agreement may allow a key employee or remaining partners to buy out a deceased partner's interest instead of dissolving the partnership.

buzz words Slang that is native to a particular business or group, often meaningless outside the group. *Marketing* Words or phrases that reflect a current fad and so are used in advertising and promotion.

byproduct Anything incidental created in the course of doing something else. A byproduct may be an incidental benefit that grows out of a discussion or it may be a harmful substance generated in the course of a manufacturing or processing operation. Often byproducts are turned to good use, as the recovery of silver from spent photographic film or animal feed from the processing of grain.

byte *Computers* A basic data unit manipulated by the computer, usually eight bits.

by the book Descriptive of a management or operating style that adheres strictly to the rules, written or understood, often said of one with very rigid standards or of cautious management intent on avoiding liability or any hint of impropriety.

C

cable *Computer* The transmission link between devices in a computer system.

cache *Computer* A buffer, or special area of memory in the computer, for holding frequently called data.

CAD/CAM, Computer Aided Design/Computer Aided Manufacturing *Computer* A program that assists in planning and production.

CADD, Computer Aided Design and Drafting *Computer* a graphics program that assists in the creation of engineering drawings.

CAL, Computer Augmented Learning *Computer* The reinforcement of learning with the use of special computer programs.

calendar year The calendar dates from January 1 to December 31, as distinguished from **fiscal year.**

call report A record maintained by salespersons, customer service personnel, and others, of contacts with clients and prospects.

cancellation clause A provision in a contract for cancellation in certain circumstances or if certain conditions are not met, as a building contract contingent on securing financing.

capacity *Computers* The size of a computer storage device; of the ability of a computer to handle a particular task. *Law* Designating as having legal authority or competence. *Manufacturing* The potential volume of output under a given set of circumstances, as by number of shifts, number of days, total capacity or available capacity.

capital *Finance* Money or property used in the conduct of a business. See also, **assets.**

capital account *Accounting* The ledger account that represents the difference between assets and liabilities of a business.

capital asset *Finance* Property that represents a long term investment, such as buildings, land, machinery, etc.

capital budget *Finance* Moneys set aside for investment in capital assets, such as new equipment, plant expansion, etc.

capital gain *Finance* Profit from the sale of a capital asset. In the case of depreciable property, such as machinery, the profit is the difference between the sale price and the **book value** of the property.

capital improvement An addition or upgrade to equipment or building that increases its value by improving productivity or extends its useful life. *Accounting* An expense that is added to the **basis** of the asset improved and depreciated.

capital intensive Descriptive of an industry that requires a substantial investment in equipment in proportion to the amount of labor necessary for manufacturing. See also **labor intensive.**

capital investment *Finance* Cost of acquiring a business or purchasing buildings and equipment.

capitalism The economic system in which the means of production are privately owned and operated for profit that accrues to the owners.

Cartesian coordinates *Computers* Numbers that locate a point in space on a two or three dimensional array.

cash basis *Accounting* A system for reporting company finances whereby transactions are recorded as they are executed, so that *Sales* reflects only moneys received and *Expenses* only moneys paid out. See also, **accrual system.**

cash budget *Finance* An estimate of anticipated receipts and cash requirements for a specified period.

cash cow *Colloq.* Descriptive of a profitable business, one that generates a significant flow of cash with little effort.

cash discount A discount in the price of goods, offered for payment on delivery or within a brief, specified time.

cash flow statement *Finance* A summary of receipts and payments for a given period, reporting the availability or shortage of cash.

cashier's check *Finance* An instrument of payment generally considered the same as cash; it is drawn on the bank's own funds and signed by an officer of the bank.

cash order An order for merchandise accompanied by payment for that merchandise.

cash position *Accounting* The amount of cash or other assets of a company that can be readily converted to cash available at a given time.

cash reserve *Finance* Cash or readily converted securities distinct from that required for immediate needs, held for contingencies.

casual labor Descriptive of individuals who perform services on an unscheduled, part-time basis. Individuals hired for a single project, as for yard or dock work and often paid from petty cash are an example of casual labor, though changes in the tax law have made it necessary, in many cases to put the casual laborer on the payroll, especially if it is someone who is repeatedly employed.

casualty insurance Protective coverage for an individual or business against losses by a sudden, unexpected or unusual circumstance, such as fire, flood, theft, etc. See also, **liability insurance.**

casualty loss *Accounting* A property loss caused by misfortune that is not covered by insurance. The expense of the loss is booked, as by recording the book value of anything destroyed and the cost of repairs, then reducing the total loss by the amount paid on the insurance claim.

cause of action *Law* The facts in a matter and the legal grounds that form the basis of a right to seek redress in a court of law. See also, **right of action.**

caveat emptor *Latin* Let the buyer beware—an admonition to a buyer to check the merchandise, price, terms, etc. before committing to a purchase.

CD, compact disk *Computers* A digital disk from which data is read by the use of a laser.

CD ROM, compact disk read-only memory *Computers* A compact disk containing data that cannot be altered.

cell *Computers* The area that holds a unit of information, such as a *spreadsheet cell.*

central buying The purchasing of all or part of the materials and supplies for a company's outlets, divisions or departments through a main purchasing office in order to secure and control quality, price and delivery.

CEO, chief executive officer The senior executive of an organization, appointed by the board of directors, with ultimate responsibility for the attainment of corporate goals.

certificate of incorporation The legal document that attests to the existence of a corporation, stating its name, purpose, financial structure, etc.

certificate of occupancy A document issued by a local government affirming that a building complies with local codes and is fit for occupancy.

certification To confirm as authentic or true. *Labor Relations* Official recognition of a union or other bargaining agent as the authorized representative of a bargaining unit.

certified check *Finance* A check for which the issuing bank guarantees payment by certifying that there are sufficient funds available in the account on which the check is drawn to cover it.

certified mail Mail for which a record of mailing and delivery is established by the postal service; written verification may be requested by the mailer. See also **registered mail.**

certified public accountant See **CPA.**

CGA, Color Graphics Adaptor *Computers* An early standard for the display on a color monitor screen.

chain of command Informally, the hierarchical structure of a business from those with the most authority to those with the least.

chairman of the board The highest ranking officer in a corporation; one who presides over meetings of the board of directors.

character *Computer* Any of the set of letters, numbers and punctuation marks that can be duplicated from the computer keyboard.

character code *Computer* A set of binary digits that represents a specific symbol.

character pitch *Computer* The number of characters per inch of a type font.

character recognition *Computer* Identification of text or special printed symbols by any one of a number of input devices, such as a scanner.

character string *Computer* A set of characters processed as a unit.

chart *Computer* To create a graph that shows the relationships among a group of associated values; the graphic representation of those values; to diagram the steps in a procedure.

chart of accounts *Accounting* An organized list of the accounts in the **general ledger** or a **subsidiary ledger** of a company. The accounts are numbered in the order they appear on a financial statement and are listed in number order. Generally, a number series represents a class of accounts, as 1000 for assets, 2000 for liabilities, etc. with numbers for individual accounts assigned in such a manner as to leave room for future additions.

chip *Computer* A semiconductor in which an integrated circuit is formed.

chattel Any tangible, movable item of personal property.

chattel mortgage The pledge of personal property as security for an obligation, as money owed.

check A negotiable instrument, that calls for a bank to pay the amount shown from the maker's account. See also **cashier's check, certified check.**

checkoff *Labor Relations* A system whereby union dues are deducted from member's pay and paid directly to the union by the employer.

check protector A device that embosses the amount on a check making it difficult to alter. Also called a *check writer.*

check register A journal for recording checks as they are written, deposits to the checking account, and keeping a running balance of the amount in the account.

check signer A device for mechanically signing checks, used when the volume of checks would make hand signing a difficult task.

chose in action *Law* The right to sue for recovery of an intangible asset, as a debt.

churning *Law* Excessive trading in a client's account to generate commissions without concern for the client.

circuit *Computers* A complete path for the flow of electrical current that includes a power source, a conductor such as copper wire, a switch for engaging and disengaging the circuit, and a load or resistance.

civil law The body of law established by a state or nation; law protecting the rights of individuals.

click *Computers* To press and release a mouse button in order to position the cursor or make a selection.

client A customer; anyone who purchases goods or services from a company; an individual represented by a lawyer, accountant, etc.

clip art *Computers* Line art, borders, symbols, etc. saved on a computer disk that can be used to embellish a document, as a flyer or newsletter.

clone *Computers* A computer or peripheral that emulates the operation of a well-known brand, usually at less cost and often without any loss of quality.

close *Accounting* To complete the recording of transactions prior to summarizing the financial activity for an accounting period; to *close the books. Marketing* To complete a sale or sales agreement.

closed corporation *Finance, Law* A corporation whose stock is owned by one person or a few people, usually members of a family or of management.

closed loop *Computer* A programmer's error in which output modifies input, so that a final value is never reached, such as a spreadsheet formula in cell *B* that calls for the value of *A+B* and that cannot be attained, as *B* changes each time the command is executed.

closed shop *Labor Relations* An organization where only workers who are members of the union may be hired; forbidden by the Taft-Hartley act of 1947. See also, **open shop, right to work, union shop.**

closed corporation *Finance* A company, the stock of which is held by a few owners and seldom traded. See also, **closely held corporation.**

closely held corporation *Finance* A company in which most of the voting stock is held by a few shareholders although enough is publicly owned to provide a market in the stock.

closing costs *Finance* The cost of transferring ownership in real estate from seller to buyer, such as for legal fees, title search, insurance, filing fees, etc.

closing entry *Accounting* The journal entry at the end of a period to transfer the balance of an income or expense account to *earnings* in order to summarize the net difference between income and expense on owner's equity. The closing entry sets the balance of the income and expense accounts to zero, and ready to accept entries for a new period.

closing inventory *Accounting* The aggregate value of all materials and supplies on hand at the close of business at the end of an accounting period.

COBOL, common business oriented language *Computers* A high level programming language which syntax resembles spoken English and is therefore relatively easy to understand.

COD, cash on delivery The requirement that the cost for materials or services must be paid by the buyer at the time of delivery, often including a delivery charge and, if a third party is responsible for delivery and collection, often a service charge. COD terms are used mostly when the value of the sale is too small to warrant opening an account, when the sale is to a new, unknown or one time buyer, or the creditworthiness of the buyer is in question.

code A particular body of law or regulations of a political entity, as a city or state, encompassing a single subject, as for building construction or motor vehicles. *Computer* To write a program or formula in terms that the computer understands as commands or that can be translated into terms that the computer understands.

code, code word Generally, any symbol or group of symbols that represent something else. A *customer code*, for example, may tell geographic location, credit terms, type of business, etc.

code of ethics A statement of the standards of conduct to which those in a particular profession should aspire, often part of the credo of a professional society.

codicil Generally, any addition or supplement to a document. *Law* An addition to a will that adds to or alters provisions contained in the will.

coding of accounts *Accounting* The initial assignment of an identification number to each account for which financial transactions are recorded. Often used to describe the writing of account numbers on **source documents** prior to making journal entries. See also, **chart of accounts.**

coinsurance *Insurance* An insurance plan that limits the liability of the insurer, usually to a percentage of the total value of the property or of the loss; in effect, causing the insurer to cover the balance of any losses. Insurance coverage provided by more than one insurer, with each accepting a portion of the risk.

COLA, Cost of Living Adjustment A correction in wage or pension scales, usually linked to the **Consumer Price Index,** to compensate for changes in the cost of living.

cold boot *Computers* Restarting a computer that has been completely shut down.

collateral *Commerce, Finance* Property offered as security for a loan or other obligation, as buying on credit.

collect call A telephone call charged to the called party; such a call is placed through an operator who identifies the calling party and determines that the party called will accept the charges before releasing the line to the caller. See also, **person-to-person call.**

collection *Finance* The conversion of *accounts receivable* into cash. Generally, descriptive of the process of managing the receivables of a company to insure that moneys owed are collected in a timely fashion and that accounts past due are not overlooked. Turning accounts over to a company department or division, or an outside agency that specializes in collecting obligations that are past due.

collective bargaining The good faith negotiations between the bargaining agent for a group of employees and their employer or the employer's agent for the purpose of setting wage rates, fringe benefits, working conditions, etc.

collusion *Law* To conspire with another for the purpose of engaging in an illegal activity.

column *Accounting, Computers* The vertical arrangement of data in a two or three dimensional array, as for a spreadsheet.

command *Computers* A key word that activates a set of instructions for the computer. One line of program code that comprises a single instruction to the computer.

command character *Computers* A character that expresses a program control function.

command driven *Computers* Descriptive of an interactive computer program that acts on each command by the user as it is issued.

command line *Computers* The position at which instructions are entered by the user to direct processing.

commercial Descriptive of that done for profit. *Manufacturing* Designating of a lower grade or quality, that provided in bulk for reprocessing.

commercial bank *Finance* A financial institution charted by the federal government or the state in which it conducts business, allowed wide latitude in the services it may offer, specializing in commercial loans and demand deposits.

commercial credit *Finance* Open account transactions between companies doing business with each other.

commercial law *Commerce* The regulations that address the rights and responsibilities of persons engaged in commerce or trade, as the **Uniform Commercial Code.**

commercial paper *Finance* Short-term notes issued by large, financially sound corporations to cover temporary shortages in cash flow. The instrument offers cash to the issuer at interest usually below the bank rate, while the investor is afforded a safe investment for temporarily idle cash.

commercial property Real estate designed or designated for use by a commercial establishment, as a store, factory, office, etc. Acreage zoned for commercial use.

commission A fee, often a percentage of the value of a transaction, paid to an employee or outside agent for services performed, especially a salesperson. An order to perform a service, as by an independent writer, designer or architect. An agency of the government that is charged with a particular regulatory task, as the Equal Employment Opportunity Commission or the Federal Communications Commission.

commitment A promise to do something in the future, as an employer's promise of a raise or promotion when certain conditions are met; a written agreement to buy certain goods or services at a specific price. Dedication or involvement, as a company's commitment to quality.

committee A group of individuals, usually appointed, assigned to meet for a particular purpose, as a *grievance committee*, assigned to hear and judge the worth of alleged wrongs in the workplace, or a *quality committee*, charged with the ongoing review of quality control standards and testing. Membership in a committee is often rotated to assure its vitality and generate new thinking. The committee is often given broad powers to investigate and to call in outside experts. A committee appointed to address a single, specific problem and then disband is called an *ad hoc committee*.

common carrier A person or company available for hire to transport people or goods.

common law *Law* A system of jurisprudence based on custom and court precedent, as distinguished from that based on **statute.**

common stock *Finance* An equity share in the ownership of a company that gives the owner the right to participate in electing the board of directors and voting on other matters brought before the stockholders, in proportion to the number of shares held. See also, **preferred stock.**

communication buffer *Computers* A device that provides temporary storage of data to be sent or as it is being received, to allow for differences in the speed of various devices.

communication link *Computers* Hardware or software that allows the transfer of data between devices.

communication protocol *Computers* Standards for the transfer of data between devices.

communication software *Computers* A program that enables the transfer of data between modems.

community property *Law* Assets accumulated by a married couple during the time of their marriage.

commuter An individual who travels regularly between two points that are a significant distance apart. Generally used to describe an individual who lives in one community and works in another, traveling the distance between them twice each day.

company A group of people joined together for a common purpose, as a business enterprise.

company car A vehicle owned by a company for the use of employees on official business. Often a vehicle owned by the company that is assigned to a particular employee for his or her use with little or no monitoring of its use for business or personal travel.

company union *Labor Relations* A union, sometimes formed at the behest of a company, that has no affiliation with other union groups and is considered to be largely under the control of the management of the company.

comparative statement *Finance* Financial reports, such as balance sheets or income statements, for different periods shown side by side so that they might be compared and analyzed. Such as comparison is an effective management tool and is usually a part of the annual report.

comparative negligence *Law* A principle of tort law upheld in some courts that in a suit for damages, the culpability of each party can be considered, so that in an auto accident, for example, if a car that is speeding strikes another car that ran through a red light, both drivers are at fault and the court may rule that no damages can be collected by either party. Such deliberation often involves an award of partial damage when it is determined that one party was more at fault than the other.

comparison shopping The process of elimination when buying to determine which product is the best value considering price and quality—one of the principal duties of a company purchasing agent.

compatibility The quality of being able to work well together, as of company employees. *Computers* The ability of certain devices, peripherals or programs to work with a particular computer. The ability to exchange programs and data between two computers.

compensating error *Accounting* An error of the exact amount made in both the debit and credit columns, often in different accounts, so the results look correct when, in fact, they are not.

compensation Anything that counterbalances another. *Commerce* Rebate to a customer for accepting damaged goods, or reimbursement for time and trouble involved in processing faulty material. *Insurance* Reimbursement for expenses associated with medical bills, lost work time, property damage, etc. *Labor Relations* Any remuneration to an employee for services performed, including wages, salary, fringe benefits, etc. *Law* Payment of damages to correct a wrong.

compensatory time Time off allowed a worker to compensate for overtime worked in lieu of pay for the overtime.

competent Qualified or capable, usually descriptive of an employee or of a vendor. *Law* Mentally able and mature; capable of understanding the terms of, and entering into, a contractual agreement.

competition *Marketing* Those who are selling similar products in the same market. The situation in which a number of producers are striving for the business of a number of consumers, so that no one producer or consumer can significantly alter the balance of the market.

competitive bid An offer by a vendor to sell a quantity of goods at a stated price. Often a **sealed bid**, opened at a specified time and date, so that all bidders are given equal consideration.

competitive strategy *Advertising, Marketing* Descriptive of any tactics to gain advantage over competition, as by cutting prices, advertising product strengths or a competitor's weakness, etc.

complete audit *Accounting* A detailed examination of a company's books including support documents and a thorough analysis of the system of internal controls.

compiler *Computers* A program that translates a high level programming language into machine language.

component An element or part, as a clause that is a *component* of a contract or a printer that is a *component* of a computer system.

compound To increase or combine; to add something that increases, as to compound a problem by adding another negative factor.

compound interest *Finance* Interest that is earned on interest, as when interest is added to a base amount so that the base amount plus interest is the amount on which interest is earned in the next period.

comprehensive Generally, descriptive of that including all or most of the relevant factors; extensive or complete. *Advertising* A layout for print media that emulates, insofar as possible, the final ad. Often referred to as a *comp. Insurance* Descriptive of a single insurance policy that covers a number of risks for a particular asset or group of assets.

comprehensive liability *Insurance* Insurance that offers a wide range of protection for negligence, as of repair or replacement for damage to property, or medical expense for injury to an individual. *Comprehensive business liability insurance* protects the ownership of a company from liability incurred in the course of operating a business or for accidents on company property; *comprehensive personal liability insurance* protects the individual and the individual's household from personal liability on and off the individual's property.

compression *Computers* A technique of compacting data for more efficient storage or transmission.

compression utility *Computers* A program that compresses files for storage to save space and restores them as required for normal use.

compromise Any resolution to a disagreement between two or more parties in which each party gives up or modifies a demand.

comptroller, controller *Finance, Accounting* The principal accounting executive of an organization, responsible for auditing financial records and procedures.

comptroller general *Finance* Head of the General Accounting Office, that oversees the finances and accounting systems of government agencies.

comptroller of the currency *Finance* A federal office charged with the responsible for the chartering and regulation of national banks.

compulsory arbitration A means of settling a dispute between two or more parties that involves the services of a disinterested party, usually a professional mediator, who meets with those involved, then renders a decision that is binding on all. *Commerce, Labor Relations* Compulsory arbitration is usually opposed by both labor and management, but may be ordered by a court when a dispute between organizations, labor unions or an organization and a labor union is detrimental to the national economy.

compulsory insurance *Insurance* Any type of insurance that is required by law, as **workmen's compensation** or automobile liability.

compulsory retirement Obligatory retirement at a certain age mandated by company policy, an employment contract or a union contract. Federal law prohibits compulsory retirement at less than 70 years of age.

computer A device that stores and manipulates data according to instructions that it also stores.

computer art Artwork created with the aid of a computer.

computer driven Descriptive of a device controlled by a computer, as a machine that, once started, performs its tasks without further input from the operator.

computer game A program designed for amusement or instruction; often, a computer model that allows assessment of the effect of changes in a business situation.

computer graphics Charts, graphs, diagrams or pictures produced with the aid of the computer.

computer language Characters and symbols that are understood directly by the computer as commands.

computer system All of the hardware and software that make up a particular computer installation.

concession *Labor Relations* A special instance of allowing a deviation from normal terms of a contract, as a union waiver to the right to advance notice of a change in shift starting time, or an employers agreement to grant a special holiday. *Marketing* Special permission for another to sell a company's product. Special terms to a buyer, as the right to return unsold merchandise.

conciliation *Labor Relations* An attempt to convince both sides in a labor dispute to meet in an attempt to resolve their differences.

condition *Law* A clause in a contract that modifies in some way the terms of the contract based on a contingency.

conditional branch *Computers* An instruction in a computer program that is executed only if certain specific conditions are met.

conditional contract *Law* A contract that remains executory until a particular requirement is met, such as an agreement by a company to purchase equipment contingent on securing financing.

conditional sale *Marketing* An agreement to sell, as merchandise, with certain stipulations, such as a requirement that part or all of the invoice must be paid in advance, that the merchandise must be delivered by a certain date, or that the buyer need only pay for the merchandise sold and may return the rest.

conference A meeting of a group of individuals for discussion of a planned agenda. *Advertising, Marketing* A meeting to plan advertising or marketing strategy. A meeting with distributors to introduce a new product or a new marketing plan.

conference call A telephone call that links three or more parties, often at different locations.

confidence game A swindle dependent on gaining the confidence of the victim, as by tendering a phony invoice that looks official or a solicitation for an order that looks like an invoice.

configuration *Computers* The way in which a computer and peripherals are programmed and connected to function together.

confirmation Generally, corroboration or verification of something. *Accounting* Request by an auditor, sent to a client or vendor, to confirm that the amount owed to or owed by an organization as recorded on its books, is correct. *Marketing* Affirmation from a client that the specifications, delivery, price, terms, etc. contained in an order entered by the company are correct.

conflict of interest Descriptive of a situation in which self interest is at odds with duty, as of a public official who has jurisdiction over matters in which he or she has a financial interest, or a purchasing agent with a financial interest in one of his company's vendors.

conglomerate A corporation that owns controlling interest in a number of companies in unrelated industries. The merging of a number of diversified businesses.

connect time *Computers* The period during which a user is on line with a **bulletin board service, fax**, or other telephone link.

conservative Generally, descriptive of a tendency to rely on tradition or maintaining the status quo; of management that is moderate or cautious, relatively inflexible and not inclined to change. *Accounting* Tending to extra care not to overstate assets nor understate liabilities and expenses, so as to not mislead investors to believe that the financial condition of a company is better than it is.

consideration Remuneration, as a fee for a service. *Law* Inducement for a contract; something of value given to fulfill a contractual obligation.

consignee An organization or person to whom something, such as merchandise, is assigned; the name on a bill of lading to whom the thing shipped is to be delivered.

consignment *Marketing* An allocation of goods or materials sent to a client for use or sale; an assignment or allotment; goods sent to a dealer for safekeeping or sale without transfer of ownership, such goods to be paid for when they are sold or returned if not sold.

consistency *Accounting* The practice of using the same procedures and basis for recording and reporting financial transactions over a long period of time in order to make valid comparisons between accounting periods as well as reliable projections for the future. *Manufacturing, Marketing* A measure of the quality of a product in that the buyer can evaluate a single unit, batch or shipment and expect the same quality in all units received.

consolidated statements *Finance* Balance sheets, income statements, etc. that include financial data of a company and all its subsidiaries. Financial statements, as for income, that combine the results of several periods, as monthly or quarterly, into a single report for the year.

consolidation The combining of two or more organizations or an organization and its subsidiaries to form a new entity. See also, **merger.** *Finance* Reporting on the finances of a parent company and its subsidiaries as a single operating unit. Consolidation requires that all transactions between subsidiaries, or the company and subsidiaries, be eliminated.

consolidator A forwarding company that combines small rail freight shipments to make up full carloads that the railroad will accept.

consortium Generally, any alliance of individuals or companies for a common good, such as a temporary affiliation of two or more companies in an enterprise requiring shared resources or a project too large for any one of the companies to complete on its own.

constant dollars *Finance* Any method of comparing financial data for different years by adjusting for difference in the value or purchasing power of the dollar from one year to the other.

construction loan A short term obligation from the bank or other lending institution to cover building costs, often paid back with the proceeds of a loan on the finished structure.

constructive receipt The tax concept that an individual must claim income when money is made available, although it may not have been received.

consultant An individual or organization hired by another organization to provide professional advice in a specified area of expertise, as personnel management, sales, manufacturing, finance, etc.

consumer Any end user of a product; often taken to be the purchaser of a product, especially by advertisers.

consumer goods Products purchased for personal or household use.

Consumer Price Index A gauge of the changes in consumer prices, determined by a monthly survey of the cost of housing, food, etc. conducted by the Bureau of Labor Statistics.

consumer protection A body of law aimed at protecting consumers from unscrupulous sellers, shoddy merchandise, etc.

container ship A seagoing vessel that carries cargo in large, standardized containers that have been loaded with merchandise and sealed at the manufacturer's facility.

context sensitive help *Computers* A feature of some applications that display on demand, a help screen with information about the feature highlighted.

contingency fund *Accounting* Generally, moneys reserved to cover unpredictable expenses; an amount set aside in an acquisitions budget for unexpected costs, as for repairs or startup costs for equipment.

contingency plan A strategy or alternative to counteract the unexpected, though possible, such as a failure to secure financing for an acquisition, the failure of a new production method, etc.

contingent fee A charge for services based on their value, as for a company that reviews freight bills for errors or a lawyer suing for damages, each of whom charges a percentage of the money recovered.

contingent liability *Finance* An amount booked for the possible incurring of an obligation for a past event, as a pending lawsuit or disputed claim. *Law* Accountability for the acts of those who are not employees, such as the negligence of an independent agent or representative.

continuous processing *Manufacturing* Descriptive of a type of operation involved in the uninterrupted flow of a specific product, as a popular food or beverage that is processed and packaged on a line designed for that one item and no others. See also **intermittent processing.**

contra-asset account *Accounting* A ledger account that reduces the value of an asset, as *depreciation.*

contract A formal agreement between two or more persons to do something or not do something—a contract requires an offer, acceptance, and a **consideration.** Generally referring to an agreement in writing that is enforceable by law.

contractor One who agrees to provide materials or a service to another for a set fee.

contract purchasing An agreement between buyer and seller whereby materials or merchandise is priced based on delivery of specific quantities at intervals over a span of time. Such contracts are common in instances where the buyer requires large quantities and assurance of a stable price and delivery.

contribution *Accounting* The difference between selling price and variable cost of manufacturing a product; also called *contribution to overhead and profit, marginal income,* or *marginal contribution. Manufacturing* Describing the part a particular job or operation plays in the profitability of a department or in maintaining a desirable level of production.

contributory negligence *Law* The act of an injured person that provides part of the basis for the condition that caused injury, such as a vehicle that is struck when the driver ignores a red light.

contributory pension plan A pension plan in which the cost is shared by employer and employee.

control To regulate and manage, as finances or manufacturing operations.

control account *Accounting* A ledger account that summarizes **subsidiary accounts**, as *accounts receivable* is the control account for the summation of the transactions in individual client accounts.

control character *Computers* A non-printing ASCII character that issues a command to the computer.

controllable costs *Accounting* Costs that are variable and can be changed, as cost of materials or labor, distinct from most **overhead** or **fixed cost**, as rent or utilities.

controlled company *Finance* A firm that is subordinate to another company that owns a controlling interest in it, though the amount of direct control may vary depending on the policy of the parent company.

controller See **comptroller**.

controlling interest *Finance* Descriptive of influence over more than 50% of the voting shares of a company, although actual ownership may be less if there is a significant block of stock sympathetic to and voting with those in control or if a significant portion of the shares are widely held and generally not voted

conversational language *Computers* A programming language that specifies commands which are similar to a spoken language.

conversion *Computers* The changing of a data file format to make it acceptable for a different use or for insertion in a different program. *Finance* Change of a security or negotiable instrument from one form to another. *Insurance* The right to change one type of life insurance policy for another under certain conditions contained in a provision in the insurance contract. *Law* The illegal seizure of the property of another; the exchange of real property for personal property. *Manufacturing* A change in, or updating of, equipment or systems.

conversion cost The price of change, as the charge for converting securities or an insurance policy, or the expense of new equipment.

converter *Computers* Software for formatting data to use in a different program. A hardware connector that permits linking of devices that would otherwise be incompatible, such as a telephone modem.

convey *Law* To transfer, as title to property, from one person to another.

conveyance *Law* The instrument by which title to property is conveyed from one person to another; a deed.

cook the books *Accounting, Colloq.* Descriptive of an effort to misrepresent a company's financial position by falsifying records and reports.

cooling-off period *Labor Relations* An interval for seeking a settlement to an impasse in labor negotiations during which time a union may not strike nor an employer stage a lock-out mandated by a contract provision or a court order. *Law* The time during which an individual who has signed a purchase agreement may cancel the contract.

cooperative Any organization owned and operated by its members and formed for their mutual benefit—members share in the work, the expense and the profits of such an enterprise.

cooperative advertising, co-op advertising Retail advertising paid for in part by the manufacturer who usually prepares the advertising and pays an advertising allowance to the retailer based on volume. Advertising of two or more products in the same spot, normally different brands owned by the same company.

coprocessor *Computers* An auxiliary chip that augments the functions of the CPU.

copy *Computers* To make a duplicate, as of a file. To duplicate copy for insertion elsewhere in a document. A program command that makes a copy of a file and saves it in another location.

copyright *Law* Protection for the owner of a creative property, as a literary, musical or artistic work, mandated by federal law. Copyright law has been extended to protect computer programs as well. To insure protection from infringement, the copyright must be registered; any use of the material by another then gives the owner of the property the right to seek damages.

corner the market Descriptive of buying a sufficient quantity of a security or commodity so as to be able to control the price.

corona wire *Computers* The wire in an electrostatic printer that attracts toner to the surface of the paper.

corporate advertising Advertising by an organization to improve its public image as contrasted to selling its products or services.

corporate structure The organization of divisions and departments within a company, including the responsibilities of each, the lines of primary and secondary communication and the lines of authority.

corporate veil A reference to the fact that acts of the individual in a corporation are masked by the corporate entity, specifically referring to attempts at hiding individual action, often illegal, under the corporate shroud.

corporation *Law* A legal entity registered with the state that exists apart from its owners, but has certain rights normally limited to individuals, as the right to own property, incur debts, etc. The advantages of the corporate form are those of: limited liability to shareholders; easy transfer of ownership through the sale of stock; continuity, that is, the death of a shareholder or of all shareholders does not end the life of the corporation.

cosign To be one of two or more signers of a contract as testimony to acceptance of the liability.

cost The capital, time, exertion, etc. associated with a course of action. *Accounting* The amount to be paid for something, as an asset, material or service. The expense to manufacture a given item. *Law* Expenses charged to the losing party in a lawsuit.

cost accounting The collection, recording, reporting and analysis of expenses associated with the manufacture of a product.

cost allocation *Accounting* The assignment of charges for overhead, supplies, etc. to various departments, machines, etc. on a reasonable basis in order to include them in manufacturing cost.

cost analysis *Accounting* A detailed review of expenses associated with the manufacture of a particular product or an operation to study means for improvement.

cost basis *Accounting* The original price of an asset, usually the purchase price plus delivery, installation, improvements, etc., used to calculate depreciation, gain or loss on the sale of the asset, etc.

cost center *Accounting* Any unit of a company to which cost may be assigned, as a machine or department.

cost effective *Finance* Descriptive of a decision, operation or procedure that is of sufficient value to warrant its price.

cost of borrowing *Finance* Referring to the interest rate on borrowed money without regard to the amount of money to be borrowed

cost of capital *Finance* The income that a business could earn on an alternate investment of similar risk.

cost of debt *Finance* Often referring to the actual dollar cost of borrowing a specific sum of money: a factor to be considered when contemplating investment in plant or equipment that will require the use of borrowed money.

cost of distribution *Accounting* The expenses associated with moving a product from the manufacturer or distributor to the consumer. *Marketing* The expense of motivating the move from manufacturer to distributor or consumer, including advertising, price rebates, sales commissions, etc.

cost of goods sold *Accounting* An income statement subtotal that expresses the direct expense of merchandise exchanged for income, as cost of materials, direct labor, etc. *Manufacturing* The expense associated with merchandise produced over which the manager or supervisor has control. *Marketing* The expense of manufacturing a product including direct cost and a fair allocation of indirect and overhead costs.

cost of living adjustment *Labor Relations* An alteration of wages or pensions based on increases in the cost of living, often pegged to the **consumer price index**. Provisions for such adjustments are contained in government retirement plans, social security rates and in most collective bargaining agreements.

cost of sales See **cost of goods sold**, *Marketing* definition. *Marketing* Often used in the sense of the **cost of distribution**, that is, expenses that do not affect those of production, when analyzing the effectiveness of the distribution network, advertising, salespersons, etc., that are controlled by marketing.

cost plus Descriptive of an agreement to perform work at raw cost increased by an allowance for overhead and profit; such allowance is usually based on a percentage of the raw cost, a fixed rate per unit or a flat fee for the job.

cottage industry Descriptive of a small business, often operated out of the home or a storefront, characterized by a lack of structure associated with a larger company or factory. See also, **home based business**.

council A group of people assembled for discussion, deliberation, etc.

counsel Advice tendered after discussion or deliberation; to advise. *Law* A legal advisor.

counterclaim *Law* A claim by one who is being sued, brought against the one suing Usually a response to diminish the strength of the original suit, the counterclaim is, however, an independent action seeking redress.

counterfeit *Law* An imitation made with intent to defraud, as by making a cheap facsimile of a quality product and attempting to pass it off as genuine.

counteroffer *Law* An offer in response to an offer that is not acceptable; the counteroffer is viewed as a rejection of the previous offer.

covenant *Law* A deliberate, binding agreement, as a contract or a promise incidental to a contract. *Law* A formal contract.

covenant not to compete *Law* An agreement by an individual not to engage in a particular field of endeavor, usually for a specified length of time. The agreement is generally contained in a contract of employment or for the sale of a business to reasonably protect the employer or new owner's rights to trade secrets, client lists, etc. Such agreements have been declared invalid, however, when they serve to prevent the individual from making a living.

CPA, certified public accountant *Accounting, Finance* A licensed accountant who has passed certain examinations and fulfilled all other requirements of the state in which he or she is licensed. Though requirements vary from state to state, certification in one state is generally considered acceptable in any state.

cps, characters per second *Computers* A measure of the speed of a printer.

CPU, central processing unit *Computers* The integrated circuits that control the operation of a microcomputer.

craft *Labor Relations* A trade that requires special training and skill, often involving years of apprenticeship.

craft union *Labor Relations* A labor organization that has as its members only those practicing a particular trade.

crash *Computers* The halt of a computer, without hope of recovery except by rebooting, caused by a program or hardware failure. *Finance* A sudden, severe drop in stock prices brought about by a lack of investor confidence.

credit balance *Accounting* In a double entry bookkeeping system, a normal balance for a liability, equity or revenue account. See also **debit balance**. Overpayment, allowance, rebate, etc. to a customer's account that results in a balance in the customer's favor.

credit bureau *Finance* An organization that collects personal and financial data about individuals, keeps a file of the information, and furnishes reports to subscribers of their service.

credit memo, credit memorandum *Accounting* Notice to a customer that his or her obligation has been reduced, stating the reason and the amount, such as an allowance for returned or damaged goods, an error on the original invoice, etc. See also **debit memo**.

creditor *Finance* One who sells to another or loans money, expecting repayment at a later time; one to whom money is owed.

credit rating *Finance* A classification assigned an individual, organization or marketable security based on an evaluation of worth, ability to meet current financial obligations and a history of doing so. Informally, an assessment of how satisfactorily one pays bills.

credit requirements *Finance* Standards set by a bank or business that a potential debtor must meet in order to offer reasonable assurance that the debt will be paid as agreed, as for an individual borrowing from a bank or an organization seeking to buy on open account.

credit union *Finance* A cooperative financial institution established by a group of people, such as members of a labor union, for the purpose of pooling savings and loaning to members.

critical path method A technique for planning complex projects that charts each operation, assigns it a time factor, and shows lines of dependency, that is, which operations must be at least partially completed before another can be started. The critical path is the shortest possible time line through the maze of operations—controlling the critical path assures timely completion.

crop *Computers* In desktop publishing, trimming off any unwanted parts of a picture, drawing or other graphic image.

crosscheck Descriptive of a technique used to verify totals in a spreadsheet: rows and columns are summed, then the total of the columns is compared to the total of the rows to verify that they are the same.

CRT, cathode ray tube *Computers* A type of picture tube used as a computer monitor screen.

culpable At fault, or liable, as when one has been indifferent to the rights of others.

current In progress; at present. *Accounting* Descriptive of an account that is paid to date; not overdue.

current asset *Accounting, Finance* Assets that are likely to be converted in the present accounting period, as cash, accounts receivable, inventory, etc.

current cost *Accounting* Present worth of an asset, such as inventory; same as **replacement cost**.

current dollars *Finance* Descriptive of the cost of an asset that has been adjusted to reflect the changes in the value of the dollar.

current liability *Accounting* A debt that is due to be repaid within twelve months, such as accounts payable or the portion of a long-term loan that is due within the year.

current market value *Finance* The valuation of an asset at present market prices.

current ratio *Finance* A comparison of the proportion of current assets to current liabilities, a measure of a company's ability to withstand a short term setback as by a loss to inventory or accounts receivables. See also, **quick ratio**.

cursor *Computers* The line or block that marks the insertion point for text or graphics in a word processing or similar program.

cursor arrows *Computers* Arrows on the keyboard that serve to move the insertion point up, down, right or left.

cursor control key *Computers* Any key that moves the insertion point without altering the position of copy, as arrow keys, Tab, End, Home, Page Up and Page Down.

custom, customary Descriptive of practice that is usual for a particular business or industry, for example, a book printer is usually allowed to deliver, and the publisher is expected to accept, additional or less copies than those called for in an order within an agreed tolerance.

customer The buyer, or user, of a product or service.

customer service Assistance provided by an individual or a group whose duty is to maintain a line of communication between clients and elements of the company, responding to customers' requests, keeping them informed of the status of work in process, etc. In a business with a finite number of customers, customer service personnel often work closely with the sales force, and frequently act on their behalf.

cut and paste *Computers* A feature of some programs, especially for word processing, that allow copy to be removed from one location and inserted in another.

cutback The act of reducing. Any reduction, as in the labor force, scheduled overtime, or the budget for capital expenditures. A decrease in the level of production.

cutoff, cutoff date *Accounting* A time at which transactions relating to the finances of a company will no longer be considered in an accounting period, all future transactions to apply to the following period.

cycle billing *Accounting* A technique for segmenting accounts receivables so that statements sent to various groups of clients and due dates for payment are spread throughout the month. The system allows more timely posting of accounts and provides for more efficient use of resources.

cyclic, cyclical Descriptive of anything that recurs at regular intervals, as a *cyclic demand* that may describe a market for products or services that are in demand during certain seasons, or a *cyclic industry* that increases or decreases production levels at certain times of the year.

D

daily report Descriptive of any account or summary of activity that is issued every day to provide information about elements of a business that are volatile and critical to smooth operation. Such a report may provide an accounting of raw materials or finished goods inventory, production output or sales logged for the previous day, or a summary of cash received and dispersed.

daisy wheel *Computers* Designating a type of impact printer in which raised characters are mounted on a rotating wheel.

damages *Law* Money that is claimed to be owed, or that a court has ordered to be paid to, an injured party as compensation for loss suffered by negligence or deliberate action of another.

data Any information. *Computers* Information that is to be entered, that has been entered, or that is output from processing, of a computer program.

database *Computers* A set of like records containing related information, such as an *employee data base* that contains a **record** for every employee, with each item of data about the employee arranged in a **field** such as name, social security number, date of birth, date hired, etc.

data block *Computers* A selection of data based on a specific search criterion.

data conversion *Computers* An altering of selected data for transfer to a different program or format, as from a database file to a spreadsheet file.

data entry *Computers* The recording or updating of information to a computer file.

data field *Computers* Any of the areas in a database dedicated to a particular item of information, as a date or name.

data format *Computers* The type of data acceptable in a particular field, as date, number, alphameric, etc.

data link *Computers* A connection between computer systems that allows information sharing. A validation formula in a spreadsheet or database that limits entry of data into a cell or field based on a previous entry. A connection between documents containing similar information, that automatically updates all documents when one is changed.

data management *Computers* The process of recording and manipulating data in the conduct of a business.

data parsing *Computers* Breaking a data string down to its basic elements for conversion to another file format, as from database fields to spreadsheet cells.

data processing *Computers* The recording and management of significant information for a specific purpose.

data record *Computers* The set of fields that comprise a unique entry in a database file.

data set *Computers* A block or series of related database records.

data structure *Computers* The way in which a particular set of database records are organized.

data transmission *Computers* The transfer of information through a computer system or between computer systems.

data validation *Computers* A means for verifying that data in a field is of the correct type or magnitude, such as by checking for a date format.

date number *Computers* A numeric value that represents a specific date, as by the number of the day and month within a year or the number of days from a base date.

dba *doing business as* A qualifier that serves to more specifically identify a business entity; the business may be legally recorded in an individual's name or a corporate name, while dealing with the public under a name that more clearly identifies the product of service offered.

deadhead *Commerce* To operate a commercial vehicle without paying passengers or cargo, often of the return trip after making a delivery.

deadline Generally, the time by which something must be done without penalty, as the latest time for completion of a task or that an offer remains in effect.

deadlock A stalemate. *Labor Relations* Often used to describe a situation in contract bargaining wherein negotiators take an opposite or contradictory stand on an issue and neither is willing to compromise.

dead time *Manufacturing* Time during which no work is being performed. Dead time, or down time, may be caused by equipment malfunction, a lack of materials, insufficient workers to run equipment or a production line, etc. Dead time may also be scheduled, such as for preventative maintenance, shutdown for scheduled holidays, vacation, etc.

dealer *Commerce* A buyer or seller, one who trades in the marketplace. A dealer may be independent, or one who is franchised or authorized to deal in a particular product or service, advertising to the public such authorization.

debenture A document attesting that money is owed to the bearer by the issuer. *Finance* An interest-bearing bond that is issued against the general credit of an organization with no specific assets pledged. Holders of such bonds issued by a corporation are creditors and therefore entitled to payment before owners or shareholders in the event of dissolution.

debit balance *Accounting* In a double entry bookkeeping system, a normal balance for an asset or expense account. See also **credit balance**.

debit memo, debit memorandum *Accounting* Notice to a customer of a charge to his or her account, stating the reason and the amount, such as a correction to an invoice, etc. See also **credit memo**.

debt ratio Any of a number of means used to measure the soundness of an organization, as the ratio between total liabilities and net worth, or between long term liabilities and net worth.

debt retirement Generally, the repayment of moneys owed. *Finance* The plan for systematic repayment of moneys owed, usually involving the setting aside of a specific amount in each accounting period.

debt service *Finance* Descriptive of the amount set aside for the periodic payment of interest and part of the principal on outstanding obligations.

debug Generally, to remove errors in the operation of systems, processes, or equipment. *Computer* To correct the configuration of equipment or errors in a program to achieve smooth operation.

decentralization The process of removing a measure of control and decision making from a key, central location, such as a corporation's headquarters, and placing it in the hands of those closer to the element controlled. Decentralization allows the local manager or supervisor greater freedom of action and the ability to adjust more quickly to changing needs.

decertification *Labor Relations* Loss by a union of its authorization to bargain for a group of workers. Such action is taken by the National Labor Relations Board when a majority of the workers represented by the union vote that they no longer desire representation by that particular union.

declining balance, double declining balance *Accounting* A system of accelerated **depreciation** that, for tax purposes, allows a larger deduction in the earlier years. The declining balance method allows depreciation at twice the **straight line** rate on the book value of the asset for each year until salvage value is reached. For example, a van purchased for $20,000 is expected to last five years with a salvage value of $5,000 at the end of five years. An asset with a five year life is depreciated at 20%, but declining balance allows twice that, or 40%. Therefore, the first year, $8,000 is claimed for depreciation leaving a book value of $12,000. The second year, $4,800 is claimed—40% times $12,000—leaving a book value of $7,200. The third year depreciation calculates to $2,880, but only $2,200 is allowed because the book value cannot fall below the salvage value of $5,000.

dedicated *Computers* Designating of that set aside for a specific purpose, as an area in computer memory for a control function, or a telephone transmission line for a fax.

deduction *Accounting* An amount subtracted, as an adjustment to an invoice, or an allowance for calculating taxable income.

deed *Law* A written instrument that conveys title to a property.

de facto *Latin* In fact; of a condition that exists, although it may not be official, moral, or legal. See **de jure**.

default Failure to do something that is required, promised or expected; commonly, the failure to make payment of principal or interest on a loan. See also **delinquent**. *Computers* Failure to issue specific instructions for the operation of a device or program.

default configuration *Computers* Guidelines or formatting for a device or program in the absence of specific instructions by the user.

defective Imperfect or faulty, as merchandise or reasoning.

deferred Put off to a later time, often by agreement.

deferred billing An agreement whereby the bill for merchandise that is shipped is delayed for a prearranged period, such as for thirty days to allow inspection of the material when it is received, or until an agreed date, that may allow the recipient to record the purchase in a later accounting period to satisfy a budgetary requirement. Such agreements are often made when merchandise is shipped in advance of need as a convenience to the shipper who lacks warehouse space.

deferred charge *Accounting* Cost that has been incurred in the current period, but that applies to the revenues of a later period and is therefore adjusted so as to withhold from current financial reports any expense that does not apply to current revenue. Such charges may be improvements to plant or equipment that will be expensed when they are put in operation.

deferred compensation Generally, descriptive of payment or an offer of payment to an employee that is not immediately available for his or her use, such as the company share of a retirement fund, stock options, etc. *Accounting* An account for recording the cost of deferred compensation in the period it is accrued so as to match it against current revenues.

deferred income *Accounting* Income received in the current period that will actually be earned in later periods, such as prepayment for a service contract that spans several years. The amount applicable to the current year is taken as income; that for subsequent years is withheld to be matched to the period for which it is reasonable to expect that expense will be incurred.

deficit Any shortfall of cash or cash equivalent, as more liabilities than assets, or more expense than income.

defunct No longer existing; out of business.

de jure *Latin* By right; existing according to law. See **de facto**.

delegate To name or appoint one to a particular task; to allow one the necessary authority to accomplish a purpose; one so appointed. Delegating authority downward through an organization is seen as a critical element to effective management in that it allows individuals at each level to concentrate on their primary tasks with minimal oversight of those for which they are responsible that are performed at lower levels.

delimiter *Computer* A symbol such as a comma or quotation mark, used to separate elements of information in a data string.

delinquent Failure to do that required, such as making payment on a financial obligation. *Delinquent* usually implies late, with anticipation that the obligation will be met; **default** implies permanent failure of ability or intent that may require legal action by the creditor.

delivery *Commerce* The act of transporting goods or the actual transfer of goods from seller to buyer. *Law* The irrevocable transfer of ownership of goods, services, etc. It can be important to a business to establish when the actual transfer of ownership takes place in order to determine liability in case of damage. For example, goods in transit are the responsibility of the carrier, but in the event of damage, it is necessary to know who has to file a claim and bear any losses not covered by the carrier's insurance. Similarly, it is important to verify responsibility for goods that have been purchased and held by the seller for future delivery at the buyer's convenience.

demand *Finance* A request for payment or fulfillment of an obligation. *Law* To petition a court for that which is rightful. *Marketing* The anticipated traffic in a product at a given price. The volume of a product that may reasonably expect to be sold tends to vary directly, although not necessarily proportionately, with the price asked for the product. See also **demand curve**.

demand curve *Marketing* A graphic representation of the relationship between price and quantity: with price on one axis and quantity on the other, the normal demand curve traces an arc that shows higher demand at lower prices and lower demand at higher prices. Modern marketing, however, has often generated a demand that runs counter to the normal price-volume relationship by selling other features that have actually created more demand at a higher price.

demand deposit Money that is deposited in a bank and that may be withdrawn without prior notice by check, transfer, etc.

demand note An instrument of indebtedness, payment of which may be requested at any time without prior notice. Such notes are often carried by a lending institution for a financially secure business that occasionally needs additional cash flow, requiring only that interest be paid periodically, and the note itself retired as cash flow allows.

demographics *Marketing* The population statistics that relate to lifestyle such as age, education, income, etc., used by advertisers and marketers to select media and message to target the audience for a product.

demurrage *Commerce* The charge levied by a carrier for delay beyond the time normally allowed for loading or unloading.

department Any of the units into which a company is divided to group the jobs of those engaged in related tasks.

deposition *Law* Sworn testimony taken outside of court by a stenographer, to be presented in court at the proper time.

depreciable life *Accounting* The time over which a piece of equipment is to be depreciated; the anticipated useful life of a piece of equipment.

depreciation *Accounting* An allowance for the decrease in the value of an asset due to wear and tear. Any of the systems for calculating the decrease in value of an asset, as **straight line, declining balance,** etc.

deregulation The rescinding of a portion of the government regulations that pertain to a particular industry with the avowed purpose of creating a more open market with increased competition.

descending sort *Computers* An alphabetical or numerical arrangement of data from the highest to the lowest.

desktop *Computers* A set of computer accessory programs that emulate items found on a desk, as a calendar, calculator or note pad.

desktop computer *Computers* A small computer designed to fit on the top of a desk. See also **microcomputer.**

desktop publishing *Computers* The creation of graphics material, such as newsletters, flyers, charts, etc. on a microcomputer.

destructive read *Computers* A computer read-out that simultaneously erases the source file.

detail person *Marketing* A salesperson who services retailers, primarily in the grocery business, and who supervises promotions, makes certain the company's products are properly displayed, etc.

device *Computers* Any component or peripheral that is a part of a computer system.

device driver *Computers* A program that interprets instructions for the operation of a peripheral, such as a printer

diagnostic *Computers* Descriptive of a system designed to detect and isolate errors or malfunctions in a programs or equipment.

diagnostic message *Computers* An error message that indicates the source of the error.

dialog box *Computers* A panel that appears on screen as a part of a program to furnish instructions, information or to request user input.

dilution *Finance* A reduction in the book value of a share of a corporation's stock caused by an increase in outstanding shares, as by exercise of warrants or options.

digit *Computers* A symbol representing an integer in a numbering system, as 0-9 in decimal notation or 0-F in hexadecimal.

digital *Computers* Of that represented by a discrete value.

digital camera *Computers* A camera that records images in digital format for downloading and viewing on a computer screen.

digital data *Computers* Information recorded according to a system of numbers, as binary for the computer.

digital recording *Computers* The recording of sound as discrete values.

DIP, dual in-line package *Computers* Designating of an integrated circuit that can be programmed with the use of a series of toggle switches.

direct cost *Accounting* Any expense for labor, materials, overhead, etc. that can be identified directly with the manufacture of a specific product, group of products, or a service.

direct labor *Accounting* The cost of labor that can be identified directly with the manufacture of a product, group of products, or a service.

direct marketing Generally, descriptive of selling by mail, that is, addressing the selling message to a particular prospect who can order directly from the mailer. Also describes the use of the mail to deliver a selling message for a particular product that may be bought from a source other than the mailer, as a local merchant.

director Any of the members of the board of directors that guides the affairs of an organization.

directory *Computers* In a computer hierarchical file structure, a division that holds related program or data files and sub-directories.

direct overhead *Accounting* Any overhead expense that can be identified directly with the manufacturing operation, and ultimately with a specific product, group of products, or a service, such as the salary of a **line supervisor**, or the cost of the space occupied by a machine.

direct sales Sales by a manufacturer to the retailer or consumer; without benefit of a middleman, broker, or distributor.

disbursement Descriptive of money paid out to satisfy an obligation.

discharge *Finance* To free from a debt or other obligation, as by payment, or by failure of another party to a contract to meet an obligation. *Labor* To terminate or dismiss a worker.

disciplinary layoff *Labor* Suspension of a worker for violation of company rules.

disclaimer A conditional statement that limits liability of the party issuing the statement under certain conditions.

disclosure Generally, the release of any information that is significant and relevant to the matter at hand, and that may not otherwise be known to the other party, such as disclosure by a purchasing agent of the company that he or she has a financial interest in one of the company's suppliers. Disclosure avoids the appearance of wrongdoing, allowing the recipient of the information to weigh the information and act accordingly. For example, in the case of the purchasing agent who has a financial interest in a supplier, management may decide it is inconsequential, that the agent should be out of the loop in any transactions involving that particular vendor, or they may insist on **divestiture**. *Finance* The inclusion in a financial report of information describing any unusual transaction that is not apparent to the reader of the report and that materially affects the bottom line.

discount *Finance* An allowance to a buyer for prompt payment. Terms of a loan in which interest is deducted from the amount of the loan at the time it is made. *Marketing* An allowance paid to a dealer or merchant for buying in volume.

discovery *Law* Any procedure for gathering information before going to court, such as that of taking testimony in advance of trial. See also **deposition.**

discrepancy An inconsistency or abnormal variance between two or more elements.

Finance Often used to describe a variance between budgeted or anticipated cost and actual cost.

discretionary cost In an organization, an allowance for expenses that are not absolutely necessary and that can be withheld without harm to the continued operation of the organization, such as a portion of the advertising budget, certain repairs and maintenance, etc.

discretionary income See **disposable income.**

discrimination *Labor Relations* Generally, any treatment or consideration of an individual or group of individuals that differs from that accorded most others in respect to hiring, discipline, training, work assignment, promotion, etc.

dishonor *Law* Refusal to make payment, or fulfill, an obligation, as a debt or other promise.

disk *Computers* a computer storage device.

disk crash *Computers* Destruction of a disk and the data it holds as a result of the read/write head coming in contact with the surface of the disk; any disk failure, sometimes recoverable.

disk drive *Computers* The device that holds, spins and reads from, or writes to, the disk.

diskette *Computers* A floppy or removable disk.

disk formatting *Computers* A series of reference points recorded on a disk that allow orderly and rapid storage and retrieval of data.

disk fragmentation *Computers* A condition that occurs after many reads and writes to a disk in that data for a single file is scattered throughout the disk rather than being stored in contiguous sectors.

disk sector *Computers* A section of a disk track.

disk tracks *Computers* Concentric circles of a disk where data is stored.

dispatcher *Commerce* One who works for a freight company or a **consortium** of independent haulers and whose function is to control the movement of operators and vehicles for the most expeditious movement of freight.

display console *Computers* a screen where the user views data, and monitors the operation of the computer.

disposable income That portion of an individual's income left after payment for necessities; the amount of one's income that can be spent for pleasure.

dissolution A breaking up or dissolving. The termination of a business, as a corporation by vote of the stockholders, consolidation, etc.

distribution *Accounting* The assignment of income and expenses to the proper accounts. *Marketing* Descriptive of the network that moves product from manufacturer or distributor to the ultimate consumer. Statistics regarding the purchase of a product by various **demographic** groups.

distribution allowance *Marketing* A rebate offered by a manufacturer to the wholesaler, distributor, etc. for advertising and promotion.

distributor An individual or company that is responsible for moving product from the manufacturer to the retailer. The distributor may be an agent charged with dispersing a pre-sold product, as a newsstand distributor who is charged with filling store racks with current issues of magazines and returning outdated product. Or, the distributor may be a wholesaler who carries a large stock of merchandise that is sold and delivered to individual merchants.

dithered image *Computers* A pattern of black or colored dots of varying size that create the image of a full range of gray or color tones on a computer monitor screen.

diversification The venture of a company into the providing of new products or services that may or may not be related to those already provided. Diversification can be an attempt to protect or increase market share by adding related products that are carried by competitors; or it can be directed toward product areas that are entirely new to the company to offset the effect of seasonal dips, to make good use of excess cash, etc.

divestiture The act of getting rid of something, usually, to prevent a conflict of interest.

division A separated unit of a company, often operating with great autonomy, almost as a separate company.

dock *Labor* To deduct from one's pay or allowances for a particular reason, as from wages for arriving late at the job or from vacation days of the worker who has exceeded the allotted number of sick days.

document Generally, a page of data, often official. *Computers* A printed copy of information held in computer memory.

documentation Generally, instructions, verification, etc. *Computers* Information or instructions relating to a program, procedure, etc.

document reader *Computers* A device that is able to recognize an image on paper and convert it to digital data.

document retrieval *Computers* A system for identifying and retrieving data stored in the computer.

domestic corporation A corporation that operates totally within the state in which it is incorporated.

DOS, disk operating system *Computers* a program that controls all of the basic operations of the computer.

dot matrix *Computers* Printing in which characters are formed by numerous dots arranged according to the pattern established for the character.

double click *Computers* Pressing and releasing a button of a mouse twice in quick succession, used to activate a selection in some programs.

double declining balance See declining balance.

double density disk *Computers* A diskette on which data is packed in order to double its capacity.

double dipping Descriptive of having two incomes, either by holding two jobs, by collecting from two retirement funds, or by collecting from a retirement fund while holding down a full-time job. Most often used to describe individuals who receive retirement or pay from two government jobs.

double-entry bookkeeping *Accounting* The system of maintaining financial records for a company in which every entry has an offsetting entry—a system of debits and credits. For example, the purchase of goods requires an entry that adds to the value of inventory that is offset by an entry to accounts payable. The effect is to create a liability in exchange for an asset so that the net worth of the company is unchanged. The system is designed to maintain an aggregate balance that allows for detection of errors and to create an **audit trail** that allows all transactions to be traced to their source.

double-sided disk *Computers* a diskette on which data is stored on both sides.

double taxation Descriptive of the taxing of corporate profits that are distributed to shareholders as dividends where they are taxed again as income to the shareholder. The term may also be used to describe that portion of personal income that is paid out in wages to domestic help or for goods and services that will be taxed again.

double time *Labor* Twice the normal hourly labor rate; descriptive of time worked that by agreement is to paid at double the normal rate, such as work on a Sunday or holiday.

download *Computers* To load a program or data into a computer from another computer or from a storage device, such as a disk.

down payment *Commerce* An amount paid in advance of the receipt of goods. Such a payment may be a good faith deposit, insuring that goods will be picked up at a later date; a payment that cuts the lender's risk when goods are bought on credit; or the first payment for the manufacture of a custom product that will be sold for cash, in which case the down payment usually covers the immediate out of pocket cost to the supplier.

downside risk An assessment of the cost or penalty if a project or investment goes awry. Such an assessment may be made when considering an investment in new equipment or a new product line. It may also be part of the decision making process to determine a course of action, for example, weighing the cost of unpacking and repacking a warehouse full of products that are in inventory to check for a suspected minor fault against the cost of replacing those products if they are returned by the consumer.

down time See dead time.

downward compatible *Computers* Descriptive of the ability of a program to run with data or formatting created by an earlier version.

dpi, dots per inch *Computers* A measure of the quality of image from a scanner or printer; the more dots per inch, the finer the image appears to the eye.

drag *Computers* To press and hold a mouse button down while moving the cursor, thereby moving the image under the cursor.

DRAM, dynamic random access memory *Computers* Memory that must be constantly refreshed to be retained and that is erased when the power is off.

draw An allowance provided to a salesperson, often for a limited time, as personal income until commissions from sales are adequate to provide a steady income. In some cases, the draw is not charged against commissions, but is considered a subsidy for a training period. A true draw, however, is deducted from commissions at an appropriate time, and the difference paid to the salesperson. Frequently, the draw is continued, with the drawing and commission accounts reconciled periodically, as monthly or quarterly.

drive *Computers* The device that moves a disk or tape past the head that reads from, and writes to, the storage medium.

drive designation *Computers* The letter assigned to a drive in order to identify it.

driver *Computers* A program or routine that translates and conveys messages between a computer and a peripheral.

drop down menu *Computers* A program feature that presents a list of options on screen when a menu title is selected.

drop shipping *Commerce* The breaking down of a large consignment of goods for shipment directly to the customer, as a retailer or consumer. In some cases, the manufacturer may handle the drop shipping of the customer's order or the customer may accept bulk shipment and perform the drop shipping.

dry goods *Commerce* Descriptive of textiles and textile products, as clothing, bedding, thread, etc.

due care *Law* The standard of reasonable conduct that is considered in judging fault for negligence— whether or not the subject exercised due care in the maintenance of property, manufacture of a product, etc.

due process *Law* The concept of the legal system and actions taken with such system to protect the rights and liberties of the individual.

dues An amount paid to maintain membership in an organization, as a labor union. Dues are primarily to cover administrative costs, that is salaries, offices, etc. for those who run the organization, although a portion may be used to cover the cost of benefits that accrue to members, such as sickness or death benefits, legal aid, etc.

dummy Generally, an imitation or substitute for the real thing. Often, a sample submitted for approval before volume production begins, as a *dummy* book from a printer to show size and construction, or a *dummy* package to assure that the product fits and can be properly displayed.

dummy corporation A corporation formed as a holding company for another company or companies and whose only function is as a buffer between the active corporation and the true owners.

dummy invoice *Accounting* An invoice for merchandise that is made in advance of the actual invoice or as a replacement for an invoice already made. A dummy invoice may be made to cover a cash order that is to be paid before shipment: the dummy furnishes documentation required by the buyer; the actual invoice that is submitted after delivery would include freight and any additional charges not picked up on the dummy invoice.

dump *Computers* To transfer the entire contents of a file to a printer, monitor or storage device.

dumping The practice of selling goods outside of the usual distribution channels, often a foreign market, for a lower than normal price and, for a reason that brings into question the ethics of the company doing the dumping. Goods may be dumped in a foreign market because they are of an inferior quality and cannot be sold domestically. Selling at a lower price in a new market may also be an attempt to undermine competition. Dumping can also be a means to increase profit—if the setup cost for production is very high, additional units beyond those that can be sold in the domestic market at regular prices may be manufactured at a very small cost; those additional units can be dumped in a foreign market and priced much lower than the same product in the domestic market while still earning a significant profit because of their low price.

dun To press for payment.

duplication A repetition of effort; to do the same task twice. *Manufacturing* A repeat of effort, as moving materials needlessly or performing a test or inspection more than once. Unless duplication is desired, as in a repeated quality control check, it should be eliminated. *Marketing* Descriptive of advertising placed in such a way that the same audience is reached through different media or different elements of the same media.

durable goods *Marketing* Descriptive of goods that represent a major purchase for most households and that have an anticipated life span of more than a few years, as a washer, dryer, automobile, etc.

duress *Law* Conduct, as a threat, that presses one to do something against his or her will.

duty *Law* A legal or moral obligation, as a duty to bargain in good faith over the terms for a labor contract, or the duty of a manufacturer to exercise reasonable care to insure that the consumer who uses the product manufactured will not come to harm because of it.

E

early retirement Descriptive of retirement from a job before the normal retirement age or time of service. Such retirement is often an alternative to job loss in times of cutback and usually involves a reduction of monthly benefits.

earned income *Finance* Money that comes to an individual or to a company as a result of involvement in the production of goods and services, as contrasted to earnings from investment.

earnest money *Law* Cash that is tendered by a buyer to prove that he or she is in earnest about a purchase, often that of real estate. Failure to purchase, except for agreed upon contingencies, usually involves forfeiture of the deposit.

earnings *Finance* All of the money that comes to an individual or company, regardless of the source, whether **earned income** or from investment, usually as reported for tax purposes.

earnings per share *Finance* That portion of the total profit reported by a company for a specified accounting period that may be allotted to each share of common stock outstanding.

easement *Law* A right granted by agreement or law for limited use of land, such as a right of way, without change of ownership.

EBCDIC, Extended Binary Coded Decimal Interchange Code *Computers* A standard code for the numeric representation of alphanumeric characters.

echelon Originally, descriptive of troop formations at varying positions or levels. Used in business to describe the levels of authority and responsibility from the top management to the least of the workers.

echo *Computers* Command or information lines that are displayed, or echoed, on the monitor screen.

economical order quantity The amount of any material that should be ordered to make the best use of the firm's resources, taking into consideration such factors as price breaks for ordering in quantity, shelf life of the material, space required and available for warehousing, anticipated time that money will be tied up in the inventory, etc.

economic life *Accounting* The anticipated time that a particular piece of equipment can be operated economically, that is, the time until operation of the equipment costs more than it can earn.

economy of scale Descriptive of the potential savings to a company through an increase in size, market share, diversification, etc. For example, a company may make better use of its equipment or buy better equipment to double its output without increasing plant size or overhead, thereby reducing unit cost through growth.

edict Originally a decree or proclamation issued by a governmental authority; now used to describe any directive that specifies clearly a company position.

edit *Computers* To make changes, as additions or deletions, to a file or document.

edit commands *Computers* Commands in a program that facilitate the process of editing, such as *move, copy, paste,* etc.

edit key *Computers* Any of the special keyboard keys, such as *insert* or *delete,* used to edit text.

edlin *Computers* A line by line text editor available in DOS.

EDP, electronic data processing *Computers* Any manipulation of data by electronic means.

EEOC See **Equal Employment Opportunity Commission.**

efficiency Of the ability to make the best use of resources—money, labor hours, and materials—in the production of goods.

EGA, Enhanced Graphics Adapter *Computers* A standard for the display on a color monitor screen.

electronic bulletin board *Computers* A computer message center.

electronic mail *Computers* The transfer of messages, with the use of the computer, from one individual to another or to a group of specified persons.

electronic spreadsheet *Computer* A computer version of a worksheet with data organized in rows and columns.

electrostatic printer *Computer* A device that creates images through the adherence of a toner to charged portions of a receiver.

embargo *Commerce* Any restriction on trade, as of certain items for security reasons, or with a particular country for economic or political reasons.

embed *Computer* To fix an element from one document or file into another.

embedded commands *Computer* Program instructions that establish and maintain the appearance, position and special characteristics of a text or graphics element.

embedded object *Computer* A drawing, chart, sound recording, etc. that is fixed in a text based document.

embedded pointer *Computer* The link between an embedded object and its source file, as the link between a chart and its spreadsheet source data.

embezzlement *Law* The misappropriation of funds or property belonging to another, by who is legally charged with their care.

eminent domain *Law* The right of government to authorize the taking of private land for public use with **just compensation** to the owner of the land.

employee One who works for wages or salary.

employee stock ownership plan *Labor Relations* Any program designed to encourage those who work for a company to purchase stock in the company, often through payroll deduction, or loans backed by the company, in order to develop an active interest among employees in the success of the enterprise. In extreme cases, an opportunity for employees to take control of an ailing company.

employer An individual or organization that engages others to work for **wages** or **salary.**

employment agency Any organization, public or private that specializes in matching workers with available jobs. Most private agencies require a contract from job seekers and charge a fee for their services.

employment contract *Labor Relations* A formal agreement between employer and employee, often required of an individual hired for a high level or sensitive position. Such a contract may include a covenant not to disclose trade secrets nor to seek or accept employment in a competing firm for a specified period. Some companies require a contract of all new employees, stating simply that the individual has read, understands, and is willing to comply with company rules.

emulation software *Computers* A program that directs a peripheral to imitate another, usually to improve performance, as the emulation of laser quality by a dot matrix printer.

enable, enabling *Computers* Allowing or directing to operate, as by computer command. *Law* Provision in a law that gives officials the power to enforce the law.

encroach *Law* To intrude on the rights or property of another.

encryption *Computers* Jumbling or coding of sensitive data for security purposes.

encumbrance *Law* A lien or claim attached to real property

END *Computers* A program code indicating the final command.

End key *Computers* A cursor movement key that sends the cursor to the end of a line of text and, used in conjunction with other keys, to the bottom right of the screen, the bottom of the page or the end of the file.

end of page indicator *Computers* A command embedded in a document to indicate the end of a printed page; the sensor on a printer that signals the end of a sheet of paper.

endorsement *Accounting* Signature on the back of a check that verifies receipt of funds. *Advertisement* A broadcast statement, usually by a well-known celebrity, that attests to or implies approval of the quality of a product. *Insurance* A document that verifies a change or addition to an insurance policy, such as special coverage, beneficiary, etc.

endowment A gift of money or property to a person or institution, usually for a specific purpose.

enjoin To forbid to do something, usually with legal authority, such as the making of false claims about a product, or spreading derogatory rumors about a competitor.

enter *Computers* To add information, as text to a document, records to a database, etc.

Enter key *Computers* A function key used to signal the end of a block of copy or enable a selected command; also expressed as CR or carriage return or Return.

enterprise A business venture, usually implying an element of risk.

entity Generally, a thing that has being. In business, the legal form elected by the owner or owners, such as a sole proprietorship, corporation, partnership, etc.

entrepreneur One who organizes and operates a business, usually implying one who is willing to accept risk in the quest for profit.

entry-level Descriptive of a job in the lower echelons of a company or a career field; a position viewed as a proving ground for new employees.

envelope feeder *Computers* A device that attaches to the printer to allow the automatic feeding of envelopes for addressing.

environment *Computers* Referring to the type of operating system, the peripherals and programs that make up a computer system.

EOM, end of month End of an accounting or payment period.

Equal Employment Opportunity Commission A government body empowered to enforce the federal regulations against discrimination by employers or unions in hiring, training, promoting, etc.

equal opportunity employer An employer who actively seeks to end discrimination in the workplace and encourages hiring, training, promotion, etc. without regard to race, creed, color, national origin, sex, etc.

equipment Machinery used in the manufacture of goods or in the performance of a service.

equipment compatibility *Computers* The quality of computers and peripherals to share data without translation.

equipment leasing The practice of procuring equipment needed for company operations through a lease arrangement rather than through outright purchase. Such lease arrangements may be available from the manufacturer or through a third party that makes a business in financing the purchase and subsequent leasing of equipment.

equity *Accounting* The aggregate of capital paid into a business plus any retained earnings. *Finance* The market value or cost of property less any liens against that property.

erase *Computers* To delete, as a block of copy or a file, from storage.

errorlevel *Computers* In a program or batch file, a value that is tested to signal a branch.

error message *Computers* A message from an operating system or program displayed on the monitor or printer indicating that an error in processing has occurred, often citing the source of the error.

escalator clause *Commerce* A provision in a long term contract that provides for a price adjustment to cover anticipated changes in the cost of labor or materials. *Labor Relations* In a labor contract, a provision for automatic increases to cover increases in the cost of living.

escape *Computers* To discontinue processing, or to return to a previous menu or operating level.

escape character *Computers* ASCII control character 027 signaled by the Escape key and used in certain program sequences to signal the start of a printer or monitor control code.

Escape key *Computers* A function key that triggers the escape command.

escape sequence *Computers* A character string prefaced by the escape code (ASCII 027) so that computer will recognize it as a command.

escrow *Law* Something of value, as money, securities or a written instrument such as a deed, placed on deposit with a third party to be held until certain conditions are fulfilled. Escrow may be a deposit of earnest money that is held until the sales agreement is executed or abandoned; a deed that is mortgage for a real estate loan, to be returned to the rightful owner when the loan is paid or declared in default; amounts paid to the holder of a mortgage for periodic expenses such as taxes and insurance; etc.

estate *Finance, Law* Generally, all of the real and personal property that a person owns. Specifically, the nature and extent of one's ownership interest in land. All that one possesses at the time of death.

estate planning *Finance* A strategy for managing property so as to legally transfer as much as possible to one's heirs by minimizing the amount that is subject to taxes, both during life and after death.

estimated liabilities *Finance* A notation to a financial statement that recognizes a liability, the exact amount of which is unknown, as for taxes, or an award by a court that is being contested.

estimator Generally, one who estimates. A vital function in a company that produces a product or service package that is tailored to the needs of a project or client, as in advertising, construction or certain types of manufacturing, the estimator calculates the anticipated cost of the project for his or her company and the client.

estop *Law* To prevent or restrain one from a denial or claim that is contradicted by previous statements or acts by that person, or by earlier findings of a court.

ethics Generally, the study of standards of conduct and morality. In practice, ethics is descriptive of the conduct one may expect from a reasonable person under normal circumstances. In addition, many trade groups have established codes of ethics that address specific areas peculiar to their business or industry.

eviction *Law* The removal of a tenant from leased property for violation of the lease contract, as by misuse of the property, non payment of rent, etc.

exchange *Commerce* Barter. To give up one thing for another, usually of comparable value. Although exchange may refer to trading promises, or a promise for material consideration, it is most usually used in the world of commerce to describe the trading of goods or services, as a consumer who returns merchandise for replacement or for something else of similar value. The exchange of merchandise or services for money is normally viewed as a *sale*.

exchange rate *Finance* The official valuation of the currency of a nation in relation to that of other nations.

excise tax A domestic duty or levy assessed on the manufacture or trade of certain commodities.

exclusion That which need not, or cannot, be included. *Finance* A qualifier to a financial statement in which the auditor or preparer notes that certain items or transactions are not included in the report or have not been verified to the preparer's satisfaction. *Insurance* A **disclaimer** that lists items or conditions not covered by a particular insurance policy.

execute *Computer* to carry out an instruction or set of instructions. *Law* To make valid, as by signing. To complete, as by performing according to the agreement contained in a contract.

executive An administrator. Generally, anyone in a company who has significant authority and responsibility for the operation of the company. Often used to describe anyone in a company who works on salary, as opposed to an hourly wage.

executive committee A select group of high level or key management personnel in a company, often charged with the oversight of company operations and the implementation of plans to move in new directions.

executor *Law* One appointed to carry out the wishes of another for disposition of property, etc. according to the terms laid out in a will.

executory *Law* Any part of a legal contract that has not been executed, or fulfilled.

exit *Computers* A program branch that returns control to the next higher level. To leave a subroutine and return to the main application program or to leave an application and return to the operating system.

exit interview *Labor Relations* A conversation with an individual who has resigned. An exit interview may offer insight into employee attitudes about a particular job, a department, and the company in general. Learning why an employee is leaving and what might have induced him or her to stay can be helpful in efforts to retain key employees or to generally reduce turnover.

ex officio By right of office; with official standing. Descriptive of membership on a committee or other group within a company that is traditionally part of the job, so that formal appointment is not required, such as a seat on the executive committee that is normally filled by the person in the position of general manager.

expansion An enlargement or broadening of scope, as of a plant, product lines, etc.

expansion card *Computers* A board that is installed in the computer to provide additional memory or functions.

expansion slots *Computers* Positions in the computer reserved for the installation of expansion or control boards.

expected return *Finance* Anticipated profit from a business, a particular venture, an investment, etc. *Expected return on investment* or *expected rate of return* is anticipated income or profit expressed as a ratio or percentage of the amount invested.

expense *Accounting* Any cost incurred in the day to day operation of the business, such as payroll, materials, or supplies. *Finance* For tax purposes, any cost that is written off in the current period; all costs that are not capitalized, assigned to ending inventory, or in some other way deferred.

expense account *Accounting* Ledger accounts that record charges to the company for which money is paid out or for which a debt is incurred. A record of costs, usually incurred by salespersons or company executives, for travel and entertainment.

expiration The date beyond which an option cannot be exercised, or beyond which an agreement is no longer in force. *Insurance* The final date that an insurance policy is in force, although certain policies may have a provision for a grace period, or for automatic renewal under certain circumstances. *Labor Relations* The final date that a labor contract is in force, although most have a clause that provides for continuance of the contract in the absence of formal notice of termination by either party. *Law* A contingency clause in a contract that often specifies a period of time after which the contract is invalid if not executed, as a real estate contract with a stipulation that financing must be arranged within thirty days from the date of the contract. Such expiration may be extended by common consent of the parties to the contract. *Marketing* The final date for a special price offer, co-op advertising, etc. The expiration may be based on the date an order is placed, accepted, or executed.

exploitation To turn to productive use. *Exploitation* is often used in a pejorative sense, as for illegal use or use without reasonable compensation; however, it may also describe putting to productive use that which was formerly considered of no value, or the clever turning of an adverse condition into a benefit.

exposure *Finance* The maximum amount of capital that is at risk in a new venture, claim, lawsuit, etc. *Marketing* Of the appearance of a product before the public through paid advertisement, promotion, or free publicity.

expressed That which is clearly stated, as the terms of a warranty, in contrast to **implied**.

expression *Computer* A symbol or symbols that describe a mathematical operation.

express mail A special classification for letters and packages carried by the U.S. Postal Service that guarantees overnight delivery between major cities.

extended coverage *Insurance* A provision in an insurance policy that offers coverage beyond that normally included, such as a company liability policy that covers employees driving rental cars on business.

extension *Insurance* A rider that continues a policy in force beyond its normal expiration date. *Law* An agreement between the parties to a contract to allow the contract provisions to remain in force beyond the time stipulated in the contract.

external audit Generally, any review of company structure, systems or procedures by an independent party, such as a management consultant. *Finance* A review of the financial records of a company by an independent accounting firm that can render an opinion regarding the accuracy of the records.

extrapolation A technique for predicting a numerical value that is unknown based on manipulation of that which is known. For example, if the time to manufacture 5,000 units and 10,000 units of the same item, under similar circumstances, is known, and there is a setup time involved, one may determine that the time required to manufacture an additional 5,000 units is the difference between the times for 5,000 and 10,000. From this, all things remaining equal, one can predict the time it will take to manufacture any quantity.

F

fabricator One who builds or constructs. *Manufacturing* Descriptive of a manufacturing operation where component parts are formed internally before assembling or are sent to another plant for final assembly. See also **assembly plant**.

facade The front of a building on the outside, often denoting a false front that has been made especially attractive or imposing. Occasionally used to describe the appearance or manner of an individual who is known or suspected to be presenting a false front, as a kind person who appears gruff.

face *Computers* In desktop publishing, all of the styles of a type of a particular design; see also **font**.

face value *Finance* The amount for which a negotiable instrument, such as a check or bond, is written without regard to any other consideration, as creditworthiness, market value, etc. Frequently used to describe an offer, as to buy or sell, with the implication that there are other considerations that must be taken into account to determine the real value of the offer.

facility A building, area, etc. set aside for some activity, such as a manufacturing plant, warehouse, loading dock, recreation room, etc.

facsimile, fax An exact copy. *Fax* generally denotes a copy sent to a distant location by transmitting discrete data over telephone lines.

factor Generally, one who acts as an agent for another in the conduct of business, usually buying and selling. Also any of the elements that go into the production of goods and services, as capital, labor, management, and all of their constituent parts. *Finance* To buy the accounts receivable of a company at a discount, or to accept them as partial payment for a loan or advance. Factoring provides immediate cash flow or release from debt for the company while providing the factor relative security for the moneys advanced.

factory A location or building where goods are produced, assembly is performed, or material is processed.

factory overhead *Accounting* Normally, all of the expenses of a company except labor and materials that are charged directly to the product. Each company has its own system, however, so that in some, factory overhead stops at the door to the factory floor, where manufacturing operations actually take place, and the cost of offices, clerical workers, managers, etc. is calculated separately. Such costs may be referred to as *front office cost*, or *sales and administrative costs*.

failure rate *Accounting* From records kept in the cost accounting system, an analysis of the frequency and duration of equipment failure, compared to productive running time. Because equipment failure also means lost labor hours and perhaps missed deliveries, the failure rate may be a key element in justifying replacement. *Manufacturing* An analysis of units failing inspection compared to total units produced. A high failure rate may call for a review of methods, materials, etc.

Fair Credit Reporting Act *Law* Legislation enacted in 1971 to protect the consumer against circulation of inaccurate or obsolete information. Under the provisions of the act, the consumer has the right to notification by a business that it is seeking credit information, the identification of the source of a report used as the basis for denying credit, certain information from the reporting agency as to content and nature of the report, correction of erroneous information, etc.

Fair Labor Standards Act *Labor Relations* Legislation originally enacted in 1938, and administered by the Wage and Hour Division of the Department of Labor, that set basic standards for minimum wages, overtime pay, and the employment of minors. Provisions that prohibit wage differential based strictly on sex are enforced by the Equal Employment Opportunity Commission.

fair market value See **market value.**

fair rate of return *Finance* Profit level at which a public monopoly, such as a utility company, is allowed to operate as determined by government regulators. An acceptable ratio of earnings to investment that is the basis on which the management of a company may judge the worth of an expansion or other investment opportunity.

fair trade *Marketing* An arrangement whereby a retailer agrees not to sell below the price set by the manufacturer for certain brand-name items. Such agreements are now illegal in most states.

fallback That which is held in reserve for a contingency. Reference to a backup plan or option that can be put into effect if the first plan doesn't work.

false advertising *Marketing* Any information from an advertiser that is untrue or misleading, especially involving price or quality of merchandise.

fan fold paper *Computers* A continuous stream of computer paper with equally spaced feed holes along the borders, perforated between pages and folded accordion-style so as to lie flat.

fast track An accelerated career path. The *fast track* may be set up by management to bring an individual or group of individuals through a series of jobs for training to quickly reach a particular level, or it may be set by an individual who jumps from job to job, securing a promotion at each level.

fax, facsimile A copy of a document sent to a remote terminal by a fax machine or computer modem over telephone lines; to send such a copy.

fax card *Computers* A controller board in a computer that enables the transmission of a facsimile.

FDA, Food and Drug Administration An agency of the U.S. government charged with approving the safety and regulating the sale of foods, medicines, cosmetics, etc.

feasibility study Examination of a proposed venture to determine whether it is practical and potentially profitable. Depending on the project, the study may call for analysis of data from various departments within the company as well as outside consultants. For example, a proposal for development of a new product may require information about the market for the product, the plant and equipment to manufacture it, the availability and cost of materials, lines of distribution, investment required and the cost of production.

featherbedding *Labor Relations* The practice of restricting output or requiring more workers than necessary in order to protect jobs.

federalism A system of government based on the union of a number of entities in which those that are a part of the union agree to subordinate a portion of their power to the central body thus formed in certain matters of common interest.

Federal Trade Commission, FTC *Marketing* The government agency charged with the investigation of unfair trade practices, including deceptive advertising.

Federal Unemployment Tax Act Legislation that provides for cooperation between the federal and state governments in the administration of unemployment compensation.

fee Payment for professional services, licenses, etc.

feed holes *Computers* Holes along the sides of continuous feed computer paper, engaged by a sprocket wheel for feeding into the printer.

fetch *Computers* To retrieve data or a file from storage.

FICA, Federal Insurance Contributions Act Federal legislation that outlines the taxes to be paid for Social Security.

fiduciary *Law* A person or other entity that holds something in trust for another and has a legal obligation to act in the best interests of that person in all matters regarding the property thus held, as the executor of a will who is responsible for preserving assets and investing wisely, when required to do so.

field Generally, an area of endeavor, as *a career field, a business field, etc. Computers* A single fragment of information that, combined with related fields, serves to make up a **record** in a **database.** A field is usually the smallest element of significant information that one might want to use to sort or select records in a database, or to retrieve from a database. For example, in a mailing list, city, state and zip code may be included in a single field, however, each is customarily assigned to separate fields so that records can be selected by city, by state, or by zip code.

field mark *Computer* A code that signals the beginning or end of a database field.

field name *Computer* The identification of a specific field in a database record.

FIFO; first in, first out *Accounting* A system for valuing inventory that presumes materials were removed in the same order that they were entered, thus matching the cost of the oldest material with oldest revenue. In a time of rising prices, however, it has been argued that the system unfairly increases taxable income at a time when the money paid out for higher priced material is tied up in inventory. See also **LIFO.**

figurehead Descriptive of a prominent individual or seemingly important position that lacks authority or responsibility; often one that is controlled by others.

file An accumulation of stored information or documents, usually arranged by subject.

Computers A collection of data or related records that is stored as a unit. *Law* To register or place on public record, a legal document, such as a deed.

file attributes *Computers* Special nature of a file for identification or protection such as read-only, archived or hidden.

file conversion *Computers* The transfer of a file's formatting codes to allow access by another program.

file maintenance *Computers* Correcting and updating files and directories to reflect the most recent data available and purging the system of outdated files.

file management *Computers* The organization and tracking of files by the operating system and the user.

file manager *Computers* A software utility designed to simplify the task of locating and organizing files.

file name *Computers* The designation that identifies a data file.

file name extension *Computers* A tag of up to three characters following a file name that aids in identification by the operating system, a program or the user.

file protection *Computers* A file attribute that identifies a data file as read-only. Setting a device on a floppy disk to make the files on the disk read-only.

file server *Computers* A computer that stores a library of program and data files for a number of users in a network.

filter *Computers* That which refines output by sifting input according to user- or program-designated criterion. User input that restricts output to a certain class or group of information. Machine controls that eliminate extraneous signals.

finance charge *Finance* The cost for buying on credit; interest. *Law* Under federal truth in lending legislation, all of the costs associated with a loan or credit sale, such as interest, service charge, finder's fee, cost of credit report, etc.

finance company An organization that specializes in lending money to consumers or businesses, or in factoring accounts receivable.

financial analysis *Finance* The study of an organization's financial records to determine its financial condition.

financial institution A bank, insurance company, or other organization that is organized to make a profit by the investment of funds.

financial planning software *Computers* A program that assists the user in budgeting, saving, investment decisions, etc.

financial statement *Finance* Any written report that purports to show the financial condition of an individual or organization. For the individual, such a report may be a simple listing of assets and liabilities. For an organization, it may include a balance sheet, income statement, cash flow statement, a report of changes in net worth.

financing The backing of an individual or organization with loans, credit, etc.

finder's fee Generally a fee paid for bringing together the parties to a transaction, such as assisting a business in finding financing, a leasing firm, clients, etc.

finished goods inventory *Accounting* Product that is completed and ready to be sold to clients. A current asset on the balance sheet.

firm Generally used to refer to any type of business organization. *Commerce* Of that which is concluded, or not likely to change, as a *firm price* or *firm order*. *Law* Any business in which the principals are not recognized apart from it; any unincorporated business.

first in, first out See **FIFO**

first mortgage *Finance, Law* A pledging of property as security for a debt that has priority over any other liens on the same property. In the event of default, the debt owed to the holder of the first mortgage will be satisfied before any others are considered.

fiscal policy *Accounting* The plans and rules of a company that relate to budgetary and financial matters.

fiscal year *Accounting* A twelve month period, not necessarily a calendar year, chosen by the management of an organization as its financial year.

fixed asset *Accounting* Any property that is used in the production of goods and services, as buildings, machinery, etc. Any asset that cannot be readily converted to use other than that for which it was originally intended, in contrast to a **current asset**.

fixed charge *Accounting* **Overhead** that does not change regardless of whether anything is produced, such as rent or insurance.

fixed cost *Accounting* Any cost of production that does not change with quantity produced, as molds, setup charges, etc. Often used to describe the day to day cost of opening the doors and operating a business, as **overhead**.

fixed disk *Computers* A computer disk that is permanently mounted in its drive.

fixed overhead See **fixed charge**.

fixture *Accounting* Descriptive of any fitting or furniture, such as a light fixture, shelving, etc., that is affixed to a wall, ceiling, or floor in a building and that is considered thereby to be legally a part of the building.

flat *Accounting* Of that which is unchanged from one period to the next, as interest charges or an expense. *Marketing* Bought or sold at a set unit price regardless of volume.

flat rate *Marketing* A price that does not change with an increase in volume.

flex time Descriptive of a system whereby workers are given some latitude in selecting their hours of work. The intent of such a system is to relieve congestion on the roads going to and from work and to allow parents with young children to tailor their schedules to those of school or day care center.

float *Finance* The period between the time a check is drawn and the time it is actually charged to the maker's account.

floppy disk *Computers* A removable memory storage device; also, *diskette*.

floppy disk controller *Computers* The hardware and software that manages the operation of a disk drive.

flow chart A graphic illustration of the sequence of steps required to complete a task or series of tasks, as a manufacturing operation.

fluctuation Descriptive of frequent up and down movement, such as the price of materials or interest rates.

FOB or **fob, free on board** Designating delivery to a certain point by the seller without charge to the buyer. Terms of sale often specify *fob shipper's dock*, indicating that the freight is to be paid by the buyer, or *fob customer's dock,* in which case the seller pays the freight. The seller may choose to pay the freight and avoid liability for the shipment while in transit, by specifying *fob shipper, freight allowed to destination.*

font *Computers* Traditionally descriptive of one type face and style in one size. With the introduction of scalable fonts, one font often refers to a type face in a single style in a wide range of sizes.

font cartridge *Computers* A device that attaches to a printer to make additional fonts available to it.

Food and Drug Administration See **FDA**

footnote *Finance* Information at the bottom of a financial statement that explains certain items in the report, such as for the effect of pending lawsuits, taxes, etc.

forecasting An attempt to predict future events based on available information. Forecasting future sales and production needs is the first step to budgeting for orderly growth of a company.

foreclosure *Law* The loss of right to a property as the result of failure to pay as agreed on a loan secured by the property.

foreign corporation A corporation organized in a foreign country or one that is conducting business in a state other than the one in which it is chartered.

foreground *Computer* Of processing that which takes place in the view of, and usually under the control of, the computer operator. Processing that has priority over all others.

foreman A man or woman who supervises the activities of a group of workers.

forfeiture *Law* The loss of property as a result of a violation of the law, or the failure to perform or exercise a right, such as for the loss of a deposit when the right to buy is not exercised.

forgery *Law* The illegal copying or counterfeiting of a document, signature, etc.

form *Computers* A document designed for the orderly entry of data; the configuration or arrangement of data in a report.

format Generally, a standard style, or layout, of data for a letter, report, etc. *Computers* The system that allows for the orderly storage and retrieval of data on a storage device as a disk. To initialize a disk to accept data. The system by which data is held in a particular file, such as spreadsheet or database. The layout, or arrangement, of information in a document.

form feed *Computers* A command to the printer to advance the paper the length of one form or one page.

formula *Computers* A string of symbols that calculate to a value, as in a spreadsheet cell that calls for the total of the values in other specified cells, or that calculates to a logical *true* or *false* as in a conditional branch command.

FORTRAN, *formula translation Computers* The first high level programmer's language to allow program statements using mathematical notation.

fortuitous Caused by accident or by chance, as of a loss covered by insurance or that may be deducted from taxable income.

forward *Commerce* To ship; to send on to another place.

forwarding company A company that specializes in the transfer of freight, as a **consolidator** that combines small shipments to fill a rail car, or one that overseas the movement of freight for export to a foreign country.

fragmentation *Computers* The condition of being broken into parts. A condition wherein files on a disk are recorded to scattered, rather than contiguous, segments.

frame *Computers* A window on a monitor screen that provides a view of information displayed by a program.

franchise *Law* Any special right granted by the government, such as for a business to operate as a corporation. The right to market a particular product or service, granted by the company that owns the rights to the brand or trade name.

fraud *Law* Deliberate deception to influence the surrender of something of value, as money, property, or rights, by another.

freedom of contract *Law* The right to enter into an agreement or covenant with others, that may only be restricted for the public good, such as for prohibition against an agreement that threatens the safety or welfare of another.

freedom of information *Law* Of federal legislation that provides the mechanism for making documents and materials of the government available to the general public.

free enterprise The concept of allowing business to operate in a competitive environment with a minimum of regulation by the government.

free market A business environment where pricing is driven by the laws of supply and demand without restraints of government, or any other unnatural force, such as a monopoly. The buying and selling of goods free from extraneous influence such as tariffs or quotas.

free on board See fob.

freight forwarder See **forwarding company.**

friction feed *Computers* A type of printer feed, usually used for single sheets.

fringe benefits *Labor Relations* Incentives offered by an organization to attract workers or negotiated by bargaining units for their members, comprising such things as sick pay, health insurance, paid vacations, and retirement plans.

front money *Finance* Advance payments, as a down payment, or funds to start an enterprise.

front office Generally, a reference to the offices of the upper management of a company, or the offices of the manager and support services in a particular plant as contrasted to those of line foremen or support services in the factory.

FTC See **Federal Trade Commission**

fulfillment The processing of orders as they are received. Fulfillment may require merely sending an item of merchandise in return for the receipt of money or a promotional coupon. In other circumstances, such as for catalog or subscription sales, fulfillment requires the creation of a complete record of the transaction as well as selection and shipment of the items ordered.

full screen access *Computers* Descriptive of a program feature that allows editing of data anywhere on the computer monitor screen.

full service Descriptive of an organization, such as an advertising agency, a bank, a printer, etc. that purports to furnish a full range of related services in its field.

function code *Computers* Any symbol or set of symbols that generates an instruction to the computer.

function key *Computers* Where *n* equals a number, one of a set of ten or twelve keys that alone or in conjunction with Ctrl, Alt or Shift execute commands in certain programs.

FYI For your information.

G

gain *Accounting* The amount received for a property in excess of its book value.

gainful employment *Insurance* In a case of disability, an occupation suited to one who is disabled that provides earnings comparable to that pursued prior to the disabling injury or illness. *Law* An occupation that is suited to the abilities of the one employed.

garnishment *Law* A notice to an employer requiring that a portion of an employee's earnings be withheld for payment of a debt.

general contractor A person or company that enters into a contract for the construction, remodeling, etc. of a facility and accepts complete responsibility for materials, the work of sub contractors, etc.

general ledger *Accounting* A complete record of the accounts that make up the financial statements of a business. General ledger accounts are often a summary of detail from a **subsidiary ledger**, as *accounts receivable*, that represents the aggregate of all transactions from the accounts of individual customers.

general partner *Finance, Law* Any of the principals in a partnership whose liability for the debts of the firm is unlimited. See also **limited partnership.**

generic Generally, referring to an entire class or group. *Marketing* Descriptive of a product without a brand name.

GET *Computers* A program instruction to fetch data, a file or command from a non-contiguous source.

GIGO, garbage in garbage out *Computers* The axiom that the quality of information from computer processing is directly related to the quality of data entered into the computer.

glass ceiling *Colloq.* Descriptive of an invisible barrier in the ranks of a company's management above which women and minorities are not promoted.

global *Computers* Descriptive of formatting or instructions that affect all of the elements in a file or all of the files created by a program.

global search *Computers* Descriptive of a search through every directory, sub-directory or file on a disk; a command to find all occurrences of a string in a file, in a group of files or anywhere on the disk.

glut An excess; usually in reference to materials or finished goods that are available in quantities so much in excess of market demand that disposing of them will be difficult, even at reduced prices.

goal oriented A management style that is driven by the setting of specific goals and the formulating of detailed plans for reaching them.

go-between An intermediary. One who deals independently with each of two or more parties, often to clear the way for the establishment of an agreement between them.

going concern Of a company that is in operation, usually profitably. The value of a *going concern* is measured by its potential for profit in addition to the worth of its assets. *Accounting* The concept that financial transactions and records are based on the premise that the organization will continue in operation.

going private Descriptive of a business that is buying up its own stock or whose stock is being bought by a third party in sufficient quantity to eliminate a market in the stock.

going public The **initial offering**, for sale to the general public, of shares in a private company.

golden handcuffs Stock options, deferred bonuses, etc. that are part of the compensation package for a valuable employee, and that are forfeit if he or she leaves the company.

golden handshake Inducements offered to an employee to encourage early retirement.

golden parachute Part of the compensation package for a key executive of a firm targeted for takeover that provides for the payment of cash or other consideration if the executive is dismissed as a result of a takeover.

good faith Without malice or intent to deceive. *Labor Relations* Of the legal requirement that the parties representing labor and management meet to resolve disputes at a mutually agreeable time and place and with an open mind.

goods Generally, any moveable tangible property. *Manufacturing, Marketing* Merchandise that has been, or will be, produced for sale.

goodwill *Accounting* An intangible asset, the difference between the book value of a business and the price paid for that business, representing the value of established customers, reputation, etc.

GOTO *Computers* A program instruction to branch off to a new set of commands.

gouge To sell at a price that is excessive or well above fair market value.

graceful degradation *Computers* A decrease in performance of a computer that allows continued operation at a lower efficiency level or that allows an orderly shutdown without loss of data.

grace period Descriptive of a contract provision that allows additional time for renewal at the end of the contract, as of a loan or insurance policy.

graduated wage *Labor Relations* A pay scale that provides for adjustment based on length of service, quality or quantity of output, etc.

grammar checker *Computers* A program that inspects a file or document for grammatical errors, advises the user of the error and suggests alternatives.

grandfather clause *Law* A provision in a new regulation or legislation that exempts those already engaged in the activity being regulated.

grapevine *Colloq.* The rumor mill; the unofficial lines of communication within an organization.

graph *Computers* A chart that displays the relative magnitude of associated elements as bars, columns, or sections of a pie.

graphic display *Computers* The depiction of graphic elements on a computer monitor screen.

graphics capability *Computers* A computer monitor with a graphic interface that permits the depiction of picture elements on screen; a printer that has the ability to print picture elements.

gratis Free; offered without charge or other consideration.

gratuitous Given without having been requested.

grid *Computers* A pattern of columns and rows for recording data as for a spreadsheet or for positioning elements as for optical character recognition.

grievance procedure *Labor Relations* The formal process by which a worker may air a complaint against an employer or a union.

gross *Finance, Manufacturing* The total amount before adjustments, as for taxes, damaged goods, etc.

group dynamics The study of the interpersonal relationships between the members of a work group.

growth rate A comparison of change during a number of like periods for some aspect of a company, as number of employees, units produced, sales, equity, etc.

guarantee *Marketing* An assurance that an item will be repaired or replaced if it does not meet with the approval of the buyer.

guaranteed annual wage A minimum assured earnings level for certain hourly workers in a company. Such assurance is normally part of an agreement that the worker will accept overtime work or transfer to other jobs as required by production demands.

guild A medieval union, formed for the mutual protection of those engaged in a particular trade or craft. Occasionally used today to designate a union whose members are employed at a craft, as a *bookbinder's guild* or an *artist's guild*.

H

hacker *Computers* One who has acquired skill in the use of computers for personal pleasure.

halt *Computers* The untimely termination of computer processing.

hand held computer *Computers* A computer small enough to be held in the hand, often used to keep track of appointments and addresses.

handling Generally, the act and cost of moving materials or products in a manufacturing plant, placing items in inventory, removing and packing them for shipping, etc. Often, a charge for services not included in the quoted price, such as for storage and retrieval, or drop shipping of merchandise. Such a charge is often incurred when a buyer places a large custom order that is to be shipped to several destinations or at different times and the exact shipping information is not known at the time the order is placed; the seller then prices the item to be manufactured and both parties agree that additional handling costs will be billed as they are incurred. Occasionally, the term is used to describe the cost of buying on credit.

handshaking *Computers* The protocol for identification and communication between two pieces of equipment.

hang-up *Computers* A temporary halt in processing.

hard copy Descriptive of a source or substantiating document that is the basis for data entry, such as an accounting transaction, or authorization for an action, such as entry of an order. *Computers* A printout of data.

hard currency *Finance* A medium of exchange that is recognized throughout the world as relatively stable.

hard disk *Computers* A disk that is mounted with its own drive, usually installed in the computer case.

hard error *Computers* An equipment malfunction or mistake in processing caused by hardware.

hard goods *Marketing* Durable property. Normally, a reference to consumer assets with a life expectancy greater than one year, as furniture, major appliances, etc.

hard sell *Marketing* A direct sales or advertising technique that stresses the importance of buying, or agreeing to buy, immediately, often by implying that dire consequences may be the result of delay. See also **soft sell**.

hardware *Computers* The computer itself and any of the peripheral devices that are a part of the system.

Hawthorne effect The inclination of an individuals to knowingly or unknowingly alter their behavior under certain circumstances, such as when they are being monitored, or when acting in a changed set of circumstances; an important factor for consideration when doing time studies or monitoring any activity.

Hawthorne studies An extensive study of the workers at the Western Electric Company's Hawthorne plant in Cicero, Illinois, that attempted to relate a variety of elements in the workplace to improved productivity and worker satisfaction.

head *Computers* The read/write head in a disk drive. The device on an impact or ink jet printer that transfers characters to paper.

head crash *Computers* A circumstance in which the read/write head contacts the surface of the disk.

header *Computers* A headline on a document or report.

headhunter *Colloq.* A firm or the representative of a firm that specializes in placing key personnel, such as managers or sales representatives. Unlike most employment agencies that work for and collect a fee from the prospective employee, the headhunter works for and collects fees from the prospective employer. Most successful headhunters specialize, or are part of an organization that has separate divisions that specialize, in a particular industry or type of job.

health maintenance organization See HMO.

hearing A formal meeting before a judge, referee, company executive, appointed committee, etc., at which interested parties present evidence or testimony regarding the matter at hand. The purpose of the hearing may be for the party or parties conducting the hearing to enter a judgment, to recommend action, or simply to gather information for further consideration.

hearsay Something one has heard, but cannot confirm as true.

hearsay evidence *Law* Testimony that relates to something heard by a witness, but not actually observed or experienced by that witness.

hedging The avoidance of total commitment. Modifying a statement to avoid taking an uncompromising position. *Commerce* Any action taken to protect ones position, as placing a tentative order for vital materials in anticipation of need, or as protection against the failure of a primary supplier to deliver. *Finance* Any arrangement to protect cash flow, as by a line of credit to offset possible cost overruns or failure of a client to pay on time.

Help *Computers* A feature in most programs that offers guidance to the user; see also **context sensitive help**.

help screen *Computers* On screen guidance for the user, often interactive, allowing a selection of subjects about which the program offers information.

heuristic Learning by applying what is known toward solving a problem, recording the results, and using that which has been learned in the next step toward a solution. Problemsolving by the use of trial and error, in contrast to an **algorithm**.

hexadecimal *Computers* A numbering system in base sixteen used in computer notation.

hidden agenda Objectives of an individual or group that are not readily apparent. Often applied in the negative sense, as for one who critiques the work of another on the pretext of being helpful, but who really is striving to discredit the other.

hidden tax A tax that is built into the cost of an item and so not apparent to the buyer.

hierarchical Of any structural order that branches directly from the point of greatest importance through various levels of a lower order, as the organization chart of a business that proceeds from the chief executive or general manager to those on a secondary level who report to him or her, with further branches indicating those who report to second-level executives, and so on. *Computers* Of the directory structure that has as its entry point the *boot directory* containing the basic files and instructions that allow the operator to access other directories containing commands, programs, data, etc. The boot directory is *parent directory* to those at the second level, that may, in turn, hold files and be parent to directories at the next level, etc.

high level language *Computes* A programming language that is somewhat similar to spoken language.

highlighted *Computes* An element on the screen that is set apart from others by underlining, reverse video or contrasting color; of a block of copy or graphic element that has been selected for some purpose.

historical cost *Accounting* The cost of purchase or acquisition; reference to the accounting principle that requires the reporting of assets at their original cost on financial statements.

hit list *Colloq.* Those persons or things that are the target of some action. Often used in the negative sense, as a list of employees to be dismissed, the hit list may also be positive, as denoting objectives to be aggressively pursued. Such a list may be one of target accounts for sales, problems to be corrected, etc.

HMO, health maintenance organization A health insurance plan whereby a company contracts to furnish medical care to a group of workers through medical personnel and organizations with whom it has contracted for such services.

holdback Generally, of money not paid until certain conditions are met. *Accounting, Commerce* Part of an invoice that is not paid until goods have been inspected and found acceptable. *Labor* A portion of wages held be the employer as security for the return of tools, uniforms, etc. supplied to a worker. That portion of wages that is in arrears throughout the length of employment as a result of the time lag between reporting and preparing the payroll.

holding company A corporation whose only asset is the stock of a subsidiary company or companies. The holding company is usually actively involved in overseeing the management of the companies it controls, and is often instrumental in initiating inter company activities.

home based business An enterprise for profit operated from a private dwelling that also serves as a residence. In some cases work is performed in the home, such as one that produces handicrafts or repairs small appliances; in others, the work is performed outside, as for painting, plumbing, carpentry, etc.

Home key *Computers* A cursor movement key that sends the cursor to the beginning of a line of text and, used in conjunction with other keys, to the top left of the screen, the top of the page or the beginning of a file.

honor *Accounting* To accept as correct, as an invoice. *Commerce* To accept and carry out an obligation, as of a contract. *Finance* To pay when due, as of a legal debt.

honorarium A payment for services for which no fee has been set and for which there is no legal obligation, as to a public speaker.

horizontal integration Expansion of a company in its main field of endeavor or a closely allied field at the same stage of production, often through the absorption of another company. A manufacturer of wood furniture, for example, may buy out another manufacturer of furniture, or a supplier of metal brackets or cushions used in the manufacturing process. See also **vertical integration**.

hot key *Computers* A key combination that executes a macro or command that would otherwise require several key strokes.

hot line *Computers* A telephone number provided by an equipment or software manufacturer or dealer through which a user may access technical help.

house brand See **private brand**.

housekeeping *Computers* The process of deleting old files, arranging files in their proper directories and maintaining an orderly file structure for efficient operation.

housing code Of local ordinance that pertains to the maintenance of standards for safety, sanitation, etc. required for residential occupancy of a dwelling. See also **building code**.

huckster Generally, a street peddler. *Marketing* One who promotes a product, especially through mass media. *Colloq.* Often, of a salesperson whose presentation and tactics are questionable; one who lacks credibility.

human relations The study of the importance of the individual in the success of an enterprise and the interaction of personnel in the workplace. Descriptive of efforts to motivate individuals by recognition of their importance and involvement in the organization.

human resources The function of managing personnel in an organization, with responsibility for hiring, training, administration of benefit programs, maintaining records, etc.

hype *Colloq.* Often describing excessive, and perhaps unwarranted, claims. *Marketing* Extensive promotion to attract consumer interest.

hypothesis A supposition established as a basis for further investigation or discussion.

I

ICC, Interstate Commerce Commission A federal agency established in 1887 to regulate the rates and service of carriers engaged in interstate commerce.

icon *Computers* A graphic image on a monitor screen that represents a directory, file, utility, etc. and that can be selected with a mouse click.

ideal capacity The maximum output possible under theoretical conditions in which a machine or plant operates continuously with no delays or down time.

idle time *Manufacturing* A period during which there is no output of value, because of equipment malfunction, lack of materials, lack of scheduled work, etc.

IF statement *Computers* A select word in a conditional branch specifying that IF a condition exists, the first set of instructions is to be followed, otherwise, follow a different set of instructions.

illegal character *Computers* A symbol that is unacceptable in a specific situation, as those symbols not available in a particular type font or a letter placed in a database number field.

illegal instruction *Computers* A reserved word or command in a formula that is not available in that particular program.

illegal strike *Labor Relations* A strike that is in violation of the law, that has not been voted and authorized by established procedure, or that is in violation of a legal contract.

image *Marketing* The way in which a product is viewed by those in its target market or by the general public. The impression that is intended to be created by advertising or publicity.

image enhancement *Computers* Altering or improving a graphic image such as art or a photograph by use of a computer program.

imaging *Computers* To create or modify a graphic representation with the use of a computer.

impact printer *Computers* A printer that creates an image by striking the paper.

impasse Generally, a deadlock; a disagreement that cannot be resolved. *Labor Relations* In negotiations, a point on which neither side is willing to give ground, making compromise impossible.

implementation To put into practice, or carry out, as a plan.

implied Not clearly expressed; suggested, often by circumstance. *Law* That which is not clearly expressed, but that may be inferred by a reasonable person under normal circumstances.

import *Commerce* To bring into the country, often for sale, goods produced in another country. The product so imported.

import quota *Commerce* A restriction on the amount of certain goods that can be brought into the country and offered for sale, normally to protect the jobs of those in the importing country producing similar goods.

imposition That which is exacted, as a tax, or toll. *Labor Relations* The placing of an unjust burden or demand, as short notice of a requirement to work overtime. Many labor contracts place restrictions on such demands, allowing for refusal without penalty.

impound To take into custody and hold property, funds, etc. pending resolution of a legal matter, as an overdue debt.

imprint Generally, to mark in some way. *Commerce* The name of a company, or a company brand, set in a particular type face or design, often with graphic embellishment; a company logo; in effect, the company's signature. Information on the outside of a shipping carton that describes the contents, quantity, etc. *Manufacturing* To mark parts with the manufacturer's or distributor's brand by stamping, printing, etc.

improvement *Accounting* Any change in equipment, building, property, etc. that increases its book value.

impulse merchandise *Marketing* Goods likely to be bought on a whim. Such goods are most effectively sold in heavy traffic areas or near the checkout counters in a store.

imputed cost *Accounting* An expense that may be ascribed, though not actually incurred, such as the interest that would be charged if materials in inventory were purchased on credit.

imputed liability See **vicarious liability**.

inadvertent Unintentional; descriptive of that caused by oversight, usually without fixing blame.

incapacity Generally, disability or lack of fitness. *Law* Not qualified, as to enter into a contract by reason of age, mental incompetence, etc.

incentive That proffered to encourage or motivate as *incentive pay* for greater production. *Marketing* A premium, special price, etc. to encourage the purchase of a product.

incidental Of that which is secondary, or associated with something of greater importance as *incidental income* from the sale of waste.

inclusive *Computers* Incorporating as part of the whole, such as the part of a formula in which terms or values joined by the reserved word *AND*, often enclosed by parenthesis must both be considered in evaluating the formula.

income *Accounting* Moneys received for the sale of goods or services that is the primary business of a company, or from *incidental* sources.

income account The ledger accounts that relate to profit and loss, including all revenue and expense accounts.

income property Property that is held for the purpose of producing revenue by rental capital gains, or both.

income statement The financial statement that summarizes revenue, expenses, depreciation, etc. to show the income or loss from operations.

incompetent Descriptive of one who is incapable of performing his or her job properly *Law* One who is not legally capable of entering into a contract by reason of mental deficiency.

incorporate To join to something that already exists, or to merge diverse elements into a unified whole. *Law* To form a business into a corporation according to the laws of a particular state.

incremental increase *Labor* A periodic increase in wages or salary according to a set scale based on time on the job. *Marketing* A periodic increase in selling price over the term of a contract to cover anticipated additions to the cost of labor and materials.

indemnity *Insurance* Protection against losses through an insurance contract. Payment for a claim of losses covered by insurance. *Law* Legal immunity from liability by certain parties or for certain actions.

independent adjuster A claims adjuster who operates as an independent contractor for one or more insurance companies.

independent audit *Accounting* Review of a company's financial records by an accounting firm that is not affiliated in any other way with the company. It is expected that the auditor from such a company can render an unbiased opinion as to whether the company is maintaining its records according to generally accepted accounting principles.

independent contractor One who performs work for a company, and is paid as a vendor rather than an employee. Tax law sets forth a number of criteria that must be met for a worker to be considered an independent contractor: the employer cannot set hours of work, place of work, furnish a significant portion of tools to perform the job, directly supervise the work in progress, etc. The independent contractor is paid in full with no deductions for withholding or FICA; he or she is responsible for filing an estimated tax form and paying self-employment tax.

indexing *Labor Relations* Adjusting wages based on an index, such as the Consumer Price Index.

indirect cost *Accounting* Any expense for labor, materials, overhead, etc. that is not related directly to the manufacture of the product, group of products, or service that a company offers for sale.

indirect labor *Accounting* The cost of labor that is not related directly to the manufacture of the product, group of products, or service that a company offers for sale.

indirect overhead *Accounting* Any overhead expense that is not related to the manufacturing operation, as the salaries of front office personnel, the cost of office space or office supplies.

inductive reasoning A problem solving technique that draws on limited information to form a more general conclusion.

industrial advertising Promotion directed to other businesses rather than the end user, as for the sale of materials, supplies, or services required for the production of other goods or services.

industrial engineering The study and implementation of the most effective integration of the tools of production—personnel, materials, and equipment.

industrial park An area designed for occupancy by companies engaged in manufacturing and those who service such companies, such as trucking or industrial supply companies.

industrial psychology The study of behavior and motivation in the workplace. The industrial psychologist offers assistance in such areas as the selection, training and promotion processes; analyzing tasks; and the measurement and improvement of performance.

industrial relations Descriptive of the interaction between supervisors and the employees who report to them in a company. Often used to describe the relationship between the management of a company and a union.

industry Any extensive business activity, often referring to all those in a similar business, as the *housing industry* or the *automotive industry*.

industry standard Specifications that tend to be relatively uniform throughout all areas of business, such as electrical outlets, computer couplers, automobile tires, clothing sizes, etc. Such standards may be set by law or regulation of a government agency, by an independent organization such as the American National Standards Institute, or by tacit agreement among manufacturers. Industry standards may be set to establish minimum safety requirements or to offer compatibility between different brands of the same items.

inelasticity Generally, the characteristic of being inflexible or not easily adaptable. *Marketing* The condition of unvarying demand, that is, a product for which demand does not increase appreciably when the price is lowered, nor does demand fall off when the price is increased.

inflation A general increase in price levels, particularly of necessities, that decreases the purchasing power of a dollar.

inflation rate The rate of increase in price levels expressed as a percentage of increase or a ratio between price levels at two distinct times, often measured monthly and expressed as an annual rate.

influence The power to affect others. Have an effect on the actions or behavior of another. *Accounting* Often an expression of the relationship between ledger accounts, that is, the way in which a change in one account affects the value of others. *Marketing* Any attempt through advertising or promotion to alter or mold the behavior of the buyer. Of an individual, circumstance, etc. that does not directly initiate a purchase, but that does significantly influence the purchaser.

information Any knowledge, data, or fact. *Computers* Any data that can be stored, retrieved and manipulated by a computer.

information management *Computers* The systems and techniques involved in effectively compiling and manipulating useful data.

information processing *Computers* The manipulation of compiled data and the compilation of reports from the data.

information retrieval *Computers* Descriptive of the techniques for accessing data from storage in the form or pattern that the user desires.

infringement *Law* Any violation, disregard or breech of the rights of another, especially concerning rights at law, as of a contract, patent, copyright, etc.

in-house services Generally, of a department or departments in a company providing services peripheral to the operation of the business, that are normally supplied by outside vendors, such as an *in-house printing plant, art department, advertising agency,* etc. Such undertakings are not a part of the products or services offered for sale by a company, but may be taken on when there is no vendor who can meet the special needs of the company, or when it is determined that the tasks can be performed more economically in house.

initialize *Computers* To format a disk to accept data; to boot up a computer by loading the system files it needs to become functional.

initiative The tendency to think and take action on one's own, without instructions from another.

injunction *Law* An order by a court, to a person or organization, prohibiting an action or directing that a course of action to be stopped.

in kind Generally, the exchange or replacement of property with material that is comparable in quality and value. Also, of services that are to be performed in a like or similar fashion.

ink jet *Computers* Of a high-quality printer that forms images on paper or other material by squirting minuscule jets of ink in patterns determined by the computer.

innovation Of the introduction of new ideas or concepts.

innovation strategy The management concept that constantly looks to new technology, methods, etc. for improvements in product, service, or performance.

in-pack *Marketing* Of a premium that is included in the package with the product, such as a toy or small book in a box of cereal. See also **on-pack**.

input Generally, anything that is put in, as an investment in an enterprise, or new information and ideas brought into a discussion. *Computers* Any information conveyed to a computer or peripheral from the keyboard, a disk or other memory device, or an external source, such as a telephone line for storage or processing.

input buffer *Computers* The area of computer memory that accepts and stores input for transfer to its destination.

input device *Computers* Any equipment linked to the computer that enters source data, such as a keyboard, an optical scanner or a modem.

input/output, I/O *Computers* A reference to the conventions for transmitting data between a computer and its peripherals or an external device.

inside information *Financial* Information that has not been made public, available only to an **insider**, and that may impact on the value of an investment, as by an offer for a takeover, or a dramatic change in company finances or prospects. Securities and exchange commission rules forbid trading on the basis of such information.

insider *Financial* One who by reason of his or her position has access to information about a company or investment that is not available to the stockholders or to the general public.

insider trading *Financial* Illegal trading in a stock based on **inside information**.

insolvency *Financial* The condition of being unable to meet ones debts; **bankruptcy**.

inspection Generally, a careful examination. *Manufacturing* Examination of materials as they are received to confirm that they meet required specifications. Examination of a product at various stages of production to confirm that a certain standard of quality is being maintained. Such inspection may be the ongoing responsibility of personnel on an assembly line, or it may be that of independent quality control personnel. See also, **quality control**.

installation *Computers* The process of setting up and configuring a computer system or program; the computer system so installed.

installment contract Generally, any agreement that calls for periodic performance at regular intervals, as the payment of debt, shipment of merchandise, providing of a service, etc. *Finance* A credit arrangement whereby interest for the period of a contract is calculated on and combined with: the cost of goods purchased, state and local sales taxes, delivery charges, etc., less any down payment; the total is then divided into equal payments, or installments, to be paid over the life of the agreement. Most automobiles are purchased on an installment contract.

institution A firmly entrenched tradition or practice. A public organization, as a bank, corporation, library, hospital, etc.

institutional advertising Of the promotion of an organization's image in contrast to the selling of a product. Such promotion may stress a concern for quality, community involvement, or the part a company plays in contributing to goods and services furnished by others. Institutional advertising has been found to be an employee morale booster in communities where the organization maintains a facility for supplying goods and services that are not readily identifiable in the final product.

instruction *Computers* A direction to the computer to set a parameter or execute an operation.

instruction code *Computers* The language understood by a particular computer or program.

instruction format *Computers* The syntax required by a particular program for issuing a command.

insurability *Insurance* Of that which may or may not be insured; of the qualities that determine whether a thing may be insured. Insurability of an employee under a company's life or medical plan, for example, may be limited for a new employee past a certain age. Insurability of a structure against certain hazards may be limited, as well, by the age of the building or its location.

insurable interest *Insurance* An expression of the interest of the policy holder in the unaltered continuance of the existence of the insured. One may only have an insurable interest if benefit is derived from the existence of the person or property insured and such benefit would be terminated if the insured ceased to exist. Life insurance on an individual, for example, may be protection to insure repayment of a debt, or to indemnify one for loss of affection. Insurance against property loss may cover indemnification for the loss of the use of the property, for the cost of replacement, or to provide income that would have been enjoyed if the property had continued in existence.

insurance A system of protection against losses that provides for payments by those who seek such protection to those who agree to provide compensation in the event of a loss. Such losses are clearly specified in a contract as to type and amount of compensation. Payments for protection, or premiums, are based on the amount of coverage and risk factors, such as the age of an individual in the case of life insurance, or type of structure in the case of insurance on a structure.

insured Covered by insurance. Of a person or property that is protected by insurance. Of the policy holder; one who is protected from loss. *Colloq.* Of that which is virtually certain; assured.

insured mail A type of protection offered by the postal service in which the sender is compensated to the extent of the declared value of the contents of a letter or package that is lost or damaged in transit.

insurer The person or company that, for a fee, agrees to protect another against a monetary loss.

intangible asset *Accounting* Descriptive of items on the company books that have value, but are without substance, such as goodwill, trademarks, copyrights, patents, etc.

integrated circuit *Computers* An electronic device that is comprised of a number of connected circuit elements formed on a single chip of semiconductor material; a microprocessor.

integrated software *Computers* A package that combines several functions in a single program, such as one that features word processing, spreadsheet, and a database manager. Word processing and spreadsheet programs often contain a graphics program that makes it possible to add charts or artwork to enhance the visual impact of reports.

integrated system *Computers* A combination of computers, programs, and peripherals that are designed to work together.

integration The bringing together or blending of otherwise disparate elements. The merging of the operation of two companies, divisions or departments, often under a single manager.

integrity The quality of being sound or complete, as the *integrity* of information. Honesty or high moral standards, as shown in business dealings.

interactive processing, interactive program *Computers* Processing of data that takes place as commands are entered by the operator and, once processing is completed, the processor waits for a new command to be entered, as contrasted to **batch processing**.

interest *Finance* A share or claim in a venture, usually expressed as a portion or percentage of the total investment. The cost of borrowing, usually expressed as a flat amount or an annual percentage of the outstanding balance of a loan.

interface *Computers* Hardware or software that forms a link between devices and allows them to communicate with each other.

interim audit *Finance* A review of a company's financial records for a period that is not the end of the fiscal year. Such an audit may be conducted prior to the issuing of an **interim statement**, or in anticipation of the annual audit.

interim statement *Finance* A financial report that covers a part of the year, such as a quarterly report. Such reports often lack the detail and precision of the annual report, but serve primarily as a means to keep shareholders apprised of company activities and performance.

interleaving *Computers* A routine that directs the computer to switch between applications, thus appearing to run both at the same time, such as printing in the background while accepting new data entered in the foreground.

interlocking directorates Descriptive of two or more companies that have one or more members of their board of directors in common.

interlocutory *Law* A decision handed down during the course of a court action, pending final disposition of the suit.

intermediary Generally, one who serves as an emissary or arbitrator, such as a **head hunter** or **mediator**.

intermittent processing *Manufacturing* Descriptive of a type of operation that involves the production of a variety of goods, such as a print shop where once the required quantity of an item is produced, the equipment is shut down to be prepared for the production of a fixed quantity of the next item. See also **continuous processing**.

internal audit *Accounting* A review of a company's financial records and the system for maintaining them by an individual appointed for that purpose from within the company. The internal audit may be to seek out the cause of discrepancies in accounts, or simply to confirm that standard policy and procedure as set by management are being followed. *Manufacturing* A review of operations by an individual or group from within the company to assess the effectiveness of systems and to recommend how they might be improved.

internal storage *Computers* Memory for the storage of data that is built into, and directly accessible by, the computer.

internship A training, or introductory period for a new, usually young, executive, during which time the subject may be exposed to a number of different jobs in various departments in order to become familiar with the company.

interrupt *Computers* A control signal that directs the computer to halt processing on one level and move to another.

interrupt priority *Computers* The order of precedence in which signals are processed, for example, input from the keyboard usually has priority over background printing.

Interstate Commerce Commission See **ICC**.

in the black *Colloq.* Descriptive of a business, department, product, etc. that is showing a profit.

in the red *Colloq.* Descriptive of a business, department, product, etc. that is showing a loss.

in transit *Commerce* Descriptive of goods that are out of the hands of the shipper and on the way to their destination.

inventory *Accounting* An asset comprised of all materials, supplies, finished goods or goods in some stage of processing that are owned by a company, whether located physically on the premises of that company, in transit, or in the hands of a distributor who has them on consignment.

inventory control The system by which inventory is managed. The recording of goods as they are received and as they are dispersed, so that an inventory balance may be maintained and periodically checked against a physical count.

inventory turnover The frequency with which the usual order quantity of an item, or items, is dispensed over a given period; one of the factors used to determine the optimum order quantity. A comparison of the cost of goods sold during an accounting period with the average cost of inventory, which may be expressed as the number of times that inventory is replaced during the period or the average length of time that goods are held in inventory.

invoice *Accounting* A bill; a detailed list of charges for goods or services that is sent to the purchaser.

involuntary conversion Condemnation; the taking of private property for public use. See also **just compensation**.

irregular A product with a cosmetic fault that does not impair function, such as an appliance with blistered paint or clothing with a pull in the fabric; such items are often sold through special outlets as seconds.

iteration A repetition. *Computers* A programming technique that causes an operation to be repeated until a certain condition is met, as in a search of a database file where successive lines are read until a match is found or the end of the file is reached.

itinerant worker A laborer who moves from place to place to find temporary employment, often a farm worker.

J

job A particular type of work, as a trade or vocation; see also **job description**. A position or place of employment. A specific task or set of tasks that, taken together, achieve a particular purpose, as *the job of mowing the lawn*. *Manufacturing* A production unit that comprises all of the goods produced to fill a specific order for a client; see also **job order**.

job action *Labor Relations* A demonstration by employees to press for the acceptance of certain demands, often by refusing to work overtime, or by strict adherence to work rules that causes a slowing down of production.

jobber *Commerce* One who buys goods from a manufacturer or importer for resale to a dealer or merchant. *Manufacturing* A company that produces goods to order, each production lot covered by a **job order**. See also **job shop**.

job classification An ordering of jobs in a company or industry that takes into account the level of knowledge and skill required for the job so as to group like jobs and establish a wage range for each group.

job cost *Accounting* All of the expense for labor, materials, and overhead, tracked by recording workers' time, materials invoices, etc., that is attributable to a particular job order for a client.

job description *Labor Relations* A detailed definition of a specific position or type of work within a company or an industry, including education and experience required, duties and responsibilities of the person filling the position, etc.

job entry *Manufacturing* All of the related tasks necessary to place work into production, such as by confirming prices and specifications, creating a **job jacket**, requisitioning materials, confirming production schedules, setting up a file to record costs, etc.

job jacket *Manufacturing* A specification sheet that identifies a particular job order and contains such information as the name of the client, goods to be produced, quantity to be produced, materials required, delivery date, etc., often printed on, or attached to, an envelope or folder to hold drawings, notes, samples, etc. Also called a *job ticket*.

job lot *Commerce* An assortment of merchandise, often of textiles, containing a variety of colors, sizes, styles, etc. Frequently used in reference to **irregulars**.

job order *Manufacturing* Authorization to produce a set quantity of a particular product for a specific customer. The merchandise so authorized.

job placement The process of matching individuals to jobs for which they are suited. The processing may take place within a company, by the personnel or human resources department, or within an industry or labor market by an employment agency.

job processing *Accounting* A cost accounting system in which items are manufactured in a **job lot** of a particular size or quantity and costs are accumulated for each job. See also **batch processing**. *Computers* The execution of a task or series of tasks for processing data.

job shop *Manufacturing* Descriptive of a company that operates on a job order system, that is, all work done must be authorized by a **job order** containing all of the necessary information about the goods to be manufactured or the services to be performed.

job ticket See **job jacket**.

joint account *Finance* Of a bank or brokerage account set up by two or more persons. Such an account may be set up to allow any one of the participants to authorize a transaction, or the signature of all may be required.

joint liability *Law* Of those relationships in which there is a shared responsibility for the payment of a debt or other obligation.

jointly and severally *Law* A type of joint liability in which the parties to a contract may be held accountable as a group, or separately as individuals, that is, each member has unlimited liability up to the total outstanding amount of the obligation.

joint tenancy *Law* Ownership of property by two or more persons, with ownership passing to the survivor or survivors in the event of the death of one of the owners. Also called *joint tenancy with the right of survivorship, joint tenants but not tenants in common*, etc. depending on the requirements of the laws of the state in which the agreement is drawn. See also **tenancy in common**.

joint venture An agreement by two or more individuals or companies to join forces and share responsibility for a project that could not be accomplished singly. Such an agreement is normally for the duration of a single project and ends when the project is completed. Also, the project undertaken.

journal Generally, a record of information and events, as recorded by an individual, or in a publication for those engaged in a scientific, academic or professional field of endeavor. *Accounting* The original record of transactions that are summarized to report the financial activities and changes in a company.

journal entry, journalize *Accounting* The recording, in a journal, of the financial transactions of a company.

journeyman A skilled worker who has completed the apprenticeship required for recognition and acceptance as a proficient craftsman.

judgment lien *Law* A court order that allows a creditor to lay claim to property in order to satisfy a debt.

junior partner A partner with a subordinate interest in a firm; one who plays a limited role in the management of the company and is eligible for a limited share of profits.

junk bond *Finance* A bond that pays a high yield to compensate for a relatively higher risk factor.

just compensation *Law* Reasonable damages paid to one who sustains a loss as the result of an **involuntary conversion**.

justifiable That which can be shown to be reasonable. *Law* Of an act, or failure to act, that can be excused by reason of an action, or lack of action, on the part of another, as the withholding of payment when merchandise is not delivered.

justification *Accounting* A report that defends or advocates an expenditure, such as for a new machine, and that points out benefits of increased production or reduced cost, how the acquisition is to be financed, etc. *Computers* In word processing, the spacing of text so that it is lined up at both side margins; also called *full justification*.

K

kerning *Computers* In word processing or desktop publishing, descriptive of proportional spacing between typeset characters.

keyboard *Computers* A panel of buttons containing the alphabet, numbers and various symbols used as the primary device for entering data into a computer.

keyboard lockout *Computers* A program feature that prevents further entry from the keyboard while the computer is processing. A security device to prevent access to the computer by unauthorized users

keypad *Computers* A small, special purpose keyboard with a limited number of buttons.

key person insurance Protection against the loss of the services of a principle in a business. Such protection may seek to compensate survivors for the reduction in the value of their investment when the services of the insured are lost, or it may be to provide cash flow to keep the business operating during an adjustment period.

keying The practice of linking a variable to a standard, such as linking a wage or price increase in a contract to the Consumer Price Index. *Marketing* Coding that is printed on a coupon in a flyer, mailer, or space advertisement in order to link the response to the source.

key word *Computers* A word or set of words in a program or formula that indicate the operation to be performed.

kickback An illegal payment to an individual for approving a purchase, contract, etc. *Labor Relations* An illegal payment demanded of an employee by an employer or union in return for job security.

kicker *Colloq.* An added incentive, as a premium offered with the purchase of a consumer product, or special services or credit terms offered in conjunction with an industrial contract.

kill *Colloq.* Generally, to end or terminate, as a project or proposal.

killing *Colloq.* Descriptive of an abnormally high profit on a transaction.

kilobyte, KB *Computers* One thousand bytes.

kiting *Finance* To alternately write and deposit checks between two or more bank accounts, taking advantage of the **float**. The alteration of a check illegally to increase its face value.

kudos Recognition or praise for a job well done.

L

labeling requirements Federal and state regulations that require warning labels on containers of poisons and other hazardous substances.

labor Work; the physical effort required to accomplish a task. Those who work for wages, in contrast to *management*. A reference to labor unions collectively.

labor agreement The terms and conditions of a contract between labor and management. The contract so joined.

labor dispute A disagreement between labor and management that may arise in the course of negotiating a contract or in the interpretation of a contract.

labor force Collectively, the workers on a job; those employed by a company; or those of the nation, defined by age, who are employed or seeking employment.

labor intensive Descriptive of a business, industry, product, or service in which the cost of production is largely for workers, that is, the production of goods or services that do not lend themselves to automation. See also **capital intensive**.

labor relations See **industrial relations**.

labor union An organization authorized to negotiate pay scales, fringe benefits, working conditions, etc. with an employer as the sole representative of a group of workers comprising a bargaining unit.

laissez-faire *French* The concept that business should be allowed to operate with a minimum of government control or regulation.

LAN, local area network *Computers* A group of computers that are linked to share common programs, data, output devices, etc.

land Real property that can be conveyed by deed.

land locked A section of real property that does not have direct access to a public thoroughfare, and must be reached by an easement through adjacent land.

landlord One who owns land that is leased to others.

landmark Generally, a marker that fixes the boundary of land or a prominent feature that serves to identify a locality. *Law* A ruling that establishes an important precedent.

land-office business *Colloq.* Descriptive of a very busy trade.

language *Computers* A precise system of vocabulary and syntax for writing programs; *absolute* or *machine* language refers to instructions that can be understood directly by the computer; an *artificial* or *high level* language more closely emulates spoken English to make programming easier.

lapse *Insurance* The termination of a policy for failure to pay the premium. *Law* The termination or loss of a right because of some contingency, as a loss of property through failure to maintain or pay taxes.

laptop computer *Computer* A small computer with built-in monitor and keyboard that is between a **desktop computer** and a **notebook computer** in size. See also **microcomputer**.

laser, light amplification by stimulated emission of radiation *Computers* A device that emits intense light of a precise wavelength.

laser disk *Computers* A storage disk that is read using laser technology.

laser printer *Computers* An electrostatic printer that creates a high quality image with the use of laser technology.

last in, first out See LIFO.

law Generally, the rules of conduct laid down and enforced by governing authority. The study of the rules of conduct established by legislation and by custom or tradition.

law of supply and demand The theory that in a free market, the relationship between supply and demand will directly affect price and the quantity available at that price.

layoff *Labor* The removal of an employee from the payroll, usually temporary, during a time of reduced demand.

lcl or **LCL, less than carload** A classification for shipments that are too small to require a full rail car and are to be held for combining with other small shipments going in the same direction before a car can be dispatched.

LCD, liquid crystal display *Computers* a monitor screen that uses liquid crystals to create an image.

lead time Generally, the lapsed time required for a sequence of events. *Manufacturing* The time required for delivery of a product, from the placing of the order to shipping. *Marketing* The time required to plan and implement an advertising campaign, from conception to placement of the advertising. The time between insertion of a print ad and the print date. The time required to bring a new product to market, from concept to distribution.

leasehold improvement *Accounting* Enhancement of leased property, as by constructing offices or production areas, installing lighting, etc. Once attached to the property, the improvements are considered part of the property and cannot be removed except for further improvement; however, the cost of labor and fixtures may be entered on the books as an asset and depreciated.

leave of absence *Labor Relations* A time away from work, usually for an extended period without pay. A leave of absence presumes a return to the same or a comparable position at the end of the leave. An individual may take leave, for example, to serve for a time as a political appointee.

ledger *Accounting* The book of final entry for accounting transactions, summarized from journal entries and forming the data that makes up the financial reports of an organization.

legal entity *Law* An individual or organization that is recognized as being able to enter into a contract and that may be sued for failure to perform.

legal right *Law* Any privilege, interest or claim that is protected by law.

legal tender *Law* Money that may be offered to satisfy a debt and that must be accepted by the debtor as proper payment.

lender An individual or institution that makes a business in providing funds to others for a fee.

less than carload See lcl.

let To lease or hire out a building or equipment to another. To award a contract for goods or services. *Law* An obstruction or hindrance.

letter of credit *Commerce, Finance* An instrument issued by a bank to guarantee the credit of a buyer up to a specified amount, usually to protect the buyer in international trade.

letter quality *Computers* Descriptive of a printer image that emulates the quality of a good typewriter.

leverage *Finance* The use of borrowed money to finance expansion and increase the profitability of a company. The relation of debt to equity in a company; the higher the long term debt, the greater the leverage.

leveraged buyout *Finance* The purchase of a corporation using borrowed funds that are largely secured by the assets of the firm being purchased.

levy The assessment and collection of taxes or other fees. The amount so assessed.

liability Any legal obligation, as money owed, or a judgment requiring the payment of compensation for damages. Anything that works to ones disadvantage. *Accounting* Any of the debts of an individual or business.

liability insurance Protective coverage for an individual or business against losses suffered by claims of injury to a third party including those arising from negligence, as for damage caused by a company's product or injury to a visitor in the company's plant. See also, **casualty insurance**.

libel *Law* A tort wrong that consists of printing, or causing to be printed, any material that is slanderous, or that would in any way cause a person to be held in contempt or ridiculed. See also **slander**.

license Generally, a official granting of permission to do something, as to marry, conduct a business, practice a profession, etc. *Manufacturing* The granting of permission, usually for a royalty fee, to use a patented process and, in some cases, to advertise such use, as a clothing manufacturer who uses a well-known process to waterproof garments. Permission by a seller, for a buyer and user of brand name materials, to use the name to promote the buyer's product, as a photo processing company that promotes its use of a brand name print paper. *Marketing* An agreement that allows the use of copyrighted material for the promotion or decoration of a product, as a cartoon character on a child's lunch box.

lien *Law* A legal claim on property as the security for a debt.

LIFO; last in, first out *Accounting* A system for valuing inventory that presumes materials are removed in the reverse of the order that they are entered, thus matching the cost of the newest material with oldest revenue. In a time of rising prices it has been argued that this system properly reports a lower taxable income while minimizing the amount of money tied up in inventory. See also **FIFO**.

limited distribution *Marketing* Restricting the sale of a product to certain markets or to certain outlets within a market, often to control the way in which the product is sold, as by maintaining an **image** of exclusivity in order to maximize profit.

limited liability Generally, the restriction of possible losses from business reverses. In a partnership, the loss of a *limited partner* is restricted to the amount invested. Losses to the investors in a corporation are limited to the amount invested as well, unless an officer or shareholder has personally guaranteed an obligation of the corporation.

limited partnership A type of business firm in which certain partners have a financial interest, but play no active part in the operation of the organization; known as *limited partners*, their liability for company debts is limited to the capital they have invested. A limited partnership must have at least one **general partner**.

limiting Descriptive of that which restricts. *Computers* A device that, because of its slower speed or capacity, restricts the processing speed of the entire system. *Law* Of legislation that restricts or restrains, as of liability to the shareholders in a corporation or the powers of a municipality.

line Of those involved directly in company output. *Colloq.* Common term for the **production line**. *Marketing* The range of goods produced by a company, or stocked by a wholesaler or merchant.

line management Supervisory personnel who oversee line functions, such as the production manager, plant manager, etc.

line of credit *Finance* An agreement by a financial institution to loan money as needed by a business up to a certain amount.

line personnel *Manufacturing* Those persons who work on a production line.

line printer *Computers* A high speed printer that prints a full line of copy at one time.

line supervisor *Manufacturing* One who directly supervises production employees, as a foreman, or floor walker.

link *Computers* The connection between two computers or a computer and peripherals. The connection between an embedded object and its source that permits updating in one instance to update all instances of the object.

linked documents *Computers* Records or files that are connected so that data from one will be automatically entered in another, such as billing records that are automatically added to the accounts receivable file.

liquid asset *Accounting, Finance* Cash or an asset that can be readily converted into cash.

liquidate *Finance* To dispose of, as a debt or other obligation by payment. To convert assets into cash. To settle the accounts of a business, as when it is being closed down.

liquidity *Finance* The ability of a business to meet its current obligations from cash on hand and assets that can be readily converted into cash.

list maintenance Of the process of adding, deleting and correcting entries to a **mailing list**. Considering that twenty percent of most lists change in the course of a year, list maintenance is critical to avoid wasting money and effort in mailing to non-existent addresses. In addition, a statistical analysis of the ratio of returns to pieces mailed may indicate that a particular list is targeting the wrong audience when, in fact, the figures are skewed by the number of dead listings.

list price *Marketing* The price quoted before discounts, sales, etc. The manufacturer's suggested retail price.

litigant *Law* A party involved in a lawsuit.

litigation *Law* Involvement in a lawsuit.

load *Computers* To call up a program or data to the computer's main memory from a storage device.

loan *Finance* A business transaction in which one party furnishes money or other assets to another in return for the promise of return or repayment plus an additional fee for profit.

lobbyist One who makes a business of influencing the members of a legislative or government administrative body as the representative of a special interest group.

local *Labor Relations* The local chapter of a labor union.

lockbox A post office box to which receivables are sent. The box number is listed on invoices as the address to which payment should be sent. The lockbox is used to separate receivables from the rest of the company's mail, to make processing more efficient, or to provide a centralized drop for a company that has facilities at more than one location. A company that sells its accounts receivables may prefer to conceal the fact by having payments sent to the **factor** in care of a lockbox in the company name. A financial institution that has loaned money against a company's receivables may also require a lockbox under their control; payments received are reported to the company and credited to its account.

locked in *Colloq.* Of that which is not likely to change under present circumstances, as a buyer who is dependent on a particular supplier because of that supplier's ability to deliver, or an agreement that has had all of the points of contention resolved.

lockout *Computers* Denial of access to the computer by a security system. In a program temporary denial of access to commands during processing. *Labor Relations* Action by an employer to bar employees from working until an agreement has been reached, as for a labor contract.

logic Generally, correct or orderly reasoning. *Computers* The use of symbols in a formula to test the relationship between elements.

logic circuit *Computers* Computer circuitry that controls logic functions.

logic formula *Computers* A group of symbols that calculates to a logical *true* or *false*, as for a conditional branch.

logic operator *Computers* A symbol used in logic formulas.

log in, log on *Computers* To type in the password that allows access to the computer.

logo, logotype A distinguishing trademark or signature used by a company, often to identify its brands of merchandise.

long-range planning The process of setting budgets and goals for the achievement of future broad objectives, that is distinctive for its lack of detail. Long range planning involves setting objectives, and intermediate goals to reach those objectives, while maintaining a measure of flexibility in order to adjust for changes in business climate, technology, etc.

long-term contract Generally, any agreement, such as for labor, sales or the leasing of property that covers a period of more than one year.

long-term liability *Accounting, Finance* Any obligation, or portion of an obligation, that is not due for payment within twelve months. According to accepted accounting procedure, a debt that is to be paid in installments over a period of more than one year is reported as a long-term liability, except for the amount that is due in the current year.

lookup table *Computers* A set of variables arranged in a two dimensional array.

loop *Computers* A set of program instructions that are executed until a specific condition is met.

loop ender *Computers* A value expressed in a loop instruction to signal a branch and prevent unnecessary iterations of the loop.

loop feedback *Computers* The output value that modifies input for the next iteration of a loop instruction.

loophole *Law* A legal means of avoidance or escape, as from the provisions of a contract, or of an ordinance.

loosely coupled *Computers* Descriptive of computers that are connected, but that operate independently of one another.

loss leader *Marketing* Merchandise that is offered at a discount in order to attract customers in the hope that they will buy other goods as well.

low-ball *Marketing* To offer a price that is expected to be well below that of any other supplier, often to overcome all other considerations or resistance by a prospect who has a solid relationship with a competitor. While low-balling is a legitimate tactic to secure an order and the opportunity to prove that one is able to perform, companies often find themselves less willing to accept the loss once the order is placed and may seek to recoup their profits with overpriced extra charges.

lower of cost or market *Accounting* The conservative reporting of an asset value, that is, if the market value of an asset drops below its **book value**, the cost may be adjusted downward on financial reports to reflect the loss.

low grade Generally of inferior quality, as stocks, merchandise, etc.

lump sum distribution A single payment in full of an obligation that is normally expected to be doled out over time, as of an annuity or retirement fund.

luxury tax A tax on goods that are not considered a necessity.

M

machine dependent *Computers* A program or device that can only function on a particular computer or type of computer.

machine error *Computers* A program error caused by an equipment malfunction.

machine language *Computers* Instructions that can executed directly by a computer. Such instructions are extremely efficient and executed rapidly, but are very detailed, written in binary code and requiring a program statement for each machine action, so that programs are very difficult to write. Most programs are written in any one of a number of artificial languages that each have their own vocabulary and syntax, that somewhat emulate spoken English. The program so written must then be compiled, or translated, into machine language before being executed.

machine loading, machine loaded *Manufacturing* Of equipment that, once prepared for operation, automatically loads materials, parts, etc. for processing, such as an automatic camera in a design or print shop that loads a sheet of film for each shot by cutting it from a master roll. Of a type of production control or scheduling that takes into account the machines used in processing, the order in which they are used, and time required of each to process an order; delivery schedule is then determined by the availability of equipment when it is needed.

machine readable *Computers* Of a set of characters or symbols that can be read directly into a computer, usually by a scanner.

macro *Computers* A set of instructions that are executed by a single command or with a hot key combination.

magnetic disk *Computers* A computer storage medium. A hard disk or floppy disk.

mail fraud The use of the postal service to deliver material that is designed to deceive or to swindle the recipient, as by false claims for a product or an invoice for a product that was not ordered or sent.

mailing list A collection of names and addresses of individuals or organizations set up in such a manner that they can be used to address materials to be sent through the mail. A mailing list may be of customers, prospects, vendors, etc. and may be the property of the mailer or rented from an organization that trades in such lists. Rented lists vary greatly in value and cost of rental, based on their source, ranging from census tract lists that purport to include everyone living in a particular area, to those who fit a given **demographic** profile, to active buyers of mail order products. See also **list maintenance**.

mail merge *Computers* A program feature that combines a mailing list with the body of a letter.

mainframe *Computers* Of a large, fixed base computer that supports hundreds of users. The demand for such computers has fallen off as minicomputers and microcomputers grow more powerful and able to support multiple users and networks.

main memory *Computers* The internal memory of a computer from which programs are run.

maintenance The maintaining of buildings and equipment in good repair. See also **preventive maintenance**.

majority Of more than half, as a *majority* of the stockholders. *Law* Of the time when one reaches legal age.

majority shareholder A stockholder who owns more than half of the voting stock in a company and thus has a controlling interest. Often of a group that owns, or controls the votes of, more than half of the outstanding voting shares.

maker A person who signs or authorizes a transaction, as one who issues a check or signs a promissory note.

make-work Descriptive of a task that serves no purpose other than that of giving an otherwise idle person something to do.

malfeasance *Law* Committing that which is unlawful; wrongdoing. See also **nonfeasance**.

malicious mischief The deliberate vandalism or destruction of the property of another.

malingerer One who feigns illness or injury to avoid work.

manage To control or direct, as an enterprise or a group of workers.

management agreement An **employment contract**. A contract between two companies engaged in a **joint venture** stipulating individual company responsibility and compensation for directing various phases or elements of the venture. A contract to direct certain aspects of a company's operations, usually joined with a company that specializes in such services, such as for accounting, human resources, training programs, etc.

management by exception The managerial concept that focuses attention on those events deviating from an acceptable pattern, such as a machine report that lists only those operations that produced below standard, or the posting of statements only to clients whose accounts are in arrears.

management by objective An administrative process whereby supervisors and workers jointly set goals and meet periodically to evaluate progress.

management consultant An individual or organization that specializes in the study and evaluation of the operation of other companies, for the purpose of offering advice to improve output, cut cost, reduce waste, etc. Generally, management consultants specialize in a particular phase of operations, such as accounting and finance, materials handling, marketing and distribution, or labor relations, or in a particular industry, such as textiles, or printing.

management information system See **MIS**.

management prerogative Of those rights that the leadership of an organization holds to be theirs exclusively and not subject to collective bargaining, such as the scheduling of work or introduction of new processes.

mandate Generally, any commission or order to do something. *Law* A directive from a higher court to a lower one. Any contract that gives one the power to act for another.

mandatory Required; of that which is compulsory and not open to negotiation. *Labor Relations* Of the requirements for being hired, such as taking and passing a physical examination; for continued employment, such as obeying company rules or submitting to and passing a periodic test for the detection of controlled substances; and for being terminated, as by reaching retirement age. *Marketing* Of laws and regulations that govern the marketing of goods, such as requirements for special labeling on certain products.

man-hour A general term to express the output of one person in one hour on a particular job or operation. Professional services, such as those of an outside accountant or lawyer, are usually based on estimated or actual man-hours. *Manufacturing* An expression of output often used to determine the cost of a project or the number of persons required for completion on time.

manufacturer's software *Computers* A system program or driver that is supplied by the original equipment manufacturer for a specific piece of equipment.

manufacturing The process of constructing or fabricating a product, especially by machine and in large quantities.

manufacturing cost *Accounting* The cost to fabricate a product, including direct materials, direct labor and factory overhead.

margin *Accounting* Anticipated or actual profit; the difference between **manufacturing**

cost and selling price.

marginal cost *Accounting* The cost of one additional unit of production, often expressed as variable cost.

marginal producer Of a product or company that is barely able to show a profit at the current price or volume level.

marginal revenue *Accounting* The increase in revenue from one additional unit of output. See also **marginal cost**.

marginal utility The satisfaction or utility gained from the consumption of one additional unit.

margin of profit Ratio of profit to sales, usually expressed as a percentage.

markdown A reduction in the selling price of goods. Sometimes, descriptive of a batch or assortment of goods that are odd sizes or out of style and are being sold off at a reduced price to clear inventory

market Generally, of any opportunity or potential opportunity to buy or sell; buyers and sellers meeting to trade. Any specific locale where goods are bought and sold.

marketability Of that which can be sold or is fit to be sold. *Finance* The ease with which an asset, such as stocks or real estate, can be converted to cash.

market analysis *Finance* Of any attempt to predict the future value of an investment, as a stock or bond, based on company performance or industry trends. *Marketing* Techniques for studying the characteristics and extent of the market for a product or group of products to predict future trends in order to formulate plans for expansion, diversification, etc.

market area *Marketing* The realm in which there is a demand or anticipated potential demand for a product, such as a geographic locale, a consumer group that fits a particular demographic profile, an industry, etc.

marketing All aspects of the advertising, merchandising and selling of goods and services.

marketing concept The strategy for promoting and selling a specific product or group of products, such as by identification with a particular lifestyle, by emphasis on benefits to users of the product, etc.

marketing director One who oversees all aspects of the marketing of a company's products, and to whom all personnel or departments responsible for marketing functions report.

market penetration *Marketing* The extent to which a particular product dominates or fails to dominate a market or market segment. A strategy intended to secure a larger share of a market or market segment by such means as aggressive advertising, promotion, etc.

marketplace Generally, anywhere that goods are traded, although it may refer to a specific location or segment of a market. Often referring figuratively to the world of trade.

market potential *Marketing* The total value of goods or services that may be sold in a particular market or in all markets. For an individual supplier, *market potential* may be regarded as unrealized sales, that is, sales by the competition in the market area. *Market potential* may also refer to a market that has not been exploited, as by a new use for a product.

market price Generally, the current prevailing price at which a product is being traded, or the price determined by supply and demand as contrasted to a price set by company policy.

market profile The configuration of data that describes the prospective individual or organizational buyer or user of a product, as by lifestyle, type of business, etc.

market research Investigation into the characteristics of a potential market, such as location, size, etc., and those in the market, such as age, education, income level, etc.

market segmentation Dividing the market for a product into separate categories according to such factors as geographic location, individual or company buyer, end use, age of user, etc. Such segmentation allows for efficient and effective advertising, promotion, customer service, etc.

market share *Marketing* The portion of the total market, or market segment, controlled by a particular company, usually expressed as a percentage of the total market.

market value *Finance* The price that goods in inventory or equipment would bring if offered for sale at a given time.

markup *Marketing* An amount added to the cost of goods to cover overhead and profit, usually expressed as a percentage of cost.

mass media Of communication systems that reach a very large audience, as radio, television, certain publications, etc.

mass production *Manufacturing* Of the fabrication of large quantities of goods on automated equipment.

matching *Accounting* The concept of financial reporting that strives for the pairing of revenue with the expenses associated with the generation of that revenue.

material Generally, a thing of significance or physical presence. The substances that, with labor and overhead, go into the cost of a project or the manufacture of a product. *Law* That which may be of sufficient importance to influence a judgment.

material budget *Manufacturing* A list of those supplies, or the cost of supplies, that have been allocated for a project or the fabrication of a batch of goods.

material cost *Accounting* The actual cost of supplies used for a particular project or in the fabrication of a batch of goods. Depending on company policy, the cost may be the amount invoiced by the vendor, or it may include some overhead for storage and handling, often applied as a percentage of the invoiced value.

materials handling Any manipulation and recording of the disposition of supplies in the plant, including the receiving, storing, and movement of raw goods; the moving, packing, shipping, and storage of finished goods; and disposal of waste.

math coprocessor *Computers* A chip that works in conjunction with the CPU to perform high speed arithmetic calculations.

mathematical operator A symbol that governs an arithmetic computation.

matrix *Computers* A pattern for comparison of elements in optical character recognition. A two dimensional array.

maturity *Finance* Of the due date of an obligation.

maxim A brief expression of a general rule, truth, or principle.

mechanic's lien *Law* A security on property granted to one who has furnished labor or materials for the improvement of the property.

mechanization *Manufacturing* The performance of tasks by machine. Of the conversion of operations from handwork to machine.

media Plural of medium. All of the means of communicating with the general public, as radio, television, publications, etc. *Marketing* All of the means of communication that carry advertising in addition to entertainment, news, etc.

media blitz *Marketing* Saturation advertisement of a product in a market or markets that comprises numerous ads in all media designed to reach as many people as possible in the market area.

media event *Marketing* A public appearance or happening that has been staged to garner publicity through the news media.

mediation *Labor Relations* Intervention in a dispute between labor and management by a third party, often a government official. The findings of a **mediator** are not binding.

mediator *Labor Relations* A person who attempts to assist parties to a dispute in reaching a settlement, often one who specializes in such service.

medium Singular of **media**.

megabyte, MB *Computers* One million bytes.

megahertz, MHz *Computers* One million cycles per second.

memo, memorandum A short note written by one as a reminder or something or as a record of events. An informal communication, usually between parties within a company. *Accounting* A preliminary document, as a *memo billing* sent with a shipment of goods. A notice or directive that authorizes some action, as the return of damaged or disputed goods. *Law* A brief, preliminary statement of the terms of an agreement or contract.

memory *Computers* A device in which data can be stored and accessed at a later time. *ROM* or *read-only memory* refers to an area of storage where the data is permanently imprinted, that is, it can be read, but not altered, as that which is built into the computer to control its basic functions. *RAM* or *random access memory* is dynamic volatile memory that must be constantly refreshed to be retained, as the area in a computer where programs are loaded for execution; *random access* refers to very fast memory of which any part can be addressed independent of the previous access. *Permanent memory* or *permanent storage* refers to memory in the computer, or on a removable device such as a disk, where data is stored; data may be changed by the operator and the memory is not dynamic, so that it is not lost when the power is off.

memory card *Computers* A computer add-on that provides additional storage.

memory resident *Computers* Descriptive of a program or utility that is loaded in RAM. See also TSR.

menu *Computers* Generally, a reference to a list of options from which the user can select

menu driven *Computers* Descriptive of a program that is easy to learn and use because it affords the user the option of selecting program options from a list, in contrast to those programs that require the user to learn numerous commands.

menial One who is a servant or servile, or a person who is employed in a lowly position. Of the tasks performed by such a person.

merchandise Things bought and sold. The act of buying and selling. *Marketing* To advertise or promote the sale of goods.

merchandise allowance Payment, or credit on account, for goods that have been returned.

merchandising *Marketing* Promoting the sale of goods through advertising and publicity, proper display and support at the point of sale, programs for discounting to buyers or consumers, etc.

merchandising allowance *Marketing* A standard offer by a manufacturer or distributor to share a portion of the cost of local advertising or promotion with the retailer.

merchant One engaged in the business of buying and selling goods at a profit, especially a shopkeeper who sells at retail.

merge Generally, to absorb, or join together, often with a loss of identity of the elements as they existed before the merge, as of two companies. See also **merger**. *Computers* To combine, as a file or database. See also **mail merge**.

merged sort *Computers* To combine and arrange in a particular order, as alphabetically, sets of database files.

merger A blending of two or more companies by **acquisition**, in which one company purchases others and they are absorbed into the parent company, or by **consolidation**, in which a new corporation is formed to absorb the merging companies.

merit pay, merit raise *Labor Relations* An addition to a standard wage that is awarded for outstanding performance on the job.

metered mail Mail that is stamped by a postage meter.

methods study Examination, usually by a third party, of the established systems, formal and informal, for accomplishing tasks throughout a company. The purpose of such a study is to find and eliminate the pockets of waste caused by miscommunication, misdirection, etc. through formalizing procedures that require more uniform action or results, and eliminating any structures or rules that are outdated or tend to make a task more complicated or difficult than it needs to be.

metric system A decimal system of weights and measures in which the basic unit of weight is the gram, of measure is the meter, and of capacity is the liter.

metropolitan area The broad region that includes a city and the surrounding area that is economically linked to it.

microcomputer A computer that is operated by a single integrated circuit called a **microprocessor**. Various types of the microcomputer are the **desktop computer**, laptop computer and notebook computer.

microprocessor An **integrated circuit** that holds the complete central processing unit for a microcomputer.

MIDI, musical instrument digital interface *Computers* The protocol for interaction between a digitized musical instrument and a computer.

middleman *Commerce, Marketing* One who purchases goods from a manufacturer to sell to a retailer or direct to the consumer.

middle management Generally a reference to those who hold administrative positions somewhere between top management and line supervisors.

migratory worker One who moves from place to place to find work, as an agricultural worker who follows the harvest.

milk *Colloq.* To exploit a situation for gain, such as by eating in the finest restaurants to take advantage of an expense account.

mill *Accounting, Finance* One tenth of a cent; from the Latin for thousandth, or one thousandth of a dollar.

mineral rights An agreement that conveys privilege to remove oil or other resources from the land and sell them for profit. Ownership of mineral rights may be held or conveyed separately from ownership of the land itself.

minicomputer *Computer* A small computer that is between a **mainframe** and a **microcomputer** in size, and that is designed to support multiple users. Mainframes, in many instances, are being replaced by powerful new minicomputers, which in turn are increasingly being replaced by networked microcomputers.

minimum wage *Labor Relations* The lowest hourly rate that can be paid to a worker who is covered by a contract, in a particular job classification. *Law* The lowest hourly rate that can be paid to a worker according to the provisions of federal or state law, usually in reference to the federal Fair Labor Standards Act that sets a minimum rate for those workers covered.

minor *Law* Of one who has not reached **majority** as specified by the law of the state governing. One who is a minor faces certain restrictions of action, such as for entering into marriage or joining the armed forces without consent.

minority interest Of the portion of a company owned by those who, in the aggregate, hold less than half of a company's voting stock.

minutes The record of transactions at a meeting, especially those of a corporation, scheduled to conduct official business, as a shareholder's meeting or a meeting of the board of directors.

MIS, management information system *Computers* An organization's facilities for gathering, storing, and managing data for use in decision making.

misdemeanor *Law* Any minor transgression, such as failure to comply with a local ordinance, that carries a relatively light penalty.

mismanagement The failure to properly fulfill administrative duties either through neglect or malice. Mismanagement may refer simply to poor performance in directing a single, small project or it may be far more serious, as in the misappropriation of company funds.

MIS, management information system *Computers* A system designed to provide timely and accurate reports for management to use as an aid in decision-making. Such a system requires correlation and integration of information gathering, data entry, and data processing.

misrepresentation Generally, false or misleading information. *Marketing* A statement or implication in product advertising, whether by accident or malice, that may cause injury to a buyer and become the basis for litigation, as by claiming a product is safe when, in fact, it contains chemicals that can cause illness.

mistake Generally, an error. *Law* An act or failure to act that may be grounds to revoke a contract, or dismiss a charge of liability against another.

mitigation A moderation or making less severe. *Law* A petition to a court for a reduction of damages on the basis of evidence that the injured party is not entitled to the full amount of the damages.

mix Generally, a blending of diverse elements. In business, often a reference to the proportion of each element in a total. *Finance* A factor in predicting a company's future strength and prospects, as by judging what the product mix will be based on anticipated demand and predicting profitability based on that mix, for example, a company's prospects may be declining despite anticipated sales increases if demand for its most profitable line is falling as the demand for less profitable items increases. *Manufacturing* Of the relative quantity of each of the company's products that is to be produced in a given period, especially as it influences the allocation of resources in order to manufacture them efficiently. *Marketing* Of the share of each of the company's products sold in each market, an important factor in planning promotion. Of the relative amount of advertising placed with each medium for a particular campaign, especially as it relates to heavy reliance on one.

mixed media See **multimedia**.

mixed signals *Colloq.* Unclear indicators of what is correct, especially those based on contradictory messages or reports. For example, reports of increasing demand for a product in a market where the number of persons fitting the demographic profile of a user is declining.

mnemonics Techniques for aiding memory. *Computers* Commands designated so as to make remembering their function easier, as *Q* for *quit*, or *P* for *print*.

modeling The process of formulating a mathematical representation that can be manipulated to show the consequence of change. For example, one might use a model of the income statement for the previous year to illustrate what the results would have been if the product mix were changed, if a product had been dropped, etc. as an aid to planning. Budgets for future periods can then be manipulated to test the effect of changes in product mix, addition of new equipment, changes in the cost of materials, etc.

modem *Computers* Modulator/demodulator; a device that converts electronic signals, especially the conversion of discrete data from a computer to analog data for transmission by telephone lines that is converted back to discrete data by the receiver.

momentum Generally, the driving force of a thing in motion. Descriptive of a condition in which the strength of movement is seen as an influence on the tendency to continue moving in the same direction, as by a strengthening economy.

monetary *Finance* Of that which concerns money.

money *Finance* In general, any medium of exchange that has recognized value, as coined or printed currency, bank notes, checks, precious metals, property, etc.

monitor Generally, anything or anyone that observes, regulates, or supervises. *Computers* A video screen that allows the user to view processing and interact with the computer. A program that oversees and manages the operation of other programs.

monopoly Sole control of a particular line of goods or services in a given market or the means to control distribution and price

moonlighting Having a second job, full- or part-time, in addition to a regular job.

morale A spirit of confidence; the mental state of a person or group in relation to a positive mental attitude.

moral obligation Of a commitment that will be honored because it is the right thing to do and represents the way in which reasonable people deal with one another rather than because of a legal requirement.

mortgage *Finance* The pledge of real estate as collateral for the payment of a loan.

mortgage insurance Any protection for the lender, or mortgagee, against loss, such as restitution for damages to the property, for damages resulting from foreclosure, or from the death of the mortgagor.

motion study An examination of the flow of work, material, etc. on an assembly line or throughout a manufacturing plant in order to make production more cost effective.

motivation The inner drive that causes one to act in a certain manner.

motivational research *Labor Relations* The study and analysis of those things that influence, or are of the greatest importance, to workers so that they might be used to encourage better performance on the job. *Marketing* Studies that attempt to determine what might influence a consumer to buy a particular product.

motor freight Trucks or trucking lines in contrast to the railroad.

mouse *Computers* A device for extremely rapid and random movement of the cursor on a monitor screen. In addition, some mouses can be programmed, so that a mouse button in combination with other keys can execute a series of keystrokes.

multimedia *Computers* Of the combining of sound and video images in a computer program or presentation. *Marketing* Of an advertising or promotional campaign that utilizes more than one medium, as television, radio and direct mail, often with messages that reinforce one another.

multinational corporation Of a corporation that operates production plants or branches in more than one country.

multiplexer *Computers* A system that manages signals between two or more devices simultaneously.

multitasking *Computers* The ability of a CPU to execute two or more programs or routines at the same time, either by independent processing or by **interleaving**.

multi-user system *Computers* A system designed to mange input and output from several terminals at the same time.

Murphy's law The maxim that if there is anything that can go wrong, it will, named for the engineer who originally expressed the sentiment in 1949.

N

national bank *Finance* A bank chartered by the federal government through the Comptroller of the Currency.

national brand *Marketing* A product that is widely distributed, in contrast to a local or regional brand.

Natural Bureau of Standards A government agency established in 1901 that conducts the research that is the basis for a national system of weights and measures, and performs other services for science and industry in the realm of testing and evaluation.

nationalization The confiscation of private assets by a government.

Nation Labor Relations Act *Labor Relations* Federal regulation that officially recognized collective bargaining by providing for the supervision of representative elections and outlawed unfair labor practices by employers.

Nation Labor Relations Board *Labor Relations* Agency created by the National Labor Relations Act that monitors the dealings between employers and the representatives of employees.

natural monopoly Generally, an enterprise that dominates a market because of conditions that limit the entry of other producers. One who raises a crop that will only grow in a limited part of the country, or who manufactures a product that is protected by patent, enjoys a natural monopoly. Such a monopoly may be legislated when it is in the public good, as by granting the right for a public utility to operate in a particular area.

natural resources Those materials that are gleaned from nature.

near letter quality, NLQ *Computers* A designation of the ability of a printer to emulate the quality of reproduction one would expect from a typewriter.

negative cash flow *Accounting* A condition characterized by a period during which a business paid out more cash than it received. A negative cash flow for a single period does not necessarily indicate a problem, as it may simply reflect a higher than normal level of credit sales in relation to expenditures and the company may have adequate cash or credit line to cover the shortfall. In addition, a period of rapid expansion may require buying from new vendors with whom credit has not been established, so that the proportion of expenditures to receipts is out of line. Over the longer term, however, a negative cash flow may indicate a failure to react quickly to increases in cost, improper management of accounts receivable, etc.

negligence *Law* The failure to exercise **due care** that results in injury or damages to another.

negotiable instrument A written agreement that contains a promise to pay a specific sum on demand or at a fixed time in the future and that can be transferred easily from one party to another.

negotiated price Any charge for goods or services that is arrived at by agreement between buyer and seller, often occasioned by special needs of the buyer, as for extended credit, special packaging or a custom product, or by conditions, such as the sellers desire to break into a market or a need for additional volume.

negotiation Generally, a bargaining or conferring. *Commerce* Bargaining between buyer and seller to arrive at a mutually agreeable price and terms. *Finance* The transfer of a **negotiable instrument** from one party to another. *Labor Relations* Bargaining in an attempt to reach agreement on the terms of a labor contract. *Marketing* Bargaining with media representatives to derive the best exposure for a favorable price.

nepotism *Labor Relations* Preferential treatment to relatives, especially in their appointment to lucrative positions in a company or department. Many companies bar or place restrictions on the hiring of those who are related in order to avoid the problems that such hiring can create.

net Of that which remains after deductions, as *sales* less *returns and allowances*, *profit* after deduction of *taxes*, *shipping weight* after deduction for *wrapping* or *container*, etc. The strict definition of similar items, as *net sales* or *net profit*, often vary from one company to another, and sometimes from one report to another, depending on how the term is being used, company policy, etc.

net assets *Accounting, Finance* The value of all of a company's assets, less liabilities. Also known as *owner's equity* or *net worth*.

net asset value *Finance* Generally, the book value of a share of stock, especially as applied to a mutual fund, calculated by deducting the value of **intangible assets** from **net assets** and dividing by the number of outstanding shares.

net cost The original cost of an asset less anything realized from its disposition, usually of an asset that is being sold or traded in, as the first step to determining profit or loss on the transaction for tax purposes.

net income *Accounting, Finance* Generally, revenue less all expenses; net profit or loss. Often a provisional amount, that is, qualified on a financial report as *before sales* expense, before administrative cost, before taxes, etc.

net loss Accounting, Finance A loss recorded on the income statement after allowance for taxes, extraordinary charges, etc.

net profit Accounting, Finance Profit after allowance for taxes, extraordinary charges, etc.

net quick assets Finance The amount by which quick assets, that is, cash, accounts receivable and marketable securities, exceed current liabilities. In effect, it is a measure of a company's ability to meet its current obligations with easily convertible assets if sales were to dry up.

net realizable value *Accounting* The amount that might be obtained from the sale of an asset after deducting any expenses associated with the sale, such as the cost of making the asset salable.

net sales *Accounting, Financing* Revenue less any returns and allowances.

network Generally, any group of persons or things that are connected with each other for some purpose. In business, often used to express an informal system of contacts that may be of help from time to time. *Computers* A number of computers, terminals, printers, scanners, plotters, or other peripherals that are connected in such a way that they can communicate with each other.

network server *Computers* A computer that stores and manages programs and data for other computers in the network.

net worth *Accounting, Finance* The value of all of an individual or a company's assets, less their liabilities. Also known as *owner's equity*.

new issue *Finance* Of stocks or bonds being sold by a corporation for the first time. *New issue* may refer to an initial offering by a private company that is **going public**, or an addition issue to secure operating capital or funds for expansion, by a public company.

niche Generally, a place that is especially suited to the thing in it. *Marketing* Of a particular market or specialty area where a company finds it profitable to concentrate its efforts. Niche marketing offers a concentration of clients in an atmosphere of limited competition.

no-fault insurance Of a type of protection, mandated by law in certain states, wherein losses to all parties, as in an automobile accident, are covered with no regard to who is at fault.

noise *Computers* A reference to extraneous and undesirable signals that interfere with transmission.

nolo contendere *Law* A plea allowed a defendant in a criminal case, in which the charges are not contested, but without admission of guilt.

nominal Generally, descriptive of that which is in name only; sometimes, an expression of that which is so slight as to be, virtually, in name only.

nominal damages *Law* A small award in recognition that a wrong was done when there is no proof of significant recoverable damages.

nominal wage A wage stated as an amount paid, without consideration of purchasing power.

nonconforming use *Law* Utilization of a parcel of land in a manner that is not in keeping with the local zoning ordinance, such as for a commercial enterprise that is located in a residential area, that occurs when the use existed before the restrictive ordinance was passed.

noncontributory *Insurance* Of a company medical, life, or retirement plan that is funded completely by the employer.

noncontrollable cost *Accounting* Of expenses that are not influenced or may be influenced only marginally by a particular individual or set of circumstances. Such costs are removed from consideration, for example, when evaluating the performance of a supervisor who cannot be held accountable for the cost of rent or utilities.

nondestructive read *Computers* Access of a data file while maintaining a copy of the file in storage.

nonfeasance *Law* Failure to do that which duty requires. See also **malfeasance**.

nonperformance *Law* Failure to perform according to agreement, as a contract.

non printing character *Computers* A command or formatting character in a computer document.

nonproductive Generally, of that which does not contribute to output, often of that which is wasteful of resources. *Accounting* Descriptive of those functions that cannot be directly identified with the fabrication of goods or the providing of service; overhead.

nonprofit Of an organization that is not formed for the express purpose of making a profit for its investors. Such an organization is often formed for some humanitarian, scientific or educational purpose, as a hospital or foundation, and is usually exempt from taxes.

nonrecurring *Accounting, Finance* Of a line item on a financial report that is unique and not expected to occur again, such as for income from the sale of equipment, or a one-time charge associated with the cost of a lawsuit.

nonvoting stock *Finance* Of preferred or other special issue stock that does not qualify the shareholder to have vote in corporate elections.

norm Normal; within the realm of standard practice, behavior, achievement, etc. the fabrication of goods or the providing of service; overhead.

normal price *Commerce* The price at which a particular product or service is traded when there is no fluctuation attributable to excess supply or demand.

normal profit *Finance* The profit level at which a producer will continue in business without significant change. A higher profit level attracts competition that will have the effect of lowering profit; a lower profit level may make other investments more attractive to the producer.

normal spoilage *Manufacturing* Wasted material or rejected product that is expected and unavoidable in a fabricating or manufacturing operation under usual conditions.

normal wear and tear *Accounting* Of that which is intended to be covered by depreciation allotted for the gradual decrease in value of equipment; there is no provision for unexpected damage to the equipment.

no-strike clause *Labor Relations* A provision in a labor contract stipulating that the workers will not strike as long as the employer lives up to the terms of the contract.

notary, notary public A public official who is authorized to authenticate documents, take depositions, perform marriages, etc.

notation *Computers* The system of words, symbols, mnemonics, etc. used to write computer programs.

note *Finance* A written promise acknowledging a debt and specifying the terms for repayment.

notebook computer *Computers* A portable computer with a monitor screen and keyboard contained in a single unit; the smallest of the general purpose computers. See also **microcomputer.**

notes payable *Accounting, Finance* Obligations in the form of debts due to others as shown on the balance sheet.

notes receivable *Accounting, Finance* An asset on the balance sheet in the form of debts due from others.

not for profit See **nonprofit.**

notice to quit *Law* Notification to a tenant that rental property is to be vacated.

nuisance *Law* A condition that poses or may pose a danger to others, or that interferes with the free use of one's property.

null and void *Law* That cannot be legally enforced; invalid, as the terms of a contract that are contrary to law.

number cruncher One capable of carrying out a project that involves a large number of complex calculations, generally descriptive of an accountant, often with the aid of a computer.

O

objective Without bias or personal prejudice. Intent or purpose, as of a marketing plan.

object linking and embedding, OLE *Computers* Connecting text or graphics data between documents and applications—linking implies that a change of data in one position changes all occurrences of the same data.

obligation *Law* A duty, as to pay a debt according to an agreement. The contract or other document that outlines the terms of such an agreement.

obsolescence The condition of being outdated or useless because of advancing technology.

occupation One's trade or profession.

occupational disease An affliction that is associated with those who engage in a particular type of work.

occupational hazard Conditions associated with certain jobs that expose the workers to the danger of injury on the job.

OCR, optical character recognition *Computers* Any of the systems or techniques for reading characters or symbols from hard copy and translating them into digital data for manipulation, such as a system that accepts input from a retail store checkout scan of product labels to ring up the sale, adjust inventory, etc. A program capability that involves reading graphic text from a hard copy or computer file, and translating it into characters that can be manipulated by the user.

octal A numbering system in base eight.

OEM, original equipment manufacturer *Commerce, Computers* The manufacturer, as contrasted to the distributor, of a particular product.

off-brand *Marketing* A product that emulates a popular brand, often of inferior quality and less expensive.

offer An expression of interest as the first step toward entering into an agreement. That which is presented for consideration. To present for sale, or bid on that which is for sale.

office automation *Computers* Use of the computer to assist in the tasks associated with running a business, such as bookkeeping, inventory control, maintaining mailing lists, etc.

office management The organization and administration of a company's offices.

off-line *Computers* Of peripheral equipment that is not turned on or that is not directly connected to or controlled by the computer. Of data that is not entered directly into the computer, but rather to a storage device, such as a tape, which is then processed by the computer.

offset *Accounting* That which sets off or balances as the offsetting credit and debit entries to the ledger. *Finance, Law* The right of a bank to confiscate deposited funds to cover a loan that is in default, called the *right of offset.*

offshore *Financial* Of any financial organization that has its headquarters outside the U.S. Of subsidiaries of U.S. firms that operate outside the U.S. to avoid heavy regulation.

off the books *Colloq.* Transactions, such as barters or payments for labor, that are not recorded in order to avoid taxes.

old boy network *Colloq.* Of the relationship that exists between certain groups of men who favor each other in business transactions and shut others out.

oligopoly A market that is dominated by a few large suppliers, as for automobiles.

ombudsman A public official or representative of a private organization who investigate the complaints of private citizens.

on account *Accounting, Finance* A payment made to partly liquidate a debt. A sale on credit, or charged to the client's account.

on consignment *Marketing* Of goods that are delivered to a merchant for sale; unsold goods are returned to the manufacturer or wholesaler.

on demand *Finance* Of a note or other obligation without a fixed payment date and for which payment may be requested at the pleasure of the holder of the obligation.

one-time buyer *Marketing* A purchaser of advertising who is contracting for a limited number of spots or insertions and is therefore not eligible for volume discounts.

on-line *Computers* Of data entry or peripherals that are connected directly to the main computer. Of equipment that is turned on.

on order Goods that have been requisitioned, but not yet received.

on-pack *Marketing* Of a premium that is attached to the outside of the package containing a product. Many marketers have reservations about the effectiveness of the on-pack because of the tendency of the premium to disappear before the product is sold. See also **in-pack.**

on-sale date *Marketing* The day on which a dated publication is to go on sale, and any remaining copies of the previous issues are to be returned to the distributor. The day on which a new product is placed on sale, often coordinated with an advertising and promotion campaign.

on speculation *Marketing* Preliminary studies, artwork, presentations, etc. prepared by an advertising agency at no charge in the hopes of securing business.

on-the-job training Learning a trade while working at it, often part of a formal training program.

op code, operation code *Computers* A symbol or set of characters that directs the computer to execute a command.

open *Computers* Of a file that has been copied from memory storage to **RAM** and is available to the user for updating or editing.

open account *Accounting* Descriptive of a client's account that contains unpaid charges. *Marketing* Sales terms that allow the client to buy on credit.

open bidding Tendering a price for goods, services, a project, etc. that is open to negotiation. See also **sealed bid.**

open-end contract *Commerce* A contract to furnish goods or services of an indefinite quantity for an unspecified period, providing for termination after proper notice by either party. *Labor Relations* A labor contract that has no fixed termination date, but a provision that calls for opening negotiations at the request of either party after proper notification.

open house In real estate, a means of showing property that is kept open to prospective buyers for inspection on specified dates. *Marketing* A means of promoting a company or its goods, especially the introduction of a new product, by creating a media event around a tour of the company facilities for prospective clients and a group of dignitaries or celebrities.

open order *Commerce* An order that has not been filled or canceled.

open shop *Labor Relations* An organization where workers are free to choose to become members of the union or not. In an open shop, non-union workers are employed under the same conditions as union workers and, though they lack the advocacy of the union when filing a grievance, share most of the same benefits as union members. See also, **closed shop, right to work, union shop.**

open stock *Commerce* Descriptive of merchandise that is kept in stock by a merchant, wholesaler, or manufacturer. Often of merchandise that can be purchased singly or as part of a set, such as china, cutlery, or crystal.

operating budget Estimated expenditures for transacting company business at the level of production forecast by the sales projection for a given period.

operating cycle A characteristic model of business activity in which cash or other assets are converted into inventory and ultimately into a product or service that is, in turn, sold for cash or other assets. The length of time from the purchase of raw materials for production until they are sold as finished goods.

operating expense *Accounting* The costs incurred in the normal conduct of a business, as distinguished from **capital investment**, the cost to acquire the means of production, or any extraordinary expenses.

operating income *Accounting* Revenues generated in the course of supplying the goods and services that are the stock in trade of a business.

operating loss *Accounting* Losses sustained in the normal conduct of business, that do not include any unusual losses, as from the sale of equipment, from a court order to pay damages, etc.

operating profit *Accounting* Profits resulting from the normal conduct of business, that do not proceed from any extraordinary transactions, as the sale of an asset, a windfall judgment, etc.

operating system Generally, the procedures and practices that determine the manner in which an organization conducts its affairs. *Computers* The program that provides a platform for the control of the functions of the computer, such as DOS, OS/2, etc.

operation Generally, any procedure or activity that is one of a series of similar activities serving to reach an objective, as *the painting operation* in an automobile assembly plant. The series of actions taken as a whole, as *a manufacturing operation*. Sometimes, referring to the site where such activities take place.

opinion Generally, an expression of that which is not certain, but which seems probable or likely valid. In business, it is often the valuation or judgment of an expert hired for examination of a particular matter, as the statement of an auditor after reviewing the company financial records. *Law* A formal statement by the court regarding the law that has bearing on a case.

opinion leader *Marketing* Descriptive of one who influences a number of others in the selection of goods and whose endorsement of a product is, therefore, highly valued.

opportunity cost Generally, a means to compare the differences in return one might expect from the selection among alternative investments; the amount that is forfeit by selecting one alternative over another. *Accounting* Potential income that is lost by resources committed to accounts receivable, inventory, etc. *Finance* In the evaluation of investment, as for new equipment or buildings, the amount that is forfeit by not committing resources to the best alternative investment.

opt Generally, to choose or select, as to opt for an alternative. To *opt out* is to decline, or back out, as of a commitment, membership, etc.

optical character recognition *Computers* Any of the systems or techniques for reading characters or symbols from hard copy and translating them into digital data for manipulation, such as a system that accepts input from a retail store checkout scan of product labels to ring up the sale, adjust inventory, etc. A program capability that involves reading graphic text from a hard copy or computer file, and translating it into characters that can be manipulated by the user.

optimal Descriptive of a course of action or solution to a problem that presents the best return for the least risk.

optimization Generally, to make the best use of, to get the most out of, or to accumulate as much as possible of something. Making the best use of facilities so as to maximize profit or output.

optimum capacity The volume of production in a manufacturing operation that results in the lowest unit cost. See also, **ideal capacity**.

option The right to choose or the act of choosing. Any of a number of alternatives or alternative courses of action available to one who must make a decision. *Computers* Any of the features of a program or application available to the user. *Finance* The right, acquired for consideration, to buy or sell an asset at an agreed price within a specified period. If the option is not executed within the specified time, it expires and the owner of the option forfeits the cost of the option. *Insurance* Any of the choices that may be made for exemptions or additional coverage that are not an integral part of the basic coverage of an insurance policy. *Marketing* Any feature that is not a standard part of a product or service, but that may be included for an extra charge.

oral contract An agreement that is not documented in writing. In most cases, oral contracts are valid, but are difficult to enforce because of the difficulty in establishing precise wording and intent.

order Generally, of a logical sequence or the act of arranging in logical sequence. *Commerce* Authorization to fabricate or provide a product or service for an agreed price. The goods or services so provided. *Computers* A program or application feature that arranges data in a sequence according to the user's instructions. *Law* A charge or command from a court or jurisdiction.

order entry *Commerce* The process of recording an order and performing the necessary tasks to assure that the order is filled. The procedure for order entry varies greatly from one company to another and from one industry to another. For example, an order for merchandise from a catalog house may require only an entry to the client's account, a warehouse order that authorizes picking, packing, and shipping of the merchandise, and a subsequent confirmation of shipping charges to post to the client's account. On the other hand, an order for custom fabricated goods may require the preparation of work orders for the plant, purchase orders and requisitions for materials, confirmation of delivery dates, etc.

order form *Commerce* A pre-printed form used to submit a request for merchandise from a wholesaler or manufacturer. *Marketing* In direct mail marketing, the form filled out by a client to request merchandise. Such forms are designed to simplify the process for the client, often requiring only that options be checked off and designed so that the order form itself becomes the mailer that conveys the order to the seller.

order number *Commerce* An identification number used to track a request for merchandise and the charges associated with it.

ordinance *Law* A statute or regulation enacted by a government body, especially of a municipality.

ordinary and necessary Descriptive of an expense that qualifies as deductible for income tax purposes, and that implies the expenditure was not frivolous or for personal gain.

ordinary course of business A conditional qualifier descriptive of any activity that is necessary and incidental to the conduct of business, and that by implication excludes any activity that does not so qualify.

ordinary life *Insurance* An insurance policy that provides a death benefit as well as a cash surrender value that builds throughout the life of the policy and is paid out at a specified age or after a number of years in force.

organization An association of individuals joined together for a specific purpose, as a business, social club, charity, etc.

organizational structure The manner is which the offices and lines of authority or a company or other establishment are arranged.

organization chart A graphic representation of the positions, departments, etc. in an organization and the lines of authority and communication between them.

organization cost, organization expense *Accounting* The costs to start a business or form a legal corporation, such as for legal fees, registration fees, franchise costs, etc. An intangible asset account that is carried on the company's books and may be amortized.

organized labor *Labor Relations* Collectively, the labor unions that engage in collective bargaining for their members.

orientation program Any program for introduction or familiarization with a company, environment, etc. Often referring to a briefing of new employees, orientation may be as simple as a tour of the office or plant, or it may be a series of meetings to familiarize an employee with every facet of the company's operation and his or her part in it.

original cost *Accounting* The purchase price of an asset plus all of the costs associated with bringing it on line, including shipping costs, modifications, testing, etc.

original entry *Accounting* The first recording of a financial transaction in a journal which may also contain an explanation or authorization for the entry.

original equipment Tools, supplies, parts, etc. that are sold to a fabricator to be joined to, and sold as part of, the final product, as the tires on a car or a monitor sold with a computer.

original equipment manufacturer Designating of one who makes a product that is furnished to another for resale to the consumer as an independent device or as part of another product.

OS/2, Operating System 2 *Computers* A program that controls all of the basic operations of the computer.

other expense *Accounting* An income statement account that reports extraordinary cost, that is, charges not associated with the normal conduct of business, or that would normally be matched against revenues of another period.

other income *Accounting* An income statement account that reports extraordinary revenue, that is, income not associated with the normal conduct of business, such as for a manufacturer receiving income for the sale of equipment or the rental of property.

outlet A location for distribution to the consumer, as a store or market. Sometimes, a shop that sells the goods, often seconds, of a particular manufacturer. Originally such outlet stores were located near a manufacturer or on the manufacturer's premises; however, increased popularity has prompted their establishment throughout the country, often in malls dedicated to such outlet stores.

out-of-pocket cost Generally, descriptive of expenses that have not been budgeted, or those for minor, miscellaneous items. *Accounting* Indicating of the direct costs of manufacturing, often used as the basis for the decision to accept a contract at a marginal price level. *Marketing* A miscellaneous allowance in a promotional budget to cover incidental expenses.

out of stock Descriptive of merchandise that is not immediately available when sought by a buyer. *Out of stock* implies a temporary condition that will be corrected by a reorder, a shipment in transit, or restocking by the manufacturer, rather than that the item is no longer available.

output The quantity of production achieved by a fabricator. *Computers* The results of processed data. Output may take such forms as personalized letters produced by combining copy for a standard letter with information contained in a database, financial or other reports for management, the checks and backup reports that make up a payroll, a production schedule, etc.

output device *Computers* A peripheral unit that delivers information to the user, such as a printer or plotter.

outside director Any member of the board of directors who is not employed by the company, often a lawyer, other professional, or business leader whose diverse opinions and contacts are of value to the firm.

outsourcing Buying the products or services of another firm, usually for a component of the buyer's product. Frequently used to designate only the purchase of goods or services to supplement in-house production when a company facility is **overbooked**.

outstanding *Finance* Designating of a debt that has not been paid or collected, or an instrument that has not been presented for payment, as a check.

overage *Accounting, Finance* The amount that a budget value is exceeded, such as for the expense of a project, or the materials required to produce an order. *Manufacturing* Excess product fabricated, as for a custom order.

overbooked Generally, of a condition in which a hotel, airline, etc. that has accepted reservations for more space than they have available. *Manufacturing* Often expressing a condition in which a manufacturing operation accepts more orders than it can fill in a timely fashion, either because of poor planning or unexpected production delays.

overdraft *Finance* A withdrawal, or attempt to withdraw, from a bank account, an amount in excess of the balance in the account.

overextended Of a business that has expanded its means of production in anticipation of an increase in demand that does not materialize, or one that is caught up in a growing market and expands to accommodate it without properly preparing for additional cash needs. *Finance* A situation in which one has made financial commitments or been allowed credit in excess of the ability to pay.

overflow *Computers* A condition in which the result of calculations is too large to be accommodated by a program, so that the number is truncated or an error condition is created.

overhead *Accounting* The costs, mostly fixed, that do not relate to a specific product or operation, such as rent, utilities, or administration. *Computers* Volatile memory that is used by various operating and utility functions, and is therefore not available for programs. Of the amount of volatile memory required by an application or utility.

overkill *Colloq.* That which is excessive. *Manufacturing* The extravagant allocation of resources to accomplish a task, resulting in needless extra expense. *Marketing* Excessive promotion of a product that wastes advertising dollars. Excessive claims for a product that may actually reduce sales because the buyer does not consider them believable.

overload *Computers* A condition that can cause a crash, brought on by an attempt to transfer more data than memory can hold, or transferring data faster than the CPU can process it.

overqualified *Labor Relations* Of one who is engaged in, or applying for, a type of work that does not require his or her level of education, experience, or competence. Employers are often reluctant to hire those who are overqualified because of concern that they may not adjust to the drop in status, and that they will leave as soon as more suitable employment becomes available.

overrun *Accounting, Finance* The amount by which a budgeted item exceeds projection, as a *cost overrun. Manufacturing* Surplus production beyond that called for by the order and that may not be readily sold.

oversold *Manufacturing* Of production facilities that cannot deliver the amount of goods by the date promised, either because of poor planning or unexpected delays. *Marketing* Of a prospect lavished with too much attention or a product for which extravagant claims are made, either of which may create concern about credibility, and cause a drop in sales.

overtime pay A premium for work beyond the normal daily or weekly hours set by law or contract; most hourly workers are covered by Federal law that decrees a minimum of a 50% premium over base pay for work beyond forty hours in one week, while union contracts often call for fewer regular time hours and a premium of 100% in certain situations.

overvalued *Accounting* Of an asset, such as inventory or a patent that is recorded on the books at a cost that is in excess of its market value.

overwrite *Computers* To save information to storage already occupied, thus obliterating the old data.

owner-operator Of one who owns and manages a business. Often used to describe a truck driver who operates his or her own rig and contracts for work through a service or another carrier.

owners' equity *Finance* The total value of the owners' interest in a business. The **net assets** of a company.

P

pack *Computers* The compression of data for more efficient use of disk storage space.

package *Computers* A desktop system that includes a computer, monitor, printer, programs, etc. Two or more programs sold as a unit. *Labor Relations* Descriptive of the aggregate of benefits, wages and fringes, that make up a collective bargaining agreement. *Marketing* The pieces that make up a direct mail packet, taken as a unit.

packaged goods Consumer products packaged for sale by the manufacturer.

packaged software *Computers* A program that is available on the open market, adaptable to a variety of uses.

packing list An accounting of the material contained in a shipment. An inventory of the contents of a package.

padding *Colloq.* Uncalled-for additions, often for personal gain, as in cheating on an expense account. *Marketing* Embellishing the claims for a product in advertising.

page *Computers* A unit of memory used by the computer to manipulate data in storage. A single sheet of output from the printer.

pagination *Computers* The numbering of printed pages in a document or file.

paid-in capital *Finance* Money paid by investors in exchange for stock.

paper *Finance* Generally, notes or other obligations.

paper feeder *Computers* The device that controls the flow of paper through the printer.

parallel *Computers* Descriptive of operations that occur simultaneously.

parallel interface *Computers* A multichannel interface that allows the transfer of a full computer word at one time.

parallel port *Computers* A connection on the computer for communicating with a peripheral device, such as a printer.

parallel processing *Computers* Processing of two or more tasks simultaneously by a computer.

parameter *Computers* A limit or characteristic, as of a program or operating system.

parent company A company that has ownership or control of another company or companies. Ownership of a subsidiary may be incidental to the operation of a parent company, or it may be its only purpose. See also **holding company.**

parse *Computers* To break down into parts, as in separating the elements of a data string from a database into columns for a spreadsheet.

partition *Computers* A divider, as on a disk for file management or for processing a database sort.

partnership *Law, Finance* An organization owned by two or more persons who are individually responsible for the debts of the partnership. See also, **limited partnership.**

password *Computers* A series of characters or symbols by which a user gains access to a computer, application or file.

past due *Finance* Of any note or obligation that has not been paid by the due date.

patent *Law* An official public document that grants a special right or privilege; usually, of the exclusive right to manufacture, or to profit from the manufacture, of an invention for a specified period of time.

patent pending Statement issued after a claim for patent is filed so as to serve notice of such filing during the time that a patent search is being conducted to determine whether the invention is indeed unique and patentable according to law.

paternalistic Of the nature of a father. Descriptive of a company whose management tends to take a fatherly interest in the employees.

path *Computers* The course followed by the computer in seeking programs and files.

patron One who supports or encourages; a benefactor. In business, a regular client.

pattern recognition *Computers* The technique used by a program to identify elements through comparison with a standard matrix as in optical character recognition.

pay *Accounting* To render to an individual or company, that which is due for goods or services rendered, etc. To discharge a debt or other obligation by reimbursement.

payback, payback period *Accounting, Finance* The time required to recoup the investment in a project. Basically, payback is calculated by dividing the amount of the investment by the amount of money the investment will return each year. Various methods, however, take differing views in calculating the amount of money returned. For example, a simple payback for investment in manufacturing equipment may discount profit on the goods produced during the payback period, considering it as part of the return, whereas a marginal payback may deduct profits, as well as the interest that could be earned on the money invested from the return, thus arriving at a longer payback period.

payee The one to whom a payment is made or to whom a debt is owed.

payer The one pays money owed or is obligated to pay at some time in the future.

payload *Commerce* Any commodity carried by truck, train, airplane, etc. The portion of a cargo that is producing revenue.

payout *Accounting* Any disbursement of funds.

pay period *Accounting* The interval for which salaries or wages are calculated and paid. Customarily, wages are paid daily or weekly, while salaries are often weekly, bi-weekly, semi-monthly, or monthly.

payroll *Accounting* The total paid out by a company for salaries and wages during a given period. The total cost to a company for labor, including amounts paid out to workers, plus deductions for withholding tax, FICA, insurance, pension fund, union dues, etc., and the employer's contribution to FICA, unemployment insurance, medical or retirement benefits, etc.

payroll register *Accounting* A complete record of payroll for all employees, including current and accumulated, regular and overtime hours, sick pay, vacation pay, deductions, etc.

PC, personal computer Generally, a small computer used by a single person, although it may be networked with other computers or file servers. *Personal computer* has been commonly synonymous with *desktop computer*, but new, powerful, laptop and notebook computers are increasingly becoming the machine of choice for a personal computer.

peak Descriptive of the time or period of greatest activity, such as the primary buying season for a particular product.

pecuniary *Financial* Involving money, as *pecuniary damages* that is monetary compensation for injury.

peddler An itinerant salesperson who deals in a variety of merchandise. *Colloq.* Any salesperson.

penalty *Finance* A charge for the late payment of a debt or other obligation. In some loan or mortgage contracts, or in the absence of a prepayment clause in a loan or mortgage contract, a charge for repaying before the maturity date. A charge for early withdrawal of an investment. *Law* Punishment imposed by a court, as for commission of a crime or a negligent act. That which is forfeited by not exercising a right, as the payment for an option to buy or sell.

pencil pusher *Colloq.* An office worker.

penny stock *Finance* Speculative shares commonly trading for less than one dollar. Gen

Generally, a term of disparagement, although some have achieved investment grade over time.

pension fund *Finance* Money accumulated for the payment of pensions to workers after retirement, mostly invested in a number of stocks and bonds, seeking the best return to fill cash needs in the future.

pension plan *Finance* A program established by a company, labor union or other organization that provides income for workers after retirement. Such programs typically are financed to a greater or lesser extent by both employers and employees.

per annum By or for the year; annually.

per capita For each person, such as *per capita income* that is the total income of a particular group of people, a nation, etc. divided by the number of persons in the group.

perceived value *Marketing* The apparent worth to the observer of a thing regardless of actual material value, as a consumer product. *Perceived value* can be an important element in the pricing of consumer goods, when a small change may make a product more attractive to the buyer, and lead to an increase in sales and profits.

per diem By the day; for each day, as an allowance for expenses.

perfect competition *Finance* A condition in the marketplace wherein no buyer or seller has the power to dominate or significantly influence the price of a product or service.

perfected Amended or modified to the point that further improvement is impossible. In actual use, often an expression of that which has been developed to the point of being satisfactory for the use intended, as a product or a process.

performance Generally, an act or accomplishment. *Law* Fulfillment of an obligation, especially for duty specified by a contract. *Finance* Of the return achieved by an investment. *Manufacturing* Of the quality of operation, such as for employees or equipment.

performance bond *Finance* A third party guarantee of the satisfactory completion of a contract; in the event of default the **surety** agrees to take over the contract or to pay damages up to the limit of the bond.

period *Accounting* An interval of time between events, as an accounting period of approximately thirty days. The number of intervals into which an event is divided, as twelve accounting periods in the year.

period cost *Accounting* An indirect expense that is linked to time rather than units of production, as utilities, rent, administrative expense, etc.

periodic costing *Accounting* A system of calculating the cost of goods and services by measuring expenses for an accounting period, such as a month, against the number of units processed or delivered during that time. Periodic costing is most effective for measuring the performance of a company, division, or department that produces a standard product that does not vary appreciably from one day to the next.

peripheral *Computers* A device that is connected to a computer and controlled by it.

peripheral program *Computers* A utility; a program that adds to the capabilities of a computer or another program, such as a memory manager or grammar checker.

perjury *Law* Willfully telling a lie while under oath. In some jurisdictions, any false swearing in a legal document.

perk *Colloq.* Perquisite. A privilege, fringe benefit, etc. accorded to one in a particular position in the organization, or for all above a certain level in the hierarchical structure of a company, such as a company car or private office.

permanent financing Long-term debt, such as bonds, or equity financing, as for stock.

permanent memory *Computers* A storage medium, such as a computer disk, that retains its memory when power is off.

permit A license or other document giving permission, as for building, conducting a business, etc.

perpetual inventory A system for recording goods transferred to, and removed from, inventory, with a running total showing the effect of each transaction. Some systems also track goods on order or in process, and those that have been promised or allotted for a purpose, so that in addition to an accounting of goods on hand, the inventory record contains notice of anticipated changes for the near future. Such a system allows for the reordering of goods when the amount in inventory plus the amount on order drops below a certain level. Periodically, the book inventory is confirmed or adjusted by a physical count of the stock on hand.

perquisite See perk.

per se *Law* By itself; requiring no further proof to establish existence, as negligence that is clearly a breach of duty, and does not require evidence of the existence of the duty.

person *Law* An individual or corporation that has certain legal rights and obligations.

personal computer See PC.

personal injury Damage to an individual, such as invasion of privacy, slander, or bodily harm, in contrast to property damage.

personal liability The exposure, or potential exposure, of all of one's assets to the claims of another, especially for the obligations of a business. Shareholders in a corporation and limited partners are normally protected, as their exposure is limited to their investment. General partners and owners of an unincorporated business, however, are personally responsible for the debts and other obligations of the company.

personal property *Law* Assets owned that can be moved, in contrast to real property and those attachments to real property that cannot be removed without damage to the property.

personnel Collectively, the individuals employed by an organization; those who make up a company's work force.

personnel administration See **personnel management**.

personnel department The office or unit within an organization that is responsible for the screening, hiring, testing, training, etc. of job candidates as well as other administrative tasks associated with the work force, such as posting notices as required by law or at the direction of management, maintenance of each employee's personnel file, tracking eligibility for benefits and keeping records of participation, filing claims, etc. In addition, the personnel department may be responsible for other programs, such as for safety or health, or the publication of a company newsletter.

personnel management The study and implementation of programs for attracting, screening, training, and retaining good employees of the type and number required by the company.

person-to-person call A telephone call placed to a particular person; such a call is place through an operator who determines that the person called is on the line before releasing the line to the caller. See also, **collect call**.

persuasion *Marketing* The process of influencing people to buy a product or service.

Peter Principle The maxim that "every employee tends to rise to his level of incompetence" first stated by Dr. Lawrence J. Peter.

petition *Law* A formal appeal to a court stating the particulars that are seen as cause for judicial action and containing a request for such action .

petty cash *Accounting* An amount of cash that is usually kept in an office to pay incidental expenses or reimburse employees for out-of-pocket costs.

physical inventory An actual count of materials, supplies, finished goods, etc. that are on hand in a storage area or on the shop floor, often taken to confirm the amount shown by a **perpetual inventory** system

picketing *Labor Relations* A demonstration by those attempting to publicize a dispute and garner support, often in connection with labor negotiations.

piece work Descriptive of labor performed by an individual whose wage is at least in part determined by the level of output.

piercing the corporate veil *Law* A court action that denies the protection of the corporate entity to certain officers or representatives of a corporation who are held accountable for their actions when, for example, they formed the corporation in order to perpetuate fraud.

piggyback *Commerce* The transporting of truck trailers on rail cars for long distance hauls.

pilferage The stealing of small amounts of goods, as by losses of goods in transit, or the misappropriation of company property by an employee.

PIM, personal information manager *Computers* A utility program that provides a means to record data important to an individual, such as a note pad or address book.

pin feed *Computers* A device that feeds a continuous form through a printer by engaging a series of holes along the edges of the form; same as *tractor feed* or *sprocket feed*.

pirated software *Computers* Programs obtained outside of the normal or legal channels.

pixel *Computers* Picture element; a basic component of a computer graphic.

placement Generally, of the installation or disposition of a person or thing. *Labor Relations* Finding employment for an individual who is out of work. Finding the proper position in a company for a candidate for employment. *Marketing* Securing a specific location for an advertisement, as on a particular page or segment of a publication.

plan B *Colloq.* An often hypothetical alternative to a plan.

planned obsolescence *Manufacturing* Fabricating a product with more emphasis on low cost than on durability. *Marketing* Promoting a newer style of an existing product in hopes of convincing the buyer to disregard utility and discard the older model for a newer one.

plant *Accounting* The assets of a company used in the manufacture of goods. The area that is set aside for manufacturing a product, as distinctive from the office area.

pleading *Law* The statement of facts that establish a cause of action in a court of law.

pledge *Law* The transfer of property as security for a debt or other obligation.

plow back *Colloq.* To return profit to a company as working capital or for the acquisition of assets to support the growth of the organization.

plotter *Computers* A computer peripheral that produces charts or graphs as output.

point *Finance* In the trading of stocks, equal to one dollar. In describing interest rates, such as for a bond or mortgage, equal to one percent.

point-of-purchase *Marketing* Of an advertising display placed in the area where merchandise is sold, as in a store or a store window.

point-of-sale See **point-of-purchase**.

point of sale system *Computers* A computer network that accepts input from remote terminals located at a retailer's cash register and uses the data to perform a variety of tasks such as creating sales reports, updating inventory records, etc.

point and click *Computers* The act of selecting an object by moving the mouse cursor to it, then pressing and releasing the mouse button.

poison pill *Finance* Any strategy by a company targeted for takeover that makes it less attractive to the prospective buyer.

pollution Generally, that which makes impure or unclean. In industry, usually descriptive of effluence that is a by-product or residue from a manufacturing process and that is contaminating the environment.

Ponzi scheme An illegal program to defraud investors, whereby part of the money paid into the program is used to pay high initial returns in order to attract more money that is partly paid out, etc. until the operator disappears.

port *Computers* Any of the connections to a computer that enable the transfer of data.

portal-to-portal pay Wages that accrue from the time the worker leaves home or shop until he or she returns, often of a worker such as a plumber or electrician who normally travels to the client's site to work.

portfolio *Finance* All of the stock, bonds, and other securities held by a particular individual or institutional investor at one time.

posting *Accounting* The recording of a financial transaction in a journal or ledger.

power of attorney *Law* An instrument in writing that attests to the authority of one to act in the place of another in certain circumstances, as for the sale of property.

power surge *Computers* A sudden increase in line voltage that can interfere with communications and is potentially damaging to the elements of a computer and the data stored. Such damage can usually be avoided by the use of a **surge protector**.

practical capacity *Manufacturing* The largest volume of product that can be manufactured efficiently when taking into consideration normal delays as for equipment malfunction, employee absence, etc.

pre-billing *Accounting* The practice of tendering an invoice for goods or services before delivery, that may be normal procedure in certain types of business, or as in the case of a client without approved credit when the seller requests payment in advance for part or all of the invoice. In other cases, a seller may bill in advance of delivery with the agreement of the client in order to protect cash flow, or the client may request invoicing in order to show the payable in the current accounting period, as for a government agency working within a strict budget allocation system. Such billing, when recorded on the company's books as revenue requires offsetting entries for anticipated cost in order to match cost and revenue for the period.

predatory pricing *Marketing* Lower than normal pricing of a product as a device to gain entrance to a market or gain a larger share of the market.

preexisting use *Law* Of a property located in an area for which zoning has changed, but which is exempted from the new regulations to the extent that the property existed for other use prior to the effective date of the new ordinance.

preferred stock *Finance* An equity share in the ownership of a company that has preference over common stock in the payment of dividends and in the distribution of assets in event of dissolution. Preferred stock does not entitle the holder to vote for the members of the board of directors.

premises *Law* A general term for buildings and land whose specific meaning varies with the context in which it is used. In respect to a worker, for example, it may mean anywhere that he or she is sent in the course of performing a job.

premium *Insurance* The amount paid as a lump sum or periodically to keep protection in force. *Marketing* Of the relative quality of a product. A gift, bonus, or reward offered to a prospect as an incentive to buy.

premium pay *Labor Relations* Generally, any addition to the regular wage scale, as overtime pay, shift differential, etc.

prepackaged *Marketing* Of a product that is packed and marked by the manufacturer, often to the retailer's specifications, so that it may be sold to the consumer without opening or altering the package in any way.

prepaid Of that which is paid in advance. *Commerce* Indicating of freight charges that have been paid or are to be paid by the shipper directly to the carrier. Reimbursement for such charges is a matter between buyer and seller.

prepaid expense *Accounting* Of a periodic expense that has been documented in the financial records of the company, whether or not actually paid, and that applies to a future accounting period. Such an expense is carried on the balance sheet as a current asset.

prepayment clause *Finance* A designation in a loan agreement that sets forth the terms for payment prior to the due date of the loan, such as for penalty, computation of interest, etc.

preprocessing *Computers* Configuring data before it is entered into a program, such as by checking for invalid data, or by converting spreadsheet rows to comma separated values for entering into a database.

presentation Generally, that which is submitted, conferred, or shown. In business, frequently a well-prepared speech accompanied by visuals, intended to sell a product or idea to a large group of people. *Law* Producing a negotiable instrument of debt for acceptance or payment; *presentment*.

present value *Finance* Of the current worth of a sum to be received in the future; the amount of money that would have to be invested at a fixed rate to yield a certain amount within a particular length of time.

presort Of mail that is sorted by zip code and bagged by the mailer, and which is then carried by the postal service at a reduced rate.

press kit A package containing press releases and related material that is generally disseminated to publicize an event.

prestige pricing *Marketing* The practice of increasing the price of a product to a level that engenders, or maintains, in the mind of the consumer, the perception of quality. The practice in a retail establishment of stocking only those goods that by their price create a perception of quality.

presumption *Law* The assumption of fact based on the knowledge of other facts.

pretax *Accounting, Finance* Of final amounts, such as profit, that have not be adjusted for taxes.

preventive maintenance *Manufacturing* The practice of, or a system for, regularly servicing equipment that is not malfunctioning in the hope of preventing or delaying malfunction.

price *Commerce* Variously, the amount of money or other consideration asked for something, or the amount for which it is traded. In the case of goods or services offered at a discount, for example, the price quoted as a normal selling price must be the price at which a significant quantity of the goods or services were sold.

price discrimination *Marketing* Offering goods for sale to a merchant at a higher or lower price than that quoted to others in similar circumstances.

priced out of the market *Marketing* Of goods or services that are priced too high to sell in a particular market, often of those that have increased in price over time.

price-earnings ratio *Finance* A comparison of the cost of a share of stock at a given time to the annual proceeds per share for the company.

price fixing Generally, any combination of manufacturers, retailers, or of retailers and manufacturers that serves to interfere with the pricing of goods and services. *Law* Under federal antitrust laws, any conspiracy that interferes with the freedom of merchants and their right to price goods or services according to their best judgment.

prima facie *Law* On its face or at first view, that is, apparent at a glance or not requiring further evidence to prove existence, credibility, etc.

primary market *Market* The geographical location or group of buyers that comprises the main area of sales for a product.

prime rate *Finance* The interest rate that a bank charges its most creditworthy clients. Most interest rates are described in terms of the amount over the prime rate.

principal *Commerce* Any of the main parties to a transaction, as a landlord and tenant. *Finance, Law* An amount of money that is owed or on which interest is paid. *Law* One who has committed or aided in the commission of a crime. One who has directed or allowed another to act as his or her agent.

principle A fundamental doctrine, or truth.

print advertising *Marketing* Any material that promotes a company, product, service, etc. in a periodical, such as a newspaper, magazine, etc.

print buffer *Computers* An area of memory reserved for holding data to be transmitted to the printer, allowing operation in the background while other processing is taking place.

print control character *Computers* Any of the symbols that control the operation or output of the printer, as for line spacing, double width characters, etc.

printed circuit *Computers* A circuit created by applying a conductor to an insulated board.

printer fonts *Computers* Type fonts built into a printer or a printer cartridge.

printout *Computers* The printed result of data processing, such as mailing labels, reports, etc.

priority mail A classification used by the postal service for the sending of parcels by first class mail.

prior period adjustment *Finance* A balance sheet item that corrects an error in reporting for the previous accounting period, entered for the purpose of correcting retained earnings and duly noting that it is not a reflection of activities for the current period.

private brand *Merchandising* A trademark name that is owned by a wholesaler or retail chain and usually sold by no other. Most major food chains have their own line or lines of private brands, also called **house brand**.

private enterprise See free enterprise.

private sector Of the segments of the economy that include households and business, and exclude government.

privatization The process of making private, as by buying back the stock of a public company, or turning over a government enterprise to private interests.

probability The likelihood that a thing will happen.

probation *Labor Relations* A trial period or one of testing, as a trial period for a new employee, or disciplinary period for a permanent employee as a last resort before dismissal.

proceeds *Finance* The net funds received from a sale, investment, business venture, etc.

process A particular means of doing something, or the act of doing something following a prescribed method. *Law* A writ directing appearance or compliance.

processing The act of doing something in a prescribed fashion. *Computers* The manipulation of data by the computer.

procurement The process of buying materials and supplies, hiring workers, etc.

product *Colloq.* Commercial goods collectively, as those from a particular company or industry. *Manufacturing* That which is produced; the output of manufacturing or fabrication.

product class *Commerce* A broad grouping of goods that are used by a particular class of buyer, as *household products* or *industrial products*, or a group of goods designed for similar use that are generally considered to be interchangeable, differing only in brand name, quality, appearance, etc.

product costing *Accounting* The recording and analysis of expenses related to the production of goods so as to establish a manufacturing cost.

product development The evaluation and testing of ideas for the creation of new merchandise or improvements to existing goods.

product differentiation *Marketing* A technique for the promotion and marketing of a product that calls for stressing the way in which it is different from competing products.

product fit *Manufacturing* The way in which the fabrication of a new item adapts to the existing equipment and systems. *Marketing* Placement of new product promotion and sales into that of the line of existing products, for example, whether it is to be merged into a product group, or become an upscale version of an existing item.

production capacity *Manufacturing* Any of a number of criteria for determining the maximum output of an operation or manufacturing plant.

production control *Manufacturing* The process, or the department that implements the process, of scheduling materials, machine time, manpower, etc. for the manufacture of orders on hand in a timely fashion.

production line *Manufacturing* A manufacturing technique that involves a series of contiguous stations, each of which performs a portion of the work required for the manufacture or assembly of a product, or part of a product.

productivity *Manufacturing* Descriptive of the level of the output of a manufacturing operation, production line, or machine relative to a standard.

product liability *Law* The principle in the law of torts that one who manufactures or sells a product is responsible for exercising reasonable care to insure that the product is not only safe to be used as intended, but that there is no other inherent danger in possessing the product and that if a defective product is sold, liability may be incurred when there is harm to the buyer as the result of those defects.

product line *Marketing* A group of items that are similar, such as for hair care or car care, directed toward a particular audience, and manufactured by a single producer or distributor.

product manager *Marketing* One who is responsible for the marketing of a product or a line of similar products for a company. See also **brand manager**.

product mix *Marketing* Of the variety of items that are sold by a company.

product positioning *Marketing* Strategic placement of a manufactured item in the mind of a potential buyer through advertising, as by stressing quality, price, style, etc.

profession Of a vocation that requires considerable training and intellect, as medicine, law, engineering, etc. Collectively, all of those who pursue any such vocation. *Colloq.* Any occupation.

profit *Accounting* Money left in a business or for distribution to shareholders after all costs and charges have been deducted from sales.

profitability *Accounting* Generally, a measure of earnings in relation to sales or assets. Often a measure of the return on a machine or manufacturing operation.

profit center *Accounting* A segment of a business that produces a profit on its own, as a division or subsidiary, or one that contributes to profit, as a department or machine.

profit margin *Accounting* A ratio of income to sales.

pro forma Literally, according to form. *Accounting, Finance* Financial statements that represent events anticipated, as the start of a new business or major changes in an existing one.

program An orderly procedure for accomplishing something, as an *employee training program*. *Computers* A set of instructions for the processing of data.

program compatibility *Computers* Descriptive of the ability of programs to work together or to share data.

programmable *Computers* Descriptive of a device whose function can be altered by the user.

programmable function key *Computers* A function key to which a command or series of commands may be assigned.

programmable mouse *Computers* A computer mouse that may be assigned commands that are executed by the mouse buttons in conjunction with keyboard keys.

programmer *Computer* One who writes instructions for a computer to accomplish a specific task.

programming language *Computers* A precise system of vocabulary and syntax for writing instructions for the computer; a high level language.

program package *Computers* All of the files and manuals needed to run a particular program. Descriptive of the qualities of a program. A set of applications, as for accounting functions, that make up a program.

projection A prediction or estimate of future results based on experience.

promissory note *Finance* A promise in writing to pay a specified amount by a certain date to a particular party or to the bearer of the note.

promoter One who advocates a cause, or finances and organizes an activity. *Law* One who drafts a plan and sets out to raise the capital to start a corporation.

promotion allowance *Marketing* An agreed amount paid to a merchant or distributor by a manufacturer for advertising or promotion of a product, often in relation to the amount of the product purchased.

prompt *Computers* A cursor; a highlight on the monitor screen that indicates where the next character will be entered. A program query or instruction.

property That which is owned, as real estate, personal goods, etc.

property line The boundary of a plot of real estate.

property rights *Law* The right to ownership and profits from land or other possessions.

property tax Assessment by a municipality on the owners of real estate.

proportional spacing *Computers* In desktop publishing, descriptive of the display of type so that the white space between characters is approximately the same regardless of the width of the character itself.

proprietary software *Computers* Packaged software that is sold with the provision that the seller retains ownership and the buyer purchases only the license to use the software subject to the provisions of a licensing agreement.

proprietorship A business enterprise owned by one person.

pro rata In proportion.

prorate *Accounting* To distribute proportionally, as the allocation of expense to match it with the proper period or revenue.

pros and cons Of the reasons for or against a proposal.

prospect *Marketing* A possible customer; one who may be interested in a particular product.

prospectus Generally, information about an enterprise or institution, often one that is new, describing features, attractions, etc. *Finance, Law* A document disclosing the financial condition of a corporation, required by law to be furnished to each prospective purchaser of the firm's securities.

protected field *Computers* A block of text, formula, etc. in a computer program that cannot be altered, usually user-defined.

protected files *Computers* Read-Only files; computer memory that may be read, but that cannot be altered.

protectionism A policy that advocates restricting the importation of foreign goods in order to protect domestic production.

protocol *Computers* The conventions governing the transfer of data between a computer and peripherals, or another computer.

proviso *Law* A condition, stipulation, or clarification in a contract, statute, etc.

proximate cause *Law* That which directly effects a result and without which such result would not have occurred.

proxy Generally the authority to act for another. *Law, Finance* The empowerment, or one who is empowered, to vote the shares of another at a stockholder's meeting.

proxy statement *Finance* Information that is required by Securities and Exchange Commission regulations to be given to each shareholder prior to corporate elections.

prudence The quality of exercising sound judgment.

prudent man rule *Law* The standard for judging that a trustee who is allowed latitude in investment decisions has acted properly to preserve the principal and seek a reasonable return on investment.

public accountant A licensed accountant who performs professional accounting services for the general public. Licensing requirements are not as stringent as for a **certified public account**, a designation that is more prestigious; however, the public accountant is qualified to perform most of the same tasks.

public corporation A corporation formed by a political entity for a specific purpose, such as that of a municipality, water district, postal service, etc.

public domain *Law* Comprising all of the lands and waters owned by the United States and the states individually, as distinguished from that owned by individuals or corporations. Of information that may be derived by anyone and that is not subject to copyright.

public interest Generally descriptive of that which is considered not to be disruptive or threatening to the safety of the general public. *Public interest* encompasses a very broad sense of values and is most usually defined by the negative, that is, those things that are *contrary* to public interest, in which context may be placed a broad category of offenses to an individual or to society collectively.

publicity *Marketing* That part of promotion dealing with efforts to make the public take notice of a person, product, company, etc.

public land See **public domain**.

publicly held *Finance* Of a corporation whose shares are owned by a broad range of investors.

public offering *Finance* A proposition for the sale of securities to a broad range of investors.

public policy An official attitude regarding a matter of public interest that may impact on the conduct of business, introduction of legislation, etc.

public record Generally, government documents that are readily available to the community, such as records of real estate transaction, court actions, etc.

public relations Of the wide dissemination of information intended to cast a favorable light on a person, company, or situation.

public sector *Finance* Of that part of the economy relating to government and governmental bodies, as contrasted to business or households.

public service advertising Free advertising that is directed to the common good, as by government or private welfare agencies promoting health or safety.

public utility A privately owned, government supervised, corporation that sells services to the public, such as for electricity or water.

public works Projects for the benefit of the public, sponsored by a government body, such as the construction of schools or roads.

punitive damages *Law* Payment in addition to compensation for actual losses, levied as a punishment in cases of willful or malicious misconduct.

purchase Generally, to obtain for a price. That which is obtained for a price. *Law* To acquire property in exchange for valuable consideration.

purchase order A document that authorizes a vendor to furnish goods or services as outlined in the document and for an agreed price.

purchasing agent One who is responsible for obtaining materials, supplies, services, etc. that are required in the normal operation of business.

purchasing power The value of money based on the goods and services that it can buy.

pure competition Descriptive of an ideal condition in which there are many buyers and sellers of a stable product so that none can cause undue influence on the supply or demand; where there is easy access to, and departure from, the market; and there is no collaboration to fix prices, supplies, etc.

pyramiding Generally, the extended use of **leverage** to promote expansion. *Finance* The use of unrealized profits in an investment to secure financing for purchasing further investments. *Law* Any scheme that attempts to defraud by creating an impression of worth where little or none exists, such as a **Ponzi scheme**. *Marketing* A marketing plan in which non-exclusive rights to distribute a line of consumer products are sold along with the products.

Q

qualified endorsement *Finance* A signature on the back of a check or other negotiable that transfers the payment to another, or that restricts the condition of payment, such as *for deposit only*.

qualified opinion *Accounting, Finance* An auditor's comment as to any limitation, reservation or exception that is taken to the financial statement, as for the possible effects of pending litigation or tax liability.

qualified prospect *Marketing* An individual or organization that has been identified by lifestyle, need, etc. as a prospective buyer for a particular product. Often used as well to describe one who has the authority and the resources to buy.

quality Any of the distinctive characteristics of a thing, often implying rank or grade.

quality control *Manufacturing* Of the efforts to maintain a grade of product that adheres to a certain standard, set by company policy, engineering specifications, etc. The responsibility for controlling quality is normally divided between production personnel and those of an independent department or unit within the company. Production workers have an ongoing obligation to monitor the quality of goods as they are produced, whereas the quality control unit is often responsible for more detailed testing of incoming materials and finished goods, collecting statistical data and reporting on failure rates, etc.

quantity discount *Marketing* A rebate, offered by a manufacturer, distributor, etc., for the purchase of multiple units of an item in an attempt to create additional sales and based on the premise that the rebate reflects a saving in **handling** cost.

quarterly Every three months, as a periodic financial reports, etc.

quasi contract *Law* An informal contract, said to exist when in the normal course of business, a service that is not specifically contracted is performed in conjunction with that contracted. When such performance is of clear benefit to the buyer, the seller is entitled to compensation, such as for the replacement of a worn part that affects the smooth operation of an automobile engine when the buyer contracted for a tune-up.

query language *Computers* Formal program notation for requesting specific data, as from a database.

queue *Computers* A list of files or data batches for processing, such as those to be printed out.

quick assets *Finance* Cash and those assets that can be readily turned into cash such as accounts receivable, or marketable securities.

quick ratio *Finance* A comparison of **quick assets** with current liabilities, a measure of an organization's ability to quickly liquidate current liabilities.

quid pro quo *Law* Literally, what for what, or the giving of something for something. **Consideration**, as that which each party to a contract is given in return for that which each gives.

quitclaim deed A document relinquishing ones claim to a property without acknowledging that such a claim ever existed. A quitclaim deed, therefore, does not convey clear title.

quota Generally, an amount or share that is assigned. *Manufacturing* The number of units of production expected from a manufacturing operation, an assembly line, a group of workers, a machine, etc. *Marketing* The number or value of units expected to be sold by an individual, in a particular market, or in total during a given period. In a time of shortage, the number of units allocated to each client or to a particular market.

quotation A statement of the price at which an item or group of items is offered for sale. Response to an inquiry that may be a simple statement of price or one that includes a detailed description of the item or items.

QWERTY keyboard *Computers* A keyboard with letters arranged the same as those on a typewriter.

R

racket *Colloq.* Any dishonest practice. Often, any means of earning money with relative ease. *Law* Obtaining money illegally, as by extortion or fraud; *racketeering*.

rack jobber *Marketing* A wholesaler who sells a variety of convenience merchandise and who maintains the display for such merchandise in the customer's store or outlet.

raider *Finance* A person or corporation who threatens to take control of a company by a controlling interest in its stock.

RAM, random access memory *Computers* Very fast memory that can be accessed independent of the previous access. Such memory is used to temporarily hold the programs and data being processed; such memory is lost when the computer is shut down.

random sampling *Manufacturing* Selection of a number of items in which each choice is independent of all previous choices, that is, there is no pattern to the selection. A system of random sampling is normally used for quality control testing on the theory that a regularly placed sample, such as the first of each batch of one hundred, or regularly timed, as selected at a certain time of the day, is more likely to exhibit a pattern of defects that does not mirror the pattern one might find if all were inspected.

range *Computers* All of the values that a variable may assume. In a spreadsheet or database, user-defined limits of data affected by a command.

rank and file Generally, blue collar workers, or employees who are not a part of management. *Labor Relations* The dues paying member of a union.

rate card *Marketing* A schedule of media rates showing cost for single insertion, discounts for multiple insertion, etc. and other information pertinent to placing an ad, such as mechanical requirements, etc.

rate of return See **return on investment**

rat race *Colloq.* Of the level of activity and stress involved in building a career or just making a living, often disparagingly, as of rats racing on a wheel and going nowhere.

raw data *Computer, Marketing* Descriptive of information that has been collected, but that has not been catalogued or analyzed.

raw material *Accounting, Manufacturing* Ingredients, components, or goods that are to be converted to a finished product.

read-only *Computers* Of a file or other section of memory that can be accessed, but not changed.

read/write head *Computers* The device in a disk drive that reads from and writes to the storage disk.

real estate *Finance, Law* Land and anything fixed to the surface, as a building, fence, trees, etc., and that which is beneath, as minerals, or above.

real property Same as **real estate**.

realtor One who acts as agent for those who wish to buy or sell real estate.

reasonable *Law* A subjective quality by which actions are often judged, especially in cases of tort liability, as for *reasonable care*, that is the caution expected of one in a particular set of circumstances, or of a *reasonable person*, that is one who exercises a measure of intelligence and judgment required by society for protection of their common interests.

rebate *Marketing* An amount refunded or deducted from an invoice for goods or services as a reward for a volume purchase, reimbursement for promotional expense, etc. Occasionally, an illegal **kickback**.

recall The calling back of a faulty product for refund, replacement, or repair by a manufacturer, sometimes ordered by a government agency when public safety is a consideration.

receipt *Commerce* A document drawn by a seller or shipper, with copies for the buyer or receiver, that attests to payment or delivery or both.

receivables *Accounting* The aggregate of all the claims for payment due a company.

receiver *Finance, Law* One who is appointed by a court to oversee and preserve property that is the subject of litigation, usually **insolvency**. In such cases, the receiver takes possession, but not title, of the entity and manages its affairs as a going concern pending final disposition.

receiving record *Commerce* A document, register, or account of goods delivered to a warehouse, retail store, manufacturing plant, etc. In some instances, a document is prepared with detailed information about each shipment received; in others, a single document contains a list of a shipments received for the day with any variances noted on the shipping papers, that are attached as the source documents. In all cases, receiving records are used to verify invoices as they are received.

reciprocity An exchange for mutual benefit. *Commerce* Often, an informal agreement whereby two or more companies offer mutual courtesy, as by each selling their products to the other.

reclamation *Manufacturing* The process of making or recovering useful products from waste, as by processing used photographic film to recover the silver. See also **recycling**.

reconciliation *Accounting* A balancing, so as to bring into agreement, such as for ledger accounts or a bank statement.

record Any documenting of a transaction; the transaction so documented. *Accounting* To make an entry into the journals or ledgers of a company. *Computers* A unique set of information in a database. See also **field**.

recoup To regain something or an equivalent, as the amount of an investment, or of a loss. *Law* To hold back a portion, or reduce the amount, of a claim with valid reason for doing so, such as proof of an earlier payment against the claim.

recourse *Finance, Law* The right to pursue a judgment that is not limited to the property held as security, against one who defaults on a debt.

recovery *Accounting* The residual value of an asset after it has been fully depreciated. The recouping of overhead expense by allocation to various profit centers. *Law* The establishment of a due and just debt by action of a court.

recruitment *Labor Relations* The process of attracting, screening, and hiring personnel.

recycling Reprocessing that which is considered waste to make it into a usable product, most common for plastic, paper and glass that are recycled for use in making special grades of the same product. See also **reclamation**.

redlining *Finance, Law* Illegal discrimination against borrowers living in certain neighborhoods.

red tape *Colloq.* Of the elaborate procedures or forms required to accomplish a task, often through a government agency.

reference check *Labor Relations* The process of verifying the information on an employment application as to places of previous employment, time of employment, reason for leaving, etc. as well as to learn as much as possible about the applicant.

referral Generally, the directing of information to another. Often a recommendation, as for employment, use of a product, etc.

refinance *Finance* To restructure debt or obligations to better suit a person or company's needs, as by extending the term, increasing the principal, etc.

reformat *Computers* To change the style of a body of text, as by altering margins, type face, etc. To convert a file for use by a different application.

refresh *Computers* To revive or renew volatile memory so as to maintain or record changes, such as by redrawing the image on the monitor screen.

refund *Finance* To refinance an obligation, usually to save interest charges. *Marketing* To reimburse a buyer for returned merchandise, or for a promotional **rebate**.

refusal *Commerce, Law* The right of a buyer to reject that which is furnished under a contractual agreement.

registered check *Finance* A check issued by a bank for a client who sets aside funds in the amount of the check.

registered mail Mail that may be insured, and that is signed for by each postal employee handling it and by the recipient, verification of delivery furnished by the postal service. See also, **certified mail**.

regulated industry A business that is subject to government oversight, such as a local utility that is restricted as to the amount of profit it can make and that must seek approval for rate increases.

regulation An ordinance, statute, or law that governs or controls conduct.

regulatory agency A governmental body, acting in the public interest, responsible for the supervision or restraint of an activity.

relational database *Computers* A database that is associated with another, usually be a common field, so that information may be drawn from both and combined in a report.

relational operator *Computers* That which associates two entities, as a common field in a database. A mathematical symbol that represents the relationship between two values, such as $>$ (greater than), $<$ (less than), $=$ (equal to), etc.

release *Finance* Being freed from an obligation, as by discharging a debt; a document that is proof of such discharge. *Law* The giving up of a right or claim, by action or a written instrument, such as permission by the owner of a copyrighted work that allows quotation or use of such a work.

reliability Of the quality of a thing to do that which is expected of it or for which it is intended. *Accounting* Of the confidence level of an auditor that financial records and accounting procedures are in accordance with accepted practice. *Finance* Of the extent to which financial reports are free of error or bias. *Marketing* In direct mail marketing, the ability of a particular mailing list or package to garner the anticipated level of return. In advertising, emphasis on the durability of a product.

remainder Generally, that which is left. *Commerce* Of a dealer who specializes the buying of excess product for resale at greatly reduced prices to other dealers or directly to the consumer, called *remaindering*.

remedy *Law* The means by which a court attempts to right, or compensate for, a wrong.

remit *Finance* To pay, as to satisfy a debt. *Law* To submit a matter for consideration.

remote *Computers* Descriptive of a terminal, data collection point, computer, or peripheral that is not in the immediate area of the host computer.

remote access *Computers* Connecting, as by modem over telephone lines, and interacting, with a computer or peripheral that is at a distance.

remote entry system *Computers* A data entry terminal that is located at a significant distance from the host computer.

remuneration *Labor Relations* Any pay or compensation for work performed, whether direct, as wages, or indirect, as fringe benefits.

renege To fail to honor an agreement or promise.

renegotiate To reopen a contract in hope of reaching agreement on more favorable terms. *Labor Relations* To revise the terms of a labor agreement in accordance with a **reopener provision** in contrast to establishing a new contract, usually because of changing conditions or the passage of time.

renewable resource Of a natural resource that replaces over time if properly managed, such as a forest.

renewal option A right to keep a contract in force if certain options are met.

rent Payment for the use of property. Income or profit earned from the ownership of land.

rent control Local regulations that establish a maximum rent that may be charged for certain dwellings, or the maximum increase allowed from one lease period to another.

reopener provision *Labor Relations* A clause in a collective bargaining agreement that allows either party to exercise the right to **renegotiate** certain parts of the contract before its expiration, usually if certain conditions are met, such as an excessive increase in the **Consumer Price Index.**

reorder point In a system for **inventory control,** the level established for placing an order to restock.

reorganization Generally, a change in the structure of an organization, such as financial, or by revising the lines of authority and responsibility so as to improve performance. *Finance* The restructuring of a company after filing for bankruptcy, while it works out a plan for repayment of outstanding debt. *Law* The restructuring of a firm as by merger, acquisition, consolidation, etc.

rep *Colloq.* A representative, as for sales or customer service.

repairs and maintenance *Accounting* An expense item for the work required to maintain property in useful condition without extending its life.

repeat sales *Marketing* Of the tendency of buyers to reorder a product by brand name, an important factor in successful advertising and marketing.

replacement cost *Accounting* Price of a comparable asset in the current market; same as **current cost.** *Insurance* A provision in some policies that provides protection up to the replacement cost of an asset regardless of **original cost** or **book value.**

report Generally, an accounting or summarizing of data; the data so summarized; presentation, orally or written, of organized data. *Computers* A document on disk, or a hard copy that summarizes the output from data processing.

repossession *Law* The reclaiming of a possession by the seller for non-payment.

representation *Marketing* Claims made for a product in advertising.

repudiation *Law* The statement of refusal to fulfill a duty or obligation as required by contract. Such refusal is not a **breach** unless the other party to the contract treats it as such and sues for damages.

requisition In business, a formal request for supplies or materials; the document used to request such materials.

resale value *Accounting* The price that an asset would bring if offered for sale, in contrast to or **residual value.**

rescission *Law* The act of canceling a contract and return of the parties to their condition prior to the making of the contract, as by agreement of the parties to the contract, by their actions, or by court decree.

research A systematic investigation and analysis of the data compiled about a specific subject, such as for a new process, the market for a product, etc.

reserved word, reserved symbol *Computers* A word or symbol in a programming language that has a special meaning.

reserve for bad debts *Accounting* An amount set aside for anticipated bad debts, credits, etc., usually as a percentage of *sales*. A reasonable reserve for bad debts serves to reduce profits and, for reporting purposes, to represent more accurately the financial position of a company.

residual value *Accounting* The value of an asset after accumulated depreciation has been deducted; the **book value,** as distinct from **actual cost** or **market value.** The scrap value of an asset, deducted before calculating **depreciation.**

resolution A formal statement of intent or opinion, often formulated by a group, as a board of directors, a committee, union group, etc. *Computers* Of the fineness of the detail of an image as on a monitor screen or output from a printer.

resource allocation The appropriation of personnel, money, equipment, etc. for the accomplishment of a product. Often a designation of the assignment of limited resources to the accomplishment of a variety of tasks according to importance.

resources All that is available for use, especially to accomplish a task, such as the personnel and equipment available to a manufacturer. *Computers* The sum of all the capabilities of a computer system determined by its hardware and software configuration.

restitution *Law* The act of correcting a wrong by attempting to restore the conditions that existed before the wrong was committed; payment to an injured party to correct a wrong; or payment by a party that committed a wrong in order to prevent **unjust enrichment** to that party.

restraint of trade *Law* Any act or agreement that tends to restrict free competition, as by **price fixing,** allocation of a market among suppliers, etc., and that operates to the detriment of buyers of goods or services.

restrictive covenant *Law* A stipulation in a real estate contract that places limits on the way in which land may be used or of the type of building that may be built thereon, etc.

retail *Marketing* Of the sale of goods in small quantities directly to the consumer.

retail display allowance *Marketing* A payment or rebate offered by a manufacturer to a retailer in consideration for improved positioning of the manufacturer's product on the retailer's shelves.

retained earnings *Accounting, Finance* Part of shareholder's equity representing accumulated profits that have been kept in the business. A balance sheet account for recording such equity.

retainer *Law* A fee paid to insure availability of services, as an advance payment to a professional, such as an attorney, to insure his or her availability for consultation from time to time, or commitment to take on a particular lawsuit.

retirement plan Any strategy for assuring a continued income after retiring from a job or career; usually, a program sponsored by an employer for the employees of the company.

retroactive Descriptive of that having effect on something that occurred prior to its existence or enactment, as a *retroactive pay increase* in a collective bargaining agreement that stipulates an increase in wages that is to take affect in the past and therefore requires adjustment of all wages paid since that time.

return *Finance* Of the income or profit from an investment or the sale of merchandise. *Marketing* The exchange of goods for like merchandise or a refund. The amount of response to a direct mail marketing campaign.

return on investment, ROI *Finance* The income expected to be realized from any investment, regardless of size, made by the company in plant facilities, equipment, etc. expressed as a percentage of the investment. In many companies, return on investment is the primary yardstick by which investment decisions are made and by which the performance of a manager is measured.

revenue Income from a particular source or collectively.

reversal A change of fortune, such as a drop in sales or income. *Law* The setting aside, or vacating, by a court, of a judgment of a lower court.

reverse discrimination *Labor, Law* The exclusion of a particular race or class of people in order to provide employment to those who have traditionally been the target of discrimination.

reversing entry *Accounting* The entry that zeroes out an account, literally reversing the total of the entries for a prior period, in order to begin recording data for the new period.

reverse video *Computers* The display, on a monitor screen, of dark characters on a light background.

revocable trust *Finance* An agreement for deeding property to another, while receiving income from the property.

revolving credit *Finance* An agreement whereby a client may borrow up to a set limit, often requiring periodic payments against the outstanding balance, and allowing additional borrowing as the balance is reduced.

rider *Insurance* An addition to an insurance policy that supplements or in some way modifies coverage of the basic policy.

right of action *Law* The right to bring suit in a court of law, as to protect a right or correct a wrong. See also, **cause of action.**

right of refusal A privilege granted by agreement, or for consideration, that gives one an opportunity to buy or bid on something before all others, or to meet any other bid. Also called *right of first refusal.*

right of rescission *Law* The privilege of a buyer to cancel a credit contract, without penalty, within three working days from that of the signing of the contract.

right of survivorship *Finance* A type of ownership that provides for the transfer of a decedent's interest in jointly held property to the survivor. See also **joint tenancy, tenancy in common.**

right to work *Labor Relations, Law* Of the state laws that make illegal any stipulation in a collective bargaining agreement that requires membership in a union as a condition for securing or continuing employment. See also **closed shop, open shop, union shop.**

risk management *Finance* Procedures to protect assets of a business or its potential for future profit against possible losses or to minimize losses if they occur, especially in reference to a specific venture or undertaking.

robotics *Manufacturing* The science that deals with the study, design, fabrication, and application of machines to perform certain repetitive or dangerous tasks that would otherwise have to be performed by human labor.

ROI See return on investment.

role playing *Labor Relations* A technique used in training or human relations in which participants portray and act out the part of others in order to recognize their own reactions to a situation, to better understand why others act as they do, and to learn the appropriate behavior for such situation.

rolling stock *Commerce* Carriers of freight, as truck trailers, rail cars, etc., generally, collectively, of all such conveyances owned by a particular company.

ROM, read-only memory *Computers* Of permanent memory, such as that stored on a compact disk, that can be accessed to be used by the computer or viewed by the operator, but that cannot be altered in any way.

root directory *Computers* The primary directory in a **hierarchical** file structure containing the command and system configuration files.

routine *Computers* A set of computer instructions that performs a particular task.

routing *Commerce* The means by which goods will be conveyed from place to place, as by truck or rail, by a particular carrier, or by a specific route.

royalty *Commerce, Law* An amount charged or paid for the use of a property owned by another, such as for an invention or literary work. Such royalty may be a lump sum payment, an amount per unit, or a percentage of revenue, and may be limited as to quantity, time, exclusivity, etc.

rubber check *Colloq., Finance* A check that is no good, that is, one drawn on an account that does not contain sufficient funds to cover it.

run *Commerce* Of a particular batch of merchandise, often, presumed to have all been fabricated during the same period. *Computer* Of the operation of a program or the processing of data. One pass through a set of data to be processed. *Manufacturing* Of the quantity of goods to be produced at one time or in series.

running cost *Accounting* The cost of operating a machine or production line, including **direct labor** and **direct overhead**, usually related to units produced or hours of operation.

run time *Computers* The interval required for a computer to perform a specific task or series of tasks, such as a mail merge. *Manufacturing* The period required to machine one unit of production, or a number of units that comprise a particular job or production lot.

S

sack *Colloq.* To dismiss, as an employee.

salary Compensation, at fixed intervals, such as weekly, monthly, etc. for services rendered, especially for those working in a clerical or professional capacity.

sale *Law* An agreement or contract for the transfer of a product or service from seller to buyer for a specified amount of money.

sales analysis *Marketing* The compilation and study of sales by product, region, profitability, etc. so as to determine the means to generate the most profit from a company's advertising and sales efforts.

sales budget A projection of anticipated sales for all of a company's products during a number of fixed periods in the future by product or product type, so as to anticipate needs in terms of workers, cash flow, etc.

sales contract A formal agreement between buyer and seller as to the terms and conditions of a sale.

sales forecast A salesperson's projection of anticipated sales for some period in the future, such as for a month or a year.

sales incentive Any device used to encourage buying or selling, as a premium or special price offered to buyers, or an extra commission, bonus, prize, etc. offered to members of the sales force.

sales pitch *Colloq.* sales presentation.

sales presentation A formal demonstration by a salesperson to a prospective buyer, explaining the benefits, qualities, etc. of a particular product or service and ending with a request for an order.

sales promotion *Marketing* The office or function for encouraging the buying and selling of certain goods and services through special programs. A program designed to increase the sales of a product or service, by motivating salespersons, distributors, prospects, etc.

sales quota The amount of a product, in units or dollars, that a salesperson is expected to sell during a given period.

salvage value *Accounting* The value of an asset after it has been fully depreciated; *scrap value.*

sampling *Manufacturing* The random taking of product from an assembly line or manufacturing unit for testing. The testing of random samples. *Marketing* Testing of a product by a panel of consumers to get their reaction and suggestions. Offering small packages of a product to consumers in hopes of inducing them to buy more.

saturation *Manufacturing* Of a condition in which no additional units of product can be manufactured without increasing investment. *Marketing* Of a condition in there is no longer a market for a product because all prospective buyers own the product. Sometimes used to describe a condition in which satisfactory coverage of a market is achieved, that is, every possible distributor carries the product.

scalable font *Computers* Descriptive of a type font that a computer program can reproduce in a wide range of sizes.

scale *Labor* Of a wage that is the normal rate paid for that particular position.

scanner *Computers*, Of an optical device that reads and records images for processing by a computer. *Marketing* Of a device that reads markings on a product or product label for recording of a sale, inventory, etc.

schedule A projected or planned sequence of events. *Manufacturing* A projection of the timing of events in the manufacture of a product, such as dates for receipt of materials or parts, start of fabrication, shipping date, etc.

scrap value *Accounting* The value of an asset after it has been fully depreciated; *salvage value.*

screen *Computers* The area on a monitor that displays information from the computer.

screen blanker *Computers* A program that prevents burning an image into a monitor screen by blacking it out after a specified period of inactivity.

screen refresh *Computers* Constant renewal of the monitor screen to provide an image that does not flicker.

screen saver *Computers* A **screen blanker** that displays a random, moving pattern on the screen.

scrolling *Computers* Movement of the image on a monitor screen to view elements outside its borders.

sealed bid *Commerce* An offer by a vendor that must be sealed when tendered and not disclosed until all bids from all vendors participating in the bidding are opened at a set time and place. A system used by the federal, state and local governments, and public utilities, to insure that the selection process is honest and impartial; bids are publicly opened and recorded, with contracts awarded to the lowest priced qualified bidder.

search *Computers* A feature in some programs that locates a word or phrase in text files, records in a data base file, or a particular file.

search firm A company that specializes in locating key personnel for prospective employers.

seasonal discount *Marketing* The tendency of certain products or services to drop in price during the off season, such as for clothing or a resort hotel.

seasonal employee One who is employed only for a certain time of the year to match increased needs or demand during that period, as a sales clerk during the Christmas shopping period.

seasonal fluctuation Regular variation in the level of activity for a business during certain seasons.

secondary boycott *Labor Relations* The practice of placing pressure on a business to cease its trading with another business that is the source of a grievance.

second mortgage *Finance* The pledging of a property that is already mortgaged. In case of default, the holder of the first mortgage has precedence for claim against default.

secured creditor *Finance* A creditor who is protected against loss by the pledge or assets.

secured debt *Finance* Indebtedness that is guaranteed by a pledge of assets.

securities *Finance* Written instruments that are evidence of a right to a share in money, property, income, etc.

securities analyst *Finance* One who makes a study of a company or an industry in order to assess the worth of investments.

security *Finance* Anything that is pledged as surety for the repayment of a loan.

security agreement *Commerce* An agreement between buyer and seller that attests to the seller's retention of interest in that which is sold until the buyer has paid for it.

seed money *Finance* Initial capital raised to start a company or venture.

selective distribution *Marketing* The selling of a product in a restricted market, often because the product is fragile and does not ship well, or only to certain dealers who agree to conform to the manufacturer's standards for promotion, pricing, etc.

self-employed Of one who works at his or her own business.

self liquidator *Marketing* Descriptive of a premium offered, or that can be offered at a price that completely covers the cost and distribution of the item.

self mailer *Marketing* A direct mail package that is self-contained, that is it does not require a separate outer envelope to carry it.

self-service *Marketing* Descriptive of a retail outlet in which the buyer performs most of the functions that would otherwise be provided by store personnel.

seller's market *Marketing* Descriptive of a condition in which there is a shortage of merchandise, excess demand, or few sellers, often marked by high prices and profits.

selling cost *Accounting* The cost of advertising and promotion to attract the interest of potential buyers of a retail product. Frequently, the cost of maintaining a sales force, including salaries, commissions, travel and entertainment expenses, etc., for a company that sells to manufacturers or distributors.

semiannual Twice a year; descriptive of that which occurs every six months.

semimonthly Twice a month, often of a pay period.

semi-variable cost *Accounting* Cost, such as floor supervision, that may vary with the level of production, but not directly with the number of units produced

seniority Of time on a job or the ranking of employees in terms of the amount of time in service to a particular company or on a particular job. Of the priority or privilege extended to one based on length of service. For example, those of greater seniority are often allowed to state their preference of job or shift assignment, and insofar as possible, are given those assignments over one of lesser seniority.

sequential Ordered; one after another. *Computers* Descriptive of data, files, etc. arranged or accessed in a particular order.

sequential search *Computers* A system for locating data that involves an ordered progression through data or files until the search object is found.

serial interface *Computers* A single line connector that transmits data sequentially, one bit at a time.

serial port *Computers* A connection on the computer for communicating with a peripheral device.

server *Computers* A computer that stores and manages programs and data for other computers or terminals in a network.

service Generally, of that which one does that is of benefit to another. *Commerce* Descriptive of a company that deals in acts of assistance to another company or for an individual, as for consulting, cleaning, etc. *Labor Relations* Of the length of time an individual has been employed by a company. See also **seniority.**

service charge A fee for things done, often in conjunction with other costs, as that of packaging or shipping a product, maintaining a record of transactions, etc.

service department A designated group or section in a company that performs tasks for the buyer, such as wrapping packages, repairing appliances, etc.; or for other departments in the company, such as equipment repair and maintenance, cleaning, etc.

setback A problem or reversal in a business, a project, etc. that temporarily slows or halts forward progress. The amount by which the boundaries of a building fall short of the property line, often a minimum set by local ordinance. A type of architecture in which each floor or certain floors fall short of the boundary of the floor below, creating a stair step arrangement.

settle Generally, to satisfy an obligation. *Finance* To pay off an outstanding loan. *Law* To resolve a dispute without litigation.

settlement *Law* Generally, the resolution of a matter without going to court.

setup *Manufacturing* The time required to make an assembly line or machine ready to run, or begin fabrication of a particular product.

severance *Labor Relations* Dismissal from a job. Pay given to an employee who has been dismissed, implying that the dismissal was without prejudice or not the fault of the employee.

sexual differential *Labor Relations* A variance in a rate of pay that has no basis except the sex of the recipient, generally against the law although subtle differences in job description or title allow it to continue in some instances.

sexual harassment *Labor Relations* Unwelcome verbal or physical advances of a sexual nature, often by a superior, so that the harassment is intimidating as well.

shakeup *Colloq.* Descriptive of a condition within a company or department marked by significant change in personnel or procedures.

share Generally, a portion of something. *Finance* A vested interest in a company or enterprise, as a share of stock.

shared resources *Computers* Descriptive of a situation in which devices or peripherals serve two or more computers or terminals.

shareholder *Finance* One who owns shares, or has an interest in an enterprise.

shareware *Computers* Non-commercial software, usually available on a trial basis.

shell corporation *Finance* A company that is incorporated with no significant assets or apparent business purpose, often a corporation formed prior to establishing a business plan and raising capital, or to mask fraudulent activities.

shift differential Compensation to an employee over base pay for working what are considered to be less desirable hours, the second or third shift.

shrink pack A thin plastic wrap that adheres tightly to the product it contains, often mounted on a rigid backing, less expensive than **blister pack** to produce.

shop floor collection *Accounting, Computers* A system for tracking employee time and production cost from data entered by the employee directly to a station located on the shop floor. Some systems require detailed entry by the employee, while others record time automatically and read a **bar code** on the employee's time card and on the work order.

shop steward *Labor Relations* A union representative, usually a part of, and elected by, the members of the group of workers that he or she serves, and who is responsible for handling grievances, collecting dues, and conducting other union business on company property and often, company time.

shortcut key *Computers* A combination of a character or function key with a shift key, used to quickly execute a command or series of commands.

shortfall Generally, any deficiency or result that does not meet expectations or needs. *Accounting* An amount of cash received that is less than expected or less than that needed to meet expenses for a given period. *Marketing* Periodic sales that do not meet expectations.

short term *Accounting* Of a period less than one year, or that which is due to be converted in less than one year, as *short term assets* that include *receivables* for which payment is expected, or *short term liabilities* that include *loans* that are due within the year.

shrinkage Usually of inventory that is less than the amount recorded by the **inventory control** system, often as a result of **pilferage,** recording errors, or errors in count when issuing supplies.

shutdown *Manufacturing* Cessation of operations due to a lack of orders, materials, workers, etc.

sick leave *Labor Relations* Time allowed for absence caused by illness, often with pay, set by company policy or the terms of a collective bargaining agreement. Extended leave granted in unusual circumstances to an employee who faces a long recuperation period, often without pay, but containing the implied promise of a job on return.

silent partner *Colloq.* Informal description of one who has no investment in a business, but who has been, or continues to be, of great service, as by offering information or advice, garnering prospects, etc. *Finance* One who has invested in, or loaned money to, a business, and who takes no active part in the running of the business; **general partner**.

simple interest *Finance* Interest that is calculated only on the principal or amount borrowed, in contrast to compounded interest that is applied to the principal plus any accumulated interest charges.

simultaneous processing *Computers* The processing, by a computer, of two or more tasks at the same time.

site audit *Finance* An examination of financial records that is conducted at the offices of the company being examined.

slander *Law* A statement to another that defames the character or reputation of a third party. See also **libel**.

slot *Computers* A position in a computer frame designed to hold a controller board.

slowdown A deliberate or incidental retarding of progress, as a job action by workers who proceed in a deliberate, methodical fashion so as to reduce output, or of the downturn of a business cycle.

slump A sudden, sharp decline in business activity.

small business Generally, of a business that employs less than 100 workers.

small claims court *Law* An informal court for hearing cases involving relatively minor claims, usually for $500 or less.

social contract A general concept of the relationship between persons and entities which holds that all have an obligation to respect the rights of the other.

social security Of the programs under the jurisdiction of the federal government that provide benefits for retirement, disability, unemployment, etc.

soft goods Nondurable goods such as textiles.

soft market *Finance* Of the slow movement in the trading of certain securities. *Marketing* Of a temporary decline in the demand for a product.

soft sell *Marketing* Direct selling or advertising that extols the value of a product, or equates the product with a better lifestyle, romance, etc. and leaves the buyer to make a decision on his or her own. A sales message that follows the old salesman's admonition of *be bright, be brief, and be gone.*

software *Computers* Any program, such as an application, system file, device driver, etc. that furnishes instructions to the computer.

software documentation *Computers* Instructions to the user for the loading and operation of software.

software utilities *Computers* Programs that assist in the operation of the computer as by improving performance, managing files, etc.

sole proprietorship A business that is owned by one person who has unlimited liability for the debts of the business.

solvency *Finance* Of the ability of a company to meet its obligations as they become due.

sort *Computers* To place data or files in a predetermined order, as alphabetical, by number, by date, by size, etc.

sort field *Computers* In a database file, the field on which the sort is based.

sound driver *Computers* The program that controls the recording, manipulation and reproduction of sound in a multimedia computer.

source data *Computers* Data that has been entered into the computer for manipulation.

source documents *Accounting* Hard copies of orders, sales tickets, invoices, etc. that are the backup for journal entries. *Computers* Any reference that is the basis for data entered into the computer.

space *Accounting* Of the square footage of a plant or department that is the basis for allocating overhead expenses. *Marketing* Of advertising in publications that is priced according to the square inches of space or portion of that is contracted.

special order *Manufacturing* A request for the fabrication of a product that is to be manufactured to the buyer's specifications.

specialty advertising *Marketing* Generally, a reference to premiums that are imprinted with a manufacturer or brand name, such as pens, paper weights, etc.

specialty shop A retail establishment that sells products geared to a particular use or consumer.

specifications *Manufacturing* A written record of an order, containing a complete description of the work to be done, materials required, etc.

speculation *Finance* Investment in an enterprise in the hope of making a profit.

speech recognition *Computers* Of the ability of a computer to accept and act on voice commands.

speech synthesis *Computers* The emulation of the human voice by a computer.

speed key *Computers* A combination of a character or function key with a shift key, used to execute a command or a series of commands.

spell checker *Computers* A feature of some word processing programs that provides verification of spelling in documents.

spike *Colloq.* A momentary sharp increase in electrical current that may damage electronic equipment, especially a computer or its memory. *Computers* A program feature that permits a number of independent elements to be removed from a document to be inserted elsewhere as a unit.

spin-off *Finance* An action that separates a division of a corporation to form a private company.

split See **stock split.**

split screen *Computers* A program feature that permits viewing different sets of data on the monitor screen at the same time.

split shift *Labor* Of a daily work schedule divided into two distinct parts with several hours of unpaid time between them.

spokesperson One who speaks for an entity, by way of press releases, product endorsements, etc.

spooler *Computers* A hardware device, or software, that transfers and stores computer output, such as data to be printed, for processing at a later time.

spot advertising *Marketing* Advertising, usually in broadcast media, that is limited to certain stations, times, etc. in contrast to network advertising.

spot check *Manufacturing* A random sampling of product from a machine or assembly line to confirm that quality requirements are being met.

spreadsheet *Accounting* Data that is arranged in a table or rows and columns, as for a financial report that compares results for several periods. *Computers* A program that aids in the preparation of reports by allowing automatic calculation, linking so that all amounts affected by the change or a single value are updated when that value is changed, etc.

sprocket feed *Computers* A device on a printer that feeds a continuous form through the printer by engaging a series of holes along the edges of the form; same as *pin feed* or *tractor feed.*

stack *Computers* An area of memory in RAM reserved for temporary storage of data.

staff Sometimes, collectively, all of the workers in a company. Often used to designate only those who support the workers in **line** positions, such as clerks or schedulers who are not directly involved in the production of goods or services.

stake *Colloq.* Of the amount one has invested in a company or enterprise. Often, a reference to one's portion of the total investment.

standard *Accounting* Of costs, as for materials, labor, etc., that conform to expectations or experience. *Manufacturing* The criterion for quality and quantity by which the performance of a machine, assembly line or crew is measured. Descriptive of material or a product that is fabricated to a usual set of specifications.

standard industrial classification A numbering system used by the federal government to identify and catalogue companies by the type of product or service which they provide.

standardization *Manufacturing* The adoption of specifications for size, quality, etc. that allow the interchanging of certain parts in different products, or the furnishing of raw materials and parts by different suppliers.

standing order *Marketing* A request by a buyer for the periodic delivery of a specified quantity of product at an agreed price unless otherwise instructed.

startup costs *Accounting, Finance* The cost to set up and begin operating a business.

statement *Accounting* A summary of transactions, as for a customer's purchases and payments in the course of a month. *Computer* A line in a program that comprises a single instruction. *Finance* A report of a company's financial transactions, as a **cash flow statement.**

statistical analysis The evaluation of a body of numerical data relating to a particular subject.

statistical sampling The process of selecting elements of data to be analyzed.

stats, statistics Numerical data that is collected, processed, and analyzed as an aid to decision making, such as for those involving demographics of the consumers of a product or quality deviation of samples from a production line.

status quo Generally, the existing state of affairs or that which existed at a particular time. *Law* Of the state that existed before a conflict, and to which condition the court seeks to return the contesting parties.

statute *Law* An ordinance or regulation; a law passed by a legislative body.

statute of limitations *Law* Any law that sets a time during which parties must take action to enforce their rights or forever more forfeit them.

step Any one of a series of related actions.

stet *Let it stand*—a printer's mark to indicate that copy, however otherwise marked, is not to be changed.

steward See **shop steward.**

stewardship Acting in a responsible manner as relates to the preservation, investment, etc. of funds that have been entrusted to ones care.

stiff *Colloq.* To avoid paying or to refuse to pay. That is excessive, as a price or a penalty.

stipend Any periodic payment, as for services, a pension, etc. A salary.

stipulation A reserve clause in a contract *Law* An agreement or concession between parties to a legal proceeding, generally in writing. A stipulation differs from a **contract** in that it does not require a **consideration.**

stock *Commerce* Merchandise that is normally kept on hand by a particular business for sale to its clients. *Finance* Shares representing capital investment in a company.

Manufacturing Raw materials that are to be used in the manufacture or fabrication of a product.

stock certificate *Finance* A document issued as evidence of an equity position in a company.

stockholder *Finance* One who owns shares of stock in a company.

stockholders' equity *Finance* The net worth of a corporation; the value of the stockholders' investment in a company

stock in trade *Commerce* The goods or services that a particular company supplies. The technique, type of service, or style, that is characteristic of a company or its personnel.

stock option *Finance* The right to buy or sell a stock at a certain price within a specified period. *Labor Relations* A type of compensation in which an employee is given the right to buy company stock at a certain price within a specified period. Such plans are normally offered to those in the upper levels of management on the theory that if they do their jobs well, the price of the stock will rise and increase the value of the option.

stockpile *Commerce* To accumulate materials, supplies or finished goods in anticipation of a shortage or price increase.

stock split *Finance* Increasing the number of shares of a company's stock without diluting the equity or earnings of the shareholders by replacing each share with two or more shares that together are worth the same as the original share. A stock split tends to increase trading because it makes the shares more accessible to those who have less to invest.

stonewalling *Colloq.* To be evasive, or to obstruct, as by withholding information.

storage *Computers* The area in a computer, as a hard disk, or an external device, as a diskette or tape, where copies of program and data files are kept for future use.

storage capacity *Computers* The volume of data, expressed in bytes, that can be contained in a storage device.

store *Commerce* An establishment that stocks goods for sale to consumers, or that is the base of operations for the sale of goods or services.

store brand *Marketing* A brand of merchandise that is associated with a particular retailer, and that is prepared, packaged, labeled, etc. to meet the retailer's specifications.

straight-line depreciation *Accounting* The most common form of **depreciation** for general accounting reports, whereby the annual depreciation for an asset is calculated by deducting salvage value from the cost of the asset and dividing by the anticipated life. For example, a van used in the business is purchased for $20,000 and is expected to have a useful life of five years at the end of which time it will be worth $5,000. Subtracting $5,000, the salvage value, from $20,000, the cost, leaves $15,000 to depreciate; $15,000 divided by five, the number of years over which it is to be depreciated, gives a total of $3,000 per year that may be claimed for depreciation.

straight time Of the standard rate of pay determined by law, company policy, or a collective bargaining agreement, without addition of **shift differential, overtime pay**, etc.

strategic planning The formulation of a strategy for company operations in terms of products, markets, long-term profitability, etc.

straw boss *Manufacturing* A group leader on a production line, often an individual of limited authority, but who sets the pace of the line.

strike *Labor Relations* Refusal by the members of a bargaining unit in a company to continue working in an attempt to pressure the employer to settle a grievance or reach agreement on a contract. *Law* Any unified action by a group of people calculated to pressure an individual or entity to meet certain demands, as by workers who refuse to work overtime, or tenants who act together in withholding rent until improvements are made.

strike benefits *Labor Relations* Any payment or other assistance to employees who are on strike, as from the union strike fund, food stamps, unemployment compensation, etc.

strikebreaker *Labor Relations* Anyone who accepts employment to replace a worker who is on strike.

string *Computers* A series of characters or symbols processed as a unit.

struck work Goods that are produced by strikebreakers or by a company that contracts with one that is on strike.

structure A building used for the offices or manufacturing plant of a company. The organization of the lines of authority, responsibility and communication throughout the various departments and divisions that make up a company.

subcontractor *Manufacturing* One who accepts the responsibility for producing all or part of a project booked by a principal contractor or another subcontractor. A subcontractor may be engaged to perform work that a primary contractor is too busy to do or a portion of a project that requires special skills or capabilities that the primary contractor does not have. See also **joint venture**.

subliminal advertising *Marketing* Of a visual message projected on a motion picture or television screen in short bursts so that it is received below the level of consciousness, that is without the receiver's awareness. Such messages have been declared illegal.

subsidiary *Finance* A company that is more than fifty percent owned by another company to which it is subordinate.

subsidiary ledger *Accounting* A record of like accounts, as for *accounts receivable*, entered from the *accounts receivable journal* which detail supports the entries to the subsidiary ledger. The entries to the subsidiary ledger, in turn, support the entry to *accounts* *receivable* in the **general ledger**.

subsidy Compensation or other incentive paid to individuals, companies, etc. to assist in their continuance or growth, as for the poor, farmers, and certain industries

substandard wage *Labor Relations* A rate of pay that is below subsistence level, the legal minimum, or the average for a particular business or industry.

substantive law *Law* Statute that defines and regulates rights and duties and that may give right to a **cause of action**.

substitution effect *Marketing* The theory that a drop in the price of a product will cause buyers to substitute it for another product and that a price increase will cause buyers to look for a substitute.

suffix *Computers* An addendum to a computer file name, separated from the name by a period, that aids in identifying the file contents, as *.SYS* for a system file, *.TXT* for a text file, etc.

suggested retail price *Marketing* The selling price for a product, suggested by the manufacturer.

suggestion system *Labor Relations* A formal procedure whereby employees can offer ideas for improvements in company operations, ranging from a suggestion box where opinions are submitted in writing, to periodic open meetings where those attending are invited to present their ideas to a suggestion panel for consideration, often including a system of cash awards based on the value of the idea.

summarize To abbreviate by discarding unnecessary detail; to condense data by totaling like elements.

sunshine laws *Law* State and federal regulations requiring that certain meetings of regulatory bodies and legislators, and the records of such meetings, be made open to the public.

superfund A federal fund designated for the cleanup of hazardous waste areas.

superintendent An executive responsible for the operation of a manufacturing plant, a department or section within the plant, etc.

Super VGA *Computers* Of a technology that creates a monitor display of higher resolution than VGA.

supervisor Anyone who is directly responsible for overseeing the work of an individual or a group.

supplemental agreement *Law* Anything that is added to a contract to correct a deficiency.

supplemental budget *Accounting* An additional periodic allocation to adjust a budget allowance, such as for additional supplies and labor when the production requirements for a period are greater than anticipated.

supplier One who supplies materials, supplies or services to a manufacturer, or consumer goods to a wholesaler or retailer.

support services *Computers* Ongoing help available to the computer user from hardware or software manufacturers or vendors, usually via a toll free hot line or bulletin board.

surety *Law* One who agrees to guarantee payment for the debts or default of another.

surety bond *Finance* An agreement containing a third party guarantee that damages owed up to a certain amount will be paid if the purchaser of the bond does not fulfill the obligations of a contract. See also, **performance bond**.

surge protector *Computers* A device that interfaces between computers or peripherals and their power sources to protect the devices from sudden surges in line voltage.

survey *Marketing* The systematic gathering of information from users in order to learn how to improve a product or service.

survivorship *Law* The right of a person who owns property in joint tenancy with another to full ownership of the property when the other person dies.

suspense account *Accounting* An account used for the temporary recording of a transaction that is not yet clearly defined, on the premise that it is better to have the amount stand out than to record it incorrectly. Payment for an insurance or damage claim, for example, may require study to determine allocation of the amount.

suspension *Labor Relations* A procedural or disciplinary layoff, usually without pay.

sweat equity *Colloq.* Occasionally of physical improvements to a property made by a proprietor who does his own carpentry, plumbing, etc. Usually of the contribution of long hours and hard work that builds volume and goodwill.

sweatshop *Manufacturing* Descriptive of a business characterized by a labor force that works long hours for low wages under substandard conditions.

sweepstakes *Marketing* A lottery to promote the sale of a product or service, in which participants are not required to wager or to buy, but only to sign up for eligibility to win.

sweetheart contract *Labor Relations* A collective bargaining agreement that is the result of collusion between company management and union officials, and that is not in the best interests of the members of the bargaining unit.

swing shift *Colloq.* The work shift between the day and night, roughly mid-afternoon until around midnight; second shift. Occasionally describing the changing schedule of a worker from shift to shift in a twenty-four hour, seven day a week operation.

switch See **bait and switch**.

symbol *Computers* Any of the characters available from the computer keyboard. A program defined element, as a mark or word, that represents a command or instruction.

symbolic logic *Computers* The use of symbols in a formula to test the relationship between elements.

symbolic name *Computers* A label that identifies a program, a file, a data field, a range of data, etc.

symbolic pricing *Marketing* Establishment of a selling price for a product that in artificially high to place it in a particular consumer niche.

sympathy strike *Labor Relations* A strike by a union not involved in a dispute, in order to shop solidarity with another union that is involved.

syndicate An association of two or more individuals or companies to share in a project or enterprise, often one that they could not, or would not, attempt singly.

syntax *Computers* The precise structure of a programming language required of one writing instructions for a computer.

synthesizer *Computers* An electronic device for producing sound from digital data.

system Any orderly arrangement of related data, rules, tasks, devices, etc. that serves to form a logical whole.

system backup *Computers* A reserved copy of all of the program and data files in a computer. A second set of hardware that can replace the primary hardware in the event of equipment failure.

system disk *Computers* A disk that contains the basic files the computer needs to operate.

system prompt *Computers* The symbols or characters on a monitor screen that indicate the command line where instructions to the operating system are to be typed.

system resources *Computers* All of the elements unique to a particular computer system, as peripheral devices, type of CPU, memory, etc.

systems analyst *Computers, Manufacturing* One accomplished in the study of complex sets of tasks, especially in a particular area of specialization, and who can recommend means for improvement.

system software *Computers* The programs that control the operation of the computer and its peripherals.

T

table *Computers* An orderly arrangement of related data in rows and columns; a two dimensional array.

table lookup *Computers* To locate a variable as a function of two values in a two dimensional array.

take delivery *Commerce* To personally or through an agent, as a receiving clerk, accept materials, supplies, merchandise, etc. sent by another. To *take delivery* implies that the goods are essentially those that were ordered, that they are acceptable as to condition with any exceptions noted on the bill that was signed to acknowledge delivery, and that the receiver intends to pay for the goods.

takeover The acquisition of one company by another through outright purchase or by acquiring over fifty percent of the outstanding stock of the firm.

tangible asset, tangible property *Accounting, Finance, Law* Descriptive of equity that is corporeal, that is, it can be seen and felt, in contrast to an **intangible asset**, such as a copyright or franchise. In some instances, especially law, *tangible property* refers to personal property, or that which can be carried or moved, in contrast to **real estate** or buildings.

take inventory *Accounting* To count and make a record of all items in storage, as materials, supplies, finished goods, etc., usually at the end of an accounting period to verify the numbers in a **perpetual inventory** and to valuate the inventory or reporting on the financial statements.

take stock Occasionally, to take a physical count of material in inventory. In more common usage, to pause and reflect; to consider a situation carefully before making a decision.

tape backup *Computers* A reserve copy of computer programs and data on magnetic tape.

tape drive *Computers* A device that reads and writes data to magnetic tape for storage, often used for the backup system of a mini or microcomputer.

target market *Marketing* Organizations that fit a particular set of criteria and are therefore viewed as potential buyers for a product or service. Individuals who, because they fit a particular demographic or psychographic profile are considered good prospects for the sale of certain goods or services.

target price *Manufacturing* The cost for which a product must be fabricated in order to conform to the company's profit goals. *Marketing* The price at which a product will find a market, and therefore, the price that includes the cost of the product, advertising, profit, etc. at which it must be brought to market.

tariff *Colloq.* Any bill or charge. *Commerce* A tax on imported goods, or the rate of such tax. The rate schedule for a truck or rail line.

task Generally, work, usually one of a number of acts that make up an undertaking, or sometimes an undertaking involving some difficulty, depending on the context in which it is used.

task management A technique for control that divides a complex job into a series of tasks, each of which is analyzed and revised to achieve optimum performance before integration with other tasks.

tax court *Law* An independent federal agency that hears appeals of disputes between taxpayers and the Internal Revenue Service.

tax deferred *Finance* Of any investment whose earnings are exempt from tax until some time or action in the future.

tax evasion *Law* The deliberate, illegal avoidance of taxes by nonpayment or under payment. *Avoidance* alone is not illegal in that it may designate a legal means of minimizing taxes.

tax exempt *Law* That which is not subject to tax, as the income from interest on state and local bonds.

tax incentive *Finance* Of the nature of certain taxes that encourage investment, as by depreciation allowances, capital gains, etc.

tax planning *Finance* An analysis of tax and investment options in order to determine the best combination of minimize taxes.

tax shelter *Finance, Law* An investment providing tax credits or deductions that can be used to offset other income, thus "sheltering" it from taxes.

tax year Any contiguous twelve month period in the life of a company or other entity, usually a calendar year, although a company may elect to coincide with a **fiscal year** that begins at any time as long as it does not change from year to year.

team management A system for the administration of a project that places the decision-making in the hands of a group of individuals often with different specialties that compliment each other, and that are necessary to the project. Such a system may be used to develop and implement a marketing plan for a new product or to set up a new plant or production line.

teaser ad *Marketing* An advertisement designed to attract the attention of the public without revealing the product, generally one of a series of ads in a program that culminates in a **media blitz** promoting the product.

technological unemployment *Labor Relations* The loss of jobs in a business or industry due to advancing technology that has made a product obsolete; that has replaced laborers with machines; or that has changed the character of a job so that those who usually perform certain tasks are no longer qualified.

telecommunications Communication by wire, especially, telephone lines for the transmission of voice, facsimile, and computer data.

telemarketing *Marketing* Use of the telephone for any phase of the promotion and sale of a product, that includes conducting a telephone survey, making an appointment for a salesman to call, ascertaining interest in a product or service so that additional information can be sent through the mail, any attempt to secure an order over the telephone, or the acceptance of orders for merchandise promoted elsewhere, as in print or on television.

tenancy *Law* The right to the possession and use of real estate, as by ownership or lease.

tenancy in common *Law* Ownership of property by two or more persons, with ownership share passing to the heirs of any owner who dies. See also **joint tenancy**.

tenement *Colloq.* A multiple dwelling that offers few amenities, or that is run down. *Law* Generally, any structure attached to the land, or a dwelling place for a tenant.

tenure *Labor Relations* The right of continued employment to one who is gainfully employed by a company or other entity, often by virtue of time in the position, guaranteed by a collective bargaining agreement. See also **seniority**. *Law* A right to hold, as property or a position.

term Generally, a specific length of time or a condition, as for the period that a contract is in force and the contingencies regarding its execution.

terminal *Computers* A device, minimally comprising a keyboard and a viewing screen, that allows the user to interact with the computer by entering instructions or information and monitoring the processing.

termination *Labor Relations* The conclusion of employment, whether by the employer or employee.

term life insurance *Insurance* An insurance policy paying death benefits that is in force for a specific period, at the end of which time it may be renewed, usually requiring renegotiation of the cost of the protection.

terms *Finance* The details, as interest rate and repayment schedule, of a loan. See also, **term**.

territory Generally, of an geographical area; often, referring to the scope of one's expertise or responsibility. *Marketing* Of the geographic area, type of client, etc. that is covered by a salesperson.

test Generally, an examination or trial. *Computers* To subject to diagnostics or sample problems to ascertain that a hardware device or program is working properly. *Manufacturing* Of experimentation with materials, supplies or methods to determine the most effective combination to achieve cost and quality objectives. *Marketing* Of experimentation with advertising or marketing strategies to determine the most economical, effective, or profitable means to sell a product.

testimonial *Marketing* A statement by a well-known personality attesting to the value of a product.

test market *Marketing* An area selected for experimentation with various advertising, pricing, or distribution plans for a product.

text editor *Computer* A type of word processor with limited formatting capabilities, usually used for writing or editing programs

think tank *Colloq.* An organization whose members are engaged in the intensive study and evaluation of problems or projects in order to offer advice to businesses or governmental bodies.

three dimensional array *Computers* An ordered group of like elements, aligned in rows, columns and layers.

three dimensional graphics *Computers* The simulation, on a computer monitor screen, of a three dimensional object.

thrift shop *Marketing* An outlet that specializes in discounted merchandise, often used.

tickler A reminder, or system of reminders, for directing attention to some important matter at an appropriate time, such as a set of dated files in which are stored information about those things that require action by a particular day or week. *Computer* A **TSR** program for the recording of appointments or other matters of importance, and that pops up at the beginning of a day or at the required time during the day to remind the user of meetings, etc.

tie-in *Marketing* Of special advertising or promotions that are associated with an ongoing campaign. Of a product that is associated in advertising or point-of-sale displays with another, related product, such as featuring a cooler for sale in conjunction with the sale of cold beverages, often with a special price on the purchase of both items.

tight ship Of a company or department that is run according to a set of strict regulations; often of the supervisor, who is cited as *running a tight ship*.

time and a half *Labor Relations* A reference to the rate of pay for working overtime; of the period worked for that rate. *Law* Pay rate mandated by federal law for working over forty hours in a week.

time and motion study *Manufacturing* A careful examination the time required, and the nature of each worker's movements, to complete a task, or a series of tasks, for the purpose of determining how to make them more efficient and productive.

time card *Manufacturing* A document that records the starting and stopping time for each employee. Often used also to record the times spent on various tasks or jobs during the day as part of a **job cost** system.

timekeeper *Accounting* One who reviews and records the data from time cards for payroll and cost accounts. Infrequently, one who records the starting and ending times of workers for a company, department or work crew.

time management A program for organizing ones tasks to make the best use of available time.

time-sharing *Computers* A system for utilization of a computer, usually a **mainframe**, by a number of users. Often a service provided by an outside firm to a number of companies that require the use of a large computer, but cannot justify its purchase. The increasing power and decreasing price of minicomputers has made the practice less common than in the past.

timetable Generally, a schedule of times for the occurrence of certain events, as the arrival and departure of public transportation. *Marketing* A schedule for coordinating specific events in a program of advertising, promotion, introduction of a new product, etc.

title *Law* The right of possession, especially for real estate.

tokenism The practice of hiring a few minority workers to counter claims of discrimination.

top down management A corporate style wherein all decisions are made at the top and then sifted down through the ranks.

topping out Of anything that has reached its peak, as the popularity of a product.

tort *Law* A wrong stemming from an act, or failure to act, in a prudent manner, that is not criminal and that is, however, grounds for a civil suit.

total cost *Accounting* The entire expense, that is, material, labor and overhead, required to fabricate a product.

total debt *Accounting, Finance* The sum of all the money owed by an organization, whether in the short or long term.

total fixed cost *Accounting, Finance* The sum of all expenses for a given period that do not vary with units of production; in effect, the cost to keep the doors of a business open during that period if nothing is produced.

total revenue *Accounting, Finance* The entire amount of income received, or owed, to a company during a given period, from any source and for any purpose.

touch terminal *Computers* A device that allows selection or entry of data by touching areas of the monitor screen.

tour *Labor Relations* Of the hours an employee is scheduled to work. Occasionally, of the time spent working for a company by one is no longer employed there.

tout *Colloq., Marketing* To promote or extol the virtues of a product.

tracer, tracking *Commerce* An inquiry or effort to seek the whereabouts of a lost package or shipment.

trackball *Computers* A hand held device, similar to a mouse, but with a fixed base holding a sphere that is manipulated to move the cursor.

tractor feed *Computers* Of a device that guides continuous-feed paper through a printer using holes that are punched into strips along the side of the paper.

trade *Commerce* Collectively, all those engaged in a similar business of line of work. *Manufacturing* Generally, a means of making a living; an occupation. Once used to refer only to skilled workers.

trade advertising *Marketing* Advertising and promotion that targets industrial users of a product.

trade association An alliance of those engaged in the same, or closely related, lines of business, usually formed for the pursuit of any cause that is seen to be in the best interests of its member, as for education and training, public relations, influencing legislation, etc.

trade magazine A periodical that is directed to the interests of those in a particular line of business.

trademark A design, symbol, etc., usually protected by registration, used by a company to distinguish its products or services from those of its competitors.

trade name The name used by a company for doing business, that is not necessarily the name under which the corporation is organized; see also **dba.** A name used by a company for its products or services; a **trademark.**

trade reference *Accounting* The name of a company doing business with a prospective buyer, given to a seller by the buyer as a credit reference, and often in the same business as the seller.

trade secret Any information from within a company that, in the hands of a competitor, would work to cause harm to the company, or to aid the competitor.

trade show A gathering of exhibitors whose purpose is to display and promote their products and services to prospective buyers who represent companies in related lines of business.

trade union *Labor Relations* Originally, a bargaining unit of those engaged in a particular craft; now generally used to designate any labor union.

transaction Any activity associated with trading or the carrying on of business; a business deal. *Law* The completion of any arrangement related to business between two or more persons.

transaction file *Accounting, Computers* A record of recent transactions, used to update a master file, such as a recording of daily sales used to update the sales account, receivables, cash account, inventory, etc.

transaction terminal *Computers* A device that permits remote input of data directly to the computer, such as on a shop floor or at a cash register.

transfer *Computers* To move data or files from one location, storage device or computer to another.

transient Temporary; passing or changing with time. *Computers* Interim, as a file that is created by a program while it is processing, then deleted when processing is completed. *Finance* Of an upswing or downturn in business that is temporary. *Labor Relations* Of the work force in a seasonal business.

translate *Computers* To convert data from one format or program to another. To convert signals from one format to another, as from analog to digital input.

transmission *Computers* The transfer of signals between elements of a computer system.

transmission speed *Computers* The rate at which data can be sent and received.

transmittal *Finance* A document that lists, and serves as verification of, items being transferred, such as for negotiable instruments, stock certificates, etc., especially for materials that are not ordinarily copied.

transparent *Computers* Descriptive of computer processing that is taking place in the background, not under the direct supervision of, or apparent to, the user.

transportation *Commerce* Any conveyance for moving people or things. Collectively, of a type of conveyance or all means of conveyance.

travel and entertainment *Accounting, Marketing* The expenses, usually associated with sales or marketing activities, that are incurred for travel to visit clients, attend trade shows, etc., and for the entertaining of clients, in the normal course of business.

treasurer *Finance* The officer who is responsible for management of the funds of an organization, and in a public corporation, for maintaining a market in its securities.

treasury stock *Finance* Shares of a company's stock that have been bought back by the company.

tree diagram A graphic representation of a tree-like structure that shows the relationship of positions in a corporation, a sequence of events, the directory structure of computer files, etc. that emanates from a single point and branches out through various levels, often depicted inverted so that the point of origin is at the top of the diagram.

trend Of conditions or events with a tendency to continue in a particular direction, as for style changes, the movement of sales, or cost increases. Recognizing and coping with trends in an important factor in long range planning.

trespass *Law* Interference with the rights of an owner to use property as he or she sees fit. Such trespass may be entry on to the land by the trespasser, the removal of property or the depositing of property, as trash.

trial and error Problem solving by attempting a solution and observing the results, often used in test marketing to determine the best means to promote a promote a product.

trial balance *Accounting* A worksheet that is a listing of ledger accounts at the end of an accounting period to be sure that all balance prior to closing the books.

trial offer *Marketing* A proposal to a prospective buyer that permits the use or inspection of a product without charge for a specified period; a technique for getting the attention of first time buyers.

troubleshooter *Colloq.* One who specializes in analyzing and solving problems.

truncation Generally, the contraction of a number by cutting off a non significant portion. *Computers* The compression of a result of calculation that is too long for a program to record.

truth in lending *Law* Federal regulation requiring that those applying for credit be given comprehensive information about the dollar amount and the annual rate of the interest. In addition, when real property is pledged as security, the buyer must be allowed three working days in which to cancel the transaction.

TSR, terminate and stay resident *Computers* Of a utility program, such as an appointment calendar, that can be loaded into memory and called up as needed.

turkey *Colloq.* Of something that does not perform to expectations, as an investment or a person.

turnaround, turn the corner *Colloq.* An improvement in the fortunes of a company, a venture, or an operation.

turnkey *Computers, Manufacturing* Of a system or other project that is designed to the client's specifications and that is thoroughly tested and ready to operate before being turned over to the client.

turnover *Labor Relations* Of the rate of change in the labor force, often a measure of worker satisfaction, effectiveness of the selection and screening process, etc. *Marketing* Of the frequency with which the product moves from the shelves to the consumer.

tutorial *Computers* An adjunct to a program that teaches the user how to use the program.

two dimensional array *Computers* An ordered group of like elements, formed in rows and columns.

tycoon A person of wealth and power who is prominent in industry or in financial circles.

type ahead buffer *Computers* An area of memory that stores key strokes entered faster than they can be processed.

U

ultra vires *Latin* Beyond the power of. *Law* Of corporate action or involvement that is outside the realm of activities specified in its charter, and that may give rise to action for withdrawal of its charter.

unauthorized strike *Labor Relations* Any form of **strike**, as a walkout, work slowdown, refusal to work overtime, etc. by members of a bargaining unit that has not been duly sanctioned by their union.

unbundle *Computers* To separately price, and offer for sale, the various parts, as a computer, monitor, keyboard, printer, programs, etc., of a system that are normally sold as a unit. *Marketing* To break down the invoice from an advertising or promotional agency, such as for charges to place advertisements in various media, creative and design costs, artwork, copy preparation, etc.

uncollected funds *Finance* Of capital that has been pledged and not yet paid, such as for checks that have been drawn, but that have not yet been charged against the account from which drawn.

underapplied *Accounting* Of charges that have not been fully recovered, such as for **overhead** in a **cost accounting** system. For example, if overhead were allocated on the basis of the number of units produced or the number of operating hours, any reduction in units produced or hours of operation would leave a portion of overhead cost that is not applied to the cost of the product. A similar situation occurs when the actual cost of overhead exceeds that on which the budget and allocation of overhead is based.

underabsorption See **underapplied**.

underemployed *Labor Relations* Of one who is engaged in a type of work that does not require his or her level of education, experience, or competence, a condition that often exists when there are more workers than there are available jobs. Within a company, a worker faced with layoff may exercise the right to bump another with less seniority, and thus wind up with a lower level job. *Manufacturing* Of a plant, production line, machine, etc. that is not being fully utilized.

underground economy Descriptive of activity that is not reported for tax purposes, such as bartering for goods or services, payments **off the books**, or dealing in illegal substances.

underpaid *Labor Relations* Of one who has been shorted in a particular pay period, such as for an error in reported hours, wage rate, etc. Of one who is working for a wage that is less than the legal rate, that originally agreed to by the employer, that specified in a contract, or that which is the normal rate for the job in that market.

under the counter Of payment that is made **off the books**, or not recorded. Such payment may be to simply avoid the paperwork involved in putting a casual worker on the payroll, but more often the term is used to describe payments that are illegal, as for a bribe or to avoid taxes.

undervalued *Accounting* Of an asset that is carried on the books at a figure that is far less than its true worth. *Finance* Of a security, as a company stock, that is trading at less than its apparent worth, often because of a slow market.

undiscounted list *Marketing* Of a published schedule of prices that shows only the full wholesale or retail rates for merchandise. Such lists, or catalogs, are often prepared by a manufacturer or wholesaler for wide distribution; individual distributors or merchants are then assigned a discount rate at which they may purchase.

undivided interest *Law* In property that is jointly owned, the right of each of the owners to use and possession of the entire property. The right to profits from the property, or proceeds from its sale, are shared according to each owner's undivided interest, but each has a right to possession of the whole.

undue influence *Law* Control or authority wielded by one party to a transaction over the other and that transcends the free will of the other in relation to the transaction.

unearned income *Accounting* Advance payments for which goods or services have not yet been furnished. *Finance* For tax purposes, income for other than personal services, as investment or interest income.

unemployable *Labor Relations* Generally, of one who is habitually unemployed, often for lack of skill or education, or because of inability to adjust to the restrictions imposed by most jobs, as by arriving on time every day. Many such *unemployables* are simply unsuited to the type of jobs they have been seeking, or that are available in their market area.

unemployment Generally, the state of not being used. The condition of being without steady work to provide income or the percentage of those who are without work.

unemployment compensation *Labor Relations* Any payment to subsidize those who are out of work. The federal and state programs that offer regular payments over a set period of time to those without work.

unencumbered *Finance* Of an asset that is owned free and clear, without **lien**.

unfair competition *Law, Marketing* Any attempt in advertising to mislead or defraud a buyer, such as by misrepresenting the cost or quality of a product, by representing a product as that of another, by infringing on the patents or copyrights of another, etc.

unfair labor practice *Labor Relations, Law* Any action of an employer or a labor union that restricts the rights of any member of a bargaining unit, as by coercion, discrimination, refusal to bargain, etc.

Uniform Commercial Code *Commerce* A set of rules adopted by most states to standardize the regulation of transactions involving the sale of merchandise, shipping documents, negotiable instruments, stock transfers, etc.

uninterruptible power supply *Computers* A sophisticated backup power supply that automatically furnishes power to a computer system when the primary power source is interrupted, permitting continued operation or an orderly shutdown.

union See **labor union**.

union shop *Labor Relations* An organization where workers are required to be members of a union; non-union workers may be hired, but are required to join the union within a specified period as a condition of continued employment, a practice outlawed in several states. See also, **closed shop, open shop, right to work**.

unit cost *Accounting* The expenditure for one unit of production, including for materials, labor and overhead.

Universal Product Code A distinctive number set that identifies a specific product, represented as a **bar code**, for use with an automated system that records sales, adjusts inventory, etc.

unjust enrichment *Law* Of the principle in law that requires one who has profited unfairly at the expense of another to make restitution.

unrecorded expense *Accounting* Of a cost that has been incurred, but not recognized at the end of an accounting period, usually because an invoice was not received.

unrecovered cost *Accounting* In a **cost accounting** system, an expense that has not been properly matched to the activity that produced it.

unsecured *Finance* Of a loan or debt that does not have an asset pledged as collateral for payment.

unskilled *Labor Relations* Descriptive of a worker who does not possess any special abilities, or a job that does not require special knowledge or training.

up and running *Computers* Descriptive of computers and peripherals that are on line and functioning properly.

update Generally, to add new information. A document, report, etc. that contains the latest information available. *Computers* Of a newer version of an existing program that offers new features, or corrects problems in the original version.

up front *Accounting* Of that which is paid or takes place in advance, as the down payment on an order.

upgrade An improvement, as of quality. *Marketing* Of a sale in which the buyer is moved to the purchase of a larger quantity, of better quality, etc.

upkeep *Manufacturing* Of the care and maintenance of equipment.

upscale *Marketing* Generally, descriptive of those products or markets characterized by higher than average prices, and often, better quality.

upswing *Finance* A change toward increased demand for a product, or an improvement in the economy as a whole.

up time *Computers* The period that a computer is on line and functioning properly.

upward compatibility *Computers* Descriptive of features built into a computer that permit upgrading.

upwardly mobile *Marketing* Descriptive of a demographic group that is likely to experience a steady improvement in status, income, standard of living, etc.

useful life *Accounting* The length of time before an asset costs more to keep in operating condition than it earns.

user friendly *Computer* Of an operating system or program that requires minimal training of users, and that is intuitive, making use easier.

user group *Computers* A special interest group that meets to share information about a particular program or computers in general.

user hot line *Computers* A telephone number provided by an equipment or software manufacturer or dealer through which a user may access technical help.

usury The practice of loaning money at an excessive rate of interest. *Law* Interest that is excessive, and, perhaps, unlawful.

utility The quality of being useful; that which is useful. *Accounting* Generally, the expenses for public utilities, as gas, water, electricity, etc. *Computers* A program that assists in the operation or management of the computer, peripheral devices, or other programs, etc.

utter *Law* The passing, or attempt to pass, a forged instrument, as a check.

V

vacation pay *Labor Relations* Income paid to an employee for the time he or she is on vacation, usually one to four weeks a year depending on the employee's length of service.

valid Descriptive of that which is recognized, or having legal force.

valuable consideration *Law* Inducement for a contract; something of value given to fulfill a contractual obligation.

valuation An estimate of the worth or cost of a thing, as a machine.

value The equivalent worth of a thing in money or some other medium of exchange. *Accounting* The amount at which assets are recorded and reported. *Marketing* The price at which goods are sold. The relative worth of goods to a buyer.

value added *Accounting* The amount by which the cost of goods are increased as the result of processing; a system that accounts for such cost. *Finance* The contribution to the worth of goods by a manufacturer or fabricator, determined by the difference between the cost of materials and the selling price.

value judgment An estimate of a situation, worth, etc. based on insight and intuition.

variable That which is subject to change. *Accounting* Descriptive of expenses that change with level of activity. *Computers* An element in a program that varies with input. *Marketing* Descriptive of those things that can affect the demand for a product.

variable budget *Accounting* A scale listing anticipated cost for various levels of output or activity. A schedule of those expenses that change with the level of volume or activity.

variable cost *Accounting* Cost, as labor and materials, associated with a unit of production and that varies directly with the number of units produced. Cost, such as floor supervision, that may vary with the level of production, but not directly with the number of units produced; also called **semi-variable cost.**

variable expense *Accounting* Expenses that change with the level of activity or production.

variable interest rate *Finance* A charge for the use of borrowed money that, by agreement, may be changed over the life of a loan, with the change usually pegged to some index.

variable name *Computers* A label that represents an element that can assume a changing value, such as a range of cells in a spreadsheet.

variable pricing *Marketing* The practice of charging different prices to different buyers, usually at the retail level, where a buyer and seller may haggle over price. On the wholesale level, variable pricing may exist, but usually must be based on some cost factor, such as packaging, volume, etc.

variance Generally, the qualification or quantification of difference. *Accounting* The difference between budgeted and actual expenses, sales, earnings, etc. *Law* In zoning, exemption from a zoning ordinance granted by the appropriate authority to one who would suffer undue and unnecessary hardship if the ordinance were strictly enforced.

vendor Generally, one who sells; a supplier of goods or services.

venture An endeavor that implies an element of risk, as in starting a business where the possibility of loss exists with the possibility of gain.

venture capital *Finance* Money or other assets loaned to start a business or invested in a business. Such loans often carry an interest rate that is higher than that for a going business in recognition of the extra element of risk.

vertical integration Expansion of a company into a new level or levels in the manufacture and distribution of its primary products. A manufacturer of furniture, for example, may acquire a company that supplies lumber or fabric for the furniture, or may expand to set up a chain of retail stores to sell the furniture produced. See also **horizontal integration.**

vested *Law* Absolute, as of a right that is not contingent on any act or event.

vested rights *Labor Relations* Of the absolute claim of an employee to the benefits of a pension plan at normal retirement age or to election of a lump sum payment as provided for in the plan if separated from the company prior to retirement. Vesting generally requires a minimum time of service with the company sponsoring the plan.

VGA, video graphics array *Computers* A standard for high resolution display on a color monitor screen.

vicarious liability *Law* Responsibility placed on one for the actions of another, as a damage claim against an employer for injury caused by his or her employee while on the job.

See also imputed liability.

video card *Computers* A board in the computer that controls the display on the monitor.

violation *Law* An act that is disruptive to normal order, or contrary to law.

virtual memory *Computers* An extension of the computer's main memory in disk storage.

virus *Computers* Unauthorized instructions in the computer that disrupt its normal operation.

vocabulary *Computers* The collection of reserved words that are acceptable for use in a particular programming language.

vocational rehabilitation *Labor Relations* A program for upgrading skills or learning new ones so as to be more employable, such as a company program for retraining employees who have been displaced by automation.

voice activated *Computers* Of a computer or computer program that responds to voice commands.

void *Law* Having no legal force; invalid

voidable *Law* Of a contract that is defective and that may be canceled without recourse.

volatile Descriptive of that which may change quickly and unexpectedly, as a particular market in goods, or the tone of labor negotiations. *Computers* Of memory that must be constantly refreshed to be retained and that is erased when the power is off.

volume A quantity or amount, as of the number of units produced, or the dollar amount of business.

volume discount *Marketing* A price reduction, or special price, based on the number of units purchased.

voluntary bankruptcy *Finance, Law* An action wherein a company or other entity that is insolvent petitions the court for protection from its creditors in anticipation that, operating under the direction of the court, it may preserve its assets for the benefit of creditors and stockholders alike.

voting stock *Finance* Shares in a company that entitle the shareholder to a single vote in corporate elections for each share of stock held.

voucher *Accounting* A form for the control of the processing of charges and disbursements: invoices received are assigned a numbered voucher on which is recorded data about the invoice required for processing and payment. *Commerce* A document that serves as evidence to a transaction or authority to make such a transaction, such as for the receipt or shipment of goods.

W

wage The amount of money paid an employee for work, usually based on an hourly rate.

wage bracket The range of wage rates or salaries paid for a particular type of work.

wage scale A listing of the wages paid for all of the jobs or job levels covered by a collective bargaining agreement, or by company policy.

waiver *Law* The voluntary relinquishing of a right; a document attesting to such relinquishing.

waiver of premium *Insurance* A provision in an insurance policy, as for illness or disability, that keeps the policy in force without payment of further premiums.

walkout Generally, a sudden departure to protest, as for those attending a meeting. *Labor Relations* A strike by workers to protest a contract violation, pressure for settlement of a grievance, etc.

want ad *Colloq.* A classified advertisement in the newspaper, especially those listing opportunities for employment.

warehouse receipt *Law* A formal document of title that is a receipt for goods issued by a person or business that deals in the storage of such goods. In certain cases, a warehouse receipt may be a negotiable instrument in that it entitles the bearer to possession of the goods it lists, and that its sale constitutes delivery of those goods.

warranty *Insurance* Assurance by one who is contracting for protection that conditions related to the risk are as stated, or will be amended to conform, such as for the installation of smoke alarms or a sprinkler system. *Law* A guarantee that property or goods described in a contract are correctly represented and that they will be replaced or repaired if found deficient. *Marketing* A guarantee to a consumer of the quality of merchandise for sale, usually with provision for repair or replacement of defective items within a specified period from the date of purchase.

waste *Law* Improper use or negligence of land by one rightfully in possession that significantly reduces the value to another who owns an interest in the land. *Manufacturing* Material that is no longer useful; a byproduct of fabrication, to be discarded.

wasted circulation *Marketing* Advertising in a market where a product is not available.

waybill *Commerce* A document that accompanies a shipment of goods, listing the shipper, destination, routing, and a description of the goods being conveyed.

wealth Generally, of anything in profusion. *Finance* Collectively, the monetary value of the assets belonging to a person, business, country, etc.

wear and tear *Accounting* Descriptive of the normal use of a product that causes a reduction in its value over time.

white collar crime *Colloq.* Designating illegal acts by one in a position of responsibility, such as stock fraud, bribery, or embezzlement.

white collar worker *Colloq.* Generally, descriptive of one who works in an office, or at a at a profession.

white elephant Generally, of that which is of no value to its owner, often maintained at great expense and, occasionally, of that which may have value to another.

wholesaler *Commerce* Usually, one who buys from a manufacturer in very large quantities and sells to retailers in somewhat smaller lots.

wildcat strike See **unauthorized strike.**

windfall, windfall profit *Accounting* An often sudden, unexpected benefit, as by the purchase of materials or goods for resale at an especially low price.

window *Computers* A viewing area on the monitor screen.

window dressing *Accounting, Finance* Any information or presentation of financial data that makes results appear better than they are. *Marketing* Product packaging to make to appear more valuable than it is.

withholding *Accounting* The amounts held back from a worker's wage or salary for income taxes, insurance, union dues, etc.

word processor *Computers* A small computer with self-contained monitor and printer that is designed to function as a typewriter, used to generate correspondence, reports, etc., often with a spelling or grammar checker, and the ability to save data to memory built into the machine or on a floppy disk. A computer program designed for the production of typeset documents, often with a variety of features or the capacity to add them, such as a spell and grammar checker, insertion and editing of graphics, a large collection of type fonts, etc.

word wrap *Computers* A feature of a word processor or word processor program that provides for the continuation of copy on a new line when one line is filled, relieving the user of the need to manually divide the lines of copy.

workaholic *Colloq.* One who is obsessive about work or abnormally attached to keeping busy.

work experience Collectively, one's knowledge and talents. A list of previous employers, usually asked of prospective employees, and including such information as dates of employment, wage rate, reason for leaving, etc.

work flow *Manufacturing* Generally, of the path that materials, work in process, and finished goods follow through the various stages of production. A diagram, or graphic representation, of the progress of product in a manufacturing operation.

workforce Collectively, all of those working in a company or other entity, a geographic area, etc.

working capital *Accounting, Finance* The excess of current assets, cash and items such as accounts receivable or inventory that are expected to be converted into cash in the near future, over current liabilities, those obligations owing and due within one year. Occasionally, descriptive of only assets that can used to pay or pledge for obligations, such as cash and accounts receivable.

working poor Those who work for minimum wage, earning just enough to buy necessities, and who lack to education or skills to improve their lot.

work in process, work in progress *Accounting* An item of inventory that represents the labor and material costs assigned to goods that are not completed. *Manufacturing* Product for which fabrication has not yet begun or is only partly completed, representing the workload ahead of a department or operation.

workload *Manufacturing* Collectively, all of the work that has yet to be completed, often within a specified period. The specific work assigned to a person, machine, assembly line, etc., or the amount of such work that can be completed by the entity.

workmen's compensation *Insurance* A state mandated insurance that reimburses workers injured on the job. Requirements vary from state to state, but generally the worker is reimbursed for medical expense, disability and lost wages.

work order *Manufacturing* A document for tracking work through a plant, that contains the identity of the customer, a description of the work, and detailed instructions for its completion. A request to a service department to perform a specific task, as for maintenance on a machine.

work permit *Labor Relations* A document that authorizes a legal alien to work for a specific period of time.

work rules *Labor Relations* Regulations regarding conditions in the workplace, conduct expected of employees and supervisors, etc., often part of a collective bargaining agreement. Sometimes, rules set forth by the company governing procedures, as for safety, tardiness, reporting of injuries, etc.

worksheet *Accounting* A collection of preliminary data to be used in the preparation of financial reports; a spreadsheet or trial balance.

work simplification *Manufacturing* The process of studying production methods in order to reduce the time, effort and cost to produce a product or perform a task.

work station *Computers* One of a number of desktop computers or terminals that are linked to other users, a mainframe, minicomputer, or file server, and peripherals such as printers, plotters, etc. *Manufacturer* Any of a number of points on an assembly line where a worker is positioned to perform a task involved in the fabrication of a product.

work stoppage *Labor Relations* A protest, usually by a group of workers in concert; a **strike** or **walkout.**

worth *Finance* The value of an asset. *Labor Relations* A measure of a worker's contribution to the value of a manufactured product or a service. The comparable value of the services of a particular worker, or of any worker doing a particular job.

writ *Law* A legal document that directs one in a course of action.

write protected *Computers* Descriptive of a storage disk or other device that may be accessed, but not changed. See also **read-only**.

WYSIWYG, what you see is what you get *Computers* descriptive of an accurate representation of type and graphics on a monitor screen.

Y

year-end *Accounting, Finance* The end of an accounting period, often, but not necessarily, the end of a calendar year. See also **fiscal year**.

year-to-date *Accounting* The sum of the accounting periods from the beginning of the current **fiscal year** until the end of the most recent accounting period, usually in reference to accumulated amounts, as sales, expenses, etc.

yellow dog contract *Labor Relations* A contract between an employer and employee that contains a provision precluding membership in a labor union. Such a contract is prohibited in most states and not enforceable in federal courts.

yes man *Colloq.* One who always strives to agree with his or her superiors; a toady.

Z

zero defects A program designed to promote a disposition toward perfection in performance among employees, often with a system of rewards for excellence.

zip code A post office system of numbering delivery areas in order to speed the sorting of mail.

zone Any area, specifically bounded, that is distinct from others in some way.

zoning The dividing of a geographical area into distinct sections, as of a city, usually to restrict their use.

zoning ordinance *Law* A regulation that limits the use of a section of land to specific purpose or bars certain activities in the section, as land set aside for residential dwellings that prohibits industrial development.

MEDICAL DICTIONARY

abdomen, abdominal cavity That part of the human body comprising the lower portion of the **trunk**, defined by the lower section of the backbone and the muscles of the back, and abdominal muscles at the sides and front. The diaphragm forms the top of the cavity and the pelvic basin forms the bottom.

The abdominal cavity contains several important organs: the **liver** in the upper right portion; the stomach and the spleen in the upper left portion; the small and large intestines in the lower portion; the kidneys, one on each side in the back; and the urinary bladder in the pelvic region. There are also major blood vessels and other smaller organs in the abdominal cavity.

abduction Descriptive of the movement of a limb or part of a limb away from the midline of the body, as, for example, when the arm is lifted away from the side of the body. Similarly, separation of the fingers or toes is called abduction.

Certain muscles involved in such movement are referred to as *abductors*. See also, **adduction**.

aberrant Deviating from the usual or normal, as behavior in a mental patient.

ablation Separation or removal of a part of the body by surgery.

ablution Washing of the body.

abnormal Descriptive of that which is unusual; not conforming to the normal.

abrade To wear down by rubbing, as the skin.

abrasion An injury caused by rubbing the surface of the skin.

abscess A swollen, inflamed area of body tissue, often tender or painful, in which pus has gathered.

The abscess is the result of the body's natural response to bacterial infection or an irritant, such as a splinter. **Leukocytes**, or white blood cells gather in the area to fight the infection: as the dead bacteria, dead leukocytes, etc. build up to form **pus**, they create pressure and discomfort results. Pressing along the line of least resistance, the abscess pushes toward the surface. Eventually the abscess will burst of its own accord, but may be lanced by a doctor. It is inadvisable to attempt to puncture the abscess before it is ready, as such action may spread the infection.

absorption The process of assimilating food or other substances into the body. Absorption may take place by a number of means, as through the gastro-intestinal tract, through the skin, or through the mucous membranes of the eyes, nose, etc.

Food and drink taken by mouth pass through the esophagus to the stomach, and finally to the small intestine where the bulk of absorption of food takes place.

Many drugs are absorbed in the same way: taken by mouth, they are carried to the small intestine where they pass through the intestinal wall and enter the bloodstream. Drugs can also be absorbed through the skin and the mucous membranes.

Light rays are absorbed by the body through the skin.

accommodation The adjustment of the lens of the eyes to adapt to available light so as to see clearly in bright or subdued light, and to distinguish objects that are near and those that are far away.

When looking at a close object, the lens of the eye thickens and becomes more convex in order to focus the light from that object on the **retina**; for a distant object, the lens contracts to bring the light from the object into focus.

Over the years, the lens may lose some of its elasticity, limiting the ability to focus, often evidenced by the tendency to hold reading matter further away or the need to wear glasses for reading.

Achilles tendon The tendon that attaches the heel to the muscles of the calf of the leg.

acne An inflammation of the sebaceous glands, or oil-secreting organs, of the skin, manifested by eruptions of hard, inflamed pimples. The condition is most common among teenagers. The oil, sebum, is a fatty substance that normally helps maintain the texture of the skin.

Increased production of androgens, or male sex hormones, in both males and females during puberty causes the sebaceous glands to become especially active and secrete large amounts of sebum that is unusually thick. This sebum has a tendency to block the glands and hair follicles. When this occurs, the follicles become clogged with sebum and cellular debris.

Usually the condition is only alleviated by time, fading as the individual reaches adulthood. Washing gently with a mild soap and water often helps by removing some of the bacteria and debris. Medication is sometimes effective for reducing symptoms, as is exposure to sunlight that tends to dry up the eruptions.

acoustic nerve The nerve that serves the ear.

acquired Descriptive of that which is developed or modified by environmental influence, in contrast to that which is inherited.

acquired immune deficiency syndrome See **AIDS**

acrophobia An excessive dread of high places. Some fear of heights is natural as part of the human defense mechanism in consideration of the possible consequences of falling. Acrophobia, however, is an unreasonable magnification of this normal fear, as the acrophobic may be terrified even in a high place where the possibility of falling is nil. Acrophobia can be disabling when it precludes work or social functions that involve going above the ground floor of a building.

ACTH AdrenoCorticoTropic Hormone; an essential hormone produced by the pituitary gland, that lies at the base of the brain. ACTH provides the link between the pituitary gland and the cortex, or covering, of the adrenal glands that secretes vital hormones essential for maintaining the body's biochemical balance.

See also, **endocrinology**.

acupuncture The ancient technique of inserting the tips of long needles into the skin and manipulating them to relieve pain or treat disease.

acute Sudden or severe, although of short duration, as contrasted to *chronic*.

Addison's disease A condition that occurs when the adrenal glands cease to function properly and fail to produce adequate quantities of the hormones called steroids.

The symptoms of Addison's disease are weakness, fatigue, and increased pigmentation of the skin. Further symptoms may include weight loss, dehydration, low blood pressure, and nausea.

adduction Descriptive of the movement of a limb or part of a limb toward the midline of the body, as, for example, when an outstretched arm is brought back to the side of the body. Similarly, bringing a separated finger or toe back to its normal position is called adduction.

The muscles involved in such movement are referred to as *adductors*. See also, **abduction**.

adenitis Inflammation of a lymph gland or node. The lymph glands are scattered throughout the body, mainly concentrated at the side of the neck, in the armpits and in the groin, to aid the body in defending against infection.

adenocarcinoma A common form of cancerous tumor, originating in glandular tissue, mainly in the stomach, large intestine, gallbladder, pancreas, uterus or prostate gland. They may also start in the breast or lungs.

If not detected and treated promptly, adenocarcinomas commonly spread to other parts of the body via the blood or lymphatic systems The secondary tumor formed by such spreading to another site has the same appearance as that of the original tumor, aiding in further diagnosis if the location of the original tumor is unknown.

adenoids A mass of lymphoid tissue located at the entrance to the throat, above the tonsils. The adenoids contain specialized white blood cells that help provide protection against diseases of the respiratory system.

The adenoids may become enlarged by throat infections as the tonsils do, and sometimes, as a result of repeated infections or allergies, they remain enlarged, obstructing the nasal passage. There is some reluctance to remove them by surgery, however, because of the protective nature of their function and the fact that they begin to shrink away at an early age, so that they are usually gone during adolescence.

adenoma A benign, or non-malignant tumor originating in glandular tissue, as contrasted to **adenocarcinoma**.

An adenoma is usually harmless, although it may cause discomfort or pain. It remains isolated and will not spread or destroy other tissue.

adenosis Disease of a gland, particularly the abnormal development of glandular tissue.

adipose tissue Fatty tissue that occurs throughout the body, mainly directly under the skin, acting as an insulation and a source of energy. It is thickest in those parts of the body most liable to sudden trauma, such as the buttocks and feet where it acts as a shock absorber.

Adipose tissue in bone marrow supports the arteries and veins; in the joints and muscles, it deters injury from sudden shock; it provides cushion and support for the heart and lungs; keeps the intestines warm; and protects the kidneys from shock.

An excess of adipose tissue can be dangerous, particularly around the heart or lungs where it adds weight to the organ and restricts its movement.

adjuvant A substance added to a medication to intensify its action.

adrenal gland One of the two glands that each lie above a kidney and secrete hormones to control certain functions of the body.

Hormones from the adrenal glands assist in the maintenance of the body's fluid balance, enhance the body's ability to cope with stress, and are vital to the body's metabolism and sexual development.

aerobe A microorganism that requires oxygen to sustain life.

aftercare Care or treatment of one who is convalescing from an illness, operation, etc.

agoraphobia An irrational dread of open or public places; a fear of leaving a place considered safe, as the home, manifested by a feeling of panic, often accompanied by a rapid heartbeat, sweating and trembling.

AIDS Acquired Immune Deficiency Syndrome, a disease that attacks the body's immune system, rendering it unable to fight disease.

AIDS is caused by a microorganism called the human immunodeficiency virus (HIV), transmitted in body fluids through sexual intercourse, the use of non sterile hypodermic needles, and contact with infected blood. A pregnant woman also may transmit the disease to the fetus.

Early symptoms include low grade fever, swollen lymph nodes, fatigue, weight loss, and diarrhea. The AIDS victim suffers from an impaired immune system, and thus is susceptible to many diseases, including various cancers, skin infections, and fungal infections. Many of the victims develop a cancer known as Kaposi's sarcoma, which often appears as purplish bumps on the skin.

Some individuals may unknowingly be carriers without exhibiting any symptoms of the disease. Blood tests can indicate exposure to the disease, although not all individuals with positive test results will contract AIDS.

It is possible to limit the potential for exposure to the virus, as by restricting the number of one's sexual partners, using condoms, and avoiding contact with hypodermic needles or blood that may be contaminated. It is common practice to give blood in advance of elective surgery, so that any transfusions will be of one's own blood although thorough testing has virtually eliminated contamination in the blood supply. There is no evidence to indicate that the virus is transmitted through casual contacts.

albinism A condition characterized by a lack of natural pigment in the skin, causing an unnaturally pale appearance. The victim has a low tolerance for exposure to the sun and may exhibit an excessive sensitivity to bright light.

albumin One of the two major proteins of the blood, formed in the liver from ingested food.

Albumin is water-soluble and found in various forms in animals, egg white and vegetables.

See also, **globulin.**

albuminuria The presence of **albumin** in the urine, often a sign of kidney malfunction. **Proteinuria** is virtually the same as albuminuria, since albumin is the only protein detected in significant amounts in the urine.

alcohol *Alcohol* refers to any of a class of organic compounds containing one or more hydroxyl groups, as *ethyl alcohol*, obtained by the fermentation of sugar, used in medicine and beverages, or *methyl alcohol*, synthesized from carbon monoxide and hydrogen, used as a fuel, solvent, etc.; a colorless, volatile liquid.

alcoholism A disease caused by the excess consumption of alcoholic beverages.

Small doses of alcohol cause a feeling of relaxation, some loss of inhibitions and stimulation of the appetite due to an increase in the flow of gastric juices. Larger doses can impair speech and muscular coordination, and may irritate the stomach lining. A very large amount can produce severe depression of the central nervous system and may be fatal.

Regular ingestion of large quantities of alcohol can create a dependency and have injurious effects on the organs of the body, especially of the liver.

alkalosis An excessive concentration of alkali, or bicarbonate, in the body fluids.

Metabolic alkalosis normally is the result of the loss of hydrochloric acid from the stomach caused by protracted vomiting or taking an excessive amount of antacids for an upset stomach. Usually, the condition is alleviated when the kidneys have enough fluid to adjust the amount of alkali in the blood.

Respiratory alkalosis is caused by excessive exhalation of carbon dioxide, usually caused by hysterical over breathing that can often be corrected by breathing into a paper bag so that carbon dioxide breathed out is breathed in again.

Alkalosis may be characterized by dizziness and jerky muscular contractions.

allergen Any substance that causes an allergic response in the body's immune system.

allergy Excessive sensitivity to a substance, as pollen, feathers, or dust, or a chemical, such as a detergent, cosmetic or drug.

Allergy is the cause of hay fever and hives, and may be the cause of many cases of asthma, eczema and sinusitis.

Allergic reactions are an exaggeration of the normal immune response to bacteria, virus, etc. Normally, the body responds to invasion by forming antibodies to fight the invader. The allergic response is similar, except that the antibodies react with the allergen, or invader substance, to cause the body to release chemicals that create undesirable side affects. Allergic reactions are most common in the respiratory tract and the skin, though they may also affect the digestive system.

allergy and immunology The study of the diagnosis and treatment of disorders that relate to the body's ability to resist threatening substances.

Immunologists, for example, may search for ways to prevent cancer by modifying the immune system to reject cancerous growth or to bring about selective operation of the immune system so that the body will accept an organ transplant.

Immunologists who deal with allergies are concerned with identifying environmental irritants that cause symptoms, and devising treatment. Allergies may be alleviated by a change of environment to eliminate the irritant, the use of drugs to relieve symptoms, or a program of desensitization that involves the injection of minute amounts of the irritant to make the immune system less sensitive to it.

Alzheimer's disease A disease caused by presenile brain atrophy. Atrophy, or shrinking, of the brain may be expected in old age; *presenile brain atrophy* is the premature shrinking of the brain that causes slowing of the mental processes, beginning with forgetfulness and progressing to irrationality.

The first symptoms are small memory lapses, usually involving lack of recall for recent events. As they grow more serious, a person may forget the name of a close relative or friend, get lost traveling between familiar places, misplace articles, recheck tasks that has been done, or repeatedly ask questions that have already been answered.

As the disease grows worse, Alzheimer victim becomes confused, frustrated, and irritable. Endless repetition of unnecessary actions is also characteristic of the disease. Some victims may become extremely agitated with little or no provocation.

amblyopia Defective eyesight without any apparent defect of the eye. The condition may be temporary or permanent and it may be partial or result in total blindness in the affected eye.

Amblyopia may be caused by poisons in the system, as from alcohol, tobacco, lead, arsenic compounds, petroleum derivatives, etc. Strokes often cause some loss of vision when there is damage to the portion of the brain that controls eyesight.

amenorrhea A lack of menstruation. *Primary amenorrhea* refers to a condition in which menstruation has never occurred. *Secondary amenorrhea* refers to a cessation of menstruation in a woman who has previously been menstruating.

Secondary amenorrhea is probably most commonly caused by pregnancy and lactation. It may also be due to anemia brought on by heavy menstrual blood loss in the past, ovarian failure, certain pituitary diseases, an emotional disturbance or even a distinctive change in life style.

amentia Mental retardation; a congenital mental deficiency. See also, **dementia**.

amino acid Any of the group of organic compounds that form the basic constituents of protein.

amnesia A loss of memory that may be temporary or permanent, caused by damage to the brain or psychological reaction.

An injury to the head that involves loss of consciousness may result in some loss of memory. Often the memories of a period before and after the injury are blanked out. The memory may return as the victim recovers from the injury, but parts of memory may never be recovered. Similar loss of memory can occur in the case of severe **trauma**, or injury, that does not involve the head.

Abrupt memory loss without injury or illness is usually the result of a psychological disorder; a person wandering aimlessly with no recollection of name or address is probably suffering from *hysterical amnesia* brought on by emotional stress.

Disease or injury can affect short-term or long-term memory, or both.

Normally, there is no recollection of infancy, but memory for most of one's life is, for the most part, continuous. In old age, the memory of recent events may be faulty, while memories from the distant past remain intact. Short-term memory loss is also a symptom of chronic alcoholism and some brain diseases such as Alzheimer's.

amniocentesis Drawing off a sample of the amniotic fluid from the womb of a pregnant woman in order to examine it.

The amniotic fluid is the medium in which the fetus lies and contains some cells from the fetus that can be analyzed to detect a number of abnormalities.

amputation The cutting off of a part of the body, usually a limb or part of a limb.

Amputation may be the result of an accident, as in an automobile or industrial plant, or it may be part of a surgical procedure necessitated by injury or disease.

anabolism The conversion of food into living tissue by the body; part of the total metabolic process. See also, **catabolism**.

analgesia Relief from pain without loss of consciousness.

Analgesics, or drugs that produce analgesia, are of three types: those that act directly on the source of the pain, those that act on the brain, and those that are specific, that is, they act on a particular illness or disease.

The most common analgesics are those in the first group, such as acetaminophen or aspirin, used to combat relatively mild pain. In addition to its analgesic action, aspirin is known for its ability to reduce fever and inflammation; for some, however, it may cause an upset stomach or some other reaction. Acetaminophen is milder, but is not as effective for reducing fever or inflammation.

The second group, far more potent and with a potential for abuse and addiction, are dispensed only by prescription. They include substances such as morphine, methadone and codeine.

The analgesics in the third group, as noted above, act on specifics, such as a migraine or a certain types of neuralgia.

Analgesia can also be uncontrolled, as from a disease of the sensory system or from an overdose of alcohol.

anaphylactic shock A severe reaction of the body to certain vaccines, antibiotics, insect stings or other antigens that may cause a state of total collapse.

Normally the body reacts to the presence of an **antigen**, or foreign substance, by creating an **antibody**, or compound, that can render the foreign substance harmless. In some persons, sensitivity to certain antigens triggers a reaction that is harmful and can be dangerous. Such sensitivity is cumulative, in that subsequent attacks are worse than the previous attack.

Anaphylactic shock is most readily evidenced by difficulty in breathing, and failure to act quickly may prove fatal—the victim requires immediate medical attention.

Any significant reaction to a shot or an insect bite should be quickly brought to the attention of a physician.

androgen A substance that promotes the development of secondary male characteristics

anemia A shortage of red blood cells or a deficiency in hemoglobin, the pigment in red blood cells that carries oxygen.

The symptoms of anemia are not distinctive, and the condition may not be detected unless it is severe. The sufferer may experience fatigue, shortness of breath, rapid heart rate, headaches, loss of appetite, dizziness, and weakness. Very severe cases of anemia may exhibit swollen ankles, a rapid weak pulse and pale clammy skin.

Anemia can be caused by inadequate materials for the manufacture of red blood cells, the inability of bone marrow to manufacture the cells, excessive or untimely destruction of the cells, or inherited abnormalities.

A lack of raw materials, such as iron, vitamin B_{12}, or folic acid can inhibit the production of hemoglobin. Iron, for example, may be lost in excessive bleeding, or be unavailable in a diet lacking in dark green vegetables, egg yolk, meat, seafood, or dried beans. Illness or disease may render the body unable to absorb the vital materials even though they are present.

The function of the bone marrow may be inhibited by disease, exposure to radioactivity, or drugs.

Red blood cells may be destroyed by excessive bleeding, disease, infection, or a mismatched blood transfusion.

In inherited, or congenital conditions, there is an abnormality in the red blood cell that inhibits effective function, such as sickle cell anemia, in which the blood cells cannot carry sufficient oxygen to the body and are inclined to break down easily.

Conditions such as bleeding ulcers, cancer, and alcoholism are likely to cause one or more types of anemia.

anesthesia A diminished or lost sense of feeling, especially the sensations of pain and touch. Anesthesia can be brought on by disease, trauma, damage to the nervous system, or the action of drugs.

Anesthesia usually refers to the administering of a drug to produce a reduced state of sensitivity in order to perform a surgical operation, or to the drug so administered.

anesthesiology The science of the administration of drugs to reduce or limit sensitivity. The anesthesiologist specializes in administering those drugs that limit sensation, or the body's ability to sense pain.

aneurysm A bulge, or swelling, in an artery that has been weakened by disease or injury. The primary danger associated with an aneurysm is that of rupture of the blood vessel, causing internal bleeding that can prove fatal.

Aneurysms occur most often in: the aorta, the largest artery in the body; the artery behind the knee; and the arteries at the base of the brain. The aneurysm may be detected in the abdomen as a pulsating mass that is very tender, and at the back of the knee, one that is painful. In a neck artery, there may be interference with nerves serving the eye, causing double vision, as well as a pulsating sound that the victim may detect.

A dissecting aneurysm is one in which the blood runs between the walls of the artery, sometimes eventually reentering the main vessel. A dissecting aneurysm in the chest will cause severe pain in the area and often symptoms resembling a heart attack. In the abdomen, pain may be severe in the area and radiate to the back, accompanied by a loss of blood to the legs.

angina pectoris A dull pressure or pain in the center of the chest that may be accompanied by a burning sensation not unlike indigestion and may radiate down the left arm; an indication that the heart muscle is not getting enough oxygen during a period of stress or exertion

The pain of an attack of angina pectoris is usually not as severe as that of a heart attack, and the heart muscles are not damaged. The pain will usually recede quickly if the victim stops all activity and rests. Although an attack of angina is not a heart attack, the experience indicates that the individual is probably a likely candidate for heart attack.

A number of conditions can prevent the heart muscle from getting enough blood to supply adequate oxygen. The most common condition is narrowing of the coronary artery due to **atherosclerosis**. Physical or mental stress can hasten the onset of the condition. whatever the suspected cause, a physician should be consulted.

Angina is usually treated by altering lifestyle to reduce stress and strain on the heart. Smoking, overeating and overexertion should be avoided. Regular exercise is necessary, but it should be tailored to the condition, avoiding those activities that place sudden, severe demands on the heart.

angiography An x ray examination of blood vessels that have been injected with a substance that is opaque to x rays in order to make them visible on the x-ray plate or viewing screen. This technique is also used in the diagnosis of tumors, especially of the brain.

angioma A tumor made up of mostly blood and lymph vessels.

angioplasty Any of a number of surgical techniques for the repairing of damaged blood vessels.

ankylosis A condition characterized by stiffness or immobility of a joint caused by fusion of its parts as a consequence of injury or surgery.

anorexia nervosa *Anorexia* is a lack of appetite, or desire for food; *anorexia nervosa* is an *aversion* to food.

The condition usually begins as an attempt to lose weight, but is then carried to extremes The individual continues to lose weight, and may suffer from severe vitamin and mineral deficiency. The condition is often worsened by vomiting, the use of purgatives and excessive exercise. If allowed to continue the victim will literally starve to death, while convinced that his or her diet is adequate.

anthrax An infectious disease that commonly infects cattle, goats or sheep and can be transmitted to man. Humans contract the infection from the spores that survive in contaminated wool, hair or hides. Hygienic methods of handling these raw materials have diminished the spread of the disease.

Infection can affect the skin, where it is characterized by itching pustules that turn black as the infection spreads. The infection also has a tendency to attack the lungs.

antibody A chemical compound produced by the body to combine with and neutralize a particular foreign substance, called an **antigen**, entering the body.

The antibody created in reaction to a particular antigen is a unique one, effective only in defense against that antigen. Its purpose is to overcome an attack of infectious matter and to stand ready to ward off future attacks.

The first time a particular bacteria invades, the body formulates an antibody. By the time the infection has run its course, there are often enough of the specific antibodies remaining in the blood to ward off the second attack, perhaps for life. Such is the basis for immunization, that which introduces dead or weakened bacteria into the body so that it will develop the necessary antibodies while experiencing few or none of the symptoms of the disease.

antigen Any substance the immune system identifies as a potential threat that starts the reaction leading to the production of a special **antibody**.

Antigens are contained in bacteria and viruses, blood from an incompatible blood group, and sera injected into the body for the treatment or prevention of infectious diseases.

antipyretic Any medication that tends to reduce fever, such as aspirin.

antiseptic Any substance that inhibits the action of bacteria.

antitoxin A substance that neutralizes a specific toxin that is released by bacteria.

anuria Lack of urination caused by kidney failure or by a blockage.

anxiety Fear or apprehension about some future possibility.

Anxiety is a normal response to anything that is of concern, the outcome of which is uncertain, as a first day of school or a trip to the dentist. It may, however, become excessive and irrational. Concern about making a good impression when meeting people, for example, is a form of anxiety; such anxiety is unhealthy, however, when apprehension is so great that one refuses to meet new people. Excessive anxiety about pollution, auto accidents, etc. can trap one in the home without hope of reprieve.

aorta The main artery of the body, that extends from the left ventricle of the heart to begin the distribution of blood throughout the rest of the body.

aphagia A lack of ability to swallow.

aphasia Partial or total loss of the ability to speak coherently, especially to connect words and ideas, as from a stroke or other illness.

apnea A temporary stopping of breathing.

apoplexy, See stroke

appendicitis Inflammation of the appendix, a small growth at the end of the large intestine, near its juncture with the small intestine.

The appendix serves no apparent purpose and the operation is quite simple. An infected appendix, however, can burst, with serious consequences.

Appendicitis usually produces a dull or sharp pain in the abdomen that may be intensified by coughing, sneezing, or even moving. This is usually accompanied by a feeling of nausea and constipation, although diarrhea is not infrequent. As the pain becomes constant, it may move to the lower right side of the abdomen over the appendix or even to the back. The area around the appendix may become very tender. At this stage the appendix is likely to become so swollen that it bursts, infecting the surrounding organs and creating a potentially life threatening situation.

Symptoms vary from person to person, as does the location of the appendix. When there is severe abdominal pain that persists, consult a physician as quickly as possible.

arteriosclerosis Any condition in which the walls of the arteries are thickened and made rigid, making them unable to process an adequate supply of blood. Commonly called *hardening of the arteries*. See also, **atherosclerosis**.

arthritis Any inflammation of the **joints**.

Arthritis causes swelling, pain, and stiffness in the joints. Damp weather, emotional stress excess weight, and abuse of the joints at work or play can make symptoms more pronounced.

The onset of arthritis is brought about by damage to the smooth surfaces where two bones join caused by injury, a progressive wearing away with age, or illness, such as crystal deposits from gout or tumors that push the joint out of position. The most common cause is *rheumatoid arthritis* which causes inflammation in the synovium, a thin membrane that lines and lubricates the joint. The inflammation ultimately destroys the elastic tissue that lines the joint, the cartilage. The cartilage is replaced by scar tissue, and the joint becomes swollen, deformed and painful.

The most effective treatment for arthritis includes drug therapy, exercise, and rest. Aspirin is the drug most commonly prescribed for arthritis—two or three tablets several times a day may reduce inflammation and relieve pain. Non aspirin pain relievers may also be effective. Daily exercise is important to preserve mobility in the arthritic joints. Moist heat is often recommended reduce pain and improve mobility.

arthroplasty The surgical repair or replacement of a joint.

In some cases where joints have become stiff and painful as the result of disease or injury, the joint may be excised by cutting away the damaged portions of bone. Such surgery leaves scar tissue to fill the gap and although the pain is relieved, the joint may be unstable.

In other cases, it is possible to replace the joint or a portion of the joint that has been excised. Replacement surgery has been particularly successful in the replacement of the hip joint.

asbestosis An inflammation of the lungs caused by the inhalation of asbestos particles.

Certain types of the mineral *asbestos* do not burn or conduct heat or electricity, and are therefore used in the making of heat and fire resistant products, and insulation. Asbestosis is commonly contracted by those who work with asbestos or in some other way are exposed to fine particle of asbestos in the air.

The asbestos particles irritate the lungs and cause shortness of breath and coughing. The victim may also suffer loss of appetite, weight loss, and bouts of fatigue. After a time, often many years, the sufferer is likely to contract tuberculosis and cancer.

ascorbic acid See **Vitamin C**

asepsis The condition of being completely free of germs.

asphyxia Suffocation; a lack of oxygen in the blood caused by interference with respiration, usually involving loss of consciousness.

Drowning is probably the most common cause of asphyxia when water blocks the passage of air to the lungs. The air passage may also be shut off by accidental inhalation of food, blockage of the throat by swelling from an infection, or strangulation.

Other causes include the inhalation of air that contains too little oxygen, air containing poison gases, and electric shock.

asthenia A loss or lack of body strength or stamina.

asthma A respiratory disorder characterized by difficulty in breathing.

Asthma attacks may be set off by an allergy, infection, overexertion, inhaling cold air, or stress. In normal breathing, air enters the lungs and is expelled through the tiny bronchioles at the end of the bronchi. The asthmatic's difficulty in breathing is caused by sensitivity of the bronchioles that brings about constriction or clogging of the tubes so that spent air cannot be properly expelled, hindering the inhalation of fresh air.

Asthma attacks are unpredictable: they may last from a few minutes to a week or more; they may occur regularly or only once in a few years; they may be mild or extremely severe.

astigmatism A condition of the eye in which imperfect curvature of the cornea or lens prevents the image on the retina to focus clearly.

In normal vision, objects are focused sharply onto the retina. When the surfaces have an incorrect curvature, the focus is distorted and parts of the image appear blurred. Although the blurring may not be apparent, the eye may constantly readjust to correct the image, causing them to tire quickly, one of the primary symptoms of astigmatism.

ataxia Lack of muscle coordination.

Ataxia may be congenital, that is, existing from birth, or caused by injury or disease of the central nervous system. It is characterized by irregular movements of the body that are unsteady or clumsy, as an awkward manner of walking, with feet wide apart or a lack of balance

atherosclerosis A condition of the arteries in which blood flow is blocked by fatty deposits.

Atherosclerosis is the most common form of **arteriosclerosis**, or hardening of the arteries, and a major contributor to heart attacks and strokes.

Formation begins when the concentration of fats that are necessary to proper function of the body and always present in the bloodstream is greatly increased and begin to form fatty streaks on the artery wall. The streaks attract nodules of cholesterol. Scar tissue forms under the nodules and attracts calcium deposits that create a hard material called plaque. The lining of plaque restricts the ability of the arteries to expand and contract properly and interferes with the flow of blood. Clots may form, further restricting the flow of blood, and in extreme cases, cutting it off entirely.

Atherosclerosis is not usually apparent until the arteries leading to a vital organ are blocked or closed off completely. Symptoms then relate to the organ that has been cut off—stoppage of blood to the heart, for example, will trigger a heart attack; closing off arteries to the head may cause dizziness, blindness or a stroke.

Aside for treatment of the symptoms caused by atherosclerosis, and surgical procedure to bypass clogged arteries, the only treatments for the disease itself are probably of greater value in prevention, such as those of losing weight, reducing cholesterol in the diet, avoiding smoking and exercising in moderation.

athlete's foot A fungal infection of the foot.

Athlete's foot is characterized by an itching, burning, or stinging feeling, especially between the toes where the skin often reddens and cracks. Peeling of the skin may occur, as well.

Treatment generally involves any of a number of salves, powders or liquids available from the drugstore without a prescription.

Athlete's foot can usually be prevented by eliminating the warm, moist environment in which the fungus thrives. The key is to dry feet well, especially between the toes, after taking a shower; change socks often and rotate shoes, especially in the hot, humid summer months; and use powder to keep the feet dry. Because athlete's foot is contagious, if it's not possible to avoid public showers, as in a health club, clogs should be worn in the shower and the feet dusted with an anti-fungal powder afterwards. In spite of caution, athlete's foot may easily be contracted and will often recur. If recurrence is frequent and severe, a physician should be consulted to verify that the problem is not caused by infection with similar symptoms, such as an allergic reaction to chemicals in the shoes.

atrophy The degeneration or wasting away of an organ or part of the body, as from disease or disuse.

auscultation Listening, as with a stethoscope to sounds within the body; sometimes, referring to the study of such sounds.
There are sounds made within the body, especially by the heart and lungs, that are characteristic of normal operation. By listening, or auscultation, the physician, with the aid of a stethoscope for amplification, is able distinguish those sounds from others that may be indicators of malfunction.

autism A condition characterized by a preoccupation with fantasy and lack of concern for reality.
An early sign of autism is indifference to those who give care; an infant may not respond to affection or being picked up. There may be little or no interest in learning to eat, use the toilet or speak, though there is no difficulty in learning to walk.
Autistic children may have an excellent memory and a high level of intelligence, but no apparent concern or desire to interact with those around them. Change, such as rearranging furniture, is upsetting to them. It would appear that their perception of the everyday world is distorted and perhaps frightening, so that they seek protection in that which is familiar.

autoimmune disease Any of a number of diseases that cause the body's immune system to produce antibodies to attack healthy tissue in the body.

autopsy Examination of a body after death.
The autopsy, also known as a *postmortem examination* or *necropsy*, is conducted by a *pathologist* who dissects the body, usually to determine the cause of death. Permission for the examination may be granted by a close relative, although such examination may be required in the case of death by violence or that of a suspicious nature, depending on state law.
The examination is very methodical, from a thorough survey of the outer surfaces to careful examination of each organ, and includes taking samples of tissue and of the contents of the body, as urine, blood, undigested food, etc. that are kept for laboratory analysis.

backbone See **spinal column.**

bacteria Any of a class of one-celled microscopic organisms, smaller than yeasts and larger than viruses, with a primitive nucleus, that multiplies by splitting in two and is able to multiply outside a living cell.
Not all bacteria are harmful and some are especially useful, as those that live in the intestines and aid in digestion, those that enrich the soil, or those used for making wine, beer, cheese, etc.
Those bacteria that produce disease are called *pathogenic*. They cause disease by invading tissue and then reproducing to destroy their surroundings, or by releasing toxins that poison the body.
Destructive bacteria are usually transmitted by direct contact, by contact with contaminated matter or by insects. Normally, the body is able to protect itself from invasion by harmful bacteria, but occasionally requires the assistance of antibiotics that destroy the organisms or prevent their multiplication.

bariatrics The study and treatment of obesity.
In addition to establishing dietary guidelines, the bariatrician is concerned with analyzing data related to the condition of being overweight or underweight in order to separate hard scientific evidence from myths about the problem.

battered-child syndrome Physical abuse of a child by a parent, guardian, baby sitter, or anyone else in a position of trust
Abuse is often deliberate and repeated, and may be provoked by a seemingly inconsequential act.
In additional to physical injuries, the child may be deprived of food or comfort, and suffer psychological damage as a result of the abuse.

bedsores Ulcerated sores on the body of person who is bedridden for an extended period; also called *pressure sores* or *decubitus ulcers.*
When the small blood vessels that nourish the skin and underlying tissue are compressed for an extended period, they cease to function and the tissue dies. Continued pressure can cause a spread of the condition to a large area and the formation of an ulcer that may become infected.
Treatment of bedsores, like prevention, requires relief of the pressure; the patient must be allowed to recuperate on an air bed or in a net hammock.

Bell's palsy A partial or total paralysis of one side of the face.
Bell's palsy is characterized by a lop-sided appearance to the face, mainly due to drooping of the mouth in affected side. Believed to be caused by inflammation of the nerve

controlling the facial muscles, the onset of the disease is rapid. Recovery usually occurs in about a week, although it is not always complete.

bends A painful condition in which nitrogen bubbles in the blood block the flow of blood to tissues; a symptom of decompression sickness or caisson disease.

The bends may be experienced by those moving too quickly from areas of high pressure to areas of lower pressure, as deep sea divers.

Nitrogen, present in the atmosphere, dissolves in the blood. The amount of nitrogen from the lungs that dissolves in the blood increases as pressure increases. The reverse is also true, that as the pressure decreases, the nitrogen moves from the blood to the lungs, but the process takes longer, so that if a diver surfaces too rapidly, nitrogen bubbles remain in the blood where they form air locks.

benign Descriptive of a tumor that is not malignant, that is, one that is expected to be of little or no harm to the body.

beriberi A vitamin deficiency disease caused by a lack of thiamine.

Beriberi affects the circulation and the nervous system and in severe cases may cause heart failure.

bile A yellow fluid produced by the liver to aid in the digestion, especially of fats.

Bile works in the intestine to break down fat into tiny globules that can be passed through the walls of the small intestine into the bloodstream, to provide fuel for the body.

Bile is produced continuously in the liver and stored in the gallbladder until food is ingested, at which time the bile is emptied into the intestine.

If the flow of bile is interrupted because the liver is not functioning properly or because of stoppage, digestion is impaired. Such condition can cause jaundice, a yellowing of the skin and eyes. Although jaundice is not a disease in itself it is symptomatic of a potentially severe problem and should be referred to a physician.

biopsy Removal of a small specimen of tissue for examination and diagnosis.

biotin See **Vitamin B complex**

birth defect Descriptive of an abnormality that is present at birth.

A birth defect may be *genetic*, that is, inherited from one or both parents, or it may be acquired during pregnancy or at birth.

bleeder Descriptive of a person who bleeds excessively, even from an otherwise insignificant wound.

There are some conditions, such as hemophilia, or those caused by a side affect of medication, etc. that do not allow normal clotting to occur. Persons suffering from such conditions may be in danger of bleeding to death even from the slightest wounds. This free bleeding may be internal as well as external, a condition that warrants close observation for shock. After applying compress bandages or gauze, the person should be rushed to the nearest hospital where medical treatment can be quickly administered.

blister A collection of fluid, as serum or blood under the outer layer of skin.

A blister may be caused by friction, as from the foot rubbing against the lining of a shoe; by heat, as from a burn; or by a caustic chemical.

An unbroken blister is little more than a petty annoyance if properly tended once the source of irritation is removed; however, a broken blister must be kept clean to prevent infection. Severe blistering should be referred to a physician for medication.

blood A fluid that runs throughout the body by way of the arteries, veins and capillaries.

Blood is composed of serum or plasma, red cells, white cells, and platelets. Plasma is a fluid that carries the blood cells and transports nutrients to all tissues. It also transports waste products resulting from tissue activity to the organs for excretion. Red cells give color to the blood and carry oxygen. White cells aid in defending the body against infection. Platelets are essential to the formation of the blood clots necessary to stop bleeding.

One-fifteenth to one-twelfth of the body weight is blood. A person weighing one hundred fifty pounds will have approximately ten to twelve pints of blood. If the tissues do not receive blood, they will die from lack of oxygen. The loss of two pints of blood by an adult, or eight to ten percent of the total contained in the body, usually is serious. The loss of three pints over a short time, one to two hours, may be fatal. The loss of four pints or more will require blood transfusions to prevent death. At certain points in the body, fatal hemorrhages may occur in a very short time. The cutting of the two principal blood vessels in the neck, the principal blood vessels in the arms, or the principal blood vessels in the thighs may cause hemorrhage that will prove fatal in one to three minutes or even less. Rupture of the main trunk blood vessels of the chest and abdomen may prove fatal in less than thirty seconds.

The loss of blood can cause a state of physical shock that occurs because there is insufficient blood flowing through the tissues of the body to provide food and oxygen.

blood clot The gelatinous material formed to stem the flow of blood when a blood vessel is injured.

Normally, the lining of a blood vessel allows the blood to flow without change in its chemistry; however, when a blood vessel is ruptured and the blood comes into contact with foreign tissue, clotting begins. *Platelets* in the blood, triggered by the contact, release a chemical that begins a chain reaction involving a number of protein constituents in the blood, ending with the conversion of fibrinogen, a soluble material, to fibrin, that is insoluble. The fibrin is laid down in fine strands that collect white and red cells to form a clot.

blood vessels Any of the passageways that carry blood: the arteries, veins and capillaries.

Oxygenated blood is carried from the heart by a large artery called the aorta. Smaller arteries branch off from this large artery, and those arteries in turn branch off into still smaller arteries. These arteries divide and subdivide until they become very small, ending in threadlike vessels known as capillaries, which extend into all the organs and tissues.

After the blood has furnished nourishment and oxygen to the tissues and organs of the body, it takes on waste products, particularly carbon dioxide. The blood returns to the heart by a system of vessels called veins. The veins connect with the arteries through the capillaries.

Very small veins join, forming larger veins, which in turn join until the very largest veins return the blood to the heart. Blood passing through the kidneys is cleared of nonvolatile waste products. When the blood from the body reaches the heart, carbon dioxide and other volatile waste products contained in the blood are eliminated and the oxygen needed by the body is replaced. The heart pumps the blood delivered by the veins into the lungs, where it flows through another network of capillaries. There, the carbon dioxide and other volatile waste products are exchanged for oxygen through the walls of air cells. The blood is thereby oxygenated and ready to be returned to the heart, which recirculates it throughout the body.

The time required for the blood to make one complete circulation of the body through miles of blood vessels is approximately seventy-five seconds in an adult at rest.

boil A painful inflammation of the skin caused by bacterial infection; a furuncle.

When **bacteria** enter the skin through a hair follicle and multiply while producing toxins, they in turn are attacked by white blood cells, or **leukocytes** whose job it is to protect the body from such invasion. As the white blood cells consume the bacteria and destroy the infection, a pustule that comprises the center of a boil may form. The pustule is made up of white blood cells and cells destroyed by the bacteria that are trapped in the hair follicle. When the pustule pushes to the surface of the skin and erupts, the boil will drain and heal.

Boils are most often formed on the neck, face, or back, but they can be located anywhere on the skin. As they grow, they become red and hot; pressure exerted on surrounding nerves can cause considerable discomfort.

No attempt should be made to burst a boil prematurely by squeezing, as it may erupt under the skin and create new infection. Normally, the boil will mature on its own; however, frequent applications of a warm wet towel may hasten the process. Care should be taken to keep the area clean, especially after the boil erupts, in order to prevent spread of infection. A particularly severe boil or the presence of numerous boils may be symptomatic of other problems and should be referred to a physician.

When a group of boils connects below the surface of the skin, the formation is called a **carbuncle.**

botulism A type of food poisoning caused by a bacterium found in improperly canned or preserved food.

In addition to the classic symptoms of food poisoning—nausea, vomiting, and abdominal cramps—toxin produced by the bacteria interferes with the transmission of nerve impulses and can cause irregularities in vision, followed by paralysis of the arms and difficulty breathing. Botulism can be fatal, so an early diagnosis and referral to a physician is critical.

breastbone A bone at the front of the chest that travels downward from the collarbone and to which the ribs are attached; the sternum.

bronchitis Inflammation of the bronchi, or air passages of the lung.

When the bronchial tubes, the air passages between the windpipe and the lungs, become infected and swollen, the glands in the mucous membrane that lines the tubes increase the secretion of mucus. The cough characteristic of bronchitis is an attempt to expel the excess fluid. In extreme cases, the infection may extend to the lungs and develop into *bronchopneumonia.*

Short term bronchitis, often following an attack of the common cold or influenza is called *acute bronchitis.* Bronchitis caused by repeated irritation from recurring infection, smoke, dust or other environmental effluence, is termed *chronic bronchitis.* Either condition is overcome only when the source of irritation has been removed.

Cigarette smoking is a primary cause of chronic bronchitis. Tobacco smoke interferes with the action of the hairlike fibers that push mucus from the lungs, allowing the mucus and irritants trapped by the mucus to remain in the lungs.

In addition to the characteristic cough, one who contracts acute bronchitis may experience flu-like symptoms: slight fever, a feeling of general malaise, aching muscles, etc. Treatment usually involves rest, steam inhalations and, if necessary, antibiotics to prevent further infection.

Chronic bronchitis often leads to permanent damage of the lungs and heart, and so should be left to the care of a physician.

brucellosis An infection caused by the bacterium *Brucella* contracted from cattle, hogs or goats.

Also known as *undulant fever* or *Malta fever,* brucellosis is primarily contracted by persons in contact with animals or involved in meat processing, but it can also be transmitted in unpasteurized milk.

Symptoms of the disease are similar to those for influenza: fever, headache, chills, and listlessness. The name *undulant fever* comes from a tendency of the condition to undulate, or move in waves, that is, bouts of the fever alternate with periods without symptoms.

bubonic plague A highly contagious epidemic disease transmitted by the bite of infected rat fleas.

The name *bubonic* derives from a symptom of the disease: a bubo, or swelling, of lymph glands, especially in the armpit or groin. Similarly, a characteristic bleeding into the skin that causes dark blotches gave rise to the name *Black Death.*

The disease is now generally limited to unsanitary tropical areas, but there are occasional outbreaks in the western parts of the United States that are controlled by modern drugs.

bursitis Inflammation of a bursa, a small sac that cushions the juncture between moving parts as bones, tendons, etc.

The bursa contains a lubricating fluid that serves to eliminate friction and promote smooth movement of the joints. The swelling and tenderness from inflammation can cause such severe discomfort that movement is impossible.

Bursitis can be *chronic*, caused by repeated or constant stress on a joint, most commonly the elbow, shoulder or knee; or *acute*, caused by sudden trauma.

Immobilizing the joint may allow healing to take place, especially in the case of acute bursitis. Chronic bursitis is usually characterized by permanent damage frequently accompanied by calcium deposits that may render the joint immobile. Moist heat or cold compresses may ease the pain and aspirin or other pain relievers can also be effective. Surgery may be advised in extreme cases.

bypass To skirt or circumvent, as a graft that passes around a clogged section of artery.

An artery narrowed by **atherosclerosis** places an added burden on the organ or tissue it services that can lead to further damage. In addition, there is the possibility that a blood clot will close the vessel completely, with catastrophic results. In many cases the problem can be resolved by grafting a section taken from another part of the body or by implanting a man-made device to circumvent the damaged section of the natural vessel.

cachexia A weakened, emaciated state of the body caused by prolonged illness.

calcification The abnormal accumulation of calcium salts in body tissue.

calculus A solidified mass, as a stone, that may be formed in the kidneys, gallbladder or other organs of the body.

callus A thickened growth of the skin; a callosity.

A callus is generally seen as protection to an area of the skin subjected to abnormal friction or pressure, as on parts of a laborer's hands or on the bottoms of the feet.

A callus may become so thick that the skin is inflexible and cracks, causing discomfort. In such a case, it may be necessary to remove the source of friction and consult a physician if discomfort is extreme. There are non-prescription medications that will soften the callosity, but removal at home should be considered carefully because of the danger of infection.

cancer Any type of malignant growth.

Normal cells reproduce in a methodical manner in accordance with genetic coding; cancerous growth is uncontrolled, spreading throughout the body, destroying or replacing normal cells.

Cancer cells have the unique ability to propagate outside the organ where they originate; the cells may be carried in the blood or lymphatic channels to other parts of the body where they attack healthy tissue.

While there is no single preventative for cancer, the risk of exposure may be lessened by avoiding known *carcinogens*, or cancer causing agents. Most cancer is treatable, so that early warning is also one of the best lines of defense. Symptoms to look for are: radical changes in bowel or bladder function; a wound that does not heal; unusual bleeding or discharge; chronic indigestion; a thickening lump anywhere on the body; any significant change in body function or formation.

canker sore An ulcerated sore, usually of the lips or lining of the mouth.

Canker sores are not contagious, and may be induced by fever, allergy, or injury to the mouth, as from ill-fitting dentures.

cardiology The study of the heart and circulatory system especially diagnosis and treatment of disorders.

capillaries Extremely tiny blood vessels that connect the arteries and the veins.

carbohydrate Any of a number of natural compounds that produce heat and energy, comprising the bulk of organic matter on earth.

carbuncle A large boil formed from the interconnection of several boils.

Carbuncles cause severe pain associated with throbbing, possible fever and a feeling of malaise.

carcinogen Any substance that promotes the formation of a cancerous growth.

carcinoma Any of the malignant cancerous growths of the cells that line organs.

cardiology The branch of medicine concerned with the study, diagnosis and treatment of the diseases and disorders of the heart.

cardiovascular system The complex that circulates blood to all cells.

The cardiovascular system is made up of tubes called vessels, liquid contents called blood, and the pump which is the heart. These vessels are able to dilate and constrict. The size of the vessels is changed by signals transmitted through nerve pathways from the nervous system to the muscles in the blood vessel walls.

When the body is in its normal state there is enough blood to fill the system completely—approximately ten to twelve pints (for a person weighing 150 pounds). The pumping action of the heart supplies all parts of the body with blood.

Food and oxygen are transported to each part of the body and waste products are removed through this system.

carpal tunnel syndrome Numbness, pain and weakness associated with compression of the *median nerve* at the wrist.

The finger tendons and the median nerve are contained in a tunnel formed by the carpal bones and the sturdy membrane that stretches over them. Any swelling of tissue within the tunnel can put pressure on the median nerve that controls the thumb, index finger, and middle finger.

Carpal tunnel syndrome may originate with pregnancy, a sprain or fracture of the wrist, arthritis, or any condition that tends to produce swelling or distortion of the wrist. The condition may be acquired or made worse by any activity that requires constant or repetitive twisting of the hand and wrist. Many cases are caused by long hours of working at a computer keyboard that requires keeping the hands at an unnatural angle.

The pain resulting from the condition has been known to run up the arm, into the shoulder and even the neck. Eventually, the sufferer may be unable to make a fist as the fingers weaken and the muscles atrophy.

The first step to recovery is to alleviate the pressure on the nerve by removing the cause; in severe cases, surgery may be necessary to prevent permanent damage. In extreme cases, that is, where treatment has been delayed, full recovery may not be possible.

carrier An otherwise healthy individual who carries an infecting organism without evidence of symptoms, and who can infect others.

cartilage The tough connective tissue between bones.

In the embryo, cartilage forms the skeleton that is later changed into bone. In the adult, the cartilage serves primarily to reduce friction in the joints and also functions as a cushion.

catabolism The breaking down of complex substances by the body to provide energy; part of the total metabolic process. See also, **anabolism**.

cataleptic One who suffers from periodic bouts of immobility characterized by muscular rigidity, an apparent suspension of awareness and, sometimes, loss of consciousness.

cataphasia A condition characterized by frequent repetition of the same words or phrases.

cataract A cloudiness or haziness of the lens of the eye that degrades vision.

In normal vision, the lens of the eye is clear and serves to direct light into the eye. When the lens becomes more or less opaque, the light is diffused, blurring the vision.

To correct the condition, the defective lens may be surgically removed, and replaced by an implant, special glasses or contact lenses.

catatonia A phase of schizophrenia characterized by periods of muscular rigidity and withdrawal alternating with periods of agitation.

catheter A hollow tube inserted into the body for the injection or withdrawal of fluids.

cerebral palsy Any of a number of conditions marked by impaired muscle control.

Cerebral palsy is caused by nerve or brain damage, usually occurring around the time of birth.

Early signs of the condition may be convulsions, partial paralysis of face muscles, or slow development of motor functions, as sitting, crawling or standing. Later symptoms may range from a simple lack of coordination to the inability to move normally. The damage that causes cerebral palsy may also cause a number of other conditions, such as mental retardation, or learning and behavioral disorders.

chemotherapy Treatment of disease with the use of chemicals.

chest The chest is formed by twenty-four ribs, twelve on each side, that are attached in the back to **vertebrae**. The seven upper pairs of ribs are attached to the **breastbone** in front by **cartilage**. The next three pairs of ribs are attached in front by a common cartilage to the seventh rib instead of the breastbone. The lower two pairs of ribs, known as the floating ribs, are not attached in front.

chest cavity The chest cavity is cone-shaped, formed by the upper part of the spinal column, or backbone, at the back, the ribs on the sides, and the ribs and breastbone in front. The diaphragm, a thin, muscular partition at the bottom of the chest cavity, separates the chest cavity and the abdominal cavity. The diaphragm is dome-shaped and lower in the back than in the front.

The lungs and the heart occupy most of the chest cavity. The heart lies between the lungs in the center of the chest behind the breastbone. It is positioned slightly to the left side, making the left lung smaller than the right. In addition to the heart and the lungs, the chest cavity contains the esophagus or food pipe that extends from the back of the throat down through the diaphragm to the stomach, the trachea or windpipe that extends to the lungs, and several major blood vessels.

chickenpox A highly contagious eruptive viral disease.

Chickenpox is so easily contracted that almost everyone is affected in childhood. The disease is spread by contact with an infected person or anything that has been contaminated by an infected person. The virus that causes chickenpox is the same virus that causes shingles, and chicken pox may also be contracted from a person who has shingles. Chickenpox usually appears as an itchy rash of small red spots around the trunk. The spots quickly develop into larger blisters that spread throughout the body. Within a few days, the blisters burst and form a crust.

With few exceptions, the greatest danger from chickenpox is the potential for infection or scarring from aggressive rubbing of the itching blisters. Children may need to wear mittens, especially at night, to keep from scratching.

Treatment consists mainly of alleviating the symptoms, especially the annoying itch; applications of a soothing lotion may help. Daily warm baths will aid in clearing the rash and reduce the risk of infection. Aspirin should not be administered, because taking aspirin during a viral infection has been associated with bouts of **Reye's syndrome**, a far more serious infection.

Usually, one attack of chickenpox is enough to insure immunity from further infection for life.

chilblain Swelling of the skin due to exposure to cold.

The condition is seldom seen in areas where indoor heating and outdoor clothing are adequate to protect against winter cold and dampness.

Chilblains appear as itchy patches of red, swollen skin on the extremities that usually recede within a few days. A chronic condition can develop, however, with a discoloration of the skin accompanied by blisters that are painful and leave scars when they heal.

chill Shivering, and a sense of being cold, often associated with a sudden increase in body temperature.

A chill often heralds the onset of infection, caused by a temporary disorder of the nerve centers that regulate body temperature. Typically, the chill develops as fever rises and may recur intermittently until the fever breaks.

chiropody The science that deals with diseases, irregularities and injuries of the foot; see **podiatry**

cholera Any of various intestinal diseases transmitted in contaminated food or water, characterized by fever, vomiting, diarrhea, and dehydration.

cholesterol A component of animal fat, blood, nerve tissue, and bile, necessary to a healthy body, but that may be harmful in excess, as in the formation of **atherosclerosis**.

chromosomes The body of genetic material contained in the nucleus of a cell, the basic unit that makes up all living things.

Chromosomes carry the genes that transmit the characteristics of a parent to a child, and through each cell throughout life, inasmuch as all cells in the body are created by division from the initial fertilized ovum, or egg.

cicatrix The fibrous tissue remaining after a wound has healed; a scar.

circadian rhythm Descriptive of the repetitive physiological processes of the body as they relate to the twenty-four hour cycle of the earth's rotation.

Everyone has a so-called *internal clock* that maintains a cyclic pattern of body processes coinciding more or less with a twenty-four hour day, as for the rising and falling of temperature, blood pressure, etc.

circulatory system The functions and organs that carry blood to and from all parts of the body, consisting of the **heart** and **blood vessels**.

Through the blood vessels, **blood** is circulated throughout the body under pressure supplied by the pumping action of the heart.

cirrhosis A disease of the liver in which healthy cells are destroyed and replaced by fibrous tissue.

Cirrhosis is the result of attempts by the liver to correct damage after sudden massive infection, as by acute **hepatitis**; over a period of months or years, as by chronic hepatitis or blockage of the bile ducts; or over a much longer period, as by alcohol abuse, the most common cause of cirrhosis.

Treatment for the condition mainly involves correcting the cause, as by removing blockage or discontinuing the ingestion of alcohol, then improving the diet to accommodate the damaged liver, as by large doses of vitamins and frequent small meals to reduce strain on the liver.

claudication Limping or lameness, especially that caused by restriction of the flow of blood to the leg muscles, as by **atherosclerosis**.

claustrophobia A morbid fear of being in a confined space or enclosed area.

cleft lip, cleft palate A birth defect in which a part or all of the upper structure of the mouth is split.

If it is not corrected, the deformity can cause difficulty with speech and hearing; however, the most immediate problem may be feeding—the infant with a cleft lip or palate may not be able to suckle.

Often a special device or an appliance can be used to facilitate feeding until the time considered suitable by the physician to attempt corrective surgery.

clot See **blood clot**

clubfoot A birth defect in which the foot is turned inward or otherwise twisted.

Early correction may involve manipulation and the use of casts or other devices to gradually correct the position of the foot. Some surgery may be required to lengthen the

Achilles tendon or correct the ankle joint. If early attempts at correction are not successful, or not undertaken, extensive surgery may be required.

coagulation The transformation of a liquid into a soft, congealed mass, as in clotting.

cocaine A narcotic used as a local anesthetic, effective when applied to mucous membrane, that is addictive when inhaled. See also, **codeine.**

coccyx A small bone that forms the lower extremity of the spinal column.

codeine An opium derivative, used for the relief of pain, similar to morphine, but not as addictive.

cod-liver oil Fish oil that is rich in vitamins A and D, often taken as a dietary supplement.

cold sore A viral infection that causes small blisters to appear about the area of the mouth, usually following an illness accompanied by fever.

colostomy A surgical procedure in which an opening is created in the wall of the abdomen and joined to an opening in the large intestine to allow the elimination of body waste.
A colostomy may be created to correct a condition caused by obstruction or disease.
Waste discharged through the opening is collected in a disposable bag that must be changed by the wearer. Once the diet is properly regulated, the colostomy causes little restriction of normal activities.

compress A pad, often of cloth, used to apply heat, moisture, or medication.

compulsion An irresistible desire, often irrational and repetitive, to do something.

concretion A hard, inorganic mass in the body, as a kidney stone; a calculus.

concussion An injury to the brain caused by sudden shock, as a sharp blow to the head.
A simple concussion, brought about by the brain striking the inside of the skull, may result in bruising brain tissue, bleeding inside the skull, and possible loss of consciousness. Unconsciousness may last a few minutes or a few hours; a longer period usually indicates more serious damage. Other symptoms of a concussion are feelings of nausea, dizziness, and headache that may last for several days. There may also be a loss of memory for a period just prior to the injury until several hours after.
Any signs of more serious injury, as an open wound, partial paralysis anywhere in the body or sharply dilated pupils should be referred to a physician.
Normally, rest is all that is required for recuperation. The victim should relax, avoid any medication stronger than aspirin and, if vomiting occurs, avoid solid food. Sleep ought to be postponed for several hours to be certain that no unusual symptoms arise and, once allowed to sleep, the victim should be awakened every two hours to give his or her name and location so as to confirm that there are no complications.
Consult a physician if a headache grows more severe, vision becomes blurred or there is any other abnormality of the eyes, and in case of spasms or staggering.

congenital Existing from birth; descriptive of a condition present at birth and that is not hereditary.

congestion An abnormal accumulation of body fluid, especially one that tends to clog.

conjunctivitis An inflammation of the conjunctiva, the membrane that covers the outer surface of the eyeball and lines the inner surface of the eyelid.
Conjunctivitis is often caused by the invasion of microorganisms and may be contracted by dust, smoke, or chemicals. Those with allergies are often victims.
The condition is characterized by redness of the eye, burning or itching, and a sensitivity to light. There is often periodic tearing and a discharge of pus.
Treatment varies with the cause of the disease and its severity. The eye should be rested and protected from bright light as much as possible; if eyelids are held closed by dry discharge, it can be softened by gentle bathing in warm water. Care should be taken to isolate handkerchiefs, towels, etc. used by the subject, as conjunctivitis is highly contagious.

connective tissue Fibrous tissue that serves to connect the cells and support the organs of the body.

contact dermatitis An inflammation of the skin caused by direct contact with an irritant.
Contact dermatitis may be caused by any of a number of substances, such as detergent, hair coloring, cosmetics, household cleaners, or by plants, such as poison ivy and poison oak.
Contact with an irritant to which the subject is sensitive may cause redness, swelling, blistering, burning, itching, or tenderness in the area of contact.
Identifying the offending substance may be a simple process of elimination or it may require the assistance of a doctor who can test for allergies. The infection may clear when the substance is avoided; more severe cases should be referred to a doctor for medication.

contagion The spread of disease, directly or indirectly, from one person to another.

contaminated Descriptive of that which is unclean, often in reference to food or water infected by bacteria.

contusion A bruise or injury that does not break the skin.

convulsion Sudden, involuntary contractions or spasms of the muscles.

coronary bypass See **bypass**

corticosteroids Any of the hormones produced in the cortex of the adrenal glands.
More than 30 corticosteroids regulate essential processes in the body.
One group, the mineralocorticoids, help maintain the salt and water balance in the body. A second group, the glucocorticoids, help regulate the use of sugars and proteins. The third group, androgens, stimulate the development of secondary male sex characteristics.

cough Sudden, noisy expulsion of air from the lungs.

Coughing is a defensive reflex that clears the lungs of excess mucus or irritating matter. The cough will persist as long as the condition that causes it, but it may be suppressed by soothing liquids or drugs that act on the cough reflex.

CPR CardioPulmonary Resuscitation; the use of artificial ventilation, that is, mouth-to-mouth breathing and external heart compression, or rhythmic pressure on the breastbone, to revive one who has suffered cardiac arrest.

cretinism A severe congenital thyroid deficiency.

The infant suffering from cretinism exhibits retarded physical and mental development that, if diagnosed early, may be treated and cured.

crib death The sudden, unexplained, death of an apparently healthy infant; sudden infant death syndrome or SIDS.

croup An inflammation of the larynx.

A condition mostly confined to children, the croup causes swelling of the larynx, or voice box, so that breathing becomes difficult. A characteristic barking cough is the result of air forced through the swollen larynx. Breathing may be further impaired if mucus blocks the windpipe and bronchi that connect to the lungs. Immediate medical attention is critical, because the swelling may close off the passage completely.

In the meantime, calm the child—an attack of croup is frightening and fear can only make the symptoms worse. If possible, sit in a bathroom with the hot shower running—the warm, moist air should ease the symptoms. Similar results may be obtained with the use of a humidifier or by breathing over a container of hot water with a tent fashioned from a towel over the head; however, resting in a parent's arms in the steamy atmosphere of a bathroom is probably most soothing.

cyst An abnormal sac containing liquid or semiliquid waste material.

Cysts often do not cause symptoms and are therefore not treated; one that causes pressure or other problems may be surgically removed.

decortication Removal of the outer layer of an organ.

defibrillation A technique to correct fibrillation, an abnormal heartbeat.

Fibrillation is commonly caused by a heart attack, when part of the heart quivers or acts independently of the normal heartbeat. The heart is not then able to pump blood through the body and death will result if the condition is not corrected.

Protracted exposure to the cold or a severe electrical shock can also cause fibrillation.

dehydration Loss of water from the body; the condition produced by loss of water or deprivation of water from body tissue.

Dehydration may be caused by the inability to take in water due to illness or disease, or by loss of water from vomiting, diarrhea, uncontrolled secretion of urine, or excessive sweating.

A serious side affect of dehydration is the critical loss of salt from the body. Unchecked dehydration may result in death in a matter of days.

delirium A temporary mental disorder characterized by excitement, confusion and hallucinations.

Delirium may be brought on by any of a number of traumatic conditions, as by infection, drugs, withdrawal of certain drugs or alcohol, high fever, etc.

Condition of the subject may undergo abrupt radical change with varying frequency, as from a state of agitated restlessness to one of serenity and comprehension.

delirium tremens (DTs) Disordered perception brought on by trauma associated with alcoholism.

Delirium tremens may be triggered by a bout of excessive alcohol consumption, by the consumption of alcohol in conjunction with other drugs, even those that would be otherwise innocuous, or by withdrawal of alcohol after a period of excess consumption.

The victim may suffer distinctive tremors, frightening hallucinations, rapid pulse, periods of profuse sweating, an overwhelming feeling of terror, extreme agitation.

delusion A belief maintained in spite of irrefutable evidence to the contrary.

Delusion may be part of a psychotic episode in which perception is altered to cause irrational interpretation of an ordinary event. In such cases, there may not be even a remote connection between the event and the interpretation.

On another level, delusion may be formed from hallucination or an elaborate scheme of rationalization that, although connected, has no basis in reality.

Delusion may also be related to depression, as in feelings of hypochondria or guilt, where the subject has negative feelings relating to personal condition, fortunes, or worthiness that are not supported in fact.

dementia Mental impairment or deficiency caused by injury or disease.

Dementia may be associated with senility, **Alzheimer's disease**, a blood clot or tumor of the brain, etc.

A loss of memory, especially for recent events, is the most common symptom of dementia.

The condition can progress to a stage where the subject suffers severe degradation or total destruction of intellectual powers, deprivation of emotional control, and a complete personality transformation.

See also, **amentia.**

dentistry The work of one whose profession is the care of the teeth and the surrounding tissue.

Dentistry involves the diagnosis and treatment of the diseases and disorders of the mouth, as well as prevention of those conditions.

Routine dental care is normally provided by a general practitioner who is qualified to recommend a specialist, if one is needed. Among the specialized fields of dentistry are: *orthodontia*, concerned with the straightening of teeth; *periodontia*, that deals with diseases of the gums; *prosthodontia*, the replacement of missing teeth; *endodontia*, focusing on diseases of the pulp and root canal surgery; and *exodontia*, dealing with the extraction of teeth.

dermatitis Any inflammation of the skin.

Dermatitis may be caused by any of a number of substances, such as detergent, hair coloring, cosmetics, or household cleaners; by plants, such as poison ivy and poison oak; or by ingesting certain foods or medications, etc.

Contact with an irritant to which the subject is sensitive may cause redness, swelling, blistering, burning, itching, or tenderness in the area of contact.

Identifying an offending substance may be a simple process of elimination or it may require the assistance of a doctor to run tests for allergies. The infection may clear when the substance is avoided; more severe cases can require medication.

Some forms of dermatitis are a secondary symptom of diseases affecting other parts of the body and others, such as *exfoliative dermatitis* that causes the shedding of skin and hair, must be referred to a physician for proper diagnosis and cure.

dermatology The study of diseases and disorders of the skin.

Because of the relationship between diseases of the skin and allergies or other diseases (see **dermatitis**), the dermatologist must have a thorough knowledge of diseases that relate to dermatitis and of allergies.

diabetes mellitus A condition in which the body is not able to satisfactorily process ingested sugar.

Body and brain cells need many different types of nourishment, one of which is sugar. The circulatory system carries sugar and transfers it to the cells with the aid of a chemical substance called insulin. The pancreas, located in the abdominal cavity, manufactures insulin. When the insulin production and sugar are in balance, the body functions normally. An individual suffering from a reduction in the production of insulin is said to have diabetes mellitus.

As a result of this imbalance, the body is adversely affected; however, a great many diabetics lead healthy, normal lives through a program of balanced diet and medication. When the diabetic's condition is not controlled, certain disorders may occur.

The major adverse reactions to insulin imbalance are *diabetic coma* and *insulin shock*.

diabetic coma A state of stupor or lethargy leading to coma, brought on by an inadequate supply of insulin.

This imbalance that triggers diabetic coma is generally due to a diabetic not taking the proper medication; a diabetic ingesting more sugar than the available insulin can accommodate; a person contracting an infection that affects insulin production; or sustained vomiting or fluid loss.

The signs of someone progressing into diabetic coma are warm and dry skin, sunken eyes, rapid and labored breathing, rapid and weak pulse, excessive urination accompanied by extreme thirst, nausea and vomiting, abdominal pain, a state of confusion and disorientation that is similar to drunkenness. Eventually the condition leads to a coma state, thus the term *diabetic coma*.

diagnosis The process of identifying a disease by careful examination of symptoms.

dialysis The process of removing waste matter and maintaining the electrolyte balance of the blood by diffusion.

Normally, dialysis is performed by the kidneys. One who suffers kidney failure, whether temporary or permanent, must have the blood cleansed by the use of an artificial kidney machine. The blood from a tube implanted in an artery is circulated through the machine where it comes in contact with a thin membrane that separates the blood from a solution containing a precise concentration of electrolytes. By the process of osmosis, the tendency of certain fluids to diffuse through a membrane from a stronger to a weaker solution, the wastes are passed through the membrane to the solution and electrolytes are passed from the solution to the blood. The blood cells, too large to pass through the membrane, are not affected and the revitalized blood is returned to the subject's body through a tube implanted in a vein.

diaphragm The muscular partition in the body that separates the chest cavity and the abdominal cavity.

digestion The process of breaking down food into those substances that can be used by the body and those that are to be discharged as waste.

Digestion begins in the mouth where food is ground by the teeth and mixed with saliva. The saliva both moistens food for easier passage, and begins the breakdown of starches. The food is passed down the throat, through the esophagus and into the stomach, at which point it is combined with digestive juices to partly liquefy it for passage into the small intestine. In the duodenum, the first section of the small intestine, bile from the liver aids in the absorption of fat and digestive juices from the pancreas further facilitate the digestion and absorption of food. Anything that is not absorbed into the bloodstream from the small intestine is passed on to the large intestine for discharge from the body.

diphtheria An acute, highly contagious disease that affects the tonsils, airways and larynx.
Diphtheria bacteria destroy the outer layer of mucous membrane in the throat or larynx. The principal mark of the disease is a grayish membrane over the throat formed from dead cells, bacteria, etc.
Diphtheria is transmitted by drops of moisture from the nose and throat of an infected person, often a carrier who is not aware of the presence of the disease.
Symptoms of the disease include sore throat, hoarseness, a rasping cough and fever. Children may be nauseous, with chills and a headache in addition to other symptoms. The characteristic membrane may vary in color or not appear at all; however, if it does form, it may detach and block off the victim's air supply. Because of the danger, sufferers need to be hospitalized where they can recuperate under close supervision.
The disease may be complicated by inflammation of the heart muscles or nerves.

dislocation Twisting out of normal position, as a bone.
Where two or more bones come together to form a joint, they are held in place by bands of strong, fibrous tissue called ligaments. Of the three types of joint, those that are immovable, those with limited motion, and those that are freely movable, the freely movable joints—those of the lower jaw, the shoulders, the elbows, the wrists, the fingers, the hips, the knees, the ankles, and the toes, are the ones most commonly dislocated.
When one or more of the bones forming a joint slip out of normal position, the ligaments holding the bones are stretched and sometimes torn loose. Fractures are often associated with dislocations. Dislocation may result from force applied at or near the joint, a sudden muscular contraction, twisting strains on joint ligaments, or a fall where the force of landing is transferred to a joint.
Some general symptoms of dislocations are a rigidity and loss of function, deformity, pain, swelling, tenderness, and discoloration. Resetting a dislocation is not a trivial matter—the victim should be placed in a doctor's care as quickly as possible.

diverticulosis, diverticulitis A *diverticulum* is a small sac or pouch; *diverticulosis* is the existence of *diverticula* (plural form of diverticulum) on the wall of the bowel.; *diverticulitis* is an inflammation of the diverticula.
It is possible, though not proven, that diverticula are formed when a lack of roughage in the diet causes the muscle layer in the wall of the colon to overwork or when those muscles are weakened by age, so that pressure in the colon forces the intestinal lining through the weak spots in the wall. Generally, diverticulosis exhibits no symptoms; however, waste matter may become trapped in the diverticula and reduce the flow of blood to the walls, paving the way for diverticulitis.
In addition to discomfort and pain in the abdomen, diverticulitis may lead to the formation of a fistula, or unnatural channel, between the colon and the bladder or another organ, infecting it as well.

DNA, RNA *DNA* is deoxyribonucleic acid, the basic component of living tissue that holds the genetic information to insure the inheritance and transmission of chromosomes and genes
RNA is ribonucleic acid, that carries the genetic information from DNA for the synthesis of protein in the cell.

DT's See **delirium tremens**

duodenal ulcer An ulcer, or open sore affecting the duodenum, the first section of the small intestine.
A *peptic ulcer* is an infection in any part of the digestive tract exposed to pepsin, a digestive juice. A *duodenal ulcer* is a type of peptic ulcer occurring in the duodenum when its lining is attacked by the action of digestive juices to which it is normally impervious.
Though unconfirmed, the cause of the ulcer may be excessive secretions of digestive juices by the stomach brought about by diet or medication.
The ulcer may remain undetected as for lack of symptoms, but usually will cause some discomfort of the abdomen, such as a burning sensation, within an hour of two of eating. The presence of the ulcer needs to be confirmed by a physician who can prescribe medication, but treatment may simply require avoiding foods that cause distress as well as those that stimulate the secretion of digestive fluids, such as caffeinated beverages and alcohol

dysentery An inflammation of the colon characterized by pain, cramps and diarrhea.
The infection, caused by bacteria, *bacillary dysentery,* or amoebae, *amoebic dysentery*, is spread through poor hygiene, as by contaminated food.

dyslexia Any of a number of reading, writing or learning disorders in one who is otherwise of normal intelligence.
Most symptoms relate to lack of a sense of direction or position; for example, letters in a word or words in a sentence may be read or written out of their normal order, or there may be difficulty matching names with their respective images.

dyspepsia Indigestion; impaired digestion.
Belching, stomach pains, a feeling that the stomach is over full, a sour taste, and even nausea, are all signs of indigestion, usually brought about by poor dietary habits. Ingesting fatty foods, rich foods, spicy foods, an excess of alcohol, or irregular meals all make one a prime candidate for dyspepsia.
Dyspepsia is quite common and seldom causes more than temporary discomfort;

however, if it is chronic, that is, occurs regularly after meals or frequently causes sleep to be interrupted, it may be warning of a more serious condition.

eczema Any inflammatory disease of the skin.
Eczema may manifest itself in redness, burning or itching, blistering, the discharge of serous matter, and crusts or scabs.

edema Swelling caused by the accumulation of fluid in the tissues.

embolism Blockage of a blood vessel by an obstruction called an embolus.
A common form of embolus is a blood clot or plaque from a clogged artery or heart valve. An air embolus may develop if an excessive amount of air is admitted during an intravenous injection, during surgery, or in moving between an area of high pressure and an area of lower pressure (see **bends**).
An embolism reduces the supply of blood to the area where it occurs causing tissue damage. Discomfort or pain may be the main symptom of an embolism with others depending on the location, as an embolism in a brain artery that emulates the symptoms of a stroke.

emphysema A lung condition in which the air spaces in the lungs are enlarged.
Emphysema often develops from the inflammation, swelling and excessive mucus production associated with bronchitis or other disease that traps air in the lungs. The result is a loss of effectiveness in moving air in and out of the lungs, putting extra strain on the heart.
Emphysema is characterized by shortness of breath. Difficulty in breathing may be accompanied by a persisting, painful cough. Sufferers of emphysema tire quite easily, largely a result of the energy required just to get enough air.

encephalitis Inflammation of the brain.
Encephalitis may be caused by bacteria or parasites, but most commonly is the result of a virus, either as a direct effect or complication from an infection.
Some of the viruses are carried by mosquitoes while others are associated with childhood diseases, as measles, mumps, or chicken pox—children are the main victims of the disease.

endocarditis Inflammation of the valves or lining of the heart.

endocrinology The study of the endocrine system and its functions as well as the diagnosis and treatment of its disorders.
The endocrine system is comprised of the glands that secrete vital hormones into the bloodstream, including the pituitary, adrenal, thyroid, pancreas, ovaries, and testes.
The hormones secreted by these glands travel throughout the body to control and combine a number of body functions. Growth abnormalities, diabetes and other diseases may be attributed to disorders of the endocrine system.

enteritis Inflammation of the intestinal tract.
Enteritis is most commonly found as a bacterial or viral infection in the small intestine as the result of the consumption of contaminated food or water.

epidemiology The study of the onset, recurrence, pattern of distribution, and control of disease.
Epidemiology deals with the communication of disease in general, the relationship between certain diseases and the conditions under which they flourish, and means of prevention, such as vaccines.
The epidemiologist is also concerned with non-infectious diseases that are widespread or of questionable origin, such as the relationship between certain illnesses and environmental pollution, or toxic substances in foods or other products.

epilepsy A neurological disorder that causes recurring seizures.
Commonly, epilepsy has no apparent cause, although in some cases it may be traced to a source, such as a tumor that forms pressure on the brain, an injury to the brain, or disorder caused by drugs.
Seizures may be so mild as to go virtually unnoticed or so severe that they can result in serious harm. The subject may be aware of an impending seizure by a tingling sensation in the extremities accompanied by distortion in the senses of sight and smell, as be seeing flashing lights and perceiving bad odors. The seizure may be marked by sitting motionless, as though daydreaming; moving or behaving in a repetitive or inappropriate manner; or by convulsions. A convulsive attack may cause the subject to cry out, stiffen and fall unconscious, lose urinary and bowel control, or exhibit jerking, spastic or thrashing movements. Convulsions are usually followed by deep sleep and no recollection of the seizure.
The epileptic may be treated by correcting any physical disorder and prescribing medication. Non-medical treatment is limited to monitoring the seizure: make the subject comfortable by loosening clothing if necessary or placing a pillow under the head; protect the subject from inhaling vomit or otherwise suffocating; make no attempt to pry open the mouth or insert anything into the mouth of a person who is having a convulsion.
Epilepsy cannot be prevented, but the seizures may be controlled by medication, allowing the epileptic to lead a normal life.

esophagus The food pipe, that extends from the throat, through the chest, ending at the stomach.

excretory systems Those parts of the body concerned with the separation and elimination of waste products.

Several different systems serve to eliminate waste products that enter the body or are formed within it. The residue of food taken into the digestive system, mainly indigestible materials, together with secretions from various glands emptying into the intestines, is gathered in the lower portion of the large intestine and eliminated through the rectum as feces.

Surplus water, carrying dissolved salts that are excess in the system or form a waste product, is extracted by the kidneys, collected in the bladder, and expelled as urine.

Carbon dioxide and certain volatile products carried by the blood are exchanged in the lungs for oxygen and pass from the body in exhaled air.

The skin contains many small organs known as sweat glands. They range from 400 to 2,800 per square inch over different parts of the body. These glands are important in eliminating heat, excess fluid, and dissolved waste products from the body.

Life and health depend on the body giving off its waste products. Interference with the normal functioning of any of the excretory systems results in illness and may even cause death.

extrasystole An abnormal contraction of the heart.

Normally, the heart beats in a regular rhythm; an extrasystole is a contraction of the heart caused by a signal emanating from somewhere other than the heart's natural pacemaker. The extrasystole may be detected as a skip, flutter, or extra beat. It may be experienced periodically, triggered by stress or excitement, or it may be recurring, as a symptom of heart disease or reaction to drugs. Whether the extrasystole is a matter for concern depends on its cause, frequency, and the general health of the subject, for example triggered by stress in one with a heart condition, the extrasystole may lead to more serious problems. Prolonged symptoms, as well, should be referred to a physician.

extremities Descriptive of arms and legs including their joining to the trunk of the body.

The *upper extremity* consists of thirty-two bones. The collarbone is a long bone, the inner end of which is attached to the breastbone and the outer end is attached to the shoulder blade at the shoulder joint. The collarbone lies just in front of and above the first rib. The shoulder blade is a flat triangular bone which lies at the upper and outer part of the back of the chest and forms part of the shoulder joint. The arm bone extends from the shoulder to the elbow. The two bones of the forearm extend from the elbow to the wrist. There are eight wrist bones, five bones in the palm of the hand, and fourteen finger bones, two in the thumb and three in each finger.

The *lower extremity* consists of thirty bones. The thigh bone, the longest and strongest bone in the body, extends from the hip joint to the knee; its upper end is rounded to fit into the socket in the pelvis, and its lower end broadens out to help form part of the knee joint. This flat triangular bone can be felt in front of the knee joint. The two bones in the leg extend from the knee joint to the ankle. There are seven bones in the ankle and back part of the foot, five long bones in the front part of the foot, and fourteen toe bones.

febrile Descriptive of body temperature that is above normal; feverish.

fever blisters An eruption about the mouth accompanying a cold or fever; cold sore or herpes simplex.

fistula An abnormal duct or passageway in the body.

A fistula may be congenital or the complication of an infection.

food allergy Excessive sensitivity to a particular food that is otherwise considered safe to eat.

A food allergy exists when the immune system reacts to a particular food or to a substance in the food by manufacturing antibodies. The foods that most commonly trigger an immune system reaction are dairy products, seafood, chocolate, tomatoes, strawberries, and citrus fruits.

A food reaction is usually manifested by digestive disorders, as cramps, nausea, vomiting, or diarrhea; however, hives, rash, nasal congestion, headache, or **anaphylactic shock** may also be symptoms.

When a food allergy is suspected, the offending substance can often be pinpointed by the process of elimination, that is, sampling or excluding foods one at a time to determine if symptoms recur. It is prudent to maintain a record of all foods eaten during this time as the reaction or lack of reaction may be the result of consuming certain foods in combination.

food poisoning Acute distress caused by food containing toxins or bacteria.

Food poisoning is the result of ingesting a subsistence that in its natural state contains poison, as certain wild mushrooms and plants, or one that has been contaminated, as food that has been improperly stored.

Cramps, diarrhea and vomiting are most commonly associated with food poisoning, but symptoms in some cases may be more severe, causing difficulty in breathing, blurred vision or paralysis. Any symptoms that are excessive or that persevere should be treated by a physician.

fracture Any break or crack in a bone.

Fractures can be divided into two classifications: *an open, or compound fracture* in which the bone is broken and an open wound is present often with the end of the broken bone protruding from the wound; *a closed, or simple fracture* in which no open wound is present, but there is a broken or cracked bone.

Broken bones, especially the long bones of the upper and lower extremities, often have sharp, sawtooth edges so that even slight movement may cause the sharp edges to cut into blood vessels, nerves, or muscles. Careless or improper movement can convert a closed fracture into an open fracture, causing damage to surrounding blood vessels or nerves

If the broken ends of the bone extend through an open wound, there is little doubt that the victim has suffered a fracture; however, the bone does not always extend through the skin, so it is well to be able to recognize other signs that a fracture exists, such as pain or tenderness in the area, deformity or irregularity of the affected area, loss of function, discoloration, and swelling.

Any fracture or suspected fracture should be referred to a physician, as improper healing can have serious consequences.

friable Descriptive of that which is easily pulverized.

frostbite Tissue damage caused by extreme cold.

Frostbite is most likely to occur when the wind is blowing, rapidly drawing heat from the body. The nose, cheeks, ears, toes, and fingers are the body parts most frequently frostbitten. As a result of exposure to cold, the blood vessels constrict causing the blood supply to the chilled parts to decrease and depriving the tissues of the warmth they need.

The signs and symptoms of frostbite are not always apparent to the sufferer, because frostbite has a numbing effect.

Frostbite goes through the following stages: the affected area will feel numb; the skin turns red, then dead white or blue-white; eventually the skin and underlying tissue is firm to the touch.

Treatment for the early stage of frostbite involves placing the affected part close to the body for warmth without rubbing. In the later stages, there is severe, perhaps permanent, damage to the tissue so that it must not be rubbed, it should be lightly covered for protection, and heat should not be applied. The subject should seek medical attention immediately; if skin is frozen, it should remain so until the subject is hospitalized as thawing is extremely painful. Avoid anything that may constrict blood vessels, such as smoking, coffee, tea or hot chocolate.

fulminating Descriptive of the onset of a disease that is rapid and severe.

furuncle See boil

gallstones Hardened masses formed in the gallbladder or in the bile duct leading from the gallbladder to the small intestine.

Gallstones, formed from cholesterol, blood, bile, and other substances, may produce no symptoms or they can cause pain in the abdomen, indigestion, especially after eating fatty foods, or nausea. Sometimes the stones pass into the intestine and are excreted.

If the stones become trapped in the bile duct, the pain is much more severe and may be accompanied by chills, fever, vomiting and jaundice, especially if the flow of bile is blocked.

gangrene Death of body tissue.

Gangrene is usually caused by a reduction or complete absence of blood to a section of tissue, although bacterial infection that destroys tissue may play a critical part in its formation.

Gangrene may be the result of burns, freezing, physical injury, a blood clot, bacteria or any other condition that interferes with the flow of blood and destroys tissue.

gastroenteritis Inflammation of the lining of the stomach and intestines.

Gastroenteritis is often the result of infection by bacteria or virus, but may also be caused by reaction to certain foods or drugs, by food poisoning, or by over consumption of alcohol.

The onset of gastroenteritis may be signaled by a feeling of discomfort in the abdomen, gas pains, cramps, nausea or diarrhea. Usually all that is required to alleviate the symptoms is rest, plenty of liquids and a temporary bland diet. Medical care may be required if symptoms persist in order to rule out a more serious condition. Excessive vomiting and diarrhea that may lead to dehydration also requires medical attention, especially for infants.

gastroenterology The branch of medicine that deals with the study, diagnosis and treatment of diseases and disorders of the stomach and intestines.

gene Any of the units that occur in the chromosome and carry the traits that are passed on from parent to child

generic Of a class or group—descriptive of drugs and other products that are prescribed and sold by their scientific name; a product that tends to be less expensive than one sold by brand name.

genetic Descriptive of characteristics that may be inherited; distinctive from *congenital*, that is dating from birth.

genetic disorder A disease or malformation that may be passed from one generation to another.

In some cases, the link is clearly established, as when a conditions is associated with a particular chromosome; in others, the association is established only by observation, as the tendency of a particular condition to occur in succeeding generations of a family.

germ Generally, a reference to those microorganisms, especially bacteria, that are capable of producing disease.

German measles A mild, contagious, viral infection; rubella.

The most serious problem associated with German measles is the likelihood of birth defect when the virus has been contracted during pregnancy.

gerontology The study of the aging process and the diseases and disabilities associated with it.

gingivitis Inflammation of the gums.

Gingivitis is usually due to a combination of poor diet and poor dental hygiene, although it may be caused by vitamin deficiency or as a complication of a disease.

The discomfort and minor bleeding associated with gingivitis may be alleviated by reducing the intake of sugar and alcohol, increasing the intake of vitamin C, and improving dental hygiene. In some cases, it is necessary for a dental surgeon to cut away damaged portions of the gum.

gland Any organ that secretes a substance to be used elsewhere in the body.

glaucoma A disorder of the eye caused by increased pressure within the eyeball.

Normally, fluid in the eyeball is under slight pressure that is carefully regulated. When fluid fails to drain and maintain a constant pressure, the buildup causes damage to the structure.

Glaucoma may be linked to other diseases of the eye or to the use of certain drugs.

Acute glaucoma is rare. The symptoms are so intense as to be impossible to ignore: extreme pain and a sudden blurring of vision. Deterioration by chronic glaucoma, on the other hand, is free of pain and so very gradual that it may go unnoticed for a long time. Initially, there may be some loss of peripheral vision without any other symptoms, followed by blurred vision, difficulty in adjusting to bright lights or darkness, and slight pain around the eye, symptoms that may be sporadic.

Most eye examinations include a check for glaucoma in order to catch it in the early stages when it can be treated most effectively.

globulin Any of several simple proteins that comprise one of the two major protein groups of the blood, insoluble in water. See also, **albumin**.

glossitis Inflammation of the tongue.

Glossitis may be specific, as an injury to the tongue or it may be symptomatic of another disorder, as a disease or vitamin deficiency.

The symptoms of glossitis vary considerably, depending on the cause. Some of the manifestations are redness, swelling, white patches, and ulcers.

Severe acute glossitis produced by infection, burns, or injury can bring about pain and swelling that causes the tongue to project into the throat, obstructing the airway. In severe cases, chewing, swallowing, or speaking may be impaired.

glucose A form of sugar found naturally in honey, fruit, and in the blood.

glycemia The presence of sugar in the blood. See also **hyperglycemia, hypoglycemia**.

glycogen A form of carbohydrate, found mainly in the muscles and in the liver, that is changed into glucose to meet the body's demands.

goiter Enlargement of the thyroid gland that appears as a swelling at the side or front of the neck.

Goiter may be caused by a diet deficient in the iodine necessary for the production of thyroid hormone; by an excess of foods that inhibit the production of thyroid hormone, as cabbage or soya; or by a cause unknown.

The swelling is the result of a futile attempt by the gland to produce more hormone by enlarging the cells within the gland.

gout Inflammation of a joint caused by excess uric acid in the bloodstream.

Gout is the result of the body's inability to properly process uric acid, a chemical normally found in the blood and urine. Excess uric acid may crystallize and be deposited in the skin, joints and kidneys.'

An attack of gout is the body's response to the crystal deposits. The initial attack is usually concentrated in a single joint; subsequent attacks may involve several joints. Attacks are very painful and the area becomes extremely sensitive, followed by redness, warmth and swelling.

A physician should be consulted for treatment, even when the symptoms disappear within a day or two, because the condition tends to reappear with increasing frequency, duration and severity.

graft Living tissue that is taken from a body to be surgically implanted in another part of the body or in another body. See also **transplant**.

gynecology The branch of medicine concerned with the diagnosis and treatment of disorders of the female reproductive system.

hallucination A false sense of perception.

A hallucination can affect the senses of sight, hearing, taste, or smell; they range from something as simple as a flash of light to a detailed and clearly identifiable sight or sound.

Hallucinations may be symptomatic of a mental disorder or the result of physical illness. Recurring and often terrifying hallucinations may accompany high fever, alcoholism, drug abuse or severe injury. Disease or a tumor of the brain may cause hallucinations related to a particular sense depending on the area of the brain affected.

hay fever An allergy to pollen manifested by cold-like symptoms; pollinosis.

Hay fever is a short-lived, seasonal, allergic reaction to the pollen of a particular plant or group of plants.

Common symptoms of hay fever include itchy watery eyes, sneezing, a watery discharge from the nose, headache, irritability, a feeling of tiredness, insomnia, coughing, and wheezing.

A number of over-the-counter remedies are available to the sufferer including antihistamines that counteract the histamine released by the body in reaction to the allergen, corticosteroids that reduce inflammation, and eye drops to relieve itching and redness. Severe cases may warrant consultation with a physician who can prescribe desensitization shots that induce the body to develop a tolerance to the allergen.

head The upper part of the human body, housing the brain and organs for sight, hearing, smell and taste, joined to the trunk by the neck.

The head is composed of twenty-two bones, eight that are closely united to form the skull, a bony case that encloses and protects the brain; fourteen other bones form the face. The only movable joint in the head is the lower jaw.

heart The heart is a hollow, muscular organ about the size of a fist, lying in the lower central region of the chest cavity. By the heart's pumping action, blood is under pressure and in constant circulation throughout the body. In a healthy adult at rest, the heart contracts between sixty and eighty times a minute; in a child, eighty to a one hundred times per minute. The effect of these contractions can be noted by the pulse, a spurt of blood through an artery. The pulse is most easily felt over the carotid artery on either side of the neck.

heart attack A sudden diminishing of the heart's ability to function; myocardial infarction. Like all living tissue, the muscles of the heart require oxygen-rich blood to function. A heart attack occurs when the blood supply to the heart is cut off by damage or blockage to the coronary artery that delivers blood to the heart muscle.

Diseases of the heart and blood vessels are the leading cause of death in the United States. Some of the early signs of a heart attack are uncomfortable pressure, squeezing, fullness, or dull pain in the center of the chest; pain radiating into the shoulders, arm, neck or jaw; sweating; nausea; dizziness; shortness of breath; or a feeling of weakness. The symptoms may come and go, leaving the impression that they are attributable to another cause such as indigestion.

Certain factors have been identified as increasing an individual's risk of some form of cardiovascular disease. There are some factors over which a person has no control, such as sex, race, age and heredity; however, there are factors that can be controlled, such as diet, weight, smoking, physical condition, etc.

heart murmur An abnormal heart sound that can usually be detected only with the aid of a stethoscope.

Generally, heart murmurs are harmless, but they can be early indicators of heart disease or a structural abnormality, such as a hole in the wall between the chambers of the heart, or incomplete closure or obstruction of a valve.

A heart murmur may be congenital, or the result of disease.

heat cramps Severe cramps caused by severe loss of salt.

Heat cramps mostly affect those who work or play a hot environment and perspire profusely; the perspiration causes a loss of salt from the body and if there is inadequate replacement, the body will then suffer from cramps, often accompanied by a feeling of faintness.

The symptoms can usually be relieved by moving to a cooler area and drinking a commercial electrolyte solution or a teaspoon of salt and as much sugar as possible dissolved in a quart of water.

heat exhaustion A condition caused by prolonged exposure to a hot environment.

Heat exhaustion occurs most commonly to persons not accustomed to hot weather, those who are overweight, and those who perspire excessively.

Loss of water and salt through sweating causes mild shock evidenced by pale and clammy skin, rapid and shallow breathing, rapid and weak pulse, nausea, weakness, dizziness, or headache.

One suffering from heat exhaustion should be moved to a cool, but not a cold place and wiped with cool, wet compresses on the face and head; if fainting seems likely, lie down with feet elevated eight to twelve inches.

heat stroke A state of collapse brought on by exposure to heat; sunstroke.

Heat stroke is a sudden onset of illness from exposure to high temperature, often the direct rays of the sun. Physical exertion and high humidity contribute to the incidence of heat stroke.

The most dangerous characteristic of heat stroke is high body temperature caused by a disturbance in the heat regulating mechanism of the body. The sufferer can no longer sweat, and this causes a rise in body temperature. This illness is most common in the elderly, alcoholics, obese persons, and those on medication.

Symptoms exhibited by a victim of heat stroke are: skin that is flushed, very hot, and very dry; pulse that is strong and rapid, but may become weaker and rapid as the condition worsens; respiration that is rapid and deep, followed by shallow breathing; high temperature; a loss of consciousness and, possibly, convulsions.

It is most important to lower body temperature as quickly as possible; failure to do so may result in permanent brain damage or death. In addition the subject should be:

moved to a cool, but not cold, environment and all clothing removed; wrapped in a cool, moist sheet and fanned or immersed in cool water or wiped with cool compresses; transported to a medical facility as rapidly as possible, continuing cooling enroute.

hematemesis Vomiting of blood.

Hematemesis may be caused by a simple irritation of the stomach, as by aspirin or over-indulgence in alcohol, or it may be an indication of more serious illness, such as ulcers or cancer.

hematology The study of blood, blood-forming organs, and related diseases.

Hematology is concerned with the diagnostic techniques for exploring disease processes through the examination of blood and bone marrow samples, as well as the workings, disorders and diseases of the blood and blood-forming organs themselves

hematoma A swelling make up of blood, usually clotted; a bruise.

A hematoma is usually the direct result of trauma, although the blood may come from a vessel that is fragile or damaged by disease. Most hematomas heal without treatment, but there is a danger of infection, especially around the nose and eyes. Any unusual behavior or complaint of headaches several days after an injury should be referred to a physician.

In cases of severe trauma, internal hematomas may develop. These too, will usually heal without treatment, although injuries to the head carry the possibility of belated symptoms of headache, drowsiness or paralysis that signal more serious injury that must be treated quickly.

hemoglobin The substance in red blood cells that enables them to carry oxygen and gives them their color.

hemophilia A hereditary disease in which improper clotting of blood puts the sufferer in danger of a severe loss of blood from a minor cut or injury.

hemorrhage The escape of blood from an artery, vein or capillary.

Hemorrhage often refers to considerable loss of blood, or uncontrolled bleeding. Normally, when blood vessels are torn or broken, the blood quickly forms clots, stemming the flow; however, when serious injury or disease, such as hemophilia, peptic ulcer, or cancer is involved, the body's normal clotting mechanism may malfunction or prove inadequate.

The seriousness of hemorrhage depends on the location and amount of bleeding. Severe hemorrhage may cause rapid pulse, dizziness, a drop in blood pressure, a rise in pulse rate, and clammy or sweaty skin. Blood in the stool, urine, or vomitus may be an indication of internal bleeding and should be reported to a physician as quickly as possible.

hepatitis Inflammation of the liver.

Hepatitis usually refers to one of a number of viral infections, characterized by jaundice. The most common are hepatitis A or *infectious hepatitis* and hepatitis B or *serum hepatitis*, both of which attack cells in the liver.

Hepatitis A is transmitted through contaminated food, water or contact with the stool of an infected person. The infection may be so mild as to be without symptoms, although the infection can still be passed on to others.

Hepatitis B virus enters the bloodstream through contact with contaminated blood or other body fluids. The virus can exist in most body fluids, including blood, saliva, semen, urine, and tears; thus, it may be transmitted by sexual contact or, infrequently, by casual contact.

Hepatitis may cause fatigue, joint and muscle pain, loss of appetite, nausea, vomiting, and diarrhea or constipation, accompanied by a low grade fever. As the disease progresses, the liver may enlarge and become tender. The characteristic jaundice is caused by the accumulation of bile pigment in the blood that turns the skin and the whites of the eyes yellow.

The disappearance of jaundice generally signals the start of recovery from hepatitis A; the hepatitis B virus, however, may persist for years or even a lifetime.

Any suspicion of hepatitis infection requires medical attention to avoid permanent liver damage. Although there is no cure, the physician can recommend a diet and life style that minimizes strain on the liver.

heredity The transmission of characteristics from parent to offspring.

Each characteristic that may be transmitted is conveyed by a gene, the primary unit of heredity. Genes are arranged on chromosomes in a precise order and every human cell is comprised of forty-six chromosomes arranged in twenty-three pairs.

On inception, the two halves of the chromosomes that are to join split and reunite; thus one half of the new chromosome that will make up a unique new individual comes from each parent.

It is this pairing of chromosomes and the genes they carry that determine the characteristics of the offspring—basically, if the characteristic carried by the genes of both parents are the same, such as for color of eyes or hair, that characteristic will be carried by the offspring; if they are different, then the dominant trait is manifest, as for brown eyes over blue; however, the offspring will always carry the brown-blue pair of genes, so that such a person might mate with another person with a brown-blue pairing and the random splitting of the chromosomes can cause a blue-blue pairing in their offspring.

Other features that are inherited, as the tendency to develop certain diseases are not so clearly defined by a single gene.

hernia The protrusion of a body part through a defect in the wall that surrounds it.

A hernia may be congenital, or it may develop when muscle walls are weakened by strain or disease.

herpes Any of a number of acute viral infections that are characterized by clusters of small blisters on the skin or mucous membrane.

Herpes simplex is a recurring form of herpes that usually affects the area around the mouth or the genitals. *Herpes zoster*, see **shingles.**

hiatal hernia The protrusion of the stomach above the diaphragm; a hiatus or diaphragmatic hernia.

The diaphragm divides the chest cavity and the abdominal cavity. Normally, the esophagus passes through the diaphragm and connect to the stomach below. A hiatal hernia occurs when a portion of the stomach protrudes up into the chest cavity through the passageway used by the esophagus.

hiccup, hiccough A sudden intake of air checked by closure of the glottis causing a sound typical to the condition.

The hiccup originates with irritation to a nerve that causes an involuntary spasm of the muscle of the diaphragm. The spasm causes a sharp intake of air that is stopped by the sudden closing of the glottis at the back of the throat. This sudden stop produces the characteristic jerk and sound.

The irritation to the phrenic nerve is usually caused by eating or drinking too fast. Unless an attack persists, the hiccup is of little significance.

Although cures for the hiccups abound, some rather bizarre, the most effective cure is holding the breath for as long as possible so as to suppress the response of the diaphragm.

hirsutism Growth of hair that is excessive or that appears in unusual areas.

hives An allergic condition characterized by itchy blotches or welts; urticaria.

Hives may be caused by allergens in food, as tomatoes, strawberries, etc.; certain drugs; bacteria; animal hair; or the environment, as exposure to cold or the sun.

An outbreak of hives may last less than an hour or continue for weeks, often subsiding, then reappearing from time to time. A mild attack is merely annoying, but more serious attacks may be accompanied by fever or nausea and even difficulty in breathing if the respiratory tract is infected. Treatment generally involves administering antihistamines.

Hodgkin's disease A malignant disease of the lymphatic system; a type of lymphoma.

The cancer tends to attack lymph glands throughout the body and often spreads to neighboring organs.

hormone A substance secreted by a gland and that is carried elsewhere to influence the function of specific cells or organs.

host Any living thing, as a person, animal, plant, or organ, that offers a suitable environment to shelter a parasite, infection, etc.

hydrophobia See **rabies**

hyperglycemia An excess of sugar in the blood, as in **diabetes mellitus.**

hypertension High blood pressure.

Blood flowing through the arteries at a pressure that is higher than normal places extra stress on the artery walls that can damage them and interfere with the blood supply to the heart, kidneys, and brain, causing heart attack, kidney failure, or stroke.

Hypertension exhibits no distinctive symptoms: headache, fatigue, dizziness, ringing in the ears, frequent nosebleeds, etc. caused by high blood pressure are all symptoms that may be attributable to other causes.

To test for hypertension, a physician checks the blood pressure using a sphygmomanometer, a device with an inflatable cuff that is wrapped around the subject's arm and a gauge to indicate pressure.

Blood pressure is expressed as two readings: the *systolic* that is the pressure during a contraction of the heart; and the *diastolic* that is the pressure between beats. The cuff is inflated to stop the flow of blood through the artery and then gradually deflated so that with the use of a stethoscope, the physician can determine the pressure at which the first pulse is heard and, as the cuff continues to deflate, the pressure at which the stream of blood passing through the artery is heard. Normal adult pressure is about 120/80 although some variance from that standard is not abnormal. Both readings are of value to the physician in making a diagnosis.

Hypertension responds well to treatment; a minor variation from normal may require simply a change in lifestyle: weight loss, reduction of stress, a program of regular exercise, and a limitation of the intake of sodium. For more severe cases, medication may be prescribed.

hyperthyroidism Any of the disorders that involve over activity of the thyroid gland.

The output of thyroid hormone is regulated by the thyroid gland's reaction to thyroid-stimulating hormone, produced in the pituitary gland when thyroid hormone is needed.

Hyperthyroidism occurs when the thyroid is no longer sensitive to this regulating mechanism, that is, thyroid hormone is produced even in the absence of thyroid-stimulating hormone.

Thyroid hormone is involved in a number of processes throughout the body, such as the regulation of body temperature, growth, fertility, and the conversion of food to energy. Such involvement portends a variety of symptoms, such as overheating, weight loss coupled with increased appetite, a reduction or cessation of menstruation, rapid heart beat, hyperactivity and tremors.

Hyperthyroidism can be treated with a variety of medications, depending on the specific condition.

hyperventilation Abnormally rapid or deep breathing, causing an excessive loss of carbon dioxide, that can make one light-headed or dizzy, or cause a loss of consciousness.

hypnosis A passive state induced by suggestion.

A hypnotic state is brought about by having a subject in a quiet environment concentrate while a hypnotist quietly urges acceptance of the receptive state of mind.

Although not everyone can be hypnotized, and hypnotism is not often encountered in orthodox medicine, it has been successfully used in the suppression of pain certain symptoms, and the altering of harmful lifestyle patterns, such as smoking.

hypoallergenic Descriptive of anything that is less likely than another similar product to cause an allergic reaction, often claimed of certain soaps and cosmetics.

hypochondria Abnormal preoccupation with one's health.

Hypochondria may be a concern for health in general, imagining symptoms that change from time to time, usually after assurance by a physician that nothing is wrong, or obsession with a particular ailment or disease, or the condition of a specific organ.

hypoglycemia An abnormal lack of sugar in the blood.

Normally, during digestion, insulin secreted by the pancreas reduces the level of blood sugar, called glucose, by enabling the body cells to absorb it.

Reactive hypoglycemia is triggered by the ingestion of food and occurs when too much insulin is secreted during digestion causing the cells over absorb it from the blood.

Fasting hypoglycemia is caused by inadequate conversion of carbohydrates into glucose, over absorption of glucose by the body, or an insulin producing tumor that does not respond to normal stimuli. At risk from fasting hypoglycemia are heavy drinkers whose sugar storage and release system in the liver is upset by alcohol or those who have not eaten for an extended period

Either type of hypoglycemia can cause fatigue, nervousness, inability to concentrate, dizziness, confusion, headache, hunger pangs, or visual impairment.

hypotension Unusually low blood pressure.

Although high blood pressure can be a serious problem that leads to complications, in most cases low blood pressure is not threatening nor does it require treatment.

It is normal for blood pressure to vary, depending on factors such as age, sex, etc. Infrequently, a medical problem, such as certain types of heart disease, cause low blood pressure; in such cases, treatment of the condition corrects the hypotension.

One recurring symptom of hypotension may be that of dizziness when rising quickly from a sitting or reclining position. Normally, when such a move is made, the blood vessels contract to prevent a sudden loss of blood to the brain; however, for the sufferer of hypotension, this mechanism may not work properly, and he or she may find it necessary to rise slowly.

hypothalamus A part of the brain that lies above the pituitary gland and regulates many body functions.

Through the pituitary gland, the hypothalamus affects the activities of the thyroid, pancreas, parathyroids, adrenals and sex glands. It is involved with the control of body temperature, sexual function, weight, fluid balance and blood pressure.

hypothermia An abnormally low body temperature.

Hypothermia is a general cooling of the entire body—the inner core of the body is chilled, so that the body cannot generate heat to stay warm.

The condition usually occurs from immersion in cold water, but may be produced by exposure to extremely low air temperatures or to temperatures between thirty and fifty degrees Fahrenheit accompanied by wind and rain. Also contributing to hypothermia are fatigue, hunger, and poor physical condition.

Exposure begins when the body loses heat faster than it can be produced. When the body is chilled, it passes through several stages: the urge to move about and exercise in order to stay warm; shivering as an involuntary effort by the body to preserve normal temperature in the vital organs; deprivation of judgment and reasoning powers; feelings of apathy, listlessness, indifference, and sleepiness; a loss of muscle coordination. Cooling becomes more rapid as the internal body temperature is lowered; eventually hypothermia will cause coma and death.

hypothyroidism A condition caused by under activity of the thyroid gland.

Thyroid hormone is involved in a number of processes throughout the body (see **hyperthyroidism**).

Hypothyroidism may be the result of a congenital defect, inflammation of the thyroid gland, or a deficiency of thyroid-stimulating hormone that causes insufficient production of thyroid hormone by the thyroid gland.

Those with hypothyroidism may be overweight, easily tired, intolerant of cold, suffer dry hair and skin, etc.

hypoxia A condition caused by a lack of oxygen in the body.

A lack of oxygen in the body may be caused by a lack of sufficient oxygen in the air breathed, as in mountain climbing or flying at high altitude; disease of the lungs that prevents oxygen from reaching the blood; or a reduction in blood circulating to the lungs due to heart failure or an obstruction of blood vessels in the lung.

hysteria Any excessive emotional state.

A psychiatric condition in which one responds to anxiety or threat with uncontrolled emotional or physical reaction, as by extreme emotional outbursts, blindness, loss of speech, etc.

idiosyncrasy That which is unusual in a person, as a mannerism, or reaction to a particular food.

ileostomy A surgical procedure in which an opening is created in the wall of the abdomen and joined to an opening in the ileum, or lower part of the small intestine, to allow the elimination of body waste.

An ileostomy is created when the colon has been removed because of injury or disease, such as cancer.

Waste discharged through the opening is collected in a disposable bag that must be changed by the wearer. Once the diet is properly regulated, the ileostomy causes little restriction of normal activities.

immune response The body's reaction to any invading organism.

Whenever the body is exposed to a foreign element, an antibody is fashioned, specific to that element, and designed to surround and disable it. The immune response comprises the body's most effective defense against disease.

Once antibodies have been produced, they not only fend off the attack, but remain in the blood to protect against the next attack. So effective are these antibodies, that a second attack seldom occurs, that is, it is stopped before the infection can take hold, as in the case of chicken pox or measles virus where a single attack virtually guarantees immunity from a second attack for life.

This abiding presence of antibodies in the blood is the basis for immunization as well—the body is exposed to weakened or dead cells for which it forms antibodies that remain in the system. Some diseases require so-called booster shots, because the antibodies are known to lose their effectiveness after a time.

In some cases, antibodies are detrimental, as in the case of allergies, transplants and transfusions.

In the case of an allergic reaction, the immune system over reacts in the presence of a substance to which the body is especially sensitive, causing unpleasant symptoms, such as itching skin, runny nose, coughing and sneezing, or watery eyes.

An allergic reaction may be so mild as to go unnoticed, or it can be so severe as to be life threatening. Of particular concern is the severe reaction called *anaphylactic shock*, often caused by insect bites, that may cause difficulty in breathing. Each attack triggers a new response, so that subsequent attacks are usually worse than the previous one.

In the case of a transplant, that is, the deliberate introduction of foreign tissue into the body, there is an attempt to destroy the intruder, making it necessary to introduce drugs to suppress the immune system. Such drugs present the additional hazard of leaving the body open to infection by other organisms that are not beneficial.

Transfused blood must be of the same type as the recipient's blood so that the immune system will not attempt to destroy it.

immune system See **allergy and immunology**

impetigo A highly contagious eruptive infection of the skin, most common in children.

incontinence Inability to control the passage of urine and stool, most often found in infants and the elderly.

Incontinence may be an indication of some other condition, such as an obstruction, infection, or other illness.

indigestion Impaired digestion; dyspepsia.

Belching, stomach pains, a feeling that the stomach is over full, a sour taste, and even nausea, are all signs of indigestion, usually brought about by poor dietary habits. Ingesting fatty foods, rich foods, spicy foods, an excess of alcohol, or irregular meals all make one a prime candidate for dyspepsia.

Indigestion is quite common and seldom causes more than temporary discomfort; however, if it is chronic, that is, occurs regularly after meals or frequently causes sleep to be interrupted, it may be warning of a more serious condition, such as ulcers and should be referred to a physician for diagnosis.

infection The presence of an organism, such as a bacterium or virus that can have a harmful effect on the body.

Indicating any organism that can cause disease.

The disease caused by such organism.

inflammation Redness and swelling, accompanied by heat and pain.

Inflammation is the way that living tissue responds to infection—it is symptomatic of the body's protective mechanism at work.

influenza A contagious viral infection of the upper respiratory tract.

Influenza is characterized by symptoms similar to a cold, often accompanied by a fever, chills, aching muscles, headache, and a feeling of general malaise.

The flu is unique in its ability to circumvent the immune system, that is, once a population has been infected, the structure of the virus changes so that existing antibodies are not effective in fighting the next attack.

Because influenza spreads so rapidly throughout a community, it has been surmised that the virus is transmitted by airborne particles from an infected person.

Influenza is unpleasant, but seldom serious except for those with a condition that is aggravated by flu symptoms, as a respiratory infection or heart condition.

Treatment for the flu is basically the same as for a bad cold; bed rest, extra fluids, and aspirin or aspirin substitute to reduce fever and muscle aches.

An association has been established between administering aspirin for a viral infection and Reye's syndrome in children; therefore, aspirin should not be given to a child with influenza.

ingest To take into the body by eating or absorbing.

inositol See **vitamin B complex**

insect bites and stings Although an insect bite or sting may be only a minor unpleasantness to most, those who have an allergic reaction to insect venom may suffer serious consequences.

An abnormal reaction to insect venom may be exhibited as swelling, tenderness and even a loss of feeling in the area of the bite that can be followed by shortness of breath, a rapid heartbeat, coughing, wheezing, and dizziness. In extreme cases, **anaphylactic shock**, a severe, potentially fatal, reaction can occur.

Unfortunately, as with most allergies, the reaction tends to grow more severe with subsequent attacks, so that one who has had a bad reaction would be prudent to avoid situations where the attack might be repeated, such as mowing the lawn, walking in the woods, etc.

Protection from severe allergic reaction may be accomplished with desensitization shots that help the body build up a tolerance. They comprise a series of shots with gradually increased doses of extract.

insulin A hormone produced in the cells of the pancreas essential for body cells to absorb sugar.

Lack of an adequate insulin supply retards the absorption of sugar, causes it to build up in the bloodstream and leads to **diabetes mellitus**; an excess of insulin can cause over absorption by the cells and create a low level of sugar in the blood called **hypoglycemia**, that can lead to **insulin shock**.

insulin shock An abnormal condition that occurs when there is an excess amount of insulin in the body.

Insulin aids in the absorption of sugar by the body cells. Too much insulin in relation to the amount of sugar available causes over absorption by the cells and a corresponding reduction of the level of sugar in the blood. When that level is too low, there is a reaction called *insulin shock*.

The prime causes of the condition are: not eating, so that not enough sugar has been taken in; taking too much insulin; or over exercising, thus burning sugar too fast.

The sufferer of insulin shock may experience a personality change, such as becoming confused or combative, headache, profuse perspiration, rapid weak pulse, dizziness, and cold, clammy skin. Eventually the condition leads to convulsions and unconsciousness.

One suffering from insulin shock requires immediate medical attention. Symptoms may be relieved temporarily by taking sugar in the form of orange juice, a candy bar, soft drinks, or several packets of sugar mixed with orange juice. The amount of sugar doesn't matter as the attending physician will balance the need for sugar against insulin production. It may be difficult to distinguish between a victim with insulin shock and one progressing into diabetic coma. When in doubt, administer sugar—giving sugar to a victim with too much blood sugar doesn't make any significant difference, but giving sugar to a victim in insulin shock can save a life.

internist A physician who specializes in the diagnosis and non surgical treatment of disease.

intestines The lower part of the alimentary canal, extending from the stomach to the anus; the large and small intestines.

ischemia A deficiency of blood in an organ or part of the body.

Ischemia is caused by obstruction of the blood vessels that supply an organ or area of the body. Such obstruction may be the result of narrowing, compression, or damage from conditions such as a blood clot or **atherosclerosis** and causes oxygen loss that leads to tissue death in the affected area.

jaundice A condition caused by bile pigments in the blood, characterized by a yellowing of the skin and other tissue.

joint The juncture of two or more bones.

There are three types of joints: *immovable joints*, such as those in the skull, *joints with limited motion*, such as those of the ribs and lower spine, *freely movable joints*, such as the knee, ankle, elbow, etc.

The bones are held in place by strong white bands, called ligaments, extending from one bone to another and entirely around the joint. A smooth membrane that lines the end of the cartilage and the inside of the ligaments secretes a fluid that keeps the joints lubricated.

kidney One of a pair of abdominal organs that removes water and waste matter from the blood and excretes them as urine.

kidney failure Descriptive of the condition that exists when the kidneys cease normal function, causing the buildup of toxic substances within the body.

Kidney failure may have any of numerous causes, such as: blockage of the urinary tract, as by kidney stones; an adverse reaction to medication; infectious disease that attacks the kidney; heart attack; severe dehydration; serious injury; or a congenital condition, one that exists from birth.

Kidney failure may be acute, when there is a sudden malfunction that causes a buildup of toxins within the body in a matter of hours, or it may be chronic, that is, a malfunction of the kidneys that grows progressively worse, with a gradual buildup of toxins, that may occur over a span of months or years.

The most common symptom of kidney failure is a reduction in the output of urine that causes an accumulation of fluid in the tissues. As the body becomes more toxic, the subject experiences constant fatigue, loss of appetite, diarrhea, nausea and difficulty in breathing. If the condition remains untreated, coma and death will follow.

kidney stone A mineral formation lodged in the urinary tract; a calculus.

Kidney stones are formed when excess minerals, such as calcium, are present and concentrate into a hard lump. They may exist without causing discomfort, or they may cause blockage that can interfere with normal function and cause considerable discomfort.

Excess calcium in the system may come from ingesting foods that have a high calcium content or those rich in vitamin D, that aids in the absorption of calcium, or from calcium released by fractured bones. Other factors may also contribute to the formation of kidney stones: uric acid may crystallize into stones; urine retained as the result of infection can contain a concentration of elements that can solidify.

When a stone becomes large enough, or becomes positioned so that it causes notice, it may cause considerable pain in the area, frequent and painful urination, blood in the urine, nausea, or chills and fever. A stone that becomes lodged in the ureter, the channel from the kidney to the bladder, can produce severe pain in the back, abdomen and groin. In any incidence of these symptoms, immediate medical attention is required.

Kidney stones that are too small to be noticed may still cause damage to delicate tissues in the urinary tract.

laceration A ragged cut or wound.

laryngitis Inflammation of the larynx.

The larynx is the voice box located in the upper part of the respiratory tract. Infection of the larynx is manifested by a hoarse or grating voice, or occasionally, a complete loss of speech.

Laryngitis may be caused an infection, such as that accompanying a cold or flu, from irritation of the mucous membrane of the larynx, as by smoking, dust, or air pollution, or from straining the voice.

In addition to altered speech, the laryngitis sufferer may also experience a scratchy feeling in the throat and pain when speaking.

The best treatment for laryngitis is a total resting of the vocal cords and, if necessary, throat spray, aspirin, or acetaminophen to relieve discomfort.

Persistent or frequent recurrence may be symptomatic of a more serious condition, and should be referred to a physician for diagnosis.

Legionnaires' disease A severe bacterial infection of the respiratory tract.

The disease gets its name from what was thought to be its first outbreak—in 1976, among those attending a convention of the American Legion in Philadelphia. Subsequently, earlier outbreaks of the disease were identified, however.

Onset of the disease may be mild, emulating the onset of influenza. Later symptoms are similar to those of any respiratory infection: coughing, shortness of breath, chest and abdominal pain, headache, fever, nausea, vomiting, and diarrhea.

Although outbreaks of the disease are infrequent, because of its life-threatening nature, it should be suspected in any respiratory infection that gets progressively worse over a period of several days, especially among the elderly or chronically ill.

leprosy A mildly contagious, chronic bacterial infection that causes loss of sensation.

lesion An alteration in the condition of tissue, that may be caused by injury, disease, abnormal growth, etc.

lethargy An unnatural lack of energy; sluggishness.

leukemia Any of a number of deadly diseases of the white blood cells and bone marrow.

Leukemia originates in the bone marrow, causing excessive production of white blood cells, many of which are immature or damaged. These ineffective white blood cells reduce the body's ability to fight infection while crowding out the red blood cells that carry oxygen throughout the body and platelets, that are necessary for clotting.

leukocyte Any of the colorless cells found in the blood, lymph, or tissues, vital to the body's defense against disease or infection; a white blood cell.

ligament Tough fibrous tissue that holds bones together at a joint and supports body organs.

lipoma A benign tumor of fatty tissue.

liver The largest gland in the body, located in the upper part of the abdominal cavity.

The liver performs a number of functions, including the manufacture of substances necessary for blood clotting, the processing of nutrients absorbed by the small intestine, and the removal of toxic substances from the blood.

lockjaw See tetanus

lumbago Rheumatic pain in the lower back; often used to describe any back pain.

lymphocyte A variety of white blood cell that develops in lymphatic tissue.

Lymphocytes are extremely important to the body's immune system—they identify the characteristics of **antigens**, produce the antibodies to combine with and destroy them, and direct immune responses.

malady Any condition that exhibits symptoms of illness or disease.

malaise A general feeling of discomfort or physical decline that may indicate the onset of disease.

malignant Descriptive of that which is a danger to health and well-being; likely to cause death.

mastoid bone The bone directly behind the ear.

mastoiditis A bacterial infection of the air cells in the mastoid bone.

Mastoiditis is usually caused by the spread of infection from the middle ear. In severe cases, the infection is in danger of reaching the interior of the skull.

measles A contagious viral disease common among children; rubeola.

The virus may be spread by moisture from the nose of throat of an infected person who is usually contagious for several days before symptoms are apparent and up to six days after the rash appears.

Early symptoms are similar to those of a cold—runny nose, congestion, sneezing, watery eyes, coughing and fever. After several days there is a sensitivity to bright light, the fever drops, and characteristic spots may appear in the mouth. Soon after, the fever rises and a rash appears, usually about the face, neck, and behind the ears before spreading over the entire body. The rash first appears as red spots; as they multiply, they grow together to form irregular blotches. Usually within days, the fever subsides and the condition improves.

Although the disease is relatively mild, anyone contracting measles should be placed under a doctor's care in order to avoid complications such as **pneumonia, encephalitis**, ear infection, **bronchitis**, etc.

As with all viral infections, aspirin should not be administered to children because of the link that has been established with **Reye's syndrome**.

melanoma A tumor, usually malignant, of cells containing dark pigment.

Meniere's disease A disorder of the inner ear caused by a buildup of fluid.

The canals, or labyrinth, of the inner ear serve to control balance and equilibrium by noting movements of the head and sending the information to the brain. Any disruption of this function can cause dizziness, nausea, vomiting, and distorted perception of surroundings, as when furniture appears to be spinning around a room.

Meniere's disease results from an increase in pressure from a buildup of fluid that distorts and, sometimes ruptures, the lining of the walls in the inner ear.

A mild attack may last less than an hour or several days, then disappear. Attacks may recur at intervals of weeks or months.

Severe attacks, that make normal movement impossible, require confinement to a bed. In the case of such attacks, bizarre illusions may accompany any head movement, the subject may suffer migraine headaches and some loss of hearing.

middle ear infection The middle ear serves to transfer sound vibrations to the inner ear and to protect the eardrum from rupture by equalizing the inside pressure with that on the outside of the body. Such equalization is made possible by the *eustachian tube* that connects the middle ear with the upper part of the throat.

The eustachian tube that protects the hearing is also the culprit that makes the middle ear susceptible to infection—most ailments of the middle ear are caused by virus or bacteria in the nose or throat that travel to the ear through the eustachian tube.

A middle ear infection can cause a severe throbbing pain, hearing loss, fever, dizziness, nausea, or vomiting. In extreme cases, the pressure against the eardrum may cause it to burst, relieving the pressure and attendant pain, but creating a danger of spreading the infection.

Because of the danger of hearing loss and spreading infection, a physician should be consulted in any case of ear infection.

mononucleosis A contagious viral disease that attacks the lymph nodes; infectious mononucleosis.

Mononucleosis is characterized by a sore throat, fever, swollen glands, and a feeling of weakness. The onset of the infection is so subtle that it appears to be no more than a simple cold; however, a sore throat that persists for more than a week, with swollen glands in the throat and neck accompanied by fever and weakness may be a sign of mononucleosis.

The usual treatment for the condition is rest and lots of liquids until temperature returns to normal. As strength returns, a resumption of normal activity should have no ill effects. Generally, mononucleosis is uncomplicated, although occasionally the infection spreads to the liver or spleen. Signs of its spread are **jaundice** and pain or tenderness in the abdomen. Either condition should be referred to a physician.

multiple sclerosis A chronic disease of the nervous system.

The condition is the result of random destruction of the *myelin sheaths* that insulate nerve cells.

Multiple sclerosis usually affects young adults, causing weakness or paralysis in parts of the body, blurred vision, muscle spasms or incontinence. The disease then commonly goes into remission that may last several years, but recurring attacks can cause increasing disability.

For some, the condition does not become severe; for others, over time, extensive nerve damage causes a loss of muscle control that precludes living a normal life.

mumps A contagious viral disease most common among children.

An attack of mumps may begin with fever, headache, sore throat or earache followed by the characteristic painful swelling of the salivary glands that may cause difficulty in eating.

Other glands and organs may become infected and swollen as well, such as the testes, ovaries, pancreas, liver, etc.

muscle Tissue made up of fibers that have the ability to contract.

It is through the contraction of muscle that all movements of the body are produced.

Voluntary muscles, also known as striated muscles are, with one notable exception, consciously controlled by the individual.

Involuntary muscles, also known as smooth muscles, such as those found in the blood vessels, digestive system, respiratory system, etc. are not under conscious control.

The exception to this ordering of muscles is a group of heart muscles that are striated, but controlled by the motor nerves rather than the conscious will.

myasthenia gravis A neuromuscular disorder characterized by a slow and progressive paralysis.

Neuromuscular is a reference to nerves and muscular. Myasthenia gravis is a condition caused by a failure of muscles to receive messages transmitted by the nerves, causing paralysis, although the muscles do not atrophy, or waste away.

Signs of the disease usually show up first in the face as paralysis of the eye muscles that causes squinting or double vision, sagging of the cheeks, and difficulty in talking, chewing, or swallowing. The arms and legs may be affected, causing difficulty in walking or in the accomplishment of everyday tasks, like lifting a fork. Eventually, breathing may be impaired.

The severity of symptoms varies from day to day and even throughout the day, with a tendency to be more oppressive at night.

There is usually no cure for myasthenia gravis, although there are drugs that can restore nerve transmission and improve muscle strength.

narcolepsy A disorder characterized by sudden, uncontrolled lapses into deep, but brief, sleep.

Attacks may be related to another condition, although they often occur with no other symptoms: the subject simply falls into a deep sleep and awakens refreshed.

nausea A feeling that one wants to vomit.

Nausea may be brought on by anything that interferes with the normal flow of nutriments through the digestive tract, whether direct, as in the case of reaction to tainted food or infection, or indirect, as by an emotional or psychological response.

Nausea may be manifested as discomfort or a burning sensation in the abdomen or chest, excessive secretion of saliva, sweating, blurred vision or feelings of weakness.

necrosis Death of tissue in the midst of healthy tissue.

Necrosis takes place when cells are destroyed by infection or when they are cut off from their blood supply. It may occur in an area of the body served by vessels that have been injured or blocked, in areas of the heart following a heart attack, or in the midst of a tumor that has outgrown its blood supply.

neoplasm Any abnormal growth of body cells or tissue; a tumor.

nephrology The branch of medicine that deals with the diagnosis and treatment of kidney disorders.

nervous system The network of cells that receive and transmit signals to coordinate the various parts of the body and the organs controlling the body functions.

The main parts of the nervous system consist of the brain and spinal cord. The brain is a collection of nerve centers. Leaving the brain, the nerves join to the spinal cord, pass through the opening in the center of the backbone or spinal column and branch off to all parts and organs of the body.

There are mainly two types of nerves entering and leaving the spinal cord: sensory nerves that convey sensations such as heat, cold, pain, and touch from different parts of the body to the brain; and motor nerves that convey impulses from the brain to the muscles causing movement.

The nervous system consists of two separate systems by function: the voluntary and the involuntary. The *voluntary nervous system* is under control of the will, that is, movements and actions that are deliberate. The *involuntary nervous system* is a series of nerve centers in the chest and abdominal cavity along the spinal column. Each of these nerve centers is connected with the spine and the brain and controls vital organs and vital functions. This system is not under control of the will; through it involuntary muscles are stimulated to function without regard to the state of consciousness.

neuralgia Descriptive of any pain along the course of a nerve.

The cause of neuralgia is not always apparent, although in some cases there may be evidence of inflammation or damage. The condition may be slight and fleeting, or it may involve a severe pain or one that is longer lasting.

Shingles, or *herpes zoster* is characterized by intense pain and infection along the course of a nerve.

Sciatica, caused by pressure on the sciatic nerve, is experienced as an ache or a recurring tingling sensation in the buttock and along the back of the thigh.

Carpal tunnel syndrome causes tingling in the fingers that may progress to pain running up the arm as a result of pressure on the large nerve that passes through the wrist.

Treatment for these and other conditions that cause neuralgia varies with the cause, location and severity of the condition.

neuritis Any inflammation of a nerve.

Neuritis may be brought on by infection, by pressure on the nerve, by exposure to toxins, by loss of the nerve's blood supply or by a lack of vital substances in the diet.

Neuritis can cause discomfort that ranges from tingling to severe pain, a loss of sensation and muscle control, or even paralysis.

Treatment for neuritis varies depending on the cause.

neurology The branch of medicine concerned with the diagnosis and treatment of disorders that have an effect on the nervous system.

The nervous system comprises the brain, the spinal cord and the network of peripheral nerves that flows throughout the body.

neurosis An emotional or psychological disorder.

Usually manifested by anxiety or depression, neurosis is commonly caused by the inability to adjust to the ordinary stresses of life.

neurotransmitter A substance that transmits nerve impulses between nerve cells.

The basic unit of the nervous system is the nerve cell, or neuron. At the ends of each nerve cell are numerous sacs containing neurotransmitter chemicals that are released by nerve impulses traveling through the nerve cell. Upon their release, the neurotransmitters jump to the next nerve cell to stimulate the production of an impulse in that nerve cell to carry the signal on.

nosebleed Bleeding from the nose caused by a rupture in the vessels in the inner lining of the nose.

Nosebleeds are usually caused by a blow to the nose, repeatedly blowing the nose, or long periods of breathing dry air. Occasionally they may be symptomatic of a more serious condition, as high blood pressure or a tumor.

Most nosebleeds can be stopped by leaning forward to avoid swallowing blood and pinching the soft portion of the nose for a few minutes, or by applying cold packs to the bridge of the nose.

Nosebleeds that are difficult to stop or recur regularly should be referred to a physician.

obesity The condition of being significantly overweight.

obsession That which engages a person's consciousness to an abnormal degree.

Obsession may take the form of irrational concerns, repetitive actions, doubts, or fears that the subject cannot avoid or dismiss.

Obsessions may be linked, as in the case of one who repeatedly checks to see that the doors are locked because of an obsession with security.

An obsession may be a symptom of a psychiatric illness or of a brain disorder.

obstetrics/gynecology *Obstetrics* is the branch of medicine that deals with conditions related to pregnancy and childbirth. *Gynecology* is concerned with the diagnosis and treatment of disorders of the female reproductive system.

Because of the close relationship between the two fields, they are often practiced as a single specialty.

occult blood Blood in such small quantities that it cannot be easily detected.

Occult blood is usually descriptive of blood passed off in the feces that cannot be detected except under a microscope. Such blood is often a sign of bleeding in the gastrointestinal tract.

oliguria An abnormal reduction in the passage of urine.

Oliguria may be a sign of kidney failure or other disease.

oncology The study of the cause and treatment of abnormal tissue growth.

Oncology deals with tumors, particularly those that are malignant, or cancerous. Because of the close association with cancers of the blood, many oncologists are also hematologists, qualified to deal with diseases of the blood.

ophthalmology The branch of medical science that deals with the study of the functions of the eye as well as the diagnoses, and treatment of diseases and injuries to the eye.

The ophthalmologist, who is a physician, may also qualify as a surgeon who can reattach retinas, remove cataracts, etc.

There are several non-medical fields that deal with the eyes, such as the *optometrist,* who tests the eyes for fitting out with corrective lenses, the *optician,* who fashions the lenses and fits glasses or contact lenses according to the prescription from the ophthalmologist or optometrist, and the *ocularist,* who fashions and fits artificial eyes.

ophthalmoplegia Weakness or paralysis of the muscles of the eye.

Ophthalmoplegia affects the muscles that control eye movements as well as dilation and contraction of the pupil. It can be caused by any condition that impacts on the muscles or the nerves that control them, as a head injury, stroke, tumor, etc.

opium An addictive narcotic, obtained from the juice of the opium poppy

Opium is the source of morphine, heroin, codeine and other medicinal compounds.

Opium engenders a feeling of euphoria, relieves pain and hunger, and, in time, brings about drowsiness and sleep; however, the addictive nature of opium is so strong that most users become physically and emotionally dependent on the drug.

orthodontia The branch of dentistry that deals with the correcting of irregularities of the teeth.

orthopedics The branch of medicine that deals with disease and injury of the muscles, bones, and joints.

ossification The transformation of soft tissue into bone or bone-like tissue.

osteoarthritis A degenerative disease of the joints.

Osteoarthritis is generally associated with age, and is most prevalent in joints weakened by a prior injury or disease, or those subjected to unusual stress, as lower body weight-bearing joints, especially among the overweight.

The condition is caused by loss of the cartilage that normally protects the ends of the bones: as the space between the bones narrows, they may grate to cause wear or displacement of the bone and ultimately, inflammation, swelling, pain, and stiffness in the joint.

osteoma A benign tumor comprised of bone.

An osteoma is seldom troublesome unless it is positioned to cause pressure on a nerve. The growth may appear anywhere in the body, but is most often attached to a normal bone, especially of the skull and the lower jaw.

osteomalacia Softening of the bones.

Osteomalacia is caused by a lack of vitamin D, that is necessary for the absorption and utilization of calcium in the body.

Vitamin D is formed in the skin from exposure to sunlight and is available in the diet in dairy products, many of which are fortified with vitamin D, and in fish oils, that are rich in vitamin D. In some areas, a lack of winter sunlight to aid in the formation of vitamin D contributes greatly to the deficiency; however, regular doses of cod liver oil, available in capsules, can overcome the problem.

The deficiency of vitamin D may also be caused by any condition that inhibits its absorption even though it is present, or by an increased requirement for the vitamin, as in pregnancy.

Osteomalacia causes pain and tenderness in the bones, and may lead to bone fractures and weakness of the muscles.

osteoporosis A condition marked by a decrease in calcium content of the bones.

As the body ages, the bones thin to some extent; when there is an abnormal lack of calcium available to the body, the process is hastened and the bones become especially susceptible to fracture.

The onset of osteoporosis may escape notice, or it may cause pain in the lower back, often following the fracture of a vertebra. Such fractures tend to be patterned, so that over a period of time, subsequent fracturing of vertebrae may lead to deformity of the spine and difficulty walking that can make one susceptible to further injury. Osteoporosis is a leading factor in the numerous hip injuries among the elderly.

The best defense is a carefully monitored program of light exercise that strengthens the muscles supporting bones that have become weakened by the disease. Diet is also any important factor, especially one that provides adequate vitamin D and calcium to promote the formation of bone.

osteosarcoma A malignant tumor of the bone.

Osteosarcoma may infect any bone but usually occurs in the long bones of the arm or leg. Most common in children and young adults, the malignancy typically spreads to the lungs which is usually fatal.

otorhinolaryngology The medical specialty that combines the study, diagnosis and treatment for diseases of the ears, nose and throat.

Because of the linkage of the passages between the ears, nose and throat—the ears and throat are linked by the eustachian tubes; the nose and throat meet at the nasopharynx—infections in one organ are commonly spread to another or to all.

otosclerosis A growth of spongy bone in the ear that causes progressive deafness.

In otosclerosis, the stapes, one of the bones in the middle ear that transmits sound waves to the inner ear, is overgrown and immobilized, so that the transmission of sound vibrations is impaired.

The condition may be corrected by a surgical procedure in which the stapes is replaced—a very delicate procedure that carries some risk of failure.

oxygen A colorless, odorless gas that occurs free in the atmosphere.

Oxygen, essential to the body, is absorbed from the lungs into the bloodstream, where it is carried by the hemoglobin in the red blood cells to be discharged to the tissues.

The brain is most sensitive to organ deprivation and is permanently damaged if its supply is cut off for more than a few minutes.

pacemaker A network of muscle fibers in the right ventricle of the heart that control the rhythm of the heartbeat; an artificial device that stimulates heart action and regularizes the heartbeat by the periodic discharge of electrical impulses.

It is the function of the natural pacemaker in the heart to cause it to beat at a regular tempo that allows for the proper flow of blood through it. When that natural function is impaired by injury or disease, an artificial pacemaker may be implanted in the heart to take over the function.

pain Severe discomfort that may be physical, as that caused by disease or injury, or emotional, as that caused by grief or depression.

The mechanics of pain are not thoroughly understood, but it is pain that assists greatly in the diagnosis of disease or injury as by location, type, or duration of the pain.

palate The roof of the mouth, that consists of a firm *hard palate* in the front and a fleshy *soft palate* in the back, toward the throat.

palliative Descriptive of medication that alleviates pain or other symptoms, but does not have the power to heal.

palpitation Rapid beating, especially of the heart.

palsy Any of a number of diseases characterized by tremors, weakness of the muscles, or an odd gait and attitude; paralysis.

pancreas A large gland located near the stomach at the back of the abdominal cavity that secretes enzymes to aid in digestion and hormones to regulate the level of sugar in the blood.

Enzymes produced by the pancreas are released to the small intestine to help break down carbohydrates, proteins and fats.

Hormones produced in the pancreas include insulin, that aids body cells in the utilization of glucose, or blood sugar, and glucagon, that prompts the liver to release stored sugar into the blood.

paralysis Impairment or loss of muscle function.

Paralysis may be caused by disease or injury to the muscle itself or to the part of the nervous system that directs it and may range in severity from impairing a single muscle or nerve to affecting a large part of the body.

Disease of the muscle itself commonly leads to weakness, rather than total paralysis, although in certain forms of *muscular dystrophy*, the disease can cause severe and ultimately fatal paralysis.

Any blockage of impulses from the nerves to the muscles, whether caused by direct injury or by disease may cause either weakness or lead to total paralysis, depending on the condition. Recovery, too, depends on the underlying cause, as in some situations there is total remission while in others there is virtually no hope for recovery.

paranoia A mental disorder characterized by delusions of persecution and grandeur.

Paranoia is characterized by suspicions that otherwise innocent acts are direct personal attacks, coupled with an exaggerated feeling of self worth that the subject feels is unrecognized or unjustly ignored by others.

paraplegia Paralysis of the lower part of the body.

Paraplegia, usually caused by damage to the spinal cord, may affect only the use of the lower limbs, or it may encompass the lower trunk as well causing dysfunction of the bladder and rectum.

parasites A plant or animal that lives in or on another from which it gains sustenance or protection without returning any benefit, and perhaps doing harm to its host.

Parkinson's disease A nervous disorder characterized primarily by tremor, muscle rigidity and a jerky gait.

The condition may be marked by uncontrollable shaking, difficulty in starting to move, a stooped posture and expressionless face. Shaking may be more noticeable with tension or excitement, or when resting. In the later stages, speech, eating and writing become more difficult.

Parkinson's disease is progressive; it may be present in a mild form for years with little change, or it can lead to severe disability within a few years.

pasteurization The process of heating a liquid to maintain a temperature of 60° to 70°C. for about forty minutes.

Pasteurization destroys organisms that cause fermentation, thus retarding spoilage of the liquid, as well as those that cause disease in humans, such as the bacteria that causes tuberculosis.

patch test A test to determine sensitivity to specific irritants.

Allergy, or excessive sensitivity to a substance such as pollen, feathers, or dust, or a chemical, such as a detergent, cosmetic or drug, is the cause of hay fever and hives, and may be the cause of many cases of asthma, eczema and sinusitis.

When the cause of an allergic reaction is not apparent, a patch test may be used to determine the irritant or irritants that are causing the reaction. The patch test is administered by applying a small patch of an irritant to the skin and checking for a reaction in one to two days. Because of the large number of possibilities, several irritants are usually tested at one time. Testing continues with different sets until it is determined which irritants cause a reaction, and treatment can begin.

pathology The branch of medical science that deals with the nature of diseases.

Pathology is concerned with determination of the causes, symptoms and effects of disease as well as the means by which the spread of a disease may be limited.

There are a number of specialties within that of pathology. Best known, perhaps, is forensic pathology, which is charged with the gathering of information, as from an autopsy, to be used as evidence in a court of law.

pediatrics The branch of medical science that deals with the diseases and care of children.

pellagra A disease caused by a deficiency of niacin.

Niacin is a part of the complex of B vitamins, present in meat, eggs, vegetables and fruit. Signs of pellagra are reddening of exposed skin, loss of appetite, and irritability. The condition is common among alcoholics.

pelvis The pelvis is a basin-shaped bony structure at the lower portion of the **trunk**. The pelvis is below the movable **vertebrae of the spinal column**, which it supports, and above the lower limbs, upon which it rests. Four bones compose the pelvis: the two bones of the backbone and the wing-shaped hip bones on either side. The pelvis forms the floor of the **abdominal cavity** and provides deep sockets in which the heads of the thigh bones fit.

peptic ulcer Descriptive of any erosion, or open sore, in the area of the digestive tract exposed to pepsin.

Pepsin is an enzyme formed in the stomach that aids in the digestion of proteins. Although unconfirmed, it is believed that peptic ulcers are the result of excessive excretions of pepsin irritating the walls of the lower end of the esophagus, the stomach, or the duodenum, the first portion of the small intestine. Natural weakness in the wall of the stomach may also contribute to the problem, as does stress and heredity.

The onset of ulcers may be subtle, exhibiting symptoms that can be taken for indigestion; however, when the symptoms appear after every meal, during stress, and occasionally, just before meals, a physician should be consulted.

pericarditis Inflammation of the pericardium, the membrane that surrounds the heart.

Pericarditis may be associated with other infections or diseases, such as pneumonia or a heart attack, or it may be caused by bacteria that enters the body through an open wound. The condition is marked by chest pains that intensify with breathing, coughing or lying down. Other illnesses with similar symptoms are equally serious; therefore, any incident of chest pain should be referred to a physician.

A condition called *constrictive pericarditis* occurs when inflammation causes thickening of the pericardium that restricts heart action. The condition is marked by difficulty breathing, swollen neck veins and accumulation of fluid in the legs.

periodontics The branch of dentistry that deals with the treatment of diseases and disorders of the periodontium, that is, the gum and tissues surrounding and supporting the teeth.

peritonitis Inflammation of the peritoneum, the membrane that lines the abdominal cavity.

Peritonitis is caused when one of the hollow organs of the abdomen is perforated, when infection is spread from an inflamed organ, or when the abdominal cavity is breached by a wound from the outside.

The condition is characterized by intense pain and the abdominal wall becomes tender and rigid. There may be nausea, vomiting, and dehydration. Peritonitis is extremely serious and requires immediate medical attention.

pertussis See **whooping cough**

phantom limb syndrome The illusion by an amputee that the missing limb is still in place.

The individual may experience feelings of touch, heat, cold, pain, etc. Usually the sensations disappear as the subject recuperates, but they may last for a considerable time or reappear without notice, especially feelings of pain.

pharmaceutics, pharmacy The craft of the precise preparation and dispensing of medicines according to the instructions of a licensed physician.

In addition, the pharmacist has the knowledge to advise on the use of non-prescription medications.

pharmacology The study and acquired knowledge of the nature and action of drugs.

pharyngitis Inflammation of the pharynx, the passage that connects the back of the mouth and nose with the larynx and esophagus; sore throat.

phlebitis Painful inflammation of a vein evidenced by swelling and sensitivity in the area of the inflammation.

pituitary gland A tiny organ located just beneath the base of the brain that produces a number of hormones that direct the functions of other glands and organs throughout the body.

platelets Disk-shaped structures in the blood that play a critical part in clotting; thrombocytes.

Normally, the lining of a blood vessel allows the blood to flow without change in its chemistry; however, when a blood vessel is ruptured and the blood comes into contact with foreign tissue, clotting begins. *Platelets* in the blood, triggered by the contact, release a chemical that begins a chain reaction involving a number of protein constituents in the blood, ending with the conversion of fibrinogen, a soluble material, to fibrin, that is insoluble. The fibrin is laid down in fine strands that collect white and red blood cells to form a clot.

pleurisy Inflammation of the pleura, the membranes that cover the outer surface of the lungs and the inner surface of the chest cavity.

The pleurae, lubricated by pleural fluid, serve to reduce the friction of chest members moving against one another as the lungs expand and contract.

Pleurisy frequently occurs as a secondary complication of a respiratory tract infection, such as pneumonia, though there are other causes.

Dry pleurisy describes the condition where the infected pleurae rub against each other; *wet pleurisy* is characterized by a condition in which fluid from the infected tissue fills the space between the pleurae or, effectively, between the lungs and the wall of the chest cavity. In either case, breathing is painful and difficult. Breathing capacity may be especially reduced in the case of wet pleurisy because the fluid in the chest cavity tends to compress the lungs.

In addition to severe chest pains that force shallow breathing, there is usually fever and a painful cough.

pneumonia Inflammation of the lungs, in which the air sacs in the lungs, the alveoli, fill with fluid and white blood cells.

Pneumonia is classified primarily according to the location of the inflammation: *lobar pneumonia* is a type of pneumonia that is usually confined to one section, or lobe, of the lung; *double pneumonia* is a condition that affects both lungs; *bronchial pneumonia* is concentrated in and about the bronchi, the airways that connect the windpipe and the air cells of the lungs; *walking pneumonia* is descriptive of a relatively mild condition that may not be readily identified as a lung infection.

Pneumonia may be caused by bacteria, virus, fungi or other microorganisms. Any foreign matter, such as a chemical, food or vomit, that is inhaled may carry an agent that causes infection. Any type of drug or disease that inhibits the immune system may make one increasingly susceptible to an attack of pneumonia.

Pneumonia commonly occurs when resistance is lowered, as by another infection, or a disease that affects the entire body. It may be brought on when the body's defenses are strained from fighting the ravages of a cold, influenza, emphysema, asthma, etc.

Any condition that requires confinement to bed for a long period increases susceptibility to pneumonia, especially in the elderly.

Pneumonia is usually characterized by chest pain, fever, coughing, and difficulty in breathing. Pneumonia caused by a viral infection may be preceded and accompanied by the symptoms normally associated the a cold or flu. Other forms of pneumonia may strike suddenly with chills, shivering, an abrupt rise in temperature, shallow breathing, and the discharge of dark yellow or bloody sputum.

General treatment for pneumonia should be with the advice of a physician, and usually involves bed rest, plenty of fluids and a soft diet. If the condition is secondary to another, treatment of the primary condition is important in order to strengthen the body's immune system. Bacterial pneumonia may be treated with antibiotics.

In very serious cases, or where there is continued labored breathing, hospital care may be necessary.

podiatry The science that deals with diseases, irregularities and injuries of the foot; chiropody.

Not all problems of the feet require a specialist, but some, such as correction of a deformity occurring at birth, should be in the hands of one likely to be most knowledgeable about the latest techniques.

The podiatrist often fills a special need by performing normal foot care that the elderly or incapacitated cannot perform for themselves, and by the knowledge and treatment of those conditions that most effect the elderly.

poisoning The introduction into the body of any substance in a quantity that is harmful or destructive.

Poisoning may be deliberate or it may be accidental. It may be caused by an otherwise non-toxic or even beneficial substance, as a medication in combination with another substance, or in a large quantity or *overdose*, that makes it harmful. It may come in the form a pollutant in the air or a bacterial growth in tainted food.

Poisoning can produce unpleasant symptoms, such as abdominal cramps, nausea, vomiting, sweating, or a feeling of weakness. It can also cause delirium, loss of consciousness, difficulty in breathing, blindness, paralysis and death.

Certain poisons may be neutralized or passed off by the body while others, ingested in small quantities accumulate in the system until they become damaging. Some cases of poisoning have no lasting effect while others cause scarring or other conditions that remain and may get worse in time.

Treatment for poisoning may be as simple as cleansing the offending substance from the body or administering an antidote, or it may require extended treatment to correct the resulting damage.

poliomyelitis An inflammation of the spinal cord that can cause paralysis; infantile paralysis; polio.

Poliomyelitis is a viral infection, spread by inhalation or ingestion of dust or fecal matter, that can reach epidemic proportions.

Infection initially causes discomfort or cramps in the muscles, sore throat, and a stiffness in the neck and spine. Symptoms may recede within a few days or they may spread throughout the system, causing paralysis, atrophy of the muscles and, in some cases, permanent disability.

Immunization is so widespread that it has been practically eradicated in the United States.

polyp A projecting growth of mucous membrane, usually not malignant.

proctology The branch of medical science that deals with diseases and disorders of the anus and rectum.

prognosis A prediction of the probable course of a disease or disability and the forecast for recovery.

prosthesis An artificial device that replaces a natural part of the body.

The most common prosthetic device is one that replaces missing teeth: dentures, false teeth, partial plates, etc.

Other prosthetic devices include artificial limbs; replacement joints, as for the hip, knee, elbow, etc.; replacement valves for the heart; and replacement lenses for the eye. Some devices are strictly cosmetic, such as an artificial eye that has no function except to replace an eye lost to disease or injury.

proteinuria The presence of protein in the urine. **Albuminuria** is virtually the same as proteinuria, since albumin is the only protein detected in significant amounts in the urine.

psoriasis A chronic skin disease characterized by reddish patches of skin with silvery scales.

Psoriasis is not contagious.

psychiatry The branch of medicine dealing with the diagnosis and treatment of mental and emotional diseases and disorders.

The *psychiatrist* is a medical doctor with training in psychology and is therefore authorized to prescribe medication as a part of therapy; the *psychologist*, on the other hand, does not have a medical degree and thus cannot prescribe drugs.

In addition to the treatment of *psychoses*, that is, severe mental disorders, psychiatry is involved in the treatment and rehabilitation of those suffering from behavioral disorders, anxiety, depression, addiction, etc.

psychology The science that deals with human behavior; the study of mental and emotional processes.

psychosis A severe personality disorder in which contact with reality is seriously impaired.

Psychosis may be the result of malfunction of the mind without apparent organic cause, or it may be caused by injury or disease.

psychosomatic Descriptive of a physical ailment that originates in a mental or emotional disorder.

pulmonary medicine The branch of medicine that deals with the study, diagnosis, and treatment of diseases and disorders of the lungs.

Pulmonary medicine is concerned with the care and treatment of such diseases as cancer of the lungs, tuberculosis, pneumonia, bronchitis, pleurisy, and emphysema.

purpura The presence of blood in the skin or mucous membranes.

Purpura is caused by defects in the walls of capillaries that have not been sealed off by platelets.

The condition is evidenced by tiny red or purple spots appearing on the surface of the skin or mucous membrane.

pus A yellowish-white fluid in which dead leukocytes, dead tissue, etc. are suspended; the result of an infection.

quarantine The isolation of those who have been exposed to a communicable disease.

The purpose of a quarantine is to limit exposure to a dangerous, communicable disease so as to prevent its spread to others, especially when there is danger of an epidemic, or rapid spread throughout the community.

Quarantine is not necessarily limited to those who show signs of being infected. Once there is exposure to certain diseases, an individual who is susceptible may be infected and not show symptoms for a time, although the disease can be passed on to another. That period of incubation varies depending on the disease. By isolating the person or persons for the longest known incubation time of the disease, there is reasonable assurance that the infection has not been passed on.

rabies An infectious, fatal, viral disease of animals that can be transmitted to man.

The rabies virus is contained in the animal's saliva; humans usually contract the disease from the bite of an infected animal.

Early symptoms of the disease are depression, restlessness and fever followed by a period of hyperactivity, abnormal salivation and painful spasms of the muscles in the throat. Usually, the victim develops an aversion to water, being unable to drink despite an irrepressible thirst. An untreated case is usually fatal in three to ten days.

To avoid rabies infection, treatment of any possible exposure should be prompt. After a bite, or any exposure of an open wound to animal saliva, the area should be completely washed with soap and water, and swabbed with an antiseptic, then seek medical help.

A domestic animal that does not exhibit symptoms should be confined and observed. A wild animal or any animal that shows symptoms of being rabid should only be captured by an experienced professional.

radiation therapy The treatment of disease by the use of radioactive materials.

Such treatment may be by material contained in a device that can be inserted directly into the tissues or a body cavity, or in an injection, or as a drink.

radiology The branch of medicine that treats of the use of radioactive substances in the diagnosis and treatment of disease.

Diagnostic radiology is mainly involved with the use of X rays to reproduce an images of part of the body on X-ray film. To improve the quality of the image and the subsequent analysis, special dyes called *contrast media* may be used in certain circumstances. Radiologists also use sound waves or magnetic impulses to create images.

Radiation oncology is a special field concerned with the application of radiation as a treatment for cancer.

rash A skin eruption, usually red spots or patches, often with minor irritation, as itching.

A rash may be symptomatic of a number of conditions, including blocked sweat glands, allergy, viral or bacterial infection, etc.

reflex An automatic, involuntary, or learned response to a stimulus.

Most of the actions of the body that allow it to function normally are reflex actions, such as the release of perspiration to adjust body heat, the secretion of digestive juices when food is ingested, or the adjustment of the eye to accommodate available light.

Many such reflexes are conscious, or controllable; for example, the reflex that closes the eye when an object is brought near may be overcome to allow examination by a physician.

Many reflexes are learned as well: experience often dictates whether one ducks or tries to catch a thrown object.

The failure of the body to respond in a normal or expected way to stimuli may also be a sign of disruption in the neural function.

respiration Inhaling and exhaling; the exchange of oxygen and carbon dioxide between the outside air and the lungs.

respiratory arrest A cessation of breathing.

Breathing may stop as a result of a variety of serious accidents. The most common causes of respiratory arrest are overdose of narcotics; electric shock, which can cause paralysis of the nerve centers that control breathing and stop or alter the regular beat of the heart; suffocation or drowning, a form of suffocation, in which air to the lungs is cut off by water or spasms of the larynx; poisonous gas, such as carbon monoxide, sulfur dioxide, oxides of nitrogen, ammonia, or hydrogen cyanide; head injuries, and heart problems.

respiratory system The system by which oxygen is taken into the body and carbon dioxide discharged; the nose, throat, larynx, trachea, bronchi and lungs.

Oxygen enters the body through respiration, the breathing process. Oxygen is essential to human life; all living tissue depends on the oxygen that is carried by the blood. Any interference with breathing causes oxygen depletion throughout the entire body.

During respiration, when air is taken into the lungs and forced out the air passes through the nose, throat, and windpipe. The air is warmed and moistened in the nose. The moist hairs and mucous membrane of the nose filter out much of the dust and foreign matter in inhaled air.

The throat is a continuation of the nose and mouth. At its lower end are two openings, one in front of the other: the opening in front, the trachea or windpipe, leads to the lungs; the one behind, the esophagus or food pipe, leads to the stomach. At the top of the windpipe is a flap, the epiglottis, that closes over the windpipe during swallowing to keep food or liquid from entering.

As the windpipe extends into the chest cavity toward the lungs, it divides into the two bronchial tubes, one going to each lung. The lungs are two cone-shaped bodies that are soft, spongy, and elastic. Each lung is covered by a closed sac called the pleura. The inside of the lungs communicates freely with the outside air through the windpipe.

Within the lungs, the bronchial tubes branch out like limbs of a tree, until they become very small. The bronchial tubes end in a group of air cells, or *alveoli* that resemble a very small bunch of grapes. Around each of the air cells is a fine network of small blood vessels or capillaries. Through the thin walls of the air cells, the blood in these capillaries exchanges carbon dioxide, other waste matter, and the by-products of tissue activity from all over the body for a supply of oxygen from the air breathed into the air cells. The discarded carbon dioxide and waste matter leave the air cells in exhaled air.

During breathing, the chest muscles and diaphragm expand the chest cavity, so that the air pressure within the chest cavity becomes less than that outside. Air rushes in to balance the pressure, filling the lungs.

During inhalation the ribs are raised and the arch of the diaphragm falls and flattens, increasing the capacity of the chest cavity, and causing air to enter. In exhalation, an act normally performed with slight muscular action, the ribs fall to their normal position, the arch of the diaphragm rises, decreasing the capacity of the chest cavity, and air is forced out.

If any air gets through the chest wall or if the lung is punctured so that air from the outside can fill the chest cavity, the lungs will not fill. This is because the air pressure is equal outside and inside the chest cavity. Thus, no suction is created for inhaling.

Breathing is an act which usually is automatic and one over which a person exerts only a limited degree of control. The amount of air breathed and frequency of breathing vary according to whether the person is at rest or engaged in work or exercise. At rest, a healthy adult breathes about fifteen times a minute and takes in twenty-five to thirty cubic inches of air per breath. Each breath moves about one-half liter (500 cc, or one pint) of air. During strenuous work, the breathing rate and amount inhaled may increase several times.

retina The light-sensitive organ at the back of the eye that receives images from the lens that are transmitted through the optic nerve to the brain.

Reye's syndrome A serious disease in which inflammation of the brain is coupled with liver damage.

Reye's syndrome is a rare condition that usually infects children recovering from a viral infection, such as chicken pox. A relationship has been established between the disease and the administering of aspirin for a viral infection; no exact cause for the disease is known.

The onset of the infection is characterized by sudden vomiting, hyperactivity or sleepiness, and confusion. Convulsions and coma may follow.

Immediate diagnosis is essential as the first few days of the disease are usually the most critical.

rheumatic fever An infectious disease characterized by swelling of the joints and inflammation of heart valves.

Rheumatic fever, most common in children, is brought about by an allergic reaction following a bacterial infection of the throat.

The condition is evidenced by painful inflammation and swelling as the joints of the ankles, knees, and wrists are infected one by one; the development of large, irregular skin rashes; and fever. Inflammation of the valves of the heart may cause permanent damage due to the formation of scar tissue that prevents the valves from opening and closing properly. Problems of the heart may surface years after the initial infection when the overworked heart becomes enlarged.

Any time a throat infection is followed within a few weeks by fever and inflammation of the joints, rheumatic fever should be considered, and a physician should be consulted.

rheumatic heart disease A complication of an attack of **rheumatic fever.**

Rheumatic fever, as noted above, may cause inflammation of the heart valves that results in the formation of scar tissue. The valves thus damaged may function without symptoms of impairment for years or even decades.

Heart murmur is a common symptom caused by blood flowing past a damaged valve. Although it is possible for the heart to compensate for the damage so that there is no serious disability, significant problems may occur. The scarring can cause a narrowing of the valve that restricts the flow of blood. Blood clots may form to further restrict the flow of blood out of the heart and lead to a number of symptoms associated with the deprivation of oxygen in the organs of the body.

Under the care of a physician, a program of regular exercise and proper diet can, in most cases, minimize the effects of rheumatic heart disease.

rheumatology The branch of medicine that deals with the study, diagnosis, and treatment of rheumatic diseases, that is, those concerned with connective tissue, as bones and muscles.

Rh factor A specific antigen that is present in some blood.

An antigen is a potentially harmful substance in the body that starts the reaction leading the body to produce a special **antibody** to neutralize it. Antigens commonly are introduced into the body by invading bacteria or other infecting agents.

The Rh, or rhesus, factor, named for the monkey in which it was first discovered, is found in certain blood, designated *Rh-positive. Rh-negative* blood is that blood lacking the Rh factor.

If Rh-positive blood is introduced into the bloodstream of one who has Rh-negative blood, antibodies are produced, because the Rh-negative immune system is unfamiliar with the Rh factor and views it as an invader.

Mixing of the different bloods can come about in two ways: by the transfusion of Rh-positive blood to an Rh-negative person, or through the mixing of the blood of an Rh-negative mother with that of a child who has inherited Rh-positive blood from the father. In either case, the Rh factor in the Rh-positive blood will cause the Rh-negative system to form antibodies to trap and destroy the offending Rh factor. Such action causes the formation of clumps in the blood that can create a stoppage that will result in death.

As with all allergies, the first exposure may not cause a serious reaction because of the time required for the body to form anti-bodies. The second transfusion or pregnancy, however, when the antibodies are already present in the blood and the immune system is ready to produce more, will almost always cause severe complications.

Careful typing of blood and the development of a substance that disables the Rh antibodies have made complications from Rh incompatibility relatively rare.

rickets A deficiency disease of children that often causes bone deformity.

Those who contract rickets tend to exhibit swollen joints or distortion of limbs and other deformities caused by softened and irregular bone growth that is the result of insufficient vitamin D to aid in the absorption of calcium and its merging into bone.

Vitamin D is formed in the skin from exposure to sunlight and is available in the diet in dairy products, many of which are fortified with vitamin D, and in fish oils that are rich in vitamin D. In some areas, a lack of winter sunlight to aid in the formation of vitamin D contributes greatly to the deficiency; however, regular doses of cod liver oil, available in capsules, can overcome the problem.

rigor mortis Stiffening of the muscles after death.

ringworm A contagious, fungal infection of the skin.

Ringworm often appears as round patches that leave red rings; hence, its name.

Ringworm may appear in a variety of forms, on various areas of the body, as the scalp, the trunk, or the groin. Athlete's foot is also a type of ringworm.

The fungus is transmitted by direct contact with an infected person or by contact with a contaminated object, such as an article of clothing, a towel, or a hair brush. Such personal items should be discarded or cleaned with a detergent to prevent spread of the infection.

Although ringworm is more of an inconvenience than a threat, it is similar to other skin infections that may be more serious and therefore should be referred to a physician.

Rocky Mountain spotted fever An infectious disease transmitted by wood ticks.

The microorganism that causes Rocky Mountain spotted fever is a parasite harbored by small animals, such as, dogs, rabbits, chipmunks, squirrels, etc., from which it is spread to man. Despite its name, the disease is not limited to the Rocky Mountain area, but may occur in other parts of the United States, and in other countries as well.

Infection produces chills and fever, painful muscles and joints, and skin eruptions.

rosacea A chronic disease characterized by reddening of the facial skin and often accompanied by pustules.

In severe cases, the nose may become red, swollen, and marked by large pores and blood vessels near the surface of the skin.

Cause of the condition is uncertain, but it has been linked to excessive consumption of caffeine in coffee, tea, cola, etc., and alcohol.

rubella A mild, contagious, viral infection; German measles.

The onset of rubella is characterized by a runny nose, swollen glands in the neck, and a low grade fever. Small red spots become visible on the face and neck within a few days, then quickly disappear as the rash spreads over the entire body. The second rash also lasts only a few days, but swelling of the glands may persist for a bit longer.

The most serious problem associated with rubella is the likelihood of birth defect after the virus has been contracted during pregnancy.

rubeola See **measles**

salmonella A bacterium that is the cause of a type of food poisoning.

Salmonella is generally contracted by eating foods, such as meat, chicken or eggs, that have been contaminated with the bacteria.

The condition causes cramps, nausea and diarrhea. Although generally mild, lasting only a few days, salmonella can be extremely serious in the very young, the elderly, or one who is already ill. Such cases should be referred to a physician promptly.

sarcoma Any of a number of malignant tumors that originate in connective tissue, such as bone or muscle.

scabies A contagious skin disease caused by a burrowing mite.

Intense itching is induced by the mite burrowing into the skin to lay her eggs, generally in the area of the wrist, fingers, genitals or feet.

Medication is available to relieve itching and promote healing. The disease may be spread by close contact; therefore, anyone associating with an infested person should be treated for the condition as well.

scarlet fever A highly contagious bacterial infection.

Scarlet fever gets its name from a characteristic scarlet rash covering the body that accompanies the fever and sore throat.

The condition is customarily treated with antibiotics accompanied by bed rest and a diet that contains lots of fluids.

scar tissue Connective tissue that has formed to replace normal tissue damaged by disease or injury.

schizophrenia A type of mental illness characterized by a withdrawal from reality.

Schizophrenia generally begins in adolescents or young adults, and may be evidenced by withdrawal, hallucinations, or discussions with a nonexistent third party with references to the subject as though he or she were not there.

sciatica Descriptive of severe pain in the lower back extending along the path followed by the sciatic nerve down the length of the back of the thigh.

scoliosis An abnormal curvature of the spine.

Usually, the condition occurs late in life, resulting from disease of the bones or muscles supporting the spinal column; however, it may be a congenital malformation of the vertebrae that can be corrected, at least in part, by surgery.

scurvy A disease caused by a deficiency of vitamin C.

Vitamin C performs a number of functions for the body, but is especially important in the formation of connective tissue that seals wounds, the activation of enzymes important to healing, and the prevention of clotting.

The more serious symptoms of scurvy such as anemia, general weakness, and internal hemorrhaging that can be attributed to a vitamin C deficiency are rare today, but the more obvious symptoms such as bleeding gums and slow healing are not.

Vitamin C cannot be synthesized, it is not stored in the body, and is often destroyed by other substances, such as certain medications or drugs; therefore, it should be a regular part of the diet or taken as a dietary supplement.

sebaceous cyst A swelling formed by the retention of sebum when the duct of a sebaceous gland is obstructed.

The sebaceous glands secrete sebum, an oily substance, that aids in protecting the skin. A gland that continues to produce sebum when the duct is blocked, fills and becomes distended with the substance. Frequently, the cyst will infect, burst, and expel its contents; one that does not can be surgically removed.

seizure A sudden attack of any kind, as by an epileptic fit, heart attack, convulsions, or a stroke.

senility A condition that encompasses the governing factors and infirmities of old age.

Senility may be used to describe simply the condition of being old, but is more often used to express infirmities, especially the decline in mental faculties.

Senility may be characterized by memory lapse, especially for recent events; slowed speech; inability to concentrate; lethargy; lack of concern about personal appearance; lack of ability to perform routine daily tasks; loss of appetite; anxiety; insensitivity to others; irritability; or withdrawal. Severe mental decline may be manifest in impulsive or inappropriate behavior; incontinence; inability to walk; etc.

In general, these conditions are progressive, that is, once begun, they continue to grow worse, a decline that may be rapid or extended over a period of many years.

septic Descriptive of that in which bacteria or other infectious substance is present.

shingles A painful viral infection of the nerves; herpes zoster.

Caused by the same virus as chicken pox, shingles is characterized by itching, painful blistering along the course of the infected nerve.

Treatment for shingles involves mainly medication to reduce the pain, and warm baths to bath the skin and prevent infection.

shock The effects of inadequate circulation of the blood throughout the body.

The *nervous system* plays an important role in shock. The various parts of the body and the organs controlling the body functions are coordinated by the nervous system, consisting mainly of the brain and spinal cord. Nerves leaving the brain go into the spinal cord, pass through the opening in the center of the backbone, or spinal column, and branch off to all parts and organs of the body. There are two principal types of nerves entering and leaving the spinal cord—sensory nerves that convey sensations such as heat, cold, pain, and touch from different parts of the body to the brain; and motor nerves that convey impulses from the brain to the muscles, causing movement.

The involuntary nervous system is a series of nerve centers in the chest and abdominal cavity along the spinal column. Each of these nerve centers is connected with the spine and the brain and controls vital organs and functions.

The *cardiovascular system* is the system that circulates blood to all cells. Food and oxygen are transported to each part of the body and waste products are removed through this system. When the body is in its normal state there is enough blood to fill the system completely—approximately ten to twelve pints for a person weighing 150 pounds. The pumping action of the heart supplies all parts of the body with blood.

Shock is the failure of this system to provide adequate blood to every part of the body. The collapse of the cardiovascular system may be caused by any of three conditions: blood is lost due to hemorrhaging; vessels dilate and there is insufficient blood to fill them; the heart fails to act properly as a pump and circulate the blood.

No matter what the reason for the collapse, the results are the same: an insufficient blood flow to provide adequate nourishment and oxygen to all parts of the body. The body process may slow down, reducing circulation and, without nourishment, organs begin to die, especially the brain.

The state of shock may develop rapidly or it may be delayed until hours after the event that triggers it. Shock occurs to some degree after every injury. It may be so slight as not to be noticed; or so serious that it results in death.

Some of the major causes of shock are: severe or extensive injuries; severe pain; loss of blood; severe burns; electrical shock; certain illnesses; allergic reactions; poisoning inhaled, ingested, or injected; exposure to extremes of heat and cold; emotional stress; substance abuse.

The signs and symptoms of shock are both physical and emotional: dazed look; paleness in light skinned individuals and ashen or grayish color in dark skinned individuals; nausea and vomiting; thirst; weak, rapid pulse; cold, clammy skin; shallow, irregular, labored breathing; pupils dilated; eyes dull and lackluster; cyanosis, or a bluish tinge to the skin, in the late stages of shock.

The most important reaction that occurs in shock is a decided drop in normal blood flow, believed to be caused by the involuntary nervous system losing control over certain small blood vessels in the abdominal cavity. This is one of the reasons the victim is nauseous.

As a large amount of blood fills the dilated vessels within the body, decreased circulation near the surface causes the skin to become pale, cold, and clammy. Other areas suffer as a result of the drop in circulation; the eyes are dull and lackluster and pupils may be dilated.

In the body's effort to fill the dilated blood vessels, less blood returns to the heart for recirculation. To overcome the decreased volume and still send blood to all parts of the body, the heart pumps faster but pumps a much lower quantity of blood per beat. Therefore, the pulse is rapid and weak.

The brain suffers from this decreased blood supply and does not function normally; the victim's powers of reasoning, thinking, and expression are dulled. The victim may exhibit: weakness and helplessness; anxiety; disorientation or confusion; unconsciousness, in the late stages of shock.

SIDS See **crib death**

sigmoidectomy Surgical removal of the final section of the large intestine that connects to the rectum.

sinusitis Inflammation of the sinus.

The sinuses are cavities in the bones of the face that are lined with mucous membrane. Normally, they are kept clear by draining into the nasal passages, but if there is any obstruction to the passage of mucus, they may become infected.

Commonly, sinusitis is associated with congestion from allergies, cold, or flu, but infection may also be caused by injury, swimming, or an abscessed tooth.

Symptoms of the infection vary, but they are often similar to the cold or flu: congestion, chills, fever, sore throat, and headache. For some sufferers, the most incapacitating symptom is a characteristic, severe headache that causes pain about the back of the head and the eyes. The sinus itself may appear puffy and swollen, and be tender to the touch.

Medication and moist heat are the most effective means for promoting drainage to relieve the pressure and remove the source of the infection. In extreme cases, surgery may be necessary to correct the condition.

skeleton The framework of bone that supports the softer body parts.

The human skeleton is composed of approximately two hundred bones, classified according to shape as long, short, flat, and irregular. The skeleton forms a strong flexible framework for the body. It supports and carries the soft parts, protects vital organs from injury, gives attachment to muscles and tendons, and forms joints to allow movement.

There are three major divisions of the human skeleton: the head, trunk and extremities.

The head is composed of twenty-two bones, eight that are closely united to form the skull, a bony case that encloses and protects the brain; fourteen other bones form the face. The only movable joint in the head is the lower jaw.

The trunk is composed of fifty-four bones and is divided into upper and lower parts by a muscular partition known as the diaphragm.

The upper portion of the trunk is the chest, its cavity, and organs. The spinal column, or backbone, is made up of thirty-three segments that are composed of vertebrae joined by strong ligaments and cartilage to form a flexible column that encloses the spinal cord. The chest is formed by twenty-four ribs, twelve on each side, that are attached to the back to vertebrae. The seven upper pairs of ribs are attached to the breastbone in front by cartilage. The next three pairs of ribs are attached in front by a common cartilage to the seventh rib instead of the breastbone. The lower two pairs of ribs, known as the floating ribs, are not attached in front.

The lower part of the trunk is the abdomen, its cavity, and organs. The pelvis is a basin-shaped bony structure at the lower portion of the trunk below the movable vertebrae of the spinal column, which it supports, and above the lower limbs, upon which it rests. Four bones compose the pelvis, the two bones of the backbone and the wing-shaped hip bones on either side. The pelvis forms the floor of the abdominal cavity and provides deep sockets in which the heads of the thigh bones fit.

The upper extremity consists of thirty-two bones. The collarbone is a long bone, the inner end of which is attached to the breastbone and the outer end is attached to the shoulder blade at the shoulder joint. The collarbone lies just in front of and above the first rib. The shoulder blade is a flat triangular bone which lies at the upper and outer part of the back of the chest and forms part of the shoulder joint. The arm bone extends from the shoulder to the elbow. The two bones of the forearm extend from the elbow to the wrist. There are eight wrist bones, five bones in the palm of the hand, and fourteen finger bones, two in the thumb and three in each finger.

The lower extremity consists of thirty bones. The thigh bone, the longest and strongest bone in the body, extends from the hip joint to the knee; its upper end is rounded to fit into the socket in the pelvis, and its lower end broadens out to help form part of the knee joint. This flat triangular bone can be felt in front of the knee joint. The two bones in the leg extend from the knee joint to the ankle. There are seven bones in the ankle and back part of the foot, five long bones in the front part of the foot, and fourteen toe bones.

skin The external covering of the body.

Although the outer layer of skin, or epidermis, is made up of layers of cells that primarily serve to protect, it also contains the cells that determine skin color. The epidermis constantly changes; as new layers are formed, old ones are shed. The layer of skin below the epidermis is the dermis. The dermis contains the blood vessels, nerves, and specialized structures such as sweat glands, that help to regulate body temperature, and hair follicles. The fat and soft tissue layer below the dermis is called the subcutaneous.

The skin has many protective functions. Skin is watertight and keeps internal fluids in while keeping germs out. A system of nerves in the skin carries information to the brain. These nerves transmit information about pain, external pressure, heat, cold, and the relative position of various parts of the body.

The skin is one of the more important organs of the body. The loss of a large part of the skin will result in death unless it can be replaced.

sleep A natural state of rest characterized by a lack of voluntary thought or movement.

During sleep, the body passes through a number of alternating states between that of being almost awake and of REM, or rapid eye movement, that is deep sleep.

It is during REM sleep, so named because of the characteristic erratic movements of the eyeballs, that dreams occur.

slipped disk Descriptive of the displacement of the disk of cartilage between the vertebrae; herniated disk; ruptured disk.

smallpox A highly contagious viral disease.

Smallpox is characterized by high fever and the emergence of red spots, first on the face and then spreading to the entire upper body. After a day or two, the spots become pustules that may leave pockmarks on the face or neck.

Although it was once a leading causes of death throughout the world, smallpox has been virtually eradicated.

smell Descriptive of the function of the olfactory nerves; to detect odor or aroma.

sneeze An involuntary action characterized by the sudden emission of air forcibly through the nose and mouth; a protective mechanism for expelling irritants from the respiratory system.

spasm The sudden, involuntary contraction of a muscle, that may be repeated for a time.

speech The ability to create unique sounds for the sole purpose of communicating thought.

sphygmomanometer Any device used for measuring blood pressure.

The most common sphygmomanometer is a device with an inflatable cuff that is wrapped around the subject's arm and a gauge to indicate pressure.

Blood pressure is expressed as two readings: the *systolic* that is the pressure during a contraction of the heart; and the *diastolic* that is the pressure between beats. The cuff is inflated to stop the flow of blood through the artery and then gradually deflated so that with the use of a stethoscope, the physician can determine the pressure at which the first pulse is heard and, as the cuff continues to deflate, the pressure at which the stream of blood passing through the artery is heard. Normal adult pressure is about 120/80 although some variance from that standard is not abnormal. Both readings are of value to the physician in making a diagnosis.

spinal column The spinal column, or backbone, is made up of thirty-three segments that are composed of **vertebrae** joined by strong **ligaments** and **cartilage** to form a flexible column that encloses the **spinal cord**.

spinal cord The network of nerve tissue that extends through the spinal column.

Nerves leaving the brain connect to the spinal cord, pass down through the spinal column, the opening in the center of the spine, and branch off to all parts and organs of the body.

There are mainly two types of nerves entering and leaving the spinal cord: sensory nerves that convey sensations such as heat, cold, pain, and touch from different parts of the body to the brain; and motor nerves that convey impulses from the brain to the muscles causing movement.

spine The human spine consists of 29 bones, called vertebrae, that provide the basis of a firm, flexible frame for the trunk of the body, and encases the spinal cord and its nerve roots.

The spinal vertebrae are separated and protected from each other by disks of cartilage that absorb the impact of any stress on the vertebrae as in walking or running.

spleen An abdominal organ that has several functions, primarily those of removing worn out or abnormal blood cells from circulation and in the manufacture of antibodies.

sporadic Recurring at irregular intervals.

sporotrichosis A chronic infection caused by a fungus that exists in soil and decaying vegetation.

Sporotrichosis commonly enters the body through ingestion or inhalation. The infection is usually limited to eruptions on the skin, but may involve the lymph glands.

sprain An injury due to stretching or tearing ligaments or other tissues at a joint.

A sprain is caused by a sudden twist or stretch of a joint beyond its normal range of motion. It may be a minor injury, causing pain and discomfort for only a few hours, or it may require weeks of medical care before normal use is restored.

A sprain is manifested by pain on movement, swelling, tenderness, and discoloration. At first the joint will probably be more comfortable if it is bandaged to limit movement and help keep the swelling down, but as soon as possible the joint should be moved and used. Sprains present basically the same signs as a closed fracture. If it is not possible to determine whether an injury is a fracture or a sprain, it should be treated as a fracture and referred to a physician.

spur A pointed outgrowth on a bone, caused by illness or injury.

sputum Saliva, often mixed with other material, as mucus, that is spit from the mouth.

Excess mucus in the respiratory tract, usually the result of irritation or infection, stimulates nerve endings that set up a cough reflex to eject the offending material.

stammer To involuntarily hesitate or falter when speaking.

The condition is usually readily overcome by speech therapy that focuses mainly on relaxation and proper breathing.

sterilization Any condition that inhibits or destroys reproductive capability .

Sterilization may be caused by disease, disability or surgical procedure.

In men, surgical sterilization is called a vasectomy, a relatively simple procedure that involves cutting through the tubes that carry sperm from the testes to the urethra.

In women, the most common procedure is cutting or blocking the fallopian tubes that carry the egg from the ovaries to the uterus.

sternum See **breastbone**.

stimulant Anything that has the effect of increasing the activity of a process or organ.

stomach The organ in the digestive system that is located between the esophagus, that delivers ingested food, and the duodenum, the first part of the small intestine. The stomach mainly churns ingested food and mixes it with digestive juices before passing it on to the duodenum for further digestion and absorption.

strain An injury to a muscle or a tendon caused by stretching or overexertion.
In severe cases muscles or tendons are torn and the muscle fibers are stretched. Strains are commonly caused by a sudden, unusual or unaccustomed movement.
A strain may cause intense pain, moderate swelling, painful or difficult movement, and, sometimes, discoloration. Generally, rest is all that is required to allow the body to replace damaged tissue; however, severe or persisting discomfort should be referred to a physician for diagnosis.

strangulation Constriction that cuts off a vital flow, as of air to the lungs or blood to an organ.

strep throat A bacterial infection of the throat.
Strep throat may cause chills and fever, and swelling of the lymph glands.

stress Any force or influence that tends to distort the normal physical or mental state.
Physically, stress is produced by normal body action, as that of the vertebrae against the disks that separate them when one is walking or running, or by abnormal stimulation, such as disease, injury, extreme ambient temperatures, etc. Mentally or emotionally, a certain amount of stress is inherent in every conscious thought or decision. Stress is recognized as a condition, however, only when it is sufficiently intense as to be beyond the ability of the body's regulating mechanisms to cope with it.
Stress may be brought on by any number of conditions that vary with the individual. For most, major lifetime events, such as loss of a job or the death of a loved one may trigger an extreme response that manifests itself in the onset or worsening of a mental or physical disorder. Others may attach special importance to less significant events and overreact to them, as an adolescent who regularly suffers asthma attacks before examinations in school.

stricture An abnormal constricting of a passage that prevents normal function.

stroke The sudden disruption of blood supply to an area of the brain; apoplexy.
Stoke may be caused by a clot formed somewhere else in the body that travels through the bloodstream to block an artery leading to the brain or in the brain, by cerebral hemorrhage brought on by the bursting of an artery in the brain, or by rupture of an **aneurysm** in an artery leading to the brain.
Those who suffer from both **hypertension** and **atherosclerosis** are the most likely candidates for a stroke, as both conditions weaken and damage the arteries. Lifestyle can also affect one's likelihood of suffering a stroke—smoking and high cholesterol levels are both significant contributing factors.
The consequence of a stroke is the loss of function in those areas of the body controlled by the affected area of the brain. Such loss of function, such as memory, sensory perception or motor skills, may be temporary, or it may be permanent.

sty A common infection of the sebaceous gland of the eyelash.
The sebaceous glands secrete sebum, an oily substance that aids in protecting the skin. The gland may become infected and pass the infection on to the hair follicle to which it is attached. The infection causes redness, swelling, and often, tenderness in the area. The sty may mature and burst, expelling its contents.
A sty will normally run its course without special treatment. Discomfort may be eased by relaxing the eye with occasional warm compresses and by wearing dark glasses. A child with a sty should be cautioned against touching or rubbing the eye and warned of the possibility that matter from the eye may dry during sleep, making the eyelid difficult to open on awakening—a frightening experience. In such cases, the matter is easily dissolved with a warm, moist compress.

subconscious Descriptive of those mental processes that occur without conscious recognition or with reduced perception, as those that are instinctive or reactive.

subdural hematoma A blood clot in the skull, beneath the outer covering of the brain

sublimation The suppression of base instincts to adapt to socially acceptable behavior.

subliminal Descriptive of that which is below the level of consciousness.

sudden infant death syndrome See **crib death**

sudden death The immediate and unexpected cessation of respiration and functional circulation.
The term *sudden death* is synonymous with cardiopulmonary arrest or heart-lung arrest. In the definition, the terms *sudden and unexpected* are extremely important. The death of a person with an organic disease such as cancer, or who is under treatment for a chronic heart condition and has gradual but progressive loss of heart function, cannot be correctly classified as *sudden death*. Cardiac arrest, when the heart stops pumping blood, may occur suddenly and unexpectedly for any number of reasons, such as heart attack, electric shock, asphyxiation, suffocation, drowning, allergic reaction, choking, or severe injury
A person is considered clinically dead the moment the heart stops beating and breathing ceases. However, the vital centers of the central nervous system within the brain may remain viable for four to six minutes more. Irreversible brain damage begins to occur to human brain cells somewhere between four and six minutes after oxygen has been excluded. This condition is referred to as biological death. Resuscitation in the treatment of sudden death depends upon this grace period of four to six minutes. After that period,

even though the heart might yet be restarted, the chance of return to a normal functional existence is lessened.

suffocation Any condition that inhibits the flow of air into the lungs.

suicide The conscious taking of one's own life.

sunburn Inflammation and discoloration of the skin caused by excessive exposure to the ultraviolet rays of the sun.

Despite the extreme discomfort of sunburn, most cases need only be treated with applications of medicated ointment to help restore the moisture balance in the skin. Extreme cases, however, can involve serious damage to the skin and loss of body moisture. Any sunburn victim who suffers from chills, fever, or nausea should be placed in the care of a physician.

Regular exposure to the ultraviolet rays of the sun has been linked to cancer and other skin diseases; therefore, one who is subject to such exposure should consider the use of a sun blocking lotion for protection.

superficial Near the surface; descriptive of that which expresses only limited intrusion, as a superficial wound.

suppurative Descriptive of the formation or presence of pus, as in a wound.

suture To join together the edges of an open wound by stitching; the stitch used to join the edges of a wound.

symptom A characteristic indicator of a disease or infection, either evident to the examiner or a sensation described by the subject, that, taken with other indicators, forms the basis for a diagnosis.

syncope Loss of consciousness caused by a temporary interruption in the flow of blood to the brain; fainting.

syndrome A number of indicators that, taken together, form a pattern for diagnosis.

synesthesia The alteration or transference of impressions from one sense to another, commonly that of smell or taste perceived as a visual color image.

synovial fluid The fluid present in the joints to lubricate the synovial membrane.

synovial membrane The membrane of the joints that, with synovial fluid, reduces the friction between two or more joined bones.

tachycardia Abnormally rapid heartbeat, caused by disease, medication, drugs, exercise, or emotional distress.

tantrum Uncontrollable rage or temper.

tapeworm A long, thin, flat worm that survives in the intestinal tract.

Tapeworms can cause weight loss and anemia in spite of a healthy appetite

taste That one of the senses stimulated by contact with the tastes buds in the mouth.

Basically, the taste buds allow one to distinguish among four different characteristics—sweet, sour or acid, salty and bitter. The distinctive taste of a specific substance is a combination of the sensory perception of the taste buds, its aroma, and its texture.

tendinitis Inflammation of a tendon.

Although tendinitis may be associated with disease, it is most usually the result of physical activity.

One who engages in athletics or physical labor without proper conditioning or preparation is a candidate for a variety of injuries, including tendinitis.

Tendinitis is manifested in pain and tenderness in the affected area, which is relieved by resting.

tendon The tough, fibrous connective tissue by which muscle is joined to bone.

teratoma A tumor comprised of embryonic tissue.

tetanus An infectious disease associated with severe muscle contraction; lockjaw

The tetanus bacteria enter the body through an open wound and produce a toxin that commonly infects the muscles of the jaw, producing steady contractions that cause the jaw to become fixed in a tightly closed position.

The disease may affect other muscles, as well, and in some cases, the contractions become so severe that they are extremely painful.

The disease may be treated with drugs to counteract the infection and others to relax the muscles.

Prevention requires prompt cleansing of puncture wounds and immunization with the tetanus vaccine.

tetany A disease caused by a lack of calcium in the blood.

Tetany is commonly associated with parathyroid disease or a lack of vitamin D in the diet. The condition causes muscle spasms and violent twitching, especially of the extremities.

thalamus A part of the brain involved in the transmission of sensory messages.

therapeutics The branch of medicine concerned with the treatment of disease.

thermography A technique for determining variance in temperature with the aid of an infrared camera.

Infrared rays from a source vary with the amount of heat given off. An infrared camera, capable of photographing infrared ray patterns, can produce an image showing the relative amounts of infrared emitted from various areas, thus allowing a diagnostician to detect areas of abnormal growth or activity.

thiamine See **vitamin B complex**

thirst An intuitive desire for fluid.

In order to maintain normal function, the body needs constant replenishment of fluids to replace those lost through the action of the lungs, sweat glands and kidneys. A number of conditions, such as stress, heavy exercise, or hemorrhage or disease can increase the need for fluids.

The need for fluids is signaled by a dry feeling in the throat and mouth, because moisture evaporates rapidly from those areas when the body lacks water.

thoracotomy A surgical opening of the chest, or thorax, for diagnostic purposes or for corrective surgery.

thrombosis Coagulation of blood; the process of forming a blood clot in the heart or a blood vessel.

thrombus A blood clot that forms in the heart or a blood vessel.

thrush A fungal infection, most often affecting children, that is characterized by the formation of white patches and ulcers on the mouth and throat.

thymus A lymph gland located in the upper part of the chest cavity, or thorax; thymus gland.

thyroid gland A gland located in front of the throat that secretes hormones for regulating the body's development and metabolism.

Thyroid hormone is involved in a number of processes throughout the body, such as the regulation of body temperature, growth, fertility, and the conversion of food to energy.

tic An intermittent, involuntary spasm or twitch, usually of the facial muscles.

tick Any of a number of parasitic mites that feed on the blood of their host.

Ticks attach themselves to the skin of humans and animals, carrying and transmitting a number of diseases, such as Rocky Mountain spotted fever.

To avoid further damage to body tissue and the risk of infection, a tick should not be pulled or rubbed off; removal is best accomplished by covering it with salad oil or by touching it with a lighted cigarette that will cause it to back off.

tinnea See **ringworm**

tinnitus A buzzing or ringing in the ear.

Tinnitus may be caused by blockage of the Eustachian tubes, excessive wax in the ears, or a disorder of the auditory nerves.

tissue Any of a number of distinctive materials, comprised of like cells, that make up the structures of the body, such as connective tissue.

tonsillectomy A surgical procedure for the removal of the tonsils.

tonsillitis Infection or inflammation of the tonsils.

The tonsils are two small, lymph glands located on each side of the throat at the back of the mouth.

Tonsillitis is usually evidenced by a sore throat, fever and difficulty in swallowing. Often, there is evidence of swelling and inflammation of the organ. Treatment generally involves rest, relieving symptoms, and sometimes, antibiotics to clear the infection. The tonsils are seldom surgically removed except in extreme conditions.

topical Descriptive of that designated for a particular part of the body, as the applying of a medication.

torso The trunk of the human body.

torticollis Wryneck; a contraction of the muscles on one side of the neck that causes the neck to twist and the head to incline to one side.

toxemia A condition in which toxins are in the blood and thereby spread throughout the system.

toxin Any of a variety of matter produced by microorganisms that cause infection and disease in humans.

trachea The tube that extends from the larynx to the bronchi in the respiratory tract; the windpipe.

tracheotomy A surgical incision in the front of the neck into the trachea.

A tracheotomy is performed when injury or disease causes an obstruction in the windpipe or makes it necessary to remove the larynx.

transplant To transfer an organ or tissue; the organ or tissue so transferred.

Transplants range from those of the cornea of the eye, to skin grafts, to those of organs and tissues, many yet in the experimental stage.

The overriding problem with transplants is one of rejection—the body's immune system builds antibodies to destroy the unfamiliar tissue—so that immunosuppressive drugs are necessary to suspend this reaction. There is danger also in the use of such drugs as they make the body vulnerable to other infection that can be life threatening.

The cornea carries no blood, and so poses no threat; the grafting of skin from one part of the body to another part of the same body poses no threat. One of the more common transplants, that of a kidney, has been most successful when the donor is a close relative who most nearly matches the tissue of the recipient.

The transplant of other organs, such as the heart, liver, or pancreas, have been undertaken with mixed results. There have been transplants of artificial devices, and even organs or tissue from other species. Undoubtedly, there will be failures, but undoubtedly, too, there will be great successes.

trauma A sudden affliction, either physical or psychological.

In the practice of medicine, *trauma* is generally descriptive of physical injury or the physical symptoms of **shock**.

In psychiatry, it is used to describe a distressing emotional experience that is difficult for the subject to deal with, and that may produce a lasting effect, as neurosis.

tremor An involuntary shaking of a part of the body.

triage A system of assigning a priority to the treatment of victims in a medical emergency based on such factors as urgent need and the chance for survival.

trunk Descriptive of the main part of the human body comprising all except the **head** and the **extremities**. The trunk is composed of fifty-four bones and divided into upper and lower parts by a muscular partition known as the **diaphragm**.

The upper portion of the trunk is the **chest**, its cavity, and organs. The lower part of the trunk is the **abdomen**, its cavity, and organs.

tuberculosis A bacterial infection characterized by the formation of tubercles.

The body's immune system cannot destroy the bacterium that cause tuberculosis; therefore it encloses them in small nodules called tubercles. As a result, the invading organism remains in the body, although it is prevented from causing infection.

The majority of those infected by tuberculosis will not experience symptoms, as the bacteria remain dormant in the body. Of those who do experience symptoms, not all will do so immediately after being infected. In many cases, the tuberculosis lies dormant and becomes active only when the body is weakened by some other disease.

Tuberculosis usually acts on the lungs, but it can infect other parts of the body, such as the kidneys, spine, or digestive tract.

Tuberculosis is contagious, spread by bacteria from the coughing or sneezing of an infected person. Anyone in contact with a tuberculosis sufferer should consult a physician for testing.

The symptoms of tuberculosis are not distinctive from other infections—in the early stages, they involve fever, fatigue and weight loss; later there may be chest pains, shortness of breath and spots of blood in coughed up sputum—however, any signs of blood in the lungs should be referred to a physician regardless of the suspected cause.

tumor Any growth of new tissue that is independent of its surroundings. A tumor may be **benign** or **malignant**.

turgid Descriptive of that which is swollen or abnormally distended.

ulcer Descriptive of an erosion, or open sore; any area of skin or mucous membrane that is lacking its normal protective cover and, usually, is inflamed.

Ulcers may occur as **bedsores** on the lower back caused by extended confinement to bed, as sores of the feet or legs associated with diabetes or varicose veins, in the digestive tract such as a **peptic ulcer**, etc.

ultrasound The technique of using high frequency sound waves to record an image of internal tissue that cannot be detected by X rays.

The sound waves are focused into beams that are deflected differently by tissues of varying density so that the existence and position of the tissue can be recorded to produce a visual image.

Ultrasound is a valuable tool in detection and diagnosis, such as the formation and position of gallstones, or irregularities in blood vessels. It can also be used for examination of the fetus during pregnancy, as it produces no harmful emission of radiation.

undulant fever See **brucellosis**

urinary bladder The organ or sac that receives, holds and discharges urine.

urology The branch of medicine that deals with the study, diagnosis and treatment of diseases and disorders of the urogenital tract, or the urinary tract and reproductive system.

urticaria An allergic condition characterized by itchy blotches or welts; hives.

Urticaria may be caused by allergens in food, as tomatoes, strawberries, etc.; certain drugs; bacteria; animal hair; or the environment, as exposure to cold or the sun.

An outbreak may last less than an hour or continue for weeks, often subsiding, then reappearing from time to time. A mild attack is merely annoying, but more serious attacks may be accompanied by fever or nausea and even difficulty in breathing if the respiratory tract is infected. Treatment generally involves administering antihistamines.

varicose veins A condition characterized by swollen, knotted blood vessels, usually in the legs.

Blood returning to the heart from the legs is pushed against gravity; therefore, the veins in the legs have a special valve to keep the blood from running backward. If a vein is weakened from obesity, lack of exercise, long stretches of sitting or standing, etc., it stretches and the valves are not allowed to close properly. Blood then leaks backward and gathers in pools that further weaken the vein.

Varicose veins may be temporary, as in the case of pregnancy when they are caused by the strain of carrying the additional weight, or when long periods of sitting or standing are not part of the normal lifestyle. In such cases, resumption of normal activity and exercise may cause them to return to normal.

The condition is obvious, as it develops close to the skin and appears as twisting, bulging lines that run down the legs, often with dark blue spots or sections. Often the ankles swell and the skin in the affected area becomes dry and itchy. In severe cases there may be shooting pains and cramps, especially at night.

Varicose veins are not serious in themselves, but they may allow the formation of clots or inflammation that can cause a more serious problem.

vein Any of the numerous vessels that carry blood back to the heart

vertebrae The bones or segments that make up the spinal column and through which the spinal cord passes. *Vertebrae* is plural; *vertebra* is singular.

vertigo A disorder in which dizziness is accompanied by a sensation of moving and the feeling that one's surroundings are moving as well.

virulent Descriptive of that which can overcome the body's defenses and cause infection; often powerful and rapid in its advance; malignant.

vitamin Any of a number of organic substances that are essential for the normal growth and functioning of the body.

Most vitamins are derived from various food sources and some are synthesized in the body.

vitamin A Obtained primarily from green leafy vegetables, eggs, butter, milk, liver, and fish liver oils, vitamin A is essential to proper formation of cells of the skin and mucous membranes, and for night vision.

vitamin B complex B vitamins are divided into several constituents:

Thiamine, or *Vitamin B_1* is available mainly in yeast, whole grain, meat, eggs, and potato. Thiamine is important to promote growth and in the proper functioning of nerves.

Riboflavin, or *Vitamin B_2* may be obtained from milk, eggs, cheese, liver, and meats; it promotes growth and aids in the body cells' metabolism.

Vitamin B_6 is contained in whole grains, fish, liver, and yeast. It is important in the metabolism of protein and the production of antibodies to fight infection.

Vitamin B_{12} is available from milk, eggs, liver and meat. It is important in the metabolism of fat and sugar; in the production of blood; and for normal growth and neurological function.

Niacin, or *nicotinic acid*, that is obtainable from yeast, liver, meat, and whole grains, aids in the metabolism of sugar and is vital to proper function of the intestines.

Folic acid, obtained from green leafy vegetables, giblets, and liver, aids in the metabolism of sugar and amino acids, the components of protein.

Pantothenic acid, obtainable from green leafy vegetables and meat, is essential to cell growth.

Biotin, found in yeast, egg and liver is essential for normal growth.

Choline, found in green leafy vegetables and meat, is essential to the metabolism of fat.

Inositol, from green leafy vegetables and meat, is linked to the metabolism of cholesterol

Vitamin C Vitamin C, or *ascorbic acid* is obtained mainly from citrus fruit, such as oranges, lemons or grapefruit, and from potatoes or tomatoes. Vitamin C is vital to the function of blood vessels, healing and the production of connective tissue.

Vitamin D Found mainly in fish liver oil and in fortified milk, vitamin D can also be formed on the skin from sunlight. It is essential to the metabolism of calcium and important to normal formation of teeth and bones.

Vitamin E Obtained from cold-pressed oils, wheat germ and whole grains, vitamin E is linked to a number of functions in the body including the manufacture of blood and to fertility.

Vitamin K Available from leafy green vegetables and fish, vitamin K is necessary for the blood to clot normally.

vitiligo A condition in which there is an absence of natural pigment in sections of the skin or hair that appear as whitish or light patches.

vomit To expel the contents of the stomach forcibly through the mouth.

wart A small, dry growth on the skin.

A wart is not malignant or, in most cases, harmful in any other way. The condition is caused by a virus that causes enlargement of the cells of the skin.

wean To teach a baby to consume foods other than mother's milk or formula.

wheeze Difficulty in breathing that is accompanied by a whistling sound.

whooping cough An infectious disease of the respiratory system that affects the mucous membranes lining the air passages. Primarily a disease of children, it is characterized by a series of coughs followed by an intake of breath that causes a whooping sound.

X rays High frequency electromagnetic radiation that is capable of penetrating some solid objects, of destroying tissue by extended exposure, and of creating an image on a photographic plate or a fluorescent screen.

X rays are used to create images of body parts for study and diagnosis.

yellow fever An often fatal viral infection contracted by the bite of an infected mosquito. Yellow fever attacks the liver and kidneys, and causes chills, fever, jaundice, and internal hemorrhaging.

yellow jaundice See **jaundice**

zoonosis Any disease in animals that can be transmitted to man.

zoster Herpes zoster. See **shingles.**

WEBSTER'S
SPELLER

This Webster's Speller is designed as a
Quick Reference Guide to spelling
and proper word hyhenation.

Words that contain double dashes (--)
between letters indicates a hyphenated word.

Single dashes (-) indicates syllabic division.

aard-vark	ab-duc-tor	ab-laut	a-bove-board
aard-wolf	ab-duct-ing	a-blaze	ab-ra-ca-dab-ra
a-back	a-beam	a-ble	abrad-ant
ab-a-ca	a-bed	a-bler	a-brade
abac-te-ri-al	ab-er-rance	a-blest	a-brad-ed
ab-a-cus	ab-er-ran-cy	a-bly	a-brad-er
ab-a-cus-es	ab-er-rant	a-ble-bod-ied	a-bra-sion
ab-a-ci	ab-er-rant-ly	a-bloom	a-bra-sive
a-baft	ab-er-ra-tion	ab-lu-tion	a-bra-sive-ly
abaft-ment	ab-er-ra-tion-al	ab-lu-tion-ar-y	ab-re-act
abaft-ed	a-bet	ab-ne-gate	a-breast
ab-a-lo-ne	a-bet-ted	ab-ne-gat-ed	a-bridge
a-ban-don	a-bet-ting	ab-ne-gat-ing	a-bridged
aban-doned	a-bet-ment	ab-ne-ga-tor	a-bridg-ing
aban-don-er	a-bet-tor	ab-ne-ga-tion	a-bridg-ment
aban-don-ment	a-bet-ter	ab-nor-mal	a-bridge-ment
a-base	a-bey-ance	ab-nor-mal-ly	a-broach
a-based	abey-ant	ab-nor-mal-i-ty	a-broad
a-bas-ing	ab-hor	ab-nor-mal-i-ties	ab-ro-gate
a-base-ment	ab-horred	a-board	ab-ro-gat-ed
a-bash	ab-hor-ring	a-bode	ab-ro-gat-ing
a-bash-ment	ab-hor-er	a-boil	ab-ro-ga-tion
a-bate	ab-hor-rence	a-bol-ish	ab-rupt
a-bat-ed	ab-hor-rent	a-bol-ish-a-ble	abrupt-ness
a-bat-ing	ab-hor-rent-ly	a-bol-ish-er	abrupt-ly
a-bat-a-ble	a-bide	a-bol-ish-ment	ab-scess
a-bate-ment	a-bid-er	ab-o-li-tion	ab-scessed
aba-tis	a-bi-ded	ab-o-li-tion-ism	ab-scise
ab-at-oir	a-bid-ing	a-b-oma-sum	ab-sci-sin
ab-ax-i-al	a-bid-ance	a-b-oma-sal	ab-scis-sa
ab-ba-cy	a-bid-ing	a-bom-i-na-ble	ab-scis-sas
ab-ba-tial	a-bid-ing-ly	a-bom-i-na-bly	ab-scis-sae
ab-bess	ab-i-gail	a-bom-i-nate	ab-scis-sion
ab-bey	a-bil-i-ty	a-bom-i-nat-ed	ab-scond
ab-beys	a-bil-i-ties	a-bom-i-na-tion	ab-scond-er
ab-bot	abi-o-log-i-cal	a-bom-i-na-tor	ab-sence
ab-bre-vi-a-tion	ab-ject	ab-o-rig-i-ne	ab-sent
ab-bre-vi-ate	ab-ject-ly	ab-o-rig-i-nal	ab-sent-ly
ab-bre-vi-at-ed	ab-ject-ness	ab-o-rig-i-nal-ly	ab-sen-tee
ab-bre-vi-at-ing	ab-jec-tion	a-born-ing	ab-sen-tee-ism
ab-bre-vi-a-tor	ab-ju-ra-tion	a-bort	ab-sent-mind-ed
ab-di-cate	ab-jure	a-bort-er	ab-sent-mind-ed-ly
ab-di-cat-ed	ab-jured	a-bor-ti-fa-cient	ab-sinthe
ab-di-cat-ing	ab-jur-ing	a-bor-tion	ab-so-lute
ab-di-ca-tion	ab-ju-ra-tion	a-bor-tion-ist	ab-so-lute-ly
ab-do-men	ab-jur-er	a-bor-tive	ab-so-lu-tion
ab-dom-i-nal	ab-late	a-bor-tive-ness	ab-so-lut-ism
ab-dom-i-nal-ly	ab-lat-ed	a-bor-tive-ly	ab-so-lut-ist
ab-duce	ab-lat-ing	a-bound	ab-so-lut-ize
ab-duct	ab-la-tion	a-bout	ab-solve
ab-duc-tion	ab-la-tive	a-bout-face	ab-solved

ab-solv-ing
ab-sorb
ab-sorb-er
ab-sorb-a-bil-i-ty
ab-sorb-a-ble
ab-sorb-tive
absorbance
ab-sor-ben-cy
ab-sor-bent
ab-sorb-ing
ab-sorp-tance
ab-sorp-tion
ab-stain
ab-stain-er
ab-sten-tion
ab-sti-nence
ab-sti-nent
ab-ste-mi-ous
ab-ste-mi-ous-ly
ab-sten-tion
ab-sti-nence
ab-stract
ab-stract-ly
ab-strac-tion
ab-strac-tive
ab-stract-ed
ab-stract-ed-ly
ab-strac-tion-ism
ab-strac-tion-ist
ab-struse
ab-struse-ly
ab-stru-si-ty
ab-surd
ab-surd-i-ty
ab-surd-ly
ab-surd-ism
ab-sur-di-ty
a-bub-ble
a-build-ing
a-bud-dance
a-bun-dant
a-bun-dant-ly
a-buse
a-bused
a-bus-ing
a-bus-er
a-bu-sive
a-bu-sive-ly
a-but
a-but-ter
a-but-ted

a-but-ting
abu-ti-lon
a-but-ment
a-but-tals
a-but-ting
a-buzz
a-bye
a-bysm
a-bys-mal
a-bys-mal-ly
a-byss
a-bys-sal
a-ca-cia
ac-a-deme
ac-a-de-mia
ac-a-dem-ic
ac-a-dem-i-cal-ly
ac-a-dem-i-cal
acad-e-mi-cian
ac-a-dem-i-cism
a-cad-e-my
a-cad-e-mies
a-can-thus
a-can-thus-es
a-can-thi
a cap-pel-la
ac-a-rid
acar-pel-ous
ac-a-rus
acatalectic
acau-les-cent
ac-cede
ac-ced-ed
ac-ced-ing
ac-ce-le-ran-do
ac-cel-er-ate
ac-cel-er-at-ed
ac-cel-er-at-ing
ac-cel-er-a-tive
ac-cel-er-at-ing-ly
ac-cel-er-a-tion
ac-cel-er-a-tive
ac-cel-er-a-tor
ac-cel-er-om-e-ter
ac-cent
ac-cent-less
ac-cen-tu-al
ac-cen-tu-al-ly
ac-cen-tu-ate
ac-cen-tu-at-ed
ac-cen-tu-at-ing

ac-cen-tu-a-tion
ac-cept
ac-cept-ing-ly
ac-cept-ance
ac-cept-er
ac-cept-or
ac-cept-a-ble
ac-cept-a-bil-i-ty
ac-cept-a-bly
ac-cept-a-ble-ness
ac-cep-tance
ac-cep-tant
ac-cep-ta-tion
ac-cept-ed
ac-cept-ed-ly
ac-cep-tor
ac-cess
ac-ces-si-ble
ac-ces-si-bil-i-ty
ac-ces-si-bly
ac-ces-sion
ac-ces-sion-al
ac-ces-so-ri-al
ac-ces-so-ry
ac-ces-so-ri-ly
ac-ciac-ca-tu-ra
ac-ci-dence
ac-ci-dent
ac-ci-dent-ly
ac-ci-den-tal
ac-ci-den-tal-ly
ac-ci-dent--prone
ac-cip-i-ter
ac-cip-i-trine
ac-claim
ac-claim-er
ac-cla-ma-tion
ac-clam-a-to-ry
ac-cli-mate
ac-cli-mat-ed
ac-cli-mat-ing
ac-cli-ma-tion
ac-cli-ma-tize
ac-cli-ma-tized
ac-cli-ma-tiz-er
ac-cli-ma-tiz-ing
ac-cliv-i-ty
ac-cliv-i-ties
ac-co-lade
ac-com-mo-date
ac-com-mo-dat-ed

ac-com-mo-dat-ing
ac-com-mo-da-tive
ac-com-mo-dat-er
ac-com-mo-da-tion
ac-com-pa-nist
ac-com-pa-ny
ac-com-pa-nied
ac-com-pa-ny-ing
ac-com-pa-nies
ac-com-plice
ac-com-plish
ac-com-plish-a-ble
ac-com-plish-ment
ac-com-plish-er
ac-com-plished
ac-cord
ac-cord-ance
ac-cord-ing
ac-cord-ing-ly
ac-cor-dant
ac-cor-dant-ly
ac-cor-di-on
ac-cor-di-on-ist
ac-cost
ac-couche-ment
ac-cou-cheur
ac-count
ac-count-a-ble
ac-count-a-bil-i-ty
ac-count-a-bly
ac-count-an-cy
ac-count-ant
ac-coun-tant-ship
ac-count-ing
ac-cou-tre-ment
ac-cred-it
ac-cred-i-table
ac-cred-i-ta-tion
ac-crete
ac-creting
ac-creted
ac-cre-tion
ac-cre-tive
ac-cre-tion-ary
ac-cru-al
ac-crue
ac-crued
ac-cru-ing
ac-cru-a-ble
ac-crue-ment
ac-cul-tur-ate

ac-cul-tur-ating
ac-cul-tur-ated
ac-cul-tur-a-tion
ac-cul-tur-a-tion-al
ac-cul-tur-a-tive
ac-cum-u-late
ac-cum-u-lat-ed
ac-cum-u-lat-ing
ac-cum-u-la-tion
ac-cu-mu-la-tive
ac-cu-mu-la-tive-ly
ac-cum-u-la-tor
ac-cu-ra-cy
ac-cu-ra-cies
ac-cu-rate
ac-cu-rate-ly
ac-cu-rate-ness
ac-curs-ed
ac-curst
ac-curs-ed-ly
ac-cus-al
ac-cu-sa-tion
ac-cu-sa-tive
ac-cu-sa-to-ry
ac-cuse
ac-cus-er
ac-cus-ed
ac-cus-ing
ac-cu-sa-tion
ac-cu-sa-to-ry
ac-cus-tom
ac-cus-tom-a-tion
ac-cus-tomed
ac-cus-tomed-ness
ace-dia
a-cel-da-ma
a-cel-lu-lar
acen-tric
aceph-a-lous
a-ce-quia
a-cerb
ac-er-bate
acer-bic
ac-er-bi-ty
ac-er-o-la
ac-er-ose
ac-er-vate
ac-er-vate-ly
ac-er-va-tion
ac-e-tab-u-lar-ia
ac-e-tab-u-lum

ac-e-tab-u-lar
ac-e-tal
ac-et-al-de-hyde
ac-et-amide
ac-et-amin-o-phen
ac-et-an-i-lide
ac-e-tate
a-ce-tic
a-cet-i-fy
a-cet-i-fied
a-cet-i-fy-ing
a-ce-ti-fi-ca-tion
a-ce-ti-fi-er
ac-e-tone
ac-e-ton-ic
ac-e-to-phe-net-i-din
a-ce-tous
ace-tyl
a-cet-y-late
a-cet-y-lat-ing
a-cet-y-lat-ed
a-cet-y-la-tion
a-cet-y-la-tive
a-ce-tyl-cho-line
a-ce-tyl-cho-lin-ic
a-cet-y-lene
a-cet-y-le-nic
ache
ached
ach-ing
a-chene
a-chieve
a-chiev-ed
a-chiev-ing
a-chiev-a-ble
a-chiev-er
a-chieve-ment
a-chla-myd-e-ous
a-chlor-hy-dric
a-chon-drite
a-chon-drit-ic
ach-ro-mat-ic
ach-ro-ma-tic-i-ty
ach-ro-ma-tize
achro-ma-tism
a-cic-u-la
a-cic-u-late
a-cic-u-lar
ac-id
ac-id-ness
ac-id-ly

ac-id-ic
a-cid-i-fy
a-cid-i-fied
a-cid-i-fy-ing
a-cid-i-fi-ca-tion
a-cid-i-fi-er
ac-i-dim-e-ter
a-cid-i-ty
ac-i-do-phile
ac-i-do-phil-ic
ac-i-do-sis
ac-i-dot-ic
a-cid-u-late
acid-o-phile
ac-i-do-phil-ic
ac-i-do-sis
a-cid-u-lat-ed
a-cid-u-lat-ing
a-cid-u-la-tion
acid-u-late
a-cid-u-lent
a-cid-u-lous
ac-i-nar
ac-i-nus
ac-i-nous
ac-knowl-edge
ac-knowl-edged
ac-knowl-edg-ing
ac-me
ac-ne
ac-ned
a-cock
a-cold
ac-o-lyte
ac-o-nite
a-corn
a-cous-tic
a-cous-ti-cal
a-cous-ti-cal-ly
a-cous-tics
ac-quaint
ac-quaint-ance
ac-qui-esce
ac-qui-esc-ed
ac-qui-esc-ing
ac-qui-es-cence
ac-qui-es-cent
ac-qui-es-cent-ly
ac-quire
ac-quired
ac-quir-ing

ac-quir-er
ac-quit
ac-quit-ted
ac-quit-ting
ac-quit-tal
a-cre
a-cre-age
ac-rid
acrid-i-ty
ac-ri-mo-ni-ous
ac-ri-mo-ni-ous-ly
ac-ri-mo-ny
ac-ro-bat
ac-ro-bat-ic
ac-ro-nym
ac-ro-pho-bi-a
a-crop-o-lis
a-cros-tic
a-cros-ti-cal-ly
a-cryl-ic
ac-ry-lo-ni-trile
act-ing
ac-tin-ia
ac-tin-i-an
ac-tin-ic
ac-tin-i-cal-ly
ac-tin-ism
ac-tin-i-um
ac-ti-nom-e-ter
ac-ti-nom-e-try
ac-ti-no-mor-phic
ac-ti-no-mor-phy
ac-ti-no-my-ces
ac-ti-no-my-ce-tal
ac-ti-no-my-co-sis
ac-ti-no-my-cot-ic
ac-ti-non
ac-ti-no-zo-an
ac-tion
ac-tion-a-ble
ac-tion-a-bly
ac-ti-vate
ac-ti-vat-ed
ac-ti-vat-ing
ac-ti-va-tion
ac-ti-va-tor
ac-tive
ac-tive-ly
ac-tiv-ism
ac-tiv-ist
ac-tiv-i-ty

ac-tiv-i-ties
ac-tor
ac-tress
ac-tu-al
ac-tu-al-ly
ac-tu-al-i-ty
ac-tu-al-i-ties
ac-tu-al-ize
ac-tu-al-ized
ac-tu-al-iz-ing
ac-tu-al-i-za-tion
ac-tu-ar-y
ac-tu-ar-ies
ac-tu-ar-i-al
ac-tu-ate
ac-tu-at-ed
ac-tu-at-ing
ac-tu-a-tion
ac-tu-a-tor
a-cu-i-ty
a-cu-i-ties
a-cu-men
a-cu-mi-nate
ac-u-punc-ture
a-cute
a-cute-ly
a-cut-er
a-cy-clic
ac-yl
ad-age
a-da-gio
ad-a-mant
ad-a-mant-ly
ad-a-man-tine
a-dapt
a-dapt-er
a-dapt-ed-ness
a-dapt-a-ble
a-dapt-a-bil-i-ty
ad-ap-ta-tion
ad-ap-ta-tion-al
ad-ap-ta-tion-al-ly
a-dap-tive
a-dap-tive-ly
a-d-ap-tiv-i-ty
add
add-a-ble
add-i-ble
ad-dax
ad-dax-es
ad-dend

ad-den-dum
ad-den-da
ad-der
ad-dict
ad-dic-tion
ad-dict-ed
ad-dic-tive
ad-di-tion
ad-di-tion-al
ad-di-tion-al-ly
ad-di-tive
ad-di-tive-ly
ad-di-tiv-i-ty
ad-dle
ad-dress
ad-dress-er
ad-dress-ee
ad-dress-a-ble
ad-duce
ad-duc-ing
ad-duced
ad-duc-er
ad-duct
ad-duc-tion
ad-duc-tive
a-de-lan-ta-do
a-demp-tion
ad-e-nine
ad-e-ni-tis
ad-e-noid
ad-e-noi-dal
ad-e-no-ma
aden-o-sine
a-dept
a-dept-ly
ad-e-qua-cy
ad-e-quate
ad-e-quate-ly
ad-here
ad-hered
ad-her-ing
ad-her-ence
ad-her-ent
ad-her-ent-ly
ad-he-sion
ad-he-sion-al
ad-he-sive
ad-he-sive-ly
ad-he-sive-ness
ad hoc
ad ho-mi-nem

ad-i-a-bat-ic
a-dieu
ad in-fi-ni-tum
a-di-os
ad-i-pose
ad-i-pos-i-ty
ad-ja-cen-cy
ad-ja-cen-cies
ad-ja-cent
ad-ja-cent-ly
ad-jec-tive
ad-jec-ti-val
ad-join
ad-join-ing
ad-journ
ad-journ-ment
ad-judge
ad-judged
ad-judg-ing
ad-ju-di-cate
ad-ju-di-cat-ed
ad-ju-di-cat-ing
ad-ju-di-ca-tion
ad-ju-di-ca-tor
ad-junct
ad-junc-tive
ad-jure
ad-jured
ad-jur-ing
ad-ju-ra-tion
ad-ju-ra-to-ry
ad-jur-er
ad-just
ad-just-a-ble
ad-just-er
ad-jus-tor
ad-just-ment
ad-ju-tan-cy
ad-ju-tant
ad lib
ad libbed
ad lib-bing
ad-man
ad-men
ad-min-is-ter
ad-min-is-ter-ing
ad-min-is-tered
ad-min-is-trate
ad-min-is-trat-ing
ad-min-is-trated
ad-min-is-tra-tion

ad-min-is-tra-tive
ad-min-is-tra-tor
ad-mi-ral
ad-mi-ral-ty
ad-mire
ad-mired
ad-mir-ing
ad-mi-ra-tion
ad-mi-rer
ad-mis-si-ble
ad-mis-si-bil-i-ty
ad-mis-sion
ad-mis-sive
ad-mit
ad-mit-ted
ad-mit-ting
ad-mit-ted-ly
ad-mit-tance
ad-mix
ad-mix-ture
ad-mon-ish
ad-mon-ish-er
ad-mo-ni-tion
ad-mon-i-to-ry
ad-mon-ish-ing-ly
ad-mon-ish-ment
a-do
a-do-be
ad-o-les-cence
ad-o-les-cent
ad-o-les-cent-ly
a-dopt
a-dopt-a-ble
a-dop-tion
a-dop-tive
a-dore
a-dored
a-dor-ing
a-dor-a-ble
ad-o-ra-tion
a-dorn
a-dorn-ment
a-doze
ad-re-nal
ad-re-nal-ly
a-dren-a-line
a-drift
a-droit
a-droit-ly
ad-sorb
ad-sor-bent

ad-sorp-tion
ad-u-late
ad-u-lat-ed
ad-u-lat-ing
ad-u-la-tor
ad-u-la-to-ry
a-dult
a-dult-hood
a-dul-ter-ate
a-dul-ter-at-ed
a-dul-ter-at-ing
a-dul-ter-ant
a-dul-ter-a-tion
a-dul-ter-y
a-dul-ter-ies
a-dul-ter-er
a-dul-ter-ous
ad-um-brate
ad-um-brat-ed
ad-um-brat-ing
ad va-lo-rem
ad-vance
ad-vanced
ad-vanc-ing
ad-vance-ment
ad-van-tage
ad-van-taged
ad-van-tag-ing
ad-van-ta-geous
ad-van-ta-geous-ly
ad-vent
ad-ven-ti-tious
ad-ven-tive
ad-ven-ture
ad-ven-tured
ad-ven-tur-ing
ad-ven-tur-er
ad-ven-ture-some
ad-verb
ad-ver-bi-al
ad-ver-sar-y
ad-ver-sar-ies
ad-verse
ad-verse-ly
ad-verse-ness
ad-ver-si-ty
ad-ver-si-ties
ad-vert
ad-vert-ence
ad-vert-ent

ad-ver-tise
ad-ver-tised
ad-ver-tis-ing
ad-ver-tis-er
ad-ver-tise-ment
ad-vice
ad-vise
ad-vised
ad-vis-ing
ad-vis-a-bil-i-ty
ad-vi-sor
ad-vis-ed-ly
ad-vise-ment
ad-vi-so-ry
ad-vo-ca-cy
ad-vo-ca-cies
ad-vo-cate
ad-vo-cat-ed
ad-vo-cat-ing
ad-vo-ca-tion
ae-gis
ae-on
aer-ate
aer-at-ed
aer-at-ing
aer-a-tion
aer-a-tor
aer-en-chy-ma
aer-i-al
aer-i-al-ly
aer-i-al-ist
aer-ie
aer-i-fy
aer-i-fi-ca-tion
aer-obe
aero-me-chan-ics
aero-naut-ics
aero-nau-ti-cal
aero-nau-tic
aero-pause
aer-o-plane
aer-o-sol
aero-sol-ize
aero-sol-iza-tion
aero-sol-iz-ing
aero-sol-ized
aer-o-space
aero-sphere
aero-stat
aero-stat-ics
aes-thete

aes-thet-ic
aes-thet-i-cal-ly
aes-thet-i-cal
afar
afeard
af-fa-ble
af-fa-bil-i-ty
af-fa-bly
af-fair
af-fect
af-fect-ing
af-fect-ing-ly
af-fec-tive
af-fec-ta-tion
af-fect-ed
af-fect-ed-ly
af-fect-ed-ness
af-fec-tion
af-fec-tion-ate
af-fec-tion-ate-ly
af-fer-ent
af-fer-ent-ly
af-fi-ance
af-fi-anced
af-fi-anc-ing
af-fi-da-vit
af-fil-i-ate
af-fil-i-at-ed
af-fil-i-at-ing
af-fin-i-ty
af-fin-i-ties
af-firm
af-firm-a-ble
af-firm-a-bly
af-fir-ma-tion
af-firm-a-tive
af-fix
af-fix-a-ble
af-fix-ment
af-fix-a-tion
af-fla-tus
af-flict
af-flic-tion
af-flu-ence
af-flu-ent
af-flu-ent-ly
af-fray
af-fri-cate
af-fric-a-tive
af-fri-ca-tion
af-front

af-ghan
afield
afire
aflame
af-la-tox-in
afloat
aflut-ter
afoot
afore
afore-men-tioned
afore-said
afore-thought
a for-ti-o-ri
afoul
afraid
afreet
afresh
af-ter
af-ter-ef-fect
af-ter-glow
af-ter--hours
af-ter-life
af-ter-most
af-ter-noon
af-ter-taste
af-ter-thought
af-ter-time
af-ter-ward
af-ter-wards
again
against
agape
aga-pe-ic
agar
ag-ate
ag-ate-ware
aga-ve
agaze
age
aged
ag-ing
age-ing
aged
age-less
age-long
agen-cy
agen-cies
agen-da
agen-da-less
agent
agen-tial

ag-glom-er-ate
ag-glom-er-at-ed
ag-glom-er-at-ing
ag-glom-er-a-tion
ag-glom-er-a-tive
ag-glu-ti-nate
ag-glu-ti-nat-ed
ag-glu-tin-at-ing
ag-glu-ti-na-tion
ag-glu-ti-na-tive
ag-gran-dize
ag-gran-dized
ag-gran-diz-ing
ag-gran-dize-ment
ag-gran-diz-er
ag-gra-vate
ag-gra-vat-ed
ag-gra-vat-ing
ag-gra-va-tion
ag-gre-gate
ag-gre-gat-ed
ag-gre-gat-ing
ag-gre-ga-tion
ag-gre-ga-tive
ag-gress
ag-gress-ive
ag-gress-ive-ly
ag-gress-ive-ness
ag-gres-sor
ag-gres-sion
ag-grieve
ag-grieved
ag-griev-ing
aghast
ag-ile
ag-ile-ly
agil-i-ty
agin-ner
agio
ag-i-tate
ag-i-tat-ed
ag-i-tat-ing
ag-i-tat-ed-ly
ag-i-ta-tion
ag-i-ta-tor
ag-i-ta-tion-al
agleam
aglow
agly-con
ag-nail
ag-nate

ag-na-tion
ag-nat-i-cal-ly
ag-nat-ic
ag-nize
ag-niz-ing
ag-nized
ag-no-men
ag-nom-i-na
ag-nos-tic
ag-nos-ti-cism
agog
ag-o-nal
agon-ic
ag-o-nist
ag-o-nis-tic
ag-o-nis-ti-cal-ly
ag-o-nis-ti-cal
ag-o-nize
ag-o-nized
ag-o-niz-ing
ag-o-niz-ing-ly
ag-o-ny
ag-o-nies
ag-o-ra-pho-bia
ag-o-ra-pho-bic
ag-o-ra-pho-bi-ac
agrar-i-an
agrar-i-an-ism
agree
agreed
agree-ing
agree-a-bil-i-ty
agree-a-ble
agree-a-ble-ness
agree-a-bly
agree-ment
ag-ri-busi-ness
ag-ri-cul-ture
ag-ri-cul-tur-al
ag-ri-cul-tur-ist
agron-o-my
ag-ro-nom-ic
ag-ro-nom-i-cal
agron-o-mist
ag-ro-nom-i-cal-ly
aground
ague
agu-ish-ly
agu-ish
aha
ahead

ahem
ahoy
aide-de-camp
ai-grette
ai-guille
ai-guil-lette
ai-ki-do
ail
ail-ing
ail-ment
ai-lan-thus
ai-ler-on
aim-less
air-less
air-less-ness
air-borne
air-brush
air-con-di-tion
air-con-di-tioned
air con-di-tion-er
air con-di-tion-ing
air-craft
air-field
air-mail
air-man
air-men
air-plane
air-port
air pres-sure
air-sick-ness
air-space
air-wave
airy
air-i-er
air-i-est
air-i-ness
air-i-ly
aisle
ajar
akim-bo
akin
al-a-bas-ter
al-a-bas-trine
a la carte
alack
alac-ri-ty
alac-ri-tous
alarm
alarm-ing
alarm-ing-ly
alarm-ist

alarm-ism
alas
alate
alat-ed
al-ba-core
al-ba-cores
al-ba-tross
al-ba-tross-es
al-be-do
al-be-it
al-bi-no
al-bi-nos
al-bi-nism
al-bum
al-bu-men
al-bu-min
al-bu-mi-nous
al-che-my
al-che-mist
al-che-mize
al-che-miz-ing
al-che-mized
al-co-hol
al-co-hol-ic
al-co-hol-ism
al-co-hol-i-cal-ly
al-cove
al-de-hyde
al-de-hy-dic
al-der
al-der-man
al-der-man-ic
ale-a-to-ry
alee
alert
alert-ness
alert-ly
ale-wife
ale-wives
al-ex-an-drine
al-ex-an-drite
alex-ia
al-fal-fa
al-fil-a-ria
al-for-ja
al-fres-co
al-ga
al-gae
al-gal
al-goid
al-ge-bra

al-ge-bra-ic
al-ge-bra-ic-al
al-ge-bra-ic-al-ly
al-ge-bra-ist
al-go-rithm
al-go-rith-mic
ali-as
ali-as-es
al-i-bi
al-i-bi-ing
al-i-bied
alien
alien-a-ble
alien-a-bil-i-ty
alien-ate
alien-at-ed
alien-at-ing
alien-ator
alien-ist
alien-ism
ali-form
alight
alight-ed
alit
alight-ing
alight-ment
align
align-ment
alike
al-i-ment
al-i-men-tal
al-i-men-tal-ly
al-i-men-ta-tion
al-i-men-ta-ry
al-i-mo-ny
al-i-mo-nies
aline-ment
al-i-quant
al-i-quot
alive
alive-ness
al-ka-li
al-ka-lies
al-ka-lis
al-ka-line
al-ka-lin-i-ty
al-ka-lize
al-ka-lized
al-ka-liz-ing
al-ka-li-za-tion
al-ka-loid

al-ka-loi-dal
all-Amer-i-can
all-a-round
al-lay
al-layed
al-lay-ing
al-lay-er
al-le-ga-tion
al-lege
al-leged
al-leg-ing
al-lege-a-ble
al-leg-ed-ly
al-le-giance
al-le-go-ry
al-le-go-ries
al-le-gor-ic
al-le-gor-i-cal
al-le-gor-i-cal-ly
al-le-gor-ist
al-le-gret-to
al-le-gro
al-le-gros
al-ler-gen
al-ler-gen-ic
al-ler-gy
al-ler-gies
al-ler-gic
al-ler-gist
al-le-vi-ate
al-le-vi-at-ed
al-le-vi-at-ing
al-le-vi-a-tion
al-le-vi-a-tor
al-le-vi-a-tive
al-le-vi-a-to-ry
al-ley
al-leys
al-li-ance
al-lied
al-li-ga-tor
all--in-clu-sive
al-lit-er-ate
al-lit-er-at-ed
al-lit-er-at-ing
al-lit-er-a-tive
al-lit-er-a-tive-ly
al-lit-er-a-tive-ness
al-lit-er-a-tion
al-lo-ca-ble
al-lo-cate

al-lo-cat-ed
al-lo-cat-ing
al-lo-ca-tion
al-lo-cu-tion
al-log-a-mous
al-log-a-my
al-lo-ge-ne-ic
al-lo-graph
al-lo-graph-ic
al-lom-er-ism
al-lom-er-ous
al-lo-path
al-lop-a-thy
al-lo-path-ic
al-lo-path-i-cal-ly
al-lop-a-thist
al-lo-phone
al-lo-phon-ic
al-lo-pu-ri-nol
al-lo-ste-ric
al-lo-ste-ri-cal-ly
al-lot
al-lot-ted
al-lot-ting
al-lot-ment
al-lot-ta-ble
al-lot-ter
al-lo-trope
al-lo-trop-ic
al-lo-trop-cal-ly
al-lot-ro-py
al-lot-ro-pism
al-lo-trope
al-lo-trop-ic
al-lo-trop-i-cal-ly
al-low
al-low-a-ble
al-low-a-bly
al-low-ed-ly
al-low-ance
al-low-anced
al-low-anc-ing
al-loy
all--pow-er-ful
all--pur-pose
all right
all-spice
al-lude
al-lud-ed
al-lud-ing
al-lure

al-lured
al-lur-ing
al-lure-ment
al-lur-er
al-lur-ing-ly
al-lu-sion
al-lu-sive
al-lu-sive-ly
al-lu-sive-ness
al-lu-via
al-lu-vi-al
al-lu-vi-um
al-lu-viums
al-ly
al-lies
al-lied
al-ly-ing
al-ma mat-er
al-ma-nac
al-man-dine
al-man-dite
al-mighty
al-mighti-ness
al-mond
al-mo-ner
al-most
alms-giv-er
alms-giv-ing
alms-house
al-ni-co
al-oe
aloft
alo-ha
alone
alone-ness
along
along-shore
along-side
aloof
aloof-ly
aloof-ness
al-o-pe-cia
al-paca
al-pen-glow
al-pen-stock
al-pes-trine
al-pha
al-pha-bet
al-pha-bet-ic
al-pha-bet-i-cal
al-pha-bet-i-cal-ly

al-pha-bet-i-za-tion
al-pha-bet-ize
al-pha-bet-ized
al-pha-bet-iz-ing
al-ready
al-so
al-tar
al-ter
al-ter-a-bil-ity
al-ter-a-ble
al-ter-ant
al-ter-a-tion
al-ter-a-tive
al-ter-cate
al-ter-cat-ing
al-ter-cat-ed
al-ter-ca-tion
al-ter e-go
al-ter-nate
al-ter-nat-ed
al-ter-nat-ing
al-ter-nate-ly
al-ter-na-tion
al-ter-na-tive
al-ter-na-tive-ly
al-ter-na-tive-ness
al-ter-na-tor
al-though
al-tim-e-ter
al-tim-e-try
al-ti-pla-no
al-ti-tude
al-to
al-to-cu-mu-lus
al-to-gether
al-to-re-lie-vo
al-to-stra-tus
al-tru-ism
al-tru-is-tic
al-tru-is-ti-cal-ly
al-tru-ist
al-lu-mi-na
alu-mi-nate
alu-mi-nif-er-ous
al-u-min-i-um
alu-mi-nous
alu-mi-num
alum-na
alum-nae
alum-nus
alum-ni

al-ve-o-lar
al-ve-o-lus
al-ve-o-li
al-ways
alys-sum
am ain
am al-gam
amal-gam-a-ble
amal-gam-ate
amal-gam-at-ed
amal-gam-at-ing
amal-gam-a-tion
aman-u-en-ses
aman-u-en-ses
am-a-ryl-lis
am ass
amass-ment
amass-er
am-a-teur
am-a-teur-ism
am-a-teur-ish
am-a-teur-ish-ly
am-a-teur-ish-ness
am-a-tive
am-a-tive-ness
am-a-tive-ly
am-a-to-ry
am-au-ro-sis
am aze
amazed
amaz-ing
amaz-ed-ly
amaz-ed-ness
amaze-ment
amaz-ing-ly
am-bas-sa-do-ri-al
am-ber
amber-gris
am-ber-jack
am-bi-dex-trous
am-bi-dex-trous-ly
am-bi-dex-ter-i-ty
am-bi-ance
am-bi-ence
am-bi-ent
am-big-u-ous
am-big-u-ous-ly
am-big-u-ous-ness
am-bi-gu-i-ty
am-bit
am-bi-tion

am-bi-tion-less
am-bi-tious
am-bi-tious-ly
am-bi-tious-ness
am-biv-a-lence
am-biv-a-lent
am-biv-a-lent-ly
am-bi-ver-sion
am-bi-ver-sive
am-bi-vert
am-ble
am-bled
am-bling
am-bler
am-blyg-o-nite
am-bly-opia
am-bo-cep-tor
am-bro-sia
am-bro-sial-ly
am-bro-sial
am-bro-type
ambs-ace
am-bu-la-crum
am-bu-lance
am-bu-la-to-ry
am-bu-lant
am-bu-late
am-bu-lat-ed
am-bu-lat-ing
am-bu-la-tion
am-bus-cade
am-bus-cad-ed
am-bus-cad-ing
am-bus-cad-er
am-bush
am-bush-ment
am-bush-er
ameba
amel-io-rate
amel-io-rat-ed
amel-io-rat-ing
amel-io-ra-ble
amel-io-ra-tion
amel-ior-a-tive
amel-io-ra-tor
amen
ame-na-ble
ame-na-bil-i-ty
ame-na-ble-ness
ame-na-bly
amend

amend-a-ble
amend-er
amend-ment
amends
amend-i-ty
amend-i-ties
amerce
amerced
amerc-ing
amerce-a-ble
amerce-ment
amerce-er
Amer-i-ca
Amer-i-can
Amer-i-cana
Amer-i-can-ism
am-e-thyst
am-e-thys-tine
am-e-tro-pia
am i-a-ble
ami-a-bil-i-ty
ami-a-bly
ami-a-ble-ness
am i-ca-ble
am-i-ca-bil-i-ty
am-i-ca-bly
am-i-ca-ble-ness
am-ice
am id
amidst
am-ide
amid-ic
amid-ships
ami-go
am ine
amino acid
ami-no-ac-id-uria
ami-no-py-rine
am ir
am iss
am-i-to-sis
am-i-tot-ic
am-i-tot-i-cal-ly
am-i-ty
am-me-ter
am-mi-no
am-mon-nia
am-mon-ic
am-mo-ni-ac
am-mo-ni-um
am-mu-ni-tion

am-ne-sia
am-ne-sic
am-nes-tic
am-nes-ty
am-ni-on
am-ni-ons
am-ni-on-ic
am-nia
am-ni-ot-ic
a-moe-ba
a-moe-bae
a-moe-bas
a-moe-bic
a-moe-ban
a-moe-boid
a-mok
a-mong
a-mongst
a-mon-til-la-do
a-mor-al
a-mo-ral-i-ty
a-mor-al-ism
a-mor-al-ly
amo-ret-to
am-or-ist
am-o-rous
am-o-rous-ly
am-o-rous-ness
a-mor-phism
a-mor-phous
a-mor-phous-ness
a-mor-phous-ly
am-or-tize
am-or-tized
am-or-tiz-ing
am-or-ti-za-tion
am-or-tiz-able
a-mount
a-mour
am-per-age
am-pere
am-per-sand
am-phet-a-mine
am-phib-ia
am-phib-i-an
am-phib-i-ous
am-phib-i-ous-ly
am-phib-i-ous-ness
am-phi-the-a-ter
am-phi-the-at-ric
am-pho-ra

am-phe-rae
am-phe-ras
am-ple
am-pler
am-plest
am-ple-ness
am-ply
am-pli-fy
am-pli-fied
am-pli-fy-ing
am-pli-fi-ca-tion
am-pli-fi-er
am-pli-tude
am-pul
am-pu-tate
am-pu-tat-ed
am-pu-tat-ing
am-pu-ta-tion
am-pu-tee
a-muck
am-u-let
a-muse
a-mused
a-mus-ing
a-muse-ment
a-mus-ed
am-yl-ase
a-nach-ro-nism
a-nach-ro-nis-tik
a-nach-ro-nous
an-a-con-da
an-aer-obe
an-aes-the-sia
an-aes-thet-ic
an-a-gram
an-a-gram-mat-ic
ana-gram-ma-tize
ana-gram-ma-tized
a-nal
an-a-lects
an-al-ge-sic
al-a-log
an-a-log-i-cal
an-a-log-i-cal-ly
a-nal-o-gize
a-nal-o-gized
a-nal-o-giz-ing
a-nal-o-gy
a-nal-o-gies
a-nal-o-gous
a-nal-y-sis

a-nal-y-ses
an-a-lyst
an-a-lyt-ic
an-a-lyt-ics
an-a-lyze
an-a-lyzed
an-a-lyz-ing
an-a-lyz-a-ble
an-a-ly-za-tion
an-a-lyz-er
an-a-pest
an-a-pes-tic
an-ar-chism
an-ar-chis-tic
an-ar-chy
an-ar-chic
an-ar-chi-cal
a-nath-e-ma
a-nath-e-mas
a-nath-e-ma-tize
a-nath-e-ma-tized
a-nath-e-ma-tiz-ing
a-nat-o-mize
a-nat-o-mized
a-nat-o-mizing
a-nat-o-mi-za-tion
a-nat-o-my
a-nat-o-mies
an-a-tom-i-cal
an-a-tom-i-cal-ly
a-nat-o-mist
an-ces-tor
an-ces-tral
an-ces-tress
an-ces-try
an-chor
an-chor-age
an-cho-ress
an-cho-rite
an-cho-vy
an-cient
an-cient-ly
an-cient-ness
an-cil-lary
an-dan-te
and-i-ron
an-dro-gen
an-drog-y-nous
an-drog-y-ny
an-dros-ter-one
an-ec-dote

an-ec-dot-age
an-ec-do-tal
an-ec-dot-ist
a-ne-mia
a-ne-mic
an-e-mom-e-ter
an-e-mom-e-try
a-nem-o-ne
an-er-oid
an-es-the-sia
an-es-thet-ic
an-es-the-tize
an-es-the-tized
an-es-the-tiz-ing
an-eu-rysm
an-eu-rism
an-eu-rys-mal
a-new
an-ga-ry
an-gel
an-gel-ic
an-gel-i-cal
an-gel-i-cal-ly
an-gel-i-ca
an-ger
an-gi-na
an-gi-na pec-to-ris
an-gi-o-sperm
an-gi-o-sper-mous
an-gle
an-gler
an-gle-worm
an-gling
an-go-ra
an-gos-tu-ra bark
an-gry
an-gri-ly
an-gri-ness
ang-strom u-nit
an-guish
an-gu-lar
an-gu-lar-i-ty
an-gu-lar-ly
an-hy-dride
an-hy-drous
an-i-line
an-i-mad-vert
an-i-mad-ver-sion
an-i-mal
an-i-mal-cule
an-i-mal-cu-lar

an-i-mal-ism
an-i-mal-i-ty
an-i-mal-ize
an-i-mal-ized
an-i-mal-iz-ing
an-i-mate
an-i-mat-ed
an-i-mat-ing
an-i-ma-tion
a-ni-ma-to
an-i-mism
an-i-mis-tic
an-i-mos-i-ty
an-i-mus
an-i-on
an-ise
an-i-seed
an-i-sette
an-kle
an-kle-bone
an-klet
an-ky-lose
an-ky-losed
an-ky-los-ing
an-ky-lo-sis
an-ky-lot-ic
an-nal-ist
an-nal-is-tic
an-nals
an-neal
an-ne-lid
an-nel-i-dan
an-nex
an-nex-a-tion
an-nex-a-tion-ist
an-ni-hi-late
an-ni-hi-lat-ed
an-ni-hi-lat-ing
an-ni-hi-la-tion
an-ni-hi-la-tor
an-ni-ver-sa-ry
an-ni-ver-sa-ries
an-no Dom-i-ni
an-no-tate
an-no-tat-ed
an-no-tat-ing
an-no-ta-tion
an-no-ta-tor
an-nounce
an-nounced
an-nounc-ing

an-nounce-ment
an-nounc-er
an-noy
an-noy-ance
an-noy-er
an-nu-al
an-nu-i-ty
an-nu-i-tant
an-nul
an-nulled
an-nul-ling
an-nul-ment
an-nu-lar
an-nu-lar-i-ty
an-nu-lar-ly
an-nu-late
an-nu-let
an-nu-lus
an-nu-lus-es
an-nun-ci-a-tion
an-nun-ci-ate
an-nun-ci-at-ed
an-nun-ci-at-ing
an-nun-ci-a-tor
an-ode
an-od-ic
an-o-dyne
a-noint
a-noint-er
a-noint-ment
a-nom-a-ly
a-nom-a-lism
a-nom-a-lous
a-nom-a-lous-ly
an-o-mie
an-o-my
an-o-nym
a-non-y-mous
an-o-nym-i-ty
a-non-y-mous-ly
a-noph-e-les
an-oth-er
an-ox-ia
an-ser-ine
an-swer
an-swer-a-ble
ant-ac-id
an-tag-o-nist
an-tag-o-nism
an-tag-o-nis-tic
an-tag-o-nize

an-tag-o-nized
an-tag-o-niz-ing
ant-arc-tic
an-te
an-ted
an-te-ing
ant-eat-er
an-te--bel-lum
an-te-ced-ence
an-te-ced-ent
an-te-cede
an-te-ced-ed
an-te-ced-ing
an-te-cham-ber
an-te-choir
an-te-date
an-te-dat-ed
an-te-dat-ing
an-te-di-lu-vi-an
an-te-lope
an-te-lopes
an-te me-rid-i-em
an-ten-na
an-ten-nae
an-ten-nas
an-te-pe-nult
an-te-ri-or
an-te-room
an-them
an-ther
an-ther-id-i-um
an-thol-o-gy
an-thol-o-gies
an-thol-o-gist
an-thol-o-gize
an-thol-o-giz-ing
an-tho-zo-an
an-thra-cene
an-thra-cite
an-thra-cit-ic
an-thrax
an-thra-ces
an-thro-poid
an-thro-pol-o-gy
an-thro-po-log-ic
an-thro-pol-o-gist
an-thr-pom-e-try
an-thro-po-met-ric
an-ti-air-craft
an-ti-bi-o-sis
an-ti-bi-ot-ic

an-ti-bod-y
an-ti-bod-ies
an-tic
an-ti-christ
an-tic-i-pate
an-tic-i-pat-ed
an-tic-i-pat-ing
an-tic-i-pa-tion
an-tic-i-pa-tive
an-tic-i-pa-to-ry
an-ti-cler-i-cal
an-ti-cler-i-cal-ism
an-ti-cli-max
an-ti-cli-mac-tic
an-ti-cli-nal
an-ti-cline
an-ti-cy-clone
an-ti-dote
an-ti-dot-al
an-ti-fed-er-al
an-ti-fed-er-al-ist
an-ti-fed-er-al-ism
an-ti-freeze
an-ti-gen
an-ti-he-ro
an-ti-his-ta-mine
an-ti-log-a-rithm
an-ti-ma-cas-sar
an-ti-mis-sile
an-ti-mo-ny
an-ti-pas-to
an-ti-pa-thy
an-ti-phon
an-tiph-o-nal
an-ti-pode
an-ti-quar-i-an
an-ti-quar-y
an-ti-quar-ies
an-ti-quate
an-ti-quat-ed
an-ti-quat-ing
an-ti-quat-ed
an-tique
an-tiqed
an-tiq-uing
an-tique-ly
an-tiq-ui-ty
an-tiq-ui-ties
an-ti-Sem-i-tism
an-ti-sep-sis
an-ti-sep-tic

an-ti-se-rum
an-ti-slav-er-y
an-ti-so-cial
an-tith-e-sis
 an-tith-e-ses
an-ti-thet-i-cal
an-ti-tox-in
 an-ti-tox-in
an-ti-trust
ant-ler
ant-ler-ed
an-to-nym
an-trum
an-tra
a-nus
an-vil
 anx-i-e-ty
 anx-i-e-ties
 anx-ious
an-y
an-y-bod-y
 an-y-bod-ies
an-y-how
an-y-more
an-y-one
an-y-place
an-y-thing
an-y-way
an-y-where
an-y-wise
a-or-ta
 a-or-tas
 a-or-tae
 a-or-tal
 a-or-tic
a-pace
a-pache
a-part
a-part-heid
a-part-ment
ap-a-thy
 ap-a-thet-ic
 ap-a-thet-i-cal-ly
ape
a-per-ri-tif
ap-er-ture
a-pex
 a-pex-es
 a-pi-ces
 ap-i-cal
a-pha-sia

a-phe-li-on
 a-phe-lia
a-phid
a-phis
 a-phi-des
aph-o-rism
 aph-o-rist
aph-ro-dis-i-ac
a-pi-an
a-pi-ar-i-an
a-pi-a-rist
a-pi-ary
 a-pi-ar-ies
a-pi-cul-ture
 a-pi-cul-tur-al
 a-pi-cul-tur-ist
a-piece
ap-ish
 ap-ish-ly
 ap-ish-ness
a-plomb
a-poc-a-lypse
 a-poc-a-lyp-tic
a-poc-o-pe
a-poc-ry-phal
ap-o-gee
a-po-lit-i-cal
a-pol-o-get-ics
 a-pol-o-gist
a-pol-o-gize
 a-pol-o-gized
 a-pol-o-giz-ing
 a-pol-o-gy
 a-pol-o-gies
ap-o-plec-tic
ap-o-plex-y
a-port
a-pos-ta-sy
 a-pos-ta-sies
a-pos-tate
 a-pos-ta-tize
 a-pos-ta-tized
 a-pos-to-tiz-ing
a pos-te-ri-o-ri
a-pos-tle
 a-pos-tle-ship
a-pos-to-late
ap-os-tol-ic
 ap-os-tol-i-cal
a-pos-tro-phe
a-poth-e-cary

a-poth-e-car-ies
ap-o-thegm
 ap-o-phthegm
 ap-o-theg-mat-ic
a-poth-e-o-sis
 a-poth-e-o-ses
 a-poth-e-o-size
 a-poth-e-o-sized
ap-pall
 ap-palled
 ap-pal-ling
ap-pa-rat-us
 ap-pa-rat-us-es
ap-par-el
ap-par-ent
ap-pa-ri-tion
 ap-pa-ri-tion-al
ap-peal
 ap-peal-a-ble
 ap-peal-er
ap-pear
 ap-pear-ance
ap-pease
 ap-peased
 ap-peasing
 ap-pease-ment
 ap-peas-a-ble
 ap-peas-er
ap-pel-lant
 ap-pel-late
 ap-pel-la-tion
 ap-pel-la-tive
ap-pend
 ap-pen-dage
 ap-pend-ant
ap-pen-dec-to-my
ap-pen-di-ci-tis
ap-pen-dix
 ap-pen-dix-es
 ap-pen-di-ces
ap-per-cep-tion
 ap-per-cep-tive
ap-per-tain
ap-pe-tite
ap-pe-tiz-er
 ap-pe-tiz-ing
ap-plaud
 ap-plause
ap-ple
ap-ple-jack
ap-pli-ance

ap-pli-ca-ble
 ap-pli-ca-bil-i-ty
 ap-pli-ca-ble-ness
ap-pli-cant
ap-pli-ca-tion
ap-pli-ca-tive
ap-pli-ca-to-ry
ap-pli-ca-tor
ap-plied
ap-ply
 ap-ply-ing
ap-point
 ap-point-a-ble
 ap-point-ee
 ap-point-er
 ap-point-ment
ap-por-tion
 ap-por-tion-ment
ap-pose
 ap-posed
 ap-pos-ing
ap-po-site
 ap-po-si-tion
 ap-po-si-tion-al
ap-pos-i-tive
ap-praise
 ap-prais-al
 ap-praised
 ap-praiser
 ap-prais-ing
ap-pre-ci-a-ble
 ap-pre-ci-a-bly
ap-pre-ci-ate
 ap-pre-ci-at-ed
 ap-pre-ci-at-ing
 ap-pre-ci-a-tion
 ap-pre-ci-a-tive
ap-pre-hend
 ap-pre-hen-si-ble
 ap-pre-hen-sion
 ap-pre-hen-sive
ap-pren-tice
 ap-pren-tic-ed
 ap-pren-tic-ing
 ap-pren-tice-ship
ap-prise
 ap-prised
 ap-pris-ing
ap-prize
ap-proach
 ap-proach-a-bil-i-ty

ap-proach-a-ble	ar-bi-trar-i-ly	ar-dent-ly	ar-mor-er
ap-pro-ba-tion	**ar-bi-trate**	**ar-dor**	ar-mor-y
ap-pro-ba-tive	ar-bi-trat-ed	**ar-du-ous**	ar-mor-ies
ap-pro-ba-to-ry	ar-bi-trat-ing	ar-du-ous-ly	**arm-pit**
ap-pro-pri-ate	ar-bi-tra-ble	**ar-e-a**	**ar-my**
ap-pro-pri-at-ed	ar-bi-tra-tor	ar-e-al	ar-mies
ap-pro-pri-at-ing	ar-bi-tra-tion	**ar-e-a-way**	**ar-ni-ca**
ap-pro-pri-ate-ly	**ar-bor**	**a-re-na**	**a-ro-ma**
ap-pro-pri-a-tor	**ar-bo-re-al**	**a-re-o-la**	**ar-o-mat-ic**
ap-pro-pri-a-tion	**ar-bo-res-cent**	a-re-o-lae	ar-o-mat-i-cal
ap-pro-pri-a-tive	**ar-bo-re-ta**	a-re-o-las	**a-round**
ap-prox-i-mate	ar-bo-re-tum	**ar-gent**	**a-rouse**
ap-prox-i-mate-ly	ar-bo-re-tums	**ar-gen-tine**	a-roused
ap-prox-i-ma-tion	**ar-bor-vi-tae**	**ar-gil**	a-rous-ing
ap-pur-te-nance	**ar-bu-tus**	**ar-gon**	**ar-peg-gi-o**
ap-pur-te-nant	**arc**	**ar-go-sy**	ar-peg-gi-os
ap-ri-cot	arced	ar-go-sies	**ar-raign**
a-pri-o-ri	arc-ing	**ar-got**	ar-raign-ment
a-pron	**ar-cade**	ar-got-ic	**ar-range**
ap-ro-pos	**ar-cane**	**ar-gue**	ar-ranged
apt	**arch**	ar-gued	ar-rang-er
apt-ly	arch-ly	ar-gu-ing	ar-rang-ing
apt-ness	**ar-cha-ic**	ar-gu-a-ble	ar-range-ment
ap-ter-ous	**ar-cha-ism**	ar-gu-er	**ar-rant**
ap-ti-tude	**ar-cha-ist**	ar-gu-ment	ar-rant-ly
aq-ua	**ar-cha-is-tic**	ar-gu-men-ta-tion	**ar-ras**
aq-uas	**arch-du-cal**	ar-gu-men-ta-tive	**ar-ray**
aq-uae	**arch-duke**	**ar-gyle**	**ar-rear**
a-qua-cul-ture	**arch-en-e-my**	ar-gyll	**ar-rest**
aq-ua-ma-rine	arch-en-e-mies	**a-ri-a**	ar-rest-er
aq-ua-naut	**arch-er**	**ar-id**	ar-rest-or
aq-ua-plane	ar-cher-y	a-rid-i-ty	**ar-ri-val**
aquar-ia	**ar-che-type**	**a-right**	**ar-rive**
aquar-i-um	ar-che-typ-al	**a-rise**	ar-rived
aquar-i-ums	ar-che-typ-i-cal	a-rose	ar-riv-ing
a-quat-ic	**arch-fiend**	a-ris-en	**ar-ro-gant**
aq-ua-tint	**ar-chi-e-pis-co-pal**	a-ris-ing	ar-ro-gat-ed
aq-ue-duct	**ar-chi-pel-a-goes**	**ar-is-toc-ra-cy**	ar-ro-gat-ing
a-que-ous	ar-chi-pel-a-gos	ar-is-toc-ra-cies	ar-ro-ga-tion
aq-ui-line	**ar-chi-tect**	aris-to-crat	**ar-row**
ar-a-besque	**ar-chi-tec-ton-ic**	aris-to-crat-ic	**ar-row-head**
ar-a-ble	**ar-chi-tec-ture**	**a-rith-me-tic**	**ar-row-root**
a-rach-nid	**ar-chi-trave**	a-rith-met-i-cal	**ar-roy-o**
a-rach-ni-dan	**ar-chive**	a-rith-me-ti-cian	ar-roy-os
ar-ba-lest	ar-chi-val	**ar-ma-da**	**ar-se-nal**
ar-ba-lest-er	ar-chi-vist	**ar-ma-dil-lo**	**ar-se-nate**
ar-ba-list	**ar-chon**	**ar-ma-ment**	**ar-se-nic**
ar-bi-ter	**arch-priest**	**ar-ma-ture**	**ar-son**
ar-bi-tral	**arch-way**	**ar-mi-stice**	ar-son-ist
ar-bit-ra-ment	**arc-tic**	**ar-moire**	**ar-te-ri-al**
ar-bi-trar-y	**ar-dent**	**ar-mor**	**ar-ter-y**

ar-ter-ies
ar-te-sian well
art-ful
  art-ful-ly
ar-thri-tis
  ar-thrit-ic
ar-thro-pod
  ar-throp-o-dal
  ar-throp-o-dous
ar-ti-choke
ar-ti-cle
ar-tic-u-lar
ar-tic-u-late
  ar-tic-u-lat-ed
  ar-tic-u-lat-ing
  ar-tic-u-late-ly
  ar-tic-u-lar-tor
  ar-tic-u-la-tion
ar-te-fact
  ar-ti-fact
ar-ti-fice
  ar-tif-i-cer
ar-ti-fi-cial
  ar-ti-fi-ci-al-i-ty
  ar-ti-fi-cial-ly
ar-til-ler-y
  ar-til-ler-ist
ar-ti-san
art-ist
ar-tiste
  ar-tis-tic
  ar-tis-ti-cal-ly
art-ist-ry
art-y
as-bes-tos
  as-bes-tus
as-cend
  as-cend-ance
  as-cend-ence
  as-cend-an-cy
  as-cend-en-cy
as-cend-ant
  as-cend-ent
as-cen-sion
as-cent
as-cer-tain
  as-cer-tain-a-ble
  as-cer-tain-ment
as-cet-ic
  as-cet-is-al
  as-cet-i-cism

as-cot
as-cribe
  as-cribed
  as-crib-ing
  as-crib-a-ble
a-sep-sis
a-sep-tic
a-sex-u-al
  a-sex-u-al-i-ty
  a-sex-u-al-ly
a-shamed
  a-sham-ed-ly
ash-en
ash-lar
  ash-ler
a-shore
ash-y
a-side
as-i-nine
a-skance
a-skew
a-slant
a-slope
a-so-cial
as-par-a-gus
as-pect
as-pen
as-per-i-ty
as-perse
  as-persed
  as-pers-ing
as-per-sion
as-phalt
  as-phal-tic
as-pho-del
as-phyx-ia
  as-phyx-i-ate
  as-phyx-i-at-ed
  as-phyx-i-a-tion
as-pic
as-pi-dis-tra
as-pir-ant
as-pi-rate
  as-pi-rat-ed
  as-pi-rat-ing
  as-pi-ra-tion
  as-pi-ra-tor
as-pire
  as-pired
  as-pir-ing
  as-pir-er

as-pi-rin
as-sail
  as-sail-a-ble
  as-sail-ant
as-sas-sin
as-sas-si-nate
  as-sas-si-nat-ed
  as-sas-si-na-tion
as-sault
as-say
  as-say-er
as-sem-blage
as-sem-ble
  as-sem-bled
  as-sem-bling
  as-sem-bler
as-sem-bly
  as-sem-blies
as-sem-bly-man
  as-sem-bly-men
as-sent
  as-sent-er
as-sert
  as-sert-er
  as-ser-tion
as-ser-tive
  as-ser-tive-ly
as-sess
  as-sess-a-ble
  as-sess-ment
  as-sess-or
as-set
as-si-du-i-ty
as-sid-u-ous
  as-sid-u-ous-ly
  as-sid-u-ous-ness
as-sign
  as-sign-a-bil-i-ty
  as-sign-a-ble
  as-sign-a-bly
as-sig-na-tion
as-sign-ee
  as-sign-ment
as-sist
  as-sist-ance
as-sis-tant
as-size
as-so-ci-ate
  as-so-ci-at-ed
  as-so-ci-at-ing
  as-so-ci-a-tion

as-so-nance
as-sort
  as-sor-ted
  as-sort-ment
as-sume
  as-sumed
  as-sum-ing
  as-sump-tion
as-sur-ance
as-sure
  as-sured
  as-sur-ing
  as-sur-er
  as-sur-ed-ly
as-ter
as-ter-isk
a-stern
as-ter-oid
  as-ter-oi-dal
asth-ma
  asth-mat-ic
a-stig-ma-tism
  as-tig-mat-ic
a-stir
as-ton-ish
  as-ton-ish-ing
  as-ton-ish-ment
as-tound
  as-tound-ing
a-strad-dle
as-tra-khan
as-tral
a-stray
a-stride
as-trin-gent
  as-trin-gen-cy
as-tro-dome
as-tro-labe
as-trol-o-gy
  as-trol-o-ger
  as-tro-log-ic
  as-tro-log-i-cal
as-tro-naut
  as-tro-nau-tics
  as-tro-nau-ti-cal
as-tro-nom-ic
  as-tro-nom-i-cal-ly
as-tron-o-my
  as-tron-o-mer
as-tro-phys-ics
  as-tro-phys-i-cist

as-tute
 as-tute-ly
a-sun-der
a-sy-lum
a-sym-me-try
 asym-met-ric
 asym-met-ri-cal
 asym-met-ri-cal-ly
at-a-vism
 at-a-vist
 at-a-vis-tic
a-tax-ia
 a-tax-ic
at-el-ier
a-thirst
ath-lete
 ath-let-ic
 ath-let-ics
a-thwart
a-tilt
at-las
 at-las-es
at-mos-phere
at-oll
at-om
ato-nal-i-ty
 ato-nal
a-tone
 a-toned
a-top
a-tri-um
a-tro-cious
 a-tro-cious-ly
a-troc-i-y
 a-troc-i-ties
at-ro-phy
 at-ro-phies
 at-ro-phied
at-ro-pine
at-tach
 at-tach-a-ble
 at-tach-ment
at-tack
at-tain
 at-tain-a-ble
 at-tain-a-bil-i-ty
 at-tain-ment
at-tain-der
at-taint
at-tar
at-tempt

at-tempt-a-ble
at-tend
at-tend-ance
at-tend-ant
at-ten-tion
at-ten-tive
at-ten-u-ate
 at-ten-u-at-ed
 at-ten-u-at-ing
 at-ten-u-a-tion
at-test
 at-tes-ta-tion
at-tic
at-tire
 at-tired
 at-tir-ing
at-ti-tude
at-ti-tu-di-nize
 at-ti-tu-di-nized
at-tor-ney
at-tract
 at-trac-tive
 at-tract-or
 at-trac-tion
at-tri-bute
 at-tri-but-ed
 at-tri-but-ing
 at-tri-bu-tion
 at-trib-u-tive
at-tri-tion
at-tune
 at-tuned
 at-tun-ing
a-typ-i-cal
 a-typ-ic
 a-typ-i-cal-ly
au-burn
au cou-rant
auc-tion
 auc-tion-eer
au-da-cious
 au-dac-i-ty
au-di-ble
 au-di-bly
au-di-ence
au-di-o
au-di-o-vis-u-al
au-dit
au-di-tion
au-dit-or
au-di-to-rium

au-di-to-ry
au-ger
aug-ment
 aug-ment-a-ble
 aug-men-ta-tion
 aug-ment-a-tive
au-grat-in
au-gur
 au-gu-ry
 au-gu-ries
au-gust
 au-gust-ly
auk
aunt
au-ra
 au-ras
 au-rae
au-ral
 au-ral-ly
au-re-ate
au-re-ole
au-re-voir
au-ri-cle
au-rif-er-ous
au-ro-ra
aus-cul-tate
 aus-cul-tat-ed
 aus-cul-tat-ing
 aus-cul-ta-tion
aus-tere
 aus-ter-i-ty
 aus-ter-i-ties
aus-tral
au-then-tic
 au-then-ti-cat-ed
 au-then-ti-cat-ing
 au-then-ti-ca-tion
au-thor
au-thor-i-tar-i-an
 au-thor-i-ta-tive
au-thor-i-ty
 au-thor-i-ties
au-thor-ize
 au-thor-ized
 au-thor-iz-ing
 au-thor-i-za-tion
au-thor-ship
au-to au-toc-ra-cy
 au-toc-ra-cies
au-to-crat
 au-to-crat-ic

au-to-crat-i-cal
au-toc-ra-cy
 au-toc-ra-cies
au-to-graph
au-to-mat
au-to-mat-ic
au-to-ma-tion
au-to-mate
 au-to-mat-ed
 au-to-mat-ing
au-tom-a-tism
au-tom-a-ton
 au-tom-a-tons
 au-tom-a-ta
au-to-mo-bile
au-to-mo-tive
au-to-nom-ic
 au-to-nom-i-cal-ly
au-ton-o-mous
 au-ton-o-mous-ly
au-ton-o-my
 au-ton-o-mies
 au-ton-o-mist
au-top-sy
au-to-sug-ges-tion
au-tumn
 au-tum-nal
aux-il-ia-ry
 aux-il-ia-ries
a-vail
 a-vail-a-bil-i-ty
 a-vail-ably
av-a-lanche
 av-a-lanched
 av-a-lanch-ing
a-vant-garde
av-a-rice
 av-a-ri-cious
 av-a-ri-cious-ly
a-vast
av-a-tar
a-ve
a-venge
 a-venged
 a-veng-ing
 a-veng-er
av-e-nue
a-ver
 a-verred
a-ver-ment
av-er-age

av-er-aged	ba-by	bac-te-ri-cide	bak-sheesh
av-er-ag-ing	ba-bies	bac-te-ri-ci-dal	bak-shish
a-verse	ba-bied	bac-te-ri-ol-o-gy	bal-a-lai-ka
a-verse-ly	ba-by-ing	bac-te-ri-ol-o-gist	bal-ance
a-ver-sion	bac-ca-lau-re-ate	bac-te-ri-o-phage	bal-anced
a-vi-a-tion	bac-ca-rat	bad	bal-anc-ing
a-vi-a-tor	bac-cha-nal	bade	bal-anc-er
av-id	bac-cha-na-li-an	badge	bal-brig-gan
a-void	bac-chant	badged	bal-co-ny
a-vow	bac-chant-te	badg-ing	bal-co-nies
a-wait	bach-e-lor	badg-er	bald
a-wake	bach-e-lor-hood	bad-i-nage	bald-ness
a-wak-en	bac-il-lar-y	bad-land	bal-der-dash
awe	bac-cil-lus	bad-lands	bald-head
awe-some	bac-cil-li	bad-ly	bal-dric
awe-struck	back-bite	bad-min-ton	bale
aw-ful	back-bit	bad-tem-pered	baled
aw-ful-ly	back-bit-ten	baf-fle	bal-ing
aw-ful-ness	back-bit-er	baf-fled	ba-leen
awhile	back-board	baf-fling	bale-ful
awk-ward	back-fire	baf-fler	bale-ful-ly
awk-ward-ly	back-fired	bag	balk
awn	back-fir-ing	bagged	balk-er
awned	back-gam-mon	bag-ging	bal-kan-ize
awn-ing	back-ground	ba-gasse	bal-kan-ized
awry	back-hand	bag-a-telle	bal-kan-iz-ing
ax	back-hand-ed	ba-gel	bal-kan-i-za-tion
ax-es	back-ing	bag-gage	balk-y
ax-i-al	back-lash	bag-gy	balk-i-er
ax-i-al-ly	back-log	bag-gi-er	balk-i-est
ax-i-om	back-slide	bag-gi-est	bal-lad
ax-i-o-mat-ic	back-slid	bag-man	bal-lade
ax-i-o-mat-i-cal	back-slid-den	bagn-io	bal-lad-eer
ax-is	back-slid-ing	bag-pipe	bal-lad-ry
ax-es	back-slid-er	bag-pi-per	bal-last
ax-le	back-spin	bah	ball-bear-ing
azal-ea	back-stop	bail	bal-le-ri-na
az-i-muth	back-stroke	bail-iff	bal-let
az-i-muth-al	back-talk	bail-i-wick	bal-lis-tic
az-ure	back-up	bails-man	bal-lis-tics
	back-ward	bails-men	bal-lis-ti-cian
B	back-wards	bairn	bal-loon
	back-wash	bait	bal-lot
bab-bitt	back-water	bake	bal-lot-ed
bab-ble	back-woods	baked	bal-lot-ing
bab-bled	back-woods-man	bak-ing	ball-room
bab-bling	ba-con	bak-er	bal-ly-hoo
bab-bler	bac-ter-ia	bak-er-y	balm
ba-bel	bac-ter-i-um	bak-er-ies	balm-y
ba-boon	bac-te-ri-al	bak-ing pow-der	balm-ier
ba-bush-ka	bac-te-ri-al-ly	bak-ing so-da	balm-i-est

balm-i-ly
ba-lo-ney
bal-sa
bal-sam
bal-us-ter
bal-us-trade
bam-bi-no
bam-bi-nos
bam-boo
ban
banned
ban-ning
ba-nal
ba-nal-i-ty
ban-nan-a
band-age
band-aged
band-ag-ing
ban-dana
ban-dan-na
ban-deau
ban-deaux
ban-de-role
ban-dit
ban-dits
ban-dit-ti
ban-dit-ry
band-mas-ter
band-o-leer
ban-do-lier
bands-man
bands-men
band-stand
band-wa-gon
ban-dy
ban-died
ban-dy-ing
ban-dy--leg-ged
bane-ful
ban-ful-ness
ban-gla-desh
ban-gle
ban-ish
ban-ish-ment
ban-i-ster
ban-jo
bank
bank-er
bank-ing
bank-note
bank-rupt

bank-rupt-cy
bank-rupt-cies
ban-ner
banns
ban-quet
ban-quet-ter
ban-quette
ban-tam
ban-tam-weight
ban-ter
ban-ter-er
ban-ter-ing-ly
ban-yan
ban-zal
ba-o-bab
bap-tism
bap-tis-mal
bap-tist
bap-tist-ery
bap-tis-ter-ies
bap-tize
bap-tized
bap-tiz-er
bap-tiz-ing
bar
barred
bar-ring
bar-bar-ic
bar-ba-rism
bar-bar-i-ty
bar-bar-i-ties
bar-ba-rize
bar-ba-rized
bar-ba-riz-ing
bar-ba-rous
bar-be-cue
bar-be-cued
bar-be-cu-ing
bar-ber
bar-ber-ry
bar-ber-ries
bar-ber-shop
bar-bi-tal
bar-bi-tu-rate
bar-bi-tur-ic
bar-busse
bar-ca-role
bard
bare
bar-er
bar-est

bare-back
bare-faced
bare-foot
bare-hand-ed
bare-ly
bar-gain
bar-gain-er
barge
barg-ed
barg-ing
bar-i-tone
bar-i-um
bar-keep-er
bar-ken-tine
bark-er
bar-ley
bar-maid
bar-man
bar-men
bar-mitz-vah
barm-y
bar-na-cle
barn-storm
barn-storm-er
barn-storm-ing
barn-yard
bar-o-graph
ba-rom-et-er
bar-o-met-ric
bar-o-met-ric-al
bar-on
ba-ro-ni-al
bar-on-age
bar-on-ess
bar-on-et
bar-on-et-age
bar-on-et-cy
bar-o-ny
bar-o-nies
ba-roque
barque
bar-quen-tine
bar-rack
bar-ra-cu-da
bar-ra-cu-das
bar-rage
bar-raged
bar-rag-ing
bar-ra-try
bar-ra-tries
bar-ra-tor

bar-ra-trous
bar-rel
bar-reled
bar-relled
bar-rel-ling
bar-ren
bar-ren-ly
bar-ren-ness
bar-rette
bar-ri-cade
bar-ri-cad-ed
bar-ri-cad-ing
bar-ri-er
bar-ring
bar-ri-o
bar-ri-os
bar-ris-ter
bar-room
bar-row
bar-ten-der
bar-ter
bar-ter-er
ba-sal
ba-salt
base-ment
bash-ful
bash-ful-ly
ba-sic
ba-si-cal-ly
ba-sil
ba-sil-i-cia
bas-i-lisk
ba-sin
ba-sis
bas-ket
bas-ket-ball
bas-ket-ry
bas-re-lief
bas-si-net
bas-tard
baste
bast-ed
bast-ing
bas-tille
bas-ti-on
bas-ti-oned
bat
bat-ted
bat-ting
bat-ter
batch

bate
 bat-ed
 bat-ing
bathe
 bathed
 bath-ing
 bath-er
 bath-i-nette
ba-thos
bath-y-scaphe
bath-y-sphere
ba-tik
ba-tiste
bat-on
bat-ten
bat-ter
bat-tery
bat-tle
 bat-tled
 bat-tling
bat-tle dore
bat-tle-field
bat-tle-ment
bat-ty
 bat-ti-er
 bat-ti-est
bau-ble
bawd-y
 bawd-i-er
 bawd-i-est
bay-o-net
 bay-o-net-ted
 bay-o-net-ing
bay-ou
ba-zaar
ba-zoo-ka
beach
bea-con
bead
 bead-ed
 bead-like
bead-y
 bead-i-er
 bead-i-est
beak
 beaked
 beak-er
beam
 beam-ed
bear
 bear-ing

bear-a-ble
bear-a-bly
bear-er
beard
 beard-ed
 beard-less
bear-skin
beast
 beast-li-ness
 beast-ly
 beast-li-er
 beast-li-est
beat
 beat-en
 beat-ing
 beat-er
be-a-tif-ic
be-at-i-fy
 be-at-i-fied
 be-at-i-fi-ca-tion
be-at-i-tude
beat-nik
beau
 beaus
 beaux
beau geste
beau-te-ous
 beau-te-ous-ly
 beau-ti-cian
beau-ti-fy
 beau-ti-fied
 beau-ti-fy-ing
 beau-ti-fi-ca-tion
 beau-ti-fi-er
 beau-ti-ful
beau-ty
beaux-arts
bea-ver
be-calm
beck-on
be-cloud
be-come
 be-com-ing
 be-com-ing-ly
bed
 bed-ded
 bed-ding
be-daub
be-daz-zle
 be-daz-zled
 be-daz-zling

be-daz-zle-ment
bed-bug
bed-clothes
be-deck
be-dev-il
 be-dev-iled
 be-dev-il-ing
 be-dev-il-ment
be-dew
bed-fast
bed-fel-low
be-dim
 be-dimmed
 be-dim-ming
bed-lam
bed-pan
be-drag-gle
 be-drag-gled
 be-drag-gling
bed-rid-den
bed-rock
bed-room
bed-sore
bed-spread
bed-spring
bed-time
bee-bread
beech
beef
beef-eat-er
beef-steak
beef-y
 beef-i-er
 beef-i-est
bee-hive
bee-line
beer-y
 beer-i-er
 beer-i-est
beest-ings
bees-wax
bee-tle
 bee-tled
 bee-tling
bee-tle-browed
be-fall
 be-fall-en
 be-fall-ing
be-fit
 be-fit-ted
 be-fit-ting

be-fog
 be-fogged
 be-fog-ging
be-fore
be-fore-hand
be-foul
be-friend
be-fud-dle
 be-fud-dled
 be-fud-dling
beg
 beg-ged
 beg-ging
be-get
 be-get-ten
 be-got
 be-got-ten
beg-gar
 beg-gar-dom
 beg-gar-hood
 beg-gar-ly
be-gin
 be-gan
 be-gun
 be-gin-ning
 be-gin-ner
be-go-ni-a
be-grime
 be-grimed
 be-grim-ing
be-grudge
 be-grudged
 be-grudg-ing
 be-grudg-ing-ly
be-guile
 be-guiled
 be-guil-ing
 be-guil-er
be-half
be-have
 be-haved
 be-hav-ing
 be-hav-ior
 be-hav-ior-ism
 be-hav-ior-ist
 be-hav-ior-is-tic
be-head
be-he-moth
be-hest
be-hind
be-hind-hand

be-hold	bel-ly-ing	ben-i-son	be-spat-ter
be-hold-ing	bel-ly-ache	ben-ny	be-speak
be-hold-er	bel-ly-ach-ing	ben-nies	be-speak-ing
be-hold-en	bel-ly-but-ton	be-numb	best
be-hoove	be-long	bent	bes-tial
be-hooved	be-long-ings	ben-zene	bes-tial-ly
be-hoov-ing	be-loved	ben-zine	bes-ti-al-i-ty
beige	be-low	ben-zo-ate	bes-ti-al-i-ties
be-ing	belt	ben-zo-in	be-stir
be-la-bor	belt-ed	ben-zol	be-stirred
be-lat-ed	belt-way	be-queath	be-stir-ring
be-lat-ed-ly	be-lu-ga	be-quest	be-stow
be-lat-ed-ness	be-mire	be-rate	be-stow-al
be-lay	be-mired	be-rat-ed	be-strew
be-lay-ed	be-mir-ing	be-rat-ing	be-stride
be-lay-ing	be-moan	be-reave	be-strid-den
belch	be-muse	be-reaved	be-strid-ing
bel-dam	be-mused	be-reav-ing	bet
be-lea-quer	be-mus-ing	be-reft	bet-ted
bel-fry	bench	be-ret	bet-ting
bel-fries	bend	ber-ga-mot	be-ta
be-lie	bend-ing	ber-i-ber-i	be-take
be-lied	bend-er	berke-li-um	be-tak-en
be-ly-ing	be-neath	ber-ry	be-tak-ing
be-lief	ben-e-dict	ber-ries	be-ta rays
be-lieve	ben-e-dic-tion	ber-ried	be-ta-tron
be-lieved	ben-e-fac-tion	ber-ry-ing	be-tel
be-liev-ing	ben-e-fac-tor	ber-serk	beth-el
be-liev-a-ble	ben-e-fac-tress	berth	be-tide
be-liev-er	ben-e-fice	ber-tha	be-tid-ed
be-lit-tle	ben-e-ficed	ber-yl	be-tid-ing
be-lit-tled	ben-e-fic-ing	be-ryl-li-um	be-to-ken
be-lit-tling	be-nef-i-cence	be-seech	be-tray
bel-la-don-na	be-nef-i-cent	be-seeched	be-tray-al
bell-boy	be-ne-fi-cial	be-seech-ing	be-tray-er
bell bouy	ben-e-fi-cial-ly	be-seech-ing-ly	be-troth
belle	ben-e-fi-ci-ar-ies	be-set	be-troth-al
belles let-tres	ben-e-fit	be-set-ting	be-troth-ed
bell-hop	ben-e-fit-ed	be-shrew	bet-ter
bel-li-cose	ben-e-fit-ing	be-side	bet-ter-ment
bel-li-cos-i-ty	be-nev-o-lence	be-sides	bet-tor
bel-lig-er-ence	be-nev-o-lent	be-siege	be-tween
bel-lig-er-en-cy	be-nev-o-lent-ly	be-sieged	be-twixt
bel-li-ger-ent	be-night-ed	be-sieg-ing	bev-el
bel-lig-er-ent-ly	be-nign	be-sieg-er	bev-eled
bel-low	be-nig-ni-ty	be-smear	bev-el-ing
bel-lows	be-nig-ni-ties	be-smirch	bev-er-age
bell-weth-er	be-nign-ly	bes-om	bev-y
bel-ly	be-nig-nant	be-sot	bev-ies
bel-lies	be-nig-nan-cies	be-sot-ted	be-wail
bel-lied	be-nig-nan-cy	be-sot-ting	be-ware

be-wil-der
  be-wil-der-ing-ly
  be-wil-der-ment
be-witch
  be-witch-er
  be-witch-ery
  be-witch-ing
  be-witch-ing-ly
  be-witch-ment
be-yond
be-zique
bi-an-nu-al
bi-as
  bi-ased
  bi-as-ing
bi-ax-i-al
  bi-ax-i-al-ly
bi-be-lot
Bi-ble
  Bib-li-cal
  Bib-li-cal-ly
  bib-li-og-ra-phy
  bib-li-og-ra-phies
  bib-li-o-graphic
bib-li-o-ma-ni-a
  bib-li-o-ma-ni-ac
bib-li-o-phile
bib-u-lous
bi-cam-er-al
bi-car-bo-nate
bi-ce-te-nary
  bi-cen-te-nar-ies
bi-cen-ten-ni-al
bi-ceps
bi-chlo-ride
bick-er
bi-con-cave
bi-con-vex
bi-cus-pid
  bi-cus-pi-dal
  bi-cus-pi-date
bi-cy-cle
  bi-cy-cled
  bi-cy-cling
  bi-cy-cler
  bi-cy-clist
bid
  bid-den
  bid-da-ble
  bid-der
  bid-dy

bid-dies
bide
  bid-ed
  bid-ing
bi-en-ni-al
  bi-en-ni-al-ly
bier
bi-fid
bi-fo-cal
  bi-fo-cals
bi-fur-cate
  bi-fur-cat-ed
  bi-fur-cat-ing
  bi-fur-ca-tion
big
  big-ger
  big-gest
  big-a-my
  big-a-mies
  big-a-mist
  big-a-mous
  big-heart-ed
  big-horn
  bight
  big-no-ni-a
  big-ot
  big-ot-ed
  big-ot-ed-ly
  big-ot-ry
  big-ot-ries
bi-jou
  bi-joux
  bi-ju-gous
bi-ki-ni
bi-lat-er-al
  bi-lat-er-al-ly
bil-ber-ry
  bil-ber-ries
bilge
bil-i-ary
bi-lin-gual
bil-ious
bilk
bill
  bil-led
  bil-ling
  bil-la-bong
  bill-board
  bil-let
  bil-let-doux
  bill-fold

bill-hook
bil-liards
bil-lings-gate
bil-lion
  bil-lion-are
  bil-lionth
bil-low
  bil-low-y
  bil-low-ier
  bil-low-i-est
bil-ly goat
bi-met-al-lism
  bi-met-al-list
  bi-me-tal-lic
bi-month-ly
  bi-month-lies
bi-na-ry
bi-nate
bin-au-ral
bind
  bind-ing
bind-er
bind-ery
  bind-er-ies
binge
  bin-go
bin-na-cle
bi-noc-u-lar
bi-no-mi-al
bio-chem-is-try
  bio-chem-i-cal
  bio-chem-ist
bi-o-cide
bi-o-e-col-o-gy
bi-o-gen-e-sis
  bi-o-ge-net-ic
  bi-og-ra-phy
  bi-og-ra-pher
  bi-o-graph-ic
  bi-o-graph-i-cal
  bi-o-graph-i-cal-ly
bi-ol-o-gy
  bi-o-log-i-cal
  bi-ol-o-gist
bi-o-met-rics
bi-o-nom-ics
bi-o-phys-ics
  bi-o-phys-i-cal
  bi-o-phys-i-cist
bi-op-sy
  bi-op-sies

bi-o-sphere
bi-o-tin
bi-par-ti-san
bi-par-tite
  bi-par-ti-tion
bi-ped
  bi-ped-al
bi-plane
bi-po-lar
  bi-po-lar-i-ty
birch
  birch-en
bird-bath
bird-brain
  bird-brained
bird-call
bird-ie
bird-lime
bird-man
bird's-eye
bi-ret-ta
birth-day
birth-mark
birth-place
birth-right
birth-stone
bis-cuit
bi-sect
  bi-sec-tion
  bi-sec-tor
  bi-sex-u-al
bish-op
  bish-op-ric
bis-muth
bi-son
bisque
bis-ter
  bis-tered
bis-tro
  bis-tros
bi-sul-fide
bitch
bite
  bit-ten
  bit-ing
  bit-ing-ly
bit-stock
bit-ter
  bit-ter-ish
  bit-ter-ly
  bit-ter-ness

bit-tern	blame-less-ness	blem-ish	blood pres-sure
bit-ter-root	blame-wor-thy	blench	blood re-la-tion
bit-ters	blame-wor-thi-ness	blend	blood-shed
bit-ter-sweet	blanch	blend-ed	blood-shot
bi-tu-men	blanc-er	blend-ing	blood-stone
bi-tu-mi-nous coal	blanch-ing	blend-er	blood-suck-er
bi-va-lent	blanc-mange	bless	blood-thirst-y
bi-va-lence	bland	bless-ed	blood-thirst-i-ly
bi-valve	bland-ly	bles-sing	bloody
bi-val-vu-lar	bland-ness	bless-ed-ness	blood-i-er
biv-ou-ac	blan-dish	blind	blood-i-est
biv-ou-acked	blan-dish-er	blind-ing	blood-ied
biv-ou-ack-ing	blan-dish-ment	blind-ing-ly	blood-y-ing
bi-week-ly	blank	blind-ly	blood-i-ly
bi-week-lies	blank-ly	blind-ness	blood-i-ness
bi-year-ly	blank-ness	blind-fold	bloom-ers
bi-zarre	blan-ket	blind-man's bluff	bloom-ing
bi-zarre-ly	blare	blink-er	bloom-ing-ly
bi-zarre-ness	blared	bliss	bloop-er
blab	blar-ing	bliss-ful	blos-som
blab-bed	blar-ney	bliss-ful-ly	blot
blab-bing	blas-pheme	bliss-ful-ness	blot-ted
blab-ber	blas-phemed	blis-ter	blot-ting
blab-ber-mouth	blas-phem-ing	blis-ter-y	blotch
black-ball	blas-phem-er	blithe	blotchy
black-ber-ry	blas-phem-ies	blithe-ly	blot-ter
black-ber-ries	blas-phe-my	blithe-some	blow
black-bird	blast-ed	blithe-some-ly	blown
black-board	bas-tu-la	blitz-krieg	blow-ing
black-en	blat	bliz-zard	blow-er
black-guard	blat-ted	block	blow-fly
black-head	blat-ting	block-er	blow-flies
black-ing	bla-tant	block-ade	blow-gun
black-jack	bla-tan-cy	block-ad-ed	blow-hole
black-list	bla-tant-ly	block-ad-ing	blow-out
black-mail	blath-er	block-ad-er	blow-pipe
black-out	blaze	block-bus-ter	blow-torch
black-smith	blazed	block-head	blow-up
black-snake	blaz-ing	block-house	blow-y
black-top	bla-zer	block-ish	blowz-y
blad-der	bleach	block-ish-ly	blub-ber
blade	bleach-er	blocky	blub-bery
blad-ed	bleak	blond	blu-cher
blame	bleak-ly	blood-curd-ling	bludg-eon
blamed	bleak-ness	blood bank	blue
blam-ing	blear	blood-ed	blu-er
blam-a-ble	bleary	blood-hound	blu-est
blame-a-ble	blear-i-ness	blood-less	blue-ness
blame-ful	bleed	blood-less-ly	blue-bell
blame-less	bleed-ing	blood-less-ness	blue-ber-ry
blame-less-ly	bleed-er	blood-let-ting	blue-ber-ries

blue-bird
blue-blood-ed
blue-bon-net
blue-coat
blue-col-lar
blue-fish
blue-grass
blue-jac-ket
blue-nose
blue-pen-cil
blue-print
blu-et
blu-ing
blun-der
blun-der-er
blun-der-ing-ly
blun-der-buss
blunt
blunt-ly
blunt-ness
blur
blur-red
blur-ring
blur-ry
blush
blushed
blush-ing
blush-ing-ly
blus-ter
blus-ter-er
blus-ter-ing-ly
blus-ter-ous
blus-ter-y
bo-a
board-er
board-walk
boast
boas-ter
boast-ful
boast-ful-ness
boast-ing-ly
boat-house
boat-man
boat-swain
bob
bob-bed
bob-bing
bob-bin
bob-ble
bob-bled
bob-bling

bob-by-pin
bob-cat
bob-o-link
bob-sled
bob-tail
bob-white
bock
bode
bod-ed
bod-ing
bod-ice
bod-i-ly
bod-kin
bod-y
bod-ied
bod-y-ing
bod-y-guard
bog
bog-gy
bog-ging
bo-gey
bog-gle
bog-gled
bog-gling
bog-gler
bo-gus
bo-gy
boil-er
bois-ter-ous
bois-ter-ous-ly
bois-ter-ous-ness
bo-la
bo-las
bold
bold-ly
bold-ness
bold-face
bo-le-ro
bol-lix
boli-worm
boll weevil
bo-lo
bo-lo-gna
bo-lo-ney
bol-ster
bol-ster-er
bolt
bolt-ed
bolt-er
bom-bard
bom-bard-ment

bom-bar-dier
bom-bast
bom-bas-tic
bom-bas-ti-cal-ly
bomb-er
bomb-proof
bomb-shell
bomb-sight
bo-na fide
bo-nan-za
bon-bon
bond-age
bond-ed
bond-man
bond-men
bonds-men
bone
boned
bon-ing
bone-head
bon-er
bon-fire
bon-go
bon-gos
bon-gies
bon-ho-mie
bo-ni-to
bon-net
bon-ny
bon-sai
bo-nus
bo-nus-es
bon voy-age
bon-y
bon-i-er
bon-i-est
boo
booed
boo-ing
boo-by
boo-bies
boo-by trap
boo-dle
boo-hoo
boo-hooed
boo-hoo-ing
book
book-bind-er
book-case
book-end
book-ie

book-ish
book-ish-ness
book-keep-ing
book-keep-er
book-let
book-mak-er
book-mark
book-mo-bile
book-plate
book-sell-er
book-sell-ing
book-stall
book-worm
boo-me-rang
boon docks
boon-dog-gle
boor
boor-ish
boor-ish-ness
boost
boost-er
boot-black
boot-ee
boot-jack
boot-leg
boot-legged
boot-leg-ging
boot-leg-ger
boot-less
boot-less-ly
boot-less-ness
boot-lick
boot-lick-er
boo-ty
boo-ties
booze
booz-er
booz-y
booz-i-er
booz-i-est
bo-rax
bor-der
bor-der-ed
bor-der-ing
bor-der-land
bor-der-line
bore
bored
bor-ing
bor-er
bo-re-al

bore-dom

bo-ric

bo-ron

bor-ough

bor-row

  bor-row-er

borsch

bosh

bosk-y

bos-om

boss-ism

boss-y

  boss-i-er

  boss-i-est

bo-sun

bot-a-ny

  bo-tan-i-cal

  bot-a-nist

  bot-a-nize

botch

  botchy

  botch-i-er

  botch-i-est

both-er

  both-er-some

bot-tle

  bot-tled

  bot-tling

  bot-tle-ful

  bot-tler

bot-tle-neck

bot-tom

  bot-tom-less

bot-u-lism

bou-doir

bouf-fant

bough

bought

bouil-lon

boul-der

boul-e-vard

bounce

  bounced

  bounc-ing

bound

bound-a-ry

  bound-a-ries

bound-er

bound-less

  bound-less-ness

boun-te-ous

boun-te-ous-ness

boun-ti-ful

boun-ty

  boun-ties

bou-quet

bour-bon

bour-geois

bour-geoi-sie

bou-tique

bou-ton-niere

bo-vine

bow-el

bow-ery

bow-ie

bow-ing

bowl

bow-leg

  bow-leg-ged

  bowl-er

bow-line

bow-ling

bow-man

  bow-men

bow-string

box

  box-ful

  box-fuls

box-car

box-er

box-ing

box of-fice

boy

  boy-hood

  boy-ish

  boy-ish-ly

boy-cott

boy-friend

boy-sen-ber-ry

  boy-sen-ber-ries

brace

  bra-ced

  brac-ing

brace-let

brac-er

bra-ces

brack-en

brack-et

brack-ish

  brack-ish-ness

bract

brae

brag

  brag-ged

  brag-ging

  brag-gart

braid

  braid-er

  braid-ing

braille

brain-child

brain-less

brain-pow-er

brain-storm

  brain-storm-ing

  brain-wash-ing

brain-y

  brain-i-er

  brain-i-est

braise

  braised

  brais-ing

bram-ble

  bram-bly

branch

  branch-ed

brand

  brand-er

  brand-ish

brand-new

bran-dy

  bran-dies

  bran-died

  bran-dy-ing

bra-sier

bras-se-rie

  bras-se-ries

bras-siere

brassy

  brass-i-er

  brass-i-est

brat

  brat-tish

  brat-ty

bra-va-do

brave

  braved

  brav-ing

  brav-ery

bra-vo

  bra-vos

bra-vu-ra

brawl

braw-ler

brawn

  brawny

  brawn-i-er

bra-zen

bra-zier

breach

bread

  bread=ed

  breadth-ways

break

  break-ing

  break-a-ble

  break-age

brak-er

breath

breathe

  breathed

  breath-ing

  breath-er

breath-ing

breath-tak-ing

  breath-tak-ing-ly

breathy

  breath-i-er

  breath-i-est

breech-es

breech-load-er

bred

breed

  breed-ing

breeze

  breezy

  breez-i-er

  breez-i-est

breth-ren

bre-vet

  bre-vet-ted

  bre-vet-ting

  bre-vi-a-ry

  bre-vi-a-ries

brev-i-ty

bri-ar

  bri-ary

bribe

  bribed

  brib-ing

  brib-a-ble

birb-ery

  brib-er-ies

  bric-a-brac

brick-lay-er
brick-lay-ing
brick-work
bride
  brid-al
bride-groom
brides-maid
bridge
bri-dle
  bri-dled
  bri-dling
brief
  brief-ly
  brief-ing
bri-er
bri-gade
bri-a-dier
brig-an-tine
bright
  bright-ly
  bright-en
bril-liance
  bril-lian-cy
  bril-liant
brim
  brimmed
  brim-ming
  brim-stone
brine
briny
bring
  bring-ing
brink
bri-oche
bri-quet
  bri-quette
brisk
  brisk-ly
bris-ket
bris-tle
  bris-tled
britch-es
brit-tle
broach
  broached
  broach-ing
broad-cast
  broad-cast-ed
  broad-cast-ing
  broad-cloth
broad-mind-ed

broad-side
bro-cade
  bro-cad-ed
  bro-cad-ing
broc-co-li
bro-chure
broil-er
bro-ken
bro-ker
bro-ker-age
bro-mide
bro-mine
bron-chi
  bron-chi-al
  bron-chi-tis
  bron-chue
bron-co
  bron-cos
  bron-to-saur
bronze
  bronz-ed
  bronz-ing
brooch
brood
  brood-ing
brook
broom-stick
broth-el
broth-er
broth-er-in-law
  broth-ers-in-law
  broth-er-ly
brow-beat
  brow-beat-en
  brow-beat-ing
brown
brown-ie
browse
  browsed
  brows-ing
bru-in
bruise
  bruis-ed
  bruis-er
  bruis-ing
brunch
bru-net
brusque
bru-tal
  bru-tal-i-ty
  bru-tal-ize

bru-tal-ized
  bru-tal-iz-ing
  bru-tal-i-za-tion
  brut-ish
bub-ble
  bub-bled
  bub-bling
  bub-bler
bu-bon-ic plague
buc-ca-neer
buck-board
buck-et
  buck-et-ed
  buck-et-ing
buck-eye
buck-le
buck-tooth
  buck-teeth
  buck-toothed
  buck-wheat
bu-col-ic
bud
  bud-ded
  bud-ding
  bud-dy
budge
budg-et
buff-er
buf-fet
  buf-fet-ed
  buf-fet=ing
  bug-a-boo
bug-gy
  bug-gi-er
  bug-gi-est
bu-gle
  bu-gled
  bu-gling
  bu-gler
build
  build-er
  build-ing
  built--in
built-up
bulb
bul-ba-ceous
bul-bar
bul-bous
bulge
  bulged
  bulg-ing

bulgy
bulk-head
bulk-y
  bulk-i-er
  bulk-i-est
  bulk-i-ly
bul-let
bul-le-tin
bul-let-proof
bull-fight
  bull-fight-er
  bull-fight-ing
  bull-finch
bul-lion
bull-pen
bull's-eye
bul-ly
  bul-lies
  bul-lied
  bul-ly-ing
bul-rush
bul-wark
bum
  bum-mer
  bum-mest
  bum-ble-bee
bump-er
bump-kin
bump-tious
  bump-y
  bump-i-er
  bump-i-est
bunch
  bunchy
bun-co
bun-combe
bun-dle
  bun-dled
  bun-dling
  bun-ga-low
bun-gle
  bun-gled
  bun-gling
  bun-gler
  bun-ion
bunk-er
bunk-house
bun-ko
bun-kum
bun-ny
  bun-nies

bun-ting
bu-oy
buoy-an-cy
buoy-ant
buoy-ant-ly
bur-ble
bur-den
bur-den-some
bur-dock
bu-rette
burg-er
bur-gess
bur-glar
bur-glar-ize
bur-glar-ized
bur-glar-iz-ing
bur-gla-ries
bur-gla-ry
bur-gle
bur-gled
bur-gling
bur-i-al
bur-lap
bur-lesque
bur-lesqued
bur-les-quing
bur-les-quer
bur-ly
bur-li-er
bur-li-est
burn
burn-ed
burnt
burn-ing
burn-a-ble
burn-er
bur-nish
bur-nish-er
bur-noose
burn-sides
burp
burr
burred
bur-ring
bur-ro
bur-ros
bur-row
bur-row-er
bur-sa
bur-sae
bur-sal

bur-sar
bur-sa-ri-al
bur-sa-ry
bur-sa-ries
bur-si-tis
burst
burst-ing
burst-er
bur-y
bur-ied
bur-y-ing
bus-boy
bus-by
bus-bies
bushed
bu-shi-do
bush-ing
bush-man
bush-men
bush-mas-ter
bush-whack
bush-whack-er
bush-whack-ing
bush-y
bush-i-er
bush-i-est
bus-i-ly
busi-ness
busi-ness-like
busi-ness-man
busi-ness-men
busi-ness-wom-an
bus-kin
bus-kined
bus-tard
bus-tle
bus-tled
bus-tling
bus-tler
bus-y
bus-i-er
bus-i-est
bus-ied
bus-y-ing
bu-ta-di-ene
bu-tane
butch-er
butch-ery
butch-er-ies
but-ler
butte

but-ton
but-tress
bu-ty-ric
bux-om
buy
bought
buy-ing
buz-zard
by-gong
by-law
byte

C

ca-bal
ca-balled
ca-ball-ing
cab-a-la
cab-a-lis-tic
cab-a-lis-ti-cal
ca-bal-le-ro
ca-ba-na
cab-a-ret
ca-ble
ca-bled
ca-bling
ca-ble-gram
cab-o-chon
ca-boo-dle
ca-boose
cab-ri-o-let
cach-a-lot
cache
cached
cach-ing
ca-chet
ca-cique
cack-le
ca-coph-o-ny
ca-coph-o-nies
cac-tus
cac-tus-es
cac-ti
cad
cad-dish
ca-dav-er
ca-dav-er-ous
cad-die
cad-died
cad-dis fly
cad-dy

cad-dies
ca-dence
ca-den-za
ca-det
cadge
cadged
cadg-ing
cad-mi-um
ca-dre
ca-du-ce-us
ca-du-cei
cea-su-ra
cae-su-rae
ca-fe
caf-e-te-ria
caf-feine
caf-tan
cage
caged
cai-man
cairn
cais-son
cai-tiff
ca-jole
cake
caked
cal-a-bash
cal-a-boose
cal-a-mine
ca-lam-i-ty
ca-lam-i-ties
ca-lam-i-tous
cal-cic
cal-ci-fy
cal-ci-fied
cal-ci-fy-ing
cal-ci-fi-ca-tion
cal-ci-mine
cal-cite
cal-ci-um
cal-cu-la-ble
cal-cu-la-bil-i-ty
cal-cu-late
cal-cu-lat-ed
cal-cu-lat-ing
cal-cu-la-tion
cal-cu-la-tor
cal-cu-lus
cal-cu-lus-es
cal-dron
cal-en-dar

cal-i-ber
cal-i-brate
cal-i-brat-ed
cal-i-brat-ing
cal-i-bra-tion
cal-i-co
cal-i-coes
cal-i-per
ca-liph
cal-iph-ate
cal-is-then-ics
cal-lig-ra-pher
cal-lig-ra-phy
call-ing
cal-li-o-pe
cal-lous
cal-loused
cal-low
cal-lus
cal-lus-es
calm
ca-lor-ic
cal-o-rie
cal-o-ries
cal-o-rif-ic
cal-u-met
cal-um-ny
calve
calved
ca-lyp-so
ca-lyp-sos
ca-lyx
ca-lyx-es
cal-y-ces
ca-ma-ra-de-rie
cam-ber
cam-bi-um
cam-bric
cam-el
cam-era
cam-i-sole
cam-ou-flage
cam-ou-flaged
cam-ou-flag-ing
cam-paign
cam-pa-ni-le
cam-pa-ni-les
camp-er
cam-phor
cam-pus
cam-pus-es

camp-y
cam-shaft
can
canned
can-ning
ca-nal
ca-naled
ca-nal-ing
ca-nard
ca-nar-y
can-can
can-cel
can-celed
can-cel-ing
can-cel-la-tion
can-cer
can-de-la-brum
can-did
can-di-da-cy
can-di-da-cies
can-di-date
can-died
can-dle
can-dor
can-dy
can-dies
can-dy-ing
cane
ca-nine
can-is-ter
can-ker
can-ker-ous
can-na-bis
canned
can-ner
can-nery
can-ner-ies
can-ni-bal
can-non
can-not
can-ny
can-nier
ca-noe
can-on
ca-non-i-cal
can-on-ize
can-on-ized
can-on-i-za-tion
can-o-py
can-ta-loup
can-ta-loupe

can-ta-lope
can-tan-ker-ous
can-ta-ta
can-teen
can-ti-cle
can-ti-lev-er
can-to
can-tos
can-ton
can-tor
can-vas
can-yon
ca-pa-bil-i-ty
cap-pa-bil-i-ties
ca-pa-ble
ca-pa-bly
ca-pa-cious
ca-pac-i-tate
ca-pac-i-tat-ed
ca-pac-i-tat-ing
ca-pac-i-ty
ca-pac-i-ties
ca-per
ca-pi-as
cap-il-lar-i-ty
cap-il-lar-y
cap-il-lar-ies
cap-i-tal
cap-i-ta-tion
ca-pit-u-late
ca-pit-u-lat-ed
ca-pit-u-lat-ing
ca-pit-u-la-tor
ca-pon
ca-pote
ca-price
ca-pri-cious
ca-pri-cious-ly
cap-ri-ole
cap-ri-oled
cap-ri-ol-ing
cap-size
cap-stone
cap-sule
cap-su-lar
cap-tain
cap-tain-cy
cap-tion
cap-tious
cap-tious-ness
cap-ti-vate

cap-tive
cap-tiv-i-ty
cap-tiv-i-ties
cap-tor
cap-ture
cap-tured
cap-tur-ing
cap-tur-er
car-a-cole
car-a-coled
car-a-col-ing
car-a-cul
ca-rafe
car-a-van
car-a-van-sa-ry
car-a-van-sa-ries
car-a-vel
car-a-way
car-bide
car-bo-hy-drate
car-bo-lat-ed
car-bol-ic
car-bon
car-bo-na-ceous
car-bo-nate
car-bo-na-tion
car-bon di-ox-ide
car-bon-if-er-ous
car-bon-ize
car-bon-ized
car-bon-iz-ing
car-bon-i-za-tion
car-boy
car-bun-cle
car-bu-re-tor
car-cass
car-cin-o-gen
car-cin-o-gen-ic
car-ci-no-ma
car-ci-no-mas
car-ci-no-ma-ta
car-da-mom
car-di-ac
car-di-gan
car-di-nal
car-di-o-graph
car-di-og-ra-phy
ca-reen
ca-reer
care-ful
care-ful-ly

care-less
  care-less-ly
  care-less-ness
ca-ress
  ca-ress-ing-ly
car-et
care-worn
car-go
  car-gos
car-hop
car-i-bou
car-i-ca-ture
  car-i-ca-tured
  car-i-ca-tur-ing
  car-i-ca-tur-ist
car-ies
car-il-lon
  car-il-lonned
  car-i-lon-ning
car-mine
car-nage
car-nal
  car-nal-i-ty
  car-nal-ly
car-na-tion
car-nel-ian
car-ni-val
car-ni-vore
  car-niv-o-rous
  car-niv-o-rous-ly
car-om
ca-rot-id
ca-rous-al
ca-rouse
  ca-roused
  ca-rous-ing
  ca-rous-er
car-ou-sel
car-pen-ter
  car-pen-try
car-pet
car-pet-ing
car-pus
car-riage
car-ri-ole
car-rot
car-roty
car-ry
  car-ried
  car-ry-ing
cart

cart-age
carte-blanche
car-tel
car-ti-lage
  car-ti-lag-i-nous
car-tog-ra-phy
  car-tog-ra-pher
  car-to-graph-ic
car-ton
car-toon
  car-toon-ist
car-tridge
cart-wheel
car-vel
car-y-at-ld
  car-y-at-ids
  car-y-at-i-des
ca-sa-ba
cas-cade
  cas-cad-ed
  cas-cad-ing
ca-sein
case-mate
  case-mat-ed
case-ment
  case-ment-ed
case-work
  case-work-er
cash-ew
cash-mere
cas-ing
ca-si-no
cas-ket
cas-sette
cas-si-no
cas-sock
  cas-socked
cas-so-wary
  cas-so-war-ies
cast
  cast-ing
cas-ta-net
cast-a-way
caste
cas-tel-lat-ed
cast-er
cas-ti-gate
  cas-ti-gat-ed
cast i-ron
cas-tle
cas-tor

cas-trate
  cas-trat-ed
  cas-trat-er
  cas-tra-tion
cas-u-al
cas-u-al-ty
  cas-u-al-ties
cas-u-ist
  cas-u-ist-ic
  cas-u-ist-ry
  cas-u-ist-ries
cat-a-clysm
  cat-a-cly-mal
cat-a-comb
cat-a-falque
cat-a-lep-sy
  cat-a-lep-tic
cat-a-log
  cat-a-loged
  cat-a-log-ing
  cat-a-log-er
ca-tal-pa
ca-tal-y-sis
  ca-tal-y-ses
  cat-a-lyt-ic
cat-a-lyst
cat-a-lyze
  cat-a-lyzed
  cat-a-lyz-ing
cat-a-ma-ran
cat-a-pult
ca-tarrh
ca-tas-tro-phe
  cat-as-troph-ic
catch
  caught
  catch-ing
catch-er
catch-up
cat-e-chism
  cat-e-chis-mal
cat-e-chiz
cat-e-chu-men
cat-e-gor-i-cal
  cat-e-gor-i-cal-ly
cat-e-go-ry
  cat-a-go-ries
  cat-e-gor-ize
  cat-e-gor-ized
  cat-e-gor-iz-ing
ca-ter

ca-ter-er
cat-er-pil-lar
ca-ter-waul
cat-fish
  cat-fish-es
cat-gut
ca-thar-sis
  ca-thar-ses
  ca-thar-tic
ca-the-dral
cath-e-ter
cat-i-on
cat-nap
  cat-napped
  cat-nap-ping
cat-nip
cat's-paw
cat-sup
cat-tail
cat-tle
cat-ty
  cat-tier
  cat-ti-est
  cat-ti-ly
  cat-ti-ness
cat-ty-cor-ner
cau-cus
  cau-cus-es
  cau-cused
  cau-cus-ing
cau-dal
cau-date
  cau-dat-ed
cau-dle
caul-dron
cau-li-flow-er
caulk
  caulk-er
caus-al
  caus-al-ly
cau-sal-i-ty
  cau-sal-i-ties
cause-way
caus-tic
  caus-ti-cal-ly
cau-ter-ize
  cau-ter-ized
  cau-ter-iz-ing
  cau-ter-i-za-tion
cau-ter-y
  cau-ter-ies

cau-tion
 cau-tion-ary
cau-tious
cav-al-cade
cav-a-lier
 cav-a-lier-ly
cav-al-ry
cave
ca-ve-at
cav-ern
 cav-ern-ous
cav-ier
cav-il
 cav-iled
 cav-il-ing
cav-i-ty
 cav-i-ties
ca-vort
cay-enne
cay-man
 cay-mans
cay-use
ce-cum
ce-dar
cede
 ced-ed
 ced-ing
ce-dil-la
ceil-ing
cel-an-dine
cel-a-brant
cel-e-brate
 cel-e-brat-ed
 cel-e-brat-ing
 cel-e-bra-tion
 cel-e-bra-tor
ce-leb-ri-ty
 ce-leb-ri-ties
ce-ler-i-ty
cel-er-y
ce-les-tial
ce-li-ac
cel-i-ba-cy
 cel-i-bate
cel-lar
cel-lo
 cel-los
 cel-list
cel-lo-phane
cel-lu-lar
cel-lule

cel-lu-lose
ce-ment
cem-e-ter-y
ce-no-bite
cen-o-taph
cen-ser
cen-sor
 cen-so-ri-al
 cen-sor-ship
cen-so-ri-ous
 cen-so-ri-ous-ly
 cen-so-ri-ous-ness
cen-sure
 cen-sured
 cen-sur-ing
 cen-sur-er
cen-sus
 cen-sus-es
 cen-sused
 cen-sus-ing
cen-tare
cen-taur
cen-te-nar-i-an
cen-te-na-ry
 cen-te-nar-ies
cen-ten-ni-al
cen-ter
cen-ti-are
cen-ti-grade
cen-ti-gram
cen-ti-li-ter
cen-ti-me-ter
cen-tral
 cen-tral-ize
 cen-tral-ized
 cen-tral-iz-ing
cen-trif-u-gal
cen-tri-fuge
cen-trip-e-tal
cen-tu-ri-an
cen-tu-ry
 cen-tu-ries
ce-ram-ic
 ce-ram-ics
ce-re-al
cer-e-bel-lum
cer-e-bral
cer-e-brum
cer-e-mo-ni-al
 cer-e-mo-no-al-ism
cer-e-mo-ny

cer-e-mo-nies
ce-rise
ce-ric
 ce-ri-um
cer-tain
cer-tain-ty
 cer-tain-ties
cer-tif-i-cate
 cer-tif-i-ca-tion
cer-ti-fy
 cer-ti-fied
 cer-ti-fy-ing
cer-ti-tude
ce-ru-le-an
cer-vi-cal
cer-vix
 cer-vix-es
 cer-vi-ces
ces-sa-tion
ces-sion
cess-pool
ce-ta-cean
 ce-ta-ceous
chafe
 chafed
 chaf-ing
chaf-er
chaff
 chaf-fer
 chaff-er-er
cha-grin
 cha-grined
 cha-grin-ing
chain re-ac-tion
chair-man
 chair-men
chaise-longue
chal-et
chal-ice
chalk
 chalky
chal-lenge
 chal-lenged
 chal-leng-ing
cham-ber
cham-ber-maid
cha-me-le-on
cham-ois
cham-pagne
cham-pi-on
 cham-pi-on-ship

chance-ful
chan-cel-lor
chanc-y
 chanc-i-er
 chanc-i-est
chan-de-lier
change
 changed
 chang-ing
 chang-a-ble
chan-nel
chan-ti-cleer
cha-os
cha-ot-ic
cha-pa-re-jos
chap-ar-ral
cha-peau
 cha-peaux
chap-el
chap-e-ron
chap-fall-en
chap-lain
chap-let
chap-ter
char
 charred
 char-ring
char-ac-ter
char-ac-ter-is-tic
char-ac-ter-ize
 char-ac-ter-ized
 char-ac-ter-iz-ing
 char-ac-ter-iz-er
cha-rade
char-coal
charge
 charged
 charg-ing
 charg-er
char-i-ot
 char-i-ot-eer
cha-ris-ma
char-i-ta-ble
 char-i-ta-ble-ness
 char-i-ta-bly
char-i-ty
 char-i-ties
cha-riv-a-ri
char-la-tan
 char-la-tan-ism
char-ley horse

charm	check-mat-ing	chest-i-er	chi-nos
char-nel	**check-out**	chest-i-est	**chi-noi-se-rie**
char-ter	**check-point**	**chev-ron**	**chintz-y**
char-treuse	**check-room**	**chew**	chintz-i-er
char-wom-an	**check-up**	chew-er	chintz-i-est
chary	**ched-dar**	chi-a-ro-scu-ro	**chip**
char-i-er	**cheek-bone**	**chi-can-ery**	chipped
char-i-est	**cheek-y**	cha-can-er-ies	chip-ping
chase	cheek-i-er	**chi-chi**	**chip-munk**
chased	cheek-i-est	**chick-a-dee**	**chip-per**
chas-ing	cheek-i-ness	**chic-ken**	**chi-rog-ra-pher**
chas-er	**cheer-ful**	**chic-ken-heart-ed**	**chi-rog-ra-phy**
chasm	cheer-ful-ly	**chic-le**	**chi-rop-o-dist**
chas-sis	cheer-ful-ness	**chic-o-ry**	**chi-ro-prac-tic**
chaste	**cheer-lead-er**	chic-o-ries	**chi-ro-prac-tor**
chaste-ly	**cheer-less**	**chide**	**chis-el**
chas-ten	cheer-less-ly	chid-ed	chis-eled
chas-tise	cheer-less-ness	**chief**	chis-el-ing
chas-tised	**chee-y**	chief-ly	chis-el-er
chas-tis-ing	cheer-i-er	**chief-tain**	**chit-chat**
chas-tis-ment	cheer-i-est	**chif-fon**	**chi-tin**
chas-tis-er	cheer-i-ly	**chif-fo-nier**	**chit-ter-ling**
chas-ti-ty	cheer-i-ness	**chi-gnon**	**chiv-al-ry**
chat	**cheese-burg-er**	**chil-blain**	chiv-al-ries
chat-ted	**cheese-cake**	**chil-dren**	chiv-al-ric
chat-ting	**cheese-cloth**	**child-bear-ing**	chiv-al-rous
cha-teau	**chees-y**	**child-birth**	chiv-al-rous-ly
cha-teaux	chees-i-er	**child-hood**	chiv-al-rous-ness
chat-e-laine	chees-i-est	**child-ish**	**chlo-rine**
chat-tel	chees-i-ness	child-ish-ly	**chlo-ro-form**
chat-ter	**chee-tah**	child-like	**clo-ro-phyll**
chat-ter-box	**chem-i-cal**	**chili**	**chock-full**
chat-ty	chem-i-cal-ly	chil-ies	**choc-o-late**
chat-ti-er	**che-mise**	**chill**	**choice**
chat-ti-est	**chem-ist**	chill-ing-ly	choice-ly
chat-ti-ly	**chem-is-try**	**chill-y**	choice-ness
chat-ti-ness	**chem-o-ther-a-py**	chill-i-er	**choir-boy**
chauf-feur	**che-nille**	chill-i-est	**choke**
chau-vin-ist	**cher-ish**	chill-i-ness	choked
chau-vin-ism	**che-root**	**chi-me-ra**	chok-ing
chau-vin-is-tic	**cher-ry**	**chi-mer-ic**	chok-er
cheap	cher-ries	chi-mer-i-cal	**chol-er**
cheap-ly	**cher-ub**	chi-mer-i-cal-ly	**chol-era**
cheap-ness	cher-ubs	chi-mer-i-cal-ness	**chol-er-ic**
cheap-en	cher-u-bim	**chim-ney**	**cho-les-te-rol**
cheap-skate	che-ru-bic	**chim-pan-zee**	**choose**
cheat	**cher-vil**	**chin**	chose
check-er-board	**chess-man**	chinned	cho-sen
check-list	chess-men	chin-ning	choos-ing
check-mate	**chest-nut**	**chi-na**	**choos-y**
check-mat-ed	**chest-y**	**chi-no**	choos-i-er

choos-i-est
chop
chopped
chop-ping
chop-per
chop-pi-ness
chop-py
chop-pi-er
chop-i-est
chop-sticks
chop su-ey
cho-ral
cho-ral-ly
cho-rale
chord
chord-al
cho-rea
cho-re-og-ra-phy
cho-re-og-ra-pher
cho-re-o-graph-ic
cho-ric
chor-is-ter
chor-tle
chor-tled
chor-tling
cho-rus
cho-rus-es
cho-rused
cho-rus-ing
chos-en
chow-der
chow mein
chrism
Christ
chris-ten
chris-ten-ing
Chris-tian
Chis-ti-an-i-ty
Chris-ti-an-i-ties
Christ-mas
chro-mate
chro-mat-ic
chro-mat-i-cal-ly
chro-mat-ics
chro-ma-tin
chro-mic
chro-mi-um
chro-mo
chro-mus
chro-mo-some
chro-mo-sphere

chron-ic
chron-i-cal-ly
chron-i-cle
chron-i-cled
chron-i-cling
chron-i-cler
chron-o-log-i-cal
chro-no-lo-gy
chro-nol-o-gies
chro-nol-o-gist
chro-nom-e-ter
chron-o-met-ric
chrys-a-lis
chry-sa-lis-es
chry-sal-i-des
chrys-o-lite
chub-by
chub-bi-er
chub-bi-est
chub-bi-ness
chuck-full
chuck-le
chuck-led
chuck-ling
chuk-ker
chum-my
chum-mi-er
chum-mi-est
chunk
chunky
chunk-i-er
chunk-i-est
church
church-li-ness
church-ly
church-go-er
church-man
church-men
church-war-den
church-yard
churl-ish
churl-ish-ly
churl-ish-ness
churn-er
chut-ney
chutz-pah
ci-bo-ri-um
ci-bo-ria
ci-ca-da
ci-ca-das
ci-ca-dea

cic-a-trix
cic-a-tri-ces
cic-a-trize
cic-a-trized
cic-a-triz-ing
cic-e-ro-ne
ci-der
ci-gar
cig-a-rette
cil-ia
cil-i-ar-y
cil-i-ate
cin-cho-na
cinc-ture
cin-der
cin-e-ma
cin-e-mas
cin-e-mat-ic
cin-e-ma-to-graph
cin-e-rar-i-um
cin-na-bar
cin-na-mon
cinque-foil
ci-on
ci-pher
cir-ca
cir-ca-di-an
cir-cle
cir-cled
cir-cling
cir-clet
cir-cuit
cir-cu-i-tous
cir-cu-i-tous-ly
cir-cu-i-tous-ness
cir-cu-lar
cir-cu-lar-ize
cir-cu-lar-ized
cir-cu-lar-iz-ing
cir-cu-lar-i-za-tion
cir-cu-la-tion
cir-cu-late
cir-cu-lat-ed
cir-cu-lat-ing
cir-cu-la-tive
cir-cu-la-tor
cir-cu-la-to-ry
cir-cum-cise
cir-cum-cised
cir-cum-cis-ing
cir-cum-cis-er

cir-cum-ci-sion
cir-cum-fer-ence
cir-cum-fer-en-tial
cir-cum-flex
cir-cum-flu-ent
cir-cum-fuse
cir-cum-fus-ing
cir-cum-fu-sion
cir-cum-lo-cu-tion
cir-cum-lo-cu-to-ry
cir-cum-scribe
cir-cum-scribed
cir-cum-scrib-ing
cir-cum-scrib-er
cir-cum-scrip-tion
cir-cum-scrip-tive
cir-cum-spect
cir-cum-stance
cir-cum-stan-tial
cir-cum-vent
cir-cum-ven-tion
cir-cum-ven-tive
cir-cus
cir-cus-es
cir-rho-sis
cir-rhot-ic
cir-rus
cis-tern
cit-a-del
cite
cit-ed
cit-ing
ci-ta-tion
cith-a-ra
cit-i-zen
cit-i-zen-ship
cit-i-zen-ry
cit-i-zen-ries
cit-rate
cit-ric
cit-ron
cit-ron-el-la
cit-rus
cit-tern
city
cit-ies
ci-ty-state
civ-et
civ-ic
civ-ics
civ-il

ci-vil-ian
ci-vil-i-ty
 ci-vil-i-ties
civ-i-li-za-tion
civ-i-lize
 civ-i-lized
 civ-i-liz-ing
clab-ber
claim
 claim-a-ble
 claim-ant
 claim-er
clair-voy-ance
 clair-voy-ant
clam
 clammed
 clam-ming
clam-bake
clam-bar
clam-my
 clam-mi-er
 clam-mi-est
 clam-mi-ly
 clam-mi-ness
clam-or
 clam-or-ous
clan
 clan-nish
clan-des-tine
clang-or
 clang-or-ous
clans-man
 clans-men
clap
 clapped
 clap-ping
clap-board
clap-per
clap-trap
claque
clar-et
clar-i-fy
 clar-i-fied
 clar-i-fy-ing
 clar-i-fi-ca-tion
clar-i-net
 clar-i-net-ist
clar-i-on
clar-i-ty
class-a-ble
clas-sic

clas-si-cal
 clas-si-cal-ly
clas-si-cism
 clas-si-cist
clas-si-fy
 clas-si-fied
 clas-si-fy-ing
 clas-si-fi-er
 clas-si-fi-ca-tion
class-mate
class-room
class-y
 class-i-er
 class-i-est
clat-ter
clause
 claus-i-cle
claus-tro-pho-bia
clav-i-chord
clav-i-cle
cla-vier
clay
 clay-ey
clay-more
clean-cut
clean-er
clean-ly
 clean-li-er
 clean-li-est
 clean-li-ness
cleanse
 cleansed
 cleans-ing
 cleans-er
clean-up
clear
 clear-ly
 clear-ness
clear-ance
clear-cut
clear-ing
clear-sight-ed
cleav-age
cleave
 cleaved
 cleav-ing
cleav-er
clef
cleft
clem-en-cy
 clem-ent

clere-sto-ry
 clere-sto-riees
cler-gy
 cler-gies
cler-gy-man
 cler-gy-men
cler-ic
 cler-i-cal
 cler-i-cal-ism
 cler-i-cal-ist
clev-er
 clev-er-ly
 clev-er-ness
clev-is
 clev-is-es
clew
cli-ent
cli-en-tele
cliff-hang-er
cli-mac-ter-ic
cli-mate
 cli-mat-ic
 cli-mat-i-cal
climb
 climb-a-ble
 climb-er
clinch-er
cling
 cling-ing
 cling-ing-ly
 cling-er
clin-ic
 clin-i-cal
 clin-i-cal-ly
clink-er
clip
 clipped
 clip-ping
clip-per
clique
 cliqu-ey
 cliqu-ish
clit-o-ris
clo-a-ca
 clo-a-cae
 clo-a-cal
clob-ber
clock-wise
clock-work
clod
 clod-dish

clod-dy
clog
 clog-ged
 clog-ging
clois-ter
 clois-tral
close
 closed
 clos-ing
 clos-est
 close-ly
 close-ness
close-fist-ed
close-mouthed
clos-et
 clos-et-ed
 clos-et-ing
close-up
clo-sure
clot
 clot-ted
 clot-ting
clothe
 clothed
 cloth-ing
clothes-horse
clothes-line
clothes-pin
cloth-ier
cloth-ing
clo-ture
cloud-burst
cloud-y
 cloud-i-er
 cloud-i-est
 cloud-i-ly
 cloud-i-ness
clo-ven
clo-ver
clo-ver-leaf
clown
 clown-ish
cloy
 cloy-ing-ly
club
 clubbed
 club-bing
club-foot
club-house
clump
 clumpy

clum-sy
clum-si-er
clum-si-est
clum-si-ly
clum-si-ness
clus-ter
coach-man
coach-men
co-ag-u-late
co-ag-u-lat-ed
co-ag-u-lat-ing
co-ag-u-la-tion
co-a-lesce
co-a-lesced
co-a-les-cing
co-a-les-cence
co-a-les-cent
co-a-li-tion
coarse
coars-er
coars-est
coars-en
coarse-ly
coast-er
coast-line
coat-ing
co-au-thor
coax
coax-ing-ly
co-balt
cob-ble
cob-bled
cob-bling
cob-bler
cob-ble-stone
co-bra
cob-web
cob-webbed
cob-web-by
co-ca
co-caine
coc-cyx
coc-cy-ges
coc-cyg-e-al
coch-le-a
cock-ade
cock-a-too
cock-crow
cock-er span-iel
cock-eyed
cock-fight

cock-le
cock-le-bur
cock-le-shell
cock-ney
cock-neys
cock-pit
cock-roach
cocks-comb
cock-sure
cock-tail
cocky
cock-i-er
cock-i-est
cock-i-ness
co-coa
co-co-nut
co-coon
cod
cod-fish
cod-dle
cod-dled
cod-dling
code
cod-ed
cod-ing
co-deine
codg-er
cod-i-cil
cod-i-fy
cod-i-fied
cod-i-fy-ing
cod-i-fi-ca-tion
cod-liv-er oil
co-ed
co-ed-u-ca-tion
coe-len-ter-ate
co-e-qual
co-erce
co-erced
co-er-cing
co-er-ci-ble
co-er-cion
co-er-cive
co-ex-ist
co-ex-ist-ence
co-ex-ist-ent
cof-fee
cof-fee-house
cof-fee-pot
cof-fer
cof-fin

co-gent
co-gen-cy
co-gent-ly
cog-i-tate
cog-i-tat-ed
cog-i-tat-ing
cog-i-ta-ble
cog-i-ta-tive
cog-nac
cog-nate
cog-ni-tion
cog-ni-tive
cog-ni-zance
cog-ni-zant
cog-wheel
co-hab-it
co-hab-i-ta-tion
co-here
co-hered
co-her-ing
co-her-ent
co-her-ence
co-her-en-cy
co-her-ent-ly
co-he-sion
co-he-sive
co-hes-sive-ly
co-hes-sive-ness
co-hort
coif-feur
coif-fure
coif-fured
coif-fur-ing
coin-age
co-in-cide
co-in-cid-ed
co-in-cid-ing
co-in-ci-dence
co-in-ci-den-tal
co-in-ci-den-tal-ly
co-i-tion
co-i-tus
co-i-tal
coke
coked
cok-ing
co-la
col-an-der
cold-blood-ed
cole-slaw
col-ic

col-icky
col-i-se-um
co-li-tis
col-lab-o-rate
col-lab-o-rat-ed
col-lab-o-rat-ing
col-lab-o-ra-tion
col-lab-o-ra-tor
col-lage
col-lapse
col-lapsed
col-laps-ing
col-lap-si-ble
col-lar
col-lar-bone
col-late
col-lat-ed
col-lat-ing
col-la-tion
col-la-tor
col-lat-er-al
col-league
col-lect
col-lect-i-ble
col-lec-tor
col-lect-ed
col-lec-tion
col-lec-tive
col-lec-tive-ly
col-lect-tiv-i-ty
col-lec-tiv-ism
col-lec-tiv-ize
col-lec-tiv-iz-ing
col-lec-tiv-i-za-tion
col-lege
col-le-gi-al
col-le-gian
col-le-giate
col-lide
col-lid-ed
col-lid-ing
col-li-sion
col-li-mate
col-li-mat-ed
col-li-mat-ing
col-li-ma-tion
col-lo-cate
col-lo-cat-ed
col-lo-cat-ing
col-lo-ca-tion
col-loid

col-lo-qui-al
col-lo-qui-al-ly
col-lo-qui-al-ism
col-lo-quy
col-lo-quies
col-lu-sion
col-lu-sive
co-logne
co-lon
colo-nel
co-lo-ni-al
co-lo-ni-al-ism
co-lo-ni-al-ist
col-o-nist
col-o-nade
col-o-ny
col-o-nies
col-o-nize
col-o-nized
col-o-niz-ing
col-o-niz-er
col-o-ni-za-tion
col-or
col-or-er
col-or-less
col-or-a-tion
col-or-blind
col-or-blind-ness
col-or-cast
col-ored
col-or-fast
col-or-ful
col-or-ing
co-los-sal
co-los-sus
co-los-si
colt-ish
col-um-bine
col-umn
co-lum-nar
co-lumned
col-um-nist
co-ma
co-mas
co-ma-tose
com-bat
com-bat-ed
com-bat-ing
com-bat-ant
com-ba-tive
comb-er

com-bi-na-tion
com-bi-na-tion-al
com-bi-na-tive
com-bine
com-bined
com-bin-ing
com-bin-a-ble
com-bin-er
com-bo
com-bos
com-bust-ti-ble
com-bus-ti-bil-i-ty
con-bus-tion
com-bus-tive
come
com-ing
come-back
co-me-di-an
co-me-di-enne
come-down
com-e-dy
com-e-dies
come-ly
come-li-ness
come-on
com-er
com-et
come-up-pance
com-fort
com-fort-a-ble
com-fort-a-bly
com-fort-er
com-fy
com-fi-er
com-fi-est
com-ic
com-i-cal
com-ing
com-i-ty
com-i-ties
com-ma
com-mas
com-mand
com-man-dant
com-man-deer
com-mand-er
com-mand-er-ship
com-mand-ment
com-man-do
com-man-dos
com-mem-o-rate

com-mem-o-rat-ed
com-mem-o-rat-ing
com-mem-o-ra-ble
com-mence
com-menced
com-menc-ing
com-mence-ment
com-mend
com-mend-a-ble
com-mend-a-bly
com-men-da-tion
com-mend-a-to-ry
com-men-su-rate
com-ment
com-men-tary
com-men-tar-ies
com-men-ta-tor
com-merce
com-mer-cial
com-mer-cial-ism
com-mer-cial-ize
com-mer-cial-ized
com-mie
com-mis-er-ate
com-mis-er-at-ed
com-mis-er-at-ing
com-mis-er-a-tion
com-mis-er-a-tive
com-mis-sar
com-mis-sar-y
com-mis-sar-ies
com-mis-sion
com-mis-sioned
com-mis-sion-er
com-mit
com-mit-ted
com-mit-ting
com-mit-ment
com-mit-tee
com-mit-tee-man
com-mode
com-mo-di-ous
com-mod-i-ty
com-mod-i-ties
com-mo-dore
com-mon
com-mon-al-ty
com-mon-al-ties
com-mon-place
com-mons
com-mon-wealth

com-mo-tion
com-mu-nal
com-mu-nal-i-ty
com-mune
com-muned
com-mun-ing
com-mu-ni-cant
com-mu-ni-cate
com-mu-ni-cat-ed
com-mu-ni-cat-ing
com-mu-ni-ca-ble
com-mu-ni-ca-tive
com-mu-ni-ca-tion
com-mun-ion
com-mun-ism
com-mun-ist
com-mu-ni-ty
com-mu-ni-ties
com-mu-nize
com-mu-nized
com-mu-niz-ing
com-mu-ta-tion
com-mu-ta-tor
com-mute
com-mut-ed
com-mut-ing
com-mut-a-ble
com-mut-er
com-pact
com-pan-ion
com-pan-ion-a-ble
com-pan-ion-ship
com-pa-ny
com-pa-nies
com-par-a-ble
com-par-a-bil-ity
com-par-a-tive
com-pare
com-pared
com-par-ing
com-par-i-son
com-part-ment
com-part-men-tal
com-part-ment-ed
com-pass
com-pas-sion
com-pas-sion-ate
com-pat-ible
com-pat-i-bly
com-pat-i-bil-i-ty
com-pa-tri-ot

com-peer
com-pel
 com-pelled
 com-pel-ling
com-pem-di-ous
 com-pen-di-um
com-pen-sate
 com-pen-sat-ed
 com-pen-sat-ing
 com-pen-sa-tive
 com-pen-sa-tor
 com-pen-sa-to-ry
com-pen-sa-tion
com-pete
 com-pet-ed
 com-pet-ing
com-pet-i-tor
 com-pe-tence
 com-pe-ten-cy
com-pe-tent
com-pe-ti-tion
com-pet-i-tive
com-pile
 com-piled
 com-pil-ing
 com-pi-la-tion
com-pla-cence
 com-pla-cen-cy
 com-pla-cent
com-plain
com-plain-ant
com-plaint
com-plai-sance
 com-plai-sant
com-plect-ed
com-ple-ment
 com-ple-men-tal
 com-ple-men-ta-ry
com-plete
 com-plet-ed
 com-plet-ing
 com-plet-a-ble
com-ple-tion
com-plex
com-plex-ion
 com-plex-ioned
com-plex-i-ty
 com-plex-i-ties
com-pli-ance
 com-pli-an-cy
 com-pli-ant

com-pli-cate
 com-pli-cat-ed
 com-pli-cat-ing
 com-pli-ca-tion
com-plic-i-ty
 com-plic-i-ties
com-pli-ment
com-ply
 com-plied
 com-ply-ing
com-po-nent
com-port
com-port-ment
com-pose
 com-posed
 com-pos-ing
com-pos-er
com-pos-ite
com-po-si-tion
com-post
com-po-sure
com-pote
com-pound
com-pre-hend
 com-pre-hend-i-ble
 com-pre-hen-si-bly
com-pre-hen-sion
com-pre-hen-sive
com-press
 com-presed
 com-press-i-ble
 com-press-i-bil-ity
com-pres-sion
com-pres-sor
com-prise
 com-prised
 com-pris-ing
com-pro-mise
 com-pro-mised
 com-pro-mis-ing
comp-trol-ler
com-pul-sion
com-pul-sive
com-pul-so-ry
com-punc-tion
com-pute
 com-put-ed
 com-put-ing
 com-pu-ta-tion
com-pu-ter
 com-put-er-ize

com-put-er-ized
com-put-er-iz-ing
com-rade
 com-rade-ship
com-sat
con
 conned
 con-ning
con-cave
con-ceal
 con-ceal-a-ble
 con-ceal-ment
con-cede
 con-ced-ed
 con-ced-ing
con-ceit
 con-ceit-ed
con-ceive
 con-ceived
 con-ceiv-ing
 con-ceiv-a-ble
 con-ceiv-a-bly
con-cen-trate
 con-cen-tra-ted
 con-cen-trat-ing
 con-cen-tra-tive
 con-cen-tra-tion
con-cen-tric
 con-cen-tri-cal
 con-cen-tric-i-ty
con-cept
 con-cep-tu-al
con-cep-tion
 con-cep-tive
con-cep-tu-al-ize
 con-cep-tu-al-ized
 con-cep-tu-al-iz-ing
con-cern
 con-cerned
 con-cern-ing
con-cert
con-cert-ed
con-cer-ti-na
con-cert-mas-ter
con-cer-to
con-ces-sion
con-ces-sion-aire
conch
 conchs
con-cil-i-ate
 con-cil-i-at-ed

con-cil-i-at-ing
con-cil-i-a-tion
con-cil-i-a-to-ry
con-cise
 con-cise-ness
 con-cise-ly
con-clave
con-clude
 con-clud-ed
 con-clud-ing
con-clu-sion
con-clu-sive
con-coct
 con-coc-tion
con-com-i-tant
 con-com-i-tance
con-cord
 con-cord-ance
 con-cord-ant
con-course
con-crete
 con-cret-ed
 con-cret-ing
con-cre-tion
 con-cre-tive
con-cu-bine
con-cur
 con-curred
 con-cur-ring
 con-cur-rence
 con-cur-rent
con-cus-sion
 con-cus-sive
con-demn
 con-dem-na-ble
 con-dem-na-tion
 con-dem-na-to-ry
con-dense
 con-densed
 con-dens-ing
 con-den-sa-ble
 con-den-sa-tion
 con-dens-er
con-de-scend
 con-de-scend-ing
 con-de-scen-sion
con-di-ment
con-di-tion
 con-di-tion-al
 con-di-tion-er
 con-di-tion-ed

con-dole
con-doled
con-dol-ing
con-do-la-to-ry
con-do-ler
con-do-lence
con-dom
con-do-min-i-um
con-done
con-doned
con-don-ing
con-do-na-tion
con-dor
con-duce
con-duced
con-duc-ing
con-duct
con-duct-i-bil-i-ty
con-duct-i-ble
con-duct-ance
con-duc-tion
con-fer-ence
con-fer-en-tial
con-fess
con-fess-ed-ly
con-fes-sion
con-fes-sion-al
con-fes-sor
con-fet-ti
con-fi-dant
con-fi-dante
con-fide
con-fid-ed
con-fid-ing
con-fi-dence
con-fi-dent
con-fi-den-tial
con-fig-u-ra-tion
con-fig-u-ra-tion-al
con-fine
con-fined
con-fin-ing
con-fine-ment
con-firm
con-firm-a-ble
con-fir-ma-tion
con-fir-ma-tive
con-fir-ma-to-ry
con-fir-med
con-firm-ed-ly
con-firm-ed-ness

con-fis-cate
con-fis-cat-ed
con-fis-cat-ing
con-fis-ca-tion
con-fis-ca-tor
con-fis-ca-to-ry
con-fla-gra-tion
con-flict
con-flict-ing
con-flic-tive
con-flic-tion
con-flu-ence
con-flu-ent
con-flux
con-form
con-form-ist
con-form-ism
con-form-a-ble
con-form-a-bly
con-form-ance
con-for-ma-tion
con-form-i-ty
con-form-i-ties
con-found
con-found-ed
con-found-ed-ly
con-front
con-fron-ta-tion
con-fuse
confused
con-fus-ing
con-fus-ed-ly
con-fus-ed-ness
con-fu-sion
con-fute
con-futed
con-fut-ing
con-fu-ta-tion
con-ga
con-gas
con-geal
con-geal-ment
con-gen-ial
con-ge-ni-al-i-ty
con-gen-ial-ly
con-gen-i-tal
con-ger
con-ge-ries
con-gest
con-ges-tion
con-ges-tive

con-glom-er-ate
con-glom-er-at-ing
con-glom-er-a-tion
con-grat-u-late
con-grat-u-lat-ed
con-grat-u-lat-ing
con-grat-u-la-tor
con-grat-u-la-to-ry
con-grat-u-la-tion
con-gre-gate
con-gre-gat-ed
con-gre-gat-ing
con-gre-ga-tion
con-gre-ga-tion-al
con-gress
con-gres-sion-al
con-gress-man
con-gress-men
con-gress-wom-an
con-gress-wom-en
con-gru-ent
con-gru-ent-ly
con-gru-ence
con-gru-en-cy
con-gru-en-cies
con-gru-i-ty
con-gru-i-ties
con-gru-ous
con-gru-ous-ly
con-ic
con-i-cal
co-ni-fer
con-jec-ture
con-jec-tured
con-jec-tur-ing
con-jec-tur-al
con-join
con-joint
con-joint-ly
con-ju-gal
con-ju-gal-ly
con-ju-gate
con-ju-gat-ed
con-ju-gat-ing
con-ju-ga-tion
con-ju-ga-tive
con-junc-tion
con-junc-tive
con-jur-a-tion
con-jure
con-jured

con-jur-ing
con-jur-er
con-nect
con-nec-tor
con-nec-tion
con-nec-tive
con-nip-tion
con-nive
con-nived
con-niv-ing
con-niv-ance
con-nois-seur
con-note
con-not-ed
con-not-ing
con-no-ta-tion
con-no-ta-tive
con-nu-bi-al
con-ni-bi-al-ly
con-quer
con-quer-a-ble
con-quer-or
con-quest
con-quis-ta-dor
con-quis-ta-dors
con-quis-ta-dor-es
con-san-quin-i-ty
con-science
con-sci-en-tious
con-sci-en-tious-ly
con-scious
con-scious-ly
con-scious-ness
con-script
con-scrip-tion
con-se-crate
con-se-crat-ed
con-se-crat-ing
con-se-cra-tive
con-se-cra-tion
con-sec-u-tive
con-sec-u-tive-ly
con-sen-sus
con-sent
con-sent-er
con-se-quence
con-se-quent
con-se-quent-ly
con-se-quen-tial
con-se-quen-tial-l
con-ser-va-tion

con-ser-va-tion-al
con-ser-va-tion-ist
con-serv-a-tive
con-serv-a-tism
con-serv-a-tive-ly
con-serv-a-to-ry
con-serv-a-to-ries
con-serve
con-served
con-serv-ing
con-serv-a-ble
con-serv-er
con-sid-er
con-sid-er-a-ble
con-sid-er-a-bly
con-sid-er-ate
con-sid-er-a-tion
con-sid-er-ing
con-sign
con-sign-er
con-sign-or
con-sign-ment
con-sign-ee
con-sist
con-sist-en-cy
con-sist-en-cies
con-sist-ence
con-sist-ent
con-sist-ent-ly
con-sis-to-ry
con-sis-to-ries
con-so-la-tion
con-sol-a-to-ry
con-sole
con-soled
con-sol-ing
con-sol-a-ble
con-sol-i-date
con-sol-i-dat-ed
con-sol-i-dat-ing
con-sol-i-da-tion
con-so-nant
con-so-nance
con-so-nant-ly
con-so-nan-tal
con-sort
con-sor-ti-um
con-sor-tia
con-spic-u-ous
con-spic-u-ous-ly
on-spire

con-spired
con-spir-ing
con-spir-a-cy
con-spir-a-cies
con-spir-a-tor
con-spir-a-to-ri-al
con-spir-er
con-spir-ing-ly
con-sta-ble
con-sta-ble-ship
con-stab-u-lar-y
con-stab-u-lar-ies
con-stant
con-stan-cy
con-stant-ly
con-stel-la-tion
con-ster-na-tion
con-sti-pate
con-sti-pa-tion
con-stit-u-en-cy
con-stit-u-en-cies
con-stit-u-ent
con-sti-tute
con-sti-tu-tion
con-sti-tu-tion-al
con-strain
con-strain-a-ble
con-strained
con-straint
con-strict
con-stric-tive
con-stric-tion
con-stric-tor
con-struct
con-struc-tor
con-struc-tion
con-struc-tion-al
con-struc-tive
con-struc-tive-ly
con-struc-tive-ness
con-strue
con-strued
con-stru-ing
con-stru-a-ble
con-stru-er
con-sul
con-su-lar
con-sul-ship
con-su-late
con-sult
con-sul-ta-tion

con-sult-ant
con-sume
con-sumed
con-sum-ing
con-sum-a-ble
con-sum-er
con-sum-mate
con-sum-mat-ed
con-sum-mat-ing
con-sum-mate-ly
con-sum-ma-tion
con-sump-tion
com-sump-tive
con-tact
con-ta-gion
con-ta-gious
con-ta-gious-ness
con-tain
con-tain-a-ble
con-tain-er
con-tain-ment
con-tam-i-nate
con-tam-i-nat-ed
con-tam-i-nat-ing
con-tam-i-nant
con-tam-i-na-tion
con-tam-i-na-tive
con-tam-i-na-tor
con-tem-plate
con-tem-plat-ed
con-tem-plat-ing
con-tem-pla-tion
con-tem-pla-tive
con-tem-po-rar-y
con-tem-po-rar-ies
con-tempt
con-tempt-i-ble
con-tempt-i-bly
con-temp-tu-ous
con-temp-tu-ous-ly
con-tend
con-tend-er
con-tent
con-tent-ment
con-tent-ed
con-tent-ed-ly
con-tent-ed-ness
con-ten-tion
con-ten-tious
con-ten-tious-ly
con-ten-tious-ness

con-ter-mi-ous
con-test
con-test-a-ble
con-test-er
con-test-ant
con-text
con-tig-u-ous
con-ti-gu-i-ty
con-ti-gu-i-ties
con-tig-u-ous-ly
con-tig-u-ous-ness
con-ti-nence
con-ti-nen-cy
con-ti-nent
con-ti-nent-ly
con-ti-nen-tal
con-tin-gent
con-tin-gen-cies
con-tin-gent-ly
con-tin-u-al
con-tin-u-al-ly
con-tin-u-ance
con-tin-ue
con-tin-ued
con-tin-u-ing
con-tin-u-a-tion
con-tin-u-er
con-ti-nu-i-ty
con-ti-nu-i-ties
con-tin-u-ous
con-tin-u-ous-ly
con-tin-u-um
con-tin-ua
con-tort
con-tor-tion
con-tor-tive
con-tor-tion-ist
con-tour
con-tra-band
can-tra-cep-tive
con-tra-cep-tion
con-tract
con-tract-ed
con-tract-i-ble
con-trac-tu-al
con-trac-tion
con-trac-tive
con-trac-tile
con-trac-tor
con-tra-dict
con-tra-dict-a-ble

con-tra-dic-tion
con-tra-dic-to-ry
con-tra-dis-tinc-tion
con-trail
con-tral-to
con-tral-tos
con-tral-ti
con-trap-tion
con-tra-pun-tal
con-tra-ri-wise
con-tra-ry
con-tra-ries
con-tra-ri-ly
con-tra-ri-ness
con-trast
con-trast-a-ble
con-trast-ing-ly
con-tra-vene
con-tra-vened
con-tra-ven-ing
con-tra-ven-er
con-tra-ven-tion
con-trib-ute
con-trib-ut-ed
con-trib-ut-ing
con-trib-ut-a-ble
con-trib-u-tor
con-trib-u-tory
con-tri-bu-tion
con-trite
con-trite-ly
con-trite-ness
con-tri-tion
con-trive
con-triv-ed
con-triv-ing
con-triv-ance
con-trol
con-trolled
con-trol-ling
con-trol-la-ble
con-trol-ler
con-trol-ler-ship
con-tro-ver-sy
con-tro-ver-sies
con-tro-ver-sal
con-tro-ver-sial-ly
con-tro-vert
con-tu-me-ly
con-tu-me-lies
con-tuse

con-tused
con-tus-ing
con-tu-sion
co-nun-drum
cov-va-lesce
con-va-lesced
con-va-les-cing
con-va-les-cence
con-va-les-cent
con-vec-tion
con-vene
con-vened
con-ven-ing
con-ven-er
con-ven-ience
con-ven-ient
con-ven-ient-ly
con-vent
con-ven-tion
con-ven-tion-al
con-ven-tion-al-ist
con-ven-tion-al-ize
con-verge
con-verged
con-verg-ing
con-ver-gence
con-ver-gen-cy
con-ver-gent
con-ver-sant
con-ver-sa-tion
con-ver-sa-tion-al
c on-verse
con-versed
con-vers-ing
con-verse-ly
con-ver-sion
con-vert
con-vert-er
con-vert-i-ble
con-vert-i-bil-i-ty
con-vert-i-bly
con-vex
con-vex-ly
con-vex-i-ty
con-vey
con-vey-a-ble
con-vey-ance
con-vey-er
con-vey-or
con-vict
con-vic-tion

con-vic-tion-al
con-vince
con-vinced
con-vinc-ing
con-vinc-er
con-vinc-i-ble
con-viv-i-al
con-viv-i-al-i-ty
con-viv-i-al-ly
con-vo-ca-tion
con-vo-ca-tion-al
con-voke
con-voked
con-vok-ing
con-vok-er
con-vo-lute
con-vo-lut-ed
con-vo-lut-ing
con-vo-lute-ly
con-vo-lu-tion
con-voy
con-vulse
con-vulsed
con-vuls-ing
con-vul-sion
con-vul-sive
con-vul-sive-ly
co-ny
coo
cooed
coo-ing
coo-ing-ly
cook-book
cook-er-y
cook-e-ries
cook-out
cool
cool-ish
cool-ly
cool-ness
cool-ant
cool-er
coo-lie
coo-lies
coon-skin
coop-er
coop-er-age
co-op-er-ate
co-op-er-at-ed
co-op-er-at-ing
co-op-er-a-tion

co-op-er-a-tive
co-op-er-a-tive-ly
co-opt
co-op-ta-tion
co-or-di-nate
co-or-di-nat-ed
co-or-di-nat-ing
co-or-di-nate-ly
co-or-di-na-tor
co-or-di-na-tion
coo-tie
cop
copped
cop-ping
cope-stone
co-pi-lot
co-pi-ous
co-pi-ous-ly
co-pi-ous-ness
cop-out
cop-per
cop-per-y
cop-per-head
cop-per-plate
cop-pice
cop-ra
copse
cop-u-la
cop-u-las
cop-u-lae
cop-u-lar
cop-u-late
cop-u-lat-ed
cop-u-lat-ing
cop-u-la-tion
cop-u-la-tive
cop-u-la-tive-ly
copy
cop-ies
cop-ied
cop-y-ing
cop-y-book
cop-y-cat
cop-y-ist
cop-y-right
co-quet
co-quet-ted
co-quet-ting
co-quet-ry
co-quet-ries
co-quette

co-quet-tish	cor-o-net-ed	**cor-rode**	cost-li-est
co-quet-tish-ly	**cor-po-ral**	cor-rod-ed	cost-li-ness
cor-a-cle	**cor-po-rate**	cor-rod-ing	**cost--plus**
cor-al	cor-po-rate-ly	cor-rod-i-ble	**cos-tume**
cor-bel	cor-po-ra-tive	**cor-ro-sion**	cos-tumed
cord-age	**cor-po-ra-tion**	**cor-ro-sive**	cos-tum-ing
cor-date	cor-po-rat-ism	**cor-ru-gate**	**cos-tum-er**
cor-date-ly	**cor-po-re-al**	cor-ru-gat-ed	**co-sy**
cor-dial	cor-po-re-al-i-ty	cor-ru-gat-ing	co-si-er
cor-dial-i-ty	cor-po-re-al-ness	cor-ru-ga-tion	cos-i-est
cor-dial-ness	**corps**	**cor-rupt**	**co-te-rie**
cor-dial-ly	**corpse**	cor-rupt-er	**co-ter-mi-nous**
cor-dil-le-ra	**corps-man**	cor-rup-ti-ble	**co-til-lion**
cord-ite	corps-men	cor-rup-ti-bil-i-ty	**cot-tage**
cor-don	**cor-pu-lent**	cor-rupt-ly	**cot-ter**
cor-do-van	cor-pu-lence	cor-rupt-ness	**cot-ton**
cor-du-roy	cor-pu-len-cy	cor-rup-tion	cot-ton-y
cord-wood	**cor-pus**	**cor-sage**	**cot-ton-mouth**
core	**cor-pus-cle**	**cor-sair**	**cot-ton-seed**
cored	cor-pus-cu-lar	**cor-set**	**cot-ton-tail**
cor-ing	**cor-ral**	cor-set-ed	**cot-ton-wood**
co-re-la-tion	cor-ralled	**cor-tex**	**couch**
co-re-spond-ent	cor-ral-ling	cor-ti-ces	**coun-cil**
co-ri-an-der	**cor-rect**	**cor-ti-cal**	coun-cil-or
cor-ker	cor-rect-a-ble	**cor-ti-sone**	coun-cil-man
cork-screw	cor-rect-i-ble	**co-run-dum**	coun-cil-lor-ship
corn-cob	cor-rect-ness	**co-sig-na-to-ry**	**count**
cor-nea	cor-rec-tor	**cos-met-ic**	count-a-ble
cor-ne-al	**cor-rec-tion**	**cos-mic**	**count-down**
cor-ner	cor-rec-tion-al	cos-mi-cal-ly	**coun-te-nance**
cor-ner-stone	**cor-rec-tive**	**cos-mog-o-ny**	coun-te-nanced
cor-net	**cor-re-late**	cos-mog-o-nies	coun-te-nanc-ing
cor-net-ist	cor-re-lat-ed	cos-mo-gon-ic	coun-te-nanc-er
corn-flow-er	cor-re-lat-ing	cos-mog-o-nist	**count-er**
cor-nice	**cor-re-la-tion**	**cos-mog-o-ny**	**coun-ter-act**
corn-starch	**cor-rel-a-tive**	cos-mog-o-nist	coun-ter-ac-tion
cor-nu-co-pi-a	**cor-re-spond**	**cos-mog-ra-phy**	coun-ter-ac-tive
corn-y	cor-re-spond-ing	cos-mog-ra-phies	**coun-ter-at-tack**
corn-i-er	cor-re-spond-ing-ly	cos-mog-ra-pher	**coun-ter-charge**
conr-i-est	**cor-re-spond-ence**	cos-mo-graph-ic	coun-ter-charged
co-rol-la	**cor-re-spond-ent**	**cos-mol-o-gy**	coun-ter-char-ging
cor-ol-lar-y	**cor-ri-dor**	cos-mol-o-gies	**coun-ter-claim**
cor-ol-lar-ies	**cor-ri-gi-ble**	cos-mo-log-ic	coun-ter-claim-ant
co-ro-na	cor-ri-gi-bil-i-ty	cos-mol-o-gist	**coun-ter-cul-ture**
co-ro-nas	cor-ri-gi-bly	**cos-mo-naut**	**coun-ter-feit**
co-ro-nae	**cor-rob-o-rate**	**cos-mo-pol-i-tan**	coun-ter-feit-er
cor-o-nar-y	cor-rob-o-rat-ed	cos-mo-pol-i-tan-ism	**coun-ter-mand**
cor-o-na-tion	cor-rob-o-rat-ing	**cos-mop-o-lite**	**coun-ter-meas-ure**
cor-o-ner	cor-rob-o-ra-tion	**cos-mos**	**coun-ter-pane**
cor-o-ner-ship	cor-rob-o-ra-tive	**cost-ly**	**coun-ter-part**
cor-o-net	cor-rob-o-ra-to-ry	cost-li-er	**coun-ter-point**

coun-ter-poise
coun-ter-poised
coun-ter-pois-ing
coun-ter-sign
coun-ter-sink
coun-ter-sank
coun-ter-sunk
coun-ter-spy
coun-ter-spies
coun-ter-weight
coun-tees
count-less
coun-tri-fied
coun-try
coun-tries
coun-try-man
coun-try-men
coun-try-wom-an
coun-try-wom-en
coun-try-side
coun-ty
coun-ties
coup
coups
coup-le
coup-led
coup-ling
coup-ler
cou-pon
cour-age
cou-ra-geous
cour-i-er
course
coursed
cours-ing
cours-er
cour-te-ous
cour-te-ous-ly
cour-te-sy
cour-te-sies
court-house
cour-ti-er
court-ly
court-li-er
court-li-est
court-mar-tial
courts-mar-tial
court-mar-tialed
court-room
court-ship
cous-in

cous-in-hood
cous-in-ly
cou-tu-rier
cov-e-nant
cov-e-nan-ter
cov-e-nan-tor
cov-er-age
cov-er-all
cov-er-let
cov-ert
cov-ert-ly
cov-ert-ness
cov-er-up
cov-et
cov-et-a-ble
cov-et-er
cov-et-ous
cov-et-ous-ly
cov-ey
cow-ard
cow-ard-ly
cow-ard-ice
cow-boy
cow-er
cow-er-ing-ly
cow-hide
cowl
cowled
cow-lick
cow-man
cow-men
co-work-er
cow-poke
cow-ry
cow-rie
cow-ries
cox-swain
coy
coy-ly
coy-o-te
coz-en
coz-en-age
coz-en-er
crab
crabbed
crab-bing
crab-by
crack-down
crack-er
crack-ing
crack-le

crack-led
crack-ling
crack-up
cra-dle
cra-dled
cra-dling
crafts-man
crafts-man-ship
crafty
craft-i-er
craft-i-est
craft-i-ly
craft-i-ness
crag
crag-ged
crag-gy
crag-gi-ness
cram
crammed
cram-ming
cram-mer
cran-ber-ry
cran-ber-ries
crane
craned
cran-ing
cra-ni-um
cra-ni-ums
cra-nia
cra-ni-al
cra-ni-ate
cra-ni-al-ly
crank-case
crank-shaft
crank-y
crank-i-er
crank-i-est
crank-i-ly
crank-i-ness
cran-ny
cran-nies
cran-nied
crash-land
crass
crass-ly
crass-ness
crate
crat-ed
crat-ing
cra-ter
cra-ter-al

cra-tered
cra-vat
crave
craved
crav-ing
crav-er
crav-ing-ly
craw-fish
crawl
crawl-y
crawl-ing-ly
crawl-er
cray-fish
cray-on
craze
craz-ing
cra-zy
cra-zi-er
cra-zi-est
cra-zi-ly
cream-er
cream-er-y
cream-er-ies
cre-ate
cre-at-ed
cre-at-ing
cre-a-tion
cre-a-tion-al
cre-a-tive
cre-a-tive-i-ty
cre-a-tor
crea-ture
cre-dence
cre-den-za
cred-i-ble
cred-i-bil-i-ty
cred-i-bly
cred-it
cred-it-a-ble
cred-it-a-bil-i-ty
cred-it-a-bly
cred-i-tor
cre-do
cre-dos
cred-u-lous
creek
creel
cre-ma-to-ry
cre-ma-to-ri-um
cre-o-sote
crepe

creped
crep-ing
cre-pus-cu-lar
cres-cen-do
cres-cent
crest
crest-ed
crest-less
crest-fall-en
cre-tin-ism
cre-tonne
crev-ice
crew-el
crib
cribbed
crib-bing
crib-ber
crib-bage
crick-et
crim-i-nal
crim-i-nal-i-ty
crim-i-nal-ly
crim-i-nol-o-gy
crim-i-nol-o-gist
crimpy
crimp-i-er
crimp-i-est
crim-son
cringe
cringed
cring-ing
crin-kle
crin-kled
crin-kli-est
crip-ple
crip-pled
crip-pling
cri-sis
cri-ses
criss-cross
cri-te-ri-on
cri-te-ria
crit-ic
crit-i-cal
crit-i-cal-ly
crit-i-cal-ness
crit-i-cism
crit-i-cize
crit-i-cized
crit-i-ciz-ing
crit-i-ciz-a-ble

cri-tique
crit-er
croak-y
croak-i-er
croak-i-est
crois-sant
cro-ny
cro-nies
crook-ed
croon-er
crop
cropped
crop-ping
crop-per
cro-quette
cross-bar
cross-bow
cross-bred
cross-breed
cross-breed-ing
cross-coun-try
cross-cut
cross-ex-am-ine
cross-ex-am-ined
cross-ex-am-in-ing
cross-ing
cross-pol-li-nate
cross-pur-pose
cross-ref-er-ence
cross-stitch
cross-ways
crotch-ety
crotch-et-i-ness
crouch
croup
croupy
crou-pi-er
crou-ton
crow-bar
crow's--foot
crow's--feet
crow's--nest
cru-cial
cru-ci-al-i-ty
cru-cial-ly
cru-ci-ble
cru-ci-fix
cru-ci-fix-ion
cru-ci-form
cru-ci-fy
cru-ci-fied

cru-ci-fy-ing
crude
crud-er
crud-est
crude-ly
crude-ness
cru-di-ty
cru-di-ties
cru-el
cru-el-ly
cru-et
cruise
cruised
cruis-ing
cruis-er
crul-ler
crum-ble
crum-bled
crum-bling
crum-bly
crunchy
crunch-i-er
crunch-i-est
cru-sade
cru-sad-er
crush-er
crush-ing
crush-ing-ly
crus-ta-cean
crust-y
crust-i-er
cry
cried
cry-ing
cry-ba-by
cry-o-gen-ics
cry-o-sur-gery
crypt
crypt-al
crypt-a-nal-y-sis
crypt-ic
cryp-ti-cal
cryp-ti-cal-ly
cryp-to-gram
cryp-to-graph
cryp-tog-ra-phy
cryp-to-graph-ic
cryp-tog-ra-pher
crys-tal
crys-tal-line
crys-tal-lize

crys-tal-lized
crys-tal-liz-ing
crys-tal-liz-er
crys-tal-liz-a-ble
crys-tal-li-za-tion
cub-by
cub-bies
cu-bic
cu-bi-cle
cu-bit
cuck-old
cuck-old-ry
cudg-el
cudg-eled
cudg-el-ing
cui-sine
cul-de-sac
culs-de-sac
cu-li-nary
cul-mi-nant
cul-mi-nate
cul-mi-nat-ed
cul-mi-nat-ing
cul-mi-na-tion
cu-lottes
cul-pa-ble
cul-pa-bil-i-ty
cul-pa-bly
cul-prit
cult
cul-tic
cul-ti-vate
cul-ti-vat-ed
cul-ti-vat-ing
cul-ti-va-tion
cul-ti-va-ble
cul-ti-vat-a-ble
cul-ti-va-tor
cul-tur-al
cul-ture
cul-tured
cul-tur-ing
cul-vert
cum-ber
cum-ber-some
cum-brance
cum lau-de
cum-mer-bound
cum-mu-late
cum-mu-lat-ed
cum-mu-lat-ing

cum-mu-la-tion
cum-mu-la-tive
cu-ne-i-form
cum-ni-lin-gus
cun-ning
cun-ning-ly
cup-board
cup-ful
cup-fuls
cu-pid-i-ty
cu-po-la
cur-a-ble
cur-a-bil-i-ty
cur-a-bly
cu-rate
cur-a-tive
cu-ra-tor
cu-ra-to-ri-al
cu-ra-tor-ship
curb-ing
curb-stone
cur-dle
cur-dled
cur-dling
cure
cured
cur-ing
cure-all
cur-few
cu-ria
cu-ri-ae
cu-ri-al
cu-rie
cu-ri-o
cu-ri-os
cu-ri-os-i-ty
cu-ri-os-i-ties
cu-ri-ous
cu-ri-um
curl
curl-er
curl-i-cue
curly
curl-i-er
curl-i-est
cur-rant
cur-ren-cy
cur-ren-cies
cur-rent
cur-ric-u-lum
cur-ric-u-lums

cur-ric-u-la
cur-ri-c-u-lar
cur-rish
cur-ry
cur-ries
cur-ri-er
cur-ry-comb
curse
cur-sive
cur-sive-ly
curt
cur-tail
cur-tail-ment
cur-tain
curt-sy
curt-sies
curt-sied
curt-sy-ing
cur-va-ceous
cur-va-ture
curve
cruved
curv-ing
curv-ed-nesss
cur-vi-lin-e-ar
cush-ion
cush-y
cush-i-er
cush-i-est
cus-pid
cus-pi-dal
cus-pi-date
cus-pi-dor
cuss-ed
cuss-ed-ly
cuss-ed-ness
cus-tard
cus-to-dian
cus-to-di-an-ship
cus-to-dy
cus-to-dies
cus-to-di-al
cus-tom
cus-tom-ary
cus-tom-ar-ies
cus-tom-ar-i-ly
cus-tom-ar-i-ness
cus-tom-built
cus-tom-er
cus-tom-ize
cus-tom-ized

cus-tom-iz-ing
cus-tom-made
cu-ta-ne-ous
cu-ti-cle
cut-lery
cut-let
cut-ting
cut-ting-ly
cut-tle
cut-up
cy-an-ic
cy-cle
cy-clic
cy-cli-cal
cy-cli-cal-ly
cy-clom-e-ter
cy-clone
cy-clo-rama
cy-clo-ram-ic
cy-clo-tron
cyg-net
cyl-in-der
cy-lin-dric
cy-lin-dri-cal
cym-bal
cym-bal-ist
cyn-ic
cyn-i-cism
cyn-i-cal
cyn-i-cal-ly
cy-no-sure
cy-pher
cy-press
cyst
cys-tic
cys-tic fi-bro-sis
cy-tol-o-gy
cy-tol-o-gist
czar
czar-e-vitch
cza-ri-na

D

dab
dabbed
dab-bing
dab-ble
dab-bled
dab-bing
dab-bler

dac-tyl
dac-tyl-ic
dad-dy--long-legs
daf-fo-dil
daf-fy
daf-fi-er
daf-fi-est
dag-ger
da-guerre-o-type
dahl-ia
dai-ly
dai-lies
dain-ty
dain-ti-er
dain-ti-est
dain-ties
dain-ti-ly
dai-qui-ri
dair-y
dair-ies
dair-y-man
dair-y-men
da-is
dai-sy
dai-sies
dal-ly
dal-lied
dal-ly-ing
dal-li-ance
dam-age
dam-aged
dam-ag-ing
dam-age-a-ble
dam-a-scene
dam-a-scened
dam-a-scen-ing
dam-ask
damn
dam-na-ble
dam-na-ble-ness
dam-na-bly
dam-na-tion
damned
damp-en
damp-er
dam-sel
dam-son
dan-de-li-on
dan-der
dan-dle
dan-dled

dan-dling
dan-druff
dan-dy
dan-dies
dan-di-er
dan-di-est
dan-dy-ism
dan-ger
dan-ger-ous
dan-ger-ous-ly
dan-gle
dan-gled
dan-gling
dan-gler
dank
dank-ly
dank-ness
dan-seuse
dan-seus-es
dap-per
dap-ple
dap-pled
dap-pling
dare
dared
dar-ing
dare-dev-il
dar-ing-ly
dark
dark-ish
dark-ly
dark-en
dark-ling
dark-room
dar-ling
dar-ling-ly
darn-er
dart-er
dash-board
dash-ing
das-tard
das-tard-li-ness
das-tard-ly
da-ta
date
dat-ed
dat-ing
dat-a-ble
dat-er
date-less
date-line

da-tive
da-tum
daub
daub-er
daugh-ter
daugh-ter-ly
daugh-ter--in--law
daugh-ters--in--law
daunt-less
daunt-less-ly
daunt-less-ness
dau-phin
dav-en-port
dav-it
daw-dle
daw-dled
daw-dling
daw-dler
dawn
day-break
day-dream
day-dream-er
day-light
day-time
daze
dazed
daz-ing
daz-ed-ly
daz-zle
daz-zled
dea-con
dea-con-ry
dea-con-ship
dea-con-ess
dead-beat
dead-en
dead-en-er
dead-end
dead-line
dead-lock
dead-ly
dead-li-er
dead-li-est
dead-li-ness
dead-pan
dead-wood
deaf
deaf-ly
deaf-ness
deaf-en
deaf-en-ing-ly

deaf-mute
deal
dealt
deal-ing
deal-er
dean-ship
dear
dear-ly
dearth
death
death-less
death-ly
death-blow
death-trap
death-watch
de-ba-cle
de-bar
de-barred
de-bar-ring
de-bar-ment
de-bark
de-bar-ka-tion
de-base
de-based
de-bas-ing
de-base-ment
de-bas-er
de-bate
de-bat-ed
de-bat-ing
de-bat-a-ble
de-bat-er
de-bauch
de-bauch-er
de-bauch-ment
de-bauch-ery
de-bauch-er-ies
deb-au-chee
de-ben-ture
de-bil-i-tate
de-bil-i-tat-ed
de-bil-i-tat-ing
de-bil-i-ta-tion
de-bil-i-ty
de-bil-i-ties
deb-it
deb-o-nair
de-bris
debt-or
de-bunk
de-bunk-er

de-but
deb-u-tante
de-cade
dec-a-dent
dec-a-dence
dec-a-dent-ly
dec-a-gon
dec-a-gram
dec-a-he-dron
dec-a-he-drons
de-cal
de-camp
de-camp-ment
de-cant
de-cant-er
de-cap-i-tate
de-cap-i-tat-ed
de-cap-i-tat-ing
de-cap-i-ta-tion
dec-a-pod
de-cath-lon
de-cay
de-crease
de-creased
de-ceit
de-ceit-ful
de-ceit-ful-ly
de-ceit-ful-ness
de-ceive
de-ceived
de-ceiv-ing
de-ceiv-er
de-ceiv-ing-ly
de-ceiv-a-ble
de-cel-er-ate
de-cel-er-at-ed
de-cel-er-at-ing
de-cel-er-a-tion
de-cen-cy
de-cen-cies
de-cen-ni-al
de-cen-ni-al-ly
de-cent
de-cent-ly
de-cen-tral-ize
de-cen-tral-ized
de-cen-tral-iz-ing
de-cep-tion
de-cep-tive
de-cep-tive-ly
de-cep-tive-ness

dec-i-bel
de-cide
 de-cid-ed
 de-cid-ing
 de-cid-a-ble
 de-cid-ed-ly
de-cid-u-ous
 de-cid-u-ous-ly
dec-i-mal
dec-i-mate
 dec-i-mat-ed
 dec-i-mat-ing
 dec-i-ma-tion
de-ci-pher
 de-ci-pher-a-ble
de-ci-sion
de-ci-sive
 de-ci-sive-ly
 de-ci-sive-ness
deck-le edge
de-claim
 dec-la-ma-tion
 de-clam-a-tory
de-clas-si-fy
 de-clas-si-fied
 de-clas-si-fy-ing
de-clen-sion
dec-li-na-tion
de-cline
 de-clined
 de-clin-ing
 de-clin-a-ble
de-cliv-i-ty
 de-cliv-i-ties
de-code
 de-cod-ed
 de-cod-ing
 de-cod-er
de-com-pose
 de-com-posed
 de-com-pos-ing
 de-com-po-si-tion
de-com-press
 de-com-pres-sion
de-con-tam-i-nate
de-con-trol
 de-con-trolled
 de-con-trol-ling
de-cor
dec-o-rate
 dec-o-rat-ed

dec-o-rat-ing
dec-o-ra-tion
dec-o-ra-tive
dec-o-ra-tive-ly
dec-o-ra-tor
dec-o-rous
 dec-o-rous-ly
de-co-rum
de-coy
de-crease
 de-creased
 de-creas-ing
 de-creas-ing-ly
de-cree
 de-creed
 de-cree-ing
de-crep-it
 de-crep-i-tude
 de-crep-it-ly
de-cre-scen-do
 de-cre-scen-dos
de-cry
 de-cried
 de-cry-ing
 de-cri-al
ded-i-cate
 ded-i-cat-ed
 ded-i-cat-ing
 ded-i-ca-to-ry
 ded-i-ca-tive
 ded-i-ca-tion
de-duce
 de-duc-i-ble
de-duct
 de-duct-i-ble
de-duc-tion
 de-duc-tive
 de-duc-tive-ly
deep
 deep-ly
 deep-ness
deep-en
deep-root-ed
deep-seat-ed
deer-skin
de-es-ca-late
 de-es-ca-lat-ed
 de-es-ca-lat-ing
 de-es-ca-la-tion
de-face
 de-faced

de-fac-ing
de-face-ment
de-fac-er
de fac-to
de-fame
 de-famed
 de-fam-ing
 def-a-ma-tion
 de-fam-a-to-ry
 de-fam-er
de-fault
 de-fault-er
de-feat
de-feat-ism
 de-feat-ist
def-e-cate
 def-e-cat-ed
 def-e-cat-ing
 def-e-ca-tion
de-fect
de-fec-tion
 de-fec-tor
de-fec-tive
 de-fec-tive-ly
 de-fec-tive-ness
de-fend
 de-fend-er
de-fend-ant
de-fense
 de-fense-less
 de-fense-less-ly
 de-fense-less-ness
 de-fen-si-ble
 de-fen-si-bil-i-ty
 de-fen-si-bly
de-fen-sive
 de-fen-sive-ly
de-fer
 de-ferred
 de-fer-ring
 de-fer-ment
def-er-ence
 def-er-en-tial
 def-er-en-tial-ly
de-fi-ance
 de-fi-ant
 de-fi-ant-ly
de-fi-cient
 de-fi-cien-cy
 de-fi-cien-cies
 de-fi-cient-ly

def-i-cit
de-file
 de-filed
 de-fil-ing
de-fine
 de-fined
 de-fin-ing
 de-fin-er
 de-fin-a-ble
 de-fin-a-bly
def-i-nite
 def-i-nite-ly
 def-i-nite-ness
def-i-ni-tion
de-fin-i-tive
 de-fin-i-tive-ly
de-flate
 de-flat-ed
 de-flat-ing
 de-fla-tion
 de-fla-tion-ary
de-flect
 de-flec-tion
 de-flec-tive
 de-flec-tor
de-flow-er
de-fo-li-ate
 de-fo-li-at-ed
 de-fo-li-at-ing
de-for-est
 de-for-est-a-tion
de-form
 de-for-ma-tion
 de-formed
de-form-i-ty
 de-form-i-ties
de-fraud
de-fray
 de-fray-al
 de-fray-ment
 de-fray-a-ble
de-frost
 de-frost-er
deft
 deft-ly
 deft-ness
de-funct
de-fy
 de-fied
 de-fy-ing
 de-fi-er

de-gen-er-ate
de-gen-er-at-ed
de-gen-er-at-ing
de-gen-er-ate-ly
de-gen-er-a-cy
de-gen-er-a-tion
de-gen-er-a-tive
de-grade
de-graded
de-grad-ing
deg-ra-da-tion
de-gree
de-his-cence
de-his-cent
de-hy-drate
de-hy-drat-ed
de-hy-drat-ing
de-hy-dra-tion
de-i-fy
de-i-fied
de-i-fy-ing
de-i-fi-ca-tion
de-i-fi-er
deign
de-ist
de-ism
de-is-tic
de-is-ti-cal
de-i-ty
de-i-ties
de-ject-ed
de-jec-ted-ly
de-jec-tion
de ju-re
de-lay
de-lay-er
de-lec-ta-ble
de-lec-ta-ble-ness
de-lec-ta-bly
de-lec-ta-tion
del-e-gate
del-e-gat-ed
del-e-gat-ing
del-e-ga-tion
de-lete
de-let-ed
de-let-ing
de-le-tion
del-e-te-ri-ous
de-lib-er-ate
de-lib-er-at-ed

de-lib-er-at-ing
de-lib-er-ate-ly
de-lib-er-ate-ness
de-lib-er-a-tion
de-lib-er-a-tive
de-lib-er-a-tor
del-i-ca-cy
del-i-ca-cies
del-i-cate
del-i-cate-ly
del-i-cate-ness
del-i-ca-tes-sen
de-li-cious
de-li-cious-ly
de-li-cious-ness
de-lim-it
de-lim-i-ta-tion
de-lin-e-ate
de-lin-e-at-ed
de-lin-e-at-ing
de-lin-e-a-tion
de-lin-e-a-tor
de-lin-quent
de-lin-quen-cy
de-lin-quen-cies
de-lir-i-um
de-lir-i-ums
de-lir-ia
de-lir-i-ous
de-lir-i-ous-ly
de-liv-er
de-liv-er-a-ble
de-liv-er-er
de-liv-er-ance
de-liv-ery
de-liv-er-ies
de-louse
de-loused
de-lous-ing
del-phin-i-um
del-ta
del-toid
de-lude
de-lud-ed
de-lud-ing
de-lud-er
de-lu-sive
de-lu-so-ry
de-lu-sive-ly
del-uge
del-uged

del-ug-ing
de-lu-sion
de-luxe
delve
delved
delv-ing
dem-a-gogue
dem-a-gogu-ery
dem-a-gog-ic
dem-a-gog-i-cal
de-mand
de-mand-er
de-mar-ca-tion
de-mean
de-mean-or
de-ment-ed
de-men-tia
de-mer-it
dem-i-god
de-mise
de-mised
de-mis-ing
dem-i-tasse
de-mo-bi-lize
de-mo-bi-lized
de-mo-bi-liz-ing
de-mo-bi-li-za-tion
de-moc-ra-cy
de-moc-ra-cies
dem-o-crat
dem-o-crat-ic
dem-o-crat-i-cal-ly
de-moc-ra-tize
de-moc-ra-tized
de-moc-ra-tiz-ing
de-mog-ra-phy
de-mog-ra-pher
dem-o-graph-ic
de-mol-ish
de-mol-ish-er
dem-o-li-tion
de-mon
de-mon-ic
de-mon-e-tize
de-mon-e-tized
de-mon-e-tiz-ing
de-mon-e-ti-za-tion
de-mo-ni-ac
de-mo-ni-a-cal
de-mon-ol-o-gy
de-mon-ol-o-gist

dem-on-strate
dem-on-strat-ed
dem-on-strat-ing
de-mon-stra-ble
de-mon-stra-bly
dem-on-stra-tion
de-mon-stra-tive
de-mon-stra-tive-ly
dem-on-stra-tor
de-mor-al-ize
de-mor-al-ized
de-mor-al-iz-ing
de-mor-al-i-za-tion
de-mor-al-iz-er
de-mote
de-mot-ed
de-mot-ing
de-mo-tion
de-mur
de-murred
de-mur-ring
de-mur-ral
de-mur-er
de-mur-est
de-mure-ly
de-mure-ness
de-mur-rage
de-nat-u-ral-ize
de-nat-u-ral-ized
de-nat-u-ral-iz-ing
de-na-ture
de-na-tured
de-na-tur-ing
den-drite
den-dro-lite
den-drol-o-gy
den-e-ga-tion
de-ni-al
de-ni-er
den-im
den-i-zen
de-nom-i-nate
de-nom-i-nat-ed
de-nom-i-nat-ing
de-nom-i-na-tion
de-nom-i-na-tive
de-nom-i-na-tor
de-note
de-not-ed
de-not-ing
de-no-ta-tion

de-noue-ment
de-nounce
dense
den-si-ty
 den-si-ties
den-tal
den-tate
den-ti-frice
den-tin
den-tist
den-tist-ry
den-ti-tion
den-ture
de-nude
 de-nud-ed
 de-nud-ing
 den-u-da-tion
de-nun-ci-ate
 de-nun-ci-at-ed
 de-nun-ci-at-ing
 de-nun-ci-a-tion
 de-nun-ci-a-to-ry
de-ny
 de-nied
 de-ny-ing
de-o-dor-ant
 de-o-dor-ize
 de-o-dor-ized
 de-o-dor-iz-ing
de-part
de-part-ed
de-part-ment
 de-part-men-tal
de-par-ture
de-pend
 de-pend-ence
de-pend-a-ble
 de-pend-a-bly
 de-pend-a-bil-i-ty
de-pend-en-cy
 de-pend-en-cies
de-pend-ent
de-pict
 de-pic-tion
de-plete
 de-plet-ed
 de-plet-ing
de-plor-a-ble
 de-plor-a-bly
de-plore
 de-plored

de-plor-ing
de-ploy
 de-ploy-ment
de-po-nent
de-pop-u-late
 de-pop-u-lat-ed
 de-pop-u-la-tion
de-port
 de-por-ta-tion
de-port-ment
de-pose
 de-posed
 de-pos-ing
 de-pos-a-ble
de-pos-it
 de-pos-i-tor
dep-o-si-tion
de-pos-i-to-ry
7de-pot
de-prave
 de-praved
 de-prav-ing
 de-prav-i-ty
dep-re-cate
 dep-re-cat-ed
 dep-re-cat-ing
 dep-re-cat-ing-ly
 dep-re-ca-tion
 dep-re-ca-to-ry
de-pre-ci-ate
 de-pre-ci-at-ed
 de-pre-ci-at-ing
 de-pre-ci-a-tion
 de-pre-ci-a-to-ry
 de-pre-ci-a-tor
dep-re-date
 dep-re-dat-ed
 dep-re-dat-ing
 dep-re-da-tion
de-press
de-pres-sant
de-pressed
de-pres-sion
de-prive
 de-prived
 de-priv-ing
 dep-ri-va-tion
depth
de-pute
 de-put-ed
 de-put-ing

dep-u-tize
 dep-u-tized
dep-u-ty
 dep-u-ties
de-rail
 de-rail-ment
de-range
 de-ranged
 de-rang-ing
 de-range-ment
der-e-lict
 der-e-lic-tion
de-ride
 de-rid-ed
 de-rid-ing
de-ri-sion
de-ri-sive
 de-ri-sive-ly
 de-ri-so-ry
der-i-va-tion
de-riv-a-tive
de-rive
 de-rived
 de-riv-ing
 de-riv-a-ble
der-ma
 der-mal
der-ma-tol-o-gy
 der-ma-to-log-i-cal
 der-ma-tol-o-gist
der-mis
der-o-gate
 der-o-gat-ed
 der-o-gat-ing
 der-o-ga-tion
de-rog-a-to-ry
 de-rog-a-to-ri-ly
der-rick
der-rin-ger
der-vish
des-cant
de-scend
 de-scend-a-ble
de-scend-ant
de-scent
de-scribe
 de-scribed
 de-scrib-ing
 de-scriba-ble
 de-scrib-er
de-scrip-tion

de-scrip-tive
 de-scrip-tive-ly
 de-scrip-tive-ness
de-scry
des-e-crate
 des-e-crat-ed
 des-e-crat-ing
 des-e-cra-tion
de-seg-re-gate
 de-seg-re-gat-ed
 de-seg-re-gat-ing
des-ert
de-sert
 de-sert-er
 de-ser-tion
des-ha-bille
des-ic-cate
 des-ic-cat-ed
 des-ic-cat-ing
 des-ic-ca-tion
 des-ic-ca-tive
de-sid-er-a-tum
de-sign
des-ig-nate
 des-ig-nat-ed
 des-ig-nat-ing
 des-ig-na-tion
 des-ig-na-tive
 des-ig-na-tor
de-sign-ed-ly
de-sign-er
de-sign-ing
de-sire
 de-sired
 de-sir-ing
 de-sir-a-ble
 de-sir-a-bil-i-ty
 de-sir-a-bly
 de-sir-ous
de-sist
des-o-late
 des-o-lat-ed
 des-o-lat-ing
 des-o-late-ly
 des-o-la-tion
de-spair
 de-spair-ing
 de-spair-ing-ly
des-per-a-do
 des-per-a-does
des-per-ate

des-per-ate-ly
des-per-ate-ness
des-per-a-tion
des-pi-ca-ble
des-pi-ca-bly
de-spise
de-spised
de-spis-ing
de-spite
de-spoil
de-spoil-er
de-spo-li-a-tion
de-spond
de-spond-en-cy
de-spond-ence
de-spond-ent
de-spond-ent-ly
des-pot
des-pot-ic
des-pot-i-cal-ly
des-pot-ism
des-sert
des-ti-na-tion
des-tine
des-tined
des-tin-ing
des-ti-ny
des-ti-nies
des-ti-tute
des-ti-tu-tion
de-stroy
de-stroy-er
de-struc-tion
de-struct-i-ble
de-struct-i-bil-i-ty
de-struc-tive
de-struc-tive-ly
de-struc-tive-ness
des-ue-tude
des-ul-to-ry
des-ul-to-ri-ly
de-tach
de-tach-a-ble
de-tached
de-tach-ment
de-tail
de-tailed
de-tain
de-tain-ment
de-tain-er
de-tect

de-tect-a-ble
de-tec-tion
de-tec-tive
de-tec-tor
de-ten-tion
de-ter
de-terred
de-ter-ring
de-ter-gent
de-te-ri-o-rate
de-te-ri-o-rat-ed
de-te-ri-o-rat-ing
de-te-ri-o-ra-tion
de-ter-mi-na-ble
de-ter-mi-nant
de-ter-ni-nate
de-ter-mi-na-tion
de-ter-mi-na-tive
de-ter-mine
de-ter-mined
de-ter-min-ing
de-ter-min-er
de-ter-mined
de-ter-mined-ly
de-ter-min-ism
de-ter-min-ist
de-ter-rent
de-ter-rence
de-test
de-tes-ta-tion
de-throne
de-throned
de-tour
de-tract
de-trac-tion
de-trac-tor
det-ri-ment
det-ri-men-tal
det-ri-men-tal-ly
de-tri-tus
deuce
deu-te-ri-um
de-val-u-ate
de-val-u-at-ed
de-val-u-at-ing
de-val-u-a-tion
dev-as-tate
dev-as-tat-ed
dev-as-tat-ing
dev-as-ta-tion
de-vel-op

de-vel-op-ment
de-vel-op-er
de-vi-ate
de-vi-at-ed
de-vi-at-ing
de-vi-ant
de-vi-a-tion
de-vice
de-vi-ous
de-vi-ous-ly
de-vise
de-vised
de-vis-ing
de-vis-a-ble
de-vis-al
de-vi-see
de-vi-sor
de-void
de-volve
de-volved
de-volv-ing
dev-o-lu-tion
de-vote
de-vot-ing
de-vot-ed
de-vot-ed-ly
dev-o-tee
de-vo-tion
de-vo-tion-al
de-vour
de-vour-er
de-vour-ing-ly
de-vout
de-vout-ly
de-vout-ness
dew-drop
dew-lap
dewy
dew-i-er
dew-i-est
dew-y-eyed
dex-ter-ous
dex-ter-ous-ly
dex-trose
di-a-be-tes
di-a-bet-ic
di-a-bol-ic
di-a-bol-i-cal
di-a-bol-i-cal-ly
di-a-crit-ic
di-a-crit-i-cal

di-a-crit-i-cal-ly
di-a-dem
di-ag-nose
di-ag-nosed
di-ag-nos-ing
di-ag-no-sis
di-ag-no-ses
di-ag-nos-tic
di-ag-nos-ti-cian
di-ag-o-nal
di-ag-o-nal-ly
di-a-gram
di-a-gramed
di-a-gram-ing
di-a-gram-mat-ic
di-a-gram-mat-i-cal
di-al
di-aled
di-al-ing
di-a-lect
di-a-lec-tal
di-a-lec-tic
di-a-lec-ti-cal
di-a-lec-ti-cian
di-a-logue
di-am-e-ter
di-a-met-ric
di-a-met-ric-al
di-a-met-ric-al-ly
dia-mond
dia-per
di-aph-a-nous
di-a-phragm
di-ar-rhea
di-a-ry
di-as-to-le
di-as-tol-ic
di-a-ther-mic
di-a-tom
di-a-ton-ic
dib-ble
dib-bled
dib-bling
di-chot-o-my
di-chot-o-mous
di-cho-tom-ic
dic-tate
dic-ta-tion
dic-ta-tor
dic-ta-to-ri-al
dic-ta-to-ri-al-ly

dic-tion-ary
dic-tum
di-dac-tic
di-dac-ti-cally
di-er-e-ses
di-e-tary
di-e-tet-ic
di-e-tet-i-cal
di-e-tet-i-cal-ly
di-e-tet-ics
di-e-ti-cian
dif-fer-ence
dif-fer-enced
dif-fer-en-cing
dif-fer-ent
dif-fer-ent-ly
dif-fer-en-tial
dif-fer-en-tial-ly
dif-fer-en-ti-ate
dif-fer-en-ti-at-ed
dif-fi-cult
dif-fi-cult-ly
dif-fi-dence
dif-fi-dent
dif-fi-dent-ly
dig-ger
dig-gings
dig-it-al
dig-i-tal-is
dig-ni-fied
dig-ni-fy
dig-ni-fy-ing
dig-ni-tary
dig-ni-tar-ies
dig-ni-ty
di-gress
di-gres-sion
di-gres-sive
di-he-dral
di-lap-i-dat-ed
di-lap-i-da-tion
dil-a-ta-tion
di-late
di-lat-ed
di-lat-ing
di-lat-a-ble
di-la-tion
dil-a-to-ry
dil-a-to-ri-ly
di-lem-ma
dil-et-tan-te

dil-et-tan-tes
dil-i-gence
dil-i-gent
dil-i-gent-ly
dil-ly-dal-ly
di-lute
di-lut-ed
di-lut-ing
di-men-sion
di-men-sion-al
di-min-ish
di-min-ish-a-ble
di-min-u-en-do
di-min-u-en-dos
dim-i-nu-tion
di-min-u-tive
di-min-u-tive-ness
dim-ple
dim-pled
dim-pling
din-er
di-nette
din-ghy
din-ghies
din-ner
di-no-saur
di-o-cese
di-oc-e-san
di-o-ram-a
diph-the-ri-a
di-plo-ma
di-plo-ma-cy
di-plo-ma-cies
dip-lo-mat
dip-lo-mat-ic
dip-lo-mat-i-cal-ly
dip-per
dip-so-ma-nia
dip-so-ma-ni-ac
di-rect
di-rect-ness
di-rec-tion
di-rec-tion-al
di-rec-tive
di-rect-ly
di-rec-tor
di-rec-to-ri-al
di-rec-tor-ship
di-rec-to-rate
di-rec-to-ry

di-rec-to-ries
dis-a-buse
dis-a-bused
dis-a-bus-ing
dis-ad-van-tage
dis-ad-van-taged
dis-af-fect
dis-af-fec-tion
dis-af-fect-ed
dis-a-gree
dis-a-gree-ing
dis-a-gree-a-ble
dis-a-gree-ment
dis-al-low
dis-al-low-ance
dis-ap-pear
dis-ap-pear-ance
dis-ap-point
dis-ap-point-ment
dis-ap-pro-ba-tion
dis-ap-prove
dis-ap-prov-al
dis-arm
dis-ar-ma-ment
dis-ar-range
dis-ar-ranged
dis-ar-rang-ing
dis-ar-ray
dis-as-sem-ble
dis-as-ter
dis-as-trous
dis-as-trous-ly
dis-a-vow
dis-a-vow-al
dis-band
dis-band-ment
dis-be-lieve
dis-be-lief
dis-be-liev-er
dis-burse
dis-bursed
dis-burs-ing
dis-burs-er
dis-cern-ing
dis-cern-ment
dis-charge
dis-charged
dis-charg-ing
dis-char-ger
dis-ci-ple

dis-ci-ple-ship
dis-ci-pline
dis-ci-plines
dis-ci-pli-nary
dis-claim-er
dis-close
dis-closed
dis-clos-er
dis-clo-sure
dis-coid
dis-col-or
dis-col-or-a-tion
dis-com-fit
dis-com-fi-ture
dis-com-fort
dis-com-mode
dis-com-mod-ing
dis-com-pose
dis-com-posed
dis-com-pos-ing
dis-con-cert
dis-con-cert-ed
dis-con-nect
dis-con-nec-tion
dis-con-so-late
dis-con-tent
dis-con-tent-ed
dis-con-tin-ue
dis-con-tin-ued
dis-con-tin-u-ing
dis-con-tin-u-ous
dis-cord
dis-cord-ance
dis-count
dis-cour-age
dis-cour-ag-ing
dis-course
dis-coursed
dis-cours-ing
dis-cour-te-ous
dis-cour-te-sy
dis-cov-er
dis-cov-er-a-ble
dis-cov-er-er
dis-cov-er-y
dis-cov-er-ies
dis-cred-it
dis-cred-it-a-bly
dis-creet
dis-crep-an-cy

dis-crep-an-cies
dis-crete
dis-cre-tion
dis-cre-tion-ary
dis-crim-i-nate
dis-crim-i-nate-ly
dis-crim-i-na-tor
dis-cur-sive
dis-cur-sive-ly
dis-cur-sive-ness
dis-cus
dis-cus-es
dis-cuss
dis-cus-sion
dis-dain
dis-dain-ful
dis-dain-ful-ly
dis-ease
dis-eased
dis-em-bark
dis-em-body
dis-em-bod-ied
dis-em-bod-y-ing
dis-en-chant
dis-en-cum-ber
dis-en-fran-chise
dis-en-gage
dis-en-gaged
dis-en-gag-ing
dis-en-tan-gle
dis-en-tan-gled
dis-en-tan-gling
dis-es-tab-lish
dis-fa-vor
dis-fig-ure
dis-fig-ured
dis-fig-ur-ing
dis-fig-ure-ment
dis-gorge
dis-gorged
dis-gorg-ing
dis-grace
dis-graced
dis-grac-ing
dis-grace-ful
dis-grace-ful-ly
dis-gust
dis-gust-ed
dis-gust-ing
dis-ha-bille

dis-har-mo-ny
dis-heart-en
dis-hev-eled
dis-hon-est
dis-hon-est-ly
dis-hon-es-ties
dis-hon-or
dis-hon-or-a-ble
dis-il-lu-sion
dis-in-cline
dis-in-clined
dis-in-fect
dis-in-her-it
dis-in-te-grate
dis-in-ter-es-ted
dis-junc-tion
dis-loy-al
dis-loy-al-ty
dis-o-be-di-ence
dis-or-der-ly
dis-o-ri-ent
dis-pos-a-ble
dis-qual-i-fy
dis-qui-et
dis-re-spect
dis-re-spect-ful
dis-rup-tive
dis-sat-is-fy
dis-sat-is-fy-ing
dis-sem-blance
dis-sem-i-nate
dis-sem-i-nat-ing
dis-sem-i-na-tor
dis-sent
dis-ser-tate
dis-ser-ta-ting
dis-serv-ice
dis-si-dent
dis-sim-i-lar
dis-sim-i-lar-i-ty
dis-sim-i-late
dis-si-pate
dis-so-nance
dis-so-nant
dis-suade
dis-tance
dis-tem-per
dis-til-late
dis-till-ery
dis-tin-guish
dis-tract

dis-tract-ing
dis-trib-ute
dis-trib-ut-ed
dis-tri-bu-tion
dis-tri-u-tor
dis-u-nite
di-van
di-verge
di-ver-gence
di-ver-gent
di-verse
di-ver-sion
div-i-dend
di-vi-sor
di-vulge
do-a-ble
doc-tor-ate
doc-u-ment
dod-der
dog-ma
dog-mat-ic
dol-drums
dol-or-ous
dol-phin
do-mes-tic
do-mes-ti-cate
dom-i-cile
dom-i-nance
dom-i-nant
dom-i-neer
do-min-ion
dor-mant
dor-mer
dor-mi-to-ry
dos-age
dos-si-er
dou-ble-faced
douche
dow-el
down-ward-ly
doz-ing
doz-en
drag-on
dra-per-y
drib-ble
drill-ing
dri-ly
driv-el
driz-zle
drom-e-dar-y
drop-per

dross
drought
drowned
drowse
drowsed
drows-ing
drow-si-ness
drudge
drug-gist
dru-id
drum-mer
drunk-ard
drunk-en
dry-ad
du-al
du-al-i-ty
du-al-ism
du-al-ist
du-al-is-tic
du-bi-ous
du-cal
duch-ess
duck-ling
dun-geon
du-nage
du-o-de-nal
du-pli-cate
du-pli-cat-ing
du-pli-ca-tor
du-plic-i-ty
du-ra-ble
du-ra-bil-ity
du-ra-bly
dur-ance
du-ra-tion
du-ti-a-ble
du-ti-ful
du-ti-ful-ly
dwarf
dwarf-ish
dwin-dle
dye-stuff
dy-ing
dy-nam-ic
dy-nam-i-cal
dy-nam-i-cal-ly
dy-na-mism
dy-na-mite
dyne
dys-en-tery
dys-func-tion

E

ea-ger
 ea-ger-ly
 ea-ger-ness
ea-gle
ea-gle eyed
ea-glet
earl-dom
ear-ly
 ear-li-er
 ear-li-est
ear-mark
ear-muff
earn
 earn-er
ear-nest
 ear-nest-ly
earn-ings
ear-ring
earth-en
earth-ly
 earth-li-er
 earth-li-est
earth-quake
earth-y
ear-wax
ease
 eased
 eas-ing
ea-sel
ease-ment
eas-i-ly
 eas-i-ness
east-er-ly
east-ern
east-ward
eas-y
 eas-i-er
 eas-i-est
eas-y-go-ing
eat
ebb
eb-on-y
 eb-on-ies
e-bul-lience
 e-bul-lient
 e-bul-li-tion
ec-cen-tric
 ec-cen-tri-cal-ly

ec-cen-tric-i-ty
 ec-cen-tric-i-ties
ec-cle-si-as-tic
 ec-cle-si-as-ti-cal
 ec-cle-si-as-ti-cal-ly
ech-e-lon
e-chi-no-derm
ech-o
e-cho-ic
e-clair
ec-lec-tic
 ec-lec-ti-cal-ly
 ec-lec-ti-cism
e-clipse
 e-clipsed
 e-clips-ing
e-clip-tic
e-col-o-gy
 e-c-o-log-ic
 e-c-o-log-i-cal
 e-col-o-gist
e-co-nom-ic
 e-co-nom-i-cal
 e-co-nom-ics
e-con-o-mist
e-con-o-mize
 e-con-o-mized
 e-con-o-miz-ing
 e-con-o-miz-er
e-con-o-my
 e-con-o-mies
ec-o-sys-tem
ec-ru
ec-sta-sy
 ec-sta-sies
ec-stat-ic
 ec-stat-i-cal
ec-to-morph
 ec-to-mor-phic
ec-to-plasm
ec-u-men-i-cal
ec-u-men-ic
 ec-u-men-i-cal-ly
 ec-u-men-ism
ec-ze-ma
e-de-ma
 e-de-ma-ta
e-den-tate
edg-y
ed-i-ble
e-dict

ed-i-fice
ed-i-fy
 ed-i-fied
 ed-i-fy-ing
 ed-i-fi-ca-tion
ed-it
e-di-tion
ed-i-tor
 ed-i-tor-ship
ed-i-to-ri-al
 ed-i-to-ri-al-ly
 ed-i-to-ri-al-ize
 ed-i-to-ri-al-lized
ed-u-cate
 ed-u-cat-ed
 ed-u-cat-ing
 ed-u-ca-ble
 ed-u-ca-tor
ed-u-ca-tion
 ed-u-ca-tion-al
e-duce
 e-duced
 e-duc-ing
 e-duc-i-ble
 e-duc-tion
eel
ee-rie
 ee-ri-er
 ee-ri-est
 ee-ri-ly
ef-fect
 ef-fec-tive
 ef-fec-tive-ness
 ef-fec-tive-ly
ef-fec-tu-al
 ef-fec-tu-al-i-ty
ef-fec-tu-ate
 ef-fec-tu-at-ed
 ef-fec-tu-at-ing
ef-fem-i-nate
 ef-fem-i-na-cy
 ef-fem-i-na-cies
 ef-fem-i-nate-ly
ef-fete
ef-fi-ca-cious
ef-fi-ca-cy
 ef-fi-ca-cies
ef-fi-cien-cy
 ef-fi-cien-cies
ef-fi-cient
 ef-fi-cient-ly

ef-fi-gy
 ef-fi-gies
ef-flo-resce
ef-flu-ent
 ef-flu-ence
ef-flu-vi-um
 ef-flu-via
 ef-flu-vi-ums
 ef-flu-vi-al
ef-fron-ter-y
 ef-fron-ter-ies
ef-ful-gent
 ef-ful-gence
ef-fuse
 ef-fused
 ef-fus-ing
ef-fu-sion
ef-fu-sive
 ef-fu-sive-ly
egal-i-tar-i-an
 egal-i-tar-i-an-ism
egg-nog
egg-plant
e-go
 e-gos
e-go-cen-tric
e-go-ism
 e-go-ist
 e-go-is-tic
 e-go-tism
e-go-tis-tic
 e-go-tis-ti-cal
e-gre-gious
 e-gre-gious-ly
e-gress
e-gret
ei-der-down
eight
 eighth
eight-ball
eight-fold
eight-y
 eight-ies
 eight-i-eth
ei-ther
e-jac-u-late
 e-jac-u-lat-ed
 e-jac-u-lat-ing
 e-jac-u-la-tion
e-ject
 e-jec-tion

e-ject-ment
e-jec-tor
eke
eked
ek-ing
e-lab-o-rate
e-lab-o-rat-ed
e-lab-o-rat-ing
e-lab-o-rate-ly
e-lab-o-ra-tion
e-lapse
e-lapsed
e-laps-ing
e-las-tic
e-las-ti-cal-ly
e-las-tic-i-ty
e-late
e-lat-ed
e-lat-ing
e-la-tion
el-bow
el-bow-room
el-der
eld-er-ship
el-der-ly
eld-er-li-ness
eld-est
e-lect
e-lec-tion
e-lec-tion-eer
e-lec-tive
e-lec-tor
e-lec-tor-ate
e-lec-tric
e-lec-tri-cal
e-lec-tri-cal-ly
e-lec-tri-cian
e-lec-tric-i-ty
e-lec-tri-fy
e-lec-tri-fied
e-lec-tri-fy-ing
e-lec-tri-fi-ca-tion
e-lec-tro-cute
e-lec-tro-cut-ed
e-lec-tro-cut-ing
e-lec-tro-cu-tion
e-lec-trode
e-lec-tro-dy-nam-ics
e-lec-trol-y-sis
e-lec-tro-lyze
e-lec-tro-lyzed
e-lec-tro-lyz-ing

e-lec-tro-lyte
e-lec-tro-lyt-ic
e-lec-tro-mag-net
e-lec-tro-mag-net-ism
e-lec-tro-mag-net-ic
e-lec-tron
e-lec-tron-ic
e-lec-tron-ics
e-lec-tron-i-cal-ly
e-lec-tro-plate
e-lec-tro-plat-ed
e-lec-tro-plat-ing
e-lec-tro-ther-a-py
e-lec-trum
el-ee-mos-y-nar-y
el-e-gant
el-e-gance
el-e-gan-cy
el-e-gant-ly
el-e-ment
el-e-men-tal
el-e-men-tal-ly
el-e-men-ta-ry
el-e-men-ta-ri-ly
el-e-phant
el-e-phan-tine
el-e-vate
el-e-vat-ed
el-e-vat-ing
el-e-va-tion
el-e-va-tor
e-lev-en
e-lev-enth
elf
e-lic-it
el-i-gi-ble
el-i-gi-bil-i-ty
el-i-gi-bly
e-lim-i-nate
e-lim-i-nat-ed
e-lim-i-nat-ing
e-lim-i-na-tion
e-lim-i-na-tor
e-lite
e-lit-ism
e-lit-ist
e-lix-ir
el-lipse
el-lip-sis
el-lip-ses
el-lip-ti-cal

el-lip-tic
el-lip-ti-cal-ly
el-o-cu-tion
el-o-cu-tion-ary
el-o-cu-tion-ist
e-lon-gate
e-lon-gat-ed
e-lon-gat-ing
e-lon-ga-tion
e-lope
el-o-quence
el-o-quent
el-o-quent-ly
else-where
e-lu-ci-date
e-lu-ci-dat-ed
e-lu-ci-dat-ing
e-lu-ci-da-tion
e-lu-ci-da-tor
e-lude
e-lud-ed
e-lud-ing
e-lu-sion
e-lu-sive
e-lu-sive-ly
elv-ish
e-ma-ci-ate
e-ma-ci-at-ed
e-ma-ci-at-ing
e-ma-ci-a-tion
em-a-nate
em-a-nat-ed
em-a-nat-ing
em-a-na-tion
e-man-ci-pate
e-man-ci-pat-ed
e-man-ci-pat-ing
e-man-ci-pa-tor
em-balm
em-balm-er
em-balm-ment
em-bank-ment
em-bar-go
em-bar-goes
em-bar-goed
em-bar-go-ing
em-bark
em-bar-ka-tion
em-bark-ment
em-bar-rass
em-bar-rass-ing-ly

em-bar-rass-ment
em-bas-sy
em-bas-sies
em-bat-tle
em-bat-tled
em-bat-tling
em-bat-tle-ment
em-bed
em-bed-ded
em-bed-ding
em-bel-lish
em-bel-lish-ment
em-ber
em-bez-zle
em-bez-zled
em-bez-zling
em-bez-zle-ment
em-bez-zler
em-bit-ter
em-bit-ter-ment
em-blem
em-blem-at-ic
em-blem-at-i-cal
em-bod-y
em-bod-ied
em-bod-y-ing
em-bod-i-ment
em-bold-en
em-bo-lism
em-bo-lus
em-bos-om
em-boss
em-boss-ment
em-bou-chure
em-brace
em-braced
em-brac-ing
em-broi-der
em-broi-dery
em-broi-der-ies
em-broil
em-broil-ment
em-bry-o
em-bry-os
em-bry-on-ic
em-bry-ol-o-gy
em-cee
em-ceed
em-cee-ing
e-mend
em-er-ald
e-merge

e-merged	em-pire	en-cap-su-lat-ing	en-dan-ger-ment
e-merg-ing	em-pir-i-cal	en-cap-sule	en-dear
e-mer-gence	em-pir-i-cal-ly	en-case	en-dear-ment
e-mer-gent	em-pir-i-cism	en-cased	en-dea-vor
e-mer-gen-cy	em-pir-i-cist	en-cas-ing	en-dem-ic
e-mer-gen-ies	em-place-ment	en-ceinte	en-dem-i-cal
e-mer-i-tus	em-ploy	en-ceph-a-li-tis	en-dem-i-cal-ly
em-er-y	em-ploy-a-ble	en-ceph-a-lit-ic	end-ing
e-met-ic	em-ploy-ee	en-ceph-a-lon	end-less
em-i-grant	em-ploy-er	en-ceph-a-la	end-less-ly
em-i-grate	em-ploy-ment	en-chant	end-most
em-i-grat-ed	em-por-i-um	en-chant-er	en-do-crine
em-i-grat-ing	em-po-ri-ums	en-chant-ress	en-do-cri-nol-o-gy
em-i-gra-tion	em-po-ria	en-chant-ing	en-do-crin-o-log-ic
em-i-nence	em-pow-er	en-chant-ing-ly	en-do-crin-o-log-i-ca
em-i-nent	em-press	en-chant-ment	en-do-cri-nol-o-gist
em-i-ent-ly	emp-ty	en-chi-la-da	en-dog-e-nous
em-i-nent do-main	emp-ti-er	en-cir-cle	en-do-sperm
em-is-sary	emp-ti-est	en-cir-cled	en-dow
em-is-sar-ies	emp-tied	en-cir-cling	en-dow-ment
e-mis-sion	emp-ty-ing	en-cir-cle-ment	en-due
e-mis-sive	emp-ti-ly	en-clave	en-dued
e-mit	emp-ti-ness	en-close	en-du-ing
e-mit-ted	emp-ty--hand-ed	en-closed	en-dur-ance
e-mit-ting	emp-ty--head-ed	en-clos-ing	en-dure
e-mit-ter	e-mu	en-clo-sure	en-dured
e-mol-lient	em-u-late	en-code	en-dur-ing
e-mol-u-ment	em-u-lat-ed	en-cod-ed	en-dur-a-ble
e-mote	em-u-lat-ing	en-cod-ing	en-dur-a-bly
e-mot-ed	em-u-la-tion	en-co-mi-ast	end-ways
e-mot-ing	e-mul-si-fy	en-com-pass	en-e-ma
e-mo-tive	e-mul-si-fied	en-com-pass-ment	en-e-my
emo-tion	e-mul-si-fy-ing	en-core	en-e-mies
emo-tion-al	e-mul-si-fi-ca-tion	en-coun-ter	en-er-get-ic
emo-ton-al-ly	e-mul-si-fi-er	en-cour-age	en-er-get-i-cal
emo-tion-al-ism	emul-sion	en-cour-aged	en-er-get-i-cal-ly
em-pan-el	emul-sive	en-cour-ag-ing	en-er-gize
em-pa-thize	en-a-ble	en-cour-ag-ing-ly	en-er-gized
em-pa-thized	en-a-bled	en-croach	en-er-giz-ing
em-pa-thiz-ing	en-a-bling	en-croach-er	en-er-gi-zer
em-pa-thy	en-act	en-croach-ment	en-er-gy
em-pa-thet-ic	e-nam-el	en-crust	en-er-gies
em-path-ic	e-nam-eled	en-crus-ta-tion	en-er-vate
em-per-or	e-nam-el-ing	en-cum-ber	en-er-vat-ed
em-pha-sis	e-nam-el-er	en-cum-brance	en-er-vat-ing
em-pha-ses	e-nam-el-ware	en-cy-clo-pe-di-a	en-er-va-tion
em-pha-size	en-am-or	en-cy-clo-pe-dic	en-fee-ble
em-pha-sized	en-am-ored-ness	en-cy-clo-pe-di-cal	en-fee-bled
em-pha-siz-ing	en-camp	en-cy-clo-pe-di-cal-ly	en-fee-bling
em-phat-ic	en-camp-ment	en-cyst	en-fee-ble-ment
em-phat-i-cal-ly	en-cap-su-late	en-dan-ger	en-fi-lade
em-phy-se-ma	en-cap-su-lat-ed		en-fi-lad-ed

en-fi-lad-ing
en-fold
en-fran-chise
en-fran-chised
en-fran-chis-ing
en-fran-chise-ment
en-gage
en-gaged
en-gag-ing
en-gage-ment
en-gen-der
en-gine
en-gi-neer
en-gorge
en-gorged
en-gorg-ing
en-gorge-ment
en-grave
en-graved
en-grav-ing
en-grav-er
en-gross
en-grossed
en-gross-er
en-gross-ing
en-gross-ing-ly
en-gross-ment
en-gulf
en-gulf-ment
en-hance
en-hanced
en-hanc-ing
en-hance-ment
enig-ma
en-ig-mat-ic
en-ig-mat-i-cal
en-ig-mat-i-cal-ly
en-join
en-join-er
en-join-ment
en-large
en-larged
en-larg-ing
en-large-a-ble
en-larg-er
en-large-ment
en-light-en
en-light-en-ment
en-list
en-list-ed
en-list-ment

en-liv-en
en-liv-en-er
en-mesh
en-mi-ty
en-mi-ties
en-no-ble
en-no-bled
en-no-bling
en-no-ble-ment
en-no-bler
en-nui
e-nor-mi-ty
e-nor-mi-ties
e-nor-mous
e-nor-mous-ly
e-nor-mous-ness
e-nough
en-plane
en-planed
en-plan-ing
en-rage
en-raged
en-rag-ing
en-rap-ture
en-rap-tured
en-rap-tur-ing
en-rich
en-rich-er
en-rich-ment
en-roll
en-roll-ment
en route
en-sconce
en-sconced
en-sconc-ing
en-sem-ble
en-shrine
en-shrin-ing
en-shroud
en-sign
en-si-lage
en-si-laged
en-si-lag-ing
en-slave
en-slaved
en-slav-ing
en-slave-ment
en-slav-er
en-snare
en-snared
en-snar-ing

en-snare-ment
en-snar-er
en-snar-ing-ly
en-sue
en-sued
en-su-ing
en-su-ing-ly
en-sure
en-sured
en-sur-ing
en-sur-er
en-tail
en-tail-er
en-tail-ment
en-tan-gle
en-tan-gled
en-tan-gling
en-tan-gle-ment
en-tan-gler
en-tente
en-ter
en-ter-a-ble
en-ter-i-tis
en-tr-prise
en-ter-pris-ing
en-ter-pris-ing-ly
en-ter-tain
en-ter-tain-er
en-ter-tain-ing
en-ter-tain-ing-ly
en-ter-tain-ment
en-thrall
en-thralled
en-thrall-ing
en-thrall-ment
en-throne
en-throned
en-thron-ing
en-throne-ment
en-thuse
en-thused
en-thus-ing
en-thu-si-asm
en-thu-si-ast
en-thu-si-as-tic
en-thu-si-as-ti-cal-ly
en-tice
en-ticed
en-tic-ing
en-tice-ment
en-tic-er
en-tic-ig-ly

en-tire
en-tire-ly
en-tire-ness
en-tire-ty
en-tire-ties
en-ti-tle
en-ti-tled
en-ti-tling
en-ti-tle-ment
en-ti-ty
en-ti-ties
en-to-mol-o-gy
en-to-mol-o-gies
en-to-mo-log-ic
en-to-mo-log-i-cal
en-to-mo-log-i-cal-ly
en-to-mol-o-gist
en-tou-rage
en-trails
en-train
en-train-er
en-trance
en-trance-way
en-tranced
en-tranc-ing
en-trance-ment
en-tranc-ing-ly
en-trant
en-trap
en-trapped
en-trap-ping
en-trap-ment
en-treat
en-treat-ing-ly
en-treat-ment
en-treat-y
en-tree
en-trench
en-trench-ment
en-tre-pre-neur
en-tre-pre-neur-i-al
en-tre-pre-neur-ship
en-tro-py
en-trust
en-trust-ment
en-try
en-tries
en-twine
en-twined
en-twin-ing
e-nu-mer-ate
e-nu-mer-at-ed

e-nu-mer-at-ing
e-nu-mer-a-tion
e-nu-mer-a-tive
e-nu-mer-a-tor
e-nun-ci-ate
e-nun-ci-at-ed
e-nun-ci-at-ing
e-nun-ci-a-tion
e-nun-ci-a-tive
e-nun-ci-a-tor
en-u-re-sis
en-u-ret-ic
en-vel-op
en-vel-oped
en-vel-op-ing
en-vi-a-ble
en-vi-a-ble-ness
en-vi-a-bly
en-vi-ous
en-vi-ous-ly
en-vi-ous-ness
en-vi-ron
en-vi-ron-ment
en-vi-ron-men-tal
en-vi-ron-men-tal-ly
en-vi-rons
en-vis-age
en-vis-aged
en-vis-ag-ing
en-vi-sion
en-voy
en-vy
en-vies
en-vied
en-vy-ing
en-vi-er
en-vy-ing-ly
en-zyme
en-zy-mat-ic
en-zy-mat-i-cal-ly
e-on
ep-au-let
e-phed-rine
e-phem-er-al
e-phem-er-al-ness
e-phem-er-al-ly
ep-ic
ep-i-cal
ep-i-cen-ter
ep-i-cure
epi-cu-re-an
ep-i-dem-ic

ep-i-dem-i-cal-ly
ep-i-der-mis
ep-i-der-mal
ep-i-der-mic
ep-i-glot-tis
ep-i-gram
ep-i-logue
ep-i-log
epis-co-pa-cy
epsi-co-pa-cies
epis-co-pal
epis-co-pa-lian
epis-co-pa-lian-ism
epis-co-pate
ep-i-sode
ep-i-sod-ic
ep-i-sod-i-cal
ep-i-sod-i-cal-ly
e-pis-te-mol-o-gy
e-psi-te-mo-log-i-cal
e-pis-te-mol-o-gist
e-pis-tle
e-pis-to-lar-y
ep-i-taph
ep-i-taph-ic
ep-i-taph-ist
ep-i-thet
ep-i-thet-ic
ep-i-thet-i-cal
e-pit-o-me
epit-o-mize
epit-o-mized
epit-o-miz-ing
ep-och
ep-och-al
ep-ox-y
ep-ox-y res-in
ep-si-lon
eq-ua-ble
eq-ua-bil-i-ty
eq-ua-ble-ness
eq-ua-bly
e-qual
e-qualed
e-qual-ling
e-qual-ly
e-qual-ness
e-qual-i-tar-i-an
e-qual-i-tar-i-an-ism
e-qual-i-ty
e-qual-i-ties
e-qual-ize

e-qual-ized
e-qual-iz-ing
e-qual-i-za-tion
e-qual-iz-er
e-qua-nim-i-ty
e-quate
e-quat-ed
e-quat-ing
e-qua-tion
e-qua-tion-al
e-qua-tion-al-ly
e-qua-tor
e-qua-to-ri-al
e-qua-to-ri-al-ly
e-ques-tri-an
e-ques-tri-enne
e-qui-dis-tance
e-qui-dis-tant
e-qui-dis-tant-ly
e-qui-lat-er-al
e-qui-li-brate
e-qui-li-brat-ed
e-qui-li-brat-ing
e-qui-li-bra-tion
e-qui-l-bra-tor
e-qui-lib-ri-um
e-qui-lib-ri-ums
e-qui-lib-ria
e-quine
e-qui-noc-tial
e-qui-nox
e-quip
e-quipped
e-quip-ping
e-quip-per
eq-ui-page
e-quip-ment
e-qui-poise
eq-ui-ta-ble
eq-ui-ta-ble-ness
eq-ui-ta-bly
eq-ui-ty
eq-ui-ties
e-quiv-a-lance
e-quiv-a-len-cy
e-quiv-a-lent
e-quiv-a-lent-ly
e-quiv-o-cal
e-quiv-o-cal-ly
e-quiv-o-cal-ness
e-quiv-o-cate
e-quiv-o-cat-ed

e-quiv-o-cat-ing
e-quiv-o-ca-tor
e-quiv-o-ca-tion
e-ra
e-rad-i-cate
e-rad-i-cat-ed
e-rad-i-cat-ing
e-rad-i-ca-ble
e-rad-i-ca-tion
e-rad-i-ca-tive
e-rad-i-ca-tor
e-rase
e-rased
e-ras-ing
e-ras-a-bil-i-ty
e-ras-a-ble
e-ras-er
e-ras-ure
e-rect
e-rect-a-ble
e-rect-er
e-rec-tive
e-rect-ly
e-rect-ness
e-rec-tile
e-rec-til-i-ty
e-rec-tion
e-rec-tor
er-go
er-mine
e-rode
e-rod-ed
e-rod-ing
e-rog-e-nous
e-ro-sion
e-rot-ic
e-rot-i-cal-ly
e-rot-i-cism
err
err-ing-ly
er-rand
er-rant
er-rant-ly
er-rat-ic
er-rat-i-cal-ly
er-ra-tum
er-ra-ta
er-ro-ne-ous
er-ro-ne-ous-ly
er-ro-ne-ous-nes
er-ror
er-ror-less

er-satz
erst-while
er-u-dite
 er-u-dite-ly
 er-u-dite-ness
er-u-di-tion
e-rupt
 e-rup-tion
 e-rup-tive
 e-rup-tive-ly
 e-rup-tive-ness
es-ca-lade
 es-ca-lad-ed
 es-ca-lad-ing
 es-ca-lad-er
es-ca-late
 es-ca-lat-ed
 es-ca-lat-ing
 es-ca-la-tion
es-ca-la-tor
es-cal-lop
es-ca-pade
es-cape
 es-caped
 es-cap-ing
 es-cap-er
es-ca-pee
es-cap-ist
 es-cap-ism
es-carp-ment
es-chew
 es-chew-al
es-chew-er
s-cort
s-cri-toire
s-crow
s-cutch-eon
s-cutch-eoned
soph-a-gus
s-o-ter-ic
s-o-ter-i-cal
s-o-ter-i-cal-ly
s-pal-ier
s-pe-cial
 s-pe-cial-ly
 s-pe-cial-ness
s-pi-o-nage
s-pla-nade
s-pouse
 s-poused
 s-pous-ing
 s-pous-er

es-pous-al
es-pres-so
es-prit
es-prit de corps
es-py
 es-pied
 es-py-ing
es-quire
 es-quired
 es-quir-ing
es-say
 es-say-er
 es-say-ist
es-sence
es-sen-tial
 es-sen-ti-al-i-ty
 es-sen-tial-ly
 es-sen-tial-ness
es-tab-lish
 es-tab-lish-er
 es-tab-lish-ment
es-tate
es-teem
es-thete
 es-thet-ic
es-ti-ma-ble
 es-ti-ma-ble-ness
 es-ti-ma-bly
es-ti-mate
 es-ti-mat-ed
 es-ti-mat-ing
 es-ti-ma-tive
 es-ti-ma-tor
es-ti-ma-tion
es-trange
 es-tranged
 es-trang-ing
 es-trange-ment
 es-tran-ger
es-trus
es-tu-ar-y
 es-tu-ar-ies
 es-tu-ar-i-al
etch
 etch-er
 etch-ing
e-ter-nal
 e-ter-nal-ly
e-ter-ni-ty
e-ter-nize
 e-ter-nized
 e-ter-niz-ing

e-ter-ni-za-tion
eth-a-nol
e-ther
e-the-re-al
 e-the-re-al-i-ty
 e-the-re-al-ly
 e-the-re-al-ness
e-the-re-al-ize
 e-the-re-al-ized
 e-the-re-al-iz-ing
 e-the-re-al-i-za-tion
eth-ic
 eth-i-cal
 eth-i-cal-ly
 eth-ics
eth-nic
 eth-ni-cal
 eth-ni-cal-ly
eth-nol-o-gy
eth-yl
eti-ol-o-gy
 eti-o-log-ist
 eti-o-log-i-cal
 eti-o-log-i-cal-ly
et-i-quette
e-tude
et-y-mol-o-gy
 et-y-mol-o-gies
 et-y-mo-log-ic
 et-y-mo-log-i-cal
 et-y-mol-o-gist
eu-ca-lyp-tus
 eu-ca-lyp-tus-es
 eu-ca-lyp-ti
eu-gen-ic
eu-lo-gise
 eu-lo-gized
 eu-lo-giz-ing
 eu-lo-gis-tic
 eu-lo-gis-ti-cal-ly
eu-nuch
eu-phe-mism
 eu-phe-mist
 eu-phe-mis-tic
 eu-phe-mis-ti-cal
 eu-phe-mis-ti-cal-ly
eu-phe-mize
 eu-phe-mized
 eu-phe-miz-ing
eu-pho-ni-ous
 eu-pho-ni-ous-ly
eu-re-ka

eu-tha-na-sia
e-vac-u-ate
 e-vac-u-at-ed
 e-vac-u-at-ing
 e-vac-u-a-tion
 e-vac-u-a-tive
 e-vac-u-a-tor
e-vac-u-ee
e-vade
 e-vad-ed
 e-vad-ing
 e-vad-a-ble
 e-vad-er
 e-vad-ing-ly
e-val-u-ate
 e-val-u-at-ed
 e-val-u-at-ing
 e-val-u-a-tion
 e-val-u-a-tor
ev-a-nes-cent
 ev-a-nes-cence
 ev-a-nes-cent-ly
e-van-gel
 evan-gel-i-cal
 evan-gel-ic
 evan-gel-i-cal-ism
 evan-gel-i-cal-ly
 evan-gel-i-cal-ness
evan-ge-lism
 evan-ge-lis-tic
 evan-ge-lis-ti-cal-ly
evan-ge-list
evan-ge-lize
 evan-ge-lized
 evan-ge-liz-ing
 evan-ge-li-za-tion
 evan-ge-liz-er
e-va-sion
e-va-sive
 e-va-sive-ly
 e-va-sive-ness
e-ven
 e-ven-ly
 e-ven-ness
e-ven-hand-ed
eve-ning
e-vent
e-vent-ful
 event-ful-ly
 event-ful-ness
e-ven-tu-al
 e-ven-tu-al-ly

e-ven-tu-al-i-ty
e-ven-tu-al-i-ties
e-ven-tu-ate
e-ven-tu-at-ed
e-ven-tu-at-ing
ev-er
ev-er-green
ev-er-last-ing
ev-er-last-ing-ly
ev-er-last-ing-ness
ev-er-more
e-vert
e-ver-si-ble
e-ver-sion
eve-ry
eve-ry-body
eve-ry-day
eve-ry-one
eve-ry-thing
eve-ry-where
e-vict
e-vic-tion
e-vic-tor
ev-i-dence
ev-i-denced
ev-i-denc-ing
ev-i-dent
ev-i-dent-ly
ev-i-den-tial
ev-i-den-tial-ly
e-vil
e-vince
e-vinced
e-vinc-ing
e-vin-ci-ble
e-vis-cer-ate
e-vis-cer-at-ed
e-vis-cer-at-ing
e-vis-cer-a-tion
e-voke
e-voked
e-vok-ing
ev-o-ca-tion
ev-o-lu-tion
ev-o-lu-tion-al
ev-o-lu-tion-ary
ev-o-lu-tion-ism
ev-ol-lu-tion-ist
e-volve
e-volved
e-volv-ing
e-volv-a-ble

e-volve-ment
e-volv-er
ew-er
ex-ac-er-bate
ex-ac-er-bat-ed
ex-ac-er-bat-ing
ex-ac-er-ba-tion
ex-act
ex-act-a-ble
ex-ac-tor
ex-act-ing
ex-act-ing-ly
ex-act-ing-ness
ex-act-i-tude
ex-act-ly
ex-ag-ger-ate
ex-ag-ger-at-ed
ex-ag-ger-at-ing
ex-ag-ger-a-tion
ex-ag-ger-a-tor
ex-am
ex-am-i-na-tion
ex-am-ine
ex-am-ined
ex-am-in-ing
ex-am-ple
ex-am-pled
ex-am-pling
ex-as-per-ate
ex-as-per-at-ed
ex-as-per-at-ing
ex-as-per-a-tion
ex-ca-vate
ex-ca-vat-ed
ex-ca-cat-ing
ex-ca-va-tion
ex-ca-va-tor
ex-ceed
ex-ceed-ing
ex-ceed-ing-ly
ex-cel
ex-celled
ex-cel-ling
ex-cel-lence
ex-cel-len-cy
ex-cel-len-cies
ex-cel-lent
ex-cel-lent-ly
ex-cel-si-or
ex-cept
ex-cept-ing
ex-cep-tion

ex-cep-tion-a-ble
ex-cep-tion-al
ex-cerpt
ex-cess
ex-ces-sive
ex-ces-sive-ly
ex-change
ex-changed
ex-chang-ing
ex-change-a-bil-i-ty
ex-change-a-ble
ex-chan-ger
ex-cheq-uer
ex-cise
ex-cised
ex-cis-ing
ex-cis-a-ble
ex-ci-sion
ex-cit-a-ble
ex-cit-a-bil-i-ty
ex-cit-a-bly
ex-ci-ta-tion
ex-cite
ex-cit-ed
ex-cit-ing
ex-cit-ed
ex-cit-ed-ly
ex-cit-ed-ness
ex-cite-ment
ex-cit-ing
ex-cit-ing-ly
ex-claim
ex-cla-ma-tion
ex-clam-a-to-ry
ex-clam-a-to-ri-ly
ex-clude
ex-clu-sion
ex-clu-sive
ex-clu-sive-ly
ex-clu-sive-ness
ex-clu-siv-i-ty
ex-com-mu-ni-cate
ex-co-ri-ate
ex-co-ri-at-ed
ex-co-ri-at-ing
ex-co-ri-a-tion
ex-cre-ment
ex-cre-men-tal
ex-cres-cence
ex-cres-cent
ex-cre-ta
ex-cre-tal

ex-crete
ex-cret-ed
ex-cret-ing
ex-cre-tion
ex-cru-ci-ate
ex-cru-ci-at-ed
ex-cru-ci-at-ing
ex-cru-ci-at-ing-ly
ex-cru-ci-a-tion
ex-cur-sive
ex-cur-sive-ly
ex-cur-sive-ness
ex-cus-a-to-ry
ex-cuse
ex-e-cra-ble
ex-e-cra-ble-ness
ex-e-cra-bly
ex-e-cra-tion
ex-e-cute
ex-e-cut-ed
ex-e-cut-ing
ex-e-cut-a-ble
ex-e-cut-er
ex-e-cu-tion
ex-e-cu-tion-er
ex-ec-u-tive
ex-ec-u-tive-ly
ex-ec-u-tor
ex-ec-u-tor-ship
ex-e-ge-sis
ex-em-pli-fy
ex-em-pli-fied
ex-em-pli-fy-ing
ex-em-pli-fi-a-ble
ex-em-pli-fi-ca-tio
ex-empt
ex-emp-tion
ex-er-cise
ex-er-cised
ex-er-cis-ing
ex-er-cis-er
ex-ert
ex-er-tion
ex-fo-li-ate
ex-fo-li-at-ed
ex-fo-li-at-ing
ex-fo-li-a-tion
ex-hal-la-tion
ex-hale
ex-haled
ex-hal-ing
ex-hal-ant

ex-haust
ex-hib-it
ex-hib-it-a-ble
ex-hib-i-tor
ex-hib-i-to-ry
ex-hi-bi-tion
ex-hi-bi-tion-ism
ex-hi-bi-tion-ist
ex-hi-bi-tion-is-tic
ex-hil-a-rate
ex-hort
ex-hor-ta-tive
ex-hor-ta-to-ry
ex-hort-er
ex-hort-ing-ly
ex-hor-ta-tion
ex-hume
ex-humed
ex-hum-ing
ex-i-gen-cy
ex-i-gen-cies
ex-i-gent
ex-i-gent-ly
ex-ile
ex-iled
ex-ist
ex-ist-ence
ex-ist-ent
ex-is-ten-tial
ex-is-ten-tial-ly
ex-it
ex li-bris
ex-o-dus
ex of-fi-ci-o
ex-og-a-my
ex-og-a-mous
ex-og-e-nous
ex-og-e-nous-ly
ex-on-er-ate
ex-or-bi-tant
ex-or-bi-tance
ex-or-bi-tant-ly
ex-o-tic
ex-ot-i-cal-ly
ex-ot-i-cism
ex-pand
ex-pand-er
ex-panse
ex-pan-si-ble
ex-pan-sion
ex-pan-sion-ism

ex-pan-sion-ist
ex-pan-sive
ex-pan-sive-ly
ex-pan-sive-ness
ex-pa-ti-ate
ex-pa-ti-at-ed
ex-pa-ti-at-ing
ex-pa-ti-a-tion
ex-pa-tri-ate
ex-pa-tri-at-ed
ex-pa-tri-at-ing
ex-pa-tri-a-tion
ex-pect
ex-pect-a-ble
ex-pect-a-bly
ex-pect-ing-ly
ex-pect-an-cy
ex-pect-an-cies
ex-pect-ant
ex-pect-ant-ly
ex-pec-ta-tion
ex-pec-to-rate
ex-pec-to-rat-ed
ex-pec-to-rat-ing
ex-pec-to-ra-tion
ex-pe-dite
ex-pe-dit-ed
ex-pe-dit-ing
ex-pe-dit-er
ex-pe-di-tion
ex-pe-di-tion-ary
ex-pe-di-tious
ex-pe-di-tious-ly
ex-pel
ex-pelled
ex-pel-ling
ex-pend
ex-pend-a-ble
ex-pend-a-bil-i-ty
ex-pend-i-ture
ex-pense
ex-pen-sive
ex-pen-sive-ly
ex-pe-ri-en-tial
ex-pe-ri-en-tial-ly
ex-per-i-ment
ex-per-i-men-ta-tion
ex-per-i-men-tal
ex-per-i-men-tal-ism
ex-per-i-men-tal-ist
ex-per-i-men-tal-ly
ex-pert

ex-pert-ly
ex-pert-ness
ex-per-tise
ex-pi-ra-tion
ex-pir-a-to-ry
ex-pire
ex-pired
ex-pir-ing
ex-plain
ex-plain-a-ble
ex-plain-er
ex-pla-na-tion
ex-plan-a-to-ry
ex-plan-a-to-ri-ly
ex-ple-tive
ex-pli-ca-ble
ex-pli-cate
ex-pli-cat-ed
ex-pli-cat-ing
ex-pli-ca-tion
ex-pli-ca-tive
ex-pli-ca-tor
ex-plic-it
ex-plic-it-ly
ex-plic-it-ness
ex-plode
ex-plod-ed
ex-plod-ing
ex-plod-er
ex-ploit
ex-ploit-a-ble
ex-ploi-ta-tion
ex-ploit-er
ex-ploit-ive
ex-plore
ex-plo-ra-tion
ex-plor-a-to-ry
ex-plor-er
ex-plo-sion
ex-plo-sive
ex-plo-sive-ly
ex-plo-sive-ness
ex-po-nent
ex-po-nen-tial
ex-po-nen-tial-ly
ex-port
ex-port-a-ble
ex-por-ta-tion
ex-port-er
ex-pose
ex-posed
ex-pos-ing

ex-pos-er
ex-po-si-tion
ex-pos-i-tor
ex-pos-i-to-ry
ex post fac-to
ex-pos-tu-late
ex-po-sure
ex-pound
ex-pound-er
ex-press
ex-press-er
ex-press-i-ble
ex-pres-sion
ex-pres-sive
ex-pres-sive-ly
ex-pres-sive-ness
ex-press-ly
ex-press-way
ex-pro-pri-ate
ex-pro-pri-at-ing
ex-pro-pri-a-tor
ex-pro-pri-a-tion
ex-pul-sion
ex-pul-sive
ex-punge
ex-pur-gate
ex-pur-ga-to-ry
ex-pur-ga-to-ri-al
ex-qui-site
ex-qui-site-ly
ex-qui-site-ness
ex-tant
ex-tem-po-rize
ex-tem-po-rized
ex-tem-po-riz-ing
ex-tem-po-riz-er
ex-tend
ex-tend-i-bil-i-ty
ex-tend-i-ble
ex-tend-ed
ex-tend-ed-ly
ex-tend-ed-ness
ex-tend-er
ex-ten-si-ble
ex-ten-si-bil-i-ty
ex-ten-sion
ex-ten-sion-al
ex-ten-sive
ex-ten-sive-ly
ex-ten-sive-ness
ex-tent
ex-ten-u-ate

ex-te-ri-or
  ex-te-ri-or-ly
ex-ter-mi-nate
  ex-ter-mi-nat-ed
  ex-ter-mi-nat-ing
  ex-ter-mi-na-tion
ex-ter-nal
  ex-ter-nal-ly
ex-tinct
ex-tinc-tion
ex-tin-guish
  ex-tin-guish-a-ble
  ex-tin-guish-er
  ex-tin-guish-ment
ex-tir-pate
  ex-tir-pat-ed
  ex-tir-pat-ing
  ex-tir-pa-tion
  ex-tir-pa-tive
ex-tol
  ex-tol-ler
  ex-tol-lingly
  ex-tol-ment
ex-tort
  ex-tor-ter
  ex-tor-tive
ex-tor-tion
ex-tra
ex-tract
  ex-tract-a-ble
  ex-trac-tive
ex-trac-tion
ex-tra-cur-ric-u-lar
ex-tra-dite
ex-tra-ne-ous
  ex-tra-ne-ous-ly
  ex-tra-ne-ous-ness
ex-traor-di-nary
  ex-traor-di-nar-i-ly
ex-trap-o-late
  ex-trap-o-lat-ed
  ex-trap-o-lat-ing
  ex-trap-o-la-tion
ex-tra-sen-so-ry
ex-trav-a-gance
  ex-trav-a-gan-cy
ex-trav-a-gant
  ex-trav-a-gant-ly
ex-trav-a-gan-za
ex-treme
  ex-treme-ly
  ex-treme-ness

ex-trem-ist
  ex-trem-ism
  ex-trem-i-ty
  ex-trem-i-ties
ex-tri-cate
  ex-tri-cat-ed
  ex-tri-cat-ing
  ex-tri-ca-ble
  ex-tri-ca-tion
ex-trin-sic
ex-tro-vert
  ex-tro-ver-sion
ex-trude
ex-u-ber-ance
ex-u-ber-ant
  ex-u-ber-ant-ly
ex-ude
  ex-ud-ed
  ex-ud-ing
  ex-u-da-tion
ex-ult
  ex-ult-ant
  ex-ult-ant-ly
  ex-ul-at-tion
  ex-ult-ing-ly
ex-ur-ban-ite
eye
  eyed
  eye-ing
eye-ball
eye-glass
  eye-glass-es
eye-hole
eye-let
eye-lid
eye-o-pen-er
  eye-o-pen-ing
eye-wit-ness
ey-rie
  ey-ry
  ey-ries

F

fa-ble
  fa-bled
fab-ric
fab-ri-cate
  fab-ri-cated
  fab-ri-cat-ing
  fab-ri-ca-tion
fab-u-lous

fab-u-lous-ness
fa-cade
  fa-cades
face
  faced
  fac-ing
face card
face--lift
fac-et
fa-ce-tious
  fa-ce-tious-ly
fa-cial
  fa-cial-ly
fac-ile
  fac-ile-ly
  fac-ile-ness
fa-cil-i-tate
fa-cil-i-ty
  fac-ing
fac-sim-i-le
fact
fac-tion
  fac-tion-al
  fac-tion-al-ly
fac-ti-tious
  fac-ti-tious-ly
fac-ti-tious-ness
fac-tor
fac-to-ry
  fac-to-ries
fac-to-tum
fac-tu-al
fac-ul-ty
fad
  fad-dish
  fad-dist
fade
  fad-ed
  fad-ing
fa-er-ie
  fa-ery
  fa-er-ies
fag
  faggged
  fag-ging
fag-got
fag-ot
Fahr-en-heit
fail-ing
  fail-ing-ly
fail-safe

fail-ure
faint
  faint-ly
  faint-ness
faint-heart-ed
fair
  fir-ness
fair-ground
fair-ly
fair-mind-ed
fair--trade
fair-y
  fair-ies
fair-y-like
fair-y tale
faith
faith-ful
faith-ful-less
fake
  faked
  fak-ing
  fak-er
fal-con
fal-con-ry
fall
  fall-en
  fall-ing
fal-la-cious
  fal-la-cious-ly
fal-la-cy
fall-guy
fal-li-ble
  fal-li-bly
fail-ing star
fall-out
fal-low
  fal-low-ness
false
  fals-er
  fals-est
false-hood
fal-si-fy
  fal-si-fied
  fal-si-fy-ing
  fal-si-fi-er
fal-si-ty
fal-ter
  fal-ter-er
  fal-ter-ing-ly
fame
famed
fa-mil-ial

fa-mil-iar
fa-mil-iar-ly
fa-mil-i-ar-i-ty
fa-mil-iar-ize
fa-mil-iar-ized
fa-mil-iar-iz-ing
fam-ily
fam-i-lies
fam-ine
fam-ish
fam-ished
fa-mous
fa-mous-ly
fan
fan-like
fan-ner
fa-nat-ic
fa-nat-i-cal
fa-nat-i-cism
fa-nat-i-cize
fa-nat-i-cized
fan-ci-er
fan-ci-ul
fan-ci-ful-ly
an-cy
fan-cies
fan-ci-ly
fan-ci-ness
an-cy-work
an-fare
ang
anged
an-light
an-tas-tic
an-tas-ti-cal
an-ta-sy
an-ta-sies
ar
ar-ther
ar-thest
r-a-way
rce
arced
arc-ing
r-ci-cal
ar-ci-cal-ly
re
red
ar-ing
re-well
r-fetched
-flung

farm
farm-er
farm-hand
farm-house
farm-ing
farm-yard
far-off
far-reach-ing
far-reach-ing-ly
far-see-ing
far-sight-ed
far-sight-ed-ly
far-ther
far-ther-most
far-thest
fas-ci-a
fas-ci-ae
fas-ci-cle
fas-ci-cled
fas-ci-nate
fas-ci-nat-ed
fas-ci-nat-ing
fas-ci-na-tion
fas-cism
fas-cist
fa-scis-tic
fash-ion
fash-ion-ble
fast
fas-ten
fas-ten-er
fas-ten-ing
fas-tid-i-ous
fas-ti-di-ous-ly
fat
fat-ter
fat-test
fa-tal
fa-tal-ly
fa-tal-ism
fa-tal-ist
fa-tal-i-ty
fa-tal-i-ties
fate
fat-ed
fat-ing
fate-ful
fate-ful-ly
fate-ful-ness
fa-ther
fa-ther-hood
fa-ther-ly

fa-ther-in-law
fa-thers-in-law
fa-ther-land
fath-om
fath-om-a-ble
fath-om-less
fa-tique
fa-tiqued
fa-tiq-uing
fat-i-ga-ble
fat-ten
fat-ten-er
fa-tu-i-ty
fa-tui-ties
fat-u-ous
fat-u-ous-ly
fau-cet
fault
fault-find-er
fault-find-ing
fault-less
fault-less-ly
fault-less-ness
fault-y
fault-i-er
fault-i-est
fault-i-ly
fau-na
fau-nas
fau-nae
faux pas
fa-vor
fa-vor-ing-ly
fa-vor-a-ble
fa-vor-ably
fa-vored
fa-vored-ly
fa-vored-ness
fa-vor-ite
fa-vor-it-ism
fawn
faze
fazed
faz-ing
fe-al-ty
fear
fear-ful
fear-ful-ly
fear-less
fear-less-ly
fea-si-ble
fea-si-bil-i-ty

fea-si-bly
feast
feat
feath-er
fea-thered
feath-er-bed-ding
fea-ture
fea-tured
fea-tur-ing
fea-ture-ness
fe-brile
fe-ces
fe-cal
feck-less
fe-cund
fe-cun-di-ty
fe-cun-date
fe-cun-dat-ed
fe-cun-da-tion
fed-er-al
fed-er-al-ism
fed-er-li-ist
fed-er-al-ize
fed-er-al-ized
fed-er-al-iz-ing
fed-er-al-i-za-tion
fed-er-al-ly
fed-er-ate
fed-er-at-ed
fed-er-at-ing
fed-er-a-tion
fee
fee-ble
fee-bler
fee-blest
fee-bly
fee-ble-mind-ed
fee-ble-mind-ed-ness
feed-back
feel
feel-ing
feel-er
feel-ing
feel-ing-ly
feel-ing-ness
feign
feigned
feign-ed-ly
feign-er
feign-ing-ly
feint
feist-y

feist-i-er	fern-er-ies	fet-ish-is-tic	fidg-et
feist-i-est	**fe-ro-cious**	**fet-lock**	fidg-ety
fe-lic-i-tate	fe-ro-cious-ly	**fet-ter**	**field-er**
fe-lic-i-tat-ed	fe-ro-ci-ty	**fet-tle**	**field-glass**
fe-lic-i-tat-ing	**fer-ret**	**fe-tus**	**fiend**
fe-lic-i-ta-tion	fer-ret-er	fe-tus-es	fiend-ish
fe-lic-i-tous	**fer-ro-con-crete**	**feud**	fiend-ish-ly
fe-lic-i-tous-ly	**fer-ro-mag-net-ic**	feud-ist	fiend-ish-ness
fe-lic-i-ty	**fer-ru-gi-nous**	**feu-dal**	**fierce**
fe-lic-i-ties	**fer-rule**	**feu-dal-ism**	fierce-ly
fe-line	**fer-ry**	**feu-dal-ist**	fierce-ness
fe-line-ly	fer-ries	feu-dal-is-tic	**fier-y**
fe-line-i-ty	fer-ry-boat	**feu-dal-i-za-tion**	fier-i-er
fell	fer-ry-man	**feu-dal-ize**	fier-i-est
fel-la-ti-o	**fer-tile**	feu-dal-ized	fier-i-ly
fel-low	fer-tile-ly	feu-dal-iz-ing	**fier-i-ness**
fel-low-ship	fer-tile-ness	**fe-ver**	**fif-teen**
fe-lon	**fer-til-i-ty**	**fe-ver blis-ter**	**fif-teenth**
fel-o-ny	**fer-ti-li-za-tion**	**fe-ver-ish**	**fifth**
fel-o-nies	**fer-ti-li-za-tion-al**	fe-ver-ish-ly	**fif-ti-eth**
fe-lo-ni-ous	**fer-ti-lize**	fe-ver-ish-ness	**fif-ty**
fe-lo-ni-ous-ly	fer-ti-lized	**fe-ver-ous**	fif-ties
fe-male	fer-ti-liz-ing	**fe-ver-ous-ly**	**fight**
fem-i-nine	fer-ti-liz-a-ble	**few**	**fight-er**
fem-i-nine-ly	**fer-ti-liz-er**	**few-ness**	**fig-ment**
fem-i-nine-ness	**fer-vent**	**fez-zes**	**fig-u-ra-tion**
fem-i-nin-i-ty	fer-ven-cy	**fi-as-co**	**fig-u-ra-tive**
fem-i-nism	**fer-vid**	fi-as-cos	fig-u-ra-tive-ly
fem-i-nist	fer-vid-ly	fi-as-coes	fid-u-ra-tive-ness
fem-i-nis-tic	fer-vid-ness	**fi-at**	**fig-ure**
fem-i-nize	**fer-vor**	**fib**	fig-ured
fem-i-nized	**fes-ter**	**fi-ber**	fig-ur-ing
fem-i-niz-ing	**fes-ti-val**	fi-bered	fig-ur-er
fe-mur	**fes-tive**	**fi-ber-board**	**fig-ure-head**
fe-murs	fes-tive-ly	**fi-ber-glass**	**fig-ur-ine**
fem-o-ra	fes-tive-ness	**fi-bril**	**fil-a-ment**
fem-o-ral	**fes-tiv-i-ty**	**fi-bril-la-tion**	fil-a-men-ta-ry
fen	**fes-toon**	**fi-broid**	fil-a-ment-ed
fen-ny	fes-toon-ery	**fi-brous**	fil-a-men-tous
fen-ni-er	fes-toon-er-ies	**fib-u-la**	**filch**
fen-ni-est	**fe-tal**	fib-u-las	**file**
fence	**fetch**	fib-u-lae	filed
fecned	**fetch-er**	**fick-le**	fil-ing
fenc-ing	**fetch-ing**	fick-le-ness	**fi-let**
fenc-er	fetch-ing-ly	**fic-tion**	**fi-let mi-gnon**
fen-der	**fete**	fic-tion-al	**fil-i-al**
fe-ral	**fet-id**	fic-tion-al-ly	fil-i-al-ly
fer-ment	fet-id-ly	**fic-ti-tious**	**fil-i-bus-ter**
fer-ment-a-ble	fet-id-ness	**fid-dle**	**fil-i-gree**
fer-men-ta-tion	**fet-ish**	fid-dler	fil-i-greed
fern	**fet-ish-ism**	fid-dled	fil-i-gree-ing
fern-er-y	fet-ish-ist	**fi-del-i-ty**	fil-lings

fill-er
fil-let
fill-ing
fil-lip
fil-ly
fil-lies
film-strip
film-y
film-i-er
film-i-est
film-i-ness
fil-ter
filth
filth-i-ness
filthy
filth-i-er
filth-i-est
fin
finned
fin-ning
fin-less
fin-like
fi-na-gled
fi-na-gling
fi-na-gler
fi-nal
fi-na-le
fi-nal-ist
fi-nal-i-ty
fi-nal-i-ties
fi-nal-ize
fi-nal-ized
fi-nal-iz-ing
fi-nal-ly
fi-nance
fi-nanced
fi-nanc-ing
fi-nan-cial
fi-nan-cial-ly
fin-an-cier
finch
find
found
find-ing
find-er
fine
fin-er
fin-est
fine-ly
fine-ness
fin-er-y
fin-er-ies

fi-nesse
fi-nessed
fi-ness-ing
fin-ger
fin-ger-bowl
fin-ger-ing
fin-ger-nail
fin-ger-print
fin-i-al
fin-i-cal
fin-i-cal-ly
fin-ick-y
fin-ick-ing
fin-is
fin-is-es
fin-ish
fin-ished
fin-ish-er
fi-nite
fi-nite-ly
fi-nite-ness
fire
fired
fir-ing
fir-er
fire-arm
fire-ball
fire-brand
fire-bug
fire-crack-er
fire-fight-er
fire-fly
fire-flies
fire-man
fire-place
fire-plug
fire-pow-er
fire-proof
fire-side
fire-trap
fire-wa-ter
fire-wood
fire-works
fir-ing-squad
firm
firm-ly
firm-ness
fir-ma-ment
first-born
first-hand
first-ling
first-ly

first-rate
first-string
fis-cal
fis-cal-ly
fish-er
fish-er-man
fish-er-men
fish-er-y
fish-er-ies
fish-hook
fish-ing
fish-wife
fish-wived
fish-y
fish-i-er
fish-i-est
fis-sle
fis-sion
fis-sure
fis-sured
fis-sur-ing
fist-ic
fist-i-cuff
fit
fit-ter
fit-test
fit-ted
fit-ting
fit-ly
fit-ness
fit-ful
fit-ful-ly
fit-ful-ness
fit-ting
fit-ting-ly
fit-ting-ness
five-fold
five-and-ten
fix
fix-a-ble
fixed
fix-ed-ly
fix-er
fix-a-tion
fix-a-tive
fix-ings
fix-i-ty
fix-i-ties
fix-ture
fiz-zle
fiz-zled
fiz-zling

fiz-zy
fiz-zi-er
fiz-zi-est
flab-ber-gast
flab-by
flab-bi-er
flab-bi-est
flab-bi-ly
flab-bi-ness
flac-cid
flag
flagged
flag-ging
flag-el-lant
flag-el-lat-ed
flag-el-lat-ing
flag-el-la-tion
fla-gi-tious
flag-on
flag-pole
flag-rank
fla-grant
fla-grant-ly
flag-ship
flag-stone
flail
flair
flake
flaked
flak-ing
flak-y
flak-i-er
flak-i-est
flak-i-ness
flam-boy-ant
flam-boy-ance
flam-boy-an-cy
flam-boy-ant-ly
flame
flamed
falm-ing
flam-ing-ly
flam-ma-ble
flange
flank
flank-er
flan-nel-ette
flap
flapped
flap-ping
flap-per
flap-jack

flare
flared
flar-ing
flare-up
flash-back
flash-light
flash-i-er
flash-i-est
flash-i-ly
flash-i-ness
flask
flat
flat-ly
flat-ted
flat-ting
flat-ness
flat-car
flat-foot
flat-foot-ed
flat-foot-ed-ly
falt-ten
flat-ten-er
flat-ter
flat-ter-er
flat-ter-ing-ly
flat-ter-y
flat-ter-ies
flat-u-lent
flat-u-lence
flat-u-len-cy
flat-u-lent-ly
flat-ware
flaunt
flaunt-er
flaunt-ing-ly
flanty
flaunt-i-er
flaunt-i-est
flau-tist
fla-vor
fla-vored
fla-vor-less
fla-vor-ing
flaw-less
fla-zen
flax-seed
flay-er
flea-bite
flea-bit-ten
fleck
flec-tion
fledge

fledged
fledg-ing
fledg-ling
flee
fled
flee-ing
fleece
fleeced
fleec-ing
fleec-y
fleec-i-er
fleec-i-est
fleec-i-ness
fleet
fleet-ly
fleet-ness
fleet-ing
fleet-ing-ly
fleet-ing-ness
flesh-ly
flesh-li-er
flesh-li-est
flesh-pots
flesh-y
flesh-i-ert
flesh-i-est
flesh-i-ness
flex-i-ble
flex-i-bil-i-ty
flex-i-bly
flex-ion
flex-or
flex-ure
fib-ber-ti-gib-bet
flick-er
flick-er-ing
fli-er
flight
flight-less
flight-y
flight-i-er
flight-i-est
flight-i-ly
flight-i-ness
flim-flam
flim-flammed
flim-flam-ming
firm-sy
firm-si-er
firm-si-est
firm-si-ly
firm-si-ness

flinch
flinch-er
flinch-ing-ly
fin-ders
fling
flung
fling-ing
flint-y
flint-i-er
flint-i-est
flint-i-ness
flip
flipped
flip-ping
flip-flop
flip-pant
flip-pan-cy
flip-pant-ly
flip-per
flirt-er
flir-ta-tion
flir-ta-tious
flit
flit-ted
flit-ting
flit-ter
float-a-ble
float-a-tion
float-er
float-ing
floc-cu-lent
floc-cu-lence
flocked
flood-gate
flood-light
flood-lit
floor-ing
floor-walk-er
floo-zy
floo-zies
flop
flopped
flop-ping
flop-per
flop-house
flop-py
flop-pi-er
flop-pi-est
flop-pi-ly
flo-ra
flo-ras
flo-rae

flo-ral
flo-res-cence
flo-res-cent
flo-ret
flo-ri-cul-ture
flo-ri-cul-tur-al
flo-ri-cul-tur-ist
flor-id
flo-rid-i-ty
flor-id-ly
flor-id-ness
flo-rist
floss
flossy
floss-i-er
floss-i-est
flo-ta-tion
flo-til-la
flot-sam
flounce
flounced
flounc-ing
floun-der
flour-y
flour-i-er
flour-i-est
flour-ish
flou-rish-ing
flow-er
flow-ered
flow-er-ing
flow-ery
flow-er-i-ness
flub
flubbed
flub-bing
fluc-tu-ate
fluc-tu-at-ed
fluc-tu-at-ing
fluc-tu-a-tion
flue
flu-ent
flu-ency
flu-ent-ly
fluff
fluff-i-ness
fluff-y
fluff-i-er
fluff-i-est
flu-id
flu-id-ly
flu-id-ness

fluke	fo-cus-es	fon-dler	for-bade
fluky	fo-cus-ing	fond-ly	for-bid-den
fluk-i-er	fo-cus-er	fond-ness	for-bid-ding
fluk-i-est	**fod-der**	**fon-due**	**force-ful**
flum-mer-y	**foe-tus**	**food-stuff**	force-ful-ly
flum-mer-ies	foe-tal	**fool-er-y**	**for-ceps**
flun-ky	**fog**	fool-er-ies	**for-ci-ble**
flunk-ies	fogged	**fool-har-dy**	for-ci-bly
flu-o-resce	fog-ging	fool-har-di-ness	**ford-a-ble**
flu-o-resced	**fog-gy**	**fool-proof**	**fore-arm**
flu-o-resc-ing	fog-gi-er	**fools-cap**	**fore-bear**
flu-o-res-cence	fog-gi-est	**foot-age**	**fore-bode**
flu-o-res-sent	fog-gi-ly	**foot-ball**	fore-bod-ed
flur-ry	fog-gi-ness	**foot-board**	fore-bod-ing
flur-ries	**fog-horn**	**foot-can-dle**	fore-bod-er
flur-ried	**fo-gy**	**foot-ed**	**fore-brain**
flur-ry-ing	fo-gies	**foot-fall**	**fore-cast**
flus-ter	fo-gy-ish	**foot-hill**	fore-cast-ed
flute	**foi-ble**	**foot-hold**	fore-cast-ing
flut-ed	**fold-er**	**foot-ing**	fore-cast-er
flut-ing	**fol-de-rol**	**foot-lights**	**fore-close**
flut-ist	**fo-li-a-ceous**	**foot-loose**	fore-closed
flut-ter	**fo-li-age**	**foot-note**	fore-clos-ing
flut-ter-er	**fo-li-ate**	foot-not-ed	fore-clo-sure
flut-ter-ing-ly	fo-li-at-ed	foot-not-ing	**fore-fa-ther**
flut-tery	fo-li-at-ing	**foot-path**	**fore-fin-ger**
flut-ter-i-er	fol-li-a-tion	**foot-print**	**fore-foot**
flut-ter-i-est	**fo-li-o**	**foot-sore**	fore-feet
flux-ion	fo-li-os	**foot-step**	**fore-front**
fly-brown	fol-li-oed	**foot-stool**	**fore-gath-er**
fly-by-night	fo-li-o-ing	**foot-wear**	**fore-go**
fly-er	**folk-lore**	**foot-work**	fore-went
fly-ing	folk-lor-ist	**foo-zle**	fore-gone
fly-leaf	**flok-sy**	foo-zled	fore-go-ing
fly-leaves	flok-si-er	foo-zling	**fore-ground**
fly-pa-per	flok-si-est	**fop**	**fore-hand**
fly-speck	flok-si-ness	fop-pery	**fore-hand-ed**
fly-wheel	**folk-ways**	fop-per-ies	fore-hand-ed-ness
foal	**fol-li-cle**	fop-pish	**fore-head**
foam	fol-lic-u-lar	fop-pish-ly	**for-eign**
foam-i-ness	**fol-low**	fop-pish-ness	for-eign-er
foam-y	**fol-low-er**	**for-age**	for-eign-ness
foam-i-er	**fol-low-ing**	for-aged	**fore-leg**
foam-i-est	**fol-ly**	for-ag-ing	**fore-lock**
fob	fol-lies	**for-ay**	**fore-man**
fobbed	**fo-ment**	**for-bear**	fore-men
fob-bing	fo-men-ta-tion	for-bore	**fore-most**
fo-cal	fo-ment-er	for-borned	**fo-ren-sic**
fo-cal-ize	**fon-dant**	for-bear-ing	**fore-or-dain**
fo-cal-lized	**fon-dle**	for-bear-ance	**fore-quar-ter**
fo-cal-iz-ing	fond-led	for-bear-ing-ly	**fore-run**
fo-cus	fon-dling	**for-bid**	fore-ran

fore-run-ning	for-giv-en	for-ti-fi-er	frac-tion-al
fore-run-ner	for-giv-ing	**for-tis-si-mo**	**frac-tious**
fore-see	for-giv-a-ble	**for-ti-tude**	frac-tious-ly
fore-saw	for-give-ness	**fort-night**	**frac-ture**
fore-seen	for-giv-er	**for-night-ly**	frac-tured
fore-see-ing	**for-go**	for-night-lies	frac-tur-ing
fore-see-a-ble	for-went	**for-tress**	**frag-ile**
fore-se-er	for-gone	**for-tu-i-tous**	fra-gil-i-ty
fore-shad-ow	for-go-ing	for-tu-i-tous-ly	**frag-ment**
fore-shad-ow-er	for-go-er	for-tu-i-tous-ness	frag-ment-al
fore-sight	**fork-loft**	**for-tu-nate**	frag-men-ter-i-ness
fore-sight-ed	**for-lorn**	for-tu-nate-ly	frag-men-tary
fore-sight-ed-ness	for-lorn-ly	**for-tune**	**frag-men-ta-tion**
fore-skin	for-lorn-ness	**for-tune-tell-er**	**frag-ment-ize**
for-est	**for-mal**	for-tune-tell-ing	frag-ment-ized
fore-stall	for-mal-ly	**for-ty**	frag-ment-iz-ing
for-est-a-tion	**for-mal-ism**	for-ties	**fra-grance**
for-es-ter	**for-mal-i-ty**	**for-ty-nin-er**	fra-grant
for-es-try	for-mal-i-ties	**fo-rum**	fra-grant-ly
fore-taste	**for-mal-ize**	fo-rums	**frail**
fore-tast-ed	for-mal-ized	fo-ra	frail-ty
fore-tast-ing	for-mal-iz-ing	**fos-sil**	frail-ness
fore-tell	for-mal-i-za-tion	**fos-sil-ize**	**frame**
fore-told	**for-mat**	fos-sil-ized	framed
fore-tell-ing	**for-ma-tion**	fos-sil-iz-ing	fram-ing
fore-tell-er	**form-a-tive**	fos-sil-i-za-tion	fram-er
fore-thought	**for-mer**	**fos-ter**	**frame-up**
for-ev-er	**for-mer-ly**	fos-tered	**frame-work**
for-ev-er-more	**for-mi-da-ble**	fos-ter-ing	**franc**
fore-warn	for-mi-da-bly	**fought**	**fran-chise**
fore-word	**form-less**	**fou-lard**	fran-chised
for-feit	form-less-ly	**found**	**frank-furt-er**
for-feit-er	**for-mu-la**	**foun-da-tion**	**frank-in-cense**
for-fei-ture	for-mu-las	foun-da-tion-al	**fran-tic**
for-gath-er	for-mu-lae	**found-er**	fran-ti-cal-ly
forge	**for-mu-lar-y**	**found-ling**	**fra-ter-nal**
forged	for-mu-lar-ies	**found-ry**	fra-ter-nal-ly
forg-ing	**for-mu-late**	found-ries	**fra-ter-ni-ty**
forg-er	for-mu-lat-ed	**foun-tain**	fra-ter-ni-ties
for-ger-y	for-mu-lat-ing	**foun-tain-head**	**frat-er-nize**
fog-er-ies	for-mu-la-tion	**four-flush-er**	**frat-ri-cide**
for-get	for-mu-la-tor	**four-square**	frat-ri-cid-al
for-got	**fort**	**four-teen**	**fraud-u-lent**
for-got-ten	**forte**	four-teenth	fraud-u-lence
for-get-ting	**forth-com-ing**	**fourth**	**fraught**
for-get-ta-ble	**forth-right**	fourth-ly	**fraz-zle**
for-get-ter	forth-right-ness	**fowl**	fraz-zled
for-get-ful	**forth-with**	fowl-er	fraz-zling
for-get-ful-ly	**for-ti-fi-ca-tion**	**foy-er**	**freak**
for-get-ful-ness	**for-ti-fy**	**fra-cas**	freak-ish
for-give	for-ti-fied	fra-cas-es	**freck-le**
for-gave	for-ti-fy-ing	**frac-tion**	freck-led

freck-li-er

free
fre-er
free-ly
free-bie
free-boot-er
free-dom
free-lance
free-lanced
free-lanc-ing
free-spoken
free-spo-ken-ness
free-stone
free-think-ing
free-way
freeze
froze
fro-zen
freez-ing
freez-er
fre-net-ic
fre-net-i-cal-ly
fren-zy
fren-zies
fren-zied
fren-zy-ing
fre-quen-cy
fre-quen-cies
fre-quent
fre-quent-er
fre-quent-ly
fresh
fresh-ly
fresh-ness
fresh-en
fresh-en-er
fresh-et
fresh-man
fresh-men
fret
fret-ted
fret-work
fri-ary
fri-ar-ies
fric-as-see
fric-as-seed
fric-tion
fric-tion-al
friend
friend-less
friend-ly
friend-li-er

friend-li-est
frieze
fright-ful
fright-ful-ly
frig-id
fri-gid-i-ty
frig-id-ly
frig-id-ness
frilly
frill-i-er
frill-i-est
fringe
fringed
fring-ing
frip-pery
frip-per-ies
frisky
frisk-i-er
fit-ter
friv-o-lous
fri-vol-i-ty
frizz
friz-zi-ness
friz-zi-er
friz-zle
friz-zled
friz-zling
frol-ic
frol-ick-ed
frol-ick-ing
frol-ic-some
front-age
fron-tal-ly
fron-tier
frost
frost-ed
frost-ing
frost-y
frost-i-er
froth
frothy
froth-i-er
froth-i-est
frou-frou
fro-ward
frown
frown-ing-ly
frow-zy
frow-zi-er
fro-zen
fro-zen-ly
fro-zen-ness

fruc-ti-fy
fruc-ti-fied
fruc-ti-fy-ing
fruc-ti-fi-ca-tion
fru-gal
fru-gal-i-ty
fru-gal-i-ties
fru-gal-ly
fruit-ful
fruit-ful-ly
fru-i-tion
fruit-less-ly
fruity
frump
frump-ish
frump-i-est
frus-trate
frus-trat-ed
frus-trat-ing
frus-tra-tion
fry-er
fud-dle
fud-dled
fud-dling
fudge
fudged
fudg-ing
fu-el
fu-eled
fu-el-ing
fu-gi-tive
fu-gi-tive-ly
ful-crum
ful-crums
ful-cra
ful-fill
ful-filled
ful-fil-ling
ful-fil-ment
full
full-ness
ful-ly
full-back
ful-mi-nate
ful-mi-nat-ed
ful-mi-nat-ing
ful-mi-na-tion
ful-some
ful-some-ly
fu-mi-gate
fu-mi-gat-ed
fu-mi-gat-ing

func-tion
func-tion-less
func-tion-al
func-tion-al-ly
func-tion-ary
func-tion-ar-ies
fun-da-men-tal
fun-da-men-tal-ly
fun-da-men-tal-ism
fun-da-men-tal-ist
fu-ner-al
fu-ner-re-al
fun-gi-cide
fun-gi-cid-al
fun-gi-cid-al-ly
fun-gous
fun-gus
fun-gi
fun-gus-es
funic-u-lar
funk-y
funk-i-er
funk-i-est
fun-nel
fun-neled
fun-nel-ing
fur
furred
fur-ring
fur-bish
fu-ri-ous
fu-ri-ous-ly
fur-long
fur-lough
fur-nace
fur-nish
fur-nish-ings
fur-ni-ture
for-row
fur-ry
fur-ri-er
fur-ri-est
fur-ther
fur-ther-more
fur-ther-most
fur-thest
fur-tive
fur-tive-ly
fu-ry
fu-ries
fuse
fused

fus-ing
fu-see
fu-se-lage
fu-si-bil-i-ty
fu-si-ble
fu-si-form
fu-si-lade
fu-si-lad-ed
fu-si-lad-ing
fu-sion
fussy
fuss-i-er
fuss-i-est
fuss-i-ly
fus-tian
fus-ty
fu-tile
fu-til-i-ty
fu-til-i-ties
fu-ture
fu-tur-is-tic
fu-tu-ri-ty
fuzz-y
gab
gabbed
gab-ber
gab-ar-dine
gab-ble
gab-bled
gab-bler
gab-by
gab-bi-er
gab-bi-est
ga-ble
ga-bled
ga-bling
gad
gad-ded
gad-ding
gad-a-bout
gad-fly
gad-flies
gad-get
gad-get-ry
gaffe
gaf-fer
gag
ga-ga
gai-e-ty
gai-e-ties
gai-ly
gain-ful

gain-say
gain-said
gain-say-ing
gait
ga-la
ga-lac-tic
gal-ax-y
gal-a-xies
gal-lant
gal-lant-ry
gal-lant-ries
gal-ler-y
gal-ler-ies
gal-ley
gal-li-cism
gal-li-mau-fry
gal-li-mau-fries
gall-ing
gal-li-vant
gal-lon
gal-lop
gal-lows
gal-lows-es
gall-stone
ga-loot
ga-lore
gal-van-ic
gal-va-nism
gal-va-nize
gal-va-nized
gal-va-nom-e-ter
gam-bit
gam-ble
gam-bled
gam-bling
gam-bol
gam-brel
game
gam-er
gam-est
gamed
gam-ing
game-keep-er
game-some
game-ster
gam-ete
ga-met-ic
gam-in
gam-ma
gam-mon
gam-ut
gam-y

gam-i-er
gam-i-est
gam-i-ly
gam-i-ness
gan-der
gang-land
gan-gling
gan-gli-on
gan-glia
gan-gli-ons
gan-gly
gan-gli-er
gan-gli-est
gang-plank
gan-grene
gan-grened
gan-gren-ing
gan-gre-nous
gang-ster
gang-way
gant-let
gan-try
gan-tries
gap
gapped
gap-ping
gar-bage
gar-ble
gar-bled
gar-bling
gar-den
gar-gan-tu-an
gar-gle
gar-gled
gar-gling
gar-goyle
gar-ish
gar-land
gar-ment
gar-nish
gar-nish-ee
gar-nish-ee-ing
gar-nish-ment
gar-ni-ture
gar-ret
gar-ri-son
gar-rote
gar-rot-ed
gar-rot-ing
gar-rot-er
gar-ru-lous
gar-ter

gas-ket
gas-lit
gas-o-line
gas-ser
gas-sy
gas-si-er
gas-si-est
gas-tric
gas-ti-tis
gas-tro-in-tes-ti-nal
gas-tron-o-my
gas-tro-nom-ic
gas-tro-nom-i-cal
gas-tro-nom-i-cal-ly
gas-works
gate-crash-er
gate-crash-ing
gate-house
gate-keep-er
gate-post
gate-way
gath-er
gath-er-ing
gauche
gau-cho
gaud-y
gaud-i-er
gaud-i-est
gaud-i-ly
gaunt-let
gauze
gauz-i-er
gauz-i-est
gauzy
gay-e-ty
gaze
gazed
gaz-er
gaz-ing
ga-ze-bo
ga-ze-bos
ga-ze-boes
ga-zelle
ga-zette
gaz-et-teer
gear-ing
gear-shift
gear-wheel
gee
geed
gee-ing
gee-zer

gei-sha
gel
gelled
gel-ling
gel-a-tin
gel-lat-i-nous
ge-la-tion
geld
geld-ed
geld-ing
gelt
gel-id
gem
gemmed
gem-ming
gem-ol-o-gy
gem-o-log-i-cal
gem-ol-o-gist
gem-stone
gen-darme
gen-der
gene
ge-ne-al-o-gy
ge-ne-a-log-i-cal
ge-ne-al-o-gist
gen-er-al
gen-er-al-is-si-mo
gen-er-al-is-si-mos
gen-er-al-ist
gen-er-al-i-ty
gen-er-al-i-ties
gen-er-ate
gen-er-at-ed
gen-er-at-ing
gen-er-a-tive
gen-er-a-tive-ly
gen-er-a-tion
gen-er-a-tor
ge-ner-ic
ge-ner-i-cal
ge-ner-i-cal-ly
gen-er-ous
gen-er-os-i-ty
gen-er-os-i-ties
gen-e-sis
ge-net-ic
ge-net-i-cal-ly
ge-net-ics
ge-net-i-cist
gen-ial
ge-ni-al-i-ty
ge-nie

ge-nies
ge-nii
gen-i-tal
gen-i-ta-lia
gen-i-tals
gen-ius
gen-ius-es
gen-o-cide
gen-o-ci-dal
gen-re
gen-teel
gen-tian
gen-tile
gen-til-i-ty
gen-til-i-ties
gen-tle
gen-tler
gen-tlest
gen-tly
gen-tle-folk
gen-tle-man
gen-tle-men
gen-tle-wom-an
gen-tle-wom-en
gen-try
gen-u-flect
gen-u-flec-tion
gen-u-flec-tor
gen-u-ine
ge-nus
gen-e-ra
ge-nus-es
ge-o-cen-tric
ge-o-cen-tri-cal-ly
ge-o-chem-is-try
ge-o-chem-i-cal
ge-o-chem-ist
ge-ode
ge-o-des-ic
ge-o-gra-phy
ge-o-gra-phies
ge-o-gra-pher
ge-o-gra-phic
ge-o-graph-i-cal
ge-o-met-ric
ge-om-e-try
ge-om-e-tries
ge-o-phys-ics
ge-o-phys-i-cal
ge-o-phys-i-cist
ge-o-pol-i-tic
ge-o-pol-i-tics

ge-o-pol-o-tic
ge-o-po-lit-i-cal
ge-o-po-lit-i-cal-ly
ge-o-ther-mal
ger-bil
ger-i-at-ric
ger-i-at-rics
ger-i-a-tri-cian
ger-i-at-rist
ger-mane
ger-mi-cide
ger-mi-cid-al
ger-on-tol-o-gy
ger-on-tol-o-gist
ger-ry-man-der
ger-und
ges-so
ges-tate
ges-tat-ed
ges-tat-ing
ges-ta-tion
ges-tic-u-late
ges-tic-u-lat-ed
ges-tic-u-lat-ing
ges-tic-u-la-tion
ges-tic-u-la-tive
ges-tic-u-la-to-ry
ges-tic-u-la-tor
ges-ture
ges-tured
ges-tur-ing
ges-tur-er
ge-sund-heit
get-a-way
gew-gaw
gey-ser
ghast-ly
ghast-li-er
ghast-li-est
ghast-li-ness
gher-kin
ghet-to
ghe-tos
ghet-toes
ghoul
gi-ant
gib-ber-ish
gib-bon
gibe
gib-er
gib-ing-ly
gib-let

gid-dy
gid-di-er
gid-di-est
gid-di-ly
gid-di-ness
gi-gan-tic
gi-gan-tism
gig-gle
gig-gled
gig-gling
gig-gler
gig-gly
gig-gli-er
gig-gli-est
gig-o-lo
gild-ed
gilt-edged
gim-crack
gim-let
gim-mick
gin-ger
gin-ger-bread
gin-ger-ly
gin-ger-li-ness
gin-ger-snap
gin-ger-y
ging-ham
gird-er
gir-dle
gir-dled
gir-dling
girl-hood
girl-ish
girth
gist
give
gave
giv-en
giv-ing
give-and-take
give-a-way
giz-zard
gla-cial
gla-cier
glad
glad-der
glad-dest
glad-ly
glad-ness
glad-den
glad-i-a-tor
glad-i-a-to-ri-al

glad-i-o-lus	glib-ly	glove	god-child
glad-i-o-lus-es	glib-ness	gloved	god-chil-dren
glad-i-o-la	**glide**	glov-ing	god-daugh-ter
glad-some	glid-ed	**glow**	god-son
glam-or-ize	glid-ing	glow-er	**god-dess**
glam-or-ized	**glim-mer**	glow-ing	**god-fa-ther**
glam-or-iz-ing	**glimpse**	**glow-worm**	**god-head**
glam-or-i-za-tion	glimpsed	**glu-cose**	**god-less**
glam-or-i-zer	**glis-san-do**	**glue**	god-less-ness
glam-or-ous	glis-san-di	glued	**god-like**
glam-or-ous-ly	glis-san-dos	glu-ing	**god-ly**
glam-or-ous-ness	**glis-ten**	**glum**	god-li-er
glam-our	**glit-ter**	glum-mer	god-li-est
glance	**gloam-ing**	glum-mest	god-li-ness
glanced	**gloat**	**glut**	**god-mo-ther**
glanc-ing	gloat-er	glut-ted	**god-par-ent**
glan-du-lar	gloat-ing	glut-ting	**god-send**
glare	**glob**	**glu-ten**	**go-get-ter**
glared	**glo-bal**	**glu-ti-nous**	**gog-gle**
glar-ing	glob-al-ly	**glut-ton**	gog-gled
glar-i-ness	**globe-trot-ter**	**glut-ton-ous**	gog-gling
glar-y	globe-trot-ting	glut-tony	**gog-gle-eyed**
glar-i-er	**glob-u-lar**	**glyc-er-in**	**gog-gles**
glar-i-est	**glob-ule**	glyc-er-ine	**go-ing**
glass-blow-ing	**glock-en-spiel**	**glyc-er-ol**	**goi-ter**
glass-blow-er	**gloom-y**	**gnarl**	**gold-brick**
glass-ful	gloom-i-er	gnarled	**gold-en**
glass-ware	gloom-i-est	gnarly	**gold-smith**
glass-y	gloom-i-ly	gnarl-i-er	**go-nad**
glass-i-er	gloom-i-ness	gnarl-i-est	**gon-do-la**
glass-i-est	**glo-ri-fy**	**gnash**	**gon-do-lier**
glass-i-ly	glo-ri-fied	**gnat**	**gon-er**
glass-i-ness	glo-ri-fy-ing	**gnaw**	**gon-or-rhea**
glau-co-ma	glo-ri-fi-ca-tion	gnawed	**goo-ber**
glaze	glo-ri-fi-er	gnaw-ing	**good-by**
glazed	**glo-ri-ous**	**gneiss**	good-bye
glaz-ing	glo-ri-ous-ly	**gnome**	**good-for-noth-ing**
gla-zier	glo-ri-ou-ness	**gnu**	**good-heart-ed**
gleam	**glo-ry**	gnus	**good-ish**
gleam-ing	glo-ries	**goad-ed**	**good-look-ing**
gleam-y	glo-ried	**go-a-head**	**good-ly**
glean	glo-ry-ing	**goal-keep-er**	good-li-er
glean-er	**glos-sa-ry**	**goat-ee**	good-li-est
glean-ing	**glos-sa-ries**	**goat-herd**	**good-na-tured**
glee	**glossy**	**goat-skin**	**good-ness**
glee-ful	gloss-i-er	**gob-ble**	**good-tem-pered**
glee-ful-ly	gloss-i-est	gob-bled	**good-y**
glee-ful-ness	gloss-i-ly	gob-bling	good-ies
glen-gar-ry	gloss-i-ness	**gob-ble-dy-ween**	**goof-off**
glib	**glot-tis**	**gob-let**	**goof-y**
glib-ber	glot-tis-es	**gob-lin**	goof-i-er
glib-best	glot-ti-des	**go-cart**	goof-i-est

goof-i-ness
goose-ber-ry
goose-ber-ries
gore
gored
gor-ing
gorge
gorged
gorg-ing
gor-geous
gor-geous-ly
gor-geous-ness
gor-y
gor-i-er
gor-i-est
gos-ling
gos-pel
gos-sa-mer
gos-sa-mery
gos-sa-mer-i-er
gos-sa-mer-i-est
gos-sip
gos-sip-ing
gos-sipy
gouge
gouged
goug-ing
goug-er
gou-lash
gourd
gour-met
gour-mets
gout
gouty
gout-i-er
gout-i-est
gov-ern
gov-ern-a-ble
gov-ern-ess
gov-ern-ment
gov-ern-men-tal
gov-er-nor
gov-er-nor-ship
gow-and
gowned
grab
grabbed
grab-bing
grab-ber
grace
graced
grac-ing

grace-ful
grace-ful-ly
grace-ful-ness
grace-less
gra-cious
gra-da-tion
grade
grad-ed
grad-ing
grad-er
gra-di-ent
grad-u-al
grad-u-al-ly
grad-u-al-ness
grad-u-ate
grad-u-at-ed
grad-u-at-ing
grad-u-ation
graf-fi-to
graf-fi-ti
graft
graft-age
graft-er
graft-ing
gra-ham
grain
grain-y
grain-i-er
grain-i-est
grain-i-ness
gram
gram-mar
gram-mar-i-an
gram-mat-i-cal
gram-mat-i-cal-ly
gra-na-ry
gra-na-ries
grand
grand-ly
grand-child
grand-daugh-ter
gran-dee
gran-deur
grand-fa-ther
gran-dil-o-quence
gran-dil-o-quent
gran-di-ose
gran-di-ose-ly
grand-moth-er
grand-par-ent
grand-son
grand-stand

grange
grang-er
gran-ite
gra-nat-ic
gran-ny
gran-nies
gran-u-lar
gran-u-lar-i-ty
gran-u-late
gran-u-lat-ed
gran-u-lat-ing
gran-u-la-tion
gran-ule
grape-fruit
grape-vine
graph-ic
graph-i-cal
graph-i-cal-ly
graph-ite
graph-ol-o-gy
graph-ol-o-gist
grap-nel
grap-ple
grap-pled
grap-pling
grap-pler
grass
grass-y
grass-i-er
grass-i-est
grass-hop-per
grass-land
grate
grat-ed
grat-ing
grate-ful
grate-ful-ly
grate-ful-ness
grat-i-fy
grat-i-fied
grat-i-fy-ing
gra-tis
grat-i-tude
gra-tu-i-tous
gra-tu-i-ty
gra-tu-i-ties
grave
graved
grav-en
grav-ing
grav-er
grave-ly

grave-ness
grav-el
grav-eled
grav-el-ing
grav-el-ly
grave-stone
grave-yard
grav-i-tate
grav-i-tat-ed
grav-i-tat-ing
grav-i-ta-tion
grav-i-ta-tion-al
grav-i-ty
grav-i-ties
gra-vy
grav-ies
gray
gray-ly
gray-ness
gray-ling
graze
grazed
graz-ing
grease
greas-ed
greas-ing
greas-y
greas-i-er
greas-i-ness
great
great-ly
great-coat
great-heart-ed
greed-y
greed-i-er
greed-i-est
greed-i-ly
greed-i-ness
green-back
green-er-y
green-er-ies
green-gro-cer
green-horn
green-house
green-hous-es
green-ing
green-ish
green-ish-ness
green-sward
greet
greet-er
greet-ing

gre-gar-i-ous
gre-gar-i-ous-ly
gre-gar-i-ous-ness
grem-lin
gren-a-dier
gren-a-dine
grey
grey-ly
grey-ness
grid-dle
grid-dle-cake
grid-i-ron
grief
griev-ance
grieve
grieved
griev-ing
griev-ous
griev-ous-ly
grif-fin
grif-fon
grill
gril-lage
grille
grill-room
grim
grim-mer
grim-mest
grim-ly
grim-ness
grim-ace
grim-aced
grim-ac-ing
grime
grimed
grim-ing
grim-y
grim-i-er
grim-i-est
grim-i-ly
grim-i-ness
grin
grin-ned
grin-ning
grin-ner
grind
ground
grind-ing
grind-er
grind-stone
grin-go
grin-gos

grip
gripped
grip-ping
gripe
griped
grip-er
grippe
gris-ly
gris-li-er
gris-li-est
gris-li-ness
gris-tle
gris-tly
gris-tli-er
gris-tli-est
grit
grit-ted
grit-ting
grit-ty
grit-ti-er
grit-ti-est
grit-ti-ly
grit-ti-ness
griz-zled
griz-zly
griz-zli-er
griz-zli-est
griz-zlies
groan
groan-er
gro-cer
gro-cer-y
gro-cer-ies
grog-gy
grog-gi-er
groin
grom-met
groom
groove
grooved
groov-er
groov-y
groov-i-er
groov-i-est
grope
groped
grop-ing
gros-grain
gross
gross-es
gross-ness
gro-tesque

gro-tesque-ly
gro-tesque-ness
grot-to
grot-toes
grot-tos
grouch
grouchy
grouch-i-er
grouch-i-est
ground-er
ground-less
ground-less-ly
ground-less-ness
ground-ling
ground-nut
ground-work
group-ie
grouse
groused
grous-ing
grous-er
grov-el
grov-eled
grov-el-er
grow
grow-ing
grow-er
growl
growl-er
grown-up
growth
grub
grubbed
grub-bing
grub-ber
grub-by
grub-bi-er
grub-bi-est
grub-stake
grub-staked
grub-stak-ing
grudge
grudged
grudg-ing
grudg-ing-ly
gru-el
gru-el-ing
grue-some
grue-some-ly
gruff
gruff-ly
gruff-ness

grum-ble
grum-bled
grum-bling
grum-bler
grump-y
grump-i-er
grump-i-ness
grunt
grunt-er
grunt-ing
gua-no
gua-nos
guar-an-tee
guar-an-teed
guar-an-tee-ing
guar-an-tor
guar-an-ty
guar-an-ties
guar-an-ty-ing
guard-ed
guard-ed-ly
guard-house
guard-i-an
guards-man
guards-men
gua-va
gu-ber-na-to-ri-al
gudg-eon
guer-ril-la
gue-ril-la
guess
gues-ser
guess-work
guest
guf-faw
guid-ance
guide
guid-ed
guid-ing
guide-book
guide-post
gui-don
guid-hall
guile
guile-ful
guile-ful-ly
guile-less
guile-less-ly
guil-to-tine
guil-lo-tined
guil-lo-tin-ing
guilt

guilt-less

guilt-less-ly

guilt-y

guilt-i-er

guilt-i-ness

guin-ea

guise

gui-tar

gui-tar-ist

gul-let

gul-li-ble

gul-li-bil-i-ty

gul-li-bly

gum

gummed

gum-ming

gum-bo

gum-bos

gum-drop

gum-my

gum-mi-er

gum-mi-est

gump-tion

gum-shoe

gum-shoed

gun

gunned

gun-ning

gun-boat

gun-fight

gun-fight-er

gun-fire

gun-man

gun-men

gun-ner

gun-ner-y

gun-ny

gun-nies

gun-ny-bag

gun-pow-der

gun-stock

gun-wale

gup-py

gup-pies

gur-gle

gur-gling

gu-ru

gush-er

gush-ing

gush-y

gush-i-er

gush-i-est

gus-set

gus-ta-to-ry

gus-to

gut-ter

gut-tur-al

gut-tur-al-ly

guz-zle

guz-zled

guz-zling

guz-zler

gym-na-si-um

gym-na-si-ums

gym-na-sia

gym-nast

gym-nas-tic

gym-nas-tics

gy-ne-col-o-gy

gy-ne-co-log-ic

gy-ne-co-log-i-cal

gy-ne-col-o-gist

gyp

gypped

gyp-ping

gyp-sum

gyp-sy

gyp-sies

gy-ral

gy-rate

gy-rat-ed

gy-rat-ing

gy-ra-tion

gy-ra-tor

gy-ra-to-ry

gyr-fal-con

gy-roi-dal

gy-rom-e-ter

gy-ro-plane

gy-ro-scope

gy-ro-scop-ic

gy-rose

gy-rus

gyve

gyved

gyv-ing

H

hab-da-lah

ha-be-as cor-pus

hab-er-dash-er

hab-er-dash-ery

hab-er-dash-er-ies

ha-bil-i-ment

hab-it

hab-it-a-ble

ha-bi-tant

hab-i-ta-tion

ha-bit-u-al

ha-bit-u-al-ly

ha-bit-u-al-ness

ha-bit-u-ate

ha-bit-u-at-ed

ha-bit-u-at-ing

ha-bit-u-a-tion

ha-ci-en-da

ha-ci-en-das

hack-le

hack-led

hack-ling

hack-ney

hack-neyed

hack-saw

hadn't

had-ron

hae-mo-glo-bin

hae-mo-phil-i-a

haft

ha-gar

hag-gard

hag-gard-ly

hag-gle

hag-gled

hag-gling

hag-gler

ha-gi-ol-o-gy

hag-i-ol-o-gies

hag-i-ol-o-gist

hag-rid-den

haik

hai-ku

hail-fel-low

hail-stone

hail-storm

hair-breadth

hair-brush

hair-cut

hair-do

hair-dress-er

hair-dress-ing

hair-line

hair-pin

hair-split-ter

hair-split-ting

hair-spring

hair-y

hair-i-er

hair-i-est

ha-la-tion

hal-cy-on

hale

haled

hal-ing

half-back

half-baked

half-breed

half-caste

half-heart-ed

half-heart-ed-ly

half hour

half--life

half-lives

half--mast

half--moon

half note

half step

half-tone

half-track

half-truth

half-way

half--wit

half--wit-ted

hal-i-but

hal-i-to-sis

hall-mark

hal-lo

hal-low

hal-lowed

hal-lu-ci-nate

hal-lu-ci-nat-ed

hal-lu-ci-nat-ing

hal-lu-ci-na-tion

hal-lu-ci-na-to-ry

hal-lu-cin-o-gen

hal-lu-cin-o-gen-ic

hal-lux

hall-way

halo-phile

halt

halt-ing

halt-ing-ly

hal-ter

hal-ter-break

halve

halved

halv-ing

halv-ers

halves	hand-spring	hard-cov-er	har-vest
hal-yard	hand-to-hand	hard-en	har-ves-ter
ham-burg-er	hand--to--mouth	hard-en-er	has--been
ham-let	hand-work	hard hat	hash-ish
ham-mer	hand-writ-ing	hard-head-ed	hash-eesh
ham-mer-head	handy	hard-heart-ed	hasn't
ham-mer-less	hand-i-er	har-di-hood	has-sle
ham-mock	hand-i-est	har-di-ness	has-sled
ham-my	handy-man	hard-ly	has-sling
ham-mi-er	handy-men	har-di-er	has-sock
ham-mi-est	hang	har-di-est	has-ten
hamp-er	hung	har-di-ly	hasty
ham-ster	hanged	hare-brained	hast-i-er
ham-string	hang-ing	hare-lip	hast-i-est
ham-strung	hung-ar	har-em	hatch-ery
ham-string-ing	hang-dog	har-le-quin	hatch-er-ies
hand-bag	hang-er	har-lot	hatch-et
hand-ball	hang-er--on	har-lot-ry	hatch-way
hand-bill	hang-man	harm-ful	hate
hand-book	hanf-men	harm-ful-ly	hat-ed
hand-cuff	hang-nail	harm-ful-ness	hat-ing
hand-ed	hang-out	harm-less	hat-er
hand-ful	hang-o-ver	harm-less-ly	hate-ful
hand-fuls	hang--up	harm-less-ness	hate-ful-ly
hand-i-cap	hank-er	har-mon-ic	hate-ful-ness
hand-i-capped	han-som	har-mon-i-cal-ly	ha-tred
hand-i-cap-ping	hap-haz-ard	har-mon-i-ca	hat-ter
hand-i-cap-per	hap-haz-ard-ly	har-mon-ics	haugh-ty
hand-i-craft	hap-haz-ard-ness	har-mo-ni-ous	haugh-ti-er
hand-i-ly	hap-less	har-mo-ni-ous-ly	haugh-ti-est
handi-ness	hap-less-ly	har-mo-nize	haugh-ti-ly
hand-i-work	hap-ly	har-mo-nized	haught-ti-ness
han-ker-chief	hap-pen	har-mo-niz-ing	haunch
han-dle	hap-pen-ing	har-mo-ny	haunch-es
han-dled	hap-pen-stance	har-mo-nies	haunt-ed
han-dling	hap-pi-ness	har-ness	haunt-ing
han-dler	hap-py	harp-ist	hau-teur
han-dle-bar	hap-pi-er	har-poon	ha-ven
hand-made	hap-pi-est	harp-si-chord	have--not
hand-maid-en	hap-pi-ly	har-py	haven't
hand--me--down	hap-py--go--lucky	har-pies	hav-er-sack
hand-out	hara-kiri	har-que-bus	havers
hand-pick	ha-rangue	har-ri-dan	hav-oc
hand-picked	ha-rangued	har-row	hawk
hand-rail	ha-rangu-ing	har-row-ing	hawk-ish
hand-shake	ha-rass	har-ry	haw-ser
hand-some	ha-rass-ment	har-ried	hay-loft
hand-som-er	har-bin-ger	har-ry-ing	hay-mak-er
hand-som-est	har-bor	harsh	hay-mow
hand-some-ly	hard--bit-ten	harsh-ly	hay-seed
hand-some-ness	hard--boiled	harsh-ness	hay-stack
hand-spike	hard--core	har-um-scar-um	hay-wire

haz-ard	health-i-est	**hec-to-li-ter**	**hel-er--skel-ter**
haz-ard-ous	health-i-ness	**hec-to-me-ter**	**hem**
haz-ard-ous-ly	**heaped**	**hedge**	hemmed
haze	**hear**	hedged	hem-ming
hazed	heared	hedg-ing	**he--man**
haz-ing	hear-ing	hedg-er	**he--men**
ha-zel	hear-er	**he-do-nism**	**hemi-sphere**
ha-zel-nut	**hear-ken**	he-do-nist	hemi-spher-ic
hazy	**hear-say**	he-do-nis-tic	hemi-sper-i-cal
ha-zi-er	**hearse**	**hee-haw**	**hem-lock**
ha-zi-est	**heart-ache**	**hefty**	**he-mo-glo-bin**
ha-zi-ly	**heart-break**	heft-i-er	**he-mo-phil-ia**
ha-zi-ness	heart-break-ing	heft-i-est	**hem-or-rhage**
head-ache	**heart-brok-en**	**he-ge-mo-ny**	hem-or-rhag-ing
head-band	**heart-burn**	he-ge-mo-nies	hem-or-rhag-ic
head-dress	**heart-en**	heg-e-mon-ic	**hem-or-rhoid**
head-er	**heart-felt**	**he-gi-ra**	hem-or-rhoid-al
head-first	**hearth-stone**	**hcif-er**	**hemp-en**
head-fore-most	**heart-less**	**height-en**	**hem-stitch**
head-gear	heart-less-ly	height-en-er	**hence-forth**
head-hunt-er	heart-less-ness	**hei-nous**	**hench-man**
head-ing	**heart-rend-ing**	hei-nous-ly	**hench-men**
head-land	**heart-sick**	**heir-ess**	hench-man-ship
head-less	**heart-strings**	**heir-loom**	**hen-na**
head-light	**heart--to--heart**	**heist**	**hen-peck**
head-line	**hearty**	**he-li-cop-ter**	**hep-a-ti-tis**
head-lined	heart-i-er	**he-li-um**	**her-ald**
head-lin-ing	heart-i-est	**he-lix**	he-ral-dic
head-long	heart-i-ly	he-li-ces	**her-ald-ry**
head-mas-ter	heart-i-ness	he-lix-es	her-ald-ries
head-mis-tress	**heat-ed**	**hell--bent**	**herb-age**
head-most	**heat-er**	**hell-cat**	**her-biv-o-rous**
head--on	**heath**	**hel-lion**	**Her-cu-le-an**
head-piece	**hea-then**	**hell-ish**	**herd-er**
head-quar-ters	**heave**	hell-ish-ly	**herds-man**
head-set	heaved	hell-ish-ness	herds-men
head-stone	heav-ing	**hel-lo**	**here-af-ter**
head-strong	**heav-en**	hel-los	**he-red-i-tary**
head-wait-er	**heav-en-ly**	**helm**	he-red-i-tar-i-ly
head-wa-ter	**heav-en-ward**	helm-less	**he-red-i-ty**
head-way	heav-en-wards	**hel-met**	he-red-i-ties
head-wind	**heavy--du-ty**	hel-met-ed	**here-in**
heady	**heavy--hand-ed**	**helms-man**	**here-of**
head-i-er	**heavy-weight**	helms-men	**her-e-sy**
head-i-est	**heck-le**	**help-er**	her-e-sies
head-i-ly	heck-led	**help-ful**	**her-e-tic**
head-i-ness	heck-ling	help-ful-ly	he-ret-i-cal
heal-er	heck-ler	help-ful-ness	he-ret-i-cal-ly
health-ful	**hect-are**	**help-ing**	**here-to**
health-ful-ly	**hec-tic**	**help-less**	**here-to-fore**
healthy	hec-ti-cal-ly	help-less-ly	**here-upon**
health-i-er	**hec-to-gram**	**help-mate**	**here-with**

her-i-ta-ble
her-i-ta-bil-i-ty
her-i-ta-bly
her-i-tage
her-maph-ro-dite
her-maph-ro-dit-ic
her-maph-ro-dit-ism
her-met-ic
her-met-i-cal
her-met-i-cal-ly
her-mit
her-mit-age
her-nia
her-ni-al
her-ni-a-tion
he-ro
he-roes
he-ro-ic
he-ro-ical
he-ro-ical-ly
her-o-in
her-o-ine
her-o-ism
her-on
her-ring-bone
her-ring-boned
her-ring-bon-ing
her-self
hes-i-tant
hes-i-tan-cy
hes-i-tan-cies
hes-i-tant-ly
hes-i-ta-tion
het-ero-dox
het-ero-doxy
het-er-o-ge-neous
het-er-o-ge-ne-ity
het-er-o-ge-neous-ly
het-ero-sex-u-al
het-ero-sex-u-al-i-ty
hew
hewed
hewn
hexa-gon
hex-ag-o-nal
hex-ag-o-nal-ly
hey-day
hey-dey
hi-a-tus
hi-a-tus-es
hi-ba-chi
hi-ber-nate

hi-ber-nat-ed
hi-ber-nat-ing
hi-ber-na-tion
hi-bis-cus
hic-cup
hic-cuped
hic-cup-ing
hid-den
hid-den-ness
hide
hid
hid-den
hid-er
hide-bound
hid-eous
hid-eous-ly
hid-eous-ness
hide-out
hi-er-ar-chy
hi-er-ar-chies
hi-er-ar-chal
hi-er-ar-chic
hi-er-ar-chi-cal
hi-er-ar-chi-cal-ly
hi-ero-glyph
hi-ero-glyph-ic
hi-ero-glyph-i-cal
hi-ero-glyph-i-cal-ly
hi--fi
high-ball
high-born
high-boy
high-brow
high-browed
high-brow-ism
high-er--up
high-fa-lu-tin
high-fa-lu-ting
high--flown
high--grade
high--hand-ed
high--hand-ed-ly
high--hand-ed-ness
high--hat
high--land
high--light
high--mind-ed
high--mind-ed-ly
high--mind-ed-ness
high-ness
high--pressure
high--pressured

high--pressur-ing
high school
high seas
high--spir-it-ed
high--spir-it-ed-ly
high--spir-it-ed-ness
high--strung
high-tail
high--tension
high--toned
high-way
high-way-man
high-way-men
hi-jack
hi-jack-er
hi-jack-ing
hike
hiked
hik-ing
hik-er
hi-lar-i-ous
hi-lar-i-ous-ly
hi-lar-i-ous-ness
hi-lar-i-ty
hill-bil-ly
hill-bil-lies
hill-ock
hill-side
hill-top
hilly
hill-i-er
hill-i-est
him-self
hin-der
hin-der-er
hind-most
hind-quar-ter
hin-drance
hind-sight
hinge
hinged
hing-ing
hint-er
hint-ing-ly
hin-ter-land
hipped
hip-pie
hip-po
hip-pos
hip-po-drome
hip-po-pot-a-mus
hip-po-pot-a-mus-es

hip-po-pot-a-mi
hire-ling
hir-sute
hir-sute-ness
hiss
hiss-er
his-ta-mine
his-ta-min-ic
his-to-ri-an
his-tor-ic
his-tor-i-cal
his-tor-i-cal-ly
his-tor-i-cal-ness
his-to-ry
his-to-ries
his-tri-on-ic
his-tri-on-i-cal
his-tri-on-i-cal-ly
his-tri-on-ics
hit
hit-ting
hit--and--run
hitch
hitch-er
hitch-hike
hitch-hiked
hitch-hik-ing
hitch-hik-er
hith-er-to
hive
hived
hiv-ing
hoary
hoar-i-er
hoar-i-est
hoar-i-ness
hoard
hoard-er
hoard-ing
hoar-frost
hoarse
hoarse-ly
hoars-en
hoarse-ness
hoax
hoax-er
hob-ble
hob-bled
hob-bling
hob-by
hob-bies
hob-by-horse

hob-gob-lin
hob-nail
hob-nail-ed
hob-nob
hob-nobbed
hob-nob-bing
ho-bo
ho-boes
ho-bos
ho-bo-ism
hock-er
hock-ey
ho-cus-po-cus
hodge-podge
hoe
hoed
hoe-ing
hoe-down
hog
hogged
hog-ging
hog-gish
hog-gish-ly
hog-gish-ness
hogs-head
hog--tie
hog--tied
hog--ty-ing
hog-wash
hoi pol-loi
hoist-er
ho-kum
hold-er
hold-ing
hold-out
hold-over
hold-up
hole
holed
hol-ing
holey
hol-i-day
ho-li-ness
Hol-land
hol-ler
hol-low
hol-low-ly
hol-low-ness
hol-ly
hol-lies
hol-ly-hock
hol-mi-um

ho-lo-caust
ho-lo-gram
hol-o-graph
hol-ster
ho-ly
ho-li-er
ho-li-est
ho-lies
hom-age
hom-bre
hom-bres
home-com-ing
home-less
home-less-ness
home-ly
home-li-er
home-li-est
home-li-ness
home-made
hom-er
home-sick
home-sick-ness
home-spun
home-stead
home-stead-er
home-ward
home-wards
home-work
homey
hom-i-er
hom-i-est
hom-i-ness
hom-i-cide
hom-i-let-ics
hom-i-ly
hom-i-lies
homing pigeon
hom-i-ny
ho-mo-ge-neous
ho-mo-ge-ne-ity
ho-mo-ge-neous-ness
ho-mog-e-nize
ho-meg-e-nized
ho-mog-e-niz-ing
ho-mo-graph
ho-mol-o-gous
ho-mol-o-gy
ho-mol-o-gies
hom-onym
hom-onym-ic
ho-mo-phone
ho-mo-pho-nic

ho-mo-sex-u-al
ho-mo-sex-u-al-i-ty
hone
honed
hon-ing
hon-est
hon-est-ly
hon-es-ty
hon-es-ties
hon-ey
hon-eys
hon-eyed
hon-ied
hon-ey-ing
hon-ey-bee
hon-ey-comb
hon-ey-moon
hon-ey-moon-er
hon-ey-suck-le
hon-ey-suck-led
hon-ky--tonk
hon-or
hon-or-able
hon-or-ably
hon-o-rar-i-um
hon-o-rar-i-ums
hon-o-rar-ia
hon-or-ary
hon-or-if-ic
hood-ed
hood-lum
hoo-doo
hoo-doo-ism
hood-wink
hood-wink-er
hoo-ey
hoof
hoofs
hooves
hoofed
hooked
hook-er
hook-up
hoo-li-gan
hoo-li-gan-ism
hoop
hooped
hoop-like
hoop-la
hoo-ray
hoose-gow
hoot

hoot-er
hoot-ing-ly
hop
hopped
hop-ping
hop-er
hope-ful
hope-ful-ly
hope-ful-ness
hope-less
hope-less-ly
hope-less-ness
hop-head
hop-per
hop-scotch
horde
hord-ed
hord-ing
ho-ri-zon
hor-i-zon-tal
hor-i-zon-tal-ly
hor-mone
hor-mon-al
horn
horned
horn-like
horny
horn-i-er
horn-i-est
hor-net
horn-swog-gle
horn-swog-gled
horn-swog-gling
hor-rol-o-gy
ho-rol-o-ger
ho-rol-o-gist
horo-scope
hor-ren-dous
hor-ren-dous-ly
hor-ri-ble
hor-ri-bly
hor-rid
hor-rid-ly
hor-rid-ness
hor-ri-fy
hor-ri-fied
hor-ri-fy-ing
hor-ri-fi-ca-tion
hor-ror
horse
hors-es
horsed

hors-ing	**hos-til-i-ty**	**hob-bub**	hum-ble-ness
horse-back	hos-til-i-ties	**huck-le-ber-ry**	hum-bly
horse-fly	**hos-tler**	huck-le-ber-ries	**hum-bug**
horse-flies	**hot**	**huck-ster**	hum-bugged
horse-hair	hot-ter	**hud-dle**	hum-bug-ging
horse-laugh	hot-test	hud-dled	hum-bug-ger
horse-men	hot-ly	hud-dling	hum-bug-gery
horse-man-ship	**hot-bed**	hud-dler	**hum-ding-er**
horse-wom-an	**hot--blood-ed**	**huffy**	**hum-drum**
horse-wom-en	**ho-tel**	huff-i-er	**hu-mer-us**
horse opera	**hot-head**	huff-i-est	**hu-mid**
horse-play	hot-head-ed	huff-i-ly	hu-mid-ly
horse-pow-er	hot-head-ed-ness	huff-i-ness	**hu-mid-i-fy**
horse-rad-ish	**hot-house**	**hug**	hu-mid-i-fied
horse-shoe	**hot-shot**	hugged	hu-mid-i-fy-ing
horse-sho-er	**hound**	hug-ging	hu-mid-i-fi-er
horse-whip	hound-er	hug-ger	**hu-mid-i-ty**
horse-whipped	**hour-glass**	**huge**	**hum-ming-bird**
horse-whip-ping	**hour-ly**	hug-er	**hum-mock**
hors-ey	**house**	hug-est	hum-mocky
horsy	hous-es	huge-ly	hum-mock-i-er
hors-i-er	housed	huge-ness	hum-mock-i-est
hors-i-est	hous-ing	**hu-la**	**hu-mor**
hors-i-ly	**house-boat**	**hulk-ing**	**hu-mor-ist**
hors-i-ness	**house-bro-ken**	**hul-la-ba-loo**	hu-mor-is-tic
hor-ta-to-ry	house-break	**hum**	**hu-mor-ous**
hor-ti-cul-ture	house-broke	hummed	hu-mor-ous-ly
hor-ti-cul-tur-al	house-break-ing	hum-ming	hu-mor-ous-ness
hor-ti-cul-tur-ist	**house-fly**	hum-mer	**hump**
ho-san-na	**house-hold**	**hu-man**	humped
hose	**house-keep-er**	hu-man-ness	humpy
hos-es	house-keep-ing	**hu-mane**	hump-i-er
hosed	**house-maid**	hu-mane-ly	hump-i-est
hos-ing	**house-warm-ing**	hu-man-ness	**hump-back**
ho-siery	**house-wife**	**hu-man-ism**	**hu-mus**
hos-pice	house-wives	hu-man-ist	**hunch-back**
hos-pi-ta-ble	house-wife-ly	hu-man-ist-ic	hunch-backed
hos-pi-ta-bly	house-wif-ery	**hu-man-i-tar-i-an-ism**	**hun-dred**
hos-pi-tal	**house-work**	**hu-man-i-ty**	**hun-ger**
hos-pi-tal-i-ty	hous-ing	hu-man-i-ties	**hun-gry**
hos-pi-tal-i-ties	**hov-el**	**hu-man-ize**	hun-gri-er
hos-pi-tal-iza-tion	hov-eled	hu-man-ized	hun-gri-est
hos-pi-tal-ize	hov-el-ing	hu-man-iz-ing	hun-gri-ly
hos-pi-tal-ized	**hov-er**	hu-man-i-za-tion	hun-gri-ness
hos-pi-tal-iz-ing	hov-er-er	hu-man-iz-er	**hunt**
hos-tage	hov-er-ing	**hu-man-kind**	hunt-er
hos-tel	**how-ev-er**	**hu-man-ly**	hunt-ing
hos-tel-ry	**how-it-zer**	**hum-ble**	hunt-ress
hos-tel-ries	howl-er	hum-bler	hunts-man
host-ess	**how-so-ev-er**	hum-blest	hunts-men
hos-tile	**hoy-den**	hum-bled	**hur-dle**
hos-tile-ly	hoy-den-ish	hum-bling	hur-dled

hur-dling
hur-dler
hur-dy--gur-dy
hur-dy--gur-dies
hurl-er
hurl-y--burl-y
hurl-y--burl-ies
hur-rah
hur-ri-cane
hur-ry
hur-ried
hur-ry-ing
hur-ried-ly
hur-ry-ing-ly
hurt-ful
hurt-ful-ly
hurt-ful-ness
hurt-ing
hur-tle
hur-tled
hur-tling
hurt-less
hus-band
hus-band-er
hus-band-less
hus-band-ly
hus-band-man
hus-band-ry
hush
husk-er
husk-ing
husky
husk-i-er
husk-i-est
husk-i-ly
husk-i-ness
husk-ies
hus-sar
hus-sy
hussies
hus-tings
hus-tle
hus-tled
hus-tling
hus-tler
hutch
hut-ment
huz-zah
huz-za
hy-a-cinth
hy-a-cin-thine
hy-a-line

hy-a-lite
hy-a-loid
hy-a-lo-plasm
hy-brid
hy-brid-ism
hy-brid-i-ty
hy-brid-ize
hy-brid-ized
hy-brid-iz-er
hy-brid-iz-ing
hy-brid-i-za-tion
hy-da-thode
hy-da-tid
hy-dra
hy-dras
hy-dae
hy-dral-azine
hy-dran-gea
hy-drant
hy-dra-ted
hy-dra-ting
hy-dra-tion
hy-dra-tor
hy-drau-lic
hy-drau-li-cal-ly
hy-drau-lics
hy-dro-car-bon
hy-dro-chlo-ric acid
hy-dro-dy-nam-ics
hy-dro-dy-na-mic
hy-dro-elec-tric
hy-dro-gen
hy-drog-e-nous
hy-dro-ly-sis
hy-drom-e-ter
hy-dro-met-ric
hy-dro-met-ri-cal
hy-drom-e-try
hy-dro-pho-bia
hy-dro-plane
hy-dro-plan-er
hy-dro-plan-ing
hy-dro-pon-ics
hy-dro-ther-a-py
hy-dro-ther-a-pist
hy-drous
hy-drox-ide
hy-drox-yl
hy-dro-zo-an
hy-e-na
hy-giene
hy-gien-ic

hy-gien-i-cal-ly
hy-gien-ist
hy-men
hy-me-ne-al
hy-me-ne-al-ly
hym-nal
hy-per-bo-la
hy-per-bo-le
hy-per-bo-lize
hy-per-bo-lized
hy-per-bo-liz-ing
hy-per-bol-ic
hy-per-crit-i-cal
hy-per-crit-i-cal-ly
hy-per-sen-si-tive
hy-per-sen-si-tiv-i-ty
hy-per-sex-u-al
hy-per-sex-u-al-ity
hy-per-ten-sion
hy-per-thy-roid-ism
hy-phen
hy-phen-ate
hy-phen-at-ed
hy-phen-at-ing
hyp-no-sis
hyp-not-ic
hyp-no-tism
hyp-no-tist
hyp-no-tize
hyp-no-tized
hyp-no-tiz-ing
hy-po
hy-po-chon-dria
hy-po-chon-dri-ac
hy-poc-ri-sy
hy-poc-ri-sies
hyp-o-crite
hy-po-der-mic
hy-po-sen-si-tize
hy-po-sen-si-tized
hy-po-sen-si-tiz-ing
hy-po-ten-sion
hy-pot-e-nuse
hy-poth-e-cate
hy-poth-e-cat-ed
hy-poth-e-cat-ing
hy-poth-e-ca-tion
hy-poth-e-ca-tor
hy-poth-e-sis
hy-poth-e-ses
hy-poth-e-size
hy-poth-e-siz-ing

hy-po-thet-i-cal
hy-po-thet-i-cal-ly
hyp-ox-emia
hyp-ox-ia
hyp-sog-ra-phy
hy-son
hys-sop
hys-ter-ec-to-my
hys-ter-ec-to-mies
hys-ter-e-sis
hys-te-ria
hys-ter-ic
hys-ter-i-cal
hys-ter-i-cal-ly
hys-ter-ics

I

iamb
iat-ric
ibid
ibi-dem
ibis
ibis-es
ice-boat
ice--cream
ice-man
ice-men
ice--skate
icon
icon-o-clasm
icon-o-clas-tic
icon-o-clast
ide-al-ize
ide-al-ized
ide-al-iz-ing
ide-al-i-za-tion
ide-al-ly
idem
iden-ti-cal
iden-ti-cal-ly
iden-ti-fi-a-ble
iden-ti-fy-ing
iden-ti-fi-a-bly
iden-ti-fi-ca-tion
iden-ti-fy
iden-ti-fied
iden-ti-fy-ing
iden-ti-fi-er
iden-ti-ty
iden-ti-ties
ides

id-i-o-cy
id-i-o-cies
id-i-om
id-i-o-mat-ic
id-i-o-mat-i-cal-ly
id-i-o-syn-cra-sy
id-i-o-syn-cra-sies
id-i-o-syn-crat-ic
id-i-ot
id-i-ot-ic
id-i-ot-i-cal-ly
idle
idol
idol-ize
idyll
idyl-lic
idyl-lic-al-ly
ig-ne-ous
ig-nite
ig-ni-tion
ig-no-ble
ig-no-bil-i-ty
ig-no-bly
ig-no-ra-mus
ig-no-rant
ig-no-rance
ig-no-rant-ly
ig-nore
ig-nored
ig-nor-ing
igua-na
ill--ad-vised
ill--ad-vis-ed-ly
ill--bred
il-le-gal
il-le-gal-i-ty
il-le-gal-ly
il-leg-i-ble
il-leg-i-bil-i-ty
il-leg-i-bly
il-le-git-i-mate
il-le-git-i-ma-cy
il-le-git-i-ma-cies
il-le-git-i-mate-ly
ill--fat-ed
ill--fa-vored
ill--got-ten
il-lib-er-al
il-lic-it
il-lim-it-able
il-lit-er-a-cy
il-lit-er-a-cies

il-lit-er-ate
ill-ness
il-log-i-cal
ill-starred
ill-tem-pered
ill-tem-pered-ly
il-lu-mi-na-tion
il-lu-mine
il-lu-mined
il-lu-min-ing
ill-use
il-lu-sion
il-lu-sive
il-lu-sive-ly
il-lu-sive-ness
il-lus-trate
il-lus-trat-ed
il-lus-trat-ing
il-lus-tra-tion
il-lus-tra-tive
il-lus-tra-tive-ly
il-lus-tra-tor
il-lus-tri-ous
il-lus-tri-ous-ly
im-age
im-aged
im-ag-ing
im-age-a-ble
im-ag-er
im-ag-ery
im-ag-eries
im-ag-eri-al
imag-in-able
imag-in-able-ness
imag-in-ably
imag-i-nary
imag-i-nar-ies
imag-i-nar-i-ly
imag-i-nar-i-ness
imag-i-na-tion
imag-i-na-tion-al
imag-i-na-tive
imag-i-na-tive-ly
imag-ine
imag-ined
imag-in-ing
im-bal-ance
im-be-cile
im-be-cil-ic
im-be-cile-ly
im-be-cil-i-ty
imbed

imbed-ded
im-bed-ding
im-bibe
im-bro-glio
im-brue
im-brued
im-bru-ing
im-i-ta-ble
im-i-tate
im-i-tat-ed
im-i-tat-ing
im-i-ta-tor
im-i-ta-tion
im-i-ta-tive
im-mac-u-late
im-mac-u-la-cy
im-mac-u-late-ly
im-ma-te-ri-al
im-ma-te-ri-al-ness
im-ma-te-ri-al-i-ty
im-ma-te-ri-al-ize
im-ma-ture
im-ma-ture-ly
im-ma-ture-ness
im-ma-tu-ri-ty
im-meas-ur-a-ble
im-meas-ur-a-bly
im-me-di-a-cy
im-me-di-a-cies
im-me-di-ate
im-me-di-ate-ly
im-me-di-ate-ness
im-me-mo-ri-al
im-me-mo-ri-al-ly
im-mense
im-mese-ly
im-mese-ness
im-men-si-ty
im-merge
im-merged
im-merse
im-mersed
im-mers-ing
im-mer-sion
im-mi-grant
im-mi-grat-ed
im-mi-gra-tion
im-mi-gra-tor
im-mi-nent
im-mi-nence
im-mo-bile
im-mo-bil-i-ty

im-mo-bi-lize
im-mod-er-ate
im-mod-er-ate-ly
im-mod-er-ate-ness
im-mod-est
im-mod-est-ly
im-mod-es-ty
im-mo-late
im-mo-lat-ed
im-mo-lat-ing
im-mo-la-tion
im-mo-la-tor
im-mor-al
im-mor-al-ist
im-mo-ral-i-ty
im-mor-al-ly
im-mor-tal
im-mov-a-ble
im-mov-a-bli-i-ty
im-mov-a-bly
im-mune
im-mu-ni-ty
im-mu-ni-ties
im-mu-nize
im-mu-nized
im-mu-niz-ing
im-mu-ni-za-tion
im-mu-nol-o-gy
im-mure
im-mured
im-mur-ing
im-mu-ta-ble
im-mu-ta-bil-i-ty
im-mu-ta-bly
im-pact
im-pac-tion
im-pact-ed
im-pair
im-pair-er
im-pair-ment
im-pa-la
im-pal-as
im-pal-ae
im-pal-pa-ble
im-pal-pa-bil-i-ty
im-pal-pa-bly
im-pan-el
im-pan-eled
im-pan-el-ing
im-part
im-par-tial
im-par-ti-al-i-ty

im-par-tial-ly
im-pass-able
im-pass-abil-i-ty
im-pass-able-ness
im-pass-ably
im-passe
im-pas-si-ble
im-pas-si-bil-i-ty
im-pas-si-bly
im-pas-sion
im-pas-sioned
im-pas-sioned-ly
im-pas-sive
im-pas-sive-ly
im-pas-sive-ness
im-pas-siv-i-ty
im-pa-tience
im-pa-tient
im-pa-tient-ly
im-peach
im-peach-a-ble
im-peach-ment
im-pec-ca-ble
im-pec-ca-bil-i-ty
im-pec-ca-bly
im-pe-cu-nious
im-pe-cu-nious-ly
im-pe-cu-nious-ness
im-pede
im-ped-ed
im-ped-ing
im-ped-i-ment
im-pel
im-pelled
im-pel-ling
im-pend
im-pend-ing
im-pen-e-tra-bil-i-ty
im-pen-e-tra-ble
im-pen-e-tra-ble-ness
im-pen-e-tra-bly
im-pen-i-tent
im-pen-i-tence
im-pen-i-tent-ly
im-per-cep-ti-ble
im-per-cep-ti-bil-i-ty
im-per-cep-tive
im-per-cep-tive-ness
im-per-fect
im-per-fect-ly
im-per-fect-ness
im-per-fec-tion

im-pe-ri-al
im-pe-ri-al-ly
im-pe-ri-al-ism
im-pe-ri-al-ist
im-pe-ri-al-is-tic
im-pe-ri-al-is-ti-cal-ly
im-per-il
im-per-iled
im-per-il-ing
im-per-il-ment
im-pe-ri-ous
im-pe-ri-ous-ly
im-pe-ri-ous-ness
im-per-ish-able
im-per-ish-abil-i-ty
im-per-ish-able-ness
im-per-ish-ably
im-per-ma-nence
im-per-ma-nen-cy
im-per-ma-nent
im-per-ma-nent-ly
im-per-me-able
im-per-me-abil-i-ty
im-per-me-able-ness
im-per-me-ably
im-per-son-al
im-per-son-al-i-ty
im-per-son-al-i-ties
im-per-son-al-ly
im-per-son-ate
im-per-son-at-ed
im-per-son-at-ing
im-per-son-a-tion
im-per-son-ator
im-per-ti-nent
im-per-ti-nence
im-per-ti-nent-ly
im-per-turb-able
im-per-turb-ably
im-per-vi-ous
im-per-vi-ous-ly
im-per-vi-ous-ness
im-pe-ti-go
im-pet-u-os-i-ty
im-pet-u-ous
im-pet-u-ous-ly
im-pet-u-ous-ness
im-pe-tus
im-pe-tus-es
im-pi-ety
im-pi-eties
im-pinge

im-pinged
im-ping-ing
im-pinge-ment
im-ping-er
im-pi-ous
im-pi-ous-ly
im-pi-ous-ness
im-pla-ca-ble
im-pla-ca-bil-i-ty
im-pla-ca-ble-ness
im-pla-ca-bly
im-plant
im-plan-ta-tion
im-plant-er
im-plau-si-ble
im-plau-si-bly
im-plau-si-bil-i-ty
im-ple-ment
im-ple-men-tal
im-ple-men-ta-tion
im-pli-cate
im-pli-cat-ed
im-pli-cat-ing
im-pli-ca-tion
im-plic-it
im-plic-it-ly
im-plic-it-ness
im-plode
im-plod-ed
im-plod-ing
im-plo-sion
im-plo-sive
im-ply
im-plied
im-ply-ing
im-po-lite
im-po-lite-ly
im-po-lite-ness
im-pol-i-tic
im-pol-i-tic-ly
im-pon-der-a-ble
im-pon-der-a-bil-i-ty
im-pon-der-a-bly
im-pone
im-poned
im-port
im-port-a-ble
im-port-er
im-por-tance
im-por-tant
im-por-tant-ly
im-por-ta-tion

im-por-tu-nate
im-por-tu-nate-ly
im-por-tune
im-por-tuned
im-por-tun-ing
im-pose
im-posed
im-pos-ing
im-pos-ter
im-po-si-tion
im-pos-si-bil-i-ty
im-pos-si-bil-i-ties
im-pos-si-ble
im-pos-si-bly
im-post
im-pos-tor
im-pos-ture
im-po-tence
im-po-ten-cy
im-po-tent
im-po-tent-ly
im-pound
im-pound-age
im-pov-er-ish
im-pov-er-ish-ment
im-prac-ti-ca-ble
im-prac-ti-ca-bil-i-ty
im-prac-ti-ca-ble-ness
im-prac-ti-ca-bly
im-prac-ti-cal
im-pre-cate
im-pre-cat-ed
im-pre-cat-ing
im-pre-ca-tion
im-preg-na-ble
im-preg-na-bil-i-ty
im-preg-na-bly
im-pre-sa-rio
im-pre-sa-ri-os
im-press
im-press-er
im-press-i-ble
im-press-ment
im-pres-sion
im-pres-sion-ist
im-pres-sion-a-ble
im-pres-sion-a-bly
im-pres-sion-ism
im-pres-sion-ist
im-pres-sion-is-tic
im-pres-sive
im-pres-sive-ly

im-pres-sive-ness	in-ac-tiv-i-ty	in-ca-pac-i-tat-ing	in-clined
im-pri-ma-tur	**in-ad-e-quate**	**in-ca-pac-i-ty**	in-clin-ing
im-print	in-ad-e-qua-cies	in-ca-pac-i-ties	in-clin-er
im-print-er	in-ad-e-qua-cy	**in-car-cer-ate**	**in-clude**
im-pris-on	**in-ad-e-quate-ly**	in-car-cer-at-ed	in-clud-ed
im-pris-on-ment	**in-ad-mis-si-ble**	in-car-cer-at-ing	in-clud-ing
im-prob-a-bil-i-ty	in-ad-mis-si-bly	in-car-cer-a-tion	in-clud-a-ble
im-prob-a-ble	**in-ad-ver-tence**	**in-car-nate**	in-clu-sion
im-prob-a-ble-ness	**in-ad-ver-ten-cy**	in-car-nat-ed	**in-clu-sive**
im-prob-a-bly	**in-ad-ver-tent**	in-car-nat-ing	in-clu-sive-ly
im-promp-tu	in-ad-ver-tent-ly	**in-car-na-tion**	in-clu-sive-ness
im-prop-er	**in-alien-a-ble**	**in-cen-di-ary**	**in-cog-ni-to**
im-prop-er-ly	in-alien-a-bly	in-cen-di-aries	in-cog-ni-tos
im-prop-er-ness	**in-am-o-ra-ta**	**in-cense**	**in-co-her-ence**
im-pro-pri-ety	in-am-o-ra-tas	in-censed	**in-co-her-ent**
im-pro-pri-eties	**in-an-i-mate**	in-ceas-ing	in-co-her-ent-ly
im-prove-ment	**in-ap-pro-pri-ate**	**in-cen-tive**	**in-come**
im-prov-i-dence	in-ap-pro-pri-ate-ly	**in-cep-tion**	**in-com-ing**
im-prov-i-dent	in-ap-pro-pri-ate-ness	**in-ces-sant**	**in-com-men-su-ra-ble**
im-prov-i-dent-ly	**in-apt**	in-ces-sant-ly	in-com-men-su-ra-bly
im-pro-vi-sa-tion	**in-apt-ti-tude**	**in-cho-ate**	**in-com-men-su-rate**
im-pro-vi-sa-tion-al	in-apt-ly	in-cho-ate-ly	**in-com-mo-di-ous**
im-pro-vise	in-apt-ness	in-cho-ate-ness	**in-com-pa-ra-ble**
im-pro-vised	**in-ar-tic-u-late**	**in-ci-dence**	in-com-pa-ra-bly
im-pro-vis-ing	in-ar-tic-u-late-ly	**in-ci-dent**	**in-com-pat-i-bil-i-ty**
im-pro-vis-er	in-ar-tic-u-late-ness	**in-ci-den-tal**	**in-com-pat-i-ble**
im-pru-dence	**in-as-much as**	in-ci-den-tal-ly	in-com-pat-i-bly
im-pru-dent	**in-at-ten-tion**	**in-cin-er-ate**	**in-com-pe-tence**
im-pru-dent-ly	**in-at-ten-tive**	in-cin-er-at-ed	**in-com-pen-ten-cy**
im-pugn	in-at-ten-tive-ly	in-cin-er-at-ing	**in-com-pe-tent**
im-pugn-er	**in-au-gu-ral**	in-cin-er-a-tion	in-com-pe-tent-ly
im-pulse	**in-au-gu-rate**	**in-cin-er-a-tor**	**in-com-plete**
im-pul-sion	in-au-gu-rat-ed	**in-cip-i-ent**	in-com-plete-ly
im-pul-sive	in-au-gu-rat-ing	in-cip-i-ent-ly	in-com-plete-ness
im-pu-ni-ty	**in-au-gu-ra-tion**	**in-cise**	in-com-ple-tion
im-pure	**in-aus-pi-cious**	in-cised	**in-com-pre-hen-si-b**
im-pure-ly	in-aus-pi-cious-ly	in-cis-ing	in-com-pre-hen-si-bl
im-pure-ness	**in-board**	**in-ci-sion**	in-com-pre-hen-sion
im-pu-ri-ty	**in-born**	**in-ci-sive**	**in-con-ceiv-able**
im-pu-ri-ties	**in-bred**	in-ci-sive-ly	in-con-ceiv-ably
in-a-bil-i-ty	in-breed	in-ci-sive-ness	**in-con-clu-sive**
in-ac-ces-si-ble	in-breed-ing	**in-ci-sor**	in-con-clu-sive-ly
in-ac-ces-si-bil-i-ties	**in-cal-cu-la-ble**	**in-cite**	in-con-clu-sive-ness
in-ac-ces-si-ble-ness	in-cal-cu-la-bly	in-cit-ed	**in-con-gru-ity**
in-ac-ces-si-bly	**in-can-des-cent**	in-cit-ing	**in-con-gru-ous**
in-ac-cu-rate	in-can-des-cence	in-cite-ment	in-con-gru-ous-ly
in-ac-cu-rate-ly	in-can-des-cent-ly	in-cit-er	in-con-gru-ous-ness
in-ac-cu-ra-cy	**in-can-ta-tion**	**in-clem-en-cy**	in-con-gru-i-ties
in-ac-cu-ra-cies	**in-ca-pa-ble**	**in-clem-ent**	**in-con-se-quen-tial**
in-ac-tion	in-ca-pa-bly	in-clem-ent-ly	in-con-se-quen-tial-
in-ac-tive	**in-ca-pac-i-tate**	**in-cli-na-tion**	**in-con-sid-er-able**
in-ac-tive-ly	in-ca-pac-i-tat-ed	**in-cline**	in-con-sid-er-ably

in-con-sid-er-ate
in-con-sid-er-ate-ly
in-con-sid-er-ate-ness
in-con-sis-tent
in-con-sist-ent-ly
in-con-sol-able
in-con-sol-able-ness
in-con-sol-ably
in-con-spic-u-ous
in-con-spic-u-ous-ly
in-con-stant
in-con-stan-cy
in-con-stan-cies
in-con-stant-ly
in-con-test-able
in-con-test-abil-i-ty
in-con-ti-nence
in-con-ti-nen-cy
in-con-ti-nent
in-con-ti-nent-ly
in-con-trol-la-ble
in-con-tro-vert-ible
in-con-ve-nience
in-con-ve-nien-cy
in-con-ve-nient
in-con-ve-nient-ly
in-con-ven-ienc-ing
in-con-vert-ible
in-con-vert-ibly
in-cor-po-rate
in-cor-po-rat-ed
in-cor-po-rat-ing
in-cor-po-ra-tion
in-cor-po-ra-tor
in-cor-po-re-al
in-cor-rect
in-cor-rect-ly
in-cor-ri-gi-ble
in-cor-ri-gi-bil-i-ty
in-cor-ri-gi-ble-ness
in-cor-ri-gi-bly
in-cor-rupt-ible
in-cor-rupt-ibil-i-ty
in-cor-rupt-ible-ness
in-cor-rupt-ibly
in-crease
in-creased
in-creas-ing
in-creas-able
in-creas-ing-ly
in-cred-i-ble
in-cred-i-bil-i-ty

in-cred-i-ble-ness
in-cred-i-bly
in-cre-du-li-ty
in-cred-u-lous
in-cred-u-lous-ness
in-cred-u-lous-ly
in-cre-ment
in-cre-men-tal
in-crim-i-nate
in-crim-i-nat-ed
in-crim-i-nat-ing
in-crim-i-na-tion
in-crim-i-na-tor
in-crim-i-na-to-ry
in-crust
in-crus-ta-tion
in-cu-bate
in-cu-bat-ed
in-cu-bat-ing
in-cu-ba-tion
in-cu-ba-tor
in-cu-bus
in-cu-bus-es
in-cul-cate
in-cul-cat-ed
in-cul-cat-ing
in-cul-ca-tion
in-cul-ca-tor
in-cul-pate
in-cul-pat-ed
in-cul-pat-ing
in-cul-pa-tion
in-cum-ben-cy
in-cum-ben-cies
in-cum-bent
in-cum-bent-ly
in-cur
in-curred
in-cur-ring
in-cur-able
in-cur-a-bil-i-ty
in-cur-a-ble-ness
in-cur-a-bly
in-cur-sion
in-cur-sive
in-debt-ed
in-debt-ed-ness
in-de-cen-cy
in-den-cies
in-de-cent
in-de-cent-ly
in-de-ci-sion

in-de-ci-sive
in-de-ci-sive-ly
in-de-ci-sive-ness
in-deed
in-de-fat-i-ga-ble
in-de-fat-i-ga-bil-i-ty
in-de-fat-i-ga-ble-ness
in-de-fat-i-ga-bly
in-def-i-nite
in-def-i-nite-ly
in-def-i-nite-ness
in-del-i-ble
in-del-i-bil-ity
in-del-i-ble-ness
in-del-i-bly
in-del-i-ca-cy
in-del-i-cate
in-del-i-cate-ness
in-del-i-cate-ly
in-dem-ni-fi-ca-tion
in-dem-ni-fy
in-dem-ni-fied
in-dem-ni-fy-ing
in-dem-ni-fi-er
in-dem-ni-ty
in-dem-ni-ties
in-dent
in-den-ta-tion
in-dent-ed
in-den-ture
in-den-tured
in-den-tur-ing
in-de-pen-dence
in-de-pen-den-cy
in-de-pen-dent
in-de-pen-dent-ly
in-de-scib-able
in-de-scrib-abil-ity
in-de-scrib-able-ness
in-de-scrib-ably
in-de-struc-ti-ble
in-de-struc-ti-bil-i-ty
in-de-struc-ti-ble-ness
in-de-struc-ti-bly
in-det-mi-na-cy
in-de-ter-mi-nate
in-de-ter-mi-nat-ly
in-de-ter-mi-na-tion
in-dex
in-dex-er
in-dex-es
in-di-ces

in-di-cate
in-di-cat-ed
in-di-cat-ing
in-di-ca-tion
in-dic-a-tive
in-dic-a-tive-ly
in-di-ca-tor
in-di-ca-tory
in-dict
in-dict-a-ble
in-dict-er
in-dict-or
in-dict-ment
in-dif-fer-ence
in-dif-fer-ent
in-dif-fer-ent-ist
in-dif-fer-ent-ly
in-dig-e-nous
in-dig-e-nous-ly
in-dig-e-nous-ness
in-di-gent
in-di-gent-ly
in-di-gest-ed
in-di-gest-ible
in-di-gest-ibil-i-ty
in-di-gest-ible-ness
in-di-ges-tion
in-di-ges-tive
in-dig-nant
in-dig-nant-ly
in-dig-na-tion
in-dig-ni-ty
in-dig-ni-ties
in-di-go
in-di-goes
in-di-gos
in-di-rect
in-di-rect-ly
in-di-rect-ness
in-dis-creet
in-dis-creet-ly
in-dis-creet-ness
in-dis-crete
in-dis-cre-tion
in-dis-crim-i-nate
in-dis-crim-i-nate-ly
in-dis-crim-i-nat-ing
in-dis-crim-i-na-tion
in-dis-pens-able
in-dis-pens-able-ness
in-dis-pens-abil-i-ty
in-dis-pens-ably

in-dis-pose
in-dis-posed
in-dis-pos-ing
in-dis-po-si-tion
in-dis-sol-u-ble
in-dis-sol-u-bil-i-ty
in-dis-sol-u-ble-ness
in-dis-sol-u-bly
in-di-um
in-di-vid-u-al
in-di-vid-u-al-ly
in-di-vid-u-al-ism
in-di-vid-u-al-ist
in-di-vid-u-al-is-tic
in-di-vid-u-al-i-ty
in-di-vid-u-al-i-ties
in-di-vid-u-al-ize
in-di-vid-u-al-ized
in-di-vid-u-al-iz-ing
in-doc-tri-nate
in-doc-tri-nat-ed
in-doc-tri-nat-ing
in-doc-tri-na-tion
in-doc-tri-na-tor
in-do-lence
in-do-lent
in-do-lent-ly
in-dom-i-ta-ble
in-dom-i-ta-bil-i-ty
in-dom-ita-ble-ness
in-dom-i-ta-bly
in-door
in-doors
in-du-bi-ta-ble
in-du-bi-ta-bil-i-ty
in-dubi-ta-ble-ness
in-du-bi-tab-ly
in-duce
in-duced
in-duce-ment
in-duc-er
in-duc-i-ble
in-duc-ing
in-duct
in-duct-ee
in-duc-tion
in-duc-tive
in-dulge
in-dulged
in-dulg-ing
in-dul-gence
in-dul-gent

in-dul-gent-ly
in-dus-tri-al
in-dus-tri-al-ly
in-dus-tri-al-ness
in-dus-tri-al-ism
in-dus-tri-al-ize
in-dus-tri-al-ist
in-dus-tri-al-i-za-tion
in-dus-tri-al-ized
in-dus-tri-al-iz-ing
in-dus-tri-ous
in-dus-tri-ous-ly
in-dus-try
in-dus-tries
ine-bri-ate
ine-bri-at-ed
ine-bri-at-ing
ine-bri-a-tion
ine-bri-ety
in-ed-u-ca-ble
in-ef-fa-ble
in-ef-fa-bil-i-ty
in-ef-fa-ble-ness
in-ef-fa-bly
in-ef-fec-tive
in-ef-fec-tive-ly
in-ef-fec-tive-ness
in-ef-fec-tu-al
in-ef-fec-tu-al-i-ty
in-ef-fec-tu-al-ly
in-ef-fec-tu-al-ness
in-ef-fi-cient
in-ef-fi-cien-cy
in-ef-fi-cien-cies
in-ef-ffi-cient-ly
in-el-i-gi-ble
in-el-i-gi-bil-i-ty
in-el-i-gi-bly
in-e-luc-ta-ble
in-ept
in-ept-i-tude
in-ept-ly
in-ept-ness
in-e-qual-i-ty
in-eq-ui-ta-ble
in-eq-ui-ty
in-eq-ui-ties
in-ert
in-ert-ly
in-ert-ness
in-er-tia
in-er-tial

in-es-cap-a-ble
in-es-cap-a-ble
in-es-ti-ma-ble
in-es-ti-ma-bly
in-ev-i-ta-ble
in-ev-i-ta-bil-i-ty
in-ev-i-ta-ble-ness
in-ev-i-ta-ble-ness
in-ev-i-ta-bly
in-ex-haust-i-ble
in-ex-haust-i-bil-i-ty
in-ex-haust-i-ble-ness
in-ex-haust-i-bly
in-ex-o-ra-ble
in-ex-o-ra-bil-i-ty
in-ex-o-ra-ble-ness
in-ex-o-ra-bly
in-ex-pe-ri-ence
in-ex-pe-ri-enced
in-ex-pert
in-ex-per-ly
in-ex-pert-ness
in-ex-pe-ri-ence
in-ex-pe-ri-enced
in-ex-pert
in-ex-pert-ly
in-ex-pert-ness
in-ex-pi-a-ble
in-ex-pi-a-ble-ness
in-ex-pi-a-bly
in-ex-pli-ca-ble
in-ex-pli-ca-bil-i-ty
in-ex-pli-ca-ble-ness
in-ex-pli-ca-bly
in-fal-li-ble
in-fal-i-bil-i-ty
in-fal-li-ble-ness
in-fal-li-bly
in-fa-mous
in-fa-mous-ly
in-fa-mous-ness
in-fa-my
in-fa-mies
in-fan-cy
in-fan-cies
in-fant
in-fant-hood
in-fant-like
in-fan-tile
in-fan-tine
in-fan-til-i-ty
in-fan-try

in-fan-tries
in-fan-try-man
in-fan-try-men
in-fat-u-ate
in-fat-u-at-ed
in-fat-u-at-ing
in-fat-u-at-ed-ly
in-fat-u-a-tion
in-fect
in-fect-ed-ness
in-fect-er
in-fect-or
in-fec-tion
in-fec-tious
in-fec-tious-ly
in-fec-tious-ness
in-fec-tive
in-fer
inferred
in-fer-ring
in-fer-a-ble
in-fer-a-bly
in-fer-ence
in-fer-er
in-fe-ri-or
in-fe-ri-or-i-ty
in-fe-ri-or-ly
in-fer-nal
in-fer-no
in-fer-nos
in-fest
in-fes-ta-tion
in-fest-er
in-fi-del
in-fi-del-i-ty
in-fi-del-i-ties
in-field
in-field-er
in-fight-ing
in-fight-er
in-fil-trate
in-fil-trat-ed
in-fil-trat-ing
in-fil-tra-tion
in-fil-tra-tive
in-fil-tra-tor
in-fi-nite
in-fi-nite-ly
in-fi-nite-ness
in-fin-i-tude
in-fin-i-tes-i-mal
in-fin-i-tes-i-mal-ty

in-fin-i-tive
in-fin-i-tive-ly
in-fin-i-ty
in-fin-i-ties
in-firm
in-firm-lly
in-firm-ness
in-fir-ma-ry
in-fir-ma-ries
in-fir-mi-ty
in-fir-mi-ties
in-flame
in-flamed
in-flam-ing
in-flam-er
in-flam-ma-ble
in-flam-ma-bil-i-ty
in-flam-ma-ble-ness
in-flam-ma-bly
in-flam-ma-tion
in-flam-ma-to-ry
in-flate
in-flat-ed
in-flat-ing
in-flat-a-ble
in-flat-ed-ness
in-fla-tor
in-flat-er
in-fla-tion
in-fla-tion-ary
in-fla-tion-ism
in-fla-tion-ist
in-flect
in-flec-tion
in-flec-tion-al
in-flec-tion-al-ly
in-flec-tion-less
in-flec-tive
in-flec-tor
in-flex-i-ble
in-flex-i-bil-i-ty
in-flex-i-ble-ness
in-flex-i-bly
in-flict
in-flict-a-ble
in-flict-er
in-flict-or
in-flic-tion
in-flic-tive
in-flu-ence
in-flu-enced
in-flu-enc-ing

in-flu-ence-a-ble
in-flu-enc-er
in-flu-en-tial
in-flu-en-tial-ly
in-flu-en-za
in-flu-en-zal
in-flu-en-za-like
in-flux
in-form
in-formed
in-for-mer
in-for-mal
in-for-mal-i-ty
in-for-mal-ly
in-form-ant
in-for-ma-tion
in-for-ma-tion-al
in-for-ma-tive
in-for-ma-tive-ly
in-for-ma-tive-ness
in-for-ma-to-ry
in-frac-tion
in-fran-gi-ble
in-fran-gi-bil-i-ty
in-fran-gi-ble-ness
in-fran-gi-bly
in-fra-red
in-fra-struc-ture
in-fre-quent
in-fre-quen-cy
in-fre-quent-ly
in-fringe
in-fringed
in-fring-ing
in-fringe-ment
in-fring-er
in-fu-ri-ate
in-fu-ri-at-ed
in-fu-ri-at-ing
in-fu-ri-at-ing-ly
in-fu-ri-a-tion
in-fuse
in-fused
in-fus-ing
in-fus-er
in-fus-i-bil-i-ty
in-fus-i-ble
in-fu-sion
in-fu-sive
in-gen-ious
in-gen-ious-ly
in-gen-ious-ness

in-gest
in-ges-tion
in-ges-tive
in-glo-ri-ous
in-glo-ri-ous-ly
in-glo-ri-ous-ness
in-got
in-grain
in-grained
in-grate
in-gra-ti-ate
in-gra-ti-at-ed
in-gra-ti-at-ing
in-gra-ti-a-tion
in-grat-i-tude
in-gre-di-ent
in-group
in-grow-ing
in-grown
in-growth
in-gulf
in-hab-it
in-hab-it-a-ble
in-hab-i-ta-tion
in-hab-it-er
in-hab-it-ed
in-hab-it-ant
in-hal-ant
in-ha-la-tion
in-ha-la-tor
in-hale
in-haled
in-hal-ing
in-hal-er
in-here
in-hered
in-her-ing
in-her-ence
in-her-ent
in-her-ent-ly
in-he-sion
in-her-it
in-her-i-tor
in-her-i-tance
in-hib-it
in-hib-i-tive
in-hib-o-to-ry
in-hib-i-ter
in-hib-it-or
in-hi-bi-tion
in-hos-pi-ta-ble
in-hos-pi-tal-i-ty

in-hu-man
in-hu-man-i-ty
in-hu-mane
in-im-i-cal
in-im-i-ta-ble
in-iq-ui-ty
in-iq-ui-ties
in-iq-ui-tous
in-i-tial
in-i-tialed
in-i-tial-ing
in-i-tial-ly
in-i-ti-ate
in-i-ti-at-ed
in-i-ti-at-ing
in-i-ti-a-tion
in-i-ti-a-tor
in-i-ti-a-tive
in-ject
in-jec-tion
in-jec-tor
in-ju-di-cious
in-junc-tion
in-junc-tive
in-jur
in-jured
in-jur-ing
in-ju-ri-ous
in-ju-ry
in-ju-ries
in-jus-tice
ink-blot
ink-ling
inky
in-law
in-lay
in-laid
in-lay-ing
in-let
in-me-mo-ri-an
in-most
in-nards
in-nate
in-ner
in-ner-most
in-ner-sole
in-ner-vate
in-ner-vat-ed
in-ner-vat-ing
in-ner-va-tion
in-nerve
in-ning

inn-keep-er	in-sa-ti-ate	in-so-cia-ble	in-sti-tu-tion-al-ism
in-no-cence	in-scribe	in-so-cia-bil-i-ty	in-sti-tu-tion-al-ize
in-no-cent	in-scru-ta-ble	in-so-cia-bly	in-sti-tu-tion-al-ized
in-no-cent-ly	in-scru-ta-bil-i-ty	in-so-far	in-struct
in-noc-u-ous	in-scru-ta-bly	in-sole	in-struc-tion
in-no-vate	in-seam	in-so-lent	in-struc-tive
in-no-vat-ed	in-sect	in-so-lence	in-struc-tor
in-no-vat-ing	in-sec-ti-cide	in-sol-u-ble	in-stru-ment
in-no-va-tion	in-sec-ti-cid-al	in-sol-u-bil-i-ty	in-stru-men-tal
in-no-va-tive	in-se-cure	in-sol-u-bly	in-stru-men-ta-list
in-no-va-tor	in-se-cu-ri-ty	in-solv-a-ble	in-stru-men-ta-tion
in-nu-en-do	in-sem-i-nate	in-sol-vent	in-sub-or-di-nate
in-nu-en-dos	in-sem-i-nat-ed	in-sol-ven-cy	in-sub-or-di-na-tion
in-nu-en-does	in-sem-i-nat-ing	in-som-nia	in-sub-stan-tial
in-nu-mer-a-ble	in-sem-i-na-tion	in-som-ni-ac	in-sub-stan-ti-al-i-ty
in-nu-mer-ous	in-sen-sate	in-so-much	in-suf-fer-a-ble
in-nu-mer-a-bly	in-sen-si-ble	in-spect	in-suf-fer-a-bly
in-ob-serv-ance	in-sen-si-tive	in-spec-tion	in-suf-fi-cient
in-ob-serv-ant	in-sen-si-tiv-i-ty	in-spec-tor	in-suf-fi-cien-cy
in-ob-serv-ant-ly	in-sen-ti-ent	in-spi-ra-tion	in-su-lar
in-oc-u-lant	in-sep-a-ra-ble	in-spi-ra-tion-al	in-su-lar-i-ty
in-oc-u-late	in-sep-a-ra-bil-i-ty	in-spire	in-su-late
in-oc-u-lat-ed	in-sep-a-ra-bly	in-spir-ing	in-su-lat-ed
in-oc-u-lat-ing	in-sert	in-spir-it	in-su-lat-ing
in-oc-u-la-tion	in-sert-er	in-sta-ble	in-su-la-tion
in-oc-u-la-tor	in-ser-tion	in-sta-bil-i-ty	in-su-la-tor
in-oc-u-lum	in-set	in-stall	in-su-lin
in-of-fen-sive	in-set-ting	in-stan-ta-ne-ous	in-sult
in-op-er-a-ble	in-shore	in-stant-ly	in-sop-port-a-ble
in-op-er-a-tive	in-side	in-state	in-sup-press-i-ble
in-op-por-tune	in-sid-er	in-stat-ed	in-sur-ance
in-op-por-tun-i-ty	in-sid-i-ous	in-stat-ing	in-sure
in-or-di-nate	in-sight	in-state-ment	in-sured
in-pa-tient	in-sight-ful	in-stead	in-sur-ing
in-pour	in-sig-nia	in-step	in-sur-er
in-put	in-sig-nif-i-cant	in-sti-gate	in-sur-gent
in-quest	in-sig-nif-i-cance	in-sti-gat-ed	in-sur-gence
in-qui-e-tude	in-sin-cere	in-sti-gat-ing	in-sur-gen-cy
in-quire	in-sin-cer-i-ty	in-sti-ga-tion	in-sur-mount-a-ble
in-quiry	in-sin-cer-i-ties	in-sti-ga-tor	in-sur-rec-tion
in-quir-ies	in-sin-u-ate	in-still	in-sur-rec-tion-ary
in-qui-si-tion	in-sin-u-at-ed	in-stinct	in-sus-cep-ti-ble
in-qui-si-tive	in-sin-u-at-ing	in-stinc-tive	in-tact
in-quis-i-tor	in-sin-u-a-tor	in-stinc-tu-al	in-take
in-road	in-sin-u-a-tion	in-stinc-tive-ly	in-tan-gi-ble
in-rush	in-sip-id	in-sti-tute	in-tan-gi-bil-i-ty
in-sane	in-si-pid-i-ty	in-sti-tut-ed	in-tan-gi-bly
in-san-i-ty	in-sip-id-ness	in-sti-tut-ing	in-te-ger
in-san-i-ties	in-sist	in-sti-tut-er	in-te-gral
in-sa-tia-ble	in-sist-ence	in-sti-tu-tor	in-te-gral-ly
in-sa-tia-bil-i-ty	in-sist-ent	in-sti-tu-tion	in-te-grate
in-sa-tia-bly	in-so-bri-e-ty	in-sti-tu-tion-al	in-te-grat-ed

in-te-grat-ing
in-te-gra-tion
in-te-gra-tion-ist
in-teg-ri-ty
in-tel-lect
in-tel-lec-tu-al
in-tel-lec-tu-al-ism
in-tel-li-gence
in-tel-li-gent
in-tel-li-gent-ly
in-tel-li-gent-sia
in-tel-li-gi-ble
in-tel-li-gi-bil-i-ty
in-tel-li-gi-bly
in-tem-per-ance
in-tem-per-ate
in-tend
in-tend-er
in-tend-ed
in-tense
in-tense-ly
in-tense-ness
in-ten-si-fy
in-ten-si-fied
in-ten-si-fy-ing
in-ten-si-fi-ca-tion
in-ten-si-fi-er
in-ten-sion
in-ten-si-ty
in-ten-si-ties
in-ten-sive
in-ten-sive-ly
in-ten-sive-ness
in-tent
in-ten-tion
in-ten-tion-al
in-ten-tion-al-ly
in-ten-tioned
in-ter
in-ter-act
in-ter-ac-tion
in-ter-breed
in-ter-bred
in-ter-cede
in-ter-ced-ed
in-ter-ced-ing
in-ter-ced-er
in-ter-cept
in-ter-cep-ter
in-ter-cept-or
in-ter-cep-tion
in-ter-cep-tive

in-ter-ces-sion
in-ter-change
in-ter-changed
in-ter-chang-ing
in-ter-chang-a-ble
in-ter-chng-a-bil-i-ty
in-ter-chang-a-bly
in-ter-col-le-gi-ate
in-ter-com
in-ter-com-mun-i-cate
in-ter-con-nect
in-ter-con-nec-tion
in-ter-con-ti-nen-tal
in-ter-course
in-ter-cul-tur-al
in-ter-cur-rent
in-ter-de-part-men-tal
in-ter-de-pend-ent
in-ter-de-pend
in-ter-de-pend-ence
in-ter-de-pend-en-cy
in-ter-dict
in-ter-dic-tion
in-ter-dis-ci-pli-nary
in-ter-est
in-ter-est-ed
in-ter-est-ed-ly
in-ter-est-ing
in-ter-face
in-ter-fa-cial
in-ter-faith
in-ter-fere
in-ter-ga-lac-tic
in-ter-im
in-te-ri-or
in-ter-ject
in-ter-jec-tion
in-ter-jec-to-ry
in-ter-ly-er
in-ter-leaf
in-ter-leaves
in-ter-leave
in-ter-leaved
in-ter-leav-ing
in-ter-line
in-ter-lined
in-ter-lin-ing
in-ter-link
in-ter-lock
in-ter-lo-cu-tion
in-ter-loc-u-tor
in-ter-loc-u-to-ry

in-ter-lop-er
in-ter-lude
in-ter-nar
in-ter-na-ry
in-ter-mar-ry
in-ter-mar-ried
in-ter-mar-ry-ing
in-ter-mar-riage
in-ter-me-di-ary
in-ter-me-di-ar-ies
in-ter-me-di-ate
in-ter-me-di-at-ed
in-ter-me-di-at-ing
in-ter-me-di-a-tion
in-ter-me-di-a-tor
in-ter-mi-na-ble
in-ter-min-gle
in-ter-min-gledd
in-ter-min-gling
in-ter-mis-sion
in-ter-mis-sive
in-ter-mit
in-ter-mix
in-ter-mix-ture
in-tern
in-ter-ship
in-ter-nal
in-ter-nal-ly
in-ter-na-tion-al
in-ter-na-tion-al-i-ty
in-ter-na-tion-al-ize
in-ter-na-tion-al-ized
in-ter-na-tion-al-ism
in-tern-ee
in-tern-ist
in-tern-ment
in-ter-of-fice
in-ter-pen-e-trate
in-ter-pen-e-tra-tion
in-ter-plan-e-tary
in-ter-play
in-ter-po-late
in-ter-pose
in-ter-posed
in-ter-pos-ing
in-ter-pos-er
in-ter-po-si-tion
in-ter-pret
in-ter-pret-a-ble
in-ter-pret-er
in-ter-pre-tive
in-ter-pre-ta-tion

in-ter-pre-ta-tion-al
in-ter-pre-ta-tive
in-ter-ro-gate
in-ter-ro-gat-ed
in-ter-ro-gat-ing
in-ter-ro-ga-tion
in-ter-ro-ga-tion
in-ter-ro-ga-tion-al
in-ter-rog-a-tive
in-ter-ro-ga-tor
in-ter-rupt
in-ter-rup-tion
in-ter-rup-tive
in-ter-rupt-er
in-ter-rupt-or
in-terr-scho-las-tic
in-ter-sect
in-ter-sec-tion
in-ter-space
in-ter-spaced
in-ter-spac-ing
in-ter-state
in-ter-stel-lar
in-ter-tid-al
in-ter-twine
in-ter-twined
in-ter-twin-ing
in-ter-ur-ban
in-ter-val
in-ter-vence
in-ter-view
in-ter-view-er
in-ter-weave
in-ter-wove
in-ter-weav-ing
in-ter-wo-ven
in-tes-tate
in-tes-tine
in-tes-ti-nal
in-ti-mate
in-ti-mat-ed
in-ti-mat-ing
in-ti-mate-ly
in-ti-ma-tion
in-tim-i-date
in-tim-i-dat-ed
in-tim-i-dat-ing
in-tim-i-da-tion
in-tim-i-da-tor
in-ti-tled
in-ti-ling
in-to

in-tol-er-a-ble	in-un-da-tor	**in-vi-ta-tion**	**ir-rec-on-cil-a-ble**
in-tol-er-a-bly	**in-vade**	in-vi-ta-tion-al	**ir-re-cov-er-a-ble**
in-tol-er-ant	**in-val-id**	**in-vo-ca-tion**	**ir-re-duc-i-ble**
in-tol-er-ance	in-va-lid-i-ty	**in-voice**	**ir-ref-u-ta-ble**
in-tomb	**in-va-lid-ism**	**in-voke**	**ir-re-gard-less**
in-to-mate	**in-val-u-a-ble**	in-voked	**ir-reg-u-lar**
in-to-nat-ed	**in-var-i-a-ble**	in-vok-ing	ir-reg-u-lar-i-ty
in-to-nat-ing	in-var-i-a-bil-i-ty	**in-vol-un-tary**	**ir-rel-e-vant**
in-to-na-tion	**in-var-i-ant**	in-vol-un-tar-i-ly	ir-rel-e-vance
in-tone	in-var-i-ance	**in-vo-lute**	ir-rel-e-van-cy
in-toned	**in-va-sion**	**in-vo-lu-tion**	**ir-re-li-gion**
in-ton-ing	in-va-sive	**in-volve**	ir-re-li-gious
in-ton-er	**in-vec-tive**	in-volved	**ir-re-mis-si-ble**
in-tox-i-cant	**in-ven-tion**	in-volv-ing	**ir-re-mov-a-ble**
in-tox-i-cate	**in-ven-tive**	in-volve-ment	**ir-rep-a-ra-ble**
in-tox-i-cat-ed	in-ven-tive-ness	in-volv-er	**ir-re-plac-a-ble**
in-tox-i-cat-ing	**in-ven-to-ry**	**in-vul-ner-a-ble**	**ir-re-press-i-ble**
in-tox-i-ca-tion	in-ven-to-ries	**in-ward**	ir-re-press-i-bil-i-ty
in-trac-ta-ble	in-ven-to-ried	in-wards	ir-re-press-i-bly
in-trac-ta-bil-i-ty	in-ven-to-ry-ing	in-ward-ly	**ir-re-proach-a-ble**
in-tra-mu-ral	**in-verse**	**in-waeve**	**ir-re-sist-i-ble**
in-tra-mu-ral-ly	**in-ver-sion**	**in-wrought**	ir-re-sist-i-bil-i-ty
in-tran-si-gent	**in-vert**	**io-dine**	**ir-res-o-lute**
in-tran-si-gence	**in-ver-te-brate**	**ion**	ir-res-o-lu-tion
in-tran-si-tive	**in-vert-ed**	ion-ic	**ir-re-spec-tive**
in-tra-state	**in-vest**	**ion-o-sphere**	**ir-re-spon-si-ble**
in-tra-ve-nous	in-ves-tor	**iota**	ir-re-spon-si-bil-i-ty
in-trench	**in-ves-ti-gate**	**ip-so fac-to**	**ir-re-spon-sive**
in-trep-id	in-ves-ti-gat-ed	**iras-ci-ble**	**ir-re-triev-a-ble**
in-tre-pid-i-ty	in-ves-ti-gat-ing	iras-ci-bil-i-ty	ir-re-triev-a-bil-i-ty
in-trique	in-ves-ti-ga-tion	iras-ci-bly	ir-re-trieev-a-bly
in-tri-quing	in-ves-ti-ga-tor	**irate**	**ir-rev-o-ca-ble**
in-trin-sic	**in-ves-ti-ture**	**ir-i-des-cent**	ir-rev-o-ca-bil-i-ty
in-trin-si-cal	**in-vest-ment**	ir-i-des-cence	**ir-ri-gate**
in-trin-si-cal-ly	**in-vet-er-ate**	**irid-i-um**	ir-ri-gat-ed
in-tro-spect	**in-vid-i-ous**	**iris**	**ir-ri-ta-ble**
in-tro-spec-tion	**in-vig-or-ate**	**irk-some**	**ir-ri-tant**
in-tro-spec-tive	in-vig-or-at-ed	**iron**	**ir-ri-tate**
in-tro-ver-sion	in-vig-or-at-ing	iron-er	**ir-rupt**
in-tro-ver-sive	in-vig-or-ant	**iron-clad**	**is-land**
in-tro-vert	in-vig-or-a-tion	**iron-ic**	**isle**
in-tro-vert-ed	in-vig-or-a-tor	iron-i-cal	**iso-bar**
in-trude	**in-vin-ci-ble**	**iron-smith**	**iso-gloss**
in-trust	in-vin-ci-bil-i-ty	**iron-ware**	**iso-late**
in-tu-it	in-vin-ci-bly	**iron-work**	iso-lat-ed
in-tu-i-tion	**in-vi-o-la-ble**	iron-work-er	**iso-met-ric**
in-tu-i-tion-al	in-vi-o-la-bil-i-ty	**iro-ny**	**ison-o-my**
in-tu-i-tive	in-vi-o-la-bly	iro-nies	**iso-ton-ic**
in-un-date	**in-vi-o-late**	**ir-rad-i-ca-ble**	**is-su-ance**
in-un-dat-ed	**in-vis-i-ble**	**ir-ra-tion-al**	**is-sue**
in-un-dat-ing	in-vis-i-bil-i-ty	ir-ra-tion-al-i-ty	**item**
in-un-da-tion	in-vis-i-bly	**ir-re-claim-a-ble**	**it-er-ate**

ivo-ry

J

jab
jabbed
jab-bing
jab-ber
jab-ber-er
jac-a-mar
jac-a-ram-da
jack-al
jack-ass
jack-boot
jack-et
jack-et-ed
jack-ham-mer
jack-knife
jack-kives
jack-knifed
jack-knif-ing
jack--o'--lan-tern
jack-pot
jackrab-bit
jac-o-net
jac-quard
jade
jad-ed
jad-ing
Jaf-fa
jag
jag-ged
jag-ging
jag-uar
jail-bird
jail-break
jail-er
ja-lopy
ja-lop-ies
jal-ou-sie
jam
jammed
jam-ming
jam-mer
jamb
jam-bo-ree
jan-gle
jan-gled
jan-gling
jan-gler
jan-gly
jan-i-tor

jan-i-to-ri-al
jar
jar-ful
jarred
jar-ring
jar-di-niere
jar-red
jar-gon
jar-gon-ize
jas-mine
jas-sid
jaun-dice
jaun-diced
jaun-dic-ing
jaunt
jaun-ty
jaun-ti-er
jaun-ti-est
jaun-ti-ly
jaun-ti-ness
jav-e-lin
jaw-bone
jaw-break-er
jay-gee
jay-walk
jay-walk-er
jazz
jazz-ist
jazz-man
jazzy
jazz-i-er
jazz-i-est
jazz-i-ly
jazz-i-ness
jeal-ous
jeal-ous-ies
jeep
jeer-er
je-hu
jel-li-fy
jel-li-fies
jel-li-fy-ing
jel-ly
jel-lied
jel-lies
jel-ly-ing
jel-ly-like
jel-ly bean
jel-ly-fish
jen-ny
jen-nies
jeop-ar-dy

jeop-ar-dize
jeop-ar-dized
jeop-ar-diz-ing
jerk
jerk-er
jerk-i-ly
jerk-y
jerk-i-er
jerk-i-est
jer-kin
jer-sey
jes-sa-mine
jest-er
jest-ing
Je-sus
jet
jet-ted
jet-ting
jet-lin-er
jet-port
jet-pro-polled
jet-sam
jet-ti-son
jet-ty
jet-ties
jew-el
jew-eled
jew-el-ing
jew-el-er
jew-el-ry
jibe
jibed
jib-ing
jig
jigged
jig-ging
jig-ger
jig-gle
jig-gled
jig-gling
jig-gly
jig-saw
jilt-er
jim-dan-dy
jim-my
jim-mies
jim-mied
jim-my-ing
jin-gle
jin-gled
jin-gling
jinx

jit-ney
jit-neys
jit-ter
jit-ters
jit-tery
jit-ter-bug
jit-ter-bugged
job
jobbed
job-bing
job-ber
job-hold-er
jock-ey
jock-eys
jock-ey-ing
jock-strap
jo-cose
jo-cos-i-ty
jo-cund
jo-cun-di-ty
jodh-pur
jog
jogged
jog-ging
jog-ger
jog-gle
jog-gled
jog-gling
join-able
join-er
joint
joint-ed
joint-ly
joist
joke
joked
jok-ing
joke-ster
jok-ing-ly
jok-er
jolt
jolt-er
jolt-ing-ly
jolty
jon-quil
jos-tle
jos-tled
jos-tling
jos-tler
jot
jott-ed
joule

jour-nal	**juke-box**	jut-ting	**ket-tle**
jour-nal-ism	**ju-lep**	jute	**ket-tle-drum**
jour-nal-ist	**ju-li-enne**	**ju-ve-nes-cence**	**key**
jour-na-lis-tic	**Ju-lius**	ju-ve-nes-cent	keyed
jour-nal-ize	**Ju-ly**	**ju-ve-nile**	**key-board**
jour-ney	**jum-ble**	ju-ve-nil-i-ty	**key-hole**
jour-ney-man	jum-bled	**jux-ta-pose**	**key-note**
jour-ney-men	jum-bling	jux-ta-posed	**key-stone**
joust	**jum-bo**	jux-ta-pos-ing	**kha-ki**
jo-vi-al	jum-bos	jux-ta-po-si-tion	khak-is
jo-vi-al-i-ty	**jump**		**kha-lif**
jowl	jump-ing	**K**	**khan**
jowled	jumpy		**kib-butz**
jowy	**jump-er**	**ka-bob**	kib-but-zim
joy-ful	**jump--off**	**kai-ser**	**ki-bitz-er**
joy-less	**junc-tion**	**ka-lei-do-scope**	**ki-bosh**
joy-ous	**junc-ture**	ka-lei-do-scop-ic	**kick-off**
joy-ride	**jun-gle**	**ka-mi-ka-ze**	**kid**
ju-bi-lant	**jun-ior**	**kan-ga-roo**	**kid-nap**
ju-bi-lance	**ju-ni-per**	**ka-olin**	**kid-ney**
ju-bi-lan-cy	**junk**	ka-oline	kid-neys
ju-bi-lar-i-an	junk-man	**ka-pok**	**kill-deer**
ju-bi-la-tion	junky	**ka-put**	**kill-ing**
ju-bi-late	**jun-ket**	**ka-ra-te**	**kill-joy**
ju-bi-lat-ed	**junk-ie**	**kar-ma**	**kiln**
ju-bi-lat-ing	**jun-ta**	kar-mic	**kilo**
ju-bi-lee	**Ju-pi-ter**	**ka-ty-did**	kil-os
judge	**ju-ris-dic-tion**	**kay-ak**	**kilo-cy-cle**
judged	ju-ris-dic-tion-al	**kay-o**	**ki-lo-gram**
judg-ing	**ju-ris-pru-dence**	**kedge**	**ki-lo-me-ter**
judge-ment	ju-ris-pru-den-tial	kedged	**ki-lo-ton**
judge-men-tal	**ju-ris-pru-dent**	kedg-ing	**kil-o-watt**
ju-di-ca-ture	**ju-rist**	**keel-haul**	**kilt**
ju-di-cial	**ju-ris-tic**	**keel-son**	**ki-mo-no**
ju-di-cia-ry	**ju-ror**	**keen-ly**	**kin-der-gar-ten**
ju-di-cious	**ju-ry**	keen-ness	**kin-dle**
Ju-dith	ju-ries	**keep-ing**	kin-dled
ju-do	ju-ry-man	**keep-sake**	kin-dling
jug	**just**	**keg-ler**	**kind-ly**
jugged	just-ly	**kelp**	kind-li-er
jug-gin	just-ness	**ken-nel**	kind-li-est
jug-ful	**jus-tice**	ken-neled	**kin-dred**
jug-gler	jus-tice-less	ken-nel-ing	**kin-e-mat-ic**
ju-gate	jus-tice-like	**ke-no**	**kin-e-scope**
jug-u-lar	jus-ti-fi-ca-tion	**ker-a-tin**	**ki-net-ic**
jug-u-lum	**jus-ti-fy**	**ker-chief**	ki-net-ics
ju-gum	jus-ti-fied	**ker-mis**	**kin-folk**
juice	jus-ti-fy-ing	**ker-nel**	**king-bird**
juic-i-er	jus-ti-fi-a-ble	**ker-o-sene**	**king-dom**
juic-i-est	jus-tif-i-ca-tory	**kes-trel**	**king-ly**
juic-i-ly	**jut**	**ketch-up**	**king-pin**
ju-jit-su	jut-ted	**ke-tone**	**king--size**

king--sized
kink-y
kink-i-er
kink-i-est
kins-folk
kins-man
kins-men
kins-wom-an
ki-osk
kip-per
kir-mess
kis-met
kiss-a-ble
kiss-er
kitch-en
kitch-en-ette
kite
kit-ed
kit-ing
kitsch
kit-ten
kit-ten-ish
kit-ten-ish-ly
kit-ty
kit-ties
kit-ty--cor-ner
ki-wi
klatch
klatsch
klep-to-ma-nia
klep-to-ma-ni-ac
knack
knap-sack
knave
knav-ery
knav-ish
knav-ish-ly
knead
knee
kneed
knee-ing
knee-cap
knee--deep
kneel
knelt
kneel-ing
kneel-er
knee-pan
knell
knick-knack
knife
knives

knifed
knif-ing
knife-like
knight
knight-hood
knight-ly
knit
knit-ted
knit-ting
knit-ter
knob
knobbed
knob-by
knob-bi-er
knob-bi-est
knock
knock-a-bout
knock-down
knock-er
knock--knee
knock--kneed
knock-out
knoll
knot
knot-ted
knot-ting
knot-like
knot-ty
knot-hole
knout
know
knew
known
know-ing
know-a-ble
know-er
know--how
know-ing-ly
knowl-edge
knowl-edge-able
know--noth-ing
knuck-le
knuck-led
knuck-ling
ko-ala
ko-bold
ko-el
ko-gas-in
kohl-ra-bi
kohl-ra-bies
ko-la
ko-lin-sky

ko-lin-skies
kook
kooky
kook-i-er
kook-i-est
kook-a-bur-ra
ko-peck
ko-ru-na
ko-sher
kou-mis
kow-tow
kro-na
kro-ne
kryp-ton
ku-dos
ku-miss
kum-quat

L

la-bel
la-beled
la-bel-ing
la-bel-er
la-bi-al
la-bi-al-ly
la-bi-ate
la-bi-o-den-tal
la-bi-um
la-bia
la-bor
la-bor-er
lab-o-ra-to-ry
la-bored
la-bo-ri-ous
la-bo-ri-ous-ly
la-bo-ri-ous-ness
la-bor-sav-ing
la-bur-num
lab-y-rinth
lab-y-rin-thine
lab-y-rin-thi-an
lace
lac-er-ate
lac-er-at-ed
lac-er-at-ing
lac-er-a-tion
lace-wing
la-ches
lach-ry-mal
lach-ry-mose
lach-ry-mose-ly

lac-ing
lack-a-dai-si-cal
lack-a-dai-si-cal-ly
lack-ey
lack-lus-ter
la-ci-nia
la-con-ic
la-con-i-cal-ly
lac-quer
lac-quer-er
la-crosse
lac-tate
lac-tat-ed
lac-tat-ing
lac-ta-tion
lac-te-al
lac-tic
lac-tose
la-cu-na
la-cu-nas
la-cu-nae
lad-der
lad-die
lade
lad-ed
lad-en
lad-ing
la-dle
la-dled
la-dling
la-dy
la-dy-bug
la-dy-fin-ger
la-dy--in--wait-ing
la-dy-like
la-dy-love
lag
lagged
lag-ging
la-ger
lag-gard
la-gniappe
la-goon
la-ic
la-i-cal
la-i-cal-ly
lair
laird
la-i-ty
la-i-ties
lake-side
lal-la-tion

la-lop-a-thy	**lan-quish**	las-sos	**lav-a-to-ry**
lam	lan-quish-ing	las-soes	lav-a-to-ries
lammed	lan-quish-ing-ly	las-so-er	**lav-en-der**
lam-ming	**lan-quor**	**last-ing**	**lav-ish**
la-ma	lan-guor-ous	last-ing-ly	lav-ish-ly
la-ma-sery	lan-guor-ous-ly	**last-ly**	la-vish-ness
la-ma-ser-ies	**lan-o-lin**	**latch-key**	**law-abid-ing**
lam-baste	**lan-tern**	**late**	**law-break-er**
lam-bast-ed	**lan-tha-num**	lat-er	law-break-ing
lam-bast-ing	**lan-yard**	lat-est	**law-ful**
lam-ben-cy	**la-pel**	late-ness	law-ful-ly
lam-bent	**lap-ful**	**late-ly**	law-ful-ness
lam-bent-ly	lap-fuls	**la-tent**	**law-less**
lam-bre-quin	laps-ful	la-ten-cy	law-less-ly
lamb-skin	**lap-i-dary**	la-tent-ly	law-less-ness
lame	lap-i-dar-ies	**lat-er-al**	**law-mak-er**
la-ment	**lap-in**	lat-er-al-ly	law-mak-ing
lam-en-ta-ble	**lap-pet**	**la-tex**	**lawn**
lam-en-ta-bly	**lapse**	la-tex-es	**law-ren-ci-um**
lam-en-ta-tion	lapsed	**lathe**	**law-suit**
lam-i-na	laps-ing	**lath-er**	**law-yer**
lam-i-nae	**lar-board**	lath-er-er	**lax**
lam-i-nas	**lar-ce-ny**	lath-ery	lax-i-ty
lam-i-nate	lar-ce-nies	**lath-ing**	lax-ly
lam-i-nat-ed	lar-ce-nous	**lat-i-tude**	lax-ness
lam-i-nat-ing	**larch**	lat-i-tu-di-nal	**lax-a-tive**
lam-i-na-tion	**lar-der**	**lat-i-tu-di-nar-i-an**	**lay-er**
lam-poon	**large**	**la-trine**	**lay-ette**
lam-prey	larg-er	**lat-ter**	**lay-man**
lam-preys	larg-est	**lat-tice**	lay-men
lance	**large-ly**	lat-tied	**lay-off**
lanced	**lar-gess**	lat-tic-ing	**lay-out**
lanc-ing	**lar-ghet-to**	**lat-tice-work**	**lay-over**
lance-wood	lar-ghet-tos	**laud-able**	**laze**
lan-dau	**larg-ish**	laud-ably	lazed
land-ed	**lar-go**	**lau-da-num**	laz-ing
land-ing	lar-gos	**lau-da-to-ry**	**la-zy**
land-la-dy	**lar-i-at**	lau-da-tive	la-zi-er
land-la-dies	**lar-rup**	**laugh**	la-zi-est
land-locked	**lar-va**	**laugh-ter**	la-zi-ly
land-lord	lar-vae	**launch**	**la-zy-bones**
land-lub-ber	lar-val	launch-er	**lea**
land-own-er	**lar-yn-gi-tis**	**laun-der**	**leach**
land-own-ing	**lar-ynx**	laun-der-er	**lead**
land-own-er-ship	lar-ynx-es	laun-dress	lead-ing
land-slide	lar-ynx-ges	**laun-der-ette**	**lead-en**
land-ward	**la-ryn-ge-al**	**laun-dry**	lead-en-ly
land-wards	**las-civ-i-ous**	laun-dries	**lead-er**
lang syne	las-ci-v-i-ous-ly	**lau-re-ate**	lead-er-less
lan-gauge	**las-sie**	**lau-rel**	lead-er-ship
lan-quid	**las-si-tude**	**la-va**	**leaf-age**
lan-quid-ly	**las-so**	**la-a-liere**	**leafy**

leaf-i-er
leaf-i-est
leaque
leaqued
leaqu-ing
leak
leak-age
leak-i-ness
leaky
leak-i-er
leak-i-est
lean
lean-ly
lean-ness
lean-ing
lean--to
lean--tos
leap
leaped
leapt
leap-ing
leap-er
leap-frog
learn
learn-ed
learnt
learn-ing
learn-er
learn-ed-ly
learn-ed-ness
lease
leased
leas-ing
leash
least-wise
least-ways
leath-er
leath-er-neck
leath-ery
leave
left
leav-ing
lev-er
leav-en
leaves
leave-talk-ing
lech-er
lech-er-ous
lech-er-ous-ly
lech-ery
lech-er-ies
lec-tern

lec-ture
lec-tured
lec-tur-ing
lec-tur-er
ledge
ledg-er
leech
leek
leer-ing-ly
leery
lee-ward
lee-way
left--hand-ed
left--hand-ed-ly
left--hand-ed-ness
left-ist
left-over
left--wing
left--wing-er
leg
legged
leg-ging
leg-a-cy
leg-a-cies
le-gal
le-gal-ly
le-gal-ist
le-gal-is-tic
le-gal-i-ty
le-gal-i-ties
le-gal-ize
le-gal-ized
le-gal-iz-ing
le-gal-i-za-tion
leg-ate
leg-a-tee
le-ga-tion
le-ga-to
leg-end
leg-end-ary
leg-er-de-main
leg-gy
leg-gi-er
leg-gi-est
leg-horn
leg-i-ble
leg-i-bil-i-ty
leg-i-bly
le-gion
le-gion-ary
le-gion-ar-ies
le-gion-naire

leg-is-late
leg-is-lat-ed
leg-is-la-tive
leg-is-la-tor
leg-is-la-tion
leg-is-la-ture
le-git
le-git-i-mate
le-git-i-mat-ed
le-git-i-mat-ing
le-git-i-ma-cy
le-git-i-mate-ly
le-git-i-mist
le-git-i-mize
le-git-i-mized
le-git-i-miz-ing
le-gume
le-gu-mi-nous
lei
leis
lei-sure
lei-sure-ly
lei-sure-li-ness
leit-mo-tif
lem-ming
lem-on
lem-on-ade
le-mur
lend
lent
lend-ing
lend-er
length
length-en
length-wise
lengthy
length-i-er
length-i-est
length-i-ly
length-i-ness
le-nient
le-ni-ence
le-ni-en-cy
le-ni-ent-ly
len-i-tive
len-i-ty
lens
len-til
len-to
le-o-nine
leop-ard
leop-ard-ess

le-o-tard
lep-er
lep-i-dop-ter-ous
lep-re-chaun
lep-ro-sy
lep-rous
les-bi-an
les-bi-an-ism
le-sion
les-see
less-en
les-sor
least
let-down
le-thal
le-thal-ly
leth-ar-gy
leth-ar-gies
le-thar-gic
le-thar-gi-cal
let-ter
let-ter-ed
let-ter-head
let-ter-ing
let-ter--per-fect
let-ter-press
let-tuce
let-up
leu-ke-mia
leu-ko-cyte
lev-ee
lev-el
lev-eled
lev-el-ing
lev-el-er
lev-el-ly
lev-el-ness
lev-el-head-ed
lev-el-head-ed-ness
lev-er
lev-er-age
le-vi-a-than
lev-i-tate
lev-i-tat-ed
lev-i-tat-ing
lev-i-ta-tion
lev-i-ty
levy
lev-ies
lev-ied
lev-y-ing
lewd

lewd-ly	li-cens-ing	**light-ly**	**lim-it-ed-ness**
lewd-ness	li-cen-see	**light--mind-ed**	**lim-ou-sine**
lex-i-cog-ra-phy	li-cens-er	light--mind-ed-ly	**limp**
lex-i-cog-ra-pher	**li-cen-ti-ate**	light--mind-ed-ness	limp-er
lex-i-co-graph-ic	**li-cen-tious**	**light-ning**	limp-ing-ly
lex-i-co-graph-i-cal	li-cen-tious-ly	**light-weight**	limp-ly
lex-i-con	li-cen-tious-ness	**light--year**	limp-ness
li-a-bil-i-ty	**li-chee**	**lig-nite**	**lim-pet**
li-a-bil-i-ties	**li-chen**	**like**	**lim-pid**
li-a-ble	**lic-it**	liked	lim-pid-i-ty
li-ai-son	**lick-e-ty--split**	lik-ing	lim-pid-ly
li-ar	**lick-spit-tle**	lik-a-ble	lim-pid-ness
li-ba-tion	**lic-o-rice**	lik-a-ble-ness	**lin-age**
li-bel	**lid-ded**	lik-a-ble-ness	**lin-den**
li-beled	**lief**	**like-li-hood**	**line**
li-bel-ing	**liege**	**like-ly**	lined
li-bel-er	**lien**	like-li-er	lin-ing
li-bel-ous	**lieu**	like-li-est	**lin-e-age**
li-bel-ous-ly	**lieu-ten-an-cy**	**like--mind-ed**	**lin-eal**
lib-er-al	**lieu-ten-ant**	lik-en	**lin-ea-ment**
lib-er-al-ly	**life-blood**	**like-ness**	**lin-ear**
lib-er-al-ness	**life-boat**	**like-wise**	lin-ear-ly
lib-er-al-ism	**life-guard**	lik-ing	**line-back-er**
lib-er-al-i-ty	**life-less**	**li-lac**	line-back-ing
lib-er-al-i-ties	life-less-ly	**lilt-ing**	**line-man**
lib-er-al-ize	life-less-ness	**lily**	line-men
lib-er-al-ized	**life-like**	lil-lies	**lin-en**
lib-er-al-iz-ing	**life-line**	**lil-y--liv-ered**	**lin-er**
lib-er-al-i-za-tion	**lif-er**	**li-ma**	**line-up**
lib-er-ate	**life-sav-er**	**limb**	**lin-ger**
lib-er-at-ed	**life--size**	**limb-er**	lin-ger-er
lib-er-at-ing	**life--style**	lim-ber-ness	lin-ger-ing-ly
lib-er-a-tion	**life-time**	**lim-bo**	**lin-ge-rie**
lib-er-a-tor	**life-work**	**lime**	**lin-go**
lib-er-tar-i-an	**lift-off**	limed	lin-goes
lib-er-tine	**lig-a-ment**	lim-ing	**lin-gua fran-ca**
lib-er-tin-ism	**lig-a-ture**	limy	**lin-qual**
lib-er-ty	lig-tured	lim-i-er	lin-qual-ly
lib-er-ties	lig-a-tur-ing	lim-i-est	**lin-quist**
li-bid-i-nous	**light-en**	lime-like	**lin-quis-tic**
li-bid-i-nous-ly	**light-er**	**lime-light**	lin-quis-tics
li-bid-i-nous-ness	**light-fin-gered**	lime-light-er	lin-quis-ti-cal
li-bi-do	**light-foot-ed**	**lim-er-ick**	lin-quis-ti-cal-ly
li-bid-in-al	light-foot-ed-ly	**lime-stone**	**lin-i-ment**
li-brar-i-an	**light-head-ed**	**lim-it**	**lin-ing**
li-brary	light-head-ed-ly	**lim-it-a-ble**	**link**
li-brar-ies	light-head-ed-ness	**lim-i-ta-tive**	linked
li-bret-to	**light-heart-ed**	**lim-i-ter**	link-er
li-bret-tos	light-heart-ed-ly	**lim-it-less**	**link-age**
li-bret-ist	light-heart-ed-ness	**lim-i-ta-tion**	**lin-net**
li-cense	**light-house**	**lim-it-ed**	**li-no-leum**
li-censed	**light-ing**	lim-it-ed-ly	**lin-seed**

lint	**li-tchi**	**liv-ery**	**lock-er**
linty	li-tchis	liv-er-ies	**lock-et**
lint-i-er	**li-ter**	liv-er-ied	**lock-jaw**
lint-i-est	**lit-er-a-cy**	liv-er-y-man	**lock-out**
lin-tel	**lit-er-al**	liv-er-y-men	**lock-smith**
li-on	lit-er-al-i-ty	**live-stock**	**lock-up**
li-on-ess	lit-er-al-ness	**liv-id**	**lo-co**
li-on-like	lit-er-al-ly	li-vid-i-ty	**lo-co-mo-tion**
li-on-heart-ed	**lit-er-ary**	liv-id-ness	**lo-co-mo-tive**
li-on-ize	lit-er-ar-i-ly	liv-id-ly	**lo-co-weed**
li-on-ized	lit-er-ar-i-ness	**liv-ing**	**lo-cus**
li-on-iz-ing	**lit-er-ate**	liv-ing-ly	lo-ci
li-on-i-za-tion	lit-er-ate-ly	liv-ing-ness	**lo-cust**
li-on-iz-er	**lit-e-ra-ti**	**liz-ard**	**lo-cu-tion**
lip-py	**lit-er-a-ture**	**lla-ma**	**lode-stone**
lip-pi-er	**lithe**	**lla-no**	**lodge**
lip-pi-est	lithe-some	lla-mos	lodged
lip-stick	lithe-ly	**loamy**	lodg-ing
liq-ue-fy	lithe-ness	**loath**	lodg-er
liq-ue-fied	**lith-i-um**	loath-ness	**lofty**
liq-ue-fy-ing	**lith-o-graph**	**loathe**	loft-i-er
liq-ue-fac-tion	lith-o-gra-pher	loathed	loft-i-est
liq-ue-fi-able	lith-o-graph-ic	loath-ing	loft-i-ly
liq-ue-fi-er	lith-o-graph-i-cal-ly	loath-ing-ly	**lo-gan-ber-ry**
li-queur	**li-thog-ra-phy**	**loath-some**	lo-gan-ber-ries
liq-uid	**lit-i-gate**	loath-some-ly	**log-a-rithm**
li-quid-i-ty	lit-i-gat-ed	loath-some-ness	log-a-rith-mic
li-quid-ness	lit-i-gat-ing	**lob**	log-a-rith-mi-cal
li-quid-ly	lit-i-ga-tion	lobbed	log-a-rith-mi-cal-ly
liq-ui-date	lit-i-ga-tor	lob-bing	**log-book**
liq-ui-dat-ed	**lit-ter**	**lobe**	**loge**
liq-ui-dat-ing	**lit-ter-bug**	lo-bar	**log-ger**
liq-ui-da-tion	**lit-tle**	lo-bate	**log-ger-hed**
liq-ui-da-tor	lit-tler	lobed	**log-ic**
liq-uor	lit-tlest	**lob-ster**	lo-gi-cian
lisle	**lit-to-ral**	**lo-cal**	**log-i-cal**
lisp	**lit-ur-gy**	lo-cal-ly	log-i-cal-i-ty
lisp-ing-ly	lit-ur-gies	**lo-cale**	log-i-cal-ly
lis-some	lit-ur-gist	**lo-cal-i-ty**	**lo-gis-tic**
lis-some-ly	lit-ur-gic	lo-cal-i-ties	lo-gis-tics
lis-some-ness	li-tur-gi-cal	**lo-cal-i-ties**	lo-gis-ti-cal
list	**liv-able**	**lo-cal-ize**	**loin-cloth**
list-ed	live-able	lo-cal-ized	**loi-ter**
list-er	**live-li-hood**	lo-cal-iz-ing	loi-ter-er
list-ing	**live-long**	lo-cal-i-za-tion	**lol-li-pop**
lis-ten	**live-ly**	**lo-cate**	**lone-ly**
lis-ten-er	live-li-er	lo-cat-ed	lone-li-er
list-less	live-li-est	lo-cat-ing	lone-li-est
list-less-ly	**liv-en**	lo-ca-tor	lone-li-ly
list-less-ness	liv-en-er	**lo-ca-tion**	**lon-er**
lit-a-ny	**liv-er**	**loch**	**lone-some**
lit-a-nies	**liv-er-wurst**	**lock-able**	lone-some-ly

lone-some-ness	lo-tus-es	lu-cu-brat-ed	**lurk**
lon-gev-i-ty	**loud**	lu-cu-brat-ing	lurk-er
long-ing	loud-ly	lu-cu-bra-tion	lurk-ing-ly
long-ing-ly	loud-ness	lu-cu-bra-tor	**lus-cious**
lon-gi-tude	**loud-mouthed**	**lu-di-crous**	lus-cious-ly
lon-gi-tu-di-nal	**loud-speak-er**	lu-di-crous-ly	**lust**
lon-gi-tu-di-nal-ly	**lounge**	**lug-gage**	lust-ful
long-lived	lounged	**lug-ger**	lust-ful-ly
long--play-ing	loung-ing	**lug-sail**	lust-er
long-shore-man	loung-er	**lu-gu-bri-ous**	lusty
long-shore-men	**louse**	lu-gu-bri-ous-ly	**lut-ist**
long--suf-fer-ing	lice	**luke-warm**	**lux-u-ri-ant**
long--term	**lou-ver**	luke-warm-ly	lux-u-ri-ance
long--wind-ed	lou-vered	**lull-a-by**	lux-u-ri-an-cy
long--wind-ed-ly	**love**	lull-a-bies	lux-u-ri-ant-ly
long-wise	loved	**lum-ba-go**	**lux-u-ri-ate**
look-out	lov-ing	**lum-bar**	lux-u-ri-at-ed
loose	lov-able	**lum-ber**	lux-u-ri-at-ing
loos-er	**love-lorn**	lum-ber-ing-ly	lux-u-ri-a-tion
loos-est	**lov-er**	lum-ber-er	**lux-u-ri-ous**
loos-en	**lov-ing**	**lum-ber-ing**	lux-u-ri-ous-ly
loot-er	loving-ly	**lum-ber-jack**	**lux-u-ry**
lop	**low-er**	**lum-ber-man**	lux-u-ries
looped	**low-er-case**	lum-ber-men	**ly-ce-um**
lop-ping	**low-er-ing**	**lu-men**	**ly-ing**
lope	low-er-ing-ly	**lu-mi-nary**	**ly-ing--in**
loped	**low-ery**	lu-mi-nar-ies	**lymph**
lop-ing	**low--key**	**lu-mi-nes-cence**	lym-phoid
lop-er	low--keyed	lu-mi-nes-cent	**lym-phat-ic**
lop-sid-ed	**low-ly**	**lu-mi-nous**	**lynch**
lo-qua-cious	low-li-er	lu-mi-nos-i-ty	lynch-er
lo-qua-cious-ly	low-li-est	lu-mi-nous-ly	lynch-ing
lo-quac-i-ty	**loy-al**	**lum-mox**	**lynx**
lo-quac-i-ties	loy-al-ist	**lumpy**	lynx-es
lord-ly	loy-al-ly	**lu-na-cy**	lynx-eyed
lord-li-er	loy-al-ties	lu-na-cies	**lyre**
lord-li-est	**loz-enge**	**lu-nar**	**ly-ric**
lord-ship	**lu-au**	**lu-nate**	lyr-i-cal
lor-gnette	**lub-ber**	**lu-na-tic**	lyr-i-cal-ly
lor-ry	lub-ber-ly	**lunch**	**ly-ser-gic acid**
lor-ries	**lu-beak**	lunch-er	**ly-sine**
lose	**lu-bri-cate**	**lun-cheon**	
lost	lu-bri-cat-ed	**lunge**	**M**
los-ing	lu-bri-cat-ing	lunged	
los-a-ble	lu-bri-ca-tion	lung-ing	**ma-ca-bre**
los-er	**luck**	**lu-pine**	ma-ca-bre-ly
lot	luck-i-er	**lurch**	**mac-ad-am**
lo-tion	luck-i-est	**lure**	**mac-ad-am-ize**
lot-tery	**lu-cra-tive**	lured	mac-ad-am ised
lot-ter-ies	lu-cra-tive-ly	lur-ing	mac-ad-am-iz-ing
lot-to	**lu-cre**	**lu-rid**	mac-ad-am-i-za-tic
lo-tus	**lu-cu-brate**	lu-rid-ly	**ma-caque**

mac-a-ro-ni
ma-caw
mace
 maced
 mac-ing
mac-er-ate
 mac-er-at-ed
 mac-er-at-ing
 mac-er-a-tion
 mac-er-a-tor
ma-chete
mach-i-nate
ma-chine
ma-chin-ery
 ma-chin-er-ies
ma-chin-ist
mack-er-el
mack-i-naw
mack-in-tosh
 mac-in-tosh
mac-ro-cosm
 mac-ro-cos-mic
 mac-ro-cos-mi-cal-ly
ma-cron
mad
 mad-der
 mad-ly
 mad-ness
mad-am
 mes-dames
mad-cap
mad-den
 mad-den-ing
 mad-den-ing-ly
mad-e-moi-selle
 mes-de-moi-selles
made-up
mad-house
mad-man
 mad-men
ma-dras
mad-ri-gal
 mad-ri-gal-ist
mael-strom
mae-stro-so
mag-a-zine
ma-gen-ta
mag-got
 mag-goty
mag-ic
 mag-i-cal
 mag-i-cal-ly

ma-gi-cian
mag-is-te-ri-al
 mag-is-te-ri-al-ly
 mag-is-te-ri-al-ness
mag-is-tra-cy
 mag-is-tra-cies
mag-is-trate
mag-ma
 mag-mas
 mag-ma-ta
 mag-mat-ic
mag-nan-i-mous
 mag-nan-i-mous-ly
 mag-na-nim-i-ty
 mag-na-nim-i-ties
mag-nate
mag-ne-sia
 mag-ne-sian
mag-ne-sium
mag-net
 mag-net-ic
 mag-net-i-cal-ly
mag-net-ism
mag-net-ize
 mag-net-ized
 mag-net-iz-ing
 mag-net-iz-a-ble
 mag-net-i-za-tion
 mag-net-iz-er
mag-ne-to
 mag-ne-tos
mag-ne-tom-e-ter
 mag-ne-to-met-ric
 mag-ne-tom-e-try
mag-nif-i-cent
 mag-nif-i-cence
 mag-nif-i-cent-ly
mag-ni-fy
 mag-ni-fied
 mag-ni-fy-ing
 maf-ni-fi-a-ble
 mag-ni-fi-ca-tion
 mag-ni-fi-er
mag-ni-tude
mag-no-lia
mag-num
mag-uey
ma-ha-ra-jah
ma-ha-ra-ni
ma-hat-ma
 ma-hat-ma-ism
ma-hoe

ma-hog-a-ny
 ma-hog-a-nies
ma-hout
maid-en
mail-a-ble
mail-box
mail-man
 mail-men
maim
 maim-er
main-land
 main-land-er
main-ly
main-mast
main-sail
main-tain
 main-tain-a-ble
main-te-nance
maize
maj-es-ty
 maj-es-ties
 ma-jes-tic
 ma-jes-ti-cal
ma-jol-i-ca
ma-jor
ma-jor-do-mo
 ma-jor-do-mos
ma-jor-i-ty
 ma-jor-i-ties
make
 mak-a-ble
 mak-er
 mak-ing
make-shift
make-up
mal-a-dapt-ed
mal-ad-just-ment
 mal-ad-just-ed
mal-ad-min-is-ter
mal-adroit
 mal-adroit-ly
 mal-adroit-ness
mal-a-dy
 mal-a-dies
mal-aise
mal-a-prop
mal-a-prop-ism
ma-lar-ia
 ma-lar-i-al
 ma-lar-i-an
 ma-lar-i-ous
ma-lar-key

mal-con-tent
male-dict
male-dic-tion
 male-dic-to-ry
male-frac-tion
male-frac-tor
ma-lev-o-lent
 ma-lev-o-lence
 ma-lev-o-lent-ly
mal-fea-sance
 mal-fea-sant
mal-for-ma-tion
 mal-formed
mal-func-tion
mal-ice
 ma-li-cious
 ma-li-cious-ly
ma-lign
 ma-lign-er
 ma-lign-ly
ma-lig-nant
 ma-lig-nan-cy
 ma-lig-nan-cies
 ma-lig-nant-ly
ma-lin-ger
 ma-lin-ger-er
mal-lard
mal-lea-ble
 mal-lea-bil-i-ty
mal-let
ma-low
mal-nour-ished
mal-nu-tri-tion
mal-oc-clu-sion
mal-odor
 mal-odor-ous
 mal-odor-ous-ly
mal-prac-tice
 mal-prac-ti-tion-er
malt
 malty
 malt-i-er
mal-treat
 mal-treat-ment
mam-ma
 ma-ma
mam-mal
 mam-ma-li-an
mam-mam-ries
mam-mon
mam-moth
mam-my

mam-mies	man-gi-er	ma-no-ri-al	**mar-gin**
man	man-gi-est	**manpow-er**	**mar-gi-nal**
manned	man-gi-ly	**man-sard**	mar-gi-na-lia
man-ning	**man-han-dle**	**man-ser-vant**	mar-gin-al-i-ty
man-a-cle	man-han-dled	**man-sion**	mar-gin-al-ly
man-a-cled	man-han-dling	**man-sized**	**mar-gin-ate**
man-a-cling	**man-hole**	**man-slaugh-ter**	mar-gin-ated
man-age	**man-hood**	**man-slay-er**	mar-gin-at-ing
man-aged	**man--hour**	**man-til-la**	mar-gin-a-tion
man-a-ging	**man-hunt**	**man-tle**	**mar-gue-rite**
man-age-a-ble	man-hunt-er	man-tled	**mar-i-cul-ture**
man-age-a-bil-i-ty	**ma-nia**	man-tling	**mari-gold**
man-age-a-bly	man-ic	**man-trap**	**mar-i-jua-na**
man-age-ment	**ma-ni-ac**	**man-u-al**	**ma-rim-ba**
man-ag-er	ma-ni-a-cal	man-u-al-ly	**ma-ri-na**
man-ag-er-ship	ma-ni-a-cal-ly	**man-u-fac-ture**	**mar-i-nade**
man-a-ge-ri-al	**man-ic-de-pres-sive**	man-u-fac-tured	mar-i-nad-ed
man-a-ge-ri-al-ly	**man-i-cure**	man-u-fac-tur-ing	mar-i-nad-ing
man-a-tee	man-i-cur-eed	man-u-fac-tur-a-ble	mar-i-na-tion
man-da-la	man-i-cur-ing	man-u-fac-tur-al	**mar-i-nate**
man-da-rin	man-i-cur-ist	man-u-fac-tur-er	mar-i-nat-ed
man-date	**man-i-fest**	**ma-nure**	mar-i-nat-ing
man-dat-ed	man-i-fest-er	**manu-script**	mar-i-na-tion
man-dat-ing	man-i-fest-ly	**many**	**ma-rine**
man-da-to-ry	**man-i-fes-ta-tion**	**man-y-sid-ed**	**mar-i-ner**
man-da-to-ries	**man-i-fes-to**	**map**	**mar-i-o-nette**
man-da-to-ri-ty	man-i-fes-tos	**mapped**	**mar-i-tal**
man-di-ble	man-i-fes-toes	map-ping	**mar-i-time**
man-dib-u-lar	**man-i-fold**	map-per	**mar-jo-ram**
man-dib-u-lary	**man-i-kin**	**ma-ple**	**marked**
man-dib-u-late	man-a-kin	**mar**	mark-ed-ly
man-do-lin	man-ni-kin	marred	**mark-er**
man-do-lin-ist	**ma-nila**	mar-ring	**mar-ket**
man-drakes	ma-nil-la	**ma-ra-ca**	mar-ket-er
man-drill	**ma-nip-u-late**	**mar-a-schi-no**	**mar-ket-able**
man-eat-er	**man-kind**	**mar-a-thon**	mar-ket-abil-i-ty
man-eat-ing	**man-ly**	**ma-raud**	**mar-ket-ing**
ma-neu-ver	man-li-er	ma-raud-er	**mar-ket-place**
ma-neu-ver-a-nil-i-ty	man-li-est	**mar-ble**	**mark-ing**
ma-neu-ver-a-ble	**man--made**	mar-bled	**marks-man**
ma-neu-ver-er	**man-na**	mar-bling	marks-men
man-ga-nese	**man-ne-quin**	mar-ble-ize	marks-man-ship
mange	**man-ner**	mar-ble-ized	**mar-lin**
man-ger	**man-nered**	mar-ble-iz-ing	**mar-ma-lade**
man-gle	**man-ner-ism**	mar-bly	**mar-mo-set**
man-gled	**man-ner-ly**	**mar-cel**	**mar-mot**
man-gling	man-ner-li-ness	mar-celled	**ma-roon**
man-go	**man-nish**	mar-cel-ling	**mar-quee**
man-goes	**man--of--war**	**march-er**	**mar-quis**
man-gos	men--of--war	**mar-chio-ness**	mar-quis-es
man-grove	**ma-nom-e-ter**	**mare's tail**	mar-quess
man-gy	**man-or**	**mar-ga-rine**	**mar-quise**

mar-quis-es	ma-son-ries	mat-ted	ma-tron-ly
mar-riage	**masque**	mat-ting	**mat-ter**
mar-riage-able	**mas-quer-ade**	**mat-a-dor**	**mat-ter-of-course**
mar-riage-abil-i-ty	mas-quer-ad-ed	**match-book**	**mat-ter--of--fact**
mar-ried	mas-quer-ad-ing	**match-mak-er**	mat-ter--of-fact-ly
mar-row	mas-quer-ad-er	match-mak-ing	mat-ter--of--fact-ness
mar-rowy	**mas-sa-cre**	**mate**	**mat-ting**
mar-row-bone	mas-sa-cred	mat-ed	**mat-tress**
mar-ry	mas-sa-cring	mat-ing	**mat-u-rate**
mar-ried	mas-sa-cre	mate-less	mat-u-rat-ed
mar-ry-ing	**mas-sage**	**ma-te-ri-al**	mat-u-rat-ing
mar-shall	mas-saged	ma-te-ri-al-ly	mat-u-ra-tion
mar-shaled	mas-sag-ing	**ma-te-ri-al-ism**	**ma-ture**
mar-shal-ing	mas-sag-er	ma-te-ri-al-ist	**ma-tur-i-ty**
marsh-mal-low	mas-sag-ist	ma-te-ri-al-is-tic	**mat-zo**
marshy	**mas-seur**	ma-te-ri-al-is-ti-cal-ly	mat-zoth
marsh-i-er	**mas-sause**	**ma-te-ri-al-ize**	mat-zos
marsh-i-est	mas-seus-es	ma-te-ri-al-ized	**maud-lin**
marsh-i-ness	**mas-sive**	ma-te-ri-al-iz-ing	**mau-so-le-um**
mar-su-pi-al	**mass-pro-duce**	**ma-te-ri-el**	mau-so-le-ums
mar-tial	mass-pro-duced	**ma-ter-nal**	mau-so-lea
mar-tin	mass-pro-duc-ing	ma-ter-nal-ism	**mauve**
mar-ti-ni	mass-pro-duc-er	ma-ter-nal-is-tic	**mav-er-ick**
mar-ti-nis	mass-pro-duc-tion	ma-ter-nal-ly	**mawk-ish**
mar-tyr	**massy**	**ma-ter-ni-ty**	**max-im**
mar-tyr-ize	masss-i-er	ma-ter-ni-ties	**max-i-mal**
mar-tyr-ized	mass-i-est	**math-e-mat-i-cal**	max-i-mal-ly
mar-tyr-iz-ing	mass-i-ness	math-e-mat-ic	**max-i-mize**
mar-tyr-dom	**mas-tec-to-my**	math-e-mat-i-cal-ly	max-i-mized
mar-vel	mas-tec-to-mies	**math-e-ma-ti-cian**	max-i-miz-ing
mar-veled	**mas-ter**	**math-e-mat-ics**	**max-i-mum**
mar-vel-ing	**mas-ter-ful**	**ma-tin**	max-i-mums
mar-vel-ous	**mas-ter-mind**	mat-in-al	max-i-ma
mar-vel-ous-ly	**mas-ter-piece**	**mat-i-nee**	**may-be**
mar-zi-pan	**mas-tery**	**ma-tri-arch**	**may-flow-er**
mas-cara	mas-ter-ies	ma-tri-ar-chal-ism	**may-fly**
mas-cu-line	**mast-head**	ma-tri-ar-chy	may-flies
mas-cu-line-ness	**mas-tic**	ma-tri-ar-chies	**may-hem**
mas-cu-lin-i-ty	**mas-ti-cate**	**ma-tri-cide**	**may-on-naise**
mas-cu-lin-ize	mas-ti-ca-ted	**ma-tric-u-lant**	**may-or**
mas-cu-lin-ized	mas-ti-ca-ting	**ma-tric-u-late**	may-or-al
mas-cu-lin-iz-ing	mas-ti-ca-ble	ma-tric-u-lat-ed	**may-or-al-ty**
mash-er	mas-ti-ca-tion	ma-tric-u-lat-ing	may-or-al-ties
mask	mas-ti-ca-tor	ma-tric-u-la-tion	**maze**
mask-like	**mas-tiff**	**ma-tri-lin-eal**	mazed
masked	**mast-odon**	**mat-ri-mo-ny**	maz-ing
mas-och-ism	**mas-toid**	mat-ri-mo-nies	**ma-zy**
mas-och-ist	**mas-tur-bate**	mat-ri-mo-ni-al	ma-zi-er
mas-och-is-tic	mas-tur-bat-ed	**ma-trix**	ma-zi-est
ma-son	mas-tur-bat-ing	ma-tri-ces	ma-zi-ly
ma-son-ic	mas-tur-ba-tion	ma-trix-es	ma-zi-ness
ma-son-ary	**mat**	**ma-tron**	**mead-ow**

mead-ow-lark
mea-ger
 mea-ger-ly
 mea-ger-ness
meal-time
meal-worm
mealy
 meal-i-er
 meal-i-est
 meal-i-ness
meal-y-mouthed
mean
 mean-ing
 mean-ly
 mean-ness
me-an-der
mean-ing-ful
 mean-ing-ful-ly
mean-ing-less
 mean-ing-less-ly
 mean-ing-less-ness
meant
mean-time
mean-while
mea-sles
mea-sly
 mea-sli-er
 mea-sli-est
meas-ur-a-ble
 meas-ur-a-bil-i-ty
 meas-ur-a-bly
meas-ure
 meas-ur-er
mea-sured
mea-sure-ment
meaty
 meat-i-er
 meat-i-est
 meat-i-ness
mec-ca
me-chan-ic
mech-a-nism
mech-a-nis-tic
 mech-a-nis-ti-cal-ly
mech-a-nize
 mech-a-nized
 mech-a-niz-ing
 mech-a-ni-za-tion
 mech-a-niz-er
med-al
 med-aled
 med-al-ing

me-dal-ic
me-dal-lion
med-dle
 med-dled
 med-dling
 med-dler
med-dle-some
me-dia
me-di-al
me-di-an
 me-di-an-ly
me-di-ate
 me-di-at-ed
 me-di-at-ing
me-di-a-tion
 me-di-a-tive
 me-di-a-to-ry
me-di-a-tor
med-ic
med-i-ca-ble
 med-i-ca-bly
med-i-cal
 med-i-cal-ly
me-di-ca-ment
med-i-cate
 med-i-cat-ed
 med-i-cat-ing
med-i-ca-tion
me-dic-i-nal
 me-dic-i-nal-ly
med-i-cine
 med-i-cined
 med-i-cin-ing
med-i-co
me-di-e-val
 me-di-e-val-ism
me-di-o-cre
me-di-oc-ri-ty
 me-di-oc-ri-ties
med-i-tate
 med-i-tat-ed
 med-i-tat-ing
 med-i-tat-ing-ly
 med-i-ta-tor
med-i-ta-tion
 med-i-ta-tive
Med-i-ter-ra-ne-an
me-di-um
 me-dia
 me-di-ums
med-ley
 med-leys

meet-ing
meet-ing-house
meg-a-city
 meg-a-cit-ies
meg-a-cy-cle
meg-a-lo-ma-nia
 meg-a-lo-ma-ni-ac
 meg-a-lo-ma-ni-a-cal
meg-a-lop-o-lis
 meg-a-lo-pol-i-tan
mega-phone
 mega-phoned
 mega-phon-ing
mega-ton
mega-watt
mei-o-sis
 mei-ot-ic
mel-a-mine
mel-an-cho-lia
 mel-an-cho-li-ac
mel-an-choly
 mel-an-chol-ies
 mel-an-chol-ic
 mel-an-chol-i-cal-ly
 mel-an-chol-i-ty
 mel-an-chol-i-ness
mel-a-nin
mel-a-no-ma
 mel-a-no-mas
 mel-a-no-ma-ta
me-lee
me-lio-rate
 me-lio-rat-ed
 me-lio-rat-ing
 me-lio-ra-ble
 me-lio-ra-tion
 me-lio-ra-tor
mel-lif-lu-ous
 mel-lif-lu-nt
 mel-lif-lu-ous-ly
mel-low
me-lo-de-on
melo-dra-ma
 melo-dra-mat-ic
 melo-dra-mat-i-cal-ly
 melo-dra-mat-ics
mel-o-dy
 mel-o-dies
 me-lod-ic
 me-lod-i-cal-ly
 me-lo-di-ous
 me-lo-di-ous-ness

mel-on
melt
 melt-ed
 melt-ing
 melt-a-bil-i-ty
 melt-a-ble
 melt-er
mem-ber
 mem-bered
 mem-ber-less
mem-ber-ship
mem-brane
 mem-bra-nous
me-men-to
 me-men-tos
 me-men-toes
memo
mem-oir
mem-o-ra-bil-ia
mem-o-ra-ble
 mem-o-ra-bly
mem-o-ran-dum
 mem-o-ran-dums
 mem-o-ran-da
me-mo-ri-al
 me-mo-ri-al-ly
me-mo-ri-al-ize
 me-mo-ri-al-ized
 me-mo-ri-al-iz-ing
 me-mo-ri-al-i-za-tion
 me-mo-ri-al-iz-er
 me-mo-ri-al-ly
mem-o-rize
 mem-o-rized
 mem-o-riz-ing
 mem-o-riz-a-ble
 mem-o-ri-za-tion
mem-o-ry
 mem-o-ries
men-ace
 men-aced
 men-ac-ing
me-nag-er-ie
mend
 mend-able
men-da-cious
 men-da-cious-ly
 men-da-cious-ness
men-dac-i-ty
men-de-le-vi-um
men-di-cant
me-ni-al

me-ni-al-ly
me-nin-ges
men-in-gi-tis
me-nis-cus
me-nis-cus-es
me-nis-ci
men-o-pause
men-o-pau-sal
me-nor-ah
men-sal
men-ses
men-stru-al
men-stru-a-tion
men-stru-ate
men-stru-at-ed
men-stru-at-ing
men-sur-a-ble
men-tal
men-tal-ly
men-tal-i-ty
men-tal-i-ties
men-thol
men-tho-lat-ed
men-tion
men-tion-a-ble
men-tion-er
men-tor
menu
me-ow
mep-ro-bam-ate
mer-can-tile
mer-can-til-ism
mer-can-til-ist
mer-ce-nary
mer-ce-nar-ies
mer-ce-nar-ily
mer-cer-ize
mer-cer-ized
mer-cer-iz-ing
mer-chan-dise
mer-chan-dised
mer-chan-dis-ing
mer-chan-dis-er
mer-chant
mer-chant-man
mer-chant-men
mer-cu-ri-al
mer-cu-ry
mer-cu-ries
mer-cy
mer-cies
mer-ci-ful

mer-ci-ful-ly
mer-ci-less
mere-ly
mer-e-tri-cious
mer-e-tri-cious-ly
mer-e-tri-cious-ness
merge
merged
merg-ing
mer-gence
merg-er
me-rid-i-an
me-rid-i-o-nal
me-ringue
mer-it
mer-i-ted
mer-it-ed-ly
mer-it-less
mer-i-to-ri-ous
mer-maid
mer-man
mer-men
mer-ri-ment
mer-ry
mer-ri-er
mer-ri-est
mer-ri-ness
mer-ry--go--round
mer-ry-mak-er
mer-ry-mak-ing
me-sa
mes-cal
mes-dames
mes-de-moi-selles
mesh-work
me-si-al
mes-mer-ism
mes-mer-ic
mes-mer-i-cal-ly
mes-mer-ist
mes-mer-ize
mes-mer-ized
mes-mer-iz-ing
mes-mer-i-za-tion
mes-mer-iz-er
mes-o-morph
mes-o-mor-phic
mes-o-mor-phism
mes-o-mor-phy
me-son
mes-o-sphere
mes-quite

mess
mess-i-ly
mess-i-ness
messy
mess-i-er
mess-i-est
mes-sage
mes-sen-ger
mes-ti-zo
me-tab-o-lism
met-a-bol-ic
met-a-bol-i-cal
me-tab-o-lize
me-tab-o-lized
me-tab-o-liz-ing
met-al
met-aled
met-al-ing
met-al-ize
met-al-ized
met-al-iz-ing
me-tal-lic
me-tal-li-cal-ly
met-al-loid
met-al-lur-gy
met-al-lur-gic
met-al-lur-gi-cal
met-al-lur-gi-cal-ly
met-al-lur-gist
met-al-work
met-al-work-er
met-al-work-ing
meta-mor-phism
meta-mor-phic
meta-mor-phose
meta-mor-phosed
meta-mor-phos-ing
meta-mor-pho-sis
meta-mor-pho-ses
met-a-phor
met-a-phor-ic
met-a-phor-i-cal
meta-phys-ic
meta-phys-ics
meta-phys-i-cal
meta-tar-sus
meta-tar-si
meta-tar-sal
meta-zo-an
meta-zo-al
meta-zo-ic
mete

met-ed
met-ing
me-te-or
me-te-or-ic
me-te-or-ite
me-te-or-it-ic
me-te-or-oid
me-te-o-rol-o-gy
me-te-o-ro-log-i-cal
me-te-o-rol-o-gist
me-ter
met-es-trus
meth-a-done
meth-ane
meth-a-nol
meth-od
me-thodi-cal
me-thodi-cal-ly
meth-od-ize
meth-od-ized
meth-od-iz-ing
meth-od-iz-er
meth-od-ol-o-gy
meth-od-ol-o-gies
meth-od-o-log-i-cal
meth-od-ol-o-gist
me-tic-u-lous
me-tic-u-los-i-ty
me-tic-u-lous-ly
met-ric
met-ri-cal
met-ri-cal-ly
met-ri-fi-ca-tion
met-ro
met-ro-nome
met-ro-nom-ic
me-trop-o-lis
met-ro-pol-i-tan
met-ro-pol-i-tan-ism
met-tle
met-tle-some
mez-za-nine
mez-zo
mi-as-ma
mi-as-mas
mi-as-ma-ta
mi-as-mat-ic
mi-as-mic
mi-ca
mi-crobe
mi-cro-bi-al
mi-cro-bi-an

mi-cro-bic	mid-sum-mer	milk-man	mind-less-ly
mi-cro-bi-ol-o-gy	mid-term	milk-men	mind-less-ness
mi-cro-bi-o-log-i-cal	mid-way	milk-weed	min-er
mi-cro-bi-ol-o-gist	mid-wife	mill-board	mine-field
mi-cro-copy	mid-wives	mil-len-ni-um	min-er-al
mi-cro-cop-ies	mid-wife-ry	mil-len-nia	min-er-al-ize
mi-cro-cosm	mid-year	mil-len-ni-al	min-er-al-ized
mi-cro-cos-mos	mien	mil-ler	min-er-al-iz-ing
mi-cro-cos-mic	mighty	mil-let	min-er-al-i-za-tion
mi-cro-cos-mi-cal	might-i-er	mil-li-am-pere	min-er-al-o-gy
mi-cro-film	might-i-est	mil-li-bar	min-er-al-og-ical
mi-cro-gram	might-i-ly	mil-li-gram	min-er-al-o-gist
mi-cro-groove	might-i-ness	mil-li-li-ter	min-e-stro-ne
mi-crom-e-ter	mi-graine	mil-li-me-ter	mine-sweep-er
mi-crom-e-try	mi-grant	mil-li-mi-cron	mine-sweep-ing
mi-cro-mi-cron	mi-grate	mil-li-ner	min-gle
mi-cro-min-ia-ture	mi-grat-ed	mil-li-nery	min-gled
mi-cro-mil-li-me-ter	mi-grat-ing	mill-ing	min-gling
mi-cron	mi-gra-tion	mil-lion	min-i-a-ture
mi-crons	mi-gra-tor	mil-lionth	min-i-a-tur-ize
mi-cra	mi-gra-to-ry	mill-lion-aire	min-i-a-tur-ized
mi-cro-or-gan-ism	mi-la-dy	mil-li-sec-ond	min-i-a-tur-iz-ing
mi-cro-phone	mi-la-dies	mill-pond	min-i-a-tur-i-za-tion
mi-cro-phon-ic	mild	mill-run	min-im
mi-cro-pho-to-graph	mild-ly	mill-stone	min-i-mal
mi-cro-read-er	mild-ness	mill-stream	min-i-mal-ly
mi-cro-scope	mil-dew	mi-lord	min-i-mize
mi-cro-scop-i-cal	mil-dewy	milt	min-i-mized
mi-cro-scop-i-cal-ly	mile-age	mime	min-i-miz-ing
mi-cros-co-py	mil-er	mimed	min-i-mi-za-tion
mi-cros-co-pist	mile-stone	mim-ing	min-i-miz-er
mi-cro-sec-ond	mi-lieu	mim-er	min-i-mum
mi-cro-wave	mi-lieus	mim-e-o-graph	min-i-mums
mid-day	mil-i-tant	mim-ic	min-i-ma
mid-dle	mil-i-tan-cy	mim-icked	min-ing
mid-dles	mil-i-tant-ness	mim-ick-ing	min-ion
mid-dling	mil-i-ta-rism	mim-i-cal	min-is-ter
mid-dle--aged	mil-i-ta-ris-tic	mim-i-cal	min-is-te-ri-al
mid-dle-man	mil-i-ta-ris-ti-cal-ly	mim-ick-r	min-is-trant
mid-dle-men	mil-i-ta-rize	mim-ic-ry	min-is-tra-tion
mid-dle-most	mil-i-ta-rized	mim-ic-ries	min-is-tries
mid-dle-weight	mil-i-ta-riz-ing	min-able	min-now
mid-dy	mil-i-ta-ri-za-tion	mine-able	mi-nor
mid-dies	mil-i-tary	min-e-ret	mi-nor-i-ty
midg-et	mil-i-tar-i-ly	mince	mi-nor-i-ties
mid-land	mi-li-tia	minced	min-strel
mid-night	milk	minc-ing	mint-age
mid-sec-tion	milk-er	minc-er	mint-er
mid-ship	milky	minc-ing-ly	min-u-end
mid-ship-man	milk-i-er	mince-meat	mi-nus
mid-ship-men	milk-i-est	mind-ed	mi-nus-cule
midst	milk-maid	mind-less	min-ute

min-ut-ed

min-ut-ing

mi-nut-er

mi-nut-est

min-ute-man

min-ute-men

mi-nu-tia

mi-nu-ti-ae

minx

mir-a-cle

mi-rac-u-lous

mi-rage

mire

mired

mir-ing

mir-ror

mirth

mirth-ful

mirth-ful-ly

mirth-ful-ness

mirth-less

mis-ad-ven-tage

mis-ad-vise

mis-ad-vised

mis-ad-vis-ing

mis-al-li-ance

mis-an-thrope

mis-an-tho-pist

mis-an-throp-ic

mis-an-throp-i-cal

mis-an-thro-py

mis-ap-ply

mis-ap-plied

mis-ap-ply-ing

mis-ap-pli-ca-tion

mis-ap-pre-hend

mis-ap-pre-hen-sion

mis-ap-pro-pri-ate

mis-ap-pro-pri-at-ed

mis-ap-pro-pri-at-ing

mis-ap-pro-pri-a-tion

mis-be-have

mis-be-haved

mis-be-hav-ing

mis-be-hav-er

mis-be-ha-vior

mis-cal-cu-late

mis-cal-cu-lat-ed

mis-cal-cu-lat-ing

mis-cal-cu-la-tion

mis-cal-cu-la-tor

mis-call

mis-car-riage

mis-car-ry

mis-car-ried

mis-car-ry-ing

mis-ce-ge-na-tion

mis-ce-ge-net-ic

mis-cel-la-neous

mis-cel-la-ny

mis-cel-la-nies

mis-chance

mis-chief

mis-chie-vous

mis-chie-vous-ly

mis-chie-vous-ness

mis-ci-ble

mis-ci-bil-i-ty

mis-con-ceive

mis-con-ceived

mis-con-ceiv-ing

mis-con-ceiv-er

mis-con-cep-tion

mis-con-duct

mis-con-strue

mis-con-strued

mis-con-stru-ing

mis-con-struc-tion

mis-count

mis-cre-ant

mis-cue

mis-cued

mis-cu-ing

mis-deal

mis-dealt

mis-deal-ing

mis-deed

mis-de-mean-or

mis-di-rect

mis-di-rec-tion

mis-do

mis-did

mis-done

mis-do-ing

mis-em-ploy

mis-em-ploy-ment

mi-ser

mi-ser-li-ness

mi-ser-ly

mis-er-a-ble

mis-er-a-ble-ness

mis-er-a-bly

mis-ery

mis-er-ies

mis-fea-sance

mis-fire

mis-fired

mis-fir-ing

mis-fit

mis-fit-ted

mis-fit-ting

mis-for-tune

mis-giv-ing

mis-gov-ern

mis-gov-ern-ment

mis-guide

mis-guid-ed

mis-guid-ing

mis-guid-ance

mis-han-dle

mis-han-dled

mis-han-dling

mis-hap

mish-mash

mis-in-form

mis-in-form-ant

mis-in-form-er

mis-in-for-ma-tion

mis-in-ter-pret

mis-in-ter-pre-ta-tion

mis-in-ter-pret-er

mis-judge

mis-judged

mis-judg-ing

mis-judg-ment

mis-lay

mis-laid

mis-lay-ing

mis-lead

mis-led

mis-lead-ing

mis-lead-er

mis-man-age

mis-man-aged

mis-man-ag-ing

mis-man-age-ment

mis-match

mis-mate

mis-mat-ed

mis-mat-ing

mis-name

mis-named

mis-nam-ing

mis-no-mer

mi-sog-a-my

mi-sog-y-ny

mi-sog-y-nist

mi-sog-y-nous

mis-place

mis-placed

mis-plac-ing

mis-place-ment

mis-play

mis-print

mis-pri-sion

mis-prize

mis-prized

mis-priz-ing

mis-pro-nounce

mis-pro-nounced

mis-pro-nouc-ing

mis-pro-nun-ci-a-tion

mis-quote

mis-quoted

mis-quot-ing

mis-quo-ta-tion

mis-read

mis-read-ing

mis-rep-re-sent

mis-rep-re-sen-ta-tion

mis-rep-re-sen-ta-tive

mis-rule

mis-ruled

mis-rul-ing

mis-sal

mis-shape

mis-shaped

mis-shap-ing

mis-shap-en

mis-sile

miss-ing

mis-sion

mis-sion-ary

mis-sion-ar-ies

mis-sive

mis-spell

mis-spelled

mis-spel-ling

mis-spend

mis-spent

mis-spend-ing

mis-state

mis-stat-ed

mis-stat-ing

mis-state-ment

mis-step

mist

mist-i-ly

mist-i-ness	miz-pah	mod-es-ties	**mol-ly-cod-dle**
mis-ta-a-ble	**miz-zen**	**mod-i-cum**	mol-ly-cod-dled
mis-take	**mne-mon-ic**	**mod-i-fi-ca-tion**	mol-ly-cod-dling
mis-took	**mne-mon-ics**	**mod-i-fy**	molt
mis-tak-en	**moa**	mod-i-fied	moult
mis-tak-ing	**mob**	mod-i-fy-ing	molt-er
mis-tak-en-ly	mobbed	mod-i-fi-a-ble	**mol-ten**
mis-tak-er	mob-bing	mod-i-fi-er	mol-ten-ly
mis-tle-toe	mob-bish	**mod-ish**	**mo-lyb-de-num**
mis-tral	**mo-bile**	mod-ish-ly	**mo-ment**
mis-treat	mo-bil-i-ty	mod-ish-ness	**me-men-tary**
mis-treat-ment	**mo-bi-lize**	**mo-diste**	mo-men-tar-i-ly
mis-tress	mo-bi-lized	**mod-u-late**	**mo-men-tous**
mis-tri-al	mo-bi-liz-ing	mod-u-lat-ed	mo-men-tous-ly
mis-trust	mo-bi-li-za-tion	mod-u-lat-ing	**mo-men-tum**
mis-trust-ful	**mob-ster**	**mod-u-la-tion**	**mon-arch**
mis-trust-ful-ly	**moc-ca-sin**	mod-u-la-tor	mo-nar-chal
mis-trust-ing-ly	**mo-cha**	mod-u-la-to-ry	mo-nar-chal-ly
misty	**mock**	**mod-ule**	**mo-nar-chi-cal**
mist-i-er	mock-er	**mod-u-lar**	mo-nar-chic
mist-i-est	mock-ing-ly	**mo-gulmo-hair**	mo-nar-chi-cal-ly
mis-un-der-stand	**mock-ery**	**moi-ety**	**mon-ar-chism**
mis-un-der-stood	mock-er-ies	moi-eties	mon-ar-chist
mis-un-der-stand-ing	**mock-ing-bird**	**moil**	mon-ar-chis-tic
mis-us-age	**mock-up**	moil-er	**mo-nas-tic**
mis-use	**mod-al**	moil-ing-ly	**mo-nas-ti-cal**
mis-used	mo-dal-i-ty	**mois-ten**	mo-nas-ti-cal-ly
mis-us-ing	mod-al-ly	moist-en-er	**mo-nas-ti-cism**
mis-us-er	**mod-el**	**mo-lar**	**mon-au-ral**
mis-val-ue	mod-eled	**mo-las-ses**	mon-au-ral-ly
mis-val-ued	mod-el-ing	**mold**	**mon-e-tary**
mis-val-u-ing	mod-el-er	mold-able	mon-e-tar-i-ly
mi-ter	**mod-er-ate**	mold-er	**mon-e-tize**
mi-tre	mod-er-at-ed	**mold-board**	mon-e-tized
mi-ti-cide	mod-er-at-ing	**mold-ing**	mon-e-tiz-ing
mi-ti-cid-al	mod-er-ate-ly	**moldy**	mon-e-ti-za-tion
mit-i-gate	mod-er-ate-ness	mold-i-er	**mon-ey**
mit-i-gat-ed	**mod-er-a-tion**	mold-i-est	**mon-ey-chang-er**
mit-i-gat-ing	**mod-er-a-tor**	mold-i-ness	**mon-ey-eyed**
mit-i-ga-tion	mod-er-a-tor-ship	**mol-e-cule**	mon-ied
mit-i-ga-tive	**mod-ern**	**mole-hill**	**mon-ey--mak-er**
mit-i-ga-tor	**mod-ern-ism**	**mole-skin**	mon-ey--mak-ing
mit-i-ga-to-ry	mod-er-ist	**mo-lest**	**mon-ger**
mi-to-sis	mod-er-ist-ic	mo-les-ta-tion	**mon-goose**
mi-tral	mod-er-ize	mo-lest-er	mon-gooses
mit-ten	**mod-ern-ize**	**mol-li-fy**	**mon-grel**
mix	mod-ern-ized	mol-li-fied	**mon-i-ker**
mixed	mod-ern-iz-ing	mol-li-fy-ing	**mo-ni-tion**
mix-ing	mod-ern-iz-er	mol-i-fi-ca-tion	**mon-i-tor**
mix-er	mod-ern-i-za-tion	mol-li-fi-er	mon-i-to-ri-al
mix-ture	**mod-est**	mol-li-fy-ing-ly	**monk**
mix-up	mod-est-ly	**mol-lusk**	monk-ish
	mod-est-ty		

monk-ish-ly	mo-nop-o-liz-er	moon-i-est	mor-phol-o-gist
mon-key	mo-nop-o-ly	moor-ing	mor-row
mon-keys	mo-nop-o-lies	moot-ness	mor-sel
mon-keyed	mono-rail	mop	mor-tal
mon-key-ing	mon-o-syl-lab-ic	mopped	mor-tal-ly
mon-key-shine	mon-o-syl-lab-i-cal-ly	mop-ping	mor-tal-i-ty
mon-chro-mat-ic	mon-o-syl-la-ble	mop-pet	mor-tal-i-ties
mon-o-chrome	mon-o-the-ism	mo-raine	mor-tar
mon-o-chro-mic	mon-o-the-ist	mo-rain-al	mort-gage
mon-o-chro-mi-cal	mon-o-the-is-tic	mo-rain-ic	mort-gaged
mon-o-chro-mi-cal-ly	mon-o-the-is-ti-cal-ly	mor-al	mort-gag-ing
mon-o-chrom-ist	mon-o-tone	mor-al-ly	mort-gag-ee
mon-o-cle	mo-not-o-nous	mo-rale	mort-gag-er
mon-o-cled	mo-not-o-nous-ly	mor-al-ist	mor-ti-cian
mon-o-cli-nal	mo-not-o-nous-ness	mor-al-is-tic	mor-ti-fy
mon-o-cline	mo-not-o-ny	mo-ral-i-ty	mor-ti-fied
mon-o-cli-nal-ly	mone-treme	mo-ral-i-ties	mor-ti-fy-ing
mon-o-cli-nous	mono-type	mor-al-ize	mor-ti-fi-ca-tion
mon-o-dist	mon-o-typ-er	mor-al-ized	mor-tise
mon-o-dy	mon-o-typ-ic	mor-al-iz-ing	mor-tised
mon-o-dies	mon-o-va-lent	mor-al-i-za-tion	mor-tising
mo-nod-ic	mon-o-va-lence	mor-al-iz-er	mort-main
mo-noe-cious	mon-o-va-len-cy	mo-rass	mor-tu-ary
mo-noe-cious-ly	mon-ox-ide	mor-a-to-ri-um	mor-tu-ar-ies
mo-nog-a-my	mon-sei-gneur	mor-a-to-ri-ums	mo-sa-ic
mo-nog-a-mist	mes-sei-gneurs	mor-a-to-ria	Mo-ses
mo-nog-a-mous	mon-sieur	mo-ray	mo-sey
mon-o-gram	mon-soon	mor-bid	mo-seyd
mon-o-grammed	mon-ster	mor-bid-ly	mo-sey-ing
mon-o-gram-ming	mon-stros-i-ty	mor-bid-i-ty	mosque
mon-o-gram-mat-ic	mon-stro-i-ties	mor-bid-ness	mos-qui-to
mon-o-graph	mon-strous	mor-dant	mos-qui-toes
mo-nog-ra-pher	mon-strous-i-ties	mor-dan-cy	mos-qui-tos
mon-o-graph-ic	mon-tage	mor-dant-ly	moss
mon-o-lith	month-ly	more-over	most-ly
mon-o-logue	month-lies	mo-res	mo-tel
mon-o-log	mon-u-ment	mor-ga-nat-ic	mo-tet
mon-o-logu-ist	mon-u-men-tal	mor-ga-nat-i-cal-ly	moth-ball
mon-o-log-ist	mon-u-men-tal-ly	morque	moth-eat-en
mon-o-ma-nia	mooch	mor-i-bund	moth-er
mon-o-ma-ni-ac	mooch-er	mo-ri-on	moth-er-hood
mon-o-ma-ni-a-cal	moon-beam	morn-ing	moth-er-in-law
mon-o-met-al-lism	moon-light	morn-ing glo-ry	moth-er-ly
mon-o-me-tal-lic	moon-light-er	morn-ing glo-ries	mo-tif
mo-no-mi-al	moon-light-ing	mo-roc-co	mo-tile
mon-nu-cle-o-sis	moon-scape	mo-rose	mo-til-i-ty
mon-o-pho-nic	moon-shine	mo-rose-ly	mo-tion
mono-plane	moon-shiner	mor-pheme	mo-tion-less
mo-nop-o-lize	moon-stone	mor-phine	mo-ti-vate
mo-nop-o-lized	moon-struck	mor-phol-o-gy	mo-ti-vat-ed
mo-nop-o-liz-ing	moony	mor-pho-log-ic	mo-ti-vat-ing
mo-nop-o-li-za-tion	moon-i-er	mor-pho-log-i-cal	mo-ti-va-tion

mo-tive	mov-a-bly	mul-ti-tu-di-nous-ly	mu-sette
mot-ley	move	mum-ble	mu-se-um
mo-tor	moved	mum-mer	mush-room
mo-tor-bike	mov-ing	mum-mery	mu-sic
mo-tor-boat	move-ment	mum-mi-fy	mu-si-cal
mo-tor-bus	mov-ie	mum-mi-fied	mu-si-cal-ly
mo-tor-cade	mow	mum-mi-fy-ing	mu-si-cale
mo-tor-cy-cle	mox-ie	mum-mi-fi-ca-tion	mu-si-cian
mo-tor-cy-cling	mu-ci-lage	mum-my	musk
mo-tor-cy-clist	mu-ci-lag-i-nous	mum-mics	musky
mo-tor-ist	muck	mum-mied	musk-i-er
mo-tor-ize	mucky	mum-my-ing	misk-i-est
mo-tor-ized	mu-cous	munch	mus-ket
mo-tor-iz-ing	mu-cos-i-ty	munch-er	mus-ke-teer
mo-tor-i-za-tion	mu-cus	mun-dane	musk-mel-on
mo-tor-man	mu-ez-zin	mun-dane-ly	musk-rat
mo-tor-men	muf-fin	mu-nic-i-pal	mus-lin
mound	muf-ti	mu-nic-i-pal-ly	muss
mount	mug	mu-nic-i-pal-i-ty	mussy
mount-able	mugged	mu-nif-i-cent	muss-i-er
mount-er	mug-ging	mu-nif-i-cence	mus-sel
moun-tain	mug-ger	mu-nif-i-cent-ly	mus-tache
moun-tain-eer	mug-gy	mu-ni-tion	mus-tang
moun-tain-ous	mug-gi-er	mu-ral	mus-ter
moun-te-bank	mug-gi-est	mu-ral-ist	mus-ty
mount-ing	mu-lat-to	mur-der	mus-ti-er
mourn	mu-lat-toes	mur-der-er	mus-ti-est
mourn-er	mul-ber-ry	mur-der-ess	mus-ti-ly
mourn-ful	mul-ber-ries	mur-der-ous	mu-ta-ble
mourn-ful-ly	mulch	mur-der-ous-ly	mu-ta-bil-i-ty
mourn-ing	mu-le-teer	mu-ri-at-ic ac-id	mu-ta-bly
mourn-ing-ly	mul-ish	murky	mu-tant
mouse	mul-ish-ly	murk-i-er	mu-ta-tion
moused	mul-let	murk-i-est	mu-tate
mous-ing	mul-li-gan	murk-i-ly	mu-tat-ed
mous-er	mul-li-ga-taw-ny	mur-mur	mu-tat-ing
mous-tache	mul-lion	mur-rain	mu-ta-tion-al
mousy	mul-lioned	mus-cat	mute
mous-i-er	mul-ti-far-i-ous	mus-ca-tel	mut-ed
mous-i-est	mul-ti-far-i-ous-ly	mus-cle	mu-ti-late
mouth	mul-ti-lat-er-al	mus-cled	mu-ti-ny
mouthed	mul-ti-ple	mus-cling	mu-ti-nies
mouth-er	mul-ti-i-cand	mus-cle--bound	mu-ti-nied
mouth-ful	mul-ti-pli-ca-tion	mus-cu-lar	mu-ti-nous
mouth-fuls	mul-ti-plic-i-ty	mus-cu-lar-i-ty	mut-ter
mouth-piece	mul-ti-pli-er	mus-cu-lar-ly	mut-ter-er
mouthy	mul-ti-ply	mus-cu-la-ture	mut-ton
mouth-i-er	mul-ti-plied	mus-cu-lo-skel-e-tal	mu-tu-al
mouth-i-est	mul-ti-ply-ing	muse	mu-tu-al-i-ty
mou-ton	mul-ti-pli-a-ble	mused	mu-tu-al-ly
mov-able	mul-ti-tude	mus-ing	muz-zle
mov-a-bil-i-ty	mul-ti-tu-di-nous	mus-ing-ly	my-col-o-gy

my-col-o-gist
my-na
my-nah
my-o-pia
my-op-ic
myr-i-ad
myr-mi-don
myrrh
myr-tle
mys-te-ri-ous
mys-te-ri-ous-ly
mys-tery
mys-ter-ies
mys-tic
mys-ti-cal
mys-ti-cal-ly
mys-ti-cism
mys-ti-fy
mys-ti-fied
mys-ti-fy-ing
mys-ti-fi-ca-tion
mys-tique
myth
myth-ic
myth-i-cal
myth-i-cal-ly
myth-i-cist
myth-i-cize
my-thol-o-gy
my-thol-o-gies
myth-o-log-ic
myth-o-log-i-cal
my-thol-o-gist

N

na-stur-tium
nas-ty
nas-ti-er
nas-ti-est
na-tal
na-tion
na-tion-hood
na-tion-al
na-tion-al-ly
na-tion-al-ism
na-tion-al-ist
na-tion-al-is-tic
na-tion-al-i-ty
na-tion-al-i-ties
na-tion-al-ize
na-tion-al-ized

na-tion-al-iz-ing
na-tion-al-i-za-tion
na-tion-wide
na-tive
na-tive-ly
na-tiv-i-ty
na-tiv-i-ties
nat-ty
nat-ti-er
nat-u-ral
nat-u-ral-ly
nat-u-ral-ness
nat-u-ral-ism
nat-u-ral-ist
nat-u-ral-is-tic
nat-u-ral-ized
nat-u-ral-iz-ing
nat-u-ral-i-za-tion
na-ture
naught
naugh-ty
naugh-ti-er
naugh-ti-est
nau-sea
nau-se-ate
nau-se-at-ed
nau-se-at-ing
nau-seous
nau-seous-ly
nau-ti-cal
nau-ti-cal-ly
nau-ti-lus
nau-ti-lus-es
nau-ti-li
na-val
na-vel
nav-i-ga-ble
nav-i-gate
nav-i-gat-ed
nav-i-gat-ing
nav-i-ga-tion
nav-i-ga-tion-al
nav-i-ga-tor
na-vy
na-vies
near
near-ly
near-ness
near-by
neat
neat-ly
neat-ness

neb-bish
neb-u-la
nec-es-sary
nec-es-sar-ies
nec-es-sar-i-ly
ne-ces-si-tate
ne-ces-si-ta-ting
ne-ces-si-ty
ne-ces-si-ties
neck-er-chief
neck-ing
neck-lace
neck-tie
ne-crol-o-gy
ne-crol-o-gies
nec-ro-man-cy
nec-ro-man-cer
ne-cro-sis
ne-crot-ic
nec-tar
nec-tar-ine
need-ful
need-ful-ly
need-ful-ness
nee-dle
nee-dled
nee-dling
nee-dle-like
nee-dler
nee-dle-point
need-less
need-less-ly
nee-dle-work
nee-dle-work-er
needy
need-i-er
need-i-est
need-i-ness
ne'er--do--well
ne-far-i-ous
ne-far-i-ous-ly
ne-far-i-ous-ness
ne-gate
ne-ga-ted
ne-ta-ting
ne-ga-tion
neg-a-tive
neg-a-tive-ly
neg-a-tive-ness
neg-a-tive-i-ty
neg-a-tiv-ism
ne-glect

ne-glec-ter
ne-glec-tor
ne-glect-ful-ness
ne-glect-ful
ne-glect-ful-ly
neg-li-gee
neg-li-gent
neg-li-gence
neg-li-gent-ly
neg-li-gi-ble
neg-li-gi-bly
neg-li-gi-bil-i-ty
ne-go-tia-ble
ne-go-tia-bil-i-ty
ne-go-ti-ate
ne-go-ti-at-ed
ne-go-ti-at-ing
ne-go-ti-a-tion
ne-go-ti-a-tor
neigh-bor
neigh-bor-ing
neigh-bor-ly
neigh-bor-li-ness
neigh-bor-hood
nei-ther
nem-e-sis
nem-e-ses
neo-clas-sic
neo-clas-si-cism
neo-lith-ic
ne-ol-o-gism
ne-ol-o-gy
ne-on
ne-o-phyte
ne-pen-the
ne-pen-the-an
neph-ew
ne-phri-tis
ne-phrit-ic
nep-o-tism
nep-o-tist
nep-tu-ni-um
nerve
nerved
nerv-ing
nerve-less
nerve--rack-ing
nerve--wrack-ing
ner-vous
ner-vous-ly
ner-vous-ness
nervy

nerv-i-er	new-born	night-fall	ni-tro-glyc-er-in
nerv-i-est	new-com-er	night-gown	ni-trous ox-ide
nerv-i-ness	new-el	night-hawk	nit-ty-grit-ty
nes-tle	new-fan-gled	night-in-gale	nit-wit
nes-tled	new-ly	night-ly	no-be-li-um
nes-tling	new-ly-wed	**night-mare**	no-bil-i-ty
nes-tler	news-boy	night-mar-ish	no-bil-i-ties
net	news-cast	night-shade	no-ble
net-ted	news-cast-er	night-shirt	no-body
net-ting	news-pa-per	night-time	noc tur-nal
neth-er	news-pa-per-man	ni-hil-ism	noc-turne
neth-er-most	news-print	ni-hil-ist	node
net-tle	news-reel	ni-hil-is-tic	nod-al
net-tled	news-stand	**nim-ble**	nod-ule
net-tling	newsy	nim-bler	nod-u-lar
net-work	news-i-er	nim-blest	no-el
neu-ral	news-i-est	nim-ble-ness	nog-gin
neu-ral-ly	newt	nim-bly	noise
neu-ral-gia	nex-us	**nim-bus**	noised
neu-ral-gic	ni-a-cin	**nin-com-poop**	nois-ing
neu-ras-the-nia	nib-ble	nine-pin	noise-less
neu-ra-then-ic	nib-bled	nine-teen	no-mad
neu-ri-tis	nib-bling	nine-teenth	no-mad-ic
neu-rit-ic	nib-bler	nine-ty	no-mad-i-cal-ly
neu-rol-o-gy	nib-lick	nine-ties	no-mad-ism
neu-ro-log-i-cal	nice	nine-ti-eth	nom de plume
neu-rol-o-gist	nic-er	nin-ny	noms de plume
neu-ron	nic-est	nin-nines	no-men-cla-ture
neu-ron-ic	nice-ly	ninth	nom-i-nal
neu-ro-sis	nice-ness	nip	nom-i-nal-ly
neu-ro-ses	nice-ty	nipped	nom-i-nee
neu-rot-ic	nice-ties	nip-ping	non-age
neu-rot-i-cal-ly	niche	nip-per	nonce
neu-ter	nick-el	nip-ple	non-cha-lant
neu-tral	nick-el-ode-on	nip-py	non-cha-lance
neu-tral-i-ty	nick-name	nip-pi-er	non-cha-lant-ly
neu-tral-ly	nick-named	nip-pi-est	non-com
neu-tral-ism	nick-nam-ing	nir-va-na	non-com-bat-ant
neu-tral-ist	nic-o-tine	nit	non-com-mit-tal
neu-tral-ize	nic-o-tin-ic	nit-ty	non-com-mit-tal-ly
neu-tral-ized	niece	nit-ti-er	non-con-duc-tor
neu-tral-iz-ing	nif-ty	nit-ti-est	non-con-duc-ing
neu-tral-i-za-tion	nif-ti-er	ni-ter	non-con-form-ist
neu-tral-iz-er	nif-ti-est	nit-pick	non-con-form-i-ty
neu-tri-no	nig-gard	ni-trate	non-de-script
neu-tron	nig-gard-li-ness	ni-trat-ed	non-en-ti-ty
nev-er	nig-gard-ly	ni-trat-ing	non-en-ti-ties
nev-er-more	nigh	ni-tra-tion	none-the-less
nev-er-the-less	nigh-er	ni-tra-tor	non-in-ter-ven-tio
new	nigh-est	ni-tric	non-met-al
new-ish	night-cap	ni-tro-gen	non-me-tal-lic
new-ness	night-dress	ni-trog-e-nous	non-pa-reil

non-par-ti-san
non-par-ti-san-ship
non-plus
non-plused
non-plus-ing
non-prof-it
non-res-i-dent
non-res-i-dence
non-res-i-den-cy
non-res-i-den-cies
non-re-stric-tive
non-sec-tar-i-an
non-sense
non-sen-si-cal
non-sen-si-cal-ly
non se-qui-tur
non-stop
non-union
non-union-ism
non-union-ist
non-vi-o-lence
non-vi-o-lent
non-vi-o-lent-ly
noo-dle
noon
noon-day
noon-time
nor-mal
nor-mal-cy
nor-mal-i-ty
nor-mal-ly
nor-mal-ize
nor-mal-ized
nor-mal-iz-ing
nor-mal-i-za-tion
north-east
north-east-ern
north-east-er
north-er
north-ern
north-ern-most
north-ern-er
north-ward
north-wards
north-ward-ly
north-west
nose
nosed
nos-ing
nose-gay
nos-tal-gia
nos-tal-gic

nos-tril
nos-trum
no-ta-ble
no-ta-rize
no-ta-rized
no-ta-riz-ing
no-ta-ri-za-tion
no-ta-ry
no-ta-ries
no-ta-tion
no-ta-tion-al
notch
notched
note
not-ed
not-ed
not-ed-ly
note-wor-thy
note-wor-thi-ness
noth-ing
noth-ing-ness
no-tice
no-ticed
no-tic-ing
no-tice-a-ble
no-tice-a-bly
no-ti-fy
no-ti-fied
no-ti-fy-ing
no-ti-fi-ca-tion
no-ti-fi-er
no-tion
no-to-ri-ous
no-to-ri-ous-ly
no-to-ri-e-ty
no-trump
nought
nour-ish
nour-ish-er
nour-ish-ing
nour-ish-ment
no-va
no-vas
nov-el
nov-el-ist
nov-el-is-tic
nov-el-ette
nov-el-ty
nov-el-ties
no-ve-na
no-ve-nae
nov-ice

no-vi-tiate
no-where
no-wise
nox-ious
nox-ious-ly
noz-zle
nu-ance
nub-bin
nu-bile
nu-cle-ar
nu-cle-us
nu-cle-us-es
nu-clei
nudge
nudged
nudg-ing
nudg-er
nud-ism
nud-ist
nug-get
nui-sance
null
nul-li-ty
nul-li-ties
nul-li-fy
nul-li-fied
nul-li-fy-ing
nul-li-fi-ca-tion
nul-li-fi-er
num-ber
num-ber-er
num-ber-less
numb-skull
nu-mer-al
num-er-al-ly
nu-mer-ate
nu-mer-at-ed
nu-mer-at-ing
nu-mer-a-tion
nu-mer-a-tor
nu-mer-i-cal
nu-mer-i-cal-ly
nu-mer-ous
nu-mer-ous-ly
nu-mis-mat-ics
nu-mis-mat-ic
nu-mis-mat-i-cal
nu-mis-ma-tist
num-skull
nun-cio
nun-ci-os
nun-nery

nun-ner-ies
nup-tial
nup-tial-ly
nurse
nursed
nurs-ing
nurs-er
nurse-maid
nurs-ery
nurs-er-ies
nut
nut-ted
nut-ting
nut-crack-er
nut-hatch
nut-meg
nu-tri-ent
nu-tri-ment
nu-tri-tion
nu-tri-tion-al
nu-tri-tion-al-ly
nu-tri-tion-ist
nu-tri-tious
nu-tri-tious-ly
nu-tri-tive
nu-tri-tive-ly
nut-shell
nut-ty
nut-ti-er
nut-ti-est
nuz-zle
nuz-zled
nuz-zling
ny-lon
nymph
nym-phal
nym-pho-ma-nia
nym-pho-ma-ni-ac

O

oaf
oaf-ish
oaf-ish-ly
oak-en
oa-kum
oar
oared
oars-man
oars-men
oar-lock
oa-sis

oa-ses	oblig-ing	**ob-sti-nate**	**oc-cu-py**
oat-en	oblig-er	ob-sti-na-cy	oc-cu-pied
oath	**ob-lique**	ob-sti-na-cies	oc-cu-py-ing
oat-meal	ob-liqued	ob-sti-nat-ly	oc-cu-pi-er
ob-bli-ga-to	ob-liqu-ing	**ob-strep-er-ous**	**oc-cur**
ob-bli-ga-tos	ob-lique-ly	ob-strep-er-ous-ly	oc-curred
ob-du-rate	**oblit-er-ate**	**ob-struct**	oc-cur-ring
ob-du-ra-cy	oblit-er-at-ed	ob-struc-tive	oc-cur-rence
ob-du-rate-ly	oblit-er-at-ing	ob-struc-tor	oc-cur-rent
obe-di-ence	oblit-er-a-tion	**ob-struc-tion**	**ocean**
obe-di-ent	oblit-er-a-tive	ob-struc-tion-ism	oce-an-ic
obe-di-ent-ly	**obliv-i-on**	ob-struc-tion-ist	**ocean-og-ra-phy**
obei-sance	obliv-i-ous	**ob-tain**	ocean-og-ra-pher
obei-sant	obliv-i-ous-ly	ob-tain-a-ble	ocean-o-graph-ic
obe-lisk	**ob-long**	ob-tain-er	**oce-lot**
obese	**ob-lo-quy**	ob-tain-ment	**ocher**
obese-ness	ob-lo-quies	**ob-trude**	ocher-ous
obes-i-ty	**ob-nox-ious**	ob-trud-ed	ochery
obey	ob-nox-ious-ly	ob-trud-ing	**o'clock**
obey-er	**oboe**	ob-trud-er	**oc-ta-gon**
ob-fus-cate	**obo-ist**	ob-tru-sion	oc-tag-o-nal
ob-fus-ca-ted	**ob-scene**	ob-tru-sive	oc-tag-o-nal-ly
ob-fus-ca-ting	ob-scene-ly	**ob-tuse**	**oc-ta-he-dron**
ob-fus-ca-tion	ob-scen-ity	ob-tuse-ly	oc-ta-he-drons
obit	ob-scen-i-ties	**ob-verse**	oc-ta-he-dra
obit-u-ary	**ob-se-qui-ous**	ob-verse-ly	oc-ta-he-dral
obit-u-ar-ies	ob-se-qui-ous-ly	**ob-vi-ate**	**oc-tane**
ob-ject	**ob-se-quy**	ob-vi-ated	**oc-tave**
ob-ject-less	ob-se-quies	ob-vi-at-ing	**oc-ta-vo**
ob-ject-or	**ob-serv-able**	ob-vi-a-tion	**oc-tet**
ob-jec-tion	ob-serv-ably	ob-vi-a-tor	**oc-to-ge-nar-i-an**
ob-jec-tion-a-ble	**ob-ser-vance**	**ob-vi-ous**	oc-tog-e-nary
ob-jec-tion-a-bly	**ob-ser-vant**	ob-vi-ous-ly	**oc-to-pus**
ob-jec-tive	ob-ser-vant-ly	**oc-ca-sion**	**oc-u-lar**
ob-jec-tive-ly	**ob-ser-va-tion**	oc-ca-sion-al	oc-u-lar-ly
ob-jec-tive-ness	ob-ser-va-tion-al	oc-ca-sion-al-ly	**oc-u-list**
ob-jec-tiv-i-ty	**ob-ser-va-to-ry**	**oc-ci-dent**	**odd**
ob-jur-gate	ob-ser-va-to-ries	oc-ci-den-tal	odd-ly
ob-jur-gat-ed	**ob-sess**	**oc-clude**	odd-ness
ob-jur-gat-ing	ob-ses-sive	oc-clud-ed	**odd-ball**
ob-jur-ga-tion	ob-ses-sive-ly	oc-clud-ing	**odd-i-ty**
ob-jur-ga-to-ry	**ob-ses-sion**	oc-clu-sive	odd-i-ties
ob-late	ob-sid-i-an	**oc-clu-sion**	**od-ic**
ob-late-ly	**ob-so-les-cent**	**oc-cult**	**odi-ous**
ob-late-ness	ob-so-les-cence	**oc-cult-ism**	odi-ous-ly
ob-li-gate	ob-so-les-cent-ly	oc-cult-ist	**odi-um**
ob-li-gat-ed	**ob-so-lete**	**oc-cu-pan-cy**	**odom-e-ter**
ob-li-gat-ing	ob-sta-cle	oc-cu-pan-cies	**odor**
ob-li-ga-tion	**ob-ste-tri-cian**	oc-cu-pant	odored
ob-lig-a-to-ry	ob-stet-rics	**oc-cu-pa-tion**	odor-less
oblige	ob-stet-ric	oc-cu-pa-tion-al	odor-ous
obliged	ob-stet-ri-cal	oc-cu-pa-tion-al-ly	odor-ous-ly

odor-if-er-ous	ogling	omit-ting	**ooze**
odor-if-er-ous-ly	**ogre**	**om-ni-bus**	oozed
od-ys-sey	ogre-ish	om-ni-bus-es	oo-zi-er
oe-di-pal	**ohm**	**om-nip-o-tence**	oo-zi-est
of-fal	ohm-ic	om-nip-o-tent-ly	oo-zi-ness
off-beat	ohm-age	**om-ni-pres-ence**	ooz-ing
off--col-or	ohm-me-ter	**om-ni-pres-ent**	oo-zy
of-fend	**oil-cloth**	om-ni-pres-ent-ly	**opac-i-ty**
of-fend-er	**oil-er**	**om-ni-science**	opac-i-ties
of-fense	**oil-skin**	om-ni-scient	**opal**
of-fense-less	**oily**	om-ni-scient-ly	**opal-es-cence**
of-fen-sive	oil-i-er	**om-ni-vore**	opal-es-cent
of-fen-sive-ly	oil-i-est	**om-niv-o-rous**	**opaque**
of-fen-sive-ness	oil-i-ness	om-niv-o-rous-ly	opaque-ly
of-fer	**oint-ment**	om-niv-o-rous-ness	opaque-ness
of-fer-er	**okra**	**onan-ism**	**open**
of-fer-ing	**old**	onan-ist	open-er
of-fer-to-ry	old-en	onan-is-tic	open-ly
of-fer-to-ri-al	old-er	**once--over**	open-ness
of-fer-to-ries	old-est	**on-com-ing**	**open--air**
off-hand	old-ish	**oner-ous**	**open door**
off-hand-ed-ly	old-ness	oner-ous-ly	**open--end**
off-hand-ed-ness	**old--fash-ioned**	oner-ous-ness	**open--eyed**
of-fice	**old-ster**	**one-self**	**open-hand-ed**
of-fice-hold-er	**old--time**	**one--sid-ed**	open-hand-ed-ly
of-fi-cer	old--tim-er	one--sid-ed-ly	**open house**
of-fi-cial	**old--world**	one--sid-ed-ness	**open-ing**
of-fi-cial-dom	**ole-ag-i-nous**	**one-time**	**open--mind-ed**
of-fi-cial-ism	ole-ag-i-nous-ly	**one--track**	open--mind-ed-ly
of-fi-cial-ly	ole-ag-i-nous-ness	**one--way**	**open-mouthed**
of-fi-ci-ate	**oleo**	**on-go-ing**	**open ses-a-me**
of-fi-ci-at-ed	oleo-mar-ga-rine	**on-ion**	**open-work**
of-fi-ci-at-ing	**ol-fac-tion**	on-ion-like	**opera**
of-fi-ci-a-tion	**ol-fac-to-ry**	on-iony	op-er-at-ic
of-fi-ci-a-tor	ol-fac-to-ries	**on-ion-skin**	op-er-at-i-cal-ly
of-fi-cious	**oli-garch**	**on--line**	**op-er-a-ble**
of-fi-cious-ly	**oli-gar-chic**	**on-look-er**	op-er-a-bil-i-ty
of-fi-cious-ness	oli-gar-chi-cal	on-look-ing	op-er-a-bly
off-ing	**oli-gar-chy**	**on-ly**	**opera glass**
off-set	oli-gar-chies	**on-o-mato-poe-ia**	**opera house**
off-set-ting	**oli-gop-oly**	on-o-mato-poe-ic	**op-er-ate**
off-shoot	**ol-ive**	on-o-mato-po-et-ic	op-er-at-ed
off-shore	**om-buds-man**	**on-rush**	op-er-at-ing
off-side	om-buds-men	on-rush-ing	**op-er-a-tion**
off-spring	**om-elet**	**on-set**	op-er-a-tive
off-stage	**omen**	**on-shore**	op-er-a-tive-ly
off--the--cuff	**om-i-nous**	**on-slaught**	**op-er-a-tor**
of-ten	om-i-nous-ly	**onto-**	**op-er-et-ta**
of-ten-times	om-i-nous-ness	**onus**	**oph-thal-mic**
ogle	**omis-sion**	**on-ward**	oph-thal-mo-log-ic
ogled	**omit**	**on-yx**	oph-thal-mol-o-gist
ogler	omit-ted	**oo-dles**	oph-thal-mol-o-gy

opi-ate	op-ti-miz-ing	or-dain-ment	orig-i-nat-ed
opine	**op-ti-mum**	**or-deal**	orig-i-nat-ing
opined	op-ti-ma	**or-der**	orig-i-na-tion
opin-ing	**op-tion**	or-dered	orig-i-na-tive
opin-ion	op-tion-al	or-der-li-ness	orig-i-na-tive-ly
opin-ion-at-ed	op-tion-al-ly	or-der-ly	orig-i-na-tor
opin-ion-at-ed-ly	**op-tom-e-trist**	**or-di-nal**	**or-i-son**
opi-um	**op-tom-e-try**	**or-di-nance**	**or-na-ment**
opos-sum	op-to-met-ric	**or-di-nari-ly**	or-na-men-tal
op-po-nent	op-to-met-ri-cal	**or-di-nary**	or-na-men-ta-tion
op-por-tune	**op-u-lence**	or-di-nari-ness	**or-nate**
op-por-tune-ly	**op-u-lent**	**or-di-na-tion**	or-nate-ly
op-por-tune-ness	op-u-lent-ly	**ord-nance**	or-nate-ness
op-por-tun-ism	**opus**	**or-dure**	**or-nery**
op-por-tun-ist	opus-es	**oreg-a-no**	or-ner-i-ness
op-por-tun-is-tic	**or-a-cle**	**or-gan**	**or-ni-thol-o-gy**
op-por-tu-ni-ty	orac-u-lar	**or-gan-dy**	or-ni-tho-log-ic
op-por-tu-ni-ties	orac-u-lar-i-ty	**or-gan-ic**	or-ni-tho-log-i-cal
op-pos-able	orac-u-lar-ly	or-gan-i-cal-ly	or-ni-tho-log-i-cal-ly
op-pos-a-bil-i-ty	**oral**	**or-gan-ism**	or-ni-thol-o-gist
op-pose	oral-ly	or-gan-is-mal	**oro-tund**
op-posed	**or-ange**	or-gan-is-mic	oro-tun-di-ty
op-pos-er	**or-ange-ade**	**or-gan-ist**	**or-phan**
op-pos-ing	**orang-utan**	**or-ga-ni-za-tion**	or-phan-hood
op-pos-ing-ly	**orate**	or-gan-i-za-tion-al	**or-phan-age**
op-po-site	orat-ed	**or-ga-nize**	**orth-odon-tics**
op-po-site-ly	orat-ing	or-ga-niz-able	orth-odon-tic
op-po-si-tion	**ora-tion**	or-ga-nized	orth-odon-tist
op-po-si-tion-al	**or-a-tor**	or-ga-niz-er	**or-tho-dox**
op-press	or-a-tor-i-cal	or-ga-niz-ing	or-tho-dox-ly
op-pres-si-ble	or-a-tor-i-cal-ly	or-ga-niz-a-ble	or-tho-dox-ness
op-pres-sor	**or-a-to-rio**	**or-gasm**	**or-tho-doxy**
op-pres-sion	or-a-to-ri-os	or-gas-mic	or-tho-dox-ies
op-pres-sive	**or-a-to-ry**	**or-gi-as-tic**	**or-tho-gen-ic**
op-pres-sive-ly	**or-bic-u-lar**	or-gi-as-ti-cal-ly	**or-thog-o-nal**
op-pres-sive-ness	or-bic-u-lar-i-ty	**or-gy**	or-thog-o-nal-ly
op-pro-bri-ous	or-bic-u-lar-ly	or-gies	**or-thog-ra-phy**
op-pro-bri-ous-ly	**or-bic-u-late**	**ori-ent**	or-tho-graph-ic
op-pro-bri-um	**or-bit**	**Ori-en-tal**	or-tho-graph-i-cal
op-tic	or-bit-al	**ori-en-tal-ism**	or-tho-graph-i-cal-ly
op-ti-cal	or-bit-er	ori-en-tal-ist	or-thog-ra-phies
op-ti-cal-ly	**or-chard**	ori-en-tal-ly	or-thog-ra-pher
op-ti-cian	**or-ches-tra**	**ori-en-tate**	**or-tho-pe-dic**
op-tics	or-ches-tral	ori-en-tat-ed	or-tho-pe-dics
op-ti-mal	or-ches-tral-ly	ori-en-tat-ing	or-tho-pe-dist
op-ti-mism	**or-ches-trate**	**ori-en-ta-tion**	**os-cil-late**
op-ti-mist	or-ches-trat-ed	**or-i-fice**	os-cil-lat-ed
op-ti-mis-tic	or-ches-trat-ing	**ori-ga-mi**	os-cil-lat-ing
op-ti-mis-ti-cal-ly	or-ches-tra-tion	**orig-i-nal**	os-cil-la-tion
op-ti-mize	**or-chid**	orig-i-nal-i-ty	os-cil-la-tor
op-ti-mi-za-tion	**or-dain**	orig-i-nal-ly	os-cil-la-to-ry
op-ti-mized	or-dain-er	**orig-i-nate**	**os-cil-lo-scope**

os-cu-late
  os-cu-lat-ed
  os-cu-lat-ing
  os-cu-la-tion
  os-cu-la-to-ry
os-mi-um
os-mose
  os-mosed
  os-mos-ing
os-mo-sis
  os-mot-ic
  os-mot-i-cal-ly
os-prey
os-si-fy
  os-si-fied
  os-si-fi-er
  os-si-fy-ing
os-ten-si-ble
  os-ten-si-bly
os-ten-sive
  os-ten-sive-ly
os-ten-ta-tion
os-ten-ta-tious
  os-ten-ta-tious-ly
os-te-op-a-thy
  os-teo-path
  os-teo-path-ic
  os-teo-path-i-cal-ly
os-tra-cism
os-tra-cize
  os-tra-cized
  os-tra-ciz-ing
os-trich
oth-er
  oth-er-ness
oth-er-wise
oth-er-world
  oth-er-world-ly
oti-ose
  oti-ose-ly
  oti-os-i-ty
ot-ter
ot-to-man
ought
ounce
our-self
our-selves
oust-er
out-bid
  out-bid-den
  out-bid-ding
  out-bid-der

out-board
out-bound
out-brave
  out-braved
  out-brav-ing
out-break
out-build-ing
out-burst
out-cast
out-come
out-cry
  out-cries
out-dat-ed
out-dis-tance
  out-dis-tanced
  out-dis-tanc-ing
out-do
  out-did
  out-do-ing
  out-done
out-door
out-er
out-er-most
outer space
out-face
  out-faced
  out-fac-ing
out-field
  out-field-er
out-flank
out-fox
out-grow
  out-grew
  out-grow-ing
  out-grown
out-growth
out-guess
out-ing
out-land-ish
  out-land-ish-ly
out-last
out-law
  out-law-ry
out-lay
  out-laid
  out-lay-ing
out-let
out-line
  out-lined
  out-lin-ing
out-live
  out-lived

  out-liv-ing
out-look
out-ly-ing
out-mod-ed
out-num-ber
out--of--date
out-post
out-put
out-rage
  out-raged
  out-rag-ing
out-ra-geous
  out-ra-geous-ly
out-range
  out-ranged
  out-rang-ing
out-rank
out-rig-ger
out-right
out-run
  out-ran
  out-run-ning
out-set
out-shine
  out-shin-ing
  out-shone
out-side
out-sid-er
out-smart
out-spo-ken
  out-spo-ken-ly
out-stand-ing
  out-stand-ing-ly
out-strip
  out-stripped
  out-strip-ping
out-ward
  out-ward-ly
  out-wards
out-weigh
out-wit
  out-wit-ted
  out-wit-ting
ova
oval
  oval-ly
ova-ry
  ovar-i-an
  ova-ries
ovate
ova-tion
ov-en

over
over-act
over-age
over-all
over-awe
  over-awed
  over-aw-ing
over-bear-ing
  over-bear-ing-ly
over-blown
over-board
over-build
  over-build-ing
  over-built
over-cast
over-charge
  over-charged
  over-charg-ing
over-coat
over-come
  over-came
over-con-fi-dence
  over-con-fi-dent
over-do
  over-did
  over-do-ing
  over-done
over-dose
  over-dos-age
over-draft
over-draw
  over-draw-ing
  over-drawn
  over-drew
over-drive
over-due
over-em-pha-sis
  over-em-pha-size
  over-em-pha-sized
  over-em-pha-sizing
over-es-ti-mate
  over-es-ti-mat-ed
  over-es-ti-mat-ing
  over-es-ti-ma-tion
over-flow
  over-flowed
  over-flowing
  over-flown
over-gen-er-ous
over-grow
  over-grew
  over-grow-ing

over-grown
over-growth
over-hand
over-hand-ed
over-hang
over-hang-ing
over-hung
over-haul
over-haul-ing
over-head
over-land
over-lap
over-lapped
over-lap-ping
over-lay
over-laid
over-lay-ing
over-look
over-lord
over-ly
over-much
over-night
over-pass
over-play
over-pow-er
over-pow-er-ing
over-reach
over-ride
over-rid-den
over-rid-ing
over-rode
over-rule
over-ruled
over-rul-ing
over-run
over-seas
over-see
over-saw
over-see-ing
over-seen
over-seer
over-shad-ow
over-shoe
over-shoot
over-shoot-ing
over-shot
over-sight
over-sim-pli-fy
over-sim-pli-fi-ca-tion
over-sim-pli-fied
over-sim-pli-fy-ing
over-size

over-sleep
over-sleep-ing
over-slept
over-spread
over-spread-ing
over-stay
over-step
over-stepped
over-step-ping
over-strung
over-stuff
overt
overt-ly
over-tax
over--the--coun-ter
over-time
over-tone
over-ture
over-turn
over-view
over-ween-ing
over-ween-ing-ly
over-weight
over-whelm
over-whelm-ing
over-wrought
ovi-duct
ovip-a-rous
ovip-ar-ous-ly
ovoid
ovoi-dal
ovule
ovu-lar
ovum
ova
owe
owed
ow-ing
owl-ish
own-er
ox-al-ic ac-id
ox-bow
ox-en
ox-ford
ox-i-da-tion
ox-i-da-tive
ox-i-dant
ox-ide
ox-i-dize
ox-i-dized
ox-i-diz-ing
ox-y-a-cet-y-lene

ox-y-gen
ox-y-gen-ate
ox-y-gen-at-ed
ox-y-gen-at-ing
ox-y-gen-a-tion
oys-ter
ozone

P

pab-u-lum
pace
paced
pac-ing
pac-er
pace-mak-er
pa-cif-ic
pa-cif-i-ca-tion
pa-cif-i-ca-tor
pa-cif-i-ca-to-ry
pac-i-fi-er
pac-i-fism
pac-i-fist
pac-i-fy
pac-i-fied
pac-i-fy-ing
pack-age
pack-ag-er
pack-er
pack-et
pack-ing
pad
pad-ded
pad-ding
pad-dle
pad-dock
pad-dy
pad-dies
pad-lock
pae-an
pe-an
pe-gan
pe-gan-ism
pag-eant
pag-ent-ry
pag-i-nate
pag-i-nat-ed
pag-i-nat-ing
pa-go-da
pains-tak-ing
pains-tak-ing-ly
paint-er

pais-ley
pa-ja-mas
pal-ace
pal-at-a-ble
pal-at-a-bil-i-ty
pal-at-a-bly
pal-ate
pa-la-tial
pa-la-tial-ly
pal-a-tiner
pa-lat-i-nate
pa-lav-er
pale
pa-le-on-tol-o-gy
pa-le-on-to-log-ic
pa-le-on-to-log-i-cal
pal-ette
pal-imp-sest
pal-in-drome
pal-ing
pal-i-sade
pal-i-sad-ed
pal-i-sad-ing
pal-la-di-um
pall-bear-er
pal-let
pal-li-ate
pal-li-at-ed
pal-li-at-ing
pal-li-a-tion
pal-lid
pal-lor
palm
pal-ma-ceous
pal-mate
pal-mate-ly
palm-er
palm-is-try
palm-ist
pal-o-mi-no
pal-o-mi-nos
pal-pa-ble
pal-pa-bil-i-ty
pal-pa-bly
pal-pate
pal-pat-ed
pal-pat-ing
pal-ter
pal-ter-er
pal-try
pal-tri-er
pal-tri-est

pam-pas
pam-pe-an
pam-per
pam-per-er
pam-phlet
pan-a-ce-a
pan-a-ce-an
pa-nache
pan-cake
pan-cre-as
pan-cre-at-ic
pan-dem-ic
pan-de-mo-ni-um
pan-der
pan-el
pan-eled
pan-el-ing
pan-el-ist
pang
pan-ic
pan-icked
pan-ick-ing
pan-nier
pan-ier
pan-ta-loon
pan-the-ism
pan-the-is-tic
pan-the-on
pan-ther
pan-ties
pan-to-mime
pan-to-mimed
pan-try
pan-tries
pant-suit
pant-y-hose
pa-pa
pa-pa-cy
pa-pa-cies
pa-pal
pa-per
pa-per-er
pa-pery
pa-per-back
pa-pil-la
pa-pil-pae
pa-poose
pap-ri-ka
pa-py-rus
par-a-ble
par-a-digm
par-a-dig-mat-ic

par-a-dise
par-a-di-si-a-cal
par-a-dox
par-a-dox-i-cal
par-af-fin
par-a-gon
par-a-graph
par-a-graph-er
par-a-keet
par-al-lax
par-al-al-lac-tic
par-al-lel
par-al-leled
par-al-lel-ing
par-al-lel-o-gram
pa-ral-y-sis
pa-ral-y-ses
par-a-lyt-ic
par-a-lyze
par-a-lyzed
par-a-lyz-ing
par-a-me-cium
par-a-med-ic
pa-ram-e-ter
par-a-mount
par-a-mount-cy
par-a-mount-ly
par-amour
para-noia
para-noid
par-a-pet
par-a-pher-nal-ia
para-phrase
para-phrased
para-phras-ing
para-ple-gia
para-ple-gic
para-psy-chol-o-gy
par-a-site
par-a-sit-ic
para-sol
par-a-sym-pa-thet-ic
para-thi-on
para-troop-er
para-ty-phoid
par-boil
par-cel
par-celed
par-cel-ing
parch-ment
par-don
par-don-a-ble

par-don-a-bly
pare
pared
par-ing
par-e-gor-ic
par-ent
pa-ren-tal
par-ent-age
pa-ren-the-sis
pa-re-sis
pa-ret-ic
par-fait
pa-ri-ah
par-i-mu-tu-el
par-ish
pa-rish-ion-er
par-i-ty
par-ka
par-lance
par-lay
par-lay-ed
par-lay-ing
par-ley
par-leyed
par-ley-ing
par-lia-ment
par-lia-men-tar-ian
par-lia-men-ta-ry
par-lor
pa-ro-chi-al
par-o-dy
par-o-dies
par-o-died
pa-role
pa-roled
par-ot-id
par-ox-ysm
par-ox-ys-mal
par-quet
par-queted
par-quet-ing
par-quet-ry
par-rot
par-rot-like
par-roty
parse
par-si-mo-ny
par-si-mo-ni-ous
par-si-mo-ni-ous-ly
pars-ley
pars-nip
par-son-age

par-take
par-took
par-tak-en
part-ed
par-the-no-gen-e-sis
par-tial
par-tial-ly
par-tial-i-ty
par-tial-i-ties
par-tic-i-pant
par-tic-i-pate
par-tic-i-pat-ed
par-tic-i-pat-ing
par-ti-cip-i-al
par-ti-ci-ple
par-ti-cle
par-ti--col-ored
par-tic-u-lar
par-tic-u-lar-ly
par-tic-u-lar-i-ties
par-tic-u-lar-ize
par-tic-u-lar-ized
par-tic-u-lar-iz-ing
par-tic-u-late
part-ing
par-ti-san
par-ti-san-ship
par-tite
par-ti-tion
par-ti-tive
part-ly
part-ner
part-ner-ship
par-tridge
par-tridg-es
part--time
par-tu-ri-ent
par-tu-ri-tion
par-ty
par-ties
par-ve-nu
pas-chal
pa-sha
pass-able
pass-ably
pas-sen-ger
pass-er-by
pass-ers-by
pass-ing
pas-sion
pas-sion-ies
pas-sion-ate

pas-sion-ate-ly
pas-sive
pas-ta
paste
pas-ted
pas-ting
paste-board
pas-tel
pas-teur-ize
pas-teur-ized
pas-teur-iz-ing
pas-teur-i-za-tion
pas-tille
pas-time
pas-tor
pas-to-ral
pas-to-ral-ly
pas-tor-ate
pas-tra-mi
past-ry
pas-tries
pas-ture
pas-ty
past-i-er
past-i-est
pat-ent
pa-ten-cy
pat-ent-ly
pat-en-tee
pat-er-nal
pat-ter-nal-ly
pa-ter-nal-ism
pa-ter-ni-ty
pa-thet-ic
path-find-er
pa-thol-o-gy
pa-thos
pa-tience
pa-tient
pa-tient-ly
pat-i-na
pa-tio
pa-tios
pa-tri-arch
pa-tri-ar-chy
pa-tri-ar-chies
pa-tri-cian
pat-ri-mo-ny
pat-ri-mo-nies
pa-tri-ot
pa-tri-ot-ic
pa-tri-ot-ism

pa-trol
pa-trolled
pa-trol-ling
pa-trol-man
pa-trol-men
pa-tron
pa-tron-ess
pa-tron-age
pa-tron-ize
pa-tron-ized
pa-tron-iz-ing
pa-tron-iz-ing-ly
pat-ro-nym-ic
pat-sy
pat-sies
pat-ter
pat-tern
pat-terned
pat-ty
pat-ties
pau-ci-ty
paunch
pau-per
pau-per-ism
pause
paused
paus-ing
pa-vil-ion
pawn
pawn-er
pawn-bro-ker
pay-a-ble
pay-off
peace
peace-able
peace-ably
peace-ful
peace-ful-ly
peach
pea-cock
peak-ed
pea-nut
pearl
pear-ly
peas-ant
peas-ant-ly
peaty
peb-ble
pe-can
pec-ca-dil-lo
pec-ca-dil-loes
pec-ca-dil-los

peck-er
pec-tin
pec-to-ral
pec-u-late
pec-u-lat-ed
pec-u-lat-ing
pe-cu-liar
pe-cu-liar-ly
pe-cu-li-ar-i-ty
pe-cu-li-ar-i-ties
pe-cu-ni-ary
ped-a-go-gue
ped-a-go-gy
ped-al
ped-aled
ped-al-ing
ped-dle
ped-es-tal
pe-des-tri-an
pe-des-tri-an-ism
pe-di-at-ric
pe-di-at-rics
pe-di-a-tri-cian
pe-di-at-rist
ped-i-cure
ped-i-cur-ist
ped-i-gree
ped-i-greed
ped-i-ment
ped-i-men-tal
ped-i-ment-ed
pe-dom-e-ter
peep-hole
peer
peer-less
peer-less-ly
peeve
peeved
peev-ing
pee-vish
pee-vish-ly
pee-wee
pe-jo-ra-tive
pe-jo-ra-tive-ly
pe-koe
pel-let
pell--mell
pel-lu-cid
pel-lu-cid-i-ty
pel-lu-cid-ly
pelt-er
pelt-ry

pel-vis
pel-vis-es
pel-ves
pel-vic
pem-mi-can
pem-i-can
pe-nal
pe-nal-ize
pe-nal-ized
pe-nal-iz-ing
pen-al-ty
pen-al-ties
pen-ance
pen-chant
pen-cil
pend-ant
pend-ent
pend-en-cy
pend-ent-ly
pend-ing
pen-du-lous
pen-du-lous-ly
pen-du-lum
pen-a-tra-ble
pen-a-tra-bil-i-ty
pen-a-tra-bly
pen-e-trate
pen-e-trat-ed
pen-e-trat-ing
pen-e-tra-tion
pen-i-cil-lin
pen-in-su-la
pen-in-su-lar
pe-nis
pen-i-tent
pen-i-tence
pen-i-ten-tial
pen-i-ten-tia-ry
pen-i-ten-tia-ries
pen-knife
pen-knives
pen-man-ship
pen-nant
pen-non
pen-ny
pen-nies
pen-ny an-te
pe-nol-o-gy
pe-no-log-i-cal
pe-nol-o-gist
pen-sion
pen-sive

pen-sive-ly
pen-ta-gon
pen-tag-o-nal
pen-tag-o-nal-ly
pen-tam-e-ter
pen-tath-lon
pent-up
pe-nult
pe-nul-ti-ma
pe-nul-ti-mate
pe-nu-ri-ous
pe-nu-ri-ous-ly
pen-u-ry
pe-on
pe-on-age
pe-o-ny
pe-on-ies
peo-ple
pep
pepped
pep-ping
pep-per
pep-pery
pep-py
pep-pi-er
pep-pi-est
pep-sin
pep-tic
per-am-bu-late
per-am-bu-la-tor
per an-num
per-cale
per cap-i-ta
per-ceive
per-ceived
per-ceiv-ing
per-ceiv-a-ble
per-cent
per-cent-age
per-cen-tile
per-cep-ti-ble
per-cep-ti-bil-i-ty
per-cep-ti-bly
per-cep-tion
per-cep-tion-al
per-cep-tu-al
per-cep-tu-al-ly
perch
per-co-late
per-co-lat-ed
per-co-lat-ing
per-co-la-tion

per-co-la-tor
per-cus-sion
per-cus-sion-ist
per di-em
per-di-tion
per-e-gri-nate
pe-remp-to-ry
pe-remp-to-ri-ly
pe-ren-ni-al
pe-ren-ni-al-ly
per-fec-tion
per-fec-tion-ist
per-fect-ly
per-fi-dy
per-fid-i-ous
per-fid-i-ous-ly
per-fo-rate
per-fo-rat-ed
per-force
per-form
per-form-a-ble
per-form-er
per-for-mance
per-fume
per-fumed
per-func-to-ry
per-func-to-ri-ly
per-haps
per-i-gee
per-i-ge-al
per-i-ge-an
peri-he-li-on
peri-he-lia
per-il
per-il-ous
per-il-ous-ly
pe-rim-e-ter
per-i-met-ic
per-i-met-ri-cal
pe-ri-od
pe-ri-od-ic
pe-ri-o-dic-i-ty
pe-ri-od-i-cal
pe-ri-od-i-cal-ly
pe-riph-ery
pe-riph-er-ies
pe-riph-er-al
pe-riph-er-al-ly
per-i-phrase
peri-scope
peri-scopic
peri-scop-i-cal

per-ish
per-ish-able
per-ish-abil-i-ty
per-ish-ably
peri-stal-sis
peri-stal-ses
peri-style
peri-to-ne-um
peri-to-ne-ums
peri-to-nea
peri-to-ne-al
peri-to-ni-tis
peri-wig
peri-win-kle
per-jure
per-jured
per-jur-ing
per-jur-er
per-ju-ry
per-ju-ries
perky
perk-i-er
perk-i-est
per-ma-nent
per-me-able
per-me-abil-i-ty
per-me-ably
per-mis-si-ble
per-mis-si-bil-i-ty
per-mis-si-bly
per-mis-sion
per-mis-sive
per-mis-sive-ly
per-mu-ta-tion
per-ni-cious
per-ni-cious-ly
per-ora-tion
per-ox-ide
per-ox-id-ed
per-ox-id-ing
per-pen-dic-u-lar
per-pen-dic-u-lar-i-ty
per-pen-dic-u-lar-ly
per-pe-trate
per-pe-trat-ed
per-pe-trat-ing
per-pe-tra-tion
per-pe-tra-tor
per-pet-u-al
per-pet-u-al-ly
per-pet-u-ate
per-pet-u-at-ed

per-pet-u-at-ing
per-pet-u-a-tion
per-pet-ua-tor
per-pe-tu-ity
per-pe-tu-ities
per-plex
per-plexed
per-plex-ing
per-plex-ing-ly
per-plex-ed-ly
per-plex-i-ty
per-plex-i-ties
per-qui-site
per-se-cute
per-se-cut-ed
per-se-cut-ing
per-se-cu-tive
per-se-cu-tor
per-se-cu-tion
per-se-vere
per-se-vered
per-se-ver-ing
per-sse-ver-ance
per-se-ver-ing-ly
per-si-flage
per-sim-mon
per-sist
per-sist-ence
per-sis-ten-cy
per-sist-ent
per-sist-ent-ly
per-snick-e-ty
per-son
per-son-able
per-son-age
per-son-al-i-ty
per-son-al-i-ties
per-son-al-ize
per-son-al-ized
per-son-al-iz-ing
per-son-al-ly
per-so-na non gra-ta
per-son-ate
per-son-at-ed
per-son-at-ing
per-son-a-tion
per-son-a-tor
per-son-i-fy
per-son-i-fied
per-son-i-fy-ing
per-son-i-fi-ca-tion
per-son-i-fi-er

per-son-nel	per-ver-si-ty	**pe-tu-nia**	**phi-al**
per-spec-tive	**per-ver-sion**	**pew-ter**	**phi-lan-der**
per-spec-tive-ly	**per-vert**	**pey-o-te**	phi-lan-der-er
per-spi-ca-cious	**per-vi-ous**	pey-o-tes	**phi-lan-thro-py**
per-spi-ca-cious-ly	per-vi-ous-ness	**pha-lanx**	phi-lan-thro-pies
per-spi-cac-i-ty	**pes-si-mism**	pha-lanx-es	phil-an-throp-ic
per-spi-cu-i-ty	pes-si-mist	pha-lang-es	phil-an-throp-i-cal
per-spic-u-ous	pes-si-mist	**pal-lus**	phi-lan-thro-pist
per-spic-u-ous-ly	pes-si-mis-tic	pal-li	**phi-late-ly**
per-spi-ra-tion	pes-si-mis-ti-cal-ly	pahl-lus-es	phil-a-tel-ic
per-spire	**pes-ter**	phal-lic	phil-a-tel-i-cal
per-spired	**pest-hole**	**phan-tasm**	phi-lat-e-list
per-spiring	**pest-i-cide**	phan-tas-ma	**phil-har-mon-ic**
per-suade	**pes-tif-er-ous**	phan-tas-mal	**phil-o-den-dron**
per-suad-ed	pes-tif-er-ous-ly	phan-tas-mic	phil-o-den-drons
per-suad-ing	**per-ti-lence**	**phan-tas-ma-go-ria**	phil-o-den-dra
per-suad-a-ble	pes-ti-len-tial	phan-tas-ma-go-ri-al	**phi-log-o-gy**
per-suad-er	**pes-ti-lent**	phan-tas-ma-gor-ic	phi-lol-o-gist
per-sua-sion	pes-ti-lent-ly	**phan-ta-sy**	phi-lol-o-ger
per-sua-sive	**pes-tle**	phan-ta-sies	phil-o-lo-gi-an
per-sua-sive-ly	pes-tled	**phan-tom**	phil-o-log-i-cal
per-sua-sive-ness	pes-tling	**phar-aoh**	phil-o-log-ic
pert	**pet-al**	**phar-ma-ceu-ti-cal**	phil-o-log-i-cal-ly
pert-ly	pet-aled	phar-ma-cue-tic	**phi-los-o-pher**
pert-ness	pet-cock	phar-ma-ceu-ti-cal-ly	**phil-o-soph-i-cal**
per-tain	**pe-ter**	**phar-ma-cue-tics**	phil-o-soph-ic
per-ti-na-cious	**pet-i-ole**	**phar-ma-cist**	phil-o-soph-i-cal-ly
per-ti-na-cious-ly	**pe-tite**	**phar-ma-col-o-gy**	**phi-los-o-phize**
per-ti-nac-i-ty	pe-tite-ness	phar-ma-co-log-ic	phi-los-o-phized
per-ti-nent	**pet-it four**	phar-ma-co-log-i-ca	phi-los-o-phiz-ing
per-ti-nence	**pe-ti-tion**	phar-ma-col-o-gist	phi-los-o-phiz-er
per-ti-nen-cy	pe-ti-tion-ary	**phar-ma-co-poe-ia**	**phi-los-o-phy**
per-ti-nent-ly	pe-ti-tion-er	phar-ma-co-poe-ial	phi-los-o-phies
per-turb	**pe-trel**	**phar-ma-cy**	**phil-ter**
per-turb-a-ble	**pet-ri-fy**	phar-ma-cies	phil-tered
per-tur-ba-tion	pet-ri-fied	**phar-ynx**	phil-ter-ing
pe-ruke	pet-ri-fy-ing	pha-ryn-ges	**phle-bi-tis**
pe-ruse	pe-tri-fac-tion	pha-ryn-ge-al	phle-bit-ic
pe-rused	**pe-tro-chem-is-try**	pha-ryn-gal	**phle-bot-o-my**
pe-rus-ing	pe-tro-chem-i-cal	**phase**	phle-bot-o-mist
pe-rus-al	**pet-rol**	phased	**phlegm**
pe-rus-er	**pet-ro-la-tum**	phas-ing	**phleg-mat-ic**
per-vade	**pe-trol-leum**	pha-sic	phleg-mat-i-cal
per-vad-ed	**pet-ti-coat**	**pheas-ant**	phleg-mat-i-cal-ly
per-vad-ing	**pet-tish**	**phe-no-bar-bi-tal**	**phlox**
per-vad-er	pet-tish-ly	**phe-nol**	**pho-bia**
per-va-sion	pet-tish-ness	phe-nol-ic	pho-bic
per-va-sive	**pet-ty**	**phe-nom-e-non**	**phoe-be**
per-va-sive-ly	**pet-u-lant**	phe-nom-e-na	**phoe-nix**
per-verse	pet-u-lance	phe-nom-e-nons	**phone**
per-verse-ly	pet-u-lan-cy	phe-nom-e-nal	phoned
per-verse-ness	pet-u-lant-ly	phe-nom-e-nal-ly	phon-ing

pho-neme
pho-ne-mic
pho-net-ic
pho-net-ics
pho-net-i-cal
pho-net-i-cal-ly
phon-ic
phon-ics
pho-no-graph
pho-no-graph-ic
pho-no-graph-i-cal-ly
pho-nol-o-gy
pho-nol-o-gies
pho-no-log-ic
pho-no-log-i-cal
pho-no-log-i-cal-ly
pho-nol-o-gist
pho-ny
pho-ni-er
pho-ni-est
pho-nies
pho-ni-ness
phos-phate
phos-pho-res-cence
phos-pho-resce
phos-pho-resced
phos-pho-resc-ing
phos-pho-res-cent
phos-pho-res-cent-ly
phos-pho-rus
pho-to
pho-tos
pho-to-copy
pho-to-cop-ies
pho-to-cop-ied
pho-to-cop-y-ing
pho-to-e-lec-tric
pho-to-en-grav-ing
pho-to-en-grave
pho-to-en-graved
pho-to-en-grav-er
pho-to-flash
pho-to-gen-ic
pho-to-graph
pho-to-graph-er
pho-tog-ra-phy
pho-to-graph-ic
pho-to-graph-i-cal
pho-to-graph-i-cal-ly
pho-to-gra-vure
pho-to--off-set
pho-to-stat

pho-to-stat-ed
pho-to-stat-ing
pho-to-stat-ic
pho-to-syn-the-sis
phrase
phrased
phras-ing
phras-al
phrase-ol-o-gy
phre-net-ic
phre-nol-o-gy
phre-nol-o-gist
phy-lac-tery
phy-lac-ter-ies
phy-log-e-ny
phy-lo-gen-e-sis
phy-lo-ge-net-ic
phy-lo-gen-ic
phy-log-e-nist
phy-lu
phys-ic
phys-icked
phys-ick-ing
phys-i-cal
phys-i-cal-ly
phy-si-cian
phys-ics
phys-i-cist
phys-i-og-no-my
phys-i-og-no-mies
phys-i-og-nom-ic
phys-i-og-nom-i-cal
phys-i-og-no-mist
phys-i-og-ra-phy
phys-i-o-graph-ic
phys-i-o-graph-i-cal
phys-i-ol-o-gy
phys-i-o-log-ic
phys-i-o-log-i-cal
phys-i-o-log-i-cal-ly
phys-i-ol-o-gist
phys-i-o-ther-a-py
phy-sique
pi-a-nis-si-mo
pi-an-ist
pi-ano
pia-nos
pi-ano-forte
pi-az-za
pi-ca
pic-a-dor
pic-a-resque

pic-a-yune
pic-a-yun-ish
pic-ca-lil-li
pic-co-lo
pic-co-los
pic-co-lo-list
pick-ax
picked
pick-er-el
pick-et
pick-et-er
pick-ing
pick-le
pick-led
pick-ling
pick-pock-et
pick-up
picky
pick-i-er
pick-i-est
pic-nic
pic-nicked
pic-nick-ing
pic-nick-er
pic-to-ri-al
pic-to-ri-al-ly
pic-ture
pic-tured
pic-tur-ing
pic-tur-esque
pic-tur-esque-ly
pid-dle
pid-dled
pid-dling
pid-gin
pie-bald
piece
piec-er
piece-meal
piece-work
piece-worker
pied
pier
pierce
pierc-ed
pierc-ing
pierc-ing-ly
pi-etism
pi-etis-tic
pi-etis-ti-cal
pi-ety
pi-eties

pif-fle
pig
pigged
pig-ging
pi-geon
pe-geon-hole
pi-geon-holed
pi-geon-hol-ing
pi-geon--toed
pig-gish
pig-ish-ly
pig-gis-ness
pig-head-ed
pig-head-ed-ly
pig-head-ed-ness
pig-ment
pig-men-tary
pig-men-ta-tion
pig-pen
pig-skin
pig-sty
pig-sties
pig-tail
pike
piked
pik-ing
pik-er
pi-las-ter
pil-chard
pile
piled
pil-ing
pil-fer
pil-fer-age
pil-fer-er
pil-grim
pil-grim-age
pil-grim-aged
pil-grim-ag-ing
pil-lage
pil-laged
pil-lag-ing
pil-lag-er
pil-lar
pill-box
pil-lion
pil-lo-ry
pil-lo-ries
pil-lo-ry-ing
pil-low
pil-low-case
pi-lot

pi-lot-age
pi-lot-less
pi-lot-house
pi-men-to
pi-men-tos
pim-ple
pim-pled
pim-ply
pin
pinned
pin-ning
pin-afore
pince-nez
pin-cers
pinch
pinch-er
pinch-beck
pin-cush-ion
pin-dling
pine
pine-like
piney
pin-ing
pi-ne-al
pine-ap-ple
pin-feath-er
pin-feath-ered
pin-feath-ery
pin-fold
pin-head
pin-head-ed
pin-hole
pin-ion
pink-eye
pink-ie
pinko
pink-os
pink-oes
pin-na
pin-nas
pin-nae
pin-nal
pin-na-cle
pin-na-cled
pin-na-cling
pi-nate
pin-nate-ly
pin-na-tion
pi-noch-le
pi-noc-le
pin-point
pin-prick

pin-set-ter
pin-tail
pin-tailed
pin-tle
pin-to
pin-tos
pin-up
pin-wheel
pin-worm
pi-o-neer
pi-ous
pi-ous-ly
pi-ous-ness
pip
pipped
pip-ping
pipe-line
pipe-lined
pipe-lin-ing
pip-er
pip-ing
pip-it
pip-pin
pip-squek
pi-quant
pi-quan-cy
pi-quant-ly
pique
piqued
pi-quing
pi-ra-cy
pi-ra-cies
pi-ra-nha
pi-rate
pi-rat-ed
pi-rat-ing
pi-rat-i-cal
pi-rat-i-cal-ly
pi-roque
pir-ou-ette
pir-ou-et-ted
pir-ou-et-ting
pi-sci-cul-ture
pis-ta-chio
pis-ta-chi-os
pis-til
pis-til-late
pis-tol
pis-toled
pis-tol-ing
pis-ton
pit

pit-ted
pit-ting
pitch--blake
pitch-blend
pitch-er
pitch-fork
pitchy
pitch-i-er
pitch-i-est
pit-e-ous
pit-e-ous-ly
pit-fall
pith
pith-i-er
pith-i-est
pith-i-ly
piti-a-ble
piti-anle-ness
piti-a-bly
piti-ful
piti-ful-ly
piti-ful-ness
piti-less
piti-less-ly
pit-man
pit-men
pit-tance
pi-tu--tar-ies
pity
pit-ies
pit-ied
pit-y-ing
pit-y-ing-ly
piv-ot
piv-ot-al
piv-ot-al-ly
pix-i-lat-ed
pixy
pix-ie
pix-ies
piz-za
piz-ze-ria
piz-zi-ca-to
place-a-ble
plac-a-bil-i-ty
plac-a-bly
plac-ard
pla-cate
pla-cat-ed
pla-cat-ing
pla-ca-tion
pla-ca-tive

pla-ca-to-ry
place
placed
plac-ing
pla-ce-bo
pla-ce-bos
pla-ce-boes
place-ment
pla-cen-ta
pla-cen-tas
pla-cen-tae
pla-cen-tal
plac-er
plac-id
pla-cid-i-ty
plac-id-ness
pla-gal
pla-gia-rism
pla-gia-rized
pla-gia-riz-ing
pla-gia-riz-er
pla-gia-ry
pla-gia-ries
plaque
plaqued
pla-quing
pla-quer
pla-guy
pla-guey
pla-gui-ly
plaid
plain
plain-ly
plain-ness
plain-song
plain-spo-ken
plain-tiff
plain-tive
plain-tive-ly
plait
plait-ing
plan
planned
plan-ning
plan-less
plan-ner
plane
planed
plan-ing
plan-er
plan-et
plan-e-tar-i-um

plan-e-tar-i-ums	pla-ton-i-cal-ly	pleat-ed	plow-a-ble
plan-e-tar-ia	pla-toon	pleat-er	plow-er
plan-e-tary	plat-ter	plebe	plow-man
plan-e-toid	platy-pus	ple-be-ian	plow-share
plan-ish	platy-pus-es	pleb-i-scite	pluck
plan-ish-er	platy-pi	pledge	pluck-er
plank-ing	plau-dit	pledged	plucky
plank-ton	plau-si-ble	pledg-ing	pluck-i-er
plank-ton-ic	plau-si-bil-i-ty	pledg-ee	pluck-i-est
plant	plau-si-bly	pledg-er	pluck-i-ly
plant-able	play-act	ple-na-ry	pluck-i-ness
plant-like	play-act-ing	pleni-po-ten-tia-ry	plug
plan-tain	play-back	pleni-po-ten-tia-ries	plugged
plan-ta-tion	play-bill	plen-i-tude	plug-ging
plant-er	play-boy	plen-te-ous	plug-ger
plaque	play-er	plen-te-ous-ly	plum-age
plasm	play-ful	plen-ti-ful	plumb-er
plas-ma	play-ful-ly	plen-ti-ful-ly	plumb-ing
plas-mic	play-ful-ness	plen-ty	plume
plas-mat-ic	play-go-er	pleth-o-ra	plumed
plas-ter	play-ground	ple-thor-ic	plum-ing
plas-ter-er	play-house	pleu-ra	plume-like
plas-ter-ing	play-hous-es	pleu-rae	plumy
plas-ter-work	play-let	pleu-ral	plum-i-er
plas-ter-board	play-mate	pleu-ri-sy	plum-i-est
plas-tered	play--off	pleu-rit-ic	plum-met
plas-tic	play-pen	plex-us	plump
plas-ti-cal-ly	play-thing	plex-us-es	plump-er
plas-tic-i-ty	play-time	pli-able	plump-ly
plas-ti-ciz-er	play-wright	pli-a-bil-i-ty	plump-ness
plat	pla-za	pli-a-ble-ness	plun-der
plat-ted	plea	pli-a-bly	plun-der-er
plat-ting	plead	pli-ant	plun-der-ous
plate	plead-ed	pli-an-cy	plunge
plat-ed	plead-ing	pli-ant-ness	plunged
plat-ing	plead-a-ble	pli-ant-ly	plung-ing
plat-er	plead-er	pli-ca-tion	plung-er
pla-teau	pleas-ant	pli-ers	plunk-er
pla-teaus	pleas-ant-ly	plight	plu-ral
pla-teaux	pleas-ant-ness	plink	plu-ral-ly
plate-ful	pleas-ant-ry	plod	plu-ral-ize
plate-fuls	pleas-an-trioes	plod-ded	plu-ral-ized
plate-let	please	plod-ding	plu-ral-iz-ing
plat-form	pleased	plod-der	plu-ral-ism
plat-i-num	pleas-ing	plop	plu-ral-ist
plat-i-tude	pleas-ing-ly	plopped	plu-ral-is-tic
plat-i-tu-di-nal	pleas-ing-ness	plop-ping	plu-ral-i-ty
plat-i-tu-di-nous	plea-sur-a-ble	plot	plu-ral-i-ties
plat-i-tu-di-nize	plea-sur-able-ness	plot-ted	plush
plat-i-tu-di-nized	plea-sur-ably	plot-ting	plush-i-ness
plat-i-tu-di-niz-ing	pleas-ure	plot-ter	plushy
pla-ton-ic	pleat	plow	plush-i-er

plush-i-est
plu-toc-ra-cy
plu-tac-ra-cies
plu-ta-crat
plu-to-cart-ic
plu-to-ni-um
plu-vi-al
ply
plied
ply-ing
ply-wood
pneu-mat-ic
pneu-mat-i-cal-ly
pneu-mat-ics
pneu-mo-nia
pneu-mon-ic
poach
poach-er
pock-et
pock-et-book
pock-et-ful
pock-et-knife
pock-et-knives
pock-mark
pock-marked
pod
pod-ded
pod-ding
pod-like
podgy
podg-i-er
podg-i-est
po-di-trist
po-di-a-try
po-di-um
po-dia
po-di-ums
po-esy
po-esies
po-et
po-et-ess
po-et-ize
po-et-ized
po-et-iz-ing
po-et-iz-er
po-et lau-re-ate
po-ets lau-re-ate
po-et-ry
po-go
po-grom
poi-gnant
poi-gnan-cy

poi-gnant-ly
poin-set-tia
point--blank
point-ed
point-ed-ly
point-ed-ness
point-er
poin-til-lism
poin-til-list
point-less
poise
poised
pois-ing
poi-son
poi-son-er
poi-son-ing
poi-son-ous
poi-son--pen
poke
poked
pok-ing
pok-er
poky
pok-i-er
pok-i-est
pok-i-ly
pok-i-ness
po-lar
po-lar-i-ty
po-lar-i-ties
po-lar-i-za-tion
po-lar-ize
po-lar-ized
po-lar-iz-ing
po-lar-iz-a-ble
po-lar-iz-er
pole
poled
pol-ing
pole-less
pole-cat
po-lem-ic
po-lem-i-cal
po-lem-i-cal-ly
po-lem-i-cist
po-lem-ics
pole-star
po-lice
po-liced
po-lic-ing
pol-i-cy
pol-i-cies

pol-i-o-my-e-li-tis
pol-ish
pol-ish-er
po-lite
po-lite-ly
po-lite-ness
pol-i-tic
po-lit-i-cal
po-lit-i-cal-ly
pol-i-ti-cian
po-lit-i-cize
po-lit-i-cized
po-lit-i-ciz-ing
pol-i-tick
pol-i-tick-er
pol-i-tics
pol-i-ty
pol-i-ties
pol-ka
pol-kaed
pol-ka-ing
poll
poll-ee
poll-er
pol-len
pol-li-nate
pol-li-nat-ed
pol-li-nat-ing
pol-li-na-tion
pol-li-na-tor
pol-li-wog
poll-ster
pol-lu-tant
pol-lute
pol-lut-ed
pol-lut-ing
pol-lu-ter
pol-lu-tion
po-lo
po-lo-ist
pol-o-naise
po-lo-ni-um
pol-ter-geist
poly-an-dry
poly-an-drous
poly-chro-mat-ic
poly-chrome
poly-es-ter
poly-eth-yl-ene
polyg-a-mist
polyg-a-my
polyg-a-mous

poly-glot
poly-gon
polyg-o-nal
polyg-o-nal-ly
poly-graph
poly-graph-ic
po-lyg-y-ny
po-lyg-y-nous
poly-he-dron
poly-he-drons
poly-he-dra
poly-he-dral
poly-mer
po-ly-mer-ize
po-ly-mer-ized
po-ly-mer-iz-ing
po-lym-er-ism
po-lym-er-i-za-tion
pol-y-mor-phism
pol-y-mor-phic
pol-y-mor-phous
poly-no-mi-al
pol-yp
poly-phon-ic
po-lyph-ony
poly-sty-rene
poly-syl-lab-ic
poly-syl-lab-i-cal-ly
poly-syl-la-ble
poly-tech-nic
poly-the-ism
poly-the-ist
poly-the-is-tic
poly-the-is-ti-cal
poly-un-sat-u-rat-ed
pom-ace
po-made
po-mad-ed
po-mad-ing
pome-gran-ate
pom-mel
pom-meled
pom-mel-ing
pom-pa-dour
pom-pon
pomp-ous
pom-pos-i-ty
pom-pous-ly
pon-cho
pon-der
pon-der-a-ble
pon-der-er

pon-der-ous
  pon-der-ous-ly
  pon-der-ou-ness
pon-iard
pon-tiff
pon-tif-i-cal
  pon-tif-i-cal-ly
pon-tif-i-cate
  pon-tif-i-cat-ed
  pon-tif-i-cat-ing
pon-toon
po-ny
  po-nies
  po-nied
  po-ny-ing
po-ny-tail
poo-dle
pool-room
poor
  poor-ish
  poor-ly
pop-corn
pop-ery
  pop-ish
pop-eyed
pop-gun
pop-in-jay
pop-lar
pop-lin
pop-per
pop-py
  pop-pies
  pop-pied
pop-py-cock
pop-u-lace
pop-u-lar
  pop-u-lar-ly
pop-u-lar-i-ty
pop-u-lar-ize
  pop-u-lar-ized
  pop-u-lar-iz-ing
  pop-u-lar-i-za-tion
  pop-u-lar-iz-er
pop-u-late
  pop-u-lat-ed
  pop-u-lat-ing
pop-u-la-tion
pop-u-lism
  pop-u-list
pop-u-lous
  pop-u-lous-ly
por-ce-lain

por-cine
por-cu-pine
pore
  pored
  por-ing
pork-er
por-nog-ra-phy
  por-nog-ra-pher
  por-no-graph-ic
  por-no-graph-i-cal-ly
po-rous
  po-rous-i-ty
  po-rous-ly
  po-rous-ness
por-poise
  por-pios-es
por-ridge
port-a-ble
  port-a-bil-i-ty
  port-a-bly
por-tage
  por-taged
  por-tag-ing
por-tal
por-tend
por-tent
  por-ten-tous
por-ter
por-ter-house
port-fo-lio
  port-fo-lios
port-hole
por-ti-co
  por-ti-coes
  por-ti-cos
por-tion
  por-tion-less
port-ly
  port-li-er
  port-li-est
por-trait
  por-trat-ist
por-trai-ture
por-tray
  por-tray-er
por-tray-al
pose
  posed
  pos-ing
pos-er
po-suer
pos-it

po-si-tion
  po-si-tion-al
  po-si-tion-er
pos-i-tive
  pos-i-tive-ly
  pos-i-tive-ness
pos-i-tiv-ism
pos-i-tron
pos-se
pos-sess
  pos-ses-sor
pos-sessed
pos-ses-sion
pos-ses-sive
  pos-ses-sive-ly
  pos-ses-sive-ness
pos-si-bil-i-ty
pos-si-ble
pos-si-bly
pos-sum
post-age
post-box
post-date
  post-dat-ed
  post-dat-ing
post-er
pos-te-ri-or
  pos-te-ri-or-i-ty
pos-ter-i-ty
post-grad-u-ate
post-haste
post-hu-mous
  post-hu-mous-ly
post-lude
post-man
  post-men
post-mark
post-mas-ter
  post-mis-tress
post me-ri-di-em
post-mor-tem
post-na-sal
post-na-tal
  post-na-tal-ly
post-paid
post-par-tum
post-pone
  post-poned
  post-pon-ing
  post-pon-a-ble
  post-pone-ment
  post-pon-er

post-scipt
pos-tu-lant
pos-tu-late
  pos-tu-lat-ed
  pos-tu-lat-ing
  pos-tu-la-tion
  pos-tu-la-tor
pos-ture
  pos-tured
  pos-tur-ing
  pos-tur-al
  pos-tur-er
post-war
po-sy
  po-sies
pot
  pot-ted
  pot-ting
po-ta-ble
pot-ash
po-tas-si-um
po-ta-to
  po-ta-toes
pot-bel-ly
  pot-bel-lied
pot-boil-er
po-tent
  po-ten-cy
  po-tent-ly
po-ten-tate
po-ten-tial
  po-ten-ti-al-i-ty
  po-ten-tial-ly
pot-hole
po-tion
pot-luck
pot-pour-ri
pot-sherd
pot-tage
pot-ter
pot-tery
  pot-ter-ies
pot-ty
  pot-ties
pot-ty--chair
pouch
  pouched
  pouchy
  pouch-i-er
  pouch-i-est
poul-tice
  poul-ticed

poul-tic-ing
poul-try
pounce
pounced
pounc-ing
pound-age
pound--fool-ish
pour
pour-a-ble
pour-er
pout
pov-er-ty
pov-er-ty--strick-en
pow-der
pow-dery
pow-er
pow-er-boat
pow-er-ful
pow-er-ful-ly
pow-er-ful-ness
pow-er-house
pow-er-less
Pow-ha-tan
pow-wow
prac-ti-ca-ble
prac-ti-ca-bil-i-ty
prac-ti-ca-bly
prac-ti-cal
prac-ti-cal-i-ty
prac-ti-cal-ly
prac-tice
prac-ti-tio-ner
prae-di-al
pre-di-al
prag-mat-ic
prag-mat-i-cal
prag-mat-i-cal-ly
prag-ma-tism
prag-ma-tist
prag-ma-tis-tic
prai-rie
praise
praised
prais-ing
prais-er
praise-wor-thy
praise-wor-thi-ly
praise-wor-thi-ness
pra-line
prance
pranced
pranc-ing

pranc-er
prank
prank-ish
prank-ster
prate
prat-ed
prat-ing
prat-er
prat-ing-ly
prat-fall
prat-tle
prat-tled
prat-tling
prat-tler
prat-tling-ly
prawn
prawn-er
pray-er
pray-er-ful
preach
prach-er
preach-ify
preach-ified
preach-ify-ing
preach-ment
preachy
preach-i-er
preach-i-est
pre-ad-o-les-cence
pre-ad-o-les-cent
pre-am-ble
pre-ar-range
pre-ar-ranged
pre-ar-rang-ing
pre-ar-range-ment
pre-as-signed
pre-can-cel
pre-can-celed
pre-can-cel-ing
pre-can-cel-la-tion
pre-car-i-ous
pre-car-i-ous-ly
pre-car-i-ous-ness
pre-cau-tion
pre-cau-tion-ary
pre-cede
pre-ced-ed
pre-ced-ing
prec-e-dence
prec-e-dent
pre-cept
pre-cep-tive

pre-cep-tor
pre-cep-to-ri-al
pre-ces-sion
pre-ces-sion-al
pre-cinct
pre-cious
pre-ci-os-i-ty
pre-cious-ness
prec-i-pice
pre-cip-i-tous
pre-cip-i-tant
pre-cip-i-tant-ly
pre-cip-i-tate
pre-cip-i-tat-ed
pre-cip-i-tat-ing
pre-cip-i-ta-tive
pre-cip-i-ta-tor
pre-cip-i-ta-tion
pre-cip-i-tous
pre-cip-i-tous-ly
pre-cise
pre-cise-ness
pre-ci-sion
pre-ci-sion-ist
pre-clude
pre-clud-ed
pre-clud-ing
pre-clu-sion
pre-clu-sive
pre-co-cious
pre-coc-cious-ly
pre-coc-cious-ness
pre-coc-i-ty
pre-cog-ni-tion
pre-cog-ni-tive
pre-con-ceive
pre-con-ciev-ed
pre-con-ceiv-ing
pre-con-cep-tion
pre-cook
pre-cur-sor
pre-cur-so-ry
pre-date
pred-a-tor
pred-a-to-ry
pred-a-to-ri-ly
pre-dawn
pre-de-ces-sor
pre-des-ti-nate
pre-des-ti-nat-ed
pre-des-ti-nat-ing
pre-des-ti-na-tion

pre-des-tine
pre-des-tined
pre-des-tin-ing
pre-de-ter-mine
pre-de-ter-mined
pre-de-ter-min-ing
pre-de-ter-mi-na-tion
pred-i-ca-ble
pred-i-ca-bil-i-ty
pre-dic-a-ment
pred-i-cate
pred-i-cat-ed
pred-i-cat-ing
pred-i-ca-tion
pred-i-ca-tive
pre-dict
pre-dict-a-ble
pre-dict-a-bly
pre-dict-a-bil-i-ty
pre-dic-tion
pre-dic-tive
pre-di-lec-tion
pre-dis-po-si-tion
pre-dis-pose
pre-dis-posed
pre-dis-pos-ing
pre-dom-i-nant
pre-dom-i-nance
pre-dom-i-nan-cy
pre-dom-i-nate
pre-dom-i-nat-ed
pre-dom-i-nat-ing
pre-dom-i-na-tion
pre-em-i-nent
pre-em-i-nence
pre-empt
pre-emp-tor
pre-emp-tion
pre-emp-tive
preen-er
pre-ex-ist
pre-ex-ist-ence
pre-ex-ist-ent
pre-fab-ri-cate
pre-fab-ri-cat-ed
pre-fab-ri-cat-ing
pre-fab-ri-a-tion
pref-ace
pref-aced
pref-ac-ing
pref-a-to-ry
pre-fer

pre-ferred
pre-fer-ring
pre-fer-rer
pref-er-a-ble
pre-fer-a-bil-i-ty
pref-er-a-bly
pref-er-ence
pref-er-en-tial
pref-er-en-tial-ly
pre-fer-ment
pre-fix
pre-flight
pre-form
preg-n-able
preg-na-bil-i-ty
preg-nan-cy
preg-nan-cies
preg-nant
pre-heat
pre-hen-sile
pre-hen-sil-i-ty
pre-his-tor-ic
prej-u-dice
prej-u-diced
prej-u-dic-ing
prej-u-di-cial
prej-u-di-cial-ly
prel-ate
prel-ate-ship
prel-a-ture
pre-lim-i-nar-y
pre-lim-i-nar-ies
pre-lim-i-nar-i-ly
prel-ude
prel-uded
prel-ud-ing
pre-ma-ture
pre-na-tu-ri-ty
pre-med-i-cal
pre-med-i-tate
pre-med-i-tat-ed
pre-med-i-ta-tion
pre-men-stru-al
pre-mier
pre-mier-ship
pre-miere
prem-ise
prem-ised
prem-is-ing
pre-mi-um
pre-mo-ni-tion
pre-mon-i-to-ry

pre-mon-i-to-ri-ly
pre-na-tal
pre-na-tal-ly
pre-oc-cu-pa-tion
pre-oc-cu-py
pre-oc-cu-pied
pre-oc-cu-py-ing
prep-a-ra-tion
pre-par-a-to-ry
pre-par-a-to-ri-ly
pre-plan
pre-planned
pre-plan-ning
pre-pon-der-ant
pre-pon-der-ance
pre-pon-der-an-cy
pre-pon-der-ant-ly
pre-pon-der-ate
pre-pon-der-at-ed
pre-pon-der-at-ing
pre-pon-der-at-ing-ly
pre-pon-der-a-tion
prep-o-si-tion
prep-o-si-tion-al
pre-pos-sess
pre-pos-sess-ing
pre-pos-sess-ing-ly
pre-pos-ter-ous
pre-puce
pre-pu-tial
pre-re-cord
pre-re-ui-site
pre-rog-a-tive
pres-age
pres-aged
pres-ag-ing
pres-ag-er
pres-by-ter-y
pres-by-ter-ies
pre-school
pre-script
pre-scrip-tion
pre-scrip-tive
pre-sea-son
pres-ence
pre-sent
pre-sent-er
pres-ent
pre-sent-a-ble
pre-sent-a-bil-i-ty
pre-sent-a-ble-ness
pre-sent-a-bly

pres-en-ta-tion
pres-ent-day
pres-ent-ly
pre-serv-a-tive
per-serve
pre-served
pre-serv-ing
pre-serv-a-ble
pres-er-va-tion
pre-serv-er
pre-side
pre-sid-ed
pre-sid-ing
pre-sid-er
pres-i-den-cy
pres-i-den-cies
pres-i-dent
pres-i-den-tial
press-board
press-ing
pres-sure
pres-sured
pres-sur-ing
press-work
pres-ti-dig-i-ta-tion
pres-ti-dig-i-ta-tor
pres-tige
pres-tig-ious
pres-to
pe-sum-a-ble
pre-sum-a-bly
pre-sump-tion
pre-sump-tive
pre-sum-tu-ous
pre-sup-pose
pre-sup-posed
pre-sup-pos-ing
pre-sup-po-si-tion
pre-tend
pre-tend-ed
pre-tend-er
pre-tense
pre-ten-sion
pre-ten-tious
pre-ten-tious-ness
pre-test
pre-text
pret-ti-fy
pret-ti-fied
pret-ti-fy-ing
pret-ti-fi-ca-tion
pret-zel

pre-vail
pre-vail-ing
prev-a-lent
prev-a-lence
pre-vent
pre-vent-a-ble
pre-vent-a-bil-i-ty
pre-vent-er
pre-ven-tion
pre-view
pre-vi-ous
pre-war
prey
prey-er
price-less
prick-er
prick-le
prick-ly
prick-li-er
prick-li-est
prick-li-ness
pride
prid-ed
prid-ing
pride-ful
pri-er
priest
priest-ess
priest-hood
pri-ma-cy
pri-ma-cies
pri-ma don-na
pri-ma don-nas
pri-mal
pri-ma-ri-ly
pri-ma-ry
pri-mar-ies
pri-mate
prime
primed
prim-ing
prime me-rid-i-an
prim-er
pr-me-val
prim-i-tive
pri-mo-gen-i-tor
pri-mo-gen-i-ture
pri-mor-di-al
pri-mor-di-al-ly
primp
prim-rose
prince-ly

pro-pelled
pro-pel-ling
pro-pel-lant
pro-pel-ler
pro-pend
propense
pro-pen-si-ty
pro-pen-si-ties
prop-er
prop-er-dirt
prop-er-tied
prop-er-ty
pro-phage
pro-phase
proph-e-cy
proph-e-cies
proph-e-sy
proph-e-sied
proph-e-sy-ing
proph-et
pro-phet-ic
pro-phet-i-cal-ly
Proph-ets
pro-phy-lax-is
pro-pin-qui-ty
pro-pi-o-nate
pro-pi-ti-ate
pro-pi-ti-at-ed
pro-pi-ti-a-tion
pro-pi-ti-a-tion
pro-pi-tia-to-ry
pro-pi-tious
pro-pi-tious-ly
pro-plas-tid
prop-man
prop-o-lis
pro-pone
pro-po-nent
pro-por-tion
pro-por-tion-a-ble
pro-por-tion-a-bly
pro-por-tion-al
pro-por-tion-al-i-ty
pro-por-tion-ate
pro-por-tion-at-ed
pro-por-tion-at-ing
pro-pos-al
pro-pose
pro-posed
prop-o-si-tion
prop-o-si-tion-al
pro-pos-i-tus

pro-pound
pro-pound-er
pro-prae-tor
pro-pran-o-lol
pro-pri-e-tary
pro-pri-e-tar-ies
pro-pri-etor
pro-pri-e-tor-ship
pro-pri-ety
pro-prio-cep-tion
pro-prio-cep-tive
pro-prio-cep-tor
pro-pto-sis
pro-pul-sion
pro-pul-sive
pro-rate
pro-rat-ed
pro-sa-ic
pro-sa-i-cal-ly
pro-scrip-tion
pro-srip-tive
prose
pros-e-cute
pros-e-cute-a-ble
pros-e-cu-tion
pros-e-cu-tor
pros-pect
pros-pec-tor
pro-spec-tive
pro-spec-tus
pros-per-i-ty
pros-per-ous
pros-tate
pros-the-sis
pros-the-ses
pros-thet-ic
pros-thet-ics
pros-the-tis
prosth-odon-tics
prosth-odon-tist
pros-ti-tute
pros-trate
pros-trat-ing
pros-tra-tor
pros-tra-tive
pro-tag-o-nist
pro-te-an
pro-tect
pro-tect-ing
pro-tec-tive
pro-tec-tor
pro-tec-tion

pro-tec-tion-ism
pro-tec-tion-ist
pro-tec-tor-ate
pro-tein
pro-test
prot-es-ta-tion
pro-tist
pro-tis-tan
pro-to-col
pro-ton
pro-to-plasm
pro-to-plas-mic
pro-to-type
pro-to-typ-i-cal
pro-to-typ-ic
pro-to-typ-i-cal-ly
pro-to-zo-an
pro-to-zo-ic
pro-tract
pro-trac-tion
pro-trac-tive
pro-trac-tile
pro-trac-tor
pro-trude
pro-trud-ed
pro-trud-ing
pro-tru-sion
pro-tru-sive
pro-tu-ber-ance
pro-tu-ber-ant
proud
proud-ly
prov-erb
pro-ver-bi-al
pro-ver-bi-al-ly
prov-i-dence
prov-i-den-tial
prov-i-dent
prov-ince
pro-vin-cial
pro-vin-cial-ism
pro-vi-sion
pro-vi-sion-er
pro-vi-sion-al
pro-vi-sion-ary
prov-o-ca-tion
pro-voc-a-tive
pro-voc-a-tive-ly
pro-voc-a-tive-ness
pro-vost
prow-ess
prowl

prowl-er
prox-i-mal
prox-i-mate
prox-i-mate-ly
prox-im-i-ty
proxy
prox-ies
prude
pru-dence
pru-dent
pru-den-tial
prud-ish
prune
pruned
prun-ing
psalm-book
psalm-ist
pseu-do
pseud-onym
pseud-on-y-mous
pseu-do-preg-nan-cy
pseu-do-preg-nant
pseu-do-sci-ence
pseu-do-sci-en-tif-ic
pshaw
psil-o-cy-bin
pso-ri-a-sis
pso-ri-at-ic
psych
psyched
psych-ing
psy-che-del-ic
psy-chi-a-trist
psy-chi-a-try
psy-chi-at-ric
psy-chi-at-ri-cal-ly
psy-chic
psy-chi-cal
psy-chi-cal-ly
psy-cho
psy-cho-anal-y-sis
psy-cho-an-a-lyt-ic
psy-cho-an-a-lyt-i-cal
psy-cho-bi-ol-o-gy
psy-cho-bi-o-log-ic
psy-cho-bi-o-log-i-cal
psy-cho-dra-ma
psy-cho-dy-nam-ic
psy-cho-dy-nam-ics
psy-cho-gen-e-sis
psy-cho-ge-net-ic
psy-cho-gen-ic

psy-cho-gen-i-cal-ly
psy-cho-log-i-cal
psy-cho-log-ic
psy-cho-log-i-cal-ly
psy-chol-o-gist
psy-chol-o-gy
psy-cho-mo-tor
psy-cho-neu-ro-sis
psy-cho-neu-rot-ic
psy-cho-path
psy-cho-pa-thol-o-gy
psy-cho-path-o-log-ic
psy-chop-a-thy
psy-cho-path-ic
psy-cho-path-i-cal-ly
psy-cho-ther-a-py
psy-cho-ther-a-pist
pto-maine
pu-ber-ty
pu-bes-cence
pu-bes-cen-cy
pu-bes-cent
pu-bic
pub-lic
pub-lic-ly
pub-li-ca-tion
pub-li-cist
pub-li-ci-ty
pub-li-cize
pub-li-cized
pub-li-ciz-ing
pub-lish
pub-lish-a-ble
pub-lish-er
puce
puck-er
pud-ding
pud-dle
pud-dled
pud-dling
pueb-lo
pueb-los
pu-er-ile
pu-er-il-i-ty
puff
puffy
puff-er
pu-gi-lism
pu-gi-list
pu-gi-lis-tic
pug-na-cious
pug-nac-i-ty

pulke
puked
puk-ing
pull-back
pul-let
pul-ley
pul-mo-nary
pulp
pul-pit
pulp-wood
pul-sate
pul-sat-ed
pul-sat-ing
pul-sa-tion
pul-sa-tor
pul-sa-to-ry
pulse
pulsed
puls-ing
pul-ver-ize
pu-ma
pu-mas
pum-ice
pu-mi-ceous
pum-mel
pum-per-nick-el
pump-kin
pun
punned
pun-ning
punch
punch-er
punc-tu-al
punc-tu-ate
punc-tu-at-ed
punc-tu-at-ing
punc-tu-a-tor
punc-tu-a-tion
punc-ture
punc-tured
punc-tur-ing
pun-dit
pun-gent
pun-gen-cy
pun-gent-ly
pun-ish
pun-ish-able
pun-ish-ment
pu-ni-tion
pu-ni-tive
pun-kah
pun-kie

pun-kin
pun-ster
punt-er
pu-ny
pu-ni-er
pu-ni-est
pun-ty
pu-ny
pup
pupped
pup-ping
pu-par-i-um
pu-pil
pep-pet-ry
pup-pet-ries
pure
pure-ly
pur-ga-tive
pur-ga-to-ry
pur-ga-to-ries
pur-ga-to-ri-al
purge
purged
pu-ri-fy
pur-ism
pur-ist
pu-ris-tic
pu-ri-ty
purl
pur-loin
pur-loin-er
pur-port
pur-port-ed
pur-port-ed-ly
pur-pose
pur-posed
pur-pos-ing
pur-pose-ly
pur-pos-ive
purse
pursed
purs-ing
purs-er
pur-su-ant
pur-sue
pur-sued
pur-su-ing
pur-suit
pur-sy
pu-ru-lent
pu-ru-lence
pu-ru-len-cy

pur-vey
pur-vey-or
pur-vey-ance
pur-view
push
push-er
push-ful
push-ing
push-over
push-up
pushy
pu-sil-lan-i-mous
pu-sil-la-nim-i-ty
pu-sal-lan-i-mous-ly
pus-sy
pussy-foot
pussy-wil-low
pus-tule
pus-tu-lar
pus-tu-late
pu-ta-tive
pu-ta-tive-ly
put--on
pu-tre-fac-tion
pu-tre-fy
pu-tre-fied
pu-tre-fy-ing
pu-trid
pu-trid-i-try
putt
putt-ed
putt-ing
putt-er
put-ter-er
put--up
puz-zle
puz-zle-ment
py-lon
pyr-a-mid
py-ra-mi-dal
py-ric
py-ro-ma-nia
py-ro-ma-ni-ac
py-ro-ma-ni-a-cal
py-ro-tech-nics
py-ro-tech-nic
py-ro-tech-ni-cal
py-thon
py-tho-ness
py-uria
pyx
pyx-id-i-um

Q

quack-ery
 quack-er-ies
quad-ran-gle
 quad-ran-gu-lar
quad-rant
 quad-ran-tal
quad-ra-phon-ic
quad-rate
 quad-rat-ed
 quad-rat-ing
qua-drat-ic
 qua-drat-i-cal-ly
qua-drat-ics
quad-ra-ture
quad-ri-lat-er-al
qua-drille
qua-dril-lion
 qua-dril-lionth
qua-droon
quad-ru-ped
 quad-ru-pe-dal
qua-dru-ple
 qua-dru-pled
 qua-dru-pling
qua-dru-plet
qua-dru-pli-cate
 qua-dru-pli-cat-ed
 qua-dru-pli-cat-ing
quaff
 quaff-er
quag-mire
 quag-mired
 quag-miry
quail
quaint
quake
qual-i-fi-ca-tion
qual-i-fied
 qual-i-fied-ly
qual-i-fy
 qual-i-fy-ing
 qual-i-fi-a-ble
 qual-i-fier
qual-i-ta-tive
qual-i-ty
 qual-i-ties
qualm
 qualm-ish

quan-da-ry
 quan-dar-ies
quan-ti-fy
 quan-ti-fy-ing
 quan-ti-fi-ca-tion
quan-ti-ta-tive
quan-ti-ty
 quan-ti-ties
quan-tum
 quan-ta
quar-an-tine
 quar-an-tin-able
quar-rel
 quar-reled
 quar-rel-ing
 quar-rel-er
quar-rel-some
quar-ri-er
quar-ry
 quar-ries
 quar-ried
 quar-ry-ing
quart
quar-ter
quar-ter-back
quar-ter-ing
quar-ter-ly
 quar-ter-lies
quar-ter-mas-ter
quar-tet
quartz
quash
qua-si
qua-ter-na-ry
qua-train
qua-ver
 quav-er-ing-ly
 qua-very
quay
quea-sy
 quea-si-er
 quea-si-est
 quea-si-ly
queen
quell
 quell-er
quench
 quench-able
 quench-er
que-ry
 que-ries

que-ried
quest
ques-tion
 ques-tion-er
ques-tion-able
 ques-tion-ably
ques-tion-naire
queue
 queued
 queu-ing
quib-ble
quick
quick-en
 quick-en-er
quick--freeze
quick--wit-ted
 quick--wit-ted-ly
qui-es-cent
 qui-es-cence
qui-et
 qui-et-ly
 qui-et-ter
qui-e-tude
quill
quilt
 quilt-ing
quince
quin-til-lion
quin-tu-ple
 quin-tu-pled
 quin-tu-pling
quin-tu-plet
quip
 quipped
 quip-ping
quirk
 quirky
quis-ling
quit
 quit-ed
 quit-ing
quit-claim
quite
quit-er
quiv-er
quix-ot-ic
quiz
quiz-zi-cal
 quiz-zi-cal-ly
quoin
quoit

quon-dam
quo-rum
quo-ta
quot-able
 quot-a-bil-i-ty
quo-ta-tion
quote
quo-tid-i-an
quo-tient

R

rab-bet
 rab-bet-ted
 rab-bet-ting
rab-bi
 rab-bis
ra-bin-ate
rab-bin-i-cal
 rab-bin-i-al-ly
rab-bit
rab-ble
 rab-bled
 rab-bling
ra-bid
 ra-bid-ly
ra-bies
rac-coon
race-horse
ra-ceme
rac-er
ra-ce-ric
ra-ce-ri-za-tion
race-track
ra-chis
 ra-chis-es
 rach-i-des
ra-cial
 ra-cial-ism
 ra-cial-ly
rac-ism
 ra-cial-ism
 rac-ist
rack-et
rack-e-teer
ra-con-teur
racy
 rac-i-ly
ra-dar
ra-di-al
 ra-di-al-ly

ra-di-ance	raked	**ra-pi-er**	rat-ti-est
ra-di-an-cy	rak-ing	**rap-ine**	**rau-cous**
ra-di-ant	**rake--off**	**rap-pel**	rau-cous-ly
ra-di-ate	rak-ish	**rap-proche-ment**	**rav-age**
ra-di-at-ed	rak-ish-ly	**rap-scal-lion**	rav-aged
ra-di-at-ing	**ral-li-form**	**rap-to-ri-al**	**rave**
ra-di-a-tion	**ral-ly**	**rap-ture**	**rav-el**
ra-di-a-tor	ral-lied	rap-tur-ous	**ra-ven**
rad-i-cal	**ram**	**rare**	**rav-en-ous**
rad-i-cal-ly	rammed	rar-er	rav-en-ous-ly
rad-i-cal-ism	**ram-ble**	rar-est	**ra-vine**
ra-dio	ram-bled	**rare-bit**	**rav-i-o-li**
ra-dio-ac-tive	ram-bling	**rar-efy**	**rav-ish**
ra-dio-ac-tive-i-ty	**ram-bler**	rar-efied	rav-ish-ment
ra-dio-gram	**ram-bunc-tious**	rar-efy-ing	**rav-ish-ing**
ra-dio-graph	**ram-bu-tan**	**rare-ly**	**raw**
ra-diog-ra-phy	**ram-i-fi-ca-tion**	**rar-i-ty**	**raw-hide**
ra-di-ol-o-gy	**ram-i-fy**	rar-i-ties	**ray-on**
ra-di-ol-o-gist	ram-i-fied	**rash**	**raze**
rad-ish	ram-i-fy-ing	**ra-so-ri-al**	razed
ra-di-um	**ram-page**	**rasp**	raz-ing
ra-di-us	ram-paged	**rasp-ber-ry**	**ra-zor**
ra-dii	ram-pag-ing	**rat-able**	**raz-zle--daz-zle**
ra-di-us-es	**ram-pan-cy**	**ratch-et**	**re-act**
ra-don	**ram-pant**	**rate**	re-ac-tive
raf-fia	ram-pant-ly	rat-ed	**re-ac-tion**
raf-fi-nose	**ram-part**	rat-ing	**re-ac-tion-ary**
raff-ish	**ram-rod**	**rath-er**	re-ac-tion-ar-ies
raf-fle	**ram-shack-le**	**rat-icide**	**re-ac-ti-vate**
raf-fled	**ranch-er**	**rat-i-fy**	re-ac-ti-vat-ed
raf-fling	**ran-cid**	rat-i-fi-ca-tion	re-ac-ti-vat-ing
raft	ran-cid-i-ty	**ra-tio**	**re-ac-tor**
raft-er	**ran-cor**	ra-tios	**read-able**
rag	ran-cor-ous	**ra-ti-o-ci-na-tion**	**read-er**
rag-ged	**ran-dom**	**ra-tion**	**read-ing**
rag-gle	ran-dom-ly	**ra-tio-nal**	**re-ad-just**
rail-ing	**range**	ra-tio-nal-i-ty	re-ad-just-ment
rail-lery	ranged	ra-tio-nal-ly	**ready--made**
rail-ler-ies	rang-ing	**ra-tion-able**	**re-agent**
rail-road	**rang-er**	**ra-tio-nal-ism**	**re-al**
rail-road-er	**rangy**	**ra-tio-nal-ize**	**re-al-ism**
rail-road-ing	rang-i-er	ra-tio-nal-iz-ing	re-al-ist
rail-way	rang-i-est	ra-tio-nal-i-za-tion	re-al-is-tic
rai-ment	**ran-sack**	**rat-line**	re-al-is-ti-cal-ly
rain-bow	**rant-er**	**rat-tan**	**re-al-ly**
rain-fall	**ran-u-la**	**rat-tle**	**realm**
rainy	**rape**	rat-tled	**Re-al-tor**
raise	rap-ist	rat-tling	**re-al-ty**
raised	**ra-phe**	**rat-tle-snake**	**ream-er**
rai-sin	**raph-ide**	**rat-ty**	**re-an-i-mate**
rake	**rap-id**	rat-ti-er	re-an-i-mat-ed

re-an-i-mat-ing
re-an-i-ma-tion
reap-er
re-ap-pear
re-ap-pear-ance
re-ap-por-tion
re-ap-por-tion-ment
rear ad-mir-ral
re-arm
re-ar-ma-ment
re-ar-range
re-ar-ranged
re-ar-rang-ing
re-ar-range-ment
rear-ward
rea-son
rea-son-er
rea-son-able
rea-son-abil-i-ty
rea-son-able-ness
rea-son-ably
rea-son-ing
re-as-sem-ble
re-as-sem-bled
re-as-sem-bling
re-as-sem-bly
re-as-sume
re-as-sump-tion
re-as-sure
re-as-sured
re-as-sur-ing
re-as-sur-ance
re-as-sur-ing-ly
re-bate
re-bat-ed
re-bat-ing
re-bat-er
reb-el
re-bel
re-belled
re-bel-ling
re-bel-lion
re-bel-lious
re-bel-lious-ly
re-birth
re-born
re-bound
re-buff
re-build
re-built
re-build-ing

re-buke
re-bus
re-bus-es
re-but
re-but-tal
re-cal-ci-trant
re-cal-ci-trance
re-cal-ci-tran-cy
re-call
re-cant
re-can-ta-tion
re-ca-pit-u-late
re-cap-ture
re-cap-tured
re-cede
re-ced-ed
re-ced-ing
re-ceipt
re-ceiv-able
re-ceive
re-ceiv-ed
re-ceiv-ing
re-ceiv-er
re-ceiv-er-ship
re-cent
re-cent-ly
re-cen-cy
re-cep-ta-cle
re-cep-tion
re-cep-tion-ist
re-cep-tive
re-cess
re-ces-sion
re-ces-sion-ary
re-ces-sion-al
re-ces-sive
re-charge
re-charg-ed
re-charg-ing
rec-i-pe
re-cip-i-ent
re-cip-i-ence
re-cip-i-en-cy
re-cip-ro-cal
re-cip-ro-cal-ly
re-cip-ro-cate
rec-i-proc-i-ty
re-cit-al
rec-i-ta-tion
rec-i-ta-tive
re-cite

re-cited
re-cit-ing
reck-less
reck-less-ly
reck-on
re-claim
rec-la-ma-tion
re-cline
re-clined
rec-luse
rec-og-ni-tion
re-cog-ni-zance
rec-og-nize
rec-og-nized
rec-og-niz-ing
rec-og-niz-a-ble
re-coil
re-coil-less
re-col-lect
re-col-lect
re-col-lec-tion
rec-om-mend
rec-om-mend-able
rec-om-mend-er
rec-om-men-da-tion
rec-om-pense
rec-om-pensed
rec-om-pens-ing
rec-on-cile
rec-on-ciled
rec-con-dite
re-con-di-tion
re-con-firm
re-con-nais-sance
re-con-noi-ter
re-con-noi-tered
re-con-noi-ter-ing
re-con-sid-er
re-con-sid-er-a-tion
re-con-struct
re-con-struc-tion
re-cord
re-cord-er
re-count
re-coup
re-course
re-cov-er
re-cov-ery
re-cov-er-ies
rec-re-ant
re-cre-ate

re-cre-at-ed
re-cre-at-ing
re-cre-a-tion
rec-re-ation
rec-re-ation-al
re-crim-i-nate
re-crim-i-nat-ed
re-crim-i-nat-ing
re-cruit
re-cruit-er
re-cruit-ment
rec-tal
rect-an-gle
rect-an-gu-lar
rec-ti-fi-er
rec-ti-fy
rec-ti-fied
rec-ti-fy-ing
rec-ti-fi-ca-tion
rec-ti-lin-ear
rec-ti-tude
rec-tor
rec-to-ry
rec-to-ries
rec-tum
rec-tums
rec-ta
re-cum-bent
re-cum-ben-cy
re-cum-bent-ly
re-cu-per-ate
re-cur
re-cur-ring
re-cur-rence
re-cur-rent
red-bird
red--blood-ed
re-dec-o-rate
re-dec-o-rat-ed
re-dec-o-ra-tion
re-ded-i-cate
re-ded-i-cat-ed
re-ded-i-ca-tion
re-deem
re-deem-able
re-deem-er
re-demp-tion
re-demp-tive
red--hand-ed
red--hot
re-di-rect

re-di-rec-tion	ref-er-ee	re-fur-bish	re-gret-ta-bly
red--let-ter	ref-er-ence	re-fus-al	re-gret-er
red--neck	ref-er-enced	re-fuse	re-gret-ful
re-do	ref-er-enc-ing	re-fused	re-gret-ful-ly
red-o-lence	ref-er-en-dum	re-fus-ing	reg-u-lar
red-o-len-cy	ref-er-en-dums	ref-use	reg-u-lar-i-ty
red-o-lent	ref-er-en-da	re-fute	reg-u-late
re-dou-ble	ref-er-ent	re-gain	reg-u-lat-ed
re-dou-bled	re-fill	re-gal	reg-u-lat-ing
re-dou-bling	re-fill-able	re-gal-ly	reg-u-la-tive
re-doubt-able	re-fine	re-gale	reg-u-la-tor
re-doubt-ably	re-fined	re-galed	reg-u-la-to-ry
re-dound	re-fin-ing	re-gal-ing	reg-u-la-tion
re-dress	re-fine-ment	re-ga-lia	re-gur-gi-tate
red-start	re-fin-ery	re-gard	re-gur-gi-tat-ed
re-duce	re-fin-er-ies	re-gard-ful	re-gur-gi-tat-ing
re-duc-tion	re-fin-ish	re-gard-ing	re-gur-gi-ta-tion
re-dun-dance	re-fit	re-gard-less	re-ha-bil-i-tate
re-dun-dant	re-fit-ted	re-gard-less-ly	re-ha-bil-i-tat-ed
re-du-pli-cate	re-fit-ting	re-gat-ta	re-ha-bil-i-tat-ing
re-du-pli-cat-ed	re-flect	re-gen-cy	re-ha-bil-i-ta-tion
re-du-pli-ca-tion	re-flec-tion	re-gen-cies	re-ha-bil-i-ta-tive
red-wood	re-flec-tive	re-gen-er-ate	re-hash
re-echo	re-flec-tive-ly	re-gen-er-at-ed	re-hears-al
re-ech-oed	re-flec-tive-ness	re-gen-er-at-ing	re-hearse
reedy	re-flec-tor	re-gen-er-a-vy	re-hearsed
reed-i-er	re-flex	re-gen-er-a-tion	re-hears-ing
reef-er	re-flex-ive	re-gen-er-a-tive	re-hears-er
re-elect	re-for-est	re-gent	reign
re-elec-tion	re-for-est-a-tion	re-grime	re-im-burse
re-em-pha-sie	re-form	reg-i-men	re-im-bursed
re-em-pha-sized	re-form-a-tory	reg-i-ment	re-im-burs-ing
re-em-pha-siz-ing	re-fract	reg-i-men-tal	re-im-burse-meny
re-en-force	re-frac-tive	reg-i-men-ta-tion	rein
re-en-forced	re-frac-tion	re-gion	re-in-car-na-tion
re-en-forc-ing	re-frac-to-ry	re-gion-al	rein-deer
re-en-force-ment	re-frac-to-ri-ly	re-gion-al-ly	re-in-force
re-en-list	re-frain	reg-is-ter	re-in-forced
re-en-list-ment	re-fresh	reg-is-tered	re-in-forc-ing
re-en-ter	re-fresh-ing	reg-is-trant	re-in-force-ment
re-en-trance	re-fresh-ment	reg-is-trar	re-in-state
re-en-try	re-frig-er-ant	reg-is-tra-tion	re-in-stat-ed
re-en-tries	re-frig-er-ate	reg-is-try	re-in-stat-ing
re-es-tab-lish	re-frig-er-at-ed	reg-is-tries	re-in-state-ment
re-es-tab-lish-ment	re-frig-er-a-tor	re-gress	re-it-er-ate
re-ex-am-ine	re-fu-el	re-gres-sion	re-it-er-at-ed
re-ex-am-i-na-tion	ref-uge	re-gres-sor	re-it-er-at-ing
re-fec-to-ry	ref-u-gee	re-gret	re-it-er-a-tion
re-fec-to-ries	re-ful-gence	re-gret-ted	re-ject
re-fer	re-ful-gent	re-gret-ting	re-jec-tion
re-fer-ral	re-fund	re-gret-ta-ble	re-joice

re-joiced
re-joic-ing
re-joic-er
re-joic-ing-ly
re-join
re-join-der
re-ju-ve-nate
re-ju-ve-nat-ed
re-ju-ve-nat-ing
re-ju-ve-na-tion
re-ju-ve-na-tor
re-kin-dle
re-kin-dled
re-kin-dling
re-lapse
re-lapsed
re-laps-ing
re-laps-er
re-late
re-lat-ed
re-lat-ing
re-lat-er
re-lat-or
re-la-tion
re-la-tion-al
re-la-tion-ship
rel-a-tive
rel-a-tive-ly
rel-a-tiv-ism
rel-a-tiv-ist
rel-a-tiv-is-tic
rel-a-tiv-i-ty
rel-a-tiv-ize
re-la-tor
re-lax
re-lax-er
re-lax-ation
re-lay
re-laid
re-lay-ing
re-lay
re-layed
re-lay-ing
re-lease
re-leas-ed
re-leas-ing
re-leas-a-ble
re-leas-er
rel-e-gate
rel-e-gat-ed
rel-e-ga-tion

re-lent
re-lent-less
rel-e-vant
rel-e-vance
rel-e-van-cy
rel-e-vant-ly
re-li-able
re-li-abil-i-ty
re-li-able-ness
re-li-ably
re-li-ance
re-li-ant
rel-ic
re-lief
re-leive
re-liev-ed
re-liev-ing
re-liev-able
re-liev-er
re-li-gion
re-li-gi-os-i-ty
re-li-gious
re-lin-quish
rel-ish
re-live
re-lived
re-liv-ing
re-lo-cate
re-lo-ct-ed
re-lo-cat-ing
re-lo-ca-tion
re-luc-tance
re-luc-tant
re-ly
re-lied
re-ly-ing
re-main
re-main-der
re-mand
re-mark
re-mark-able
re-mark-able-ness
re-mark-ably
re-me-di-a-ble
re-me-di-al
rem-e-dy
rem-e-dies
rem-e-died
rem-e-dy-ing
re-mem-ber
re-mem-brance

re-mind
re-mind-er
re-mind-ful
rem-i-nisce
rem-i-nisced
rem-i-nisc-ing
rem-i-nis-cence
rem-i-nis-cent
re-miss
re-mis-sion
re-mit
re-mit-ted
re-mit-ting
re-mit-tance
rem-nant
re-mod-el
re-mon-strance
re-mon-strate
re-mon-strat-ed
re-mon-strat-ing
re-morse
re-morse-ful
re-morse-ful-ly
re-morse-less
re-mote
re-mot-er
re-mot-est
re-mount
re-mov-able
re-mov-al
re-move
re-moved
re-mov-ing
re-mu-ner-ate
re-mu-ner-at-ed
re-mu-ner-at-ing
re-mu-ner-a-tion
re-nais-sance
re-na-scence
re-na-scent
rend
rend-er
ren-dez-vous
ren-dez-voused
ren-dez-vous-ing
ren-di-tion
ren-e-gade
re-nege
re-neged
re-neg-ing
re-new

re-new-al
ren-net
re-nounce
re-nounced
re-nounc-ing
ren-o-vate
ren-o-vat-ed
ren-o-vat-ing
ren-o-va-tion
re-nown
re-nowned
rent-al
re-nun-ci-a-tion
re-or-ga-ni-za-tion
re-or-ga-nize
re-or-ga-niz-ed
re-or-gan-iz-ing
re-pair
re-pair-man
re-pair-men
rep-a-ra-ble
rep-a-ra-tion
rep-ar-tee
re-pa-tri-ate
re-pa-tri-at-ed
re-pay
re-paid
re-pay-ing
re-pay-ment
re-peal
re-peat
re-peat-able
re-peat-ed
re-peat-er
re-pel
re-pelled
re-pel-ling
re-pel-lent
re-pent
re-pent-ance
re-pen-tant
re-per-cus-sion
rep-er-toire
rep-er-to-ry
rep-er-to-ries
rep-e-ti-tion
rep-e-ti-tious
re-pet-i-tive
re-place
re-placed
re-plac-ing

re-plac-able
re-place-ment
re-plen-ish
re-plete
re-ple-tion
rep-li-ca
re-ply
re-plied
re-ply-ing
re-plies
re-port
re-port-ed-ly
re-port-er
rep-or-to-ri-al
re-pose
re-posed
re-pos-ing
re-pose-ful
re-pos-i-to-ry
re-pos-i-tor-ies
re-pos-sess
re-pos-ses-sion
rep-re-hend
rep-re-hen-si-ble
rep-re-sent
rep-re-sen-ta-tion
rep-re-sen-ta-tive
re-press
re-pres-sion
re-prieve
re-prieved
re-priev-ing
rep-ri-mand
re-print
re-pris-al
re-proach
re-proach-ful
rep-ro-bate
rep-ro-ba-tion
re-pro-duce
re-pro-duced
re-pro-duc-ing
re-pro-duc-tion
re-pro-duc-tive
re-proof
re-prove
re-proved
re-prov-ing
rep-tile
rep-til-ian
re-pub-lic

re-pub-li-can
re-pub-li-can-ism
re-pu-di-ate
re-pu-di-at-ed
re-pu-di-at-ing
re-pu-di-a-tion
re-pu-di-a-tion-ist
re-pugn
re-pug-nan-cy
re-pug-nant
re-pulse
re-pulsed
re-puls-ing
re-pul-sion
re-pul-sive
rep-u-ta-ble
rep-u-ta-bly
rep-u-ta-bil-i-ty
rep-u-ta-tion
re-pute
re-put-ed
re-put-ing
re-put-ed-ly
re-quest
re-qui-em
re-quire
re-quired
re-quir-ing
re-quire-ment
req-ui-site
re-quit-al
re-quite
re-quit-ed
re-quit-ing
re-run
re-run-ning
re-sale
re-scind
res-cue
res-cued
res-cu-ing
res-cu-er
re-search
re-search-er
re-sem-blance
re-sem-ble
re-sem-bled
re-sem-bling
re-sent
re-sent-ful
re-sent-ment

re-ser-va-tion
re-serve
re-served
re-serv-ing
re-serv-ist
res-er-voir
re-set
re-set-ting
re-side
re-sid-ed
re-sid-ing
res-i-dence
res-i-den-cy
res-i-den-cies
res-i-dent
res-i-den-tial
re-sid-u-al
res-i-due
re-sign
res-ig-na-tion
re-signed
re-sil-ient
re-sil-ience
re-sil-ien-cy
res-in
res-in-ous
re-sist
re-sist-er
re-sist-ible
re-sist-ance
re-sis-tant
re-sist-less
re-sis-tor
res-o-lute
res-o-lu-tion
re-solve
re-solved
re-solv-ing
res-o-nance
res-o-nant
res-o-nate
res-o-nat-ed
res-o-nat-ing
res-o-na-tor
re-sort
re-sound
re-sound-ing
re-source
re-source-ful
re-spect
re-spect-ful

re-spect-ful-ly
re-spect-able
re-spect-a-bil-i-ty
re-spect-ing
re-spec-tive
re-spec-tive-ly
res-pi-ra-tion
res-pi-ra-to-ry
res-pi-ra-tor
re-spire
re-spired
re-spir-ing
re-spite
re-splend-ant
re-splend-ence
re-spond
re-spon-dent
re-sponse
re-spon-si-bil-i-ty
re-spon-si-bil-i-ties
re-spon-si-ble
re-spon-sive
res-tau-rant
rest-ful
res-ti-tu-tion
res-tive
rest-less
res-to-ra-tion
re-stor-a-tive
re-store
re-stored
re-stor-ing
re-strain
re-straint
re-strict
re-strict-ed
re-strict-ed-ly
re-stric-tion
re-stric-tive
re-sult
re-sul-tant
re-sume
re-sumed
re-sum-ing
re-sump-tion
re-sur-gence
re-sur-gent
res-ur-rect
res-ur-rec-tion
re-sus-ci-tate
re-sus-ci-tat-ed

re-sus-ci-tat-ing
re-sus-ci-ta-tion
re-sus-ci-ta-tor
re-tail
re-tail-er
re-tain
re-tainer
re-take
re-took
re-tak-en
re-tak-ing
re-tal-i-ate
re-tal-i-at-ed
re-tal-i-at-ing
re-tal-i-a-tion
re-tard
re-tard-ant
re-tar-da-tion
re-tard-ed
re-ten-tion
re-ten-tive
ret-i-cence
ret-i-cent
ret-i-nue
re-tire
re-tired
re-tir-ing
re-tire-ment
re-tool
re-tort
re-touch
re-trace
re-traced
re-trac-ing
re-tract
re-trac-tion
re-trac-tor
re-trac-tile
re-tread
re-treat
re-trench
re-trench-ment
re-tri-al
ret-ri-bu-tion
re-trieve
re-trieved
re-triev-ing
re-triev-er
ret-ro-ac-tive
ret-ro-grade
ret-ro-grad-ed

ret-ro-grad-ing
ret-ro-gress
ret-ro-gees-sion
ret-ro-ges-sive
ret-ro--rock-et
ret-ro-spect
ret-ro-spec-tion
ret-ro-spec-tive
re-turn
re-turn-able
re-turn-ee
re-union
re-unite
re-unit-ed
re-unit-ing
rev
rev-ved
rev-ving
re-vamp
re-veal
rev-eil-le
rev-el
rev-el-er
rev-e-la-tion
rev-el-ry
rev-el-ries
re-venge
re-venged
re-veng-ing
re-venge-ful
rev-e-nue
rev-e-nu-er
re-ver-ber-ate
re-ver-ber-at-ed
re-ver-ber-at-ing
re-ver-ber-a-tion
re-vere
re-vered
re-ver-ing
rev-er-ence
rev-er-enced
rev-er-enc-ing
rev-er-end
rev-er-ent
rev-er-en-tial
rev-er-ie
re-ver-sal
re-verse
re-versed
re-vers-ing
re-vers-i-ble

re-ver-sion
re-vert
re-view
re-view-er
re-vile
re-viled
re-vil-ing
re-vise
re-vised
re-vis-ing
re-vi-sion
re-vi-sion-ist
re-vi-sion-ism
re-viv-al
re-viv-al-ist
re-vive
re-vived
re-viv-ing
rev-o-ca-ble
rev-o-ca-tion
re-voke
re-voked
re-vok-ing
re-volt
rev-o-lu-tion
rev-o-lu-tion-ary
rev-o-lu-tion-ar-ies
rev-o-lu-tion-ist
rev-o-lu-tion-ize
rev-o-lu-tion-ized
rev-o-lu-tion-iz-ing
re-volve
re-volved
re-volv-ing
re-volv-er
re-vue
re-vul-sion
re-write
re-wrote
re-writ-ten
re-writ-ting
rhap-sod-ic
rhap-sod-i-cal
rhap-sod-i-cal-ly
rhap-so-dize
rhap-so-dized
rhap-so-diz-ing
rhap-so-dy
rhap-so-dies
rhap-so-dist
rhea

rhe-ni-um
rheo-stat
rhe-tor
rhet-o-ric
rhe-tor-i-cal
rhet-o-ri-cian
rheum
rheu-mat-ic
rheu-mat-i-cal-ly
rheu-ma-tism
rhine-stone
rhi-no
rhi-noc-er-os
rhi-noc-er-os-es
rhi-zome
rho-di-um
rho-do-den-dron
rhom-bic
rhom-boid
rhom-boi-dal
rhom-bus
rhom-bus-es
rhom-bi
rhu-barb
rhyme
rhymed
rhym-ing
rhyme-ster
rhythm
rhyth-mic
rhyth-mi-cal
rhyth-mi-cal-ly
rib
ribbed
rib-bing
rib-ald
rib-ald-ry
rib-ald-ries
rib-bon
ri-bo-fla-vin
rib-bo-nu-cle-ase
rice
riced
ric-ing
rich-es
rich-less
rick-ets
rick-ety
rick-et-i-er
rick-et-i-est
rick-shaw

ric-o-chet
rid
 rid-ded
 rid-ding
rid-dance
rid-dle
 rid-dled
 rid-dling
ride
 rid-den
 rid-ding
ride-er
ridge
 ridged
 ridg-ing
ridge-pole
rid-i-cule
 rid-i-culed
 rid-i-cul-ing
ri-dic-u-lous
rif-fle
 rif-fled
 rif-fling
riff-raff
rig
 rigged
 rig-ging
rig-ger
righ-teous
right-ful
right-hand
right--hand-ed
right-ism
rig-id
 ri-gid-i-ty
rig-ma-role
rig-or
rig-or-ous
rile
 riled
 ril-ing
rim
rime
ring-er
ring-lead-er
ring-let
ring-mas-ter
ring-worm
rinse
 rinsed
 rins-ing

ri-ot-ous
rip
ripped
rip-ping
rip-per
ri-par-i-an
rip-en
rip--off
rip-ple
 rip-pled
 rip-pling
rip-saw
rip-tide
rise
 rose
 ris-en
 ris-ing
ris-er
ris-i-ble
 ris-i-bil-i-ty
rit-u-al
rit-u-al-ism
 rit-u-al-ist
 rit-u-al-is-tic
 rit-u-al-is-ti-cal-ly
ritzy
 ritz-i-er
 ritz-i-est
ri-val
ri-val-ry
 ri-val-ries
riv-er
riv-er-side
riv-et
 riv-et-er
riv-i-era
riv-u-let
roach
road-ster
road-way
roast-er
rob
 robbed
 rob-bing
rob-ber
rob-bery
 rob-ber-ies
robe
 robed
 rob-ing
rob-in

ro-bot
ro-bust
rock-er
rock-et
rock-et-ry
rocky
 rock-i-er
 rock-i-est
ro-co-co
ro-dent
ro-deo
 ro-de-os
roe-buck
roent-gen
rog-er
roque
 ro-guish
 ro-guish-ly
roqu-ery
 roqu-er-ies
roist-er
roll-er
roll-er bear-ing
roll-er coast-er
roll-er skate
rol-lick
 rol-lick-ing
roll-ing pin
ro-ly--po-ly
 ro-ly--po-lies
ro-maine
ro-mance
 ro-manced
 ro-manc-ing
ro-man-tic
ro-man-ti-cism
ro-man-ti-cize
 ro-man-ti-ciz-ing
romp-er
roof-ing
rook-ery
 rook-er-ies
rook-ie
room-er
room-ful
room-mate
roomy
 room-i-er
 room-i-est
 room-i-ly
room-i-ness

roos-ter
root-stock
rope
 roped
 rop-ing
ropy
 rop-i-er
 rop-i-est
ro-sa-ry
 ro-sa-ries
ro-se-ate
rose-bud
rose--col-ored
rose-mary
 rose-mar-ies
ro-sette
ros-in
ros-ter
ros-trum
 ros-tra
 ros-trums
ro-ta-ry
 ro-tar-ies
ro-tate
 ro-tat-ed
 ro-tat-ing
ro-ta-tion
ro-tis-ser-ie
ro-tor
rot-ten
ro-tund
 ro-tun-di-ty
 ro-tun-di-ties
ro-tun-da
rouge
 rouged
 roug-ing
rough-age
rough--and--tum ble
rough-en
rough-house
rough-neck
rough-shod
rou-lette
round-er
round-ish
round-up
rouse
 roused
 rous-ing
rous-er

roust	rue-ful-ly	rus-tic	sac-ri-lege
roust-a-bout	ruff	rus-ti-cate	sac-ri-le-gious
rout	ruffed	rus-ti-cat-ed	sc-ro-il-li-ac
route	ruf-fi-an	rus-ti-cat-ing	sac-ro-sanct
rout-ed	ruf-fle	rus-ti-ca-tion	sac-ro-sanc-i-ty
rout-ing	ruf-fled	rus-tle	sac-rum
rout-er	ruf-fling	rus-tled	sac-rums
rou-tine	rug-ged	rus-tling	sac-ra
rou-tin-ize	rug-ged-ly	rus-tler	sa-cral
rou-tin-ized	rug-ged-ness	rust-proof	sad-den
rou-tin-iz-ing	ru-in	rus-ty	sad-dle
row-boat	ru-in-ation	rust-i-er	sad-dled
row-dy	ru-in-ous	rust-i-est	sad-dling
row-dies	rule	rut	sad-dle-backed
row-di-er	ruled	rut-ted	sad-dle-bag
row-di-est	rul-ing	rut-ting	sad-ism
roy-al-ist	rul-er	ru-ta-ba-ga	sad-ist
roy-al-ty	rum-ba	ru-the-ni-um	sa-dis-tic
roy-al-ties	rum-baed	ruth-less	sad-o-mas-o-chism
rub-ber	rum-ba-ing	ruth-less-ly	sad-o-mas-o-chist
rub-bery	ru-mi-nant	rut-ty	sa-fa-ri
rub-ber-ize	rum-mage		sa-fa-ris
rub-ber-ized	rum-maged		safe
rub-ber-iz-ing	rum-mag-ing		saf-er
rub-ber-neck	rum-mag-er		saf-est
rub-bish	rum-my		safe--con-duct
rub-bish-ly	rum-mies		safe-crack-er
rub-ble	ru-mor	**S**	safe-crack-ing
rub-bly	ru-mor-mon-ger		safe--de-pos-it
rub-bli-er	rum-ple		safe-guard
rub-bli-est	rum-pled		safe-keep-ing
rub-down	rum-pling	sa-ber	safe-ty
ru-bel-la	rum-pus	sa-ber-toothed ti-ger	safe-ties
ru-be-o-la	run	sa-ble	safe-ty match
ru-bi-cund	run-ning	sab-o-tage	safe-ty pin
ru-bid-i-um	run-about	sab-o-taged	safe-ty valve
ru-bric	run-around	sab-o-tag-ing	safe-ty zone
ru-by	run-away	sab-o-teur	saf-flow-er
ru-bies	run-ner	sa-bra	sag
ruck-sack	run-ner--up	sac-cha-rin	sagged
ruck-us	run-ny	sac-er-do-tal	sag-ging
rud-der	run-ni-er	sa-chet	sa-ga
rud-dy	run-ni-est	sack-cloth	sa-ga-cious
rud-di-er	run-off	sack-ful	sa-gac-i-ty
rud-di-est	run--on	sack-fuls	sage
rud-di-ly	run--through	sack-ing	sag-er
rude	run-way	sac-ra-ment	sag-est
ru-di-ment	rup-ture	sac-ra-men-tal	sage-brush
ru-di-ment-al	rup-tured	sa-cred	sail-er
ru-di-men-ta-ry	rup-tur-ing	sa-cred-ly	sail-fish
rue-ful	ru-ral	sa-cred-ness	sail-ing
		sac-ri-fice	
		sac-ri-ficed	
		sac-ri-fic-ing	
		sac-ri-fic-er	
		sac-ri-fi-cial	

sail-or
saint
  saint-hood
saint-ed
saint-ly
  saint-li-er
  saint-li-est
sa-ke
sal-a-ble
  sal-a-ble
  sal-a-bil-i-ty
  sal-a-bly
sa-la-cious
sal-ad
sal-a-man-der
sa-la-mi
sal-a-ry
  sal-a-ries
sales-man
  sales-men
sales-man-ship
sales-per-son
  sales-peo-ple
sales-room
sa-li-ent
  sa-li-ence
  sa-li-en-cy
  sa-li-ent-ly
sa-line
  sa-lin-i-ty
sa-li-va
  sal-i-vary
sal-low
  sal-low-ish
salm-on
sa-lon
sa-loon
salt-cel-lar
sal-tine
salt-shak-er
salt-wa-ter
salt-wort
salt-y
  salt-i-er
  salt-i-est
  salt-i-ness
sa-lu-bri-ous
sal-u-tar-y
sal-u-ta-tion
sa-lu-ta-to-ry
  sa-lu-ta-to-ries

sa-lute
  sa-luted
  sa-lut-ing
  sa-lut-er
sal-va-tion
salve
  salved
  salv-ing
  salv-or
sam-ba
  sam-baed
  sam-ba-ing
same-ness
sam-o-var
sam-ple
  sam-pled
  sam-pling
sam-pler
san-a-to-ri-um
sanc-ti-fy
  sanc-ti-fied
  sanc-ti-fy-ing
  sanc-ti-fi-ca-tion
  sanc-ti-fi-er
sanc-ti-mo-ny
  sanc-ti-mo-ni-ous
sanc-tion
  sanc-tion-a-ble
  sanc-tion-er
sanc-ti-ty
  sanc-ti-ties
sanc-tu-ary
  sanc-tu-ar-ies
sanc-tum
  sanc-ta
san-dal
san-dal-wood
sand-bag
  sand-bagged
sand-bank
sand-blast
sand-box
sand-cast
  sand-cast-ed
  sand-cast-ing
sand-lot
sand-man
  sand-men
sand-pa-per
sand-pi-per
sand-stone

sand-wich
sane
  san-er
  san-est
  sane-ly
sang-froid
san-gui-nary
san-quine
  san-quine-ly
san-i-tar-i-um
  san-i-tar-i-ums
  san-i-tar-ia
san-i-tary
  san-i-tar-i-ly
san-i-ta-tion
san-i-tize
  san-i-tized
  san-i-tiz-ing
san-i-ty
sap
  sapped
  sap-ping
sap-head
  sap-head-ed
sa-pi-ent
  sa-pi-ence
  sa-pi-en-cy
sap-less
sap-ling
sa-pon-i-fy
  sa-pon-i-fied
  sa-pon-i-fy-ing
sap-per
sap-phire
sap-phism
sap-py
  sap-pi-er
  sap-pi-est
sap-suck-er
sap-wood
sa-ran
sar-casm
  sar-cas-tic
  sar-cas-ti-cal-ly
sar-co-ma
  sar-co-mas
  sar-co-ma-ta
sar-coph-a-gus
  sar-coph-a-gus-es
sar-dine
sar-don-ic

  sar-don-i-cal-ly
sar-gas-sum
sa-ri
  sa-ris
sa-rong
sar-sa-pa-ril-la
sar-to-ri-al
sa-shay
sas-sa-fras
sas-sy
  sas-si-er
  sas-si-est
sa-tan-ic
  sa-tan-i-cal
sa-tan-ism
  sa-tan-ist
satch-el
sate
  sat-ed
  sat-ing
sa-teen
sat-el-lite
sa-ti-a-ble
  sa-ti-a-bly
  sa-ti-a-bil-i-ty
sa-ti-ate
  sa-ti-at-ed
  sa-ti-at-ing
  sa-ti-a-tion
sa-ti-e-ty
sat-in
  sat-iny
sat-ire
sa-tir-i-cal
  sa-tir-i-cal-ly
sat-i-rist
sat-i-rize
  sat-i-rized
  sat-i-riz-ing
  sat-i-riz-er
sat-is-fac-tion
sat-is-fac-to-ry
  sat-is-fa-to-ri-ly
sat-is-fy
  sat-is-fied
  sat-is-fy-ing
  sat-is-fi-a-ble
  sat-is-fi-er
  sat-is-fy-ing-ly
sat-u-rate
  sat-u-rat-ed

sat-u-rat-ing
sat-u-ra-tion
sat-ur-na-li-a
sat-ur-nine
sa-tyr
sa-tyr-ic
sauce
sauced
sauc-ing
sau-cer
sau-cy
sau-er-bra-ten
sau-er-kraut
sau-na
saun-ter
saun-ter-er
sau-sage
sau-sage-like
sav-age
sav-age-ry
sav-age-ries
sa-van-na
sa-vant
save
saved
sav-ing
sav-er
sav-ior
sa-voir-faire
sa-vor
sa-vor-er
sa-vory
sa-vor-i-er
sa-vor-i-est
sav-vy
saw-buck
saw-dust
sawed--off
saw-horse
saw-mill
saw-toothed
saw-yer
sax-o-phone
sax-o-phon-ist
say
said
say-ing
say-a-ble
say-er
say-s-o
scab

scabbed
scab-bing
scab-bard
sca-bies
scaf-fold
sac-fold-ing
sca-lar
scal-a-wag
scald
scald-ing
scale
scaled
scal-ing
scale-less
scamp
scamp-er
scan
scan-dal
scan-dal-ize
scan-dal-ized
scan-dal-iz-ing
scan-dal-mon-ger
scan-dal-ous
scan-sion
scant
scant-ness
scan-ties
scanty
scant-i-er
scant-i-est
scape-goat
scape-grace
scap-u-la
scap-u-las
scap-u-lae
scar
scarred
scar-ring
scarce
scar-ci-ty
scare-crow
scare-mon-ger
scarf
scarfs
scarf-skin
scar-i-fy
scar-i-fied
scar-i-fy-ing
scar-let
scarp
scary

scar-i-er
scar-i-est
scat
scat-ted
scat-ting
scathe
scat-o-log-i-cal
scat-ter
scat-ter-a-ble
scat-ter-er
scav-enge
scav-enged
scav-eng-ing
scav-en-ger
sce-nar-i-o
sce-nar-i-os
sce-nar-ist
scen-ery
scen-er-ies
sce-nic
sce-ni-cal
scent
scent-ed
scep-ter
scep-tered
scep-ter-ing
sched-ule
sched-ul-ed
sched-ul-ing
sche-ma-tize
sche-ma-tized
sche-ma-tiz-ing
scheme
schem-er
schem-ing
scher-zo
scher-zos
scher-zi
schism
schis-mat-ic
schis-mat-i-cal
schist
schizo
schiz-os
schiz-oid
schiz-o-phre-ni-a
schiz-o-phren-ic
schle-miel
schmaltz
schmaltzy
schmo

schnapps
schnau-zer
schnit-zel
schnook
schnor-kel
schnoz-zle
schol-ar
schol-ar-ly
schol-ar-li-ness
schol-ar-ship
scho-las-tic
scho-las-ti-cal
scho-las-ti-cism
school board
school bus
school-child
school-chil-dern
school-ing
school-mas-ter
school-teach-er
school-teach-ing
school-work
schoon-er
schuss
schwa
sci-at-ic
sci-ence
sci-en-tif-ic
sci-en-tif-i-cal-ly
sci-en-tist
scim-i-tar
scin-tig-ra-phy
scin-til-la
scin-til-lant
scin-til-late
scin-til-lat-ed
scin-til-lat-ing
scin-til-la-tion
sci-on
scis-sor
scle-ra
scle-rot-i-ca
scle-ro-sis
scle-ro-ses
scle-rot-ic
scle-rous
scoff
scoff-er
scoff-ing-ly
scold
scold-er

scold-ing
scol-lop
sconce
scone
scoop
scoot-er
scope
scorch
scorched
scorch-ing
scorch-er
score
scored
scor-ing
score-less
scor-er
score-board
score-keep-er
scorn
scorn-er
scorn-ful
scot-free
scot-tie
scoun-drel
scoun-drel-ly
scour
scour-er
scourge
scourged
scourg-ing
scourg-er
scour-ing
scout-ing
scout-mas-ter
scowl
scowl-er
srab-ble
scrab-bled
scrab-bling
scrab-bler
scrag
scragged
scrag-ging
scrag-gly
scrag-gli-er
scrag-gli-est
scrag-gy
scrag-gi-er
scrag-gi-est
scram
scrammed

scram-ming
scram-ble
scram-bled
scram-bling
scram-bler
scrap
scrapped
scrap-ping
scrap-book
scrape
scrap-per
scrap-py
scrap-pi-er
scrap-pi-est
scrap-pi-ly
scratch
scratch-a-ble
scratch-er
scratch-y
scratch-i-er
scratch-i-est
scratch-i-ly
scratch-i-ness
scrawl
scrawn-y
scrawn-i-er
scrawn-i-est
screamer
scream-ing-ly
screech
screech-er
screen
scrren-a-ble
screen-er
screen-play
screw
screw-driv-er
screw-y
screw-i-er
screw-i-est
scrib-ble
scrib-bled
scrib-bling
scrib-bler
scribe
scribed
scrib-ing
scrib-al
scrim
scrim-mage
scrim-mag-ing

scrimp-y
scrimp-i-er
scrimp-i-est
script
scrip-tur-al
scrip-ture
script-writ-er
scroll-work
scrooge
scro-tum
scro-ta
scrounge
scroung-er
scrub
scrubbed
scrub-bing
scrub-ber
scrub-by
scrub-bi-er
scrub-bi-est
scrub-wom-an
scrub-wom-en
scruffy
scruff-i-er
scruff-i-est
scrump-tious
scru-ple
scru-bled
scru-bling
scru-pu-lous
scru-pu-los-i-ty
scru-pu-lous-ly
scru-ta-ble
scru-ti-nize
scru-ti-nized
scru-ti-ny
scru-ti-nies
scu-ba
scud
scud-ded
scud-ding
scuf-fle
scuf-fled
scuf-fling
scul-ler-y
scul-ler-ies
sculp-tor
sculp-ture
sculp-tur-ed
sculp-tur-ing
sculp-tur-al

scum
scummed
scum-ming
scur-ri-lous
scur-ril-i-ty
scur-ril-i-ties
scur-ry
scur-ri-ed
scur-ry-ing
scur-vy
scut-tle
scut-tled
scut-tling
scut-tle-butt
scythe
scythed
scyth-ing
sea-bed
sea-coast
sea-drome
sea-far-ing
sea-far-er
sea-food
sea gull
sea horse
seal
seal-er
sea-lam-prey
sea legs
sea lev-el
seal-ing wax
sea li-on
seal-skin
seam
seam-er
sea-maid
sea-man
sea-men
sea-man-ship
seam-stree
seam-y
seam-i-er
seam-i-est
sea ot-ter
sea-plane
sea-port
search
search-a-ble
search-er
search-ing
search-light

search war-rant	se-cret-ing	seed-i-er	sel-dom
sea-scape	se-cre-tion	seed-i-est	se-lect
sea ser-pent	se-cre-tive	see-ing	se-lect-ed
sea-shell	se-cre-to-ry	seek	se-lec-tor
sea-shore	se-cre-to-ries	sought	se-lec-tion
sea-sick	sec-tar-i-an	seek-ing	se-lec-tive
sea-sick-ness	sec-tar-i-an-ism	seem-ing	se-lec-tiv-i-ty
sea-side	sec-tion	seem-ing-ness	se-le-ni-um
sea-son	sec-tion-al	seem-ly	self-a-base-ment
sea-son-er	sec-tor	seep	self-ab-ne-ga-tion
sea-son-a-ble	sec-to-ri-al	seepy	self-a-buse
sea-son-al	sec-u-lar	seep-i-er	self--ad-dressed
sea-son-al-ly	sec-u-lar-ism	seep-i-est	self--adjusting
sea-son-ing	sec-u-lar-ize	seep-age	self-adjust-ment
seat-ing	sec-u-lar-ized	se-er	self-ad-ministered
sea ur-chin	sec-u-lar-iz-ing	seer-ess	self--as-sur-ance
sea-ward	se-cure	seer-suck-er	self--cen-tered
sea-weed	se-cured	see-saw	self--cen-tered-ness
sea-wor-thy	se-cur-ing	seethe	self--col-lect-ed
sea-wor-thi-ness	se-cu-ri-ty	seethed	self--com-mand
se-ba-ceous	se-cu-ri-ties	seeth-ing	self--com-posed
se-cant	se-dan	seg-ment	self--con-fessed
se-cede	se-date	seg-men-tal	self--con-fi-dence
se-ced-ed	se-dat-ed	seg-men-tary	self--con-fi-dent
se-ced-ing	se-dat-ing	seg-men-ta-tion	self--con-scious
se-ced-er	se-da-tion	seg-re-gate	self--con-scious-ne
se-ces-sion	sed-a-tive	seg-re-gat-ed	self--con-tained
se-ces-sion-ist	sed-en-tary	seg-re-gat-ing	self--con-trol
se-clude	sed-en-tar-i-ness	seg-re-ga-tion	self--con-trolled
se-clud-ed	sedge	seg-re-ga-tion-sit	self--cor-rect-ing
se-clud-ing	sed-i-ment	sei-gneur	self--crit-i-cal
se-clu-sion	sed-i-men-tal	seine	self--crit-i-cism
se-clu-sive	sed-i-men-ta-ry	seined	self--de-cep-tion
sec-ond	sed-i-men-ta-tion	sein-ing	self--de-cep-tive
sec-ond-ar-y	se-di-tion	seis-mic	self--de-fense
sec-ond-ar-i-ly	se-di-tion-ary	seis-mal	self--de-ni-al
sec-ond--best	se-di-tious	seis-mi-cal	self--de-ny-ing
sec-ond--class	se-duce	seis-mi-cal-ly	self--de-ter-min-
sec-ond-quess	se-duced	seis-mo-graph	self--dis-ci-pline
sec-ond-hand	se-duc-ing	seis-mog-ra-pher	self--dis-ci-pline
sec-ond-rate	se-duc-er	seis-mo-graph-ic	self--ed-u-cate-e
sec-ond--sto-ry man	se-duc-tive	seis-mog-ra-phy	self--ed-u-ca-tion
se-cre-cy	se-duc-tive-ness	seis-mol-o-gy	self--ef-fac-ing
se-cre-cies	sed-u-lous	seis-mo-log-ic	self--em-ployed
se-cret	se-du-li-ty	seis-mo-log-i-cal	self--em-ploy-m
sec-re-tar-i-at	sed-u-lous-ness	seis-mol-o-gist	self--es-teem
sec-re-tary	seed-bed	seize	self--ev-i-dent
sec-re-tar-ies	seed-case	seized	self--ev-i-dence
sec-re-tar-i-al	seed-ing	seiz-ing	self--ex-plan-a-
se-crete	seed-pod	seiz-er	self--ex-pres-si
se-cret-ed	seedy	sei-zure	self--ex-pres-siv

self--ful-fill-ing
self--ful-fill-ment
self--gov-ern-ment
self--gov-erned
self--gov-ern-ing
self--help
self--im-age
self--im-por-tance
self--im-por-tant
self--im-posed
self--im-prove-ment
self--in-duced
self--in-dul-gence
self--in-dul-gent
self--in-flict-ed
self--in-ter-est
self--in-ter-est-ed
self-ish
self-ish-ness
self--kow-ledge
self--less
self-less-ness
self--love
self--lov-ing
self--made
self--per-pet-u-at-ing
self-per-pet-u-a-tion
self--pity
self--pit-y-ing
self--pol-li-na-tion
self--pos-sessed
self--pos-sess-ed-ly
self--pos-ses-sion
self--pres-er-va-tion
self--pro-pelled
self--pro-pel-ling
self--re-al-i-za-tion
self--re-li-ance
self--re-li-ant
self--re-spect
self--re-spect-ing
self--re-straint
self--re-strain-ing
self--right-eous
self--right-eous-ness
self--sac-ri-fice
self--sac-ri-fic-ing
self--same
self--sat-is-fied
self--sat-is-fac-tion
self--sat-is-fy-ing

self--ser-vice
self--serv-ing
self--start-er
self--start-ing
self--styled
self--suf-fi-cient
self--suf-fic-ing
self--suf-fi-cien-cy
self--sup-port
self--sup-port-ing
self--taught
self--will
self--willed
sell
sell-ing
sell-er
sell-out
sel-vage
sel-vaged
se-man-tics
se-man-tic
se-man-ti-cal
se-man-ti-cal-ly
sem-a-phore
sem-a-phor-ed
sem-a-phor-ing
sem-blance
se-men
se-mes-ter
sem-i-an-nu-al
sem-i-an-nu-al-ly
sem-i-ar-id
sem-i-au-to-mat-ic
sem-i-cir-cle
sem-i-cir-cu-lar
sem-i-clas-si-cal
sem-i-clas-sic
sem-i-co-lon
sem-i-con-duc-tor
sem-i-con-duct-ing
sem-i-con-scious
sem-i-con-sious-ness
sem-i-de-tached
sem-i-fi-nal
sem-i-fi-nal-ist
sem-i-flu-id
sem-i-for-mal
sem-i-gloss
sem-i-liq-uid
sem-i-month-ly
sem-i-nal

sem-i-nal-ly
sem-i-nar-y
sem-i-nar-ies
sem-i-nar-ian
sem-i-of-fi-cial
sem-i-of-fi-cial-ly
sem-i-per-ma-nent
sem-i-per-me-a-ble
sem-i-pre-cious
sem-i-pri-vate
sem-i-pro-fes-sion-al
sem-i-pro
sem-i-pub-lic
sem-i-skilled
sem-i-sol-id
sem-i-trail-er
sem-i-trop-ic
sem-i-trop-i-cal
sem-i-trop-ics
sem-i-vow-el
sem-i-week-ly
sem-i-week-lies
sem-i-year-ly
sen-a-ry
sen-ate
sen-a-tor
sen-a-tor-ship
sen-a-to-ri-al
sen-a-to-ri-al-ly
send--off
se-nile
se-nil-i-ty
sen-ior
sen-ior-i-ty
sen-na
sen-sate
san-sa-tion
sen-sa-tion-al
sen-sa-tion-al-ly
sen-sa-tion-al-ism
sense
sensed
sens-ing
sense-less
sense-less-ness
sen-si-bil-i-ty
sen-si-ble-ness
sen-si-ble
sen-si-ble-ness
sen-si-bly
sen-si-tive

sen-si-tiv-i-ty
sen-si-tiv-i-ties
sen-si-tize
sen-si-tized
sen-si-tiz-ing
sen-si-ti-za-tion
sen-si-tizer
sen-sor
sen-so-ry
sen-so-ri-al
sen-su-al
sen-su-al-i-ty
sen-su-al-ly
sen-su-al-ism
sen-su-al-ist
sen-su-al-ize
sen-su-al-ized
sen-su-al-iz-ing
sen-su-al-i-za-tion
sen-su-ous
sen-tence
sen-tenced
sen-tenc-ing
sen-tient
sen-ti-ment
sen-ti-men-tal
sen-ti-men-tal-ly
sen-ti-men-til-i-ty
sen-ti-men-tal-i-ties
sen-ti-men-tal-ist
sen-ti-men-tal-ize
sen-ti-men-tal-ized
sen-ti-men-tal-iz-ing
sen-ti-nel
sen-ti-neled
sen-ti-nel-ing
sen-try
sen-tries
se-pal
se-paled
se-palled
sep-a-ra-ble
sep-a-ra-bil-i-ty
sep-e-ra-bly
sep-a-rate
sep-a-rat-ed
sep-a-rat-ing
sep-a-ra-tion
sep-a-ra-tist
sep-a-ra-tism
sep-a-ra-tive

sep-a-ra-tor	se-ri-al	set-back	sex-i-est
se-pi-a	se-ri-al-ly	set-in	shab-by
sep-sis	se-ri-al-ist	set-off	shab-bi-er
sep-ses	se-ri-al-i-za-tion	set-ter	shab-bi-est
sep-ten-ni-al	se-ri-al-ize	set-ting	shab-bi-ly
sep-tet	se-ri-al-ized	set-tle	shack-le
sep-tic	se-ri-al-iz-ing	set-tled	shack-led
sep-ti-cal-ly	se-ries	set-tling	shack-ling
sep-tic-i-ty	se-ri-ous	set-tle-ment	shack-ler
sep-tu-a-ge-nar-i-an	se-ri-ous-ly	set-tler	shade
sep-tum	se-ri-ous-ness	set-to	shad-ed
sep-ta	se-ri-ous--mind-ed	set-up	shad-ing
sep-tu-ple	se-ri-us--mind-ed-ly	sev-en	shade-less
sep-tu-pled	ser-mon	sev-enth	shad-ow
sep-tu-pling	ser-mon-ize	sev-en-teen	shad-ow-box
sep-ul-cher	ser-mon-ized	sev-en-teenth	shad-owy
sep-u-chered	ser-mon-iz-ing	sev-en-ty	shad-y
sep-u-cher-ing	se-rol-o-gy	sev-en-ti-eth	shad-i-er
se-pul-chral	se-ro-log-ic	sev-er	shad-i-est
se-quel	se-ro-log-i-cal	sev-er-a-bil-i-ty	shad-i-ly
se-quence	se-rol-o-gist	sev-er-a-ble	shaft-ing
se-quent	se-rous	sev-er-al	shag
se-quen-tial	ser-pent	sev-er-al-ly	shagged
se-quen-tial-ly	ser-pen-tine	sev-er-al-fold	shag-ging
se-ques-ter	ser-rate	sev-er-ance	shag-gi-ly
se-ques-tered	ser-rat-ing	se-vere	shake
se-ques-tra-ble	ser-ra-tion	se-ver-er	shak-en
se-ques-tra-tion	se-rum	se-ver-est	shak-ing
se-quin	se-rums	se-vere-ness	shake-down
se-quined	se-ra	se-ver-i-ty	shak-er
se-quoi-a	serv-ant	se-ver-i-ties	shake-up
se-ra-pe	serve	sew	shak-y
ser-aph	served	sew-age	shak-i-er
ser-aphs	serv-ing	sew-ing	shak-i-est
ser-a-phim	serv-er	sew-ing ma-chine	shak-i-ly
se-raph-ic	serv-ice	sex-less	shal-lot
ser-e-nade	serv-iced	sex-ol-o-gy	shal-low
ser-e-nad-ed	serv-ic-ing	sex-o-log-i-cal	shal-low-ness
ser-e-nad-ing	serv-ice-a-ble	sex-ol-o-gist	sham
ser-e-nad-er	serv-ice-a-bil-i-ty	sex-tant	shammed
ser-en-dip-i-ty	serv-ice-a-ble-ness	sex-tet	sham-ming
ser-en-dip-i-tous	serv-ice-a-bly	sex-ton	sha-man
se-rene	serv-ice-man	sex-tu-ple	sha-man-ism
se-rene-ness	ser-vile	sex-tu-pled	sha-man-ist
se-ren-i-ty	ser-vil-i-ty	sex-tu-pling	sham-bles
se-ren-i-ties	ser-vile-ness	sex-tu-plet	shame
serf	ser-vi-tude	sex-u-al	shamed
serge	ser-vo-mech-an-ism	sex-u-al-ly	sham-ing
ser-geant	ses-a-me	sex-u-al-i-ty	shame-faced
ser-geant at arms	ses-qui-cen-ten-ni-al	sex-y	shame-fac-ed-ly
ser-geant ma-jor	ses-sion	sex-i-er	shame-ful

shame-ful-ly
shame-ful-ness
sham-mer
sham-my
sham-poo
sham-pooed
sham-poo-ing
sham-poo-er
sham-rock
shan-tey
shan-ties
shan-ty-town
shape
shaped
shap-ing
shap-a-ble
shap-er
shape-less
shape-ly
shape-li-ier
shape-li-est
share
shared
shar-ing
shar-er
share-crop-per
share-crop
share-cropped
share-crop-ping
share-hold-er
shark-skin
sharp-en
sharp-en-er
sharp-er
sharp-eyed
sharp-ie
sharp-shoot-er
sharp-shoot-ing
sharp-tongued
sharp-wit-ted
sharp-wit-ted-ly
sharp-wit-ted-ness
shat-ter
shat-ter-proof
shave
shaved
shav-ing
shav-er
shawl
sheaf
sheaves

shear
sheared
shear-ing
shear-er
sheath
sheath-less
sheathe
sheathed
sheath-ing
sheath-er
shed
shed-ding
sheen
sheeny
sheen-i-er
sheep-dog
sheep-herd-er
sheep-herd-ing
sheep-ish
sheep-skin
sheer
sheer-ly
sheet-ing
sheik
shelf
shelves
shell
shelled
shel-lac
shel-lacked
shel-lack-ing
shell-fire
shell-fish
shell shock
shel-ter
shel-ter-er
shelve
shelved
shelv-ing
she-nan-i-gan
shep-herd
shep-herd-ess
sher-bet
sher-iff
sher-ry
sher-ries
shib-bo-leth
shield
shield-er
shift
shift-er

shift-less
shift-y
shift-i-er
shift-i-est
shift-i-ly
shil-ly--shal-ly
shil-ly-shal-lied
shil-ly-shal-ly-ing
shim-mer
shim-mery
shim-mer-i-er
shim-mer-i-est
shim-my
shim-mies
shim-mied
shim-my-ing
shin
shinned
shin-ning
shin-bone
shin-dig
shine
shined
shone
shin-ing
shin-er
shin-gle
shin-gled
shin-gling
shin-gler
shin-gles
shin-ing
shin-ing-ly
shin-ny
shin-nied
shin-ny-ing
shin-y
shin-i-er
shin-i-est
ship
shipped
ship-ping
ship-a-ble
ship-board
ship-build-er
ship-build-ing
ship-mate
ship-ment
ship-per
ship-yard
shirk

shirker
shirt-tail
shirt-waist
shish ke-bab
shiv-er
shiv-ery
shiv-er-i-er
shiv-er-i-est
shoal
shock-er
shock-ing
shod-dy
shod-di-er
shod-di-ly
shod-di-ness
shoe-horn
shoe-lace
shoe-mak-er
sho-er
shoe-string
shoo--in
shoot
shot
shoot-ing
shoot-er
shop
shopped
shop-ping
shop-keep-er
shop-lift-er
shop-lift-ing
shop-per
shop-talk
shop-worn
shore
shore-line
short
short-ly
short-ness
short-age
short--change
short--changed
short--chang-ing
short-com-ing
short-cut
short-cut-ting
short-en
short-en-er
short-en-ing
short-hand
short--hand-ed

short--lived
short--sight-ed
 short--sight-ed-ly
 short--sight-ed-ness
short--tem-pered
short--term
short-wave
short--wind-ed
shot-gun
 shot-gunned
 shot-gun-ning
shoul-der
shoul-der blade
shout-er
shout-ing
shove
 shoved
 shov-ing
 shov-er
shov-el
 shov-eled
 shov-el-ing
shov-el-ful
show
 showed
 shown
 show-ing
show-bill
show-boat
 show-case
 show-cased
 show-cas-ing
show-down
show-er
 show-ery
show-man
 show-men
 show-man-ship
show-off
show-piece
show-place
show-room
show-y
 show-i-er
 show-i-est
 show-i-ly
shrap-nel
shred
 shred-ded
 shred-ding
 shred-der

shrew
shrewd
 shrewd-ly
 shrewd-ness
shrew-ish
shriek
shrill
 shirl-ly
shrimp
shrine
 shrined
 shrin-ing
shrink
 shrunk-ed
 shrink-a-ble
 shrink-er
shrink-age
shriv-el
 shriv-eled
 shriv-el-ing
shroud
shrub-bery
 shrub-ber-ies
shrub-by
 shrub-bi-er
 shrub-bi-est
shrug
 shrugged
 shrug-ging
shuck-er
shud-der
 shud-dery
suf-fle
 shuf-fled
 shuf-fling
 shuf-fler
shuf-fle-board
shun
 shunned
 shun-ning
 shun-ner
shunt
 shunt-er
shut-down
shut-eye
shut-in
shut-off
shut-out
shut-ter
shut-tle
 shut-tled

shut-tling
shut-tle-like
shy
 shi-er
 shy-est
 shy-ness
shy-ster
sib-i-lant
 sib-i-lance
sib-ling
sick
 sicked
 sick-ing
sick-bed
sick-en
 sick-en-ing
sick-ish
sick-le
sick-ly
 sick-li-er
 sick-li-est
sick-ness
sick-room
side-arm
side-board
 sid-ed
side-kick
side-line
 side-lined
 side-lin-ing
side--long
side-show
side-split-ting
side-step
 side-step-ped
 side-step-ping
side-swipe
 side-swiped
 side-swip-ing
side-track
side-ways
 sid-ing
si-dle
 si-dled
 si-dling
siege
si-en-na
si-er-ra
si-es-ta
sieve
 sieved

siev-ing
sift-er
sift-ings
sigh-er
sight-ed
sight-less
sight-ly
sight-read
 sight-read-ing
sight-see-ing
 sight-see-er
sig-nal
 sig-naled
 sig-nal-ing
 sig-nal-er
sig-nal-man
 sig-nal-men
sig-na-to-ry
 sig-na-to-ries
sig-na-ture
sign-board
sig-net
sig-nif-i-cance
sig-nif-i-cant
sig-ni-fi-ca-tion
sig-ni-fy
 sig-ni-fied
 sig-ni-fy-ing
 sig-ni-fi-a-ble
 sig-ni-fi-er
sign-post
si-lage
si-lence
 si-lenced
 si-lenc-ing
 si-lenc-er
si-lent
si-lent part-ner
sil-hou-ette
 sil-hou-et-ted
 sil-hou-et-ting
sil-ic-a
sil-i-con
sil-i-cone
silk-en
silk-like
silk-weed
silk-worm
silk-y
 silk-i-er
 silk-i-est

silk-i-ly
sil-ly
sil-li-er
sil-li-est
sil-li-ness
si-lo
si-los
si-loed
si-lo-ing
silt
sil-ta-tion
silt-y
silt-i-er
silt-i-est
sil-ver
sil-ver-fish
sil-ver-fox
sil-ver-ware
sil-ver-y
sim-i-an
sim-i-lar
sim-i-lar-i-ty
sim-i-lar-i-ties
sim-i-le
si-mil-i-tude
sim-mer
si-mon-ize
si-mon-ized
si-mon-iz-ing
sim-pa-ti-co
sim-per
sim-per-er
sim-per-ing-ly
sim-ple
sim-pler
sim-plest
sim-ple-ness
sim-ple--mind-ed
sim-ple sen-tence
sim-ple-ton
sim-plex
sim-plic-i-ty
sim-plic-i-ties
sim-pli-fy
sim-pli-fied
sim-pli-fy-ing
sim-pli-fi-ca-tion
sim-pli-fi-er
sim-plism
sim-plis-tic
sim-plis-ti-cal-ly

sim-ply
sim-u-late
sim-u-lat-ed
sim-u-lat-ing
sim-u-la-tion
sim-u-la-tive
sim-u-la-tor
si-mul-cast
si-mul-cast-ing
si-mul-ta-ne-ous
si-mul-ta-ne-ous-ly
si-mul-ta-ne-i-ty
sin
sinned
sin-ning
sin-cere
sin-cer-i-ty
si-ne-cure
si-ne qua non
sin-ew
sin-ew-y
sin-ful
sin-ful-ly
sin-ful-ness
sing
sing-ing
sing-a-ble
singe
singed
singe-ing
sing-er
sin-gle
sin-gled
sin-gling
sin-gle-ness
sin-gle-brest-ed
sin-gle--hand-ed
sin-gle-hand-ed-ly
sin-gle--mind-ed
sin-gle--mind-ed-ly
sin-gle--space
sin-gle--spaced
sin-gle--spac-ing
sin-gle-ton
sin-gle--track
sin-gly
sing-song
sin-gu-lar
sin-gu-lar-i-ty
sin-gu-lar-i-ties
sin-is-ter

sin-is-ter-ness
sink-a-ble
sink-er
sink-hole
sin-less
sin-ner
sin-u-ate
sin-u-at-ed
sin-u-at-ing
sin-u-ous
sin-u-os-i-ty
sin-u-ous-ness
si-nus
si-nus-i-tis
sip
sipped
sip-ping
sip-per
si-phon
sire
sired
sir-ing
si-ren
sir-loin
sis-sy
sis-sies
sis-si-fied
sis-sy-ish
sis-ter
sis-ter-li-ness
sis-ter-ly
sis-ter-in-law
sis-ters-in-law
si-tar
sit-in
sit-ter
sit-ting
sit-u-ate
sit-u-at-ed
sit-u-at-ing
sit-u-a-tion
six--pack
six--shoot-er
six-teen
six-teenth
sixth
six-ty
six-ti-eth
siz-a-ble
siz-a-ble-ness
siz-a-bly

size
sized
siz-ing
siz-zle
siz-zled
siz-zling
siz-zler
skate
skat-ed
skat-ing
skat-er
ske-dad-dle
ske-dad-dled
ske-dad-dling
skein
skel-e-ton
skel-e-tal
skep-tic
skep-ti-cal
skep-ti-cism
sketch
sketch-er
sketch-book
sketch-y
sketch-i-er
sketch-i-est
sketch-i-ly
skew-er
skew-ness
ski
skied
ski-ing
ski-er
skid
skid-ded
skid-ding
skid-der
skilled
skil-let
skill-ful
skill-ful-ly
skill-ful-ness
skim
skimmed
skim-ming
skim-mer
skimp
skimp-i-ly
skimp-y
skimp-i-er
skimp-i-est

skin	slak-ing	slea-zi-est	**slim**
skinned	**sla-lom**	**sled**	slim-mer
skin-ning	**slam**	sled-ded	slim-mest
skin--deep	slammeed	sled-ding	slimmed
skin dive	slam-ming	sled-der	slim-ming
skin div-ing	**slam-bang**	**sledge**	slim-ness
skin div-er	**slan-der**	sledged	**slime**
skin-flint	slan-der-er	sledg-ing	slimed
skin-less	slan-der-ous	**sleek**	slim-ing
skin-ner	**slang**	sleek-er	**slimy**
skin-ny	slang-i-er	sleek-ness	slim-i-er
skin-ni-er	slang-i-est	**sleep-er**	slim-i-est
skin-ni-est	**slant**	**sleep-less**	slim-i-ly
skin-tight	slant-ways	sleep-less-ness	**sling-er**
skip-per	slant-wise	**sleep-walk**	**sling-shoot**
skir-mish	**slap**	sleep-walk-er	**slink-y**
skir-mish-er	slapp-ed	sleep-walk-ing	slink-i-er
skirt-er	slap-ping	**sleep-y**	slink-i-est
skirt-ing	slap-per	sleep-i-er	**slip**
skit-ter	**slap-dash**	sleep-i-est	slipped
skit-tish	**slap-hap-py**	sleep-i-ly	slip-ping
skiv-vy	slap-hap-pi-er	**sleep-y-head**	**slip-cov-er**
skiv-vies	slap-hap-pi-est	**sleet**	**slip-knot**
skoal	**slap-stick**	sleet-y	**slip--on**
skul-dug-ger-y	**slash-er**	sleet-i-ness	**slip-o-ver**
skulk-er	**slash-ing**	**sleeve**	**slip-page**
skull-cap	**slat**	sleeved	**slip-per**
skunk	slat-ted	sleev-ing	**slip-per-y**
sky	slat-ting	sleeve-less	slip-per-i-er
skies	**slate**	**sleigh**	slip-per-i-est
skied	slat-ed	sleigh-er	**slip-py**
sky-ing	slat-ing	**sleight**	**slip-shod**
sky-blue	**slath-er**	**slen-der**	**slip-stick**
sky-cap	**slat-tern**	slen-der-ness	**slip-up**
sky-div-ing	slat-tern-ly	**slen-der-ize**	**slit**
sky-rock-et	**slaugh-ter**	slen-der-ized	slit-ting
sky-svap-er	slaugh-ter-er	slen-der-iz-ing	slit-ter
sky-ward	**slaugh-ter-house**	**sleuth**	**slith-er**
sky-way	**slave**	**slice**	slith-ery
sky-writ-ing	slaved	sliced	**sliv-er**
sky-writ-er	slav-ing	slic-ing	sliv-er-er
slab	**slav-er**	slic-er	sliv-er-like
slabbed	**slav-er-y**	**slick-er**	**slob-ber**
slab-bing	**slav-ish**	**slick-ness**	slob-ber-er
slack	sla-vish-ly	**slide**	slob-ber-ing-ly
slack-ness	**slay**	slid	**sloe--eyed**
slack-en	slain	slid-ing	**slo-gan**
slack-er	slay-ing	slid-er	slo-gan-eer
slack-jawed	slay-er	**slight**	**slop**
slake	**slea-zy**	slight-er	slopped
slaked	slea-zi-er	slight-ing	slop-ping

slope
 sloped
 slop-ing
 slop-er
slop-py
 slop-pi-er
 slop-pi-est
 slo-pi-ly
 slop-pi-ness
slosh-y
 slosh-i-er
 slosh-i-est
slot
 slot-ted
 slot-ting
sloth
 sloth-ful
 sloth-ful-ly
slouch
 slouch-er
 slouch-i-ly
 slouch-i-ness
 slouch-y
 slouch-i-er
 slouch-i-est
slough
 slough-y
 slough-i-er
 slough-i-est
slov-en
slov-en-ly
 slov-en-li-ness
slow-down
slow--mo-tion
slow-poke
slow--wit-ted
sludge
 slug-y
 sludg-i-er
 sludg-i-est
slug
 slugged
 slug-ging
 slug-ger
slug-gard
 slug-gard-li-ness
slug-gish
 slug-gish-ness
sluice
 sluiced
 sluic-ing

slum
 slummed
 slum-ming
slum-ber
 slum-ber-er
slum-ber-ous
slur
 slurred
 slur-ring
slush
 slush-i-ness
 slush-y
 slush-i-er
 slush-i-est
slut
 slut-tish
sly
smack
 smack-ing
small--mind-ed
 small--mind-ed-ness
small-pox
small--time
 small--tim-er
smart
 smart-ness
smart al-eck
 smart-al-eck-y
smart-en
smash
 smash-ing
smash--up
smat-ter
 smat-ter-er
 smat-ter-ing
smear
 smear-er
smear-y
 smear-i-er
 smear-i-est
smell
 smelled
 smel-ling
 smell-er
 smell-y
 smell-i-er
 smell-i-est
smelt
smelt-er
 smelt-ery
smid-gen

snile
 smil-er
 smil-ing-ly
smirch
smirk
 smirk-er
 smirk-ing-ly
smite
 smote
 smit-ten
 smit-ting
 smit-er
smith-er-eens
smit-ten
smock-ing
smog-gy
 smog-gi-er
 smog-gi-est
smoke
 smoked
 smok-ing
 smoke-less
smoke-house
 smok-er
 smoke-stack
 smok-ing jack-et
smok-y
 smok-i-er
 smok-i-est
 smok-i-ly
smol-der
smooth
 smooth-er
 smooth-ness
smooth-en
smooth-ie
smoth-er
 smoth-er-y
 smoth-er-i-er
 smoth-er-i-est
smudge
 smudged
 smudg-ing
 smudg-i-ly
smug
 smug-ger
 smug-gest
 smug-ly
 smug-ness
smug-gle
 smug-gled

 smug-gling
 smug-gler
smut
 smut-ted
 smut-ting
smut-ty
 smut-ti-er
 smut-ti-est
 smut-ti-ly
sna-fu
 sna-fued
 sna-fu-ing
snag
 snagged
 snag-ging
 snag-gy
snag-gle-tooth
 snag-gle-teeth
 snag-gle-toothed
snail
 snail-like
 snail-paced
snake
snake-bite
snake-skin
snak-y
 snak-i-er
 snak-i-est
snap
 snapped
 snap-ping
snap-back
snap-drag-on
snap-per
snap-pish
 snap-pish-ness
snap-py
 snap-pi-er
 snap-pi-est
 snap-pi-ly
snap-shot
snare
 snared
 snar-ing
 snar-er
snarl
 snarl-er
 snarl-y
 snarl-i-er
 snarl-i-est
snatch

snatch-i-er	snob-bish	snubbed	**so-cial-ize**
snatch-i-est	snob-bish-ness	snub-bing	so-cial-ized
snatch-i-ly	**snoop**	snub-ber	so-cial-iz-ing
snaz-zy	snoop-y	**snub-by**	so-cial-i-za-tion
snaz-zi-er	snoop-i-er	snub-bi-er	so-cial-iz-er
snaz-zi-est	snoop-i-est	snub-bi-est	**so-ci-e-ty**
sneak-er	snoop-er	snub-bi-ness	so-ci-e-ties
sneak-ing	**snoot-y**	snub--nosed	so-ci-e-tal
sneak-y	snoot-i-er	**snuf-fle**	**so-ci-o-ec-o-nom-ic**
sneak-i-er	snoot-i-est	**snuff-y**	**so-ci-ol-o-gy**
sneak-i-est	snoot-i-ly	snuff-i-er	so-ci-ol-o-log-i-cal
sneak-i-ly	snoot-i-ness	snuff-i-est	so-ci-ol-o-gist
sneer	**snooze**	**snug**	**so-ci-o-po-lit-i-cal**
sneer-er	snoozed	**snug-gle**	**sock-et**
sneer-ing-ly	snooz-ing	snug-gled	**sod**
sneeze	snooz-er	snug-gling	sod-ded
sneezed	**snore**	**soak**	sod-ding
sneez-ing	snored	soak-age	**so-da**
sneez-er	snor-ing	soak-er	**so-dal-i-ty**
sneez-y	snor-er	soak-ing-ly	so-dal-i-ties
sneez-i-er	**snor-kel**	**so--and--so**	**sod-den**
sneez-i-est	**snort**	**soap-box**	sod-den-ness
snick-er	snort-er	**soap-suds**	**so-di-um**
snif-fle	**snot-ty**	**soap-y**	**sod-om-y**
snif-fled	snot-ti-er	soap-i-er	**so-ev-er**
snif-fling	snot-ti-est	soap-i-est	**so-fa**
snif-fler	**snout**	**soap-i-ly**	**soft**
snif-fy	snout-ed	soap-i-ness	soft-ness
snif-fi-er	snout-y	**soar-er**	**soft-ball**
snif-fi-est	snout-i-er	**sob**	**soft--boiled**
snif-fi-ly	snout-i-est	sobbed	**sof-ten**
snif-ter	**snow-ball**	sob-bing	sof-ten-er
snip	**snow-blow-er**	sob-ber	**soft--head-ed**
snipped	**snow-bound**	**so-ber**	**soft--heart-ed**
snip-ping	**snow-cap**	so-ber-ing-ly	soft--heart-ed-ness
snip-per	**snow-drift**	so-ber-ness	**soft ped-al**
snipe	**snow-fall**	**so-bri-e-ty**	soft-ped-aled
sniped	**snow-flake**	**so-bri-quet**	soft-ped-al-ing
snip-ing	**snow-man**	**so--called**	**soft--shell**
snip-er	snow-men	**soc-cer**	**soft--shoe**
snip-py	**snow-mo-bile**	**so-cia-ble**	**soft--spok-en**
snip-pi-er	**snow-plow**	so-cia-bil-i-ty	**soft-ware**
snip-pi-est	**snow-shoe**	so-cia-bly	**soft-wood**
snip-pi-ly	snow-shoed	**so-cial**	**soft-y**
snitch-er	snow-shoe-ing	so-ci-al-i-ty	sof-ties
sniv-el	**snow-suit**	so-cial-ly	**sog-gy**
sniv-eled	**snow--white**	**so-cial-ism**	sog-gi-er
sniv-el-ing	**snow-y**	**so-cial-ist**	sog-gi-est
sniv-el-er	snow-i-er	so-cial-is-tic	sog-gi-ly
snob	snow-i-est	so-cial-is-ti-cal-ly	sog-gi-ness
snob-ber-y	**snub**	**so-cial-ite**	**so-journ**

so-journ-er
sol-ace
sol-aced
sol-ac-ing
sol-ac-er
so-lar
so-lar-i-um
so-lar-i-ums
so-lar-ia
so-lar-ize
so-lar-ized
so-lar-iz-ing
so-lar-i-za-tion
sol-der
sol-der-er
sol-dier
sol-dier-y
sol-e-cism
sole-ly
sol-emn
sol-emn-ly
sol-emn-less
so-lem-ni-ty
so-lem-ni-ties
sol-em-nize
sol-em-nized
sol-em-niz-ing
sol-em-ni-za-tion
sole-ness
so-lic-it
so-lic-i-ta-tion
so-lic-i-tor
so-lic-i-tous
so-lic-i-tous-ness
so-lic-i-tude
sol-id
so-lid-i-ty
sol-id-ness
sol-i-dar-i-ty
sol-i-dar-i-ties
so-lid-i-fy
so-lid-i-fied
so-lid-i-fy-ing
so-lid-i-fi-ca-tion
so-lil-o-quize
so-lil-o-quized
so-lil-o-quiz-ing
so-lil-o-quist
so-lil-o-quy
so-lil-o-quies
sol-i-taire

sol-i-tar-y
sol-i-tar-ies
sol-i-tar-i-ly
sol-i-tar-i-ness
sol-i-tude
so-lo
so-loed
so-lo-ing
so-lo-ist
sol-stice
sol-u-ble
sol-u-bil-i-ty
sol-u-bly
sol-ute
so-lu-tion
solve
solved
solv-ing
solv-a-ble
solv-a-bil-i-ty
solv-er
sol-vent
sol-ven-cy
so-mat-ic
so-ma-to-type
som-ber
som-ber-ly
som-ber-ness
som-bre-ro
som-bre-ros
some-bod-y
some-bod-ies
some-day
some-how
some-place
som-er-sault
some-thing
some-time
some-times
some-way
some-what
some-where
sosm-nam-bu-late
som-no-lent
som-no-lence
som-no-len-cy
so-nar
so-na-ta
song-bird
song-fest
song-ster

song-stress
song-writ-er
son-ic
son--in--law
sons--in--law
son-net
son-ny
son-nies
so-no-rous
so-nor-i-ty
so-no-rous-ness
soon-er
soothe
soothed
sooth-ing
sooth-er
sooth-say-er
sooth-say-ing
soot-y
soot-i-er
soot-i-est
soot-i-ly
sop
sopped
sop-ping
soph-ist
soph-ism
so-phis-tic
so-phis-ti-cal
so-phis-ti-cate
so-phis-ti-cat-ed
so-phis-ti-cat-ing
so-phis-ti-ca-tion
so-phis-ti-ca-tor
soph-ist-ry
soph-ist-ries
soph-o-more
soph-o-mor-ic
soph-o-mor-i-cal
soph-o-mor-i-cal-ly
sop-o-rif-ic
sop-py
sop-pi-er
sop-pi-est
so-pran-o
so-pran-os
sor-cer-er
sor-cer-ess
sor-cer-y
sor-cer-ies
sor-cer-ous

sor-did
sor-did-ness
sore
sor-er
sor-est
sore-ly
sore-ness
sore-head
sore-head-ed
sor-ghum
so-ror-i-ty
so-ror-i-ties
sor-rel
sor-row
sor-row-er
sor-row-ful
sor-ry
sor-ri-er
sor-ri-est
sor-ri-ly
sort-a-ble
sort-er
sor-tie
so--so
sot
sot-ted
sot-tish
sot-tish-ness
sot-vo-vo-ce
sought
soul-ful
soul-ful-ly
soul-ful-ness
soul-less
soul-searching
sound
sound-a-ble
sound-ly
sound-ness
sound-box
sound-er
sound-ing
sound-less
sound-less-ly
sound-proof
soup-y
soup-i-er
soup-i-est
sour
sour-ish
sour-ness

sour-ball	**spa-ghet-ti**	speak-ing	**spec-u-late**
source	**span**	speak-a-ble	spec-u-lat-ed
souse	spanned	**speak-eas-y**	spec-u-lat-ing
soused	span-ning	speak-eas-ies	spec-u-la-tion
sous-ing	**span-gle**	**speak-er**	spec-u-la-tive
south-bound	span-gled	speak-er-ship	spec-u-la-tor
south-east	span-gling	**spear-er**	**speech-i-fy**
south-east-er	**span-iel**	**spear-head**	speech-i-fie
south-east-er-ly	**spank-er**	**spear-mint**	speech-i-fy-ing
south-east-ern	**spank-ing**	**spe-cial**	**speech-less**
south-east-ward	**spar**	spe-cial-ly	speech-less-ness
south-east-ward-ly	sparred	**spe-cial-ist**	**speed**
south-er	spar-ring	**spe-cial-ize**	speed-ed
south-er-ly	**spare**	spe-cial-ized	speed-ing
south-ern	spared	spe-cial-iz-ing	speed-er
south-ern-most	spar-ing	spe-cial-i-za-tion	speed-ster
south-ern-er	spar-er	**spe-cial-ty**	**speed-boat**
south-paw	spar-est	spe-cial-ties	speed-boat-ing
south-ward	spar-a-ble	**spe-cie**	**speed-om-e-ter**
south-ward-ly	spare-ness	**spe-cies**	**speed--up**
south-west	**spare-rib**	**spec-i-fia-ble**	**speed-way**
south-west-er	**spar-ing**	**spe-cif-ic**	**speed-y**
south-west-ern	spar-ing-ness	spe-cif-i-cal-ly	speed-i-er
south-west-ern-er	**spark-er**	spec-i-fic-i-ty	speed-i-est
south-west-ward	**spar-kle**	**spec-i-fi-ca-tion**	speed-i-ly
south-west-ward-ly	spar-kled	**spec-i-fy**	speed-i-ness
sou-ve-nir	spar-kling	spec-i-fied	**spe-le-ol-o-gy**
sov-er-eign	**spar-kler**	spec-i-fy-ing	spe-le-ol-o-gist
sov-er-eign-ty	**spar-row**	spec-i-fi-er	**spell**
sov-er-eign-ties	**spar-row-grass**	**spec-i-men**	spelled
so-vi-et	**sparse**	**spe-cious**	spell-ing
sow-er	spars-er	spe-ci-os-i-ty	**spell-bind**
soy-bean	spars-est	spe-ci-os-i-ties	spell-bouns
space	**spasm**	spe-cious-ness	spell-bind-ing
spaced	**spas-mod-ic**	**speck-le**	spell-bind-er
spac-ing	spas-mod-i-cal	speck-led	**spell-er**
space-less	spas-mod-i-cal-ly	speck-ling	**spe-lun-ker**
spac-er	**spas-tic**	**spec-ta-cle**	**spend**
space-craft	spas-ti-cal-ly	spec-ta-cled	spent
space-man	**spat**	**spec-tac-u-lar**	spend-ing
space-men	spat-ted	spec-tac-u-lar-ly	spend-a-ble
space-ship	spat-ting	**spec-ta-tor**	spend-er
space-walk	**spa-tial**	**spec-ter**	**spend-thrift**
spa-cious	spa-cial	**spec-tral**	**sper-ma-cet-i**
spa-cious-ness	spa-ti-al-i-ty	**spec-tro-scope**	**sper-mat-ic**
spade	spa-tial-ly	spec-tro-scop-ic	**sper-ma-to-zo-on**
spad-ed	**spat-ter**	spec-tro-scop-i-cal	sper-ma-to-zo-a
spad-ing	**spat-u-la**	spec-tros-co-py	sper-ma-tozo-ic
spade-ful	**spawn**	**spec-trum**	**spew-er**
spad-er	**speak**	spec-tra	**sphag-num**
spade-work	spok-en	spec-trums	**sphere**

sphered
spher-ing
spher-ic
sphe-ric-i-ty
sphe-roid
sphe-roi-dal
sphinc-ter
sphin-ter-ic
sphinx
sphinxes
sphin-ges
spice
spiced
spi-cule
spic-u-lar
spic-u-late
spic-y
spic-i-er
spic-i-esst
spic-i-ly
spi-der
spi-der-y
spiel
spiel-er
spi-er
spiff-y
spiff-i-er
spiff-i-est
spig-ot
spike
spiked
spik-ing
spik-y
spik-i-er
spik-i-est
spill
spilled
spill-ing
spil-lage
spill-way
spin
spun
spin-ning
spin-ach
spi-nal
spi-nal-ly
spin-dle
spin-dled
spin-dling
spin-dle-legs
spin-dle-leg-ged

spin-dly
spin-dli-er
spin-dli-est
spine-less
spin-et
spin-na-ker
spin-ner
spin-ning wheel
spin--off
spi-nose
spi-nous
spin-ster
spin-y
spin-i-ness
spi-ra-cle
spi-ral
spi-raled
spired
spir-ing
spir-it
spir-it-ed
spir-it-ism
spir-ir-ist
spir-it-less
spir-it-les-ness
spir-i-tous
spir-it-u-al
spir-it-u-al-ly
spir-it-u-al-ism
spir-it-u-al-ist
spir-it-u-al-is-tic
spir-it-u-al-i-ty
spir-it-u-al-i-ties
spir-it-u-al-ize
spir-it-u-al-ized
spir-it-u-al-iz-ing
spir-it-u-al-i-za-tion
spir-it-u-ous
spir-it-u-os-i-ty
spi-ro-chete
spit
spat
spit-ting
spit-ter
spite
spit-ed
spit-ing
spite-ful
spit-fire
spit-tle
spit-toon

splash
splash-er
splashy
splash-i-er
splash-i-est
splash-i-ly
splash-board
splat-ter
splay-foot
splay-feet
splay-foot-ed
spleen
spleen-ful
splen-did
splen-dif-er-ous
sple-net-ic
splice
spliced
splic-er
splin-ter
splin-tery
split
split-ting
split-a-ble
split-ter
split--lev-el
split--sec-ond
splotch
spotch-y
splotch-i-er
splotch-i-est
splurge
splurged
splurg-ing
splut-ter
splut-ter-er
spoil
spoil-ed
spoil-ing
spoil-age
spoil-er
spoil-sport
spoke
spoked
spok-ing
spo-ken
spokes-man
spokes-men
spokes-wom-an
spokes-wom-en
sponge

sponged
spong-ing
spong-er
spon-gy
spon-gi-er
spon-gi-est
spon-sor
spon-sor-ship
spon-ta-ne-i-ty
spon-ta-ne-i-ties
spon-ta-ne-ous
spon-ta-ne-ous-ly
spook-ish
spook-y
spook-i-er
spook-i-est
spook-i-ly
spoon-er-ism
spoon-er-is-tic
spoon--fed
spoon--feed
spoon--feed-ing
spoon-ful
spoon-fuls
spo-rad-ic
spo-rad-i-cal
spo-rad-i-cal-ly
spo-ran-gi-um
spo-ran-gia
spore
spored
spor-ing
sport
sport-ing
sport-ing-ly
spor-tive
sports-cast
sports-cast-er
sports-man
sports-wear
sports-writ-er
sport-y
sport-i-er
sport-i-est
sport-i-ly
spot
spot-ted
spot-ting
spot-less
spot-less-ly
spot-light

spot-ted
spot-ted fe-ver
spot-ter
spot-ty
spot-ti-er
spouse
spout
spout-er
sprain
sprawl
spray
spread-ing
spread--ea-gle
spread--ea-gled
spread--ea-gling
spread-er
sprig
sprigged
sprig-ging
spright-ly
spright-li-er
spright-li-est
spring
spring-ing
spring-board
spring--clean-ing
spring-time
spring-y
spring-i-er
sprin-kle
sprin-kled
sprin-kling
sprink-ler
sprint
sprint-er
sprock-et
spruce
spruc-er
spruc-est
spruced
spruc-ing
spry
spry-er
spry-est
spry-ly
spue
spued
spu-ing
spume
spumed
spum-ing

spum-ous
spunk-y
spunk-i-er
spunk-i-ness
spur
spurred
spur-ring
spu-ri-ous
spu-ri-ous-ness
spurner
spurt
spurt-er
spur-tive
sput-nik
sput-ter
sput-ter-er
spu-tum
spu-ta
spy
spies
spied
spy-ing
spy-glass
squad-ron
squal-id
squal-id-ly
squal-id-ness
squall
squally
squall-i-er
squall-i-est
squal-or
squan-der
squan-der-er
square
squared
squar-ing
square-ly
square-ness
square-dance
square-danced
square-danc-ing
squar-ish
squar-ish-ly
squash
squash-er
squash-es
squash-y
squash-i-er
squash-i-est
squat

squat-ted
squat-ting
squat-ly
squat-ter
squat-ty
squat-ti-er
squat-ti-est
squawk
squawk-er
sqauwk-y
squawk-i-er
squawk-i-est
squeak
squeal
squeal-er
squeam-ish
squeam-ish-ly
squeam-ish-ness
squee-gee
squeeze
squeez-ed
squeez-ing
squeez-er
squelch
squelch-er
squib
squid
squig-gle
squig-gled
squig-gling
squint--eyed
squire
squired
squir-ing
squirm
squirmy
squirm-i-er
squirm-i-est
squir-rel
squirt
squirt-er
stab
stabbed
stab-bing
stab-ber
sta-bil-i-ty
sta-bil-i-ties
sta-bi-lize
sta-bi-lized
sta-bi-liz-ing
sta-bi-li-za-tion

sta-bi-liz-er
sta-ble
sta-bled
stac-ca-to
stack-er
sta-di-um
staff-er
stag
stagged
stag-ging
stage-coach
stage-hand
stage--struck
stag-ger
stag-ger-cr
stag-ger-ing
stag-nant
stag-nan-cy
stag-nate
stag-nat-ed
stag-nat-ing
stag-na-tion
stag-y
stag-i-er
stag-i-est
stag-i-ly
stain
stain-a-ble
stained
stain-er
stained glass
stain-less
stair-case
stair-way
stair-well
stake
staked
stak-ing
stake-hold-er
sta-lac-tite
sta-lag-mite
stalk
stalled
stal-lion
stal-wart
stal-wart-ness
sta-men
sta-mens
stam-i-na
stam-mer
stam-mer-ing-ly

stamp-er
stance
stand
stand-ing
stand-er
stand-ard
stand-ard-ize
stand-ard-ized
stand-by
stnad-ee
stand--in
stand--off-ish
stand--off-ish-ness
stand-out
stand-pipe
stand-point
stand-still
sta-nine
stan-za
stan-za-ic
staph-y-lo-coc-cus
sta-ple
sta-pled
sta-pling
sta-pler
star
star-board
star-dom
stare
stared
star-fish
star-gazed
star-gaz-ing
star-let
star-light
star-ling
star-ry
star-ri-er
star-ri-est
star-ry--eyed
star-span-gled
start-er
star-tle
star-tled
star-tling
star-tling-ly
star-va-tion
starve
starved
starv-ing
a-sis

state
stat-ed
stat-ing
stat-a-ble
state-craft
state-hood
state-less
state-less-ness
state-ly
state-li-er
state-li-est
state-ment
state-room
state-side
states-man
states-men
states-man-like
states-man-ship
stat-ic
stat-ics
sta-tion
sta-tion-ar-y
ssta-tion-er
sta-tion-er-y
stat-ism
stat-ist
sta-tic-tic
sta-tis-ti-cal
sta-tic-ti-cal-ly
stat-is-ti-cian
sta-tis-tics
sta-tor
stat-u-ar-y
stat-u-ar-ies
stat-ue
stat-u-esque
stat-u-ette
stat-ure
sta-tus
stat-ute
staunch
stave
staved
stav-ing
stay
stay-ed
stay-ing
stay-er
stead-fast
stead-fast-ly
stead-y

steam-boat
steam-er
steam-fit-ting
steam-roll-er
steam-ship
steam-y
steam-i-er
steam-i-est
steam-i-ly
ste-a-tite
sted-fast
steel-head
steel-works
steel-work-er
steel-y
steel-i-er
steel-yard
steep
steep-ly
steep-en
stee-ple
stee-ple-chase
stee-ple-chas-er
stee-ple-jack
steer
steer-a-ble
steer-er
steer-age
stein
stem
stemmed
stem-ware
stem-wind-er
stem-wind-ing
sten-cil
sten-ciled
sten-cil-ing
ste-nog-ra-pher
ste-nog-ra-phy
sten-o-graph-ic
sten-o-raph-i-cal-ly
sten-to-ri-an
step
stepped
step-ping
step-broth-er
step-child
step-child-ren
step-daugh-ter
step-fa-ther
step-lad-der

step-moth-er
step-par-ent
stepped-up
step-sis-ter
step-son
ster-e-o
ster-e-os
ster-e-o-phon-ic
ster-e-o-phon-i-cal-ly
ster-e-o-scope
ster-e-o-scop-ic
ster-e-o-type
ster-e-o-typed
ster-e-o-typ-ing
ster-ile
ste-ril-i-ty
ster-i-lize
ster-i-lized
ster-i-liz-ing
ster-i-li-za-tion
ster-i-li-zer
ster-ling
stern
stern-ly
stern-ness
ster-num
ster-na
ster-nums
stern-wheel-er
ster-oid
steth-o-scope
steth-o-scop-ic
ste-ve-dore
ste-ve-dored
ste-ve-dor-ing
ste-ward
stew-ard-ness
stick-er
stick-ing
stick-le-back
stick-ler
stick-pin
stick-up
stick-y
stick-i-er
stick-i-est
stiff
stiff-ly
stiff-ness
stiff-en
stiff-en-er

stiff--necked	**stir**	**store-keep-er**	**stran-ger**
sti-fle	stirred	**store-room**	**stran-gu-la-tion**
sti-fled	stri-ring-ly	**sto-ried**	strn-gu-late
sti-fling	**stir-rup**	**storm-y**	stran-gu-lat-ed
sti-fler	**stitch**	storm-i-er	stran-gu-lat-ing
sti-fling-ly	stitch-er	storm-i-est	**strap**
stig-ma	**stock-ade**	storm-i-ly	srapped
stig-mas	stock-ad-ed	storm-i-ness	**stra-te-gic**
stig-ma-ta	stock-ad-ing	**sto-ry**	str-te-gi-cal-ly
stig-ma-tic	**stock-brok-er**	sto-ries	**strat-e-gy**
stig-mat-i-cal-ly	**stock-hold-er**	sto-ry-ing	strat-e-gies
stig-ma-tize	**Stock-holm**	**sto-ry-book**	strat-e-gist
stig-ma-tized	**stock-ing**	**sto-ry-tell-er**	**strat-i-fi-ca-tion**
stig-ma-tiz-ing	**stock-yard**	stor-y-tell-ing	**strat-i-fy**
sti-let-to	**stodg-y**	**stout**	strat-i-fied
sti-let-tos	stodg-i-er	stout-ly	strat-i-fy-ing
sti-let-toes	stodg-i-est	stout-ness	**stra-to-cu-mu-lus**
still-birth	stodg-i-ly	**stout--heart-ed**	**strat-o-sphere**
still-born	**sto-ic**	**stove**	strat-o-spher-ic
still life	**sto-i-cal**	stoved	**stra-tum**
still-ness	**stoke**	stov-ing	-stra-ta
stilt-ed	stoked	**stove-pipe**	stra-tums
stilt-ed-ly	stok-ing	**stow-age**	**stra-tus**
stim-u-lant	stok-er	**stow-a-way**	stra-ti
stim-u-late	**stol-id**	**stra-bis-mus**	**straw-ber-ry**
stim-u-lat-ed	sto-lid-i-ty	**strad-dle**	straw-ber-ries
stim-u-lat-ing	stol-id-ly	strad-dled	**stream-er**
stim-u-la-tive	**sto-ma**	strad-dler	**stream-line**
stim-u-lus	sto-ma-ta	**strafe**	stream-lined
stim-u-li	sto-mas	strafed	stream-lin-ing
sting-er	**stom-ach**	straf-ing	**street-car**
sting-ing-ly	**stom-ach-er**	**strag-gle**	**street-walk-er**
stin-gy	**stone-ma-son**	strag-gled	street-walk-ing
stin-gi-er	stone-ma-son-ry	strag-gling	**strength-en**
stin-gi-est	**stone-wall**	strag-gler	strength-en-er
stin-gi-ly	**ston-y**	**strag-gly**	**stren-u-ous**
stin-gi-ness	ston-i-er	strag-gli-er	stren-u-os-i-ty
stink	ston-i-est	strag-gli-est	stren-u-ous-ly
stink-ing	ston-i-ly	**straight-en**	**strep-to-coc-cus**
stink-er	**stop**	straight-en-er	strep-to-coc-ci
stink-y	stopped	**straight-for-ward**	strep-to-coc-cal
stink-i-er	**stop-light**	straight-for-ward-ly	strep-to-coc-cic
stink-i-est	**stop-o-ver**	**straight-way**	**strep-to-my-cin**
stint-er	**stop-page**	**strain-er**	**stress**
sti-pend	**stop-per**	**strait-en**	stress-ful
stip-ple	**stop-watch**	**strait-jack-et**	stress-ful-ly
stip-u-late	**stor-age**	**strait-laced**	stress-ful-ness
stip-u-lat-ed	**store**	**strange**	**stretch**
stip-u-lat-ing	stored	strang-er	stretch-a-bil-i-ty
stip-u-la-tion	stor-ing	strang-est	stretch-a-ble
stip-u-la-to-ry	**store-house**	strang-ly	**stri-a**

stri-ae
stri-ate
stri-at-ed
stri-at-ing
strick-en
strict
strict-ly
strict-ness
stric-ture
stride
strid-den
strid-ding
stri-dent
strid-u-la-tion
strife
strife-ful
strife-less
string
strung
string-ing
strin-gent
strin-gen-cy
strin-gent-ly
string-y
string-i-er
string-i-est
strip
stripped
strip-ping
stripe
striped
strip-ing
strip-ling
strip-per
strip-tease
strip-teas-er
stro-bo-scope
stro-bo-scop-ic
stro-bo-scop-i-cal-ly
stroke
stroked
strok-ing
stroll-er
strong
strong-ish
strong-ly
strong--arm
strong-box
strong-hold
strong-mind-ed
strong-mind-ed-ly

strong-mind-ed-ness
stron-ti-um
stron-tic
strop
stropped
strop-ping
struc-tur-al
struc-tur-al-ly
struc-ture
struc-tured
struc-tur-ing
struc-ture-less
strug-gle
strug-gled
strum
strum-mer
strum-pet
strut
strut-ting
strych-nine
strych-nia
strych-nic
stub-born
stub-born-ly
stub-born-ness
stuck--up
stud
stud-ded
stud-ding
stu-dent
stud-ied
stud-ied-ly
stud-ied-ness
stu-di-o
stu-di-os
stu-di-ous
stu-di-ous-ly
stud-ies
stud-y-ing
stuff-er
stuff-ing
stuff-y
stul-ti-fy
stul-ti-fied
stul-ti-fy-ing
stul-ti-fi-ca-tion
stul-ti-fi-er
stum-ble
stump
stump-er
stumpy

stun-ning
stunt
stunt-ed
stunt-ed-ness
stu-pe-fy
stu-pe-fied
stu-pe-fy-ing
stu-pen-dous
stu-pen-dous-ly
stu-por
stu-por-ous
stur-dy
stur-di-er
stur-di-est
stur-geon
stut-ter
stut-ter-er
stut-ter-ing-ly
style
styled
styl-ing
styl-er
styl-ish
styl-ish-ly
sty-lus-es
sty-li
sty-mie
sty-mies
sty-mied
sty-mie-ing
styp-tic
styp-ti-cal
styp-tic-i-ty
sub
subbed
sub-bing
sub-al-tern
sub-arc-tic
sub-as-sem-bly
sub-as-sem-blies
sub-as-sem-bler
sub-base-ment
sub-chas-er
sub-class
sub-com-mit-tee
sub-con-scious
sub-con-scious-ly
sub-con-ti-nent
sub-con-ti-nen-tal
sub-con-tract
sub-con-trac-tor

sub-cul-ture
sub-cul-tur-al
sub-cu-ta-ne-ous
sub-cu-ta-ne-ous-ly
sub-ded-u-tante
sub-di-vide
sub-di-vid-ed
sub-di-vid-ing
sub-di-vid-a-ble
sub-di-vid-er
sub-di-vi-sion
sub-di-vi-sion-al
sub-due
sub-dued
sub-en-try
sub-en-tries
sub-freez-ing
sub-group
sub-head
sub-hu-man
sub-ject
sub-jec-tion
sub-jec-tive
sub-jec-tive-ly
sub-jec-tive-ness
sub-jec-tiv-i-ty
sub-join
sub-ju-gate
sub-ju-gat-ed
sub-ju-gat-ing
sub-ju-ga-tion
sub-ju-ga-tor
sub-junc-tive
sub-lease
sub-leased
sub-leas-ing
sub-let
sub-let-ting
sub-li-mate
sub-li-mat-ed
sub-li-mat-ing
sub-li-ma-tion
sub-lime
sub-lim-i-nal
sub-lim-i-nal-ly
sub-lim-i-ty
sub-lim-i-ties
sub-ma-chine gun
sub-mar-gin-al
sub-ma-rine
sub-merge

sub-merged	sub-stance	suc-cinct	sug-gest-er
sub-mer-gi-ble	sub-stand-ard	suc-cinct-ly	sug-gest-i-ble
sub-merse	sub-stan-tial	suc-cinct-ness	sug-ges-tion
sub-mersed	sub-stan-ti-al-i-ty	suc-cor	sug-ges-tive
sub-mer-sion	sub-stan-tial-ly	suc-cor-er	sug-ges-tive-ly
sub-mers-i-ble	sub-stan-tive	suc-co-tash	sug-ges-tive-ness
sub-mi-cro-scop-ic	sub-stan-ti-val	suc-co-bus	suit-a-ble
sub-mis-sion	sub-stan-tive-ly	suc-cu-bi	suit-a-bil-i-ty
sub-mis-sive	sub-sti-tute	suc-cu-lent	suit-case
sub-mis-sive-ly	sub-sti-tut-ed	suc-cu-lence	suite
sub-mis-sive-ness	sub-sti-tut-ing	suc-cu-len-cy	suit-ing
sub-mit	sub-sti-tu-tion	suc-cu-lent-ly	suit-or
sub-mit-ted	sub-stra-tum	suc-cumb	sul-fa
sub-mit-ting	sub-stra-ta	suck-er	sul-fa-nil-a-mide
sub-nor-mal	sub-stra-tums	suck-le	sul-fate
sub-nor-mal-i-ty	sub-struc-ture	suck-led	sul-fide
sub-or-di-nate	sub-teen	suck-ling	sul-fur
sub-or-di-nat-ed	sub-tend	su-crose	sul-fu-ric
sub-or-di-na-tive	sub-ter-fuge	suc-tion	sul-fur-ous
sub-orn	sub-ter-ra-ne-an	sud-den-ly	sul-fur-ous-ly
sub-or-na-tion	sub-ter-ra-ne-ous	sud-den-less	sulk-y
sub-orn-er	sub-ter-ra-ne-an-ly	suds-y	sul-ly
sub-poe-na	sub-ter-ra-ne-ous-ly	suds-i-er	sul-lied
sub-poe-naed	sub-ti-tle	suds-i-est	sul-ly-ing
sub-poe-na-ing	sub-tle	sue	sul-tan
sub-scribe	sub-tle-ness	sued	sul-tan-ic
sub-scribed	sub-tle-ty	su-ing	sul-tan-a
sub-scrib-ing	sub-tle-ties	su-er	sul-tan-ess
sub-scrib-er	sub-tly	suede	sul-tan-ate
sub-scrip-tion	sub-tra-hend	su-et	sul-try
sub-se-quent	sub-trop-i-cal	su-ety	sul-tri-er
sub-se-quence	sub-trop-ic	suf-fer-ance	sul-tri-est
sub-se-quent-ly	sub-trop-ics	suf-fice	sum
sub-ser-vi-ent	sub-ur-bia	suf-ficed	su-mac
sub-ser-vi-ence	sub-ver-sion	suf-fic-ing	sum-ma-rize
sub-ser-vi-en-cy	sub-ver-sion-ary	suf-fic-er	sum-ma-rized
sub-side	sub-ver-sive	suf-fi-cien-cy	sum-ma-ry
sub-sid-ed	sub-ver-sive-ly	suf-fi-cien-cies	sum-ma-ries
sub-sid-ing	sub-ver-sive-ness	suf-fi-cient	sum-mar-i-ly
sub-sid-ence	sub-vert	suf-fi-cient-ly	sum-ma-tion
sub-sid-i-ar-y	sub-vert-er	suf-fix	sum-ma-tion-al
sub-sid-i-ar-ies	sub-way	suf-fo-cate	sum-mer
sub-si-dize	suc-ceed	suf-fo-cat-ed	sum-mery
sub-si-dized	suc-ceed-er	suf-fo-cat-ing	sum-mer-house
sub-si-diz-ing	suc-ces-sion	suf-frage	sum-mit
sub-si-dy	suc-ces-sion-al	suf-fra-gette	sum-mons
sub-si-dies	suc-ces-sion-al-ly	suf-fuse	sum-mons-es
sub-sist	suc-ces-sive	suf-fused	sump-tu-ar-y
sub-sist-ence	suc-ces-sive-ly	suf-fus-ing	sump-tu-ous
sub-soil	suc-ces-sive-ness	sug-ar-coat	sump-tu-ous-ly
sub-son-ic	suc-ces-sor	sug-gest	sun

sunned
sun-ning
sun-bathe
sun-bon-net
sun-burn
sun-burned
sun-burnt
sun-dae
sun-der
sun-der-ance
sun-di-al
sun-dries
sun-dry
sunk-en
sun-light
sun-rise
sun-shine
sun-shiny
sun-spot
sun-stroke
sun-up
sup
supped
su-per
su-per-a-bun-dant
su-per-a-bun-dance
su-per-an-nu-ate
su-perb
su-perb-ly
su-per-car-go
su-per-car-goes
su-per-charge
su-per-charg-er
su-per-cil-i-ous
su-per-cil-i-ous-ly
su-per-e-go
su-per-e-rog-a-to-ry
su-per-fi-cial
su-per-fi-ci-al-i-ty
su-per-fi-ci-al-i-ties
su-per-high-way
su-per-hu-man
su-per-hu-man-i-ty
su-per-hu-man-ly
su-per-im-pose
su-per-im-posed
su-per-im-pos-ing
su-per-in-tend
su-per-in-tend-en-cy
su-per-in-tend-ent
su-pe-ri-or

su-pe-ri-or-i-ty
su-pe-ri-or-ly
su-per-la-tive
su-per-la-tive-ly
su-per-man
su-per-mar-ket
su-per-nal
su-per-nal-ly
su-per-nat-u-ral
su-per-nu-mer-ar-y
su-per-nu-mer-ar-ies
su-per-pow-er
su-per-scribe
su-per-scib-ing
su-per-scrip-tion
su-per-script
su-per-sede
su-per-sed-ed
su-per-sed-ing
su-per-son-ic
su-per-son-i-cal-ly
su-per-star
su-per-sti-tion
su-per-sti-tious
su-per-sti-tious-ly
su-per-struc-ture
su-per-vene
su-per-vened
su-per-ven-ing
su-per-ven-tion
su-per-vise
su-per-vised
su-per-vis-ing
su-per-vi-sion
su-pine
su-pine-ly
sup-per
sup-plant
sup-plan-ta-tion
sup-plant-er
sup-ple
sup-pler
sup-plest
sup-ple-ment
sup-ple-men-tal
sup-pli-ant
sup-pli-ant-ly
sup-pli-cant
sup-ply
sup-port
sup-port-a-ble

sup-port-er
sup-por-tive
sup-pose
sup-po-si-tion
sup-po-si-tion-al
sup-pos-i-to-ry
sup-press
sup-pres-sion
sup-pres-sor
su-pra-re-nal gland
su-prem-a-cy
su-prem-a-cies
su-prem-a-cist
su-preme
su-preme-ly
sur-cease
sur-charge
sur-charged
sur-charg-ing
sur-cin-gle
sure
sur-er
sur-est
sure-ly
sure--fire
sure--foot-ed
sure--foot-ed-ly
sure-ty
sure-ties
sure-ty-ship
surf
surfy
surf-i-er
sur-face
sur-faced
sur-fac-ing
surf-board
surf-board-er
sur-feit
sur-feit-er
sur-geon
sur-ger-y
sur-ger-ies
sur-gi-cal
sur-ly
sur-mise
sur-mised
sur-mis-ing
sur-mount
sur-mount-a-ble
sur-name

sur-pass
sur-pass-a-ble
sur-pass-ing
sur-plice
sur-plus
sur-plus-age
sur-prise
sur-prised
sur-pris-ing
sur-re-al-ism
sur-re-al-ist
sur-re-al-is-tic
sur-ren-der
sur-rep-ti-tious
sur-rep-ti-tious-ly
sur-rey
sur-reys
sur-ro-gate
sur-ro-gat-ed
sur-ro-gat-ing
sur-round
sur-round-er
sur-round-ing
sur-tax
sur-veil-lance
sur-veil-lant
sur-vey
sur-vey-ing
sur-vey-or
sur-viv-al
sur-vive
sur-vived
sur-viv-ing
sur-vi-vor
sus-cep-ti-ble
sus-cep-ti-bil-i-ty
sus-cep-ti-bly
sus-pect
sus-pend
sus-pend-er
sus-pense
sus-pense-ful
sus-pen-sion
sus-pi-cious
sus-pi-cious-ly
sus-tain
sus-tain-a-ble
sus-tain-er
sus-tain-ment
sus-te-nance
su-ture

su-ze-rain
su-ze-rain-ly
svelte
svelte-ly
swad-dle
swad-dled
swad-dling
swain
swain-ish
swal-low
swal-low-er
swal-low-tail
swa-mi
swa-mis
swamp
swampy
swank
swank-i-ly
swan's--down
swap
swapped
swap-ping
sward
swarth-y
swarth-i-er
swarth-i-est
swat
swathe
swathed
swath-ing
swat
sway-a-ble
sway-er
sway-back
sway-backed
swear-word
sweat
sweat-er
sweat-shop
sweep
swept
sweep-ing
sweep-er
sweep-stakes
sweet
sweet-ish
sweet-ly
sweet-heart
sweet-meat
sweet-talk
swell-head

swel-ter
swel-ter-ing
swerve
swerved
swerv-ing
swift
swift-ly
swim-ming
swim-ming-ly
swin-dle
swin-dled
swin-dling
swin-dler
swipe
swiped
swip-ing
swirl
swish
swish-er
switch
switch-er
switch-blade
switch-board
switch--hit-ter
swiv-el
swiv-eled
swiv-el-ing
swiz-zle
sword
sword-fish
sword-play
sword-play-er
swords-man
swords-man
swords-man-ship
syc-a-more
syc-o-phant
syc-o-phan-cy
syc-o-phan-tic
syl-lab-bic
syl-lab-i-cate
syl-lab-i-cat-ed
syl-lab-i-cat-ing
syl-lab-i-ca-tion
syl-la-bus
syl-la-bus-es
syl-la-bi
syl-lo-gism
sul-lo-gis-tic
sylph-like
syl-van

sym-bi-o-sis
sym-bi-ot-ic
sym-bi-ot-i-cal-ly
sym-bol
sym-bol-ic
sym-bol-i-cal
sym-bol-ism
sym-bol-ist
sym-me-try
sym-me-tries
sym-pa-thize
sym-pa-thized
sym-pa-thiz-ing
sym-pa-thiz-er
sym-pa-thy
sym-pa-thies
sym-pho-ny
sym-pho-nies
sym-phon-ic
sym-po-si-um
sym-po-sia
sym-po-si-ums
symp-tom
syn-a-gogue
syn-gog-al
syn-gog-i-cal
syn-apse
sync
synced
sync-ing
syn-chro-nism
syn-chro-nis-tic
syn-chro-nis-ti-cal
syn-chro-nis-ti-cal-ly
syn-chro-nize
syn-chro-nized
syn-chro-niz-ing
syn-chro-ni-za-tion
syn-chro-nous
syn-chro-nous-ly
syn-di-cate
syn-di-cat-ed
syn-di-cat-ing
syn-drome
syn-drom-ic
syn-od
syn-od-al
syn-o-nym
syn-no-nym-ic
syn-no-nym-i-cal
syn-no-nym-i-ty

syn-on-y-mous
syn-on-y-mous-ly
syn-on-y-my
syn-on-y-mies
syn-op-sis
syn-op-ses
syn-op-ti-cal
syn-tac-tic
syn-tac-ti-cal
syn-tac-ti-cal-ly
syn-tax
syn-the-sis
syn-the-ses
syn-the-sist
syn-the-size
syn-the-sized
syn-the-siz-ing
syn-the-ic
syn-thet-i-cal
syn-thet-i-cal-ly
syph-i-lis
syph-i-lit-ic
sy-ringe
sy-ringed
sy-ring-ing
syr-up
syr-upy
syr-up-i-er
syr-up-i-est
sys-tem
sys-tem-at-ic
sys-tem-at-i-cal
sys-tem-a-tize
sys-tem-a-tized
sys-tem-a-tiz-ing
sys-tem-a-ti-za-tion
sys-tem-a-tiz-er
sys-tem-ic
sys-tem-i-cal-ly
sys-to-le
sys-tol-ic

T

tap
tab-er-na-cle
ta-ble
ta-ble-spoon
tab-leau
tab-let

tab-loid
ta-boo
tab-u-lar
 tab-u-lar-ly
ta-chom-e-ter
tac-it
 tac-it-ly
tack
 tack-er
tack claw
tacki-ness
tack-le
ta-co
tac-tic
 tac-tic-al
 tac-tic-ian
tad
tad-pole
taf-fe-ta
 taf-fet-ized
taff-rail
tag
 tag-ger
tail
tail-gate
tai-lor
taint
take
talc
tale
tal-ent
 tal-ent-ed
tal-ent scout
tall
 tall-ish
tal-low
 tal-low
tal-ly
tal-on
 tal-on-ed
tam-bou-rine
tame
 tame-ly
tam-per
tan
 tan-dem
tang
 tangy
tan-gent

tan-gen-cy
tan-gen-tial
tan-ger-ine
tan-gi-ble
tan-gi-bil-ity
tan-gle
tanglement
tan-go
tan-kard
tan-ta-lize
 tan-ta-lizer
 tan-ta-liz-ingly
tan-ta-lum
tan-trum
tap
tape
ta-per
tap-es-try
tap-i-o-ca
taps
tar-dy
 tar-di-ness
tar-get
tar-iff
tar-nish
 tar-nish-able
tar-ot
tar-pau-lin
tar-ry
tart
 tart-ly
 tart-ness
tar-tan
tar-tar
 tar-tar-ic
task
tas-sel
taste
 taste-ful
 taste-less
tat-ter
tat-tle
 tat-tler
tattle-tale
tat-too
 tat-too
 tat-too-er
taught
taut
 taut-ly

taut-ness
tau-tol-o-gy
tav-ern
 tav-ern-er
tax
 tax-able
 tax-a-tion
tax--ex-empt
tax shel-ter
tax-i
 taxi-cab
tax-i-der-my
 tax-i-derm-ist
tea
teach
 teach-ing
 teach-able
 teach-er
team
 team-ster
tear
 teary
tease
 teaser
tech-ne-tium
tech-ni-cal
 tech-ni-cal-ly
tech-nique
tech-nol-o-gy
te-dious
 te-dious-ly
tee
teem
teens
teeth
tele-cast
tele-graph
 tele-graph-er
 tele-graph-ic
te-lep-a-thy
 te-lep-a-thic
 te-lep-a-thist
tele-phone
 tele-phoner
tele-pho-to
 tele-pho-to-graph
tele-scope
 tele-scopic
tele-thon
tele-vi-sion

tel-ex
tel-lu-ri-um
tem-per
 tem-per-able
tem-per-a-ment
 tem-per-a-ment-al
tem-per-ance
tem-per-ate
 tem-per-ate-ly
tem-per-a-ture
tem-pest
tem-ple
tem-po
tem-po-rary
tempt
 tempt-er
ten
te-na-cious
 te-na-cious-ly
ten-ant
tend
ten-den-cy
ten-der
 ten-der-ly
 ten-der-ness
ten-der-loin
ten-don
ten-dril
 ten-dril-ed
ten-nis
ten-or
tense
ten-sion
 ten-sion-al
tent
ten-ta-cle
ten-ta-tive
 ten-ta-tive-ly
ten-ure
te-pee
tep-id
 tep-id-ly
ter-bi-um
ter-cen-ten-a-ry
term
ter-mi-nal
ter-mi-nate
 ter-mi-nation
ter-mite

ter-race
ter-rain
ter-ra-pin
ter-res-tri-al
ter-ri-ble
ter-ri-bly
ter-ri-er
ter-rif-ic
ter-rif-ical-ly
ter-ri-fy
ter-ri-fied
ter-ri-fying
ter-ri-to-ry
ter-ri-to-rial
ter-ri-to-rial-ly
ter-ror
ter-ror-ism
terse
test
test-er
tes-ta-ment
tes-ta-ment-ary
tes-tate
tes-ti-fy
tes-ti-fier
tes-ti-mo-ni-al
tes-ti-mo-ny
tes-tis
test tube
test--tube baby
tet-a-nus
teth-er
text
text-book
tex-tile
tex-ture
tex-tural
tex-tural-ly
thal-li-um
than
thank
thank-ful
thank-ful-ly
thank-ful-ness
thank-less
thanks
that
thatch
thaw

the
the-atre
the-at-ri-cal
the-at-ri-cals
theft
their
the-ism
them
theme
the-matic
them-selves
then
thence
thence-forth
thence-for-ward
the-oc-ra-cy
the-oc-rat
the-ol-o-gy
the-ol-o-gian
the-o-rize
the-o-re-ti-cian
the-o-ri-za-tion
the-o-rist
the-o-ry
ther-a-peu-tics
ther-a-peu-tist
ther-a-py
ther-a-pist
there
there-abouts
there-after
there-by
there-fore
there-from
there-in
ther-mal
ther-mom-e-ter
ther-mom-e-tric
ther-mo-plas-tic
ther-mo-stat
ther-mo-stat-ic
the-sau-rus
these
the-sis
they
they'd
they'll
they're
they've
thick

thick-ly
thick-ness
thick-en
thief
thieve
thigh
thim-ble
thim-ble-ful
thin
thin-ly
thin-ness
thing
think
think-able
think-er
third
thirst
thirst-y
thir-teen
this
this-tle
thith-er
thong
tho-rax
tho-racic
tho-ri-um
thorn
thorn-y
thor-ough
thor-ough-ness
thor-ough-ly
thor-ough-bred
thor-ough-fare
those
though
thought
thought-ful
thought-less
thou-sand
thrash
thrash-er
thread
thread-y
thread-bare
threat
threat-en
three
thresh
thresh-old
threw

thrice
thrift
thrift-i-ly
thrift-i-ness
thrift-y
thrill
thrill-ing
thrill-ing-ly
thrive
throat
throb
throm-bo-sis
throng
throt-tle
through
through-out
throw
thru
thrush
thrust
thru-way
thud
thug
thug-gish
thumb
thump
thun-der
thun-der-bolt
thun-der-cloud
thun-der-show-er
thus
thwack
thwart
thy
thyme
thy-roid
thy-rox-ine
ti-ara
tick
tick-et
tick-le
tick-ler
tidal wave
tid-bit
tide
tid-ings
ti-dy
ti-di-ly
ti-di-ness

tie
tier
 tier-ed
ti-ger
tiger-eye
tight
tight-en
 tight-en-er
tight-rope
tights
tile
till
 till-er
tilt
tim-ber
time
time--shar-ing
time tri-al
tim-id
tinc-ture
tin-der
tin-der-box
tine
tinge
tin-gle
 tin-gly
tink-er
tin-ny
tin-sel
tint
ti-ny
tip
tip-ple
tip-sy
 tip-si-ness
ti-rade
tire
tire-less
 tire-less-ly
tis-sue
ti-ta-ni-um
tithe
 tither
tit-il-late
 tit-il-lat-ing
ti-tle
toad
 toad-stool
toast

toast-y
toast-er
to-bac-co
to-bog-gan
 to-bog-gan-ist
to-day
tod-dle
 tod-dler
tod-dy
toe
tof-fee
to-geth-er
 to-geth-er-ness
toil
 toil-some
toi-let
toi-lette
to-ken
tol-er-ate
 tol-er-a-tion
 tol-er-ance
 tol-er-ant
toll
tom-a-hawk
to-ma-to
tom-boy
 tom-boy-ish
tomb-stone
tom-cat
to-mor-row
ton
tone
tongs
tongue
ton-ic
ton-sil
ton-sil-lec-to-my
tool
tooth
 tooth-ed
 tooth-less
top
to-paz
top-coat
top-ic
top-most
to-pog-ra-phy
top-ple
top-sy--tur-vy

torch
tor-ment
 tor-ment-ing-ly
 tor-ment-or
tor-na-do
tor-pe-do
tor-pid
 tor-pid-ity
 tor-pid-ly
tor-rent
 tor-rent-ial
tor-rid
 tor-rid-ly
tor-sion
 tor-sion-al
tor-so
tort
tor-toise
tor-tu-ous
 tor-tu-ous-ness
to-tal
 to-tal-ly
 to-tal-i-tar-i-an
 to-tal-i-tar-i-an
tote
to-tem
tot-ter
tou-can
touch
 touch-able
tough
 tough-ly
 tough-ness
tou-pee
tour
 tour-ism
 tour-ist
tour-na-ment
tour-ni-quet
tou-sle
tout
 tout-er
tow
to-ward
tow-el
tow-er
 tow-er-ing
town
town-ship
tox-e-mi-a

tox-ic
tox-in
toy
trace
 trace-able
 trace-ably
 trac-er
track
 track-able
 track-er
tract
trac-tion
trac-tor
trade
 trade-able
trade-mark
trade--off
tra-di-tion
 tra-di-tion-al
 tra-di-tion-al-ly
tra-duce
 tra-duce-ment
 tra-ducer
traf-fic
trag-e-dy
trail
trail-er
trait
trai-tor
tra-jec-to-ry
tram-mel
 tram-mel-er
tramp
tram-ple
 tram-pler
tram-po-line
 tram-po-lin-ist
trance
tran-quil
 tran-quil-lity
 tran-quil-ly
 tran-quil-ize
tran-scend
 tran-scend-ent
 tran-scend-ence
tran-scribe
tran-script
tran-scrip-tion
trans-fer
 trans-fer-able

trans-fer-ence

trans-fig-ure

trans-fig-ura-tion

trans-fix

trans-fix-ion

trans-form

trans-for-mable

trans-for-ma-tion

trans-for-mer

trans-fuse

trans-fus-ion

trans-fus-er

trans-gress

trans-gress-ion

trans-gress-or

trans-gres-sive

tran-sient

tran-sient-ly

tran-sit

trans-late

trans-la-tion

tran-sla-tor

trans-lu-cent

trans-mis-sion

trans-mit

trans-miss-ible,

trans-mitt-able

trans-mitt-er

trans-mute

trans-mu-ta-tion

tran-som

trans-par-ent

trans-par-ency

trans-par-ent-ly

tran-spire

trans-plant

trans-plant-able

trans-pose

trans-sex-u-al

trap

tra-peze

trap-shoot-ing

trau-ma

tra-vail

trav-el

trav-el-er

tra-ver-ser

trawl

tray

treach-er-ous

treach-er-ous-ly

treach-ery

tread

treas-ure

treas-ur-er

treas-ur-y

treat

treat-able

treat-er

treat-ment

treb-le

tre-foil

trek

trel-lis

trem-ble

trem-bler

trem-bly

tre-men-dous

trem-or

trench

trench-er

trend

trend-set-ter

tres-pass

tri-al

tri-an-gle

tri-an-gu-lar-i-ty

tribe

trib-u-la-tion

trib-un-al

trib-ute

tri-ceps

trick

trick-y

trick-er-y

trick-le

tri-col-or

tri-col-or-ed

tri-cy-cle

tri-dent

tried

tri-en-ni-al

tri-en-ni-al-ly

trill

tril-lion

trim

tri-ni-tro-tol-u-ene

trin-ket

tri-o

trip-le

trip-let

trip-li-cate

tri-pod

trite

tri-umph

tri-umph-ant

tri-umph-ant-ly

triv-i-al

trol-ley

trom-bone

troop

troop-er

tro-phy

trop-ic

trop-i-cal

trop-i-cal-ly

tro-pism

tro-po-sphere

trot

troth

trou-ble

trou-bler

trou-bling-ly

trough

trounce

troupe

trout

trow-el

trow-el-er

tru-ant

truce

truck

truck-er

trudge

true

true-ness

trump

trum-pet

trunk

truss

trust

trust-er

trust-less

truth

truth-ful

truth-ful-ly

try

try-ing

tryst

tsu-na-mi

tub

tu-ba

tube

tu-ber

tu-ber-cu-lo-sis

tuck

tuft

tug

tu-i-tion

tu-lip

tum-ble

tum-bler

tu-mult

tu-mul-tu-ous

tu-na

tun-dra

tune

tune-ful

tung-sten

tu-nic

tun-nel

tur-ban

tur-bine

tur-bu-lent

tur-bu-lent-ly

tu-reen

turf

tur-key

tur-moil

tur-nip

turn-key

turn-off

turn-over

tur-pen-tine

tur-quoise

tur-ret

tur-tle

tur-tle-neck

tusk

tus-sle

tu-tor

tut-ti--frut-ti

tu-tu

tux-e-do

twain

tweed

twee-zers

twelve
twen-ty
twice
twid-dle
twig
twi-light
twill
twin
twine
twinge
twing-ed
twin-kle
twirl
twist
twist-er
twit
twitch
twit-ter
twit-ter-y
two-fold
ty-coon
tyke
type
type-face
type-writ-er
ty-phoid
ty-phoon
typ-i-cal
typ-i-cal-ly
typ-i-fy
typ-i-fy-ing
typ-ist
ty-po
ty-ran-no-sau-rus
tyr-an-ny

U

ubiq-ui-tous
ubiq-ui-tary
ubiq-ui-tous-ly
ubiq-ui-ty
ud-der
ug-ly
ug-li-er
ug-li-est
ukase
uku-le-le
ul-cer
ul-cer-ous

ul-cer-ate
ul-cer-at-ed
ul-na
ul-nae
ul-ster
ul-te-ri-or
ul-te-ri-or-ly
ul-ti-mate
ul-ti-mate-ly
ul-ti-ma-tum
ul-ti-ma-tums
ul-ti-ma-ta
ul-tra
ul-tra-con-serv-a-tive
ul-tra-high
ul-tra-ma-rine
ul-tra-son-ic
ul-tra-vi-o-let
ul-u-late
ul-u-lat-ed
ul-u-lat-ing
um-ber
um-bil-i-cal
um-bra
um-bras
um-brae
um-brage
um-bra-geous
um-brel-la
umi-ak
um-laut
um-pire
um-pired
um-pir-ing
ump-teen
ump-teenth
un-a-bashed
un-a-bash-ed-ly
un-a-ble
un-a-bridged
un-ac-cep-t-able
un-ac-cept-ed
un-ac-com-pa-nied
un-ac-count-able
un-ac-count-a-bly
un-ac-cus-tomed
un-ac-quaint-ed
un-a-dorned
un-a-dul-ter-at-ed
un-a-dul-ter-at-ed-ly
un-ad-vised

un-ad-vis-ed-ly
un-af-fect-ed
un-af-fect-ed-ly
un-a-fraid
un--Amer-i-can
unan-i-mous
una-nim-i-ty
unan-i-mous-ly
un-an-swer-able
un-an-swered
un-ap-pe-tiz-ing
un-ap-pre-ci-at-ed
un-ap-pre-ci-a-tive
un-armed
un-a-shamed
un-asked
un-a-spir-ing
un-as-sail-able
un-as-sail-ably
un-as-sailed
un-at-tached
un-at-tain-able
un-at-tained
un-at-tend-ed
un-au-thor-ized
un-a-vail-a-ble
un-a-vail-a-bil-i-ty
un-a-vail-a-bly
un-a-void-a-ble
un-a-void-a-bil-i-ty
un-a-void-ably
un-a-ware
un-backed
un-bal-anced
un-bar
un-barred
un-bar-ring
un-bear-able
un-bear-ably
un-beat-en
un-beat-able
un-be-com-ing
un-be-com-ing-ly
un-be-lief
un-be-liev-able
un-be-liev-ably
un-be-liev-er
un-be-liev-ing
un-be-liev-ing-ly
un-bend
un-bend-ing

un-bi-ased
un-bi-ased-ly
un-bid-den
un-bind
un-bound
un-bind-ing
un-blem-ished
un-bolt
un-bolt-ed
un-born
un-bos-om
un-bound
un-bound-ed-ly
un-bowed
un-bread-able
un-bri-dle
un-bri-dled
un-bri-dling
un-bro-ken
un-bro-ken-ly
un-buck-le
un-buck-led
un-bur-den
un-but-ton
un-but-toned
un--called--for
un-can-ny
un-can-ni-er
un-can-ni-est
un-can-ni-ly
un-cap
un-capped
un-cap-ping
un-ceas-ing
un-ceas-ing-ly
un-cer-e-mo-ni-ous
un-cer-e-mo-ni-ous-ly
un-cer-tain
un-cer-tain-ly
un-cer-tain-ty
un-cer-tain-ties
un-chal-lenged
un-change-able
un-change-ably
un-changed
un-chang-ing
un-char-i-ta-ble
un-char-i-ta-bly
un-chart-ed
un-chris-tian
un-cir-cum-cised

un-civ-il
un-civ-il-ly
un-civ-i-lized
un-class-i-fi-able
un-clas-si-fied
un-cle
un-clean
un-clean-ly
un-clear
un-cloak
un-clut-tered
un-coil
un-com-fort-able
un-com-fort-ably
un-com-mit-ted
un-com-mon
un-com-mon-ly
un-com-pre-hend-ing
un-com-pro-mis-ing
un-com-pro-mised
un-con-cern
un-con-cerned
un-con-di-tion-al
un-con-di-tion-al-ly
un-con-firmed
un-con-nect-ed
un-con-nect-ed-ly
un-con-quer-a-ble
un-con-quered
un-con-scion-able
un-con-scion-ably
un-con-scious
un-con-scious-ly
un-con-scious-ness
un-con-sti-tui-tion-al
un-con-strained
un-con-test-ed
un-con-trol-la-ble
un-con-trol-la-bly
un-con-trolled
un-con-ven-tion-al
un-con-ven-tion-al-ly
un-count-ed
un-cou-ple
un-cou-pled
un-cou-pling
un-couth
un-couth-ly
un-cov-er
un-cov-ered
unc-tion

unc-tu-ous
unc-tu-os-i-ty
unc-tu-ous-ly
un-curl
un-cut
un-daunt-ed
un-daunt-ed-ly
un-de-ceive
un-de-ceived
un-de-ceiv-ing
un-de-ceiv-a-ble
un-de-cid-ed
un-de-cid-ed-ly
un-de-cid-ed-ness
un-de-fined
un-de-fin-a-ble
un-de-mon-stra-tive
un-de-ni-a-ble
un-de-ni-a-bly
un-de-nied
un-de-pend-able
un-de-pend-a-bil-i-ty
un-der
un-der-a-chiev-er
un-der-a-chiev-ment
un-der-act
un-der-age
un-der-arm
un-der-bel-ly
un-der-car-riage
un-der-charge
un-der-charged
un-der-charg-ing
un-der-class-man
un-der-class-men
un-der-clothes
un-der-coast
un-der-cur-rent
un-der-cut
un-der-cut-ting
un-der-de-vel-oped
un-der-de-vel-op-ing
un-der-dog
un-der-done
un-der-es-ti-mate
un-der-es-ti-mat-ed
un-der-es-ti-mat-ing
un-der-es-ti-ma-tion
un-der-foot
un-der-gar-ment
un-der-go

un-der-went
un-der-gone
un-der-grad-u-ate
un-der-ground
un-der-growth
un-der-lie
un-der-lay
un-der-lain
un-der-ly-ing
un-der-line
un-der-lined
un-der-lin-ing
un-der-ling
un-der-mine
un-der-mined
un-der-min-ing
un-der-min-er
un-der-most
un-der-neath
un-der-priv-i-leged
un-der-rate
un-der-rat-ed
un-der-rat-ing
un-der-score
un-der-scored
un-der-scor-ing
un-der-sea
un-der-sec-re-tary
un-der-sec-re-tar-ies
un-der-sell
un-der-sold
un-der-ell-ing
un-der-sell-er
un-der-shirt
un-der-shot
un-der-side
un-der-signed
un-der-stand
un-der-stood
un-der-stand-ing
un-der-stand-a-ble
un-der-stand-a-bly
un-der-state
un-der-stat-ed
un-der-stat-ing
un-der-state-ment
un-der-stood
un-der-study
un-der-stud-ied
un-der-stud-y-ing
un-der-stud-ies

un-der-take
un-der-took
un-der-tak-en
un-der-tak-ing
un-der-tak-er
un-der-the-coun-ter
un-der-tone
un-der-tow
un-der-wa-ter
un-der-weight
un-der-write
un-der-wrote
un-der-writ-ten
un-der-writ-er
un-de-sir-a-ble
un-de-sir-a-bil-i-ty
un-de-sir-a-bly
un-de-ter-mined
un-dies
un-dip-lo-mat-ic
un-dip-lo-mat-i-cal-ly
un-dis-ci-plined
un-dis-closed
un-dis-posed
un-dis-tin-guished
un-di-vid-ed
un-doubt-ed
un-doubt-ed-ly
un-doubt-ing
un-due
un-du-lant
un-du-late
un-du-lat-ed
un-du-lat-ing
un-du-la-tion
un-du-ly
un-dy-ing
un-earth
un-earth-ly
un-easy
un-eas-i-er
un-eas-i-est
un-ease
un-eas-i-ly
un-eas-i-ness
un-em-ployed
un-em-ploy-ment
un-e-qual
un-e-qual-ly
un-e-qual-ed
un-e-quiv-o-cal

un-e-quiv-o-cal-ly
un-err-ing
un-err-ing-ly
un-eth-i-cal
un-eth-i-cal-ly
un-e-ven
un-e-ven-ly
un-e-ven-ness
un-ex-cep-tion-able
un-ex-pect-ed
un-ex-pect-ed-ly
un-fail-ing
un-fail-ing-ly
un-faith-ful
un-faith-ful-ly
un-faith-ful-ness
un-fa-mil-iar
un-fa-mil-i-ar-i-ty
un-fa-mil-iar-ly
un-fast-en
un-fas-ten-a-ble
un-fas-ten-er
un-fath-om-a-ble
un-fa-vor-a-ble
un-fa-vor-a-bly
un-feel-ing
un-feel-ing-ly
un-feigned
un-feign-ed-ly
un-fet-ter
un-fet-tered
un-fin-ished
un-fit
un-fit-ly
un-fit-ness
un-fit-ting
un-flat-ter-ing
un-flinch-ing
un-flinch-ing-ly
un-fold
un-for-get-ta-ble
un-for-get-ta-bly
un-for-giv-a-ble
un-for-tu-nate
un-for-tu-nate-ly
un-found-ed
un-found-ed-ness
un-friend-ly
un-friend-li-er
un-friend-li-est
un-friend-li-ness

un-frock
un-furl
un-gain-ly
un-gain-li-ness
un-gird
un-gird-ed
un-gird-ing
un-glazed
un-god-ly
un-god-li-er
un-god-li-est
un-god-li-ness
un-gov-ern-able
un-gov-ern-ably
un-gra-cious
un-gra-cious-ly
un-gra-cious-ness
un-gram-mat-i-cal
un-gram-mat-i-cal-ly
un-grate-ful
un-grate-ful-ly
un-grate-ful-ness
un-guard-ed
un-guard-ed-ly
un-guent
un-gu-late
un-ham-pered
un-hand
un-handy
un-hand-i-er
un-hand-i-est
un-hap-py
un-hap-pi-er
un-hap-pi-est
un-hap-pi-ly
un-hap-pi-ness
un-harmed
un-healthy
un-health-i-er
un-health-i-ly
un-heard
un-heed-ed
un-heed-ful
un-heed-ing
un-hinge
un-hinged
un-hing-ing
un-hitch
un-ho-ly
un-ho-li-er
un-ho-li-est

un-hol-li-ly
un-ho-li-ness
un-hook
un-horse
un-horsed
un-hors-ing
un-hur-ried
un-hurt
uni-cam-er-al
uni-cam-er-al-ly
uni-cel-lu-lar
uni-corn
uni-fi-ca-tion
uni-form
uni-formed
uni-form-i-ty
uni-form-ly
uni-fy
uni-fied
uni-fy-ing
uni-fi-er
uni-lat-er-al
uni-lat-er-al-ism
uni-lat-er-al-ly
un-imag-in-able
un-im-pair-ed
un-im-peach-able
un-im-peach-a-bly
un-im-por-tance
un-im-por-tant
un-im-proved
un-in-hib-it-ed
un-in-hib-it-ed-ly
un-in-ter-est-ed
un-in-ter-est-ing
un-ion
un-ion-ism
un-ion-ist
un-ion-ize
un-ion-ized
un-ion-iz-ing
un-ion-i-za-tion
unique
unique-ly
unique-ness
uni-son
unit
unite
unit-ed
unit-ing
unit-er

uni-ty
uni-ties
uni-valve
uni-valved
uni-val-vu-lar
uni-ver-sal
uni-ver-sal-i-ty
uni-ver-sal-ly
uni-ver-sal-ness
uni-ver-sal-ize
uni-ver-sal-ized
uni-ver-sal-iz-ing
uni-verse
uni-ver-si-ty
uni-ver-si-ties
un-just
un-just-ly
un-kempt
un-kind
un-kind-ness
un-kind-ly
un-known
un-law-ful
un-law-ful-ly
un-law-ful-ness
un-learn
un-learned
un-learn-ing
un-learn-ed
un-learn-ed-ly
un-leash
un-less
un-let-ter-ed
un-like
un-like-ness
un-like-ly
un-like-li-er
un-like-li-est
un-like-li-ness
un-lim-ber
un-lim-it-ed
un-load
un-load-er
un-lock
un-looked--for
un-make
un-made
un-mak-ing
un-mak-er
un-man
un-manned

un-man-ning
un-mask
un-mean-ing
un-mean-ing-ly
un-men-tion-able
un-mer-ci-ful
un-mer-ci-ful-ly
un-mis-tak-able
un-mis-tak-a-bly
un-mit-i-gat-ed
un-mit-i-gat-ed-ly
un-nat-u-ral
un-nat-u-ral-ly
un-nat-u-ral-ness
un-nec-es-sary
un-nec-es-sar-i-ly
un-nerve
un-nerved
un-nerv-ing
un-num-bered
un-ob-jec-tion-able
un-or-gan-ized
un-pack
un-par-al-leled
un-par-don-able
un-pleas-ant
un-pleas-ant-ly
un-pleas-ant-ness
un-plumbed
un-pop-u-lar
un-pop-u-lar-i-ty
un-pop-u-lar-ly
un-prec-e-dent-ed
un-prec-e-dent-ed-ly
un-prin-ci-pled
un-print-able
un-pro-fes-sion-al
un-pro-fes-sion-al-ly
un-qual-i-fied
un-qual-i-fied-ly
un-ques-tion-able
un-ques-tion-ably
un-ques-tioned
un-quote
un-quot-ed
un-quot-ing
un-rav-el
un-rav-eled
un-rav-el-ing
un-rav-el-ment
un-read

un-re-al
un-rea-son-able
un-rea-son-ably
un-rea-son-ing
un-re-fined
un-re-gen-er-ate
un-re-lat-ed
un-re-lent-ing
un-re-lent-ing-ly
un-re-mit-ting
un-re-serve
un-re-served
un-re-serv-ed-ly
un-rest
un-ri-valed
un-roll
un-ruf-fled
un-ru-ly
un-ruy-li-er
un-ru-li-est
un-sad-dle
un-sad-dled
un-sad-dling
un-said
un-sa-vory
un-say
un-say-ing
un-scathed
un-schooled
un-scram-ble
un-scram-bled
un-scram-bling
un-screw
un-scru-pu-lous
un-scru-pu-lous-ly
un-seal
un-sea-son-able
un-sea-son-ably
un-seat
un-seem-ly
un-set-tle
un-set-tled
un-set-tling
un-sheathe
un-sheathed
un-sheath-ing
un-shod
un-sight-ly
un-sight-li-er
un-sight-li-est
un-skilled

un-skill-ful
un-skill-ful-ly
un-snap
un-snapped
un-snap-ping
un-snarl
un-so-phis-ti-cat-ed
un-so-phis-ti-cat-ed-ly
un-so-phis-ti-ca-tion
un-sound
un-sound-ly
un-spar-ing
un-spar-ing-ly
un-speak-a-ble
un-speak-a-bly
un-sta-ble
un-sta-bly
un-steady
un-stead-i-er
un-stead-i-est
un-stead-i-ly
un-stop
un-stopped
un-stop-ping
un-strung
un-stud-ied
un-sung
un-tan-gle
un-tan-gled
un-tan-gling
un-taught
un-think-able
un-think-ing
un-think-ing-ly
un-ti-dy
un-tie
un-tied
un-ty-ing
un-til
un-time-ly
un-time-li-ness
un-to
un-told
un-touch-a-ble
un-touch-a-bly
un-to-ward
un-to-ward-ly
un-truth
un-tu-tored
un-used
un-u-su-al

un-u-su-al-ly
un-u-su-al-ness
un-ut-ter-able
un-ut-ter-ably
un-var-nished
un-veil
un-wary
un-war-i-ly
un-well
un-whole-some
un-whole-some-ly
un-will-ing
un-will-ing-ly
un-will-ing-ness
un-wind
un-wound
un-wind-ing
un-wise
un-wise-ly
un-wit-ting
un-wit-ting-ly
un-wont-ed
un-wont-ed-ly
un-wor-thy
un-wor-thi-ly
un-wor-thi-ness
un-wrap
un-wrapped
un-wrap-ping
un-yield-ing
up-beat
up-braid
up-braid-er
up-braid-ing
up-com-ing
up-coun-try
up-date
up-dat-ed
up-dat-ing
up-end
up-grade
up-grad-ed
up-grad-ing
up-heav-al
up-heave
up-heaved
up-heav-ing
up-hill
up-hold
up-held
up-hold-ing

up-hol-ster
up-hol-ster-er
up-hol-stery
up-keep
up-land
up-lift
up-most
up-on
up-per
up-per--class
up-per-cut
up-per-cut-ting
up-per-most
up-pish
up-pish-ly
up-pi-ty
up-raise
up-raised
up-rais-ing
up-rear
up-right
up-right-ly
up-right-ness
up-ris-ing
up-roar
up-roar-i-ous
up-set
up-set-ting
up-shot
up-side
up-stage
up-staged
up-stag-ing
up-stairs
up-stand-ing
up-start
up-take
up-to-date
up-town
up-trend
up-turn
up-ward
up-ward-ly
ura-ni-um
ur-ban
ur-bane
ur-bane-ly
ur-ban-i-ty
ur-ban-ize
ur-ban-ized
ur-ban-iz-ing

ur-ban-i-za-tion
ur-chin
urea
ure-al
ure-ter
ure-thra
ure-thrae
ure-thras
ure-thral
ur-gent
ur-gen-cy
ur-gen-cies
ur-gent-ly
uric
uri-nal
uri-nal-y-sis
uri-nal-y-ses
uri-nary
uri-nar-ies
uri-nate
urine
urol-o-gy
uro-log-ic
uro-log-i-cal
urol-o-gist
us-able
us-ably
us-abil-i-ty
us-age
use
use-ful
use-ful-ly
ush-er
usu-al
usu-al-ly
usurp
usur-pa-tion
usurp-er
usu-ry
usu-ries
usu-ri-ous
uten-sil
uter-us
ut-eri
util-i-tar-ian
util-i-ty
util-i-ties
uti-lize
uti-lized
uti-liz-ing
uti-li-za-tion

ut-most
ut-ter
ut-ter-a-ble
ut-ter-er
ut-ter-ance
ut-ter-most
uvu-la
uvu-las
uvu-lae
ux-o-ri-ous
ux-o-ri-ous-ly

V

va-can-cy
va-can-cies
va-cant
va-cant-ly
va-cate
va-cat-ed
va-cat-ing
va-ca-tion
vac-ci-nate
vac-ci-nat-ed
vac-ci-nat-ing
vac-ci-na-tion
vac-cine
vac-il-late
vac-il-lat-ed
vac-il-lat-ing
vac-il-la-tion
vac-il-la-tor
va-cu-i-ty
va-cu-i-ties
vac-u-ous
vac-u-ous-ly
vac-u-um
vac-u-ums
vac-ua
vac-u-um--packed
va-gi-na
va-gi-nas
va-gi-nae
vag-i-nal
va-grant
va-gran-cy
va-gran-cies
va-grant-ly
vague
vague-ly

vain
vain-ly
vain-ness
vain-glo-ry
vain-glo-ries
vain-glo-ri-ous
val-ance
val-e-dic-to-ry
val-e-dic-to-ries
va-lence
va-len-cy
val-en-tine
va-let
val-iant
val-iant-ly
val-id
val-id-ly
val-i-date
val-i-dat-ed
val-i-dat-ig
val-i-da-tion
va-lid-i-ty
va-lid-i-ties
va-lise
val-ley
val-leys
val-or
val-or-ous
val-u-able
val-u-ably
val-u-a-tion
val-u-a-tion-al
val-ue
val-ued
val-u-ing
val-ue-less
valve
valve-less
val-vu-lar
va-moose
vam-pire
vam-pir-ic
vam-pir-ism
va-na-di-um
van-dal
van-dal-ism
van-dal-ize
van-dal-ized
van-dal-iz-ing
vane
vaned

vane-less
van-guard
va-nil-la
van-ish
van-ish-er
van-i-ty
van-i-ties
van-quish
van-quish-a-ble
van-quish-er
van-tage
vap-id
va-pid-i-ty
vap-id-ly
va-por
va-por-er
va-por-ish
va-por-ize
va-por-ized
va-por-iz-ing
va-por-i-za-tion
va-por-iz-er
va-por-ous
va-por-opus-ly
va-que-ro
va-que-ros
var-i-able
var-i-abil-i-ty
var-i-ably
var-i-ance
var-i-ant
var-i-a-tion
var-i-a-tion-al
var-i-col-ored
var-i-cose
var-ied
var-ied-ness
var-ie-gate
var-ie-gat-ed
var-ie-gat-ing
var-ie-ga-tion
var-ie-ga-tor
va-ri-etal
va-ri-etal-ly
va-ri-ety
va-ri-e-ties
var-i-ous
var-i-ous-ly
var-nish
var-nish-er
var-si-ty

var-si-ties
vary
var-ied
vary-ing
var-i-er
vary-ing-ly
vas-cu-lar
vas-cu-lar-i-ty
va-sec-to-my
va-sec-to-mies
vas-o-mo-tor
vas-sal
vas-sal-age
vast-ness
vat
vat-ted
vat-ting
vaude-ville
vault
vault-ed
vault-er
vault-ing
vaunt
vaunt-er
vaunt-ing-ly
vec-tor
vec-to-ri-al
veer-ing
veg-e-ta-ble
veg-e-tal
veg-e-tar-i-an
veg-e-tar-i-an-ism
veg-e-tate
veg-e-tat-ed
veg-e-tat-ing
veg-e-ta-tion
veg-e-ta-tion-al
veg-e-ta-tive
ve-he-ment
ve-he-mence
ve-he-men-cy
ve-hi-cle
ve-hic-u-lar
veil
veiled
veil-ing
vein
veiny
vein-i-er
vein-i-est
vein-ing

vel-lum
ve-loc-i-ty
ve-loc-i-ties
vel-our
ve-lum
ve-la
vel-vet
vel-vet-ed
vel-ve-teen
vel-vety
vel-vet-i-er
vel-vet-i-est
ve-nal
ve-nal-i-ty
ve-nal-ly
ve-na-tion
ve-na-tion-al
vend-er
vend-or
ven-det-ta
vend-i-ble
vend-i-bil-i-ty
ve-neer
ve-neer-er
ve-neer-ig
ven-er-able
ven-er-abil-i-ty
ven-er-ably
ven-er-ate
ven-er-a-tion
ven-er-a-tor
ve-ne-re-al
venge-ance
venge-ful
venge-ful-ness
ve-ni-al
ve-ni-al-i-ty
ve-ni-al-ness
ve-ni-al-ly
ven-i-son
ven-om
ven-om-ous
ve-nous
ve-nous-ly
vent
vent-ed
vent-ing
ven-ti-late
ven-ti-lat-ed
ven-ti-lat-ing
ven-ti-la-tion

ven-ti-la-tor
ven-tral
ven-tral-ly
ven-tri-cle
ven-tril-o-quism
ven-tri-lo-qui-al
ven-tril-o-quist
ven-tril-o-quize
ven-tril-o-quized
ven-tril-o-quiz-ing
ven-ture
ven-ture-some
ven-tur-ous
ve-ra-cious
ve-rac-i-ty
ve-rac-i-ties
ve-ran-da
ver-bal
ver-bal-ly
ver-bal-ize
ver-bal-ized
ver-bal-iz-er
ver-ba-tim
ver-bi-age
ver-bose
ver-bose-ness
ver-bo-ten
ver-dant
ver-dan-cy
ver-dict
ver-di-gris
ver-dure
ver-dured
ver-dur-ous
verge
verged
verg-ing
ver-i-fi-ca-tion
ver-i-fy
ver-i-fied
ver-i-fy-ing
ver-i-fi-abil-i-ty
ver-i-fi-able
ver-i-fi-er
veri-si-mil-i-tude
veri-ta-ble
veri-ta-bly
ver-i-ty
ver-i-ties
ver-meil
ver-mic-u-lar

ver-mic-u-late
ver-mic-u-lat-ed
ver-mi-fuge
ver-mil-ion
ver-min
ver-min-ous
ver-mouth
ver-nac-u-lar
ver-nac-u-lar-ism
ver-nal
ver-nal-ly
ver-sa-tile
ver-sa-til-i-ty
versed
ver-si-fy
ver-si-fied
ver-si-fy-ing
ver-si-fi-er
ver-si-fi-ca-tion
ver-sion
ver-sion-al
ver-sus
ver-te-bra
ver-te-brae
ver-te-bral
ver-te-bral-ly
ver-te-brate
ver-tex
ver-tex-es
ver-ti-cal
ver-ti-cal-i-ty
ver-ti-cal-ly
ver-ti-go
ver-ti-goes
ver-tig-i-nes
ves-i-cant
ves-i-ca-to-ry
ves-i-ca-to-ries
ves-i-cate
ves-i-cat-ed
ves-i-cat-ing
ves-i-ca-tion
ves-i-cle
ve-sic-u-lar
ves-pers
ves-sel
ves-tal
vest-ed
ves-ti-bule
ves-ti-buled
ves-ti-bul-ing

ves-tib-u-lar
ves-tige
ves-tig-i-al
ves-tig-i-al-ly
vest-ment
vest-pock-et
ves-try
ves-tries
vet
vet-ted
vet-ting
vet-er-an
vet-er-i-nar-i-an
vet-er-i-nary
ve-to
vex
vex-er
vex-ing-ly
vex-a-tion
vex-a-tious
vexed
via
vi-a-ble
vi-a-bil-i-ty
vi-a-bly
vi-a-duct
vi-al
vi-and
vi-brant
vi-bran-cy
vi-brate
vi-brat-ed
vi-bra-tion
vi-bra-to
vi-bra-tos
vi-bra-tor
vi-bra-to-ry
vi-bur-num
vic-ar
vic-ar-ship
vic-ar-age
vi-car-i-ous
vi-car-i-ous-ly
vice ad-mi-ral
vice--con-sul
vice--pres-i-dent
vice-roy
vice-roy-al
vice ver-sa
vi-cin-i-ty
vi-cin-i-ties

vi-cious
vi-cious-ly
vi-cis-si-tude
vic-tim
vic-tim-ize
vic-tim-ized
vic-tim-iz-ing
vic-tor
vic-to-ri-ous
vic-to-ri-ous-ly
vic-to-ry
vic-to-ries
vict-ual
vid-eo
view-er
view-less
view-point
vig-il
vig-i-lance
vig-i-lant
vig-i-lan-te
vi-gnette
vig-or
vig-or-ous
vig-or-ous-ly
vi-king
vile
vil-i-fy
vil-i-fied
vil-i-fi-ca-tion
vil-la
vil-lain
vil-lain-ous
vil-lainy
vil-lain-ies
vil-lein
vil-lous
vil-lus
vil-li
vin-ci-ble
vin-ci-bil-i-ty
vin-di-cate
vin-di-cat-ed
vin-di-cat-ing
vin-dic-tive
vin-dic-tive-ly
vin-dic-tive-ness
vin-e-gar
vin-e-gary
vine-yard
vi-nous

vin-tage
vint-ner
vi-nyl
vi-ol
vi-o-la
vi-o-list
vi-o-la-ble
vi-o-la-bil-i-ty
vi-o-late
vi-o-lat-ed
vi-o-la-tion
vi-o-lence
vi-o-lent
vi-o-let
vi-o-lin
vi-o-lin-ist
vi-o-lon-cel-lo
vi-o-lon-cel-list
vi-per
vi-ra-go
vi-ral
vir-eo
vir-e-os
vir-gin
vir-gin-al
vir-gin-i-ty
vir-gule
vir-ile
vi-ril-i-ty
vi-rol-o-gy
vi-rol-o-gist
vir-tu-al
vir-tue
vir-tu-os-i-ty
vir-tu-os-i-ties
vir-tu-o-so
vir-tu-ous
vir-tu-ous-ly
vir-u-lence
vir-u-len-cy
vir-u-lent
vi-rus
vi-rus-es
vi-sa
vis-age
vis-cera
vis-cer-al
vis-cid
vis-cid-ly
vis-cos-i-ty
vis-cos-i-ties

vis-count
vis-count-cy
vis-count-ship
vis-count-ess
vis-cous
vis-i-bil-i-ty
vis-i-bil-i-ties
vis-i-ble
vi-sion
vi-sion-ary
vi-sion-ar-ies
vis-it
vis-i-tant
vis-lt-a-tion
vis-it-ing
vis-i-tor
vi-sor
vis-ta
vi-tal
vi-tal-i-ty
vi-tal-i-ties
vi-tal-ize
vi-tal-ized
vi-tal-iz-ing
vi-tal-i-za-tion
vi-tals
vi-ta-min
vi-ti-ate
vit-re-ous
vit-re-os-i-ty
vit-ri-fy
vit-ri-fied
vit-ri-fy-ing
vit-ri-fi-a-ble
vit-ri-fi-ca-tion
vit-ri-ol
vit-ri-ol-ic
vi-tu-per-ate
vi-tu-per-at-ed
vi-tu-per-at-ing
vi-tu-per-a-tion
vi-va
vi-va-cious
vi-vac-i-ty
vi-vac-i-ties
viv-id
viv-i-fy
viv-i-fied
viv-i-fy-ing
vi-vip-ar-ous
vivi-sec-tion

vix-en
vi-zier
vi-zor
vo-cab-u-lar-y
vo-cab-u-lar-ies
vo-cal
vo-ca-tion
vo-ca-tion-al
vo-cif-er-ous
vod-ka
voice-print
void-able
vol-a-tile
vol-a-til-i-ty
vol-can-ic
vol-can-i-cal-ly
vol-ca-no
vol-ca-noes
vol-ca-nos
vo-li-tion
vol-ley
vol-leys
vol-ley-ball
volt-age
vol-ta-ic
volt-me-ter
vol-u-ble
vol-u-bly
vol-u-bil-i-ty
vol-ume
vo-lu-mi-nous
vo-lu-mi-nous-ly
vol-un-tary
vol-un-tar-i-ly
vol-un-teer
vo-lup-tu-ary
vo-lup-tu-ar-ies
vo-lup-tu-ous
vom-it
voo-doo
vo-ra-cious
vo-rac-i-ty
vor-tex
vor-tex-es
vor-ti-ces
vo-ta-ry
vor-ta-ries
vot-er
vo-tive
vouch-er
vouch-safe

vouch-safed
vouch-saf-ing
vow-el
voy-age
voy-aged
voy-ag-ing
voy-ag-er
vo-ya-geur
vo-yeur
vo-yeur-ism
voy-eur-is-tic
vul-can-ite
vul-gar
vul-gar-ism
vul-gar-i-ty
vul-gar-i-ties
vul-gar-ize
vul-gar-ized
vul-gar-iz-ing
vul-gate
vul-ner-a-ble
vul-ner-a-bly
vul-pine
vul-ture
vul-va
vul-vae
vul-vas

W

wab-ble
wab-bled
wab-bling
wacky
wack-i-er
wack-i-est
wack-i-ly
wad
wad-ded
wad-ding
wade
wad-ed
wad-ing
wad-er
waf-er
waf-fle
wag
wagged
wag-ging
wag-ger

wag-gish
wage
waged
wag-ing
wa-ger
wag-gery
wag-ger-ies
wag-gle
wag-gled
wag-gling
wag-on
wag-on-er
wain-scot
wain-scot-ing
wain-wright
waist-band
waist-coat
waist-line
wait-er
wait-ing
wait-ress
waive
waived
waiv-ing
waiv-er
wake
waked
wok-en
wak-ing
wake-ful
wake-ful-ly
wak-en
wale
waled
wal-ing
walk-a-way
walk-er
walk-ie-talk-ie
walk-out
walk-o-ver
walk-up
walk-way
wal-al-by
wal-la-bies
wall-board
wal-let
wall-eye
wall-eyed
wall-flow-er
wal-lop
wall-to-wall

wal-nut	wary	wa-ter-llogged	weak-en
wal-rus	war-i-er	Wa-ter-loo	weak-kneed
wal-rus-es	war-i-est	wa-ter main	weak-ling
wam-pum	war-i-ly	wa-ter-man	weak-ly
wan	wash-able	wa-ter-men	weak-li-er
wan-ner	wash-ba-sin	wa-ter-mark	weak-li-est
wan-nest	wash-board	wa-ter-mel-on	weak-mind-ed
wan-ness	wash-bowl	wa-ter moc-ca-sin	weak-ness
wan-der	wash-cloth	wa-ter-proof	wealthy
wan-der-lust	wash-er	wa-ter-re-pel-lent	wealth-i-er
wane	wash-ing	wa-ter-shed	wealth-i-est
waned	wash-out	wa-ter-side	wealth-i-ly
wan-ing	wash-room	wa-ter ski	wean
wan-gle	wash-stand	wa-ter-skied	weap-on
wan-gled	wash-tub	wa-ter-ski-ing	weap-on-ry
wan-gling	wasn't	wa-ter-spout	wear
wan-gler	wasp	wa-ter-tight	wear-ing
want-ing	wasp-ish	wa-ter-way	wea-ri-some
wan-ton	wasp-ish-ly	wa-ter-works	wea-ry
wa-pi-ti	was-sail	wa-tery	weath-er
wa-pi-ties	wast-age	watt-age	weath-er--beat-en
war-ble	waste	watt-hour	weath-er-cock
war-bled	wast-ed	wat-tle	weath-er-man
war-bling	wast-ing	wat-tled	weath-er-men
war-bler	waste-ful	wat-tling	weath-er-proof
war-den	waste-ful-ly	wave	weather vane
war-den-ship	waste-ful-ness	waved	weave
ward-er	waste-bas-ket	wav-ing	weaved
ward-robe	waste-land	wave-length	wov-en
ware-house	waste-pa-per	wave-let	weav-ing
war-fare	wast-er	wa-ver	weav-er
war-head	wast-rel	wav-y	web
war-horse	watch-dog	wav-i-er	webbed
war-like	watch-ful	wav-i-est	web-bing
war-lock	watch-man	wav-i-ly	web-foot
warm	watch-men	wax	web-foot-ed
warm-er	watch-tow-er	waxed	wed-ding
warm-est	watch-word	wax-ing	wedge
warm--blood-ed	wa-ter	wax-en	wedged
warm-heart-ed	wat-er-buck	wax-wing	wedg-ing
war-mon-ger	wa-ter-col-or	wax-work	wed-lock
warmth	wa-ter-course	waxy	weedy
warn-ing	wa-ter-cress	wax-i-er	weed-i-er
war-path	wa-ter-fall	wax-i-est	weed-i-est
war-rant	wa-ter-foul	way-far-er	week-day
war-ran-ty	wa-ter-front	way-far-ing	week-end
war-ran-ties	wa-ter-less	way-lay	week-ly
war-ren	wa-ter lev-el	way-laid	weep-ing
war-ri-or	wa-ter lily	way-lay-ing	wee-vil
war-ship	wa-ter lil-ies	way-side	weigh
war-time	wa-ter line	way-ward	weight

weighty	whal-ing	**whim-per**	whizzed
weight-i-er	**whale-boat**	**whim-si-cal**	whiz-zing
weight-i-est	**whale-bone**	**whim-sy**	whiz-zes
weight-i-ly	**whal-er**	whim-sies	**whoa**
weird	**wharf**	**whine**	**who-ev-er**
weird-er	wharves	whined	**whole-heart-ed**
weird-est	**what-ev-er**	whin-ing	**whole-sale**
wel-come	**what-not**	**whin-ny**	whole-saled
wel-comed	**what-so-ev-er**	whin-nied	whole-sal-ing
wel-com-ing	**wheat**	whin-nying	whole-sal-er
wel-fare	**wheat-en**	whin-nies	**whole-some**
well--be-ing	**whee-dle**	**whip**	**whole-wheat**
well-born	whee-dled	whipped	**whol-ly**
well--bred	whee-dling	whip-ping	**whom-ev-er**
well--dis-posed	whee-dler	**whip-lash**	**whom-so-ev-er**
well--done	**wheel and ax-le**	**whip-per-snap-per**	**whoop-ing**
well--found-ed	**wheel-bar-row**	**whip-pet**	**whop-per**
well--groomed	**wheel-chair**	**whip-poor-will**	**whop-ping**
well--ground-ed	**wheeled**	**whir**	**whorled**
well--known	**wheel-house**	whirred	**whose-so-ev-er**
well--mean-ing	**wheel-wright**	whir-ring	**who-so-ev-er**
well--nigh	**wheeze**	**whirl-i-gig**	**wick-ed**
well--off	wheezed	**whirl-pool**	**wick-er**
well--read	wheez-ing	**whirl-wind**	**wick-er-work**
well--spo-ken	**wheezy**	**whisk-er**	**wick-et**
well-spring	wheez-i-er	**whis-key**	**wide**
well--thought--of	wheez-i-est	whis-ky	wid-er
well--timed	wheez-i-ly	whis-keys	wid-est
well--to--do	**whelm**	whis-kies	**wide--awake**
well--wish-er	**whelp**	**whis-per**	**wide--eyed**
well--worn	**whence-so-ev-er**	**whist**	**wid-en**
wel-ter	**where-abouts**	**whis-tle**	**wide-spread**
wel-ter-weight	**where-as**	whis-tled	**wid-geon**
were-wolf	**where-by**	whis-tling	**wid-ow**
were-wolves	**where-fore**	**whis-tler**	**wid-ow-er**
west-bound	**where-in**	**white**	**wid-ow-hood**
west-er-ly	**where-on**	whit-er	**width**
west-ern	**where-so-ev-er**	whit-est	**wield-er**
west-ern-er	**where-to**	whit-ish	**wieldy**
west-ern-ize	**where-up-on**	**white--col-lar**	**wie-ner**
west-ern-ized	**wher-ev-er**	**white-fish**	**wig-gle**
west-ern-iz-ing	**where-with**	**whit-en**	wig-gled
west-ern-i-za-tion	**where-with-al**	**white-wash**	wig-gling
west-ern-most	**wher-ry**	**white water**	wig-gly
west-ward	wher-ries	**whith-er**	wig-gli-er
wet	**whet**	**whit-ing**	**wig-gler**
wet-ter	whet-ted	**whit-tle**	**wig-wag**
wet-test	whet-ting	whit-tled	wig-wagged
wet-back	**wheth-er**	whit-tling	wig-wag-ging
whale	**whet-stone**	whit-tler	**wig-wam**
whaled	**whch-ev-er**	**whiz**	**wild-cat**

wild-cat-ted
wild-cat-ting
wild-cat strike
wil-der-ness
wild-fire
wild-fowl
wild--goose chase
wild-life
wild-wood
wile
wiled
wil-ing
wil-i-ly
wil-i-ness
willed
will-ful
wil-lies
will-ing
will--o'--the--wisp
wil-low
wil-lowy
wil-ly--nil-ly
wim-ble
wim-ple
win
win-ning
wince
winced
winc-ing
wind
wound
wind-ing
wind-bag
wind-break
wind-ed
wind-fall
wind-flow-er
win-dow
wind-row
wind-shield
wind-storm
wind-up
wind-ward
windy
wind-i-er
wind-i-est
wine
wined
win-ing
win-ery
win-er-ies

wine-skin
winged
win-ner
win-ning
win-some
win-ter
win-ter-gree
win-ter-ize
win-ter-ized
win-ter-iz-ing
win-ter-i-za-tion
win-try
wipe
wiped
wip-ing
wire-haired
wire-les
wire-tap
wiry
wir-i-er
wir-i-est
wis-dom
wise
wis-er
wis-est
wise-acre
wise-crack
wish-bone
wish-ful
wishy-washy
wisp
wispy
wis-ter-ia
wist-ful
witch-craft
witch-ery
witch-er-ies
witch-ing
with-draw
with-er
with-ered
with-er-ing
with-hold
with-held
with-hold-ing
with-in
with-out
with-stand
with-stood
with-stand-ing
wit-less

wit-ness
wit-ted
wit-ti-cism
wit-ting
wit-ting-ly
wiz-ard
wi-zard-ly
wi-zard-ry
wiz-en
wiz-ened
wob-ble
woe-be-gone
woe-ful
wolf-hound
wolf-ram
wol-ver-ine
wom-an
wom-en
wom-an-ly
wom-an-hood
womb
wom-bat
wom-en-folk
won-der
won-der-ful
won-der-land
won-der-ment
won-drous
wont-ed
wood-bine
wood-cut-ter
wood-ed
wood-en
wood-land
wood-man
wood-men
wood-peck-er
wood-shed
woods-man
woods-men
wood-wind
wood-work
woody
wood-i-er
wood-i-est
woof-er
wool-en
wool-gath-er-ing
wool-ly
wool-li-er
wool-li-est

wool-ly-head-ed
woozy
wooz-i-er
wooz-i-est
word-book
word-ing
word-less
word-less-ly
work-a-ble
work-a-bil-i-ty
work-a-day
work-bench
work-book
work-day
worked-up
work-er
work-horse
work-house
work-ing
work-ing-man
work-ing-men
work-man
work-men
work-man-like
work-man-ship
work-ta-ble
world-ly
world-li-er
world-li-est
world-ly--wise
world-wide
worm--eat-en
worm-wood
wormy
worm-i-er
worm-i-est
worn--out
wor-ri-some
wor-ry
wor-ried
wor-ry-ing
wor-ries
wor-ry-wart
wors-en
wor-ship
wor-ship-ful
wor-sted
worth-less
worth-while
wor-thy
wor-thi-er

wor-thi-est
wor-thi-ness
would--be
wouldn't
wound-ed
wraith
wran-gle
wran-gled
wran-gling
wrath-ful
wreak
wreath
wreathe
wreathed
wreath-ing
wreck-age
wreck-er
wrench
wres-tle
wres-tled
wres-tling
wretch-ed
wrig-gle
wrig-gled
wrin-kle
wrin-kled
wrin-kling
wrist-band
write
wrote
writ-ten
writ-ing
write-in
writ-er
writhe
writhed
writh-ing
wrong-do-er
wrong-do-ing
wronged
wrong-ful
wrong-head-ed
wrought
wry
wri-er
wri-est
wry-ly

X

X chro-mo-some

xe-bec
xe-non
xen-o-pho-bia
X-ray
x-sec-tion
xy-lem
xy-lo-phone
xy-lose

Y

yacht
yacht-ing
yachts-man
yachts-men
yak
yam
yank
Yan-kee
yap
yapped
yap-ping
yard-age
yard-arm
yard-mas-ter
yard-stick
yarn
yar-row
yawn
year
year-book
year-ling
year-long
year-ly
yearn
yearn-ing
year--round
yeast
yeasty
yeast-i-er
yeast-i-est
yel-low
yel-low-ish
yel-low-bird
yel-low fe-ver
yel-low-ham-mer
yel-low jack-et
yelp
yen

yenned
yen-ning
yeo-man
yeo-men
ye-shi-va
ye-shi-vas
yes-ter-day
yes-ter-year
ye-ti
yew
yield
yield-ing
yip
yipped
yip-ping
yo-del
yo-deled
yo-del-ing
yo-del-er
yo-ga
yo-gic
yo-gi
yo-gis
yo-gurt
yoke
yoked
yok-ing
yo-kel
yolk
yon-der
yore
young
young-ling
young-ster
your-self
your-selves
youth-ful
yowl
yt-ter-bi-um
yt-tri-um
yuc-ca
yule-tide
yum-my
yum-mi-er
yum-mi-est

Z

za-ny
za-nies

za-ni-er
za-n-est
za-ni-ly
zeal-ot
zeal-ous
ze-bra
ze-bras
ze-bu
ze-nith
zeph-yr
zep-pe-lin
ze-ro
ze-ros
ze-roes
zest
zesty
zest-i-er
zest-i-est
zig-zag
zig-zagged
zig-zag-ging
zinc
zing
zin-nia
zip
zipped
zip-ping
zip-per
zip-py
zip-pi-er
zip-pi-est
zir-con
zir-con-ni-um
zith-er
zo-di-ac
zo-di-a-cal
zom-bie
zom-bi
zon-al
zone
zoned
zon-ing
zoo
zoos
zo-ol-o-gy
zo-o-log-i-cal
zo-o-log-i-cal-ly
zo-ol-o-gist
zuc-chi-ni
zwie-back
zy-gote

ENGLISH/SPANISH DICTIONARY

a *indef. article* una; un
a-back *adv.* atras
a-ban-don *v.* abandonar
ab-bey *n.* monasterio
ab-bre-vi-a-tion *n.* abreviación
ab-di-cate *v.* abdicar
ab-do-men *n.* abdomen
a-bil-i-ty *n.* habilidad
ab-nor-mal *adj.* anormal
a-bol-ish *v.* abolir
a-bout *prep.* sobre; alrededor de
a-bove *prep.* sobre; encima de
a-bra-sion *n.* abrasión
ab-rupt *adj.* brusco
ab-so-lute *adj.* completo; absoluto
ab-solve *v.* absolver
ab-sorb *v.* absorber
ab-stract *v.* abstraer
a-bun-dant *adj.* abundante
ac-a-dem-ic *adj.* academico
a-cad-e-my *n.* academia
ac-cel-er-ate *v.* acelerar
ac-cent *n.* acento
ac-cept *v.* recibir
ac-ces-si-ble *adj.* accesible
ac-ci-dent *n.* accidente
ac-com-pa-ny *v.* acompanar
ac-com-plish *v.* cumplir; acabar
ac-cord *n.* acuerdo
ac-cor-di-on *n.* acordéon
ac-count *v.* explicar
ac-cus-tom *v.* acostumbrar
a-chieve *v.* acabar
ac-quaint *v.* enterar
ac-quire *v.* adquirir
a-cross *prep.* a traves de
act *v.* fingir; hacer
ac-tion *n.* acción
ac-ti-vate *v.* activar
ac-tive *adj.* activo
ac-tu-al *adj.* actual; real
a-dapt *v.* adaptar
add *v.* sumar; anadir
ad-di-tion *n.* adición

ad-e-quate *adj.* suficiente
ad-ja-cent *adj.* adyacente
admin-is-ter *v.* administrar
ad-min-is-tra-tion *n.* administración
ad-mire *v.* admirar
ad-mit *v.* confesar; admitir
ad-vance *v.* avanzar
ad-ven-ture *n.* aventura
ad-verb *n.* adverbio
ad-ver-sar-y *n.* adversario
ad-ver-tise *v.* publicar
ad-vise *v.* avisar
ad-vo-cate *v.* abogar
aer-ate *v.* airear
aes-thet-ic *adj.* estetico
a-far *adv.* lejos
af-fair *n.* amorosa
af-fec-ta-tion *n.* afectación
af-fec-tion *n.* afeccion
af-fin-i-ty *n.* afinidad
af-firm-a-tive *n.* aserción
af-flic-tion *n.* aflicción
af-flu-ence *n.* afluencia
af-ter *prep.* detras de
af-ter-noon *n.* tarde
af-ter-ward *adv.* despues
a-gain *adv.* otra vez
a-gainst *prep.* contra
a-ged *adj.* viejo
ag-gra-vate *v.* agravar
ag-gres-sion *n.* agresión
ag-gres-sive *adj.* agresivo
a-gil-i-ty *n.* agilidad
a-go *adj.* pasado
a-gree *v.* acordar
a-gree-ment *n.* acuerdo
a-ground *adv.* encallado
a-head *adv.* al frente
aid *n.* ayuda
aim *v.* aspirar
air *n.* aire
air-plane *n.* avion
air-port *n.* aeropuerto
a-larm *n.* alarma
al-bi-no *n.* albino
al-co-hol *n.* alcohol
a-lert *adj.* alerte
al-ge-bra *n.* algebra
al-ien *n.* extranjero

a-like *adj.* semejante
al-i-men-ta-ry *adj.* alimenticio
a-live *adj.* activo
all *adj.* todo
al-le-ga-tion *n.* alegación
al-ler-gy *n.* alergia
al-le-vi-ate *v.* calmar
al-li-ga-tor *n.* caiman
al-low *v.* dar; permitir
al-low-ance *n.* ración; permision
al-lure *v.* tentar
al-lu-sion *n.* alusion
al-most *adv.* casi
a-lone *adj.* solo
al-pha-bet *n.* alfabeto
al-so *adv.* también; ademas
al-read-y *adv.* ya
al-ter-a-tion *n.* alteración
al-ter-ca-tion *n.* altercación
al-ter-nate *v.* alternar
al-though *conj.* aunque
al-to-geth-er *adv.* en total
al-ways *adv.* siempre
a-maze *v.* asombrar
a-maze-ment *n.* sorpresa
am-bas-sa-dor *n.* embajador
am-bi-tion *n.* ambición
am-biv-a-lence *n.* ambivalencia
am-bu-late *v.* andar
a-me-na-ble *adj.* docil
A-mer-i-can *adj.* americano
a-mi-a-ble *adj.* amable
am-nes-ty *n.* amniastia
a-mong *prep.* en medio de
am-o-rous *adj.* amoroso
am-ple *adj.* abundante
am-pli-fy *v.* amplificar
a-muse-ment *n.* pasatiempo
an *indef. article* una; un; uno
an-al-ge-sic *adj.* analgesico
an-ces-tor *n.* antepasado
an-cient *adj.* antiguo

and *conj.* y
an-gel *n.* angel
an-gry *adj.* enfadado
an-i-mal *n.* animal
an-i-mate *v.* dar vida
an-i-ma-tion *n.* animación
an-i-mos-i-ty *n.*
  animosidad
an-kle *n.* tobillo
an-nex-a-tion *n.* anexión
an-ni-hi-late *v.* aniquilar
an-ni-hi-late *v.*
  aniquilar
an-ni-ver-sa-ry *n*
  . aniversario
an-nounce *v.* proclamar
an-nounce-ment *n.*
  anuncio
an-noy-ance *n.* fastidio
an-nun-ci-ate *v.* anunciar
an-nun-ci-a-tion *n.*
  anunciacion
an-oth-er *adj., pron.* otro
an-swer *v.* contestar;
  responder
ant *n.* hormiga
an-tag-o-nize *v.* contender
ant-arc-tic *adj.* antartico
an-te-lope *n.* antilope
an-te-ri-or *adj.* anterior
an-ti-bi-ot-ic *n.*
  antibiotico
an-ti-bod-y *n.* anticuerpo
an-tic-i-pate *v.* esperar
an-tic-i-pa-tion *n.*
  expectacion
an-tique *adj.* antiguo
an-ti-so-cial *adj.* antisocial
anx-ious *adj.* impaciente
an-y *adj., pron.* alguno;
  algun
an-y-bod-y *pron.* alguien
an-y-one *pron.* alguien;
  alguno
an-y-thing *pron.* algo
a-part-ment *n.*
  apartamento
ape *n.* mono
a-pol-o-gize *v.* disculparse
ap-pa-rel *n.* ropa
ap-peal *n.* apelacion

ap-pear *v.* parecer
ap-pear-ance *n.* apariencia
ap-pen-dix *n.* apendice
ap-pe-tite *n.* gana
ap-plaud *v.* aplaudir
ap-ple *n.* manzana
ap-pli-ca-tion *n.*
  aplicación
ap-ply *v.* aplicar
ap-praise *v.* valorar
ap-pre-hend *v.* entender
ap-pre-hen-sion *n.*
  aprenhension
ap-proach *v.* aproximarse
ap-prov-al *n.* aprobación
ap-prove *v.* aprobar
ap-prox-i-mate *v.*
  aproximar
A-pril *n.* abril
a-quar-i-um *n.* acuario
ar-bi-trar-y *adj.* arbitrario
ar-bi-trate *v.* arbitrar
ar-chi-tect *n.* arquitecto
ar-chi-tec-ture *n.*
  arquitectura
arc-tic *adj.* artico
a-re-na *n.* arena
ar-gue *v.* razonar
ar-gu-ment *n.* disputa
ar-id *adj.* arido
a-ris-to-crat *n.* aristocrata
a-rith-me-tic *n.* aritmetica
arm *n.* brazo
arm-ful *n.* brazado
arm-pit *n.* sobaco
ar-my *n.* ejercito
ar-o-mat-ic *adj.* aromatico
a-round *adv.* alrededor
ar-range-ment *n.* orden
ar-rest *v.* detener
ar-rive *v.* llegar
ar-ro-gant *adj.* arrogante
art *n.* arte
ar-tic-u-late *v.* articular
ar-tic-u-la-tion *n.*
  articulacion
ar-ti-fi-cial *adj.* artificial
art-ist *n.* artista
as *conj., adv.* como
as-cen-sion *n.* ascensión
as-cribe *v.* atribuir

a-shamed *adj.*
  avergonzado
ask *v.* rogar; preguntar
a-sleep *adv., adj.* dormido
as-pi-rin *n.* aspirina
as-sault *v.* atacar
as-sem-ble *v.* juntar
as-sem-bly *n.* asamblea
as-sign *v.* asignar
as-sign-ment *n.* asignación
as-sim-i-late *v.* asimilar
as-sist *v.* ayudar
as-sist-ance *n.* ayuda
asth-ma *n.* asma
asth-mat-ic *adj.* asmatico
as-ton-ish *v.* asombrar
as-ton-ish-ment *n.*
  asombro
as-trol-o-gy *n.* astrologia
as-tron-o-my *n.*
  astronomia
at *prep.* a; en
ath-lete *n.* atleta
ath-let-ic *adj.* atletico
at-om *n.* atomo
a-tom-ic *adj.* atomico
a-top *prep.* sobre
at-tach *v.* pegar; sujetar
at-tack *v.* atacar
at-tempt *v.* intentar
at-tend *v.* asistir
at-ten-tion *n.* atención
at-tract *v.* atraer
at-trac-tion *n.* atracción
a-typ-i-cal *adj.* atipico
au-di-ence *n.* publico
au-di-tion *n.* audición
au-di-to-ry *adj.* auditivo
Au-gust *n.* agosto
aunt *n.* tia
au-then-tic-i-ty *n.*
  autenticidad
au-thor *n.* autor
au-thor-i-ty *n.* autoridad
au-thor-ize *v.* autorizar
au-to-bi-og-ra-pher *n.*
  autobiografo
au-to-bi-og-ra-phy *n.*
  autobiografia
au-to-mat-ic *adj.*
  automatico

a-venge v. vengar

av-e-nue n. avenida

av-er-age adj. medio

a-vert v. apartar

a-wait v. esperar

a-wake v. despertar(se)

a-way adv. lejos

aw-ful adj. horrible

awk-ward adj. embarazoso

B

ba-boon n. mandril

ba-bush-ka n. pañuelo

ba-by n. nino

bach-e-lor n. soltero

back n. espalda

back-ward adv. atras

ba-con n. tocino

bac-ter-i-um n. bacteria

bad adj. malo

bag n. bolso; saco

bag-gage n. equipaje

bail v. afianzar

bake v. cocer en horno

bak-er n. panadero

bak-ing n. cocción

bal-ance n. equilibrio

bald adj. calvo

ball n. pelota

bal-lad n. balada

bal-le-ri-na n. bailarina

bal-let n. ballet

bal-loon n. globo

bal-lot n. votación

balm n. balsamo

ban v. prohibir

ba-nan-a n. platano

band-age v. vendar

ban-dit n. bandido

bang v. golpear

ban-ish v. desterrar

bank n. banco

bank-er n. banquero

bap-tism n. bautismo

bar v. excluir

bar-ber n. peluquero

bar-ber-shop n. peluqueria

bare adj. desnudo, v. des nudar

bare-ly adv. simplemente

barge n. gabarra

bar-i-um n. bario

bark v. ladrar, n. ladrido

barn n. granero

ba-rom-et-er n. barometro

bar-on n. baron

bar-on-ess n. baronesa

bar-rel n. barril

bar-ri-cade n. barricada

base-ball n. beisbol

ba-sic adj. basico

ba-sil-i-ca n. basilica

bas-ket n. cesta

bas-ket-ball n. baloncesto

bat v. golpear, n. maza

bath n. bano

bathe v. banar(se)

bat-tle v. luchar, n. lucha

bay n. bahia

be v. estar; ser

beach n. playa

beak n. pico

beam n. rayo

bear n. oso

beat v. vencer; golpear

beat-en adj. derrotado

beau-ti-ful adj. hermoso

beau-ty n. belleza

be-cause conj. porque

be-come v. hacer(se)

bed n. cama

bed-room n. alcoba

bee n. abeja

bee-hive n. colmena

beer n. cerveza

be-fit v. convenir

be-fore prep. antes de, adv. delante

beg v. pedir

be-gin v. comenzar

be-gin-ning n. comienzo

be-hav-ior n. compor tamiento

be-hind adv. atras; detras, prep. detras de

be-ing n. ser

be-liev-a-ble adj. creible

be-lieve v. creer

bell n. cascabel

bel-lig-er-ent adj. beligerante

be-long-ings n. pertenencias

be-low adv. abajo, prep. debajo de

belt n. cinturon

bench n. banco

be-neath prep. debajo de

ben-e-dic-tion n. bendición

be-nef-i-cent adj. benefico

ben-e-fi-cial adj. beneficioso

be-nev-o-lence n. benevolencia

be-side prep. cerca

be-sides prep. ademas de

best adj. mejor

bes-tial adj. bestial

be-tray v. revelar

be-tray-al n. traición

bet-ter adv., adj. mejor

be-tween adv. en medio, prep. entre

bev-er-age n. bebida

be-yond prep. despues de

Bi-ble n. Biblia

Bil-li-cal adj. biblico

bib-li-og-ra-phy n. bibliog rafia

bi-cy-cle n. bicicleta

bi-cy-clist n. biciclista

big adj. grande

big-a-my n. bigamia

bike n. bicicleta

bill n. pico; cuenta

bill-board n. cartelera

bil-liards n. billar

bil-lion n. billon

bind v. encuadernar; atar

bi-og-ra-pher n. biografo

bi-o-graph-ic adj. biografico

bi-og-ra-phy n. biografia

bi-ol-o-gy n. biologia

bi-plane n. biplaño

bird n. pajaro

birth n. nacimiento

birth-day *n.* cumpleanos
bi-sect *v.* bisecar
bi-sec-tion *n.* bisección
bish-op *n.* obispo
bit *n.* pedazo
bite *v.* picar
bit-ter-ness *n.* rencor
bi-zarre *adj.* raro
black *adj.* negro
black-en *v.* difamar
blad-der *n.* vejiga
blame *v.* culpar
blank *n., adj.* blanco
blan-ket *n.* manta
blast *v.* destruir, *n.* explo
 sion
blem-ish *v.* manchar
bless *v.* bandecir
bless-ing *n.* bendición
blind *v.* cegar, *adj.* ciego
blind-ness *n.* ceguera
bliss *n.* felicidad
blis-ter *v.* ampollar(se)
block *n.* manzana
block-ade *adj.* bloqueo
block-age *n.* obstrucción
blond *adj.* rubio
blood *n.* sangre
blood-y *adj.* sangriento
bloom *v.* florecer
blouse *n.* blusa
blow *v.* inflar; soplar
blue *adj.* azul
blunt *adj.* abrupto
blush *n.* sonrojo
board *n.* consejo
boat *n.* barco
bod-y *n.* cuerpo
bois-ter-ous *adj.* ruidoso
bold *adj.* descarado
bomb *n.* bomba
bom-bard-ment *n.*
 bombar deo
bone *n.* hueso
bon-y *adj.* huesudo
book *n.* libro
boom *n.* prosperidad
boot *n.* bota
bore *v.* aburrir
born *adj.* nacido
bor-row *v.* apropiarse

boss *n.* jefe
bo-tan-ic *adj.* botanico
bot-a-ny *n.* botanica
both *adj.* los dos
bot-tle *n.* botella
bough *n.* rama
boul-e-vard *n.* avenida
bounce *v.* rebotar
bound *v.* saltar
boun-te-ous *adj.*
 abundante
bou-quet *n.* ramo
box-er *n.* boxeador
box-ing *n.* boxeo
boy *n.* chico
brack-et *n.* corchete
brain-y *adj.* listo
brake *v.* frenar
branch *n.* rama
brave *adj.* valiente
bra-zen *adj.* descarado
bread *n.* pan
break *v.* quebrar; romper
break-age *n.* rotura
break-fast *n.* desayuno
breath *n.* respiració_
bribe *v.* cohechar
bride *n.* novia
bridge *n.* puente
brief *adj.* breve
bright *adj.* brillante
bright-ness *n.* lustre
bril-liant *adj.* brillante
bring *v.* traer
brisk *adj.* vigoroso
bro-ken *adj.* roto;
 quebrado
bronze *n.* bronce
brook *n.* arroyo
broom *n.* escoba
broth-er *n.* hermano
broth-er-hood *n.*
 fraternidad
broth-er-in-law *n.* cuando
brow *n.* ceja
brown *adj.* moreno
bruise *n.* contusión
brush *n.* cepillo
bru-tal *adj.* brutal
budg-et *v.* presupuestar
buf-fa-lo *n.* bufalo

bug *n.* bicho
build *v.* construir
build-ing *n.* construcción
bull *n.* toro
bump *n.* choque
bunch *n.* racimo
bun-ny *n.* conejito
bu-reauc-ra-cy *n.*
 burocracia
bu-reau-crat *n.* burocrata
bur-glar *n.* ladron
bur-glar-ize *v.* robar
burn *v.* incendiar
burnt *adj.* quernado
bur-ro *n.* burro
burst *v.* romper
bus *n.* autobus
bush *n.* arbusto
busi-ness *n.* oficio
but *conj.* pero
but-ter *n.* mantequilla
but-ter-fly *n.* mariposa
buy *v.* comprar
buy-er *n.* comprador
by *adv.* cerca, *prep.* cerca
 de; por

C

cab *n.* taxi
ca-bal *n.* cabala
cab-a-la *n.* cabala
cab-a-ret *n.* cabaret
cab-bage *n.* col
cab-driv-er *n.* taxista
cab-in *n.* cabana
cab-i-net *n.* gabinete
cab-i-net-mak-er *n.*
 ebanista
cab-i-net-work *n.*
 ebanisteria
ca-ble *n.* cable
ca-ble-gram *n.*
 cablegrama
ca-ca-o *n.* cacao
ca-chet *n.* cacareo
cac-tus *n.* cacto
ca-dav-er *n.* cadaver
ca-dav-er-ous *adj.* cadav-
 erico
cad-die *n.* caddy

ca-dence *n.* cadencia
ca-det *n.* cadete
cad-mi-um *n.* cadmio
ca-du-ce-us *n.* caduceo
ca-fe *n.* cafe
caf-e-te-ri-a *n.* cafeteria
caf-feine *n.* cafeina
caf-tan *n.* tunica
cage *n.* jaula
ca-jole *v.* engatusar
cake *n.* pastel
cal-a-bash *n.* calabaza
cal-a-mine *n.* calamina
ca-lam-i-ty *n.* calamidad
cal-ci-fi-ca-tion *n.* cal
    cificacion
cal-ci-fy *v.* calcificar
cal-ci-um *n.* calcio
cal-cu-late *v.* calcular
cal-cu-lat-ed *adj.*
    intencional
cal-cu-lat-ing *adj.*
    calculador
cal-cu-la-tion *n.* calculo
cal-cu-la-tor *n.*
    calculadora
cal-dron *n.* caldera
cal-en-dar *n.* calendario
cal-i-ber *n.* calibre
cal-i-brate *v.* calibrar
cal-i-bra-tion *n.*
    calibración
cal-i-co *n.* calico
cal-i-per *n.* calibrador
ca-liph *n.* califa
cal-is-then-ics *n.*
    calistenia
ca-lix *n.* caliz
call *v.* llamar
call-er *n.* cisitante
cal-lig-ra-pher *n.*
    caligrafo
cal-lig-ra-phy *n.* caligrafia
call-ing *n.* vocación
cal-lous *v.* encallecerse
cal-low *adj.* inmaturo
cal-lus *n.* callo
calm *v.* calmar(se); *n.*
    calma
calm-ness *n.* tranquilidad
ca-lor-ic *adj.* calorico

cal-o-rie *n.* caloria
ca-lum-ni-ate *v.* calumniar
cal-va-ry *n.* calvario
cal-lyx *n.* caliz
ca-ma-ra-der-ie *n.* cama-
    raderia
cam-bi-um *n.* cambium
cam-el *n.* camello
ca-mel-lia *n.* camelia
cam-e-o *n.* camafeo
cam-er-a *n.* camara
cam-ou-flage *n.* camuflaje
camp *v.* acampar
cam-paign *n.* campana
camp-er *n.* campista
cam-phor *n.* alcanfor
can *v.* poder
ca-nar-y *n.* canario
can-cel *v.* cancelar; matar;
    anular
can-cel-la-tion *n.* can
    celacion
can-cer *n.* cancer
can-cer-ous *adj.* canceroso
can-des-cent *adj.*
    candente
can-did *adj.* franco
can-di-da-cy *n.*
    candidatura
can-di-date *n.* candidato
can-died *adj.* escarchado
can-dle *n.* cirio; vela
can-dle-hold-er *n.*
    candelero
can-dle-stick *n.* candelero
can-dor *n.* franqueza
can-dy *n.* azucar
cane *n.* cana; baston
ca-nine *adj.* canino
can-is-ter *n.* lata
canned *adj.* enlatado
can-ni-bal *n.* canibal
can-ni-bal-ism *n.* cani-
    balismo
can-ni-bal-is-tic *adj.*
    canibal
can-non *n.* conon
ca-noe *n.* canoa
ca-non-i-za-tion *n.*
    canoni- zacion
can-on-ize *v.* canonizar

can-ta-loupe *n.* cantalupo
can-teen *n.* cantina
can-vas *n.* lona
can-yon *n.* canon
cap *n.* tapa
ca-pa-bil-i-ty *n.* capacidad
ca-pa-ble *adj.* capaz
ca-pa-cious *adj.* espacioso
ca-pac-i-ty *n.* capacidad
ca-per *n.* cabriola
cap-il-lar-y *n.* capilar
cap-i-tal *n., adj.* capital
cap-i-tal-ism *n.*
    capitalismo
cap-i-tal-ist *n.* capitalista
cap-i-tal-is-tic *adj.*
    capitalista
cap-i-tal-i-za-tion *n.*
    capitalizacion
cap-i-tal-ize *v.* capitalizar
cap-i-tal-ly *adv.* ad
    mirablemente
cap-i-tol *n.* capitolio
ca-pit-u-late *v.* capitular
ca-price *n.* capricho
ca-pri-cious *adj.*
    caprichoso
cap-sule *n.* capsula
cap-tain *n.* capitan
cap-tion *n.* subtitulo
cap-tious *adj.* capcioso
cap-ti-vate *v.* cautivar
cap-ti-va-tion *n.* encanto
cap-tive *adj.* cautivo
cap-tiv-i-ty *n.* cautividad
cap-tor *n.* capturador
cap-ture *v.* capturar
car *n.* coche
car-a-mel *n.* caramelo
car-at *n.* quilate
car-a-van *n.* caravana
car-bide *n.* carburo
car-bine *n.* carabina
car-bo-hy-drate *n.* car
    bohifrato
car-bon *n.* carbono
car-bon-ate *v.* carbonatar
car-bun-cle *n.* carbunco
car-bu-re-tor *n.*
    carburador

car-cin-o-gen-ic *adj.* can cerigeno

card *n.* tarjeta

car-di-ac *adj.* cardiaco

car-di-nal *adj.* cardinal

car-di-o-gram *n.* car diograma

car-di-ol-o-gy *n.* cardiologia

care *v.* cuidar

ca-reer *n.* carrera

care-free *adj.* des- preocupado

care-ful *adj.* cuidadoso

care-less *adj.* espontaneo; descuidado

ca-ress *n.* caricia

care-tak-er *n.* portero

car-go *n.* carga

car-i-ca-ture *n.* caricatura

car-nage *n.* carniceria

car-nal *adj.* carnal

car-ni-val *n.* carnaval

car-ni-vore *n.* carnivoro

car-niv-o-rous *adj.* carnivoro

ca-rous-al *n.* jarana

car-ou-sel *n.* carrusel

car-pen-try *n.* carpinteria

car-pet *n.* alfombra

car-riage *n.* carruaje

car-ri-er *n.* carrero

car-rot *n.* zanahoria

car-ry *v.* lograr; llevar

car-sick *adj.* mareado

cart *n.* carro

cart-age *n.* acarreo

car-tel *n.* cartel

car-ti-lage *n.* cartilago

cart-load *n.* carretada

car-toon *n.* tira

car-toon-ist *n.* caricaturista

car-tridge *n.* cartucho

carve *v.* esculpir

carv-ing *n.* escultura

case *n.* caja

cahs *n.* efectivo

cash-ew *n.* anacardo

cash-ier *n.* cajero

cash-mere *n.* cachemira

ca-si-no *n.* casino

cask *n.* barril

cas-se-role *n.* cacerola

cas-sette *n.* casete

cast *v.* dar; fundir; echar

cas-ta-nets *n.* castanuelas

caste *n.* casta

cas-ti-gate *v.* castigar

cas-tle *n.* castillo

cas-trate *v.* castrar

cas-tra-tion *n.* castración

ca-su-al *adj.* casual

cas-u-al-ly *adv.* casualmente

ca-su-ist-ry *n.* casuistica

cat *n.* gato

ca-tab-o-lism *n.* catabolismo

cat-a-log *n.* catalogo

cat-a-lyst *n.* catalizador

cat-a-lyt-ic *adj.* catalitico

cat-a-lyze *v.* catalizar

cat-a-pult *n.* catapulta

cat-a-ract *n.* catarata

ca-tas-tro-phe *n.* catastrofe

cat-a-stroph-ic *adj.* catastrofico

cat-a-ton-ic *adj.* catatonico

catch *v.* prender; coger

catch-er *n.* receptor

catch-ing *adj.* contagioso

catch-y *adj.* capcioso

cat-e-chism *n.* catecismo

cat-e-gor-ic *adj.* categorico

cat-e-gor-i-cal-ly *adv.* cate- goricamente

cat-e-go-rize *v.* clasificar

cat-e-go-ry *n.* categoria

cat-er-pil-lar *n.* oruga

cat-er-waul *v.* chillar

ca-thar-sis *n.* catarsis

ca-the-dral *n.* catedral

cath-ode *n.* catodo

cath-o-lic *adj.* catolico

ca-thol-i-cism *n.* catolicismo

cat-nip *n.* nebeda

cat-tail *n.* espadana

cat-tle *n.* ganado

cat-tle-man *n.* ganadero

cau-li-flow-er *n.* coliflor

cau-sa-tion *n.* causalidad

caus-a-tive *adj.* causativo

cause *n.* razon; causa

cause-way *n.* elevada

caus-tic *adj.* caustico

cau-ter-ize *v.* cauterizar

cau-tion *v.* amonestar

cau-tion-ar-y *adj.* preventivo

cau-tious *adj.* cauteloso

cav-al-ry *n.* caballeria

cave *n.* cueva

cav-ern *n.* caverna

cav-ern-ous *adj.* cavernoso

cav-i-ty *n.* cavidad

ca-vort *v.* cabriolar

cay *n.* cayo

cease *v.* suspender

cease-less *adj.* continuo

ce-dar *n.* cedro

cede *v.* ceder

ceil-ing *n.* techo

cel-e-brant *n.* celebrante

cel-e-brate *v.* celebrar

cel-e-brat-ed *adj.* celebre

cel-e-bra-tion *n.* celebración

ce-leb-ri-ty *n.* celebridad

cel-er-y *n.* apio

ce-les-tial *adj.* celestial

cel-i-ba-cy *n.* celibato

cel-i-bate *adj.* celibe

cell *n.* celda

cel-lar *n.* sotano

cel-lo-phane *n.* celofan

cel-lu-lar *adj.* celular

cel-lu-loid *n.* celuloide

cel-lu-lose *n.* celulosa

ce-ment *n.* cemento

cem-e-ter-y *n.* cementerio

cen-ser *n.* insensario

cen-sor *n.* censor

cen-so-ri-ous *adj.* cen surador

cen-sor-ship *n.* censura

cen-sure *v.* censurar

cen-sus *n.* censo

cent *n.* centavo

cen-taur *n.* centauro

cen-ten-ni-al *adj.*
centenario

cen-ter *n.* centro

cen-ti-grade *adj.*
centigrado

cen-ti-gram *n.* centiframo

cen-ti-li-ter *n.* centilitro

cen-ti-me-ter *n.*
centimetro

cen-tral *adj.* central

cen-tral-ize *v.*
centralizar(se)

cen-tric *adj.* centrico

cen-trif-u-gal *adj.*
centrifugo

cen-tu-ry *n.* siglo

ce-phal-ic *adj.* cefalico

ce-ram-ic *adj.* ceramico

ce-re-al *n.* cereal

cer-e-bral *adj.* cerebral

cer-e-brum *n.* cerebro

cer-e-mo-ni-al *adj.*
ceremonial

cer-e-mo-ni-ous *adj.*
ceremonioso

cer-e-mo-ny *n.* ceremonia

cer-tain *adj.* seguro; cierto

cer-tain-ly *adv.*
ciertamente

cer-tain-ty *n.* certeza

cer-ti-fi-a-ble *adj.*
certificable

cer-tif-i-cate *n.* certificado

cer-ti-fi-ca-tion *n.* cer
tificacion

cer-ti-fied *adj.* certificado

cer-ti-fy *v.* certificar

cer-ti-tude *n.* certidumbre

cer-vix *n.* cerviz

ces-sa-tion *n.* cesación

ces-sion *n.* cesion

chafe *v.* frotar; rozar

cha-grin *v.* desilusionar

chair *n.* silla

chair-man *n.* presidente

chair-man-ship *n.*
presiden cia

chair-wo-man *n.*
presidenta

cha-let *n.* chalet

chal-ice *n.* caliz

chalk *n.* tiza

chalk-board *n.* pizarra

chal-lenge *v.* desafiar

chal-leng-er *n.* desafiador

cham-ber-lain *n.*
chambelan

cha-me-leon *n.* camaleon

champ *n.* campeon

cham-pagne *n.* champana

cham-pi-on *n.* campeon

cham-pi-on-ship *n.* cam
peonato

chance *n.* oportunidad;
casualidad

chan-cel-ler-y *n.*
cancilleria

chan-cel-lor *n.* canciller

change *v.* transformar;
cam biar

change-a-ble *adj.*
cambiable

change-o-ver *n.* cambio

chang-er *n.* cambiador

chan-nel *n.* canal

chant *n.* canto

cha-os *n.* caos

cha-ot-ic *adj.* caotico

chap-el *n.* capilla

chap-er-one *n.* carabina

chap-lain *n.* capellan

chap-ter *n.* capitulo

char-ac-ter *n.* caracter

char-ac-ter-is-tic *n.* carac
teristica

char-ac-ter-ize *v.* carac
terizar

char-coal *n.* carboncillo

charge *v.* pedir; cargar

cha-ris-ma *n.* carisma

char-i-ta-ble *adj.*
caritativo

char-i-ty *n.* caridad

charm *n.* encanto

charm-er *n.* encantador

charm-ing *adj.* encantador

chart *v.* trazar

char-ter *n.* carta

chase *v.* perseguir

chaste *adj.* casto

chas-ten *v.* castigar

chas-tise *v.* castigar

chas-ti-ty *n.* castidad

chat *v.* charlar

chat-ter *v.* charlar

chau-vin-ist *n.* chauvinista

chau-vin-is-tic *adj.*
chauvinista

cheap *adj.* barato

cheap-en *v.* degradar(se)

cheap-ly *adv.* barato

cheap-ness *n.* tacaneria

cheat *v.* enganar

cheat-er *n.* tramposo

cheat-ing *adj.* tramposo

check *n.* cheque; parada;
cuenta

check-book *n.* chequera

check-ered *adj.* a cuadros

cheek *n.* mejilla

cheep *adj.* piada

cheer *v.* alegrar; alentar

cheer-ful *adj.* alegre

cheer-i-ly *adv.*
alegremente

cheer-less *adj.* triste

cheese *n.* queso

cheese-cake *n.* quesadilla

chef *n.* cocinero

chem-i-cal *n.* quimico

chem-ist *n.* quimico

chem-is-try *n.* quimica

che-mo-ther-a-py *n.*
quimioterapia

cher-ish *v.* abrigar; querer

cher-ry *n.* cerezo

cher-ub *n.* querubin

che-ru-bic *adj.* querubico

chess *n.* ajedrez

chest *n.* pecho

chest-nut *n.* castanañ

chew *v.* masticar

chew-ing *n.* masticación

chick-en *n.* pollo

chick-pea *n.* garbanzo

chief *n.* jefe

chif-fon *n.* chifon

child *n.* hijo; nino

child-birth *m.* parto

child-ish *adj.* aninado

child-like *adj.* infantil

chil-i *n.* chile
chill *n.* frio
chill-ing *adj.* frio
chime *n.* carillon
chim-ney *n.* chimenea
chim-pan-zee *n.*
chimpance
chin *n.* barba
chi-na *n.* china
chip *n.* astilla; *v.* astillar
chip-per *adj.* jovial
chi-ro-prac-tor *n.*
quiroprac tico
chirp *v.* gorjear
chis-el *n.* cincel
chis-el-er *n.* cincelador
chiv-al-rous *adj.* cabal
leresco
chiv-al-ry *n.*
caballerosidad
chive *n.* cebollino
chlo-ride *n.* cloruro
chlo-rine *n.* cloro
chlo-ro-phyll *n.* clorofila
choc-o-late *n.* chocolate
choice *adj.* selecto; *n.*
preferencia
choir *n.* coro
choke *v.* ahogar; atorar;
estrangular
chol-er-a *n.* colera
chol-er-ic *adj.* colerico
cho-les-ter-ol *n.* colesterol
chomp *v.* ronzar
choose *v.* escoger
choos-ing *n.* seleccion
chop *v.* cortar
cho-ral *n.* coral
cho-re-og-ra-pher *n.*
coreo- grafo
cho-re-og-ra-phy *n.*
coreo- grafia
cho-sen *adj.* escogido
chow *n.* comida
Christ *n.* Cristo
chris-ten *v.* bautizar
chris-ten-ing *n.* bautismo
Chris-tian *n.* cristiano
Chris-ti-an-i-ty *n.* cris
tianismo
Christ-mas *n.* Navidad

chro-mat-ic *adj.*
cromatico
chrome *n.* cromo
chro-mi-um *n.* cromo
chro-mo-some *n.* cro-
mosoma
chron-ic *adj.* cronico
chron-i-cle *n.* cronica
chron-o-log-ic *adj.*
cronologico
chro-nol-o-gy *n.*
cronologia
chrys-a-lis *n.* crisalida
chry-san-the-mum *n.*
crisan temo
chum *n.* companero
chunk *n.* trozo
church *n.* iglesia
church-man *n.* clerigo
churn *n.* mantequera
chute *n.* conducto; rampa
ci-ca-da *n.* cigarra
ci-der *n.* sidra
ci-gar *n.* puro
cig-a-rette *n.* cigarrillo
cinch *n.* cincha
cin-der *n.* carbonilla
cin-e-ma *n.* cine
cin-e-mat-ic *adj.* filmico
cin-e-ma-tog-ra-phy *n.*
cinematografia
cin-na-mon *n.* canela
ci-pher *v.* cifrar
cir-cle *n.* ciclo
cir-cuit *n.* circuito
cir-cu-lar *adj.* circular
cir-cu-late *v.* circular
cir-cu-lat-ing *adj.*
circulante
cir-cu-la-tion *n.*
circulacion
cir-cum-cise *v.* circuncidar
cir-cum-cised *adj.*
circunciso
cir-cum-ci-sion *n.*
circuncision
cir-cum-fer-ence *n.* circun
ferencia
cir-cum-nav-i-gate *v.*
circun navegar

cir-cum-scribe *v.* cir
cunscribir
cir-cum-spect *adj.* circun-
specto
cir-cum-stance *n.* circun-
stancia
cir-cum-stan-tial *adj.*
circun- stancial
cir-cus *n.* circo
cir-rho-sis *n.* cirrosis
cir-rus *n.* cirro
cis-tern *n.* cisterna
cit-a-del *n.* ciudadela
ci-ta-tion *n.* citación
cite *v.* citar
cit-i-zen *n.* ciudadano
cit-i-zen-ship *n.*
ciudadania
cit-rus *adj.* citrico
cit-y *n.* ciudad
civ-et *n.* civeta
civ-ic *adj.* civico
civ-il *adj.* civil
ci-vil-ian *n.* civil
ci-vil-i-ty *n.* civilidad
civ-i-li-za-tion *n.*
civilización
civ-i-lize *v.* civilizar
claim *v.* merecer; reclamar
clair-voy-ance *n.*
clarividen cia
clair-voy-ant *adj.*
clarividente
clam *n.* almeja
clam-or *n.* clamor
clam-or-ous *adj.*
clamoroso
clamp *n.* abrazadera
clan *n.* clan
clan-gor *n.* estruendo
clap *v.* aplaudir
clap-per *n.* badajo
clap-ping *n.* aplausos
clar-et *n.* clarete
clar-i-fi-ca-tion *n.*
clarificacion
clar-i-fy *v.* clarificar
clar-i-net *n.* clarinete
clar-i-on *adj.* sonoro
clar-i-ty *n.* claridad
clash *v.* entrechocarse

class *n.* clase
clas-sic *adj.* clasico
clas-si-cal *adj.* clasico
clas-si-cism *n.* clasicismo
clas-si-cist *n.* clasicista
clas-si-fi-ca-tion *n.* clasificacion
clas-si-fied *adj.* clasificado
clas-si-fy *v.* clasificar
class-y *adj.* elegante
clause *n.* clausula
claus-tro-pho-bi-a *n.*
claustrofobia
clav-i-chord *n.* clavicordio
clav-i-cle *n.* clavicula
claw *n.* garra
clay *n.* arcilla
clean *v.* limpiar
clean-cut *adj.* definido
clean-er *n.* limpiador
clean-ing *n.* limpieza
clean-li-ness *n.* limpieza
cleanse *v.* limpiar
cleans-er *n.* limpiador
clear *adj.* despejado;
transparente
clear-cut *adj.* claro
clear-ing *n.* claro
clear-ly *adv.* claramente
cleav-age *n.* division
cleave *v.* adherir; partir
cleav-er *n.* cuchillo
clem-en-cy *n.* clemencia
cler-gy *n.* clero
cler-gy-man *n.* clerigo
cler-ic *adj.* clerigo
cler-i-cal *adj.* clerical
clerk *n.* oficinista
clev-er *adj.* listo
clev-er-ness *n.* inteligencia
cli-ent *n.* cliente
cli-mac-tic *adj.*
culminante
cli-mate *n.* clima
cli-mat-ic *adj.* climatico
cli-max *n.* climax
climb *v.* trepar
climb-er *n.* alpinista
climb-ing *adj.* trepador
clin-ic *n.* clinica
clin-i-cal *adj.* clinico

cli-ni-cian *n.* clinico
clip *v.* cortar
cloak *n.* manto
clock *n.* reloj
clog *n.* atasco
clois-ter *n.* claustro
clone *n.* clon
close *v.* cerrar
closed *adj.* cerrado;
vedado
close-down *n.* cierre
close-ly *adv.* atentamente;
de cerca
close-ness *n.* proximidad
close-out *n.* liquidacion
clos-et *n.* armario
clos-ing *n.* cierre
clot *n.* coagulo
cloth *n.* tela
clothe *v.* arropar
clothes *n.* ropa
cloth-ing *n.* ropa
cloud *n.* nube
cloud-burst *n.* aguacero
cloud-y *adj.* nuboso
clout *n.* bofetada
clo-ver *n.* trebol
clown *n.* payaso
club *n.* palo; trebol
clue *n.* pista
clump *n.* grupo
clum-sy *adj.* pesado
coach *n.* vagon; coche
coach-man *n.* cochero
co-ag-u-late *v.*
coagular(se)
co-ag-u-la-tion *n.*
coagulación
coal *n.* carbon
co-a-lesce *v.* unirse
co-a-li-tion *n.* coalicion
coarse *adj.* tosco
coars-en *v.* vulgarizar
coarse-ness *n.* aspereza
coast *n.* costa
coast-al *adj.* costero
coast-er *n.* trineo
coat *n.* pelo
coat-ed *adj.* banado
coat-ing *n.* capa; bano
coat-tail *n.* faldon

coax *v.* engatusar
coax-ing *n.*
engatusamiento
cob *n.* elote
co-balt *n.* cobalto
cob-bler *n.* zapatero
co-bra *n.* cobra
cob-web *n.* telarana
co-caine *n.* cocaina
coc-cyx *n.* coccix
cock *n.* gallo
cock-ade *n.* escarapela
cock-a-too *n.* cacatua
cock-i-ness *n.* presuncion
cock-le *n.* berberecho
cock-pit *n.* cancha
cock-roach *n.* cucaracha
cock-tail *n.* coctel
co-coa *n.* cacao
co-coa-nut *n.* coco
co-coon *n.* capullo
code *n.* codigo
co-de-fend-ant *n.*
coacusado
co-deine *n.* codeina
cod-fish *n.* bacalao
cod-i-fy *v.* codificar
co-di-rec-tion *n.*
codireccion
co-ef-fi-cient *n.*
coeficiente
co-erce *v.* coercer
co-er-cion *n.* coercion
co-ex-ist *v.* coexistir
co-ex-is-tence *n.*
coexistencia
co-ex-ten-sive *adj.*
coextenso
cof-fee *n.* cafe
cof-fer *n.* cofre
cof-fin *n.* ataud
cog *n.* diente
cog-i-tate *v.* meditar
cog-nac *n.* conac
cog-ni-tion *n.* cognición
cog-ni-zance *n.*
conocimiento
cog-ni-zant *adj.* enterado
co-hab-it *v.* cohabitar
co-here *v.* adherirse
co-her-ence *n.* coherencia

co-her-ent *adj.* coherente
co-he-sion *n.* cohesion
co-he-sive *adj.* cohesivo
co-hort *n.* compañero
coil *n.* rollo
coin *v.* acunar; *n.* moneda
co-in-cide *v.* coincidir
co-in-ci-dence *n.*
  coinciden cia
co-in-ci-den-tal *adj.* coin
  cidente
co-la *n.* cola
col-an-der *n.* colador
cold *n., adj.* frio
cold-blood-ed *adj.*
  impasible
cold-heart-ed *adj.*
  insensible
cold-ness *n.* frialdad
col-ic *n.* colico
col-i-se-um *n.* coliseo
co-li-tis *n.* colitis
col-lab-o-rate *v.* colaborar
col-lab-o-ra-tion *n.*
  colaboracion
col-lab-o-ra-tion-ist *n.*
  colaboracionista
col-lab-o-ra-tive *adj.*
  cooperativo
col-lab-o-ra-tor *n.*
  colaborador
col-lage *n.* collage
col-laspe *v.* desplomarse;
  caerse
col-laps-i-ble *adj.* plegable
col-lar *n.* cuello
col-lar-bone *n.* clavicula
col-late *v.* colacionar
col-lat-er-al *adj.* colateral
col-league *n.* colega
col-lect *v.* recoger; reunir;
  coleccionar
col-lect-ed *adj.* sosegado
col-lec-tion *n.* coleccion
col-lec-tive *adj.* colectivo
col-lec-tiv-ist *n.*
  colectivista
col-lec-tiv-ize *v.*
  colectivizar
col-lec-tor *n.* colector
col-lege *n.* colegio

col-le-gian *n.* estudiante
col-le-giate *adj.*
  universitario
col-lide *v.* chocar
col-li-sion *n.* choque
col-loid *n.* coloide
col-lo-qui-al *adj.* familiar
col-lo-qui-um *n.* cologuio
col-lo-quy *n.* coloquio
col-lude *v.* confabularse
col-lu-sion *n.*
  confabulación
co-logne *n.* colonia
co-lon *n.* colon
colo-nel *n.* coronel
co-lo-ni-al *adj.* colonial
co-lo-ni-al-ist *n.*
  colonialista
col-o-nist *n.* colonizador
col-o-ni-za-tion *n.*
  colonización
col-o-nize *v.* colonizar
col-o-niz-er *n.* colonizador
col-on-nade *n.* columnata
col-o-ny *n.* colonia
col-or *v.* colorear; *n.* color
col-or-a-tion *n.* coloración
col-ored *adj.* coloreado
col-or-ful *adj.* pintoresco
col-or-ing *n.* coloración
col-or-less *adj.* incoloro
co-los-sal *adj.* colosal
co-los-sus *n.* coloso
co-los-to-my *n.*
  colostomia
col-umn *n.* columna
col-umn-ist *n.* columnista
co-ma *n.* coma
co-ma-tose *adj.* comatoso
comb *v.* peinar, *n.* peine
com-bat *v.* conbatir
com-bat-ant *n.*
  combatiente
com-bat-ive *adj.*
  combativo
com-bi-na-tion *n.*
  combinación
com-bine *v.* combinar
com-bo *n.* conjunto
com-bus-ti-ble *adj.*
  conbus tible

com-bus-tion *n.*
  combustion
come *v.* llegar; venir
come-back *n.* replica
co-me-di-an *n.*
  comediante
co-me-di-enne *n.*
  comedianta
com-e-dy *n.* comedia
come-on *n.* incentivo
com-et *n.* cometa
com-fort *v.* consolar
com-fort-a-ble *adj.*
  confortable
com-fort-er *n.* consolador
com-ic *adj.* comico
com-i-cal *adj.* comico
com-ing *adj.* venidero
com-ma *n.* coma
com-mand *n.* mando; *v.*
  mandar
com-man-dant *n.*
  comandante
com-mand-er *n.*
  comandante
com-mand-ing *adj.*
  imponente
com-man-do *n.* comando
com-mem-o-rate *v.*
  conmemorar
com-mem-o-ra-tion *n.*
  conmemoración
com-mence *v.* comenzar
com-mence-ment *n.*
  comienzo
com-mend *v.* encomendar
com-men-da-tion *n.*
  recomendacion
com-men-su-rate *adj.*
  proporcionado
com-ment *n.* observación
com-men-tar-y *n.*
  comentario
com-men-tate *v.* comentar
com-merce *n.* comercio
com-mer-cial *adj.*
  comercial
com-mer-cial-ism *n.*
  comercialismo
com-mer-cial-ize *v.*
  comercializar

com-mis-er-ate v.
compadecerse

com-mis-sar n. comisario

com-mis-sar-y n.
economato

com-mis-sion v. encargar;
n. comision

com-mis-sion-er n. com
isario

com-mit v. entregar

com-mit-ment n. com
promiso

com-mit-tal n. obligación

com-mit-ee n. comite

com-mode n. comoda

com-mo-dore n.
comodoro

com-mon adj. comun

com-mon-place adj. or
dinario

com-mon-wealth n. com
unidad

com-mo-tion n. tumulto

com-mu-nal adj. comunal

com-mune v. comulgar

com-mu-ni-ca-ble adj.
comunicable

com-mu-ni-cate v.
comunicar(se)

com-mu-ni-ca-tion n.
comunicación

com-mu-ni-ca-tive adj.
comunicativo

com-nu-ca-tor n. com
unicante

com-mun-ion n.
comunion

com-mu-nism n.
comunismo

com-mun-ist n. comunista

com-mu-nis-tic adj.
comunista

com-mu-ni-ty n.
comunidad

com-mu-ta-tion n.
conmutacion

com-mu-ta-tive adj.
conmutativo

com-mute v. conmutar

com-pact adj. compacto

com-pan-ion n.
companero

com-pan-ion-ship n.
companerismo

com-pa-ny n. compania

com-pa-ra-ble adj.
comparable

com-par-a-tive adj.
comparativo

com-pare v. comparar

com-par-i-son n.
comparación

com-part-ment n.
compartimiento

com-pass n. compas

com-pas-sion n.
compasion

com-pas-sion-ate adj.
compasivo

com-pat-i-ble adj.
compatible

com-pa-tri-ot n.
compatriota

com-pel v. compeler

com-pel-ling adj.
incontestable

com-pen-sate v.
compensar

com-pen-sa-tion n.
conpensacion

com-pete v. competir

com-pe-tence n.
competencia

com-pe-tent adj.
competente

com-pe-ti-tion n.
competencia

com-pet-i-tive adj.
competitivo

com-pet-i-tor n.
competidor

com-pi-la-tion n.
compilacion

com-plie v. compilar

com-plain v. quejarse

com-plain-ant n.
demandante

com-plaint n. queja

com-plai-sant adj.
complaciente

com-ple-ment n.
complemento

com-ple-men-ta-ry adj.
complementario

com-plete adj. completo

com-ple-tion n.
terminación

com-plex adj. complejo

com-plex-ion n. caracter

com-pli-nance n.
conformidad

com-pli-ant adj.
obediente

com-pli-cate v. complicar

com-pli-cat-ed adj.
complicado

com-pli-ca-tion n.
complicacion

com-plic-i-ty n.
complicidad

com-pli-ment n. honor;
elogio

com-pli-men-ta-ry adj.
elogioso

com-ply v. obedecer

com-po-nent n.
componente

com-port-ment n.
comportamiento

com-pose v. redactar

com-posed adj. tranquilo

com-pos-er n. compositor

com-pos-ite adj.
compuesto

com-po-si-tion n.
composicion

com-po-sure n. serenidad

com-pound adj.
compuesto

com-pre-hend v.
comprender

com-pre-hen-si-ble adj.
comprensible

com-pre-hen-sion n.
comprension

com-pre-hen-sive adj.
comprensivo; general

com-press n. compresa

com-pressed adj.
comprimido

com-pres-sion *n.*
compresion

com-prise *v.* constar de;
comprender

com-pro-mise *n.*
compromiso; *v.*
componer

com-pro-mis-ing *adj.*
comprometedor

com-pul-sive *adj.*
obsesivo

com-pul-so-ry *adj.*
compulsorio

com-pu-ta-tion *n.* calculo

com-pute *v.* computar

com-put-er *n.* computador

com-put-er-ize *v.*
computarizae

com-rade *n.* camarada

con *adv.* contra

con-cave *adj.* concavo

con-ceal *v.* ocultar

con-cede *v.* conceder

con-ceit-ed *adj.* vanidoso

con-ceiv-a-ble *adj.*
concebible

con-ceive *v.* concebir

con-cen-trate *v.*
concentrar(se)

con-cen-tra-tion *n.*
concentracion

con-cen-tric *adj.*
concentrico

con-cept *n.* concepto

con-cep-tion *n.*
concepción

con-cep-tu-al *adj.*
conceptual

con-cern *v.* concernir

con-cerned *adj.*
preocupado

con-cern-ing *prep.* acerca
de

con-cert *n.* concierto

con-cet-ed *adj.* conjunto

con-cer-to *n.* concierto

con-ces-sion *n.* concesión

con-cil-i-ate *v.* conciliar

con-cil-i-a-tion *n.* con
ciliacion

con-cise *adj.* conciso

con-clude *v.* concluir

con-clu-sion *n.* conclusión

con-clu-sive *adj.*
concluyente

con-coc-tion *n.* confección

con-cord *n.* concordia

con-crete *adj.* concreto

con-cur *v.* concurrir

con-cur-rence *n.*
concurrencia

con-cur-rent *adj.*
concurrente

con-cus-sion *n.* concusión

con-dem-na-ble *adj.* con
denable

con-den-sa-tion *n.*
condensación

con-dense *v.*
condensar(se)

con-dens-er *n.*
condensador

con-de-scend-ing *adj.*
condescendiente

con-di-ment *n.*
condimento

con-di-tion *v.* condicionar

con-done *v.* condoñar

con-duc-tor *n.* cobrador

con-fed-er-a-cy *n.*
confederación

con-fed-er-a-tion *n.*
confederacion

con-fer *v.* oferenciar

con-fess *v.* confesar

con-fide *v.* confiar

con-fi-dence *n.* confianza

con-fi-den-tial *adj.*
confidencial

con-firm *v.* confirmar

con-flict *v.* chocar

con-form-i-ty *n.*
conformidad

con-fron-ta-tion *n.*
confrontación

con-fuse *v.* confundir

con-fu-sion *n.* confusión

con-gest *v.* acumular

con-ges-tion *n.* congestión

con-glom-er-a-tion *n.*
conglomeración

con-grat-u-la-tion *n.*
felicitación

con-gre-gate *v.*
congregar(se)

con-junc-tion *n.*
cónjunción

con-jure *v.* conjurar

con-nect *v.* conectar

con-no-ta-tion *n.*
connotación

con-note *v.* connotar

con-sec-u-tive *adj.*
consecutivo

con-serv-a-to-ry *n.*
conservatorio

con-serve *v.* conservar

con-sid-er *v.* considerar

con-sid-er-a-tion *n.*
consideración

con-sist *v.* consistir

con-sol-i-date *v.*
consolidar

con-sol-i-da-tion *n.*
consolidación

con-stan-cy *n.* constancia

con-stant *adj.* continuo

con-sti-tu-tion *n.*
constitución

con-struc-tion *n.*
construcción

con-sult *v.* consultar

con-sume *v.* consumir

con-sump-tion *n.*
consunción

con-tain *v.* contener

con-tam-i-na-tion *n.*
contaminación

con-tem-plate *v.* proyectar

con-tem-po-rar-y *n.*
contemplación

con-tend *v.* afirmar;
contender

con-ti-nen-tal *adj.*
continental

con-tin-gen-cy *n.*
contingencia

con-tin-ue *v.* seguir;
continuar

con-trac-tion *n.*
contracción

con-tra-dict *v.* contradecir

con-trast v. contrastar	**course** n. plato; dirección	**crin-kle** v. arrugar(se)
con-tri-bu-tion n. contribución	**cous-in** n. prima; primo	**crip-ple** v. mutilar
con-trol v. dirigir; controlar	**cov-er** n. cubierta, v. cubrir	**cri-sis** n. crisis
		crisp adj. crespo
con-va-lesce v. convalecer	**cow** n. vaca	**crisp-y** adj. crujiente
con-ven-tion n. convención	**cow-boy** n. vaquero	**crit-ic** n. critico
	coy-o-te n. coyote	**crit-i-cal** adj. critico
con-verge v. convergir	**crab** n. cangrejo	**crit-i-cism** n. critica
con-ver-sa-tion n. conversación	**crack-er** n. galleta	**crit-i-cize** v. criticar
	cra-dle v. mercer	**cri-tique** n. critica
con-verse v. conversar	**crash** n. choque; estallido	**croc-o-dile** n. cocodrilo
con-ver-sion n. conversión	**crate** n. cajon	**cro-cus** n. azafran
con-vey v. llevar	**cra-ter** n. crater	**crook** n. angulo; baculo
con-vic-tion n. convicción	**crave** v. ansiar	**crook-ed** adj. corvo
con-vince v. convencer	**crav-ing** n. anhelo	**crop** n. fusta; cultivo
con-vul-sion n. convulsión	**crawl** v. gatear; arrastrarse	**cross-beam** n. traviesa
cook n. cocinero, v. cocinar	**cray-on** n. pastel	**cross-bow** n. ballesta
	craze v. enloquecer	**cross-cur-rent** n. contracor riente
cook-ie n. galleta	**crazed** adj. loco	
cool adj. fresco	**cra-zy** adj. loco	**cross-ex-am-ine** v. interrogar
co-or-di-nate v. coordinar	**cream** n. crema	
co-or-di-na-tion n. coordinación	**cream-y** adj. cremoso	**cross-word puz-zle** n. cruci grama
	crease v. doblar	
cop-per n. cobre	**cre-ate** v. producir; crear	**crouch** v. acuclillarse
cop-y v. copiar	**cre-a-tion** n. creación	**cross** v. cruzar, n. cruz
cor-dial-i-ty n. cordialidad	**cre-a-tive** adj. creador	**crow** v. cacarear
corn n. maiz	**cre-a-tiv-i-ty** n. originalidad	**crowd** n. gentio; multitud
cor-po-ral adj. corporal		**crowd-ed** adj. concurrido
cor-po-ra-tion n. corporación	**cre-a-tor** n. creador	**crown** n. corona
	crea-ture n. criatura	**crown-ing** n. coronación
cor-pu-lent adj. gordo	**cre-dence** n. credito	**cru-ci-ble** n. crisol
cor-pus-cu-lar adj. corpuscular	**cre-den-tial** n. credencial	**cru-ci-fix** n. crucifijo
	cred-i-ble adj. creible	**cru-ci-fix-ion** n. crucifixión
cor-ral v. acorralar	**cred-it** n. credito; reconocimiento	
cor-rect v. corregir		**cru-ci-fy** v. crucificar
cor-rec-tion n. corrección	**cred-it-a-ble** adj. loable	**crude** adj. tosco; ordinario; crudo
cor-re-spond v. escribir	**cred-u-lous** adj. credulo	
cor-re-spond-ence n. correspondencia	**creed** n. credo	**crude-ness** n. tosquedad
	creep-y adj. espeluznante	**cru-el** adj. cruel
cor-rode v. corroer	**cre-mate** v. incinerar	**cru-el-ty** n. crueldad
cor-ro-sion n. corrosión	**cre-ma-tion** n. incineración	**cruise** v. navegar
cor-rup-tion n. corrupcion		**crumb** n. migaja
cos-met-ic n. cosmetico	**crepe** n. crespon	**crum-ble** v. desmigajar(se)
cos-mic adj. cósmico	**cres-cent** n. medialuna	**crum-ple** v. estrujar(se)
cost v. costar, n. precio	**crest** n. cresta	**crunch-y** adj. crujiente
couch n. sofá	**cre-tin** n. cretiño	**cru-sade** n. cruzada
count n. cuenta, v. contar	**crew** n. equipo	**cru-sad-er** n. cruzado
coun-try n. campo; pais	**crib** n. pesebre	**crush** v. aplastar
cou-ple n. pareja	**crick-et** n. grillo	**crust** n. costra; corteza
cou-ra-geous adj. valiente	**crime** n. crimen	**crus-ta-cean** n. crustaceo
	crim-i-nal n., adj. criminal	**crust-y** adj. costroso

cry v. llorar

crypt n. cripta

crys-tal n. cristal

crys-tal-line adj. cristaliño

crys-tal-lize v. cristalizar(se)

crys-tal-log-ra-phy n. cristalografia

cube n. cubo

cu-bic adj. cubico

cu-bi-cle n. compartimiento

cub-ist n. cubista

cu-cum-ber n. pepiño

cud-dle v. abrazar(se)

cue n. taco

cu-li-nar-y adj. culinario

cul-mi-nate v. culminar

cul-pa-ble adj. culpable

cul-prit n. culpable

cult n. culto

cul-ti-vate v. cultivar

cul-ti-va-tion n. cultivo

cul-ti-va-tor n. cultivador

cul-tur-al adj. cultural

cul-ture n. cultura

cul-tured adj. culto

cum-ber v. embarazar

cum-ber-some adj. embarazoso

cu-mu-late v. acumular

cu-mu-la-tive adj. acumulativo

cun-ning adj. habil; astuto

cup n. taza

cup-ful n. taza

cur-a-ble adj. curable

curb n. bordillo

curd n. cuajada

cure n. cura

cu-ri-os-i-ty n. curiosidad

cu-ri-ous adj. curioso

curl v. enrollar(se); rizar(se)

cur-ren-cy n. moneda

cur-rent n., adj. corriente

cur-rent-ly adj. actualmente

curse n. desgracia; maldicion

curs-ed adj. maldito

cur-sor n. cursor

cur-tain n. telon

cur-va-ture n. curvatura

curve n. curva

curved adj. curvo

cus-to-di-an n. custodio

cus-to-dy n. custodia

cus-tom n. costumbre

cus-tom-ar-i-ly adv. acostumbrado

cut adj. cortado; n. cortadura; v. cortar

cu-ta-ne-ous adj. cutaneo

cute adj. mono

cu-ti-cle n. cuticula

cut-ler-y n. cubiertos

cy-a-nide n. cianuro

cy-cle n. ciclo

cy-clic adj. ciclico

cy-clist n. ciclista

cy-clone n. ciclón

cyl-in-der n. cilindro

cy-lin-dri-cal adj. cilindrico

cym-bal n. cimbalo

cyn-i-cal adj. cinico

cyn-i-cism n. cinismo

cy-press n. cipres

cyst n. quiste

cys-tic adj. enquistado

cys-ti-tis n. cistitis

cy-to-plasm n. citoplasma

czar n. zar

cza-ri-na n. zariña

D

dad n. papa

dai-ly adj. diario

dain-ty adj. delicado

dair-y-man n. lechero

dam v. represar, n. presa

dam-age v. danar; perjudicar

damp adj. humedo

dance n. baile, v. bailar

dan-cer n. bailador

dan-ger n. peligro

dan-ger-ous adj. peligroso

dare v. arriesgarse

dar-ing n. atrevimiento

dark n. oscuridad, adj. oscuro

dark-en v. oscurecer

dark-ness n. oscuridad

dash v. precipitarse; romper

date n. cita; fecha

daugh-ter n. hija

daugh-ter-in-law n. nuera

day n. dia

day-time n. dia

daz-zle v. deslumbrar

dead adj. muerto

deaf adj. sordo

deaf-en v. ensordecer

deaf-ness n. sordera

deal-er n. tratante

death n. muerte

de-bate v. debatir

de-bil-i-tate v. debilitar

de-bil-i-ta-tion n. debilitacion

debt n. deuda

debt-or n. deudor

dec-a-dence n. decadencia

dec-a-dent adj. decadente

de-cease v. morir

de-ceased adj. muerto

De-cem-ber n. diciembre

de-cent adj. decente

de-cide v. decidir

de-cid-ed adj. decidido

de-cid-ed-ly adv. decididamente

dec-i-mal n. decimal

dec-la-ra-tion n. declaración

de-clare v. declarar

de-cline v. rehusar

de-com-po-si-tion n. descomposición

dec-o-ra-tor n. decorador

de-crease v. disminuir(se)

de-duc-tion n. descuento

deep adj. profundo

deep-en v. intensificar

de-fect n. defecto

de-fec-tion n. defección

de-fec-tive adj. defectuoso

de-fend v. defender

de-fend-ant n. demandado

de-fi-cien-cy *n.*
deficiencia

de-flate *v.* desinflar

de-fla-tion *n.* desinflación

de-form *v.* desfigurar;
deformar

de-form-i-ty *n.*
deformidad

de-gen-er-ate *v.* degenerar

de-grade *v.* degradar

de-gree *n.* rango

de-hy-drate *v.* deshidratar

de-hy-dra-tion *n.*
deshidratacion

de-lete *v.* tachar

de-lib-er-ate *v.* deliberar

de-li-cious *adj.* delicioso

de-light-ful *adj.*
encantador

de-liv-er *v.* entregar

de-liv-er-y *n.* entrega

de-mand *v.* demandar;
exigir

de-moc-ra-cy *n.*
democracia

dem-o-crat *n.* democrata

dem-o-crat-ic *adj.*
democratico

dem-on-strate *v.*
demostrar

dem-on-stra-tion *n.*
demostracion

de-mor-al-ize *v.* des
moralizar

de-nom-i-na-tion *n.*
denominacion

de-nom-i-na-tor *n.*
denominador

de-note *v.* denotar

de-nounce *n.* denunciar

dense *adj.* denso

den-si-ty *n.* densidad

den-tist *n.* dentista

de-nun-ci-ate *v.* denunciar

de-nun-ci-a-tion *n.*
denuncia

de-par-ture *n.* salida

de-pend-en-cy *n.* depen
dencia

de-port *v.* deportar

de-por-ta-tion *n.* depor
tacion

de-prave *v.* depravar

de-praved *adj.* depravado

de-pres-sion *n.* desaliento

depth *n.* fondo

de-rive *v.* derivar(se)

de-scend *v.* bajar; de
scender

de-scribe *v.* describir

de-scrip-tion *n.*
descripción

de-serve *v.* merecer

des-ig-na-tion *n.*
nombramiento

de-sire *v.* desear

de-spair *v.* desesperar

de-spite *prep.* a pesar de

des-sert *n.* postre

de-stroy *v.* destruir

de-struct-i-ble *adj.*
destructible

de-struc-tion *n.*
destruccion

de-tain *v.* retener

de-ter *v.* disuadir

de-ter-mi-na-tion *n.*
determinación

de-ter-mine *v.* resolver;
determinar

de-test-a-ble *adj.*
detestable

de-val-u-a-tion *n.*
devaluación

dev-as-tate *v.* devastar

dev-as-ta-tion *n.* devas
tacion

de-vel-op *v.* desenvolver

dev-il *n.* diablo

de-vote *v.* dedicar

de-vour *v.* devorar

di-a-be-tes *n.* diabetes

di-a-bet-ic *adj.* diabetico

di-ag-nose *v.* diagnosticar

di-ag-no-sis *n.* diagnostico

di-al *v.* marcar

di-a-logue *n.* dialogo

di-a-ry *n.* diario

dic-ta-tor *n.* dictador

dic-tion-ar-y *n.* diccionaio

die *v.* morir

dif-fer-ence *n.* diferencia

dif-fer-ent *aj.* diferente

dif-fi-cult *adj.* dificil

dif-fi-cul-ty *n.* dificultad

dif-fu-sion *n.* difusion

dig *n.* excavacion, *v.*
extraer

di-ges-tion *n.* digestion

dig-it *n.* dedo

dig-ni-fy *v.* dignificar

di-lem-ma *n.* dilema

dil-i-gence *n.* diligencia

dil-i-gent *adj.* diligente

di-lute *v.* diluir

di-lu-tion *n.* dilución

dim *adj.* oscuro

di-min-ish *v.*
disminuir(se)

dine *v.* cenar

din-ner *n.* cena

di-plo-ma-cy *n.*
diplomacia

dip-lo-mat *n.* diplomatico

dip-lo-mat-ic *adj.*
diplomatico

di-rect *v.* dirigir, *adj.*
directo

di-rec-tion *n.* dirección

di-rec-tor *n.* director

dis-a-ble *v.* inutilizar

dis-ap-pear *v.* desaparecer

dis-ap-pear-ance *n.*
desaparicion

dis-as-trous *adj.*
desastroso

dis-a-vow *v.* desconocer

dis-charge *v.* despedir

dis-ci-pli-nar-y *adj.* dis
ciplinario

dis-ci-pline *v.* disciplinar,
n. castigo

dis-con-nect *v.*
desconectar

dis-con-tin-u-ous *adj.*
discontinuo

dis-cov-er *v.* descubrir

dis-crep-an-cy *n.*
discrepancia

dis-cus-sion *n.* discusión

dis-ease *n.* enfermedad

dis-guise *n.* disfraz, *v.* dis
frazar

dish *n.* plato

dis-hon-or *v.* deshonrar

dis-hon-or-a-ble *adj.*
deshonroso

dis-in-fect-ant *n.*
desinfectante

dis-in-ter-est *n.* desinteres

disk *n.* disco

dis-lo-cate *v.* dislocar

dis-lo-ca-tion *n.*
dislocación

dis-o-bey *v.* desobedecer

dis-or-der *n.* desorden

dis-pense *v.* dispensar

dis-play *n.* demostrar

dis-pute *n.* disputa, *v.*
disputar

dis-qual-i-fy *v.*
descalificar

dis-solve *v.* disolver(se)

dis-suade *v.* disuadir

dis-sua-sion *n.* disuasion

dis-tance *n.* distancia

dis-tant *adj.* distante

dis-till *v.* destilar

dis-till-er-y *n.* destileria

dis-tinc-tion *n.* distincion

dis-tin-guish *v.* distinguir

dis-tract *v.* distraer

dis-trac-tion *n.* distracción

dis-tri-bu-tion *n.*
distribución

dis-turb *v.* perturbar

dis-turb-ance *n.* disturbio

di-verge *v.* divergir

di-ver-gence *n.*
divergencia

di-ver-sion *n.* diversion

di-ver-si-ty *n.* diversidad

di-vert *v.* divertir

di-vide *v.* dividir(se)

di-vin-i-ty *n.* divinidad

diz-zy *adj.* mareado

do *v.* cumplir; hacer

doc-tor *n.* medico

doc-u-ment *n.* documentar

dog *n.* perro

dog-mat-ic *adj.* dogmatico

doll *n.* muneca

dol-lar *n.* dolar

do-mes-tic *adj.* domestico

do-mes-ti-cate *v.*
domesticar

dom-i-na-tion *n.*
dominación

don *v.* ponerse

do-nate *v.* donar

do-nor *n.* donante

door *n.* puerta

dor-mi-to-ry *n.* dormitorio

dou-ble *v.* doblar(se)

doubt *n.* duda, *v.* dudar

down *prep., adv.* abajo

doz-en *n.* doceña

drag-on *n.* dragon

dra-ma *n.* drama

dra-mat-ic *adj.* dramatico

dram-a-tist *n.* dramaturgo

draw *v.* sacar; dibujar; ar
rastrar

dream *v.* sonar, *n.* sueño

dream-er *n.* sonador

dredge *v.* dragar

dress *n.* vestido, *v.*
vestir(se)

drink *n.* bebida, *v.* beber

drive *v.* manejar; empujar;
conducir

drow-sy *adj.* sonoliento

drug *n.* droga

drunk *adj.* borracho

drunk-ard *n.* borracho

drunk-en *adj.* borracho

du-al-i-ty *n.* dualidad

duck *n.* pato

dull *adj.* embotado; torpe

dumb *adj.* mudo

du-pli-cate *adj.* duplicado,
v. duplicar

du-pli-ca-tion *n.*
duplicacion

du-ra-tion *n.* duracion

dur-ing *prep.* durante

du-ty *n.* derechos

dwell *v.* habitar

dy-nam-ic *adj.* dinamico

dy-nam-i-cal *adj.*
dinamico

dys-en-ter-y *n.* disenteria

E

each *adv.* para cada uno,
adj. cada

ea-ger *adj.* impaciente

ea-ger-ness *n.* ansia

ea-gle *n.* aguila

ea-glet *n.* aguilucho

ear *n.* oido; oreja

ear-li-ness *n.* precocidad

ear-ly *adj.* primitivo *adv.,*
adj. temprano

earn *v.* merecer

earn-ings *n.* sueldo

ear-ring *n.* pendiente

earth *n.* mundo; tierra

earth-ly *adj.* mundano

earth-quake *n.* terremoto

ease *v.* facilitar, *n.*
facilidad

eas-i-ly *adv.* facilmente

eas-i-ness *n.* facilidad

east *n.* este

east-ern *adj.* del este

eas-y *adj.* facil

eat *v.* gastar; comer

ec-cen-tric *adj.* excentrico

ec-cen-tric-i-ty *n.*
excentricidad

e-clipse *v.* eclipsar

e-clip-tic *adj.* ecliptico

e-col-o-gist *n.* ecologo

e-col-o-gy *n.* ecologia

e-co-nom-ic *adj.*
economico

e-con-o-mist *n.*
economista

e-con-o-mize *v.*
economizar

e-con-o-my *n.* economia

edge *n.* filo

ed-i-fi-ca-tion *n.*
edificacion

ed-i-fy *v.* edificar

ed-it *v.* editar

e-di-tion *n.* edicion

ed-i-tor *n.* editor

ed-i-to-ri-al-ist *n.*
editorialista

ed-u-cate *v.* educar

ed-u-ca-tion *n.* educacion

ef-fect v. efectuar, n. resultado

ef-fer-ves-cence n. efervescencia

ef-fer-ves-cent adj. efervescente

ef-fi-cien-cy n. eficiencia

ef-fi-cient adj. eficiente

ef-fort n. esfuerzo

ef-fu-sion n. efusion

egg n. huevo

e-go-tist n. egotista

eight adj. ocho

eight-een adj. dieciocho

eighth adj. octavo

eight-y adj. ochenta

ei-ther adv. tampoco; tam bien, adj. cualquier

e-late v. alegrar

el-bow n. codo

e-lect v. elegir

e-lec-tion n. eleccion

e-lec-tive adj. electivo

e-lec-tri-cian n. electricista

e-lec-tric-i-ty n. electricidad

el-e-gant adj. elegante

el-e-men-ta-ry adj. elemental

el-e-phant n. elefante

el-e-vate v. elevar

el-e-va-tion n. elevacion

e-lev-en adj. once

el-i-gi-bil-i-ty n. elegibilidad

e-lim-i-nate v. eliminar

e-lim-i-na-tion n. eliminación

e-man-ci-pate v. emancipar

e-man-ci-pa-tion n. emancipación

em-er-ald n. esmeralda

e-merge v. salir

e-mer-gence n. salida

em-i-grate v. emigrar

em-i-gra-tion n. emigración

em-i-nent adj. eminente

e-mit v. emitir

e-mo-tion n. emoción

em-pire n. imperio

em-ploy v. emplear

em-ploy-ee n. empleado

emp-ty v. vaciar, adj. desocupado

e-mul-sion n. emulsion

en-chant v. encantar

en-chant-ing adj. encantador

en-cy-clo-pe-dia n. enciclopedia

end n. final; fin

end-ing n. fin

en-dorse v. endosar

en-dorse-ment n. endoso

en-dure v. durar

en-e-my n. enemigo

en-er-get-ic adj. energico

en-er-gy n. energia

en-gage v. engranar; apalabrar

en-gage-ment n. obligación

en-gi-neer n. ingeniero

en-gi-neer-ing n. ingenieria

Eng-lish n. ingles

en-joy v. disfrutar

en-joy-ment n. disfrute

e-nor-mous adj. enorme

e-nough adv. bastante

en-slave v. entrar

en-ter-tain-ment n. espectaculo

en-thu-si-asm n. entusiasmo

en-thu-si-ast n. entusiasta

en-tire adj. entero

en-tire-ly adv. totalmente

en-trance n. entrada

en-trust v. entregar

en-try n. partida; entrada

en-vel-op v. envolver

en-zyme n. enzima

ep-i-dem-ic n. epidemia

ep-i-sode n. episodio

ep-och n. epoca

e-qual v. igualar, n. igual

e-qual-i-ty adj. igualdad

e-qual-ly adv. igualmente

e-quip-ment n. equipo

e-quiv-a-lent adj. equivalente

e-ra n. era

e-rase v. borrar

e-ras-er n. borrador

e-rect v. erigir

e-rec-tion n. erección

e-ro-sion n. erosion

er-u-di-tion n. erudición

e-rup-tion n. erupción

es-cort v. acompanar, n. acompanante

es-pe-cial adj. especial

es-pe-cial-ly adv. especialmente

es-sen-tial adj. esencial

es-thet-ic adj. estetico

es-ti-mate v. estimar

e-ter-nal adj. eterno

e-ter-nal-ly adv. eternamente

e-ter-ni-ty n. eternidad

eth-i-cal adj. etico

eu-lo-gize v. elogiar

eu-lo-gy n. elogio

eu-pho-ri-a n. euforia

eu-phor-ic adj. euforico

e-vac-u-a-tion n. evacuación

e-vade v. evadir

e-val-u-ate v. evaluar

e-val-u-a-tion n. evaluación

e-vap-o-rate v. evaporar(se)

e-vap-o-ra-tion n. evaporación

e-va-sion n. evasion

eve n. vispera

e-ven adj. igualar

e-ven-tu-al-i-ty n. eventualidad

eve-ry adj. todo

ev-i-dence n. evidencia

e-vil n. mal

ev-o-lu-tion n. evolución

ex-act adj. exacto

ex-ag-ger-a-tion n. ex ageracion

ex-al-ta-tion n. exaltacion

ex-am-ine *v.* examinar
ex-am-ple *n.* ejemplo
ex-ca-va-tion *n.*
excavación
ex-ceed *v.* superar; exceder
ex-cel-lence *n.* excelencia
ex-cel-lent *adj.* excelente
ex-cep-tion *n.* excepcion
ex-ces-sive *adj.* excesivo
ex-cite *v.* excitar
ex-claim *v.* exclamar
ex-cla-ma-tion *n.*
exclamacion
ex-cuse *v.* excusar;
perdonar
ex-er-cise *n.* ejercicio
ex-hi-bi-tion *n.* exposición
ex-hort *v.* exhortar
ex-ile *n.* exilado; destierro
ex-ist *v.* existir
ex-ist-ence *n.* existencia
ex-it *n.* salida
ex-o-tic *adj.* exotico
ex-pan-sion *n.* expansion
ex-pect-an-cy *n.* expec
tacion
ex-pec-ta-tion *n.* expec
tacion
ex-pe-di-tion *n.*
expedición
ex-pel *v.* expulsar
ex-pe-ri-ence *v.*
experimentar
ex-per-i-ment *n.*
experimento
ex-pire *v.* terminar
ex-pla-na-tion *n.*
explicación
ex-plo-ra-tion *n.*
exploracion
ex-plor-er *n.* explorador
ex-plo-sion *n.* explosion
ex-por-ta-tion *n.*
exportacion
ex-press *v.* expresar
ex-pres-sion *n.* expresion
ex-pres-sive *adj.*
expresion
ex-tend *v.* extender
ex-ten-sion *n.* extension
ex-te-ri-or *adj.* exterior

ex-tinct *adj.* extinto
ex-tinc-tion *n.* extincion
ex-tra *n.* extra
ex-tra-or-di-nar-y *adj.*
extraordinario
ex-treme *adj.* extremo
ex-ul-ta-tion *n.* exultación
eye *n.* ojo

F

fa-ble *n.* fabula
fab-ric *n.* tela
fab-ri-cate *v.* inventar
fab-u-lous *adj.* fabuloso
face *n.* cara
fa-cial *adj.* facial
fa-cil-i-tate *v.* facilitar
fa-cil-i-ty *n.* facilidad
fact *n.* hecho
fac-tion *n.* facción
fac-tor *n.* factor
fac-to-ry *n.* fabrica
fac-ul-ty *n.* facultad
fail *v.* acabar; faltar
fail-ure *n.* fracaso
faint-ness *n.* debilidad
fair *adj.* justo; rubio
faith *n.* fe
faith-ful *adj.* fiel
fake *n.* impostura
fal-con *n.* halcon
fall *v.* caer(se)
false *adj.* falso
false-hood *n.* mentira
false-ly *adv.* falsamente
fal-si-fy *v.* falsificar
fal-si-ty *n.* falsedad
fame *n.* fama
fa-mil-iar *adj.* familiar
fa-mil-i-ar-i-ty *n.*
familiaridad
fam-i-ly *n.* familia
fa-mous *adj.* famoso
fan *n.* aficionado
fan-cy *n.* fantasia
fan-tas-tic *adj.* fan
fan-ta-sy *n.* fantasia
far *adv.* lejos
farm *n.* granja
fas-ci-nate *v.* fascinar

fast *adj.* rapidamente;
rapido
fat *adj.* gordo
fa-tal *adj.* fatal
fa-tal-i-ty *n.* fatalidad
fate *n.* suerte
fa-ther *n.* padre
fa-ther-in-law *n.* suegro
fa-tigue *n.* fatiga
fault *n.* culpa; falta
fa-vor *n.* favor
fa-vor-a-ble *adj.* favorable
fear *n.* miedo
fear-ful *adj.* temeroso
fear-some *adj.* temible
feath-er *n.* pluma
feath-er-y *adj.* plumoso
Feb-ru-ar-y *n.* febrero
fed-er-al *adj.* federal
fed-er-a-tion *n.* federación
feed *v.* alimentar
feel *v.* sentir(se)
feel-ing *n.* emoción
fe-lic-i-ty *n.* felicidad
fe-line *adj.* felino
fell *v.* talar
fel-on *n.* criminal
fel-o-ny *n.* crimen
fe-male *n.* hembra
fem-i-nine *adj.* femenino
fe-mur *n.* femur
fence *v.* esgrimir
fenc-ing *n.* esgrima
fer-men-ta-tion *n.* fermen
tacion
fe-ro-ci-ty *n.* ferocidad
fer-tile *adj.* fecundo; fertil
fer-til-i-ty *n.* fecundidad
fer-ti-lize *v.* fertilizar
fes-ti-val *n.* fiesta
fes-tive *adj.* festivo
feu-dal-ism *n.* feudalismo
fe-ver *n.* fiebre
few *adj.* pocos
fib *v.* mentir
fi-brous *adj.* fibroso
fic-tion *n.* ficcion
fic-ti-tious *adj.* ficticio
fi-del-i-ty *n.* fidelidad
field *n.* prado; campo
fif-teen *adj.* quince

fifth *adj.* quinto

fif-ty *adj.* cincuenta

fight *v.* pelear; luchar, *n.* pelea; lucha

fig-ure *n.* tipo; figura

fill *v.* llenar

film *n.* pelicula

fi-nal *adj.* final

fi-nal-ist *n.* finalista

fi-nal-i-ty *n.* finalidad

fi-nal-ly *adv.* finalmente

fi-nan-cial *adj.* financiero

find *v.* hallar; encontrar

fin-ger-nail *n.* uña

fire *n.* fuego

fire-crack-er *n.* petardo

fire-man *n.* bombero

fire-place *n.* hogar

fi-rm *adj.* firme

fir-ma-ment *n.* firmamento

firm-ly *adv.* firmemente

first *adj.* primero

fish *n.* pez

fish-er-man *n.* pescador

fish-ery *n.* pesquera

fis-sion *n.* fisión

fit *v.* probar; acomodar, *adj.* adecuado

five *adj.* cinco

fix *v.* arreglar

flag *n.* bandera

flame *n.* llama; *v.* flamear

flap *v.* ondear

flat *adj.* plano; llano

fla-vor *n.* sabor

flea *n.* pulga

flee *v.* fugarse; huir

flex-i-ble *adj.* flexible

flight *n.* vuelo

flood *n.* diluvio

flo-ral *adj.* floral

flor-id *adj.* florido

flo-rist *n.* florista

flour *n.* harina

flow-er *n.* flor

flu-id *adj.* fluido

flu-o-res-cent *adj.* fluores cente

flute *n.* flauta

flut-ter *n.* aleteo, *v.* revolotear

fly *v.* volar, *n.* mosca

fo-cus *v.* enfocar

fog *n.* niebla

fold *v.* plegar; doblar

folk *n.* gente

fol-li-cle *n.* foliculo

fol-low *v.* perseguir; seguir

fol-low-er *n.* seguidor

fond-ly *adv.* afectuosamente

food *n.* alimento

foot *n.* pata; pie

foot-ball *n.* futbol

foot-step *n.* paso

for *conj.* pues, *prep.* para; por

for-bid *v.* prohibir

force *v.* forzar, *n.* fuerza

fore-arm *n.* antebrazo

fore-head *n.* frente

for-eign *adj.* extranjero

for-eign-er *n.* extranjero

for-est *n.* bosque

fore-tell *v.* predecir

for-feit *v.* perder

for-get *v.* olvidar(se)

for-get-ful *adj.* olvidadizo

for-give *v.* perdonar

fork *n.* tenedor

for-mal-i-ty *n.* formalidad

for-ma-tion *n.* formación

for-mu-la *n.* formula

fort *n.* fuerte

for-ti-fi-ca-tion *n.* fortificacion

for-tune *n.* fortuna

for-ty *adj.* cuarenta

for-ward *adv.* adelante

fos-sil *n.* fosil

foul *adj.* sucio

foun-da-tion *n.* fundación

foun-tain *n.* fuente

four *adj.* cuarto

four-teen *adj.* catorce

fourth *adj.* cuarto

fox *n.* zorra

frac-tion *n.* fracción

frac-ture *v.* quebrar, *n.* frac tura

frag-ile *adj.* frágil

frag-ment *n.* fragmento

fra-grant *adj.* oloroso

frank-ly *adv.* francamente

frank-ness *n.* franqueza

fran-tic *adj.* frenetico

fra-ter-ni-ty *n.* fraternidad

free *v.* libertar, *adj.* libre

free-dom *n.* libertad

French *n., adj.* frances

fre-quen-cy *n.* frecuencia

fre-quent *adj.* frecuente

fresh *adj.* fresco

fresh-en *v.* refrescar

fric-tion *n.* fricción

Friday *n.* viernes

friend *n.* amigo, amiga

friend-ly *adj.* amistoso

frig-id *adj.* frio

frog *n.* rana

from *prep.* desde; de

front *n.* frente

fron-tal *adj.* frontal

frown *n.* ceno

fru-gal *adj.* frugal

fruit *n.* fruta

frus-trate *v.* frustrar

frus-tra-tion *n.* frustración

fry *v.* freir

fu-gi-tive *n., adj.* fugitivo

full *adj.* completo; lleno

ful-ly *adv.* completamente

func-tion *v.* funcionar

func-tion-al *adj.* funcional

fun-da-men-tal *adj.* fundamental

fun-ny *adj.* comico

fur *n.* piel

fu-ri-ous *adj.* furioso

fur-ni-ture *n.* mueblaje

fur-ther *adj., adv.* mas lejos

fu-tile *adj.* inutil

fuzz *n.* pelusa

G

gai-e-ty *n.* alegria

gai-ly *adv.* alegremente

gain *v.* ganar

gal-ax-y *n.* galaxia

gal-lant-ry *n.* galanteria

gal-ler-y *n.* galeria

gal-lon *n.* galon

game *n.* partido; juego

gap *n.* hueco

ga-rage *n.* garaje

gar-bage *n.* basura

gar-den *n.* jardin

gar-nish *v.* adornar

gas *n.* gasolina

gas-e-ous *adj.* gaseous

gas-o-line *n.* gasolina

gas-tric *adj.* gastrico

gate *n.* puerta

gath-er *v.* fruncir; reunir

gaze *v.* mirar

ga-zette *n.* gaceta

gear *v.* engraner

gene *n.* gen

ge-ne-al-o-gy *n.* genealogia

gen-er-al *adj.* general

gen-er-al-i-ty *n.* generalidad

gen-er-al-ize *v.* generalizar

gen-er-tion *n.* generador

gen-er-os-i-ty *n.* generosidad

gen-er-ous *adj.* generoso

gen-i-tal *adj.* genital

gen-ius *n.* genio

gen-tle-man *n.* caballero

gen-tly *adv.* suavemente

ge-o-gra-pher *n.* geógrafo

ge-o-gra-phy *n.* geografia

ge-ol-o-gy *n.* geologia

ge-o-met-ric *adj.* geométrico

ger-mi-nate *v.* germinar

ger-mi-na-tion *n.* germinación

ges-ture *n.* gesto

get *v.* lograr; obtener

ghost *n.* fantasma

giant *adj.* gigantesco

gi-gan-tic *adj.* gigantesco

gi-raffe *n.* jirafa

girl *n.* chica; niña

give *v.* entregar; dar

gla-cial *adj.* glacial

gla-cier *n.* glaciar

glad *adj.* alegre

glad-ness *n.* alegria

glance *v.* rebotar; mirar

glide *v.* deslizarse

glob-ule *n.* globulo

gloom *n.* tristeza

gloom-y *adj.* melancolico

glo-ri-fy *v.* glorificar

glo-ri-ous *adj.* glorioso

glove *n.* guante

glue *v.* encolar

gnaw *v.* roer

go *v.* ir

goat *n.* cabra

God *n.* Dios

god-daugh-ter *n.* ahijada

god-fa-ther *n.* padrino

god-moth-er *n.* madrina

god-son *n.* ahijado

gold *n.* oro

golf *n.* golf

good *adj.* bueno

goose *n.* ganso

gov-ern *v.* gobernar

gov-er-nor *n.* gobernador

grace *n.* gracia

gra-cious *adj.* agradable

gra-da-tion *n.* gradación

grad-u-al *adj.* gradual

gram *n.* gramo

gram-mat-i-cal *adj.* gramatical

grand *adj.* magnifico; grandioso

grand-daugh-ter *n.* nieta

grand-fa-ther *n.* abuelo

grand-moth-er *n.* abuela

grand-son *n.* nieto

grant *v.* conferir; otorgar

grape *n.* uva

graph-ic *adj.* grafico

grass *n.* hierba

grass-hop-per *n.* saltamontes

gus-to *n.* entusiasmo

gym *n.* gimnasio

gym-nast *n.* gimnasta

gym-nas-tic *adj.* gimnastico

gy-ne-col-o-gy *n.* ginecologia

H

hab-it *n.* costumbre

hab-i-tat *n.* habitación

hab-i-ta-tion *n.* habitación

hail *n.* granizo, *v.* granizar

hall *n.* sala

halt *v.* parar

ham *n.* jamón

ham-burg-er *n.* hamburguesa

ham-mer *v.* martillar, *n.* martillo

hand *n.* mano

hand-some *adj.* hermoso

hang *v.* pegar; colgar

hap-pen *v.* pasar

hap-pen-ing *n.* acontecimiento

hap-pi-ly *adv.* alegremente

hap-pi-ness *n.* alegria

hap-py *adj.* feliz

har-bor *n.* puerto

hard *adj.* firme

har-dy *adj.* robusto

harm *v.* dañar

harm-ful *adj.* dañino

har-mo-ni-ous *adj.* armonioso

har-mo-ny *n.* armonia

harsh *adj.* severo

harsh-ness *n.* severidad

har-vest *v.* cosechar

hat *n.* sombrero

hatch *v.* empollar, *n.* portezuela

hatch-et *n.* machado

hate *n.* odio, *v.* odiar

hate-ful *adj.* odioso

have *v.* tener

hawk *n.* halcon

haz-ard *v.* arriesgar, *n.* azar

he *pron.* el

head *n.* cabeza

health *n.* salud

hear *v.* oir

hear-ing *n.* oido

heart *n.* corazón

hearth *n.* hogar

heat *v.* calentar, *n.* calor
heat-er *n.* calentador
heav-en *n.* cielo
heav-y *adj.* fuerte
heel *n.* talon
height *n.* altura
height-en *v.* elevar
heir *n.* heredero
heir-ess *n.* heredera
hel-i-cop-ter *n.*
helicoptero
hell *n.* infierno
hel-lo *int.* hola
help *n.* ayuda, *v.* ayudar
help-ful *adj.* util
hem-i-sphere *n.*
hemisferio
hem-i-spher-ic *adj.*
hemisferico
hemp *n.* cañamo
hen *n.* gallina
her-ald-ry *n.* heraldica
herb *n.* hierba
here *adv.* aqui
he-red-i-tar-y *adj.*
hereditario
he-red-i-ty *n.* herencia
her-ni-a *n.* hernia
he-ro *n.* heroe
he-ro-ic *adj.* heroico
her-o-ine *n.* heroina
hes-i-tant *adj.* vacilante
hes-i-tate *v.* vacilar
hex-ag-o-nal *adj.*
hexagonal
hide *v.* ocultar(se)
high *adj.* alto
hike *n.* caminata
hill *n.* colina
him-self *pron.* el mismo
hin-der *v.* impedir
hip *n.* cadera
his *pron.* suyo
his-to-ri-an *n.* historiador
his-tor-ic *adj.* historico
hit *n.* golpe, *v.* golpear
hoax *n.* engaño
hold *v.* contener; tener
hol-low *adj.* vacio
home *n.* casa
hom-i-cide *adj.* homicidio

hom-i-ly *n.* homilia
hon-est *adj.* honrado
hon-ey *n.* miel
hon-or *v.* honrar, *n.* honor
hon-or-a-ble *adj.*
honorable
hop *n.* salto, *v.* saltar
hope *v.* desear, *n.*
esperanza
hor-i-zon-tal *adj.*
horizontal
hor-mone *n.* hormona
hor-ri-ble *adj.* horrible
hor-ror *n.* horror
horse *n.* caballo
hos-pi-tal *n.* hospital
hos-pi-tal-i-ty *n.*
hospitalidad
host-ess *n.* huéspeda
hos-tile *adj.* hostil
hos-til-i-ty *n.* hostilidad
hot *adj.* caliente
ho-tel *n.* hotel
hour *n.* hora
house *n.* casa
how *adv.* cómo
hug *v.* abrazar
huge *adj.* enorme
hu-man *n.* humano
hu-man-i-ty *n.* humanidad
hu-mid *adj.* humedo
hu-mid-i-ty *n.* humedad
hu-mil-i-ate *v.* humillar
hu-mil-i-a-tion *n.*
humillación
hu-mor *n.* complacer
hun-dred *adj.* ciento
hun-ger *n.* hambre
hunt *v.* cazar
hunt-er *n.* cazador
hus-band *n.* esposo
hy-dro-gen *n.* hidrogeno
hy-giene *n.* higiene
hymn *n.* himno
hyp-no-tize *v.* hipnotizar
hyp-o-crite *n.* hipocrita
hy-poth-e-sis *n.* hipotesis
hys-ter-ic *adj.* histérico

I

I *pron.* yo
ice *n.* hielo
ice-berg *n.* iceberg
ice cream *n.* helado
i-cy *adj.* helado
i-de-a *n.* idea
i-de-al *adj.* ideal
i-de-al-ize *v.* idealizar
i-den-ti-fi-ca-tion *n.*
identificación
i-den-ti-fy *v.* identificar
i-den-ti-ty *n.* identidad
id-i-ot *n.* idiota
i-dol *n.* idolo
i-dol-ize *v.* idolatrar
if *conj.* si
ig-no-rance *n.* ignorancia
ig-no-rant *adj.* ignorante
ill *adj.* enfermo
il-leg-i-ble *adj.* ilegible
il-le-git-i-mate *adj.*
ilegitimo
ill-ness *n.* enfermedad
il-lu-sion *n.* ilusion
il-lus-trate *v.* ilustrar
im-ag-i-nar-y *adj.*
imaginario
im-ag-i-na-tion *n.*
imaginación
im-ag-ine *v.* imaginar
im-i-tate *v.* imitar
im-ma-ture *adj.* inmaturo
im-mense *adj.* inmenso
im-mer-sion *n.* inmersion
im-mi-grate *v.* inmigrar
im-mi-gra-tion *n.* in
migracion
im-mor-al *adj.* inmoral
im-mu-ni-ty *n.* inmunidad
im-peach *v.* acusar
im-pel *v.* impulsar
im-pe-ri-ous *adj.*
imperioso
im-per-son-al *adj.* imper
sonal
im-plore *v.* implorar
im-po-lite *adj.* descortes
im-por-tance *n.*
importancia
im-por-tant *adj.*
importante

im·pose v. imponer
im·pos·tor n. impostor
im·prac·ti·cal adj.
  impracticable
im·press v. imprimir
im·pres·sion n. impresion
im·print v. imprimir
im·prove v. mejorar
im·prove·ment n. mejora
im·pro·vise v. improvisar
im·pulse n. impulso
in adv. dentro, prep.
  durante, en
in·a·bil·i·ty n. inhabilidad
in·ca·pac·i·tate v. in
  capacitar
inch n. pulgada
in·ci·den·tal adj.
  incidental
in·cin·er·ate v. incinerar
in·ci·sion n. incisión
in·cite v. incitar
in·cli·na·tion n.
  inclinación
in·clu·sion n. inclusión
in·com·pa·ra·ble adj.
  incomparable
in·com·pe·tent adj.
  incompetente
in·com·plete adj.
  incompleto
in·cor·rect adj. incorrecto
in·crease v. crecer,
  acrecentar
in·crim·i·nate v.
  incriminar
in·de·cen·cy n. indecencia
in·de·cent adj. indecente
in·def·i·nite adj.
  indefinido
in·dent v. mellar
in·den·ta·tion n. mella
in·de·pend·ence n.
  independencia
in·de·pend·ent adj.
  independiente
in·di·cate v. indicar
in·di·ca·tion n. indicación
in·dif·fer·ent adj.
  indiferente

in·di·ges·tion n.
  indigestion
in·dir·ect adj. indirecto
in·dis·cre·tion n.
  indiscrecion
in·di·vid·u·al n. individuo
in·doors adv. dentro
in·dus·tri·al adj.
  industrial
in·er·tia n. inercia
in·ev·i·ta·ble adj.
  inevitable
in·fa·my n. infamia
in·fan·cy n. infancia
in·fect v. infectar
in·fec·tion n. infeccion
in·fe·ri·or adj. inferior
in·fi·del·i·ty n. infidelidad
in·fin·i·ty n. infinidad
in·flam·ma·ble adj.
  inflamable
in·flate v. inflar
in·fla·tion n. inflación
in·form v. informar
in·for·ma·tion n.
  información
in·for·ma·tive adj.
  informativo
in·fuse v. infundir
in·fu·sion n. infusion
in·gre·di·ent n.
  ingrediente
in·hab·it v. habitar
in·her·it·ance n. herencia
in·hi·bi·tion n. inhibición
in·i·ti·ate v. iniciar
in·i·ti·a·tion n. iniciación
in·ject v. inyectar
in·jec·tion n. inyección
ink n. tinta
inn n. posada
in·ner adj. interior
in·no·cent adj. inocente
in·oc·u·late v. inocular
in·oc·u·la·tion n.
  inoculación
in·scribe v. inscribir
in·scrip·tion n.
  inscripción
in·sect n. insecto
in·ser·tion n. insercion

in·side n. interior
in·sip·id adj. insipido
in·sist v. insistir
in·so·lence n. insolencia
in·so·lent adj. insolente
in·spec·tion n. inspección
in·spi·ra·tion n.
  inspiración
in·stant n. instante
in·sti·gate v. instigar
in·sti·tu·tion n. institución
in·struc·tion n.
  instrucción
in·su·lin n. insulina
in·te·grate v. integrar
in·te·gra·tion n.
  integración
in·tel·lect n. intelecto
in·tel·lec·tu·al adj.
  intelectual
in·tel·li·gence n.
  inteligencia
in·tel·li·gent adj.
  inteligente
in·tense adj. intenso
in·ten·si·ty n. intensidad
in·ten·tion n. intención
in·ter·cede v. interceder
in·ter·cept v. interceptar
in·ter·est n. interes
in·te·ri·or adj. interior
in·ter·mis·sion n.
  intermisión
in·ter·nal adj. interior
in·ter·na·tion·al adj.
  internacional
in·ter·pose v. interponer
in·ter·ro·gate v. interrogar
in·ter·ro·ga·tion n.
  interrogacion
in·ter·rup·tion n.
  interrupción
in·ter·sec·tion n.
  intersección
in·ter·vene v. intervenir
in·ti·mate v. intimar
in·tim·i·date v. intimidar
in·to prep. en
in·tol·er·ant adj.
  intolerante
in·to·na·tion n. entonación

in-trep-id *adj.* intrepido
in-tri-cate *adj.* intrincado
in-tro-duce *v.* introducir
in-tro-duc-tion *n.*
  introducción
in-vade *v.* invadir
in-va-lid *adj.* invalido
in-va-sion *n.* invasion
in-ven-tion *n.* invención
in-vert *v.* invertir
in-vest *v.* investir
in-ves-ti-gate *v.* investigar
in-ves-ti-ga-tion *n.*
  investigación
in-vis-i-ble *adj.* invisible
in-vi-ta-tion *n.* invitacion
in-vite *v.* invitar
i-on *n.* ion
i-ron *v.* planchar, *n.*
  plancha
i-ro-ny *n.* ironia
ir-ra-di-ate *v.* irradiar
ir-ra-tion-al *adj.* irraciónal
ir-reg-u-lar *adj.* irregular
ir-re-spon-si-ble *adj.*
  irresponsable
is-land *n.* isla
isle *n.* isla
is-sue *v.* publicar; salir, *n.*
  resultado; emision
it *pron.* le; la; lo; ello; ella;
  el
i-tin-er-ar-y *n.* itinerario
i-vy *n.* hiedra

J

jab *v.* golpear
jack-al *n.* chacal
jack-ass *n.* burro
jack-et *n.* chaqueta
jade *n.* jade
jag-uar *n.* jaguar
jail *v.* encarcelar, *n.* carcel
Jan-u-ar-y *n.* enero
jar *n.* jarra
jas-mine *n.* jazmin
jave-lin *n.* jabalina
jazz *n.* jazz
jeal-ous *adj.* celoso
jeop-ar-dize *v.* arriesgar
jer-sey *n.* jersey

jew-el *n.* joya
jew-el-er *n.* joyero
jew-el-ry *n.* joyas
job *n.* trabajo
join *v.* unir(se)
jour-nal *n.* periodico
jour-nal-ism *n.*
  periodismo
jour-nal-ist *n.* periodista
jour-ney *v.* viajar, *n.* viaje
joy-ous *adj.* alegre
judge *n.* juez; *v.* juzgar
ju-di-cial *adj.* judicial
juice *n.* jugo
July *n.* julio
jump *n.* salto, *v.* saltar
jump-er *n.* saltador
June *n.* junio
ju-rist *n.* jurista
ju-ry *n.* jurado
jus-ti-fy *v.* justificar

K

ka-lei-do-scope *n.*
  calidoscopio
kan-ga-roo *n.* canguro
keep *v.* detener; tener;
  cumplir
keg *n.* cuñete
ken-nel *n.* perrera
ker-chief *n.* pañuelo
ket-tle *n.* tetera
key *n.* llave
kid-ney *n.* riñón
kill *v.* matar
kil-o-gram *n.* kilogramo
kil-o-me-ter *n.* kilómetro
kind *adj.* bueno; *n.* genero
kind-ly *adj.* bondadoso
kind-ness *n.* benevolencia
king *n.* rey
king-dom *n.* reino
kiss *n.* beso; *v.* besar
kitch-en *n.* cocina
kit-ten *n.* gatito
knee *n.* rodilla
knife *v.* acuchillar, *n.*
  cuchillo
knight *n.* caballero
knock *v.* golpear

knot *v.* anudar
knowl-edge *n.* saber

L

la-bi-al *adj.* labial
la-bor *v.* trabajar, *n.*
  trabajo
lab-o-ra-to-ry *n.*
  laboratorio
la-bo-ri-ous *adj.* laborioso
lac-er-ate *v.* lacerar
lac-er-ation *n.* laceración
lac-quer *n.* laca
lac-tic *adj.* lactico
lad *n.* chico
lad-der *n.* escalera
la-dy *n.* dama
la-goon *n.* laguna
lake *n.* lago
lamb *n.* cordero
lam-en-ta-tion *n.*
  lamentacion
lam-i-nate *v.* laminar
lamp *n.* lampara
land *v.* pais; tierra
lan-guage *n.* lenguaje
lan-tern *n.* linterna
large *adj.* grande
lass *n.* muchacha
last *adv.* finalmente; *adj.*
  final
late *adv.* tarde
lat-i-tude *n.* latitud
laugh *n.* risa, *v.* reir(se)
laugh-ing *adj.* risueño
laugh-ter *n.* risa
la-va *n.* lava
law *n.* derecho; ley
lay-er *n.* estrato
la-zy *adj.* perezoso
lead *v.* mandar; conducir
lead-er *n.* lider
leaf *n.* hoja
league *n.* liga
lean *adj.* magro
learn *v.* aprender
least *adv.* menos, *adj.*
  menor
leave *v.* salir; dejar; irse
left *adj.* izquierdo

leg *n.* pierna
le-gal *adj.* legal
le-gal-i-ty *n.* legalidad
leg-end *n.* leyenda
leg-end-ar-y *adj.*
   legendario
leg-is-late *v.* legislar
leg-is-la-tion *n.* legislación
le-git-i-mate *adj.* legitimo
lem-on *n.* limon
lem-on-ade *n.* limonada
leop-ard *n.* leopardo
less *adv., adj.* menos
les-son *n.* lección
let *v.* dejar; permitir
let-ter *n.* carta
let-tuce *n.* lechuga
li-a-bil-i-ty *n.* obligación
lib-er-al *adj.* liberal
lib-er-ate *v.* libertar
lib-er-ty *n.* libertad
li-brar-y *n.* biblioteca
lie *v.* mentir; acostarse
life *n.* vida
lift *v.* levantar(se); elevar
light *n.* lampara; luz
light-ly *adv.* ligeramente
like *n.* gusto, *v.* gustar
like-ness *n.* semejanza
li-lac *n.* lila
lil-y *n.* lirio
lim-bo *n.* limbo
lime *n.* lima
lim-it *v.* limitar
lim-ou-sine *n.* limusina
line *v.* alinear; rayar, *n.*
   raya; linea
li-on *n.* león
lip *n.* labio
liq-uid *n.* liquido
liq-ui-date *v.* liquidar
liq-uor *n.* licor
list *n.* lista
lit-er-al *adj.* literal
lit-er-ar-y *adj.* literario
lit-er-a-ture *n.* literatura
lit-tle *n., adj., adv.* poco,
   adj. pequeno
live *v.* vivir
liz-ard *n.* lagarto
lob-ster *n.* langosta

lo-cal *adj.* local
lo-cal-i-ty *n.* localidad
lo-cate *v.* encontrar
lone *adj.* solitario
lone-ly *adj.* solo
long *adj.* largo
look *n.* mirada, *v.* buscar;
   mirar
loose *v.* soltar, *adj.*
   disoluto; suelto
lost *adj.* perdido
lo-tion *n.* locion
lot-ter-y *n.* loteria
loud *adj.* alto
love *v.* amar; querer, *n.*
   amor
love-ly *adj.* hermoso
low *adv., adj.* bajo, *adv.*
   abajo
low-er *v.* bajar
loy-al *adj.* fiel
loy-al-ty *n.* fidelidad
lu-bri-cant *n.* lubricante
lu-bri-cate *v.* lubricar
luck *n.* suerte
lug-gage *n.* equipaje
lum-ber *n.* leno
lu-nar *adj.* lunar
lunch *v.* almorzar, *n.* al
   muerzo
lus-ter *n.* lustre
lux-u-ry *n.* lujo
lyr-ic *adj.* lirico

M

ma-ca-bre *adj.* macabro
mac-a-ro-ni *n.* macar
   rones
mac-a-roon *n.* mostachon
ma-chaw *n.* guacamayo
mac-er-ate *v.* macerar(se)
ma-chet-e *n.* machete
mach-i-nate *v.* maquinar
mach-i-na-tion *n.*
   maquinacion
ma-chine *n.* maquina
ma-chine-gun *n.* ametral
   lar
ma-chin-er-y *n.*
   maquinaria

ma-chin-ist *n.* maquinista
mack-er-el *n.* caballa
mac-ra-me *n.* macrame
mac-ro-bi-ot-ics *n.*
   macrobiotica
mac-ro-cosm *n.*
   macrocosmo
mac-ro-scop-ic *adj.*
   macroscopico
mad *adj.* furioso
mad-cap *adj.* alocado
mad-den *v.* enloquecer
mad-den-ing *adj.*
   enloquecedor
made-up *adj.* incentado
mad-ness *n.* locura
mag-a-zine *n.* revista
mag-got *n.* gusano
mag-ic *n.* magia
mag-i-cal *adj.* mágico
ma-gi-cian *n.* mago
mag-is-te-ri-al *adj.*
   magistral
mag-is-trate *n.* magistrado
mag-nate *n.* magnate
mag-ne-si-um *n.*
   magnesio
mag-net-ic *adj.* magnetico
mag-net-ism *n.*
   magnetismo
mag-net-ize *v.* magnetizar
mag-ni-fi-ca-tion *n.*
   ampliacion
mag-nif-i-cence *n.*
   magnificencia
mag-nif-i-cent *adj.*
   magnifico
mag-ni-fi-er *n.*
   amplificador
mag-ni-fy *v.* aumentar
mag-ni-tude *n.* magnitud
mag-num *n.* magnum
ma-hog-a-ny *n.* caoba
maid *n.* soltera
mail *n.* correo
mail-box *n.* buzon
main-tain *v.* mantener
main-te-nance *n.*
   mantenimiento
ma-jes-tic *adj.* majestuoso
maj-es-ty *n.* majestad

ma-jor *adj.* mayor

ma-jor-i-ty *n.* mayoria

make *v.* ganar; crear; hacer

mak-er *n.* fabricante

mak-ing *n.* fabricacion

mal-a-dy *n.* dolencia

ma-lar-i-a *n.* malaria

mal-con-tent *adj.*
malcontento

male *adj.* masculino;
macho

mal-e-dic-tion *n.*
maldición

ma-lev-o-lence *n.*
malevolencia

ma-lev-o-lent *adj.*
malévolo

mal-func-tion *v.*
funcionarmal

mal-ice *n.* malicia

ma-li-cious *adj.* malicioso

ma-lig-nan-cy *n.*
malignidad

ma-lig-nant *adj.* maligno

mall *n.* alameda

mal-le-a-ble *adj.* maleable

mal-nour-ished *adj.*
desnutrido

mal-nu-tri-tion *n.*
desnutrición

malt *n.* malta

mal-treat *v.* maltratar

mal-treat-ment *n.*
maltratamiento

mam-mal *n.* mamifero

mam-ma-li-an *adj.*
mamifero

mam-ma-ry *adj.* mamario

man *n.* hombre

man-age *v.* manejar

man-age-a-ble *adj.*
manejable

man-age-ment *n.* gerencia

man-da-rin *n.* mandarin

man-date *n.* mandato

man-da-to-ry *adj.*
mandante

man-do-lin *n.* mandolina

ma-neu-ver *v.* maniobrar

ma-neu-ner-a-ble *adj.*
maniobrable

man-ga-nese *n.*
manganeso

man-gle *v.* mutilar

man-go *n.* mango

man-hood *n.* madurez

ma-ni-a *n.* mania

ma-ni-ac *adj.* maniático

man-i-cure *n.* manicura

man-i-cur-ist *n.* manicuro

man-i-fest *adj.* manifiesto

man-i-fes-ta-tion *n.*
manifes tacion

man-i-fes-to *n.* manifiesto

ma-ni-kin *n.* maniquí

ma-nip-u-late *v.*
manipular

ma-nip-u-la-tion *n.*
manipulacion

ma-nip-u-la-tive *adj.*
demanipuleo

ma-nip-u-la-tor *n.*
manipulador

man-li-ness *n.* hombria

man-ly *adj.* masculino

man-ne-quin *n.* maniqui

man-ner *n.* manera

man-nered *adj.*
amanerado

man-ner-ism *n.*
amaneramiento

man-nish *adj.* hombruno

man-tel *n.* manto

man-tle *n.* manto

man-u-al *adj.* manual

man-u-fac-ture *n.*
manufactura

man-u-fac-tured *adj.*
manufacturado

man-u-fac-tur-ing *adj.*
manufacturero

man-u-script *n.*
manuscrito

man-y *adj.* muchos

map *n.* mapa

ma-ple *n.* arce

map-mak-er *n.* cartografia

mar *v.* desfigurar

mar-a-thon *n.* maraton

ma-raud-er *n.*
merodeador

mar-ble *n.* marmol

mar-bled *adj.* jaspeado

mar-bling *n.* marmoración

march *v.* marchar

March *n.* marzo

mar-ga-rine *n.* margarina

mar-gin *s.* margen

mar-gin-al *adj.* marginal

mar-i-gold *n.* maravilla

ma-ri-na *n.* marina

mar-i-nate *v.* marinar

ma-rine *n.* marino

mar-i-ner *n.* marinero

mar-i-tal *adj.* marital

mar-i-time *adj.* marítimo

mark *n.* marca

marked *adj.* marcado

mark-er *n.* marcador

mar-ket *v.* vender; *n.*
mercado

mar-ket-a-ble *adj.*
vendible

mar-ket-er *n.* vendedor

mark-ing *n.* marca

mar-ma-lade *n.*
mermelada

ma-roon *v.* abandonar

mar-quis *n.* marques

mar-riage *n.* matrimonio

mar-ried *adj.* casado

mar-row *n.* medula

mar-ry *v.* casar(se)

marsh *n.* pantano

mar-shal *n.* mariscal

marsh-y *adj.* pantanoso

mar-su-pi-al *adj.*
marsupial

mart *n.* mercado

mar-tial *adj.* marcial

mar-tyr *n.* martir

mar-tyr-dom *n.* martirio

mar-vel *s.* maravilla

mar-vel-lous *adj.*
maravilloso

mas-cot *n.* mascota

mas-cu-line *adj.*
masculion

mas-och-ism *n.* maso
quismo

mas-quer-ade *n.*
mascarada

mas-ter *n.* maestro

mas-ti-cate *v.* masticar

ma-te-ri-al *adj., n.*
material

ma-ter-nal *adj.* maternal

ma-ter-ni-ty *n.*
maternidad

math *n.* matematicas

math-e-mat-ics *n.*
matematicas

ma-ture *v.* madurar, *adj.*
maduro

May *n.* mayo

may *v.* poder

me *pron.* mi; me

meal *n.* comida

mean *v.* intentar

meas-ure *v.* medir

meas-ure-ment *n.*
medición

me-chan-ic *n.* mecánico

me-chan-i-cal *adj.*
mecánico

med-al *n.* medalla

me-di-ate *v.* mediar

med-i-cal *adj.* medico

med-i-ca-tion *n.*
medicación

med-i-cine *n.* medicina

med-i-tate *v.* meditar

med-i-ta-tion *n.*
meditación

meet *v.* reunirse;
encontrar(se)

mel-o-dy *n.* melodia

mel-on *n.* melon

mem-ber *n.* miembro

mem-o-ra-ble *adj.*
memorable

men-tal *adj.* mental

men-tion *v.* mencionar, *n.*
mencion

mer-cu-ry *n.* mercurio

mer-it *v.* merecer

mer-ry *adj.* festivo

mes-sage *n.* comunicación

mes-sen-ger *n.* mensajero

met-al *n.* metal

me-te-or-ol-o-gy *n.*
meteorologia

meth-od *n.* metodo

mi-crobe *n.* microbio

mi-cro-phone *n.*
microfono

mi-cro-scope *n.*
microscopio

mid-dle *n., adj.* medio

mid-night *n.* medianoche

mi-grate *v.* emigrar

mil-i-tar-y *adj.* militar

mi-li-tia *n.* milicia

milk *n.* leche

mil-lion *n.* millon

mil-lion-aire *n.* millonario

mind *v.* obedecer, *n.*
mente

min-er-al *n.* mineral

min-is-ter *n.* ministro

mi-nor *adj.* menor

mi-nor-i-ty *n.* minoria

mi-nus *prep.* menos

mir-a-cle *n.* milagro

mi-rac-u-lous *adj.*
milagroso

mir-ror *n.* espejo

mis-chie-vous *adj.*
malicioso

miss *v.* perder

mis-sion *n.* misión

mis-sion-ar-y *n.* misionero

mis-take *v.* equivocar(se)

mis-ter *n.* senor

mis-treat *v.* maltratar

mit-i-gate *v.* mitigar

mit-ten *n.* mitón

mix *n.* mezcla, *v.*
mezclar(se)

mix-ture *n.* mezcla

mod-el *v.* modelar, *n.*
modelo

mod-er-ate *v.* moderar,
adj. moderado

mod-ern *n.* moderno

mod-est *adj.* modesto

mod-i-fi-ca-tion *n.*
modificación

mod-i-fy *v.* modificar

mod-u-late *v.* modular

moist *adj.* humedo

mold *v.* moldear, *n.* molde

mol-e-cule *n.* molecula

mol-lusk *n.* molusco

mom *n.* mama

mo-ment *n.* momento

mon-as-ter-y *n.*
monasterio

Mon-day *n.* lunes

mon-ey *n.* dinero

mon-i-tor *n.* monitor

mon-key *n.* mono

mon-o-gram *n.*
monograma

mo-no-tone *n.* monotonia

mo-not-o-nous *adj.*
monotono

mon-ster *n.* monstruo

month *n.* mes

moon *n.* luna

mop *n.* estropajo

mor-al *adj.* moral

more *n., adv., adj.* mas

morn-ing *n.* manana

mor-tal *n., adj.* mortal

mor-tal-i-ty *n.* mortalidad

mor-tu-ar-y *n.* mortuorio

mos-qui-to *n.* mosquito

most *adj.* muy; mas

moth *n.* polilla

moth-er *n.* madre

moth-er-hood *n.*
maternidad

moth-er-in-law *n.* suegra

mo-tor-cy-cle *n.*
motocicleta

montain *n.* montana

mouse *n.* raton

mouth *n.* boca

move *v.* mundar; mover

mov-ie *n.* película

Mr. *n.* señor

Mrs. *n.* señora

Ms. *n.* senora

much *adj.* muy, *n., adv.,*
adj. mucho

mul-ti-ple *adj.* multiple

mul-ti-pli-ca-tion *n.* multi
plicacion

mul-ti-ply *v.* multiplicar

mu-nic-i-pal *adj.*
municipal

mus-cle *n.* musculo

mus-cu-lar *adj.*
musculoso

mu-sic *n.* musica

mu-si-cal *adj.* musical
mu-si-cian *n.* musico
must *v.* deber
mus-tache *n.* bigote
mu-ti-late *v.* mutilar
my *adj.* mi
my-self *pron.* yo mismo
mys-ter-y *n.* misterio
myth *n.* mito
my-thol-o-gy *n.* mitología

N

nab *v.* prender
nag *n.* jaca
nail *v.* clavar, *n.* clavo
name *v.* apellido; nombre
nap-kin *n.* servilleta
nar-cot-ic *n.* narcotico
nar-rate *v.* narrar
nar-ra-tion *n.* narración
nar-ra-tive *adj.* narrativo
na-sal *adj.* nasal
na-tal *adj.* natal
na-tion *n.* nation
na-tion-al *n., adj.* naciónal
na-tiv-i-ty *n.* natividad
nat-u-ral *adj.* natural
na-ture *n.* genero;
  naturaleza
nau-se-a *n.* nausea
nau-ti-cal *adj.* nautico
na-val *adj.* naval
nav-i-ga-ble *adj.*
  navegable
nav-i-gate *v.* navegar
nav-i-ga-tion *n.*
  navegación
near *prep.* cerca de, *adv.*
  cerca, *adj.* próximo
nec-es-sar-y *adj.* necesario
ne-ces-si-tate *v.* necesitar
ne-ces-si-ty *n.* necesidad
need *v.* necesitar
neg-a-tive *n.* negativa
ne-go-ti-a-tion *n.*
  negociación
neigh-bor-hood *n.* barrio
nei-ther *pron.* ninguno,
  conj. tampoco; ni
neph-ew *n.* sobrino

nerv-ous *adj.* nervioso
neu-tral *n., adj.* neutral
neu-tral-i-ty *n.*
  neutralidad
neu-tral-ize *v.* neutralizar
nev-er *adv.* jamas; nunca
new *adj.* nuevo
new-ly *adv.* nuevamente
news *n.* nuevas
next *adj.* próximo
nice *adj.* agradable; amable
nick-el *n.* niquel
niece *n.* sobrina
night *n.* noche
night-time *n.* noche
nine *adj.* nueve
nine-teen *adj.* diecinueve
nine-ty *adj.* noventa
ninth *adj.* noveno
no *n., adv.* no
no-bod-y *n., pron.* nadíe
noise *n.* ruido
nois-y *adj.* ruidoso
none *pron.* nadie; nada
noon *n.* mediodia
nor *conj.* ni
nor-mal *adj.* normal
nor-mal-ly *adv.*
  normalmente
north *n.* norte
north-east *n.* nordeste
north-west *n.* noroeste
nose *n.* nariz
not *adv.* no
no-ta-ble *adj.* notable
no-ta-tion *n.* notacion
note *v.* notar, *n.* nota
no-ti-fy *v.* notificar
no-tion *n.* nocion
no-to-ri-ous *adj.* notorio
No-vem-ber *n.* noviembre
now *adv.* ahora
nu-cle-ar *adj.* nuclear
nude *n., adj.* desnudo
num-ber *v.* numerar, *n.*
  numero
nu-mer-i-cal *adj.*
  numerico
nu-mer-ous *adj.* numeroso
nut *n.* nuez
nu-tri-tion *n.* nutrición

O

oak *n.* roble
oar *n.* remo
o-a-sis *n.* oasis
o-be-di-ence *n.* obediencia
o-bese *adj.* obeso
o-bey *v.* obedecer
ob-jec-tion *n.* objeción
ob-jec-tive *n., adj.*
  objetivo
ob-li-gate *v.* obligar
ob-li-ga-tion *n.* obligación
o-blige *v.* obligar
ob-long *adj.* oblongo
ob-scene *adj.* obsceno
ob-scu-ri-ty *n.* oscuridad
ob-ser-va-tion *n.* obser
  vacion
ob-sti-nate *adj.* obstinado
ob-struct *v.* obstruir
ob-tain *v.* obtener
oc-ca-sion *n.* ocasión
oc-ca-sion-al *adj.* ocasiónal
oc-cu-pa-tion *n.*
  ocupación
oc-cur *v.* ocurrir
o-cean *v.* oceáno
oc-ta-gon *n.* octagono
Oc-to-ber *n.* octubre
odd *adj.* raro
odd-i-ty *n.* rareza
o-di-ous *adj.* odioso
of *prep.* de
off *adv.* fuera
of-fer *n.* ofrecimiento, *v.*
  ofrecer
of-fice *n.* oficina
of-fi-cer *n.* oficiál
of-fi-cial *n., adj.* oficiál
oil *n.* aceite
oil-y *adj.* aceitoso
old *adj.* anciano; viejo
o-mis-sion *n.* omisión
on *prep.* sobre
once *n., adv.* una vez
on-ion *n.* cebolla
on-ly *adj., adv.* solo
on-to *prep.* sobre; en
o-pac-i-ty *n.* opacidad

o-pal *n.* opalo

o-pen *v.* abrir, *adj.* abierto

o-pen-ing *n.* abertura

o-per-a *n.* opera

op-er-a-tion *n.* operación

o-pin-ion *n.* opinion

op-por-tune *adj.* oportuno

op-por-tu-ni-ty *n.* opor tunidad

op-po-site *adj.* opuesto

op-ti-cal *adj.* optico

op-tion *n.* opción

or *conj.* o; o sea

o-ral *adj.* oral

or-ange *adj.* anaranjado, *n.* naranja

o-ra-tion *n.* oracion

or-ches-tra *n.* orquesta

or-der *n.* orden

or-di-nar-y *adj.* ordinario

or-gan-ism *n.* organismo

or-gan-i-za-tion *n.* or ganizacion

or-gan-ize *v.* organizar

o-rig-i-nal *adj.* original

o-rig-i-nate *v.* originar

os-ten-ta-tion *n.* ostentacion

oth-er *prep.* el otro, *adj.* otro

ounce *n.* onza

our *adj.* nuestro

our-selves *pron.* nosotros

out *prep.* fuera de, *adv.* fuera

out-er *adj.* externo

out-fit *n.* traje

out-line *v.* bosquejar, *n.* bosquejo

out-side *adv.* fuera, *n.* ex terior

out-ward *adj.* exterior

o-va-ry *n.* ovario

o-va-tion *n.* ovación

ov-en *n.* horno

o-ver *adj.* otra vez, *prep.* sobre; encima de

o-ver-lap *v.* solapar

o-ver-night *adj.* de noche

o-ver-sight *n.* olvido

o-ver-turn *v.* volcar

o-ver-weight *adj.* gordo

owe *v.* tener deudas

owl *n.* buho

own *v.* reconocer

ox-ide *n.* oxido

ox-y-gen *n.* oxigeno

oys-ter *n.* ostra

P

pa *n.* papá

pace *n.* paso

pa-cif-ic *adj.* pacifico

pac-i-fism *n.* pacifismo

pac-i-fy *v.* pacificar

pack *n.* fardo

pack-age *n.* paquete

pact *n.* pacto

pad *n.* almohadilla

pad-dle *n.* canalete

pad-lock *n.* candado

pa-gan *n.* pagano

page *n.* página

pag-eant *n.* espectaculo

pa-go-da *n.* pagoda

pail *n.* cubo

pain *v.* doler; *n.* dolor

pain-ful *adj.* doloroso

pains-tak-ing *a.* laborioso; esmerado

paint *n.* pintura, *v.* pintar

paint-ing *n.* pintura

pair *n.* pareja; par

pa-jam-as *n.* pijama

pal-ace *n.* palacio

pal-ate *n.* paladar

pale *a.* palido; claro

pa-le-on-tol-o-gy *n.* paleontologia

pal-ette *n.* paleta

pal-i-sade *n.* palizada

pall *v.* perder su sabor

pal-lid *palido*

pal-lor *n.* palidez

palm *n.* palma

palm-is-try *n.* quiromancia

pal-pa-ble *adj.* palpable

pal-pi-ta-tion *n.* palpitación

pal-try *a.* miserable

pam-per *v.* mimar

pam-phlet *n.* folleto

pan *n.* cazuela

pan-a-ce-a *n.* panacea

pan-cake *n.* hojuela

pan-cre-as *n.* pancreas

pan-de-mo-ni-um *n.* pandemonium

pane *n.* hoja de vidrio

pan-el *n.* panel

pang *n.* punzada; dolor

pan-han-dle *v.* mendigar

pan-ic *n.* terror

pan-o-ram-a *n.* panorama

pan-sy *n.* pensamiento

pant *n., pl.* pantalones

pan-the-ism *n.* panteismo

pan-ther *n.* pantera

pan-to-mime *n.* pantomima

pan-try *n.* despensa

pa-pa *n.* papa

pa-pa-cy *n.* papado; pon tificado

pa-per *n.* papel

pa-pier-ma-che *n.* cartón piedra

pa-poose *n.* crio

pa-py-rus *n.* papiro

par *n.* par

par-a-ble *n.* parábola

par-a-chute *n.* paracaídas

pa-rade *n.* parada

par-a-dise *n.* paraiso

par-a-dox *n.* paradoja

par-af-fin *n.* paraffin

par-a-graph *n.* parrafo

par-al-lel *a.* paralelo

pa-ral-y-sis *n.* parálisis

par-a-lyze *v.* paralizar

par-ram-e-ter *n.* parametro; limite

par-a-noi-a *n.* paranoia

par-a-pher-nal-ia *n.* arreos

par-a-phrase *n.* parafrasis

par-a-site *n.* parásito

par-a-troop-er *n.* paracaidista

parcel *n.* paquete; bulto

parch *v.* secar

parch-ment *n.* pergamino
par-don *n.* perdón, *v.*
  perdonar
pare *v.* cortar
par-ent *n.* madre; padre
par-ren-the-sis *n.*
  parentesis
pa-ri-ah *n.* paria
par-ish *n.* parroquia
park *v.* aparcar, *n.* parque
par-ley *v.* parlamentar
par-lia-ment *n.*
  parlamento
par-lor *n.* sala de recibo
pa-ro-chi-al *a.* parroquial;
  estrecho
par-o-dy *n.* parodia
pa-role *n.* libertad bajo
  palabra
par-ox-ysm *n.* paroxismo
par-rot *n.* loro
par-ry *v.* parar
par-sley *n.* perejil
par-son *n.* clérigo
part *v.* separar(se);
  partir(se), *n.* parte
par-take *v.* tomar parte
par-tial *adj.* parcial
par-tial-i-ty *n.* parcialidad
par-tic-i-pant *a.* participe
par-tic-i-pate *v.* participar
par-tic-i-pa-tion *n.* par
  ticipacion
par-ti-ci-ple *n.* participio
par-ti-cle *n.* partículo
par-tic-u-lar *adj.*
  particular
par-tic-u-lar-i-ty *n.*
  particion; tabique
part-ing *a.* despendida
par-ti-san *n.* partidario
par-ti-tion *n.* partición;
  tabique
part-ner *n.* socio
par-tridge *n.* perdiz
par-ty *n.* fiesta
pass *v.* aprobar; pasar
pas-sage *n.* pasaje;
  travesia; pasadizo
pas-sen-ger *n.* pasajero;
  viajero

pas-sion *n.* pasión
pas-sion-ate *a.* apasionado
pas-sive *adj.* pasivo
pass-port *n.* pasaporte
pass-word *n.* santo y sena
past *n., adj.* pasado
paste *n.* enguido; pasta
paste-board *n.* carton
pas-teur-i-za-tion *n.*
  pasteurizacion
pas-teur-ize *v.* pasteurizar
pas-time *n.* pasatiempo
pas-tor *n.* pastor
pas-try *n.* pasteles
pas-ture *n.* pasto
pat *n.* golpecito; pastelillo
patch *n.* pedazo
pat-ent *n.* patente
pa-ter-nal *adj.* paterno
pa-ter-ni-ty *n.* paternidad
path *n.* senda
pa-thet-ic *a.* patético
pa-thol-o-gy *n.* patología
pa-tience *n.* paciencia
pa-tient *a.* paciente
pa-ti-o *n.* patio
pa-tri-ar-chy *n.*
  patriarcado
pat-ri-mo-ny *n.*
  patrimonio
pa-tri-ot *n.* patriota
pa-trol *v.* patrullar
pa-tron *n.* cliente
pat-tern *n.* patrón
pau-per *n.* pobre
pause *n.* pausa
pave *v.* empedrar; pavimen
  tar
pave-ment *n.* pavimento
pa-vil-ion *n.* pabellon
paw *v.* manosear, *n.* pata
pawn *v.* empenar
pay *v.* pagar; ser
  provechoso
pay-roll *n.* nomina
pea *n.* guisante
peace *n.* paz
peace-ful *a.* tranquilo
peach *n.* melocoton
pea-cock *n.* pavo real;
  pavon

peak *n.* pico; cumbre
peal *v.* repicar
pea-nut *n.* cachuete
pear *n.* pera
pearl *n.* perla
peas-ant *n.* campesino
pab-ble *n.* guijarro
pec-ca-dil-lo *n.* pecadillo
pe-cu-liar *adj.* peculir
pe-cu-li-ar-i-ty *n.*
  peculiaridad
ped-al *n.* pedal
ped-dle *v.* vender por las
  calles
ped-dler *n.* buhonero
ped-es-tal *n.* pedestal
pe-des-tri-an *n.* peaton
ped-i-gree *n.* genealógia
peel *v.* pelar
peer *n.* par
peg *n.* clavija; estaca
pel-let *n.* bolita; pella
pelt *n.* piel
pel-vis *n.* pelvis
pen *n.* pluma
pe-nal *a.* penal
pen-al-ty *n.* pena; castigo
pen-cil *n.* lápiz
pend-ant *n.* pendiente
pend-ing *adj.* pendiente
pen-du-lum *n.* péndulo
pen-e-trate *v.* penetrar
pen-i-cil-in *n.* penicilina
pen-in-su-la *n.* península
pen-i-tent *n.* penitente
pen-i-ten-tia-ry *n.*
  presidio
pen-ny *n.* centavo
pen-sion *n.* pensión
pen-sive *adj.* pensativo
pen-ta-gon *n.* pentágono
pe-on *n.* peon
pe-o-ny *n.* peonía
peo-ple *n.* gente; pueblo
pep-per *n.* pimienta;
  pimiento
pep-per-mint *n.* menta
per *prep.* por
per-ceive *v.* percibir
per-cent *n.* por ciento
per-cent-age *n.* porcentaje

per-cep-tion *n.* percepción
perch *n.* percha; perca
per-di-tion *n.* perdición
per-en-ni-al *a.* perenne
per-fect *adj.* perfecto
per-fec-tion *n.* perfección
per-fo-rate *v.* perforar
per-form *v.* efectuar;
    hacer; representar
per-for-mance *n.*
    representación; función
per-fume *n.* perfume
per-il *n.* peligro
pe-rim-e-ter *n.* perimetro
pe-ri-od *n.* periodo
pe-ri-od-i-cal *adj.*
    periódico
pe-riph-er-y *n.* periferia
per-i-scope *n.* periscopia
per-ish *v.* perecer
per-jure *v.* perjurar(se)
per-ju-ry *n.* perjurio
per-ma-nent *a.*
    permanente
per-mis-sion *n.* permiso
per-mit *v.* permitir; tolerar
per-pen-dic-u-lar *adj.* per
    pendicular
per-pet-u-al *a.* perpetuo;
    continuo
per-plex *v.* confundir
per-se-cute *v.* perseguir
per-se-cu-tion *n.*
    persecución
per-sist *v.* persistir
per-son *n.* persona
per-son-al-i-ty *n.*
    personalidad
per-son-nel *n.* personal
per-spec-tive *n.*
    perspectiva
per-spi-ra-tion *n.* sudor
per-suade *v.* persuadi
per-spire *v.* sudar
per-ver-sion *n.* perversión
pe-ti-tion *n.* peticion
phar-ma-cy *n.* farmacia
phi-los-o-phy *n.* filosofía
pho-bi-a *n.* fobia
pho-to-cop-y *n.* fotocopia
pho-to-graph *n.* foto

pho-tog-ra-phy *n.*
    fotografia
phrase *n.* frase
phys-i-cal *adj.* fisico
phy-si-cian *n.* medico
pi-an-o *n.* piano
pick *v.* picar; elegir
pic-ture *n.* foto; cuadro;
    pelicula
pie *n.* pastel
piece *n.* pedazo
pig *n.* cerdo
pi-geon *n.* paloma
pil-lar *n.* pilar
pine *n.* pino
pink *adj.* rosado
pipe *n.* pipa
pis-tol *n.* pistola
pit-y *n.* lastima
place *v.* poner, *n.*
    posición; sitio
plac-id *adj.* placido
plague *n.* plaga
plain *adj., n.* llano
plan *v.* planear, *n.* plano
plane *n.* avion; plano
plan-et *n.* planeta
plant *v.* plantar, *n.* planta
plas-ma *n.* plasma
plas-tic *n., adj.* plastico
plate *n.* plato
play *v.* tocar; jugar, *n.*
    juego
plea *n.* defensa
plead *v.* suplicar; defender
pleas-ure *n.* placer
plen-ti-ful *adj.* abundante
plen-ty *n.* abundancia
plum *n.* ciruela
plum-age *n.* plumaje
plu-ral *n., adj.* plural
pock-et *n.* bolsillo
po-em *n.* poema
po-et *n.* poeta
po-et-ic *adj.* poético
point *n.* punto
po-lice *n.* policía
po-lit-i-cal *adj.* politico
pol-i-ti-cian *n.* politico
pol-i-tics *n.* politicia
pol-lu-tion *n.* polución

pomp-ous *adj.* pomposo
pond *n.* estanque
po-ny *n.* jaca
pool *n.* piscina
poor *adj.* pobre
pop-u-lar *adj.* popular
pop-u-late *v.* poblar
pop-u-la-tion *n.* población
port *n.* puerto
por-tion *n.* parte
pose *v.* plantear
po-si-tion *n.* posición
pos-i-tive *adj.* positivo
pos-sess *v.* poseer
pos-ses-sion *n.* posesión
pos-si-bil-i-ty *n.*
    posibilidad
pos-si-ble *adj.* posible
post *n.* poste; puesto;
    correo
post-age *n.* porte;
    franqueo
post-card *n.* tarjeta
post-er *n.* cartel
pos-te-ri-or *adj.* posterior
post-man *n.* cartero
post-mark *n.* matasellos
post me-rid-i-em *a.*
    postmeridiano
post-mor-tem *n.* autopsia
post-pone *v.* alazar
post-script *v.* posdata
pos-ture *n.* postura
pot *n.* olla; tiesto
po-tas-si-um *n.* potasio
po-ta-to *n.* patata
po-tent *a.* potente; fuerte
po-ten-tial *adj.* potencial
po-tion *n.* posion
pot-ter-y *n.* alfareria
pouch *n.* bolsa
poul-try *n.* aves de corral
pound *n.* libra
pour *v.* diluviar
pout *v.* hace puncheros
pov-er-ty *n.* pobreza
pow-der *n.* polvo
pow-er *n.* fuerza; poder
pow-er-ful *a.* potente;
    poderoso
prac-ti-cal *adj.* práctico

practice *v.* practicar;
ejercer

prag-mat-ic *a.* pragmatico

pari-rie *n.* pradera

praise *v.* alabar

prank *n.* travesura

pray *v.* rezar

prayer *n.* oración

preach *v.* predicar

pre-am-ble *n.* preambulo

pre-cau-tion *n.* precaución

pre-dede *v.* preceder

prec-e-dent *n.* precedente

pre-cint *n.* recinto; distrito
electoral

pre-cious *adj.* precioso

prec-i-pice *n.* precipicio

pre-cip-i-ta-tion *n.*
precipitacion

pre-cise *a.* preciso; exacto

pre-co-cious *a.* precoz

pre-cur-sor *n.* precursor

pred-e-ces-sor *n.*
predecesor

pre-des-ti-na-tion *n.*
predestinación.

pre-dic-a-ment *n.* apuro

pre-dict *v.* pronosticar

pre-dic-tion *n.* pronóstico

pre-dom-i-nant *a.*
predominante

pref-ace *n.* prologo;
prefacio

pre-fer *v.* preferir

pref-er-ence *n.*
preferencia

pre-fix *n.* prefijo

preg-nan-cy *n.* embarazo

preg-nant *adj.*
embarazada

pre-his-tor-ic *adj.*
prehistorico

prej-u-dice *n.* prejuicio

pre-lim-i-nar-y *n.*
preliminar

pre-lude *n.* preludio

pre-med-i-tate *v.*
premeditar

pre-miere *n.* estreno

pre-mi-um *n.* prima

pre-mo-ni-tion *n.*
presentimiento

pre-oc-cu-pied *adj.*
preocupado

prep-a-ra-tion *n.*
preparacion

pre-pare *v.* preparar(se)

prep-o-si-tion *n.*
preposición

pre-pos-ter-ous *a.*
absurdo

pre-req-ui-site *a.*
requisito previo

pre-rog-a-tive *n.*
prerrogativa

pre-scribe *v.* prescribir

pre-scrip-tion *n.* recenta

pres-ence *n.* presencia

pres-ent *adj.* presente, *v.*
presentar, *n.* regalo

pres-en-ta-tion *n.* presen
tacion

pre-serv-a-tive *a.* preserv
ativo

pre-serve *v.* preservar; con
servar

pre-side *v.* presidir

pres-i-dent *n.* presidente

press *n.* prensa; imprenta

pres-sure *n.* presión;
urgencia

pres-ti-gid-i-ta-tion *n.*
prestidigitación

pres-tige *n.* prestigio

pre0sume *v.* presumir;
suponer

pre-tend *v.* pretender

pre-tense *n.* pretexto

pret-ty *a.* guapo; bonito;
mono

pre-vail *v.* prevalecer;
predominar

pre-vent *v.* impedir

pre-vi-ous *a.* previo

prey *n.* presa

price *n.* precio

price-less *a.* inapreciable

prick *v.* punzar

pride *n.* orgullo

priest *n.* sacerdote

prim *a.* estirado

pri-ma-ry *adj.* primario

prime *adj.* primero

prim-i-tive *adj.* primitivo

pri-mo-gen-i-ture *n.*
primogeniture

prince *n.* principe

prin-cess *n.* princesa

prin-ci-pal *n., adj.*
principal

prin-ci-pal-i-ty *n.*
principado

prin-ci-ple *n.* principio

print *v.* imprimir

print-ing *n.* imprenta

pri-or *a.* anterior

pri-or-i-ty *n.* prioridad

pri-or-y *n.* priorato

prism *n.* prism

pris-on *n.* carcel

pri-va-cy *n.* soledad

pri-vate *adj.* privado

priv-i-lege *n.* privilegio

prize *n.* premio

prob-a-bil-i-ty *n.*
probabilidad

prob-a-ble *a.* probable

probe *n.* sonda

prob-lem *n.* problema

pro-ce-dure *n.*
procedimiento

pro-ceed *v.* proceder

proc-ess *n.* proceso

pro-claim *v.* proclamar

pro-cliv-i-ty *n.*
proclividad; inclinación

pro-cras-ti-nate *v.* dilatar;
aplazar

pro-cure *v.* obtener; al
cahuetear

prod *v.* ponzar

prod-i-gal *a.* prodigo

pro-d-i-gy *n.* prodigio

pro-duce *v.* producir

prod-uct *n.* producto

pro-fane *a.* profano

pro-fan-i-ty *n.* profanidad

pro-fes-sion *n.* profesión

pro-fes-sor *n.* profesora;
profesor

pro-fi-cien-cy *n.* pericia

pro-file *n.* perfil

prof-it *n.* ganancia; beneficio
pro-found *a.* profundo
pro-fuse *a.* profuso
pro-fu-sion *n.* profusion
prog-e-ny *n.* progenie
prog-no-sis *n.* pronostico
pro-gram *n.* programa
prog-ress *n.* progreso; desarrollo
pro-gres-sive *a.* progresivo
pro-hib-it *v.* prohibir
pro-hi-bi-tion *n.* prohibición
pro-ject *n.* proyecto, *v.* proyectar
pro-jec-tile *n.* proyectile
pro-lif-ic *adj.* prolifico
pro-logue *n.* prolongar
pro-long *v.* prolongar
prom-i-nent *a.* prominente
pro-mis-cu-ous *a.* promiscuo; libertino
prom-ise *v.* prometer, *n.* promesa
prom-on-to-ry *n.* promontorio
pro-mote *v.* promover; fomenter; ascender
pro-mo-tion *n.* promoción
prompt *a.* puntual; pronto
pro-noun *n.* pronombre
pro-nounce *v.* pronunciar(se)
pro-nounced *a.* marcado
pro-nun-ci-a-tion *n.* pronun ciacion
proof *n.* prueba
proof-read-er *n.* corrector de pruebas
prop *n.* apoyo
prop-a-gan-da *n.* propaganda
pro-pel *v.* propulsar
pro-pel-ler *n.* helice
pro-pen-si-ty *n.* propensión; inclinacion
prop-er *a.* propio; apropiado; decente

prop-er-ty *n.* propiedad
proph-e-cy *n.* profeciz
proph-e-sy *v.* profetizar
proph-et *n.* profeta
pro-phy-lac-tic *a.* profilatico
pro-pi-tious *a.* propicio
pro-por-tion *n.* proporción
pro-pose *v.* proponer(se); declararse
prop-o-si-tion *n.* proposición; propuesta
pro-pri-e-tor *n.* propietario
pro-pri-e-ty *n.* corrección; decoro
pro-scribe *v.* proscribir
prose *n.* prosa
pros-e-cute *v.* proseguir
pros-pect *n.* perspectiva
pros-per *v.* prosperar
pros-per-i-ty *n.* prosperidad
pros-ti-tute *n.* prostituta; ramera
pros-trate *v.* postrar(se); derribar
pro-tag-o-nist *n.* protagonista
pro-tect *v.* proteger
pro-tein *n.* proteina
pro-test *n.* protesta, *v.* protestar
pro-to-col *n.* protocolo
pro-ton *n.* proton
pro-to-plasm *n.* protoplasma
pro-trude *v.* salir fuera
proud *a.* orgulloso; arrogante
prove *v.* probar
pro-verb *n.* proverbio
pro-vide *v.* proveer
prov-ince *n.* provincia
pro-vi-sion *n.* provision
pro-voc-a-tive *a.* provocativa; provocador
pro-voke *v.* provocar
prow *n.* proa
prox-y *n.* poder; apoderado

prude *n.* gasmona
prune *n.* ciruela pasa
pry *v.* meterse; fisgonear
psalm *n.* salmo
pseu-do-nym *n.* seudonimo
psych-e-del-ic *a.* psiquedelico
psy-chi-a-trist *n.* psiquiatra
psy-chi-a-try *n.* psiquiatría
psy-cho-a-nal-y-sis *n.* psicoanalisis
psy-cho-an-a-lyze *v.* psicoanalizar
psy-cho-log-i-cal *adj.* psicológico
psy-chol-o-gy *n.* psicología
psy-cho-sis *n.* psicosis
pto-maine *n.* ptomaina
pub *n.* taberna
pu-ber-ty *n.* pubertad
pub-lic *n., adj.* público
pub-li-ca-tion *n.* publicación
pub-lish *v.* publicar
pub-lish-er *n.* editor
puck-er *v.* arrugar
pud-ding *n.* pudin
pud-dle *n.* charco
puff *v.* soplar; inflar
pug-na-cious *a.* pugnaz
puke *v.* vomitar
pull *v.* tirar; arrastrar
pul-ley *n.* polea
pul-mo-nar-y *a.* pulmonar
pulp *n.* pulpa
pul-pit *n.* púlpito
pulse *n.* pulso
pul-ver-ize *v.* pulverizar
pum-ice *n.* piedra pómez
pump *n.* bomba
pump-kin *n.* calabaza
pun *n.* juego de palabras o vocablos
punch *v.* punzar
punc-tu-al *adj.* puntual
punc-tu-a-tion *n.* puntuación

punc-ture *n.* pinchazo
pun-ish *v.* castigar
pu-ny *a.* encanijado
pu-pa *n.* crisalida
pu-pil *n.* estudiante; pupila
pup-pet *n.* titere
pur-chase *v.* comprar
pure *adj.* puro
pur-ga-to-ry *n.* purgatorio
pu-ri-fy *v.* purificar
pu-ri-tan *n.* puritano
pur-ple *adj.* purpureo
pur-pose *n.* fin; proposito;
resolucion
purr *n.* ronreneo
purse *n.* bolsa
pur-sue *v.* perseguir
pur-suit *n.*
perseguimiento; busca;
ocupación
pus *n.* pus
push *v.* empujar; apretar
puss-y *n.* gatito
put *v.* meter; poner(se)
pu-tre-fy *v.* pudrir
pu-trid *a.* odrido
put-ty *n.* masilla
pyr-a-mid *n.* piramide
pyre *n.* pira
py-thon *n.* pitón

Q

quack *v.* graznar; *n.*
graznido
quad-ran-gle *n.*
cuadrangulo
quad-rant *n.* cuadrante
quad-rate *adj.* cuadrante
quad-rat-ic *adj.*
cuadratico
quad-ri-ceps *n.* cuadriceps
quad-ri-lat-er-al *n., adj.*
cuadrilatero
quad-ri-ple-gi-a *n.*
cuadriplejia
quad-ri-ple-gic *adj.*
cuadriplejico
quad-ru-ple *v.*
cuadruplicar(se)
quag-mire *n.* pantano

quail *n.* codorniz
quake *v.* temblar
qual-i-fi-ca-tion *n.*
calificacion
qual-i-fied *adj.* acreditado;
capacitado
qual-i-fi-er *n.* calificativo
qual-i-fy *v.* habilitar
qual-i-fy-ing *adj.*
eliminatoria
qual-i-ta-tive *adj.*
cualitativo
qual-i-ty *n.* calidad
qualm *n.* duda
quan-ti-ta-tive *adj.* cuan
titativo
quan-ti-ty *n.* cantidad
quar-an-tine *n.*
cuarentena
quar-rel *n.* riña
quar-rel-er *n.* pendenciero
quar-rel-some *adj.*
pendeciero
quar-ry *n.* cantera
quart *n.* cuarto
quar-ter *n.* cuarto
qua-ter-deck *n.* alcazar
quar-ter-ly *adj.* trimestral
quar-tet *n.* cuarteto
quartz *n.* cuarzo
qua-ver *v.* temblar
queen *n.* reina
quench *v.* matar; apagar
quench-a-ble *adj.* apagar
ques-tion *n.* pregunta
quick *adj.* listo; rapido
qui-et *adj.* silencioso
quit *v.* dejar; irse
quo-ta-tion *n.* cita
quote *v.* citar

R

rab-bi *n.* rabino
rab-bit *n.* conejo
rab-ble *n.* chusma
rab-id *adj.* rabioso
ra-bies *n.* rabia
rac-coon *n.* mapache
race *v.* correr de prisa, *n.*
raza

rac-er *n.* corredor
race-track *n.* pista
ra-cial *adj.* racial
rac-ism *n.* racismo
ra-cist *n.* racista
rack *n.* potro
rack-et *n.* raqueta
rac-y *adj.* picante
ra-dar *n.* radar
ra-di-al *adj.* radial
ra-di-ance *n.* resplandor
ra-di-ant *adj.* radiante
ra-di-ate *v.* radiar; emitir;
brillar
ra-di-a-tion *n.* radiación
ra-di-a-tor *n.* radiador
rad-i-cal *n., adj.* radical
rad-i-cle *n.* radicula
ra-di-o *n.* radio
ra-di-o-ac-tive *adj.*
radiactivo
ra-di-o-ac-tiv-i-ty *n.*
radiactividad
ra-di-o-broad-cast *v.*
radiar
ra-di-o-gram *n.*
radiograma
ra-di-o-graph *n.*
radiografia
ra-di-ol-o-gist *n.*
radiologo
ra-di-ol-o-gy *n.* radiologia
rad-ish *n.* rabano
ra-di-um *n.* radio
ra-di-us *n.* radio
ra-don *n.* radon
raff-ish *adj.* ostentoso
raf-fle *n.* rifa
raft *n.* balsa
raft-er *n.* cabrio
rag *n.* trapo
rage *v.* enfurecerse
rag-ged *adj.* desigual
raid *v.* atacar
rail *n.* carril
rail-ing *n.* baranda
rail-road *n.* ferrocarril
rail-way *n.* ferrocarril
rain *v.* llover, *n.* lluvia
rain-bow *n.* arco iris
rain-coat *n.* impereable

rain-drop *n.* gota de lluvia

rain-fall *n.* precipitación

rain-wear *n.* ropa impermeable

rain-y *adj.* lluvioso

raise *v.* criar; ;evantar

raised *adj.* repujado

rai-sin *n.* pasa

rake *v.* restrillar, *n.* rastro

ral-ly *n.* reunión, *v.* reunir(se)

ram *n.* carnero

ram-ble *v.* divagar

ram-bler *n.* vagabundo

ram-bunc-tious *adj.* al borotador

ram-i-fi-ca-tion *n.* ramificación

ramp *n.* rampa

ram-page *n.* alboroto

ramp-ant *adj.* destartalado

ranch *n.* hacienda

ranch-er *n.* hacendado

ran-cid *adj.* rancio

ran-cor *n.* rencor

ran-cor-ous *adj.* rencoroso

ran-dom *adj.* fortuito

range *v.* colocar; alinear

rang-er *n.* guardabosques

rank *n.* rango; fila

rank-ing *adj.* superior

ran-kle *v.* enconarse

ran-sack *v.* saquear

ran-som *v.* rescatar, *n.* rescate

rant *v.* vociferar

rap *v.* golpear

ra-pa-cious *adj.* rapaz

ra-pac-i-ty *n.* rapacidad

rape *v.* violar, *n.* violación

rap-id *adj.* rapido

ra-pid-i-ty *n.* rapidez

rap-ine *n.* rapiña

rap-ist *n.* violador

rap-port *n.* relación

rapt *adj.* absorto

rap-ture *n.* rapto

rap-tur-ous *adj.* extasiado

rare *adj.* poco; raro

rar-e-fied *adj.* refinado

rar-e-fy *v.* enrarecer(se)

rar-ing *adj.* impaciente

rar-i-ty *n.* rareza

ras-cal *n.* bribón

rash *n.* erupcion

rash-er *n.* tocino

rasp-ber-ry *n.* frambuesa

rasp-y *adj.* aspero

rat *n.* rata

rate *v.* tasar, *n.* razón

rath-er *adv.* un poco

rat-i-fy *v.* ratificar

rat-ing *n.* popularidad; clasificacion

ra-tio *n.* proporción

ra-ti-oc-i-nate *v.* raciocinar

ra-tion *n.* racion

ra-tion-al *adj.* racional

ra-tion-ale *n.* explicación; raxon

ra-tion-al-i-ty *n.* racionalidad

ra-tion-al-i-za-tion *n.* racionalización

ra-tion-al-ize *v.* racionalizar

ra-tion-ing *n.* racionamiento

rat-tle *n.* ruido

rat-trap *n.* ratonera

raun-chy *adj.* sucio

rav-age *v.* destruir, *n.* estrago

rave *v.* delirar

rav-el *v.* deshilar(se)

ra-ven *n.* cuervo

ra-ven-ous *adj.* coraz

ra-vine *n.* barranco

rav-ing *adj.* extraordinario

rav-ish *v.* raptar

rav-ish-ing *adj.* encantador

raw *adj.* novato; crudo

ray *n.* rayo

ray-on *n.* rayón

reach *n.* alcance, *v.* extenderse; alargar

re-act *v.* reaccionar

re-ac-tion *n.* reacción

re-ac-tion-ar-y *n.* reaccionario

re-ac-tor *n.* reactor

read *v.* decir; leer

read-ing *n.* lección

re-ad-just *v.* reajustar

read-y *adj.* pront; listo

re-al *adj.* real

re-al-i-ty *n.* realidad

re-al-ize *v.* realizar

re-al-ly *adv.* realmente

realm *n.* reino

ream *n.* resma

rea-son *v.* razonar, *n.* razon

rea-son-a-ble *adj.* razonable

reb-el *adj., n.* rebelde

re-bel-lion *n.* rebelión

re-buke *n.* reprimenda

re-call *v.* retirar; hacer

re-cant *v.* retractar(se)

re-cede *v.* retroceder

re-ceipt *n.* ingresos

re-ceive *v.* acoger; recibir

re-cent *adj.* reciente

re-cep-ta-cle *n.* receptaculo

re-cep-tion *n.* recepción

re-cess *n.* nicho

re-ces-sion *n.* retroceso

rec-i-pe *n.* receta

re-cip-ro-cal *adj.* reciproco

re-cit-al *n.* recital

rec-i-ta-tion *n.* recitación

re-cite *v.* recitar

reck-on *v.* considerar

re-claim *v.* reclamar

re-cline *v.* recostar(se)

rec-luse *n.* recluso

rec-og-ni-tion *n.* reconocimiento

rec-om-pense *n.* recom pensa

rec-on-cile *v.* reconcinar

re-con-struct *v.* reconstruir

re-cord *n.* disco, *v.* registrar

re-couse *n.* recurso

re-cov-er *v.* recobrar

re-cruit *n.* recluta**

rec-tan-gle *n.* rectangulo
rec-ti-fy *v.* rectificar
re-cu-per-ate *v.* recuperar
re-cu-per-a-tion *n.* recuperación
red *adj.* rojo
red-dish *adj.* rojizo
re-deem *v.* redimir
re-demp-tion *n.* redención
re-do *v.* rehacer
re-duce *v.* disminuir; reducir
re-duc-tion *n.* reducción
reef *n.* escollo
reek *n.* olor
re-fer *v.* referir(se)
ref-er-ee *n.* arbitro
ref-er-ence *n.* referencia
re-fill *v.* rellenar
re-fine *v.* refinar
re-fin-er-y *n.* refinería
re-flect *v.* reflejar
re-flec-tion *n.* reflejo
re-flex *adj.* reflejo
re-flex-ive *adj.* reflexive
re-form *n.* reforma, *v.* reformarse
re-form-a-to-ry *n.* reformatorio
re-fract *v.* refractar
re-frain *v.* refrenar
re-fresh *v.* refrescar
re-fresh-ment *n.* refresco
re-frig-er-ate *v.* refrigerar
ref-uge *n.* refugio
ref-u-gee *n.* refugiado
re-fund *n.* reembolso
re-fuse *v.* rehusar
re-gain *v.* recobrar
re-gard *v.* considerar
re-gen-er-ate *v.* regenerar
re-gent *n.* regente
re-gime *n.* regimen
reg-i-men *n.* regimen
reg-i-ment *n.* regimiento
re-gion *n.* región
reg-is-ter *v.* registrar, *n.* registro
re-gret *n.* sentimiento
reg-u-lar *adj.* regular
reg-u-la-tion *n.* regulación

re-ha-bil-i-tate *v.* rehabilitar
re-ha-bil-i-ta-tion *n.* rehabilitacion
re-hearse *v.* ensayar
reign *v.* reinar, *n.* reinado
re-im-burse *v.* reembolsar
rein *n.* rienda
re-in-car-na-tion *n.* reencar nacion
re-in-force *v.* reforzar
re-it-er-ate *v.* reiterar
re-ject *v.* rechazar
re-lapse *n.* recaida, *v.* rein cidir
re-late *v.* relatar
re-lat-ed *adj.* afin
re-la-tion *n.* relación
re-lax *v.* relajar
re-lease *n.* descargo
re-lent *v.* ceder
re-li-a-ble *adj.* confiable
rel-ic *n.* reliquia
re-lief *n.* alivio
re-lieve *v.* aliviar
re-li-gion *n.* religión
re-li-gious *adj.* religioso
rel-ish *n.* apetencia, *v.* gustar
re-ly *v.* contar; confiar
re-main *v.* quedar(se)
rem-e-dy *n.* remedio
re-mem-ber *v.* acordarse de
re-mem-brance *n.* recuerdo
re-mind *v.* recordar
rem-i-nis-cence *n.* reminiscencia
re-miss *adj.* descuidado
re-mit *v.* remitir
re-mit-tance *n.* remesa
re-morse *n.* remordimiento
re-mote *adj.* remoto
re-move *v.* apartar(se); quitar(se)
ren-ais-sance *n.* renacimiento
rend *v.* hander
ren-der *v.* volver

red-dez-vous *v.* reunirse
ren-e-gade *n.* renegado
re-new *v.* renovar(se)
re-nounce *v.* renunciar
re-nown *n.* renombre
rent *v.* alquilar, *n.* alquiler
re-pair *v.* remendar; reparar
re-pay *v.* pagar; recompensar
re-peat *v.* repetir(se)
re-pel *v.* repeler
re-per-cus-sion *n.* repersución
rep-er-toire *n.* repertorio
re-place *v.* reponer
re-ply *n.* respuesta
re-port *v.* informar
rep-re-hen-si-ble *adj.* reprensible
rep-re-sen-ta-tion *n.* representación
re-press *v.* reprimir
rep-ri-mand *v.* reprender
rep-roach *n.* reproche
re-pro-duce *v.* reproducir
rep-tile *n.* reptil
re-pub-lic *n.* república
re-pulse *n.* repulsa
rep-u-ta-tion *n.* reputación
re-quest *v.* rogar
re-quire *v.* necesitar; exigir
res-cue *n.* rescate
re-search *v.* investigar
re-sent *v.* resentirse de
res-er-va-tion *n.* reservación
re-serve *v.* reservar
re-side *v.* vivir; residir
res-i-dent *n., adj.* residente
re-sign *v.* resignarse
res-ig-na-tion *n.* resignación
res-in *n.* resina
re-sist *v.* resistir
re-sist-ance *n.* resistencia
res-o-lu-tion *n.* resolucion
re-solve *v.* resolver(se)

re-sort *n.* recurso
re-source *n.* recurso
re-spect *n.* respeto
re-spect-a-ble *adj.*
respetable
re-spect-ful *adj.*
respetuoso
re-spect-ing *prep.*
respecto
re-spec-tive *adj.*
respectivo
res-pi-ra-tion *n.*
respiración
res-pi-ra-tor *n.* respirador
res-pi-ra-to-ry *adj.*
respiratorio
re-spire *v.* respirar
res-pite *n.* respiro
re-splen-dent *adj.*
resplandeciente
re-spond *v.* responder
re-spon-dent *adj.*
resplandeciente
re-sponse *n.* respuesta
re-spon-si-bil-i-ty *n.*
responsabilidad
re-spon-si-ble *adj.*
responsable
rest *n.* descansar
res-tau-rant *n.* restaurante
rest-ful *adj.* sosegado
res-ti-tute *v.* restituir
res-ti-tu-tion *n.*
restitución
rest-less *adj.* inquieto
res-to-ra-tion *n.*
restauración
re-store *v.* restaurar
re-strain *v.* refrenar
re-strict *v.* restringir
re-stric-tion *n.* restricción
re-sult *n.* resultado, *v.*
resultar
re-sus-ci-tate *v.* resucitar
re-tain *v.* retener
re-tard *v.* retardar
ret-i-na *n.* retina
re-tire *v.* retirarse
re-tract *v.* retractar(se)
re-trieve *v.* recobrar

ret-ro-ac-tive *adj.*
retroactivo
re-turn *v.* volver
re-un-ion *n.* reunión
re-veal *v.* revelar
rev-e-la-tion *n.* revelación
re-venge *v.* vengar(se)
re-verse *adj.* inverso
re-view *n.* resena
re-vise *v.* repasar; revisar
re-vi-sion *n.* revision
re-vive *v.* revivir
re-voke *v.* revocar
rev-o-lu-tion *n.*
revolución
rev-o-lu-tion-ary *n., adj.*
revolucionario
re-volve *v.* revolverse
re-volv-er *n.* revolver
re-ward *n.* recompensa
rhap-so-dy *n.* rapsodia
rhe-tor-i-cal *adj.* retorico
rheu-mat-ic *adj.*
reumatico
rheu-ma-tism *n.*
reumatismo
rhyme *v.* rimar, *n.* rima
rhythm *n.* ritmo
rib *n.* costilla
rib-bon *n.* cinta
rice *n.* arroz
rich *adj.* fertil; rico
rid *v.* librar(se)
rid-dle *n.* acertijo
ride *v.* montar
rid-i-cule *v.* ridiculizar
ri-dic-u-lous *adj.* ridículo
ri-fle *n.* rifle
right *adj.* exacto; derecho
rig-id *adj.* rigido
rig-or-ous *adj.* riguroso
rind *n.* piel
ring *v.* sonar, *n.* anillo
rink *n.* pista
rip *v.* arrancar; rasgar
ripe *adj.* maduro
rise *v.* subir; levantarse
risk *n.* riesgo
rite *n.* rito
rit-u-al *n., adj.* ritual
ri-val-ry *n.* rivalidad

riv-er *n.* rio
roach *n.* cucaracha
road *n.* camino
roar *v.* rugir
rob *v.* robar
robe *n.* bata
ro-bust *adj.* robusto
rock *n.* roca
ro-dent *n.* roedor
roll *n.* rollo; lista
ro-mance *n.* amorio
ro-man-tic *adj.* romántico
ro-man-ti-cism *n.*
romanticismo
roof *n.* tejado
room *n.* sitio; cuarto
roost-er *n.* gallo
root *n.* raíz
rope *n.* cuerda
rose *n.* rosa
ros-y *adj.* rosado
ro-tate *v.* girar
rough *adj.* tosco; aspero
rou-lette *n.* ruleta
round *prep.* alrededor de,
adj. redondo
route *n.* ruta
rou-tine *n.* rutina
roy-al-ty *n.* realeza
rub *v.* rozar; fregar
rub-bish *n.* basura
ru-by *n.* rubi
rud-der *n.* timón
rude *adj.* tosco; rudo
ru-di-ment *n.* rudimento
rug *n.* alfombra
ru-in *v.* arruinar, *n.* ruina
rule *v.* gobernar, *n.* regla
rul-er *n.* regla
rum *n.* ron
ru-mor *n.* rumor
run *v.* correr
run-ning *adj.* corriente
ru-ral *adj.* rural
rust *n.* orín
rus-tic *adj.* rustico
ruth-less *adj.* despiadado
rye *n.* centeno

S

Sab-bath *n.* domingo
sa-ber *n.* sable
sa-ble *n.* cabellína
sab-o-tage *v.* sabotear, *n.* sabotaje
sac-cha-rin *n.* sacrina
sack *n.* saco
sac-ra-ment *n.* sacramento
sacred *adj.* sagrado
sac-ri-fice *v.* sacrificar, *n.* sacrificio
sac-ri-lege *n.* sacrilegio
sad *adj.* triste
sad-den *v.* entristecer
sad-dle *v.* ensillar
sad-ism *n.* sadismo
sa-fa-ri *n.* safari
safe *adj.* seguro
safe-ty *n.* seguridad
sag *v.* combar(se)
sa-ga *n.* saga
sage *n., adj.* sabio
sail *v.* nevegar, *n.* vela
sail-or *n.* marinero
saint *n., adj.* santo
sake *n.* consideración; motivo
sal-ad *n.* ensalada
sal-a-man-der *n.* salamandra
sal-a-ry *n.* salario
sale *n.* venta
sa-line *n.* salino
sa-li-va *n.* saliva
sal-low *n.* cetrino
sal-ly *n.* salida
salm-on *n.* salmón
sa-lon *n.* salón
sa-loon *n.* salón
salt *n.* sal
sal-u-tar-y *adj.* saludable
sal-u-ta-tion *n.* saludo
sa-lute *v.* sakudar
sal-vage *n.* salvamento
sal-va-tion *n.* salvación
salve *n.* unguento
sal-vo *n.* salva
same *adj.* mismo
sam-ple *v.* probar
san-a-to-ri-um *n.* sanatorio

sanc-ti-fy *v.* santificar
sanc-tion *n.* sanción
sanc-ti-ty *n.* santidad
sanc-tu-ar-y *n.* santuario
sand *n.* arena
san-dal *n.* sandalia
sand-stone *n.* arenisca
sand-wich *n.* bocadillo
sand-y *adj.* arenoso
sane *adj.* sano
san-gui-nar-y *a.* sanguinario
san-i-tar-i-um *n.* sanatorio
san-i-tar-y *adj.* sanitario
san-i-ta-tion *n.* instalación sanitaria
san-i-ty *n.* juicio sano
sap *n.* savia
sa-pi-ent *a.* sabio
sap-phire *n.* zafiro
sar-casm *n.* sarcasmo
sar-cas-tic *adj.* sarcastico
sar-coph-a-gus *n.* sarcofago
sar-dine *n.* sardina
sa-ri, sa-ree *n.* sari
sash *n.* faja
sas-sy *adj.* descarado
sa-tan *n.* Satanas
sa-tan-ic *a.* satanico
sate *v.* saciar; dsatisfacer
sat-el-lite *n.* satelite
sa-ti-ate *v.* saciar
sat-in *n.* raso
sa-tire *n.* satira
sat-is-fac-tion *n.* satisfacción
sat-is-fy *v.* satisfacer
sat-u-rate *v.* saturar
Sat-ur-day *n.* sabado
sa-tyr *n.* satiro
sauce *n.* salsa
sau-cer *n.* platillo
sau-sage *n.* salchicha
sav-age *n.; adj.* salvaje
save *v.* ahorrar; salvar
sav-ing *n.* economia
sav-ior *n.* salvador
sa-vor *n.* sabor
saw *n.* sierra
sax-o-phone *n.* saxofón

say *v.* decir
say-ing *n.* dicho
scab *n.* costra
scaf-fold *n.* andamio
scald *v.* escaldar
scale *n.* escala
scal-lop *n.* venera; feston
scalp *n.* pericraneo
scal-pel *n.* escalpelo
scan *v.* escundrinar
scan-dal *n.* escandalo
scan-dal-ize *v.* escandalizar
scant *adj.* escaso
scant-y *adj.* escaso
scape-goat *n.* cabeza de turco
scar *n.* cicatriz
scarce *adj.* escaso
scare *v.* asustar
scare-crow *n.* espantajo; espantapajaros
scarf *n.* bufanda
scar-let *n.* escarlata
scat-ter *v.* esparcir
scav-en-ger *n.* basurero
scene *n.* vista; escena
scen-er-y *n.* paisaje
scent *n.* pista; olor
sched-ule *n.* horario
scheme *v.* intrigar
schism *n.* cisma
schiz-o-phre-ni-a *n.* esquizofrenia
schol-ar *n.* erudito; alumno
schol-ar-ship *n.* erudición; beca
scho-las-tic *adj.* escolar
school *n.* escuela
sci-ence *n.* ciencia
sci-en-tist *n.* cientifico
scim-i-tar *n.* cimitarra
scis-sors *n.* tijeras
scoff *v.* mofarse
scold *v.* reganar
scoop *n.* paleta
scoot-er *n.* patinete
scope *n.* alcance
scorch *v.* chamuscar
score *n.* cuenta

scorn *n.* desden

scor-pi-on *n.* escorpión

scotch *v.* frustrar

scoun-drel *n.* canalla

scour *v.* fregar; recorrer

scout *n.* explorador

scowl *v.* poner mal gesto

scrag-gy *a.* escarnado

scram-ble *v.* revolver

scrap *n.* fragmento; sobras

scrape *v.* raer

scratch *v.* rayar; rasgunar; rascar

scrawl *n.* garrabatos; garrapatos

scream *n.* grito

screen *n.* biombo; pantalla

screw *v.* atornillar, *n.* tornillo

scrib-ble *v.* garrapatear

scrim-mage *n.* arrebatina

script *n.* letra cursiva; guion

scrip-ture *n.* Sagrada Escritura

scroll *n.* rollo de pergamino

scrub *v.* fregar

scru-ple *n.* escrupulo

scru-ti-nize *v.* escundrinar

scru-ti-ny *n.* escrutinio

scuf-fle *v.* pelear

sculp-tor *n.* escultor

sculp-ture *v.* esculpir, *n.* escultura

scum *n.* espuma

scur-ry *v.* darse prisa

scur-vy *n.* escorbuto

scut-tle *v.* echar a pique

scythe *n.* guadana

sea *n.* mar

seal *n.* foca

seal *n.* sello *v.* cerrar

seam *n.* costura

sea-man *n.* marinero

seam-stress *n.* costurera

seam-y *à.* asqueroso

se-ance *n.* sesión de espiritistas

sea-port *n.* puerto de mar

sear *v.* marchitar; chamuscar

search *v.* buscar

sea-shore *n.* orilla del mar

sea-sick-ness *n.* mareo

sea-son *n.* estación

sea-son-ing *n.* condimento

seat *v.* sentar, *n.* asiento

sea-weed *n.* alga marina

se-clude *v.* aislar

se-clu-sion *n.* retiro

sec-ond *n., adj.* segundo

sec-ond-ar-y *adj.* secundario

sec-ond-hand *a.* de segunda mano

sec-ond-rate *a.* inferior

se-cre-cy *n.* secreto

se-cret *n., adj.* secreto

sec-re-tar-y *n.* secretario

se-crete *v.* secretar; ovultar

se-cre-tion *n.* secrecion

sect *n.* secta

sec-tion *n.* seccion

sec-tor *n.* sector

sec-u-lar *adj.* secular

se-cure *adj.* seguro

se-cu-ri-ty *n.* seguridad

se-date *adj.* sosegado

sed-a-tive *n.* sedativo

sed-en-tar-y *a.* sedentario

sed-i-ment *n.* sedimento

se-di-tion *n.* sedicion

se-duce *v.* seducir

se-duc-tion *n.* seduccion

see *v.* percebir; ver

seed *n.* semilla; simiente

seed-y *a.* desharrapado

seek *v.* buscar; solicitar

seem *v.* parecer

seem-ly *a.* decoroso; correcto

seep *v.* rezumarse

se-er *n.* profeta

seg-ment *n.* segmento

seg-re-gate *v.* segregar

seg-re-ga-tion *n.* segregacion

seis-mo-graph *n.* sismografo

seize *v.* apoderarse de; asir

sei-zure *n.* asimiento

sel-dom *adv.* ramente

se-lect *adj.* selecto, *v.* elegir

se-lec-tion *n.* seleccion

self *n.* See **my-self, yourself**

self-cen-tered *a.* egocentrico

self-com-mand *n.* dominio de si mismo

self-con-fi-dence *n.* confianza en si mismo

self con-scious *a.* timido

self-control *n.* dominio de si mismo

self-ev-i-dent *a.* patente

self-ex-plan-a-to-ry *a.* evidente; obvio

self-gov-ern-ment *n.* autonomia

self-im-por-tance *n.* presun cion

self-ish *a.* egoista; inter esado

self-less *a.* desinteresado

self-re-li-ance *n.* confianza en si mismo

self-same *a.* mismo

self-suf-fi-cient *adj.* inde pendiente

self-will *n.* terquedad

sell *v.* vender

se-man-tics *n.* semantica

sem-blance *n.* parecido; apariencia

se-men *n.* semen

se-mes-ter *n.* semestre

sem-i-cir-cle *n.* semicirculo

sem-i-co-lon *n.* punto y coma

sem-i-fi-nal *adj.* semifinal

sem-i-nar *n.* seminario

sem-i-nar-y *n.* seminario

sem-i-of-fi-cial *adj.* semiofi cial

sem-i-pre-cious *adj.* semi precioso

sem-i-week-ly *a.* bisemanal

sen-ate *n.* senado
sen-a-tor *n.* senador
send *v.* mandar; enviar
se-nile *adj.* senil
sen-ior *adj.* superior
sen-ior-i-ty *n.* antiguedad
sen-sa-tion *n.* sensacion
sense *v.* percibir, *n.* sentido
semse-less *a.* sin sentido; insensato
sen-si-bil-i-ty *n.* sensibilidad
sen-si-ble *adj.* razonable
sen-si-tive *adj.* delicado
sen-si-tiv-i-ty *n.* delicadeza
sen-so-ry *adj.* sensorio
sen-su-al *adj.* sensual
sen-su-ous *adj.* sensorio
sen-tence *n.* frase
sen-ti-ment *n.* sentimiento
sen-ti-nel *n.* centinela
sen-try *n.* centinela
se-pal *n.* sepalo
sep-a-rate *v.* separar(se)
sep-a-ra-tion *n.* separacion
Sep-tem-ber *n.* septiembre
sep-tic *adj.* septico
sep-ul-cher *n.* sepulcro
se-quel *n.* resultado
se-quence *n.* sucesion
sequestered *a.* aislado
se-ques-ter *v.* separar; aislar
se-quin *n.* lentejuela
ser-aph *n.* serafin
ser-e-nade *n.* serenata
se-rene *n.* sereno
se-ren-i-ty *n.* serenidad
serf *n.* siervo
ser-geant *n.* sargento
se-ri-al *a.* en serie
se-ries *n.* serie
se-ri-ous *adj.* serio
ser-mon *n.* sermon
ser-pent *n.* serpiente
se-rum *n.* suero

serv-ant *n.* serviente; servidor
serve *v.* servir
serv-ice *n.* servicio
serv-ice-man *n.* militar
ser-vile *a.* servil
ses-sion *n.* sesion
set *v.* fijar; poner(se)
set-back *n.* reves
set-ting *n.* engaste
set-tle *v.* arreglar; resolver
set-tle-ment *n.* colonizacion
set-tler *n.* colono
seven *adj., n.* siete
sev-en-teen *adj.* diecisiete
sev-enth *n., adj.* septimo'
sev-en-ty *n., adj.* setenta
sev-er *v.* cortar
sev-er-al *a.* varios; diversos
se-vere *adj.* severo
se-ver-i-ty *n.* severidad
sew *v.* coser
sew-er *n.* albanal
sex *n.* sexo
sex-tet *n.* sexteto
sex-u-al *adj.* sexual
sex-y *a.* provocativo
shab-by *a.* raido; en mal es tado
shack *n.* choza
shack-le *n.* grillete
shade *v.* sombrear, *n.* sombra
shad-ing *n.* degradacion
shad-ow *n.* sombra
shadowy *a.* umbroso; vago
shad-y *adj.* sombreado
shaft *n.* eje; pozo
shag-gy *adj.* velludo
shake *v.* estrechar; temblar
shak-y *a.* poso profundo
sham *v.* fingir(se), *adj.* fin gido
sham-bles *n.* desorden
shame *n.* verguenza
shame-less *al* desvergon zado
sham-poo *n.* champu
shan-ty *n.* choza

shape *v.* formar, *n.* forma
shape-ly *a.* bien formado
share *n.* parte
shark *n.* tiburon
sharp *adj.* vivo; cortante
sharp-en *v.* afilar; sacar punta
shat-ter *v.* hacer(se) pedazos
shave *v.* afeitar(se)
shav-er *n.* maquina de afeitar
shawl *n.* chal
she *pron.* ella
shears *n.* tijeras grandes
shed *v.* quitarse; verter
sheen *n.* lustre
sheep *n.* oveja
sheep-ish *a.* timido
sheer *adj.* escarpado
sheet *n.* sabana; hoja; lamina
sheik, sheikh *n.* jeque
shelf *n.* estante
shell *n.* cascara
shel-lac, shel-lack *n.* goma laca
shell-fish *n.* marisco
shel-ter *n.* refugio
shep-herd *n.* pastor
sher-bet *n.* sorbete
sher-iff *n.* sheriff
sher-ry *n.* jerez
shield *n.* escudo
shift *v.* mover(se); cambiar
shil-ly-shal-ly *v.* vacilar
shim-mer *v.* rielar
shin *n.* espinilla
shine *v.* pulir; brillar
shin-gle *n.* ripia; tejamanil
shin-y *adj.* brillante
ship *n.* barco
ship-ment *n.* embarque; envio
ship-shape *a.* en buen orden
ship-wreck *n.* naufragio
shirk *v.* evitar; esquivar
shirt *n.* camisa
shiv-er *v.* temblar

shock *n.* susto; choque; postracion nerviosa

shod-dy *a.* de pacotilla; falso

shoe *n.* zapato

shoe-horn *n.* calzador

shoe-lace *n.* cordon

shoot *v.* espigar; disparar

shoot-ing *n.* tiro; caza con escopeta

shoot-ing star *n.* estrella fugaz

shop *n.* taller; tienda

shop-keep-er *n.* tendero

shore *n.* playa

short *adj.* breve; corto

short-age *n.* deficienca; escasez

short cir-cuit *n.* corto circuito

short-com-ing *n.* defecto

short-cut *n.* atajo

short-en *v.* acortar(se)

short-hand *n.* taquigrafía

short-lived *a.* de breve duración

short-tem-pered *a.* de mal genio

shot *n.* tiro; tirador

shot-gun *n.* escopeta

should *aux. v. past form of* **shall**

shoul-der *n.* hombro

shout *v.* gritar, *n.* grito

shov-el *n.* pala

show *v.* mostrar(se)

show-er *v.* ducharse, *n.* ducha

show-man *n.* director de espectaculos

shred *v.* hacer tiras

shrew *n.* arpia

shrewd *a.* sagaz; prudente

shriek *n.* chillar

shril *a.* estridente

shrimp *n.* camarón

shrine *n.* relicario

shrink *v.* encoger(se)

shriv-el *v.* encoger(se); secar(se)

shroud *n.* mortaja

shrub *n.* arbusto

shrub-ber-y *n.* arbustos

shrug *v.* encogerse de hombros

shud-der *v.* extremecerse

shuf-fle *v.* arrastrar los pies; *(cards)* barajar

shun *v.* evitar; apartarse de

shut *v.* cerrar(se)

shut-ter *n.* contraventana

shut-tle *n.* lanzadera

shy *adj.* timido

sic *v.* atacar

sick *adj.* enfermo

sick-en *v.* enfermar(se)

sick-le *n.* hoz

sick-ness *n.* enfermedad

side *n.* partido; lado

side-burns *n.* patillas

side-long *a.* lateral

side-track *v.* desviar

side-walk *n.* acera

side-ways *adv.* oblicuamente

siege *n.* sitio; cerco

sieve *n.* coladera; tamiz

sift *v.* tamizar

sigh *n.* suspiro, *v.* suspirar

sight *n.* visión; vista

sight-less *adj.* ciego

sight-see-ing *n.* visita de puntos de interes

sign *n.* signo; senal

sig-nal *n.* senal

sig-na-ture *n.* firma

sig-nif-i-cance *n.* significación

sig-ni-fy *v.* significar

si-lence *n.* silencio

si-lent *adj.* silencioso

sil-hou-ette *n.* silueta

sil-ic-a *n.* silice

sil-i-con *n.* silicio

silk *n.* seda

silk-y *adj.* sedoso

sil-ly *adj.* bobo

si-lo *n.* silo

silt *n.* sedimento

sil-ver *n.* plata

sil-ver-smith *n.* platero

sil-ver-ware *n.* vajilla de plata

sim-i-an *a.* simico

sim-i-lar *adj.* similar

sim-i-lar-i-ty *n.* semejanza

sim-mer *v.* hervir a fuego lento

sim-per *v.* sonreirse afectadamente

sim-ple *adj.* simple; facil

sim-pli-fy *v.* simplificar

sim-ply *adv.* sencillamente

sim-u-late *v.* simular

si-mul-ta-ne-ous *a.* simultaneo

sin *n.* pecado; transgresion

since *conj.* puesto que, *prep.* despues; desde

sin-cere *adj.* sincero

sin-cer-i-ty *n.* sinceridad

si-ne-cure *n.* sinecura

sin-ew *n.* tendón

sing *v.* cantar

sing-er *n.* cantante

sin-gle *adj.* único; soltero

sin-gle-hand-ed *a.* sin ayuda

sin-gu-lar *adj.* singular

sin-is-ter *adj.* siniestro

sink *v.* hundir(se)

sin-ner *n.* pecador

si-nus *n.* seno

sip *n.* sorbo, *v.* sorber

sir *n.* señor

sire *n.* padre

si-ren *n.* sirena

sir-loin *n.* solomillo

sis-ter *n.* hermana

sis-ter-in-law *n.* cuñada

sit *v.* sentar(se)

site *n.* sitio

sit-u-a-tion *n.* situacion

six *adj., n.* seis

six-teen *adj., n.* dieciséis

sixth *n., adj.* sexto

six-ty *adj., n.* sesenta

size *n.* talla

siz-zle *v.* chisporrotear

skate *v.* patinar

skel-e-ton *n.* esqueleto

skep-tic *n.* esceptico**

skep-ti-cal *adj.* esceptico
ski *v.* esquiar
skill *n.* destreza; habilidad
skil-let *n.* sarten
skin *n.* piel
skin-ny *adj.* flaco
skirt *n.* falda
skull *n.* cráneo
skunk *n.* mofeta
sky *n.* cielo
sky-scrap-er *n.* rascacielos
slack-en *v.* aflojar
slacks *n.* pantalones
slan-der *v.* calumniar, *n.* calumnia
slap *v.* pegar
slaugh-ter *v.* matar
slave *n.* esclavo
slav-er-y *n.* esclavitud
slay *v.* matar
sled *n.* trineo
sleep *v.* dormir
sleeve *n.* manga
sleigh *n.* trineo
slen-der *adj.* delgado
slice *v.* tajar, *n.* tajada
slide *v.* deslizarse
slim *adj.* delgado
slip-per *n.* zapatilla
slip-per-y *adj.* resbaladizo
slit *v.* cortar
slope *v.* inclinar(se), *n.* inclinación
slow *adj.* torpe; lento
slow-ly *adv.* despacio
smack *v.* pegar
small *adj.* paqueño
smart *adj.* listo; fresco
smell *v.* oler
smile *n.* sonrisa, *v.* sonreir(se)
smoke *v.* fumar, *n.* humo
smooth *adj.* suave
snail *n.* caracol
snake *n.* culebra
snap-shot *n.* foto
sneeze *n.* estornudo, *v.* estornudar
snore *n.* ronquido, *v.* roncar
snow *v.* nevar, *n.* nieve

so *conj.* por tanto, *adv.* así; tan
soak *v.* remojar
soap *n.* jabón
so-ber *adj.* sobrio
soc-cer *n.* futbol
so-cia-ble *adj.* sociable
so-cial *adj.* social
so-cial-ism *n.* socialismo
so-cial-ize *v.* socializar
so-ci-e-ty *n.* sociedad
so-di-um *n.* sodio
so-fa *n.* sofa
soil *v.* manchar, *n.* tierra
so-lar *adj.* solar
sol-dier *n.* soldado
sole-ly *adv.* solamente
sol-emn *adj.* solemne
so-lic-it *v.* solicitar
sol-id *n., adj.* solido
sol-i-dar-i-ty *n.* solidaridad
sol-i-tar-y *adj.* solitario
sol-u-ble *adj.* soluble
so-lu-tion *n.* solución
solve *v.* resolver
sol-vent *adj.* solvente
som-ber *adj.* sombrio
some *pron.* algunos, *adj.* alguno
some-bo-dy *pron.* alguien
some-day *adv.* algun dia
some-one *pron.* alguién
some-thing *n.* algo
some-times *adv.* a veces
son *n.* hijo
song *n.* canción
son-in-law *n.* yerno
soon *adv.* pronto
soothe *v.* calmar
so-pran-o *n.* soprano
sor-did *adj.* vil
sor-ry *adj.* triste
so-so *adv.* así así
soul *n.* alma
sound *n.* ruido
soup *n.* sopa
sour *adj.* agrio
south *n.* sur
south-east *n.* sudeste
south-ern *adj.* del sur

south-west *n.* sudoeste
sov-er-eign *n., adj.* soberano
space *v.* espaciar, *n.* espacio
spa-cious *adj.* espacioso
spa-ghet-ti *n.* espagueti
spasm *n.* espasmo
spas-mod-ic *adj.* espasmodico
spas-tic *adj.* espastico
spat-u-la *n.* espatula
speak *v.* decir; hablar
spear *n.* lanza
spe-cial *adj.* especial
spe-cial-ist *n.* especialista
spe-cial-ize *v.* especializar(se)
spe-cial-ty *n.* especialidad
spe-cies *n.* especie
spe-cif-ic *adj.* especifico
spec-i-fy *v.* especificar
spec-ta-cle *n.* espectaculo
spec-tac-u-lar *adj.* espectacular
speech-less *adj.* mudo
speed *v.* apresurarse; acelerar
spell *v.* deletrear
spell-bind *v.* encantar
spell-ing *n.* ortografia
spend *v.* gastar
sperm *n.* esperma
sperm-whale *n.* cachalote
sphere *n.* esfera
spher-i-cal *adj.* esferico
spice *n.* especia
spic-y *adj.* picante
spi-der *n.* arana
spill *v.* verter(se)
spin-ach *n.* espinaca
spi-nal *adj.* espinal
spine *n.* espinazo
spi-ral *adj., n.* espiral
spir-it *n.* espiritu
spir-it-u-al *adj.* espiritual
spir-it-u-al-ism *n.* espiritismo
spit *v.* escupir
spite *n.* rencor
splin-ter *n.* astilla

split *v.* dividir; separarse
spoil *v.* echar(se); estropear(se)
spo-ken *adj.* hablado
sponge *n.* esponja
spon-gy *adj.* esponjoso
spon-ta-ne-i-ty *n.* espontaneidad
spon-ta-ne-ous *adj.* espontaneo
spoon *n.* cuchara
spoon-ful *n.* cucharada
spo-rad-ic *adj.* esporadico
spore *n.* espora
sport *n.* deporte
sports-man *n.* deportista
spot *n.* mancha
spot-ty *adj.* manchado
spouse *n.* esposa; esposo
spread *v.* diseminar
spring *n.* primavera, *v.* saltar
spring-time *n.* primavera
spruce *n.* picea
spu-ri-ous *adj.* espurio
spy *v.* espiar
squad-ron *n.* escuadron
squal-id *adj.* desalinado
square *adj., n.* cuadrado
squeak *n.* chirrido, *v.* chillar
sta-bil-i-ty *n.* estabilidad
sta-ble *adj.* estable
sta-di-um *n.* estadio
stage *n.* etapa
stain *n.* mancha
stair *n.* escalón
stair-way *n.* escalera
stamp *n.* sello
stam-pede *n.* estampida
stand *v.* colocar
stand-ing *adj.* derecho
sta-ple *n.* grapa
sta-pler *n.* grabadora
star *n.* estrella
star-less *adj.* sin estrellas
star-ry *adj.* estrellado
start *v.* comenzar; empezar
state *n.* estado
stat-ic *adj.* estatico

sta-tion *n.* estación
sta-tis-tic *n.* estadistico
stat-ue *n.* estatua
stay *v.* quedar(se)
steal *v.* robar
steam *v.* empanar, *n.* vapor
steam-y *adj.* vaporoso
stem *n.* tallo
step *n.* escalera
step-broth-er *n.* hermanastro
step-daugh-ter *n.* hijastra
step-fa-ther *n.* padrastro
step-moth-er *n.* madrastra
step-sis-ter *n.* hermanastra
step-son *n.* hijastro
ste-ril-i-ty *n.* esterilidad
stick *n.* palo
stick-y *adj.* viscoso
stiff *adj.* rigido
still *adj.* tranquilo
stim-u-lant *n.* estimulante
stim-u-late *v.* estimular
stink *v.* hedor
stip-u-late *v.* estipular
stip-u-la-tion *n.* estipulación
stock-ing *n.* media
sto-i-cal *adj.* estoico
stom-ach *n.* estomago
stone *n.* piedra
stop *v.* terminar
stop-light *n.* semaforo
store *n.* almacen; tienda
stork *n.* cigüeña
storm *n.* tempestad
sto-ry *n.* piso; historia
stove *n.* estufa
straight *adj.* directo
strange *adj.* extraño; raro
stra-te-gic *adj.* estrategico
strat-e-gy *n.* estrategia
straw *n.* pajilla
straw-ber-ry *n.* fresa
stream *n.* arroyo
street *n.* calle
strength *n.* vigor; fuerza
strict *adj.* estricto
strike *v.* atacar; golpear
string *n.* cordel

stripe *n.* raya
striped *adj.* rayado
strong *adj.* robusto; fuerte
struc-tur-al *adj.* estructural
stu-dent *n.* estudiante
stu-di-o *n.* estudio
stud-y *v.* estudiar
stu-pen-dous *adj.* estupendo
stu-pid *adj.* estupido
style *n.* modo; estilo
sub-di-vide *v.* subdividir
sub-ject *adj., n.* sujeto
sub-jec-tive *adj.* subjetivo
sub-lease *v.* subarrendar
sub-let *v.* subarrendar
sub-li-mate *v.* sublimar
sub-li-ma-tion *n.* sublimación
sub-merge *v.* sumergir(se)
sub-mis-sion *n.* sumision
sub-nor-mal *adj.* anormal
sub-scribe *v.* subscribir(se)
sub-scrip-tion *n.* subscripción
sub-stance *n.* esencia; substancia
sub-stan-tial *adj.* substancial
sub-sti-tute *n.* substituto, *v.* substituir
sub-tract *v.* substraer
sub-urb *n.* suburbio
sub-way *n.* metro
suc-ceed *v.* suceder
suc-ces-sion *n.* sucesión
suc-ces-sor *n.* sucesor
such *adv.* tan, *pron., adj.* tal
suc-tion *n.* succión
suf-fer *v.* sufrir
suf-fi-cien-cy *n.* suficiencia
suf-fo-ca-tion *n.* sofocacion
sug-ar *n.* azucar
sug-ar-y *adj.* azucarado
sug-gest *v.* sugerir
sug-ges-tion *n.* sugestión

suit *n.* traje
sum *v.* sumar, *n.* suma
sum-ma-ry *adj.* sumario
sum-mer *n.* verano
sun *n.* sol
Sun-day *n.* domingo
sun-down *n.* puesta del sol
sun-flow-er *n.* girasol
sun-glass-es *n.* gafas de sol
sun-light *n.* luz del sol
sun-rise *n.* salida del sol
su-per-fi-cial *adj.* superficiál
su-per-in-tend *v.* superentender
su-pe-ri-or *n., adj.* superior
su-pe-ri-or-i-ty *n.* superioridad
su-per-mar-ket *n.* supermercado
su-per-sti-tion *n.* superstición
su-per-sti-tious *adj.* supersticioso
su-pine *adj.* supino
sup-per *n.* cena
sup-ple-ment *n.* suplemento
sup-pli-cate *v.* suplicar
sup-pose *v.* suponer
sup-pres-sion *n.* supresión
su-prem-a-cy *n.* supremacia
su-preme *adj.* supremo
sure *adj.* seguro
sure-ly *adv.* seguramente
sur-face *n.* superficie
sur-geon *n.* cirujano
sur-ger-y *n.* cirugía
sur-name *n.* apellido
sur-prise *v.* sorprender, *n.* sorpresa
sur-vive *v.* sobrevivir
sus-cep-ti-ble *adj.* susceptible
sus-pend *v.* suspender
sus-pen-sion *adj.* suspensión

sus-pi-cious *adj.* sospechoso
sus-tain *v.* sustentar
swan *n.* cisne
swap *v.* cambiar
swat *v.* matar
swear *v.* jurar
sweat *n.* sudor, *v.* sudar
sweat-y *adj.* sudoroso
sweet *adj.* dulce
swim *n.* natación, *v.* nadar
swim-mer *n.* nadador
switch *v.* cambiar
sword *n.* espada
syl-la-ble *n.* silaba
sym-bol *n.* simbolo
sym-bol-ic *adj.* simbolico
sym-bol-ism *n.* simbolismo
sym-bol-ize *v.* simbolizar
sym-me-try *n.* simetría
sym-pa-thy *n.* simpatia
syn-di-cate *v.* sindicar
syn-o-nym *n.* sinonimo
syn-on-y-mous *adj.* sinonimo
syn-thet-ic *adj.* sintetico
sys-tem *n.* sistema
sys-tem-a-tize *v.* sis tematizar

T

tab *n.* cuenta
tab-er-nac-le *n.* tabernáculo
ta-ble *n.* mesa
ta-ble-spoon-ful *n.* cucharada
tab-let *n.* tableta
ta-boo, ta-bu *a.* tabú
tab-u-lar *adj.* tabular
tab-u-late *v.* tabular
tac-it *a.* tácito
tac-i-turn *adj.* taciturno
tack *n.* tachuela; virada
tack-le *n.* equipo; carga
tact *n.* tacto
tac-tics *n.* tactica
tad-pole *n.* renacuajo
taf-fe-ta *n.* tafetan
taf-fy *n.* caramelo
tag *n.* etiqueta; marbete

tail *n.* cola; rabo
tai-lor *n.* sastre
taint *v.* inficionar(se); corromper(se)
take *v.* coger; tomar; sacar
take-off *n.* despegue
tal-cum pow-der *n.* polvo de talco
tale *n.* cuenta
tal-ent *n.* talento
tal-ent-ed *adj.* talentoso
tal-is-man *n.* talismán
talk *v.* decir; hablar
talk-a-tive *adj.* hablador
tall *a.* alto
tal-low *n.* sebo
tal-ly *n.* cuenta
tal-on *n.* garra
tam-bou-rine *n.* pandereta
tame *a.* domesticado; manso; soso
tam-per *v.* estropear; falsificar
tan *v.* curtir; tostar
tan-dem *adv.* en tandem
tang *n.* sabor fuerte
tan-gent *n., adj.* alto
tan-ge-rine *n.* naranja mandarina o tangerina
tan-gi-ble *adj.* tangente
tan-gle *v.* enredar(se)
tan-go *n.* tango
tank *n.* tangible
tan-ta-lize *v.* atormentar
tan-ta-mount *a.* equivalente
tan-trum *n.* rabieta; berrinche
tap *n.* grifo; golpecito
tape *n.* tanque
ta-per *v.* afilar
tap-es-try *n.* tapiz
tape-worm *n.* cinta
tap-i-o-ca *n.* tenia
ta-pir *n.* tapir
tar *v.* alquitranar; embrear
ta-ran-tu-la *n.* tapioca
tar-dy *adj.* tarantula
tar-get *n.* blanco
tar-iff *n.* tardio

tar-nish v. deslustrar(se);
   empanar
tar-ry v. tardar; detenerse
tart n. tarifa
tar-tar n. tártaro
task n. tarea; labor
task-mas-ter n. capataz
tas-sel n. borla
taste n. sabor
tast-y adj. sabroso
tat-ter n. andrajo
tat-tered a. harapiento;
   andrajoso
tat-too n. tatuaje
taunt n. mofa; sarcasmo;
   escarnio
taut a. tieso; tirante
tav-ern n. taberna
taw-dry a. charro
taw-ny a. leonado
tax n. impuesto;
   contribución; carga
tax-i n. taxi
tax-i-cab n. taxi
tea n. te
tea-bag n. sobre de te;
   muneca de té
teach v. instruir
teach-er n. maestro;
   profesora; profesor
tea-cup n. taza para te
tea-ket-tle n. tetera
team n. equipo
team-mate n. compañero
   de equipo
team-ster n. camionero;
   camionista
team-work n. cooperación
tea-pot n. tetera
tear n. lágrima
tear v. rasgar(se);
   romper(se)
tease v. tomar el pelo;
   atormentar
tea-spoon n. cucharilla
tea-spoon-ful n.
   cucharadita
tech-ni-cal adj. técnico
tech-ni-cian n. tecnico
tech-nol-o-gy n.
   tecnología

te-di-ous adj. tedioso
tel-e-gram n. telegrama
tel-e-graph n. telegrafo
te-leg-ra-phy n. telegrafía
tel-e-phone n. telefono
tel-e-scope n. telescopio
tel-e-vi-sion n. televisión
tell v. mandar; decir
tem-per-a-ment-al adj.
   temperamental
tem-per-a-ture n. fiebre
tem-pes-tu-ous adj.
   tempestuoso
tem-ple n. templo
tem-po n. tiempo
tem-po-ral adj. temporal
temp-ta-tion n. tentación
ten adj., n. diez
tend v. tender
ten-den-cy n. tendencia
ten-der-ly adv.
   tiernamente
ten-don n. tendón
ten-nis n. tenis
tense v. tensar, adj. tenso
ten-sion n. tensión
ter-mi-nal adj., n.
   terminal
ter-mi-nate v. terminar
ter-mi-nol-o-gy n.
   terminología
ter-rain n. terreno
ter-res-tri-al adj. terrestre
ter-ri-ble adj. terrible
ter-rif-ic adj. terrifico
ter-ror n. terror
ter-ror-ism n. terrorismo
ter-ror-ist n. terrorista
test v. examinar, n.
   examen
tes-ti-fy v. testificar
text n. texto
tex-ture n. textura
than conj. de; que
thanks n. gracias
that adj. aquella; aquel;
   esa; ese
the def. art. la; le; las; los;
   lo
the-a-ter n. teatro

them pron. las; les; los;
   ellas; ellos
then adv. luego; entonces
the-ol-o-gy n. teologia
the-o-rize v. teorizar
the-o-ry n. teoria
there adv. ahí; allí; allá
ther-mal adj. termal
ther-mom-e-ter n. ter
   mometro
the-sau-rus n. tesauro
these pron. estas; estos
they pron. ellas; ellos
thick adj. denso
thief n. ladrón
thigh n. muslo
thin adj. escaso; delgado
thing n. cosa
think v. creer; pensar
third adj. tercero
thirst n. sed
thir-teen n., adj. trece
thir-ty n., adj. treinta
this adj. esta; este, pron.
   esto; esta; este
thorn n. espina
thorn-y adj. espinoso
thor-ough adj. completo
though adv. sin embargo,
   conj. aunque
thought-ful adj. pensativo
thou-sand n., adj. mil
threat-en v. amenazar
three n., adj. tres
throat n. garganta
throne n. trono
through prep. por
throw v. lanzar; echar
thumb n. pulgar
Thurs-day n. jueves
tib-i-a n. tibia
tick-le v. cosquillear
tide n. marea
ti-gar n. tigre
till prep. hasta
tim-ber n. madero
time n. hora; tiempo; vez
tim-id adj. timido
tim-id-i-ty n. timidez
tip n. propina
tire v. cansar(se)

tired *adj.* cansado

tire-some *a.* molesto

tis-sue *n.* tisu

ti-tan-ic *adj.* titanico

tithe *n.* diezmo

ti-tle *v.* titular, *n.* titulo

tit-ter *v.* reir a medias

tit-u-lar *a.* titular

TNT, T.N.T. *n.* explosívo

to *adv., prep.* hacia, *prep.* hasta; a

toad *n.* sapo

toad-stool *n.* hongo; hongo venenoso

toast *v.* tostar; brindar

to-bac-co *n.* tabaco

to-bog-gan *n.* tobogan

to-day *n., adv.* hoy

toe *n.* dedo del pie

tof-fee, tof-fy *jn.* caramelo

to-ga *n.* toga

to-geth-er *adv.* juntos

toil *v.* trabajar asiduamente; afanarse

toi-let *n.* retrete; water; tacado

toi-let-ry *n.* articulo de tocador

to-ken *n.* indicio; prenda; señal

tol-er-a-ble *a.* tolerable; regular

tol-er-ance *n.* tolerancia

tol-er-ant *a.* tolerante

tol-er-ate *v.* permitir; tolerar

toll *n.* peaje

to-ma-to *n.* tomate

tomb *n.* tumba

tomb-stone *n.* lapida sepulcral

to-mor-row *adv., n.* mañana

ton *n.* tonelada

tone *n.* tono; tendencia

tongs *n.* tenazas

tongue *n.* lengua

ton-ic *n.* tonico

to-night *adv.* esta noche

ton-nage *n.* tonelaje

ton-sil *n.* amigdala; tonsila

ton-sil-li-tis *n.* amigdalitis

too *adv.* además; también

tool *n.* herramienta

tooth *n.* diente

tooth-ache *n.* dolor de muelas

tooth-brush *n.* cepillo de dientes

top *n.* tapa

to-paz *n.* topacio

top-coat *n.* sobretodo

top-hat *n.* chistera

top-ic *n.* tema

top-i-cal *adj.* topico

to-pop-ra-phy *n.* topografía

top-ple *v.* venirse abajo

top-sy-tur-vy *adv.* patas arri ba

torch *n.* antorcha; hacha

tor-ment *v.* atormentar

tor-na-do *n.* tormento

tor-pe-do *n.* torpedo

tor-rent *n.* torrente

tor-rid *a.* torrido

tor-so *n.* torso

tor-toise *n.* tortuga

tor-tu-ous *a.* tortuoso

tor-ture *v.* torturar

toss *v.* echar

tot *n.* nene; nena

to-tal *n., adj.* total

to-tal-i-tar-i-an *a.* totalitario

to-tal-ly *adv.* totalmente

tote *v. inf.* llevar

to-tem *n.* tótem

tot-ter *v.* bambolearse

touch *v.* tocar(se)

touch-y *a.* irritable

tough *adj.* difícil

tough-en *v.* endurecer(se); hacer(se)

tour *n.* viaje; excursión

tour-ism *n.* turismo

tour-ist *n.* turista

tour-na-ment *n.* torneo

tour-ni-quet *n.* torniquete

tou-sle *v.* despeinar

tow *v.* llevar a remolque

to-ward *prep.* cerca de

tow-el *n.* toalla

tow-er *n.* torre

town *n.* pueblo; ciudad

tox-ic *a.* tóxico

tox-in *n.* toxina

toy *n.* juguete

trace *n.* indicio; huella; rastro

tra-che-a *n.* tráquea

track *n.* via; pista; senda

tract *n.* extensión; tratado

trac-tor *n.* tractor

trade *v.* comerciar

trade-mark *n.* marca de fabrica; marca registrado

trade un-ion *n.* sindicato

tra-di-tion *n.* tradición

tra-di-tion-al *adj.* tradiciónal

tra-duce *v.* calumniar

traf-fic *n.* tráfico

trag-e-dy *n.* tragedia

trag-ic *adj.* trágico

trail *v.* arrastrar(se); rastrear

trail-er *n.* remolque

train *n.* tren

trait *n.* caracteristica; rasgo

trai-tor *n.* traidor

tra-jec-to-ry *n.* trayectoria

tramp *v.* andar con pasos pesados

tram-ple *v.* pisotear

trance *n.* arrobamiento; es tado hipnotico

tran-quil *adj.* tranquilo

tran-quil-li-ty *n.* tranquilidad

tran-quil-lize *v.* tranquilizar

tran-quil-iz-er *n.* tran quilizante

trans-act *v.* despachar

trans-ac-tion *n.* transacción

tran-scend *v.* sobresalir

tran-scribe *v.* transcribir

tran-script *n.* trasunto

tran-scrip-tion *n.* transcripción

trans-fer *v.* transferir;
trasladar

trans-fer-ence *n.*
transferencia

trans-form *v.* transformar

trans-for-ma-tion *n.*
transcripción; copia

trans-form-er *n.* transfor
mador

trans-fu-sion *n.*
transfusión

trans-gress *v.* traspasar;
pecar

trans-gres-sion *n.*
transgresion

tran-sient *a.* transitorio;
pasajero

tran-sis-tor *n.* transistor

tran-sit *n.* transito

tran-si-tion *n.* transito

tran-si-tive *a.* transiotivo

tran-si-to-ry *adj.*
transitorio

trans-late *v.* traducir

trans-la-tion *n.* traducción

trans-lu-cent *a.*
translucido

trans-mis-sion *n.*
transmision

trans-mit *v.* transmitir

trans-mit-ter *n.*
transmisor

tran-som *n.* travesano

trans-par-ent *a.*
transparente

tran-spire *v.* transpirar;
suceder

trans-plant *v.* trasplantar

trans-port *n.* transporte, *v.*
transportar

trans-por-ta-tion *n.*
transporte

trans-pose *v.* transponer

trans-verse *a.* transversal

trap *v.* entrampar

tra-peze *n.* trapecio

trash *n.* basura

trau-ma *n.* trauma

trau-mat-ic *adj.*
traumatico

trav-el *v.* viajar

trea-son *n.* traición

treas-ure *n.* tesoro

treas-ur-er *n.* tesorero

treas-ur-y *n.* tesoro

treat *v.* tratar

trea-tise *n.n* tratado

treat-ment *n.* tratamiento

trea-ty *n.* tratado; pacto

tre-ble *a.* triple

tree *n.* arbol

trek *v.* caminar

trel-lis *n.* enrejado;
espaldera

trem-ble *v.* temblar

tre-men-dous *a.* tremendo

trem-or *n.* temblor

trench *n.* foso; trinchera

tri-al *n.* prueba

tri-an-gle *n.* triángulo

tri-an-gu-lar *adj.*
triangular

tri-bu-nal *n.* tribunal

trib-ute *n.* tributo

trick *n.* trucio; trampa;
engano

trick-le *v.* gotear

tri-cy-cle *n.* triciclo

tried *adj.* probado

tri-fle *n.* bagatela

tri-fling *a.* sin importanciá

trig-ger *n.* gatillo

trig-o-nom-e-try *n.*
trigonometriá

tril-lion *n.* billón

trim *v.* guarnecer

trin-ket *n.* dije

tri-o *n.* trió

trip *n.* viaje

tri-ple *v.* triplicar(se)

trip-let *n.* trillizo

trip-li-cate *v.* triplicar

tri-pod *n.* tripode

trite *a.* gastado

tri-umph *n.* triunfo

tri-um-phant *adj.*
triunfante

triv-i-al *a.* trivial; frivolo

triv-i-al-i-ty *n.* trivialidad

trol-ley *n.* tranvia

trom-bone *n.* trombón

troop *n.* tropa; escuadron

troop-er *n.* soldado de
caballería

tro-phy *n.* trofeo

trop-ic *n.* trópico

trop-i-cal *adj.* tropical

trot *v.* ir al trote; hacer
trotar

trou-ba-dour *n.* trovador

trou-ble *v.* molestar(se)

trou-ble-some *a.* molesto

trough *n.* abrevadero

troupe *n.* compania

trou-sers *n.* pantalones

trous-seau *n.* ajuar

trout *n.* trucha

trow-el *n.* paleta;
desplantador

tru-ant *n.* novillero

truce *n.* tregua

truck *n.* camión

true *adj.* verdadero

tru-ly *adv.*
verdaderamente;
realmente

trump *n.* triumfo

trum-pet *n.* trompeta

trun-cate *v.* truncar

trunk *n.* tronco; baul

trus *v.* empaquetear

trust *v.* esperar, *n.*
fideicomiso

trus-tee *n.* fideicomisario

trust-wor-thy *a.*
fidedigno; confiable

trust-y *adj.* seguro

truth *n.* verdad

trugh-ful *a.* veraz

try *v.* probar

try-ing *a.* dificil; penoso

tryst *n.* cita

T-shirt *n.* camiseta

tub *n.* baño; tina

tu-ba *n.* tuba

tube *n.* tubo

tu-ber-cu-lo-sis *n.*
tuberculosis

tuck *v.* alforzar

Tues-day *n.* martes

tuft *n.* copete

tug *v.* tirar con fuerza;
remolcar

tug-boat *n.* remolcador
tu-i-tion *n.* ensenanza
tu-lip *n.* tulipan
tum-ble *v.* caer(se)
tum=bler *n.* volteador; vaso
tu-mor *n.* tumor
tu-mult *n.* tumulto
tu-mul-tu-ous *a.* tumultuoso
tu-na *n.* atun
tun-dra *n.* tundra
tune *n.* aire; afinación
tu-nic *n.* tunica
tun-nel *n.* tunel
tur-ban *n.* turbante
tur-bid *adj.* turbido
tur-bine *n.* turbina
tur-bu-lence *n.* turbulenciá; confusion
tur-bu-lent *adj.* turbulento
tu-reen *n.* sopera
turf *n.* cesped
tur-key *n.* pavo
tur-moil *n.* tumulto
turn *v.* volver(se); girar
turn-coat *n.* traidor
tur-nip *n.* nabo
turn-out *n.* ocncurrencia; producción
turn-pike *n.* autopista de peaje
turn-stile *n.* torniquete
tur-pen-tin *n.* trementina
tur-quoise *n.* turquesa
tur-ret *n.* turrecilla
tur-tle *n.* tortuga
tusk *n.* colmillo
tus-sle *n.* agarrada
tu-te-lage *n.* tutela
tu-tor *n.* tutor
tux-e-do *n.* smoking
TV *n.* televisión
twang *n.* tanido; timbre nasal
tweed *n.* mezcla de lana
tweez-ers *n.* bruselas
twelfth *adj.* duodecimo
twelve *adj., n.* doce
twen-ty *adj., n.* veinte
twice *adv.* dos veces

twig *n.* ramita
twi-light *n.* crepusculo
twill *n.* tela cruzada
twin *adj., n.* gemelo
twine *n.* guita; bramante
twinge *n.* dolor agudo
twin-kle *v.* centellear
twirl *v.* girar; piruetear
twist *v.* torcer(se)
twitch *v.* crisparse
twit-ter *v.* gorjear
two *adj., n.* dos
two-faced *a.* falso; hipoocrita
ty-coon *n.* magnate
type *n.* tipo
type-write *v.* escribir a maquina
type-writ-er *n.* maquína de escribir
ty-phoid *n.* fiebre tifoidea
ty-phoon *n.* tifón
ty-phus *n.* tifus
typ-i-cal *adj.* tipico
typ-i-fy *v.* simbolizar
typ-ist *n.* mecanografo
ty-pog-ra-phy *n.* tipografía
ty-ran-ni-cal *a.* tiránico; despotico
tyr-an-nize *v.* tiranizar
tyr-an-ny *n.* tirania

U

u-biq-ui-tous *adj.* ubicuo
u-biq-ui-ty *n.* ubicuidad
ud-der *n.* ubre
ug-li-ness *n.* fealdad
ug-ly *adj.* feo
u-ku-le-le *n.* ukelele
ul-cer *n.* úlcera
ul-cer-ate *v.* ulcerar(se)
ul-cer-ous *adj.* ulceroso
ul-na *n.* cúbito
ul-te-ri-or *adj.* ulterior
ul-ti-mate *adj.* último
ul-ti-ma-tum *n.* ultimatum
ul-tra *adj.* excesivo
ul-tra-mod-ern *adj.* ultramoderno

ul-tra-son-ic *adj.* ultrasonico
ul-tra-sound *n.* ultrasonido
ul-tra-vi-o-let *adj.* ultravioleta
ul-u-late *v.* ulular
um-bil-i-cal *adj.* umbilical
um-bil-i-cus *n.* ombligo
um-brel-la *n.* paraguas
um-pire *n.* arbitro
ump-teen *a.* muchos
un-a-bashed *a.* desvergonzado; descarado
un-a-ble *adj.* incapaz
un-a-bridged *adj.* no abreviado
un-ac-cent-ed *adj.* sin acento
un-ac-cept-a-ble *adj.* inaceptable
un-ac-count-a-ble *adj.* inexplicable
un-ac-cus-tomed *adj.* no acostumbrado
un-ac-knowl-edged *adj.* no econocido
un-a-dorned *adj.* sin adorno
un-a-dul-ter-at-ed *adj.* no adulterado
un-af-fect-ed *adj.* sin afectación
un-a-fraid *adj.* sin temor
un-aid-ed *adj.* sin ayuda
un-am-big-u-ous *adj.* sin ambiguedad
u-nan-i-mous *adj.* unanime
un-an-swer-a-ble *adj.* incontestable
un-ap-proach-a-ble *adj.* inaccesible
un-armed *adj.* desarmado
un-as-sail-a-ble *adj.* inexpugnable
un-as-sist-ed *adj.* sin ayuda
un-as-sum-ing *a.* modesto; sencillo
un-at-tached *adj.* suelto

un-at-tend-ed *adj.*
desatendido
un-at-trac-tive *adj.*
inatractivo
un-au-thor-ized *adj.* sin
autorización
un-a-void-a-ble *adj.*
inevitable
un-a-ware *adj.* ignorante
un-a-wares *adv.* de
improviso
un-bal-anced *adj.*
desequilibrado
un-beat-a-ble *adj.*
invencible
un-beat-en *adj.* invicto
un-be-com-ing *a.* que
sienta mal
un-be-lief *n.* incredulidad
un-be-liev-a-ble *adj.*
increible
un-be-liev-er *n.* descreido
un-be-liev-ing *adj.*
incredulo
un-bend *v.* desencorvar;
aflojar
un-bend-ing *adj.*
inflexible
un-bi-ased *a.* imparcial
un-bind *v.* desatar
un-blem-ished *adj.* puro
un-born *a.* no nacido
un-bos-om *v.* revelar
un-bound-ed *adj.*
ilimitado
un-bowed *adj.* recto
un-break-a-ble *adj.*
irrompible
un-breath-a-ble *adj.*
irrespirable
un-bri-dled *adj.*
desenfrenado
un-bro-ken *adj.* inviolado;
sin romper
un-buck-le *v.* deshebillar
un-bur-den *v.* descargar
un-bot-ton *v.*
desabotonar(se)
un-caged *adj.* suelto
un-called-for *a.*
inmerecido

un-can-ny *a.* extraño;
misterioso
un-cap *v.* destapar
un-ceas-ing *adj.* incesante
un-cer-e-mo-ni-ous *a.*
informal
un-cer-tain *adj.* indeciso
un-cer-tain-ty *n.*
incertidumbre
un-change-a-ble *adj.*
inalterable
un-changed *adj.*
inalterado
un-chang-ing *adj.*
invariable
un-chart-ed *adj.*
desconocido
un-civ-il *adj.* incivil
un-civ-i-lized *adj.*
incivilizado
un-clad *adj.* desnudo
un-clasp *v.* separar
un-cle *n.* tío
un-clean *adj.* sucio
un-clear *adj.* confuso
un-clog *v.* desatascar
un-com-fort-a-ble *adj.*
incomodo
un-com-mon *adj.* raro
un-com-mu-ni-ca-tive *a.*
poco comunicativo
un-com-pro-mis-ing *a.*
inflexible
un-con-cern *n.*
indiferencia
un-con-nect-ed *adj.*
inconexo
un-con-scious *adj.*
inconsciente
un-con-sid-ered *adj.*
inconsiderado
un-con-trolled *adj.*
desenfrenado
un-cooked *adj.* crudo
un-count-ed *adj.*
innumerable
un-cross *v.* descruzar
un-de-cid-ed *adj.* indeciso
un-der-es-ti-mate *v.*
subestimar

un-der-ground *adj.*
subterraneo
un-der-line *v.* subrayar
un-der-neath *adv.* debajo,
prep. bajo
un-der-wear *n.* ropa
interior
un-do *v.* desatar
un-fin-ished *adj.*
incompleto
unn-fold *v.* extender; abrir
u-ni-form *n.* uniforme
un-ion *n.* unión
u-ni-ted *adj.* unido
u-ni-ver-sal *adj.* universal
un-luck-y *adj.* desdichado
un-rest *n.* inquietud
un-sa-vor-y *adj.*
desagradable
un-seem-ly *adj.*
indecoroso
un-skilled *adj.* inexperto
un-so-phis-ti-cat-ed *adj.*
candido
un-sta-ble *adj.* inestable
un-stead-y *adj.* inseguro
un-til *prep.* hasta
un-truth-ful *adj.*
mentiroso
un-u-su-al *adj.* raro
un-wrap *v.* desenvolver
up *prep.* subiendo, *adj.*
ascendente, *adv.*
acabado; arriba
up-hill *adj.* ascendente
up-hol-ster-y *n.* tapiceria
up-on *prep.* sobre; encima
de
up-per *adj.* alto
up-per-cut *n.* gancho
up-roar *n.* alboroto
up-set *n.* trastorno; *v.*
volcar
up-stairs *adj.* arriba
u-ra-ni-um *n.* uranio
U-ra-nus *n.* Urano
ur-ban *adj.* urbano
urge *n.* impulso, *v.* incitar
ur-gent *adj.* urgente
u-rine *n.* orina
urn *n.* urna

us *pron.* nosotras; nosotros; nos
use *n.* uso, *v.* utilizar; usar
use-less *adj.* inútil
u-su-al *adj.* usual
u-ten-sil *n.* utensilio
utilitarian *n.* utilitario
u-til-i-ty *n.* utilidad
u-til-ize *v.t.* utilizar
ut-ter-ance *n.* expresion
u-ter-us *n.* utero
uxorious *a.* uxorio; gurromino

V

va-can-cy *n.* vacante
va-cant *adj.* vacío
va-ca-tion *n.* vacación
vac-ci-nate *v.* vacunar
vac-ci-na-tion *n.* vacunacion
vac-cine *n.* vacuna
vac-il-late *n.* vacilar
vac-il-la-tion *n.* vacilacon; fluctuación
va-cu-i-ty *n.* vacuidad
vac-u-um *n.* vacio
va-gar-y *n.* capricho
va-grant *n.* vagabundo
vague *adj.* incierto; vago
vain *adj.* vano
vale *n.* valle
val-e-dic-to-ry *n.* discurso de despedida
val-en-tine *n.* novia o novio en el dia de San Valentine
val-id *adj.* valido
val-i-date *v.* validar
va-lid-i-ty *n.* validez
va-lise *n.* maleta
val-ley *n.* valle
val-or *n.* valor; valentia
val-u-a-ble *a.* valioso; costoso; precioso
val-u-a-tion *n.* valuación
val-ue *v.* valuar, *n.* valor
valve *n.* valvula
vam-pire *n.* vampiro

van *n.* vanguardia; camion de mudanzas
van-dal *n.* vandalo
van-dal-ism *n.* vandalismo
vane *n.* veleta
van-guard *n.* vanguardia
va-nil-la *n.* vainilla
van-ish *v.* desaparecer
van-i-ty *n.* vanidad
van-quish *v.* vencer; conquistar
van-tage *n.* ventaja; provecho
vap-id *a.* insipido
va-por *n.* vapor
va-por-ize *v.* vaporizar(se)
va-por-ous *a.* vaporoso
var-i-a-bil-i-ty *n.* variabilidad
var-i-a-ble *n., adj.* variable
var-i-a-tion *n.* variación
var-i-cose *a.* varicoso
var-ied *adj.* variado
va-ri-e-ty *n.* variedad
var-i-ous *adj.* variado
var-nish *n.* barniz
var-si-ty *n.* equip principal de una universidad
var-y *v.* variar; desviarse; cam biar
vase *n.* jarrón
vast *adj.* vasto
veal *n.* ternera
veg-e-ta-ble *n.* legumbre
veg-e-tar-i-an *n.* vegetariano
veg-e-tate *v.* vegetar
veg-e-ta-tion *n.* vegetacion
ve-hi-cle *n.* vehículo
vein *n.* vena
ve-loc-i-ty *n.* velocidad
ve-nal-i-ty *n.* venalidad
vend *v.* vender
ven-er-a-ble *adj.* venerable
ven-er-a-tion *n.* veneración
ve-ni-al *adj.* venial
ven-om *n.* veneno

ven-om-ous *adj.* venenoso
ven-ti-late *v.* ventilar
ven-tral *adj.* ventral
ven-tri-cle *n.* ventrículo
ven-ture-some *adj.* aventurero
Ve-nus *n.* Venus
ve-ra-cious *adj.* veraz
verb *n.* verbo
ver-bal *adj.* verbal
ver-bose *adj.* verboso
ver-bos-i-ty *n.* verbosidad
ver-dict *n.* veredicto
ver-i-fy *v.* verificar
ver-mouth *n.* vermut
ver-nal *adj.* vernal
ver-sa-til-i-ty *n.* adaptabilidad
verse *n.* versiculo
ver-sion *n.* versión
ver-te-bra *n.* vertebra
ver-te-brate *adj.* vertebrado
ver-ti-cal *adj.* vertical
ver-y *adj.* mismo, *adv.* muy
ves-sel *n.* vaso
vest *n.* chaleco
vet *n.* veterinario
vet-er-an *adj., n.* veterano
vet-er-i-nar-i-an *n.* veterinario
vet-er-i-nar-y *adj., n.* veterinario
vi-brant *adj.* vibrante
vi-brate *v.* oscilar
vi-bra-tion *n.* vibración
vic-ar *n.* vicario
vi-car-i-ous *a.* substituto
vice *n.* vicio
vice-pres-i-dent *n.* vicepresidente
vice-roy *n.* virrey
vice ver-sa *adv.* viceversa
vi-cin-i-ty *n.* vecindad
vi-cious *a.* depravado; vicioso; cruel
vic-tim *n.* victima
vic-tim-ize *v.* hacer victima

vic-to-ri-ous *adj.*
  victorioso
vic-to-ry *n.* victoria
view *v.* ver, *n.* escena
vig-i-lance *n.* vigilancia
vig-or *n.* vigor
vig-or-ous *adj.* vigoroso
vil-lage *n.* aldea
vin-di-cate *v.* vindicar
vine *n.* vid
vin-e-gar *n.* vinagre
vi-o-la *n.* viola
vi-o-la-tion *n.* violación
vi-o-lent *adj.* violento
vi-o-let *adj.* violado
vi-o-lin *n.* violín
vir-ile *adj.* viril
vi-ril-i-ty *n.* virilidad
vir-tu-al *adj.* virtual
vir-tu-al-ly *adv.*
  virtualmente
vir-u-lent *adj.* virulento
vi-rus *n.* virus
vis-cos-i-ty *n.* viscosidad
vis-count *n.* vizconde
vis-count-ess *n.*
  vizcondesa
vise *n.* tornillo
vis-i-bil-i-ty *n.* visibilidad
vis-i-ble *a.* visible;
  conspicuo
vi-sion *n.* visión
vi-sion-ar-y *n.* visionario
vis-it *n.* visita, *v.* visitar
vis-it-a-tion *n.* visitación
vi-sor *n.* visera
vis-u-al *adj.* visual
vis-u-al-ize *v.* representarse
  en la mente
vi-tal *adj.* vital
vi-tal-i-ty *n.* vitalidad
vi-ta-min *n.* vitamina
vit-re-ous *a.* vitreo
vit-ri-ol *n.* vitriolo
vi-tu-per-ate *v.* vituperar
vi-va-cious *a.* vivaz;
  animado; vivaracho
vi-vac-i-ty *n.* vivacidad;
  animacion
viv-id *adj.* intenso; vivo
vix-en *n.* arpia; zorra

vo-cab-u-lar-y *n.*
  vocabulario
vo-cal *adj.* vocal
vo-cal-ist *n.* cantante
vo-ca-tion *n.* vocación
vod-ka *n.* vodka
vogue *n.* moda; boga
voice *n.* voz
void *a.* nulo; vacio
vol-can-ic *adj.* volcanico
vol-ca-no *n.* volcan
vo-li-tion *n.* voluntad;
  volicion
vol-ley *n.* descarga; voleo
volt *n.* voltio
volt-age *n.* voltaje
vol-u-ble *a.* hablador
vol-ume *n.* cantidad;
  volumen
vol-un-tar-y *adj.*
  voluntario
vol-un-teer *n.* voluntario
vo-lup-tu-ar-y *n.*
  voluptuoso
vo-lup-tu-ous *a.*
  voluptuoso
vom-it *n.* vomito, *v.*
  vomitar
vom-it-ing *n.* vomito
voo-doo *n.* vodu
vo-ra-cious *a.* voraz
voracity *n.* voracidad
vor-tex *n.* vortice
votary *n.* devoto;
  partidario
vote *v.* votar, *n.* voto
vo-ter *n.* votante
vot-ing *n.* votacion
vo-tive *a.* votivo; exvoto
vouch *v.i.* afirmar
vouch-er *n.* comprobante
vow-el *n.* vocal
voy-age *v.* viajar, *n.* viaje
vul-gar *adj.* vulgar
vul-gar-ize *v.* vulgarizar
vul-ner-a-ble *a.*
  vulnerable
vul-ture *n.* buitre

W

wack-y *a.* loco; chiflado
wad *n.* fajo; taco; rollo;
  bolita
wad-dle *v.* anadear
wade *v.* vadear; pasar con
  dificultad
wag *v.* menear(se)
wage *n.* salario
wag-er *v.* apostar
wag-on *n.* carro
waif *n.* nino abandonado
wail *v.* lamentarse; sollozar
wain-scot *n.* friso de
  madera
waist *n.* cintura
waist-coat *n.* chaleco
waist-line *n.* talle
wait *n.* espera, *v.* esperar
wait-er *n.* camarero
wait-ress *n.* camarera
waive *v.* renunciar a; aban
  donar
waiv-er *n.* renuncia
wake *v.* despertar(se)
wake-ful *a.* vigilante
wak-en *v.* despertar(se)
walk *n.* caminata, *v.*
  caminar; andar
walk-out *n.* huelga
walk-o-ver *n.* triunfo facil
wall *n.* pared
wall-board *n.* carton de
  yeso
wal-let *n.* cartera
wal-lop *v.* zurrar
wal-low *v.* revp;carse
wall-pa-per *n.* papel
  pintado
wal-nut *n.* nogal
wal-rus *n.* morsa
waltz *n.* vals
wan *a.* palido
wan-der *v.* desviarse
wan-der-lust *n.* deseo de
  viajar
wane *v.* disminuir;
  menguar
want *v.* querer; requerir;
  desear
want-ing *a.* deficiente**

wan-ton *a.* lascivo; desenfrenado

war *v.* guerrear, *n.* guerra

war-ble *v.* trinar

war-cry *n.* grito de guerra

ward *v.* desviar

war-den *n.* guardián; alsaide

ward-robe *n.* guardarropa; vestuario

ware *n.* mercancias

ware-house *n.* almacén

war-fare *n.* guerra

war-lock *n.* hechicero

warm *v.* calentar(se), *adj.* caluroso; caliente

warm-heart-ed *a.* afectuoso

war-mong-er *n.* belicista

warmth *n.* calor

warn *v.* advertir

warn-ing *n.* advertencia; aviso

warp *v.* albearse; pervertir

war-rant *n.* autorizacion; garantia

war-ran-ty *n.* garantia

war-ren *n.* conejera

war-ri-or *n.* guerrero

wart *n.* verruga

war-y *a.* cauteloso

was *pret of* be

wash *v.* lavar(se)

wash-cloth *n.* paño para lavarse

wash-er *n.* lavadora

wash-ing *n.* lavado

wash-room *n.* lavabo

wash-stand *n.* lavamanos

wash-tub *n.* tin o cuba de lavar

wasp *n.* avispa

wast-age *n.* desgaste; merma

waste *n.* perdida, *v.* desperdiciar

wast-rel *n.* derrochador

watch *n.* reloj, *v.* mirar; observar

watch-ful *a.* vigilante; desvelado

watch-man *n.* vigilante

watch-word *n.* santo y sena

wa-ter *n.* agua

wa-ter-col-or *n.* acuarela

wa-ter-course *n.* corriente

wa-ter-fall *n.* cascada

wa-ter-fowl *n.* ave acuantica

wa-ter-front *n.* terreno rebereno

wa-ter lil-y *n.* nenufar

wa-ter-logged *a.* anegado

wa-ter-mark *n.* nivel de agua; filigrana

wa-ter-mel-on *n.* sandia

wa-ter-proof *a.* impermeable

wa-ter-side *n.* orilla del agua

wa-ter sof-ten-er *n.* ablandador quimico de agua

wa-ter-spout *n.* tromba marina; mangua

wa-ter-tight *a.* estanco; seguro

wa-ter-way *n.* canal

wa-ter-y *adj.* insipido

watt *n.* vatio

wave *v.* ondular, *n.* onda

wa-ver *v.* oscilar; vacilar

wav-y *a.* ondulado

wax *n.* cera

wax-en *a.* de cara; palido

wax-work *n.* figura de cera

way *n.* camino; modo; direccion

way-far-er *n.* viajero

way-lay *v.* asaltar

way-side *n.* borde del camino

way-ward *a.* voluntarioso; travieso

we *pron.* nosotras; nosotros

weak *adj.* debil

weak-en *v.* debilitar(se)

weak-ling *n.* alfenique

weak-ly *a.* achacoso

weak-mind-ed *a.* sin voluntad

weak-ness *n.* debilidad

wealth *n.* riqueza

wealth-y *adj.* rico

wean *v.* destetar

weap-on *n.* arma

weap-on-ry *n.* armas

wear *v.* desgastar(se); llevar

wear-ing *adj.* penoso

wea-ri-some *a.* fastidioso

wea-ry *a.* fatigado; aburrido

wea-sel *n.* comadreja

weath-er *n.* tiempo

weath-er-beat-en *a.* curtido pro la intemperie

weath-er-glass *n.* barometro

weath-er-man *n.* pronosticador de tiempo

weave *v.* tejido

web *n.* tela

web-bing *n.* cincha

wed *v.* casar(se)

wed-ding *n.* boda

wedge *n.* cuña

wed-lock *n.* matrimonio

Wednes-day *n.* miércoles

wee *a.* paqueñito

weed *v.* escardar

week *n.* semana

week-day *n.* dia laborable o de trabajo

week-end *n.* fin de la semana

week-ly *a.* semanal

weep *v.* llorar

wee-vil *n.* gorgojo

weigh *v.* pesar

weight *n.* pesa

weight-y *adj.* pesado

weird *adj.* extrano

wel-come *adj.* agradable

weld *v.* soldar

wel-fare *n.* bienestar

well *adv.* pues, *n.* fuente

well-be-ing *n.* bienestar

well-bred *a.* bien criado

well-dis-posed *a.* bien dispuesto

well-known *adj.* famoso

well-off *a.* adimerado

well-read *a.* leido

well-thought-of *a.* bien mirado

well-timed *a.* oportuno

well-to-do *a.* acaudalado

welt *n.* verdugon

wel-ter *v.* revolcar(se)

wench *n.* moza

were *pret. of* be

were-wolf *n.* hombre que puede transformarse en lobo

west *n.* oeste

west-ern *adj.* occidental

wet *v.* mojar(se)

whack *v.* golpear

whale *n.* ballena

whale-bone *n.* ballena

wharf *n.* muelle

what *pron.* qué; lo que; cual

what-ev-er *pron.* todo lo qué

what-not *n.* estante; juguetero

wheat *n.* trigo

whee-dle *v.* engatusar; halagar

wheel *n.* rueda

wheel-bar-row *n.* carretilla

wheel-chair *n.* silla de ruedas

wheeze *v.* respirar asmaticamente

when *conj.* cuando

whence *adv.* de donde; de que

when-ev-er *adv.* siempre que

where *conj., adv.* donde, *adv.* adonde

where-a-bouts *n.* paradero

where-as *conj.* visto que

where-up-on *adv.* con lo cual

wher-ev-er *adv.* dondequiera

wheth-er *conj.* si

whey *n.* suero de la leche

which *pron.* lo que; cual; la; le

which-ev-er *pron.* cualquiera

whiff *n.* olorcillo

while *conj.* mientras

whim *v.* lloriquear

whim-per *v.* lloriquear

whim-si-cal *a.* caprichoso

whine *v.* gimotear

whin-ny *n.* relincho

whip *v.* batir

whir *v.* zumbar; batir

whirl *v.* girar repidamente

whirl-pool *n.* remolino

whirl-wind *n.* torbellino

whisk-ers *n.* barbas; bigotes

whis-key *n.* whisky

whis-per *n.* cuchicheo, *v.* cuchichear

whis-tle *v.* silbar

white *n., adj.* blanco

white-col-lar *a.* oficinesco

whit-en *v.* blanquear

white-wash *n.* jalbeque

whith-er *conj.* adonde

whit-tle *v.* cortar poco a poco

whiz *v.* silbar; rehilar

who *pron.* la; el; lo; quién; que

who-ev-er *pron.* quienquiere que

whole *n., adj.* todo

whole-heart-ed *a.* sincero; incondicional

whole-sale *n.* venta al por menor

whole-some *a.* saludable

whol-ly *adv.* completamente

whom *pron.* a quién

whom-ev-er *pron.* a quien quiera

whoop *n.* alarido

whore *n.* puta; prostituta

whose *pron.* cuyo

why *n.* porqué

wick *n.* mecha

wick-ed *adj.* malicioso

wick-er *a.* de mimbre

wide *adj.* ancho

wide-a-wake *a.* despabilado

wid-en *v.* ensanchar(se)

wide-spread *a.* extendido; difuso

wid-ow *n.* viuda

wid-ow-er *n.* viudo

width *n.* anchura

wield *v.* ejercer; mandar; manejar

wife *n.* esposa

wig *n.* peluca

wig-gle *v.* menear(se); cimbrearse

wild *adj.* descabellado

wild boar *n.* jabali

wil-der-ness *n.* yermo; desierto

wile *n.* ardid

will *v.* querer

will-ful *a.* voluntarioso; terco; premeditado

will-ing *a.* dispuesto; com planciente

wil-low *n.* sauce

wil-low-y *a.* esbelto

wil-ly-nil-ly *adv.* de grado o por fuerza

wilt *v.* marchitar(se)

win *n.* victoria, *v.* lograr; ganar

wince *v.* estremecerse; respingar

winch *n.* torno

wind *n.* viento

wind *v.* arrollar(se)

wind-fall *n.* ganacia inesperada

wind-mill *n.* molino de viento

win-dow *n.* ventana

win-dow-pane *n.* cristal

wind-shield *n.* parabrisas

wind-y *adj.* ventoso

wine *n.* vino

win-er-y *n.* lagar; candiotera

wing *n.* ala

wink *v.* guinar; pestanear

win-ner *n.* ganador

win-ning *n.* ganancias

win-ter *n.* invierno

win-try *adj.* invernal

wipe *v.* enjugar; secar; borrar

wire *n.* alambre

wir-ing *n.* instalación de alambres

wir-y *a.* nervudo

wis-dom *n.* sabiduria

wise *adj.* acertado; sabio

wish *n.* deseo, *v.* desear

wish-ful *adj.* deseoso

wit *n.* sal

witch *n.* bruja

witch-craft *n.* brujeria

with *prep.* con

with-draw-al *n.* retirada

with-drawn *a.* ensimismado

with-hold *v.* retener

with-in *adv.* dentro

with-out *adv.* por fuera

with-stand *v.* resistir

wit-ness *n.* testigo

wi-ti-cism *n.* dicho gracioso

wit-ty *a.* salado; ingenioso

wiz-ard *n.* hechicero

wob-ble *v.* bambolear; bailar

woe *n.* aflicción; infortunio

wolf *n.* lobo

wom-an *n.* mujer

wom-an-kind *n.* sexo femenino

womb *n.* matriz

wom-en's rights *n.* derechos de la mujer

won-der *v.* asombrarse

won-der-ful *adj.* maravilloso

wood *n.* madera

wood-en *a.* de madera; sin expresion

wood-land *n.* monte

wood-peck-er *n.* picamaderos

wood-y *adj.* lenoso

wool *n.* lana

wool-ly *adj.* lanudo

word *n.* palabra

work *v.* trabajar, *n.* obra; trabajo

work-er *n.* trabajador

work-shop *n.* taller

world *n.* mundo

world-wide *a.* mundial

worm *n.* gusano

worn *adj.* usado

worrier *n.* aprensivo; pesimista

wor-ry *v.* inquietar(se)

wors-en *v.* empeorar

wor-ship *v.* venerar

worth *n.* valor

worth-less *adj.* despreciable

wound *v.* herir

wrap *v.* envolver

wreck *v.* naufragar, *n.* ruina

wrin-kle *v.* arrugar(se), *n.* ar ruga

wrist *n.* muñeca

write *v.* escribir

writ-er *n.* escritora; escritor

writ-ing *n.* escrito

wrong *adj.* equivocado

wrong-ful *a.* injusto; falso

wrong-head-ed *a.* terco

wrought *a.* forjado; trabajado

wry *a.* torcido; ironico; mueca

X

x-ray *v.* radiografiar, *n.* radiografia

Y

yank *v.* sacar de un tirón

Yan-kee *n.* yanqui

yard *n.* yarda

yard-goods *n.* tejidos

yard-stick *n.* vara de medir

yarn *n.* hilaza

yar-row *n.* milenrama

yawn *n.* bostezo, *v.* bostezar

ye *pron.* vosotros

yea *adv.* sí

year *n.* año

year-ling *n.* primal

year-ly *adv.* anualmente

yearn *v.* suspirar; anhelar

yearn-ing *n.* anhelo

yeast *n.* levadura

yell *n.* grito, *v.* gritar

yel-low *n., adj.* amarillo

yes *adv.* sí

yes-ter-day *n.* ayer

yet *adv.* todavía

yew *n.* tejo

yield *v.* rendir(se)

yolk *n.* yema

yon-der *adv.* allí; allá

yore *n.* antaño

you *pron.* vosotras; vosotros; tu

young *adj.* joven

young-ster *n.* jovencito

your *adj.* sus; tus; vuestras; vuestros

yours *pron.* tu; vos; vosotros; vosotras

your-self *pron.* usted mismo; tu mismo

youth *n.* jovenes

youth-ful *adj.* juvenil

Z

zeal *n.* ardor

zeal-ous *adj.* celoso

ze-bra *n.* cebra

ze-nith *n.* cenit

ze-ro *n.* cero

ze-ro hour *n.* hora de ataque

zest *n.* gusto

zone *n.* zona

zoo *n.* zoo

zo-o-log-i-cal *adj.* zoologico

ENGLISH/FRENCH
DICTIONARY

a, art. un, m., une f.
aardvark, n. aardvark, m.
abacus, n. abaque m.
abandon, vb. abandonner
abandon, n. abandon m.
abandoned, adj. abandonné
abate, vb. diminuer
abatement, n. diminution f.
abbey, n. abbaye
abbreviate, vb. abréger
abbreviation, n.
  abréviation f.
abdicate, vb. abdiquer
abdomen, n. abdomen m.
abominal, adj. abdominal
abduct, vb. enlever
abductor, n. ravisseur m.
abettor, n. aide m.
  complice m.
abeyance, n. suspension f.
abide, vb. (tolerate)
  supporter; (remain)
  demeurer; **(a. by the law)**
  respecter la loi
ability, n. talent m.
abject, adj. abject
able, adj. capable; (to be
  able) pouvoir
able-bodied, adj. fort,
  robuste
ably, adv. capablement
aboard, adv. à bord
abode, n. demeure f.
abolish, vb. abolir
abolishment, n.
  abolissement m.
abominate, vb. abominer
abomination, n.
  abomination f.
abortion, n. avortement m.
abortive, adj. abortif,
  manqué
abound, vb. abonder
  (de or en)
about, adv. (approxi-
  mately) à
peu près; autour
above, adv. au-dessus; prep.
  au-dessus de; plus de
abrasive, adj. abrasif m.
abreast, adv. de front
abroad, adv. à l'étranger

abrupt, adj. (hasty) brusque
abscess, n. abcès m.
absence, n. absence f.
absent, adj. absent
absolute, adj. absolu
absolutely, adv. absolument
absolution, n. absolution f.
absolve, vb. absoudre
absorb, vb. absorber
absorbed, adj. absorbé
absorbent, adj. abosor-
  bant m.
absorbing, adj. absorbant
absorption, n. absorption
abstinence, n. abstinence f.
abstract, adj. abstrait
absurd, adj. absurde
abundance, n. abondance f.
abundant, adj. abondant
abuse, n. abus m.
abusive, adj. (insulting)
  injurieux
abut, vb. aboutir (à)
abyss, n. abîme m.
academic, adj. académique
academy, n. académie f.
accede, vb. consentir
accelerate, vb. accélérer
accelerator, n.
  accélérateur m.
accent, n. accent m.
accept, vb. accepter
acceptance, n. acceptation f.
access, n. accès, abord m.
accessory, n. accessoire m.
accident, n. accident m.
accidental, adj. accidentel
acclaim, vb. acclamer
acclamation, n. acclamation f.
acclimate, vb. acclimater
accomodate, vb. (lodge)
  loger; (oblige) obliger
accompany, vb.
  accompagner
accomplish, vb. accomplir
accomplished, adj.
  accompli, achevé
accord, n. accord,
  rapport m.
accordance, n. accord m.

accordingly, adv. en
  conséquence
account, n. compte m.
accountant, n. compt-
  able m.
accounting, n.
  comptabilité f.
accretion, n.
  accroissement m.
accumulate, v.t. accumuler
accumulation, n.
  entassement m.
accumulative, adj. (chose)
  qui s'accumule
accuracy, n. précision f.
accurate, adj. précis
accusative, n. and adj.
  accusatif m.
accuse, v.t. accuser
accustom, v.t. accoutumer
ace, n. as m.
acetate, n. acétate m.
acetylene, n. acétylène m.
ache, n. douleur f.
achieve, vb. exécuter
achievement, n.
  accomplissement m.
acid, adj. acide m.
acidity, n. acidité f.
acknowledge, vb.
  reconnaître
acne, n. acné f.
acorn, n. gland m.
acquaint, vb. informer (de)
acquaintance, n.
  connaissance f.
acquainted, adj. connu,
  familier (avec)
acquiesce(in), vb.
  acquiescer (à)
acquire, vb. acquérir
acquit, vb. acquitter
acre, n. arpten m., acre f.
acrid, adj. âcre
acrobat, n. acrobate
across, prep. à travers
act, n. acte m. vb. jouer
acting, n. jeu m.
action, n. action f.
active, adj. actif, agile, alerte
activity, n. activité f.
actor, n. acteur m.

actress, n. actrice f.

actual, adj. réel

actually, adv. réellement, en effet

actuate, vb. mettre en action, animer

acupuncture, n. acuponcture f.

acutely, adv. vivement

acuteness, n. finesse f.

adapt, v.t. adapter

adaptable, adj. adaptable

adaptability, n. faculté d'adaptation f.

adaptation, n. adaptation f.

adapter, n. qui adapte

add, v.t ajouter; additionner

adder, v. vipère f.

addict, n. personne adonnée à f.

addition, n. addition f.

additional, adj. additionnel

address, n. adresse m.

adenoid, adj. and n. adénoïde f.

adept, adj. habile adepte

adequacy, n. suffisance f.

adequate, adj. suffisant

adhere, vb. adhérer

adherent, n. adhérent m.

adhesion, n. adhésion f.

adieu, n. and adv. adieu

adjective, n. adjectif m.

adjoin, vb. adjoindre

adjourn, vb. ajourner

adjunct, n. and adj. adjoint, accessoire m.

adjust, vb. ajuster, arranger, régler

adjuster, n. ajusteur m.

adjustment, n. ajustement accommodement m.

administer, vb. administrer

administration, n. administration f.

administrative, adj. administratif

administrator, n. administrateur m.

admirable, adj. admirable

admiral, n. amiral m.

admiration, n. admiration f.

admire, vb. admirer

admirer, n. admirateur m.

admiringly, adv. avec admiration

admission, n. (entrance) entrée f.

admit, vb. laisser entrer

admittance, n. accès m.

admonish, vb. réprimander

adolescence, n. adolescence f.

adolescent, adj. and n. adoles- cent m., adolescente f.

adopt, vb. adopter

adoption, n. adoption f.

adorable, adj. adorable

adoration, n. adoration f.

adore, vb. adorer

adorn, vb. orner

adult, adj. and n. adulte m.f.

adulterer, n. adultère m.

adulteress, n. femme adultère f.

adultery, n. adultère m.

advance, v.t. avancer, faire

advanced, adj. avancé

advancement, n. avancement m.

advantage, n. avantage m.

advantageous, adj. avantageux

advent, n. venue f.; (eccles.) Avent m.

adventure, n. aventure f.

adventurer, n. aventurier m.

adventurous, adj. aventureux

adverb, n. adverbe m.

adverse, adj. adverse

advert, vb. faire allusion (à)

advertise, vb. annoncer

advertisement, n. annoncer

advertising, n. publicité f.

advice, n. conseil m.

advise, vb. conseiller

advocate, n. avocat m.

aerate, vb. aérer

aeration, n. aération f.

aerial, adj. aérien

aerie, n. aire f.

aesthetic, adj. esthétique

afar, adv. loin, de loin

affair, n. affaire f.

affect, vb. toucher, intéresser

affected, adj. maniéré

affecting, adj. touchant, émouvant

affection, n. affection f.

affiance, vb. fiancer

affidavit, n. déclaration par écrit sous serment attestation f.

affiliate, vb. affilier

affinity, n. affinité f.

affirm, vb. affirmer

affirmation, n. affirmation f.

affix, vb. apposer

afflict, vb. affliger (de)

affliction, n. affliction f.

affluence, n. affluence, opulence f.

affluent, adj. affluent, opulent

afford, vb. donner, fournir

affront, n. affront m.

afloat, adv. à flot

afraid, adj. effrayé pris de peur

Africa, n. l' Afrique f.

after, prep. après; sur, à la suite de

afternoon, n. après-midi m.f.

afterward, adv. ensuite

again, adv. encore

against, prep. contre

age, n. âge m.

ageless, adj. toujours jeune

agency, n. agence f.

agenda, n. ordre du jour, agenda m.

agent, n. agent m.

aggravate, vb. aggraver

aggravation, n. aggravation f., agacement m.

aggregate, adj. global

aggression, n. agression f.

aggressive, adj. agressif

aggressor, n. agresseur m.

aghast, adj. consterné

agitate, vb. agiter, exciter

agitator, n. agitateur m.

ago, adv. passé, il y a

agonized, v.t. torturer

agony, n. angoisse, agonie f.

agree, vb. être d'accord

agreeable, adj. agréable

agreeably, adv.
agréablement

agreement, n. accord m.

agriculture, n. agriculture f.

ahead, adv. and interj. en
avant

aid, n. aide, assistance f.

AIDS, n. (acaronym) -
acquired immune
deficiency syndrome - le
SIDA (syndrome
d'immuno- déficience
acquise)

ail, vb. être souffrant

ailment, n. indisposition f.

aim, n. point de mire, but m.

air, n. air, vent m., brise f.

airbag, n. sac à air m.

airborne, adj. aéroporté

air-condition, vb. climatiser

air-conditioning, n.
climatisation f.

aircraft, n. avion, les
avions, m., pl.

air gun, n. fusil à vent

airliner, n. avion m.

air mail, n. poste aérienne f.

airplane, n. avion m.

air pollution, n. pollution
de l'air f.

airport, n. aéroport m.

air pressure, n. pression
d'air f.

air sickness, n. mal de l'air

airtight, adj. imperméable à
l'air

airy, adj. ouvert à l'air; aéré

aisle, n. bas-côté m.

ajar, adv. entr'ouvert

akin, adj. allié (à). parent
(de)

alarm, n. alarme, alerte f.

albino, n. albinos m.

album, n album m.

alcohol, n. alcool m.

alcoholic, adj. alcoolique

alert, adj. alerte

algebra, n. algèbre f.

alibi, n. alibi m.

alien, adj. etranger

align, vb. aligner

alike, adj. semblable; adv.
également

alive, adj. vivant, envie

alkali, n. alcali m.

alkaline, adj. alcalin

all, adj. tout m. sg., toute
f. sg., tous m., pl, toutes
f., pl;
adv. and pron. tout; surtout;
tout d'un coup

allay, vb. apaiser

allegation, n. allégation f.

allege, vb. alléguer

allegiance, n. fidélité f.

allergy, n. allergie f.

alleviate, vb. soulager

alley, n. ruelle f.

alliance, n. alliance f.

allied, adj. allié

alligator, n. alligator m.

allocate, vb. assigner

allot, vb. répartir

allotment, n. partage m.

allow, vb. permettre;
admettre

allowance, n. allocation,
ration

alloy, n. alliage m.

allure, vb. séduire

allusion, n. allusion f.

ally n. allié m.

alamanc, n. almanach m.

almond, n. amande f.

aloft, adv. en haut, en l'air

alone, adj. seul, solitaire

along, adv. le long de

aloud, adv. à haute voix

alphabet, n. alphabet m.

alphabetical, adj.
alphabétique

Alps, n. les Alpes f., pl.

already, adv. déja

also, adv. aussi

altar, n. autel m.

alter, vb. changer

alteration, n. modification f.

alternate, vb. alterner, faire
alternativement

alternative, n. alternative f.

although, conj. bien que

altitude, n. altitude f.

altogether, adv. tout à fait

alum, n. alun m.

aluminium, n. alumi-
nium m.

always, adv. toujours

amalgam, n. amalgame m.

amass, vb. amasser

amateur, n. amateur m.

amaze, vb. étonner

amazement, n. stupeur f.

amazing, adj. étonnant

ambassador, n.
ambassadeur m.

amber, n. ambre m.

ambidextrous, adj.
ambidextre

ambition, n. ambition f.

ambitious, adj. ambitieux

ambulance, n. ambulance f.

ambulatory, adj.
ambulatoire

ambush, n. embuscade f.

amend, vb. amender

amenity, n. aménité f.,
agrément m.

America, n. l'Amérique f.

American, adj. américain,
n.; Américain m.

amethyst, n. améthyste f.

amid, prep. au milieu de

amiss, adv. mal, en
mauvaise part

amity, n. amitié f.

ammonia, n. ammoniaque f.

amnesty, n. amnistie f.

among, prep. parmi, entre

amount, n. somme,
(quantity) quantité f.

ampere, n. ampère m.

amphibious, adj. amphibie

amphitheatre, n.
amphithéâtre m.

ample, adj. ample

amplify, vb. amplifier

amputate, n. amputer

amputee, n. amputé m.

amuse, vb. amuser

an, art. un m., une f.

analysis, n. analyse f.

analyst, n. analyste m.

analyze, vb. analyser

anatomy, n. anatomie f.

ancestor, n. ancêtres m., pl.

ancestral, adj. d'ancêtres,
héréditaire

ancestry, n. ancêtres m., pl.

anchor, vb. ancre f.

anchorage, n. mouillage,
ancrage m.

anchovy, n. anchois m.

ancient, adj. ancien m.

and, conj. et

anecdote, n. anecdote f.

anemia, n. anémie f.

anesthetist, n.
anesthésiste m.

anew, adv. de nouveau

angel, n. ange m.

anger, n. colère f.

angle, n. angle m.

angry, adj. fâché

anguish, n. angoisse f.

animal, n. and adj.
animal m.

animate, vb. animer

animation, n. animation f.

animosity, n. animosité f.

anise, n. anis m.

ankle, n. cheville f.

annals, n., pl. annales f., pl.

annex, n. dépendance f.

annexation, n. annexation f.

annihilate, vb. anéantir

anniversary, n.
anniversaire m.

annotate, vb. annoter

annotation, n. annotation f.

announce, vb. annoncer

announcement, n.
annonce f.

announcer, n. annonciateur

annoy, vb. (vex) contrarie

annoyance, n. contrariété f.

annual, adj. annuel

annuity, n. annuité f.

annul, vb. annuler

anoint, vb. oindre

anonymous, adj. anonyme

another, adj. and pron. un
autre m., une autre f.

answer, vb. répondre; n.
réponse f.

ant, n. fourmi f.

antagonize, vb. eveiller
l'antagonisme

antarctic, adj.
antarctique m.

antelope, n. antilope f.

antenna, n. antenne f.

anterior, adj. antérieur

anthem, n. hymne m.

anthrax, n. anthrax m.

antic, n. bouffonerie f.

anticipate, vb. anticiper;
prévoir

anticipation, n.
anticipation f.

antidote, n. antidote m.

antinomy, n. antinomie f.

antipathy, n. antipathie f.

antique, n. antique m.;
(antique dealer)
antiquaire m.

antiquity, n. antiquité f.

antiseptic, adj. and n.
antiseptique m.

antisocial, adj. antisocial

antler, n. andouiller m.

anvil, n. enclume f.

anxiety, n. anxiété f.

anxious, adj. inquiet m.

any, adj. du, de la

anybody, pron. (somebody)
quelq'un

anyhow, adv. de toute facon

anyone, pron. quelqu'un,
chacun, qui que ce soit

anything, pron. quelque
chose m.

anywhere, adv. n'importe où

apart, adv. à part

apartheid, n. ségrégation f.

apartment, n. logement m.

apathy, n. apathie f.

ape, n. singe m.

apex, n. sommet m.

apiece, adv. chacun

apologize, vb. s'excuser,
faire des excuses

apology, n. excuses f., pl.

apostle, n. apôtre m.

appal, vb. épouvanter

apparatus, n. appareil m.

apparel, n. habillement,
vêtement m.

apparent, adj. apparent

appeal, n. appel m.; vb. en
appeler (de)

appear, vb. apparaître

appearance, n. apparition f

appease, vb. apaiser,
pacifier

appeaser, n. personne qui
apaise

appendage, n. accessoire m

appendectomy, n.
appendéctomie f.

appendicits, n.
appendicite f.

appendix, n. appendice m

appetite, n. appétit m.

appetizer, n. apéritif m.

applaud, vb. applaudir

applause, n.
applaudissements m., pl

apple, n. pomme f.

applesauce, n. compote de
pommes f.

appliance, n. appareil m.

applicant, n. postulant m

application, n. demande

applied, adj. appliqué

apply, vb. appliquer (à),
s'appliquer

appoint, vb. nommer;
désigner

appointment, n.
nomination f.

apposition, n. apposition

appraisal, n. évaluation

appraise, n. expert m.

appreciable, adj.
appréciable

appreciate, vb. apprécier
estimer

appreciation, n.
appréciation f.

apprehend, vb. saisir,
arrêter

apprehension, n.
arrestation f.

apprehensive, adj.
  intelligent
approach, n. approche f.
approbation, n.
  approbation f.
approval, n. approbation f.
approve, vb. approuver
approximate, adj.
  approximatif
approximately, adv.
  approximative-
  ment, à peu pres
apricot, n. abricot m.
April, n. avril m.
apron, n. tablier m.
apt, adj. sujet, enclin,
  porté (à)
aptitude, n. aptitude f.
aquarium, n. aquarium m.
aquatic, adj. aquatique
aqueduct, n. aqueduc m.
aqueous, adj. aqueux
arab, n. Arabe m.f. adj.
  arabe
arabic, adj. and n. arabe m.
arbiter, n. arbitre m.
arbitrary, adj. arbitraire
arbitrate, vb. arbitrer
arbitration, n. arbitrage m.
arbitrator, n. arbitre m.
arbor, n. arbre m.
arc, n. arc m.
arcade, n. arcade f.
arch, n. arc m.; (of bridge)
  arche f. adj. espiègle
archbishop, n.
  archevêque m.
archduke, n. archiduc m.
archer, n. archer m.
archery, n. tir à l'arc m.
architect, n. architecte m.
architecture, n.
  architecture f.
archives, n. archives f., pl.
archway, n. voûte f.,
  passage (sous une
  voûte) m.
arctic, adj. arctique
ardor, n. ardeur f.
area, n. aire; région,
  surface f.

area code, n. indicatif
  interurbain m.
arena, n. arène f.
argue, vb. argumenter
argument, n. argument m.;
  (dispute) discussion f.
arid, adj. aride
arise, vb. s'élever;
  provenir de
aristocracy, n. aristocratie f.
aristocrat, n.
  aristocrate m.f.
arithmetic, n.
  arthimétique f.
ark, n. arche f.
arm, n. bras m.; arme f. vb.
  armer
arm-chair, n. fauteuil m.
armed forces, n. forces
  armées f., pl.
armful, n. brassée f.
armhole, n. emmanchure f.
armistice, n. armistice m.
armor, n. armure f.
armpit, n. aisselle f.
arms, n. armes f., pl.
army, n. armée f.
aroma, n. arome m.
aromatic, adj. aromatique
around, adv. autour; prep.
  autour de
arouse, vb. soulever;
  réveiller
arraign, vb. accuser,
  poursuivre en justice
arrange, vb. arranger, réler
arrangement, n.
  arrangement m.
array, vb. ranger
arrest, n. arrestation f.;
  arrêts m., pl.
arrival, n. arrivée f.
arrive, vb. arriver
arrogant, adj. arrogant
arrogate, vb. attribuer
  injustement
arrow, n. flèche f.
arrowhead, n. pointe de
  flèche f. arsenal, n.
  arsenal m.
arsenic, n. arsenic m.
arson, n. crime

d'incendie m.
art, n. art m.; beauxarts
arterial, adj. artériel
artery, n. artère f.
artful, adj. artificieux; adroit
arthritis, n. arthrite f.
article, n. article m.
artillery, n. artillerie f.
artist, n. artiste m.
artistic, adj. artistique
artistry, n. habileté f.
as, adv. comme; aussi...que;
  conj. de facon à;
  pendant que
asbestos, n. asbeste m.
ascend, vb. monter
ascendancy, n. ascendant m.
ascendant, adj. ascendant,
  supérieur
ascertain, vb. s'assurer
ascetic, n. ascétique m.
ascribe, vb. attribuer
ash, n. cendre f.; (tree)
  frêne m.
ashamed, adj. honteux,
  confus
ashore, adv. à terre;
  débarquer
Asia, n. l'Asie f.
Asian, n. Asiatique m.f.; adj.
  asiatique
aside, adv. de côte
ask, vb. demander à; inviter
askance, adv. de travers,
  obliquement
asleep, adj. endormi
asparagus, n. asperges f., pl.
aspect, n. aspect m.
asphalt, n. asphalte m.
asphyxiate, vb. asphyxier
aspirant, n. aspirant m.,
  candidat m.
aspiration, n. aspiration f.
aspirator, n. aspirateur m.
aspire, vb. aspirer
ass, n. âne m., ânesse f.
assail, vb. assaillir
assailant, n. assaillant m.
assassin, n. assassin m.
assassination, n.
  assassinat m.
assault, n. assaut m.

assay, n. essai m., vérification, épreuve f. vb. essayer

assemblage, n. assemblage m.

assemble, vb. assembler

assembly, n. assemblée f.

assert, vb. affirmer

assess, vb. evaluer, imposter

assets, n., pl. actif m.

assign, vb. assigner

assignable, adj. assignable, transférable

assignation, n. assignation f., rendezvous m.

assignment, n. attribution, assignation

assistance, n. aide f.

assistant, n. qui aide, auxiliaire

associate, vb. associe

association, n. association f.

assort, vb. assortir

assorted, adj. assorti

assortment, n. assortiment, m.

assume, vb. prendre sur soi

assuming, adj. prétentieux, arrogant

assumption, n. supposition f.

assurance, n. assurance f.

assure, vb. assurer

aster, n. aster m.

asterisk, n. astérisque m.

astern, adv. à l'arrière, sur l'arrière

asteroid, n. astéroïde m.

asthma, n. asthme m.

astonish, vb. étonner

astonishment, n. étonnement m.

astound, vb. étonner, ébahir

astride, adv. à califourchon

astringent, n. and adj. astringent m.

astrology, n. astrologie f.

astronaut, n. astronaute m.

astronomy, n. astronomie f.

at, prep. à, en, dans; contre

atheist, n. athée

athlete, n. athlète m.

athletic, adj. athlétique

Atlantic, adj. atlantique

atlas, n. atlas m.

atomsphere, n. atmospère f.

atom, n. atome m.

atomic, adj. atomique

atomic bomb, n. bombe atomique f.

atonement, n. expiation f.

atrocity, n. atrocité f.

atrophy, n. atrophie f.

attach, vb. attcher

attaché, n. attaché m.

attachment, n. attachment

attack, n. attaque f.

attain, vb. atteindre

attainment, n. acquisition f.

attempt, n. tentative f.

attend, vb. soigner; servir; assister

attendance, n. service m.; présence f.

attention, n. attention f.

attentive, adj. attentif

attest, vb. attester

attic, n. grenier m.

attire, n. costume m.

attitude, n. attitude f.

attorney, n. avoué m.

attract, vb. attirer

attraction, n. attraction f.

attractive, adj. attrayant

attribute, n. attribut m.

attune, vb. accorder

auction, n. enchère

auctioneer, n. commissairepriseur m.

audacity, n. audace f.

audible, adj. intelligible

audience, n. auditoire m.

audit, vb. verifier (des comptes); n. vérfication des comptes

audition, n. audition f.

auditor, n. vérificateur m.

auditorium, n. salle f.

auditory, adj. auditif

August, n. août m.

aunt, n. tante f.

Australia, n. l'Australie f.

authentic, adj. authentique

authenticity, n. authenticité f.

author, n. auteur m.

authority, n. authorité f.

authorization, n. autorisation f.

authorize, vb. autoriser

auto, n. auto f.

autobiography, n. autobiographie f.

autogrpah, n. autographe m.; vb. autographier

automatic, adj. automatique

automatically, adv. automatiquement

automobile, n. automobile f.

autopsy, n. autopsie f.

autumn, n. automne m.

auxiliary, adj. auxiliaire m.

avail, vb. servir

available, adj. disponible

avenge, vb. venger

avenue, n. avenue f.

average, n. moyenne f. adj moyen

averse, adj. opposé

aversion, n. aversion f.

avert, vb. détourner

aviation, n. aviation f.

aviator, n. aviateur m.

avid, adj. avide

avoid, vb. éviter

avow, vb. avouer

await, vb. attendre

awake, vb. éveill

award,, n. prix m.; senten f.; vb. dècerner

away, adv. loin; absnt

awful, adj. terrible

awhile, adv. pendant quelque temps

awkward, adj. gauche; embarrassant

awning, n. tente f.

axe, n. hache f.

axis, n. axe m.

axle, n. arbre, essieu

azure, n. azur m.

B

babble, vb. babiller

babe, n. enfant m.f.

baboon, n. babouin m.

baby, n. bébé m.

bachelor, n. célibataire m.

back n. dos m.; vb. reculer; adv. en arrière

backbone, n. épine dorsale f.

background, n. fond m.

backhand, adj. donné avec le revers de la main

backward, adv. en arrière

backwardness, n. état arriéré m.

backwater, n. eau stagnante f.

bacon, n. lard m.

bacterium n. bactérie f.

bad, adj. mauvais; mechant

baffle, vb. déconcerter

bag, n. sac m.; (suitcase) valise f.

baggage, n. bagage m.

bagpipe, n. cornemuse f.

bail, n. caution f. vb. vider

baliff, n. huissier m.

bait, n. appât m.

bake, vb. faire cuire au four

baker, n. boulanger m.

bakery, n. boulangerie f.

baking, n. cuisson f.

balance, n. équilibre, solde m.; balance f. vb. balancer, peser

balcony, n. balcon m.

baldness, n. calvitie f.

bale, n. balle f.

balk, vb. frustrer

ball, n. balle f., boule f., bal m.

ballad, n. romance f.; ballade f.

ballast, n. lest m.

ball bearing, n. roulements à billes m.

ballerina, n. ballerine f.

ballet, n. ballet m.

balloon, n. ballon m.

ballot, n. scrutin m.

balm, n. baume m.

balmy, adj. embaumé

balsam, n. baume m.

balustrade, n. balustrade f.

bamboo, n. bambou m.

ban, n. ban m. vb. metre au ban

banal, adj. banal

banana, n. banane f.

band, n. bande f.

bandage, n. bandeau m.

bandanna, n. foulard m.

bandbox, n. carton m.

bandit, n. bandit m.

bandsman, n. musicien m.

bandstand, n. kiosque á musique m.

baneful, adj. pernicieux

bang, vb. frapper violemment; n. coup m.

banish, vb. bannir

banishment, n. bannissement m.

banister, n. rampe, f.

bank, n. rivage m.

bankbook, n. livret de banque m.

banker, n. banquier m.

banking, n. banque f.

bank note, n. billet de banque m.

bankrupt, adj. failli, en faillite m.

bankruptcy, n. faillie f.

banner, n. bannière f.

banquet, n. banquet m.

banter, n. badinage m.; vb. badiner, railler

baptism, n. baptême m.

baptismal, adj. batismal

Baptist, n. Baptiste m.

baptistery, n. baptistère m.

baptize, vb. baptiser

bar, n. bar, barreau m.

barb, n. barbillon m.

barbarism, n. barbarie f., (gramm.) barbarisme m.

barber, n. coiffeur m.

barbiturate, n. barbiturate m.

bare, adj. nu; vb. découvrir

bareback, adv. à dos nu

barefoot, adv. nu-pieds

barely, adv. à peine

bareness, n. nudité f.

bargain, n. marché m.

bargain, vb. marchander

barge, n. chaland m.

bark, n. (tree) écorce f.; (dog) aboiement m.; vb. (dog) aboyer

barley, n. orge f.

barn, n. (grain) grange f.; (live-stock) étable f.

barnacle, n. (shellfish) anatife m.; (goose) barnache f.

barometer, n. baromètre m.

barometric, adj. barométrique

baron, n. baron m.

baroness, n. baronne f.

baronial, adj. baronnial, seigneurial

baroque, adj. baroque m.

barrack, n. caserne f.

barrel, n. baril m.

barren, adj. stérile

barrenness, n. stérilité f.

barricade, n. barricade f.

barrier, n. barrière f.

barter, n. troc m.

base, n. base f.; adj. bas m.

baseball, n. base-ball m.

basement, n. sous-sol m.

bashful, adj. timide

bashfully, adv. timidement

bashfulness, n. timidité f.

basic, adj. fondamental

basin, n. cuvette f., bassin m.

basis, n. base f.

bask, vb. se chauffer

basket, n. panier m., corbeille f.

bass, n. basse f; (fish) bar m.

bassinet, n. bercelonnette f.

bassoon, n. basson m.

bastard, n. bâtard m.

baste, vb. arroser; (sewing) faufiler

bat, n. (animal) chauve-souris f.; (baseball) batte f.

batch, n. fournée f.

bate, vb. rabattre

bath, n. bain m.
bathe, vb. se baigner
bather, n. baigneur m.
baton, n. bâton m.
battalion, n. bataillon m.
batter, n. (cooking) pâte f.
battery, n. batterie
battle, n. bataille f.
battle, vb. lutter
battlefield, n. champ de bataile m.
battleship, n. cuirassé m.
bawl, vb. brailler
bayonet, n. baïonnette f.
bazaar, n. bazar m.
be, vb. être
beach, n. plage f.
beacon, n. phare m.
bead, n. perle f.
beak, n. bec m.
beaker, n. gobelet m., coupe f.
beam, n. putre f., rayon m.; vb. rayonner
beaming, adj. rayonnant
bean, n. haricot m.
bear, n. ours m.; vb. porter, supporter, enfanter
beard, n. barbe f.
bearer, n. porteur m.
bearing, n. maintien, coussinet, relèvement m.
beast, n. bête f.
beat, vb. battre; n. battement m.
beaten, adj. battu
beatify, vb. béatifier
beating, n. battement m., rossée f.
beau, n. galant m.
beautiful, adj. beau m.
beaver, n. castor m.
because, conj. parce que
beckon, vb. faire signe (à)
become, vb. devenir
becoming, adj. convenable
bed, n. lit m.
bedclothes, n. les draps et couvertures f., pl.
bedridden, adj. alité
bedroom, n. chambre à

coucher f.
bedside, n. bord du lit m.
bedspread, n. dessus de lit m.
bedstead, n. bois de lit m.
bedtime, n. l'heure du coucher
bee, n. abeille f.
beef, n. boeuf m.
beehive, n. ruche f
beer, n. bière f.
beeswax, n. cire jaune f.
beet, n. betterave f.
beetle, n. scarabée m.
befit, vb. convenir à
befitting, adj. convenable
before, adv. en avant, avant; prep. devant, avant
beforehand, adv. d'avance
befriend, vb. seconder, aider
beg, vb. mendier, prier
beggar, n. mendiant m.
begin, vb. commencer
beginner, n. commençant m.
beginning, n. commencement m.
beguile, vb. tromper, séduire
behalf, n. de la part de, en faveur de
behave, vb. se conduire
behavior, n. conduite f.
behind, n. derrière m.
behold, vb. voir; interj. voici
beige, adj. beige m.
being, n. être m.
belated, adj. attardé
belch, vb. éructer
belfry, n. clocher, beffori m.
Belgian, n. Belge m.f.; adj. beige
Belgium, n. Belgique f.
belief, n. croyance, confiance f.
believable, adj. croyable
believe, vb. croire
believer, n. croyant m.
bell, n. cloche, clochette f.
bellboy, n. chasseur m.
bellow, vb. mugir
bellows, n., pl. soufflet m.

belly, n. ventre m.
belongings, n., pl. effets m., pl.
beloved, adj. and n. chéri m.
below, prep. en aval, au-dessous de
belt, n. ceinture f.
bench, n. banc m.
bend, vb. plier, courber tourner
beneath, prep. sous, au-dessous
benediction, n. bénédiction f.
benefactor, n. bienfaiteur m.
beneficent, adj. beinfaisant
beneficial, adj. salutaire
beneficiary, n. bénéficiaire m.
benefit, n. bienfait, profit m.
benevolent, adj. bienveillant
benign, adj. bénin m. bénigne f.
bent, n. penchant m.
bequeath, vb. léguer
bequest, n. legs m.
bereave, vb. priver (de)
bereavement, n. privation f., perte f., deuil m.
beseech, vb. supplier, implorer
beside, prep. à côté de
besides, adv. en outre
besiege, vb. assiéger
best, adj. le meilleur; adv. le mieux
bestial, adj. bestial
bestir, vb. remuer
bestow, vb. accorder
bet, n. pari m.; vb. parier
betray, vb. trahir
betroth, vb. fiancer
betrothal, n. fiancailles f., pl.
better, adj. en biseau; vb. bi aiser
beverage, n. boisson f.
bewilder, vb. égarer
bewildering, adj. découtant
bewilderment, n. égarement m.
bewitch, vb. ensorceler

beyond, adv. au delà; prep. au delà de

biannual, adj. semestriel

bias, n. biais m.

bib, n. bavette f.

Bible, n. Bible f.

biblical, adj. biblique

bibliography, n. bibliographie f.

biceps, n. biceps m.

bicker, vb. se quereller, se chamailler

bicycle, n. bicyclette f.

bicyclist, n. cycliste m.

bid, n. enchère f., appel m.; vb. ordonner, inviter

bidder, n. enchérisseur m.

bide, vb. demeurer, attendre

bier, n. corbillard m., civière f.

bifocal, adj. bifocal

big, adj. grand

bigamy, n. bigamie f.

bigot, n. bigot m.

bigotry, n. bigoterie f.

bilateral, adj. bilatéral

bile, n. bile f.

bilingual, adj. bilingue

bilious, adj. bilieux

bill, n. addition, note f., billet m.

billet, n. (mil.) billet de logement m.

billiard, adj. de billard

billion, n. billion m.

billow, n. grande vague, lame f.

bi-monthly, adj. bimensuel

bin, n. coffre m.

bind, vb. lier; (books) relier

bindery, n. atelier de reliure m.

binding, n. (book) reliure f.; adj. obligatoire

binocular, adj. binoculaire

biochemistry, n. biochimie f.

biography, n. biographie f

biological, adj. biologique

biology, n. biologie f.

biped, n. bipède m.

bird, n. oiseau m.

birth, n. naissance f.

birth control, n. limitation des naissances f.

birthday, n. anniversaire m.

birthplace, n. lieu de naissance m.

birth rate, n. natalité f.

birthright, n. droit d'aînesse m.

biscuit, n. biscuit; petit four m.

bishop, n. évêque m.

bison, n. bison m.

bitch, n. chienne f.

bite, n. morsure f.; vb. mordre

biting, adj. mordant, piquant

bitterly, adv. amèrement, avec amertume

bitterness, n. amertume f.

bivouac, n. bivouac m.

biweekly, adj. and adv. (de) tous les quinze jours

black, adj. noir

blackberry, n. mûre

blackboard, n. tableau noir m.

blackmail, n. chantage m.

black-market, n. marché noir m.

blackout, n. blackout m.

blacksmith, n. forgeron m.

bladder, n. vessie f.

blade, n. lame f., brin m.

blame, n. blâme m.; vb. blâmer

blameless, adj. innocent, sans tache

blanch, vb. blanchir; pâlir

bland, adj. doux, aimable

blank, n. blanc m., vide m; adj. blanc m., blance f., vide

blanket, n. couverture f.

blast, n. (wind) rafale f.; (mine) explosion f.

blaze, n. flambée f.; vb. flamber

blazing, adj. enflammé, flamboyant

bleach, vb. blanchir

bleak, adj. morne

bleakness, n. froidure f.

bleed, vb. saigner

blemish, n. defaut m.

blend, n. mélange m.; vb. mêler

blended, adj. mélangé

bless, vb. bénir

blessed, adj. béni, saint

blessing, n. bénédiction f.

blight, vb. flétrir, détruire, nieller, brouir; n. brouissure f.

blind, n. store m.; adj. aveugle

blindness, n. cécité f.

blink, vb. clignoter

bliss, n. béatitude f.

blissful, adj. bienheureux

blissfully, adv. heureusement

blister, n. ampoule f.

blithe, adj. gai, joyeux

blizzard, n. tempête de neige f.

bloat, vb. boursoufle

block, n. bloc m.; vb. bloquer

blockade, n. blocus m.

blond, adj. and n. blond m.

blood, n. sang m.

bloodhound, n. limier m.

bloodless, adj. exsangue

bloodshed, n. effusion de sang f.

bloodshot, adj. injecté de sang

bloody, adj. sanglant

bloom, n. fleur f.; vb. fleurir

blooming, n. floraison f.; adj. fleurissant

blossom, n. fleur f.

blot, n. tache f.; vb. tacher

blotch, n. tache f.

blotchy, adj. tacheté

blouse, n. blouse f.

blow, n. coup m.; vb. souffler

blue, adj. bleu

blueprint, n. dessin négatif m.

bluff, n. bluff m.

blunder, n. bévue f.

blunt, adj. émoussé; brusque

bluntly, adv. brusquement

bluntness, n. brusquerie f.

blur, vb. barbouiller

blush, n. rougeur f.; vb. **rougir**

boar, n. sanglier m.

board, n. plance, pension f.

boast, vb. se vanter

boaster, n. vantard m.

boastful, adj. vantard m.

boat, n. bateau m.

boathouse, n. garage (à beaux) m.

bob, vb. (hair) couper court

bode, vb. présager

bodice, n. corsage m.

bodily, adj. corporel

body, n. corps m.

boil, vb. bouillir; intr., faire bouillir; n. furoncle m.

boiler, n. chaudière f.

boisterous, adj. bruyant

bold, adj. hardi

boldface, adj. caractères, impudent

boldly, adv. hardiment

boldness, n. hardiesse f.

bolster, n. traversin m.

bolt, n. verrou m.; vb. verrouiller

bomb, n. bombe f.

bombard, vb. bombarder

bombardier, n. **bombardier m.**

bond, n. lien m., obliation f.

bondage, n. servitude f.

bone, n. os m.

boneless, adj. sans os

bonfire, n. feu de joie m.

bonnet, n. chapeau m.

bonus, n. boni m.

bony, adj. osseux

book, n. livre m.

bookcase, n. bibliothèque f.

bookkeeper, n. teneur de livres m.

bookkeeping, n. compt-

abilite f.

booklet, n. opuscule m.

bookseller, n. libraire m., bougquiniste m.

boon, n. bienfait m.

boor, n. rustre m.

boorish, adj. rustre

boost, vb. pousser

boot, n. bottine f.

bootblack, n. cireur m.

booth, n. baraque f., cabine f.

booty, n. butin m.

border, n. bord m., **frontière f.**

border-line, adj. touchant

bore, vb. forer, ennuyer

boredom, n. ennui m.

boring, adj. ennuyeux

born, adj. né; vb. naître

borrower, n. emprunteur m.

bosom, n. sein m.

boss, n. patron m.; vb. diriger

bossy, adj. autoritaire

botanical, adj. botanique

botany, n. botanique f.

botch, n. pustule f.; vb. ravauder

both, adj. and pron. tous les deux

bother, n. ennui m.

bothersome, adj. importun

bottle, n. bouteille f.

bottom, n. fond m.

bottomless, adj. sans fond

boulder, n. grosse pierre f.

boulevard, n. boulevard m.

bounce, vb. rebondir

bound, n. borne f., bound m.; vb. borner, bondir

boundary, n. frontière f.

boundless, adj. sans bornes, illimité

bound, n. largesse, prim f.

bouquet, n. bouquet m.

bow, n. arc m., archet m., révérence f., avant m.

bowels, n., pl. entrailles f., pl.

bowl, n. bol m.; vb. jouer aux boules

box, n. boîte f.

boxer, n. boxeur m.

boxing, n. la boxe f.

boy, n. garcon m.

boycott, vb. boycotter

boyhood, n. enfance, adolescence f.

brace, vb. fortifier; n. vilebrequin m., paire f., **couple m.**

bracelet, n. bracelet m.

bracket, n. console f., crochet m.

brag, vb. se vanter

braid, n. tresse f.; galon m.; vb. tresser, natter

brain, n. cerveau m.; cervelle f.

brake, n. frein m.

bran, n. son m.

branch, n. branche f.

brand, n. marque f.

brandy, n. eau-de-vie f.

brass, n. cuivre jaune

brassiere, n. soutiengorge m.

brat, n. marmot m.

bravado, n. bravade f.

brave, adj. courageux

bravery, adv. courageusement

brawl, n. rixe f.

bray, vb. braire

brazen, adj. effronté

Brazil, n. le Brésil m.

breach, n. infraction f.; (mil.) brèche f.

bread, n. pain m.

breadth, n. largeur f.

break, n. rupture f., interruption f.; vb. rompre, briser casser

breakable, adj. fragile

breakage, n. cassure, rupture f.

breakfast, n. petit **déjeuner m.**

breast, n. poitrine f., sein m.

breath, n. haleine f., souffle m.

breathe, vb. respirer

breathless, adj. essoufflé

breathlessly, adv. en haletant

breed, vb. élever

breeder, n. éleveur m.

breeding, n. éducation f., élevage m.

breeze, n. brise (de houille) f.

breezy, adj. venteux, dégagé

brevity, n. brièveté f.

brew, vb. brasser, faire de la bière

brewery, n. brasserie f.

brick, n. brique f.

bridal, adj. nuptial

bride, n. nouvelle mariée f.

bridegroom, n. nouveau marié m.

bridesmaid, n. demoiselle d'honneur f.

bridge, n. pont m., passerelle f., bridge m.

bridle, n. bride f.

brief, adj. bref m.

brief case, n. serviette f.

briefly, adv. brièvement

briefness, n. brièveté f.

brigade, n. brigade f.

bright, adj. brillant

brighten, vb. faire briller

brightness, n. éclat m.

brilliance, n. brillant, éclat m.

brilliant, adj. brillant

brim, n. bord m.

bring, vb. apporter, amener, porter

brink, n. bord m.

brisk, adj. vif

brisket, n. poitrine

briskly, adv. vivement

briskness, n. vivacité f.

bristle, n. soie f.

British, adj. britannique

brittle, adj. fragile

broad, adj. large

broadcast, adj. radiodiffusé

broadcaster, n. speaker m.

broadly, adv. largement

brocaded, adj. de brocart

broil, vb. griller

broiler, n. gril m.

broker, n. courtier m.

brokerage, n. courtage m.

bronchitis, n. bronchite f.

bronze, n. bronze m.

brooch, n. broche f.

brood, n. couvée f.; vb. couver

brook, n. ruisseau m.

broom, n. balai m.

broth, n. bouillon m.

brother, n. frère m.

brotherhood, n. fraternité f.

brotherly, adj. fraternel

brown, adj. brun

browse, vb. brouter; feuilleter

bruise, n. meurtrissure f.; vb. meurtrir

brunette, adj. and n. brune f.

brunt, n. choc m.

brush, n. brosse f.

brushwood, n. broussailles f., pl.

brutality, n. brutalité f.

brutalize, vb. abrutir

brute, n. brute f.

bubble, n. bulle f.; vb. bouillonner

buck, n. daim, mâle m.

bucket, n. seau m.

buckle, n. boucle f.

bud, n. bourgeon m.; vb. bourgeonner

budge, vb. bouger

budget, n. budget m.

buffalo, n. buffle m.

buffet, n. buffet m.

buffoon, n. bouffon m.

bug, n. insecte m.

bugle, n. clairon m.

build, vb. bâtir

builder, n. entrepreneur m., constructeur m.

building, n. bâtiment m.

bulb, n. ampoule f., bulbe m.

bulge, n. bosse f.

bulkhead, n. cloison étanche f.

bulky, adj. encombrant

bull, n. taureau m.

bulldog, n. bouledogue m.

bulldozer, n. machine à refouler f.

bullet, n. balle f.

bulletin, n. bulletin m.

bully, n. matamore m.

bulwark, n. rempart m.

bum, n. fainéant m.

bump, n. coup m., bosse f.; vb. cogner

bumper, n. pare-choc m.

bun, n. petit pain rond (au lait) m.

bunch, n. botte f.

bundle, n. paquet m.

bungle, vb. bousiller

bunion, n. oignon m.

bunk, n. couchette f.

bunny, n. lapin m.

bunting, n. drapeaux m., pl.

buoy, n. bouée f.

buoyant, adj. leger, flottant

burden, n. fardeau m.

burdensome, adj. onéreux

bureau, n. bureau m., commode f.

burglar, n. cambrioleur m.

burglarize, vb. cambrioler

burglary, n. vol avec effraction m., cambriolage m.

burial, n. enterrement m.

burly, adj. de forte carrure

burn, vb. brûler

burner, n. bec m., brûleur m.

burning, adj. brûlant

burrow, n. terrier m.

burst, vb. éclater

bury, vb. enterrer

bus, n. autobus m.

bush, n. buisson m.

bushel, n. boisseau m.

bushy, adj. buissonneux

busily, adv. activement

business, n. affaire f.; affaires f., pl.

businesslike, adj. pratique

busy, adj. occupé

but, conj. mais, sauf (except)

butcher, n. boucher m.

butler, n. maître d'hôtel m.

butt, n. bout m.

butter, n. beurre m.

buttercup, n. bouton d'or m.

butterfly, n. papillon m.
buttock, n. fesse f.
button, n. bouton m.
buttonhole, n. boutonnière f.
buttress, n. contrefort m.
buy, vb. acheter
buyer, n. acheteur m.
buzz, n. bourdonnement m.
buzzard, n. buse f.
by, prep. par, près de (near to)
bylaw, n. règlement local m.
by-pass, n. route

C

cab, n. **taxi, fiacre m.**
cabaret, n. **cabaret m.**
cabbage, n. chou m.
cabin, n. cabane, cabine f.
cable, n. cable m.; vb. câbler
cactus, n. cactus m.
cad, n. goujat m.
café, n. café m.
caffeine, n. caféine f.
cage, n. cage f.
cake, n. gâteau m.
calamity, n. calamité f.
calcium, n. calcium m.
calculable, adj. calculable
calculate, vb. calculer
calculus, n. calcul m.
calendar, n. calendrier m.
calf, n. veau m.
caliber, n. calibre m.
calico, n. calicot m.
call, n. appel m.,
   visite f.; vb. **appeler,**
   faire visite à
calligraphy, n. calligraphie f.
calling, n. vocation, profession f.
callousness, n. insensibilité f.
callow, adj. blanc-bec
callus, n. callosité f.
calm, adj. calme; vb. calmer
calmly, adv. avec calme
calmness, n. tranquilité f.
caloric, adj. calorique
calore, n. calorie f.

calumniate, vb. calomnier
Calvary, n. Calvaire m.
calve, vb. vêler
calyx, n. calice m.
camel, n. chameau m.
camellia, n. camélia m.
cameo, n. camée m.
camera, n. appareil m.
camouflage, vb. camoufler
camp, n. camp, camping m.; vb. camper
campaign, n. campagne f.
camper, n. campeur m.
campus, n. terrains d'un collège or d'une université m., pl.
can, n. boîte f., bidon m.; vb. pouvoir
Canada, n. le Canada m.
canal, n. canal m.
canapé, n. canapé m.
canary, n. serin m.
cancel, vb. annuler, biffer
cancellation, n. annulation f.
cancer, n. cancer m.
candelabrum, n. candélabre m.
candid, adj. sincère
candidate, n. candidat m.
candidly, adv. franchement
candidness, n. candeur f.
candied, adj. candi
candle, n. bougie f.
candlestick, n. chandelier m.
candour, n. sincérité f
candy, n. bonbon m.
cane, n. canne f.
canine, adj. canin
canister, n. boîte à thé f.
canker, n. chancre m.
canned, adj. conservé en boites
cannery, n. conserverie f.
cannibal, n. cannibale m.f.
cannon, n. canon, m.
cannonade, n. canonnade f.
canny, adv. avisé, rusé
canoe, n. canot m.

canon, n. chanoine m., canon (rule) m.
canonical, adj. canonique
canonize, vb. canoniser
canopy, n. dais m.
can't, vb. ne pas pouvoir
cantaloup, n. melon m., cantaloup m.
canteen, n. cantine f., bidon m
canter, n. petit galop f.; vb. aller au petit galop
canvas, n. toile f.
canvass, n. solicitation f.; vb. solliciter
canyon, n. gorge f., défilé m.
cap, n. bonnet m., casquette f.
capability, n. capacité f.
capable, adj. capable
capably, adv. capablement
capacity, n. capacité f.
cape, n. bond m., câpre f.; vb. bondir
capital, n. capital m., capitale f.
capitalism, n. capitalisme m.
capitalization, n. capitalisation f.
capitalize, vb. capitaliser
capon, n. capon m.
capsule, n. capsule f.
captain, n. capitaine m.
captivate, vb. captiver
captive, adj. and n. captif m
captivity, n. captivité f.
capture, n. capture f.; vb. capturer
car, n. voiture f., wagon m.
carafe, n. carafe f.
caramel, n. caramel m.
carat, n. carat m.
caravan, n. caravane f.
caraway, n. carvi, cumin m
carbohydrate, n. carbohydrate m.
carbon, n. carbone m.
carbon dioxide, n. acide carbo-

nique m.

carbon monoxide, n. oxyde de
carbone m.

carbon paper, n. papier carbone m.

carburetor, n. carburateur m.

card, n. carte f.

cardboard, n. carton m.

cardiac, adj. cardiaque

cardigan, n. gilet de tricot m.

cardinal, n. cardinal m.

care, n. souci m.; attention f.; prendre soin de.; vb soucier de

career, n. carrière f.

carefree, adj. insouciant

careful, adj. soigneux

carefully, adv. soigneusement

carefulness, n. soin m., attention f.

careless, adj. insouciant

caress, n. caresse f.; vb. caresser

cargo, n. cargaison

caries, n. carie f.

carillon, n. carillon m.

carload, n. voiturée f.

carnal, adj. charnel

carnation, n. incarnat m.

carol, n. noël m.

carpenter, n. charpentier m.

carpet, n. tapis m.

carpeting, n. pose de tapis f.

carriage, n. voiture f., maintien m., transport m.

carrier, n. porteur m., messager m.

carrot, n. carotte m.

carrousel, n. carrousel m.

carry, vb. porter, continuer, exécuter

cart, n. **charrette f.**

cartel, n. cartel m.

carter, n. charretier m.

cartilage, n. cartilage m.

carton, n. carton m.

cartoon, n. dessin satirique

m.

carve, vb. sculpter, découper

carver, n. découpeur m., sculp- teur m.

carving, n. découpage m., sculpture f.

cascade, n. cascade f.

case, n. cas m., cause f., caisse f., eui m., en tout cas (in any case)

cash, n. espèces f., pl.; (C.O.D.) livraison contre remboursement f.

cashier, n. caissier m.

cashmere, n. cachemire m.

casino, n. casino m.

cask, n. tonneau m.

casket, n. cassette f.

casserole, n. casserole f.

cassette, n. cassette f.

cast, n. coup m., trempe f., distribution f., **moulage m.**

castaway, n. naufragé m., reje-té m.

caste, n. caste f.

caster, n. fondeur m.

castle, n. château m.

castoff, adj. abondonné

casual, adj. casuel, insouciant

casualness, n. nonchalance f.

casualties, n. pertes f., pl.

cat, n. chat m., chatte f.

cataclysm, n. cataclysme m.

catacomb, n. catacombe f.

catalogue, n. catalogue m.

cataract, n. cataracte f.

catastrophe, n. catastrophe f.

catch, vb. attraper, saisir

catcher, n. qui attrape

catchy, adj. facile à retenir

categorical, adj. catégorique

category, n. catégorie f.

cater, vb. pourvoir (à)

caterpillar, n. chenille f.

catgut, n. corde à boyau f.

cathedral, n. cathédrale f.

Catholicism, n. catholicisme m.

catsup, n. sauce piquante f.

cattle, n. bétail m., bestiaux m., pl.

cattleman, n. éleveur de bétail m.

cauliflower, n. choufleur m.

cause, n. cause f.

causeway, n. chaussée f.

caution, n. prudence f.

cautious, adj. prudent

cavalier, adj. and n. cavalier m.

cavalry, n. cavalerie f.

cave, n. caverne f.

cavern, n. caverne f.

caviar, n. caviar m.

cavity, n. cavité f.

cease, vb. cesser (de)

cedar, n. cèdre m.

ceiling, n. plafond m.

celebrant, n. célébrant

celebrate, vb. célébrer

celebration, n. célébration f.

celebrity, n. célébrité f.

celery, n. céleri m.

celestial, adj. céleste

celibacy, n. célibat m.

cell, n. cellule f.

cellar, n. cave f.

cellophane, n. cellophane f.

cellular, adj. cellulaïre

cellulose, n. cellulose f.

cement, n. ciment m.; vb. cimenter

cemetery, n. cimetière m.

censor, n. censeur m.; vb. censurer

censorship, n. censure f.

censure, n. censure f.

census, n. recensement m.

cent, n. cent

center, n. centre m.

centerfold, n. pages centrales f., pl.

centerpiece, n. pièce de milieu f.

centigrade, adj. centigrade

centigrade thermometer, n. thermomètre centigrade m.

central, adj. central

centralize, vb. centraliser

century, n. siècle m.

ceramic, adj. céramique

ceramics, n. céramique f.

cereal, adj. and n. céréale f.

cerebral, adj. cérébral

ceremonial, adj. and n. cérémonial m.

ceremony, n. cérémonie f.

certain, adj. certain

certainly, adv. certainement

certainty, n. certitude f.

certificate, n. certificat m.; acte de naissance

certification, n. certification f.

certified, adj. certifié, diplôme, breveté

certifier, n. qui certifie

certify, vb. certifier

certitude, n. certitude f.

cervical, adj. cervical

cervix, n. cervix m.

cessation, n. cessation, suspension f.

cession, n. cession f.

cesspool, n. fosse d'aisances f.

chafing dish, n. réchaud m.

chagrin, n. chagrin m.

chain, n. chaîne f.

chair, n. chaise f., **fauteuil m.**

chairman, n. président m.

chairperson, n. président m., présidente f.

chairwoman, n. présidente f.

chalice, n. calice m.

chalk, n. craie f.

challenge, vb. défier, contester

challenger, n. qui fait un défi, prétendant m.

chamber, n. chambre f.

chamberlain, n. chambellan m.

champ, vb. ronger, mâcher

champion, n. champion m.

championship, n. championnat m.

chance, n. chance f., par hasard m.

chancel, n. sanctuaire, choeur m.

chancellor, n. chancelier m.

chandelier, n. lustre m.

change, n. chagement m.

changeable, adj. changeant

changer, n. changeur m.

channel, n. canal m.

chant, n. chant m.; vb. chanter

chaos, n. chaos m.

chap, n. gercure f., gars m.

chapel, n. chapelle f.

chaperon, n. duègne f.; chaperon m.

chaplain, n. aumônier m.

chapter, n. chapitre m.

character, n. caractère, personnage, rôle m.

characterize, vb. caractériser

charcoal, n. charbon (m.) de bois

charge, n. charge f. prix, soin m.; vb. charger, charger de; demander

charger, n. grand plat, cheval de bataille m.

charitable, adj. charitable

charitably, adv. charitablement

charity, n. charité f.

charm, n. charme m. vb. charmer

charmer, n. charmeur, enchanteur m.

charming, adj. charmant

charred, adj. carbonisé

chart, n. carte f.; grapique m.

chase, n. chasse f.; vb. chasser

chaser, n. chasseurm., ciseleur m.

chasm, n. abime m.

chassis, n. chassis m.

chaste, adj. chaste

chastise, vb. châtier

chastity, n. chasteté f.

chat, n. causette f.; vb. causer

chateau, n. château m.

chattel, n. bien, meuble m.

chatter, n. vavardate m.; vb. vavarder

chatterbox, n. vavard m.

chauffeur, n. chauffeur m.

cheap, adj. bon marché, de peu de valeur

cheapen, vb. déprécier

cheapness, n. bon **marché m., bas prix m., basse qualité f.**

cheat, vb. tromper, tricher

cheater, n. tricheur, trompeur m.

check, n. frein m., vérification f., ticket m., addition f., chèque

checker, n. enregistreur m., contrôleur m.

cheek, n. joue f.

cheerfully, adv. gaiement, de bon coeur

cheerfulness, n. gaieté f., bonne humeur f.

cheerless, adj. triste, morne, sombre

cheery, adj. gai, joyeux

cheese, n. fromage m.

cheesecloth, n. gaze f.

chemical, adj. chimique

chemically, adv. chimiquement

chemist, n. chimiste m.f.

chemistry, n. chimie f.

chemotherapy, n. chimiothérapie f.

chenille, n. chenille f.

cherish, vb. chérir

cherry, n. cerise f.

chess, n. échecs m., pl.

chessman, n. pièce f.

chest, n. coffre m., **poitrine f.**

chestnut, n. châtaigne f.

chevron, n. chevron m.

chew, vb. mâcher

chic, adj. chic

chick, n. poussin m.

chicken, n. poulet m.

chicken-pox, n. varicelle f.

chicle, n. chiclé m.

chief, n. chef m.; adj. principal

chiefly, adv. surtout, principalement

chieftain, n. chef de clan m.

chiffon, n. chiffon m.

chilblain, n. engelure f.

child, n. enfant m.f.

childbirth, n. enfantement m.

childhood, n. enfance f.

childish, adj. enfantin

childlessness, n. puérilité f., enfantillage m.

childlike, adj. comme un enfant, en enfant

Chile, n. le Chili m.

chili, n. piment m.

chill, n. froid m., frisson m. vb. refroidir

chilly, adj. un peu froid

chime, n. carillon m.; vb. carillonner

chimney, n. cheminée f.

chimpanzee, n. chimpanzé m.

chin, n. menton m.

China, n. la Chine f.

china, n. porcelaine f.

chinchilla, n. chinchilla m.

chintz, n. perse f.

chip, n. éclat m., frites f., pl.

chipmunk, n. tamias m.

chiropractor, n. chiropracteur m.

chirp, vb. pépier, gazouiller

chisel, vb. ciseler; n. ciseau m.

chivalry, n. chevalerie f.

chive, n. ciboulette f.

chlorine, n. chlore m.

chocolate, n. chocolat m.

choice, n. choix m.

choir, n. choeur m.

choke, vb. étouffer

choker, n. foulard m.

choose, vb. choisir

chop, n. côtelette f.; vb. couper

chopper, n. couperet m.

chopstick, n. baguette f., bâtonnet m.

choral, adj. choral

chord, n. accord m.

chorus, n. choeur m.

christen, vb. baptiser

christening, n. baptême m.

Christian, adj. and n. chrétien m.

Christianity, n. christianisme m.

Chirstmas, n. Noël m.

chronic, adj. chronique

chronicle, n. chronique f.

chronological, adj. chronologique

chrysalis, n. chrysalide f.

chrysanthemum, n. chrysanthème m.

chubby, adj. joufflu

chuckle, vb. rire tout bas

chum, n. camarade, copain m.

chummy, adj. familier, intime

chunk, n. gros morceau m.

chunky, adj. en gros morceaux

church, n. église f.

churchman, n. homme d'église m., ecclésiastique m.

churchyard, n. cimetière m.

churn, vb. baratter

chute, n. glissière f.

chutney, n. chutney m.

cicada, n. cigale f.

cider, n. cidre m.

cigar, n. cigare m.

cigarette, n. cigarette f.

cilia, n. cils m., pl.

ciliary, adj. ciliaire

cinch, n. c'est facile

cinchona, n. quinquina m.

cinder, n. cendre f.

cinema, n. cinéma m.

cinematic, adj. cinematographique

cinnamon, n. cannelle f.

cipher, n. chiffre m., zéro m.

circle, n. cercle m.; vb. entourer (de)

circuit, n. circuit m.

circular, adj. circulaire

circulation, n. circulation f.

circulator, n. circulateur m.

circumcise, vb. circoncire

circumcision, n. circoncision f.

circumference, n. circonférence f.

circumscribe, vb. circonscrire

circumstance, n. circonstance f., moyens m., pl.

circus, n. cirque m.

citation, n. citation f.

cite, vb. citer

citizen, n. citoyen m.

citizenry, n. touse les citoyens m., pl.

citizenship, n. droit de cité

citric acid, n. acide citrique m.

city, n. ville f., cité f.

civic, adj. civique

civil, adj. civil, poli, (civil servant) fonctionnaire m.

civilization, n. civilisation f.

civilize, vb. civiliser

clad, adj. habilié, vêtu

claim, n. demande f., droit m.; vb. demander

clairvoyance, n. clairvoyance f.

clairvoyant, n. voyant m.

clam, n. palourde f., mollusque m.

clamber, vb. grimper

clammy, adj. visqueux, moite

clamor, n. clameur f.

clamorous, adj. bruyant

clan, n. clan m., clique f.

clap, vb. (applaud) applaudir

clapboard, n. bardeau m.

clapper, n. claqueur m., battant (of a bell) m.

claque, n. claque f.

claret, n. vin rouge de Bordeaux m.

clarify, vb. (lit.) clarifier; (fig.) éclaircir

clarinet, n. clarinette f.

clarion, n. clairon m.

clarity, n. clarté f.

clash, vb. choquer, s' entrechoquer; n. choc m.

clasp, n. agrafe, étreinte f.; vb. agrafer, étreindre

class, n. classe f.

classification, n. classification f.

classify, vb. classifier, classer

classroom, n. salle de classe f.

clatter, n. burit m.

clause, n. clause f.

claw, n. griffe f.

claw-hammer, n. marteau à dent m.

clay, n. argile, glaise f.

clean, adj. propre; vb. nettoyer

clean-cut, adj. net, fin

cleanse, vb. nettoyer, curer

cleanser, n. chose qui nettoie f., détersif, cureur m.

clear, adj. clair, net, lucide

clearing, n. éclaircissement m.

clearly, adv. clairement, nettement

clearness, n. clarté f., neteté f.

cleat, n. fer m., (naut.) taquet m.

cleavage, n. fendage m., scisson f.

cleaver, n. fendeur m., fendoir m., couperet m.

cleft, n. fente f.

clemency, n. clémence f.

clench, vb. serrer

clergy, n. clergé m.

clergyman, n. ecclésiastique m.

clerical, adj. clerical, de bureau

clerk, n. employé m., commis m.

clever, adj. habile

cleverness, n. adresse f.

clew, n. fil m.

cliché, n. cliché m.

click, n. cliquetis m., déclic m.; vb. cliqueter

client, n. client m.

cliff, n. falaise f.

climax, n. comble m.

climb, n. montée f.; vb. monter, grimper

climber, n. grimpeur m., ascensioniste m.

clinch, vb. river; conclure

cling, vb. s'accrocher

clinic, n. clinique f.

clip, vb. couper; n. pince f.

clipping, n. coupure f.

clique, n. clique f.

clock, n. (large) horloge f., (small) pendule f.

clockwise, adv. dans le sens des aiguilles d'une montre

clockwork, n. mouvement d'horlogerie m.

clod, n. motte de terre f.

clog, b. entraver

clone, n. reproduction exacte f.

close, adj. clos, bien fermé

closely, adv. de près, étroitement

closeness, n. proximité, exactitude f.

closet, n. cabinet, **boudoir m.**

clot, n. caillot m.

cloth, n. étoffe f.

clothe, vb. vêtir, habiller

clothes, n. habits m., pl.

clothespin, n. pince f.

clothier, n. drapier m. tailleur m.

clothing, n. vêtements m.,

pl.

cloud, n. nuage m.

cloudburst, n. rafale de pluie f.

cloudless, adj. sans nuage

cloudy, adj. nuageux, couvert

clout, n. morceau m., piece f.

clove, n. clou de girofle m.

clover, n. trèfle m.

clown, n. bouffon m.

cloy, vb. rassasier

club, n. massues f., **cercle m.**

clubfoot, n. pied bot m.

clue, n. fil m.

clumsy, adj. gauche

cluster, n. groupe m., grappe f., bouquet m.; vb. se grouper

clutch, n. griffe f., embrayage m.

clutter, vb. encombrer

coach, n. carrosse m., voiture f.

coal, n. charbon m., houille f.

coalition, n. coalition f.

coarse, adj. grossier

coarseness, n. gorssièreté f.

coast, n. côte f.

coastal, adj. de la côte, littoral

coaster, n. caboteur m., dessous de carage m.

coast guard, n. gardecôtes m.

coat, n. habit; m. couche f.

coating, n. couche f., enduit m., étoffe pour **habits f.**

coax, vb. cajoler

cobalt, n. cobalt m.

cobblestone, n. pierre du pavé f.

cobra, n. cobra m.

cobweb, n. toile d'araignée f

cocaine, n. cocaine f.

cockroach, n. blatte f.

cocky, adj. suffisant

cocoa, n. cacao m.

cocoon, n. cocon m.

cod, n. morue f.

coddle, vb. dorloter

code, n. code m.

codeine, n. codéine f.

codfish, n. morue f.

coerce, vb. contraindre

coffee, n. café m.

coffin, n. cercueil m.

cog, n. dent f.

coherent, adj. cohérent

coiffure, n. coiffure f.

coin, n. pièce de monnaie

coincide, vb. coïncider

coincidence, n. coïncidence f.

coincident, adj. coïncident

colander, n. passoire f.

cold, n. froid m., rhume m.

cold-blooded, adj. de sang froid

coldness, n. froideur f.

collaborate, vb. collaborer

collapse, vb. s'effrondrer, s'affaisser

collar, n. col m.; (dog) collier m.

collarbone, n. clavicule f.

collate, vb. collationner, comparer

collation, n. collation f., comparaison f., repas froid m.

colleague, n. collègue m., f.

collect, vb. rassembler

collection, n. collection, collecte f.

collective, adj. collectif

collectively, adv. collectifement

collector, n. collectionneur m., contrôleur m.

college, n. collège m., université f.

collegiate, adj. de collège, collégial

collide, vb. se heurter

collision, n. collision f.

collusion, n. collusion f., con-

nivence f.

colon, n. deux points m., pl.

colonel, n. colonel m.

colonial, adj. colonial

colonist, n. colon m.

colonization, n. colonisation f.

colonize, vb. coloniser

colony, n. colonie f.

color, n. couleur f.

colored, adj. coloré, de couleur, colorie

colorful, adj. coloré, pittoresque

coloring, n. coloris m., couleur f.

colossal, adj. colossal

colt, n. poulain m.

colter, n. coutre m.

column, n. colonne f.

coma, n. com m.

comb, n. peigne m.

combat, n. combat m.

combination, n. combinaison f.

combustible, adj. and n. combustible m.

combustion, n. combustion f.

come, vb. venir; arriver; recontrer; partir; revenir; descendre; entrer

comedian, n. comédien m.

comedy, n. comédie f.

comely, adj. avenant

comet, n. comète f.

comfort, n. consolation f., confort m.

comfortable, adj. commode, confortable

comforter, n. consolateur m.

comfortless, adj. sans consolation, inconsolable, désolé

coming, n. venue, arrivée, approche f.

comma, n. virgule f.

command, n. commandement m.

commandeer, vb.

réquisitioner

commemorate, vb. commémorer

commemorative, adj. commémoratif

commence, vb. commencer

commencement, n. commencement, début

commend, vb. recommander, louer

commendable, adj. louable, recommandable

comment, n. commentaire m.

commerce, n. commerce m.

commercial, adj. commercial

commission, n. commission; perpétration f.

commissioner, n. commissaire m.

commit, vb. commettre

commitment, n. engagement m.

committee, n. comité m.

commodity, n. produit m., commodité f., denrée f.

common, adj. commun, vulgaire

commonly, adv. communément, ordinairement

commonplace, n. lieu-commun m.

commonwealth, n. état m.

communicate, vb. communiquer

communication, n. communication f.

communion, n. communion f.

community, n. communauté f.

commuter, n. voyageur de banlieue m.

compact, adj., serré, compact

compactness, n. compacité f.

companion, n compagnon m., compagne f.

m., compagne f.

companionship, n. camaraderie f.

company, n. compagnie f.

comparable (with,) adj.
comparable (à)

comparatively, adv. com-
parativement, relative-
ment

compare, vb. comparer

comparison, n. comparaison f.

compartment, n. compartiment m.

compass, n. (naut.) boussole
f.; (geom.) compas m.

compassion, n. compassion f.

compassionate, adj. compatissant

compatible, adj. compatible

compel, vb. forcer

compensate, vb. compenser

compensation, n. compensation f.

compete, vb. rivaliser

competence, n.
compétence f.

competent, adj. capable

competently, adv. conven-
ablement, avec
compétence

competition, n. concurrence f.

competitor, n. concurrent m.

compile, vb. compiler

complacency, n. contentement m.

complacent, adj. content de
soi-même

complacently, adv. avec un
air (un ton) suffisant

complain, vb. se plaindre

complainer, n. plaignant m.,
réclameur m.

complainingly, adv. d'une
manière plaignante

complaint, n. plainte f.

complement, n.
complément m.

complete, adj. complet

completely, adv.
complètement, tout à fait

completeness, n. état complet m., perfection f.

completion, n.
achèvement m.

complex, adj. and n. com-
plexe m.

complexion, n. teint m.

complexity, n. com-
plexité f.

compliance, n. acquiesce-
ment m.

compliant, adj. complaisant,
accommodant

complicate, vb. compliquer

complicity, n. complicité f.

compliment, n . compliment m.

complimentary, adj. flat-
teur, de félicitations

component, adj. and n.
composant m.

comport, vb. s'accorder
(avec)

compose, vb. composer

composer, n. composi-
teur m.

composite, adj. composé

composition, n. composition f.

compost, n. compost m.,
terreau m.

composure, n. calme m.,
tranquilité f.,
slang-froid m.

compound, n. composé m.,
composition f.

comprehend, vb. comprendre

comprehensible, adj.
compréhen- sible, inteligi-
ble

comprehension, n.
compréhension f.

comprehensive, adj.
compréhensif

compress, n. compresse f.

compressed, adj. comprimé

compression, n. compres-

sion f.

compressor, n. com-
presseur m

comprise, vb. comprendre

compromiser, n. compro-
metteur m.

compulsion, n. contrainte f.

compulsive, adj. coercitif,
obligatoire

compulsory, adj. obligatoire

compunction, n. componc-
tion f.

computation, n. supputa-
tion f.

compute, vb. supputer

computer, n. ordinateur m.

computerize, vb. informa-
tiser

computer science, n. infor-
matique f.

comrade, n. camarade m.f.

concave, adj. concave

conceal, vb. cacher

concede, vb. concéder

conceivably, adv. d'une
manière concevable

conceive, vb. concevoir

concentrate, vb. concentre

concept, n. concept m.

conception, n. conception f

concern, n. affxiété, intérêt
soin, souci m.

concerning, prep. concer-
nant

concert, n. concert m.

concession, vb. concession f.

concise, adj. concis

concisely, adv. avec concision, succinctement

conciseness, n. concision f.

conclave, n. conclave m.

conclude, vb. conclure

conclusion, n. conclusion f

conclusive, adj. concluant

concord, n. concorde f.

concordat, n. concordat m

concourse, n. councours m
affluence f.

concrete, n. béton m.

concur, vb. concourir, être

d'accord

oncurrence, m. assentiment m.

oncurrent, adj. concourant

ondemn, vb. condamner

ondemnable, adj. condamnable

ondensation, n. condensation f.

ondense, vb. condenser

ondenser, n. condenseur m.

ndiment, n. condiment m., assaisonnement m.

ndition, n. condition f.

nditional, adj. and n. conditionnel m.

nditionally, adv. conditionanellement

ndolence, n. condoléance f.

ndominium, n. condominium m.

nducive, adj. favorable

nduct, n. conduite f.

nductivity, n. conductivité f.

nductor, n. conducteur, receveur (d'orchestre) m.

nduit, n. conduit, tuyau m.

ne, n. cône m.

nfection, n. confection f.;(sweet) bonbon m.

nfectioner, n. confiseur m.

nfectionery, n. confiserie f.

nfederate, adj. and n. confédéré m.

nfer, vb. conférer

nference, n. entretien m.

nfess, vb. avouer

nfession, n. confession f.

nfessional, n. confessional m.

nfessor, n. confesseur m.

nfetti, n. confetti m.

nfidant, n. confident m.

nfidence, n. confiance f.

nfident, adj. confiant

confidently, adv. avec confiance

confine, vb. confiner; limiter

confirm, vb. confirmer

confirmation, n. confirmation f.

confirmed, adj. invétéré, incorrigible

confiscate, vb. confisquer

conflagration, n. conflagration f., incendie m.

conflict, n. conflit m.

conform, vb. conformer

conformation, n. conformation, conformité f.

conformer, n. conformiste m.

conformist, n. conformiste m.

conformity, n. conformité f.

confront, vb. confronter

confuse, vb. confondre

confusion, n. confusion f.

congenial, adj. sympathique, convenable

congential, adj. congénital

congestion, n. (med.) congestion f.; (traffic) encombrement m.

congratulate, vb. féliciter de

congratulation, n. félicitation f.

congregate, vb. rassembler

congregation, n. assemblée f.

congress, n. congrès m.

conjecture, n. conjecture f.

conjunction, n. conjonction f.

conjunctive, adj. conjonctif

connect, vb. joindre

connection, n. connexion f.

conquer, vb. conquérir

conqueror, n. conquérant m.

conquest, n. conquête f.

conscience, n. conscience f.

conscious, adj. conscient

consciously, adv. sciem-

ment, en parfaite connaissance

consciousness, n. conscience f.

conscript, adj. and n. conscrit m.

conscription, n. conscription f.

consecrate, vb. consacrer

consecration, n. consécration f.

consecutive, adj. consécutif

consecutively, adv. consécutivement, de suite

consensus, n. consensus m., assentiment général m.

consent, n. consentement m.

consequence, n. conséquence f.

consequent, adj. conséquent

consequential, adj. conséquent, logique

consequently, adv. par conséquent

conservation, n. conservation f.

conservatism, n. conservatisme m.

conservative, adj. conservateur

conservatively, adv. d'une manière conservatrice

conservatory, n. conservatoire m.

conserve, vb. conserver

consider, vb. considérer

considerable, adj. considérable

considerably, adv. considérablement

considerate, adj. plein d'égards

considerately, adv. avec égards, avec indulgence

consideration, n. considération f.

considering, prep. vu que, attendu que

consign, vb. consigner

consignment, n. expédition, consignation f.

consistency, n. consistance f.

consistent, adj. consistant

consolation, n. consolation f.

console, vb. consoler

consolidate, vb. consolider

consonant, n. consonne f.

conspicuous, adj. en évidence

conspiracy, n. conspiration f.

conspirator, n. conspirateur m.

conspire, vb. conspirer

constant, adj. constant

constipation, n. constipation f.

constituent, adj. constituant

constitute, vb. constituer

constitution, n. constitution f.

constrain, vb. contraindre

constraint, n. contrainte f.

constrict, vb. resserrer

construct, vb. construire

construction, n. construction f.

constructive, adj. constructif

constructor, n. constructeur m.

consul, n. consul m.

consult, vb. consulter

consultation, n. consultation f.

consume, vb. consumer

consumer, n. consommateur m.

consummate, adj. consommé

consumption, n. consommation; (med.) phtisie f.

consumptive, adj. poitrinaire, tuberculeux

contact, n. contact m.

contagious, adj. contagieux

contain, vb. contenir

container, n. récipient m.

contaminated, adj. contaminé

contemplation, n. contemplation f.

contemplative, adj. contemplatif

contemporary, adj. contemporain

contempt, n. mépris m.

contemptuous, adj. méprisant

contend, vb. lutter, soutenir

contender, n. compétiteur m., concurrent m.

content, n. contentement m.

contention, n. contention, lutte f.

contentment, n. contentement m.

contest, n. lutte f., concours m. contestant, n. concurrent m.

context, n. contexte m.

contiguous, adj. contigu

continent, adj. and n. continent m.

continental, adj. continental

contingency, n. contingence f.

contingent, adj. contingent

continuation, n. continuation f.

continue, vb. continuer

continuous, adj. continu

continouously, adv. continûment, sans interruption

contort, vb. tordre, défigurer

contour, n. contour m.

contraband, n. contrebande f.

contraception, n. procédés anticonceptionnels m., pl.

contract, n. contrat m.

contracted, adj. contracté, resserré

contraction, n. contraction f.

contractor, n. entrepreneur m.

contradict, vb. contredire

contradictable, adj. qui peut

être contredit

contradiction, n. contradiction f., démenti m.

contraption, n. machin m.

contrast, n. contraste m.

contribute, vb. contribuer

contribution, n. contribution f.

contributor, n. contribuant m.

contributory, adj. contribuant

contrite, adj. contrit, pénitent

contrition, n. contrition f.

contrive, vb. inventer, imaginer, arranger

control, n. autorité f.

controllable, adj. vérifiabl gouvernable

controller, n. contrôleur m

controversy, n. controverse f.

contusion, n. contusion f.

convalescence, n. convalecence f.

convalescent, adj. convale cent

convenience, n. convenance f., commodité f.

convenient, adj. commode

convent, n. couvent m.

conventional, adj. conven tionnel

converge, vb. converger

convergent, adj. converge

conversation, n. conversation f.

converse, vb. converser

convert, vb. convertir

converter, n. convertis seur m.

convertible, adj. convertible, convertissable

convex, adj. convexe

convey, vb. transporter, transmettre

conveyance, n. transport

convict, n. forçat m.; vb. condamner

conviction, n. conviction

persuasion f.

convince, vb. convaincre

convincing, adj. convain-
cant

convicingly, adv. d'une
manière confaincante

convival, adj. jovial, joyeux

convocation, n. convoca-
tion f.

convoy, n. convoi m.

convulsion, n. convulsion f.

convulsive, adj. convulsif

cook n. cuisinier m.; vb.
cuire, intr. faire cuire

cookbook, n. livre de cuisine m.

cookie, n. gâteau sec m.

cool, adj. frais m., fraîche f.

cooler, n. rafraîchissoir m.

coolness, n. fraîcheur f.

co-operate, vb. coopérer

co-operation, n.
coopération f.

co-operative, n. coopérative
f. adj. coopératif

co-ordiante, vb. coordonner

co-ordination, n. coordination f.

cop, n. flic m.; vb. attraper,
pincer

copier, n. machine à
copier f.

copious, adj. copieux

copper, n. cuivre m.

copy, n. copie f.; vb. copier

copyright, n. droit d'auteur
m., pl.

coquette, n. coquette f.

coral, n. corail m., pl.
coraux

cord, n. corde f.

cordial, adj. and n. cor-
dial m.

cordiality, n. cordialité f.

cordially, adv. cordialement

cordon, n. cordon m.

corduroy, n. velours
côtelé m.

core, n. coeur m.

cork, n. liège, bouchon m.

corkscrew, n. tire-bouchon

m.

corn, n. maïs m.

cornea, n. cornée f.

corner, n. coin m.

cornerstone, n. pierre angulaire f.

cornet, n. cornet m.

cornice, n. corniche f.

coronary, adj. coronaire

coronation, n. couron-
nement m.

coroner, n. coroner m.

coronet, n. (petite)
couronne f.

corporal, n. (mil.) capo-
ral m.

corporate, adj. de corporation

corporation, n. corpora-
tion f.

corps, n. corps m.

corpse, n. cadavre m.

corpulent, adj. corpulent,
gros

corpuscle, n. corpuscule m.

corral, n. corral m.

correct, adj. correct; vb.
corriger

correction, n. correction f.

corrective, adj. de correction, correctif

correctly, adv. correctment,
justement

correctness, n. correction f.

correlate, vb. être en
corrélation; intr. mettre en
corrélation

correspond, vb. corre-
spondre

correspondence, n corre-
spondance f.

correspondent, n. corre-
spondant m.

corridor, n. couloir m.

corrode, vb. corroder

corrosion, n. corrosion f.

corrugate, vb. rider, plisser

corrupt, adj. corrompu; vb.
corrompre

corruptible, adj. corruptible

corruption, n. corruption f.

corruptive, adj. corruptif

corsage, n. corsage m.

corset, n. corset m.

corvette, n. corvette f.

cosmetic, adj. and n.
cosmétique m.

cosmic, adj. cosmique

cosmopolitan, adj. and n.
cosmopolite m.f.

cosmos, n. cosmos m.

cost, n. coût; vb. coûter

costly, adj. coûteux

costume, n. costume m.

costumer, n. costumier m.

cost, n. prix, frais m.

cottage, n. chaumière f.

cotton, n. coton m.

cottonseed, n. graine de
coton f.

couch, n. divan m.

cough, n. toux f.; vb. tousser

could, vb. pouvait, pourrait

council, n. conseil m.

councilman, n. con-
seiller m.

counsel, n. conseil m.; vb.
conseiller

counselor, n. conseiller m.

count, n. compte, comte m.;
vb. compter

counter, n. comptoir m.;
adv. à l'encontre de

counteract, vb. neutraliser

counteraction, n. action
contraire f.

counterfeit, adj. faux m.,
fausse f.; vb. contrefaire

counterpart, n. contre-
partie f.

countess, n. comtesse f.

countless, adj. innombrable

country, n. pays m., cam-
pagne, patrie f.

county, n. comté m.

coupé, n. coupé m.

couple, n. couple f.; vb. coupler

coupon, n. coupon m.

courage, n. courage m.

courageous, adj. courageux

courier, n. courrier m.

course, n. cours m., bien en-
tendu route f., service m.
court, n. cour f.; vb. faire la
cour à
courteous, adj. courtois
courtesy, n. courtoisie f.
courthouse, n. palais de
jusitice m.
courtier, n. courtisan m.
courtroom, n. salle d'audience f.
courtship, n. cour f.
cousin, n. cousin m., cou-
sine f.
covenant, n. pacte m.
cover, vb. couvrir, voiler,
déguise; cacher
coverage, n. couverture f.
covering, n. couvertue f.,
enveloppe f.
covet, vb. convoiter
cow, n. vache f.
coward, n. lâche m.
cower, vb. se blottir
cowhide, n. peau de vache f.
coy, adj. timide
cozy, adj. confortable
crab, n. crabe m.
crab apple, n. pomme
sauvage f.
crack, vb. fendre, fêler,
casser; n. fente, fissure f.
cracked, adj. fendu, fêlé
cracker, n. biscuit m.
cracking, n. craquement,
claquement m.
crackup, n. crach m.
cradle, n. berceau m.
craft, n. habileté f., métier
m., embarcation f.
craftsman, n. artisan m.
craftsmanship, n. habilté,
technique f.
crafty, adj. rusé, astucieux
cram, vb. remplir, farcir
cramp, n. crampe f., cram-
pon m.
cranberry, n. canneberge,
airelle f.
crane, n. grue f.
cranium, n. crâne m.

crank, n. manivelle f.
cranky, adj. d'humeur difficile
crash, n. faire un grand
fracas
crate, n. caisse f.
crater, n. cratère m.
craven, adj. lâche, poltron
craving, n. désir ardent, besoin impérieux m.
crawl, vb. ramper, se trainer
crayon, n. pastel m.
crazed, adj. fou, dément
crazy, adj. fou m. folle f.
cream, n. crème f.
creamy, adj. crémeux, de
crème
crease, n. pli m .; vb.
frois ser
create, vb. créer
creation, n. création f.
creative, adj. créateur m.,
créatrice f.
creator, n. créateur m.,
créatrice f.
creature, n. créature f.
credible, adj. croyable
credit, n. crédit; honneur m.
creditable, adj. estimable
creditably, adv. honorable-
ment
creditor, n. créancier m.
creed, n. croyance f.;
credo m.
creek, n. ruisseau m.
creep, vb. ramper; se glisser
cremate, vb. incinérer
crematory, n.
crématorium m.
crepe, n. crêpe m.
crescent, n. croissant m.
crest, n. crête, f.
crew, n. équipage m.,
équipe f.
crib, n. lit d'enfant m.,
mangeoire f.
cricket, n. (insect) gril-
lon m.
crier, n. crieur, huissier m.
crime, n. crime m.
criminal, adj. criminel

criminology, n. criminolo-
gie f.
crimson, adj. and n.
cramoisi m.
cringe, vb. faire des
courbettes, se lapir, s'humilier
crinkle, n. pli m., sinu-
osité f.
cripple, n. estropié m.; vb.
estropier
crisis, n. crise f.
crisp, adj. cassant, croquan
croustillant
crispness, n. frisure f.
crisscross, adj. and adv. en
trecroisé
critic, n. critique m.
critical, adj. critique
criticism, n. critique f.
criticize, vb. critiquer
critique, n. critique f.
croak, vb. coasser, croasse
crochet, vb. broder au cro
chet; crochet n.
crock, n. pot de terre m.
crockery, n. faënce f.
crocodile, n. crocodile m.
crone, n. vieille femme f.
crony, n. vieux camarade,
compère m.
crook, n. escroc, voleur m
crooked, adj. tortu
croon, vb. chantonner, fre
donner
crop, n. récolte f.
croquette, n. croquette f.
cross, n. croix f.; adj. mat
sade; vb. croiser, se
signer, rayer
crossbreed, n. race
croisée f.
cross-examine, vb. contr
examiner
cross-eye, adj. louche
cross-fertilization, n.
croisement m.
cross-purpose, n. opposi
tion, contradiction f.; r
lentendu m.
cross section, n. coupe

travers f.

crossword puzzle, n. mots croisés m., pl.

crotch, n. fourche f., fourchet m.

crouch, vb. s'accroupir

croup, n. croupe f.; (med.) croup m.

croupier, n. croupier m.

crouton, n. croûton m.

crow, n. corneille f.; chant du coq m.

crowd, n. foule f.

crowded, adj. encombré

crown, n. couronne, calotte f., sommet m.; vb. couronner

crucial, adj. crucial

crucifix, n. crucifix m.

crucifixion, n. crucifixion f.; crucifiement m.

crucify, vb. crucifier

crude, adj. grossier, imparfait, fruste

cruel, adj. cruel

cruise, n. croisière f.

cruiser, n. croiseur m.

crumbs, n. miette, mie f.

crumble, vb. émietter

crunch, vb. croquaer broyer

crusade, n. croisade f.

crush, vb. écraser

crust, n. croûte f.

crutch, n. béquille f.

cry, n. cri m.; vb. crier, pleurer

crying, adj. criant

cryosurgery, n. cryochirurgle f.

crypt, n. crypte f.

crystal, n. cristal m.

crysallize, vb. cristalliser

cub, n. petit m.

Cuba, n. le Cuba m.

Cuban, n. Cubain m.; adj. cubain

cube, n. cube m.

cubic, adj. cubique

cubicle, n. compartiment m., cabine f.

cubic measure, n. mesures de volume f., pl.

cubism, n. cubisme m.

cucumber, n. concombre m.

cud, n. bol alimentaire m.; panse, chique f.

cuddle, vb. serrer

cue, n. réplique f.; mot m.

cuff, n. poignet m.

cuisine, n. cuisine f.

culinary, adj. culinaire, de cuisine

cull, vb. cueillir, recuellir

culprit, n. accusé m., accusée f.

cult, n. culte m.

cultivate, vb. cultiver; adj. cultivable

cultivated, adj. cultivé

cultivation, n. culture f.

cultivator, n. cultivateur m.

cultural, adj. cultural, agricole, culturel

culture, n. culture f.

culvert, n. ponceau, petit aqueduc

cumbersome, adj. encombrant

cunning, n. ruse, adresse, finesse f.

cup, n. tasse, coupe f.; gobelet, godet m.

cupful, n. tasse, pleine tasse f.

cupboard, n. armoire f.

cupel, n. coupelle f.

Cupid, n. Cupidon m.

curable, adj. guérissable, curable

curator, n. conservateur, administrateur m.

curb, n. gourmette f.; bord, frein m. vb. mettre la gourmette à

curd, n. lait caillé, caillé m.; vb. cailler, figer

curdle, vb. cailler

cure, n. guérison f.; remède m.; vb. guérir

curfew, n. couvre-fue m.

curio, n. curiosité f.

curiosity, n. curiosité f.; antiaqaire m.

curious, adj. curieux

curl, n. boucle f.; vb. friser

curling, n. frisure

curly, adj. risé, bouclé

currant, n. groseille f.

currency, n. monnaie f.

current, adj. and n. courant m.

currently, adv. couramment

curriculum, n. programme d'études, plan d'études m.

curry, n. cari m.

curse, n. malédiction f.; juron m., fléau m.; vb. maudire; hurer

cursed, adj. maudit

cursor, n. curseur m.

curt, adj. brusque, bref, sec

curtail, vb. raccourcir

curtain, n. rideau m.; courtine f.

curve, n. courbe f.; vb. courber

cushion, n. clussin m.

cuspidor, n. crachoir m.

custard, n. crème f.

custodian, n. gardien m.

custody, n. garde, détention f.

custom, n. coutume f.

customary, adj. habituel

customer, n. client m.

cute, adj. gentil m., gentille f.

cuticle, n. cuticule f.

cutlery, n. coutellerie f.

cutlet, n. côtelette f.

cutthroat, n. coupe-jarret m.

cutting, n. incision f.; adj. incisif, tranchant

cutty, adj. court

cycle, n. cycle m.; vb. faire de la bicyclette

cyclist, n. cycliste m.

cyclone, n. cyclone m.

cylinder, n. cylindre m.

dab, n. coup léger m.;
tape f.; vb. toucher
légèrement
dad, n. papa m.
daffodil, n. narcisse m.
daily, adj. quotidient, journalier
dainty, adj. délicat, friand
dairy, n. laiterie f.
daisy, n. marguerite f.
dam, n. digue f.
damage, n. dommage m.;
vb. endommager
damp, adj. humide
dampen, vb. humecter
dance, n. danse f.; vb.
danser
dandruff, n. pellicules f., pl.
danger, n. danger m.
dangerous, adj. dangereux
dangle, vb. intr. pendiller
Danish, adj. and n.
danois m.
dare, vb. oser
dark, adj. sombre
darken vb. obscurcir
darling, adj. and n.; chéri m.
dart, n. dard m.; pince f.
dash, n. fougue f.; trait m.;
vb. lancer, détruire, se
précipiter
data, n. données f., pl.
data processing, n. élabora-
tion f.
date, n. date f.; rendezvous m.
daughter, n. fille f.
daughter-in-law, n. belle-
fille f.
daunt, vb. intimider
dauntless, adj. intrépide, in-
domptable
dawn, n. aube f.
day, n. jour m.; journée f.
daylight, n. lumière du
jour f.
daylight-saving time, n.
l'heure d'éte f.
daze, vb. étourdir
deacon, n. diacre m.

dead, adj. mort
dead end, n. cul de sac m.;
impasse f.
deadline, n. ligne de délimi-
tation f.
deadlock, n. impasse f.
deadly, adj. mortel
deaf, adj. sourd
deafen, vb. assourdir
deaf-mute, adj. sourd-muet
deafness, n. surdité f.
dealer, n. marchand m.
dean, n. doyen
dear, adj. and n. cher m.
dearly, adv. chèrement
death, n. mort f.
deathless, adj. impérissable
deathly, adj. mortel
debacle, n. débâcle f.
debase, vb. avilir
debatable, adj. discutable
debate, n. débat m.
debater, n. orateur par-
lemen- taire, argumenta-
teur m.
debentue, n. obligation f.
debiliate, vb. débiliter,
affai- blir
debit, n. débit m.
debonair, adj. courtois et
jovial
debris, n. débris m., pl.
debt, n. dette f.
debtor, n. débiteur m.
debunk, vb. dégonfler
debut, n. deut m.
debutante, n. débutante f.
decade, n. période de dix
ans f.
decadence, n. décadence f.
decaffeinated, adj.
décaféiné
decanter, n. carafe f.
decay, n. décadence f.
deceased, adj. dunt
deceit, n. tromperie f.
deceitful, adj. trompeur
deceive, vb. tromper
deceiver, n. imposteur
December, n. décembre m.

decency, n. décence f.
decent, adj. décent
deception, n. tromperie,
duperie f.
deceptive, adj. décevant,
tromppeur
decide, vb. décider
decided, adj. de_idé,
prononcé
decimal, adj. décimal
decimate, vb. décimer
decipher, vb. déchiffrer
decision, n. décision f.
decisive, adj. décisif
deck, n. pont, paquet m.
declaim, vb. déclamer
declare, vb. déclarer
decline, vb. décliner
decompose, vb. décomposer
decor, n. décor m.
decorate, vb. décorer
decoration, n. décoration f.
decorative, adj. décoratif
decorator, n. décorateur m.
decoy n. leurre m.; vb.
leurrer
decrease, n. diminution
f.; vb. diminuer
dedication, n. dédicace f.
deduce, vb. déduire
deduct, vb. déduire
deduction, n. déduction
deed, n. action f.; (law) acte
notarié m.
deep, adj. profond
deepen, vb. approfondir
deeply, adv. profondément
deer, n. cerf m.
deface, vb. défigurer
default, n. défaut m.
defeat, n. défaite f.; vb.
vaincre
defect, n. défaut m.
defection, n. défection f.
defective, adj. défectueux
defend, vb. défendre
defendant, n. défendeur m.
defender, n. défenseur m.
defense, n. défense f.
defenseless, adj. sans
défense

defensive, adj. défensif
defer, vb. différer, déférer
deference, n. déférence f.
defiant, adj. de défi
deficiency, n. insuffisance f.
deficient, adj. insuffisant
deficit, n. deficit m.
defile, vb. souiller
define, vb. définir
definite, adj. défini
definitely, adv. d'une
    manière derminée
definition, n. définition f.
definitive, adj. définitif
deflate, vb. dégonfler
deflation, n.
    dégonflement m.
deflect, vb. faire dévier,
    détourner
deform, vb. déformer
deformity, n. difformité f.
defraud, vb. frauder
defray, vb. payer
defrost, vb. déglacer
defroster, n. déglaceur m.
deft, adj. adroit
defy, vb. défier
degenerate, vb. dégénérer
degrade, vb. dégrader
degree, n. degré m.
dehydrate, vb. déshydrater
deify, vb. déifier
deign, vb. daigner
dejected, adj. abattu
dejection, n. abattement m.
delay, n. retard m.; vb. re-
    tarder
delegate, n. délégué m.; vb.
    déléguer
delegation, n. délégation f.
delete, vb. rayer, vigger
deliberate, adj. délibéré;
    vb. délibérer
deliberately, adv. de propos
    délibére
deliberation, n.
    délibération f.
deliberative, adj. délibératif
delicacy, n. délicatesse f.
delicate, adj. délicate

delicious, adj. délicieux
delight, n. délices f., pl.; vb.
    enchanter
delightful, adj. charmant
delinquency, n. délit m.
delinquent, adj. and n.
    délinquant m.
delirious, adj. délirant
deliver, vb. délivrer
deliverance, n. délivrance f.
delivery, n. accouchement,
    débit m.; livraison, distri-
    bution f.
delude, vb. tromper
delusion, n. illusion f.
deluxe, adv. de luxe
demand, n. demande f.; vb.
    demander
demean, vb. comporter
demeanor, n. maintien m.
demerit, n. démérite m.
demise, n. décès m., mort f.
demobilize, vb. démobiliser
democracy, n. démocratie f.
democrat, n. démocrate m.f.
demorcratic, adj.
    démocratique
demolish, vb. démolir
demonstrate, vb. dontrer
demonstration, n.
    démonstration f.
demonstrative, adj.
    démonstratif
demonstrator, n.
    démonstrateur m.
demoralize, vb. démoraliser
demote, vb. réduire à un
    grade inférieur
demure, adj. posé, d'une
    modestie affectée
den, n. antre, repaire m.
denial, n. dénégation f.;
    refus m.
Denmark, n. Danemark m.
denominator, n.
    dénominateur m.
denote, vb. dénoter
denounce, vb. dénoncer
dense, adj. dense, bête
density, n. densité f.
dent, n. bosselure f.

dental, adj. dentair, dental
dentist, n. dentiste m.
denture, n. dentier,
    râtelier m.
denude, vb. dénuder
deny, vb. nier
deodorant, n.
    désodorisant m.
deodorize, vb. désodoriser,
    désinfecter
depart, vb. partir, s'en aller,
    quitter
department,n. départe-
    ment, ministère, grand
    magasin m.
deparmental, adj.
    départemental
departure, n. départ m.
dependability, n. confiance
    que l'on inspire f.
dependable, adj. digne de
    confiance
dependence, n. dépendance,
    confiance f.
dependent, adj. dépendant
depict, vb. peindre
depiction, n. description f.
deplorable, adj. déplorable
deplore, vb. déplorer
deport, vb. déporter
deportation, n.
    déportation f.
depose, vb. déposer
deposit, n. dépôt m.; vb.
    déposer
depositor, n. déposant m.
deprecate, vb.
    désapprouver,
    s'opposer à
depreciate, vb. déprécier
depress, vb. abaisser, abattre
depression, n. dépression,
    crise f.;
    abattement m.
depth, n. profoundeur f.
deputy, n. délégué,
derail, vb. dé_ailler
derange, vb. déranger
derive, vb. dériver
dermatology, n. dermatolo-
    gie f.

derrick, n. grue f.

descend, vb. descendre

descendant, n. descendant m.

descent, n. descente f.

describe, vb. décrire

description, n. description f.

desert, n. désert, mérite m.; vb. déserter

deserter, n. déserteur m.

desertion, n. abandon m.; désertion f.

deserve, vb. mériter

deserving, adj. méritoire, de mérite

design, n. dessein, projet m.; vb. dessiner

designate, vb. désigner

designation, n. désignation f.

designer, n. dessinateur m.

designing, adj. intrigant, artificieux

desirable, adj. désirable

desire, n. désir m.; vb. désirer

desist, vb. cesser

desk, n. bureau, pupitre m.

desolate, adj. désolé

despair, n. désespoir m.; vb. désespérer

desperate, adj. désespéré

despicable, adj. méprisable

despise, vb. mépriser

despite, prep. en dépti de

despondent, adj. découragé

despot, n. despote m.

desser, n. desser m.

destination, n. destination f.

destine, vb. destiner

destiny, n. destin m.

destitute, adj. dénué, indigent

destitution, n. destitution f.

destroy, vb. détruire

destroyer, n. destructeur, contre-torpilleur m.

destructible, adj. destructible

destruction, n. destruction f.

destructive, adj. destructif

detach, vb. détacher

detachment, n. détachement m.

detail, n. détail m.

detain, vb. retenir, détenir

detect, vb. découvrir

detection, n. découverte f.

detective, n. agent de la police secrète, roman policier m.

detention, n. détention f.

detergent, n. détersif m.

deteriorate, vb. détériorer

determine, vb. déterminer

determined, adj. déterminé

deterrent, n. and adj. préventif m.

detest, vb. détester

detour, n. détour m.

devastate, vb. dévaster

develop, vb. développer

developer, n. révélateur m.

development, n. développement m.

device, n. expédient m.

devil, n. diable m.

devise, vb. combiner, tramer

devote, vb. consacrer

devotee, n. dévot m.; dévote f.

devotion, n. dévotion f.; dévouement m.

devour, vb. dévorer

devout, adj. dévot

dew, n. rosée f.

dexterity, n. destérité f.

dexterous, adj. adroit

diabetes, n. diabète m.

diagnose, vb. diagnostiquer

diagnosis, n. diagnose f.

diagnostic, adj. diagnostique

diagonally, adv. diagonalement

diagram, n. diagramme m.

dial, n. cadran m.; vb. composer

dialect, n. dialecte m.

dialogue, n. dialogue m.

diameter, n. diamètre m.

diamond, n. diamant m.

diaper, n. couche f.

diaphragm, n. diaphragme m.

diarrhea, n. diarrhée f.

diary, n. journal m.

dice, n. dés m., pl.

dictaphone, n. machine à dicter f.

dictate, vb. dicter

dictation, n. dictée f.

dictator, n. dictateur m.

dictorial, adj. dictatorial

dictatorship, n. dictature f.

diction, n. diction f.

dictionary, n. dictionnaire m.

die, n. dé m.; vb. mourir

diet, n. régime m.

dietary, adj. diététique

dietetics, n. diététique f.

dietitian, n. diététicien m.

difference, n. différence f.

different, adj. différent

differential, adj. différentiel

difficult, adj. difficile

difficulty, n. difficulté f.

diffuse, adj. diffus

diffusion, n. diffusion f.

dig, vb. bêcher, creuser

digest, vb. digérere

digestible, adj. digestible

digestion, n. digestion f.

digestive, adj. and n. digestif m.

digital, adj. digital

digitalis, n. digitaline f.

dignified, adj. plein de dignité

dignify, vb. honorer, élever

dignity, n. dignité f.

digress, vb. faire une digression

digression, n. digression f.

dilate, vb. dilater

dilatory, adj. dilatoire, lent, négligent

dilemma, n. dilemme m.

dilettante, n. dilettante, amateur m.

diligence, n. diligence f.
diligent, adj. diligent
dill, n. aneth m.
dilute, vb. diluer
dim, adj. faible, terne
dime, n. un dixième de dollar m.
dimension, n. dimension f.
diminish, vb. diminuer
dimness, n. faiblesse, obscurité f.
dimple, n. fossette f.
dine, vb. diner
dingy, adj. défraîchi; terne
dinner, n. diner m.
dinosaur, n. dinosaurien m.
dip, vb. plonger
diptheria, n. diphtérie f.
diploma, n. diplôme m.
diplomacy, n. diplomatie f.
diplomat, n. diplomate m.
diplomatic, adj. diplomatique
dipper, n. cuiller à pot f.
dire, adj. affreux
direct, vb. diriger, addresser; adj. direct
direction, n. direction f.; instructions f., pl.
directly, adv. directement
directness, n. rectitude, ranchise f.
director, n. directeur m.
directory, n. annuaire m.
dirt, n. saleté f.
dirty, adj. sale
disabiltiy, n. incapacité f.
disable, vb. mettre hors de combat
disabled, adj. invalide
disadvantage, n. désavantage m.
disagree, vb. être en désaccord
disagreeable, adj. désagréable
disagreement, n. désaccord m.
disappear, vb. disparaître
disapperance, n. disparition f.

disappoint, vb. désappointer
disappointment, n. désappointement m.
disapproval, n. désapprobation f.
disapprove, vb. désapprouver
disarmament, n. désarmement m.
disarray, n. désarroi, désordre m.
disassemble, vb. démonter, déassembler
disaster, n. désastre m.
disavow, vb. désavouer
disband, vb. congédier
disbelieve, vb. ne pas croire, refuser de croire
discern, vb. discerner
discerning, adj. judicieux, éclaire
discharge, n. décharge f.; (mil.) congé m.; vb. décharger; congédier
discipline, n. discipline f.
disclaim, vb. désvouer, nier
disclaimer, n. désavouer m.
disclose, vb. révéler
disco, adj. disco
discolor, vb. décolorer
discomfiture, n. féfaite, déroute f.
discomfort, n. malaise m.
disconnect, vb. désunir
discontent, n. mécontentement m.
discontented, adj. mécontent
discontinue, vb. discontinuer
discord, n. discorde f.
discordant, adj. discordant, endésaccord
discotheque, n. discothèque f.
discount, n. escompte m.; remise f.
discourage, vb. décourager
discouragement, n. découragement m.

discourse, n. discours m.
discourteous, adj. impoli
discourtesy, n. impolitesse f.
discover, vb. découvrir
discovery, n. découverte f.
discreditable, adj. déshonorant, peu honorable
discrepancy, n. contradiction f.
discretion, n. discrétion f.
discriminate, vb. distinuer
discrimination, n. discernement, jugement m.
discuss, vb. discuter
discussion, n. discussion f.
disdain, n. dédain m.
disdainful, adj. dédaigneux
disease, n. maladie f.
disembark, vb. débarquer
disenchantment, n. désenchantement m.
disengage, vb. dégager
disentangle, vb. démêler
disfavor, n. défaveur f.
disfigure, vb. defigurer, enlai dir
disgrace, n. disgrâce f.
disgraceful, adj. honteux
disgruntled, adj. mécontent, de mauvaise humeur
disguise, n. déguisement m.
dish, n. plat m.; vb. (to do the dishes) laver la vaisselle
dishonest, adj. malhonnête(té)
dishonor, n. déshonneur m.
dishonorable, adj. déhonorant
disinfect, vb. désinfecter
disinfectant, n. désinfectant m.
disinherit, vb. déshériter
disjointed, adj. désarticulé, disloqué
disk, n. disque m.
dislike, n. aversion f.; vb. ne pas aimer
dislocate, vb. disloquer
dislodge, vb. déloger

disloyal, adj. infidele

dismay, n. consternation f.

dismember, vb. démembrer

dismiss, vb. congédier

dismount, vb. descendre

disobedience, n. désobéissance f.

disobey, vb. désobéir à

disorder, n. désordre m.

disorderly, adj. désordonné

disown, vb. désavouer

disparate, adj. disparate

disparity, n. inégalité f.

dispatch, n. expédition, promptitude, dépêche f.

dispatcher, n. expéditeur m.

dispel, vb. dissiper

dispensable, adj. dont on peut se passer

dispense, vb. distribuer, dispenser

dispersal, n. dispersion f.

disperse, vb. disperser

displace, vb. déplacer

displacement, n. déplacement m.

display, n. exposition f.; étalage m.; vb. étaler

displease, vb. déplaire à

disposal, n. disposition f.

dispose, vb. disposer

disposition, n. disposition, f.; caractère m.

disproportion, n. disproportion f.

disprove, vb. réfuter

disputable, adj. contestable, disputable

dispute, n. discussion, dispute f.

disqualify, vb. disqualifier

disregard, n. insouciance f.

disrespect, n. irrevérence f.

disrespectful, adj. irrespectueux

disrobe, vb. déshabiller, dévêtir

disrupt, vb. faire éclater, rompre

dissatisfaction, n. mécontentement m.

dissatisfy, vb. mécontenter

dissect, vb. disséquer

disservice, n. mauvais service rendu m.

dissimilar, adj. dissemblable

dissipate, vb. dissiper

dissipated, adj. dissipé

dissociate, vb. déassocier, dissocier

dissolute, adj. dissolu

dissolution, n. dissolution f.

dissolve, vb. dissoudre

dissonant, adj. dissonant

distance, n. distance f.

distant, adj. distant

distaste, n. dégoût m.

distasteful, adj. désagréable

distend, vb. dilater, gonfler

distill, vb. distiller

distillery, n. distillerie f.

distinct, adj. distinct

distinction, n. distinction f.

distinctive, adj. dinstinctif

distinctly, adv. distinctement

distinguish, vb. distinguer

distinguished, adj. distingué

distract, vb. distraire; affoler

distracted, adj. affolé, bouleversé

distraction, n. distraction; folie f.

distraught, adj. affolé, éperdu

distress, n. détresse f.; vb. affliger

distribute, vb. distribuer

distribution, n. distribution f.

distributor, n. distributeur m.

district, m. contrée f.

distrust, n. méfiance f.

disturb, vb. déranger

disturbance, n. dérangement m.

ditch, n. fossé m.

diver, n. plongeur m.

divergence, n. divergence f.

diverse, adj. divers

diversion, n. divertissement m.

diversity, n. diversité f.

divert, vb. détourner, divertir

divide, vb. diviser

divided, adj. divisé, séparé

divine, adj. divin

divinity, n. divinité f.

divisible, adj. divisible

division, n. division f.

divorce, n. divorce m.; vb. divrocer

dizziness, n. vertige m.

dizzy, adj. pris de vertige

do, vb. faire

docile, adj. docile

dock, n. bassin m.

docket, n. registre, bordereau m.

doctor, n. docteur m.

doctrine, n. doctrine f.

document, n. document m.

documentary, adj. documentaire

dodge, vb. esquiver, éluder

doe, n. daine f.

dog, n. chien m.

doghouse, n. chenil m.

doleful, adj. lugubre

doll, n. poupée f.

dollar, n. dollar m.

dolphin, n. dauphin m.

domain, n. domaine m.

dome, n. dôme m.

domestic, adj. domestique

domicile, n. domicile m.

dominance, n. dominance, prédominance f.

dominate, vb. dominer

domination, n. domination f.

dominion, n. domination f.

donate, vb. donner

donation, n. donation f.

done, vb. fait

donkey, n. âne m.

doom, vb. condamner

door, n. porte f.; concierge

m.f.
dormitory, n. dortoir m.
dosage, n. dosage m.
dose, n. dose f.
dot, n. point m.
double, adj. and n. double m.
double-breasted, adj. croisé
doubt, n. doute m.
doubtful, adj. douteux
doubtless, adv. sans doute
dough, n. pâte f.
doughnut, n. pet de nonne m.
dove, n. colombe f.
down, n. duvet m.
downfall, n. chute f.
downhill, n. descente f.
downpour, n. averse f.
downright, adv. tout à fait
downstairs, adv. en bas
downtown, adv. en ville
downy, adj. duvetuex
doze, vb. sommeiller
dozen, n. douzaine f.
drab, adj. gris, terne
draft, n. dessin, courant d'air m. (mil.) conscription f.
draftsman, n. dessinateur m.
drafty, adj. plein de courante d'air
drag, vb. traîner
dragnet, n. drague, seine f.; chalut m.
dragon, n. dragon m.
drain, vb. drainer
drainage, n. drainage m.
dram, n. drachme, goutte f.
drama, n. drame m.
dramatic, adj. dramatique
dramatist, n. dramaturge m.
dramatize, vb. dramatiser
drape, vb. draper
drapery, n. draperie f.
drastic, adj. drastique
draught, n. traction f.; trait m.
draw, vb. dessiner
drawbridge, m. pont-levis m.

drawer, n. tiroir m.
drawing, n. dessin m.
dray, n. camion m.
drayman, n. camionneur m.
dread, n. crainte f.
dreadful, adj. affreux
dream, n. rêve m.
dreamer, n. rêveur m.
dreamy, adj. rêveur m., rêveuse f.
dreary, adj. morne
dredge, vb. draguer
drench, vb. tremper
dress, vb. habiller, vêtir, parer, orner
dresser, n. commode f.
dressing, n. toilette f.; pansement m.
dressmaker, n. couturière f.
drier, n. sécheur, dessécheur m.
drift, vb. dériver
driftwood, n. bois flottant m.
drill, n. foret, exercice m.; vb. forer
drink, n. boisson f.; vb. boire
drip, vb. dégoutter
drive, n. promenade en voiture f.
driver, n. chauffeur m.
drizzle, n. bruine f.; vb. bruiner
droop, vb. pencher
drop, n. goutte f.; vb. laisser tomber
dropsy, n. hydropisie f.
drought, n. sécheresse f.
drove, n. troupeau m.
drown, n. noyer
drowse, vb. s'assoupir
drowsy, adj. somnolent
drudge, vb. s'éreinter
drug, n. drogue f.
druggist, n. pharmacien m.
drum, n. tambour, tympan m.
drummer, n. tambour m.
drunk, adj. ivre
drunkard, n. ivrogne m.

dry, adj. sec m.; sèche f.
dryness, n. sécheresse f.
dual, adj. double
duck, n. canard m.
duct, n. conduit m.
ductile, adj. ductile
duel, n. duel m.
duelist, n. duelliste m.
duet, n. duo m.
duke, n. duc m.
dull, adj. ennuyeux
dullard, n. lourdaud m.
dullness, n. monotonie f.
dumb, adj. muet m., muette f.
dummy, n. mannequin m., mort m.
dump, n. voirie f.
dumping, n. boulette (de pâte) f.
dum, vb. importuner, talonner
dunce, n. crétin m.
dune, n. dune f.
dungeon, n. cachot m.
duplex, adj. double
duplicate, n. double m.; vb. faire le double de
duplication, n. duplication f.
duplicity, n. duplicité f.
durable, adj. durable
durability, n. durabilité f.
duration, n. durée f.
duress, n. contrainte, coercition f.
during, prep. pendant
dusk, n. crépuscule m.
dusky, adj. sombre
dust, n. poussière f.; vb. épousseter
dusty, adj. poussiéreux
Dutch, adj. and n. hollandais m.
Dutchman, n. Hollandais m.
dutiful, adj. respectueux, fidèle
dutifully, adv. ave soummission
duty, n. devoir, dorit m.;

être de service

duty-free, adj. exempt de droits

dwarf, adj. and n., nain m.

dwell, vb. demeurer

dwindle, vb. diminuer

dye, n. teinture f.

dyer, n. teinturier m.

dynamic, adj. dynamique

dynamics, n. dynamique f.

dynamite, n. dynamite f.

dynamo, n. dynamo f.

dynasty, n. dynastie f.

dyslexia, n. dyslexie f.

dyspepsia, n. dyspepsie f.

dyspeptic, adj. dyspeptique

E

each, adj. chaque; pron. chacun m.

eager, ad. ardent, vif

eagerness, n. empressement m.

eagel, n. aigle m.; (mil.) aigle f.

ear, n. oreille f.

eardrum, n. tympan m.

earl, n. comte m.

early, adj. matinal, premier

earn, vb. gagner

earnest, adj. sérieux

earphone, n. casque m.

earring, n. boucle d'oreille f.

earth, n. terre f.

earthly, adj. terrestre

earthquake, n. tremblement de terre

ease, n. aise f.; avec facilité

easel, n. chevalet m.

easily, adv. largement, facilement

easiness, n. aisance, facilité f.

east, n. est m.

Easter, n. Pâques m.

eastern, adj. de l'est, oriental

eastward, adv. vers l'est

easy, adj. facile, aise

eat, vb. manger

ebb, n. reflux, déclin m.

ebony, n. ébène m.

eccentric, adj. excentrique

eccentricity, n. excentricité f.

ecclesiastic, adj. and n. ecclé- siastique m.

ecclesiastical, adj. ecclésiastique

echelon, n. échelon m.

echo, n. écho m.

eclipse, n. éclipse f.

ecological, adj. écologique

ecology, n. écologie f.

economic, adj. économique

economical, adj. économe

economics, n. éconoimie politque f.

economist, n. économiste m.

economize, vb. économiser

economy, n. économie f.

ecstasy, n. extase f.; transport m.

eczema, n. eczéma m.

edge, n. bord, fil m.

edging, n. pose, bordure f.

edgy, adj. d'un air agacé

edibile, adj. comestible

edict, n. edit m.

edition, édition f.

editor, n. éditeur, rédacteur m.

editorial, n. article de fond m.

educate, vb. elever, instruire

education, n. éducation f.

educator, n. éducateur m.

eel, n. anguille f.

effect n. effet m.; vb. effectuer

effective, adj. efficace, effectif

effectivenss, n efficacité f.

efficacy, n. efficacité f.

efficiency, n. compétence f.; rende ment m.

efficient, adj. capable

effort, n. effort m.

effortless, adj. sans effort

effusive, adj. démonstratif

egg, n. oeue m.; (boiled) oeuf á la coque; (fried) oeuf sur le plat; (hard-boiled) oeuf dur

eggplant, n. aubergine f.

Egypt, n. l Égypte m.

Egyptian, n. Égyptien m.; adj. égyptien

eight, adj. and n. huit m.

eighteen, adj. and n. dix-huit m.

eighteenth, adj. and n. dix-huitième, m.f.

eight, adj. and n. huitième m.f.

eighty, adj. and n. quatre-vingts m.

either, pron. l'un ou l'autre m.; conj. ou, soit

eject, vb. rejeter, émettre

ejection, n. expulsion, éjection f.

elaborate, adv. minutieux.; vb. élaborer

elapse, vb. s'écouler

elastic, adj. and n. élastique m.

elasticity, n. élasticité f.

elate, vb. exalter, transporter

elated, adj. exalté

elbow, n. coude m.

elder, adj. and n. aîné m.

elderly, adj. d'un certain âge

elect, vb. élire

election, n. élection f.

elective, adj. électif

electorate, n. électorat m., les votants m., pl.

electric, electrical, adj. électrique

electrician, n. électricien m.

electricity, n. électricité f.

electrocute, vb. électrocuter

electron, n. électron m.

electronics, n. électronique f.

elegance, n. élégance f.

elegant, adj. élégant

elegiac, adj. élégiaque

elegy, n. élégie f.

element, n. élément m.

elementary, adj. élémentaire

elephant, n. éléphant m.

elevate, vb. élever

elevation, n. élévation f.

elevator, n. ascenseur m.

eleven, adj. and n. onze m.

eleventh, adj. and n. onzième m.f.

elf, n. elfe m.

elfin, adj. d'elfe

elicit, vb. tirer, faire jaillir

eligibility, n. éligibilité f.

eligible, adj. éligible

eliminate, vb. éliminer

elimination, n. élimination f.

elixir, n. élixir m.

elk, n. élan m.

elm, n. orme m.

elope, vb. s'enfuir

eloquence, n. éloquence f.

eloquent, adj. éloguent

eloquently, adv. d'une manière éloquente

else, adj. autre, quelqu'un d'autre

elsewhere, adv. ailleurs

elucidate, vb. élucider, éclaircir

elude, vb. éluder

elusive, adj. évasif, insaisissable

emaciated, adj. émacié

emancipate, vb. émanciper

emancipation, n. émancipation f.

emasculate, vb. émasculer

embalm, vb. embaumer

embankment, n. levée f.

embargo, n. embargo m.

embark, vb. embarquer

embarrass, vb. embarrasser

embarrassing, adj. embarrassant

embarrassment, n. embar-

ras m.

embassy, n. ambassade f.

embellish, vb. embellir

embellishment, n. embellissement m.

ember, n. braise f., charbon ardent m.

embezzle, vb. détourner

embitter, vb. aigrir, envenimer

emblazon, vb. blasonner

emblem, n. emblème m.

embody, vb. incarner, incorporer

emboss, vb. graver en relief, travailler en boasse

embrace, n. reinte f.

embroider, vb. broder

embroidery, n. broderie f.

embryo, n. embryon m.

emerald, n. émeraude f.

emerge, vb. émerger

emergency, n. circonstance critique f.

emery, n. émeri m.

emigrant, n. émigrant m.

emigrate, vb. émigrer

emigration, n. émigration f.

eminence, n. éminence f.

emit, vb. émettre

emolument, n. traitement m.

emotion, n. émotion f.

emotional, adj. émotif, émotionnable

emperor, n. empereur m.

emphasis, n. force f.; accent m.

emphasize, vb. mettre en relief

emphatic, adj. énergique

empire, n. empire m.

employ, vb. employer

employee, n. employé m.

employer, n. patron m.

employment, n. emploi m.

empress, n. impératrice f.

emptiness, n. vide m.

empty, adj. vide, à vide

emulate, vb. émuler

enable, vb. mettre à

même (de)

enact, vb. ordonner, arrêter

enactment, n. promulgation f.; acte législatif m.

enamel, n. émail m.

encephalitis, n. encéphalite f.

enchant, vb. enchanter

enchanting, adj. ravissant

enchantment, n. enchantement m.

enclose, vb. enclore, clore

enclosure, n. action de clore, clôture

encompass, vb. entourer

encounter, vb. rencontrer f.

encourage, vb. encourager

encouragement, n. encouragement m.

encroach, vb. empiéter

encyclopedia, n. encyclopédie f.

end, n. fin, extrémité f.; bout, but, objet m.

endanger, vb. mettre en danger

endear, vb. rendre cher

endearment, n. charme, attrait m.

endeavor, n. effort m.; vb. tâcher, essayer

endemic, adj. endémique

ending, n. terminaison, désinence f.

endless, adj. sans fin, perpétuel

endorse, vb. endosser, appuyer

endorsement, n. endossement, approbation m.

endowment, n. dotation, fondation f.

endurance, n. résistance f.

endure, vb. supporter

enduring, adj. durable

enema, n. lavement m.

enemy, adj. and n ennemi m.

energetic, adj. énergique

energy, n. énergie f.

enfold, vb. envelopper

enforce, vb. imposer, exécuter

enforcement, n. exécution f.

enfranchise, vb. affranchir, accorder le droit de vote

engage, vb. engager, retenir, prendre, louer

engaged, adj. fiancé, occupé

engagement, n. engagement m.; fiancailles f., pl.

engaging, adj. attrayant, séduisant

engine, n. machine, locomotive f.; moteur m.

engineer, n. ingénieur, mécanicien m.; (mil.) soldat du génie m.

engineering, n. génie m.

England, n. l'Angleterre f.

English, adj. and n. anglais m.

engrave, vb. graver

engraver, n. graveur m.

engraving, n. gravure f.

enhance, vb. rehausser

enjoy, vb. jouir de, s'amuser

enjoyable, adj. agréable

enjoyment, n. jouissance f.

enlarge, vb. agrandir

enlargement, n. agrandissement m.

enlarger, n. agrandisseur, amplificateur m.

enligthen, vb. éclairer

enlightenment, n. éclaircissement m.

enlist, vb. enrôler

enmity, n. inimitié f.

enormous, adj. enorme

enough, adj. and adv. assez

enrage, vb. faire enrager

enrich, vb. enrichir

ensemble, n. ensemble m.

entail, vb. entraîner, imposer

entangle, vb. empêtrer

enter, vb. entrer dans

enterprise, n. enteprise f.

enterprising, adj. entreprenant

entertain, vb. amuser, recevoir

entertainment, n. hospitalité

enthusiasm, n. enthousiasme m.

entice, vb. attirer

entire, adj. entier

entirely, adv. entièrement

entitle, vb. donner droit à, intituler

entrails, n. entrailles f., pl.

entrance, n. entrée f.

entrap, vb. attraper, prendre au piège

entreat, vb. supplier

entry, n. entrée, inscriphon f.

enumerate, vb. énumérer

enunication, n. énonciation f.

envelop, vb. envelopper

envelope, n. enveloppe f.

enviable, adj. enviable

envious, adj. envieux

environment, n. milieu m.

envoy, n. envoyé m.

envy, n. envie f.; vb. envier

epic, n. épopée f.; adj. épique

epilepsy, n. épliepsie f.

epilogue, n. épilogue m.

epoch, n. époque f.

equable, adj. uniforme, régulier

equal, adj. égal, être à la hauteur de

equality, n. égalité f.

equalize, vb. égaliser

equate, vb. égaler, mettre en equation

equation, n. équation f.

equator, n. équateur m.

equilibrium, n. équilibre m.

equip, vb. équiper

equipment, n. equipment m.

equitable, adj. équitable, juste

equity, n. équité f.

equivalent, adj. and n.

équivalent m.

era, n. ère f.

eradicate, vb. déraciner

erase, vb. effacer

eraser, n. gomme f.

erect, adj. droit

erection, n. érection, construction f.

erectness, n. attitude droite f.

erode, vb. éroder, ronger

erosion, n. érosion f.

erosive, adj. érosif

erotic, adj. érotique

err, vb. errer

errand, n. course f.

errant, adj. errant

erratic, adj. irrégulier, excentrique

erring, adj. égaré dévoyé

erroneous, adj. erroné

error, n. erreur f.

erudite, adj. érudit

erudition, n. érudition f.

erupt, vb. entrer en éruption

eruption, n. éruption f.

escalate, vb. escalader

escalator, n. escalier roulant m.

escape, n. fuite f.; vb. échapper

escort, n. (mil.) escorte f.; cavalier m.

esculent, adj. comestible

esoteric, adj. ésotérique

especial, adj. spécial

espionage, n. espionnage m.

espouse, vb. éspouser, embrasser

Eskimo, n. Esquimau m.

esquire, n. écuyer m.

essay, n. essai m.; épreuve f.

essence, n. essence f.

essential, adj. essentiel

essentially, adv. essentiellement

establish, vb. établir

establishment, n. établissement m.

estate, n. état, rang m.; propriété f.

esteem, n. estime f.; vb. estimer

estimate, n. estimation, évaluation f.

estimation, n. jugement m.

estrange, vb. aliéner

etching, n. gravure à l'eauforte f.

eternal, adj. éternel

eternity, n. éternité f.

ether, n. éther m.

ethical, adj. moral

ethics, n. éthique f.

Ethiopia, n. l' Ethiopie f.

ethnic, adj. ethnique

etiquette, n. étiquette f.

eucalyptus, n. eucalyptus m.

eugenic, adj. eugénésique

eugneics, n. eugénisme m.; eugénique f.

Europe, n. l'Europe f.

European, adj. Européen m.

euthanasia, n. euthanasie f.

evacuate, vb. évacuer

evade, vb. éluder

evaluate, vb. évaluer

evaluation, n. évaluation f.

evangelist, n. évangéliste m.

evaporate, vb. évaporer

evaporation, n. évaporation f.

evasion, n. subterfuge f.

eve, n. veille f.

even, adj. égal, régulier

evening, n. soir m.; soirée f.

event, n. événement, cas m.

eventful, adj. plein d'événements

ever, adv. toujours; jamais

evergreen, adj. toujours vert

everlasting, adj. eternel, perétuel

every, adj. chaque, tous les m.; toutes les f.

everybody, everyone, pron. tout le monde

everyday, adj. de tous le jours, journalier

everything, n. tout m.

everywhere, adv. partout

evict, vb. évincer, expulser

eviction, n. éviction, expulsion f.

evidence, n. évidence, preuve f.

evident, adj. évident

evidently, adv. évidemment

evil, n. mal m.

evoke, vb. évoquer

evolution, n. évolution f.

evolve, vb. évoluer, développer

ewe, n. agnelle f.

exact, adj. exact

exacting, adj. exigeant

exactly, adv. exactement

exaggerated, adj. exagéré

exaggeration, n. exagération f.

exalt, vb. exalter, élever

exaltation, n. exaltation f.

examination, n. examen m.

examine, vb. examiner

example, n. exemple m.

exasperate, vb. exaspérer

exasperation, n. exaspération f.

exceed, vb. excéder

exceedingly, adv. extrêmement

excel, vb. exceller

excellence, n. excellence f.

excellent, adj. excellent

except, vb. excepter, exclure; prep. excepté, sauf

exception, n. exception f.

exceptional, adj. exceptionnel

excerpt, n. extrait m.

excess, n. excès, excédent, surpoids m.

excessive, adj. excessif

exchange, n. échange, troc m.

exchangeable, adj. échangeable

excise, n. contribution indirecte, régie f.

excitable, adj. émotionnable,

excitable

excite, vb. exciter

excitement, n. agitation f.

exclaim, vb. s'écrier

exclamation, n. exclamation f.

exclude, vb. exclure(de)

exclusion, n. exclusion f.

exclusive, adj. exclusif, sélect

excommunicate, vb. excommunnier

excortate, vb. excorier, écorcher

excruciating, adj. atroce, affreux

exculpate, vb. disculper, exonérer

excursion, n. excursion f.

excusable, adj. excusable

excuse, n. excuse f.

execute, vb. exécuter

execution, n. exécution f.

executive, adj. and n. exécutif m.

executor, n. exécuteur m.

exemplify, vb. expliquer par des exemples

exempt, adj. exempt; vb exempter

exercise, n. exercice m.; vb. exercer

exert, vb. employer, s'efforcer de

exertion, n. effort m.

exhale, vb. exhaler

exhaust, n. échappement m.; vb. épuiser

exhaustion, n. épuisement m.

exhaustive, adj. complet, approfondi

exhibit, vb. exposer, montrer

exhibition, n. exposition f.

exhilarate, vb. égayer

exhort, vb. exhorter

exhortation, n. exhortion f.

exhume, vb. exhumer

exile, n. exil, exilé m.; vb. exiler

exist, vb. exister

existence, n. existence f.

existent, adj. existant

exit, n. sortie f.

exodus, n. exode m.

exorcise, vb. exorciser

exotic, adj. exotique

expand, vb. étendre, déployer

expanse, n. étendue f.

expansion, n. expansion f.

expansive, adj. expansif

expatriate, vb. expatrier

expect, vb. s'attendre à, attendre

expectancy, n. attente f.

expectation, n. attente, espérance f.

expediency, n. convenance f.

expedient, n. expédient m.

expedite, vb. activer, accélérer

expedition, n. expédition f.

expel, vb. expulser

expend, vb. dépenser, épuiser

expenditure, n. dépense f.

expense, n. dépnse f.; frais m., pl.

expensive, adj. coûteux, cher

experienced, adj. expérimenté

experiment, n. expérience f.

experimental, adj. expérimental

expert, adj. and n. expert m.

expiate, vb. expier

expiration, n. expiration f.

expire, vb. expirer

explain, vb. expliquer

explanation, n. explication f.

explanatory, adj. explicatif

explicit, adj. explicite

explode, vb. éclater

exploitation, n. exploitation f.

exploration, n. exploration f.

exploratory, adj. exploratif

explore, vb. explorer

explorer, n. explorateur m.

explosion, n. explosion f.

explosive, adj. and n. explosif m.

exponent, n. interprète m.

export, n. exportation f.; vb. exporter

expose, vb. exposer

exposition, n. exposition

exposure, n. exposiiton f.

expound, vb. exposer

express, adj. exprès; vb. exprimer

expression, n. expression f.

expressive, adj. expressif

expressly, adv. expressément

expressman, n. agent de messageries m.

expropriate, vb. exproprier

expulsion, n. expulsion f.

expunge, vb. effacer, rayer

exquisite, ajd. exquis

extant, adj. existant

extend, vb. étendre, prolonger

extension, n. extension f.

extensive, adj. étendu

extensively, adv. d'une manière étendue

extent, n. étendue f.

extenuate, vb. exténuer, atténuer

exterior, adj. and n. extérieur m.

exterminate, vb. exterminer

extermination, n. extermination f.

external, adj. externe

extinct, adj. éteint

extinction, n. extinction f.

extinguish, vb. éteindre

extirpate, vb. extirper

extol, vb. vanter

extort, vb. extorquer

extortion, n. extorsion f.

extra, adj. supplémentaire, en sus, extraordinaire

extract, n. extraire

extraction, n. extraction, origine f.

extraordinary, adj. extraordinaire

extravagance, n. extravagance, prodigalité f.

extravagant, adj. extravagant, prodigue

extravaganza, m. oeuvre fantaisiste f.

extreme, adj. and n. extrême m.

extremity, n. extrémite f.

exuberant, adj. exubérant

exude, vb. exsuder

exult, vb. exulter

exultant, adj. exultant, joyeux

eye, n. oiel m.; yeux m., pl.

eyeball, n. bulbe de l'oeil m.

eyebrow, n. sourcil m.

eyeglass, n. lorgnon m.

eyeglasses, n. lunettes f., pl.

eyelash, n. cil n.

eyelid, n. paupière f.

eyesight, n. vue f.

eyewitness, n. temoin oculaire m.

F

fable, n. fable f.

fabric, n. construction f.

fabricate, vb. fabriquer

fabulous, adj. fabuleux

face, n. figure f.; vb. faire face à

facet, n. facette f.

facial, adj. facial

facing, n. revêtement, revers m.

facsimile, n. fac-similé m.

fact, n. fait m.; en effet (in fact)

faction, n. faction f.

factual, adj. effectif, positif

fad, n. marotte f.

fade, vb. se faner, se décolorer,

s'évanouir

fail, vb. manquer, faillir

faint, adj. faible, défaillant

fair, n. foire m.; adj. beau m., belle f.; blond, juste; passable

fairly, adj. honnêtement, impartialement

fairness, n. honnêteté f.

faith, n. foi f.

faithful, adj. fidèle

fake, vb. truquer

faker, n. truqueur m.

falcon, n. faucon m.

fall, n. chute f.; (month) aut# omme m.

fallen, adj. tombé déchu

fallout, n. pluie radioactive f.

fallow, adj. en jachère

false, adj. faux m.; fausse f.n. mensonge m.

fame, n. renommée f.

familiar, adj. familier

familiarity, n. familiarité f.

familiarize, vb. familiariser

family, n. famille f.

famished, adj. affamé

famous, adj. célèbre

fan, n. éventail, ventilateur m.

fancy, n. fantaisie f.; vb. se figurer

fanfare, n. fanfare f.

fantastic, adj. fantastique

fantasy, n. fantaisie f.

far, adv. loin, jusqu'ici, autant que, beaucoup, de beaucoup

faraway, adj. lointain

fare, n. prix m.; chère f.; vb. aller

farewell, interj. and n. adieu m.

far-fetched, adj. forcé

farm, n. ferme f.

farmer, n. fermier m.

farmhouse, n. maison de ferme f.

farming, n. culture f.

far-sighted, adj. clairvoyant

farther, adj. plus éloigné; adv. plus loin

fascinate, vb. fasciner

fashion, n. mode, manière f.

fast, n. jeûne m.; adj. rapide, en avance, en avance; vb. jeûner; adv. vite, ferme

fasten, vb. attacher

fastening, n. attache f.

fat, adj. gras m.; grasse f.

fatal, adj. fatal, mortel

fatality, n. fatalité f.

fatally, adv. fatalement, mortellement

fate, n. destin m.

father, n. père m.

fatherhood, n. paternité f.

father-in-law, n. beaupère m.

fatherless, adj. sans père

fatherly, adj. paternel

fatigue, n. fatigue f.

fatten, vb. engraisser

fatty, adj. graisseux

faucet, n. robinet m.

fault, n. faute f.; défaut m.

faultless, adj. sans défaut

faulty, adj. défectueux

favor, n. faveur f.; vb. favoriser

favorable, adj. favorable

favored, adj. favorisé

favorite, adj. and n. favori, m.; favorite f.

fawn, n. faon m.

fear n. crainte, peur f.; vb. craindre, avoir peur de

fearful, adj. craintif; effrayant

fearless, adj. intrépide

feasible, adj. faisable

feast, n. fête f.; festin m.

feather, n. plume f.

feathered, adj. emplumé

feature, n. trait m.

February, n. février m.

federal, adj. fédéral

federation, n. fédération f.

fedor, n. chapeau mou m.

fee, n. honoraires m.pl.; frais

m., pl.

feeble, adj. faible

feed, n. nourriture f.; vb. nourrir

feel, vb. sentir, tâter

feeling, n. sentiment m.

feline, adj. félin

fell, adj. funeste

fellow, n. homme, garçon, compagnon m.

fellowship, n. camaraderie, bourse universitaire f.

felon, n. criminel m.

felony, n. crime m.

felt, n. feutre m.

female, n. femme, femelle f.; adj. féminin, femelle

feminine, adj. féminin

femininity, n. féminéité f.

fence, n. clôture f.; vb. enclore, fair de l'escrime

fencing, n. escrime f.

fender, n. garde-boue; garde-feu m.

fern, n. fougère f.

ferry, n. passage en bac; bac m.

fertile, adj. fertile

fertility, n. fertilité f.

fertilization, n. fertilisation f.

fertilize, vb. fertiliser

fervent, adj. fervent

festival, n. fête f.

festive, adj. de fête

festoon, n. feston m.; vb. festonner

fetal, adj. foetal

fetch, vb. aller chercher, apporter

fetching, adj. attrayant

fete, vb. fêter

fetter, n. lien m.; chaîne f.; vb. enchaîner

fetus, n. foetus m.

feud, n. inimitié f.; fief m.

feudalism, n. régime féodal m.

fever, n. fièvre f.

feverish, adj. fiévreux, fébrile

feverishly, adv. fébrilement, fiévreusement

few, adj. peu de, quelques

fiancé, n. fiancé m.

fiasco, n. fiasco m.

fiat, n. décret m.

fib, n. petit mensonge m.

fiber, n. fibre f.

fickle, adj. volage

fiction, n. fiction f.; romans m., pl.

fictional, adj. de romans

fictitious, adj. fictif, imaginaire

fiddle, n. violon m.; vb. jouer du violon

fidelity, n fidélité f.

field, n. champ m.

fiendish, adj. diabolique, infernal

fierce, adj. féroce

fiery, adj. ardent

fiesta, n. fête f.

fife, n. fifre m.

fifteen, adj. and n. quinze m.

fifteenth, adj. and n. quinzième m.

fifth, adj. and n. cinquième m.

fifty, adj. and n. cinquante m.

fig, n. figue f.

fight, n. combat m.; lutte, dispute f.; vb. combattre, se disputer

fighter, n. combattant m.

figment, n. invention f.

figurative, adj. figuré

figuratvely, adj. au figuré

figure, n. figure, tournure f.; chiffre m. vb. figurer, calculer

figured, adj. à dessin

figurehead, n. homme de paille m.

filament, n. filament m.

filch, vb. escamoter

file, n. lime, file, liasse f.; archives f., pl.; classeur m.

fill, vb. remplir

filling, n. remplissage m.

film, n. film m.; pellicule f.

filter, n. filtre m.; vb. filtrer

fin, n. nageoire f.

final, adj. final

finale, n. finale m.

finally, adv. finalement, enfin

finance, n. finance f.; vb. financer

financial, adj. financier

find, vb. trouver

fine, n. amende, belle f.; fin.; vb. mettre à l'amende; adj. beau m.

finery, n. parure f.

finesse, n. finesse f.; vb. finasser

finger, n. doigt m.

fingernail, n. ongle m.

fingerprint, n. empreinte digitale f.

finish, vb. finir

finite, adj. fini

Finland, n. la Finlande f.

Finn, n. Finladais, **Finnois m.**

fire, n. feu, incendie m.

fire alarm, n. avertisseur d'incendie m.

firearm, n. arme à feu f.

fire escape, n. échelle de sauvetage f.

fire extinguisher, n. extincteur m.

fireman, n. pompier m.

fireplace, n. cheminée f.

fireproof, adj. à l'épreuve du feu

firewood, n. bois de chauffage m.

fireworks, n. feu d'artifice m.

firm, n. maison de commerce f.

firmness, n. fermeté f.

first, adj. premier; adv. d'abord

first aid, n. premiers secours m., pl.

first-class, adj. de premier ordre

first-hand, adj. de première main

fiscal, adj. fiscal

fish, n. poisson m.; vb. pêcher

fisherman, n. pêcheur m.

fishing, n. pêche f.

fist, n. poing m.

fit, n. accès m.; adj. convenable, capable, propre à

fitful, adj. agité, irrégulier

fitness, n. convenance, santé physique f.; à-propos m.

fitting, n. convenable, à propos, juste

five, adj. and n. cinq m.

fix, vb. fixer, attacher, établir, arrêter

fixed, adj. fixe

fixture, n. meuble à demeure

flabby, adj. flasque

flag, n. drapeau m.; dalle f.

flagon, n. flacon m.

flagpole, n. mât de drapeau m.

flagrant, adj. flagrant

flagrantly, adv. d'une manière flagrante

flair, n. flair m.

flamboyant, adj. flamboyant

flame, n. flamme f.; vb. flamboyer

flaming, adj. flamboyant

flamingo, n. flamant m.

flank, n. flanc m.

flannel, n. flanelle f.

flap, n. coup, battant m.; patte f.; vb. battre

flare, vb. flamboyer

flash, n. éclair m.

flashlight, n. flash m.

flashy, adj. voyant

flask, n. gourde f.

flat, n. appartement m.; adj. plat m.

flatness, n. égalité f.; aplatissement m.

flatten, vb. aplatir

flatter, vb. flatter

flattery, n. flatterie f.

flaunt, vb. parader, étaler

flavor, n. saveur f.;
  armoe m.

flavoring, n. assaisonnement m.

flavorless, adj. fade

flaw, n. défaut m.

flawless, adj. sans défaut,
  parfait

flawlessly, adv. d'une
  manière impeccable

flax, n. lin m.

flea, n. puce f.

flee, vb. s'enfuir

fleece, n. toison f.

fleecy, adj. laineux, mouton-
  neux

fleet, n. flotte f.

fleeting, adj. tugitif

flesh, n. chair f.

flexibility, n. flexibilité f.

flexible, adj. flexible

flicker, vb. trembloter, vaciller

flier, n. aviateur m.

flight, n. vol m.; fuite f.

flinch, vb. reculer, broncher

fling, vb. jeter

flint, n. pierre à briquet;
  silex m.

flirt, vb. flirter

flirtation, n. flirt m.

float, vb. flotter

flock, n. troupeau m.; vb. ac-
  courir

flog, vb. fouetter

flood, n. inondation f.

floodlight, n. lumière à
  grand flots f.

floor, n. plancher, parquet,
  carreau m.

flooring, n. plancer, par-
  quet m.

flop, n. coup mat m.

floral, adj. floral

florist, n. fleuriste m.f.

flounder, n. flet m.

flour, n. fairne f.

flourish, vb. prospérer

flow, vb. couler

flower, n. fleur f.

flowerpot, n. pot à fleurs m.

flue, n. tuyau de
  cheminée m.

fluency, n. facilité f.

fluent, adj. courant

fluid, adj. and n. fluide m.

flunk, vb. coller, recaler

flourescent lamp, n. lampe
  flourescente f.

flurry, n. agitation f.

flush, n. rougeur, chasse f.

flute, n. flûte f.

flutter, n. voltigement m.
  palpiter

fly, n. mouche f.

foam, n. écume f.

focal, adj. focal

focus, n. foyer m.

foe, n. ennemi m.

fog, n. brouillard m.

foggy, adj. brumeux

foil, n. feuille f.

foist, vb. fourrer

fold, n. pli m.

folder, n. prospectus m.

foilage, n. feuillage m.

folio, n. in-folio m.

folk, n. gens m.f., pl.

folklore, n. folk-lore m.

follow, vb. suivre

follower, n. disciple m.

folly, n. folie f.

fond, adj. tendre; vb. aimer

fondant, n. fondant m.

fondle, vb. caresser

fondly, adv. tendrement

fondness, n. tendresse f.

food, n. nourriture f.

fool, n. sot, bête m.; sotte f.

foot, n. pied m.

footage, n. métrage m.

football, n. fottball,
  ballon m.

footing, n. pled, point d'appui m.

footnote, n. note f.

footprint, n. empreinte de

pas f.

footstep, n. pas m.

footstool, n. tabouret m.

footwork, n. jeu de pieds m.

for, prep. paour; conj. car

forage, n. fourrage m.; vb.
  fourrager

forbear, vb. s'abstenir de,
  montrer de la patience

forbearance, n. patience f.

forbid, vb. défendre (à)

forbidding, adj. rébarbatif

force, n. force f.

forced, adj. force

forceful, adj. énergique

forcefulness, n. énergie,
  vigueur f.

forceps, n. forceps m.

forcible, adj. forcé

ford n. gué m.; vb. traverser
  à gué

forearm, n. avant-bras m.

forebears, n. ancêtres m.,pl.

forecast, n. prévision f.; vb.
  prévoir

forecastle, n. gailard m.

foreclose, vb. exclure, for-
  clore

forefather, n. ancêtre m.

forefinger, n. index m.

foregone, adj. décidé
  d'avance

foreground, n. premier
  plan m.

forehead, n. front m.

foreign, adj. étranger

foreigner, n. étranger m.

foreleg, n. jambe
  antérieure f.

foremost, adj. premier

forensic, adj. judiciaire

foresee, vb. prévoir

foresight, n. prévoyance f.

forest, n. forêt f.

forestall, vb. anticiper, de-
  vancer

forester, n. forestier m.

foretell, vb. prédire

forever, adv. pour toujours

forevermore, adv. à jamais

forfeit, vb. forfaire

forfeiture, n. perte par confiscation, forfaiture f.

forge, n. forge f.; vb. forger, contrefaire

forger, n. faussaire, falsificateur m.

forgery, n. faux m.

forget, vb. oublier

forgetful, adj. oublieux

forgive, vb. pardonner (à)

forgiveness, n. pardon m.

forgo, vb. renoncer à

fork, n. fourchette, fourche f.

forlorn, adj. désespéré; abandonné

formal, adj. formel

formally, adv. formellement

format, n. format m.

formation, n. formation f.

formative, adj. formatif, formateur

former, adj. précédent; pron. le premier

formerly, adv. autrefois, jadis, auparavant

formula, n. formule f.

forsake, vb. abandonner

fort, n. fort m.

forth, adv. en avant

forthcoming, adv. à venir

forthwith, adv. sur-le-champ

fortitude, n. courage m.

fortress, n. forteresse f.

fortunate, adj. heureux

fortune, n. fortune f.

forty, adj. and n. quarante m.

forward, adj. en avant, avancé, hardi

forwardness, n. empressement m.; effronterie f.

fossil, n. fossile m.

foster, vb. nourrir

foul, adj. sale, malpropre, dégoûtant

found, vb. fonder

foundation, n. foundation f.; fondement m.

founder, n. foundateur m.

fountain, n. fontaine f.

four, adj. and n. quatre m.

four-in-hand, n attelage à quatre m.

fourscore, adj. quatre-vingts

foursome, n. à quatre

fourteen, adj. and n. quatorze m.

fourth, adj. and n. quatrième m.

fowl, n. volaille f.

fox, n. renard m.

foxglove, n. digitale f.

foxhole, n. renardière f.

foxy, adj. rusé

foyer, n. foyer m.

fraction, n. fraction m.

fracture, n. fracture f.

fragile, adj. fragile

fragment, n. fragment m.

fragmentary, adj. fragmentaire

fragrance, n. parfum m.

fragrant, adj. parfumé

frail, adj. frêle

frailty, n. faiblesse f.

frame, n. cadre m.; structure f.

frame-up, n. coup monté m.

framework, n. charpente f.

France, n. la France f.

franchise, n. droit de vote m.

frank, adj. franc m.; franche f.

frankincense, n. encens m.

frankly, adv. franchement

frankness, n. franchsie f.

frantic, adj. frénétique

fraternal, adj. fraternel

fraternally, adv. fraternellement

fraternity, n. fraternité f.

fraud, n. fraude f.; imposteur m.

fraudulent, adj. frauduleux

fraudulently, adv. frauduleusement

fraught, adj. chargé(de), plein, gros

fray, n. bagarre f.

freak, n. caprice, phénomène m.

freckle, n. tache de rousseur f.

freckled, adj. taché de rousseur

free, adj. libré; gratuit; vb. libérer, affranchir

freedom, n. liberté f.

freeze, vb. geler

freezer, n. glacière f.; congélateur m.

freight, n. fret m.

French, adj. and n. français m.

frenzy, n. frénésie f.

frequency, n. fréquence f.

frequent, adj. fréquent, fréquenter

frequently, adv. fréquemment

fresco, n. fresque f.

fresh, adj. frais, récent, nouveau m.

freshen, vb. refraichir

freshman, n. étudiant de première année m.

freshness, n. fraîcheur f.

fret, n. fermentation

fretful, adj. chagrin

fretfulness, n. irritabilité f.

friction, n. friction f.

Friday, n. vendredi m.

friend, n. ami m.; amie f.

friendless, adj. sans amis

friendliness, n. disposition amicale f.

friendly, adj. amical

friendship, n. amitié f.

frighten, vb. effrayer

frigid, adj. glacial

frill, n. volant m.

frilly, adj. froncé, ruché

frisky, adj. folâtre

frivolous, adj. frivole

frog, n. grenouille f.

frolic, vb. folâtrer

from, prep. de, depuis

front, n. front, devant m.

frontage, n. étendue de devant f.

fronteir, n. frontière f.

frost, n. gelée f.

frosting, n. glacage m.

frosty, adj. gelé, glacé

frown, vb. forncer les sourcils

frowzy, adj. mal tenu, peu soigné

frozen, adj. gelé

frugal, adj. frugal

frugalty, n. frugalité f.

fruit, n. fruit m.

fruitful, adj. fructueux **fructification** f.

fruitless, adj. infructueux

frustrate, vb. faire échouer

frustration, n. frustration f.

fry, vb. frire, faire frire

fryer, n. casserole f.

fuchsia, n. fuchsia m.

fudge, n. travail bâclé m.

fuel, n. combustible m.

fugitive, adj. fugitif

fugue, n. fugue f.

fulfill, vb. accomplir

fulfillment, n. accomplissement m.

full, adj. plein

fullback, n. arrière m.

fully, adv. pleinement

fumble, vb. tâtonner

fume, n. fumée f.

fumigage, vb. desinfecter

fumigator, n. fumigateur m.

fun, n. amusement m.; plaisanterie drôlerie f.

function, n. fonction f.

fund, n. fonds m.

fundamental, adj. fondamental

funeral, n. funérailles f., pl.

fungus, n. fongus m.

funnel, n. entonnoir m.; cheminée f.

funny, adj. drôle

fur, n. fourrure f.

furious, adj. furieux

furlong, n. furlong m.

furnace, n. fourneau m.

furnish, vb. fournir,

meubler

furniture, n. meubles m.,pl.

furred, adj. fourré

furrier, n. fourreur m.

furrow, n. sillon m.

furry, adj. qui ressemble à la fourrure

further, adv. plus éloigné

furthermore, adv. en outre

fury, n. furie f.

fuse, vb. fondre

fuselage, n. fuselage

fusion, n. fusion f.

fuss, n. faire des histoires

fussy, adj. difficile

futile, adj. futile, vain, frivole

future, n. avenir m.

fuzz, n. duvet, flou m.

G

gab, vb. **jaser**

abardine, n. **gabardine** f.

gable, n. pignon m.

gadget, n. truc m.

gag, n. blague, bobard f., bâilon m.; vb. bâilonner

gain, n. gain m.; vb. gagner

gainful, adj. profitable, rémunérateur

gait, n. allure f.

gala, n. fête de gala f.

galaxy, n. galaxie, assemblée brillante f.

gale, n. grand vent m.

gall, n. fiel m.; écorchure f.

gallant, adj. vaillant, galant

gall bladder, n. vésicule du fiel f.

galley, n. galère, cuisine, galée f.

gallon, n. gallon m.

gallows, n. potence f.

gallstone, n. calcul **biliaire m.**

galore, adv. à foison, à profusion

galosh, n. galoche f.

galvanize, vb. galvaniser

gamble, n. jeu de hasard m.

gambler, n. joueur m.

gambling, n. jeu m.

gambler, n. joueur m.

gambling, n. jeu

gambol, n. gambade f.; vb. gamboler

game, n. jeu, gibier m.

gamely, adv. courageusement, crânement

gameness, n. courage m.; crânerie f.

gander, n. jars m.

gang, n. bande, équipe f.

gangling, adj. dégingandé

gangrene, n. gangrène f.

gangrenous, adj. gangreneux

gangster, n. gangster m.

gangway, n. passage, passavant m.

gap, n. ouverture f.

garage, n. garage m.

garb, n. vêtement, costume m.; vb. vêtir, habiller

garbage, n. ordures f., pl.

garble, vb. tronquer, altérer

garden, n. jardin m.

gardener, n. jardinier m.

gardenia, n. gardénia m.

gargle, n. gargarisme m; vb. se gargarlser

gargoyle, n. gargouille f.

garsih, adj. voyant

garland, n. guirlande f.

garlic, n. ail m.

garment, n. vêtement m.

garner, vb. mettre en grenier

garnet, n. grenat m.

garnish, vb. garnir

garnishee, n. tiers-saisi m.

garnishment, n. saisiearrêt f.

garret, n. mansarde f.

garrison, n. garnison f.

garrote, n. garrotte f.; vb. garrotter

garrulous, adj. bavard, loquace

garter, n. jarretière f.

gas, n. gaz m.

gaseous, adj. gazeux

gash, n. coupure, entaille f.; vb. couper, entailler

gasket, n. garcette f.

gasless, adj. sans gaz

gas mask, n. masque à gaz m.

gasoline, n. essence f.

gasp, vb. sursauter, haleter

gassy, adj. gazeux, bavard

gastric, adj. gastrique

gastric juice, n. suc gastrique m.

gastritis, n. gastrite f.

gastronomically, adv. d'une manière gastronomique

gastronomy, n. gastronomie f.

gate, n. porte, barriére, grille f.

gateway, n. porte, entrée f.

gather, vb. rassembler, recueillir

gathering, n. rasemblement m.

gaudy, adj. voyant

gaunt, adj. décharné

gauntlet, m. gantelet m.

gauze, n. gaze f.

gavel, n. marteau m.

gawky, adj. dégingandé

gaze, vb. regarder fixement

gazette, n. gazette f.

gear, n. appareil, engrenage m.;

gearing, n. engrenage m.

gearshift, n. changement de vitesse m.

gelatin, n. gélatine f.

gelding, n. animal châtré m.

gem, n. pierre précieuse f.

gender, n. genre m.

gene, m. déterminant d'hérédité m.

general, adj. and n. général m.

generalize, vb. généraliser

generally, adv. généralement

generate, vb. engendrer, générer

generation, n. génération f.

generic, adj. gémérique

generous, adj. généreux

generously, adv. généreusement

genetic, adj. génétique

genetics, n. génétique f.

genial, adj. sympathique

genially, adv. affablement

genital, adj. génital

genitals, n. organes génitaux m., pl.

genius, n. génie m.

genteel, adj. de bon ton

gentle, n. gentil m.; adj. doux m., douce f.

gentleman, n. monsieur m.

gentleness, n. douceur f.

gently, adv. doucement

gentry, n. petite noblesse f.

genuine, adj. véritable

genuinely, adv. véritablement

genuineness, n. authenticité f.

genus, n. genre m.

geography, n. géographie f.

geometry, n. géomètrie f.

geranium, n. géranium m.

germ, n. germe m.

German, n. Allemand m.; allemand m. adj. allemand

German measles, n. rougeole bénigne f.

Germany, n. l'Allemagne f.

germicide, n. microbicide m.

germinage, vb. germer

gestate, vb. enfanter

gestation, n. gestation f.

gesticulate, vb. gesticuler

gesticulation, n. gesticulation f.

gesture, n. geste m.

get, vb. obtenir, recevoir, prendre, devenir, arriver, entrer, descendre

getaway, n. fuite f.

geyser, n. geyser m.

ghastly, adj. horrible

ghost, n. revenant m.

ghoul, n. goule f.; vampire m.

giant, n. géant m.

gibberish, n. baragouin m.

gibbon, n. gibbon m.

gibe, n. railerie f.; vb. railler

giblet, n. abatis m.

giddy, adj. étourdi

gift, n. don, cadeau m.

gifted, adj. doué

gigantic, adj. géant, gigantesque

giggle, vb. rire nerveusement, glousser

glid, vb. dorer

gill, n. ouïes f., pl.

gilt, n. dorure f.; adj. doré

gimlet, n. vrille f.

gin, n. genièvre m.

ginger, n. gingembre m.

gingersnap, n. biscuit au gingembre m.

gingham, n. guingan m.

giraffe, n. girafe f.

gird, vb. ceindre

girder, n. support m.

girdle, n. gaine f.

girl, n. fille, jeune fille f.

girlish, adj. de jeune fille

gist, n. fond m.; essence f.

give, vb. donner, rendre, céder, distribuer, **renoncer à**

given, adj. donné

giver, n. donneur m.

gizzard, n. gésier m.

glace, adj. glacé

glacial, adj. glaciaire

glacier, n. glacier m.

glad, adj. heureux

glade, n. clairère, éclaircie f.

gladly, adv. volontiers

gladness, n. joie f.

glamour, n. éclat m.

glance, n. coup d'oeil m.

gland, n. glande f.

glare, n. clarté f.; regard enflammé m.; vb. briller, jeter des regards

glaring, adj. éclatant, flagrant, voyant, manifeste

glass, n. verre m.

glasses, n. lunettes f., pl.

glassful, n. verre m.; verrée f.

glassware, n. verrerie f.

glassy, adj. vitreux

glaucoma, n. glaucome m.

glaze, n. lustre m.; vb. vitrer

glazier, n. vitrier m.

gleam, n. lueur f.; vb. luire

glee, n. allégresse f.

gleeful, adj. joyeux, allègre

glen, n. vallon, ravin m.

glide, vb. glisser, planer

glider, n. planeur m.

glimpse, vb. entrevoir

glitter, vb. étinceler

globe, n. globe m.

globular, adj. globulaire, globuleux

globule, n. globule m.

gloom, n. ténèbres f., pl.; tristesse f.

gloomy, adj. sombre

glorify, vb. glorifier

glorious, adj. glorieux, radieux

glory, n. gloire f.

gloss, lustre, vernis m.; glose f.; vb. lustrer, glacer

glossary, n. glossaire m.

glossy, adj. lustré, glacé

glove, n. gant m.

glow, n. lumière, chaleur f.

glowing, adj. embrasé, rayonnant

glowingly, adv. en termes chaleureux

glucose, n. glucose m.

glue, n. colle forte f.; vb. coller

glum, adj. maussade

glumness, n. air maussade m.; tristesse f.

glutionous, adj. glutineux

glutton, n. gourmand m.

gluttonous, adj. gourmand, goulu

glycerin, n. glycérine f.

gnarl, n. loupe f.; noeud m.

gnash, vb. grincer

gant, n. moucheron m.

gnaw, vb. ronger

go, vb. aller

goal, n. but m.

goat, n. chèvre f.

goatee, n. barbiche f.

goatskin, n. peau de chèvre f.

gobble, n. avaleur, dindon m.; vb. gober, avaler

goblet, n. gobelet m.

goblin, n. gobelin, lutin m.

God, n. Dieu m.

godchild, n. filleul m.

goddess, n. déesse f.

godfather, n. parrain m.

godless, adj. athée, impie, sans Dieu

godlike, adj. comme un dieu; divin

godly, adj. dévot, pieux, saint

godmother, n. marraine f.

goiter, n. goitre m.

gold, n. or m.

golden, adj. d'or

goldenrod, n. solidage m.

goldsmith, n. orfèvre m.

golf, n. golf m.

gondola, n. gondole f.

gone, adj. disparu, parti

gonorrhea, n. gonorrhée f.

good, n. bien m.; adj. bon m., bonne f.

good-bye, n. and interj. **adieu m.**

good-hearted, adj. qui a bon coeur, compatissant

good-humored, adj. de bonne humeur, plein de bonhomie

good-natured, adj. au bon naturel, accommodant

goodness, n. bonté f.

good will, n. bonne volonté f.

goose, n. oie f.

gooseberry, n. groseille verte f.

gore, n. chanteau, soufflet m.; vb. corner

gorge, n. gorge f.

gorgeous, adj. splendide

gorilla, n. gorille m.

gory, adj. sanglant, ensanglanté

gospel, n. évangile m.

gossip, n. bavardage m.; vb.

bavarder

Gothic, adj. gothique

gouge, n. gouge f.; vb. gouger

gourmet, n. gourmet m.

govern, vb. gouverner

governess, n. gouvernante f.

government, n. gouvernement m.

govermental, adj. gouvernemental

governor, n. gouvernant m.

gown, n. robe f.

grab, vb. saisir

grace, n. grâce f.

graceful, adj. graceiux

gracefully, adv. avec grâce

gracious, adj. gracieux

grackle, n. mainate m.

grade, n. grade m.; qualité f.; vb. classer

gradually, adv. graduellement

graduate, vb. raduer, prendre ses grades

graft, n. corruption f.

grail, n. graal m.

grain, n. grain m.

gram, n. gramme m.

grammar, n. grammaire f.

grammar school, n. école primaire f.

grammatical, adj. grammatical

grand, adj. grandiose

grandchild, n. petit-fils m.; petite-fille f.

granddaughter, n. petite-fille f.

grandee, n. grand m.

grandeur, n. grandeur f.

grandfather, n. grand-père m.

grand jury, n. jury d'accusation m.

grandly, adv. grandement, magnifiquement

grandmother, n. grand'mère f.

grandson, n. petit-fils m.

grandstand, n. grande tribune f.

granite, n. granit m.

granny, n. bonne-maman f.

gran, n. concession f, subvention f.; vb. accorder; admettre

granule, m. granule m.

grape, n. raisin m.

grapefruit, n. pamplemousse f.

grapevine, n. treille f.

graph, n. courbe f.

graphic, adj. graphique, pittoresque

graphite, n. graphite m.

grasp, n. prise f.; vb. saisir

grass, n. herbe f.

grasshopper, n. sauterelle f.

grate, n. grille f.

grateful, adj. reconnaissant

gratify, vb. contenter, satisfaire

grating, n. grille f.; vb. grincant, discordant

gratitude, n. gratitude f.

gratuity, n. pourboire m.

grave, n. tombe f.; adj. grave

gravel, n. gravier m.

gravely, adv. gravement, sérieusement

gravestone, n. pierre sépulcrale, tombe f.

graveyard, n. cimetière m.

gravitate, vb. graviter

gravitation, n. gravitation f.

gravity, n. gravité f.

gravure, n gravure f.

gravy, n. jus m.

gray, adj. gris

grayish, adj. grisâtre

graze, vb. paître

grazing, n. graisse f.; vb. graisser

great, adj. grand

greatness, n. grandeur f.

Greece, n. la Grèce f.

greediness, n. gourmandise f.

greedy, adj. gorumand

Greek, n. Grec m.; adj. grec m., grecque f.

green, adj. vert

greenhouse, n. serre f.

greet, vb. saluer

greeting, n. salutation f.; accueil m.

gregarious, adj. grégaire

grenade, n. grendade f.

greyhound, n. lévrier m.

grid, n. gril m.

griddle, n. gril m.

gridiron, n. gril m.

grief, n. chagrin m.

grievance, n. grief m.

grieve, vb. affliger, chagriner

grievous, adj. douloureux

grill, n. gril m.; vb. griller

grim, adj. inistre

grimace, n. grimace f.

grime, n. saleté, noirceur f.

grin, n. large sourire m.

grind, vb. moudre, aiguiser

grip, n. prise f.

gripe, vb. saisir, empoigner, grogner

grisly, adj. hideux, horrible

gristle, n. cartilage m.

grit, n. grès, sable m.

groan, n. gémissement m.; vb. gémir

grocer, n. épicier m.

grocery, n. épicerie f.

groin, n. aine f.

groom, n. palefrenier, nouveau marié m.

groove, n. rainure f.

grope, vb. tâtonner

gross, adj. gros m.; grosse f.

grossness, n. grossièreté, énormite f.

grostesque, adj. and n. grotesque m.

grouch, n. maussaderie f.

ground, n. terre f.

grouse, n. tétras m.; vb. grogner

grove, n. bocage, bosquet m.

grovel, vb. ramper, se vautrer

grow, vb. croitre, grandir, devenir, cultiver

growl, vb. grogner

grown, adj. fait, grand

grownup, adj. and n. grand m.,

adulte m.f.

growth, n. croissance f.

growl, vb. grogner

grown, adj. fait

grown-up, adj. fait, grand

growth, n. croissance f.

grub, n. larve f.; ver blanc m.

gruel, n. gruau m.

gruesome, adj. lugubre, terrifiant

grumble, adj. bourru, morose; n. grondeur

grumbling, n. murmure m.

grunt, n. grogenement m.

guarantee, n. garantie f.; vb. garantir

guaranty, n. garantie f.

guard, n. garde f.; vb. garder

guarded, adj. prudent, circonspect, réserve

guardian, n. gardien m.

guardsman, n. garde m.

guava, n. goyave f.

guerrilla, n. guérilla f.

guess, n. conjecture f.

guesswork, n. conjecture

guest, n. invité m.

guidance, n. direction f.

guide, n. guide m.

guidebook, n. guide m.

guidepost, n. poteau indicateur m.

guilt, n. culpabilité f.

guiltly, adv. criminellement

guiltless, adj. innocent

guilty, adj. coupable

guinea pig, n. cobaye m.

guitar, n. guitare f.

gulch, n. ravin m.

gulf, n. golfe m.

gull, n. mouette f.

gulp, n. goulée f.

gum, n. gomme f.

gun, n. canon m.

gunboat, n. canonnière f.

gunman, n. partisan armé, voleur arme, bandit m.

gunshot, n. portée de fusil f.

gush, n. jailissement m.

gusto, n. goût m., délectation,

verve f.

gut, n. boyau, intestin m.

gutter, n. gouttière f.

guzzle, vb. ingurgiter, boire avidement

gym, n. gymnase m.

gymnasium, n. gymnase m.

gymnast, n. gymnaste m.

gymnastic, adj. gymnastique

gymnastics, n. gymnastique f.

gynecology, n. gynécologie f.

gypsy, n. gitane m.f.

H

habeas corpus, n. habeas corpus m.

habiliment, n. habillement m.

habit, n. coutume, habitude f.

habitat, n. habitat m.

habitation, n. habitation f.

habitual, adj. habituel

hack, vb. hacher, tailler en pièces

haddock, n. aigle fin m.

hail, n. grêle f; vb. grêler

hailstorm, n. tempète de grêle f.

hair, n. cheveux m., pl.; chevelure f.

haircut, n. coupe de cheveux f.

hairdo, n. coiffure f.

hairpin, n. épingle à cheveux f.

hale, adj. sain

half, n. motié f.

halfback, n. demi-arrière m.

halfway, adv. à mi-chemin

half-wit, n. niais, sot m.

halibut, n. flétan m.

hall, n. salle f.; vestibule m.

hallow, vb. sanctifier

halloween, n. la veille de la

hallway, n. vestibule m.

halo, n. auréole f.

halt, n. halte f.

halter, n. licou m.; longe, corde f.

halve, vb. diviser en deux, partager en deux

ham, n. jambon m.

hammer, n. marteau m.

hammock, n. hamac m.

hamper, n. pannier m.

hamstring, vb. couper le jarret à, couper les moyens à

hand, n. main f.

handcuff, n. menotte f.; vb. mettre les menottes à

handful, n. poitnée f.

handicap, n. handicap, désavan tage m.

handicraft, n. métier m.

handiwork, n. main-d'o euvre f.

handkerchief, n. mouchoir m.

handle, n. manche m.; vb. manier

handmade, adj. fait à la main, fabriqué à la main

handmaid, n. servante f.

hand organ, n. orgue portatif, orgue de Barbarie m.

handout, n. aumône f.; compte rendu, communiqué à la presse m.

handsome, adj. beau m.; belle f.

handwriting, n. écriture f.

handy, adj. adroit, commode, sous la main

hang, vb. pendre

hanging, n. suspension, pendaison f.

hangman, n. bourreau m.

hangnail, n. envie f.

hang-over, n. reste, reliquat m.

hank, m. échevau m.; torchette f.

hanker, vb. désirer vivement, convoiter

haphazard, adv. au hasard

happen, vb. arriver, se

trouver

happening, n. événement m.

happily, adv. heureusement

happiness, n. bonheur m.

happy, adj. heureux

harass, vb. harceler, tracasser

harbor, n. asile, port m.

hard, adj. dur, difficile; adv. fort

harden, vb. durcir

hardly, adv. durement, à peine

hardness, n. dureté, difficulté f.

hardship, n. privation f.

hardware, n. quincaillerie f.

hardy, adj. robuste

hare, n. lièvre m.

harelip, n. bec-de-lièvre m.

harem, n. harem m.

hark, vb. prêter l'oreille à

harlot, n. prostituée, fill de joie f.

harm, n. mal m.

harmful, adj. nuisible

harmless, adj. inoffensif

hamronic, adj. harmonique

harmonious, adj. harmonieux

harmonize, vb. harmoniser

harmony, n. harmonie f.

harness, n. harpon m.

harrow, vb. herser, tourmenter

harry, vb. harceler

harsh, adj. rude

harshness, n. rudesse f.

harvest, n. moisson f.

hash, n. hachis m.

hasn't, vb. n'a pas

hassle, vb. harceler

haste, n. hâte f.

hasten, vb. hâter

hasty, adj. précipité

hat, n. chapeau m.

hatch, vb. couver

hatchery, n. établissement de pisiculture m.

hatchet, n. hachette f.

hate, vb. haïr, détester

hateful, adj. odieux

hatred, n. haine f.

haul, vb. trîner

haunt, vb. hanter

have, vb. avoir

haven't, n. n'ont pas

havoc, n. ravage m.

hawk, n. faucon m.

hawker, n. colporteur, marchand ambulant m.

hay, n. foin m.

hay fever, n. fièvre des foins f.

hayloft, n. fenil, grenier m.

haystack, n. meule de foin f.

hazard, n. hasard m.

haze, n. petite brume

hazel, n. noisetier, coudrier m.

hazy, adj. brumeux, nébuleux

he, pron. il; lui, celui

head, n. tête f.

headache, n. mal de tête m.

headband, n. bandeau m.

headgear, n. garniture de tête, coiffure f.

heading, n. rubrique f.

headlight, n. phare, projecteur m.

headmaster, n. directeur, principal m.

head-on, adj. and adv. de front

headquarters, n. (mil.) quartier général m.

headstone, n. pierre angulaire f.

heady, adj. capiteux, emporté

heal, vb. guérir

health, n. santé f.

healthful, adj. salubre

healthy, adj. sain

heap, n. tas m.

hear, vb. entendre

hearing, n. audition, ouïe f.

hearse, n. corbillard m.

heart, n. coeur m.

heartache, n. chagrin m.; peine de coeur f.

heartbreak, n. déchirement decoeur m.

heartbroken adj. qui a le coeur brisé

heartburn, n. brûlures d'estomac, aigreur f., pl.

heartsick, adj. qui a la mort dans l'âme

hearty, adj. cordial

heat, n. chaleur f.

heated, adj. chaud, chauffé, animé

heatstroke, n. coup de chaleur m.

heavenly, adj. céleste, divin

heavy, adj. lourd

heavyweight, n. poids lourd m.

Hebrew, n. hébreu m.

heckle, vb. embarrasser de questions

hectare, n. hectare m.

hedge, n. haie f.

hedgehog, n. hérisson m.

heed, n. attention f.

heel, n. talon m.

hefty, adj. fort, solide, costaud

heifer, n. génisse f.

height, n. hauteur f.

heir, n. héritier m.

heirloom, n. meuble de famille m.

helicopter, n. hélicoptère m.

helium, n. hélium m.

hell, enfer m.

hello, interj. allô (au téléphone)

helm, n. gouvernail, timon m.

helmet, n. casque m.

help, n. aide, assistance f.; secours m.

helper, n. aide m.f.

helpful, adj. serviable, utile

helping, n. portion, secourable f.

helpless, adj. délaisse, impuissant

hem, n. ourlet m.; vb. ourler

hemisphere, n. hémisphère m.

hemlock, n. ciguë f.

hemoglobin, n. hémoglobine f.

hemorrhoid, n. hémmorroïde f.

hemp, n. chanvre m.

hen, n. poule f.

hence, adv. d'ici, de là

henceforth, adv. désormais

henchman, n. homme de confiance, acolyte, satellite m.

henna, n. henné m. teindre au henné

her, adj. son, sa, ses

herald, n. héraut m.

heraldic, adj. héraldique

herb, n. herbe f.

herd, n. troupeau m.

here, adv. ici, voici

hereabout, adv. ici; voici, que voici

hereafter, adv. dorénavant

hereby, adv. par ce moyen, par ceci

hereditary, adj. héréditaire

herein, adv. cienclus

heretic, n. hérétique m.f.

heritage, n. héritage, partrimoine m.

hermit, n. ermite m.

hernia, n. hernie f.

hero, n. héros m.

heroic, adj. héroïque

heroin, n. héroïne f.

heroism, n. héroïsme m.

heron, n. héron m.

herpes, n. herpès m.

herring, n. hareng m.

herringbone, n. arête de hareng f.

hers, pron. le sien m.; la sienne f.

herself, pron. le sien m.; la sienne f.

hertz, n. hertz m.

hesitancy, n. hésitation, incertitude f.

hesitant, adj. hésitant, irrésolu

hesitate, vb. hésiter

hesitation, n. hésitation f.

heterosexual, adj. hétérosexuel

hew, vb. couper, tailler

hexagon, n. hexagone m.

hiatus, n. lacune f.

hibernate, vb. hiberner, hiverner

hibernation, n. hibernation f.

hiccup, n. hoquet m.

hickory, n. noyer blanc d'Amerique m.

hide, vb. cacher; n. peau f.

hideous, adj. hideux

high, adj. haut

highbrow, n. intellectuel m.

high fidelity, n. haute fidélité f.

highland, n. haute terre f.

highlight, n. clou m.

highly, adv. extrèmement

high-minded, adj. à l'esprit élevé, généreux

high school, n. lycée m.

high tide, n. marée haute f.

highway, n. grande route f.

hijacker, n. pirate de l'air m.

hike, n. aller à pied

hilarious, adj. hilare

hill, n. colline f.

him, pron. le, lui, celui

himself, pron. lui-même

hinder, vb. gêner, empêcher

hindquarter, n. arrière-main, arrière-train m.

hindrance, n. empêchement, obstacle m.; entrave f.

Hindu, n. Hindou m.; adj. hindou

hinge, n. gond m.

hip, n. hanche f.

hippopotamus, n. hippopotame m.

hire, vb. louer, engager

his, adj. son m., sa f., ses pl.; pron. le sien m.; la sienne

Hispanic, adj. hispanique

historian, n. historien m.

historic, adj. historique

historical, adj. historique

history, n. histoire f.

hit, n. coup, succès m.; vb. frapper

hitch, n. anicroche f.; vb. accrocher

hither, adv. ici.; adj. le plus rapproché

hive, n. ruche f.

hives, n. éruption, varicelle, pustuleuse, urticaire f.

hoard, n. amas m.; vb. amasser; thésauriser

hoarse, adj. enroué

hoax, n. mystification f.

hobo, n. vagabond m., clochard m., ouvrier ambulant m.

hock, n. jarret m.

hockey, n. hockey m.

hod, n. auge f.

hog, n. proc m.

hoist, n. treuil m.; grue f.; vb. hisser

hold, n. prise, cale f.; vb. tenir, contenir, retainir, arrêter, détenir

holdup, n. arrêt m., coup à main arméem.; suspension f.

hole, n. trou m.

holiday, n. jour, de fête m.

holiness, n. sainteté f.

Holland, n. les Pays-Bas m., pl.

hollow, adj. and n. creux m.

holly, n. houx m.

holocaust, n. holcauste m.

hologram, n. hologramme m.

holster, n. étui m.

holy, adj. saint

Holy Spirit, n. Saint-Esprit m.

homage, n. hommage m.

home, n. maison f.; foyer domestique, chez-soi m.

homeland, n. patrie f.

homeless, adj. sans foyer, sans asile, sans abri

homely, adj. laid

homemade, adj. fait à la maison

homesick, adj. nostalgique

homestead, n. ferme f.; bien de famille m.

homework, n. ravail fait à la maison m.; devoirs m., pl.

homocide, n. homicide m.

homonym, n. homonyme m.

homosexual, n. and adj. homosexuel m.

Honduras, n. l' Honduras m.

hone, vb aiguiser, faffiler

honest, adj. honnête

honestly, adv. honnêtement, de bonne foi

honesty, n. honnêteté f.

honey, n. miel m.

honeybee, n. abeille domestique f.

honeycomb, n. rayon de miel m.; vb. cribler, affouiller

honeymoon, n. lune de miel f.

honeysuckle, n. chèvrefeuille m.

honor, n. honneur m.

honorable, adj. honorable

honorary, adj. honoraire

hood, n. capuchon m.; capote f.

hoof, n. sabot m.

hook, n. cro, homeçon m.

hooked, adj. crochu, recourbé

hoop, n. cercle m.

hoot, n. ululation f.

hop, n. houblon m. vb. sautiler

hope, n. espérance f., espoir

hopeful, adj.. plein d'espoir

hopeless, adj. désespéré

hoplessness, n. désespoir, état désespéré m.

hopscotch, n. marelle f.

horde, n. horde f.

horizon, n. horizon m.
horizontal, adj. horizontal
hormone, n. hormone f.
horn, n. corne f.; cor m.
hornet, n. frelon m.
horoscope, n. horoscope m.
horrendous, adj. horrible, horripilant
horrible, adj. horrible
horrid, adj. affreux
horrify, vb. horrifier
horror, n. horreur f.
horse, n. cheval m.
horsepower, n. puissance en chevaux f.
horseradish, n. raifort m.
horseshoe, n. fer à cheval m.
horsewhip, n. cravache f.
hose, n. tuyau m.; bas m., pl.
hosiery, n. bonneterie f.
hospitable, adj. hospitalier
hospital, n. hôpital m.
hospitality, n. hospitalité f.
hospitalization, n. hospitalisation f.
hospitalize, vb. hospitaliser
host, n. hôte m.
hostage, n. otage m.
hostel, n. hôtellerie, auberge f.
hostess, n. hôtesse f.
hostile, adj. hostile
hot, adj. chaud
hot dog, n. saucisse chaude
hotel, n. hôtel m.
hound, n. chien de chasse m.
hour, n. heure f.
hourglass, n. sablier m.
hourly, adv. à chaque heure
house, n. maison, chambre f.
housefly, n. mouche domestique f.
household, n. famille f.; ménage m.
housekeeper, n. gouvernante f.
housewife, n. ménagère f.
housework, n. ménage m.
hover, vb. planer

hovercraft, n. aéroglisseur m.
how, adv. comment; de quelle façon; (how much) combien
however, adv. de quelque manière que, quelque...que
howl, vb. hurler
hub, n. moyeu, centre m.
huckleberry, n. airelle f.
huddle, n. tas confus, fouillis m.
hue, n. couleur f.
huff, n. emportement m., accès de colère m.
hug, n. étreinte f.
huge, adj. énorme
hulk, n. carcasse f., ponton m.
hull, n. coque f.; corps m.
hullabaloo, n. vacarme m.
hum, vb. bourdonner, fredonner
human, humane, adj. humain
humanism, n. humanisme m.
humanitarian, adj. humanitaire
humanities, n. humanités f., pl.
humanity, adv. humainement
humble, adj. humble
humbug, n. blague, tromperie, fumisterie f.
humid, adj. humide
humidify, vb. humidifier
humidor, n. boîte à cigares f.
humiliate, adj. humilier
humiliation, n. humiliation f.
humility, v. humilité f.
humor, n. humour m.; humeur f.
humorous, adj. humoristique, drôle
hump, n. bosse f.
humus, n. humus, ter-

reau m.
hunch, n. bosse f, pressentiment m.; vb. arrondir, voûter
hunchback, n. bossu m.
hundred, adj. and n. cent m.
hundredth, n. and adj. centième m.
Hungarian, n. Hongrois m.; hongrois f. (language) hongrois m.
Hungary, n. l'Hongrie f.
hunger, n. faim f.
hungry, adj. affamé
hunk, n. gros morceau m.
hunt, vb. chasser
hunter, n. chassuer m.
hunting, n. chasse f.
hurl, vb. lancer
hurricane, n. ouragan m.
hurry, n. hâte, précipitation, confusion f.
hurt, vb. faire du mal; n. mal m.
hurtle, vb. se choquer, se heurter
husband, n. mari m.
hush, n. calme, silence m.
husky, adj. cossu, rauque, enroué
hustle, vb. bousculer, (se)presser
hut, n. cabane f.
hutch, n. huche f.; clapier m.
hybrid, n. hybride m.
hydrant, n. prise d'eau, bouche d'incendie f.
hydraulic, adj. hydraulique
hydrogen, n. hydrogène m.
hyena, n. hyène f.
hygiene, n. hygiène f.
hymn, n. hymne, hymne m.f.
hymnal, n. hymnaire, receuil d'hymnes m.
hypen, n. trait d'union m.
hyphenate, vb. mettre un trait d'union à
hypnotism, n. hypnotisme m.

hynotoize, vb. hynotiser
hysteria, n. hystérie f.

I

I, pron. je, moi
iamble, adj. iambique
Iberia, n. l' Ibérie f.
ice, n. glace f.
ice cream, n. glace f.
icing, n. glacé m.
icon, icone f.
idea, n. idée f.
ideal, adj. and n. idéal m.
identical, adj. identique, même
identification, n. identification f.
ideology, n. idéologie f.
idiocy, n. idiotie f.
idiom, n. idiome, idiotisme m.
idiot, adj. and n. idiot m.; imbécile m.f.
idle, adj. désoeuvré, paresseux
idleness, n. oisiveté f.
idol, n. idole f.
idyl, idylle f.
idylic, adj. idyllique
if, conj. si
ignorance, n. ignorance f.
ignorant, adj. ignorant
ignore, vb. feindre d'ignorer
ill, n. mal; adj. malade
illegal, adj. illégal
illegitimate, adj. illégitime
illicit, adj. illicite
illiteracy, n. analphabétisme m.
illiterate, adj. illettré
illness, n. maladie f.
illogical, adj. illogique
illuminate, vb. illuminer
illumination, n. illumination, enluminure f.
illusion n. illusion f.
illusive, adj. illusoire
illustrative, adj. explicatif,

qui éclaircit
illustrious, adj. illustre
ill will, adj. mauvais vouloir m.; malveillance f.
image, n. image f.
imagery, n. images f., pl.; language figuré m.
imaginative, adj. imaginatif
imagine, vb. imaginer
imam, n. imam m.
imbecile, n. imbécile m.
imitate, vb. imiter
imitation, n. imitation f.
immanent, adj. immanent
immature, adj. pas mûr, prématuré
immediate, adj. immédiate
immense, adj. immense
immerse, vb. immerger, plonger
immigrant, n. immigrant, immigré m.
immigrate, vb. immigrer
imminent, adj. imminent
immobile, adj. fixe, immobile
immoral, adj. immoral
immortal, adj. and n. immortel m.
immunity, n. exemption, immunité f.
immunize, vb. immuniser
impact, n. choc, impact m.
impale, vb. empaler
impart, vb. donner, communiquer, transmettre
impartial, adj. impartial
impatience, n. impatience f.
impatient, adj. impatient
impede, vb. entraver, empêcher
impediment, n. entrave, empêchement f. **obstacle m.**
impel, vb. pousser, forcer
impenetrable, adj. impénétrable
impenitent, adj. impénitent
imperative, n. impératif m.; adj. urgent, **impérieux**

imperceptible, adj. imperceptible
imperfect, adj. and n. imparfait m.
imperial, adj. impérial
impersonate, vb. personnifier, représenter
impertinence, n. impertinence f.
impervious, adj. impénétrable
impetuous, adj. impétueux
impetus, n. élan m.; vitesse, acquise f.
implacable, adj. implacable
implant, vb. inculquer, implanter
implement, n. outil m.
implicate, vb. impliquer, entremêler
implication, n. implication f.
implicit, adj. implicite
implied, adj. implicite, tacite
implore, vb. implorer
imply, vb. impliquer
impolite, adj. impoli
imoponderable, adj. impondérable
import, n. portée, signification f.
importance, n. importance f.
important, adj. important
importation, n. imporation f.
importune, vb. importuner
impose, vb. imposer
imposition, n. imposition f.
impossible, adj. impossible
impotence, n. impuissance f.
impotent, adj. impuisant
impoverish, vb. appauvrir
impregnate, vb. imprégner, féconder
impressrio, n. imprésario m.
impress, vb. imprimer(à)
impression, n. impression f.
impressive, adj. impression-

nant

imprison, emprisonner

improbable, adj. improbable

impromptu, adv. adj. and n. impromptu m

improper, adj. inconvenant

improve, vb améliorer

improvement, n. amélioration f.

improvise, vb. improviser

impugn, vb. attaquer, contester, impugner

impulse, n. impulsion f.

impulsion, n. impulsion f.

impunity, n. impunité f.

impure, adj. impur

impurity, n. impureté f.

impute, vb. imputer

in, prep. en, dans, à, par, pour

inadvertent, adj. inattentif, négligent

inalienable, adj. inaliénable

inaugural, adj. inaugural

incandescence, n. incandescence f.

incandescent, adj. incandescent

incapacitate, vb. rendre incapable

incarcerate, vb. incarcérer

incarnate, vb. incarner

incendiary, n. incendiaire m.

incense, n. encens m.

incentive, n. stimulant, aiguillon m.

inception, n. commencement m.

incest, n. inceste m.

inch, n. pouce m.

incident, n. incident m.

incinerator, n. incinérateur m.

incipient, adj. naissant

incision, n. incision, entaille f.

incisive, adj. incisif, tranchant

incisor, n. incisive f.

incite, vb. inciter, instiguer

incline, vb. incliner

include, vb. renfermer

inclusive, adj. inclusif

incognito, adj. and adv. incognito

income, n. revenu m.

incomparable, adj. incomparable

inconvenience, n. inconvénient m.

incorporate, vb. incorporer

incorrigible, adj. incorrigible

increase, n. augmentation f.

incredible, adj. incroyable

incredulous, adj. incrédule

incriminate, vb. incriminer

incumbent, n. titulaire, bénéficiaire m.

incur, vb. encourir

incurable, adj. incurable

indeed, adv. en effet

indefatigable, adj. infatigable, inlassable

indefinite, adj. indéfini

indefinitely, adv. indéfiniment

indelible, adj. indélébile, ineffaçable

indemnity, n. garantie, indemnité, f.; dédommagment m.

indent, vb. denteler, découper, entailler

independence, n. indépendance f.

independent, adj. indépendant

in-depth, adj. profond

index, n. index m.

India, n. l'Inde f.

indicate, vb. indiquer

indication, n. indication f.

indicative, adj. and n. indicatif m.

indicator, n. indicateur m.

indict, vb. accuser, inculper

indifference, adj. indifférent

indigenous, adj. indigène

indigent, adj. indigent, pauvre

indigestion, n. dyspepsie, indigestion f.

indignant, adj. indigné

indignity, n. indignité f.; affront m.

indirect, adj. indirect

indiscreet, adj. indiscret

indiscretion, n. imprudence f.

indispensable, adj. indispensable

indisposed, adj. souffrant

individual, n. individuel, isolé

indoctrinate, vb. endoctriner

indolent, adj. indolent, paresseux

indorse, vb. endosser, sanctionner

induce, vb. persuader, produire

induct, vb. installer, conduire

inductive, adj. inductif

indulge, vb. contenter, favoriser

indulgent, adj. indulgent

industry, n. industrie, assiduité f.

ineligible, adj. inéligible

inept, adj. inepte, mal à propos

inert, adj. inerte, apathique

inertia, n. inertie f.

inevitable, adj. inévitable

inexplicable, adj. inexplicable

infallible, adj. infallible

infamous, adj. infâme

infamy, n. infamie f.

infance, n. enfance f.

infant, n. enfant m.f.; bébé m.

infantile, adj. enfantin, enfantile

infantryman, n. soldat d'infanterie m.

infatuated, adj. infauté, entiché

infect, vb. infecter

infection, n. infection f.

infectious, adj. infectieux

infer, vb. duire

inference, m. inférence f.

inferior, adj. and n. inférieur m.

infernal, adj. infernal

inferno, n. enfer m.

infest, vb. infester

infidelity, n. infidélité f.

infiltrate, vb. infiltrer

infinite, adj. and n. infini m.

infinity, n. infinité f.

infirm, adj. infirme, faible, maladif

inflame, vb. enflammer

inflate, vb. gonfler

inflict, vb. infliger

infliction, n. infliction; peine f.

influenca, n. influence f.

influential, adj. influent

influenze, n. grippe, influenza f.

inform, vb. informer

information, n. renseignements m., pl.

infringe, vb. enfreindre, violer

infuriate, vb. rendre furieux

ingenious, adj. ingénieux

ingredient, n. ingrédient m.

inhabit, vb. habiter

inhale, vb. inhaler, aspirer

inherent, adj. inhérent

inherit, vb. hériter

inhibit, vb. arrêter, empêcher

inhuman, adj. inhumain, barbare

inimical, adj. enemi, hostile, défavorable

inimitable, adj. inimitable

iniquity, n. iniquité f.

initial, n. initiale f.

initiate, vb. commencer, initier

initiation, n. commencement, début m.; **initiation** f.

initiative, n. initiative f.

inject, vb. injecter

injection, n. injection f.

injure vb. nuire blesser, abimer

injurious, adj. nuisible, injurieux

injury, n. person préjudice m.; blessure f.

injustice, n. injustice f.

ink, n. encre f.

inland, adj. and n. intérieur m.

inmate, n. habitant, pensionnaire m.

inn, n. suberge f.

innocence, n. innocence f.

innocent, adj. innocent

innocuous, adj. inoffensif

innovation, n. innovation f.

innumerable, adj. innombrable

inoculate, vb. inoculer

inquest, n. enquête f.

inquire, vb. se renseigner

insane, adj. fou m.; folle f.

insanity, n. folie, démence f.

inscribe, vb. inscrire, graver

inscription, n. inscription f.

insect, n. insecte m.

inseparable, adj. inséparable

insert, vb. insérer

inside, n. dedans m.

insidious, adj. insidieux

insight, n. perspicacité, pénétration f.

insignia, n. insignes m., pl.

insignificant, adj. insignifiant

insinuate, vb. insinuer

insinuation, n. insinuation f.

insipid, adj. insipide, fade

insist, vb. insister

insistence, n. insistance f.

insistent, adj. qui insiste, importun

insolence, n. insolence f.

insolent, adj. insolent

insomnia, n. insomnie f.

inspect, vb. examiner, inspecter

inspection, n. inspection f.

inspector, n. inspecteur m.

inspiration, n. inspiration f.

inspire, vb. inspirer

install, vb. installer

instance, n. exemple m.

instant, n. instant m.

instantaneous, adj. instantané

instantly, adv. à l'instant

instead, adv. au lieu de cela

instigate, vb. instiguer

instill, vb. instiller, faire pénétrer, inculquer

instinct, n. instinct m.

instinctive, adj. instinctif

institute, vb. instituer

instruct, vb. instruire

instruction, n. instruction f.

instructor, n. (mil.) instructeur, m.; chargé de cours m.

instrument, n. instrument m.

insufficient, adj. insuffisant

insular, adj. insulaire

insulate, vb. isoler

insulation, n. isolement m.

insulin, n. insuline f.

insult, vb. insulter

insuperable, adj. insurmontable

insurance, n. assurance f.

insure, vb. assurer

insurgent, adj. and n. insurgé m.

intact, adj. intact

integral, adj. intégrant

integrate, vb. intégrer, compléter, rendre entier

integrity, n. intégrité f.

intellect, n. esprit; intellect m.

intellectual, adj. and n. intellectuel m.

intelligent, adj. intelligent

intelligible, adj. intelligible

intend, vb. avoir l'intention de

intense, adj. intense

intensive, adj. intensif

intention, n. intention f.

intercede, vb. intervenir, intercéder

intercept, vb. intercepter, capter

interdict, vb. interdire, prohiber

interest, n. intérêt m.

interesting, adj. intéressant

interface, n. entreface f.

interfere, vb. intervenir

interim, adv. entre temps, en attendant

interject, vb. lancer, émettre

interjection, n. interjection f.

interlude, n. intermède, interlude m.

intermarry, vb. se marier

interment, n. enterrement m.

intermittent, adj. intermittent

intern, n. interne m.

internal, adj. interne

international, adj. international

interne, n. interne m.

interpret, vb. interpréter

interpretation, n. interprétation f.

interpreter, n. interprète m.f.

interrogate, n. interroger, questionner

interrogation, n. interrogation f.

interrupt, vb. interrompre

intersect, vb. entrecouper, intersecter

intersection, n. intersection f.

intersperse, vb. entremêler, parsemer

interval, n. intervalle m.

intervene, vb. intervenir

intervention, n. intervention f.

interview, n. entrevue f.

intestine, n. intestin m.

intimacy, n. intimité f.

intimate, adj. intime

intimidate, vb. indimider

into, prep. en, à, dans

intonation, n. intonation f.

intone, vb. entonner, psalmodier

intoxicate, vb. enivrer

intravenous, adj. intraveineux

intrepid, adj. intrépide, brave, courageux

intricate, adj. compliqué

intrigue, n. intrigue f.

intrinsic, adj. intrinsèque

introduce, vb. introduire

introspection, n. introspection f; recueillement m.

introver, n. introverti m.

intrude (on), vb. importuner

intruder, n. intrus m.

intuition, n. intuition f.

inundate, vb. inonder

invade, vb. envahir

invader, n. envahisseur m.

invalid, adj. and n. infirme m.f.

invariable, adj. invariable

invasion, n. invasion f.

invective, n. invective f.

invent, vb. inventer

invention, n. invention f.

inventor, n. inventeur m.

invest, vb. investir, placer

investigation, n. investigation f.

investment, n. placement m.

invidious, adj. odieux, haïssable, ingrat

invigorate, vb. fortifier, vivfier

invincible, adj. invincible

invisible, adj. invisible

invitation, n. invitation f.

invite, vb. inviter

invocation, n. invocation f.

invoice, n. facture f.

invoke, vb. invoquer

involuntary, adj. involontaire

involve, vb. impliquer, entraîner

iodine, n. iode m.

Iraq, n. l'Irak m.

irate, adj. en colère, furieux

Ireland, n. l'Irlande f.

iris, n. iris m.

Irish, adj. irlandais

irk, vb. ennuyer

iron, n. fer m.

irony, n. ironie f.

irrational, adj. irrationnel, abusrde

irrefutable, adj. irréfutable, irrécusable

irregular, adj. irrégulier

irrelevant, adj. non pertient, hors de propos

irresistible, adj. irrésistible

irresponsible, adj. irresponsable

irreverent, adj. irrévérent, irrévérencieux

irrevocable, adj. irrévocable

irrigate, vb. irriguer, arroser

irrigation, n. irrigation f.

irritability, n. irritabilité f.

irritant, n. irritant m.

irritate, vb. irriter

Islam, n. Islam m.

island, n. île f.

isolate, vb. isoler

isolation, n. isolement m.

isosceles, adj. isoscèle

Israel, n. l'Israël m.

issuance, n. délivrance f.

issue, n. issue, question, émission f.; résultat m.

it, pron. il m.; elle f.; le m., la f., lui

Italy, n. l'Italie f.

itch, n. démangeaison f.

item, n. articlé; détail m.

itinerant, adj. ambulant

its, adj. son m.; sa f.; ses pl. pron. le sien m.; la

sienne f.

itself, pron. lui-même m.; ellemême f.

ivory, n. ivoire m.

ivy, n. lierre m.

J

jab, n. coup de pointe, coup sec m.

jackal, n. chacal m.

jackass, n. âne, idiot m.

jacket, n. veston m.; jaquette f.

jacknife, n. couteau de poche m.

jade, n. rosse, haridelle f.

jaded, adj. surmené, éreinté

jaged, adj. déchiqueté, entaillé

jaguar, n. jaguar m.

jail, n. prison f.

jailer, n. gardien, geôlier m.

jam, n. foule, presse, confiture f.

jamb, n. jambage, chambranle m.

janitor, n. concierge, portier m.

January, n. janvier m.

Japan, n. le Japon m.

Japanese, n. Japonais

jar, n. pot, son discordant m.

jargon, n. jargon m.

jasmine, n. jasmin m.

jaundice, n. jaunisse f.

jaunt, n. petite excursion, balade f.

javelin, n. javelot m.; javeline f.

jaw, n. mâchoire f.

jay, n. geai m.

jazz, n. jazz m.

jealous, adj. jaloux

jealousy, n. jalousie f.

jeans, n. jeans m., pl.

jeer, n. raillerie, moquerie, huée f.

jelly, n. gelée f.

jellyfish, n. méduse f.

jeopardize, vb. exposer au danger, mettre en danger, hasarder

jeopardy, n. danger m., péril m.

jerk, n. saccade f.

jerky, adj. saccadé, coupé

jersey, n. jersey, tricot de laine m.

Jerusalem, n. Jérusalem m.

jester, n. railleur, farceur, bouffon m.

Jesus, n. Jésus m.

jet, n. jet, jet d'eau m.

jettison, n. jet à la mer m.

jetty, n. jetée f.; môle m.

Jew, n. Juif m.; Jive f.

jewel, n. bijou m.

jeweler, n. bijoutier, jouaillier m.

jewelry, n. bijouterie f.

Jewish, adj. juif m.; jive f.

jib, n. loc m.

jiffy, n. instant, clin d'oeil m.

jig, n. gigue f.; calibre, gabarit m.

jilt, vb. délaisser

jingle, n. tintement m., cliquetis m.

jinx, n. porte-malheur m.

jittery, adj. trés nerveux

job, n. travail; emploi m.

jobber, n. intermédiaire, marchandeur m.

jockey, n. jockey m.

jocular, adj. facétieux, jovial

jocund, adj. enjoué

jodhpurs, n. pantation d'équitation m.

jog, n. coup, cahot m.; secousse f.

joggle, n. petite secousse f.

join, vb. joindre, se jondre à

joiner, n. menuisier m.

joint, n. joint m.; adj. commun

jointly, adv. ensemble, conjointement

joist, n. solive, poutre f.

joke, n. plaisanterie f.; vb. plaisanter

joker, n. farceur, blagueur, joker m.

jolly, adj. joyeux

jolt, n. cahot, choc m.; secousse f.; vb. cahoter, secouer, ballotter

jonquil, n. jonquille f.

jostle, vb. coudoyer

journal, n. journal m.

journalism, n. journalisme m.

journalist, n. journaliste m.

journey, n. voyage m.; vb. voyager

jovial, adj. jovial, gai

jowl, n. mâchoire f.

joy, n. joie f.

joyful, adj. joyeux

jubilant, adj. réjoui, jubilant, exultant

jubilee, n. jubilé m.

Judaism, n. judaïsme m.

judge, n. juge m.

judgement, n. jugement m.

judicial, adj. judiciaire

judiciary, adj. judiciaire

judicious, adj. judicieux, sensé

jug, n. cruche f.

juggle, vb. jongler

jugular, adj. jugulaire

juice, n. jus m.

juicy, adj. juteux

July, n. juillet m.

jumble, n. brouillamini, fouillis m.

jump, n. saut m.; vb. sauter

junction, n. jonction f.; embranchement m.

juncture, n. jointure, jonction, conjoncture f.

June, n. juin m.

jungle, n. jungle, brousse f.

junior, adj. and n. cadet, subalterne m.

juniper, n. genévrier, genièvre m.

junk, n. rebut m.

junket, n. jonchée f.; festin m.

jurisdiction, n. juridiction f.

jurist, n. juriste, légiste m.

juror, n. juré, membre du jury m.

jury, n. jury m.

just, adj. juste

justice, n. justice f.

justifiable, adj. justifiable, justifié

justification, n. justification f.

justify, vb. justifier

jut, vb. faire saillie

jute, n. jute m.

juvenile, adj. juvénile

K

kale, n. chou m.

kaleidoscope, n. kaléidoscope m.

kangaroo, n. kangourou m.

karat, n. carat m.

karate, n. karaté m.

keen, adj. aiguisé, aigu, pénétrant

keep, vb. tenir, garder, continuer à

keeper, n. gardien m.

keepsake, n. souvenir m.

keg, n. caque f.; barillet m.

kennel, n. chenil m.

kercheif, n. fichu, mouchoir m.

kernel, n. grain m.; amande f.

kerosene, n. pétrole m.

ketchup, n. sauce piquante à

kettle, n. bouilloire f.

key, n. clef, clé f.

keyhole, n. entrée de clef f.

khaki, n. kaki m.

kick, n. coup de pied m.

kid, n. gosse m.f., chevreau m.

kidnap, vb. enlever de vive force

kidnaper, n. auteur de l'enlévement m.

kidney, n. rein, rognon m.

kidney bean, n. haricot nain m.

kill, vb. tuer

killer, n. tueur, meurtrier m.

kiln, n. four, séchoir m.

kilocycle, n. kilocycle m.

kilowatt, n. kilowatt m.

kilt, n. kilt m.

kimono, n. kimonoi m.

kin, n. parent m.

kind, n. genre m.

kindergarten, n. jardin dénfants m.

kindle, vb. allumer

kindling, n. allumage m.

kindness, n. bonté f.

kindred, n. parenté f.

kinetic, adj. cinétique

king, n. roi m.

kiss, n. baiser m.; vb. baiser, embrasser

kitchen, n. cuisine f.

kite, n. cer-volant m.

kitten, n. petit chat m.

knack, n. tour de main m.

knapsack, n. havresac m.

knead, vb. pétrir, malaxer

knee, n. genou m.

kneecap, n. genouillère f.

knife, n. couteau m.

knock, n. coup m.

knot, noeud m.

know, vb. savoir, connaître

knowing, adj. intelligent, instruit

knowledge, n. connaissance f.

knuckle, n. articulation du doigt, jointure

kodak, n. kodak m.

Korea, n. la Corée f.

kosher, adj. cachir, cacher

L

label, n. étiquette m.

labor, n. travail m.; ouvriers m., pl.

laboratory, n. laboratoire m.

laborer, n. travailleur m.

laborious, adj. laborieux

labor union, n. syndicat m.

laburnum, n. cytise m.

labyrinth, n. labyrinthe m.

lac, n. gomme-laque

lace, n. dentelle f.; cordon, point, lacet m.

lacerate, vb. lacérer, déchirer

laceration, n. lacération f.

lack, n. manque, besoin, défaut m.; vb. manquer de

lackadaisical, adj. affecté, minaudier; apathique

lacking, adj. manquant (de)

laconic, adj. laconique

lacquer, n. laque m.

lacrosse, n. crosse canadienne f.

lactic, adj. lactique

lactose, n. lactose f.

lacy, adj. de dentelle

lad, n. garcon, jeune homme

ladder, n. échelle f.

lade, vb. charger (de); jeter

lady, n. dame f.

lading, n. chargement m.

ladle, n. cuiller à pot

lady, n. dame f.

ladybug, n. coccinelle f.

lad, repris de justice

lagoon, n. lagune f.

laid, adj. vergé

laid-back, adj. décontracté

lair, n. tanière f., repaire m.

laissez faire, n. laissez faire m.

laity, n. les laïques m., pl.

lake, n. lac m.

lamb, n. agneau m.

lamb's wool, n. laine d'agneau

lambent, adj. qui effeure;

qui rayonne doucement

lame, adj. boiteux

lament, vb. se lamenter; pleurer

lamentable, adj. lamentable, déplorable

lamentation, n. lamentation f.

laminate, vb. laminer, écacher

lamp, n. lampe f.

lamplighter, n. allumeur m.

lamp post, n. lampadaire m.

lampoon, n. pasquinade f.

lance, n. lance f.

lancer, n. lancier m.

land, n. terre f.

landholder, n. propriétaire foncier m.

landing, n. débarquement, mise à terre m.

landlord, n. propriétaire m.f.

landmark, n. borne f.

landscape, n. paysage m.

landslide, n. éboulement m.

landward, adv. vers la terre

lane, n. senteir m.; ruelle f.

language, n. langue f.; langage m.

languid, adj. languissant

languish, vb. languir

languor, n. langueur f.

lank, adj. grand et maigre

lanolin, n. lanoline f.

lantern, n. lanterne f.

lap, n. genoux m., pl.

lapel, n. revers m.

lapin, n. lapin m.

lapse, n. laps m.;faute f.

larceny, n. larcin, vol m.

lard, n. saindoux m.

large, adj. grand

largely, adv. en grande partie

largo, n. largo m.

lariat, n. lasso m.

lark, n. aloutette f.

larkspur, n. pied d'alouette, delphinium m.

larva, n. larve f.

laryngitis, n. laryngite f.

larynx, n. larynx m.

lascivious, adj. lascif

laser, n. laser m.

lash, n. lanière f.; coup de fouet m.

lass, n. jeune fille f.

lassitude, n. lassitude f.

lasso, n. lasso m.

last, adj. dernier; enfin

lasting, adj. durable

latch, n. loquet m.

latchet, n. cordon de soulier m.

late, adj. and adv. tard; en retard; feu; dernier

lately, adv. dernièrement

latecomer, n. retardataire

latent, adj. latent, caché

lateral, adj. latéral

lath, n. latte f.

lathe, n. tour m.

lather, n. mousse f.; écume f.

Latin, n. Latin m.; latin m.

latitude, n. latitude f.

latrine, n. latrine f.

latten, n. fer-blanc, laiton

latter, adj. and pron. dernier

lattice, n. treillis m.

laud, vb. louer

laudable, adj. louable

laudanum, n. laudanum m.

laudatory, adj. élogieux

laugh, n. rire m.

laughable, adj. risible

laugher, n. rieur m.

laughing, adj. rieur, enjoué

laughter, n. rire m.

launch, vb. lancer; mettre à la mer

launder, n. blanchir

laundry, n. buanderie

laundryman,n. blanchiesseur m.

laureate, adj . and n. lauréat m.f.

laurel, n. laurier m.

lava, n. lave f.

lavatory, n. lavabo m.

lave, vb. laver, baigner

lavender, n. lavande f.

lavish, adj. prodigue; somptueux

lavishly, adv. prodigalement

lavishness, n. prodigalité f.

law, n. loi f.; droit m.

lawful, adj. légal

lawless, adj. sans loi

lawn, n. peolouse f.

lawsuit, n. procès m.

lawyer, n. avocat; avoué; jurisconsulte m.

lax, adj. lâche, mou, relâche

laxative, n. laxatif m.

laxity, n. relâchement m.

lay, vb. poser

layer, n. couche f.

layman, n. laïque m.

lazy, adj. paresseux

lead, n. plomb m.; mine f.

leaden, adj. de plomb

leaser, n. chef m.

leaf, n. feuille f.

leaflet, n. feuillet m.

league, n. ligue f.; lieue f.

leak, n. fuite f.; voie d'eau f.

leakage, n. fuite d'eau f.

leaky, adj. qui coule, qui fait eau

lean, adj. s'appuyer, s'incliner, pencher, inckiner

leap, vb. sauter

leap year, n. année bissextile f.

learn, vb. apprendre

learned, adj. savant, docte

learning, n. science, instruction f.

lease, n. bail m.

leash, n. laisse, attache f.

least, n. permission f.

leaven, n. levain m.; vb. faire lever

lecherous, adj. lascif, libertin

lecture, n. conférence f

lecturer, n. conférencier m

ledge, n. bord m.

ledger, n. grand livre m.

leech, n. sangsue f.

leek, n. poireau m

leeward, adj. and adv. sous le vent

left, adj. and n. gauche f.; à gauche

leftist, n. gaucher m.

leg, n. jambe f.; patte f.

legacy, n. legs m.

legal, adj. légal

legality, n. légalité f.

legalization, légalisation

legalize, vb. rendre; egal

legally, adv. légalement

legate, vb. léguer

legation, n. légation

legend, légende f.

legendary, adj. légendaire

legible, adj. lisible

legion, n. légion f.

legionary, adj. de légion

legislate, vb. faire les lois

legislation, n. législation f.

legislator, n. législateur m.

legislature, n. législature f.

legitimate, adj. légitime

legume, n. légume m.

leisure, n. loisir m.

leisurely, adv. à loisir

lemon, n. citron m.

lemonade, n. limonade f.

lend, vb. prêter

lenght, n. longueur; durée f.

lengthen, vb. allonger

lengthwise, adv. en long

lengthy, adj. assez long

lenient, adj. indulgent

lens, n. lentille f.; objectif m.

Lent, n. carême m.

Lenten, adj. de carême

Lentil, n. lentile f.

lento, adv. lento

leopard, n. léopard m.

leper, n. lépreux m.

leprosy, n. lèpre f.

lesbian, n. lesbienne f.

lesion, n. lesion f.

less, adj. moindre; moins de

lesser, adj. moindre

lesson, n. lecon f.

lest, conj. de peur que

let, vb. laisser; louer

letdown, n. décaption f.

lethal, adj. mortel

lethargic, adj. léthargique

lethargy, n. léthargie f.

letter, n. lettre f.

letterhead, n. en-tête de lettre m.

lettuce, n. laitue f.

levee, n. lever m.

level, adj. égal

lever, n. levier m.

levy, n. levée f.

lewd, adj. impudique

lexicon, n. lexique m.

liability, n. responsibilité f.

liable, adj. responsable de sujet à

liar, n. menteur m.

libation, n. libation f.

libel, n. diffamation f.

libelous, adj. diffamatoire

liberal, adj. libéral; généreux

liberalism, n. libéralisme m.

liberality, n. libéralité f.

liberate, vb. libérer

libertine, n. libre-penseur m.

liberty, n. liberté f.

libidinous, adj. libidneux

libido, n. libido m.

librarian, n. bibliothécaire m.

library, n. bibliothèque f.

libretto, n. livret m.

licnese, n. permis m.; patente f.

licentious, adj. licencieux

lick, vb. lécher

licorice, n. réglisse f.

lid, n. couvercle m.

lie, n. mensonge m.; vb. mentir

lien, n. privilège m.

lieutenant, n. lieutenant m.

life, n. vie f.

lifeguard, n. garde du corps m.

life insurance, n. assurance sur la vie f.

lifeless, adj. sns vie

life preserver, n. appareil de sauvetage m.

lifetime, n. vie f., vivant m.

lift, vb. lever

ligament, n. ligament m.

ligature, n. ligature f.

light, n. lumière f.; adj.léger; clair

lighten, vb. alléger; éclairer

lighthouse, n. phare m.

lightly, adv. légèrement

lightness, n. légèreté f.

lightning, n. éclair m.

lignite, n. lignite m.

likable, adj. agréable

like, adj. pareil; même, égal; vb. aimer bien, trouver bon

likelihood, n. probabilité f.

likely, adj. probable

liken, vb. comparer

likeness, n. ressemblance f.

likewise, adv. de même

lilac, n. lilas m.

lily, n. lis; muguet m.

limb, n. membre m.; grosse branche f.

limber, adj. souple, flexible

limbo, n. limbes m., pl.

lime, n. chaux f; lime f.

limelight, n. lumière oxhydrique f.

limestone, n. pierre à chaux f., calcaire m.

limit, n. limite f.

limitation, n. limitation f.

limitless, adj. sans limite

limousine, n. limousine f.

limp, adj. flasque

limpid, adj. limpide

linden, n. tilleul m.

line, n. ligne f.

lineage, n. lignée, race f.

lineal, adj. inéaire

linen, n. toile f.; linge m.

linger, vb. s'attarder

lingerie, n. lingerie f

liniment, n. liniment m.
lining, n. doublure f.
link, n. chaînon, anneau m.
linoleum, n, linoléum m.
linseed, n. graine de lin f.
lint, n. charpie f.
lion, n. lion m.
lip, n. lèvere f.
liquefy, vb. liquéfirer
liqueur, n. liqueur f.
liquid, adj. and n. liquide m.
liquidate, vb. liquider
liquidation, n. liquidation f.,
   acquittement m.
liquor, n. boisson alco
   olique f.
lisle, n. fil d'Ecosse m.
lisp, vb. zézayer
list, n. liste f.
listen, vb. écouter
listless, adj. inattentif
litany, n. litanie f.
literacy, n. degré d'aptitude
   à lire et à écrire m.
literal, adj. litéral
literary, adj. littéraire
literate, adj. lettré
literature, n. littérature f.
lithe, adj. flexible, pliant
lithograph, vb. lithogra-
   phier
lithography, n. litho gra-
   phie f.
litiant, n. plaideur m.
litigation, n. litige m.
litmus, n tournesoil m.
litter, n. litière f.; fouillis m.
little, n. and adv. peu m.;
   adj. petit
liturgical, adj. liturgique
liturgy, n. liturgie f.
live, vb. vivre
lively, adj. vif m., vive f.
liven, vb. animer, activer
liver, n. foie m.
livery, n. livrée f.
livestock, n. bétail m.
livid, adj. livide, blême
lizard, n. lézard m.
llama, n. lama m.

lo, interj. voilà
load, n. charge f.; fardeau m.
loaf, n. pain m.
loafer, n. fainéant m.
loam, n. terre grasse f.
loan, n. prêt m.; emprunt m.
loath, adj. fâché, peiné
loathing„ n. déoût m.
loathsome, adj. dégoûtant
lobby, n. vestibule m.
lobe, n. lboe m.
lobster, n. hoimard m.
local, adj. local
locale, n. localité, scène f.
locality, n. localité f.
localize, vb. localiser
location, n. placement m.
lock, n. serrure f.; mèche f.
locker, n. armoire f.
locket, n médallion m.
lockjaw, n. teanos m.
locksmith, n. serrurie m.
locomotive, n. locomotive f.
lode, n. filon m.
lodge, vb. loger
lodger, n. locataire m.
lodging, n. logement m.
loft, n. grenier m.
lofty, adj. élevé; hautain
log, n. bûche f.; loch m.
loge, n. loge f.
logic, n. logique f.
logical, adj. logique
loins, n. reins m., pl.
loiter, vb. fiâner
lollipop, n. sucre d'orge m.
London, n. Londres m.
lone, adj. solitaire; délaissé
lonely, adj. isolé
loneliness, n. solitude f.
long, adj. long m., longue f.
longevity, n. longévté f.
loom, n. métier m.
loop, n. boucle f.
loophole, n. meurtrière f.
loose, adj. lâche
loosen, vb. desserrer
loot, n. butin m.
lop, vb. élaguer, ébrancher
loquacious, adj. loquace

lord, n. seigneur m; lord m.
lordship, n. seigneurie f.
lose, vb. perdre
loss, n. perte f.
lot, n. sort m.; terrain m.
lotion, n. lotion f.
lottery, n. loterie f.
lotus, n. lotus, lotos m.
loud, adj. fort; bruyant
lounge, n. sofa; hall m.
louse, n. pou m.
lout, n. rustre m.
louver, n. auvent m.
lovable, adj. aimable
love, n. amour m.
lovely, adj. beau m., belle f.
lover, n. amoureux m.
low, adj. bas m., basse f.
lower, vb. baisser
lowly, adj. humble
loyal, adj. loyal
loyalist, n. loyaliste m.
loyalty, n. loyauté f.
lozenge, n. pastille f.
lubricant, n. lubrifiant m.
lubricate, vb. lubrifier
lucid, adj. lucide
luck, n. chance f.
lucky, adj. heureux
lucrative, adj. lucratif
ludicrous, adj. risible
lug, vb. trainer, tirer
luggage, n. bagages m., pl.
lukewarm, adj. tiede
lull, n. moment de calme m.
lullaby, n. berceuse f.
lumbago, n. lumbago m.
lumber, n. bois de charpente m.
luminous, adj. lumineux
lump, n. masse f.
lumpy, adj. grumeleux
lunacy, n. foile f.
lunar, adj. lunaire
lunatic, n. aliéné m.
lunch, n. déjeuner m.
luncheon, n. déjeuner m.
lung, n. poumon m.
lunge, n. embardée f.
lure, vb. leurrer; attirer

lurid, adj. blafard, sombre

lurk, vb. se cacher

luscious, adj. délicieux

lush, adj. luxuriant

lust, n. luxure f.

luster, n. lustre m.

lustful, adj. lascif, sensuel

lustrous, adj. brillant, lustré

lusty, adj. vigoureux

lute, n. luth m.

Lutheran, n. Luthérien m.

luxuriant, adj. exubérant

luxurious, adj. luxueux

luxury, n. luxe m.

lying, n. mensonge m.

lymph, n. lymphe f.

lynch, vb. lyncher

lyre, n. lyre f.

lyric, adj. lyrique

lyricixm, n. lyrisme m.

M

macaroni, n. macaroni m.

machine, n. machine f.

machine gun, n. mi-
trailleuse f.

machinery, n. machiniste
m.

machismo, n. phallocratie f.

macho, adj. phallocrate

mackerel, n. maquereau m.

mackinaw, n. mackinaw m.

mad, adj. fou m., folle f.

madam, n. madame f.

madcap, n. and adj.
écervelé

madden, vb. exaspérer

made, adj. fait, fabriqué

mafia, n. mafia f.

magazine, n. revue f.

magic, n. magie f.

magician, n. magicien m.

magistrate, n. magistrat m.

magnanimous, adj. mag-
nanime

magnate, n. magnat m.

magnesium, n .
magnésium m.

magnet, n. aimant m.

magnetic, adj. magnétique

magnificance, n. maginifi-
cence f.

magnificent, adj. magni-
fuque

magnify, vb. grossir

magnitue, n grandeur f.

mahogany, n. acajou m.

maid, n. bonne f.

maiden, adj. de jeune fille

mail, n. courrier m.

mailman, n. facteur m.

maim, vb. estropier, mutiler

main, adj. principal

mainframe, n. partie cen-
trale d'un infomrateur f.

mainland, n. continent m.

mainspring, n. grand ressort
m.; mobile essentiel m.

maintain, vb. maintenir;
soutenir

maintenance, n. entre-
tien m.

maize, n. maïs m.

majestic, adj. majestueux

majesty, n. majesté f.

major, n. commandant m.

majority, n. majorité f.

make, n. fabrication

maker, n. fabricant m.

makeshift, n. pis aller

make-up, n. maquillage m.

malady, n. maladie f.

malaria, n. malaria f.

male, adj. and n. mâle m.

malevolent, adj. maleveil-
lant

malice, n. méchanceté f.

malicious, adj. méchant

malign, vb. calomnier

malignant, adj. malin m.,
maligne f.

malleable, adj. malléable

malnutirition, n. sousali-
mentation f.

malpractice, n. méfait m.

malt, n. malt m.

mammal, n. mammifère m.

man, n. homme m.

manage, vb. diriger, mener,
conduire

management, n. direction f.

manager, n. directeur,
ménager m.

mandate, n. mandat m.

mandatory, adj. obligatoire

mandolin, n. mandoline f.

mane, n. crinière f.

maneuver, n. manoeuvre f.

manganese, n.
manganèse m.

manger, n. mangeoire f.

mangle, vb. mutiler

manhood, n. virilité f.

mania, n. manie; folie f.

maniac, adj. and n. fou m.,
folle f.

manicure, n. manucure m.f;
soin des ongles m.

manifest, adj. manifeste

manifesto, n. manifeste m.

manifold, adj. divers, multiple

manipulate, vb. manipuler

mankind, n. genre
humain m.

manly, adj. viril

manner, n. manière f.;
moeurs f., pl.

mannerism, n. maniérisme,
m., affectation f.

mansion, n. château;
hôtel m.

manslaughter, n. homicide
involontaire m.

mantel, n. manteau m.;
tablette f.

mantle, n. manteau f.

manual, adj. and n.
manuel m.

manufacture, n. manufac-
ture f.; produit m.

manufacturer, n.
fabricant m.

manure, n. fumier m.

manuscript, adj. and n.
manuscrit m.

many, adj. beaucoup de,
bien

map, n. carte
géographique f.

maple, n. érable m.

mar, vb. gâter

marble, n. marbre m.

march, n. march f.;

March, n. mars m.

mare, n. jument f.

margarine, n. marge f.

marijuana, n. marijuana f.

marine, n. marine f.; fuslier marin m.

mariner, n. marin m.

marionette, n. marionnette f.

marital, adj. matrimonial

maritime, adj. maritime

mark, 1. n. marque f.; but m.; point m.; vb. marquer

market, n. marché m.

market place, n. place due marché f.

marmalade, n. confiture f.

maroon, adj. and n. rouge foncé m. vb. abandonner

marquee, n. marquise f.

marquis, n. marquis m.

marriage, n. mariage m.

married, adj. marié

marrow, n. moelle f.

marry, vb. épouser; se marier

marsh, n. marais m.

marshal, n. maréchal m.

marshmallow, n. guimauve f. bonbon à la guimauve

martial, adj. martial

martinet, n. officier strict sur la discipline m.

martyr, n. martyr m.

martyrdom, n. martyre m.

marvel, n. merveille f.; vb. s'étonner de.

marvelous, adj. merveilleux

mascara, n. mascara m.

mascot, n. mascotte f.

masculine, adj. masculin

mash, n. purée f.

mask,, n. masque m.; vb. masquer

mason, n. macon m.

masquerate, n. mascarade f., bal masqué m.

mass, n. masse f.

Mass, n. messe f.

massacre, n. massacre m. vb. massacrer

massage, n. massage m.

masseur, n. masseur m.

massive, adj. massif

mass metting, n. réunion f.

mast, n. mât m.

master, n. maître m.; vb. maîtriser

masterpiece, n. chef-d'oeuvre m.

mastery, n. maîtrise f.

masticate, vb. mâcher

mat, n. paillasson m.

match, n. allumette f.; **égal m.; mariage m.; vb. assortir**

mate, n. camarade m.f; compaguon m.; compagne f.; officier m.

material, n. matière; étoffe f.; adj. matériel

materialism, n. matérialisme m.

maternal, adj. maternel

maternity, n. maternité f.

mathematical, adj. mathématique

mathematics, n. mathématiques f., pl.

matinee, n. matinée f.

matriarch, n. femme qui porte les chausses f.

matrimony, n. mariage m.

matron, n. matrone f.

matter, n. matière f.; suiet m.; affaire f.; vb. importer

mattress, n. matelas m.

mature, adj. mûr.; vb. mûrir

maturity, n. maturité f.; échéance f.

maudlin, adj. larmoyant

mausoleum, n. mausolée m.

maxim, n. maxime f.

maximum, n. maximum m.

may, vb. pouvoir

May, n. mai m.

maybe, adv. peut-être

mayhem, n. mutilation f.

mayonnaise, n. mayonnaise f.

mayor, n. maire m.

maze, n. labyrinthe m.

me, pron. me; moi

meadow, n. prée m.; prairie f.

meager, adj. maigre

meal, n. repas m.; farine f.

mean, n. moyenne f.; moyens m.,pl.; moyen m.; adj. humble; avare; vb. vouloir dire; se proposer

meaning, n. sens m.

meantime adv. sur ces entrefaites

measles, n. rougeole f.

measure, n. mesure f.; vb. mesurer

measurement, n. **mesurage m.**

meat, n. viande f.

mechanic, n. mecanicien m.

mechanical, adj. mécanique

mechanism, n. **mécanisme m.**

mechanize, vb mécaniser

medal, n. médaille f.

meddle, vb. se mêler

media, n. organes de communication m., pl

median, n. médian

mediate, vb. agir en médiateur

medical, adj. médical

medicate, vb. médicamenter

medicine, n. médecine m.

medieval, adj. médiéval

mediocre, adj. médiocre

mediocrity, n. médiocrité f.

meditate, vb. méditer

meditation, n. méditation f.

Mediterranean, n. Méditerranée f.

medium, n. milieu; intermédiaire; médium m.

medley, n. mélange m.

meek, adj. doux m., douce f.

meekness, n. douceur f.

meet, vb. rencontrer; faire la connaissance de; faire

face à

meeting, n. réunion f.

megahertz, n. mégahertz m.

megaphone, n. mégaphone m.

melancholy, n. mélancolie f.

mellow, adj. moelleux

melodous, adj. mélodieux

melodrama, n. mélodrame m.

melody, n. mélodie f.

melon, n. melon m.

melt, vb. fondre

meltdown, n. fusion f.

member, n. membre m.

membrane, n. membrane f.

memnto, n. mémento m.

meoir, n mémoire m.

memorable, adj. mémorable

memorandum, n. mémorandum m.

memorial, n. souvenir, monument m. adj. commémoratif

memorize, vb. apprendre par coeur

memory, n. mémoire f.

meance, n. menace; vb. meancer

menagerie, n. ménagerie f.

mend, vb. raccommoder; corriger

mendacious, adj. menteur

mendicant, n. and adj. mendiant m.

menial, adj. servile

menstruation, n. menstruation f.

menswear, n. habillements masculins m., pl.

mental, adj. ental

mentality, n. mentalité f.

menthol, n. menthol m.

mention, n. mention f.; vb. mentionner; il n'yu a pas de qoi

menu, n. menu m.

mercantile, adj. mercantile

mercenary, adj. and n. mercenaire m.

merchandise, n. marchandise f.

merchant, n. négociant m.; adj. marchand

merchant marine, n. marine marchande f.

merciful, adj. miséricordieux

merciless, adj. impitoyable

mercury, n. mercure m.

mercy, n. miséricorde f.; à la merci de

mere, adj. simple

merely, adv. simplement

merge, vb. fusionner

merger, n. fusion f.

merit, n. mérite m.; vb. mériter

meritorious, adj. méritant; méritoire

mermaid, n. sirène f.

merriment, n. gaieté f.

merry, adj. gai

merry-go-round, n. carrousel m.

mesh, n. maille f.

mesmerize, n. magnétiser

mess, n. fouillis m.; gâchis ml; (mil.) popote f.; vb. gâcher

message, n. message m.

messenger, n. messager m.

messy, adj. malpropre

metabolism, n. métabolisme m.

metal, n. métal m.

metallic, adj. métallique

metamorphosis, n. métamorphose f.

metaphysics, n. metaphysique f.

meteor, n. météore m.

meter, n. mètre m.; compteur m.

method, n. méthode f.

meticulous, adj. méticuleux

metric, n. métrique

metropolis, n. métropole f.

metroplitan, adj. métropolitain

mettle, n. ardeur f.

Mexican, n. Mexicain m.

Mexico, n. Mexique m.

mezzanine, n. mezzanine f.

microbe, n. microbe m.

microfiche, n. microfiche f.

microfilm, n. microfilm m.

microform, n. microforme f.

microphone, n. microphone m.

microscope, n. microscope m.

microscopic, adj. microscopique

mid, adj. du milieu, moyen

middle, n. milieu m.

middle-aged, adj. d'un certain âge

Middle Ages, n. moyen âge m.

middle class, n. classe moyenne f.

midget, n. nain m.

midnight, n. minuit m.

midriff, n. diaphragme m.

midwife, n. sage-femme f.

mien, n. mine f., air m.

might, n. puissance f.

mighty, adj. puissant

migrate, vb. emigrer

migration, n. migration f.

mild, adj. doux m., douce f.

mildew, n. rouille f.

mile, n. mille m.

mileage, n. kilométrage m.

milestone, n. bourne routière f.

militarism, n. militarisme m.

military, adj. militaire

militia, n. milice f.

milk, n. lait m.

milkman, n. laitier m.

milky, adj. laiteux

mill, n. moulin m.; filature f.; usine f.; vb. moudre; fourmiller

miller, n. meunier m.

millimeter, n. millimètre m.

milliner, n. modiste f.

millinery, n. modes f., pl.

million, n. million m.

millionaire, adj. and n. million naire m.f.

mimic, n. mime, imitateur m.; adj. mimique; vb. imiter

mince, vb. hacher

mind, n. eprit m.; avis m.; envie f.; vb. faire attention à; écouter; s'occuper de; prendre garde; garder; n'importe

mindful, adj. attentif

mine, n. mine f.; pron. le mien m., la mienne f.

mine field, n. champ de mines m.

miner, n. mineur m.

mineral, adj. and n. minéral m.

mine sweeper, n. dragueur de mines m.

mingle, vb. mêler

minature, n. miniature f.

miniaturize, vb. miniaturiser

minimize, vb. réduire au minimum

minimum, n. minimum m.

minimum wage, n. salaire minimum m.

mining, n. exploitation minière f., pose de mines f.

minister, n. ministre m.

ministry, n. ministlere m.

mink, n. vison m.

minnow, n vairon m.

minor, adj. and n. mineur m.

minority, n. minorité f.

minstrel, n. ménestrel m.

mint, n. la monnaie f.; vb. frapper

minute, n. minute f.; adj. minuscule; minutieux

miracle, n. miracle m.

miraculous, adj. miraculeux

mirage, n. mirage m.

mire, n. boue f., bourbier m.

mirror, n. miroir m.

mirth, n. gaieté f.

misadventure, n. mésaventure f., contretemps m.

misappropriate, vb. détourner, dépréder

misbehave, vb. se mal conduire

miscellaneous, adj. divers

mischief, n. mal m.; malice f.

mischievous, adj.. expiègle; méchant

misconstrue, vb. mal interpréter, tourner en mal

misdemeanor, n. délit m.

miser, n. avare m.f.

miserable, adj. malheureux; misérable

miserly, adj. avare

misery, n. souffranc; misère f.

misfit, n. vêtement manqué m.; inadapté m., inapte m.

misfortune, n. malheur m.

misgiving, n. doute m.

mishap, n. mésaventure f.

mislead, vb. romper, égarer

misplace, vb. mal placer

mispronounce, vb. mal prononcer, estropier

miss, vb manquer; vous me manquez

Miss, n. mademoiselle f.

missile, n. projectile, m.

mission, n. mission f.

missionary, adj. and n. missionnaire m.f.

misspell, vb. mal orthographier

mist, n. brume f.

mistake, n. erreur f.; vb. comprendre mal; se tromper

mister, n. monsieur m.

mistletoe, n. gui m.

mistreat, vb. maltraiter

mistress, n. maîtresse f.

mistrust, n. méfiance f.; vb. se méfier de

misty, adj. brumeux

misunderstand, vb. mal comprendre

misuse, vb. faire mauvais usage; maltraiter

mite, n. denier m., obole f.

mitigate, vb. adoucir

mitten, n. moufle f.

mix, vb. mêler

mixture, n. mélange m.

mix-up, n . émbrouillement m.

moan, n. gémissement m.

moat, n. fossé m.

mob, n. foule; populace f.

mobile, adj. mobile

mobilization, n. mobilisation f.

mobilize, vb. mobiliser

mock, vb. se moquer de; singer

mockery, n. moquerie f.

mod, adj. à la mode

mode, n. mode m.

model, n. modèle m.

moderate, adj. modéré; vb. modérer

moderation, n. modératon f.

modern, adj. moderne

modernize, vb. moderniser

modest, adj. modeste

modesty, n. modestie f.

modify, vb. modifier

modish, adj. à la mode

modulate, vb moduler

moist, adj. moite

moisten, vb. humecter

moisture, n. humidité f.

molar, n. and adj. molaire f.

molasses, n. mélasse f.

mold, n. moule m.; moisissure f.; vb. mouler

moldy, adj. moisi

mole, n. taupe f.; grain de beauté m.

molecule, n. molécule f.

molest, vb. molester

mollify, vb. adoucir, apaiser

molten, adj. fondu, coulé

moment, n. moment m.

momentary, adj. momentané

momentous, adj. important

monarch, n. monarque m.

monarchy, n. monarchie f.

monastery, n. monastère m.

Monday, n. lundi m.

monetary, adj. monétaire

money, n. argent m.; monnaie f.

mongre. n. métis m.

monitor, n. moniteur m.

monk, n. moine m.

monkey, n. singe m.

monologue, n. monologue m.

monoplane, n. monoplan m.

monopolize, vb. monopoliser

monopoly, n. monopole m.

monosyllable, n. monosyllabe m.

monotone, n. monotone m.

monotonous, adj. monotone

monotony, n. monotonie f.

monsoon, n. mousson f.

monster, n. monstre m.

monstrosity, n. monstruosité f.

monstrous, adj. onstrueux

month, n. mois m.

monthly, adj. mensuel

monument, n. monument m.

monumnetal, adj. monumental

mood, n. humeur f.; mode m.

moody, adj. de mauvaise humeur

moon, n. lune f.

moonlight, n. clair de lune m.

moor, n. lande f.

mooring, n. amarrage m.

moot, adj. discutable

mop, n. balai à laver m.

moped, n. cyclomoteur m

moral, n. morale f.; moralité f.

morale, n. moral m.

moralist, n. moraliste m.f.

morality, n. moralité fl; morale f.

morally, adv. moralement

morbid, adj. morbide

more, adj. and adv. plus; plus de

moreover, adv. de plus

mores, n. moeurs f., pl

morgue, n. morgue f.

morning, n. matain m.; matinée f.;

moron, n. idiiot

morose, adj. morose

Morse code, n. l'alphabet Morse m.

morsel, n. morceau m.

mortal, adj. and n. mortel m.

mortality, n. mortailité f.

mortar, n. mortier m.

mortgage, n. hypothèque f.

mortician, n. entrepreneur de pompes funèbres m.

mortify, vb. mortifier

mortuary, adj. mortuaire

mossaaic, n. mosaaïque f.; adj. en mosaïque

Moscow, n. Moscou m.

Moslem, adj. and n. musulman m.

mosquito, n. moustique m.

moss, n. mousse f.

most, n. le plus.; adj. le plus; la plupart.

mostly, adv. pur la plupart; la plupart du temps

moth, n. mite f.

mother, n. mère f.

mother-in-law, n. belle-mère f.

motif, n. motif m.

motion, n. mouvement m.; signe m.

motionless, adj. immobile

motion-picture, n. film m.

motivate, vb. motiver

motive, n. motif m.

motor, n. moteur m.

motorboat, n. canot automobile m.

motorist, n. automo-

biliste m.

motto, n. devise f.

mound, n. tertre m.

mount, n. mont m.; monture

mountain, n. montagne f.

mountaineer, n. montagnard m.

mountainous, adj. montagneux

mountebank, n. saltimbanque m., charlatan m.

mourn, vb. pleurer

mournful, adj. triste

mourning, n. deuil m.

mouse, n. souris f.

mouth, n. bouche f.

mouthpiece, n. embouchure f., embout m.

movable, adj. mobile

move, vb. mouvoir, tr.; remuer; bouger; émouvoir

movement, n. mouvement m.

moving, n. déménagement m.

mow, vb. faucher; tondre

much, adj. pron. and adv. beáucoup de; trop; tant

mucilage, n. mucilage m.

muck, n. fumier n.

mucous, adj. muqueux

mud, n. boue f.

mud-bank, n. de vase m.

muddle, vb. brouiller, troubler

muddler, n. brouillon m.

muddy, adj boueux

muff, n. manchon m.

muffin, n. petit pan m.

muffle, vb. emmitoufler

mug, n. gobelet, pot m.

mulatto, n. mulâtre m.

mulberry, n. mûre f.

mukch, n. paillis m.

mule, n. multet m.

mull, n. cap promontoire m.

muller, n. molette

multariculate, adj. multicapsulaire

multicoloured, adj. multi-
colore

multinational, adj. multinational

multiple, adj. multiple m.

multiplication, n. multiplication f.

multiplicty, n. multi-
plicité f.

multiply, vb. multiplier

multitude, n. multitude f.

mum, n. maman f.

mumble, vb. marmotter

mummer, n. mime

mummification, n. momi-
fication f.

mummy, n. momie;
maman f.

mumps, n. oreilons m., pl.

munch, vb. mâcher

mundane, adj. mondain

mungoose, n. mangouste f.

municipal, adj. municipal

munificent, adj. munificent

munition, n. munition f.

mural, n. peinture murale f.

murder, n. meurtre m.

murderer, n. meutrtrier m.

murmur, n. murmure m.;
vb. murmurer

muscle, n. muscle m.

muscular, adj. musculaire;
musculeux

muse, n. muse f.; vb.
méditer

museum, n. musée m.

mush, n. brouillage m.

mushroom, n.
champignon m.

music, n. musique f.

musical, adj. musical; musi-
cient

musician, n. musicien m.

Muslim, adj. and n. musulman m.

muslin, n. mousseline f.

must, vb. devoir; falloir

mustache, n. moustache f.

mustard, n. moutarde f.

muster, vb. rassembler

musty, adj. moisi, suranné

mutation, n. mutation f.

mute, adj. muet

mutilitate, vb. mutiler

mutiny, vb. mutinerie f.

mutter, vb. grommeler

mutton, n. mouton m.

mutual, adj. mutuel

muzzle, n. muselière f.

my, adj. mon m., ma f.,
mes pl.

myopia, n. myopie f.

myuriad, n. myriade f.

myrtle, n. myrte m.

myself, pron. moi-même;
moi

mystagogue, n. mysta-
gogue m.

mysterious, adj. mystérieux

mystery, n. mystère m.

mystic, adj. mystique; initié,
magicien

mystical, adj. mystique

mystify, vb mystifier

myth, n. mythe m.

mythical, adj. mythique

mythology, n. mythologie f.

N

nab, vb. happer, pincer,
saisir

nag, vb. gronder

nail, n. ongle; clou m.

nail-brush, n. brosse à ongles f.

nail-file, n. lime à ongles f.

naïve, adj. naïf m. naïve f.

naked, adj. nu, à nu

name, n. nom m.

named, adj. nommé
désigné

nameless, adj. sans nom,
anonyme

name-plate, n. plaque f.

namesake, n. homonyme m.

nanny, n. bonne d'enfant

nap, n. peitit somme m.

nape, n. nuque f.

napkin, n. serviette f.

napkin ring, rond de servi-
ett m.

narcissus, n. narcisse m.

narcotic, adj. and n. narco-
tique m.

narrate, vb. raconter

narration, narration f.

narrative, n. récit, narré m.

narrator, n. narrateur m.

narrow, adj. étroit

narrow minded, adj. à
l'esprit étroit

nasal, adj. nasal, du nez

nasty, adj. désagréable

natal, adj. natal

nation, n. nation f.

national, national m.

nationalism, n. mational-
isme m.

nationalist, n. national-
iste m.

nationalize, vb. nationaliser

native, n. natif m.;
indigène m.f.

nativity, n. naissance f.

natural, adj. naturel

naturalism, n. natural-
isme m.

naturalist, n. naturaliste m.

naturalize, vb. naturaliser

naturalness, n. naturel m.

nature, n. nature f.

naught, n. néant, rien

naughty, adj. méchant

nausea, n. nausée f.

nauseous, adj. nauséeux

nauseousness, n. nature
nauséabonde f.

nautical, adj. marin, nau-
tique

naval, adj. naval

nave, n. nef f.

navel, n. nombril m.

navigable, adj. navigable

navigate, vb. naviguer

navigation, n. navigation f.

navigator, n. navigateur m.

navy, n. marine f.

nay, adv. non; bien plus

near, adj. proche.; adv. prés.

nearly, adv. de près;

presque

nearness, n. proximité

near-sighted, adj. myope

neat, adj. propre, soigné

neatness, n. propreté f.

nebula, n. nébuleuse f.

nebulous, adj. nébuleux

necessary, adj. nécessaire

necessitate, vb. nécessiter

necessity, n. nécessité f.

neck, n. cou; goulot m.

necklace, n. cravate f.

nectar, n. nectar m.

need, n. besoin m.

needful, adj. nécessaire

needfully, adv.
nécessairement

needle, n. aiguille f.

needle point, n. pointe d'aiguille f.

needless, adj. inutile

needlessness, n. inutilité f.

needs, adv. nécessairement

needy, adj. nécessiteux

nefarious, adj. inlame

negative, adj. négatif

neglect, n. négligence f.

negligee, n. négligée f.

negligent, adj. négligent

negligible, adj. négligeable

negotiate, vb. négocier

negotiation, n.
négociation f.

neigh, vb. hennir

neighbor, n. voisin;
prochain m.

neighborhood, n. voisinage m.

neither, adj. and pron. ni
l'un ni l'autre

neon, n. néon m.

neophyte, n. néophyte m.

neoplasm, n. n'eoplasme m.

nephew, n. neveu m.

nepotism, n. népotisme m.

Neptune, n. Neptune m.

nerve, n. nerf m.

nerve cell, n. cellule
nerveuse f.

nerve racking, adj. horripi-

lant

nervous, adj. nerveux

nest, n. nid m.

nest egg, n. nichet m.

nesting, adj. nicheur

nestle, vb. se nicher

net, n. filte m.; adj. net m.,
nette f.

Netherlands, (the) n. les
Pays Bas m., pl.
Hollande f.

network, n. réseau m.

neuraliga, n. névralgie f.

neurology, n. neurologie f.

neurotic, adj. and n.
nevrosé m.

neuter, adj. neutre

neutral, adj. and n.
neutre m.

neutralize, vb. neutraliser

neutron, n. neutron m.

never, adv. jamais

nevertheless, adv.
néanmoins

new, adj. nouveau m., nouvelle; neuf m., neuve f.

newel, n. tout flambant neuf

news, n. nouvelle f.

newsboy, n. vendeur de
jouirnaux m.

newscast, n. journal parlé
m.; informations f., pl.

newspaper, n. journal m.

newsreel, n. film d'actualité m.

New Testament, n. le Nouveau Testament m.

new year, n. nouvel an m.

next, adj. prochain; adv. ensuite

nexus, n. connexion f.

nib, n. bec m.; pointe f.

nibble, vb. grignoter

nice, adj. bon, agréable

niceness, n. goût
agréable m.

nick, n. entaille f.

nickel, n. nickel m.

nickname, n. surnom m.

nicotine, n. nicotine f.

niece, n. nièce f.

nifty, adj. pimpant

night, n. nuit f.; soir m.

night cap, n. bonnet de nuit

night club, n. boite de nuit
f., établissement
de nuit m.

nightgown, n. chemise de
nuit f.

nightingale, n. rossignol m.

nightly, adv. tous les soirs;
toutes le nuits

nightmare, n. cauchemar m.

nimble, adj. agile

nine, adj. and n. neuf m.

nineteen, adj. and n. dixneuf m.

ninety, adj. and n. quatrevingt-dix m.

ninth, adj. and n.
neuvième m.

nip, n. pincement m.,
pince f.

nipple, n. mamelon m.

nitrogen, n. nitrogène m.

no, adj. pas de interj., adv.
non

nob, n. caboche f.

nobility, n. noblesse f.

noble, adj. noble

nobleman, n. gentilhomme m.

nobleness, n. noblesse f.

nobly, adv. noblement

nobody, pron. personne

nocturnal, adj. nocturne

nocturnally, adv. nocturnement

nod, n. signe de la tête m.

node, n. noeud m.

nohow, adv. en aucune
facon

noise, n. bruit m.

noiseless, adj. silencieux

noisome, n. puant, fétide

noisy, adj. bruyant

nomad, n. nomade m. and f.

nominal, adj. nominal

nominate, vb. nommer;
désigner

nomination, n. nomination;
présentation f.

nominee, n. personne
nommée f., candidat
choisi m.
nonability, n. inhabilité
non acceptance, n. nonac-
ceptation f.
nonaligned, adj. non-aligné
nonchalant, adj. nonchalant
noncombatant, adj. and n.
noncombattant m.
noncommissioned, adj. sans
brevet
noncommittal, adj. qui
n'engage à rien
nondescript, adj.
indéfinissable
none, pron. aucun
nonentity, n. nullité f.
non-proliferation, n. non-
prolifértion m.
non-resident, n. and adj.
nonrésident m.
nonsense, n. abusrdité f.
non-stop, adj. sans arrêt
noodles, n. nouilles f., pl.
nook, n. coin m., recon m.
noon, n. midi m.
noonday, n. midi m.
noose, n. noeud coulant m.
nor, conj. ni; ni...ne
norm, norme f.
normal, adj. normal
normality, n. normalité f.
normalize, vb. normaliser
normally, adv. normalement
north, n. nord m.
northeast, n. nord-est m.
northern, adj. du nord
North Pole, n. pole nord m.
northwest, n. nord-ouest m.
Norway, n. Norvège f.
Norwegian, n.
Norvégien m.
nose, n. nez m.
nosebleed, n. saignement de
nez m.
nose dive, n. vol piqué m.
nosalgia, n. nostalgie f.
nostalgic, adj. nostalgique
nostril, n. narine f.;
naseau m.

nostrum, n. panacée f.,
remède de chariatan m.
nosy, adj. fouinard
not, adv. pas
notability, n. notabilité f.
notable, adj. and n. no-
table m.
notary, n. notaire m.
notation, n. notation
notch, n. coche, encoche
note, n. note f.; billet m.
notebook, n. carnet m.
noted, adj. célèbre
notepaper, n . papier à
notes m.
noteworthy, adj. remar-
quable, mémorable
nothing, pron. rien
notice, n. avis m.; attention
f.; préavis m.
noticeable, adj. remar-
quable; apparent
notification, n. notification f.
notify, vb. avertir
notion, n. idée f.
notoriety, n. notoriété f.
notorious, adj. notoire
notwithstanding, adv. tout
de même
noun, n. substnatif m.
nourish, vb. nourrir
nourishment, n. nourrit-
ure f.
novel, n. roman m.
novelist, n. romancier m.
novelty, n. nouveauté f.
November, n. novembre m.
novice, n. novice m.f.
now, adv. maintenant; à
présent
nowhere, adv. nulle part
nozzle, n. ajutage m.
nuance, n. nuance f.
nuclear, adj. nucléaire
nude, adj. nu; le nu m.
nugget, n. pépite f.
nuisance, n. ennui m.;
peste f.
null, adj. nul
number, n. nombre;

chiffre m.
numerical, adj. numérique
numerous, adj. nombreux
num, n. religieuse f.
nuncho, n. nonce m.
nuptial, adj. nuptial
nurse, n. garde-malade m.
or f.
nursery, n. chambre des en-
fants f.; pépinière f.
nurture, n. nourriture f.; vb.
nourrir
nut, n. noix f.; écrou m.
nutcracker, n. casse-
noix m.
nutrition, n. nutrition f.
nutritious, adj. nutrifif
nutshell, n. coquille de
noix f.
nylon, n. nylon m.
nymph, n. nymphe f.

O

oak, n. chême m.
oar, n. rame f.
oasis, n. oasis f.
oath, n. serment m.; juron
m.
oatmeal, n. farine d'avoine f
oats, n. avoine f.
obodurate, adj. obstiné teu
obedience, n. obéissance f.
obedient, adj. obéissant
obeisance, n. salut m.
obedient, adj. obéissant
obeisance, n. salut m.
obelisk, n. obélisque m.
obey, vb. obéir à
obituary, n. nécrologe m.
object, n. objet m.
objection, n. objection f.
objectionable, adj.
répréhensible
objective, adj. and n. objectif m.
obligation, n. obligation f.
obligatory, adj. obligatoire
oblige, vb. obliger

oblivion, n. oubli m.
obnoxious, adj. odieux
obscene, adj. obscène
obscure, adj. obscur
obsequious, adj. obsequieux
observance, n. observance f.
observation, n. observation f.
observe, vb. observer
observer, n. observateur m.
obsession, n. obsession f.
obsolete, adj. désuet
obstacle, n. obstacle m.
obstetrician, n. médecin-aocoucheur m.
obstinate, adj. obsitiné
obstroperous, adj. tapageur
obstruct, vb. obstruer
obstruction, n. obstructin f.
obtain. vb. obtenir
obtrude, vb. mettre en avant
obviate, vb. prévenir, éviter
obvious, adj. évident
occasion, n. occasion f.
occasional, adj. de temps en temps
occult, adj. occulte
occupant, n. occupant m.
occupation, n. occupation f.; métier m.
occupy, vb. occuper
occur, vb. avoir lieu; se présenter à l'esprit
occurrence, n. occurrence f.
ocean, n. océan m.
octagon, n. octogone m.
octave, n. octave f.
October, n. octobre m.
octopus, n. poulpe m.
ocular, adj. oculaire
oculist, n. oculiste f.
odd, adj. impair; dépariellé; bizarre
oddity, n. singularité f.
odds, n. inégalitef., cote f.
odious, adj. odieux
odor, n. odeur f.
of, prep de
off, adv. à...de distance; trompu; prep. de

offend, vb. offenser; enfreindre la loi
offender, n. offenseur; délinquant m.
offense, n. offense f.; délit m.
offensive, n. offensive f.; adj. offensif; offensant
offer n. offre f.; vb. offrir
offering, n. offre, offrande f.
office, n. office m.; fonctions f., pl; bureau m.
officer, n. (mil) officier; fonctionnaire m.
official, adj. officiel
officiate, vb. officier
officious, adj. officieux
offshore, adv. au large
offspring, n. descendant m.
often, adv. souvent
oil, n. huile f.
oilcloth, n. toile cirée f.
oily, adj. huileux
ointment, n. onguent m.
okay, interj. très bien
old, adj. vieux m.
old-fashioned, adj. démodé
Old Testament, n. l'Ancien Testament m.
olfactory, adj. olfactif
oligarchy, n. oligarchie f.
olive, n. olivier m.; olive f.
omelet, n. omelette f.
omen, n. présage m.
ominous, adj. de mauvais augure
omission, n. omission f.
omit, vb. omettre
omnibus, n. omnibus m.
omnipotent, adj. omnipotent, tout-puissant
on, prep. sur
once, adv. une fois; autrefois
one, adj. un, seul, m.
oneself, pron. soi-mème; se
one-sided, adj. unilatéral
onion, n. oignon m.
only, adj. seul; adv. seulement
onslaught, n. assaut m.
onward, adj. and adv. en

avant
opal, n. opale f.
opaque, adj. opaque
open, adj. ouvert; vb. ouvrir
opening, n. ouverture f.
opera, n. opéra m.
opera glasses, n. jumelles f., pl.
operate, vb. opérer; actionner
operatic, adj. d'opéra
operation, n. opération f.; fonctionnement m.
operator, n. opérateur m.
operetta, n. opérette f.
opinion, n. opinion f.
opponent, n. adversaire m.f.
opportunism, n. opportunisme m.
opportunity, n. occasion f.
oppose, vb. (put in opposition) opçposer; (resit) s'opposer à
opposite, 1. adj. opposé. **2.** adv. vis-à-vis. **3.** prep. en face de
opposition, n. oppoisiiton f
oppress, vb. opprimer
oprression, n. oppression f
oppressive, adj. oppressif; (heat, etc.) accablant
optic, adj. optique
optician, n. opticien m
optimism, n. optimisme m
optimistic, adj. optimiste
option, n. option f.
optional, adj. facultatif
optometry, n. optométrie f.
opulent, adj. opulent, riche
or, conj. ou; ni
oracle, n. oracle m.
oral, adj. oral
orange, n. orange f.
orangeade, n. orangeade f.
oration, n. discours m.
orator, n. orateur m.
oratory, n. art oratoire m.
orbit, n. orbite f.
orchard, n. verger m.
orchestra, n. orchestre m.
orchid, n. orchhidée f.

ordain, vb. ordonner

ordeal, n. épreuve f.

order, n. ordre m.; commande f.; vb. ordonner; commander

orderly, adj. ordonné

ordinance, n. ordannance f.

ordinary, adj. and n. ordinaire m.

ordination, n. ordinatiion f.

ore, n. minerai m.

organ, n. orgue m.; organe m.

organdy, n. organdi m.

organic, adj. organique

organism, n. organisme m.

organist, n. organiste m.f.

organization, n. organisation f.

organize, vb. organiser

orgy, n. orgie f.

orient, vb. orienter

Orient, n. Orient m.

Oriental, n. Oriental m.

orientation, n. orientation f.

origin, n. origine f.

original, adj. original; originel

originality, n. originalité f.

ornament, n. ornement m.

ornamental, adj. ornemental

ornate, adj. orné

ornithology, n. ornithologie f.

orphan, n. orphelin m.

orphanage, n. orphelinat m.

orthodox, adj. orthodoxe

orthopedics, n. orthopédie f.

osmosis, n. osmose f.

ostensible, adj. prétendu

ostentation, adj. plein d'ostentation

ostracize, vb. ostraciser

ostrich, n. autruch f.

other, adj. and pron. autre

otherwise, adv. autrement

ought, vb. devoir

ounce, n. once f.

our, adj. notre

ours, pron. le nôtre m.

ourself, pron. nous-même;

ouster n. éviction f.

out, adv. dehors

outbreak, n. commencement m.

outburst, n. éruption f.

outcast, n. paria m.

outcome, n. résultat m.

outdoors, adv. dehors

outer, adj. extérieur

outfit, n. équipement m.

outgrowth, n. conséquence f.

outing, n. promenade f.

outlandish, adj. bizarre

outlaw, vb. proscrire

outlet, n. issue f.

outline n. contour m.

out-of-date, adj. suranné

output, n. rendement m.

outrage, n. outrage m.

outrageous, adj. outrageant

outrank, vb. occuper un rang supérieur

outright, adv. complètement

outrun, vb. dépasser

outside, adv. dehors; prep. en dehors de

outskirts, n. extrémité; bords f., pl.

outspread, vb. étendre, déployer

outstanding, adj. non payé

outstay, vb. rester plus longtemps que

outstretched, adj. étendue, tendu

outwalk, vb. marcher plus vite que

outward, adj. extérieur, du dehors

outwardly, adv. extérieurement

outwardness, objectivité f.

outwear, durer plus longtemps que

oval, adj. and no. ovale m.

ovation, n. ovation f.

oven, n. four m.

over, prep. sur; au-dessus de; au delà de; plus de; adv. partout

overbearing, adj. arrogant

overcoat, n. pardessus m.

overcome, vb. vaincre; succomber à

overdue, adj. arriéré, échu

overflow, vb. déborder

overhaul, vb. examiner en détail, remettre au point

overhead, adj. général; adv. en haut

overkill, n. exagération rhétorique f.

overlook, vb. avoir vue sur; négliger

overnight, adv. pendant la nuit

overpower, vb. subjuguer; accabler

overrule, vb. décider contre

overrun, vb. envahir

oversee, vb. surveiller

oversight, n. inadvertance f.

overstuffed, adj. rembourré

overt, adj. manifeste

overtake, vb. rattraper; arriver à

overthrow, vb. renverser

overtime, n. heures supplémentaires f., pl.

overture, n. ouverture f.

overturn, vb. renverser

overview, n. vue d'ensemble f.

overweight, n. excédent m.

overwhelm, vb. accabler (de)

owe, vb. devoir

owing, adj. dû

owl, n. hibou m.

own, adj. propre; posséder

owner, n. propriétaire m.f.

ox, n. boeuf m.

oxide, oxyde m.

oxygen, n. oxygène m.

oxygen mask, n. masque d'oxygène m.

oyster, n. huître f.

ozone, n. ozone m.

P

pace, n. pas m.; allure f.;
vb. arpenter
pacific, adj. pacifique
Pacific Ocean, n. océan
Pacifique m.
pacify, vb pacifier
pack, n. paquet m.; bande f.;
vb emballer; entasser
package, n. paquet m.
pact, n. pacte, contrat m.
pad, n. bourrelet m.; tampon
m.; bloc m.
paddle, n. pagaie f.
pagan, adj. and n. païen m.
page, n. page f.; page m.
pageant, n. spectacle m.
pagoda, n. pagode f.
pail, n. seau m.
pain, n. douleur; peine f.
painful, adj. douloureux
painstaking, adj. soigneux
paint, n. peinture f.; vb.
pendre
painter, n. peintre m.
painting, n. peinture f.
pair, n. apire f.
pajamas, n. pyjama m.
palace, n. palais m.
palate, n. palais m.
pale, adj. pâle
paleness, n. pâleur f.
palette, n. palette f.
pall, n. drap funéraire m.;
vb. s'affadir
pallbearer, n. porteur m.
pallid, adj. pâle, blème
palm, n. palmier m.; palme;
paume f.
paltry, adj. mesquin
pamper, vb. choyer
pamphlet, n. brochure f.
pan, n. casserole f.
panacea, n. panacée f.
pancake, n. crêpe f.
pane, n. vitre f.
panel, n. panneau m.
panic, n. panique f.
panorama, n. panorama m.

pant, vb. haleter
pantomime, n. pan-
tomime m.
pantry, n. office f.
pants, n. pantalon m.
panty hose, n. collant m.
papal, adj. papal
paper, n. papier m.
papberback, n. livre
broché m.
par, n. pair m., égalité f.
parable, n. parabole f.
parachute, n. parachute m.
parade, n. parade f.
paradise, n. paradis m.
paradox, n. paradoxe m.
paragraph, n. alinéa m.
parakeet, n. pettruche f.
parallel, n. paralléle f.
(line); adj. parallèle
paralyze, vb. paralyser
paramedic, n. assistant
médical m.
parameter, n. paramètre m.
paramount, adj. souverain
paraphrase, vb. paraphraser
parasite, n. parasite m.
parcel, n. paquet; colis
postal m.
parch, vb. dessécher
parchment, n. par-
chemin m.
pardon, n. pardon m.
pare, vb. peler (fruit)
parent, n. père m.; mère f.;
parents (parents) m., pl.
parcentage, n. naissance f.
parenthesis, n. parenthèse f.
park, n. parc m.; vb. sta-
tionner
parley, n. conférence f.,
pourparler m.
parliament, n. parlement m.
parliamentary, adj. par-
lementaire
parlor, n. petit salon m.
parochial, adj. paroissial; de
clocher
parody, n. parodie f.
parole, n. parole f.; vb.
libérer conditinellment

paroxysm, n. paroxysme m.
parrot, n. perroquet m.
parsley, n. persil m.
parson, n. pasteur m.
part, n. partie; part f.; vb.
diviser; partager; se
séparer
partial, adj. partiel; partial
participant, adj. and n. participant m.
participant, adj. and n. participant m.
participate, vb. participer
particle, n. particule f.
particular, n. détail m.; adj.
particulier; exigeant
parting, n. séparation;
raie f.
partition, n. partage m. cloi
son f.
partner, n. associé m.
party, n. parti m.; réception
f.; groupe m.
pass, vb. passer; passer par
passable, adj. traversable,
passsable, assez on
passage, n. passage m.
passenger, n. voyageur; air
passager m.
passion, n. passion f.
passionate, adj. passionné
passive, adj. and passif m.
passport, n. passeport m.
past, adj. and n. passé m.;
prep. au delà de; plus de
quartre heures et demie
paste, n. pâte f.; colle f.; vl
coller
pasteurize, vb. pasteuriser
pastime, n. passe-temps m
pastor, n pasteur m.
pastry, n. pâtisserie f.
pasture, n. pâturage m.
pasty, adj. empâte, pâteux
pat, vb. taper
patch, n. pièce f.; vb.
rapiécer
patchwork, n. ouvrage fai
de pièces disparate sm
patent, n. brevet d'invention m.

paternal, adj. paternel

paternity, n. paternité f

path, n. sentier m.

pathetic, adj. pathétique

pathology, n. pathologie f.

pathos, n. pathétique m.

patience, n. patience f.

pateint, n. malade m.f.; adj. patient

patio, n. patio m.

patriarch, n. patriarche m.

patriot, n. patriote m.f.

patriotic, adj. patriotique

patriotism, n. patriotisme m.

patrol, n. patrouille f.

patrolman, n. agent, patrouilleur m.

patron, n. protecteur; client m.

patronize, vb. protèger

pattern, n. modèle; dessin m.

pauper, n. indigent, pauvre, mendiant m.

pause, n. pause f.

paver, vb. paver

pavement, n. pavé m.; trottoir m.

pavillion, n. pavillon m.

paw, n. patte f.

pawn, n. pion m.; vb. mettre en gage, engager

pay, n. salaire m.; vb. payer

payment, n. payement m.

pea, n. pois m.

peace, n. paix f.

peaceable, n. paicifique

peach, n. pêche f.

peacock, n. paon m.

peak, n. sommet, m.

peal, n. retentissement m.; vb. sonner, retentir

peanut, n. arachide f.

pear, n. poire f.

pearl, n. perle f.

peasant, n. paysan m.

pebble, n. cailou m.

peck, vb. becqueter

peculiar, adj. particulier; singulier

pecuniary, adj. pécuniaire

pedagogue, n . pedagagoue m.

pedagogy, n. pagogie f.

pedal, n. pédale f.

pedant, n. pédant m.

peddle, vb. colporter

peddler, n. colporteur m.

pedestal, n. piedestal m.

pedestrian, n. piéton m.

pediatrician, n. pédiatre m.

pedigree, n. généalogie f.

peek, n. coup d'oeil furtif m.; vb. regarder à la dérobée

peel, n. pelure f.; vb. peler

peep, vb. regarder furtivement

peer, n. pair m., pareil m.; vb. scruter, regarder

peg, n. cheville f.

pelt, n. peau, fourrure f.; vb. lancer, jeter

pelvis, n. bassin m.

pen, n. plume f.

penalty, n. peine f.

penance, n. pénitence f.

penchant, n. penchant m.

pencil, n. crayon m.

pending, prerp. pendant

penetrate, vb. énétrer

penetration, n. pénétration f.

peninsula, n. penninsule f.

penitent, adj. pénitent, contrit

penny, n. sou m.

pension, n. pension f.

pensive, adj. pensif

people, n. gens m.f, pl; peuple m.

pepper, n. poivre m.

perambulator, n. voiture d'enfant f.

perceive, vb. apercevoir

percent, pour cent

percentage, n. pourcentage m.

perceptible, adj. perceptible

perception, n. perception f.

perch, n. perchoir m.;

perche f.

perdition, n. perte f.

peremptory, adj. péremptoire

pernnial, adj. perpétuel; vivace

perfect, adj. parfait

perfection, n. perfection f.

perforation, n. perforation f.

perform, vb. accomplir; jouer

performance, n. accomplissement m.; représentation f.

perfume, n. parfum m.

perfunctory, adj. fait pur la forme, superficiel

perhaps, adv. peut-être

peril, n. péril m.

perilous, adj. périlleux

perimeter, n. périmètre m.

period, n . période f.; point m.

periodic, adj. périodique

periodical, n. périodique m.

periphery, n. périphérie f.

perish, vb. périr

perishable, adj. périssable

perjury, n. parjure m.

permanent, adj. permanent

permeate, vb. filtrer

permissable, adj. admissible

permission, n. permission f.

permit, n. permis m.; vb. permettre

pernicious, adj. pernicieux

perpendicular, adj. perpendiculaire, vertical

perpetrate, vb. perpétrer

perpetual, adj. perpétuel

perplex, vb. mettre dans la perplexité

perplexity, n. perplexité f., embarras m.

persecute, vb. persécuter

persecution, n. persécution f.

perseverance, n. persévérance f.

persevere, vb. persévérer

persist, vb. persister
persistent, adj. persistant
person, n. personne f.
personage, n. personnage m.
personal, adj. personnel
personality, n. personnalité f.
personally, adv. personnellement
personnel, n. personnel m.
perspective, n. perspective f.
perspiration, n. transpiration f.
perspire, vb. transpirer
persuade, vb. persuader
persuasive, adj. persuasif
pertain, vb. appartenir
pertinent, adj. pertinent
perturb, vb. troubler
pervade, vb. pénétrer
perverse, adj. entêté
perversion, n. perversion f.
pessimism, n. pessimisme m.
pestilence, n. pestilence f.
pet, n. animal familier m.
petal, n. pétale m.
petition, n. pétition f.
petroleum, n. pétrole m.
petticoat, n. jupon m.
petty, adj. insignifiant
phantom, n. fantôme m.
pharmacist, n. pahrmacien m.
pharmacy, n. pharmacie f.
phase, n. phase f.
phenomenal, adj. phénoménal
phenomenon, n. phénomène m.
philosopher, n. philosophe m.
philosophy, n. philosophie f.
phobia, n. phobie f.
phonograph, n. phongraphe m.
photocopier, n. photo-

copieur m.
photocopy, n. photocopie f.
photograph, n. photographie f.
phrase, n. phrase f.
physical, adj. physique
physician, n. médecin m.
physics, n. physique f.
pianist, n. pianiste m.f.
piano, n. piano m.
pick, vb. choisir; cueillir
pickles, n. conserves (f., pl.) au vinaigre
picnic, n. pique-nique m.
picture, n. tableau m.; **film m.**
picturesque, adj. pittoresque
pie, n. tarte f.
piece, n. morceau m.
pier, n. jetée f.; quai m.
pierce, vb. percer
piety, n. pieté f.
pig, n. cochon m.
pigeon, n. pigeon m.
pigeonhole, n. case f.
pile, n. pieu; tas m.; vb. entasser
pilgrim, n. pèlerin m.
pilgrimage, n. pèlerinage m.
pill, in pilule f.
pillar, n. pilier m.
pillow, n. oreiller m.
pilkot, n. pilote m.
pimple, n. bouton m.
pin, n. épingle f.; vb. épingler
pinch, vb. pincer
pine, n. pin m.; vb. languir
pineapple, n. ananas m.
pink, adj. and n. rose m.
pinnacle, n. pinacle m.
pint, n. pinte f.
pioneer, n. pionnier m.
pipe, n. tuyau m.; pipe f.
piper, n. joueur de cornemuse m.
piquant, adj. piquant
pirate, n. pirate m.
pistol, n, pistolet m.

piston, n. piston m.
pit, n. fosse f.
pitch, n. poix f.; jet m.; hauteur f.; ton m.; vb. lancer
pitcher, n. cruche f.; lanceur m.
pitfall, n. trappe f.
pitiful, adj. pitoyable
pitless, adj. impitoyable
pity, n. pité f; quel dommage; vb. plaindre
pivot, n. pivot m., axe m.
pizza, n. pizza f.
place, n. endroit m.; lieu m.; vb. mettre
placid, adj. placide
plague, n. peste f.; fléau m.
plaid, n. plaid; tartan m.
plain, n. plaine f.; adj. clair; simple; quelconque
plaintiff, n. demandeur m.
plan, n. plan m.; vb. faire le plan de
plane, n. plan
planet, n. planète f.
plant, n. plante f.; vb. planter
plantation, n. plantation f.
planter, n. planteur m.
plasma, n. plasma m.
plaster, n. plâtre m.
plastic, adj. plastique
plate, n. plaque, assiette f.
plateau, n. plateau m.
platform, n. plate-forme f.; quai m.
platter, n. plat m.
plausible, adj. plausible
play, n. jeu m.; piece de théâtre f.; vb. jouer; jouer à; jouer de
player, n. jouer, acteur m.
playful, adj. enjoué
playground, n. terrain de jeu m.
playmate, n. camarade de jeu m.f.
playwright, n. dramaturge m.
plea, n. défense, excuse f.
plead, vb. plaider; alléguer

pleasant, adj. agréable

please, vb. plaire à; contenter; s'il vous plaît

pleasure, n. plaisir m.

pleat, n. pli m.

pledge, n. gage, engagement m.

plentiful, adj. abondant

plenty, n. abondance f.

pliable, adj. pliable

pliers, n. pinces f., pl.

plight, n. ètat m.

plot, n. intrigue f.; complot m.

plow, n. charrue f.; vb. labourer

pluck, n. courage m.

plug, n. tampon m.; prise de courant f.

plum, n. prune f.

plumber, n. plombier m.

plume, n. panache m.

plump, adj. grassouillet

plunder, vb. piller

plunge, n. plongeon m.

plural, adj. and. pluriel m.

plus, n. plus m.

pneumonia, n. pneumonie f.

poach, vb. pocher

poacher, n. braconnier m.

pocket, n. poche f.

pocketbook, n. sac à main m.

poem, n. poésie, poème f.

poet, n. poète m.

poetic, adj. poétique

poetry, n. poésie f.

poignant, adj. poignant

point, n. point m.

pointed, adj. pointu; mordant

poise, n. équilibre m.

poison, n. poison m.; vb. empoisonner

poisonous, adj. empoisonné

Poland, n. Pologne f.

polar, adj. polarie

Pole, n. Polonais m.

pole, n. pôle m.; perche f.

police, n. police f.

policeman, n. agent de police m.

policy, n. politique, police f.

Polish, adj. and n. polonais m.

polish, vb. polir; cirer

polite, adj. poli

politic, adj. politique

politician, n. politicien m.

politics, n. politique f.

poll, n. scrutin m.

pollen, n. polen m.

pollute, vb. polluer

polygamy, n. polygamie f.

pomp, n. pompe f.

pompous, adj. pompeux

pond, n. ètan m.

ponder, n. refléchir

ponderous, adj. pesant

pony, n. poney m.

pool, n. mare, piscine f.

poor, adj. pauvre

pop, n. petit burit sec m.

pope, n. pape m.

popular, adj. populaire

popularity, n. popluarité f.

population, n. population f.

pore, n. pore m.; vb. s'absorber dans

pork, n. porc m.

pornography, n. pornographie f.

porous, adj. preux

port, n. port, bâbord, porto m.

portable, adj. portatif

portal, n. portail m.

portfolio, n. portefeuille m.

portion, n. portion f.

portrait, n. portrait m.

portray, vb. peindre; dépeindre

Portugal, n. Portugal m.

Portuguese, n. Portugais m.; portugais m.

pose, n. pose f.

position, n. position f.

positive, n. positif m.

possession, n. possession f.

possibility, n. possibilité f.

possible, adj. possible

possibly, adv. il est possible

post, n. poste f.; poteau, poste m.

postage, n. affranchissement m.

postal, adj. postal

post card, n. carte postale f.

poster, n. affiche f.

posterior, adj. postérieur

posterity, n. postérité f.

post office, n. bureau de poste m.

postpone, vb. remettre

postscript, n. post-scrptum m.

posture, n. posture f.

pot, n. pot m.; marmite f.

potato, n. pomme de terre f.

potent, adj. puissant

potential, adj. and n. potentiel m.

pottery, n. poterie f.

pouch, n. sac m.

poultry, n. volaile f.

pound, n. livre f.

pour, vb. verser; tomber à verse

poverty, n. pauvreté f.

powder, n. pouvoir m.

powerful, adj. puissant

powerless, adj. impuissant

practical, adj. pratique

practiccally, ad. pratiquement

practice, n. exercice m.; habitude f.; pratique f.; vb. pratiquer

practiced, adj. expérimenté

prairie, n. savane f.

praise, n. éloge m.; vb. louer

prank, n. fredaine f.

pray, vb. prier

prayer, n. prière f.

preach, n. prêcher

preacher, n. prédicatuer m.

precarious, adj. précaire

precaution, n. précaution f.

precede, vb. précéder

precept, n. précepte m.
precious, adj. précieux
precipice, n. précipice m.
precipitate, vb. précipiter
precise, adj. précis
precision, n. précision f.
preclude, vb. empêcher
precocious, adj. précoce
predecessor, n.
    prédécesseur m.
predict, vb. prédire
predispose, vb. prédisposer
prefabricate, vb.
    préfabriquer
preface, n. préface f.
prefer, vb. préférer
preferable, adj. préférable
preference, n. préférence f.
prefix, n. préfixe m.
pregnant, adj. enceinte
prejudice, n. préjugé m.
preliminary, adj.
    préliminaire
prelude, n. prélude m.
premature, adj. prématuré
premeditate, vb. préméditer
premier, n . premier min-
    istre m.
première, n. première f.
premise, n. lieux m., pl.;
    prémisse f.
premium, n. prix m.
preparation, n.
    préparation f.;
    préparatifs m., pl.
preparatory, adj.
    préparatoire
prepare, vb. preparer
preponderant, adj.
    prépondérant
preposition, n.
    préposition f.
preposterous, adj. absurde
prerequisite, n. nécesité
    préalable f.
prescribe, vb. prescrire
prescription, n. prescirp-
    tion, ordannance f.
presence, n. présence f.
present, adj and n. présent
    m.; vb. présenter

presentable, adj.
    présentable
presentation, n.
    présentation f.
presently, adv. tout à l'heure
preservative, adj. and n.
    préservatif m.
preserve, n. confiture f.; vb.
    préserver
preside, vb présider
president, n. président m.
press, n. presse f.; vb.
    presser
pressure, n. pression f.
prestige, n. prestige m.
presume, vb. présumer
presumptuous, adj.
    présomptueux
pretend, vb. prétendre;
    simuler
pretense, n . faux sem-
    blant m.
prentionious, adj.
    préntentieux
pretext, n. prétexte m.
pretty, adj. joli
prevail, vb. prévaloir
prevalent, adj. répandu
prevent, vb. empêcher;
    prévenir
prevention, n.
    empêchement m.
preventive, adj. préventif
previous, adj. antérieur
prey, n. proie f.
price, n. prix m.
priceless, adj. inestimable
prick, n. piqûre f.
pride, n. orgueil m.
priest, n. prêtre m.
prim, adj. affecté
primary, adj. premier; pri-
    maire
prime, n. combine m.; adj.
    premier, de première
    qualite
primitive, adj. primitif
prince, n. prince m.
princess, n. princesse f.
principal, adj. principal
principle, n. principe m.

print, n. empreinte, impres-
    sion, épreuve f.; vb. im-
    primer
prinout, n. feuille imprimée
    produite par un ordina-
    teur f.
priority, n. priorité f.
prism, n. prisme m.
prison, n. prison f.
prisoner, n. prisonnier m.
privacy, n. retraite f.
private, adj. particullier
    prive
privation, n. privation f.
privilege, n. privilège m.
prize, n. prix m.
probability, n. probabilité f.
probable, adj. probable
probe, vb. sonder
problem, n. problème m.
procedure, n. procédé m.
proceed, vb. procéder;
    avancer
process, n. procédé m.
procession, n. cortège m.;
    procession f.
proclaim, vb. proclamer
proclamation, n. proclama-
    tion f.
procure, vb. procurer
prodigal, adj. and n.
    prodigue m.
prodigy, n. prodige m.
produce, vb. produire
product, n. produit m.
production, n. production f.
productive, adj. productif
profane, adj. profane
profess, vb. professer
profession, n. profession f.
professional, adj. profes-
    sionnel
professor, n. professeur m.
proficient, adj. capable
profile, n. profil m.
profit, n. profit m.
profitable, adj. profitable
profound, adj. profond
profuse, adj. profus;
    prodigue
program n. programme m.

progress, n. progrès m.; marche f.

progressive, adj. progressif

prohibit, vb. defendre

prohibition, n. défense f.

prohibitive, adj. prhibitif

project, n. projet m.; vb. projeter; faire saillie

projecction, n. projection, saillie f.

projector, n. projecteur m.

proliferation, n. prolifération f.

prolong, vb. prolonger

prominent, adj. sailant

promiscuous, adj. s ans distinction

promise, n. promesse f.

promote, vb. promouvoir; encourager

promotion, n. promotion f.

prompt, adj. prompt

pronoun, n. pronoum m.

pronounce, vb. prononcer

pronunciation, n. prononciation f.

proof, n. preuve, épreuve f.

prop, n. appui

propaganda, n. propagande f.

propagate, vb. propager

propeller, n. helice f.

proper, adj. propre; convenable

property, n. propriété f.

prophecy, n. prophétie f.

prophesy, vb. prophétiser

prophet, n. prophète m.

prophetic, adj. prophétique

proportion, n. proportion f.

proportionate, adj. proportionné

proposal, n. proposition, demande en mariage f.

propose, vb. propser

proposition, n. proposition; affaire f.

proprietor, n. propriétaire m.f.

prosaic, adj. prosaique

proscribe, vb. proscrire

prose, n. prose f.

prosecute, vb. poursuivre

prospect, n. perspective f.

prospective, adj. en perspective

prosper, vb. prospérer

prosperity, n. prospérité f.

prosperous, adj. prospère

prostitue, n. prostituée f.

prostrate, adj. prosterné

protect, vb. protéger

protection, n. protection f

protective, adj. protecteur.

protector, n. protecteur m.

protégé n. protégé m.

protein, n. protéine f.

protest, n. protestation f.; protêt m.; vb. protester

Protestant, adj. and n. protestant m.

protocol, n. protocole m.

protrude, vb. saillir

prove, vb. prouver; éprouver

proverb, n. proverbe m.

provide, vb. pourvoir, fournir

providence, n. prévoyance; providence f.

province, n. province f.

provincial, adj. and n. provincial m.

provision, n. provision f.

provocation, n. provocation f.

provoke, vb. provoquer; irriter

prowess, n. prouesse f.

prowl, vb. rôder

proximity, n. proximité f.

prudence, n. prudence f.

prudent, adj. prudent

prune, n. pruneau m.

Prussia, n. Prusse f.

psalm, n. psaume m.

psychitry, n. psychiatrie f.

psychology, n. psychologie f.

psychological, adj. psychologique

public, n. public m.; adj.

public m., publique f.

publicaton, n. publication f.

publicity, n. oublicité f.

publish, vb. publier

publsiher, n. éditeur m.

pudding, n. pouding m.

puddle, n. flaque f.

puff, n. bouffée f.

pull, vb. tirer

pulley, n. poulie f.

pulp, n. pulpe f.

pulpit, n. chaire f.

pulsar, n. pulsar m.

puisate, vb. battre

pulse, n. pouls m.

pump, n. pompe f.; vb. pomper

pumpkin, n. potiron m.

pun, n. calembour m.

punch, n. poincon; coup de point m.; pounch m.; vb. percer; gourmer

punctual, adj. ponctuel

punctuate, vb. ponctuer

puncture, n. piqûre f.

punish, vb. punir

punishment, n. punition f.

pupil, n. élève m.f.; pupille f.

puppet, n. marionnette f.

puppy, n. petit chien m.

purchase, n. achat m.; vb. acheter

pure, adj. pur

puree, n. purée f.

purge, vb. purger

purify, vb. purifier

purity, n. pureté f.

purple, adj. violet

purpose, n. but m.; à propos

purse, n. bourse f.

pursue, vb. poursuivre

pursuit, n. poursuite; occupation f.

push, n. poussée f.; vb. pousser

put, vb. mettre

puzzle, n. problème m.; vb. embarrasser

pyramid, n. pyramide f.

Q

quack, n. charlatan,

quackery, n. charlatanisme m.

quackish, adj. de charlatan

quad, cadrat m.

quadrangle, n. quadrilatère m.

quadraphonic, adj. quadriphonique

quaestor, n. questeur

quag, n. fondrière f.

quail, n. caille f.

quaint, adj. étrange

quake, vb. trembler

Quaker, n. Quakeresse f., Quakeress n.

quaking, n. tremblement m.

quakingly, adv. en tremblant

qualifiable, adj. qualifiable

qualification, n. réseve; compétence; qualification f.

qualify, vb. qualifier; modifier

qualifying, adj. qualificatif

quality, n. qualité f.

qualm, n. scrupule m.

quandary, n. embarras m.

quantitative, n. quantité

quantity, n. quantité f.

quantum, n. montant, quantum m.

quarnatine, n. quarantaine f.

quarrel, n. querelle f.

quarreller, n. querelleur m.

quarrelling, n. querelle f.

quarry, n. carrière f.

quart, n. quart de gallon m.

quartan, n. fièvre quarte f.

quarter, n. quart, quartier m.

quarterly, adj. trimestriel

quartet, n. quatuor m.

quartz, n. quartz m.

quasar, n. quasar m.

quaver, vb. chevroter

quavering, n. trille, tremolo m.; cadence f.

quay, n. quai m.; vb. garnir de quais

queasiness, n. nausées f., pl.

queasy, adj. sujet à des nausées

queen, n. reine f.

queen bee, n. reine-abeille f.

queer, adj. bizarre, étrange, drôle

quell, vb. réprimer

queller, n. personne qui réprime f.

quench, vb. éteindre; étancher

quenchable, adj. extinguible

quencher, n. personne f.

querulous, adj. plaintiff, maussade

querulously, adv. d'un ton dolent en se plaignant

query, n. question f.

quest, n. recherche f.

question, n. question f.; vb. interroger; mettre en doute

questionable, adj. douteux

questionary, n. questionnaire m.

questioner, n. questionneur m.

questioning, n. questions f., pl.

question mark, n. point d'interrogation m.

questionnaire, n. questionnaire m.

quibble, n. argutie, chicane f.

quick, adj. rapide; vif; adv. vite

quicken, vb. accélérer

quickening, adj. vivifiant, qui ranime

quiet, n. tranquillité f.; adj. tranquille

quietness, n. tranquillement

quill, n. (for writing) plume d'oie f.

quilling, n. tuyautage m.

quilt, n. courtepointe f.

quilting, adj. quinaire

quiaine, n. quinine f.

quint, n. quinte f.

quintain, n. quintaine f.

quinte, n. quinte f.

quip, n. mot piquant m.

quirk, n. sarcasme m.

quit, vb. quitter, abandonner

quite, adv. tout à fait

quitter, n. personne qui quitte f.

quiver, vb. trembloter

quivering, n. tremblement m.

quiz, n. petit examen m.; vb. exaiminer

quizzing, n. raillerie f.

quoin, n. coin m.

quoit, n. palet

quorum, n. quorum m.

quota, n. quote-part f.; contingent m.

quotation, n. citation f; cote f.

quote, vb. citer

R

rabbi, n. rabbin m.

rabbit, n. lapin

rabble, n. tourbe f.

rabid, adj. enragé

rabies, n. rage, hydropgobie f.

race, n. (people) race f.; vb. lutter à la course

race course, n. terrain de course m.

race-track, n. piste f.

rack, n. râtelier, (torture) chevalet de torture m.

racket, n. (tennis) raquette f.; (noise) tintamarre m.

racking, n. soutirage (of liquors) m.

racoon, n. raton laveur m.

racy, adj. qui a un goût de terroir

radar, n. radar m.

raddle, n. ocre rouge f.

radiant, adj. radieux

radiate, vb. irradier

radiation, n. rayonnement m.

radiator, n. radiateur m.

radical, adj. and n. radical m.

radicalism, n. radicalisme m.

radicular, adj. radiculaire

radio, n. télègraphi e sans fil f.

radioactive, adj. radio-actif

radiogram, n. combiné radioélectrophone m.

radish, n. radis m.

radium, n. radium m.

radius, n. rayon m.

raffle, n. loterie, tombola f.

raft, n. radeau m.

rafter, n. chevron m.

rafting, n. flottage en train m.

rag, n. chiffon m.

ragamuffin, n. gueux, polisson

rage, n. rage, fureur f.

ragged, adj. en haillons

ragweed, n. ambrosie f.

raid, n. (police) descente f.

rail, n. barre f.

railroad, n. chemin de fer m.

railway, n. chemin de fer m.

raiment, n. vêtement m.

rain, n. pluie f.; vb. pleuvoir

rainbow, n. arc-en-ciel m.

raincoat, n. imperméable m.

rainfall, n. chute de pluie f.

rainy, adj. pluvieux

raise, vb. (bring up,) élever; (lift) lever; cultiver

raisin, n. raisin sec m.

raising, n. action de lever f.

rajah, n. raja m.

rake, n. râteau m.; vb. râteler

raking, n. ratissage m.

rally, n. ralliement, rassemblement m.

ram, n. bélier m.

ramble, vb. rôder; (speech) divaguer

ramble, n. excursionniste m.

ramification, n. ramification f.

rammer, n. pilon m.

ramp, n. rampe f.

rampart, n. rempart m.

ramrod, n. baguette f.

ramshackle, adj. qui tombe en ruines

ranch, n. ranch m.

rancid, adj. rance

randem, n. attelage á trois chevaux en fléche

random, n. hassard m.

range, n. étendue, chaine, portée f.

ranger, n. garde-forestier m.

rank, n. rang m.; vb. ranger

ransack, vb. fouiller; (pillage) saccager

ransom, n. rancon f.

rant, n. déclamation extravagante f.

rap, n. coup m.; vb. frapper

rapid, adj. and n. rapide m.

rapper, n. frappeur, râfleur d'antiquités m.

rapture, n. ravissement m.

rare, adj. rare

rarely, adv. rarement

rascal, n. coquin m.

rask, n. éruption f.; adj. téméraire

raspberry, n. framboise f.

rat, n. rat m.

rate, n. taux m.; vitiesse f.

rather, adv. plutôt

ratify, vb. ratifier

ration, n. ration f.

rational, adj. raisonnable

rattle, n. (toy) hochet, (noise) fracas m.

rave, vb. délirer; (rave about) s'extasier sur

raven, n. corbeau m.

raw, adj. cru

ray, n. rayon m.

rayon, n. rayonne f.

razor, n. rasoir m.

reach, n. portée f.; vb. atteindre; étendre; arriver à

react, vb. réagir

reaction, n. reaction f.

reactionary, adj. réactionnaire

read, vb. lire

reader, n. (person) lecteur m.

readily, adv. promptement

ready, adj. prêt

real, adj. réel

realist, n. réaliste m.f.

reality, n. réalité f.

realization, n. réalisation f.

realize, vb. s'apercevoir de; realiser

really, adv. vraiment

realm, n. royaume m.

reap, vb. moissonner

rear, n. queue f.; adj. situe à l'arrière

reason, n. raison.; vb. raisonner

reasonable, adj. raisonnable

reassure, vb. rassurer

rebate, n. rabais m.

rebel, adj. and n. rebelle m.f

rebellion, n. rébellion f.

rebellious, adj. rebelle

rebirth, n. renaissance f.

rebound, n. rebond m.

rebuke, n. réprimande f.; vb. réprimander

rebuttal, n. réfutation f.

recall, vb. (remember) se

rappeler

reced, vb. s'éloigner

receipt, n. quittance f.

receive, vb. recevoir

receiver, n. (phone) récepteur m.

recent, adj. récent

receptacle, n. réceptacle m.

reception, n. réception f.; accueil m.

receptive, adj. réceptif

recess, n. recoin m.; vacances f., pl.; récréation f.

recipe, n. recette f.

reciprocate, vb. payer de retour

recite, vb. réciter

reckless, adj. téméraire

reckon, vb. compter

reclaim, v. défricher

recline, vb. reposer

recognition, n. reconnaissance f.

recognize, vb. reconnaître

recoil, vb. reculer

recollect, vb. se rappeler

recommend, vb. recommander

recommendation, n. recommandation f.

recompense, n . récompense f.

reconcile, vb. réconcilier

record, n. registre, antécédents m.; mention f.; vb. enregistrer

record player, n. tournedisques m.

recount, vb. raconter

recover, vb. recouvrer; se rétablir

recovery, n. recouvrement, rétablissement m.

recruit, n. recrue f.; vb. recruter

rectangle, n. rectangle m.

rectify, vb. rectifier

recuperate, vb. se rétablir, intr

recur, vb. revenir

recycle, vb. recycler

red, adj. and n. rouge m.

redeem, vb. racheter

redemption, n. rachat m.

redress, n. justice f.; vb. redresser, téparer; faire justice à

reduce, vb. réduire

reduction, n. réductin, (of price) remise f.

reed, n. roseau m.; (music) anche f.

reef, n. récif m.

reel, n. bobine f.

refer, vb. référer

referee, n. arbitre m.

reference, n. référence f.

refill, vb. remplir

refine, vb. raffiner

refinement, n. raffinement m.

reflect, vb. rléchir

reflection, n. rlexion f.

reform, n. féforme f.; vb. réformer

reformation, n. réforme f.

refractory, adj. réfractaire

refrain from, vb. se retenir de

refresh, vb. rafraîchir

refreshment, n. rafraîchissement m.

refrigerator, n. frigidaire m.

refuge, n. refuge m.

refugee, n. réfugié m.

refund, n. remobursement m. vb. rembourser

refusal, n. refus m.

refuse, n. rebut m.; vb. refuser

refute, vb. réfuter

regain, vb. regagner

regal, adj. royal

regard, n. égard m.; amitiés f., pl.; vb. regarder

regardless, adj. sans se soucier de

regent, adj. and n. régent m.

regime, n. régime m.

regiment, n. régiment m.

region, n. région f.

register, n. registre m.; vb.

enregistrer; recommander

registration, n. enregistrement m.

regret, n. regret m.; vb. regretter

regular, adj. régulier

regularity, n. regularité f.

regulate, vb. régler

regulation, n. réglement m.

regulator, n. régulateur m.

rehabilitate, vb. réhabiliter

rehearse, vb. répéter

reign, n. règne m.; vb.régner

rein, n. rêne f.

reindeer, n. renne m.

reinforce, vb. renforcer

reinforcement, n. renfort m.

reject, vb. rejeter

rejoice, vb. réjouir

rejoin, vb. rejoindre; (reply) répliquer

relapse, n. rechute f.

relate, vb. raconter; se rapporter (à) (relate to) entrer en rapport avec

relation, n. relation f.; (relatvie) parent m.

relative, n. parent m. adj. relatif

relax, vb. relâcher

relay, n. relais m.; vb. relayer

release, n. déliverance f.; vb. libérer

relent, vb. se laisser attendrir

relevant, adj. pertinent

reliabiltiy, n. sûreté f.

reliable, adj. digne de confiance

reliant, adj. confiant

relic, n. relique f.

relief, n. (ease) soulagement, (help) secours, (projection) relief m.

relieve, vb. (ease) soulager; secourir

religion, n. religion f.

religious, adj. religieux

relinquish, vb. abandonner

relish, n. goût m.; vb. goûter

reluctant, adj . peu disposé (à)

rely upon, vb. compter sur

remain, vb. rester

remainder, n. reste m.

remark, n. remarque f.; vb. remarquer

remarkable, adj. remarquable

remedy, n. remède m.; vb. rémédier à

remember, vb. se souvenir de

remembrance, n. souvenir m.

reminisce, vb. raconter ses souvenirs

remit, vb. remettre

remnant, n. reste, vestige, coupon m.

remorse, n. remords m.

remote, adj. éloigné; vague

removable, adj. transportable

removal, n. enlèvement m.

remove, vb. enlever

rend, vb. déchirer

render, vb. rendre

rendezvous, n. rendezvous m.

rendw, vb. renouveler

renewal, n. renouvellement m.

renounce, vb. renoncer à; répudier

renovate, vb. renouveler

renown, n. renommée f.

rent, n. réparation f.; vb. réparer

repay, vb. rendre; (refund) reimbourser

repeat, vb. répéter

repel, vb. repousser

repent, vb. se repentir

repentance, n. repentir m.

repertoire, n. répertoire m.

repetition, n. répétition f.

replace, vb. replacer; (take the place of) remplacer

reply, n. réponse f.; vb. répondre

report, n. rapport m.; vb. rapporter

repose, n. repos m.

represent, vb. représenter

representation, n. représentation f.

repress, vb. réprimer

reprimand, n. réprimande f.

reproach, n. reproche m.; vb. faire des reproches à

reproduce, vb. reproduire

reproduction, n. reporduction f.

reproof, n. réprimande f.

reprove, vb. réprimander

reptile, n. reptile m.

republic, n. république f.

republican, adj. and n. républicain m.

repulsive, adj. répulsif

reputation, n. réputation f.

repute, n. renom m.; vb. réputer

request, n. requête f.; vb. demander

require, vb. exiger

requirement, n. exigence f.

requisite, adj. nécessaire

requisition, n. réquisition f.

rescue, n. délivrance f.; vb. délivrer

research, n. recherche f.

resemble, vb. ressembler à

resent, vb. être froissé de

reservation, n. réserve

reserve, n. réserve f.; vb. réserver

reservoir, n. réservoir m.

reside, vb. résider

residence, n. résidence f.

resident, n. habitant m.; adj. résidant

resign, vb. résigner; se démettre (de)

resignation, n. résignation, démission f.

resist, vb. résister (à)

resistance, n. résistance f.

resolute, adj. résolu

resolution, n. résolution f.

resolve, vb. résoudre

resonant, adj. résonnant

resound, vb. résonner

resource, n. ressource f.

respect, n. repsect, (reference) rapport m.; vb. respecter ·

respectable, adj. respectable

respectful, adj. respectueux

respective, adj. respectif

respiration, n. respiration f.

respite, n. répit m.

respond, vb. répondre

response, n. réponse f.

responsibility, n. responsabilité f.

responsible, adj. responsable

rest, n. repos, (remainder) reste m.; les autres m.f., pl.2. vb. se reposer

restaurant, n. restaurant m.

restful, adj. qui repose

restless, adj. (anxious) inquiet

restoration, n. restauration f.

restore, vb. remettre; (repair) restaurer

restrain, vb. contenir

restraint, n. contrainte f.

restrict, vb. restreindre

result, n. résultat m.; vb. résulter

resume, vb. reprendre

résumé, n. résumé m.

resurrect, vb. ressusciter

retail, n. détail m.

retain, vb. retenir

retaliate, vb. user de représailles

retard, vb. retarder

reticent, adj. réservé

retina, n. retine f.

retire, vb. se retirer

retort, n riposte f.

retreat, n. retraite f.; vb. se retirer

retrieve, vb. recouvrer

retrospect, n. renvoi, (in

retrospect) coup d'oeil rétrospectif m.

return, n. retour m.; recettes f., pl.; vb. rendre; (go back) retourner; (come back) revenir

reunion, n. réunion f.

reveal, vb. révéler

revel, vb. s'ébattre

revelation, n. révélation f.

revelry, n. bacchanale f.

revenge, n. vengeance f.; vb. se venger

revenue, n. revenu m.

revere, vb. révérer

reverence, n. révérence f.

reverend, adj. révérend

reverent, adj. respectueux

reverie, n. rêverie f.

reverse, n. (opposite) contraire, re vers m.; (gear) marche (f.) arrière.; vb. renverser

revert, vb. revenir

review, n. revue f.

revise, vb. réviser

revision, n. révision f.

revival, n. renaissance f.; (religious) réveil m.

revive, vb. revivre, intr.; faire revivre

revoke, vb. révoquer

revolt, n. révolte f.; vb. se révolter

revolution, n. révolution f.

revolutionary, adj. révolutionnaire

revolve, vb. tourner

revolver, n. revolver m.

reward, n. récompense f.; vb. récompenser

rheumatism, n. rhumatisme m.

rhinoceros, n rhinocéros m.

rhubarb, n. ruhbarbe f.

rhyme, n. rime f.; vb. rimer

rhythm, n. rythme m.

rhythmical, adj. rythmique

rib, n. côte f.

ribbon, n. ruban m.

rice, n. riz m.

rich, adj. riche

rid, vb. débarrasser

riddle, n. énigme f.

ride, n. promenade f.; vb. (horse) aller à cheval; (vehicle) aller en voiture

rider, n. cavalier m.

ridge, n. crête f.

ridicule, n. ridicule m.; vb. se moquer de

ridiculous, adj. ridicule

rifle, n. fusil m.

rig, 1. n. (vesel) greéement m.; (outfit) tenue f. 2. vb. gréer

right, n. droit m.; droit; (correct, proper) juste; avoir raison bien

righteous, adj. juste

righteousness, n. justice f.

rigid, adj. rigide

rigor, n. rigueur f.

rigorous, adj. rigoureux

rim, n. bord m.; (wheel) jante f.

ring, n. anneau m.; (ornament) bague f.; (circle) cercle

rinse, vb. rincer

riot, n. émeute f.

rip, n. fente f.; vb. fendre

ripe, adj. mûr

ripen, vb. mûrir

ripoff, n. vol m.; vb. voler

ripple, n. ride f.; vb. rider

rise, n. (increase) augmentation f.; (rank) avancement m.; vb. se lever

risk, n. risque m.; vb. risquer

rite, n. rite m.

ritual, adj. rituel

rival, adj. and n. rival m.; vb. rivaliser avec

rivalry, n. rivalité f.

river, n. fleuve m.

rivet, n. rivet m.

road, n. route f.

roam, vb. errer

roar, vb. hurler; (lion) rugir; (sea) mugir; (thunder)

gronder; (laughter) éclater de

roast, n. rôti m.; vb. rôtir

rob, vb. voler

robber, n. vol m.

robe, n. robe f.

robin, n. rouge-gorge m.

robot, n. automate m.

robust, adj. robuste

rock, n. rocher m.; vb. balacner; (child) bercer

rocker, n. (chair) chaise (f.) à bascule

rocket, n. fusée f.

rocky, adj. rocheux

rod, n. verge f.

rodent, adj. and n. rongeur m.

rogue, n. coquin m.

roguish, adj. coquin

role, n. rôle m.

roll, n. rouleau, (bread) petit pain m.; (list) liste f.

roller, n. rouleau m.

Roman, n. Romain m.; adj. romain

romance, n. roman de chevalerie m.

romantic, adj. romanesquer; romantique

romp, n. tapage m.;¼ve, vb. errer (par)

rover, n. rôdeur m.

row, n. rang m.; dispute f.; vb. ramer

rowboat, n. barque f.

rowdy, adj. tapageur

royal, adj. royal

royalty, n. royauté f.; droits d'auteur m., pl.

rub, vb. frotter

rubber, n. caoutchouc m.

rubbish, n. rebuts m., pl.; (nonsesne) bêtises f., pl.

ruby, n. rubis m.

rudder, n. gouvernail m.

ruddy, adj. rouge

rude, adj. (rough) rude; (impolite) impoli

rudiment, n. rudiment m.

rue, vb. regretter

ruffian, n. bandit m.

ruffle, n. fraise f.

rug, n. tapis m.

rugged, adj. (rough) rude; (uneven) raboteux

ruin, n. règle, (authority) autorité f.;vb. gouverner

ruler, n. souverain m.; règle f.

rum, n. rhum m.

Rumania, n. Roumanie f.

Rumanian, n. (person) Roumain, (language) roumain m.; adj. roumain

rumba, n. rumba f.

rumble, vb. gronder

rumor, n. rumeur f.

run, vb. courir; marcher; déteindre; couler; s'enfuir

run-down, adj. épuisé

rung, n. échelon m.

runner, n. (person) coureur, chemin de table m.

rupture, n. rupture f.

rural, adj. rural

rush, n. (haste) hâte, ruée f.; coup, jonc m.; vb. se précipiter

Russia, n. Russie f.

Russian, 1. n. (person) Russe m.f.; (language) russe m.; adj. russe

rust, n. rouille f.; vb. rouiller

rustic, adj. rustique

rustle, n. (leaves) bruissement m.

rusty, adj. rouillé

rut, n. ormière f.

ruthless, adj, impitoyable

rye, n. seigle m.

S

Sabbath, n. sabbat m.

saber, n. sabre m.

sable. n. zibeline f.

sabotage. abotage m.; vb.

saboter

saboteur, n. saboteur m.

saccharin, n. saccharine f.

sachet, n. sachet m.

sack, n. sac m.; vb. saccager

sacrament, n. sacrement m.

sacred, adj. sacré

sacrifice, n. sacrifice m.; vb. sacrifier

sacrilege, n. sacrilège m.

sad, adj. triste

sadden, vb. attrister

saddle, n. selle f.

sadism, n. sadisme m.

safe, n. coffre-fort n.; adj sûr, (safe and sound) ain et sauf

safeguard, vb. sauvegarder

safety, n. sûretè f.

safety pin, n. épingle anglaise f.

sage, n. (plant) sauge f.

sail, n. voile f.; vb. faire voile

sailboat, adj. navigable

sailor, n. marin m.

saint, adj. and n. saint m.

salad, n. salade f.

salary, n. appointements m., pl.

sale, n. vente f.

salesman, n. vendeur m.

sales tax, n. impôt sur les ventes m.

saliva, n. salive f.

salmon, n. saumon m.

salt, n. sel m.; vb. saler

salute, n. salut m.; vb. saluer

salvage, n. sauvetage m.

salvation, n. salut m.

salve, n . onguent m.

same, adj. and pron. même; adv. dememe

sample, n. échantillon m.

sanatorium, n. sanatorium m.

sanctify, vb. sanctifier

sanction, n. sanction f.

sanctity, n. sainteté f.

sanctuary, n. sanctuaire m.

sand, n. sable m.

sandal, n. sandale f.

sandwich, n. sandwich m.

sandy, adj. sablonneux

sane, adj. sain d'esprit

sanitary, adj. sanitaire

sanitation, n. hygiène f.

sanity, n. santé d'esprit f.

Santa Claus, n. Bonhomme Noël m.

sap, n. sève f.

sapphire, n. saphir m.

sarcasm, n. sarcasme m.

sardine, n. sardine f.

sash, n. ceinture f.; (window) châsis m.

satellite, n. satellite m.

satin, n. satin m.

satire, n. satire f.

satisfaction, n. satisfaction f.

satisfactory, adj. satisfaisant

satisfy, vb. satisfaire

saturate, vb. saturer

Saturday, n. samedi m.

sauce, n. sacue f.

saucer, n. soucoupe f.

saucy, adj. impertinent

sausage, n. saucisse f.

savage, adj. and n. sauvage m.f.

save, vb. sauver; (put aside) mettre de côté; (economize) épargner

savior, n. sauveur m.

savor, n. saveur f.

savory, adj. savoureux

saw, n. scie f.; vb. scier

say, vb. dire

scab, n. croûte, gale f.

scaffold, n. échafaud m.

scald, vb. échauder

scale, n. (fish) écaille, (balance) balance, (music) gamme f.; vb. es calader

scalp, n. cuir chevelu m.; vb. scalper

scan, vb. (examine) scruter

scandal, n. scandale m.

scandalous, adj. scandaleux

Scandinavia, n. Scandinavie f.

Scandinavian, n. Scandinave m.f.; adj. scandinave

scant(y), adj. limité, faible

scar, n. cicatrice f.

scarce, adj. rare

scare, vb. elfrayer

scarf, n. écharpe f.

scarlet, adj. and n. écarlate, (scarlet fever) scarlatine f.

scathing, adj. cinglant

scatter, vb. éparpiller

scavenger, n. boueur m.

scenario, n. scénario m.

scene, n. scène f.

scenery, n. (landscape) paysage m.

scent, n. parfum m. odeur f.; vb. flairer, sentir

schedule, n. plan m.

scheme, n. plan m.

scholar, n. savant m.

scholarship, n. (school) bourse f.

school, n. école f.

sciatica, n. sciatique f.

science, n. science f.

science fiction, n. science-fiction f.

scientist, n. homme de science m.

scissors, n. ciseaux m., pl.

scoff at, vb. se moquer de

scold, vb. groner

scoop out, vb. évider

scope, n, (extent) portée, (outlet) carrilere f.

scorch, vb. roussir

score, n. (games) points m., pl.; (music) partition f.

Scotch, Scottish, adj. écossais

Scotchman, Scotsman, n. Ecossais m.

Scotland, n. Ecosse f.

scour, vb nettoyer

scourge, n. fléau m.

scout, n. éclaireur, boy-scout m.

scowl, vb. se renfrogner

scramble, vb. avancer péniblement

scrap, n. petit morceau m.; vb. mettre au rebut

scream, n. cri m.; vb. crier

screen, n. écran m.; (folding screen) paravent m.

screw, n. vis f.; vb. visser

screwdriver, n. tournevis m.

scribble, vb. griffonner

scroll, n. rouleau m.

scrub, vb. frotter

scruple, n. scrupule m.

scrupulous, adj. scrupuleux

scrutinize, vb. scruter

sculptor, n. sculpteur m.

sculpture, n. sculpture f.

scythe, n. faux f.

sea, n. mer f.

seabed, n. lit de la mer f.

seacoast, n. littoral m.

seal, n. (animal) phoque, (stamp) sceau m.; vb. sceller

seam, n. couture f.

seaport, n. port de mer m.

search, n. recherche f.; vb. chercher

seasickness, n. mal de mer m.

season, n. saison f.; vb. assaisonner

seat, n. siège m.; vb. asseoir

second, n. seconde f.; adj. second, deuxième

secondary, adj. secondaire

secret, adj. and n. secret m.

secretary, adj. secrétaire m.f.

sect, n. secte f.

section, n. section f.

sectional, adj. régional

secular, adj. (church) séculier; (time) séculaire

secure, adj. sûr.; vb. (make sure) mettre en sûreté; (make fast) fixer; (obtain) obtenir

security, n. sûreté f, caution f., (finance, pl.) valeurs

f., pl.

sedative, adj. and n . sédatif m.

seduce, vb. séduire

see, vb. voir

seed, n. semence, (vegetables, etc) graine f.

seek, vb. chercher

seem, vb. sembler

seep, vb. suinter

segment, n. segment m.

segregate, vb. séparer

seize, vb. saisir

seldom, adv. rarement

select, vb. choisir

selection, n. sélection f.

self, n. moi m., personne f.

selfish, adj. égolste

selfishness, n. égoIsme m.

sell, vb. vendre

semantics, n. sémantique f.

semester, n. semestre m.

semicircle, n. demi -cercle m..

semicolon, n. point et virgule m.

seminary, n. séminaire m.

senate, n. sénat m.

senator, n. sénateur m.

send, vb. envoyer; (send back) renvoyer

senile, adj. sénile

senior, adj.. and n. (age) ainé m., (rank) supérieur m.

senior citizen, n. personne dutroisième âge f.

sensation, n. sensation f.

sensational, adj. sensationnel

sense, n. sens m.

sensible, adj. (wise) sensé; (appreciable) sensible

sensitive, adj. sensible

sensual, adj. sensuel

sentence, n. (gramm.) phrase, (law) sentence f.

sentiment, n. sentiment m.

sentimental, adj sentimental

seperate, adj. séparé. 2. vb. séparer

separation, n. séparation f.

September, n. septembre m.

sequence, n. suite f.

serenade, n. sérénade f.

serene, adj. serein

sergeant, n. sergent m.

serial, n. roman-feuilleton m.

series, n. série f.

serious, adj. serieux

sermon, n. sermon m.

serpent, n. serpent m.

serum, n. sérum m.

servant, n. (domestic) domestique m.f; (public) employé m.

serve, vb. servir

srvice, n. service, (church) office m.

servitude, n. servitude f.

session, n. session f.

set, n. ensemble m.; adj. fixe; vb. (put) mettre; (regulate) régler; (jewels) monter; (fix) fixer, vb. intr (sun) se coucher

settle, vb. (establish) établir, (fix) fixer, (decide) décider, (arrange) arranger; (pay) payer

settlement, n. (colony) colonie f.; (accounts) règlement m.

settler, n. colon m.

seven, adj. and n. sept m.

seventeen, adj. and n. dix-sept m.

seventh, adj. and n. septième m.

seventy, adj. and n. soixantedix m.

sever, vb. séparer, couper

several, adj. and pron. plusieurs

sever, adj. sévère

severity, n. sévérité f.

sew, vb. coudre

sewer, n. égout m.

sex, n. sexe m.

sexism, n. sexisme m.

sexist, adj. sexiste

sexton, n. saacristain m.

sexual, adj. sexuel

shabby, adj. (clothes) usé; (person) mesquin

shade, n. ombre f.; (colors) nuance f.; (window) store m.; vb. ombrager

shadow, n. ombre f.

shady, adj. ombragé; (not honest) louche

shaft, n. (mine) puits m.

shaggy, adj. poilu, hirsute

shake, vb. tr. secouer, trebler; (shake hands) serrer la main à

shallow, adj. peu profond

shame, n. honte f.

shameful, adj. honteux

shampoo, n. schampooing m.

shape, n. forme f.; vb. former

share, n. part, (finance) action f.; vb. partager

shark, n. requin m.

sharp, adj. (cutting) tranchant; (clever) fin; (piercing) percant; (music) diese

sharpen, vb. aiguiser

shatter, vb. briser

shave, vb. raser

shawl, n. châle m.

she, pron elle

sheaf, n. (grain) gerbe f.

shear, vb. tondre

shears, n. cisailles f., pl.

sheath, n. étui m.

shed, n. hangar m.; vb.verser

sheep, n. mouton m.

sheet, n. (bed) drap m.; (paper, metal) feuille f.

shelf, n. rayon m.

shell, n. coquille f, carcasse f.; obus m.

shellac, n. laque f.

shelter, n. abri m.; vb.
abriter

shepherd, n. berger m.

sherbet, n. sorbet m.

sherry, n. xérès m.

shield, n. bouclier m.

shift, n. (change) changement m.; (workers) équipe f.; (expedient) expédient m.; vb. changer, (shift gears) changer de vitesse

shine, vb. briller, intr; (shoes) cirer

shiny, adj. luisant

ship, n. navire, vaisseau m.

shipment, n. envoi m.

shirk, vb esquiver

shirt, n. chemise f.

shiver, n. frisson m.; vb. frissonner

shock, n. choc m.; vb. choquer

shoe, n. soulier m.

shoelace, n. lacet m.

shoemaker, n. cordonnier m.

shoot, vb. tirer, (person) fusillier; (hit) atteindre

shop, n. boutique f.; (factory) atelier m.; vb. faire des emplettes

shore, n. rivage m.

short, adj. court

shortage, n. manque m.

shorten, vb. raccourcir

shorthand, n. sténographie f.

shot, n. coup m.

should, vb. devoir (in conditional)

shoulder, n. épaule f.

shout, n. cri m.; vb. crier

shove, vb. pousser

shovel, n. pelle f.

show, n. (exhibition) exposition, (display) paradae f.; semblant m.; vb. montrer

shower, n. averse f.

shrapnel, n. shrapnel m.

shrewed, adj. sagace

shriek, n. cir percant m.

shrill, adj. aigu

shrimp, n. crevette f.

shrine, n. châsse f.

shrink, vb. rétrécir

shroud, n. linceul m.

shrub, n. arbrisseau m.

shudder, n. frisson m.; vb. frissonner

shun, vb. fuir

shut, vb. fermer

shutter, n. volte m.

shy, adj. timide

sick, adj. malade

sickness,n. maladie f.

side, n. côte f.

sidewalk, n. trottoir m.

siege, n. siège m.

sieve, n. tamis m.

sift, vb. cribler

sigh, n. soupir m.; vb. soupirer

sight, n. vue f.; (spectacle) spectacle m.

sightseeing, n. tourisme m.

sign, n. signe m.; enseigne f.; vb. signer

signal, n. signal m.

signature, n. signature f.

significance, n. (meaning) signification, (importance) importance f.

significant, adj. sinificatif

signify, vb. signifier

silence, n. silence m.

silent, adj. silencieux

silk, n. soie f.

silken, adj. de soie

silly, adj. sot m., sotte f.

silver, n. argent m.; adj. dártent

silverware, n. argenterie f.

similar, adj. semblable

simple, adj. simple

simplicity, n. simplicité f.

simplify, vb. simplifier

simply adv. simplement

simultaneous, adj. simultané

sin, n. péché m.; vb. pécher

since, adv. prep. depuis; conj. (time) depuis que; (cause) puisque

sincere, adj. sincère

sincerity, n. sincérité f.

sinful, adj. (person) pécheur m. pécheresse f.; (act) coupable

sing, vb. chanter

singer, n. chanteur m.

single, adj. (one) seul; (particular) particulier; (not married) célibataire

singular, adj. and n. singulier m.

sinister, adj. sinistre

sink, n. evier m.; vb. enfoncer, (vessel) couler áu fond; (weaken) baisser

sinner, n. pécheur m., pécheresse f.

sinus, n. sinus m.

sip, vb. siroter

sir, n. monsieur m.; (title) Sir m.

sirloin, n. aloyau m.

sister, n. soeur f.

sister-in-law, n. belle-soeur f.

sit, vb. (sit down) s'asseoir; (be seated) être assis

site, n. emplacement m.

situate, vb. situer

situation, n. situation f.

six, adj. and n. six m.

sixteen, adj. and n. seize m.

sixteenth, adj. and n. seizième m.

sixth, adj. and n. sixième m.

sixty, adj. and n. soixante m.

size, n. grandeur, (person) taille, (shoes, gloves) pointure f.

skate, n. patin m.

skateboard, n. plance à roulettes f.

skeleton, n. squelette m.

skeptic, n sceptique m.f.

skeptical, adj. sceptique

sketch, n. croquis m.; vb.

esquisser

ski, n. ski m.; vb. faire du ski

skill, n. adresse f.

skillful, adj. adroit

skim, vb. (milk) écrémer; (book) feuilleter; (surface) effleurer

skin, n. peau f.; vb. écorcher

skip, vb. sauter

skirt, n. jupe f.

skull, n. craine m.

sky, n. ciel m.

skyscraper, n. gratte-ciel m.

slab, adj. lache

slacken, vb. (slow up) ralentir; (loosen) relâcher

slacks, n. pantalon m.

slander, n. calomnie f.; vb. calomnier

slang, n. argot m.

slant, n. inclinaison, pente f.

slap, n. claque f.

slash, n. taillade f.

slate, n. ardoise f.

slaughter, n. massacre, (animals) abbattage m.; vb. massacrer; abattre

slave, n. esclave m.f.

slavery, n. exclavage m.

slay, vb. tuer

sled, n. traineau m.

sleep, n. sommeil, (nap) somme m.; vb. dormir

sleepy, adj. qui a envie de dormir

sleet, n. neige à moitié fondue f.

sleeve, n. manche f.

sleigh, n. traneau m.

slender, adj. mince; svelte

slice, n. tranche f.

slide, n. glissade f.; (microscope) lamelle f.; vb. glisser

slight, adj. léger; mince

slim, adj. svelte

sling, n. fronde, écharpe f.; vb. lancer; suspendre

slip, n. glissade f.; (mistake) faux pas m.; vb. glisser;

(err) faire une faute

slipper, n. pantoufle f.

slippery, adj. glissant

slit, n. fente f.; vb. fendre

slogan, n. mot d'ordre m.; (politics) cri de guerre m.

slope, n. pente f.; vb. incliner

slot, n. fente f.

slow, adj. lent, tardif

slowness, n. lenteur f.

sluggish,m adj. paresseux

slumber, vb. sommeiller

sly, adj. (crafty) fusé

smack, n. (a bit) spoupoon, (noise) claquement m.

small, adj. petit

smallpox, n. petite vérole f.

smart, adj. (clever) habile, (stylish) élegant; vb. cuire

smash, vb. briser

smear, n. tache f.; vb salir

smell, n. odeur f.; vb. sentir

smelt, n. éperlan, m; vb. fondre

smile, n. vb. sourire m.

smite, vb. frapper

smoke, n. fumée f.; vb. fumer

smolder, vb. couver

smooth, adj. lisse; vb. lisser

smother, vb. étouffer

smuggle, vb. faire passer en contregande

snack, n. cass-croute m.

snag, n. obstacle caché m.

snail, n. escargot m.

snake, n. serpent m.

snap, n. (bite) coup de ents, (sound) coup sec m.; vb. (with teeth) happer; (sound) faire claquer

snapshot, n. cliché m.

snare, n. pilege m.

snarl, vb. grogner

snatch, vb. saisir

sneak, vb. se glisser furtivement

sneer, vb ricaner

sneeze, n. éternuement m.; vb. ternuer

snob, n. snob m.

snopre, vb. ronfler

snow, n. neige f.; vb. neiger

snug, adj. confortable

so, adv. si; tellement; (thus) ainsi

soak, vb. tremper

soap, n. savon m.

soar, vb. prendre son essor

sob, n. sanglot m.; vb. sangloter

sober, adj. sobre; (sedate) sérieux; (not intoxicated) qui n'est pas ivre

sociable, adj. sociable

social, adj. social

socialism, n. socialisme m.

socialist, adj. and n. socialiste m.f.

society, n. société f.

sociology, n. sociologie f.

sock, n. chaussette f.

socket, n. douille f.

sod, n. motte f.

soda, n. soude, (soda water) eau de Seltz f.

sofa, n. canapé m.

soft, adj. doux m., douce, (yielding) mou m., molle f.

soften, vb. amollir

soil, n. terrori m.; vb. souiller

sojours, n. séjour m.; vb. séhjourner

solace, n. consolation f.

solar, adj. solaire

soldier, n. soldat m.

sole, n. (shoe) semelle, (fish) sike f.

soilemn, adj. solennel

solemnity, n. solennité f.

solicit, vb. solliciter

solicitous, adj. empressé

solid, adj. and n. solide n.

solidity, n. solidité f.

solitary, adj. solitaire

solitude, n. solitude f.

solo, n. solo m.

solution, n. solution f.

solve, vb. résoudre

solvent, adj. dissolvant

somber, adj. sombre

some, adj. quelque m. or f.

somebody, someone, pron. quelqu'un

something, pron. quelque chose m.

some time, adv. (past) autrefois; (future) quelque jour

sometimes, adv. quelquefois

somewhat, adv. quelque peu

somewhere, adv. quelque part

son, n. fils m.

song, n. chant m.; chanson f.

son-in-law, n. gendre m.

soon, adv. bientôt, tôt

soot, n. suie f.

soothe, vb. calmer

sophisticated, adj. blasé

soprano, n. soprano m.

sordid, adj. sordide

sore, adj. douloureux, endolori, susceptible

sorrow, n. douleur f.

sorrowful, adj. affligé, triste

sorry, adj. fâché, désolé

sort, n. sorte f.; vb. trier

soul, n. âme f.

sound, adj. en bon état, bon; ; vb. sonner, retentir

soup, n. potage n.

sour, adj. aigre

source, n. source f.

south, n. sud m.

southeast, n. sud-est m.

southern, adj. du su

South Pole, n. pôle sud m.

southwest, n. soud-ouest m.

souvenir, n. souvenir m.

sow, vb. semer

space, n. espace m.

space shuttle, n. navette spatiale f.

spacious, adj. spacieux

spade, n. bêche f.; (cards) pique m.

Spain, n. Espagne f.

span, n. empan m.; (bridge) travée f.

Spaniard, n. Espagnol m.

Spanish, adj. and n. expagnol m.

spank, vb. fesser

spanking, n. fessée f.

spare, adj. (in reserve) de réserve; vb. épargner

spark, n. étincelle f.

sparkle, vb. étinceler

sparrow, n. moineau m.

spasm, n. spasme m.

speak, vb. parler

speaker, n. (public) orateur m.

special, adj. spécial

specialist, n. spécialiste m.f.

specialty, n. spécialité f.

species, n. espèce f.

specific, adj. spécifique

specify, vb. specifier

specimient, n. spécimen m.

spectacle, n. spectacle m.

spectacular, adj. spectaculaire

spectator, n. spectateur m.

speculate, vb. spéculer

speculation, n. spéculation f.

speech, n. (address) discours m.; (utterance) parole f.

speed, n. vitesse f.

speedy, adj. rapide

spell, n. charme m.; (period) période f.; vb. épeler

spend, vb. (money) dépenser; (time) passer

sphere, n. sphère f.

spice, n. épice f.

spider, n. araignée f.

spike, n. pointe f.

spill, vb. répandre

spin, vb. (thread) filer; tourner

spinach, n. épinards m., pl.

spine, n. épine dorsale f.

spiral, n. spirale f.; adj. spiral

spirit, n. esprit m.

spiritual, adj. spirituel

spirtiualism, n. spiritisme m.

spit, n. crachat m., salive f.

spite, n. dépit m.

splash, vb. éclabousser

splendid, adj. splendide

splendor, n. splendeur f.

splinter, n. éclat m.

split, vb. fendre

spoil, n. butin m.; vb. gâter

sponge, n. éponge f.

sponsor, n. (law) garant m.

spontaneous, adj. spontané

spontaneity, n. spontanéité f.

spool, n. bobine f.

spoon, n. cuiller f.

spoonful, n. cuillerée f.

sporadic, adj. sporadique

sport, n. sport, (fun) jeu m.

spot, n. (stain) tache f.; (place) endroit m.; vb. tacher; (recognize) reconnaitre

spouse, n. époux m., épouse f.

spout, n. (eapot, etc.) bec m.; vb. jailir

sprain, n. entorse f.

sprawl, vb. s'étaler

spray, n. (sea) embrun m.

spead, n. étendue f.; vb. étendre

spree, n. fiare la noce

sprightly, adj. éveillé

spring, n. (season) printemps m.; source f.; vb. (leap) sauter; (water) jailir

sprinkle, vb. asperger

spry, adj. alerte

spur, n. éperon m.; vb. éperonner

spurious, adj. faux m.

spurn, vb. repousser

spurt, n. jet m.; vb. jaillir

spy, n. espion m.

squad, n. escouade f.

squadron, n. escardron m.

squalid, adj. misérable

squall, n. rafale f.

squander, vb. gaspiller

square, n. (geom.) carré m.; adj. carré

squat, vb. s'accroupir

squeak, vb. crier

squeeze, vb. serrer, presser

squirrel, n. écureuil m.

squirt, vb. seringuer

stab, vb. poignarder

stability, n. stabilité f.

stable, n. écurie f.; adj. stale

stack, n. (hay) meule f.(chimney) souche f.

staff, n. bâton, (personnel) personnel m.

stage, n.

stagflation, n. staglation f.

stagger, vb. (totter) chanceler

stagnant, adj. stagnant

stain, n. tache f.; vb. (spot) tacher; (color) teinter

stairs, n. escalier m.

stake, n. (post) pieu m.; vb. mettre au je, parier

stale, adj. (bread) rassis

stalk, n. tige f.

stall, n. (stable, church) stalle f.

stamina, n. vigueur f.

stammer, vb. gégayer

stamp, n. timbre-poste (postage) m.; vb. (letter) timbrer; (with foot) frapper du pied

stampede, n. sauve-qui-peut n.

stand, n. (position) position, (resistance) résistance f.; vb. (put) poser; (endure) supporter

standard, n. (flag) étendard, (measure, etc.) étalon, (living, etc.) niveau m.

star, n. étoile, (movie) vedette f.

strach, n. amidon m.

stare, vb. regarder fixement

stark, adj. pur

start, n. (beginning) commencement, tressaillement m.; vb.

commencer tressaillir
startle, vb. effrayer
starvation, n. faim f.
starve, vb. intr. mourir de
faim
state, n. état m.; vb.
déclarer
statement, n. déclaraton f.
statesman, n. homme
d'état m.
static, adj. statique
station, n. (railroad) gare,
(bus, subway) station f.
stationary, adj. stationnaire
stationery, n. papeterie f.
statistics, n. statistique f.
statue, n. statue f.
stay, vb. rester
steady, adj. ferme; soutenu
steak, n. bifteck m.
steal, vb. voler
steam, n. vapeur f.
steamboat, n. bateau à
vapeur m.
steamship, n. vapeur n.
steel, n. acier m.
steep, adj. raide
steeple, n. clocher m.
steer, n. jeune boeuf m.; vb.
gouverner
stem, n. (plant) tige f.
stenographer, n.
sténographe m.f.
stenography, n,
sténographie f.
step, n. pas m.; (stairs)
marche f.
sterophonic, adj.
stéréophonique
sterile, adj. stérile
stern, adj. sévère
stethoscope, n.
stéthoscope m.
stew, n. ragoût m.
steward, n. (airline) garcon m.
stewardess, n. (airline)
hôtesse de l'air f.
stick, n. bâton m.; vb.
(paste) colle
sticky, adj. gluant

stiff, adj. raide
stiffness, n. raideur f.
stifle, vb. étouffer
still, adj. tranquille; adv.
encore; conj. cependant
stillness, n. tranquilité f.
stimulant, n. stimulant m.
stimulate, vb. stimuler
stimulus, n. stimulant m.
sting, n. piqûre.; vb. (prick)
piquer, (smart) cuire
stingy, adj. mesquin
stir, vb. remuer; bouger; n.
mouvement m.
stitch, n. (sewing) point m.;
(knitting) maille f.; vb.
coudre
stock, n. marchandises f.,
pl.; (finance)
valeurs f., pl.
stockbroker, n. agent de
change m.
stock exchange, n.
Bourse f.
stocking, n. bas m.
stole, n. étole f.
stomach, n. estomac m.
stone, n. pierre f.
stool, n. excabeau m.
stoop, vb. se pencher
stop, n. arrêt m.; vb. arrêter,
(prevent) empêcher (de);
(cease) cesser
storage, n. emmagasi-
nage m.
store, n. (shop) magasin m.;
(supply) provision f.; vb.
emmagasiner
storm, n. orage m.
stormy, adj. orageux
story, n. histoire f.; (floor)
étage m.
stouts, adj. gros m. grosse f.
stove, n. fourneau m.
straight, adj. and adv. droit
straighten, vb. redresser
strain, n. effort m.; vb.
(stretch) tendre; (filter)
passer
strait, n. (geographical)
détroit m.

strand, n. plage f.
strange, adj. étrange; (foreign) étranger
stranger, n. éttranger m.
strangle, vb. étrangler
strap, n. courroie f.
strategic, adj. stratégique
strategy, n. stratégie f.
straw, n. paille f.
strawberry, n. fraise f.
stray, adj. égaré
streak, n. raie f.; vb. rayer
stream, n. courant m.;
(small friver) ruisseau m.
streamline, vb. caréner
street, n. rue f.
strength, n. force f.
strengthen, vb. fortifier
strenuous, adj. énergique
streptococcus, n. strepto-
coque m.
stress, n. force, tension f.;
(gramm.) accent m.; vb.
accentuer
stretch, vb. étendre
stretcher, n. brancard m.
strict, adj. strict
stride, n. enjambée f.
strife, n. lutte f.
strike, n. grève f.; vb. frapper; (match) allumer;
(clock) sonner; (workers)
se mettre en grève
string, n. ficelle, (music)
corde f.
string bean, n. haricot
vert m.
strip, n. bande f.; vb.
dépouiller
stripe, n. bande f.; (mil.)
galon m.
strive, vb. s'efforcer (de)
stroke, n. coup m.; vb. caresser
stroll, n. tour m.
strong, adj. fort
structure, n structure f.
struggle, n. lutte f.; vb. lutter
stub, n. souche f.
stubborn, adj. opiniâtre, ob-

stiné, têtu

student, n. étudiant m.

studio, n. atelier m.

studious, adj. studieux

study, n. étude f.; (room) cabine de travail m.; vb. étudier

stuff, n. (materials) matériaux, n., pl.; (textile) étoffe f.; vb. bourrer

stuffing, n. bourre, (cooking) farce f.

stumble, vb. trébucher

stump, n. (tree) souche f.

stum, vb. étourdir

stunt, n. tour de force m.

stupid, adj. stupide

stupidity, n stupidité f.

sturdy, adj. virgoureux

stutter, vb. bégayer

style, n. style m.

stylish, adj. élégant

subconscious, adj. cubconxcient

subdue, vb. subjuguer

subject, n. sujet m.; adj. (people, country) assujetti; (liable) sujet; vb. assujettir

sublimate, vb. sublimer

sublime, adj. sublime

submarine, n. sousmarin m.

submerge, vb. submerger

submission, n. soumission f.

submit, vb. soumettre

subnormal, adj. sous-normal

subscribe, vb. (consent, support) souscrire; (to paper, etc.) s'abonner

subscription, n. souscription f.; abonnement m.

subsequent, adj. subséquent

subsidy, n. subvention f.

substance, n. substance f.

substantial, adj. substantiel

substitute, n. remplacant m.; vb substituer

substitution, n. substitutionf.

subterfuge, n. subterfuge, fauxfuyant m.

subtle, adj. subtil

subract, vb. soustraire

suburb, n. faubourg m.

subversive, adj. subversif

subway, n. métro (politain) m.

succeed, vb. (come after) succéder à; (be successful) réussir (à)

success, n. succes m.

successful, adj. heureux

succession, n. succession

successive, adj. successif

successor, n. successeur m.

succumb, vb. succomber

such, adj. tel, pareil

suck, vb. sucer

suction, n. succion f.

sudden, adj. soudain

sue, vb. poursuivre

suffer, vb. souffrir

suffice, vb. suffire

sufficient, adj. suffisant

suffocate, vb. suffoquer

sugar, n. sucre m.

suggest, vb. suggérer

suggestion, n. suggestion f.

suicide, n. suicide m.; vb. (commit suicide) se suicider

suit, n. (law) procès, (clothes) complet m.; (cards) couleur f.; vb. convenir (à)

suitable, adj. convenable

suitcase, n. valise f.

sum, n. somme f.

summary, n. résumé, abrége m.; adj. sommaire, immédiat

summer, n. été m.

summon, vb. (call together) convoquer

sumn, n. soleil m.

sunburn, n. hâle m.

Sunday, n. dimance m.

sunny, adj. ensoleillé

sunshine, n. soleil m.

superb, adj. superbe

superficial, adj. superficiel

superfluous, adj. superflu

superintendent, n. surveillant m.

superior, adj. and n. supérieur m.

superiority, n. supériorité f.

supernatural, adj. and n. surnaturel m.

supersede, vb. remplacer

superstar, n. superstar m.

superstition, n. superstition f.

superstitious, adj. superstitieux

supervise, vb. surveiller

supper, n. souper m.

supplement, n. supplément m.

supply, n. approvisionnement m.; (provision) provision f.; vb. fournir (de)

support, n. appui m.; vb. soutenir; (bear) supporter; (back up) appuyer

suppose, vb. supposer

suppress, vb. supprimer

suppression, n. suppression f.

supreme, adj. supréme

sure adj. sûr

surface, n. surface f.

surge, n. houle f.

surgeon, n. chirurgien m.

surgery, chirurgie f.

surpass, vb. surpasser

surplus, n. surplus m.

surprise, n. surprise f.; vb. surprendre

surrender, vb. rendre

surround, vb. entourer

survey, vb. contempler; (investigate) examiner

survival, n. survivance f.

survive, vb. survivre

susceptible, adj. susceptible (de)

suspect, vb. soupconner

suspend, vb. suspendre

suspense, n. incertitude f.

suspension, n. suspension f.

sujspicion, n. soupcon m.

sustain, vb. soutenir

swallow, n. (bird) hirondelle f.; vb. avaler

swamp, n. marais m.

swan, n. cygne m.

swarm, n. essaim m.

sway, n. (rule) domination, (motion) oscillation f. ; vb. gouverner

swear, n. jurer

sweat, n. sueur f.; vb. suer

Sweden, n. Suèdois m.

Sweden, n. Suède f.

Swedish, adj. and n. suédois m.

sweep, n. (bend) courbe f.; (movement) mouvement m. circulaire vb. balayer

sweepstakes, n. poule f.

sweet, adj. doux m., douce f.; sucré

sweeten, vb. sucrer

sweetener, n. adoucidssant m.

sweetheart, n. amant m., amante f.

sweetness, n. couceur f.

sweet potato, n. patate f.

swell, vb. bonfler, enfler

swollen, vb. enfler, s'enfler

swelling, n. enflure, bouffissure f.

swelter, vb. étouffer de chaleur

swerve, vb. s'écarter, se détourner

swift, adj. rapide

swiftly, adv. vite, rapidement n.

swiss, vb. nager

swindle, vb. escroquer

swine, n. cochon m.

swing, vb. balancer

Swiss, n. Suisse m.; adj. suisse, helvétique

switch, n. (electric) interrupteur m.

Switzerland, n. Suisse f.

sword, n. épée f.

syllable, n. syllable f.

symbol, n. symbole m.

symbolic, adj. sybolique

sympathetic, adj. compatisstant

sympathy, n. compassion f.

symphony, n. symphonie f.

symptom, n. symptôme m.

syndicate, n. syndicat m.

syndrome, n. syndrome m.

synonym, n. synonyme m.

synthetic, adj. synthétique

syrup, n. sirop m.

system, n. système m.

T

table, n. table f.

tablecloth, n. nappe f.

tablespoon, n. cuiller à bouche f.

tablet, n. tablette f.

tabling, n. assemblage m.

taboo, n. and adj. tabou m.

tabular, adj. arrangé en tableaux

tack, n. (nail) brouqette f.; vb. clouer

tackiness, n. viscosité f.

tacking, n. cloutage m.

tackle, n. attirail m.; apparaux *m,pl*. v.a. saisir a bras le corps

tackler, n. plaqueur m.

tackling, n. gréement m.

tacky, adj. collant, visqueur

tact, n. tact m.

tactful, adj. plein de tact

tactless, adj. sans tact

tadpole, n. têtard m.

taffeta, n. taffetas m.

tag, n. étiquette f.

tall, n. queue f.

tailor, n. tailleur m.

take, vb. prendre; (lead) conduire; (carry) porter

tale, n. conte m.

talent, n. talent m.

talk, n. conversation f.; vb parler

talkative, adj. bavard

tall, adj. grand

tame, adj. (animal) apprivoisé

tamper, vb. toucher à

tan, n. (leather) tan m.; (skin) hâle m.

tangible, adj. tangible

tangle, n . embrouillement m.

tank, n. réservoir, (mil.) char (d'assaut) m.

tap, n. (water) robinet m.; (knock) petit coup m.; vb. frapper legèrement

tape, n. ruban m.

tape recorder, n. magnétophone m.

tapestry, n. tapisserie f.

tar, n. goudron m.

target, n. cible f.

tariff, n. tarif m.

tarnish, vb. ternir

task, n. tâche f.

taste, n. goût m.; vb. goûter

tasty, adj. savoureux

taut, adj. raide

tavern, n. taverne f.

tax, n. impôt m.; vb. imposer

taxi, n. taxi m.

taxpayer, n. contribuable m.

tea, n. thé m.

teach, vb. enseigner; (to do) apprendre à

teacher, n. instituteur, (school) professeur m.

team, n. (animals) attelage m..; (people) équipe f.

teapot, n. théière f.

tear, n. larme, (rip) déchirure f.; vb. déchirer

tease, vb. taquiner

teaspoon, n. cuiller à thé f.

technical, adj. technique

technique n. technique f.

telegram, n. télégramme m.

telegraph, n. télégraphe m.

telephone, n. téléphone m.; vb. téléphoner

telescope, n. télescope m.

television, n. télévision f.
tell, vb. dire; (story, etc.) raconter
teller, n. (bank) caissier m.
temper, n. (humor) humeur f.; (anger) colère, (metals) trempe f.
temperence, n. tempérance f.
temperate, adj. (habit) sorbre; (climate) tempéré
temperature, n. température f.
tempest, n. tempête f.
temple, n. temple m.; (forehead) tempe f.
temporary, adj. temporaire
tempt, vb. tenter
temptation, n. tentation f.
ten, adj. and n. dix m.
tenant, n. locataire m.f.
tend, vb. tendre, intr.; (care for) soigner
tendency, n. tendance f.
tender, adj. tendre
tendernes, n. tendresse f.
tendon, n. tenon m.
tennis, n. tennis m.
tenor, n. (music) ténor m.
tense, adj. tendu
tension, n. tension f.
tent, n. tente f.
tentative, adj. tentatif, expérimental
tenth, adj. and n. dixième m.
term, n. terme m.; (school) trimestre m.; (conditions) conditions f., pl.
terrible, adj. terrible
terrify, vb. terrifier
territory, n. territoire m.
terror, n. terreur f.
test, n. épreuve f.; vb. mettre àl'épreuve
testament, n. testatment m.
testify, vb. témoigner (de); (declare) affirmer
testimony, n. témoignage m.
text, n. texte m.
textile, adj. textile

texture, n. texture f.
than, conj. que; de (between numbers)
thank, vb. remercier; merci
thankful, adj. reconnaissant
that, (those, pl.) adj. ce cet m., cette f., ces, pl.; demonstrative pron. celuilà m.,celle-là f., ceux-là m., pl.; conj. que; (purpose) pour que
the, art. le m., la f., les, pl.
theater, n. théâtre m.
theft, n. vol m.
their, adj. leur sg., leurs pl.
theirs, pron. le leur m., la leur f., les teurs pl.
them, pron. eux m., elles f.; les (direct), leur (indirect)
theme, n. thème m.
themselves, pron euxmèmes m., elles-mémes f.; (reflexive) se
then, adv. alors; (after that) ensuite
thence, adv. (place) de là; (reason) pour cette raison
theology, n. théologie f.
theoretical, adj. théorique
theory, n. théorie f.
therapy, n. thérapie f.
there, adv. là, y; il; en cela
therefore, adv. donc
thermometer, n. thermomètre m.
they, pron. ils m., elles f.
thick, adj. épais
thicken, vb. épaissir
thickness, n. épasseur f.
thief, n. voleur m.
thigh, n. cuisse f.
thimble, n. dé m.
thin, adj. mince
thing, n. chose f.
thinker,n. penseur m.
third, n. tiers m.; adj. troisième
thirst, n. soif f.
thirsty, adj. avoir soif
thirteen, adj. and n. treize m.

thirty, adj. and n. trente m.
this, sg. (these, pl.) adj. ce, cet m., cette f., ces pl.; demonstrative pron. celuici m.f. ceux-ci m., pl., celles-ci f.,pl.
thorough, adj. complet, entier
though, conj. quoique
thought, n. pensée f.
thoughtful, adj. pensif
thousand, adj. and n. mille m.
thread, n. fil m.
threat, n. meancc f.
threaten, vb menacer
three, adj. and n. trois m.
thrift, n. économie f.
thrill, n. tressaillement m.; vb. tressaillir, intr.; faire frémir
thrive, vb. prospérer
throat, n. gorge f.
throne, n. trône m.
through, prep and adv. à travers; avoir fini
throughout, adv. partout
throw, vb. jeter
thrust, vb. ousser
thumb, n. pouce m.
thunder, n. tonnerre m.; vb. tonner
Thursday, n. jeudi m.
thus, adv. ainsi
ticket, n. billet m.
tickle, vb. chatouiller
ticklish, adj. chatouilleux
tide, n. marée f.
tidy, adj. (person) ordonné; en bon ordre
tie, n. lien m.; cravate f.; vb. attacher; (bind) lier; (knot) nouer
tier, n. gradin m.
tiger, n. tigre m.
tight, adj. serré; (drunk) gris
tighten, vb. serrer
tile, n. (roof) tuile f.
till prep. jusqu'a; conj. jusqu'a ce que
tilt, vb. pencher

time, n. temps m.; (occasion) fois f.; (clock) heure f.; (what time is it?) quelle heure est-il?

timid, adj. timide

timidity, n. timidité f.

tin, n. étain m.

tint, n. teinte f.

tiny, adj. tout petit

tip, n. (money) pourboire m.; (end) bout m.

tired, adj. fatigué

tissue, n. tissu m.

title, n. titre m.

to, prep à, de

tobacco, n. tabac m.

today, adv. aujourd'hui

toe, n. orteil m.

together, adv. ensemble

toil, vb. travailler dur

toilet, n. toilette f.

token, n témoignage, (coin) jeton m.

tolerance, n. tolérance f.

tolerate, vb. tolérer

tomato, n. tomate f.

tomb, n. tombeau m.

tomorrow, adv. demain

ton, n. tonne f.

tone, n. ton m.

tongue, n. langue f.

tonic, adj. and n. tonique m.

tonight, adv. cette nuit; (evening) ce soir

tonsil, n. amygdale f.

too, adv. trop; (als) aussi

tool, n. outil m.

tooth, n. dent m.

toothache, n. mal de dents m.

toothbrush, n. brosse (f.) á dents

top, n. (mountain, etc.) sommet, table) dessus m.

topcoat, n. pardessus m.

topic, n. sujet m.

torch, n. torche f.

torment, n. tourment m.; vb. tourmenter

torrent, n. torrent m.

torture, n. torture f.; vb. tor-turer

toss, vb. (throw) jeter; s'agiter

total, adj. and n. total m.

tough, adj. dur

tour, n. tour m.

tourist, n. touriste m.f.

tournament, n. tournoi m.

tow, vb. remorquer

toward, prep. (place, time) vers; (feelings, etc.) en-vers

towel, n. serviette f.

tower, n. tour f.

town, n. ville f.

toy, n. jouet m.

trace, n. trace f.

track, n. piste f.; (railroad) voie f.

tract, n. (space) étendue f.

tractor, n. tracteur m.

trade, n. commerce, (job) métier m.; vb. commercer

tradition, n. tradition f.

traffic, n. circulation f.

tragedy, n. tragédie f.

tragic, adj tragique

trail, n. trace f.

train, n. train m.; (dress)

tramp, n. (steps) bruit de pas; (person) chem-ineau m.

tranquil, adj. tranquille

transaction, n. opération f.

transfer, n. transport m.; (ticket) billet de corre-spondance m.; vb. transférer

transform, vb. transformer

transfusion, n. transfusion f.

transition, n. transition f.

translate, vb. traduire

transmit, vb. transmettre

transparent, adj. transparent

transport, n. transport m.; vb. transporter

transsexual, adj. transsexuel

transvestite, adj. travesti

trap, n. piège m.; vb. prendre au piège

trash, n. (rubbish) rebut m.

travel, n. voyage m.; vb. voyager

traveler, n. voyageur m.

traveler's check, n. chèque de voyage n.

tray, n. plateau m.

treacherous, adj. traître

tread, vb. marcher

treason, n. trahison f.

treasure, n. trésor m.

treasurer, n. trésorier m.

treasury, n. trésor m.

treat, vb. traiter

treatment, n. traitement m.

treaty, n. traité m.

tree, n. arbre m.

tremble, vb. trembler

tremendous, adj. terrible

trench, n. tranchée f.

trend, n. tendance f.

trespass, vb. empiéter

triage, n. présélection f.

trial, n. (law) procès m.; (test) épreuve f.

triangle, n. triangle m.

tribulation, n. tribulation f.

tributary, n. (river) affluent m.; adj tributaire

tribure, n. tribut m.

trick, n. ruse f.; vb. duper

tricky, adj. astucieux

trifle, n. bagatelle f.

trigger, n. détente f.

trim, adj. soigne.; vb. (put in order) arranger; (adorn) garnir; tailer

trinket, n. breloque f.

trip, n. voyage m.; vb. trébucher

triple, adj. and n. triple m.

trite, adj rebatu

triumph, n. triomphe m.

triumphant, adj. triomphant

trivial, adj. trivial

trolley-car, n. tramway m.

troop, n. troupe f.

trophy, n. trophée m.

tropic, n. tropique m.

trot, n. trot m.; vb. intr. trot-ter

trouble, n. (misfortune) malheur m.; (difficulty) difficulté f.; dérangement m.; vb. (worry) inquiéter, déranger

troublesome, adj. gênant

trough, n. auge f.

trousers, n. pantalon m.

trousseau, n. trousseau m.

trout, n. truite f.

truce, n. trève f.

truck, n. camion m.

true, adj vrai

truly, adv. vraiment

trumpet, n. trompette f.

trunk, n. (clothes) malle f.; (body, tree) tronc m.

trust, n. confiance f.; (business) trust m.; vb. se confier à; (entrust) confier

trustworthy, adj. digne de confiance

truth, n. vérité f.

truthful, adj. sincère

try, vb. essayer; (law) mettre en jugement

tryst, n. rendez-vous m.

tub, n. baignoire f.

tube, n. tube m.

tuberculosis, n. tuberculose f.

tuck, n. (fold) pli m.

Tuesday, n. mardi m.

tug, n. (boat) remorqueur m.; vb. (pull) tirer

tuition, n. (prix de l') enseignement m.

tuilip, n. tulipe f.

tumble, vb (fall) tomber

tumor, n. tumeur f.

tummult, n. tumulte m.

tujms, n. thon m.

tune, n. air m.; (concord harmony) accord m.; vb. accorder

tunnel, n. tunnel m.

turban, n. turban m.

turf, n. gazon m.

Turk, n. Turc m., Turque f.

turkey, n. dindon m.

Turkey, n. Turquie f.

turmoil, n. tumulte m.

turn, n. tour m.; (road) détour m.; vb. tourner

turnip, n. navet m.

turret, n. tourelle f.

turtle, n. tortue f.

tutor, n. précepteur m.

twelfth, adj. and n. douzième m.

twelve, adj. and n. douze m.

twentieth, adj. and n. vingtiéme m.

twenty, adj. and n. vingt m.

twice, adv. deux fois

twig, n. brindile f.

twilight, n. crépuscule m.

twin, adj. and n. jumeau m., jumelle f.

twine, n. ficelle f.

twinkle, vb. scintiller

twist, vb. tordre

two, adj. and n. deux m.

type, n. type m.; (printing) caractère m.; vb. taper à la machine

typhoid fever, n. fièvre typhoide f.

typical, adj. typique

typist, n. dactyl o (graphe) m.f.

tyranny, n. tyrannie f.

tyrant, n. tyran m.

U

udder, n. mamelle f.

ugliness, n. laideur f.

ugly, adj. laid

ulcer, n. ulcère m.

ulterior, adj. ultérieur

ultimate, adj. dernier

umbrella, n. parapluie m.

umpire, n. arbitre m.f.

unable, adj. incapable; (u.to) dans l'impossibilité de

unanimous, adj. unanime

uncertain, adj. incertain

uncle, n. oncle m.

unconscous, n. inconscient m. ; adj. (aware) inconscient; (faint) sans connaissance

uncover, vb. découvrir

under, prep. sous.; adv. audessous,

underestimate, vb. sous-estimer

undergo, vb. subir

underground, adj. souterrain

underline, vb. souligner

underneath, adv. en dessous

undershirt, n. gilet de dessous m.

understand, vb. comprendre

undertake, vb. entreprendre

underwear, n. vêtements de dessous m., pl.

undo, vb. défaire

undress, vb. déshabiller

uneasy, adj. gêné

uneven, adj. inégal

unexpected, adj. nattendu

unfair, adj. injuste

unfit, adj. peu propre (à)

unfold, vb. déplier

unforgettable, adj. inoubliable

unfortunate, adj. malheureux

unhappy, adj. malheureux

unicorn, n. licorne f.

unidentified, adj. peu idiomatique

uniform, adj. and n. uniforme m.

uniformity, n. uniformité f.

uniformly, adv. uniformément

unify, vb. unifier

union, n. union f.

unique, adj. unique

unisex, adj. unisexuel

unit, n. unité f.

unite, vb. unir

United Nations, n. Nations

Unies f., pl.

United States, n. les États-Unis m., pl.

unity, n. unité f.

universal, adj. universel

universe, n. univers m.

university, n. université f.

unleaded, adj. sans plomb

unless, conj. à moins que...ne

unlike, adj. dissemblable

unload, vb. décharger

unlock, vb. ouvrir

untie, vb. dénouer

until, conj. jusqu'à ce que

unusual, adj. insolite

up, prep. vers le haut de, au haut

uphold, vb. soutenir

upon, prep. sur

upper, adj. supérieur

upright, adj. droit

uproar, n. vacarme m.

upset, vb. renverser

upstairs, adv. en haut

uptight, adj. tendu

upward, adj. dirigé en haut; adv. en montant

urge, vb. (beg) prier

urgency, n. urgence f.

urgent, adj. urgent

us, pron. nous

use, n. usage m.; vb. employer, se servir de

useful, adj. utile

useless, adj. inutile

usher, n. huissier m.

usual, adj. usuel

utensil, n. ustensile m.

utmost, n. le plus, tout son possible; adj. (greatest) le plus grand

utter, adj. absolu; vb. prononcer; (cry) pousser

utterance, n. emmission f.

uvula, n. luette, uvule f.

V

vacancy, n. vide m., vacance f.

vacant, adj. vide

vacate, vb. quitter, évacuer

vacation, n. vacances f.,pl.

vaccinate, vb. vacciner

vaccine, n. vaccin m.

vacuum, n. vide m.; (vacuum cleaner) aspirateur m.

vagrant, adj. vagabond

vague, adj. vague

vain, adj. vain

valiant, adj. vaillant

valid, adj. valide

valley, n. vallée f.

valuable, adj. de valeur

value, n. valeur f.; vb. évaluer

valve, n. soupape f.

vanilla, n. vanille f.

vanish, vb. s'évanouir

vanity, n. vanité f.

vanquish, vb. vaincre

vapor, n. vapeur f.

varied, adj. varié

variety, n. variété f.

various, adj. divers

varnish, n. vernis m.; vb. lernir

vary, vb. varier

vasectomy, n. vasectomie f.

vast, adj. vaste

vault, n. voûite f.

vegetable, n. légume m.

vehicle, n. véhicule m.

veil, n. voile m.

vein, n. veine f.

velvet, n. velours m.

vengeance, n. vengeance f.

vent, n. ouverture f.

venture, n. aventure f.; vb. hasarder

verb, n. verbe m.

verdict, n. verdict m.

verify, vb. vérifier

verse, n. vers m., pl.

version, n. version f.

vertical, adj. vertical

very, adv. très

vessel, n. vaisseau m.

vest, n. gilet m.

veteran, n. vétéran m.

veto, n. véto m.

vibrate, vb. vibrer

vibration, n. vibration f.

vicinity, n. voisinage m.

vicious, adj. méchant

victim, n. victime f.

victor, n. vainqueur m.

view, n. vue f.

village, n. village m.

villain, n. scélérat m.

vine, n. vigne f.

vinegar, n. vinaigre m.

vintage, n. vendange, (year of wine) année f.

violence, n. violence

violent, adj. violent

violet, n. violette f.; adj. violet

violin, n. violon m.

virgin, n. vierge f.

virtual, adj. virtuel, defait

virus, n. virus m.

visible, adj. visible

vision, n. vision f.

visit, n. visite f.; vb. visiter

visitor, n. visiteur m.

visual, adj. visuel

vital, adj. vital

vitamin, n. vitamine f.

vocabulary, n. vocabulaire m.

vocal, adj. vocal

voice, n. voix f.

void, adj. (law) nul

volcano, n. volcan m.

volume, n. volume m.

volunteer, n. volontaire m.; vb. s'engager

vomit, vb. vomir

vote, n. vote m.; vb. voter

vow, n. voeu m.

vowel, n. voyelle f.

voyage, n. voyage m.

vulgar, adj. vulgaire

vulnerable, adj. vulnérable

W

wade, vb. traverser à gué

waffle, n. gaufre (américaine) f.

wag, vb. agiter

wage, vb. (war) faire la guerre

wages, n. salaire m.

wagon, n. chariot m.

wall, vb. gémir

waist, n. taille f.

wait (for), vb. attendre

waiter, n. garçon m.

wake, vb. éveiller, réveiller

walk, n. promenade f.; vb. marcher; (take a walk) se promener

wall, n. mur m.

wallcovering, n. tenture f.

wallet, n. portefeuille m.

wallpaper, n. papier peint m.; papier à tapisser m.

walnut, n. noix f.

walrus, n. morse m.

waltz, n. valse f.

wander, vb. errer

want, n. besoin m.; vb. vouloir

war, n. guerre f.

ward, n. (hospital) salle f.; (charge) pupille m.f.

ware, n. marchandises f., pl.

warm, adj. chaud, avoir chaud; vb. chauffer

warmth, n. chaleur f.

warn, vb. avertir

warning, n. avertissement m.

warp, vb. détourner

warrant, n. mandat m.; vb. garantir

wash, vb. laver

wasp, n. guêpe f.

waste, n. perte f. gaspillage m., prodigalité f.

watchful, adj. vigilant

watchman, n. gardien m.

water, n. eau f.

waterbed, n. aqualit m.

waterproof, adj. imperméable

wave, n. vague f.;

(sound) onde f.; permanente; vb. agiter, (hair) on- duler

waver, vb. vaciller

wavy, adj. ondoyant, onduleux

wax, n. cire f.

way, n. (road) chemin m.; (distance) distance, manière f.; côté m.

we, pron. nous

weak, adj. faible

weaken, vb. affaiblir

weakness, n. faiblesse f.

wealth, n. richesse f.

wealthy, adj. riche

weapon, n. arme f.

wear, vb. porter

weary, adj. las fatigué

weasel, n. belette f.

weather, n. temps m.

weave, vb. tisser

weaver, n. tisserand m.

web, n. (fabric) tissu m.; (spider) toile f.

wedding, n. noces f., pl.; adj. de noces, de mariage

wedge, n. coin m.

Wednesday, n. mercredi m.

weed, n. mauvaise herbe f.

week, n. semaine f.

weekday, n. jour de semaine m.

week-end, n. week-end m., fin de semaine f.

weekly, adj. hebdomadaire

weep, vb. pleurer

weigh, vb. peser

weight, n. poids m.

weird, adj. mystérieux

welcome, adj. bienvenu

welfare, n. bien-être m.

well, n. (water) puits m.; adv. bien

well-known, adj. bien connu

west, n. ouest m.

western, adj. de l'ouest

wet, adj. mouillé; (weather) pluvieux; vb. mouiller

whale, n. baleine f.

what, adj. quel m.; pron. ce qui (subject), ce que (object), qu'est-ce qui, quoi, qu'est-ceque

wheat, n. blé m.

wheel, n. roue f.

when, conj quand

whenever, conj. toutes les fois que

where, con. où

wherever, conj. partout où

whether, conj. soit que; (if) si

which, adj. quel, pron. (relative) qui; lequel; (interrogative) lequel

whichever, pron. n'importe lequel

while, conj. pendant que; (whereas) tandis que

whim, n. caprice m.; lubie f.

whip, n. fouet m.; vb. fouetter, battre

whirl, vb. faire tourner, tourner

whirlpool, n. tourbillon d'eau m.

whirlwind, n. tourbillon de vent m.

whisker, n. (man) favori m.; (animals) moustache.

whiskey, n. whiskey m.

whisper, vb. chuchoter

whistle, n. siflet m.; vb. sifler

white, adj. blanc m., blanche f.

who, pron. qui, qu'est-cequi

whoever, pron. qui que cr soit, quiconque

whole, adj. entier

wholesale, adj. and adv. en gros

wholesome, adj. sain

wholly, adv. entièrement

whom, pron. que; lequel; qui est-ce que

whose, pron. dont; de qui; duquel m., de laquelle f.,

desquels m., pl.

why, adv. pourquoi

wicked, adj. méchant f.

wide, adj. large

widow, n. veuve f.

widower, n. veuf m.

width, n. largeur f.

wife, n. femme f.

wild, adj. sauvage

wilderness, n. désert m.

wildlife, n. faune f.

will, n. volonté f.; testament m.; vb. vouloir; (bequeath) léguer

win, vb. gagner

wind, n. vent m.

window, n. fenêtre, (shop) devanture f.

windy, adj. venteux

wine, n. vin m.

wing, n. aile f.

wink, n. clin d'oeil m.; vb. clignoter

winner, n. gagnant m.

winter, n. hiver m.

wipe vb. essuyer

wire, n. fil de fer m.

wireless, adj. sans fil

wisdom, n. sagesse f.

wise, adj. sage

wish, n. désir m.; vb. désirer

wit, n. esprit m.

with, prep. avec

withdraw, vb. retirer

wither, vb. flétrir

withhold, vb. refuser

within, adv. dedans

without, prep. sans

witness, n. toin m.

witty, adj. spirituel

wizard, n. sorcier m.

woe, n. malheur m.

woman, n. femme f.

womb, n. matrice f.

wonder, vb. se demander; (be surprised) être étonné

wonderful, adj. merveilleux

wood, n. bois m.

wooden, adj. de bois

wool, n. laine f.

woolen, adj. de laine

word, n. mot m.

work, n. travail m.; vb. travailler

worker, n. travailleur m.

workman, n. ouvrier m.

world, n. monde m.

worm, n. ver m.

worn, adj. usé

worry, n. souci m.; vb. tracasser, préoccuper

worse, adj. pire; adv. pis

worship, n. culte m.; vb. adorer

worth, n. valeur f.; vb. valoir; adj. valant, qui méritre

worthless, adj. indigne; (without value) sans valeur

worthy, adj. digne

would, vb. vouloir

wound, n. blessure f.; vb. besser

wrap, vb. envelopper

wrath, n. courroux m.

wreath, n. couronne f.

wreck, n. (ship) naufrage m.; (remains) débris m., pl.

wrestle, vb. lutter

wretched, adj. misérable

wring, vb. tordre

wrinkle, n. ride f.; vb. rider, plisser

wrist, n. poignet m.

write, vb. écrire

write-off, n. annulation, non-valeur f.

writer, n. écrivain m.

written, adj. écrit, par écrit

wrong, adj. faux m., fausse f.;

X

x-rays, n. rayons X m., pl.

xylophone, n. xylophone m.

Y

yacht, n. yacht m.

yam, n. igname f.

yard, n. (house) cour f.; (lumber) chantier, (measusre) yard m.

yarn, n. fil m.

yawn, n. bâilement m.; vb. bâiler

year, n. and m.; (duration) année f.

yearly, adj. annuel

yearn for, vb. soupirer après

yell, vb. hurler

yellow, adj. and n. jaune m.

yes, adv. oui

yesterday, adv. hier

yet, adv. encore; conj. néanmoins

yield, vb. (resign) céder; produire

yoke, n. joug m.

yolk, n. jaune m.

you, pron. vous

young, adj. jeune

your, adj. votre sg., vos pl.; ton m.sg., ta f.sg., tes pl.

yours, pron. le vôtre; le tien m., la tienne f.

yourself, pron. vousmême; toi-même; vous, te

youth, n. jeunesse f.

youthful, adj. (young) jeune; (of youth) de jeunesse

Z

zap, vb. frapper d'une facon soudaine et inattendue

zeal, n. zèle m.

zealous, adj. zélé

zebra, n. zre m.

zero, n. zéro m.

zest, n. entrain m.; (taste) saveur f.

zip code, n. code postal m.

zone, n. zone f.

zoo, n. jardin zoologique

A GUIDE TO FIRST AID TECHNIQUES

CONTENTS

Importance of First Aid

Sudden illness or injury can often be serious unless proper care is administered promptly. **First aid** is immediate attention to one suffering from illness or injury.

First aid does not replace the physician, but assists the victim until proper medical assistance can be obtained. One of the most important principles of first aid is to obtain medical assistance in all cases of serious injury. Even seemingly minor injuries should be examined by a physician if there is any question of proper treatment or possibility of complication.

The urgent need for quick action in responding to life-threatening situations makes it important for everyone to be able to give proper emergency care until a victim can be transported to a medical facility.

When first aid is properly administered, it can often restore natural breathing and circulation, control bleeding, reduce the severity of shock, protect injuries from infection or other complications, and help conserve the victim's strength. If prompt steps are taken and medical aid is obtained, the victim's chances of recovery are greatly improved.

The principal aims of first aid are:

- ♦ Relief of life-threatening conditions
- ♦ Protection from further injury and complications
- ♦ Arrangement of transportation for the victim to a medical facility in such a manner as not to complicate the injury or subject the victim to unnecessary discomfort
- ♦ Making the victim as comfortable as possible to conserve strength

First aiders must be able to take charge of a situation, keep calm while working under pressure, and organize others to do likewise. By demonstrating competence and using well-selected words of encouragement, first aiders should win the confidence of others nearby and do everything possible to reassure the apprehensive victim.

During the first few minutes following an injury, the injured person has a better chance of full recovery if there is someone nearby trained in first aid. Everyone should be able to give effective assistance until an injured person can receive professional medical care.

A Short Course in Anatomy

To grasp first aid procedures and effectively administer effective first aid, it is necessary to know something about the anatomy and the physiology of the human body. Anatomy refers to structure and physiology refers to the functions of the body.

The body is composed of solids, such as bones and tissue; and fluids, such as blood, and the secretions of various glands, organs and membranes.

The principal regions of the body are:

- • head
- • neck
- • chest
- • abdomen
- • upper and lower extremities

For the purposes of this book, the upper extremity from one shoulder to the elbow will be referred to as the upper arm or simply the arm. The portion from the elbow to the wrist will be called the forearm; the portion of the lower extremity from the hip to the knee will be called the thigh; and the portion from the knee to the ankle, the leg.

SKELETON

The human skeleton is composed of approximately two hundred bones, which are classified according to shape as long, short, flat, and irregular bones. The skeleton forms a strong flexible framework for the body. It supports and carries the soft parts, protects vital organs from injury, gives attachment to muscles and tendons, and forms joints to allow movement.

There are three major divisions of the human skeleton:

- The head
- The trunk or main part of the body
- The upper and lower extremities or limbs

HEAD

The head is composed of twenty-two bones, eight that are closely united to form the skull, a bony case that encloses and protects the brain; fourteen other bones form the face. The only movable joint in the head is the lower jaw.

TRUNK

The trunk is composed of fifty-four bones and divided into upper and lower parts by a muscular partition known as the diaphragm.

The upper portion of the trunk is the chest, its cavity, and organs. The spinal column, or backbone, is made up of thirty-three segments that are composed of vertebrae joined by strong ligaments and cartilage to form a flexible column that encloses the spinal cord. The chest is formed by twenty-four ribs, twelve on each side, that are attached in the back to vertebrae. The seven upper pairs of ribs are attached to the breastbone in front by cartilage. The next three pairs of ribs are attached in front by a common cartilage to the seventh rib instead of the breastbone. The lower two pairs of ribs, known as the floating ribs, are not attached in front.

The lower part of the trunk is the abdomen, its cavity, and organs. The pelvis is a basin-shaped bony structure at the lower portion of the trunk. The pelvis is below the movable vertebrae of the spinal column, which it supports, and above the lower limbs, upon which it rests. Four bones compose the pelvis, the two bones of the backbone and the wing-shaped hip bones on either side. The pelvis forms the floor of the abdominal cavity and provides deep sockets in which the heads of the thigh bones fit.

EXTREMITIES

The upper extremity consists of thirty-two bones. The collarbone is a long bone, the inner end of which is attached to the breastbone and the outer end is attached to the shoulder blade at the shoulder joint. The collarbone lies just in front of and above the first rib. The shoulder blade is a flat triangular bone which lies at the upper and outer part of the back of the chest and forms part of the shoulder joint. The arm bone extends from the shoulder to the elbow. The two bones of the forearm extend from the elbow to the wrist. There are eight wrist bones, five bones in the palm of the hand, and fourteen finger bones, two in the thumb and three in each finger.

The lower extremity consists of thirty bones. The thigh bone, the longest and strongest bone in the body, extends from the hip joint to the knee; its upper end is rounded to fit into the socket in the pelvis, and its lower end broadens out to help form part of the knee joint. This flat triangular bone can be felt in front of the knee joint. The two bones in the leg extend from the knee joint to the ankle. There are seven bones in the ankle and back part of the foot, five long bones in the front part of the foot, and fourteen toe bones.

Most fractures and dislocations occur to the bones and joints of the extremities.

JOINTS AND LIGAMENTS

Two or more bones coming together form a joint.

There are three types of joints:

1. Immovable joints, such as those in the skull
2. Joints with limited motion, such as those of the ribs and lower spine
3. Freely movable joints, such as the knee, ankle, elbow, etc.

Freely movable joints are those most commonly injured and of most concern in first aid. The ends of bones forming a movable joint are covered by cartilage.

The bones are held in place by strong white bands, called ligaments, extending from one bone to another and entirely around the joint. A smooth membrane that lines the end of the cartilage and the inside of the ligaments secretes a fluid that keeps the joints lubricated.

MUSCLES AND TENDONS

Bones, the framework of the body, are mostly covered with flesh and muscle tissue which give the body its shape and contour.

There are two types of muscles:

1. Voluntary muscles: those that are consciously controlled, such as muscles of the arms and legs.
2. Involuntary muscles: those that are not consciously controlled, such as muscles of the heart and those that control digestion and breathing.

Strong, inelastic, fibrous cords called tendons attach the muscles to the bones. The muscles cause the bones to move by flexing or extending.

SKIN

The skin is far more than a protective covering for the body. Although the outer layer of skin, or epidermis, is made up of layers of cells that primarily serve to protect, it also contains the cells that determine skin color. The epidermis constantly changes; as new layers are formed, old ones are shed. The layer of skin below the epidermis is the dermis. The dermis contains the blood vessels, nerves, and specialized structures such as sweat glands, that help to regulate body temperature, and hair follicles. The fat and soft tissue layer below the dermis is called the subcutaneous.

The skin has many protective functions. Skin is watertight and keeps internal fluids in while keeping germs out. A system of nerves in the skin carries information to the brain. These nerves transmit information about pain, external pressure, heat, cold, and the relative position of various parts of the body.

The skin is one of the most important organs of the body. The loss of a large part of the skin will result in death unless it can be replaced. Skin often provides important information to the first aider concerning the victim's condition, such as pale, sweaty skin that may indicate shock.

CHEST CAVITY

The chest cavity is cone-shaped, formed by the upper part of the spinal column or backbone at the back, the ribs on the sides, and the ribs and breastbone in front. The diaphragm, a thin, muscular partition at the bottom of the chest cavity separates the chest cavity and the abdominal cavity. The diaphragm is dome-shaped and lower in the back than in the front.

The lungs and the heart occupy most of the chest cavity. The heart lies between the lungs in the center of the chest behind the breastbone. It is positioned slightly to the left side, making the left lung smaller than the right. In addition to the heart and the lungs, the chest cavity contains the esophagus or food pipe that extends from the back of the throat down through the diaphragm to the stomach, the trachea or windpipe that extends to the lungs, and several major blood vessels.

ABDOMINAL CAVITY

The abdominal cavity is in the lower portion of the trunk, formed by the lower portion of the backbone, the muscles in the back and abdominal muscles at the sides and front. The diaphragm forms the top of the cavity and the pelvic basin forms the bottom.

The abdomen contains several important organs: the liver in the upper right portion; the stomach and the spleen in the upper left portion; the small and large intestines in the lower portion; the kidneys, one on each side in the back; and the urinary bladder in the pelvic region. There are also major blood vessels and other organs in the abdominal cavity.

EXCRETORY SYSTEMS

Several different systems serve to eliminate waste products that enter the body or are formed within it. The residue of food taken into the digestive system, mainly indigestible materials, together with secretions from various glands emptying into the intestines, is gathered in the lower portion of the large intestine and eliminated through the rectum as feces.

Surplus water, carrying dissolved salts that are excess in the system or form a waste product, is extracted by the kidneys, collected in the bladder, and expelled as urine.

Carbon dioxide and certain volatile products carried by the blood are exchanged in the lungs for oxygen and pass from the body in exhaled air.

The skin contains many small organs known as sweat glands. They range from 400 to 2,800 per square inch over different parts of the body. These glands are important in eliminating heat, excess fluid, and dissolved waste products from the body.

Life and health depend on the body giving off its waste products. interference with the normal functioning of any of the excretory systems results in illness and may even cause death.

RESPIRATORY SYSTEM

Oxygen enters the body through respiration, the breathing process. Oxygen is essential to human life; all living tissue depends on oxygen that is carried by the blood. Any interference with breathing causes oxygen depletion throughout the entire body. Knowledge of the respiratory system and the organs concerned with respiration will greatly aid in understanding artificial ventilation.

During respiration, when air is taken into the lungs, called inhalation, and forced out, called exhalation, the air passes through the nose, throat, and windpipe. The air is warmed and moistened in the nose. The moist hairs and mucous membrane of the nose filter out much of the dust and foreign matter in inhaled air.

The throat is a continuation of the nose and mouth. At its lower end are two openings, one in front of the other: the opening in front, the trachea or windpipe, leads to the lungs; the one behind, the esophagus or food pipe, leads to the stomach. At the top of the windpipe is a flap, the epiglottis, that closes over the windpipe during swallowing to keep food or liquid from entering.

As the windpipe extends into the chest cavity toward the lungs, it divides into the two bronchial tubes, one going to each lung. The lungs are two cone-shaped bodies that are soft, spongy, and elastic. Each lung is covered by a closed sac called the pleura. The inside of the lungs communicates freely with the outside air through the windpipe.

Within the lungs, the bronchial tubes branch out like limbs of a tree, until they become very small. The bronchial tubes end in a group of air cells (alveoli) resembling a very small bunch of grapes. Around each of the air cells is a fine network of small blood vessels or capillaries. Through the thin walls of the air cells, the blood in these capillaries exchanges carbon dioxide, other waste matter, and the by-products of tissue activity from all over the body for a supply of oxygen from the air breathed into the air cells. The discarded carbon dioxide and waste matter leave the air cells in exhaled air.

During breathing, the chest muscles and diaphragm expand the chest cavity, so that the air pressure within the chest cavity becomes less than that outside. Air rushes to balance the pressure filling the lungs.

Breathing consists of two separate acts: inhalation, enlarging the chest cavity so air is drawn into the lungs, and exhalation, decreasing the size of the chest cavity so air is forced out of the lungs.

During inhalation the ribs are raised and the arch of the diaphragm falls and flattens, increasing the capacity of the chest cavity, and causing air to enter. In exhalation, an act normally performed with slight muscular action, the ribs fall to their normal position, the arch of the diaphragm rises decreasing the capacity of the chest cavity, and air is forced out.

If any air gets through the chest wall or if the lung is punctured so that air from the outside can fill the chest cavity, the lungs will not fill. This is because the air pressure is equal outside and inside the chest cavity. Thus, no suction is created for inhaling.

Breathing is an act which usually is automatic and one over which a person exerts only a limited degree of control. The amount of air breathed and frequency of breathing vary according to whether the person is at rest or engaged in work or exercise. At rest, a healthy adult breathes about fifteen times a minute and takes in twenty-five to thirty cubic inches of air per breath. Each breath moves about one-half liter (500 cc, or one pint) of air. During strenuous work, the breathing rate and amount inhaled may increase several times.

CIRCULATORY SYSTEM

The circulatory system, that carries blood to and from all parts of the body, consists of the heart and blood vessels. Through the blood vessels, blood is circulated throughout the body under pressure supplied by the pumping action of the heart.

Blood

Blood is composed of serum or plasma, red cells, white cells, and platelets. Plasma is a fluid that carries the blood cells and transports nutrients to all tissues. It also transports waste products resulting from tissue activity to the organs for excretion. Red cells give color to the blood and carry oxygen. White cells aid in defending the body against infection. Platelets are essential to the formation of the blood clots necessary to stop bleeding.

One-fifteenth to one-twelfth of the body weight is blood. A person weighing one hundred fifty pounds will have approximately ten to twelve pints of blood. If the tissues do not receive blood, they will die from lack of oxygen. The loss of two pints of blood by an adult, or eight to ten percent of the total contained in the body, usually is serious. The loss of three pints over a short time, one to two hours, may be fatal. The loss of four pints or more will require blood transfusions to prevent death. At certain points in the body, fatal hemorrhages may occur in a very short time. The cutting of the two principal blood vessels in the neck, the principal blood vessels in the arms, or the principal blood vessels in the thighs may cause hemorrhage that will prove fatal in one to three minutes or even less. Rupture of the main trunk blood vessels of the chest and abdomen may prove fatal in less than thirty seconds.

The loss of blood causes a state of physical shock. This occurs because there is insufficient blood flowing through the tissues of the body to provide food and oxygen. All processes of the body are affected. When a person is in shock, vital body functions slow down. If the conditions causing shock are not reversed, death may occur.

Blood Vessels

Oxygenated blood is carried from the heart by a large artery called the aorta. Smaller arteries branch off from this large artery, and those arteries in turn branch off into still smaller arteries. These arteries divide and subdivide until they become very small, ending in threadlike vessels known as capillaries, which extend into all the organs and tissues.

After the blood has furnished the necessary nourishment and oxygen to the tissues and organs of the body, it takes on waste products, particularly carbon dioxide. The blood returns to the heart by a different system of blood vessels known as veins. The veins are connected with the arteries through the capillaries.

Very small veins join, forming larger veins, which in turn join until the very largest veins return the blood to the heart. Blood passing through the kidneys is cleared of nonvolatile waste products. When the blood from the body reaches the heart, carbon dioxide and other volatile waste products contained in the blood must be eliminated and the oxygen needed by the body is replaced. The heart pumps the blood delivered to it by the veins into the lungs, where it flows through another network of capillaries. There, the carbon dioxide and other volatile waste products are exchanged for oxygen through the delicate walls of air cells. The blood is thereby oxygenated and ready to return to the heart, which recirculates it throughout the body.

The time taken for the blood to make one complete circulation of the body through miles and miles of blood vessels is approximately seventy-five seconds in an adult at rest.

Heart

The heart is a hollow, muscular organ about the size of a fist, lying in the lower central region of the chest cavity. By the heart's pumping action, blood is under pressure and in constant circulation throughout the body. In a healthy adult at rest, the heart contracts between sixty and eighty times a minute; in a child, eighty to a one hundred times per minute. The effect of these contractions can be noted by the pulse, a spurt of blood through an artery. The pulse is most easily felt over the carotid artery on either side of the neck.

General Procedures

No two situations requiring first aid are the same; however, the following procedures are generally applicable:

- Take charge or follow instructions! If you are first at the scene, instruct someone to obtain medical help and others to assist as directed. If you arrive after someone else has taken charge, do as you are asked by the person in charge.
- Secure the scene. Ask someone to remove or mark any hazards.
- If several people have been injured, decide upon priorities in caring for each of the victims.
- Make a primary survey of the victim.
- Care for life-threatening conditions.
- Make a secondary survey of victim.
- Care for all injuries in order of need.
- Keep the injured person or persons lying down.
- Loosen restrictive clothing if necessary.
- Cover victim to keep warm and dry.
- Keep onlookers away from the victim.
- When necessary, improvise first aid materials using whatever is available.
- Cover all wounds completely.
- Prevent air from reaching burned surfaces as quickly as possible by using a suitable dressing.
- Remove small, loose foreign objects from a wound by brushing away from the wound with a piece of sterile gauze.
- **Do not** try to remove embedded objects.
- Place a bandage compress and a cover bandage over an open fracture without undue pressure before applying splints.
- Support and immobilize fractures and dislocations.
- Except for lower jaw dislocations, leave the reduction of fractures or dislocations to a doctor.
- Unless absolutely necessary, never move a victim until fractures have been immobilized.
- Test a stretcher before use, and carefully place an injured person on the stretcher.
- Carry the victim on a stretcher, without any unnecessary rough movements.

EVALUATING THE SITUATION

First aiders should take charge with full recognition of their own limitations and, while caring for life-threatening conditions, direct others briefly and clearly as to exactly what they should do and how to secure assistance. Information should be gathered to determine the extent of the injuries. This information can be obtained from:

- Friends, relatives or bystanders
- What you are able to observe at the scene
- The victim, if he or she is conscious
- What you observe about the victim

PATIENT ASSESSMENT

Primary Survey

Many conditions may be life-threatening, but three in particular require immediate action:
- Respiratory arrest
- Circulatory failure
- Severe bleeding

Respiratory arrest and/or circulatory failure can set off a chain of events that will lead to death. Severe and uncontrolled bleeding can lead to an irreversible state of shock in which death is inevitable. Death may occur in a very few minutes if an attempt is not made to help the victim in these situations. Before caring for lesser injuries, the first aider should follow the ABC method to check for life-threatening conditions:

A) Airways—Establish responsiveness, position the victim, and to ensure adequate breathing, an open airway must be established and maintained. If there are no signs of breathing, artificial ventilation must be given immediately.

B) Bleeding—Make a careful and thorough check for any bleeding. Control serious bleeding by using proper methods.

C) Circulation—If a victim experiences circulatory failure, a person *trained* in cardiopulmonary resuscitation (CPR) should check for a pulse, and if none is detected, start CPR at once.

In making the primary survey, **do not** move the victim any more than is necessary to support life. Rough handling or any unnecessary movement might cause additional pain and aggravate serious injuries that have not yet been detected.

Secondary Survey

When the life-threatening conditions have been controlled, the secondary survey should begin. The secondary survey is a head-to-toe examination to check **carefully** for any additional unseen injuries that can cause serious complications. This is conducted by examining for the following:

- Neck - Examine for neck injury—tenderness, deformity, medical identification necklace, etc. Spine fractures, especially in the neck area may accompany head injuries. Gently feel and look for any abnormalities. If a spinal injury is suspected, stop the secondary survey until the head can be stabilized. Follow these same precautions for any suspected spinal injury.
- Head - Without moving the head, check for blood in the hair, scalp lacerations, and contusions. Gently feel for possible bone fragments or depressions in the skull. Loss of fluid or bleeding from the ears and nose is an indication of possible skull fracture.
- Chest - Check the chest for cuts, impaled objects, fractures, and penetrating (sucking) wounds by observing chest movement. When the sides are not rising together or one side is not moving at all, there may be lung and rib damage.
- Abdomen - Gently feel the abdominal area for cuts, penetrations, and impaled objects, observing for spasms and tenderness.
- Lower back - Feel for deformity and tenderness.
- Pelvis - Check for grating, tenderness, bony protrusions, and depressions in the pelvic area.
- Genital region - Check for any obvious injury.
- Lower extremities - Check for discoloration, swelling, tenderness and deformities which are sometimes present with fractures and dislocations. Paralysis in the legs indicates a fractured back.
- Upper extremities - Check for discoloration, swelling, tenderness, and deformities which are sometimes present with fractures and dislocations. Paralysis in the arms and legs indicates a fractured neck. Check for a medical identification bracelet.
- Back surfaces - Injuries underneath the victim are often overlooked. Examine for bony protrusions, bleeding, and obvious injuries.

If the victim is conscious, explain that you are going to perform the head-to-toe survey and inform him or her what you are going to do. Be reassuring at all times.

Besides being trained in proper first aid methods, all first aiders should know what first aid equipment is available at home, at work, in the car, etc. The equipment should be checked periodically.

Artificial Ventilation

At the top of the windpipe is a flap, the epiglottis, which closes over the windpipe during swallowing to keep food or liquid from entering it. When a person is unconscious, the flap may fail to respond; therefore, no solids or liquids should be given by mouth, since they may enter the windpipe and lungs and cause suffocation or serious complications. If an unconscious person is lying on his or her back, the tongue is apt to fall against the back of the throat and interfere with air reaching the lungs. Sometimes it may block the throat entirely.

When a person is unconscious or breathing with difficulty, the head-tilt/chin-lift maneuver should be used to open the airway. **This procedure is not recommended for a victim with possible neck or spinal injuries.**

CAUSES OF RESPIRATORY ARREST

Breathing may stop as a result of a variety of serious accidents. The most common causes of respiratory arrest are overdoses of narcotics, electric shock, drowning, suffocation, poisonous gases, head injuries, and heart problems.

Electric Shock

The chance of accidental contact with electrical current is a common hazard in the home as the result of faulty wiring, etc. and in many industrial plants. Any electric current can be dangerous. Electricity can cause paralysis of the nerve centers that control breathing and stop or alter the regular beat of the heart.

The symptoms of electric shock are sudden loss of consciousness, impairment or absence of respiration or circulation, weak pulse, and sometimes burns. Breathing may be so weak and shallow that it cannot be detected.

If the victim is free from contact with the electric current, begin first aid at once. If the victim is still in contact with the current, rescue the victim at once, being careful not to come in contact with the current. Every second of delay in removing a person from contact with an electric current lessens the chance of resuscitation. In all cases, remove the current from the victim or the victim from the current promptly. Start artificial ventilation or CPR at once, if necessary.

Drowning

Remove a victim of drowning from the water as quickly as possible. Begin artificial ventilation immediately without taking the time to remove water which may be in the respiratory tract.

Drowning is a form of suffocation. The supply of air to the lungs has been cut off completely by water or spasm of the larynx. This cutoff does not create an immediate lack of oxygen in the body. There is a small reserve in the air cells of the lungs, in the blood and in some of the tissue that can sustain life for up to six minutes or longer at low temperatures. Because this reserve is exhausted relatively quickly, it is important to start artificial ventilation as soon as possible.

Suffocation

Always rescue a suffocation victim as quickly as possible. Symptoms of suffocation in an unconscious person are: the lips, fingernails, and ear lobes become blue or darker in color; the pulse becomes rapid and weak; breathing stops; and the pupils of the eyes become dilated. The cause may be a blocked windpipe preventing air from getting into the lungs. Artificial ventilation is of no value until blockage is removed.

Dangerous Gases

Several noxious or toxic gases encountered in everyday life can cause asphyxiation. These gases include carbon monoxide, sulfur dioxide, oxides of nitrogen, ammonia, hydrogen cyanide, and cyanogen compounds.

Persons should be aware of the early warning signs of exposure so gases may be detected before asphyxiation occurs. Headache, nausea, and tearing of the eyes are the three most common symptoms of the presence of dangerous gases. Rescuers should take care to protect themselves. Unless the surrounding air is good, take the victim to pure air immediately and begin artificial ventilation at once.

Nontoxic gases, such as carbon dioxide and methane, may also cause suffocation by displacing oxygen.

PRINCIPLES OF ARTIFICIAL VENTILATION

Artificial ventilation is the process for causing air flow in and out of the lungs when natural breathing has ceased or when it is very irregular or inadequate.

When breathing has ceased, the body's oxygen supply is cut off; brain cells start to die within four to six minutes. This can cause irreversible brain damage and if breathing is not restored, death will occur. In some cases the heart may continue to beat and circulate blood for a short period after a person stops breathing. If artificial ventilation is started within a short time after respiratory arrest, the victim has a good chance for survival.

Certain general principles must always be kept in mind when administering artificial ventilation by any method:

- ◆ Time is of prime importance; every second counts.
- ◆ **Do not** take time to move the victim unless the accident site is hazardous.
- ◆ **Do not** delay ventilation to loosen the victim's clothing or warm the victim. These are of secondary importance to getting air into the victim's lungs.
- ◆ Perform head-tilt/chin-lift method for opening airway, which will bring the tongue forward.
- ◆ Remove any visible foreign objects from the mouth.
- ◆ An assistant should loosen any tight fitting clothing in order to promote circulation and go or send for help.
- ◆ Use a blanket, clothing or other material to keep the victim warm and dry.
- ◆ Maintain a steady, constant rhythm while giving artificial ventilation. Be sure to look for rise and fall of the chest and look, listen, and feel for return air. If none, look for upper airway obstruction.
- ◆ Continue artificial ventilation until one of the following occurs:
  - ◆ Spontaneous breathing resumes
  - ◆ You are relieved by a qualified person
  - ◆ A doctor pronounces the victim dead
  - ◆ You are exhausted and physically unable to continue
- ◆ **Do not** fight the victim's attempts to breathe.
- ◆ Once the victim recovers, constantly monitor the victim's condition because breathing may stop again.
- ◆ Keep the victim lying down.
- ◆ Treat the victim for physical shock.

METHODS OF ARTIFICIAL VENTILATION

The first thing to do when finding an unconscious person is to establish unresponsiveness by tapping on the shoulder and asking "Are you OK?" Place the victim on his or her back. Open the airway by using the head-tilt/chin-lift method. Remove any visible foreign objects from the mouth. To assess the presence or absence of spontaneous breathing in a victim, the rescuer should place his or her ear near the victim's mouth and nose while maintaining the open airway position. Look toward the victim's body and while observing the victim's chest, the rescuer should:

- ◆ **LOOK** for the chest to rise and fall;
- ◆ **LISTEN** for air escaping during exhalation;
- ◆ **FEEL** for the flow of air.

If the chest does not rise and fall and no air is heard or felt, the victim is not breathing. This assessment should take only three to five seconds. If it is determined that the victim is not breathing, begin artificial ventilation.

Mouth-to-Mouth Ventilation

Mouth-to-mouth ventilation is by far the most effective means of artificial ventilation for use on a victim of respiratory arrest.

- ♦ Open the airway. The most common cause of airway obstruction in an unconscious victim is the tongue. The tongue is attached to the lower jaw; moving the jaw forward lifts the tongue away from the back of the throat and opens the airway.
  - ♦ Kneel at the victim's side with knee nearest the head opposite the victim's shoulders.
  - ♦ Use the **head-tilt/chin-lift maneuver** (if no spinal injury exists) to open airway. Place one of your hands on the forehead and apply gentle, firm, backward pressure using the palm of your hand. Place the fingertips of your other hand under the chin. The fingertips are used to bring the chin forward and to support the jaw.
- ♦ Pinch the nose closed. Inhale deeply and place your mouth over the victim's mouth (over mouth and nose with children) making sure of a tight seal. Give two full breaths into the air passage watching for the chest to rise after each breath.
- ♦ Keep the victim's head extended at all times.
- ♦ Remove your mouth between breaths and let the victim exhale.
- ♦ Feel and listen for the return flow of air, and look for fall of the victim's chest.

If neck injury is suspected, use modified jaw-thrust.
- ♦ Place victim on his or her back.
- ♦ Kneel at the top of victim's head, resting on your elbows.
- ♦ Reach forward and gently place one hand on each side of victim's chin, at the angles of the lower jaw.
- ♦ Push the victim's jaw forward, applying most of the pressure with your index fingers.
- ♦ **Do not** tilt or rotate the victim's head.

Repeat this procedure giving one breath twelve times per minute for an adult, fifteen times per minute for a small child. For an infant, give gentle puffs of air from the mouth twenty times per minute .

Mouth-to-Nose Ventilation

In certain cases, mouth-to-nose ventilation may be required. The mouth-to-nose technique is similar to mouth-to-mouth except that the lips are sealed by pushing the lower jaw against the upper jaw and air is forced into the victim by way of the nose.

Mouth-to-Stoma Ventilation

Persons who have undergone a laryngectomy (surgical removal of the larynx) have a permanent stoma (opening) that connects the trachea directly to the skin. The stoma is recognized as an opening at the front base of the neck. When such an individual requires rescue breathing, direct mouth-to-stoma ventilation is performed. The rescuer's mouth is sealed around the stoma, and air is blown into it until the chest rises. When the rescuer's mouth is removed from the stoma, permit the victim to exhale.

Other persons may have a temporary tracheostomy tube in the trachea. To ventilate these persons, seal the victim's mouth and nose by the rescuer's hand or by a tightly fitting face mask to prevent leakage of air when the rescuer blows into the tracheostomy tube.

GASTRIC DISTENTION

One problem that may occur during artificial ventilation is the accumulation of air in the victim's stomach. Air in the stomach can cause two problems:
- • Reduction in the volume of air that enters the lungs because the diaphragm is farther forward than normal
- • Vomiting

To reduce distention, proceed as follows:
- ◆ Reposition the victim's head to provide a better airway.
- ◆ Limit ventilation force and volume.
- ◆ If vomiting occurs, turn the victim on his or her side if no spinal injury is present.
- ◆ **Do not** press on the stomach unless suction equipment is available and you have been trained to use it, otherwise material from the stomach may become lodged in the lungs.

OBSTRUCTED AIRWAY

An obstruction in the airway can cause unconsciousness and respiratory arrest. There are many factors that can partially or fully obstruct the airway, such as gum, tobacco, or loose dentures. Foreign body obstruction sometimes occurs during eating. A variety of foods can cause choking, but meat is the most common.

When the airway is completely obstructed, the victim is unable to speak, breath, or cough and will clutch the neck. Some people will use the universal distress signal for choking—a hand raised to the neck with fingers extended around the neck in one direction, the thumb in the other direction as though attempting to choke oneself. If the person is choking, movement of air will be absent. Unconsciousness will result due to lack of oxygen and death will follow quickly if prompt action is not taken.

Conscious Victim, Sitting or Standing

- ◆ Determine if obstruction of airway is partial or complete.
- ◆ If partial obstruction, that is, there is some exchange of air, encourage victim to cough.
- ◆ If there is no air exchange, stand behind the victim and place your arms around the victim's waist.
- ◆ Grasp one fist in your other hand and position the thumb side of your fist against the middle of the victim's abdomen just above the navel and well below the rib cage.
- ◆ **Do not** squeeze victim.
- ◆ Press your fist into the victim's abdominal area with a quick upward thrust.
- ◆ Repeat the procedure if necessary.

Chest Thrust, Conscious Victim

The chest thrust is another method of applying the manual thrust when removing an obstruction from the airway. Use this method on a pregnant victim or when the rescuer is unable to wrap his or her arms around the victim's waist, as in gross obesity.

- ◆ When the conscious victim is standing or sitting, position yourself behind him or her and slide your arms under the armpits, so that you encircle the chest.
- ◆ Make a fist with one hand and place the thumb side of this fist on the victim's sternum.
- ◆ Make contact with the midline of the sternum about two to three finger-widths above the lower tip of the sternum.
- ◆ Grasp the fist with your other hand and press with a quick backward thrust.
- ◆ Repeat thrusts until the obstruction is expelled or the victim becomes conscious.

Victim Alone

The victim of an obstructed airway who is alone may use his or her own fist as described previously, or bend over the back of a chair and exert downward pressure.

Unconscious Victim

When you attempt to give artificial ventilation and you feel resistance, that is, the air is not getting in, the victim's airway is probably obstructed. The most common cause of airway obstruction in an unconscious person is the tongue falling back into the airway, which can be corrected by using the head-tilt/chin-lift maneuver. When the airway is obstructed by a foreign body, the obstruction must be cleared or ventilation will be ineffective.

Abdominal Thrust, Victim Lying Down

♦ Position victim on his or her back, face up.
♦ Straddle victim's hips, if possible.
♦ Place the heel of one hand against the middle of the victim's abdomen between the rib cage and the navel with fingers pointing toward the victim's chest.
♦ Place your other hand on top of the first.
♦ Move your shoulders directly over the victim's abdomen.
♦ Press into the victim's abdominal area with a quick upward thrust.
♦ Do six to ten thrusts.
♦ Follow with opening mouth and finger sweep.
♦ Attempt artificial ventilation.
♦ Repeat the procedures until obstruction is cleared.

Chest Thrust, Victim Lying Down

Apply the chest thrust method to remove an obstruction from a pregnant or obese victim.

♦ Position the victim on his or her back.
♦ Open the airway.
♦ Kneel close to the victim.
♦ Place the heel of one hand on the lower half of the breast bone about one to one and one-half inches above the tip (xiphoid process) with fingers elevated. The heel of the hand must be parallel to the breast bone.
♦ Place the other hand on top of and parallel to the first hand.
♦ With your shoulders directly over your hands, exert a downward thrust. Keep elbows straight by locking them.
♦ Do six to ten thrusts.
♦ Follow with opening mouth and finger sweep.
♦ Attempt artificial ventilation.
♦ Repeat the procedure until obstruction is cleared.

Manual Removal

Whenever a foreign object is in the victim's mouth, the rescuer should remove it with the fingers. Manual thrusts may dislodge the obstruction, but not expel it. The rescuer should turn the victim face up, open the victim's mouth with the cross-finger technique or tongue-jaw lift if necessary, and clear the obstruction with a finger sweep.

Tongue-Jaw Lift

Open victim's mouth by grasping both the tongue and lower jaw and lifting.

Cross-Finger Technique

♦ Cross your thumb under your index finger.
♦ Brace your thumb and finger against the victim's upper and lower teeth.
♦ Push your fingers apart to separate the jaws.

Finger Sweep

♦ Open the victim's jaws with one hand.
♦ Insert the index finger of your other hand down the inside of the cheek and into the throat to the base of the tongue.
♦ The index finger is then swept across the back of the throat in a hooking action to dislodge the obstruction.
♦ Grasp and remove the foreign object when it comes within reach.

Cardiopulmonary Resuscitation (CPR)

Cardiopulmonary resuscitation (CPR) involves the use of artificial ventilation (mouth-to-mouth breathing) and external heart compression (rhythmic pressure on the breastbone). **These techniques must be learned through training and supervised practice. Courses are available through the American Heart Association and American Red Cross.** Incorrect application of external heart compressions may result in complications such as damage to internal organs, fracture of ribs or sternum, or separation of cartilage from ribs. (Rib fractures may occur when compressions are being correctly performed but this is not an indication to stop compression.) **Application of cardiopulmonary resuscitation when not required could result in cardiac arrest, so never practice these skills on another person.** When CPR is properly applied, the likelihood of complications is minimal and acceptable in comparison with the alternative—death.

SUDDEN DEATH

Sudden death is the immediate and unexpected cessation of respiration and functional circulation. The term *sudden death* is synonymous with cardiopulmonary arrest or heart-lung arrest. In the definition, the terms *sudden and unexpected* are extremely important. The death of a person with an organic disease such as cancer, or who is under treatment for a chronic heart condition and has gradual but progressive loss of heart function, cannot be correctly classified as *sudden death*. Cardiac arrest, when the heart stops pumping blood, may occur suddenly and unexpectedly for any number of reasons:

- Heart attack
- Electric shock
- Asphyxiation
- Suffocation
- Drowning
- Allergic reaction
- Choking
- Severe injury

A person is considered clinically dead the moment the heart stops beating and breathing ceases. However, the vital centers of the central nervous system within the brain may remain viable for four to six minutes more. Irreversible brain damage begins to occur to human brain cells somewhere between four and six minutes after oxygen has been excluded. This condition is referred to as biological death. Resuscitation in the treatment of sudden death depends upon this grace period of four to six minutes. After that period, even though the heart might yet be restarted, the chance of return to a normal functional existence is lessened. In sudden death, start CPR even if the four-to-six minute mark has been passed. However, the urgency of reestablishing the oxygenation system of the body, that is, ventilation and circulation, within the four-to-six minute grace period cannot be overemphasized.

HEART ATTACK

Diseases of the heart and blood vessels are the leading cause of death in the United States. Over 540,000 people die annually from heart attacks. Of these, approximately 350,000 die outside the hospital within the first two hours of the arrest.

Recognition of the early warning signs is extremely important. The following are the early warning signs of an impending heart attack:

- Uncomfortable pressure, squeezing, fullness, or dull pain in the center of the chest lasting for more than minutes
- Pain may radiate into the shoulders, arm, neck or jaw.,

- Sweating
- Nausea
- Shortness of breath
- Feeling of weakness
- Pale and sick looking

A person need not exhibit all these symptoms to have a heart attack. The symptoms of heart attack may come and go, often leading the victim to attribute these symptoms to another cause such as indigestion.

RISK FACTORS

Certain factors have been identified as increasing an individual's risk of some form of cardiovascular disease. Some factors a person has no control over, such as sex, race, age and heredity. However, people can do a tremendous amount to improve their physical condition and reduce the chance of cardiovascular disease.

RECOGNIZING THE PROBLEM

The person who initiates emergency heart-lung resuscitation has two responsibilities:
- To apply emergency measures to keep the clinically dead victim biologically alive
- To be sure the victim receives proper medical care

When sudden death occurs, the rescuer must act immediately upon recognition of heart failure. In order to prevent biological death, the rescuer must be able to do the following:
- Recognize rapidly the apparent stoppage of heart action and respiration.
- Provide artificial ventilation to the lungs.
- Provide artificial circulation of the blood.

In addition to performing CPR, the rescuer must summon help in order that an ambulance and/or a physician may be called to the scene.

CPR PROCEDURE FOR SINGLE RESCUER

The CPR procedures should be learned and practiced on a training mannequin under the guidance of a qualified instructor. The step by step procedure for cardiopulmonary resuscitation is as follows:
- **Establish unresponsiveness.** Gently shake the victim's shoulder and shout, "Are you OK?" The individual's response or lack of response will indicate to the rescuer if the victim is just sleeping or unconscious.
- **Call for help.** Help will be needed to assist in performing CPR or to call for medical help.
- **Position the victim.** If the victim is found in a crumpled up position and/or face down, the rescuer must roll the victim over; this is done while calling for help.
    - When rolling the victim over, take care that broken bones are not further complicated by improper handling. Roll the victim as a unit so that the head, shoulders, and torso move simultaneously with no twisting.
    - Kneel beside the victim, a few inches to the side.
    - The arm nearest the rescuer should be raised above the victim's head.
    - The rescuer's hand closest to the victim's head should be placed on the victim's head and neck to prevent them from twisting.
    - The rescuer should use the other hand to grasp under the victim's arm furthest from rescuer. This will be the point at which the rescuer exerts the pull in rolling the body over.
    - Pull carefully under the arm, and the hips and torso will follow the shoulders with minimal twisting.
    - Be sure to watch the neck and keep it in line with the rest of the body.
    - The victim should now be flat on his or her back.

- **A-Airway. Open the airway.** The most common cause of airway obstruction in an unconscious victim is the tongue.
  - Use the head-tilt/chin-lift maneuver to open airway. (This maneuver is not recommended for a victim with possible neck or spinal injuries.)
- **B-Breathing. Establish breathlessness.** After opening the airway establish breathlessness.
  - Turn your head toward the victim's feet with your cheek close over the victim's mouth (3 to 5 seconds).
  - **Look** for a rise and fall in the victim's chest.
  - **Listen** for air exchange at the mouth and nose.
  - **Feel** for the flow of air.

Sometimes opening and maintaining an open airway is all that is necessary to restore breathing.

- **Provide artificial ventilation.**
  - If the victim is not breathing give two full breaths by mouth-to-mouth, mouth-to-nose, or mouth-to-stoma ventilation.
  - Allow for lung deflation between each of the two ventilations.
- **C-Circulation. Check for pulse.** Check the victim's pulse to determine whether external cardiac compressions are necessary.
  - Maintain an open airway position by holding the forehead of the victim.
  - Place your fingertips on the victim's windpipe and then slide them towards you until you reach the groove of the neck. Press gently on this area (carotid artery).
  - Check the victim's carotid pulse for at least five seconds but no more than ten seconds.
  - If a pulse is present, continue administering artificial ventilation once every five seconds or twelve times a minute. If not, make arrangements to send for trained medical assistance and begin CPR.
- **Perform cardiac compressions.**
  - Place the victim in a horizontal position on a hard, flat surface.
  - Locate the bottom of the rib cage with the index and middle fingers of your hand closest to patient's feet.
  - Run your index finger up to or in the notch where the ribs meet the sternum (breastbone).
  - Place your middle finger in notch and index finger on sternum.
  - Place the heel of the other hand on the sternum next to the index finger in the notch in the rib cage.
  - Place the hand used to locate the notch at the rib cage on top and parallel to the hand which is on the sternum.
  - Keep the fingers off the chest, by either extending or interlocking them.
  - Keep the elbows in a straight and locked position.
  - Position your shoulders directly over the hands so that pressure is exerted straight downward.
  - Exert enough downward pressure to depress the sternum of an adult one and one-half to two inches.
  - Each compression should squeeze the heart between the sternum and spine to pump blood through the body.
  - Totally release pressure in order to allow the heart to refill completely with blood.
  - Keep the heel of your hand in contact with the victim's chest at all times.
  - Make compressions down and up in a smooth manner.
- Perform fifteen cardiac compressions at a rate of eighty to one hundred per minute, counting "one and, two and, three and," .... to fifteen.
- Use the head-tilt/chin-lift maneuver and give two full breaths (artificial ventilation).
- Repeat cycle four times (fifteen compressions and two ventilations).

♦ After the fourth cycle, recheck the carotid pulse in the neck for a heartbeat (five to ten seconds).
♦ If breathing and heartbeat are absent, resume CPR (fifteen compressions and two ventilations).
♦ Stop and check for heartbeat every few minutes thereafter.
♦ Never interrupt CPR for more than five seconds except to check the carotid pulse or to move the victim.

CHILD RESUSCITATION

Some procedures and rates differ when the victim is a child. Between one and eight years of age, the victim is considered a child. The size of the victim can also be an important factor. A very small nine-year-old victim may have to be treated as a child. Use the following procedures when giving CPR to a child:

♦ Establish unresponsiveness by the shake and shout method.
♦ Open the airway using the head-tilt/chin-lift method.
♦ Establish breathlessness (three to five seconds).
♦ If the victim is not breathing, give two breaths.
♦ Check the carotid pulse for at least five seconds.
♦ Perform cardiac compressions.
    ♦ Place the victim in a horizontal position on a hard, flat surface.
    ♦ Use the index and middle fingers of your hand closest to the patient's feet to locate the bottom of the rib cage.
    ♦ Place your middle finger in notch and index finger on sternum.
    ♦ The heel of the other hand is placed on the sternum next to the index finger in the notch in the rib cage.
    ♦ The fingers must be kept off the chest by extending them.
    ♦ Elbow is kept straight by locking it.
    ♦ The shoulders of the rescuer are brought directly over the hand so that pressure is exerted straight downward.
    ♦ Exert enough pressure downward with one hand to depress the sternum of the child one to one and one-half inches.
    ♦ Compress at a rate of eighty to one hundred times per minute. Ventilate after every five compressions.

INFANT RESUSCITATION

If the victim is younger than one year, it is considered an infant and the following procedures apply:

♦ Establish unresponsiveness by the shake and shout method.
♦ Open the airway; take care not to overextend the neck.
♦ Establish breathlessness (three to five seconds).
♦ Cover the infant's mouth and nose to get an airtight seal.
♦ Puff cheeks, using the air in the mouth to give two quick ventilations.
♦ Check the brachial pulse for five seconds.
♦ To locate the brachial pulse:
    ♦ Place the tips of your index and middle fingers on the inner side of the upper arm.
    ♦ Press slightly on the arm at the groove in the muscle.
♦ If heartbeat is absent, begin CPR at once:
    ♦ Place the index finger just under an imaginary line between the nipples on the infant's chest. Using the middle and ring fingers, compress chest one-half to one inch.
    ♦ Compress at the rate of at least one hundred times per minute.
    ♦ Ventilate after every five compressions.

TRANSPORTING THE VICTIM

Do not interrupt CPR for more than five seconds unless absolutely necessary. However, when CPR is being performed and the victim must be moved for safety or transportation reasons, **do not** interrupt CPR for more than thirty seconds.

When moving a victim up or down a stairway, provide victim with effective CPR before interruption. Move the victim as quickly as possible and resume CPR at next level.

TERMINATION OF CPR

Under normal circumstances CPR may be terminated under one of four conditions:
- The victim is revived
- Another person trained in CPR relieves you
- The person performing CPR becomes exhausted and cannot continue
- A doctor pronounces the victim dead

Controlling Bleeding

Hemorrhaging or Bleeding

Hemorrhaging or bleeding is the escape of blood from an artery, vein, or capillary.

Bleeding from an Artery

Arterial bleeding is characterized by bright red blood that spurts from a wound. The blood in the arteries is pumped directly from the heart, and spurts at each contraction. Having received a fresh supply of oxygen, the blood is bright red.

Bleeding from a Vein

When dark red blood flows from a wound in a steady stream, a vein has been cut. The blood, having given up its oxygen and received carbon dioxide and waste products in return is dark red.

Bleeding from Capillaries

Blood from cut capillaries oozes. There is usually no cause for alarm as relatively little blood is lost. Usually direct pressure with a compress applied over the wound will cause the formation of a clot. When large skin surface is involved, the threat of infection may be more serious than the loss of blood.

"BLEEDERS"

There are some conditions, such as hemophilia, or those caused by a side affect of medication, etc. that do not allow normal clotting to occur. Some persons may be in danger of bleeding to death even from the slightest wounds. This free bleeding may be internal as well as external, a condition that warrants close observation for shock. In addition to applying compress bandages or gauze, rush the person to the nearest hospital where medical treatment can be quickly administered.

METHODS OF CONTROLLING BLEEDING

Most bleeding can be easily controlled. External bleeding can usually be suppressed by applying direct pressure to the open wound. Direct pressure permits normal blood clotting to occur.

In cases of severe bleeding, the first aider may be upset by the appearance of the wound and the emotional state of the victim. Remember that a small amount of blood emerging from a wound spreads and appears as a lot of blood. It is important for the first aider to keep calm, keep the victim calm and do what is necessary to relieve the situation.

When it is necessary to control bleeding, use the following methods:
- Direct pressure with sterile bandage, if available
- Elevation
- Pressure points
- Direct Pressure
- Tourniquet, if necessary (**as a last resort only**)

Direct Pressure

The best all around method of controlling bleeding is to apply pressure directly to the wound. This is best done by placing gauze or the cleanest material available against the bleeding point and applying firm pressure with the hand until a cover bandage can be applied. The cover bandage knot should be tied over the wound unless otherwise indicated. The bandage supplies direct pressure and should not be removed until the victim is examined by a physician. When air splints or pressure bandages are available, they may be used over the heavy layer of gauze to supply direct pressure.

Bleeding that continues after the bandage is in place indicates that not enough pressure has been applied. In such cases, **do not remove the original dressing.** Use the hand to put more pressure on the wound over the bandage, or apply a second bandage. Either method should control the bleeding.

In severe bleeding, if gauze or other suitable material is not available, the bare hand should be used to apply direct pressure immediately. This will control most bleeding.

Elevation

Elevating the bleeding part of the body above the level of the heart will slow the flow of blood and speed clotting. For example, bleeding from a cut on the hand or arm will be slowed by raising the arm over the head. In the case of a foot wound, the victim should lie down with the leg propped up.

Use elevation with direct pressure when there are no fractures or fractures have been splinted and it will cause no pain or aggravation to the injury.

Pressure Points

Arterial bleeding can be controlled by applying pressure with the finger at *pressure points*. Pressure points are places over a bone where arteries are close to the skin. Pressing the artery against the underlying bone can control the flow of blood to the injury. There are twenty-six pressure points on the body, thirteen on each side, situated along main arteries.

In cases of severe bleeding where direct pressure is not adequate to control the bleeding, digital pressure must be used. **Use pressure points with caution,** as indirect pressure may cause damage to the limb as a result of an inadequate flow of blood. When the use of indirect pressure at a pressure point is necessary, **do not** substitute indirect pressure for direct pressure on the wound; use both direct and indirect pressure. Hold the pressure point only as long as necessary to stop the bleeding. Indirect pressure should be reapplied if bleeding recurs.

The *temporal pressure point*, located slightly above and to the side of the eye, is used to control arterial bleeding from a scalp or head wound. It is important that this point be used for brief periods only; as it can cut off blood to the brain and cause damage if held over thirty seconds.

The *facial pressure point* will help slow the flow of blood from a cut on the face. It should be used only for a minute or two. The pressure point is located in the "notch" along the lower edge of the bony structure of the jaw.

When there is bleeding from the neck, locate the trachea at the midline of the neck. Slide your fingers toward the site of the bleeding in the neck and feel for the pulsations of the carotid artery. Place your fingers over the artery, with your thumb behind the patient's neck. Apply pressure by squeezing your fingers toward your thumb. This action will compress the carotid artery against the trachea.

There are few occasions for using the *carotid pressure point*. **Do NOT use this method unless it is a part of your training.** If profuse bleeding from the neck is not controlled by direct pressure, you may have to use this technique. **NEVER apply pressure to both sides of the neck at the same time.** Take great care not to apply heavy pressure to the trachea. Stay alert because the patient may become faint or unconscious. Assume that the cervical spine has been injured and take all necessary steps to avoid excessive movement of the patient's head, neck, and back while you control profuse bleeding. **CAUTION: Maintain pressure for only a few seconds without releasing, since you are shutting off a large supply of oxygenated blood to the brain.**

The *subclavian pressure point* is located deep behind the collar bone in the "sink" of the shoulder. To reach it, you must push your thumb through the thick layer of muscle at the top of the shoulder and press the artery against the collar bone. It should be used only in extreme cases, such as amputation of the arm.

For wounds just above the elbow, the *axillary pressure point* is effective. Here, the artery just under the upper arm is pressed against the bone from underneath.

One of the most effective and most used pressure points for cuts on the lower arm is the *brachial point* at the elbow. Locate this pressure point in a groove on the inside of the arm and the elbow. To apply pressure, grasp the middle of the victim's arm with the thumb on the outside of the arm and the fingers on the inside. Press the fingers toward the thumb. Use the flat inside surface of the fingers, not the fingertips. This inward pressure closes the artery by pressing it against the arm bone.

The *radial pressure point* is located on the forearm close to the wrist on the thumb side of the hand and the *ulnar pressure point* is located on the little finger side of the wrist. The radial pressure point may be used for controlling bleeding at the wrist. Both pressure points must be used at the same time to control bleeding of the hand.

The *femoral artery* is often used to control severe bleeding from a wound on the lower extremity and the amputation of the leg. The pressure point is located on the front, center part of the crease in the groin area. This is where the artery crosses the pelvic basin on the way into the lower extremity. To apply pressure, position the victim flat on his or her back, if possible. Place the heel of one hand directly on the pressure point and apply the small amount of pressure needed to close the artery. If bleeding is not controlled, it may be necessary to press directly over the artery with the flat surface of the fingertips and apply additional pressure on the fingertips with the heel of the other hand.

The *popliteal pressure point* at the back of the knee is the most effective point for controlling bleeding from a wound on the leg. The artery passes close to the surface of the skin, over the large bones in the knee joint.

The *dorsalis pedis pressure point* controls the bleeding in the lower foot and toes. It is found on the top of the foot.

Tourniquet

A tourniquet is a device used to control severe bleeding. It is used as an absolute last resort after all other methods have failed. First aiders should thoroughly understand the dangers and limitations of its use.

A tourniquet should normally be used only for life-threatening hemorrhage that cannot be controlled by other means. A tourniquet may be dangerous. Improper use of a tourniquet by inexperienced, untrained persons may cause tissue injury or even death. Use a tourniquet when there is a loss of a limb or to completely shut off the entire blood supply to a limb. The pressure device itself often cuts into or injures the skin and underlying tissue. it is only required when large arteries are severed, in cases of partial or complete severance of a limb, and when bleeding is uncontrollable.

The standard tourniquet usually is a piece of web belting about thirty-six inches long, with a buckle or small device to hold it tightly in place when applied. A tourniquet can be improvised from a strap, belt, suspender, handkerchief, towel, necktie, cloth, or other suitable material. An improvised tourniquet should be at least two inches wide to distribute pressure over tissues. **NEVER use wire, cord, or anything that will cut into the flesh.** A cravat bandage may be used as a tourniquet.

The procedure for application of a tourniquet is as follows:

- While the proper pressure point is being held to temporarily control the bleeding, place the tourniquet between the heart and wound, with sufficient uninjured flesh between the wound and tourniquet.
- In using an improvised tourniquet, wrap the material tightly around the limb twice and tie in a half knot on the upper surface of the limb.
- Place a short stick or similar sturdy object at the half knot and tie a full knot.
- Twist the stick to tighten the tourniquet **only until the bleeding stops.**
- Secure the stick in place with the base ends of the tourniquet, another strip of cloth or suitable material.

Precautions:

- **Do not shield a tourniquet from view.**
- **Make a written note of the tourniquet's location and the time it was applied and attach the note to the victim's clothing. Alternatively, make a "T" on the victim's forehead.**

- Get the victim to a medical facility as soon as possible.
- Once the tourniquet is tightened, it should not be loosened except by or on the advice of a doctor. The loosening of a tourniquet may dislodge clots and result in sufficient loss of blood to cause severe shock and death.

INTERNAL BLEEDING

Internal bleeding in the chest or abdominal cavities usually results from a hard blow or certain fractures. Internal bleeding is usually not visible, but it can be very serious, even fatal. internal bleeding may be determined by any or all of the following signs and symptoms:

- Pain, tenderness, swelling, or discoloration where injury is suspected
- Abdominal rigidity or muscle spasms
- Bleeding from mouth, rectum, or other natural body openings
- Showing symptoms of shock:
  - Dizziness, without other symptoms - dizziness when going from lying to standing may be the only early sign of internal bleeding
  - Cold and clammy skin
  - Eyes dull, vision clouded, and pupils enlarged Weak and rapid pulse
  - Nausea and vomiting
  - Shallow and rapid breathing
  - Thirst
  - Weak and helpless feeling

Emergency care for internal bleeding requires securing and maintaining an open airway, and treating for shock. **Never give the victim anything by mouth.**

Transport anyone suspected of having any internal bleeding to professional medical help as quickly and safely as possible. Keep an injured person on his or her side when blood or vomit is coming from the mouth. Place the victim with chest injuries on the injured side if no spinal injuries are suspected. Transport the victim gently.

NOSEBLEEDS

Nosebleeds are more often annoying than life threatening. They are more common during cold weather, when heated air dries out the nasal passages.

First aid for nosebleeds is simple:

- Keep the victim quietly seated, leaning forward if possible.
- Gently pinch the nostrils closed.
- Apply cold compresses to the victim's nose and face.
- If the person is conscious, it may be helpful to apply pressure beneath the nostril above the lip.
- Instruct victim not to blow his or her nose for several hours after bleeding has stopped or clots could be dislodged and start the bleeding again.

Nosebleeds that cannot be controlled through these measures may signal a more severe condition, such as high blood pressure. The victim should see a physician. Anyone who suffers a nosebleed after an injury should be examined for possible facial fractures.

If a fractured skull is suspected as the cause of a nosebleed, **do not** attempt to stop the bleeding. To do so might increase the pressure on the brain. Treat the victim for a fractured skull.

Shock

Medically, *shock* is the term used to describe the effects of inadequate circulation of the blood throughout the body. Shock may result from a variety of causes and can cause irreversible harm to the victim.

NERVOUS SYSTEM

The nervous system plays an important role in shock. The various parts of the body and the organs controlling the body functions are coordinated by the nervous system. This system consists of two separate systems by function: the voluntary and the involuntary.

The main parts of the nervous system consist of the brain and spinal cord. The brain is a collection of nerve centers. Leaving the brain, the nerves go into the spinal cord and pass down through the opening in the center of the backbone or spinal column and branch off to all parts and organs of the body.

There are mainly two types of nerves entering and leaving the spinal cord: sensory nerves that convey sensations such as heat, cold, pain, and touch from different parts of the body to the brain; and motor nerves that convey impulses from the brain to the muscles causing movement.

The involuntary system is a series of nerve centers in the chest and abdominal cavity along the spinal column. Each of these nerve centers is connected with the spine and the brain and controls vital organs and vital functions. This system is not under control of the will; through it involuntary muscles are stimulated to function without regard to our state of consciousness.

The cardiovascular system is the system that circulates blood to all cells. Food and oxygen are transported to each part of the body and waste products are removed through this system.

The cardiovascular system is made up of tubes called vessels, liquid contents called blood, and the pump which is the heart. These vessels are able to dilate and constrict. The size of the vessels is changed by signals transmitted through nerve pathways from the nervous system to the muscles in the blood vessel walls.

When the body is in its normal state there is enough blood to fill the system completely— approximately ten to twelve pints (for a person weighing 150 pounds). The pumping action of the heart supplies all parts of the body with blood.

Shock is the failure of this system to provide enough circulation of blood to every part of the body.

The collapse of the cardiovascular system may be caused by any of three conditions:

1. Blood is lost.
2. Vessels dilate and there is insufficient blood to fill them.
3. The heart fails to act properly as a pump and circulate the blood.

No matter what the reason for the collapse, the results are the same: an insufficient blood flow to provide adequate nourishment and oxygen to all parts of the body. The body process may slow down, reducing circulation and, without nourishment, organs begin to die, especially the brain.

CAUSES OF SHOCK

The state of shock may develop rapidly or it may be delayed until hours after the event that triggers it. Shock occurs to some degree after every injury. It may be so slight as not to be noticed; or so serious that it results in death in cases where the injuries received ordinarily would not prove fatal.

Some of the major causes of shock are as follows:

- Severe or extensive injuries
- Severe pain
- Loss of blood
- Severe burns
- Electrical shock
- Certain illnesses
- Allergic reactions
- Poisoning inhaled, ingested, or injected
- Exposure to extremes of heat and cold
- Emotional stress
- Substance abuse

The signs and symptoms of shock are both physical and emotional. Shock may be determined by any or all of the following conditions:

- Dazed look
- Paleness in light skinned individuals and ashen or grayish color in dark skinned individuals

- Nausea and vomiting
- Thirst
- Weak, rapid pulse
- Cold, clammy skin
- Shallow, irregular, labored breathing
- Pupils dilated
- Eyes dull and lackluster
- Cyanosis, or a bluish tinge to the skin, in the late stages of shock

Some of the reactions known to take place within the body in cases of shock bear directly on the symptoms presented. The most important reaction that occurs in shock is a decided drop in normal blood flow, believed to be caused by the involuntary nervous system losing control over certain small blood vessels in the abdominal cavity. This is one of the reasons the victim is nauseous.

As a large amount of blood fills the dilated vessels within the body, decreased circulation near the surface causes the skin to become pale, cold, and clammy. Other areas suffer as a result of the drop in circulation; the eyes are dull and lackluster and pupils may be dilated.

In the body's effort to fill the dilated blood vessels, less blood returns to the heart for recirculation. To overcome the decreased volume and still send blood to all parts of the body, the heart pumps faster but pumps a much lower quantity of blood per beat. Therefore, the pulse is rapid and weak.

The brain suffers from this decreased blood supply and does not function normally; the victim's powers of reasoning, thinking, and expression are dulled. The victim may exhibit the following:

- Weak and helpless feeling
- Anxiety
- Disorientation or confusion
- Unconsciousness, in the late stages of shock

FIRST AID TREATMENT FOR SHOCK

While life threatening, shock is a serious condition which is reversible if recognized quickly and treated effectively. Always maintain an open airway and ensure adequate breathing; control any bleeding.

First aid for the victim of physical shock is as follows:

- Keep the victim lying down, if possible. Make sure that the head is at least level with the body. Elevate the lower extremities if the injury will not be aggravated and there are no abdominal or head injuries. It may be necessary to raise the head and shoulders if a person is suffering from a head injury, sunstroke, heart attack, stroke, or shortness of breath due to a chest or throat injury. However, it should be noted that if an accident was severe enough to roduce a head injury there may also be spinal damage. If in doubt, keep the victim flat.
- Provide the victim with plenty of fresh air.
- Loosen any tight clothing (neck, chest, and waist) in order to make breathing and circulation easier.
- Handle the victim as gently as possible and minimize movement.
- Keep the victim warm and dry by wrapping in blankets, clothing or other available material. These coverings should be placed under as well as over the victim to reduce the loss of body heat. Keep the victim warm enough to be comfortable. The objective is to maintain as near normal body temperature as possible—not to add heat.
- Do not give the victim anything by mouth.
- The victim's emotional well-being is just as important as his or her physical well-being. Keep calm and reassure the victim. Never talk to the victim about his or her injuries. Keep onlookers away from the victim as their conversation regarding the victim's injuries may be upsetting.

ANAPHYLACTIC SHOCK

Various technical terms describe different types of shock. At least one of these, anaphylactic shock, is given special emphasis because it is a life-threatening emergency which requires rapid treatment.

Anaphylactic shock is a sensitivity reaction. It occurs when a person contacts something to which he or she is extremely allergic. People who are subject to anaphylactic shock should carry emergency medical identification at all times.

A person can contact substances that can cause anaphylactic shock by eating fish or shellfish, berries, or oral drugs such as penicillin. Insect stings (yellow jackets, wasps, hornets, etc.) or injected drugs can cause a violent reaction, as well as inhaled substances such as dust or pollen.

Sensitivity reactions can occur within a few seconds after contact with the substance. Death can result within minutes of contact; therefore, it is important that the first aider recognize the signs and symptoms of anaphylactic shock:

- Itching or burning skin
- Hives covering a large area
- Swelling of the tongue and face
- Severe difficulty in breathing
- Tightening or pain in the chest
- Weak pulse
- Dizziness
- Convulsion
- Coma

Anaphylactic shock is an emergency that requires medication to counteract the allergic reaction. If the victim carries any medication to counteract the allergy, help the victim take the medicine.

Arrange for transportation to a medical facility as quickly as possible because anaphylactic shock can be fatal in less than fifteen minutes. Notify the hospital as to what caused the reaction, if known. Maintain an open airway. If necessary, provide artificial ventilation and CPR and treat for physical shock.

FAINTING

Fainting is a temporary loss of consciousness due to an inadequate supply of oxygen to the brain and is a mild form of shock. Fainting may be caused by the sight of blood, exhaustion, weakness, heat, or strong emotions such as fright, joy, etc. Some people faint more easily than others.

The signs and symptoms of fainting may be any or all of the following:

- The victim may feel weak and dizzy, and may see spots.
- The face becomes pale and the lips blue in both light and dark skinned people.
- The forehead is covered with cold perspiration.
- The pulse is rapid and weak.
- The breathing is shallow.

The first aid for fainting is as follows:

- If the person feels faint, the initial response might be sitting with the head between the knees.
- Have the victim lie down with the head lower than the feet.
- If the victim is unconscious for any length of time, something may be seriously wrong. Arrange for transportation to a medical facility.
- Treat the victim for physical shock.
- Maintain an open airway.
- **Do not** give stimulants.

TreatingWounds

OPEN WOUNDS

An *open wound* refers to any break in the skin. When the skin is unbroken, it affords protection from most bacteria or germs; however, germs may enter through even a small break in the skin, and an infection may develop. Any open wound should receive prompt medical attention. If germs have been carried into an open wound by the object causing the break in the skin, the flow of blood will sometimes wash out the germs; but, as will be explained later, some types of wounds do not bleed freely.

Breaks in the skin range from pin punctures or scratches to extensive cuts, tears, or gashes. An open wound may be the only surface evidence of a more serious injury such as a fracture, particularly in the case of head injuries involving fracture of the skull. In first aid, open wounds are divided into six classifications: Abrasions, amputations, avulsions, incisions, lacerations, and punctures.

Abrasions

Abrasions are caused by rubbing or scraping. These wounds are seldom deep, but a portion of the skin has been damaged, leaving a raw surface with minor bleeding. The bleeding in most abrasions is from the capillaries. Abrasions are easily infected due to the top layer of skin being removed leaving the underlying skin exposed.

Amputations

An amputation involves the extremities. When an amputation occurs, the fingers, toes, hands, feet, or limbs are completely cut through or torn off which causes jagged skin and exposed bones. Bleeding may be excessive or the force that amputates a limb may close off torn vessels, limiting the amount of bleeding. A clean cut amputation seals off vessels and minimizes bleeding. A torn amputation usually bleeds heavily.

Avulsions

An avulsion is an injury that tears an entire piece of skin and tissue loose or leaves it hanging as a flap. This type of wound usually results when tissue is forcibly separated or torn from the victim's body. There is great danger of infection and bleeding. Body parts that have been wholly or partly torn off may sometimes be successfully reattached by a surgeon.

Incisions

Wounds produced by a sharp cutting edge, such as a knife or razor, are referred to as incised wounds. The edges of such wounds are smooth without bruising or tearing. If such a wound is deep, large blood vessels and nerves may be severed. Incised wounds bleed freely, and are often difficult to control.

Lacerations

Lacerated wounds are those with rough or jagged edges. The flesh has been torn or mashed by blunt instruments, machinery, or rough edges such as a jagged piece of metal.

Because the blood vessels are torn or mashed, these wounds may not bleed as freely as incised wounds. The ragged and torn tissues, with the foreign matter that is often forced or ground into the wound make it difficult to determine the extent of the damage. The danger of infection is great in lacerations.

Punctures

Puncture wounds are produced by pointed objects such as needles, splinters, nails, or pieces of wire that pass through the skin and damage tissue in their path. The small number of blood vessels cut sometimes prevents free bleeding. The danger of infection in puncture wounds is great due to this poor drainage.

There are two types of puncture wounds:
- A *penetrating puncture wound* causes injured tissues and blood vessels whether it is shallow or deep.
- A *perforating puncture wound* has an entrance and exit wound. The object causing the injury passes through the body and out to create an exit wound which in many cases is more serious than the entrance wound.

FIRST AID FOR OPEN WOUNDS

The chief duties of a first aider in caring for open wounds are to stop bleeding and to prevent germs from entering the wound. If germs do not enter, there will be much less chance of infection and the wound will heal quickly.

♦ Carefully cut or tear the clothing so that the injury may be seen.
♦ If loose foreign particles are around the wound, wipe them away with clean material. **Always wipe away from the wound, not toward it.**
♦ **Do not** attempt to remove an object impaled in the wound. Serious bleeding and other damage may occur if the object is removed. Stabilize the object with a bulky dressing.
♦ **Do not** touch the wound with your hands, clothing, or anything that is not clean, if possible.
♦ Place a sterile bandage compress or gauze, when available, over the wound and tie in place.
♦ Dressings should be wide enough to completely cover the wound and the area around it.
♦ Protect compresses, or gauze dressings with a cover bandage made from a cravat or triangular bandage. Place outer dressings on all open wounds except for wounds of the eye, nose, chin, finger and toe, or compound fractures of the hand and foot when splints are applied. Either use a cravat bandage or triangular bandage to cover the entire dressing.
♦ Unless otherwise specified, tie the knots of the bandage compress and outer dressing over the wound on top of the compress pad to help in checking the bleeding. However, when an open fracture is involved, tie away from wound.
♦ Keep victim quiet and lying still. Any movement will increase circulation which could restart bleeding.
♦ Reassure the victim to ease emotional reaction.
♦ Treat for shock.

FIRST AID DRESSINGS AND BANDAGES

First aid materials for dressings and bandages include:
- Bandage compress
- Gauze
- Roller bandage
- Adhesive compress
- Triangular bandage
- Cravat bandage

Bandage Compress

A bandage compress is a special dressing intended to cover open wounds. It consists of a pad made of several thicknesses of gauze attached to the middle of a strip of gauze. Pad sizes range from one to four inches. Bandage compresses usually come folded so that the gauze pad can be applied directly to the open wound with virtually no exposure to the air or fingers. The strip of gauze at either side of the gauze pad is folded back so that it can be opened and the bandage compress tied in place with no disturbance of the sterile pad. The gauze of a bandage compress may be extended to twice its normal size by opening up folded gauze. Unless otherwise specified, all bandage compresses and all gauze dressings should be covered with an open triangular cravat or roller bandage.

Gauze

Gauze is used in several ways to apply first aid dressings. Plain gauze may be used in place of a bandage compress to cover large wounds and wounds of the trunk. Plain gauze of various sizes is supplied in packets. In cases of profuse bleeding or where bulk is required to stabilize embedded objects, use several layers of gauze. Care should be taken not to touch the portion of the gauze that is to be placed in contact with the wound.

Gauze Roller Bandage

The gauze roller bandage is a self-adhering form-fitting bandage. It can be made secure with several snug overlapping wraps then tied in place.

Adhesive Compress

An adhesive compress is a self-adhering bandage that has gauze to cover the wound and a sticky backing which holds to the victim's skin.

Triangular Bandage

A standard triangular bandage is made from a piece of cloth approximately forty inches square by folding the square diagonally and cutting along the fold. It is easily applied and can be handled so that the part to be applied over wound or burn dressings will not be soiled.

A triangular bandage does not tend to slip off once it is correctly applied. It is usually made from unbleached cotton cloth, although any kind of cloth will do. In emergencies, a triangular bandage can be improvised from a clean handkerchief, a clean piece of shirt, etc.

The triangular bandage is also used to make improvised tourniquets, to support fractures and dislocations, to apply splints, and to form slings. If a regular-size bandage is found to be too short when a dressing is applied, it can be lengthened by tying another bandage to one end.

Cravat Bandages

A triangular bandage may be used open or folded. When folded, it is known as a cravat. A cravat bandage is prepared as follows:

- Make a one inch fold along the base of the triangular bandage.
- Bring the point (apex) to the center of the folded base, placing the point underneath the fold, to make a *wide cravat* bandage.
- A *medium cravat* is made by folding lengthwise along a line midway between the base and the new top of the bandage, in effect, folding the wide cravat bandage in half lengthwise.
- A *narrow cravat* is made by repeating the folding.

This method has the advantage that all bandages can be folded to a uniform width, or the width may be varied to suit the purpose for which it is to be used. To complete a dressing, the ends of the bandage are tied securely.

SQUARE KNOT

Unless otherwise specified, all knots or ties mentioned in this manual should be tied in a square knot.

To tie a square knot, take an end of the bandage in each hand, pass the end in the right hand over and around the end in the left and tie a single knot. Then pass the end now in the left hand over the end in the right hand, and complete the knot. Each loose end, after the second knot is tied, will be doubled back and lying against itself with the other end wrapped around it. The rule to remember in tying a square knot is right over left, then left over right.

This knot can be untied easily by converting it into a slip knot. Grasp one tail of the bandage in one hand, hold the bandage with the other hand, and pull the tail under the knot rolls. Release the tail, and with the free hand grasp the knot, holding it firmly; with the other hand, pull the bandage away from the knot.

SLINGS

Slings are used to support injuries of the shoulder, upper extremities or ribs. In an emergency they may be improvised from belts, neckties, scarves, or similar articles. Bandages should be used if available.

Triangular Bandage Sling

Tie a triangular bandage sling as follows:

- Place one end of the base of an open triangular bandage over the shoulder on the injured side.
- Allow the bandage to hang down in front of the chest so that the apex, or point, will be behind the elbow of the injured arm.
- Bend the arm at the elbow with hand slightly elevated (four to five inches).
- Bring the forearm across the chest and over the bandage.
- Carry the lower end of the bandage over the shoulder on the uninjured side and tie at uninjured side of the neck, being sure the knot is at the side of the neck.

♦ Twist the apex of the bandage, and tuck it in at the elbow.

The hand should be supported with the fingertips exposed, whenever possible, to permit detection of interference with circulation.

Cravat Bandage Sling

Tie a cravat bandage sling as follows:

♦ Place one end over the shoulder on the injured side.
♦ Allow the bandage to hang down in front of the chest.
♦ Bend the arm at the elbow with hand slightly elevated four to five inches.
♦ Bring the forearm across the chest and over the bandage.
♦ Carry the lower end of the bandage over the injured arm to the shoulder on the uninjured side and tie at uninjured side of neck.

Basket Sling

A useful sling for transporting or handling a victim with a suspected neck injury or an unconscious victim whose arms may create difficulties, can be made with an open triangular bandage as follows:

♦ Place an open triangular bandage across the chest with the apex down.
♦ Fold the arms over one another on the bandage. Bring the ends of the base together and tie.
♦ Cross the apex over the folded arms and tie to the knotted ends of the base.

PRINCIPLES OF BANDAGING

♦ Bandage wounds snugly, but not too tightly. Too tight a bandage may damage surrounding tissue or interfere with the blood supply, especially if swelling occurs. A bandage tied too loosely may slip off the wound.
♦ In bandaging the arms or the legs, leave the tips of the fingers or toes uncovered where possible to detect any interference with circulation.
♦ If the victim complains that the bandage is too tight, loosen it and make it comfortable, but snug. Unless otherwise specified, all knots should be tied over open wounds to help control bleeding.
♦ If bandages become saturated with blood, apply additional bandages or dressings. **Do not** remove original dressing.

DRESSINGS FOR WOUNDS

The following dressings are recommended for covering wounds:

Scalp, Temple, Ear, or Face

To dress an open wound for the scalp, temple, ear, or face, proceed as follows:

♦ Apply the pad of a bandage compress over the wound.
♦ Carry one end under the chin, and the other over the top of the head.
♦ Cross at the temple in front of the ear on the side opposite the injury.
♦ Bring one end around the front of the head and the other end low around the back of the head.
♦ Tie on or near the compress pad.
♦ Cover the compress with a cravat bandage applied in the same manner.

If the wound is on the cheek or the front of the face, cross the bandage compress and cravat bandage behind the ear, on the side opposite the injury; bring the ends around the forehead and back of the head, and tie.

Extensive Wounds of the Scalp

A wound or wounds involving a large area of the scalp may be dressed by covering the injury with a piece of gauze or a large bandage compress.

♦ Apply the pad of a sterile compress to the wound.
♦ Carry one end under the chin and the other end over the top of the head.
♦ Cross the ends at the temple.
♦ Carry one end around the forehead.

♦ Pass the other end around the back of the head and tie on the opposite side of the face.
♦ Next apply a triangular bandage over the head with the base snugly across the forehead, just above the eyebrows and the apex of the bandage at the back of the neck.
♦ Bring the two ends of the bandage around the head just above the ears.
♦ Cross under the bony prominence on the back of the head.
♦ Return the ends to the middle of the forehead.
♦ Tie just above the eyebrows.
♦ Fold up the apex and tuck it in snugly over the crossed ends at the back of the head.

When gauze is used, take care to keep it in place while the cover bandage is being applied.

Forehead or Back of Head

To dress an open wound of the forehead or back of the head, proceed as follows:
♦ Apply the pad of a sterile bandage compress over the injury.
♦ Hold the compress in place by passing the ends of the compress around the head above the ears, and tying over the compress pad.
♦ Apply the center of a cravat bandage over the pad, take the ends around the head, cross them, and tie over the compress pad.

Eye Injuries

Objects embedded in the eye should be removed only by a doctor. Such objects must be protected from accidental movement or removal until the victim receives medical attention.
♦ Tell the victim that both eyes must be bandaged to protect the injured eye.
♦ Encircle the eye with a gauze dressing or other suitable material.
♦ Position a cup or cone over the embedded object. The object should not touch the top or sides of the cup. It may be necessary to make a hole in the bottom of the cup if the object is longer than the cup.
♦ Hold the cup and dressing in place with a bandage compress or roller bandage that covers both eyes. It is important to bandage both eyes to prevent movement of the injured eye.
♦ Never leave the victim alone, as the victim may panic with both eyes covered. Keep in hand contact so the victim will always know someone is there.
♦ Stabilize the head with sand bags or large pads and always transport the victim on his or her back.
♦ Ensure that the victim does not tamper with the dressing or embedded object.

This procedure should also be used for lacerations and other injuries to the eyeball.

After a serious injury, the eyeball may be knocked out of the socket. No attempt should be made to put the eye back into the socket. The eye should be covered with a moist dressing and a protective cup without applying pressure to the eye. A bandage compress or roller bandage that covers both eyes should be applied. Transport the victim face up with the head immobilized.

For all injuries to and around the upper or lower lid of the eye, use a sterile bandage compress as follows:
♦ Place the center of a bandage compress over the injured eye.
♦ Carry the end on the injured side below the ear to the back of the head.
♦ Carry the other end above the ear on the opposite side.
♦ Tie toward the injured side below the bony prominence on the back of the head.
♦ Bring both ends over the top of the head, passing the longer end under the dressing at the temple on the uninjured side.
♦ Slide it in front of the uninjured eye and pull it tightly enough to raise the dressing above the uninjured eye.
♦ Tie to the other end on top of the head.

Nose

To bandage a wound to the nose, proceed as follows:
♦ Split the tails of a bandage compress.

- Apply the pad of the compress to the wound.
- Pass the top tails, one to each side of the head below the ears and tie at the back of the neck.
- Pass the bottom tails, one to each side of the head above the ears and tie at the back of the head.

Chin

In order to tie a bandage for a wound on the chin, proceed as follows:
- Split the tails of a bandage compress. Apply the pad of the compress to the wound.
- Pass the top tails, one to each side of the neck, below the ears and tie at the back of the neck.
- Pass the bottom tails, one to each side of the head in front of the ears and tie at the top of the head.

Neck or Throat

To bandage a wound on the neck or throat, proceed as follows:
- Apply the pad of a sterile bandage compress to the wound.
- Pass the ends around the neck, and tie over the wound.
- Place the center of cravat bandage over the compress.
- Pass the ends of the cravat bandage around the neck, cross them, bring them around the neck again, and tie loosely.
- Use hand pressure over the wound for control of excessive bleeding.

Shoulder

In order to tie a bandage for a wound of the shoulder, proceed as follows:
- Apply the pad of a bandage compress over the wound. Bring the ends under the armpit.
- Cross, carry to the top of the compress, cross, carry one end across the chest and one end across the back, and tie in the opposite armpit over a pad.
- Place the apex of a triangular bandage high up on the shoulder. Place the base, along which a hem has been folded, below the shoulder on the upper part of the arm, carry the ends around the arm and tie them on the outside.
- To hold the bandage in position, place the center of a cravat bandage under the opposite armpit; carry the ends to the shoulder over the apex of the first bandage; tie a single knot; then fold the apex over and complete the knot.
- Place the forearm in a triangular bandage sling.

Armpit

To dress a wound of the armpit, proceed as follows:
- Apply the pad of a bandage compress over the wound. Lift the arm only high enough to apply compress, as further damage may occur to lacerated nerves which are close to the surface.
- Carry the ends over the shoulder and cross.
- Carry one end across the chest and the other end across the back.
- Tie under the opposite arm over a pad.
    > **If there is severe bleeding,** place a hard object over the pad of the compress and push it well up into the armpit, holding the pads in place by a cravat bandage.
- Place the center of a cravat bandage over the wound.
- Bring the ends over the shoulder, crossing them; then pass the ends around the chest and back and tie them under the opposite arm. Next bring the arm down and secure it firmly against the chest wall by a cravat bandage passed around the arm and chest. Tie securely on the opposite side over a pad.
- Place the forearm in a triangular sling.

Arm, Forearm, and Wrist

To bandage wounds of the arm, forearm, and wrist, proceed as follows:
- Apply the pad of a sterile bandage compress over the wound.

♦ Pass the ends several times around the arm and tie them over the pad.
♦ Place the center of a cravat bandage over the pad.
♦ Pass the ends around the arm, cross them, continue around the arm and tie over the pad.
♦ Place the forearm and hand in a triangular sling.

Elbow

To dress a wound of the elbow, proceed as follows:
♦ Start with joint in a slightly bent position.
♦ Apply the pad of a bandage compress over the wound.
♦ Pass the ends of the bandage around the elbow and carry them around the arm just above the elbow.
♦ Cross them and carry them around the forearm just below the elbow.
♦ Tie at a point below the elbow.

Cover with a cravat bandage as follows:
♦ Place the center of the cravat bandage over the point of the elbow.
♦ Pass the ends around and cross them above the point of the elbow.
♦ Carry them around the arm and cross again at the bend of the elbow.
♦ Carry around the forearm, and tie just below the point of the elbow.
♦ Immobilize the upper extremity by placing the forearm in a triangular sling.

Palm or Back of Hand

To dress a wound of the palm or back of the hand, proceed as follows:
♦ Apply the pad of a bandage compress over the wound.
♦ Pass the ends several times around the hand and wrist.
♦ Tie over the pad.
♦ Place the center of a cravat bandage over the pad.
♦ Cross the ends at the opposite side of the hand.
♦ Pass one end around the little finger side of the hand.
♦ Pass the other end between the thumb and forefinger, taking the ends to the wrist.
♦ Cross the ends and continue around the wrist, crossing at the back of the wrist.
♦ Cross again at the inside of the wrist.
♦ Tie at the back of the wrist.
♦ Place the forearm and hand in a triangular bandage sling.

Extensive Wounds of the Hand

Control arterial bleeding of the hand.
To dress extensive wounds of the hand, proceed as follows:
♦ Apply gauze or a bandage compress over the wound.
♦ When there are multiple wounds of fingers, separate the fingers with gauze.
♦ If a bandage compress is used, pass the ends several times around the hand and wrist.
♦ Tie them over the pad.

Cover the hand with a triangular bandage as follows:
♦ Place the base on the inner side of the wrist.
♦ Bring the apex down over the back of the hand.
♦ Cross the ends (little finger side first) over the back of the hand and wrist.
♦ Wrap around wrist, ending in tie on back of wrist.
♦ Bring the apex down over the knot and tuck it under.
♦ Place the forearm and hand in a triangular bandage sling.
♦ If there is swelling, elevate and apply ice.

Finger

To dress a wound of the finger, proceed as follows:
♦ Apply the pad of a small bandage compress over the wound.
♦ Pass the ends several times around the finger and tie over the pad.
♦ A small adhesive compress may be used instead of a bandage compress for a wound of the finger or a wound on the end of the finger. A bent finger should be dressed bent and not fully extended.

♦ If more than one finger is injured, cover with an open triangular bandage as for extensive wounds of the hand.

Chest or Back Between Shoulder Blades

To dress a wound on the chest or back between the shoulder blades, proceed as follows:
♦ Place the pad of the compress over the wound so that the ends are diagonally across the chest or back.
♦ Carry one end over the shoulder and under the armpit. Carry the other end under the armpit and over the shoulder. Tie the ends over the compress.

Cover the compress and chest or back with a triangular bandage as follows:
♦ Place the center of the base at the lower part of the neck.
♦ Allow the apex to drop down over the chest or back, as appropriate.
♦ Carry the ends over the shoulders and under the armpits to the center of the chest or back.
♦ Tie with the apex below the knot.
♦ Turn the apex up and tuck it over the knot.

Back, Chest, Abdomen, Or Side

To tie a bandage for the back, chest, abdomen, or side, proceed as follows:
♦ Apply the pad of a sterile bandage compress or sterile gauze over the wound. If a sterile bandage compress is used, take the ends around the body (one end across the back and the other across the abdomen or chest and tie on the side).
♦ Cover with a proper size cravat bandage by placing the center of the bandage on the side nearest the injury.
♦ Take the ends across the back and abdomen or chest and tie on the opposite side.

NOTE: If air is being sucked into the lungs through a wound in the chest, cover the wound immediately with a nonporous material, such as plastic wrap, wax paper, or your hand; then dress the wound. Transport the victim to a medical facility as quickly as possible.

Protruding Intestines

To dress a wound in which the victim's intestines are protruding, proceed as follows:
♦ Place the victim on his or her back with something under the knees to raise them and help relax the abdominal muscles.
♦ **Do not** try to re-place the intestines; leave the organ on the surface.
♦ Cover with aluminum foil, plastic wrap, or a moist dressing.
♦ Cover lightly with an outer dressing. This will help preserve heat.

Lower Abdomen, Back, or Buttocks

To dress a wound of the lower part of the abdomen, the lower part of the back or the buttocks, proceed as follows:
♦ Apply a pad made from several layers of sterile gauze; in the absence of gauze, the pad of a sterile compress may be placed over the wound and held in place by passing the ends around the body and tying them.
♦ Cover the gauze or bandage compress with two triangular bandages:
  ♦ Tie the apexes in the crotch.
  ♦ Bring the base of one bandage up on the abdomen.
  ♦ Pass the ends around to the back and tie.
  ♦ Pass the ends of the other bandage around to the front and tie.

Groin

To dress a wound of the groin, proceed as follows:
♦ Apply the pad of a bandage compress over the wound.
♦ Carry the ends to the hip and cross.
♦ Carry the ends across to the opposite side of the body and tie.

Cover the compress with two cravat bandages tied together as follows:
♦ Place the center of one of the cravat bandages over the pad and follow the compress in such a manner as to cover it entirely.

♦ Continue with the other cravat bandage around the entire body a second time and tie.

Crotch

To bandage a wound of the crotch, proceed as follows:

♦ Cover wound with sterile gauze.
♦ Pass a narrow cravat bandage around the waist and tie in front, leaving the ends to hang free.
♦ Pass a second cravat bandage under the knot of the first cravat bandage.
♦ Pass the two ends of the second cravat bandage between the thighs and bring one end around each hip.
♦ Tie to the ends of the cravat bandage tied around the body.

Hip

To dress a wound of the hip, proceed as follows:

♦ Split the tails of a bandage compress.
♦ Place the pad over the wound.
♦ Pass the top tails around the body.
♦ Tie over the opposite hip.
♦ Pass the ends of the bottom tails around thigh and cross on inside of thigh.
♦ Continue around the thigh, tying on the outside.

Cover with a triangular bandage as follows:

♦ Place the base of a triangular bandage on the thigh with the apex pointing up; bring the ends of the base around the thigh, and tie.
♦ Pass a second cravat bandage around the body at the waist and tie a single knot over the apex of the triangular bandage.
♦ Fold the apex over the knot and complete tying the knot.

Thigh or Leg

To tie a bandage for a wound of the thigh or leg, proceed as follows:

♦ Apply the pad of a bandage compress over the wound.
♦ Pass the ends around the injured extremity and tie over the pad.
♦ Place the center of a cravat bandage over the compress, pass the ends around the injured part, cross them, bring them around again, and tie over the pad.

Knee

To dress a wound of the knee, proceed as follows:

♦ Apply the pad of a sterile bandage compress over the wound.
♦ Cross the ends at the back of the knee and return to the front of the knee.
♦ Tie firmly over the pad, if possible.
♦ Place the center of a cravat bandage over the pad.
♦ Bring the ends of the bandage around each side of the leg.
♦ Cross them at the back of the knee, pull them forward, and tie them above the knee.

Ankle

To dress a wound of the ankle, proceed as follows:

♦ Apply the pad of a bandage compress to the wound.
♦ Carry the ends to the top of the instep and cross.
♦ Carry the ends around the bottom of the foot and cross over the instep again.
♦ Pass the ends around the ankle and tie over the pad.
♦ Place the center of a cravat bandage over the compress.
♦ Carry the ends to the top of the instep, cross.
♦ Cross the ends under the foot, bring back to the top of the instep and cross.
♦ Carry the ends around the ankle and tie over the pad.

Foot

To dress a wound of the foot proceed as follows:

♦ Apply the pad of a bandage compress to the wound.

♦ Carry the ends around the foot and ankle.
♦ Tie over the pad.
♦ Place the center of a cravat bandage over the compress.
♦ Carry the ends around the foot and ankle, ending in a tie as near the front of the ankle as possible.

Extensive Wounds of Foot or Toes

First, control arterial bleeding of the foot.
To dress extensive wounds of the foot and toes, proceed as follows:

♦ Apply gauze or the pad of a large bandage compress over the wound and tie it in place.
♦ Place the base of a triangular bandage on the back of the ankle.
♦ Bring the apex under the sole of the foot, over the toes, back over the instep, and up the leg to a point above the ankle in front.
♦ Pass the end on the little toe side over the instep, then the other end over the instep, and continue around the ankle with both ends and tie in front.
♦ Bring the apex down over the knot and tuck in under the knot.

Toe

To dress a wound of the toe, proceed as follows:

♦ Apply the pad of a small bandage compress over the wound.
♦ Pass the ends around the toe several times and tie over the pad.
♦ Instead of a bandage compress a small adhesive compress may be used for a wound of the toe or a wound on the end of the toe.
♦ When there are multiple wounds of the toes, separate the toes with gauze. Cover with a triangular bandage as described for extensive wounds of the foot.

CLOSED WOUNDS

Closed wounds are injuries where the skin is not broken, but damage occurs to underlying tissues. These injuries may result in internal bleeding from damage to internal organs, muscles, and other tissues. Closed wounds are classified as follows:

• Bruises
• Ruptures or hernias

Bruises

Bruises are caused by an object striking the body or the body coming into contact with a hard object, for example in a fall or a bump. The skin is not broken, but the soft tissue beneath the skin is damaged. Small blood vessels are ruptured, causing blood to seep into surrounding tissues. This produces swelling. The injured area appears red at first, then darkens to blue or purple. When large blood vessels have been ruptured or large amounts of underlying tissue have been damaged, a lump may develop as a result of the blood collecting within the damaged tissue. This lump is called a hematoma or blood tumor.
The symptoms of a bruise are as follows:

• Immediate pain
• Swelling
• Rapid discoloration
• Later, pain or pressure on movement

The first aid for bruises is as follows:

♦ To limit swelling and reduce pain, apply an ice bag, a cloth wrung out in cold water, or a chemical cold pack.
♦ Elevate the injured area and place at complete rest.
♦ Check for fractures and other possible injuries.
♦ Treat for shock.

Severe bruises should have the care of a doctor.

Ruptures or Hernias

The most common form of rupture or hernia is a protrusion of a portion of an internal organ through the wall of the abdomen. Most ruptures occur in or just above the groin, but they may occur at other places over the abdomen. Ruptures result from a combination of weakness of the tissues and muscular strain.

The symptoms of a rupture are as follows:

- Sharp, stinging pain
- Feeling of something giving away at the site of the rupture
- Swelling
- Possible nausea and vomiting

The first aid for an individual who has suffered a rupture is as follows:

♦ Place the victim on his or her back with the knees well drawn up.
♦ Place a blanket or similar padding under the knees.
♦ Place the center of a cravat under the padding, bring the ends above the knees and tie.
♦ Place the center of two cravat bandages tied together at the ends on the outside of the thighs and pass the ends around the thighs, cross under the blanket, bring the ends around the legs just above the ankles and tie.
♦ Never attempt to force the protrusion back into the cavity.
♦ Place cold application to injured area.
♦ Cover with a blanket.
♦ The victim should be transported lying down with the knees drawn up.

FOREIGN BODIES

Foreign Bodies in the Eye

Foreign bodies such as particles of dirt, dust, or fine pieces of metal may enter the eye and lodge there. If not removed, they can cause discomfort, inflammation and possibly, infection.

Through an increased flow of tears, nature limits the possibility of harm by dislodging many of these substances. **Do not** let the victim rub the eye. Rubbing may scratch the delicate eye tissues or force sharp objects into the tissues. This makes removal of the object difficult. The first aider should not attempt to remove foreign bodies. It is always much safer to send the person to a physician.

To remove a foreign body on the inside of the eyelid, proceed as follows:

♦ Pull upper eyelid down over the lower eyelashes.
♦ Lift eyelid and remove object with sterile gauze.

The first aid for a foreign body on the eye that is not on the cornea or imbedded is as follows:

♦ Flush the eye with clean water, if available, for 15 minutes. If necessary, hold the eyelids apart.
♦ Often a foreign body lodged under the upper eyelid can be removed by drawing the upper lid down over the lower lid; as the upper lid returns to its normal position, the under surfaces will be drawn over the lashes of the lower lid and the foreign body removed by the wiping action of the eyelashes.
♦ A foreign body on the surface of the eye may also be removed by grasping the eyelashes of the upper lid and turning the lid over a cotton swab or similar object. The particle may then be carefully removed from the eyelid with the corner of a piece of sterile gauze.

If a foreign body becomes lodged in the eyeball, **do not** attempt to disturb it, as it may be forced deeper into the eye and result in further damage. Place a bandage compress over both eyes. Keep the victim calm and get medical help.

Foreign Bodies in the Ear

Small insects, pieces of rock, or other material may become lodged in the ear. Children sometimes put other objects, such as kernels of corn, peas, buttons or seeds in their ears. Such objects as seeds absorb moisture and swell in the ear, making their removal difficult and often causing inflammation.

The first aid for foreign bodies in the ear is as follows:

♦ **Do not** insert pins, match sticks, pieces of wire or other objects in the ear to dislodge foreign bodies because this may damage the tissue lining of the ear or perforate the ear drum.

- In the case of insects, turn the victim's head to the side and put several drops of warm olive oil, mineral oil, or baby oil in the ear; then let the oil run out and the drowned insect may come out with it. **Do not** try to flush out objects with water.
- Consult a physician if a foreign body cannot be easily removed.

Foreign Bodies in the Nose

Foreign bodies in the nose usually can be removed without difficulty, but occasionally the services of a physician are required.

The first aid for a foreign body in the nose is as follows:

- Induce sneezing by sniffing snuff or pepper, or tickling the opposite nostril with a feather. This will usually dislodge a foreign body in the nose.
- **Do not** blow the nose violently or with one nostril held shut.
- **Do not** attempt to dislodge the foreign body with a hairpin or similar object. This method may damage tissues of the nasal cavity or push the foreign body into an inaccessible place.

Foreign Bodies in the Stomach

Foreign bodies such as pins coins, nails, and other objects are sometimes swallowed accidentally. Except for pins, nails, or other sharp objects, foreign objects that are swallowed usually cause no great harm.

The first aid for a foreign body in the stomach is as follows:

- **Do not** give anything to induce vomiting or bowel movement.
- Consult a physician immediately.

Burns and Scalds

CLASSIFICATION OF BURNS

Burns may be classified according to extent and depth of damage as follows:

- First degree
  Minor

  Burned area is painful.
  Outer skin is reddened.
  Slight swelling is present.

- Second degree
  Moderate

  Burned area is painful.
  Underskin is affected. Blisters may form.
  The area may have a wet, shiny appearance because of exposed tissue.

- Third degree
  Critical

  Insensitive due to the destruction of nerve endings.
  Skin is destroyed.
  Muscle tissues and bone underneath may be damaged.
  The area may be charred, white, or grayish in color.

Burns may also be classified according to cause. The four major types of burns by cause are as follows:

- Chemical
- Thermal
- Electrical
- Radiation

The seriousness of a burn or scald is influenced by the extent of the body surface involved, as well as by the depth to which the tissue has been penetrated. It is generally assumed that where two-thirds of the surface of the body is injured by a second degree burn or scald, death will usually follow, but a much smaller area injured by a third-degree burn can also cause death.

Burns can do more damage than injure the skin. Burns can damage muscles, bones, nerves, and blood vessels. The eyes can be burned beyond repair. The respiratory system structures can be damaged, with possible airway obstruction, respiratory failure, and respiratory arrest. In addition to the physical damage caused by burns, victims also may suffer emotional and psychological problems that could last a lifetime.

Shock is very severe when burns are extensive and may cause death in a few hours.

FIRST AID FOR BURNS

The first aid given to a burn victim largely depends on the cause of the burn and the degree of severity.

Emergency first aid for burns or scalds should primarily be:

♦ Exclusion of air from the burned area
♦ Relief of the pain that immediately follows burns
♦ Minimizing the onset of shock
♦ Prevention of infection.

Remove all clothing from the injured area, but cut around any clothing that adheres to the skin and leave it in place. Keep the patient covered, except the injured part, since there is a tendency to chill.

First aid dressings for burns and scalds should be free of grease or oil. The use of greases or oils in the treatment of burns makes it necessary to cleanse the burned or scalded areas with a solvent before medical treatment can begin. This delays the medical treatment and is very painful.

Be careful when dressing burns and scalds. Burned and scalded surfaces are subject to infection the same as open wounds and require the same care to prevent infection. **Do not** break blisters intentionally.

Never permit burned surfaces to be in contact with each other, such as areas between the fingers or toes, the ears and the side of the head, the undersurface of the arm and the chest wall, the folds of the groin, and similar places.

Cover bandages should be loose enough to prevent pressure on burned surfaces. Swelling often takes place after burn dressings have been applied, so check them frequently to see that they are not too tight. Watch for evidence of shock and treat if it is present.

In cases of severe burns, remove the victim to the hospital as quickly as possible. The victim will probably require an anesthetic so that ordinarily nothing should be given by mouth.

In addition to the general principles listed, certain other principles must be followed when giving first aid for specific types of burns.

Chemical Burns of the Eyes

Frequently chemical substances, especially lime, cement, caustic soda, or acids or alkalis from storage batteries get into the eyes. The treatment is to wash the eyes freely with clean water. To do this, have the victim lie down, hold the eyelids open with the fingers and pour the water into the inner corner of the eyes from a pitcher or other container. Use plenty of water and wash the eyes thoroughly, being sure the water actually flows across the eyes. **Do not** put neutralizing solution in the eyes. Cover both eyes with moistened sterile gauze pads and secure in place. Chemical burns of the eyes should receive the attention of an eye specialist as soon as possible.

Chemical Burns

General first aid for chemical burns is as follows:

♦ Remove all clothing containing the chemical agent.
♦ **Do not** use any neutralizing solution, unless recommended by a physician.
♦ Irrigate with water for at least 15 minutes, use potable water if possible.
♦ Treat for shock.
♦ Transport to a medical facility.

First aid for dry chemical (alkali) burns is an exception to the general first aid for chemical burns because mixing water with dry alkali creates a corrosive substance. The dry alkali should be brushed from the skin and water should then be used in very large amounts.

Minor Thermal Burns

General first aid for minor thermal burns is as follows:
- ♦ Use cool, moist applications of gauze or bandage material to minimize blistering.
- ♦ Treat for physical shock.

If the victim has thermal burns on the eyelids, apply moist, sterile gauze pads to both eyes and secure in place.

Moderate or Critical Thermal Burns

General first aid for more serious thermal burns is as follows:
- ♦ **Do not** use cold applications on extensive burns; cold could cause chilling.
- ♦ Cover the burn with a clean, dry dressing.
- ♦ Treat for shock.
- ♦ Transport to a medical facility.

Electrical Burns

General first aid for electrical burns is as follows:
- ♦ Conduct a primary survey, as cardiac and respiratory arrest can occur in cases of electrical burns.
- ♦ Check for points of entry and exit of current.
- ♦ Cover burned surface with a clean dressing.
- ♦ Splint all fractures. (Violent muscle contractions caused by the electricity may result in fractures.)
- ♦ Treat for physical shock.
- ♦ Transport to a medical facility.

Respiratory failure and cardiac arrest are the major problems caused by electrical shock and **not** the burn. Monitor pulse and breathing while preparing victim for transportation.

Radiation Burns

Radiation presents a hazard to the rescuer as well as the victim. A rescuer who must enter a radioactive area should stay for as short a time as possible. Radiation is undetectable by the human senses and the rescuer, while attempting to aid the victim, may receive a fatal dose of radiation without realizing it. Notify experts immediately of possible radioactive contamination.

Burns of the Face, Head, and Neck

Any burn of the face is dangerous since it may involve injury to the airway or the eyes. When applying gauze for burns of the face or head, avoid covering the nostrils as the victim may already be having respiratory problems. Victims with respiratory illnesses will be placed in greater jeopardy when exposed to heated air or chemical vapors. Victims with other health problems such as heart disease, kidney disease, or diabetes will react more severely to burn damage. Treat all burns as more serious if accompanied by other injuries.

To dress a burn of the face or head, proceed as follows:
- ♦ Apply several layers of gauze to the burned area and ensure that the gauze is placed between raw surfaces of ears and head.
- ♦ Loosely apply a cravat bandage around the forehead to secure layers of gauze for the upper part of the face.
- ♦ Loosely apply a second cravat bandage around the chin to secure layers of gauze for the lower part of the face.

If the neck only is burned:
- ♦ Dress it by applying gauze or other burn dressing.
- ♦ The burn dressing should be applied in several layers and covered with a cravat bandage the same as for wounds and bleeding of the neck.
- ♦ Burn dressings should always be applied loosely.

Burns to the Back

For burns to the back, apply gauze in several layers and ensure that it covers all burned surfaces including between the arm and chest wall and in the armpit. Cover the gauze dressings with a cover dressing as follows:

♦ Split the apex of a triangular bandage just far enough to tie around the front of neck.
♦ Place the base of bandage around the lower part of the back and tie in front.
♦ Dress small burns of the back loosely with a triangular or cravat bandage as for wounds and bleeding between shoulders or wounds of the back as the injury may indicate.

Burns on the Chest

For burns on the chest, apply gauze in several layers and ensure that it covers all burned surfaces including between the arm and chest wall and in the armpit. Cover the gauze dressing with a cover dressing as follows:

♦ Split the apex of a bandage just enough to tie at the back of neck.
♦ Place base of bandage around the waist and tie in back.
♦ Dress small burns of the chest loosely with a triangular cravat bandage as for wounds and bleeding between the shoulders or wounds of the chest as the injury may indicate.

Treatment of all Other Burns

Burn dressings should be loosely covered with a bandage as described for a wound and bleeding of the part or parts involved.

Sprains, Strains, and Fractures

The musculoskeletal system is composed of all the bones, joints, muscles, tendons, ligaments, and cartilages in the body. The makeup of the musculoskeletal system is subject to injury from sprains, strains, fractures and dislocations.

SPRAINS

Sprains are injuries due to stretching or tearing ligaments or other tissues at a joint. They are caused by a sudden twist or stretch of a joint beyond its normal range of motion.

Sprains may be minor injuries, causing pain and discomfort for only a few hours. In severe cases, however, they may require many weeks of medical care before normal use is restored.

The symptoms of a sprain are as follows:

• Pain on movement
• Swelling
• Tenderness
• Discoloration

Sprains present basically the same signs as a closed fracture. If you cannot determine whether the injury is a fracture or a sprain, treat it as a fracture.

The first aid for sprains is as follows:

♦ Elevate the injured area and place it at complete rest.
♦ Reduce swelling and relieve pain by applying an ice bag, a cloth wrung in cold water or a chemical cold pack. **Caution: Never use ice in direct contact with the skin; always wrap it in a towel or other material.**
♦ If swelling and pain persist, take the victim to the doctor.

The ankle is the part of the body most commonly affected by sprains. When the ankle has been sprained and the injured person must use the foot temporarily to reach a place for further treatment, the following care should be given:

- ♦ Unlace the shoe, but do not remove it.
- ♦ Place the center of a narrow cravat bandage under the foot in front of the heel of the shoe.
- ♦ Carry the ends up and back of the ankle, crossing above the heel, then forward, crossing over the instep, and then downward toward the arch to make a hitch under the cravat on each side, just in front of the heel of the shoe.
- ♦ Pull tightly and carry the ends back across the instep.
- ♦ Tie at the back of the ankle.

STRAINS

A strain is an injury to a muscle or a tendon caused by overexertion. In severe cases muscles or tendons are torn and the muscle fibers are stretched. Strains are caused by sudden movements or overexertion.
The symptoms of a strain are as follows:

- • Intense pain
- • Moderate swelling
- • Painful and difficult movement
- • Sometimes, discoloration

The first aid care for a strain is as follows:

- ♦ Place the victim in a comfortable position.
- ♦ Apply a hot, wet towel.
- ♦ Keep the injured area at rest.
- ♦ Seek medical attention.

FRACTURES

A fracture is a broken or cracked bone. For first aid purposes fractures can be divided into two classifications:

- • Open, or compound fracture. The bone is broken and an open wound is present. Often the end of the broken bone protrudes from the wound.
- • Closed, or simple fracture. No open wound is present, but there is a broken or cracked bone.

Broken bones, especially the long bones of the upper and lower extremities, often have sharp, sawtooth edges; even slight movement may cause the sharp edges to cut into blood vessels, nerves, or muscles, and perhaps through the skin. Careless or improper handling can convert a closed fracture into an open fracture, causing damage to surrounding blood vessels or nerves which can make the injury much more serious. A person handling a fracture should always keep this in mind. Damage due to careless handling of a closed fracture may greatly increase pain and shock, cause complications that will prolong the period of disability, and endanger life through hemorrhage of surrounding blood vessels.

If the broken ends of the bone extend through an open wound, there is little doubt that the victim has suffered a fracture. However, the bone does not always extend through the skin, so the person administering first aid must be able to recognize other signs that a fracture exists.

The general signs and symptoms of a fracture are as follows:

- • Pain or tenderness in the region of the fracture
- • Deformity or irregularity of the affected area
- • Loss of function (disability) of the affected area
- • Moderate or severe swelling
- • Discoloration
- • Information from the victim who victim may have felt the bone snap or break.

Be careful when examining injured persons, particularly those apparently suffering from fractures. For all fractures the first aider must remember to maintain an open airway, control bleeding and treat for shock. Do not attempt to change the position of an injured person until he or she has been examined and it has been determined that movement will not complicate the injuries. If the victim is lying down, it is far better to attend to the injuries with the victim in that position and with as little movement as possible. If fractures are present, make any necessary movement in such a manner as to protect the injured part against further injury.

SPLINTS

Use splints to support, immobilize, and protect parts with injuries such as known or suspected fractures, dislocations or severe sprains. When in doubt, treat the injury as a fracture and splint it. Splints prevent movement at the area of the injury and at the nearest joints. Splints should immobilize and support the joint or bones above and below the break.

Many types of splints are available commercially. Easily applied and quickly inflated plastic splints give support to injured limbs. Improvised splints may be made from pieces of wood, broom handles, newspapers, heavy cardboard, boards, magazines, or similar firm materials.

Certain guidelines should be followed when splinting:

- ◆ Gently remove all clothing from around any suspected fracture or dislocation.
- ◆ Do not attempt to push bones back through an open wound.
- ◆ Do not attempt to straighten any fracture.
- ◆ Cover open wounds with a sterile dressing before splinting.
- ◆ Pad splints with soft material to prevent excessive pressure on the affected area and to aid in supporting the injured part.
- ◆ Pad under all natural arches of the body such as the knee and wrist.
- ◆ Support the injured part while splint is being applied.
- ◆ Splint firmly, but not so tightly as to interfere with circulation or cause undue pain.
- ◆ Support fracture or dislocation before transporting victim.
- ◆ Elevate the injured part and apply ice when possible.

Use inflatable splints to immobilize fractures of the lower leg or forearm. When applying inflatable splints (non-zipper type), follow these guidelines:

- ◆ Put splint on your own arm so that the bottom edge is above your wrist.
- ◆ Help support the victim's limb or have someone else hold it.
- ◆ Hold injured limb, and slide the splint from your forearm over the victim's injured limb.
- ◆ Inflate by mouth only to the desired pressure. The splint should be inflated to the point where your thumb would make a slight indentation.
- ◆ Do not use an inflatable plastic splint with an open fracture with protruding bones.

For a zipper-type air splint, lay the victim's limb in the unzippered air splint, zip it and inflate. Traction cannot be maintained with this type of splint.

Change in temperature can affect air splints. Going from a cold area to a warm area will cause the splint to expand or vice versa, therefore, it may be necessary to deflate or inflate the splint until proper pressure is reached.

AREAS OF FRACTURE

Skull

A fracture may occur to any area of the skull and is considered serious due to possible injury to the brain. Injuries to the back of the head are particularly dangerous since a fractured skull may result without a visible wound to the scalp. The victim of a skull fracture may exhibit any or all of the following symptoms:

- • Loss of consciousness for any length of time
- • Difficulty in breathing
- • Clear or blood-tinged fluid coming from the nose and/or ears
- • Partial or complete paralysis
- • Pupils of unequal size
- • Speech disturbance
- • Convulsions
- • Vomiting
- • Impaired vision or sudden blindness

Consider all serious injuries to the head as possible fractures of the skull. A person with a skull fracture may also have an injury to the neck and spine.

The first aid for a skull fracture is as follows:

♦ Stabilize the head as you open the airway using the modified jaw-thrust maneuver.
♦ Check breathing - restore if necessary.
♦ Check pulse.
♦ Control bleeding from the scalp with minimal pressure and dress the wound; tie the knots of the bandage away from injured area. Do not try to control bleeding from ears or nose.
♦ Keep the victim quiet and lying down.
♦ Maintain an open airway.
♦ Immobilize head, neck, and back on backboard.
♦ Elevate the head end of the stretcher.
♦ Never give a stimulant.
♦ Keep the victim warm and treat for shock.
♦ Pad around the fractured area and under the neck to keep victim's head from resting on suspected fracture.

Spinal Column

The spinal column consists of bones called vertebrae. Each vertebra surrounds and protects the spinal cord and specific nerve roots.

Fracture of the spinal column may occur at any point along the backbone between its junction with the head at the top and with the pelvic basin below. Where portions of the broken vertebrae are displaced, the spinal cord may be cut, or pressure may be put on the cord.

Spinal cord injuries can result in paralysis or death, because they cannot always be corrected by surgery and the spinal cord has very limited self healing powers. Thus, it is extremely important for the person giving first aid to be able to recognize the signs of spinal column damage.

The following signs and symptoms are associated with spinal injuries:

• Pain and tenderness at the site of the injury
• Deformity
• Cuts and bruises
• Paralysis

First, check the lower extremities for paralysis. If the victim is conscious, use the following method:

♦ Ask the victim if he or she can feel your touch on his or her feet.
♦ Ask the victim to wiggle his or her toes.
♦ Ask the victim to press against your hand with his or her feet.

Second, check the upper extremities for paralysis. If the victim is conscious, use the following method:

♦ Ask the victim if he or she can feel your touch to his or her hands.
♦ Ask the victim to wiggle his or her fingers.
♦ Ask the victim to grasp your hand and squeeze.

If the victim is unconscious, perform the following tests for paralysis:

♦ Stroke the soles of the feet or ankles with a pointed object; if the spinal cord is undamaged, the feet will react.
♦ Stroke the palms of the hands with a pointed object; if the spinal cord is undamaged, the hands will react.

Treat all questionable injuries to the spinal column, even in the absence of signs of paralysis, as a fracture of the spinal column. The initial care that the victim receives at the scene of the accident is extremely important. Proper care, not speed, is essential. Improper care or handling could result in paralysis or death. The first aid for an individual with a fractured spinal column uses fifteen bandages as follows:

♦ If a broken-back splint is used, pad each long board with a blanket.
♦ Stabilize the head, immobilizing it in line with the rest of the body. Maintain stabilization until after the victim is secured to a splint, stretcher, or other hard, flat surface which provides firm support. Do not move victim until completely immobilized.
♦ Use a blanket or padding around the head and neck. Fold to make a strip about six inches wide and long enough to run along the side of the head from the

shoulder to the head, across the top of the head and down the other side to the shoulder.

♦ Pass first bandage around the forehead padding and splint, and tie on the outer side of splint.
♦ Pass second bandage around the splint and padding at the chin, and tie on the outer side of splint.
♦ Pass third bandage around the body and well up in the armpits and tie on outer side of splint.
♦ Pass fourth bandage around the body and splint at the lower part of the chest and tie on the outer side of the splint.
♦ Pass the fifth bandage around the body and splint at the hips, and tie on the outer side of the splint.
♦ Pass the center of the sixth bandage well up on the shoulder, passing one end between the long boards under the neck, continuing under the crosspiece, completing the tie at the upper edge of splint under the armpit.
♦ Tie the seventh bandage in the same manner around the other shoulder.
♦ Pass the eighth bandage around one hip and crotch and crosspiece between long boards and tie on outer side of splint.
♦ Apply ninth bandage in the same manner around the other hip.
♦ Apply tenth bandage around the upper part of one thigh and the long board and tie on the outer side of the splint.
♦ Apply eleventh bandage on the other side in the same manner.
♦ Pass twelfth bandage around the leg and long board just below the knee and tie on the outer side of the splint.
♦ Apply thirteenth bandage on the other side in the same manner.
♦ Pass the fourteenth bandage around one ankle and the long board, and tie on the outer side of the splint.
♦ Apply fifteenth bandage on the other side in the same manner.
♦ Use enough people to safely lift the victim as a unit and place the victim on his or her back on the splint or stretcher.
♦ Lift victim only high enough to slide the splint or stretcher underneath.
♦ Secure the victim to the splint or stretcher so that the entire body is immobilized.
♦ Cover with a blanket and treat for shock.

Nose

A broken nose is a very common type of fracture and may result from any hard blow. The symptoms of a broken nose are as follows:

• Deformity of the bridge of the nose
• Pain
• Bleeding
• Swelling

Treat any blow to the nose that causes bleeding as a fracture.
The first aid care for a broken nose is as follows:

♦ Apply a bandage compress if there is an open fracture.
♦ Take the victim to the doctor.

Upper Jaw

In fractures of the upper jaw or cheekbone, where there is an open wound, treat as for an open wound of the face, but do not tie bandage knots over wounds. If there is no open wound, a dressing is not necessary, but take the victim to a doctor.

Lower Jaw

The symptoms of a fracture of the lower jaw are as follows:

• The mouth is usually open.
• Saliva mixed with blood flows from the mouth.
• The teeth of the lower jaw may be uneven, loosened, or knocked out.
• Talking is painful and difficult.

The first aid for a fracture of the lower jaw is as follows:

♦ Maintain a clear airway.

♦ Gently place the jaw in a position so that the lower teeth rest against the upper teeth, if possible.
♦ Place the center of a cravat bandage over the front of the chin and pass the ends around the back of the head and tie, leaving the ends long.
♦ Place the center of a second cravat bandage under the chin, pass the ends over the cheeks to the center of the top of the head and tie, leaving the ends long.
♦ Bring the ends of the two bandages together and tie separately. Do not tie too tightly.
♦ Transport the victim on his or her side to allow drainage if no spinal injury is suspected.

Collarbone

Fracture of the collarbone frequently is caused by a fall with the hand outstretched or by a blow to the shoulder. The symptoms of a fractured collarbone are as follows:

• Pain in the area of the shoulder
• Partial or total disability of the arm on the injured side
• The injured shoulder tends to droop forward.
• The victim frequently supports the arm on the injured side at the elbow or wrist with the other hand.

Support the fracture until the following dressings have been applied:

♦ Place padding between the arm and the victim's side.
♦ Put the arm on the injured side in a triangular sling with the hand elevated about four to five inches.
♦ Secure the arm on the injured side to the body with a medium cravat. Center the bandage on the outside of the arm. Carry the bandage across the chest and back. Tie over a pad on the uninjured side of the body.

Shoulder Blade

Fracture of the shoulder blade is not a common injury. It is sometimes caused by a direct blow to the shoulder blade and usually results in a closed fracture with little displacement. Symptoms are as follows:

• Pain and swelling at the fracture
• Inability to swing the arm back and forth from the shoulder

To support a fracture of the shoulder blade proceed as follows:

♦ Place the forearm in a triangular sling.
♦ Bind the arm securely to the chest with a wide cravat bandage extending from the point of the shoulder downward by carrying one end across the chest and the other end across the back.
♦ Tie over a pad under the opposite armpit.

Upper Arm

Fracture of the upper portion of the arm is recognized by the following symptoms:

• Swelling
• Deformity
• Inability to use the arm below the point of the fracture.

In order to immobilize a fracture of the upper third of the arm proceed as follows:

♦ Have an assistant support the fracture on both sides of the break.
♦ Bind the arm to the rib cage with a wide cravat bandage that is tied over a pad under the opposite armpit.
♦ Place the forearm in a cravat bandage sling.

Do not pull the forearm up too high because this will increase pain.

Lower Arm, Elbow, Forearm, or Wrist

Take extreme care when dealing with a fractured elbow, as the fracture may cause extensive damage to surrounding tissues, nerves, and blood vessels. Improper care and handling of a fractured elbow could result in a permanent disability.

The symptoms of a fractured elbow are as follows:

• Extreme pain
• Extensive discoloration around elbow
• Swelling

- Deformity
- Bone may be visible or projecting from the wound.

The first aid for a fractured elbow in a straight position is as follows:

- Do not bend, straighten, or twist the arm in any direction.
- If available, apply an inflatable plastic splint.
- If an inflatable plastic splint is not available, use a splint long enough to reach from one inch below the armpit to one inch beyond the tip of the middle finger.
- While the fracture is being supported, pad to conform to the deformity and place splint on the inner side of the arm.
- Place the center of the first cravat bandage on the outside of the arm at the upper end of the splint, cross on the inside of the arm over the splint, pass the ends one or more times around the arm and splint, and tie on the outside.
- Place the centers of the second and third cravat bandages on the arm just above and below the elbow, and apply in a similar manner.
- Center the fourth cravat bandage on the back of the wrist. Pass the ends around and cross on the splint under the wrist, bring one end up around the little finger side, and cross over the back of the hand and down between the forefinger and thumb. Pass the other end up over the thumb, cross it over the back of the hand down around the little finger side, then cross both ends on the splint and tie on top of the hand.
- Tie a fifth cravat bandage around the splint, arm and body to prevent movement during transportation.

If the arm is bent, immobilize in a bent position by making an L-shaped splint for the forearm and wrist from two pieces of board one-half inch thick and four inches wide. One piece should be long enough to extend from one inch below the armpit to the point of the elbow and the other long enough to extend from the point of the elbow to one inch beyond the end of the middle finger. Immobilize the limb to the splint in the following manner:

- Fasten the boards together securely to form an L-shaped splint.
- Pad the splint.
- While an assistant supports the fracture on both sides of the break apply the splint to the inner side of the arm and forearm after placing the forearm across the chest.
- Use four cravat bandages to hold the splint in place.
- Place the center of the first cravat bandage on the outside of the arm at the upper end of the splint, pass around the arm one or more times, and tie on the arm.
- Place the centers of the second and third cravat bandages on the arm and forearm, respectively, passing around one or more times and tying on the arm.
- Apply the fourth cravat bandage by placing the center of the bandage on the back of the wrist, passing the ends around and crossing on the splint under the wrist. Take one end up around the little finger side, passing over the back of the hand and down between the forefinger and thumb. Pass the other end up over the thumb, and cross it over the back of the hand down around the little finger side; then cross both ends on the splint and tie on top of the hand.
- Place the arm in a cravat bandage sling.

Fractures of the forearm and wrist are usually less painful than fractures of the arm, shoulder blade, or elbow. The symptoms of a fractured forearm and wrist are as follows:

- Pain
- Tenderness
- Severe deformity, especially if both bones of the forearm are broken

If available, use a plastic inflatable splint to immobilize the forearm or wrist.

Hand and Fingers

Fractures of the hand usually result from a direct blow. The symptoms of a fracture of the hand are as follows:

- Acute pain
- Tenderness
- Swelling
- Discoloration

- Enlarged joints

If available, use a plastic inflatable splint for immobilization.

Use a board splint if a plastic inflatable splint is not available. To immobilize a fractured hand with a board splint, proceed as follows:

♦ Apply a well-padded splint about one-half inch thick, four inches wide, and long enough to reach from the point of the elbow to one inch beyond the end of the middle finger.

♦ Place padding in the palm of the hand and under the wrist.

♦ Carry one end around the little finger side across the back of the hand and wrist and the other end around the thumb side across the back of the hand and wrist.

♦ Cross the ends on the inside of the wrist, bring them to the back of the wrist and tie.

♦ Bring the apex down over the knot and tuck it under.

♦ Place the forearm in a cravat bandage sling.

♦ Apply the splint to the inside of the forearm and hand with one cravat and one triangular bandage.

♦ Place the center of the cravat on the outside of the forearm just below the elbow; pass it around the forearm one or more times; tie it on the outside of the forearm.

♦ Place the base of a triangular bandage under the splint at the wrist; bring the apex around the end of the splint over the hand to a point above the wrist.

♦ Carry one end around the little finger side across the back of the hand and wrist and the other end around the thumb side across the back of the hand and wrist.

♦ Cross the ends on the inside of the wrist, bring them to the back of the wrist and tie.

♦ Bring the apex down over the knot and tuck it under.

♦ Place the forearm in a cravat bandage sling.

Finger

The symptoms of a fracture of the finger is as follows:

- Pain
- Swelling
- Deformity

The first aid for a fractured finger is as follows:

♦ Place a narrow padded splint under the broken finger and palm of the hand.

♦ Pass a narrow strip of cloth around the splint and palm of the hand; tie over the splint.

♦ Pass a narrow strip of cloth around the finger and the splint above the fracture; tie over the splint.

♦ Pass a narrow strip of cloth around the finger and the splint below the fracture; tie over the splint.

♦ Place the hand in a narrow cravat bandage sling.

Rib

Fracture of a rib usually is caused by a direct blow or a severe squeeze. A fracture can occur at any point along the rib. The symptoms of a fractured rib are as follows:

- Severe pain on breathing
- Tenderness over the fracture
- Deformity
- Inability to take a deep breath

Cravat bandages will immobilize fractured ribs. Place the bandages in the following order:

♦ Apply padding over injured ribs.

♦ Apply two medium cravat bandages around the chest firmly enough to afford support, centering the cravats on either side of the pain.

♦ Upon exhalation, tie the knots over a pad on the opposite side of the body. If the cravat bandages cause more pain, loosen them.

♦ Support the arm on the injured side in a sling.

♦ Treat for shock as it is usually severe.

♦ Secure medical treatment.

Wrap the chest gently when the ribs are depressed or frothy blood comes from the victim's mouth. These may be indications of a punctured lung. Place the victim in a semi-prone position (if no neck or spine injury exists) with the injured side down. This will allow more room for expansion of the uninjured lung.

Pelvis or Hip

Fracture of the pelvis or hip usually results from a squeezing type injury through the hips or from a direct blow. Use extreme care when handling an individual with a fracture of the pelvis or hip because there is a possibility of associated internal injuries to the digestive, urinary, or genital organs. The symptoms of a fractured pelvis or hip are as follows:

- Pain in the pelvic region
- Discoloration
- Unable to raise his or her leg
- Inward rotation of foot and leg on affected side

To support the pelvic region before the victim is transported proceed as follows:

- Maintain support of the pelvic region with hands at the sides of the hips until two wide bandages have been applied.
- Place the center of a wide cravat bandage over one hip, the upper edge extending about two inches above the crest of the hip bone.
- Pass the ends around the body and tie over a pad on the opposite hip.
- Place the center of a second wide cravat bandage over the opposite hip, the upper edge extending about two inches above the crest of the hipbone.
- Pass the ends around the body and tie on the first bandage.
- Lift the victim only high enough to place him or her on a firm support, preferably a broken back splint.
- When a broken back splint is used, secure the body to the splint with eight cravat bandages as follows:
- Pass the first cravat bandage around the splint and the upper part of the chest, well up in the armpits and tie on one side near the splint.
- Pass the second cravat bandage around the splint and the lower part of the chest and tie near the splint.
- Pass the third and fourth cravat bandages around the splint and each thigh just below the crotch and tie on the outside near the splint.
- Pass the fifth and sixth cravat bandages around splint and each leg, just below the knee and tie on the outside near the splint.
- Pass the seventh and eighth cravat bandages around the splint and each ankle, and tie on the outside near the splint.
- Cover the victim with a blanket and treat for shock.
- Get the victim to the doctor or hospital.

Thigh or Knee

If a fracture of the thigh or knee is open, dress the wound. If the fracture is at the knee joint and the limb is not in a straight position, make no attempt to straighten the limb. Splint in line of deformity. Attempts to straighten the limb may increase the possibility of permanent damage. Improvise a way to immobilize the knee as it is found, using padding to fill any space. Use the utility splint stretcher or a similar support to immobilize fractures of the knee or thigh. Before placing the victim on the stretcher, it should be well padded and tested. Additional padding will also be necessary for the natural arches of the body. Raise the victim carefully for placement on the stretcher while the fracture is supported from the underside on both sides of the break.

Apply the splint with bandages. All bandages should be tied on the injured side near the splint.

- Tie the first bandage around the body and splint under the armpits.
- Tie the second around the chest and splint and the third around the hips and splint.
- Tie the fourth and fifth bandages on the injured leg just below the crotch at the thigh and above the knee, respectively, (above and below fracture) and tie on the injured side near the splint.
- Tie the sixth and seventh bandages on the injured leg below the knee and at the ankle.

- ♦ An additional bandage at the ankle on the uninjured side may be needed for additional support.
- ♦ The victim should be transported on a regular stretcher or stretcher board.

When using a stretcher board, it should be well padded and the bandages applied in normal order. On some types of stretcher boards it may be necessary to tie both lower limbs together with each of the last four cravat bandages. To prevent movement of the legs, pad well between the legs before applying the cravats.

Any improvised splint for the thigh or knee should be long enough to immobilize the hip and the ankle.

Kneecap

A splint suitable for a broken back may also be used for a fracture of the kneecap. Dress any open wound first. The splint should be well padded with additional padding under all natural body arches. Support the fracture from the top and on both sides and carefully raise the victim to place the prepared and tested splint underneath.

Apply the splint with seven cravat bandages. Tie all bandages on the injured side near the splint, except the fifth and sixth bandages which tie on top.

- ♦ Tie three bandages around the body and the splint; one just below the armpits, one around the chest, and one around the hips.
- ♦ Tie the fourth bandage around the thigh and splint just below the crotch.
- ♦ Place the center of the fifth bandage just above the kneecap, bring the ends under the thigh and splint, and bring ends over the leg above the kneecap, but do not tie.
- ♦ Place the center of the sixth bandage just below the kneecap, bring the ends under the leg and splint up over the thigh and tie above the knee over the fifth bandage.
- ♦ Pull the ends of the fifth bandage tight and tie below the knee over the sixth bandage.
- ♦ The seventh bandage is tied around the ankle and splint.
- ♦ An additional bandage at the ankle and thigh on the uninjured side may be needed for additional support.

Transport the victim on a regular stretcher. Any stretcher board used for this type of injury should be the type of board which is prepared for individual bandaging of each lower extremity. Otherwise, the bandages would be applied as for fracture of thigh or knee. Any improvised splint for the kneecap should be long enough to immobilize the hip and the ankle.

Leg or Ankle

If the fracture is open, dress the wound before splinting. When it is necessary to remove a shoe or boot because of pain from swelling of the ankle or for any other reason, the removal must be carefully done by unlacing or cutting the boot to prevent damage to the ankle. In the absence of severe swelling or bleeding it may be wise to leave the boot on for additional support.

The splint for a fracture of the leg or ankle should reach from against the buttocks to beyond the heel. Place a well-padded splint under the victim while the leg is supported on both sides of the fracture. Tie the bandages on the outer side, near the splint as follows:

- ♦ Pass the end of the first bandage around the inner side of the thigh at the groin, pass it over the thigh under the splint, and tie.
- ♦ Pass two bandages around the thigh and splint, one at the middle of the thigh and the other just above the knee and tie.
- ♦ Place additional padding around the knee and ankle.
- ♦ Place a padded splint on the outer side of the leg.
- ♦ Pass a fourth bandage around the leg, the padding, and the splint just below the knee and tie; pass a fifth bandage just above or below the fracture and tie. **Do not** tie over fracture.
- ♦ Pass the center of a sixth bandage around the instep and bring the ends up each side of the ankle.
- ♦ Cross the ends on top and pass them around the ankle and splint.
- ♦ Cross the ends under the splint, return to the top of the ankle, cross and carry down each side of the ankle and tie under the instep.

When using an inflatable plastic splint, roll up or cut away the clothing from the limb to a point above the upper end of the splint. The splint should be long enough to immobilize the knee as well as the ankle (Figure 8-32). Cover open wounds with gauze, but they need not be bandaged because the splint will form an airtight cover for such wounds. After the splint is applied, pressure from the inflated splint will help control any bleeding that may develop. Apply the splint while supporting the fracture on both sides. Close and inflate the splint.

Ankle or Foot

To make an improvised splint for the ankle or foot, proceed as follows:

- ♦ Carefully fold a blanket or pillow around the ankle and foot.
- ♦ Tie the first bandage around the leg above the ankle.
- ♦ Tie the second bandage around the ankle.
- ♦ Tie the third bandage below the ankle.
- ♦ Place padding between the ankles and extend the padding above the knees.
- ♦ Place the fourth bandage around knees and tie.
- ♦ Place the fifth bandage below knees and tie.
- ♦ Place the sixth bandage around ankles and tie.

Crushed Bones of Foot or Toes

When caring for a fracture of the foot or toes, leave a boot or shoe in place if possible and support the injured foot. Use extreme care if it is necessary to remove any type of footwear. If a damaged protective cap of a safety boot has become embedded in the foot, do not remove the boot.

It should be noted that it may be impossible to use an inflatable splint with the shoe on. If footwear is removed, carefully dress any open wounds before applying a splint.

Immobilize a fracture of the foot or toes as follows:

- ♦ Place a well-padded splint, about four inches wide and long enough to extend from one-half inch beyond the heel to one-half inch beyond the big toe, on the bottom of the foot.
- ♦ Start the center of a cravat bandage around the ankle from the back just above the heel. Cross over the arch and carry under the foot and splint. Cross under the splint and bring the ends to the back of the heel. Cross at the back of the heel, carry the ends around the ankle and tie in front.
- ♦ Start the center of a second bandage on top of the toes, carry the ends around the foot and splint several times, then tie on top of the foot.

An air splint specifically made for the foot and ankle or an improvised splint made from a blanket or pillow as in caring for a fractured ankle may be used.

DISLOCATIONS

Where two or more bones come together they form a joint. The bones forming a joint are held in place by bands of strong, fibrous tissue known as ligaments. There are three varieties of joints: immovable joints, joints with limited motion, and freely movable joints. The first aider is concerned particularly with the freely movable joints—the lower jaw, the shoulders, the elbows, the wrists, the fingers, the hips, the knees, the ankles, and the toes. These are the joints most commonly dislocated.

A dislocation is when one or more of the bones forming a joint slip out of normal position. The ligaments holding the bones in proper position are stretched and sometimes torn loose. Fractures are often associated with dislocations.

Dislocations may result from the following:

- Force applied at or near the joint
- Sudden muscular contractions
- Twisting strains on joint ligaments
- Falls where the force of landing is transferred to a joint

Some general symptoms of dislocations are as follows:

- Rigidity and loss of function
- Deformity
- Pain
- Swelling
- Tenderness

- Discoloration

General First Aid for Dislocations

A first aider does not have the skill necessary to reduce dislocations. Inexperience in manipulating the joints can further damage the ligaments, blood vessels and nerves found close to joints. With one exception (the lower jaw) only a physician should reduce a dislocation. The victim experiences pain which justifies one reduction attempt.

Splint and/or dress the affected joint in line of deformity in which you find it. Obtain medical help.

Lower Jaw

The symptoms of a dislocated lower jaw are as follows:

- Pain
- Open mouth
- Rigid jaw
- Difficulty in speaking

If medical aid is not available for some time, reduce the dislocation as follows:

- ◆ Place thumbs in the victim's mouth, resting them well back on each side of the lower teeth.
- ◆ Seize the outside of the lower jaw with the fingers. Press first downward and forward.
- ◆ When the jaw starts into place, slip the thumbs off the teeth to the inside of the cheeks.
- ◆ Remove thumbs from mouth.
- ◆ Place the center of a cravat bandage over the front of the chin.
- ◆ Carry the ends to the back of the head and tie.
- ◆ Center another bandage under the victim's chin, bring the ends to the top of the head and tie.
- ◆ Bring the ends of both bandages together and tie them separately.

NOTE: If the reduction attempt is not successful, do not make repeated attempts to reduce the dislocation and do not apply a dressing. Secure medical treatment.

Shoulder

The shoulder joint usually is dislocated by falls or blows directly on the shoulder or by falls on the hand or elbow. The symptoms of a dislocated shoulder are as follows:

- The elbow stands off one or two inches from the body.
- The arm is held rigid.
- The shoulder appears flat.
- A marked depression is evident beneath the point of the shoulder.
- Pain and swelling are present at the site of the injury.
- The victim cannot bring the elbow in contact with the side.

While the arm is being supported in the position in which it was found, immobilize the shoulder in the following manner:

- ◆ Place the point of a wedge-shaped pad (approximately four inches wide and one to three inches thick) between the arm and the body.
- ◆ Tape or tie the pad in place.
- ◆ Place the center of a medium width cravat on the outside of the arm just above the elbow.
- ◆ Carry one end across the chest and the other end across the back.
- ◆ Tie on the opposite side over a pad.
- ◆ Place the arm in a triangular bandage sling.

Elbow

Dislocation occurs at the elbow joint as a result of a blow at the joint or occasionally by a fall on the hand. It usually can be recognized by these symptoms:

- Deformity at the joint
- Inability to bend the limb at the joint
- Great pain

The elbow must be immobilized in the line the deformity is found. While the elbow is being supported, proceed as follows:

♦ Prepare and pad a splint, straight, L-shaped, or a modification of the latter depending on the position of the arm, long enough to reach from one inch below the armpit to one inch beyond the tip of the middle finger.

♦ Pad splint to conform to the deformity, and place on the inside of the arm.

♦ Place the center of the first cravat bandage on the outside of the arm at the upper end of the splint, cross on the inside of the arm over the splint, pass the ends one or more times around the arm and splint, and tie on the outside.

♦ Place the center of the second cravat bandage on the arm just above the elbow and apply in a similar manner.

♦ Place the center of the third cravat bandage on the forearm just below the elbow, and apply in a similar manner.

♦ Place the center of the fourth cravat bandage on the back of the wrist, passing the ends around and crossing on the splint under the wrist, bring one end up around the little finger side, and cross over the back of the hand and down between the forefinger and thumb. Pass the other end up over the thumb, cross it over the back of the hand down around the little finger side, then cross both ends on the splint and tie on the top of the hand.

♦ Bind the limb to the body or place the forearm in a cravat bandage sling (depending on the position of the arm).

Wrist

Dislocation of the wrist usually occurs when the hand is extended to break the force of a fall. It is difficult, however, to distinguish between a dislocation and a fractured wrist. Treat a suspected dislocated wrist the same as a fractured wrist.

Finger

The usual symptoms of a dislocated finger are as follows:

• Inability to bend at dislocation
• Deformity of the joint
• Shortening of the digit
• Pain and swelling

Do not attempt to reduce the dislocation. immobilize the digit by using small pads as for any deformity and splinting, or by tying the injured member to the one next to it. Obtain medical treatment.

Hip

Dislocation of the hip usually results from falling onto the foot or knee. It may also be caused by a direct blow when the thigh is at an angle with the spine. While supporting the dislocation in the line of deformity, carefully raise the victim only high enough to be placed on a well-padded and tested splint or stretcher board suitable for a broken back. Support is necessary until the splint or stretcher board is applied.

The symptoms of a dislocated hip are as follows:

• Intense pain
• Lengthening or shortening of the leg, with the foot turned in or out
• Pain and swelling at the joint

The first aid for a dislocated hip is:

♦ Make a pad of clothing, blankets, or other material large enough to support the limb in the line of deformity. (The affected leg will be turned either inward or outward.)

♦ Place a small pad between the feet.

♦ Pass the first cravat bandage around the splint, the upper part of the chest, and tie the ends of the bandage on the injured side near the splint.

♦ Pass the second cravat bandage around the splint and lower part of the chest and tie the ends of the bandage on the injured side near the splint.

♦ Pass the third cravat bandage around the splint and the body at the hips, and tie on the injured side near the splint.

♦ Pass the fourth cravat bandage around the splint and the thigh just above the knee, and tie on the injured side near the splint.

♦ Pass the fifth cravat bandage around the splint and the ankles, and tie on the injured side near the splint.
♦ Pass the sixth cravat bandage over the insteps, cross the ends under the soles of the feet, and bring them back to the insteps, tying loosely.
♦ If the victim is unconscious, the forearms should be placed in a basket sling.

Knee

Dislocation of the knee results from direct force applied at the knee or from a fall on the knee. The symptoms of the dislocation are as follows:
• Deformity
• Inability to use the knee Great pain
While supporting the dislocation, apply a splint as for fracture of the thigh, using either a broken back splint or a stretcher board. Place extra padding of blankets, clothes, or similar material to conform to the deformity.

Ankle

Dislocation of the ankle may show several types of deformity. Bones are almost always broken. There is a marked deformity at the joint. As a rule, there is rapid and marked swelling and great pain. While supporting the dislocation, apply an improvised splint as for a fracture of the ankle or foot, and add padding to conform to the deformity. Use an air splint long enough to immobilize the knee or use a blanket or pillow to splint the leg or ankle. Use additional cravats for anchoring to broken back splint.

Toe

The symptoms of a dislocated toe are as follows:
• Inability to bend at dislocation
• Deformity of the joint
• Shortening of the digit
• Pain and swelling
Do not attempt to reduce the dislocation. Immobilize the digit by using small pads as for any deformity and splinting it by tying the injured member to the one next to it.

Transporting the Injured

After receiving first aid, an injured person often requires transportation to a medical facility. Under special circumstances like those in mining accidents, the victim needs to be transported to a place accessible to ambulance personnel. The first aider is responsible for seeing that the victim is transported in such a manner as to prevent further injury and is not subjected to additional pain or discomfort. Improper handling and careless transportation often add to the original injuries, increase chance of shock, and endanger life.

Under normal circumstances, **do not** move a victim until a thorough examination has been made and first aid has been given. Move a seriously injured person in a position that is least likely to aggravate injuries. Various methods for carrying a victim can be used in emergencies, but the stretcher is the preferred method of transportation. Use other means of transportation when a stretcher is unavailable or impractical.

TWO-PERSON SEAT CARRY

The two-person seat carry is a technique for transporting a victim in a seat fashioned from the rescuers' arms. It provides for speedy removal and can be used when the victim must be moved through narrow passageways. **Do not** use this technique when there is indication of damage to the spinal column or any injury that could be aggravated by such handling of the victim.

THREE-PERSON CARRY

Use the three-person lift and carry to move an injured person a short distance, through narrow passageways, or when a stretcher is not available. Also use this lift when an injured person is being placed on or removed from a stretcher.

This lift requires three persons, and a fourth is desirable. Lifting must be done on command of one person.

To perform the three-person lift and carry, proceed as follows:

- Three rescuers kneel beside the victim on the least injured side, if possible.
- One bearer, opposite the victim's shoulders, supports the victim's neck and shoulders.
- One bearer, opposite the victim's hips, supports the victim's thighs and small of the back.
- The other bearer, opposite the victim's knees, supports the victim's knees and ankles.
- On command, the bearers slowly lift, keeping the victim's body level, until they can come to rest on the knee nearest the victim's feet.
- On command, the bearers slowly raise the victim on his or her side so that the victim rests in the bend of their elbows and is held closely to their chests.
- When the command is given, all bearers rise in unison.
- The bearers can then, when commanded, move the victim.

FOUR-PERSON LOG ROLL

This technique for moving a person with spinal injuries requires four persons, one who acts as captain. To perform the four-person log roll, proceed as follows:

- The rescuer who is acting as captain applies stabilization to the neck and head as he or she opens the airway using the modified jaw-thrust maneuver.
- Place a stretcher board parallel to the victim.
- Three rescuers (one at the shoulders, one at the waist, and one at the knees) kneel at the victim's side opposite the board, leaving room to roll the victim towards them while one rescuer maintains stabilization of the neck and head.
- The shoulder level rescuer extends the victim's arm over the head on the side to which the victim will be rolled (the side toward the rescuers).
- The shoulder level rescuer then reaches across the victim and places one hand under victim's shoulder and the other hand under victim's upper arm.
- The waist level rescuer reaches across and places one hand on the victim's waist and the other hand under victim's buttocks.
- The knee level rescuer reaches across and places one hand under the victim's knees and the other hand under the mid calf.
- Command is given to roll victim as a unit onto his or her side.
- Command is given for waist level rescuer or bystander to pull spine board into position against victim.
- Command is given to roll victim in unison onto the stretcher board.
- Place rolled blankets beside head and neck for additional protection and secure head to board with cravat bandages.
- Secure the victim to the splint or stretcher so that the entire body is immobilized.

STRADDLE SLIDE

Another technique for moving a person with a spinal injury onto a long board is the straddle slide. Three persons handle the victim and the fourth person slides the board into place. To perform the straddle slide move, proceed as follows:

- One rescuer, standing at the head of the victim, bending at the waist, maintains an open airway with the modified jaw-thrust and applies stabilization to the neck and head.
- The second rescuer straddles the victim, facing toward the head. Bending at the waist, the rescuer grips the victim's arms just below the shoulders.
- A third rescuer also faces and straddles the victim. Bending at the waist, the rescuer places his or her hands on the sides of the victim's waist. (The legs of

the three rescuers must be spread sufficiently to allow the passage of the long board between them.)
♦ A fourth rescuer positions the board at the victim's head in line with his or her body.
♦ On a signal from the commanding rescuer, the rescuers lift the victim just high enough to allow the fourth rescuer to slide the board under victim.
♦ On command, the rescuers gently lower the victim onto the board. Support must be maintained until victim is secured.

STRETCHERS

Test any stretcher to determine serviceability immediately before placing an injured person on it. Place an uninjured person, weighing as much or more than the victim, face down on the stretcher. Lift the stretcher waist high and lower it to the ground. Pad stretcher with a blanket or similar material after it has been tested. Due to possible deterioration of canvas stretchers, take extra precautionary measures when testing the stretcher.

Canvas Stretcher

The canvas stretcher consists of canvas stretched between two poles. The poles are long enough to afford handholds for the bearers at each end.

Basket Stretcher

Various types of basket stretchers are also used to transport the injured. After the victim has been secured by means of straps and foot braces, the basket may be transported even in a vertical position.

Stretcher Board or Spine Board

A stretcher board or spine board is made from a wide board approximately one and one-half inches thick, or from laminated plywood about three-quarter inch thick. The length is usually about seventy-eight inches and the width eighteen inches. Slots about one inch wide are placed along the edges. Pass cravat bandages through these slots to secure the victim to the board. The slots also serve as handholds. Some variations have additional slots in the center of the boards so that each leg may be secured separately to the board. The aluminum stretcher is similar to the wooden board except that it folds in half.

Scoop Stretcher

The scoop stretcher is another means for lifting and transporting a victim. Because of its two piece construction, its prime advantage is a minimum of body movement in placing the victim on the stretcher. Both sides of the victim must be accessible to use this type of stretcher. Slide the frame halves under the victim from either side. Prevent pinching the victim or catching the clothing between the stretcher halves by lifting the victim by the clothes as the stretcher is being closed. In cases of spinal injury, pelvis, hip, or thigh fractures, use a spine board or broken-back splint.

Improvised Stretchers

A satisfactory stretcher may be improvised with a blanket, canvas, or a strong sheet, and two poles or pieces of pipe, seven to eight feet long. To construct an improvised stretcher using two poles and a blanket, proceed as follows:
♦ Place one pole about one foot from the center of the unfolded blanket.
♦ Fold the short side of the blanket over the pole.
♦ Place the second pole on the two thicknesses of the blanket about two feet from the first pole and parallel to it.
♦ Fold the remaining side of the blanket over the second pole. When the victim is placed on the blanket, the weight of the body secures the folds.
Use cloth bags or sacks for stretcher beds. Make holes in the bottoms of the bags or sacks, and pass the poles through them. Use enough bags or sacks to give the required length of the bed. Also make a stretcher from three or four coats or jackets. Turn the sleeves inside out with the jacket fastened and the sleeves inside the coat. Place a pole through each sleeve.

STRETCHER TRANSPORTATION

When transporting a victim on a canvas stretcher, take care to see that the crosspieces are locked in place.

When lifting a victim for stretcher transportation it is preferable to have four or more persons to lift. If only four persons are available and a spinal injury is not suspected, the following method is recommended:

- ♦ Each of the four bearers rests on the knee nearest the victim's feet. Three of the bearers position themselves on the victim's least injured side, at the victim's knees, at the hips, and at the shoulders. The fourth bearer is positioned at the victim's hips on the opposite side from the others.
- ♦ The hands of the bearer at the shoulders are placed under the victim's neck and shoulders.
- ♦ The hands of the bearer at the knees are placed under victim's knees and ankles.
- ♦ The other two bearers, across from each other, place their hands under the victim's pelvis and the small of the back.
- ♦ The four bearers slowly lift the victim, keeping the body level.
- ♦ The victim is rested on the knees of the three bearers on the same side.
- ♦ The fourth bearer places the stretcher under the victim.
- ♦ The bearer who has placed the stretcher assumes his or her original position.
- ♦ The victim is gently lowered to the stretcher and covered with a blanket.
- ♦ The bearers position themselves, one at each end and one at each side of the stretcher, facing the victim.
- ♦ All bearers grasp and lift the stretcher.
- ♦ The two bearers in the center shift one hand toward the victim's feet and support this end, while the bearer at the victim's feet turns around to a marching position.
- ♦ The victim is usually transported feet first so that the bearer at the victim's head can constantly monitor the victim's condition.

Environmental Emergencies

HYPOTHERMIA

Hypothermia is a general cooling of the entire body. The inner core of the body is chilled so the body cannot generate heat to stay warm. This condition can be produced by exposure to low temperatures or to temperatures between thirty and fifty degrees Fahrenheit with wind and rain. Also contributing to hypothermia are fatigue, hunger, and poor physical condition.

Exposure begins when the body loses heat faster than it can be produced. When the body is chilled, it passes through several stages:

- The initial response of a victim exposed to cold is to build a fire and to voluntarily exercise in order to stay warm. The fire can also signal rescuers if the victim is lost.
- As the body tissues are cooled, the victim begins to shiver as a result of an involuntary adjustment by the body to preserve normal temperature in the vital organs. These responses drain the body's energy reserves.
- Cold reaches the brain and deprives the victim of judgment and reasoning powers.
- The victim experiences feelings of apathy, listlessness, indifference, and sleepiness.
- The victim does not realize what is happening.
- The victim looses muscle coordination.

- Cooling becomes more rapid as the internal body temperature is lowered. Eventually hypothermia will result in a coma. The victim will have a very slow pulse and very slow respiration. If cooling continues the victim will die.
- The victim of hypothermia may not recognize the symptoms and deny that medical attention is needed; therefore, it is important to judge the symptoms rather than what the victim says. Even mild symptoms of hypothermia need immediate medical care.

First aid for a victim of hypothermia is as follows:

- ♦ Get the victim out of the elements (wind, rain, snow, cold, etc.)
- ♦ Remove all wet clothing.
- ♦ Wrap the victim in blankets. Be certain the blankets are under, as well as over, the victim. Maintain the victim's body heat by building a fire or placing heat packs, electric heating pads, hot water bottles, or even another rescuer in the blankets with the victim. (**Do not warm the victim too quickly.**)
- ♦ If the victim is conscious, give warm liquids to drink. If the victim is conscious, try to keep the victim awake.
- ♦ CPR is indicated if the victim stops breathing and the heart stops beating.
- ♦ Get the victim to a medical facility as soon as possible.
- ♦ Remember to handle the victim gently. In extreme cases rough handling may result in death.

FROSTBITE

Frostbite results from exposure to severe cold. It is more likely to occur when the wind is blowing, rapidly taking heat from the body. The nose, cheeks, ears, toes, and fingers are the body parts most frequently frostbitten. As a result of exposure to cold, the blood vessels constrict. Thus the blood supply to the chilled parts decreases and the tissues do not get the warmth they need.

The signs and symptoms of frostbite are not always apparent to the victim. Since frostbite has a numbing effect, the victim may not be aware of it until told by someone else.

Frostbite goes through the following stages:

Frostnip

- The affected area will feel numb to the victim.
- The skin becomes red, then white during frostnip.

Treatment for frostnip is as follows:

- ♦ Place hand over frost nipped part.
- ♦ Place frost nipped fingers in armpit.

Superficial Frostbite

- As exposure continues the skin becomes white and waxy.
- The skin is firm to touch, but underlying tissues are soft.
- The exposed surface becomes numb.

The treatment for superficial frostbite is as follows:

- ♦ Remove the victim from the environment.
- ♦ Apply a steady source of external warmth.
- ♦ **DO NOT RUB AREA.**
- ♦ Cover the area with a dry, sterile dressing (when dressing foot or hand, pad between toes and fingers).
- ♦ Splint if dealing with an extremity.
- ♦ Transport to the hospital.

As area thaws, it may become a mottled blue and blisters will develop.

Deep Frostbite

- If freezing is allowed to continue, all sensation is lost, and the skin becomes a "dead" white, yellow-white, or mottled blue-white.
- The skin is firm to touch as are the underlying tissues.

Treatment for deep frostbite is as follows:

- ♦ Leave it frozen until victim reaches hospital.
- ♦ Dress, pad, and splint frostbitten extremities. (When dressing injury, pad between fingers and toes.)

♦ Transport the victim to a hospital.
♦ If there is a delay in transport, rewarming may be done at the site. Place the affected part in water bath of 100 to 105 degrees. Apply warm cloths to areas that cannot be submerged. An extreme amount of pain is associated with rewarming.
♦ Rewarming is complete when the area is warm and red or blue in color and remains so after removal from the bath. **DO NOT REWARM IF THERE IS A POSSIBILITY OF REFREEZING.**

General Rules for Treating Frostbite

♦ Apply loose, soft, sterile dressings to affected area. Splint and elevate the extremity.
♦ Give the victim warm fluids containing sugar to drink if he or she does not have an altered level of consciousness.
♦ **DO NOT RUB, CHAFE, OR MANIPULATE FROSTBITTEN PARTS.**
♦ **DO NOT USE HOT WATER BOTTLES OR HEAT LAMPS.**
♦ **DO NOT PLACE THE VICTIM NEAR A STOVE OR FIRE, BECAUSE EXCESSIVE HEAT CAN CAUSE FURTHER TISSUE DAMAGE.**
♦ **DO NOT ALLOW THE VICTIM TO SMOKE, BECAUSE NICOTINE CONSTRICTS THE BLOOD VESSELS.**
♦ **DO NOT ALLOW THE VICTIM TO DRINK COFFEE, TEA, OR HOT CHOCOLATE BECAUSE THESE SUBSTANCES WILL CAUSE THE BLOOD VESSELS TO CONSTRICT.**
♦ **DO NOT ALLOW VICTIM TO WALK IF THE FEET ARE FROSTBITTEN.**

HEAT STROKE

Heat stroke is a sudden onset of illness from exposure to the direct rays of the sun or too high temperature without exposure to the sun. Physical exertion and high humidity definitely contribute to the incidence of heat stroke.

The most important characteristic of heat stroke is the high body temperature which is caused by a disturbance in the heat-regulating mechanism of the body. The person can no longer sweat, and this causes a rise in body temperature.

This illness is more common in the elderly. Alcoholics, obese persons, and those on medication are also very susceptible to heat stroke.

The signs and symptoms of heat stroke are as follows:

• The skin is flushed, very hot, and very dry. (Perspiration is usually absent.)
• The pulse is usually strong and rapid, but may become weak and rapid as the victim's condition worsens.
• The respiration is rapid and deep, followed by shallow breathing.
• The body temperature can reach 108 degrees.
• The victim rapidly loses consciousness and may experience convulsions.

Care should be centered around lowering the body temperature as quickly as possible. Failure to do this will result in permanent brain damage or death.

The care for heat stroke is as follows:

♦ Maintain an open airway.
♦ Move the victim to a cool environment. Remove all clothing.
♦ Wrap the victim in a cool, moist sheet and use a fan to cool the victim.
♦ Immerse the victim in cool water if the above treatment is not feasible.
♦ Use cool applications if neither of above treatments are feasible.
♦ Transport the victim to the hospital as rapidly as possible, continuing cooling enroute.

HEAT EXHAUSTION

Heat exhaustion occurs in individuals working in hot environments. It is brought about by the loss of water and salt through sweating. This loss of fluid will cause mild shock.

This illness occurs most commonly to persons not accustomed to hot weather, those who are overweight, and those who perspire excessively. The signs and symptoms of heat exhaustion are as follows:

• The skin is pale and clammy.

- The skin shows evidence of profuse perspiration.
- Breathing is rapid and shallow.
- The pulse is rapid and weak.
- The victim may complain of nausea, weakness, dizziness, and/or headache.

The first aid for heat exhaustion is as follows:

- Move the victim to a cool and comfortable place, but **do not** allow chilling.
- Try to cool the victim by fanning or wiping the face with a cool, wet cloth.
- Loosen the victim's clothing.
- If fainting seems likely, have the victim lie down with feet elevated eight to twelve inches.
- Treat the victim for shock.

HEAT CRAMPS

Heat cramps affect people who work in a hot environment and perspire. The perspiration causes a loss of salt from the body and if there is inadequate replacement, the body will then suffer from cramps.

Signs and symptoms of heat cramps are as follows:

- The presence of profuse perspiration is evident.
- The victim complains of muscle cramps, painful spasms in the legs or abdomen.
- The victim may feel faint.

First aid for heat cramps is as follows:

- Move the victim to a cool environment.
- If the victim is conscious, give sips of cool salt and sugar water (one teaspoon of salt plus as much sugar as the person can stand, per quart of water) or a commercial electrolyte solution.

Medical Emergencies

DIABETIC EMERGENCIES

Body and brain cells need many different types of nourishment, one of which is sugar. The circulatory system carries sugar and transfers it to the cells with the aid of a chemical substance called insulin. The pancreas, located in the abdominal cavity, manufactures insulin. When the insulin production and sugar are in balance, the body functions normally. An individual suffering from an imbalance in the production of insulin is said to have diabetes mellitus. As a result of this imbalance, the body is adversely affected. However, a great many diabetics lead healthy, normal lives through a program of balanced diet and medication. When the diabetic's condition is not controlled, certain disorders may occur. The major adverse reactions to insulin imbalance are diabetic coma and insulin shock.

Diabetic Coma

Diabetic coma is a result of an inadequate insulin supply. This imbalance is generally due to a diabetic not taking the proper medication; a diabetic ingesting more sugar than the insulin can accommodate; a person contracting an infection which affects insulin production; or a person vomiting or sustaining fluid loss.

The signs and symptoms of someone progressing into diabetic coma are as follows:

- Warm and dry skin
- Sunken eyes
- Rapid and labored breathing
- Rapid and weak pulse
- Excessive urination
- Extreme thirst

- Nausea and vomiting
- Abdominal pain
- Sickly sweet odor of acetone (similar to nail polish remover or spoiled fruit) on the breath
- A state of confusion and disorientation that is similar to drunkenness
- Eventually a coma state, thus the term diabetic coma

The first aid for the victim progressing into a diabetic coma is as follows:

- ♦ Watch for vomiting.
- ♦ Maintain an open airway.
- ♦ Treat the victim for shock.
- ♦ Transport the victim to a medical facility as quickly as possible.

Insulin Shock

Insulin shock results when there is a shortage of sugar relative to the amount of insulin in the body. The prime reasons for the condition are that the victim has not eaten, so that not enough sugar has been taken in; the victim has taken too much insulin; or the victim has over exercised, thus burning sugar too fast.

The signs and symptoms of insulin shock are as follows:

- The victim experiences a personality change in the early stages. Victims may become confused or combative.
- Headache
- Profuse perspiration
- Rapid, weak pulse
- Dizziness
- Cold, clammy skin
- Eventually convulsions and unconsciousness
- Normal or shallow respiration

The first aid for insulin shock is as follows:

- ♦ If the victim is conscious, sugar can be administered in the form of orange juice, a candy bar, soft drinks, or several packets of sugar mixed with orange juice. Don't worry about the amount of sugar given to the victim, as the doctor will balance the need for sugar against insulin production when the victim arrives at the hospital.
- ♦ If the victim is unconscious, a sprinkle of granulated sugar can be placed under the tongue.
- ♦ The victim should be transported to a medical facility for continuing care as quickly as possible.

If you cannot distinguish between a victim with insulin shock and a victim progressing into diabetic coma, give sugar to the victim. Giving sugar to a victim with too much blood sugar doesn't make any significant difference to victim outcome, but giving sugar to a victim in insulin shock can save a life.

EPILEPTIC SEIZURES

Epilepsy is a neurological disorder, usually of known origin, resulting in recurring seizures. Grand mal and petit mal are the types of seizures which may occur. Of these two, grand mal is more severe.

The petit mal attack is characterized by the following:

- Only partial loss of consciousness, if any, occurs.
- The victim remains aware of what is going on nearby.
- The victim may experience minor convulsive movements of the eyes or extremities.

The signs and symptoms of a grand mal seizure are as follows:

- The victim may have a premonition or aura before the attack occurs.
- Loss of consciousness occurs.
- The victim's body becomes rigid, and then convulsions occur.
- During the seizure, the victim may lose bowel and bladder control.
- The face is usually pale before the seizure and becomes cyanotic (bluish) during the seizure.
- Severe spasms of the jaw muscles sometimes occur, causing the tongue to be bitten.

- Breathing may be loud and labored with a peculiar hissing sound or it may stop altogether during the seizure.
- The victim may froth at the mouth.

The seizure only lasts for a few minutes. The victim usually will be unconscious for a period of time after the seizure. After the seizure the victim will usually be very tired and sleepy.

If the victim does not regain consciousness after the seizure and begins to experience more convulsions, the patient is in a more critical situation.

The following first aid for a victim of an epileptic seizure should be given as necessary:

- The victim should be kept calm. **Do not** restrain the victim.
- Protect the victim from injury by moving objects that could cause harm.
- **Do not** place anything in the victim's mouth during the seizure.

When the seizure is over, do the following:

- Maintain an open airway.
- Allow the victim to rest.
- Protect the victim from stress or embarrassment.

STROKE

A stroke occurs when the blood supply carrying oxygen to the brain is cut off due to a blockage or rupture of a blood vessel. The effects of a stroke on the brain can be temporary or permanent, and range from slight to severe.

Cerebral thrombosis is a blockage of the cerebral artery by a clot which forms inside the artery.

Cerebral hemorrhage occurs when a diseased artery in the brain ruptures and floods the surrounding tissue with blood.

Cerebral embolism occurs when a wandering blood clot (embolus) carried in the blood stream becomes lodged in one of the cerebral blood vessels.

The signs and symptoms of a stroke are as follows:

- The victim may have a decreased level of consciousness or be totally unconscious.
- Respiration is usually slow with a snoring sound caused by the tongue falling back into the airway.
- Pupils are unequal in size.
- Paralysis or weakness on one side of the body or face is present.
- The victim loses the ability to speak, or the victim's speech is slurred.

The first aid for a stroke victim is as follows:

- Maintain an open airway.
- Keep the tongue or saliva from blocking the air passage.
- **Do not** give the victim anything by mouth.
- Keep the victim lying down with the head and shoulders raised to alleviate some of the pressure on the brain. If the victim is unconscious, place the victim on the affected side to allow fluids to drain.
- **Do not** move the victim any more than necessary.
- Keep the victim quiet and calm.
- Reassure the victim, who may be quite anxious or nervous.
- Obtain medical care as soon as possible.

DRUG ABUSE

Drugs may be classified as uppers, downers, narcotics, mind-affecting (hallucinogens), or volatile chemicals.

Uppers are stimulants that affect the nervous system to excite the user.

Downers are depressants that affect the central nervous system and relax the user.

Narcotics affect the nervous system and change many of the normal activities of the body and often produces an intense state of excitement or distortion of the user's senses.

Volatile chemicals are depressants acting upon the central nervous system.

It is important for the first aider to be able to detect possible drug abuse at the overdose level and to relate certain signs to certain types of drugs. You will use basically the same care for all drug abuse victims and that care will not change unless you are ordered to do something by a poison control center.

Signs of Drug Abuse

Drug abuse and drug overdose signs and symptoms can vary from one victim to another, even for the same drug. The scene, bystanders, and the victim may be your only sources for finding out if you are dealing with drug abuse and the substance involved. When questioning the victim and bystanders, ask if the victim has been taking any medications rather than using the word *drugs*.

The following significant signs and symptoms are related to specific drugs:

- **Uppers:** Excitement, increased pulse and breathing rates, rapid speech, dry mouth, dilated pupils, sweating, and the complaint of having gone without sleep for long periods.
- **Downers:** Sluggish, sleepy victim lacking typical coordination of body movements and speaking with slurred speech. Pulse and breathing rates are low, often to the point of a true emergency.
- **Mind-affecting drugs;** Fast pulse rate, dilated pupils, and a flushed face. The victim often "sees" things, has little concept of real time, and may not be aware of the true environment. Often, the victim makes no sense when speaking.
- **Narcotics:** Reduced rate of pulse and breathing, often has a lower skin temperature. The pupils are constricted, muscles are relaxed, and sweating is heavy. The victim is very sleepy and may go into a coma.
- **Volatile chemicals:** Dazed or showing temporary loss of contact with reality. The victim may go into a coma. The inside of the nose and mouth may show swollen membranes. The victim may complain of a "funny numb feeling" or "tingling" inside the head.

Some of the above symptoms are similar to other medical emergencies previously discussed.

Care for Drug Abuse Victims

When providing care for drug abuse victims, you should:

- Summon help so that an ambulance or a physician may be called to the scene.
- Monitor breathing and be alert for respiratory arrest.
- Talk to the victim to gain confidence and to maintain the level of consciousness.
- Protect the victim from further harm.
- Treat for shock.
- Continue to reassure the victim throughout all phases of care.

NOTE: You should always be alert and ready to protect yourself since many drug abusers appear calm at first and then become violent as time passes. If the victim creates an unsafe scene and you are not a trained law enforcement officer, GET OUT and find a safe place until the police arrive.

POISONS

Poisons are any substances which act to produce harmful effects on the normal body processes. There are four ways in which these substances may enter the body:

- Ingestion (eating or drinking)
- Inhalation (nose and mouth)
- Injection (body tissues or blood stream)
- Absorption (through the skin)

Poisoning by Ingestion

The chief causes of poisoning by ingestion are as follows:

- Overdose of medication (intentional or accidental). This includes the combining of drugs and alcohol.
- Household cleaners, chemicals and medications left within the reach of children
- Original labels left on containers that are now used to store poisons
- Improperly stored food

The signs and symptoms of poisoning by ingestion are as follows:

- Nausea, vomiting, and diarrhea
- Severe abdominal pains or cramps

- Altered respiration and pulse rates
- Corroded, burned, or destroyed tissues of the mouth
- Unusual odors on the breath
- Stains around the mouth

The following is first aid for poisoning by ingestion:

- Call the poison control center.
- The control center may indicate to dilute the substance by giving the victim milk or water or induce vomiting so that the substance is removed from the stomach. Vomiting will prevent absorption into the circulation system.
- Vomiting should **NOT** be induced in the following cases:
    - If the victim has swallowed a strong acid or alkali which would cause further damage when vomited.
    - If a petroleum product has been swallowed, because it can be easily inhaled into the lungs and cause pneumonia
    - If the victim is unconscious or semiconscious because the victim may inhale the vomit into the lungs
    - If the victim is convulsing
    - If the victim has a serious heart problem

Check with the poison control center to determine the best method to induce vomiting. The victim should be sitting and leaning forward to prevent vomit from going into the lungs. Collect the vomit and take it to the hospital with the victim, along with the poison's container.

Poisoning by Inhalation

Certain toxic or noxious gases may stop respiration by a direct poisoning effect or by preventing the transport of oxygen by the red blood cells. Such gases are encountered in mining, oil drilling, and similar industries. They include sulfur dioxide, the oxides of nitrogen, ammonia, hydrogen sulfide, hydrogen cyanide, and carbon monoxide.

The signs and symptoms of inhaled poisons are as follows:

- Shortness of breath
- Coughing
- Cyanosis (bluish color)
- Cherry red color if dealing with carbon monoxide poisoning

To provide first aid for poisoning by inhalation, proceed as follows:

- Remove the victim to fresh air as quickly as possible. The rescuer should not risk entering a hazardous atmosphere without proper personal protective equipment.
- Maintain an open airway.
- In appropriate cases, initiate artificial ventilation or cardiopulmonary resuscitation.
- Treat the victim for shock.

Carbon Monoxide

Carbon monoxide, a product of incomplete combustion is probably the most common of the poisonous gases. Overexposure can be fatal. Carbon monoxide causes asphyxia because it combines with the hemoglobin of the blood much more readily than oxygen does. The blood, therefore, carries less and less oxygen from the lungs to the body tissues. The first symptoms of asphyxia appear when a thirty percent blood saturation level has been reached.

The signs and symptoms of carbon monoxide poisoning are as follows:

- Headache
- Dizziness
- Yawning
- Fainting
- Weakness
- Bright, cherry red color
- Lips and earlobes may possibly turn bluish in color
- Nausea and vomiting

To provide first aid for carbon monoxide poisoning proceed as for any other inhalation poisoning.

Poisoning by Absorption

Many substances in the form of gases, fumes, mists, liquids, and dusts cause poisoning or irritation of the skin when they come into contact with it. Underlying tissues (hair follicles, oil glands, sweat glands) may also be affected. The normal structure of the skin is changed and irritation and inflammation occur. Usually, inflammation does not progress rapidly, but gradually, after continued exposure to the cause. Persons who note changes in the normal texture of their skin or continued irritation of the skin should seek medical advice before a chronic condition develops. Needless discomfort can be prevented by early medical care.

The first aid for the victim of contact poisoning is as follows:

♦ Remove contaminated clothing.
♦ Flood the contaminated area with plenty of water.
♦ If dealing with a dry poison, brush as much off as possible before washing the area with water.
♦ Watch the person for signs of shock and changes in respiration.

Poisoning by Injection

Poisons can enter the skin by means of injections or bites of animals, poisonous snakes, and insects. Some people may have an allergic reaction to a nonpoisonous insect bite or drug which may result in anaphylactic shock.

First aid is aimed at minimizing the travel of the poison to the heart. General first aid for poisons injected into the skin is as follows:

♦ Keep the person calm, quiet, and at rest.
♦ All jewelry (bracelets, rings, watches, etc.) should be removed from the bitten extremity, in case of swelling.
♦ Apply a constricting bandage above and below the bite at the edge of the swelling, loosely enough to slide a finger under the bandage. The pulse should be checked periodically below the bite; bandages are only to be used as a constriction, not as a tourniquet.
♦ Transport the victim to a medical facility while keeping the victim as calm and as still as possible.

Bites of Animals

Any warm-blooded animal may suffer from rabies. If a person is bitten by an animal, always suspect the animal to be rabid until it is proven otherwise. The saliva from a rabid animal enters the wound caused by the bite, transmitting the disease to the victim. If possible the animal should be captured or identified and held for medical observation.

First aid for animal bites is as follows:

♦ Control bleeding.
♦ Wash the wound with soap and water and rinse with alcohol.
♦ Dress and bandage the wound. Splint if dealing with an extremity.
♦ Take the victim to a medical facility as quickly as possible.

Snakebites

Coral snakes, copperheads, rattlesnakes, and water moccasins are the four types of poisonous snakes in the United States.

The signs and symptoms of a snakebite are as follows:

• A sharp, stinging pain with one or more puncture marks in the area
• Swelling, discoloration, and pain in the bitten area.

As the poison goes through the body, other symptoms develop such as:

• Weakness
• Nausea and vomiting
• Weak and rapid pulse
• Respiratory distress
• Shock

The first aid for snakebites is as follows:

♦ Begin care at once.
♦ Keep the victim lying down and quiet with the injured part immobile and lower than the rest of the body.

- ◆ Remove all rings, watches, and bracelets from the extremity.
- ◆ Apply constricting bands above and below the area. The constricting bands should be tight enough to slow down surface circulation but not so tight as to cut off arterial flow.
- ◆ Treat for shock.
- ◆ Apply an ice pack to the wound **only** if the poison control center or a physician advises to do so. **Do not** cut into the bite and suction or squeeze unless you are directed to do so by a physician. **NEVER** suck the venom from the wound using your mouth.
- ◆ **Do not** give the victim anything by mouth.
- ◆ Identify the snake if possible. If the snake can be killed, take it to the hospital with the victim.
- ◆ Monitor vital signs while transporting victim to a medical facility.
- ◆ For persons who frequent regions infested with poisonous snakes, it is recommended that a snakebite kit be carried.

Insect Bites and Stings

Many insects bite or sting, but few can cause serious symptoms by themselves, unless of course, the person is allergic to them. However, some insects transmit diseases. For example, certain types of mosquitoes transmit malaria, yellow fever, and other diseases; certain types of ticks transmit spotted or Rocky Mountain fever; and certain types of biting flies transmit tularemia or rabbit fever.

Occasionally, stinging or biting insects that have been feeding on or have been in contact with poisonous substances can transmit this poison at the time of the sting or bite.

Persons who have experienced serious reactions from previous insect bites should be urged to secure any possible immunization or have an antidote readily available to prevent more serious reactions from future insect bites and stings.

The signs and symptoms of insect bites and stings are as follows:

- • The stings of bees and the bites of mosquitoes, ticks, fleas, and bedbugs usually cause only local irritation and pain in the region stung or bitten.
- • Moderate swelling and redness may occur and some itching, burning, and pain may be present.

The first aid for insect bites and stings is as follows:

- ◆ The sting area should be inspected to determine whether the stinger is still left in the body. If it is, remove it in order to prevent further injection of toxin. The stinger should be carefully scraped off the skin, rather than grasped with tweezers, so as not to squeeze toxin into the body.
- ◆ Application of ice or ice water to the bite helps to slow absorption of toxin into the blood stream. A paste of baking soda and water can also be applied to the bite.
- ◆ The victim should be observed for signs of an allergic reaction. For people who are allergic, maintain an open airway and get the victim to medical help as quickly as possible.

Bites and Stings of Spiders, Centipedes, Tarantulas, and Scorpions

The effect of stings and bites of spiders, centipedes, tarantulas, and scorpions in some instances are much more severe than those of the insects previously mentioned. They may cause alarming symptoms.

The signs and symptoms of these bites are as follows:

- • Generally, the bite consists of two small pinpoint punctures of the skin and produce local swelling and redness with a smarting, burning pain.
- • Exhaustion, sweating, and nausea may appear.
- • Pain or cramping may develop in the back, shoulders, chest, and limbs.
- • In some instances the symptoms are mild and subside within six to twelve hours, but occasionally they are severe and can cause a state of collapse.

The **black widow spider** is a moderately large, glossy black spider with very fine hairs over the body, which give it a silky appearance. On the abdomen is a characteristic red or crimson marking in the form of an hourglass. Only the female is poisonous; the male, which is smaller, is harmless.

The **brown recluse spider** injects a venom which causes a limited destruction of red blood cells and certain other blood changes. The victim may develop chills, fever, joint pains, nausea, and vomiting. A rash may also develop within twenty-four to forty-eight hours.

Tarantulas are hairy spiders. Those found in the southwestern United States are not poisonous, but occasionally a victim will have an allergic reaction to the injected venom. Tarantulas coming into the country in imported fruit may be poisonous. Their bites may cause marked pain and local redness with swelling. Death is extremely rare.

Most species of **scorpions** in this country do not inject a toxin that is generally harmful to humans. The sting may result in local swelling and discoloration, similar to a wasp sting, and may sometimes cause allergic reactions. The sting of the more dangerous species of scorpions causes little or no swelling or discoloration, but locally there will be a tingling or burning sensation. Considerable discomfort may ensue. Death, although unlikely, occurs occasionally in infants and young children and might conceivably occur in older persons. The poison acts mainly on the nervous system.

The first aid for an allergic reaction to bites and stings of spiders, centipedes, tarantulas and scorpions is as follows:

♦ Apply constricting band between the bite or sting and the heart if the bite is on an extremity.
♦ Apply a cold pack on the area.
♦ Keep the victim quiet to retard absorption of the poison into the circulatory system.
♦ If the bite is on an extremity, splint it and keep it lower than the heart.
♦ Get the victim to medical help as quickly as possible.

Poison Ivy, Poison Oak, and Poison Sumac

These poisonous plants grow as vines or shrubs, from ankle to shoulder high. The poison comes mainly from their leaves but also may come from bruising their roots, stems, and berries. The smoke from burning brush containing these plants has been known to carry the poisons a considerable distance.

The signs and symptoms of this kind of skin poisoning are as follows:

• A red rash, with some swelling, itching and burning, followed by formation of blisters of various sizes filled with blood serum.
• The symptoms appear on the exposed skin surfaces, usually the hands, wrists and arms, six hours to several days after exposure.
• The blisters may fill with pus or contaminated fluid. When they break, crusts and scabs are formed. Considerable fluid may exude from broken blisters.
• When the affected area is large and the inflammation is severe, there may be fever, headache, and general body weakness.

The first aid for the victim of such poisoning is as follows:

♦ Contaminated clothing and jewelry should be removed.
♦ Wash the area with soap and water.
♦ A lotion may be applied to ease the victim's discomfort, if the rash is mild.
♦ If a severe reaction appears, seek medical help.